The
Encyclopedia
of
Prayer
and
Praise

The
Encyclopedia
of
Prayer
and
Praise

Compiled and edited by

Mark Water

 HENDRICKSON
PUBLISHERS

The Encyclopedia of Prayer and Praise
Hendrickson Publishers, Inc.
P.O. Box 3473
Peabody, Massachusetts 01961-3473

Copyright © 2004 John Hunt Publishing Ltd., UK
Text copyright: © 2004 Mark Water

Designed by Jim Weaver Design, Basingstoke, UK
Cover design by Hendrickson Publishers, Inc., USA

ISBN 1-56563-280-x

First printing – April 2004

Typeset in Albertina

Cover Art: Stained Glass in St. Peter's Anglican Church
Credit: © Roger De La Harpe; Gallo Images/CORBIS

Printed by the Maple-Vail Book Manufacturing Group, USA

Acknowledgements

All Bible quotations are from the New International Version unless otherwise stated.

New King James Version. Copyright © 1982 by Thomas Nelson, Inc. All rights reserved.

New International Version. Copyright © 1973, 1978, 1984 by International Bible Society. Used by permission of Zondervan Publishing House. All rights reserved.

The New Revised Standard Version. Copyright 1989, Division of Christian Education of the National Council of the Churches of Christ in the United States of America

Scripture quotations from the Revised Standard Version of the Bible, © 1973 by the Division of Christian Education, National Council of Churches.

The Message. Copyright © 1993, 1994, 1995, 1996. Used by permission of NavPress Publishing Group.

O Lord, open my lips,
and my mouth will declare your praise.

King David Psalm 51.15

Give thanks to the Lord, for he is good;
his love endures forever.

King David Psalm 118.1

How this book is organized

The Encyclopedia of Prayer and Praise is divided into two parts, and includes a number of tools to help navigate through the book and find the text you want.

◪ General table of contents for the whole book, which lists the major sections in each part, is found on p. xi

◪ Part One: Individual Prayers by Topic
   • Detailed table of contents, p. 3, which breaks down each section into subsections
   • Indexes
      ○ Index of authors and sources, p. 369
      ○ Index of subjects, p. 375
      ○ Appendix of biographical information, p. 381

◪ Part Two: Historical Works on Prayer and Collected Prayers
   • Detailed table of contents, p. 393, which breaks down each section into subsections
   • Part Two is not indexed – instead, each section in Part One begins with a list of cross-references to sections in Part Two which address the same topic.

Contents

Contents

Introduction

The breath of prayer – the very air of Christian living – prayer lies within the inmost being. It may be a sigh, or a well-articulated paragraph, a brief poem, or a prolonged cry. Christian prayers can never be exhausted. This encyclopedia sets out to bring together some of the most helpful prayers and teaching about prayer of the past two millennia. Over the past 50 years we have been very well served with books of contemporary prayers. Rather than duplicate such material, the emphasis of *The Encyclopedia of Prayer and Praise* is the rich, and often neglected, heritage of classic Christian prayers.

Scope

The encyclopedia confines itself to *Christian* prayers. Prayers of other faiths are outside the scope of this book.

Christian prayers

Many weird and wonderful prayers are included in some books but a helpful distinction to make about Christian prayers is that they are addressed to God the Father, or God the Son, or God the Holy Spirit. This encyclopedia only includes prayers addressed to one of the Trinity. It excludes prayers addressed to saints or angels.

Topics covered

Perhaps the best guide to the subjects that should be in a prayer book is given by the prayers in the Bible, and in particular the book of Psalms, and Jesus' and Paul's prayers. There every mood and human experience are set before God. By setting out to include such a range of subjects this encyclopedia has many prayers on topics which have often been neglected in the past.

This, of course, means that numerous prayers which were rightly thought of as being Jewish prayers, before the Christian era, are now viewed as being "Christian" prayers. In common with other books of prayers this encyclopedia includes many prayers that have been based on the psalms and from other sections of the Bible, but it also includes some of the psalms in Coverdale's traditional, and timeless, English.

Who's in, who's out?

As long as the prayer is addressed to God and is Christian in its content it was eligible for inclusion. Not all individuals whose prayers are included here may have been remembered as outstanding Christians, but if someone wrote an edifying Christian prayer it is a candidate for inclusion. The vast majority of prayers included are by pious Christians of previous generations. So prayers from Peter Abelard, Aelred of Rievaulx, Aethelwold, Alcuin, Cecil Frances Alexander, Henry Alford, Alfred the Great, Ambrose, to Charles and John Wesley, Susanna Wesley, Brooke Foss Westcott, John Greenleaf Whittier, William III, William Williams, Catherine Winkworth, George Wither, Christopher Wordsworth, Francis Xavier, and Sir Christopher Yelverton are all included. Prayers have also been drawn from the writings of some of the most famous Christians down the ages: the apostle John, Cyprian of Cathage, Augustine of Hippo, Bede the historian, Anselm of Canterbury, Martin Luther, Teresa of Avila, John Donne, Jonathan Edwards, George Müller, and Dietrich Bonhoeffer. *The Encyclopedia of Prayer and Praise* may be able to lay claim to being one of the largest collections of classic Christian prayers ever published, and most probably the largest collection published in the 21st century.

Contemporary prayers

This encyclopedia includes many hundreds of contemporary prayers. One unique collection of contemporary prayers is published in its entirety, for the first time, in this encyclopedia. It consists of a prayer for each day and was written at the turn of the millennium in America. *Prayer Prescription for every day of the year*, by Donna L. Hammond, is a collection of original Christian prayers "intended for use as part of a daily devotional."

Prayers for young children

There is a collection of more than 100 prayers which have been written to pray with young children.

Prayers for young people

The young people's prayer collection includes many informal prayers written in the form of a conversation, often in the style of Brother Lawrence.

Teaching on prayer

In addition to the prayers themselves, this book includes extracts of classic Christian teaching on prayer, and prayer collections which have been culled from many sources, from the pages of the Bible onwards. It is easy to forget that the problems about prayer faced today by many people have been wrestled over by saintly Christians in the past. As early as the 3rd century, Origen was tackling many such difficulties. In the fourth chapter of his book entitled *Prayer*, Origen focuses on one of the perennial "problems" about prayer, under the heading: "Answer to objections: man's freewill and God's foreknowledge."

Perhaps the most respected writing on prayer, in a reasonably short compass, to come from the Reformers, is the section about prayer in John Calvin's *The Institutes of Christian Religion*. This is included in full.

There are many examples among the feature pages of more down-to-earth approaches to prayer. Perhaps the most famous of these is *Practicing the Presence of God*, by Brother Lawrence. Even though this is fairly long it has been included in its entirety.

Collections of prayers

Another element in *The Encyclopedia of Prayer and Praise* is its collections of prayers. These are a number of prayers by one person, or, occasionally, by a group of people.

Meditation

Many aspects of prayer are explored in *The Christian Encyclopedia of Prayer*, both in its prayers and in its extracts of teaching about prayer. One such approach to prayer is meditation.

Until quite recent times, Christian mediation played little part in the lives of many Christians as it was regarded with deep suspicion. This may have been because the word "meditation" was so often linked with non-Christian activities. The fact that meditation was such an important part of the prayer life of the psalmist seems to have been overlooked. Not infrequently, the psalmist meditated on God's law and on God's creation: "But his delight is in the law of the Lord, and on his law he meditates day and night" (Psalm 2:1); "Oh, how I love your law! I meditate on it all day long" (Psalm 119:97); "... I will meditate on your wonderful works" (Psalm 145:5); "I will meditate on all your works and consider all your mighty deeds" (Psalm 77:12). The psalmist even prayed, "May my mediation be pleasing to him [God]" (Psalm 104:34). Over the past few decades there has been a noticeable return to the simplicity of biblical meditations based on reading the Bible.

Christian meditation has been defined in a variety of different ways: "By meditation is meant the process in which you deliberately turn over in your heart whatsoever you have read or heard, earnestly ruminating and thereby kindling your affections and enlightening your understanding" (Geert Zerbolt); "All good meditative prayer is a conversion of our entire self to God. The whole purpose of meditation is to deepen consciousness of the basic relationship of the creature to the Creator, and of the sinner to the Redeemed" (Thomas Merton).

Until the 11th century Christian meditation was linked very strongly to *lectio divina*, (holy reading). As the mind applies itself to the word of God, so it is sustained and stimulated by the sacred text. Many passages in Scripture were used as the basis for meditation by Augustine, William Thierry, and, most famously of all, by Anselm. Meditations and prayer became fused in the hearts and minds of such people.

From the 15th century onwards meditations resulted in a vast array of beautiful literature from the pens of the spiritual leaders of the time: Ignatius of Loyola, Francis de Sales, Dom Augustine Baker; and from Anglican and Puritan divines of the 17th century, such as Andrewes, Donne, Hall, Baxter, and Bunyan, and of the 18th century with William Law and John Wesley. Some of these meditations have been included in this encyclopedia.

Enriching your own prayer life

Few Christians would claim that they are masters of their own prayer life. Most acknowledge their lack in this area. The vast collection of prayers and wide range of teaching about prayer in *The Encyclopedia of Prayer and Praise* aims to enrich our own praying and meditation. Breathe in and breathe out of these pages a life-line to God. May these words become your own.

Part One:
Individual Prayers by Topic

Detailed Contents, Part One

Preparing to Pray

SEEKING GOD

O Good Jesus, let your voice sound in my ears
so that my heart and mind and inmost soul
may learn of your love, and the very depths of
my heart be joined to you who are my greatest
delight and joy.

Aelred of Rievaulx, 1109–67

Lord, teach me to seek you, and reveal yourself to me as I seek you. For I cannot seek you
unless you first teach me and I cannot find you
unless you first reveal yourself to me.

Ambrose, c.339–397

O Almighty and ever living God, heavenly
Father, to whom it is manifestly known, how
inconstant and wandering the minds of men
are, in any good actions; and how easily we
suffer ourselves to be carried away from the
contemplation of thee, by diversity of distractions, and unseasonable thoughts, which take
hold of us, in the time of our devotions and
prayers unto thee; who also, by thine only
begotten Son Christ Jesus, didst prescribe unto
his disciples a form of prayer to be offered
up to thee, and hast derived the same from
them to us. Behold me, most wretched sinner,
wholly depraved and corrupt, entreating thee,
by the same Son, that for his sake thou wouldest infuse thy Holy Spirit into me, which may
adopt me into the number of thine elect: that it
may teach me how I ought to pray, according
to thy holy will: that it may allay all troublesome and wandering thoughts in me, while
I offer up my prayers and praises unto thee:
suffer me not to serve thee with my lips, and
be absent in heart from thee: but create a right
spirit within me, that I being sensible of all
thy graces and comforts, may with a joyful

and holy zeal, perform my duty to thee: that so, my prayers and desires may appear before thee; and in thy Son's name, I may effectually be heard, and my petitions may be granted, to the glory and honor of thy most holy name, and the endless comfort of mine own soul, through the same, our only Lord and Savior Jesus Christ. Amen.

Lancelot Andrewes, 1555–1626

O supreme and unapproachable light, O holy and blessed truth, how far Thou art from me who am so near to Thee! How far art Thou removed from my vision, although I am so near to Thine! Everywhere Thou art wholly present and I see Thee not. In Thee I move and in Thee I have my being and cannot come to Thee. Thou art within me and about me and I feel Thee not.

Anselm, 1033–1109

Give us grace, almighty Father, to address you with all our hearts as well as with our lips. You are everywhere present: from you no secrets can be hidden. Teach us to fix our thoughts on you, reverently and with love, so that our prayers are not in vain, but are acceptable to you, now and always, through Jesus Christ our Lord.

Jane Austen, 1775–1817

Almighty God, Lord of angels and all creation, Who dwell on high yet care for the lowly, Who search the heart and know every hidden thing, eternal and unchanging Light, we trust in Your great mercy to hear the prayers offered from our unclean lips.

Basil the Great, c.330–379

Father,
give us wisdom to perceive you,
intellect to understand you,
diligence to seek you,
patience to wait for you,
eyes to behold you,
a heart to meditate on you
and a life to proclaim you,
through the power of the Spirit
of our Lord Jesus Christ.

Benedict, 480–543

O Lord, take away all coldness, all wanderings of thoughts, and fix our souls upon thee and thy love, O merciful Lord and Savior, in this our hour of prayer.

E.W. Benson, 1829–96

O, God, help us to pray and concentrate our thoughts on you. We cannot do this alone. In us there is darkness, but in you there is light. We are lonely, but you leave us not. We are feeble in heart, but with you there is peace. In us there is bitterness, but with you there is patience. We do not understand your ways, but you know the way for us. Help us, O God, through Jesus Christ our Savior. Amen.

Dietrich Bonhoeffer, 1906–45

Almighty God, which hast promised to hear the petitions of them that ask in thy son's name, we beseech thee mercifully to incline thine ears to us that have made now our prayers and supplications unto thee, and grant that those things which we have faithfully asked according to thy will, may effectually be obtained to the relief of our necessity, and to the setting forth of thy glory: Through Jesus Christ our Lord.

Book of Common Prayer, 1549

Almighty God, the fountain of all wisdom, who knowest our necessities before we ask, and our ignorance in asking: we beseech thee to have compassion upon our infirmities, and those things, which for our unworthiness we dare not, and for our blindness we cannot ask, vouchsafe to give us for the worthiness of thy son Jesus Christ our Lord. Amen.

Book of Common Prayer, 1549

Assist us mercifully, O Lord, in these our supplications and prayers, and dispose the way of thy servants, toward the attainment of everlasting salvation, that among all the changes and chances of this mortal life, they may ever be defended by thy most gracious and ready help; through Christ our Lord. Amen.

Book of Common Prayer, 1549

Father, enable our minds to rise to your ineffable dwelling place. Let us find the light and direct the eyes of our soul to you. Dispel the mists and the opaqueness of the earthly mass, and shine out with your splendor. You are the serene and tranquil abode of those who persevere in their goal of seeing you. You are at the same time the beginning, the vehicle, the guide, the way and the goal.

Severinus Boethius, c.480–524

My Lord Jesus Christ, hear my prayer, even though it may be that I have by my deeds done nothing to deserve it, yet do it because you are true God and worthy. Make my heart burning with the fire of your love, so that everything that is in it which is against you becomes like ashes in the blowing wind.

Bridget of Sweden, 1303–73

Almighty God, from whom every good prayer comes, deliver us, when we draw close to you, from coldness of heart and wandering thoughts, that with steadfast thought and kindled desire we may worship you in the faith and spirit of Jesus Christ our Lord.

William Bright, 1824–1901

My God, my God, let me for once look on thee
As though nought else existed, we alone!
And as creation crumbles, my soul's spark
Expands till I can say: Even for myself
I need thee and I feel thee and I love thee.

Robert Browning, 1812–89

Bestow upon us fullness in our need,
Love towards God,
The affection of God,
The smile of God,
The wisdom of God.
The grace of God,
The fear of God,
And the will of God
To do in the world of the Three,
As angels and saints
Do in heaven;
Each shade and light,
Each day and night,
Each time in kindness,
Give Thou us Thy Spirit.

Carmina Gadelica

God, Listen to my prayer
Bend to me Thine ear,

Let my supplications and my prayers
Ascend to Thee upwards,
Come, Thou King of Glory,
To protect me down,
Thou King of life and mercy
With the aid of the Lamb,
Thou Son of Mary Virgin
To protect me with power,
Thou Son of the lovely Mary
Of purest fairest beauty.

Carmina Gadelica

O God,
I am as one hungry for rice,
parched as one thirsty for tea.
Fill my so empty heart.
Amen.

Chinese prayer

I am not worthy, Lord and Master, that you should come under the roof of my soul: nevertheless, since you desire, O lover of mankind, to dwell within me, I am bold to draw near. You invite me to open the door which you alone have made, that entering in there you may bring light into my darkened mind: I do believe that you will do this.

For you did not throw out the prostitute when she came with tears, neither did you reject the tax collector when he repented, nor did you reject the thief when he sought to enter your kingdom, nor did you reject the persecutor when he repented. But you treated all who came to you in penitence as your friends. You alone are to be blessed, now and for ever.

John Chrysostom, c.347–407

Lord, I know not what I ought to ask of you. You only know what I need. You know me better than I know myself. O Father, give to your child what he himself knows not how to ask. Teach me to pray. Pray yourself in me.

F. Fénelon, 1651–1715

Spare me that I may not
labor without birth,
sigh without tears,
meditate without voice,
cloud without rain,
struggle without reaching,
call without being heard,

implore without being heeded,
groan without being comforted,
beg without being helped,
smolder without aroma,
see you without being fulfilled.

Gregory of Narek, 951–1003

Holy Spirit dwell in me, that I may become
    prayer.
Whether I sleep or wake, eat or drink, labor
    or rest, may the fragrance of prayer rise
    effortlessly, in my heart.
Purify my soul and never leave me, so that
    my heart and mind may, with voices full of
    sweetness, sing in secret to God.

Isaac the Syrian (7th century)

O sweetest love of God, too little known,
whoever has found you will be at rest.
Let everything change, O my God,
that I may rest in you.
How sweet to me is your presence,
you who are the sovereign good!
I will draw near to you in silence,
and will uncover your feet,
that it may please you to unite me with
    yourself,
making my soul your bride.
I will rejoice in nothing until I am in your
    arms;
O Lord, I beseech you, leave me not for a
    moment.

John of the Cross, 1542–91

Holy God, teach me this day how to worship!
May my soul be upon its knees! May I discern
Thy Presence, and be filled with holy reverence
and fear! Teach me to pray. Amen.

J.H. Jowett, 1864–1923

Lord, teach us how to pray aright,
With reverence and with fear;
Though dust and ashes in thy sight,
We may, we must draw near.

James Montgomery, 1771–1854

O thou by whom we come to God,
The Life, the Truth, the Way,
The path of prayer thyself hast trod:
Lord, teach us how to pray.

James Montgomery, 1771–1854

We perish, if we cease from prayer;
O grant us power to pray;
And when to meet thee we prepare,
Lord, meet us by the way.

James Montgomery, 1771–1854

Everlasting God! The Three-One and Thrice
Holy! In deep reverence would I with veiled
face worship before the holy mystery of Thy
Divine Being. And if it please Thee, O most
glorious God, to unveil aught of that mystery,
I would bow with fear and trembling, lest I sin
against Thee, as I meditate on Thy glory.

Andrew Murray, 1828–1917

Blessed Jesus! In whom as the Son the path of
prayer has been opened up, and who givest
us assurance of the answer, we beseech Thee,
teach Thy people to pray. O let this each day
be the sign of our sonship, that, like Thee,
we know that the Father heareth us always.
Amen.

Andrew Murray, 1828–1917

I am bending my knee
In the eye of the Father who created me,
In the eye of the Son who purchased me,
In the eye of the Spirit who cleansed me,
In friendship and affection.
Through Thine own Anointed One, O God,
Father, in Thy mysterious Presence kneeling,
Fain would our souls feel all Thy kindling
    love;
For we are weak, and need some deep
    revealing
Of trust and strength and calmness from
    above.

J.H. Newman, 1801–90

Give me grace, O my Father, to be utterly
ashamed of my own reluctance to pray. Rouse
me from sloth and coldness, and make me
desire you with my whole heart. Teach me to
love meditation, sacred reading, and prayer.
Teach me to love what which must engage my
mind for all eternity.

J.H. Newman, 1801–90

Savior of every life, your voice makes itself
heard even at the heart of our contradictions.
You tell us: Be opened! And when we are

almost without words, we may discover that a single word is enough in order to pray.

Brother Roger of Taizé, b.1915

O Lord, I do not know what to ask of You.
    You alone know what are my true needs.
You love me more than I myself know how
    to love.
Help me to see my real needs which are
    concealed from me.
I do not dare to ask either for a cross or for
    consolation.
I can only wait on You. My heart is open to
    You.
Visit and help me, for the sake of Your great
    mercy.
Strike me and heal me; cast me down and
    raise me up.
I worship in silence Your holy will and Your
    unsearchable ways.
I offer myself as a sacrifice to You.
I have no other desire than to fulfill Your will.
Teach me to pray. Pray You Yourself in me.
Amen.

Metropolitan Philaret, 1782–1867

O Lord seek us, O Lord find us
In Thy patient care,
Be Thy love before, behind us,
Round us everywhere.
Lest the god of this world blind us,
Lest he bait a snare,
Lest he forge a chain to bind us,
Lest he speak us fair,
Turn not from us, call to mind us,
Find, embrace us, hear.
By Thy love before, behind us,
Round us everywhere.

Christina Rossetti, 1830–94

O almighty God, the searcher of all hearts, who has declared that who draw near to you with their lips when their hearts are far from you are an abomination to you: cleanse, we beseech you, the thoughts of our hearts by the inspiration of your Holy Spirit, that no wandering, vain, or idle thoughts may put out of our minds that reverence and godly fear that becomes all those who come into your presence.

Jonathan Swift, 1667–1745

Holy Jesus, give me the gift and spirit of prayer.

Jeremy Taylor, 1613–67

Open, Lord my inward ear;
And bid my heart rejoice!

Bid my quiet spirit hear
Thy comfortable voice.
Never in the whirlwind found,
Or where the earthquakes rock the place;
Still and silent is the sound,
The whisper of Thy grace.
From the world of sin, and noise,
And hurry, I withdraw;

For the small and inward voice
I wait with humble awe.
Silent am I now, and still,
Dare not in Thy presence move;
To my waiting soul reveal
The secret of Thy love.

Charles Wesley, 1707–88

Each moment draw from earth away
My heart, that lowly waits thy call;
Speak to my inmost soul, and say,
"I am thy Love, thy God, thy All!"
To feel thy power, to hear thy voice,
To taste thy love, be all my choice.
Amen

John Wesley, 1707–88

IN SILENCE AND STILLNESS

O Lord, the Scripture says, "There is a time for
    silence and a time for speech."
Savior, teach me the silence of humility,
the silence of wisdom,
the silence of love,
the silence of perfection,
the silence that speaks without words,
the silence of faith.
Lord teach me to silence my own heart that I
    may listen to the gentle movement of the
    Holy Spirit within me and sense the depths
    which are of God.

Source unknown, Frankfurt prayer, 16th century

Almighty, beneficent, loving God of all, Creator of everything visible and invisible, Savior and Restorer, Provider and Pacifier, O mighty Spirit of the Father, we entreat you with open arms and pray with sighs and cries standing before your awe-inspiring presence.

Gregory of Narek, 951–1003

Let all mortal flesh keep silent, and with fear
   and trembling stand;
Ponder nothing earthly-minded, for with
   blessing in his hand,
Christ our God to earth descendeth, our full
   homage to command.

Liturgy of St James

Lift up our souls, O Lord, to the pure, serene light of your presence; that there we may breathe freely, there repose in your love, there may be at rest from ourselves, and from there return, arrayed in your peace, to do and bear what will please you; for your holy name's sake.

E.B. Pusey, 1800–82

Dear Lord and Father of mankind,
Forgive our foolish ways!
Reclothe us in our rightful mind;
In purer lives your service find,
In deeper reverence, praise.

Breathe through the heats of our desire
Thy coolness and thy balm;
Let sense be dumb, let flesh retire;
Speak through the earthquake, wind, and fire,
O still small voice of calm!

J.G. Whittier, 1807–92

Praise, Confession, and Thanksgiving

Related entries in Part Two

Extracts of classic Christian teaching on prayer, and prayer collections
Augustine Baker, Holy Wisdom, Or Directions for the Prayer of Contemplation
Augustine of Hippo: When You Pray
A.A. Bonar: Praise
Thomas Boston: How the Spirit Enables Us to Pray
Thomas Boston: Praying in the Name of Christ
John Calvin: On Prayer
Stephen Charnock: A Discourse of Delight in Prayer
John Chrysostom: Jesus Praying for Himself
John Chrysostom: Rejoice
P.T. Forsyth: The Soul of Prayer
William Gurnall: Prayer and Thanksgiving
Martin Luther: Table Talk
F. B. Meyer: The Way into the Holiest
Origen: The Content of Prayer and the Recipient of Prayer
J.C. Ryle: A Call to Prayer
Jeremy Taylor: Holy Living
Tertullian: On Prayer
B.B. Warfield: Prayer as a Means of Grace
Alexander Whyte: Imagination in Prayer

Stories about prayer and people who prayed
A.T. Pierson: George Müller of Bristol

PRAISE

General prayers of praise

Great art Thou, O Lord, and greatly to be praised; great is Thy power, and Thy wisdom is infinite. Thee would we praise without ceasing. Thou callest us to delight in Thy praise, for Thou hast made us for Thyself, and our hearts find no rest until we rest in Thee; Who with the Father and the Holy Ghost all glory, praise, and honor be ascribed, both now and for evermore. Amen.

Augustine of Hippo, 354–430

Lord, whether prosperity smile or adversity frown, let your praise be ever in my mouth.

Augustine of Hippo, 354–430

Fairest Lord Jesus, Ruler of all nature,
O Thou of God and man the Son,
Thee will I cherish, Thee will I honor,
Thou, my soul's glory, joy and crown.

Fair are the meadows, fairer still the
    woodlands,
Robed in the blooming garb of spring;
Jesus is fairer, Jesus is purer,
Who makes the woeful heart to sing.

Fair is the sunshine,
Fairer still the moonlight,
And all the twinkling starry host;
Jesus shines brighter, Jesus shines purer
Than all the angels heaven can boast.

All fairest beauty, heavenly and earthly,
Wondrously, Jesus, is found in Thee;
None can be nearer, fairer or dearer,
Than Thou, my Savior, art to me.

Beautiful Savior! Lord of all the nations!
Son of God and Son of Man!
Glory and honor, praise, adoration,
Now and forever more be Thine.

Author unknown, German Jesuits, 17th century,
translated by Joseph A. Seiss, 1873

The King of love my Shepherd is,
Whose goodness faileth never,
I nothing lack if I am His
And He is mine forever.

Where streams of living water flow
My ransomed soul He leadeth,
And where the verdant pastures grow,
With food celestial feedeth.

Perverse and foolish oft I strayed,
But yet in love He sought me,
And on His shoulder gently laid,
And home, rejoicing, brought me.

In death's dark vale I fear no ill
With Thee, dear Lord, beside me;
Thy rod and staff my comfort still,
Thy cross before to guide me.

Thou spread'st a table in my sight;
Thy unction grace bestoweth;
And O what transport of delight
From Thy pure chalice floweth!

And so through all the length of days
Thy goodness faileth never;
Good Shepherd, may I sing Thy praise
Within Thy house forever.

H.W. Baker, 1821–77

Fill Thou my life, O Lord my God,
In every part with praise,
That my whole being may proclaim
Thy being and Thy ways.
Not for the lip of praise alone,
Nor e'en the praising heart
I ask, but for a life made up
Of praise in every part!

Fill every part of me with praise;
Let all my being speak
Of Thee and of Thy love, O Lord,
Poor though I be, and weak.
So shalt Thou, Lord, from me, e'en me,
Receive the glory due;
And so shall I begin on earth
The song forever new.

So shall each fear, each fret, each care
Be turned into a song,
And every winding of the way
The echo shall prolong;
So shall no part of day or night
From sacredness be free;
But all my life, in every step

Be fellowship with Thee.

Horatius Bonar, 1808–82

No coward soul is mine,
No trembler in the world's storm-troubled
    sphere:
    I see Heaven's glories shine,
And faith shines equal, arming me from fear.

O God within my breast,
Almighty, ever-present Deity!
    Life – that in me has rest,
As I – undying Life – have Power in Thee!

Vain are the thousand creeds
That move men's hearts: unutterably vain;
    Worthless as withered weeds,
Or idlest froth amid the boundless main,

To waken doubt in one
Holding so fast by thine infinity;
    So surely anchored on
The steadfast rock of immortality.

With wide-embracing love
Thy spirit animates eternal years,
    Pervades and broods above,
Changes, sustains, dissolves, creates, and
    rears.

Though earth and man were gone,
And suns and universes ceased to be,
    And Thou wert left alone,
Every existence would exist in Thee.

There is not room for Death,
Nor atom that his might could render void:
    Thou – Thou art Being and Breath,
And what Thou art may never be destroyed.

Emily Brontë, 1818–48, her last poem

Take my life, and let it be
Consecrated, Lord, to thee;
    Take my moments and my days,
Let them flow in ceaseless praise.

Frances Ridley Havergal, 1836–70

Glory to you, O Champion of all Loves, who
for our sake endured the cross, encountered
the enemy and tasted death. Glory be to you, O
King of all Kings, who for our salvation wrestled with principalities and powers, subdued
the forces of hell and won the greatest of all
victories. To you be all praise, all glory and all
love; now and for ever. Amen.

Thomas Ken, 1637–1711

Let our mouth be filled with thy praise, O
Lord, that we may sing of thy glory, for that
thou hast counted us worthy to partake of thy
holy, divine, immortal and life-giving mysteries: preserve thou us in thy holiness, that we
may learn of thy righteousness all the day long.
Alleluia, Alleluia, Alleluia.

Liturgy of John Chrysostom and Basil the Great

O All-Transcendent God, what words can
hymn your praises? No word does you justice.
What mind can probe your secret? No mind
can encompass you. You are alone beyond
the power of speech, yet all that we speak
stems from you. You are alone beyond the
power of thought, yet all that we can conceive
springs from you. All things proclaim you,
those endowed with reason and those bereft
of it. All the expectation and pain of the world
coalesces in you. All things utter a prayer to
you, a silent hymn composed by you. You
sustain everything that exists, and all things
move together to your orders. You are the
goal of all that exists. You are one and you are
all, yet you are none of the things that exist
– neither a part nor the whole. You can avail
yourself of any name; how shall I call you, the
only unnameable? All-transcendent God!

Gregory of Nazianzen, 329–389

1   God of mercy, God of grace,
2   Show the brightness of Thy face:
3   Shine upon us, Savior, shine,
4   Fill Thy church with light Divine;
5   And Thy saving health extend,
6   Unto earth's remotest end.

7   Let Thy people praise Thee, Lord;
8   Be by all that live adored;
9   Let the nations shout and sing,
10 Glory to their Savior King;
11 At Thy feet their tributes pay,
12 And Thy holy will obey.

13 Let the people praise Thee, Lord;

14   Earth shall then her fruits afford;
15   God to man His blessing give,
16   Man to God devoted live;
17   All below, and all above,
18   One in joy, and light, and love.

H.F. Lyte, 1793–1847, based on Psalm 67

Praise to the Lord, the Almighty, the King of
    creation!
O my soul, praise Him, for He is thy health
    and salvation!
All ye who hear, now to His temple draw near;
Praise Him in glad adoration.

Joachim Neander, 1650–80,
translated by Catherine Winkworth

Strengthen, O Lord, our weakness in your
compassion, and comfort and help the needs
of our soul in your loving kindness. Waken our
thoughts from sleep, and lighten the weight of
our limbs; wash us and cleanse us from the
filth of our sins.

Nestorian Liturgy, 5th/6th century

O good Lord Jesus Christ, I pray that you will
open my mouth, so that I may praise you, and
give you thanks for all your goodness towards
me: and I beseech you to keep it from all vain
talk, and from all other ways of offending you.

Primer, 1557

Lord, keep me always near to you.
Let nothing separate me from you, let nothing
    keep me back from you.
If I fall, bring me back quickly to you, and
    make me hope in you, trust in you, and
    love you for ever.

E.B. Pusey, 1800–82

O Lord Jesus Christ, Wisdom and Word of
God, dwell in our hearts, we beseech thee, by
thy most Holy Spirit, that out of the abundance of our hearts our mouths may speak
thy praise.

Christina Rossetti, 1830–94

O infinite God, center of my soul, convert me
powerfully unto thee, that in thee I may take
rest, for thou didst make me for thee, and my
heart is unquiet till it be united to thee.

Thomas Traherne, 1636–74

O for a thousand tongues to sing
My great Redeemer's praise,
The glories of my God and King,
The triumphs of His grace!

Charles Wesley, 1707–88

Come, Almighty to deliver,
Let us all Thy life receive;
Suddenly return and never,
Never more Thy temples leave.
Thee we would be always blessing,
Serve Thee as Thy hosts above,
Pray and praise Thee without ceasing,
Glory in Thy perfect love.

Charles Wesley, 1707–88

I'll praise him while he lends me breath;
And when my voice is lost in death,
Praise shall employ my nobler powers;
My days of praise shall ne'er be past,
While life, and thought, and being last,
Or immortality endures.

John Wesley, 1703–91

I thank you, O God, for the relief and satisfaction of mind that come with the firm assurance
that you govern the world; for the patience
and resignation to your providence that are
afforded as I reflect that even the tumultuous
and irregular actions of the sinful are, nevertheless, under your direction, who are wise,
good and omnipotent, and have promised
to make all things work together for good to
those who love you.

Susanna Wesley, 1669–1742

Teach us, O Lord, to love you, to trust you and
for ever to praise you. Let us exalt your name
both in the day and in the night. Let us serve
you both in the house of prayer and in the
world about us. Let us ascribe to you with all
your saints both wisdom and majesty, both
honor and glory, world without end. Amen.

Henry Vaughan, 1621–95

Praise and prayers to the One God in Three, the Trinity

We pray to you, O Lord, who are the supreme Truth, and all truth is from you. We beseech you, O Lord, who are the highest Wisdom, and all the wise depend on you for their wisdom. You are the supreme Joy, and all who are happy owe it to you. You are the Light of minds, and all receive their understanding from you. We love, we love you above all. We seek you, we follow you, and we are ready to serve you. We desire to dwell under your power for you are the King of all. Amen.

King Alfred the Great, 849–899

Blessing and honor, thanksgiving and praise
 more than we can utter,
 more than we can conceive,
be unto you, O most holy and glorious Trinity,
 Father, Son and Holy Spirit,
by all angels, all people, all creatures
 for ever and ever. Amen and Amen.

Lancelot Andrewes, 1555–1626

O supreme Lord, most secret and most present, most beautiful and strong! What shall I say, my God, my life, my holy joy? What shall anyone say when he speaks to you?

Augustine of Hippo, 354–430

O Lord in whom all things live,
who commanded us to seek you,
who are always ready to be found:
to know you is life,
to serve you is freedom,
to praise you is our soul's delight.
We bless you and adore you,
we worship you and magnify you,
we give thanks to you for your great glory,
through Jesus Christ our Lord.

Augustine of Hippo, 354–430

O Lord our God, we believe in Thee, the Father and the Son and the Holy Spirit. For the Truth would not say, Go, baptize all nations in the name of the Father and of the Son and of the Holy Spirit, unless Thou wast a Trinity. Nor wouldest thou, O Lord God, bid us to be baptized in the name of Him who is not the Lord God. Nor would the divine voice have said, Hear, O Israel, the Lord thy God is one God, unless Thou wert so a Trinity as to be one Lord God. And if Thou, O God, wert Thyself the Father, and wert Thyself the Son, Thy Word Jesus Christ, and the Holy Spirit your gift, we should not read in the book of truth, "God sent His Son;" nor wouldest Thou, O Only-begotten, say of the Holy Spirit, "Whom the Father will send in my name"; and, "Whom I will send to you from the Father." Directing my purpose by this rule of faith, so far as I have been able, so far as Thou hast made me to be able, I have sought Thee, and have desired to see with my understanding what I believed; and I have argued and labored much. O Lord my God, my one hope, hearken to me, lest through weariness I be unwilling to seek Thee, "but that I may always ardently seek Thy face." Do Thou give strength to seek who hast made me find Thee, and hast given the hope of finding Thee more and more. My strength and my infirmity are in Thy sight: preserve the one, and heal the other. My knowledge and my ignorance are in Thy sight; where Thou hast opened to me, receive me as I enter; where Thou hast closed, open to me as I knock. May I remember Thee, understand Thee, love Thee. Increase these things in me, until Thou renewest me wholly. I know it is written, "In the multitude of speech, thou shalt not escape sin." But O that I might speak only in preaching Thy word, and in praising Thee! Not only should I so flee from sin, but I should earn good desert, however much I so spake. For a man blessed of Thee would not enjoin a sin upon his own true son in the faith, to whom he wrote, "Preach the word: be instant in season. out of season." Are we to say that he has not spoken much, who was not silent about Thy word, O Lord, not only in season, but out of season? But therefore it was not much, because it was only what was necessary. Set me free, O God, from that multitude of speech which I suffer inwardly in my soul, wretched as it is in Thy sight, and flying for refuge to Thy mercy; for I am not silent in thoughts, even when silent in words. And if, indeed, I thought of nothing save what pleased Thee, certainly I would not ask Thee to set me free from such multitude of speech. But many are my thoughts, such as Thou knowest, "thoughts of man, since they are vain."

Grant to me not to consent to them; and if ever they delight me, nevertheless to condemn them, and not to dwell in them, as though I slumbered. Nor let them so prevail in me, as that anything in my acts should proceed from them; but at least let my opinions, let my conscience, be safe from them, under Thy protection. When we shall have come to Thee, these very many things that we speak, and yet come short, will cease; and Thou, as One, wilt remain "all in all." And we shall say one thing without end, in praising Thee in One, ourselves also made one in Thee. O Lord the one God, God the Trinity, whatever I have said in these books that is of Thine, may they acknowledge who are Thine; if anything of my own, may it be pardoned both by Thee and by those who are Thine. Amen.

*Augustine of Hippo, 354–430,
conclusion to his book, On the Trinity*

Glory be to the Father, and to the Son, and to the Holy Spirit, as it was in the beginning, is now, and ever shall be, world without end. Amen.

Author unknown

Father, forgive us,
Jesus, redeem us,
Holy Spirit, renew us.

Author unknown

I am giving thee worship with my whole life,
I am giving thee assent with my whole power,
I am giving thee praise with my whole tongue,
I am giving thee honor with my whole
    utterance,
I am giving thee reverence with my whole
    understanding,
I am giving thee offering with my whole
    thought,
I am giving thee praise with my whole fervor,
I am giving thee humility in the blood of the
    Lamb.
I am giving thee love with my whole devotion,
I am giving thee adoration with my whole
    desire,
I am giving thee love with my whole heart,
I am giving thee affection with my whole being.
I am giving thee my existence with my whole
    mind,

I am giving thee my soul, O God of all gods.

Early Scottish prayer

Keep me, O Lord, while I tarry on this earth, in a daily serious seeking after thee, and in a believing affectionate walking with thee; that, when thou comest, I may be found not hiding my talent, nor serving my flesh, nor yet asleep with my lamp unfurnished; but waiting and longing for my Lord, my glorious God, for ever and ever.

Richard Baxter, 1615–91

O all ye Works of the Lord, bless ye the Lord:
    praise him, and magnify him for ever.
O ye Angels of the Lord, bless ye the Lord:
    praise him, and magnify him for ever.
O ye Heavens, bless ye the Lord: praise him,
    and magnify him for ever.
O ye Waters that be above the firmament,
    bless ye the Lord: praise him, and magnify
    him for ever.
O all ye Powers of the Lord, bless ye the Lord:
    praise him, and magnify him for ever.
O ye Sun and Moon, bless ye the Lord: praise
    him, and magnify him for ever.
O ye Stars of heaven, bless ye the Lord: praise
    him, and magnify him for ever.
O ye Showers and Dew, bless ye the Lord:
    praise him, and magnify him for ever.
O ye Winds of God, bless ye the Lord: praise
    him, and magnify him for ever.
O ye Fire and Heat, bless ye the Lord: praise
    him, and magnify him for ever.
O ye Winter and Summer, bless ye the Lord:
    praise him, and magnify him for ever.
O ye Dews and Frosts, bless ye the Lord:
    praise him, and magnify him for ever.
O ye Frost and Cold, bless ye the Lord: praise
    him, and magnify him for ever.
O ye Ice and Snow, bless ye the Lord: praise
    him, and magnify him for ever.
O ye Nights and Days, bless ye the Lord: praise
    him, and magnify him for ever.
O ye Light and Darkness, bless ye the Lord:
    praise him, and magnify him for ever.
O ye Lightnings and Clouds, bless ye the Lord:
    praise him, and magnify him for ever.
O let the Earth bless the Lord: yea, let it praise
    him, and magnify him for ever.
O ye Mountains and Hills, bless ye the Lord:

praise him, and magnify him for ever.
O all ye Green Things upon the earth, bless
    ye the Lord: praise him, and magnify him
    for ever.
O ye Wells, bless ye the Lord: praise him, and
    magnify him for ever.
O ye Seas and Floods, bless ye the Lord: praise
    him, and magnify him for ever.
O ye Whales, and all that move in the waters,
    bless ye the Lord: praise him, and magnify
    him for ever.
O all ye Fowls of the air, bless ye the Lord:
    praise him, and magnify him for ever.
O all ye Beasts and Cattle, bless ye the Lord:
    praise him, and magnify him for ever.
O ye Children of Men, bless ye the Lord: praise
    him, and magnify him for ever.
O let Israel bless the Lord: praise him, and
    magnify him for ever.
O ye Priests of the Lord, bless ye the Lord:
    praise him, and magnify him for ever.
O ye Servants of the Lord, bless ye the Lord:
    praise him, and magnify him for ever.
O ye Spirits and Souls of the Righteous, bless
    ye the Lord: praise him, and magnify him
    for ever.
O ye holy and humble Men of heart, bless ye
    the Lord: praise him, and magnify him for
    ever.
O Ananias, Azarias, and Misael, bless ye the
    Lord: praise him, and magnify him for
    ever.
Glory be to the Father, and to the Son: and to
    the Holy Ghost;
As it was in the beginning, is now, and ever
    shall be: world without end. Amen.
    Benedicite, omnia opera, Book of Common Prayer

Spirit, give me of Thine abundance
Father, give me of Thy wisdom,
Son, give me in my need,
Jesus beneath the shelter of Thy shield.
    Carmina Gadelica

Now to the Father who created each creature,
Now to the Son who paid ransom for His
    people,
Now to the Holy Spirit, Comforter of might :
Shield and save us from every wound;
Be about the beginning and end of our race,
Be giving us to sing in glory,

In peace, in rest, in reconciliation,
Where no tear shall be shed, where death
    comes no more.
Where no tear shall be shed, where death
    comes no more.
    Carmina Gadelica

God, and Spirit, and Jesus,
From the crown of my head
To the soles of my feet;
Come I with my reputation,
Come I with my testimony,
Come I to Thee, Jesu –
Jesu, shelter me.
    Carmina Gadelica

O Eternal God! O Eternal Trinity! Through the union of Thy divine nature Thou hast made so precious the Blood of Thine Only-begotten Son! O eternal Trinity, Thou art as deep a mystery as the sea, in whom the more I seek, the more I find; and the more I find, the more I seek. For even immersed in the depths of Thee, my soul is never satisfied, always famished and hungering for Thee, eternal Trinity, wishing and desiring to see Thee, the True Light.

O eternal Trinity, with the light of understanding I have tasted and seen the depths of Thy mystery and the beauty of Thy creation. In seeing myself in Thee, I have seen that I will become like Thee. O eternal Father, from Thy power and Thy wisdom clearly Thou hast given to me a share of that wisdom which belongs to Thine Only-begotten Son. And truly hast the Holy Spirit, who proceedeth from Thee, Father and Son, given to me the desire to love Thee.

O eternal Trinity, Thou art my maker and I am Thy creation. Illuminated by Thee, I have learned that Thou hast made me a new creation through the Blood of Thine Only-begotten Son because Thou art captivated by love at the beauty of Thy creation.

O eternal Trinity, O Divinity, O unfathomable abyss, O deepest sea, what greater gift could Thou givest me then Thy very Self? Thou art a fire that burns eternally yet never consumes, a fire that consumes with Thy heat my self-love. Again and again Thou art the fire who taketh away all cold heartedness and illuminateth the mind by Thy light, the light with which Thou hast made me to know Thy truth.

By this mirrored light I know Thou are the highest good, a good above all good, a fortunate good, an incomprehensible good, an unmeasurable good, a beauty above all beauty, a wisdom above all wisdom, for Thou art wisdom itself, the food of angels, the fire of love that Thou givest to man.

Thou art the garment covering our nakedness. Thou feedest our family with Thy sweetness, a sweetness Thou art from which there is no trace of bitterness. O Eternal Trinity! Amen.

Catherine of Siena, 1347–80

Holy, holy, holy, Most Holy One, our fathers' Father, God of Abraham, God of Isaac, God of Jacob, God of the apostles, God of the prophets, God of virgins, God of those who live as they ought to live, God of those who believe, God and Father of our Lord Jesus Christ, Who is Thy Son: humbly we call upon Thee.

Humbly we make our prayers unto Thee, O Son, the Only Begotten, proceeding from the Father's lips before the world had taken shape, born – O mystery – from the womb of Mary, the holy virgin. Grant, we pray, that we may make progress in the spiritual life, that holy desire may increase in us and that we may be sound of heart; for souls reborn in the bath that brings salvation ought to stay immune from sin, the work of the flesh. We ask that there may be no stain on our faith, no perversity in our minds, no weakness in our devotion, no relaxation in our pursuit of good works or in our love. Rather, may we be strong members of Thy holy Church.

Unto Thee do we bend our knees and bow our heads, before whom the angels and archangels, the martyrs in their thousands, the choir of apostles and the glorious prophets jump for joy; to whom all the birds sing praises; whom every tongue confesses in heaven, on earth and in the world below; whose existence is felt even by things without feeling. Thou alone dost exist, and apart from Thee and outside of Thee no one exists.

We pray Thee, Lord, all-powerful Father, seen of none but the Son and served by angels and archangels; we pray Thee, Lord and Father, to grant us spiritual integrity, absolute purity, real devotion and holy, reasonable, pure,

impartial consciences, strengthened by faith against the wiles of the world. Arm our hearts against the dangers that come to us from the Devil and against the enticements of the flesh. May we not be caught in the deadly toils of the Enemy, the violent, the blood-loving: may we bear intact the seal of eternal salvation.

Drive away from us all the uncleanness of the world and all the insinuations of the Devil. May the Devil be caught in a trap and brought low; may we master him and put him out of our way, like Thy holy angel Raphael, who drove out of Thy servant Sara the wickedest of wicked spirits, Asmodeus.

As Thou didst stand by Tobias, so in Thy kindness stand by me. As Thou showed mercy to the three young men in the furnace and to Daniel, so, in Thy kindness, show mercy to us Thy servants.

Thou raised the dead to life, gavest sight to the blind, hearing to the deaf, speech to the dumb; Thou hast enabled the lame to walk and Thou madest lepers whole.

Deal with us Thy servants as Thou dealt with them, for we believe with all our minds that Thou wast born, that Thou didst suffer and that Thou wilt come to judge the living and the dead.

Stand by us, as Thou stoodest by Thine apostles in prison, by Thecla at the stake, by Paul under persecution and by Peter on the waves.

From the seven thrones where Thou sittest at the Father's right hand, look down on us and deliver us from eternal death and destruction. O supremely One: Father in the Son, Son in the Father, and Holy Spirit: through the Holy Spirit and with Him, in holy Church, honor, virtue, splendor, majesty, power, blessing and immortality are Thine now and always will be, for all eternity, through all the endless ages. Amen.

Cyprian, c.200–258

Holy Lord, holy Father, holy God, mine own holy God: who is greater than Thee? I give Thee thanks and praise, God of Abraham, God of Isaac, God of Jacob, God of our fathers, God of the apostles, God of the prophets, God of the martyrs.

God of the living, Thou hast existed before the world was given shape. Thou wilt come and judge the living and the dead. Thou art the true God; the ceremonial seat upon which Thou sittest is formed of cherubim and seraphim. Thou lookest out into the depths.

Thou seest everything before it comes into being; Thou hast the power to destroy things and to set them up again; Thou canst make the dry land green.

Thou rulest supreme, Lord, over all that is. Deliver me from this world and answer my prayer, as Thou answered the children of Israel in the land of Egypt – and even so, they did not trust Thee, or Thy servant Moses, either.

What do I not deserve for my sins? When Thou decidest to break the earth in pieces, in what cleft rock shall I hide from Thy might? To what mountain shall I say, "Fall on me," to what hill, "Hide me from the Lord I fear," when Thou comest to shatter the earth? Help me, Lord, I beg Thee. Do not judge me by what I have done: I have not obeyed Thy directions at all.

Answer my prayer, as Thou answered Jonas when he prayed to Thee from the whale's belly; yes, answer me as Thou answered him, and bring me from death to life. The Ninevites did penance in the Lord's sight in hair shirts and ashes. I too confess my sins to Thee; have mercy on me too, for Thou lovest men to repent.

David said: "Lord, for the honor of Thy name efface the record of my sins." I too beg Thy majesty to efface the record of mine.

Answer my prayer, as Thou answered when the three young men Ananias, Azarias and Misael, prayed to Thee from the red-hot furnace and Thou sent Thy angel with a shower of dew to frustrate the designs of Nebuchadnezzar, who was ruling the kingdom at the time; for Thou art the King of kings and Lord of lords, Thou alone hast immortality and dwellest in unapproachable light, which no man has ever seen or ever can see.

Answer my prayer, as Thou answered Daniel when he prayed unto Thee from the lion-pit and Thou sent Habacuc, the prophet, who brought him his dinner and said: "Eat the dinner that the Lord has sent thee"; to which Daniel replied: "The Lord will not forsake those who seek Him."

Answer my prayer, as Thou answered Tobias and Sara when they prayed unto Thee in the courtyard of their house and the angel Raphael offered their prayers for them. Answer my prayers too and admit my petitions to Thine holy presence; send Thine holy angel at once to take my sins away, as he took the unclean spirit from Sara, Raguel's daughter; and give light to my mind, as Thou gavest it to the eyes of Tobias.

Answer my prayer, as Thou answered Susanna when she fell into the hands of the elders and prayed for deliverance. Deliver me from this world, for purity of conscience is a delight unto Thee.

Answer my prayer, as Thou answered Ezechias, the king of Juda, and took away his sickness. Take away the sickness from my flesh, and increase my faith as Thou increased the length of his life by fifteen years. Deliver me from this world as Thou delivered Thecla from the amphitheater; deliver me from all weakness of the flesh.

I make my petitions unto Thee, majestic Father, who in this the last of the ages hast shown us Thy mercy by sending us Jesus Christ, Thy Son, our Lord and Savior, born of Mary the virgin through the Holy Spirit, as Gabriel said he would be – Jesus Christ, through whom Thou hast freed us from the danger of imminent death.

Unto Thee too I make my petitions, Son of the living God, who have done so many wonders. At Cana in Galilee Thou changed water into wine, for Israel's sake; Thou opened the eyes of the blind, gave hearing to the deaf, restored to paralytics the use of their limbs, loosened stammering tongues, healed the possessed, enabled the lame to run like deer, cured a woman of a flux of blood, raised the dead to life, walked on the sea itself and prescribed a limit for it; "To this point," Thou saidst, "thou shalt come, and here thou shalt break with all thy force." To Thee I pray, Son of the living God, for the forgiveness of all my sins, unto Thee who art in heaven, the Son in the Father, as the Father is in Thee, and was and will be eternally.

The throne upon which Thou sittest is formed of cherubim and seraphim. Around Thee angels stand, and archangels, their numbers numberless, in awe and fear of our glory and power. "Holy, holy, holy," they say, "is the Lord God of Sabaoth."

Thou Thyself madest a bargain with us when Thou saidst: "Ask, and the gift will come; knock, and the door shall be opened to you. Whatever you ask my Father in my name, I ask my Father to give you." I ask, then, and I expect the gift to come; I seek, and I expect to find; I knock, and I expect the door to be opened to me; I ask in Thy name, and I expect Thee to ask the Father to give me what I ask. For the honor of Thy name I am ready to offer the sacrifice of my blood and to undergo any torture that may be inflicted on me.

Thou hast always listened to me, Lord, Thou art my defender: defend me from my enemy. May Thine angel of light protect me, for Thou hast said: "What you confidently ask in prayer will be given you."

Men are all unreliable, but Thou art true to Thy word. Thou hast promised, Lord, and Thou hast the power, to give me that heavenly Sacrament of Thine which will make me fit to see the faces of Thy saints. May Thy Spirit work in me and Thy will be done in me, for I have promised to be Thine all the days of my life.

Thou gavest a supremely valid testimony when Thou suffered at Pontius Pilate's hands, Thou wast crucified, Thou went down to hell, Thou drewest death's sting. Death was beaten, our enemy the Devil was beaten.

Thou rose from the dead and appeared to Thine apostles, Thou sittest at the right hand of the Father, Thou wilt come to judge the living and the dead. Thou art assured of the mastery: deliver me from the power of him that would injure my soul. By the virtue of Thy name, deliver me from the power that works against me and give me the means of overcoming my enemy.

Thou art a powerful protector, and when our prayers and petitions come from the heart, Thou makest Thyself their advocate. Intercede for my sins day and night; bring my prayers before Thy Father.

And Thou, Lord, holy Father, be kind to me; look at my prayers in a favorable light, as Thou looked at Abel's offerings. In Thy kindness, deliver me from eternal fire and punishment and from all the other torments Thou hast in store for the wicked. I ask it through the good and blessed Jesus Christ, our Savior, through whom may praise and power and glory be Thine throughout all ages. Amen.

Cyprian, c. 200–258

Most exalted Trinity, divinity above all knowledge, whose goodness passes understanding, who guides Christians to divine wisdom; direct our way to the summit of your mystical oracles, most incomprehensible, most lucid and most exalted, where the simple and pure and unchangeable mysteries of theology are revealed in the darkness, clearer than light; a darkness that shines brighter than light, that invisibly and intangibly illuminates with splendors of inconceivable beauty the soul that sees not. Let this be my prayer.

Dionysius the Pseudo-Areopagite, c.500

O Lord God, almighty, immortal, invisible, the mysteries of whose being are unsearchable; accept, we beseech thee, our praises for the revelation which thou hast made of thyself, Father, Son, and Holy Spirit, three persons and one God; and mercifully grant that, ever holding fast this faith, we may magnify thy glorious name; who livest and reignest, one God, world without end.

John Dowden, 1840–1910

Glory to the Father, our Creator, and to the Son, our Savior, and to the Holy Spirit, our Restorer, unto unending and indelible eternity.

Ephraem, c.306–378

Unchanging and Unchangeable, before angelic eyes,
The Vision of the Godhead in its tranquil beauty lies;
And, like a city lighted up all gloriously within,
Its countless lusters glance and gleam, and sweetest worship win.
On the Unbegotten Father, awful well-spring of the Three,
On the Sole Begotten Son's coequal Majesty.
On Him eternally breathed forth from Father and from Son.
The spirits gaze with fixed amaze, and unreckoned ages run.

Chorus:
Myriad, myriad angels raise
Happy hymns of wondering praise,

Ever through eternal days,
Before the Holy Trinity,
One Undivided Three!

Still the Fountain of the Godhead giveth forth
    eternal being:
Still begetting, unbegotten, still His own
    perfection seeing,
Still limiting His own loved Self with His dear
    coequal Spirit,
No change comes o'er that blissful Life, no
    shadow passeth near it.
And beautiful dread Attributes, all manifold
    and bright,
Now thousands seem, now lose themselves in
    one self-living light;
And far in that deep Life of God, in harmony
    complete,
Like crowned kings, all opposite perfections
    take their seat.

And in that ungrowing vision nothing
    deepens, nothing brightens,
But the living Life of God perpetually lightens;
And created life is nothing but a radiant
    shadow fleeing
From the unapproached lusters of that
    Unbeginning Being;
Spirits wise and deep have watched that
    everlasting Ocean,
And never o'er its lucid field bath rippled
    faintest motion;
In glory undistinguished never have the Three
    seemed One,
Nor ever in divided streams the Single
    Essence run.

There reigns the Eternal Father, in His lone
    prerogatives,
And, in the Father's Mind, the Son, all self-
    existing, lives,
With Him, their mutual jubilee, that deepest
    depth of love,
Life-giving Life of two-fold source, the many
    gifted Dove!
O Bountiful! O Beautiful! can Power or
    Wisdom add
Fresh features to a life, so munificent and glad?
Can even uncreated Love, ye angels! give a hue
Which can ever make the Unchanging and
    Unchangeable look new?

The Mercy of the Merciful is equal to Their
    might,
As wondrous as Their Love, and as Their
    Wisdom bright!
As They, who out of nothing called creation
    at the first,
In everlasting purposes Their own design had
    nursed, –
As They, who in their solitude, Three Persons,
    once abode,
Vouchsafed of Their abundance to become
    creation's God, –
What They owed not to Themselves They
    stooped to owe to man,
And pledged Their glory to him, in an
    unimaginable plan.

See! deep within the glowing depth of that
    Eternal Light.
What change hath come, what vision new
    transports angelic sight?
A creature can it be, in uncreated bliss?
A novelty in God? Oh what nameless thing
    is this?
The beauty of the Father's Power is o'er it
    brightly shed,
The sweetness of the Spirit's Love is unction
    on its head;
In the wisdom of the Son it plays its wondrous
    part,
While it lives the loving life of a real Human
    heart!

A Heart that hath a Mother, and a treasure of
    red blood,
A Heart that man can pray to, and feed upon
    for food!
In the brightness of the Godhead is its
    marvelous abode,
A change in the Unchanging, creation
    touching God!
Ye spirits blest, in endless rest, who on that
    Vision gaze,
Salute the Sacred Heart with all your
    worshipful amaze,
And adore, while with ecstatic skill the Three
    in One ye scan,
The Mercy that hath planted there that blessed
    Heart of Man!

All tranquilly, all tranquilly, doth that Blissful

Vision last,
And Its brightness o'er immortalized creation
    will it cast;
Ungrowing and unfading, Its pure Essence
    doth it keep,
In the deepest of those depths where all are
    infinitely deep;
Unchanging and Unchangeable as It hath ever
    been,
As It was before that Human heart was there
    by angels seen,
So is it at this very hour, so will it ever be,
With that Human Heart within It, beating hot
    with love of me!

Chorus:
Myriad, myriad angels raise
Happy hymns of wondering praise,
Ever through eternal days,
Before the Holy Trinity,
One Undivided Three!
          Frederick William Faber, 1814–63

O Trinity supreme in being,
O Unity without beginning,
the hosts of angels sing thy praises,
trembling before thee.
Heaven, earth and the depths stand in awe of
    thee, all-holy Trinity:
men bless thee,
fire is thy servant,
all things created obey thee in fear.
        Festal Menaion, Greek Orthodox Church

You are holy, Lord, the only God,
and your deeds are wonderful.
You are strong.
You are great.
You are the most high.
You are almighty.
You, holy Father are King of heaven and earth.
You are three and one, Lord God, all Good.
You are Good, all Good, supreme Good,
Lord God, living and true.
You are love. You are wisdom.
You are humility. You are endurance.
You are rest. You are peace.
You are joy and gladness.
You are justice and moderation.
You are all our riches, and you suffice for us.
You are beauty.

You are gentleness.
You are our protector.
You are our guardian and defender.
You are our courage. You are our haven and
    our hope.
You are our faith, our great consolation.
You are our eternal life, great and wonderful
    Lord,
God almighty, merciful Savior.
          Francis of Assisi, 1181–1226

Holy, holy, holy, Lord God almighty, who is
and who was and who is to come. Let us praise
and exalt him above all for ever. Worthy are
you, O Lord our God, to receive praise, glory,
honor and blessing. Let us praise and exalt
him for ever. Worthy is the lamb that was
slain to receive power and divinity, wisdom
and strength, honor, glory and blessing. Let
us praise and exalt him for ever. Let us bless
the Father, the Son, and the Holy Spirit. Let us
praise and exalt him for ever. All the works of
the Lord, now bless the Lord, Let us praise and
exalt him for ever. Praise God, all of you his
servants, and you that fear him, both small and
great. Let us praise and exalt him for ever. Let
heaven and earth praise his glory, and every
creature that is in heaven, and on earth, and
under the earth. Let us praise and exalt him for
ever. Glory to the father and to the Son, and to
the Holy Spirit, as it was in the beginning, is
now, and shall be for ever. Amen.
          Francis of Assisi, 1181–1226

Lord, I am yours,
and I must belong to no one but you.
My soul is yours,
and must live only through you.
My will is yours,
and must love only for you.
I must love you as my first cause,
since I am from you.
I must love you as my goal and rest,
since I am for you.
I must love you more than my own being,
since my being comes from you.
I must love you more than myself,
since I am all yours and all in you. Amen.
          Francis de Sales, 1567–1622

Glory be to God in the highest,

Lord of heaven and earth,
who so loved the world
as to send his only Son
to redeem us from sin,
and to obtain for us everlasting life.
All praise be to you, most gracious God,
for your infinite mercies towards us in Jesus
    Christ our Lord.

John Hamilton, 1511–71

Holy, holy, holy! Lord God Almighty!
Early in the morning our song shall rise to Thee;
Holy, holy, holy, merciful and mighty!
God in three Persons, blessèd Trinity!

Holy, holy, holy! All the saints adore Thee,
Casting down their golden crowns around the
    glassy sea;
Cherubim and seraphim falling down before
    Thee,
Who was, and is, and evermore shall be.

Holy, holy, holy! though the darkness hide
    Thee,
Though the eye of sinful man Thy glory may
    not see;
Only Thou art holy; there is none beside Thee,
Perfect in power, in love, and purity.

Holy, holy, holy! Lord God Almighty!
All Thy works shall praise Thy Name, in earth,
    and sky, and sea;
Holy, holy, holy; merciful and mighty!
God in three Persons, blessèd Trinity!

Reginald Heber, 1783–1826

Let all the world in every corner sing,
"My God and King!"
The heavens are not too high,
His praise may thither fly:
The earth is not too low,
His praises there may grow,
The church with psalms must shout,
No door can keep them out:
But, above all, the heart
Must bear the longest part.
Let all the world in every corner sing,
"My God and King!"

George Herbert, 1593–1633

Preserve us, O God, in the faith of your saints, a

faith both tried and trusted. May we enjoy both
now and for ever the eternal love of the Father,
the abiding love of the Son and the indwelling
of love of the Holy Spirit, one God in glory and
majesty, world without end. Amen

Hilary of Poitiers, 315–367

Blessing and brightness, wisdom, thanksgiving,
Great power and might to the king who rules
    over all.
Glory and honor and goodwill,
Praise and the sublime song of minstrels,
Overflowing love from every heart to the king
    of heaven and earth.
To the chosen trinity has been joined
Before all, after all, universal blessing,
Blessing and everlasting blessing,
Blessing everlasting and blessing.

Irish prayer, 9th century

Thou brightness of eternal glory,
thou comfort of the pilgrim soul,
with thee is my tongue without voice,
and my very silence speaketh unto thee.
Come, oh come, for without thee I shall have
    not joyful day or hour;
for thou art my joy,
and without thee my table is empty.
Praise and glory be unto thee;
let my mouth, my soul, and all creatures
    together,
praise and bless thee.

Thomas à Kempis, 1379–1471

In confidence of your goodness and great
mercy, O Lord, I draw near to you, as a sick
person to the Healer, as one hungry and thirsty
to the Fountain of life, a creature to the Creator,
a desolate soul to my own tender Comforter.
Behold, in you is everything that I can or
ought to desire. You are my salvation and my
redemption, my Helper and my strength.

Thomas à Kempis, 1379–1471

We are enfolded in the Father, and we are
enfolded in the Son, and we are enfolded in
the Holy Spirit. And the Father is enfolded
in us, and the Son is enfolded in us, and the
Holy Spirit is enfolded in us: almightiness, all
wisdom, all goodness: one God, one Lord.

Julian of Norwich, 1342–c.1416

O Trinity, uncreated and without beginning,
O undivided Unity, three and one,
Father, Son and Spirit, a single God:
accept this our hymn from tongues of clay
as if from mouths of flame.
The Lenten Triodion, Greek Orthodox Church

Worthy of praise from every mouth, of confession from every tongue, of worship from every creature, is your glorious name, O Father, Son, and Holy Spirit, who created the world by the word of your power, and in love wonderfully redeemed it. Wherefore with angels, and archangels, and all the company of heaven, we adore and magnify your holy name, evermore praising you, and saying:
    Holy, Holy, Holy Lord God of hosts,
    Heaven and earth are full of your praises:
    Hosanna in the highest.
Nestorian Liturgy, 5th/6th century

O Father, my hope.
O Son, my refuge.
O Holy Spirit, my protection.
Holy Trinity, glory to thee.
Office of Compline, Eastern Orthodox Church

I bind to myself the name,
the strong name of the Trinity;
by invocation of the same,
The Three in One, and One in Three.
Of whom all nature has creation;
eternal Father, Spirit, Word:
Praise to the Lord of my salvation,
Salvation is of Christ the Lord.
Patrick, c.389–c.461

Lord Jesus, think on me
That I may sing above
To Father, Spirit, and to Thee
The strains of praise and love.
Synesius of Cyrene, 375–430,
translated by Allen W. Chatfield

Glory to the Father, who has woven garments of glory for the resurrection; worship to the Son, who was clothed in them at his rising; thanksgiving to the Spirit, who keeps them for all the Saints; one nature in three, to him be praise.
Syrian Orthodox liturgy

O Lord my God, most merciful, most secret, most present, most constant, yet changing all things, never new and never old, ever in action, yet ever quiet, creating, upholding, and perfecting all, who has anything but your gift? Or what can anyone say when he speaks about you? Yet, have mercy on us, O Lord, that we may speak to you, and praise your name.
Jeremy Taylor, 1613–67,
based on Augustine of Hippo, 354–430

We praise thee, O God: we acknowledge thee
    to be the Lord.
All the earth doth worship thee: the Father
    everlasting.
To thee all Angels cry aloud: the Heavens, and
    all the Powers therein.
To thee Cherubim and Seraphim: continually
    do cry,
Holy, Holy, Holy: Lord God of Sabaoth;
Heaven and earth are full of the Majesty: of
    thy glory.
The glorious company of the Apostles: praise
    thee.
The goodly fellowship of the Prophets: praise
    thee.
The noble army of Martyrs: praise thee.
The holy Church throughout all the world:
    doth acknowledge thee;
The Father: of an infinite Majesty;
Thine honorable, true: and only Son;
Also the Holy Ghost: the Comforter.
Thou art the King of Glory: O Christ.
Thou art the everlasting Son: of the Father.
When thou tookest upon thee to deliver
    man: thou didst not abhor the Virgin's
    womb.
When thou hadst overcome the sharpness
    of death: thou didst open the Kingdom of
    Heaven to all believers.
Thou sittest at the right hand of God: in the
    glory of the Father.
We believe that thou shalt come: to be our
    Judge.
We therefore pray thee, help thy servants:
    whom thou hast redeemed with thy
    precious blood.
Make them to be numbered with thy Saints: in
    glory everlasting.
O Lord, save thy people: and bless thine
    heritage.

Govern them: and lift them up for ever.
Day by day: we magnify thee;
And we worship thy Name: ever world
   without end.
Vouchsafe, O Lord: to keep us this day
   without sin.
O Lord, have mercy upon us: have mercy
   upon us.
O Lord, let thy mercy lighten upon us: as our
   trust is in thee.
O Lord, in thee have I trusted: let me
   never be confounded.

Te Deum Laudamus, 5th century,
The Book of Common Prayer

Glory be to you, O Lord, my Creator.
Glory be to you, Jesus, my Redeemer.
Glory be to you, Holy Spirit, my Sanctifier,
   Guide and Comforter.
All love, all glory, be to the high and
   undivided Trinity, whose deeds are
   inseparable, and whose worldwide rule is
   for ever; to you, and to you alone, and to
   your Son, and to the Holy Spirit, be glory
   for ever and ever.

Thomas Wilson, 1663–1755

Great, O Lord, is your kingdom, your power
   and your glory;
great also is your wisdom, your goodness,
   your justice, your mercy;
and for all these we bless you, and will
   magnify your name for ever and ever.

George Wither, 1588–1667

Praise and prayers to God the Father

THEREFORE, O Lord, thou art not only that
than which a greater cannot be conceived, but
thou art a being greater than can be conceived.
For, since it can be conceived that there is
such a being, if thou art not this very being, a
greater than thou can be conceived. But this is
impossible.

Anselm, 1033–1109

Father, a closed heart cannot keep out your
gaze. You open it as you please in mercy or in
justice. Nothing can hide from your heart.

Augustine of Hippo, 354–430

How great was your love for us, kind Father!
You did not spare your only-begotten Son but
surrendered him for the sake of us sinners!

Augustine of Hippo, 354–430

O Thou Who at all times and at every hour
art worshiped and glorified in heaven and on
earth, O Good God, long-suffering and plenteous in mercy; Who lovest the righteous and
hast mercy on sinners; Who callest all men to
salvation through the promise of good things
to come: Do Thou, O Lord, accept our prayers
at this hour, and in Thy goodness direct our
lives to Thy commandments. Sanctify our
souls and purify our bodies. Set aright our
thoughts and purify our intentions. Make our
minds chaste and sober, and deliver us from
all afflictions, evils, pains, and passions of the
soul. And compass us round about with Thy
holy angels, that, guarded and guided by their
array, we may attain to the unity of the faith
and to the knowledge of Thine unapproachable glory: For blessed art Thou unto the ages
of ages. Amen.

Basil the Great, 330–379

I bless you, O Lord,
Though I am powerless, you strengthen my
   weakness.
You stretch forth from above your helping hand
and bring me back unto yourself.
What shall I render to you, O all-good Master,
for all the good things you have done
and continue to do for me, the sinner?
I will cease not to bless you all the days of my
   life,
my creator,
my benefactor,
and my guardian.

Excerpt from a prayer to the Almighty God
and Father who loves humankind,
Basil the Great, 330–379

Almighty and everlasting God, who dost
govern all things in heaven and earth; Mercifully hear the supplications of thy people,
and grant us thy peace all the days of our life;
through Jesus Christ our Lord. Amen.

Book of Common Prayer,
The Second Sunday after the Epiphany

O Lord, you are our Father, and we are only clay from the earth. You are our Creator, and we are the work of your hands. You are our Shepherd, we are your flock. You are our Redeemer, we are your people whom you have bought. You are our God, we are your heritage.

John Calvin, 1509–64

Thanks be to Thee, Holy Father of Glory
Father kind, ever-loving, ever-powerful,
Because of all the abundance, favor, and
   deliverance
That Thou bestowest upon us in our need.
Whatever providence befalls us as thy
   children,
In our portion, in our lot, in our path,
Give to us with it the rich gifts of Thine hand
And the joyous blessing of Thy mouth.

Carmina Gadelica

My Lord, you are my love, my honor, my
   hope, and my refuge.
You are my life, my glory, my goal, my Master,
   my Father, my love.
Amen.

Anthony Mary Claret, 1807–70

O Lord God, in whom we live and move and have our being, open our eyes that we may behold your fatherly presence always with us. Draw our hearts to you with the power of your love. Teach us to be anxious about nothing, and when we have done what you have given us to do, help us, O God our Savior, to leave the issue to your wisdom. Take from us all doubt and mistrust. Lift our hearts up to you in heaven, and make us to know that all things are possible for us through your Son our Redeemer.

B.F. Westcott, 1825–1901

Praise and prayers to God the Son

O Jesus Christ, you are my Father, my merciful God, my great King, my good Shepherd, my only Master, my best helper, my beloved friend of overwhelming beauty, my living Bread, my eternal priest. You are my guide to my heavenly home, my one true light, my holy joy, my true way, my shining wisdom, my unfeigned simplicity, the peace and harmony of my soul, my perfect safeguard, my bounteous inheritance, my everlasting salvation.

Augustine of Hippo, 354–430

My loving Lord, Jesus Christ, why have I ever loved or desired anything else in my life but you, my God? Where was I when I was not in communion with you? From now on, I direct all my desires to be inspired by you and centered on you. I direct them to press forward for they have tarried long enough, to hasten towards their goal, to seek the one they yearn for.

Augustine of Hippo, 354–430

O Jesus, let him who does not love you be accursed, and filled with bitterness. O gentle Jesus, let every worthy feeling of mine show you love, take delight in you and admire you. O God of my heart and my inheritance, Christ Jesus, may my heart mellow before the influence of your spirit and may you live in me. May the flame of your love burn in my soul. May it burn incessantly on the altar of my heart. May it glow in my innermost being. May it spread its heat into the hidden recesses of my soul and on the day of my consummation may I appear before you consumed in your love.

Augustine of Hippo, 354–430

For the gift of his Spirit,
   praise be to Christ;
for the universal church,
   praise be to Christ;
for the means of grace,
   praise be to Christ;
for the hope of glory,
   praise be to Christ;
for the triumphs of the gospel,
   praise be to Christ;
for the lives of his saints,
   praise be to Christ;
in joy and in sorrow,
   praise be to Christ;
in life and in death,
   praise be to Christ;
now and to the end of the age,
   praise be to Christ.

Author unknown

Soul of Christ, sanctify me.
Body of Christ, save me.
Blood of Christ, inebriate me.
Water from the side of Christ, wash me.
Passion of Christ, strengthen me.
O good Jesus, hear me.
Hide me within your wounds
and never allow me to be separated from you.
From the wicked enemy defend me.
In the hour of my death call me,
and bid me come to you,
so that with your saints I may praise you
for ever and ever.

Anima Christi, 14th century,
attributed to Ignatius Loyola

Christ be with me, Christ within me,
Christ behind me, Christ before me,
Christ beside me, Christ to win me,
Christ to comfort and restore me,
Christ beneath me, Christ above me,
Jesus, as a mother you gather your people to
  you:
You are gentle with us as a mother with her
  children;
Often you weep over our sins and our pride:
tenderly you draw us from hatred and
  judgment.
You comfort us in sorrow and bind up our
  wounds:
in sickness you nurse us,
and with pure milk you feed us.
Jesus, by your dying we are born to new life:
by your anguish and labor we come forth in
  joy.
Despair turns to hope through your sweet
  goodness:
through your gentleness we find comfort in
  fear.
Your warmth gives life to the dead:
your touch makes sinners righteous.
Lord Jesus, in your mercy heal us:
in your love and tenderness remake us.
In your compassion bring grace and
  forgiveness:
for the beauty of heaven may your love
  prepare us.

Anselm, 1033–1109

Jesus, Thou Joy of loving hearts,
Thou Fount of life, Thou Light of men,

From the best bliss that earth imparts
We turn unfilled to Thee again.

Bernard of Clairvaux, 1090–1153

Jesus, the very thought of thee
With sweetness fills the breast;
But sweeter far thy face to see,
And in thy presence rest.

Bernard of Clairvaux, 1090–1153,
translated by Edward Caswall, 1814–78

I heard the voice of Jesus say, "Come unto Me
  and rest;
Lay down, thou weary one, lay down Thy
  head upon My breast."
I came to Jesus as I was, weary and worn and
  sad;
I found in Him a resting place, and He has
  made me glad.

I heard the voice of Jesus say, "Behold, I freely
  give
The living water; thirsty one, stoop down, and
  drink, and live."
I came to Jesus, and I drank of that life giving
  stream;
My thirst was quenched, my soul revived, and
  now I live in Him.

I heard the voice of Jesus say, "I am this dark
  world's light;
Look unto Me, thy morn shall rise, and all thy
  day be bright."
I looked to Jesus, and I found in Him my star,
  my sun;
And in that light of life I'll walk, till traveling
  days are done.

Horatius Bonar, 1808–82

Lord Jesus Christ, pierce my soul with your love
so that I may always long for you alone, who
are the bread of angels and the fulfillment of
the soul's deepest desires. May my heart always
hunger and feed on you, so that my soul may
be filled with the sweetness of your presence.
May my soul thirst for you, who are the source
of life, wisdom, knowledge, light and all the
riches of God our Father. May I always seek and
find you, think about you, speak to you and do
everything for the honor and glory of your holy
name. Be always my hope, my peace, my refuge

and my help in whom my heart is rooted so that I may never be separated from you.

Bonaventure, c.1221–74

Almighty God, who hast given us grace at this time with one accord to make our common supplications unto thee; and dost promise, that when two or three are gathered together in thy Name thou wilt grant their requests; Fulfill now, O Lord, the desires and petitions of thy servants, as may be most expedient for them; granting us in this world knowledge of thy truth, and in the world to come life everlasting. Amen.

John Chrysostom, c.347–407

My Jesus, there is one thing I ask that I know
   you will grant.
Yes, my Jesus, I ask you for love,
for great flames of that fire
you brought down from heaven to earth.
May that sacred fire enkindle, burn, melt and
   pour me
into the mould of God's will.
Amen.

Anthony Mary Claret, 1807–70

Lord Jesus Christ, draw our hearts to yourself; bind them together in inseparable love, that we may abide in you, and you in us, and that the everlasting covenant between us may remain certain for ever. O wound our hearts with the darts of fire of your piercing love. Let them pierce through all our sloth, that we may become whole and sound. Let us have no lover but you alone; let us seek no joy or comfort except in you.

Miles Coverdale, 1488–1568

Alleluia! sing to Jesus! His the scepter, His the
   throne.
Alleluia! His the triumph, His the victory
   alone.
Hark! the songs of peaceful Zion thunder like
   a mighty flood.
Jesus out of every nation has redeemed us by
   His blood.

William C. Dix, 1837–98

Litany of the Holy Name of Jesus
Lord, have mercy on us
Christ, have mercy on us.
Lord, have mercy on us.
Jesus, hear us.
Jesus, graciously hear us.

God, the Father of heaven,[1]
God, the Son, Redeemer of the world,
God, the Holy Spirit,
Holy Trinity, one God,
Jesus, Son of the living God,
Jesus, splendor of the Father,
Jesus, brightness of eternal light,
Jesus, king of glory,
Jesus, the sun of justice,
Jesus, son of the Virgin Mary,
Jesus, amiable,
Jesus, admirable,
Jesus, the powerful God,
Jesus, father of the world to come,
Jesus, angel of the great council,
Jesus, most powerful,
Jesus, most patient,
Jesus, most obedient,
Jesus, meek and humble of heart,
Jesus, lover of chastity,
Jesus, lover of us,
Jesus, God of peace,
Jesus, author of life,
Jesus, model of all virtues,
Jesus, zealous for souls,
Jesus, our God,
Jesus, our refuge,
Jesus, father of the poor,
Jesus, treasure of the faithful
Jesus, good shepherd,
Jesus, true light,
Jesus, eternal wisdom,
Jesus, infinite goodness,
Jesus, our way and our life,
Jesus, joy of angels,
Jesus, king of patriarchs,
Jesus, master of apostles,
Jesus, teacher of the evangelists,
Jesus, strength of martyrs,
Jesus, light of confessors
Jesus, purity of virgins,
Jesus, crown of all saints,
Be merciful, Spare us, O Jesus.
Be merciful, Graciously hear us, O Jesus

From all evil,[2]
From all sin,
From Thy wrath,
From the snares of the devil,
From the spirit of fornication,
From eternal death,
From a neglect of Thy inspirations,
By the mystery of Thy holy Incarnation,
By Thy nativity,
By Thy infancy,
By Thy most divine life,[1]
By Thy labors,
By Thy agony and passion,
By Thy cross and dereliction,
By Thy languors,
By Thy death and burial,
By Thy resurrection,
By Thy ascension,
By Thy institution of the Most Holy
    Eucharist,[2]
By Thy joys,
By Thy glory,
Lamb of God, Who takes away the sins of the
    world, Spare us, O Jesus!
Lamb of God, Who takes away the sins of the
    world, Hear us, O Jesus!
Lamb of God, Who takes away the sins of the
    world, Have mercy on us, O Jesus!
Jesus, hear us.
Jesus, graciously hear us.

Let us pray.
O, Lord Jesus Christ, Who has said, 'Ask and
you shall receive, seek and you shall find,
knock and it shall be opened unto you!' mercifully attend to our supplications and grant us
the gift of your divine charity, that we may ever
love you with our whole heart and never desist
from Thy praise.
    Give us, O Lord, a perpetual respect and
love of Thy holy name; for you never cease to
govern those whom you instruct in the solidity
of Thy love. Who lives and reigns, one God,
world without end. Amen.

Responses:
[1] Have mercy on us.
[2] Deliver us, O Jesus.
                        Eastern Orthodox Church

Set our hearts on fire with love to you, O
Christ our God, that in its flame we may love
you with all our heart, with all our mind, with
all our soul and with all our strength and our
neighbors as ourselves, so that, keeping your
commandments, we may glorify you, the giver
of all good gifts.
                        Eastern Orthodox Church

It is right that man should acknowledge your
    divinity,
it is right for heavenly beings to worship your
    humanity.
The heavenly beings were amazed to see how
    small you became,
and earthly ones to see how exalted.
                        Ephrem the Syrian, c.306–378

Lord Jesus Christ, you said that you are the
    Way, the Truth, and the Life.
Help us not to stray from you, for you are the
    Way;
nor to distrust you, for you are the Truth;
nor to rest on any other than you, as you are
    the Life.
You have taught us what to believe, what to
    do, what to hope, and where to take our
    rest.
Give us grace to follow you, the Way, to learn
    from you, the Truth, and live in you, the
    Life.
                        Desiderius Erasmus, 1467–1536

We adore Thee, most holy Lord Jesus Christ,
here and in all Thy churches that are in the
whole world, and we bless Thee; because
by Thy Holy Cross Thou hast redeemed the
World. Amen.
                        Francis of Assisi, 1181–1226

O love eternal,
my soul needs and chooses you eternally.
Oh, come Holy Spirit,
and inflame our hearts with your love.
To love – or to die.
To die – and to love.
To die to all other love
in order to live in Jesus' love,
so that we may not die eternally.
But that we may live in your eternal love,
O Savior of our souls,

we eternally sing,
'Live, Jesus.
Jesus, I love.
Live, Jesus, whom I love.
Jesus, I love,
Jesus who lives and reigns forever and ever.
    Amen.'
               Francis de Sales, 1567–1622. Concluding
    prayer in his book Treatise on the Love of God

Who is like you, Jesus, sweet Jesus?
You are the light of those who are spiritually
    lost.
You are the life of those who are spiritually
    dead.
You are the liberation of those who are
    imprisoned with guilt.
You are the glory of those who hate
    themselves.
You are the guardian of those who are
    paralyzed by fear.
You are the guide of those who are bewildered
    by falsehood.
You are the peace of those who are in turmoil.
You are the prince of those who yearn to be
    led.
You are the priest of those who seek truth.
               Johann Freylinghausen, 1670–1739

Lord Jesus Christ, I adore you,
you wept over Lazarus and raised him from
    the dead;
I beg that I may gain eternal life,
and that you will cause to spring up within me
your fountain of living water,
gushing out for eternal life.
Lord Jesus Christ, I adore you,
transfixed to the cross,
wine and myrrh to quench your thirst:
I beg that your wound may be transformed
into a medicine for my soul.
Lord Jesus Christ, I adore you, laid in the tomb:
May your death be life to me.
               Gallican Formularies

Blessed is your love for mankind, my Lord
and Savior Jesus Christ. Why do you forsake
me? You alone are without sin, and your name
shows kindness and love for mankind. Show
me compassion, for you alone love mankind.
               Gregory the Illuminator, d.325

JESU is in my heart. His sacred name
Is deeply carved there; but th' other week
A great affliction broke the little frame,
Ev'n all to pieces; which I went to seek:
And first I found the corner where was J,
After, where ES, and next where U was
    graved.
When I had got these parcels, instantly
I sat me down to spell them, and perceived
That to my broken heart he was I ease you
And to my whole is JESU.
               George Herbert, 1593–1633

Lord, who am I, that You should desire so
    much to be loved by me?
And whom shall I love, if I love not You, my
    Jesus?
Here I am, Lord; dispose of me as You please.
Give me Your love; I ask nothing more.
Make me all Yours before I die.
               Alphonsus Liguori, 1696–1787

"I was an hungered and you fed me,"
you who clothed the naked ones;
"I was thirsty and you gave me drink,"
you who took the strangers in;
"You came to me in the prison,"
you who think of all good things.
Prostrate, I fall before you, Savior,
make me worthy of these words;
Keep me always in peace,
faithful to your Word.
               Grigor Magistros, c.990–1059

Christ, God of Gods, have mercy on me.
In iniquity did my mother give birth to me. I
    beg you, Savior, have mercy on me.
Wounded in sin, I fall down before you,
    Savior. Do not overlook me. Have mercy
    on me.
Sighing, the tax-collector received forgiveness
    in the temple. In his very words I too call
    out, "Have mercy on me, God."
The thief cried upon the cross: "Remember
    me, Lord." In his very words I too call out,
    "Have mercy on me, God."
Pleading, the prodigal son begged you,
    "Father, I have sinned against heaven and
    before you." In his very words I too call
    out, "Have mercy on me, God."
With the poor, Lord, grant us sobriety, by the

example of Lazarus, so that in voluntary
poverty we might be worthy with him of
the kingdom of heaven. Hear us and have
mercy on us, Christ God.

In place of the bread of deprivation, you
granted him the bread of immortality.
And contrary to the uncompassionate rich
man, you received Lazarus into the bosom
of Abraham. Hear us and have mercy on
us, Christ God.

Enlighten the eyes of our heart so we may
receive the mercy that comes from you,
Lord of mercy, lest like the rich man in the
fiery furnace, we ask to be refreshed with a
fingertip of water. Hear us and have mercy
on us, Christ God.

Together with the wakeful ones in heaven,
glorify the almighty Father, God who has
no beginning!

With angelic voice, glorify the only-begotten
Son, begotten of the Father!

And with joyous sound, glorify the Holy
Spirit, the Restorer, with unceasing voice!

God without beginning and heavenly king,
glorified by the immortal heavenly hosts,
we bless you, O Father without beginning.

You humbled yourself from the heights for
our salvation, O Liberator of bonds and
Healer of our souls. We praise you, O only-
begotten Son.

Consubstantial with the Father and glorified
with the Only-begotten, distributor of gifts
and bestower of mercy, You we glorify,
true Holy Spirit.

O Wisdom of the Father, who shined the
divine light of your Word upon the
darkness of ignorance enclosing the world,
enlighten us also.

You signified in the rich man and Lazarus
an example of the universal judgment
by handing them the contrary fates they
received.

And so we shall ask you, Lord, to save us
from the fire of sin and suffering, that we
might rest in the bosom of the righteous
patriarch.

With him, we too join the voice of the choirs
of angels singing glory in the highest to the
indivisible Holy Trinity.

Mesrob Mashtots, 5th century

Born as a son,
led forth as a lamb,
sacrificed as a sheep,
buried as a man,
he rose from the dead as a God,
for he was by nature God and man.
He is all things:
he judges, and so he is Law;
he teaches, and so he is Wisdom;
he saves, and so he is Grace;
he begets, and so he is Father;
he is begotten, and so he is Son;
he suffers, and so he is Sacrifice;
he is buried, and so he is man;
he rises again, and so he is God.
This is Jesus Christ,
to whom belongs glory for all ages.

Melito of Sardis, d.189

O my sweet Savior Christ, who in your undeserved love towards humankind so kindly suffered
the painful death of the cross, do not allow me to
be cold or lukewarm in love again towards you.

Thomas More, 1478–1535

How sweet the Name of Jesus sounds
In a believer's ear!
It soothes his sorrows, heals his wounds,
And drives away his fear.

It makes the wounded spirit whole,
And calms the troubled breast;
'Tis manna to the hungry soul,
And to the weary rest.

John Newton, 1725–1807

If ask'd, what of Jesus I think?
Though still my best thoughts are but poor,
I say, He's my meat and my drink,
My life, and my strength, and my store;
My shepherd, my husband, my friend,
My Savior from sin and from thrall;
My hope from beginning to end,
My portion, my Lord, and my all.

John Newton, 1725–1807

O Jesus, the most-good goodness,
I have done no good before you;
but grant that I may make a beginning
because of your goodness.

Nikodemos of the Holy Mountain, 18th century

At the Name of Jesus, every knee shall bow,
Every tongue confess Him King of glory now;
'Tis the Father's pleasure we should call Him
    Lord,
Who from the beginning was the mighty
    Word.

Caroline Maria Noel, 1817–77

Christ in quiet, Christ in danger,
Christ in hearts of all that love me,
Christ in mouth of friend and stranger.

Breastplate of Patrick, c.389–c.461

All hail the power of Jesus' Name! Let angels
    prostrate fall;
Bring forth the royal diadem, and crown Him
    Lord of all.
Bring forth the royal diadem, and crown Him
    Lord of all.

Edward Perronet, 1726–92

To thee, O Jesu, I direct my eyes;
to thee my hands,
to thee my humble knees;
to thee my heart shall offer sacrifice;
to thee my thoughts, who my thoughts only
    see;
to thee my self – my self and all I give;
to thee I die;
to thee I only live.

Attributed to Walter Raleigh, 1552–1618

Jesus, receive my heart,
and bring me to your love.
All my desire you are.
Kindle fire within me,
that I may receive your love,
and see your face in bliss
which will never cease,
in heaven with never an ending.

Richard Rolle, 1290–1349

My Christ! My Christ! My shield, my encircler!
Each day, each light, each dark.
My Christ! My Christ! My shield, my encircler!
Each day, each light, each dark.
Be near me, uphold me, my treasure, my
    triumph,
In my lying, in my standing, in my watching,
    in my sleeping.
Jesus, Son of Mary! My helper, my encircler!

Jesus, Son of David! My strength everlasting!
Jesus, Son of Mary! My helper, my encircler!
Jesus, Son of David! My strength everlasting!

Traditional Scottish prayer

Unite me to thyself, O adorable Victim … life
giving heavenly bread feed me; sanctify me
… reign in me, transform me to thyself; live
in me, let me live in thee, let me adore thee in
thy life giving Sacrament as my God … listen
to thee as to my Master … obey thee as my
King … imitate thee as my model … follow
thee as my shepherd … love thee as my Father
… seek thee as my physician who will heal
all the maladies of my soul… be indeed my
Way, Truth and Life… sustain me O Heavenly
Manna through the desert of this world, till I
shall behold thee unveiled in thy Glory.

Elizabeth Ann Seton, 1774–1821

Lord Jesus, make yourself to me
A living, bright reality.
More present to faith's vision keen
Than any outward object seen.

Hudson Taylor, 1832–1905

O Jesus, Whose Face is the sole beauty that
ravishes my heart, I may not behold here upon
earth the sweetness of Thy Glance, nor feel
the ineffable tenderness of Thy Kiss. I bow to
Thy Will – but I pray Thee to imprint in me
Thy Divine Likeness, and I implore Thee so to
inflame me with Thy Love, that it may quickly
consume me and I may soon reach the Vision
of Thy glorious Face in Heaven. Amen.

Thérèse of Lisieux, 1873–97

Prayers to and for God the Holy Spirit

Lord Jesus, may the fire of your Holy Spirit
consume in us all that displeases you, and
kindle in our hearts a burning zeal for the
service of our kingdom; through our Savior
Jesus Christ.

Ancient collect

Breathe in me, Holy Spirit,
that my thoughts may all be holy.
Move in me, Holy Spirit,
that my work, too, may be holy.

Attract my heart, Holy Spirit,
that I may love only what is holy.
Strengthen me, Holy Spirit,
that I may defend all that is holy.
Protect me, Holy Spirit,
that I may always be holy.

Augustine of Hippo, 354–430

Holy Spirit, powerful Consoler, sacred Bond of
the Father and the Son, Hope of the afflicted,
descend into my heart and establish in it your
loving dominion. Enkindle in my tepid soul
the fire of your Love so that I may be wholly
subject to you. We believe that when you dwell
in us, you also prepare a dwelling for the Father
and the Son. Deign, therefore, to come to me,
Consoler of abandoned souls, and Protector
of the needy. Help the afflicted, strengthen the
weak, and support the wavering. Come and
purify me. Let no evil desire take possession of
me. You love the humble and resist the proud.
Come to me, glory of the living, and hope of
the dying. Lead me by your grace that I may
always be pleasing to you. Amen.

Augustine of Hippo, 354–430

Come, Holy Ghost, our souls inspire,
And lighten with celestial fire.
Thou the anointing Spirit art,
Who dost thy sevenfold gifts impart.

Thy blessed unction from above,
Is comfort, life, and fire of love.
Enable with perpetual light
The dullness of our blinded sight.

Anoint and cheer our soiled face
With the abundance of thy grace.
Keep far our foes, give peace at home;
Where thou art guide, no ill can come.

Teach us to know the Father, Son,
And thee, of both, to be but One;
That, through the ages all along,
This may be our endless song:
  Praise to thy eternal merit,
  Father, Son, and Holy Spirit.

Author unknown. The Book of Common Prayer,
translated by John Cosin, 1594–1672, The Ordinal

Come down, O love divine, seek Thou this

soul of mine,
And visit it with Thine own ardor glowing.
O Comforter, draw near, within my heart
  appear,
And kindle it, Thy holy flame bestowing.

O let it freely burn, til earthly passions turn
To dust and ashes in its heat consuming;
And let Thy glorious light, shine ever on my
  sight,
And clothe me round, the while my path
  illuming.

Let holy charity, mine outward vesture be,
And lowliness become mine inner clothing;
True lowliness of heart, which takes the
  humbler part,
And o'er its own shortcomings weeps with
  loathing.

And so the yearning strong, with which the
  soul will long,
Shall far outpass the power of human telling;
For none can guess its grace, till he become
  the place
Wherein the Holy Spirit makes His dwelling.

Bianco of Siena, c.1367–1434,
translated by Richard F. Littledale

O God, forasmuch as without thee we are not
able to please thee; Mercifully grant, that thy
Holy Spirit may in all things direct and rule our
hearts; through Jesus Christ our Lord. Amen.

The Book of Common Prayer, Collect for the
Nineteenth Sunday after Trinity

O Lord, who hast taught us that all our doings
without charity are nothing worth; Send thy
Holy Ghost and pour into our hearts that most
excellent gift of charity, the very bond of peace
and of all virtues, without which whosoever
liveth is counted dead before thee; Grant this
for thine only Son Jesus Christ's sake.

The Book of Common Prayer, Collect for the
Sunday called Quinquagesima, or the
next Sunday before Lent

I beg you, Lord, because of my human frailty,
To send me your Spirit to enlighten me and
  enkindle your love within me,
To guide me and lead me along the right path

of Jesus Christ.
Amen.

Anthony Mary Claret, 1807–70

Almighty God, Who has given us the commandment to pray for the gift of the Holy Ghost: Most heartily we beseech Thee, through Jesus Christ our Advocate, to grant us Thy Holy Spirit, that He may quicken our hearts by Thy saving Word, and lead us into all truth, that He may guide, instruct, enlighten, govern, comfort and sanctify us unto, everlasting life; through the same Jesus Christ, Thy Son, our Lord. Amen.

*The Common Service Book of
the Lutheran Church, 1917*

O Lord God almighty, we thank you with all our hearts, for feeding our souls with the body and blood of your most dear Son. We beseech you to so illumine our minds with your Holy Spirit, that we may daily increase in faith in you, in certainty of hope in your promises, and fervency of love to you and our neighbor, to the glory and praise of your holy name.

Miles Coverdale, 1488–1568

O Holy Spirit of God, who with your holy
    breath cleanses the hearts and minds of
    people,
        comforting them when they are in
            sorrow,
        leading them when they are out of the
            way,
        kindling them when they are cold,
        knitting them together when they are at
            variance,
        and enriching them with many gifts;
        by whose working all things live:
We beseech you to maintain and daily increase
    the gifts which you have given us;
        that with your light before us and
            within us we may pass through
            this world without stumbling and
            without straying;
        who lives and reigns with the Father
            and the Son, for ever.

Desiderius Erasmus, 1467–1536

In the eye of the Father who created me,
In the eye of the Son who purchased me,

In the eye of the Spirit who cleansed me,
In friendship and affection.
Through Thine own Anointed One, O God,
Bestow upon us fullness in our need,
Love towards God,
The affection of God,
The smile of God,
The wisdom of God.
The grace of God,
The fear of God,
And the will of God
To do in the world of the Three,
As angels and saints
Do in heaven;
Each shade and light,
Each day and night,
Each time in kindness,
Give Thou us Thy Spirit.

Gaelic

Breathe on me, Breath of God;
Fill me with life anew,
That I may love what thou dost love,
And do what thou wouldst do.

Breathe on me, Breath of God,
Till I am wholly thine,
Until this earthly part of me
Glows with thy fire divine.

Breathe on me, Breath of God,
So shall I never die,
But live with thee the perfect life
Of thine eternity.

Edwin Hatch, 1835–89

Litany to the Holy Spirit
In the hour of my distress,
When temptations me oppress,
And when I my sins confess,
    Sweet Spirit comfort me!

When I lie within my bed,
Sick in heart and sick in head,
And with doubts discomforted,
    Sweet Spirit comfort me!

When the house doth sigh and weep,
And the world is drowned in sleep,
Yet mine eyes the watch do keep,
    Sweet Spirit comfort me!

When the artless Doctor sees
No one hope but of his fees,
And his skill runs on the lees,
   Sweet Spirit comfort me!

When the Tempter me pursu'th
With the sins of all my youth,
And half damns me with untruth,
   Sweet Spirit comfort me!

When the passing bell doth toll,
And the furies in a shoel
Come to fright a parting soul,
   Sweet Spirit, comfort me!

When the tapers now burn blue,
And the comforters are few,
And that number more than true,
   Sweet Spirit, comfort me!

When, God, knows, I'm tossed about,
Either with despair, or doubt;
Yet before the glass be out,
   Sweet Spirit, comfort me!

When the judgment is revealed,
And that opened which was sealed,
When to thee I have appealed,
   Sweet Spirit comfort me!

Robert Herrick, 1591–1679

O God, who has taught us that love is the fulfilling of the law: Help us by your Holy Spirit so to love you that we may always seek to do your holy will; and so to love our neighbor that we may in all things do to others as we would that they should do to us; for the sake of him who loved us and gave himself for us, your Son Jesus Christ our Lord.

W.W. How, 1823–97

O thou who camest from above,

   O God the Holy Spirit, most loving Comforter of the fainthearted, I pray that you will always turn what is evil in me into good and what is good into what is better; turn my mourning into joy, my wandering feet into the right path, my ignorance into knowledge of your truth, my lukewarmness into zeal, my fear into love, all my material good into a spiritual gift, all my earthly desires into heavenly desires, all that is transient into what lasts for ever, everything human into what is divine, everything created and finite into that sovereign and immeasurable good, which you yourself are, O my God and Savior.

Thomas à Kempis, 1379–1471

Holy Spirit, divine Consoler, I adore You as my true God, with God the Father and God the Son. I adore You and unite myself to the adoration You receive from the angels and saints.
I give You my heart and I offer my ardent thanksgiving for all the grace which You never cease to bestow on me.
O Giver of all supernatural gifts, … I beg You to visit me with Your grace and Your love and to grant me the gift of holy fear, so that it may act on me as a check to prevent me from falling back into my past sins, for which I beg pardon.
Grant me the gift of piety, so that I may serve You for the future with increased fervor, follow with more promptness Your holy inspirations, and observe Your divine precepts with greater fidelity.
Grant me the gift of knowledge, so that I may know the things of God and, enlightened by Your holy teaching, may walk, without deviation, in the path of eternal salvation.
Grant me the gift of fortitude, so that I may overcome courageously all the assaults of the devil, and all the dangers of this world which threaten the salvation of my soul.
Grant me the gift of counsel, so that I may choose what is more conducive to my spiritual advancement and may discover the wiles and snares of the tempter.
Grant me the gift of understanding, so that I may apprehend the divine mysteries and by contemplation of heavenly things detach my thoughts and affections from the vain things of this miserable world.
Grant me the gift of wisdom, so that I may rightly direct all my actions, referring them to God as my last end; so that, having loved Him and served Him in this life, I may have the happiness of possessing Him eternally in the next.
Amen.

Alphonsus Liguori, 1696–1787

Most Holy Spirit, the Paraclete, Father of the poor, Comforter of the afflicted, Light of hearts, Sanctifier of souls; behold me prostrate in Thy presence.

I adore Thee with profoundest homage: I bless Thee a thousand times, and with the Seraphim who stand before Thy throne, I also say: "Holy, holy, holy."

I firmly believe that Thou art eternal, consubstantial with the Father and the Divine Son. I hope in Thy goodness that Thou wilt deign to save and sanctify my soul. I love Thee, o Divine Love, with all my affections above all the things of this world, because Thou art Infinite Goodness, alone worthy of all love.

And since in my ingratitude and blindness to Thy holy inspirations, I have so often offended Thee by my sins, with tears in my eyes I beg Thy pardon a thousand times, and am more sorry for having offended Thee, the Sovereign Good, than for any other evil.

I offer Thee this most cold heart of mine, and I pray Thee to pierce it with a ray of Thy light, and with a spark of Thy fire, which shall melt the hard ice of my iniquities.

Thou who didst fill the soul of the most holy Mary with immense graces, and didst inflame the hearts of the Apostles with holy zeal, inflame, I beseech Thee, my heart also with Thy love.

Thou art the Divine Spirit; give me courage against all evil spirits.

Thou art Fire; enkindle in me Thy love.

Thou art Light; enlighten my mind with the knowledge of eternal things.

Thou art the Dove; give me innocence of life.

Thou art the gentle Breeze; disperse the storms of my passions. Thou art the Tongue; teach me how to bless Thee always. Thou art the Cloud; shelter me under the shadow of Thy protection.

And lastly, Thou art the Giver of all heavenly gifts; animate me, I beseech Thee, with Thy grace; sanctify me with Thy charity; enlighten me with Thy wisdom; adopt me by Thy goodness as Thy son, and save me in Thy infinite mercy; so that I may ever bless Thee, praise Thee, and love Thee; first during this life on earth, and then in heaven for all eternity. Amen.

Alphonsus Liguori, 1696–1787

Come, Creating Spirit,
Visit the minds of those who are yours,
Fill with the highest grace
The hearts of those whom you have created.

You are called Comforter and Protector,
You are God's greatest gift,
The power of life, fire, mercy,
And ointment for the soul.

You are the sevenfold gift,
The right finger of the Father,
The fulfillment of the Father's promise,
The preaching tongue.

Kindle a light in the senses,
Fill the heart with love,
Strengthen our weak bodies
With the power of patience.

Defend from the enemy,
Give peace with ourselves,
Lead us wisely,
Protect against all evil.

All knowing comes from you.
Give, that we learn to know the father, and the son,
And you as well, Spirit,
That we may believe eternally.

Glory be to the Father and to the Son,
Who rose from the dead,
And to you, Comforter and Protector,
In eternity eternally.
Amen.

Attributed to Hrabanus Maurus, c.784–856

The prayers I make will then be sweet indeed
    If thou the Spirit give by which I pray:
    My unassisted heart is barren clay,
That of its native self can nothing feed.

Michelangelo, 1475–1564

Holy Lord Jesus, the heavenly Vine of God's own planting, I beseech Thee, reveal Thyself to my soul. Let the Holy Spirit, not only in thought, but in experience, give me to know all that Thou, the Son of God, art to me as the true Vine.

Andrew Murray, 1828–1917

O Holy Ghost that givest grace where Thou wilt, come into me and ravish me to Thee; change the nature that Thou hast made with Thy honeyed gifts, that my soul fulfilled with Thy liking joy, may despise and cast away all things in this world. Spiritual gifts she may take of Thee, the Giver, and going by songful joy into undescried light she may be all melted in holy love. Burn in the center of my soul and my heart with Thy fire that on Thine altar shall endlessly burn.

Richard Rolle, 1290–1349

Holy Spirit,
as the wind is thy symbol, so forward our
   goings,
as the dove, so launch us heavenwards,
as water, so purify our spirits,
as a cloud, so abate our temptations,
as dew, so revive our languor,
as fire, so purge out our dross.

Christina Rossetti, 1830–94

Come, true light.
Come, life eternal.
Come, hidden mystery.
Come, treasure without name.
Come, reality beyond all words.
Come, person beyond all understanding.
Come, rejoicing without end.
Come, light that knows no evening.
Come, unfailing expectation of the saved.
Come, raising of the fallen.
Come, resurrection of the dead.
Come, all-powerful, for unceasingly you create, refashion and change all things by your will alone.
Come, invisible whom none may touch and handle.
Come, for you continue always unmoved, yet at every instant you are wholly in movement; you draw near to us who lie in hell, yet you remain higher than the heavens.

Come, for your name fills our hearts with longing and is ever on our lips; yet who you are and what your nature is, we cannot say or know.
Come, Alone to the alone.
Come, for you are yourself the desire that is within me.
Come, my breath and my life.
Come, the consolation of my humble soul.
Come, my joy, my glory, my endless delight.

Symeon the New Theologian, 949–1022

Heavenly Majesty, Comforter, Spirit of truth, who art everywhere present and fillest all things, treasury of good gifts and giver of life, Come and abide in us and cleanse of all impurity and save our souls, O good One.
Amen.

Symeon the New Theologian, 949–1022

The pure celestial fire to impart,
Kindle a flame of sacred love
On the mean altar of my heart.

There let it for thy glory burn,
With inextinguishable blaze;
And trembling to its source return,
In humble love and fervent praise.

Jesus, confirm my heart's desire
To work, and speak, and think for thee;
Still let me guard the holy fire,
And still stir up thy gift in me.

Ready for all thy perfect will,
My acts of faith and love repeat,
Till death thy endless mercies seal,
And make the sacrifice complete.

Charles Wesley, 1707–88

Most great and glorious Lord God, accept my imperfect repentance, and send your Spirit of adoption into my heart, that I may again be owned by you, call you Father, and share in the blessings of your children.

John Wesley, 1703–91

CONFESSION

Confession of sin

Father, I have sinned against heaven and before you; I am no longer worthy to be called your son.

Luke 15.21 NRSV

Merciful and pitiful Lord, longsuffering and full of compassion, I have sinned, Lord, I have sinned against Thee; O wretched man that I am, I have sinned, Lord, against Thee much and grievously, in observing lying vanities. I conceal nothing: I make no excuses. I give Thee glory, O Lord, this day. I denounce against myself my sins. Indeed I have sinned against the Lord, and thus and thus have I done [here he would fill in the particulars]. I have sinned and perverted that which was right and it profited me not. And what shall I now say? or with what shall I open my mouth? What shall I answer, seeing I have done it? Without plea, without excuse, self-condemned am I. I have destroyed myself. O Lord, righteousness belongeth unto Thee, but unto me confusion of face. And Thou art just in all that is brought upon me for Thou has done right, but I have done wickedly. And now, Lord, what is my hope? Art not Thou, my Lord?

Lancelot Andrewes, 1555–1626

Forgive me my sins, O Lord,
forgive me the sins of my youth and the sins
   of mine age,
the sins of my soul, and the sins of my body,
my secret and whispering sins,
my presumptuous and my crying sins,
the sins that I have done to please myself,
and the sins that I have done to please others.
Forgive me those sins which I know,
and those sins which I know not.

Author unknown, 6th century

O Thou great Fountain of the Love of God, I beseech Thee, help me, that I may die from my Vanity and Sin in the Death of my Redeemer, Jesus Christ.

Jakob Boehme, 1555–1624

Oppressed with sin and woe,
A burdened heart I bear;
Oppressed by many a mighty foe,
Yet I will not despair.

With this polluted heart,
I dare to come to thee -
Holy and mighty as thou art -
For thou wilt pardon me.

I feel that I am weak,
And prone to every sin;
But thou, who giv'st to those who seek,
Wilt give me strength within.

I need not fear my foes;
I need not yield to care;
I need not sink beneath my woes,
For thou wilt answer prayer.

In my Redeemer's name,
I give myself to thee;
And, all unworthy as I am,
My God will cherish me.

Anne Brontë, 1820–49

O Lord God, eternal and almighty Father, we acknowledge and sincerely confess before your holy majesty that we are miserable sinners, conceived and born in iniquity and sin, prone to evil, and incapable of any good work, and that in our depravity we make no end of breaking your holy commandments. We thus call down destruction on ourselves from your just judgments. Nevertheless, O Lord, we lament that we have offended you, and we condemn ourselves and our faults with true repentance, asking you to help us from wretchedness by your grace

Deign, then, O most gracious and most merciful God and Father, to bestow your mercy on us in the name of Jesus Christ your Son our Lord. Effacing our faults, and all our sinfulness, daily increase on us the gifts of your Holy Spirit, that we from our inner hearts, acknowledging our sin, may be more and more displeasing to ourselves, and become truly repentant, and that your Holy Spirit may produce in us the fruits of righteousness and holiness, through Jesus Christ, our Savior.

John Calvin, 1509–64

Before thy throne, O God, we kneel: give us a
conscience quick to feel,
A ready mind to understand the meaning of
thy chastening hand;
Whate'er the pain and shame may be, bring
us, O Father, nearer thee.

Search out our hearts and make us true; help
us to give to all their due,
From love of pleasure, lust of gold, from sins
which make the heart grow cold,
Wean us and train us with thy rod; teach us to
know our faults, O God.

For sins of heedless word and deed, for pride
ambitious to succeed,
For crafty trade and subtle snare to catch the
simple unaware,
For lives bereft of purpose high, forgive,
forgive O Lord we cry.

Let the fierce fires which burn and try, our
inmost spirits purify;
Consume the ill; purge out the shame; O God
be with us in the flame,
A newborn people may we rise, more pure,
more true, more nobly wise."
William Boyd Carpenter, 1841–1918

Merciful Father, give us grace that we may
never presume to sin; but if at any time we
offend Thy Divine Majesty, may we truly
repent and lament our offense, and by a lively
faith obtain remission of all our sins; solely
through the merits of Jesus Christ, Thy Son,
our Lord. Amen.
*The Common Service Book of
the Lutheran Church, 1917*

Almighty God, our Maker and Redeemer, we
poor sinners confess unto Thee, that we are
by nature sinful and unclean, and that we have
sinned against Thee, by thought, word, and
deed.
Wherefore we flee for refuge to Thine infinite
mercy, seeking and imploring Thy grace, for
the sake of our Lord Jesus Christ.
Evangelical Lutheran Hymn-Book, 1912

O most merciful God, who hast given Thine
Only-begotten Son to die for us, have mercy

upon us, and for His sake grant us remission of
all our sins: and by thy Holy Spirit increase in
us true knowledge of Thee, and of Thy will, and
true obedience to Thy Word, to the end that
by Thy grace we may come to everlasting life,
through Jesus Christ our Lord. Amen.
Evangelical Lutheran Hymn-Book, 1912

Save me, who have fallen into sin, for you alone
are without sin. Remove me from the mire of
my iniquity, for I am submerged forever and
ever. Save me from my enemies, for like a lion
they growl and roar, seeking to swallow me up.
Now, my Lord, flash your lightning and destroy
their power. May they fear you and be cut off
from the light of your face, since they cannot
stand in your presence, Lord, nor in the presence of those who love you. Whoever calls on
you sees the power of the sign of your Cross,
Lord, and trembles and shies away from it.
*Gregory the Illuminator, d. 325,
founder of the Armenian Church*

Almighty God, we are unworthy to come into
your presence, because of our many sins. We
do not deserve any grace or mercy from you, if
you dealt with us as we deserve. We have sinned
against you, O Lord, and we have offended you.
And yet, O Lord, as we acknowledge our sins
and offenses, so also do we acknowledge you
to be a merciful God, a loving and favorable
Father, to all who turn to you. And so we
humbly ask you, for the sake of Christ your
son, to show mercy to us, and forgive us all
our offenses. Forgive the sins of our youth, and
the sins of our old age. By your Spirit, O God,
take possession of our hearts, so that, not only
the actions of our life, but also the words of
our mouths, and the smallest thought of our
minds, may be guided and governed by you.
Through Jesus Christ our Lord, to whom, with
you and the Holy Spirit, be all honor and glory,
n now and forever. Amen.
John Knox's Liturgy of 1560

A Litany
Drop, drop, slow tears,
And bathe those beauteous feet
Which brought from Heaven
The news and Prince of Peace:
Cease not, wet eyes,

His mercy to entreat;
To cry for vengeance
Sin doth never cease.
In your deep flood
Drown all my faults and fears;
Nor let His eye
See sin, but through my tears.

Phineas Fletcher, 1582–1650

O Jesus, Who shall give to my eyes a torrent
of tears, that day and night I may weep for my
sins? I beseech Thee, through Thy bitter and
bloody tears, to move my heart by Thy divine
grace, so that from my eyes tears may flow
abundantly, and that I may weep all my days
over Thy sufferings, and still more over their
cause, my sins.

Francis of Assisi, 1181–1226

Hear me, O God!
    A broken heart
    Is my best part:
Use still thy rod,
    That I may prove
    Therein thy love.

If thou hadst not
    Been stern to me,
    But left me free,
I had forgot
    Myself and thee.

For sin's so sweet,
    As minds ill bent
    Rarely repent,
Until they meet
    Their punishment.

Who more can crave
    Than thou hast done?
    That gav'st a Son,
To free a slave
    First made of nought;
    With all since bought.

Sin, death, and hell
    His glorious name
    Quite overcame,
Yet I rebel,
    And slight the same.
But I'll come in,

Before my loss
    Me farther toss,
As sure to win
    Under his cross.

Ben Jonson, 1572–1637, from
"The Underwood," Poems of Devotion

Father, I pray Thee, cleanse me through Thy
Word. Let it search out and bring to light all
that is of self and the flesh in my religion. Let
it cut away every root of self-confidence, that
the Vine may find me wholly free to receive His
life and Spirit. O my holy Husbandman, I trust
Thee to care for the branch as much as for the
Vine. Thou only art my hope.

Andrew Murray, 1828–1917

God, my good and loving Lord, I acknowledge
all the sins which I have committed every day
in my life, whether in thought, word or deed.
I ask for forgiveness from the depths of my
heart for offending You and others and repent
of my old ways. Help me by Your grace to
change, to sin no more and to walk in the way
of righteousness and to praise and glorify Your
Name, Father, Son and Holy Spirit. Amen.

Orthodox prayer

O Lord my God, I confess that I have sinned
against You in thought, word and deed. I have
also omitted to do what Your holy law requires
of me. But now with repentance and contrition
I turn again to Your love and mercy. I entreat
You to forgive me all my transgressions and to
cleanse me from all my sins. Lord, fill my heart
with the light of Your truth. Strengthen my will
by Your grace. Teach me both to desire and to
do only what pleases You. Amen.

Orthodox prayer

Behold the prodigal! To thee I come,
To hail my Father and to seek my home.
Nor refuge could I find, nor friend abroad,
Straying in vice and destitute of God.

O let thy terrors and my anguish end!
Be thou my refuge and be thou my friend:
Receive the son thou didst so long reprove,
Thou that art the God of love!

Matthew Prior, 1664–1721

I, a poor sinner, acknowledge before you, my God and Creator, that I have terribly and in many ways sinned against you, not only outwardly, but much more with inward blindness, unbelief, doubts, despondency, impatience, pride, covetousness, envy, hatred, malice, and other sinful affections, as you, my Lord and God, know well, and I cannot deeply enough deplore. But I repent of these things, and am sorry for them, and heartily ask you for mercy, for the sake of your beloved Son Jesus Christ. Amen.

Reformed Liturgy of the Palatinate, 1585

Four things which are not in thy treasury,
I lay before thee, Lord, with this petition:
My nothingness, my wants,
my sins, and my contrition.

Robert Southey, 1774–1843

Most holy and merciful Father; We acknowledge and confess in Thy Presence: Our sinful nature prone to evil and slothful in good; And all our shortcomings and offenses against Thee. Thou alone knowest how often we have sinned: In wandering from Thy ways; In wasting Thy gifts; In forgetting Thy love. But Thou, O Lord, have pity upon us; Who are ashamed and sorry for all wherein we have displeased Thee. Teach us to hate our errors; Cleanse us from our secret faults; And forgive our sins; For the sake of Thy dear Son our Savior. And O most holy and loving Father; Send Thy purifying grace into our hearts, we beseech Thee; That we may henceforth live in Thy light and walk in Thy ways; According to the commandments of Jesus Christ our Lord. Amen.

Henry Van Dyke, 1852–1933

My God, I love you above all things
and I hate and detest with my whole soul
the sins by which I have offended you,
because they are displeasing in your sight,
who are supremely good and worthy to be loved.
I acknowledge that I should love you
with a love beyond all others,
and that I should try to prove this love to you.
I consider you in my mind as infinitely greater
than everything in the world,
no matter how precious or beautiful.
I therefore firmly and irrevocably resolve

never to consent to offend you
or do anything that may displease your
    sovereign goodness
and place me in danger of falling from your
    holy grace,
in which I am fully determined
to persevere to my dying breath. Amen

Francis Xavier, 1506–52

Seeking forgiveness

Have mercy on me, O God,
    according to your steadfast love;
according to your abundant mercy
    blot out my transgressions.
Wash me thoroughly from my iniquity,
    and cleanse me from my sin.
For I know my transgressions,
    and my sin is ever before me.
Against you, you alone, have I sinned,
    and done what is evil in your sight,
so that you are justified in your sentence
    and blameless when you pass judgment.
…Create in me a clean heart, O God,
    and put a new and right spirit within me.
Do not cast me away from your presence,
    and do not take your holy spirit from me.
…O Lord, open my lips,
    and my mouth will declare your praise.
For you have no delight in sacrifice;
        if I were to give a burnt-offering, you
            would not be pleased.
The sacrifice acceptable to God is a broken
    spirit;
        a broken and contrite heart, O God, you
            will not despise.

Psalm 51.1–4, 10–11, 15–17 NRSV

Almighty and merciful God, the fountain of all goodness, who knowest the thought of our hearts: we confess that we have sinned against Thee, and done evil in Thy sight. Wash us, we beseech Thee, from the stains of our past sins, and give us grace and power to put away all hurtful things; that, being delivered from the bondage of sin, we may bring forth fruits worthy of repentance, and at last enter into thy promised joy; through the mercy of Thy blessed Son, Jesus Christ our Lord.

Alcuin, 735–804

O God, I who presume to invoke Thy Holy Name, stand in the presence of Thy Divine Majesty: have mercy upon me, a man: a sinner smeared by the foulness of inherent impurity; forgive the unworthy priest in whose hand this oblation is seen offered: Spare O Lord one polluted by sins: in faults the foremost, in comparison to all others, and do not enter into judgment with Thy servant, for no one living is justified in Thy sight. It is true that we are weighed down in the faults and desires of our flesh: remember, O Lord, that we are flesh and there is no other source of help than Thee. O Jesus Christ, let us live. Amen.

*Ambrose, c.339–397, from the
Lorrha ("Stowe") Missal*

O Lord, my Savior, in whose power it is to remit sins, I beseech Thee say unto me, 'Loose thee from thy chains, come out of the bonds of thy sins" and when Thou sayest it, loose those cords of my errors wherewith I am entangled and bound; for, though I am the most wicked of all men, and to be abhorred by reason of my continuance in sins, yet when thou commandest, I shall be free from them. Amen.

Ambrose, c.339–397

Forgive me my sins, O Lord; forgive me the sins of my youth and the sins of my age, the sins of my soul and the sins of by body, my secret and my whispering sins, my presumptuous and my crying sins, the sins that I have done to please myself and the sins that I have done to please others. Forgive me those sins that I know and those sins which I know not; forgive them, O Lord, forgive them all of your great goodness.

Lancelot Andrewes, 1555–1626

O thou gracious and gentle and condescending God, thou God of peace, Father of mercy, God of all comfort; see, I lament before thee the evil of my heart; I acknowledge that I am too much disposed to anger, jealousy, and revenge, to ambition and pride, which often give rise to discord and bitter feelings between me and others. Too often have I thus offended and grieved both thee, O long-suffering Father, and my fellow-men. Oh forgive me this sin, and suffer me to partake of the blessing which thou

has promised to the peacemakers, who shall be called the children of God.

Johann Arndt, 1558–1621

Lord, how great is your patience. You are full of compassion and gracious, slow to anger, abounding in mercy, and true! You make your sun rise on the good and on the wicked alike; you send rain on the just and the unjust alike. You do not desire the death of sinners; you would rather that they turn from wickedness and truly live. By your patience you lead us to repentance.

Augustine of Hippo, 354–430

Eternal God, who so carest for every one of us as if thou carest for him alone, and so for all as if all were but one, blessed is the man who loveth thee and his friend in thee, and his enemy for thee, for he alone loses no one dear to him, to whom all are dear in him who never can be lost.
Amen.

Augustine of Hippo, 354–430

Forgive me, Lord, my sins
    the sins of my youth,
    the sins of the present;
    the sins I laid upon myself in an ill
       pleasure,
    the sins I cast upon others in an ill
       example;
    the sins which are manifest to all the world,
    the sins which I have labored to hide from
       mine acquaintance,
         from mine own conscience,
         and even from my memory;
    my crying sins and my whispering sins,
    my ignorant sins and my willful;
    sins against my superiors, equals, servants,
       against my lovers and benefactors,
    sins against myself, mine own body, mine
       own soul,
    sins against thee, O heavenly Father, O
       merciful Son,
       O blessed Spirit of God.

Source unknown

The hatred which divides nation from nation, race from race, class from class,
Father, forgive.

The covetous desires of men and nations
to possess what is not their own,
Father, forgive.

The greed which exploits the labors of men,
and lays waste the earth,
Father, forgive.

Our envy of the welfare and happiness of
    others,
Father, forgive.

Our indifference to the plight of the homeless
    and the refugee,
Father, forgive.

The lust which uses for ignoble ends
the bodies of men and women,
Father, forgive.

The pride which leads to trust in ourselves
and not in God,
Father, forgive.

*Author unknown, prayer on a plaque on the
altar of Coventry Cathedral, written in 1964*

Forgive the sins we have committed in knowledge or in ignorance, in thought, word, or
deed; and cleanse us, body and soul, from
every stain. Allow us to pass through the darkness of this present life watchful and alert,
always expecting the coming bright day of
Your Only-begotten Son, our Lord, God, and
Savior, Jesus Christ. He shall come in glory to
judge all people and reward us according to
our deeds.

Basil the Great, c.330–379

Almighty and most merciful Father, we have
erred and strayed from thy ways like lost sheep,
we have followed too much the devices and
desires of our own hearts, we have offended
against thy holy laws. We have left undone
those things which we ought to have done, and
we have done those things which we ought not
to have done, and there is no health in us. But
thou, O Lord, have mercy upon us miserable
offenders; spare thou them, O God, which
confess their faults; restore thou them that are
penitent, according to thy promises declared
unto mankind in Christ Jesus our Lord. And

grant, O most merciful Father, for his sake, that
we may hereafter live a godly, righteous, and
sober life, to the glory of thy holy Name.

*Book of Common Prayer, 1552,
Morning and Evening Prayer*

Grant, we beseech thee, merciful Lord, to thy
faithful people pardon and peace, that they
may be cleansed from all their sins, and serve
thee with a quiet mind; through Jesus Christ
our Lord. Amen.

*Book of Common Prayer, Collect for the
Twenty-first Sunday after Trinity*

Almighty God, Father of our Lord Jesus Christ,
Maker of all things, judge of all men; We
acknowledge and bewail our manifold sins
and wickedness, Which we, from time to time,
most grievously have committed, By thought,
word, and deed, Against thy Divine Majesty,
Provoking most justly thy wrath and indignation against us. We do earnestly repent, And
are heartily sorry for these our misdoings; The
remembrance of them is grievous unto us;
The burden of them is intolerable. Have mercy
upon us, Have mercy upon us, most merciful
Father; For thy Son our Lord Jesus Christ's
sake, Forgive us all that is past; And grant that
we may ever hereafter Serve and please thee In
newness of life, To the honor and glory of thy
Name; Through Jesus Christ our Lord. Amen.

Book of Common Prayer, The Lord's Supper

Grant, Almighty God, that, since to a perverse,
and in every way a rebellious people, thou
didst formerly show so much grace, as to
exhort them continually to repentance, and
to stretch forth thy hand to them by thy
Prophets, – O grant, that the same word
may sound in our ears; and when we do not
immediately profit by thy teaching, O cast
us not away, but, by thy Spirit, so subdue all
our thoughts and affections, that we, being
humbled, may give glory to thy majesty, such
as is due to thee, and that, being allured by
thy paternal favor, we may submit ourselves
to thee, and, at the same time, embrace that
mercy which thou offerest and presentest to
us in Christ, that we may not doubt but thou
wilt be a Father to us, until we shall at length
enjoy that eternal inheritance, which has been

obtained for us by the, blood of thine only-begotten Son. Amen.

John Calvin, 1509–64

We are guilty and polluted, O God,
In spirit, in heart, and in flesh,
In thought, in word, in act,
We are hard in Thy sight in sin.
Put Thou forth to us the power of Thy love,
Be thou leaping over the mountains of our
    transgressions,
And wash us in the true blood of conciliation,
Like the down of the mountain, like the lily of
    the lake.

Carmina Gadelica

O most merciful Father, you forgive the sins of those who truly repent: we come before your throne in the name of Jesus Christ, that for his sake alone you will have compassion on us, and not allow our sin to be a cloud between you and us.

John Colet, c.1467–1519

We beseech thee, good Lord, that it may please thee to give us true repentance; to forgive us all our sins, negligences, and ignorances; and to endue us with the grace of thy Holy Spirit, to amend our lives according to thy holy word.

Thomas Cranmer, 1489–1556, from The Litany, 1544

Master and Lord, Jesus Christ our God, You alone have authority to forgive my sins, whether committed knowingly or in ignorance, and make me worthy to receive without condemnation Your divine, glorious, pure and life-giving Mysteries, not for my punishment, but for my purification and sanctification, now and in Your future Kingdom. For You, Christ our God are compassionate and love mankind and to You we give glory with the Father and the Holy Spirit now and forever and ever. Amen.

John of Damascus, c.676–749

Forgive me, O Lord, through the merits of thine Anointed, my Savior, Jesus Christ.

John Donne, 1572–1631

Wilt Thou forgive that sin where I begun,

Which is my sin, though it were done
    before?
Wilt Thou forgive that sin through which I
    run,
    And do run still, though still I do deplore?
        When Thou hast done, Thou hast not
            done,
        For I have more.

Wilt Thou forgive that sin which I have won
    Others to sin? and made my sin their door?
Wilt Thou forgive that sin which I did shun
    A year or two, but wallowed in, a score?
        When Thou hast done, Thou hast not
            done,
        For I have more.

I have a sin of fear, that when I have spun
    My last thread, I shall perish on the shore;
Swear by Thyself, that at my death Thy Son
    Shall shine as He shines now and
        heretofore;
        And, having done that, Thou hast
            done,
        I fear no more.

John Donne, 1572–1631

Almighty God, our Heavenly Father, hath had mercy upon us, and hath given His Only Son to die for us, and for His sake forgiveth us all our sins. To them that believe on His Name, He giveth power to become the sons of God, and hath promised them His Holy Spirit. He that believeth, and is baptized, shall be saved. Grant this, Lord, unto us all.

Evangelical Lutheran Hymn-Book, 1912

Lord, from you flows true and continual kindness. You had cast us off and justly so, but in your mercy you forgave us. You were at odds with us, and you reconciled us. You had set a curse on us, and you blessed us. You had banished us from the garden, and you called us back again. You took away the fig leaves that had been an unsuitable garment, and you clothed us in a cloak of great value. You flung wide the prison gates, and you gave the condemned a pardon. You sprinkled clean water on us, and you washed away the dirt.

Gregory of Nyssa, c.335–c.395

Lord, who has form'd me out of mud,
    And hast redeem'd me through they blood,
    And sanctifi'd me to do good;

Purge all my sins done heretofore:
    For I confess my heavy score,
    And I will strive to sin no more.

Enrich my heart, mouth, hands in me,
    With faith, with hope, with charitie;
    That I may run, rise, rest with thee.

George Herbert, 1593–1633

Look upon us in your mercy, O Lord, and take away our sins. Be to us both our reward and our redeemer, and defend us against all adversities that may assault us in body or soul: through Christ our Lord. Amen.

Irenaeus, c.130–c.200

Lord, give me Grace to examine all my misspent life, in the bitterness of my Soul to confess my sins, with a broken and contrite Heart, to bewail them with utmost abhorrence to forsake them, and do thou so order my steps in thy Word, that for the time to come, no wickedness may have Dominion over me, that I may bring forth fruits meet for repentance.

Thomas Ken, 1637–1711

Out of the depths I cry to thee,
Lord God! oh hear my prayer!
Incline a gracious ear to me,
And bid me not despair:
If Thou rememberest each misdeed,
If each should have its righteous meed,
Lord, who shall stand before Thee?

Tis through Thy love alone we gain
The pardon of our sin;
The strictest life is but in vain,
Our works can nothing win,
That none should boast himself of aught,
But own in fear Thy grace hath wrought
What in him seemeth righteous.

Wherefore my hope is in the Lord,
My works I count but dust,
I build not there, but on His word,
And in His goodness trust.

Up to His care myself I yield,
He is my tower, my rock, my shield,
And for His help I tarry.

And though it linger till the night,
And round again till morn,
My heart shall ne'er mistrust Thy might,
Nor count itself forlorn.
Do thus, O ye of Israel's seed,
Ye of the Spirit born indeed,
Wait for your God's appearing.

Though great our sins and sore our wounds,
And deep and dark our fall,
His helping mercy hath no bounds,
His love surpasseth all.
Our trusty loving Shepherd He,
Who shall at last set Israel free
From all their sin and sorrow.

*Martin Luther, 1483–1546, translated
by Catherine Winkworth, 1855*

Forgive me, most gracious Lord and Father, if this day I have done or said anything to increase the pain of the world. Pardon the unkind word, the impatient gesture, the hard and selfish deed, the failure to show sympathy and kindly help where I had the opportunity, but missed it; and enable me so to live that I may daily do something to lessen the tide of human sorrow, and add to the sum of human happiness. Amen.

F.B. Meyer, 1847–1929

If my soul has turned perversely to the dark;
If I have left some brother wounded by the
    way;
If I have preferred my aims to thine;
If I have been impatient and would not wait;
If I have marred the pattern drawn out for my
    life;
If I have cost tears to those I loved;
If my heart has murmured against thy will,
O Lord, forgive.

F.B. Meyer, 1847–1929

O Good Shepherd, who laid down your life
    for the sheep, remember us:
Be propitious, and have mercy on us.
O everlasting Power and Wisdom of the
    most high God, the Word of the Father,

remember us:
Be propitious, and have mercy on us.
O Maker of the world, the Life of all, the Lord
    of angels, remember us:
Be propitious, and have mercy on us.
O Lamb of God, who for us was led as a sheep
    to the slaughter, remember us:
Be propitious, and have mercy on us.
You who was arrested, although innocent,
    mocked, given over to robbers, remember
    us:
Be propitious, and have mercy on us.
You who alone has through your death
    overcome the death our guilt, remember us:
Be propitious, and have mercy on us.

Mozarabic Breviary

Master and Lord of Heaven and Earth and King
of the ages. Deign to open the door of repentance to me, for in anguish of my heart I pray
to Thee, our true God, the Father of our Lord
Jesus Christ, the Light of the world. Look upon
me in Thy great loving-kindness and accept
my prayer. Incline Thine ear to my prayer and
forgive me all the evil that I have done by the
abuse of my free will.

Orthodox prayer

Behold, I seek rest, yet I do not find it, for I have
not received forgiveness from my conscience.
I thirst for peace, but there is no peace in me
from the dark abyss of my transgressions.
Hear, O Lord, a heart which cries to Thee.
Regard not my evil deeds, but consider the
agony of my soul and make haste to heal me
who am badly wounded.

Orthodox prayer

By the grace of Thy love for men, give me
time for repentance and deliver me from my
shameful deeds, lest I finally perish. Hear me,
O Lord, in my despair. Behold, I am bereft of
my will and of every thought of amendment.
Therefore, I have recourse to Thy compassion.
Have mercy on me, cast down and condemned
on account of my sins.

Orthodox prayer

O Lord, rescue me who am enslaved and held
by my evil deeds, as if I were shackled with
chains. Thou Alone knowest how to set pris-

oners free; and as Thou Alone knowest secret
things, Thou healest wounds that are known
by no one but seen by Thee. Therefore, being
tortured in every way by cruel pains, I cry only
to Thee, the Physician of all who are afflicted,
the Door of those who knock without, the
Way of the lost, the Light of those in darkness,
the Redeemer of those in bonds, Who ever
restrainest Thy right hand and withholdest
Thy anger prepared for sinners, but Who givest
time for repentance through Thy great love
for men.

Orthodox prayer

O Thou Who art quick to show mercy and
slow to punish, shine upon me, who have fall-
en badly, the light of Thy countenance, O Lord.
In Thy loving-kindness stretch Thy hand to me
and raise me from the depth of my transgressions. For Thou Alone art our God, Who dost
not rejoice at the destruction of sinners, and
Who dost not turn away Thy face from those
who cry to Thee with tears.

Orthodox prayer

Hear, O Lord, the voice of Thy servant who
cries to Thee, and manifest Thy light to me
who am deprived of light, and give me Thy
grace, for I have no hope whatever, that I may
always trust in Thy help and power. Turn my
weeping into joy, rend my rags and gird me
with gladness. Grant that I may rest from my
dark deeds and enjoy the morning calm with
Thy chosen, O Lord, whence all pain, sorrow
and sighing have fled away. May the door of
Thy Kingdom be opened to me, that I may
enter with those who rejoice in the light of
Thy countenance, O Lord, and that even I may
receive eternal life in Christ Jesus our Lord.

Orthodox prayer

O holy God, whose mercy and compassion
made you come from the high throne down
into this world for our salvation: mercifully forgive us all the sins we have done and
thought and said. Send us cleanness of heart
and purity of soul; restore us with your Holy
Spirit, that we may from now on live virtuously and love you with all our hearts; through
Jesus Christ your Son.

Richard Rolle, 1290–1349

Jesus Christ, have mercy on me, as you are king of majesty; and forgive all my sins that I have committed, both great and small; and bring me, if it is your will to heaven to live always with you.

Richard Rolle, 1290–1349

O merciful Lord Jesus, forget not me, as I have forgotten thee.

Christina Rossetti, 1830–94

O God, though our sins be seven, though our sins be seventy times seven, though our sins be more in number than the hairs of our head, yet give us grace in loving penitence to cast ourselves down into the depths of thy compassion.

Christina Rossetti, 1830–94

O God, who wouldest not the death of a sinner, but that he should be converted and life: forgive the sins of us who turn to thee with all our heart, and grant us the grace of eternal life, through Jesus Christ our Lord.

Early Scottish Prayer

Lord, cleanse me of my sins and have mercy on me.
You have created me; have mercy on me.
There is no way to measure my sin; have mercy on me.
Lord, forgive the many times I disobey You.
Master, I bow down before Your cross and glorify Your resurrection.
Lord, when I sin in what I say and do, have mercy on me because of Your great compassion.

Seraphim of Sarov, 1759–1833

O Lord, heal our infirmities, pardon our offences, lighten our burdens, enrich our poverty; through Christ our Lord.

Christopher Sutton, 16th century

O Lord Jesu Christ, take us to thyself, draw us with cords to the foot of thy cross; for we have no strength to come, and we know not the way. Thou art mighty to save, and none can separate us from thy love. Bring us home to thyself, for we are gone astray. We have wandered: do thou seek us. Under the shadow of thy cross let us

live all the rest of our lives, and there we shall be safe.

Frederick Temple, 1821–1902

Jesus, lover of my soul, let me to Thy bosom fly,
While the nearer waters roll, while the tempest still is high.
Hide me, O my Savior, hide, till the storm of life is past;
Safe into the haven guide; O receive my soul at last.

Other refuge have I none, hangs my helpless soul on Thee;
Leave, ah! leave me not alone, still support and comfort me.
All my trust on Thee is stayed, all my help from Thee I bring;
Cover my defenseless head with the shadow of Thy wing.

Wilt Thou not regard my call? Wilt Thou not accept my prayer?
Lo! I sink, I faint, I fall – Lo! on Thee I cast my care;
Reach me out Thy gracious hand! While I of Thy strength receive,
Hoping against hope I stand, dying, and behold, I live.

Thou, O Christ, art all I want, more than all in Thee I find;
Raise the fallen, cheer the faint, heal the sick, and lead the blind.
Just and holy is Thy Name, I am all unrighteousness;
False and full of sin I am; Thou art full of truth and grace.

Plenteous grace with Thee is found, grace to cover all my sin;
Let the healing streams abound; make and keep me pure within.
Thou of life the fountain art, freely let me take of Thee;
Spring Thou up within my heart; rise to all eternity.

Charles Wesley, 1707–88

He breaks the power of canceled sin,

He sets the prisoner free;
His blood can make the foulest clean,
His blood availed for me.

Charles Wesley, 1707–88

Lord Jesus, you were called the friend of
sinners, be my friend, for I acknowledge that
I have sinned. Forgive the wrong that I have
done and the right that I have failed to do;
my secret and my more open sins; my sins of
ignorance and my deliberate sins; sins to please
myself and sins to please others; the sins which
I remember, and the sins which I have forgotten; forgive all these, for it was for me also that
you died. My Lord and Savior. Amen.

John Wesley 1703–91

Forgive them all, O Lord:
our sins of omission and our sins of
    commission;
the sins of our youth and the sins of our riper
    years;
the sins of our souls and the sins of our
    bodies;
our secret and our more open sins;
our sins of ignorance and surprise,
and our more deliberate and presumptuous
    sins;
the sins we have done to please ourselves,
and the sins we have done to please others;
the sins we know and remember,
and the sins we have forgotten;
the sins we have striven to hide from others
and the sins by which we have offended
    others;
forgive them, O Lord, forgive them all for his
    sake,
who died for our sins and rose for our
    justification,
and now stands at your right hand to make
    intercession for us,
Jesus Christ our Lord.

John Wesley, 1703–91

Forgive me my sins, O Lord; the sins of my
present and the sins of my past, the sins of my
soul and the sins of my body, the sins which I
have done to please myself and the sins which
I have done to please others. Forgive me my
casual sins and my deliberate sins, and those
which I have tried to hide so that I have hidden

them even from myself. Forgive me them, O
Lord, forgive them all; for Jesus Christ's sake.

Thomas Wilson, 1663–1755

THANKSGIVING

General thanksgiving

I thank you, O Lord, my Lord,
for my being, my life, my gift of reason;
for my nurture, my preservation, by guidance;
for my education, my civil rights, my religious
    privileges;
for your gifts of grace, of nature, of this world;
for my redemption, my regeneration, in
    instruction in the Christian faith;
for my calling, my recalling, my manifold
    renewed recalling;
for your forbearance and long-suffering, your
    prolonged forbearance, many a time, and
    many a year;
for all the benefits I have received, and all the
    undertakings in which I have prospered;
for any good I may have done;
for the use of the blessings of this life.
… For all these and also for all other mercies,
    known and unknown, open and secret,
    remembered by me, or now forgotten,
    kindnesses received by my willingly, or
    even against my will, I praise you, I bless
    you, I thank you, all the days of my life.

Lancelot Andrewes, 1555–1626

Lord, when I look upon mine own life it seems
Thou hast led me so carefully, so tenderly,
Thou canst have attended to no one else; but
when I see how wonderfully Thou hast led
the world and art leading it, I am amazed that
Thou hast time to attend to such as I.

Augustine of Hippo, 354–430

Lord, you are never new and never old. Yet you
give new life to all things.

Augustine of Hippo, 354–430

I thank Thee, O Lord,
because Thou hast bound me in the bundle
    of life.
I thank Thee, O Lord,

because Thou hast saved me from the pit.
I thank Thee, O Lord,
because Thou hast gladdened me with thy
    Covenant.
I thank Thee, O Lord,
because Thou hast set thine eye upon me.

Dead Sea Scrolls

In spite of my unworthiness, I praise You and
I glorify You, O Lord, for Your mercy to me
is without limit. You have been my help and
my protection. May the name of Your majesty
be praised forever. To you, our God, be glory.
Amen.

Ephraem, c.306–378

Good God, many and great are the blessings
by which I am bound to Thee, and for which
I give Thee most hearty thanks; but how can I
sufficiently thank Thee for having enlightened
me with the holy faith? I tremble, O Lord,
when I compare this Thy great gift with my
own ingratitude.

Francis de Sales, 1567–1622

We give you thanks, omnipotent, ever-living
God of truth, eternal Father of our Lord Jesus
Christ, Creator of heaven and earth, of people,
and of all creatures, Sustainer of all things, Giver
of all life, order and wisdom, unfailing Source
of help: And to your Son our Lord Jesus Christ,
your Word and eternal Image: and to your Holy
Spirit, with whom you endowed the apostles
at Pentecost. We give thanks to you, O God
of holiness, and truth, wisdom and goodness,
justice and mercy, purity and loving kindness,
for with goodness and wisdom unmatched you
revealed yourself to us, sending your Son into
the world, destined to assume h human nature
and to become a sacrifice for us.

We give thanks to you, O God, for gathering your eternal church, for guarding the
ministry of your Word, for granting your Holy
Spirit, and for giving everlasting life. We thank
you, O God, because you gave us all good
things, because you alleviated and removed the
chastisement we justly deserve, because you
bestowed on us all the blessings of soul and
body. To you be all glory, honor, praise, and
thanksgiving, for ever and ever.

Philip Melanchthon, 1497–1560

We worship you, O Lord God, and give thanks
to you for your great glory and power, which
you show to your servants in your wonderful
world. All the things which we enjoy are from
your mighty hand, and you alone are to be
praised for all the blessings of the life that now
is. Make us thankful to you for all your mercies
and more ready to serve you with all our heart;
for the sake of Jesus Christ. Amen.

The Narrow Way, 1869

Almighty and merciful God, I most humbly
and heartily thank Your divine majesty for
Your loving kindness and tender mercies,
that You have heard my humble prayer, and
graciously granted me deliverance from my
trouble and misery. I pray to you to continue
granting Your helping grace, that I may lead a
life pleasing to You, that I may continually offer
to You a sacrifice of praise and thanksgiving, O
Father, Son, and Holy Spirit. Amen.

Orthodox prayer

Thank You, Lord, for Your strength and guidance in my work. You are the fulfillment of
all good things. Fill also my soul with joy and
gladness, that I may praise You always. Amen.

Orthodox prayer

Almighty God, Father of all mercies, we thine
unworthy servants do give thee most humble
and hearty thanks for all thy goodness and
loving-kindness to us, and to all men; We
bless thee for our creation, preservation, and
all the blessings of this life; but above all, for
thine inestimable love in the redemption of the
world by our Lord Jesus Christ; for the means
of grace, and for the hope of glory. And, we
beseech thee, give us that due sense of all thy
mercies, that our hearts may be unfeignedly
thankful, and that we shew forth thy praise, not
only with our lips, but in our lives; by giving up
ourselves to thy service, and by walking before
thee in holiness and righteousness all our days;
through Jesus Christ our Lord, to whom with
thee and the Holy Ghost be all honor and glory,
world without end. Amen.

*Edward Reynolds, 1599–1667, The
Book of Common Prayer, Thanksgiving*

Help us to look back on the long way that Thou

hast brought us, on the long days in which we have been served, not according to our deserts, but our desires; on the pit and the miry clay, the blackness of despair, the horror of misconduct, from which our feet have been plucked out. For our sins forgiven or prevented, for our shame unpublished, we bless and thank Thee, O God. Help us yet again and ever. So order events, so strengthen our frailty, as that day by day we shall come before Thee with this song of gratitude, and in the end we be dismissed with honor. In their weakness and their fear, the vessels of thy handiwork so pray to Thee, so praise Thee. Amen.

R.L. Stevenson, 1850–94

Almighty God:
We are so blessed.
Thank you for this food,
And for this splendid family
That you have gathered here today.

Lord, we know that everything we have
Is from you.
And that everything we are
Is from you.

Indeed, Lord–
We are so blessed.
And we are very, very thankful.
Amen.

Dr John N. Todd III, by kind permission

O God, who hast so greatly loved us and mercifully redeemed us, give us grace, that in everything we may yield ourselves, our wills, and our works, a continual thank offering unto thee, through Jesus Christ our Lord. Amen.

Westminster Directory of Worship, 1647

Thanksgiving for creation

O Lord, our Sovereign,
    how majestic is your name in all the earth!
…When I look at your heavens, the work of
    your fingers,
        the moon and the stars that you have
            established;
what are human beings that you are mindful
    of them,

mortals that you care for them?
Yet you have made them a little lower than God,
    and crowned them with glory and
        honor.

Psalm 8.1, 3–5 NRSV

All things bright and beautiful,
All creatures great and small,
All things wise and wonderful,
The Lord God made them all.

Each little flower that opens,
Each little bird that sings,
He made their glowing colors,
He made their tiny wings.

The purple-headed mountain,
The river running by,
The sunset, and the morning,
That brightens up the sky;

The cold wind in the winter,
The pleasant summer sun,
The ripe fruits in the garden,
He made them every one.

The tall trees in the greenwood,
The meadows where we play,
The rushes by the water,
We gather every day; –

He gave us eyes to see them,
And lips that we might tell,
How great is God Almighty,
Who has made all things well.

C.F. Alexander, 1818–95

O Lord how wonderful are thy works in all the world, in wisdom hast thou made them all.

Lancelot Andrewes, 1555–1626

Blessed art Thou, O Lord,
Who didst create the firmament of heaven,
    The heavens and the heavens of heavens,
        The heavenly hosts,
            Angels and archangels,
                Cherubim and seraphim:
    Waters above the heavens,
        vapors,
            exhalations,
                whereof [come]

Clouds from the end of the earth,
Lightnings, thunders,
Winds out of treasures,
storms
            rains,
dew,
hail,
snow like wool.
hoar frost like ashes,
ice as morsels:
waters under the heavens
    for drinking
    for washing.

                    Lancelot Andrewes, 1555–1626

Almighty One, in the woods I am blessed.
Happy everyone in the woods. Every tree
speaks through Thee. O God! What glory in
the woodland! On the heights is peace–peace
to serve Him.

                    Ludwig van Beethoven, 1770–1827

Now we must praise the ruler of heaven,
The might of the Lord and his purpose of
    mind,
The work of the glorious Father; for he,
God eternal, established each wonder,
He, holy creator, first fashioned the heavens
As a roof for the children of earth.
And then our guardian, the everlasting Lord,
Adorned this middle-earth for men.
Praise the almighty king of heaven.

                    Cædmon, 7th century

Father, we thank you, especially for letting me
fly this flight … for the privilege of being able
to be in this position, to be in this wondrous
place, seeing all these many startling, wonderful things that you have created.

        *L. Gordon Cooper, Jr., b.1927. Prayer while
        orbiting the earth in a space capsule*

Lord, may we love all your creation, all the
earth and every grain of sand in it. May we
love every leaf, every ray of your light. For we
acknowledge to you that all is like an ocean, all
is flowing and blending, and that to withhold
any measure of love from anything in your
universe is to withhold that same measure of
love from you.

                    Fyodor Dostoyevsky, 1821–81

For flowers that bloom about our feet,
Father, we thank Thee.
For tender grass so fresh, so sweet,
Father, we thank Thee.
For the song of bird and hum of bee,
For all things fair we hear or see,
Father in heaven, we thank Thee.

For blue of stream and blue of sky,
Father, we thank Thee.
For pleasant shade of branches high,
Father, we thank Thee.
For fragrant air and cooling breeze,
For beauty of the blooming trees,
Father in heaven, we thank Thee.

For this new morning with its light,
Father, we thank Thee.
For rest and shelter of the night,
Father, we thank Thee
For health and food, for love and friends,
For everything Thy goodness sends,
Father in heaven, we thank Thee.

                    Ralph Waldo Emerson, 1803–82

Most high, most great and good Lord, to you
belong praises, glory and every blessing; to you
alone do they belong, most high God.
    May you be blessed, my Lord, for the gift of
all your creatures and especially for our brother sun, but whom the day is enlightened. He is
radiant and bright, of great splendor, bearing
witness to you, O my God.
    May you be blessed, my Lord, for our sister
the moon and the stars; you have created them
in the heavens, fair and clear.
    May you be blessed, my Lord, for my broth-
er the wind, for the air, for cloud and calm, for
every kind of weather, for through them you
sustain all creatures.
    May you be blessed, my Lord, for our sister
water, which is very useful, humble, pure and
precious.
    May you be blessed, my Lord, for our broth-
er fire, bright, noble and beautiful, untamable
and strong, by whom you illumine the night.
    May you be blessed, my Lord, for our moth-
er the earth, who sustains and nourishes us,
who brings forth all kinds of fruit, herbs and
brightly colored flowers.
    May you be blessed, my Lord, for those who

pardon out of love for you, and who patiently bear illness and tribulation.

Happy are those who abide in peace, for through you, most high God, they will be crowned.

May you be blessed, my Lord, for our sister death of body, from whom no living person can escape. Woe to him who dies in a state of mortal sin. Happy are those who at the hour of death are found in obedience to your holy will, for the second death cannot hurt them.

Praise and bless, my Lord; give him thanks and serve him with great humility.

Francis of Assisi, 1181–1226, "Canticle of the Sun"

When I look at your heavens, according to my own lights, with these weak eyes of mine, I am certain with reservation that they are your heavens. The stars circle in the heavens, reappear year after year, each with a function and service to fulfill. And though I do not understand them, I know that you, O God, are in them.

Hilary of Poitiers, c.315–c.367

Glory be to God for dappled things –
For skies of couple-color as a brinded cow;
For rose-moles in all stipple upon the trout
    that swim;
Fresh-firecoal chestnut-falls; finches' wings;
Landscape plotted and pieced-fold, fallow and
    plough;
And all trades, their gear and tackle and trim.
All things counter, original, spare, strange;
Whatever is fickle, freckeled (who knows
    how?)
With swift, slow; sweet, sour; adazzle, dim;
He fathers-forth whose beauty is past change:
Praise him.
Gerard Manley Hopkins, 1844–89, "Pied Beauty"

Lord God through the light of nature you have aroused in us a longing for the light of grace, so that we may be raised in the light of your majesty. To you I give thanks, Creator and Lord, that you have allowed me to rejoice in your deeds. Praise the Lord you heavenly harmonies, and you who know the revealed harmonies. For from him, through him and in him, all is, which is perceptible as well as spiritual; that which we know and that which we

do not know, for there is still much to learn.
Johann Kepler, 1571–1630

O thou who coverest thy high places with the
    waters,
who settest the sand as a bound to the sea
and dost uphold all things:
the sun sings thy praises,
the moon gives thee glory,
every creature offers a hymn to thee,
his author and creator, for ever.
The Lenten Triodion, Greek Orthodox Church

Great art Thou, O Lord, and marvelous are Thy works, and there is no word which sufficeth to hymn Thy wonders. For Thou, of thine own good will, hast brought into being all things which before were not, and by Thy might Thou upholdest creation, and by Thy providence Thou orderest the world.

Orthodox liturgy

For the beauty of the earth,
For the beauty of the skies,
For the love which from our birth
Over and around us lies:
Christ, our God, to thee we raise
This our sacrifice of praise.

For the beauty of each hour
Of the day and of the night,
Hill and vale and tree and flower,
Sun and moon and stars of light:
Christ, our God, to thee we raise
This our sacrifice of praise.
F.S. Pierpoint, 1835–1917

O God, we thank you for this universe, our home; and for its vastness and richness, the exuberance of life which fills it and of which we are part. We praise you for the vault of heaven and for the winds, pregnant with blessings, for the clouds which navigate and for the constellations, there so high. We praise you for the oceans and for the fresh streams, for the endless mountains, the trees, the grass under our feet. We praise you for our senses, to be able to see the moving splendor, to hear the songs of lovers, to smell the beautiful fragrance of the spring flowers. Give us, we pray you, a heart that is open to all this joy and all this beauty, and free our souls of the blindness that comes from preoccupation with the things of life, and of the shadows of passions, to the point that we no longer see nor hear, not even when the bush at the roadside is afire with the glory of God.

Walter Rauschenbusch, 1861–1918

Thanksgiving for God's love

As yet my love is weak, my heart imperfect, and so I have great need of your strength and comfort. Visit me often, I pray, and instruct me in the way of your laws. Set me free from all evil passions, and heal my heart from all immoral desires. And thus, healed and cleansed in spirit, may I learn how blissful it is to plunge into the depths of your love.

Thomas à Kempis, 1379–1471

Let your love dissolve my hard heart. Let your love raise me above myself. Let your love reveal to me joy beyond imagination. Let my soul exhaust itself in singing the praises of your love. Let me love you more than I love myself, and let me love myself only for your sake. And let me see your love shining in the hearts of all people, that I may love them as I love you.

Thomas à Kempis, 1379–1471

Father in Heaven! You have loved us first, help us never to forget that You are love so that this sure conviction might triumph in our hearts over the seduction of the world, over the inquietude of the soul, over the anxiety for the future, over the fright of the past, over the distress of the moment. But grant also that this conviction might discipline our soul so that our heart might remain faithful and sincere in the love which we bear to all those whom You have commanded us to love as we love ourselves.

You have loved us first, O God, alas! We speak of it in terms of history as if You have only loved us first but a single time, rather than that without ceasing You have loved us first in all things and every day and our whole life through. When we wake up in the morning and turn our soul toward You – You are the first – You have loved us first; if I rise at dawn and at the same second turn my soul toward You in prayer, You are there ahead of me, You have loved me first. When I withdraw from the distractions of the day and turn my soul toward You, You are the first and thus forever. And yet we always speak ungratefully as if You have loved us first only once.

Søren Kierkegaard, 1813–55

You who are unchangeable, whom nothing changes! You who are unchangeable in love, precisely for our welfare, not submitting to any change: may we too will our welfare, submitting ourselves to the discipline of Your unchangeableness, so that we may in unconditional obedience find our rest and remain at rest in Your unchangeableness. You are not like us; if we are to preserve only some degree of constancy, we must not permit ourselves too much to be moved, nor by too many things. You on the contrary are moved, and moved in infinite love, by all things. Even that which we humans beings call an insignificant trifle, and pass by unmoved, the need of a sparrow, even this moved You; and what we so often scarcely notice, a human sigh, this moves You, You who are unchangeable! You who in infinite love do submit to be moved, may this our prayer also move You to add Your blessing, in order that there may be brought about such a change in us who pray as to bring us into conformity with Your unchangeable will, You who are unchangeable!

Søren Kierkegaard, 1813–55

My life is an instant,
    an hour which passes by;
My life is a moment
    Which I have no power to stay.
You know, O my God,
    That to love you here on earth –
      I have only today.

Thérèse of Lisieux, 1873–97

Where shall my wondering soul begin?
How shall I all to heaven aspire?
A slave redeem'd from death and sin,
A brand pluck'd from eternal fire,
How shall I equal triumphs raise,

Or sing my great Deliverer's praise?

O how shall I the goodness tell,
Father, which thou to me hast show'd?
That I, a child of wrath and hell,
I should be call'd a child of God,
Should know, should feel my sins forgiven,
Blest with this antepast of heaven!

And shall I slight my father's love?
Or basely fear his gifts to own?
Unmindful of his favors prove?
Shall I, the hallow'd cross to shun,
Refuse his righteousness to' impart,
By hiding it within my heart?

No: though the ancient Dragon rage,
And call forth all his host of war;
Though earth's self-righteous sons engage;
Them, and their god, alike I dare;
Jesus, the sinner's Friend, proclaim;
Jesus to sinners still the same.

Outcasts of men, to you I call,
Harlots, and publicans, and thieves!
He spreads his arms to' embrace you all;
Sinners alone his grace receives:
No need of him the righteous have;
He came the lost to seek and save.

Come, O my guilty brethren, come,
Groaning beneath your load of sin;
His bleeding heart shall make you room,
His open side shall take you in:
He calls you now, invites you home;
Come, O my guilty brethren, come!

For you the purple current flow'd
In pardons from his wounded side;
Languish'd for you the' eternal God;
For you the Prince of Glory died:
Believe, and all your sin's forgiven,
Only believe, and yours is heaven!
John Wesley, 1707–88

Thanksgiving for forgiveness and salvation

Gracious God of majesty and awe, I seek your protection, I look for your healing. Poor trou-bled sinner that I am, I appeal to you, the fountain of all mercy. I cannot bear your judgment, but I trust in your salvation. Lord, I show my wounds to you and uncover my shame before you. I know my sins are many and great, and they fill me with fear, but I hope in your mercies, for they cannot be numbered.
Ambrose, c.339–397

Lord Jesus Christ, eternal king, God and man, crucified for mankind, look upon me with mercy and hear my prayer, for I trust in you. Have mercy on me, full of sorrow and sin, for the depth of your compassion never ends.
Ambrose, c.339–397

May thy strong hand, O Lord, be ever my
    defense;
thy mercy in Christ, my salvation;
thy all-veritable word, my instructor;
the grace of thy life-bringing Spirit, my
    consolation
all along, and at last.
Lancelot Andrewes, 1555–1626

Too late have I loved you, O Beauty so ancient, O Beauty so new. Too late have I loved you! You were within me but I was outside myself, and there I sought you! In my weakness I ran after the beauty of the things you have made. You were with me, and I was not with you. The things you have made kept me from you – the things which would have no being unless they existed in you! You have called, you have cried, and you have pierced my deafness. You have radiated forth, you have shined out brightly, and you have dispelled my blindness. You have sent forth your fragrance, and I have breathed it in, and I long for you. I have tasted you, and I hunger and thirst for you. You have touched me, and I ardently desire your peace.
Augustine of Hippo, 354–430

Lord, you help those who turn to you. You redeem us so that we may come to you.
Augustine of Hippo, 354–430

Lord, only this do I ask of your great kindness: that you convert me totally to you and allow no obstacle to hinder me as I wend my way to you.
Augustine of Hippo, 354–430

Unto Thee will I offer up an offering of praise.
Late have I loved you,
O Beauty ever old and ever new.
You were within and I without, and there I
    sought you.
You were with me when I was not with you.
You called and cried to me, and pierced my
    deafness.
You shone and glowed, and dispelled my
    blindness.
You touched me, and I burned for your peace.

Augustine of Hippo, 354–430

Helper of all who turn to you,
Light of all who are in the dark,
Creator of all that grows from seed,
Promoter of all spiritual growth,
Have mercy, Lord, on me.
And make me a temple fit for you.
Do not look too closely at my sins,
For if you are quick to notice my faults
I shall not dare to appear before you.
In your great mercy.
In your boundless love,
Wash away my sins
By the hand of Jesus Christ,
Your only child, the chief healer of souls

Author unknown, papyrus 2nd–4th century

Lord Jesus Christ, Son of God, have mercy on
me, a sinner.

*Author unknown, known as
the "Jesus Prayer," Eastern Orthodox*

Lord, for thy tender mercies' sake, lay not our
sins to our charge, but forgive what is past and
give us grace to amend our lives; to decline
from sin and incline to virtue, that we may
walk with a perfect heart before thee, now and
evermore.

Source unknown, 16th century

Have mercy on me, O God, according to your
    loving-kindness;
        in your great compassion blot out my
            offences.
Wash me through and through from my
    wickedness and cleanse me from my sin.
Holy God,
holy and mighty,
holy immortal One,

have mercy upon me.

Source unknown, Eastern Orthodox

Lord Jesus Christ,
I admit that I am a sinner.
I believe that you died on the cross for my sins.
I now invite you to come into my life as my
    Lord and Savior.

Source unknown

We must praise Thy goodness, that Thou hast
left nothing undone to draw us to Thyself. But
one thing we ask of Thee, our God, not to cease
Thy work in our improvement. Let us tend
towards Thee, no matter by what means, and
be fruitful in good works, for the sake of Jesus
Christ our Lord. Amen.

Ludwig von Beethoven, 1770–1827

Lord, I have heard that Thou art a merciful
God, and hast ordained that Thy Son Jesus
Christ should be the Savior of the world; and
moreover, that Thou art willing to bestow
him upon such a poor sinner as I am, (and I
am a sinner indeed;) Lord, take therefore this
opportunity and magnify Thy grace in the
salvation of my soul, through Thy Son Jesus
Christ. Amen.

John Bunyan, 1628–88

O Lord God, Heavenly Father, Who by the
blessed light of Thy divine Word has led us to
the knowledge of Thy Son: We most heartily
beseech Thee so to replenish us with the grace
of Thy Holy Spirit, that we may ever walk in
the light of Thy truth, and rejoicing with sure
confidence in Christ our Savior, may in the
end be brought unto everlasting salvation;
through the same Jesus Christ, Thy Son, our
Lord, Amen.

*The Common Service Book of
the Lutheran Church, 1917*

O happy day, that fixed my choice
On Thee, my Savior and my God!
Well may this glowing heart rejoice,
And tell its raptures all abroad.

Refrain
Happy day, happy day, when Jesus washed my
    sins away!

He taught me how to watch and pray, and live
   rejoicing every day
Happy day, happy day, when Jesus washed my
   sins away.

O happy bond, that seals my vows
To Him Who merits all my love!
Let cheerful anthems fill His house,
While to that sacred shrine I move.
Refrain

It's done: the great transaction's done!
I am the Lord's and He is mine;
He drew me and I followed on;
Charmed to confess the voice divine.
Refrain

Now rest, my long divided heart,
Fixed on this blissful center, rest.
Here have I found a nobler part;
Here heavenly pleasures fill my breast.
Refrain

High heaven, that heard the solemn vow,
That vow renewed shall daily hear,
Till in life's latest hour I bow
And bless in death a bond so dear.
Refrain

Philip Doddridge, 1702–51

Lord Jesus Christ, King of Kings, You have
power over life and death. You know what is
secret and hidden, and neither our thoughts
nor our feelings are concealed from You. Cure
me of duplicity; I have done evil before You.
   Now my life declines from day to day
and my sins increase. O Lord, God of souls
and bodies, You know the extreme frailty of
my soul and my flesh. Grant me strength in
my weakness, O Lord, and sustain me in my
misery.
   Give me a grateful soul that I may never
cease to recall Your benefits, O Lord most
bountiful. Be not mindful of my many sins, but
forgive me all my misdeeds.

Ephraem, c.306–378

Almighty and eternal God, merciful Father,
who hast given to the human race Thy beloved
Son as an example of humility, obedience,
and patience, to precede us on the way of life,
bearing the cross: Graciously grant us that
we, inflamed by His infinite love, may take up
the sweet yoke of His Gospel together with
the mortification of the cross, following Him
as His true disciples, so that we shall one day
gloriously rise with Him and joyfully hear the
final sentence: "Come, ye blessed of My Father,
and possess the kingdom which was prepared
for you from the beginning," where Thou
reignest with the Son and the Holy Ghost, and
where we hope to reign with Thee, world without end. Amen.

Francis of Assisi, 1181–1226

O my adorable and loving Savior, consume my
heart with the burning fire with which Yours
is aflamed. Pour down on my soul those graces
which flow from Your love. Let my heart be
united with Yours. Let my will be conformed
to Yours in all things. May Your Will be the rule
of all my desires and actions. Amen.

Gertrude of Thüringen, 1256–1302

Redemption

Having been tenant long to a rich Lord,
Not thriving, I resolved to be bold,
And make a suit unto him, to afford
A new small-rented lease, and cancel th'old.

In heaven at his manor I him sought:
They told me there, that he was lately gone
About some land, which he had dearly bought
Long since on earth, to take possession.

I straight return'd, and knowing his great
   birth,
Sought him accordingly in great resorts;
In cities, theatres, gardens, parks, and courts:
At length I heard a ragged noise and mirth

Of thieves and murderers: there I him espied,
Who straight, Your suit is granted, and died.

George Herbert, 1593–1633

O Lord, show your mercy to me and gladden
my heart. I am like the man on the way to Jeri-
cho who was overtaken by robbers, wounded
and left for dead. O Good Samaritan, come to
my aid, I am like the sheep that went astray.
O Good Shepherd, seek me out and bring me
home in accord with your will. Let me dwell

in your house all the days of my life and praise
you for ever and ever with those who are there.

Jerome, c.342–420

And wilt Thou pardon, LORD,
A sinner such as I?
Although Thy book his crimes record
Of such a crimson dye?

So deep are they engraved, –
So terrible their fear,
The righteous scarcely shall be saved,
And where shall I appear?

My soul, make all things known
To Him Who all things sees:
That so the LAMB may yet atone
For thine iniquities.

O Thou Physician blest,
Make clean my guilty soul!
And me, by many a sin oppressed,
Restore, and keep me whole!

I know not how to praise
Thy mercy and Thy love:
But deign Thy servant to upraise,
And I shall learn above!

Joseph of the Studium, 9th century

O Lord Jesus Christ your love covers the multitude of my sins. So when I am fully aware of
my sin, when before the justice of heaven only
wrath is pronounced upon me, then you are
the only person to whom I can escape. If I try
to cover myself against the guilt of sin and the
wrath of heaven, I will be driven to madness
and despair. But if I rely on you to cover my
sins, I shall find peace and joy. you suffered
and died on the cross to shelter us from our
guilt, and take upon yourself the wrath that we
deserve. Let me rest under you, and may you
transform me into your likeness.

Søren Kierkegaard, 1813–55

Father in Heaven! Hold not our sins up against
us but hold us up against our sins so that the
thought of You when it wakens in our soul,
and each time it wakens, should not remind us
of what we have committed but of what You
did forgive, not of how we went astray but of

how You did save us!

Søren Kierkegaard, 1813–55

We thank thee, O God, the Father of our Lord
Jesus Christ, that thou hast revealed thy Son
to us, on whom we have believed, whom we
have loved, and whom we worship. O Lord
Jesus Christ, we commend our souls to thee.
O heavenly Father, we know that although we
shall in thine own good time be taken away
from this life, we shall live for ever with thee.
"God so loved the world, that he gave his only
begotten Son, that whosoever believeth in him
should not perish, but have everlasting life."
Father into thy hands we commend our spirit;
through Jesus Christ our Lord.

Martin Luther, 1483–1546

O thou that beholdest all things, we have
sinned against thee in thought, word, and
deed; blot out our transgressions, be merciful
to us sinners, and grant that our names may be
found written in the Book of Life, for the sake
of Christ Jesus our Savior.

Nerses of Clajes, 4th century

Glorious things of thee are spoken,
    Zion, city of our God!
He, whose word cannot be broken,
    Formed thee for His own abode.
On the rock of ages founded,
    What can shake thy sure repose?
With salvation's walls surrounded,
    Thou may'st smile at all thy foes.

See! the streams of living waters,
    Springing from eternal love,
Well supply thy sons and daughters,
    And all fear of want remove.
Who can faint while such a river
    Ever flows their thirst t'assuage:
Grace which, like the Lord the giver,
    Never fails from age to age?

Round each habitation hov'ring,
    See the cloud and fire appear!
For a glory and a cov'ring,
    Showing that the Lord is near:
Thus deriving from their banner
    Light by night and shade by day,
Safe they feed upon the manna

Which He gives them when they pray.

Blest inhabitants of Zion,
    Washed in the Redeemer's blood!
Jesus, whom their souls rely on,
    Makes them kings and priests to God:
'Tis His love His people raises
    Over self to reign as kings,
And as priests, His solemn praises
    Each for a thank-off'ring brings.

Savior, if of Zion's city
    I through grace a member am,
Let the world deride or pity,
    I will glory in Thy name:
Fading is the worldling's pleasure,
    All his boasted pomp and show;
Solid joys and lasting treasure
    None but Zion's children know.
                    John Newton, 1725–1807

Amazing grace! how sweet the sound
That saved a wretch like me;
I once was lost, but now am found;
Was blind, but now I see.

'Twas grace that taught my heart to fear,
And grace my fear relieved;
How precious did that grace appear,
The hour I first believed!

Through many dangers, toils and snares
I have already come:
'Tis grace that brought me safe thus far,
And grace will lead me home.

The Lord has promised good to me,
His word my hope secures;
He will my shield and portion be
As long as life endures.

Yes, when his heart and flesh shall fail,
And mortal life shall cease,
I shall profess within the veil
A life of joy and peace.

When we've been there a thousand years,
Bright shining as the sun,
We've no less days to sing God's praise
Than when we first begun.
                    John Newton, 1725–1807

O Heavenly King, the comfortor, the spirit of Truth, Who art present everywhere and fillest all things; Treasury of Blessings and Giver of Life; come and abide in us and cleanse us from every stain, and save our souls, O Gracious One.
                    Orthodox prayer

Listen, my soul: God has come to us;
Our Lord has visited us.
For my sake He was born of the Virgin Mary,
He was wrapped in swaddling clothes,
He who covers heaven with the clouds
and vests Himself with robes of light.
For my sake He was placed in the lowly
    manger,
He whose throne is the heavens and whose
    feet rest upon earth.
For my sake He was fed with His mother's
    milk,
He who feeds all creatures.
For my sake He was held in His mother's arms,
He who is borne by the Cherubim
and holds all creatures in His embrace.
For my sake He was circumcised according to
    the law,
He who is maker of the Law.
For my sake, He who is unseen
became visible and lived among men,
He who is my God.
My God became one like me, like a man;
the word became flesh,
and my Lord, the Lord of Glory,
took for my sake the form of a servant
and lived upon earth and walked upon earth
He who is the King of Heaven.
He labored, worked miracles,
conversed with men, was like a servant,
He who is the Lord of all.
He was hungry and thirsty,
He who provides food and drink for all
    creatures.
He wept, He who wipes away all tears.
He suffered and mourned,
He who is the consoler of all men.
He consorted with sinners,
He who alone is just and holy.
He who is omnipotent toiled
and had nowhere to lay His head,
He who lives in light inaccessible.
He was poor,

He who gives riches to all men.
He wandered from town to town and from
   place to place,
He who is omnipresent and fills all space.
And thus for thirty-three years and more
He lived and labored upon earth for my sake –
I who am His servant.

Tychon of Zadonsk, 18th century,
Russian Christian

Thanksgiving for the Scriptures

Lord, thy word abideth,
And our footsteps guideth,
Who its truth believeth
Light and joy receiveth.

O that we discerning
Its most holy learning,
Lord, may love and fear thee,
Evermore be near thee.

H.W. Baker, 1821–77

Father of mercies, in thy word
What endless glory shines!
For ever be thy name adored
For these celestial lines.

O may these heavenly page be
My ever dear delight,
And still new beauties may I see,
And still increasing light.

Divine instructor, gracious Lord,
Be thou for ever near;
Teach me to love thy sacred word,
And view my Savior here.

Anne Steele, 1717–78

Blessed Lord, by whose providence all holy
scriptures were written and preserved for
our instruction, give us grace to study them
this and every day with patience and love.
Strengthen our souls with the fullness of their
divine teaching. Keep us from all pride and
irreverence. Guide us in the deep tings of thy
heavenly wisdom, and of thy great mercy lead
us by thy Word unto everlasting life; through
Jesus Christ our Lord and Savior.

B.F. Westcott, 1825–1901

Thanksgiving for spiritual and material blessings

Bless the Lord, O my soul,
   and all that is within me,
   bless his holy name.
Bless the Lord, O my soul,
   and do not forget all his benefits –
who forgives all your iniquity,
   who heals all your diseases,
who redeems your life from the Pit,
   who crowns you with steadfast love and
      mercy,
who satisfies you with good as long as you live
   so that your youth is renewed like the
      eagle's.

Psalm 103.1–5 NRSV

We thank thee with all our hearts for every
gracious dispensation, for all the blessings that
have attended our lives, for every hour of
safety, health and peace, of domestic comfort
and innocent enjoyment. We feel that we have
been blessed far beyond any thing that we
have deserved; and though we cannot but
pray for a continuance of all these mercies, we
acknowledge our unworthiness of them and
implore thee to pardon the presumption of
our desires.

Jane Austen, 1775–1817

Almighty God, more generous than any
   father, we stand amazed at the many gifts
   you shower upon us.
   You give freely and willingly, always
      with regard to our ability to receive.
   You give daily gifts, teaching us to trust
      you for tomorrow.
   You give us gifts through one another,
      so that we may learn to share.
   You give through our own effort,
      respecting our independence.
How thoughtfully you offer all your gifts!
   So continue, Lord, of your goodness.

Author unknown

O God, I thank thee for all the joy I have had
in life.

Byrhtnoth, d.991

O Lord, may you be blessed for your provi-

dence and the care you have always shown me wherever I have been.
Amen.

Anthony Mary Claret, 1807–70

O God our Father, we would thank thee for all the bright things of life. Help us to see them, and to count them, and to remember them, that our lives may flow in ceaseless praise; for the sake of Jesus Christ our Lord.

J.H. Jowett, 1846–1923

We render unto thee our thanksgiving, O Lord our God, Father of our Lord and Savior Jesus Christ, by all means, at all times, in all places; for that thou hast sheltered, assisted, supported, and led us on through the time past of our life and brought us to this hour. And we pray and beseech thee, O God and loving Lord, grant us to pass this day, this year, and all the time of our life without sin, with all joy, health and salvation.

Liturgy of St Mark, 2nd century

Is not sight a jewel?
Is not hearing a treasure?
Is not speech a glory?
O my Lord, pardon my ingratitude and pity my dullness who am not sensible of these gifts. The freedom of thy bounty hath deceived me. These things were too near to be considered. Thou presented me with thy blessings, and I was not aware. But now I give thanks and adore and praise thee for thy inestimable favors.

Thomas Traherne, 1636–74

Thanksgiving for understanding

I thank thee, gracious Lord, I thank thee; because what I formerly believed by thy bounty, I now so understand by thine illumination, that if I were unwilling to believe that thou dost exist, I should not be able not to understand this to be true.

Anselm, 1033–1109

Prayers for Spiritual Growth

GRACE

GRATITUDE

GROWTH

GUIDANCE

HAPPINESS

HEALING, SPIRITUAL

HEAVEN

HOLINESS

HOPE

HUMILITY

KNOWLEDGE OF GOD

LIGHT

OBEDIENCE

PERSEVERANCE

PRAYER, HELP IN

PRESENCE OF GOD

PRIDE

PURITY

RECONCILIATION

REGENERATION

RENEWAL

REST

RESTORATION

REVERENCE

RIGHTEOUSNESS

SALVATION AND RESTORATION, SEEKING

SEEKING GOD

SELF-DENIAL

SERVING GOD

SIMPLICITY

SPEAKING

SPIRITUAL PILGRIMAGE

STEADFASTNESS

STEWARDSHIP

STRENGTH

TEMPTATION, RESISTING

TRUST

TRUTH

UNSELFISHNESS

VIRTUE

VISION OF GOD

WILL OF GOD

WISDOM

WITNESS

WORSHIP

Related entries in Part Two

Extracts of classic Christian teaching on prayer

Richard Baxter: The Saint's Everlasting Rest

John Calvin: Daniel's Prayer

Thomas à Kempis: The Imitation of Christ

Abraham Kuyper: Prayer and the Consciousness

Andrew Murray: Prayer and Fasting

Richard Sibbes: Divine Meditations

George Whitefield: The Pharisee and the Publican

THE GIFT OF THE SPIRIT

Lord Jesus, as God's Spirit came down and rested upon you, may the same Spirit rest upon us, bestowing his sevenfold gifts. First, grant us the gift of understanding, by which your precepts may enlighten our minds.

Second, grant us counsel, by which we may follow in your foot-steps on the path of righteousness.

Third, grant us courage, by which we may ward off the Enemy's attacks.

Fourth, grant us knowledge, by which we can distinguish good from evil.

Fifth, grant us piety, by which we may acquire compassionate hearts.

Sixth, grant us fear, by which we may draw back from evil and submit to what is good.

Seventh, grant us wisdom, that we may taste fully the life-giving sweetness of your love.

Bonaventure, 1217–74

THE FRUIT OF THE SPIRIT

Fruitful living

Light eternal, shine in my heart:
Power eternal, deliver me from evil:
Wisdom eternal, scatter the darkness of my ignorance:
Might eternal, pity me.
Grant that I may ever seek thy face, with all my heart and soul and strength;
and, in thine infinite mercy, bring me at last to thy holy presence, where I shall behold thy glory and possess thy promised joy.

Alcuin, 735–804

O Lord, who hast mercy upon all, take away from me my sins, and mercifully kindle in me the fire of thy Holy Spirit. Take away from me the heart of stone, and give me a heart of flesh, a heart to love and adore thee, a heart to delight in thee, to follow and to enjoy thee, for Christ's sake.

Ambrose, c.339–397

O merciful God, fill our hearts, we pray, with the graces of your Holy Spirit; with love, joy, peace, patience, gentleness, goodness, faithfulness, humility and self-control. Teach us to love those who hate us; to pray for those who despitefully use us; that we may be the children of your love, our Father, who makes the sun to rise on the evil and the good, and sends rain on the just and on the unjust. In adversity grant us grace to be patient; in prosperity keep us humble; may we guard the door of our lips; may we lightly esteem the pleasures of this world, and thirst after heavenly things; through Jesus Christ our Lord.

Anselm, 1033–1109

Bestow on me, Lord, a genial spirit and unwearied forbearance; a mild, loving patient heart; kindly looking, pleasant, friendly speech and manners in daily life; that I may give offence to no one, but as much as in me lies live in charity with all men.

Johann Arndt, 1555–1621

Make me, O my God,
humble without pretence,
cheerful without levity,
serious without dejection,
grave without moroseness,
active without frivolity,
truthful without duplicity,
fearful of thee without despair,
trustful of thee without presumption,
chaste without depravity,
able to correct my neighbor without angry
    feeling,
and by word and example to edify him
    without pride,
obedient without gainsaying,
patient without murmuring.

Thomas Aquinas, 1225–74

Grant to us your servants: to our God – a heart of flame; to our fellow men – a heart of love; to ourselves – a heart of steel.

Augustine of Hippo, 354–430

My God, I believe in you: increase my faith.
I hope in you: strengthen my hope.
I love you, and desire to love you more and
    more, and above all things, and above all

others. Bring to life my love and make me completely yours.

Author unknown

May God, who seeth all things, and who is the Ruler of all spirits and the Lord of all flesh–who chose our Lord Jesus Christ and us through Him to be a special people–grant to every soul that calleth upon His glorious and holy name, faith, fear, peace, patience, long-suffering, self-control, purity, and sobriety, to the well-pleasing of His name, through our High Priest and Protector, Jesus Christ, by whom be to Him glory, and majesty, and power, and honor, both now and for evermore. Amen.

Clement of Rome, c.30–c.95

O Lord and Master of my life,
Grant that I may not have a spirit of idleness,
of discouragement,
of lust for power,
and of vain speaking.
But bestow on me, your servant,
the spirit of chastity,
of meekness,
of patience,
and of love.
Yes, O Lord and King,
grant that I may perceive
my own transgressions,
and judge not my brother,
For you are blessed from age to age.

Ephraem, c.306–378

May I be an enemy to no one and the friend of
    what abides eternally.
May I never quarrel with those nearest me,
    and be reconciled quickly if I should.
May I never plot evil against others, and if
    anyone plot evil against me, may I escape
    unharmed and without the need to hurt
    anyone else.
May I love, seek, and attain only what is good.
May I desire happiness for all and harbor envy
    for none.
May I never find joy in the misfortune of one
    who has wronged me.
May I never wait for the rebuke of others, but
    always rebuke myself until I make reparation.
May I gain no victory that harms me or my
    opponent.

May I reconcile friends who are mad at each
other.
May I, insofar as I can, give all necessary help
to my friends and to all who are in need.
May I never fail a friend in trouble.
May I be able to soften the pain of the grief
stricken and give them comforting words.
May I respect myself.
May I always maintain control of my emotions.
May I habituate myself to be gentle, and
never angry with others because of
circumstances.
May I never discuss the wicked or what they
have done, but know good people and
follow in their footsteps.

Eusebius of Caesarea, d.c.340

Give us, O Lord, purity of lips, clean and
innocent hearts, and rectitude of action; give
us humility, patience, self-wisdom and understanding, the spirit of counsel and strength,
the spirit of knowledge and godliness, and of
thy fear; make us ever to seek thy face with all
our heart, all our soul, all our mind; grant us to
have a contrite and humbled heart in thy presence, to prefer nothing to thy love. Have mercy
upon us, we humbly beseech thee; through
Jesus Christ our Lord.

Gallican Sacramentary

Eternal God,
the light of the minds that know thee,
the life of the souls that love thee,
the strength of the wills that serve thee;
help us so to know thee that we may truly
love thee,
so to love thee that we may fully serve thee,
whom to serve is perfect freedom.

*Gelasian Sacramentary, 5th century, based on a
prayer by Augustine of Hippo, 354–430*

O Lord God, grant us always, whatever the world
may say, to content ourselves with what you say,
and to care only for your approval, which will
outweigh all worlds; for Jesus Christ's sake.

General Charles Gordon, 1833–85

King of glory, King of peace,
I will love thee:
And that love may never cease,
I will move thee.

Thou hast granted my request,
Thou has heard me:
Thou didst note my working breast,
Thou has spared me.

Wherefore with my utmost art
I will sing thee,
And the cream of all my heart
I will bring thee.

Though my sins against me cried,
Thou didst clear me;
And alone, when they replied,
Thou didst hear me.

Seven whole days, not one in seven,
I will praise thee.
In my heart, though not in heaven,
I can raise thee.

Thou grew'st soft and most with tears,
Thou relentedst.
And when Justice call'd for fears,
Thou dissentedst.

Small it is, in this poor sort
To enrol thee:
Even eternity's too short
To extol thee.

George Herbert, 1593–1633, The Temple

Give me, O Lord, I pray thee, firm faith, unwavering hope, perfect charity.
Pour into my heart the spirit of wisdom and
understanding, the spirit of counsel and spiritual strength, the spirit of knowledge and true
godliness, and the sprit of thy holy fear.
I offer up unto you my prayers and intercessions, for those especially who have in any way
hurt, grieved, or found fault with me, or who
have done me any harm or displeasure.
For all those also whom, at any time, I have
annoyed, troubled, burdened, and scandalized,
by words or deeds, knowingly or in ignorance:
that you would grant us all equally pardon
for our sins, and for our offences against each
other.
Take away from our hearts, O Lord, all
suspiciousness, indignation, anger and contention, and whatever may harm charity, and
lesson brotherly love. Have mercy, O Lord,

have mercy on those who crave for your mercy, give grace to those who stand in need of your grace, and make us such that we may be worthy to receive your grace, and go forward to life eternal.

Thomas à Kempis, 1379–1471

Guide us, teach us, and strengthen us, O Lord, we beseech thee, until we become such as thou wouldest have us be: pure, gentle, truthful, high-minded, courteous, generous, able, dutiful and useful; for thy honor and glory.

Charles Kingsley, 1819–75

Behold, Lord, an empty vessel that needs to be filled. My Lord, fill it. I am weak in the faith, strengthen me. I am cold in love; warm me and make me fervent that my love may go out to my neighbor. O Lord, help me. Strengthen my faith and trust in you.

With me, there is an abundance of sin; in you is the fullness of righteousness. Therefore I will remain with you, from whom I can receive, but to whom I may not give.

Martin Luther, 1483–1546

Give me, good Lord, an humble, lowly, quiet, peaceable, patient, charitable, kind and filial and tender mind, every shade, in fact, of charity, with all my words and all my works, and all my thoughts, to have a taste of thy holy blessed Spirit.

Thomas More, 1478–1535

Grant, I thee pray, such heat into mine heart
That to this love of thine may be equal;
Grant me from Satan's service to astart,
With whom me rueth so long to have been
    thrall;
Grant me, good Lord and Creator all,
The flame to quench of all sinful desire
And in thy love set all mine heart afire.

That when the journey of this deadly life
My silly ghost hath finishèd, and thence
Departen must without his fleshly wife,
Alone into his Lordès high presènce,
He may thee find, O well of indulgènce,
In thy lordship not as a lord, but rather
As a very tender, loving father.

Thomas More, 1478–1535

Our Father, Thou comest seeking fruit. Teach us, we pray Thee, to realize how truly this is the one object of our existence, and of our union to Christ. Make it the one desire of our hearts to be branches, so filled with the Spirit of the Vine, as to bring forth fruit abundantly.

Andrew Murray, 1828–1917

Our Father which art in Heaven, Thou art the heavenly Husbandman. And Christ is the heavenly Vine. And I am a heavenly branch, partaker of His heavenly life, to bear His heavenly fruit. Father, let the power of His life so fill me, that I may ever bear more fruit, to the glory of Thy name.

Andrew Murray, 1828–1917

O our God, we believe in thee, we hope in thee, and we love thee, because thou has created us, redeemed us, and does sanctify us. Increase our faith, strengthen our hope, and deepen our love, that giving up ourselves wholly to thy will, we may serve thee faithfully all the rest of our life; through Jesus Christ our Lord.

The Narrow Way, 1869

Praise to the Holiest in the height,
    And in the depth be praise;
In all his words most wonderful,
    Most sure in all his ways.

O loving wisdom of our God!
    When all was sin and shame,
A second Adam to the fight
    And to the rescue came.

O wisest love! that flesh and blood,
    Which did in Adam fail,
Should strive afresh against the foe,
    Should strive and should prevail.

And that a higher gift than grace
    Should flesh and blood refine,
God's presence and his very self,
    And essence all-divine.

O generous love! That he who smote
    In Man, for man, the foe,
The double agony in Man,
    For man, should undergo;

And in the garden secretly,
    And on the cross on high,
Should teach his brethren, and inspire
    To suffer and to die.

Praise to the Holiest in the height,
    And in the depth be praise;
In all his words most wonderful,
    Most sure in all his ways.
                    J.H. Newman, 1801–90

I asked the Lord, that I might grow
    In faith, and love, and every grace;
Might more of His salvation know,
    And seek more earnestly His face.

I hoped that in some favored hour
    At once He'd answer my request,
And by His love's constraining power
    Subdue my sins, and give me rest.

Instead of this, He made me feel
    The hidden evils of my heart;
And let the angry powers of hell
    Assault my soul in every part.

Yea more, with His own hand He seemed
    Intent to aggravate my woe;
Crossed all the fair designs I schemed,
    Blasted my gourds, and laid me low.

"Lord, why is this?" I trembling cried,
    "Wilt thou pursue Thy worm to death?"
"'Tis in this way," the Lord replied,
    "I answer prayer for grace and faith.

These inward trials I employ
    From self and pride to set thee free;
And break thy schemes of earthly joy,
    That thou may'st seek thy all in me."
                    John Newton, 1725–1807

Hold us fast, O Lord of Hosts, that we fall not from thee. Grant us thankful and obedient hearts, that we may increase daily in love, knowledge and fear of thee. Increase our faith, and help our unbelief; that being provided for and relieved of all our needs by thy fatherly care and providence, we may live a godly life, to the praise and good example of thy people, and after this life may reign with thee for ever;

through Jesus Christ our Savior.
                    James Pilkington, 1520–76

A Prayer for the graces of faith, hope, charity
O Lord God of infinite mercy, of infinite excellency, who hast sent thy holy Son into the world to redeem us from an intolerable misery, and to teach us a holy religion, and to forgive us an infinite debt: give me thy Holy Spirit, that my understanding and all my facilities may be so resigned to the discipline and doctrine of my Lord, that I may be prepared in mind and will to die for the testimony of Jesus, and to suffer any affliction or calamity that shall offer to hinder my duty, or tempt me to shame or sin or apostasy; and let my faith be the parent of a good life, a strong shield to repel the fiery darts of the devil, and the author of a holy hope, of modest desires, of confidence in God, and of a never-failing charity to thee, my God, and to all the world; that I may never have my portion with the unbelievers or uncharitable and desperate persons; but may be supported by the strengths of faith in all temptations, and may be refreshed with the comforts of a holy hope in all my sorrows, and may bear the burden of the Lord, and the infirmities of my neighbor, by the support of charity; that the yoke of Jesus may become easy to me, and my love may do all the miracles of grace, till from grace it swell to glory, from earth to heaven, from duty to reward, from the imperfections of a beginning and still growing love, it may arrive to the consummation of an eternal and never-ceasing charity, through Jesus Christ the Son of thy love, the author of our hope, and the author and finisher of our faith: to whom with thee, O Lord God, Father of heaven and earth, and with thy Holy Spirit, be all glory and love and obedience and dominion, now and for ever. Amen.
                    Jeremy Taylor, 1613–67

Hear our prayers, O Lord, and consider our desires. Give unto us true humility, a meek and quiet spirit, a holy and useful manner of life; bearing the burdens of our neighbors, denying ourselves, and studying to benefit others, and to please thee in all things. Grant us to be righteous in performing promises, loving to our relatives, careful of our charges; to be gentle and easy to be entreated, slow to anger, and readily prepared for every good work.

Jeremy Taylor, 1613–67

Govern all by your wisdom, O Lord, so that my soul may always be serving you according to your will, and not as I desire. Do not punish me, I pray, by granting what I want and ask, if it offends your love, which would always live in me. Let me die to myself, that I may serve you, let me live to you, who in yourself are the true Life.

Teresa of Avila, 1515–82

O most loving Jesu, pattern of charity, who makest all the commandments of the law to consist in love towards God and towards man, grant to us to love thee with all our heart, with all our mind, and all our soul, and our neighbor for thy sake; that the grace of charity and brotherly love may dwell in us, and all envy, harshness, and ill-will may die in us; and fill our hearts with feelings of love, kindness, and compassion, so that by constantly rejoicing in the happiness and good success of others, by sympathizing with them in their sorrows, and putting away all harsh judgments and envious thoughts, we may follow thee, who art thyself the true and perfect love.

Treasury of Devotion, 1869

O thou Prince of Peace, who, when thou wast reviled revilest not again, and on the cross didst pray for thy murderers, implant in our hearts the virtues of gentleness and patience, that we may overcome evil with good, for thy sake love our enemies, and as children of our heavenly Father seek thy peace, and evermore rejoice in thy love; through Jesus Christ our Savior.

Treasury of Devotion, 1869

Love

LOVE OF GOD

We love you, O our God; and we desire to love you more and more. Grant to us that we may love you as much as we desire, and as much as we ought. O dearest friend, who has so loved and saved us, the thought of whom is so sweet

and always growing sweeter, come with Christ and dwell in our hearts; that you keep a watch over our lips, our steps, our deeds, and we shall not need to be anxious either for our souls or our bodies. Give us love, sweetest of all gifts, which knows no enemy. Give us in our hearts pure love, born of your love to us, that we may love others as you love us. O most loving Father of Jesus Christ, from whom flows all love, let our hearts, frozen in sin, cold to you and cold to others, be warmed by this divine fire. So help and bless us in your Son.

Anselm, 1033–1109

O Lord our God, grant us grace to desire you with a whole heart, that so desiring you we may seek you and find you; and so finding you, may love you; and loving you, may hate those sins from which you have redeemed us, for Jesus Christ's sake.

Anselm, 1033–1109

Lord, my heart is before you. I try, but by myself I can do nothing; do what I cannot. Admit me into the inner room of your love. I ask, I seek, I knock. You have made me seek, make me receive; you have enabled me to seek, enable me to find. You have taught me to knock, open to my knock. …

I faint with hunger for your love; refresh me with it. Let me be filled with your love, rich in your affection, completely held in your care. Take me and possess me wholly, who with the Father and the Holy Spirit are alone blessed from age to age.

Anselm, 1033–1109

Fire that forever blazes and never goes out,
love that forever burns and never grows cold,
embrace me that I may love you.
I love you, Jesus with all my heart,
with all my soul, with all my strength.
O that I may love you more and that all may
    love you.
Amen.

Anthony Mary Claret, 1807–70

Lord, you are my love, my honor, my hope,
    and my refuge.
You are my glory and my goal, My Master, My
    Father.

Help me to seek nothing more than you
Nor to know anything but your holy will and
   how to fulfill it.
I want you alone, and in you, by you and for
   you all other things.
You are more than enough for me.
Make me love you as you love me and as you
   would have me love you.
Amen.

Anthony Mary Claret, 1807–70

Look on us, O Lord, and let all the darkness
of our souls disappear before the beams of
your brightness. Fill us with your holy love,
and open to us the treasures of your wisdom.
You know all our desire, so bring to perfection
what you have started, and what your Spirit
has awakened us to ask in prayer. We seek your
face, turn your face to us and show us your
glory. Then our longing will be satisfied and
our peace will be perfect.

Augustine of Hippo, 354–430

Come, Lord,
work on us,
set us on fire
and clasp us close,
be fragrant to us,
draw us to your love,
let us run to you.

Augustine of Hippo, 354–430

O God, who hast prepared for them that love
thee such good things as pass man's understanding; Pour into our hearts such love toward
thee, that we, loving thee above all things, may
obtain thy promises, which exceed all that
we can desire; through Jesus Christ our Lord.
Amen.

*Book of Common Prayer, the
Sixth Sunday after Trinity*

God, which has prepared to them that love thee,
such good things as pass all man's understanding: Pour into our hearts such love toward thee,
that we loving thee in all things, may obtain thy
promises, which exceed all that we can desire:
through Jesus Christ our Lord.

*Book of Common Prayer, 1549, Collect
for the Sixth Sunday after Trinity Sunday*

My God, I love you above all else and you
I desire as my final goal. Always and in all
things, with my whole heart, and strength I
seek you. If you do not give yourself to me, you
give nothing; if I do not find you, I find nothing. Grant me, therefore, most loving God, that
I may always love you for yourself above all
things, and seek you in all things in the present
life, so that finally I may find you and keep you
for ever in the world to come.

Thomas Bradwardine, c.1290–1349

May the power of your love, Lord Christ, fiery
and sweet as honey, so absorb our hearts as to
withdraw them from all that is under heaven.
Grant that we may be ready to die for love of
your love, as you died for love of our love.

Francis of Assisi, 1181–1226

O Love, O God, you created me, in your love
   recreate me.
O Love, you redeemed me, fill up and redeem
   for yourself in me whatever part of your
   love has fallen into neglect within me.
O Love, O God, you made me yours, as in the
   blood of your Christ purchased me, in your
   truth sanctify me.
O Love, O God, you adopted me as a
   daughter, after your own heart fashion and
   foster me.
O Love, you chose me as yours not another's,
   grant that I may cling to you with my
   whole being.
O Love, O God, you loved me first, grant that
   with my whole heart, and with my whole
   soul, and with my whole strength, I may
   love you.

Gertrude of Thüringen, 1256–1302

O Love, O God almighty, in your love confirm
   me.
O Love most wise, give me wisdom in the love
   of you.
O Love most sweet, give me sweetness in the
   taste of you.
O Love most dear, grant that I may live only
   for you.
O Love most faithful, in all my tribulations
   comfort and succor me.
O Love who is always with me, work all my
   works in me.

O Love most victorious, grant that I may
    persevere to the end in you.
                    Gertrude of Thüringen, 1256–1302

Faith will vanish into sight;
Hope be emptied in delight;
Love in heaven will shine more bright;
    Therefore give us love.
                    Christopher Wordsworth, 1807–85

All people that on earth do dwell,
    Sing to the Lord with cheerful voice;
Him serve with mirth, his praise forth tell,
    Come ye before him, and rejoice.

The Lord, ye know, is God indeed;
    Without our aid he did us make;
We are his folk, he doth us feed,
    And for his sheep he doth us take.

Oh enter then his gates with praise,
    Approach with joy his courts unto;
Praise, laud, and bless his name always.
    For it is seemly so to do.

For why, the Lord our God is good;
    His mercy is for ever sure;
His truth at all times firmly stood,
    And shall from age to age endure.
                    William Kethe, d.1593, based on Psalm 100

Ah, blessed Lord, I wish I knew how I might
best love you and please you, that my love were
as sweet to you as your love is to me.
                    Margery Kempe, c.1371–c.1432

My crucified Love, my dear Jesus! I believe
in Thee, and confess Thee to be the true Son
of God and my Savior. I adore Thee from the
abyss of my own nothingness, and I thank
Thee for the death Thou didst suffer for me,
that I might obtain the life of divine grace. My
beloved Redeemer, to Thee I owe all my salvation. Through Thee I have hitherto escaped
hell; through Thee have I received the pardon
of my sins. But I am so ungrateful, that, instead
of loving Thee, I have repeated my offenses
against Thee. I deserve to be condemned, so as
not to be able to love Thee any more: but no,
my Jesus, punish me in any other way, but not
in this. If I have not loved Thee in times past, I

love Thee now; and I desire nothing but to love
Thee with all my heart. But without Thy help I
can do nothing. Since Thou dost command me
to love Thee, give me also the strength to fulfill
this Thy sweet and loving precept. Thou hast
promised to grant all that we ask of Thee: You
shall ask whatever you will and it shall be done
unto you. Confiding, then, in this promise, my
dear Jesus, I ask, first of all, pardon of all my
sins; and I repent, above all things, because
I have offended Thee, O Infinite Goodness! I
ask for holy perseverance in Thy grace till my
death. But, above all, I ask for the gift of Thy
holy love. Ah, my Jesus, my Hope, my Love,
my All, inflame me with that love which Thou
didst come on earth to enkindle! "Tui amoris
me ignem accende." For this end, make me
always live in conformity with Thy holy will.
Enlighten me, that I may understand more and
more how worthy Thou art of our love, and
that I may know the immense love Thou hast
borne me, especially in giving Thy life for me.
Grant, then, that I may love Thee with all my
heart, and may love Thee always, and never
cease to beg of Thee the grace to love Thee in
this life; that, living always and dying in Thy
love, I may come one day to love Thee with all
my strength in heaven, never to leave off loving
Thee for all eternity.
                    Alphonsus Liguori, 1696–1787

O Love that wilt not let me go,
I rest my weary soul in thee;
I give thee back the life I owe,
That in thine ocean depths its flow
May richer, fuller be.
                    George Matheson, 1842–1906

Christ my God, set my heart on fire with love
in You, that in its flame I may love You with
all my heart, with all my mind, and with all
my soul and with all my strength, and my
neighbor as myself, so that by keeping Your
commandments I may glorify You the Giver of
every good and perfect gift. Amen.
                    Orthodox prayer

Litany of the Love of God
Lord, have mercy on us.
Christ, have mercy on us.
Lord, have mercy on us.

Christ, hear us. Christ graciously hear us.
God, the Father of heaven,
Have mercy on us.
God the Son, Redeemer of the world,
Have mercy on us.
God, the Holy Ghost,
Have mercy on us.
Holy Trinity, one God,
Have mercy on us.
Thou Who art Infinite Love,
Have mercy on us.
Thou Who didst first love me,
Have mercy on us.
Thou Who commandest me to love Thee,
Have mercy on us.

With all my heart,
I Love Thee, O My God
With all my soul,
I Love Thee, O My God
With all my mind,
I Love Thee, O My God
With all my strength,
I Love Thee, O My God
Above all possessions and honors,
I Love Thee, O My God
Above all pleasures and enjoyments,
I Love Thee, O My God
More than myself, and everything belonging
    to me,
I Love Thee, O My God
More than all my relatives and friends,
I Love Thee, O My God
More than all men and angels,
I Love Thee, O My God
Above all created things in heaven or on
    earth,
I Love Thee, O My God
Only for Thyself,
I Love Thee, O My God
Because Thou art the sovereign Good,
I Love Thee, O My God
Because Thou art infinitely worthy of being
    loved,
I Love Thee, O My God
Because Thou art infinitely perfect,
I Love Thee, O My God
Even hadst Thou not promised me heaven,
I Love Thee, O My God
Even hadst Thou not menaced me with hell,
I Love Thee, O My God

Even shouldst Thou try me by want and
    misfortune,
I Love Thee, O My God
In wealth and in poverty,
I Love Thee, O My God
In prosperity and in adversity,
I Love Thee, O My God
In health and in sickness,
I Love Thee, O My God
In life and in death,
I Love Thee, O My God
In time and in eternity,
I Love Thee, O My God
In union with that love wherewith all the saints
    and all the angels love Thee in heaven,
I Love Thee, O My God
In union with that love wherewith the Blessed
    Virgin Mary loveth Thee,
I Love Thee, O My God
In union with that infinite love wherewith
    Thou lovest Thyself eternally,
I Love Thee, O My God

Pope Pius VI, 1717–99

My God, Who dost possess in incomprehensible abundance all that is perfect and worthy
of love, annihilate in me all guilty, sensual,
and undue love for creatures. Kindle in my
heart the pure fire of Thy love, so that I may
love nothing but Thee or in Thee, until being
so entirely consumed by holy love of Thee, I
may go to love Thee eternally with the elect in
heaven, the country of pure love. Amen.

Pope Pius VI, 1717–99

Most loving Lord, give me a childlike love of
thee, which casts out all fear.

E.B. Pusey, 1800–82

O Lord, prepare my heart, I beseech thee, to
reverence thee, to adore thee, to love thee; to
hate, for love of thee, all my sins, imperfections,
shortcomings, whatever in me displeaseth
thee; and to love all which thou lovest, and
whom thou lovest. Give me, Lord, fervor of
love, shame for my unthankfulness, sorrow for
my sins, longing for thy grace, and to be wholly
united with thee. Let my very coldness call for
the glow of thy love; let my emptiness and
dryness, like a barren and thirsty land, thirst
for thee, call on thee to come into my soul,

who refreshesest those who are weary. Let my heart ache to thee and for thee, who stillest the aching heart. Let my mute longings praise thee, crave to thee, who satisfiest the empty soul, that waits on thee.

E.B. Pusey, 1800–67

O Love everlasting, enflame my soul to love God, so that nothing may burn in me but His embraces. O good Jesu, who shall grant me to feel Thee that now may neither be felt nor seen? Pour Thyself into the center of my soul. Come into my heart and fill it with Thy clearest sweetness. Moisten my mind with the hot wine of Thy sweet love, that forgetful of all ills and all troubling images, and only having Thee, I may be glad and joy in Jesu my God. Henceforward, sweetest Lord, go not from me, continually biding with me in Thy sweetness; for Thy presence only is solace to me, and Thy absence only leaves me heavy.

Richard Rolle, 1290–1349

Teach us, Lord, to fear thee without being afraid; to fear thee in love, that we may love without fear; through Jesus Christ our Lord.

Christina Rossetti, 1830–94

Grant to us, O Lord, that most excellent of all virtues, the gift of your divine love. Let love be in our thinking and our speaking, in our daily work and in the hidden places of our souls. Let love be in our friendships and in our life with those it is hard to bear. Let love be in our joys and in our sorrows, in our life and in our death. Amen.

William Temple, 1881–1944

Lord Jesus, I am not an eagle. All I have are the eyes and the heart of one. In spite of my littleness, I dare to gaze at the sun of love, and long to fly towards it.

Thérèse of Lisieux, 1873–97

Since You loved me so much as to give me Your only Son as my Savior and my Spouse, the infinite treasures of His merits are mine. I offer them to You with gladness, begging You to look upon me only in the Face of Jesus and in His heart burning with Love.

Thérèse of Lisieux, 1873–97

I love you, O my God, and my only desire is to love you until the last breath of my life. I love you, O my infinitely lovable God, and I would rather die loving you, than live without loving you. I love you, Lord, and the only grace I ask is to love you eternally … My God, if my tongue cannot say in every moment that I love you, I want my heart to repeat it to you as often as I draw breath.

John Vianney, 1786–1859

Love divine, all loves excelling,
Joy of heaven to earth come down;
Fix in us thy humble dwelling;
All thy faithful mercies crown!
Jesus, Thou art all compassion,
Pure unbounded love Thou art;
Visit us with Thy salvation;
Enter every trembling heart.

Charles Wesley, 1707–88

Thou hidden love of God, whose height,
Whose depth unfathom'd no man knows,
I see from far thy beauteous light,
Inly I sigh for thy repose;
My heart is pain'd, nor can it be
At rest, till it finds rest in thee.

Thy secret voice invites me still,
The sweetness of thy yoke to prove:
And fain I would: but tho' my will
Seem fix'd, yet wide my passions rove;
Yet hindrances strew all the way;
I aim at thee, yet from thee stray.

'Tis mercy all, that thou hast brought
My mind to seek her peace in thee;
Yet while I seek, but find thee not,
No peace my wand'ring soul shall see;
O when shall all my wand'rings end,
And all my steps to thee-ward tend!

Is there a thing beneath the sun
That strives with thee my heart to share?
Ah! tear it thence, and reign alone,
The Lord of ev'ry motion there;
Then shall my heart from earth be free,
When it hath found repose in thee.

O hide this self from me, that I
No more, but Christ in me may live;

My vile affections crucify,
Nor let one darling lust survive;
In all things nothing may I see,
Nothing desire or seek but thee.

O Love, thy sov'reign aid impart,
To save me from low-thoughted care:
Chase this self-will thro' all my heart,
Thro' all its latent mazes there:
Make me thy duteous child, that I
Ceaseless may Abba, Father, cry!

Ah no! ne'er will I backward turn:
Thine wholly, thine alone I am!
Thrice happy he who views with scorn
Earth's toys, for thee his constant flame;
O help that I may never move
From the blest footsteps of thy love!

Each moment draw from earth away
My heart that lowly waits thy call:
Speak to my inmost soul, and say,
I am thy love, thy God, thy all!
To feel thy power, to hear thy voice,
To taste thy love, be all my choice.

John Wesley, 1703–91

O God, the God of all goodness and of all
grace, who are worthy of a greater love than we
can either give or understand: fill our hearts,
we beseech you, with such love towards you
that nothing may seem too hard for us to do or
to suffer in obedience to your will; and grant
that loving you, we may become daily more
like you, and finally obtain the crown of life
which you have promised to those who love
you; through Jesus Christ our Lord.

B.F. Westcott, 1825–1901

Love is kind and suffers long,
Love is meek and thinks no wrong,
Love than death itself more strong;
    Therefore give us love.

Christopher Wordsworth, 1807–85

LOVE OF OTHERS

Blessed are those who love you, O Lord, and
love their friends in you and their enemies
because of you.

Augustine of Hippo, 354–430

Lord, inspire me with love, that I may teach
sweetness.

Augustine of Hippo, 354–430

Save us, Lord, from being self-centered in our
prayers, and teach us to remember to pray for
others. May we be so caught up in love for
those for whom we pray, that we may feel their
needs as keenly as our own, and pray for them
with imagination, sensitivity and knowledge.
We ask this in Christ's name.

John Calvin, 1509–64

O God, the well of love and Father of all, make
us so to love that we know not but to love every
man in Jesus Christ your our Lord.

Collect, 14th century

Grant me, I beseech thee, my God, in the name
of Jesus Christ thy Son, the charity which
never fails, that my light may shine, warming
my own heart and enlightening others.

Columbanus, c.550–615

Take away from our hearts, O Lord, all
    suspicion, anger,
wrath, contention, and whatever may injure
    charity and lessen
brotherly love. Have mercy, O Lord, have
    mercy on those who ask
Your mercy, give grace to those who need it,
    and make us such that
we may be worthy to enjoy Your favor and
    gain eternal life.

Thomas à Kempis, 1379–1471

To thee, O God, we turn for peace. Grant us the
blessed assurance that nothing shall deprive us
of that peace, neither ourselves, nor our foolish
earthly desires, nor my wild longings, nor the
anxious cravings of my heart.

Søren Kierkegaard, 1813–55

Set my heart on fire with the love of thee, most
loving Father, and then to do thy will, and to
obey thy commandments, will not be grievous to me. For to him that loveth, nothing is
difficult, nothing is impossible; because love is
stronger than death. Oh, may love fill and rule
my heart. For then there will spring up and
be cherished between thee and me a likeness

of character, and union of will, so that I may choose and refuse what thou dost. May thy will be done in me and by me forever.

Jacobus Horstius Merlo, 1597–1664

O God, who of thy great love to man didst reconcile earth to heaven through thine only-begotten Son: grant that we who by the darkness of our sins are turned aside from brotherly love, may be filled with his Spirit she abroad within us, and embrace our friends in thee and our enemies for thy sake; through Jesus Christ our Lord.

Mozarabic Liturgy, 7th century

Lord, thou art the living flame, burning ceaselessly with love for man. Enter into me and inflame me with thy fire so that I might be like thee.

J.H. Newman, 1801–90

O God almighty, by whom and before whom we all are brethren: grant us so truly to love one another, that evidently and beyond all doubt we may love thee; through Jesus Christ thy Son, our Lord and brother.

Christina Rossetti, 1830–94

Pour on us, O Lord, the spirit of love and brotherly-kindness; so that, sprinkled by the dew of thy benediction, we may be made glad by thy glory and grace; through Jesus Christ our Lord.

Sarum Breviary

Make us worthy, Lord,
To serve our fellow-men
Throughout the world
Who live and die in poverty and hunger.
Give them, through our hands,
This day their daily bread;
And by our understanding love,
Give peace and joy.

Mother Teresa, 1910–98

Our Father, here I am, at your disposal, your
  child,
to use me to continue your loving the world,
by giving Jesus to me and through me,
to each other and to the world.
Let us pray for each other that we allow Jesus

to love in us
and through us with the love with which his
  Father loves us.

Mother Teresa, 1910–98

Almighty and most merciful God, who hast given us a new commandment that we should love one another, give us also grace that we may fulfill it. Make us gentle, courteous, and forbearing. Direct our lives so that we may each look to the good of others in word and deed. And hallow all our friendships by the blessing of thy spirit; for his sake who loved us and gave himself for us, Jesus Christ our Lord.

B.F. Westcott, 1825–1901

O Lord, the Author and Persuader of peace, love and goodwill, soften our hard and steely hearts, warm our frozen and icy hearts, that we may wish well to one another, and may be the true disciples of Jesus Christ. And give us grace even now to begin to show that heavenly life, where there is no hatred, but peace and love everywhere, towards one another.

Ludovicus Vives, 1492–1540

Joy

My God,
I pray that I may so know you and love you
that I may rejoice in you.
And if I may not do so fully in this life
let me go steadily on
to the day when I come to that fullness …
Let me receive
That which you promised through your
  truth,
that my joy may be full

Anselm, 1033–1109

Jesus, Thou Joy of loving hearts,
Thou Fount of life, Thou Light of men,
From the best bliss that earth imparts,
We turn unfilled to Thee again.

Bernard of Clairvaux, 1090–1153

As the hand is made for holding and the eye for seeing, you have created me for joy, O God.

Share with me in finding that joy everywhere: in the violet's beauty, in the lark's melody, in the child's face, in a mother's love, in the purity of Jesus.

Gaelic prayer

Father in heaven, when the thought of you wakes in our hearts, let it not wake like a frightened bird that flies about in dismay, but like a child waking from its sleep with a heavenly smile.

Søren Kierkegaard, 1813–55

Praise, my soul, the King of heaven;
    To his feet thy tribute bring;
Ransomed, healed, restored, forgiven,
    Who like thee his praise should sing?
Praise him, praise him,
    Praise the everlasting King.

Praise him for his grace and favor
    To our fathers in distress;
Praise him still the same for ever,
    Slow to chide, and swift to bless:
Praise him, praise him,
    Glorious in his faithfulness.

Father-like he tends and spares us;
    Well our feeble frame he knows;
In his hands he gently bears us,
    Rescues us from all our foes:
Praise him, praise him,
    Widely as his mercy flows.

Angels, help us to adore him,
    Ye behold him face to face;
Sun and moon, bow down before him;
    Dwellers all in time and space,
Praise him, praise him.
    Praise with us the God of grace.

H.F. Lyte, 1793–1847,
based on Psalm 103

Lord, help us to be masters of ourselves, that we may be servants of others.

Alexander Paterson

Jesus, I am resting, resting,
In the joy of what Thou art;
I am finding out the greatness
Of Thy loving heart.
Thou hast bid me gaze upon Thee,

And Thy beauty fills my soul,
For by Thy transforming power,
Thou hast made me whole.

Jean Sophia Pigott, 1845–82

O God, fountain of love, pour your love into your souls, that we may love those whom you love with the love you give us, and think and speak about them tenderly, meekly, lovingly; and so loving our brothers and sisters for your sake, may grow in your love, and live in love and living in love may live in you; for Jesus Christ's sake.

E.B. Pusey, 1800–82

O sweet and true Joy, I pray Thee come! Come O sweet and most desired! I pray Thee come! Come O sweet and most desired! Come my Love, that art all my comfort! Glide down into a soul longing for Thee and after Thee with sweet heat. Kindle with Thy heat the wholeness of my heart. With Thy light enlighten my inmost parts. Feed me with honeyed songs of love, as far I may receive them by my powers of body and soul.

Richard Rolle, 1290–1349

WE are evil, O God, and help us to see it and amend. We are good, and help us to be better. Look down upon thy servants with a patient eye, even as Thou sendest sun and rain; look down, call upon the dry bones, quicken, enliven; recreate in us the soul of service, the spirit of peace; renew in us the sense of joy.

R.L. Stevenson, 1850–94

Grant to us, O Lord, the royalty of inward happiness, and the serenity which comes from living close to thee. Daily renew in us the sense of joy, and let the eternal Spirit of the Father dwell in our souls and bodies, filling every corner of our hearts with light and grace; so that, bearing about with us the infection of good courage, we may be diffusers of life, and may meet all ills and cross accidents with gallant and high-hearted happiness, giving thee thanks always for all things.

R.L. Stevenson, 1850–94

Lord Jesus, think on me
That, when the flood is past,

I may th'eternal brightness see
And share Thy joy at last.
Synesius of Cyrene, 375–430,
translated by Allen W. Chatfield

My Lord I love you
my God I am sorry
my God I believe in you
my God I trust you.
Help us to love one another
as you love us.
Mother Teresa, 1910–98

Joy to the world, the Lord is come!
Let earth receive her King;
Let every heart prepare Him room,
And heaven and nature sing,
And heaven and nature sing,
And heaven, and heaven, and nature sing.

Joy to the world, the Savior reigns!
Let men their songs employ;
While fields and floods, rocks, hills and plains
Repeat the sounding joy,
Repeat the sounding joy,
Repeat, repeat, the sounding joy.
Isaac Watts, 1674–1748

Peace

O God, make us children of quietness and
heirs of peace.
Clement of Alexandria, c.150–c.215

Peace, perfect peace, in this dark world of sin?
The blood of Jesus whispers peace within.

Peace, perfect peace, by thronging duties
pressed?
To do the will of Jesus, this is rest.

Peace, perfect peace, with sorrows surging
round?
On Jesus' bosom naught but calm is found.

Peace, perfect peace, with loved ones far
away?
In Jesus' keeping we are safe, and they.

Peace, perfect peace, our future all unknown?

Jesus we know, and He is on the throne.

Peace, perfect peace, death shadowing us and
ours?
Jesus has vanquished death and all its powers.

It is enough: earth's struggles soon shall cease,
And Jesus call us to heaven's perfect peace.
Edward H. Bickersteth, 1786–1850

Grant to us, Thou Savior of Glory,
The fear of God, the love of God, and His
affection.
Each day and night give us Thy peace.
Each day and night give us Thy peace.
Carmina Gadelica

The peace of the Father of joy,
The peace of the Christ of pasch,
The peace of the Spirit of grace,
To ourselves and to our children,
Ourselves and our children.
Carmina Gadelica

O God, who art Peace everlasting, whose
chosen reward is the gift of peace, and who
hast taught us that the peacemakers are thy
children, pour thy sweet peace into our souls,
that everything discordant may utterly vanish,
and all that makes for peace be sweet to us
forever.
Gelasian Sacramentary, 5th century

In peace, let us beseech the Lord
for the peace that is from above
and the salvation of our souls;
for the peace of the whole world
and of the holy churches of God
and of all men.
For our homes, that they may be holy,
and for all our pastors, teachers and
governors;
for our city (township, village) and country
and all who dwell therein;
for all that travel by land, by air, by water;
for the sick and all who need your pity and
protection.
On all, have mercy, and preserve all, O God,
by your grace:
for to you, O Lord, is due glory, honor, and
worship;

world without end.
Amen
Liturgy of St. John Chrysostom

O God, you are the unsearchable abyss of peace, the ineffable sea of love, the fountain of blessings and the bestower of affection, who sends peace to those who receive it. Open to us this day the sea of your love and water us with abundant streams from the riches of your grace and from the most sweet springs of your kindness.
Clement of Alexandria, c.150–c.215

O thou lover of mankind, send down into our hearts that peace which the world cannot give, and give us peace in this world. O King of Peace, keep us in love and charity; be our God, for we have none other beside thee; grant unto our souls the life of righteousness, that the death of sin may not prevail against us, or against any of thy people.
Walter Farquhar Hook, 1798–1875

O Lord, grant that this night
We may sleep in peace.
And that in the morning
Our awakening may also be in peace.
May our daytime
Be cloaked in your peace.
Protect us and inspire us
To think and act only out of love.
Keep far from us all evil;
May our paths be free from all obstacles
From when we go out
Until the time we return home.
Jewish prayer

O Lord, calm the waves of this heart, calm its tempest!
Calm yourself, O my soul, so that the divine can act in you!
Calm yourself, O my soul, so that God is able to repose in you,
so that his peace may cover you!
Yes, Father in heaven, often have we found that the world cannot give us peace, but make us feel that you are able to give us peace; let us know the truth of your promise: that the whole world may not be able to take away your peace.
Søren Kierkegaard, 1813–55

Lord, may I eschew evil and do good, speak peace and pursue it.
William Laud, 1573–1645, based on Psalm 34.14

O Lord, look mercifully on us, and grant that we may always choose the way of peace.
Sarum Missal, 1085

O God, who are peace everlasting, whose chosen reward is the gift of peace, and who has taught us that the peacemakers are your children: Pour your peace into our hearts, that everything discordant may utterly vanish, and that all that makes for peace be loved and sought by us always; through Jesus Christ our Lord.
Mozarabic Sacramentary

O Lord, grant unto me that with Thy peace I may greet all that this day is to bring. Grant unto me grace to surrender myself completely to Thy holy will. In every hour of this day instruct and guide me in all things. Whatever tidings I may receive during this day, do Thou teach me to accept tranquilly in the firm belief that Thy holy will governs all. Govern Thou my thoughts and feelings in all I do and say. When unforeseen things occur, let me not forget that all is sent by Thee. Teach me to behave sincerely and reasonably toward everyone, that I may bring confusion and sorrow to no one. Bestow on me, O Lord, strength to endure the fatigue of the day and to bear my part in its events. Guide Thou my will and teach me to pray, to believe, to hope, to suffer, to forgive, and to love.
Optina elders

Let us not seek *out* of thee, O Lord, what we can find only *in* thee: peace and joy and bliss. Lift up our souls above the weary round of harassing thoughts to the pure, serene atmosphere of your presence, that there we may breathe freely, there repose in your love, there be at rest from ourselves; and from there return arrayed with your peace, to do and bear what will best please you.
E.B. Pusey, 1800–82

Jesus! the name that charms our fears,
That bids our sorrows cease;

'Tis music in the sinner's ears,
'Tis life, and health, and peace.
Charles Wesley, 1707–88

Drop thy still dews of quietness
Till all our strivings cease:
Take from our lives the strain and stress,
And let our ordered lives confess
The beauty of your peace.
J.G. Whittier, 1807–92

Patience

Unite our hearts, O Lord, in bonds of affection
that we may live with one another in humility and peace. Give us patience in the time of
trial, and steadfastness in the tasks before us.
Refresh our hearts in the hour of anguish and
sustain us in the day of our need. Be to us, and
to your whole Church, both our everlasting
light and our eternal salvation; through Jesus
Christ our Lord. Amen
Bernhard Albrecht, 1569–1636

Give me patience, that I may teach discipline.
Augustine of Hippo, 354–430

O GOD, Who by the meek endurance of Thine
Only-begotten Son didst beat down the pride
of the old enemy: Help us, we beseech Thee,
rightly to treasure in our hearts what our Lord
hath of His goodness borne for our sakes; that
after His example we may bear with patience
whatsoever things are adverse to us; through
Jesus Christ, Thy Son, our Lord. Amen.
The Common Service Book
of the Lutheran Church, 1917

O God, give us patience when those who are
wicked hurt us. O how impatient and angry
we are when we think ourselves unjustly slandered, reviled and hurt! Christ suffers blows
upon his cheek, the innocent for the guilty; yet
we may not abide one rough word for his sake.
O Lord, grant us virtue and patience, power
and strength, that we may take all adversity
with goodwill, and with a gentle mind overcome it. And if necessity and thy honor require
us to speak, grant that we may do so with
meekness and patience, that the truth and thy

glory may be defended, and our patience and
steadfast continuance perceived.
Miles Coverdale, 1488–1568

O LORD, Master of my life, grant that I may
not be infected with the spirit of slothfulness
and inquisitiveness, with the spirit of ambition
and vain talking.

Grant instead to me, your servant, the spirit
of purity and of humility, the spirit of patience
and neighborly love.
Ephraem, c.306–378

O Jesus, gracious Lamb of God, I renounce
forever my impatience. Crucify, O Lord, my
flesh and its concupiscences; scourge, scathe,
and punish me in this world, do but spare
me in the next. I commit my destiny to Thee,
resigning myself to Thy holy will: may it be
done in all things!
Francis of Assisi, 1181–1226

Lord, teach me the art of patience while I am
well, and enable me to use of it when I am
sick. In that day either lighten my burden or
strengthen my back. Make me, who so often
in my health have discovered my weakness in
presuming on my own strength, to be strong
in my sickness when I solely rely on your
assistance.
Thomas Fuller, 1608–61

Lord, here I am, do with me as seems best in
Thine own eyes; only give me, I beseech Thee, a
penitent and patient spirit to expect Thee.
Amen.
William Laud, 1573–1645

Take from us, O God, all tediousness of spirit,
all impatience and unquietness. Let us possess
ourselves in patience, through Jesus Christ our
Lord.
Jeremy Taylor, 1613–67

When many are coming and going and there is
little leisure, give us grace, O heavenly Father,
to follow the example of our Lord Jesus Christ,
who knew neither impatience or spirit nor
confusion of work, but in the midst of his
labors held communion with thee, and even
upon earth was still in heaven; where he now

reigneth with thee and the Holy Spirit world
without end.

C.J. Vaughan, 1816–97

Kindness

Keep us, O God, from all pettiness. Let us be
large in thought, in word, in deed. Let us be
done with faultfinding and leave off all self-
seeking. May we put away all pretence and
meet each other face to face, without self-pity
and without prejudice. May we never be hasty
in judgment, and always be generous. Let us
always take time for all things, and make us
grow calm, serene and gentle. Teach us to put
into action our better impulses, to be straightforward and unafraid. Grant that we may realize that it is the little things of life that create
differences, that in the big things of life we are
as one. And, O Lord God, let us not forget to
be kind!

Mary Queen of Scots, 1542–87

Grant us, we beseech thee, O Lord, grace to
follow thee withersoever thou goest.

In little daily duties to which thou callest
us, bow down our wills to simple obedience,
patience under pain or provocation, strict
truthfulness of word or manner, humility and
kindness.

In great acts of duty or perfection, if thou
shouldst call us to them, uplift us to sacrifice
and heroic courage, that in all things, both
small and great, we may be imitators of thy
dear Son, even Jesus Christ our Lord.

Christina Rossetti, 1830–94

Goodness

Lord of all power and might, who art author
and giver of all good things: Graft in our hearts
the love of thy Name, increase in us true religion, nourish us with all goodness, and of thy
great mercy keep us in the same; through Jesus
Christ our Lord.

*Book of Common Prayer, Collect
for the Seventh Sunday after Trinity*

I believe, Lord, but let me believe more firmly.
I hope, Lord, but let me hope more surely.
I love, Lord, but let me love more ardently.
I repent, Lord, but let me repent more deeply.
I beg you, Lord, what do you want me to do?
Teach me to fulfill your will, for you are my
   God.
Give me an understanding heart …
To distinguish right from wrong.
Father, give me humility, meekness,
Chastity, patience and charity.
Father, teach me goodness, knowledge and
   discipline.
Father, give me your love, together with your
   grace, and I will be rich enough.

Anthony Mary Claret, 1807–70

O God, who madest me for thyself, to show
forth thy goodness in me: manifest, I humbly
beseech thee, the life-giving power of thy holy
nature within me; help me to such a true and
living faith in thee, such strength of hunger
and thirst after the birth, life and spirit of thy
holy Jesus in my soul, that all that is within
me may be turned from every inward thought
or outward work that is not of thee, thy holy
Jesus, and heavenly workings in my soul.

William Law, 1686–1761

Infinite Goodness, I esteem You above all
things; I love You with all my heart; I give
myself entirely to You. Accept my poor love,
and give me more love. May I forget all, that I
may remember only You, my love, my all.

Alphonsus Liguori, 1696–1787

Lord, since you exist, we exist. Since you are
beautiful, we are beautiful. Since you are good,
we are good. By our existence, we honor you.
By our beauty we glorify you. By our goodness we love you. Lord, through your power
all things were made. Through your wisdom
all things are governed. Through your grace
all things are sustained. Give us power to serve
you, wisdom to discern your laws, and grace to
obey those at all times.

Edmund Rich, c.1180–1240

Faithfulness

Grant, O Lord, that what we have said with our lips, we may believe in our hearts and practice in our lives; and of thy mercy keep us faithful unto the end; for Christ's sake.

John Hunter, 1849–1917

Strengthen me, O God, by the grace of your Holy Spirit; grant me to be strengthened with the might of the inner man, and to put away from my heart all useless anxiety and distress, and let me never be distracted by various longings, whether they are worthless or precious; but may I view all things as passing away, and myself as passing away with them.

Grant me prudently to avoid the one who flatters me, and patiently to bear with the one who contradicts me; for it is a mark of great wisdom not to be moved by every wind of words or to be influenced by wicked flattery; for thus we will go on securely in the course we have begun.

Thomas à Kempis, 1379–1471

Increase our faith, O merciful Father, that we do not swerve at any time from thy heavenly words, but augment in us hope and love, with a careful keeping of all thy commandments, that no hardness of heart, no hypocrisy, no concupiscence of the eye, no enticement of the world, do draw us away from thy obedience. Amen

John Knox, c.1513–72

Gentleness

Drive away the lust of gluttony, put to flight the spirit of fornication, quench the greediness of the world; give the virtue of abstinence: the love of chastity: poverty of spirit: refrain headlong wrathfulness; give gentleness in me: take away the sorrow of the world; increase ghostly joy: drive away boastfulness of mind; grant compunction of heart.

Lancelot Andrewes, 1555–1626

Gracious Lord, in whom are laid up all the treasures of knowledge and wisdom, direct me in the ways of life; remove from me the ways of death. Give me a soft and meek spirit, that I may help the succorless, and comfort the comfortless. O my dear Lord, pardon me for the neglect of this duty, and make me to redeem the time with a cheerful constancy.

The Penitent Pilgrim, 1641

God, the Father of our Lord Jesus Christ, increase in us faith and truth and gentleness, and grant us part and lot among his saints.

Polycarp, c.69–c.155

Self-control

Lord, give us hearts never to forget thy love; but to dwell therein whatever we do, whether we sleep or wake, live or die, or rise again to the life that is to come. For thy love is eternal life and everlasting rest; for this is life eternal to know thee and thy infinite goodness. O let its flame never be quenched in our hearts; let it grow and brighten, till our whole souls are glowing and shining with its light and warmth. Be thou our joy, our hope, our strength and life, our shield and shepherd, our portion for ever. For happy are we if we continue in the love wherewith thou hast loved us; holy are we when we love thee steadfastly. Therefore, O thou, whose name and essence is love, enkindle our hearts, enlighten our understanding, sanctify our wills, and fill all the thoughts of hearts, for Jesus Christ's sake.

Johann Arndt, 1555–1621

We implore thee, by the memory of thy cross's hallowed and most bitter anguish, make us fear thee, make us love thee, O Christ.

Bridget, c.460–c.528

O my God, let me walk in the way of love which knoweth not how to seek self in anything whatsoever. Let me love thee for thyself, and nothing else but in and for thee. Let me love nothing instead of thee, for to give all for love is a most sweet bargain. Let thy love work in me and by me, and let me love thee as thou wouldst be loved by me.

Gertrude More, 1606–33

ABANDONMENT

O sovereign goodness of the sovereign Providence of my God! I abandon myself forever to Thy arms. Whether gentle or severe, lead me henceforth whither Thou wilt; I will not regard the way through which Thou wilt have me pass, but keep my eyes fixed upon Thee, my God, who guidest me. My soul finds no rest without the arms and the bosom of this heavenly Providence, my true Mother, my strength and my rampart.

Therefore I resolve with Thy divine assistance, o my Savior, to follow Thy desires and Thy ordinances, without regarding or examining why Thou dost this rather than that; but I will blindly follow Thee according to Thy divine will, without seeking my own inclinations.

Hence I am determined to leave all to Thee, taking no part therein save by keeping myself in peace in Thy arms, desiring nothing except as Thou incitest me to desire, to will, to wish. I offer Thee this desire, o my God, beseeching Thee to bless it; I undertake all it includes, relying on Thy goodness, liberality, and mercy, with entire confidence in Thee, distrust of myself, and knowledge of my infinite misery and infirmity.

Amen!

Jane Frances de Chantal, 1571–1641

Father,
I abandon myself into your hands,
do with me what you will.
Whatever you may do,
I thank you.
I am ready for all.
I accept all.
Let your will be done in me and all your
    creatures.
I wish no more than this, O Lord.
Into your hands I commend my soul;
I offer it to you with all the love of my heart,
for I love you, Lord, and so need to give
    myself,
to surrender myself into your hands, without
    reserve
and with boundless confidence, for you are
    my Father.

Charles de Foucauld, 1855–1916

ABIDING

O my Noble Vine, I beseech Thee give Sap to me Thy Branch; that I may bud and grow in Thy Strength and Sap, in Thy Essence; beget in me true Strength by Thy Strength.

Jakob Boehme, 1555–1624

ACTION

O Lord, the Lord whose ways are right, keep us in thy mercy from lip-service and empty forms; from having a name that we live, but being dead.

Help us to worship Thee by righteous deeds and lives of holiness; that our prayer also may be set forth in Thy sight as the incense, and the lifting up of our hands be as an evening sacrifice.

Christina Rossetti, 1830–94

ASSURANCE

Blessèd assurance, Jesus is mine!
O what a foretaste of glory divine!
Heir of salvation, purchase of God,
Born of His Spirit, washed in His blood.
Refrain
This is my story, this is my song,
Praising my Savior, all the day long;
This is my story, this is my song,
Praising my Savior, all the day long.
Perfect submission, perfect delight,
Visions of rapture now burst on my sight;
Angels descending bring from above
Echoes of mercy, whispers of love.
Refrain
Perfect submission, all is at rest
I in my Savior am happy and blest,
Watching and waiting, looking above,
Filled with His goodness, lost in His love.
Refrain

Frances Jane (Fanny) Crosby, 1820–1915

COMMUNION WITH GOD

My spirit longs for Thee
Within my troubled breast,
Though I unworthy be
Of so divine a guest.

Of so divine a guest
Unworthy though I be,
Yet has my heart no rest
Unless it come from thee.

John Byrom, 1691–1763

God, of your goodness, give me yourself,
for you are sufficient for me.
I may not correctly ask for anything less,
to be worthy of you.
If I were to ask anything less
I should always be in need,
for in you alone do I have all.

Julian of Norwich, 1342–c.1416

O my God, may I always keep myself in your
love, by praying in the Holy Spirit. As your infinite love is always streaming in blessings on me,
so let my soul be always breathing love to you.

Thomas Ken, 1637–1711

Come, my Way, my Truth, my Life:
Such a Way as gives us breath:
Such a Truth as ends of strife:
Such a Life as killeth death.

Come, my Light, my Feast, my Strength:
Such a Light, as shows a feast:
Such a Feast, as mends in length:
Such a Strength, as makes his guest.

Come, my Joy, my Love, my Heart:
Such a Joy, as none can move:
Such a Love, as none can part:
Such a Heart, as joys in love.

George Herbert, 1593–1633

Were earth a thousand times as fair,
Beset with gold and jewels rare,
  She yet were far too poor to be
  A narrow cradle, Lord, for thee.

Ah, dearest Jesus, holy child,
Make thee a bed, soft, undefiled,

Within my heart, that it may be
A quiet chamber kept for thee.

*Martin Luther, 1483–1546,
translated by Catherine Winkworth*

O God, the Father of mercies, grant to us
always to hold fast to the spirit of adoption,
whereby we cry to you 'Father', and are called,
and are, 'your children', through Jesus Christ,
our Lord.

Roman Breviary

Teach us to pray often, that we may pray
oftener.

Jeremy Taylor, 1613–67

COMPASSION

Father, all loving and most tender, we confess
the hardness of our hearts and our want of
compassion for our neighbor. Grant us the
grace of pity, the ministry of compassion and
the gift of consoling the broken-hearted. Teach
us to love with your own forbearance and
never harshly or unlovingly to judge another;
for your own mercies' sake. Amen.

Johann Arndt, 1555–1621

O Lord, baptize our hearts into a sense of the
needs and conditions of all.

George Fox, 1624–91

Teach me to feel another's woe;
  To hide the fault I see;
That mercy I to others show,
  That mercy show to me.

Alexander Pope, 1688–1744

Christ, I see thy crown of thorns in every eye,
thy bleeding, wounded naked body in every
soul; thy death liveth in every memory; thy
wounded body is embalmed in every affection;
thy pierced feet are bathed in everyone's tears;
and it is my privilege to enter with thee into
every soul.

Thomas Traherne, 1636–74

CONFIDENCE IN GOD

It is good to mistrust ourselves, but how would that advantage us were we not to throw all our confidence on God, and to wait on His mercy? If you feel no such confidence, cease not on that account from making these acts and from saying to Our Lord: "Yet, O Lord, though I have no feeling of confidence in You, nevertheless, I know that You are my God, that I am all Yours, and that I have no hope but in Your goodness; so, I abandon myself entirely into Your Hands." It is always in our power to make these acts; although we have difficulty in performing them, still there is no impossibility. Thus we testify faithfulness to our Lord.

Francis de Sales, 1567–1622

CONTENTMENT

Two things have I required of thee, O Lord,
deny thou me not before I die;
remove far from me vanity and lies;
give me neither poverty nor riches,
feed me with food convenient for me;
lest I be full and deny thee and say, who is the
    Lord?
Or lest I be poor and steal,
and take the name of my God in vain.
Let me learn to abound, let me learn to suffer
    need,
in whatsoever state I am, therewith to be
    content.
For nothing earthly, temporal, mortal, to long
    nor to wait.
Grant me a happy life, in piety, gravity, purity,
in all things good and fair,
in cheerfulness, in health, in credit,
in competency, in safety, in gentle estate, in
    quiet;
a happy death,
a deathless happiness.

Lancelot Andrewes, 1555–1625

Almighty God, who knows our necessities before we ask, and our ignorance in asking: Set free your servants from all anxious thoughts about tomorrow; make us content with your good gifts; and confirm our faith that as we seek your kingdom, you will not allow us to lack any good thing; through Jesus Christ our Lord.

Augustine of Hippo, 354–430

I asked for knowledge – power to control
    things;
I was granted understanding – to learn to love
    persons.
I asked for strength to be a great man;
I was make weak to become a better man.
I asked for wealth to make friends;
I became poor, to keep friends.
I asked for all things to enjoy life;
I was granted all life, to enjoy things.
I cried for pity; I was offered sympathy.
I craved for healing of my own disorders;
I received insight into another's suffering.
I prayed to God for safety – to tread the
    trodden path;
I was granted danger, to lost track and find
    the Way.
I got nothing that I prayed for;
I am among all men, richly blessed.

Author unknown

He that is down needs fear no fall
He that is low, no pride:
He that is humble ever shall
Have God to be his guide.

I am content with what I have,
Little be it or much:
And, Lord, contentment still I crave,
Because thou savest such.

John Bunyan, 1628–88,
Pilgrim's Progress

O God, animate us to cheerfulness. may we have a joyful sense of our blessings, learn to look on the bright circumstances of our lot, and maintain a perpetual contentedness under thy allotments. Fortify our minds against disappointments and calamity. Preserve us from despondency, from yielding to dejection. Teach us that no evil is intolerable but a guilty conscience, and that nothing can hurt us, if with true loyalty of affection, we keep thy commandments and take refuge in thee; through Jesus Christ our Lord. Amen.

William Ellery Channing 1780–1842

Almighty God, our Heavenly Father, Who dost feed the birds and clothe the flowers, and Who carest for us as a father for his children: We beseech Thee, graciously guard us against distrust and vain over-carefulness, and help us, through Thy Holy Spirit, to live to the hallowing of Thy Name, the coming of Thy Kingdom and the doing of Thy Will, so that we may cast all our care on Thee and in unwavering faith, abide trustingly in Thee; through Jesus Christ, Thy Son, our Lord. Amen

The Common Service Book of
the Lutheran Church, 1917

Grant me, most sweet and loving Jesus, to rest in you above every creature, above all health and beauty, above all glory and honor, above all power and dignity, above all skill and shrewdness, above all riches and talents, above all joy and exultation, above all fame and praise, above all hope and promise, above all merit and desire, above all gifts that you may shower on me, above all joy or tribulation that my mind may feel or receive. And grant me to rest in you above angels and archangels, above all the heavenly host, above all things visible and invisible, and above all that you are not, my God. For you, my God, are above all.

Thomas à Kempis, 1379–1471

O Lord you know what is best for me. Let this or that be done, as you wish. Give what you will, how much you will and when you will.

Thomas à Kempis, 1379–1471

O thou divine Spirit that, in all events of life, art knocking at the door of my heart, help me to respond to thee. I would not be driven blindly as the stars over their courses. I would not be made to work out thy will unwillingly, to fulfill thy law unintelligently, to obey thy mandates unsympathetically. I would take the events of my life as good and perfect gifts from thee; I would receive even the sorrows of life as disguised gifts from thee. I would have my heart open at all times to receive thee, at morning, noon, and night; in spring, and summer and winter. Whether thou comest to me in sunshine or in rain, I would take thee into my heart joyfully. Thou art thyself more than the sunshine, thou art thyself compensation for the rain; it is thee and not thy gifts I crave; knock, and I shall open unto thee.

George Matheson, 1842–1906

O Lord, whose way is perfect,
help us always to trust in thy goodness;
    that walking with thee
    and following thee in all simplicity,
we may possess quiet and contented minds,
    and may cast all our care on thee
    who carest for us;
for thy dear Son's sake, Jesus Christ.

Christina Rossetti, 1830–94

Guide me, O Lord, in all the changes and varieties of the world; that in all things that shall happen, I may have an evenness and tranquility of spirit; that my soul may be wholly resigned to thy divinest will and pleasure, never murmuring at thy gentle chastisements and fatherly correction.

Jeremy Taylor, 1613–67

COURAGE

Lord God, that we may receive your blessing, touch our brows, touch our heads, and do not look upon us in anger. In a hard year, offer us mercy; in a year of affliction, offer us kindness; dark spirits banish from us, bright spirits bring close to us; gray spirits put away from us, good spirits draw near to us. When we are afraid, offer us courage; when we are ashamed, be our true face; be over us like a blanket, be under us like a bed of furs. Amen.

Traditional prayer from Mongolia

May he give us
all the courage that we need
to go the way he shepherds us.
That when he calls
we may go unfrightened.

If he bids us come to him
across the waters,
that unfrightened we may go.

And if he bids us climb a hill,
may we not notice that it is a hill,

mindful only of
the happiness of his company.

He made us for himself,
that we should travel with him
and see him at the last
in his unveiled beauty
in the abiding city where
he is light
and happiness
and endless home.

Bede Jarrett, 1881–1934

Make us, O blessed Master, strong in heart, full of courage, fearless of danger, holding pain and danger cheap when we lie in the path of duty. May we be strengthened with all might by thy Spirit in our hearts.

F.B. Meyer, 1847–1929

We thank Thee, Lord, for the glory of the late days and the excellent face of thy sun. We thank Thee for good news received. We thank Thee for the pleasures we have enjoyed and for those we have been able to confer. And now, when the clouds gather and the rain impends over the forest and our house, permit us not to be cast down; let us not lose the savor of past mercies and past pleasures; but, like the voice of a bird singing in the rain, let grateful memory survive in the hour of darkness. If there be in front of us any painful duty, strengthen us with the grace of courage; if any act of mercy, teach us tenderness and patience.

R.L. Stevenson, 1850–94

Grant that we here before Thee may be set free from the fear of vicissitude and the fear of death, may finish what remains before us of our course without dishonor to ourselves or hurt to others, and, when the day comes, may die in peace. Deliver us from fear and favor: from mean hopes and cheap pleasures. Have mercy on each in his deficiency; let him be not cast down; support the stumbling on the way, and give at last rest to the weary.

R.L. Stevenson, 1850–94

These are the gifts I ask of Thee,
Spirit serene:
Strength for the daily task,

Courage to face the road,
Good cheer to help me bear the traveler's load,
And, for the hours of rest that come between,
An inward joy of all things heard and seen.
These are the sins I fain
    Would have thee take away:
    Malice, and cold disdain,
    Hot anger, sullen hate,
Scorn of the lowly, envy of the great,
And discontent that casts a shadow gray
On all the brightness of the common day.

Henry Van Dyke, 1852–1933

DEDICATION

I believe that you created me:
let not the work of your hands be despised.
I believe that I am after your image and
    likeness:
let not your own likeness be defaced.
I believe that you saved me by your blood:
let not the price of the ransom be squandered.
I believe that you proclaimed me a Christian
    in your name:
let not your namesake be scorned.
I believe that you hallowed me in rebirth:
let not that consecration be despoiled.
I believe that you engrafted me into the
    cultivated olive tree:
let not the limb of your mystical body be cut
    out.
Amen.

Lancelot Andrewes, 1555–1626

O Lord, I love you. I love, I burn, I pant for you;
I trample under foot all that gives here delight.
I want to go to you.

Augustine of Hippo, 354–430

O thou, the merciful Father of spirits, the attraction of love and ocean of delights, draw up these drossy hearts unto thyself, and keep them there till they are spiritualized and refined; and second thy servant's weak endeavors, and persuade those that read these lines, to the practice of this delightful, heavenly work! O suffer not the soul of thy most unworthy servant to be a stranger to those joys which he describes to others; but keep me, while I remain on earth, in daily breathings after thee, and in a believing, affectionate walking with thee! And when thou comest, let me be found so doing; not serving my flesh, nor asleep, with my lamp unfurnished; but waiting and longing for my Lord's return! Let those who shall read these heavenly directions, not merely read the fruit of my studies, but the breathing of my active hope and love; that if my heart were open to their view, they might there read the same most deeply engraven with a beam from the face of the Son of God; and not find vanity, or lust, or pride within, when the words of life appear without; that so these lines may not witness against me; but proceeding from the heart of the writer, may be effectual, through thy grace, upon the heart of the reader, and so be the savor of life to both! Amen.

Richard Baxter, 1615–91

O Lord,
I place myself in your hands and dedicate
    myself to you.
I pledge myself to do your will in all things:
To love the Lord God with all my heart, all my
    soul, all my strength.
Not to kill, not to steal not to covet, not to
    bear false witness, to honor all persons.
Not to do to another what I should not want
    done to myself.
Not to seek after pleasures.

To love fasting.
To relieve the poor.
To clothe the naked.
To visit the sick.

To bury the dead.
To help those in trouble.
To console the sorrowing.
To hold myself aloof from worldly ways.
To prefer nothing to the love of Christ.

Not to give way to anger.
Not to foster a desire for revenge.
Not to entertain deceit in the heart.
Not to make a false peace.

Not to forsake charity.

Not to swear, lest I swear falsely.
To speak the truth with heart and tongue.
Not to return evil for evil

To do no injury, indeed, even to bear patiently
    any injury done to me.
To love my enemies.
Not to curse those who curse me but rather to
    bless them.
To bear persecution for justice's sake.

Not to be proud.
Not to be given to intoxicating drink.
Not to be an overeater.
Not to be lazy.
Not to be slothful
Not to be a detractor.

To put my trust in God.
To refer the good I see in myself to God.
To refer any evil I see in myself to myself
To fear the day of judgment.
To be in dread of hell.

To desire eternal life with spiritual longing.
To keep death before my eyes daily.
To keep constant watch over my actions.
To remember that God sees me everywhere.

To call upon Christ for defense against evil
    thoughts that arise in my heart.
To guard my tongue against wicked speech.
To avoid much speaking.
To avoid idle talk.

Not to seek to appear clever.
To read only what is good to read.
To pray often.
To ask forgiveness daily for my sins, and to
    seek ways to amend my life.

To obey my superiors in all things rightful.
Not to desire to be thought holy, but to seek
    holiness.
To fulfill the commandments of God by good
    works.

To love chastity.
To hate no one.
Not be jealous or envious of anyone.
Not to love strife.

Not to love pride.

To honor the aged.
To pray for my enemies.
To make peace after a quarrel, before the
    setting of the sun.
Never to despair of your mercy, O God of mercy.

Benedict, 480–543

O Savior, pour upon me thy Spirit of
    meekness and love,
Annihilate the selfhood in me, be thou all my
    life.
Guide though my hand, which trembles
    exceedingly, upon the rock of ages.

William Blake, 1757–1827

O Most Gracious and Deep Love of God in
Christ Jesus! I beseech Thee grant me Thy
Pearl, impress It into my Soul, and take my
Soul into Thy Arms.

Jakob Boehme, 1555–1624

In thee would we lose ourselves utterly; do in
us what thou wilt.

Jakob Boehme, 1555–1624

All for the glory of God
I want to love you, my God,
with all my heart, with all my being, with all
    my strength:
I consecrate to you my thoughts, desires,
    words and actions,
Whatever I have and whatever I can be.
Let me use what I have for your greater honor
    and glory according to your will.
Amen.

Anthony Mary Claret, 1807–70

I pray, Lord, that you enlighten my mind,
inflame my will, purify my heart, and sanctify
my soul. Amen.

Clement XI, 1649–1721

Be gracious, O Instructor, to us Thy children,
Father, Charioteer of Israel, Son and Father,
both in One, O Lord. Grant to us who obey
Thy precepts, that we may perfect the likeness
of the image, and with all our power know
Him who is the good God and not a harsh
judge. And do Thou Thyself cause that all of us

who have our conversation in Thy peace, who
have been translated into Thy commonwealth,
having sailed tranquilly over the billows of sin,
may be wafted in calm by Thy Holy Spirit, by
the ineffable wisdom, by night and day to the
perfect day; and giving thanks may praise, and
praising thank the Alone Father and Son, Son
and Father, the Son, Instructor and Teacher,
with the Holy Spirit, all in One, in whom is
all, for whom all is One, for whom is eternity,
whose members we all are, whose glory the
aeons are; for the All-good, All-lovely, All-
wise, All-just One. To whom be glory both
now and for ever. Amen.

Clement of Alexandria, c.150–c.215,
Prayer to the Pedagogus

Lord Jesus, be thou a light to my eyes,
music to my ears,
sweetness to my taste,
and full contentment to my heart.
Be thou my sunshine in the day,
my food at table,
my repose in the night,
my clothing in nakedness,
and my succor in all necessities.

John Cosin, 1594–1672

Lord Jesu, I give thee my body, my soul, my
substance, my fame, my friends, my liberty
and my life. Dispose of me and all that is mine
as it may seem best to thee and tot he glory of
thy blessed name.

John Cosin, 1594–1672

O God, the true and only life, in whom and
from whom and by whom are all good things
that are good indeed; from whom to be turned
is to fall, to whom to turn is to rise again; in
whom to abide is to dwell for ever, from whom
to depart is to die; to whom to come again is
to revive, and in whom to lodge is to live: take
away from me whatsoever thou wilt, so that
thou give me only thyself.

Thomas Dekker, c.1570–1623

Come, our Light, and illumine our darkness.
Come, our Life, and raise us from death.
Come, our Physician, and heal our wounds.
Come, Flame of divine Love, and burn up our
    sins.

Come, our King, sit upon the throne of our
hearts and reign there.
For you alone are my King and my Lord
Dimitrii of Rostov, 17th century

Wound my heart O Lord, so that afterwards
I can feel your healing touch. Break my heart
into pieces, if you will but at length condescend to bind it up.
Philip Doddridge, 1702–51

O my blessed Savior Lord Jesus, thou asketh
my love, thou desirest to have my heart ...
[and] since it is thy pleasure to have it and thy
goodness doth ask it of me saying: Give me thy
heart, I freely give it to thee.
John Fisher, 1459–1535

Lord, I pray, that the burning and delicious
ardor of your love may detach my soul from all
things which are under heaven, so that I may
die for love of your love. For you are the One
who for love of my love was prepared to die.
Francis of Assisi, 1181–1226

O innocent Jesus, having sinned, I am guilty of
eternal death, but Thou willingly dost accept
the unjust sentence of death, that I might live.
For whom, then, shall I henceforth live, if not
for Thee, my Lord? Should I desire to please
men, I could not be Thy servant. Let me, therefore, rather displease men and all the world,
than not please Thee, O Jesus.
Francis of Assisi, 1181–1226

Lord, make me an instrument of your peace.
Where there is hatred, let me sow love,
where there is injury, pardon,
where there is doubt, faith,
where there is despair, hope,
where there is darkness, light,
where there is sadness, joy.

O Divine Master, grant that we may not so
much seek
to be consoled as to console,
not so much to be understood as to
understand,
not so much to be loved as to love.
For it is in giving that we receive,
it is in pardoning that we are pardoned,

it is in dying that we are born to eternal life.
Attributed to Francis of Assisi, 1181–1226

Lord Jesus, I give you my hands to do your
work. I give you my feet to go your way. I give
you my eyes to see as you do. I give you my
tongue to speak your words. I give you my
mind that you may think in me. I give you my
spirit that you may pray in me. Above all, I give
you my heart that you may love in me your
Father and all mankind. I give you my whole
self that you may grow in me, so that it is you,
Lord Jesus, who live and work and pray in me.
The Grail Prayer

O God, worthy of an infinite love, I have
nothing which can adequately measure your
dignity, but such is my desire towards you, that
if I had all that you have, I would gladly and
thankfully give all to you.
Gertrude of Thüringen, 1256–1302

All for Jesus, all for Jesus!
All my being's ransomed powers:
All my thoughts and words and doings,
All my days and all my hours.

Refrain:
All for Jesus! All for Jesus!
All my days and all my hours;
All for Jesus! All for Jesus!
All my days and all my hours.
Mary D. James, 1810–1883

To You, my Jesus, do I consecrate all the
remainder of my life. I wish only, and I wish in
all things, that which You desire.
Alphonsus Liguori, 1696–1787

Lord, thou knowest what I want, if it be thy will
I have it, and if it be not thy will, good Lord, do
not be displeased, for I want nothing which
you do not want.
Julian of Norwich, 1342–c.1416

Blessed be your name, Lord God, who has set
before me life and death, and has invited me
to chose life. Now, Lord God, I chose life, with
all my heart. I chose you, my God, for you are
my life.

Lord, make me completely holy, that all my

spirit, soul and body may be a temple for you. Live in me, and be my God and I will be your servant.

Thomas Ken, 1637–1711

Stir us up to offer thee, O Lord, our bodies, our souls, our spirits, in all we love and all we learn, in all we plan and all we do, to offer our labors, our pleasures, our sorrows to thee; to work through them for thy kingdom, to live as those who are not their own, but bought with thy blood, fed with thy body; thine from our birth-hour, thine now, and thine for ever and ever.

Charles Kingsley, 1819–75

O Lord Jesus Christ, you have made me and redeemed me and brought me to where I now am: you know what you wish to do with me; do with me according to your will, for your tender mercies' sake.

King Henry VI, 1421–71

I take God the Father to be my God;
I take God the Son to be my Savior;
I take the Holy Ghost to be my Sanctifier;
I take the Word of God to be my rule;
I take the people of God to be my people;
And I do hereby and dedicate and yield my
    whole self to the Lord:
And I do this deliberately, freely, and for ever.
Amen.

Act of commitment taught to
Matthew Henry by his father

O King of Heaven! make Thyself also King of my heart, possess me entirely.

Alphonsus Liguori, 1696–1787

Take, Lord, and receive all my liberty,
my memory, my understanding,
and my whole will.
All that I have and call my own,
you have given to me.
I surrender it all to you
to be disposed of according to your will.
Give me only your love and your grace;
with these I will be rich enough,
and will desire nothing more.

Ignatius Loyola, 1491/1495–1556

Lord, I give and offer up unto thee myself and all that is mine, actions and words, repose and silence; only do thou preserve and guide me, and direct my hand and mind and tongue to things that are acceptable to thee, and withdraw me from anything from which it were better to abstain, by and for the sake of Jesus Christ our Lord.

William Laud, 1573–1645

O Christ, my life, possess me utterly.
Take me and make a little Christ of me.
If I am anything but Thy Father's son,
'Tis something not yet from the darkness
    won.
Oh, give me light to live with open eyes.
Oh, give me life to hope above all skies.

George MacDonald, 1824–1905

Father, into your hands I give the heart which left thee but to learn how good thou art.

George MacDonald, 1824–1905

Send out your light and your truth, that I may live always near to you, my God. Let me feel your love, that I may be as it were already in heaven, that I may do my work as the angels do theirs; and let me be ready for every work, ready to go out or go in, to stay or depart, just as you direct.

Lord, let me have no will of my own, or consider my true happiness as depending in the smallest degree on anything that happens to me outwardly, but as consisting totally in conformity to your will.

Henry Martyn, 1781–1812

Use me, my Savior, for whatever purpose and in what way you require. Here is my poor heart, any empty vessel: fill it with your grace. Here is my sinful and troubled soul: bring it to life and refresh it with your love. Take my heart for you to live in; my mouth to spread abroad the glory of your name; my love and all my powers for the advancement of your believing people; and never allow the steadfastness and confidence of my faith to abate.

D.L. Moody, 1837–99

May not a single moment of my life be spent

outside the light, love, and joy of God's presence and may not a moment without the entire surrender of my self as a vessel for Him to fill full of His Spirit and His love.

Andrew Murray, 1828–1917

O Emmanuel, O Wisdom, I give myself to thee, I trust thee wholly. Thou art wiser than I, more loving to me than I am to myself; deign to fulfill thy high purposes in me, whatever they be. Work in and through me: I am born to serve thee, to be thine, to be thy instrument. Le me be thy blind instrument. I ask not to see, I ask not to know, I ask simply to be used.

J.H. Newman, 1801–90

My God, I will put myself without reserve into your hands. What have I in heaven, and apart from you what do I want upon earth? My flesh and my heart fail, but God is the God of my heart, and my portion forever.

J.H. Newman, 1801–90

My Lord and my God, take me from all that keeps me from you.
My Lord and my God, grant me all that leads me to you.
My Lord and my God, take me from myself and give me completely to you.

Nicholas of Flue, 1417–87

O Lord, let me not henceforth desire health or life except to spend them for thee and with thee. Thou alone knowest what is good for me; do therefore what seemeth thee best. Give to me or take from me; conform my will to thine; and grant that, with humble and perfect submission, and in holy confidence, I may receive the orders of thine eternal providence; and may equally adore all that comes to me from thee, through Jesus Christ our Lord.

Blaise Pascal, 1623–62

Lorica of Patrick
I arise today
Through a mighty strength, the invocation of the Trinity,
Through a belief in the Threeness,
Through confession of the Oneness
Of the Creator of creation.

I arise today
Through the strength of Christ's birth and His baptism,
Through the strength of His crucifixion and His burial,
Through the strength of His resurrection and His ascension,
Through the strength of His descent for the judgment of doom.

I arise today
Through the strength of the love of cherubim,
In obedience of angels,
In service of archangels,
In the hope of resurrection to meet with reward,
In the prayers of patriarchs,
In preachings of the apostles,
In faiths of confessors,
In innocence of virgins,
In deeds of righteous men.

I arise today
Through the strength of heaven;
Light of the sun,
Splendor of fire,
Speed of lightning,
Swiftness of the wind,
Depth of the sea,
Stability of the earth,
Firmness of the rock.

I arise today
Through God's strength to pilot me;
God's might to uphold me,
God's wisdom to guide me,
God's eye to look before me,
God's ear to hear me,
God's word to speak for me,
God's hand to guard me,
God's way to lie before me,
God's shield to protect me,
God's hosts to save me
From snares of the devil,
From temptations of vices,
From every one who desires me ill,
Afar and anear,
Alone or in a multitude.

I summon today all these powers between me and evil,

Against every cruel merciless power that
   opposes my body and soul,
Against incantations of false prophets,
Against black laws of pagandom,
Against false laws of heretics,
Against craft of idolatry,
Against spells of women and smiths and
   wizards,
Against every knowledge that corrupts man's
   body and soul.
Christ shield me today
Against poison, against burning,
Against drowning, against wounding,
So that reward may come to me in abundance.

Christ with me, Christ before me, Christ
   behind me,
Christ in me, Christ beneath me, Christ above
   me,
Christ on my right, Christ on my left,
Christ when I lie down, Christ when I sit
   down,
Christ in the heart of every man who thinks
   of me,
Christ in the mouth of every man who speaks
   of me,
Christ in the eye that sees me,
Christ in the ear that hears me.

I arise today
Through a mighty strength, the invocation of
   the Trinity,
Through a belief in the Threeness,
Through a confession of the Oneness
Of the Creator of creation
                                      Patrick c.389–c.461

O Lord my God, rescue me from myself, and
   give me to thee;
take away from me everything which draws
   me from thee;
give me all those things which lead me to thee;
for Jesus Christ's sake.
                                      Precationes Piae, 1564

O Lord Jesu, our only health and our everlasting life, I give myself wholly unto thy will:
being sure that the thing cannot perish which
is committed unto thy mercy.
   Thou, merciful Lord, wast born for my sake:
thou didst suffer both hunger and thirst for my

sake; thou didst preach and teach, dist pray and
fast, for my sake: and finally thou gavest thy
most precious body to die and thy blood to be
shed on the cross, for my sake. Most merciful
Savior, let all these things profit me which thou
freely hast given me. O Lord, into thy hands I
commit my soul.
                                      Primer, 1559

O my soul, cease from the love of this world
and melt in Christ's love, that always it may be
sweet to thee to speak, read, write, and think
of Him; to pray to Him and ever to praise
Him. O God, my soul, to Thee devoted, desires
to see Thee! She cries to Thee from afar. She
burns in Thee and languishes in Thy love. O
Love that fails not, Thou hast overcome me!
O everlasting Sweetness and Fairness Thou
hast wounded my heart, and now overcome
and wounded I fall. For joy scarcely I live, and
nearly I die; for I may not suffer the sweetness
of so great a Majesty in this flesh that shall
undergo corruption.
                                      Richard Rolle, 1290–1349

May Jesus Christ, the King of glory, help us to
make use of all the myrrh that God sends, and
to offer him the true incense of our hearts; for
his name's sake. Amen.
                                      Johannes Tauler, 1300–61

I live, yet no true life I know,
And, living thus expectantly,
I die because I do not die.

Since this new death in life
Estranged from self my life has been,
For now I live a life unseen:
The Lord has claimed me as His own.
My heart I gave Him for His throne,
Whereon He wrote indelibly:
"I die because I do not die."

Within this prison house divine,
Prison of love whereby I live,
My God Himself to me doth give,
And liberate this heart of mine,
And, as with love I yearn and pine,
With God my prisoner I sigh:
"I die because I do not die."

How tedious is this life below,
This exile with its grief and pains.
This dungeon and these cruel chains
In which the soul is forced to go!
Straining to leave this life of woe,
With anguish sharp and deep I cry:
"I die because I do not die."

How bitter our existence ere
We come at last the Lord to meet!
For, though the soul finds loving sweet,
The waiting time is hard to bear.
Oh, from this leaden weight of care,
My God relieve me speedily,
Who die because I do not die.

I only live because I know
That death and hope is all the more secure
Since death and life together go.
death, thou life-creator, lo!
I wait upon thee, come thou nigh:
I die because I do not die.

Consider, life, love's potency
And cease to cause me grief and pain.
Reflect, I beg, that, thee to gain,
I first must lose thee utterly.
Then, death, come pleasantly to me.
Come softly: undismayed am I
Who die because I do not die.

That life, with life beyond recall,
Is truly life for evermore:
Until this present life be over
We cannot savor life at all.
So, death, retreat not at my call,
For life through death I can descry
Who die because I do not die.

O life, what service can I pay
Unto my God who lives in me
Save if I first abandon thee
That I may merit thee for aye?
Such yearning for my Spouse have I,
Dying because I do not die.

Teresa of Avila, 1515–82

Prayer of devotion
Almighty God –
Everything I have is from you – and is yours.
Everything I am – is from you.
You created me and I belong to you.

Forgive me, Lord,
For my sins and errors.

Stay with me, Father,
and help me to stay with you,

Lord, help me to know you better –
And to see you, and to hear you,
And to feel your presence,
While you are so near –
And especially when I am looking away,
And listening to the world.

Father, bless those you have given to me,
And those you will place in my path,
Every day.
Help me to be an example for them.
Allow me not only to teach them,
But to learn from them.

Help me to share with the world –
And to give to the world.
Lord, you have given me so much.

Thank you for the marvelous individuals
That you have allowed to be with me
In this life.
Bless and love them – and protect them.
And Lord, include them with your
Chosen ones.

In your Almighty Name I pray. Amen.
Dr John N. Todd III, by kind permission

Lord, I am no longer my own, but yours. Put
me to what you will, rank me with whom you
will. Let be employed by you or laid aside for
you, exalted for you or brought low by you. Let
me have all things, let me have nothing, I freely
and heartily yield all things to your pleasure
and disposal. And now, O glorious and blessed
God, Father, Son, and Holy Spirit, you are mine
and I am yours. So be it. Amen.
John Wesley, 1703–91

Take my poor heart, and let it be
Forever closed to all but thee;
Seal thou my breast, and let me wear
That pledge of love forever there.
John Wesley, 1703–91

I am no longer my own, but thine.
Put me to what thou wilt, rank me with
    whom thou wilt.
Put me to doing, put me to suffering.
Let me be employed by thee or laid aside for
    thee,
exalted for thee or brought low by thee.
Let me be full, let be have nothing.
I freely and heartily yield all things
to thy pleasure and disposal.
And now, O glorious and blessed God,
Father, Son, and Holy Spirit,
thou art mine, and I am thine. So be it.
And the covenant which I have made on
    earth,
let it be ratified in heaven. Amen.
                    The Wesleyan Covenant Prayer

Lord, be thy word my rule,
In it may I rejoice;
Thy glory be my aim,
Thy holy will my choice.

Thy promises my hope;
Thy providence my guard;
Thine arm my strong support;
Thyself my great reward.
                Christopher Wordsworth, 1807–85

DEPENDENCE ON GOD

Save us, O Lord, from the snares of a double
    mind.
Deliver us from all cowardly neutralities.
Make us to go in the paths of your
    commandments,
and to trust for our defense in your mighty
    arm alone;
through Jesus Christ our Lord.
                        R.H. Froude, 1803–36

None other lamb, none other name,
    None other hope in heaven or earth or sea,
None other hiding-place from guilt and shame,
    None beside thee!

My faith burns low, my hope burns low;
    Only my heart's desire cries out in me,
By the deep thunder of its want and woe,
    Cries out to thee.

Lord, thou art life, though I be dead;
    Love's fire thou art, however cold I be:
Nor heaven have I, nor place to lay my head,
Nor home, but thee.
                        Christina Rossetti, 1830–94

O Lord, take full possession of my heart, raise
    there your throne, and command there as
    you do in heaven.
Being created by you, let me live for you;
being created for you, le me always act for
    your glory;
being redeemed by you, let me give to you
    what is yours;
and let my spirit cling to you alone, for your
    name's sake.
                        John Wesley, 1703–91

DETACHMENT

Give me Thy grace, good Lord
to set the world at nought;
To set my mind fast upon Thee,
and not to hang upon the blast of men's mouths;
To be content to be solitary,
not to long for worldly company;
Little by little utterly to cast off the world,
and rid my mind of all the business thereof;
Not to long to hear of any worldly things,
but that the hearing of worldly phantasies
    may be to me unpleasant;
Gladly to be thinking of God,
piteously to call for His help;
To lean unto the comfort of God,
busily to labor to love Him;
To know my own vileness and wretchedness,
to be humble and meek myself under the
    mighty hand of God;
To bewail my sins passed,
for the purging of them patiently to suffer
    adversity;
Gladly to bear my purgatory here,
to be joyful of tribulations;
To walk the narrow way that leads to life,
to bear the cross with Christ;
To have the last thing in remembrance,
to have ever before my eye my death that is
    ever at hand;
To make death no stranger to me,

to foresee and consider the everlasting fire of
   hell;
To pray for pardon before the Judge come,
to have continually in mind the passion that
   Christ suffered for me;
For His benefits unceasingly to give Him
   thanks,
to buy the time again that I before have lost;
To abstain from vain conversations,
to eschew light foolish mirth and gladness;
Recreations not necessary to cut off,
of worldly substance, friends, liberty, life and
   all, to set the loss as nothing
for the winning of Christ;
To think my greatest enemies my best friends,
for the brethren of Joseph could never have
   done him so much good
with their love and favor as they did him with
   their malice and hatred.
These attitudes are more to be desired of
   every man
than all the treasure of all the princes and
   kings Christian and heathen,
were it gathered and laid together all upon
   one heap.

Thomas More, 1478–1535

DILIGENCE

O God, grant unto us that we be not unwise,
but understanding thy will: not slothful, but
diligent in thy work: that we run not as uncertainly, nor fight thy battles as those that beat
the air. Whatsoever our hand findeth to do,
may we do it with our might: that when
thou shalt call thy laborers to give them their
reward, we may so have run that we may
obtain; so have fought the good fight, as to
receive the crown of eternal life; through Jesus
Christ our Lord.

Henry Alford, 1810–71

Grant, O Lord, that as we go forth once more
to our daily labor we may remember the truths
that we learnt, and may carry out the resolutions we made on thy holy day. Keep us from
our besetting sins, and strengthen us to do thy
holy will, that we may never forget whose we

are and whom we serve; through Jesus Christ
our Lord.

W.W. How, 1823–97

Almighty God, in whose hands are all the
powers of men, grant that we may not lavish
away the life which you have given us on
useless trifles; but enable us by your Holy
Spirit so to shun sloth and negligence that
every day we may carry out the task which
you have allotted us, and obtain such success
as will most promote your glory; for the sake
of Jesus Christ.

Samuel Johnson, 1709–84

DISCERNMENT

O Lord, give us more charity, more self-denial,
more likeness to you. Teach us to sacrifice our
comforts to others, and our preferences for the
sake of doing good. Make us kindly in thought,
gentle in word, generous in deed. Teach us
that it is better to give than to receive, better to
forget ourselves than to put ourselves forward,
better to minister than to be ministered to. And
to you, the God of love, be all glory and praise,
now and for ever.

Henry Alford, 1810–71

Lord God Almighty, Shaper and Ruler of all
creatures, we pray that by your great mercy
and by the token of the holy cross you will
guide us to your will. Make our minds steadfast, strengthen us against temptation, and
keep us from all unrighteousness. Shield us
against our enemies, seen and unseen. Teach
us to inwardly love you before all things with
a clean mind and a clean body. For you are our
Maker and Redeemer, our help and comfort,
our trust and hope, for ever.

King Alfred the Great, 849–899

Grant unto me
   to bruise the serpent's head,
   to remember the last things,
   to cut off occasions [for evil],
   to be sober,
   not to sit idle,
   to refuse the evil,

to cleave to the good,
to make a covenant touching the eyes,
to bring the body into subjection,
to give oneself to prayer,
to withdraw to penitence.

Lancelot Andrewes, 1555–1626

Steer the ship of my life, good Lord, to your quiet harbor, where I can be safe from the storms of sin and conflict. Show me the course I should take. Renew in me the gift of discernment, so that I can always see the right direction in which I should go. And give me the strength and courage to choose the right course, even when the sea is rough and the waves are high, knowing that through enduring hardship and danger in your name we shall find comfort and peace.

Basil the Great, c.330–379

Almighty God, Father of our Lord Jesus Christ, establish and confirm us in your truth by your Holy Spirit. Reveal to us what we do not know; perfect in us what is lacking; strengthen us in what we know; and keep us faultless in your service; through the same Jesus Christ our Lord.

Clement of Rome, c.30–c.95

Give to us the spirit of prayer, frequent and fervent, holy and persevering; an unreprovable faith, a just and humble hope, and a never-failing charity.

John Cosin, 1594–1672

God almighty, eternal, righteous and merciful, may we poor sinners, carry out your will and always do what pleases you. May we be so inwardly purified, enlightened and alight with the fire of the Holy Spirit that we follow in the footsteps of your well-beloved Son, our Lord Jesus Christ.

Francis of Assisi, 1181–1226

O Lord Jesus, who came down from heaven to redeem us from all iniquity, we beseech you to write your word in our hearts that we may know you, and the power of your resurrection, and express it in turning from our sins. Rule in our hearts by faith, that being dead to sin and living to righteousness, we may bear the fruit

of holiness and grow in grace and in personal knowledge of you.

Henry Hammond, 1605–60

Give us, O Lord, we humbly pray, a wise, a sober, a patient, an understanding, a devout, a religious, a courageous heart; a soul full of devotion to serve you, and strength against all temptations; through Jesus Christ our Lord.

William Laud, 1573–1645

Lord Jesus Christ, fill us, we pray, with your light and life that we may show forth your wonderful glory. Grant that your love may so fill our lives that we may count nothing too small to do for you, nothing too much to give and nothing too hard to bear.

Ignatius Loyola, 1491/1495–1556

My Redeemer and my Lord,
I beseech Thee, I entreat Thee,
Guide me in each act and word,
That hereafter I may meet Thee,
Watching, waiting, hoping, yearning,
With my lamp well trimmed and burning!

Interceding
With these bleeding
Wounds upon Thy hands and side,
For all who have lived and err
Thou hast suffered, Thou hast died,
Scourged, and mocked, and crucified,
And in the grave hast Thou been buried!

If my feeble prayer can reach Thee,
O my Savior, I beseech Thee,
Even as Thou has died for me,
More sincerely
Let me follow where Thou leadest,
Let me, bleeding as Thou bleedest,
Die, if dying I may give
Life to one who asks to live,
And more nearly,
Dying thus, resemble Thee!

H.W. Longfellow, 1807–82

O Holy and ever-blessed Lord, teach us, we beseech thee, to love one another, to exercise forbearance and forgiveness towards our enemies; to recompense no man evil for evil, but to be merciful even as thou, our Father in heaven, art merciful: that so we may continually follow after thee in all our doings, and be more and more conformed to thine image and likeness.

New Church Book of Worship, 1876

O Lord Jesus Christ, who when on earth was always occupied by your Father's business: grant that we may not grow weary in well-doing. Give us grace to do all in your name. Be our beginning and end of everything: the pattern whom we follow, the Redeemer in whom we trust, the Master whom we serve, the Friend to whom we look for sympathy. May we never shrink from our duty through any fear of people; make us faithful until death; and bring us at last into the eternal presence, where with the Father and the Holy Spirit you live and reign for ever.

E.B. Pusey, 1800–82

What is before us, we know not, whether we shall live or die; but this we know, that all things are ordered and sure. Everything is ordered with unerring wisdom and unbounded love, by thee, our God, who art love. Grant us in all things to see thy hand; through Jesus Christ our Lord.

Charles Simeon, 1759–1836

Lord, I can see plainly that you are the only and the true source of wisdom, since you alone can restore faith and hope to a doubting and despairing soul. In your Son, Jesus, you have shown me that even the most terrible suffering can be beautiful, if it is in obedience to your will. And so the knowledge of your Son has enabled me to find joy in my own suffering. Lord, my dear Father, I kneel before you this day, and praise you fervently for my present sufferings, and give thanks for the measureless sufferings of the past. I now realize that all these sufferings are part of your paternal love, in which you chastise and purify me. And through that discipline I now look at you without shame and terror, because I know that you are preparing me for: your eternal kingdom.

Henry Suso, 1295–1366

May the mind of Christ my Savior
Live in me from day to day,
By his love and power controlling
All I do and say.

May the word of God dwell richly
In my heart from hour to hour,
So that all may see I triumph
Only through his power.

May the love of Jesus fill me
As the waters fill the sea;
Him exalting, self abasing,
This is victory.

Kate B. Wilkinson, 1859–1928

DISCIPLESHIP

O God, the Holy Ghost in Christ my Savior, teach me, I pray Thee, what I shall do, that I may turn to Thee. O draw me in Christ to the Father, and help me, that now and from henceforward I may go forth from Sin and Vanity, and never any more enter into them again. Stir up in me a true Sorrow for the Sins I have committed. O keep me in Thy Bonds; and let me not loose from Thee, lest the Devil sift me in my wicked Flesh and Blood, and bring me again into the Death of Death. O enlighten Thou my Spirit, that I may see the Divine Path, and walk in it continually. O take that away from me, which always turneth me away from Thee; and give me that which always turneth me to Thee; take me wholly from Myself and give me wholly to Thyself. O let me begin nothing, let me will, think, and do nothing without Thee. O Lord, how long! Indeed I am not worthy of that which I desire of Thee, I pray Thee let the Desire of my Soul dwell but in the Gates of Thy Courts; make it but a Servant of Thy Servants. O preserve it from that horrible Pit, wherein there is no Comfort or Refreshment.

Jakob Boehme, 1555–1624

O Lord, take from me what keeps me from
    Thee;
O Lord, give me what brings me to Thee;
O Lord, take myself and give me Thyself.

Nicklaus of Fleuh, 1417–87

O Jesus, Thou hast set me apart from the world; what, then, shall I seek therein? Thou hast created me for Heaven; what, then, have I to do with the world? Depart from me, deceitful world, with thy vanities! Henceforth I will follow the Way of the Cross traced out for me by my Redeemer, and journey onward to my heavenly home, there to dwell forever and ever.

Francis of Assisi, 1181–1226

O my Jesus, Thou didst bear my burden and the heavy weight of my sins. Should I, then, not bear in union with Thee, my easy burden of suffering and accept the sweet yoke of Thy commandments? Thy yoke is sweet and Thy burden is light: I therefore willingly accept it. I will take up my cross and follow Thee.

Francis of Assisi, 1181–1226

ENDURANCE

O heavenly Father, I praise and thank thee for all thy goodness and faithfulness throughout my life. Thou hast granted me many blessings. Now let me accept tribulation from thy hand. Thou wilt not lay on me more than I can bear. Thou makest all things work together for good for thy children.

*Dietrich Bonhoeffer, 1906–45,
written at Christmastime 1943, from
the prison in which he was executed*

O give us patience and steadfastness in adversity, strengthen our weakness, comfort us in trouble and distress, help us to fight; grant to us that in true obedience we may give over our own will to you our Father in all things, according to the example of your beloved Son; that in adversity we grudge not, but offer up ourselves to you without contradiction. O give us a willing and cheerful mind, that we may gladly suffer and bear all things for your sake.

Miles Coverdale, 1488–1568

Merciful God, grant us feeble people endurance in adversity. May wicked roots of envy and malice not grow in us. Pull out the wicked root of covetousness from us. Save us from being brought into temptation by Satan. Grant

us love towards friends and enemies, that we may follow in your ways, our Father, and the example of your only-begotten Son, Jesus Christ.

Miles Coverdale, 1488–1568

O good Jesu, the word of the Father, the brightness of the Father's glory, whom angels desire to behold; teach me to do your will; that guided by your good spirit, I may come to that blessed city where there is everlasting day and all are of one spirit; where there is certain security and secure eternal tranquility and quiet felicity and happy sweetness and sweet pleasantness; where you, with the Father and the Holy Spirit live and reign, world without end.

Gregory I, c.540–604

Almighty and merciful God,
who art the strength of the weak,
the refreshment of the weary,
the comfort of the sad,
the help of the tempted,
the life of the dying,
the God of patience and of all consolation;
thou knowest full well the inner weakness of our nature, how we tremble and quiver before pain, and cannot bear the cross without thy divine help and support. Help me, then, O eternal and pitying God, help me to possess my soul in patience, to maintain unshaken hope in thee, to keep that childlike trust which feels a Father's heart hidden beneath the cross; so shall I be strengthened with power according to thy glorious might, in all patience and long-suffering; I shall be enabled to endure pain and temptation, and, in the very depth of my suffering, to praise thee with a joyful heart.

Johann Habermann, 1516–90

Give me grace, good Lord
To count the world as nothing,
To set my mind firmly on you
And not to hang on what people say;
To be content to be alone,
Not to long for worldly company,
Little by little to throw off the world
    completely
And rid my mind of all its business;
Not to long to hear of any worldly things;

Gladly to be thinking of you,
Pitifully to call for your help,
To depend on your comfort,
Busily to work to love you;
To know my own worthlessness and
    wretchedness,
To humble and abase myself under your
    mighty hand,
To lament my past sins,
To suffer adversity patiently, to purge them,
Gladly to bear my purgatory here,
To be joyful for troubles;
To walk the narrow way that leads to life,
To bear the Cross with Christ,
To keep the final hour in mind,
To have always before my eyes my death,
    which is always at hand,
To make death no stranger to me,
To foresee and consider the everlasting fire of
    hell,
To pray for pardon before the judge comes;
To keep continually in mind the passion that
    Christ suffered for me,
For his benefits unceasingly to give him
    thanks;
To buy back the time that I have wasted before,
To refrain from futile chatter,
To reject idle frivolity,
To cut out unnecessary entertainments,
To count the loss of worldly possessions,
    friends, liberty and life itself as absolutely
    nothing, for the winning of Christ;
To consider my worst enemies my best
    friends,
For Joseph's brothers could never have done
    him as much good with their love and
    favor as they did with their malice and
    hatred.
Thomas More, 1478–1535

O God, the author of peace and lover of
concord, grant unto us to be so firmly established in the love of thyself, that no trials
whatsover may be able to part us from thee.
Roman Breviary

EVIL, DELIVERANCE FROM

From witches, warlocks and wurricoes,
From ghoulies, ghosties and long-leggit beasties,
From all things that go bump in the night–
Good Lord, deliver us!
Source unknown, early Cornish,
England

O thou who knowest our hearts, and who seest
our temptations and struggles, have pity upon
us, and deliver us from the sins which make
war upon our souls. Thou art all-powerful, and
we are weak and erring. Our trust is in thee, O
thou faithful and good God. Deliver us from
the bondage of evil, and grant that we may
hereafter be thy devoted servants, serving thee
in the freedom of holy love, for Christ's sake.
Eugene Bersier, 1831–89

From all blindness of heart; from pride,
    vainglory, and hypocrisy; from
    envy, hatred, and malice, and all
    uncharitableness,
Spare us, good Lord.
From fornication, and all other deadly sin; and
    from all the deceits of the world, the flesh,
    and the devil,
Spare us, good Lord.
From lightning and tempest; from
    earthquake, fire, and flood; from plague,
    pestilence, and famine; from battle and
    murder, and from sudden death,
Spare us, good Lord.
From all sedition, privy conspiracy, and
    rebellion; from all false doctrine,
    heresy, and schism; from hardness of
    heart, and contempt of thy Word and
    Commandment,
Spare us, good Lord.
By the mystery of thy holy Incarnation; by
    thy holy Nativity and Circumcision; by thy
    Baptism, Fasting, and Temptation,
Spare us, good Lord.
By thine Agony and Bloody Sweat; by thy
    Cross and Passion; by thy precious Death
    and Burial; by thy glorious Resurrection
    and Ascension, and by the Coming of the
    Holy Ghost,
Spare us, good Lord.
In all time of our tribulation; in all time of our
    prosperity; in the hour of death, and in the
    day of judgment,
Spare us, good Lord.
Book of Common Prayer, The Litany

Batter my heart, three-person'd God, for you
As yet but knock, breathe, shine, and seek to
    mend.
That I may rise and stand, o'erthrow me, and
    bend
Your force to break, blow, burn, and make me
    new.
I, like an usurp'd town, to another due
Labor to admit you, but O, to no end!
Reason, your viceroy in me, me should
    defend,
But is captiv'd and proves weak or untrue.

Yet dearly I love you, and would be loved fain,
But am betrothed unto your enemy;
Divorce me, untie, or break that knot again,
Take me to you, imprison me, for I
Except you enthrall me, never shall be free,
Nor ever chaste, except you ravish me.

John Donne, 1572–1631

O God, who art the author of peace and lover
of concord, in knowledge of whom standeth
our eternal life, whose service is perfect freedom: defend us thy humble servants in all
assaults of our enemies; that we, surely trusting in thy defense, may not fear the power of
any adversaries; through the might of Jesus
Christ our Lord.

Book of Common Prayer, Morning Prayer, 1549

O Lamb of God, who takest away the sin of the
world, look upon us and have mercy upon us;
thou who art thyself both Victim and Priest,
thyself both Reward and Redeemer, keep safe
from all evil those whom thou hast redeemed,
O Savior of the world.

Irenaeus, c.130–c.200

O deliver me from them whose words are
softer than butter, when they have war in
their heart; and from them whose words are
smoother than oil, while they are very swords.
Lord, I cast my burden upon thee, that thou
mayest sustain me, and not suffer me to fall
for ever.
Amen.

William Laud, 1573–1645

Our Father in heaven, deliver us, we pray thee,
from all manner of evil, whether it touch our

body or soul, our property or good name, and
at last, when the hour of death shall come,
grant us a blessed end and graciously take us
from this vale of sorrow to thyself in heaven,
through Jesus Christ, thy Son, our Lord.

Martin Luther, 1483–1546

O Lord, open our minds to see ourselves as
    you see us,
and from all unwillingness to know our
    weakness and our sin,
Good Lord, deliver us.

From selfishness;
from wishing to be the center of attention;
from seeking admiration;
from the desire to have our own way in all
    things;
from unwillingness to listen to others;
from resentment of criticism,
Good Lord, deliver us.

From love of power; from jealousy;
from taking pleasure in the weakness of
    others,
Good Lord, deliver us.

From the weakness of indecision; from fear of
    adventure;
from constant fear of what others are thinking
    of us; from fear of speaking what we know
    is truth,
and doing what we know is right,
Good Lord, deliver us.

From possessiveness about material things
    and people;
from carelessness about the needs of others;
from selfish use of time and money;
from all lack of generosity,
Good Lord, deliver us.

From laziness of conscience;
from lack of self-discipline; from failure to
    persevere;
from depression in failure and
    disappointment,
Good Lord, deliver us.

From failure to be truthful;
from pretence and acting a part; from

hypocrisy;
from all dishonesty with ourselves and with
    others,
Good Lord, deliver us.

From impurity in word, in thought, and in
    action;
from failure to respect the bodies and minds
of ourselves and others;
from any kind of addiction,
Good Lord, deliver us.

From hatred and anger; from sarcasm;
from lack of sensitivity and division in our
    community;
from all failure to love and to forgive,
Good Lord, deliver us.

From failure to see our sin as an affront to
    God;
from failure to accept the forgiveness of
    others,
Good Lord, deliver us.

Peter Nott, b.1933

Grant, Lord, that I may not, for one moment,
admit willingly into my soul any thought
contrary to thy love.

E.B. Pusey, 1800–82

Heavenly Father, the Father of all wisdom,
understanding, and true strength, we beseech
thee look mercifully upon thy servants, and
send thy Holy Spirit into their hearts; that
when they must join to fight in the field for
the glory of thy name, they may be defended
with the strength of thy right hand, and may
manfully stand in the confession of thy faith,
and continue in the same unto their lives' end,
through our Lord Jesus Christ.

Nicholas Ridley, c.1500–55

Lord Jesus, All-pure, purify us that we may
    behold thee.
All-holy, sanctify us that we may stand before
    thee.
All-gracious, mould us that we may please
    thee.
Very love, suffer us not to set at naught thy
    love; suffer not devil, world, flesh, to
    destroy us; suffer not ourselves to destroy

ourselves; us with whom thou strivest,
who thou desirest, whom thou lovest.

Christina Rossetti, 1830–94

Help me now, O God, to do all things in your
    sight, who sees in secret.
Shut out, O God, from my heart everything
    that offends you.
By your mighty power, repress all my
    wandering thoughts, and tread down Satan
    under my feet.

Treasury of Devotion, 1869

FAITH

Almighty God, who in thy wisdom hast so
ordered our earthly life that we needs must
walk by faith and not by sight; grant us such
faith in thee that, amidst all things that pass our
understanding, we may believe in thy fatherly
care, and ever be strengthened by the assurance that underneath are the everlasting arms;
through Jesus Christ our Lord.

Source unknown

Lord, increase my faith,
as a grain of mustard seed;
not dead,
enduring but for a time,
feigned,
masking void the law;
but a faith
working by love,
working with works,
    a supplier of virtue.
living,
overcoming the world,
most holy. Amen.

Lancelot Andrewes, 1555–1626

While faith is with me, I am best;
It turns my darkest night to day;
But, while I clasp it to my breast,
I often feel it slide away.

What shall I do if all my love,
My hopes, my toil, are cast away?
And if there be no God above
To hear and bless me when I pray?

Oh, heal me, God!
For thou alone
Canst my distracted soul relieve.
Forsake it not: it is thine own,
Through weak, yet longing to believe.

Anne Brontë, 1820–49

Almighty and Ever-living God, who has given to them that believe exceeding great and precious promises: Grant us so perfectly, and without all doubt, to believe in Thy Son Jesus Christ, that our faith in Thy sight may never be reproved. Hear us, O Lord, through the same, our Savior Jesus Christ. Amen.

The Common Service Book of the Lutheran Church, 1917

Merciful God, be thou now unto me a strong tower of defense. Give me grace to await thy leisure, and patiently to bear what you doest unto me, nothing doubting or mistrusting thy goodness towards me. Therefore do with me in all things as thou wilt: Only arm me, I beseech thee, with thy Armour, that I may stand fast; above all things taking to me the shield of faith, praying always that I may refer myself wholly to thy will, being assuredly persuaded that all thou doest cannot but be well. And unto thee be all honor and glory.

Lady Jane Grey, 1537–54, before her execution

O most merciful Father, we beseech thee, for thy mercy's sake, continue thy grace and favor towards us. Let not the sun of thy gospel ever go down out of our hearts; let thy truth abide and be established among us for ever. Help our unbelief, increase our faith, and give us hearts to consider the time of our visitation. Through faith clothe us with Christ, that he may live in us, and thy name may be glorified through us in all the world.

John Jewel, 1522–55

Teach us, O God not to torture ourselves, not to make martyrs of ourselves through stifling reflection; but rather teach us to breathe deeply in faith, through Jesus, our Lord.

Søren Kierkegaard, 1813–55

FORGIVING OTHERS

O Lord, remember not only the men and women of good will, but also those of ill will. But do not remember all the suffering they have inflicted on us; remember the fruits we have brought, thanks to this suffering – our comradeship, our loyalty, our courage, our generosity, the greatness of heart which has grown out of all this, and when they come to judgment let all the fruits which we have borne be their forgiveness.

Author unknown, prayer found near the body of a dead child in the Ravensbruck concentration camp

Lord, you return gladly and lovingly to lift up the one who offends you; and I do not turn to raise up and honor the one who angers me. Forgive me, Lord.

John of the Cross, 1542–91

O Lord Jesus, because, being surrounded with infirmities we often sin and have to ask pardon, help us to forgive as we would be forgiven; neither mentioning old offences committed against us, nor dwelling upon them in thought, nor being influenced by them in heart; but loving our brother freely, as you freely loved us. For your name's sake.

Christina Rossetti, 1830–94

Lord, enlighten us to see the beam that is in our own eye, and blind us to the mote that is in our brother's. Let us feel our offences with our hands, make them great and bright before us like the sun, make us eat them and drink them for our diet. Blind us to the offences of our beloved, cleanse them from our memories, take them out of our mouths for ever. Let all here before Thee carry and measure with the false balances of love, and be in their own eyes and in all conjunctures the most guilty. Help us at the same time with the grace of courage, that we be none of us cast down when we sit lamenting amid the ruins of our happiness or our integrity: touch us with fire from the altar, that we may be up and doing to rebuild our city: in the name and by the method of him in whose words of prayer we now conclude.

R.L. Stevenson, 1850–94

But I know Whom I have believèd,
And am persuaded that He is able
To keep that which I've committed
Unto Him against that day.

Daniel Webster Whittle, 1840–1901

GENEROSITY

O Lord and King, grant me the grace of being
aware of my sins and of not thinking evil of
those of my brethren.
For you are blessed, now and ever, and forever.
Amen.

Ephraem, c.306–378

Make us always eager, Lord, to share the good
things that we have. Grant us such a measure
of your Spirit that we may find more joy in
giving than in getting. Make us ready to give
cheerfully without grudging, secretly without
praise, and in sincerity without looking for
gratitude, for Jesus Christ's sake.

John Hunter, 1849–1917

Dearest Lord, teach me to be generous;
teach me to serve you as you deserve;
to give and not to count the cost,
to fight and not to heed the wounds,
to toil and not to see for rest,
to labor and not to seek reward,
except to know that I do your will.

Ignatius Loyola, 1491/1495–1556

O Lord Jesus Christ, who though you were rich
became poor, grant that all our desire for and
covetousness of earthly possessions may die in
us, and that the desire of heavenly things may
live and grow in us. Keep us from all idle and
vain expenses that we may always have enough
to him to him who is in need, and that we
may not give grudgingly our out of necessity,
but cheerfully. Through your merits may we
partake of the riches of your heavenly treasure.

Treasury of Devotion, 1869

GODLINESS

Almighty and Everlasting God who of Thy
great mercy in Jesus Christ, Thy Son, dost
grant us forgiveness of sin, and all things
pertaining to life and godliness: Grant us, we
beseech Thee, Thy Holy Spirit, that He may so
rule our hearts, that we, being ever mindful of
Thy fatherly mercy, may strive to mortify the
flesh, and to overcome the world; and, serving
Thee in holiness and pureness of living, may
give Thee continual thanks for all Thy goodness; through Jesus Christ, Thy Son, our Lord.
Amen.

*The Common Service Book of
the Lutheran Church, 1917*

GRACE

Hedge up my way with thorns,
that I find not the path for following vanity.
Hold thou me in with bit and bridle,
lest I fall from thee.
O Lord, compel me to come in to thee.

Lancelot Andrewes, 1555–1626

Lord, I bring the poverty of my soul to be
transformed by your beauty; the wildness of
my passions to be tamed by your love; the
stubbornness of my will to be conformed by
your commandments and the yearnings of my
heart to be renewed by your grace; both now
and for ever. Amen.

Catherine of Genoa, 1447–1510

Hark, my soul! It is the Lord;
'Tis thy Savior, hear his word;
Jesus speaks, and speaks to thee:
'Say, poor sinner, lov'st thou me?

Lord, it is my chief complaint
That my love is weak and faint;
Yet I love thee and adore,
Oh for grace to love thee more!

William Cowper, 1731–1800

O Lord, disdain not my prayer – the prayer
of a wretched sinner; sustain me with Your
grace until the end, that it may protect me as in
the past It is Your grace which has taught me
wisdom; blessed are they who follow her ways,
for they shall receive the crown of glory.

Ephraem, c.306–378

I am bending my knee
In the eye of the Father who created me,
In the eye of the Son who purchased me,
In the eye of the Spirit who cleansed me,
In friendship and affection.
Through Thine own anointed One, O God,
Bestow upon us fullness in our need,
Love towards God,
The affection of God,
The smile of God,
The wisdom of God,
The grace of God,
The fear of God,
And the will of God,
To do on the world of the Three,
As angels and saints
Do in heaven;
Each shade and light,
Each day and night,
Each time and kindness,
Give Thou us Thy Spirit.

Gaelic prayer

Lord, give me grace to use this world so as not to abuse it. Lord, grant that I may never go beyond or defraud my brother in any matter for thou art the avenger of all such.

Thomas Ken, 1637–1711

Good and gracious Lord, as you give me grace
    to acknowledge my sins, so give me grace
    in both word and heart to repent them
    and utterly forsake them. And forgive me
    those sins which my pride blinds me from
    discerning.
Glorious God, give me your grace to turn my
    back on the things of this world, and to fix
    my heart solely on you.
Give me your grace to amend my life, so that
    I can approach death without resentment,
    knowing that in you it is the gateway to
    eternal riches.
Glorious God, take from me all sinful fear, all
    sinful sorrow and self-pity, all sinful hope
    and all sinful desire. Instead give me such
    fear, such sorrow, such pity, such hope and
    such desire as may be profitable for my
    soul.
Good Lord, give me this grace, in all my fear
    and agony, to find strength in that great
    fear and agony which you, sweet Savior,

had on the Mount of Olives before your bitter passion.

Almighty God, take from me all desire for
    worldly praise, and all emotions of anger
    and revenge. Give me a humble, lowly,
    quiet, peaceable, patient, generous, kind,
    tender and compassionate mind.

Grant me, good Lord, a full faith, a firm
    hope and a fervent love, that I may desire
    only that which gives you pleasure and
    conforms to your will.
And, above all, look upon me with your love
    and your favor.

Thomas More, 1478–1535

Holy God whose nature and name is Love:
Seeing there is in Christ Jesus an infinite
    fullness of all that we can want or wish
O that we may all receive of his fullness,
    grace upon grace;
Grace to pardon our sins and subdue our
    iniquities;
Grace to justify our persons and to sanctify
    our souls;
Grace to complete that holy change,
    that renewal of our hearts,
    whereby we may be transformed
into that blessed image wherein you did create
    us;
through Jesus Christ our Lord,
who lives and reigns with you and the Holy
    Spirit,
one God, now and forever. Amen.

John Wesley, 1703–91

GRATITUDE

Lord of all mercy and goodness, suffer us not by any ingratitude or hardness of heart to forget the wonderful benefits that thou hast bestowed upon us this and every day; but grant that we may be merciful all the days of our life of the incomparable gifts which thou ever givest us through Jesus Christ our Lord.

Source unknown, early Scottish

O my God, let me with gratitude remember and confess unto Thee Thy mercies bestowed upon me. Let my bones be steeped in Thy love, and let them say, Who is like unto Thee, O Lord? "Thou hast loosed my bonds, I will offer unto Thee the sacrifice of thanksgiving."

Augustine of Hippo, 354–430

O God and Lord of the Powers, and Maker of all creation, who, because of your clemency and incomparable mercy, didst send Thine Only-Begotten Son and our Lord Jesus Christ for the salvation of mankind, and with His venerable Cross didst tear asunder the record of our sins, and thereby didst conquer the rulers and powers of darkness; receive from us sinful people, O merciful Master, these prayers of gratitude and supplication, and deliver us from every destructive and gloomy transgression, and from all visible and invisible enemies who seek to injure us. Nail down our flesh with fear of Thee, and let not our hearts be inclined to words or thoughts of evil, but pierce our souls with your love, that ever contemplating Thee, being enlightened by Thee, and discerning Thee, the unapproachable and everlasting Light, we may unceasingly render confession and gratitude to Thee: The eternal Father, with Thine Only-Begotten Son, and with Thine All-Holy, Gracious, and Life-Giving Spirit, now and ever, and unto ages of ages. Amen.

Basil the Great, c.329–379

And still, O Lord, to me impart
An innocent and grateful heart.

S.T. Coleridge, 1772–1834

Thou that hast given so much to me,
give one thing more, a grateful heart.
Not thankful when it pleases me,
as if your blessings had spare days;
but such a heart whose very pulse
may be thy praise.

George Herbert, 1593–1633

O Lord, that lends me life,
Lend me a heart replete with thankfulness.

William Shakespeare, 1564–1616

GROWTH

May God in his mercy grant that every day we may be troubled, tried, disciplined, or make some progress.

*Augustine of Hippo,
354–430*

SEND, we beseech Thee, Almighty God, Thy Holy Spirit into our hearts, that He may rule and direct us according to Thy will, comfort us in all our temptations and afflictions, defend us from all error, and lead us into all truth; that we, being steadfast in the faith, may increase in love and in all good works, and in the end obtain everlasting life; through Jesus Christ, Thy Son, our Lord. Amen.

*The Common Service Book of
the Lutheran Church, 1917*

GUIDANCE

Incline your ear, O Lord, and answer me,
    for I am poor and needy.
… Teach me your way, O Lord,
    that I may walk in your truth;
    give me an undivided heart to revere your
    name.

Psalm 86.1, 11 NRSV

O King of Glory and Lord of Valors, our warrior and our peace, who has said, 'Be of good cheer, I have overcome the world,' be victorious in us your servants, for without you we can do nothing. Grant your compassion to go before us, your compassion to come behind us: before us in our undertaking, behind us in our ending. And what will I now say, unless that your will be done, who wills that all should be save? Your will is our salvation, our glory our joy.

Alcuin, 735–804

Grant me, I beseech thee, almighty and merciful God, fervently to desire, wisely to search out, truly to acknowledge, and perfectly to fulfill, all that is well-pleasing to thee. Order thou my worldly condition to the honor and glory of thy name; and of all that thou requirest me to do, grant me the knowledge, the desire, and the ability, that I may so fulfill it as I ought, and as is expedient for the welfare of my soul

Thomas Aquinas, 1225–74

God of all goodness, grant us to desire ardently, to seek wisely, to know surely, and to accomplish perfectly your holy will, for the glory of
your name.

Thomas Aquinas, 1225–74

Lord, heal and open my eyes that I may recognize your will. Show me the road I must travel
that I may see you.

Augustine of Hippo, 354–430

Lord, hour by hour,
Be thou my Guide,
That, by thy power,
No step may slide.

Source unknown, "The Westminster Chimes"

O Lord our God, teach us to ask aright for
the right blessings. Guide the vessel of our
life towards yourself, the tranquil haven of all
storm-tossed souls. Show us the course we
should take. Renew a willing spirit within us.
Let your Spirit curb our wayward senses and
guide and enable us to what is our true good,
to keep your laws and in all our deeds always
to rejoice in your glorious and gladdening
presence. For yours is the glory and praise of
all your saints for ever and ever.

Basil the Great, c.329–379

Open our hearts, O Lord, and enlighten our
minds by the grace of your Holy Spirit, that
we may seek what is well-pleasing to your will;
and so order our doings after your commandments, that we may be found fit to enter into
your everlasting joy, through Jesus Christ our
Lord.

Bede, c.673–735

Thy way, not mine, O Lord,
However dark it be:
Lead me by thine own hand,
Choose out the path for me.

The kingdom that I seek
Is thine: so let the way
That leads to it be thine,
Else I must surely stray.

Take thou my cup, and it
With joy or sorrow fill,

As best to thee may seem;
Choose thou my good and ill.

Not mine, not mine the choice
In things or great or small;
By thou my guide, my strength,
My wisdom and my all.

Horatius Bonar, 1808–82

Lord, show me the way
And make me willing to walk therein.

Bridget of Sweden, 1303–73

We beseech you, O Lord, to enlighten our
minds and to strengthen our wills, that we may
know what we ought to do, and be enabled
to do it, through the grace of your most Holy
Spirit, and for the merits of your Son, Jesus
Christ our Lord.

William Bright, 1824–1901

God guide me with Thy wisdom
God chastise me with Thy justice,
God help me with Thy mercy,
God protect me with Thy strength.

Carmina Gadelica

Enlighten our minds, we beseech Thee, O God,
by the Spirit Who proceedeth from Thee; that,
as Thy Son has promised, we may be led into
all truth; through the same Jesus Christ, Thy
Son, our Lord. Amen.

*The Common Service Book of
the Lutheran Church, 1917*

God moves in a mysterious way,
His wonders to perform;
He plants his footsteps in the sea,
And rides upon the storm.

Deep in unfathomable mines
Of never-failing skill,
He treasures up his bright designs,
And works his sov'reign will.

Ye fearful saints, fresh courage take,
The clouds ye so much dread
Are big with mercy, and shall break
In blessings on your head.

Judge not the Lord by feeble sense,

But trust him for his grace;
Behind a frowning providence
He hides a smiling face.

His purposes will ripen fast,
Unfolding ev'ry hour;
The bud may have a bitter taste,
But sweet will be the flow'r.

Blind unbelief is sure to err,
And scan his work in vain;
God is his own interpreter,
And he will make it plain.

William Cowper, 1731–1800

Almighty God, teach us by your Holy Spirit,
what to believe, what to do, and where to take
our rest.

Desiderius Erasmus, 1467–1536

Most high, glorious God,
enlighten the darkness of our minds.
Give us a true faith, a certain hope and a
    perfect love,
so that we may always and in all things act
    according to your holy will. Amen.

Francis of Assisi, 1181–1226

O Lord, we beseech thee mercifully to receive
the prayers of thy people who call upon thee;
and grant that they may both perceive and
know what things they ought to do; and also
may have grace and power faithfully to fulfill
the same; through Jesus Christ our Lord.

Gregorian Sacramentary,
6th century

Our Father, teach us not only Thy will, but how
to do it. Teach us the best way of doing the
best thing, lest we spoil the end by unworthy
means; for the sake of Christ Jesus our Lord.
Amen.

J.H. Jowett, 1864–1923

O Lord, I am yours. Do what seems good in
    your sight,
and give me complete resignation to your will.

David Livingstone, 1813–73

O eternal God, in whose appointment our life
stands, and who has committed our work to

us. We commit our cares to you. We thank you
that we are your children, and that you have
assured us that, while we are intent upon your
will, you will heed our wants. Fill us with that
compassion for others' troubles which comes
from forgetfulness of our own; with the charity of those who know their own unworthiness; and with the glad hope of the children
of eternity. And to you, the Beginning and the
End, Lord of the living, Refuge of the dying, be
thanks and praise for ever. Amen.

James Martineau, 1805–1900

Lord, I am blind and helpless, stupid and ignorant, cause me to hear; cause me to know;
teach me to do; lead me.

Henry Martyn, 1781–1812

Lord, I thank Thee that Thy love constraineth
me. I thank Thee that, in the great labyrinth of
life, Thou waitest not for my consent to lead
me. I thank Thee that Thou leadest me by a
way which I know not, by a way which is above
the level of my poor understanding … Protect
me from the impetuous desires of my nature
– desires as short-lived as they are impetuous.
Ask me not where I would like to go; tell me
where to go; lead me in Thine own way; hold
me in Thine own light. Amen.

George Matheson, 1842–1906

O Lord, You who steadied the hand of Peter
as he began to sink on the stormy sea, if you
are with me, no one is against me. Grant to
me the shield of faith and the mighty armor of
the Holy Spirit to protect me and guide me to
do Your will. The future I put into Your hands,
O Lord, and I follow You to a life in Christ.
Amen

Orthodox prayer

If I am right, thy Grace impart
    Still in the right to stay:
If I am wrong, oh teach my heart
    To find that better way.

Alexander Pope, 1688–1744

Speak, Lord, for thy servant heareth.
Grant us ears to hear,
eyes to see,
wills to obey,

hearts to love;
then declare what thou wilt,
reveal what thou wilt,
command what thou wilt,
demand what thou wilt.

Christina Rossetti, 1830–94

Grant, O Father, that this day we may be doers of your Word, and not hearers only.

Christopher Smart, 1722–71

Lord Jesus, think on me
Nor let me go astray;
Through darkness and perplexity
Point Thou the heavenly way.

Synesius of Cyrene, 375–430,
translated by Allen W. Chatfield

I know not what the future hath
Of marvel or surprise,
Assured alone that life and death
God's mercy underlies.

J.G. Whittier, 1807–92

Lord, I am a countryman coming from my country to yours. Teach me the laws of your country, its way of life and its spirit, so that I may feel at home there.

William of St Thierry, 1085–1148

Guide me, O Thou great Redeemer,
Pilgrim through this barren land.
I am weak, but Thou art mighty;
Hold me with Thy powerful hand.
Bread of heaven, bread of heaven,
Feed me till I want no more;
Feed me till I want no more.

William Williams, 1717–91

HAPPINESS

My God, let me know and love you, so that I may find my happiness in you. Since I cannot fully achieve this on earth, help me to improve daily until I may do so to the full Enable me to know you ever more on earth, so that I may know you perfectly in heaven. Enable me to love you ever more on earth, so that I may love you perfectly in heave. In that way my joy

may be great on earth, and perfect with you in heaven.

Augustine of Hippo, 354–430

O God of truth, grant me the happiness of heaven so that my joy may be full in accord with your promise. In the meantime let my mind dwell on that happiness, my tongue speak of it, my heart pine for it, my mouth pronounce it, my soul hunger for it, my flesh thirst for it, and my entire being desire it until I enter through death in the joy of my Lord forever. Amen.

Augustine of Hippo, 354–430

HEALING, SPIRITUAL

See also: PRAYERS FOR THE CHRISTIAN CHURCH: Christian leaders, Spiritual health

Your hand, O God Almighty, is able to heal all the infirmities of my soul.

Augustine of Hippo, 354–430

HEAVEN

O only pure and sinless Lord, Who through the ineffable compassion of Thy love for men didst assume our whole nature through the pure and virgin blood of her who supernaturally conceived Thee by the coming of the Divine Spirit and by the will of the Eternal Father; O Christ Jesus, Wisdom and Peace and Power of God, Who in Thy assumption of our nature didst suffer Thy life-giving and saving Passion – the Cross, the Nails, the Spear, and Death – mortify all the deadly passions of my body. Thou Who in Thy burial didst spoil the dominions of hell, bury with good thoughts my evil schemes and scatter the spirits of wickedness. Thou Who by Thy life-giving Resurrection on the third day didst raise up our fallen first Parent, raise me up who am sunk in sin and suggest to me ways of repentance. Thou Who by Thy glorious Ascension didst deify our nature which Thou hadst assumed and didst honor it by Thy session at the right hand of the Father, make me worthy by partaking of Thy holy Mysteries of a place at Thy right hand among those who are saved. Thou Who by the descent of the Spirit, the Paraclete, didst make Thy holy Disciples worthy vessels, make me also a recipient of His coming. Thou Who art to come again to judge the World with justice, grant me also to meet Thee on the clouds, my Maker and Creator, with all Thy Saints, that I may unendingly glorify and praise Thee with Thy Eternal Father and Thy all-holy and good and life-giving Spirit, now and ever, and to the ages of ages. Amen.

Symeon the Translator, 11th century

HOLINESS

Grant, O Lord,
that Christ himself may be formed in us,
that we may conform to his image;
for his name's sake.

Lancelot Andrewes, 1555–1626

The Deeps

Lord Jesus, give me a deeper repentance, a horror of sin, a dread of its approach. Help me chastely to flee it and jealously to resolve that my heart shall be Thine alone. Give me a deeper trust, that I may lose myself to find myself in Thee, the ground of my rest, the spring of my being. Give me a deeper knowledge of Thyself as savior, master, lord, and king. Give me deeper power in private prayer, more sweetness in Thy Word, more steadfast grip on its truth. Give me deeper holiness in speech, thought, action, and let me not seek moral virtue apart from Thee. Plough deep in me, great Lord, heavenly husbandman, that my being may be a tilled field, the roots of grace spreading far and wide, until Thou alone art seen in me, Thy beauty golden like summer harvest, Thy fruitfulness as autumn plenty. I have no master but Thee, no law but Thy will, no delight but Thyself, no wealth but that Thou givest, no good but that Thou blessest, no peace but that Thou bestowest. I am nothing but that Thou makest me. I have nothing but that I receive from Thee. I can be nothing but that grace adorns me. Quarry me deep, dear Lord, and then fill me to overflowing with living water.

Author unknown, a Puritan prayer

GOD, Whose strength is made perfect in weakness: Mortify and kill all vices in us, and so strengthen us by Thy grace, that by the innocency of our lives, and the constancy of our faith even unto death, we may glorify Thy holy Name; through Jesus Christ, Thy Son, our Lord. Amen.

The Common Service Book of the Lutheran Church, 1917

O teach us to despise all vanities, to fight the battles of the Lord manfully against the flesh, the world, and the devil, to spend our time religiously and usefully, to speak gracious words, to walk always in your presence, to preserve our souls and bodies in holiness, fit for the habitation of the Holy Spirit of God.

John Cosin, 1594–1672

Help me to avoid every sin,
And the source of every sin to forsake,
And as the mist scatters on the crest of the
    hills,
May each ill haze clear from my soul, O God.

Gaelic prayer

Our Father, you called us and saved us in order to make us like your Son, our Lord Jesus Christ. Day by day, change us by the work of your Holy Spirit so that we may grow more like him in all that we think and say and do, to his glory.

Søren Kierkegaard, 1813–55

Cleanse me, O God, by the bright fountain of thy mercy, and water me with the dew of thine abundant grace, that, being purified from my sins, I may grow up in good works, truly serving thee in holiness and righteousness all the days of my life.

Private Devotions, 1560

Sanctify us, O Lord.
Baptize thy whole Church with fire, that
    the divisions soon may cease, and that it
    may stand before the world as a pillar and
    buttress of thy truth.
Sanctify us, O Lord.

Grant us all the fruits of thy Holy Spirit:
  brotherly love, joy, peace, patience,
  goodwill and faithfulness.
Sanctify us, O Lord.
May the Holy Spirit speak by the voice of thy
  servants, here and everywhere, as they
  preach thy word.
Sanctify us, O Lord.
Send thy Holy Spirit, the comforter, to all who
  face adversity, or who are the victims of
  men's wickedness.
Sanctify us, O Lord.
Preserve all nations and their leaders
  from hatred and war, and build up a >
  community among nations, through the
  power of thy Spirit.
Sanctify us, O Lord.
Holy Spirit, Lord and source of life, giver of
  the seven gifts,
Sanctify us, O Comforter.
Spirit of wisdom and understanding, Spirit of
  counsel and strength,
Sanctify us, O Comforter.
Spirit of knowledge and devotion, Spirit of
  obedience to the Lord.
Sanctify us, O Comforter.

Taizé Community

O eternal God, who has made all things subject
to mankind, and mankind for your glory; sanctify our souls and bodies, our thoughts and
our intentions, our words and actions. Let our
body be the servant of our spirit, and both
body and spirit servants of Jesus; that doing all
things for your glory here, we may be partakers
of your glory hereafter, through Jesus Christ
our Lord.

Jeremy Taylor, 1613–67

Let the remembrance of all the glory wherein I was created make me more serious and
humble, more deep and penitent, more pure
and holy before thee.

Thomas Traherne, 1637–74

HOPE

I wait for the Lord, my soul waits,
  and in his word I hope;

my soul waits for the Lord
more than those who watch for the morning,
more than those who watch for the morning.

Psalm 130.5–6 NRSV

O Israel, hope in the Lord
  from this time on and for evermore.

Psalm 131.3 NRSV

For your mercies' sake, O Lord my God, tell me
what you are to me. Say to my soul: "I am your
salvation." So speak that I may hear, O Lord;
my heart is listening; open it that it may hear
you, and say to my soul: "I am your salvation."
After hearing this word, may I come in haste to
take hold of you. Hide not your face from me.
Let me see your face even if I die, lest I die with
longing to see it. The house of my soul is too
small to receive you; let it be enlarged by you.
It is all in ruins; do you repair it. There are thing
in it – I confess and I know – that must offend
your sight. But who shall cleanse it? Or to what
others besides you shall I cry out? From my
secret sins cleanse me, O Lord, and from those
of others spare your servant. Amen.

Augustine of Hippo, 354–430

O God, who never forsakest those that hope
in thee: grant that we may ever keep that
hope which thou hast given us by thy Word
as an anchor of our souls, to preserve us sure
and steadfast, unshaken and secure in all the
storms of life; through Jesus Christ our Lord.

Source unknown

Grant, Almighty God, that as we now carry
about us this mortal body, yea, and nourish
through sin a thousand deaths within us; O
grant that we may ever by faith direct our eyes
toward heaven, and to that incomprehensible
power, which is to be manifested at the last
day by Jesus Christ our Lord, so that in the
midst of death we may hope that thou wilt
be our Redeemer, and enjoy that redemption
which he completed when he rose from the
dead, and not doubt that the fruit which he
then brought forth by his Spirit will come also
to us when Christ himself shall come to judge
the world; and may we thus walk in the fear
of thy name, that we may be really gathered
among his members, to be mane partakers of

that glory which by his death he has procured for us. Amen

John Calvin, 1509–64

O God, the author and fountain of hope, enable us to rely with confident expectation on thy promises, knowing that the trials and hindrances of the present time are not worthy to be compared with the glory that shall be revealed, and having our faces steadfastly set towards the light that shineth more and more to the perfect day; through Jesus Christ our Lord.

A Devotional Diary

In You, O Lord Jesus, have I hoped;
let me not be confounded forever.
You alone are good.
You alone are powerful.
You alone are eternal.
To you alone be honor and glory,
love and thanksgiving
forever and ever.

Peter Julian Eymard, 1811–68

The God and Father of our Lord Jesus Christ open all our eyes, that we may see that blessed hope to which we are called; that we may altogether glorify the only true God and Jesus Christ, whom he hath sent down to us from heaven; to whom with the Father and the Holy Ghost be rendered all honor and glory to all eternity.

John Jewel, 1522–71

O my God, relying upon thy infinite power and mercy, and the precious blood of my Lord and Savior Jesus Christ, I hope to obtain the forgiveness of my sins and everlasting life: and I hereby resolve, by thy grace, to perform all that thou hast revealed to me of thy holy will.

Treasury of Devotion, 1869

Come, Thou long expected Jesus
Born to set Thy people free;
From our fears and sins release us,
Let us find our rest in Thee.
Israel's strength and consolation,
Hope of all the earth Thou art;
Dear desire of every nation,
Joy of every longing heart.

Charles Wesley, 1707–88

O Lord, who art the hope of all the ends of the earth, let me never be destitute of a well-grounded hope, nor yet possessed with a vain presumption: suffer me not to think thou wilt either be reconciled to my sins, or reject my repentance; but give me, I beseech thee, such a hope as may be answerable to the only ground of hope, thy promises, and such as may both encourage and enable me to purify myself from all filthiness, both of flesh and spirit; that so, it may indeed become to me an anchor of the soul both sure and steadfast.

The Whole Duty of Man, 1658

HUMILITY

I acknowledge, Lord, and I give thanks that you have created your image in me, so that I may remember you, think of you, love you. But this image is so obliterated and worn away by wickedness, it is so obscured by the smoke of sins, that it cannot do what it was created to do, unless you renew and reform it. I am not attempting, O Lord, to penetrate your loftiness, for I cannot begin to match my understanding with it, but I desire in some measure to understand your truth, which my heart believes and loves. For I do not seek to understand in order that I may believe, but I believe in order to understand. For this too I believe, that 'unless I believe, I shall not understand.'

Anselm, 1033–1109

Give us grace to endeavor after a truly Christian spirit to seek to attain that temper of forbearance and patience of which our blessed savior has set us the highest example; and which, while it prepares us for the spiritual happiness of the life to come, will secure to us the best enjoyment of what this world can give. Incline us oh God! to think humbly of ourselves, to be severe only in the examination of our own conduct, to consider our fellow-creatures with kindness, and to judge of all they say and do with that charity which we would desire from them ourselves.

Jane Austen, 1775–1817

Litany of Humility
O Jesus, meek and humble of heart,

Hear me.
From the desire of being esteemed,
Deliver me, O Jesus.
From the desire of being loved,
Deliver me, O Jesus.
From the desire of being extolled,
Deliver me, O Jesus.
From the desire of being honored,
Deliver me, O Jesus.
From the desire of being praised,
Deliver me, O Jesus.
From the desire of being preferred to others,
Deliver me, O Jesus.
From the desire of being consulted,
Deliver me, O Jesus.
From the desire of being approved,
Deliver me, O Jesus.

From the fear of being humiliated,
Deliver me, O Jesus.
From the fear of being despised,
Deliver me, O Jesus.
From the fear of suffering rebukes,
Deliver me, O Jesus.
From the fear of being calumniated,
Deliver me, O Jesus.
From the fear of being forgotten,
Deliver me, O Jesus.
From the fear of being ridiculed,
Deliver me, O Jesus.
From the fear of being wronged,
Deliver me, O Jesus.
From the fear of being suspected,
Deliver me, O Jesus.

That others may be loved more than I,
Jesus, grant me the grace to desire it.
That others may be esteemed more than I,
Jesus, grant me the grace to desire it.
That, in the opinion of the world,
  others may increase and I may decrease,
Jesus, grant me the grace to desire it.
That others may be chosen and I set aside,
Jesus, grant me the grace to desire it.
That others may be praised and I go
  unnoticed,
Jesus, grant me the grace to desire it.
That others may be preferred to me in
  everything,
Jesus, grant me the grace to desire it.
That others may become holier than I,

provided that I may become as holy as I
  should,
Jesus, grant me the grace to desire it.
Source unknown, Litany of Humility

I asked God for strength, that I might achieve,
I was made weak, that I might learn humbly
  to obey.
I asked for health, that I might do greater
  things,
I was given infirmity, that I might do better
  things.
I asked for riches, that I might be happy,
I was given poverty, that I might be wise.
I asked for power, that I might have the praise
  of men,
I was given weakness, that I might feel the
  need of God.
I asked for all things, that I might enjoy life,
I was given life, that I might enjoy all things.
I got nothing that I asked for –
but everything that I had hoped for,
almost despite myself, my unspoken prayers
  were answered.
I am among all men most richly blessed.
*A Soldier's Prayer, written by an anonymous
  confederate soldier, in the US civil war*

Give us true humility, a meek and a quiet
spirit, a loving and a friendly, a holy and a
useful conversation, bearing the burdens of our
neighbors, denying ourselves, and studying to
benefit others, and to please thee in all things.
John Cosin, 1594–1672

O Thou who in almighty power wast weak,
and in perfect excellency wast lowly, grant
unto us the same mind. All that we have which
is our own is naught; if we have any good in
us it is wholly thy gift. O Savior, since thou,
the Lord of heaven and earth, didst humble
thyself, grant unto us true humility, and make
us like thyself; and then, of thine infinite goodness, raise us to thine everlasting glory; who
livest and reignest with the Father and the Holy
Ghost for ever and ever.
Thomas Cranmer, 1489–1556

O Lord Jesus Christ, who didst humble thyself
to become man, and to be born into the world
for our salvation: teach us the grace of humil-

ity, root out of our hearts all pride and haughtiness, and so fashion us after thy holy likeness in this world, that in the world to come we may be made like unto thee in thy eternal kingdom.

W.W. How, 1823–97

Lord, we Thy presence seek;
May ours this blessing be;
Give us a pure and lowly heart,
A temple meet for Thee.

John Keble, 1792–1866

Take from us, O God, all pride and vanity, all boasting and self-assertiveness, and give us the true courage that shows itself by gentleness; the true wisdom that shows itself by simplicity; and the true power that shows itself by modesty; through Jesus Christ our Lord.

Charles Kingsley, 1819–75

O God, who resists the proud, and gives grace to the humble: grant us the virtue of true humility, which your only-begotten Son himself gave us the perfect example; that we may never offend you by our pride, and be rejected by our self-assertion; through Jesus Christ our Lord.

Leonine Sacramentary

Eternal God, let this mind be in us which was also in Christ Jesus; that as he from his loftiness stooped to the death of the cross, so we in our lowliness may humble ourselves, believing, obeying, living and dying, for his name's sake.

Christina Rossetti, 1830–94

Give me the lowest place: not that I dare
   Ask for that lowest place, but Thou hast
      died
That I might live and share
   Thy glory by Thy side.
Give me the lowest place: or if for me
   That lowest place too high, make one more
      low
Where I may sit and see
   My God and love Thee so.

Christina Rossetti, 1830–94

Lord Jesus Christ, pattern of humility, who

emptied yourself of your glory, and took on yourself the form of a servant, root out of us all pride of boasting in our hearts, that acknowledging that we are guilty sinners, we may willing suffer contempt for your sake, and only glory in you. Not unto us, O Lord, but to your name be the praise, for your loving mercy and for your truth's sake.

Treasury of Devotion, 1869

Lord, give us a heart to turn all knowledge to thy glory and not to our own. Keep us from being deluded with the lights of vain philosophies. Keep us from the pride of human reason. Let us not think our own thoughts; but in all things acting under the guidance of the Holy Spirit, may we find thee everywhere, and live in all simplicity, humility and singleness of heart unto the Lord.

H.K. White, 1785–1806

KNOWLEDGE OF GOD

Merciful Lord, the Comforter and Teacher of Thy faithful people, increase in Thy Church the desires of which Thou hast given, and confirm the hearts of those who hope in Thee by enabling them to understand the depth of Thy promises, that all Thine adopted sons may even now behold, with the eyes of faith, and patiently wait for, the light of which as yet Thou dost not openly manifest; through Jesus Christ our Lord. Amen.

Ambrose, c.339–397

Lord Jesus, let me know myself and let me
   know you,
And desire nothing save only you.
Let me hate myself and love you.
Let me do everything for the sake of you.
Let me humble myself and exalt you.
Let me think of nothing except you.
Let me die to myself and live in you.
Let me accept whatever happens as from you.
Let me banish self and follow you,
And ever desire to follow you.
Let me fly from myself and take refuge in you,
That I may deserve to be defended by you.
Let me fear for myself, let me fear you,

And let me be among those who are chosen
   by you.
Let me distrust myself and put my trust in
   you.
Let me be willing to obey for the sake of you.
Let me cling to nothing save only to you,
And let me be poor because of you.
Look upon me, that I may love you.
Call me that I may see you,
And for ever enjoy you.

Augustine of Hippo, 354–430

O Lord God, give us your Christ, let us know
your Christ, let us see your Christ, not as the
Jews saw him, and then crucified him, but as
the angels see him and rejoice.

Augustine of Hippo, 354–430

O God, you are the Truth and the Light of my
heart. Let me listen to you and not to the darkness within me.

Augustine of Hippo, 354–430

O Lord,
I understand now that to know you only as a
   philosopher;
to have the most sublime and conscious
   speculations
concerning your essence, your attributes ,
   your providence;
to be able to demonstrate your Being from all,
or any of the works of nature;
and to discourse with the greatest elegancy
and propriety of words of your existence or
   operations,
will avail us nothing unless at the same time
   we know you experimentally, unless the
   heart perceives and knows you to be her
   supreme good,
her only happiness!

Susanna Wesley, 1669–1742

LIGHT

O God, who by your almighty word enlightens
everyone who comes into the world, enlighten,
we pray, the hearts of your servants, by the
glory of your grace, that we may always think
such things as are worthy and pleasing to your

Majesty and love you with a perfect heart,
through Jesus Christ our Lord.

Alcuin, 735–804

Pour into our hearts, Almighty God, the pure
serene light of your truth, that we may avoid
the darkness of sin, who have come to know
and fear you, the eternal Light; through Jesus
Christ our Lord.

Ambrosian Manual

O God our Father, who dost exhort us to pray,
And who dost grant what we ask, if only,
When we ask, we live a better life;
Hear me, who am trembling in this darkness,
And stretch forth Thy hand unto me;
Hold forth Thy light before me;
Recall me from my wanderings;
And, Thou being my Guide,
May I be restored to myself and Thee,
Through Jesus Christ. Amen.

Augustine of Hippo, 354–430

Lord, you are the light of my heart and the
bread in the mouth of my soul.

Augustine of Hippo, 354–430

Grant, we beseech Thee, Almighty God, that
the brightness of Thy glory may shine forth
upon us, and that the light of Thy light by the
illumination of the Holy Spirit may [make
firm] the hearts of all that have been born
anew by Thy grace; through Jesus Christ, Thy
Son, our Lord. Amen.

*The Common Service Book of
the Lutheran Church, 1917*

We beseech you, O Lord, in your loving-kindness, to pour your holy light into our souls;
that we may always be devoted to you, by
whose wisdom we were created, and by whose
providence we are governed; through Jesus
Christ our Lord.

Gelasian Sacramentary, 5th century

O Light that followest all my way,
I yield my flickering torch to thee;
My heart restores its borrowed ray,
That in thy sunshine's blaze its day
May brighter, fairer be.

George Matheson, 1842–1906

O Lord Jesus Christ, who art the very bright Sun of the world, ever rising, never going down: shine, we beseech thee, upon our spirit, that the night of sin and error being driven away by thy inward light, we may walk without stumbling, as in the day. Grant this, O Lord, who livest and reignest with the Father and the Holy Ghost for evermore.

Primer, 1559, after Erasmus, 1467–1536

O heavenly Father, the author and fountain of all truth, the bottomless sea of all understanding, send, we beseech thee, thy Holy Spirit into our hearts, and lighten our understandings with the beams of thy heavenly grace. We ask this, O merciful Father, for thy dear Son, our Savior, Jesus Christ's sake.

Nicholas Ridley, c.1500–55

O sweet and delectable light that is my Maker, uncreated; enlighten the face and sharpness of my inward eye with clearness, uncreated, that my mind, inwardly cleansed from uncleanness and made marvelous with gifts, may swiftly flee into the high gladness of love; and kindled with Thy savor, I may sit and rest, joying in Thee, Jesu. And going as it were ravished in heavenly sweetness, and made stable in the beholding of things unseen, never, save by godly things, shall I be gladdened.

Richard Rolle, 1290–1349

Open wide the window of our spirits, O Lord,
    and fill us full of light;
open wide the door of our hearts, that we
    may receive and entertain you with all our
    powers of adoration and praise.

Christina Rossetti, 1830–94

Grant us your light, O Lord: that the darkness of our hearts being done away, we may come to the true light, even Christ our Savior.

Office of Compline, Sarum Breviary

OBEDIENCE

I offer myself to Thee –
to build with me and do with me as Thou wilt.
Relieve me of the bondage of self,
That I may better do Thy will.

Take away my difficulties,
that victory over them may bear witness
to those I would help
of Thy Power,
Thy Love
and
Thy Way of Life.
May I do Thy will always!

Author unknown, used by Alcoholics Anonymous

My Creator
I am now willing that you should have all of
    me, good and bad.
I pray that you now remove from me
every single defect of character
which stands in the way of my usefulness to
    You and my fellows.
Grant me strength as I go from here to do
    your bidding.
Amen

Author unknown, used by Alcoholics Anonymous

Loving God, breath into our hearts and minds at this time your loving and guiding word. Inspire us by your Spirit, that we may hear, and later do, what you would have us hear and do. Lift us up by your still small voice within and grant us the blessing we need and we seek. We ask it in Jesus' name. Amen

Richard Baxter, 1615–91

Grant, Almighty God, that as thou hast made known thy Law, and hast also added thy gospel, in which thou callest us to thy service, and also invitest us with all kindness to partake of thy grace – O grant, that we may not be deaf, either to thy command or to the promises of thy mercy, but render ourselves in both instances submissive to thee, and so learn to devote all our faculties to thee, that we may in truth avow that the rule of a holy and religious life has been delivered to us in thy law, and that we may also firmly adhere to thy promises, lest through any of the allurements of the world, or through the flatteries and crafts of Satan, thou shouldst suffer our minds to be drawn away from that love which thou hast once for all manifested to us in thine only begotten Son, and in which thou daily confirmest us by the teaching of the Gospel, until we at length shall come to the full enjoyment of this love in that celestial inheritance, which has been purchased for us by the blood of thine only Son. Amen.

John Calvin, 1509–64

Clothe me, clothe me with yourself, eternal truth, so that I may live this earthly life with true obedience, and with the light of your most holy faith.

Catherine of Siena, 1347–80

Because you are so good, my Father,
I want nothing more than to know your holy
    will
So that I may do it;
nothing more than to love you.
Amen.

Anthony Mary Claret, 1807–70

Kindle in us the fire of your love; sow in us your fear; strengthen our weakness by your power; bind us closely to you and to each other in our firm and indissoluble bond of unity.

Clement of Alexandria, c.150–c.215

Free us from our selfish interests, and guide us, good Lord, to see thy way and to do thy will.

Charles Kingsley, 1819–75

Deliver me, Lord God, from a slothful mind, from all lukewarmness, and all dejection of spirit. I know these cannot but deaden my love for you; mercifully free my heart from them, and give me a lively, zealous, active and cheerful spirit; that I may vigorously perform whatever you command, thankfully suffer whatever you choose for me, and always be ardent to obey in all things your holy love.

John Wesley, 1703–91

Eternal God, my sovereign Lord, I acknowledge all I am, all I have, is yours. Give me such a sense of your infinite goodness that I may return to you all possible love and obedience.

John Wesley, 1703–1791

PERSEVERANCE

O God our Father, let us find grace in thy sight so as to have grace to serve thee acceptably with reverence and godly fear, and further grace not to receive thy grace in vain, not to neglect it and fall from it, and to persevere in it unto the end of our lives; through Jesus Christ our Lord.

Lancelot Andrewes, 1555–1626

Grant, Lord God, that we may cleave to thee
    without parting,
worship thee without wearying,
serve thee without failing,
faithfully seek thee,
happily find thee,
and forever possess thee,
the one only God,
blessed for all eternity.

Anselm, 1033–1109

O Lord God, when Thou givest to Thy servants to endeavor any great matter, grant us also to know that it is not the beginning, but the continuing of the same to the end, until it be thoroughly finished, which yieldeth the true glory; through Him who for the finishing of Thy work laid down his life, our Redeemer, Jesus Christ.

Source unknown, based on a saying of Sir Francis Drake, c.1540–96

Almighty God, our heavenly Father, who from your tender love towards us sinners has given us your Son, that believing in him we may have everlasting life; Grant us your Holy Spirit that we may continue steadfast in this faith to the end, and may come to everlasting life; through Jesus Christ, your Son, our Lord.

John Calvin, 1509–64

Grant, Almighty God, that as thou not only invitest us continually by the voice of thy gospel to seek thee, but also offerest to us thy Son as our mediator, through whom an access to thee is open, that we may find thee a propitious Father; O grant, that relying on thy kind invitation, we may through life exercise ourselves in prayer, and as so many evils disturb us on all sides and so many wants distress and oppress us, may we be led more earnestly to call on thee, and in the meanwhile be never wearied in this exercise of prayer; until having been heard by thee throughout life, we may at length be gathered to thine eternal kingdom where we shall enjoy that salvation which thou hast promised to us, and of which also thou daily testifiest to us by thy gospel, and be forever united to thine only-begotten Son of whom we are now members; that we may be partakers of all the blessings which he has obtained for us by his death. Amen.

John Calvin, 1509–64

O God in heaven, have mercy on us! Lord, Jesus Christ, intercede for your people, deliver us at the opportune time, preserve in us the true genuine Christian faith, collect your scattered sheep with your voice, your divine Word as Holy Writ calls it. Help us to recognize your voice, help us not to be allured by the madness of the world, so that we may never fall away from you, O Lord Jesus Christ.

Albrecht Dürer, 1471–1528

Father, keep us from vain strife of words. Grant to us constant profession of the Truth! Preserve us in a true and undefiled Faith so that we may hold fast to that which we professed when we were baptized in the Name of the Father, Son and Holy Spirit – that we may have Thee for our Father, that we may abide in Thy Son and in the fellowship of the Holy Spirit. Through Jesus Christ, Our Lord. Amen.

Hilary of Poitiers, c.315–c.367

O Lord! do teach me how real the labor of prayer is. I know how here on earth, when I have failed in an undertaking, I can often succeed by renewed and more continuing effort, by giving more time and thought: show me how, by giving myself more entirely to prayer, to live in prayer, I shall obtain what I ask.

Andrew Murray, 1828–1917

Lord Jesus, who would think that I am Thine?
    Ah, who would think
Who sees me ready to turn back or sink,
    That Thou art mine?

I cannot hold Thee fast tho' Thou art mine:
    Hold Thou me fast,
So earth shall know at last and heaven at last
    That I am Thine.

Christina Rossetti, 1830–94

Give us grace and strength to forbear and persevere. Give us courage and gaiety and a quiet mind, spare us to our friends, soften us to our enemies, bless us if it may be in all our innocent endeavors, if it may give us the strength to encounter that which is to come that we may be brave in peril, constant in tribulation temperate in wrath and in all change of fortune and down to the gates of death loyal and loving to one another.

R.L. Stevenson, 1850–94

You, O Lord, have called us to watch and pray. Therefore, whatever may be the sin against which we pray, make us careful to watch against it, and so have reason to expect that our prayers will be answered.

In order to perform this duty aright, grant us grace to preserve a sober, equal temper, and sincerity to pray for your assistance. Amen.

Susannah Wesley, 1669–1742

PRAYER, HELP IN

May I seek you, Lord, by praying to you, and let me pray to you by believing in you.

Augustine of Hippo, 354–430

Lord teach me what I need,
And teach me how to pray;
And do not let me seek thy grace,
Not meaning what I say.

John Burton, 1803–77

Strong covenant God, save us from being self-centered in our prayers, and teach us to remember to pray for others. May we be so bound up in love with those for whom we pray that we may feel their needs as acutely as our own, and intercede for them with sensitiveness, with understanding and with imagination. This we ask in Christ's name. Amen.

John Calvin, 1509–64

What various hindrances we meet
In coming to the mercy seat!
Yet who, that knows the power of prayer,
But wishes to be often there!

Prayer makes the darkened cloud withdraw,

Prayer climbs the ladder Jacob saw,
Gives exercise to faith and love,
Brings every blessing from above.

Restraining prayer, we cease to fight;
Prayer makes the Christian's Armour bright;
And Satan trembles when he sees
The weakest saint upon his knees.

While Moses stood with arms spread wide,
Success was found on Israel's side;
But when, through weariness, they failed,
That moment Amalek prevailed.

Have you no words, Ah! think again!
Words flow apace when you complain
And fill your fellow-creature's ear
With the sad tale of all your care.

Were half the breath, thus vainly spent
To heaven in supplication sent,
Your cheerful song would oftener be,
"Hear what the Lord has done for me!"
William Cowper, 1731–1800

I pray to you, Christ, Savior of the world. Look down and have mercy on me. Save me from the multitude of my transgressions, for I have disdained all the good things you have done for me since I was a child. Foolish and stupid as I am now, you fashioned me as a vessel filled with your knowledge and wisdom. Multiply in me your graces. Satisfy my hunger, quench my thirst, enlighten my darkened mind, and focus my wandering thoughts.
Ephraem, c.306–378

Grant that I may not pray alone with the mouth; help me that I may pray from the depths of my heart.
Martin Luther, 1483–1546

Blessed Lord! who ever livest to pray, Thou canst teach me too to pray; me too, to live ever to pray. In this Thou lovest to make me share Thy glory in heaven, that I should pray without ceasing, and ever stand as a priest in the presence of my God.
Andrew Murray, 1828–1917

Lord! teach me to pray. Lord Jesus! I trust Thee

for it; teach me to pray in faith. Lord! teach me this lesson of today: Every one that asketh receiveth. Amen.
Andrew Murray, 1828–1917

Lord, I do not know what to ask of You. You know better than me what my needs are. You love more than I know how to love. Help me to see clearly my real needs which I do not see. I open my heart to You. Examine and reveal to me my faults and sins. I put all trust in You. I have no other desire than to fulfill Your will. Teach me how to pray. Pray in me. Amen.
Orthodox prayer

What a Friend we have in Jesus, all our sins
  and griefs to bear!
What a privilege to carry everything to God
  in prayer!
O what peace we often forfeit, O what
  needless pain we bear,
All because we do not carry everything to
  God in prayer.

Have we trials and temptations? Is there
  trouble anywhere?
We should never be discouraged; take it to the
  Lord in prayer.
Can we find a friend so faithful who will all
  our sorrows share?
Jesus knows our every weakness; take it to the
  Lord in prayer.

Are we weak and heavy laden, cumbered with
  a load of care?
Precious Savior, still our refuge, take it to the
  Lord in prayer.
Do your friends despise, forsake you? Take it
  to the Lord in prayer!
In His arms He'll take and shield you; you will
  find a solace there.

Blessed Savior, Thou hast promised Thou wilt
  all our burdens bear
May we ever, Lord, be bringing all to Thee in
  earnest prayer.
Soon in glory bright unclouded there will be
  no need for prayer
Rapture, praise and endless worship will be
  our sweet portion there.
Joseph Medlicott Scriven, 1819–86

PRESENCE OF GOD

Lord, how exalted you are and yet the humble
   of heart are your dwelling.

Augustine of Hippo, 354–430

Grant us, Lord, to know in weakness the
   strength of your incarnation:
in pain the triumph of your passion:
in poverty the riches of your Godhead:
in reproach the satisfaction of your sympathy:
in loneliness the comfort of your continual
   presence:
in difficulty the efficacy of your intercession:
in perplexity the guidance of your wisdom;
and by your glorious death and resurrection
   bring us at last to the joy of seeing you face
   to face.

Author unknown

Eternal God, the refuge of all your children,
in our weakness you are our strength,
in our darkness our light,
in our sorrow our comfort and peace.
May we always live in your presence,
and serve you in our daily lives;
through Jesus Christ our Lord.

Boniface, c.680–c.754

Grant, Almighty God, that as thou shinest
on us by thy word, we may not be blind
at midnight, nor willfully seek darkness, and
thus lull our minds asleep: but may we be
roused daily by thy words, and may we stir up
ourselves more and more to fear thy name and
thus present ourselves and all our pursuits, as
a sacrifice to thee, that thou mayest peaceably
rule, and perpetually dwell in us, until thou
gatherest us to thy celestial habitation, where
there is reserved for us eternal rest and glory
through Jesus Christ our Lord. Amen.

John Calvin, 1509–64

God be with us
On this Thy day,
Amen.
[God be with us
On this Thy night,
Amen.]
To us and with us,
On this Thy day,

Amen.
[To us and with us,
On this Thy night,
Amen.]
It is clear to be seen of us,
Since we came into the world,
That we have deserved Thy wrath,
Amen.
O Thine own wrath,
Thou God of all,
Amen.
Grant us forgiveness,
Amen.

Carmina Gadelica

God that madest earth and heaven,
   Darkness and light,
Who the day for toil hast given,
   For rest the night;
Guard us waking, guard us sleeping,
   And when we die:
May we in thy mighty keeping
   All peaceful lie.

Reginald Heber, 1783–1826

O Lord Christ, who came that we might have
life and have it more abundantly, so come that
all shall have full opportunity to live; so come
that we may open out opportunities to all who
are dear to you because they lack and suffer
hunger. Come and break down all that hinders
life, the iron walls of grim refusal that give
life no chance. Come and give us wisdom and
patience, courage and resolution to discover
how your goodwill may verify itself to all. Give
us life that we may give out life. Come and fill
us with your own strong desire; with your own
brave hope, that all may find their way to live in
you. Give unity; give brotherhood; give peace.

H. Scott Holland, 1847–1918

Draw near to your flock, O Shepherd of Israel,
that we may rejoice at the sound of your voice;
walk through the darkest shadows at your
bidding and climb the rugged steeps under
your protection. May we come at the last to the
sight of your unclouded beauty where, in the
glory of eternal light, you are worshipped for
evermore. Amen.

Bede Jarrett, 1881–1934

Write your blessed name, O Lord, upon my heart, there to remain so indelibly engraved, that no prosperity, no adversity shall ever move me from your love. Be to be a strong tower of defense, a comforter in tribulation, a deliverer in distress, a very present help in trouble and a guide to heaven through the many temptations and dangers of this life.

Thomas à Kempis, 1379–1471

If this day I should get lost amid the perplexities of life and the rush of many duties, do thou search me out, gracious Lord, and bring me back into the quiet of thy presence.

F.B. Meyer, 1847–1929

More of thy presence, Lord, impart,
More of thine image let me bear;
Erect thy throne within my heart,
And reign without a rival there.

John Newton, 1725–1807

Lord, purge our eyes to see
Within the seed a tree,
Within the glowing egg a bird,
Within the shroud a butterfly.
Till, taught by such we see
Beyond all creatures, Thee.
And hearken to thy tender word
And hear its "Fear not; it is I."

Christina Rossetti, 1830–94

Christ, Whose glory fills the skies,
Christ, the true, the only Light,
Sun of Righteousness, arise,
Triumph o'er the shades of night;
Dayspring from on high be near;
Day-star, in my heart appear.

Dark and cheerless is the morn
Unaccompanied by Thee;
Joyless is the day's return
Till Thy mercy's beams I see;
Till they inward light impart,
Glad my eyes, and warm my heart.

Visit then this soul of mine,
Pierce the gloom of sin and grief;
Fill me, Radiancy divine,
Scatter all my unbelief;
More and more Thyself display,

Shining to the perfect day.

Charles Wesley, 1707–88

PRIDE

Show me, as my soul can bear,
    The depth of inbred sin;
    All the unbelief declare,
    The pride that lurks within;
Take me, I am yours, my Lord,
Bring into captivity
Every high aspiring thought
That would not bend the knee.

Charles Wesley, 1707–1788

PURITY

Dearest Jesus! I know well that every perfect gift, and above all others that of chastity, depends upon the most powerful assistance of Thy Providence, and that without Thee a creature can do nothing. Therefore, I pray Thee to defend, with Thy grace, chastity and purity in my soul as well as in my body. And if I have ever received through my senses any impression that could stain my chastity and purity, do Thou, Who art the Supreme Lord of all my powers, take it from me, that I may with an immaculate heart advance in Thy love and service, offering myself chaste all the days of my life on the most pure altar of Thy Divinity. Amen.

Thomas Aquinas, 1225–74

Lord, take from me this hard heart, and give me a new, clean heart of flesh and blood. You who made my heart pure, take possession of mine and make it Your home. Hold it and fill it. You, the seal of holiness, beauty of all beauties, engrave on my heart Your image and the imprint of Your mercy. Be, O God, my eternal love and my inheritance. Amen.

Baldwin, d.1190

Collect for Purity
Almighty God, unto whom all hearts be open, and all desires known, and from whom no secrets are hid: cleanse the thoughts of our hearts, by the inspiration of thy Holy Spirit:

that we may perfectly love thee, and worthily magnify thy holy name: through Christ our Lord.

Book of Common Prayer, 1549

Almighty and most merciful Father, look down on us your unworthy servants through the mediation and merits of Jesus Christ, in whom only are you well pleased. Purify our hearts by your Holy Spirit, and as you add days to our lives, so good Lord, add repentance to our days; that when we have passed this mortal life we may be partakers of your everlasting kingdom; through the merits of Jesus Christ our Lord.

King Charles I, 1600–49

O ardent fire of my God, which contains, produces, and imprints those living ardors which attract the humid waters of my soul, and dry up the torrents of earthly delights, and afterwards soften my hard self-opinionatedness, which time has hardened so exceedingly!

O consuming fire, which even amid ardent flames imparts sweetness and peace to the soul! In thee, and in none other, do we receive this grace of being reformed to the image and likeness in which we were created.

O burning furnace, in which we enjoy the true vision of peace, which tries and purifies the gold of the elect, and leads the soul to seek eagerly for its highest good, even thyself, in thy eternal truth.

Gertrude of Thüringen, 1526–c.1301

Dear heavenly Father,
Give me clean hands, clean words, and clean
    thoughts;
Help me to stand for the hard right
Against the easy wrong;
Save me from habits that harm;
Teach me to work as hard,
And play as fair in thy sight alone,
As if the whole world saw;
Forgive me when I am unkind,
And help me to forgive those who are unkind
    to me;
And keep me ready to help others.

William de Witt Hyde, 1858–1917

Blest are the pure in heart,

For they shall see our God:
The secret of the Lord is theirs;
Their soul is Christ's abode.

John Keble, 1792–1866

We beseech you, Christ Jesus, Son of God, crucified for us and risen again, have compassion on us. Intercede for us with the eternal Father. Purify us with your Holy Spirit.

Philip Melanchthon, 1497–1560

O Son of God, Lord Jesus Christ, you shield and keep us, and love purity: through your Holy Spirit, pure and spotless, kindle purity in our hearts, and incline our rulers to true devotion. Quench the demonic forces and fires of impurity that rage in our hearts.

Philip Melanchthon, 1497–1560

Lord, help me to keep my thoughts pure, my words true, and my deeds kind; that alone or with others, I shall be at one with thee.

Sarum Primer, 1558

Lord Jesus, think on me
And purge away my sin;
From earthborn passions set me free
And make me pure within.

*Synesius of Cyrene, 375–430,
translated by Allen W. Chatfield*

O God, the Father of our Savior Jesus Christ, whose name is great, whose nature is blissful, whose goodness is inexhaustible, God and Ruler of all things, who are blessed for ever; before whom stand thousands and thousands, and ten thousand times ten thousand, the hosts of holy angels and archangels; sanctify, O Lord, our souls and bodies and spirits, search our consciences, and cast out from us every evil thought, every base desire, all envy and pride, all wrath and anger, and all that is contrary to your holy will. And grant us, O Lord, Lover of men and women, with a pure heart and contrite soul to call on thee, our holy God and Father who art in heaven.

Syrian Rite

Write deeply upon our minds, O Lord God, the lesson of thy holy word, that only the pure in heart can see thee. Leave us not in the bondage of any sinful inclination. May we neither deceive ourselves with the thought that we have no sin, nor acquiesce idly in aught of which our conscience accuses us. Strengthen us by thy Holy Spirit to fight the good fight of faith, and grant that no day may pass without its victory; through Jesus Christ our Lord.

C.J. Vaughan, 1816–97

Make and keep me pure within.

Charles Wesley, 1707–88

O eternal God, who has taught us by your holy Word that our bodies are the temples of your Spirit, keep us we most humbly beseech you temperate and holy in thought, word, and deed, that at the last we, with all the pure in heart, may see you, and be make like you in your heavenly kingdom, through Christ our Lord.

B.F. Westcott, 1825–1901

RECONCILIATION

O God the Father of all
you ask every one of us to spread
love where the poor are humiliated
joy where the church is brought low
and reconciliation where people are divided
father against son, mother against daughter,
husband against wife,
believers against those who cannot believe,
Christians against their unloved fellow
    Christians.
You open this way for us,
so that the wounded body of Jesus Christ,
    your church,
may be leaven of communion for the poor of
    the earth
and the whole human family.

Brother Roger of Taizé, b.1915 and
Mother Teresa of Calcutta, 1910–98

REGENERATION

Almighty God, Who has given us Thy Only-begotten Son to take our nature upon Him: Grant that we being regenerate, and made Thy children by adoption and grace, may daily be

renewed by Thy Holy Spirit; through the same Jesus Christ, Thy Son, our Lord. Amen.

The Common Service Book of
the Lutheran Church, 1917

RENEWAL

See also: PRAYERS FOR THE CHRISTIAN CHURCH: Church fellowship, Revival

O Lord God, Heavenly Father, Who has given Thine only Son to die for our sins, and to rise again for our justification: Quicken us, we beseech Thee, by Thy Holy Spirit, unto newness of life, that, through the power of His Resurrection, we may dwell with Christ forever; Who liveth and reigneth etc. Amen.

The Common Service Book of
the Lutheran Church, 1917

REST

Lord Jesus, think on me,
With many a care oppressed;
Let me Thy loving servant be
And taste Thy promised rest.

Synesius of Cyrene, 375–430,
translated by Allen W. Chatfield

RESTORATION

The house of my soul is too small for you to come to it. May it be enlarged by you. It is in ruins: restore it. In your eyes it has offensive features, I admit it, I know it; but who will clean it up? Or to whom shall I cry other than you? "Cleanse me from my secret faults, Lord, and spare your servant from sins to which I am tempted by others" (Ps. 31.5).

Augustine of Hippo, 354–430

O Almighty, Merciful, and Gracious God and Father, with our whole heart we beseech Thee for all who have forsaken the Christian Faith; all who have wandered from any portion thereof, or are in doubt or temptation through the corruptors of Thy Word; that Thou wouldest visit them as a Father, reveal unto them their error, and bring them back from their wanderings; that they, in singleness of heart, taking pleasure alone in the pure truth of Thy Word, may be made wise thereby unto everlasting life; through Jesus Christ, Thy Son, our Lord. Amen.

The Common Service Book of
the Lutheran Church, 1917

REVERENCE

Lord, make me to have a perpetual fear and love of thy holy name; for thou never failest to help and govern them thou dost bring up in thy steadfast love. Grant this even for Jesus Christ his sake.
Amen

William Laud, 1573–1645

RIGHTEOUSNESS

Be Thou to us, O Lord, a crown of glory in the day when Thou shalt come to judge the world by fire; that Thou mayest graciously clothe us here with the robe of righteousness, and hereafter with the perfection of a glorious liberty; through Thy mercy, who livest and reignest, with the Father and the Holy Spirit, one God, world without end. Amen.

Mozarabic rite, translated by
William Bright, 1824–1901

Jesus, our Master, meet us while we walk in the way, and long to reach the heavenly country; so that, following your light we may keep the way of righteousness, and never wander away into the darkness of this world's night, while you, who are the Way, the Truth, and the Life, are shining within us; for your own name's sake. Amen.

Mozarabic prayer

SALVATION AND
RESTORATION, SEEKING

I pray thee, merciful Jesus, that as thou hast graciously granted me to drink down sweetly from the Word which tells of thee, so wilt thou

kindly grant that I may come at length to thee, the fount of all wisdom, and stand before thy face for ever.

Bede, 675–735, last words of his Ecclesiastical
History of the English People

Just as I am, without one plea
But that thy blood was shed for me,
And that thou bidd'st me come to thee,
    O Lamb of God, I come.

Just as I am, though tossed about
With many a conflict, many a doubt,
Fightings within, and fears without,
    O Lamb of God, I come.

Just as I am, poor, wretched, blind;
Sight, riches, healing of the mind,
Yea all I need, in thee to find,
    O Lamb of God, I come.

Just as I am, thou wilt receive,
Wilt welcome, pardon, cleanse, relieve:
Because thy promise I believe,
    O Lamb of God, I come.

Just as I am (thy love unknown
Has broken every barrier down),
Now to be thine, yea thine alone,
    O Lamb of God, I come.

Just as I am, of that free love
The breadth, length, depth and height to prove,
Here for a season then above,
    O Lamb of God, I come.

Charlotte Elliott, 1789–1871

O holy Jesus, meek Lamb of God; Bread that came down from heaven; light and life of all holy souls: help me to a true and living faith in you. Open yourself within me with all your holy nature and spirit, that I may be born again by you, and in you be a new creation, brought alive and revived, led and ruled by your Holy Spirit.

William Law, 1686–1761

Grant us, Lord, we beseech thee, not to mind earthly things, but to seek things heavenly; so that though we are set among scenes that

pass away, our heart and affection may steadfastly cleave to the things that endure for ever; through Jesus Christ our Lord.
Leonine Sacramentary

Teach us, dear Lord, frequently and attentively
  to consider this truth:
    that if I gain the whole world and
      lose you, in the end I have lost
      everything;
    whereas if I lose the world and gain you,
      in the end I have lost nothing.
J.H. Newman, 1801–90

SEEKING GOD

Give me yourself, O my God, give yourself to me. Behold I love you, and if my love is too weak a thing, grant me to love you more strongly. I cannot measure my love to know how much it falls short of being sufficient, but let my soul hasten to your embrace and never be turned away until it is hidden in the secret shelter of your presence. This only do I know, that it is not good for me when you are not with me, when you are only outside me. I want you in my very self. All the plenty in the world which is not my God is utter want. Amen.
Augustine of Hippo, 354–430

O Lord my God, I believe in you, Father, Son and Holy Spirit. Insofar as I can, insofar as you have given me the power, I have sought you. I became weary and I labored.

O Lord my God, my sole hope, help me to believe and never to cease seeking you. Grant that I may always and ardently seek out your countenance. Give me the strength to seek you, for you help me to find you and you have more and more given me the hope of finding you.

Here I am before you with my firmness and my infirmity. Preserve the first and heal the second.

Here I am before you with my strength and my ignorance. Where you have opened the door to me, welcome me at the entrance; where you have closed the door to me, open to my cry; enable me to remember you, to understand you, and to love you. Amen.
Augustine of Hippo, 354–430

SELF-DENIAL

Lord, take me from myself and give me to yourself.
Catherine of Siena, 1347–80

Induce me, O Jesus, to lay aside my former self and to be renewed according to Thy will and desire. I will not spare myself, however painful this should be for me: despoiled of things temporal, of my own will, I desire to die, in order to live for Thee forever.
Francis of Assisi, 1181–1226

SERVING GOD

Lord Jesus, our Savior, let us now come to you: Our hearts are cold; Lord, warm them with your selfless love. Our hearts are sinful; cleanse them with your precious blood. Our hearts are weak; strengthen them with your joyous Spirit. Our hearts are empty; fill them with your divine presence. Lord Jesus, our hearts are yours; possess them always and only for yourself.
Augustine of Hippo, 354–430

O God, who has warned us that you will require much from those to whom much is given; grant that we, whose lot is cast in so goodly a heritage, may strive together the more abundantly, by prayer, by almsgiving, by fasting, and by all appointed means, to extend to those who do not know you what we so richly enjoy; and as we have entered into the labors of others so to labor that, others may enter into ours, to the fulfillment of your holy will and the salvation of all mankind; through Jesus Christ our Lord.
Augustine of Hippo, 354–430

Almighty God, in whom we live and move and have our being, you have made us for yourself and our hearts are restless until in you they find their rest. Grant us purity of heart and strength of purpose, that no selfish passion may hinder us from knowing your will, no weakness from doing it; but that in your light we may see light clearly, and in your service we may find our perfect freedom; through Jesus Christ our Lord.
Augustine of Hippo, 354–430

Incline us, O God, to think humbly on ourselves, to be saved only in the examination of our own conduct, to consider our fellow creatures with kindness, and to judge of all they say and do with the charity which we would desire from them ourselves.

Jane Austen, 1775–1817

Lord God, the God of all goodness and grace, you are worthy of a greater love than we can give or understand: fill our hearts with such love towards you which overcomes laziness and fear, that nothing may seem too hard for us to do or to suffer as we obey you; and grant that in loving you we may become daily more like you, and may finally obtain the crown of life which you have promised to those who love you, through Jesus Christ our Lord.

Author unknown

My Lord, I have nothing to do in this world
    but to seek and serve you.
I have nothing to do with my heart and its
    affections but to breathe after you.
I have nothing to do with my tongue and pen
    but to speak to you and for you, and to
    make known your glory and your will.

Richard Baxter, 1615–91

O Lord, we most humbly beseech you to give us grace not only to be hearers of the Word, but also doers of the Word; not only to love, but also to live your gospel; not only to profess, but also to practice your blessed commandments, for the honor of your holy name.

Thomas Becon, 1512–67

My God and my Father,
may I know you and make you known;
love you and make you loved;
serve you and make you served;
praise you and make all creatures praise you.

Anthony Mary Claret, 1807–70

Teach us, gracious Lord, to begin our deeds with reverence, to go on with obedience, and to finish them in love; and then to wait patiently in hope, and with cheerful confidence to look up to you, whose promises are faithful and rewards infinite; through Jesus Christ.

George Hickes, 1642–1715

May it please you, O Lord, to enlighten my heart with the fire of your love. I offer my hands to do your work, my lips to sing your praise and my life to proclaim your glory. Look upon my neighbors in their needs and guide me and bless me as I serve you in them; for Jesus' sake. Amen.

Hildegard of Bingen, 1098–1179

My God, my Love: you are all mine, and I am all yours. Increase love in me, that with my inner heart I may taste how sweet it is to love. Let me love your more than myself, and myself only for you, and in you all that love you truly.

Thomas à Kempis, 1379–1471

Grant, O Lord, that I may be so ravished in the wonder of your love that I may forget myself and all things; may feel neither prosperity nor adversity; may not fear to suffer all the pain in the world rather than be parted from you.

O let me feel you more inwardly, and truly present with me than I am with myself, and make me most circumspect in your presence, my holy Lord.

Robert Leighton, 1611–84

Remember, O Lord, what thou hast wrought in us, and not what we deserve; and as thou hast called us to thy service, make us worthy of our calling; through Jesus Christ our Lord.

Leonine Sacramentary

O Jesus, fill me with your love now, and I pray, accept me, and use me a little for your glory. O do, do, I pray, accept me and my service, and take all the glory.

David Livingstone, 1813–73

Almighty God, the Protector of all who trust in you, without whose grace nothing is strong, nothing is holy, increase and multiply on us your mercy, that through your holy inspiration we may think the things that are right and by your power may carry them out, through Jesus Christ our Lord.

Martin Luther, 1483–1546

God has created me to do for him some definite service; he has committed some work to me which he has not committed to another. I have my mission … I am a link in a chain, a connection between people. God has not created me for nothing. I shall do good, I shall do his work; I shall be a preacher of truth in my own place, while not intending it, if I do but keep his commandments and serve him in my calling.

J.H. Newman, 1801–90

Lord, Thou sendest down rain upon the uncounted millions of the forest, and givest the trees to drink exceedingly. We are here upon this isle a few handfuls of men, and how many myriads upon myriads of stalwart trees! Teach us the lesson of the trees. The sea around us, which this rain recruits, teems with the race of fish; teach us, Lord, the meaning of the fishes. Let us see ourselves for what we are, one out of the countless number of the clans of thy handiwork. When we would despair, let us remember that these also please and serve Thee.

R.L. Stevenson, 1850–94

Oh my Lord! How true it is that whoever works for you is paid in troubles! And what a precious price to those who love you if we understand its value.

Teresa of Avila, 1515–82

O Jesus, my Love, my vocation, at last I have found it … my vocation is Love! Yes, I have found my place in the Church and it is You, o my God. who have given me this place; in the heart of the Church, my Mother, I SHALL BE LOVE.

Thérèse of Lisieux, 1873–97

O merciful God, fill our hearts, we pray, with the graces of your Holy Spirit; with love, joy, peace, patience, gentleness, goodness, faithfulness, humility and self-control.

O Lord, in confidence of your great mercy and goodness to all who truly repent and resolve to do better, I most humbly implore the grace and assistance of the Holy Spirit to enable me to become every day better.

Grant me the wisdom and understanding to know my duty, and the heart and will to do it.

Endue me, O Lord, with the true fear and love of you, and with a prudent zeal for your glory.

Increase in me the graces of charity and meekness, of truth and justice, of humility and patience, and a firmness of spirit to bear every condition with constancy of mind.

King William III, 1650–1702

SIMPLICITY

Jesus, help me to simplify my life by learning what you want me to be – and becoming that person.

Thérèse of Lisieux, 1873–97

SPEAKING

Lord, keep my tongue from evil, and my lips that they speak no guile.

*William Laud, 1573–1645,
based on Psalm 34.12*

SPIRITUAL PILGRIMAGE

Eternal Light, shine into our hearts,
eternal Goodness, deliver us from evil,
eternal Power, be our support,
eternal Wisdom, scatter the darkness of our
   ignorance,
eternal Pity, have mercy upon us;
that with all our heart and mind and strength
   we may seek they face and be brought by
   your infinite mercy to your holy presence;
   through Jesus Christ our Lord.

Alcuin, 735–804

Give us, O Lord, a steadfast heart, which no unworthy affection may drag downwards; an unconquered heart, which no tribulation can wear out; give us an upright heart, which no unworthy purpose may tempt aside. Bestow on us also, O Lord, understanding to know you, diligence to seek you, wisdom to find you and a faithfulness that may finally embrace you; through Jesus Christ our Lord.

Thomas Aquinas, 1225–74

Let the eternal God be the portion of my soul;
let heaven be my inheritance and hope;
let Christ be my Head, and my promise of
    security;
let faith be my wisdom,
and love my very heart and will,
and patient persevering obedience be my life;
and then I can spare the wisdom of the world,
because I can spare the trifles that it seeks,
and all that they are like to get by it.

Richard Baxter, 1615–91

I beseech Thee, good Jesus, that as Thou hast
graciously granted to me here on earth sweetly
to partake of the words of Thy wisdom and
knowledge, so Thou wilt vouchsafe that I may
some time come to Thee, the fountain of all
wisdom, and always appear before Thy face;
who livest and reignest, world without end.

Bede, c.673–735

O God, the protector of all that trust in thee,
without whom nothing is strong, nothing
is holy; Increase and multiply upon us thy
mercy; that, thou being our ruler and guide, we
may so pass through things temporal, that we
finally lose not the things eternal: Grant this,
O heavenly Father, for Jesus Christ's sake our
Lord. Amen.

*Book of Common Prayer, Collect for the Fourth
Sunday after Trinity*

Who would true valor see,
Let him come hither;
One here will constant be,
Come wind, come weather
There's no discouragement
Shall make him once relent
His first avow'd intent
To be a pilgrim.

Whoso beset him round
With dismal stories,
Do but themselves confound;
His strength the more is.
No lion can him fright,
He'll with a giant fight,
But he will have a right
To be a pilgrim.

He knows he at the end

Shall life inherit.
Then fancies fly away,
He'll not fear what men say;
He'll labor night and day
To be a pilgrim.

John Bunyan, 1628–88, Pilgrim's Progress

Heavenly Father, you have taught us that our
life on earth is a pilgrimage from this world
to that which is to come. Guide us on our
journey; defend us from the perils of the way;
and save us from going astray into by-path
meadow. May ours be a pilgrim's progress; and
as we press on our way may it be with a song of
praise in our hearts; and by your grace may we
endure faithfully till we reach the Celestial City
and receive your welcome home.

Based on John Bunyan's Pilgrim's Progress

Lord, I believe in you – increase my faith.
I trust in you – strengthen my trust.
I love you – let me love you more and more.
I am sorry for my sins – deepen my sorrow.
I worship you as my first beginning, I long
    for you as my last end, I praise you as my
    constant helper, and call on you as my
    loving protector.
Guide me by your wisdom, correct me with
    your justice, comfort me with your mercy,
    protect me with your power.
I offer you, Lord, my thoughts – to be fixed
    on you; my words – to have you for their
    theme; my actions – to reflect my love for
    you; my sufferings – to be endured for your
    greater glory.
I want to do what you ask of me – in the way
    you ask, for as long as you ask, because
    you ask it.
Lord, enlighten my understanding, strengthen
    my will, purify my heart, and make me
    holy.
Help me to repent of my past sins and to resist
    temptation in the future. Help me rise
    above my human weaknesses and to grow
    stronger as a Christian.
Let me love you, my Lord and my God, and
    see myself as I really am – a pilgrim in
    this world, a Christian called to respect
    and to love all whose lives I touch, those
    in authority over me or those under my
    authority, my friends and my enemies.

Help me to conquer anger with gentleness,
greed with generosity, apathy by fervor.
Help me to forget myself and reach out to
others.
Make me prudent in planning, courageous in
taking risks. Make me patient in suffering,
unassuming in prosperity.
Keep me, Lord, attentive at prayer, temperate
in food and drink, diligent in my work,
firm in my good intentions.
Let my conscience be clear, my conduct
without fault, my speech blameless, and
my life well-ordered.
Teach me to realize that this world is passing,
that my true future is the happiness of
heaven, that life on earth is short, and the
life to come eternal.
Help me prepare for death with a proper fear
of judgment, and a greater trust in your
goodness.
Lead me safely through death to the endless
joy of heaven.
Grant this through Christ our Lord. Amen

The Universal Prayer, attributed to
pope Clement XI, 1649–1721

O God our Father, help us to a deeper trust
in the life everlasting. May we feel that this
love which is now, ever shall be; this robe of
the flesh is thy gift to thy child, and, when it
is worn out, thou wilt clothe him again; t his
work of life is the work that hast given us to do,
and, when it is done, thou wilt give us more;
this love, that makes all our life so glad, flows
from thee, for thou art love, and we shall love
forever. Help us to feel how, day by day, we see
some dim shadow of the eternal day that will
break upon us at the last. May the gospel of thy
Son, the whisper of thy Spirit, unite to make
our faith in the life to come, strong and clear;
then shall we be glad when thou shalt call us,
and enter into thy glory in Jesus Christ.

Robert Collyer, 1823–1912

I am nought,
I have nought,
I seek nought
but sweet Jesus in Jerusalem.

Walter Hilton, 14th century, Pilgrim's Prayer

O Father, give perfection to beginners,

intelligence to the little ones,
and aid to those who are running their course.
Give sorrow to the negligent,
fervor of spirit to the lukewarm,
and to those who have attained a good ending.

Irenaeus, c.130–c.200

O happy band of pilgrims,
If onward ye will tread
With JESUS as your Fellow
To JESUS as your Head!

O happy, if ye labor
As JESUS did for men:
O happy, if ye hunger
As JESUS hungered then!

The Cross that JESUS carried
He carried as your due:
The Crown that JESUS weareth
He weareth it for you.

The Faith by which ye see Him,
The Hope, in which ye yearn,
The Love that through all troubles
To Him alone will turn, –

What are they, but vaunt-couriers
To lead you to His Sight?
What are they, save the effluence
Of Uncreated Light?

The trials that beset you,
The sorrows ye endure,
The manifold temptations
That Death alone can cure, –

What are they, but His jewels
Of right celestial worth?
What are they but the ladder,
Set up to Heav'n on earth?

O happy band of pilgrims,
Look upward to the skies: –
Where such a light affliction
Shall win you such a prize!

Joseph of the Studium, 9th century,
translated by J.M. Neale

Lift up our hearts, we beseech you, O Christ,
above the false show of things, above fear,

above laziness, above selfishness and covetousness, above custom and fashion, up to the everlasting truth and order that you are; that we may live joyfully and freely, in faithful trust that you are our Savior, our example, and our friend, both now and for evermore.

Charles Kingsley, 1819–75

O Lord, support us all the day long of this troublous life, until the shadows lengthen, and the evening comes, and the busy world is hushed, and the fever of life is over, and our work is done. Then, Lord, in your mercy grant us a safe lodging, and a holy rest, and peace at the last; through Jesus Christ our Lord.

Used by J.H. Newman, 1801–90.
Based on a 16th-century prayer

Let me never forget, O my God, that seasons of consolation are refreshments here, and nothing more; not our abiding state. They will not remain with us, except in heaven. Here they are only intended to prepare us for doing and suffering. I pray Thee, O my God, to give them to me from time to time. Shed over me the sweetness of thy presence, lest I faint by the way; let I find religious service wearisome, through my exceeding infirmity, and give over prayer and meditation; lest I go about my daily work in a dry spirit, or am tempted to take pleasure in it for its own sake, and not for thee. Give me thy divine consolations from time to time; but let me not rest in them. Let me use them for the purpose for which thou givest them. Let me not think it grievous, let me not be downcast, if they go. Let them carry me forward to the thought and the desire of heaven.

J.H. Newman, 1801–90

O Lord God, from whom we come, in whom we are enfolded, to whom we shall return:
Bring us in our pilgrimage through life;
    with the power of the Father protecting,
    with the love of Jesus indwelling,
    and the light of the Spirit guiding,
until we come to our ending,
in life and love eternal.

Peter Nott, b.1933

What shall befall us hereafter we know not; but

to God, who cares for all men, who will one day reveal the secrets of all hearts, we commit ourselves wholly, with all who are near and dear to us. And we beseech the same most merciful and almighty God, that for the time to come we may so bear the reproach of Christ with unbroken courage, as ever to remember that here we have no continuing city, but may seek one to come, by the grace and mercy of our Lord Jesus Christ; to whom with the Father, and the Holy Ghost, be all honor and dominion, world without end.

Matthew Parker, 1504–75

The Passionate Man's Pilgrimage

Give me my scallop-shell of quiet,
My staff of faith to walk upon,
My scrip of joy, immortal diet,
My bottle of salvation,
My gown of glory, hope's true gage;
And thus I'll take my pilgrimage.

Blood must be my body's balmer;
No other balm will there be given;
Whilst my soul, like quiet palmer,
Travelleth towards the land of heaven;
    Over the silver mountains,
    Where spring the nectar fountains:
    There will I kiss
    The bowl of bliss,
And drink mine everlasting fill
Upon every milken hill.
My soul will be a-dry before;
But, after, it will thirst no more.

From thence to heaven's Bribeless hall
Where no corrupted voices brawl,
No Conscience molten into gold,
Nor forged accusers bought and sold,
No cause deferred, nor vain spent journey,
For there Christ is the King's Attorney:
Who pleads for all without degrees,
And he hath Angels, but no fees.
When the grand twelve million Jury,
Of our sins with dreadful fury,
'Gainst our souls black verdicts give,
Christ pleads his death, and then we live,
Be thou my speaker, taintless pleader,
Unblotted Lawyer, true proceeder,
Thou movest salvation even for alms:
Not with a bribed Lawyer's palms.

And this is my eternal plea,
To him that made Heaven, Earth and Sea,
Seeing my flesh must die so soon,
And want a head to dine next noon,
Just at the stroke when my veins start and
    spread
Set on my soul an everlasting head.
Then am I ready like a palmer fit,
To tread those blest paths which before I writ.

*Walter Raleigh, 1552–1618, written when
he was a prisoner in the Tower of London,
awaiting execution. The scallop-shell was a
symbol of pilgrimage in the Middle Ages*

Fix thou our steps, O Lord, that we stagger
not at the uneven motions of the world, but
steadily go on to our glorious home; neither
censuring our journey by the weather we meet
with, nor turning out of the way for anything
that befalls us.

The winds are often rought, and our own
weight presses us downwards. Reach forth, O
Lord, thy hand, thy saving hand, and speedily
deliver us.

Teach us, O Lord, to use this transitory life
as pilgrims returning to their beloved home;
that we may take what our journey requires,
and not think of settling in a foreign country.

John Wesley, 1703–91

E Tenebris
Come down, O Christ, and help me! reach thy
    hand,
    For I am drowning in a stormier sea
    Than Simon on thy lake of Galilee:
The wine of life is split upon the sand,
My heart is in some famine-murdered land
    When all good things have perished
        utterly,
    And well I know my soul in hell must
        lie
If I this night before God's throne should
    stand.
"He sleeps perchance, or rideth to the chase,
    Like Baal, when his prophets howled
        that name
    From morn to noon on Carmel's
        smitten height."
Nay, peace, I shall behold, before the night,
    The feet of brass, the robe more white
        than flame,

The wounded hands, the weary human face.

Oscar Wilde, 1854–1900

STEADFASTNESS

Almighty and most Merciful God, Who has
appointed us to endure sufferings and death
with our Lord Jesus Christ, before we enter
with Him into eternal glory: Grant us grace
at all times to subject ourselves to Thy holy
will, and to continue steadfast in the true faith
unto the end of our lives. and at all times to
find peace and joy in the blessed hope of the
resurrection of the dead, and of the glory of the
world to come; through Jesus Christ, Thy Son,
our Lord. Amen.

*The Common Service Book of
the Lutheran Church, 1917*

STEWARDSHIP

All Glory be to thee, O Lord God, for that
portion of the good things of this Life, thou
hast been pleased to vouchsafe me; Thou Lord
hast made me thy Steward of them, and at the
great day, I must give an account to thee of my
stewardship. O make me a faithful Steward of
them, that I may give an account to thee with
joy, and not with grief.

Thomas Ken, 1637–1711

STRENGTH

To my weariness, O Lord, grant your rest; to
my exhaustion, your strength and to my tired
eyes, your healing light. Guide me, guard me
and shelter me within the shadow of your
wings and quicken me in your service with the
brightness of your glory; through Jesus Christ
our Lord. Amen.

Lancelot Andrewes, 1555–1626

God of life, there are days when the burdens we
carry chafe our shoulders and wear us down;
when the road seems dreary and endless, the
skies gray and threatening; when our lives have
no music in them and our hearts are lonely,
and our souls have lost their courage. Flood the

path with light, we beseech you; turn our eyes to the skies as they are full of promise.

Augustine of Hippo, 354–430

Lord, guard us from all danger and carry us to yourself. And you will be our strong support from childhood to old age; for when our strength is yours, we are strong.

Augustine of Hippo, 354–430

Lord Jesus Christ, King of kings, you have power over life and death. You know even things that are uncertain and obscure, and our very thoughts and feelings are not hidden from you. Cleanse me from my secret faults, and I have done wrong and you saw it. You know how weak I am, both in soul and in body. Give me strength, O Lord, in my frailty and sustain me in my sufferings. Grant me a prudent judgment, dear Lord, and let me always be mindful of your blessings. Let me retain until the end your grace that has protected me till now.

Ephraem, c.306–378

Fight the good fight with all thy might;
Christ is thy Strength, and Christ thy Right;
Lay hold on life, and it shall be
Thy joy and crown eternally.

Run the straight race through God's good
    grace,
Lift up thine eyes, and seek His face;
Life with its way before us lies,
Christ is the Path, and Christ the Prize.

Cast care aside, upon thy Guide,
Lean, and His mercy will provide;
Lean, and the trusting soul shall prove
Christ is its Life, and Christ its Love.

Faint not nor fear, His arms are near,
He changeth not, and thou art dear.
Only believe, and thou shalt see
That Christ is all in all to thee.

John Samuel Bewley Monsell, 1811–75

Father hear the prayer we offer;
    Not for ease our prayer shall be,
    But for strength that we may ever
    Live our lives courageously,
    Live our lives courageously.

Not for ever in green pastures
    Do we ask our way to be;
    But the steep and rugged pathway
    May we tread rejoicingly,
    May we tread rejoicingly.

Not for ever by still waters
    Would we idly rest and stay;
    But would strike the living fountains
    From the rocks along our way,
    From the rocks along our way.

Be our strength in hours of weakness,
    In our wanderings be our guide;
    Through endeavor, failure, danger,
    Father, be there at our side,
    Father, be there at our side.

Love M.W. Willis, 1824–1908

TEMPTATION, RESISTING

Turn my heart to your decrees,
    and not to selfish gain.
Turn my eyes from looking at vanities;
    give me life in your ways.

Psalm 119.36–37 NRSV

O God, our Father, we are exceedingly frail, and indisposed to every virtuous and noble undertaking: Strengthen our weakness, we beseech you, that we may be valiant in this spiritual war; help us against our own negligence and cowardice, and defend us from the treachery of our unfaithful hearts; for the sake of Jesus Christ our Lord.

Augustine of Hippo, 354–430

O God, by thy mercy strengthen us who lie exposed to the rough storms of troubles and temptations. Help us against our own negligence and cowardice, and defend us from the treachery of our unfaithful hearts. Succor us, we beseech thee, and bring us to thy safe haven of peace and felicity.

Augustine of Hippo, 354–430

Come to my aid, that I may not stray from the way of salvation.

Augustine of Hippo, 354–430

Eternal God and Father, help us to entrust the past to your mercy, the present to your love, and the future to your wisdom, in the name of Jesus Christ our Lord, who is the same yesterday, and today, and for ever.

Source unknown

O Lord, strengthen me against all temptations, especially the temptation of , etc.

Author unknown, The Private Devotions of William Laud

O Lord, succor, we beseech thee, us who are tempted. May nothing induce us to distrust thy care over us, nor to use thy gifts to the denial of thee, their giver. May we never presume upon thy protection when we are forsaking thy paths, and tempting thee. May we never, for the sake of any supposed gain or advancement, quench the testimony of thy Spirit or prove disloyal to thy service. Do thou so support us in all temptations that, when we have been tried, we may receive the crown of life, which thou has prepared for them that love thee.

Henry Alford, 1810–71

Strengthen my life, Lord, against every temptation, and turn my adversary away from me ashamed and confounded every time he attacks me. Strengthen every step of my mind and tongue, and every move of my body.

John Chrysostom, c.347–407

O God, Who justifiest the ungodly, and Who desirest not the death of the sinner: We humbly implore Thy Majesty, that Thou wouldest graciously assist, by Thy heavenly aid, and evermore shield with Thy protection, Thy servants who trust in Thy mercy, that they may be separated by no temptations from Thee, and, without ceasing, may serve Thee; through Jesus Christ, Thy Son, our Lord. Amen.

The Common Service Book of the Lutheran Church, 1917

Almighty and Everlasting God who, by Thy Son, has promised us forgiveness of sins and everlasting life: We beseech Thee so to rule and govern our hearts by Thy Holy Spirit, that in our daily need, and especially in all time of temptation, we may seek help from Him, and

by a true and lively faith in Thy Word obtain the same; through Jesus Christ, Thy Son, our Lord. Amen.

The Common Service Book of the Lutheran Church, 1917

God, Who makest all things to work together for good to them that love Thee: Pour into our hearts such steadfast love toward Thee, that the pure desires which by Thy Spirit have been stirred up in us, may not be turned aside by any temptation; through Jesus Christ, Thy Son, our Lord. Amen.

The Common Service Book of the Lutheran Church, 1917

Lord, our heavenly Father, who orderest in troubles, humility in comforts, constancy in temptations, and victory over all our spiritual enemies. Grant us sorrow for our sins, thankfulness for your benefits, fear of your judgment, love of your mercies, and mindfulness of your presence; now and for evermore.

John Cosin, 1594–1672

O for a closer walk with God,
  A calm and heavenly frame;
A light to shine upon the road
  That leads to the Lamb!

Return, O holy Dove, return,
  Sweet messenger of rest;
I hate the sins that made thee mourn,
  And drove thee from my breast.

The dearest idol I have known,
  Whate'er that idol be,
Help me to tear it from thy throne,
  And worship only thee.

So shall my walk be close with God,
  Calm and serene my frame;
So purer light shall mark the road
  That leads me to the Lamb.

William Cowper, 1731–1800

Lord, you know all that lies before us, both of duty and temptation. Keep us, we pray, from all things hurtful to the body and the soul. Strengthen within us all that is praiseworthy and true, and grant that nothing may come between us and your holy presence; through Jesus Christ our Lord. Amen

John Hunter, 1849–1917

Enlighten our understandings with knowledge of right, and govern our wills by thy laws, that no deceit may mislead us, no temptation corrupt us; that we may always endeavor to do good and hinder evil. Amidst all the hopes and fears of this world, take not thy Holy Spirit from us; for the sake of Jesus Christ our Lord.

Samuel Johnson, 1709–84

Our Father, may the world not mould us today, but may we be so strong as to help to mould the world; through Jesus Christ our Lord. Amen.

J.H. Jowett, 1864–1923

Lord, our heavenly Father, who orderest all things for our eternal good, mercifully enlighten our minds, and give us a firm and abiding trust in thy love and care. Silence our murmings, quiet our fears, and dispel our doubts, that rising above our afflictions and our anxieties, we may rest on thee, the rock of everlasting strength.

New Church Book of Worship, 1876

In your hearts enthrone Him; there let Him
   subdue
All that is not holy, all that is not true;
Crown Him as your Captain in temptation's
   hour;
Let His will enfold you in its light and power.

Caroline Maria Noel, 1817–77

Lord, without thee I can do nothing; with thee I can do all. Help me by thy grace, that I fall not; help me by thy strength, to resist mightily the very first beginnings of evil, before it takes hold of me; help me to cast myself at once at thy sacred feet, and lie still there, until the storm be overpast; and, if I lost sight of thee, bring me back quickly to thee, and grant me to love thee better, for thy tender mercy's sake.

E.B. Pusey, 1800–82

O my Savior, let men not fall little by little, or think myself able to bear the indulgence of any known sin because it seems so insignificant.

Keep me from sinful beginnings, lest they lead me on to sorrowful endings.

C.H. Spurgeon, 1834–92

Lord Jesus, think on me
When floods the tempest high;
When on doth rush the enemy,
O Savior, be Thou nigh!

*Synesius of Cyrene, 375–430,
translated by Allen W. Chatfield*

Blessed Lord, who was tempted in all things just as we are, have mercy on our frailty. Out of weakness give us strength. Grant us to reverence you, so that we may reverence you only. Support us in time of temptation. Make us bold in time of danger. Help us to do your work with courage, and to continue your faithful soldiers and servants to our life's end; through Jesus Christ our Lord.

B.F. Westcott, 1825–1901

O heavenly Father, subdue in me whatever is contrary to Thy holy will. Grant that I may ever study to know Thy will, that I may know how to please Thee. Grant, O God, that I may never run into those temptations which, in my prayers, I desire to avoid. Lord, never permit my trials to be above my strength.

Thomas Wilson, 1663–1755

TRUST

O Savior Christ, who leads to eternal blessedness those who commit themselves to thee: grant that we, being weak, may not presume to trust in ourselves, but may always have thee before our eyes to follow as our guide; that thee, who alone knows the way, may lead us to our heavenly desires. To thee, with the Father and the Holy Ghost, be glory for ever.

Miles Coverdale, 1488–1568

TRUTH

From the cowardice that shrinks from new
   truths,
from the laziness that is content with half-
   truth,

from the arrogance that thinks it knows all
truth,
O God of truth, deliver us.

Source unknown

O Lord God, Heavenly Father, we beseech Thee,
let Thy Holy Spirit dwell in us, that He may
enlighten and lead us into all truth, and evermore defend us from all adversities; through
Jesus Christ, Thy Son our Lord. Amen.

*The Common Service Book of
the Lutheran Church, 1917*

Lord, give us weak eyes for things which are of
no account and clear eyes for all your truth.

Søren Kierkegaard, 1813–55

Christ himself says to his Father, "Your Word
is truth." May the almighty God, our heavenly
Father, give us the love and light of truth to
shine in our hearts through his Holy Spirit,
through Jesus Christ, our Lord.

Nicholas Ridley, c.1500–1555

Arise, O sun of righteousness, upon us, with
healing in thy wings; make us children of the
light and of the day. Show us the way in which
we should walk, for unto thee, O Lord, do we
lift up our souls. Dispel our mists of ignorance
which cloud our understandings. Let no false
suggestion either withdraw our hearts from
the love of thy truth, or from the practice of
it in all the actions of our lives; for the sake of
Jesus Christ our Lord.

Thomas Sherlock, 1678–1761

Set a watch, O Lord, before my mouth, and
keep the door of my lips.
Lord, keep my tongue from evil, and my lips
that they speak no guile.

Treasury of Devotion, 1869

Almighty God who hast sent the Spirit of truth
unto us to guide us into all truth: so rule our
lives by thy power that we may be truthful in
thought and word and deed. May no fear or
hope ever make us false in act or speech; cast
out from us whatsoever loveth or maketh a lie,
and bring us all into the perfect freedom of thy
truth; through Jesus Christ our Lord.

B.F. Westcott, 1825–1901

UNSELFISHNESS

Lord, I perceive my soul deeply guilty of envy.
I would prefer your work not done than done
by someone else other than myself. Dispossess
me, Lord, of this bad spirit, and turn my envy
into holy emulation; yes, make other peoples'
gifts to be mine, by making me thankful to you
for them.

Thomas Fuller, 1608–61

Lord, teach us to understand that your Son
died to save us, not from suffering, but from
ourselves; not from injustice, far less from
justice, but from being unjust. He died that we
might live—but lives as he lives, by dying as he
died who died to himself.

George MacDonald, 1824–1905

VIRTUE

Grant that I may not fail or swerve either in
prosperity or adversity; that I be not lifted up
by the one, and cast down by the other. Let me
thank Thee in prosperity, and preserver my
patience in adversity.

Thomas Aquinas, 1225–74

Let me joy in nothing but what leads to Thee,
nor grieve for anything but what leads away
from Thee; let me neither seek to please, nor
fear to displease any but Thee alone. May all
transitory things grow vile in my eyes, O God,
and may all that is Thine be dear to me for Thy
sake, and Thou, O my God, are above them
all.

Thomas Aquinas, 1225–74

May all joy be irksome to me that is without
Thee, nor may I desire anything that is apart
from Thee. May all labor and toil delight me,
which is for Thee, and all rest be weariness,
which is not in Thee. Grant me, O God, continually to lift up my heart towards Thee, and to
bring sorrowfully to my mind my many short-
comings, with full purpose of amendment.

Thomas Aquinas, 1225–74

Make me, O God, obedient without demur,
poor without repining, chaste without stain,

patient without murmur, humble without pretence, joyous without frivolity, fearful without abjectness, truthful without disguise, given to good works without presumption, faithful to rebuke my neighbor without arrogance, and ever ready to edify him by word and example without pretension.

Thomas Aquinas, 1225–74

Give me, O God, an ever watchful heart, which no subtle speculation may lure from Thee. Give me a noble heart, which no unworthy affection can draw downwards to the earth. Give me an upright heart, which no insincere intention can warp. Give me a firm heart, which no tribulation can crush or quell. Give me a free heart, which no perverted or impetuous affection can claim for its own.

Thomas Aquinas, 1225–74

VISION OF GOD

Lord, lift up the light of your countenance on us, that in your light we may see light; the light of your grace today, and the light of your glory hereafter; through Jesus Christ our Lord.

Lancelot Andrewes, 1555–1626

O my Savior, and my God, let it come. May the hour come when my eyes are given the vision of what I already believe, and grasp what I now hope for and greet from a distance. May my spirit embrace and kiss what now with my whole might I yearn for, and be altogether absorbed in the abyss of your love. But, meanwhile, bless, my soul, my Savior, and praise his name, which is holy and full of the holiest delights.

Anselm, 1033–1109

Most loving Father, who has taught us to dread nothing except the loss of you, preserve me from faithless fears and worldly anxieties, from corrupting passions and unhallowed love of earthly treasures; and grant that no clouds of this mortal life may hide me from the light of that love which is immortal and which you have shown to us in your Son, Jesus Christ our Lord.

William Bright, 1824–1901

Be thou my vision, O Lord of my heart;
Naught be all else to me, save that thou art,
Thou my best thought, by day or by night,
Waking or sleeping, thy presence my light.

Traditional Irish

O God, grant that looking upon the face of the Lord, as into a glass, we may be changed into his likeness, from glory to glory. Take out of us all pride and vanity, boasting and forwardness; and give us the true courage which shows itself by gentleness; the true wisdom which shows itself by simplicity; and the true power which shows itself by modesty.

Charles Kingsley, 1819–75

I need Thee to teach me day by day, according to each day's opportunities and needs. Give me, O my Lord, that purity of conscience which alone can receive Thy inspirations. My ears are dull, so that I cannot hear Thy voice. My eyes are dim, so that I cannot see Thy tokens. Thou alone canst quicken my hearing, and purge my sight, and cleanse and renew my heart. Teach me to sit at Thy feet, and to hear Thy word. Amen.

J.H. Newman, 1801–90

O my God, give me thy grace so that the things of this earth and things more naturally pleasing to me, may not be as close as thou art to me. Keep thou my eyes, my ears, my heart from clinging to the things of this world. Break my bonds, raise my heart. Keep my whole being fixed on thee. Let me never lose sight of thee: and while I gaze on thee, let my love of thee grow more and more every day.

J.H. Newman, 1801–90

May the Lord Jesus place his hands on our
    eyes that we may begin to catch sight of
    the thing that are not seen more than the
    things that are seen.
May he open our eyes that they will alight
    on the things to come more than on the
    things of this age.
May he unveil the vision of our heart that it
    may contemplate God in spirit.
We ask this through our Lord Jesus Christ to
    whom belong glory and power for ever. Amen.

Origen, 185–254

WILL OF GOD

Lord, I praise Thee for this place I am in; but the wonder has begun to stir in me – is this Thy place for me? Hold me steady doing Thy will. It may be only restlessness; if so, calm me to strength that I sin not against Thee by doubting.

Oswald Chambers, 1874–1917

Cleanse our minds, O Lord, we beseech thee, of all anxious thoughts for ourselves, that we may learn not to trust in the abundance of what we have, save as tokens of thy goodness and grace, but that we may commit ourselves in faith to thy keeping, and devote all our energy of soul, mind and body to the work of thy kingdom and the furthering of the purposes of thy divine righteousness; through Jesus Christ our Lord.

Euchologium Anglicanum

The end I seek is thy Glory, O God, and my
    own happiness,
Not the happiness of the body, but of the
    mind,
which is incapable of true happiness
till renewed and sanctified,
till restored to its native liberty,
till recovered to from its lapse, an in all things
made conformable to Thy will and laws.

Susanna Wesley, 1669–1742

WISDOM

Sweet Lord, release wisdom from the seat of your greatness that it may be with us, toil with us, work with us, speak in us. May she according to your good pleasure, direct our thoughts, words, and all our works and counsels, to the honor of your Name, the profit of the community, and our salvation. Through our friend Jesus Christ, to whom; with you and Holy Spirit, be honor and glory throughout all ages. Amen.

Aelred, of Rievaulx, 1109–67

Give me grace, Lord, to be strong, prudent, just and wise in all things. Give me an exact faith, generous love and unshakeable trust in you. Fill me with the spirit of intelligence and wisdom. Let me always be considerate about other people. O perfect and eternal Light, enlighten me.

Alcuin, 735–804

Enlighten my understanding, that I may teach wisdom.

Augustine of Hippo, 354–430

O God, by whom the meek are guided in judgment, grant that the spirit of wisdom may guide me from all false choices, and that walking in your straight path I may not stumble or fall.

William Bright, 1824–1901

Almighty God, the Giver of Wisdom,
without whose help resolutions are vain,
without whose blessing study is ineffectual,
enable me, if it be Thy will, to attain such
    knowledge as may qualify me
to direct the doubtful and instruct the
    ignorant,
to prevent wrongs, and terminate contentions;
and grant that I may use that knowledge
    which I shall attain,
to Thy glory and my own salvation.

Samuel Johnson, 1709–86

Grant, O God, that we may wait patiently, as servants standing before their Lord, to know your will; that we may welcome all truth, under whatever outward forms it may be uttered; that we may bless every good deed, by whomsoever it may be done; and that we may rise above all party strife to the contemplation of the eternal Truth and Goodness; through Jesus Christ our Lord.

Charles Kingsley, 1819–75

God, give us the serenity to accept what
    cannot be changed;
give us the courage to change what should be
    changed;
give us the wisdom to distinguish one from
    the other.

Attributed to Reinhold Niebuhr,
1892–1971, also known as
The Serenity Prayer

O Lord God of time and eternity, who makes us creatures of time, that when time is over, we may attain your blessed eternity: With time, your gift, give us also wisdom to redeem the time, so our day of grace is not lost; for our Lord Jesus' sake.

Christina Rossetti, 1830–94

Thou canst make me understand,
Though I am slow of heart;
Thine, in whom I live and move,
Thine the work, the praise is Thine,
Thou art wisdom, power, and love,
And all Thou art is mine.

Charles Wesley, 1707–88

WITNESS

O Lord, who though you were rich yet for our sakes became poor, and has promised in your holy gospel that whatever is done for the least of your brethren you will receive as done to you: Give us grace, we humbly beseech you, to be always willing and ready to minister, as you enable us, to the needs of others, and to extend the blessings of your kingdom over all the world; to your praise and glory, who are God over all, blessed for ever.

Augustine of Hippo, 354–430

O Lord, grant all who contend for the faith, never to injure it by clamor and impatience; but, speaking thy precious truth in love, so to present it that it may be loved, and that men may see in it thy goodness and beauty.

William Bright, 1824–1901

O God, who to an expectant and united Church didst grant at Pentecost the gift of the Holy Spirit, and hast wonderfully brought into one fold those who now worship thee here: Grant, we beseech thee, the help of the same Spirit in all our life and worship, that we may expect great things from thee, and attempt great things for thee, and being one in thee may show to the world that thou didst send Jesus Christ our Lord, to whom, with thee and the Holy Spirit, be all honor and glory, world without end. Amen.

William Carey, 1761–1834

O Lord, give us, we beseech Thee, in the name of Jesus Christ Thy Son our Lord, that love which can never cease, that will kindle our lamps but not extinguish them, that they may burn in us and enlighten others.

Do Thou, O Christ, our dearest Savior, Thyself kindle our lamps that they may evermore shine in Thy Temple and receive unquenchable light from Thee, that will enlighten our darkness and lessen the darkness of the world.

Columba, 521–597

Lord, speak to me, that I may speak
    in living echoes of thy tone;
    as thou has sought, so let me seek
    thine erring children lost and lone.

2. O strengthen me, that while I stand
    firm on the rock, and strong in thee,
    I may stretch out a loving land
    to wrestlers with the troubled sea.

3. O teach me, Lord, that I may teach
    the precious things thou dost impart;
    and wing my words, that they may reach
    the hidden depths of many a heart.

4. O fill me with thy fullness, Lord,
    until my very heart o'erflow
    in kindling thought and glowing word,
    thy love to tell, thy praise to show.

5. O use me, Lord, use even me,
    just as thou wilt, and when, and where,
    until thy blessed face I see,
    thy rest, thy joy, thy glory share.

Frances Ridley Havergal, 1836–70

I thank you, my Creator and Lord, that you have given me these joys in your creation, this ecstasy over the deeds of your hands. I have made known the glory of your deeds to people as far as my finite spirit was able to understand your infinity. If I have said anything wholly unworthy of you, or have aspired after my own glory, graciously forgive me.

Johann Kepler, 1571–1630

Make us, O Lord, to flourish like pure lilies in the courts of your house, and to show forth to the faithful the fragrance of your good deeds, and the example of a godly life, through your mercy and grace.

Mozarabic Liturgy

O My God! Most Blessed Trinity, I desire to Love You and make you Loved, to work for the glory of Holy Church by saving souls on earth and liberating those suffering in purgatory. I desire to accomplish Your will perfectly and to reach the degree of glory You have prepared for me in Your Kingdom. I desire, in a word, to be saint, but I feel my helplessness and I beg You, O my God! to be Yourself my Sanctity!

Thérèse of Lisieux, 1873–97

My gracious Master and my God,
Assist me to proclaim,
To spread through all the earth abroad
The honors of Thy name.

Charles Wesley, 1707–88

WORSHIP

Teach me that the worship in spirit and truth is not of man, but only comes from Thee; that it is not only a thing of times and seasons, but the outflowing of a life in Thee. Teach me to draw near to God in prayer under the deep impression of my ignorance and my having nothing in myself to offer Him, and at the same time of the provision Thou, my Savior, makest for the Spirit's breathing in my child-like stammerings. I do bless Thee that in Thee I am a child, and have a child's liberty of access; that in Thee I have the spirit of Sonship and of worship in truth. Teach me, above all, Blessed Son of the Father, how it is the revelation of the Father that gives confidence in prayer; and let the infinite Fatherliness of God's Heart be my joy and strength for a life of prayer and of worship. Amen.

Andrew Murray, 1828–1917

The Christian Year

Contents

SUNDAYS

Saturday, eve of Sunday
O Lord Jesus Christ, Son of the living God, who as on this day didst rest in the sepulcher, and didst thereby sanctify the grave to be a bed of hope to thy people: Make us so to abound in sorrow for our sins, which were the cause of thy passion, that when our bodies rest in the dust, our souls may live with thee; who livest and reignest with the Father and the Holy Spirit, one God, world without end.

Office of Compline

O Lord Jesus Christ, who on the first day of the week rose again: Raise up our souls to serve the living God; and as you did also on this day send down on your apostles your most Holy Spirit, so take not the same Spirit from us, but grant that we may be daily renewed and plentifully enriched by his power; for your own mercy's sake, who lives and reigns with the Father and the Holy Spirit, ever one God, world without end.

Lancelot Andrewes, 1555–1626

Prepare us, O God, for the worship of your house, and give us grace to serve you with reverence, joy, and thanksgiving; through Jesus Christ our Lord.

Source unknown

O God, who makes us glad with the weekly remembrance of the glorious resurrection of your Son our Lord; vouchsafe us this day such a blessing through your worship, that the days which follow it may be spent in your favor; through the same Jesus Christ our Lord. Amen.

William Bright, 1824–1901

Shout joyfully to God, all the earth,
sing praise to his name,
proclaim his glorious praise.

Say to God: How tremendous your deeds are!
On account of your great strength
you enemies woo your favor.

Let the whole earth worship you,
singing praises, singing praises to your name.

Come and listen,
all you who fear God,
while I tell you what great things
he has done for me.

To him I cried aloud,
high praise was on my tongue.

From his holy temple
he heard my voice,
my entreaty reached his ears.

Bless our God, you peoples,
loudly proclaim his praise.

In him will every race
in the world be blessed;
all nations will proclaim his glory.

Blessed be the Lord, the God of Israel,
who alone does wondrous deeds.

Blessed forever be his glorious name;
may the whole world be filled with his glory.
Amen. Amen.

*Francis of Assisi, 1181–1226. Prayer for
Sundays and major feast days, to be said
at nine o'clock in the morning (Terce)*

NEW YEAR

Almighty God, by whose mercy my life has been yet prolonged to another year, grant that thy mercy may not be in vain. Let not my years be multiplied to increase my guilt, but as age advances, let me become more pure in my thoughts, more regular in my desires, and more obedient to thy laws. Let not the cares of the world distract me, nor the evils of age overwhelm me. But continue and increase thy loving kindness towards me, and when thou shalt call me hence, receive me to everlasting happiness, for the sake of Jesus Christ, our Lord.

Samuel Johnson, 1709–84

New Year's Eve
At the Close of the Year
Let hearts and tongues unite,
    And loud thanksgivings raise:

'Tis duty, mingled with delight,
  To sing the Savior's praise.

To him we owe our breath,
  He took us from the womb,
Which else had shut us up in death,
  And prov'd an early tomb.

When on the breast we hung,
  Our help was in the Lord;
'Twas he first taught our infant tongue
  To form the lisping word.

When in our blood we lay,
  He would not let us die,
Because his love had fix'd a day
  To bring salvation nigh.

In childhood and in youth,
  His eye was on us still:
Though strangers to his love and truth,
  And prone to cross his will.

And since his name we knew,
  How gracious has he been:
What dangers has he led us through,
  What mercies have we seen!

Now through another year,
  Supported by his care,
We raise our Ebenezer here,
  "The Lord has help'd thus far."

Our lot in future years
  Unable to foresee,
He kindly, to prevent our fears,
  Says, "Leave it all to me."

Yea, Lord, we wish to cast
  Our cares upon thy breast!
Help us to praise thee for the past,
  And trust thee for the rest.
                    John Newton, 1725–1807

Give us the will, O God,
to pray to thee continually,
to learn to know thee rightfully,
to serve thee always holily,
to ask thee all things needfully,
to praise thee always worthily,
to love thee always steadfastly,
to ask thy mercy heartily,
to trust thee always faithfully,
to obey thee always willingly,
to abide thee always patiently,
to use thy neighbor honestly,
to live here always virtuously,
to help the poor in misery,
to thank thee ever gratefully,
to hope for heaven's felicity,
to have faith, hope and charity.
                    Thomas Tusser, 1524–80

Father, let me dedicate
All this year to thee,
In whatever worldly state
Thou wilt have me be:
Not from sorrow, pain or care,
Freedom dare I claim;
This alone shall be my prayer,
"Glorify thy name."
                    Lawrence Tuttiett, 1825–97

THANKSGIVING DAY

Dear Lord, help us to pause to recall our nation's first Thanksgiving as we too give You thanks for our many blessings. Help us today to recognize our blessings and to realize that You are our Provider also! You have watched over our nation, and it is because of Your divine love and care that we have survived this far. Thank You, Lord, and help us each to strive to be worthy of Your amazing grace.
In Jesus' holy name we pray.
                    D. L. Hammond

Gracious Lord God, as we prepare for Thanksgiving Day tomorrow, let us prepare our hearts. As many across the nation are worshipping together, let us join together in praising You and counting our blessings, for we each have some, perhaps more than we realize – we are here! Any day that one can get out of bed is a day to be grateful. We thank You for Your sustaining grace, Your protection, and for Your presence in our lives through good times and through trying times this past year ... We pray for those in this country, and in other nations around the world, who are suffering and need Your help ... As You have blessed us, help us

to be a blessing to others, in sharing where we can, and in praying that You will sustain them and supply their needs.
In Jesus' name we pray.
Amen.

D. L. Hammond

THE SEASONS

Almighty God, Lord of heaven and earth, in whom we live and move and have our being; who does good unto all men, making your sun to rise on the evil and on the good, and sending rain on the just and on the unjust; favorably behold us your servants, who all on your name, and send us your blessing from heaven, in giving us fruitful seasons, and satisfying us with food and gladness; that both our hearts and mouths will be continually filled with your praise, giving thanks to you in your holy church; through Jesus Christ our Lord.

John Cosin, 1594–1672

HARVEST

Come, ye thankful people, come, raise the
  song of harvest home;
All is safely gathered in, ere the winter storms
  begin.
God our Maker doth provide for our wants to
  be supplied;
Come to God's own temple, come, raise the
  song of harvest home.

Henry Alford, 1810–71

We plough the fields and scatter
The good seed on the land.
But it is fed and watered
By God's almighty hand.
He sends the snow in winter,
The warmth to swell the grain,
The breezes and the sunshine,
And soft, refreshing rain:
All good gifts around us are sent from heaven
  above;
Then thank the Lord, O thank the Lord,
for all his love.

Matthias Claudius, 1740–1815

Keep, O Lord, our journey through this life free also from storm and hurt unto the end. Send down refreshing rain upon the. places that have need of it; gladden and renew through it the face of the earth, that it may delight in the refreshing drops and become green ... Bless, O Lord, the fruits of the earth, keep them for us free from disease and hurt, and prepare them for our sowing and our harvest ... Bless now also, O Lord, the crown of the year through Thy goodness for the sake of the poor among Thy people, for the sake of the widow and the orphan, for the sake of the wanderer and the newcomer and for the sake of all who trust in Thee and call upon Thy Holy Name."

Egyptian Liturgy of St Mark

THE CHRISTIAN YEAR

Advent

The Advent refrains on the Magnificat
Each may be followed by the response:
Even so, come Lord Jesus

O Wisdom, coming forth from the mouth of
  the Most High,
    and reaching mightily from one end of
      the earth
    to the other, ordering all things well:
Come and teach us the way of prudence.

O Adonai, and leader of the house of Israel,
    who appeared to Moses in the fire of
      the burning bush
    and gave him the law on Sinai:
Come and redeem us with an outstretched
  arm.

O Root of Jesse, standing as a sign to the
  people,
    before whom kings shall shut their
      mouths
    and the nations shall seek:
Come and deliver us and do not delay.

O Key of David, and scepter of the house of
  Israel,
    who opens and no one can shut,
    who shuts and no one can open:

Come and bring the prisoners from the prison
house,
  those who dwell in darkness and the
  shadow of death.

O Daystar, splendor of light eternal
 and sun of righteousness:
  Come and enlighten those who dwell in
  darkness
  and the shadow of death.

O King of the nations, and their desire,
  the corner-stone making both one:
Come and save us, whom you formed from
 the dust.

O Emmanuel, our King and Lawgiver,
  the desire of all nations and their Savior:
Come and save us, O Lord our God.

      Author unknown, 9th century

Almighty God, give us grace that we may cast
away the works of darkness, and put upon us
the Armour of light, now in the time of this
mortal life in which thy Son Jesus Christ came
to visit us in great humility; that in the last
day, when he shall come again in his glorious
majesty to judge both the quick and the dead,
we may rise to the life immortal; through him
who liveth and reigneth with thee and the Holy
Ghost, one God, now and for ever. Amen.

  Book of Common Prayer, First Sunday of Advent

O Lord Jesu Christ, who at Thy first Coming
didst send Thy messenger to prepare Thy way
before Thee; Grant that the ministers and stewards of Thy mysteries may likewise so prepare
and make ready Thy way, by turning the hearts
of the disobedient to the wisdom of the just,
that at Thy second Coming to judge the world
we may be found an acceptable people in Thy
sight, Who livest and reignest with the Father
and the Holy Spirit, ever one God, world without end. Amen

    Book of Common Prayer, Collect
    for the Third Sunday in Advent,
    attributed to John Cosin, 1594–1672

We beseech you, O Lord, to purify our
consciences by your daily visitation; that when
your Son our Lord comes, he may find in us

a mansion prepared for himself; through the
same Jesus Christ our Lord.

    Gelasian Sacramentary, 5th century

Make us, we beseech you, O Lord our God,
watchful and alert in waiting for the coming of
your Son Christ our Lord; that when he comes
and knocks, he will not find us sleeping in sin,
but awake and rejoicing in his praises; through
the same Jesus Christ our Lord.

    Gelasian Sacramentary, 5th century

Awake – again the Gospel-trump is blown –
From year to year it swells with louder tone,
From year to year the signs of wrath
Are gathering round the Judge's path,
Strange words fulfill'd, and mighty works
 achiev'd,
And truth in all the world both hated and
 believ'd.

Awake! why linger in the gorgeous town,
Sworn liegemen of the Cross and thorny
 crown?
Up from your beds of sloth for shame,
Speed to the eastern mount like flame,
Nor wonder, should ye find your King in tears
Even with the loud Hosanna ringing in his
 ears.

Alas! no need to rouse them: long ago
They are gone forth, to swell Messiah's show:
With glittering robes and garlands sweet
They strew the ground beneath his feet:
All but your hearts are there—O set to prove
True confessors in faith, worst hypocrites in
 love!

Meanwhile he paces through th' adoring
 crowd,
Calm as the march of some majestic cloud,
That o'er wild scenes of ocean-war
Holds its still course in heaven afar:
Even so, heart-searching Lord, as years roll on,
Thou keepest silent watch from thy triumphal
 throne.

Even so, the world is thronging round to gaze
On the dread vision of the latter days,
Constrain'd to own Thee, but in heart
Prepared to take Barabbas' part:

"Hosanna" now, to-morrow "Crucify,"
The changeful burden still of their rude
    lawless cry.
Yet in that throng of selfish hearts untrue
Thy sad eye rests upon thy faithful few,
Children and childlike souls are there,
Blind Bartimeus' humble prayer,
And Lazarus waken'd from his four days'
    sleep,
Enduring life again, that Passover to keep.

And fast beside the olive-border'd way
Stands the bless'd home, where Jesus deign'd
    to stay,
The peaceful home, to zeal sincere
And heavenly contemplation dear,
When Martha lov'd to wait with reverence
    meet,
And wiser Mary linger'd at thy sacred feet.

Still through decaying ages as they glide,
Thou lov'st thy chosen remnant to divide;
Sprinkled along the waste of years
Full many a soft green isle appears:
Pause where we may upon the desert road,
Some shelter is in sight, some sacred safe
    abode.

When withering blasts of error swept the sky,
And Love's last flower seem'd fain to droop
    and die,
How sweet, how lone the ray benign
On shelter'd nooks of Palestine!
Then to his early home did Love repair,
And cheer'd his sickening heart with his own
    native air.

Years roll away: again the tide of crime
Has swept thy footsteps from the favor'd
    clime.
Where shall the holy Cross find rest?
On a crown'd monarch's mailed breast:
Like some bright angel o'er the darkling scene,
Through court and camp he holds his
    heavenward course serene.

A fouler vision yet; an age of light,
Light without love, glares on the aching sight:
O who can tell how calm and sweet,
Meek Walton! shews thy green retreat,
When wearied with the tale thy times disclose,

The eye first finds thee out in thy secure
    repose?

Thus bad and good their several warnings give
Of His approach, whom none may see and
    live:
Faith's ear, with awful still delight,
Counts them like minute bells at night,
Keeping the heart awake till dawn of morn,
While to her funeral pile this aged world is
    borne.

But what are heaven's alarms to hearts that
    cower
In willful slumber, deepening every hour,
That draw their curtains closer round,
The nearer swells the trumpet's sound?
Lord, ere our trembling lamps sink down and
    die,
Touch us with chastening hand, and make us
    feel Thee nigh.
            John Keble, 1792–1866, The Christian Year

May the Lamb of God, who once came to take
    away the sins of the world, take away from
    us every stain of sin. Amen.
And may he who came to redeem what was
    lost, at his second coming not cast away
    what he has redeemed. Amen.
That, when he comes, we may have perpetual
    joy with him on whom we have believed.
    Amen.
            Mozarabic Breviary

Christmas

THE ANNUNCIATION

Christmas Eve
O Lord, we beseech Thee, incline Thine ear
to our prayers, and lighten the darkness of
our hearts by Thy gracious visitation; through
Jesus Christ our Lord.
            Gregorian Sacramentary 6th century

A Christmas dedication
Lord Jesus,
I give you my hands to do your work,
I give you my feet to go your way,
I give you my eyes to see as you do.
I give you my tongue to speak your words,

I give you my mind that you may think in me,
I give you my spirit that you may pray in me.
Above all, I give you my heart that you may
    love in me, your Father, and all mankind.
I give you my whole self that you may grow in
    me, so that it is you, Lord Jesus, who live
    and work and pray in me.
I hand over to your care, Lord my soul and
    body, my mind and thoughts, my prayers
    and hopes, my health and my work, my life
    and my death, my parents and my family,
    my friends and my neighbors, my country
    and all men. Today and always.

Lancelot Andrewes, 1555–1626

Let the just rejoice, for their Justifier is born.
Let the sick and infirm rejoice, for their Savior
    is born.
Let the captives rejoice, for their Redeemer is
    born.
Let slaves rejoice, for their Master is born.
Let free people rejoice, for their Liberator is
    born.
Let all Christians rejoice, for Jesus Christ is
    born.

Augustine of Hippo, 354–430

Almighty God, who hast given us thy only-
begotten Son to take our nature upon him,
and as at this time to be born of a pure Virgin:
Grant that we, being regenerate and made thy
children by adoption and grace, may daily be
renewed by thy Holy Spirit; through the same
our Lord Jesus Christ, who liveth and reigneth
with thee and the same Spirit ever, one God,
world without end. Amen.

Book of Common Prayer,
Collect for Christmas Day

O holy Child of Bethlehem,
Descend to us, we pray;
Cast out our sin, and enter in:
Be born in us today.
We hear the Christmas angels
The great glad tidings tell:
O come to us, abide with us,
Our Lord Emmanuel.

Phillips Brooks, 1835–93

Now the holly bears a berry
    as white as the milk.

And Mary bore Jesus,
    who was wrapped up in silk.

And Mary bore Jesus Christ
    our Savior for to be,
And the first tree in the greenwood,
    it was the holly.

Now the holly bears a berry
    as black as the coal.
And Mary bore Jesus
    who died for us all.

Now the holly bears a berry
    as blood as it is red.
Then trust we our Savior
    who rose from the dead.

Traditional Cornish carol

Merciful and most loving God, by whose
will and bountiful gift Jesus Christ our Lord
humbled himself that he might exalt humankind; and became flesh that he might restore
in us the most celestial image; and was born of
the Virgin that he might uplift the lowly: Grant
us the inheritance of the meek, perfect in us
your likeness, and bring us at last to rejoice in
beholding your beauty, and with all your saints
to glory your grace; through the same Jesus
Christ our Lord.

Gallican Sacramentary

O God, who makes us glad with the yearly
remembrance of the birth of your only Son Jesus
Christ. Grant that as we joyfully receive him for
our Redeemer, so we may with sure confidence
behold him when he comes to be our Judge;
who lives and reigns with you and the Holy
Spirit, ever one God, world without end.

Gelasian Sacramentary, 5th century

The shepherds sing: and shall I silent be?
My God, no hymn for thee?
My soul's shepherd too; a flock it feeds
Of thoughts, and words, and deeds;
The pasture is thy word; the streams, thy
    grace
Enriching all the place.
Shepherd and flock shall sing, and all my
    powers
Out-sing the daylight hours.

George Herbert, 1593–1633

Glory be to God in the highest, and on earth peace, goodwill towards men; for unto us is born this day a Savior, who is Christ the Lord. We praise you, we bless you, we glorify you, we give thanks to you, for this your greatest mercy, Lord God, heavenly King, God the Father almighty.

Thomas Ken, 1637–1711

Angels, from the realms of glory,
    Wing your flight o'er all the earth,
Ye who sang creation's story,
    Now proclaim Messiah's birth;
Come and worship,
    Worship Christ the new-born King.

Shepherds, in the field abiding,
    Watching o'er your flocks by night,
God with man is now residing,
    Yonder shines the infant-light;
Come and worship,
    Worship Christ the new-born King.

Sages, leave your contemplations,
    Brighter visions beam afar;
Seek the great Desire of nations;
    Ye have seen His natal star;
Come and worship,
    Worship Christ the new-born King.

Saints before the altar bending,
    Watching long in hope and fear,
Suddenly the Lord, descending,
    In His temple shall appear;
Come and worship,
    Worship Christ the new-born King.

Sinners, wrung with true repentance,
    Doom'd for guilt to endless pains,
Justice now revokes the sentence,
    Mercy calls you, break your chains
Come and worship,
    Worship Christ the new-born King.

James Montgomery, 1771–1854

Lord Jesus Christ, who visited this world with the presence of your incarnation, and whose coming to judgment every Christian soul expects, justify us in the day of your coming with your wonted mercy, that we, who now celebrate the festival of your incarnation, may then be joined to the company of your saints; who with the Father and the Holy Spirit, lives and reigns, one God, world without end.

Mozarabic Sacramentary

THE BIRTH OF JESUS

A great and mighty wonder!
A full and holy cure!
The Virgin bears the Infant,
With Virgin-honor pure!

The Word becomes Incarnate,
And yet remains on high:
And Cherubim sing anthems
To shepherds from the sky.

And we with them triumphant
Repeat the hymn again:
"To GOD on high be glory,
And peace on earth to men!"

While thus they sing your Monarch,
Those bright angelic bands,
Rejoice, ye vales and mountains!
Ye oceans, clap your hands!

Since all He comes to ransom,
By all be He adored,
The Infant born in Bethlehem,
The Savior and the LORD!

And idol forms shall perish,
And error shall decay,
And CHRIST shall wield His scepter,
Our LORD and GOD for aye.

Anatolius, d.458

Let your goodness, Lord, appear to us, that we, made in your image, conform ourselves to it. In our own strength we cannot imitate your majesty, power and wonder; nor is it fitting for us to try. But your mercy reaches from the heavens, through the clouds, to the earth below. You have come to us as a small child, but you have brought us the greatest of all gifts, the gift of eternal love. Caress us with your tiny hands, embrace us with your tiny arms and pierce our hearts with your soft, sweet cries.

Bernard of Clairvaux, 1090–1153

Sacred infant, all divine,
What a tender love was thine,
Thus to come from highest bliss
Down to such a world as this!

Teach, O teach us, holy child,
By thy face so meek and mild,
Teach us to resemble thee
In thy sweet humility.

Edward Caswall, 1814–78

The Child of glory, The Child of Mary,
Born in the stable, The king of all,
Who came to the wilderness
And in our stead suffered;
Happy they are counted
Who to him are near.

Celtic prayer for Christmas Day

CHRIST is born! Tell forth His fame!
CHRIST from Heaven! His love proclaim!
CHRIST on earth! Exalt His Name!
Sing to the LORD, O world, with exultation!
Break forth in glad thanksgiving, every nation!
For He hath triumphed gloriously!

Man, in God's own Image made,
Man, by Satan's wiles betrayed,
Man, on whom corruption preyed,
Shut out from hope of life and of salvation,
Today CHRIST maketh him a new creation,
For He hath triumphed gloriously!

For the Maker, when His foe,
Wrought the creature death and woe,
Bowed the Heav'ns, and came below, 4
And in the Virgin's womb His dwelling making
Became true man, man's very nature taking
For He hath triumphed gloriously!

He, the Wisdom, WORD, and Might,
GOD, and SON, and Light of light,
Undiscovered by the sight
Of earthly monarch, or infernal spirit,
Incarnate was, that we might Heav'n inherit;
For He hath triumphed gloriously!

Cosmas, the Melodist, d.c.760

Ode III
Him, of the Father's very Essence,
Begotten, ere the world began,

And, in the latter time, of Mary,
Without a human sire, made Man:
Unto Him, this glorious morn,
Be the strain outpoured!
Thou That liftest up our horn,
Holy art Thou, LORD!

The earthly Adam, erewhile quickened
By the blest breath of GOD on high,
Now made the victim of corruption,
By woman's guile betrayed to die,
He, deceived by woman's part,
Supplication poured;
Thou Who in my nature art,
Holy art Thou, LORD!

Thou, JESUS CHRIST, wast consubstantial
With this our perishable clay,
And, by assuming earthly nature,
Exaltedst it to heavenly day.
Thou, That wast as mortal born,
Being GOD adored,
Thou That liftest up our horn,
Holy art Thou, LORD!

Rejoice, O Bethlehem, the city
Whence Judah's monarchs had their birth;
Where He that sitteth on the Cherubs,
The King of Israel, came on earth:
Manifested this blest morn,
As of old time never,
He hath lifted up our horn,
He shall reign for ever!

Cosmas, the Melodist, d.c.760

Moonless darkness stands between.
Past, the Past, no more be seen!
But the Bethlehem star may lead me
To the sight of Him Who freed me
From the self that I have been.
Make me pure, Lord: Thou art Holy;
Make me meek, Lord: Thou wert lowly;
Now beginning, and always,
Now begin, on Christmas day.

Gerard Manley Hopkins, 1844–1889

All praise to Thee, eternal God,
Who, clothed in garb of flesh and blood,
Dost take a manger for Thy throne,
While worlds on worlds are Thine alone.
Hallelujah!

Once did the skies before Thee bow;
A virgin's arms contain Thee now,
While angels, who in Thee rejoice,
Now listen for Thine infant voice.
Hallelujah!

A little Child, Thou art our Guest
That weary ones in Thee may rest;
Forlorn and lowly is Thy birth
That we may rise to heaven from earth.
Hallelujah!

Thou comest in the darksome night
To make us children of the light,
To make us in the realms divine,
Like Thine own angels, round Thee shine.
Hallelujah!

All this for us Thy love hath done;
By This to Thee our love is won;
For this our joyful songs we raise
And shout our thanks in ceaseless praise.
Hallelujah!

                    Martin Luther, 1483–1546

Away in a manger, no crib for a bed,
The little Lord Jesus laid down His sweet head.
The stars in the sky looked down where He
    lay,
The little Lord Jesus, asleep on the hay.

The cattle are lowing, the Baby awakes,
But little Lord Jesus, no crying He makes;
I love Thee, Lord Jesus, look down from the
    sky
And stay by my cradle til morning is nigh.

Be near me, Lord Jesus, I ask Thee to stay
Close by me forever, and love me, I pray;
Bless all the dear children in Thy tender care,
And fit us for heaven to live with Thee there.
            Attributed to Martin Luther, 1483–1546

Praise for the Incarnation
Sweeter sounds than music knows
Charm me in Immanuel's name;
All her hopes my spirit owes
To his birth, and cross, and shame.

When he came, the angels sung,
"Glory be to God on high;"

Lord, unloose my stamm'ring tongue,
Who should louder sing than I?

Did the Lord a man become,
That he might the law fulfill,
Bleed and suffer in my room,
And canst thou, my tongue, be still?

No, I must my praises bring,
Though they worthless are and weak;
For should I refuse to sing,
Sure the very stones would speak.

O my Savior, Shield, and Sun,
Shepherd, Brother, Husband, Friend,
Ev'ry precious name in one,
I will love thee without end.
                    John Newton, 1725–1807

Love came down at Christmas,
Love all lovely, love divine;
Love was born at Christmas,
Star and angels gave the sign.

Worship we the Godhead,
Love incarnate, love divine;
Worship we our Jesus:
But wherewith for sacred sign?

Love shall be our token,
Love shall be yours and love be mine,
Love to God and to all men,
Love for plea and gift and sign.
                    Christina Rossetti, 1830–94

In the bleak mid-winter
    Frosty wind made moan,
Earth stood hard as iron,
    Water like a stone;
Snow had fallen, snow on snow,
    Snow on snow,
In the bleak mid-winter
    Long ago.

Our God, Heaven cannot hold Him,
    Nor earth sustain;
Heaven and earth shall flee away
    When He comes to reign:
In the bleak mid-winter
    A stable-place sufficed
The Lord God Almighty
    Jesus Christ.

Enough for Him whom cherubim
    Worship night and day,
A breastful of milk
    And a mangerful of hay;
Enough for Him whom angels
    Fall down before,
The ox and ass and camel
    Which adore.

Angels and archangels
    May have gathered there,
Cherubim and seraphim
    Throng'd the air,
But only His mother
    In her maiden bliss
Worshipped the Beloved
    With a kiss.

What can I give Him,
    Poor as I am?
If I were a shepherd
    I would bring a lamb,
If I were a wise man
    I would do my part,
Yet what I can I give Him; –
    Give my heart.

Christina Rossetti, 1830–94

Hark! The herald angels sing,
"Glory to the newborn King;
Peace on earth, and mercy mild,
God and sinners reconciled!"
Joyful, all ye nations rise,
Join the triumph of the skies;
With th'angelic host proclaim,
"Christ is born in Bethlehem!"
Refrain
Hark! the herald angels sing,
"Glory to the newborn King!"

Christ, by highest heav'n adored;
Christ the everlasting Lord;
Late in time, behold Him come,
Offspring of a virgin's womb.
Veiled in flesh the Godhead see;
Hail th'incarnate Deity,
Pleased with us in flesh to dwell,
Jesus our Emmanuel.
Refrain

Hail the heav'nly Prince of Peace!
Hail the Sun of Righteousness!
Light and life to all He brings,
Ris'n with healing in His wings.
Mild He lays His glory by,
Born that man no more may die.
Born to raise the sons of earth,
Born to give them second birth.
Refrain

Charles Wesley, 1707–88

Epiphany

May our Lord Jesus Christ bless you, who of old on this day gloriously appeared to the shepherds in the manger. Amen.

May he himself protect and defend us in all things, who for us mercifully took upon himself our human infancy. Amen.

And may he, who is our Lord and Savior, graciously keep us until eternity.

Mozarabic Breviary

Almighty and everlasting God, who hast made known the incarnation of thy Son by the bright shining of a star, which when the wise men beheld they adored thy majesty and presented costly gifts: Grant that the star of thy righteousness may always shine in our hearts, and that for our treasure we may give to thy service ourselves and all that we have; through the same Jesus Christ our Lord.

Gelastian Sacramentary

O God, our loving Father, help us rightly to remember the birth of Jesus, that we may share in the song of the angels, the gladness of the shepherds and the worship of the wise men. May Christmas morning make us happy to be your children and Christmas evening bring us to our beds with grateful thoughts, forgiving and forgiven, for Jesus' sake.

R.L. Stevenson, 1850–94

Jesus' life

O God, whose blessed Son was manifested that he might destroy the works of the devil, and make us the sons of God, and heirs of eternal life; Grant us, we beseech thee, that, having this hope, we may purify ourselves, even as he is pure; that, when he shall appear again with power and great glory, we may be made like unto him in his eternal and glorious kingdom; where with thee, O Father, and thee, O Holy Ghost, he liveth and reigneth, ever one God, world without end.

Book of Common Prayer, 1662, Collect for
the Sixth Sunday after the Epiphany

PRESENTATION OF JESUS IN THE TEMPLE

O God, who made the most glorious name of our Lord Jesus Christ, your one and only Son, to be exceeding sweet and supremely lovable to your faithful servants: Mercifully grant that all who devoutly venerate this name of Jesus on earth may in this life receive your holy comfort, and in the life to come receive your unending joy; through the same Jesus Christ our Lord.

Sarum Missal, 1085

ASH WEDNESDAY

Almighty and everlasting God, who hatest nothing that thou hast made and dost forgive the sins of all them that are penitent: Create and make in us new and contrite hearts, that we, worthily lamenting our sins, and acknowledging our wretchedness, may obtain of thee, the God of all mercy, perfect remission and forgiveness; through Jesus Christ our Lord. Amen.

Book of Common Prayer, First
day of Lent, Ash Wednesday

LENT

To Keep a True Lent
Is this a Fast, to keep
　　The larder lean?
　　And clean
From fat of veals and sheep?

Is it to quit the dish
　　Of flesh, yet still
　　To fill
The platter high with fish?

Is it a fast an hour,
　　Or ragg'd to go,
　　Or show
A down-cast look and sour?

No: 'tis a Fast to dole
　　Thy sheaf of wheat
　　And meat
Unto the hungry soul.

It is to fast from strife
　　And old debate,
　　And hate;
To circumcise thy life.

To show a heart grief-rent;
　　To starve thy sin,
　　Not bin;
And that's to keep thy Lent.

Robert Herrick, 1591–1679

PALM SUNDAY

Jesus, hastening for the world to suffer,
Enters in, Jerusalem, to thee:
With His Twelve He goeth forth to offer
That free sacrifice He came to be.

They that follow Him with true affection
Stand prepared to suffer for His Name:
Be we ready then for man's rejection,
For the mockery, the reproach, the shame.

Now, in sorrow, sorrow finds its healing:
In the form wherein our father fell,
CHRIST appears, those quick'ning Wounds
　　revealing,
Which shall save from sin and death and hell.

Now, Judaea, call thy Priesthood nigh thee!
Now for Deicide prepare thy hands!
Lo! thy Monarch, meek and gentle by thee!
Lo! the Lamb and Shepherd in thee stands!

To thy Monarch, Salem, give glad greeting!
Willingly He hastens to be slain
For the multitude His entrance meeting
With their false Hosanna's ceaseless strain.
"Blest is He That comes," they cry,
"On the Cross for man to die!"

Andrew of Crete, 660–732

Almighty and everlasting God, who, of thy tender love towards mankind, hast sent thy Son, our Savior Jesus Christ, to take upon him our flesh, and to suffer death upon the cross, that all mankind should follow the example of his great humility; Mercifully grant, that we may both follow the example of his patience, and also be made partakers of his resurrection; through the same Jesus Christ our Lord. Amen.

Book of Common Prayer, Palm Sunday

Ride on! ride on in majesty!
Hark! all the tribes 'Hosanna' cry:
O Savior meek, pursue Thy road
With palms and scattered garments strowed.

Ride on! ride on in majesty!
In lowly pomp ride on to die:
O Christ, Thy triumphs now begin
O'er captive death and conquered sin.

Ride on! ride on in majesty!
The winged squadrons of the sky
Look down with sad and wondering eyes
To see the approaching sacrifice.

Ride on! ride on in majesty!
Thy last and fiercest strife is nigh;
The Father on His sapphire throne
Awaits His own anointed Son.

Ride on! ride on in majesty!
In lowly pomp ride on to die;
Bow thy meek head to mortal pain,
Then take, O God, Thy power and reign.

H.H. Milman, 1791–1868

As on this day we keep the special memory of our Redeemer's entry into the city, so grant, O Lord, that now and ever he may triumph in our hearts. Let the king of peace and glory enter in, and let us lay ourselves and all we are in full joyful homage before him; through the same Jesus Christ our Lord.

Handley C.G. Moule, 1841–1920

Refrain:
All glory, laud and honor,
To Thee, Redeemer, King,
To Whom the lips of children
Made sweet hosannas ring.

Thou art the King of Israel,
Thou David's royal Son,
Who in the Lord's Name comest,

The King and Blessèd One.
Refrain

The company of angels
Are praising Thee on High,
And mortal men and all things
Created make reply.
Refrain

The people of the Hebrews
With palms before Thee went;
Our prayer and praise and anthems
Before Thee we present.
Refrain

To Thee, before Thy passion,
They sang their hymns of praise;
To Thee, now high exalted,
Our melody we raise.
Refrain

Thou didst accept their praises;
Accept the prayers we bring,
Who in all good delightest,
Thou good and gracious King.
Refrain

Theodulph of Orleans, c.750–820,
translated by J.M. Neale

PASSION OF CHRIST

The cross is the hope of Christians
the cross is the resurrection of the dead
the cross is the way of the lost
the cross is the savior of the lost
the cross is the staff of the lame
the cross is the guide of the blind
the cross is the strength of the weak
the cross is the doctor of the sick
the cross is the aim of the priests
the cross is the hope of the hopeless
the cross is the freedom of the slaves
the cross is the power of the kings
the cross is the water of the seeds
the cross is the consolation of the bondsmen
the cross is the source of those who seek water
the cross is the cloth of the naked.
We thank you, Father, for the cross.

Litany of the Cross

TO THE FEET

O Savior of the world, I cry to Thee; O Savior,

suffering God, I worship Thee; O wounded beauteous Love, I kneel to Thee; Thou knowest, Lord, how I would follow Thee, If of Thyself Thou give Thyself to Me.

Thy Presence I Believe; O come to me! Behold me prostrate, Jesus; look on me! How beautiful Thou art! O turn to me! O in Thy tender mercy turn to me, And let Thy untold pity pardon me!

With trembling love and feat I worship Thee; I kiss the grievous nails which entered Thee, And think on those dire wounds which tortured Thee, And, grieving, lift my weeping eyes to Thee, Transfixed and dying all for love of me!

O wondrous grace! O gracious charity! O love of sinners in such agony! Sweet Father of the poor! O who can be Unmoved to witness this great mystery, – The Healer smitten, hanging on a tree?

O gentle Jesus, turn Thee unto me; What I have broken do Thou bind in me, And what is crooked make Thou straight in me; What I have lost restore Thou unto me, And what is weak and sickly heal in me.

O Love! with all my strength I seek for Thee; Upon and in thy Cross I look for Thee; With sorrow and with hope I turn to Thee, – That through Thy Blood new health may come to me, That washed therein Thy love may pardon me.

O take my heart, Thou Loved One; let it be Transfixed with those dear wounds for love of Thee, O wound it, Jesus, with pure love of Thee; And let it so be crucified with Thee, that it may be forever joined to Thee.

Sweet Jesus, loving God, I cry to Thee; Thou guilty, yet I come for love of Thee; O show Thyself, dear Savior, kind to me! Unworthy as I am, O turn to me, Nor at thy sacred Feet abandon me!

Dear Jesus, bathed in tears, I kneel to Thee; In shame and grief I lift my eyes to Thee; Prostrate before Thy Cross I bow to Thee, And thy dear Feet embrace; O look on me, Yea, from Thy Cross, O look, and pardon me.

O my Beloved, stretched against that Thee, Whose arms divine are now enfolding me, whose gracious Heart is now upholding me, – O my Beloved, let me wholly be Transformed, forgiven, one alone with Thee!

TO THE KNEES

O Jesus, King of Saints, I worship Thee; O hope of sinners, hail! I rest on Thee; True God, true man, Thou hangest on the Tree Transfixed, with quivering flesh and shaking knees, A criminal esteemed, – I worship Thee.

Alas, how poor, how naked, wilt Thou be! How hast Thou stript Thyself for love of me, How made Thyself a gazing-stock to be! Not forced, but, O my God! How willingly In all Thy limbs Thou sufferest on that Tree!

Thy Precious Blood wells forth abundantly From all Thy open wounds incessantly; All bathed therein, O God, in agony Thou standest on the Cross of infamy, Awaiting the appointed hour to die.

O infinite, O wondrous majesty! O terrible, unheard-of poverty! Ah, who, returning so great charity, I willing, Jesus, thus to give for Thee His blood for Thine, in faithful love for Thee?

O Jesus, how shall I, then, answer Thee, Who am so vile, and have not followed Thee? Or how repay the love that loveth me With such sublime, such awful charity Transfixed, from double death to set me free?

O Jesus, what Thy love hath been for me! O Jesus, death could never conquer Thee! Ah, with what loving care Thou keepest me Enfolded in Thine arms, lest I should be, By death of sin, a moment torn from Thee!

Behold, O Jesus, how for love of Thee, With all my soul I trembling cling to Thee, And Thy dear Knees embrace. O pity me! Thou knowest why – in pity bear with me, And overlook the shame that covers me!

O let the Blood I worship flow on me, That what I do may never anger Thee; The Blood which flows at every pore from Thee Each imperfection may it wash from me, That I may undefiled and perfect be.

O force me, best Beloved, to draw to Thee, Transfixed and bleeding on the shameful Tree, Despised and stretched in dying agony! All my desire, O Lord, is fixed on Thee; O call me, then, and I will follow Thee.

I have no other love, dear Lord, but Thee; Thou art my first and last; I cling to Thee. It is no labor, Lord; love sets me free; Then heal me, cleanse me, let me rest on Thee, For love is life, and life is love – in Thee.

TO THE HANDS

Hail, holy Shepherd! Lord, I worship Thee, Fatigued with combat, steeped in misery; Whose sacred Hands, outstretched in agony, All pierced and dislocated on the Tree, Are fastened to the wood of infamy.

Dear holy Hands, I humbly worship ye, With roses filled, fresh blossoms of that Tree; The cruel iron enters into ye, While open gashes yield unceasingly The Precious stream down-dropping from the Tree.

Behold, Thy Blood, O Jesus, flows on me – The price of my salvation falls on me; O ruddy as the rose, it drops on me. Sweet Precious Blood, it wells abundantly From both Thy sacred Hands to set me free.

My heart leaps up, O Jesus, unto Thee; Drawn by those nail-pierced Hands it flies to Thee; Drawn by those Blood-stained Hands stretched out for me, My soul breaks out with sighing unto Thee, And longs to slake its thirst, O Love, in Thee.

My God, what great stupendous charity – Both good and bad are welcomed here by Thee! The slothful heart Thou drawest graciously, The loving one Thou callest tenderly, And unto all a pardon grantest free.

Behold, I now present myself to Thee, Who dost present thy bleeding Hands to me; The sick Thou healest when they come to Thee; Thou canst not, therefore, turn away from me, Whose love Thou knowest, Lord, is all for Thee.

O my Beloved, fastened to the Tree, Draw, by Thy love, my senses unto Thee; My will, my intellect, my memory, And all I am, make subject unto Thee, In whose dear arms alone is liberty.

O draw me for Thy Cross' sake to Thee; O draw me for Thy so wide charity; Sweet Jesus, draw my heart in truth to Thee, O put an end to all my misery, And crown me with Thy Cross and victory!

O Jesus, place Thy sacred Hands on me, With transport let me kiss them tenderly, With groans and tears embrace them fervently; And, O for these deep wounds I worship Thee; And for the blessed drops that fall on me!

O dearest Jesus, I commend to Thee Myself and all I am, most perfectly; Bathed in Thy Blood, behold, I live for Thee; O, may Thy blessed Hands encompass me, And in extremity deliver me!

TO THE SIDE

O Jesus, highest Good, I yearn for Thee; O Jesus, merciful, I hope in Thee, Whose sacred Body hands upon the Tree, Whose limbs, all dislocated painfully, Are stretched in torture, all for love of me!

Hail, sacred Side of Jesus! Verily The hidden spring of mercy lies in Thee, The source of honeyed sweetness dwells in Thee, The fountain of redemption flows from Thee, The secret well of love that cleanses me.

Behold, O King of Love, I draw to Thee; If I am wrong, O Jesus, pardon me; Thy love, Beloved, calls me lovingly, As I with blushing cheek gaze willingly Upon the living wound that bleeds for me.

O gentle opening, I worship Thee; O open door and deep, I look in Thee; O most pure stream, I gaze and gaze on Thee: More ruddy than the rose, I draw to Thee; More healing than all health, I fly to Thee.

More sweet than wine Thine odor is for me; The poisoned breath of sin it drives from me; Thou art the draught of life poured out for me. O ye who thirst, come, drink thereof with me; And Thou, sweet wound, O open unto me.

O red wound open, let me draw to Thee, And let my throbbing heart be filled from Thee! Ah, see! My heart, Beloved, faints for Thee. O my Beloved, open unto me, That I may pass and lose myself in Thee.

Lord, with my mouth I touch and worship Thee, With all the strength I have I cling to Thee, With all my love I plunge my heart in Thee, My very life-blood would I drawn from Thee, – O Jesus, Jesus! Draw me into Thee!

How Sweet Thy savor is! Who tastes of Thee, O Jesus Christ, can relish naught but Thee; Who tastes Thy living sweetness lives by Thee; All else is void – the soul must die for Thee; So faints my heart, – so would I die for thee.

I languish, Lord! O let me hide in Thee! In Thy sweet Side, my Love, O bury me! And may the fire divine consuming Thee Burn in my heart where it lies hid in Thee, Without a fear reposing peacefully!

When in the hour of death Thou callest me, O Love of loves, may my soul enter Thee; May my last breath, O Jesus fly to Thee; So no fierce beast may drive my heart from Thee, But in Thy Side may it remain with Thee!

TO THE BREAST

O God of my salvation, hail to Thee! O Jesus, sweetest Love, all hail to Thee! O venerable Breast, I worship Thee; O dwelling-place of love, I fly to Thee, With trembling touch adore and worship Thee.

Hail, throne of the Most Holy Trinity! Hail, ark immense of tender charity! Thou stay of weakness and infirmity, Sweet rest of weary souls who rest on Thee, Dear couch of loving ones who lean on Thee!

With reverence, O Love, I kneel to Thee, O worthy to be ever sought by me; Behold me, Jesus, looking unto Thee. O, set my heart on fire, dear Love, from Thee, And burn it in the flame that burns in Thee.

O make my breast a precious home for thee, A furnace of sweet love and purity, A well of holy grief and piety; Deny my will, conform it unto Thee, That grace abundant may be mine in Thee.

Sweet Jesus, loving Shepherd, come to me; Dear Son of God and Mary, come to me; Kind Father come, let Thy Heart pity me, And cleanse the fountain of my misery In that great fountain of Thy clemency.

Hail, fruitful splendor of the Deity! Hail, fruitful figure of Divinity! From the full treasure of Thy charity, O pour some gift in Thy benignity Upon the desolate who cry to Thee!

Dear Breast of most sweet Jesus, mine would be All Thine in its entire conformity; Absolve it from all sin, and set it free, That it may burn with ardent charity, And never, never cease to think on Thee.

Abyss of wisdom from eternity, The harmonies of angels worship Thee; Entrancing sweetness flows, O Breast, from thee; John tasted it as he lay rapt on Thee; O grant me thus that I may dwell in Thee!

Hail, fountain deep of God's benignity! The fullness of the immense Divinity Hath found at last a creature home in Thee. Ah, may the counsel that I learn from Thee All imperfection purify in me!

True temple of the Godhead, hail to Thee! O draw me in Thy gracious charity, Thou ark of

goodness, full of grace for me. Great God of all, have mercy upon me, And on Thy right hand keep a place for me.

TO THE FACE

Hail, bleeding Head of Jesus, hail to Thee! Thou thorn-crowned Head, I humbly worship Thee! O wounded Head, I lift my hands to Thee; O lovely Face besmeared, I gaze on Thee; O bruised and livid Face, look down on me!

Hail, beauteous Face of Jesus, bent on me, Whom angel choirs adore exultantly! Hail, sweetest Face of Jesus, bruised for me – Hail, Holy One, whose glorious Face for me Is shorn of beauty on that fatal Tree!

All strength, all freshness, is gone forth from Thee: What wonder! Hath not God afflicted Thee, And is not death himself approaching Thee? O Love! But death hath laid his touch on Thee, And faint and broken features turn to me.

O have they thus maltreated Thee, my own? O have they Thy sweet Face despised, my own? And all for my unworthy sake, my own! O in Thy beauty turn to me, my own; O turn one look of love on me, my own!

In this Thy Passion, Lord, remember me; In this Thy pain, O Love, acknowledge me; The honey of whose lips was shed on me, The milk of whose delights hath strengthened me Whose sweetness is beyond delight for me!

Despise me not, O Love; I long for Thee; Contemn me not, unworthy though I be; But now that death is fast approaching Thee, Incline Thy Head, my Love, my Love, to me, To these poor arms, and let it rest on me!

The holy Passion I would share with Thee, And in Thy dying love rejoice with Thee; Content if by this Cross I die with Thee; Content, Thou knowest, Lord, how willingly Where I have lived to die for love of Thee.

For this Thy bitter death all thanks to Thee, Dear Jesus, and Thy wondrous love for me! O gracious God, so merciful to me, Do as Thy guilty one entreateth Thee, And at the end let me be found with Thee!

When from this life, O Love, Thou callest me, Then, Jesus, be not wanting unto me, But in the dreadful hour of agony, O hasten, Lord, and be Thou nigh to me, Defend, protect, and O deliver me.

When Thou, O God, shalt bid my soul be free, Then, dearest Jesus, show Thyself to me! O condescend to show Thyself to me, – Upon Thy saving Cross, dear Lord, to me, – And let me die, my Lord, embracing Thee!

TO THE SACRED HEART

Hail, sacred Heart of God's great Majesty! Hail, sweetest Heart, my heart saluteth Thee! With great desire, O Heart, I seek for Thee, And faint for joy, O Heart, embracing Thee; Then give me leave, O Love, to speak to Thee.

With what sweet love Thou languishedst for me! What pain and torment was that love to Thee! How didst Thou all Thyself exhaust for me! How hast Thou wholly given Thyself to me, That death no longer might have hold of me!

O bitter death and cruel! Can it be Thou darest so to enter greedily Into that cell divine? O can it be The Life of life, that lives there gloriously, Should feel thy bite, O death, and yield to thee?

For Thy death's sake which Thou didst bear for me, When Thou, O sweetest Heart, didst faint for me, O Heart most precious in its agony, See how I yearn, and longing turn to Thee! Yield to my love, and draw me unto Thee!

O sacred Heart, beloved most tenderly, Cleanse Thou my own; more worthy let it be, All hardened as it is with vanity; O make it tender, loving, fearing Thee, And all its icy coldness drive from me.

O sinner as I am, I come to Thee; My very vitals throb and call for Thee; O Love, sweet love, draw hither unto me! O Heart of Love, my heart would ravished be, And sicken with the wound of love for Thee!

Dilate and open, Heart of love, for me, And like a rose of wondrous fragrance be, Sweet Heart of love, united unto me; Anoint and pierce my heart, O Love, with Thee, How can he suffer, Lord, who loveth Thee?

O Heart of Love, who vanquished is by Thee Knows nothing, but beside himself must be; No bounds are set to that sweet liberty, No moderation, – he must fly to Thee, Or die he must of many deaths for Thee.

My living heart, O Love, cries out for Thee; With all its strength, O Love, my soul loves Thee; O Heart of Love, incline Thou unto me, That I with burning love may turn to Thee, And with devoted breast recline on Thee!

In that sweet furnace let me live for Thee, Nor let the sleep of sloth encumber me; O let me sing to Thee and weep to Thee, Adore, and magnify, and honor Thee, And always take my full delight in Thee.

Thou Rose of wondrous fragrance, open wide, And bring my heart into Thy wounded Side, O sweet heart, open! Draw Thy loving bride, All panting with desires intensified, And satisfy her love unsatisfied.

Unite my heart, O Jesus, unto Thine, And let Thy wounded love be found in mine. Ah, if my heart, dear love, be made like Thine O will it not be pierced with darts divine, the sweet reproach of love that thrills through Thine?

O Jesus, draw my heart within Thy Breast, That it may be by Thee alone possessed. O Love, in that sweet pain it would find rest, In that entrancing sorrow would be blest, And love itself in joy upon Thy Breast.

Behold, O Jesus, how it draws to Thee! O call it, that it may remain in Thee! See with what large desire it thirsts for Thee! Reprove it not, O Love; it loves but Thee: Then bid it live – by one sweet taste of Thee!

Bernard of Clairvaux, 1090–1153, Rhythmical Prayer to the Sacred Members of Jesus Hanging on the Cross

Monday of Holy Week

Grant, we beseech you, Almighty God, that we, who amid so many adversities do fail through our own infirmities, may be restored through the Passion and Intercession of your Only-begotten Son, Who lives and reigns, with you and the Holy Ghost, ever One God, world without end. Amen.

The Common Service Book of the Lutheran Church, 1917

Wednesday of Holy Week

Grant, we beseech you, Almighty God, that we, who for our evil deeds are continually afflicted, may mercifully be relieved by the Passion of your Only-begotten Son, Who lives and reigns with you and the Holy Ghost, ever One God, world without end. Amen.

The Common Service Book of the Lutheran Church, 1917

O Sacred Head surrounded
By Crown of piercing thorn!
O bleeding Head, so wounded,
Reviled and put to scorn!
Death's pallid hue comes o'er Thee,
The glow of life decays,
Yet angel hosts adore Thee
And tremble as they gaze.

I see Thy strength and vigor
All fading in the strife,
And death, with cruel rigor,
Bereaving Thee of life;
O agony and dying!
O love to sinners free!
Jesus, all grace supplying,
O turn Thy face on me!

In this Thy bitter Passion,
Good Shepherd, think of me,
With Thy most sweet compassion,
Unworthy though I be;
Beneath Thy Cross abiding,
Forever would I rest,
In Thy dear love confiding,
And with Thy presence blest.

Bernard of Clairvaux, 1090–1153

O Jesus Christ! Eternal Sweetness to those who love Thee, joy surpassing all joy and all desire, Salvation and Hope of all sinners, Who hast proved that Thou hast no greater desire than to be among men, even assuming human nature at the fullness of time for the love of men, recall all the sufferings Thou hast endured from the instant of Thy conception, and especially during Thy Passion, as it Was decreed and ordained from all eternity in the Divine plan.

Remember, O Lord, that during the Last Supper with Thy disciples, having washed their feet, Thou gavest them Thy Most Precious Body and Blood, and while at the same time Thou didst sweetly console them, Thou didst foretell them Thy coming Passion.

Remember the sadness and bitterness which Thou didst experience in Thy Soul as Thou Thyself bore witness saying: "My Soul is sorrowful even unto death."

Remember all the fear, anguish and pain that Thou didst suffer in Thy delicate Body before the torment of the Crucifixion, when,

after having prayed three times, bathed in a sweat of blood, Thou wast betrayed by Judas, Thy disciple, arrested by the people of a nation Thou hadst chosen and elevated, accused by false witnesses, unjustly judged by three judges during the flower of Thy youth and during the solemn Paschal season.

Remember that Thou wast despoiled of Thy garments and clothed in those of derision; that Thy Face and Eyes were veiled, that Thou wast buffeted, crowned with thorns a reed placed in Thy Hands, that Thou was crushed with blows and overwhelmed with affronts and outrages.

In memory of all these pains and sufferings which Thou didst endure before Thy Passion on the Cross, grant me before my death true contrition, a sincere and entire confession, worthy satisfaction and the remission of all my sins. Amen

My sweet Lord Jesus Christ, have mercy on me, a sinner.

Jesus, son of God, born of the Virgin Mary, crucified to save mankind, reigning now in Heaven, have mercy on us.

Bridget of Sweden, 1303–73

Almighty and Everlasting God, Who have sent your Son, our Savior Jesus Christ, to take upon Him our flesh, and to suffer death upon the Cross, that all mankind should follow the example of His great humility: Mercifully grant that we may both follow the example of His patience, and also be made partakers of His resurrection; through the same Jesus Christ, your Son, our Lord, Who lives and reigns with and the Holy Ghost, ever One God, world without end. Amen.

*The Common Service Book of
the Lutheran Church, 1917*

Christ's cross over this face, and thus over my ear. Christ's cross over this eye. Christ's cross over this nose.

Christ's cross to accompany me before. Christ's cross to accompany me behind me. Christ's cross to meet every difficulty both on hollow and hill.

Christ's cross eastwards facing me. Christ's cross back towards the sunset. In the north, in the south, increasingly may Christ's cross straightway be.

Christ's cross up to broad Heaven. Christ's cross down to earth. Let no evil or hurt come to my body or my soul.

Christ's cross over me as I sit. Christ's cross over me as I lie. Christ's cross be all my strength until we reach the King of Heaven.

From the top of my head to the nail of my foot, O Christ, against every danger I trust in the protection of the cross.

Till the day of my death, going into this clay, I shall draw without – Christ's cross over this face.

Celtic prayer

"Take up your cross," the Savior said,
"If you would my disciple be;
Deny yourself, forsake the world,
And humbly follow after me."

Take up your cross – let not its weight
Fill your weak spirit with alarm;
His strength shall bear your spirit up,
And brace your heart, and nerve your arm.

Take up your cross, nor heed the shame
Nor let your foolish pride rebel;
Your Lord for you the cross endured
To save your soul from death and hell.

Take up your cross, then, in his strength,
And calmly every danger brave;
He'll guide us to a better home,
And lead to victory o'er the grave.

Take up your cross and follow Christ
Nor think till death to lay it down;
For only they who bear the cross
May hope to win the glorious crown.

To you, great Lord, the One in Three,
All praise for evermore ascend;
And grant us in our rest to see
The heavenly life that knows no end.

C.W. Everest, 1814–77

Restorer of the universe, who clothed us with your glorious light, on whom the soldiers spread the crimson mantle of reproach; remove from me the rags of sin stained with the horrible blood and clothe me anew with my former robe.

They bent the knee mocking you, heavenly King, they inflicted blows on your crowned head and hit you with the reed, and so did I stoop down to earth, obeying the will of the evil one. Let me not become the object of his game but lift me up again.

The mob surrounded you physically following the verdict of the judge, and you received blows on your skull for the sake of the skull of the first-born man. By virtue of the baptismal font restore me to health, the one needlessly afflicted from head to toe.

In lieu of the sacred and shining ornament which you placed on Aaron's head, the tillers of Israel's vineyard placed a crown of thorns on you. Take away from me the thorn of sin with which the enemy has inflicted me, and heal the lacerated wound so that the scars of sin may be eradicated.

They gave you the gall to drink, the vinegar to the thirsty. You drank of it willingly, so that the fruits of bitterness might become sweet. Take away the bitterness of the venom which has been injected in the recesses of my soul and thus may your love be sweetened therein.

In lieu of the tree that ushered in death, once planted in paradise, you lifted the wood of the Cross, raising it on Golgotha. Lift up my soul submerged in sin, O Lifter of the heaviest burden, as you lifted up the sheep upon your shoulder. Take my soul up from earth to its promised place.

At the third hour on Friday you, Lord, were nailed to the Cross, loosening the shackles of the first-born man and binding the enemy. Strengthen me beneath the shadow of your life-giving Sign and enlighten me with its light from the rising of the sun.

The gates of the Edenic paradise were opened to the blessed thief, his petition being granted according to his faith. Grant me also, Lord, with him to hear the same response: "Today you shall be with me in Eden, your first homeland."

Nerses the Gracious, 1102–73. In Armenian, the initial letters of this hymn form an acrostic spelling of the author's name (Nerses)

O Jesus, Who in Thy cruel Passion didst become the "Reproach of men and the Man of Sorrows," I worship Thy Divine Face. Once it shone with the beauty and sweetness of the Divinity: now for my sake it is become as the face of a leper. Yet in that disfigured Countenance I recognize Thy infinite Love, and I am consumed with the desire of loving Thee and of making Thee loved by all mankind. The tears that streamed in such abundance from Thy Eyes are to me as precious pearls which I delight to gather, that with their infinite worth I may ransom the souls of poor sinners.

Thérèse of Lisieux, 1873–97

You did undertake for me,
    For me to death were sold;
Wisdom in a mystery
    Of dying love unfold;
Teach the lesson of your cross,
Let me die with you to reign;
All things let me count but loss,
That you, I may regain.

Charles Wesley, 1707–88

MAUNDY THURSDAY

Lord Jesus Christ, who when thou wast able to institute thy holy sacrament at the Last Supper, didst wash the feet of the apostles, and teach us by thy example the grace of humility: cleanse us, we beseech thee, from all stain of sin, that we may be worthy partakers of thy holy mysteries; who livest and reignest with the Father and the Holy Ghost, one God, world without end.

Office of the Royal Maundy in Westminster Abbey

GOOD FRIDAY

My God, my God, why have you forsaken me?
    Why are you so far from helping me,
        from the words of my groaning?
O my God, I cry by day, but you do not answer;
    and by night, but find no rest.
Yet you are holy,
    enthroned on the praises of Israel.
In you our ancestors trusted;
    they trusted, and you delivered them.
To you they cried, and were saved;
    in you they trusted, and were not put to
        shame.
But I am a worm, and not human;

scorned by others, and despised by the
    people.
All who see me mock at me;
    they make mouths at me, they shake
        their heads;
'Commit your cause to the Lord; let him
    deliver-
        let him rescue the one in whom he
            delights!'
Yet it was you who took me from the womb;
    you kept me safe on my mother's
        breast.
On you I was cast from my birth,
    and since my mother bore me you have
        been my God.
Do not be far from me,
    for trouble is near
    and there no one to help.

Psalm 22.1–11 NRSV

Lord, you go alone to your sacrifice. You offer yourself to death, whom you have come to destroy. What can we miserable sinners plead, who know that for the deeds that we have done you do atone? Ours is the guilt, Lord. Why then must you suffer torture for our sins? Make our hearts so to share in your passion, that our fellow-suffering may invite your mercy. This is that night of tears, and the three days of sadness, until the day dawns with the risen Christ, bringing joy to those who mourn. May we so suffer with you, Lord, that we make take part in y our glory, so that our three days of mourning passes away and becomes your Easter joy.

Peter Abelard, 1079–1142

There is a green hill far away
Outside a city wall,
Where the dear Lord was crucified,
Who died to save us all.

We may not know, we cannot tell
What pains he had to bear;
But we believe it was for us
He hung and suffered there.

C.F. Alexander, 1823–95

O Lord, who thy dear life didst give
    For us in narrow grave to lie,
Teach us to die that we may live,

To live that we may never die.

C.F. Alexander, 1823–95

Lord Jesus Christ, who for the redemption of the world ascended the wood of the cross, and the whole world was turned into darkness, grant us always that light, both in body and soul, whereby we may attain to everlasting life; who with the Father and the Holy Spirit live and reign, one God, world without end.

Ambrosian Manual

Dying, let me still abide
Jesu, grant me this, I pray,
Ever in thy heart to stay;
Let me evermore abide
Hidden in thy wounded side.

If the evil one prepare,
Or the world, a tempting snare,
I am safe when I abide
In thy heart and wounded side.

If the flesh, more dangerous still,
Tempt my soul to deeds of ill,
Naught I fear when I abide
In thy heart and wounded side.

Death will come one day to me;
Jesu, cast me not from thee:
Dying let me still abide
In thy heart and wounded side.

Latin, 17th century, translated by
H.W. Baker, 1821–77

Fence me about, O Lord, with the power of your honorable and life-giving cross, and preserve me from every evil.

Source unknown, Eastern Orthodox

Jesus, poor and abject, unknown and despised, have mercy upon me, and let me not be ashamed to follow thee.

O Jesus, hated, calumniated, and persecuted, have mercy upon me, and make me content to be as my master.

O Jesus, blasphemed, accused, and wrongfully condemned, have mercy upon me, and teach me to endure the contradiction of sinners.

O Jesus, clothed with a habit of reproach and shame, have mercy upon me, and let me not seek my own glory.

O Jesus, insulted, mocked, and spit upon, have mercy upon me, and let me not faint in the fiery trial.

O Jesus, crowned with thorns and hailed in derision;

O Jesus, burdened with our sins and the curses of the people;

O Jesus, affronted, outraged, buffeted, overwhelmed with injuries, griefs and humiliations;

O Jesus, hanging on the accursed tree, bowing the head, giving up the ghost, have mercy upon me, and conform my whole soul to be thy holy, humble, suffering Spirit.

Author unknown

Litany of the Passion

Lord, have mercy on us.
Christ, have mercy on us.
Lord, have mercy on us.
Christ, hear us. Christ, graciously hear us.

God, the Father of heaven,[1]
God, the Son, Redeemer of the world,
God, the Holy Ghost,
Holy Trinity, one God,
Jesus, the Eternal Wisdom,
Jesus, sold for thirty pieces of silver,
Jesus, prostrate on the ground in prayer,
Jesus, strengthened by an angel,
Jesus, in Thine agony bathed in a bloody sweat,
Jesus, betrayed by Judas with a kiss,
Jesus, bound by the soldiers,
Jesus, forsaken by your disciples,

Jesus, brought before Annas and Caiphas.[1]
Jesus, struck in the face by a servant,
Jesus, accused by false witnesses,
Jesus, declared guilty of death,
Jesus, spat upon,
Jesus, blindfolded,
Jesus, smitten on the cheek,
Jesus, thrice denied by Peter,
Jesus, delivered up to Pilate,
Jesus, despised and mocked by Herod,
Jesus, clothed in a white garment,
Jesus, rejected for Barabbas,
Jesus, torn with scourges,
Jesus, bruised for our sin,

Jesus, esteemed a leper,
Jesus, covered with a purple robe,
Jesus, crowned with thorns
Jesus, struck with a reed upon the head,
Jesus, demanded for crucifixion by the Jews,
Jesus, condemned to an ignominious death,
Jesus, given up to the will of Thine enemies,
Jesus, loaded with the heavy weight of the cross,
Jesus, led like a sheep to the slaughter,
Jesus, stripped of your garments,
Jesus, fastened with nails to the cross,
Jesus, reviled by the malefactors,
Jesus, promising paradise to the penitent thief,
Jesus, commending St. John to your Mother
    as her son,
Jesus, declaring yourself forsaken by your
    Father,
Jesus, in your thirst given gall and vinegar to
    drink,
Jesus, testifying that all things written
    concerning Thee were accomplished,
Jesus, commending your spirit into the hand
    of your Father,[1]
Jesus, obedient even to the death of the cross,
Jesus, pierced with a lace,
Jesus, made a propitiation for us,
Jesus, taken down from the cross,
Jesus, laid in the sepulcher,
Jesus, rising gloriously from the dead,
Jesus, ascending into heaven,
Jesus, our advocate with the Father,
Jesus, sending down on your disciples the
    Holy Ghost, the Paraclete,
Jesus, exalting your Mother above the choirs
    of angels,
Jesus, Who shalt come to judge the living and
    the dead,
Be merciful, Spare us, O Lord.
Be merciful, Graciously hear us, O Lord.
From all evil,
From all sin,
From anger, hatred, and every evil will,
From war, famine, and pestilence,
From all dangers of mind and body,
From everlasting death,
Through your most pure conception,
Through your miraculous nativity,
Through your humble circumcision
Through your baptism and holy fasting,
Through your labors and watchings,
Through your cruel scourging and crowning,

Through your thirst, and tears, and nakedness,
Through your precious death and cross,
Through your glorious resurrection and
    ascension,
Through your sending forth the Holy Ghost,
    the Paraclete,[2]
In the day of judgment,
We sinners beseech Thee, hear us.

That Thou would spare us,[3]
That Thou would pardon us,
That Thou would vouchsafe to bring us to
    true penance,
That Thou would vouchsafe mercifully to
    pour into our hearts the grace of the Holy
    Spirit,
That Thou would vouchsafe to defend and
    propagate your holy Church,
That Thou would vouchsafe to preserve and
    increase all societies assembled in your
    holy name,
That Thou would vouchsafe to bestow upon
    us true peace,
That Thou would vouchsafe to give us
    perseverance in grace and in your holy
    service,
That Thou would vouchsafe to deliver us from
    unclean thoughts, the temptations of the
    devil, and everlasting damnation,
That Thou would vouchsafe to unite us to the
    company of your saints,
That Thou would vouchsafe graciously to hear
    us,
Lamb of God, Who takest away the sins of the
    world, Spare us, O Lord.
Lamb of God, Who takes away the sins of the
    world, Graciously hear us, O Lord.
Lamb of God, Who takes away the sins of the
    world, Have mercy on us, O Lord.
Christ, hear us; Christ, graciously hear us.

V. We adore Thee, O Christ, and praise Thee:
R. Because by your holy cross Thou hast
    redeemed the world

Let us Pray
Almighty and eternal God, Who hast appointed Thine only-begotten Son the Savior of the
world, and hast willed to be appeased with
His blood, grant that we may so venerate this
price of our salvation, and by its might be so

defended upon earth from the evils of this present life, that in heaven we may rejoice in its everlasting fruit. Who lives and reigns with Thee in the unity of the Holy Ghost, world without end. Amen.

Responses:
1 Have mercy on us.
2 Lord Jesus, deliver us.
3 We beseech Thee, hear us.
Source unknown, Litany of the Passion

Man of Sorrows! what a name
For the Son of God, Who came
Ruined sinners to reclaim.
Hallelujah! What a Savior!

Bearing shame and scoffing rude,
In my place condemned He stood;
Sealed my pardon with His blood.
Hallelujah! What a Savior!

Guilty, vile, and helpless we;
Spotless Lamb of God was He;
"Full atonement!" can it be?
Hallelujah! What a Savior!

Lifted up was He to die;
"It is finished!" was His cry;
Now in heav'n exalted high.
Hallelujah! What a Savior!

When He comes, our glorious King,
All His ransomed home to bring,
Then anew His song we'll sing:
Hallelujah! What a Savior!
Philip Paul Bliss, 1838–76

Fifteen prayers of Bridget
1st Prayer
O Jesus! You have proved that You have no greater desire than to be among men, even assuming human nature at the fullness of time for the love of men. I recall all the sufferings of Your life especially Your Passion.

I remember, O Lord, that during the Last Supper with Your disciples, having washed their feet, You gave them Your Most Precious Body and Blood, and, while consoling them You foretold Your coming Passion.

I remember the sadness and bitterness which You experienced in Your Soul as You said, My Soul is sorrowful even unto death.

I remember all the fear, anguish and pain that You did suffer in Your delicate Body before the torment of the Crucifixion, when, after having prayed three times, bathed in a sweat of blood, You were betrayed by Judas, arrested by the people of a nation You had chosen and elevated, accused by false witnesses and unjustly judged by three judges.

I remember that You were despoiled of Your garments and clothed in those of derision, that Your Face and Eyes were covered, that You were beaten, crowned with thorns, a reed placed in Your Hands, that You were crushed with blows and overwhelmed with insults and outrages. In memory of all these pains and sufferings which You endured before Your Passion on the Cross, grant me before my death a true contrition, a sincere and entire confession, worthy satisfaction and the remission of all my sins. Amen.

2nd Prayer
O Jesus! I remember the horror and sadness which You endured when Your enemies surrounded You, and by thousands of insults, spits, blows, lacerations and other unheard-of cruelties tormented You. In consideration of these torments and insulting words, I beg You to deliver me from all my enemies, visible and invisible, and to bring me, under Your protection, to the perfection of eternal salvation. Amen.

3rd Prayer
O Jesus! I remember the very bitter pain You did suffer when the executioners nailed Your Sacred Hands and Feet to the Cross by blow after blow with big blunt nails, and, not finding You in a sad enough state, to satisfy their cruelty they enlarged Your Wounds, and added pain to pain, stretching Your Body on the Cross and dislocated Your Bones by pulling Them on all sides. I beg of You by the memory of this most loving suffering of the Cross to grant me the grace to love You. Amen.

4th Prayer
O Jesus! I Remember the bruises You suffered and the weakness of Your Body, which was distended to such a degree that never was there

pain like Yours. From the crown of Your Head to the soles of Your Feet there was not one spot on Your Body which was not in torment. Yet, for getting all Your sufferings, You did not cease to pray to Your Heavenly Father for Your enemies, saying: Father, forgive them, for they know not what they do.

Through this great mercy and in memory of this suffering, grant that the remembrance of Your most bitter Passion may effect in us a perfect contrition and the remission of all our sins. Amen.

5th Prayer

O Jesus! I remember the sadness which You experienced when, foreseeing those who would be damned for their sins, You suffered bitterly over these hopeless, lost and unfortunate sinners.

Through this abyss of compassion and pity and especially through the goodness which You displayed to the good thief when You said to him, This day you will be with Me in Paradise, I beg of You that at the hour of my death to show me mercy. Amen.

6th Prayer

O Jesus! I remember the grief which You suffered when, like a common criminal, You were raised and fastened to the Cross, when all Your relatives and friends abandoned You, except Your Beloved Mother who remained close to You during Your agony and Whom You entrusted to Your faithful disciple when You said,

Woman, behold Your son. Son behold your Mother.

I beg You by the sword of sorrow which pierced the soul of Your Holy Mother, to have compassion on me in all my afflictions and tribulations, both of body and spirit, and to assist me in all my trials and especially at the hour of my death. Amen.

7th Prayer

O Jesus! I remember Your profound gesture of love from the Cross when You said, I thirst, and Your suffering from the thirst for the salvation of the human race. I beg You to inflame in our hearts the desire to tend toward perfection in all our actions and to extinguish in us all worldly desires. Amen.

8th Prayer

O Jesus! I remember the bitterness of the gall and vinegar which You tasted on the Cross for love of us. Grant us the grace to receive worthily Your Precious Body and Blood during our life and at the hour of our death that It may be a remedy of consolation for our souls. Amen.

9th Prayer

O Jesus! I remember the pain You endured when, immersed in an ocean of bitterness at the approach of death, insulted, outraged by the people, You cried out in a loud voice that You were abandoned by Your Father, saying: My God, My God, why have You forsaken Me? Through this anguish I beg You not to abandon me in the terrors and pains of my death. Amen.

10th Prayer

O Jesus! I remember that for our sakes You were immersed into an abyss of suffering. In consideration of the enormity of Your Wounds, teach me to keep, through pure love, Your Commandments, which are a wide and easy path for those who love You. Amen.

11th Prayer

O Jesus! I remember Your Wounds which penetrated to the very marrow of Your Bones and to the depth of Your Being. Draw me away from sin and hide me in Your Wounds. Amen.

12th Prayer

O Jesus! I remember the multitude of Wounds which afflicted You from Head to Foot, torn and reddened by the spilling of Your Precious Blood. O great and universal pain which You suffered in Your Flesh for love of us! What is there You could have done for us which You have not done?

May the fruit of Your sufferings be renewed in my soul by the faithful remembrance of Your Passion and may Your love increase in my heart each day until I see You in eternity, You Who are the treasury of every real good and joy, which I beg You to grant me in Heaven. Amen.

13th Prayer

O Jesus! I remember the pain You endured when all Your strength, both moral and physical, was entirely exhausted; You bowed Your Head, saying: It is consummated.

Through this anguish and grief, I beg You to have mercy on me at the hour of my death, when my mind will be greatly troubled and my soul will be in anguish. Amen.

14th Prayer

O Jesus! I remember the simple and humble recommendation You made of Your Soul to Your Eternal Father, saying, "Father, into Your Hands I commend My Spirit," and when, Your Body all torn and Your Heart broken, You expired. By this precious death, I beg You to comfort me and give me help to resist the devil, the flesh and the world, so that, being dead to the world, I may live for You alone. I beg of You at the hour of my death to receive me. Amen.

15th Prayer

O Jesus! I remember the abundant outpouring of Blood which You shed. From Your Side, pierced with a lance by a soldier, Blood and Water poured forth until there was not left in Your Body a single Drop; and finally the very substance of Your Body withered and the marrow of Your Bones dried up.

Through this bitter Passion and through the outpouring of Your Precious Blood, I beg You to pierce my heart so that my tears of penance and love may be my bread day and night. May I be entirely converted to You; may my heart be Your perpetual resting place; may my conversation be pleasing to You; and may the end of my life be so praiseworthy that I may merit Heaven and there with Your saints praise You forever. Amen.

Bridget, c.460–c.528

Almighty God, we beseech you graciously to behold this your family, for which our Lord Jesus Christ was contented to be betrayed, and given up into the hands of wicked men, and to suffer death upon the Cross; through the same Jesus Christ, your Son, our Lord, Who lives and reigns with you and the Holy Ghost, ever One God, world without end. Amen.

*The Common Service Book of
the Lutheran Church, 1917*

Merciful and everlasting God, who has not spared your only Son, but delivered Him up for us all, that He might bear our sins upon the Cross: Grant that our hearts may be so fixed with steadfast faith in Him that we may not fear the power of any adversaries; through the same Jesus Christ, your Son, our Lord. Amen.

*The Common Service Book of
the Lutheran Church, 1917*

Almighty and everlasting God who has willed that your Son should bear for us the pains of the Cross that you might remove from us the power of the adversary, [the Devil]: Help us so remember and give thanks for our Lord's Passion that we may obtain remission of sin and redemption from everlasting death; through the same Jesus Christ, your Son, our Lord. Amen.

*The Common Service Book of
the Lutheran Church, 1917*

Lord, by this sweet and saving sign,
Defend us from our foes and thine.

Jesus, by thy wounded feet,
    Direct our path aright:
Jesus, by thy nailed hands,
    Move ours to deeds of love:
Jesus, by thy pierced side,
    Cleanse our desires:
Jesus, by thy crown of thorns,
    Annihilate our pride:
Jesus, by thy silence,
    Shame our complaints:
Jesus, by thy parched lips,
    Curb our cruel speech:
Jesus, by thy closing eyes,
    Look on our sin no more:
Jesus, by thy broken heart,
    Knit ours to thee.

And by this sweet and saving sign,
Lord, draw us to our peace and thine.

Richard Crashaw, 1613–49

My song is love unknown,
My Savior's love to me,
Love to the loveless shown,
That they might lovely be.
O, who am I,

That for my sake
My Lord should take
Frail flesh, and die?

He came from his blest throne,
Salvation to bestow:
But men made strange, and none
The longed-for Christ would know.
But O, my Friend,
My Friend indeed,
Who at my need
His life did spend!

Sometimes they strew his way,
and his sweet praises sing;
Resounding all the day
hosannas to their King;
Then 'Crucify!'
is all their breath,
And for his death
they thirst and cry.

Why, what hath my Lord done?
What makes this rage and spite?
He made the lame to run,
he gave the blind their sight.
Sweet injuries!
Yet they at these
Themselves displease,
and 'gainst him rise.

They rise, and needs will have
my dear Lord made away;
A murderer they save,
the Prince of Life they slay.
Yet cheerful he to suffering goes,
That he his foes
from thence might free.

Sometimes they strew his way,
and his sweet praises sing;
Resounding all the day
hosannas to their King;
Then 'Crucify!'
is all their breath,
And for his death
they thirst and cry.

Why, what hath my Lord done?
What makes this rage and spite?
He made the lame to run,

he gave the blind their sight.
Sweet injuries!
Yet they at these
Themselves displease,
and 'gainst him rise.

They rise, and needs will have
my dear Lord made away;
A murderer they save,
the Prince of Life they slay.
Yet cheerful he to suffering goes,
That he his foes
from thence might free.

Here might I stay and sing,
No story so divine;
Never was love, dear King,
Never was grief like thine!
This is my Friend,
In whose sweet praise
I all my days
Could gladly spend.

Samuel Crossman, c.1624–83

The Cross

The Cross, my seal in baptism, spread below
Doth by that form into an anchor grow,
Crosses grow anchors, bear as thou should'st
    do
Thy cross, and that cross grows an anchor too.
But he that makes our crosses anchors thus
Is Christ, Who there is crucified for us.

*John Donne, 1572–1631. John Donne wrote these
words to go with a signet ring that he gave to Isaak
Walton. On the ring was an engraving of Christ
crucified with the cross in the shape of an anchor*

The Dream of the Rood

Hear while I tell about the best of dreams
Which came to me the middle of one night
While humankind were sleeping in their beds.
It was as though I saw a wondrous tree
Towering in the sky suffused with light...
... the best
Of woods began to speak these words to me:
'It was long past – I still remember it -
That I was cut down at the copse's end,
Moved from my roots. Strong enemies there
    took me,
Told me to hold aloft their criminals,
Made me a spectacle. Men carried me

Upon their shoulders, set me on a hill,
A host of enemies there fastened me.
And then I saw the Lord of all mankind
Hasten with eager zeal that He might mount
Upon me. I durst not against God's word
Bend down or break, when I saw tremble all
The surface of the earth. Although I might
Have struck down all the foes, yet stood I fast.
Then the young hero (who was God almighty)
Got ready, resolute and strong in heart.
He climbed onto the lofty gallows-tree,
Bold in the sight of many watching men,
When he intended to redeem mankind.
I trembled as the warrior embraced me.
But still I dared not bend down to the earth,
Fall to the ground. Upright I had to stand.
A rood I was raised up; and I held high
The noble King, the Lord of heaven above.
I dared not stoop. They pierced me with dark
    nails;
The scars can still be clearly seen on me,
The open wounds of malice. Yet might I
Not harm them. They reviled us both
    together.
I was made wet all over with the blood
Which poured out from His side, after He had
Sent forth His spirit. And I underwent
Full many a dire experience on that hill.
I saw the God of hosts stretched grimly out.
Darkness covered the Ruler's corpse with
    clouds,
His shining beauty; the shadows passed
    across,
Black in the darkness. All creation wept,
Bewailed the King's death; Christ was on the
    cross.
And yet I saw men coming from afar,
Hastening to the Prince. I watched it all.'

Author unknown. 8th-century poem and
meditation on the death of Christ presented
from the point of view of the rood (or cross) on
which Christ was crucified

I give you glory, O Christ, because you, the
    Only-begotten, the Lord of all, underwent
    the death of the Cross to free my sinful
    soul from the bonds of sin. What shall I
    give to you, O Lord, in return for all this
    kindness?
Glory to you, O Lord, for your love, for your
    mercy, for your patience.

Glory to you, for forgiving us all our sins,
    for coming to save our souls, for your
    incarnation in the Virgin's womb.
Glory to you, for your bonds, for receiving the
    cut of the lash, for accepting mockery.
Glory to you, for your crucifixion, for your
    burial, for your resurrection.
Glory to you, for your resurrection, for being
    preached to men, for being taken up
    heaven.
Glory to you who sit at the Father's right hand
    and will return in glory.
Glory to you for willing that the sinner be
    saved through your great mercy and
    compassion.

Ephraem, c.306–378

O Lord, you received affronts without number
    from your blasphemers, yet each day you
    free captive souls from the grip of the
    ancient enemy.
You did not avert your face from the spittle
    of perfidy, yet you wash souls in saving
    waters.
You accepted your scourging without
    murmur, yet through your meditation you
    deliver us from endless chastisements.
You endured ill-treatment of all kinds, yet
    you want to give us a share in the choirs of
    angels in glory everlasting.
You did not refuse to be crowned with thorns,
    yet you save us from the wounds of sin.
In your thirst you accepted the bitterness of
    gall, yet you prepare yourself to fill us with
    eternal delights.
You kept silence under the derisive homage
    rendered you by your executioners, yet you
    petition the Father for us although you are
    his equal in divinity.
You came to taste death, yet you were the
    Life and had come to bring it to the dead.
    Amen.

Gregory I, c.540–604

The death of Christ
O my chief good,
How shall I measure out thy blood?
How shall I count what thee befell,
    And each grief tell?

Shall I thy woes
Number according to thy foes?
Or, since one star show'd thy first breath,
    Shall all thy death?

    Or shall each leaf
Which falls in Autumn, score a grief?
Or cannot leaves, but fruit, be signe
    Of the true vine?

    Then let each hour
Of my whole life one grief devour;
That thy distress through all may run,
    And be my sun.

    Or rather let
My several sins their sorrows get;
That, as each beast his cure doth know,
    Each sin may so....
                    George Herbert, 1593–1633, The Temple

The Sacrifice

O all ye, who pass by, whose eyes and mind
To worldly thing are sharp, but to be blind;
To me, who took eyes that I might find you:
Was ever grief like mine?

...Mine own Apostle, who the bag did bear,
Though he had all I had, did not forbear
To sell me also, and to put me there:
Was ever grief like mine?

For thirty pence he did my death devise,
Who at three hundred did the ointment prize,
Not half so sweet as my sweet sacrifice:
Was ever grief like mine?

Therefore my soul melts, and my heart's dear
    treasure
Drops blood (the only beads) my words to
    measure:
"O let this cup pass, if it be thy pleasure:"
Was ever grief like mine?

These drops being temper'd with a sinner's
    tears,
A balsam are for both the Hemispheres,
Curing all wounds, but mine; all, but my fears:
Was ever grief like mine?

... Arise, arise, they come! Look how they run!

Alas! what haste they make to be undone!
How with their lanterns do they seek the sun:
Was ever grief like mine?

With clubs and staves they seek me, as a thief,
Who am the way of truth, the true relief,
Most true to those who are my greatest grief:
Was ever grief like mine?

Judas, dost thou betray me with a kiss?
Canst thou find hell about my lips? and miss
Of life, just at the gates of life and bliss?
Was ever grief like mine?

See, they lay hold on me, not with the hands
Of faith, but fury; yet at their commands
I suffer binding, who have loosed their bands:
Was ever grief like mine?

All my disciples fly, fear puts a bar
Betwixt my friends and me. They leave the
    star,
That brought the wise men of the East from
    far:
Was ever grief like mine?

...They bind, and lead me unto Herod: he
Sends me to Pilate. This makes them agree;
But yet friendship is my enmity:
Was ever grief like mine?

Herod and all his bands do set me light,
Who teach all hands to war, fingers to fight,
And only am the Lord of hosts and might:
Was ever grief like mine?

Herod in judgment sits, while I do stand;
Examines me with a censorious hand:
I him obey, who all things else command:
Was ever grief like mine?

The Jews accuse me with despitefulness;
And vying malice with my gentleness,
Pick quarrels with their only happiness:
Was ever grief like mine?

I answer nothing, but with patience prove
If stony hearts will melt with gentle love.
But who does hawk at eagles with a dove?
Was ever grief like mine?

...Hark how they cry aloud still, "Crucify:
It is not fit he live a day," they cry,
Who cannot live less than eternally:
Was ever grief like mine?

Pilate a stranger holdeth off; but they,
Mine own dear people, cry, "Away, away,"
With noises confused frighting the day:
Was ever grief like mine?

Yet still they shout, and cry, and stop their ears,
Putting my life among their sins and fears,
And therefore wish "My blood on them and
    theirs:"
Was ever grief like mine?

...They choose a murderer, and all agree
In him to do themselves a courtesy;
For it was their own cause who killed me:
Was ever grief like mine?

And a seditious murderer he was:
But I the Prince of Peace; peace that doth pass
All understanding, more than heaven doth
    glass:
Was ever grief like mine?

...Ah, how they scourge me! yet my
    tenderness
Doubles each lash: and yet their bitterness
Winds up my grief to a mysteriousness:
Was ever grief like mine?

They buffet me, and box me as they list,
Who grasp the earth and heaven with my fist.
And never yet, whom I would punish, miss'd:
Was ever grief like mine?

Behold, they spit on me in scornful wise;
Who with my spittle gave the blind man eyes,
Leaving his blindness to mine enemies:
Was ever grief like mine?

My face they cover, though it be divine.
As Moses' face was veiled, so is mine,
Lest on their double-dark souls either shine:
Was ever grief like mine?

Servants and abjects flout me; they are witty:
"Now prophesy who strikes thee," is their
    ditty.

So they in me deny themselves all pity:
Was ever grief like mine?

And now I am deliver'd unto death,
Which each one calls for so with utmost
    breath,
That he before me well-nigh suffereth:
Was ever grief like mine?

Weep not, dear friends, since I for both have
    wept,
When all my tears were blood, the while you
    slept:
Your tears your own fortunes should be kept:
Was ever grief like mine?

The soldiers lead me to the common hall;
There they deride me, they abuse me all:
Yet for twelve heavenly legions I could call:
Was ever grief like mine?

Then the scarlet robe they me array;
Which shows my blood to be the only way,
And cordial left to repair man's decay:
Was ever grief like mine?

Then on my head a crown of thorns I wear;
For these are all the grapes Zion doth bear,
Though I my vine planted and water'd there:
Was ever grief like mine?

So sits the earth's great curse in Adam's fall
Upon my head; so I remove it all
From th' earth unto my brows, and bear the
    thrall:
Was ever grief like mine?

Then with the reed they gave to me before,
They strike my head, the rock from whence
    all store
Of heavenly blessings issue evermore:
Was ever grief like mine?

They bow their knees to me, and cry, 'Hail, King'
Whatever scoffs or scornfulness can bring,
I am the floor, the sink, where they it fling:
Was ever grief like mine?

Yet since man's scepters are as frail as reeds,
And thorny all their crowns, bloody their
    weeds;

I, who am Truth, turn into truth their deeds:
Was ever grief like mine?

The soldiers also spit upon that face
Which angels did desire to have the grace,
And Prophets once to see, but found no place:
Was ever grief like mine?

Thus trimmed, forth they bring me to the rout,
Who "Crucify him," cry with one strong
   shout.
God holds his peace at man, and man cries
   out:
Was ever grief like mine?

They lead me in once more, and putting then
Mine own clothes on, they lead me out again.
Whom devils fly, thus is he toss'd of men:
Was ever grief like mine?

And now weary of sport, glad to engross
All spite in one, counting my life their loss,
They carried me to my most bitter cross:
Was ever grief like mine?

My cross I bear myself, until I faint:
Then Simon bears it for me by constraint,
The decreed burden of each mortal Saint:
Was ever grief like mine?

"O all ye how pass by, behold and see:"
Man stole the fruit, but I must climb the tree;
The tree of life to all, but only me:
Was ever grief like mine?

Lo, here I hang, charged with a world of sin,
The greater world o' the two; for that came in
By words, but this by sorrow I must win:
Was ever grief like mine?

Such sorrow, as if sinful man could feel,
Or feel his part, he would not cease to kneel,
Till all were melted, though he were all steel:
Was ever grief like mine?

But, "O my God, my God!" why leav'st thou
   me,
The Son, in whom thou dost delight to be?
"My God, my God"
Never was grief like mine?

Shame tears my soul, my body many a wound;
Sharp nails pierce this, but sharper that
   confound;
Reproaches, which are free, while I am bound:
Was ever grief like mine?

Now heal thyself, Physician; now come down.
Alas! I did so, when I left my crown
And Father's smile for you, to feel his frown:
Was ever grief like mine?

In healing not myself, there doth consist
All that salvation, which ye now resist;
Your safety in my sickness doth subsist:
Was ever grief like mine?

Betwixt two thieves I spend my utmost
   breath,
As he that for some robbery suffereth.
Alas! what have I stolen from you? death:
Was ever grief like mine?

A king my title is, prefix'd on high;
Yet by my subjects I'm condemn'd to die
A servile death in servile company:
Was ever grief like mine?

They gave me vinegar mingled with gall,
But more with malice: yet, when they did call,
With Manna, Angels' food, I fed them all:
Was ever grief like mine?

They part my garments, and by lot dispose
My coat, the type of love, which once cured
   those
Who sought for help, never malicious foes:
Was ever grief like mine?

Nay, after death their spite shall farther go;
For they will pierce my side, I full well know;
That as sin came, so Sacraments might flow:
Was ever grief like mine?

But now I die; now all is finished.
My woe, man's weal: and now I bow my head:
Only let others say, when I am dead,
Never was grief like mine.
            George Herbert, 1593–1633, The Sacrifice

Rex Tragicus
Put off thy robe of purple, then go on

To the sad place of execution:
Thine hour is come; and the tormentor stands
Ready, to pierce thy tender feet, and hands.
Long before this, the base, the dull, the rude,
Th' inconstant and unpurged multitude
Yawn for thy coming; some ere this time cry,
How he defers, how loath he is to die!
Amongst this scum, the soldier with his spear,
And that sour fellow, with his vinegar,
His sponge, and stick, do ask why thou dost
    stay?
So do the scurf and bran too: Go thy way,
Thy way, thou guiltless Man, and satisfy
By thine approach, each their beholding eye.
Not as a thief, shalt thou ascend the mount,
But like a person of some high account:
The cross shall be thy stage; and thou shalt
    there
The spacious field have for thy theatre.
Thou art that Roscius, and that marked-out
    man,
That must this day act the tragedian,
To wonder and affrightment: Thou art He,
Whom all the flux of nations comes to see;
Not those poor thieves that act their parts
    with Thee:
Those act without regard, when once a King,
And God, as thou art, comes to suffering.
No, no, this scene from thee takes life and
    sense,
And soul and spirit, plot and excellence.
Then begin, great King! ascend thy throne,
And thence proceed to act thy passion
To such a height, to such a period raised,
As hell, and earth, and heaven may stand
    amazed.
God, and good angels guide thee; and so bless
Thee in thy several parts of bitterness;
That those, who see thee nailed unto the tree,
May (though they scorn Thee) praise and pity
    Thee.
And we (Thy lovers) while we see Thee keep
The laws of action, will both sigh and weep;
And bring our spices, and embalm Thee dead;
That done, we'll see Thee sweetly buried.

Robert Herrick, 1591–1679, Rex Tragicus, or Christ
Going to his Cross. The poet, as he watches the scene
in his imagination, addresses Christ

His Savior's Words, Going to the Cross

Have, have ye no regard, all ye
Who pass this way, to pity me
Who am a man of misery?

A man both bruis'd, and broke, and one
Who suffers not here for mine own
But for my friends' transgression?

Ah! Zion's Daughters, do not fear
The Cross, the Cords, the Nails, the Spear,
The Myrrh, the Gall, the Vinegar,

For Christ, your loving Savior, hath
Drunk up the wine of God's fierce wrath;
Only, there's left a little froth,

Less for to taste, than for to shew
What bitter cups had been your due,
Had He not drank them up for you.

Robert Herrick, 1591–1679

It is a thing most wonderful,
Almost too wonderful to be,
That God's own Son should come from
    heaven,
And die to save a child like me.

And yet I know that it is true:
He chose a poor and humble lot,
And wept, and toiled, and mourned, and died
For love of those who loved him not.

But even could I see him die,
I could but see a little part
Of that great love, which, like a fire,
Is always burning in his heart.

It is most wonderful to know
His love for me so free and sure;
But 'tis more wonderful to see
My love for him so faint and poor.

And yet I want to love thee, Lord;
O light the flame within my heart,
And I will love thee more and more,
Until I see thee as thou art.

W.W. How, 1823–97

O my Savior, lifted
From the earth for me,
Draw me in thy mercy
Nearer unto thee.

Lift my earth-bound longings,
Fix them, Lord, above;
Draw me with the magnet
Of thy mighty love.

And I come, Lord Jesus,
Dare I turn away?
No, thy love hath conquered,
And I come today.

W.W. How, 1823–97

My God, my Love: you are all mine, and I am all yours. Increase love in me, that with my inner heart I may taste how sweet it is to love. Let me love your more than myself, and myself only for you, and in you all that love you truly.

Thomas à Kempis, 1379–1471

O Lord Jesus, forasmuch as your life was despised by the world, grant us so to imitate you, even though the world despises us, that with your image always before our eyes, we may learn that only the servants of the cross can find the way of genuine happiness and true light. Hear us and save us, Lord Jesus.

Thomas à Kempis, 1379–1471

O Christ, give us patience and faith and hope as we kneel at the foot of thy Cross, and hold fast to it. Teach us by thy Cross that however ill the world may be, the Father so loved us that he spared not thee.

Charles Kingsley, 1819–75

May our dear Lord Jesus Christ show you his hands and his side, and with his love put joy into your hearts, and may you behold and hear only him until you find your joy in him.

Martin Luther, 1483–1546

O Cross that liftest up my head,
I dare not ask to fly from thee;
I lay in dust life's glory dead,
And from the ground there blossoms red
Life that shall endless be.

George Matheson, 1842–1906

O Lord Jesus Christ, Son of the living God, who at this evening hour didst rest in the sepulcher and didst thereby sanctify the grave to be a bed of hope to thy people: make us so to abound in sorrow for our sins, which were the cause of thy passion, that when our bodies lie in the dust, our souls may live with thee; who livest and reignest with the Father and the Holy Spirit, one God, world without end.

Office of Compline

Rock of ages, cleft for me,
Let me hide myself in Thee!
Let the water and the blood,
From Thy riven side which flowed,
Be of sin the double cure;
Cleanse me from its guilt and pow'r.

Not the labors of my hands
Can fulfill Thy law's demands:
Could my zeal no respite know,
Could my tears for ever flow,
All for sin could not atone:
Thou must save, and Thou alone!

Nothing in my hand I bring,
Simply to Thy Cross I cling;
Naked, come to Thee for dress;
Helpless, look to Thee for grace;
Foul, I to the fountain fly:
Wash me, Savior, or I die!

While I draw this fleeting breath –
When my eye-strings break in death –
When I soar through tracts unknown –
See Thee on Thy throne-throne –
Rock of ages, cleft for me,
Let me hide myself in Thee.

A.M. Toplady, 1740–78

The first ten stations of the cross

First station: Jesus is condemned to death
O innocent Jesus, who with wonderful submission wast for our sakes condemned to die. Grant that we may bear in mind that our sins were the false-witnesses; our blasphemies, backbitings, and evil speakings were the cause of thy accepting with gladness the sentence of the impious judge. O may this thought touch our hearts and make us hate those sins which caused thy death.

Second station: Jesus receives his cross
O blessed Jesus, grant us by virtue of thy cross and bitter passion, cheerfully to submit to and

willingly to embrace all the trials and difficulties of this our earthly pilgrimage, and may we be always ready to take up our cross daily and follow thee.

Third station: Jesus falls under the weight of the cross
O Jesus, who for our sins didst bear the heavy burden of the cross and didst fall under its weight, may the thought of thy sufferings, make us watchful against temptation, and do thou stretch out thy sacred hand to help us lest we fall into any grievous sin.

Fourth station: The cross is laid upon Simon of Cyrene
O Jesus! I thank thee, that thou has permitted me to suffer with thee, may it be my privilege to bear my cross may I glory in nothing else; by it may the world be crucified unto me, and I unto the world, may I never shrink from suffering, but rather rejoice, if I be counted worthy to suffer for thy name's sake.

Fifth station: Jesus speaks to the women of Jerusalem
O Lord Jesus, we mourn and will mourn both for thee and for ourselves; for thy sufferings, and for our sins which caused them. Oh, teach us so to mourn, that we may be comforted, and escape those dreadful judgments prepared for all those who reject or neglect them.

Sixth station: Jesus is stripped of his garments
O Lord Jesus! Thou didst suffer shame for our most shameful deeds. Take from us, we beseech thee, all false shame, conceit, and pride, and made us so to humble ourselves in this life, that we may escape everlasting shame in the life to come.

Seventh station: Jesus is nailed to the cross
O Jesus! Crucified for me, subdue my heart with thy holy fear and love, and since my sins were the cruel nails that pierced thee, grant that in sorrow for my past life I may pierce and nail to thy cross all that offends thee.

Eighth station: Jesus hangs on the cross
O Jesus! we do devoutly embrace that honored cross, where thou didst love us even unto death. In thy death is all our hope. Henceforth let us live only unto thee, so that whether we live or die we may be thine.

Ninth station: Jesus is taken down from the cross
O Lord Jesus, grant that we may never refuse that cross, which thou hast laid upon us: who willed not to be taken down from the cross, until thou hadst accomplished the work which thou camest to do.

Tenth station: Jesus is laid in the sepulcher
O Jesus, most compassionate Lord, we adore thee dead and enclosed in the holy sepulcher. We desire to enclose thee within our hearts, that, united to thee, we may rise to newness of life, and by the gift of final perseverance die in thy grace.

Treasury of Devotion, 1869

O Lord, in your great mercy, keep us from forgetting what you have suffered for us in body and soul. May we never be drawn by the cares of this life from Jesus our Friend and Savior, but daily may live nearer to his cross.

Hedley Vicars, 1826–55

When I survey the wondrous Cross,
    On which the Prince of glory died,
My richest gain I count but loss,
    And pour contempt on all my pride.

Forbid it, Lord, that I should boast
    Save in the death of Christ my God;
All the vain things that charm me most,
    I sacrifice them to his blood.

See from his head, his hands, his feet,
    Sorrow and love flow mingled down;
Did e'er such love and sorrow meet,
    Or thorns compose so rich a crown?

His dying crimson like a robe,
    Spreads o'er his body on the Tree;
Then am I dead to all the globe,
    And all the globe is dead to me.

Were the whole realm of nature mine,
    That were a present far too small;
Love so amazing, so divine,

Demands my soul, my life, my all.

Isaac Watts, 1674–1748

EASTER EVE

God, who did enlighten this most holy night with the glory of the Lord's Resurrection: Preserve in all your people the spirit of adoption which you has given, so that renewed in body and soul they may perform unto you a pure service; through Jesus Christ, your Son, our Lord. Who lives and reigns with you and the Holy Ghost, ever One God, world without in end. Amen.

*The Common Service Book of
the Lutheran Church, 1917*

EASTER

My Dancing Day

Tomorrow shall be my dancing day:
I would my true love did so chance
to see the legend of my play,
To call my true love to my dance:

*Sing O my love, O my love, my love, my love;
This have I done for my true love.*

Then was I born of a virgin pure,
Of here I took fleshly substance;
Thus was I knit to man's nature,
To call my true love to my dance:
Sing O my love …

In a manger laid and wrapped I was,
So very poor, this was my chance,
Betwixt an ox and a silly poor ass,
To call my true love to my dance:
Sing O my love …

Then afterwards baptized I was;
The Holy Ghost on me did glance,
My Father's voice heard from above,
To call my true love to my dance:
Sing O my love …

Into the desert I was led,
Where I fasted without substance;
The devil bade me make stones my bread,
To call my true love to my dance:
Sing O my love …

For thirty pence Judas me sold,

His covetousness for to advance;
"Mark whom I kiss, the same do hold,"
The same is he shall lead the dance.
Sing O my love …

Before Pilate the Jews me brought,
Where Barabbas had deliverance;
They scourged me and set me at nought,
Judged me to die to lead the dance:
Sing O my love …

Then on the cross hanged I was,
Where a spear to my heart did glance;
There issued forth both water and blood,
To call my true love to my dance:
Sing O my love …

Then down to hell I took my way
For my true love's deliverance,
And rose again on the third day,
Up to my true love and the dance:
Sing O my love …

Then up to heaven I did ascend,
Where now I dwell in sure substance,
On the right hand of God, that man
May come unto the general dance:
Sing O my love …

Author unknown, 15th century

Almighty and everlasting God, who has sent your Son, our Savior Jesus Christ, to take upon Him our flesh, and to suffer death upon the Cross, that all mankind should follow the example of His great humility:

Mercifully grant that we may both follow the example of His patience, and also be made partakers of His resurrection; through the same Jesus Christ, your Son, our Lord, Who lives and reigns with and the Holy Ghost, ever One God, world without end. Amen.

*The Common Service Book of
the Lutheran Church, 1917*

Almighty God, who, through your only-begotten Son, Jesus Christ, has overcome death, an opened unto us the gate of everlasting life: We humbly beseech you, that, a you put into our minds good desires, so by your continual help we may bring the same to good effect through Jesus Christ, your Son, our Lord, Who lives and reigns with you and the Holy Ghost, ever One God world without end. Amen.

*The Common Service Book of
the Lutheran Church, 1917*

Grant, we beseech you, almighty God, that we who celebrate your Paschal Feast, kindled with heavenly desires, may ever thirst for the Fountain of Life, Jesus Christ, your Son, our Lord, Who lives and reigns with you and the Holy Ghost, ever One God world without end. Amen.

*The Common Service Book of
the Lutheran Church, 1917*

Grant, we beseech you, almighty God, that we who celebrate the solemnities of the Lord's Resurrection, may by the renewal of your Holy Spirit rise again from the death of the soul; through the same Jesus Christ, your Son, our Lord. Amen.

*The Common Service Book of
the Lutheran Church, 1917*

'Tis the Day of Resurrection:
Earth! tell it out abroad!
The Passover of gladness!
The Passover of GOD!
From Death to Life Eternal, –
From this world to the sky,
Our CHRIST hath brought us over,
With hymns of victory.

Our hearts be pure from evil,
That we may see aright
The LORD in rays eternal
Of Resurrection-Light:
And, listening to His accents,
May hear, so calm and plain,
His own – All Hail! – and hearing,
May raise the victor strain!

Now let the Heav'ns be joyful!
Let earth her song begin!
Let the round world keep triumph,
And all that is therein:
Invisible and visible
Their notes let all things blend, –
For CHRIST the LORD hath risen, –
Our joy that hath no end.

John Damascene, c. 780

Hail thee, festival day! blest day that art
    hallowed for ever;
Day whereon Christ arose, breaking the
    kingdom of death.
(Repeat as refrain, after choir sings each stanza.)

Lo, the fair beauty of the earth, from the death
    of the winter arising!
Every good gift of the year now with its
    Master returns:
Refrain

He who was nailed to the cross is Lord and the
    ruler of all men;
All things created on earth sing to the glory
    of God:
Refrain

Daily the loveliness grows, adorned with the
    glory of blossom;
Heaven her gates unbars, flinging her increase
    of light:
Refrain

Rise from the grave now, O Lord, who art
    author of life and creation.
Treading the pathway of death, life thou
    bestowest on man:
Refrain

God the All-Father, the Lord, who rulest the
    earth and the heavens,
Guard us from harm without, cleanse us from
    evil within:
Refrain

Jesus the health of the world, enlighten our
    minds, thou Redeemer,
Son of the Father supreme, only begotten of
    God:
Refrain

Spirit of life and power, now flow in us, fount
    of our being,
Light that dost lighten all, life that in all dost
    abide:
Refrain

Praise to the Giver of good! Thou Love who
    art author of concord,

Pour out thy balm on our souls, order our
    ways in thy peace:
Refrain
V.H. Fortunatus, 530–609

O God, who by your One and only Son has
overcome death and opened to us the gate of
everlasting life; grant, we pray, that those who
have been redeemed by his passion may rejoice
in his resurrection, through the same Christ
our Lord.
Gelasian Sacramentary, 5th century

By fruit, the ancient Foe's device
Drove Adam forth from Paradise:
CHRIST, by the cross of shame and pain,
Brought back the dying Thief again:
"When in Thy kingdom, LORD," said he,
"Thou shalt return, remember me!"

Thy Holy Passion we adore
And Resurrection evermore:
With heart and voice to Thee on high,
As Adam and the Thief we cry:
"When in Thy kingdom Thou shalt be
"Victor o'er all things, think of me!"

Thou, after three appointed days,
Thy Body's Temple didst upraise:
And Adam's children, one and all,
With Adam, to New Life didst call:
"When Thou," they cry, "shalt Victor be
"In that Thy kingdom, think of me!"

Early, O CHRIST, to find Thy Tomb,
The weeping Ointment-bearers come:
The Angel, clothed in white, hath said,
"Why seek the Living with the dead?
"The LORD of Life hath burst death's chain,
"Whom here ye mourn and seek in vain."

The Apostles, on Thy Vision bent,
To that appointed mountain went:
And there they worship when they see,
And there the message comes from Thee,
That every race beneath the skies
They should disciple and baptize.

We praise the FATHER, GOD on High,
The Holy SON we magnify:
Nor less our praises shall adore

The HOLY GHOST, for evermore;
This grace, Blest TRINITY, we crave;
Thy suppliant servants hear and save.
Germanicus, 634–734

It is only right, with all the powers of our
heart and mind, to praise You Father and your
Only-Begotten Son, Our Lord Jesus Christ.
Dear Father, by your wondrous condescension
of Loving-Kindness toward us, your servants,
you gave up your Son. Dear Jesus you paid
the debt of Adam for us to the Eternal Father
by your Blood poured forth in Loving-Kindness. you cleared away the darkness of sin by
your magnificent and radiant Resurrection.
You broke the bonds of death and rose from the
grave as a Conqueror. You reconciled Heaven
and earth. Our life had no hope of Eternal
Happiness before you redeemed us. Your Resurrection has washed away our sins, restored our
innocence and brought us joy. How inestimable
is the tenderness of your Love!

We pray you, Lord, to preserve your servants in the peaceful enjoyment of this Easter
happiness. We ask this through Jesus Christ
Our Lord, Who lives and reigns with God The
Father, in the unity of the Holy Spirit, forever
and ever. Amen.
Gregory I, c.540–604

Easter Wings

Lord, who createdst man in wealth and store,
Though foolishly he lost the same,
Decaying more and more,
Till he became
Most poor:

With thee
Oh let me rise
As larks, harmoniously,
And sing this day thy victories:
Then shall the fall farther the flight in me.

My tender age in sorrow did begin:
And still with sickness and shame
Thou did'st so punish sin,
That I became
Most thin

With thee
Let me combine,

And feel this day the victory,
For, if I imp my wing on thine,
Affliction shall advance the flight in me.
George Herbert, 1593–1633, The Temple

I got me flowers to strew thy way;
I get me boughs off many a tree:
but thou wast up by break of day,
And brought'st thy sweets along with thee.

The Sun arising in the East,
Though he give light, and th' East perfume;
If they should offer to contest
With thy arising, they presume.

Can there be any day but this,
Though many suns to shine endeavor?
We count three hundred, but we miss:
There is but one, and that one ever.
George Herbert, 1593–1633, The Temple

Rise, heart; thy Lord is risen. Sing his praise
Without delays,
Who takes thee by the hand, that thou
likewise
With him may'st rise:
That, as his death calcinèd thee to dust,
His life may make thee gold, and much more,
Just.

Awake, my lute, and struggle for thy part
With all thy art.
The cross taught all wood to resound his name
Who bore the same.
His stretchèd sinews taught all strings, what
key
Is best to celebrate this most high day.

Consort both heart and lute, and twist a song
Pleasant and long:
Or since all music is but three parts vied,
And multiplied;
O let thy blessed Spirit bear a part,
And make up our defects with his sweet art.
George Herbert, 1593–1633, The Temple

Almighty and everlasting God, Who hast
preserved me by Thy fatherly care through all
the years of my past life, and now permittest
me again to commemorate the sufferings and
merits of our Lord and Savior Jesus Christ,
grant me so to partake of this holy rite, that the
disquiet of my mind may be appeased, that my
faith may be increased, my hope strengthened,
and my life regulated by Thy Will. Make me
truly thankful for that portion of health which
Thy mercy has restored, and enable me to use
the remains of life to Thy glory and my own
salvation. Take not from me, O Lord, Thy Holy
Spirit. Extinguish in my mind all sinful and
inordinate desires. Let me resolve to do that
which is right, and let me by Thy help keep my
resolutions. Let me, if it is best for me, at last
know peace and comfort, but whatever state
of life Thou shalt appoint me, let me end it by
a happy death, and enjoy eternal happiness in
Thy presence, for the sake of Jesus Christ our
Lord. Amen.
Samuel Johnson, Easter, 1770

Almighty God, who through the death of your
Son has destroyed sin and death, and by his
resurrection has restored innocence and everlasting life, that we may be delivered from the
dominion of the devil, and our mortal bodies
raised up from the dead: Grant that we may
confidently and whole-heartedly believe this,
and, finally, with your saints, share in the joyful
resurrection of the just; through the same
Jesus Christ, your Son, our Lord.
Martin Luther, 1483–1546

Jesus Christ is risen today, Alleluya!
Jesus Christ is risen to-day, Alleluya!
Our triumphant holy day, Alleluya!
Who did once, upon the Cross, Alleluya!
Suffer to redeem our loss. Alleluya!

Hymns of praise then let us sing, Alleluya!
Unto Christ, our heavenly King, Alleluya!
Who endured the Cross and grave, Alleluya!
Sinners to redeem and save. Alleluya!

But the pains that he endured, Alleluya!
Our salvation have procured; Alleluya!
Now above the sky he's King, Alleluya!
Where the angels ever sing. Alleluya!
*Lyra Davidica, 1708, translated from
a 14th-century manuscript*

May the Lord Jesus Christ, who, dying for the
salvation of the whole world, rose this day

from the dead, mortify you from your sins by his resurrection. Amen.

And may he, who, by the gibbet of the cross destroyed the rule of death, grant you a portion in the life of blessedness. Amen.

So that you, who celebrate this day of his resurrection with joy in this world, may attain the company of the saints in the heavenly kingdom. Amen.

Through the aid of his mercy, who with God the Father and the Holy Spirit lives and reigns one God, world without end. Amen.

Mozarabic Sacramentary

Litany of the resurrection

Lord, have mercy.
Lord, have mercy.
Christ, have mercy.
Christ, have mercy.
Lord, have mercy.
Lord, have mercy.
Christ, hear us.
Christ, graciously hear us.

God the Father of Heaven, have mercy on us.
God the Son, Redeemer of the world, have
    mercy …
God the Holy Ghost,
Holy Trinity, one God,
Jesus, Redeemer of mankind,
Jesus, Conqueror of sin and Satan,
Jesus, triumphant over Death.,
Jesus, the Holy and the Just,
Jesus, the Resurrection and the Life,
Jesus, the Giver of grace,
Jesus, the Judge of the world,

Who didst lay down Thy life for Thy sheep,
    have mercy on us.
Who didst rise again the third day,
Who didst manifest Thyself to Thy chosen,
Visiting Thy blessed Mother,
Appearing to Magdalen while she wept,
Sending Thy angels to the holy women,
Comforting the Eleven,
Saying to them, Peace,
Breathing on them the Holy Ghost,
Confirming the faith of Thomas,
Committing Thy flock to Peter,
Speaking of the Kingdom of God,

We sinners, beseech Thee, hear us.
That we may walk in newness of life, we
    beseech Thee hear us.
That we may advance in the knowledge of Thee,
That we may grow in grace,
That we may ever have the bread of life,
That we may persevere unto the end,
That we may have confidence before Thee at
    Thy coming,
That we may behold Thy face with joy,
That we may be placed at Thy right hand in
    the judgment.
That we may have our lot with the saints,

Lamb of God, who takest away the sins of the
    world,
Spare us, O Lord.
Lamb of God, who takest away the sins of the
    world,
Graciously hear us, O Lord..
Lamb of God, who takest away the sins of the
    world,
Have mercy on us.

Christ, hear us.
Christ, graciously hear us.
Lord, have mercy.
Christ, have mercy.
Lord, have mercy.

Christ is risen, Alleluia.
He is risen indeed, and hath appeared unto
    Simon, Alleluia.

J.H. Newman, 1801–90

O God, who by Thy only-begotten Son hast
    overcome death, and
opened on us the way to eternal life,
    vouchsafe, we beseech Thee,
so to confirm us by Thy grace, that we may in
    all things walk after
the manner of those who have been redeemed
    from their sins,
through the same Jesus Christ our Lord.
    Amen.

J.H. Newman, 1801–90

We glorify Thy divine condescension, and praise Thee, O Christ. Thou wast born from the Virgin and didst remain inseparably with the Father. Thou didst suffer as man, and didst voluntarily endure the Cross. Thou didst rise from the grave, coming forth from it as from a bridal chamber, in order to save the world. O Lord, glory to Thee.

Orthodox Liturgy

Litany of the resurrection
Lord, have mercy.
Lord, have mercy.
Christ, have mercy.
Christ, have mercy.
Lord, have mercy.
Lord, have mercy.
Christ, hear us.
Christ, graciously hear us.

God the Father of Heaven, have mercy on us.
God the Son, Redeemer of the world, have mercy …
God the Holy Ghost,
Holy Trinity, one God,
Jesus, Redeemer of mankind,
Jesus, Conqueror of sin and Satan,
Jesus, triumphant over Death.,
Jesus, the Holy and the Just,
Jesus, the Resurrection and the Life,
Jesus, the Giver of grace,
Jesus, the Judge of the world,

Who didst lay down Thy life for Thy sheep, have mercy on us.
Who didst rise again the third day,
Who didst manifest Thyself to Thy chosen,
Visiting Thy blessed Mother,
Appearing to Magdalen while she wept,
Sending Thy angels to the holy women,
Comforting the Eleven,
Saying to them, Peace,
Breathing on them the Holy Ghost,
Confirming the faith of Thomas,
Committing Thy flock to Peter,
Speaking of the Kingdom of God,

We sinners, beseech Thee, hear us.
That we may walk in newness of life, we beseech Thee hear us.
That we may advance in the knowledge of Thee,
That we may grow in grace,
That we may ever have the bread of life,
That we may persevere unto the end,
That we may have confidence before Thee at

Thy coming,
That we may behold Thy face with joy,
That we may be placed at Thy right hand in the judgment.
That we may have our lot with the saints,

Lamb of God, who takest away the sins of the world,
Spare us, O Lord.
Lamb of God, who takest away the sins of the world,
Graciously hear us, O Lord …
Lamb of God, who takest away the sins of the world,
Have mercy on us.
Christ, hear us.
Christ, graciously hear us.
Lord, have mercy.
Christ, have mercy.
Lord, have mercy.

Christ is risen, Alleluia.
He is risen indeed, and hath appeared unto Simon, Alleluia.

Let us pray.

O God, who by Thy only-begotten Son hast overcome death, and opened for us the way to eternal life, vouchsafe, we beseech Thee, so to confirm us by Thy grace, that we may in all things walk after the manner of those who have been redeemed from their sins, through the same Jesus Christ our Lord. Amen

J.H. Newman, 1801–90

Easter Monday
Out in the rain a world is growing green,
    On half the trees quick buds are seen
Where glued-up buds have been.
Out in the rain God's Acre stretches green,
    Its harvest quick tho' still unseen:
For there the Life hath been.

If Christ hath died His brethren well may die,
    Sing in the gate of death, lay by
This life without a sigh:
For Christ hath died and good it is to die;
    To sleep when so He lays us by,
Then wake without a sigh.

Yea, Christ hath died, yea, Christ is risen again:
  Wherefore both life and death grow plain
To us who wax and wane;
For Christ Who rose shall die no more again:
  Amen: till He makes all things plain
Let us wax on and wane.

Christina Rossetti, 1830–94

Most glorious Lord of Life, that on this day
Didst make thy triumph over death and sin;
And, having harrowed hell, didst bring away
Captivity, thence captive, us to win:
This joyous day, dear Lord, with joy begin;
And grant that we, for whom thou didst die,
Being with thy dear blood clean washed from
  sin,
May live for ever in felicity.
And that thy love, we weighing worthily,
May likewise love thee for the same again;
And for thy sake, that all like dear didst buy,
With love may one another entertain!
  So let us love, dear Lord, like as we ought.
  – Love is the lesson which the Lord us
    taught.

Edmund Spenser, 1552–99

Christ, the Lord, is risen today, Alleluia!
Sons of men and angels say, Alleluia!
Raise your joys and triumphs high, Alleluia!
Sing, ye heavens, and earth, reply, Alleluia!

Love's redeeming work is done, Alleluia!
Fought the fight, the battle won, Alleluia!
Lo! the Sun's eclipse is over, Alleluia!
Lo! He sets in blood no more, Alleluia!

Vain the stone, the watch, the seal, Alleluia!
Christ hath burst the gates of hell, Alleluia!
Death in vain forbids His rise, Alleluia!
Christ hath opened paradise, Alleluia!

Lives again our glorious King, Alleluia!
Where, O death, is now thy sting? Alleluia!
Once He died our souls to save, Alleluia!
Where thy victory, O grave? Alleluia!

Soar we now where Christ hath led, Alleluia!
Following our exalted Head, Alleluia!
Made like Him, like Him we rise, Alleluia!
Ours the cross, the grave, the skies, Alleluia!

Hail, the Lord of earth and heaven, Alleluia!
Praise to Thee by both be given, Alleluia!
Thee we greet triumphant now, Alleluia!
Hail, the resurrection day, Alleluia!

King of glory, Soul of bliss, Alleluia!
Everlasting life is this, Alleluia!
Thee to know, Thy power to prove, Alleluia!
Thus to sing and thus to love, Alleluia!

Hymns of praise then let us sing, Alleluia!
Unto Christ, our heavenly King, Alleluia!
Who endured the cross and grave, Alleluia!
Sinners to redeem and save. Alleluia!

But the pains that He endured, Alleluia!
Our salvation have procured, Alleluia!
Now above the sky He's King, Alleluia!
Where the angels ever sing. Alleluia!

Jesus Christ is risen today, Alleluia!
Our triumphant holy day, Alleluia!
Who did once upon the cross, Alleluia!
Suffer to redeem our loss. Alleluia!

Charles Wesley, 1707–88

Love's redeeming work is done;
Fought the fight, the battle won:
Lo, our Sun's eclipse is o'er!
Lo, he sets in blood no more.

Vain the stone, the watch, the seal,
Christ has burst the gates of hell;
Death in vain forbids his rise;
Christ has opened Paradise.

Lives again our glorious King;
Where, O death, is now thy sting?
Dying once, he all doth save;
Where thy victory, O grave?

Charles Wesley, 1707–88

ASCENSION

Grant, we beseech thee, Almighty God, that
like as we do believe thy only-begotten Son
our Lord Jesus Christ to have ascended into
the heavens; so we may also in heart and mind
thither ascend, and with him continually dwell,
who liveth and reigneth with thee and the Holy
Ghost, one God, world without end. Amen.

Book of Common Prayer, Ascension Day

O God, the King of glory, who hast exalted thine only Son Jesus Christ with great triumph unto thy kingdom in heaven; We beseech thee, leave us not comfortless; but send to us thine Holy Ghost to comfort us, and exalt us unto the same place whither our Savior Christ is gone before, who liveth and reigneth with thee and the Holy Ghost, one God, world without end. Amen.

*The Book of Common Prayer, Collect
for Sunday after Ascension Day*

Almighty and merciful God, into whose gracious presence we ascend, not by the frailty of the flesh but by the activity of the soul: Make us always by your inspiration to seek after the courts of the heavenly city, where our Savior Christ has ascended, and by your mercy confidently to enter them, both now and hereafter; through the same Jesus Christ our Lord.

Leonine Sacramentary

O Christ, the King of Glory, who through the everlasting gates didst ascend to thy Father's throne, and open the kingdom of heaven to all believers: Grant that, while you reign in heaven, we may not be bowed down to the things of earth, but that our hearts may be lifted up where you, our redemption, have gone ahead; who with the Father and the Holy Spirit lives and reigns, ever one God, world without end.

Mozarabic Sacramentary

Hail the day that sees Him rise, Alleluia!
To His throne above the skies, Alleluia!
Christ, awhile to mortals given, Alleluia!
Reascends His native heaven, Alleluia!

Charles Wesley, 1707–88

The coming of the Holy Spirit/Pentecost

*See also: Praise, Confession, and Thanksgiving,
Prayers to and for God the Holy Spirit, p 28*

Almighty God, eternal Father of our Lord Jesus Christ, creator of heaven and earth and mankind, one with your Son and the Holy Spirit, have mercy on us. Justify us through your Son, Jesus Christ, and sanctify us with your Holy Spirit. Establish, guard and guide your church, O God.

Philip Melanchthon, 1497–1560

Grant, we beseech thee, almighty and merciful God, that the Holy Ghost may come upon us, and by his gracious in-dwelling, may make us a temple of his glory; through Jesus Christ our Lord. Amen.

Treasury of Devotion, 1869

Trinity Sunday

Praise be to thee, O God the Father, who didst create all things by thy power and wisdom, and didst so love the world as to give thy Son to be our Savior.

Praise be to thee, O God the Son, who wast made man like unto us in all things, sin except, and wast delivered for our offences and raised again for our justification.

Praise be to thee, O God the Holy Spirit, who dost lead us into all truth, and dost shed abroad the love of God in our hearts.

All praise and glory be to thee, O God, Father, Son, and Holy Spirit, for ever and ever.

Author unknown

Thanks be to you, O God, for revealing
  yourself to humankind, and for sending
  your messengers in every generation.
Thanks be to you for the first apostles of
  Christ, sent into all the world to preach the
  gospel;
for those who brought the good news to our
  land;
for all who, in ages of darkness, kept alive
  the light, or in times of indifference were
  faithful to their Lord's command;
for all your followers in every age who have
  given their lives for the faith;
for those in our own day who have gone to
  the ends of the earth as heralds to your
  love;
for the innumerable company who now
  praise you from every race and nation and
  language.
With these and the whole company of heaven
  we worship you; through Jesus Christ our
  Lord.

Author unknown

God the Father bless me, Christ guard me, the Holy Spirit enlighten me, all the days of my life! The Lord be the defender and guardian of my soul and my body, now and always, world without end. Amen.

The Book of Cerne, 9th century

The right hand of the Lord preserve me
 always to old age!
The grace of Christ perpetually defend me
 from the enemy!
Direct, Lord, my heart into the way of peace.
Lord God, deliver and help me.

Aethelwold, c.908–984

Almighty and everlasting God, who hast given unto us thy servants grace, by the confession of a true faith to acknowledge the glory of the eternal Trinity, and in the power of thy Divine Majesty to worship the Unity; We beseech thee, that thou wouldst keep us steadfast in this faith, and evermore defend us from all adversities, who livest and reignest, one God, world without end. Amen.

Book of Common Prayer, Collect for Trinity Sunday

A Litany
   The Father
Father of Heaven, and Him, by whom
It, and us for it, and all else for us
   Thou mad'st, and govern'st ever, come
And re-create me, now grown ruinous:
   My heart is by dejection, clay,
   And by self-murder, red.
From this red earth, O Father, purge away
All vicious tinctures, that new fashionèd
I may rise up from death, before I'm dead.

   The Son
   O Son of God, who seeing two things,
Sin and death, crept in, which were never
   made,
   By bearing one, tried'st with what stings
The other could Thine heritage invade;
   O be Thou nail'd unto my heart,
   And crucified again.
Part not from it, though it from Thee would
   part,
But let it be, by applying so Thy pain,
Drown'd in Thy blood, and in Thy passion
   slain.

   The Holy Ghost
   O Holy Ghost, whose temple I
Am, but of mud walls, and condensèd dust,
   And being sacrilegiously
Half wasted with youth's fires, of pride and
   lust,
   Must with new storms be weather-beat;
   Double in my heart Thy flame,
Which let devout sad tears intend; and let
(Though this glass lanthorn, flesh, do suffer
   main)
Fire, Sacrifice, Priest, Altar be the same.

John Donne, 1572–1631 from A Litanie

May God the Father bless you, who created all
 things in the beginning. Amen.
May the Son bless you, who for our salvation
 came down from his throne on high.
 Amen.
May the Holy Spirit bless you, who rested as a
 dove on the Christ in Jordan. Amen.
May he sanctify you in the Trinity and unity
 whose coming to judgment all nations
 look for. Amen.
Which may he deign to grant, the Father, the
 Son, and the Holy Spirit, one God, world
 without end. Amen.

Gallican Sacramentary

Almighty and everlasting God, who dost kindle the flame of thy love in the hearts of the saints, grant unto us the same faith and power of love; that, as we rejoice in their triumphs, we may profit by their examples, through Jesus Christ our Lord.

Gothic missal

The coming of the kingdom

Eternal God, in whose perfect kingdom no sword is drawn but the sword of righteousness, and no strength known but the strength of love: we pray thee so mightily to shed and spread abroad thy Spirit, that all peoples and ranks may be gathered under one banner, of the Prince of Peace; as children of one God and Father of all; to whom be dominion and glory now and for ever.

Source unknown

Almighty God, our heavenly Father, to forget whom is to stumble and fall, to remember whom is to rise again: we pray thee to draw the people of this country to thyself. Prosper all efforts to make known to them thy truth, that many may learn their need of thee and thy love for them; so that thy Church and kingdom may be established among us to the glory of thy Name; through Jesus Christ our Lord.

Randall T. Davidson, 1848–1930

Brothers, this Lord Jesus shall return again,
With His Father's glory, with His angel train;
For all wreaths of empire meet upon His brow,
And our hearts confess Him King of glory
   now.

Caroline Maria Noel, 1817–1877

Prayers for Everyday Life

John Bunyan: On Praying in the Spirit
Francis de Sales: Introduction to the Devout Life
Madame Guyon: A Short and Very Easy Method of Prayer
Brother Lawrence: The Practice of the Presence of God
Andrew Murray: With Christ in the School of Prayer
R.A. Torrey: Praying in the Spirit
George Whitefield: Intercession: Every Christian's Duty

PRAYERS FOR TIMES OF LIFE

Birth of a baby

O Almighty, Everlasting God and Father, Creator of all things, Who by Thy grace, through Thy Son, our Lord, makest the anguish of our human birth a holy and salutary cross: We pray Thee, o gracious Father, Lord and God, that Thou wouldest preserve and guard the work of Thine own hand; forsake not them who cry to Thee in sore travail, but deliver them out of all their pains, to their joy, and to the glory of Thy goodness; through Jesus Christ, Thy Son, our Lord. Amen.

*The Common Service Book of
the Lutheran Church, 1917*

Babies

O Lord God, in whose hands are the issues of life, we thank thee for thy gifts to us at this time. We thank thee for the life given, and the life preserved. And as thou hast knit together life and love in one fellowship, so we pray thee to grant that with this fresh gift of life to us, there may be given an increase of love one to another; through Jesus Christ our Lord.

William Boyd Carpenter, 1841–1918

School and student days

Good Lord, you have refreshed our souls with the streams of knowledge; lead in us at last to yourself, the source and spring of knowledge.

Alcuin, 735–804

O God, our heavenly Father, by whose Spirit people are taught knowledge, who gives wisdom to all who ask you: Grant your blessing, we beseech you, on this school, and help us in the work you have given us to do. Enable us all to work diligently, not with eye-service, but in singleness of heart, remembering that without you we can do nothing, and that in your fear is the beginning of wisdom; through Jesus Christ our Lord.

F.D. Maurice, 1805–72

Lord and Savior, true and kind,
Be the master of my mind:
Bless and guide and strengthen still
All my powers of thought and will.

While I ply the scholar's task,
Jesus Christ, be near I ask:
Help the memory, clear the brain,
Knowledge still to seek and gain.

Handley C.G. Moule, 1841–1920

The unmarried

Jesus my Lord, Who became man and graced us with the beauty of Your life and with the example of faith, purity and love; help me, I pray, to love You with all my mind, heart and soul, and to live according to Your teachings. Strengthen me when temptations strike, that I may remain pure in thought and steadfast in virtue, doing only things that are pleasing to You. Guide me to live Your will and not my own as I look to the future. Grant me faith, courage and love, that I may serve You in holiness all the days of my life. Amen.

Orthodox prayer

Widow or widower

Lord Jesus Christ, Who through your mercy, resurrected the only son of the widow in Nain; I pray to You in need and all alone, putting my hope in God and asking for help. O You who fulfill our every need and complete everything we lack, grant me faith, courage, love and understanding of Your Will. Amen.

Orthodox prayer

Growing old

The right hand of the Lord preserve me always to old age. The grace of Christ perpetually defend me from the enemy. Lord, direct my heart in the way of peace. Lord God, come quickly and deliver me. Amen.

Aethelwod, c.908–984

Lord,
Thou knowest better than I know myself,
that I am growing older and will some day be
    old.
Keep me from the fatal habit of thinking I
    must say something
on every subject and on every occasion.
Release me from craving to straighten out
    everybody's affairs.
Make me thoughtful but not moody;
helpful but not bossy.
With my vast store of wisdom, it seems a pity
    not to use it all,
but Thou knowest, Lord,
that I want a few friends at the end.

Keep my mind free from the recital of endless
    details;
give me the wings to get to the point.
Seal my lips on my aches and pains.
They are increasing,
and love of rehearsing them is becoming
    sweeter as the years go by.
I dare not ask for grace enough to enjoy the
    tales of others' pains,
but help me to endure them with patience.

I dare not ask for improved memory,
but for a growing humility,
and a lessening cocksureness

when my memory seems to clash with the
    memory of others.
Teach me the glorious lesson that occasionally
    I may be mistaken.
Keep me reasonably sweet.
I do not want to be a saint
(some of them are so hard to live with)
but a sour old person is one of the crowning
    works of the devil.
Give me the ability to see good things in
    unexpected places
and talents in unexpected people.
And give me, O Lord,
the grace to tell them so.

Author unknown, 17th-century nun

O Lord, evening is at hand, furnish it with brightness. As day has its evening so also has life; the even of life is age, age has overtaken me, furnish it with brightness. Cast me not away in the time of age; forsake me not when my strength fails me. Do thou make, do thou bear, do thou carry and deliver me. Abide with me, Lord, for it is toward evening, and the day is far spent of this fretful life. Let thy strength be made perfect in my weakness.

Lancelot Andrewes, 1555–1626

Lord, our God, we are in the shadow of your wings. Protect us and bear us up. You will care for us as if we were little children, even to our old age. When you are our strength we are strong, but when we are our own strength we are weak. Our good always lives in your presence, and we suffer when we turn our faces away from you. We now return to you, O Lord, that we may never turn away again.

Augustine of Hippo, 354–430,
as he contemplated old age

Grow old along with me!
The best is yet to be,
The last of life, for which the first was made:
Our times are in his hand
Who saith "A whole I planned,
Youth shows but half; trust God: see all nor
    be afraid!"

Robert Browning, 1812–89

Lord, be merciful now that my life is approaching its end, and the evening awaits me. There is not enough time for me to cleanse myself of my sins, for they are so many. Heal me while I am still on earth, and I shall be truly healthy. In your mercy, move me to repent so that I shall not be ashamed when I meet you in heaven.

Macarius of Egypt, c.300–c.390

Lord, thank you that in your love you have taken from me all earthly riches, and that you now clothe me and feed me through the kindness of others. Lord, thank you, that since you have taken from me my sight, you serve me now with the eyes of others.

Lord, thank you that since you have taken away the power of my hands and my heart, you serve me through the hands and hearts of others. Lord, I pray for them. Reward them for with your heavenly love, that they may faithfully serve and please you until they reach their happy end.

Mechtild of Magdeburg, 1210–97

I spent my youth thinking of you and loving you. Now, may my growing up be to your honor, my aging be blessed by you, and my death be turned to life by you, that you may be my nurturer and manager throughout my life.

John Sarkavag Vardapetca. 1050–1129

Facing death

Oh, what their joy and their glory must be, those endless Sabbaths the blessed ones see; crowns for the valiant, for weary ones rest: God shall be all, and in all ever blest.

Truly Jerusalem name we that shore, vision of peace that brings hope evermore; wish and fulfillment shall severed be ne'er, nor the thing prayed for come short of the prayer.

There, where no trouble distraction can bring, we the sweet anthems of Zion shall sing, while for thy grace, Lord, their voices of praise thy blessed people eternally raise.

Now, in the meantime, with hearts raised on high, we for that country must yearn and must sigh,

seeking Jerusalem, dear native land, through the long exile on Babylon's strand.

Low before him with our praises we fall, of whom, and in whom, and through whom are all; of whom, the Father; and in whom, the Son; through whom, the Spirit, with both ever one.

Peter Abelard, 1079–1144, translated by J.M. Neale, 1818–66

Look, God, I have never spoken to you,
And now I want to say, 'How do you do?'
And see, God, they told me you did not exist,
And I, like a fool, believed all this.
Last night, from a shell-hole, I saw your sky,
I figured that they had told me a lie.
Had I taken time before to see things you had
    made,
I'd sure have known they weren't calling a
    spade a spade.

I wonder, God, if you would shake my poor
    hand?
Somehow I feel you would understand.
Strange I had to come to this hellish place
Before I had time to see your face.
Well, I guess, there isn't much more to say,
But I'm glad, God, that I met you today.
The zero hour will soon be here,
But I'm not afraid to know that you're near.
The signal has come – I shall soon have to go,
I like you lots – this I want you to know.
I am sure this will be a horrible fight;
Who knows? I may come to your house
    tonight.
Though I wasn't friendly to you before,
I wonder, God, if you'd wait at your door?
Look, I'm shedding tears – me shedding tears!
Oh! I wish I'd known you these long, long
    years.
Well, I have to go now, dear God. Good bye,
But now that I've met you I'm not scared to
    die.

Author unknown. Lines discovered on the dead body of an American soldier killed in North Africa in the Second World War, 1944

O blessed Jesu, most mighty lion, king immortal and victorious, have mind of the sorrow that thou sufferedst when all the powers of thine heart and body for feebleness failed thee utterly, and when thou saidst, inclining thine head thus: 'It is all done'. For mind of thine anguish and sorrow blessed Jesu, have mercy on me in my last end, when my soul shall be anguished and my spirit troubled. Amen

Bridget of Sweden, 1303–73

O God, give me of thy wisdom,
O God, give me of thy mercy,
O God, give me of thy fullness,
And of thy guidance in face of every strait.

O God, give me of thy holiness,
O God, give me of thy shielding,
O God, give me of thy surrounding,
And of thy peace in the knot of my death.

In Mine Eternity
God to enfold me,
God to surround me,
God in my speaking,
God in my thinking.

God in my sleeping,
God in my waking,
God in my watching,
God in my hoping.

God in my life,
God in my lips,
God in my soul,
God in my heart.

God in my sufficing,
God in my slumber,
God in mine ever-living soul,
God in mine eternity.

Carmina Gadelica

O give me of thy surrounding,
And of thy peace at the hour of my death!

Celtic

O Jesus, be mindful of your promise; think on us your servants; and when we leave this world, speak these loving words to our souls: "Today you will be with me in joy." O Lord Jesus Christ, remember us your servants who trust in you, when our tongue cannot speak, when our eyes cannot see and when our ears

cannot hear. Let our soul always rejoice in you, and be joyful about your salvation, which you have bought for us through your death.

Miles Coverdale, 1488–1568

O Lord Jesu, who art the only health of all men living, and the everlasting life of those who die in thy faith: I give myself wholly unto thy will, being sure that the thing cannong perish which is committed unto thy mercy.

Thomas Cromwell, 1485–1540, before his execution

Bring us, O Lord God, at our last awakening into the house and gate of heaven, to enter that gate and dwell in that house, where there shall be no darkness nor dazzling, but one equal light; no noise nor silence, but one equal music; no fears nor hopes, but one equal possession; no ends nor beginnings, but one equal eternity; in the habitations of your glory and dominion, world without end.

John Donne, 1572–1631

Lord Jesus Christ, true Man and God
Who borest anguish, scorn, the rod,
And didst at last upon the tree,
To bring thy Father's grace to me;
I pray thee, through that bitter woe,
Let me, a sinner, mercy know.

When comes the hour of failing breath,
And I must wrestle, Lord, with death,
Then come, Lord Jesus, came with speed,
And help me in my hour of need.
Lead me from this dark vale beneath,
And shorten then the pangs of death.

Joyful my resurrection be;
Thou in the judgment plead for me,
And hide my sins, Lord, from thy face,
And give me life, of thy dear grace.
I trust in Thee, O blessed Lord,
And claim the promise of thy Word.

Paul Eber, 1557, translated
Catherine Winkworth, 1858

O loving Christ, draw me, a weakling, after thyself; for if thou dost not draw me I cannot follow you. Give me a brave and alert spirit. If my body is weak, may thy grace go before me, come alongside me and follow me. Without thine help I can do nothing, least of all go to a painful death for thine honor. Give me a ready spirit, a fearless heart, a right faith, a firm hope, and a perfect love, that for thy sake I may lay down my life with patience and joy.

John Huss, c.1369–1415, lying in chains in prison

Lord, bless all means that are used for my recovery, and restore me to my health in your good time; but if you have appointed that it should be otherwise, your blessed will be done. Draw me away from an affection for things below, and fill me with an ardent desire for heaven. Lord, fit me your yourself, and then call me to those joys unspeakable and full of glory, when it pleases you, and that for the sake of your only Son, Jesus, my Savior.

Thomas Ken, 1637–1711

Lord, I am coming as fast as I can, I know I must pass through the shadow of death before I can come to see thee, but it is but umbra mortis, a mere shadow of death, a little darkness upon nature, but thou by thy merits and passion hast broke through the jaws of death; so Lord receive my soul, and have mercy upon me, and bless this Kingdome with peace and with plenty, and with brotherly love and charity, that there may not be this effusion of Christian blood amongst them, for Jesus Christ's sake, if it be thy will.

William Laud, 1573–1645, on the scaffold

Make my service acceptable to Thee while I live, and my soul ready for Thee when I die.

William Laud, 1573–1645

Make me all Yours before I die.

Alphonsus Liguori, 1696–1787

Abide with me; fast falls the eventide;
The darkness deepens; Lord, with me abide!
When other helpers fail, and comforts flee,
Help of the helpless, O abide with me.

Swift to its close ebbs out life's little day;
Earth's joys grow dim, its glories pass away;
Change and decay in all around I see;
O thou who changest not, abide with me.

I need thy presence every passing hour;
What but thy grace can foil the tempter's power?
Who like thyself my guide and stay can be?
Through cloud and sunshine, O abide with me.

I fear no foe with thee at hand to bless;
Ills have no weight, and tears no bitterness.
Where is death's sting? where, grave, thy victory?
I triumph still, if thou abide with me.

Hold thou thy cross before my closing eyes;
Shine through the gloom, and point me to the skies:
Heaven's morning breaks, and earth's vain shadows flee;
In life, in death, O Lord, abide with me!

H.F. Lyte, 1793–1847

From death to life: from sorrow to joy: from a vale of misery to a paradise of mercy.
I know that my Redeemer liveth, and that I shall be raised again in the last day.
I shall walk before the Lord in the land of the living.
In thee, O Lord, have I trusted: let me never be confounded.
Into thy hands I comment my spirit: for thou has redeemed me, O Lord, thou God of truth.
Thou art my helper and Redeemer: make no long tarrying, O my God.
Come, Lord Jesu, come quickly.
Lord Jesus, receive my sprit.

Meditations and Prayers, compiled by John Cosin, 1594–1672

Good Lord,
give me the grace so to spend my life,
that when the day of my death shall come,
though I may feel pain in my body,
I may feel comfort in soul;
and with faithful hope in thy mercy,
in due love towards thee
and charity towards the world,
I may, through thy grace,
part hence into thy glory.

Thomas More, 1478–1535

Even such is time, that takes in trust
Our youth, our joys, our all we have,
And pays us but with earth and dust;
Who in the dark and silent grave,
When we have wandered all our ways
Shuts us the story of our days;
But from this earth, this grave, this dust,
My God shall raise me up, I trust.

Walter Raleigh, 1552–1618, written on the
fly-leaf of his Bible the night before he was
executed at the Tower of London

O Lord Jesus Christ, Son of the living God, who
at the ninth hour of the day, with outstretched
hands and bowed head, commended your spirit
to God the Father, and by your death unlocked
the gates of paradise: Mercifully grant that in
the hour of our death our souls may come to
the true paradise, which is yourself; who lives
and reigns God, world without end.

Office of None

O my most blessed and glorious Creator, who
has fed me all my life, and redeemed me from
all evil; seeing it is your merciful pleasure to
take me out of this frail body, and to wipe away
all tears from my eyes, and all sorrows from
my heart, I do with all humility and willingness consent and submit myself wholly to your
sacred will.

My most loving Redeemer, into your saving
and everlasting arms I comment my spirit; I
am ready, my dear Lord, and earnestly expect
and long for your good pleasure. Come quickly, and receive the soul of your servant who
trusts in you.

Henry Vaughan, 1622–95

Finish, then, Thy new creation;
Pure and spotless let us be.
Let us see Thy great salvation
Perfectly restored in Thee;
Changed from glory into glory,
Till in heaven we take our place,
Till we cast our crowns before Thee,
Lost in wonder, love, and praise.

Charles Wesley, 1707–88

When I tread the verge of Jordan,
Bid my anxious fears subside;
Death of deaths, and hell's destruction,

Land me safe on Canaan's side.
Songs of praises, songs of praises,
I will ever give to Thee;
I will ever give to Thee.

William Williams, 1717–91

Bereavement

God of all compassion, in your unending love
and mercy for us your turn the darkness of
death into the dawn of new life. Show compassion to your people in their sorrow.

Be our refuge and our strength to lift us
from the darkness of this grief to the peace and
light of your presence.

Your son, our Lord Jesus Christ, by dying
for us, conquered death and by rising again,
restored life.

May we then go forward eagerly to meet
him, and after our life on earth be reunited
with our brothers and sisters where every tear
will be wiped away.

Author unknown

Almighty God, Father of all mercies and giver
of all comfort, deal graciously, we pray, with
those who mourn, that casting every care on
you, they may the consolation of your love;
through Jesus Christ our Lord.

Author unknown

We give them back to thee, dear Lord, who
gavest them to us. Yet as thou didst not lose
them in giving, so we have not lost them by
their return. For what is thine is ours always,
if we are thine.

Author unknown, Quaker prayer

May the cry of widows, orphans and destitute
children enter into thine ears, O most loving
Savior. Comfort them with a mother's tenderness, shield them from the perils of this world,
and bring them at last to thy heavenly home.

John Cosin, 1594–1672

Death is nothing at all; I have only slipped
  away into the next room.
I am I and you are you, whatever we were to
  each other we are still.
Call me by my old familiar name, speak to me
  in the easy way which we always used.

Put no difference in your tone; wear no forced
air of solemnity or sorrow.
Laugh as we always laughed at little jokes
together.
Pray, smile, think of me, pray for me.
Let my name be ever the household word that
it always was, let it be spoken without the
effort, without the trace of a shadow in it.
Life means all that it ever meant, it is the same
as it ever was; there is absolutely unbroken
continuity.
What is death but a negligible accident? Why
should I be out of mind because I am out
of sight?
I am but waiting for you, for an interval
somewhere very near, just around the
corner.
All is well.
Nothing is past; nothing is lost. One brief
moment and all will be as before.

Henry Scott Holland,
1847–1918

O Lord of all worlds, we bless your name for
all those who have entered into their rest, and
reached the promised land where you are seen
face to face. Give us grace to follow in their
footsteps, as they followed in the footsteps of
your holy Son. Keep alive in us the memory of
those dear to ourselves whom you have called
to yourself; and grant that every remembrance
which turns our hearts from things seen to
things unseen may lead us always upwards to
you, until we come to our eternal rest; through
Jesus Christ our Lord.

F.J.A. Hort, 1828–92

We give back to you, O God, those whom you
gave to us. You did not lose them when you
gave them to us, and we do not lose them by
their return to you. Your dear Son has taught
us that life is eternal and love cannot die, so
death is only a horizon, and a horizon is only
the limit of our sight. Open our eyes to see
more clearly and draw us close to you that we
may know that we are nearer to our loved ones,
who are with you. You have told us that you are
preparing a place for us: prepare us, that where
you are we may be always, O dear Lord of life
and death.

William Penn, 1644–1718

FAMILIES AND FRIENDS

Lord and Savior, You have taught us to honor
our fathers and mothers, and to show love
and obedience toward them. From the depth
of my heart I fervently pray to You, Jesus, my
God: hear my prayer. Bless my parents who
have raised me up with the help of Your grace.
Protect them from evil, harm and sickness.
Grant them faith, health and joy. Bless all their
works that they may give You honor and glory
all the days of their lives. Amen

Orthodox prayer

Parting from a friend
To-day we go forth separate, some of us to
pleasure, some of us to worship, some upon
duty. Go with us, our guide and angel; hold
Thou before us in our divided paths the mark
of our low calling, still to be true to what small
best we can attain to. Help us in that, our
maker, the dispenser of events – Thou, of the
vast designs, in which we blindly labor, suffer
us to be so far constant to ourselves and our
beloved.

R.L. Stevenson, 1850–94

For our absent loved ones we implore thy
loving-kindness. Keep them in life, keep them
in growing honor; and for us, grant that we
remain worthy of their love. For Christ's sake,
let not our beloved blush for us, nor we for
them. Grant us but that, and grant us courage
to endure lesser ills unshaken, and to accept
death, loss, and disappointment as it were
straws upon the tide of life.

R.L. Stevenson, 1850–94

Birthdays and anniversaries

Happy birthday to you,
Happy birthday to you,
Happy birthday dear __,
God bless you today.

Author unknown

My Jesus, my King, my Life, my All; I again
dedicate my whole self to Thee. Accept me, and
grant, O gracious Father, that ere this year is
gone I may finish my task. In Jesus' name I ask

it. Amen, so let it be.

David Livingstone, 1813–73. His Last Journals,
March 19, 1872, his birthday

Homes and parents

O Lord, whose will it is that, next to thyself, we should hold our parents in highest honor, it is not the least of our duties to beseech thy goodness towards them. Preserve, I pray thee, my parents and home in the love of thy church and in health of body and mind; grant that through me no sorrow may befall them; and finally, as they are kind to me, so be thou to the, who art the supreme Father of all.

Desiderius Erasmus 1467–1536

Father of all mankind, make the roof of my house wide enough for all opinions, oil the door of my house so it opens easily to friend and stranger and set such a table in my house that my whole family may speak kindly and freely around it.

Source unknown, Hawaii

The Sacred Three
My fortress be
Encircling me
Come and be round
My hearth, my home.

Traditional Hebridean chant

Bless This House, O Lord we pray
Make it safe by Night and Day.
Bless these Walls, so firm and stout
Keeping want and Trouble out.

Bless the Roof and Chimneys tall.
Let Thy Peace lie over all.

Bless this Door that it may prove
Ever open to Joy and Love

Bless these Windows shining bright
Letting in God's heavenly Light.

Bless the folks who dwell within,
Keep them pure and free from Sin.

Bless us all that one day we

May dwell, O Lord, on high with Thee.

Author unknown

O heavenly Father, shed forth thy blessed Spirit richly on all members of this household. Make each one of us an instrument in thy hands for good. Purify our hearts, strengthen our minds and bodies, fill us with mutual love. Let no pride, no self-conceit, no rivalry, no dispute, ever spring up among us. Make us earnest and true, wise and prudent, giving no just cause for offence; and may thy holy peace rest upon us this and every day, sweetening our trials, cheering us in our work, and keeping us faithful to the end; through Jesus Christ, our Lord.

Church Guild, 19th century

Visit we beseech thee most gracious Father, this family and household with thy protection. Let thy blessing descend and rest on all who belong to it. Guide us here, and hereafter bring us to thy glory; through Jesus Christ our Lord.

J.C. Ryle, 1816–1900

Heavenly Father, we beseech thee to look in thy mercy upon this household. Grant that ever member of it may be taught and guided of thee. Bless the relations and friends of each of us; thou knowest their several necessities; and prosper our efforts to advance thy kingdom at home and abroad; for our Lord Jesus Christ's sake.

A.C. Taut, 1811–82

Inspire and strengthen us by your Holy Spirit,
    O Lord God, to seek your will and uphold
    your honor in all things:
in the purity and joy of our homes,
in the trust and fellowship of our common
    life,
in daily service of the good,
after the pattern and in the power of your
    Son, our Lord and Savior, Jesus Christ.

Jeremy Taylor, 1613–67

O eternal God, our most merciful Lord and gracious Father, thou art my guide, the light of mine eyes, the joy of my heart, the author of my hope, and the object of my love and worshipping, thou relievest all my needs, and determinest all my doubts, and art an eternal fountain of blessing, open to all thirsty and weary souls that come and cry to thee for mercy and refreshment. Have mercy upon thy servant, and relieve my fears and sorrows, and the great necessities of my family; for thou alone, O Lord, canst do it.

Jeremy Taylor, 1613–67

Death of a child

O God, to me who am left to mourn his departure, grant that I may not sorrow as one without hope for my beloved who sleeps in you; but, as always remembering his courage, and the love that united us on earth, I may begin again with new courage to serve you more fervently who are the only source of true love and true fortitude; that when I have passed a few more days in this valley of tears and this shadow of death, supported by your rod and staff, I may see him face to face, in those pastures and beside those waters of comfort where I believe he already walks with you. O Shepherd of the sheep, have pity on this darkened soul of mine.

E.W. Benson, 1829–96, on the death of his young son Martin

O God, you have dealt very mysteriously with us. We have been passing through deep waters; our feet were well-nigh gone, But though you slay us, yet we will trust in you … You have reclaimed your lent jewels. Yet, O Lord, shall I not thank you now? I will thank you not only for the children you have left to us, but for those you have reclaimed. I thank you for the blessing of the last ten years, and for all the sweet memories of these lives … I thank you for the full assurance that each has gone to the arms of the Good Shepherd, whom each loved according to the capacity of her years. I thank you for the bright hopes of a happy reunion, when we shall meet to part no more. O Lord, for Jesus Christ's sake, comfort our desolate hearts.

A.C. Taut, 1811–82, five of his six children died of scarlet fever in one month, in 1856

Children

Blessed Lord Jesus, Who has taught us that we must be as the little children in order to come to Thy Kingdom, and Who didst love and bless them most tenderly: Grant that our children may be drawn unto Thee by Thy good Spirit and ever kept in Thy service, so that walking in Thy way, they may ever show forth Thy praise and be one with us in the confession of Thy holy Name; Who livest, etc. Amen.

The Common Service Book of the Lutheran Church, 1917

Almighty God and heavenly Father, we thank you for the children which you have given us; give us also grace to train them in your faith, fear and love; that as they advance in years they may grow in grace, and may hereafter be found in the number of your elect children; through Jesus Christ our Lord.

John Cosin, 1594–1672

Bless my children with healthy bodies, with good minds, with the graces and gifts of your Spirit, with sweet dispositions and holy habits, and sanctify them throughout their bodies and souls and spirits, and keep them blameless until the coming of the Lord Jesus.

Jeremy Taylor, 1613–67

Gentle Jesus, meek and mild,
Look upon a little child
Make me gentle as Thou art,
Come and live within my heart.
Take my childish hand in Thine,
Guide these little feet of mine.
So shall all my happy days,
Sing their pleasant song of praise
And the world shall always see
Christ, the Holy Child, in me.

Charles Wesley, 1707–88

Neighbors

Holy Father, we commend into your hands our family and our friends, our neighbors and our benefactors. Strengthen and confirm all faithful people and convert all sinners into your ways of goodness and love. Rouse the careless, raise the fallen, heal the sick, and grant your peace to the dying; and all for your own love's sake. Amen.

B.F. Westcott, 1825–1901

Lord, Thou hast taught us that all who come our way are our neighbors. But hear our prayer for those with whom we come in daily contact because they live close to us. Help us to be good neighbors to them. Give us the grace to ignore petty annoyances and to build on all that is positive in our relationship, that we may love them as we love ourselves, with genuine forbearance and kindness.

B.F. Westcott, 1825–1901

Family

We pray for the safety and welfare of our own family and friends wheresoever dispersed, beseeching thee to avert from them all material and lasting evil of body or mind; and may we by the assistance of thy holy spirit so conduct ourselves on earth as to secure an eternity of happiness with each other in thy heavenly kingdom. Grant this most merciful Father, for the sake of our blessed savior in whose holy name and words we further address thee.

Jane Austen, 1775–1817

For the joy of human love,
Brother, sister, parent, child,
Friends on earth and friends above,
For all gentle thoughts and mild.

Refrain:
Lord of all, to Thee we raise,
This our hymn of grateful praise.

F.S. Pierpoint, 1835–1917

Lord, behold our family here assembled.
We thank you for this place in which we
    dwell,
for the love accorded us this day,
for the hope with which we expect the
    morrow;
for the health, the work, the food and the
    bright skies
that make our lives delightful;
for our friends in all parts of the earth.
Give us courage and gaiety and the quiet
    mind.
Spare us to our friends, soften us to our
    enemies.
Bless us, if it may be, in all our innocent
    endeavors;

if it may not, give us the strength to endure
    that which is to come
that we may be brave in peril, constant in
    tribulation,
temperate in wrath and in all changes of
    fortune
and down to the gates of death, loyal and
    loving to one another.
We beseech of you this help and mercy for
    Christ's sake.

R.L. Stevenson, 1850–94

O Lord, fill us with your Holy Spirit, that we may firmly believe in Jesus Christ, and love him with all our hearts. Wash our souls in his precious blood. Make us to hate sin and to be holy in thought, word and deed. Help us to be faithful wives and loving mothers. Bless us and all who belong to the Mother's Union; unite us in love and prayer, and teach us to train our children for heaven. Pour out your Holy Spirit on our husbands and children. Make our homes, homes of peace and love, and may we so live on earth, that we may live with you for ever in heaven; for Jesus Christ's sake.

Mary Sumner, 1828–1921

O God, you are present with your faithful people in every place, mercifully hear our prayers for those we love who are now separated from us. Watch over them, we pray, and protect them in anxiety, danger and temptations; and assure both them and us that you are always near and that we are one with you for ever; through Jesus Christ our Lord.

F.B. Westcott, 1825–1901

Friends

O blessed Lord, who has commanded us to love one another, grant us grace that having received your undeserved bounty, we may love everyone in you and for you. We pray for your clemency for everyone; but especially for the friends whom your love has give us. Love them, O fountain of love, and make them love you with all their heart, that they may will and speak and do those things only which are pleasing to you.

Anselm, 1033–1109

O God, our heavenly Father, who hast commanded us to love one another as thy children, and has ordained the highest friendship in the bond of thy Spirit, we beseech thee to maintain and preserve us always in the same bond, to thy glory, and our mutual comfort, with all those to whom we are bound by any special tie, either of nature or of choice; that we may be perfected together in that love which is from above, and which never faitheth when all other things shall fail. Send down the dew of thy heavenly grace upon us, that we may have joy in each other that passeth not away; and, having lived together in love here, according to thy commandment, may live for ever together with them, being made one in thee, in thy glorious kingdom hereafter, through Jesus Christ our Lord.

John Austin, 1613–69

Lord God, who by the grace of your Holy Spirit has poured out your love into the hearts of your faithful people: Mercifully grant to those whom we love health of body and soul; that they may serve you with all their strength and gladly fulfill all your good pleasure; through Jesus Christ our Lord.

Gregorian Sacramentary 6th Century

Grant, O Lord, that we may keep a constant guard on our thoughts and passions, that they may never lead us into sin; that we may live in perfect love with all humankind, in affection to those who love us, and in forgiveness to those, if any there are, who hate us. Give us good and virtuous friends. In the name of our blessed Lord and Savior Jesus Christ.

Warren Hastings, 1732–1818

And, Oh my brethren,
O kind and affectionate hearts,
O loving friends,
should you know anyone whose lot it has been,
by writing or by word of mouth,
in some degree to help you thus to act;
if he has ever told you
what you knew about yourselves,
or what you did not know;
has read to you your wants or feelings,
and comforted you by the very reading;
has made you feel that there was a higher life

than this daily one,
and a brighter world than that you see;
or encouraged you,
or sobered you,
or opened a way to the inquiring,
or soothed the perplexed;
if what he had said or done
has ever made you take interest in him,
and feel well inclined toward him;
remember such a one in time to come,
though you hear him not,
and pray for him,
that in all things he may know God's will,
and at all times he may be ready to fulfill it.

J.H. Newman, 1801–90

DIFFICULTIES AND TROUBLE

Anxiety

In these our days so perilous,
Lord, peace in mercy send us;
No God but thee can fight for us,
No God but thee defend us;
Thou our only God and Savior.

Martin Luther, 1483–1546

Set free, O Lord, the souls of your servants from all restlessness and anxiety. Give us that peace and power which flow from you. Keep us in all perplexity and distress, that upheld by your strength and stayed on the rock of your faithfulness we may abide in you now and evermore.

Francis Paget, 1851–1911

Lord God, may I be troubled by nothing,
Frightened by nothing.
Everything changes,
But you don't change.
Patience obtains everything.
I shall want nothing if
I possess you.
You alone, God, are all I need.

Teresa of Avila, 1515–82

Being over-tired

O heavenly Father, in whom we live and move and have our being, we humbly pray thee so to guide and govern us by thy Holy Spirit, that in all the cares and occupations of our daily life we may never forget thee, but remember that we are ever walking in thy sight; for thine own name's sake.

Ancient Collect

Good Jesus, strength of the weary, rest of the restless, by the weariness and unrest of your sacred cross, come to me who am weary that I may rest in you.

E.B. Pusey, 1800–82

O Lord, who art as the Shadow of a great Rock in a weary land, who beholdest thy weak creatures weary of labor, weary of pleasure, weary of hope deferred, weary of self; in thine abundant compassion, and unutterable tenderness, bring us, I pray thee, unto thy rest.

Christina Rossetti, 1830–94

Difficulties

O most loving Shepherd, in the deepest of all waters we will trust you. In the darkest of all valleys we will rejoice in your presence. In the worst of our days we shall rest at peace in your arms. In the most troubled of our nights we shall be comforted by your saints. Amen.

Archibald Campbell Taut, 1811–82

Lord Jesus, think on me
Amid the battle's strife;
In all my pain and misery
Be Thou my Health and Life.

Synesius of Cyrene, 375–430,
translated by Allen W. Chatfield

Stress

Lord, teach us to number our days, that we may apply our hearts to wisdom.
Lighten, if it is your will, the pressures of this world's cares.
Above all, reconcile us to your will, and give us a peace which the world cannot take away; through our Savior Jesus Christ.

Thomas Chalmers, 1780–1847

The God of love my shepherd is,
And he that doth me feed:

While he is mine, and I am His,
What can I want or need?

He leads me to the tender grass,
Where I both feed and rest;
Then to the streams that gently pass:
In both I have the best.

Or if I stray, he doth convert,
And bring my mind in frame:
And all this not for my desert,
But for his holy name.

Yea, in death's shady, black abode
Well may I walk, not fear:
For thou art with me, and thy rod
To guide, thy staff to bear.

Nay, thou dost make me sit and dine,
Even in my enemies' sight;
My head with oil, my cup with wine
Runs over day and night.

Surely they sweet and wondrous love
Shall measure all my days;
And as it never shall remove,
So neither shall my praise.

George Herbert, 1593–1633, The Temple

Blessed Jesus, you are always near in times of stress.
Although we cannot feel your presence you are close.
You are always there to help and watch over us.
Nothing in heaven or on earth can separate you from us.

After Margery Kempe, c.1373–c.1440

Depression

I believe
    that thou didst create me:
        the workmanship of thy hands
            despise not.
    that I am after thine image and likeness:
        thy likeness
            suffer not to be blotted out.
    that thou didst redeem me in thy blood:
        the price of the ransom
            suffer not to perish.

that thou didst make me a Christian after
   thine own name:
      thine own namesake
think not scorn of.
that thou didst hallow me in regeneration:
   thine own hallowed thing
      destroy not.
that thou didst engraft me in the good
   olive tree:
   the member of the body mystical
      cut not off.
O think upon thy servant as concerning thy
   word,
   wherein thou hast caused me to put my
   trust.
My soul hath longed for thy salvation
   and I have a good hope because of thy
   word.
     Be thou my hope
       yet and yet again
     and my portion in the land of the living.

Lancelot Andrewes, 1555–1626,
translated by F.E. Brightman

Shine from the cross to me, then all is peace;
Shine from the throne, then all my troubles
   cease;
Speak but the word, and sadness quits my soul;
Touch but my hand with thine, and I am
   whole.

Horatius Bonar, 1808–82

Ah, Lord, my prayers are dead, my affections
dead, and my heart is dead: but thou art a living
God and I bear myself upon thee.

William Bridge, 1600–70

As pants the hart for cooling streams,
When heated in the chase,
So longs my soul, O God, for Thee
And Thy refreshing grace.

For Thee, my God, the living God,
My thirsty soul doth pine;
O, when shall I behold Thy face,
Thou majesty divine?

Why restless, why cast down, my soul?
Hope still; and thou shalt sing
The praise of Him Who is thy God,
Thy health's eternal spring.

To Father, Son, and Holy Ghost,
The God Whom we adore,
Be glory as it was, is now,
And shall be evermore.

Nahum Tate, 1652–1715, and Nicholas Brady,
1639–1726, Psalm 42

O my God! Source of all mercy! I acknowledge your sovereign power. While recalling the wasted years that are past, I believe that you, Lord, can in an instant turn this loss to gain. Miserable as I am, yet I firmly believe that you can do all things. Please restore to me the time lost, giving me your grace, both now and in the future, that I may appear before you in "wedding garments."

Teresa of Avila, 1515–82

Tragedy

In you, O Lord, I seek refuge;
    do not let me ever be put to shame;
    in your righteousness deliver me.
Incline your ear to me;
    rescue me speedily.
Be a rock of refuge for me,
    a strong fortress to save me.
… Into your hand I commit my spirit;
    you have redeemed me, O Lord, faithful
    God.

Psalm 31.1–2, 5 NRSV

Eternal God, our heavenly Father, who loves us with an everlasting love: Help us now to wait on you with reverent and submissive hearts, that we, through patience and comfort of the Scriptures, may have hope, and be lifted above our distress into the light and peace of your presence; through Jesus Christ our Lord.

Author unknown

O Joy that seekest me through pain,
I cannot close my heart to thee;
I trace the rainbow through the rain,
And feel the promise is not vain,
That morn shall tearless be.

George Matheson, 1842–1906

Illness and suffering

O God, the Father of lights, from whom comes

down every good and perfect gift: mercifully look upon our frailty and infirmity, and grant us such health of body as you know is neeedful for us; that both in body and soul we may evermore serve you with all our strength; through Jesus Christ our Lord.

John Cosin, 1594–1672

Send me any chastisement, but deprive me not of the power of loving You.

Alphonsus Liguori, 1696–1787

Times of darkness and difficulty

O Savior of the world, the Son, Lord Jesus: stir up thy strength and help us, we humbly beseech thee.

By thy cross and precious blood thou hast redeemed us: save us and help us, we humbly beseech thee.

Thou didst save thy disciples when ready to perish: hear us and save us, we humbly beseech thee.

Let the pitifulness of thy great mercy loose us from our sins, we humbly beseech thee.

Make it appear that thou art our Savior and mighty deliverer: O save us, that we may praise thee, we humbly beseech thee.

Draw near, according to thy promise from the throne of thy glory: look down and hear our crying, we humbly beseech thee.

Come again, and dwell with us, O Lord Christ Jesus: abide with us forever, we humbly beseech thee.

And when thou shalt appear with power and great glory: may we be make like unto thee in thy glorious kingdom.

Thanks be to thee, O Lord: Hallelujah.

Source unknown, 12th century

We humbly beseech thee, O Father, mercifully to look upon our infirmities; and for the glory of thy Name turn from us all those evils that we most righteously have deserved; and grant that in all our troubles we may put our whole trust an confidence in thy mercy, and evermore serve thee in holiness and pureness of living, to thy honor and glory; through our only Mediator and Advocate, Jesus Christ our Lord.

Book of Common Prayer, Litany, 1549

O Lord, enlighten my heart, which evil desire has darkened. O Lord, help me to think about what is good.

John Chrysostom, c.347–407

O my God I thank you and I praise you for accomplishing your holy and all-lovable will without any regard for mine.

With my whole heart, in spite of my heart, do I receive this cross I feared so much!

It is the cross of your choice, the cross of your love. I venerate it; nor for anything in the world would I wish that it had not come, since you willed it.

I keep it with gratitude and with joy, as I do everything that comes from your hand; and I shall strive to carry it without letting it drag, with all the respect and all the affection which your works deserve.

Francis de Sales, 1567–1622

My stock lies dead, and no increase
Doth my dull husbandry improve:
O let thy graces without cease
Drop from above!

If still the Sun should hide his face,
Thy house would but a dungeon prove,
Thy works night's captives: O let grace
Drop from above!

The dew doth every morning fall;
And shall the dew outstrip thy Dove?
The dew, for which grass cannot call,
Drop from above!

Death is still working like a mole,
And digs my grave at each remove:
Let grace work too, and on my soul
Drop from above!

Sin is still hammering my heart
Unto a hardness, void of love:
Let suppling grace, to cross his art,
Drop from above!

O come! for thou dost know the way.
Or if to me thou wilt not move,
Remove me where I need not say-
Drop from above!

George Herbert, 1593–1633, The Temple

My spirit is dry within me because it forgets to feed on you.

> *John of the Cross, 1542–91*

Holy Spirit, Lord of light,
  From the clear celestial height
  Thy pure beaming radiance give.
Come, thou Father of the poor,
  Come with treasure which endure,
  Come thou light of all that live!
Thou of all consolers best.
  Thou the soul's delightful guest,
  Dost refreshing peace bestow.
Thou in toil art comfort sweet,
  Pleasant coolness in the heat,
  Solace in the midst of woe.
Light immortal, light divine,
  Visit thou these hearts of thine,
  And our inmost being fill.
If thou take thy grace away
  Nothing pure in man will stay;
  All his good is turned to ill.
Heal our wounds, our strength renew.
  On our dryness pour thy dew,
  Wash the stains of guilt away.
Bend the stubborn heart and will;
  Melt the frozen, warm the chill;
  Guide the steps that go astray.
Thou on us, who ever more
  Thee confess and thee adore,
  With thy sevenfold gifts descend:
Give us comfort when we die,
  Give us life with thee on high;
  Give us joys that never end.

> *Attributed to Stephen Langton, 1151–1228,*
> *translated by E. Caswall, 1814–78*

Grant, we beseech thee, O Lord our God, that in whatever dangers we are placed we may call upon thy name, and that when deliverance is given us from on high we may never cease from thy praise; through Jesus Christ our Lord.

> *Leonine Sacramentary*

Lord Jesus Christ, who according to the will of the Father, through the co-operation of the Holy Ghost, hast by Thy death given life to the world: deliver me.

> *Margaret of Scotland,*
> *c.1045–92*

Lead, kindly Light, amid the encircling gloom,
  Lead Thou me on!
The night is dark, and I am far from home -
  Lead Thou me on!
Keep Thou my feet; I do not ask to see
The distant scene – one step enough for me.

I was not ever thus, nor pray'd that Thou
  Shouldst lead me on.
I loved to choose and see my path, but now
  Lead Thou me on!
I loved the garish day, and, spite of fears,
Pride ruled my will: remember not past years.

So long Thy power hath blest me, sure it still
  Will lead me on,
O'er moor and fen, o'er crag and torrent, till
  The night is gone;
And with the morn those angel faces smile
Which I have loved long since, and lost
  awhile.

> *J.H. Newman, 1801–90*

My dear Lord, though I am so very weak that I have not strength to ask you for suffering as a gift, at least I will beg from you grace to meet suffering well when you in your love and wisdom brings it on me. Let me bear pain, reproach, disappointment, slander, anxiety, suspense, as you want me to, O my Jesus, and as you by your own suffering have taught me, when it comes.

> *J.H. Newman, 1801–90*

All will be well, and all will be well, and all manner of things will be well.

> *Julian of Norwich, 1342–c.1416*

Now thank we all our God,
With heart and hand and voices,
Who wondrous things has done,
In whom his world rejoices;
Who from our mother's arms
Has blessed us on our way
With countless gifts of love
And still is ours today.

O may this bounteous God
Through all our life be near us,
With ever joyful hearts
And blessed peace to cheer us;

And keep us in his grace,
And guide us when perplexed,
And free us from all ills
In this world and the next.
                    Martin Rinkart, 1586–1649,
                    translated by Catherine Winkworth

I have no wit, no words, no tears;
    My heart within me like a stone
    Is numbed too much for hopes or fears;
        Look right, look left, I dwell alone;
I lift mine eyes, but dimmed with grief
        No everlasting hills I see;
My life is in the falling leaf:
    O Jesus, quicken me.

My life is like a faded leaf,
    My harvest dwindled to a husk;
Truly my life is void and brief
    And tedious in the barren dusk;
My life is like a frozen thing,
    No bud nor greenness can I see:
Yet rise it shall – the sap of Spring;
    O Jesus, rise in me.

My life is like a broken bowl,
    A broken bowl that cannot hold
One drop of water for my soul
    Or cordial in the searching cold;
Cast in the fire the perished thing,
    Melt and remold it, till it be
A royal cup for Him my King:
    O Jesus, drink of me.
                    Christina Rossetti, 1830–94

Though waves and storms go o'er my head,
Though strength and health and friends be
    gone,
Though joys be withered all, and dead,
Though every comfort be withdrawn,
On this my steadfast soul relies, –
Father! Thy mercies never dies.
                    Johann A. Rothe, 1799–1867

Lord Jesus, think on me,
And purge away my sin;
From earthborn passions set me free,
And make me pure within.

Lord Jesus, think on me,
With care and woe oppressed;

Let me thy loving servant be,
And taste thy promised rest.

Lord Jesus, think on me,
Nor let me go astray;
Through darkness and perplexity
Point thou the heavenly way.

Lord Jesus, think on me,
Than when the flood is past,
I may the eternal brightness see,
And share thy joy at last.
                    Synesius, 375–430, translated
                    A.W. Chatfield, 1808–96

Through all the changing scenes of life,
In trouble and in joy,
The praises of my God shall still
My heart and tongue employ.
                    Nahum Tate, 1652–1715, and
                    Nicholas Brady, 1639–1726

O God, our Help in ages past,
Our Hope for years to come,
Our Shelter from the stormy blast,
And our eternal Home!

Beneath the shadow of Thy throne
Thy saints have dwelt secure;
Sufficient is Thine arm alone,
And our defense is sure.

Before the hills in order stood,
Or Earth received her frame,
From everlasting Thou art God,
To endless years the same.

Thy Word commands our flesh to dust:
'Return, ye sons of men!'
All nations rose from earth at first
And turn to earth again.

A thousand ages in Thy sight
Are like an evening gone;
Short as the watch that ends the night
Before the rising sun.

The busy tribes of flesh and blood,
With all their cares and fears,
Are carried downward by the flood,
And lost in following years.

Time, like an ever rolling stream,
Bears all its sons away;
They fly forgotten as a dream
Dies at the opening day.

Like flowery fields the nations stand,
Pleased with the morning light;
The flowers beneath the mower's hand
Lie withering ere 'tis night.

Our God our help in ages past,
Our hope for years to come,
Be Thou our guard while life shall last,
And our eternal Home.

Isaac Watts, 1674–1748

Grant, Lord God, that in the middle of all the discouragements, difficulties and dangers, distress and darkness of this mortal life, I may depend on your mercy, and on this build my hopes, as on a sure foundation. Let your infinite mercy in Christ Jesus deliver me from despair, both now and at the hour of death.

Thomas Wilson, 1663–1755

Doubt

Through the night of doubt and sorrow
Onward goes the pilgrim band,
Singing songs of expectation,
Marching to the promised land.

*Bernhardt Ingemann, 1789–1862,
translated by S. Baring-Gould, 1834–1924*

When surrounded with doubts from every direction, we who are defiled in heart and are in need to listen, look up to you, O High Priest Jesus, who experienced our weak nature.
For our sake you became bearer of sin that we may become righteous for you.
For our sake you became earthly that we may become heavenly.
For our sake you became bread that we, by partaking of you, may be sanctified.
Grant your aggrieved body to be sanctifying food to all hearts. Pour out the stream of your blood in sinless drops for the joy of sinlessness among humankind. Lower the anchor of your Cross to us strugglers in the sea of this world and lift us up to you.

We fell short of grace, cover us.
We retracted from work, forgive us.
We grope in darkness, enlighten us.
We have become lax in faith, restore us.
You are hope. You are light. You are life. You are forgiveness itself. You are, indeed, immortality. Those who have put their trust in you are waiting for your grace. Those who have joined themselves to your body are longing to obtain redemption from you. You are their redeemer Priest, who has purchased his flock with his blood.
Consider us all. When faced with uncertainties, comfort us through what you have done for us. Calm our anguish through your peace. Let us rest from our labors in your mansions, where you have gone and which, O Lord, you have promised. Make those who are yours worthy to glorify you there, always, with the Father and the Holy Spirit. Amen.

Nersess Lambronac'i, 1153–1198

Jesus, your light is shining within us,
let not my doubts and my darkness speak to me;
Jesus, your light is shining within us,
let my heart always welcome your love.

Brother Roger, b.1915

Financial problems

Let nothing disturb you
nothing frighten you,
all things are passing;
patient endurance
attains all things.
One whom God possesses
lacks nothing,
for God alone suffices.

Bookmark of Teresa of Avila, 1515–82

Times of change

Be, Lord, within me to strengthen me,
without me to preserve me,
over me to shelter me,
beneath me to support me,
before me to direct me,
behind me to bring me back,

and round about me to fortify me.

Lancelot Andrewes, 1555–1626

Thank you, Lord Jesus, that you will be our hiding place whatever happens.

Corrie ten Boom, 1892–1983

EVERYDAY LIFE

Employment/Study

O Lord, give your blessing, we pray, to our daily work, that we may do it in faith and heartily, as to the Lord and not to men.

All our powers of body and mind are yours, and we devote them to your service. Sanctify them, and the work in which we are engaged; and, Lord, so bless our efforts that they may bring forth in us the fruits of true wisdom.

Teach us to seek after truth and enable us to gain it; and grant that while we know earthly things, we may know you, and be known by you, through and in your Son Jesus Christ.

Thomas Arnold, 1795–1842

The Students' Psalm
The Lord is my shepherd, I shall not flunk;
He keepeth me from lying down when I
   should be studying.
He leadeth me beside the water cooler for a
   study break;
He restores my faith in study guides.
He leads me to better study habits
For my grades' sake.

Yea, tho' I walk through the valley of
   borderline grades,
I will not have a nervous breakdown;
For thou art with me;
My prayers and my friends, they comfort me.

Thou givest me the answers in moments of
   blankness;
Thou anointest my head with understanding,
My test paper runneth over with questions I
   recognize.

Surely passing grades and flying colors shall
   follow me
All the days of examinations;

And I shall not have to dwell in this
   University/College/Polytech Forever !
Amen.

Author unknown

O God, give us work
   till our life shall end,
and give us life
   till our work is done.

Author unknown

God give me work
Till my life shall end,
And life
Till my work is done.

*Source unknown, inscribed on the
grave of Winifred Holtby, 1898–1935*

O Lord Jesus Christ, only-begotten Son of thine eternal Father, thou hast said that without thee we can do nothing. O Lord, I embrace with faith and with my whole heart and soul what thou hast said. Help me, a sinner, to finish the work which I now undertake for thee; in the name of the Father, and of the Son, and of the Holy Spirit.

Source unknown, Eastern Orthodox

Help us to put away laziness, be full of courage, and be found doing His work ready to enter His glorious kingdom with joy. You are the true light of every creature, and to You all creation sings.

Basil the Great, c.330–379

Prevent us, O Lord, in all our doings with thy most gracious favor, and further us with thy continual help; that in all our works begun, continued, and ended in thee, we may glorify thy holy Name, and finally by thy mercy obtain everlasting life; through Jesus Christ our Lord. Amen.

Book of Common Prayer, 1549, The Lord's Supper

O Lord, I do not pray for tasks equal to my strength: I ask for strength equal to my tasks.

Phillips Brooks, 1835–93

O Lord, who art the fountain of all wisdom and learning, since thou of thy special goodness hast granted that my youth is instructed in good arts which may assist me to honest and holy living, grant also, by enlightening my mind, which otherwise labors under blindness, that I may be fit to acquire knowledge; strengthen my memory faithfully to retain what I may have learned: and govern my heart, that I may be willing and even eager to profit, lest the opportunity which thou now givest me be lost through my sluggishness. Be pleased therefore to infuse thy Spirit into me, the Spirit of understanding, of truth, judgment, and prudence, lest my study be without success, and the labor of my teacher be in vain.

John Calvin, 1509–64

In whatever kind of study I engage, enable me to remember to keep its proper end in view, namely, to know thee in Christ Jesus thy Son; and may every thing that I learn assist me to observe the right rule of godliness. And seeing thou promisest that thou wilt bestow wisdom on babes, and such as are humble, and the knowledge of thyself on the upright in heart, while thou declarest that thou wilt cast down the wicked and the proud, so that they will fade away in their ways, I entreat that thou wouldst be pleased to turn me to true humility, that thus I may show myself teachable and obedient first of all to thyself, and then to those also who by thy authority are placed over me. Be pleased at the same time to root out all vicious desires from my heart, and inspire it with an earnest desire of seeking thee. Finally, let the only end at which I aim be so to qualify myself in early life, that when I grow up I may serve thee in whatever station thou mayest assign me.

John Calvin, 1509–64

May my work be faithful;
May my work be honest;
May my work be blessed;
May my work bless others;
May my work bless you.
May the wealth and work of the world be
    available to all and for the exploitation of
    none.

Celtic Prayer

Lord, hear; Lord, forgive; Lord, do.
Hear what I speak not; forgive what I speak
    amiss; do what I leave undone;

that, not according to my word or my deed,
    but according to thy mercy and truth, all
    may issue to thy glory and to the good of
    thy kingdom.

Maria Hare, 1798–1870

The Elixir

Teach me, my God and King,
    In all things thee to see,
And what I do in any thing,
    To do it as for thee.

Not rudely, as a beast,
    To run into an action;
But still to make thee prepossest,
    And give it his perfection.

A man that looks on glass,
    On it may stay his eye;
Or if he pleaseth, through it pass,
    And then the heaven espy.

All may of thee partake:
    Nothing can be so mean,
Which with this tincture (for thy sake)
    Will not grow bright and clean.

A servant with this clause
    Makes drudgery divine:
Who sweeps a room, as for thy laws,
    Makes that and th' action fine.

This is the famous stone
    That turneth all to gold:
For that which God doth touch and own
    Cannot for less be told.

George Herbert, 1593–1633, The Temple

O Lord, renew our spirits and draw our hearts to yourself, that our work may not be to us a burden but a delight. Let us not serve you with the spirit of bondage like slaves, but with freedom and gladness, delighting in you and rejoicing in your work, for Jesus Christ's sake.

Benjamin Jenks, 1647–1724

O Lord, in whose hands are life and death, by whose power I am sustained, and by whose mercy I am spared, look down upon me with pity. Forgive me that I have until now so much neglected the duty which thou hast assigned to me, and suffered the days and hours of which I must give account to pass away without any endeavor to accomplish thy will. Make me to remember, O God, that every day is thy gift and ought to be used according to your command. Grant me, therefore, so to repent of my negligence, that I may obtain mercy from thee, and pass the time which thou shalt yet allow me in diligent performance of thy commands, through Jesus Christ.

Samuel Johnson, 1709–84

Almighty God, our heavenly Father, without whose help labor is useless, without whose light search in vain, invigorate my studies and direct my enquiries, that I may through due diligence and right discernment establish myself and others in your holy faith. Take not, O Lord, your Holy Spirit from me, let not evil thoughts have dominion in my mind. Let me not linger in ignorance and doubt, but enlighten and support me for the sake of Jesus Christ our Lord.

Samuel Johnson, 1709–84

O God, who has ordained that whatever is to be desired should be sought by labor, and who, by your blessing, brings honest labor to good effect, look with mercy on my studies and endeavors. Grant me, O Lord, to desire only what is lawful and right; and afford me calmness of mind and steadiness of purpose, that I may so do your will in this short life, as to obtain happiness in the world to come, for the sake of Jesus Christ our Lord.

Samuel Johnson, 1709–84, written in his private register when he was 67 year old, on July 25, 1775

O Father, light up the small duties of this day's life. May they shine with the beauty of Thy countenance. May we believe that glory may dwell in the commonest task. For the sake of Jesus Christ our Lord we ask it. Amen.

J.H. Jowett, 1864–1923

O God, who has commanded that no one should be idle, give us grace to employ our talents and faculties in the service appointed for us; that, whatever our hand finds to do, we may do it with our might.

James Martineau, 1805–1900

The things, good Lord, that we pray for, give us the grace to labor for.

Thomas More, 1478–1535

Almighty God, our Help and Refuge, who knows that we can do nothing right without Your guidance and help; direct me by Your wisdom and power, that I may accomplish this task and, whatever I do according to Your divine will, so that it may be beneficial to me and others and to the glory of Your holy Name. Amen.

Orthodox prayer

My Lord and Savior, You became man and labored with Your hands until the time of Your ministry. Bless me as I begin this work. Help me to bring it to completion. Lord, enlighten my mind and strengthen my body, that I may accomplish my task according to Your will. Guide me to bring about works of goodness to Your service and glory. Amen.

Orthodox prayer

Lord Jesus Christ, my God, You have said, "Apart from me You can do nothing." In faith I embrace Your words, Lord, and I entreat Your goodness. Help me to carry out the work I am about to begin, and to bring it to completion. To You I give glory, Father, Son and Holy Spirit. Amen.

Orthodox prayer

Christ my Lord, the Giver of light and wisdom, who opened the eyes of the blind man and transformed the fishermen into wise heralds and teachers of the gospel through the coming of the Holy Spirit, shine also in my mind the light of the grace of the Holy Spirit. Grant me discernment, understanding and wisdom in learning. Enable me to complete my assignments and to abound in every good work, for to You I give honor and glory. Amen.

Orthodox prayer

Before study
Most blessed Lord, send the grace of Your Holy Spirit on me to strengthen me that I may learn well the subject I am about to study and by it become a better person for Your glory, the comfort of my family and the benefit of Your

Church and our Nation. Amen.

Orthodox prayer

After study

I thank You, Lord our God, that again on this occasion You have opened my eyes to the light of Your wisdom. You have gladdened my heart with the knowledge of truth. I entreat You, Lord, help me always to do Your will. Bless my soul and body, my words and deeds. Enable me to grow in grace, virtue and good habits, that Your name may be glorified, Father, Son and Holy Spirit, now and forever. Amen.

Orthodox prayer

Give us grace, O Lord, to work while it is day, fulfilling diligently and patiently whatever duty thou appointest us; doing small things in the day of small things, and great labors if thou summon us to any; rising and working, sitting still and suffering, according to thy word. God with us, and we will go, but if thou go not with us, send us not; go before us, if thou put us forth; let us hear thy voice when we follow. Hear us, we beseech thee, for the glory of thy great name.

Christina Rossetti, 1830–94

Wherever I am, whatever I do, thou, Lord,
    seest me.
O keep me in thy fear all the day long.

Treasury of Devotion, 1869

Forth in your name, O Lord, I go,
My daily labor to pursue,
You, only you, resolved to know
In all I think, or speak or do.

The task your wisdom has assigned
O let me cheerfully fulfill,
In all my works your presence find,
And prove your good and perfect will.

Charles Wesley, 1707–88

O Lord, let us not live to be useless, for Christ's sake.

John Wesley, 1703–91

Travel

May the Lord keep our going out and our coming in from this time on and for evermore.

After Psalm 121.8 NRSV

Go forth in peace,
for you have followed the good road.
Go forth without fear,
for he who created you has made you holy,
has always protected you,
and loves you as a mother.
Blessed be you, my God, for having created
    me.

Clare of Assisi, 1194–1253

Leader to life, Path to truth, our Lord Jesus
    Christ;
You led Joseph to Egypt,
and the people of Israel through the Red Sea;
and Moses to Mount Sinai,
and his people to the land of promise.
And you traveled with Cleopas and his
    companion to Emmaus. Now, I pray you,
    Lord, lead me and my companions
to travel in peace on the journey before us.
Save us from the visible and invisible enemy
and lead us safely to the place we are headed.
For you are our way and our truth and our
    life.
Glory and worship to you now and always
and unto the ages of ages. Amen.

Hovhannes Garnets'i, c.1180–1245

Lord Jesus Christ my God, be my Companion, guide and protector during my journey. Keep me from all danger, misfortune and temptation. By Your divine power grant me a peaceful and successful journey and safe arrival. In You I place my hope and trust and You I praise, honor and glorify, together with Your Father and Holy Spirit now and forever and ever. Amen.

Orthodox prayer

O Savior, who hast journeyed with [Luke and] Cleopas to Emmaus, journey with thy servants as they now set out upon their way, and defend them from all evil.

Orthodox prayer [The Bible account of Jesus' resurrection appearance on the road to Emmaus, Luke 24.13–35, only identifies Cleopas, the other traveler is unnamed.]

Lord Jesus, You traveled with the two disciples after the resurrection and set their hearts on fire with Your grace. Travel also with me and gladden my heart with Your presence. I know, Lord, that I am a pilgrim on this earth, seeking the citizenship which is in heaven. During my journey surround me with Your holy angels and keep me safe from seen and unseen dangers. Grant that I may carry out my plans and fulfill my expectations according to Your will. Help me to see the beauty of creation and to comprehend the wonder of Your truth in all things. For You are the way, the truth and the life, and to You I give thanks, praise and glory forever. Amen.

Orthodox prayer

Prayers for People in Special Need

THE DISABLED

O God, who are the Father of lights, and with whom there is no darkness at all: we thank you for the good gift of sight which you have given us, and we pray that you will fill us with your own compassion for those who do not have it. Direct and prosper the efforts that are made for their welfare. Reveal to them by your Spirit the things which eyes have not seen, and comfort them with the hope of the light everlasting, to which, of your great mercy, we ask you to bring us all; through Jesus Christ our Savior.
Arthur W. Robinson, 1856–1928

THE DYING

My Lord God, even now I accept at Thy hand, cheerfully and willingly, with all its anxieties, pains and sufferings, whatever kind of death it shall please Thee to be mine.
Pope Pius X, 1835–1914

["My Prayer for Bob Tanner," by his physician – and his friend, Dr. John Todd. Bob Tanner died on July 21, 2000; as a result of carcinoma of the colon. He lived for more than seven productive years after the initial diagnosis. The prayer was meant to be read out loud.]

Almighty God – I am praying again, for my friend, Bob Tanner.

I pray, Lord, that you will bless Bob Tanner; and love him, and guide him, and comfort him – as he goes through whatever travail you may have planned for him. Lord, strengthen Bob, and allow him to see your presence – your hand, your purpose, your intention – in all of this distress that you have allowed to befall him.

215

Lord, forgive Bob for whatever errors he may have committed, and for whatever "flaws" you may have recorded in your "book", concerning his actions and his performance, during his journey in this world – the journey that you assigned to him.

Almighty God, my hope is that you will cure Bob of this disease that has infested him. Lord, I accept your sovereignty in all matters of human existence, both in this World, and in the life-to-come – in the Kingdom of Heaven. I know that with one word, "Heal", you have the power to remove Bob's illness. My prayer is that you will speak that word, now, Lord; and that you will cause this dreadful illness to disappear … and to be gone from Bob's body, forever.

Lord, help Bob to understand that you "discipline" your favorite sons. My prayer is that you will include Bob among those whom you love the most … those that you protect, and favor … and I pray that you will allow Bob to sense – to know within his very "soul" – that you are in him … and with him.

We remember, Lord, and we understand, that you created each of your people for your plan, and your purpose – and for your pleasure. You caused Bob Tanner to come into this world … to be born into this life … for a reason – for your own plan. Don't leave him now, please, Lord. Allow Bob to become free of his illness, so that he can complete the work that you have assigned to him, and so that he may finish those activities for which you created him.

Almighty God, I do not pray that you will swap my earthly and humanly requests for the divine plan and purpose that you have for Bob. I do pray, however, that you will empower Bob to tolerate his illness … and to see you, peacefully, in whatever you have in your design for him.

And Lord, in Bob's continuing spiritual development, let there be a growing trust in you … to complement his faith in you.

And, most of all, I pray that you will accept Bob, to be among your "chosen" ones, for eternity – in the company of God's people … both now, and in the life-to-come.

Father, help all of us – your people – to remember that "it is not for this life only that the Christ has given us hope".

Lord – in your Book of Truth, your Bible, you say the following words, to comfort your people … and to instruct us about yourself. Help us always to recall your counsel:

1 Corinthians 15.19 (NEB) If it is for this life only that the Christ has given us hope, we of all men are most to be pitied.

2 Corinthians 4.16–18 (NRSV) So we do not lose heart. Even though our outer nature is wasting away, our inner nature is being renewed, day by day. For this slight momentary affliction is preparing us for an eternal weight of glory, beyond all measure, because we look not at what can be seen, but at what cannot be seen; for what can be seen is temporary, but what cannot be seen is eternal.

Colossians 3.1,2 (NRSV) So if you have been raised with Christ, seek the things that are above, where Christ is, seated at the right hand of God. Set your minds on things that are above, not on things that are on earth.

2 Corinthians 5.6–9 (NRSV) So we are always confident; even though we know that while we are at home in the body, we are away from the Lord – for we walk by faith – not by sight. Yes, we do have confidence; and we would rather be away from the body, and at home with the Lord. So whether we are at home or away, we make it our aim to please Him.

Philippians 3.20,21 (NRSV) Our citizenship is in heaven; and it is from there that we are expecting a Savior, the Lord Jesus Christ. He will transform the body of our humiliation, that it may be conformed to the body of His glory, by the power that also enables Him to make all things subject to Himself.

Hebrews 11.13, 16 All of these died in faith without having received the promises – but from a distance, they saw and greeted them. They confessed that they were strangers and foreigners on the earth … But as it is, they desire a better country – that is, a heavenly one. Therefore God is not ashamed to be called their God – indeed, He has prepared a city for them.

Matthew 10.29 Jesus speaking: "Never a sparrow falls … apart from the will of my Father."

Almighty God, I pray this prayer in your

holy and all-powerful name. Amen.

Dr. John N. Todd III, prayer written, April
24th 1997, by kind permission

THE FEARFUL

Blessed are all your saints, our God and King, who have traveled over life's tempestuous sea, and have arrived in the harbor of peace and felicity. Watch over us who are still in our dangerous voyage; and remember those who lie exposed to the rough storms of trouble and temptations. Frail is our vessel, and the ocean is wide; but as in your mercy you have set our course, so steer the vessel of our life toward the everlasting shore of peace, and bring us at length to the quiet haven of our heart's desire, where you, O our God, are blessed, and live and reign for ever and ever.

Augustine of Hippo, 354–430

For yours is salvation,
and from you is redemption,
and by your right hand is restoration,
and your finger is fortification.
Your command is justification.
Your mercy is liberation.
Your countenance is illumination.
Your face is exultation.
Your spirit is benefaction.
Your anointing oil is consolation.
A dew drop of your grace is exhilaration.
You give comfort.
You make us forget despair.
You lift away the gloom of grief.
You change the sighs of our heart into
    laughter.

Gregory of Narek, 951–1003

Grant calmness and control of thought to those who are facing uncertainty and anxiety: let their heart stand fast, believing in the Lord. Be thou all things to all men, knowing each one and his petition, each house and its need, for the sake of Jesus Christ.

Russian Liturgy, 6th century

THE POOR

O Lord God, as the heavens are high above the earth, so are Thy ways above our ways, and Thy thoughts above our thoughts. For wise and holy purposes best known to Thyself, Thou hast seen fit to deprive me of all earthly relatives; but when my father and mother forsook me, then Thou did take me up. I desire to thank Thee, that I am this day a living witness to testify that Thou art a God, that will ever vindicate the cause of the poor and needy, and that Thou hast always proved Thyself to be a friend and father to me. O, continue Thy loving kindness even unto the end; and when health and strength begin to decay, and I, as it were, draw nigh unto the grave, O then afford me Thy heart-cheering presence, and enable me to rely entirely upon Thee. Never leave me nor forsake me, but have mercy upon me for Thy great name's sake. And not for myself alone do I ask these blessings, but for all the poor and needy, all widows and fatherless children, for the stranger in distress; and may they call upon Thee in such manner as to be convinced that Thou art a prayer-hearing and prayer-answering God; and thine shall be the praise, forever. Amen.

Maria W. Stewart, 1803–79

THE PERSECUTED

O God
We remember not only our son but also his
    murderers;
Not because they killed him in the prime of
    his youth and made our hearts bleed and
    our tears flow,
Not because with this savage act they have
    brought further disgrace on the name of
    our country among the civilized nations of
    the world;
But because through their crime we now
    follow thy footsteps more closely in the
    way of sacrifice.
The terrible fire of this calamity burns up all
    selfishness and possessiveness in us;
Its flame reveals the depths of depravity and
    meanness and suspicion, the dimension
    of hatred and the measure of sinfulness in

human nature;
It makes obvious as never before our need to
    trust in God's love as shown in the cross of
    Jesus and his resurrection;
Love which makes us free from hate towards
    our persecutors;
Love which brings patience, forbearance,
    courage, loyalty, humility, generosity,
    greatness of heart;
Love which more than ever deepens our
    trust in God's final victory and his eternal
    designs for the Church and for the world;
Love which teaches us how to prepare
    ourselves to face our own day of death.
O God
Our son's blood has multiplied the fruit of the
    Spirit in the soil of our souls;
So when his murderers stand before thee on
    the day of judgment
Remember the fruit of the Spirit by which
    they have enriched our lives.
And forgive.

*Hassan Dehqani-Tafti. This prayer was
written by Bishop Hassan Dehqani-Tafti of
Iran, on the martyrdom of his son*

I am the wheat of God, and am ground by the
teeth of the wild beasts, that I may be found the
pure bread of God ... I long after the Lord, the
Son of the true God and Father, Jesus Christ.
Him I seek, who died for us and rose again ... I
am eager to die for the sake of Christ. My love
has been crucified, and there is no fire in me
that loves anything. But there is living water
springing up in me, and it says to me inwardly:
Come to the Father.

Ignatius of Antioch, c.35–c.107

Father, make us more like Jesus. Help us to bear
difficulty, pain, disappointment and sorrows,
knowing that in your perfect working and
design you can use such bitter experiences to
shape our characters and make us more like
our Lord. We look with hope for that day when
we shall be wholly like Christ, because we shall
see him as he is. Amen.

Ignatius of Antioch, ? –c.107, before his martyrdom

REFUGEES

O Lord, we bring before you the distress and
dangers of peoples and nations, the pleas of
the imprisoned and the captive, the sorrows
of the grief-stricken, the needs of the refugee,
the impotence of the weak, the weariness of
the despondent, and the diminishments of the
aging. O Lord, stay close to all of them. Amen.

Anselm, 1033–1109

THE SAD

Lord, remember all who are single and lonely.
Lord, remember all who cannot sleep,
Do not want to sleep or sleep fitfully.
Lord, remember all people in relationships -
The sacrifices, the getting on together,
The space or lack of it.
Lord, remember all who feel downtrodden,
Victimized or unfairly treated.
Lord, remember all who find no point,
Value or meaning in living.

Finally Lord, remember any who suffer,
No matter what form the suffering takes,
And may it bear fruit
Even if this fruit is unknown to the sufferer
Or known only in hindsight.

Author unknown

THE SICK

Prayer for the Sick
Watch, O Lord, with those who wake, or
    watch, or weep tonight, and give your
    angels charge over those who sleep.
Tend your sick ones, O Lord Christ.
Rest your weary ones.
Bless your dying ones.
Soothe your suffering ones.
Pity your afflicted ones.
Shield your joyous ones.
And for all your love's sake. Amen.

Augustine of Hippo, 354–430

Almighty God, and Heavenly Father, whose
providence orders all things both in heaven
and earth; we humble ourselves before Thee

with the deepest reverence; acknowledging that even in your severest dispensations you have gracious designs towards us. We beseech Thee to look down in Your wonted goodness and mercy upon this Your servant, upon whom You have laid your afflicting hand. Sanctify Your fatherly correction to him (or her), and grant that he may receive it with meekness and bear it with patience. Suffer him not, O Lord, to murmur or repine at the severity of his trials; but let all Your visitations be so blessed to him, by the consolations of Your Holy Spirit, that they may be the means of weaning him more and more from the world of sin, of setting his affections on things above, and not on things on the earth, and of bringing him nearer to Thee in true devotion of heart. We know, O Heavenly Father, that You do not willingly afflict and grieve the children of men; and that of Your goodness You have caused this sickness to befall Your servant [or have allowed it]. O grant him such a measure of Your grace, as may enable him cheerfully to submit his will to Yours, and to regard this visitation as a paternal chastisement from You, to promote his spiritual good. And if, in the days of health and prosperity, he has at any time and in any manner forgotten You, and turned aside from Your holy way; O merciful God, let not his past faults provoke You to turn Your face from him, now that he flies unto You in this his time of trouble. Shut not up Your tender mercies in displeasure, but for the merits of Your dear Son, and through His all-prevailing intercession, pardon all his sins, and restore him to Your love and favor. Support him, O Lord, under all his pains and infirmities; perfect his repentance; increase and strengthen his faith; incite his obedience; and expand his charity. Lay not more upon him than You wilt enable him to bear, and with the temptations that You permit to assail him, do You, according to Your promise, provide a way for his escape.

Bless the means which are being employed for his relief; and recovery; grant that they may be such, and so directed that they may bring about, in Your good time, that desirable result. But if You hast otherwise determined, grant, we beseech You, that the more the outward man decay, so much the more the inner man may be strengthened and renewed by Your Holy Spirit; and give him grace so to take Your visitation, that after this painful life is ended, he may dwell with You, in life everlasting, through the merits and mediation of our blessed Lord and Savior, Jesus Christ. Amen.

Manual of Devotions, 1863

A prayer for a dangerously ill person

O Lord our God, we approach Your presence, who alone can succor and save, beseeching you to look down in pity upon this Your servant, here lying in great weakness of body, under Your chastening hand. We know, O Lord, that with You are the issues of life and of death; that with You nothing is impossible; that if you will You can even yet raise him (or her) up, heal all his infirmities, and restore him to health. In entire submission to Your righteous will, we beg this mercy at Your hands. Spare him, O good Lord, and grant him a longer continuance among us. But whatever You have determined, let his soul be precious in Your sight. Give him true repentance for all the sins, ignorance, and negligence of his past life, and a lively faith in Jesus Christ. Wash his soul with the precious blood of Your dear Son, and sanctify it by and adorn it with the graces of Your Holy Spirit, that it may be cleansed from all its defilements, and be presented pure and blameless and without spot before You, in the great Day of Your power. Fit him, we pray You, for whatever in Your wise providence You hast appointed for him, whether life or death; that it may be unto him to live unto Christ, and if to die, that to die may be gain; and that in all things he may find cause to praise and glorify Your holy name. If You should be graciously pleased to raise him from his bed of languishing, grant that he may lead the residue of his life in Your fear and to Your glory. Or if You hast otherwise determined, prepare him for the hour of his departure; defend him from his spiritual enemies; finish all that is wanting in the work of his salvation; support and comfort him in his last agonies; make his end easy and peaceful; and fill him with an hope full of immortality. Finally, O Lord, receive him into the arms of Your unspeakable mercy, into the glorious state of Your saints in light, and give him a resurrection unto eternal life in Your heavenly kingdom. All which we ask, in the name, and through the merits and mediation of our Advocate and Redeemer, Jesus Christ. Amen.

Manual of Devotions, 1863

O most mighty God and merciful Father, we most humbly beseech thee, if it be thy good pleasure, to continue to us that singular benefit which thou hast given us in the friendship of thy servant, our dear brother, who now lieth on the bed of sickness. Let him abide with us yet awhile for the furtherance of our faith; yet awhile spare him, that he may live to thy honor and our comfort. Thou hast made him a great help and furtherance of the best things among us. O Lord, we beseech thee, restore to us our dear brother, by restoring him to health.

Nicholas Ferrar, 1592–1637, written when George Herbert was gravely ill

I lie here on a cot, struck down by evil,
sinking in a mattress of disease and torment,
like the living dead yet able to speak.
O kind Son of God,
have compassion upon my misery.

Gregory of Narek, 951–1003

Almighty and most merciful Father, whose loving kindness is over all thy works; behold, visit and relieve this thy servant who is grieved with sickness. Grant that the sense of her weakness may add strength to her faith, and seriousness to her repentance. And grant that, by the help of thy Holy Spirit, after the pains and labors of this short life, we may all obtain everlasting happiness, through Jesus Christ our Lord: for whose sake hear our prayers.

Samuel Johnson, 1709–86, prayed as he left a very ill friend

Jesus Christ, my Lord and Savior, You became man and died on the cross for our salvation. You healed people of sickness and affliction through Your love and compassion. Visit me, Lord and grant me strength to bear this sickness with which I am afflicted, with patience, submission to Your will and trust in Your loving care. I pray that You will bless the means used for my recovery and those who administer them. Grant that my sickness may be to my spiritual benefit and that I may live the rest of

my life more faithfully according to Your will. For You are the source of life and healing and to You I give praise and glory, now and forever. Amen.

Orthodox prayer

Heavenly Father, physician of our souls and bodies, Who have sent Your only-begotten Son and our Lord Jesus Christ to heal every sickness and infirmity, visit and heal also Your servant (name) from all physical and spiritual ailments through the grace of Your Christ. Grant him (her) patience in this sickness, strength of body and spirit, and recovery of health. Lord, You have taught us through Your word to pray for each other that we may be healed. I pray, heal Your servant (name) and grant to him (her) the gift of complete health. For You are the source of healing and to You I give glory, Father, Son and Holy Spirit. Amen.

Orthodox prayer

We pray for the sick, grant them health and raise them up from their sickness and let them have perfect health of body and soul, for you are the Savior and Benefactor, you are Lord and King of all. Amen.

Serapion, d.360

Thanksgiving after recovery from illness
Almighty God and heavenly Father, You are the fountain of life and healing. I bless Your holy name and offer to You thanks for having delivered me from sickness and restored me to health. Grant me Your eternal grace, I pray, that I may live a new life in true obedience to You. Guide me to do Your will in all things devoting my life to Your service. Thus living for You may I be found worthy of Your kingdom, where You dwell in glory with Your Son and Your Holy Spirit forever. Amen.

Orthodox prayer

O Lord God Jesus Christ, the Life and strength of all that put their hope in You, Whose mercies are numberless, and the treasury goodness that is infinite, we give thanks to You for the blessings which You have bestowed., and we humbly beseech You to continue Your goodness toward us. As You have been well pleased to restore us to our bodily health, so do imbue our souls with all the heavenly graces, perseverance in good works, and prepare us by Your blessings in this life for the enjoyment of eternal happiness in the Life to come. For to You are due all glory, honor, and worship, as also to Your Eternal Father and Your All-holy Good and Life-creating Spirit, both now and forever, and to the ages of ages. Amen.

Orthodox prayer

Three prayers used by Dean Jonathan Swift for Stella in her last sickness, 1727

1

Almighty and most gracious Lord God, extend, we beseech Thee, Thy pity and compassion toward this Thy languishing servant; teach her to place her hope and confidence entirely in Thee; give her a true sense of the emptiness and vanity of all earthly things; make her truly sensible of all the infirmities of her life past, and grant to her such a true sincere repentance as is not to be repented of. Preserve her, O Lord, in a sound mind and understanding during this Thy visitation; keep her from both the sad extremes of presumption and despair. If Thou shalt please to restore her to her former health, give her grace to be ever mindful of that mercy, and to keep those good resolutions she now makes in her sickness, so that no length of time nor prosperity may entice her to forget them. Let no thought of her misfortunes distract her mind, and prevent the means toward her recovery, or disturb her in her preparations for a better life. We beseech thee also, O Lord, of Thy infinite goodness, to remember the good actions of this Thy servant; that the naked she hath clothed, the hungry she hath fed, the sick and the fatherless whom she hath relieved, may be reckoned according to Thy gracious promise, as if they had been done unto Thee. Hearken, O Lord, to the prayers offered up by the friends of this Thy servant in her behalf, and especially those now made by us unto thee. Give Thy blessing to those endeavors used for her recovery; but take from her all violent desire either of life or death, further than with resignation to Thy holy will. And now, O Lord, we implore Thy gracious favor toward us here met together. Grant that the sense of this Thy servant's weakness may add strength to our faith; that we,

considering the infirmities of our nature and the uncertainty of life, may by this example be drawn to repentance before it shall please Thee to visit us in like manner. Accept these prayers, we beseech Thee, for the sake of Thy dear Son Jesus Christ, our Lord, who, with Thee and the Holy Ghost, liveth and reigneth, ever one God, world without end. Amen.

2 Written October 17, 1727

Most merciful Father, accept our humblest prayers in behalf of this Thy languishing servant; forgive the sins, the frailties, and infirmities of her life past. Accept the good deeds she hath done in such a manner that, at whatever time Thou shalt please to call her, she may be received into everlasting habitations. Give her grace to continue sincerely thankful to Thee for the many favors Thou hast bestowed upon her, the ability and inclination and practice to do good, and those virtues which have procured the esteem and love of her friends and a most unspotted name in the world. O God, Thou dispensest Thy blessings and Thy punishments as it becometh infinite justice and mercy; and since it was Thy pleasure to afflict her with a long, constant, weakly state of health, make her truly sensible that it was for very wise ends, and was largely made up to her in other blessings more valuable and less common. Continue to her, O Lord, that firmness and constancy of mind wherewith Thou hast most graciously endowed her, together with that contempt of worldly things and vanities that she has shown in the whole conduct of her life. O All-powerful Being, the least motion of whose will can create or destroy a world, pity us, the mournful friends of Thy distressed servant, who sink under the weight of her present condition, and the fear of losing the most valuable of our friends. Restore her to us, O Lord, if it be Thy gracious will, or inspire us with constancy and resignation to support ourselves under so heavy an affliction. Restore her, O Lord, for the sake of those poor who, by losing her, will be desolate, and those sick who will not only want her bounty, but her care and tending; or else, in Thy mercy, raise up some other in her place with equal disposition and better abilities. Lessen, O Lord, we beseech Thee, her bodily pains, or give her a double strength of mind to support them. And if Thou wilt soon take her to Thyself, turn our thoughts rather upon that felicity which we hope she shall enjoy, than upon that unspeakable loss we shall endure. Let her memory be ever dear unto us, and the example of her many virtues, as far as human infirmity will admit, our constant imitation. Accept, O Lord, these prayers, poured from the very bottom of our hearts, in Thy mercy, and for the merits of our blessed Savior. Amen.

3 Written November 6, 1727

O merciful Father, who never afflictest Thy children but for their own good, and with justice, over which Thy mercy always prevaileth, either to turn them to repentance, or to punish them in the present life in order to reward them in a better; take pity, we beseech Thee, upon this Thy poor afflicted servant, languishing so long and so grievously under the weight of Thy hand. Give her strength, O Lord, to support her weakness, and patience to endure her pains without repining at Thy correction. Forgive every rash and inconsiderate expression which her anguish may at any time force from her tongue, while her heart continueth in an entire submission to Thy will. Suppress in her, O Lord, all eager desires of life, and lessen her fears of death by inspiring into her an humble yet assured hope of Thy mercy. Give her a sincere repentance for all her transgressions and omissions, and a firm resolution to pass the remainder of her life in endeavoring to her utmost to observe all Thy precepts. We beseech Thee likewise to compose her thoughts, and preserve to her the use of her memory and reason during the course of her sickness. Give her a true conception of the vanity, folly, and insignificance of all human things, and strengthen her so as to beget in her a sincere love of Thee in the midst of her sufferings. Accept and impute all her good deeds, and forgive her all those offences against Thee which she hath sincerely repented of or through the frailty of memory hath forgot. And now, O Lord, we turn to Thee in behalf of ourselves and the rest of her sorrowful friends. Let not our grief afflict her mind, and thereby have an ill effect on her present distemper. Forgive the sorrow and weakness of those among us who sink under the grief and terror of losing so dear and useful a friend. Accept and pardon our most earnest prayers and wishes for her longer continuance in this evil world, to do what Thou art pleased to call Thy service, and is only her bounden duty, that she may be still a comfort to us and to all others who will want the benefit of her conversation, her advice, her good offices, or her charity. And since Thou hast promised that where two or three are gathered together in Thy name Thou wilt be in the midst of them to grant their request, O gracious Lord, grant to us who are here met in Thy name that those requests, which in the utmost sincerity and earnestness of our hearts we have now made in behalf of this Thy distressed servant and of ourselves, may effectually be answered, through the merits of Jesus Christ our Lord. Amen.

Jonathan Swift, 1667–1745

In hospital

O God, make the door of this house wide enough to receive all who need human love and fellowship, and a heavenly Father's care; and narrow enough to shut out all envy, pride and hate. Make its threshold smooth enough to be no stumbling-block to children, nor to straying feet, but rugged enough to turn back the tempter's power: make it a gateway to thine eternal kingdom.

Thomas Ken, 1637–1711, inscribed on St Stephen's Walbrook, London

Prayers asking for healing

Lord, I am not worthy that thou shouldest come under my roof, but speak the word only and my soul shall be healed. Amen.

Author unknown

O Lord, holy Father, creator of the universe, author of its laws, you can bring the dead back to life, and heal those who are sick. We pray for our sick brother that he may feel your hand upon him, renewing his body and refreshing his soul. Show to him the affection in which you hold all your creatures.

Dimma, 7th century

Heal my soul, O God, for I have sinned, grievously sinned against thee, and by my sins have provoked thee, who art the God of Mercy, to anger. O Heal my backsliding, and love me freely, and take away mine iniquity, and receive me graciously, and turn thine anger from me.

Thomas Ken, 1637–1711

I humbly pray to thee, O Lord, for my Bodily Cure; but because I know I may be eternally happy hereafter without Health of Body here, I pray for it with a resolution, to acquiesce in thy good pleasure, shouldst thou think fit to deny it. But, O my God, when I pray for the Cure of my Soul, I resolve I will not be denied, I will never give over importuning thee, till thou givest me that Godly sorrow, which worketh repentance to salvation, not to be repented of, till thou hast begun to kindle thy love in my Heart.

Thomas Ken, 1637–1711

O Lord God of our salvation, to whom no sickness is incurable, we pray that in your compassion you will drive way from your servants, who look for your heavenly medicine, all illness; show forth in them the might of your healing power, and make them whole both in body and soul; through Jesus Christ our Lord.

Mozarabic Psalter

Thanksgiving for recovery

Great and Mighty God, who bringest down to the grave, and bringest up again; we bless you for your great goodness, in having heard and answered our prayers, and in having turned our heaviness into joy, and mourning into gladness, by restoring this Your servant to some degree of his (or her) former health. Blessed be your name, that you did not forsake him in his sickness; but did visit him with comforts from above; did support him in patience and submission to Your will; and at last did send him seasonable relief. Inspire

his soul with a grateful sense of Your mercy, and with an holy purpose to requite it, by giving himself up in all his future days, heartily to Your service. Perfect, we beseech You, Your gracious goodness towards him; prosper the means employed for his cure; that being restored to health of body, vigor of mind, and cheerfulness of spirit, he may be able to go to your house of prayer, to offer You an oblation with great gladness; and to bless Your holy name for all Your loving kindness and tender mercy towards him, through Jesus Christ our Lord. Amen.

Manual of Devotions, 1863

THE SUICIDAL

Lord thank you for creating me.
Lord, thank you for spurning my attempted
  refusals of life.
Lord, thank you even for my weaknesses
Because it is through them that I learn
  humility,
The need of your grace
And not daring to compare myself to you!

Author unknown

Lord, remember all those who felt
That they had no-one to turn to
For whatever reason
Like shame, real or imagined
And took their own lives.
Please, please have mercy on them.

Author unknown

Lord, remember all those
Who feel tempted to suicide
And give them a reason to live.
Even if it is the wrong reason,
It can be changed later.
Finally Lord, I thank you that
You see the whole picture.
Teach us not to judge on just a part.

Author unknown

Global Prayers

Related entries in Part Two

Extracts of classic Christian teaching on prayer

John Chrysostom: Homily on the Lord's Prayer
Cyprian: The Lord's Prayer
A.A. Hodge: The Communion of Saints
Origen: Our Father in Heaven
R.A. Torrey: Prayer and Revival
Thomas Watson: The Lord's Prayer
John Wesley: Upon Our Lord's Sermon on the Mount

Stories about prayer and people who prayed
John B. Gough: Touching Incidents and Remarkable Answers to Prayer

PEOPLE IN NEED

God of love, whose compassion never fails;
we bring before you the troubles and perils of
    people and nations,
the sighing of prisoners and captives,
the sorrows of the bereaved,
the necessities of strangers,
the helplessness of the weak,
the despondency of the weary,
the failing powers of the aged.
O Lord, draw near to each;
for the sake of Jesus Christ our Lord.

Anselm, 1033–1109

May thy mercy be extended over all mankind,
bringing the ignorant to the knowledge of thy
truth, awakening the impenitent, touching the
hardened. Look with compassion upon the
afflicted of every condition, assuage the pangs
of disease, comfort the broken in spirit.

Jane Austen, 1775–1817

We offer up our prayers unto thee, O most
gracious God and most merciful Father, for all
men in general, that as thou art pleased to be
acknowledged the Savior of the whole human
race by the redemption accomplished by Jesus
Christ thy Son, so those who are still strangers
to the knowledge of him, and immersed in
darkness, and held captive by ignorance and
error, may, by thy Holy Spirit shining upon
them, and by thy gospel sounding in their ears,
be brought back to the right way of salvation,
which consists in knowing thee the true God
and Jesus Christ whom thou hast sent. We beg
that those on whom thou hast deigned already
to bestow the favor of thy grace, and whose
minds thou hast enlightened by the knowledge
of thy word, may daily profit more and more,
being enriched with thy spiritual blessings, so
that we may all together, with one heart and
mouth, worship thee, and pay due honor, and
yield just service to thy Christ, our Lord, and
King, and Lawgiver.

John Calvin, 1509–64

We beg you, Lord, to help and defend us.
Deliver the oppressed,
have compassion on the despised,
raise the fallen,

reveal yourself to the needy,
heal the sick,
bring back those who have strayed from you,
feed the hungry,
lift up the weak,
remove the prisoners' chains.
May every nation come to know that you are
    God alone,
that Jesus is your Son,
that we are your people, the sheep of your
    pasture.

Clement of Rome, c.30–c.95

Lord God, graciously comfort and care for all
who are imprisoned, hungry, thirsty, naked,
and miserable; also all widows, orphans, sick,
and sorrowing. In brief, give us our daily bread,
so that Christ may abide in us and we in him
for ever, and that with him we may worthily
bear the name of Christian.

Martin Luther, 1483–1546

Almighty God, the Father of mercies and God
of all comfort, come to my help and deliver me
from this difficulty that besets me. I believe
Lord, that all trials of life are under Your care
and that all things work for the good of those
who love You. Take away from me fear, anxiety and distress. Help me to face and endure
my difficulty with faith, courage and wisdom.
Grant that this trial may bring me closer to You
for You are my rock and refuge, my comfort
and hope, my delight and joy. I trust in Your
love and compassion. Blessed is Your name,
Father, Son and Holy Spirit, now and forever.
Amen.

Orthodox prayer

O God, our help in time of need, Who are
just and merciful, and Who inclines to the
supplications of His people. Look down upon
me and have mercy on me and deliver me
from the trouble that now besets me. Deal
with us not according to our iniquities, but
according to Your manifold mercies, for we
are the works of Your hands, and You know
our weaknesses. I pray to you to grant me
Your divine helping grace, and endow me with
patience and strength to endure my hardships
with complete submission to Your Will. Only
You know our misery and sufferings, and to

You, our only hope and refuge, I flee for relief and comfort, trusting in Your infinite love and compassion, that in due time, when You know best, You will deliver me from this trouble, and turn my distress into comfort. We then shall rejoice in Your mercy, and exalt and praise Your Holy Name, O Father, Son and Holy Spirit, both now and forever and to the ages of ages. Amen

Orthodox prayer

Relieve and comfort, O Lord, all the persecuted and afflicted; speak peace to troubled consciences; strengthen the weak; confirm the strong; instruct the ignorant; deliver the oppressed; relieve the needy; and bring us all, by the waters of comfort and in the ways of righteousness, to the kingdom of rest and glory, through Jesus Christ our Lord.

Jeremy Taylor, 1613–67

People suffering from drought

O God heavenly father, which by thy son Jesus Christ, hast promised to all them that seek thy kingdom, and the righteousness thereof, all things necessary to the bodily sustenance: send us (we beseech thee) in this our necessity, such moderate rain and showers, that we may receive the fruits of the earth, to our comfort and to thy honor; Through Jesus Christ our Lord.

Book of Common Prayer, 1549

For Fair Weather

O Lord God, which for the sin of man didst once drown all the world, except eight persons, and afterward of thy great mercy didst promise never to destroy it so again: We humbly beseech thee, that although we for our iniquities have worthily deserved this plague of rain and waters, yet, upon our true repentance, thou wilt send us such weather whereby we may receive the fruits of the earth in due season, and learn both by the punishment to amend our lives, and by the granting of our petition to give thee praise and glory: Through Jesus Christ our Lord.

Book of Common Prayer, 1549

Victims of war

Comfort, O Lord, we pray thee, all who are mourning the loss of those who laid down their lives in war. Be with them in their sorrow, support them in their loneliness. Give them faith to look beyond the troubles of this present time, and to know that neither life nor death can separate us from thy love which is in Christ Jesus our Lord.

Author unknown

In memory of those who made the supreme sacrifice, O God, make us better men and women, and give us peace in our time; through Jesus Christ our Lord.

Author unknown

THE NATIONS OF THE WORLD

Social justice

O Lord, our heavenly Father. High and Mighty, King of Kings and Lord of Lords, who dost from the Throne behold all the dwellers on earth and reignest with power supreme and control over all kingdoms, empires and governments; look down in mercy we beseech Thee on these American States, who have fled to Thee from the rod of the oppressor, and thrown themselves on Thy gracious protection desiring henceforth to be dependent only on Thee. To Thee they have appealed for the righteousness of their cause. To Thee do they look up for that countenance and support which Thou alone canst give. Take them therefore Heavenly Father under Thy nurturing care. Give them wisdom in counsel and valor in the field. Defeat the malicious designs of our cruel adversaries. Convince them of the unrighteousness of their cause, and if they persist in their sanguinary purpose, O let the voice of thine own unerring justice, sounding in their hearts, constrain them to drop their weapons of war from their unnerved hands in the day of battle. Be Thou present, O God of wisdom and direct the counsels of this honorable Assembly. Enable them to settle things on the best and surest foundation; that the scent of blood may speedily be closed, that order, harmony and peace may be effectually restored, and truth and justice and religion and piety may prevail and flourish among Thy people. Preserve the health of their bodies, and the vigor of their minds; shower down on them and the millions they represent such temporal blessings as Thou seest expedient for them in this world, and crown them with everlasting glory in the world to come. All this we ask in the name of and through the merits of Jesus Christ, Thy Son, our Savior. Amen.

J. Duche, First prayer in Congress, December 17, 1711

Almighty God, we make our earnest prayer that Thou wilt keep the United States in Thy Holy protection; and Thou wilt incline the hearts of the citizens to cultivate a spirit of subordination and obedience to government; and entertain a brotherly affection and love for one another and for their fellow citizens of the United States at large. And finally that Thou wilt most graciously be pleased to dispose us all to do justice, to love mercy, and to demean ourselves with that charity, humility, and pacific temper of mind which were the characteristics of the Divine Author of our blessed religion, and without a humble imitation of whose example in these things we can never hope to be a happy nation. Grant our supplication, we beseech Thee, through Jesus Christ our Lord, Amen.

George Washington, 1732–99

Strengthen us, O God, to relieve the oppressed, to hear the groans of poor prisoners, to reform the abuses of all professions; that many be made not poor to make a few rich; for Jesus Christ's sake.

Oliver Cromwell, 1599–1658

Medical care and research

O Lord Jesus Christ, who went about doing good and healing all kinds of sickness: give strength, wisdom and gentleness to all your ministering servants, our doctors, surgeons and nurses; that always bearing your presence with them, they may not only heal but bless, and shine as lamps of hope in the darkest hours of distress and fear; who lives and reigns

with the Father and the Holy Spirit, ever one God world without end.

Church Missionary Society, 1899

Education

Grant, O Lord, to all students, to know what is worth knowing, to love what is worth loving, to praise what delights you most, to value what is precious in your sight and to reject what is evil in your eyes. Grant them true discernment to distinguish between different things. Above all, may they search out and do what is most pleasing to you; through Jesus Christ our Lord.

Thomas à Kempis, 1379–1471

Almighty Father, grant that our universities and colleges may be houses of faith and fruitful study; and that their students may so learn truth as to bear its light along all their ways, and so learn Christ as to be found in him; who liveth and reigneth with thee and the Holy Spirit, one God, world without end.

King's College, Cambridge

The arts

O God, who by thy Spirit in our hearts dost lead men to desire your perfection, to seek for truths and to rejoice in beauty: illuminate and inspire, we beseech thee, all thinkers, writers, artists and craftsmen; that, in whatsoever is true and pure and lovely, thy name may be hallowed and thy kingdom come on earth; through Jesus Christ our Lord.

Prayer found in St. Anselm's Chapel, Canterbury

CHRISTIAN WRITERS
O Lord the one God, God the Trinity, whatever I have said in these books that is of Thine, may they acknowledge who are Thine; if anything of my own, may it be pardoned both by Thee and by those who are Thine. Amen.

Augustine of Hippo, 354–430,
conclusion to his book, On the Trinity

Our nation

Almighty God, Who has given us a land, wherein we are free to read and hear Thy Word, to confess Thy Name, and to labor together for the extension of Thy Kingdom: Grant, we beseech Thee, that the liberty vouchsafed unto us, may be continued to our children and our children's children, and that the power of the Gospel may here abound, to the blessing of all the nations of the earth, and to Thine eternal glory; through Jesus Christ, Thy Son, our Lord. Amen.

The Common Service Book of the Lutheran Church, 1917

O God, Who by Thy Providence didst lead our forefathers to this land wherein they found refuge from oppression and freedom to worship Thee: We beseech Thee, ever to guide our Nation in the way of Thy truth and peace, so that we may never fail in the blessing which Thou has promised to that people whose God is the Lord; through Jesus Christ, Thy Son, our Lord. Amen.

The Common Service Book of the Lutheran Church, 1917

Rulers, governments, and leaders

A Prayer for The President of the United States, and all in Civil Authority

O Lord, our heavenly Father, the high and mighty Ruler of the universe, who dost from thy throne behold all the dwellers upon earth; Most heartily we beseech thee, with thy favor to behold and bless thy servant THE PRESIDENT OF THE UNITED STATES, and all others in authority; and so replenish them with the grace of thy Holy Spirit, that they may always incline to thy will, and walk in thy way. Endue them plenteously with heavenly gifts; grant them in health and prosperity long to live; and finally, after this life, to attain everlasting joy and felicity; through Jesus Christ our Lord. Amen.

American Book of Common Prayer, 1928

O merciful Father in heaven, Who holds in your hand all the might of man, and Who has ordained the powers that be for the punishment of evil-doers, and for the praise of them that do well, and of Whom is all rule and authority in the kingdoms of the world: We humbly beseech Thee, graciously regard your servants, the President of the United States, the Governor of this [State], our Judges and Magistrates, and all the Rulers of the earth. May all that receive[power]bear it according to your commandment. Enlighten and defend them by your Name, O God. Grant them wisdom and understanding, that, under their peaceable governance, your people maybe guarded and directed in righteousness, quietness, and unity. Protect and [help them], O God of our salvation, that we, with them, may show forth the praise of Thy Name; through Jesus Christ, Thy Son, our Lord. Amen.

The Common Service Book of the Lutheran Church, 1917

Almighty God, our Heavenly Father, Whose mercies are new unto us every morning, and Who, though we have in no wise deserved Thy goodness, dost abundantly provide for all our wants of body and soul: Give us, we pray Thee, Thy Holy Spirit, that we may heartily acknowledge Thy merciful goodness toward us, give thanks for all Thy benefits, and serve Thee in willing obedience; through Jesus Christ, Thy Son, our Lord. Amen.

The Common Service Book of the Lutheran Church, 1917

Almighty God, maker of all things, thou hast placed thy creatures necessary for our use in diverse lands: grant that all peoples and nations, needing one another, may be knit together in one bond of mutual service, to share their diverse riches; through Jesus Christ our Lord. Amen.

Author unknown, 16th century

Almighty God, who rulest over all the kingdoms of the world, and dost order them according to thy good pleasure: We yield thee unfeigned thanks, for that thou wast pleased, as on this day, to set thy Servant our Sovereign Lady, Queen Elizabeth, upon the Throne of this Realm. Let thy wisdom be her guide, and let thine arm strengthen her; let truth and justice, holiness and righteousness, peace and charity, abound in her days; direct all her counsels and endeavors to thy glory, and the welfare of her subjects; give us grace to obey her cheerfully for conscience sake, and let her always possess the hearts of her people; let her reign be long and prosperous, and crown her with everlasting life in the world to come; through Jesus Christ our Lord. Amen.

Book of Common Prayer, Accession Service

O God, who providest for thy people by thy power, and rulest over them in love: Vouchsafe so to bless thy Servant our Queen, that under her this nation may be wisely governed, and thy Church may serve thee in all godly quietness; and grant that she being devoted to thee with her whole heart, and persevering in good works unto the end, may, by thy guidance, come to thine everlasting kingdom; through Jesus Christ thy Son our Lord, who liveth and reigneth with thee and the Holy Ghost, ever one God, world without end. Amen.

Book of Common Prayer, Accession Service, 14th century

Almighty God,
Give us, we pray, the power to discern clearly right from wrong and allow all our words and actions to be governed thereby and by the laws of this land."

Dwight D. Eisenhower, 1890–1969

O God, almighty Father, King of kings and Lord of lords, grant that the hearts and minds of all who go out as leaders before us, the statesmen, the judges, the men of learning and the men of wealth, may be so filled with the love of thy laws and of that which is righteous and life-giving, that they may be worthy stewards of thy good and perfect gifts; through Jesus Christ our Lord.

Knights of the Garter prayer

Lord, preserve thy people. Maintain righteous government everywhere, so that all things may take place in an orderly way and peace may not be destroyed by revolution or secret enmity, nor the eternal good order be corrupted by debased living or disturbed by other offenses. Amen.

Martin Luther, 1483–1546

Almighty God, from whom all thoughts of truth and peace proceed, kindle, we pray, in the hearts of all people the true love of peace, and

guide with your pure and peaceable wisdom those who take counsel for the nations of the earth; that in tranquility your kingdom may go forward, till the earth is filled with the knowledge of your love; through Jesus Christ our Lord.

Francis Paget, 1851–1911

Almighty God, by whom alone kings reign and princes decree justice and from whom alone cometh all wisdom and understanding: we thine unworthy servants, here gathered together in thy name, do most humbly beseech thee to send down thy heavenly wisdom from above, to direct and guide us in all our consultations; and grant that, we having thy fear always before our eyes and laying aside all private interests, prejudices and partial affections, the result of all our counsels may be the glory of thy blessed name, the maintenance of true religion and justice, the safety, honor and happiness of the Sovereign, the public welfare, peace and tranquility of the realm and the uniting and knitting together of the hearts of all persons and estates within the same in true Christian love and charity towards one another; through Jesus Christ our Lord.

Christopher Yelverton, House of Commons prayer, composed c.1578, until 2000 prayed at every sitting of the House of Commons

Tolerance

O! Thou God of all beings, of all worlds, and
of all times,
We pray, that the little differences in our
clothes,
in our inadequate languages,
in our ridiculous customs,
in our imperfect laws,
in our illogical opinions,
in our ranks and conditions which
are so disproportionately important to us
and so meaningless to you,
that these small variations
that distinguish those atoms that we call men,
one from another,
may not be signals of hatred and persecution.

*François-Marie Arouet
de Voltaire, 1694–1778*

Peace

Almighty God and Creator, You are the Father of all people on the earth. Guide, I pray, all the nations and their leaders in the ways of justice and peace. Protect us from the evils of injustice, prejudice, exploitation, conflict and war. Help us to put away mistrust, bitterness and hatred. Teach us to cease the storing and using of implements of war. Lead us to find peace, respect and freedom. Unite us in the making and sharing of tools of peace against ignorance, poverty, disease and oppression. Grant that we may grow in harmony and friendship as brothers and sisters created in Your image, to Your honor and praise. Amen.

Orthodox prayer

THE ENVIRONMENT

Pets

O Lord Jesus Christ, who has taught us that without the knowledge of our Father in heaven no sparrow falls to the ground, help us to be very kind to all animals and our pets. May we remember that you will one day ask us if we have been good to them. Bless us as we take care of them; for your sake.

Author unknown

Animals

O God, grant us a deeper sense of fellowship with all living things, our little brothers and sisters to whom in common with us you have given this earth as home. We recall with regret that in the past we have acted high-handedly and cruelly in exercising our domain over them. Thus, the voice of the earth which should have risen to you in song has turned into a groan of travail. May we realize that all these creatures also live for themselves and for you – not for us alone. They too love the goodness of life, as we do, and serve you better in their way than we do in ours. Amen.

Basil the Great, c.329–379

Hear our humble prayer, O God, for our friends the animals, especially for animals who are suffering; for any that are hunted or lost or deserted or frightened or hungry; for all that must be put to death. We entreat for them all thy mercy and pity and for those who deal with them we ask a heart of compassion, gentle hands and kindly words. Make us ourselves to be true friends to animals and so to share the blessing of the merciful.

Albert Schweitzer, 1875–1965

FOR ALL PEOPLE TO KNOW GOD

Lord Jesus, who didst stretch out thine arms of love on the hard wood of the cross, that all men might come within the reach of thy saving embrace, clothe us in thy Spirit, that we, stretching for our hands in loving labor for others, may bring those who know thee not, to the knowledge and love of thee, who with the Father and the Holy Ghost livest and reignest one God.

C.H. Brent, 1862–1929

O God, who hast made of one blood all nations of men for to dwell on the face of the earth, and didst send thy blessed Son, Jesus Christ, to preach peace to them that are afar off, and to them that are nigh; grant that all the peoples of the world may feel after thee and find thee; hasten, O God, the fulfillment of thy promise to pour out thy Spirit upon all flesh, through Jesus Christ our Lord.

George Cotton, 1813–66

I pray to you, Lord God of Abraham, Isaac and Jacob, Father of our Lord Jesus Christ. You are infinite in mercy, and it is y our will that we should learn to know you. You created heaven and earth, you rule over all. You are the true, the only God, and there is no other god above you. Grant, through our Lord Jesus Christ and the working of the Holy Spirit, that all may come to know you, for you alone are God. Let them draw strength from you and be kept from all teaching that is heretical or godless.

Irenaeus, c.130–c.200

Daily Prayers

THE LORD'S PRAYER

Our Father, which art in heaven, Hallowed
be thy Name. Thy kingdom come. Thy will
be done in earth, As it is in heaven. Give us
this day our daily bread. And forgive us our
trespasses, As we forgive them that trespass
against us. And lead us not into temptation,
But deliver us from evil. For thine is the kingdom, The power, and the glory, For ever and
ever. Amen.

Book of Common Prayer

Upon The Lord's Prayer.
Our Father which in heaven art,
Thy name be always hallowed;
Thy kingdom come, thy will be done;
Thy heavenly path be followed
By us on earth as 'tis with thee,
We humbly pray;
And let our bread us given be,
From day to day.

Forgive our debts as we forgive
Those that to us indebted are:
Into temptation lead us not,

But save us from the wicked snare.
The kingdom's thine, the power too,
We thee adore;
The glory also shall be thine
For evermore.

John Bunyan, 1628–88

O Lord God, *our Father in heaven*, we your unworthy children on earth pray that you will look on us in your mercy, and give us your grace; that *your holy name* may be sanctified among us and in all the world, through the pure and sincere teaching of the Word, and through earnest charity in our daily living and our conversation. Root out from us all false teaching and evil living, so that your name is not slandered.

Let *your kingdom come*, and be great. May all sinful, blind people who are in the devil's grip be brought to the knowledge of the true faith in Jesus Christ your Son.

Strengthen us, Lord, with your Spirit, to do and to suffer *your will* both in life and death, so that our will may always be broken, offered and put to death.

And *give us our daily bread*. Preserve us from covetous desire so that we may be assured of having the abundance of all good things.

Forgive us our trespasses, as we forgive those who offend us, that our heart may have a sure and glad conscience, and that we may never fear, or be afraid of any sin.

Lead us not into temptation, but help us through your Spirit to subdue the flesh, to despise the world with its vanities, and to overcome the devil with all his cunning attacks.

And finally, *deliver us from all evil*, physical and spiritual, temporal and eternal.

Miles Coverdale, 1488–1568

Our Father, who art in heaven

In whom we live, and move, and have our being; grant that I and all Christians may live worthy of this glorious relation, and that we may not sin, knowing that we are accounted as yours. We are your by adoption; make us yours by the choice of our will.

Hallowed by your name

O God, whose name is great, wonderful, and holy, grant that I and all your children may glorify you, not only with our lips but in our lives; that others, seeing our good works, may glorify our Father who is in heaven.

Your kingdom come

May the kingdoms of the world become the kingdoms of our Lord and of his Christ. And may all that own you for their King, become your faithful subjects, and obey your laws. Dethrone, Lord God, and destroy Satan and his kingdom, and enlarge the kingdom of grace.

Your will be done, in earth, as it is in heaven

We adore your goodness, Lord God, in making your will known to us in your holy Word. May this your Word be the rule of our will, of our desires, of our lives and actions. May we always sacrifice our will to yours, be pleased with all your choice for ourselves and others, and adore your providence in the government of the world.

Give us this day our daily bread

Heavenly Father, who knows what we need, give us the necessities and comforts of this life with your blessing; but above all, give us the bread which nourishes us for eternal life. Lord God, who gives everyone life and breath and all things, give us grace to be generous to those in need, from what you have given us which is more than our daily bread.

And forgive us our trespasses as we forgive those who trespass against us

Make us truly aware of your goodness and mercy and patience towards us, that we may from our hearts forgive everyone who has sinned against us. May my enemies always have a place in my prayers, and in your mercy.

And lead us not into temptation

Support us, heavenly Father, through all our trials, and grant that they may bear the peaceful fruits of righteousness.

But deliver us from evil

From all sin and wickedness, from our spiritual enemy, from the temptations and traps of the evil world, and from everlasting death, good Lord deliver us.

Thomas Wilson, 1663–1755

Our Father, which in Heaven art,
    We sanctify thy Name;
Thy Kingdom come, thy will be done,
    In Heaven and Earth the same.
Give us this day, our daily bread,
    And us forgive thou so,
As we on them that us offend,
    Forgiveness do bestow.
Into temptation lead us not,
    And us from evil free,
For thine the Kingdom, Power and Praise,
    Is and shall ever be.

George Wither, 1588–1667

DAILY PRAYERS

Lord, I hand over to your care, my soul and
body, my prayers and my hopes, my health and
my work, my life and my death, my parents
and my family, my friends and my neighbors,
my country and all people. Today and always.

Lancelot Andrewes, 1555–1626

O Lord, to be turned from you is to fall, to be
turned to you is to rise, and to stand in you is to
abide for ever. Grant us in all our duties your help,
in all our perplexities your guidance, in all our
dangers your protection, and in all our sorrows
your peace; through Jesus Christ our Lord.

Augustine of Hippo, 354–430

Grant us grace, almighty Father, so to pray as
to deserve to be heard.

Jane Austen, 1775–1817

Although things are not perfect
Because of trial or pain
Continue in thanksgiving
Do not begin to blame.
Even when the times are hard
Fierce winds are bound to blow
God is forever able
Hold on to what you know.
Imagine life without His love
Joy would cease to be
Keep thanking Him for all the things
Love imparts to thee.
Move out of "Camp Complaining"
No weapon that is known
On earth can yield the power

Praise can do alone
Quit looking at the future
Redeem the time at hand
Start every day with worship
To "thank" is a command.
Until we see Him coming
Victorious in the sky
We'll run the race with gratitude
Xalting God most high
Yes, there will be good times and yes some
    will be bad, but …
Zion waits in glory … where none are ever sad!
Amen !!!

Author unknown, Alphabet prayer

Just a closer walk with Thee,
Grant it, Jesus, is my plea,
Daily walking close to Thee,
Let it be, dear Lord, let it be.

Author unknown

O Lord, forgive what I have been, sanctify what
I am, and order what I shall be.

Author unknown

God with me lying down
God with me rising up,
God with me in each ray of light,
Nor I a ray of joy without Him,
Nor one ray without Him.

Carmina Gadelica

Christ with me sleeping,
Christ with me waking,
Christ with me watching,
Every day and night,
Each day and night.

Carmina Gadelica

God with me protecting,
The Lord with me directing,
The Spirit with me strengthening,
For ever and for evermore,
Ever and evermore, Amen.
Chief of chiefs, Amen.

Carmina Gadelica

May I speak each day according to Thy justice
Each day may I show Thy chastening, O God;
May I speak each day according to Thy
    wisdom,

Each day and night may I be at peace with
Thee.

Carmina Gadelica

Each day may I count the causes of Thy mercy,
May I each day give heed to Thy laws;
Each day may I compose to Thee a song,
May I harp each day Thy praise, O God.

Carmina Gadelica

May I each day give love to Thee, Jesu,
Each night may I do the same;
Each day and night, dark and light,
May I laud Thy goodness to me, O God.

Carmina Gadelica

Thanks be to you, my Lord Jesus Christ,
for all the benefits you have won for me.
For all the pains and insults you have borne
for me.
O most merciful Redeemer, Friend, and
Brother,
may I know you more clearly,
love you more dearly,
and follow you more nearly,
day by day.

Richard of Chichester, 1197–1253

My time is in your hands, O Lord
1. O Lord, deprive me not of your heavenly
   blessings;
2. O Lord, deliver me from eternal torment;
3. O Lord, if I have sinned in my mind or
   thought, in word deed, forgive me.
4. O Lord, deliver me from every ignorance
   and inattention, from a petty soul and a
   stony, hard heart;
5. O Lord, deliver me from every temptation;
6. O Lord, lighten my heart darkened by evil
   desires;
7. O Lord, I, being a human being, have
   sinned; you, being God, forgive me in
   your loving kindness, for you know the
   weakness of my soul.
8. O Lord, send down your grace to help me,
   that I may glorify your holy name;
9. O Lord Jesus Christ, write my the name of
   your servant in the Book of Life, and grant
   me a blessed end;
10. O Lord my God, even if I have done
    nothing good in your sight, yet grant me,

your grace, that I may make a start doing
good.
11. O Lord, sprinkle on my heart the dew of
    your grace;
12. O Lord of heaven and earth, remember
    me, your sinful servant, with my cold and
    impure heart, in your kingdom.
13. O Lord, receive me in repentance;
14. O Lord, do not leave me;
15. O Lord, save me from temptation;
16. O Lord, grant me pure thoughts;
17. O Lord, grant me tears of repentance,
    remembrance of death, and the sense of
    peace;
18. O Lord, make me remember to confess
    my sins;
19. O Lord, grant me humility, love, and
    obedience;
20. O Lord, grant me tolerance, magnanimity,
    and gentleness;
21. O Lord, implant in me the root of all
    blessings: the reverence of you in my
    heart;
22. O Lord, grant that I may love you with all
    my heart and soul, and that I may obey
    your will in all things;
23. O Lord, shield me from evil people, devils
    and passions;
24. O Lord, you know your creation and what
    you have planned for it; may your will
    also be fulfilled in me, a sinner, for you are
    blessed for ever more. Amen.

*John Chrysostom, c.347–407, according
to the hours of the day and night*

God guide me with your wisdom,
God chastise me with your justice,
God help me with your mercy,
God protect me with your strength,
God shield me with your shade,
God fill me with your grace,
For the sake of your anointed Son.

Gaelic prayer

My dearest Lord,
be thou a bright flame before me,
be thou a guiding star above me,
be thou a smooth path beneath me,
be thou a kindly shepherd behind me,
today – tonight – and forever.

Columba, 521–597

Alone with none but you, my God,
I journey on my way.
What need I fear, when you are near
O king of night and day?
More same am I within your hand
Than if a host did round me stand.

Columba, 521–597

Keep us, Lord, so awake in the duties of our callings that we may sleep in your peace and wake in your glory.

John Donne, 1572–1631

Almighty and most merciful God, the Father of our Lord Jesus Christ: We give Thee thanks for all Thy goodness and tender mercies, especially for the gift of Thy dear Son, and for the revelation of Thy will and grace: and we beseech Thee so to implant Thy Word in us, that in good and honest hearts we may keep it, and bring forth fruit by patient continuance in well doing.

Most heartily we beseech thee so to rule and govern Thy Church universal, with all its pastors and ministers, that it may be preserved in the pure doctrine of Thy saving Word, whereby faith toward Thee may be strengthened, and charity increased in us toward all mankind.

Grant also health and prosperity to all that are in authority, especially to the President [and Congress] of the United States, the Governor [and Legislature] of this Commonwealth, and to all our Judges and Magistrates; and endue them with grace to rule after Thy good pleasure, to the maintenance of righteousness, and to the hindrance and punishment of wickedness, that we may lead a quiet and peaceable life, in all godliness and honesty.

May it please Thee also to turn the hearts of our enemies and adversaries, that they may cease their enmity, and be inclined to walk with us in meekness and in peace.

All who are in trouble, want, sickness, anguish of labor, peril of death, or any other adversity, especially those who are in suffering for Thy

Name and for Thy truth's sake, comfort, O God, with Thy Holy Spirit, that they may receive and acknowledge their afflictions as the manifestation of Thy fatherly will.

And although we have deserved Thy righteous wrath and manifold punishments, yet, we entreat Thee, O most merciful Father, remember not the sins of our youth, nor our many transgressions; but out of Thine unspeakable goodness, grace and mercy, defend us from all harm and danger of body and soul. Preserve us from false and pernicious doctrine, from war and bloodshed, from plague and pestilence, from all calamity by fire and water, from hail and tempest, from failure of harvest and from famine, from anguish of heart and despair of Thy mercy, and from an evil death. And in every time of trouble, show Thyself a very present Help, the Savior of all men, and especially of them that believe.

Cause also the needful fruits of the earth to prosper, that we may enjoy them in due season. Give success to the Christian training of the young, to all lawful occupations on land and sea, and to all pure arts and useful knowledge; and crown them with Thy blessing.

(Here special Supplications, Intercessions, and Prayers may be made.)

These, and whatsoever other things Thou wouldest have us ask of Thee, O God, vouchsafe unto us for the sake of the bitter sufferings and death of Jesus Christ, Thine only Son, our Lord and Savior, who liveth and reigneth with Thee and the Holy Ghost, ever one God, world without end.

Evangelical Lutheran Hymn-Book

Our Father, each day is a little life, each night a tiny death; help us to live with faith and hope and love. Lift our duty above drudgery; let not our strength fail, or the vision fade, in the heat and burden of the day. O God, make us patient and pitiful one with another in the fret and jar of life, remembering that each fights a hard fight and walks a lonely way. Forgive us, Lord, if we hurt our fellow souls; teach us a gentler tone, a sweeter charity of words, and a more healing touch. Sustain us, O God, when we must face sorrow; give us courage for the day and hope for the morrow. Day unto day may we lay hold of thy hand and look up into thy face, whatever befall, until our work is finished and the day is done. Amen.

Francis of Assisi, 1181–1226

O Lord, lift up the light of your countenance on us; let your peace rule in our hearts, and may it be our strength and our song in the house of our pilgrimage. We commit ourselves to your care and keeping; let your grace be mighty in us, and sufficient for us, in all the duties of the day. Keep us from sin. Give us the rule over our own spirits, and guard us from speaking unadvisedly with our lips. May we live together in holy love and peace, and under your blessing in this life and for evermore.

Matthew Henry, 1662–1714

To thee, O Master that lovest all men, I hasten on rising from sleep; by thy mercy I go forth to do thy work, and I pray to thee: help me at all time, in everything; deliver me from every evil thing of this world and from every attack of the devil; save me and bring me to thine eternal kingdom. For thou art my Creator, the Giver and Provider of everything good; in thee is all my hope, and to thee I ascribe glory, now and ever, and to the ages of ages.

Attributed to Macarius of Egypt, c.300–c.390

My faith looks up to thee,
Thou Lamb of Calvary,
    Savior divine;
Now hear me while I pray,
Take all my guilt away,
O let me from this day
    Be wholly thine.

Ray Palmer, 1808–87

In this hour of this day, fill us, O Lord, with your mercy, that rejoicing throughout the whole day, we may take delight in your praise; through Jesus Christ our Lord.

Sarum Missal, 1085

Remember, Christian soul, that you have today, and every day of your life:
    God to glorify,
    Jesus to imitate,
    a soul to save,
    a body to mortify,
    sins to repent of,
    virtues to acquire,
    hell to avoid,
    heaven to gain,
    eternity to prepare for,

time to profit by,
neighbors to edify,
the world to despise,
devils to combat,
passions to subdue,
death, perhaps, to suffer,
judgment to undergo.

Christopher Smart, 1722–71

Help of all who seek help from thee, can it be better to keep silence about my necessities, hoping that thou wilt relieve them? No, indeed; for thou, my Lord and my joy, knowing how many they must be, and how it will alleviate them if we speak to thee of them, dost bid us pray to thee of them, and say that thou wilt not fail to give.

Teresa of Avila, 1515–82

On hearing a clock strike
My time is in your hands, O Lord.

Treasury of Devotion, 1869

MORNING PRAYERS

Let me hear of your steadfast love in the
    morning,
    for in you I put my trust.
Teach me the way I should go,
    for to you I lift up my soul.

Psalm 143.8, 10 NRSV

Thou who sendest forth the light, createst the morning, makest the sun to rise on the good and on the evil: enlighten the blindness of our minds with the knowledge of the truth: lift Thou up the light of thy countenance upon us, that in thy light we may see light, and, at the last, in the light of grace the light of glory.

Lancelot Andrewes, 1555–1626

Glory be to Thee, O Lord, glory to Thee.
Glory to Thee who givest me sleep to recruit
    my weakness,
and to remit the toils of this fretful flesh.

To this day and all days,
a perfect, holy, peaceful, healthy, sinless course,
Vouchsafe O Lord.
The Angel of peace, a faithful guide,

guardian of souls and bodies,
to encamp around me,
and ever to prompt what is salutary,
Vouchsafe O Lord.
Pardon and remission of all sins and of all
    offences
Vouchsafe O Lord.
To our souls what is good and convenient,
    and peace to the world,

Repentance and strictness
for the residue of our life,
and health and peace to the end,
Vouchsafe O Lord.
Whatever is true, whatever is honest,
whatever just, whatever pure,
whatever lovely, whatever of good report,
if there be any virtue, if any praise,
such thoughts, such deeds,
Vouchsafe O Lord.

A Christian close, without sin, without shame,
and, should it please Thee, without pain,
and a good answer
at the dreadful and fearful judgment-seat
of Jesus Christ our Lord,
Vouchsafe O Lord.

Confession
Essence beyond essence, Nature increate,
Framer of the world,
I set Thee, Lord, before my face,
and I lift up my soul unto Thee.
I worship Thee on my knees,
and humble myself under Thy mighty hand.
I stretch forth my hands unto Thee,
my soul gaspeth unto Thee as a thirsty land.
I smite on my breast and say with the
    Publican,
God be merciful to me a sinner, the chief of
    sinners;
to the sinner above the Publican,
be merciful as to the Publican.

Father of mercies,
I beseech Thy fatherly affection,
despise me not an unclean worm,
a dead dog, a putrid corpse,
despise not Thou the work of Thine own
    hands,
despise not Thine own image

though branded by sin.
Lord, if Thou wilt, Thou canst make me clean,
Lord, only say the word, and I shall be
    cleansed.
And Thou, my Savior Christ,
Christ my Savior,
Savior of sinners, of whom I am chief,
despise me not, despise me not, O Lord,
despise not the cost of Thy blood,
who am called by Thy Name;
but look on me with those eyes
with which Thou didst look upon
Magdalene at the feast,
Peter in the hall,
the thief on the wood;
that with the thief I may entreat Thee humbly.
Remember me, Lord, in Thy kingdom;
that with Peter I may bitterly weep and say,
O that mine eyes were a fountain of tears
that I might weep day and night;
that with Magdalene I may hear Thee say,
Thy sins be forgiven thee,
and with her may love much, for many sins
    yea manifold
have been forgiven me.
And Thou, All-holy, Good, and Life-giving
    Spirit,
despise me not, Thy breath,
despise not Thine own holy things;
but turn Thee again, O Lord, at the last,
and be gracious unto Thy servant.

Commendation
Blessed art Thou, O Lord,
Our God, the God of our Fathers;
Who turnest the shadow of death into the
    morning;
and lightenest the face of the earth;
Who separatest darkness from the face of the
    light;
and banishest night and bringest back the day;
Who lightenest mine eyes,
that I sleep not in death;
Who deliverest me from the terror by night,
from the pestilence that walketh in darkness;
Who drivest sleep from mine eyes,
and slumber from mine eyelids;
Who makest the outgoings of the morning
and evening to praise Thee;
because I laid me down and slept and rose up
    again,

for the Lord sustained me; because I waked
    and beheld,
and my sleep was sweet unto me.
Blot out as a thick cloud my transgressions,
and as a cloud my sins;
grant me to be a child of light, a child of the
    day,
to walk soberly, holily, honestly, as in the day,
vouchsafe to keep me this day without sin.
Thou who upholdest the falling and liftest the
    fallen,
let me not harden my heart in provocation,
or temptation or deceitfulness of any sin.
Moreover, deliver me to-day
from the snare of the hunter
and from the noisome pestilence;
from the arrow that flieth by day,
from the sickness that destroyeth in the noon
    day.
Defend this day against my evil,
against the evil of this day defend Thou me.
Let not my days be spent in vanity,
nor my years in sorrow.
One day teileth another,
and one night certifies another.
O let me hear Thy loving-kindness betimes
in the morning,
for in Thee is my trust;
shew Thou me the way that I should walk in,
for I lift up my soul unto Thee.
Deliver me, O Lord, from mine enemies,
for I flee unto Thee.
Teach me to do the thing that pleaseth Thee,
    for Thou art my God:
let Thy loving Spirit lead me forth into the
    land of righteousness.
Quicken me, O Lord, for Thy Name's sake,
and for Thy righteousness' sake bring my soul
    out of trouble:
remove from me foolish imaginations,
inspire those which are good and pleasing in
    Thy sight.
Turn away mine eyes lest they behold vanity :
let mine eyes look right on,
and let mine eyelids look straight before me.
Hedge up mine ears with thorns
lest they incline to undisciplined words.
Give me early the ear to hear,
and open mine ears to the instruction of Thy
    oracles.
Set a watch, O Lord, before my mouth,

and keep the door of my lips.
Let my word be seasoned with salt,
that it may minister grace to the hearers.
Let no deed be grief unto me nor offence of
    heart.
Let me do some work
for which Thou wilt remember me, Lord,
for good,
and spare me according to the greatness
of Thy mercy.
Into Thine hands I commend my spirit, soul,
    and body,
which Thou hast created, redeemed,
regenerated,
O Lord, Thou God of truth:
and together with me
all mine and all that belongs to me.
Thou hast vouchsafed them to me,
Lord, in Thy goodness.
Guard us from all evil,
guard our souls,
I beseech Thee, O Lord.
Guard us without falling,
and place us immaculate
in the presence of Thy glory
in that day.
Guard my going out and my coming in
henceforth and for ever.
Prosper, I pray Thee, Thy servant this day, and
    grant him mercy
in the sight of those who meet him.
O God, make speed to save me,
O Lord, make haste to help me. o turn Thee
    then unto me,
and have mercy upon me;
give Thy strength unto Thy servant,
and help the son of Thine handmaid.
Show some token upon me for good,
that they who hate me may see it and be
    ashamed,
because Thou, Lord, hast holpen me
and comforted me.

Lancelot Andrewes, 1555–1626

Blessed are thou, O Lord our God, the God of
our fathers, who turnest the shadow of death
into the morning; who hast lightened mine
eyes that I sleep not in death.

O Lord, blot out as a night-mist mine iniquities. Scatter my sins as a morning cloud.
Grant that I may become a child of the light,

and of the day. Vouchsafe to keep me this day without sin. Uphold me when I am falling, and lift me up when I am down. Preserve this day from any evil of mine, and me from the evils of the day. Let this day add some knowledge, or good deed, to yesterday.

Oh, let me hear thy loving-kindness in the morning, for in thee is my trust. Teach me to do the thing that pleaseth thee, for thou art my God. Let thy loving Spirit lead me forth into the land of righteousness.

Lancelot Andrewes, 1555–1626

Lord God, you have sent out your light, created the morning, and have made the sun to rise on the good and the evil; enlighten the blindness of our minds with the knowledge of the truth. Pour out the light of your countenance on us, that in your light we may see light, and, at the last, see the light of your grace and the light of your glory.

Lancelot Andrewes, 1555–1626

We commend to you, O Lord,
our souls and our bodies,
our minds and our thoughts,
our prayers and our hopes,
our health and our work,
our life and our death;
our parents and brothers and sisters,
our benefactors and friends,
our neighbors, our countrymen,
and all Christian people,
this day and always.

Lancelot Andrewes, 1555–1626

O Lord, thou knowest how busy I must be this day. If I forget thee, do not thou forget me.

General Lord Astley, 1579–1652,
before the battle of Edgehill

O Lord our God, as thou hast in mercy preserved us to the beginning of another day, enable us by thy grace to live to thee, and to set our affections on things above, not on things upon the earth. Pour into our minds the light of thy truth and cause us to rejoice in thy word. Shed abroad thy love in our hearts, and bestow upon us abundantly the peace and comfort of thy Holy Spirit; for the sake of Jesus Christ our Lord.

Isaac Ashe, 19th century

Grant unto us, O Lord, this day
  to walk with you as Father,
  to trust in you as Savior,
  to worship you as Lord;
  that all our works may praise you
  and our lives may give you glory.

Author unknown

I call upon you, O Lord, and in the morning you hear me. In the morning I offer you my prayer, watching and waiting. I lift my heart to you, O Lord, to be strengthened for this day. Be with me in all I do, my God; guide me in all my ways. I will carry some burdens today; some trials will be mine. So I wait for your help, Lord, lest I stumble and fall. I will do my work, Father, the work begun by your Son. He lives in me and I in Him; may his work today be done. Amen.

Source unknown

Bless me, O God, the Father, Son, and Holy Ghost, Thou only True God. I thank Thee through Jesus Christ our Lord and Savior, for the Preservation of me, and for all other Benefits. I now commend myself, both Soul and Body, and all that Thou hast set me to do in my Employment and Calling, into Thy Protection. Be Thou the Beginning of my Conceptions, my Undertakings, and all my Doings. Work Thou so in me, that I may begin all Things to the Glory of Thy Name, and accomplish them in Thy Love for the Good and Service of my Neighbor. Send Thy holy Angel along with me, to turn the Temptations of the Devil and corrupt Nature away from me. Preserve me from the Malice of evil Men; make all my Enemies reconcilable to me, and bring my Mind into Thy Vineyard, that I may labor in my Office and Employment, and behave as Thy obedient Servant therein. Bless me, and all that I am to go about and do this Day, with the Blessing of Thy Love and Mercy. Continue Thy Grace and Love in Jesus Christ upon me, and give me a Mind cheerfully to follow Thy Leading and execute Thine Appointment. Let Thy Holy Spirit guide me in my Beginning, and my Progress, on to my Last End, and be the Willing, Working, and Accomplishing of all in me. Amen.

Jakob Boehme, 1555–1624

Help us, O God,
to serve thee devoutly
and the world busily.
May we do our work wisely,
give succor secretly,
go to our meat appetitely,
sit thereat discreetly,
arise temperately,
please our friend duly,
go to our bed merrily
and sleep surely,
for the joy of our Lord Jesus Christ.

After a translation by Sulpicius,
c.363–c.420, printed by Wynkyn de
Worde in 1500

Help us this day, O God, to serve thee devoutly, and the world busily. May we do our work wisely, give succor secretly, go to meat appetitely, sit thereat discreetly, arise temperately, please our friend duly, go to bed merrily, and sleep surely; for the joy of our Lord, Jesus Christ.

Traditional

Lord, let us learn from the experience of today the lessons which thou meanest today to teach.

Clement Bailhache, 1856–1924

My Father, for another night
Of quiet sleep and rest,
For all the joy of morning light,
Your holy name be blest.

H.W. Baker, 1821–77

Heavenly Father, I most heartily thank thee, that it has pleased thy fatherly goodness to take care of me this night past. I most entirely beseech thee, most merciful Father, to show the same kindness toward me this day, in preserving my body and soul; that I may neither think, breathe, speak, nor do anything that may be displeasing to thy fatherly goodness, dangerous to myself, or hurtful to my neighbor; but that all my doings may be agreeable to your most blessed will, which is always good; that they may advance thy glory, answer to my vocation, and profit my neighbor, whom I ought to love as myself; that, whenever thou callest me hence, I may be found the child not

of darkness but of light; through Jesus Christ our Lord.

Thomas Becon, 1512–67

O Lord, our heavenly Father, almighty and ever living God, which hast safely brought us to the beginning of this day: defend us in the same with thy mighty power; and grant that this day we fall into no sin, neither run into any kind of danger, but that all our doings may be ordered by thy governance, to do always that is righteous in thy sight: through Jesus Christ our Lord.

Book of Common Prayer, 1549,
Matins, Collect for Grace

God be in my head,
and in my understanding;
God be in my eyes,
and in my looking;
God be in my mouth,
and in my speaking;
God be in my heart,
and in my thinking;
God be at my end,
and at my departing.

Book of Hours, 1514

O Lord, who has brought us through the darkness of night to the light of the morning, and who by your Holy Spirit illumines the darkness of ignorance and sin: We beseech you, from your loving kindness, pour your holy light into our souls; that we may always be devoted to you, by whose wisdom we were created, by whose mercy we were redeemed, and by whose providence we are governed; to the honor and glory of your great name.

Book of Hours, 1864

My God, my Father and Preserver, who of thy goodness hast watched over me during the past night, and brought me to this day, grant also that I may spend it wholly in the worship and service of thy most holy deity. Let me not think, or say, or do a single thing which tends not to thy service and submission to thy will, that thus all my actions may aim at thy glory and the salvation of my brethren, while they are taught by my example to serve thee. And as thou art giving light to this world for the purposes of external life by the rays of the sun, so enlighten my mind by the effulgence of thy Spirit, that he may guide me in the way of thy righteousness. To whatever purpose I apply my mind, may the end which I ever propose to myself be thy honor and service. May I expect all happiness from thy grace and goodness only. Let me not attempt anything whatever that is not pleasing to thee.

Grant also, that while I labor for the maintenance of this life, and care for the things which pertain to food and raiment, I may raise my mind above them to the blessed and heavenly life which thou hast promised to thy children. Be pleased also, in manifesting thyself to me as the protector of my soul as well as my body, to strengthen and fortify me against all the assaults of the devil, and deliver me from all the dangers which continually beset us in this life. But seeing it is a small thing to have begun, unless I also persevere, I therefore entreat of thee, O Lord, not only to be my guide and director for this day, but to keep me under thy protection to the very end of life, that thus my whole course may be performed under thy superintendence. As I ought to make progress, do thou add daily more and more to the gifts of thy grace until I wholly adhere to thy Son Jesus Christ, whom we justly regard as the true Sun, shining constantly in our minds. In order to my obtaining of thee these great and manifold blessings, forget, and out of thy infinite mercy, forgive my offences, as thou hast promised that thou wilt do to those who call upon thee in sincerity.

John Calvin, 1509–64

Thanks be to Thee, Jesus Christ
Who brought'st me up from last night,
To the gladsome light of this day,
To win everlasting life for my soul,
Through the blood Thou didst shed for me.

Carmina Gadelica

Praise be to Thee, O God, for ever,
For the blessings Thou didst bestow on me –
My food, my speech, my work, my health.

Carmina Gadelica

O God, who broughtst me from the rest of
    last night

Unto the joyous light of this day,
Be Thou bringing me from the new light of
    this day
Unto the guiding light of eternity.
Oh! from the new light of this day
Unto the guiding light of eternity.

Carmina Gadelica

My Lord, I am ready on the threshold of this
    new day to go forth armed with thy power,
    seeking adventure on the high road, to
    right wrong,
to overcome evil, to suffer wounds and endure
    pain if need be,
but in all things to serve thee bravely,
    faithfully, joyfully that at the end of the
    day's labor, kneeling for thy blessing, thou
    mayest find no blot upon my shield. Amen.

From Chester Cathedral

O you most holy and ever-loving God, we thank you once more for the quiet rest of the night that has gone by, for the new promise that has come with this fresh morning, and for the hope of this day. While we have slept, the world in which we live has swept on, and we have rested under the shadow of your love. May we trust you this day for all the needs of the body, the soul, the spirit. Give us this day our daily bread. Amen.

Robert Collyer, 1823–1912

Grant us, O Lord, to pass this day in gladness and peace, without stumbling and without stain, that reaching the eventide victorious over all temptation through Thy ever present aid we may praise Thee, the Eternal God, Who dost govern all things and art blessed for evermore; through Jesus Christ, Thy Son, our Lord. Amen.

*The Common Service Book of
the Lutheran Church, 1917*

We praise Thee, we sing hymns to Thee, we bless Thee; we glorify Thee, we worship Thee by Thy great High Priest; Thee who art the true God, who art the One Unbegotten, the only inaccessible Being. For Thy great glory, O Lord and heavenly King, O God the Father Almighty, O Lord God, the Father of Christ the immaculate Lamb, who taketh away the sin of the world, receive our prayer, Thou that sittest upon the cherubim. For Thou only art holy, Thou only art the Lord Jesus, the Christ of the God of all created nature, and our King, by whom glory, honor, and worship be to Thee.

Didache, 1st century

We give thee hearty thanks, O God, for the rest of the past night and for the gift of a new day with its opportunities of pleasing thee. Grant that we so pass its hours in the perfect freedom of thy service, that at eventide we may again give thanks unto thee: through Jesus Christ our Lord.

Eastern Church, 3rd century, Daybreak Office

My God, I give you this day.
I offer you, now,
all of the good that I shall do
and I promise to accept,
for love of you,
all of the difficulty that I shall meet.
Help me to conduct myself during this day
in a way that pleases you.

Francis de Sales, 1567–1622

Thanks to Thee, O God, that I have risen
    today,
To the rising of this life itself;
May it be to Thine own glory, O God of every
    gift,
And to the glory, aid Thou my soul
With the aiding of Thine own mercy,
Even as I clothe my body with wool,
Cover Thou my soul with the shadow of Thy
    wing.

Gaelic prayer

Lord! Make our heart Your temple in which You live. Grant that every impure thought, every earthly desire might be like the idol Dagon – each morning broken at the feet of the Ark of the Covenant. Teach us to master flesh and blood and let this mastery of ourselves be our bloody sacrifice in order that we might be able to say with the Apostle: "I die every day."

Søren Kierkegaard, 1813–55

On rising
My God! I adore You, I love You with my
    whole heart.

I thank You for all Your benefits, especially for having preserved me during the past night.

Alphonsus Liguori, 1696–1787

O Lord our God, who hast chased the slumber from our eyes, and once more assembled us to lift up our hands unto thee and to praise thy just judgments, accept our prayers and supplications, and give us faith and love. Bless our coming in and our going out, our thoughts, words, and works, and let us begin this day with the praise of the unspeakable sweetness of thy mercy. Hallowed by thy name. They kingdom come; through Jesus Christ our Lord.

Greek Liturgy, 3rd century

Most Holy Trinity, have mercy upon us.
O Lord, cleanse us from our sins.
O Master, pardon our iniquities.
O Holy One, visit and heal our infirmities,
for thy name's sake.

Morning prayer, Greek Orthodox Church

O Lord, prepare us for all the events of the day; for we know not what a day may bring forth. Give us grace to deny ourselves; to take up our cross daily, and to follow in the steps of our Lord and Master.

Matthew Henry, 1662–1714

Matins
    I cannot open mine eyes,
    But thou art ready there to catch
    My morning-soul and sacrifice:
Then we must needs for that day make a match.

    My God, what is a heart?
    Silver, or gold, or precious stone,
    Or star, or rainbow, or a part
Of all these things, or all of them in one?

    My God, what is a heart,
    That thou shouldst it so eye, and woo,
    Pouring upon it all thy art,
As if that thou hadst nothing else to do?

    Indeed, man's whole estate
    Amounts (and richly) to serve thee:
    He did not heaven and earth create,
Yet studies them, not Him by whom they be.

Teach me thy love to know;
  That this new light, which now I see,
  May both the work and workman show:
Then by a Sunbeam I will climb to thee.
                    George Herbert, 1593–1633, The Temple

Make me remember, O God, that every day is
thy gift, and ought to be used according to thy
command, through Jesus Christ our Lord.
                              Samuel Johnson, 1709–84

Hues of the rich unfolding morn,
That, ere the glorious sun be born,
By some soft touch invisible
Around his path are taught to dwell; –

Thou rustling breeze so fresh and gay,
That dancest forth at opening day,
And brushing by with joyous wing,
Wakenest each little leaf to sing; –

Ye fragrant clouds of dewy steam,
By which deep grove and tangled stream
Pay, for soft rains in season given,
Their tribute to the genial heaven; –

Why waste your treasures of delight
Upon our thankless, joyless sight;
Who day by day to sin awake,
Seldom of heaven and you partake?

Oh! timely happy, timely wise,
Hearts that with rising morn arise!
Eyes that the beam celestial view,
Which evermore makes all things new!

New every morning is the love
Our wakening and uprising prove;
Through sleep and darkness safely brought,
Restored to life, and power, and thought.

New mercies, each returning day,
Hover around us while we pray;
New perils past, new sins forgiven,
New thoughts of God, new hopes of heaven.

If on our daily course our mid
Be set to hallow all we find,
New treasures still, of countless price,
God will provide for sacrifice.

Old friends, old scenes, will lovelier be,
As more of heaven in each we see:
Some softening gleam of love and prayer
Shall dawn on every cross and care.

As for some dear familiar strain
Untir'd we ask, and ask again,
Ever, in its melodious store,
Finding a spell unheard before;

Such is the bliss of souls serene,
When they have sworn, and steadfast mean,
Counting the cost, in all to espy
Their God, in all themselves deny.

O could we learn that sacrifice,
What lights would all around us rise!
How would our hearts with wisdom talk
Along Life's dullest dreariest walk!

We need not bid, for cloister'd cell,
Our neighbor and our work farewell,
Nor strive to wind ourselves too high
For sinful man beneath the sky:

The trivial round, the common task,
Would furnish all we ought to ask;
Room to deny ourselves; a road
To bring us, daily, nearer God.

Seek we no more; content with these,
Let present Rapture, Comfort, Ease,
As heaven shall bid them, come and go: –
The secret this of Rest below.

Only, O Lord, in thy dear love
Fit us for perfect Rest above;
And help us, this and every day,
To live more nearly as we pray.
                  John Keble, 1792–1866, The Christian Year

And help us, this day and every day,
To live more nearly as we pray.
                              John Keble, 1792–1866

New every morning is the love
Our wakening and uprising prove;
Through sleep and darkness safely brought,
Restored to live, and power, and thought.

New mercies, each returning day,
Hover around us while we pray;
New perils past, new sins forgiven,
New thoughts of God, new hopes of heaven.

If on our daily course our mind
Be set to hallow all we find,
New treasures still, of countless price,
God will provide for sacrifice.

The trivial round, the common task,
Would furnish all we ought to ask,
Room to deny ourselves, a road
To bring us daily nearer to God.

Only, O Lord, in thy dear love
Fit us for perfect rest above;
And help us this and every day
To live more nearly as we pray.
John Keble, 1792–1866

At the start of a day
Who can tell what a day may bring forth?
Cause me therefore, gracious God,
to live every day as if it were to be my last,
for I know not but that it may be such.
Cause me to live now as I shall wish I had done
when I come to die.
O grant that I may not die with any guilt on my
conscience, or any known sin unrepented of,
but that I may be found in Christ,
who is my only Savior and Redeemer
Thomas à Kempis, 1379–1471

Awake, my soul, and with the sun
Thy daily stage of duty run;
Shake off dull sloth, and early rise
To pay thy morning sacrifice.

Redeem thy misspent time that's past;
Live this day as if 'twere thy last;
T'improve thy talent take due care:
'Gainst the great day thyself prepare.

Let all thy converse be sincere,
Thy conscience as the noonday clear;
Think how all-seeing God thy ways
And all thy secret thoughts surveys.

Influenced by the light divine
Let thy own light in good works shine:

Reflect all heaven's propitious ways,
In ardent love and cheerful praise.

Wake, and lift up thyself, my heart,
And with the angels bear thy part,
Who all night long unwearied sing
Glory to the eternal king.

I wake, I wake, ye heavenly choir;
May your devotion me inspire,
That I like you my age may spend,
Like you may on my God attend.

May I like you in God delight,
Have all day long my God in sight,
Perform like you my Maker's will;
Oh may I never more do ill!

Had I your wings, to heaven I'd fly;
But God shall that defect supply,
And my soul, winged with warm desire,
Shall all day long to heaven aspire.

Glory to Thee who safe has kept,
And hath refreshed me whilst I slept.
Grant, Lord, when I from death shall wake,
I may of endless light partake.

I would not wake, nor rise again,
Even heaven itself I would disdain,
Wert not Thou there to be enjoyed,
And I in hymns to be employed.

Heaven is, dear Lord, where'er Thou art:
Oh never, then, from me depart;
For to my soul 'tis hell to be
But for one moment without Thee.

Lord, I my vows to Thee renew;
Disperse my sins as morning dew;
Guard my first springs of thought and will,
And with Thyself my spirit fill.

Direct, control, suggest, this day,
All I design, or do, or say,
That all my powers, with all their might,
In Thy sole glory may unite.
Thomas Ken, 1637–1711

We give thanks to you, heavenly Father, through
Jesus Christ your dear Son, that you have

protected us through the night from all danger and harm; and we beseech you to preserve and keep us, this day also, from all sin and evil; that in all our thoughts, words and deeds, we may serve and please you. In your hands we commend our bodies and souls, and all that is ours. Let your holy angel guard us, that the wicked one may have no power over us.

Martin Luther, 1483–1546, his morning prayer

You are the life-giving Power and the Source of immortality, Christ God, our Savior. You have granted us to rise in the middle of the night and to confess to you regarding your statutes and righteousness. And now we ask you, Lord our God, make us vigilant and ready with your saints at the morning hour, and giving thanks with them, let us glorify you with the Father and the Holy Spirit. Now and always and unto the ages of ages. Amen.

John Mantakuni, c.420–490

We give you thanks, O Lord our God, who have awakened us from restful sleep by the grace of your mercy. Awaken our minds in righteousness for you, Lord our God, so that our eyes may see your salvation. May your divinity come and abide in us, and may your mercy shelter and protect your servants. By day and by night and at all times make us, your servants, reflect always on the love of your commandments, in thanksgiving to glorify the Father and the Son and the Holy Spirit. Now and always and unto the ages of ages. Amen.

John Mantakuni, c.420–490

Eternal God, who committest to us the swift and solemn trust of life; since we know not what a day may bring forth, but only that the hour for serving thee is always present, may we wake to the instant claims of thy holy will; not waiting for tomorrow, but yielding today. In all things draw us to the mind of Christ, that thy lost image may be traced again, and thou mayest own us as at one with him and thee.

James Martineau, 1805–1900

Almighty, eternal God, Father of our Lord Jesus Christ, creator of heaven and earth and mankind, together with your Son, our Lord Jesus Christ, your Word and Image, and with

your Holy Spirit: Have mercy on us, and forgive us all our sins for you Son's sake, whom you have made our Mediator. Guide and sanctify us by your Holy Spirit, who was poured out on the apostles. Grant that we may truly know and praise you throughout eternity.

Philip Melanchthon, 1497–1560, his morning prayer

May the Lord Jesus Christ, who is the splendor of eternal Light, remove from your hearts the darkness of night. Amen.
May he drive far from you the snares of the crafty enemy, and always give to guard you the angel of light. Amen.
That you may rise to your morning praises, kept safe in him, in whom consists all the fullness of your salvation. Amen.

Mozarabic Psalter

Enlighten the darkness of our minds, stretch forth your helping hand, confirm and give us strength; that we may arise and confess you and glorify you without ceasing all the days of our life, O Lord of all.

Nestorian Liturgy, 5th/6th century

O my God, make me happy this day in thy service. Let me do nothing, say nothing, desire nothing, which is contrary to thy will. Give me a thankful spirit, and a heart full of praise for all that thou hast given me, and for all thou hast withheld from me.

Ashton Oxenden, 1808–92

O Day-spring, Sun of righteousness,
    Shine forth with light for me!
Treasure of mercy, let my soul thy hidden
    riches see!

Thou before whom the thoughts of men lie
    open in thy sight,
Unto my soul, now dark and dim, grant
    thoughts that shine
with light!

O Father, Son and Holy Ghost, Almighty One
    in Three,
Care-taker of all creatures, have pity upon me!

Awake O Lord, awake to help, with grace and
    power divine;

Awaken those who slumber now, like
   heaven's host to shine!

O Lord and Savior, life-giver, unto the dead
   give life,
And raise up those that have grown weak and
   stumbled in the
strife!

O skilful Pilot! Lamp of light, that burnest
   bright and clear!
Strength and assurance grant to me, now hid
   away in fear!

O thou that makest old things new, renew me
   and adorn;
Rejoice me with salvation, Lord, for which I
   inly mourn.

Giver of good, unto my sins be thy forgiveness
   given!
Lead thy disciples, heavenly King, unto the
   flocks of heaven!

Nerses the Gracious, 1102–73

I rise today with the power of God to guide
   me,
the might of God to uphold me,
the wisdom of God to teach me,
the eye of God to watch over me,
the ear of God to hear me,
the word of God to give me speech,
the hand of God to protect me,
the path of God to lie before me,
the shield of God to shelter me,
the host of God to defend me
      against the snares of the devil and the
         temptations of the world,
      against every man who meditates injury
         to me,
whether far or near.

Breastplate of Patrick, c.389–c.461

Lord, give me the strength to greet the coming
day in peace. Help me in all things to rely
on Your holy will. Reveal Your will to me
every hour of the day. Bless my dealings with
all people. Teach me to treat all people who
come to me throughout the day with peace
of soul and with firm conviction that Your
will governs all. In all my deeds and words

guide my thoughts and feelings. In unexpected
events, let me not forget that all are sent by
you. Teach me to act firmly and wisely, without
embittering and embarrassing others. Give me
the physical strength to bear the labors of this
day. Direct my will, teach me to pray, pray in
me. Amen.

Metropolitan Philaret, 1782–1867

Lord God, the Father, what thou hast created;
Lord God, the Son, what thou hast redeemed;
Lord God, the Holy Ghost, what thou hast
hallowed, I commend into thy hands. To thy
holy name let honor, glory, praise, and thanks
be given in the morning hour, and in all eternity. Amen.

Johann Friedrich Starck

The day returns and brings us the petty round
of irritating concerns and duties. Help us
to play the man, help us to perform them
with laughter and kind faces, let cheerfulness
abound with industry. Give us to go blithely on
our business all this day; bring us to our resting
beds weary and content and undishonored;
and grant us in the end the gift of sleep.

R. L. Stevenson, 1850–94

All this day, O Lord, let me touch as many lives
as possible for thee; and every life I touch, do
thou by thy Spirit quicken, whether through
the word I speak, the prayer I breathe, or the
life I live.

Mary Sumner, 1828–1921

In thy name, O Lord Jesus Christ, do I rise from
sleep: do thou bless, guide, and guard me, and
lead me to everlasting life.
Amen.

Treasury of Devotion, 1869

Lord, that which we have prayed against this
morning, suffer us not to have done before the
evening.

C.J. Vaughan, 1816–97

Most blessed Trinity, and one eternal God, as
you have today woken me up from physical
sleep, so wake up my soul from the sleep of
sin; and as you have strengthened my through
sleep, so after death give me life; for death to

me is but to sleep with you; to whom be all glory, wisdom, majesty, dominion, and praise, now and always.

Henry Vaughan, 1622–95

Morning Prayer
Almighty God, and most merciful father, who didst command the children of Israel to offer daily sacrifice to thee, that thereby they might glorify and praise thee for thy protection both night and day; receive, O Lord, my morning sacrifice which I now offer up to thee; I yield thee humble and hearty thanks that thou has preserved me from the dangers of the night past, and brought me to the light of this day, and the comforts thereof, a day which is consecrated to thine own service and for thine own honor. Let my heart, therefore, Gracious God, be so affected with the glory and majesty of it, that I may not do mine own works, but wait on thee, and discharge those weighty duties thou requirest of me; and since thou art a God of pure eyes, and wilt be sanctified in all who draw near unto thee, who doest not regard the sacrifice of fools, nor hear sinners who tread in the courts, pardon, I beseech thee, my sins, remove them from thy presence, as far as the east is from the west, and accept of me for the merits of thy son Jesus Christ, that when I come into thy temple, and compass thine alter, my prayers may come before thee as incense; and as thou wouldst hear me calling upon thee in my prayers, so give me grace to hear thee calling on me in thy word, that it may be wisdom, righteousness, reconciliation and peace to the saving of my soul in the day of the Lord Jesus. Grant that I may hear it with reverence, receive it with meekness, mingle it with faith, and that it may accomplish in me, gracious God, the good work for which thou has sent it. Bless my family, kindred, friends and country, be our God & guide this day and for ever for his sake, who lay down in the Grave and arose again for us, Jesus Christ our Lord, Amen.

George Washington, 1732–99

EVENING PRAYERS

I will both lie down and sleep in peace;
    for you alone, O Lord, make me like down in safety.

Psalm 4.8 NRSV

Holy Lord, almighty and eternal Father, thank you for your mercy that has protected me throughout this day. Let me pass through this night peacefully and with a pure mind and body, that rising with purity in the morning, I may serve you gratefully.

Alcuin, 735–804

The day is past and over;
All thanks, O LORD, to Thee!
I pray Thee, that offenceless
The hours of dark may be.
O Jesu! keep me in Thy sight,
And save me through the coming night!
The joys of day are over:
I lift my heart to Thee;
And call on Thee, that sinless
The hours of sin may be.
O Jesu! make their darkness light,
And save me through the coming night!
The toils of day are over:
I raise the hymn to Thee;
And ask that free from peril
The hours of fear may be.
O Jesu! keep me in Thy sight,
And guard me through the coming night!
Lighten mine eyes, O SAVIOR,
Or sleep in death shall I,
And he, my wakeful tempter,
Triumphantly shall cry:
"He could not make their darkness light,
Nor guard them through the hours of night!"
Be Thou my soul's preserver,
O GOD! for Thou dost know
How many are the perils
Through which I have to go:
Lover of men! O hear my call,
And guard and save me from them all!

Anatolius, d.458

Let me think upon thy Name in the night season, and keep thy law: let the evening prayer go up unto Thee, and thy pity come down unto us, O Thou which givest songs in the night, which makest the outgoings of the morning and evening to praise Thee, which givest thy beloved wholesome sleep.

Lancelot Andrewes, 1555–1626

The day is gone,
and I give Thee thanks, O Lord.

Evening is at hand,
make it bright unto us.
As day has its evening so also has life;
the even of life is age, age has overtaken me,
make it bright unto us.
Cast me not away in the time of age;
forsake me not when my strength faileth me.
Even to my old age be Thou He,
and even to hoar hairs carry me ;
do Thou make, do Thou bear, do Thou carry
    and deliver me.
Abide with me, Lord, for it is toward evening,
and the day is far spent of this fretful life.
Let Thy strength be made perfect in my
    weakness.

Day is fled and gone, life too is going, this
    lifeless life.
Night cometh, and cometh death, the
    deathless death.
Near as is the end of day, so too the end of life.
We then, also remembering it, beseech of
    Thee for the close of our life,
that Thou wouldest direct it in peace,
Christian, acceptable, sinless, shameless,
and, if it please Thee, painless, Lord, O Lord,
gathering us together under the feet of Thine
    Elect,
when Thou wilt, and as Thou wilt, only
    without shame and sins.
Remember we the days of darkness, for they
    shall be many, lest we be cast into outer
    darkness.
Remember we to outstrip the night doing
    some good thing.
Near is judgment;
a good and acceptable answer at the dreadful
    and fearful judgment-seat of Jesus Christ
    vouchsafe to us, O Lord.
By night I lift up my hands in the sanctuary,
    and praise the Lord.
The Lord hath granted His loving-kindness in
    the day time;
and in the night season did I sing of Him,
and made my prayer unto the God of my life.
As long as I live will I magnify Thee on this
    manner,
and lift up my hands in Thy Name.
Let my prayer be set forth in Thy sight as the
    incense,
and let the lifting up of my hands be an

evening sacrifice.
Blessed art Thou, O Lord, our God, the God of
    our fathers,
who hast created the changes of days and
    nights,
who givest songs in the night,
who hast delivered us from the evil of this day
who hast not cut off like a weaver my life,
nor from day even to night made an end of
    me.

Confession
Lord,
as we add day to day, so sin to sin.
The just falleth seven times a day; and I, an
    exceeding sinner,
seventy times seven; a wonderful, a horrible
    thing, O Lord.
But I turn with groans from my evil ways,
and I return into my heart, and with all my
    heart I turn to Thee,
O God of penitents and Savior of sinners;
and evening by evening I will return
in the innermost marrow of my soul;
and my soul out of the deep crieth unto Thee.
I have sinned, O Lord, against Thee,
heavily against Thee; alas, alas, woe is me!
for my misery. I repent, o me!
I repent, spare me, O Lord, I repent, o me, I
    repent,
help Thou my impenitence.
Be appeased, spare me, O Lord;
be appeased, have mercy on me ;
I said, Lord, have mercy upon me,
heal my soul, for I have sinned against Thee.
Have mercy upon me, O Lord, after Thy great
    goodness,
according to the multitude of Thy mercies do
    away mine offences.
Remit the guilt, heal the wound, blot out the
    stains,
clear away the shame, rescue from the
    tyranny,
and make me not a public example.
o bring Thou me out of my trouble, cleanse
    Thou me from secret faults,
keep back Thy servant also from
    presumptuous sins.
My wanderings of mind and idle talking
lay not to my charge.
Remove the dark and muddy flood

of foul and wicked thoughts.
O Lord, I have destroyed myself;
whatever I have done amiss, pardon
    mercifully.
Deal not with us after our sins,
neither reward us after our iniquities.
Look mercifully upon our infirmities;
and for the glory of Thy All-holy Name,
turn from us all those ills and miseries,
which by our sins, and by us through them,
are most righteously and worthily deserved.

Commendation

To my weariness, O Lord, vouchsafe Thou
    rest,
to my exhaustion
renew Thou strength.
Lighten mine eyes that I sleep not in death.
Deliver me from the terror by night,
the pestilence that walketh in darkness.
    Supply me with healthy sleep,
and to pass through this night without Fear.
o keeper of Israel, who neither slumberest nor
    sleepest,
guard me this night from all evil,
guard my soul, O Lord.
Visit me with the visitation of Thine own,
reveal to me wisdom in the visions of the
    night.
If not, for I am not worthy, not worthy, at
    least, o loving Lord,
Let sleep be to me a breathing time as from
    toil, so from sin.
Yea, O Lord, nor let me in my dreams imagine
    what may anger Thee,
what may defile me.
Let not my loins be filled with illusions,
yea, let my reins chasten me in the night
    season,
yet without grievous terror.
Preserve me from the black sleep of sin;
all earthly and evil thoughts put to sleep
    within me.
Grant to me light sleep, rid of all imaginations
fleshly and satanical.
Lord, Thou knowest how sleepless are mine
    unseen foes,
and how feeble my wretched flesh,
Who madest me ;
shelter me with the wing of Thy pity;
awaken me at the fitting time, the time of

prayer;
and give me to seek Thee early,
for Thy glory and for Thy service.

Into Thy hands, O Lord, I commend myself,
    my spirit, soul, and body:
Thou didst make, and didst redeem them;
and together with me, all my friends and all
    that belongs to me.
Thou hast vouchsafed them to me, Lord,
in Thy goodness.
Guard my lying down and my rising up,
from henceforth and for ever.
Let me remember Thee on my bed, and search
    out my spirit;
let me wake up and be present with Thee;
let me lay me down in peace, and take my rest:
for it is Thou, Lord, only that makest me dwell
    in safety.

Lancelot Andrewes, 1555–1626

Take us, we pray thee, O Lord of our life, into
thy keeping this night and for ever. O thou
light of lights, keep us from inward darkness;
grant us so to sleep in peace, that we may arise
to work according to thy will; through Jesus
Christ our Lord.

Lancelot Andrewes, 1555–1626

O Lord our God, keep us in peace during this
night and at all times. Keep our hearts and
thoughts secure in holy reverence for you. So
that we may be protected at all times from the
snares of the enemy. And let us offer blessing
and glory to the Father and to the Son and to
the Holy Spirit, now and forever and unto the
ages of ages. Amen.

Armenian prayer

Before we go to rest, we would commit
ourselves to God's care through Christ,
beseeching him to forgive us for all our sins
of this day past, and to keep alive his grace in
our hearts, and to cleanse us from all sin, pride,
harshness, and selfishness, and to give us the
spirit of meekness, humility, firmness, and
love. O Lord, keep thyself present to us ever,
and perfect thy strength in our weakness. Take
us and ours under thy blessed care, this night
and evermore; through Jesus Christ our Lord.

Thomas Arnold, 1795–1842

An Evening Prayer (1)

Look with Mercy on the Sins we have this day committed, and in Mercy make us feel them deeply, that our Repentance may be sincere, and our resolutions steadfast of endeavoring against the commission of such in future. Teach us to understand the sinfulness of our own Hearts, and bring to our knowledge every fault of Temper and every evil Habit in which we have indulged to the discomfort of our fellow-creatures, and the danger of our own Souls. May we now, and on each return of night, consider how the past day has been spent by us, what have been our prevailing Thoughts, Words, and Actions during it, and how far we can acquit ourselves of Evil. Have we thought irreverently of Thee, have we disobeyed Thy commandments, have we neglected any known duty, or willingly given pain to any human being? Incline us to ask our Hearts these questions Oh! God, and save us from deceiving ourselves by Pride or Vanity.

Jane Austen, 1775–1817

Give us a thankful sense of the Blessings in which we live, of the many comforts of our lot; that we may not deserve to lose them by Discontent or Indifference.

Jane Austen, 1775–1817

Be gracious to our Necessities, and guard us, and all we love, from Evil this night. May the sick and afflicted, be now, and ever thy care; and heartily do we pray for the safety of all that travel by Land or by Sea, for the comfort & protection of the Orphan and Widow and that Thy pity may be shewn upon all Captives and Prisoners.

Jane Austen, 1775–1817

Above all other blessings Oh! God, for ourselves, and our fellow-creatures, we implore Thee to quicken our sense of thy Mercy in the redemption of the World, of the Value of that Holy Religion in which we have been brought up, that we may not, by our own neglect, throw away the salvation thou hast given us, nor be Christians only in name. Hear us Almighty God, for His sake who has redeemed us, and taught us thus to pray.

Jane Austen, 1775–1817

An Evening Prayer (2)

Almighty God! Look down with mercy on Thy servants here assembled and accept the petitions now offered up unto Thee. Pardon oh! God the offences of the past day. We are conscious of many frailties; we remember with shame and contrition, many evil thoughts and neglected duties; and we have perhaps sinned against Thee and against our fellow-creatures in many instances of which we have no remembrance. Pardon oh God! whatever thou has seen amiss in us, and give us a stronger desire of resisting every evil inclination and weakening every habit of sin. Thou knowest the infirmity of our nature, and the temptations which surround us.

Jane Austen, 1775–1817

Be Thou merciful, oh Heavenly Father! to creatures so formed and situated. We bless Thee for every comfort of our past and present existence, for our health of body and of mind and for every other source of happiness which Thou hast bountifully bestowed on us and with which we close this day, imploring their continuance from Thy Fatherly goodness, with a more grateful sense of them, than they have hitherto excited. May the comforts of every day, be thankfully felt by us, may they prompt a willing obedience of Thy commandments and a benevolent spirit toward every fellow-creature.

Jane Austen, 1775–1817

Have mercy oh gracious Father! upon all that are now suffering from whatsoever cause, that are in any circumstance of danger or distress. Give them patience under every affliction, strengthen, comfort and relieve them.

Jane Austen, 1775–1817

To Thy goodness we commend ourselves this night beseeching Thy protection of us through its darkness and dangers. We are helpless and dependent; graciously preserve us. For all whom we love and value, for every friend and connection, we equally pray; however divided and far asunder, we know that we are alike before Thee, and under Thine eye. May we be equally united in Thy faith and fear, in fervent devotion towards Thee, and in Thy merciful protection this night. Pardon oh

Lord! the imperfections of these our prayers, and accept them through the mediation of our Blessed Savior, in whose Holy words, we further address Thee.

Jane Austen, 1775–1817

Father of Heaven! whose goodness has brought us in safety to the close of this day, dispose our hearts in fervent prayer. Another day is now gone, and added to those, for which we were before accountable. Teach us almighty father, to consider this solemn truth, as we should do, that we may feel the importance of every day, and every hour as it passes, and earnestly strive to make a better use of what thy goodness may yet bestow on us, than we have done of the time past.

Jane Austen, 1775–1817

Keep us O Heavenly Father from evil this night. Bring us in safety to the beginning of another day and grant that we may rise again with every serious and religious feeling which now directs us.

Jane Austen, 1775–1817

Yours, O Lord, is the day, yours also is the night; cover our sins with your mercy as you cover the earth with darkness; and grant that the Sun of Righteousness may always shine in our hearts, to chase away the darkness of all evil thoughts; through Jesus Christ our Lord.

Author unknown

Abide with us, O good Lord, through the night, guarding, keeping, guiding, sustaining, sanctifying, and with thy love gladdening us, that in thee we may ever live, and in thee may die; through Jesus Christ our Lord.

E.W. Benson, 1829–96

I lift my Heart to Thee, O God, Thou Fountain of Eternal Life, and give Thee Thanks through Jesus Christ, Thy Beloved Son, our Lord and Savior, for having protected and preserved me this Day from all Mischief that might have befallen me. I commend to Thy Disposal my Condition and Employment, together with the Work of my Hands, and humbly repose them on Thee. So fill my Soul with Thy Spirit, that neither the grand Enemy, the Devil, nor any other evil Influence or Desire, may find Harbor therein. Let my Mind only delight in Thee in Thy Temple, and let Thy good Angel stay with me, that I may rest safely in Thy Power, and under Thy Protection. Amen.

Jakob Boehme, 1555–1624

Lighten our darkness, we beseech thee, O Lord, and by thy great mercy, defend us from all perils and dangers of this night, for the love of thy only Son, our Savior Jesus Christ.

Book of Common Prayer, 1549, Evensong, Collect for Aid against all Perils

Lord God, who hast given man the night for rest, as thou hast created the day in which he may employ himself in labor, grant, I pray, that my body may so rest during this night that my mind cease not to be awake to thee, nor my heart faint or be overcome with torpor, preventing it from adhering steadfastly to the love of thee. While laying aside my cares to relax and relieve my mind, may I not, in the meanwhile, forget thee, nor may the remembrance of thy goodness and grace, which ought always to be deeply engraven on my mind, escape my memory. In like manner, also, as the body rests may my conscience enjoy rest. Grant, moreover, that in taking sleep I may not give indulgence to the flesh, but only allow myself as much as the weakness of this natural state requires, to my being enabled thereafter to be more alert in thy service. Be pleased to keep me so chaste and unpolluted, not less in mind than in body, and safe from all dangers, that my sleep itself may turn to the glory of thy name. But since this day has not passed away without my having in many ways offended thee through my proneness to evil, in like manner as all things are now covered by the darkness of the night, so let every thing that is sinful in me lie buried in thy mercy. Hear me, O God, Father and Preserver, through Jesus Christ thy Son.

John Calvin, 1509–64

I lie down to-night,
With the Triune of my strength,
With the Father, with Jesus,
With the Spirit of might.

Carmina Gadelica

May the Light of lights come
To my dark heart from thy place;
May the Spirit's wisdom come
To my heart's tablet from my Savior.
Be the peace of the Spirit mine this night,
Be the peace of the Son mine this night,
Be the peace of the Father mine this night,
The peace of all peace be mind this night,
Each morning and evening of my life.

Celtic prayer

O Lord Jesus Christ, our Watchman and
Keeper, take us to thy care; grant that, our
bodies sleeping, our minds may watch in
thee, and be made merry by some sight of
that celestial and heavenly life, wherein thou
art the King and Prince, together with the
Father and the Holy Spirit, where thy angels
and holy souls be most happy citizens. Oh
purify our souls, keep clean our bodies, that
in both we may please thee, sleeping and
waking, for ever.

Christian Prayers, 1566

Lord our God,
as we keep watch with you this night
we commend all people
and their lives to you.
We remember in particular all those who are
    working,
those who in their suffering cannot sleep,
those who use the night to do evil,
those who are afraid of the day about to
    dawn.
May they all come out into the light of your
    Day.
We ask you this, through Jesus, our Lord.

Cistercian Vigil Prayer

Holy Father, keep us in your truth;
holy Son, protect us under the wings of your
    cross;
holy Spirit, make us temples and dwelling
    places for your glory;
grant us your peace all the days of our lives,
    O Lord.

Compline,
Maronite Church

Visit, we beseech thee, O Lord, this place, and
drive from it all the snares of the enemy; let
your holy angels dwell here to preserve us in
peace; and may your blessing be on us evermore; through Jesus Christ our Lord.

Compline, Roman Breviary

Look down, O Lord, from your heavenly
throne, illuminate the darkness of this night
with your celestial brightness, and from the
sons of light banish the deeds of darkness;
through Jesus Christ our Lord.

Compline, Roman Breviary

Be present, O merciful God, and protect us
through the silent hours of this night, so that
we who are wearied by the changes and chances of this fleeting world, may repose on your
eternal changelessness; through Jesus Christ
our Lord.

Compline, Roman Breviary

Save us, O Lord, while waking, and guard us
while sleeping: that awake we may watch with
Christ, and asleep we may rest in peace.

Compline, Sarum Breviary

Preserve me, Lord, while I am waking, and
defend me while I am sleeping, that my soul
may continually watch for you, and both body
and soul may rest in your peace for ever.

John Cosin, 1594–1672

We praise Thee, we sing hymns to Thee, we
bless Thee for Thy great glory, O Lord our King,
the Father of Christ the immaculate Lamb,
who taketh away the sin of the world. Praise
becomes Thee, hymns become Thee, glory
becomes Thee, the God and Father, through
the Son, in the most holy Spirit, for ever and
ever. Amen.

Didache, 1st century

Lord Jesus Christ, you welcomed the children
who came to you, accept also from me, this
evening prayer. Shelter me under the shadow
of your wings, that in peace I may lie down
and sleep. When you wake me up may I live for
you, for you alone are full of mercy.

Eastern Orthodox Church

May the angels watch me
    As I lie down to sleep.

May angels guard me
    As I sleep alone.
Gaelic blessing

Lord, you commanded peace:
    you gave peace.
You bequeathed peace;
    give us your peace from heaven.
Make this day peaceful,
    and the remaining days of our life.
Gaelic prayer

Evensong
      Blest be the God of love,
Who gave me eyes, and light, and power this
    day,
      Both to be busy and to play.
    But much more blest be God above,

      Who gave me sight alone,
Which to himself he did deny;
      For when he sees my ways, I die:
    But I have got his Son, and he hath
      none.

      What have I brought thee home
For this thy love? have I discharged the debt,
      Which this day's favor did beget?
    I ran; but all I brought, was foam.

      Thy diet, care, and cost
Do end in bubbles, balls of wind;
      Of wind to thee whom I have crost,
But balls of wild-fire to my troubled mind.

      Yet still thou goest on,
And now with darkness closest weary eyes,
    Saying to man, *It doth suffice:*
    Henceforth repose; your work is done.

      Thus in thy Ebony box
Thou dost enclose us, till the day
    Put our amendment in our way,
And give new wheels to our disorded clocks.

      I must, which shows more love,
The day or night: that is the gale, this
    th'harbour;
    That is the walk, and this the arbor;
    Or that the garden, this the grove.

    My God, thou art all love.
    Not one poor minute 'escapes thy
      breast,
    But brings a favor from above;
And in this love, more than in bed, I rest.
George Herbert, 1593–1633, The Temple

O Almighty Lord, Word of the Father, Jesus Christ, Who are Yourself perfect: for the sake of Your great mercy never depart from me, Your servant, but ever abide in me.

O Jesus, Good Shepherd of Your sheep, do not let me fall into the revolt of the serpent, nor leave me to the will of Satan, for the seed of corruption is in me. O Lord God Whom we worship, O Holy King Jesus, preserve me while I sleep with Your unchanging light, Your Holy Spirit, by Whom You sanctified Your disciples. Grant, O Lord, even to me, Your unworthy servant, Your salvation upon my bed; enlighten my mind with the light of the understanding of Your holy Gospel, my soul with the love of Your Cross, my heart with the purity of Your Word, my body with Your passionless passion.

Keep my thoughts in Your humility, and rouse me in good time to glorify You. For You are glorified above all, with Your eternal Father and with the most Holy Spirit, now and ever and unto ages of ages. Amen.
Ignatius of Antioch, c.35–c.107

'Tis gone, that bright and orbed blaze,
Fast fading from our wistful gaze;
Yon mantling cloud has hid from sight
The last faint pulse of quivering light.

In darkness and in weariness
The traveler on his way must press,
No gleam to watch on tree or tower,
Whiling away the lonesome hour.

Sun of my soul! Thou Savior dear,
It is not night if Thou be near:
Oh may no earth-born cloud arise
To hide Thee from thy servant's eyes.

When round thy wondrous works below
My searching rapturous glance I throw,
Tracing out Wisdom, Power, and Love,
In earth or sky, in stream or grove; –

Or by the light thy words disclose
Watch Time's full river as it flows,
Scanning thy gracious Providence,
Where not too deep for mortal sense: –

When with dear friends sweet talk I hold,
And all the flowers of life unfold; –
Let not my heart within me burn,
Except in all I Thee discern.

When the soft dews of kindly sleep
My wearied eyelids gently steep,
Be my last thought, how sweet to rest
For ever on my Savior's breast.

Abide with me from morn till eve,
For without Thee I cannot live:
Abide with me when night is nigh,
For without Thee I dare not die.

Thou Framer of the light and dark,
Steer through the tempest thine own ark:
Amid the howling wintry sea
We are in port if we have Thee.

The Rulers of this Christian land,
'Twixt Thee and us ordained to stand, –
Guide Thou their course, O Lord, aright,
Let all do all as in thy sight.

Oh by thine own sad burthen, borne
So meekly up the hill of scorn,
Teach Thou thy Priests their daily cross
To bear as thine, nor count it loss!

If some poor wandering soul of thine
Have spurn'd, to-day, the voice divine,
Now, Lord, the gracious work begin;
Let her no more lie down in sin.

Watch by the sick: enrich the poor
With blessings from thy boundless store:
Be every mourner's sleep to-night
Like infant's slumbers, pure and light.

Come near and bless us when we wake,
Ere through the world our way we take:
Till in the ocean of thy love
We lose ourselves in heaven above.
John Keble, 1792–1866, The Christian Year

Forgive me, Lord, for thy dear Son,
The ill that I this day have done,
That with the world, myself, and thee
I, ere I sleep, at peace may be.

Teach me to live, that I may dread
The grave as little as my bed;
Teach me to die, that so I may
Rise glorious at the awful day.

O may my soul on thee repose,
And with sweet sleep mine eyelids close,
Sleep that may me more vigorous make
To serve my God when I awake.

When in the night I sleepless lie,
My soul with heavenly thoughts supply;
Let no ill dreams disturb my rest,
No powers of darkness me molest.
Thomas Ken, 1637–1711

Glory to thee, my God, this night
for all the blessings of the light;
keep me, O keep me, King of kings,
beneath thy own almighty wings.
Thomas Ken, 1637–1711

O Lord, I cry unto thee, hearken unto me, O God. Thou holdest my eyes waking: I am so feeble that I cannot speak: and in the night season my soul refuseth comfort; yet even then give me grace especially, that I may commune with mine own heart, and search out my spirits, and compose them in thee, that I may rise to serve thee.
Amen.
William Laud, 1573–1645

Into your hands, O Lord, we commend our souls and bodies, beseeching you to keep us this night under your protection and to strengthen us for your service tomorrow, for Christ's sake.
William Laud, 1613–67

Abide with us, O Lord, for it is toward evening and the day is far spent; abide with us, and with your whole church. Abide with us in the evening of the day, in the evening of life, in the evening of the world. Abide with us and with all your faithful ones, O Lord, in time and eternity.

Lutheran Manuel of Prayer

O Eternal God, King of all creation, Who have granted me to attain to this hour, forgive me the sins which I have committed this day in thought, word, and deed; and cleanse, O Lord, my humble soul from every stain of flesh and spirit.

Grant me, O Lord, to pass through the sleep of this night in peace, that when I rise from my bed I may please Your holy Name all the days of my life, and conquer the enemies, both corporeal and incorporeal, that contend against me.

Deliver me, O Lord, from the vain thoughts that stain me, and from evil desires.

For Thine is the kingdom and the power and the glory of the Father and of the Son and of the Holy Spirit, now and ever and unto ages of ages.

Macarius of Egypt,
c.300–c.390

Grant, Lord, to keep us this evening without sin. Blessed are You O Lord, God of our fathers, and praised and glorified is Your Name for ever. Amen. Lord, let Your mercy come upon us, O Lord, for we have trusted in You. Blessed are You O Lord, teach me Your commandments. Blessed are You O Master, make me to understand Your commandments. Blessed are You, O Holy One, enlighten me with Your commandments. Lord, Your love endures forever; Do not turn away from the work of Your hands. To You belong praise, song; and glory, to the Father, and the Son, and the Holy Spirit, both now and forever and to the ages of ages. Amen.

Orthodox prayer

Now that the day has ended, I thank you Lord, and I ask that the evening and the night be sinless. Grant this to me, O Savior, and save me.

Orthodox prayer

Lord, God our Father, if during this day I have sinned in word, deed or thought forgive me in Your goodness and love. Grant me peaceful

sleep; protect me from all evil and awake me in the morning that I may glorify you, Your Son and Your Holy Spirit now and forever and ever. Amen.

Orthodox prayer

We come before Thee, O Lord, in the end of thy day with thanksgiving.

Our beloved in the far parts of the earth, those who are now beginning the labors of the day what time we end them, and those with whom the sun now stands at the point of noon, bless, help, console, and prosper them.

Our guard is relieved, the service of the day is over, and the hour come to rest. We resign into thy hands our sleeping bodies, our cold hearths, and open doors. Give us to awake with smiles, give us to labor smiling. As the sun returns in the east, so let our patience be renewed with dawn; as the sun lightens the world, so let our loving-kindness make bright this house of our habitation.

R.L. Stevenson, 1850–94

Lord, receive our supplications for this house, family, and country. Protect the innocent, restrain the greedy and the treacherous, lead us out of our tribulation into a quiet land.

Look down upon ourselves and upon our absent dear ones. Help us and them; prolong our days in peace and honor. Give us health, food, bright weather, and light hearts. In what we meditate of evil, frustrate our will; in what of good, further our endeavors. Cause injuries to be forgot and benefits to be remembered.

Let us lie down without fear and awake and arise with exultation. For his sake, in whose words we now conclude.

R.L. Stevenson, 1850–94

Go with each of us to rest; if any awake, temper them the dark hours of watching; and when the day returns, return to us, our sun and comforter, and call us up with morning faces and with morning hearts, eager to labor, eager to be happy, if happiness should be our portion, and if the day be marked for sorrow, strong to endure it.

R.L. Stevenson, 1850–94, written
on the eve of his unexpected death

Into your hands, O Lord, I commend my spirit, for you have redeemed me, O Lord, the God of truth. I will lay down in peace, and take my rest, for it is you Lord only who make me live in safety.

Treasury of Devotion, 1869

Evening Prayer

O most Glorious God, in Jesus Christ my merciful and loving Father, I acknowledge and confess my guilt, in the weak and imperfect performance of the duties of this day. I have called on thee for pardon and forgiveness of sins, but so coldly and carelessly, that my prayers are become my sin and stand in need of pardon. I have heard thy holy word, but with such deadness of spirit that I have been an unprofitable and forgetful hearer, so that, O Lord, thou I have done thy work, yet it hath been so negligently that I may rather expect a curse than a blessing from thee. But, O God, who art rich in mercy and plenteous in redemption, mark not, I beseech thee, what I have done amiss; remember that I am but dust, and remit my transgressions, negligences and ignorances, and cover them all with the absolute obedience of thy dear Son, that those sacrifices which I have offered may be accepted by thee, in and for the sacrifice of Jesus Christ offered upon the cross for me; for his sake, ease me of the burden of my sins, and give me grace that by the call of the Gospel I may rise from the slumber of sin into newness of life. Let me live according to those holy rules which thou has this day prescribed in thy holy word; make me to know what is acceptable in thy sight, and therein to delight, open the eyes of my understanding, and help me thoroughly to examine myself concerning my knowledge, faith and repentance, increase my faith, and direct me to the true object Jesus Christ the way, the truth and the life, bless O Lord, all the people of this land, from the highest to the lowest, particularly those whom thou hast appointed to rule over us in church & state. Continue thy goodness to me this night. These weak petitions I humbly implore thee to accept and answer for the sake of thy Dear Son Jesus Christ our Lord, Amen.

George Washington, 1732–99

And now, O blessed Redeemer, our rock, our hope, and only sure defense, to thee do we cheerfully commit both our soul and body. If thy wise providence see fit, grant that we may rise in the morning, refreshed with sleep, and with a spirit of activity for the duties of the day, but whether we wake here or in eternity grant that our trust in thee may remain sure, and our hope unshaken, through Jesus Christ our Lord.

H.K. White, 1785–1806

PRAYERS FOR MEALS

See also: Children's prayers and young people's prayers: Meal times

Graces for before or after meals

For health and strength and daily food,
We praise your name, O Lord.

Author unknown

Lord make us thankful for these and all thy mercies.
We ask thee, O Lord, to provide for the needs of others, and to give us thankful hearts.

Author unknown

We bless Thee, Lord for this our food,
For life and health and every good
May we are more blessed than we deserve,
live less for self and more to serve

Robert Burns, 1759–96

We give thanks, O God and Father, for the many mercies which thou of thy infinite goodness art constantly bestowing upon us; both in that by supplying all the helps which we need to sustain the present life, thou showest that thou hast a care even of our bodies, and more especially in that thou hast deigned to beget us again to the hope of the better life which thou hast revealed to us by thy holy gospel. And we beseech thee not to allow our minds to be chained down to earthly thoughts and cares, as if they were buried in our bodies. Rather cause that we may stand with eyes upraised in expectation of thy Son Jesus Christ, till he appear from heaven for our redemption and salvation.

John Calvin,
1509–64

For food in a world where many walk in
hunger;
For faith in a world where many walk in fear;
For friends in a world where many walk alone;
We give you humble thanks O Lord.

Canadian grace

God, our Father, in a world where many are
lonely,
we thank you for friendship.
In a world where many are despairing,
we thank you for hope
In a world that many find meaningless,
we thank you for faith
In a world where many are hungry,
we thank you for this food.

Canadian grace

Thou art blessed, O Lord, who nourishest me from my youth, who givest food to all flesh. Fill our hearts with joy and gladness, that having always what is sufficient for us, we may abound to every good work, in Christ Jesus our Lord, through whom glory, honor, and power be to Thee for ever. Amen.

Didache, 1st century

Give us grace, O Lord,
to be ever thankful for Thy providence,
with hearts always ready
to provide for the needs of others.

Francis of Assisi, 1181–1226

Blessed be Thou,
Lord God of the universe,
who bringest forth bread from the earth
and makest glad the hearts of men.

Hebrew prayer

Let us, with a gladsome mind,
Praise the Lord, for He is kind,
All living things He doth feed
His full hand supplies their need.

John Milton,
1608–74

Come, Lord Jesus, our guest to be
And bless these gifts
Bestowed by Thee.
And bless our loved ones everywhere,
And keep them in Your loving care.

Moravian blessing

To God who gives our daily bread
A thankful song we raise,
And pray that he who sends us food
May fill our hearts with praise.

Thomas Tallis, 1510–85

Bless me, O Lord, and let my food strengthen me to serve you, for Jesus Christ's sake.

Isaac Watts, 1674–1748

Give me a good digestion, Lord,
And also something to digest;
But when and how that something comes
I leave to thee, who knowest best.

Give me a healthy body, Lord;
Give me the sense to keep it so;
And a heart that is not bored
Whatever work I have to do.

Give me a healthy mind, good Lord;
That finds the good that dodges sight;
And seeing sin, is not appalled,
But seeks a way to put it right.

Give me a point of view, good Lord,
Let me know what it is, and why,
Don't let me worry overmuch
About the thing that's known as 'I'.

Give me a sense of humor, Lord,
Give me the power to see a joke,
To get some happiness from life,
And pass it on to other folk.

Refectory Grace, Chester Cathedral. Written
by Thomas Henry Basil Webb while a
schoolboy at Winchester College. He was
killed in 1917 on the Somme, aged 19

Graces for before meals

The head of the table says:
O Christ our God, bless this food and this

drink of your servants with a spiritual blessing, and make us healthy in soul and body; so that as we enjoy the food our bodies require in the modesty appropriate to our religious calling, we may share in your infinite blessings, and in the kingdom of heaven, together with your saints. So that in thanksgiving, we may glorify you, with the Father and with the all-holy Spirit, now and always and unto the ages of ages. Amen.
All respond:
     Let us eat this meal in peace, which the Lord has given us as a gift. Blessed is the Lord for all his gifts. Amen.

Armenian prayer

Bless O Lord before we dine,
each dish of food, each glass of wine,
And make us evermore aware,
how much O Lord, we're in Thy care.

Author unknown

Bless O Lord this food [these gifts] to our use
and us to thy loving service;
and keep us ever mindful
of the needs of others. Amen.

Author unknown

From thy hand cometh every good,
We thank thee for our daily food.
And with it Lord, thy blessing give,
And to thy glory may we live. Amen.

Author unknown

Bless us, O Lord and these Thy gifts
Which we are about to receive
From Thy bounty, through Christ our Lord.
Amen.

*Author unknown, traditional
blessing before a meal*

Midday meal

Bless us, O Lord and these Thy gifts
Which we are about to receive
From Thy bounty, through Christ our Lord.
May the King of everlasting glory make us partakers of the heavenly table. Amen.

*Author unknown, traditional
blessing before a midday meal*

Evening meal

Bless, O Lord, this food to our use and us in your service, and keep us mindful of the needs of others; for Christ's sake.

Author unknown

Bless, O Lord, your gifts to our use
and us to your service;
In Jesus' name we ask it.
Amen.

Author unknown

Bless us, O Lord and these Thy gifts
Which we are about to receive
From Thy bounty, through Christ our Lord.
May the King of everlasting glory lead us to the banquet of life eternal. Amen.

*Author unknown, traditional
blessing before an evening meal*

Blessèd are you, Lord God of creation.
Generously you give us of the fruits of the earth to delight and nourish us.
Bless this meal and strengthen us in your service; through Christ our Lord.

Author unknown

Blessed art Thou, Lord of all Creation.
Through your goodness we have these gifts for our use,
the fruit of your bounty and the work of human hands.
As they become part of our substance may they give you honor and glory. Amen.

Author unknown

Come, Lord Jesus, and be our Guest,
Our morning joy, our evening rest,
And with our daily bread impart
Your love and peace to every heart.
Amen.

Author unknown

Come Lord Jesus, be our guest,
and let this food to us be blessed. Amen.

Author unknown

For what we are about to receive may the Lord make us truly thankful.

Author unknown

Lord, bless this food to our bodies
And our bodies to your service. In Jesus' name,
Amen.

Author unknown

The Lord bless this food for our use and us in
His service and help us to remember the needs
of others.

Author unknown

This happy meal,
will better be:
If we, O Lord, Remember Thee.

Author unknown

We thank you, O Lord, for these your gifts, and
we beseech you to grant that, whether we eat
or drink, or whatsoever we do, all may be done
to your glory. Amen.

Author unknown

The Selkirk Grace
Some hae meat and canna eat,
And some would eat that want it;
But we hae meat, and we can eat,
Sae let the Lord be thankit.

*Robert Burns, 1759–96, can be
sung to "Auld Lang Syne"*

O Lord, in whom is the source and inexhaustible fountain of all good things, pour out thy
blessing upon us, and sanctify to our use the
meat and drink which are the gifts of thy kindness towards us, that we, using them soberly
and frugally as thou enjoinest, may eat with a
pure conscience.

Grant, also, that we may always both with
true heartfelt gratitude acknowledge, and with
our lips proclaim thee our Father and the giver
of all good, and, while enjoying bodily nourishment, aspire with special longing of heart
after the bread of thy doctrine, by which our
souls may be nourished in the hope of eternal
life, through Christ Jesus our Lord.

John Calvin, 1509–64

Be present at our table, Lord,
Be here and everywhere ador'd,
These creatures bless and grant that we
May feast in paradise with thee.

*John Cennick, 1718–55. Josiah Wedgwood, 1674–
1748, gave a teapot with these words on it to John
Wesley. This grace was often used by Methodists*

Bless our house,
Bless our table,
Bless the whole wide world,
and teach us to take everything
gratefully from Thy hand O Lord.

Danish grace

All that we have,
Is all a gift.
It comes, O God, from you;
We thank you for it.

German grace

Christ, bread of life,
Come and bless this food.
Amen.

Hispanic Lutheran grace

Bless, O Lord, this food we are about to eat;
and we pray you, O God, that it may be good
for our body and soul; and if there be any poor
creature hungry or thirsty walking along the
road, send them into us that we can share the
food with them, just as you share your gifts
with all of us.

Irish grace

May the blessing of the five loaves and the
two fishes which God shared out among the
five thousand be ours. May the King who
did the sharing bless our sharing and our
co-sharing.

Irish grace

May this food restore our strength, giving new
energy to tired limbs, now thoughts to weary
minds. May this drink restore our souls, giving
new vision to dry spirits, new warmth to cold
hearts. And once refreshed, may we give new
pleasure to you, who gives us all.

Irish grace

Let us lift our eyes toward the sanctuary of
    heaven
and bless the Lord.
Blessed art Thou, O Lord our God, King of the
    Universe,

who has sanctified us with Thy
   commandments
and brought forth this food from the earth.
                Traditional Jewish blessing before meals

For these and all Thy mercies given,
We bless and praise Thy Name, O Lord,
May we receive them with thanksgiving,
Ever trusting in Thy Word,
To Thee alone be honor, glory,
Now and henceforth for evermore.
Amen.
                From the "Laudi Spirituali",
                The Laud Spiritual, 1545

Lord God, Heavenly Father, bless us and these
your gifts, which we receive from your generous hand, through Jesus Christ, our Lord.
Amen.
                Martin Luther, 1483–1546

Come, Lord Jesus, be our guest,
And may our meal by you be blest. Amen.
                Attributed to Martin Luther, 1483–1546

Lord, bless our meal, and the friendship of the
table.
                Royal Navy grace

Thou O Lord, bless our meal today,
and may Thy spiritual Presence fill us with
   gratitude
for these abundant blessings.
                Scottish grace

In Jesus' name to the table we go
God bless the food we receive
To God the honor, us the gain
So we have food in Jesus' name. Amen.
                Swedish grace

We praise Thee, O God, who bringest forth
   food from the earth,
And wine that makes glad the heart of man
And we humbly beg Thee, Lord,
to look down from Heaven upon the souls
   that are hungry,
and to fill them with all good things.
                University of Durham grace

Let us be thankful for whatever

light, laughter, food and affection and
   friendship
that may come our way,
and let us be mindful equally
of those who at this festive season
or some future moment
may be sadly without any or all
of these good and golden things.
                Welsh grace

Blessing to God, for ever blest
To God the master of the feast,
Who hath for us a table spread,
and with his daily bounties feed;
May He with all his gifts impart,
the crown of all – a thankful heart.
                Charles Wesley 1707–88

Graces for after meals

The head of the table says:
   Glory to you, Lord. Glory to you, King of
glory, for you have given us the food of joy
and have filled our hearts out of the fullness of
your all-satisfying mercy. Fill us now with your
Holy Spirit, so that we may please you and not
be ashamed. For you will come and reward
us each according to our deeds. And you are
worthy of glory, dominion and honor, now
and always and unto ages of ages. Amen.
All respond:
   May Christ our God, who has fed us
and filled us, make the fullness of this table
constant and abundant. Glory to him forever.
Amen.
                Armenian prayer

For what we have received may the Lord make
us truly thankful.
                Author unknown

For these and for all thy gifts, we give Thee
thanks, O Lord.
                Author unknown

O Lord, give us thankful hearts.
                Author unknown

We give thee thanks, almighty God, for these
and all thy mercies, who livest and reignest,

world without end.
Amen.

Author unknown

We give you thanks, O Lord, for all these gifts
which we have received from thy bounty
through Christ our Lord.
Amen.

Traditional English grace

We thank thee, O Lord, for this food and for all
thy Mercies.

Author unknown

We thank you, O Christ our God, that you have
satisfied us with your earthly gifts; deprive
us not of your heavenly kingdom, but as you
came among your disciples, O Savior, and gave
them peace, come to us and save us.

Eastern Orthodox

Latin graces

LATIN GRACES BEFORE MEALS
Benedic, Domine, dona tua,
quae de largitate sumus sumpturi.
Bless, O Lord, your gifts,
which from your bounty we are about to
    receive.

8th-century English blessing

Benedic, Domine, nobis et donis tuis quae ex
largitate tua sumus sumpturi; et concede ut,
ab iis salubriter enutriti, tibi debitum obsequium praestare valeamus, per Jesum Christum dominum nostrum; mensae caelestis nos
participes facias, Rex aeternae gloriae.
    Bless, O Lord, both us and these Thy gifts,
which, of Thy bounty, we are about to receive;
and grant that being by them wholesomely fed,
we may be able to render that worship which
is Thy due, through Jesus Christ our Lord; at
whose celestial table may we be partakers, O
King of everlasting glory.

Gonville and Caius College, Cambridge

Benedic, Domine, nos et dona tua,
quae de largitate tua sumus sumpturi,
et concede, ut illis salubriter nutriti

tibi debitum obsequium praestare valeamus,
per Christum Dominum nostrum.
Bless, O Lord, us and your gifts,
which from your bounty we are about to
    receive,
and grant that, healthily nourished by them,
we may render you due obedience,
through Christ our Lord.

*Grace, Queens' College,
Cambridge*

Benedic nobis,
Domine Deus,
atque eis donis tuis,
quae de tua largitae sumus sumpturi.
Bless us
Lord God,
and these Thy gifts
which of Thy bounty
we are about to receive.

Winchester College grace

Benedic Domine, nos et dona tua,
qui de tua largitate sumus sumpturi,
per Christum Dominum nostrum. Amen.
Bless Lord, us, and these thy gifts,
which of thy goodness we are about to enjoy,
through Christ our Lord. Amen.

*Grace said at evening meals at
Emmanuel College, Cambridge*

Domine Deus, quicquid appositum est aut
apponetur, Christus dignetur benedicere. In
nomine Patris et Filii et Spiritus Sancti. Amen.
Lord God, this food which is before us and that
which is to come, may Christ deign to bless. In
the name of the Father and of the Son and of
the Holy Spirit. Amen.

*Grace said at evening meals at
Trinity Hall, Cambridge*

Oculi omnium in te sperant Domine
et tu das escam illorum in tempore
    opportuno.
Aperis tu manum tuam
et imples omne animal benedictione.
The eyes of all look to you, O Lord,
and you give them their food in due time.
You open your hand
and fill every living thing with your blessing.

Author unknown

LATIN GRACE BEFORE DINNER
Benedictus benedicat.
May the Blessed One give a blessing.
Traditional English grace

LATIN GRACE AFTER DINNER
Benedicto benedicatur.
Let praise be given to/by the Blessed One.
Traditional English grace

PRAYERS FOR READING THE BIBLE

Take away, O Lord, the veil of my heart
while I read the scriptures.
Lancelot Andrewes, 1555–1626

Glory be to thee, O Lord,
for that thou didst create not only the visible
        light,
but the light invisible,
that which may be known of God, the law
        written in the heart;
give us a mind to perceive this light in
        the oracles of prophets,
        the melody of psalms,
        the prudence of proverbs,
        the experience of histories,
and the life and love of our Lord Jesus Christ,
for his sake.
Lancelot Andrewes, 1555–1626

Instruct me, Lord, and command what you
will. But first heal me and open my ears that I
may hear your words.
Augustine of Hippo, 354–430

Blessed Lord, who hast caused all holy Scriptures to be written for our learning: grant that we may in such wise hear them, read, mark, learn, and inwardly digest them, that by patience and comfort of thy holy Word, we may embrace and ever hold fast the blessed hope of everlasting life, which thou hast given us in our Savior Jesus Christ.
Book of Common Prayer, 1549,
Collect, Second Sunday in Advent

Most gracious God, our heavenly Father, in whom alone dwells all the fullness of light and wisdom, enlighten our minds by your Holy Spirit to truly understand your Word. Give us grace to receive it reverently and humbly. May it lead us to put our whole trust in you alone, and so to serve and honor you that we may glory your holy name and encourage others by setting a good example.
John Calvin, 1509–64

Grant us, merciful God, knowledge and true understanding of your word, that we may know what your will is, and also may show in our lives those things that we do know; so that we may not only be knowers of your word, but also doers of your word, through our Lord and Savior Jesus Christ.
Author unknown,
King Henry VIII's Primer

Gracious God and most merciful Father, who has given us the rich and precious jewel of your holy word: assist us with your Spirit so that your word may be written in our heart for our everlasting comfort, to reform us, to renew us to be like your own image, to build us up in the perfect heavenly virtues. Grant this, heavenly Father, for the sake of Jesus Christ.
The Geneva Bible, attributed
to King Edward VI

Lord, you have given us your Word as a light to shine on our path; grant that we may so meditate on that Word, and follow its teaching, that we may find in it the light that shines more and more until the perfect day; through Jesus Christ our Lord.
Jerome, c.342–420

O Lord Jesus, let not your word become a judgment on us, lest we heat it and do not do it, or believe it and do not obey it.
Thomas à Kempis, 1379–1471

Break Thou the bread of life, dear Lord, to me,
As Thou didst break the loaves beside the sea;
Beyond the sacred page I seek Thee, Lord;
My spirit pants for Thee, O living Word!
Mary Artemesia Lathbury, 1841–1913

Teach me, my Lord Jesus, instruct me, that

I may learn from you what I ought to teach about you.

William Laud, 1573–1645

Master who loves us, shine Your eternal light in our hearts that we may better know you. Help us to fully understand Your gospel message. Instill in us respect for Your holy commandments, that by overcoming our worldly desires we might life a spiritual life of thoughts and deeds which pleases You. We ask this of You, O Christ our god, for You are the light of our souls and bodies and You we glorify with Your eternal Father and Your all-holy good and life-giving Spirit now and forever. Amen.

Orthodox prayer

Shine within my heart, loving Master, the pure light of Your divine knowledge, and open the eyes of my mind that I may understand Your teachings. Instill in me also reverence for Your blessed commandments, so that having conquered sinful desires I may pursue a spiritual way of life, thinking and doing all those things that are pleasing to You. For You, Christ my God, are my light, and to You I give glory together with Your Father and Your Holy Spirit, now and forever. Amen.

The liturgy of John Chrysostom, 4th century

O Lord, Thy Word is before us, give us a meek, and a reverent and teachable mind, while we read and study it. Be Thou, O blessed Spirit, our Teacher. Shine, O Lord, upon Thine own sacred page and make it clear to us. What we see not, show us, and where we are wrong, correct us. Bring home some portion to our soul, and thus make us wise unto salvation, through Jesus Christ our Savior.

Ashton Oxenden, 1808–92

PROTECTION

Be gracious to our prayers, O Merciful God, and guard Thy people with loving protection; that they who confess Thine only begotten Son as God, born in our bodily flesh, may never be corrupted by the deceits of the devil; through the same Jesus Christ our Lord. Amen.

Ambrose, c.339–397

God Almighty bless us with his Holy Spirit this day;
guard us in our going out and coming in;
keep us always steadfast in his faith,
free from sin and safe from danger;
through Jesus Christ our Lord.

Author unknown

Almighty Lord and everlasting God, vouchsafe, we beseech thee, to direct, sanctify, and govern, both our hearts and bodies, in the ways of thy laws, and in the works of thy commandments: that through thy most mighty protection, both here and ever, we may be preserved in body and soul; through our Lord and savior Jesus Christ. Amen.

Book of Common Prayer, 1549

O God, from whom all holy desires, all good counsels, and all just works do proceed: Give unto thy servants that peace which the world cannot give; that both our hearts may be set to obey thy commandments, and also that by thee we, being defended from the fear of our enemies, may pass our time in rest and quietness; through the merits of Jesu Christ our Savior.

Book of Common Prayer, 1549,
Evensong, Second Collect

Grant, O Lord, that we may live in your fear,
die in your favor,
rest in your peace,
rise in your power,
reign in your glory;
for your own beloved Son's sake,
Jesus Christ our Lord.

William Laud, 1573–1645

My Heavenly Father, I thank you, through Jesus Christ, your beloved Son, that you kept me safe from all evil and danger last night. Save me, I pray, today as well, from every evil and sin, so that all I do and the way that I live will please you. I put myself in your care, body and soul and all that I have. Let your holy angels be with me, so that the evil enemy will not triumph over me. Amen.

Martin Luther, 1483–1546

The Lord preserve my going out and my

coming in: from this time forth for evermore.
O give your angels charge over me, to keep me
in all my ways.
Order my steps according to your word, so
shall no wickedness have dominion over me.

Treasury of Devotion, 1869

Prayers for The Christian Church

A.B. Bruce: Training of the Twelve
John Newton: Public Prayer
C.H. Spurgeon: The Prayer of Jabez

Prayer collections
Book of Common Prayer: Collection of Prayers
The Genevan Book of Order
Collection of prayers in the Orthodox tradition

CHURCH LIFE

Baptism/Thanksgiving for a birth

May the Lord of his great mercy bless you,
and give you understanding of his wisdom
    and grace.
May he nourish you with the riches of the
    catholic faith,
and make you persevere in all good works.
May he keep your steps from wandering,
and direct you into the paths of love and
    peace.

Source unknown

O almighty and eternal God, most merciful
Father, as the just live by faith, and as it is
impossible for anyone to please you without
belief; we pray that you will grant to this child
the gift of faith, in which you will seal and
assure his heart in the Holy Spirit, according to
the promise of your Son; that the inner regeneration of the Spirit may be truly represented
by the outward baptism, and that the child
may be buried with Christ into death, and be
raised up from death by Christ, to the praise of
your glory and the edifying of *his* neighbor.

Miles Coverdale, 1488–1568

To adults

O Almighty and eternal God, Thou, who hast
according to thy severe judgment punished the
unbelieving and unrepentant world with the
flood, and hast according to thy great mercy
saved and protected believing Noah and his
family; Thou, who hast drowned the obstinate
Pharaoh and his host in the Red Sea, and hast
led thy people Israel through the midst of the
Sea upon dry ground, by which baptism is
signified – we beseech thee, that Thou wilt be
pleased of thine infinite mercy, graciously to
look upon this person, and incorporate him
by thy Holy Spirit into thy Son Jesus Christ,
that he may be buried with him into his death,
and be raised with him in newness of life; that
he may daily follow him, joyfully bearing his
cross, and cleave unto him in true faith, firm
hope, and ardent love; that he may with a
comfortable sense of thy favor, leave this life,
which is nothing but a continual death, and at
the last day, may appear without terror before
the judgment seat of Christ thy Son, through
Jesus Christ our Lord, who with thee and the
Holy Ghost, one only God, lives and reigns
forever. Amen.

Liturgy of the Reformed Church

To adults

Almighty God and merciful Father, we thank
and praise thee, that thou hast forgiven us and
our children all our sins, through the blood of
thy Son Jesus Christ, and received us through
thy Holy Spirit, as members of thine only
begotten Son, and adopted us to be thy children, and sealed and confirmed the same unto
us by holy baptism. We beseech thee, through
the same Son of thy love, that thou wilt be
pleased always to govern this baptized person
by thy Holy Spirit, that he may lead a Christian
and godly life, and increase and grow up in the
Lord Jesus Christ, that he may acknowledge
thy fatherly goodness and mercy, which thou
hast shown to him and to us, and live in all
righteousness, under our only Teacher, King,
and High Priest, Jesus Christ; and that he may
manfully fight against and overcome sin, the
devil and his whole dominion, to the end that
he may eternally praise and magnify thee, and
thy Son Jesus Christ together with the Holy
Ghost, the one only true God. Amen.

Liturgy of the Reformed Church

O Lord, holy Father, almighty, everlasting God, from whom all the light of truth comes: We pray that in your eternal and most tender goodness, you will bestow your blessing on this your servant, N., and enlighten *him* with the light of your knowledge. Purify and sanctify *him*, and give *him* true knowledge that he may be worthy to come to the grace of your baptism, that he may have a firm hope, true guidance, and holy teaching, and that he may so come to the grace of your baptism, through Christ our Lord.

Martin Luther, 1483–1546

Almighty God, the Father of our Lord Jesus Christ, who has given you new birth through water and the Holy Spirit, and has forgiven you all your sin, strengthen you with his grace to life everlasting. Amen. Peace be with you.

Martin Luther, 1483–1546, blessing after a baptism

Infant baptism

O Lord God, eternal and omnipotent Father, since it hath pleased thee of thy infinite mercy to promise us that thou wilt be our God, and the God of our children, we pray that it may please thee to confirm this grace in the child before thee, born of parents whom thou hast called into thy Church; and as it is offered and consecrated to thee by us, do thou deign to receive it under thy holy protection, declaring thyself to be its God and Savior, by forgiving it the original sin of which all the race of Adam are guilty, and thereafter sanctifying it by thy Spirit, in order that when it shall arrive at the years of discretion it may recognize and adore thee as its only God, glorifying thee during its whole life, so as always to obtain of thee the forgiveness of its sins. And in order to its obtaining such graces, be pleased to incorporate it into the communion of our Lord Jesus Christ, that it may partake of all his blessings as one of the members of his body. Hear us, O merciful Father, in order that the baptism, which we communicate to it according to thy ordinance, may produce its fruit and virtue, as declared to us by the gospel.

John Calvin, 1509–64

To Infants of Believers

O Almighty and eternal God, Thou, who hast according to thy severe judgment punished the unbelieving and unrepentant world with the flood, and hast according to thy great mercy saved and protected believing Noah and his family; Thou, who hast drowned the obstinate Pharaoh and his host in the Red Sea, and hast led thy people Israel through the midst of the Sea upon dry ground, by which baptism was signified – we beseech thee, that Thou wilt be pleased of thine infinite mercy, graciously to look upon these children, and incorporate them by thy Holy Spirit, into thy Son Jesus Christ, that they may be buried with him into his death, and be raised with him in newness of life; that they may daily follow him, joyfully bearing their cross, and cleave unto him in true faith, firm hope, and ardent love; that they may, with a comfortable sense of thy favor, leave this life, which is nothing but a continual death, and at the last day, may appear without terror before the judgment seat of Christ thy Son, through Jesus Christ our Lord, who with thee and the Holy Ghost, one only God, lives and reigns forever. Amen.

Liturgy of the Reformed Church

To Infants of Believers

Almighty God and merciful Father, we thank and praise thee, that Thou hast forgiven us, and our children, all our sins, through the blood of thy beloved Son Jesus Christ, and received us through thy Holy Spirit as members of thine only begotten Son, and adopted us to be thy children, and sealed and confirmed the same unto us by holy baptism; we beseech thee, through the same Son of thy love, that Thou wilt be pleased always to govern these baptized children by Thy Holy Spirit, that they may be piously and religiously educated, increase and grow up in the Lord Jesus Christ, that they then may acknowledge thy fatherly goodness and mercy, which Thou hast shown to them and us, and live in all righteousness, under our only Teacher, King and High Priest, Jesus Christ; and manfully fight against, and overcome sin, the devil and his whole dominion, to the end that they may eternally praise and magnify thee, and thy Son Jesus Christ, together with the Holy Ghost, the one only true God. Amen.

Liturgy of the Reformed Church

Confirmation

O God, the good of all goodness and of all grace, who art worthy of a greater love than we either give or understand, fill our hearts, we beseech thee, with such love toward thee, that nothing may seem too hard for us to do or to suffer in obedience to thy will; and grant that thus loving thee we may become daily more like thee, and finally obtain the crown of life which thou has promised to those that love thee; through Jesus Christ our Lord.

Source unknown, 19th century

O Jesus, thou hast promised
    To all who follow thee,
That where thou art in glory
    There shall thy servant be;
And, Jesus, I have promised
    To serve thee to the end;
O give me grace to follow,
    My Master and my Friend.

O let me see thy footmarks,
    And in them plant mine own:
My hope to follow duly
    Is in thy strength alone.
O guide me, call me, draw me,
    Uphold me to the end;
And then in heaven receive me,
    My Savior and my Friend!

J.E. Bode, 1816–74

Defend, O Lord, this thy Child [or this thy Servant] with thy heavenly grace, that *he* may continue thine for ever; and daily increase in thy Holy Spirit more and more, until he come unto thy everlasting kingdom. Amen.

Book of Common Prayer, the Order of Confirmation

Come, Holy Spirit, and daily increase in these your servants your many gifts of grace; the spirit of wisdom and understanding, the spirit of counsel and strength, the spirit of knowledge and true godliness; and fill them with the spirit of your holy fear, now and evermore.

Gelasian Sacramentary

The Lord's Supper

Preparing for the Lord's Supper

Lord Jesus Christ, I approach your banquet table in fear and trembling, for I am a sinner, and dare not rely on my own worth but only on your goodness and mercy. I am defiled by many sins in body and soul, and by my unguarded thoughts and words.

Ambrose, c.339–397

Praise to you, saving sacrifice, offered on the wood of the cross for me and for all mankind. Praise to the noble and precious blood, flowing from the wounds of my crucified Lord Jesus Christ and washing away the sins of the whole world. Remember, Lord, your creature, whom you have redeemed with your blood. I repent my sins, and I long to put right what I have done. Merciful Father, take away all my offenses and ins; purify me in body and soul, and make me worthy to taste the holy of holies.

Ambrose, c.339–397

May your body and blood, which I intend to receive, although I am unworthy, be for me the remission of my sins, the washing away of my guilt, the end of my evil thoughts, and the rebirth of my better instincts. May it incite me to do the works pleasing to you and profitable to my health in body and soul, and be a firm defense against the wiles of my enemies.

Ambrose, c.339–397

O merciful Lord Jesus, I confess myself to be a most grievous and wretched sinner, not worthy to approach into thy presence, altogether unfit and unmeet to receive thee under the roof of my soul, in respect of the stains and pollutions thereof, and that it is not decked and fitted, with such good graces, as thy majesty and presence requireth, and therefore am afraid to come near unto thee: yet, O Lord, considering thy comfortable saying, that thou dost nor desire the death of a sinner, but that he should turn unto thee and live; and thy blessed invitation, how lovingly, with the arms of thy mercy stretched out, thou hast called all, that are heavily oppressed with the burden of their sins, to come to thee for comfort and ease. And lastly, thy usual practice, in pitying and relieving those which were cast down with the thought of their misdeeds; as the Thief on the Cross, Mary Magdalen, the Woman taken in Adultery, the Publican, Peter and Paul, I am comforted and emboldened to come unto thee, assuredly trusting, that thou wilt of thy goodness supply my defects, and make me a worthy receiver of the high mystery and benefit of thy blessed Sacrament, whereof of myself I am altogether unworthy. Stretch out thy right hand, O sweet Jesus, to me thy poor servant, and give out of thy rich store-house of mercy what I want; that thereby I may be made a living temple to thee, and an acceptable habitation for thine honor to abide in: and grant, that being cleansed by thy mercy and goodness, I may, by thy grace and power, persevere in all godliness of conversation, to the end of my days, and attain to that blessed place, where thou reignest, with the Father and Holy Spirit, world without end. Amen.

Lancelot Andrewes, 1555–1626

Before Holy Communion
Almighty, everlasting God, I draw near to the sacrament of your only-begotten Son, our Lord Jesus Christ.
I who am sick approach the physician of life.
I who am unclean come to the fountain of mercy;
blind, to the light of eternal brightness;
poor and needy to the Lord of heaven and earth.
Therefore, I pray, that you will, in your endless mercy,
heal my sickness, cleanse my defilement, enlighten my blindness, enrich my poverty, and clothe my nakedness.
Then shall I dare to receive the bread of angels,
the King of kings and Lord of lords,
with reverence and humility, contrition and love,
purity and faith, with the purpose and intention necessary for the good of my soul ...

Thomas Aquinas, 1225–74

Jesu! Shepherd of the sheep!
Thy true flock in safety keep.
Living Bread! Thy life supply;
Strengthen us, or else we die;
Fill us with celestial grace:
Thou, who feedest us below!

Source of all we have or know!
Grant that with Thy Saints above,
Sitting at the Feast of Love,
We may see Thee face to face. Amen

Thomas Aquinas, 1225–74

As the night-watch looks for the morning, so do our eyes wait for you, O Christ.

As watchmen look for the morning, so do we look for you, O Christ; come with the dawning of the day, and make yourself known to us in the breaking of the bread; for you are our God for ever and ever.

Author unknown, A prayer for the evening before the Lord's Supper

Thou, Lord Almighty, hast created all things for the sake of thy name and hast given food and drink for men to enjoy, that they may give thanks to thee; but to us thou hast vouchsafed spiritual food and drink and eternal life through Jesus, thy Servant. Above all, we give thee thanks because thou art mighty. To thee be the glory for evermore.

Author unknown, Christian prayer, c.100

O Christ, our only Savior, so live within us that we may go from here with the light of hope in our eyes, and the fire of inspiration on our lips, your Word on our tongues, and your love in our hearts. Amen.

G.C. Bunion

Prayer of Humble Access
We do not presume to come to this thy table (O merciful Lord) trusting in our own righteousness, but in thy manifold and great mercies: we be not worthy so much as to gather up the crumbs under thy table: but thou art the same Lord whose property is always to have mercy: Grant us therefore (gracious Lord) so to eat the flesh of thy dear Son Jesus Christ, and to drink his blood in these holy Mysteries, that we may continually dwell in him, and he in us, that our sinful bodies may be made clean by his body, and our souls washed through his most precious blood.

Book of Common Prayer, 1549

Almighty God, who in your great mercy have gathered us into your visible Church: Grant that we may not turn from the purity of your worship, but that we may so honor you, both in spirit and in action, that your name may be glorified in us, and we may be true members of your only-begotten Son, Jesus Christ our Lord. Amen.

Book of Common Worship of the Presbyterian Church in the United States of America, 1906

Almighty God, our heavenly Father, we call your name, praying that it will please you to turn away from our many terrible sins, by which we have never stopped deserving your anger. And because we are not worthy to appear before your sovereign majesty, we pray that you will see us in your beloved Son Jesus Christ, and accept the merit of his death in satisfaction for all our offenses, and that in him we may be pleasing in your eyes. Pour out your Holy Spirit upon us, enlightening our minds with true understanding of your word. And give us your grace, so that as we receive your truth into our hearts with humility and awe, we may be led to place all our trust in you, living to serve and worship you, to the glory of your holy name. And since you have chosen to count us among your people, help us to give you the love and honor that we owe to you, as children to our Father, and as servants to our Lord.

John Calvin, 1509–64

As our Lord Jesus Christ, not content with having once offered his body and blood upon the cross for the forgiveness of our sins, has also destined them to us as nourishment for eternal life, so grant us of thy goodness, that we may receive this great blessing with true sincerity of heart and ardent desire, and endued with sure faith, enjoy together his body and blood, or rather himself entire, just as He himself, while He is true God and man, is truly the holy bread of heaven that gives us life, that we may no longer live in ourselves, and after our own will, which is altogether depraved, but he may live in us, and conduct us to a holy, happy, and ever-during life, thus making us truly partakers of the new and eternal covenant, even the covenant of grace; and in feeling fully persuaded that thou art pleased to be for ever a propitious Father to

us, by not imputing to us our offences, and to furnish us, as dear children and heirs, with all things necessary as well for the soul as the body, we may pay thee endless praise and thanks, and render thy name glorious both by words and deeds. Fit us, then, on this day thus to celebrate the happy remembrance of thy Son: grant also that we may exercise ourselves therein, and proclaim the benefits of his death, that thus receiving new increase and strength for faith and every other good work, we may with greater confidence profess ourselves thy children, and glory in thee our Father.

John Calvin, 1509–64

Lord, Jesus Christ my God, forgive the faults and sins which I, Your unworthy servant have committed from my youth to this day and hour, whether knowingly or in ignorance, whether by words, deeds, intentions or thoughts and whether by habit or through any of my senses. By the prayers of Your pure and Virgin Mother, make me worthy without condemnation to receive Your precious, immortal and life-giving Mysteries for the forgiveness of sins and eternal life. May the Eucharist sanctify, enlighten, strengthen and heal my soul and body and thus destroy my evil thoughts, intentions and prejudices. For Yours, Christ our God, is the Kingdom, the power, the glory, the honor and worship with the Father and the Holy Spirit, now and forever and ever. Amen.

John Chrysostom, c.347–407

Welcome to the Table
   This is the feast of heav'nly wine,
      And God invites to sup;
   The juices of the living vine
      Were pressed, to fill the cup.

   Oh, bless the Savior, ye that eat,
      With royal dainties fed;
   Not heav'n affords a costlier treat,
      For Jesus is the bread!

The vile, the lost, he calls to them,
   Ye trembling souls appear!
The righteous, in their own esteem,
   Have no acceptance here.

Approach, ye poor, nor dare refuse
    The banquet spread for you;
    Dear Savior, this is welcome news,
    That I may venture too.

If guilt and sin afford a plea,
    And may obtain a place;
    Surely the Lord will welcome me,
    And I shall see his face!
        William Cowper, 1731–1800, Olney Hymns

Preparing for the Lord's Supper

O Lord and Master, Jesus Christ, our God, Fountain of life and immortality, Creator of all things visible and invisible; Consubstantial and Coeternal Son of the eternal Father, who in thine exceeding great love didst become incarnate in the latter days, and was crucified for us ungrateful and wicked children, and by thine own Blood didst renew our nature corrupted by sin; Do thou, O Immortal King, receive me, a repentant sinner; incline thine ear unto me and hear my prayer. I have sinned, O Lord, I have sinned against heaven and before thee, and I am not worthy to lift up my eyes to the majesty of thy glory, for I have affronted thy goodness, and broken thy commandments, and disobeyed thy laws. But thou, O Lord most loving, long-suffering and merciful, hast not given me over to perish in my sin, but dost ever await my return. For, O Thou who lovest mankind, thou hast said, by thy Prophet, that thou hast no pleasure in the death of a sinner, but rather that he should turn from his wickedness and live. Thou dost not desire, O Master, to destroy the works of thy hands or that they should perish, but willets that all men should be saved and come to the knowledge of the Truth. Wherefore I, although unworthy both of heaven and of earth and of this temporary life, even I, a wretched sinner who had given myself over to every evil desire, despair not of salvation, though I have been wholly subject to sin, a slave to passion, and have defiled thine image within me, who am thy creation and thy work; but trusting in thine infinite compassion, draw nigh unto thee. Receive me, O Lord, thou that lovest mankind, as thou didst receive the sinful woman, the thief, the publican and the prodigal son. Take away the heavy burden of my sins, O Thou that takest away the sins of the world, and healest the infirmities of men, and callest all that are weary and heavy laden to thyself and givest them rest; thou that camest not to call the righteous but sinners to repentance, cleanse thou me from all stain of body and soul and teach me to fulfill holiness in thy fear, that with the witness of my conscience pure, I may receive a portion of thy Holy Gifts, and be united to thy Holy Body and Precious Blood, and may have thee, with thy Father and Holy Spirit, dwelling and abiding in me. And grant, O Lord Jesus Christ, my God, that the partaking of thy precious and Life-giving Mysteries may not be to my condemnation, nor may not through the weakness of my soul and body be received unworthily; but grant that, even unto my last breath, I may partake of a portion of thy Holy Gifts without condemnation, unto the Communion of thy Holy Spirit, as a preparation for eternal Life and for a good defense at thy dread Judgment Seat; so that I, together with all thine elect, may also receive those incorruptible good things which thou hast prepared for them that love thee, O Lord; in whom thou art glorified forever. Amen.
        Basil the Great, c.330–379

O Lord, I know that I am unworthy to receive thy Holy Body and Precious Blood; I know that I am guilty, and that I eat and drink condemnation to myself, not discerning the Body and Blood of Christ my God. But trusting in thy loving-kindness I come unto thee who hast said: He that elated my Body and trinket my Blood shall dwell in me and I in him. Therefore, O Lord, have compassion on me and make not an example of me, thy sinful servant. But do unto me according thy great mercy, and grant that these Holy Gifts may be for me unto the healing, purification, enlightenment, protection, salvation and sanctification of my soul and body, and to the expulsion of every evil imagination, sinful deed or work of the Devil. May they move me to reliance on thee and to love thee always, to amend and keep firm my life; and be ever in me to the increase of virtue, to the keeping of the Holy Spirit, and as a good defense before thy dread Judgment Seat, and for Life Eternal. Amen.
        Basil the Great, c.330–379

Almighty and ever living God, we most

heartily thank thee, for that thou hast vouchsafed to feed us in these holy Mysteries, with
the spiritual food of the most precious body
and blood of thy son our savior Jesus Christ,
and hast assured us (duly receiving the same)
of thy favor and goodness towards us, an
that we be very members incorporate in thy
Mystical body, which is the blessed company
of all faithful people, and heirs through hope
of thy everlasting kingdom, by the merits of
the most precious death and passion of thy
dear son. We therefore most humbly beseech
thee, o heavenly father, so to assist us with
thy grace, that we may continue in that holy
fellowship, and do all such good works, as
thou hast prepared for us to walk in: through
Jesus Christ our Lord, to whom with thee and
the holy ghost, be all honor and glory, world
without end. Amen.

Book of Common Prayer, 1549

We do not presume to come to this thy table (o
merciful Lord) trusting in our own righteousness, but in thy manifold and great mercies:
we be not worthy so much as to gather up the
crumbs under thy table: but thou art the same
lord whose property is always to have mercy:
Grant us therefore (gracious Lord) so to eat
the flesh of thy dear son Jesus Christ, and to
drink his blood in these holy Mysteries, that
our sinful bodies may be made clean by his
body, and our souls washed through his most
precious blood. Amen.

Book of Common Prayer, 1549

And now, O Father, mindful of the love
That bought us, once for all, on Calvary's tree,
And having with us Him that pleads above,
We here present, we here spread forth to Thee,
That only offering perfect in Thine eyes,
The one true, pure, immortal sacrifice.

Look, Father, look on His anointed face,
And only look on us as found in Him;
Look not on our misusing of Thy grace,
Our prayer so languid, and our faith so dim;
For lo! between our sins and their reward,
We set the passion of Thy Son our Lord.

And then for those, our dearest and our best,
By this prevailing presence we appeal;

O fold them closer to Thy mercy's breast!
O do Thine utmost for their souls' true weal!
From tainting mischief keep them white and
    clear,
And crown Thy gifts with strength to
    persevere.

And so we come; O draw us to Thy feet,
Most patient Savior, Who canst love us still!
And by this food, so awful and so sweet,
Deliver us from every touch of ill:
In Thine own service make us glad and free,
And grant us nevermore to part with Thee.

William Bright, 1824–1901

O Lord my God, I know that I am not worthy
or sufficient that Thou shouldest come under
the roof of the house of my soul, for all is
desolate and fallen, and Thou hast not with me
a place fit to lay Thy head. But as from the highest heaven Thou didst humble Thyself for our
sake, so now conform Thyself to my humility.
And as Thou didst consent to lie in a cave and
in a manger of dumb beasts, so also consent to
lie in the manger of my unspiritual soul and to
enter my defiled body. And as Thou didst not
disdain to enter and dine with sinners in the
house of Simon the Leper, so consent also to
enter the house of my humble soul which is
leprous and sinful. And as Thou didst not reject
the woman, who was a harlot and a sinner like
me, when she approached and touched Thee,
so also be compassionate with me, a sinner,
as I approach and touch Thee, and let the live
coal of Thy most holy Body and precious
Blood be for the sanctification and enlightenment and strengthening of my humble soul
and body, for a relief from the burden of my
many sins, for a protection from all diabolical
practices, for a restraint and a check on my evil
and wicked way of life, for the mortification
of passions, for the keeping of Thy commandments, for an increase of Thy divine grace, and
for the advancement of Thy Kingdom. For it
is not insolently that I draw near to Thee, O
Christ my God, but as taking courage from
Thy unspeakable goodness, and that I may
not by long abstaining from Thy communion
become a prey to the spiritual wolf. Therefore,
I pray Thee, O Lord, Who alone art holy, sanctify my soul and body, my mind and heart, my

emotions and affections, and wholly renew me. Root the fear of Thee in my members, and make Thy sanctification indelible in me. Be also my helper and defender, and guide my life in peace. Amen.

John Chrysostom, c.347–407

O Lord and Master Jesus Christ, our God, who alone hath power to forgive the sins of men, do thou, O Good One who lovest mankind, forgive all the sins that I have committed in knowledge or in ignorance, and make me worthy to receive without condemnation thy divine, glorious, immaculate and life-giving Mysteries; not unto punishment or unto increase of sin; but unto purification, and sanctification and a promise of thy Kingdom and the Life to come; as a protection and a help to overthrow the adversaries, and to blot out my many sins. For thou art a God of Mercy and compassion and love toward mankind, and unto Thee we ascribe glory together with the Father and the Holy Spirit; now and ever, and unto ages of ages. Amen.

John Chrysostom, c.347–407

I believe, O Lord, and I confess that thou art truly the Christ, the Son of the living God, who didst come into the world to save sinners, of whom I am chief. And I believe that this is truly thine own immaculate Body, and that this is truly thine own precious Blood. Wherefore I pray thee, have mercy upon me and forgive my transgressions both voluntary and involuntary, of word and of deed, of knowledge and of ignorance; and make me worthy to partake without condemnation of thine immaculate Mysteries, unto remission of my sins and unto life everlasting. Amen. Of thy Mystic Supper, O Son of God, accept me today as a communicant; for I will not speak of thy Mystery to thine enemies, neither will I give thee a kiss as did Judas; but like the thief will I confess thee: Remember me, O Lord, in thy Kingdom. Not unto judgment nor unto condemnation be my partaking of thy Holy Mysteries, O Lord, but unto the healing of soul and body.

John Chrysostom, c.347–407

O Lord God, who has left unto us in a wonderful Sacrament a memorial of your Passion:

Grant, we beseech you, that we may so use this Sacrament of your Body and Blood, that the fruits of your redemption may continually be manifest in us; Who lives and reigns with the Father and the Holy Ghost, ever One God, world without end. Amen.

The Common Service Book of the Lutheran Church, 1917

I stand before the gates of thy Temple, and yet I refrain not from my evil thoughts. But do thou, O Christ my God, who didst justify the publican, and hadst mercy on the Canaanite woman, and opened the gates of Paradise to the thief; open unto me the compassion of thy love toward mankind, and receive me as I approach and touch thee, like the sinful woman and the woman with the issue of blood; for the one, by embracing thy feet received the forgiveness of her sins, and the other by but touching the hem of thy garment was healed. And I, most sinful, dare to partake of thy whole Body. Let me not be consumed but receive me as thou didst receive them, and enlighten the perceptions of my soul, consuming the accusations of my sins; through the intercessions of Her that without stain gave Thee birth, and of the heavenly Powers; for thou art blessed unto ages of ages. Amen.

John of Damascus, c.676–749

Lord Jesus Christ, since you have taught us that we do not live by bread alone; feed us now and evermore with the bread which comes down from heaven, even your own self, our Savior and our Redeemer. Amen.

John Dowden, 1840–1910

We give thanks to Thee, Almighty God, that Thou hast refreshed us through this salutary gift; and we beseech Thee, that of Thy mercy Thou wouldest strengthen us through the same in faith toward Thee and in fervent love toward one another, through Jesus Christ, Thy dear Son, our Lord, who liveth and reigneth with Thee, and the Holy Ghost, ever one God, world without end.

Evangelical Lutheran Hymn-Book

Prayer in preparation for the Lord's Supper

Glory be to Thee, O Lord, who makest Thine

own Body and Blood to become our spiritual food, to strengthen and refresh our souls.

Glory be to Thee, O Lord, who by this heavenly food dost mystically unite us to Thyself; for nothing becomes one with our bodies more than the bodily food we eat, which turns into our very substance, and nothing makes us to become one with Thee more, than when Thou vouchsafes to become the very food of our souls!

Glory be to Thee, O Lord, who by this immortal food dost nourish our souls to live the life of grace here, and dost raise us up to life everlasting hereafter! Lord, do Thou evermore give us this bread! Amen, Amen.

Thomas Ken, 1637–1711, Manual
for Winchester Scholars

O Father of Mercy, and God of all consolation, since all creatures acknowledge and confess you as Governor and Lord: It becomes us, whom you have made with your own hands, at all times to honor and magnify your divine majesty. First, because you have created us in your own image and likeness: But above all because you have freed us from that everlasting death and damnation, into which the power of evil drew the human race through sin, from bondage to which neither man nor angel was able to make us free. We praise you, O Lord, that you, who are rich in mercy, and infinite in goodness, have provided our redemption in your only and well-beloved Son, who in your true love you gave to be made a man like us in all things, sin excepted, to receive in his body the punishment of our transgression, by his death to make satisfaction to your justice, and through his resurrection to destroy the power of death; and so to bring life to the world again.

John Knox, c.1513–72

O Lord, we acknowledge that no creature is able to comprehend the length and breadth, the depth and height of your most excellent love, which moved you to show mercy where none was deserved, to promise and give life where death had been victorious, to receive us in your grace when we could do nothing but rebel against your justice. O Lord, the blind dullness of our nature will not allow

us sufficiently to weigh your ample benefits; yet, nevertheless, at the commandment of Jesus Christ our Lord, we present ourselves at this his table, which he has left to be used in remembrance of his death, until his coming again: to declare and witness before the world, that by him alone we have received liberty and life; that by him alone acknowledge us to be your children and heirs; that by him alone we may come near to the throne of your grace; that by him alone we are may in your spiritual kingdom eat and drink at his table, with whom we will eat one day in heaven, and by whom our bodies shall be raised up again from the dust, and shall be placed with him in that endless joy, which you, O Father of mercy, have prepared for your chosen ones before the foundation of the world was laid. And these most immeasurable benefits we acknowledge and confess to have received from your free mercy and grace, by your only beloved Son Jesus Christ: for which, therefore, we your congregation, moved by your Holy Sprit, give you all thanks, praise, and glory, for ever and ever. Amen.

John Knox, c.1513–72

Most merciful Father, we offer to you all praise, thanks, and glory, that in your great mercy, it has pleased you to grant us, who are miserable sinners, so excellent a gift and treasure, as to receive us into the fellowship and company of your dear Son Jesus Christ our Lord. You delivered him to death for us, and now you have given him to us as food and nourishment for eternal life. And now we pray, O heavenly Father, that you will never permit us to become so ungrateful as to forget your wonderful benefits; but imprint and lock them in our hearts, so that we may grow and increase more and more in true faith each day, and that we may continually use our faith in all kinds of good work; and O Lord, make us strong in every difficulty, so that we may constantly stand in the confession of faith, glorifying you in our lives, you who are God over all things, and blessed for ever. So be it. Amen.

John Knox, c.1513–72

O most merciful God and Father, we beseech thee, that Thou wilt be pleased in this Supper (in which we celebrate the glorious remembrance of the bitter death of thy beloved Son Jesus Christ) to work in our hearts through the Holy Spirit, that we may daily more and more with true confidence, give ourselves up unto thy Son Jesus Christ, that our afflicted and contrite hearts, through the power of the Holy Ghost, may be fed and comforted with his true body and blood; yea, with him, true God and man, that only heavenly bread; and that we may no longer live in our sins, but he in us, and we in him, and thus truly be made partakers of the new and everlasting covenant of grace. That we may not doubt but Thou wilt forever be our gracious Father, nevermore imputing our sins unto us, and providing us with all things necessary, as well for the body as the soul, as thy beloved children and heirs; grant us also thy grace, that we may take up our cross cheerfully, deny ourselves, confess our Savior, and in all tribulations, with uplifted heads expect our Lord Jesus Christ from heaven, where he will make our mortal bodies like unto his most glorious body, and take us unto him in eternity.

Liturgy of the Reformed Church

O Lord, our merciful Father, we ask you to look upon us who are gathered here in your presence now, and shed upon us a congregation, and upon each of us individually, the helpful spirit of your grace, so that all our thoughts and desires now may be such that you can approve and satisfy them, and that in our worship we may each be aware that we have come into your presence. Amen.

Alexander Maclaren, 1826–1910

As watchmen wait for the morning, so do our souls long for you, O Christ. Come with the dawning of the day, and make yourself known to us in the breaking of bread; for you are our God for ever and ever.
Amen.

Mozarabic liturgy, 7th century

O Thou living fruit, Thou sweet blossom, Thou delicious paradise apple of the blooming fatherly heart, Thou sweet vine of Cyprus in the vineyard of Egad, who will give me to receive Thee so worthily this day that Thou

shalt desire to come to me, to dwell with me, and never to separate from me! O unfathomable good, that fillest heaven and earth, incline Thyself graciously this day, and despise not Thy poor creature. Lord, if I am not worthy of Thee, yet do I stand in need of Thee. Ah, gentle Lord, art Thou not He who with one word created heaven and earth? Lord, with one word canst Thou restore health to my sick soul. O Lord, do unto me according to Thy grace, according to Thy infinite mercy, and not according to my deserts. Yes, Thou art the innocent Paschal Lamb, which at this day is still offered up for the sins of all mankind. Ah, Thou sweet-tasting bread of heaven, which contains all sweet tastes according to the desire of everyone's heart, make the hungry mouth of my soul to rejoice in Thee this day; give me to eat and to drink; strengthen, adorn, and unite me interiorly to Thee. Ah, Eternal Wisdom, come down so powerfully this day into my soul, that all my enemies may be driven out of her, all my crimes be melted away, and all my sins be forgiven. Enlighten my understanding with the light of true faith. Inflame my will with Thy sweet love. Cheer up my mind with Thy glad presence, and give virtue and perfection to all my powers. Watch over me at my death, that I may enjoy Thy beatific vision in eternal bliss. Amen.

Henry Suso, 1295–1366

From sullied lips,
From an abominable heart,
From an unclean tongue,
Out of a polluted soul,
Receive my prayer, O my Christ.
Reject me not,
Nor my words, nor my ways,
Nor even my shamelessness,
But give me courage to say
What I desire, my Christ.
And even more, teach me
What to do and say.
I have sinned more than the harlot
Who, on learning where Thou wast lodging,
Bought myrrh,
And dared to come and anoint
Thy feet, my Christ,
My Lord and my God.
As Thou didst not repulse her

When she drew near from her heart,
Neither, O Word, abominate me,
But grant me Thy feet
To clasp and kiss,
And with a flood of tears
As with most precious myrrh
Dare to anoint them.
Wash me with my tears
And purify me with them, O Word.
Forgive my sins
And grant me pardon.
Thou knowest the multitude of my evil-
doings,
Thou knowest also my wounds,
And Thou seest my bruises.
But also Thou knowest my faith,
And Thou beholdest my willingness,
And Thou headrest my sighs.
Nothing escapes Thee, my God,
My Maker, my Redeemer,
Not even a tear-drop,
Nor part of a drop.
Thine eyes know
What I have not achieved,
And in Thy book
Things not yet done
Are written by Thee.
See my depression,
See how great is my trouble,
And all my sins
Take from me, O God of all,
That with a clean heart,
Trembling mind
And contrite spirit
I may partake of Thy pure
And all-holy Mysteries
By which all who eat and drink Thee
With sincerity of heart
Are quickened and deified.
For Thou, my Lord, hast said:
"Whoever eats My Flesh
And drinks My Blood
Abides in Me
And I in Him."
Wholly true is the word
Of my Lord and God.
For whoever partakes of Thy divine
And deifying Gifts
Certainly is not alone,
But is with Thee, my Christ,
Light of the Triune Sun

Which illumines the world.
And that I may not remain alone
Without Thee, the Giver of Life,
My Breath, my Life,
My Joy,
The Salvation of the world,
Therefore I have drawn near to Thee
As Thou seest, with tears
And with a contrite spirit.
Ransom of my offences,
I beseech Thee to receive me,
And that I may partake without
condemnation
Of Thy life-giving and perfect Mysteries,
That Thou mayest remain as Thou hast said
With me, thrice-wretched as I am,
Lest the tempter may find me
Without Thy grace
And craftily seize me,
And having deceived me, may seduce me,
From Thy deifying words.
Therefore I fall at Thy feet
And fervently cry to Thee:
As Thou receives the Prodigal
And the Harlot who drew near to Thee,
So have compassion and receive me,
The profligate and the prodigal,
As with contrite spirit
I now draw near to Thee.
I know, O Savior, that no other
Has sinned against Thee as I,
Nor has done the deeds
That I have committed.
But this again I know
That not the greatness of my offences
Nor the multitude of my sins
Surpasses the great patience
Of my God,
And His extreme love for men.
But with the oil of compassion
Those who fervently repent
Thou dost purify and enlighten
And makest them children of the light,
Sharers of Thy Divine Nature.
And Thou dost act most generously,
For what is strange to Angels
And to the minds of men
Often Thou tellest to them
As to Thy true friends.
These things make me bold, my Christ,
These things give me wings,

And I take courage from the wealth
Of Thy goodness to us.
And rejoicing and trembling at once,
I who am straw partake of fire,
And, strange wonder!
I am ineffably bedewed,
Like the bush of old
Which burnt without being consumed.
Therefore with thankful mind,
And with thankful heart,
And with thankfulness in all the members
Of my soul and body,
I worship and magnify
And glorify Thee, my God,
For Thou art blessed,
Now and throughout the ages.

Symeon the New Theologian, 949–1022

Behold I approach for Divine Communion.
O Creator, let me not be burnt by
   communicating,
For Thou art Fire which burns the unworthy.
But purify me from every stain.

Symeon the Translator, 11th century

Holy, holy, holy Lord God Almighty, who are and
were, and are to come: We, who are not worthy
of the least of your mercies, humbly present
ourselves in your presence. We come to you, our
Creator and Redeemer, with honor, adoration,
and praise. Enable us by your good Spirit to attend
with undistracted minds, with reverence and awe,
to the holy duties to which you are calling us
today. Allow us, we pray, to come with humble
boldness into the holy of holies, by the new and
living way into your presence Christ has made
ready for us through his sacrifice. Teach us from
your word. May we read it with wise and understanding hearts. Prepare us to sing your praises
with music in our hearts, and to offer you acceptable worship. Teach us to pray; inspire us with a
spirit of devotion; enable us to exercise faith in
every moment of our worship. And let all we do
be done to the Glory of the Father, and of the Son,
and of the Holy Spirit, one God; and graciously
accept us, through Jesus Christ our Lord. Amen.

*Synod of New York and Philadelphia's proposed
revision of the Directory for Worship, 1787*

After receiving the Lord's Supper

If all the creatures in the world should offer
themselves together with me to praise thee, O
Lord, yet is it certain that we could not give thee
sufficient thanks for the least of thy mercies; and
if together we cannot sufficiently praise thee for
the least, how much less can I alone perform so
great a duty, for such inestimable blessings, as I
have at this time received; for vouchsafing to visit
me, comfort me, and honor me with acceptance
and admittance to thy blessed table. If Elizabeth,
the mother of John Baptist, upon the Virgin
Mary's entrance to her house) said, Whence is
it that the Mother of my Lord should come to
me? What shall I say, whom the Lord himself
hath visited and united to him, by his blessed
Sacrament, being a vessel and receptacle of all
impurity, who hath so often offended, despised
and neglected him? King David wondered why
God should so esteem of, or visit man; but I
wonder much more, why he should be made
man for man, abide with him, suffer death for
him, and give himself to him for spiritual food.
Solomon, after he had built a temple to God,
reasoned thus: But will God dwell indeed on
the earth? Behold the heaven of heavens cannot
contain thee, how much less this house, that
I have builded? May not I much more marvel,
that God will not disdain to come and abide in
this my poor and wretched soul? What greater
benefit or grace, what greater argument of his
love is there, can there be showed to me? Oh my
soul, if thou wouldest but thoroughly conceive
the happiness that cometh to thee by this holy
Sacrament, then consider and well weigh, what
benefits it bringeth with it. By it the sons of men
are made the sons of God, and all that is earthly
or carnal in us is mortified, that the Deity may
live and abide with us. What therefore, O my
Lord, shall I do? What thanks shall I render to
thee? With what fervency shall I love thee? For
if thou, so mighty a Lord, hast vouchsafed to
love me, poor wretched creature, how should it
be, but that I should return love again to thee?
And how shall I express my love better, than
in forbearing those things which thou dost
abhor, and following those things which thou
dost command? Give, O Lord, to this end thy
concomitant grace to me, whereby I may return
a reciprocal love to thee, and love those things,
which are acceptable to thee, and avoid those
things, which are to thee unpleasing.

Lancelot Andrewes, 1555–1626

Give me a heart, which may love thee with so true, faithful, and constant affection, as that nothing under the sun may separate me from the love of thee. Let me not follow the love of the world, or delight in the vanities of it any longer: but give me power to kill and quench all other love and desires, and to love thee only, desire thee only, and only think of thee, and thy commandments: that all my affections and thoughts may be fixed on thee; that in all temptations and adversities, I may have recourse to thee only, and receive all comfort from thee alone, who livest and reignest, one God, world without end. Amen.

Lancelot Andrewes, 1555–1626

I give Thee thanks, O holy Lord, Father almighty, eternal God, who hast vouchsafed, not for any merit of mine, but solely out of the condescension of Thy mercy, to satisfy me a sinner, Thine unworthy servant, with the precious Body and Blood of Thy Son our Lord Jesus Christ. I pray that this holy Communion be not to me a condemnation unto punishment, but a saving plea unto forgiveness. May it be unto me the Armour of faith and the shield of good will. May it be the emptying out of my vices, the extinction of all concupiscence and lust, the increase of charity and patience, of humility and obedience, and of all virtues; a strong defense against the snares of all enemies, visible and invisible; the perfect quieting of all my evil impulses, both fleshly and ghostly; a firm cleaving unto Thee, the one true God; and a pledge of a blessed destiny. And I beseech Thee, that Thou wouldst vouchsafe to bring me, a sinner, to the ineffable banquet, where Thou, with Thy Son and the Holy Ghost, art to Thy saints true light, fullness of content, eternal joy, gladness without alloy and perfect bliss. Through the same Christ our Lord. Amen.

Thomas Aquinas, 1225–74

O Master, Christ our God, King of the ages, and maker of all things: I thank thee for all the good things which thou hast bestowed upon me, and for this partaking of thine immaculate and life-giving Mysteries. Wherefore I pray thee, who art good and lovest mankind: Keep me under thy protection, and in the shadow of thy wings; and grant unto me with a pure conscience and even unto my last breath, to partake of thy holy Mysteries, unto remission of sins and unto life everlasting. For thou art the Bread of Life, the Fountain of holiness, the Giver of good things, and unto thee we ascribe Glory: to the Father, and to the Son, and to the Holy Spirit; now and ever, and unto ages of ages. Amen.

Basil the Great, c.330–379

Lord, enthroned in heavenly splendor,
First begotten from the dead,
You alone, our strong Defender,
Now lift up Your people's head.

Refrain:
Alleluia! Alleluia! Alleluia!
Jesus, true and living Bread!
Jesus, true and living Bread!

Here our humblest homage pay we,
Here in loving reference bow;
Here for faith's discernment pray we,
Lest we fail to know You now.
Refrain

Though the lowliest form doth veil Thee
As of old in Bethlehem,
Here as there Thine angels hail Thee,
Branch and Flower of Jesse's stem.
Refrain

Paschal Lamb, Your offering finished
Once for all when You were slain,
In its fullness undiminished
Shall forevermore remain.
Refrain

Great High Priest of our profession,
Through the veil Thou wentest in,
By Thy mighty intercession,
Grace and peace for us to win.
Refrain

Life imparting heavenly Manna,
Smitten Rock with streaming side,
Heaven and earth with loud hosanna
Worship You, the Lamb Who died.
Refrain

George Hugh Bourne, 1840–1928

We offer you immortal praise and thanks, heavenly Father, for the great blessing which you have conferred on us miserable sinners, in allowing us to partake of your Son Jesus Christ, whom was handed over to die for us, and now gives us the food of everlasting life. So we dedicate the rest of our lives to advance your glory and build up our neighbors, through the same Jesus Christ your Son, who, in the unity of the Holy Spirit, lives with you and reigns for ever.

John Calvin, 1509–64

O Lord, my God, I am not worthy that you should come into my soul, but I am glad that you have come to me because in your loving kindness you desire to dwell in me you ask me to open the door of my soul, which you alone have created, so that you may enter into it with your loving kindness and dispel the darkness of my mind. I believe that you will do this for you did not turn away Mary Magdalene when she approached you in tears. Neither did you withhold forgiveness from the tax collector who repented of his sins or from the good thief who asked to be received into your kingdom. Indeed, you numbered as your friends all who came to you with repentant hearts. O God, you alone are blessed always, now, and forever.

John Chrysostom, c.347–407

We give thanks to you, almighty God, that you have refreshed us with this salutary gift; and we pray that in your mercy you will strengthen our faith in you, and in fervent love towards one another; through Jesus Christ, your dear Son, our Lord, who lives and reigns with you and the Holy Spirit, ever one God, world without end.

Martin Luther, 1483–1546

Lord, I am indeed unworthy that you should come under my roof, but I need and long for your help and grace that I may walk in the right path. Therefore, I come to you, trusting only in the comforting words which I have heard, which you invite me with to your table and say to me, who is so unworthy, that I will receive forgiveness of my sins through your body and blood, if I eat and drink of this sacrament. Amen! Dear Lord, I do not doubt that your Word is true, and relying on this promise I eat and drink with you. Let it happen to me according to your will and Word.

Martin Luther, 1483–1546

O Thou who willingly dost give thy flesh to me as food, Thou who art a Fire, consuming the unworthy, Consume me not, O my Creator; But rather pass through all my body parts, Into all my joints, my reins, my heart. Burn thou the thorns of all my transgressions, Cleanse my soul, and hallow thou my thoughts. Make firm my knees, and my bones likewise; Enlighten as one my five senses, Establish me wholly in thy fear; Ever shelter me, and guard and keep me From every soul-corrupting deed and word, Chasten me, purify me, and control me; Adorn me, teach me, and enlighten me. Show me to be a Tabernacle of thy Spirit only, And in no wise the dwelling-place of sin, That from me, thy habitation, through the entrance of thy Communion, Every evil deed and every passion may flee as from fire.

Symeon the Translator, 11th century

May thy holy Body, O Lord Jesus Christ our God, be unto me for life eternal, and thy precious Blood unto remission of my sins. May this Eucharist be unto me for joy, health, and gladness; and at thy dread Second Coming make me, a sinner, worthy to stand at the right hand of thy glory. Amen.

Symeon the Translator, 11th century

We give you thanks, O heavenly Father, who has delivered us from the power of darkness and transferred us into the kingdom of your Son; grant, we pray, that as by his death he has recalled us to life, so by his presence abiding in us he may raise us to joys eternal; through the same Jesus Christ our Lord.

Mozarabic Sacramentary

In this Holy Sacrifice,
may we be redeemed
by the precious Body and Blood
of our Savior Jesus Christ:
may our lives be made new in him.

In this Holy Eucharist,
in humble thanksgiving
for the life, suffering and resurrection
of our Lord,

may we offer to him
ourselves, our souls and bodies.

In this Holy Communion,
may we be one in the mystical Body of Christ,
united in loving fellowship
with out Lord,
his saints in heaven,
and our fellow Christians everywhere.

In this Holy Communion,
may we be one with all humanity;
may we offer the joy and sorrow,
the good and evil
of all creation.

In this Holy Memorial of the Last Supper,
may we remember with penitence and joy
his great love for us sinners;
may we offer to him our sacrifice
of praise and thanksgiving.

In this Holy Mystery,
may we abide him
and he in us.

Peter Nott, b.1933

O Thou, who didst manifest thyself in the breaking of bread to thy disciples at Emmaus: Grant us ever through the same blessed sacrament of thy presence to know thee, and to love thee more and more with all our hearts. Abide with us, O Lord, that we may every abide in thee; for thy tender mercy's sake.

E.B. Pusey, 1800–82

Blessed Jesus, who art about to come to us thy unworthy servants in the blessed sacrament of thy body and blood, prepare our hearts, we beseech thee, for thyself. Grant us that repentance for our past sins, that faith in the atonement made for them by thee upon the cross, that full purpose of amendment of life, that perfect love to thee and to all men, which shall fit us to receive thee. Lord, we are not worthy that thou shouldest come under our roof, much less that we should receive thee into ourselves; but since thou didst not disdain to be laid in a manger amidst unclean beasts, so vouchsafe to enter into our souls and bodies, unclean though they be through many sins

and defilements.
Lord, come to us that thou mayest cleanse us.
Lord, come to us that thou mayest heal us.
Lord, come to us that thou mayest strengthen us.

And grant that having received thee, we may never be separated from thee by our sins, but may continue thine for ever, till we see thee face to face in thy heavenly kingdom, where, with the Father and the Holy Ghost, thou livest and reignest, ever one God, world without end.

Treasury of Devotion, 1869

A prayer just before receiving the bread and the wine
Jesus Christ, the Lamb, the Branch, the bright and Morning Star, the Bread of life that came down from heaven, have mercy upon me. It is Thy promise that whoever eateth Thy Flesh and drinketh Thy Blood shall have eternal life in him, and Thou wilt raise him up at the last day. Behold, O God, I am now coming to Thee, O Thou fountain of purgation! Thou well of living waters, wash me clean.

Henry Vaughan, 1622–95, The Mount of Olives

Almighty God, who has given your only Son to die for us: Grant that we who have been united in the communion of his most precious Body and Blood may be so cleansed from our past sins, and so strengthened to follow the example of his most holy life, that we may hereafter enjoy everlasting fellowship with you in heaven, through him who loved us and gave himself for us, the same Jesus Christ our Lord.

B.F. Westcott, 1825–1901

Here, O my Lord, I see thee face to face;
Here would I touch and handle things unseen,
Here grasp with firmer hand the eternal grace,
And all my weariness upon thee lean.

Here would I feed upon the bread of God,
Here drink with thee the royal wine of heaven;
Here would I lay aside each earthly load,
Here taste afresh the calm of sin forgiven.

Mine is the sin, but thine the righteousness;
Mine is the guilt, but thine the cleansing blood;

Here is my robe, my refuge, and my peace -
Thy blood, thy righteousness, O Lord, my
    God.

Horatius Bonar, 1808–82

Marriage

May God be with you and bless you.
May you see your children's children.
May you be poor in misfortune, rich in
    blessings.
May you know nothing but happiness
From this day forward.

Author unknown, traditional wedding blessing

God, all mighty, all good, and all wise, who
from the beginning didst foresee that it was
not good for man to be alone, and therefore
didst create him a help meet for him, and hast
ordained that two should be one, we beg of
thee, and humbly request, that since it has
pleased thee to call these persons to the holy
state of marriage, thou wouldst deign, of thy
grace and goodness to give and send them thy
Holy Spirit, in order that they may live holily
in true and firm faith, according to thy good
will, surmounting all bad affections, edifying
each other in all honesty and chastity, giving
thy blessing to them as thou didst to thy
faithful servants Abraham, Isaac, and Jacob,
that having holy lineage they may praise and
serve thee, teaching them, and bringing them
up to thy praise and glory, and the good of
their neighbor, through the advancement and
exaltation of thy holy gospel Hear us, Father of
Mercy, through our Lord Jesus Christ, thy very
dear Son. Amen.

John Calvin, 1509–64

Our Lord fill you with all graces, and anoint
you with all good, to live together long and
holily.

John Calvin, 1509–64

The Lord sanctify and bless you, the Lord pour
the riches of his grace upon you, that you may
please him and live together in holy love to
your lives' end. Amen.

John Knox, c.1513–72

Almighty God, Thou, who dost manifest thy
goodness and wisdom in all thy works and ordinances; and from the beginning hast said, that
it is not good that man be alone and therefore
hast created him a help meet to be with him,
and ordained that they who were two should
be one, and who dost also punish all impurity;
we pray thee, since Thou hast called and united
these two persons in the holy state of marriage,
that Thou wilt give them thy Holy Spirit, so that
they in true love and firm faith may live holy
according to thy divine will and resist all evil.
Wilt Thou also bless them as Thou hast blessed
the believing fathers, thy friends and faithful
servants, Abraham, Isaac and Jacob; in order
that they as coheirs of the covenant which Thou
hast established with these fathers, may bring
up their children, which Thou wilt be pleased to
give them, in the fear of the Lord, to the honor of
thy holy name, to the edification of thy Church
and to the extension of the holy gospel. Hear us,
Father of all mercy, for the sake of Jesus Christ,
thy beloved Son, our Lord, in whose name we
conclude our prayer: Our Father which is in
heaven. Hallowed be thy name. Thy kingdom
come. Thy will be done in earth, as it is in
heaven. Give us this day our daily bread. And
forgive us our debts, as we forgive our debtors.
And lead us not into temptation, but deliver
us from evil: For thine is the kingdom, and the
power and the glory, for ever. Amen. Hearken
now to the promise of God, from Psalm 128:
"Blessed is every one that feareth the Lord, that
walketh in his ways. For thou shalt eat the labor
of thine hands: happy shalt thou be, and it shall
be well with thee. Thy wife shall be as a fruitful
vine by the sides of thine house; thy children
like olive plants round about thy table. Behold,
that thus shall the man be blessed that feareth
the Lord. The Lord shall bless thee out of Zion:
and thou shalt see the good of Jerusalem all the
days of thy life; yea, thou shalt see thy children's
children, and peace upon Israel." The Lord our
God replenish you with his grace, and grant that
ye may long live together in all godliness and
holiness. Amen.

Liturgy of the Reformed Church

Funerals

Of old thou hast created me from nothing,
and honored me with thy divine image;
but when I disobeyed thy commandment,
thou hast returned me to the earth whence I
    was taken.
Lead me back again to thy likeness,
refashioning my ancient beauty.

Greek Orthodox Church, the Funeral Service

Ordination

Almighty God, our Heavenly Father, who hast
purchased to Thyself an Universal Church by
the precious Blood of Thy dear Son, Mercifully
look upon the same, and at this time so guide
and govern the minds of Thy servants, the
Bishops and Pastors of Thy flock, that they may
lay hands suddenly on no man, but faithfully
and wisely make choice of fit persons to serve
in the sacred Ministry of thy Church. And
to those which shall be ordained to any holy
function give Thy grace and Heavenly benediction; that both by their life and doctrine they
may set forth Thy glory and set forward the
salvation of all men; through Jesus Christ our
Lord. Amen.

Book of Common Prayer, first Ember Collect,
attributed to John Cosin, 1594–1672

Commissioning for ministry in the church

Almighty God, Who makest all things in heav-
en and earth to serve Thy gracious will: We
commit to Thy care and protection these Thy
servants whom we send forth in Thy Name;
fulfill the promise made through Thy Son to be
with them at all times, whatever be the perils
they may meet, or the trials they may undergo;
bless them with Thy continual favor; give them
many souls as the reward of their labor; and in
every hour of conflict, uncertainty and doubt
strengthen and uphold them, and give them
Thy peace; through Jesus Christ, Thy Son, our
Lord. Amen.

The Common Service Book of
the Lutheran Church, 1917

O God, be present with us always, dwell within
our heart. With your light and your Spirit
guide our souls, our thoughts, and all our
actions, that we may teach your Word, that
your healing power may be in us and in your
worldwide church.

Philip Melanchthon, 1497–1560

Pastors

O Almighty God, Who by Thy Son Jesus Christ,
didst give to Thy holy Apostles many excellent
gifts, and comrnandedst them earnestly to
feed Thy flock: Make, we beseech Thee, all
Pastors diligently to preach Thy holy Word,
and the people obediently to follow the same,
that they may receive the crown of everlasting
glory; through Jesus Christ, Thy Son, our Lord.
Amen.

The Common Service Book of
the Lutheran Church, 1917

Almighty and Gracious God, the Father of our
Lord Jesus Christ, Who has commanded us to
pray that Thou wouldest send forth laborers
into Thy harvest: Of Thine infinite mercy give
us true teachers and ministers of Thy Word,
and put Thy saving Gospel in their hearts
and on their lips, that they may truly fulfill
Thy command, and preach nothing contrary
to Thy Holy Word; that we, being warned,
instructed, nurtured, comforted and strengthened by Thy heavenly Word, may do those
things which are well-pleasing to Thee, and
profitable to us; through Jesus Christ, Thy Son,
our Lord. Amen.

The Common Service Book of
the Lutheran Church, 1917

Sundays

O Lord God, Heavenly Father, we beseech Thee
so to rule and guide us by Thy Holy Spirit,
that we hear and receive Thy Holy Word with
our whole heart and hallow Thy Holy Day, in
order that through Thy Word we also may be
sanctified, learn to place all our trust and hope
in Jesus Christ Thy Son, and following Him, be
led safely through all evil, until through Thy

grace, we come to everlasting life; through the same Jesus Christ, Thy Son, our Lord. Amen.

Worship preparation

Eternal, Almighty, and most gracious God: heaven is your throne, and earth is your foot-stool; holy and reverend is your name; you are praised by the angels of heaven, and in the gathering of your church on earth. Despite our unworthiness, you have invited us through our Mediator, Jesus Christ, to present ourselves and our prayers to you. Receive us graciously. Help us by your Spirit. Let us stand in awe of you. Put your law into our hearts, and write it on our minds. Let your word come to us in power, and help us receive it in love, with attentive, reverent, and teachable minds. Through your word, allow us to taste the flavor of eternal life. Make us fervent in prayer and joyful in praise. Help us serve you this day without distraction, that we may find that a day in your courts is better than a thousand elsewhere, and that it is good for us to come near to God; through Jesus Christ our Lord and Savior. Amen.

Richard Baxter, 1615–91

After worship

Accept, O God, the worship of our hearts and of our lips, and give us grace to glorify you in our lives, for the sake of Jesus Christ our Lord.

Source unknown

O God, whose nature and property is ever to have mercy and to forgive, receive our humble petitions; and though we be tied and bound with the chain of our sins, yet let the pitiful-ness of thy great mercy loose us; for the honor of Jesus Christ, our Mediator and Advocate. Amen.

Book of Common Prayer, Prayers and Thanksgivings

Grant, we beseech thee, almighty God, that the words which we have heard this day with our outward ears may, through thy grace, be so grafted inwardly in our hearts that they may bring forth in us the fruit of good living, to the honor and praise of thy name, through Jesus

Christ our Lord.

Gelasian Sacramentary, 5th century

Almighty God, bestow on us the meaning of words, the light of understanding, the nobility of diction and the faith of the true nature. And grant that what we believe we may also speak.

Hilary of Poitiers, c.315–c.367

O gracious Lord, since thou hast promised that, where two or three are gathered together in thy name, thou wilt be in the midst of them to grant their requests: grant to us who are met in thy name that those requests which in the utmost sincerity of our hearts we have now made, may effectually be answered; through the merits of Jesus Christ our Lord.

Jonathan Swift, 1667–1745

Preaching and preachers

O Savior of the world, who art little known and loved less by the world, especially through the fault of Thy ministers; Thou who didst give up Thy life for the salvation of souls – I beseech Thee through the merits of Thy Passion, to enlighten and inflame so many priests who might convert sinners and sanctify the entire earth if they preached Thy Word with humil-ity and simplicity, as Thou and Thy disciples preached it.

But, alas!, they do not do so; they preach themselves and not Thee, and thus the world is full of preachers and in the meantime hell is crowded with souls.

O Lord, repair this mighty ruin which preachers cause in Thy Church, and if it be necessary, humble, I pray Thee, as an example to others, by some visible sign, those priests who for their own glory adulterate Thy holy Word, that they may amend, and they may not thus obstruct the spiritual profit of the people.

Thus I hope, thus I pray. Amen.

Alphonsus Liguori, 1696–1787

Offertory prayers

Blessed be thou, O Lord God, for ever and ever;

for all things come of thee, and of thy own do I now give thee.

1 Chronicles 29

All things come from you, and of your own do we give you. Accept and bless, O God our Father, these our gifts, and pour out on us the spirit of your own abundant giving; that as we have freely received, so we may freely give, to the glory of your name; through Jesus Christ our Lord.

Author unknown

Grant, we beseech you, Almighty God, that these our gifts, being dedicated to your service, may be used for your glory and the good of your Church and people; through Jesus Christ our Lord.

Author unknown

O most merciful and gracious God, from whose open hand we all have received much: We ask you to accept this offering of your people. Remember in your love those who have brought it. Remember also those persons and purposes for which it is given. So follow this sacrifice with your blessing that it may promote peace and good will, and advance the kingdom of our Lord and Savior Jesus Christ, in whose name we pray; Amen.

Book of Common Worship of the Presbyterian Church U.S.A., 1906

Pulpit prayers

Give us grace, O Lord, not only to hear your Word with our ears, but also to receive it into our hearts and to show it in our lives; for the glory of your great name.

Author unknown

Turn we to the Lord God, the Father Almighty, and with pure hearts offer to Him, so far as our meanness can, great and true thanks, with all our hearts praying His exceeding kindness, that of His good pleasure He would deign to hear our prayers, that by His Power He would drive out the enemy from our deeds and thoughts, that He would increase our faith, guide our understandings, give us spiritual thoughts, and

lead us to His bliss, through Jesus Christ His Son our Lord, who liveth and reigneth with Him, in the Unity of the Holy Spirit, one God, for ever and ever. Amen.

Augustine of Hippo, 354–430, the prayer he often used after his sermons and lectures

O Lord, uphold me, that I may uplift you; and may the words of my mouth, and the meditation of our hearts, be acceptable in your sight, O Lord, our strength and our redeemer.

Author unknown

O Lord, open to us your Word, and our hearts to your Word, that we may know you better and love you more; for your mercy and for your truth's sake.

Author unknown

O Almighty and ever-living Lord God! Majesty, and Power, and Brightness, and Glory! How shall we dare to appear before thy face, who are contrary to thee, in all we call thee? for we are darkness, and weaknesse, and filthinesse, and shame. Misery and sin fill our days: yet art thou our Creatour, and we thy work: Thy hands both made us, and also made us Lords of all thy creatures; giving us one world in our selves, and another to serve us: then did'st thou place us in Paradise, and wert proceeding still on in thy Favors, untill we interrupted thy Counsels, disappointed thy Purposes, and sold our God, our glorious, our gracious God for an apple. O write it! O brand it in our foreheads for ever: for an apple once we lost our God, and still lose him for no more; for money, for meat, for diet: But thou Lord, art patience, and pity, and sweetnesse, and love; therefore we sons of men are not consumed. Thou hast exalted thy mercy above all things; and hast made our salvation, not our punishment, thy glory: so that then where sin abounded, not death, but grace superabounded; accordingly, when we had sinned beyond any help in heaven or earth, then thou saidest, Lo, I come! then did the Lord of life, unable of himselfe to die, contrive to do it. He took flesh, he wept, he died; for his enemies he died; even for those that derided him then, and still despise him. Blessed Savior! many waters could not quench thy love! nor no pit overwhelm it. But though the streams of thy blood were currant through darkness, grave, and hell; yet by these thy conflicts, and seemingly hazards, didst thou arise triumphant, and therein mad'st us victorious. Neither doth thy love yet stay here! for, this word of thy rich peace, and reconciliation, thou hast committed, not to Thunder, or Angels, but to silly and sinful men: even to me, pardoning my sins, and bidding me go feed the people of thy love.

Blessed be the God of Heaven and Earth! who only doth wondrous things. Awake therefore, my Lute, and my Viol! awake all my powers to glorifie thee! We praise thee! we bless thee! we magnifie thee for ever! And now, O Lord! in the power of thy Victories, and in the ways of thy Ordinances, and in the truth of thy Love, Lo, we stand here, beseeching thee to bless thy word, wherever spoken this day throughout the universal Church. O make it a word of power and peace, to convert those who are not yet thine, and to confirm those that are: particularly, bless it in this thy own Kingdom, which thou hast made a Land of light, a store-house of thy treasures and mercies: O let not our foolish and unworthy hearts rob us of the continuance of this thy sweet love: but pardon our sins, and perfect what thou hast begun. Ride on Lord, because of the word of truth, and meekness. and righteousness; and thy right hand shall teach thee terrible things. Especially, bless this portion here assembled together, with thy unworthy Servant speaking unto them: Lord Jesu! teach thou me, that I may teach them; Sanctifie, and enable all my powers, that in their full strength they may deliver thy message reverently, readily, faithfully, & fruitfully. O make thy word a swift word, passing from the ear to the heart, from the heart to the life and conversation: that as the rain returns not empty, so neither may thy word, but accomplish that for which it is given. O Lord hear, O Lord forgive! O Lord, hearken. and do so for thy blessed Son's sake, in whose sweet and pleasing words, we say, Our Father, &c.

George Herbert, 1593–1633

O Lord, whom to know is to live, I beseech you to increase in me the knowledge of your truth. In the truth which I know, establish me; whatever I ought to know, teach me; in truths in which I waver, strengthen me; in things in which I am deceived, correct me; in things hard to understand, guide me; and from untruths deliver me. Send out your light and your truth, and let them lead me, until I know as I am known.

After Fulgentius Ruspensis, 468–533,
known as his "Preacher's Prayer"

A Prayer after Sermon
Blessed be God! and the Father of all mercy! who continueth to pour his benefits upon us. Thou hast elected us, thou hast called us, thou hast justified us, sanctified, and glorified us: Thou wast born for us, and thou livedst and diedst for us: Thou hast given us the blessings of this life, and of a better. O Lord! thy blessings hang in clusters, they come trooping upon us! they break forth like mighty waters on every side. And now Lord, thou hast fed us with the bread of life: so man did eat Angels food: O Lord, bless it: O Lord, make it health and strength unto us; still striving & prospering so long within us, until our obedience reach the measure of thy love, who hast done for us as much as may be. Grant this dear Father, for thy Son's sake, our only Savior: To whom with thee, and the Holy Ghost, three Persons, but one most glorious, incomprehensible God, be ascribed all Honor, and Glory, and Praise, ever. Amen.

George Herbert, 1593–1633

Opening and closing a meeting

May God give us light to guide us, courage to support us, and love to unite us, now and always.

Author unknown

Grant, we beseech you, merciful Lord, that the words we have said and sung with our lips we may believe in our hearts and show in our lives, to your honor and glory; through Jesus Christ our Lord.

Author unknown

Heavenly Father, be pleased to accept and bless all that we have offered to you in this act of worship; and give us grace to show your praise not only with our lips, but in our lives; through Jesus Christ our Lord.

Author unknown

Be with us, Lord God, as we go back into the world.
May the lips which have sung your praises always speak the truth.
May the ears that have heard your Word be shut to what is evil.
May the feet that have brought us to your house always walk in your ways;
through Jesus Christ our Lord.

Author unknown

Sanctify, O Lord, both our coming in and our going out; and grant that when we leave your h house we may not leave your presence, but may abide evermore in your love; through our Lord and Savior Jesus Christ.

Author unknown

Accept, O Lord, the praise we bring to you; pardon the imperfections of our worship; write on our hearts your holy Word; and give us grace to love and serve and praise you all our days; through Jesus Christ our Lord.

Author unknown

Heavenly Father, as we meet now in your presence,
we ask you to open our ears to hear your voice,
to open our lips to sing your praise,
and to open our hearts to love you more and more;
for Christ our Savior's sake.

Author unknown

Sanctify, O Lord, our hearts and minds, and inspire our praise; and give us grace to glorify you alike in our worship and in our work; through Jesus Christ our Savior.

Author unknown

Almighty God, who hast promised to hear the petitions of them that ask in thy Son's Name: we beseech thee mercifully to incline thine ears to us that have now made our prayers and supplications unto thee; and grant that those things, which we have faithfully asked according to thy will, may effectually be obtained, to the relief of our necessity, and to the setting forth of thy glory; through Jesus Christ our Lord.

Book of Common Prayer, 1549,
Post-Communion Collect

Holy Spirit, you make alive; bless also this our gathering, the speaker and the hearer; fresh from the heart it shall come, by your aid, let it also go to the heart.

Søren Kierkegaard, 1813–55

Let your mighty outstretched arm, O Lord God, be our defense; you mercy and loving kindness in Jesus Christ, your dear Son, our salvation; your all true word our instruction; the grace of your life-giving Spirit our comfort and consolation, to the end and in the end; through the same Jesus Christ our Lord.

John Knox, Book of Common Order, 1564

Retreats

O Lord Jesu Christ, who didst say to thine apostles, come ye apart into a desert place and rest awhile, for there were many coming and going; grant, we beseech thee, to thy servants here gathered together, that they may rest awhile at this present time with thee. May they so seek thee, whom their souls desire to love, that they may both find thee, and be found of thee.

And grant such love and such wisdom to accompany the words which shall be spoken in thy name, that they may not fall to the ground, but may be helpful in leading them onward through the toils of their pilgrimage, to that rest which remaineth to the people of God; where, nevertheless, they rest not day and night from thy perfect service; who with the Father and the Holy Spirit, livest and reignest ever one God, world without end.

R.M. Benson, 1824–1915

CHURCH FELLOWSHIP

Children

Almighty and Everlasting God, Who dost will that not one of these little ones should perish, and has sent Thine Only Son to seek and to save that which was lost, and through Him has said, Suffer the little children to come unto Me, and forbid them not, for of such is the kingdom of God: Most heartily we beseech Thee so to bless and govern the children of Thy Church, by Thy Holy Spirit, that they may grow in grace and in the knowledge of Thy Word; protect and defend them against all danger and harm, giving Thy holy Angels charge over them; through Jesus Christ, Thy Son, our Lord. Amen.

*The Common Service Book of
the Lutheran Church, 1917*

Local church

O merciful God, bless this particular church in which I live; make it, and all its members of it, sound in faith, and holy in life, that they may serve thee, and thou bless them, through Jesus Christ our Lord. Amen.

*Author unknown, The Private
Devotions of William Laud*

Grant, we beseech Thee, Almighty God, unto Thy Church, Thy Holy Spirit, and the wisdom which cometh down from above, that Thy Word, as becometh it, may not be bound, but have free course and be preached to the joy and edifying of Christ's holy people, that in steadfast faith we may serve Thee, and in the confession of Thy Name abide unto the end: through Jesus Christ, Thy Son, our Lord. Amen.

*The Common Service Book of
the Lutheran Church, 1917*

Worldwide church

For the Catholic Church:
  for the churches throughout the world:
  their truth, unity and stability to wit:
  in all let charity thrive, truth live:
  for our own church:
  that the things that are wanting therein be

supplied,
  that are not right be set in order.

Lancelot Andrewes, 1555–1626

O Author of all consolation, we commend to thee all of thy people whom thou chastisest in various ways: those afflicted by pestilence, famine, or war; individuals also pressed by poverty, or imprisonment, or disease, or exile, or any other suffering in body or mind, that wisely considering that the end which thou hast in view is to bring them back into the right path by thy rod, they may be imbued with the sense of thy paternal love, and repent with sincere purpose of heart, so as to turn unto thee with their whole mind, and being turned, receive full consolation, and be delivered from all their evils.

John Calvin, 1509–64

Lord God of all times and places, we pray for your Church, which is set today amid the perplexities of a changing order, and face to face with new tasks. Baptize her afresh in the life-giving spirit of Jesus. Bestow upon her a great responsiveness to duty, a swifter compassion with suffering, and an utter loyalty to your will. Help her to proclaim boldly the coming of your kingdom. Put upon her lips the ancient gospel of her Lord. Fill her with the prophets' scorn of tyranny, and with a Christlike tenderness for the heavy laden and downtrodden. Bid her cease from seeking her own life, lest she lose it. Make her valiant to give up her life to humanity, that, like her crucified Lord, she may mount by the path of the cross to a higher glory; through the same Jesus Christ our Lord. Amen.

Walter Rauschenbusch, 1861–1918

Christians in heaven

All shall be Amen and Alleluia.
We shall rest and we shall see,
We shall see and we shall know,
We shall know, and we shall love,
We shall love and we shall praise.
Behold our end which is no end.

Augustine of Hippo, 354–430

For all the saints, who from their labors rest,

Who Thee by faith before the world confessed,
Thy Name, O Jesus, be forever blessed.
Alleluia, Alleluia!

W.W. How, 1823–97

Glory to God, and praise and love
Be ever, ever given,
By saints below and saints above,
The church in earth and heaven.

Charles Wesley, 1707–88

Revival

Revive Thy work, O Lord,
Thy mighty arm make bare;
Speak with the voice that wakes the dead,
And make Thy people hear.

Revive Thy work, O Lord,
Disturb this sleep of death;
Quicken the smold'ring embers now
By Thine almighty breath.

Revive Thy work, O Lord,
Create soul-thirst for Thee;
And hungering for the Bread of Life
O may our spirits be.

Revive Thy work, O Lord,
Exalt Thy precious Name;
And, by the Holy Ghost, our love
For Thee and Thine inflame.

Revive Thy work, O Lord,
Give Pentecostal showers;
The glory shall be all Thine own,
The blessing, Lord, be ours.

Albert Midlane, 1825–1909

PERSECUTED CHRISTIANS

O God of all power, you called from death
the great pastor of the sheep, our Lord Jesus:
comfort and defend the flock which he has
redeemed through the blood of the everlasting
covenant. Increase the number of true preachers; enlighten the hearts of the ignorant; relieve
the pain of the afflicted, especially of those
who suffer for the testimony of the truth; by

the power of our Lord Jesus Christ.

John Knox, c.1513–72

They did not nail him then, but simply bound
him. And he, placing his hands behind him,
and being bound like a distinguished ram
[taken] out of a great flock for sacrifice, and
prepared to be an acceptable burnt-offering
unto God, looked up to heaven, and said,

O Lord God Almighty, the Father of thy
beloved and blessed Son Jesus Christ, by whom
we have received the knowledge of Thee, the
God of angels and powers, and of every creature, and of the whole race of the righteous who
live before thee, I give Thee thanks that Thou
hast counted me, worthy of this day and this
hour, that I should have a part in the number
of Thy martyrs, in the cup of thy Christ, to the
resurrection of eternal life, both of soul and
body, through the incorruption [imparted] by
the Holy Ghost. Among whom may I be accepted this day before Thee as a fat and acceptable
sacrifice, according as Thou, the ever-truthful
God, hast fore-ordained, hast revealed beforehand to me, and now hast fulfilled. Wherefore
also I praise Thee for all things, I bless Thee,
I glorify Thee, along with the everlasting and
heavenly Jesus Christ, Thy beloved Son, with
whom, to Thee, and the Holy Ghost, be glory
both now and to all coming ages. Amen.

Polycarp, c.69–c.155

MISSION AND MISSIONARIES

O Lord, who has warned us that you will
require much from those to whom much is
given: Grant that we, whose lot is cast in so
goodly a heritage, may strive together the more
abundantly, by our prayers, our labors and our
gifts, to extend to those who do not know what
we so richly enjoy; and as we have entered into
the labors of others, so to labor that others
may enter into ours, to the fulfillment of your
holy will and the salvation of all humankind;
through Jesus Christ our Lord.

Author unknown, 5th century

Lord, from whom all good things do come;
grant us thy humble servants, that by thy holy
inspiration we may think those things that

be good, and by thy merciful guiding may perform the same: through our Lord Jesus Christ.

Book of Common Prayer, 1549, Collect
for the fifth Sunday after Easter

O God, who didst so love the world as to give Thine Only-begotten Son, that whosoever believeth in Him should not perish, but have everlasting life: Look with compassion upon the [people] who know Thee not, and on the multitudes that are scattered as sheep having no shepherd; and so bestow upon us Thy grace, that we, with all Thy believing people, may be the messengers of Thy Gospel, seek them that are lost, and restore them unto Thee; that they, being gathered out of all places whither they have wandered, may be strengthened, nurtured, protected and guided by the true Shepherd and Bishop of souls, Jesus Christ, Thy Son, unto Whom, with Thee and the Holy Ghost be honor and power, dominion and glory, world without end. Amen.

The Common Service Book of
the Lutheran Church, 1917

Almighty God, Heavenly Father, Who, through Thy Son, Jesus Christ, has given commandment unto Thy people to go into all the world and preach the Gospel to every creature: Grant us a ready will to obey Thy Word; and as we have entered into the labors of other men [and women], help us to serve Thee, that others may enter into our labors; and that we with them, and they with us, may attain unto everlasting life; through the same Jesus Christ, Thy Son, our Lord. Amen.

The Common Service Book of
the Lutheran Church, 1917

Thy Kingdom come, O God,
Thy rule, O Christ, begin;
Break with Thine iron rod
The tyrannies of sin.

Where is Thy reign of peace,
And purity, and love?
When shall all hatred cease,
As in the realms above?

When comes the promised time

That war shall be no more –
Oppression, lust, and crime,
Shall flee Thy face before?

We pray Thee, Lord, arise,
And come in Thy great might;
Revive our longing eyes,
Which languish for Thy sight.

Men scorn Thy sacred Name,
And wolves devour Thy fold;
By many deeds of shame
We learn that love grows cold.

O'er heathen lands afar
Thick darkness broodeth yet:
Arise, O Morning Star,
Arise, and never set!

Lewis Hensley, 1824–1905

Dear Jesus,
Help us to spread your fragrance everywhere
    we go.
Flood our souls with your Spirit and life.
Penetrate and possess our whole being so
    utterly
that our lives may only be a radiance of yours.
Shine through us
and be so in us
that every soul we come in contact with
may feel your presence in our soul.
Let them look up and see no loner us
but only Jesus.
Stay with us
and then we shall begin to shine as you shine,
so to shine as to be light to others.
The light, O Jesus, will be all from you.
None of it will be ours.
It will be your shining on others through us.
Let us thus praise you in the way you love best
by shining on those around us.
Let us preach you without preaching
not by words, but by our example
by the catching force
the sympathetic influence of what we do
the evident fullness of the love our hearts bear
    to you.

Mother Teresa, 1910–98

O God of all the nations of the earth, remember the multitudes of the heathen, who, though created in thine image, have not known thee, nor the dying of thy Son their Savior Jesus Christ; and grant that by the prayers and labors of thy holy church they may be delivered from all superstition and unbelief and brought to worship thee; through him whom thou hast sent to be the resurrection and the life to all men, the same thy Son Jesus Christ our Lord.

Francis Xavier, 1506–52

UNITY

Almighty God, which dost make the minds of all faithful men to be of one will: grant unto thy people, that they may love the thing, which thou commandest, and desire that which thou dost promise, that among the sundry and manifold changes of the world, our hearts may surely there be fixed, whereas true joys are to be found: through Jesus Christ our Lord.

Book of Common Prayer, 1549, Collect for the fourth Sunday after Easter

O God the Father of our Lord Jesus Christ, our only Savior, the Prince of Peace: Give us grace seriously to lay to heart the great dangers we are in by our unhappy divisions. Take away all hatred and prejudice, and whatsoever else may hinder us from godly union and concord: that, as there is but one Body, and one Spirit, and one hope of our calling, one Lord, one faith, one baptism, one God and Father of us all; so we may henceforth be all of one heart, and of one soul, united in one holy bond of truth and peace, of faith and charity, and with one mind and one mouth glorify thee; through Jesus Christ our Lord. Amen.

Book of Common Prayer, Accession Service, 1715

Grant, Almighty God, that since under the guidance of thy Son we have been united together in the body of thy Church, which has been so often scattered and torn asunder, O grant that we may continue in the unity of faith, and perseveringly fight against all the temptations of this world, and never deviate from the right course, whatever new troubles may daily arise; and though we are exposed to many deaths, let us not be seized with fear,

such as may extinguish in our hears every hope; but may we, on the contrary, learn to raise up our eyes and minds and all our thoughts to thy great power, by which thou quickenest the dead, and raisest from nothing things which are not, so that, though we be daily exposed to ruin, our souls may ever aspire to eternal salvation, until thou at length really showest thyself to be the fountain of life, when we shall enjoy that endless felicity which has been obtained for us by the blood of thine only begotten Son our Lord. Amen.

John Calvin, 1509–64

Father, we pray for your Church throughout the world, that it may share to the full in the work of your Son, revealing you to men and reconciling men to you and to one another; that we and all Christian people may learn to love one another as you have loved us, and your Church may more and more reflect the unity which is your will and your gift, in Jesus Christ our Lord.

Chapel of Unity, Coventry Cathedral

O Lord, my God, you have created the choirs of angels and spiritual powers; you have stretched forth the heavens and established the earth, creating all that exists from nothing. You hear those who obey your will and keep your commands in holy fear. Hear my prayer and protect your faithful people, for you have established me as their unsuitable and unworthy servant. Make your people known for the unity and profession of their faith. Inspire the hearts of your people with your word and your teaching. You called us to preach the Gospel of your Christ and to encourage them to lives and works pleasing to you. I now return to you, your people, your gift to me. Direct them with your powerful right hand, and protect them under the shadow of your wings. May all praise and glorify your name, the Father, Son, and Holy Spirit. Amen.

Cyril of Alexandria, d.444

O almighty God, who has built your church on the foundations of the apostles and prophets, Jesus Christ himself being the head cornerstone: grant us to be so joined together in unity of spirit by their teaching that we may be made into a holy temple, acceptable to you, through Jesus Christ our Lord.

English Reformers, 1549

Most gracious Father, we most humbly beseech thee for thy Holy Catholic [universal] Church. Fill it with all truth; in all truth with all peace. Where it is corrupt, purge it; where it is in error, direct it; where anything is amiss, reform it; where it is right, strengthen and confirm it; where it is in need, furnish it; where it is divided and torn apart, make up its breaches, O holy One of Israel.

William Laud, 1573–1645

O God of peace, good beyond all that is good, in whom is calmness and concord: Heal the dissensions which divide us from one another, and bring us to unity of love in you; through Jesus Christ our Lord.

Liturgy of St Dionysius, 1st century

May the almighty Son of God, Jesus Christ, who prayed in deepest anguish to his eternal Father that we in him might be one, mercifully unite us all.

Philip Melanchthon, 1497–1560

Christ, from whom all blessings flow,
Perfecting the saints below,
Hear us, who your nature share,
Who your mystic body are.

Move and actuate and guide.
Diverse gifts to all divide;
Placed according to your will,
Let us all our work fulfill.

Sweetly may we all agree,
Touched with loving sympathy;
Kindly for each other care,
Every member feel its share.

Charles Wesley, 1707–88

O God, bless and preserve thy Church dispersed over the face of the earth. Restore to it unity and concord, in the acknowledgement of the Truth and the practice of righteousness. Remove out of it all errors and dissensions, that they who profess the same faith may no longer persecute and destroy one another, as it becomes brethren and those that are heirs of the same common salvation.

King William III, 1650–1702

CHRISTIAN LEADERS

Grant, O merciful God, that with malice towards none, with charity to all, with forgiveness in the right as you enable us to see the right, we may strive to finish the work we are engaged in; to bind up the nation's wounds, to care for … the widow and orphan; to do all which may achieve a just and lasting peace among ourselves and with all nations.

After Abraham Lincoln, 1809–65

Lord Jesus, merciful and patient, grant us grace, I beseech thee, ever to teach in a teachable spirit; learning along with those we teach, and learning from them whenever thou so pleasest. Word of God, speak to us, what thou wilt. Wisdom of God, instruct us, instruct by us, if and whom thou wilt. Eternal truth, reveal thyself to us, reveal thyself by us, in whatsoever measure thou wilt; that we and they may all be taught by God.

Christina Rossetti, 1830–94

Church's ministry

Lord Jesus Christ, whose arms of love were stretched wide upon the cross so that all may come within your saving embrace; stretch forth in mercy the hands of your Church today that in its ministry of compassion we may enter again into the Kingdom of your justice and grace. Amen.

Charles Henry Brent, 1862–1929

Christian workers

O faithful Father and Savior, we commend to thee in our prayers all whom thou hast appointed pastors over thy faithful, and to whose guidance thou hast committed our souls; whom, in fine, thou hast been pleased to make the dispensers of thy holy gospel; that thou wouldst guide them by thy Holy Spirit, and so make them honest and faithful ministers of thy glory, making it all their study, and directing all their endeavors to gather together all the wretched sheep which are still wandering astray, and bring them back to Jesus Christ the chief Shepherd and Prince of bishops; and that they may increase in righteousness and holiness every day; that in the meanwhile thou wouldst be pleased to rescue all thy churches from the jaws of ravening wolves and all hirelings, who are led only by a love of fame or lucre, and plainly care not for the manifestation of thy glory, and the salvation of thy flock.

John Calvin, 1509–64

Go then, beloved brother, and teach all nations, baptizing them in the name of the Father and of the Son, and of the Holy Ghost. God our heavenly Father, who has called thee to his holy ministry, enlighten thee with his Holy Spirit, strengthen thee with his hand and so govern thee in thy ministry, that thou mayest do gently and fruitfully walk therein, to the glory of his Name, and the propagation of the Kingdom of his Son Jesus Christ. Amen.

Liturgy of the Reformed Church,
Installation of Professors of Theology

Lord God, You have appointed me as a Bishop and Pastor in Your Church, but you see how unsuited I am to meet so great and difficult a task. If I had lacked Your help, I would have ruined everything long ago. Therefore, I call upon You: I wish to devote my mouth and my heart to you; I shall teach the people. I myself will learn and ponder diligently upon You Word. Use me as Your instrument – but do not forsake me, for if ever I should be on my own, I would easily wreck it all.

Martin Luther, 1483–1546

O God, the Father of the forsaken, who teaches us that love towards people is the bond of perfectness and the imitation of yourself: open our eyes and touch our hearts that we may see and do the things which belong to our peace. Strengthen us in the work which we have undertaken; give us wisdom, perseverance, faith and zeal; and in your own time and according to your pleasure prosper our work; for the love of your Son Jesus Christ our Lord.

Lord Shaftesbury, 1801–85

You are never tired, O Lord, of doing us good; let us never be weary of doing you service. But as you have pleasure in the well-being of your servants, let us take pleasure in the service of our Lord, and abound in your work and in your love and praise evermore.

John Wesley, 1703–91

Elders and deacons

Therefore, ye elders, be diligent in the government of the Church, which is committed to you, and the ministers of the Word. Be also, as watchmen over the house and city of God, faithful to admonish and to caution every one against his ruin; Take heed that purity of doctrine and godliness of life be maintained in the Church of God. And, ye deacons, be diligent in collecting the alms, prudent and cheerful in the distribution of the same: assist the oppressed, provide for the true widows and orphans, show liberality unto all men, but especially to the household of faith. Be ye all with one accord faithful in your offices, and hold the mystery of the faith in a pure conscience, being good examples unto all the people. In so doing you will purchase to yourselves a good degree, and great boldness in the faith, which is in Christ Jesus, and hereafter enter into the joy of our Lord. On the other hand, beloved Christians, receive these men as the servants of God: count the elders that rule well worthy of double honor, give yourselves willingly to their inspection and government. Provide the deacons with good means to assist the indigent. Be charitable, ye rich, give liberally, and contribute willingly. And, ye poor, be poor in spirit, and deport yourselves respectfully towards your benefactors, be thankful to them, and avoid murmuring: follow Christ, for the food of your souls, but not for bread. "Let him that has stolen (or who has been burdensome to his neighbors) steal no more: but rather let him labor, working with his hands the things which are good, that he may give to him that needeth." Each of you, doing these things in your respective callings, shall receive of the Lord, the reward of righteousness. But since we are unable of ourselves, let us call upon the name of the Lord saying: O Lord God and heavenly Father, we thank thee that it has pleased thee, for the better edification of thy Church, to ordain in it, besides the ministers of the Word, rulers and assistants, by whom thy Church may be preserved in peace and prosperity, and the indigent assisted; and that Thou hast at present granted us in this place, men, who are of good testimony, and we hope endowed with thy Spirit. We beseech thee, replenish them more and more with such gifts as are necessary, for them in their ministration; with the gifts of wisdom, courage, discretion, and benevolence, to the end that every one may, in his respective office, acquit himself as is becoming; the elders in taking diligent heed unto the doctrine and conversation, in keeping out the wolves from the sheepfold of thy beloved Son; and in admonishing and reproving disorderly persons. In like manner, the deacons in carefully receiving, and liberally and prudently distributing of the alms to the poor, and in comforting them with thy holy Word. Give grace both to the elders and deacons, that they may persevere in their faithful labor, and never become weary by reason of any trouble, pain or persecution of the world. Grant also especially thy divine grace to this people, over whom they are placed, that they may willingly submit themselves to the good exhortations of the elders, counting them worthy of honor for their work's sake; give also unto the rich, liberal hearts towards the poor, and to the poor grateful hearts towards those who help and serve them; to the end that every one acquitting himself of his duty, thy holy name

may thereby be magnified, and the kingdom of thy Son Jesus Christ, enlarged, in whose name we conclude our prayers, saying: Our Father which is in heaven. Hallowed be thy name. Thy kingdom come. Thy will be done in earth, as it is in heaven. Give us this day our daily bread. And forgive us our debts, as we forgive our debtors. And lead us not into temptation, but deliver us from evil: For thine is the kingdom, and the power and the glory, for ever. Amen.

Liturgy of the Reformed Church

Spiritual health

O thou God of peace, unite our hearts by thy bond of peace, that we may live with one another continually in gentleness and humility, in peace and unity. O thou God of patience, give us patience in the time of trial, and steadfastness to endure to the end. O thou spirit of prayer, awaken our hearts, that we may lift up holy hands to God, and cry unto him in all our distresses. O thou gentle wind, cool and refresh our hearts in all heat and anguish. Be our defense and shade in the time of need, our help in trial, our consolation when all things are against us. Come, O thou eternal light, salvation, comfort, be our light in darkness, our salvation in life, our comfort in death; and lead us in the straight way to everlasting life, that we may praise thee, forever.

Bernhard Albrecht, 1569–1636

Blessings and Doxologies

BLESSINGS

Unto God's gracious mercy and protection we commit you. The Lord bless you and keep you. The Lord make his face shine upon you, and be gracious to you. The Lord lift his countenance upon you, and give you peace.
Aaronic blessing, Numbers 6.24–26

May the God of hope fill you with all joy and peace in believing, so that you may abound in hope by the power of the Holy Spirit.
Romans 15.13 NRSV

May the grace of our Lord Jesus Christ,
and the love of God,
and the fellowship of the Holy Spirit,
be with you all.
2 Corinthians 13.14

Peace be to the brethren, and love with faith, from God the Father and the Lord Jesus Christ. Grace be with all them that love our Lord Jesus Christ in sincerity. Amen.
Ephesians 6.23–24 KJV

May the God of peace himself sanctify you entirely; and may your spirit and soul and body be kept sound and blameless at the coming of our Lord Jesus Christ.
1 Thessalonians 5.23 NRSV

Now may our Lord Jesus Christ himself and God our Father, who loved us and through grace gave us eternal comfort and good hope, comfort your hearts and strengthen them in every good work and word.
2 Thessalonians 2.16–17 NRSV

Now may the God of peace who brought again from the dead our Lord Jesus, the great shepherd of the sheep, by the blood of the eternal covenant, equip you with everything good that you may do his will, working in you that which is pleasing in his sight, through Jesus Christ; to whom be glory for ever and ever. Amen.
Hebrews 13.20–21 RSV

Grace be with you, mercy, and peace, from God the Father, and from the Lord Jesus Christ, the Son of the Father, in truth and love.
2 John 3 KJV

To him who loves us and freed us from our sins by his blood, and made us to be a kingdom, priests serving his God and Father, to him be glory and dominion for ever and ever. Amen.
Revelation 1.5–6 NRSV

May God the Father bless us; may Christ take care of us; the Holy Spirit enlighten us all the days of our life. The Lord be our defender and keeper of body and soul, both now and for ever, to the ages of ages.
Aethelwold, c.908–984

Behold, the Cross of the Lord!
Be gone, all evil powers!
The Lion of the tribe of Judah,
The Root of David, has conquered!
Alleluia, Alleluia!
St Anthony's Blessing

May the blessing of God Almighty, the Father, the Son, and the Holy Spirit, rest on us and on all our work and worship done in his name. May he give us light to guide us, courage to support us, and love to unite us, now and for evermore.

Author unknown

Bless all who worship thee,
From the rising of the sun
Unto the going down of the same.
Of thy goodness, give us;
With thy love, inspire us;
By thy spirit, guide us;
By thy power, protect us;
In thy mercy, receive us,
Now and always.

Author unknown, 5th century

Go in peace; and may the blessing of God the Father, the Son, and the Holy Spirit rest on you and remain with you, this day (*night*) and for evermore.

Author unknown

May the love of the Father enfold us,
the wisdom of the Son enlighten us,
the fire of the Spirit inflame us;
and may the blessing of the triune God rest
    on us,
and abide with us,
now and evermore.

Author unknown

The grace of our Lord Jesus Christ, and the love of God, and the fellowship of the Holy Ghost, be with us all evermore.

Book of Common Prayer

The peace of God, which passeth all understanding, keep your hearts and minds in the knowledge and love of God, and of his Son Jesus Christ our Lord: and the blessing of God Almighty, the Father, the Son, and the Holy Ghost, be amongst you and remain with you always.

*Book of Common Prayer, The Order for Holy
Communion*

The grace of God the Father and the peace of our Lord Jesus Christ, through the fellowship of the Holy Spirit, dwell with us for ever.

John Calvin, 1509–64

The Lord bless you and keep you safe. The Lord cause his countenance to shine upon you,

and be gracious to you. The Lord turn his face toward you, and bestow upon you all prosperity. AMEN.

John Calvin, 1509–64

The grace of our Lord Jesus Christ be with you, and with all everywhere that are the called of God through Him, by whom be to Him glory, honor, power, majesty, and eternal dominion, from everlasting to everlasting. Amen.

Clement of Rome, c.30–c.95

To the Holy Spirit who sanctifies us, with the Father who made and created us, and the Son who redeemed us, be given all honor and glory, world without end.

Thomas Cranmer, 1489–1556

The everlasting Father bless us with his blessing everlasting.

Thomas Cranmer, Primer, 1559

The Lord bless you and keep you.
May he show his face to you and have mercy
    on you.
May he turn his countenance to you and give
    you peace.
The Lord bless you, Brother Leo.

*Francis of Assisi, 1181–1226. Francis'
blessing to Brother Leo, which Brother Leo
always carried with him*

May the road rise to meet you,
may the wind be always at your back,
may the sun shine warm upon your face,
may the rain fall softly on your fields,
may God hold you in the hollow of his hand.

Gaelic prayer

May God, the Lord, bless us with all heavenly
    benediction, and make us pure and holy in
    his sight.
May the riches of his glory abound in us.
May he instruct us with the word of truth,
    inform us with the gospel of salvation
    and enrich us with his love, through Jesus
    Christ, our Lord.

Gelasian Sacramentary, 5th century

The Lord bless you and save you; the Lord make his face shine upon you, and be merciful unto you; the Lord turn his countenance towards you, and grant you his peace.

The Genevan Book of Order

May the grace of the Lord Jesus sanctify us and keep us from all evil; may he drive far from us all hurtful things, and purify both our souls and bodies; may he bind us to himself by the bond of love, and may his peace abound in our hearts.

Gregorian Sacramentary, 6th century

God bless all those I love,
God bless all those that love me,
God bless all those that love those that I love
And all those that love those that love me.

Jewish Prayer

Our Father, bless us all together
With the light of Your presence.
For in the light of Your presence
You give us, Lord our God,
Law and life,
Love and kindness,
Justice and mercy,
Blessing and peace.

Jewish prayer

The great Bishop of our souls, Jesus our Lord, so strengthen and assist your troubled hearts with the mighty comfort of the Holy Spirit, that neither earthly tyrants, nor worldly torments, may have power to drive you from the hope and expectation of that kingdom, which for the elect was prepared from the beginning, by our heavenly Father, to whom be all praise and honor, now and ever.

John Knox, c.1513–72

The Almighty God and Father, replenish you all with his grace, that ye may faithfully and fruitfully discharge your respective offices. Amen.

Liturgy of the Reformed Church

May the almighty God, Father of our Savior Jesus Christ, who through his gospel is gathering an eternal church among men and women, strengthen you in body and soul, and graciously keep and guide you, world without end.

Philip Melanchthon, 1497–1560

Son of God, Lord Jesus Christ, crucified on a cross for us and raised up from the grave, to you we pray. Receive us into your eternal church and keep us always. In the light of your Word, with your Holy Spirit, guide us.

Philip Melanchthon, 1497–1560

The almighty God, Father of our Lord and Savior, Jesus Christ, mercifully protect you, strengthen you, and guide you.

Philip Melanchthon, 1497–1560

The blessing of the Lord rest and remain upon
all his people,
in every land and of every tongue;
the Lord meet in mercy all who seek him;
the Lord comfort all who suffer and mourn;
the Lord hasten his coming,
and give us his people peace by all means.

Handley C.G. Moule, 1841–1920

May the Almighty Lord, who bore the
reproach of the cross, bless all this family
present here. Amen.
May he, who hung on the tree, himself lead us
to the heavenly kingdom. Amen.
May he place us at the right hand of the
Father, who was made the cause of our
peace. Amen.
Through the mercy of our God, who is
blessed and reigns, and governs all things,
world without end.

Mozarabic Breviary

May Christ the Lord, who brought back the
lost sheep on his shoulders to heaven,
cleanse you from the stain of sin. Amen.
May he, who forgave the sins of the crucified
robber, and restored him to paradise,
purify you from all sins, and enlighten you
with the presence of his brightness. Amen.
May he wipe away from you all guilt of sins,
and place you in the company of the
blessed. Amen.
Through the mercy of our God, who is
blessed and reigns, and governs all things,
world without end.

Mozarabic Breviary

May the infinite and glorious Trinity, the Father, the Son, and the Holy Spirit, direct our life in good works, and after our journey through this world, grant us eternal rest with the saints.

Mozarabic Liturgy, 7th century

May the grace of Christ our Savior,
And the Father's boundless love,
With the Holy Spirit's favor,
Rest upon us from above.

John Newton, 1725–1807

Go forth into the world in peace;
be of good courage;
hold fast that which is good;
render to no man evil for evil;
strengthen the fainthearted;
support the weak;
help the afflicted;
honor all men;
love and serve the Lord,
rejoicing in the power of the Holy Spirit.
And the blessing of God Almighty, the Father,
the Son, and the Holy Ghost, be upon you,
and remain with you for ever.

The Proposed Prayer Book, 1928

May the eternal God bless and keep us, guard
our bodies, save our souls, direct our
thoughts, and bring us safe to the heavenly
country, our eternal home, where Father,
Son and Holy Spirit ever reign, one God for
ever and ever.

Sarum Missal, 1085

May the love of the Lord Jesus draw us to
himself;
may the power of the Lord Jesus strengthen us
in his service;
may the joy of the Lord Jesus fill our souls.
May the blessing of God almighty, the Father,
the Son, and the Holy Spirit, be among you
and remain with you always.

*After William Temple,
1881–1944*

The power of the Father govern and protect
me.
The wisdom of the Son teach and enlighten
me.
The influence of the Holy Spirit renew and
quicken me.

The blessing of the everlasting and all-holy
Trinity be with me for evermore.
Amen.

Treasury of Devotion, 1869

May God the Father bless me;
Jesus Christ defend and keep me;
the power of the Holy Spirit enlighten me and
sanctify me,
this night and for ever.

Treasury of Devotion, 1869

The mighty God of Jacob be with you to
defeat his enemies, and give you the favor
of Joseph.
The wisdom and spirit of Stephen be with
your heart and with your mouth, and teach
your lips what to say, and how to answer
all things.
He is our God, if we despair in ourselves and
trust in him; and his is the glory.

William Tyndale, c.1491–1536

DOXOLOGIES

Now to the King eternal, immortal, invisible,
the only God, be honor and glory for ever and
ever. Amen.

1 Timothy 1.17 NIV

To God the Father, who has made us and all
the world;
to God the Son, who has redeemed us and all
mankind;
to God the Holy Spirit, who sanctifies us and
all the elect people of God;
to the one living and true God be all glory for
ever and ever.

Author unknown

Praise to the Father,
Praise to the Son,
Praise to the Spirit,
The Three in One.

Celtic prayer

Glory be to thee, O Lord, glory to thee, O holy
One, glory to thee, O King!

John Chrysostom, c.347–407

To God the Father, who first loved us, and
    made us accepted in the Beloved;
to God the Son, who loved us, and washed us
    from our sins in his own blood;
to God the Holy Ghost, who sheds the love of
    God abroad in our hearts:
to the one true God be all love and all glory,
    for time and eternity.

Thomas Ken, 1637–1711

Praise God, from whom all blessings flow;
Praise him, all creatures here below;
Praise him above ye heavenly host;
Praise Father, Son and Holy Ghost.

Thomas Ken, 1637–1711

To God the Father, God the Son,
And God the Spirit, Three in One,
Be honor, praise, and glory giv'n,
By all on earth, and all in heav'n.

Isaac Watts, 1674–1748

Let God the Father, and the Son,
And Spirit, be adored,
Where there are works to make him known,
Or saints to love the Lord.

Isaac Watts, 1674–1748

The God of mercy be adored,
Who calls our souls from death;
Who saves by his redeeming word,
And new-creating breath.

To praise the Father, and the Son,
And Spirit, all divine,
The One in Three, and Three in One,
Let saints and angels join.

Isaac Watts, 1674–1748

Ye angels round the throne,
And saints that dwell below,

Worship the Father, praise the Son,
And bless the Spirit too.

Isaac Watts, 1674–1748

Now to the great and sacred Three,
The Father, Son, and Spirit, be
Eternal praise and glory giv'n,
Through all the worlds where God is known,
By all the angels near the throne,
And all the saints in earth and heav'n.

Isaac Watts, 1674–1748

To God the Father's throne
Perpetual honors raise,
Glory to God the Son,
To God the Spirit praise:
With all our powers,
Eternal King,
Thy name we sing,
While faith adores.

Isaac Watts, 1674–1748

Bless us, O God the Father, who has created
    us.
Bless us, O God the Son, who has redeemed
    us.
Bless us, O God the Holy Spirit, who sanctifies
    us.
O Blessed Trinity, keep us in body, soul, and
    spirit to everlasting life.

Weimarishches Gesangbuch, 1873

Glory be to you, O God, the Father, the Maker
    of the world:
Glory be to you, O God, the Son, the
    Redeemer of humankind:
Glory be to you, O God, the Holy Spirit, the
    Sanctifier of your people.

F.B. Westcott, 1825–1901

Children's Prayers and Young People's Prayers

Young people's prayers

GOD FIRST
OTHERS NEXT
ME LAST
MY LIFE

Related entries in Part Two

Extracts of classic Christian teaching on prayer

John Bunyan: Temporal Things Spiritualized
William Scribner: Praying for Your Children

Stories about prayer and people who prayed
Author unknown: Praying hands

Helping children to pray
Author unknown: Fingers of Prayer

Children's prayers

LEARNING AND LISTENING

How to pray: the Lord's Prayer

The Lord's Prayer
Our Father in heaven,
May your name be honored,
Your kingdom come,
Your will be done,
On earth as it is in heaven.
Give us this day our daily bread.
Forgive us our sins
As we forgive the sins of others.
And lead us not into temptation,
But deliver us from evil.
For yours is the kingdom,
The power and the glory,
For ever and ever. Amen.

The Bible

As I read the Bible
Dear Lord, open my eyes that I may see
the wonderful truths in the pages of the Bible.
Amen.

Based on Psalm 119.18

Read and learn
Dear Lord,
you inspired all the Bible
    to be written for us to read;
each time we come to the Bible
    help us to:
    listen to your voice,
    read,
    note,
    learn,
    and take your message
    to our hearts,
so that we may love you
    as our Savior.
Amen.
    Based on a prayer from the Book of Common Prayer

Reading the Bible
When I listen to Bible stories,
dear Lord, help me to understand
what you are saying to me.
All my life help me to enjoy
hearing and reading the Bible.
Amen.

No Bibles
[In some countries no one is allowed to buy or
sell the Bible. If people can get a Bible they read
it secretly.]

Please help these people, dear Lord,
to be brave.
Keep them safe.
Help people who long to have Bibles
to get hold of copies.
Amen.

God speaks

Guide me

Guide me in your truth and teach me,
for you are my God and Savior.
My hope is in you all the day long.

From Psalm 25

PRAISING

I love you, O Lord

I love you, O Lord, my strength.
The Lord is my rock.
The Lord is my deliverer.
My God is my rock who keeps me totally safe.
Amen.

From Psalm 18

God is so great

I praise you, Lord,
you are very great.
You make springs flow down the
    mountainsides.
They give water to all the animals.

Based on Psalm 104

I will praise you

I will praise your greatness,
    my God and king;
I will praise your name for ever and ever.
Every day I will praise you:
I will speak about your greatness for ever and
    ever.
The Lord is great and worthy of being highly
    praised;
His greatness no one can understand.

From Psalm 145

A prayer sung in heaven

Our Lord and God!
You are worthy to receive glory,

honor, and power.
For you created all things,
and by your will
they were given existence and life.
Amen.

From Revelation 4

Fill my life

Please fill my life, O Lord my God,
    In every part with praise,
That my who being may proclaim,
    Your being and your ways.

Based on Horatius Bonar,
1808–82

The earth

For the beauty of the earth,
For the beauty of the skies,
For the love which from our birth
Over and around us lies,
    Christ, our God, to thee we raise
    This our sacrifice of praise.

F. S. Pierpoint, 1835–1917

Beauty

For the beauty of each hour
Of the day and of the night,
Hill and vale and tree and flower,
Sun and moon and stars of light,
    Christ, our God, to thee we raise
    This our sacrifice of praise.

F. S. Pierpoint, 1835–1917

The future

How good is the God we adore,
Our faithful, unchangeable Friend.
We'll praise him for all that is past
And trust him for all that's to come.

J. Hart, 1712–68

The wonderful world

Lord God,
You have made such a wonderful world:
bright stars, towering mountains,
rushing rivers,
and deep, deep seas.
We sing your praises
for your wonderful world.

Based on a 3rd-century
Egyptian prayer

THANKING

For God's love

A big thank you
Almighty God, Father of all mercies,
we your unworthy servants
do give you most humble and hearty thanks
for all your goodness
and loving-kindness to us,
and to all people.
Amen.

*Part of Edward Reynolds's prayer
called the General Thanksgiving*

Starting again
Dear Father God,
thank you for our great love.
When I do wrong things,
and am sorry – you forgive me.
You forget all about the wrong things
and you help me to start again.
Amen.

The Lord's love
Thank you, Lord,
because you are good.
Your love lasts for ever.
Amen.

Based on Psalm 107.1

Sunshine in place of clouds
Dear heavenly Father,
thank you for forgiving me
the wrong things I have done,
when I am then really sorry.
I sometimes feel that the bad things
I do are like big clouds
between you and me.
Thank you for sweeping away
these clouds so I feel
the warmth of your love,
like sunshine.
Amen.

God's child
Heavenly Father,
Thank you that you are *my* Father,
Thank I am your child,
And that you love me.
Amen.

For Jesus

Jesus loves me
Jesus loves me! This I know,
For the Bible tells me so.
Little ones to Him belong;
They are weak, but He is strong.

Refrain:
Yes, Jesus loves me!
Yes, Jesus loves me!
Yes, Jesus loves me!
The Bible tells me so.

Jesus loves me! This I know,
As He loved so long ago,
Taking children on His knee,
Saying, "Let them come to Me."
Refrain

Jesus loves me still today,
Walking with me on my way,
Wanting as a friend to give
Light and love to all who live.
Refrain

Jesus loves me! He who died
Heaven's gate to open wide;
He will wash away my sin,
Let His little child come in.
Refrain

Jesus loves me! He will stay
Close beside me all the way;
Thou hast bled and died for me,
I will henceforth live for Thee.
Refrain

Anna Bartlett Warner, 1827–1915

The whole world
Thank you, Lord Jesus,
for making the whole world.
Thank you that everything is under your
        control.
        And we can trust you each day.
Amen.

Every country
Dear Lord Jesus,
thank you, for your great love,
that you love everyone,

in every country,
in all the world.
Amen.

Being happy with Jesus
Dear Lord Jesus,
Just being with you,
Makes me most wonderfully happy.
Thank you
That I can talk to you in prayer,
At any time in the day,
And whenever I wake up at night.
Amen.

Going to school
When I wake up in the morning
    thank you, Jesus, for being there.
When I go to school each day,
    thank you, Jesus, for being there.
When I'm playing with my friends,
    thank you, Jesus, for being there.
Amen.

The Bethlehem baby
Dear Lord Jesus,
how wonderful that you were born
    as a baby in Bethlehem,
how wonderful that you grew up
    as a boy in Nazareth.
Thank you for being like one of us.
Thank you that you know all about
    falling over and tears.
Thank you that you know all about
    happy days and laughing.
Thank you that we can talk to you
    about everything.
Thank you that you understand
    about everything.
Amen.

For the Bible

Bible translators
Thank you, Lord Jesus, for all the people who
have translated the Bible into English and into
other languages. Please help Bible translators
and Bible teachers today. Help them to be
patient. Give them understanding to choose
the right words.
Amen.

A lamb
Thank you, Father,
that the Bible is like a lamp to my feet,
and a light to my path.
It shows me how I ought to live.
Amen.

Based on Psalm 119

Thank you for the Bible
Dear Father God, thank you for the Bible.
Thank you for its stories,
    its poems and songs.
Thank you that it teaches us about you.
Amen.

For animals and nature

Thank you
Lord God, sometimes in the Bible
animals were your servants.
    The big fish rescued Jonah.
    Balaam's donkey saw an angel,
and spoke to his master.
    Jesus rode a donkey into Jerusalem.
Thank you for all the animals who
    help us,
    protect us,
    and love us.
Thank you for
sheep dogs,
    guide dogs,
    horses,
    donkeys, and
    elephants.
Amen.

My pet
Dear Lord Jesus,
thank you for my pet, …
Thank you for all the hours
we spend together,
and for all the joy …
brings to me.
Amen.
(*Say your pet's name in the blanks.*)

My pet
Dear Jesus,
I just love my pet,
who's always there,

full of life,
letting me care.
Thank you, Lord Jesus.
Amen.

Puddles

Dear Lord God,
    For rain and puddles,
we thank you.
    For conkers and blackberries in hedges,
we thank you.
    For ladybirds,
we thank you.
    For snowflakes and snowballs,
we thank you.
    For … (*add your own things …*)
Amen.

The park

Thank you, Lord Jesus,
        for the park:
    for the trees and flowers,
    and the long grassy slopes.
But most of all
    thank you for the ducks on the lake.
Amen.

The sun

Lord God,
we thank you for the earth, our home:
for the wide sky and shimmering sun,
for the salt sea and running water,
for the everlasting hills
and the endless winds,
for all the trees and all the grass.
Give us hearts wide open to all your beauty.
Amen.

Based on a prayer by Walter
Rauschenbusch, 1861–1918

The Lord's kindness

Let us thank God with our mind,
Praise the Lord, for he is kind,
Chorus:
    For his mercies will endure,
    Ever faithful, ever sure.

Based on John Milton,
1608–74

For good things

Count your blessings

Count your blessings, name them one by one,
Count your blessings, see what God hath
    done!
Count your blessings, name them one by one,
And it will surprise you what the Lord hath
    done.

Johnson Oatman, Jr.,
1856–1922

Jubilate deo

Jubilate deo, jubilate deo.
Alleluia.

Author unknown

Apple seed

The Lord is good to me,
And so I thank the Lord
For giving me the things I need
The sun, the rain and the apple seed
The Lord is good to me.

And every seed that grows
Will grow into a tree.
And one day soon
There'll be apples there,
For everyone in the world to share,
The Lord is good to me.

"Johnny Appleseed",
John Chapman, 1774–1845

Variety

Dear Lord Jesus,
thank you for making all the people
in the world to be so different
from each other.
All the different languages,
all the different foods,
all the different ways of living,
all the different kinds of faces.
Thank you, Lord Jesus,
for the wonderful variety in your world.
Amen.

Singing

Dear Lord Jesus,
thank you that I can sing songs and choruses,
and so tell you how much I love you.
Amen.

Good news

Dear Lord Jesus,
I want to laugh and dance and sing –
I want to jump and twirl and spring
Up into the air – and right down.
I want to grin and act the clown –
I want to come to you and pray.
With all my heart I want to say:
Thank you for the news –
The good news we've heard today.
Amen.

Fun days at school

Heavenly Father,
often it's fun at school.
It's fun:
   – finding out about new things,
   – doing experiments,
   – singing,
   – learning to do sums and read,,
   – playing games,
   – painting and making models,
   – hearing stories.
Thank you for school.
Amen.

Thankful hearts

We thank you, then, our Father
for all thing bright and good;
the seed-time and the harvest,
our life, our health, our food:
accept the gifts we offer
for all your love imparts;
and that which you most welcome
our humble, thankful hearts.

M. Claudius, 1740–1815

Pancakes

Cooking:
Mix a pancake.
Stir a pancake.
Pop it in the pan.
Fry the pancake.
Toss the pancake.
Catch it if you can!
Thank you, Lord Jesus,
for all the fun I have
trying to cook.
Amen.

*Based on Christina Rossetti,
1830–94*

All things

Thank you, Lord Jesus,
for giving us so many things
to enjoy each day.

Based on words of St Paul

TV

Dear Lord Jesus, I love to watch TV:
   – the stories
   – the cartoons
   – the songs.
Thank you for all the people
who make the programmes.
Amen.

Books

Thank you, Lord Jesus, for books:
   – for their pictures,
   – for their stories,
   – for their poems,
   – for science books,
   – for nature books,
   – for information books.
And thank you for your book
   – the Bible
   where I learn about you.
Amen.

Today's inventions

Heavenly Father, thank you for modern
      inventions:
   – for computers,
   – for spaceships,
   – for new medicines.
May they be used wisely
to help everyone.
Amen.

Toys

Heavenly Father,
I love playing with all my toys.
Thank you for giving me
      eyes to see them,
      hands to arrange them,
      and imagination to have such fun.
Amen.

Being thankful

Lord Jesus,
thank you for all the gifts
your keep on giving us.

Give us one more thing –
a grateful heart. Amen.

Based on George Herbert, 1593–1633

For birthdays

Alleluia, Amen.
Alleluia, Amen.
Alleluia, Alleluia,
Alleluia, Amen.

Author unknown, sung to "Happy birthday"

ASKING

For forgiveness

The Jesus prayer
Lord Jesus Christ, Son of God,
have mercy on me, a sinner.
Amen.

Saying sorry
Dear Lord Jesus,
I'm sorry that I don't always
want to say, "Sorry."
Please help me to be loving,
and forgiving, as you are.
Amen.

My bad temper
Dear Father God,
I got into a bad temper today,
and then I sulked.
I'm sorry.
Amen.

Please forgive us
Dear Lord Jesus,
we are sorry that we have done
    what we should not have done.
We are sorry that we have not done
    what we should have done.
Please forgive us.
And help us to please you tomorrow.
Amen.

For family and friends

Bless my parents
Heavenly Father, bless my parents and all
those who love and care for me. Help me in
all ways to be respectful and obedient to them
according to Your will. Send down upon me
Your grace to perform all my duties carefully
and faithfully, to avoid unacceptable company
and influence and to resist all temptation
that may come my way. Help me Lord to live
a serious, good and godly life, praising You
constantly and glorifying Your holy Name.
Amen.

Orthodox prayer

Paul prays for his friends
I pray that you and all God's holy people will
be able to understand the greatness of Christ's
love.
I pray that you can understand
    how wide and
    how long and
    how high and
    how deep
that love is.
Amen.

From Ephesians 3.18

Joy from hope
May the God of hope
fill you with all joy and peace
as you trust in him,
so that you may overflow with hope
by the power of the Holy Spirit.
Amen.

Romans 15.13

When I'm greedy
Dear Jesus,
sometimes I'm greedy.
I want too much
and I grab things for myself.
I'm sorry.
Please help me to share
and to give
and to think of others.
Amen.

My Mum and Dad
Dear heavenly Father,

sometimes my Mum and Dad are so busy,
and they have such a lot to do.
Please help them.
Amen.

Home
Dear heavenly Father,
thank you for my home and family.
Please may your love be always with us,
Please may your care always protect us,
Please may your peace always surround us.
Amen.

A special "thank you"
Dear heavenly Father,
thank you especially for …
(Add your own name or names)
who always loves me,
who always has time to listen to me,
and play with me;
who always wants to help me,
and understands when I'm sad.
Amen.

For other people

People who need love
Dear Father,
I pray for those who have no one
to love them enough to pray for them.
Wherever they are,
whoever they are,
let them know that they are not forgotten.
Amen.

Francis of Assisi, 1181–1226

Disabled people
Dear Lord Jesus,
you made blind people see,
    lame people walk,
    deaf people hear.
Please specially help all people today
who can't see or hear or move about.
Give them patience, and peace,
and trust in you.
And help the rest of us to understand
how hard it is to be disabled.
Amen.

School teachers
Thank you, Lord Jesus,
for all our school teachers.
Please give them lots of patience
and lots of good ideas as they teach us.
Amen.

Refugees
Dear Lord Jesus, when you were a baby,
    You and Mary and Joseph were refugees.
When you were grown up
    you had no home of your own.
Dear Lord Jesus, be with all refugees
    and homeless people today.
Help them to find homes of their own.
And be with all people working to help
    homeless people and refugees.
Amen.

The lonely
Dear Lord Jesus,
we thank you for your promise:
"I will never leave you."
Please may lonely people
know that you are with them.
Amen.

The weak and tired
We bring before you, Lord God,
the troubles of people and nations;
the sighing of prisoners,
the sorrows of the bereaved,
the helplessness of the weak,
the feebleness of the old.
Lord God, be close to each of them.
Amen.

Based on a prayer of Anselm, 1033–1109

Healers
Thank you, Lord Jesus, for all people who are
    healers,
all the doctors and nurses,
and everybody who works in hospitals:
and for all the people who find
    new medicines and cures.
Please make them wise and loving.
Amen.

Justice
Heavenly Father, please be with all rulers and
    all judges in courts of law, all juries, all

lawyers and solicitors, and all people who
make laws.
Please help them to make wise and fair laws,
and to make good decisions.
Amen.

Persecuted people

Lord Jesus, we pray for people who are in
prison in some countries just because they
believe in you.
Please comfort them in prison.
Help Amnesty International and other
organizations who work to free people
who are in prison for standing up for what
is right and true.
Amen.

People at work

Dear Lord, we pray for all the people who
work in towns
and help to keep them going:
postmen and policewomen,
bus drivers and train drivers,
collectors of rubbish and street cleaners,
and supermarket staff.
Thank you for all the people who work
so hard so we can enjoy each day.
Amen.

Sick people

Care for your sick people,
dear Lord Jesus.
Rest your tired people,
dear Lord Jesus.
Comfort your dying people,
dear Lord Jesus.
Amen.
   Based on a prayer of Augustine of Hippo, 354–430

Wars

Dear Lord God, There are so many wars all
over the world.
Please help people to stop hating and killing.
Help them to listen to each other
and to understand each other's problems
and to work for peace.
Amen.

Some people

There are some people, Lord Jesus,
I don't like very much.

I don't feel happy
when I'm with them.
But you love them.
Please may they know your love.
Please help them.
Amen.

For planet earth

For bikes and trucks

For bikes and trucks and trains,
For buses and for planes,
For barges, yachts and boats –
For everything that floats –
And rockets off to stars –
For tractors and for cars –
Thank you, Lord.
Help travelers to keep safe –
and obey the rules and not get angry.
Amen.

Our world

Thank you, Lord Jesus, for making our
wonderful world.
Please help me to care for your world,
for the animals, for the trees,
and for the fish and the birds.
And please help us to love
the people in your world.
Amen.

For animals and birds

Animals

Let us thank God who does feed
all living creatures in their need.
Chorus:
for his mercies will endure,
ever faithful, ever sure.
   Based on John Milton, 1608–74

Insects and fish

Father God, you made our earth as a home
for:
– animals,
– birds,
– reptiles,
– insects,
– and fish,

– as well as for people.
And you told us to take care of the animals.
Please be with all farmers, scientists, vets,
zoo-keepers and circus trainers.
Help everybody to be kind to animals,
and treat them well.
Amen.

For myself

GOOD AND BAD TIMES

My pet has died
Dear Lord Jesus,
my pet had died.
You know how much
I loved, and loved him/her.
Thank you for his/her life
and all the loving days
and happy times we had together.
Amen.

I'm fed up
Dear Lord Jesus,
everything seems to be going wrong today.
I feel so fed up.
Help me to think about you,
and about your love,
and to be happy again.
Amen.

Away from home
I'm here away from home,
Lord Jesus, help me.
I am here in need,
Lord Jesus, help me.
I am here in pain,
Lord Jesus, help me.
I am here in trouble,
Lord Jesus, help me.
I am here alone,
Lord Jesus, help me.
Amen.

From a Celtic prayer

Happy days
For all the things that make me happy:
    – for adventures in the wind and rain,
    – for going head-over-heels on the grass,
dear Lord Jesus, thank you.
Amen.

It's not fair
Dear Lord Jesus, things seem so unfair!
Sometimes I feel as if
    I never get wheat I want,
    but every body else does.
Help me not to mind.
Help me to remember that
    you love me
    and give me all I need
    when I feel like this.
Amen.

You made her well
Dear Lord Jesus,
when a young girl was very ill
    you went to her,
    held her hand
    and made her well again.
Dear Lord Jesus,
I feel so sick today –
    please make me well again.
Thank you for being with me.
Thank you for loving me.
Amen.

Going to Jesus
When things are tough at school
    help me to trust you,
    Lord Jesus.
When everything goes wrong,
    help me to trust you,
    Lord Jesus.
When I feel very, very sad
    help me to trust you,
    Lord Jesus.
Amen.

My work at school
Dear Lord Jesus, sometimes my work at
    school
seems so hard to do.
Help me to do my best,
and trust you,
even when I can't do everything.
Amen.

Holidays
Tomorrow is our holiday!
Three cheers – hurrah!
    Hurrah!
    Hurrah!

I'm so excited – I can't sit still.
I'm so happy – I'm nearly ill!
Dear Lord Jesus, I've come to say,
Please take care of us on our holiday.
Amen.

When I'm afraid

Even when I go through the worst difficulties,
I will not be afraid, Lord Jesus,
for you are with me.

From Psalm 23

Jesus listens

Lord Jesus,
Thank you for always hearing my prayers,
Even when they are quick and short.
Thank you for hearing me,
Especially when I am sad.
Amen.

Sad times

Please give us, Lord Jesus,
    in all our difficulties, your help;
    in all our dangers, your protection;
    and in all our sad times,
your comfort.
Amen.

Based on Augustine of Hippo, 354–430

Storms

Dear Lord Jesus,
storms can be so scary.
The thunder is so loud.
The lightning is so bright.
But thunder and lightning are beautiful, too.
Your friends were scared,
in a storm at sea,
but you kept them safe.
Please keep me and my family
safe in storms.
Amen.

Dogs

Dear Lord Jesus,
sometimes I get scared of dogs.
Little dogs are so bouncy and yappy.
Big dogs are so tall.
Their barks are so loud.
They growl.
They have sharp teeth.
But I know you are with me.

When I see a dog,
help me to stop being frightened.
Amen.

Sharing my sadness

Thank you, Lord Jesus,
for sharing my sadness.
Thank you, Lord Jesus,
that you know all about me.
Amen.

Worries

Dear Lord Jesus, please help me, when I'm
    afraid,
and when I lie in bed at night, full of worries.
Amen.

SCHOOLDAYS

Heavenly Father, hear our prayer,
Keep us in Thy loving care,
Guard us through the live long day,
In our work and in our play.
Keep us pure and sweet and true,
In everything we say and do.

Author Unknown

Sticking up for Jesus

Dear Lord Jesus,
Help me to stand up for you at school.
Help me not to let you down by anything I say
    or do.
Help me not to be ashamed of praying to you
    or going to church.
Amen.

Difficult lessons

When my lessons are hard and I don't understand the teacher,
please help me, Lord Jesus.
Please be my guide and teacher as I learn.
Amen.

The ant

The tiny, busy ant works like crazy.
Like the ant, help me,
Lord Jesus, to be never lazy.

Based on Proverbs 6.6

My memory

Lord Jesus, please help me in all the tests and
    exams I have,

especially when I'm upset or
worried about them.
Please help me to enjoy all my work
and please give me a good memory.
Amen.

Feeling alone at school
Lord Jesus, sometimes I'm lonely at school.
The other children leave me out of their
    teams.
Help me to remember that you are my best
    friend.
You are with me in the playground.
You are sitting next to me at my desk.
Amen.

Strength
I have so much to get through today, Lord
    Jesus.
Please help me to do everything
in the strength you give me.
Amen.

In charge of my mind
Lord and Savior, true and kind,
Be the Master of my mind.
Bless and guide and strengthen still
All my powers of thought and will.
Amen.

Handley C.G. Moule, 1841–1920

If I forget you
Lord, you know how busy I will be today.
If I forget you,
Please do not forget me.
Amen.

Based on Jacob Astley, 1579–1652

School!
Dear heavenly Father, sometimes I don't want
    to go to school.
I don't want to leave my Mum, my toys, my
    pet.
Thank you that you have said,
"I will never leave you."
Please help me at school.
Amen.

See Hebrews 13.5

LOOKING AT JESUS

Christmas

What can I give?
What can I give you,
    Poor as I am?
If I were a shepherd,
    I would bring a lamb.
If I were a wise man
    I would do my part.
Yet what I can I give you –
    Give my heart.

Christina Rossetti, 1830–94

Stay with us
O holy child of Bethlehem,
    Come down to us we pray.
Cast out our sin and enter in,
    Be born in us today.
We hear the Christmas angels
    The great glad tidings tell,
O come to us, abide with us,
    Our Lord Immanuel.

Phillip Brooks, 1835–93

Come to my heart
You did leave your throne and your kingly
    crown,
When you came to earth for me:
But in Bethlehem's home there was found no
    room
For your holy nativity.
O come to my heart, Lord Jesus.
There is room in my heart for you.

E.E.S. Elliott

The joy of the angels
May the joy of the angels,
And the peace of the Lord Jesus,
Fill our hearts
At this Christmas time.
Amen.

Jesus' life

The Jesus story
Dear Lord Jesus, I love hearing about
all you said and all you did.

Thank you for my Bible
and my teachers at church.
Amen.

The miracles of Jesus
Thank you, Lord Jesus, for all your miracles:
like when the wind and the waves
were about to drown
your followers in their boat
and you calmed the sea.
Help me to trust you
whenever I am in danger.
Amen.

The children and Jesus
Dear Lord Jesus, I am so happy to know
that you took children
into your arms,
showed your love for them,
and blessed them
when you met them.
Please be with me
all through this day.
Amen.

Easter

I think about the cross
It is a thing most wonderful –
    Almost too wonderful to be –
That God's own Son should come from
   heaven
     And die to save a child like me.

And yet I know that it is true:
    He came to this poor world below,
And wept and toiled, and mourned and died,
    Only because he loved us so.

I sometimes think about the cross,
    And shut my eyes, and try to see
The cruel nails, and crown of thorns,
    And Jesus crucified for me.

And yet I want to love you, Lord,
    Help me to grow and grow in grace,
That I may love you more and more,
    Until I'm with you, face to face.
W.W. How, 1823–97

Easter
Thank you, Lord Jesus, for Easter:
   – for Easter eggs,
   – for Easter holidays,
but most of all,
   that you are alive for ever
   and with us every day.
Amen.

Easter Day
Dear Lord Jesus,
I am so happy because you did not stay dead.
On Easter Sunday
   you came alive again.
And you are alive today
   and for ever.
Amen.

Jesus my friend

With all my heart
Dear Lord Jesus, I love you with all my heart.
Thank you for loving me
   with all your heart.
Amen.

My best friend
Dear Lord Jesus,
thank you,
   that you are my best friend.
Thank you,
   that you never stop loving me.
Amen.

Jesus in heaven

When I die
Dear Father God,
thank you for promising
that all your friends will be in heaven,
with you and with Jesus,
after this life.
Amen.

The dying
Thank you, Lord Jesus, that you have already
   prepared a place
in heaven for each of us who trust you.
Please help those people who are soon to die

to know that they can live with you for ever
and ever.
Amen.

All God's people
Dear heavenly Father, thank you that in heaven
we will be with you,
and we'll meet up with all your other friends.
Amen.

Preparing a place
Lord Jesus,
you have told us that you are preparing a
place for us in heaven;
prepare us also for that happy time,
that where you are
we may be with you always.
Amen.

Based on a prayer by William Penn, 1644–1718

The dying thief
Dear Lord Jesus, thank you that you said
to the thief
who trusted in you as he died,
"Today you will be with me in paradise."
Amen.

From the Bible, Luke 23.43

Like Jesus' followers
Lord Jesus,
thank you that heaven is such a wonderful
place,
where all your followers who have died
now sing your praises.
Amen.

With Jesus, for ever
Dear Lord Jesus,
you have told us that
one day you will come again
as a great king
with your angels.
We can't wait to be with you,
and with everyone who loves you,
all together, forever.
Amen.

A new heaven
Dear Lord Jesus, we are so looking forward
to being with you in heaven.

Thank you for telling us
that in heaven there is:
– no more crying,
– no more pain,
– no more dying,
– and no more sadness,
as all these things will have gone.
Amen.

Based on the Bible, Revelation 21.1, 4

THE HOLY SPIRIT

With us
Dear heavenly Father, when Jesus went to
heaven
you sent your Holy Spirit
to be with us.
Your Spirit is the same
as Jesus being with us.
Thank you that your Spirit
is here to help us all the time.
Amen.

Rule our hearts
Lord God,
Without you
We are not able to please you;
Please may your Holy Spirit
Guide us in everything we do
And be in charge of our hearts.
Amen.

Based on a prayer from the Book of Common Prayer

Holy Spirit
Holy Spirit, hear me
When I kneel to pray.
Come to me and teach me
What I ought to say.

From a hymn by W.H. Parker, 1845–1929

JESUS' FRIENDS: THE CHURCH

Sunday
Thank you, Lord Jesus, for our Sundays.
They are always such great days.
Thank you for the church
I go to in the mornings and
for all the friends I meet there.

Thank you that I am at home
in the evenings with my family.
Amen.

Sunday school
Thank you, Lord Jesus, for my Sunday school
    and church club
and for all the times when we learn about you.
Amen.

Missionaries
Thank you, Lord Jesus, for people who have
    gone
        to other countries
        to tell others about you.
Please help them when their work is tough.
Please support them when people laugh at
    them.
Please encourage them when they feel like
    giving up.
Amen.

God's family
Thank you, heavenly Father, that everyone
    who loves you
belongs to your family – the Church.
Amen.

Love to keep us close
May the Lord Jesus give us
    light to guide us.
May the Lord Jesus give us
    courage to support us.
May the Lord Jesus give us
    love to keep us close together.
Amen.

The world
Dear Lord Jesus, it's so great
    that your followers are everywhere:
    – in sleepy villages
    – in busy towns
    – and in tall skyscrapers.
Please give your strength
    to your followers
    who feel lonely.
Amen.

Together
Dear Father God,
there are so many different churches,

and so many differing ways
of showing love to you.
Help the people in your churches
    to pray together
    and work together,
    and show your love all the time.
Amen.

Stand up for Jesus
Dear Lord Jesus,
I pray now for your followers
    who are made fun of,
    who are not allowed to:
    – go to church
    – read their Bibles
    – teach children about you.
May they know that you
    are especially close to them.
Amen.

Preachers
Dear Father God, please be with
    all preachers and ministers,
    and all Sunday school teachers
    as they teach us each week.
Help all people who:
    – sing in church choirs,
    – hand out song books,
    – read the Bible out aloud,
    – and tell us stories about Jesus.
Help them to be wise and loving
    in their work for you.
Amen.

LIVING LIKE JESUS

Serving God
Teach us, good Lord, to serve you as you
    deserve,
To give and not to count the cost,
To fight and not to heed the wounds,
To toil and not to look for rest,
To work hard and not to ask for any reward
Except to know that we are doing your will.
            Based on Ignatius Loyola, 1491/1495–1556

Lead me
Father, lead me, day by day,
Always in your own sweet way.

Teach me to be pure and true
Show me what I ought to do.
Amen.

J.P. Hopps, 1834–1919

Listening to a Bible story
May the words of my mouth
and the thoughts of my heart
be acceptable to you,
O Lord, my Rock and my Redeemer.
Amen.

Psalm 19.14

Telling others
Almighty God, give me eyes to see you,
a heart to think about you,
and a life to tell others about you.
Amen.

Based on a prayer by Benedict,
480–543

Keep going
O Lord God, when you give your servants
any great matter to accomplish, grant us also
to know that it is not the beginning but the
continuing of it until it is completely finished
which brings the true glory. Through him who,
for the completing of your work, laid down his
life for us, our Redeemer, Jesus Christ.
Amen.

Based on a saying of
Francis Drake, c.1540–96

Being useful
Lord, help me to bring peace to other people;
where there is hatred, let me bring love;
where there is injury, let me bring pardon;
where there is doubt, let be bring faith;
where there is despair, let be bring light;
where there is sadness, let me bring joy …
Amen.

Author unknown, attributed to
Francis of Assisi, 1181–1226

Showing love
Dear Lord Jesus, help me to show your love
to everyone I meet today.
Amen.

Made for God
Lord God, you made us for yourself,

and our hearts are restless
until they find rest in you.
Amen.

Augustine of Hippo, 354–430

Love is
Love is patient:
Lord Jesus, make me patient.
Love is kind:
Lord Jesus, make me kind.
Love is not proud:
Lord Jesus, make me humble.
Lord Jesus, make me like you.
Amen.

The Bible, 1 Corinthians 13

Attempt great things
Lord God, help me to attempt great things for
    you,
and to expect great things from you.
Amen.

Based on a prayer by
William Carey, 1761–1834

Love for everyone
Dear Lord Jesus,
Please may I have your love in my heart today:
Your love for everyone I speak to,
Your love even for the people I don't like.
And most of all, may I have love for you.
Amen.

The gift of love
Dear Lord,
you have told us that everything we do
is no good,
unless it is done in love
with the Spirit of Jesus
in our lives and hearts.
Give us this most wonderful gift of love.
Amen.

My hands, Jesus' hands
Jesus' hands were kind hands,
    doing good to all.
Healing pain and sickness,
    blessing children small:
Washing tired feet,
    and saving those who fall:
Jesus' hands were kind hands,
    doing good to all.

Faith, hope, love

Give me, good Lord, complete faith,
strong hope,
and lots of love.
Amen.

From Thomas More, 1478–1535

Unkind thoughts

Heavenly Father, I know you hate it
when I say unkind words,
when I do unkind things,
when I think unkind thoughts.
Please help me to be kind today.
Amen.

Like Jesus

Father God, you have made us;
Lord Jesus, you have forgiven us.
Please help us to be more like you
    in our thinking
    and in everything we do.
Amen.

Helping

Dear Lord Jesus,
when I'm asked to help at school,
or at church,
may I do it as if I'm doing it for you.
Amen.

Listening

Speak, Lord, for your servant hears.
Grant us ears to hear,
Eyes to see,
Wills to obey,
Hearts to love.
Amen.

Christina Rossetti, 1830–94

LIVING WITH JESUS

Comfort

Dear Lord Jesus, as I get older,
    some things frighten me more and more.
Please stay next to me
    throughout all my life.
Amen.

Journeys

Please keep us as we travel today, Lord Jesus.

Thank you for the excitement of getting ready
    for a journey.
Help us to remember that you come with us
    as we go.
Please bring us back home, safe and well.
Amen.

Christ beside me

Christ be with me, Christ within me.
Christ behind me, Christ before me.
Christ beside me, Christ to win me.
Christ to comfort me, and restore me.
Christ beneath me, Christ above me.
Christ to quiet me, Christ in danger.
Christ in hearts of all that love me.
Christ in mouth of friend and stranger.

From Breastplate of Patrick, translated by
C.F. Alexander, 1823–95

Praying

Dear heavenly Father, I'm so happy
that I can talk to you in prayer
– anywhere – at home, in school,
or walking along the road.
Amen.

Never leave me

Never leave me, nor forsake me,
    Always be my friend.
I need you from life's beginning,
    To its end.

Based on W.J. Mathams,
1842–1906

The Spirit of Jesus

Dear Lord Jesus, I'm so glad that you are with
    me,
        with your Spirit,
        the Holy Spirit.
Help me to live in such a way
    that I never make you sad.
Amen.

All our moments

Lord Jesus, always with us stay,
Make all our moments calm and bright,
Chase the dark night of sin away,
Spread through the world your holy light.

Translated from 12th-century Latin
by Ray Palmer, 1808–87

Hand in hand with Jesus
Dear Lord Jesus,
we put our hands
in your hand,
as we travel with you each day.
> *Based on a prayer by Augustine of Hippo, 354–430*

Friend of little children
Jesus, friend of little children,
  Be a friend to me.
Take my hand and always keep me
  Close to you.
> *Based on W. J. Mathams, 1842–1906*

Christmas
Be near me, Lord Jesus, I ask you to stay
Close by me for ever, and love me, I pray.
Bless all the dear children in your tender care,
And fit us for heaven to live with you there.
> *Martin Luther, 1483–1546*

Seeing
Lord,
make me see your glory
in every place.
Amen.
> *Michelangelo, 1475–1564*

MEAL TIMES

See also: Daily Prayers: Prayers for meals

Said graces

Food
For the Lord's service
Bless, O Lord, this food to our use
and ourselves in your service,
through Jesus Christ our Lord.
Amen.
> *Author unknown*

Bless O Lord this food to our use,
And give us thankful hearts,
Through your grace and mercy.
Amen.
> *Author unknown*

Dear Lord, thank you for this gift of food
You've placed upon our table.

And help us all to do your work
In any way we're able.
> *Author unknown, traditional children's grace*

Thank you
For every cup and plateful,
Lord, make us truly grateful.
Amen.
> *Author unknown*

Daily food
For health and strength and daily food,
We praise your name, our Lord.
Amen.
> *Author unknown*

God bless us
God bless us. (hands on head)
God bless the food. (hands around plate)
Amen. (hands folded)
> *Author unknown, traditional grace*
> *with hand movements*

God is great and God is good,
And we thank him for our food;
By his hand we must be fed,
Give us, Lord, our daily bread. Amen.
> *Author unknown*

God is great, God is good.
Let us thank him for our food. By his hands,
  we are fed.
Let us thank him for our bread.
Amen.
> *Author unknown, traditional children's grace*

God, we thank you for this food.
For rest and home and all things good.
For wind and rain and sun above.
But most of all for those we love.
> *Author unknown, traditional children's grace*

Thank the Lord, gracious Lord,
Grateful thanks to him now give,
For His truth and goodness ever, ever live.
> *Author unknown*

Daily food
Thank you, God, for rain and sun,
And all the plants that grow,
Thank you for our daily food

And friends who love us so.
Amen.

Author unknown

Bless our food and drink
God bless the poor
God bless the sick
And bless the human race.
God bless our food.
God bless our drink.
All homes, O God, embrace.

Bridget of Kildare, c.460–c.528

From the earth
Thank you, Lord God,
for bringing food from the earth
and making the hearts of your people happy.

Based on an old Jewish prayer

We thank you for our food,
Dear Jesus, kind and good.

Author unknown, traditional children's grace

We thank You for water, for sunshine, for rain,
For pineapple, taro and tall sugar cane,
For flowers and birds, for girls and for boys
For all of Your gifts, thanksgiving and joy.
Amen.

Author unknown, Hawaiian grace

Bless the creatures of the sea,
Bless this person I call me.
Bless the keys you made so grand,
Bless the sun that warms this land.
Bless the fellowship we feel,
As we gather for this meal.

The Keys Blessing

Bless our food
Come, Lord Jesus, be our guest,
And may our meal by you be blest.
Amen.

After Martin Luther, 1483–1546

For food,
For rainment,
For life,
For opportunity,
For friendship and fellowship,
We thank thee O Lord.

Philmont Grace

Strength
Bless me, dear Lord Jesus,
and let my food strengthen me
to serve you.
Amen.

Based on Isaac Watts, 1674–1748

Sung graces

Alphabet Grace
A-B-C-D-E-F-G
Thank you, God for feeding me.

Author unknown, sung to
"Twinkle twinkle little star"

Praise Ye the Lord
Allelu, Allelu, Allelu, Allelujiah
Praise ye the Lord
Allelu, Allelu, Allelu, Allelujiah
Praise ye the Lord.
Praise ye the Lord, Allelujiah
Praise ye the Lord, Allelujiah
Praise ye the Lord, Allelujiah
Praise ye the Lord

Author unknown, sung to "Praise ye the Lord"

Be Present At Our Table, Lord
Be present at our table, Lord,
Be here and everywhere adored.
These mercies bless and grant that we
May live in fellowship with Thee.

Other last lines:
May live in harmony with Thee
May feast in Paradise with Thee.
May strengthened for Thy service be.
May spend our lives in serving Thee.

Based on John Cennick, 1718–55,
sung to "Old Hundredth"

Be present here, most gracious God,
From whom all goodness springs.
Make clean our hearts, and feed our souls
On good and joyful things.

Author unknown, 1615, sung to "Dundee"

Bless our friends,
Bless our food,
Come, O Lord and sit with us.

May our talk
Glow with peace;
Come with your love to surround us.

Friendship and love
May they bloom and glow,
Bloom and glow forever.

Bless our friends,
Bless our food,
Bless all mankind forever.

> *Author unknown, traditional peace*
> *grace, sing to "Edelweiss'*

Come Lord Jesus, be our guest,
May this food by thee be blest,
May our souls by thee be fed,
Ever on the living Bread.

> *Author unknown, traditional grace,*
> *sing to "Twinkle Twinkle Little Star"*

God is great
God is great and God is good,
God is good, God is good,
Let us thank him for this food,
Alleluia.

> *Author unknown. Can be sung to*
> *the tune of "London Bridge"*

God is great, God is good,
Now we're gonna thank him for our food:
We're gonna thank him morning, noon and
   night,
We're gonna thank him cause he's out of
   sight.
Amen (chi chi chi, chi chi chi, chi chi chi)
Amen.

> *Author unknown, sing to "Rock Around the Clock"*

God is great, God is good, Alleluia
Let us thank him for our food, Alleluia.
By His hand we all are fed, Alleluia
Thank you Lord, for daily bread, Alleluia.

> *Author unknown, sing to "Michael*
> *Row The Boat Ashcre"*

Hark to the chimes,
Come bow thy head,
We thank thee, Lord,
For this good bread.

> *Author unknown, sung to "Chimes tune"*

Some have meat and cannot eat
And some have nay that want it
But we have meat and we can eat
And so the Lord we thanketh.

> *Robert Burns, 1759–96, can be*
> *sung to "Auld Lang Syne"*

GOOD MORNING PRAYERS

Grace to work

The things, good Lord, that we pray for,
give us grace to work for.
Amen.

> *Thomas More, 1478–1535*

Day by day

Day by day, dear Lord,
of you three things I pray –
to know you more clearly,
to love you more dearly,
to follow you more nearly,
day by day.
Amen.

> *Based on a prayer by Richard of*
> *Chichester, 1197–1253*

Peace

Dear Lord Jesus,
you promised your peace
to your first followers.
May I have your peace
in my life today,
and so spread peace to everyone
I meet and talk to.
Amen.

Start with me

Lord, change the world –
and begin with me.
Amen.

> *Prayer of a Chinese Christian*

Peace to others

Lord God, help me to spread a little happiness
   to all the people I meet today.
Help me to spread a little of your love
   to all the people I meet today.
Help me to spread a little peace
   to all the people I meet today.
Amen.

The power of God
I get up today with
The power of God to guide me,
The wisdom of God to teach me,
The eye of God to watch over me,
The hand of God to protect me,
And the shield of God to shelter me.
Amen.

Based on Breastplate of Patrick

Hearing
Dear Lord Jesus, when you were on earth
you spoke to your friends.
And you still speak today –
not with the voice my ears can hear,
but through:
    – the words of the Bible,
    – ideas in my mind,
    – things that happen,
    – what other people say,
    – the loving thing they do,
    – church services,
    – my pets,
    – the world you made.
Help me to hear and understand what you are
    saying.
Amen.

A new day
Thank you, Lord, for rest and sleep.
Thank you, Lord, for keeping me safe through
    the past night.
Thank you, Lord, for this new day.
Amen.

Safety
Heavenly Father, thank you for bringing us
    safely
to the beginning of this new day.
Keep us safe by your great power.
Do not let us fall into sin
or run into danger today.
Guide us in all that we do,
and help us to do what is right.
Amen.

Based on a prayer from the Book of Common Prayer

Everything I do
Teach me, Lord God,
to do everything
that I do today

as if I am doing it for you.
Amen.

George Herbert, 1593–1633

Sleep
Father God, for sleep and rest,
for morning light,
and a bright new day, thank you.
Amen.

After Henry William Baker, 1821–77

Every gift
For this new morning and its light,
For rest and shelter of the night,
For health and food, for love and friends
For every gift your good sends,
We thank you, Lord.
Amen.

Author unknown

Every day
May I remember, dear Lord,
that every day comes as a gift from you,
to be used in a way
that pleases you.
Amen.

After Samuel Johnson, 1709–1784

All good gifts
All good gifts around us
Are sent from heaven above;
Then thank the Lord, O thank the Lord,
For all his love.

Matthias Claudius, 1740–1815,
translated by J.M. Campbell

My friends
Dear Lord Jesus, thank you for all my toys
and all the games I play.
Please help me to have a happy time
as I play with my friends today.
Amen.

GOOD NIGHT PRAYERS

Matthew, Mark, Luke, and John,
Bless this bed that I lay on.
Before I lay me down to sleep,
I give my soul to Christ to keep.

Four corners to my bed,
Four angels 'round my head,
One to watch, one to pray,
And two to bear my soul away.

I go by sea, I go by land,
The Lord made me with his right hand,
If any danger come to me,
Sweet Jesus Christ, deliver me.

For he's the branch and I'm the flower,
Pray God send me a happy hour,
And if I die before I wake,
I pray the Lord my soul to take.

*Traditional children's prayer,
author unknown*

Now I lay me down to sleep,
I pray the Lord my soul to keep.
Four corners to my bed,
Four angels there aspread:
Two to foot and two to head,
And four to carry me when I'm dead.
If any danger come to me,
Sweet Jesus Christ deliver me.
And if I die before I wake,
I pray the Lord my soul to take.

*Traditional children's prayer,
author unknown*

Guard us

Save us, dear Lord, while waking,
and guard us while sleeping,
that awake we may watch with Christ
and asleep we may rest in peace.
Amen.

From Office of Compline

Bedtime prayer

Bless me Lord, this night I pray,
Keep me safe till dawn of day,
Bless my mother and my father,
Bless my sister and my brother,
Bless each little girl and boy,
Bless them all for heavenly joy.
Amen.

*Author unknown, traditional
children's bedtime prayer*

Playing

I've been playing with my best friend today,

and we've had such a great time.
Thank you, Lord Jesus.
Amen.

Loving Shepherd

Loving Shepherd of your sheep,
    May your lamb in safety sleep.
Let your angels round me stand,
    None can take me from your hand.

Based on a prayer by J. E. Leeson, 1808–82

While we sleep

Before the ending of the day,
Creator of the world, we pray,
that you with your constant care would keep
Your watch around us as we sleep.
Amen.

From the Latin, pre-8th century

God bless

The moon shines bright,
The stars give light.
God bless us all,
Both great and small.

Watch, O Lord

Watch, O Lord,
with those who wake,
or watch,
or weep tonight,
and give your angels charge
over those who sleep.
Amen.

Augustine of Hippo, 354–430

Lighten our darkness

Lighten our darkness,
Lord, we pray;
and in your great mercy defend us
from all dangers of this night,
for the love of your only Son,
our Savior, Jesus Christ. Amen.

*Based on a prayer from Evening Prayer from the
Book of Common Prayer*

Keep me safe

Lord, keep me safe this night
    and take away my fears.
May angels guard me while I sleep,
    till morning light appears.

Traditional

Fun and rest

Thank you, Lord Jesus, for the fun we have
had today.
Thank you, Lord Jesus,
for all the rest we'll enjoy tonight.
Amen.

Sleep in peace

In peace I will lie down and sleep,
For you alone, Lord,
Keep me perfectly safe.
Amen.

From Psalm 4

All through the night

Dear Father God, the nights are so dark.
There are shadows,
and noises I don't understand.
Thank you that you are
looking after me all night long.
Amen.

GOD BLESS US

God bless you

God bless all those that I love,
God bless all those that love me.
God bless all those that love those that I love,
And all those that love those that love me.
Amen.

*Words stitched on a piece of cloth,
in America, over 200 years ago*

May the Lord bless you

May the Lord bless us and take care of us:
May the Lord be kind and gracious to us:
May the Lord look on us with his favor
    and give us his peace.
Amen.

From Numbers 6

The love of Jesus

May the love of the Lord Jesus
    draw us to himself:
May the power of the Lord Jesus
    strengthen us for his service:
May the joy of the Lord Jesus
    fill our lives.
Amen.

Based on a prayer by William Temple, 1881–1944

The Lord bless you

The Lord bless you and keep you.
The Lord go with you
    to inspire and protect you.
The Lord open your ears to listen,
The Lord open your eyes to see,
The Lord open your heart to give and receive.
Amen.

In the palm of his hand

May the road rise to meet you,
May the wind be always at your back,
May the sun shine warm in your face,
The rain fall softly on your fields.
May God hold you in the palm of his hand.
Amen.

Based on a Gaelic blessing, from Ireland

The friendship of the Holy Spirit

May the grace of our Lord Jesus Christ,
the love of God,
and the friendship of the Holy Spirit,
be with us all.
Amen.

2 Corinthians 13.14

The peace of God

The peace of God, which is beyond all
    understanding,
keep our hearts and minds
in the knowledge and love of God,
and of his Son,
Jesus Christ our Lord.
Amen.

*Based on a prayer in The Book of Common
Prayer, from the 1549 Lord's Supper Service*

Bless us and keep us

May the eternal God
bless us and keep us,
protect our bodies,
save our souls,
direct our thoughts,
and bring us safely
to our home with Jesus,
to live with him for ever.
Amen.

Based on a prayer in the Sarum Breviary

Young people's prayers

GOD FIRST

Easter
A splash of color–
and you wash the morning skies.
Darkness fades.
A dash of light–
And you freshen up the earth.
Sunrise!
Lord, a new day is a marvelous thing
But life from death is something
    unimaginable.
Help me to understand
What it means
That you are alive! Alive!
Surprise me, Lord,
with the joy of the first Easter morning.

Circle me O God
Keep Faith within, Doubt out
Keep Hope within, Despair out
Keep Peace within, Anxiety out

Circle me O God
Circle me O God
Circle me O God

Author unknown

Tucked deep inside
Lord,
I remembered what you said.
I tucked your words deep inside my heart.
And just when I needed them,
there they were!
It was wonderful, Lord.
Thank you for
keeping your words in me
so that they help me
to choose the right thing.
Lord,
I will not forget your words.

See Psalm 119.1–16

Would I dance?
Would I dance?
Sure I would!
And I did.
My heart throbbed

to your rhythm, Lord,
when you asked me to dance.
Your music still plays,
and my life still sways
in praise,
my Lord,
in praise.

Rain on dry ground
Dusty land,
your air sears my throat,
burns dry the grass,
eats up my hope.
So I pray, Lord,
for rain.
In livid clouds,
in waves of storm
and rage of wind
till, heavy in silence,
the first drops hit the ground,
melt the thunder,
drum on the earth.
Rain on the dry ground,
your rain, Lord Jesus,
bringing life to my dry soul.

Feeling the wind
Lord,
everything looks beautiful,
the sun,
the birds,
the trees,
the flowers.
I feel like climbing up a hill
and running full pelt down
in the breeze
feeling the wind against my face.
What a beautiful world
you have made, Lord,
for us to enjoy.

OTHERS NEXT

Kum ba yah
Kum ba yah, my Lord, kum ba yah!
Kum ba yah, my Lord, kum ba yah!
Kum ba yah, my Lord, kum ba yah!
O Lord, kum ba yah!

Someone's laughing, Lord, kum ba yah!

Someone's laughing, Lord, kum ba yah!
Someone's laughing, Lord, kum ba yah!
O Lord, kum ba yah!

Someone's crying, Lord, kum ba yah!
Someone's crying, Lord, kum ba yah!
Someone's crying, Lord, kum ba yah!
O Lord, kum ba yah!

Someone's praying, Lord, kum ba yah!
Someone's praying, Lord, kum ba yah!
Someone's praying, Lord, kum ba yah!
O Lord, kum ba yah!

Someone's singing, Lord, kum ba yah!
Someone's singing, Lord, kum ba yah!
Someone's singing, Lord, kum ba yah!
O Lord, kum ba yah!

Kum ba yah, my Lord, kum ba yah!
Kum ba yah, my Lord, kum ba yah!
Kum ba yah, my Lord, kum ba yah!
O Lord, kum ba yah!

*Author unknown, African-American
spiritual. Kum ba yah means
"Come by here."*

Praying and loving
He prayeth well
Who loveth well
Both man and bird and beast.
He prayeth best
All things both great and small;
For the dear God
Who loveth us,
He made and loveth all.

Samuel Taylor Coleridge, 1772–1834

I cannot love millions
Lord, how do I love everybody?
Millions and millions live.
I cannot imagine them,
let alone meet them.
They must fill towns and towns.
It seems impossible to love people I can't see.
Lord,
how can I love everyone?
One,
that's it …
Help me to love each *one*;
everyone whom I meet.

Lost days
Line into line,
circle into circle;
his hands never stop moving
as he speaks.
He remembers things
I've never heard of,
and talks of a world
I'll never know.
Old, old pictures, Lord,
frayed at the edges,
are still alive in his heart,
memories of an old man
leaving a half smile
playing on his lips;
his lifetime in moments, Lord.
And the rocking chair swings,
and stiff fingers slowly fall,
and sleep is in the air.
Bless my granddad, Lord.

Life can be tough in class
Lord,
I don't know why
but school is boring.
I know my friends think so too.
Sometimes I get so bored
I get angry with the teachers.
Lord, I know I shouldn't
but … it happens,
and they always pick on me.
The others are rude too,
but they always pick on *me*.
Yeah, I know I'm to blame,
but why not someone else?
Why always me?
It's not fair …
Well, O.K., maybe it is,
but …
O Lord, please help me,
I know in my heart it's what *I* do that matters.

Life can be tough in the playground
Lord, at school
I'm bullied
because I go to church.
They pick on me and call me names.
They say I'm soft
and laugh at me.
Lord, I do believe in you.
I want to serve you,

I want to love you,
even when life is tough.
Thank you for your strength
which helps me.
Thank you for your presence
which surrounds me.
Thank you for your love
which hold me up
so that I do not fall
when life is tough.

It makes my mouth water
I wonder what it's like to be hungry,
really hungry that is.
They told us at school, Lord,
that millions are starving.
I can't imagine that.
Here,
in my town,
we just buy what we like:
cool Pepsi,
or a packet of crisps.
Oh yes, Lord—
crisps, cheese and onion flavored,
it makes my mouth water to think!
I wonder
what it's like
to be hungry, Lord.
It must be awful.
Thank you for food, Lord,
help me to have
a more grateful heart.

ME LAST

Inside myself
The skies withdraw
into the seas.
Seas melt into oceans.
All is in all, a ceaseless flow.
Lord, you know me
inside.
How I withdraw
into myself,
how I think ceaselessly about things,
how I curl up when I meet others.
Help me, Lord,

to flow outwards,
to learn to think of others,
to talk of others, to love others.
Fill me with your Spirit,
so that I overflow with you.

The color of hate
This morning, Lord,
my heart almost burst
with hate,
and the color of it crushed me:
red passion
sinking into orange,
fading into white.
Hot white,
dead white,
lifeless,
crushed.
Forgive me, Lord Jesus,
lift me up and wash me.

Love your enemies
Lord, I feel hurt inside,
and I want to kick out and scream.
Maybe he's wrong,
maybe he's right.
I don't know.
But I do know I could hurt him back.
Help me to control my anger,
help me to calm my emotions.
My heart is hard, Lord Jesus,
soften it with your still, small voice.

Cheating
I cheat, sometimes,
like Zacchaeus,
I cheat, too, Lord.
In little ways,
like not paying my bus fare,
or taking sweets from the shop.
I pretend I'm better than I am as well
and cheat myself.
Little lies turn to big lies, Lord,
little cheating will become big
if I don't stop now.
Help me, Lord Jesus,
to be like Zacchaeus
after he met you.
You changed his life,
change mine too.

See Luke 19.1–10

A creepin' up on me
He comes
A creepin' up on me.
When I least expect him,
when I'm thinking my thoughts,
when others have gone,
when I'm lying in bed,
when I'm lazing in class,
when I'm jumping for joy
and go berserk with glee–
then
sin comes a creepin' up on me,
and catches me off guard.
Lord, help me to be on guard
against temptation.

See 1 Peter 5.8

If I had a harmonica
If I had a harmonica
I'd play it to those around me
so that when they were worried
I'd bring peace.
If I had a flute
I'd play it to those around me
so that when they were depressed
I'd bring joy.
If I had a ukulele
I'd play it to those around me
so that when they were hateful
I'd bring love.
Lord, make me an instrument
of your peace, joy and love.

Violence
It's on TV, Lord,
from the news
right down through the cowboys and detectives
to Batman, even in "Tom and Jerry!"
They're all at it, Lord.
In fact there doesn't seem to be anything without it –
violence, Lord,
seems to be the way everyone talks.
Our world is violent:
countries and nations are violent,
I am violent.
Violence comes in different forms,
in actions and in words.
Forgive me, Lord Jesus, for the times
I have been violent in my treatment of others

in words or deeds.
Fill me with your gentle spirit.

MY LIFE

Dabbling with the occult
Lord, nothing can separate me from your love,
nothing *in* this world or *outside* this world,
and the devil does try
to separate us
by making ouija boards and
superstitions of all kinds look attractive.
Help me to obey you
by not getting involved with the occult.
Protect and surround me
with your presence
so that I will not dabble with this
– even in fun.

See Deuteronomy 18.11 NT 12

Yes, I do like him
To be honest, Lord,
Yes, I do like him.
And he likes me.
He hasn't actually said so
But I can tell.
He's really nice, Lord.
You'd like him!
He's kind, and helpful,
And intelligent and sporty,
and good at art –
And simply terrific at the guitar.
In fact you could say
He was re-a-lly dishy, Lord!
What do you say, Lord!
You do like him?
Oh great …
But does he like you?
Well I don't think
I mentioned that earlier, did I?
No …
One thing he did say, I forgot.
No, Lord,
He doesn't like you.
Thank you for reminding me.
Loving you is the most important
Quality that my partner must have.

Competing with others
Lord, I'm sorry

that I'm so selfish
I hate to see others do well.
I always want to be "tops"
and find it hard to be on
the losing side.
Please help me to do my best,
yet to know what my limits are.
Please help me to say, "Well done,"
to people who are better than me.
Please help me to serve you
in all that I do.

Thinking what I like
Lord,
sometimes my thoughts
stray,
they remember nasty things,
and they imagine harmful things.
Sometimes my thoughts
forget you,
they get drawn into ugly ideas,
and all that is good is forgotten.
Please help me –
help me to guide my mind,
to think of things that are pleasing to you,
things that will make me act
as if I belonged to you.

Doing what I like
Starting from today,
Lord,
I'd like to be
more thoughtful towards others.

Rules are so difficult to keep,
they seem so unnecessary,
school rules, club rules, family rules
– they are never ending.
Yet, Lord, I know that often they are
    important,
they help us to live together peacefully.
Please help me, Lord, to keep rules
and laws so that
I may be an example to others
and show that I belong to you.
I'd like to be more thoughtful towards others,
starting from today, Lord.

Saying what I like
Lord, you know how "wordy"
my tongue is so often;
so gossipy,
so twisty,
so lying,
so hurtful,
so smooth,
so flattering,
so self-important.
I use my tongue to say such awful things,
and by what I *don't* say
when I should
I harm people too.
I cannot control my tongue
but you can, Lord.
Guard my lips from
saying anything that
is displeasing to you.

Bible Prayers

Contents

OLD TESTAMENT PRAYERS

Then Jacob said, "O God of my father Abraham and God of my father Isaac, the Lord who said to me, 'Return to your country and to your family, and I will deal well with you': I am not worthy of the least of all the mercies and of all the truth which You have shown Your servant; for I crossed over this Jordan with my staff, and now I have become two companies. Deliver me, I pray, from the hand of my brother, from the hand of Esau; for I fear him, lest he come and attack me *and* the mother with the children. For You said, 'I will surely treat you well, and make your descendants as the sand of the sea, which cannot be numbered for multitude.'"

Jacob, Genesis 32.9–12 NKJV

I will sing to the Lord, for he has triumphed gloriously;
  horse and rider he has thrown into the sea.
The Lord is my strength and my might,
  and he has become my salvation;
this is my God, and I will exalt him. …
Who is like you, O Lord, among the gods?
Who is like you, majestic in holiness,
awesome in splendor, doing wonders?

Moses, Exodus 15.1–2, 11 NRSV

Moses' Intercession For His People
Then Moses returned to the Lord and said, "Oh, these people have committed a great sin, and have made for themselves a god of gold! Yet now, if You will forgive their sin – but if not, I pray, blot me out of Your book which You have written."

Moses, Exodus 32.31–32 NKJV

Then Moses said to the Lord, "See, You say to me, 'Bring up this people.' But You have not let me know whom You will send with me. Yet You have said, 'I know you by name, and you have also found grace in My sight.' Now therefore, I pray, if I have found grace in Your sight, show me now Your way, that I may know You and that I may find grace in Your sight. And consider that this nation *is* Your people."

And He said, "My Presence will go *with you*, and I will give you rest."

Then he said to Him, "If Your Presence does not go *with us*, do not bring us up from here. For how then will it be known that Your people and I have found grace in Your sight, except You go with us? So we shall be separate, Your people and I, from all the people who *are* upon the face of the earth."

So the Lord said to Moses, "I will also do this thing that you have spoken; for you have found grace in My sight, and I know you by name."

And he said, "Please, show me Your glory."

Then He said, "I will make all My goodness pass before you, and I will proclaim the name of the Lord before you. I will be gracious to whom I will be gracious, and I will have compassion on whom I will have compassion." But He said, "You cannot see My face; for no man shall see Me, and live." And the Lord said, "Here is a place by Me, and you shall stand on the rock. So it shall be, while My glory passes by, that I will put you in the cleft of the rock, and will cover you with My hand while I pass by. Then I will take away My hand, and you shall see My back; but My face shall not be seen."

Moses, Exodus 33.12–23 NKJV

So Moses made haste and bowed his head toward the earth, and worshiped. Then he said, "If now I have found grace in Your sight, O Lord, let my Lord, I pray, go among us, even though we *are* a stiff-necked people; and pardon our iniquity and our sin, and take us as Your inheritance."

Moses, Exodus 34.8–9 NKJV

So Moses cried out to the Lord, saying, "Please heal her, O God, I pray!"

Moses, Numbers 12.13 NKJV

And Moses said to the Lord: "Then the Egyptians will hear *it*, for by Your might You brought these people up from among them, and they will tell *it* to the inhabitants of this land. They have heard that You, Lord, *are* among these people; that You, Lord, are seen face to face and Your cloud stands above them, and You go before them in a pillar of cloud by day and in a pillar of fire by night. Now *if* You kill these people as one man, then the nations which have heard of Your fame will speak, saying, 'Because the Lord was not able to bring this people to the land which He swore to give them, therefore He killed them in the wilderness.' And now, I pray, let the power of my Lord be great, just as You have spoken, saying, 'The Lord is longsuffering and abundant in mercy, forgiving iniquity and transgression; but He by no means clears *the guilty,* visiting the iniquity of the fathers on the children to the third and fourth *generation.'*[£] Pardon the iniquity of this people, I pray, according to the greatness of Your mercy, just as You have forgiven this people, from Egypt even until now."

Moses, Numbers 14.13–19 NKJV

"Then I pleaded with the Lord at that time, saying: 'O Lord God, You have begun to show Your servant Your greatness and Your mighty hand, for what god *is there* in heaven or on earth who can do *anything* like Your works and Your mighty *deeds?* I pray, let me cross over and see the good land beyond the Jordan, those pleasant mountains, and Lebanon.'

Moses, Deuteronomy 3.23–25 NKJV

Therefore I prayed to the Lord, and said: 'O Lord God, do not destroy Your people and Your inheritance whom You have redeemed through Your greatness, whom You have brought out of Egypt with a mighty hand. Remember Your servants, Abraham, Isaac, and Jacob; do not look on the stubbornness of this people, or on their wickedness or their sin, lest the land from which You brought us should say, "Because the Lord was not able to bring them to the land which He promised them, and because He hated them, He has brought them out to kill them in the wilderness." Yet they *are* Your people and Your inheritance, whom You brought out by Your mighty power and by Your outstretched arm.'

Moses, Deuteronomy 9.26–29 NKJV

Then Manoah prayed to the Lord, and said, "O my Lord, please let the Man of God whom You sent come to us again and teach us what we shall do for the child who will be born."

Manoah, Judges 13.8 NKJV

Then Samson called to the Lord, saying, "O Lord God, remember me, I pray! Strengthen me, I pray, just this once, O God, that I may with one *blow* take vengeance on the Philistines for my two eyes!"

Samson, Judges 16.28 NKJV

So Hannah arose after they had finished eating and drinking in Shiloh. Now Eli the priest was sitting on the seat by the doorpost of the tabernacle of the Lord. And she *was* in bitterness of soul, and prayed to the Lord and wept in anguish. Then she made a vow and said, "O

Lord of hosts, if You will indeed look on the affliction of Your maidservant and remember me, and not forget Your maidservant, but will give Your maidservant a male child, then I will give him to the Lord all the days of his life, and no razor shall come upon his head."

Hannah, 1 Samuel 1.9–11 NKJV

And Hannah prayed and said:

"My heart rejoices in the Lord;
My horn is exalted in the Lord.
I smile at my enemies,
Because I rejoice in Your salvation.

"No one is holy like the Lord,
For *there is* none besides You,
Nor *is there* any rock like our God.

"Talk no more so very proudly;
Let no arrogance come from your mouth,
For the Lord *is* the God of knowledge;
And by Him actions are weighed.

"The bows of the mighty men *are* broken,
And those who stumbled are girded with
    strength.
Those who were full have hired themselves out
    for bread,
And the hungry have ceased *to hunger.*
Even the barren has borne seven,
And she who has many children has become
    feeble.

"The Lord kills and makes alive;
He brings down to the grave and brings up.
The Lord makes poor and makes rich;
He brings low and lifts up.
He raises the poor from the dust
And lifts the beggar from the ash heap,
To set *them* among princes
And make them inherit the throne of glory.

"For the pillars of the earth *are* the Lord's,
And He has set the world upon them.
He will guard the feet of His saints,
But the wicked shall be silent in darkness.

"For by strength no man shall prevail.
The adversaries of the Lord shall be broken in
    pieces;

From heaven He will thunder against them.
The Lord will judge the ends of the earth.
"He will give strength to His king,
And exalt the horn of His anointed."

Hannah, 1 Samuel 2.1–10 NKJV

Then King David went in and sat before the Lord; and he said: "Who *am* I, O Lord God? And what is my house, that You have brought me this far? And yet this was a small thing in Your sight, O Lord God; and You have also spoken of Your servant's house for a great while to come. *Is* this the manner of man, O Lord God? Now what more can David say to You? For You, Lord God, know Your servant. For Your word's sake, and according to Your own heart, You have done all these great things, to make Your servant know *them.* Therefore You are great, O Lord God. For *there is* none like You, nor *is there any* God besides You, according to all that we have heard with our ears. And who *is* like Your people, like Israel, the one nation on the earth whom God went to redeem for Himself as a people, to make for Himself a name – and to do for Yourself great and awesome deeds for Your land – before Your people whom You redeemed for Yourself from Egypt, the nations, and their gods? For You have made Your people Israel Your very own people forever; and You, Lord, have become their God.

"Now, O Lord God, the word which You have spoken concerning Your servant and concerning his house, establish *it* forever and do as You have said. So let Your name be magnified forever, saying, 'The Lord of hosts *is* the God over Israel.' And let the house of Your servant David be established before You. For You, O Lord of hosts, God of Israel, have revealed *this* to Your servant, saying, 'I will build you a house.' Therefore Your servant has found it in his heart to pray this prayer to You.

"And now, O Lord God, You are God, and Your words are true, and You have promised this goodness to Your servant. Now therefore, let it please You to bless the house of Your servant, that it may continue before You forever; for You, O Lord God, have spoken *it,* and with Your blessing let the house of Your servant be blessed forever."

David, 2 Samuel 7.18–29 NKJV

Then *someone* told David, saying, "Ahithophel *is* among the conspirators with Absalom." And David said, "O Lord, I pray, turn the counsel of Ahithophel into foolishness!"

David, 2 Samuel 15.31 NKJV

The Lord is my rock, my fortress, and my
    deliverer,
        my God, my rock, in whom I take refuge,
my shield and the horn of my salvation,
        my stronghold and my refuge,
my savior; you save me from violence.

David, 2 Samuel 22.1 NRSV

The spirit of the Lord speaks through me,
    his word is upon my tongue.
The God of Israel has spoken,
    the Rock of Israel has said to me:
One who rules over people justly,
    ruling in the fear of God,
is like the light of morning,
    like the sun rising on a cloudless morning,
gleaming from the rain on the grassy land.

David, 2 Samuel 23.2–4 NRSV

And David's heart condemned him after he had numbered the people. So David said to the Lord, "I have sinned greatly in what I have done; but now, I pray, O Lord, take away the iniquity of Your servant, for I have done very foolishly."

David, 2 Samuel 24.10

[17]Then David spoke to the Lord when he saw the angel who was striking the people, and said, "Surely I have sinned, and I have done wickedly; but these sheep, what have they done? Let Your hand, I pray, be against me and against my father's house."

David, 2 Samuel 24.17

Then Solomon stood before the altar of the Lord in the presence of all the assembly of Israel, and spread out his hands toward heaven; and he said: "Lord God of Israel, *there is* no God in heaven above or on earth below like You, who keep *Your* covenant and mercy with Your servants who walk before You with all their hearts. You have kept what You promised Your servant David my father; You have both spoken with Your mouth and fulfilled *it* with

Your hand, as *it is* this day. Therefore, Lord God of Israel, now keep what You promised Your servant David my father, saying, 'You shall not fail to have a man sit before Me on the throne of Israel, only if your sons take heed to their way, that they walk before Me as you have walked before Me.' And now I pray, O God of Israel, let Your word come true, which You have spoken to Your servant David my father.

"But will God indeed dwell on the earth? Behold, heaven and the heaven of heavens cannot contain You. How much less this temple which I have built! Yet regard the prayer of Your servant and his supplication, O Lord my God, and listen to the cry and the prayer which Your servant is praying before You today: that Your eyes may be open toward this temple night and day, toward the place of which You said, 'My name shall be there,' that You may hear the prayer which Your servant makes toward this place. And may You hear the supplication of Your servant and of Your people Israel, when they pray toward this place. Hear in heaven Your dwelling place; and when You hear, forgive.

"When anyone sins against his neighbor, and is forced to take an oath, and comes *and* takes an oath before Your altar in this temple, then hear in heaven, and act, and judge Your servants, condemning the wicked, bringing his way on his head, and justifying the righteous by giving him according to his righteousness.

"When Your people Israel are defeated before an enemy because they have sinned against You, and when they turn back to You and confess Your name, and pray and make supplication to You in this temple, then hear in heaven, and forgive the sin of Your people Israel, and bring them back to the land which You gave to their fathers.

"When the heavens are shut up and there is no rain because they have sinned against You, when they pray toward this place and confess Your name, and turn from their sin because You afflict them, then hear in heaven, and forgive the sin of Your servants, Your people Israel, that You may teach them the good way in which they should walk; and send rain on Your land which You have given to Your people as an inheritance.

"When there is famine in the land, pestilence *or* blight *or* mildew, locusts *or* grasshoppers; when their enemy besieges them in the land of their cities; whatever plague or whatever sickness *there is*; whatever prayer, whatever supplication is made by anyone, *or* by all Your people Israel, when each one knows the plague of his own heart, and spreads out his hands toward this temple: then hear in heaven Your dwelling place, and forgive, and act, and give to everyone according to all his ways, whose heart You know (for You alone know the hearts of all the sons of men), that they may fear You all the days that they live in the land which You gave to our fathers.

"Moreover, concerning a foreigner, who *is* not of Your people Israel, but has come from a far country for Your name's sake (for they will hear of Your great name and Your strong hand and Your outstretched arm), when he comes and prays toward this temple, hear in heaven Your dwelling place, and do according to all for which the foreigner calls to You, that all peoples of the earth may know Your name and fear You, as *do* Your people Israel, and that they may know that this temple which I have built is called by Your name.

"When Your people go out to battle against their enemy, wherever You send them, and when they pray to the Lord toward the city which You have chosen and the temple which I have built for Your name, then hear in heaven their prayer and their supplication, and maintain their cause.

"When they sin against You (for *there is* no one who does not sin), and You become angry with them and deliver them to the enemy, and they take them captive to the land of the enemy, far or near; *yet* when they come to themselves in the land where they were carried captive, and repent, and make supplication to You in the land of those who took them captive, saying, 'We have sinned and done wrong, we have committed wickedness'; and *when* they return to You with all their heart and with all their soul in the land of their enemies who led them away captive, and pray to You toward their land which You gave to their fathers, the city which You have chosen and the temple which I have built for Your name: then hear in heaven Your dwelling place their prayer and their supplication, and maintain

their cause, and forgive Your people who have sinned against You, and all their transgressions which they have transgressed against You; and grant them compassion before those who took them captive, that they may have compassion on them (for they *are* Your people and Your inheritance, whom You brought out of Egypt, out of the iron furnace), that Your eyes may be open to the supplication of Your servant and the supplication of Your people Israel, to listen to them whenever they call to You. For You separated them from among all the peoples of the earth *to be* Your inheritance, as You spoke by Your servant Moses, when You brought our fathers out of Egypt, O Lord God."

And so it was, when Solomon had finished praying all this prayer and supplication to the Lord, that he arose from before the altar of the Lord, from kneeling on his knees with his hands spread up to heaven. Then he stood and blessed all the assembly of Israel with a loud voice, saying: "Blessed *be* the Lord, who has given rest to His people Israel, according to all that He promised. There has not failed one word of all His good promise, which He promised through His servant Moses. May the Lord our God be with us, as He was with our fathers. May He not leave us nor forsake us, that He may incline our hearts to Himself, to walk in all His ways, and to keep His commandments and His statutes and His judgments, which He commanded our fathers. And may these words of mine, with which I have made supplication before the Lord, be near the Lord our God day and night, that He may maintain the cause of His servant and the cause of His people Israel, as each day may require, that all the peoples of the earth may know that the Lord *is* God; *there* is no other. Let your heart therefore be loyal to the Lord our God, to walk in His statutes and keep His commandments, as at this day."

Solomon, 1 Kings 8.22–61 NKJV

O Lord, God of Abraham, Isaac, and Israel, let it be known this day that you are God in Israel, that I am your servant, and that I have done all these things at your bidding. Answer me, O Lord, answer me, so that this people may know that you, O Lord, are God, and that you have turned their hearts back.

Elijah, on Mount Carmel, 1 Kings 18 36–37 NRSV

Then Hezekiah prayed before the Lord, and said: "O Lord God of Israel, *the One* who dwells *between* the cherubim, You are God, You alone, of all the kingdoms of the earth. You have made heaven and earth. Incline Your ear, O Lord, and hear; open Your eyes, O Lord, and see; and hear the words of Sennacherib, which he has sent to reproach the living God. Truly, Lord, the kings of Assyria have laid waste the nations and their lands, and have cast their gods into the fire; for they *were* not gods, but the work of men's hands – wood and stone. Therefore they destroyed them. Now therefore, O Lord our God, I pray, save us from his hand, that all the kingdoms of the earth may know that You *are* the Lord God, You alone."

Hezekiah, 2 Kings 19.15–19 NKJV

Oh that you would bless me and enlarge my border, and that your hand might be with me, and that you would keep me from hurt and harm!

Jabez, 1 Chronicles 4.10, NRSV

Blessed are you, O Lord, the God of our
    ancestor Israel, for ever and ever.
Yours, O Lord, are the greatness, the power,
    the glory, the victory, and the majesty;
for all that is in the heavens and on the earth
    is yours;
yours is the kingdom, O Lord, and you are
    exalted as head above all.

David, 1 Chronicles 29.10–11 NRSV

And Asa cried unto the Lord his God, and said, Lord, it is nothing with Thee to help, whether with many, or with them that have no power: help us, O Lord our God; for we rest on Thee, and in Thy name we go against this multitude. O Lord, Thou art our God; let not man prevail against Thee.

2 Chronicles 14.11 KJV

O Lord, God of our fathers, are you not the God who is in heaven? You rule over all the kingdoms of the nations. Power and might are in your hand, and no one can withstand you. O our God, did you not drive out the inhabitants of this land before your people Israel and give it forever to the descendants of Abraham your friend? They have lived in it and have built in it

a sanctuary for your Name, saying "If calamity comes upon us, whether the sword of judgment, or plague or famine, we will stand in your presence before this temple that bears your Name and will cry out to you in our distress, and you will hear us and save us." But now here are men from Ammon, Moab and Mount Seir, whose territory you would not allow Israel to invade when they came from Egypt; so they turned away from them and did not destroy them. See how they are repaying us by coming to drive us out of the possession you gave us as an inheritance. O our God, will you not judge them? For we have no power to face this vast army that is attacking us. We do not know what to do, but our eyes are upon you.

Jehoshaphat, 2 Chronicles 20.6–12

And I said: "I pray, Lord God of heaven, O great and awesome God, *You* who keep *Your* covenant and mercy with those who love You and observe Your commandments, please let Your ear be attentive and Your eyes open, that You may hear the prayer of Your servant which I pray before You now, day and night, for the children of Israel Your servants, and confess the sins of the children of Israel which we have sinned against You. Both my father's house and I have sinned. We have acted very corruptly against You, and have not kept the commandments, the statutes, nor the ordinances which You commanded Your servant Moses. Remember, I pray, the word that You commanded Your servant Moses, saying, 'If you are unfaithful, I will scatter you among the nations; but *if* you return to Me, and keep My commandments and do them, though some of you were cast out to the farthest part of the heavens, *yet* I will gather them from there, and bring them to the place which I have chosen as a dwelling for My name.' Now these *are* Your servants and Your people, whom You have redeemed by Your great power, and by Your strong hand. O Lord, I pray, please let Your ear be attentive to the prayer of Your servant, and to the prayer of Your servants who desire to fear Your name; and let Your servant prosper this day, I pray, and grant him mercy in the sight of this man."

Nehemiah, Nehemiah 1.5–11 NKJV

Then Job answered the Lord and said:

"I know that You can do everything,
And that no purpose *of Yours* can be withheld
  from You.
You asked, 'Who *is* this who hides counsel
  without knowledge?'
Therefore I have uttered what I did not
  understand,
Things too wonderful for me, which I did not
  know.
Listen, please, and let me speak;
You said, 'I will question you, and you shall
  answer Me.'
"I have heard of You by the hearing of the ear,
But now my eye sees You.
Therefore I abhor *myself,*
And repent in dust and ashes."

Job, Job 42.1–6 NKJV

"Now when I had delivered the purchase deed
to Baruch the son of Neriah, I prayed to the
Lord, saying: "Ah, Lord God! Behold, You have
made the heavens and the earth by Your great
power and outstretched arm. There is nothing
too hard for You. *You* show lovingkindness
to thousands, and repay the iniquity of the
fathers into the bosom of their children after
them – the Great, the Mighty God, whose
name *is* the Lord of hosts. *You are* great in
counsel and mighty in work, for your eyes are
open to all the ways of the sons of men, to give
everyone according to his ways and according
to the fruit of his doings. You have set signs and
wonders in the land of Egypt, to this day, and
in Israel and among *other* men; and You have
made Yourself a name, as it is this day. You
have brought Your people Israel out of the land
of Egypt with signs and wonders, with a strong
hand and an outstretched arm, and with great
terror; You have given them this land, of which
You swore to their fathers to give them – 'a land
flowing with milk and honey.' And they came
in and took possession of it, but they have not
obeyed Your voice or walked in Your law. They
have done nothing of all that You commanded
them to do; therefore You have caused all this
calamity to come upon them.

"Look, the siege mounds! They have come
to the city to take it; and the city has been
given into the hand of the Chaldeans who fight
against it, because of the sword and famine
and pestilence. What You have spoken has

happened; there You see *it!* And You have said
to me, O Lord God, 'Buy the field for money,
and take witnesses'! – yet the city has been
given into the hand of the Chaldeans.

Jeremiah, Jeremiah 32.16–25 NKJV

And I prayed to the Lord my God, and made
confession, and said, "O Lord, great and
awesome God, who keeps His covenant and
mercy with those who love Him, and with
those who keep His commandments, we have
sinned and committed iniquity, we have done
wickedly and rebelled, even by departing from
Your precepts and Your judgments. Neither
have we heeded Your servants the prophets,
who spoke in Your name to our kings and our
princes, to our fathers and all the people of
the land. O Lord, righteousness *belongs* to You,
but to us shame of face, as *it is* this day – to the
men of Judah, to the inhabitants of Jerusalem
and all Israel, those near and those far off in all
the countries to which You have driven them,
because of the unfaithfulness which they have
committed against You.

"O Lord, to us *belongs* shame of face, to our
kings, our princes, and our fathers, because
we have sinned against You. To the Lord our
God *belong* mercy and forgiveness, though we
have rebelled against Him. We have not obeyed
the voice of the Lord our God, to walk in His
laws, which He set before us by His servants
the prophets. Yes, all Israel has transgressed
Your law, and has departed so as not to obey
Your voice; therefore the curse and the oath
written in the Law of Moses the servant of God
have been poured out on us, because we have
sinned against Him. And He has confirmed His
words, which He spoke against us and against
our judges who judged us, by bringing upon
us a great disaster; for under the whole heaven
such has never been done as what has been
done to Jerusalem.

"As *it is* written in the Law of Moses, all
this disaster has come upon us; yet we have
not made our prayer before the Lord our God,
that we might turn from our iniquities and
understand Your truth. Therefore the Lord has
kept the disaster in mind, and brought it upon
us; for the Lord our God *is* righteous in all the
works which He does, though we have not
obeyed His voice. And now, O Lord our God,

who brought Your people out of the land of Egypt with a mighty hand, and made Yourself a name, as *it is* this day – we have sinned, we have done wickedly!

"O Lord, according to all Your righteousness, I pray, let Your anger and Your fury be turned away from Your city Jerusalem, Your holy mountain; because for our sins, and for the iniquities of our fathers, Jerusalem and Your people *are* a reproach to all *those* around us. Now therefore, our God, hear the prayer of Your servant, and his supplications, and for the Lord's sake cause Your face to shine on Your sanctuary, which is desolate. O my God, incline Your ear and hear; open Your eyes and see our desolations, and the city which is called by Your name; for we do not present our supplications before You because of our righteous deeds, but because of Your great mercies. O Lord, hear! O Lord, forgive! O Lord, listen and act! Do not delay for Your own sake, my God, for Your city and Your people are called by Your name."

Daniel, Daniel 9.4–19 NKJV

I called to the Lord out of my distress,
   and he answered me;
out of the belly of Sheol I cried,
   and you heard my voice.
You cast me into the deep,
   into the heart of the seas,
   and the flood surrounded me;
all your waves and your billows
   passed over me.
Then I said, 'I am driven away
   from your sight;
how shall I look again
   upon your holy temple?'
The waters closed in over me;
   the deep surrounded me;
weeds were wrapped around my head
   at the roots of the mountains.
I went down to the land
   whose bars closed upon me forever;
yet you brought up my life from the Pit,
   O Lord my God.
As my life was ebbing away,
   I remembered the Lord;
and my prayer came to you,
   into your holy temple.
Those who worship vain idols

forsake their true loyalty.
But I with the voice of thanksgiving
   will sacrifice to you;
what I have vowed I will pay.
   Deliverance belongs to the Lord!

Jonah, Jonah 2.2–9, NRSV

O Lord, I have heard of your renown,
   and I stand in awe, O Lord, of your work.

Habakkuk 3.2 NRSV

Though the fig tree does not blossom,
   and no fruit is on the vines;
though the produce of the olive fails
   and the fields yield no food;
though the flock is cut off from the fold
   and there is no herd in the stalls,
yet I will rejoice in the Lord;
   I will exult in the God of my salvation.

Habakkuk 3.17–18 NRSV

Prayers from the Psalms

You show me the path of life.
   In your presence there is fullness of joy;
   in your right hand are pleasures for
      evermore.

Psalm 16.11 NRSV

I love you, O Lord, my strength.

Psalm 18.1 NRSV

The Lord is my shepherd, I shall not want.
   He makes me lie down in green pastures;
he leads me beside still waters;
   he restores my soul.
He leads me in right paths
   for his name's sake.

Even though I walk through the darkest valley,
   I fear no evil;
for you are with me;
   your rod and your staff-
   they comfort me.

You prepare a table before me
   in the presence of my enemies;
you anoint my head with oil;
   my cup overflows.
Surely goodness and mercy shall follow me

all the days of my life,
and I shall dwell in the house of the Lord
   my whole life long.
Psalm 23 NRSV

To you, O Lord, I lift up my soul.
… Make me to know your ways, O Lord;
   teach me your paths.
Lead me in your truth, and teach me,
   for you are the God of my salvation;
   for you I wait all day long.
Be mindful of your mercy, O Lord, and of
   your steadfast love,
   for they have been from of old.
Psalm 25.1, 4–6 NRSV

The Lord is my light and my salvation;
   whom shall I fear?
The Lord is the stronghold of my life;
   of whom shall I be afraid?
… I believe that I shall see the goodness of the
   Lord
     in the land of the living.
Wait for the Lord;
   be strong, and let y our heart take
     courage;
     wait for the Lord!
Psalm 27.1, 13–14 NRSV

For with you is the fountain of life;
   in your light we see light.
Psalm 36.9 NRSV

Be merciful to me, O God, be merciful to me,
   for in you my soul takes refuge;
in the shadow of your wings I will take refuge,
   until the destroying storms pass by.
Psalm 57.1 NRSV

Hear my cry, O God;
   listen to my prayer.
From the end of the earth I call to you,
   when my heart is faint.

Lead me to the rock
   that is higher than I;
for you are my refuge,
   a strong tower against the enemy.
Psalm 61.1–3 NRSV

O God, you are my God, I seek you,

my soul thirsts for you;
my flesh faints for you,
   as in a dry and weary land where there is
     no water.
Psalm 63.1 NRSV

God be merciful unto us, and bless us: and
   shew us the light of his countenance, and
   be merciful unto us;
That thy way may be known upon earth: thy
   saving health among all nations.
Let the peoples praise thee, O God: yea, let all
   the peoples praise thee.
O let the nations rejoice and be glad: for thou
   shalt judge the folk righteously, and govern
   the nations upon earth.
Let the people praise thee, O God: yea, let all
   the people praise thee.
Then shall the earth bring forth her increase:
   and God, even our own God, shall give us
   his blessing.
God shall bless us: and all the ends of the
   world shall fear him.
Deus misereatur, Psalm 67, Book of Common Prayer

How lovely is your dwelling-place,
   O Lord of hosts!
My soul longs, indeed it faints
   for the courts of the Lord;
my heart and my flesh sing for joy
   to the living God.

Event he sparrow finds a home,
   and the swallow a nest for herself,
   where she may lay her young,
at your altars, O Lord of hosts,
   my King and my God.
Happy are those who love in your house,
   ever singing your praise.

Happy are those whose strength is in you,
   in whose heart are the highways of Zion.
As they go through the valley of Baca
   they make it a place of springs;
   the early rain also covers it with pools.
They go from strength to strength;
   the God of gods will be seen in Zion.
Psalm 84.1–7 NRSV

O come, let us sing unto the Lord: let us
   heartily rejoice in the strength of our

salvation.

Let us come before his presence with
thanksgiving: and show ourselves glad in
him with Psalms.

For the Lord is a great God: and a great King
above all gods.

In his hand are all the corners of the earth:
and the strength of the hills is his also.

The sea is his, and he made it: and his hands
prepared the dry land.

O come, let us worship and fall down: and
kneel before the Lord our Maker.

For he is the Lord our God: and we are the
people of his pasture, and the sheep of his
hand.

To day if ye will hear his voice, harden not
your hearts: as in the provocation, and as
in the day of temptation in the wilderness;

When your fathers tempted me: proved me,
and saw my works.

Forty years long was I grieved with this
generation, and said: It is a people that do
err in their heart, and they have not known
my ways.

Unto whom I sware in my wrath that they
should not enter into my rest.

Glory be to the Father, and to the Son: and to
the Holy Ghost;

As it was in the beginning, is now, and ever
shall be: world without end. Amen.

Psalm 95, Book of Common Prayer

O sing unto the Lord a new song: for he hath
done marvelous things.

With his own right hand, and with his holy
arm: hath he gotten himself the victory.

The Lord declared his salvation: his
righteousness hath he openly showed in
the sight of the heathen.

He hath remembered his mercy and truth
toward the house of Israel: and all the ends
of the world have seen the salvation of our
God.

Show yourselves joyful unto the Lord, all ye
lands: sing, rejoice, and give thanks.

Praise the Lord upon the harp: sing to the
harp with a psalm of thanksgiving.

With trumpets also and shawms: O shew
yourselves joyful before the Lord the King.

Let the sea make a noise, and all that therein
is: the round world, and that dwell therein.

Let the floods clap their hands, and let the hills
be joyful together before the Lord: for he
cometh to judge the earth.

With righteousness shall he judge the world:
and the peoples with equity.

Cantate Domino, Psalm 98, Book of Common Prayer

O be joyful in the Lord, all ye lands: serve the
Lord with gladness, and come before his
presence with a song.

Be ye sure that the Lord he is God; it is he that
hath made us, and not we ourselves: we are
his people, and the sheep of his pasture.

O go your way into his gates with
thanksgiving, and into his courts with
praise: be thankful unto him, and speak
good of his Name.

For the Lord is gracious, his mercy is
everlasting: and his truth endureth from
generation to generation.

Jubilate Deo, Psalm 100, Book of Common Prayer

PSALMS TO PRAY IN TIMES OF ANXIETY OR FEAR

A white-tailed deer drinks
    from the creek;
I want to drink God,
    deep draughts of God.
I'm thirsty for God-alive.
I wonder, "Will I ever make it —
    arrive and drink in God's presence?"
I'm on a diet of tears —
    tears for breakfast, tears for supper.
All day long
    people knock at my door,
Pestering,
    "Where is this God of yours?"

These are the things I go over and over,
    emptying out the pockets of my life.
I was always at the head of the worshiping
    crowd,
    right out in front,
Leading them all,
    eager to arrive and worship,
Shouting praises, singing thanksgiving —
    celebrating, all of us, God's feast!

Why are you down in the dumps, dear soul?
    Why are you crying the blues?
Fix my eyes on God —
    soon I'll be praising again.

He puts a smile on my face.
> He's my God.

When my soul is in the dumps, I rehearse
> everything I know of you,
From Jordan depths to Hermon heights,
> including Mount Mizar.
Chaos calls to chaos,
> to the tune of whitewater rapids.
Your breaking surf, your thundering breakers
> crash and crush me.
Then God promises to love me all day,
> sing songs all through the night!
> My life is God's prayer.

Sometimes I ask God, my rock-solid God,
> "Why did you let me down?
Why am I walking around in tears,
> harassed by enemies?"
They're out for the kill, these
> tormentors with their obscenities,
Taunting day after day,
> "Where is this God of yours?"

Why are you down in the dumps, dear soul?
> Why are you crying the blues?
Fix my eyes on God –
> soon I'll be praising again.
He puts a smile on my face.
He's my God.
> *Psalm 42 THE MESSAGE*

Clear my name, God; stick up for me
> against these loveless, immoral people.
Get me out of here, away
> from these lying degenerates.
I counted on you, God.
> Why did you walk out on me?
Why am I pacing the floor, wringing my
> hands
over these outrageous people?

Give me your lantern and compass,
> give me a map,
So I can find my way to the sacred mountain,
> to the place of your presence,
To enter the place of worship,
> meet my exuberant God,
Sing my thanks with a harp,
> magnificent God, my God.

Why are you down in the dumps, dear soul?
> Why are you crying the blues?
Fix my eyes on God –
> soon I'll be praising again.
He puts a smile on my face.
He's my God.
> *Psalm 43 THE MESSAGE*

God is a safe place to hide,
> ready to help when we need him.
We stand fearless at the cliff-edge of doom,
> courageous in seastorm and
> earthquake,
Before the rush and roar of oceans,
> the tremors that shift mountains.

Jacob-wrestling God fights for us,
God of angel armies protects us.

River fountains splash joy, cooling God's city,
> this sacred haunt of the Most High.
God lives here, the streets are safe,
> God at your service from crack of
> dawn.
Godless nations rant and rave, kings and
> kingdoms threaten,
> but Earth does anything he says.

Jacob-wrestling God fights for us,
God of angel armies protects us.

Attention, all! See the marvels of God!
> He plants flowers and trees all over the
> earth,
Bans war from pole to pole,
> breaks all the weapons across his knee.
"Step out of the traffic! Take a long,
> loving look at me, your High God,
> above politics, above everything."

Jacob-wrestling God fights for us,
God of angel armies protects us.
> *Psalm 46 THE MESSAGE*

No doubt about it! God is good –
> good to good people, good to the good-
> hearted.
But I nearly missed it,
> missed seeing his goodness.
I was looking the other way,
> looking up to the people

At the top,
    envying the wicked who have it made,
Who have nothing to worry about,
    not a care in the whole wide world.

Pretentious with arrogance,
    they wear the latest fashions in violence,
Pampered and overfed,
    decked out in silk bows of silliness.
They jeer, using words to kill;
    they bully their way with words.
They're full of hot air,
    loudmouths disturbing the peace.
People actually listen to them – can you
    believe it?
        Like thirsty puppies, they lap up their
        words.

What's going on here? Is God out to lunch?
    Nobody's tending the store.
The wicked get by with everything;
    they have it made, piling up riches.
I've been stupid to play by the rules;
    what has it gotten me?
A long run of bad luck, that's what –
    a slap in the face every time I walk out
    the door.

If I'd have given in and talked like this,
    I would have betrayed your dear
    children.
Still, when I tried to figure it out,
    all I got was a splitting headache …

Until I entered the sanctuary of God.
    Then I saw the whole picture:
The slippery road you've put them on,
    with a final crash in a ditch of delusions.
In the blink of an eye, disaster!
    A blind curve in the dark, and
    – nightmare!
We wake up and rub our eyes … Nothing.
    There's nothing to them. And there
    never was.

When I was beleaguered and bitter,
    totally consumed by envy,
I was totally ignorant, a dumb ox
    in your very presence.
I'm still in your presence,
    but you've taken my hand.

You wisely and tenderly lead me,
    and then you bless me.

You're all I want in heaven!
    You're all I want on earth!
When my skin sags and my bones get brittle,
    God is rock-firm and faithful.
Look! Those who left you are falling apart!
    Deserters, they'll never be heard from
    again.
But I'm in the very presence of God –
    oh, how refreshing it is!
I've made Lord God my home.
God, I'm telling the world what you do!
                        Psalm 73 THE MESSAGE

God, it seems you've been our home forever;
    long before the mountains were born,
Long before you brought earth itself to birth,
    from "once upon a time" to "kingdom
    come" – you are God.

So don't return us to mud, saying,
    "Back to where you came from!"
Patience! You've got all the time in the world
    – whether
        a thousand years or a day, it's all the
        same to you.
Are we no more to you than a wispy dream,
    no more than a blade of grass
That springs up gloriously with the rising sun
    and is cut down without a second
    thought?
Your anger is far and away too much for us;
    we're at the end of our rope.
You keep track of all our sins; every misdeed
    since we were children is entered in
    your books.
All we can remember is that frown on your
    face.
        Is that all we're ever going to get?
We live for seventy years or so
    (with luck we might make it to eighty),
And what do we have to show for it? Trouble.
    Toil and trouble and a marker in the
    graveyard.
Who can make sense of such rage,
    such anger against the very ones who
    fear you?

Oh! Teach us to live well!

Teach us to live wisely and well!
Come back, God – how long do we have to
wait? –
    and treat your servants with kindness
      for a change.
Surprise us with love at daybreak;
    then we'll skip and dance all the day
      long.
Make up for the bad times with some good
times;
    we've seen enough evil to last a lifetime.
Let your servants see what you're best at –
    the ways you rule and bless your
      children.

And let the loveliness of our Lord, our God,
rest on us,
    confirming the work that we do.
Oh, yes. Affirm the work that we do!
           Psalm 90 THE MESSAGE

You who sit down in the High God's presence,
    spend the night in Shaddai's shadow,
Say this: "God, you're my refuge.
    I trust in you and I'm safe!"
That's right – he rescues you from hidden
traps,
    shields you from deadly hazards.
His huge outstretched arms protect you –
    under them you're perfectly safe;
    his arms fend off all harm.
Fear nothing – not wild wolves in the night,
    not flying arrows in the day,
Not disease that prowls through the darkness,
    not disaster that erupts at high noon.
Even though others succumb all around,
    drop like flies right and left,
    no harm will even graze you.
You'll stand untouched, watch it all from a
distance,
    watch the wicked turn into corpses.
Yes, because God's your refuge,
    the High God your very own home,
Evil can't get close to you,
    harm can't get through the door.
He ordered his angels
    to guard you wherever you go.
If you stumble, they'll catch you;
    their job is to keep you from falling.
You'll walk unharmed among lions and
snakes,

and kick young lions and serpents from
    the path.
"If you'll hold on to me for dear life," says
God,
    "I'll get you out of any trouble.
I'll give you the best of care
    if you'll only get to know and trust me.
Call me and I'll answer, be at your side in bad
times;
    I'll rescue you, then throw you a party.
I'll give you a long life,
give you a long drink of salvation!"
           Psalm 91 THE MESSAGE

Oh my soul, bless God.
    From head to toe, I'll bless his holy
      name!
Oh my soul, bless God,
    don't forget a single blessing!

    He forgives your sins – every one.
    He heals your diseases – every one.
    He redeems you from hell – saves your
      life!
    He crowns you with love and mercy – a
      paradise crown.
    He wraps you in goodness – beauty
      eternal.
    He renews your youth – you're always
      young in his presence.

God makes everything come out right;
    he puts victims back on their feet.
He showed Moses how he went about his
work,
    opened up his plans to all Israel.
God is sheer mercy and grace;
    not easily angered, he's rich in love.
He doesn't endlessly nag and scold,
    nor hold grudges forever.
He doesn't treat us as our sins deserve,
    nor pay us back in full for our wrongs.
As high as heaven is over the earth,
    so strong is his love to those who fear
      him.
And as far as sunrise is from sunset,
    he has separated us from our sins.
As parents feel for their children,
    God feels for those who fear him.
He knows us inside and out,

keeps in mind that we're made of mud.
Men and women don't live very long;
    like wildflowers they spring up and
        blossom,
But a storm snuffs them out just as quickly,
    leaving nothing to show they were here.
God's love, though, is ever and always,
    eternally present to all who fear him,
Making everything right for them and their
    children
        as they follow his Covenant ways
        and remember to do whatever he said.

God has set his throne in heaven;
    he rules over us all. He's the King!
So bless God, you angels,
    ready and able to fly at his bidding,
    quick to hear and do what he says.
Bless God, all you armies of angels,
    alert to respond to whatever he wills.
Bless God, all creatures, wherever you are –
    everything and everyone made by God.

And you, oh my soul, bless God!
          Psalm 103 THE MESSAGE

I look up to the mountains;
    does my strength come from
        mountains?
No, my strength comes from God,
    who made heaven, and earth, and
        mountains.

He won't let you stumble,
    your Guardian God won't fall asleep.
Not on your life! Israel's
    Guardian will never doze or sleep.

God's your Guardian,
    right at your side to protect you –
Shielding you from sunstroke,
    sheltering you from moonstroke.

God guards you from every evil,
    he guards your very life.
He guards you when you leave and when you
    return,
he guards you now, he guards you always.
          Psalm 121 THE MESSAGE

God, investigate my life;

get all the facts firsthand.
I'm an open book to you;
    even from a distance, you know what
        I'm thinking.
You know when I leave and when I get back;
    I'm never out of your sight.
You know everything I'm going to say
    before I start the first sentence.
I look behind me and you're there,
    then up ahead and you're there, too –
    your reassuring presence, coming and
        going.
This is too much, too wonderful –
    I can't take it all in!

Is there anyplace I can go to avoid your Spirit?
    to be out of your sight?
If I climb to the sky, you're there!
    If I go underground, you're there!
If I flew on morning's wings
    to the far western horizon,
You'd find me in a minute –
    you're already there waiting!
Then I said to myself, "Oh, he even sees me in
    the dark!
    At night I'm immersed in the light!"
It's a fact: darkness isn't dark to you;
    night and day, darkness and light,
        they're all the same to you.

Oh yes, you shaped me first inside, then out;
    you formed me in my mother's womb.
I thank you, High God – you're breathtaking!
    Body and soul, I am marvelously made!
    I worship in adoration – what a
        creation!
You know me inside and out,
    you know every bone in my body;
You know exactly how I was made, bit by bit,
    how I was sculpted from nothing into
        something.
Like an open book, you watched me grow
    from conception to birth;
    all the stages of my life were spread out
        before you,
The days of my life all prepared
    before I'd even lived one day.

Your thoughts – how rare, how beautiful!
    God, I'll never comprehend them!
I couldn't even begin to count them –

any more than I could count the sand
    of the sea.
Oh, let me rise in the morning and live always
    with you!
        And please, God, do away with
            wickedness for good!
And you murderers – out of here! –
        all the men and women who belittle
            you, God,
        infatuated with cheap god-imitations.
See how I hate those who hate you, God,
        see how I loathe all this godless
            arrogance;
I hate it with pure, unadulterated hatred.
        Your enemies are my enemies!

Investigate my life, O God,
    find out everything about me;
Cross-examine and test me,
    get a clear picture of what I'm about;
See for yourself whether I've done anything
    wrong –
then guide me on the road to eternal life.
Psalm 139 THE MESSAGE

NEW TESTAMENT PRAYERS

Our Father in heaven,
    hallowed be your name.
    Your kingdom come.
    Your will be done,
        on earth as it is in heaven.
    Give us this day our daily bread.
    And forgive us our debts,
        as we also have forgiven our debtors.
    And do not bring us to the time of trial,
        but rescue us from the evil one.
Matthew 6.9–13 NRSV

My soul doth magnify the Lord: and my spirit
    hath rejoiced in God my Savior.
For he hath regarded: the lowliness of his
    handmaiden.
For behold, from henceforth: all generations
    shall call me blessed.
For he that is mighty hath magnified me: and
    holy is his Name.

And his mercy is on them that fear him:
    throughout all generations.
He hath showed strength with his arm:
    he hath scattered the proud in the
    imagination of their hearts.
He hath put down the mighty from their seat:
    and hath exalted the humble and meek.
He hath filled the hungry with good things:
    and the rich he hath sent empty away.
He remembering his mercy hath holpen
    his servant Israel: as he promised to our
    forefathers, Abraham and his seed, for ever.
Magnificat, Luke 1.46–55, Book of Common Prayer

Blessed the Lord God of Israel: for he hath
    visited and redeemed his people;
And hath raised up a mighty salvation for us:
    in the house of his servant David;
As he spake by the mouth of his holy
    Prophets: which have been since the world
    began;
That we should be saved from our enemies:
    and from the hand of all that hate us.
To perform the mercy promised to our
    forefathers: and to remember his holy
    Covenant;
To perform the oath which he sware to our
    forefather Abraham: that he would give us;
That we being delivered out of the hand of our
    enemies: might serve him without fear;
In holiness and righteousness before him: all
    the days of our life.
And thou, Child, shalt be called the Prophet
    of the Highest: for thou shalt go before the
    face of the Lord to prepare his ways;
To give knowledge of salvation unto his
    people: for the remission of their sins,
Through the tender mercy of our God:
    whereby the day-spring from on high hath
    visited us;
To give light to them that sit in darkness, and
    in the shadow of death: and to guide our
    feet into the way of peace.
Glory be to the Father, and to the Son: and to
    the Holy Ghost;
As it was in the beginning, is now, and ever
    shall be: world without end. Amen.
Benedictus, Luke 1.68–79,
The Book of Common Prayer

Glory to God in the highest heaven,

and on earth peace among those whom
he favors!

Luke 2.14 NRSV

Lord, now lettest thou thy servant depart in
peace: according to thy word.
For mine eyes have seen: thy salvation,
Which thou hast prepared: before the face of
all people;
To be a light to lighten the Gentiles: and to be
the glory of thy people Israel.

Nunc dimittis, Luke 2.29–32,
Book of Common Prayer

I thank you, Father, Lord of heaven and earth,
because you have hidden these things from
the wise and the intelligent and have revealed
them to infants; yes, Father, for such was your
gracious will.

Luke 10.21 NRSV

Father, I thank you for having heard me. I knew
that you always hear me, but I have said this
for the sake of the crowd standing here, so that
they may believe that you sent me.

John 11.41–42 NRSV

Father, if you are willing, remove this cup from
me; yet, not my will but yours be done.

Luke 22.42 NRSV

Father, glorify your name.

John 12.28 NRSV

Holy Father, keep them in your name, which
you have given me, that they may be one, even
as we are one. While I was with them, I kept
them in your name, which you have given
me; I have guarded them, and none of them is
lost but the son of perdition, that the scripture
might be fulfilled. But now I am coming to
you; and these things I speak in the world, that
they may have my joy fulfilled in themselves. I
have given them your word; and the world has
hated them because they are not of the world,
even as I am not of the world. I do not pray that
you should take them out of the world, but that
you should keep them from the evil one. They
are not of the world, even as I am not of the
world. Sanctify them in the truth; your word is
truth. As you did send me into the world, so I

have sent them into the world.

John 17.11–18 RSV

The prayers of Jesus on the cross

Father, forgive them; for they know not what
they do.

Luke 23.34 KJV

My God, my God, why hast thou forsaken
me?

Matthew 27.46 KJV

It is finished.

John 19.30 KJV

Father, into thy hands I commend my spirit.

Luke 23.46 KJV

Prayers from the book of Acts

They nominated two: Joseph Barsabbas, nick-
named Justus, and Matthias. Then they prayed,
"You, oh God, know every one of us inside
and out. Make plain which of these two men
you choose to take the place in this ministry
and leadership that Judas threw away in order
to go his own way." They then drew straws.
Matthias won, and was counted in with the
eleven apostles.

Acts 1.23–26 THE MESSAGE

As soon as Peter and John were let go, they
went to their friends and told them what the
high priests and religious leaders had said.
Hearing the report, they lifted their voices in
a wonderful harmony in prayer: "Strong God,
you made heaven and earth and sea and every-
thing in them. By the Holy Spirit you spoke
through the mouth of your servant and our
father, David:
  'Why the big noise, nations?
  Why the mean plots, peoples?
  Earth's leaders push for position,
  Potentates meet for summit talks,
  The God-deniers, the Messiah-defiers!'
"For in fact they did meet – Herod and
Pontius Pilate with nations and peoples, even

Israel itself! – met in this very city to plot against your holy Son Jesus, the One you made Messiah, to carry out the plans you long ago set in motion.

"And now they're at it again! Take care of their threats and give your servants fearless confidence in preaching your Message, as you stretch out your hand to us in healings and miracles and wonders done in the name of your holy servant Jesus."

Acts 4.23–30 THE MESSAGE

Lord Jesus, receive my spirit ... Lord, do not hold this sin against them.

Stephen, as he was being martyred.
Acts 7.59–60 NRSV

"Well, it happened just as Ananias said. After I was back in Jerusalem and praying one day in the Temple, lost in the presence of God, I saw him, saw God's Righteous Innocent, and heard him say to me, 'Hurry up! Get out of here as quickly as you can. None of the Jews here in Jerusalem are going to accept what you say about me.'

"At first I objected: 'Who has better credentials? They all know how obsessed I was with hunting out those who believed in you, beating them up in the meeting places and throwing them in jail. And when your witness Stephen was murdered, I was right there, holding the coats of the murderers and cheering them on. And now they see me totally converted. What better qualification could I have?'

"But he said, 'Don't argue. Go. I'm sending you on a long journey to outsider Gentiles.'"

Acts 22.17–21 THE MESSAGE

Prayers of Paul

What am I to do, Lord?

Acts 22.10 NRSV

I thank God through Jesus for every one of you. That's first. People everywhere keep telling me about your lives of faith, and every time I hear them, I thank him. And God, whom I so love to worship and serve by spreading the good news of his Son – the Message! – knows that every time I think of you in my prayers, which is practically all the time, I ask him to clear the way for me to come and see you.

Romans 1.8–10 THE MESSAGE

O the depth of the riches and wisdom and
    knowledge of God! How unsearchable are
    his judgments and how inscrutable his
    ways!
    'For who has known the mind of the Lord?
        Or who has been his counselor?'
    'Or who has given a gift to him,
        to receive a gift in return?'
For from him and through him and to him
    are all things. To him be the glory for ever.
    Amen.

Romans 11.33–36 NRSV

Now the God of patience and consolation grant you to be likeminded one toward another according to Christ Jesus: That ye may with one mind and one mouth glorify God, even the Father of our Lord Jesus Christ.

Romans 15:5–6 KJV

Now the God of peace be with you all. Amen.

Romans 15.33 KJV

All of our praise rises to the One who is strong enough to make you strong, exactly as preached in Jesus Christ, precisely as revealed in the mystery kept secret for so long but now an open book through the prophetic Scriptures.

Romans 16.25 THE MESSAGE

To God only wise, be glory through Jesus Christ for ever. Amen.

Romans 16.27 KJV

Blessed be the God and Father of our Lord Jesus Christ, the Father of mercies and the God of all consolation, who consoles us in all our affliction, so that we may be able to console those who are in any affliction with the consolation with which we ourselves are consoled by God.

2 Corinthians 1.3–4 NRSV

The grace of the Lord Jesus Christ, the love of God, and the communion of the Holy Spirit be with all of you.

2 Corinthians 13.14 NRSV

Grace to you and peace from God our Father and the Lord Jesus Christ, who gave himself for our sins to set us free from the present evil age, according to the will of our God and Father, to whom be the glory for ever and ever. Amen.

Galatians 1.3–4 NRSV

Brethren, the grace of our Lord Jesus Christ be with your spirit. Amen.

Galatians 6.18 KJV

Blessed be the God and Father of our Lord Jesus Christ, who has blessed us in Christ with every spiritual blessing in the heavenly places, just as he chose us in Christ before the foundation of the world to be holy and blameless before him in love.

Ephesians 1.3–4 NRSV

Glory to God in the church!
Glory to God in the Messiah, in Jesus!
Glory down all the generations!
Glory through all millennia! Oh, yes!

Ephesians 3.21 THE MESSAGE

Every time you cross my mind, I break out in exclamations of thanks to God. Each exclamation is a trigger to prayer. I find myself praying for you with a glad heart. I am so pleased that you have continued on in this with us, believing and proclaiming God's Message, from the day you heard it right up to the present. There has never been the slightest doubt in my mind that the God who started this great work in you would keep at it and bring it to a flourishing finish on the very day Christ Jesus appears.

It's not at all fanciful for me to think this way about you. My prayers and hopes have deep roots in reality. You have, after all, stuck with me all the way from the time I was thrown in jail, put on trial, and came out of it in one piece. All along you have experienced with me the most generous help from God. He knows how much I love and miss you these days. Sometimes I think I feel as strongly about you as Christ does!

So this is my prayer: that your love will flourish and that you will not only love much but well. Learn to love appropriately. You need to use your head and test your feelings so that your love is sincere and intelligent, not sentimental gush. Live a lover's life, circumspect and exemplary, a life Jesus will be proud of: bountiful in fruits from the soul, making Jesus Christ attractive to all, getting everyone involved in the glory and praise of God.

Philippians 1.3–11 THE MESSAGE

Our God and Father abounds in glory that just pours out into eternity. Yes.

Philippians 4.20 THE MESSAGE

Our prayers for you are always spilling over into thanksgivings. We can't quit thanking God our Father and Jesus our Messiah for you! We keep getting reports on your steady faith in Christ, our Jesus, and the love you continuously extend to all Christians. The lines of purpose in your lives never grow slack, tightly tied as they are to your future in heaven, kept taut by hope.

The Message is as true among you today as when you first heard it. It doesn't diminish or weaken over time. It's the same all over the world. The Message bears fruit and gets larger and stronger, just as it has in you. From the very first day you heard and recognized the truth of what God is doing, you've been hungry for more. It's as vigorous in you now as when you learned it from our friend and close associate Epaphras. He is one reliable worker for Christ! I could always depend on him. He's the one who told us how thoroughly love had been worked into your lives by the Spirit.

Be assured that from the first day we heard of you, we haven't stopped praying for you, asking God to give you wise minds and spirits attuned to his will, and so acquire a thorough understanding of the ways in which God works. We pray that you'll live well for the Master, making him proud of you as you work hard in his orchard. As you learn more and more how God works, you will learn how to do your work. We pray that you'll have the strength to stick it out over the long haul – not the grim strength of gritting your teeth but the glory-strength God gives. It is strength that endures the unendurable and spills over into joy, thanking the Father who makes us strong enough to take part in everything bright and beautiful that he has for us.

God rescued us from dead-end alleys and dark dungeons. He's set us up in the kingdom of the Son he loves so much, the Son who got us out of the pit we were in, got rid of the sins we were doomed to keep repeating.

Colossians 1.3–14 THE MESSAGE

May God our Father himself and our Master Jesus clear the road to you! And may the Master pour on the love so it fills your lives and splashes over on everyone around you, just as it does from us to you. May you be infused with strength and purity, filled with confidence in the presence of God our Father when our Master Jesus arrives with all his followers.

1 Thessalonians 3.11–13 THE MESSAGE

Now The Lord of peace himself give you peace always by all means. The Lord be with you all.

2 Thessalonians 3.16 KJV

God the blessed and only Sovereign, King of kings and Lord of lords, dwells in majesty immortal and in light unapproachable. Him no eye has seen, and no one can see. To Him be honor and eternal dominion, honor and dominion forever! Amen!

1 Timothy 6.15–16 RSV

Grace, mercy, and peace, from God the Father and Christ Jesus our Lord.

2 Timothy 1.2 KJV

The Lord Jesus Christ be with thy spirit. Grace by with you. Amen.

2 Timothy 4.22 KJV

Grace to you, and peace, from God our Father and the Lord Jesus Christ.

Philemon 3 KJV

Other New Testament prayers

Now may the God of peace, who brought back from the dead our Lord Jesus, the great shepherd of the sheep, by the blood of the eternal covenant, make you complete in everything good so that you may do his will, working among us that which is pleasing in his sight,

through Jesus Christ, to whom be the glory for ever and ever. Amen.

Hebrews 13.20–21 NRSV

Blessed be the God and Father of our Lord Jesus Christ! By his great mercy we have been born anew to a living hope through the resurrection of Jesus Christ from the dead, and to an inheritance which is imperishable, undefiled, and unfading, kept in heaven for you, who by God's power are guarded through faith for a salvation ready to be revealed in the last time.

1 Peter 1.3–5 NRSV

To him be the power for ever and ever. Amen.

1 Peter 5.11, NIV

Grace and peace be multiplied unto you through the knowledge of God, and of Jesus our Lord. According as his divine power hath given unto us all things that pertain unto life and godliness, through the knowledge of him that hath called us to glory and virtue: Whereby are given unto us exceeding great and precious promises: that by these ye might be partakers of the divine nature, have escaped the corruption that is in the world through lust.

2 Peter 1.2–4 KJV

Now to him who is able to keep you from falling, and to make you stand without blemish in the presence of his glory with rejoicing, to the only God our Savior, through Jesus Christ our Lord, be glory, majesty, power, and authority, before all time and now and for ever. Amen.

Jude 24–25 NRSV

You are worthy, our Lord and God,
      to receive glory and honor and power,
for you created all things,
      and by your will they existed and were
            created.

Revelation 4.11 NRSV

Amen! Blessing and glory and wisdom and thanksgiving and honor and power and might be to our God for ever and ever! Amen.

Revelation 7.12 NRSV

We give thanks to thee, Lord God Almighty,

who art and who wast, that thou hast taken thy
great power and begun to reign.

Revelation 11.17 rsv

Great and amazing are your deeds,
    Lord God the Almighty!
Just and true are your ways,
    King of the nations!
Lord, who will not fear
    and glorify your name?
For you alone are holy.
    All nations will come
    and worship before you.
for your judgments have been revealed.

Revelation 15.3–4 NRSV

Hallelujah! For the Lord our God the Almighty
reigns. Let us rejoice and exult and give him
the glory, for the marriage of the Lamb has
come, and his Bride has made herself ready; it
was granted her to be clothed with fine linen,
bright and pure.

Revelation 19.6–8 RSV

Even so, come, Lord Jesus.

Revelation 22.20

Short Prayers

SHORT PRAYERS

SHORT BIBLE PRAYERS

ARROW PRAYERS

SHORT PRAYERS

A short prayer finds its way to heaven.
William Langland, c.1330–c.1400

Let this day, O Lord, add some knowledge or good deed to yesterday.
Lancelot Andrewes, 1555–1626

O Lord, thou knowest how busy I must be this day. If I forget thee, do not thou forget me.
General Lord Astley, 579–1652,
before the battle of Edgehill

Lord, how exalted you are and yet the humble of heart are your dwelling.
Augustine of Hippo, 354–430

You have made us for yourself and our hearts are restless until in you they find their rest.
Augustine of Hippo, 354–430

Lord, give me what you are requiring of me.
Augustine of Hippo, 354–430

Let me die, Lord, that I may see You.
Augustine of Hippo, 354–430

O God, give me strength.
Gladys Aylward, 1902–70

Protect me, dear Lord;
My boat is so small,
And your sea is so big.
Breton fisherman's prayer

O God, I thank thee for all the joy I have had in life.
Byrhtnoth, d.991

Let our chief goal, O God, be your glory, and to enjoy you for ever.
John Calvin, 1509–64

Lord, let your glory be my goal, your word my rule, and then you will be done.
King Charles I, 1600–49

Change the world, O Lord, beginning with me.
A Chinese student

Glory to God for all things.
John Chrysostom, c.347–407

O God, make us children of quietness and heirs of peace.
Clement of Alexandria, c.150–c.215

O Lord, never allow us to think we can stand by ourselves and not need you, our greatest need.
John Donne, 1572–1631

Teach me to pray. Pray yourself in me.
F. Fénelon, 1651–1715

Lord Jesus Christ, Son of God, have mercy on me, a sinner.
The Jesus Prayer. The Eastern Orthodox Church teaches that this prayer is to be said many times regularly during the day.

My God and My All!

The Meditation Prayer of
Francis of Assisi, 1181–1226

May I die for the love of Your love, who did deign to die for the love of my love!

Francis of Assisi, 1181–1226

Free us from our selfish interests, and guide us, good Lord, to see thy way and to do thy will.

Charles Kingsley, 1819–75

Give me Scotland, or I die.

John Knox, c.1513–72

Lord, make me according to your heart.

Brother Lawrence, 1611–91

Let me never know myself apart from the living God!

D.H. Lawrence, 1885–1930

My Jesus, You alone are sufficient for me.

Alphonsus Liguori, 1696–1787

Eternal Father, for the love of Jesus Christ have pity on me.

Alphonsus Liguori, 1696–1787

My God, I wish for You alone, and nothing more.

Alphonsus Liguori, 1696–1787

May I this day give myself wholly to You.

Alphonsus Liguori, 1696–1787

Lord, give us faith that right makes might.

Abraham Lincoln, 1809–65

Give me but Your love and Your grace, and I am rich enough.

Ignatius Loyola,
1491/1495–1556

Lord, make me see your glory in every place.

Michelangelo, 1475–1564

The things, good Lord, that we pray for, give us the grace to labor for.

Thomas More, 1478–1535

I ask not to see; I ask not to know; I ask only to be used.

J.H. Newman, 1801–90

O God, help us not to despise or oppose what we do not understand.

William Penn, 1644–1718

Teach us to pray often, that we may pray oftener.

Jeremy Taylor, 1613–67

Pray God, keep us simple.

W.M. Thackeray, 1811–63

Lord, make your will our will in all things.

C.J Vaughan, 1816–97

Make and keep me pure within.

Charles Wesley, 1707–88

Jesus, strengthen my desire to work and speak and think for you.

John Wesley, 1703–91

O Lord, let us not live to be useless, for Christ's sake.

John Wesley, 1703–91

SHORT BIBLE PRAYERS

A good watchmaker is one who makes watches and prays: a good housemaid is one who sweeps and prays.

E.B. Pusey, 1800–82

Speak, for your servant is listening.

Samuel, 1 Samuel 3.10 NRSV

Let the words of my mouth and the meditation of my heart be acceptable to you, O Lord, my rock and my redeemer.

Psalm 19.14 NRSV

Wait for the Lord;
    be strong, and let your heart take courage;
    wait for the Lord!

Psalm 27.14 NRSV

O send out your light and your truth;
let them lead me;
let them bring me to your holy hill
and to your dwelling.

Psalm 43.3 NRSV

O God, you know my folly;
the wrongs I have done are not hidden
from you.

Psalm 69.5 NRSV

Be pleased, O God, to deliver me.
O Lord, make haste to help me!

Psalm 70.1 NRSV

Will you not revive us again,
so that your people may rejoice in you?

Psalm 85.6 NRSV

Bless the Lord, O my soul,
and all that is within me,
bless his holy name.

Psalm 103.1 NRSV

Lord, save me!

Peter, Matthew 14.30

Lord, help me.

A Canaanite woman, Matthew 15.25

I believe, help my unbelief!

*Father of boy possessed by
an unclean spirit, Mark 9.24*

Here am I, the servant of the Lord; let it be with
me according to your word.

Mary, Luke 1.38 NRSV

God, be merciful to me, a sinner!

Praying tax-collector, Luke 18.13

Jesus, remember me when you come into your
kingdom.

Penitent dying thief, Luke 23.42

My Lord and my God!

Thomas, John 20.28

Grace be with you.

2 Timothy 4.2

Come, Lord Jesus!

Revelation 22.20

The grace of the Lord Jesus be with all the
saints. Amen.

Revelation 22.20 NRSV

ARROW PRAYERS

Prayer may be equally with words or without:
it may be "Jesu," "my God and my all."

E.B. Pusey, 1800–82

In some theological books these prayers are
called ejaculations prayers "preces ejaculato-
riae," i.e. "the arrow prayers." This comes from
the Latin word jaculum or dart, because these
are prayers that dart up to heaven. These are
prayers that are shot up to heaven like an
arrow from a bow, or like a spear from a
soldier's hand.

Awake, O my soul, awake!
Be gracious to me, O God.
Create a clean heart in me.
Fill me with joy and gladness.
Glory to the Lamb of God.
God is worthy of our praise.
Have mercy on me, O God.
His eye is on the sparrow.
His love is everlasting.
Holy, holy, holy Lord.
Holy is the Lamb of God.
How good is the Lord to all.
I have been given mercy.
I have called you by your name.
I have grasped you by the hand.
I will never forget you.
In you I hope all day long.
In you I place all my trust.
In your love remember me.
Jesus is the Lamb of God.
Joy cometh in the morning.
Let go and let God.
Let the healing waters flow.
My cup is overflowing.
My peace is my gift to you.
Oh, that we might know the Lord!
Remember your mercies, Lord.

Taste and see that the Lord is good.
The Lord keeps the little ones.
You are my strength and my song.

Famous Prayers

Contents   FAMOUS PRAYERS

            PRAYERS OF THE FAMOUS

Related entries in Part Two

Prayer collections
George Herbert: Christian Poetry Collection

FAMOUS PRAYERS

Unto God's gracious mercy and protection we commit you. The Lord bless you and keep you. The Lord make his face shine upon you, and be gracious to you. The Lord lift his countenance upon you, and give you peace.
> *The Aaronic blessing, Numbers 6.24–26*

The Lord is my shepherd, I shall not want.
    He makes me lie down in green pastures;
he leads me beside still waters;
    he restores my soul.
He leads me in right paths
    for his name's sake.
Even though I walk through the darkest valley,
    I fear no evil;
for you are with me;
    your rod and your staff-
    they comfort me.
You prepare a table before me
    in the presence of my enemies;
you anoint my head with oil;
    my cup overflows.
Surely goodness and mercy shall follow me
    all the days of my life,
and I shall dwell in the house of the Lord
    my whole life long.
> *Psalm 23 NRSV*

My soul doth magnify the Lord: and my spirit
    hath rejoiced in God my Savior.
For he hath regarded: the lowliness of his
    handmaiden.
For behold, from henceforth: all generations
    shall call me blessed.
For he that is mighty hath magnified me: and
    holy is his Name.
And his mercy is on them that fear him:
    throughout all generations.
He hath showed strength with his arm:
    he hath scattered the proud in the
    imagination of their hearts.
He hath put down the mighty from their seat:
    and hath exalted the humble and meek.
He hath filled the hungry with good things:
    and the rich he hath sent empty away.
He remembering his mercy hath holpen
    his servant Israel: as he promised to our
    forefathers, Abraham and his seed, for ever.
> *Magnificat, Luke 1.46–55,*
> *Book of Common Prayer, 1549*

Father, if you are willing, remove this cup from me; yet, not my will but yours be done.
> *Luke 22.42 NRSV*

Father, into thy hands I commend my spirit.
> *Luke 23.46 KJV*

The grace of the Lord Jesus Christ, the love of God, and the communion of the Holy Spirit be with all of you.

2 Corinthians 13.14 NRSV

May the grace of our Lord Jesus Christ,
and the love of God,
and the fellowship of the Holy Spirit,
be with you all.

2 Corinthians 13.14

Now may the God of peace who brought again from the dead our Lord Jesus, the great shepherd of the sheep, by the blood of the eternal covenant, equip you with everything good that you may do his will, working in you that which is pleasing in his sight, through Jesus Christ; to whom be glory for ever and ever. Amen.

Hebrews 13.20–21 RSV

Blessing and honor, thanksgiving and praise
        more than we can utter,
        more than we can conceive,
be unto you, O most holy and glorious
        Trinity,
        Father, Son and Holy Spirit,
by all angels, all people, all creatures
        for ever and ever. Amen and Amen.

Lancelot Andrewes, 1555–1626

Soul of Christ, sanctify me.
Body of Christ, save me.
Blood of Christ, inebriate me.
Water from the side of Christ, wash me.
Passion of Christ, strengthen me.
O good Jesus, hear me.
Hide me within your wounds
and never allow me to be separated from you.
From the wicked enemy defend me.
In the hour of my death call me,
and bid me come to you,
so that with your saints I may praise you
for ever and ever.

The 'Anima Christi', 14th century

O Lord, thou knowest how busy I must be this day. If I forget thee, do not thou forget me.

General Lord Astley, 1579–1652,
before the battle of Edgehill

Grant me, I beseech thee, almighty and merci-

ful God, fervently to desire, wisely to search out, truly to acknowledge, and perfectly to fulfill, all that is well-pleasing to thee. Order thou my worldly condition to the honor and glory of thy name; and of all that thou requirest me to do, grant me the knowledge, the desire, and the ability, that I may so fulfill it as I ought, and as is expedient for the welfare of my soul

Thomas Aquinas, 1225–74

Grant to us your servants: to our God – a heart of flame; to our fellow men – a heart of love; to ourselves – a heart of steel.

Augustine of Hippo, 354–430

O Lord, forgive what I have been, sanctify what I am, and order what I shall be.

Author unknown

Go in peace; and may the blessing of God the Father, the Son, and the Holy Spirit rest on you and remain with you, this day (night) and for evermore.

Author unknown

O Lord, remember not only the men and women of good will, but also those of ill will. But do not remember all the suffering they have inflicted on us; remember the fruits we have brought, thanks to this suffering – our comradeship, our loyalty, our courage, our generosity, the greatness of heart which has grown out of all this, and when they come to judgment let all the fruits which we have borne be their forgiveness.

Author unknown, prayer found near the body of a
dead child in the Ravensbruck concentration camp

May the blessing of God Almighty, the Father, the Son, and the Holy Spirit, rest on us and on all our work and worship done in his name. May he give us light to guide us, courage to support us, and love to unite us, now and for evermore.

Author unknown

Bless all who worship thee,
From the rising of the sun
Unto the going down of the same.
Of thy goodness, give us;

With thy love, inspire us;
By thy spirit, guide us;
By thy power, protect us;
In thy mercy, receive us,
Now and always.

Author unknown, 5th century

May the love of the Father enfold us,
the wisdom of the Son enlighten us,
the fire of the Spirit inflame us;
and may the blessing of the triune God rest
on us,
and abide with us,
now and evermore.

Author unknown

Father,
give us wisdom to perceive you,
intellect to understand you,
diligence to seek you,
patience to wait for you,
eyes to behold you,
a heart to meditate on you
and a life to proclaim you,
through the power of the Spirit
of our Lord Jesus Christ.

Benedict, 480–543

Eternal God, the refuge of all your children,
in our weakness you are our strength,
in our darkness our light,
in our sorrow our comfort and peace.
May we always live in your presence,
and serve you in our daily lives;
through Jesus Christ our Lord.

Boniface, c.675–754

Our Father, which art in heaven, Hallowed
be thy Name. Thy kingdom come. Thy will
be done in earth, As it is in heaven. Give us
this day our daily bread. And forgive us our
trespasses, As we forgive them that trespass
against us. And lead us not into temptation.
But deliver us from evil. For thine is the kingdom, The power, and the glory, For ever and
ever. Amen.

The Book of Common Prayer, 1549

The peace of God, which passeth all understanding, keep your hearts and minds in the
knowledge and love of God, and of his Son

Jesus Christ our Lord: and the blessing of God
Almighty, the Father, the Son, and the Holy
Ghost, be amongst you and remain with you
always.

The Book of Common Prayer, 1549
The Order for Holy Communion

O God, from whom all holy desires, all good
counsels, and all just works do proceed: Give
unto thy servants that peace which the world
cannot give; that both our hearts may be set
to obey thy commandments, and also that
by thee we, being defended from the fear of
our enemies, may pass our time in rest and
quietness; through the merits of Jesu Christ
our Savior.

The Book of Common Prayer, 1549,
Evensong, Second Collect

God be in my head,
and in my understanding;
God be in my eyes,
and in my looking;
God be in my mouth,
and in my speaking;
God be in my heart,
and in my thinking;
God be at my end,
and at my departing.

Book of Hours, 1514

O Lord, convert the world – and begin with
me.

Chinese student's prayer

Almighty God, who hast given us grace at this
time with one accord to make our common
supplications unto thee; and dost promise,
that when two or three are gathered together
in thy Name thou wilt grant their requests;
Fulfill now, O Lord, the desires and petitions
of thy servants, as may be most expedient for
them; granting us in this world knowledge of
thy truth, and in the world to come life everlasting. Amen.

John Chrysostom, c.347–407

We beg you, Lord, to help and defend us.
Deliver the oppressed,
have compassion on the despised,
raise the fallen,

reveal yourself to the needy,
heal the sick,
bring back those who have strayed from you,
feed the hungry,
lift up the weak,
remove the prisoners' chains.
May every nation come to know that you are
    God alone,
that Jesus is your Son,
that we are your people, the sheep of your
    pasture.

Clement of Rome, c.30–c.95

My dearest Lord,
be thou a bright flame before me,
be thou a guiding star above me,
be thou a smooth path beneath me,
be thou a kindly shepherd behind me,
today – tonight – and forever.

Columba, 521–597

Be present, O merciful God, and protect us
through the silent hours of this night, so
that we who are wearied by the changes and
chances of this fleeting world, may repose on
your eternal changelessness; through Jesus
Christ our Lord.

Office of Compline

Save us, O Lord, while waking, and guard us
while sleeping, that awake we may watch with
Christ, and asleep we may rest in peace.

Office of Compline

Lord Jesus Christ, you said that you are the
    Way, the Truth, and the Life.
Help us not to stray from you, for you are the
    Way;
nor to distrust you, for you are the Truth;
nor to rest on any other than you, as you are
    the Life.
You have taught us what to believe, what to
    do, what to hope, and where to take our
    rest.
Give us grace to follow you, the Way, to learn
    from you, the Truth, and live in you, the
    Life.

Desiderius Erasmus, 1467–1536

Lord, make me an instrument of your peace.
Where there is hatred, let me sow love,

where there is injury, pardon,
where there is doubt, faith,
where there is despair, hope,
where there is darkness, light,
where there is sadness, joy.
O Divine Master, grant that we may not so
    much seek
to be consoled as to console,
not so much to be understood as to
    understand,
not so much to be loved as to love. For it is in
    giving that we receive,
it is in pardoning that we are pardoned,
it is in dying that we are born to eternal life.

Attributed to Francis of Assisi, 1181–1226

The Lord bless you and keep you.
May he show his face to you and have mercy
    on you.
May he turn his countenance to you and give
    you peace.
The Lord bless you, Brother Leo.

Francis of Assisi, 1181–1226
Francis' blessing to Brother Leo, which
Brother Leo always carried with him

May the road rise to meet you,
may the wind be always at your back,
may the sun shine warm upon your face,
may the rain fall softly on your fields,
may God hold you in the hollow of his hand.

Traditional Gaelic prayer

Easter Wings
Lord, who createdst man in wealth and store,
    Though foolishly he lost the same,
        Decaying more and more,
            Till he became
                Most poor:

            With thee
        Oh let me rise
    As larks, harmoniously,
And sing this day thy victories:
Then shall the fall farther the flight in me.

My tender age in sorrow did begin:
    And still with sickness and shame
        Thou did'st so punish sin,
            That I became
                Most thin

With thee
Let me combine,
And feel this day the victory,
For, if I imp my wing on thine,
Affliction shall advance the flight in me.
George Herbert, 1593–1633, The Temple

Lord Jesus Christ, Son of God, have mercy on
me, a sinner.
The Jesus Prayer

Dearest Lord, teach me to be generous;
teach me to serve you as you deserve;
to give and not to count the cost,
to fight and not to heed the wounds,
to toil and not to see for rest,
to labor and not to seek reward,
except to know that I do your will.
Ignatius Loyola, 1491/1495–1556

May the Almighty Lord, who bore the
    reproach of the cross, bless all this family
    present here. Amen.
May he, who hung on the tree, himself lead us
    to the heavenly kingdom. Amen.
May he place us at the right hand of the
    Father, who was made the cause of our
    peace. Amen.
Through the mercy of our God, who is
    blessed and reigns, and governs all things,
    world without end.
Mozarabic Breviary

God bless all those that I love;
God bless all those that love me.
God bless all those that love those that I love
And all those that love those that love me.
Jewish prayer

O Lord, support us all the day long of this troublous life, until the shadows lengthen, and the
evening comes, and the busy world is hushed,
and the fever of life is over, and our work is
done. Then, Lord, in your mercy grant us a safe
lodging, and a holy rest, and peace at the last;
through Jesus Christ our Lord.
Used by J.H. Newman, 1801–90,
based on a 16th-century prayer

God, give us the serenity to accept what
    cannot be changed;

give us the courage to change what should be
    changed;
give us the wisdom to distinguish one from
    the other.
Attributed to Reinhold Niebuhr, 1892–1971,
also known as The Serenity Prayer

I bind to myself the name,
the strong name of the Trinity;
by invocation of the same,
The Three in One, and One in Three.
Of whom all nature has creation;
eternal Father, Spirit, Word:
Praise to the Lord of my salvation,
Salvation is of Christ the Lord.
Patrick, c.389–c.461

Christ be with me, Christ within me,
Christ behind me, Christ before me,
Christ beside me, Christ to win me,
Christ to comfort and restore me,
Christ beneath me, Christ above me,
Christ in quiet, Christ in danger,
Christ in hearts of all that love me,
Christ in mouth of friend and stranger.
Breastplate of Patrick

I rise today with the power of God to guide
    me,
the might of God to uphold me,
the wisdom of God to teach me,
the eye of God to watch over me,
the ear of God to hear me,
the word of God to give me speech,
the hand of God to protect me,
the path of God to lie before me,
the shield of God to shelter me,
the host of God to defend me
against the snares of the devil and the
    temptations of the world,
against every man who meditates injury to
    me,
whether far or near.
Breastplate of Patrick

Go forth into the world in peace;
be of good courage;
hold fast that which is good;
render to no man evil for evil;
strengthen the fainthearted;
support the weak;

help the afflicted;
honor all men;
love and serve the Lord,
rejoicing in the power of the Holy Spirit.
And the blessing of God Almighty, the Father,
    the Son, and the Holy Ghost, be upon you,
    and remain with you for ever.
                        The Proposed Prayer Book, 1928

Thanks be to you, my Lord Jesus Christ,
for all the benefits you have won for me.
For all the pains and insults you have borne
    for me.
O most merciful Redeemer, Friend, and
    Brother,
may I know you more clearly,
love you more dearly,
and follow you more nearly,
day by day.
                Richard of Chichester, c.1198–1253

May the eternal God bless and keep us, guard
our bodies, save our souls, direct our thoughts,
and bring us safe to the heavenly country, our
eternal home, where Father, Son and Holy
Spirit ever reign, one God for ever and ever.
                        Sarum Breviary

I asked God for strength, that I might achieve,
I was made weak, that I might learn humbly
    to obey.
I asked for health, that I might do greater
    things,
I was given infirmity, that I might do better
    things.
I asked for riches, that I might be happy,
I was given poverty, that I might be wise.
I asked for power, that I might have the praise
    of men,
I was given weakness, that I might feel the
    need of God.
I asked for all things, that I might enjoy life,
I was given life, that I might enjoy all things.
I got nothing that I asked for –
but everything that I had hoped for,
almost despite myself, my unspoken prayers
    were answered.
I am among all men most richly blessed.
        A Soldier's Prayer, written by an anonymous
        confederate soldier, in the US civil war

We praise thee, O God: we acknowledge thee
    to be the Lord.
All the earth doth worship thee: the Father
    everlasting.
To thee all Angels cry aloud: the Heavens, and
    all the Powers therein.
To thee Cherubim and Seraphim: continually
    do cry,
Holy, Holy, Holy: Lord God of Sabaoth;
Heaven and earth are full of the Majesty: of
    thy glory.
The glorious company of the Apostles: praise
    thee.
The goodly fellowship of the Prophets: praise
    thee.
The noble army of Martyrs: praise thee.
The holy Church throughout all the world:
    doth acknowledge thee;
The Father: of an infinite Majesty;
Thine honorable, true: and only Son;
Also the Holy Ghost: the Comforter.
Thou art the King of Glory: O Christ.
Thou art the everlasting Son: of the Father.
When thou tookest upon thee to deliver
    man: thou didst not abhor the Virgin's
    womb.
When thou hadst overcome the sharpness
    of death: thou didst open the Kingdom of
    Heaven to all believers.
Thou sittest at the right hand of God: in the
    glory of the Father.
We believe that thou shalt come: to be our
    Judge.
We therefore pray thee, help thy servants:
    whom thou hast redeemed with thy
    precious blood.
Make them to be numbered with thy Saints: in
    glory everlasting.
O Lord, save thy people: and bless thine
    heritage.
Govern them: and lift them up for ever.
Day by day: we magnify thee;
And we worship thy Name: ever world
    without end.
Vouchsafe, O Lord: to keep us this day
    without sin.
O Lord, have mercy upon us: have mercy
    upon us.
O Lord, let thy mercy lighten upon us: as our
    trust is in thee.
O Lord, in thee have I trusted: let me

never be confounded.

Te Deum Laudamus, 4th/5th century,
The Book of Common Prayer

May the love of the Lord Jesus draw us to
    himself;
may the power of the Lord Jesus strengthen us
    in his service;
may the joy of the Lord Jesus fill our souls.
May the blessing of God almighty, the Father,
    the Son, and the Holy Spirit, be among you
    and remain with you always.

After William Temple, 1881–1944

Let nothing disturb you
nothing frighten you,
all things are passing;
patient endurance
attains all things.
One whom God possesses
lacks nothing,
for God alone suffices.

Bookmark of Teresa of Avila, 1515–82

PRAYERS OF THE FAMOUS

Lord God Almighty, shaper and ruler of all
creatures, we pray that by your great mercy
and by the token of the holy cross you will
guide us to your will. Make our minds steadfast, strengthen us against temptation, and
keep us from all unrighteousness. Shield us
against our enemies, seen and unseen. Teach
us to inwardly love you before all things with
a clean mind and a clean body. For you are our
Maker and Redeemer, our help and comfort,
our trust and hope, for ever.

King Alfred the Great, 849–899

Almighty God, in whom we live and move and
have our being, you have made us for yourself
and our hearts are restless until in you they find
their rest. Grant us purity of heart and strength
of purpose, that no selfish passion may hinder
us from knowing your will, no weakness from
doing it; but that in your light we may see light
clearly, and in your service we may find our
perfect freedom; through Jesus Christ our Lord.

Augustine of Hippo, 354–430

Give us grace, almighty Father, to address you
with all our hearts as well as with our lips. You
are present everywhere: from you no secrets
can be hidden.

Teach us to fix our thoughts on you, reverently and with love, so that our prayers are not
in vain, but are acceptable to you, now and
always, through Jesus Christ our Lord.

Jane Austen, 1775–1817

I beseech Thee, good Jesus, that as Thou hast
graciously granted to me here on earth sweetly
to partake of the words of Thy wisdom and
knowledge, so Thou wilt vouchsafe that I may
some time come to Thee, the fountain of all
wisdom, and always appear before Thy face;
who livest and reignest, world without end.

Bede, c.673–735

O Savior, pour upon me thy Spirit of
    meekness and love,
Annihilate the selfhood in me, be thou all my
    life.

William Blake, 1757–1827

In my Redeemer's name,
I give myself to thee;
And, all unworthy as I am,
My God will cherish me.

Anne Brontë, 1820–49

Lord,
How do I love thee? Let me count the ways.
I love thee to the depth and breadth and height
my soul can reach, when feeling out of sight
for the ends of being and of ideal grace.
I love thee to the level of every day's
most quiet need, by sun and candlelight.
I love thee purely, as they turn from praise.
I love thee with a passion put to use
in my old griefs, and with my childhood faith.
I love thee with a love I seemed to lose
with my lost saints – I love thee with the
    breath,
smiles, tears, of all my life!
And, God, if thou dost choose
I shall love thee better after death.

Elizabeth Browning, 1806–61

Grow old along with me!
The best is yet to be,

The last of life, for which the first was made:
Our times are in his hand
Who saith "A whole I planned,
Youth shows but half; trust God: see all nor
    be afraid!"

Robert Browning, 1812–89

He that is down needs fear no fall
He that is low, no pride:
He that is humble ever shall
Have God to be his guide.
I am content with what I have,
Little be it or much:
And, Lord, contentment still I crave,
Because thou savest such.

John Bunyan, 1628–88

The grace of God the Father and the peace of
our Lord Jesus Christ, through the fellowship
of the Holy Spirit, dwell with us for ever.

John Calvin, 1509–64

Almighty and most merciful Father, look
down on us your unworthy servants through
the mediation and merits of Jesus Christ, in
whom only are you well pleased. Purify our
hearts by your Holy Spirit, and as you add days
to our lives, so good Lord, add repentance to
our days; that when we have passed this mortal
life we may be partakers of your everlasting
kingdom; through the merits of Jesus Christ
our Lord.

King Charles I, 1600–49

O Christ, ruler and Lord of the world, to thee we
consecrate this land, its scepter and its power.
Guard thy land, guard it from every foe.

Emperor Constantine, c.280–337

To the Holy Spirit who sanctifies us, with the
Father who made and created us, and the Son
who redeemed us, be given all honor and glory,
world without end.

Thomas Cranmer, 1489–1556

Strengthen us, O God, to relieve the oppressed,
to hear the groans of poor prisoners, to reform
the abuses of all professions; that many be
made not poor to make a few rich; for Jesus
Christ's sake.

Oliver Cromwell, 1599–1658

Bring us, O Lord God, at our last awakening
into the house and gate of heaven, to enter into
that gate and dwell in that house, where there
shall be no darkness or dazzling, but one equal
light; no noise or silence, but one equal music;
no fears or hopes, but one equal possession;
no ends of beginnings, but one equal eternity;
in the habitation of thy glory and dominion
world without end.

John Donne, 1572–1631

O Lord God, when Thou givest to Thy servants to
endeavor any great matter, grant us also to know
that it is not the beginning, but the continuing
of the same to the end, until it be thoroughly
finished, which yieldeth the true glory; through
Him who for the finishing of Thy work laid
down his life, our Redeemer, Jesus Christ.

*Source unknown, based on a saying
of Francis Drake, c.1540–96*

O Lord God, grant us always, whatever the
world may say, to content ourselves with what
you say, and to care only for your approval, which will outweigh all worlds; for Jesus
Christ's sake.

General Charles Gordon, 1833–85

Merciful God, be thou now unto me a strong
tower of defense. Give me grace to await thy
leisure, and patiently to bear what you doest
unto me, nothing doubting or mistrusting thy
goodness towards me. Therefore do with me in
all things as thou wilt: Only arm me, I beseech
thee, with thy armor, that I may stand fast;
above all things taking to me the shield of faith,
praying always that I may refer myself wholly
to thy will, being assuredly persuaded that all
thou doest cannot but be well. And unto thee
be all honor and glory.

Lady Jane Grey, 1537–54, before her execution

Grant, O Lord, that we may keep a constant
guard on our thoughts and passions, that they
may never lead us into sin; that we may live in
perfect love with all humankind, in affection to
those who love us, and in forgiveness to those,
if any there are, who hate us. Give us good and
virtuous friends. In the name of our blessed
Lord and Savior Jesus Christ.

Warren Hastings, 1732–1818

O Lord Jesus Christ, you have made me and redeemed me and brought me to where I now am: you know what you wish to do with me; do with me according to your will, for your tender mercies' sake.

King Henry VI, 1421–71

Make me remember, O God, that every day is Thy gift and ought to be used according to Thy command, through Jesus Christ our Lord.

Samuel Johnson, 1709–1784

Take from us, O God, all pride and vanity, all boasting and self-assertiveness, and give us the true courage that shows itself by gentleness; the true wisdom that shows itself by simplicity; and the true power that shows itself by modesty; through Jesus Christ our Lord.

Charles Kingsley, 1819–75

The great Bishop of our souls, Jesus our Lord, so strengthen and assist your troubled hearts with the mighty comfort of the Holy Spirit, that neither earthly tyrants, nor worldly torments, may have power to drive you from the hope and expectation of that kingdom, which for the elect was prepared from the beginning, by our heavenly Father, to whom be all praise and honor, now and ever.

John Knox, c.1513–72

Teach me, my Lord Jesus, instruct me, that I may learn from you what I ought to teach about you.

William Laud, 1573–1645

Let me never know myself apart from the living God!

D.H. Lawrence, 1885–1930

Lord, give us faith that right makes might.

Abraham Lincoln, 1809–65

O Lord, I am yours. Do what seems good in
  your sight,
and give me complete resignation to your will.

David Livingstone, 1813–73

Almighty God, the Protector of all who trust in you, without whose grace nothing is strong, nothing is holy, increase and multiply on us your mercy, that through your holy inspiration we may think the things that are right and by your power may carry them out, through Jesus Christ our Lord.

Martin Luther, 1483–1546

O Lord my God, I have hope in thee;
O my dear Jesus, set me free.
Though hard the chains that fasten me
And sore my lot, yet I long for thee.
I languish and groaning bend my knee,
Adoring, imploring, O set me free.

Mary Queen of Scots, 1542–87,
on the eve of her execution

Lord, make me see your glory in every place.

Michelangelo, 1475–1564

Let us with a gladsome mind
Praise the Lord, for he is kind;
For his mercies shall endure,
Ever faithful, ever sure.

John Milton, 1608–1674

O my sweet Savior Christ, who in your undeserved love towards humankind so kindly suffered the painful death of the cross, do not allow me to be cold or lukewarm in love again towards you.

Thomas More, 1478–1535

O Lord, let me not henceforth desire health or life except to spend them for thee and with thee. Thou alone knowest what is good for me; do therefore what seemeth thee best. Give to me or take from me; conform my will to thine; and grant that, with humble and perfect submission, and in holy confidence, I may receive the orders of thine eternal providence; and may equally adore all that comes from thee, through Jesus Christ our Lord.

Blaise Pascal, 1623–62

The Passionate Man's Pilgrimage
Give me my scallop-shell of quiet,
My staff of faith to walk upon,
My scrip of joy, immortal diet,
My bottle of salvation,
My gown of glory, hope's true gage;
And thus I'll take my pilgrimage.

Blood must be my body's balmer;
No other balm will there be given;
Whilst my soul, like quiet palmer,
Travelleth towards the land of heaven;
Over the silver mountains,
Where spring the nectar fountains:
      There will I kiss
      The bowl of bliss,
And drink mine everlasting fill
Upon every milken hill.
My soul will be a-dry before;
But, after, it will thirst no more.

From thence to heaven's Bribeless hall
Where no corrupted voices brawl,
No Conscience molten into gold,
Nor forged accusers bought and sold,
No cause deferred, nor vain spent journey,
For there Christ is the King's Attorney:
Who pleads for all without degrees,
And he hath Angels, but no fees.

When the grand twelve million Jury,
Of our sins with dreadful fury,
'Gainst our souls black verdicts give,
Christ pleads his death, and then we live,
Be thou my speaker, taintless pleader,
Unblotted Lawyer, true proceeder,
Thou movest salvation even for alms:
Not with a bribed Lawyer's palms.

And this is my eternal plea,
To him that made Heaven, Earth and Sea,
Seeing my flesh must die so soon,
And want a head to dine next noon,
Just at the stroke when my veins start and
      spread
Set on my soul an everlasting head.
Then am I ready like a palmer fit,
To tread those blest paths which before I writ.
      Sir Walter Raleigh, 1552–1618, written when he
      was a prisoner in the Tower of London, awaiting
      execution. The scallop-shell was a symbol of
      pilgrimage in the Middle Ages

Jesus, your light is shining within us,
let not my doubts and my darkness speak to
      me;
Jesus, your light is shining within us,
let my heart always welcome your love.
      Brother Roger, b.1915

Hear our humble prayer, O God, for our friends the animals, especially for animals who are suffering; for any that are hunted or lost or deserted or frightened or hungry; for all that must be put to death. We entreat for them all thy mercy and pity and for those who deal with them we ask a heart of compassion, gentle hands and kindly words. Make us ourselves to be true friends to animals and so to share the blessing of the merciful.
      Albert Schweitzer, 1875–1965

Go with each of us to rest; if any awake, temper them the dark hours of watching; and when the day returns, return to us, our sun and comforter, and call us up with morning faces and with morning hearts, eager to labor, eager to be happy, if happiness should be our portion, and if the day be marked for sorrow, strong to endure it.
      R.L. Stevenson, 1850–94, written
      on the eve of his unexpected death

O almighty God, the searcher of all hearts, who has declared that who draw near to you with their lips when their hearts are far from you are an abomination to you: cleanse, we beseech you, the thoughts of our hearts by the inspiration of your Holy Spirit, that no wandering, vain, or idle thoughts may put out of our minds that reverence and godly fear that becomes all those who come into your presence.
      Jonathan Swift, 1667–1745

Our Father, here I am, at your disposal, your
      child,
to use me to continue your loving the world,
by giving Jesus to me and through me,
to each other and to the world.
Let us pray for each other that we allow Jesus
      to love in us
and through us with the love with which his
      Father loves us.
      Mother Teresa, 1910–98

The mighty God of Jacob be with you to defeat his enemies, and give you the favor of Joseph. The wisdom and spirit of Stephen be with your heart and with your mouth, and teach your lips what to say, and how to answer all things.

He is our God, if we despair in ourselves and
trust in him; and his is the glory.
William Tyndale, c.1491–1536

O merciful God, fill our hearts, we pray, with
   the graces of your Holy Spirit; with love,
   joy, peace, patience, gentleness, goodness,
   faithfulness, humility and self-control.
O Lord, in confidence of your great mercy
   and goodness to all who truly repent
   and resolve to do better, I most humbly
   implore the grace and assistance of the
   Holy Spirit to enable me to become every
   day better.
Grant me the wisdom and understanding to
   know my duty, and the heart and will to
   do it.
Endue me, O Lord, with the true fear and love
   of you, and with a prudent zeal for your
   glory.
Increase in me the graces of charity and
   meekness, of truth and justice, of humility
   and patience, and a firmness of spirit to
   bear every condition with constancy of
   mind.
King William III, 1650–1702

Indexes and Appendix

Index of Authors and Sources

Index of Subjects

Appendix of Biographical Information

Abelard, Peter, 1079–1144, French philosopher and theologian

Aedelwold, c.908–984, Complied a collection of 74 prayers and hymns from the ninth century, called the *Prayer Book of Aedelwold the Bishop*, and the *Book of Cerne*

Aelred, of Rievaulx, 1109–67, English Cistercian abbot

Aethelwold, c.908–984

Albrecht, Bernhard, 1569–1636

Alcuin, 735–804, English scholar and theologian

Alexander, Cecil Frances, 1823–95, Irish hymn writer

Alford, Henry, 1810–71, Dean of Canterbury

Alfred the Great, 849–899, King of Wessex

Ambrose, c.339–397, Bishop of Milan

Ambrosian Manual

Andrew of Crete, 660–732, Bishop of Crete

Andrewes, Lancelot, 1555–1626, Bishop of Chichester and then Winchester; one of the translators of the Authorized Version/ King James Version of the Bible

Anima Christi, 14th century

Anselm, 1033–1109, Archbishop of Canterbury. Scholastic theologian who defended the Christian faith by the use of reason

Anthony,c.251–c.356, Founder of Christian monasticism

Appleseed, Johnny, see Chapman, John

Aquinas, Thomas, 1225–74, Italian Dominican monk, theologian and philosopher

Arndt, Johann, 1555–1621, German Lutheran pietist

Arnold, Thomas, 1795–1842, Headmaster of Rugby School

Ashe, Isaac, 19th century

Astley, General Lord Jacob, 1579–1652, English soldier

Augustine, 354–430, Bishop of Hippo in North Africa. One of the most influential theologians in the Christian church

Austen, Jane, 1775–1817, English novelist

Austin, John, 1613–69

Aylward, Gladys, 1902–70, English missionary to China

Baillie, Joanna, 1762–1851, English poet

Baker, Henry Williams, 1821–77, English clergyman and hymn writer. Editor of *Hymns Ancient and Modern*

Baldwin, d.1190, Archbishop of Canterbury

Baring-Gould, Sabine, 1834–1924, Translator of hymns

Basil the Great, c.329–379, Bishop of Caesarea, theologian

Baxter, Richard, 1615–91, English Puritan minister and religious writer

Becon, Thomas, 1512–67, English Protestant divine

Bede, the Venerable, c.673–735, English biblical scholar and church historian

Beethoven, Ludwig van, 1770–1827, German composer

Benedict, 480–543, founder of the Benedictine order of monks

Benson, Edward White, 1829–96, Archbishop of Canterbury

Bernard of Clairvaux, 1090–1153, Cistercian monk and abbot, author of a monastic Rule and several mystical treatises

Bersier, Eugene, 1831–89, Minister of the Free Reformed Church in Paris

Bianco of Siena, c.1367–1434, hymn writer

Bickersteth, Edward H., 1825–1906, Bishop of Exeter and hymn writer

Blake, William, 1757–1827, poet and painter

Bliss, Philip Paul, 1838–76, American hymn writer

Bode, John Ernest, 1816–74, English clergyman and hymn writer

Boehme, Jakob, 1575–1626, shoemaker from Silesia who wrote down his mystical experiences

Boethius, Severinus, c.480–524, Roman statesman, writer and philosopher

Bonar, Horatius, 1808–82, Scottish Presbyterian minister

Bonaventure, c.1221–74, Franciscan theologian

Bonhoeffer, Dietrich, 1906–45, German Protestant theologian, executed for opposing the Nazis

Boniface, c.680– c.754, English missionary to Germany

Book of Common Worship of the Presbyterian Church U.S.A., 1906

Book of Common Prayer, The, 1549

Book of Common Prayer, The, 1552

Book of Common Prayer, The, 1662, Replaced service books such as the breviary and missal. Based on Cranmer's writing, first used in 1549 and re-introduced in 1662

Book of Cerne, The, 9th century,

Book of Hours, 1514

Bounds, Edward McKendree, 1835–1913, American Methodist minister and devotional writer

Bourne, George Hugh, 1840–1928, English minister and hymn writer

Bradford, John, c.1510–55

Bradwardine, Thomas, c.1290–1349, chaplain to King Edward III

Brady, Nicholas, 1639–1726, hymn writer and translator

Brent, Charles, Henry, 1862–1929, missionary Bishop of the Philippines

Breton fisherman's prayer

Breviary, a book of prayers, psalms and Bible readings used by nuns and monks

Bridge, William, 1600–70, English Puritan divine

Bridget of Kildare, c.460–c.528, Irish abbess

Bridget of Sweden, 1303–73, mystic and patron saint of Sweden, founder of the Brigittine Order

Bridges, Charles, 1794–1869

Bright, William, 1824–1901, English historian

Birgitta, see Bridget of Sweden

Brontë, Anne, 1820–49, English novelist

Brontë, Emily, 1818–48, English novelist

Brooks, Phillips, 1835–93, Bishop of Massachusetts

Browning, Elizabeth Barrett, 1806–61, English poet

Browning, Robert, 1812–89, English poet

Bruce, Alexander Balmain, 1831–99

Bunyan, John, 1628–88, English nonconformist minister and author of Pilgrim's Progress

Burns, Robert, 1759–96, Scottish bard

Burton, John, 1803–1877

Byrom, John, 1691–1763, English poet and hymn writer

Byrhtnoth, d.991, English leader of the East Saxons

Cædmon, 7th century, an English illiterate herdsman who had a dream about "the beginning of things."

Calvin, John, 1509–64, French leading Reformation theologian who settled in Geneva

Campbell, John McLeod, 1800–72, Scots theologian and author

Carey, William, 1761–1834, English missionary to India and Bible translator

Carmina Gadelica, a collection of old oral prayers poems etc from the Highlands of Scotland, collected in the 19th century

Carpenter, William Boyd, 1841–1918, chaplain to Queen Victoria

Caswall, Edward, 1814–78, English hymn writer

Catherine of Genoa, 1447–1510, Italian Franciscan tertiary

Catherine of Siena, 1347–80, Sister of the Dominican order

Cennick, John, 1718–55, supporter of John Wesley and George Whitefield and hymn writer

Cerne, Book of, 9th century

Chalmers, Thomas, 1780–1847, Scottish divine

Chambers, Oswald, 1874–1917, Scottish Bible teacher and author

Channing, William Ellery, 1780–1842, known as the father of American Unitarianism

Chapman, John, 1774–1845, known as "Johnny Appleseed", an American pioneer and folk hero

Charles I, 1600–49, English monarch

Chatfield, Allen William, 1808–96, translator of Greek Christian hymns into verse

Chester Cathedral

Christian Prayers, 1566, written by Henry Bull, a keen supporter of the Reformation

Church Guild, 19th century

Church Missionary Society, English missionary society

Chrysostom, John, c.347–407, Bishop of Constantinople, known as the "golden-mouthed" preacher

Clare of Assisi, 1194–1253, Italian cofoundress of the Order of Poor Ladies, or Clares

Claret, Anthony Mary, 1807–70, Spanish Catholic missionary

Claudius, Matthias, 1740–1815, German poet

Clement XI, 1649–1721, Pope 1700–21

Clement of Alexandria, c.150–c.215, Greek theologian

Clement of Rome, c.30–c.95, reckoned to be the fourth bishop of Rome; writer.

Coleridge, Samuel Taylor, 1772–1834, English Romantic poet

Colet, John, c.1467–1519, English theologian

Columba, 521–597, Irish missionary

Columbanus, c.550–615, Irish missionary who established Celtic monasteries throughout Gaul

Collyer, Robert, 1823–1912, English Methodist who became Unitarian minister in Chicago

Common Service Book of the Lutheran Church, The, 1917

Compline, in the monastic ritual, the last service of the day

Constantine the Great, c.280–337, Roman Emperor

Cooper, L. Gordon, b.1927, American astronaut

Cosin, John, 1594–1672, Bishop of Durham, liturgist

Cosmas, the Melodist d.c.760, Bishop of Maiuma, near Gaza

Cotton, George Edward, 1813–66, Anglican bishop of Calcutta

Coventry Cathedral

Coverdale, Miles, 1488–1568, English Bible translator and Bishop of Exeter

Cowper, William, 1731–1800, English poet and close friend of John Newton

Cranmer, Thomas, 1489–1556, Archbishop of Canterbury, main compiler of Book of Common Prayer

Crashaw, Richard, 1613–49, Puritan poet

Cromwell, Oliver, 1599–1658, English revolutionary soldier and statesman

Cromwell, Thomas, 1485–1540, English statesman

Crosby, Frances Jane, (Fanny), 1820–1915, American prolific hymn writer

Crossman, Samuel, c.1624–83, Prebendary of Bristol Cathedral

Cyril of Alexandria, d.444, Bishop of the Egyptian city of Alexandria

Damascene, John, d.c.780, poet and last but one of the Fathers of the Eastern Church

Davidson, Randall T., 1848–1930

de Chantal, Jane Frances, 1571–1641, French Catholic, foundress of the Order of the Visitation of The Blessed Virgin Mary

Dehqani-Tafti, Hassan, Anglican Bishop in Iran

Dekker, Thomas, c.1570–1623, English playwright

Devotional Diary, A

Didache, 1st century, early Christian writing

Dimitrii of Rostov, 17th century

Dimma, 7th century, Irish monk

Dionysius the Pseudo-Areopagite, c.500, Syrian mystical theologian

Dix, William Chatterton, 1837–98, English hymn writer

Doddridge, Philip, 1702–51, British nonconformist minister and hymn writer

Donne, John, 1572–1631, English poet and Dean of St Paul's Cathedral, London

John Dowden, 1840–1910, Bishop of Edinburgh

Drake, Sir Francis, c.1540–96, seaman of Elizabethan England

Dream of the Rood, The

Duche, J., 18th century, American chaplain to the Congress

Dürer, Albrecht 1471–1528, German painter and engraver

Eber, Paul, 1511–69, German Reformer

Edward VI, 1537–63, English monarch

Egyptian Liturgy of St Mark

Eisenhower, Dwight David, 1890–1969, U.S.A. President

Elliot, Emily E.S., 1836–98, Prolific English hymn writer

Elliott, Charlotte, 1789–1871, English hymn writer

Emerson, Ralph Waldo, 1803–82, American poet

English Reformers, 1549

Ephraem, c.306–378, also known as Ephrem the Syrian. Deacon and poet of the Syrian church

Ephrem, see Ephraem

Erasmus, Desiderius, 1467–1536, Dutch humanist scholar who prepared an accurate edition of the Greek New Testament

Eusebius of Caesarea, d.c.340, Bishop of Caesarea and historian

Euchologium Anglicanum

Evangelical Lutheran Hymn-Book, The, 1912

Everest, Charles William, 1814–1877, American Episcopal minister

Eymard, Peter Julian, 1811–68, French Catholic priest and spiritual writer

Fénelon, François, 1651–1715, French archbishop

Festal Menaion, Service in the Greek Orthodox Church

Ferrar, Nicholas, 1592–1637, founder of Little Gidding Community

Fisher, John, 1459–1535, English Cardinal and martyr

Fletcher, Phineas, 1582–1650, English poet

Fortunatus, V.H., 530–609, Foucauld, Charles de, 1855–1916, *French priest and missionary in the Sahara*

Fox, George, 1624–91, English preacher and founder of the Religious Society of Friends (the Quakers)

Francis of Assisi, 1181–1226, Italian founder of Franciscan order of friars

Francis de Sales, 1567–1622, Roman Catholic bishop of Geneva

Frankfurt prayer, 16th century

Freylinghausen, Johann, 1670–1739, German pastor

Froude, Richard Hurrell, 1803–36, Anglican theologian

Fuller, Thomas, 1608–61, English clergyman and historian

Gallican Formularies

Gallican Sacramentary, The

Gelasian Sacramentary, 5th century, a sacramentary (see *Sacramentary*) named after the 5th-century pope, Gelasius, but probably written by nuns at Chelles, Paris

Geneva Bible, 1599

Germanicus, 634–734, Patriarchate of Constantinople

Gertrude of Thüringen, known as Gertrude the Great, see Gertrude the Great

Gertrude the Great, 1256–c.1301, German Bendictine mystical writer

Gordon, General Charles George, 1833–85, Governor of Sudan

Gothic Missal, The

Gregorian Sacramentary, The, 6th century

Gregory I, c.540–604, pope who sent Augustine to convert the English

Gregory of Narek, 951–1003, Armenian mystic and poet

Gregory of Nazianzen, 329–89, one of the four great doctors of the church in the 4th century. Also known as Gregory the Theologian

Gregory the Illuminator, d. 325, founder of the Armenian Church

Grey, Lady Jane, 1537–54, Queen of England for nine days, before her execution

Guthrie, William, 1620–65, English Puritan

Madame Guyon, 1647–1717

Habermann, Johann, 1516–90

Hamilton, John, 1511–71, Roman Catholic Archbishop of St. Andrews, Scotland, and supporter of Mary Queen of Scots

Hammond, Henry, 1605–60, chaplain to Charles I

Hart, Joseph, 1712–68, Independent minister and hymn writer

Hastings, Warren, 1732–1818, Governor-General of Bengal

Hatch, Edwin, 1835–89, Reader in Ecclesiastical History at Oxford

Havergal, Frances Ridely, 1836–70, poet and hymn writer

Heber, Reginald, 1783–1826, Bishop of Calcutta, poet and hymn writer

Henry VI, 1421–71, English monarch

Henry VIII, 1491–1547, English monarch

Henry, Matthew, 1662–1714, Nonconformist Bible commentator

Herbert, George, 1593–1633, Anglican clergyman and religious poet

Herrick, Robert, 1591–1674, English clergyman and poet

Hickes, George, 1642–1715, Bishop of Thetford, Norfolk, England

Hilary, c.315–c.367, Bishop of Poitiers, theologian

Hildegard of Bingen, 1098–1179, German Benedictine abbess and mystic, known as "the Sybil of the Rhine"

Hilton, Walter, 14th century, English spiritual writer

Hodge, A.A., 1823–86

Holland, Henry Scott, 1847–1918, theologian and canon of St. Paul's Cathedral, London.

Hook, Walter Farquhar, 1798–1875

Hopkins, Gerard Manley, 1844–89, English poet and Jesuit priest

Hopps, John Page, 1834–1919, English Baptist pastor

Hort, F.J.A., 1828–92, English biblical scholar

How, William Walsham, 1823–97, first Bishop of Wakefield, hymn writer

Hunter, John, 1849–1917, Scottish minister
Huss, John, c.1369–1415
Bohemian theologian and martyr
Hyde, William de Witt, 1858–1917, American
 hymn writer

Ignatius, c.35 –c.107, Bishop of Antioch,
 martyred
Ignatius of Loyola, 1491/1495–1556, Spanish
 founder of the Society of Jesus (Jesuits)
Ingemann, Bernhardt, 1789–1862, Danish
 professor of literature
Irenaeus, c.130–c.200
Bishop of Lyons who opposed Gnosticism
Isaac the Syrian, 7th century

James, Mary Dagworthy, 1810–83, American
 hymn writer
Jarrett, Bede, 1881–1934, English Dominican
Jenks, Benjamin, 1647–1724, Nonconformist
 minister
Jerome, c.342–420, biblical scholar and
 translator
Jonson, Ben, 1572–1637, English poet and
 playwright
Jewel, John, 1522–71, Bishop of Salisbury
John of Damascus, c.676–749, Syrian
 theologian, last of the Greek fathers
John of the Cross, 1542–91, Spanish mystic
 and founder of the Discalced Carmelites
Johnson, Dr. Samuel, 1709–84, English writer
 and lexicographer
Joseph of the Studium, 9th century, Sicilian
 monk and poet
Jowett, J.H., 1864–1923, English
 Congregationalist preacher and writer in
 America
Julian of Norwich, 1342–c.1416, English
 anchoress of Norwich

Keble, John, 1792–1866, poetry professor and
 leader of the Oxford Movement
Kempe, Margery, c.1373–c.1432, English mystic
 and writer
Kempis, Thomas à, 1379–1471, Augustinian
 monk and reputed author of *Imitation of
 Christ*
Ken, Thomas, 1637–1711, Bishop of Bath and
 Wells
Kepler, Johannes, 1571–1630, German
 astronomer, founder of physical astronomy

Kethe, William, d.1594, Scottish minister and
 hymn writer
Kierkegaard, Søren, 1813–55, attributed as
 founder of existentialist philosophy
King's College, Cambridge
King Henry VIII's Primer
Kingsley, Charles, 1819–75, English clergyman,
 social reformer whose novels include *The
 Water Babies*
Knights of the Garter, 14th century
Knox, John, c.1513–72, Scottish Reformer,
 Chaplain to Edward VI of England, and
 main compiler of the Scottish Prayer Book
Kuyper, Abraham, 1837–1920, Dutch Calvinist
 statesman and theologian

Lambronac'i, Nersess, 1153–98, Bishop of
 Tarsus
Langland, William, c.1332–c.1400, English
 poet
Langton, Stephen, 1151–1228, Archbishop of
 Canterbury
Lathbury, Mary Artemesia, 1841–1913,
 American poet
Law, William, 1686–1761, English clergyman,
 writer and spiritual adviser
Lawrence, Brother, 1611–91, French Carmelite
 lay brother
Lawrence, D.H., 1885–1930, English writer
Laud, William, 1573–1645, Archbishop of
 Canterbury, adviser to King Charles I
Leighton, Robert, 1611–84, Scottish
 Presbyterian minister and devotional
 writer
Lenten Triodion, service in the Greek
 Orthodox Church
Leonine Sacramentary, The
Liguori, Alphonsus, 1696–1787, Italian
 churchman, Doctor of the Church
Lincoln, Abraham, 1809–65, President of
 U.S.A.
Liturgy of John Chrysostom and Basil the Great
Liturgy of St Dionysus, 1st century, this
 Liturgy (of the Syrian Jacobite Church)
 gives the doctrine of Dionysius in a
 liturgical form.
Liturgy of St James, one of the oldest liturgical
 forms of the Lord's Supper. An adapted
 version still used by Maronite and Jacobite
 Christians
Liturgy of St Mark, second century

Livingstone, David, 1813–73, Scottish medical missionary and explorer in Africa

Longfellow, Henry Wadsworth, 1807–82, American poet

Luther, Martin, 1483–1546, German monk and theologian who led the Protestant Reformation and translated the Bible into German

Lyra Davidica, 1708

Lyte, Henry Francis, 1793–1847, Anglican clergyman, perpetual curate of Lower Brixham, Devon, hymn writer

Macarius of Egypt, c.300–c.390, hermit and mystic

Macdonald, George, 1824–1905, Scottish congregational minister and writer of Christian allegories and children's stories

Maclaren, Alexander, 1826–1910, Scottish divine

Magistros, Grigor, c.990–1059, leading Armenian theologian

Mantakuni, John, c.420–490, Armenian spiritual writer

Margaret of Scotland, c.1045–92, raised in Hungray, became Queen of Scotland

Martineau, James, 1805–1900, English Unitarian theologian

Martyn, Henry, 1781–1812, scholar and pioneer missionary to India and Persia

Mary Queen of Scots, 1542–87, executed under Queen Elizabeth I

Mesrob Mashtots, 5th century, Armenian theologian and inventor of the Armenian alphabet

Mathams, Walter John, 1853–1931, English Baptist pastor

Matheson, George, 1842–1906, blind Scottish minister

Maurice, Frederick Denison, 1805–72, Anglican clergyman, leader of Christian Socialist movement

Maurus, Hrabanus, c.784–856, German scholar and theologian

Mechtild of Magdeburg, 1210–97, German mystic

Meditations and Prayers, compiled by John Cosin

Melanchthon, Philip, 1497–1560, German reformer and author of the *Augsburg Confession*

Melito of Sardis, d.189, Bishop of Sardis, and martyr

Merlo, Jacobus Horstius, 1597–1664

Meyer, F.B., 1847–1929, English Baptist minister

Michelangelo, 1475–1564, Italian painter, artist, sculptor, and inventor

Midlane, Albert, 1825–1909

Milman, Henry Hart, 1791–1868

Milton, John, 1608–74, English ecclesiastical poet and hymn writer

Missal, missals contained services of the Mass for a year

Moody, Dwight Lyman, 1837–99, American evangelist

Monsell, John Samuel Bewley, 1811–1875, Irish minister and poet

Montgomery, James, 1771–1854, Scottish hymn writer

More, Gertrude, 1606–33, English Benedictine nun

More, Thomas, 1478–1535, Lord Chancellor of England

Moule, Handley C.G., 1841–1920, Bishop of Durham

Mozarabic Breviary, see Mozarabic Liturgy

Mozarabic Liturgy, 7th century, the national liturgy of the Spanish Church, until the end of the eleventh century

Mozarabic Psalter, see Mozarabic Liturgy

Mozarabic rite, see Mozarabic Liturgy

Murray, Andrew, 1828–1917

Neale, John Mason, 1818–66, English translator of Latin and Greek hymns

Neander, Joachim

Nerses of Clajes, 4th century

Nerses the Gracious, 1102–73, Armenian bishop and poet

Nestorian Liturgy, 5th/6th century, forms of worship of the Nestorian Church

New Church Book of Worship, 1876

Newman, John Henry, 1801–90, leader of the Anglican Oxford Movement who became a Roman Catholic cardinal.

Newton, John, 1725–1807, Anglican clergyman and hymn writer

Nicholas of Flue, 1417–87, Swiss hermit

Niebuhr, Reinhold, 1892–1971, American theologian

Narrow Way, The, 1869

Nikodemos of the Holy Mountain, 18th century, Greek monk

Noel, Caroline Maria, 1817–77, English hymn writer

Nott, Peter, b.1933, Bishop of Norwich, England

Oatman, Jr., Johnson, 1856–1922, prolific writer of gospel songs

Office of None, in the monastic ritual, one of the daily religious services, originally recited at 3 p.m.

Office of the Royal Maundy in Westminster Abbey

Optina elders

Origen, 185–254, leading theologian of the Greek Church

Oxenden, Ashton, 1808–92, Canadian Anglican bishop

Paget, Francis, 1851–1911, Bishop of Oxford

Palmer, Ray, 1808–87, American Congregational minister and hymn writer

Parker, Matthew, 1504–75, Archbishop of Canterbury

Parker, William H., 1845–1929, English businessman

Pascal, Blaise, 1623–62, French mathematician, physicist and writer

Paterson, Alexander, prison reformer

Patrick, c.389–c.461, English missionary-bishop to Ireland who also evangelized Picts and Anglo-Saxons

Penitent Pilgrim, The, 1641

Penn, William, 1644–1718, English Quaker, founded Pennsylvania

Perronet, Edward, 1726–92, English minister and hymn writer

Philaret, 1782–1867, Metropolitan of Moscow

Phillips, John, 1676–1708, English poet

Pierpoint, Folliot Sandford, 1835–1917, English hymn writer

Pigott, Jean Sophia, 1845–82, Irish hymn writer

Pilkington, James, 1520–76

Pius VI, 1717–99, Pope, 1775–99

Pius X, 1835–1914, Pope, 1903–14

Polycarp, c.69–c.155, Bishop of Smyrna, knew the apostle John, burnt to death for his faith

Pope, Alexander, 1688–1744, English poet and satirist

Precationes Piae, 1564

Primer, a devotional prayer book for lay people, mainly in use before the Reformation.

Primer, 1557, see Primer

Primer, 1559, see Primer

Prior, Matthew, 1664–1721, English poet

Private Devotions, 1560

Private Devotions of William Laud, The, 1667, Prayers compiled and used by Dr William Laud

Pusey, Edward Bouverie, 1800–82, English Tractarian leader

Raleigh, Sir Walter, 1552–1618, English courtier, writer, and adventurer

Rauschenbusch, Walter, 1861–1918, American cleargyman, leading figure in Social Gospel movement

Reynolds, Edward, 1599–1667, Bishop of Norwich

Rich, Edmund, c.1180–1240, Professor at Oxford University and Archbishop of Canterbury

Richard of Chichester, 1197–1253, Bishop of Chichester

Ridley, Nicholas, c.1500–55, Protestant reformer and Bishop of London, martyred under Queen Mary

Rinkart, Martin, 1586–1649, German minister and poet

Robinson, Arthur W., 1856–1928, Canon of Canterbury

Roger, Brother, Roger Schutz, b. 1915, founder of the Taizé Community

Rolle, Richard, 1290–1349, Yorkshire hermit and spiritual writer

Roman Breviary, a book with psalms and Bible readings for daily services

Rossetti, Christina, 1830–94, devout British, Anglican poet

Rothe, Johann A., 1799–1867, German pastor

Ruspensis, Fulgentius, 468–533

Russian liturgy, 6th century

Ryle, John Charles, 1816–1900, first Anglican bishop of Liverpool

Sacramentary, a sacramentary is an early form of office book used in the Western Church, containing services and prayers

Sarum Breviary (see Sarum Missal)

Sarum Missal, 1085, a liturgy widely used in

pre-Reformation England

Sarum Primer, 1558

Serapion, d.360, hermit, who was made bishop of Thmuis, on the Nile delta

Seraphim of Sarov, 1759–1833, Russian Orthodox monk

Seton, Elizabeth Ann, 1774–1821, American Catholic educator

Shaftesbury, Lord Anthony Ashley Cooper, 1801–85, English social reformer

Shakespeare, William, 1564–1616, English poet and dramatist

Sherlock, Thomas, 1678–1761, English divine

Schweitzer, Albert, 1875–1965, humanitarian, theologian, missionary, organist, and medical doctor

Scriven, Joseph Medlicott, 1819–86, Irish hymn writer

Simeon, Charles, 1759–1836, Bible teacher and promotor of missionary work

Smart, Christopher, 1722–71, English poet

Soldier's Prayer, A

Southey, Robert, 1774–1843, English poet laureate

Spenser, Edmund, 1552–99, English poet

Spurgeon, C.H., 1834–92, English Baptist minister

Starck, Johann Friedrich, German pietist

Steele, Anne, 1717–78, English hymn writer

Stevenson, Robert Louis, 1850–94, Scottish travel writer and novelist

Stewart, Maria W., 1803–79, American abolitionist

Sulpicius, Severus, c.363–c.420, early Christian ascetic and writer

Sumner, Mary, 1828–1921, founder of the Mothers' Union

Suso, Henry, 1296–1366, German Dominican mystic

Sutton, Christopher, 16th century,

Swift, Jonathan, 1667–1745, Irish satirist, Dean of St Patrick's, Dublin

Symeon the New Thologian, 949–1022, leading Orthodox mystic

Symeon the Translator, 11th century

Synesius of Cyrene, 375–430, Bishop of Ptolemais

Syrian Rite, one of the nine main groups of the ancient Christian liturgies

Tallis, Thomas, 1505–85, influential English composer

Tate, Nahum, 1652–1715, poet laureate and translator

Tauler, Johann, 1300–61, German mystic and Dominican

Taylor, James Hudson, 1832–1905, English medical missionary who founded the China Inland Mission

Taylor, Jane, 1782–1866, English children's author and poet

Taylor, Jeremy, 1613–67, Chaplain to Archbishop Laud and King Charles I, and Bishop of Down and Connor

Temple, Frederick, 1821–1902, Archbishop of Canterbury

Temple, William, 1881–1944, Archbishop of Canterbury

ten Boom, Corrie, 1892–1983, Dutch preacher and writer who hid Jews during World War II

Teresa of Avila, 1515–82, Spanish Carmelite mystic

Teresa, Mother, of Calcutta, 1910–98, founder of the Order of the Missionaries of Charity

Tertullian, c.160–225

Thackeray, William Makepeace, 1811–63, English writer

Theodulph of Orleans, c.750–821, Hymn writer

Thérèse of Lisieux, 1873–97, French nun

Todd, III, John N., contemporary American doctor

Toplady, Augustus Montague, 1740–78 English clergyman and hymn writer

Traherne, Thomas, 1637–74 Anglican mystical poet

Treasury of Devotion, 1869, compiled by a priest who asked to remain anonymous

Tusser, Thomas, 1524–80, English agricultural writer and poet

Tuttiett, Lawrence, 1825–97, prebendary of St Ninian's Cathedral, Perth, Scotland

Tychon of Zadonsk, 18th century, Russian Christian

Tyndale, William, c.1491–1536, English reformer and Bible translator

Van Dyke, Henry, 1852–1933, American clergyman, educator, and author

Vardapetca, John Sarkavag, 1050–1129, leading Armenian theologian

Vaughan, Charles John, 1816–97, writer and

Dean of Llandaff, Wales

Vaughan, Henry, 1622–95, English poet

Vianney, John, also known as Cure of Ars, 1786–1859, French parish priest

Vicars, Captain Hedley, 1826–55, soldier killed at Sebastopol

Vives, Ludovicus, 1492–1540, Spanish scholar and friend of Erasmus

Voltaire, François-Marie Arouet de, 1694–1778, French author and philosopher

Warner, Anna Bartlett, 1827–1915, American hymn writer

Washington, George, 1732–99, President of U.S.A.

Watson,Thomas, c.1620–86

Watts, Isaac, 1674–1748, Nonconformist pastor and hymn writer

Webb, Thomas Henry Basil, 1898–1917, Englishman killed in the battle of the Somme

Wedgwood, Josiah, 1674–1748, English potter

Wesley, Charles, 1707–88, English clergyman and great hymn writer who wrote more than 7,000 hymns

Wesley, John, 1703–91, founder of Methodism

Wesley, Susanna, 1670–1742, mother of John and Charles Wesley

Westcott, Brooke Foss, 1825–1901, Bishop of Durham, leading Bible scholar

White, Henry Kirke, 1785–1806, English poet

Whitefield, George, 1714–70

Whittle, Daniel Webster, 1840–1901 American hymn writer

Whittier, John Greenleaf, Quaker poet

Whole Duty of Man, The, 1658

Wilde, Oscar, 1854–1900, Irish dramatist

Wilkinson, Kate Barclay, 1859–1928, Anglican hymnwriter

William III, 1650–1702, English monarch

Williams, William, 1717–91, Welsh minister and hymn writer

Willis, Love Maria Whitcomb, 1824–1908, American editor

Wilson, Thomas, 1663–1755, Bishop of Sodor and Man

Winkworth, Catherine, 1829–78, pioneer of women's education and translator of hymns

Wither, George, 1588–1667, English Puritan poet

Wordsworth, Christopher, 1807–85, Bishop of Lincoln, nephew of William Wordsworth

Xavier, Francis, 1506–52, Jesuit teacher and pioneer missionary to India and Japan

Yelverton, Sir Christopher, 1536–1612, English Member of Parliament

Part Two:
Historical Works on Prayer and Collected Prayers

Detailed Contents, Part Two

Extracts of Classic Christian Teaching

On Cleaving to God
Albert the Great

The nature and value of prayer, and how the heart should be recollected within itself

Since we are incapable of ourselves of any other good action whatsoever, and since we can of ourselves offer nothing to the Lord God (from whom all good things come) which is not his already, with this one exception, as he has deigned to show us both by his own blessed mouth as well as by his example, that we should turn to him in all circumstances and occasions as guilty, wretched, poor, beggarly, weak, helpless, subject servants and sons. And that we should beseech him and lay before him with complete confidence the dangers that are besetting us on all sides, completely grief-stricken in ourselves, in humble prostration of mind, in fear and love, and with recollected, composed, mature, true and naked, shamefaced affection, with great yearning and determination, and in groaning of heart and sincerity of mind.

Thus we commit and offer ourselves up to him freely, securely and nakedly, fully and in everything that is ours, holding nothing back to ourselves, in such a complete and final way, that the same is fulfilled in us as in our blessed father Isaac, who speaks of this very type of prayer, saying, Then we shall be one in God, and the Lord God will be all in all and alone in us when his own perfect love, with which he first loved us, will have become the disposition of our own hearts too. This will come about when all our love, all our desire, all our concern, all our efforts, in fact everything we think, everything we see, speak and even hope will be God, and that unity which now is of the Father with the Son, and of the Son with the Father, will be poured into our own heart and mind as well, in such a way that just as he loves us with sincere and indissoluble love we too will be joined to him with eternal and inseparable affection. In other words we shall be united with him in such a way that whatever we hope, and whatever we say or pray will be God. This therefore should be the aim, this the concern and goal of a spiritual man – to be worthy to possess the image of future bliss in this corruptible body, and in a certain measure experience in advance how the foretaste of that heavenly bliss, eternal life and glory begins in this world.

This, as I say, is the goal of all perfection, that his purified mind should be daily raised up from all bodily objects to spiritual things until all his mental activity and all his heart's desire become one unbroken prayer. So the mind must abandon the dregs of earth and press on towards to God, on whom alone should be fixed the desire of a spiritual man, for whom the least separation from that *summum bonum* is to be considered a living death and dreadful loss. Then, when the requisite peace has been established in his mind, when it is free from attachment to any carnal passion, and clings firmly in intention to that one supreme good, the Apostle's sayings are fulfilled, Pray without ceasing (1 Thessalonians 5.17), and, Pray in every place lifting up pure hands without anger or dispute (1 Timothy 2.8). For when the power of the mind is absorbed in this purity, so to speak, and is transformed from an earthly nature into the spiritual or angelic likeness, whatever it receives into itself, whatever it is occupied with, whatever it is doing, it will be pure and sincere prayer. In this way, if you continue all the time in this way it will become as easy and clear for you to remain in contemplation in your inward and recollected state, as to live in the natural state.

Attributed to Albert the Great, c.1200–80

Proslogium
or Discourse on the Existence of God

Anselm

INTRODUCTORY NOTE

In this brief work the author aims at proving in a single argument the existence of God, and whatsoever we believe of God. The author writes in the person of one who contemplates God, and seeks to understand what he believes. To this work he had given this title: Faith Seeking Understanding. He finally named it *Proslogium*, – that is, *A Discourse*.

Sidney Norton Deane

PREFACE

After I had published, at the solicitous entreaties of certain brethren, a brief work (the *Monologium*) as an example of meditation on the grounds of faith, in the person of one who investigates, in a course of silent reasoning with himself, matters of which he is ignorant; considering that this book was knit together by the linking of many arguments, I began to ask myself whether there might be found a single argument which would require no other for its proof than itself alone; and alone would suffice to demonstrate that God truly exists, and that there is a supreme good requiring nothing else, which all other things require for their existence and well-being; and whatever we believe regarding the divine Being.

Although I often and earnestly directed my thought to this end, and at some times that which I sought seemed to be just within my reach, while again it wholly evaded my mental vision, at last in despair I was about to cease, as if from the search for a thing which could not be found. But when I wished to exclude this thought altogether, lest, by busying my mind to no purpose, it should keep me from other thoughts, in which I might be successful; then more and more, though I was unwilling and shunned it, it began to force itself upon me, with a kind of importunity. So, one day, when I was exceedingly wearied with resisting its importunity, in the very conflict of my thoughts, the proof of which I had despaired offered itself, so that I eagerly embraced the

thoughts which I was strenuously repelling.

Thinking, therefore, that what I rejoiced to have found, would, if put in writing, be welcome to some readers, of this very matter, and of some others, I have written the following treatise, in the person of one who strives to lift his mind to the contemplation of God, and seeks to understand what he believes. In my judgment, neither this work nor the other, which I mentioned above, deserved to be called a book, or to bear the name of an author; and yet I thought they ought not to be sent forth without some title by which they might, in some sort, invite one into whose hands they fell to their perusal. I accordingly gave each a title, that the first might be known as, An Example of Meditation on the Grounds of Faith, and its sequel as, Faith Seeking Understanding. But, after, both had been copied by many under these titles, many urged me, and especially Hugo, the reverend Archbishop of Lyons, who discharges the apostolic office in Gaul, who instructed me to this effect on his apostolic authority – to prefix my name to these writings. And that this might be done more fitly, I named the first, *Monologium*, that is, *A Soliloquy*; but the second, *Proslogium*, that is, *A Discourse*.

CHAPTER 1

Exhortation of the mind to the contemplation of God. – It casts aside cares, and excludes all thoughts save that of God, that it may seek Him. Man was created to see God. Man by sin lost the blessedness for which he was made, and found the misery for which he was not made. He did not keep this good when he could keep it easily. Without God it is ill with us. Our labors and attempts are in vain without God. Man cannot seek God, unless God himself teaches him; nor find him, unless he reveals himself. God created man in his image, that he might be mindful of him, think of him, and love him. The believer does not seek to understand, that he may believe, but he believes that he may understand: for unless he believed he would not understand.

Up now, slight man! flee, for a little while, thy occupations; hide thyself, for a time, from thy disturbing thoughts. Cast aside, now, thy burdensome cares, and put away thy toilsome business. Yield room for some little time to God; and rest for a little time in him. Enter the inner chamber of thy mind; shut out all thoughts save

EXTRACTS OF CLASSIC CHRISTIAN TEACHING 399

that of God, and such as can aid thee in seeking him; close thy door and seek him. Speak now, my whole heart! speak now to God, saying, I seek thy face; thy face, Lord, will I seek (Psalms xxvii. 8). And come thou now, O Lord my God, teach my heart where and how it may seek thee, where and how it may find thee.

Lord, if thou art not here, where shall I seek thee, being absent? But if thou art everywhere, why do I not see thee present? Truly thou dwellest in unapproachable light. But where is unapproachable light, or how shall I come to it? Or who shall lead me to that light and into it, that I may see thee in it? Again, by what marks, under what form, shall I seek thee? I have never seen thee, O Lord, my God; I do not know thy form. What, O most high Lord, shall this man do, an exile far from thee? What shall thy servant do, anxious in his love of thee, and cast out afar from thy face? He pants to see thee, and thy face is too far from him. He longs to come to thee, and thy dwelling-place is inaccessible. He is eager to find thee, and knows not thy place. He desires to seek thee, and does not know thy face. Lord, thou art my God, and thou art my Lord, and never have I seen thee. It is thou that hast made me, and hast made me anew, and hast bestowed upon me all the blessing I enjoy; and not yet do I know thee. Finally, I was created to see thee, and not yet have I done that for which I was made.

O wretched lot of man, when he hath lost that for which he was made! O hard and terrible fate! Alas, what has he lost, and what has he found? What has departed, and what remains? He has lost the blessedness for which he was made, and has found the misery for which he was not made. That has departed without which nothing is happy, and that remains which, in itself, is only miserable. Man once did eat the bread of angels, for which he hungers now; he eateth now the bread of sorrows of which he knew not then. Alas! for the mourning of all mankind, for the universal lamentation of the sons of Hades! He choked with satiety, we sigh with hunger. He abounded, we beg. He possessed in happiness, and miserably forsook his possession; we suffer want in unhappiness, and feel a miserable longing, and alas! we remain empty.

Why did he not keep for us, when he could

so easily, that whose lack we should feel so heavily? Why did he shut us away from the light, and cover us over with darkness? With what purpose did he rob us of life, and inflict death upon us? Wretches that we are, whence have we been driven out; whither are we driven on? Whence hurled? Whither consigned to ruin? From a native country into exile, from the vision of God into our present blindness, from the joy of immortality into the bitterness and horror of death. Miserable exchange of how great a good, for how great an evil! Heavy loss, heavy grief, heavy all our fate!

But alas! wretched that I am, one of the sons of Eve, far removed from God! What have I undertaken? What have I accomplished? Whither was I striving? How far have I come? To what did I aspire? Amid what thoughts am I sighing? I sought blessings, and lo! confusion. I strove toward God, and I stumbled on myself. I sought calm in privacy, and I found tribulation and grief, in my inmost thoughts. I wished to smile in the joy of my mind, and I am compelled to frown by the sorrow of my heart. Gladness was hoped for, and lo! a source of frequent sighs!

And thou too, O Lord, how long? How long, O Lord, dost thou forget us; how long dost thou turn thy face from us? When wilt thou look upon us, and hear us? When wilt thou enlighten our eyes, and show us thy face? When wilt thou restore thyself to us? Look upon us, Lord; hear us, enlighten us, reveal thyself to us. Restore thyself to us, that it may be well with us, – thyself, without whom it is so ill with us. Pity our toilings and strivings toward thee since we can do nothing without thee. Thou dost invite us; do thou help us. I beseech thee, O Lord, that I may not lose hope in sighs, but may breathe anew in hope. Lord, my heart is made bitter by its desolation; sweeten thou it, I beseech thee, with thy consolation. Lord, in hunger I began to seek thee; I beseech thee that I may not cease to hunger for thee. In hunger I have come to thee; let me not go unfed. I have come in poverty to the Rich, in misery to the Compassionate; let me not return empty and despised. And if, before I eat, I sigh, grant, even after sighs, that which I may eat. Lord, I am bowed down and can only look downward; raise me up that I may look upward. My iniquities have gone over my head; they overwhelm me; and, like a heavy load, they weigh me down. Free me from them; unburden me, that the pit of iniquities may not close over me.

Be it mine to look up to thy light, even from afar, even from the depths. Teach me to seek thee, and reveal thyself to me, when I seek thee, for I cannot seek thee, except thou teach me, nor find thee, except thou reveal thyself. Let me seek thee in longing, let me long for thee in seeking; let me find thee in love, and love thee in finding. Lord, I acknowledge and I thank thee that thou hast created me in this thine image, in order that I may be mindful of thee, may conceive of thee, and love thee; but that image has been so consumed and wasted away by vices, and obscured by the smoke of wrong-doing, that it cannot achieve that for which it was made, except thou renew it, and create it anew. I do not endeavor, O Lord, to penetrate thy sublimity, for in no wise do I compare my understanding with that; but I long to understand in some degree thy truth, which my heart believes and loves. For I do not seek to understand that I may believe, but I believe in order to understand. For this also I believe, – that unless I believed, I should not understand.

CHAPTER 2
Truly there is a God, although the fool hath said in his heart, There is no God.

And so, Lord, do thou, who dost give understanding to faith, give me, so far as thou knowest it to be profitable, to understand that thou art as we believe; and that thou art that which we believe. And indeed, we believe that thou art a being than which nothing greater can be conceived. Or is there no such nature, since the fool hath said in his heart, there is no God? (Psalms xiv. 1). But, at any rate, this very fool, when he hears of this being of which I speak – a being than which nothing greater can be conceived – understands what he hears, and what he understands is in his understanding; although he does not understand it to exist.

For, it is one thing for an object to be in the understanding, and another to understand that the object exists. When a painter first conceives of what he will afterwards perform, he has it in his understanding, but he does not yet understand it to be, because he has not yet performed it. But after he has made the painting, he both has it in his understanding, and he understands that it exists, because he has made it. Hence, even the fool is convinced that something exists in the understanding, at least, than which nothing greater can be conceived. For, when he hears of this, he understands it. And whatever is understood, exists in the understanding. And assuredly that, than which nothing greater can be conceived, cannot exist in the understanding alone. For, suppose it exists in the understanding alone: then it can be conceived to exist in reality; which is greater.

Therefore, if that, than which nothing greater can be conceived, exists in the understanding alone, the very being, than which nothing greater can be conceived, is one, than which a greater can be conceived. But obviously this is impossible. Hence, there is no doubt that there exists a being, than which nothing greater can be conceived, and it exists both in the understanding and in reality.

CHAPTER 3
God cannot be conceived not to exist. – God is that, than which nothing greater can be conceived. – That which can be conceived not to exist is not God.

And it assuredly exists so truly, that it cannot be conceived not to exist. For, it is possible to conceive of a being which cannot be conceived not to exist; and this is greater than one which can be conceived not to exist. Hence, if that, than which nothing greater can be conceived, can be conceived not to exist, it is not that, than which nothing greater can be conceived. But this is an irreconcilable contradiction. There is, then, so truly a being than which nothing greater can be conceived to exist, that it cannot even be conceived not to exist;. and this being thou art, O Lord, our God.

So truly, therefore, dost thou exist, O Lord, my God, that thou canst not be conceived not to exist; and rightly. For, if a mind could conceive of a being better than thee, the creature would rise above the Creator; and this is most absurd. And, indeed, whatever else there is, except thee alone, can be conceived not to exist. To thee alone, therefore, it belongs to exist more truly than all other beings, and hence in a higher degree than all others. For, whatever else exists does not exist so truly, and hence in a less degree it belongs to it to exist. Why, then, has the fool said in his heart, there is no God (Psalms xiv. 1), since it is so evident, to a rational mind, that thou dost exist in the highest degree of all? Why, except that he is dull and a fool?

CHAPTER 4
How the fool has said in his heart what cannot be conceived. – A thing may be conceived in two ways: (1) when the word signifying it is conceived; (2) when the thing itself is understood As far as the word goes, God can be conceived not to exist; in reality he cannot.

But how has the fool said in his heart what he could not conceive; or how is it that he could not conceive what he said in his heart? since it is the same to say in the heart, and to conceive.

But, if really, nay, since really, he both conceived, because he said in his heart; and did not say in his heart, because he could not conceive; there is more than one way in which a thing is said in the heart or conceived. For, in one sense, an object is conceived, when the word signifying it is conceived; and in another, when the very entity, which the object is, is understood.

In the former sense, then, God can be conceived not to exist; but in the latter, not at all. For no one who understands what fire and water are can conceive fire to be water, in accordance with the nature of the facts themselves, although this is possible according to the words. So, then, no one who understands what God is can conceive that God does not exist; although he says these words in his heart, either without any or with some foreign, signification. For, God is that than which a greater cannot be conceived. And he who thoroughly understands this, assuredly understands that this being so truly exists, that not even in concept can it be non-existent. Therefore, he who understands that God so exists, cannot conceive that he does not exist.

I thank thee, gracious Lord, I thank thee; because what I formerly believed by thy bounty, I now so understand by thine illumination, that if I were unwilling to believe that thou dost exist, I should not be able not to understand this to be true.

CHAPTER 5
God is whatever it is better to be than not to be; and he, as the only self-existent being, creates all things from nothing.

What art thou, then, Lord God, than whom nothing greater can be conceived? But what art thou, except that which, as the highest of all beings, alone exists through itself, and creates all other things from nothing? For, whatever is not this is less than a thing which can be conceived of. But this cannot be conceived of thee. What good, therefore, does the supreme Good lack, through which every good is? Therefore, thou art just, truthful, blessed, and whatever it is better to be than not to be. For it is better to be just than not just; better to be blessed than not blessed.

CHAPTER 6
How God is sensible (sensibilis) *although he is not a body. – God is sensible, omnipotent, compassionate, passionless; for it is better to be these than not be. He who in any way knows, is not improperly said in some sort to feel.*

But, although it is better for thee to be sensible, omnipotent, compassionate, passionless, than not to be these things; how art thou sensible, if thou art not a body; or omnipotent, if thou hast not all powers; or at once compassionate and passionless? For, if only corporeal things are sensible, since the senses encompass a body and are in a body, how art thou sensible, although thou art not a body, but a supreme Spirit, who is superior to body? But, if feeling is only cognition, or for the sake of cognition, – for he who feels obtains knowledge in accordance with the proper functions of his senses; as through sight, of colors; through taste, of flavors, – whatever in any way cognizes is not inappropriately said, in some sort, to feel.

Therefore, O Lord, although thou art not a body yet thou art truly sensible in the highest degree in respect of this, that thou dost cognize all things in the highest degree; and not as an animal cognizes, through a corporeal sense.

CHAPTER 7
How he is omnipotent, although there are many things of which he is not capable. – To be capable of being corrupted, or of lying, is not power, but impotence. God can do nothing by virtue of impo-

tence, and nothing has power against him.
But how art thou omnipotent, if thou art not capable of all things? Or, if thou canst not be corrupted, and canst not lie, nor make what is true, false – as, for example, if thou shouldst make what has been done not to have been done, and the like. – how art thou capable of all things? Or else to be capable of these things is not power, but impotence. For, he who is capable of these things is capable of what is not for his good, and of what he ought not to do; and the more capable of them he is, the more power have adversity and perversity against him; and the less has he himself against these.

He, then, who is thus capable is so not by power, but by impotence. For, he is not said to be able because he is able of himself, but because his impotence gives something else power over him. Or, by a figure of speech, just as many words are improperly applied, as when we use "to be" for "not to be," and "to do" for what is really not to do, "or to do nothing." For, often we say to a man who denies the existence of something: "It is as you say it to be," though it might seem more proper to say, "It is not, as you say it is not." In the same way, we say, "This man sits just as that man does," or, "This man rests just as that man does"; although to sit is not to do anything, and to rest is to do nothing.

So, then, when one is said to have the power of doing or experiencing what is not for his good, or what he ought not to do, impotence is understood in the word power. For, the more he possesses this power, the more powerful are adversity and perversity against him, and the more powerless is he against them.

Therefore, O Lord, our God, the more truly art thou omnipotent, since thou art capable of nothing through impotence, and nothing has power against thee.

CHAPTER 8
How he is compassionate and passionless. God is compassionate, in terms of our experience, because we experience the effect of compassion. God is not compassionate, in terms of his own being, because he does not experience the feeling (affectus) of compassion.
But how art thou compassionate, and, at the same time, passionless? For, if thou art

passionless, thou dost not feel sympathy; and if thou dost not feel sympathy, thy heart is not wretched from sympathy for the wretched; but this it is to be compassionate. But if thou art not compassionate, whence cometh so great consolation to the wretched? How, then, art thou compassionate and not compassionate, O Lord, unless because thou art compassionate in terms of our experience, and not compassionate in terms of thy being.

Truly, thou art so in terms of our experience, but thou art not so in terms of thine own. For, when thou beholdest us in our wretchedness, we experience the effect of compassion, but thou dost not experience the feeling. Therefore, thou art both compassionate, because thou dost save the wretched, and spare those who sin against thee; and not compassionate because thou art affected by no sympathy for wretchedness.

CHAPTER 9
How the all-just and supremely just God spares the wicked, and justly pities the wicked. He is better who is good to the righteous and the wicked than he who is good to the righteous alone. Although God is supremely just, the source of his compassion is hidden. God is supremely compassionate, because he is supremely just. He saveth the just, because justice goes with them; he frees sinners by the authority of justice. God spares the wicked out of justice; for it is just that God, than whom none is better or more powerful, should be good even to the wicked, and should make the wicked good. If God ought not to pity, he pities unjustly. But this it is impious to suppose. Therefore, God justly pities.
But how dost thou spare the wicked, if thou art all just and supremely just? For how, being all just and supremely just, dost thou aught that is not just? Or, what justice is that to give him who merits eternal death everlasting life? How, then, gracious Lord, good to the righteous and the wicked, canst thou save the wicked, if this is not just, and thou dost not aught that is not just? Or, since thy goodness is incomprehensible, is this hidden in the unapproachable light wherein thou dwellest? Truly, in the deepest and most secret parts of thy goodness is hidden the fountain whence the stream of thy compassion flows.

For thou art all just and supremely just,

yet thou art kind even to the wicked, even because thou art all supremely good. For thou wouldst be less good if thou wert not kind to any wicked being. For, he who is good, both to the righteous and the wicked, is better than he who is good to the wicked alone; and he who is good to the wicked, both by punishing and sparing them, is better than he who is good by punishing them alone. Therefore, thou art compassionate, because thou art all supremely good. And, although it appears why thou dost reward the good with goods and the evil with evils; yet this, at least, is most wonderful, why thou, the all and supremely just, who lackest nothing, bestowest goods on the wicked and on those who are guilty toward thee.

The depth of thy goodness, O God! The source of thy compassion appears, and yet is not clearly seen! We see whence the river flows, but the spring whence it arises is not seen. For, it is from the abundance of thy goodness that thou art good to those who sin against thee; and in the depth of thy goodness is hidden the reason for this kindness.

For, although thou dost reward the good with goods and the evil with evils, out of goodness, yet this the concept of justice seems to demand. But, when thou dost bestow goods on the evil, and it is known that the supremely Good hath willed to do this, we wonder why the supremely just has been able to will this.

O compassion, from what abundant sweetness and what sweet abundance dost thou well forth to us! O boundless goodness of God how passionately should sinners love thee! For thou savest the just, because justice goeth with them; but sinners thou dost free by the authority of justice. Those by the help of their deserts; these, although their deserts oppose. Those by acknowledging the goods thou hast granted; these by pardoning the evils thou hatest. O boundless goodness, which dost so exceed all understanding, let that compassion come upon me, which proceeds from thy so great abundance! Let it flow upon me, for it wells forth from thee. Spare, in mercy; avenge not, in justice.

For, though it is hard to understand how thy compassion is not inconsistent with thy justice; yet we must believe that it does not oppose justice at all, because it flows from goodness, which is no goodness without justice; nay, that it is in true harmony with justice. For, if thou art compassionate only because thou art supremely good, and supremely good only because thou art supremely just, truly thou art compassionate even because thou art supremely just. Help me, just and compassionate God, whose light seek; help me to understand what I say.

Truly, then, thou art compassionate even because thou art just. Is, then, thy compassion born of thy justice? And dost thou spare the wicked, therefore, out of justice? If this is true, my Lord, if this is true, teach me how it is. Is it because it is just, that thou shouldst be so good that thou canst not be conceived better; and that thou shouldst work so powerfully that thou canst not be conceived more powerful? For what can be more just than this? Assuredly it could not be that thou shouldst be good only by requiting (*retribuendo*) and not by sparing, and that thou shouldst make good only those who are not good, and not the wicked also. In this way, therefore, it is just that thou shouldst spare the wicked, and make good souls of evil.

Finally, what is not done justly ought not to be done; and what ought not to be done is done unjustly. If, then, thou dost not justly pity the wicked, thou oughtest not to pity them. And, if thou oughtest not to pity them, thou pityest them unjustly. And if it is impious to suppose this, it is right to believe that thou justly pityest the wicked.

CHAPTER 10
How he justly punishes and justly spares the wicked. – God, in sparing the wicked, is just, according to his own nature because he does what is consistent with his goodness; but he is not just, according to our nature, because he does not inflict the punishment deserved.

But it is also just that thou shouldst punish the wicked. For what is more just than that the good should receive goods, and the evil, evils? How, then, is it just that thou shouldst punish the wicked, and, at the same time, spare the wicked? Or, in one way, dost thou justly punish, and, in another, justly spare them? For, when thou punishest the wicked, it is just, because it is consistent with their deserts; and when, on the other hand, thou sparest the wicked, it is just, not because it is compatible with their deserts, but because it is compatible with thy goodness.

For, in sparing the wicked, thou art as just, according to thy nature, but not according to ours, as thou art compassionate, according to our nature, and not according to thine; seeing that, as in saving us, whom it would be just for thee to destroy, thou art compassionate, not because thou feelest an affection (*affectum*), but because we feel the effect (*effectum*); so thou art just, not because thou requitest us as we deserve, but because thou dost that which becomes thee as the supremely good Being. In this way, therefore, without contradiction thou dost justly punish and justly spare.

CHAPTER 11
How all the ways of God are compassion and truth; and yet God is just in all his ways. – We cannot comprehend why, of the wicked, he saves these rather than those, through his supreme goodness: and condemns those rather than these, through his supreme justice.

But, is there any reason why it is not also just, according to thy nature, O Lord, that thou shouldst punish the wicked? Surely it is just that thou shouldst be so just that thou canst not be conceived more just; and this thou wouldst in no wise be if thou didst only render goods to the good, and not evils to the evil. For, he who requiteth both good and evil according to their deserts is more just than he who so requites the good alone. It is, therefore, just, according to thy nature, O just and gracious God, both when thou dost punish and when thou sparest.

Truly, then, all the paths of the Lord are mercy and truth (Psalms xxv. 10); and yet the Lord is righteous in all his ways (Psalms cxlv. 17). And assuredly without inconsistency: For, it is not just that those whom thou dost will to punish should be saved, and that those whom thou dost will to spare should be condemned. For that alone is just which thou dost will; and that alone unjust which thou dost not will. So, then, thy compassion is born of thy justice.

For it is just that thou shouldst be so good that thou art good in sparing also; and this may be the reason why the supremely Just can will goods for the evil. But if it can be comprehended in any way why thou canst will

to save the wicked, yet by no consideration can we comprehend why, of those who are alike wicked, thou savest some rather than others, through supreme goodness; and why thou dost condemn the latter rather than the former, through supreme justice.

So, then, thou art truly sensible (*sensibilis*), omnipotent, compassionate, and passionless, as thou art living, wise, good, blessed, eternal: and whatever it is better to be than not to be.

CHAPTER 12
God is the very life whereby he lives; and so of other like attributes.

But undoubtedly, whatever thou art, thou art through nothing else than thyself. Therefore, thou art the very life whereby thou livest; and the wisdom wherewith thou art wise; and the very goodness whereby thou art good to the righteous and the wicked; and so of other like attributes.

CHAPTER 13
How he alone is uncircumscribed and eternal, although other spirits are uncircumscribed and eternal. – No place and time contain God. But he is himself everywhere and always. He alone not only does not cease to be, but also does not begin to be.

But everything that is in any way bounded by place or time is less than that which no law of place or time limits. Since, then, nothing is greater than thou, no place or time contains thee; but thou art everywhere and always. And since this can be said of thee alone, thou alone art uncircumscribed and eternal. How is it, then, that other spirits also are said to be uncircumscribed and eternal?

Assuredly thou art alone eternal; for thou alone among all beings not only dost not cease to be but also dost not begin to be.

But how art thou alone uncircumscribed? Is it that a created spirit, when compared with thee is circumscribed, but when compared with matter, uncircumscribed? For altogether circumscribed is that which, when it is wholly in one place, cannot at the same time be in another. And this is seen to be true of corporeal things alone. But uncircumscribed is that which is, as a whole, at the same time everywhere. And this is understood to be true of thee alone. But circumscribed, and, at the same time, uncircumscribed is that which, when it is anywhere as a whole, can at the same time be somewhere else as a whole, and yet not everywhere. And this is recognized as true of created spirits. For, if the soul were not as a whole in the separate members of the body, it would not feel as a whole in the separate members. Therefore, thou, Lord, art peculiarly uncircumscribed and eternal; and yet other spirits also are uncircumscribed and eternal.

CHAPTER 14
How and why God is seen and yet not seen by those who seek him.

Hast thou found what thou didst seek, my soul? Thou didst seek God. Thou hast found him to be a being which is the highest of all beings, a being than which nothing better can be conceived; that this being is life itself, light, wisdom, goodness, eternal blessedness and blessed eternity; and that it is every where and always.

For, if thou hast not found thy God, how is he this being which thou hast found, and which thou hast conceived him to be, with so certain truth and so true certainty? But, if thou hast found him, why is it that thou dost not feel thou hast found him? Why, O Lord, our God, does not my soul feel thee, if it hath found thee? Or, has it not found him whom it found to be light and truth? For how did it understand this, except by seeing light and truth? Or, could it understand anything at all of thee, except through thy light and thy truth?

Hence, if it has seen light and truth, it has seen thee; if it has not seen thee, it has not seen light and truth. Or, is what it has seen both light and truth; and still it has not yet seen thee, because it has seen thee only in part, but has not seen thee as thou art? Lord my God, my creator and renewer, speak to the desire of my soul, what thou art other than it hath seen, that it may clearly see what it desires. It strains to see thee more; and sees nothing beyond this which it hath seen, except darkness. Nay, it does not see darkness, of which – there is none in thee; but it sees that it cannot see farther, because of its own darkness.

Why is this, Lord, why is this? Is the eye of the soul darkened by its infirmity, or dazzled by thy glory? Surely it is both darkened in itself, and dazzled by thee. Doubtless it is both obscured by its own insignificance, and overwhelmed by thy infinity. Truly, it is both contracted by its own narrowness and overcome by thy greatness.

For how great is that light from which shines every truth that gives light to the rational mind? How great is that truth in which is everything that is true, and outside which is only nothingness and the false? How boundless is the truth which sees at one glance whatsoever has been made, and by whom, and through whom, and how it has been made from nothing? What purity, what certainty, what splendor where it is? Assuredly more than a creature can conceive.

CHAPTER 15
He is greater than can be conceived.

Therefore, O Lord, thou art not only that than which a greater cannot be conceived, but thou art a being greater than can be conceived. For, since it can be conceived that there is such a being, if thou art not this very being, a greater than thou can be conceived. But this is impossible.

CHAPTER 16
This is the unapproachable light wherein he dwells.

Truly, O Lord, this is the unapproachable light in which thou dwellest; for truly there is nothing else which can penetrate this light, that it may see thee there. Truly, I see it not, because it is too bright for me. And yet, whatsoever I see, I see through it, as the weak eye sees what it sees through the light of the sun, which in the sun itself it cannot look upon. My understanding cannot reach that light, for it shines too bright. It does not comprehend it, nor does the eye of my soul endure to gaze upon it long. It is dazzled by the brightness, it is overcome by the greatness, it is overwhelmed by the infinity, it is dazed by the largeness, of the light.

O supreme and unapproachable light! O whole and blessed truth, how far art thou from me, who am so near to thee! How far removed art thou from my vision, though I am so near to thine! Everywhere thou art wholly present, and I see thee not. In thee I move, and in thee I have my being; and I cannot come to thee.

Thou art within me, and about me, and I feel thee not.

CHAPTER 17

In God is harmony, fragrance, sweetness, pleasantness to the touch, beauty, after his ineffable manner.

Still thou art hidden, O Lord, from my soul in thy light and thy blessedness; and therefore my soul still walks in its darkness and wretchedness. For it looks, and does not see thy beauty. It hearkens, and does not hear thy harmony. It smells, and does not perceive thy fragrance. It tastes, and does not recognize thy sweetness. It touches, and does not feel thy pleasantness. For thou hast these attributes in thyself, Lord God, after thine ineffable manner, who hast given them to objects created by thee, after their sensible manner; but the sinful senses of my soul have grown rigid and dull, and have been obstructed by their long listlessness.

CHAPTER 18

God is life, wisdom, eternity, and every true good. – Whatever is composed of parts is not wholly one; it is capable, either in fact or in concept, of dissolution. In God wisdom, eternity, etc., are not parts, but one, and the very whole which God is, or unity itself, not even in concept divisible.

And lo, again confusion; lo, again grief and mourning meet him who seeks for joy and gladness. My soul now hoped for satisfaction; and lo, again it is overwhelmed with need. I desired now to feast, and lo, I hunger more. I tried to rise to the light of God, and I have fallen back into my darkness. Nay, not only have I fallen into it, but I feel that I am enveloped in it. I fell before my mother conceived me. Truly, in darkness I was conceived, and in the cover of darkness I was born. Truly, in him we all fell, in whom we all sinned. In him we all lost, who kept easily, and wickedly lost to himself and to us that which when we wish to seek it, we do not know; when we seek it, we do not find; when we find, it is not that which we seek.

Do thou help me for thy goodness' sake! Lord, I sought thy face; thy face, Lord, will I seek; hide not thy face far from me (Psalms xxvii. 8). Free me from myself toward thee. Cleanse, heal, sharpen, enlighten the eye of my mind, that it may behold thee. Let my soul recover its strength, and with all its understanding let it strive toward thee, O Lord. What art thou, Lord, what art thou? What shall my heart conceive thee to be?

Assuredly thou art life, thou art wisdom, thou art truth, thou art goodness, thou art blessedness, thou art eternity, and thou art every true good. Many are these attributes: my straitened understanding cannot see so many at one view, that it may be gladdened by all at once. How, then, O Lord, art thou all these things? Are they parts of thee, or is each one of these rather the whole, which thou art? For, whatever is composed of parts is not altogether one, but is in some sort plural, and diverse from itself; and either in fact or in concept is capable of dissolution.

But these things are alien to thee, than whom nothing better can be conceived of. Hence, there are no parts in thee, Lord, nor art thou more than one. But thou art so truly a unitary being, and so identical with thyself, that in no respect art thou unlike thyself; rather thou art unity itself, indivisible by any conception. Therefore, life and wisdom and the rest are not parts of thee, but all are one; and each of these is the whole, which thou art, and which all the rest are.

In this way, then, it appears that thou hast no parts, and that thy eternity, which thou art, is nowhere and never a part of thee or of thy eternity. But everywhere thou art as a whole, and thy eternity exists as a whole forever.

CHAPTER 19

He does not exist in place or time, but all things exist in him.

But if through thine eternity thou hast been, and art, and wilt be; and to have been is not to be destined to be; and to be is not to have been, or to be destined to be; how does thine eternity exist as a whole forever? Or is it true that nothing of thy eternity passes away, so that it is not now; and that nothing of it is destined to be, as if it were not yet?

Thou wast not, then, yesterday, nor wilt thou be to-morrow; but yesterday and to-day and to-morrow thou art; or, rather, neither yesterday nor to-day nor to-morrow thou art; but simply, thou art, outside all time. For yesterday and to-day and to-morrow have no existence, except in time; but thou, although nothing exists without thee, nevertheless dost not exist in space or time, but all things exist in thee. For nothing contains thee, but thou containest all.

CHAPTER 20
He exists before all things and transcends all things, even the eternal things. – The eternity of God is present as a whole with him; while other things have not yet that part of their eternity which is still to be, and have no longer that part which is past.

Hence, thou dost permeate and embrace all things. Thou art before all, and dost transcend all. And, of a surety, thou art before all; for before they were made, thou art. But how dost thou transcend all? In what way dost thou transcend those beings which will have no end? Is it because they cannot exist at all without thee; while thou art in no wise less, if they should return to nothingness? For so, in a certain sense, thou dost transcend them. Or, is it also because they can be conceived to have an end; but thou by no means? For so they actually have an end, in a certain sense; but thou, in no sense. And certainly, what in no sense has an end transcends what is ended in any sense. Or, in this way also dost thou transcend all things, even the eternal, because thy eternity and theirs is present as a whole with thee; while they have not yet that part of their eternity which is to come, just as they no longer have that part which is past? For so thou dost ever transcend them, since thou art ever present with thyself, and since that to which they have not yet come is ever present with thee.

CHAPTER 21
Is this the age of the age, or ages of ages? – The eternity of God contains the ages of time themselves, and can be called the age of the age or ages of ages.

Is this, then, the age of the age, or ages of ages? For, as an age of time contains all temporal things, so thy eternity contains even the ages of time themselves. And these are indeed an age, because of their indivisible unity; but ages, because of their endless immeasurability. And, although thou art so great, O Lord, that all things are full of thee, and exist in thee;

yet thou art so without all space, that neither midst, nor half, nor any part, is in thee.

CHAPTER 22
He alone is what he is and who be is. – All things need God for their being and their well-being.

Therefore, thou alone, O Lord, art what thou art; and thou art he who thou art. For, what is one thing in the whole and another in the parts, and in which there is any mutable element, is not altogether what it is. And what begins from non-existence, and can be conceived not to exist, and unless it subsists through something else, returns to non-existence; and what has a past existence, which is no longer, or a future existence, which is not yet, – this does not properly and absolutely exist.

But thou art what thou art, because, whatever thou art at any time, or in any way, thou art as a whole and forever. And thou art he who thou art, properly and simply; for thou hast neither a past existence nor a future, but only a present existence; nor canst thou be conceived as at any time non-existent. But thou art life, and light, and wisdom, and blessedness, and many goods of this nature. And yet thou art only one supreme good; thou art all-sufficient to thyself, and needest none; and thou art he whom all things need for their existence and well-being.

CHAPTER 23
This good is equally Father, and Son, and Holy Spirit. And this is a single, necessary Being, which is every good, and wholly good, and the only good. – Since the Word is true, and is truth itself, there is nothing in the Father, who utters it, which is not accomplished in the Word by which he expresses himself. Neither is the love which proceeds from Father and Son unequal to the Father or the Son, for Father and Son love themselves and one another in the same degree in which what they are is good. Of supreme simplicity nothing can be born, and from it nothing can proceed, except that which is this, of which it is born, or from which it proceeds.

This good thou art, thou, God the Father; this is thy Word, that is, thy Son. For nothing, other than what thou art, or greater or less than thou, can be in the Word by which thou dost express thyself; for the Word is true, as thou art truthful. And, hence, it is truth itself, just as thou art; no other truth than thou; and thou art of so simple a nature, that of thee nothing can be born other than what thou art. This very good is the one love common to thee and to thy Son, that is, the Holy Spirit proceeding from both. For this love is not unequal to thee or to thy Son; seeing that thou dost love thyself and him, and he, thee and himself, to the whole extent of thy being and his. Nor is there aught else proceeding from thee and from him, which is not unequal to thee and to him. Nor can anything proceed from the supreme simplicity, other than what this, from which it proceeds, is.

But what each is, separately, this is all the Trinity at once, Father, Son, and Holy Spirit; seeing that each separately is none other than the supremely simple unity, and the supremely unitary simplicity which can neither be multiplied nor varied. Moreover, there is a single necessary Being. Now, this is that single, necessary Being, in which is every good; nay, which is every good, and a single entire good, and the only good.

CHAPTER 24
Conjecture as to the character and the magnitude of this good. – If the created life is good, how good is the creative life!
And now, my soul, arouse and lift up all thy understanding, and conceive, so far as thou canst, of what character and how great is that good! For, if individual goods are delectable, conceive in earnestness how delectable is that good which contains the pleasantness of all goods; and not such as we have experienced in created objects, but as different as the Creator from the creature. For, if the created life is good, how good is the creative life! If the salvation given is delightful, how delightful is the salvation which has given all salvation! If wisdom in the knowledge of the created world is lovely, how lovely is the wisdom which has created all things from nothing! Finally, if there are many great delights in delectable things, what and how great is the delight in him who has made these delectable things.

CHAPTER 25
What goods and how great, belong to those who

enjoy this good. – Joy is multiplied in the blessed from the blessedness and joy of others.
Who shall enjoy this good? And what shall belong to him, and what shall not belong to him? At any rate, whatever he shall wish shall be his, and whatever he shall not wish shall not be his. For, these goods of body and soul will be such as eye hath not seen nor ear heard, neither has the heart of man conceived (Isaiah lxiv. 4; 1 Corinthians ii. 9).

Why, then, dost thou wander abroad, slight man, in thy search for the goods of thy soul and thy body? Love the one good in which are all goods, and it sufficeth. Desire the simple good which is every good, and it is enough. For, what dost thou love, my flesh? What dost thou desire, my soul? There, there is whatever ye love, whatever ye desire.

If beauty delights thee, there shall the righteous shine forth as the sun (Matthew xiii. 43). If swiftness or endurance, or freedom of body, which naught can withstand, delight thee, they shall be as angels of God, – because it is sown a natural body; it is raised a spiritual body (1 Corinthians xv. 44) – in power certainly, though not in nature. If it is a long and sound life that pleases thee, there a healthful eternity is, and an eternal health. For the righteous shall live for ever (Wisdom v. 15), and the salvation of the righteous is of the Lord (Psalms xxxvii. 39). If it is satisfaction of hunger, they shall be satisfied when the glory of the Lord hath appeared (Psalms xvii. 15). If it is quenching of thirst, they shall be abundantly satisfied with the fatness of thy house (Psalms xxxvi. 8). If it is melody, there the choirs of angels sing forever, before God. If it is any not impure, but pure, pleasure, thou shalt make them drink of the river of thy pleasures, O God (Psalms xxxvi. 8).

If it is wisdom that delights thee, the very wisdom of God will reveal itself to them. If friendship, they shall love God more than themselves, and one another as themselves. And God shall love them more than they themselves; for they love him, and themselves, and one another, through him, and he, himself and them, through himself. If concord, they shall all have a single will.

If power, they shall have all power to fulfill their will, as God to fulfill his. For, as God will have power to do what he wills, through himself, so they will have power, through him, to do what they will. For, as they will not will aught else than he, he shall will whatever they will; and what he shall will cannot fail to be. If honor and riches, God shall make his good and faithful servants rulers over many things (Luke xii. 42); nay, they shall be called sons of God, and gods; and where his Son shall be, there they shall be also, heirs indeed of God, and joint-heirs with Christ (Romans viii. 17).

If true security delights thee, undoubtedly they shall be as sure that those goods, or rather that good, will never and in no wise fail them; as they shall be sure that they will not lose it of their own accord; and that God, who loves them, will not take it away from those who love him against their will; and that nothing more powerful than God will separate him from them against his will and theirs.

But what, or how great, is the joy, where such and so great is the good! Heart of man, needy heart, heart acquainted with sorrows, nay, overwhelmed with sorrows, how greatly wouldst thou rejoice, if thou didst abound in all these things! Ask thy inmost mind whether it could contain its joy over so great a blessedness of its own.

Yet assuredly, if any other whom thou didst love altogether as thyself possessed the same blessedness, thy joy would be doubled, because thou wouldst rejoice not less for him than for thyself. But, if two, or three, or many more, had the same joy, thou wouldst rejoice as much for each one as for thyself, if thou didst love each as thyself. Hence, in that perfect love of innumerable blessed angels and sainted men, where none shall love another less than himself, every one shall rejoice for each of the others as for himself.

If, then, the heart of man will scarce contain his joy over his own so great good, how shall it contain so many and so great joys? And doubtless, seeing that every one loves another so far as he rejoices in the other's good, and as, in that perfect felicity, each one should love God beyond compare, more than himself and all the others with him; so he will rejoice beyond reckoning in the felicity of God, more than in his own and that of all the others with him.

But if they shall so love God with all their heart, and all their mind, and all their soul, that still all the heart, and all the mind, and all the soul shall not suffice for the worthiness of this love; doubtless they will so rejoice with all their heart, and all their mind, and all their soul, that all the heart, and all the mind, and all the soul shall not suffice for the fullness of their joy.

CHAPTER 26
Is this joy which the Lord promises made full? – The blessed shall rejoice according as they shall love; and they shall love according as they shall know.

My God and my Lord, my hope and the joy of my heart, speak unto my soul and tell me whether this is the joy of which thou tellest us through thy Son: Ask and ye shall receive, that your joy may be full (John xvi. 24). For I have found a joy that is full, and more than full. For when heart, and mind, and soul, and all the man, are full of that joy, joy beyond measure will still remain. Hence, not all of that joy shall enter into those who rejoice; but they who rejoice shall wholly enter into that joy.

Show me, O Lord, show thy servant in his heart whether this is the joy into which thy servants shall enter, who shall enter into the joy of their Lord. But that joy, surely, with which thy chosen ones shall rejoice, eye hath not seen nor ear heard, neither has it entered into the heart of man (Isaiah lxiv. 4; 1 Corinthians ii. 9). Not yet, then, have I told or conceived, O Lord, how greatly those blessed ones of thine shall rejoice. Doubtless they shall rejoice according as they shall love; and they shall love according as they shall know. How far they will know thee, Lord, then! and how much they will love thee! Truly, eye hath not seen, nor ear heard, neither has it entered into the heart of man in this life, how far they shall know thee, and how much they shall love thee in that life.

I pray, O God, to know thee, to love thee, that I may rejoice in thee. And if I cannot attain to full joy in this life may I at least advance from day to day, until that joy shall come to the full. Let the knowledge of thee advance in me here, and there be made full. Let the love of thee increase, and there let it be full, that here my joy may be great in hope, and there full in truth. Lord, through thy Son thou dost command, nay, thou dost counsel us to ask; and thou dost promise that we shall receive, that our joy may be full. I ask, O Lord, as thou dost counsel through our wonderful Counselor. I will receive what thou dost promise by virtue of thy truth, that my joy may be full. Faithful God, I ask. I will receive, that my joy may be full. Meanwhile, let my mind meditate upon it; let my tongue speak of it. Let my heart love it; let my mouth talk of it. Let my soul hunger for it; let my flesh thirst for it; let my whole being desire it, until I enter into thy joy, O Lord, who art the Three and the One God, blessed for ever and ever. Amen.

St Anselm, 1033–1109, translated
by Sidney Norton Deane, 1903

When You Pray
Augustine of Hippo

"And when ye pray," says He, "ye shall not be as the hypocrites are; for they love to pray standing in the synagogues and in the corners of the streets, that they may be seen of men." And here also it is not the being seen of men that is wrong, but doing these things for the purpose of being seen of men; and it is superfluous to make the same remark so often, since there is just one rule to be kept, from which we learn that what we should dread and avoid is not that men know these things, but that they be done with this intent, that the fruit of pleasing men should be sought after in them. Our Lord Himself, too, preserves the same words, when He adds similarly, "Verily I say unto you, They have received their reward"; hereby showing that He forbids this,-the striving after that reward in which fools delight when they are praised by men.

"But when ye pray," says He, "enter into your bed-chambers." What are those bed-chambers but just our hearts themselves, as is meant also in the Psalm, when it is said, "What ye say in your hearts, have remorse for even in your beds"? "And when ye have shut the doors," says He, "pray to your Father who is in secret." It is a small matter to enter into our bed-chambers if the door stand open to the unmannerly, through which the things that are outside profanely rush in and assail our inner man. Now we have said that outside are all temporal and visible things, which make

their way through the door, i.e. through the fleshly sense into our thoughts, and clamorously interrupt those who are praying by a crowd of vain phantoms. Hence the door is to be shut, i.e. the fleshly Sense is to be resisted, so that spiritual prayer may be directed to the Father, which is done in the inmost heart, where prayer is offered to the Father which is in secret. "And your Father," says He, "who seeth in secret, shall reward you." And this had to be wound up with a closing statement of such a kind; for here at the present stage the admonition is not that we should pray, but as to how we should pray. Nor is what goes before an admonition that we should give alms, but as to the spirit in which we should do so, inasmuch as He is giving instructions with regard to the cleansing of the heart, which nothing cleanses but the undivided and single-minded striving after eternal life from the pure love of wisdom alone.

"But when ye pray," says He, "do not speak much, as the heathen do; for they think that they shall be heard for their much speaking." As it is characteristic of the hypocrites to exhibit themselves to be gazed at when praying, and their fruit is to please men, so it is characteristic of the heathen, i.e. of the Gentiles, to think they are heard for their much speaking. And in reality, every kind of much speaking comes from the Gentiles, who make it their endeavor to exercise the tongue rather than to cleanse the heart. And this kind of useless exertion they endeavor to transfer even to the influencing of God by prayer, supposing that the Judge, just like man, is brought over by words to a certain way of thinking. "Be not ye, therefore, like unto them," says the only true Master. "For your Father knoweth what things are necessary for you, before ye ask Him." For if many words are made use of with the intent that one who is ignorant may be instructed and taught, what need is there of them for Him who knows all things, to whom all things which exist, by the very fact of their existence, speak, and show themselves as having been brought into existence; and those things which are future do not remain concealed from His knowledge and wisdom, in which both those things which are past, and those things which will yet come to pass, are all present and cannot pass away?

But since, however few they may be, yet there are words which He Himself also is about to speak, by which He would teach us to pray; it may be asked why even these few words are necessary for Him who knows all things before they take place, and is acquainted, as has been said, with what is necessary for us before we ask Him? Here, in the first place, the answer is, that we ought to urge our case with God, in order to obtain what we wish, not by words, but by the ideas which we cherish in our mind, and by the direction of our thought, with pure love and sincere desire; but that our Lord has taught us the very ideas in words, that by committing them to memory we may recollect those ideas at the time we pray.

But again, it may be asked (whether we are to pray in ideas or in words) what need there is for prayer itself, if God already knows what is necessary for us; unless it be that the very effort involved in prayer calms and purifies our heart, and makes it more capacious for receiving the divine gifts, which are poured into us spiritually. For it is not on account of the urgency of our prayers that God hears us, who is always ready to give us His light, not of a material kind, but that which is intellectual and spiritual: but we are not always ready to receive, since we are inclined towards other things, and are involved in darkness through our desire for temporal things. Hence there is brought about in prayer a turning of the heart to Him, who is ever ready to give, if we will but take what He has given; and in the very act of turning there is effected a purging of the inner eye, inasmuch as those things of a temporal kind which were desired are excluded, so that the vision of the pure heart may be able to bear the pure light, divinely shining, without any setting or change: and not only to bear it, but also to remain in it; not merely without annoyance, but also with ineffable joy, in which a life truly and sincerely blessed is perfected.

Augustine of Hippo, 354–430

The Kneeling Christian

Author unknown

CONTENTS

PREFACE

A traveler in China visited a heathen temple on a great feast-day. Many were the worshipers of the hideous idol enclosed in a sacred shrine. The visitor noticed that most of the devotees brought with them small pieces of paper on which prayers had been written or printed. These they would wrap up in little balls of stiff mud and fling at the idol. He enquired the reason for this strange proceeding, and was told that if the mud ball stuck fast to the idol, then the prayer would assuredly be answered; but if the mud fell off, the prayer was rejected by the god. We may smile at this peculiar way of testing the acceptability of a prayer. But is it not a fact that the majority of Christian men and women who pray to a Living God know very little about real prevailing prayer? Yet prayer is the key which unlocks the door of God's treasure-house. It is not too much to say that all real growth in the spiritual life – all victory over temptation, all confidence and peace in the presence of difficulties and dangers, all repose of spirit in times of great disappointment or loss, all habitual communion with God – depend upon the practice of secret prayer. This book was written by request, and with much hesitancy. It goes forth with much prayer. May He Who said, "Men ought always to pray, and not to faint," "teach us to pray."

CHAPTER 1: GOD'S GREAT NEED

"God wondered." This is a very striking thought! The very boldness of the idea ought surely to arrest the attention of every earnest Christian man, woman and child. A wondering God! Why, how staggered we might well be if we knew the cause of God's "wonder"! Yet we find it to be, apparently, a very little thing. But if we are willing to consider the matter carefully, we shall discover it to be one of the greatest possible importance to every believer on the Lord Jesus Christ. Nothing else is so momentous – so vital – to our spiritual welfare. God "wondered that there was no intercessor" (Isa. lix. 16) – 'none to interpose" (R.V., marg.). But this was in the days of long ago, before the coming of the Lord Jesus Christ "full of grace and truth" – before the outpouring of the Holy Spirit, full of grace and power, "helping our infirmity," "Himself making intercession for us" and in us (Rom. viii. 26). Yes, and before the truly amazing promises of our Savior regarding prayer; before men knew very much about prayer; in the days when sacrifices for their sins loomed larger in their eyes than supplication for other sinners.

Oh, how great must be God's wonder today! For how few there are among us who know what prevailing prayer really is! Every one of us would confess that we believe in prayer, yet how many of us truly believe in the power of, prayer? Now, before we go a step farther, may the writer most earnestly implore you not to read hurriedly what is contained in these chapters. Much – very much – depends upon the way in which every reader receives what is here recorded. For everything depends upon prayer. Why are many Christians so often defeated? Because they pray so little. Why are many church-workers so often discouraged and disheartened? Because they pray so little. Why do most men see so few brought "out of darkness to light" by their ministry? Because they pray so little. Why are not our churches simply on fire for God? Because there is so little real prayer. The Lord Jesus is as powerful today as ever before. The Lord Jesus is as anxious for men to be saved as ever before. His arm is not shortened that it cannot save: but He cannot stretch forth His arm unless we pray more – and more really. We may be assured of this – the secret of all failure is our failure in secret prayer. If God "wondered" in the days of Isaiah, we need not be surprised to find that in the days of His flesh our Lord "marveled." He marveled at the unbelief of some – unbelief which actually prevented Him from doing any mighty work in their cities (Mark vi. 6). But we must remember that those who were guilty of this unbelief saw no beauty in Him that they should desire Him, or believe on Him.

What then must His "marvel" be today, when He sees amongst us who do truly love and adore Him, so few who really "stir themselves up to take hold of God" (Isa. lxiv. 7). Surely there is nothing so absolutely astonishing as a practically prayerless Christian? These are eventful and ominous days. In fact, there are many evidences that these are "the last days" in which God promised to pour out His Spirit – the Spirit of supplication – upon all flesh (Joel ii. 28). Yet the vast majority of professing Christians scarcely know what "supplication" means; and very many of our churches not only have no prayer-meeting, but sometimes unblushingly condemn such meetings, and even ridicule them. The Church of England, recognizing the importance of worship and prayer, expects her clergy to read prayers in Church every morning and evening. But when this is done, is it not often in an empty church? And are not the prayers frequently raced through at a pace which precludes real worship? "Common prayer," too, often must necessarily be rather vague and indefinite. And what of those churches where the old-fashioned weekly prayer-meeting is retained? Would not "weakly" be the more appropriate word? C. H. Spurgeon had the joy of being able to say that he conducted a prayer-meeting every Monday night "which scarcely ever numbers less than from a thousand to twelve hundred attendants." My brothers, have we ceased to believe in prayer? If you still hold your weekly gathering for prayer, is it not a fact that the very great majority of your church members never come near it? Yes, and never even think of coming near it. Why is this? Whose fault is it? "Only a prayer-meeting" – how often we have heard the utterance! How many of those reading these words really enjoy a prayer-meeting? Is it a joy or just a duty? Please forgive me for asking so many questions and for pointing out what appears to be a perilous weakness and a lamentable shortcoming in our churches. We are not out to criticize – far less to condemn. Anybody can do that. Our yearning desire is to stir up Christians "to take hold of" God, as never before. We wish to encourage, to enhearten, to uplift. We are never so high as when we are on our knees. Criticize? Who dare criticize another? When we look back upon the past and remember how much prayerlessness there has been in one's own life, words of criticism of others wither away on the lips. But we believe the time has come when a clarion call to the individual and to the Church is needed – a call to prayer.

Now, dare we face this question of prayer? It seems a foolish query, for is not prayer a part and parcel of all religions? Yet we venture to ask our readers to look at this matter fairly and squarely. Do I really believe that prayer is a power? Is prayer the greatest power on earth, or is it not? Does prayer indeed "move the Hand that moves the world"? Do God's prayer-commands really concern Me? Do the promises of God concerning prayer still hold good? We have all been muttering "Yes – Yes – Yes" as we read these questions. We dare not say "No" to any one of them. And yet – ! Has it ever occurred to you that our Lord never gave an unnecessary or an optional command? Do we really believe that our Lord never made a promise which He could not, or would not, fulfill? Our Savior's three great commands for definite action were: – Pray ye Do this Go ye! Are we obeying Him? How often His command, "Do this," is reiterated by our preachers today! One might almost think it was His only command! How seldom we are reminded of His bidding to "Pray" and to "Go." Yet, without obedience to the "Pray ye," it is of little or no use at all either to "Do this" or to "Go." In fact, it can easily be shown that all want of success, and all failure in the spiritual life and in Christian work, is due to defective or insufficient prayer. Unless we pray aright we cannot live aright or serve aright. This may appear, at first sight, to be gross exaggeration, but the more we think it over in the light Scripture throws upon it, the more convinced shall we be of the truth of this statement. Now, as we begin once more to see what the Bible has to say about this mysterious and wonderful subject, shall we endeavor to read some of our Lord's promises, as though we had never heard them before.

What will the effect be? Some twenty years ago the writer was studying in a Theological College. One morning, early, a fellow-student – who is today one of England's foremost missionaries – burst into the room holding an open Bible in his hands. Although he was preparing for Holy Orders, he was at that time only a young convert to Christ. He had gone up to the University "caring for none of these things." Popular, clever, athletic – he had already won a place amongst the smart set of his college, when Christ claimed him. He accepted the Lord Jesus as a personal Savior, and became a very keen follower of his Master. The Bible was, comparatively, a new book to him, and as a result he was constantly making "discoveries." On that memorable day on which he invaded my quietude he cried excitedly – his face all aglow with mingled joy and surprise –" "Do you believe this? Is it really true?" "Believe what?" I asked, glancing at the open Bible with some astonishment. "Why, this – " and he read in eager tones St. Matthew xxi. 21, 22: "'If ye have faith and doubt not … all things whatsoever ye shall ask in prayer, believing, ye shall receive.' Do you believe it? Is it true?" "Yes," I replied, with much surprise at his excitement, "of course it's true – of course I believe it." Yet, through my mind there flashed all manner of thoughts! "Well, that's a very wonderful promise," said he. "It seems to me to be absolutely limitless! Why don't we pray more?" And he went away, leaving me thinking hard. I had never looked at those verses quite in that way. As the door closed upon that eager young follower of the Master, I had a vision of my Savior and His love and His power such as I never had before. I had a vision of a life of prayer – yes, and "limitless" power, which I saw depended upon two things only – faith and prayer. For the moment I was thrilled. I fell on my knees, and as I bowed before my Lord what thoughts surged through my mind – what hopes and aspirations flooded my soul! God was speaking to me in an extraordinary way. This was a great call to prayer. But – to my shame be it said – I heeded not that call. Where did I fail? True, I prayed a little more than before, but nothing much seemed to happen. Why? Was it because I did not see what a high standard the Savior requires in the inner life of those who would pray successfully? Was it because I had failed to measure up my life to the "perfect love" standard so beautifully described in the thirteenth chapter of the first Epistle to the Corinthians? For, after all, prayer is not just putting into action good resolutions "to pray." Like David, we need to cry, "Create in me a clean heart, O God" (Psa. li) before we can pray aright. And the inspired words of the Apostle of Love need to be heeded today as much as ever before: "Beloved, if our heart condemn us not, we have boldness toward God; and [then] whatsoever we ask, we receive of Him" (1 John iii. 21). "True – and I believe it." Yes, indeed, it is a limitless promise, and yet how little we realize it, how little we claim from Christ. And our Lord "marvels" at our unbelief. But if we could only read the Gospels for the first time, what an amazing book it would seem! Should not we "marvel" and "wonder"?

And today I pass on that great call to you. Will you give heed to it? Will you profit by it? Or shall it fall on deaf ears and leave you prayerless? Fellow-Christians, let us awake! The devil is blinding our eyes. He is endeavoring to prevent us from facing this question of prayer. These pages are written by special request. But it is many months since that request came. Every attempt to begin to write has been frustrated, and even now one is conscious of a strange reluctance to do so. There seems to be some mysterious power restraining the hand. Do we realize that there is nothing the devil dreads so much as prayer? His great concern is to keep us from praying. He loves to see us "up to our eyes" in work – provided we do not pray. He does not fear because we are eager and earnest Bible students – provided we are little in prayer. Someone has wisely said, "Satan laughs at our toiling, mocks at our wisdom, but trembles when we pray." All this is so familiar to us – but do we really pray? If not, then failure must dog our footsteps, whatever signs of apparent success there may be. Let us never forget that the greatest thing we can do for God or for man is to pray. For we can accomplish far more by our prayers than by our work. Prayer is omnipotent; it can do anything that God can do! When we pray God works. All fruitfulness in service is the outcome of prayer – of the worker's prayers, or of those who are holding up holy hands on his behalf. We all know how to pray, but perhaps many of us need to cry as

the disciples did of old, "Lord, teach us to pray." O Lord, by Whom ye come to God, The Life, the Truth, the Way, The path of prayer Thyself hast trod; Lord, teach us now to pray.

CHAPTER 2: ALMOST INCREDIBLE PROMISES
"When we stand with Christ in glory, looking o'er life's finished story," the most amazing feature of that life as it is looked back upon will be its prayerlessness. We shall be almost beside ourselves with astonishment that we spent so little time in real intercession. It will be our turn to "wonder." In our Lord's last discourse to His loved ones, just before the most wonderful of all prayers, the Master again and again held out His kingly golden scepter and said, as it were, "What is your request? It shall be granted unto you, even unto the whole of My kingdom!" Do we believe this? We must do so if we believe our Bibles. Shall we just read over very quietly and thoughtfully one of our Lord's promises, reiterated so many times? If we had never read them before, we should open our eyes in bewilderment, for these promises are almost incredible. From the lips of any mere man they would be quite unbelievable. But it is the Lord of heaven and earth Who speaks; and He is speaking at the most solemn moment of His life. It is the eve of His death and passion. It is a farewell message. Now listen! "Verily, verily I say unto you, he that believeth on Me, the works that I do shall he do also; and greater works than these shall he do: because I go unto the Father. And whatsoever ye shall ask in My name, that will I do, that the Father may be glorified in the Son. If ye shall ask anything in My name, that will I do" (John xiv. 13, 14). Now, could any words be plainer or clearer than these? Could any promise be greater or grander? Has anyone else, anywhere, at any time, ever offered so much? How staggered those disciples must have been! Surely they could scarcely believe their own ears. But that promise is made also to you and to me. And, lest there should be any mistake on their part, or on ours, our Lord repeats Himself a few moments afterwards. Yes, and the Holy Spirit bids St. John record those words again. "If ye abide in Me, and My words abide in you, ask whatsoever ye will, and it shall be done unto you. Herein is My Father glorified, that ye bare

much fruit; and so shall ye be My disciples" (John xv. 7, 8).

These words are of such grave importance, and so momentous, that the Savior of the world is not content even with a threefold utterance of them. He urges His disciples to obey His command "to ask." In fact, He tells them that one sign of their being His "friends" will be the obedience to His commands in all things (verse 14). Then He once more repeats His wishes: "Ye did not choose Me, but I chose you, and appointed you, that ye should go and bear fruit, and that your fruit should abide: that whatsoever ye shall ask the Father, in My name, He may give it you" (John xv. 16). One would think that our Lord had now made it plain enough that He wanted them to pray; that He needed their prayers, and that without prayer they could accomplish nothing. But to our intense surprise He returns again to the same subject, saying very much the same words. "In that day ye shall ask Me nothing" – i.e., "ask Me no question" (R.V., marg.) – "Verily, verily I say unto you, if ye ask anything of the Father, He will give it you in My name. Hitherto have ye asked nothing in My name: ask, and ye shall receive, that your joy may be fulfilled" (John xvi. 23, 24). Never before had our Lord laid such stress on any promise or command – never! This truly marvelous promise is given us six times over. Six times, almost in the same breath, our Savior commands us to ask whatsoever we will. This is the greatest – the most wonderful – promise ever made to man. Yet most men – Christian men – practically ignore it! Is it not so? The exceeding greatness of the promise seems to over-whelm us. Yet we know that He is "able to do exceeding abundantly above all that we ask or think" (Eph. iii. 20). So our blessed Master gives the final exhortation, before He is seized, and bound, and scourged, before His gracious lips are silenced on the cross, "Ye shall ask in My name ... for the Father Himself loveth you" (verse 26). We have often spent much time in reflecting upon our Lord's seven words from the cross. And it is well we should do so. Have we ever spent one hour in meditating upon this, our Savior's sevenfold invitation to pray? Today He sits on the throne of His Majesty on high, and He holds out to us the scepter of His power. Shall

we touch it and tell Him our desires? He bids us take of His treasures. He yearns to grant us "according to the riches of His glory," that we may "be strengthened with power through His Spirit in the inner man." He tells us that our strength and our fruitfulness depend upon our prayers. He reminds us that our very joy depends upon answered prayer (John xvi. 24).

And yet we allow the devil to persuade us to neglect prayer! He makes us believe that we can do more by our own efforts than by our prayers – by our intercourse with men than by our intercession with God. It passes one's comprehension that so little heed should be given to our Lord's sevenfold invitation – command – promise! How dare we work for Christ without being much on our knees? Quite recently an earnest Christian "worker" – a Sunday-school teacher and communicant – wrote me, saying, "I have never had an answer to prayer in all my life." But why? Is God a liar? Is not God trustworthy? Do His promises count for naught. Does He not mean what He says? And doubtless there are many reading these words who in their hearts are saying the same thing as that Christian worker. Payson is right – is Scriptural – when he says: "If we would do much for God, we must ask much of God: we must be men of prayer." If our prayers are not answered – always answered, but not necessarily granted – the fault must be entirely in ourselves, and not in God. God delights to answer prayer; and He has given us His word that He will answer. Fellow-laborers in His vineyard, it is quite evident that our Master desires us to ask, and to ask much. He tells us we glorify God by doing so!

Nothing is beyond the scope of prayer which is not beyond the will of God – and we do not desire to go beyond His will. We dare not say that our Lord's words are not true. Yet somehow or other few Christians really seem to believe them. What holds us back? What seals our lips? What keeps us from making much of prayer? Do we doubt His love? Never! He gave His life for us and to us. Do we doubt the Father's love? Nay. "The Father Himself loveth you," said Christ when urging His disciples to pray. Do we doubt His power? Not for a moment. Hath He not said, "All power hath been given unto Me in heaven and on earth. Go ye … and lo, I am with you alway …"? (Matt. xxviii. 18–20). Do we doubt His wisdom? Do we mistrust His choice for us? Not for a moment. And yet so very few of His followers consider prayer really worth while. Of course, they would deny this – but actions speak louder than words. Are we afraid to put God to the test? He has said we may do so. "Bring Me the whole tithe into the storehouse … and prove Me now herewith, saith the Lord of Hosts, if I will not open you the windows of heaven, and pour you out a blessing that there shall not be room enough to receive it" (Mal. iii. 10). Whenever God makes us a promise, let us boldly say, as did St. Paul, I believe God (Acts xxvii. 25), and trust Him to keep His word. Shall we begin today to be men of prayer, if we have never done so before? Let us not put it off till a more convenient season.

God wants me to pray. The dear Savior wants me to pray. He needs my prayers. So much – in fact, everything – depends upon prayer. How dare we hold back? Let every one of us ask on our knees this question: "If no one on earth prayed for the salvation of sinners more fervently or more frequently than I do, how many of them would be converted to God through prayer ?" Do we spend ten minutes a day in prayer? Do we consider it important enough for that? Ten minutes a day on our knees in prayer – when the Kingdom of Heaven can be had for the asking! Ten minutes? It seems a very inadequate portion of our time to spend in taking hold of God (Isa. lxiv. 7)! And is it prayer when we do "say" our prayers, or are we just repeating daily a few phrases which have become practically meaningless, whilst our thoughts are wandering hither and thither? If God were to answer the words we repeated on our knees this morning should we know it? Should we recognize the answer? Do we even remember what we asked for? He does answer. He has given us His word for it. He always answers every real prayer of faith. But we shall see what the Bible has to say on this point in a later chapter. We are now thinking of the amount of time we spend in prayer. "How often do you pray?" was the question put to a Christian woman. "Three times a day, and all the day beside," was the quick reply. But how many are there like that? Is prayer to me

just a duty, or is it a privilege – a pleasure – a real joy – a necessity? Let us get a fresh vision of Christ in all His glory, and a fresh glimpse of all the "riches of His glory" which He places at our disposal, and of all the mighty power given unto Him. Then let us get a fresh vision of the world and all its needs. (And the world was never so needy as it is today.) Why, the wonder is not that we pray so little, but that we can ever get up from our knees if we realize our own need; the needs of our home and our loved ones; the needs of our pastor and the Church; the needs of our city – of our country – of the heathen and Mohammedan world! All these needs, can be met by the riches of God in Christ Jesus.

St. Paul had no doubt about this – nor have we. Yes! "My God shall supply all your need according to His riches in glory, in Christ Jesus" (Phil. iv. 19). But to share His riches we must pray, for the same Lord is rich unto all that call upon Him (Rom. x. 12). So great is the importance of prayer that God has taken care to anticipate all the excuses or objections we may be likely to make. Men plead their weakness or infirmity – or they declare they do not know how to pray. God foresaw this inability long ages ago. Did He not inspire St. Paul to say: "The Spirit also helpeth our infirmity, for we know not how to pray as we ought; but the Spirit Himself maketh intercession for us with groanings which cannot be uttered; and He that searcheth the hearts knoweth what is in the mind of the Spirit, because He maketh intercession for the saints according to the will of God" (Rom. viii. 26, 27). Yes. Every provision is made for us. But only the Holy Spirit can "stir us up" to "take hold of God." And if we will but yield ourselves to the Spirit's promptings we shall most assuredly follow the example of the apostles of old, who "gave themselves to prayer," and "continued steadfastly in prayer" (R.V., Acts vi. 4). We may rest fully assured of this – a man's influence in the world can be gauged not by his eloquence, or his zeal, or his orthodox, or his energy, but by his prayers. Yes, and we will go farther and maintain that no man can live aright who does not pray aright. We may work for Christ from morn till night; we may spend much time in Bible study; we may be most earnest and faithful and "acceptable" in our preaching and in our individual dealing, but none of these things can be truly effective unless we are much in prayer. We shall only be full of good works; and not "bearing fruit in every good work" (Col. i. 10). To be little with God in prayer is to be little for God in service. Much secret prayer means much public power.

Yet is it not a fact that whilst our organizing is well nigh perfect, our agonizing in prayer is well nigh lost? Men are wondering why the Revival delays its coming. There is only one thing that can delay it, and that is lack of prayer. All Revivals have been the outcome of prayer. One sometimes longs for the voice of an archangel, but what would that avail if the voice of Christ Himself does not stir us up to pray? It seems almost impertinence for any man to take up the cry when our Savior has put forth His "limitless" promises. Yet we feel that something should be done, and we believe that the Holy Spirit is prompting men to remind themselves and others of Christ's words and power. No words of mine can impress men with the value of prayer, the need of prayer, and the omnipotence of prayer. But these utterances go forth steeped in prayer that God the Holy Spirit will Himself convict Christian men and women of the sin of prayerlessness, and drive them to their knees, to call upon God day and night in burning, believing, prevailing intercession! The Lord Jesus, now in the heavenlies, beckons to us to fall upon our knees and claim the riches of His grace. No man dare prescribe for another how long a time he ought to spend in prayer, nor do we suggest that men should make a vow to pray so many minutes or hours a day. Of course, the Bible command is to "Pray without ceasing." This is evidently the "attitude of prayer" – the attitude of one's life. Here we are speaking of definite acts of prayer. Have you ever timed your prayers? We believe that most of our readers would be amazed and confounded if they did time themselves! Some years ago the writer faced this prayer question. He felt that for himself at least one hour a day was the minimum time that he should spend in prayer. He carefully noted down every day a record of his prayer-life. As time went on he met a working-man who was being much used of God. When asked to what he chiefly

attributed his success, this man quietly replied, "Well, I could not get on without two hours a day of private prayer." Then there came across my path a Spirit-filled missionary from overseas, who told very humbly of the wonderful things God was doing through his ministry. (One could see all along that God was given all the praise and all the glory.) "I find it necessary, oftentimes, to spend four hours a day in prayer," said this missionary. And we remember how the Greatest Missionary of all used sometimes to spend whole nights in prayer. Why? Our blessed Lord did not pray simply as an example to us: He never did things merely as an example. He prayed because He needed to pray. As perfect Man, prayer to Him was a necessity. Then how much more is it necessary to you and me? "Four hours a day in prayer!" exclaimed a man who is giving his whole life to Christian work as a medical missionary. "Four hours? Give me ten minutes and I'm done!" That was an honest and a brave confession – even if a sad one. Yet, if some of us were to speak out as honestly –

Now, it was not by accident that these men crossed my path. God was speaking through them. It was just another "call to prayer" from the "God of patience," who is also a "God of comfort" (Rom. xv. 5). and when their quiet message had sunk into my soul a book came into my hands, "by chance," as people say. It told briefly and simply the story of John Hyde – "Praying Hyde," as he came to be called. Just as God sent St. John the Baptist to prepare the way of our Lord at His first coming, so He sent in these last days St. John the Prayer, to make straight paths for His coming again. "Praying Hyde" – what a name! As one read of this marvelous life of prayer, one began to ask, "Have I ever prayed?" I found others were asking the same question. One lady, who is noted for her wonderful intercession, wrote me, saying, "When I laid down this book, I began to think I had never in all my life really prayed!" But here we must leave the matter. Shall we get on our knees before God and allow His Holy Spirit to search us through and through? Are we sincere? Do we really desire to do God's will? Do we really believe His promises? If so, will it not lead us to spend more time on our knees before God? Do not vow to pray "so much" a day. Resolve to pray much, but prayer, to be of value, must be spontaneous, and not from constraint. But we must bear in mind that mere resolutions to take more time for prayer, and to conquer reluctance to pray, will not prove lastingly effective unless there is a wholehearted and absolute surrender to the Lord Jesus Christ. If we have never taken this step, we must take it now if we desire to be men of prayer. I am quite certain of this fact: God wants me to pray: wants you to pray. The question is, are we willing to pray? Gracious Savior, pour out upon us the fullness of the Holy Spirit, that we may indeed become Kneeling Christians. To God your every want In instant prayer display. Pray always; pray and never faint: Pray! Without ceasing, pray.

CHAPTER 3: "ASK OF ME AND I WILL GIVE"

God wants me to pray, to be much in prayer – because all success in spiritual work is dependent on prayer. A preacher who prays little may see some results of his labors, but if he does it will be because someone, somewhere is praying for him. The "fruit" is the pray-er's – not the preacher's. How surprised some of us preachers will be one day, when the Lord shall "reward every man according to his works." "Lord! Those were my converts! It was I who conducted that mission at which so many were brought into the fold." Ah, yes – I did the preaching, the pleading, the persuading; but was it "I" who did the praying? Every convert is the result of the Holy Spirit's pleading in answer to the prayers of some believer. O God, grant that such surprise may not be ours. O Lord, teach us to pray! We have had a vision of a God pleadingly calling for prayer from His children. How am I treating that call? Can I say, with St. Paul, "I am 'not disobedient to the heavenly vision'"? Again we repeat, if there are any regrets in heaven, the greatest will be that we spent so little time in real intercession whilst we were on earth. Think of the wide sweep of prayer! "Ask of Me, and I will give thee the heathen for thine inheritance, and the uttermost parts of the earth for thy possession" (Psalm ii. 8).

Yet many people do not trouble to bring even the little details of their own lives to God in prayer, and nine out of ten Christian people never think of praying for the heathen! One is staggered at the unwillingness of Christians to pray. Perhaps it is because they have never experienced, or even heard of, convincing answers to prayer. In this chapter we are setting out to do the "impossible." What is that? We long to bring home to the heart and conscience of every reader the power of prayer. We venture to describe this as "impossible." For if men will not believe, and act upon, our Lord's promises and commands, how can we expect them to be persuaded by any mere human exhortations? But do you remember that our Lord, when speaking to His disciples, asked them to believe that He was in the Father and the Father in Him? Then he added: "If you cannot believe My bare word about this, believe Me for the very works' sake" (John xiv. 11). It was as if He said, "If My Person, My sanctified life, and My wonderful words do not elicit belief in Me, then look at My works: surely they are sufficient to compel belief? Believe Me because of what I do." Then He went on to promise that if they would believe, they should do greater works than these. It was after this utterance that He gave the first of those six wonderful promises in regard to prayer. The inference surely is that those "greater works" are to be done only as the outcome of prayer. May the disciple therefore follow the Master's method? Fellow-worker, if you fail to grasp, fail to trust our Lord's astounding promises regarding prayer, will you not believe them "for the very works' sake"? That is, because of those "greater works" which men and women are performing today – or, rather, the works which the Lord Jesus is doing, through their prayerful co-operation? What are we "out for"? What is our real aim in life? Surely we desire most of all to be abundantly fruitful in the Master's service. We seek not position, or prominence, or power. But we do long to be fruitful servants. Then we must be much in prayer. God can do more through our prayers than through our preaching.

A. J. Gordon once said, "You can do more than pray, after you have prayed, but you can never do more than pray until you have prayed." If only we would believe this! A lady in India was cast down through the failure of her life and work. She was a devoted missionary, but somehow or other conversions never resulted from her ministry. The Holy Spirit seemed to say to her, "Pray more." But she resisted the promptings of the Spirit for some time. "At length," said she, "I set apart much of my time for prayer. I did it in fear and trembling lest my fellow-workers should complain that I was shirking my work. After a few weeks I began to see men and women accepting Christ as their Savior. Moreover, the whole district was soon awakened, and the work of all the other missionaries was blessed as never before. God did more in six months than I had succeeded in doing in six years. And," she added, "no one ever accused me of shirking my duty." Another lady missionary in India felt the same call to pray. She began to give much time to prayer. No opposition came from without, but it did come from within. But she persisted, and in two years the baptized converts increased sixfold! God promised that He would "pour out the Spirit of grace and supplication upon all flesh" (Joel ii. 28). How much of that Spirit of "supplication" is ours? Surely we must get that Spirit at all costs? Yet if we are not willing to spend time in "supplication," God must perforce withhold His Spirit, and we become numbered amongst those who are "resisting the Spirit," and possibly "quenching" the Spirit. Has not our Lord promised the Holy Spirit to them that ask? (Luke xi. 13). Are not the very converts from heathendom putting some of us to shame?

A few years ago, when in India, I had the great joy of seeing something of Pandita Ramabai's work. She had a boarding-school of 1,500 Hindu girls. One day some of these girls came with their Bibles and asked a lady missionary what St. Luke xii. 49 meant – "I came to cast fire upon the earth; and what will I, if it is already kindled?" The missionary tried to put them off with an evasive answer, not being very sure herself what those words meant. But they were not satisfied, so they determined to pray for this fire. And as they prayed – and because they prayed – the very fire of heaven came into their souls. A very Pentecost from above was granted them. No wonder they continued to pray! A party of these girls upon whom God had poured the "Spirit of supplication" came to a mission house where I spent some weeks.

"May we stay here in your town and pray for your work?" they asked. The missionary did not entertain the idea with any great enthusiasm. He felt that they ought to be at school, and not "gadding about" the country. But they only asked for a hall or barn where they could pray; and we all value prayers on our behalf. So their request was granted, and the good man sat down to his evening meal, thinking. As the evening wore on, a native pastor came round. He broke down completely. He explained, with tears running down his face, that God's Holy Spirit had convicted him of sin, and that he felt compelled to come and openly confess his wrongdoing. He was quickly followed by one Christian after another, all under deep conviction of sin.

There was a remarkable time of blessing. Back-sliders were restored, believers were sanctified, and heathen brought into the fold – all because a few mere children were praying. God is no respecter of persons. If anyone is willing to conform to His conditions, He for His part will assuredly fulfill His promises. Does not our heart burn within us, as we hear of God's wonderful power? And that power is ours for the asking. I know there are "conditions." But you and I can fulfill them all through Christ. And those of us who cannot have the privilege of serving God in India or any other overseas mission, may yet take our part in bringing down a like blessing.

When the Revival in Wales was at its height, a Welsh missionary wrote home begging the people to pray that India might be moved in like manner. So the coal-miners met daily at the pit-mouth half an hour before dawn to pray for their comrade overseas. In a few weeks' time the welcome message was sent home: "The blessing has come." Isn't it just splendid to know that by our prayers we can bring down showers of blessing upon India, or Africa, or China, just as readily as we can get the few drops needed for our own little plot? Many of us will recall the wonderful things which God did for Korea a few years ago, entirely in answer to prayer. A few missionaries decided to meet together to pray daily at noon. At the end of the month one brother proposed that, "as nothing had happened," the prayer-meeting should be discontinued. "Let us each pray at home as we find it convenient," said he. The others, however, protested that they ought rather to spend even more time in prayer each day. So they continued the daily prayer-meeting for four months. Then suddenly the blessing began to be poured out. Church services here and there were broken up by weeping and confessing of sins. At length a mighty revival broke out. At one place during a Sunday evening service the leading man in the church stood up and confessed that he had stolen one hundred dollars in administering a widow's legacy. Immediately conviction of sin swept the audience. That service did not end till 2 o'clock on Monday morning. God's wondrous power was felt as never before. And when the Church was purified, many sinners found salvation. Multitudes flocked to the churches out of curiosity. Some came to mock, but fear laid hold of them, and they stayed to pray. Amongst the "curious" was a brigand chief, the leader of a robber band. He was convicted and converted. He went straight off to the magistrate and gave himself up. "You have no accuser," said the astonished official, "yet you accuse yourself! We have no law in Korea to meet your case." So he dismissed him. One of the missionaries declared, "It paid well to have spent several months in prayer, for when God gave the Holy Spirit, He accomplished more in half a day than all the missionaries together could have accomplished in half a year." In less than two months, more than 2,000 heathen were converted.

The burning zeal of those converts has become a byword. Some of them gave all they had to build a church, and wept because they could not give more. Needless to say, they realized the power of prayer. Those converts were themselves baptized with the "Spirit of supplication." In one church it was announced that a daily prayer-meeting would be held at 4:30 every morning. The very first day 400 people arrived long before the stated hour – eager to pray! The number rapidly increased to 600 as days went on. At Seoul, 1,100 is the average attendance at the weekly prayer-meeting. Heathen people came – to see what was happening. They exclaimed in astonishment, "The living God is among you." Those poor heathen saw what many Christians fail to see. Did not Christ say, "Where two or three are gathered together in My name, there am I in the midst of them"? (Matt. xviii. 20). What is possible in Korea is possible here. God is "no respecter" of nations. He is longing to bless us, longing to pour His Spirit upon us. Now, if we – here in this so-called Christian country – really believed in prayer, i.e., in our Lord's own gracious promises, should we avoid prayer-meetings? If we had any genuine concern for the lost condition of thousands in our own land and tens of thousands in heathen lands, should we withhold our prayers? Surely we do not think, or we should pray more. "Ask of Me – I will give," says an almighty, all-loving God, and we scarcely heed His words!

Verily, converts from heathendom put us to shame. In my journeyings I came to Rawal Pindi, in N.W. India. What do you think happened there? Some of Pandita Ramabai's girls went there to camp. But a little while before this, Pandita Ramabai had said to her girls, "If there is any blessing in India, we may have it. Let us ask God to tell us what we must do in order to have the blessing." As she read her Bible she paused over the verse, "Wait for the promise of the Father … ye shall receive power after that the Holy Ghost is come upon you" (Acts i. 4–8). "'Wait'! Why, we have never done this," she cried. "We have prayed, but we have never expected any greater blessing today than we had yesterday!" Oh, how they prayed! One prayer-meeting lasted six hours. And what a marvelous blessing God poured out in answer to their prayers. Whilst some of these girls were at Rawal Pindi, a lady missionary, looking out of her tent towards midnight, was surprised to see a light burning in one of the girls' tents – a thing quite contrary to rules. She went to expostulate, but found the youngest of those ten girls – a child of fifteen – kneeling in the farthest corner of the tent, holding a little tallow candle in one hand and a list of names for intercession in the other. She had 500 names on her list – 500 out of the 1,500 girls in Pandita Ramabai's school. Hour after hour she was naming them before God. No wonder God's blessing fell wherever those girls went, and upon whomsoever those girls prayed for.

Pastor Ding Li Mei, of China, has the names of 1,100 students on his prayer-list. Many hundreds have been won to Christ through his prayers. And so out-and-out are his converts that many scores of them have entered the Christian ministry. It would be an easy matter to add to these amazing and inspiring stories of blessing through prayer. But there is no need to do so. I know that God wants me to pray. I know that God wants you to pray. "If there is any blessing in England we may have it." Nay, more – if there is any blessing in Christ we may have it. "Blessed be the God and Father of our Lord Jesus Christ, who hath blessed us with every spiritual blessing in the heavenly places in Christ" (Eph. i. 3). God's great storehouse is full of blessings. Only prayer can unlock that storehouse. Prayer is the key, and faith both turns the key and opens the door, and claims the blessing. Blessed are the pure in heart, for they shall see God. And to see Him is to pray aright.

Listen! We have come – you and I – once more to the parting of the ways. All our past failure, all our past inefficiency and insufficiency, all our past unfruitfulness in service, can be banished now, once and for all, if we will only give prayer its proper place. Do it today. Do not wait for a more convenient time. Everything worth having depends upon the decision we make. Truly God is a wonderful God! And one of the most wonderful things about Him is that He puts His all at the disposal of the prayer of faith. Believing prayer from a wholly-cleansed heart never fails. God has given us His word for it. Yet vastly more wonderful is the amazing fact that Christian men and women should either not believe God's word, or should fail to put it to the test. When Christ is "all in all" – when He is Savior and Lord and King of our whole being, then it is really He Who prays our prayers. We can then truthfully alter one word of a well-known verse and say that the Lord Jesus ever liveth to make intercession in us. Oh, that we might make the Lord Jesus "marvel" not at our unbelief but at our faith! When our Lord shall again "marvel," and say of us, "Verily ... I have not found so great faith, no, not in Israel" (Matt. viii. 10), then indeed shall "palsy" – paralysis – be transformed into power. Has not our Lord come to "cast fire" upon us? Are we "already kindled"? Can He not use us as much as he used those mere children

of Khedgaon? God is no respecter of persons. If we can humbly and truthfully say, "To me to live is Christ" (Phil. i. 21), will He not manifest forth His mighty power in us?

Some of us have been reading about Praying Hyde. Truly, his intercession changed things. Men tell us that they were thrilled when John Hyde prayed. They were stirred to their inmost being when he just pleaded the name "Jesus! – Jesus! – Jesus!" and a baptism of love and power came upon them. But it was not John Hyde, it was the Holy Spirit of God whom one consecrated man, filled with that Spirit, brought down upon all around him. May we not all become "Praying Hydes"? Do you say "No! He had a special gift of prayer"? Very well – how did he get it? He was once just an ordinary Christian man – just like any of us. Have you noticed that, humanly speaking, he owed his prayer-life to the prayers of his father's friend? Now get hold of this point. It is one of greatest importance, and one which may profoundly affect your whole life. Perhaps I may be allowed to tell the story fully, for so much depends upon it. Shall we quote John Hyde himself? He was on board a ship sailing for India, whither he was going as a missionary. He says, "My father had a friend who greatly desired to be a foreign missionary, but was not permitted to go. This friend wrote me a letter directed in care of the ship. I received it a few hours out of New York harbor. The words were not many, but the purport of them was this: 'I shall not cease praying for you, dear John, until you are filled with the Holy Spirit.' When I had read the letter I crumpled it up in anger and threw it on the deck. Did this friend think I had not received the baptism of the Spirit, or that I would think of going to India without this equipment? I was angry. But by and by better judgment prevailed, and I picked up the letter, and read it again. Possibly I did need something which I had not yet received. I paced up and down the deck, a battle raging within. I felt uncomfortable: I loved the writer; I knew the holy life he lived, and down in my heart there was a conviction that he was right, and that I was not fit to be a missionary.... This went on for two, or three days, until I felt perfectly miserable.... At last, in a kind of despair, I asked the Lord to fill me with

the Holy Spirit; and the moment I did this …
I began to see myself, and what a selfish ambition I had." But he did not yet receive the blessing sought. He landed in India and went with a fellow-missionary to an open-air service. "The missionary spoke," said John Hyde, "and I was told that he was speaking about Jesus Christ as the real Savior from sin.

When he had finished his address, a respectable-looking man, speaking good English, asked the missionary whether he himself had been thus saved? The question went home to my heart; for if it had been asked me, I would have had to confess that Christ had not fully saved me, because I knew there was a sin in my life which had not been taken away. I realized what a dishonor it would be on the name of Christ to have to confess that I was preaching a Christ that had not delivered me from sin, though I was proclaiming to others that He was a perfect Savior. I went back to my room and shut myself in, and told the Lord that it must be one of two things: either He must give me victory over all my sins, and especially over the sin that so easily beset me, or I must return to America and seek there for some other work. I said I could not stand up to preach the Gospel until I could testify of its power in my own life. I … realized how reasonable this was, and the Lord assured me that He was able and willing to deliver me from all sin. He did deliver me, and I have not had a doubt of this since." It was then, and then only, that John Hyde became Praying Hyde. And it is only by such a full surrender and such a definite claiming to be delivered from the power of sin in our lives that you and I can be men of prevailing prayer. The point we wish to emphasize, however, is the one already mentioned. A comparatively unknown man prays for John Hyde, who was then unknown to the world, and by his prayers brings down such a blessing upon him that everyone knows of him now as "Praying Hyde."

Did you say in your heart, dear reader, a little while ago, that you could not hope to be a Praying Hyde? Of course we cannot all give so much time to prayer. For physical or other reasons we may be hindered from long-continued praying. But we may all have his spirit of prayer. And may we not all do for others what the unnamed friend did for John Hyde? Can we not pray the blessing down upon others – upon your vicar or pastor? Upon your friend? Upon your family? What a ministry is ours, if we will but enter it! But to do so, we must make the full surrender which John Hyde made. Have we done it? Failure in prayer is due to fault in the heart. Only the "pure in heart" can see God. And only those who "call on the Lord out of a pure heart" (2 Tim. ii. 22) can confidently claim answers to their prayers. What a revival would break out, what a mighty blessing would come down if only everyone who read these words would claim the fullness of the Holy Spirit now! Do you not see why it is that God wants us to pray? Do you now see why everything worth having depends upon prayer? There are several reasons, but one stands out very clearly and vividly before us after reading this chapter. It is just this: if we ask and God does not give, then the fault is with us. Every unanswered prayer is a clarion call to search the heart to see what is wrong there; for the promise is unmistakable in its clearness: "If ye shall ask anything in My name, that will I do" (John xiv. 14). Truly he who prays puts, not God, but his own spiritual life to the test! Let me come closer to Thee, Jesus, Oh, closer every day; Let me lean harder on Thee, Jesus, Yes, harder all the way.

CHAPTER 4: ASKING FOR SIGNS
"Does God indeed answer prayer?" is a question often on the lips of people, and oftener still in their inmost hearts. "Is prayer of any real use?" Somehow or other we cannot help praying; but then even pagan savages cry out to someone or something to aid them in times of danger and disaster and distress. And those of us who really do believe in prayer are soon faced with another question: "Is it right to put God to the test?" Moreover, a further thought flashes into our minds: "Dare we put God to the test?" For there is little doubt failure in the prayer-life is often – always? – due to failure in the spiritual life. So many people harbor much unbelief in the heart regarding the value and effectiveness of prayer; and without faith, prayer is vain. Asking for signs? Putting God to the test? Would to God we could persuade Christian men and women to do so. Why, what a test this would be of our own faith in

God, and of our own holiness of life. Prayer is the touchstone of true godliness. God asks our prayers, values our prayers, needs our prayers. And if those prayers fail, we have only ourselves to blame. We do not mean by this that effective prayer always gets just what it asks for. Now, the Bible teaches us that we are allowed to put God to the test.

The example of Gideon in Old Testament days is sufficient to show us that God honors our faith even when that faith is faltering. He allows us to "prove Him" even after a definite promise from Himself. This is a very great comfort to us. Gideon said unto God, "If Thou wilt save Israel by mine hand, as Thou hast said, behold, I will put a fleece of wool on the floor; and if the dew be on the fleece only … then shall I know that Thou wilt save Israel by mine hand, as Thou has said." Yet, although there was a "bowl full of water" in the fleece the next morning, this did not satisfy Gideon! He dares to put God to the test the second time, and to ask that the fleece should be dry instead of wet the following night. "And God did so that night" (Judges vi. 40). It is all very wonderful, the Almighty God just doing what a hesitating man asks Him to do! We catch our breath and stand amazed, scarcely knowing which startles us the more – the daring of the man, or the condescension of God! Of course, there is more in the story than meets the eye. No doubt Gideon thought that the "fleece" represented himself, Gideon.

If God would indeed fill him with His Spirit, why, salvation was assured. But as he wrung the fleece out, he began to compare himself with the saturated wool. "How unlike this fleece am I! God promises deliverance, but I do not feel full of the Spirit of God. No inflow of the mighty power of God seems to have come into me. Am I indeed fit for this great feat?" No! But then, it is "Not I, but God." "O God, let the fleece be dry – canst Thou still work? Even if I do not feel any superhuman power, any fullness of spiritual blessing within me: even if I feel as dry as this fleece, canst Thou still deliver Israel by my arm?" (Little wonder that he prefaced his prayer with the words, "Let not Thine anger be hot against me"!) "And God did so that night: for it was dry upon the fleece only, and there was dew on all

the ground" (verse 40). Yes, there is more in the story than can be seen at a glance. And is it not so in our own case? The devil so often assures us that our prayers cannot claim an answer because of the "dryness" of our souls. Answers to prayer, however, do not depend upon our feelings, but upon the trustworthiness of the Promiser. Now, we are not urging that Gideon's way of procedure is for us, or for anyone, the normal course of action. It seems to reveal much hesitation to believe God's Word. In fact, it looks gravely like doubting God. And surely it grieves God when we show a faith in Him which is but partial. The higher and better and safer way is to "ask, nothing doubting." But it is very comforting and assuring to us to know that God allowed Gideon to put Him to the test. Nor is this the only such case mentioned in Scripture. The most surprising instance of "proving God" happened on the Sea of Galilee. St. Peter put our Lord Himself to the test. "If it be Thou – " yet our Savior had already said, "It is I." "If it be Thou, bid me come unto Thee on the water." And our Lord said, "Come," and Peter "walked on the water" (Matt. xiv. 28, 29). But this "testing-faith" of Peter's soon failed him. "Little faith" (verse 31) so often and so quickly becomes "doubt." Remember that Christ did not reprove him for coming. Our Lord did not say, "Wherefore didst thou come?" but "Wherefore didst thou doubt?" To put God to the test is, after all, not the best method. He has given us so many promises contingent on believing prayer, and has so often proved His power and His willingness to answer prayer, that we ought, as a rule, to hesitate very much before we ask Him for signs as well as for wonders! But, someone may be thinking, does not the Lord God Almighty Himself bid us to put Him to the test? Did He not say, "Bring ye the whole tithe into the storehouse … and prove Me now herewith, saith the Lord of Hosts, if I will not open unto you the windows of heaven, and pour you out a blessing, that there shall not be room enough to receive it"? (Mal. iii. 10). Yes that is true: God does say, "Prove Me: test Me." But it is really we ourselves who are thus tested. If the windows of heaven are not opened when we pray, and this blessing of fullness-to-overflowing is not bestowed upon us, it can only be because we are not whole-tithers. When we are in very deed wholly yielded to God – when we have brought the whole tithe into the storehouse for God – we shall find such a blessing that we shall not need to put God to any test!

This is a thing we shall have to speak about when we come to the question of unanswered prayer. Meanwhile we want every Christian to ask, "Have I ever fairly tested prayer?" How long is it since you last offered up a definite prayer? People pray for "a blessing" upon an address, or a meeting, or a mission; and some blessing is certain to come, for others are also pleading with God about the matter. You ask for relief from pain or healing of sickness: but Godless people, for whom no one appears to be praying, often recover, and sometimes in a seemingly miraculous way. And we may feel that we might have got better even if no prayer had been offered on our behalf. It seems to me that so many people cannot put their finger upon any really definite and conclusive answer to prayer in their own experience. Most Christians do not give God a chance to show His delight in granting His children's petitions; for their requests are so vague and indefinite. If this is so, it is not surprising that prayer is so often a mere form – an almost mechanical repetition, day by day, of certain phrases; a few minutes' "exercise" morning and evening.

Then there is another point. Have you, when in prayer, ever had the witness borne in upon you that your request was granted? Those who know something of the private life of men of prayer are often amazed at the complete assurance which comes over them at times that their prayers are answered, long before the boon they seek is actually in their possession. One prayer-warrior would say, "A peace came over my soul. I was confident my request was granted me." He then just thanked God for what he was quite sure God had done for him. And his assurance would prove to be absolutely well founded. Our Lord Himself always had this assurance, and we should ever bear in mind that, although He was God, He lived His earthly life as a perfect Man, depending upon the Holy Spirit of God. When He stood before the opened tomb of Lazarus, before He had actually called upon the dead to come forth, He said, "Father, I thank Thee that

Thou hast heard Me. And I know that Thou hearest Me always" (John xi. 41, 42). Why, then, did He utter His thanks? "Because of the people which stand by I said it, that they may believe that Thou hast sent Me." If Christ is dwelling in our hearts by faith: if the Holy Spirit is breathing into us our petitions, and we are "praying in the Holy Ghost," ought we not to know that the Father "hears" us? (Jude 20). And will not those who stand by begin to recognize that we, too, are God-sent? Men of prayer and women of prayer will agonize before God for something which they know is according to His will, because of some definite promise on the page of Scripture. They may pray for hours, or even for days, when suddenly the Holy Spirit reveals to them in no uncertain way that God has granted their request; and they are confident that they need no longer send up any more petitions to God about the matter. It is as if God said in clear tones: "Thy prayer is heard and I have granted thee the desire of thy heart." This is not the experience of only one man, but most men to whom prayer is the basis of their life will bear witness to the same fact. Nor is it a solitary experience in their lives: it occurs again and again.

Then prayer must give place to action. God taught Moses this: "Wherefore criest thou unto Me? Speak unto the children of Israel that they go forward" (Exod. xiv. 15). We are not surprised to find that Dr. Goforth, a much-used missionary in China, often has this assurance given him that his petitions are granted. "I knew that God had answered. I received definite assurance that He would open the way." For why should anyone be surprised at this? The Lord Jesus said, "Ye are My friends, if ye do the things I command you. No longer do I call you servants; for the servant knoweth not what his lord doeth: but I have called you friends" (John xv. 14, 15). Do you think it surprising, then, if the Lord lets us, His "friends," know something of His plans and purposes? The question at once arises, does God mean this to be the experience of only a few chosen saints, or does He wish all believers to exercise a like faith, and to have a like assurance that their prayers are answered? We know that God is no respecter of persons, and therefore we know that any true believer in Him may share His mind and will. We are His friends if we do the things He commands us. One of those things is "prayer." Our Savior begged His disciples to "have faith in God" (the literal translation is "Have the faith of God"). Then, He declares, you can say to a mountain, "Be thou taken up and cast into the sea," and if you believe and doubt not, it shall come to pass. Then He gives this promise: "All things whatsoever ye pray and ask for, believe that ye have received them [that is, in heaven], and ye shall have them [on earth]" (Mark xi. 24). Now, this is exactly the experience we have been talking about. This is just what real men of prayer do. Such things naturally pass the comprehension of unbelievers. Such things are perplexing to the half-believers. Our Lord, however, desires that men should know that we are His disciples, sent as He was sent (John xvii. 18 and xx. 21). They will know this if we love one another (John xiii. 35). But another proof is provided, and it is this: if we know and they see that "God heareth us always" (John xi. 42).

Some of us at once recall to mind George Müller's wonderful prayer-life. On one occasion, when crossing from Quebec to Liverpool, he had prayed very definitely that a chair he had written to New York for should arrive in time to catch the steamer, and he was quite confident that God had granted his petition. About half an hour before the tender was timed to take the passengers to the ship, the agents informed him that no chair had arrived, and that it could not possibly come in time for the steamer. Now, Mrs. Müller suffered much from sea-sickness, and it was absolutely essential that she should have the chair. Yet nothing would induce Mr. Müller to buy another one from a shop near by. "We have made special prayer that our Heavenly Father would be pleased to provide it for us, and we will trust Him to do so," was his reply; and he went on board absolutely sure that his trust was not misplaced, and would not miscarry. Just before the tender left, a van drove up, and on the top of the load it carried was Mr. Müller's chair. It was hurried on board and placed into the hands of the very man who had urged George Müller to buy another one! When he handed it to Mr. Müller, the latter expressed no surprise, but quietly removed his hat and thanked his Heavenly Father. To this man of God such an answer to prayer was not wonderful, but natural. And do you not think that God allowed the chair to be held back till the very last minute as a lesson to Mr. Müller's friends – and to us? We should never have heard of that incident but for that delay. God does all He can to induce us to pray and to trust, and yet how slow we are to do so! Oh, what we miss through lack of faith and want of prayer! No one can have very real and deep communion with God who does not know how to pray so as to get answers to prayer.

If one has any doubt as to God's willingness to be put to the test, let him read a little book called *Nor Scrip* (Marshall, Morgan and Scott, Ltd.). Miss Amy Wilson Carmichael tells us in its pages how again and again she "proved God." One gets the impression from the book that it was no accident that led her to do so. Surely God's hand was in it? For instance, in order to rescue a Hindu child from a life of "religious" shame, it was necessary to spend a hundred rupees. Was she justified in doing so? She could help many girls for such a sum: ought she to spend it on one? Miss Wilson Carmichael felt led to pray that God would send her the round sum of a hundred rupees – no more, no less – if it was His will that the money should be spent in this way. The money came – the exact amount – and the sender of it explained that she had sat down to write a check for a broken sum, but had been impelled to make it just a hundred rupees. That happened over fifteen years ago, and since that time this same missionary has put God to the test over and over again, and He has never failed her. This is what she says: "Never once in fifteen years has a bill been left unpaid; never once has a man or woman been told when we were in need of help; but never once have we lacked any good thing. Once, as if to show what could be done if it were required, 25 pounds came by telegram! Sometimes a man would emerge from the clamoring crowd at a railway station, and slip some indispensable gift of money into the hand, and be lost in the crowd again before the giver could be identified." Is it wonderful? Wonderful! Why, what does St. John say, speaking by the Spirit of God? "And this is the boldness which we have towards Him, that if we ask anything, according to His will, He heareth us; and if we know that He heareth us, whatsoever we ask, we know that we have the petitions which we have asked of Him" (1 John v. 14, 15).

Have you and I such "boldness"? If not, why not? To call it wonderful is to show our want of faith. It is natural to God to answer prayer: normal, not extraordinary. The fact is – let us be quite honest and straightforward about it – the fact is so many of us do not believe God. We may just as well be quite candid about it. If we love God we ought to pray, because He wants us to pray, and commands us to pray. If we believe God we shall pray because we cannot help doing so: we cannot get on without it. Fellow-Christian, you believe in God, and you believe on Him (John iii. 16), but have you advanced far enough in the Christian life to believe Him; that is, to believe what He says and all He says? Does it not sound blasphemous to ask such a thing of a Christian man? Yet how few believers really believe God! – God forgive us! Has it ever struck you that we trust the word of our fellow-man more easily than we trust God's word? And yet, when a man does "believe God," what miracles of grace God works in and through him! No man ever lived who has been revered and respected by so many peoples and tongues as that man of whom we are told three times over in the New Testament that "He believed God" (Rom. iv. 3; Gal. iii. 6; James ii. 23). Yes, "Abraham believed God, and it was reckoned unto him for righteousness." And today, Christian and Jew and Moslem vie with each other in honoring his name. We implore every believer on Christ Jesus never to rest till he can say, "I believe God, and will act on that belief" (Acts xxvii. 25). But before we leave the question of testing God, we should like to point out that sometimes God leads us on "to prove Him." Sometimes God has put it into the heart of Miss Wilson Carmichael to ask for things she saw no need for. Yet she felt impelled by the Holy Spirit to ask. Not only were they granted her, but they also proved an inestimable boon. Yes, God knows what things we have need of, whether we want them or not, before we ask (Matt. vi. 8). Has not God said, "I will in no wise fail thee"? Oftentimes the temptation would come to Miss Wilson Carmichael to let others know

of some special need. But always the inner assurance would come, as in the very voice of God, "I know, and that is enough." And, of course, God was glorified. During the trying days of the war, even the heathen used to say, "Their God feeds them." "Is it not known all the country round," said a worldly heathen, "that your God hears prayer?" Oh, what glory to God was brought about by their simple faith! Why do not we believe God? Why do we not take God at His word? Do believers or unbelievers ever say of us, "We know your prayers are answered"? Ye missionaries the wide world over, listen! (Oh, that these words might reach every ear, and stir every heart!) It is the yearning desire of God – of our loving Savior Jesus Christ – that every one of us should have the same strong faith as that devoted lady missionary we are speaking about. Our loving Father does not wish any child of His to have one moment's anxiety or one unsatisfied need. No matter how great our need may be; no matter how numerous our requirements, if we only "prove Him" in the manner He bids us, we shall never have room enough to receive all the blessing He will give (Mal. iii. 10).

Oh, what peace we often forfeit !
Oh, what needless pain we bear!
All because we do not carry
Everything to God in prayer.

Or all because, when we do "carry it," we do not believe God's word. Why is it we find it so hard to trust Him? Has He ever failed us? Has He not said over and over and over again that He will grant all petitions offered out of a pure heart, "in His name"? "Ask of Me"; "Pray ye"; "Prove Me"; "Try Me." The Bible is full of answers to prayer – wonderful answers, miraculous answers; and yet somehow our faith fails us, and we dishonor God by distrusting Him! If our faith were but more simple We should take Him at His word, And our lives would be all sunshine In the bounties of our Lord. But our eye must be "single" if our faith is to be simple and our "whole body full of light" (Matt. vi. 22). Christ must be the sole Master. We cannot expect to be free from anxiety if we are trying to serve God and Mammon (Matt. vi. 24, 25). Again we are led back to the Victorious Life! When we indeed present our bodies "a living sacrifice, holy, acceptable to God" (Rom. xii. 1);

when we present our members "as servants to righteousness and sanctification" (Rom. vi. 19); then He presents Himself to us and fills us with all the fullness of God (Eph. iii. 19). Let us ever bear in mind that real faith not only believes that God can, but that He does answer prayer. We may be slothful in prayer, but "the Lord is not slack concerning His promise" (2 Peter iii. 9). Is not that a striking expression?

Perhaps the most extraordinary testing of God which that Dohnavur missionary tells us of is the following. The question arose of purchasing a rest-house in the hills near by. Was it the right thing to do? Only God could decide. Much prayer was made. Eventually the petition was offered up that if it was God's will that the house should be purchased, the exact sum of 100 pounds should be received. That amount came at once. Yet they still hesitated. Two months later they asked God to give them again the same sign of His approval of the purchase. That same day another check for 100 pounds came. Even now they scarcely liked to proceed in the matter. In a few days' time, however, another round sum of 100 pounds was received, earmarked for the purchase of such a house. Does it not flood our hearts with joy to remember that our gracious Savior is so kind? It is St. Luke the physician who tells us that God is kind (Luke vi. 35). Love is always "kind" (1 Cor. xiii. 4); and God is Love. Think over it when you pray. Our Lord is "kind." It will help us in our intercessions. He bears so patiently with us when our faith would falter. "How precious is Thy lovingkindness, O God" (Psalm xxxvi. 7); "Thy lovingkindness is better than life" (Psalm lxiii. 3). The danger is that we read of such simple faith in prayer, and say, "How wonderful!" and forget that God desires every one of us to have such faith and such prayer. God has no favorites! He wants me to pray; He wants you to pray. He allows such things to happen as we have described above, and suffers them to come to our knowledge, not to surprise us, but to stimulate us. One sometimes wishes that Christian people would forget all the man-made rules with which we have hedged prayer about! Let us be simple. Let us be natural. Take God at His word. Let us remember that "the kindness of God our Savior, and His love toward man," has appeared

(Titus iii. 4). God sometimes leads men into the prayer-life. Sometimes, however, God has to drive us into such a life. As some of us look back over our comparatively prayerless life, what a thrill of wonder and of joy comes over us as we think of the kindness and "patience of Christ" (2 Thess. iii. 5). Where should we have been without that? We fail Him, but, blessed be His name, He has never failed us, and He never will do so. We doubt Him, we mistrust His love and His providence and His guidance; we "faint because of the way"; we murmur because of the way; yet all the time He is there blessing us, and waiting to pour out upon us a blessing so great that there shall not be room to receive it. The promise of Christ still holds good: "Whatsoever ye shall ask in My name, that will I do, that the Father may be glorified in the Son" (John xiv. 14). Prayer changes things – and yet how blind And slow we are to taste and see The blessedness that comes to those Who trust in Thee. But henceforth we will just believe God.

CHAPTER 5: WHAT IS PRAYER?
Mr. Moody was once addressing a crowded meeting of children in Edinburgh. In order to get their attention he began with a question: "What is prayer?" – looking for no reply, and expecting to give the answer himself. To his amazement scores of little hands shot up all over the hall. He asked one lad to reply; and the answer came at once, clear and correct, "Prayer is an offering up of our desires unto God for things agreeable to His will, in the name of Christ, with confession of our sins and thankful acknowledgment of His mercies." Mr. Moody's delighted comment was, "Thank God, my boy, that you were born in Scotland." But that was half a century ago. What sort of answer would he get today? How many English children could give a definition of prayer? Think for a moment and decide what answer you yourself would give. What do we mean by prayer? I believe the vast majority of Christians would say, "Prayer is asking things from God." But surely prayer is much more than merely "getting God to run our errands for us," as someone puts it. It is a higher thing than the beggar knocking at the rich man's door. The word "prayer" really means "a wish

directed towards," that is, towards God. All that true prayer seeks is God Himself, for with Him we get all we need. Prayer is simply "the turning of the soul to God." David describes it as the lifting up of the living soul to the living God. "Unto Thee, O Lord, do I lift up my soul" (Psa. xxv. 1). What a beautiful description of prayer that is! When we desire the Lord Jesus to behold our souls, we also desire that the beauty of holiness may be upon us. When we lift up our souls to God in prayer it gives God an opportunity to do what He will in us and with us. It is putting ourselves at God's disposal. God is always on our side. When man prays, it is God's opportunity. The poet says: Prayer is the soul's sincere desire, Uttered or unexpressed, The motion of a hidden fire That trembles in the breast. "Prayer," says an old Jewish mystic, "is the moment when heaven and earth kiss each other."

Prayer, then, is certainly not persuading God to do what we want God to do. It is not bending the will of a reluctant God to our will. It does not change His purpose, although it may release His power. "We must not conceive of prayer as overcoming God's reluctance," says Archbishop Trench, "but as laying hold of His highest willingness." For God always purposes our greatest good. Even the prayer offered in ignorance and blindness cannot swerve Him from that, although, when we persistently pray for some harmful thing, our willfulness may bring it about, and we suffer accordingly. "He gave them their request," says the Psalmist, "but sent leanness into their soul" (Psa. cvi. 15). They brought this "leanness" upon themselves. They were "cursed with the burden of a granted prayer." Prayer, in the minds of some people, is only for emergencies! Danger threatens, sickness comes, things are lacking, difficulties arise – then they pray. Like the infidel down a coal mine: when the roof began to fall he began to pray. An old Christian standing by quietly remarked, "Aye, there's nowt like cobs of coal to make a man pray." Prayer is, however, much more than merely asking God for something, although that is a very valuable part of prayer if only because it reminds us of our utter dependence upon God. It is also communion with God – intercourse with God – talking with (not only to) God. We

get to know people by talking with them. We get to know God in like manner. The highest result of prayer is not deliverance from evil, or the securing of some coveted thing, but knowledge of God. "And this is life eternal, that they should know Thee, the only true God" (John xvii. 3). Yes, prayer discovers more of God, and that is the soul's greatest discovery. Men still cry out, "O, that I knew where I might find Him, that I might come even to His seat" (Job xxiii. 3). The kneeling Christian always "finds" Him, and is found of Him. The heavenly vision of the Lord Jesus blinded the eyes of Saul of Tarsus on his downward course, but he tells us, later on, that when he was praying in the temple at Jerusalem he fell into a trance and saw Jesus. "I ... saw him" (Acts xxii. 18). Then it was that Christ gave him his great commission to go to the Gentiles. Vision is always a precursor of vocation and venture. It was so with Isaiah. "I saw the Lord high and lifted up, and his train filled the temple" (Isa vi. 1). The prophet was evidently in the sanctuary praying when this happened. This vision also was a prelude to a call to service, "Go ..." Now, we cannot get a vision of God unless we pray. And where there is no vision the soul perishes. A vision of God!

Brother Lawrence once said, "Prayer is nothing else than a sense of God's presence" – and that is just the practice of the presence of God. A friend of Horace Bushnell was present when that man of God prayed. There came over him a wonderful sense of God's nearness. He says: "When Horace Bushnell buried his face in his hands and prayed, I was afraid to stretch out my hand in the darkness, lest I should touch God." Was the Psalmist of old conscious of such a thought when he cried, "My soul, wait thou only upon God"? (Psa. lxii. 5.) I believe that much of our failure in prayer is due to the fact that we have not looked into this question, "What is prayer?" It is good to be conscious that we are always in the presence of God. It is better to gaze upon Him in adoration. But it is best of all to commune with Him as a Friend – and that is prayer. Real prayer at its highest and best reveals a soul athirst for God – just for God alone. Real prayer comes from the lips of those whose affection is set on things above. What a man of prayer Zinzendorf was. Why?

He sought the Giver rather than His gifts. He said: "I have one passion: it is He, He alone." Even the Mohammedan seems to have got hold of this thought. He says that there are three degrees in prayer. The lowest is that spoken only by the lips. The next is when, by a resolute effort, we succeed in fixing our thoughts on Divine things. The third is when the soul finds it hard to turn away from God. Of course, we know that God bids us "ask" of Him. We all obey Him so far; and we may rest well assured that prayer both pleases God and supplies all our need. But he would be a strange child who only sought his father's presence when he desired some gift from him! And do we not all yearn to rise to a higher level of prayer than mere petition? How is it to be done? It seems to me that only two steps are necessary – or shall we say two thoughts? There must be, first of all, a realization of God's glory, and then of God's grace. We sometimes sing: Grace and glory flow from Thee; Shower, O shower them, Lord, on me. Nor is such a desire fanciful, although some may ask what God's glory has to do with prayer. But ought we not to remind ourselves Who He is to Whom we pray? There is logic in the couplet: Thou art coming to a King; Large petitions with thee bring. Do you think that any one of us spends enough time in pondering over, yes, and marveling over, God's exceeding great glory? And do you suppose that any one of us has grasped the full meaning of the word "grace"? Are not our prayers so often ineffective and powerless – and sometimes even prayerless – because we rush unthinkingly and unpreparedly into God's presence, without realizing the majesty and glory of the God Whom we are approaching, and without reflecting upon the exceeding great riches of His glory in Christ Jesus, which we hope to draw upon?

We must "think magnificently of God." May we then suggest that before we lay our petitions before God we first dwell in meditation upon His glory and then upon His grace – for He offers us both. We must lift up the soul to God. Let us place ourselves, as it were, in the presence of God and direct our prayer to the King of kings, and Lord of lords, Who only hath immortality, dwelling in light unapproachable ... to Whom be honor and power

eternal (1 Tim. vi. 16). Let us then give Him adoration and praise because of His exceeding great glory. Consecration is not enough. There must be adoration. "Holy, holy, holy, is the Lord of Hosts," cry the seraphim; "the whole earth is full of his glory" (Isa. vi. 3). "Glory to God in the highest," cries the "whole multitude of the heavenly host" (Luke ii. 14). Yet some of us try to commune with God without stopping to "put off our shoes from off our feet" (Exod. iii. 5). Lips cry "God be merciful" That ne'er cry "God be praised." O come let us adore Him! And we may approach His glory with boldness. Did not our Lord pray that His disciples might behold His glory? (John xvii. 24). Why? And why is "the whole earth full of His glory"? The telescope reveals His infinite glory. The microscope reveals His uttermost glory. Even the unaided eye sees surpassing glory in landscape, sunshine, sea and sky. What does it all mean? These things are but a partial revelation of God's glory. It was not a desire for self-display that led our Lord to pray, "Father, glorify Thy Son" ... "O Father, glorify Thou Me" (John xvii. 1, 3). Our dear Lord wants us to realize His infinite trustworthiness and unlimited power, so that we can approach Him in simple faith and trust. In heralding the coming of Christ the prophet declared that "glory of the Lord shall be revealed, and all flesh shall see it together" (Isa. xl. 5). Now we must get a glimpse of that glory before we can pray aright. So our Lord said, "When ye pray, say Our Father, Who art in heaven [the realm of glory], hallowed be Thy name." There is nothing like a glimpse of glory to banish fear and doubt. Before we offer up our petitions may it not help us to offer up our adoration in the words of praise used by some of the saints of old? Some devout souls may not need such help. We are told that Francis of Assisi would frequently spend an hour or two in prayer on the top of Mount Averno, whilst the only word which escaped his lips would be "God" repeated at intervals. He began with adoration – and often stopped there! But most of us need some help to realize the glory of the invisible God before we can adequately praise and adore Him. Old William Law said, "When you begin to pray, use such expressions of the attributes of God as will make you sensible of His greatness and power."

This point is of such tremendous importance that we venture to remind our readers of helpful words. Some of us begin every day with a glance heavenwards whilst saying, "Glory be to the Father, and to the Son, and to the Holy Ghost." The prayer, "O Lord God most holy, O Lord most mighty, O holy and merciful Savior!" is often enough to bring a solemn awe and a spirit of holy adoration upon the soul. The Gloria in Excelsis of the Communion Service is most uplifting: "Glory be to God on high and in earth peace ... We praise Thee; we bless Thee; we worship Thee; we glorify Thee; we give thanks to Thee for Thy great glory, O Lord God, heavenly King, God the Father Almighty." Which of us can from the heart utter praise like that and remain unmoved, unconscious of the very presence and wondrous majesty of the Lord God Almighty? A verse of a hymn may serve the same purpose. My God. how wonderful Thou art! Thy majesty how bright. How beautiful Thy mercy-seat In depths of burning light! How wonderful, how beautiful The sight of Thee must be; Thine endless wisdom, boundless power And awful purity. This carries us into the very heavenlies, as also do the words: Holy, holy, holy, Lord God Almighty, All Thy works shall praise Thy name In earth, and sky, and sea. We need to cry out, and to cry often, "My soul doth magnify the Lord, and my spirit hath rejoiced in God my Savior" (Luke i. 46, 47). Can we catch the spirit of the Psalmist and sing, "Bless the Lord, O my soul, and all that is within me, bless His holy name"? (Psa. ciii. 1.) "Bless the Lord, O my soul. O Lord my God, Thou art very great; Thou are clothed with honor and majesty" (Psa. civ. 1). When shall we learn that "in His temple everything saith Glory!" (Psa. xxix. 9, R.V.) Let us, too, cry, Glory! Such worship of God, such adoration and praise and thanksgiving, not only put us into the spirit of prayer, but in some mysterious way they help God to work on our behalf. Do you remember those wonderful words, "Whoso, offereth the sacrifice of thanksgiving, glorifyeth Me and prepareth a way that I may show him the salvation of God"? (Psa. l. 23, R.V., marg.) Praise and thanksgiving not only open the gates of heaven for me to approach God, but also "prepare a way" for God to bless me. St. Paul cries, "Rejoice evermore!" before he says, "Pray without ceasing." So then our praise, as well as our prayers, is to be without ceasing. At the raising of Lazarus our Lord's prayer had as its first utterance a note of thanksgiving. "Father, I thank Thee that Thou heardest Me" (John xi. 41). He said it for those around to hear. Yes, and for us to hear. You may perhaps be wondering why it is that we should specially give thanks to God for His great glory when we kneel in prayer; and why we should spend any time in thinking of and gazing upon that glory. But is He not the King of Glory? All He is and all He does is glory. His holiness is "glorious" (Exod. xv. 11). His name is glorious (Deut. xxviii. 58). His work is "glorious" (Psa. cxi. 3). His power is glorious (Col. i. 11). His voice is glorious (Isa. xxx. 30). All things bright and beautiful All creatures great and small. All things wise and wonderful, The Lord God made them all. For His glory. "For of him and through him and unto him are all things; to whom be glory for ever" (Rom. xi. 36). And this is the God who bids us come to Him in prayer. This God is our God, and He has "gifts for men" (Psa. lxviii. 18). God says that everyone that is called by His name has been created for His glory (Isa. xliii. 7). His Church is to be a "glorious" Church – holy and without blemish (Eph. v. 27). Have you ever fully realized that the Lord Jesus desires to share with us the glory we see in Him? This is His great gift to you and me, His redeemed ones. Believe me, the more we have of God's glory, the less shall we seek His gifts. Not only in that day "when he shall come to be glorified in his saints" (2 Thess. i. 10) is there glory for us, but here and now – today. He wishes us to be partakers of His glory. Did not our Lord Himself say so? "The glory which thou has given me, I have given unto them," He declares (John xvii. 22). What is God's command? "Arise, shine, for thy light is come, and the glory of the Lord is risen upon thee." Nay, more than this: "His glory shall be seen upon thee," says the inspired prophet (Isa. lx. 1, 2). God would have people say of us as St. Peter said of the disciples of old: "The Spirit of Glory and the Spirit of God resteth upon you" (1 Peter iv. 14). Would not that be an answer to most of our prayers? Could we ask for anything better? How can we get this glory? How are we to reflect it? Only as the result of prayer. It is when we pray, that the Holy Spirit takes of the things of Christ and reveals them unto us (John xvi. 15). It was when Moses prayed, "Show me, I pray thee, thy glory," that he not only saw somewhat of it, but shared something of that glory, and his own face shone with the light of it (Exod. xxxiii. 18, xxxiv. 29). And when we, too, gaze upon the "glory of God in the face of Jesus Christ" (2 Cor. iv. 6), we shall see not only a glimpse of that glory, but we shall gain something of it ourselves. Now, that is prayer, and the highest result of prayer. Nor is there any other way of securing that glory, that God may be glorified in us (Isa. lx. 21). Let us often meditate upon Christ's glory – gaze upon it and so reflect it and receive it. This is what happened to our Lord's first disciples. They said in awed tones, "We beheld his glory!" Yes, but what followed? A few plain, unlettered, obscure fishermen companied with Christ a little while, seeing His glory; and lo! they themselves caught something of that glory. And then others marveled and "took knowledge of them that they had been with Jesus" (Acts iv. 13). And when we can declare, with St. John, "Yea, and our fellowship is with the Father and with His Son Jesus Christ" (1 John i. 3), people will say the same of us: "They have been with Jesus!" As we lift up our soul in prayer to the living God, we gain the beauty of holiness as surely as a flower becomes beautiful by living in the sunlight.

Was not our Lord Himself transfigured when He prayed? And the "very fashion" of our countenance will change, and we shall have our Mount of Transfiguration when prayer has its rightful place in our lives. And men will see in our faces "the outward and visible sign of an inward and spiritual grace." Our value to God and to man is in exact proportion to the extent in which we reveal the glory of God to others. We have dwelt so much upon the glory of Him to Whom we pray, that we must not now speak of His grace. What is prayer? It is a sign of spiritual life. I should as soon expect life in a dead man as spiritual life in a prayerless soul! Our spirituality and our fruitfulness are always in proportion to the reality of our prayers. If, then, we have at all wandered away from home in the matter of prayer, let us today resolve, "I

will arise and go unto my Father, and say unto Him, Father – ." At this point I laid down my pen, and on the page of the first paper I picked up were these words: "The secret of failure is that we see men rather than God."

Romanism trembled when Martin Luther saw God. The "great awakening" sprang into being when Jonathan Edwards saw God. The world became the parish of one man when John Wesley saw God. Multitudes were saved when Whitfield saw God. Thousands of orphans were fed when George Müller saw God. And He is "the same yesterday, today, and forever." Is it not time that we got a new vision of God – of God in all His glory? Who can say what will happen when the Church sees God? But let us not wait for others. Let us, each one for himself, with unveiled face and unsullied heart, get this vision of the glory of the Lord. "Blessed are the pure in heart, for they shall see God" (Matt. v. 8). No missioner whom it has been my joy to meet ever impressed me quite as much as Dr. Wilbur Chapman. He wrote to a friend: "I have learned some great lessons concerning prayer. At one of our missions in England the audiences were exceedingly small. But I received a note saying that an American missionary … was going to pray God's blessing down upon our work. He was known as 'Praying Hyde.' Almost instantly the tide turned. The hall became packed, and at my first invitation fifty men accepted Christ as their Savior. As we were leaving I said, 'Mr. Hyde, I want you to pray for me.' He came to my room, turned the key in the door, and dropped on his knees, and waited five minutes without a single syllable coming from his lips. I could hear my own heart thumping and his beating. I felt the hot tears running down my face. I knew I was with God. Then, with upturned face, down which the tears were streaming, he said 'O God!' Then for five minutes at least he was still again; and then, when he knew that he was talking with God … there came up from the depth of his heart such petitions for men as I had never heard before. I rose from my knees to know what real prayer was. We believe that prayer is mighty, and we believe it as we never did before." Dr. Chapman used to say, "It was a season of prayer with John Hyde that made me realize what real prayer was. I owe to him more than I owe to any man for showing me what a prayer-life is, and what a real consecrated life is ... Jesus Christ became a new Ideal to me, and I had a glimpse of His prayer-life; and I had a longing which has remained to this day to be a real praying man." And God the Holy Spirit can so teach us. Oh, ye who sigh and languish And mourn your lack of power, Hear ye this gentle whisper: "Could ye not watch one hour?" For fruitfulness and blessing There is no royal road; The power for holy service Is intercourse with God.

CHAPTER 6: HOW SHALL I PRAY?

How shall I pray? Could there be a more important question for a Christian man to ask? How shall I approach the King of Glory? When we read Christ's promises regarding prayer we are apt to think that He puts far too great a power into our hands – unless, indeed, we hastily conclude that it is impossible for Him to act as He promises. He says, ask "anything," "whatsoever," "what ye will," and it shall be done. But then He puts in a qualifying phrase. He says that we are to ask in His name. That is the condition, and the only one, although, as we shall remind ourselves later on, it is sometimes couched in different words. If, therefore, we ask and do not receive, it can only be that we are not fulfilling this condition. If then, we are true disciples of His – if we are sincere – we shall take pains (infinite pains, if need be) to discover just what it means to ask in His name; and we shall not rest content until we have fulfilled that condition. Let us read the promise again to be quite sure about it. "Whatsoever ye shall ask in my name, that will I do, that the Father may be glorified in the Son. If ye shall ask anything in my name, I will do it" (John xiv. 13, 14). This was something quite new, for our Lord said so. "Hitherto ye have asked nothing in my name," but now, "ask and ye shall receive, that your joy may be full" (John xvi. 24). Five times over our Lord repeats this simple condition, "In my name" (John xiv. 13, 14; xv. 16; xvi. 23, 24, 26). Evidently something very important is here implied. It is more than a condition – it is also a promise, an encouragement, for our Lord's biddings are always His enablings. What, then, does it mean to ask in His name? We must know this at all costs, for

it is the secret of all power in prayer. And it is possible to make a wrong use of those words. Our Lord said, "Many shall come in my name, saying, 'I am Christ,' and shall deceive many" (Matt. xxiv. 5). He might well have said, "And many shall think they are praying to the Father in my name, whilst deceiving themselves." Does it mean just adding the words, "and all this we ask in the name of Jesus Christ," at the end of our prayers? Many people apparently think that it does. But have you never heard – or offered – prayers full of self-will and selfishness which ended up in that way, "for Christ's sake. Amen"? God could not answer the prayers St. James refers to in his epistle just because those who offered them added, "we ask these things in the name of our Lord Jesus Christ." Those Christians were asking "amiss" (James iv. 3). A wrong prayer cannot be made right by the addition of some mystic phrase! And a right prayer does not fail if some such words are omitted. No! It is more than a question of words. Our Lord is thinking about faith and facts more than about some formula. The chief object of prayer is to glorify the Lord Jesus. We are to ask in Christ's name "that the Father may be glorified in the Son" (John xiv. 13). Listen! We are not to seek wealth or health, prosperity or success, ease or comfort, spirituality or fruitfulness in service simply for our own enjoyment or advancement or popularity, but only for Christ's sake – for His glory.

Let us take three steps to a right understanding of those important words, "in my name."

(1) There is a sense in which some things are done only "for Christ's sake" – because of His atoning death. Those who do not believe in the atoning death of Christ cannot pray "in His name." They may use the words, but without effect. For we are "justified by His blood" (Rom. v. 9), and "we have redemption through His blood, even the forgiveness of sins" (Eph. i. 7; Col. i. 14). In these days when Unitarianism under its guileful name of Modernism has invaded all sects, it is most important to remember the place and work of the shed blood of Christ, or "prayer" – so-called – becomes a delusion and a snare. Let us illustrate this point by an experience which happened quite early in Mr. Moody's ministry. The wife of an infidel judge – a man of great

intellectual gifts – begged Mr. Moody to speak to her husband. Moody, however, hesitated at arguing with such a man, and told him so quite frankly. "But," he added, "if ever you are converted will you promise to let me know?" The judge laughed cynically, and replied, "Oh, yes, I'll let you know quick enough if I am ever converted!" Moody went his way, relying upon prayer. That judge was converted, and within a year. He kept his promise and told Moody just how it came about. "I began to grow very uneasy and miserable one night when my wife was at a prayer-meeting. I went to bed before she came home. I could not sleep all that night. Getting up early the next morning, I told my wife I should not need any breakfast, and went off to my office. Telling the clerks they could take a holiday, I shut myself up in my private room. But I became more and more wretched. Finally, I fell on my knees and asked God to forgive me my sins, but I would not say 'for Jesus' sake,' for I was Unitarian, and I did not believe in the atonement. In an agony of mind I kept praying, 'O God, forgive me my sins,' but no answer came. At last, in desperation, I cried, 'O God, for Christ's sake forgive my sins.' Then I found peace at once." That judge had no access to the presence of God until he sought it in the name of Jesus Christ. When he came in Christ's name he was at once heard and forgiven. Yes, to pray "in the name" of the Lord Jesus is to ask for things which the blood of Christ has secured – "purchased" – for us. We have "boldness to enter into the holiest by the blood of Jesus" (Heb. x. 19). There is entrance by no other way. But this is not all that those words "In my Name" mean.

(2) The most familiar illustration of coming "in the name" of Christ is that of drawing money from a bank by means of a check. I can draw from my bank account only up to the amount of my deposit there. In my own name, I can go no farther. In the Bank of England I have no money whatsoever, and can therefore draw nothing therefrom. But suppose a very wealthy man who has a big account there gives me a blank check bearing his signature, and bids me fill it in to any amount I choose. He is my friend. What shall I do? Shall I just satisfy my present need, or shall I draw as much as I dare? I shall certainly do nothing

to offend my friend, or to lower myself in his esteem. Well, we are told by some that heaven is our bank. God is the Great Banker, for "every good gift and every perfect gift is from above, and cometh down from the Father" (James i. 17). We need a "check" wherewith to "draw" upon this boundless store. The Lord Jesus gives us a blank check in prayer. "Fill it in," says He, "to any amount; ask 'anything,' 'what ye will,' and you shall have it. Present your check in My name, and your request will be honored." Let me put this in the words of a well-known evangelist of today. "That is what happens when I go to the bank of heaven – when I go to God in prayer. I have nothing deposited there; I have no credit there; and if I go in my own name I will get absolutely nothing. But Jesus Christ has unlimited credit in heaven, and He has granted me the privilege of going with His name on my checks; and when I thus go my prayers will be honored to any extent. To pray, then, in the name of Christ is to pray, not on the ground of my credit, but His." This is all very delightful, and, in a sense, very true. If the check were drawn on a Government account, or upon some wealthy corporation, one might be tempted to get all one could. But remember we are coming to a loving Father to Whom we owe all, and Whom we love with all our heart, and to Whom we may come repeatedly. In cashing our checks at the bank of heaven we desire chiefly His honor and His glory. We wish to do only that which is pleasing in His sight. To cash some of our "checks" – to answer some of our prayers – would only bring dishonor to His name, and discredit and discomfort to us. True, His resources are unlimited; but His honor is assailable. But experience makes argument unnecessary! Dear reader, have we not – all of us – often tried this method only to fail? How many of us dare say we have never come away from the bank of heaven without getting what we asked for, although we have apparently asked "in Christ's name"? Wherein do we fail? Is it because we do not seek to learn God's will for us? We must not try to exceed His will. May I give a personal experience of my own which has never been told in public, and which is probably quite unique? It happened over thirty years ago, and now I see why. It makes such a splendid illustration of what we are now trying to learn about prayer. A well-to-do friend, and an exceedingly busy one, wished to give me one pound towards a certain Objection. He invited me to his office, and hastily wrote out a check for the amount. He folded the check and handed it to me, saying, "I will not cross it. Will you kindly cash it at the bank?" On arriving at the bank I glanced at my name on the check without troubling to verify the amount, endorsed it, and handed it to a clerk. "This is rather a big sum to cash over the counter," he said, eyeing me narrowly. "Yes, I replied laughingly, "one pound!" "No," said the clerk: "this is made out for 'one thousand pounds!" And so it was! My friend was, no doubt, accustomed to writing big checks; and he had actually written "one thousand" instead of "one" pound. Now, what was my position legally? The check was truly in his name. The signature was all right. My endorsement was all right. Could I not demand the 1,000 pounds, provided there was sufficient in the account? The check was written deliberately, if hurriedly, and freely to me – why should I not take the gift? Why not? But I was dealing with a friend – a generous friend to whom I owed many deeds of lovingkindness. He had revealed his mind to me. I knew his wishes and desires. He meant to give me one pound, and no more. I knew his intention, his "mind," and at once took back the all-too-generous check, and in due time I received just one pound, according to his will. Had that donor given me a blank check the result would have been exactly the same. He would have expected me to write in one pound, and my honor would have been at stake in my doing so. Need we draw the lesson? God has His will for each one of us, and unless we seek to know that will we are likely to ask for "a thousand," when He knows that "one" will be best for us. In our prayers we are coming to a Friend – a loving Father. We owe everything to Him. He bids us come to Him whenever we like for all we need. His resources are infinite. But He bids us to remember that we should ask only for those things that are according to His will – only for that which will bring glory to His name. John says, "If we ask anything according to His will, He heareth us" (1 John v.14). So then our Friend gives us a blank check, and leaves us to fill in "anything"; but He knows that if we

truly love Him we shall never put down – never ask for – things He is not willing to give us, because they would be harmful to us. Perhaps with most of us the fault lies in the other direction. God gives us a blank check and says, Ask for a pound – and we ask for a shilling! Would not my friend have been insulted had I treated him thus? Do we ask enough? Do we dare to ask "according to His riches in glory"? The point we are dwelling upon, however, is this – we cannot be sure that we are praying "in His name" unless we learn His will for us.

(3) But even now we have not exhausted the meaning of those words, "In my Name." We all know what it is to ask for a thing "in the name" of another. But we are very careful not to allow anyone to use our name who is not to be trusted, or he might abuse our trust and discredit our name. Gehazi, the trusted servant, dishonestly used Elisha's name when he ran after Naaman. In Elisha's name he secured riches, but also inherited a curse for his wickedness. A trusted clerk often uses his employer's name and handles great sums of money as if they were his own. But this he does only so long as he is thought to be worthy of such confidence in him. And he uses the money for his master, and not for himself. All our money belongs to our Master, Christ Jesus. We can go to God for supplies in His name if we use all we get for His glory. When I go to cash a check payable to me, the banker is quite satisfied if the signature of his client is genuine and that I am the person authorized to receive the money. He does not ask for references to my character. He has no right whatever to enquire whether I am worthy to receive the money or to be trusted to use it aright. It is not so with the Bank of Heaven. Now, this is a point of greatest importance. Do not hurry over what is now to be said. When I go to heaven's bank in the name of the Lord Jesus, with a check drawn upon the unsearchable riches of Christ, God demands that I shall be a worthy recipient. Not "worthy" in the sense that I can merit or deserve anything from a holy God – but worthy in the sense that I am seeking the gift not for m own glory or self-interest, but only for the glory of God. Otherwise I may pray and not get. "Ye ask and receive not, because ye ask amiss that ye may spend it in your pleasures" (James iv. 3,

R.V.). The great Heavenly Banker will not cash checks for us if our motives are not right. Is not this why so many fail in prayer? Christ's name is the revelation of His character. To pray "in His name" is to pray in His character, as His representative sent by Him: it is to pray by His Spirit and according to His will; to have His approval in our asking, to seek what He seeks, to ask help to do what He Himself would wish to be done, and to desire to do it not for our own glorification, but for His glory alone. To pray "in His name" we must have identity of interests and purpose. Self and its aims and desires must be entirely controlled by God's Holy Spirit, so that our wills are in complete harmony with Christ's will. We must reach the attitude of St. Augustine when he, cried, "O Lord, grant that I may do Thy will as if it were my will, so that Thou mayest do my will as if it were Thy will." Child of God, does this seem to make prayer "in His name" quite beyond us? That was not our Lord's intention. He is not mocking us! Speaking of the Holy Spirit our Lord used these words: "The Comforter ... Whom the Father will send in my name" (John xiv. 26). Now, our Savior wants us to be so controlled by the Holy Spirit that we may act in Christ's name. "As many as are led by the Spirit of God, they are the sons of God" (Rom. viii. 14). And only sons can say, "Our Father." Our Lord said of Saul of Tarsus: "He is a chosen vessel unto Me to bear My name before the Gentiles and kings, and the children of Israel" (Acts ix. 15). Not to them, but before them. So St. Paul says: "It pleased God to reveal his Son in me." We cannot pray in Christ's name unless we bear that name before people. And this is only possible so long as we "abide in" Him and His words abide in us. So we come to this – unless the heart is right the prayer must be wrong. Christ said, "If ye abide in Me, and My words abide in you, ye shall ask what ye will, and it shall be done unto you" (John xv. 7).

Those three promises are really identical – they express the same thought in different words. Look at them – Ask anything in my name, I will do it (John xiv. 13, 14). Ask what ye will (if ye abide in me and my words abide in you), and it shall be done (John xv. 7). Ask anything, according to his will, we have the petitions (1 John v. 14). And we could sum

them all up in the words of St. John, "'Whatsoever we ask, we receive of him, because we keep his commandments and do the things which are pleasing in his sight" (1 John iii. 22). When we do what He bids, He does what we ask! Listen to God and God will listen to you. Thus our Lord gives us "power of attorney" over His kingdom, the kingdom of heaven, if only we fulfill the condition of abiding in Him. Oh, what a wonder is this! How eagerly and earnestly we should seek to know His "mind," His wish, His will! – How amazing it is that any one of us should by our own self-seeking miss such unsearchable riches! We know that God's will is the best for us. We know that He longs to bless us and make us a blessing. We know that to follow our own inclination is absolutely certain to harm us and to hurt us and those whom we love. We know that to turn away from His will for us is to court disaster. O child of God, why do we not trust Him fully and wholly? Here we are, then, once again brought face to face with a life of holiness. We see with the utmost clearness that our Savior's call to prayer is simply a clarion call to holiness. "Be ye holy!" for without holiness no man can see God, and prayer cannot be efficacious. When we confess that we "never get answers to our prayers," we are condemning not God, or His promises, or the power of prayer, but ourselves. There is no greater test of spirituality than prayer. The man who tries to pray quickly discovers just where he stands in God's sight. Unless we are living the Victorious Life we cannot truly pray "in the name" of Christ, and our prayer-life must of necessity be feeble, fitful and oft-times unfruitful. And "in His name" must be "according to His will." But can we know His will? Assuredly we can. St. Paul not only says, "Let this mind be in you which was in Christ Jesus ..." (Phil. ii. 5); he also boldly declares, "We have the mind of Christ" (1 Cor. ii. 16). How, then, can we get to know God's will? We shall remember that "the secret of the Lord is with them that fear him" (Psa. xxv. 14). In the first place, we must not expect God to reveal His will to us unless we desire to know that will and intend to do that will. Knowledge of God's will and the performance of that will go together. We are apt to desire to know God's will so that we may decide whether we will obey or not. Such an attitude is disastrous. "If any man willeth to do His will, he shall know of the teaching" (John vii. 17). God's will is revealed in His Word in Holy Scriptures. What He promises in His Word I may know to be according to His will. For example, I may confidently ask for wisdom, because His Word says, "If any ... lack wisdom, let him ask of God ... and it shall be given him" (James i. 5). We cannot be men of prevailing prayer unless we study God's Word to find out His will for us. But it is the Holy Spirit of God Who is prayer's great Helper.

Read again those wonderful words of St. Paul: "In the same way the Spirit also helps us in our weakness; for we do not know what prayers to offer nor in what way to offer them, but the Spirit Himself pleads for us in yearnings that can find no words, and the Searcher of hearts knows what the Spirit's meaning is, because His intercessions for God's people are in harmony with God's will" (Rom. Viii. 26, 27; Weymouth). What comforting words! Ignorance and helplessness in prayer are indeed blessed things if they cast us upon the Holy Spirit. Blessed be the name of the Lord Jesus! We are left without excuse. Pray we must: pray we can. Remember our Heavenly Father is pledged to give the Holy Spirit to them that ask Him (Luke xi. 13) – and any other "good thing" too (Matt. vii. 11). Child of God, you have often prayed. You have, no doubt, often bewailed your feebleness and slackness in prayer. But have you really prayed in His name? It is when we have failed and know not "what prayers to offer" or "in what way," that the Holy Spirit is promised as our Helper. Is it not worth while to be wholly and whole-heartedly yielded to Christ? The half-and-half Christian is of very little use either to God or man. God cannot use him, and man has no use for him, but considers him a hypocrite. One sin allowed in the life wrecks at once our usefulness and our joy, and robs prayer of its power. Beloved, we have caught a fresh glimpse of the grace and the glory of our Lord Jesus Christ. He is willing and waiting to share with us both His glory and His grace. He is willing to make us channels of blessing. Shall we not worship God in sincerity and truth, and cry eagerly and earnestly, "Lord, what shall I do?" (Acts xxii. 10, R.V.) and then, in the power of His might, do it? St. Paul once shot up that prayer to heaven; "What shall I do?" What answer did he get? Listen! He tells us in his counsel to believers everywhere just what it meant to him, and should mean to us: "Beloved, put on ... a heart of compassion, kindness, humility, longsuffering; ... above all things put on love and let the peace of Christ rule in your hearts ... Let the word of Christ dwell in you richly in all wisdom ... And whatsoever ye do, in word or deed, do all in the name of the Lord Jesus, giving thanks to God the Father through him" (Col. iii. 12–17). It is only when whatsoever we do is done in His name that He will do whatsoever we ask in His name.

Chapter 7: Must I Agonize?

Prayer is measured, not by time, but by intensity. Earnest souls who read of men like Praying Hyde are today anxiously asking, "Am I expected to pray like that?" They hear of others who sometimes remain on their knees before God all day or all night, refusing food and scorning sleep, whilst they pray and pray and pray. They naturally wonder, "Are we to do the same? Must all of us follow their examples?" We must remember that those men of prayer did not pray by time. They continued so long in prayer because they could not stop praying. Some have ventured to think that in what has been said in earlier chapters I have hinted that we must all follow in their train. Child of God, do not let any such thought – such fear? – distress you. Just be willing to do what He will have you do – what He leads you to do. Think about it; pray about it. We are bidden by the Lord Jesus to pray to our loving Heavenly Father. We sometimes sing, "Oh, how He loves!" And nothing can fathom that love. Prayer is not given us as a burden to be borne, or an irksome duty to fulfill, but to be a joy and power to which there is no limit. It is given us that we "may find grace to help us in time of need" (Heb. iv. 16, R.V.). And every time is a "time of need." "Pray ye" is an invitation to be accepted rather than a command to be obeyed. Is it a burden for a child to come to his father to ask for some boon? How a father loves his child, and seeks its highest good! How he shields that little one from any sorrow or pain or suffering! Our heavenly Father loves us infinitely more than any earthly father. The Lord Jesus loves us infinitely more than any earthly friend. God forgive me if any words of mine, on such a precious theme as prayer, have wounded the hearts or consciences of those who are yearning to know more about prayer. "Your heavenly Father knoweth," said our Lord: and if He knows, we can but trust and not be afraid. A schoolmaster may blame a boy for neglected homework, or unpunctual attendance, or frequent absence; but the loving father in the home knows all about it. He knows all about the devoted service of the little laddie in the home circle, where sickness or poverty throws so many loving tasks in his way. Our dear, loving Father knows all about us. He sees. He knows how little leisure some of us have for prolonged periods of prayer. For some of us God makes leisure. He makes us lie down (Psa. xxiii. 2) that He may make us look up. Even then, weakness of body often prevents prolonged prayer. Yet I question if any of us, however great and reasonable our excuses, spend enough thought over our prayers. Some of us are bound to be much in prayer. Our very work demands it. We may be looked upon as spiritual leaders; we may have the spiritual welfare or training of others. God forbid that we should sin against the Lord in ceasing to pray enough for them (1 Sam. xii. 23).

Yes, with some it is our very business – almost our life's work – to pray, Others – have friends who give them pain, yet have not sought a friend in Him. For them they cannot help praying. If we have the burden of souls upon us we shall never ask, "How long need I pray?" But how well we know the difficulties which surround the prayer-life of many! A little pile of letters lies before me as I write. They are full of excuses, and kindly protests, and reasonings it is true. But is that why they are written? No! No! Far from it. In every one of them there is an undercurrent of deep yearning to know God's will, and how to obey the call to prayer amid all the countless claims of life. Those letters tell of many who cannot get away from others for times of secret prayer; of those who share even bedrooms; of busy mothers, and maids, and mistresses who scarcely know how to get through the endless washing and cooking, mending and cleaning, shopping and visiting; of tired workers who are too weary to pray when the day's work is done. Child of God, our heavenly Father knows all about it. He is not a taskmaster. He is our Father. if you have no time for prayer, or no chance of secret prayer, why, just tell Him all about it – and you will discover that you are praying! To those who seem unable to get any solitude at all, or even the opportunity of stealing into a quiet church for a few moments, may we point to the wonderful prayer-life of St. Paul ? Did it ever occur to you that he was in prison when he wrote most of those marvelous prayers of his which we possess? Picture him. He was chained to a Roman soldier day and night, and was never alone for a moment. Epaphias was there part of the time, and caught something of his master's passion for prayer. St. Luke may have been there. What prayer-meetings! No opportunity for secret prayer. No! but how much we owe to the uplifting of those chained hands! You and I may be never, or rarely ever, alone, but at least our hands are not fettered with chains, and our hearts are not fettered, nor our lips.

Can we make time for prayer? I may be wrong, but my own belief is that it is not God's will for most of us – and perhaps not for any of us – to spend so much time in prayer as to injure our physical health through getting insufficient food or sleep. With very many it is a physical impossibility, because of bodily weakness, to remain long in the spirit of intense prayer. The posture in which we pray is immaterial. God will listen whether we kneel, or stand, or sit, or walk, or work. I am quite aware that many have testified to the fact that God sometimes gives special strength to those who curtail their hours of rest in order to pray more. At one time the writer tried getting up very early in the morning – and every morning – for prayer and communion with God. After a time he found that his daily work was suffering in intensity and effectiveness, and that it was difficult to keep awake during the early evening hours! But do we pray as much as we might do? It is a lasting regret to me that I allowed the days of youth and vigor to pass by without laying more stress upon those early hours of prayer. Now, the inspired command is clear enough: "Pray without ceasing" (1 Thess.

v. 17). Our dear Lord said, "Men ought always to pray, and not to faint" – "and never lose heart" (Weymouth) (Luke xviii. 1). This, of course, cannot mean that we are to be always on our knees. I am convinced that God does not wish us to neglect rightful work in order to pray. But it is equally certain that we might work better and do more work if we gave less time to work and more to prayer. Let us work well. We are to be "not slothful in business" (Rom. xii. 11). St. Paul says, "We exhort you, brethren, that ye abound more and more; and that ye... do your own business, and to work with your hands ... that ye may walk honestly ... and have need of nothing" (1 Thess. iv. 11, 12). "If any will not work, neither let him eat" (1 Thess. iii. 10). But are there not endless opportunities during every day of "lifting, up holy hands" – or at least holy hearts – in prayer to our Father? Do we seize the opportunity, as we open our eyes upon each new day, of praising and blessing our Redeemer? Every day is an Easter day to the Christian. We can pray as we dress. Without a reminder we shall often forget. Stick a piece of stamp-paper in the corner of your looking-glass, bearing the words, – "Pray without ceasing." Try it. We can pray as we go from one duty to another. We can often pray at our work. The washing and the writing, the mending and the minding, the cooking and the cleaning will be done all the better for it. Do not children, both young and old, work better and play better when some loved one is watching? Will it not help us ever to remember that the Lord Jesus is always with us, watching? Aye, and helping. The very consciousness of His eye upon us will be the consciousness of His power within us. Do you not think that St. Paul had in his mind this habitual praying rather than fixed seasons of prayer when he said, "The Lord is at hand" – i.e., is near (Weymouth). "In nothing be anxious, but in everything, by prayer and supplication, with thanksgiving, let your requests be made known unto God" (Phil. iv. 5, 6)? Does not "in everything" suggest that, as thing after thing befalls us, moment by moment, we should then and there make it a "thing" of prayer and praise to the Lord Who is near? (Why should we limit this "nearness" to the Second Advent?) What a blessed thought:

prayer is to a near-God. When our Lord sent His disciples forth to work, He said, "Lo, I am with you alway."

Sir Thomas Browne, the celebrated physician, had caught this spirit. He made a vow "to pray in all places where quietness inviteth; in any house, highway or street; and to know no street in this city that may not witness that I have not forgotten God and my Savior in it; and that no town or parish where I have been may not say the like. To take occasion of praying upon the sight of any church which I see as I ride about. To pray daily and particularly for my sick patients, and for all sick people, under whose care soever. And at the entrance into the house of the sick to say, 'The peace and the mercy of God be upon this house.' After a sermon to make a prayer and desire a blessing, and to pray for the minister." But we question if this habitual communion with our blessed Lord is possible unless we have times – whether long or brief – of definite prayer. And what of these prayer seasons? We have said earlier that prayer is as simple as a little child asking something of its father. Nor would such a remark need any further comment were it not for the existence of the evil one. There is no doubt whatever that the devil opposes our approach to God in prayer, and does all he can to prevent the prayer of faith. His chief way of hindering us is to try to fill our minds with the thought of our needs, so that they shall not be occupied with thoughts of God, our loving Father, to Whom we pray. He wants us to think more of the gift than of the Giver. The Holy Spirit leads us to pray for a brother. We get as far as "O God, bless my brother" – and away go our thoughts to the brother, and his affairs, and his difficulties, his hopes and his fears, and away goes prayer! How hard the devil makes it for us to concentrate our thoughts upon God! This is why we urge people to get a realization of the glory of God, and the power of God, and the presence of God, before offering up any petition. If there were no devil there would be no difficulty in prayer, but it is the evil one's chief aim to make prayer impossible. That is why most of us find it hard to sympathize with those who profess to condemn what they call "vain repetitions" and "much speaking" in prayer – quoting our Lord's words in His sermon on the mount. A prominent London vicar said quite recently, "God does not wish us to waste either His time or ours with long prayers. We must be business-like in our dealings with God, and just tell Him plainly and briefly what we want, and leave the matter there." But does our friend think that prayer is merely making God acquainted with our needs? If that is all there is in it, why, there is no need of prayer! "For your Father knoweth what things ye have need of before ye ask him," said our Lord when urging the disciples to pray. We are aware that Christ Himself condemned some "long prayers" (Matt. xxiii. 14). But they were long prayers made "for a pretense," "for a show" (Luke xx. 47). Dear praying people, believe me, the Lord would equally condemn many of the "long prayers" made every week in some of our prayer-meetings – prayers which kill the prayer-meeting, and which finish up with a plea that God would hear these "feeble breathings," or "unworthy utterings." But he never condemns long prayers that are sincere.

Let us not forget that our Lord sometimes spent long nights in prayer. We are told of one of these – we do not know how frequently they were (Luke vi. 12). He would sometimes rise a "great while before day" and depart to a solitary place for prayer (Mark i. 35). The perfect Man spent more time in prayer than we do. It would seem an undoubted fact that with God's saints in all ages nights of prayer with God have been followed by days of power with men. Nor did our Lord excuse Himself from prayer – as we, in our ignorance, might think He could have done – because of the pressing calls to service and boundless opportunities of usefulness. After one of His busiest days, at a time when His popularity was at its highest, just when everyone sought His company and His counsel, He turned His back upon them all and retired to a mountain to pray (Matt. xiv. 23). We are told that once "great multitudes came together to hear Him, and to be healed of their infirmities." Then comes the remark, "But Jesus himself constantly withdrew into the desert, and there prayed" (Luke v. 15, 16, Weymouth). Why? Because He knew that prayer was then far more potent than "service." We say we are too busy to pray. But the busier our Lord was, the more He prayed.

Sometimes He had no leisure so much as to eat (Mark iii. 20); and sometimes He had no leisure for needed rest and sleep (Mark vi. 31). Yet He always took time to pray. If frequent prayer, and, at times, long hours of prayer, were necessary for our Savior, are they less necessary for us? I do not write to persuade people to agree with me: that is a very small matter. We only want to know the truth. Spurgeon once said: "There is no need for us to go beating about the bush, and not telling the Lord distinctly what it is that we crave at His hands. Nor will it be seemly for us to make any attempt to use fine language; but let us ask God in the simplest and most direct manner for just the things we want … I believe in business prayers. I mean prayers in which you take to God one of the many promises which He has given us in His Word, and expect it to be fulfilled as certainly as we look for the money to be given us when we go to the bank to cash a check. We should not think of going there, lolling over the counter chattering with the clerks on every conceivable subject except the one thing for which we had gone to the bank, and then coming away without the coin we needed; but we should lay before the clerk the promise to pay the bearer a certain sum, tell him in what form we wished to take the amount, count the cash after him, and then go on our way to attend to other business. That is just an illustration of the method in which we should draw supplies from the Bank of Heaven." Splendid! But – ? By all means let us be definite in prayer; by all means let us put eloquence aside – if we have any! By all means let us avoid needless "chatter," and come in faith, expecting to receive. But would the bank clerk pass me the money over the counter so readily if there stood by my side a powerful, evil-countenanced, well-armed ruffian whom he recognized to be a desperate criminal waiting to snatch the money before my weak hands could grasp it? Would he not wait till the ruffian had gone? This is no fanciful picture. The Bible teaches us that, in some way or other, Satan can hinder our prayers and delay the answer. Does not St. Peter urge certain things upon Christians, that their "prayers be not hindered"? (1 Peter iii. 7.) Our prayers can be hindered. "Then cometh the evil one and snatcheth away that which hath been sown in the heart" (Matt. xiii. 19, R.V.).

Scripture gives us one instance – probably only one out of many – where the evil one actually kept back – delayed – for three weeks an answer to prayer. We only mention this to show the need of repeated prayer, persistence in prayer, and also to call attention to the extraordinary power which Satan possesses. We refer to Daniel x. 12, 13: "Fear not, Daniel, for from the first day that thou didst set thine heart to understand, and to humble thyself before God, thy words were heard: and I am come for thy word's sake. But the prince of the kingdom of Persia withstood me one and twenty days. But lo, Michael, one of the chief princes, came to help me." We must not overlook this Satanic opposition and hindrance to our prayers. If we were to be content to ask God only once for some promised thing or one we deemed necessary, these chapters would never have been written. Are we never to ask again? For instance, I know that God willeth not the death of a sinner. So I come boldly in prayer: "O God, save my friend." Am I never to ask for his conversion again? George Müller prayed daily – and oftener – for sixty years for the conversion of a friend. But what light does the Bible throw upon "business-like" prayers? Our Lord gave two parables to teach persistence and continuance in prayer. The man who asked three loaves from his friend at midnight received as many as he needed "because of his importunity" – or persistency (Weymouth), i.e., his "shamelessness," as the word literally means (Luke xi. 8). The widow who "troubled" the unjust judge with her "continual coming" at last secured redress. Our Lord adds "And shall not God avenge his elect which cry unto him day and night, and he is longsuffering over them?" (Luke xviii. 7, R.V.) How delighted our Lord was with the poor Syro-Phoenician woman who would not take refusals or rebuffs for an answer! Because of her continual request He said: "O woman, great is thy faith: be it unto thee even as thou wilt" (Matt. xv. 28). Our dear Lord, in His agony in Gethsemane, found it necessary to repeat even His prayer. "And he left them and went away and prayed a third time, saying again the same words" (Matt. xxvi. 44). And we find St. Paul, the apostle of prayer, asking God time after time to remove his thorn

in the flesh. "Concerning this thing," says he, "I besought the Lord thrice that it might depart from me" (2 Cor. xii. 8). God cannot always grant our petitions immediately. Sometimes we are not fitted to receive the gift. Sometimes He says "No" in order to give us something far better. Think, too, of the days when St. Peter was in prison. If your boy was unjustly imprisoned, expecting death at any moment, would you – could you – be content to pray just once, a "business-like" prayer: "O God, deliver my boy from the hands of these men"? Would you not be very much in prayer and very much in earnest? This is how the Church prayed for St. Peter. "Long and fervent prayer was offered to God by the Church on his behalf" (Acts xii. 5, Weymouth). Bible students will have noticed that the A.V. rendering, "without ceasing," reads "earnestly" in the R.V. Dr. Torrey points out that neither translation gives the full force of the Greek. The word means literally "stretched-out-ed-ly." It represents the soul on the stretch of earnest and intense desire. Intense prayer was made for St. Peter. The very same word is used of our Lord in Gethsemane: "And being in an agony he prayed more earnestly, and his sweat became as it were great drops of blood falling down upon the ground" (Luke xxii. 44). Ah! there was earnestness, even agony in prayer. Now, what about our prayers? Are we called upon to agonize in prayer? Many of God's dear saints say "No!" They think such agonizing in us would reveal great want of faith. Yet most of the experiences which befell our Lord are to be ours. We have been crucified with Christ, and we are risen with Him. Shall there be, with us, no travailing for souls? Come back to human experience. Can we refrain from agonizing in prayer over dearly beloved children who are living in sin? I question if any believer can have the burden of souls upon him – a passion for souls – and not agonize in prayer. Can we help crying out, like John Knox, "O God, give me Scotland or I die"? Here again the Bible helps us. Was there no travail of soul and agonizing in prayer when Moses cried out to God, "O, this people have sinned a great sin, and have made gods of gold. Yet now, if thou wilt forgive their sin – ; and if not, blot me, I pray thee, out of thy book"? (Exod. xxxii. 32). Was there no agonizing in prayer when St.

Paul said, "I could wish" – ("pray," R.V. marg.) – "that I myself were anathema from Christ for my brethren's sake"? (Rom. ix. 3). We may, at all events, be quite sure that our Lord, Who wept over Jerusalem, and Who "offered up prayers and supplications with strong crying and tears" (Heb. v. 7), will not be grieved if He sees us weeping over erring ones. Nay, will it not rather gladden His heart to see us agonizing over the sin which grieves Him? In fact, may not the paucity of conversions in so many a ministry be due to lack of agonizing in prayer? We are told that "As soon as Zion travailed she brought forth her children" (Isa. lxvi. 8).

Was St. Paul thinking of this passage when he wrote to the Galatians, "My little children, of whom I am again in travail until Christ be formed in you"? (Gal. iv. 19). And will not this be true of spiritual children? Oh, how cold our hearts often are! How little we grieve over the lost! And shall we dare to criticize those who agonize over the perishing? God forbid! No; there is such a thing as wrestling in prayer. Not because God is unwilling to answer, but because of the opposition of the "world-rulers of this darkness" (Eph. vi. 12, R.V.). The very word used for "striving" in prayer means "a contest." The contest is not between God and ourselves. He is at one with us in our desires. The contest is with the evil one, although he is a conquered foe (1 John iii. 8). He desires to thwart our prayers. "We wrestle not against flesh and blood, but against principalities, against the world-rulers of this darkness, against the spiritual hosts of wickedness in the heavenly places" (Eph. vi. 12). We, too, are in these "heavenly places in Christ" (Eph. i. 3); and it is only in Christ that we can be victorious. Our wrestling may be a wrestling of our thoughts from thinking Satan's suggestions, and keeping them fixed on Christ our Savior – that is, watching as well as praying (Eph. vi. 18); "watching unto prayer." We are comforted by the fact that "the Spirit helpeth our infirmities: for we know not how to pray as we ought" (Rom. viii. 26). How does the Spirit "help" us, teach us, if not by example as well as by precept? How does the Spirit "pray"? "The Spirit Himself maketh intercession for us with groanings which cannot be uttered (Rom. viii. 26). Does the Spirit "agonize" in prayer as

the Son did in Gethsemane? If the Spirit prays in us, shall we not share His "groanings" in prayer? And if our agonizing in prayer weakens our body at the time, will angels come to strengthen us, as they did our Lord? (Luke xxii. 43). We may, perhaps, like Nehemiah, weep, and mourn, and fast when we pray before God (Neh. i. 4). "But," one asks, "may not a godly sorrow for sin and a yearning desire for the salvation of others induce in us an agonizing which is unnecessary, and dishonoring to God?" May it not reveal a lack of faith in God's promises? Perhaps it may do so. But there is little doubt that St. Paul regarded prayer – at least sometimes – as a conflict (see Rom. xv. 30). In writing to the Colossian Christians he says: "I would have you know how greatly I strive for you … and for as many as have not seen my face in the flesh; that their hearts may be comforted" (Col. ii. 1, 2). Undoubtedly he refers to his prayers for them. Again, he speaks of Epaphras as one who is "always striving for you in his prayers, that ye may stand perfect, and fully assured in all the will of God" (Col. iv. 12). The word for "strive" is our word "agonize," the very word used of our Lord being "in an agony" when praying Himself (Luke xxii. 44). The apostle says again, Epaphras "hath much labor for you," that is, in his prayers. St. Paul saw him praying there in prison, and witnessed his intense striving as he engaged in a long, indefatigable effort on behalf of the Colossians.

How the Praetorian guard to whom St. Paul was chained must have wondered – yes, and have been deeply touched – to see these men at their prayers. Their agitation, their tears, their earnest supplications as they lifted up chained hands in prayer must have been a revelation to him! What would they think of our prayers? No doubt St. Paul was speaking of his own custom when he urged the Ephesian Christians and others "to stand," "with all prayer and supplication, praying at all seasons in the Spirit, and watching thereunto in all perseverance and supplication for all saints, and on my behalf … an ambassador in chains." (Eph. vi. 18–20). That is a picture of his own prayer-life, we may be sure. So then prayer meets with obstacles, which must be prayed away. That is what men mean when they talk about praying through. We must wrestle with the machinations of Satan. It may be bodily weariness or pain, or the insistent claims of other thoughts, or doubt, or the direct assaults of spiritual hosts of wickedness. With us, as with St. Paul, prayer is something of a "conflict," a "wrestle," at least sometimes, which compels us to "stir" ourselves up "to lay hold on God" (Isa. lxiv. 7). Should we be wrong if we ventured to suggest that very few people ever wrestle in prayer? Do we? But let us never doubt our Lord's power and the riches of His grace. The author of The Christian's Secret of a Happy Life told a little circle of friends, just before her death, of an incident in her own life. Perhaps I may be allowed to tell it abroad. A lady friend who occasionally paid her a visit for two or three days was always a great trial, a veritable tax upon her temper and her patience. Every such visit demanded much prayer-preparation. The time came when this "critical Christian" planned a visit for a whole week! She felt that nothing but a whole night of prayer could fortify her for this great testing. So, providing herself with a little plate of biscuits, she retired in good time to her bedroom, to spend the night on her knees before God, to beseech Him to give her grace to keep sweet and loving during the impending visit." No sooner had she knelt beside her bed than there flashed into her mind the words of Phil. iv. 19: "God shall supply all your need according to His riches in glory by Christ Jesus." Her fears vanished. She said, "When I realized that, I gave Him thanks and praised Him for His goodness. Then I jumped into bed and slept the night through. My guest arrived the next day, and I quite enjoyed her visit. No one can lay down hard and fast rules of prayer, even for himself. God's gracious Holy Spirit alone can direct us moment by moment. There, however, we must leave the matter. God is our judge and our Guide.

But let us remember that prayer is a many-sided thing. As Bishop Moule says, "True prayer can be uttered under innumerable circumstances." Very often Prayer is the burden of a sigh, The falling of a tear, The upward glancing of an eye, When none but God is near. It may be just letting your request be made known unto God (Phil. iv. 6). We cannot think that prayer

need always be a conflict and a wrestle. For if it were, many of us would soon become physical wrecks, suffering from nervous breakdown, and coming to an early grave. And with many it is a physical impossibility to stay any length of time in a posture of prayer. Dr. Moule says: "Prayer, genuine and victorious, is continually offered without the least physical effort or disturbance. It is often in the deepest stillness of soul and body that it wins its longest way. But there is another side of the matter. Prayer is never meant to be indolently easy, however simple and reliant it may be. It is meant to be an infinitely important transaction between man and God. And therefore, very often ... it has to be viewed as a work involving labor, persistence, conflict, if it would be prayer indeed." No one can prescribe for another. Let each be persuaded in his own mind how to pray, and the Holy Spirit will inspire us and guide us how long to pray. And let us all be so full of the love of God our Savior that prayer, at all times and in all places, may be a joy as well as a means of grace. Shepherd Divine, our wants relieve In this and every day; To all Thy tempted followers give The power, to watch and pray. The spirit of interceding grace Give us the faith to claim; To wrestle till we see Thy face And know Thy hidden Name.

CHAPTER 8: DOES GOD ALWAYS ANSWER PRAYER?

We now come to one of the most important questions that any man can ask. Very much depends upon the answer we are led to give. Let us not shrink from facing the question fairly and honestly. Does God always answer prayer? Of course, we all grant that He does answer prayer – some prayers, and sometimes. But does He always answer true prayer. Some so-called prayers He does not answer, because He does not hear them. When His people were rebellious, He said, "When ye make many prayers, I will not hear" (Isa. i. 15). But a child of God ought to expect answers to prayer. God means every prayer to have an answer; and not a single real prayer can fail of its effect in heaven. And yet that wonderful declaration of St. Paul: "All things are yours, for ye are Christ's" (1 Cor. iii. 21), seems so plainly and so tragically untrue for most Christians. Yet it is not so. They are ours, but so many of us do not possess our possessions. The owners of Mount Morgan, in Queensland, toiled arduously for years on its barren slopes, eking out a miserable existence, never knowing that under their feet was one of the richest sources of gold the world has ever known. There was wealth, vast, undreamt of, yet unimagined and unrealized. It was "theirs," yet not theirs. The Christian, however, knows of the riches of God in glory in Christ Jesus, but he does not seem to know how to get them.

Now, our Lord tells us that they are to be had for the asking. May He indeed give us all a right judgment in "prayer-things." When we say that no true prayer goes unanswered we are not claiming that God always gives just what we ask for. Have you ever met a parent so foolish as to treat his child like that? We do not give our child a red-hot poker because he clamors for it! Wealthy people are the most careful not to allow their children much pocket-money. Why, if God gave us all we prayed for, we should rule the world, and not He! And surely we would all confess that we are not capable of doing that. Moreover, more than one ruler of the world is an absolute impossibility! God's answer to prayer may be "Yes," or it may be "No." It may be "Wait," for it may be that He plans a much larger blessing than we imagined, and one which involves other lives as well as our own. God's answer is sometimes "No." But this is not necessarily a proof of known and willful sin in the life of the suppliant, although there may be sins of ignorance. He said "No" to St. Paul sometimes (2 Cor. xii. 8, 9). More often than not the refusal is due to our ignorance or selfishness in asking. "For we know not how to pray as we ought" (Rom. viii. 26). That was what was wrong with the mother of Zebedee's children. She came and worshiped our Lord and prayed to Him. He quickly replied, "Ye know not what ye ask" (Matt. xx. 22).

Elijah, a great man of prayer, sometimes had "No" for an answer. But when he was swept up to glory in a chariot of fire, did he regret that God said "No" when he cried out "O Lord, take away my life"? God's answer is sometimes "Wait." He may delay the answer because we are not yet fit to receive the gift we crave – as with wrestling Jacob. Do you remember the famous prayer of Augustine – "O God, make me pure, but not now"? Are not our prayers sometimes like that? Are we always really willing to "drink the cup" – to pay the price of answered prayer? Sometimes He delays so that greater glory may be brought to Himself. God's delays are not denials. We do not know why He sometimes delays the answer and at other times answers "before we call" (Isa. lxv. 24).

George Müller, one of the greatest men of prayer of all time, had to pray over a period of more than sixty-three years for the conversion of a friend! Who can tell why? "The great point is never to give up until the answer comes," said Müller. "I have been praying for sixty-three years and eight months for one man's conversion. He is not converted yet, but he will be! How can it be otherwise? There is the unchanging promise of Jehovah, and on that I rest." Was this delay due to some persistent hindrance from the devil? (Dan. x. 13). Was it a mighty and prolonged effort on the part of Satan to shake or break Müller's faith? For no sooner was Müller dead than his friend was converted – even before the funeral. Yes, his prayer was granted, though the answer tarried long in coming. So many of George Müller's petitions were granted him that it is no wonder that he once exclaimed, "Oh, how good, kind, gracious and condescending is the One with Whom we have to do! I am only a poor, frail, sinful man, but He has heard my prayers ten thousands of times." Perhaps some are asking, How can I discover whether God's answer is "No" or "Wait"? We may rest assured that He will not let us pray sixty-three years to get a "No"! Müller's prayer, so long repeated, was based upon the knowledge that God "willeth not the death of a sinner"; "He would have all men to be saved" (1 Tim. ii. 4). Even as I write, the postman brings me an illustration of this. A letter comes from one who very rarely writes me, and did not even know my address – one whose name is known to every Christian worker in England. A loved one was stricken down with illness. Is he to continue to pray for her recovery? Is God's answer "No," or is it, "Go on praying – wait"? My friend writes: "I had distinct guidance from God regarding my beloved ... that it was the will of God she should be taken ... I retired into the rest of surrender and submission to His will. I have much to praise God for." A few hours later God took that loved one to be with Him in glory. Again may we urge our readers to hold on to this truth: true prayer never goes unanswered.

If we only gave more thought to our prayers we should pray more intelligently. That sounds like a truism. But we say it because some dear Christian people seem to lay their common sense and reason aside before they pray. A little reflection would show that God cannot grant some prayers. During the war every nation prayed for victory. Yet it is perfectly obvious that all countries could not be victorious. Two men living together might pray, the one for rain and the other for fine weather. God cannot give both these things at the same time in the same place! But the truthfulness of God is at stake in this matter of prayer. We have all been reading again those marvelous prayer-promises of our Lord, and have almost staggered at those promises – the wideness of their scope, the fullness of their intent, the largeness of the one word "Whatsoever." Very well! "Let God be found true" (Rom. iii. 4). He certainly will always be "found true." Do not stop to ask the writer if God has granted all his prayers. He has not. To have said "Yes" to some of them would have spelt curse instead of blessing. To have answered others was, alas! a spiritual impossibility – he was not worthy of the gifts he sought. The granting, of some of them would but have fostered spiritual pride and self-satisfaction. How plain all these things seem now, in the fuller light of God's Holy Spirit! As one looks back and compares one's eager, earnest prayers with one's poor, unworthy service and lack of true spirituality, one sees how impossible it was for God to grant the very things He longed to impart! It was often like asking God to put the ocean of His love into a thimble-heart! And yet, how God just yearns to bless us with every spiritual blessing! How the dear Savior cries again and again, "How often would I ... but ye would not"! (Matt. xxiii. 37). The sadness of it all is that we often ask and do not receive because of our unworthiness – and then we complain because God does not answer our prayers! The Lord Jesus declares that God gives the Holy Spirit – who teaches us how to pray – just as readily as a father gives good gifts to his children. But no gift is a "good gift" if the child is not fit to use that gift. God never gives us something that we cannot, or will not, use for His glory (I am not referring to talents, for we may abuse or "bury" those, but to spiritual gifts). Did you ever see a father give his baby boy a razor when he asked for it, because he hoped the boy would grow into a man and then find the razor useful? Does a father never say to his child, "Wait till you are older, or bigger, or wiser, or better, or stronger"? May not our loving heavenly Father also say to us, "Wait"? In our ignorance and blindness we must surely sometimes say, In very love refuse Whate'er Thou seest Our weakness would abuse. Rest assured that God never bestows tomorrow's gift today. It is not unwillingness on His part to give. It is not that God is ever straitened in Himself. His resources are infinite, and His ways are past finding out. It was after bidding His disciples to ask that our Lord goes on to hint not only at His providence, but at His resources. "Look at the wild birds" (Matt. vi. 26, Moffatt); "your heavenly Father feedeth them."

How simple it sounds. Yet have you ever reflected that not a single millionaire, the wide world over, is wealthy enough to feed all "the birds of the air," even for one day? Your heavenly Father feedeth them every day, and is none the poorer for it. Shall He not much more feed you, clothe you, take care of you? Oh, let us rely more upon prayer! Do we not know that "He is a Rewarder of them that diligently seek Him"? (Hebrews xi. 6). The "oil" of the Holy Spirit will never cease to flow so long as there are empty vessels to receive it (1 Kings iv. 6). It is always we who are to blame when the Spirit's work ceases. God cannot trust some Christians with the fullness of the Holy Spirit. God cannot trust some workers with definite spiritual results in their labors. They would suffer from pride and vainglory. No! we do not claim that God grants every Christian everything he prays for. As we saw in an earlier chapter, there must be purity of heart, purity of motive, purity of desire, if our prayers are to be in His name. God is greater than His promises, and often gives more than either we desire or deserve – but He does not always do so. So, then, if any specific petition is not granted, we may feel sure that God is calling us to examine our hearts. For He has undertaken to grant every prayer that is truly offered in His name. Let us repeat His blessed words once more – we cannot repeat them too often – "Whatsoever ye shall ask in My name, that will I do, that the Father may be glorified in the Son. If ye shall ask anything in My name, that will I do" (John xiv. 13, 14). Remember that it was impossible for Christ to offer up any prayer which was not granted. He was God – He knew the mind of God – He had the mind of the Holy Spirit. Does He once say, "Father, if it be possible, let ..." as He kneels in agony in Gethsemane's garden, pouring out strong crying and tears? Yes, and "He was heard for His reverential awe" (Heb. v. 7, Dr. Moule). Surely not the "agony," but the son-like fear, gained the answer? Our prayers are heard not so much because they are importunate but because they are filial. Brother Christian, we cannot fully understand that hallowed scene of dreadful awe and wonder. But this we know – that our Lord never yet made a promise which He cannot keep, or does not mean to fulfill. The Holy Spirit maketh intercession for us (Rom. viii. 26), and God cannot say Him "Nay." The Lord Jesus makes intercession for us (Hebrews vii. 25), and God cannot say Him "Nay." His prayers are worth a thousand of ours, but it is He who bids us pray!

"But was not St. Paul filled with the Holy Spirit?" you ask, "and did he not say, 'We have the mind of Christ?' Yet he asked thrice over that God would remove the 'thorn' in his flesh – and yet God distinctly tells him He would not do so." It is a very singular thing, too, that the only petition recorded of St. Paul seeking something for his own individual need was refused! The difficulty, however, is this: Why did St. Paul, who had the "mind" of Christ, ask for something which he soon discovered was contrary to God's wishes? There are doubtless many fully-consecrated Christians reading these words who have been perplexed because God has not given some things they prayed for. We must remember that we may be filled with the Spirit and yet err in judgment or desire. We must remember, too, that we are never filled with God's Holy Spirit once for all. The evil one is always on the watch to put his mind

into us, so as to strike at God through us. At any moment we may become disobedient or unbelieving, or may be betrayed into some thought or act contrary to the Spirit of love. We have an astonishing example of this in the life of St. Peter. At one moment, under the compelling influence of God's Holy Spirit, he cries, "Thou art the Christ, the Son of the living God!" Our Lord turns, and with words of high commendation says, "Blessed art thou, Simon, for flesh and blood hath not revealed it unto thee, but My Father, which is in heaven." Yet, a very little while after, the devil gets his mind into St. Peter, and our Lord turns and says unto him, "Get thee behind me, Satan!" (Matt. xvi. 17, 23). St. Peter was now speaking in the name of Satan! Satan still "desires to have" us. St. Paul was tempted to think that he could do far better work for his beloved Master if only that "thorn" could be removed. But God knew that Paul would be a better man with the "thorn" than without it. Is it not a comfort to us to know that we may bring more glory to God under something which we are apt to regard as a hindrance or handicap, than if that undesired thing was removed? "My grace is sufficient for thee: for My power is made perfect in weakness" (2 Cor. xii. 9).

Remember that God nothing does, nor suffers to be done, but what thou would'st thyself did'st thou but see The end of all He does as well as He. St. Paul was not infallible – nor was St. Peter, or St. John; nor is the Pope or any other man. We may – and do – offer up mistaken prayers. The highest form of prayer is not, "Thy way, O God, not mine," but "My way, O God, is Thine!" We are taught to pray, not "Thy will be changed," but "Thy will be done." May we, in conclusion, give the testimony of two who have proved that God can be trusted? Sir H. M. Stanley, the great explorer, wrote: "I for one must not dare to say that prayers are inefficacious. Where I have been in earnest, I have been answered. When I prayed for light to guide my followers wisely through the perils that beset them, a ray of light has come upon the perplexed mind, and a clear road to deliverance has been pointed out. You may know when prayer is answered, by the glow of content which fills one who has flung his cause before God, as he rises to his feet. I have evidence, satisfactory to myself, that prayers are granted." Mary Slessor, the story of whose life in West Africa has surely thrilled us all, was once asked what prayer meant to her. She replied, "My life is one long, daily, hourly record of answered prayer for physical health, for mental overstrain, for guidance given marvelously, for errors and dangers averted, for enmity to the Gospel subdued, for food provided at the exact hour needed, for everything that goes to make up life and my poor service. I can testify with a full and often wonder-stricken awe that I believe God answers prayer. I know God answers prayer!"

CHAPTER 9: ANSWERS TO PRAYER

Mere human nature would choose a more startling title to this chapter. Remarkable answers – wonderful answers – amazing answers. But we must allow God to teach us that it is as natural to Him to answer prayer as it is for us to ask. How He delights to hear our petitions, and how He loves to answer them! When we hear of some wealthy person giving a treat to poverty-stricken people, or wiping out some crushing deficit in a missionary society, we exclaim, "How nice to be able to do a thing like that!" Well, if it is true that God loves us – and we know it is true – do you not think it gives Him great joy to give us what we ask? We should like, therefore, to recount one or two answers to prayer out of very many which have come to our notice, so that we may have greater boldness in coming to the Throne of Grace. God saves men for whom we pray. Try it. In talking over this question with a man of prayer a few days ago, he suddenly asked me, "Do you know St. M-'s Church, L-?" "Quite well – have been there several times." "Let me tell you what happened when I lived there. We had a prayer-meeting each Sunday before the 8 o'clock communion service. As we rose from our knees one Sunday a sidesman said, 'Vicar, I wish you would pray for my boy. He is twenty-two years old now, and has not been to church for years.' 'We can spare five minutes now,' replied the vicar. They knelt down again and offered up earnest supplication on behalf of that man. Although nothing was said to him about this, that youth came to church that same evening. Something in the sermon

convicted him of sin. He came into the vestry broken-hearted, and accepted Jesus Christ as, his Savior." On Monday morning my friend, who was working as a Church Army captain in the parish, was present at the weekly meeting of the staff. He said to the vicar, "That conversion last night is a challenge to prayer – a challenge from God. Shall we accept it?" "What do you mean?" asked the vicar. "Well," said he, "shall we single out the worst man in the parish and pray for him?" By unanimous consent they fixed upon K- as the worst man they knew. So they "agreed" in prayer for his conversion. At the end of that week, as they were conducting a Saturday night prayer-meeting in the mission hall, and whilst his very name was on their lips, the door swung open and in staggered K-, much the worse for liquor. He had never been in that mission hall before. Without thinking of removing his cap he sank on a chair near the door and buried his face in his hands. The prayer-meeting suddenly became an enquiry-room. Even as he was – in drink – he sought the Lord Who was seeking him. Nor did he ever go back. Today he is one of the finest dockyard missioners in the land.

Oh, why do we not pray for our unconverted friends? They may not listen to us when we plead with them, but they cannot hold out if we pray for them. Let two or three agree in prayer over the salvation of the worst, and then see what God will do! Tell God and then trust God. God works in a wonderful way, as well as in a "mysterious" way, His wonders to perform. Dan Crawford told us recently that when returning to his mission field after a furlough, it was necessary to make all possible haste. But a deep stream, which had to be crossed, was in flood, and no boats were available, or usable, for that matter. So he and his party camped and prayed. An infidel might well have laughed aloud. How could God get them across that river! But, as they prayed, a tall tree which had battled with that river for scores of years began to totter and fall. It fell clear across the stream! As Mr. Crawford says, "The Royal Engineers of heaven had laid a pontoon bridge for God's servants." Many young people will be reading these prayer-stories. May we remind them that God still hears the voice of the lad – yes, and the lass? (Gen. xxi. 17). For them may we be allowed to add the following story, with the earnest desire that prayer may be their heritage, their very life; and that answered prayer may be their daily experience.

Some little time ago, a Chinese boy of twelve years old, named Ma-Na-Si, a boarder in the mission school at Chefoo, went home for the holidays. He is the son of a native pastor. Whilst standing on the doorstep of his father's house he espied a horseman galloping towards him. The man – a heathen – was in a great state of perturbation. He eagerly enquired for the "Jesus-man" – the pastor. The boy told him that his father was away from home. The poor man was much distressed, and hurriedly explained the cause of his visit. He had been sent from a heathen village some miles away to fetch the "holy man" to cast a devil out of the daughter-in-law of a heathen friend. He poured out his sad story of this young woman, torn by devils, raving and reviling, pulling out her hair, clawing her face, tearing her clothes, smashing up furniture, and dashing away dishes of food. He told of her spirit of sacrilege, and outrageous impiety, and brazen blasphemy and how these outbursts were followed by foaming at the mouth, and great exhaustion, both physical and mental "But my father is not at home." the boy kept reiterating. At length the frenzied man seemed to understand. Suddenly he fell on his knees, and, stretching out his hands in desperation, cried, "You, too, are a Jesus-man; will you come?" Think of it – a boy of twelve! Yes, but even a lad, when fully yielded to his Savior, is not fearful of being used by that Savior. There was but one moment of surprise, and a moment of hesitation, and then the laddie put himself wholly at his Master's disposal. Like little Samuel of old he was willing to obey God in all things. He accepted the earnest entreaty as a call from God. The heathen stranger sprang into the saddle, and, swinging the Christian boy up behind him, he galloped away. Ma-Na-Si began to think over things. He had accepted an invitation to cast out a devil in the name of Christ Jesus. But was he worthy to be used of God in this way? Was his heart pure and his faith strong? As they galloped along he carefully searched his own heart for sin to be confessed and repented of. Then he prayed for guidance what to say and

how to act, and tried to recall Bible instances of demoniacal possession and how they were dealt with. Then he simply and humbly cast himself upon the God of power and of mercy, asking His help for the glory of the Lord Jesus. On arrival at the house they found that some of the members of the family were by main force holding down the tortured woman upon the bed. Although she had not been told that a messenger had gone for the native pastor, yet as soon as she heard footsteps in the court outside she cried, "All of you get out of my way quickly, so that I can escape. I must flee! A 'Jesus-man' is coming. I cannot endure him. His name is Ma-Na-Si." Ma-Na-Si entered the room, and after a ceremonial bow knelt down and began to pray. Then he sang a Christian hymn to the praise of the Lord Jesus. Then, in the name of the Risen Lord, glorified and omnipotent, he commanded the demon to come out of the woman. At once she was calm, though prostrate with weakness. From that day she was perfectly whole. She was amazed when they told her that she had uttered the name of the Christian boy, for she had never heard of it or read of it before, for the whole of that village was heathen. But that day was veritably a "beginning of days" to those people, for from it the Word of the Lord had free course and was glorified.

Beloved reader, I do not know how this little narrative affects you. It is one that moves me to the very depths of my being. It seems to me that most of us know so little of the power of God – so little of His overwhelming, irresistible love. Oh, what love is His! Now, every time we pray, that wonderful love envelops us in a special way. If we really loved our blessed Savior, should we not oftener seek communion with Him in prayer? Fellow Christian, is it because we pray so little that we criticize so much? Oh, let us remember that we, like our dear Savior, are not sent into the world to condemn, to judge, the world, "but that the world should be saved through Him" (John iii. 17). Will any thoughtless word of criticism of anyone move anyone nearer to Christ? Will it even help the utterer of that fault-finding to be more like the Master? Oh, let us lay aside the spirit of criticism, of blaming, of fault-finding, of disparaging others or their work. Would not

St. Paul say to us all, "And such were some of you, but ye are washed"? (2 Cor. vi. 11). Do you see what we are aiming at? All the evil dispositions and failings we detect in others are due to the devil. It is the evil one in the heart who causes those words and deeds which we are so ready to condemn and to exaggerate. Demon-possession is not unknown in England, but it takes a different form, perhaps. Our very friends and acquaintances, so kindly and lovable, are often tied and bound by some besetting sin – "whom Satan hath bound, lo, these many years." We may plead with them in vain. We may warn them in vain. Courtesy and charity – and our own failings and short-comings – forbid us standing over them like Ma-Na-Si and exercising the evil spirit! But have we tried prayer – prayer always backed up by love which cannot be "provoked"? (1 Cor. xiii. 5). God answers prayer from old and young, when there is a clean heart, a holy life, and a simple faith. God answers prayer. We are but frail and faulty servants at the best. Sincere as we may be, we shall sometimes ask amiss. But God is faithful that promised, and He will guard us from all harm and supply every need. Can I have the things I pray for? God knows best; He is wiser than His children. I can rest. "Beloved, if our heart condemn us not, we have boldness toward God; and whatsoever we ask we receive of him, because we keep his commandments, and do those things that are pleasing in his sight" (1 John iii. 21).

CHAPTER 10: HOW GOD ANSWERS PRAYER

For man fully to understand God and all His dealings with us is an utter impossibility. "O the depth of the riches both of the wisdom and the knowledge of God! How unsearchable are his judgments, and his ways past tracing out!" (Rom. xi. 33). True, but we need not make difficulties where none exists. If God has all power and all knowledge, surely prayer has no difficulties, though occasionally there may be perplexities. We cannot discover God's meth-od, but we know something of His manner of answering prayer. But at the very outset may we remind ourselves how little we know about ordinary things? Mr. Edison, whose knowledge is pretty profound, wrote in August, 1921, "We

don't know the millionth part of one per cent about anything. We don't know what water is. We don't know what light is. We don't know what gravitation is. We don't know what enables us to keep on our feet to stand up. We don't know what electricity is. We don't know what heat is. We don't know anything about magnetism. We have a lot of hypotheses, but that is all." But we do not allow our ignorance about all these things to deprive us of their use! We do not know much about prayer, but surely this need not prevent us from praying! We do know what our Lord has taught us about prayer. And we do know that He has sent the Holy Spirit to teach us all things (John xiv. 26). How, then, does God answer prayer? One way is just this: – He reveals His mind to those who pray. His Holy Spirit puts fresh ideas into the minds of praying people. We are quite aware that the devil and his angels are busy enough putting bad thoughts into our minds. Surely, then, God and His holy angels can give us good thoughts? Even poor, weak, sinful men and women can put good thoughts into the minds of others. That is what we try to do in writing! We do not stop to think what a wonderful thing it is that a few peculiar-shaped black marks on this white paper can uplift and inspire, or depress and cast down, or even convict of sin! But, to an untutored savage, it is a stupendous miracle. Moreover, you and I can often read people's thoughts or wishes from an expression on the face or a glance of the eye. Even thought transference between man and man is a commonplace today. And God can in many ways convey His thoughts to us.

A remarkable instance of this was related by a speaker last year at Northfield. Three or four years ago, he met an old whaling captain who told him this story. "A good many years ago, I was sailing in the desolate seas off Cape Horn, hunting whales. One day we were beat-ing directly south in the face of a hard wind. We had been tacking this way and that all the morning, and were making very little headway. About 11 o'clock, as I stood at the wheel, the idea suddenly came into my mind, 'Why batter the ship against these waves? There are prob-ably as many whales to the north as to the south. Suppose we run with the wind instead of against it? In response to that sudden idea

I changed the course of the ship, and began to sail north instead of south. One hour later, at noon, the look-out at the masthead shouted 'Boats ahead!' Presently we overtook four lifeboats, in which were fourteen sailors, the only survivors of the crew of a ship which had burned to the water's edge ten days before. Those men had been adrift in their boats ever since, praying God frantically for rescue; and we arrived just in time to save them. They could not have survived another day." Then the old whaler added, "I don't know whether you believe in religion or not, but I happen to be a Christian. I have begun every day of my life with prayer that God would use me to help someone else, and I am convinced that God, that day, put the idea into my mind to change the course of my ship. That idea was the means of saving fourteen lives." God has many things to say to us. He has many thoughts to put into our minds. We are apt to be so busy doing His work that we do not stop to listen to His Word. Prayer gives God the opportunity of speaking to us and revealing His will to us. May our attitude often be: "Speak, Lord, Thy servant heareth." God answers other prayers by putting new thoughts into the minds of those we pray for. At a series of services dealing with the Victorious Life, the writer one afternoon urged the congregation to "make up" their quarrels if they really desired a holy life. One lady went straight home, and after very earnest prayer wrote to her sister, with whom, owing to some disagreement, she had had nothing to do for twenty years! Her sister was living thirty miles away. The very next morning the writer of that note received a letter from that very sister asking forgiveness and seeking reconciliation. The two letters had crossed in the post. While the one sister was praying to God for the other, God was speaking to that other sister, putting into her mind the desire for reconciliation. You may say, Why did not God put that desire there before? It may be that He foresaw that it would be useless for the distant sister to write asking forgiveness until the other sister was also willing to forgive. The fact remains that, when we pray for others, somehow or other it opens the way for God to influence those we pray for. God needs our prayers, or He would not beg us to pray. A

little time back, at the end of a weekly prayer-meeting, a godly woman begged those present to pray for her husband, who would never go near a place of worship. The leader suggested that they should continue in prayer then and there. Most earnest prayers were offered up. Now, the husband was devoted to his wife, and frequently came to meet her. He did so that night, and arrived at the hall while the prayer-meeting was still in progress. God put it into his mind to open the door and wait inside – a thing he had never done before. As he sat on a chair near the door, leaning his head upon his hand, he overheard those earnest petitions. During the homeward walk he said, "Wife, who was the man they were praying for tonight?" "Oh," she replied, "it is the husband of one of our workers." "Well, I am quite sure he will be saved," said he; "God must answer prayers like that." A little later in the evening he again asked, "Who was the man they were praying for?" She replied in similar terms as before. On retiring to rest he could not sleep. He was under deep conviction of sin. Awaking his wife, he begged her to pray for him. How clearly this shows us that when we pray, God can work! God could have prompted that man to enter that prayer-meeting any week. But had he done so it is a question whether any good at all would have come from it. When once those earnest, heartfelt petitions were being offered up on his behalf God saw that they would have a mighty influence upon that poor man. It is when we pray that God can help us in our work and strengthen our resolves. For we can answer many of our own prayers. One bitter winter a prosperous farmer was praying that God would keep a neighbor from starving. When the family prayers were over, his little boy said, "Father, I don't think I should have troubled God about that." "Why not?" he asked. "Because it would be easy enough for you to see that they don't starve!" There is not the slightest doubt that if we pray for others we shall also try to help them. A young convert asked his vicar to give him some Christian work. "Have you a chum?" "Yes," replied the boy. "Is he a Christian?" "No, he is as careless as I was." "Then go and ask him to accept Christ as his Savior." "Oh, no!" said the lad, "I could never do that. Give me anything but that."

"Well," said the vicar, "promise me two things: that you will not speak to him about his soul, and that you will pray to God twice daily for his conversion." "Why, yes, I'll gladly do that," answered the boy. Before a fortnight was up he rushed round to the vicarage. "Will you let me off my promise? I must speak to my chum!" he cried. When he began to pray God could give him strength to witness. Communion with God is essential before we can have real communion with our fellow-man. My belief is that men so seldom speak to others about their spiritual condition because they pray so little for them. The writer has never forgotten how his faith in prayer was confirmed when, as a lad of thirteen, he earnestly asked God to enable him on a certain day to secure twenty new subscribers for missions overseas. Exactly twenty new names were secured before night closed in. The consciousness that God would grant that prayer was an incentive to eager effort, and gave an unwonted courage in approaching others.

A cleric in England suggested to his people that they should each day pray for the worst man or woman and then go to them and tell them about Jesus. Only six agreed to do so. On arrival home he began to pray. Then he said, "I must not leave this to my people. I must take it up myself. I don't know the bad people. I'll have to go out and enquire." Approaching a rough-looking man at a street corner, he asked, "Are you the worst man in this district?" "No, I'm not." "Would you mind telling me who is?" "I don't mind. You'll find him at No. 7, down that street." He knocked at No. 7 and entered. "I'm looking for the worst man in my parish. They tell me it might be you?" "Whoever told you that? Fetch him here, and I'll show him who's the worst man! No, there are lots worse than me." "Well, who is the worst man you know?" "Everybody knows him. He lives at the end house in that court. He's the worst man." So down the court he went and knocked at the door. A surly voice cried, "Come in!" There were a man and his wife. "I hope you'll excuse me, but I'm the minister of the chapel along the round. I'm looking for the worst man in my district, because I have something to tell him. Are you the worst man?" The man turned to his wife and said, "Lass, tell him what I said to

you five minutes ago." "No, tell him yourself." "What were you saying?" enquired the visitor. "Well, I've been drinking for twelve weeks. I've had the D.T.'s and have pawned all in the house worth pawning. And I said to my wife a few minutes ago, 'Lass, this thing has to stop, and if it doesn't, I'll stop it myself – I'll go and drown myself.' Then you knocked at the door! Yes, sir, I'm the very worst man. What have you got to say to me?" "I'm here to tell you that Jesus Christ is the greatest Savior, and that He can make out of the worst man one of the best. He did it for me, and He will do it for you." "D'you think He can do it even for me?" "I'm sure He can. Kneel down and ask Him." Not only was the poor drunkard saved from his sins, but he is today a radiant Christian man, bringing other drunken people to the Lord Jesus Christ. Surely none of us finds it difficult to believe that God can, in answer to prayer, heal the body, send rain or fair weather, dispel fogs, or avert calamities? We have to do with a God whose knowledge is infinite. He can put it into the mind of a doctor to prescribe a certain medicine, or diet, or method of cure. All the doctor's skill is from God. "He knoweth our frame" – for He made it. He knows it far better than the cleverest doctor or surgeon. He made, and He can restore. We believe that God desires us to use medical skill, but we also believe that God, by His wonderful knowledge, can heal, and sometimes does heal, without human co-operation. And God must be allowed to work in His own way. We are so apt to tie God down to the way we approve of. God's aim is to glorify His name in answering our prayers. Sometimes He sees that our desire is right, but our petition wrong.

St. Paul thought he could bring more glory to God if only the thorn in the flesh could be removed. God knew that he would be a better man and do better work with the thorn than without it. So God said No-No-No to his prayer, and then explained why! So it was with Monica, who prayed so many years for the conversion of Augustine, her licentious son. When he was determined to leave home and cross the seas to Rome she prayed earnestly, even passionately, that God would keep him by her side, and under her influence. She went down to a little chapel on the seashore to spend the night in prayer close by where the ship lay at anchor. But, when morning came, she found that the ship had sailed even while she prayed! Her petition was refused, but her real desire was granted. For it was in Rome that Augustine met the sainted Ambrose, who led him to Christ. How comforting it is to know that God knows what is best! But we should never think it unreasonable that God should make some things dependent upon our prayers. Some people say that if God really loves us He would give us what is best for us whether we ask Him or not.

Dr. Fosdick has so beautifully pointed out that God has left man many things to do for himself. He promises seedtime and harvest. Yet man must prepare the soil, sow, and till, and reap in order to allow God to do His share. God provides us with food and drink. But He leaves us to take, and eat, and drink. There are some things God cannot, or at least will not, do without our help. God cannot do some things unless we think. He never emblazons His truth upon the sky. The laws of science have always been there. But we must think, and experiment, and think again if we would use those laws for our own good and God's glory. God cannot do some things unless we work. He stores the hills with marble, but He has never built a cathedral. He fills the mountains with iron ore, but He never makes a needle or a locomotive. He leaves that to us. We must work. If, then, God has left many things dependent upon man's thinking and working, why should He not leave some things dependent upon man's praying? He has done so. "Ask and ye shall receive." And there are some things God will not give us unless we ask. Prayer is one of the three ways in which man can co-operate with God; and the greatest of these is prayer. Men of power are without exception men of prayer. God bestows His Holy Spirit in His fullness only on men of prayer. And it is through the operation of the Spirit that answers to prayer come. Every believer has the Spirit of Christ dwelling in him. For "if any have not the Spirit of Christ, he is none of his." But a man of prevailing prayer must be filled with the Spirit of God. A lady missionary wrote recently that it used to be said of Praying Hyde that he never spoke to an unconverted man but that he was soundly converted. But if he ever did fail at first

to touch a heart for God, he went back to his room and wrestled in prayer till he was shown what it was in himself that had hindered his being used by God. Yes, when we are filled with the Spirit of God, we cannot help influencing others God-ward. But, to have power with men, we must have power with God. The momentous question for you and me is not, however, "How does God answer prayer?" The question is, "Do I really pray?" What a marvelous power God places at our disposal! Do we for a moment think that anything displeasing to God is worth our while holding on to? Fellow-Christian, trust Christ wholly, and you will find Him wholly true. Let us give God the chance of putting His mind into us, and we shall never doubt the power of prayer again.

CHAPTER 11: HINDRANCES TO PRAYER

The, poet said, and we often sing:

What various hindrances we meet
In coming to the mercy-seat.

Yes, indeed, they are various. But here again, most of those hindrances are our own making. God wants me to pray. The devil does not want me to pray, and does all he can to hinder me. He knows that we can accomplish more through our prayers than through our work. He would rather have us do anything else than pray. We have already referred to Satan's opposition to prayer: Angels our march oppose Who still in strength excel Our secret, sworn, relentless foes, Countless, invisible. But we need not fear them, nor heed them, if our eyes are ever unto the Lord. The holy angels are stronger than fallen angels, and we can leave the celestial hosts to guard us. We believe that to them – the hosts of evil – we owe those wandering thoughts which so often wreck prayer. We no sooner kneel than we "recollect" something that should have been done, or something which had better be seen to at once. These thoughts come from without, and are surely due to the promptings of evil spirits.

The only cure for wandering thoughts is to get our minds fixed upon God. Undoubtedly a man's worst foe is himself. Prayer is for a child of God – and one who is living as a child of God should pray. The great question is: Am I harboring any foes in my heart? Are there traitors within? God cannot give us

His best spiritual blessings unless we fulfill conditions of trust, obedience and service. Do we not often ask earnestly for the highest spiritual gifts, without even any thought of fulfilling the necessary requirements? Do we not often ask for blessings we are not fitted to receive? Dare we be honest with ourselves, alone in the presence of God? Dare we say sincerely, "Search me, O God, and see –"? Is there anything in me which is hindering God's blessing for me and through me? We discuss the "problem of prayer"; we are the problem that needs discussing or dissecting! Prayer is all right! There is no problem in prayer to the heart which is absolutely stayed on Christ. Now, we shall not quote the usual Bible texts which show how prayer may be frustrated. We merely desire that everyone should get a glimpse of his own heart.

No sin is too small to hinder prayer, and perhaps to turn the very prayer itself into sin, if we are not willing to renounce that sin. The Moslems in West Africa have a saying, "If there is no purity, there is no prayer; if there is no prayer, there is no drinking of the water of heaven." This truth is so clearly taught in Scripture that it is amazing that any should try to retain both sin and prayer. Yet very many do this. Even David cried, long ages ago, "If I regard iniquity in my heart, the Lord will not hear" (Psa. lxvi. 18). And Isaiah says, "Your iniquities have separated between you and your God, and your sins have hid his face from you" (Isa. lix. 2). Surely we must all agree that it is sin in us, and not the unwillingness of Christ to hear, that hinders prayer. As a rule, it is some little sin, so-called, that mars and spoils the prayer-life. There may be:

(1) Doubt

Now, unbelief is possibly the greatest hindrance to prayer. Our Lord said that the Holy Spirit would convict the world of sin – "of sin because they believe not on Me" (John xvi. 9). We are not "of the world," yet is there not much practical unbelief in many of us? St. James, writing to believers, says: "Ask in faith, nothing doubting; for he that doubteth … let not that man think he shall receive anything of the Lord" (James i. 6–8). Some have not because they ask not. Others "have not" because they

believe not. Did you think it a little strange that we spent so much time over adoration and thanksgiving before we came to the "asking"? But surely, if we get a glimpse of the glorious majesty of our Lord, and the wonders of His love and grace, unbelief and doubt will vanish away as mists before the rising sun? Was this not the reason that Abraham "staggered not," "wavered not through unbelief," in that he gave God the glory due unto His name, and was therefore "fully assured that what He had promised He was able also to perform"? (Rom. iv. 20, 21). Knowing what we do of God's stupendous love, is it not amazing that we should ever doubt?

(2) Then there is Self – the root of all sin

How selfish we are prone to be even in our "good works"! How we hesitate to give up anything which "self" craves for. Yet we know that a full hand cannot take Christ's gifts. Was this why the Savior, in the prayer He first taught, coupled us with everything else? "Our" is the first word. "Our Father … give us … forgive us … deliver us …" Pride prevents prayer, for prayer is a very humbling thing. How hateful pride must be in the sight of God! It is God who gives us all things "richly to enjoy." "What hast thou that thou didst not receive?" asks St. Paul (1 Cor. iv. 7).

Surely, surely we are not going to let pride, with its hateful, ugly sister, jealousy, ruin our prayer-life? God cannot do great things for us whereby we may be glad if they are going to "turn our heads." Oh, how foolish we can be! Sometimes, when we are insistent, God does give us what we ask, at the expense of our holiness. "He gave them their request, but sent leanness into their soul" (Psa. cvi. 15). O God, save us from that – save us from self! Again, self asserts itself in criticizing others. Let this thought burn itself into your memory – the more like Jesus Christ a man becomes, the less he judges other people. It is an infallible test. Those who are always criticizing others have drifted away from Christ. They may still be His, but have lost His Spirit of love. Beloved reader, if you have a criticizing nature, allow it to dissect yourself and never your neighbor. You will be able to give it full scope, and it will never be unemployed! Is this a harsh remark?

Does it betray a tendency to commit the very sin – for it is sin – it condemns? It would do so were it spoken to any one individual. But its object is to pierce armor which is seemingly invulnerable. And no one who, for one month, has kept his tongue "from picking and stealing" the reputation of other people will ever desire to go back again to back-biting. "Love suffereth long and is kind" (1 Cor. xiii. 4). Do we? Are we? We are ourselves no better because we have managed to paint other people in worse colors than ourselves. But, singularly enough, we enhance our own spiritual joy and our own living witness for Christ when we refuse to pass on disparaging information about others, or when we refrain from "judging" the work or lives of other people. It may be hard at first, but it soon brings untold joy, and is rewarded by the love of all around. It is most hard to keep silent in the face of "modern" heresies. Are we not told to "contend earnestly for the faith which was once for all delivered unto the saints"? (Jude 3). Sometimes we must speak out – but let it always be in the spirit of love. "Rather let error live than love die."

Even in our private prayers fault-finding of others must be resolutely avoided. Read once more the story of John Hyde praying for the "cold brother." Believe me, a criticizing spirit destroys holiness of life more easily than anything else, because it is such an eminently respectable sin, and makes such easy victims of us. We need scarcely add that when a believer is filled with the Spirit of Christ. – who is Love – he will never tell others of the unchristian behavior he may discern in his friends. "He was most rude to me"; "He is too conceited"; "I can't stand that man"; and such-like remarks are surely unkind, unnecessary, and often untrue. Our dear Lord suffered the contradiction of sinners against Himself, but He never complained or published abroad the news to others. Why should we do so? Self must be dethroned if Christ is to reign supreme. There must be no idols in the heart. Do you remember what God said of some leaders of religion? "These men have taken their idols into their heart … ; should I be inquired of at all by them?" (Ezek. xiv. 3). When our aim is solely the glory of God, then God can answer our prayers. Christ Himself rather than His gifts should be our desire. "Delight thyself in the Lord and He shall give thee the petitions of thine heart" (Psa. xxxvii. 4, R.V., marg.). "Beloved, if our heart condemn us not, we have boldness toward God; and whatsoever we ask we receive of him, because we keep his commandments and do the things that are pleasing in his sight" (1 John iii. 21, 22). It is as true today as in the early days of Christianity that men ask, and receive not, because they ask amiss that they may spend it on their pleasures – .i.e., self (James iv. 3).

(3) Unlove in the heart is possibly the greatest hindrance to prayer

A loving spirit is a condition of believing prayer. We cannot be wrong with man and right with God. The spirit of prayer is essentially the spirit of love. Intercession is simply love at prayer. He prayeth best who loveth best All things both great and small; For the great God Who loveth us, He made and loveth all. Dare we hate or dislike those whom God loves? If we do, can we really possess the Spirit of Christ? We really must face these elementary facts in our faith if prayer is to be anything more than a mere form.

Our Lord not only says, "And pray for those that persecute you; that ye may be sons of your Father who is in heaven" (Matt. v. 44, 45). We venture to think that large numbers of so-called Christians have never faced this question. To hear how many Christian workers – and prominent ones, too – speak of others from whom they disagree, one must charitably suppose they have never heard that command of our Lord! Our daily life in the world is the best indication of our power in prayer. God deals with my prayers not according to the spirit and tone which I exhibit when I am praying in public or private, but according to the spirit I show in my daily life. Hot-tempered people can make only frigid prayers. If we do not obey our Lord's command and love one another, our prayers are well-nigh worthless. If we harbor an unforgiving spirit it is almost wasted time to pray. Yet a prominent Dean of one of our cathedrals was recently reported to have said that there are some people we can never forgive! If so, we trust that he uses an abridged form of the Lord's prayer. Christ taught us to say "Forgive us ... as we forgive." And He goes farther than this. He declares, "If ye forgive not men their trespasses, neither will your heavenly Father forgive your trespasses" (Matt. vi. 15). May we ever exhibit the Spirit of Christ, and not forfeit our own much-needed forgiveness. How many of our readers who have not the slightest intention of forgiving their enemies, or even their offending friends, repeated the Lord's prayer today? Many Christians have never given prayer a fair chance. It is not through conscious insincerity, but from want of thought. The blame for it really rests upon those of us who preach and teach. We are prone to teach doctrines rather than doings. Most men desire to do what is right, but they regard the big things rather than the little failings in the life of love. Our Lord goes so far as to say that even our gifts are not to be presented to God if we remember that our brother "hath ought against us" (Matt. v. 23). If He will not accept our gifts, is it likely He will answer our prayers? It was when Job ceased contending with his enemies (whom the Bible calls his "friends") that the Lord "turned his captivity" and gave him twice as much as he had before (Job xlii. 10). How slow we are – how unwilling we are – to see that our lives hinder our prayers! And how unwilling we are to act on love-lines. Yes, we desire to "win" men. Our Lord shows us one way. Don't publish abroad his wrongdoings. Speak to him alone, and "thou hast gained thy brother" (Matt. xviii. 15). Most of us have rather pained our brothers! Even the home-life may hinder the prayer-life. See what Peter says about how we should so live in the home that our "prayers be not hindered" (1 Peter iii. 1–10).

We would venture to urge every reader to ask God to search his heart once again and to show him if there is "any root of bitterness" towards anyone. We all desire to do what is pleasing to God. It would be an immense gain to our spiritual life if we would resolve not to attempt to pray until we had done all in our power to make peace and harmony between ourselves and any with whom we have quarreled. Until we do this as far as lies in our power, our prayers are just wasted breath. Unkindly feelings towards another hinder God from helping us in the way He desires. A loving life is an essential condition of believing prayer. God challenges us again, today, to become fit persons to receive His superabundant blessings. Many of us have to decide whether we will choose a bitter, unforgiving spirit, or the tender mercies and loving-kindness of our Lord Jesus Christ. Is it not amazing that any man can halt between two opinions with such a choice in the balance? For bitterness harms the bitter more than anyone else. "Whensoever ye stand praying, forgive if ye have ought against anyone; that your Father also, who is in heaven, may forgive you" (Mark xi. 25). So said the blessed Master. Must we not then either forgive, or cease trying to pray? What shall it profit a man if he gain all his time to pretend to pray, if he harbors unlove in his heart to prevent real prayer? How the devil laughs at us because we do not see this truth! We have God's word for it that eloquence, knowledge, faith, liberality, and even martyrdom profit a man nothing – get hold of it – nothing, unless his heart is filled with love (1 Cor. xiii.). "Therefore give us love."

(4) Refusal to do our part may hinder God answering our prayers

Love calls forth compassion and service at the sight of sin and suffering, both here and overseas. Just as St. Paul's heart was "stirred" – "provoked" – within him as he beheld the city full of idols (Acts xvii. 16). We cannot be sincere when we pray "Thy kingdom come" unless we are doing what we can to hasten the coming of that kingdom – by our gifts, our prayers and our service. We cannot be quite sincere in praying for the conversion of the ungodly unless we are willing to speak a word, or write a letter, or make some attempt to bring him under the influence of the Gospel. Before one of Moody's great missions he was present at a meeting for prayer asking for God's blessing. Several wealthy men were there. One began to pray that God would send sufficient funds to defray the expenses. Moody at once stopped him. "We need not trouble God about that," he said quietly, "we are able to answer that prayer!"

(5) Praying only in secret may be a hindrance

Children of a family should not always

meet their father separately. It is remarkable how often our Lord refers to united prayer – "agreed" prayer. "When ye pray, say, Our Father"; "If two of you shall agree on earth as touching anything they shall ask, it shall be done for them ... For where two or three are gathered together in my name, there am I in the midst of them" (Matt. xviii. 19, 20). We feel sure that the weakness in the spiritual life of many churches is to be traced to an inefficient prayer-meeting, or the absence of meetings for prayer. Daily matins and evensong, even when reverent and without the unseemly haste which is so often associated with them, cannot take the place of less formal gatherings for prayer, in which everyone may take part. Can we not make the weekly prayer-meeting a live thing and a living force?

(6) Praise is as important as prayer

We must enter into His gates with thanksgiving, and into His courts with praise, and give thanks unto Him and bless His name (Ps. c. 4). At one time in his life Praying Hyde was led to ask for four souls a day to be brought into the fold by his ministry. If on any day the number fell short of this, there would be such a weight on his heart that it was positively painful, and he could neither eat nor sleep. Then, in prayer he would ask the Lord to show him what was the obstacle in himself. He invariably found that it was the want of praise in his life. He would confess his sinfulness and pray for a spirit of praise. He said that as he praised God seeking souls would come to him. We do not imply that we, too, should limit God to definite numbers or ways of working; but we do cry: "Rejoice! Praise God with heart and mind and soul." It is not by accident that we are so often bidden to "rejoice in the Lord." God does not want miserable children; and none of His children has cause for misery. St. Paul, the most persecuted of men, was a man of song. Hymns of praise came from his lips in prison and out of prison: day and night he praised His Savior. The very order of his exhortations is significant. "Rejoice evermore; pray without ceasing; in everything give thanks: for this is the will of God in Christ Jesus to you" (1 Thess. v. 16–18). The will of God. Get that thought into your mind. It is not an optional thing. REJOICE:

PRAY: GIVE THANKS. That is the order, according to the will of God – for you, and for me. Nothing so pleases God as our praises – and nothing so blesses the man who prays as the praises he offers! "Delight thyself also in the Lord; and he shall give thee the petitions of thine heart" (Ps. xxxvii. 4, R.V., marg.).

A missionary who had received very bad news from home, was utterly cast down. Prayer availed nothing to relieve the darkness of his soul. He went to see another missionary, no doubt seeking comfort. There on the wall was a motto-card: "Try Thanksgiving!" He did; and in a moment every shadow was gone, never to return. Do we praise enough to get our prayers answered? If we truly trust Him, we shall always praise Him. For God nothing does nor suffers to be done But thou would'st do thyself Could'st thou but see The end of all events as well as He. One who once overheard Luther praying said, "Gracious God! What spirit and what faith is there in his expressions! He petitions God with as much reverence as if he were in the Divine presence, and yet with as firm a hope and confidence as he would address a father or a friend." That child of God seemed quite unconscious that "hindrances to prayer" existed! After all that has been said, we see that everything can be summed up under one head. All hindrance to prayer arises from ignorance of the teaching of God's Holy Word on the life of holiness He has planned for all His children, or from an unwillingness to consecrate ourselves fully to Him. When we can truthfully say to our Father, "All that I am and have is thine," then He can say to us, "All that is mine is thine."

CHAPTER 12: WHO MAY PRAY?

It is only two centuries ago that six undergraduates were expelled from the University of Oxford solely because they met together in each other's rooms for extempore prayer! Whereupon George Whitefield wrote to the Vice-Chancellor, "It is to be hoped that, as some have been expelled for extempore praying, we shall hear of some few others of a contrary stamp being expelled for extempore swearing." Today, thank God, no man in our land is hindered by his fellow-men from praying. Any man may pray – but has every man a right to pray? Does God listen to anyone? Who may pray? Is it the privilege – the right – of all men? Not everyone can claim the right to approach the King of our realm. But there are certain persons and bodies of people who have the privilege of immediate access to our sovereign. The Prime Minister has that privilege. The ancient Corporation of the City of London can at anytime lay its petition at the feet of the King. The ambassador of a foreign power may do the same. He has only to present himself at the gate of the palace of the King, and no power can stand between him and the monarch. He can go at once into the royal presence and present his request. But none of these has such ease of access and such loving welcome as the Kings own son. But there is the King of kings – the God and Father of us all.

Who may go to Him? Who may exercise this privilege – yes, this power – with God? We are told – and there is much truth in the remark – that in the most skeptical man or generation prayer is always underneath the surface, waiting. Has it the right to come forth at anytime? In some religions it has to wait. Of all the millions in India living in the bondage of Hinduism, none may pray except the Brahmins! A millionaire merchant of any other caste must perforce get a Brahmin – often a mere boy at school! – to say his prayers for him. The Mohammedan cannot pray unless he has learned a few phrases in Arabic, for his "god" only hears prayers offered in what they believe to be the holy language. Praise be to God, no such restrictions of caste or language stand between us and our God. Can any man, therefore, pray? Yes, you reply, anyone. But the Bible does not say so. Only a child of God can truly pray to God. Only a son can enter His presence. It is gloriously true that anyone can cry to Him for help – for pardon and mercy. But that is scarcely prayer. Prayer is much more than that. Prayer is going into "the secret place of the Most High," and abiding under the shadow of the Almighty (Ps. xci. 1). Prayer is a making known to God our wants and desires, and holding out the hand of faith to take His gifts. Prayer is the result of the Holy Spirit dwelling within us. It is communion with God. Now, there can scarcely be communion between a king and a rebel. What communion hath light with darkness? (2 Cor. vi. 14). In ourselves we have no right to pray. We have access to God only through the Lord Jesus Christ (Eph. iii. 18, ii. 12). Prayer is much more than the cry of a drowning man – of a man sinking in the whirlpool of sin: "Lord, save me! I am lost! I am undone! Redeem me! Save me!" Anyone can do this, and that is a petition which is never unanswered, and one, if sincere, to which the answer is never delayed. For "man cannot be God's outlaw if he would." But that is not prayer in the Bible sense. Even the lions, roaring after their prey, seek their meat from God; but that is not prayer. We know that our Lord said, "Everyone that asketh receiveth" (Matt. vii. 8.) He did say so, but to whom? He was speaking to His disciples (Matt. v. 1, 2). Yes, prayer is communion with God: the "home-life" of the soul, as one describes it. And I much question whether there can be any communion with Him unless the Holy Spirit dwells in the heart, and we have "received" the Son, and so have the right to be called "children of God" (John i. 12). Prayer is the privilege of a child. Children of God alone can claim from the heavenly Father the things which He hath prepared for them that love Him. Our Lord told us that in prayer we should call God "our Father." Surely only children can use that word? St. Paul says that it is "because ye are sons God sent forth the Spirit of His Son into our hearts, crying, 'Abba, Father'" (Gal. iv. 6). Is this what was in God's mind when, in dealing with Job's "comforters," He said, "My servant Job shall pray for you; for him will I accept"? (Job xlii. 8.) It looked as if they would not have been "accepted" in the matter of prayer. But as soon as one becomes a "son of God" he must enter the school of prayer. "Behold, he prayeth," said our Lord of a man as soon as he was converted. Yet that man had "said" prayers all his life (Acts ix. 11). Converted men not only may pray, but must pray – each man for himself, and, of course, for others. But, unless and until we can truthfully call God "Father," we have no claim to be treated as children – as "sons," "heirs of God and joint heirs with Christ" – no claim at all.

Do you say this is hard? Nay, surely it is natural. Has a "child" no privileges? But do not misunderstand me. This does not shut any man out of the kingdom of heaven. Anyone, anywhere, can cry, "God be merciful to me, a sinner!" Any man who is outside the fold of Christ, outside the family of God, however bad he may be, or however good he thinks he is, can this very moment become a child of God, even as he reads these words. One look to Christ in faith is sufficient "Look and live." God did not even say "see" – He says just look! Turn your face to God. How did those Galatian Christians become "sons of God"? By faith in Christ. "For ye are all sons of God through faith in Christ Jesus" (Gal. iii. 26). Christ will make any man a son of God by adoption and grace the moment he turns to Him in true repentance and faith. But we have no rightful claim even upon God's providence unless we are His children. We cannot say with any confidence or certainty, "I shall not want," unless we can say, with confidence and certainty, "The Lord is my Shepherd." A child, however, has a right to his father's care, and love, and protection, and provision. Now, a child can only enter a family by being born into it. We become children of God by being "born again," "born from above" (John iii. 3, 5). That is, by believing on the Lord Jesus Christ (John iii. 16). Having said all this as a warning, and perhaps as an explanation why some people find prayer an utter failure, we hasten to add that God often hears and answers prayer even from those who have no legal right to pray – from those who are not His "children," and may even deny that He exists! The Gospels tell us of not a few unbelievers who came to Christ for healing; and He never sent one away without the coveted blessing – never. They came as "beggars," not as "children." And even if "the children must first be fed," these others received the crumbs – yea, and more than crumbs – that were freely given. So today God often hears the cry of unbelievers for temporal mercies.

One case well known to the writer may be given as an illustration. My friend told me that he had been an atheist many years. Whilst an infidel, he had been singing for forty years in a church choir because he was fond of music. His aged father became seriously ill two or three years ago, and lay in great pain. The doctors were helpless to relieve the sufferer. In his distress for his father, the infidel choirman fell on his knees and cried, "O God, if there is a God, show Thy power by taking away, my father's pain!" God heard the man's piteous cry, and removed the pain immediately. The "atheist" praised God, and hurried off to his vicar to find out the way of salvation! Today he is out-and-out for Christ, giving his whole time to work for his newly-found Savior. Yes, God is greater than His promises, and is more willing to hear than we are to pray. Perhaps the most striking of all "prayers" from the lips of unbelievers is that recorded of Caroline Fry, the author of Christ Our Example. Although possessed of beauty, wealth, position and friends, she found that none of them satisfied, and at length, in her utter misery, she sought God. Yet her first utterance to Him was an expression of open rebellion to and hatred of Him! Listen to it – it is not the prayer of a "child": – "O God, if Thou art a God: I do not love Thee; I do not want Thee; I do not believe there is any happiness in Thee: but I am miserable as I am. Give me what I do not seek; give me what I do not want. If Thou canst, make me happy. I am miserable as I am. I am tired of this world; if there is anything better, give it me." What a "prayer"! Yet God heard and answered. He forgave the wanderer and made her radiantly happy and gloriously fruitful in His service.

We must remember that no man can come unashamed and with confidence to his Father in heaven unless he is living as a son of God should live. We cannot expect a father to lavish his favors upon erring children. Only a faithful and sanctified son can pray with the Spirit and pray with the understanding also (1 Cor. xiv. 15). But if we are sons of God, nothing but sin can hinder our prayers. We, His children, have the right of access to God at any time, in any place. And He understands any form of prayer. We may have a wonderful gift of speech pouring itself out in a torrent of thanksgiving, petition, and praise like St. Paul; or we may have the quiet, deep, lover-like communion of a St. John. The brilliant scholar like John Wesley and the humble cobbler like William Carey are alike welcome at the throne of grace. Influence at the court of heaven depends not upon birth, or brilliancy, or achievement, but upon humble and utter independence upon the Son of the King. Moody attributed his marvelous success to the prayers of an obscure and almost unknown invalid woman! And truly the invalid saints of England could bring about a speedy revival by their prayers. Oh, that all the shut-ins" would speak out! Do we not make a mistake in supposing that some people have a "gift" of prayer? A brilliant Cambridge undergraduate asked me if the life of prayer was not a gift, and one which very few possessed? He suggested that, just as not everyone was musical, so not everyone is expected to be prayerful! George Müller was exceptional not because he had a gift of prayer, but because he prayed. Those who cannot "speak well," as God declared Aaron could, may labor in secret by intercession with those that speak the word. We must have great faith if we are to have great power with God in prayer, although God is very gracious and oftentimes goes beyond our faith. Henry Martyn was a man of prayer, yet his faith was not equal to his prayers. He once declared that he "would as soon expect to see a man rise from the dead as to see a Brahmin converted to Christ." Would St. James say, "Let not that man think he shall receive anything of the Lord"? (James i. 7).

Now, Henry Martyn died without seeing one Brahmin accepting Christ as his Savior. He used to retire, day by day, to a deserted pagoda for prayer. Yet he had not faith for the conversion of a Brahmin. A few months back there knelt in that very pagoda Brahmins and Mohammedans from all parts of India, Burma and Ceylon, now fellow-Christians. Others had prayed with greater faith than Henry Martyn. Who may pray? We may; but do we? Does our Lord look at us with even more pathos and tenderness than when He first uttered the words, and say, "Hitherto ye have asked nothing in My name? Ask, and ye shall receive, that your joy may be full" (John xvi. 24). If the dear Master was dependent on prayer to make His work a power, how much more are we? He sometimes prayed with "strong crying and tears" (Heb. v. 7). Do we? Have we ever shed a prayerful tear? Well might we cry, "Quicken us, and we will call upon Thy name" (Ps. lxxx. 18). St. Paul's exhortation to Timothy may well be made to us all: "Stir up the gift of God which is in thee" (2 Tim. i. 6). For the Holy Spirit is prayer's great Helper. We are incapable of ourselves to translate our real needs into prayer. The Holy Spirit does this for us. We cannot ask as we ought. The Holy Spirit does this for us. It is possible for unaided man to ask what is for our ill. The Holy Spirit can check this. No weak or trembling hand dare put in motion any mighty force. Can I – dare I – move the Hand that moves the universe? No! Unless the Holy Spirit has control of me. Yes, we need Divine help for prayer – and we have it! How the whole Trinity delights in prayer! God the Father listens: the Holy Spirit dictates: the eternal Son presents the petition – and Himself intercedes; and so the answer comes down. Believe me, prayer is our highest privilege, our gravest responsibility, and the greatest power God has put into our hands. Prayer, real prayer, is the noblest, the sublimest, the most stupendous act that any creature of God can perform. It is, as Coleridge declared, the very highest energy of which human nature is capable. To pray with all your heart and strength – that is the last, the greatest achievement of the Christian's warfare on earth. "LORD, TEACH US TO PRAY!"

Unknown author

Holy Wisdom
Or
Directions for the Prayer of Contemplation
Augustine Baker

QUOTATION ON THE CONTEMPLATIVE LIFE St. Bernard, perfectly experienced in the internal ways of a contemplative life, writing to certain religious Fathers of the Carthusian Order, professing the same, excellently expresses this union in these words: "It is the duty of others (that live active lives either in the world or religion) to serve God; but it is yours to adhere inseparably unto Him. It belongs to others to believe, to know, to love, to adore God; but to you to taste, to understand, to be familiarly acquainted with, and to enjoy Him."

1. Through prayer alone we attain the end of our creation and redemption – to wit, union

with God, in which alone consists our happiness and perfection.

2. By prayer, in this place, I do not understand petition or supplication, which, according to the doctrine of the schools, is exercised principally by the understanding, being a signification of what the person desires to receive from God. But prayer here especially meant is rather an offering and giving to God whatsoever He may justly require from us – that is, all duty, love, obedience, etc.; and it is principally, yea, almost only exercised by the affective part of the soul.

3. Now prayer, in this general notion, may be defined to be an elevation of the mind to God, or more largely and expressly thus: prayer is an affectuous actuation of an intellective soul towards God, expressing, or at least implying, an entire dependence on Him as the Author and Fountain of all good, a will and readiness to give Him His due, which is no less than all love, obedience, adoration, glory, and worship, by humbling and annihilating of herself and all creatures in His presence; and lastly, a desire and intention to aspire to an union of spirit with Him.

4. This is the nature and these the necessary qualities which are all, at least virtually, involved in all prayer, whether it be made interiorly in the soul only, or withal expressed by words or outward signs.

5. Hence it appears that prayer is the most perfect and most divine action that a rational soul is capable of; yea, it is the only principal action for the exercising of which the soul was created, since in prayer alone the soul is united to God. And, by consequence, it is of all other actions and duties the most indispensably necessary.

6. For a further demonstration of which necessity we may consider:

1. That only in prayer we are joined to God, our last end, from whom when we are separated we are in ourselves, wherein our chief misery consists.

2. That by prayer grace and all good is obtained, conserved, and recovered; for God being the Fountain of all good, no good can be had but by recourse to Him, which is only by prayer.

3. That by prayer alone all exterior good things are sanctified, so as to become blessings to us.

4. That prayer does exercise all virtues, in so much as whatsoever good action is performed, it is no further meritorious than as it proceeds from an internal motion of the soul, elevating and directing it to God (which internal motion is prayer); so that whatsoever is not prayer, or is not done in virtue of prayer, is little better than an action of mere nature.

5. That there is no action with which sin is incompatible but prayer. We may, lying in our sins, give alms, fast, recite the Divine Office, communicate, obey our superiors, etc.; but it is impossible to exercise true prayer of the spirit and deliberately continue under the guilt of sin, because by prayer, a soul being converted and united to God, cannot at the same time be averted and separated from Him.

6. That by prayer alone, approaching to God, we are placed above all miseries; whereas, without prayer, the least calamity would oppress us. Therefore prayer is the proper remedy against all kinds of afflictions, guilt, remorses, etc.

7. And hence it is that all the devil's quarrels and assaults are chiefly, if not only, against prayer; the which if he can extinguish, he has all that he aims at – separating us from the fruition and adhesion to God, and therewith from all good. And hence likewise it is that the duty of prayer is enjoined after such a manner as no other duty is, for we are commanded to exercise it without intermission. We must needs pray continually and never give over.

St Bernard

QUOTATION ON PRAYER

St. Augustine said, "If thou dost continually desire (God) thou dost continually pray." He also said, "It is a special grace of God's Holy Spirit to be able to pray aright."

Certain patterns of devout exercises have an immediate impact on our hearts and actions.

1. Hail, Sweet Jesus; praise, honor, and glory be to Thee, O Christ, who for my sake hast vouchsafed to come down from Thy royal seat,

and from the mellifluous bosom of Thy Divine Father, into this valley of misery, and to be incarnate and made man by the Holy Ghost.

2. Choose, I beseech Thee, my heart for Thy dwelling-place; adorn it, replenish it with spiritual gifts, and wholly possess it.

3. O that I were able, by profound humility, to unite Thee to it, and with an ardent affection to receive Thee; and after having received Thee, to retain Thee with me!

4. O that I were so fastened unto Thee, that I might never depart or turn away my mind from Thee.

5. Hail, sweet Jesus; praise, honor, and glory be to Thee, O Christ, who hast vouchsafed to be born of Thy Virgin Mother, … in a poor stable;

6. Whom, being born, she humbly adored.

7. O that it were Thy will to be continually born in me by a new fervor of spirit,

8. And that I may be wholly burnt with the fire of Thy love!

9. O that Thou wort the only comfort, desire, and solace of my heart!

10. O that I sought after Thee alone, thought on Thee alone, and loved Thee alone!

11. Hail, sweet Jesus; praise, honor, and glory be to Thee, O Christ, who, being born in the depth of winter, didst not refuse to be swaddled in poor clothes, and weeping to be laid in a manger, and as a little infant to be nourished at Thy Mother's breast;

12. I adore Thee, most dear Redeemer, King of angels.

13. Hail, Prince of Peace, Light of the Gentiles, and most desired Savior;

14. Grant, O Lord, that I may always stand in Thy sight, truly humble and truly poor in spirit;

15. Grant that for Thy holy name's sake I may willingly endure all kinds of mortification, and may love nothing in the world besides Thee, nor wish to possess anything but Thee.

16. Hail, sweet Jesus; whom the celestial legions of angels did honor, newly born, with joyful praises; and the shepherds, devoutly seeking and finding, adored with admiration;

17. Grant that I may joyfully, without tediousness, persevere in Thy service and praises.

18. Hail, sweet Jesus, who wouldst upon the eighth day, like other children, be circumcised,

and, being yet an infant, shed Thy Precious Blood;

19. And for our singular comfort wouldst be called JESUS, which signifieth a Savior:

20. O that it would please Thee to admit me, circumcised from all bad thoughts, words, and works, into the number of Thy children!

21. Thou, O Lord, art called Jesus, that is to say, a Savior: be Thou therefore my Savior, and save me.

22. Hail, sweet Jesus, whom the sages, with a devout seeking, found by the direction of a star, and having found, most humbly adored,

23. Offering unto Thee gifts of gold, frankincense, and myrrh;

24. Grant, O Lord, that with these blessed men I may always seek and adore Thee in spirit and truth;

25. Grant that I may offer daily unto Thee the gold of bright shining charity, the frankincense of sweet-smelling devotion, and the myrrh of perfect mortification.

26. Hail, sweet Jesus, who for our sake wouldst be subject to the law, and, to give us an example of humility, wouldst be carried to the temple by Thy Blessed Mother, and be redeemed with an offering ordained for such as were poor;

27. Where just Simeon and Anna the Prophetess, rejoicing greatly at Thy presence, gave very glorious testimony of Thy dignity:

28. O that all pride were utterly thrown down in me!

29. O that all desire of human favor and itch of self-love were cooled and cured in me!

30. Hail, sweet Jesus; praise, honor, and glory be to Thee, O Christ, who, staying in the temple, wert for the space of three days with great grief sought by Thy devout Mother, and at length with great joy found by her sitting in the midst of the doctors, hearing them and proposing questions to them:

31. Would to God Thou wouldst give and communicate Thyself in such sort unto me, that I might never be separated from Thee, nor ever be deprived of Thy comfort!

32. Hail, sweet Jesus, who, for the space of thirty years remaining unknown, hast vouchsafed to be reputed the son of Joseph the carpenter and of his wife the Blessed Virgin Mary;

33. Let Thy grace, I beseech Thee, pluck up and utterly root out of the fund of my soul all pride and ambition:

34. O that I may delight to be unknown, and to be esteemed vile and base!

35. Hail, sweet Jesus, who hast not disdained to come to the river Jordan, and entering into it to be baptized by Thy servant John the Baptist;

36. I would, through Thy merits, I might become most clean and pure, even in this life.

37. Hail, sweet Jesus, who, for our sakes abiding amongst wild beasts in the desert, and fasting forty days and forty nights, and persevering in prayer, hast permitted Thyself to be tempted by Satan;

38. And overcoming him, hast been honored with the ministry and service of angels;

39. Give me grace that I may chastise and subdue my flesh, with all the vicious affections thereof;

40. Give me grace that I may constantly persevere in prayer and other spiritual exercises;

41. Let no temptation, I beseech Thee, defile me, but rather let temptations purge me and unite me unto Thee.

42. Hail, sweet Jesus, who, to the end Thou mightest gather together the dispersed children of God, hast vouchsafed to preach penance, to call disciples, and out of them to choose twelve Apostles to be eminent preachers of Thy faith;

43. Draw me after Thee, and powerfully stir up my heart to love Thee;

44. Grant that I may adhere to Thee alone. Amen.

45. Hail, sweet Jesus; praise, honor, and glory be to Thee, O Christ, who for me host suffered many afflictions, heat, cold, hunger, thirst, labors, and miseries;

46. Grant that I may receive from Thy hand cheerfully all kinds of adversity.

47. Hail, sweet Jesus, who, thirsting for the conversion of souls, hast passed whole nights in prayer,

48. Hast been wearied with traveling, last passed from country to country, from city to city, from town to town, from village to village;

49. Let Thy love make me quick and ready to all good things, that I be never slothful in Thy service;

50. Grant that everywhere I may have a zeal for Thy honor, and employ myself wholly in Thy service.

51. Hail, sweet Jesus; praise, honor, and glory be to Thee, O Christ, who, conversing with men, hast vouchsafed most willingly to comfort them, and by many miracles most mercifully to cure their maladies and diseases;

52. Give me a devout heart full of affection and compassion, whereby I may pity other men's afflictions, and may have as great feeling of their miseries as if they were my own;

53. Whereby also I may bear patiently with all men's imperfections, and to the best of my ability succor them in their necessities.

54. Hail, sweet Jesus; praise, honor, and glory be to Thee, O Christ, who hast not shunned the company of publicans and sinners, but hast afforded them Thy most loving familiarity and ready pardon of sins, to Matthew, Zacheus, Mary Magdalen, and to the woman taken in adultery, and to the rest that were repentant;

55. Grant that I may embrace all men with cheerful love and charity;

56. May readily forgive those who offend me;

57. May perfectly love those who hate me.

58. Hail, sweet Jesus, who for my soul's sake hast suffered many injuries, many blasphemies, many reproaches, and infinite abuses from those on whom Thou hadst bestowed many benefits;

59. Give me a heart truly innocent and simple, that I may sincerely love my enemies and unfeignedly pity them;

60. And rendering good for evil may, through perfect charity and meek patience, perfectly please Thee. Amen.

61. Hail, sweet Jesus; praise, honor, and glory be to Thee, O Christ, who, coming to Jerusalem in a meek and gentle manner, didst ride upon an ass, and amidst the praises which were sung by the people who came to meet Thee didst pour forth tears, bewailing the ruin of the city and destruction of those ungrateful souls:

62. O that I might never be delighted with the praises and favors of men;

63. But always be profitably employed in internal tears of compunction and devotion!

64. Hail, sweet Jesus, whom Judas, the

treacherous disciple, sold for a little money to the Jews who persecuted Thee and conspired Thy death;

65. Root out of my heart all evil desires of transitory things;

66. Grant that I may never prefer anything before Thee.

67. Hail, sweet Jesus; praise, honor, and glory be to Thee, O Christ, who in Jerusalem, according to the law, didst eat the Paschal lamb with Thy disciples, and giving them an example of humility and holy charity, kneeling upon the ground, didst wash their feet, and having washed them didst wipe them with a towel:

68. Would to God this example might pierce my heart, and utterly throw down in me all pride and loftiness!

69. Give me, O Lord, a most profound humility, by which I may without difficulty cast myself at all men's feet.

70. Hail, sweet Jesus, who with an unspeakable charity hast instituted the Sacrament of the Eucharist, and with a wonderful liberality hast in it given Thyself to us;

71. Stir up in me a desire and enkindle in the interior of my soul a vehement thirst of this most venerable Sacrament;

72. Grant that when I come to this table of life I may with a chaste affection, singular humility, and perfect purity of heart receive Thee.

73. Hail, sweet Jesus, who immediately before Thy Passion didst begin to fear, to grieve, and be sad, taking upon Thyself our weakness,

74. That by this Thy infirmity thou mayest comfort and strengthen those that tremble at the expectation of death;

75. Preserve me, I beseech Thee, as well from vicious sadness as from foolish joy;

76. Grant that all the grief I have hitherto sustained may redound to Thy glory and the remission of my sins.

77. Hail, sweet Jesus, who, falling upon the ground, prayedst unto Thy Father, and humbly offeredst up Thyself wholly unto Him, saying, "Father, Thy will be done";

78. Grant that in all necessities and tribulations I may have recourse unto Thee by prayer;

79. That I may give and resign myself wholly to Thy will;

80. That I may with a quiet mind receive all things as from Thy hands.

81. Hail, sweet Jesus; praise, honor, and glory be to Thee, O Christ, who, being in an agony, didst pray very long;

82. And being Creator of heaven and earth, the King of kings and Lord of angels, didst not disdain to be comforted by an angel;

83. Grant that in all adversity and desolation, in all tribulation and affliction, I may seek comfort from Thee only,

84. And that I may find help and assistance at Thy hand

85. O that I could in all events wholly rely on Thee,

86. And leave myself wholly to Thy Fatherly care!

87. Hail, sweet Jesus, who, by reason of the greatness and vehemency of Thy grief, hadst Thy Body moistened all over with a bloody sweat:

88. O that all the parts of my interior man would sweat out holy tears of contrition!

89. Hail, sweet Jesus, who of Thine own accord offeredst Thyself to be taken by Judas the traitor, and Thine other enemies thirsting after Thy blood, and desiring Thy death;

90. Grant, for the honor of Thy name, I may not fly adversities,

91. But may cheerfully go to meet them,

92. And joyfully receive them, as precious tokens sent from Thee;

93. And humbly and constantly endure them as long as it shall please Thee.

94. Hail, sweet Jesus, who didst lovingly kiss the traitor Judas coming deceitfully to Thee;

95. Showing, by the calmness of Thy countenance and sweetness of Thy words, that Thou didst love him;

96. Grant that I may show myself loving and mild to all my enemies;

97. That I may pardon them from my heart, howsoever they shall offend me;

98. And tolerate and love them as the ministers of Thy will and promoters of my salvation.

99. Hail, sweet Jesus, who didst permit Thine enemies most furiously to lay their sacrilegious hands upon Thee;

100. And, being cruelly bound by them, didst not revenge but mildly endure the reproaches, blasphemies, and injuries wherewith they did

most wickedly affront Thee:

101. O that, being freed from the bonds of vice, I may be fast tied to Thee with the sweet chains of love!

102. O that Thou wouldst bestow upon me the grace of true patience! Amen.

103. Hail, sweet Jesus; praise, honor, and glory be to Thee, O Christ, who didst restore and heal the ear of Malchus, one of Thy furious persecutors, cut off by Peter, Thy chief disciple;

104. That so, rendering good for evil, the riches of Thy mercy and mildness might shine forth to us;

105. Grant, I beseech Thee, that the desire of revenge may never have place in my heart;

106. Grant that I may bear intimate compassion and affection towards all such as offend me;

107. Strengthen my too great weakness, and make steadfast my too great inconstancy, with the most strong support of Thy grace.

108. Hail, sweet Jesus, who sufferedst Thyself to be led, bound as a malefactor and thief, by a troop of soldiers unto Annas, and to be presented before him.

109. O unspeakable mildness of my Redeemer!

110. Behold, whilst Thou art taken, whilst Thou art drawn, whilst Thou art haled, Thou dost not complain, Thou dost not murmur, Thou makest no resistance;

111. Grant, O Lord, that these examples of Thy virtues may shine in me to my good and everlasting glory.

112. Hail, sweet Jesus, King of heaven and earth, who, standing, humble, like a base and abject person, before the proud High-priest, didst with great modesty receive a cruel blow given Thee upon the Face by one of his servants;

113. Suppress, I beseech Thee, in me all motions of anger and wrath; dull all the stings of indignation, and extinguish all desire of revenge;

114. That, even provoked with injuries, I may not be troubled;

115. That I may not strive or make any tumult;

116. But, suffering all things with a meek and patient mind, I may render good for evil, and ever be ready to favor those who most cross

and molest me.

117. Hail, sweet Jesus; praise, honor, and glory be to Thee, O Christ, who didst suffer Thyself to be shamefully led bound to Caiphas, that Thou mightest restore us to true liberty, freeing us from the bonds of everlasting death;

118. Grant that in the very midst of derisions and contumelies I may give Thee thanks with all my heart,

119. And that by them I may be advanced in Thy love.

120. Hail, sweet Jesus, whom Peter the chief of the Apostles thrice denied; and yet Thou most mercifully lookedst upon him, and provokedst him to repentance and holy tears for his offence:

121. O that it might please Thee in like manner to look upon me with that lovely eye of Thy mercy!

122. That, with due tears of repentance, I may bewail my past sins;

123. And having bewailed them, may not hereafter any more return to them again.

124. Hail, sweet Jesus, who with a pleasing countenance and modest look, standing before the priests and the elders of the people of the Jews, didst not disdain to be falsely accused and suffer many injuries;

125. Grant that I may never utter any falsity or calumniate any man;

126. But may suffer such calumnies as are laid against me with great tranquility of heart;

127. And, referring all difficulties to Thee, with silence I may expect Thy grace and comfort.

128. Hail, sweet Jesus, who, whilst Thou didst make profession of the truth, affirming Thyself to be Son of God, yet didst Thou not disdain to be esteemed a blasphemer;

129. Grant that in all places and before all men I may stand to the truth, and in awe of the presence of Thy Divinity and Majesty I may not fear the censures and judgments of men.

130. Hail, sweet Jesus, who by the wicked Jews wast proclaimed guilty of death, and without cause condemned;

131. That by Thy unjust condemnation Thou mightest deliver us from the guilt of our sins wherewith we were justly attainted;

132. Grant that I may reject all sinister and rash suspicions;

133. That I may suffer, without any bitter-

ness of heart, all such wrongful detractions and wicked judgments as others shall devise against me;

134. And that on all occasions I may retain, by the help of Thy grace, a quiet and untroubled mind.

135. Hail, sweet Jesus; praise, honor, and glory be to Thee, O Christ, who for my sake wast made the disgrace and scorn of men, and the outcast of the people;

136. And didst not turn away Thy sacred Face, which the angels desire to behold, from the filthy spittle of Thy adversaries;

137. Grant that I may imitate Thy meekness and patience.

138. Hail, sweet Jesus, who didst vouchsafe to be most cruelly beaten and buffeted, and most unworthily reproached and reviled for my sake;

139. Grant, I beseech Thee, that I may never refuse to be despised and to be reputed base and vile,

140. And that, according to Thy permission, I may be contented to be exercised with all kinds of injuries;

141. That I may receive them, not as from men, but from Thee, and of Thy Fatherly mercy.

142. Hail, sweet Jesus, who didst permit Thyself to be mocked and scoffed, and Thy lovely Face (which to behold is the chiefest happiness), for Thy greater derision, to be blindfolded;

143. Grant that, the veil of ignorance being taken away, I may be endued with the knowledge of Thy will;

144. Imprint in my heart a continual remembrance of Thee;

145. Thou knowest, O Lord, how hard a thing it is for me to suffer, though never so small a matter;

146. Out of Thy mercy, therefore, assist my frailty, that I may not cowardly fall or faint at the coming of any adversity.

147. Hail, sweet Jesus, who didst permit Thyself (being mocked and bound) to be led to the profane tribunal of Pilate the judge, and in a disdainful manner to be presented before him, Thou Thyself being the Judge of the living and the dead;

148. Grant that I may be truly subject to my superiors and all powers over me ordained by Thee;

149. That I may obey my equals, and love and honor all men;

150. Grant that I may not fear other men's judgments of me, but may receive them with a ready and meek mind. Amen.

151. Hail, sweet, Jesus, who, standing before Pilate, didst Humbly hold Thy peace, whilst the Jews did wrongfully accuse and calumniate Thee:

152. Grant, O Lord, that I may never be troubled at other men's slandering me,

153. But that I may with silence overcome all injuries;

154. Give me the perfect grace, of humility, by which I may neither desire to be praised nor refuse to be contemned;

155. Grant that I may imitate Thy innocency and patience;

156. That I may both live well, and, living well, be contented to be ill spoken of and despised.

157. Hail, sweet Jesus, who, with great exclamations and much noise of people, like a most heinous malefactor wast drawn from tribunal to tribunal, from Pilate to Herod, through the midst of the city;

158. Grant that I may not be dejected with any injuries of my enemies,

159. And that I be not much ashamed of contempt,

160. To the end that, by Thy gracious assistance, I may possess my soul in patience.

161. Hail, sweet Jesus; praise, honor, and glory be to Thee, O Christ, who, by Thy silence condemning Herod's vain desire, wouldst not, without good cause and for a good end, delight his curious eyes by working a miracle; and didst thereby give us a lesson to avoid ostentation in the presence of great men;

162. Pour into my soul Thy spirit of profound humility;

163. Mortify and extinguish in me all tickling of vain glory:

164. Grant that I may not seek to gain the praises of men, but do all and purely for Thy honor and glory.

165. Hail, sweet Jesus, who didst not disdain to be scoffed at by Herod and his whole army, and to be clothed in a white garment, like a fool or a madman;

166. Grant that I may rather choose to be reputed base and abject with Thee than glorious with the world;

167. That I may esteem it better and more worthy to suffer disgrace for Thy love, than to shine in the vain honor of the world;

168. Grant that, knowing thoroughly my own unworthiness, I may grow base in my own conceit, and despise, reprehend, and bewail myself.

169. Hail, sweet Jesus, who, being compared with the notorious thief Barabbas, wast judged more wicked and more worthy of death than he:

170. The murderer is set at liberty, and the impious Jews demand Thy death, who art the Author of life;

171. Thou art indeed that Living Stone rejected by man but chosen by God:

172. O that I may prefer nothing before Thee, nor change Thee for anything!

173. O that I could esteem all things as dung and filth, to the end I might gain Thee!

174. Grant, O Lord, that the blot of envy may never stain my soul.

175. Hail, sweet Jesus, who, being stripped naked in the palace and bound to a pillar, didst suffer Thy naked and most immaculate Flesh to be rent with most cruel scourges, that with Thy sores Thou mightest heal our wounds:

176. O amiable Jesus, I make choice of Thee, covered with stripes, for the spouse of my soul,

177. Desiring to be inflamed and burned with the fire of Thy most sweet love;

178. Strip my heart naked, I beseech Thee, from all indecent cogitations;

179. Grant that I may now patiently suffer the scourges of Thy Fatherly correction. Amen.

180. Hail, sweet Jesus; praise, honor, and glory be to Thee, O Christ, upon whom are discharged unspeakable injuries and contumelies;

181. For they clothed Thee, the King of Glory, with a purple garment for Thy greater affront;

182. They fastened upon Thy divine head a crown of thorns;

183. They put into Thy hands a scepter of a reed, and, kneeling down in a scornful manner, saluted Thee, saying, "Hail, King of the Jews!"

184. Plant, I beseech Thee, in my heart the memory of Thy Passion;

185. Let scorn for Thy sake be my glory, and injuries and affronts my crown.

186. Hail, sweet Jesus, who didst not refuse for my sake to be beaten with a reed, to be buffeted, to be spit upon, and to be the object of all kinds of derision;

187. I beseech Thee, by Thy wounds, by Thy Blood, by Thy disgrace, and by all the grief and sorrow Thou sufferedst for me, to endow my soul with all Thy patience and graces;

188. That Thou wouldst convert me and all I have to Thy everlasting praise and glory.

189. Hail, sweet Jesus, who, being defiled with spittle, rent and disfigured with stripes, bound and wholly miserable, wast brought forth as a spectacle to the enraged people, wearing a crown of thorns and a robe of purple;

190. Grant that with my heart I may utterly tread under foot, and have in detestation, all ambition, ostentation, worldly pomp and vanity, and all earthly dignity;

191. That, by profound humility and true contempt of myself, I may incessantly run towards the glory of Thy heavenly felicity.

192. Hail, sweet Jesus, who, being declared innocent by Pilate the judge, didst not refuse to hear the furious outcries of the Jews, by which they demanded that Thou shouldst be crucified;

193. Grant that I may live innocently, and not be troubled by reason of other men's evil will towards me;

194. Give me this grace, that I may neither backbite other men, nor willingly give ear to those that do it;

195. But that still I may have a good opinion of others, and bear other men's imperfections with a true compassion;

196. And love all men for God and in God with a pure, sincere, and cordial affection.

197. Hail, sweet Jesus; praise, honor, and glory be to Thee, O Christ, who didst permit Thyself in the presence of Thy people to be unjustly condemned to the most ignominious death of the cross,

198. That Thou mightest free us from the sentence of eternal death;

199. Grant that I may seek Thy honor, and rather choose to be exercised with Thee in adversity, than by forsaking Thee to enjoy the

commodities of life.

200. Hail, sweet Jesus, who, with many disgraces and injuries offered Thee, didst carry Thy cross with great pain upon Thy sacred and torn shoulders,

201. And, being weary and breathless, didst languish under the burden;

202. Grant that, with fervent devotion, I may embrace the cross of my own abnegation,

203. And with an ardent charity imitate the example of Thy virtues,

204. And may humbly follow Thee unto death.

205. Hail, sweet Jesus, who, in that lamentable journey in which Thou wentest to Thy death, didst meekly admonish the women, that they should bewail themselves and their children;

206. Give me acceptable tears of compunction, with which I may truly bewail my sins and my own ingratitude;

207. Give me tears of devout compunction and of holy love, which may melt my hard heart, and make it grateful unto Thee,

208. That I may love Thee alone, and rest in Thee only.

209. Hail, sweet Jesus; praise, honor, and glory be to Thee, O Christ, who, having Thy shoulders bruised with the weight of the cross, didst at length arrive weary at the place of execution,

210. Where wine, mingled with gall, was offered Thee to refresh Thy languishing strength:

211. O that Thou wouldst extinguish in me the allurements of gluttony and the concupiscence of the flesh,

212. And cause in me an aversion and horror of all impure and unlawful delights;

213. And that I may eat and drink soberly to the glory of Thy name,

214. That I may hunger and thirst after Thee alone,

215. And in Thee place my delight and joy!

216. Hail, sweet Jesus, who didst not disdain to be stripped naked upon Mount Calvary in the sight of the people,

217. And to suffer a most bitter pain by Thy sores, renewed with the pulling off Thy clothes;

218. Grant that I may love poverty of spirit, and not be troubled with any worldly want;

219. Grant that by Thy example I may endure and suffer any corporal necessities or calamities whatsoever.

220. Hail, sweet Jesus, who, being naked, didst not refuse to be rudely stretched out upon the wood of the cross, and cruelly fastened with nails unto the same;

221. In this manner Thou didst suffer Thy innocent hands and delicate feet to be most grievously wounded, and all Thy sacred joints to crack and be put out of joint;

222. Grant me, O Lord, that with a faithful and grateful mind I may consider this Thy unspeakable charity, with which of Thy own accord Thou didst stretch forth Thy arms, and willingly offer Thy hands and feet to be pierced;

223. Vouchsafe, O Lord, to enlarge and extend my heart with the perfect love of Thee;

224. Pierce it, and fasten it unto Thyself with the most sweet nail of charity;

225. And all my senses, cogitations, and affections enclose only on Thee.

226. Hail, sweet Jesus; praise, honor, and glory be to Thee, O Christ, who didst hang (Thy hands and feet being pierced) three hours upon the shameful wood of the cross, and, shedding in great abundance Thy Precious Blood, didst of Thy own accord endure unspeakable torments throughout Thy whole Body;

227. Lift up, I pray Thee, upon the wood of Thy cross, my miserable soul groveling on the ground.

228. O healthful Blood, O reviving Blood!

229. O that Thou wouldst purge and thoroughly heal me, being washed with this Thy Precious Blood!

230. O that Thou wouldst offer this Thy Blood to Thy Father for a perfect satisfaction of all my iniquities!

231. Grant, I beseech Thee, that mine inward man may, with ardent affection, mentally receive the lively drops of Thy Precious Blood, and may truly "taste how sweet Thy Spirit is."

232. Hail, sweet Jesus, who wast so good even to those that were so wicked, that for the very same persons who did crucify Thee Thou didst pray unto Thy Father, saying, "Father, forgive them, for they know not what they do";

233. Give me, I beseech Thee, the grace of

true meekness and patience, by which I may, according to Thy commandment and example, love my enemies,

234. And do good to those that hate me;

235. I heartily pray unto Thee for those that hurt and persecute me.

236. Hail, sweet Jesus, who wouldst that the title written in Hebrew, Greek, and Latin (as it were the trophy of Thy victory) should be fastened to the cross, that we beholding it might courageously fight against our invisible enemies;

237. Protect me, under this title, against the wiles and deceits of the devil:

238. Teach me, under this title, to overcome all temptations, and to subdue all vices;

239. That, having by grace conquered them, I may freely praise and glorify Thy holy name. Amen.

240. Hail, sweet Jesus; praise, honor, and glory be to Thee, O Christ, whose garments the soldiers divided amongst themselves, but did leave Thy coat, which was without seam, undivided;

241. Pour down into my heart, I beseech Thee, the spirit of peace and union,

242. That I may never, through my fault, divide or trouble the concord and union of my brethren;

243. But that I may always endeavor to repair divisions and pacify troubles.

244. Hail, sweet Jesus, who, suffering upon the altar of the cross incomprehensible torments and ineffable anguishes, wert shamefully reproached and scorned by the Jews, who vomited out of their wicked mouths sundry blasphemies against Thee;

245. Grant, O Lord, that, being mindful of Thy humility, patience, and mildness, I may quietly and cheerfully suffer pain, disgrace, persecution, infamy, etc.,

246. And may remain with Thee nailed to the cross even to the end;

247. Let no violence of temptation, no storm of adversity, no tempest of contumely, hinder me from effecting my good purposes;

248. Let not death, nor life, nor things present nor to come, nor any creature separate me from Thy love.

249. Hail, sweet Jesus, who didst tolerate one of the thieves to upbraid Thee, and didst most

mercifully and bountifully promise the glory of Paradise to the other, who humbly acknowledged his own injustice, and with a devout faith confessed Thee to be his King and God;

250. Behold me, I beseech Thee, with those eyes of mercy which Thou didst cast upon the thief repentant for his sins:

251. O that, by Thy holy help and grace, I may lead a life so innocent, that I may faithfully serve Thee and purely love Thee!

252. That at the end of my life I may deserve to hear, most merciful Redeemer, that most desired voice, "This day thou shalt be with Me in Paradise."

253. Hail, sweet Jesus, who, from the cross beholding Thy most sweet Mother full of grief and tears, with inward compassion didst commend her to Thy disciple John, and again John to her, and us all in John unto Thy said Mother;

254. Grant that I may love and honor her with a most chaste and ardent affection;

255. That, having her for my Mother, I may deserve also to be acknowledged by her for her son;

256. Grant that in all necessities, and especially at the hour of my death, I may find her present assistance.

257. Hail, sweet Jesus; praise, honor, and glory be to Thee, O Christ, who in a most pitiful manner, hanging upon the cross with wide gaping wounds, didst profess Thyself to be destitute of all comfort;

258. Grant that with a firm confidence I may always have recourse to Thee, my most merciful Savior, in all adversities, temptations, and desolations,

259. And wholly distrusting myself, I may trust in Thee alone,

260. And commit and resign myself entirely to Thee;

261. Wound my soul with the remembrance of Thy wounds;

262. Imprint them in my heart, and make my spirit even drunk with Thy Sacred Blood;

263. That I may attend to Thee, and Thee only seek, find, hold, and possess.

264. Hail, sweet Jesus, who, panting upon the cross, Thy Body being drawn dry for want of Blood, becamest very thirsty, and didst burn with an unspeakable desire of our salvation;

265. Grant that I may ardently thirst after Thy honor and the salvation of souls,

266. And may with courage employ myself in this affair;

267. Grant that I may not be hindered nor entangled by any transitory thing.

268. Hail, sweet Jesus, who wouldst that a sponge dipped in vinegar and gall should be offered Thee to drink, being then thirsty even to death, that by taking thereof Thou mightest satisfy for our gluttony and leave us an example of poverty;

269. Give me grace to despise unlawful pleasures and avoid all excess in meat and drink;

270. Also to use those things moderately which Thou givest for the sustentation of the body;

271. Pacify the inordinateness of my desires, that whatsoever doth please Thee may please me, and whatsoever displeaseth Thee may be displeasing also to me.

272. Hail, sweet Jesus, most enamored of mankind, who, duly performing the work of our redemption, didst offer up Thyself upon the altar of the cross a holy sacrifice for the expiation of the sins of all men;

273. Be Thou, I beseech Thee, the scope of all my thoughts, words, and works,

274. That in all things I may with a right and simple intention seek Thy honor;

275. Grant that I may never grow cold nor faint in Thy service;

276. But that fervor of spirit may be renewed in me, and that I may daily more and more be inflamed to praise and love Thee. Amen.

277. Hail, sweet Jesus; praise, honor, and glory be to Thee, O Christ, who of Thy own accord didst embrace death, and recommending Thyself to Thy Heavenly Father, bowing down Thy venerable head, yieldedst up Thy Spirit;

278. Truly thus giving up Thy life for Thy sheep, Thou hast shown Thyself to be a good Shepherd;

279. Thou didst die, O Only-begotten Son of God; Thou died, O my beloved Savior, that I might live for ever:

280. O how great hope, how great confidence have I reposed in Thy Death and Thy Blood!

281. I glorify and praise Thy holy name, acknowledging my infinite obligations to Thee;

282. O good Jesus, by Thy bitter Death and Passion, give me grace and pardon;

283. Give unto the faithful departed rest and life everlasting.

284. Hail, sweet Jesus, at whose death the sun withdrew his light, the veil of the Temple was rent asunder, and the monuments opened;

285. O Sun of Justice, permit not, I beseech Thee, that the beams of Thy grace at any time forsake me;

286. But let them continually enlighten the inmost parts of my soul;

287. Withdraw wholly from me the veil of hypocrisy;

288. Shake the earth of my soul with wholesome repentance;

289. Rend my stony heart,

290. That, being wholly renewed, I may contemn all transitory things, and love only that which is eternal.

291. Hail, sweet Jesus, who wouldst that Thy side should be opened with a soldier's lance,

292. And out of it pour blood and water to revive and wash our souls;

293. Thou wouldst, O my best Beloved, that Thy mellifluous Heart should be wounded for me;

294. O that it might please Thee to make a most deep wound in my heart with the lance of Thy love,

295. And unite it to Thy most Sacred Heart,

296. In such manner that I may have no power to will anything but that which Thou wilt!

297. Bring in, O my Lord, bring in my soul, through the wound of Thy side, into the bosom of Thy charity and the treasure-house of Thy Divinity,

298. That I may joyfully glorify Thee, my God, crucified and dead for me. Amen.

299. Hail, sweet Jesus; praise, honor, and glory be to Thee, O Christ, who sufferedst all that the malice of men or devils could devise;

300. Behold, with as much devotion as possibly I can, I salute the five principal Wounds of Thy blessed Body.

301. Hail, ruddy, glorious, and mellifluous Wounds of my Redeemer and my King!

302. Hail, glorious seals of my reconciliation and salvation!

303. I humbly desire to abide and be hidden in

you, and be by that means secure from all evil.

304. Hail, sweet Jesus, who, being with great lamentations of Thy friends taken down from the cross, wouldst be anointed with precious ointments, wrapped in a winding-sheet, and buried where no man was buried before;

305. Bury, I beseech Thee, all my senses, all my forces, and all my affections in Thee,

306. That, being joined to Thee by efficacious love, I may become insensible in respect of all other things.

307. Hail, sweet Jesus, who hast vanquished the power of the devil …

311. Hail, sweet Jesus, who like a conqueror with glorious triumph didst arise out of Thy closed sepulcher,

312. And, revested with Thy lovely countenance, didst replenish Thy friends with new joy and gladness;

313. Grant, O Lord, that, leaving the old paths of my wicked conversation, I may walk in the newness of life,

314. And seek and savor those things which are above in heaven, and not those things which are here upon earth,

315. To the end that when Thou my life shalt appear at the last day, I may appear with Thee in glory.

316. Hail, sweet Jesus; praise, honor, and glory be to Thee, O Christ, who, forty days after Thy Resurrection, didst gloriously ascend into heaven in the sight of Thy disciples, where Thou sittest on the right hand of Thy Father, blessed for evermore:

317. O that my soul might always languish on earth, and ascend and aspire towards heaven!

318. May it hunger and thirst always after Thee!

319. Hail, sweet Jesus, who didst give Thy Holy Ghost to the elect disciples persevering together with one mind in prayer,

320. And didst send them to teach all nations throughout the whole world;

321. Cleanse, I beseech Thee, the interior of my heart;

322. Give me true purity and constancy of mind, that the Holy Ghost nay find a grateful habitation in my soul,

323. And may replenish me with the special gifts of His grace;

324. May comfort, strengthen, fill, govern, and possess me.

325. Hail, sweet Jesus, who, coming as a Judge at the last clay, wilt render unto every one according to his works, either punishment or reward;

326. O my most merciful Lord God, grant that according to Thy will I may so innocently pass the course of this miserable life,

327. That, my soul departing out of the prison of my body, I may be vested with Thy merits and virtues,

328. And be received into Thy everlasting joy,

329. And with all the Saints I may bless and praise Thee for ever.

330. Hail, sweet Jesus, whom I have most grievously offended all the days of my life;

331. Alas, I have never ceased to be ungrateful to Thee, resisting Thy grace in divers manners, and always adding new faults unto my former;

332. Behold, O my sweet Refuge; behold me, the outcast of all creatures, bringing with me nothing but bundles of sins;

333. I prostrate myself at the feet of Thy mercy, and humbly implore pardon and remission;

334. Pardon, I beseech Thee, and save me, for Thy name's sake;

335. For I believe and am assured that no sins are so grievous and heinous but, by the merits of Thy most Sacred Passion, may be forgiven and, washed away. Amen.

HOLY EXERCISES OF CONTRITION
An advice to the reader

These following Exercises of Contrition are useful and proper first, for such devout souls as, being naturally indisposed for discursive prayer, are consequently obliged to begin an internal course of prayer with such immediate acts or affections. Such, therefore, at the beginning, may do well to make these Exercises of the purgative way the entire subject of their recollections, until they find that, remorse ceasing, they are enabled for the following Exercises of Love, etc. Secondly, these Exercises may be useful also for souls that have made a greater progress in the prayer of immediate acts; but this is when, by occasion of some sin committed, they judge it fit to raise contrition in their hearts for it. In which case it will not be necessary that their whole recollection should be spent in these acts;

but it will suffice to exercise one or two of them at first, and to employ the remainder of the time in their usual former matter of prayer.

The First Exercise

1. Who will give to mine eyes a fountain of tears, that I may bewail both day and night my sins and ingratitude towards God my Creator?

2. Consider (O my soul) the multitude of the benefits that God hath bestowed upon thee, and be thou confounded and ashamed of thy wickedness and ingratitude.

3. Consider who thy Creator is, and who thou art; how He hath behaved Himself towards thee, and how thou towards Him.

4. Thou hast made me, O Lord, when I was not; and that according to Thine own image.

5. Thou from the very first instant of my being hast been My God, My Father, My Deliverer, and All my Good.

6. Thou, with the benefits of Thy providence, hast preserved my life even till this present. O, let it be spent in Thy service!

7. But because these things, O gracious Lord, cost Thee nothing, to bind me more fast to Thee, Thou wouldst need give me a present bought by Thee most dearly.

8. Thou hast come down from heaven, to seek me in all those ways in which I had lost myself. O, draw up my soul unto Thee!

9. Thou hast exalted and made noble my nature by uniting it in One Person with Thy Divinity.

10. By Thy captivity Thou hast loosed my bonds, and by delivering Thyself into the hands of sinners Thou hast delivered me from the power of the devil; and by taking upon Thee the form of a sinner Thou hast destroyed my sins.

The Second Exercise

1. These things Thou didst to allure and bind me unto Thee, and to strengthen my hope.

2. To make me detest sin, by beholding what Thou hast done and suffered to overthrow the kingdom of sin.

3. And also that, being overcome and overwhelmed with the multitude of Thy benefits, I should love Him who did so much for me, and loved me so dearly.

4. Behold, O God, Thou hast redeemed me;

but what had this availed me if I had not been baptized? Among so many infidels as are in the world Thou hast brought me to Thy Faith and Baptism.

5. There that covenant was made that Thou shouldst be mine, and I Thine; Thou my Lord, and I Thy servant; Thou my Father, and I Thy child; that Thou shouldst behave Thy. self as a Father towards me, and I as a child towards Thee.

6. What shall I say of the other Sacraments which Thou hast instituted for remedies of my evils, making a plaster for my sins of Thine own most Precious Blood!

7. Having these helps, yet have I not remained in goodness; but my wickedness hath been so great, that I have lost my first innocency.

8. And Thy mercy on the other side is so great, that Thou hast patiently hitherto expected me.

9. O my hope and Savior, how can I without tears call to my remembrance how oftentimes Thou mightest justly have bereaved me of my life?

10. To Thee, therefore, be given the glory which is due; and to me shame and confusion of face, as it is this day.

The Third Exercise

1. How many thousand souls now peradventure burn in hell, who have less sinned than I, and yet I burn not there!

2. What had become of me, if Thou hadst taken me away when Thou tookest them?

3. Who then, O Lord, bound the hands of Thy justice? who held the rod of Thy judgments when I by sinning provoked Thee?

4. What pleased Thee in me that Thou didst deal more mercifully with me than with others?

5. My sins cried unto Thee, and Thou stoppedst Thine ears. My malice every day increased against Thee, and Thy goodness every day increased towards me.

6. I was wearied in sinning, and Thou wast not wearied in expecting.

7. In the midst of my sins I received from Thee divers good inspirations, which I neglected.

8. What shall I now render, O Lord, unto Thee, for all these benefits which I have received of Thee I because Thou hast given me Thyself, what shall I render to Thee?

9. If all the lives of angels and men were mine, and that I should offer them all unto Thee as a sacrifice, what were this oblation if compared with one drop of Thy Blood, which Thou hast shed for me so abundantly?

10. Who, therefore, will give tears to mine eyes, that I may bewail my ingratitude and wicked retribution or requital of these Thy so many benefits? Help me, O Lord, and give me grace, that I may worthily bewail mine iniquities.

The Fourth Exercise

1. My God, I am Thy creature, made according to Thy image; take away from me that which I have made, and acknowledge that which Thou hast made.

2. I have bent all my forces to do Thee injury, and have offended Thee by the works of my hands.

3. The things which Thou hast given and created for me, to be employed and used for Thy service and honor, I have wrongfully and most unthankfully converted and employed the same to Thy offence and dishonor.

4. My feet have been swift to evil, and my eyes have been dissolute to vanity, and mine ears have been always open to trifles and toys.

5. My understanding, which should have contemplated Thy beauty and have meditated both day and night on Thy commandments, hath considered transitory toys and meditated day and night how to transgress Thy said commandments.

6. My will was by Thee invited to the love of celestial delights and delicacies ; but I preferred the earth before heaven.

7. Alas, what can I, a wretch, answer, if Thou enterest with me into judgment, and wilt say: I have planted thee a chosen vineyard, all true seed; how then, O strange vineyard, art thou turned in My sight into that which is depraved?

8. I have not only been ungrateful for Thy benefits, but used Thy benefits also themselves as weapons against Thee.

9. Thou hast made all creatures for my use, to allure me to love Thee; I have abused them, and of them have divers times taken occasion of sin. I have made choice rather of the gift than the Giver.

10. What shall I say? Wherefore have not all the calamities and miseries which I have known to have fallen upon other men, and touched not me, been a sufficient argument to me that my delivery from every one of them was a peculiar benefit from Thee?

The Fifth Exercise

1. But if a most strict account shall be demanded for these things which cost Thee so little, what account wilt Thou ask of those which Thou hast bought Thyself with Thy most Precious Blood?

2. My God, how have I perverted all Thy counsels for my salvation!

3. How have I violated the mystery of Thine Incarnation!

4. Thou wert made man to make me partaker of the Divine Nature. I have made myself a beast and the slave of the devil.

5. Thou hast come down to the earth to bring me to heaven; and I have not hearkened to or acknowledged this high vocation, but have persevered in wickedness and in the mire of my baseness.

6. Thou hast made me one body with Thee; and I have joined myself again with the devil.

7. Thou hast humbled Thyself even to the dust of the earth; I puff myself up with pride.

8. Thou wouldst die to kill my sins; and I, presuming in Thy said mercy, goodness, and love, have not feared to sin against Thee. What greater impiety can be imagined?

9. I have taken occasion of Thy goodness to work malice; and by that means which Thou hast used to kill sin, I have taken occasion to raise again sin in myself.

10. Because Thou wert so good, I thought I might without prejudice be evil. Woe to mine ingratitude! And because Thy benefits were so many, I thought I might without punishment render unto Thee as many injuries.

The Sixth Exercise

1. Thus have I made Thy medicines occasions of sin, and I have turned that sword, which I received of Thee to defend my-self from mine enemies, against my own bowels, and with the same murdered mine own soul.

2. Thou died, that they that now live may not live to themselves, but unto Thee.

3. O most patient Lord, who for sinners hast suffered buffets, but far more patient in suffering sinners, will this Thy patience endure for ever towards me? What shall I do, my Lord I what shall I do? I confess I am not worthy to appear in Thy sight nor to behold Thee. Whither shall I fly from Thy face?

4. Art not Thou my Father, and in very truth a Father of mercies which have no end or measure?

5. What, then, shall I do, but cast myself down at Thy feet, and humbly crave mercy? Art not Thou My Creator? My Preserver? My Redeemer? My Deliverer? My King? My Pastor? My Priest? and My Sacrifice?

6. If Thou repellest me, who will receive me? If Thou rejectest me, of whom shall I seek succor?

7. Behold, I come full of wounds; Thou canst heal me: I come all blind; Thou canst give me sight: I come all dead; Thou canst raise me: I come all full of leprosy; Thou canst make me clean.

8. Thou shalt sprinkle me, O Lord, with hyssop (with Thy Precious Blood shed for me), and I shall be made clean.

9. Thou, O God, who art able to do all things, convert me unto Thee; renew my spirit, enlighten my understanding, sanctify my will, increase my strength of body and soul, that I may depend only on Thee, fear and love Thee above all things, and serve Thee fervently; and that in all my affections hereafter I may conform myself to Thy blessed will and pleasure.

10. I beseech Thee, finally, to impart unto me Thine abundant effectual grace, by which I may be able to begin to lead a perfect and holy life, and to serve Thee perfectly and thoroughly even to the end. For therefore Thou, O my God, gavest me a being, that I may employ it in Thy service

The Seventh Exercise

1. Take pity, O Lord, take pity, O merciful Savior, of me, most miserable sinner, doing things of blame, and worthily suffering for the same.

2. If I ponder the evil which I daily commit, that which I endure is nothing in comparison of it.

3. Thou, O Lord our God, art just and full of goodness, neither is there in Thee any wickedness.

4. Because when we offend, Thou dost not unjustly and cruelly afflict us; who when we were not, hast powerfully made us; and when for our sins we were guilty of damnation, Thou hast by Thy wonderful mercy and goodness set us in the state of salvation.

5. I know, O Lord God, and am assured that our life is not governed by uncertain chances, but wholly disposed and ordered by Thy awful power and providence.

6. Wherefore I humbly beseech Thee, that Thou wilt not deal with me according to my iniquities, by which I have deserved Thine anger, but according to Thy manifold mercies which surmount the sins of the whole world.

7. Take pity on me, Thy son, whom Thou hast begotten in the great grief of Thy Passion; and do not so attend to my wickedness that Thou forget Thy goodness.

8. Is it possible for a woman to forget the child of her own womb? And though she should forget, O most loving Father, Thou hast promised not to be unmindful.

9. Truly it is better for me not to be at all, than to be without Thee, sweet Jesus.

10. It is better not to live, than to live without Thee, the only true life.

The Eighth Exercise

1. Woe to me at the Day of Judgment, when the books of our consciences shall be opened (wherein our actions are registered), when of me it shall be openly proclaimed, See here a man and his works!

2. Alas, what shall I say? I will call and cry unto Thee, O Lord my God; why am I consumed being silent?

3. Weep, O my soul, and make lamentation, as a young married woman for the death of her husband.

4. O anger of the Almighty, rush not upon me, for I cannot subsist against Thee.

5. Take pity on me, lest I despair of Thy mercy; that by despairing of myself, I may find comfort in confiding in Thee.

6. And albeit I have done that for which Thou must justly condemn me, yet Thou past not lost Thy accustomed property of showing

mercy and pity.

7. Thou, O Lord, dost not desire the death of sinners, neither dost Thou take pleasure in the perdition of those that die.

8. Nay, rather that those who were dead might live, Thou Thyself hast died; and Thy death hath been the death that was due to sinners; and they by Thy death are come to life.

9. Grant me, I beseech Thee, O Lord, that Thou living I may not die; since that Thy death hath given life, much more let Thy life give life.

10. Let Thy heavenly hand help me, and deliver me from the hands of those that hate me, lest they insult and rejoice over me, saying, We have devoured him.

The Ninth Exercise

1. How is it possible, O good Jesus, that ever any one can despair of Thy mercy? who, when we were Thine enemies, hast redeemed us with Thy Precious Blood, and hast reconciled us to God.

2. Behold, O Lord, protected by Thy mercy, I run, craving pardon, to the throne of Thy glory, calling and knocking until Thou take pity on me.

3. For if Thou past called us to pardon, even when we did not seek it, how much more shall we obtain pardon if we ask it!

4. Forget my pride provoking Thee to displeasure, and weigh my wretchedness imploring Thy favor.

5. O Savior Jesus, be Thou my succor and protection, and say unto my soul, I am thy Salvation.

6. I do presume very much on Thy bounty, because Thou Thyself dost teach us to ask, seek, and knock at the door of Thy mercy.

7. Thou therefore, O Lord, who willest me to ask, grant that I may receive. Thou dost counsel me to seek; grant me likewise to find. Thou dost teach me to knock; open unto me, knocking at the door of Thy mercy.

8. Behold, besides my heart I have nothing else to give Thee; neither can I give Thee this without Thee. Take me, therefore, and draw me unto Thee, that so I may be Thine by imitation and affection, like as I am by condition and creation, who livest and reignest world without end.

9. O Lord God Almighty, who art Trinity in Unity, who art always in all things, and wert before all things, and wilt be in all things everlastingly, one blessed God for all eternity;

10. To Thee, this and all the days of my life, I commend my soul, my body, my seeing, my hearing, taste, smell, and touching; all my cogitations, affections, words, and actions; all things that I have without and within me; my sense and understanding; my memory, faith, and belief; and my constancy in well-doing; all these I commend into the hands of Thy powerful protection, to the end that all the nights and days, hours and moments of my life, Thou mayest preserve and direct me.

The Tenth Exercise

1. If Thou, O Lord, examine my righteousness, I shall be found as a dead man, stinking through rottenness.

2. But if Thou behold me with the eye of Thy mercy, Thou wilt thereby raise me from the sepulcher of mine iniquity.

3. Whatsoever Thou hatest in me, O Lord, expel and root out of me.

4. Bestow on me, O Lord, Thy fear, compunction of heart, humility, and a conscience free from all sin.

5. Grant me grace, O Lord, that I may be always able to live in charity with my brethren.

6. Give me grace, O Lord, not to forget my own sins, or pry into the sins or doings of other men.

7. Visit me weakened; Cure me diseased.

8. Refresh me wearied; Raise me dead.

9. Grant me, O Lord, a heart that may fear Thee, a mind that may love Thee, a sense that may conceive Thee, eyes that may see Thee.

10. Give me, O Lord, discretion to be able to discern betwixt good and evil, and endue me with an understanding ever watchful.

The Eleventh Exercise

1. O most mild and merciful Lord and Savior, Son of the living God, the world's Redeemer, amongst all men and in all things I confess myself to be a miserable sinner.

2. Nevertheless I beseech Thee, most sweet and sovereign Father, that as an abject I may not be cast out of Thy favor.

3. Yea, rather, O Lord, Thou who art King of kings, and hast determined and decreed the length of each man's life, grant me a devout desire to amend mine.

4. Stir up my sluggish soul, to the end that at all times and in all things it may seek, desire, love, and fear Thee, and may put in practice that which is pleasing to Thee.

5. I most humbly and heartily beseech Thee (who art Alpha and Omega, the beginning and ending), that when the time is come I must die, Thou wilt be a mild and merciful Judge, and a perpetual protector to me against the accusations and snares of the devil, mine old adversary.

6. Admit me for ever into the society of the holy Angels and of all Thy Saints in Thy heavenly city, where Thou art blessed and praised for all eternity.

7. O hope of my heart, O strength of my soul, may it please Thy omnipotent goodness to accomplish what my wonderful great weakness doth attempt to perform, seeing Thou art my life and the scope of my intention!

8. And albeit hitherto I have not deserved to love Thee so much as I ought, yet such is my desire that I would most gladly do it.

9. Grant me to accomplish and perform Thy holy inspirations.

10. Transform, most sweet Savior, my tepidity into a most fervent love of Thee. For the only thing I desire to attain unto by this my prayer is, that I may be able to love Thee with a most ardent affection.

HOLY EXERCISES OF PURE LOVE TO GOD
The First Exercise

1. I do rejoice in all the perfections that are in Thee, O my God, as in Thy wisdom, goodness, power, and all other Thy divine prerogatives and perfections.

2. Let it please and suffice me that Thou art infinitely happy and rich (my most benign and loving Father).

3. I do rejoice at the presence of Thee, my God, in heaven (where Thou reignest as in Thy kingdom), and that Thou art there worshiped, adored, and loved by all Thy Angels and Saints.

4. So that if it were in my power, I would love and honor Thee with all that love and worship wherewith all the Angels and Saints do there love Thee.

5. I do rejoice in all the loves and services that the just men in the Church (especially the perfect) in all former ages, in the present or in the future ages have and do, or shall bear and perform towards Thee.

6. And I desire to love Thee with the love of them, and would for Thy love do and perform, if it lay in my power, all their works, as well internal as external, and would undergo all their labors, and endure all their afflictions.

7. I do heartily rejoice in all the good things that are in the elect servants of God, but especially for the wonderful gifts of the perfect, and that they are by Thee, O my God, illuminated, inflamed, and sanctified.

8. My love and desire towards Thee, O my God, is such, and so great, that if it were possible to me, and acceptable to Thee, I would of each soul (especially my own) make a kingdom of heaven, that Thou mightest be beloved and praised in so many heavens by the dwellers in them.

9. Which, if it lay in my power, should be more in number than the grass piles on the earth, the sands in the sea, or drops of water therein.

10. I do here in Thy presence, O my God, hold and repute myself as nothing; and whatsoever I have above nothing, natural or supernatural, I acknowledge it to be Thine only.

11. And because of myself I am nothing, and that my God is all good, and that all good things come only from Him, I do greatly rejoice, and with all my heart confess that I am nothing, can do nothing, and have nothing; for both my being and ability to do, and all I have, is Thine and from Thee.

The Second Exercise

1. I do here, in the presence of God, repute and judge myself the most vile of all creatures; and because I cannot feel or perceive this in myself, but rather the contrary (having a good and great opinion of myself), I do acknowledge, therefore, that I am the most proud and ungrateful of all others; and I do bewail myself as such an one.

2. O my God, I love and desire to love Thee, with a love pure and free from all respect of proper commodity and self-interest.

3. I love Thee, my Lord, with a perseverant love, purposing by the help of Thy holy grace and assistance never to be separated from Thee by sin.

4. And if I were to live for millions of years, yet would I ever remain Thy faithful servant and lover.

5. I wish all creatures would adore and serve Thee, and that infidels may be converted to Thy faith, and all sinners to a good life; and all this only for Thy supreme honor and glory.

6. I wish that neither myself nor any other had ever offended Thee, my God; and that in particular I myself had ever served Thee faithfully from the instant of my nativity.

7. I wish and desire that both I myself and all others may Hereafter serve and love Thee most faithfully, and this for the love and good-will I bear Thee.

8. I rejoice and congratulate that Thou, my Lord God, art so rich and happy, that all creatures can add no more to Thy happiness than already Thou hast;

9. Nevertheless, because Thou mayest have external honor and worship from Thy creatures, I do wish sincerely that all of them may accordingly perform their service and the worship due unto Thee the best they can.

10. I am sorry for all the sins and indignities that are, have, or shall be done unto Thee, by myself or any others.

11. And this principally and only I am sorry for, because these sins are injuries done to Thy Divine Majesty, who only art worthy to be honored and served by all Thy creatures.

12. I do joyfully accept and am glad of all that is pleasing to God, be it prosperity or adversity, sweet or bitter, and this merely for the love I bear Him.

13. I am sorry for all that doth displease God, or is contrary to His divine will or commandments, and all this only for the love of Him and His glory.

The Third Exercise

1. I congratulate with Thee, O my God, for the blessedness end all the perfections that are in Thee, and which for all eternity Thou hast ever had; as Thy omnipotence, wisdom, goodness, etc.

2. I congratulate with Thee also, and am glad that Thou art in Thyself most rich and fully sufficient both for Thyself and all creatures.

3. I likewise with Thee, O my Lord, rejoice in the sweet ordinance and disposition of heaven and earth, and for all the things which are in the marvelous creation of this world, and for all the works which Thou hast made, or shalt yet make unto the end of the world.

4. I congratulate, approve, and rejoice in all the judgments of my Lord God, as well manifest as secret: concerning the devils, and the wicked men that live in this world.

5. I congratulate and rejoice with Thee, O my God, in all the lauds and praises which the Angels and Saints in heaven and Thy servants on earth do give Thee, and for all the worship they yield unto Thee.

6. Because I find myself altogether insufficient to praise my God, I do for my help and assistance therein invite and call upon the holy angels and all creatures;

7. And with them I join my own soul, with all the powers of it, that all of them together may glorify my God for His infinite excellency.

8. I am sorry I am not perfect, and wish that (so far as it may please my God to grant) I may be perfect the more worthily to praise Thee;

9. And not out of any commodity by it to myself, but purely for the love I beat Thy Divine Majesty, who art infinitely worthy of more love and honor than all creatures that are or can be, are able to perform towards Thee.

10. Exult and rejoice and be thou delighted, O my soul, for all the excellency and good things that are in thy God.

11. I rejoice in the dignity that our Savior Christ now hath in heaven, and congratulate Him in it.

The Fourth Exercise

1. Blessed be Thy Eternal Father, O Heavenly Lord Jesus, who so abundantly bestowed these felicities on Thee;

2. do Thou blessedly and gloriously enjoy them for all eternity.

3. I praise and exalt my God for His great goodness and liberality showed towards His most faithful and elect friends.

4. I do exceedingly rejoice that since all creatures together are in no sort able to praise, Thee, my God, according to the very least

worth that is in Thee, yet Thou Thyself, and Thou only, art able sufficiently and perfectly to praise and glorify Thyself.

5. I do rejoice indeed at this, and do heartily desire Thee to do it evermore.

6. Yea, I do heartily crave of Thee that Thou mayest incessantly and most intensively praise Thyself, since Thou only art able to do it, and deservest to have it done.

7. I do congratulate and rejoice with Thee, O my Lord God, in all the works which Thou hast done; and this only because they are the works of Thy hands.

8. As for the creation of the world, Thy providence about it, Thy redemption of it; wonderfully esteeming all these works, because they are Thine.

9. And I rejoice as well in that Thou hast made a hell for the punishment of the wicked, as a heaven for the reward of the good.

10. I wish and desire, out of my love to God, that He may be praised and known of all men; and I do invite all creatures to do the same with myself.

11. I offer myself, for the love of my God, to bear and suffer all things which may be to His honor and glory; though no manner of commodity accrue to me thereby, but purely I do it out of the free love I bear, and desire to bear, towards my God.

12. Lastly, I profess that if I could desire anything wherein I might show or exercise my love towards my God, I hope (with the help of His grace) I should and would do it most cheerfully and readily out of the pure and sincere love that I bear and wish to bear towards my God, without respect of any commodity by it to myself: which God grant me to do for His glory and my happiness. Amen.

CERTAIN EXPRESSIONS OF LOVE TOWARDS GOD

To be used according to the disposition of the soul.

1. Grant me to do what Thou commandest, O my Lord, and command what Thou wilt.

2. O life of my soul!

3. Into Thy hands, O Lord, I do commend my spirit.

4. My heart is ready, O my God, my Heart is ready.

5. Lo, here I am; send me.

6. O Lord, what is there in heaven, or what upon earth, that I would have besides Thee?

7. Lord, what wilt Thou have me to do?

8. O woe is to me, that my sojourning is prolonged!

9. Thou knowest, O Lord, that I love Thee, and will bestow my life for Thee.

10. Even as the hart doth thirst after the fountain of waters, so doth my soul thirst after Thee, O God.

11. I desire to be dissolved and to be with Christ.

12. When shall I come and appear before the face of our Lord?

13. I beseech the Heavenly King to cause me (who am very much grieved for want of it) to come to the sight of Him whom I so much love.

14. Lord, if I have found favor in Thy sight, show unto me Thy face.

15. O my soul, and all that is within me, bless ye our Lord, and praise His holy name.

16. I will bless our Lord at all times, His praise shall ever be in my mouth.

17. Holy, Holy, Holy, Lord God of Sabaoth; heaven and earth are full of the majesty of Thy glory.

18. O my God, my God, look upon me; why hast Thou forsaken me?

19. O my God, my Helper, I will hope. in Thee.

20. O Lord, Thy mercy is in heaven, and Thy truth reacheth to the clouds.

21. To Thee have I lifted up mine eyes, who dwellest in heaven.

22. My Beloved is mine, and I am His.

23. Thy kingdom is a kingdom for ever, and Thy reign is for all generations and generations.

24. Thou hast wounded my heart, my Spouse, Thou hast wounded my heart.

25. I adjure you, O daughters of Jerusalem, if you shall find my Beloved, tell Him that I languish with love.

26. Come, Thou my Beloved, come.

27. Whither is thy Beloved gone? whither is thy Beloved turned aside? and we will seek Him with thee.

28. Who shall procure unto me, that I may

find Thee and kiss Thee?

29. Draw me after Thee, we shall run in the odor of Thine ointments.

30. Thou whom my soul loveth, show unto me where Thou dost eat, where Thou dost lodge.

31. Show me Thy face; let Thy voice sound in mine ears.

32. I have sought for Him whom my soul loveth; I have sought for Him, and have not found Him.

33. When I had gone a little farther, I found Him whom my soul loveth.

34. My soul melted as He spoke to me.

35. I will love Thee, O Lord, my strength, my firm foundation, my refuge, and my deliverer.

36. Enlighten mine eyes, that I may never sleep in death; lest mine enemy may come at length to say, I have prevailed against him.

37. Thou art worthy, O Lord God, to have glory and honor and power and praise.

38. Let Thy works, O Lord, confess unto Thee, and let Thy Saints praise Thee.

39. Though I were to die for it, yet I would not deny Thee.

40. I will not let Thee go till Thou hast blessed me.

41. Have mercy on me, O Lord, have mercy on me, because my soul doth confide in Thee.

42. Blessed are they who dwell in Thy house, O Lord; they praise Thee for ever and ever.

43. O all my hope!

44. O all my glory

45. O all my refuge, and all my joy

46. O life of my soul, and the pleasant repose of my spirit!

47. Mortify in me whatsoever displeaseth Thy sight, and make me according to Thy Heart.

48. Wound me, O Lord, wound the most inward part of my soul with the darts of Thy love,

49. And make me drunk with the wine of Thy perfect charity.

50. When shall all die in me which is contrary to Thee?

51. When shall I live to be no more mine own?

52. When shall nothing else live in me, but Thou, O Jesus?

53. When shall the flames of Thy love wholly consume me?

54. When shall I be altogether melted and pierced through with the wonderful efficacy of Thy sweetness?

55. When wilt Thou free me from all these impediments and distractions, and make me one spirit with Thee, that I may not any more depart from Thee?

56. O dearly beloved! O dearly beloved of my soul!

57. O sweetness of my heart!

58. O God of my soul, why guidest not Thou Thyself to Thy poor creature?

59. Thou fillest heaven and earth, and wilt Thou leave my heart empty?

60. Too late have I known Thee, O infinite goodness!

61. Too late have I loved Thee, O beauty so ancient and so new!

62. Woe to me, I have loved Thee not!

63. Blind I was that I saw Thee not.

64. Thou wert within me, and I went, seeking Thee abroad;

65. But now that I have found Thee, though late, suffer not, good Lord, that I ever leave Thee. Amen. Amen. Amen.

HOLY EXERCISES OF ACTS OF THE WILL
The First Exercise

1. My God, Thou art of a most simple being, therefore infinite in all perfections;

2. I do adore Thee with my whole heart, with most profound humility and reverence;

3. And because Thou only art most worthy of all love, I do and for ever will (through Thy grace) love Thee with a most entire and sincere love.

4. Thy being, O my God, is incomprehensibly immense, filling and penetrating all things;

5. O, teach me, therefore, so to live as being always in Thy presence;

6. Possess my heart as Thy temple, and reign in it as Thy throne.

7. I offer unto Thee, my life and all my faculties and strength, to be employed only in Thy service.

8. Thou, O my God, art alone from everlasting to everlasting; eternally and unchangeably perfect and happy.

9. O my soul, never cease to bless our infinitely great and bountiful Lord, all whose perfections and happiness shall eternally be

contemplated and enjoyed by thee.

10. O, bless our Lord, all the works of our Lord; praise Him and exalt Him for ever.

The Second Exercise

1. Great art Thou, O Lord, and great is Thy power; yea, and Thy wisdom is infinite.

2. Send, O God, out of Thy inexhaustible fountain of light, one beam into my soul, that I may perfectly see, admire, and adore all Thy most wise and secret judgments.

3. O my soul, how filthy and odious is sin, when thou lookest upon it by a divine light!

4. O, how ungrateful have I been to my most merciful God, whose infinite power and wisdom have been continually watchful over me!

5. Whom need I to fear, having a Savior infinite both in power, wisdom, and goodness?

6. Thou, my God, art good, not with this or that kind of goodness, or after such or such a manner; but simple good, without all limitation or measure.

7. O my soul, if a small shadow and appearance of good here on earth doth, with such violence, draw our affections, how ought we to love Him by whom all good is communicated to creatures!

8. My God, if I had in my heart all the capacity of loving that is in all men and angels, it were all due to Thee alone. How much more, then, ought I to employ all that little power that is in me!

9. My God, give me this proof of sincere love to Thee, to make me as well love Thee commanding as promising; as well chastising as comforting.

10. How happy were we, O my soul, if we had no other will but the will of Jesus!

The Third Exercise

1. My God, Thou art the author, end, and measure of all purity and holiness; before whom folly is fund even in the angels.

2. How infinite is Thy goodness, then, since Thou desirest that my heart may become a temple for Thy holiness to dwell in!

3. O that Thy presence would purify it from all strange and unworthy affections to creatures!

4. O that there I might have my only conversation with Thee in a holy silence and solitude!

5. O my soul, conceive if thou canst bow ugly and abominable sin (which is impurity itself) is in the eyes of our God, who is purity itself.

6. Thy divine providence, O my God, stretcheth to all creatures whatsoever; by its law all things arise, fall, move, and rest: even the very hairs of our heads are numbered by Thee.

7. O ungrateful and foolish wretch that I am, how oft have I desired and even endeavored to withdraw myself from this all-comprehending providence, having a will to live according to mine own most imprudent judgment! My God, I repent me of this from the bottom of my heart, and most humbly beg pardon of Thee.

8. From this hour my purpose, through Thy grace, is to accept and welcome all occurrences, whether pleasing or distasteful to sense, as coming from Thy heavenly providence: this shall be my comfort and stay in all my afflictions; in dangers, security; and perfect rest of mind in expectation of future events.

9. Do Thou alone, O my God, provide, determine, will, and choose for me.

10. Hast not Thou, O my God, provided for me Thine own kingdom? What, then, can make me dejected?

The Fourth Exercise

1. Who can declare the mercies of my God towards my soul? Of nothing He raised me to the dignity of an intellectual, immortal nature; from the low state of nature He exalted me to the divine state of grace; from thence He will raise me to a participation of His glory and happiness.

2. Bless thou our Lord, O my soul; and all that is in me, praise His holy name.

3. And with me let all His holy Angels and Saints sing forth the praises of my God, my most merciful and liberal Benefactor.

4. Let it suffice, O my soul, that hitherto we have been so unpardonably ungrateful.

5. My God, through Thy grace I will consecrate the remainder of my life to the glorifying of Thy holy name, directing all the powers of my body and soul to the accomplishing of Thy will and increasing of Thy glory and praise.

6. Thy right hand, O my God, is full of righteousness: Thou art a most just Judge, and with Thee is no acceptation of persons; but Thou

renderest to every one according to his works.

7. This Thy justice is as truly acceptable to me as Thy goodness.

8. Be Thou therefore exalted in the punishing of all obstinate impenitent sinners; for just and reasonable it is that Thou shouldst be feared.

9. But Thy will it is, O my God, that I should appeal from Thy tribunal of justice to that of mercy, being desirous to amend and correct all my past sins and provocations of Thee.

10. However, O my God, if Thou wilt exercise Thy justice on me, let it be in this world, that Thou mayest spare me in the next.

The Fifth Exercise

1. My God, as Thou art the Author of the being of all things, so art Thou the End also; for Thy glory all things were and are created.

2. And a great proof hereof Thou hast given to all the sons of Adam, for we see that our hearts find no rest at all whilst we adhere by affection to creatures.

3. Therefore, my God, I do here offer myself as a holocaust, to be even consumed to Thy glory.

4. I offer unto Thee my understanding, firmly to adhere to all divine verities revealed by Thee to Thy Church, renouncing all doubt or questioning of any of them; and herein my purpose irrevocable is, through Thy grace, to live and die.

5. O that it would please Thee that all mankind might know Thee, and with a firm faith confess Thee!

6. My God, I do willingly offer unto Thee my blood to seal this my faith, whensoever by Thy providence an occasion shall be presented, hoping that then Thou wilt be my strength and my salvation; and being assured that, whilst I hope in Thee, I shall not be weakened.

7. O my God, that Thou wouldst wholly possess my mind, which is Thine, and which I here offer to Thee! Fill it with good thoughts of Thee only; expel out of my memory all vain seducing objects of vanity.

8. I offer unto Thee, O my God, all my will and affections; to will, love, and desire only that which Thou willest and lovest.

9. If Thou wilt have me to be in light, be Thou ever praised; and if Thou wilt have me to be in darkness, be Thou likewise praised.

10. I renounce all propriety in myself, for I am wholly Thine, both for life and death, for time and eternity.

The Sixth Exercise

1. My God, in union with that most perfect and acceptable oblation of Thy Son my Savior Jesus Christ, I offer unto Thee my whole self entirely, and all things that belong unto me, to be employed only in Thy service and worship.

2. Let His worthiness recompense for my unworthiness, that I may obtain that for His merits which I cannot for my own.

3. I offer unto Thee my watching and my sleeps, in union with His waking from the sleep of death.

4. I offer unto Thee all my thoughts, speeches, and actions. to be sanctified and purified to Thy glory by all His most holy thoughts, words, and actions.

5. I offer unto Thee my refections, in union of that Blessed Refection in which He gave His most Precious Body and Blood to nourish the souls of His disciples.

6. I offer unto Thee all the prayers and other exercises of piety which, through Thy grace, I have or shall perform, beseeching Thee to accept them in union with those most perfect merits and heavenly prayers which Thy Son offered to Thee on Mount Olivet or elsewhere.

7. My God, I offer unto Thee all the afflictions, pains, desertions, and tribulations which I either have or ever shall suffer in union with the most bitter Passion of Thy only-begotten Son, my only Savior.

8. O most sweet and merciful Jesus, as Thou in infinite goodness didst offer Thyself unto Thy Father for the expiation of my sins, and to purchase for me an inheritance of glory, behold I here offer my whole self entirely to Thee, to be employed purely to Thy glory.

9. Do Thou likewise offer me with Thyself, Thy merits and sufferings, to Thy Heavenly Father, that my poverty may be enriched with Thy abundance, and my sins canceled by Thy merits.

10. O Holy Spirit, the greatest gift that our Heavenly Father had to bestow upon the sons of men, without whose inspiration we cannot so much as think a good thought, behold I offer my heart and my whole self unto Thee,

beseeching Thee so to purify my soul with Thy sevenfold graces that I may serve Thee with a chaste body, and please Thee with a pure heart. Amen.

The Seventh Exercise

1. My God and all my good, I am nothing, I have nothing, I can do nothing that is good as of myself; Thou art all, and all our sufficiency is from Thee only.

2. I do here humbly prostrate my soul before Thee, plunging myself in the abyss of mine own nothing.

3. How infinitely good art Thou, O my God, that vouchsafest to behold and take care of so vile, so unclean a creature as I am!

4. I beseech Thee that even for this most undeserved goodness of Thine I may yet more humble myself before Thee and all others.

5. I am content that my inexpressible vileness were known unto all, to the end that all may treat me according to my demerits, out of a just zeal to Thy glory.

6. O my God, the God of love, I would to God that as I live only in Thee and by Thee, so likewise my living may be for Thy honor and service.

7. My God, even because I am indeed nothing, and Thou alone art all, therefore will I utterly distrust and abandon myself, and securely trust in Thee only, who alone art able to supply my infinite wants and cure my defects.

8. To Thee, O Lord Jesus, is this poor and wretched soul of mine left, to Thy guard is it committed by Thy Heavenly Father; behold I cast all my care and solicitude upon Thee, both for this life and that which is to come.

9. My God, Thou alone art my love, and Thou only shalt be my fear.

10. My God, Thou hast made me unto Thee, and my heart is unquiet (and so let it be more and more) till it rest in Thee; let me find bitterness in all undue love to creatures.

HOLY EXERCISES OF RESIGNATION
Acts of general resignation

1. My God, whatsoever I have, whatsoever I can do, all this Thou hast freely bestowed on me. Behold I offer myself and all that belongs to me to Thy heavenly will. Receive, O Lord, my entire will and liberty; possess my under-standing, memory, and all my affections; only vouchsafe to bestow upon me Thy love, and I shall be rich enough; nothing more do I desire; Thou alone, O my God, sufficest me.

2. O my God and all my good, I have and do consecrate to Thy love and honor both my body and soul. Conserve them as it shall please Thee, and employ them according to Thine own will in Thy service.

3. My Lord, I here prostrate myself before Thee, to do Thee homage for what I am and may be by Thy grace.

4. My God, I beseech Thee to glorify Thyself by me, according to whatsoever manner Thou shalt please.

5. My God, hereafter I will never search any object of my affections out of Thee, since I see that all good is to be found in Thee.

6. O most desirable goodness of my God, let it be to me even as Thou wilt, O eternal, most holy, and well-pleasing will of my Savior; do Thou reign in and over all my wills and desires from this moment for ever.

7. My God and all my good, for that infinite love of Thine own self, grant that as I live in and by Thee, so may I live only to and for Thee.

8. O my soul, let us live to Him, and for Him only, that died for us; let us disengage ourselves from this base world; let us pass from sense to reason, and from reason to grace; let us enter into commerce with the angels, that our conversation may be with Jesus, that so by all manner of ways we may be His, both in life and death, in time and eternity.

9. O my soul, let us freely submit ourselves to our Lord's judgments, renouncing our own judgment; let us adore them, though we be ignorant of them. Let us most assuredly believe that He doth nothing but for our greater good. Whatsoever befalls us, let us take it willingly and thankfully from His hands, which are always full of blessings for us.

10. Let Jesus only live and reign in my heart, and let the world and all its vain desires perish.

1. Forms of particular acts of resignation

About External Goods. For the love of God, and in conformity to His will, I resign myself:

1. To be deprived of any of the clothes that I have, or may have, though never so necessary;

2. or of books;

3. or of convenient lodgings;

4. and to have those things bestowed on me from which my nature is most averted.

5. To be driven to wear clothes that seem base, unfit, or inconvenient for the season.

6. To be ill accommodated in lodging, bedding, etc.

7. To want even necessary clothes.

8. To be forced to wear such clothes as will make me appear ridiculous.

9. To want meat or drink;

10. or to have only such as is ungrateful to nature.

11. To endure crosses that in any sort, spiritually or corporally, may fall on my friends or kindred, as loss of state, infirmity, death, etc.;

12. and, on the other side, to restrain all inordinate complacency in their prosperity.

13. To endure that my friends should neglect, forget, yea, hate and persecute me.

14. To be abandoned of all creatures, so that I may have no man or thing to cleave unto, save only Thee my God, who wilt abundantly suffice me.

15. To be indifferent in what place, company, etc., I shall live;

16. yea, to live with those from whom my nature is most averted.

17. To live in all sorts of afflictions, as long as shall please Thee my God;

18. and not to yield to the motion of nature, which perhaps out of wearisomeness would fain have life at an end. But wholly to conform my will to Thy good will and pleasure;

19. yea, to take pleasure that Thy will may be fulfilled in me any way.

2. Acts of Resignation about our Good Name.

For the love of Thee my God, and in conformity to Thy will, I resign myself:

1. To suffer all manner of disgraces, contempts, affronts, infamies, slanders, etc., be they done to my face or behind my back;

2. though I have given no cause or provocations;

3. yea, after I have done the greatest kindnesses to my defamers;

4. if I have deserved them by my fault I am sorry for it and beg pardon, but am glad of this good effect of it, that it is an occasion of procuring this mortification and humiliation.

5. To suffer injuries either from superiors, equals, or inferiors.

6. To be in life or manner of my death shameful and odious to others;

7. and after death to be evil thought and evil spoken of by others;

8. yea, not to have any that will vouchsafe to pray for me;

9. yea, to be esteemed to have died in the state of eternal damnation;

10. yea, moreover, to have it expressed so to the world in a chronicle, to the shame of all that have relation to me;

11. in this life to be held for the scum of mankind, forsaken by all both in their doings and affections.

12. To be mortally persecuted by professed enemies (though I will account none such);

13. yea, by such as have had great proofs of my charity to them;

14. in sickness and other necessities to be driven to be chargeable and troublesome to others;

15. whereas I in the mean time am profitable to none at all;

16. so that all men do grow weary of me, and long to be rid of me;

17. and in this case to remain several years, yea, all my life long;

18. dying a natural death (so it be in Thy grace), to be esteemed by others to have destroyed myself;

19. and thereupon to have my body ignominiously used, buried in the highway or under the gallows, to the eternal loss of my fame and unspeakable confusion of my kindred, friends, etc.

3. Acts of Resignation about the Body.

For the love of Thee, O my God, and in conformity to Thy will, I resign myself:

1. to suffer weaknesses, sickness;

2. pains;

3. deformity;

4. horror in the sight of others, as was the case of Job and Lazarus.

5. To suffer extremity of heat or cold;

6. want of necessary sleep, and hunger or thirst;

7. indigestion;

8. torments and defects about my five senses.

9. To be affrighted with horrible and hideous sights of devils, etc.

10. To be afflicted with fearful noises.

11. To suffer scourgings, beatings, etc.

12. To be spit upon, as Thou my Savior wast.

13. To suffer incisions, torments, etc., external and internal.

14. To suffer loss of eyes, hearing, etc.; to be overtoiled with all sorts of labors;

15. and this being in feebleness of body.

16. To lose all pleasure and gust in meats and drinks.

17. To suffer any disfiguring in my face, or distortions in other parts of my body.

18. To suffer the loss of any of my members.

19. To receive harm in my imagination, and thereby to lose my perfect judgment, so as to become a fool or mad.

20. That my body should by little and little putrefy and rot away.

21. To die suddenly, or after long sickness and tokens of death.

22. To die without senses or memory, and distracted or mad.

23. To endure the agony of death, and the long torments that do accompany it.

24. To suffer the unwillingness and terror that nature feels in the separation of the soul from the body.

25. To die a natural death, or else a violent and painful one, procured by others.

26. To die at what time, in what place and manner it shall please Thee my God.

27. To die without the help of any of the Sacraments, being not able to come by them.

28. In the agony of death to endure such terror, afflictions, and temptations as the devil doth then usually procure.

29. Being dead, to want not only all decent or honorable, but even Christian burial, so as that my body may be made a prey to beasts and fowls.

4. Particular Acts of Resignation about the Soul.
For the love of God, and in conformity to His will, I do resign myself:

1. To undergo all sorts of temptations that shall please Thee my God to lay on me or permit to befall me;

2. and to suffer them to the end of my life, ever adhering to Thee.

3. To endure all manner of desolations, aridities, and in devotions.

4. To suffer all obscurity and darkness in my understanding; all coldness and dullness of affection in my will to Thee, so far as I am not able to help it;

5. in all which I renounce the seeking any solace in creatures.

6. To want all manner of gifts and graces not necessary to my salvation;

7. nor to desire inordinately nor rest with affection in supernatural contemplations, sweetnesses, or other extraordinary visits or favors.

8. To resign myself to all things, be they never so contrary to sensuality.

9. To bear with the repugnance that I find in sensuality, till with Thy grace (sooner, or later, or never) it may be brought to perfect subjection to my spirit; in the mean time suffering patiently the difficulty that is in fighting against it, or resisting the desires of it.

10. To endure all the difficulties, tediousnesses, and expectations that are in a spiritual life; also such various changes, chances, and perplexities as are in it; notwithstanding all which my purpose is (through Thy grace) to persevere and go through them all.

11. To bear with my own defectuousness, frailty, and proneness to sin; yet using my best industry, and bearing with what I cannot amend.

12. To die before I can reach to perfection.

13. To live and die in that degree of a spiritual life as shall seem good to Thee, and not according to my own will;

14. yet ever desiring and endeavoring that I may not be wanting in cooperating with Thy calls and graces.

15. To be contented to serve Thee according to that manner Thou hast provided and appointed; that is, with regard to my natural talents, complexion, etc., as likewise such supernatural helps and graces as Thou shalt afford me, and not according to the talents and gifts bestowed on others.

16. To be contented that Thou hast bestowed greater gifts on other men than on me.

17. To understand and know no more nor

no otherwise than Thy will is, and to remain ignorant in what Thou wilt have me to be ignorant of.

18. To give up and offer to Thee my God whatsoever honor and contentment may come by such knowledge; for all is Thine.

19. To want all knowledge but such as are necessary to my salvation.

20. To follow Thee by all the ways whatsoever that Thou shalt call me, externally or internally, though I cannot understand how they can lead to a good issue; so walking, as it were, blindfold.

21. To be contented that others excel me in virtues, and that they be better esteemed; yet ever desiring that I may not be wanting in my industries.

22. To be content not to know in what case I am as to my soul; nor in what degree of perfection, nor whether I go backward or forward;

23. nor to know whether I be in the state of grace; only beseeching Thee that I be industrious to please Thee.

24. To be content that another should receive the fruit of all my endeavors and actions, though never so perfect, so purely do I desire to serve Thee.

25. To endure with patience all manner of injuries;

26. and yet to be esteemed by others that I endure them against my will, without humility, with murmuring, revengefulness, and pride, and that the fear of danger or discredit only hinders me from executing such revenge.

27. To serve Thee purely for Thine own sake, so as that I would serve Thee though there had been no reward or punishment.

28. To do and suffer in this life both in soul and body what, and in what manner, and for how long as it shall please Thee my God.

29. To be content to enjoy the lowest place in heaven;

OTHER MIXED RESIGNATIONS

The reader should note that before every one of the following fifteen exercises of particular resignations there is premised a proper passage of Holy Scripture, which is the basis for the following acts of devotion.

1. *O, how good art Thou, O my God, to those that*

trust in Thee, to the soul that truly seeks Thee! What art Thou, then, to those that find Thee!

1. Whatsoever I shall suffer, O my God, by Thy ordinance, either in body or soul, and how long soever I shall suffer, I renounce all consolation but what comes from Thee.

2. My God, though Thou shouldst always hide Thy face from me, and never afford me any consolation, yet will I never cease to love, praise, and pray unto Thee.

3. For Thy sake I renounce all pleasure in eating and drinking, being resolved to make use of Thy creatures only in obedience to Thy will, and to the end thereby to be enabled to serve Thee.

4. I resign myself to abide all my lifetime among strangers; yea, or among such as have an aversion towards me, and which will never cease to molest me.

5. My God, casting myself wholly on Thy Fatherly providence, I renounce all care and solicitude for tomorrow concerning anything belonging to this life.

6. I offer unto Thee, O my God, this desire and resolution of my heart, that notwithstanding my continual in devotion, my infinite distractions and defects, etc., I will never give over the exercises of an internal life.

7. My desire is always to be in the lowest place, beneath all creatures, according to my demerit.

8. For Thy love, O my God, I renounce all inordinate affections to my particular friends or kindred.

9. I resign myself to suffer any lameness or distortedness in any of my members.

10. I resign myself to abide all my life among those that are enemies to Thy Catholic Church, and there to be in continual fears, dangers, and persecutions.

2. *Draw me, O God, we will run after Thee, because of the odor of Thy precious ointments.*

1. For Thy love, O my God, I resign myself to want necessary clothing, or to be deprived of those which I have.

2. I resign myself patiently to bear with the repugnance I find in my corrupt nature, and the difficulty in resisting the unruly passions of it. Yes, through Thy grace, my purpose is to use my best industry and vigilance against it.

3. For Thy love I renounce the seeking after all curious and impertinent knowledge.

4. I renounce all sensual contentment in sleep or other corporal refreshments, being desirous to admit no more of them than shall be necessary, and in obedience to Thy will.

5. My God, through Thy grace, neither hard usage from others, nor any mere outward corporal extremity or want, shall force me to seek a change of my present condition.

6. My God, I do consecrate myself to Thee alone, for the whole remnant of my life to pursue the exercises of an internal life, leaving the fruit and success of my endeavors to Thy holy will.

7. For Thy love, and in conformity to Thy blessed will, I resign myself to be abandoned of all creatures, so as to have none to have recourse unto but Thee only.

8. I offer myself unto Thee, with patience to suffer whatsoever Thou shalt inflict on me, and never to yield to the inclination and feebleness of nature, which perhaps out of wearisomeness would have life at an end.

9. When obedience or charity shall require it, I resign myself to go and abide in a place haunted with evil spirits, being assured that as long as I adhere to Thee they cannot hurt my soul.

10. I renounce rashness, readiness, and forwardness to judge the actions of others, employing all my severity in censuring against myself only.

3. My God and all my good, in Thy heavenly will is life; but death is mine. Not my will, therefore, but Thine be done in earth as it is in heaven.

1. For Thy love, O my God, I do resign myself to be deprived of all the gifts and privileges which in my nature I do most affect, and to see them conferred on the person for whom I have the greatest aversion.

2. I resign myself not only to want the esteem or favor of my superiors, but also to be despised, and hardly, yea, injuriously treated by them.

3. When through my own demerit I do deserve such ill usage from them, I will be sorry and humbled for my fault, and bless Thee for punishing it so easily in this life.

4. O tepidity, I do detest thee.

5. I do resign myself, and am even desirous to find such usage in this world, that I may know and feel it to be only a place of exile.

6. My God, whatsoever affliction or desertion Thou shalt suffer to befall me, through Thy grace I will neither omit, neglect, nor shorten my daily appointed recollections.

7. I offer myself to Thee, O my God, entirely to be disposed of by Thee, both for life and death. Only let me love Thee, and that is sufficient for me.

8. Whatsoever natural or other defectuousness shall be in me, either for mind or body, by which I may incur disesteem from others, I do willingly embrace such occasions of humiliation.

9. I renounce all forwardness to give counsel to others, being much rather desirous to receive it from any other.

10. I do utterly renounce all familiarity and all unnecessary conversation or correspondence with persons of a different sex.

4. My Lord Jesus, Thou who art Truth hast said, My yoke is easy and My burden light.

1. I have received from Thy hands a cross of religious penitential discipline; through Thy grace I will continue to bear it till my death, never forsaking any ways to ease it by external employments, or to escape from it, and shake it off by missions, etc.

2. For Thy love, O my God, and in conformity to Thy will, I resign myself to die when, where, and in what manner Thou shalt ordain.

3. I am content to see others make a great progress in spirit, and to do more good in Thy Church than myself.

4. I renounce all that satisfaction and false peace which is got by yielding to my inordinate passions, and not by resisting and mortifying them.

5. My God, till Thou hast humbled that great pride which is in me, do not spare to send me daily yet more and greater humiliations and mortifications.

6. I offer myself unto Thee, to suffer with patience and quietness whatsoever desolations, obscurity of mind, or deadness of affections that shall befall in a spiritual course; notwithstanding all which, through Thy grace, I will never neglect a serious tendency to Thee.

7. I am content to serve Thee with those mean

talents that Thou hast given me.

8. I yield myself to endure all manner of injuries and contempts, and yet to be esteemed by others to be impatient and revengeful.

9. I do renounce all solicitude to please others, or to gain the affections of any one to myself.

10. I do resign myself to such painful and withal base offices as my proud and slothful nature doth abhor, whensoever obedience, charity, or Thy will shall impose them on me.

5. My God, Thou art faithful, and wilt not suffer us to be tempted above that we are able; but wilt with the temptation give an issue that we may be able to bear it.

1. My God, my desire is to serve Thee gratis, like a son, and not as a mercenary.

2. I came into religion to suffer and to serve; I renounce, therefore, all desires of procuring ease, plenty, or superiority.

3. In love to Thee, O my God, I resign myself to follow Thee, by whatsoever ways, external or internal, that Thou shalt conduct me, although I be not able to understand them, nor can see how there be any good issues of them.

4. I am content to see all become weary and desirous to be rid of me.

5. I am resigned to want whatsoever gift and graces are not necessary to my salvation.

6. In love to Thee, O my God, and in submission to Thy will, I do renounce all inordinate love and correspondence with the world, that so I may attend to Thee only.

7. I resign myself to become a spectacle horrible and loathsome to men's eyes, as was Job or Lazarus.

8. I do adore and most humbly submit myself to Thy most wise and secret judgments concerning my death or future state.

9. I resign myself to suffer those most bitter pains of the stone, gout, colic, etc., if Thou shalt ordain them to fall on me.

10. I renounce all obstinacy in defending mine own opinions, and all desire of victory in discourse.

6. My God, who is like unto Thee, who hast Thy dwelling most high, yet humblest Thyself to regard the things which are (done) in heaven and earth!

1. I resign myself to abide in this place and in this present state of life wherein Thou hast put me; neither will I seek or ever procure a change for any outward sufferings till Thou shalt appoint.

2. Let all creatures scorn, abandon, and persecute me, so that Thou, O my God, wilt accompany and assist me; Thou alone sufficest me.

3. Through Thy grace I will never cease to approach nearer and nearer to Thee by prayer and abstraction from creatures.

4. I do resign myself, whensoever necessity, obedience, or charity shall require it, to visit and assist any one lying sick, though of the plague, or any other infectious or horrible disease.

5. I am contented that those who are nearest to me in blood or friendship should be so averted from me as to abhor my name.

6. I resign myself to die a natural or violent death, and as soon as it shall please Thee.

7. I offer unto Thee this desire and purpose of my heart, that I will esteem no employment to be necessary but the aspiring to a perfect union with Thee, and that I will not undertake any other business but in order to this.

8. I do heartily renounce all affection to all, even venial imperfections and the occasions of them.

9. I renounce all propriety in any dignity or office that I have or may have hereafter.

10. I desire to have no more to do with the world than if I were already dead and buried.

7. My God, it is my only good to adhere unto Thee, who art the God of my heart and my portion for ever.

1. I offer myself unto Thee to be afflicted with whatsoever temptation, external or internal, Thou shalt permit to befall me; and though I should fall never so oft, yet will I not yield to dejection of mind or despair, but will rise up as soon as by Thy grace I shall be enabled.

2. I resign myself to follow Thee, O my Lord Jesus, in the same poverty of which Thou hast given me an example, renouncing all propriety in anything, and being contented and pleased to enjoy only what shall be necessary in all kinds.

3. I resign myself not only to be disfavored by my superiors, but also to see those most favored that are most averted from me.

4. My God, although Thou shouldst kill me, yet will I never cease to hope and trust in Thee.

5. I am content not to learn or know any more than Thou wouldst have me to know.

6. I do offer myself to all manner of contradictions and injuries to be sustained from my superiors or brethren, in patience, silence, and without complaining.

7. I renounce all impatience and unquietness for my many defects and hourly imperfections.

8. I do offer unto Thee my desire and resolution never to relinquish an internal spiritual course, notwithstanding any difficulties whatsoever that shall occur in it.

9. My God, I do not desire a removal of all temptations, which show me:

10. How impossible it is to enjoy a perfect peace in this life; and,

11. How necessary unto me Thy grace and assistance is. I embrace the pain of them. Only let me not offend Thee by yielding to them.

12. For Thy love I resign myself to be deprived of all proper and certain habitation.

8. Holy, Holy, Holy, Lord God of Sabaoth! All the earth is full of Thy glory. Glory be to Thee most High.

1. For Thy love, O my God, and in conformity to Thy holy will, I resign myself unto Thee, with all that I am, have, can do, or suffer, in soul, body, goods, fame, friends, etc., both for time and eternity.

2. For Thy love I do renounce all desire of authority, especially all charge over the souls of others.

3. I am content not to learn or know more than Thou wouldst have me to know.

4. I resign myself, whensoever Thou shalt call me to it, to sacrifice my life, in what manner soever Thou shalt ordain, for the defense of Thy Catholic truth, trusting in Thy merciful promise that Thou wilt assist me in such trials.

5. My God, I am content to be blotted out of the memory of all (except those that would afflict me).

6. My God, let me be the universal object of the contempt and hatred of all creatures, so that I may love Thee and enjoy Thy presence and grace.

7. Jesus, who art the Prince of peace, and whose habitation is in peace, I offer my heart unto Thee, that Thou mayest establish a firm peace in it, calming the tempestuous passions that so oft rage in it.

8. I renounce all affection to speaking.

9. I resign myself in sickness to be burdensome and chargeable to others, so as that all should become weary and desirous to be rid of me.

10. I renounce all facility in hearkening to or believing any ill that is reported concerning others, and much more to be a disperser of such report.

9. I adore Thee, O my God, the blessed and only Potentate, King of kings and Lord of Lords, who dwellest in unapproachable light: to Thee be glory and eternal dominions. Amen.

1. I resign and offer myself unto Thee, to follow the conduct of Thy Holy Spirit in an internal life, through bitter and sweet, light and darkness, in life and death.

2. I do renounce all solicitous designs to gain the affections of superiors or of any others; with any intention thereby to procure ease or contentment to nature.

3. I do renounce all propriety in any endowments that Thou hast or shalt give me.

4. I am contented with whatsoever Thou shalt provide for my sustenance, how mean, how little, and how disgustful soever it be.

5. I resign myself in the agony of death to endure whatsoever pains, frights, or temptations Thou shalt permit to befall me, only let my spirit. always adhere to Thee.

6. My God, I do here again renew and ratify my vows of religious profession, consecrating myself and all that I have or can do to Thy glory and service only.

7. I resolve, through Thy grace, that my great and daily defects shall not destroy my peace of mind nor confidence in Thy goodness.

8. I resign myself, for the humiliation and good of my soul, to be deprived of any endowments and gifts that may any way make me be esteemed by others.

9. I resign myself in sickness to want the assistance and comfort of friends, yea, even the use of Sacraments.

10. I resign myself (yea, would be glad) to lose

all sensual pleasure in meats and drinks, if such were Thy will.

10. *Blessed is the man whose hope is only in the name of Thee my God, and that regardeth not vanities and deceitful frenzies.*

1. Though Thou shouldst always hide Thy face from me, yea, my God, although Thou shouldst kill me, yet will I never cease to approach to Thee, and to put my whole trust in Thee only.

2. I consecrate my whole life to Thee, to be spent in a continual tendency in soul to Thee; not presuming to expect any elevated contemplations or extraordinary graces, but referring to Thy holy pleasure whether I shall ever be raised above my present mean exercises.

3. I resign myself to be esteemed fit and capable only of the basest and most toilsome offices; the which if they shall be imposed upon me, I will not avoid them.

4. I resign myself to be guided only by Thee and Thy holy inspirations.

5. I resign myself to be continually tormented, and to have my sleeps broken with any kind of troublesome noises or frights, etc.

6. My God, I resign myself to Thee alone, to live and die in that state and degree of a spiritual life to which it shall seem good to Thee to bring me; only I beseech Thee, that I may not be negligent in cooperating with Thy grace and holy inspirations.

7. I resign myself to suffer the straits and tediousness of a prison, and there to be deprived of books, or any thing that may divert my mind.

8. I resign myself to suffer the extremity of heat and cold, and to want the comfort of all refreshments against heat, and of necessary clothes against cold.

9. I resign myself to be obliged to take meats and drinks loathsome to my nature.

10. I resign myself to see others, my inferiors, provided of all things, and myself only neglected.

11. *Our Lord is my light and salvation: whom, then, should I fear?*

1. There is not any spiritual exercise so displeasing or painful to my nature which I would not embrace, if I knew or did believe Thy will to be such.

2. My God, so I may die in Thy grace and holy love, I resign myself to the infamy of being reputed to have procured my own death; and that therefore my body should be ignominiously cast out, and none to have the charity to pray for my soul.

3. I resign myself to be affrighted with horrible noises, hideous apparitions, etc.

4. Through Thy grace, my God, I will not rest with affection in any of Thy gifts how sublime soever; but will only make use of them to pass by their means in to Thee, who art my only uncreated, universal, and infinite good.

5. I esteem this life to be a mere prison or place of exile.

6. My God, I offer my soul unto Thee, that Thou mayest establish a firm peace in it, not to be interrupted as now it is by every contradiction and cross.

7. I resign myself to have my superiors, and all others whom my nature would wish to be most friendly, to be in all things a continual contradiction and cross to me.

8. For Thy love I would be content rather to have no use of my tongue at all, than thus continually to offend Thee with it.

9. Let all creatures be silent before Thee, and do Thou, O my God, alone speak unto me; in Thee alone is all that I desire to know or love.

10. My God, I know that to fly Thy cross is to fly Thee that died on it; welcome, therefore, be (these) Thy crosses and trials.

12. *My God, with Thee is the fountain of life, and in Thy light we shall see light.*

1. My God, to Thee only do I consecrate the remainder of my life, purposing to account no business to be necessary, but only tendency to Thee by prayer and abnegation.

2. I resign myself, if such be Thy pleasure, even to be deprived of all use of these eyes, that are still so much delighted with vanity, curiosity, and all distracting objects.

3. O that I were nothing, that so Thou, my God, mayest be all in all!

4. I resign myself to be deprived of all certain habitation, and to live a vagabond in the world, so that none should take care of me or own me.

5. My God, my desire is to serve Thee in a state wherein I may be deprived of all propri-

ety and election in all things, as well internal as external: do Thou, my Lord, choose for me.

6. In conformity to Thy heavenly will, O my God, I do accept the pain and trouble that I feel from my continual indevotion, my unruly passions, and (almost) unremediable imperfections; and I will with patience expect Thy good time, when I shall be enabled with Thy grace to rectify them.

7. For Thy love I renounce all conversations and correspondences, which I do find to be occasions to me of falling into defects, by nourishing inordinate affection or unquietness.

8. I renounce the folly of being disquieted with seeing that others are not such as I would have them to be, since I cannot make myself such an one as I fain would.

9. I offer myself to become a fool unto all for Thee, my God.

10. So that thereby my pride may be humbled, I even beg of Thee, my God, that Thou wouldst not spare to send me crosses and contradictions.

13. *I know, my God, that Thou art the God that triest hearts and lovest simplicity, therefore in the simplicity of my heart I offer myself unto Thee.*

1. O my God, when will the time come that Thou wilt lead my soul into Thy solitude?

2. For Thy love I renounce all complacency in any kind of endowment or skill in any arts (as far as any of these are in me), consecrating all that by Thy free gift is in me to Thy glory and service only.

3. Feed me, O Lord, with the bread of tears, and give me drink in tears, according to the measure that Thou shalt think fit.

4. My God, it is Thou that hast placed me in this my present condition; and Thou only shalt displace me.

5. O tepidity, I abhor thee. My God, teach me an effectual cure and remedy against it; let not my latter end be worse than my beginning.

6. My God, I offer unto Thee my heart, that whatsoever yet unknown inordinate desires are in it, Thou mayest teach me to mortify them by any ways Thou shalt please.

7. I resign myself, in case that obedience shall unavoidably oblige me thereto, to undertake that most fearful employment of the charge of souls (in the mission, etc.).

8. For Thy love and for the mortification of sensuality, I could content to be freed from all necessity of eating and drinking, if such were Thy pleasure.

9. I offer unto Thee, my God, this desire of my heart, that at last, this day, I may begin perfectly to serve Thee, having spent so much time unprofitably.

14. *My Lord and my God, from Thee are all things, by Thee are all things, to Thee are all things: to Thee only be glory, love, and obedience for ever.*

1. My God, if Thou wilt that I be in light, be Thou blessed for it, and if Thou wilt that I be in darkness, still be Thou blessed for it. Let both light and darkness, life and death, praise Thee.

2. Blessed be Thy holy name that my heart doth not (and never may it) find rest or peace in anything that I seek or love inordinately, whilst I do not love it in Thee and for Thee only.

3. I offer unto Thee this resolution of mine, that by all lawful and fitting ways I will endeavor to avoid any office of authority.

4. I resign myself to live and abide in any state or place where I shall daily have my health or life endangered.

5. I renounce all resting affection to sensible gusts in my recollections, resolving to adhere firmly to Thee, as well in aridities as consolations.

6. Through Thy grace and assistance, O my God, no hard usage from others, nor any desire of finding any ease or contentment to my nature, shall force me to change my present condition.

7. My God, if Thou shalt so ordain or permit, I resign my body to be possessed or tormented by evil spirits, so that my spirit may always adhere by love to Thee.

8. I resign myself to take part in any calamity, disgrace, etc., that Thy Divine Providence shall permit to befall the country or community in which I live.

9. My God, I am nothing, I have nothing, I desire nothing, but Jesus, and to see Him in peace in Jerusalem.

15. *Blessed art Thou, O my God, in all Thy gifts, and holy in all Thy ways.*

1. I offer unto Thee the desire and resolu-

tion of my heart, that no employment which cannot without sin be avoided, nor much less any complacency in conversation with others, nor any unwillingness to break off conversation through impertinent civility, shall cause me to omit or shorten my daily appointed recollections.

2. Far be it from me that my peace should depend on the favor or affection of any creature, and not in subjection to Thy will only.

3. I renounce all knowledge that may hinder or distract me from the knowledge of my own defects and nothingness.

4. My God, I have neither devotion nor attention, and indeed do not deserve either; only I beseech Thee that Thou wilt accept of my sufferings.

5. My God, so that I may die in Thy holy fear and love, I resign myself to want all comforts and assistance from others, both in my death and after it, if such be Thy will.

6. My God, through Thy grace I will never voluntarily undertake any employment or study, but such as shall serve to advance my principal and most necessary business of seeking Thee by prayer, to which all other designs shall give way.

7. My God, I beseech Thee not only to forgive, but to crown with some special blessing all those that despise, depress, or persecute me, as being good instruments of Thy grace to abate pride and self-love in me.

8. Whatsoever dignity or privilege I enjoy, I am content to relinquish it whensoever it shall be Thy will; and if I were wrongfully deprived of it, I will not for the recovering endanger the loss of mine own peace or that of others.

9. I resign myself not only to suffer for mine own faults, but also the faults of my brethren.

10. My God, my desire is to live to Thee only. Place me, therefore, where Thou, wilt; give me or take from me what Thou wilt. Only let me live to Thee and with Thee; that suffices me.

A DAILY CONSTANT EXERCISE
(An extract from Blosius, *Lud. Blosius in Instit. Spirit. chapter* xi.)
1. Of Contrition.
My Lord and my God, what shall I, sinful wretch, say unto Thee? I bow the knees of my heart, acknowledging in Thy sight my manifold and grievous sins. I have sinned, O God, I have sinned and done evil before Thee. I have sinned against Thee, my most omnipotent Creator. I have sinned against Thee, my most merciful Redeemer. I have sinned against Thee, my most liberal Benefactor. Woe unto me, I have continually been most ungrateful to Thee. I am a most vile creature, dust and ashes. Be merciful, O Lord; be merciful, be merciful unto me. Behold my sorrow and contrition for my sins. O, would to God I had never offended Thee! Would to God I had never resisted and hindered the operation of Thy grace in my heart! Would to God I had always pleased Thee, and observed Thy holy will and inspirations! My purpose and firm resolution, through Thy grace, is to avoid henceforward whatsoever may offend Thee, and rather to die than willingly to provoke Thy wrath and hatred against me. Therefore, O merciful Jesus, by Thy most bitter Passion and all the merits of Thy most Sacred Humanity, I beseech Thee to pardon and blot out all my sins. Wash me with Thy Precious Blood; heal, purge, and sanctify me.

2. Reflections on the Merits and Passion of our Savior Jesus Christ
I do adore, glorify, and bless Thee, O my only Savior Jesus Christ, for all Thy unspeakable mercies and benefits. O Son of the living God, I do most humbly give thanks to Thee for that for me Thou hast vouchsafed in Thine infinite love:

1. To become man.

2. To be born in a poor stable and laid in a manger.

3. To suffer poverty with Thy poor Virgin Mother.

4. For more than thirty years to be wearied with continual labors and travails for our good.

5. Out of inexpressible anguish to sweat drops of Blood.

6. To be ignominiously apprehended by sinners, unworthily bound and arraigned before Thine enemies.

7. To be shamefully defiled with spittings, cruelly beaten, and dishonorably clothed with a white and purple garment, like a fool and a mock king.

8. To be unjustly condemned to death.

9. To be cruelly torn with whips and crowned with thorns.

10. To be most tormentingly fastened with nails to the cross.

11. To be most inhumanely presented with gall and vinegar to drink in Thy extreme thirst.

12. For me to hang naked, wounded, and condemned in inconceivable torments many hours on the cross;

13. There to shed Thy most Precious Blood, and to offer Thy life a propitiation for my sins.

14. To be sealed up in the grave, from whence, notwithstanding, Thou didst raise Thyself, conquering death for me. O blessed Jesus, my only Hope and Salvation, grant that I may love Thee with a most fervent and constant love. O wounds of my Lord, inflicted for me, I salute you. With what love were you suffered by Him! And what love do you deserve from me!

3. Acts of Humiliation

Behold, O most merciful Savior, I, a most abominable sinner, in imitation of Thy most glorious humility, do submit myself to all creatures, acknowledging myself unworthy to live on earth; and, after the example of Thy most admirable charity, I do with sincere love, according to my utmost ability, embrace all those that do afflict or persecute me. For Thy love I do renounce all iniquity and vanity, all inordinate delectations, all self-will and immortification. I do relinquish and reject all things below Thee; and above all I do make election of Thee, as my only good. I do commit and resign myself entirely to Thee. I do desire and beseech Thee that Thy most perfect and well-pleasing will may be accomplished in me and concerning me, in time and eternity. For Thy love and glory I am ready to want any consolation, and to suffer any injury, contempt, or tribulation. If such be Thy pleasure, my Heavenly Lord, let me live in the same poverty and afflictions that Thou didst suffer all Thy life long.

ADORATION, OF THE MOST BLESSED TRINITY. O most Holy, Glorious, and Ever-blessed Trinity, Father, Son, and Holy Ghost; One omnipotent, most wise, most holy, and most merciful God; I do in the profound abyss of mine own nothing adore Thee, my most gracious God.

Vouchsafe to teach and assist me, whose hope is only in Thee. O Heavenly Father, by Thine infinite power establish my memory in Thee, fill it with holy and divine thoughts; O eternal Son of Thy coeternal Father, by Thine infinite wisdom illuminate mine understanding, and adorn it with the knowledge of Thy supreme excellency and mine own incomprehensible vileness. O Holy Spirit, the most pure love of the Father and Son, by Thine infinite goodness inflame my soul with an inextinguishable ardor of divine love. O my God and all my good, O that I could love and praise Thee as perfectly and incessantly as all Thy Angels do! According to the utmost extent and capacity that Thou hast given me, I do glorify, adore, love, and magnify Thee. But because I cannot worthily praise Thee, do Thou vouchsafe to praise and glorify Thyself in and by me. If I had the love of all creatures, I would most willingly expend and employ it on Thee only.

EXPRESSIONS OF LOVE TOWARDS GOD
My Lord and my God.
O Being infinitely peaceable and infinitely amiable;
O infinite abyss of goodness, infinitely delicious and desirable;
O torrent of inestimable delectations and joys;
O my all-sufficient reward;
Thou art my only immutable good. What do I desire but Thee!
O, draw me after Thee; Inflame me with the fire of Thy most fervent love.
O my God, my God and All, Plunge me in the abyss of Thy Divinity, swallow me entirely, and make me one spirit with Thee, that Thou mayest take Thy delights in me.
Nothing but Jesus, nothing but Jesus.
O Jesus, do Thou alone live and reign in my soul.
My God, let me only love Thee, and that suffices me.

Augustine Baker, lawyer, monk, historian, mystic, 1575–1641, The Third Treatise of Prayer. First section. This writing was compiled from more than forty sources in the seventeenth century by Dom Augustine Baker, O.S.B., a monk of the English Benedictine Congregation. Edited from the Douay edition of 1657

How to Spend the Day with God

Richard Baxter

"This is the day which the LORD hath made; we will rejoice and be glad in it" Psalm 118:24.

A holy life is inclined to be made easier when we know the usual sequence and method of our duties – with everything falling into its proper place. Therefore, I shall give some brief directions for spending the day in a holy way.

Sleep

Measure the time of your sleep appropriately so that you do not waste your precious morning hours sluggishly in your bed. Let the time of your sleep be matched to your health and labor, and not to slothful pleasure.

First Thoughts

Let God have your first awaking thoughts; lift up your hearts to Him reverently and thankfully for the rest enjoyed the night before and cast yourself upon Him for the day which follows.

Familiarize yourself so consistently to this that your conscience may check you when common thoughts shall first intrude. Think of the mercy of a night's rest and of how many that have spent that night in Hell; how many in prison; how many in cold, hard lodgings; how many suffering from agonizing pains and sickness, weary of their beds and of their lives.

Think of how many souls were that night called from their bodies terrifyingly to appear before God and think how quickly days and nights are rolling on! How speedily your last night and day will come! Observe that which is lacking in the preparedness of your soul for such a time and seek it without delay.

Prayer

Let prayer by yourself alone (or with your partner) take place before the collective prayer of the family. If possible let it be first, before any work of the day.

Family Worship

Let family worship be performed consistently and at a time when it is most likely for the family to be free of interruptions.

Ultimate Purpose

Remember your ultimate purpose, and when you set yourself to your day's work or approach any activity in the world, let HOLINESS TO THE LORD be written upon your hearts in all that you do.

Do no activity which you cannot entitle God to, and truly say that he set you about it, and do nothing in the world for any other ultimate purpose than to please, glorify and enjoy Him. "Whatever you do, do all to the glory of God" (1 Corinthians 10:31).

Diligence in Your Calling

Follow the tasks of your calling carefully and diligently. Thus:

(a) You will show that you are not sluggish and servants to your flesh (as those that cannot deny it ease), and you will further the putting to death of all the fleshly lusts and desires that are fed by ease and idleness.

(b) You will keep out idle thoughts from your mind, that swarm in the minds of idle persons.

(c) You will not lose precious time, something that idle persons are daily guilty of.

(d) You will be in a way of obedience to God when the slothful are in constant sins of omission.

(e) You may have more time to spend in holy duties if you follow your occupation diligently. Idle persons have no time for praying and reading because they lose time by loitering at their work.

(f) You may expect God's blessing and comfortable provision for both yourself and your families.

(g) it may also encourage the health of your body which will increase its competence for the service of your soul.

Temptations and Things That Corrupt

Be thoroughly acquainted with your temptations and the things that may corrupt you – and watch against them all day long. You should watch especially the most dangerous of the things that corrupt, and those temptations that either your company or business will unavoidably lay before you.

Watch against the master sins of unbelief: hypocrisy, selfishness, pride, flesh pleasing and the excessive love of earthly things. Take care against being drawn into earthly mindedness and excessive cares, or covetous designs for rising in the world, under the pretence of diligence in your calling.

If you are to trade or deal with others, be vigilant against selfishness and all that smacks of injustice or uncharitableness. In all your dealings with others, watch against the temptation of empty and idle talking. Watch also against those persons who would tempt you to anger. Maintain that modesty and cleanness of speech that the laws of purity require. If you converse with flatterers, be on your guard against swelling pride.

If you converse with those that despise and injure you, strengthen yourself against impatient, revengeful pride.

At first these things will be very difficult, while sin has any strength in you, but once you have grasped a continual awareness of the poisonous danger of any one of these sins, your heart will readily and easily avoid them.

Meditation
When alone in your occupations, improve the time in practical and beneficial meditations. Meditate upon the infinite goodness and perfections of God; Christ and redemption; Heaven and how unworthy you are of going there and how you deserve eternal misery in Hell.

The Only Motive
Whatever you are doing, in company or alone, do it all to the glory of God (1 Corinthians 10: 31). Otherwise, it is unacceptable to God.

Redeeming The Time
Place a high value upon your time, be more careful of not losing it than you would of losing your money. Do not let worthless recreations, television, idle talk, unprofitable company, or sleep rob you of your precious time.

Be more careful to escape that person, action or course of life that would rob you of your time than you would be to escape thieves and robbers.

Make sure that you are not merely never idle, but rather that you are using your time in the most profitable way that you can and do

not prefer a less profitable way before one of greater profit.

Eating and Drinking
Eat and drink with moderation and thankfulness for health, not for unprofitable pleasure. Never please your appetite in food or drink when it is prone to be detrimental to your health.

Remember the sin of Sodom: "Look, this was the iniquity of your sister Sodom: She and her daughter had pride, fullness of food and abundance of idleness" – Ezekiel 16:49.

The Apostle Paul wept when he mentioned those "whose end is destruction, whose god is their belly, and whose glory is in their shame – who set their minds on earthly things, being enemies to the cross of Christ" – Philippians 3: 18–19. O then do not live according to the flesh lest you die (Romans 8:13).

Prevailing Sins
If any temptation prevails against you and you fall into any sins in addition to habitual failures, immediately lament it and confess it to God; repent quickly whatever the cost. It will certainly cost you more if you continue in sin and remain unrepentant.

Do not make light of your habitual failures, but confess them and daily strive against them, taking care not to aggravate them by unrepentance and contempt.

Relationships
Remember every day the special duties of various relationships: whether as husbands, wives, children, masters, servants, pastors, people, magistrates, subjects.

Remember every relationship has its special duty and its advantage for the doing of some good. God requires your faithfulness in this matter as well as in any other duty.

Closing the Day
Before returning to sleep, it is wise and necessary to review the actions and mercies of the day past, so that you may be thankful for all the special mercies and humbled for all your sins. This is necessary in order that you might renew your repentance as well as your resolve for obedience, and in order that you may examine

yourself to see whether your soul grew better or worse, whether sin goes down and grace goes up and whether you are better prepared for suffering, death and eternity.

May these directions be engraven upon your mind and be made the daily practice of your life.

If sincerely adhered to, these will be conducive to the holiness, fruitfulness and quietness of your life and add to you a comfortable and peaceful death.

Richard Baxter, 1615–91

The Saint's Everlasting Rest

Richard Baxter

CHAPTER 14

What use heavenly contemplation makes of consideration, the affections, soliloquy, and prayer
I. The use of consideration, and its great influence over the heart.
II. Contemplation is promoted by the affections; particularly,
  1. By love;
  2. Desire;
  3. Hope;
  4. Courage, or boldness;
  5. Joy.
III. The usefulness of soliloquy and prayer in heavenly contemplation.

Having set thy heart in tune, we now come to the music itself. Having got an appetite, now approach to the feast, and delight thy soul as with marrow and fatness. Come, for all things are now ready. Heaven and Christ, and the exceeding weight of glory, are before you. Do not make light of this invitation, nor begin to make excuses; whosoever thou art, rich or poor, though in an alms-house or hospital, though in the high-ways or hedges, my commission is, if possible, to compel you to come in; and blessed is he that shall eat bread in the kingdom of God! The manna lieth about your tents; walk out, gather it up, take it home, and feed upon it. In order to this, I am only to direct you – how to use your consideration – and affections – your soliloquy and prayer.

First. Consideration is the great instrument by which this heavenly work is carried on. This must be voluntary, and not forced. Some men consider unwillingly; so God will make the wicked consider their sins when he shall "set them in order before their eyes;" so shall the damned consider the excellency of Christ, whom they once despised, and the eternal joys which they have foolishly lost. Great is the power which consideration hath for moving the affections and impressing things on the heart; as will appear by the following particulars:

1. Consideration, as it were, opens the door between *the head and the heart*. The understanding having received truths, lays them up in the memory, and consideration conveys them from thence to the affections. What excellency would there be in much learning and knowledge, if the obstructions between the head and the heart were but opened, and the affections did but correspond to the understanding! He is usually the best scholar, whose apprehension is quick, clear and tenacious; but he is usually the best Christian, whose apprehension is the deepest and most affectionate, and who has the readiest passages, not so much from the ear to the brain, as from that to the heart. And though the Spirit be the principal cause, yet, on our part, this passage must be opened by consideration.

2. Consideration presents to the affections those things which are *most important*. The most delightful object does not entertain where it is not seen, nor the most joyful news affect him who does not hear it; but consideration presents to our view those things which were as absent, and brings them to the eye and ear of the soul. Are not Christ and glory affecting objects? Would they not work wonders upon the soul, if they were but clearly discovered, and our apprehensions of them in some measure corresponded to their worth? It is consideration that presents them to us: this is the Christian's perspective by which he can see from earth to heaven.

3. Consideration, also, presents the most important things in *the most affecting way*. It reasons the case with a man's own heart. When a believer would reason his heart to heavenly contemplation, how many argu-

ments offer themselves from God and Christ, from each of the divine perfections, from our former and present state, from promises, from present sufferings and enjoyments, from hell and heaven! Every thing offers itself to promote our joy, and consideration is the hand to draw them all out; it adds one reason to another, till the scales turn: this it does when persuading to joy, till it has silenced all our distrusts and sorrows, and our cause for rejoicing lies plain before us. If another's reasoning is powerful with us, though we are not certain whether he intends to inform or deceive us, how much more should our own reasoning prevail with us, when we are so well acquainted with our own intentions! Nay, how much more should God's reasoning prevail with us, which we are sure cannot deceive, or be deceived! Now, consideration is but the reading over and repeating God's reasons to plead with himself why he should return to his father's house, so have we to plead with our affections, to persuade them to our Father's everlasting mansions.

4. Consideration *exalts reason to its just authority.* It helps to deliver it from its captivity to the senses, and sets it again on the throne of the soul. When reason is silent, it is usually subject; for when it is asleep, the senses domineer. But consideration awakens our reason, till, like Samson, it rouses up itself, and breaks the bonds of sensuality, and bears down the delusions of the flesh. What strength can the lion exert while asleep? What is a king, when dethroned, more than another man? Spiritual reason, excited by meditation, and not fancy or fleshly sense, must judge of heavenly joys. Consideration exalts the objects of faith, and comparatively disgraces the objects of sense. The most inconsiderate men are most sensual. It is too easy and common to sin against knowledge; but against sober, strong, persevering consideration, men seldom offend.

5. Consideration makes reason *strong and active.* Before, it was a standing water, but now as a stream, which violently bears down all before it. Before, it was as the stones in the brook, but now like that out of David's sling, which smites the Goliath of our unbelief in the forehead. As wicked men continue wicked, because they bring not reason into action and exercise; so

godly men are uncomfortable, because they let their reason and faith lie asleep, and do not stir them up to action by this work of meditation. What fears, sorrows and joys will our very dreams excite! How much more, then, would serious meditation affect us!

6. Consideration can *continue* and persevere in this rational employment. Meditation holds reason and faith to their work, and blows the fire till it thoroughly burns. To run a few steps will not get a man heat, but walking an hour may; and though a sudden occasional thought of heaven will not raise our affections to any spiritual heat, yet meditation can continue our thoughts till our hearts grow warm. Thus you see the powerful tendency of consideration to produce this great elevation of the soul in heavenly contemplation.

Secondly. Let us next see how this heavenly work is promoted by the particular exercise of THE AFFECTIONS. It is by consideration that we first have recourse to the memory, and from thence take those heavenly doctrines which we intend to make the subject of our meditation; such as promises of eternal life, descriptions of the saints' glory, the resurrection, etc. We then present them to our judgment, that it may deliberately view them and take an exact survey, and determine uprightly concerning the perfection of our celestial happiness, against all the dictates of flesh and sense, and so as to magnify the Lord in our hearts, till we are filled with a holy admiration. But the principal thing is to exercise, not merely our judgment, but our faith in the truth of the promises, and of our own personal interest in them, and title to them. If we did really and firmly believe that there is such a glory, and that within a few days our eyes shall behold it, O what passion would it raise within us! What astonishing apprehensions of that life would it produce! What love, what longing would it excite within us! O how it would actuate every affection! how it would transport us with joy, upon the least assurance of our title! Never expect to have love and joy move, when faith stands still, which must lead the way. Therefore daily exercise faith, and set before it the freeness of the promise, God's urging all to accept it, Christ's gracious disposition, all the evidences of the love of Christ, his faithfulness to his engagement, and the evidences of his love in ourselves; lay all these together, and think whether they do not testify the good will of the Lord concerning our salvation, and may not properly be pleaded against our unbelief. Thus, when the judgment has determined, and faith has apprehended the truth of our happiness, then may our meditation proceed to raise our affections; and particularly love, desire, hope, courage or boldness, and joy.

1. *Love* is the first affection to be excited in heavenly contemplation; the object of it is goodness. Here, Christian, is the soul-reviving part of thy work. Go to thy memory, thy judgment and thy faith, and from them produce the excellencies of thy rest; present these to thy affection of love, and thou wilt find thyself, as it were, in another world. Speak out, and love can hear. Do but reveal these things, and love can see. It is the brutish love of the world that is blind; divine love is exceedingly quicksighted. Let thy faith take hold of thy heart, and show it the sumptuous buildings of thy eternal habitation, and the glorious ornaments of thy father's house, even the mansions Christ is preparing, and the honors of his kingdom; let thy faith lead thy heart into the presence of God, and as near as thou possibly canst, and say to it, "Behold the Ancient of Days, the Lord Jehovah, whose name is, I AM: this is he who made all the worlds with his word, who upholds the earth, who rules the nations, who disposes of all events, who subdues his foes, who controls the swelling waves of the sea, who governs the winds, and causes the sun to run its race, and the stars to know their courses. This is he who loved thee from everlasting, formed thee in the womb, gave thee this soul, brought thee forth, showed thee the light, and ranked thee with the chief of his earthly creatures; who endued thee with thy understanding, and beautified thee with thy gifts; who maintains thy life and all its comforts, and distinguishes thee from the most miserable and vilest of men. O here is an object worthy of thy love! Here shouldst thou even pour out thy soul in love! Here it is impossible for thee to love too much! This is the Lord who hath blessed thee with his benefits, 'spread thy table in the sight of thine enemies, and made thy cup overflow!' This is he whom angels and saints praise, and the heavenly host for ever magnify!" Thus do thou expatiate on the praises of God, and open his excellencies to thine heart, till the holy fire of love begins to kindle in thy breast.

If thou dost not yet feel thy love burn, lead thy heart farther, and show it the Son of the living God, whose name is "Wonderful, Counselor, the mighty God, the everlasting Father, the Prince of peace": show it the King of saints on the throne of his glory, "the First and the Last; who is, and was, and is to come: who liveth, and was dead, and behold, he liveth for evermore; who hath made thy peace by the blood of his cross," and hath prepared thee with himself a habitation of peace: his office is that of the great peace-maker; his kingdom is the kingdom of peace; his Gospel is the tidings of peace; his voice to thee now is the voice of peace! Draw near, and behold him. Dost thou not hear his voice? He that bade Thomas come near, and see the print of the nails, and put his finger into his wounds; he it is that calls to thee, "Come near, and view the Lord thy Savior, and be not faithless, but believing; peace be unto thee, fear not, it is I." Look well upon him. Dost thou not know him? It is he that brought thee up from the pit of hell, reversed the sentence of thy damnation, bore the curse which thou shouldst have borne, restored thee to the blessing thou hadst forfeited, and purchased the advancement which thou must inherit for ever. And dost thou not yet know him? His hands were pierced, his head, his side, his heart were pierced, that by these marks thou mightest always know him. Dost thou not remember when he "found thee lying in thy blood and took pity on thee, and dressed thy wounds, and brought thee home, and said unto thee, Live!" Hast thou forgotten, since he wounded himself to cure thy wounds, and let out his own blood to stop thy bleeding? If thou knowest him not by the face, the voice, the hands, thou mayst know him by that heart: that soul-pitying heart is his; it can be none but his; love and compassion are its certain signatures: this is he who chose thy life before his own; who pleads his blood before his father, and makes continual intercession for thee. If he had not suffered, what hadst thou suffered? There was but a step between thee and hell when he interposed and bore the stroke. And is not here fuel enough for thy love to feed on? Doth not thy throbbing heart stop here to ease itself, and, like Joseph, "seek for a place to weep in?" or do not the tears of thy love bedew these lines? Go on, then, for the field of love is large; it will be thy eternal work to behold and love; nor needest thou want work for thy present meditation.

How often hath thy Lord found thee, like Hagar, sitting, and weeping, and giving up thy soul for lost, and he opened to thee a well of consolation, and also opened thine eyes to see it! How often, in the posture of Elijah, desiring to die out of thy misery, hath he spread thee a table of unexpected relief, and sent thee on his work refreshed and encouraged! How often, in the case of the prophet's servant, crying out, "Alas, what shall we do, for a host doth encompass us," hath he "opened thine eyes to see more for thee than against thee!" How often, like Jonah, peevish and weary of thy life, hath he mildly said, "Doest thou well to be angry" with me, or murmur against me? How often hath he set thee on "watching and praying," repenting and believing, "and, when he hath returned, hath found thee asleep;" and yet he hath covered thy neglect with a mantle of love, and gently pleaded for thee, that "the spirit is willing, but the flesh is weak!" Can thy heart be cold when thou thinkest of this? Can it contain, when thou rememberest these boundless compassions? Thus, reader, hold forth the goodness of Christ to thy heart; plead thus with thy frozen soul, till, with David, thou canst say, "My heart was hot within me; while I was musing, the fire burned." If this will not rouse up thy love, thou has all Christ's personal excellencies to add, all his particular mercies to thyself, all his sweet and near relations to thee, and the happiness of thy everlasting abode with him. Only follow them close to thy heart. Deal with it as Christ did with Peter, when he thrice asked him, "Lovest thou me?" till he was grieved, and answered, "Lord, thou knowest that I love thee!" So grieve and shame thy heart out of its stupidity, till thou canst truly say, "I know, and my Lord knows, that I love him."

2. The next affection to be excited in heavenly contemplation, is *desire*. The object of it is goodness, considered as absent, or not yet attained. If love be warm, desire will not be cold. Think with thyself, "What have I seen! O the incomprehensible glory! O the transcendent beauty! O blessed souls that now enjoy it! who see a thousand times more clearly what I have seen at a distance, and through dark, interposing clouds. What a difference between my state and theirs! I am sighing, and they are singing; I am offending, and they are pleasing God. I am a spectacle of pity, like a Job or Lazarus; but they are perfect, and without blemish. I am here entangled in the love of the world, while they are swallowed up in the love of God. They have none of my cares and fears; they weep not in secret; they languish not in sorrows; these 'tears are wiped away from their eyes.' O happy, a thousand times happy souls! Alas, that I must dwell in sinful flesh, when my brethren and companions dwell with God! How far out of sight and reach of their high enjoyment do I here live! What poor feeble thoughts have I of God! What cold affections toward him! How little have I of that life, that love, that joy, in which they continually live! How soon doth that little depart, and leave me in thicker darkness! Now and then a spark falls upon my heart, and, while I gaze upon it, it dies, or rather, my cold heart quenches it. But they have their 'light in his light,' and drink continually at the spring of joy. Here we are vexing each other with quarrels, when they are of one heart and voice, and daily sound forth the hallelujahs of heaven with perfect harmony. O what a feast hath my faith beheld, and what a famine is yet in my spirit! O blessed souls! I may not, I dare not envy your happiness; I rather rejoice in my brethren's prosperity, and am glad to think of the day when I shall be admitted into your fellowship. I wish not to displace you, but to be so happy as to be with you. Why must I stay, and weep, and wait? My Lord is gone; He hath left this earth, and is entered into his glory: my brethren are gone; my friends are there; my house, my hope, my all is there. When I am so far distant from my God, wonder not what aileth me if I now complain: an ignorant Micah will do so for his idol, and shall not my soul do so for the living God? Had I no hope of enjoyment, I would go and hide myself in the deserts, and lie and howl in some obscure wilderness, and

spend my days in fruitless wishes; but since it is the land of my promised rest, and the state I must myself be advanced to, and my soul draws near, and is almost there, I will love and long, I will look and desire, I will be breathing, 'How long, Lord! how long wilt thou suffer this soul to pant and groan, and not open to him who waits, and longs to be with thee!'" Thus, Christian reader, let thy thoughts aspire, till thy soul longs, as David, "O that one would give me to drink of the wells of salvation!" And till thou canst say, as he did, "I have longed for thy salvation, O Lord!" And as the mother and brethren of Christ, when they could not come at him because of the multitude, sent to him, saying, "Thy mother and brethren stand without, desiring to see thee"; so let thy message to him be, and he will own thee; for he hath said, "They that hear my word, and do it, are my mother and my brethren."

3. Another affection to be exercised in heavenly contemplation, is *hope*. This helps to support the soul under sufferings, animates it in the greatest difficulties, gives it firmness in the severest trials, enlivens it in duties, and is the very spring that sets all the wheels in motion. Who would believe or strive for heaven, if it were not for the hope he hath of obtaining it? Who would pray, but for the hope of prevailing with God? If your hope dies, your duties die, your endeavors die, your joys die, and your soul dies. And if your hope be not in exercise, but asleep, it is next to dead. Therefore, Christian reader, when thou art raising thy affections to heaven, forget not to give one lift to thy hope. Think thus, and reason thus with thy own heart: "Why should I not confidently and comfortably hope, when my soul is in the hands of so compassionate a Savior, and when the kingdom is at the disposal of so bountiful a God? Did he ever discover the least backwardness to my good, or inclination to my ruin? Hath he not sworn, that 'he delights not in the death of him that dieth, but rather that he should repent and live?' Have not all his dealings witnessed the same? Did he not warn me of my danger when I never feared it, because he would have me escape it? Did he not tell me of my happiness when I had no thoughts of it, because he would have me enjoy it? How often hath he drawn me to himself and

his Christ, when I have drawn backward! How hath his Spirit incessantly solicited my heart! And would he have done all this, if he had been willing that I should perish? Should I not hope, if an honest man had promised me something in his power? And shall I not hope when I have the covenant and oath of God? It is true, the glory is out of sight; we have not beheld the mansions of the saints; but is not the promise of God more certain than our sight? We must not be saved by sight, but 'by hope; and hope that is seen is not hope; for what a man seeth, why doth he yet hope for? But if we hope for that we see not, then do we with patience wait for it.' I have been ashamed of my hope in an arm of flesh, but hope in the promise of God 'maketh not ashamed.' In my greatest sufferings I will say, 'the Lord is my portion; therefore will I hope in him. The Lord is good unto them that wait for him, to the soul that seeketh him. It is good that a man should both hope and quietly wait for the salvation of the Lord; for the Lord will not cast off for ever; but though he cause grief, yet will he have compassion, according to the multitude of his mercies.' Though I languish and die, yet will I hope; for 'the righteous hath hope in his death.' Though I must lie down in dust and darkness, yet there 'my flesh shall rest in hope.' And when my flesh hath nothing to rejoice in, yet will I 'hold fast the rejoicing of the hope firm unto the end'; for 'the hope of the righteous shall be gladness.' Indeed, if I must myself satisfy divine justice, then there had been no hope; but Christ hath 'brought in a better hope, by the which we draw nigh to God.' Or, if I had to do with a feeble creature, there were small hope; for how could he raise this body from the dust and lift me above the sun? But what is this to the Almighty Power which made the heavens and the earth out of nothing? Cannot that power which raised Christ from the dead, raise me? and that which hath glorified the Head, glorify also the members? 'Doubtless, by the blood of his covenant, God will send forth his prisoners out of the pit wherein is no water:' therefore will I 'turn to the strong hold, as a prisoner of hope.'"

4. *Courage*, or boldness, is another affection to be exercised in heavenly contemplation; it leads to resolution, and concludes in action.

When you have raised your love, desire and hope, go on, and think thus with yourself: "Will God indeed dwell with men? And is there such a glory within the reach of hope? Why then do I not lay hold upon it? Where is the cheerful vigor of my spirit? Why do I not 'gird up the loins of my mind'? Why do I not set upon my enemies on every side, and valiantly break through all resistance? What should stop me, or intimidate me? Is God with me, or against me, in the work? Will Christ stand by me, or will he not? 'If God and Christ be for me, who can be against me?' In the work of sin, almost all things are ready to help us, and only God and his servants are against us; yet how ill does that work prosper in our hands! But in my course to heaven, almost all things are against me, but God is for me; and therefore how happily does the work succeed! Do I enter upon this work in my own strength, or rather in the strength of Christ my Lord? And 'cannot I do all things through him that strengthens me?' Was he ever foiled by an enemy? He has indeed been assaulted, but was he ever conquered? Why, then, does my flesh urge me with the difficulties of the work? Is any thing too hard for Omnipotence? May not Peter boldly walk on the sea if Christ give the word of command? If he begin to sink, is it from the weakness of Christ, or from the smallness of his faith? Do I not well deserve to be turned into hell, if mortal threats can drive me thither? Do I not well deserve to be shut out of heaven, if I will be frightened from thence with the reproach of tongues? What if it were father, or mother, or husband, or wife, or the nearest friend I have in the world, if they may be called friends who would draw me to damnation, should I not forsake all that would keep me from Christ? Will their friendship countervail the enmity of God, or be any comfort to my condemned soul? Shall I be yielding to the desires of men, and only harden myself against the Lord? Let them beseech me upon their knees, I will scorn to stop my course to behold them, I will shut my ears to their cries: let them flatter or frown, let them draw out tongues and swords against me; I am resolved, in the strength of Christ, to break through and look upon them as dust. If they would entice me with preferment, even with the kingdoms of the world, I will no more

regard them than the dung of the earth. O blessed rest! O glorious state! Who would sell thee for dreams and shadows? Who would be enticed or affrighted from thee? Who would not strive, and fight, and watch, and run, and that with violence, even to the last breath, in order to obtain thee? Surely none but those that know thee not, and believe not thy glory."

5. The last affection to be exercised in heavenly contemplation, is *joy*. Love, desire, hope and courage, all tend to raise our joy. This is so desirable to every man by nature, and so essentially necessary to constitute our happiness, that I hope I need not say much to persuade you to any thing that would make your life delightful. Supposing you, therefore, already convinced that the pleasures of the flesh are brutish and perishing, that your solid and lasting joy must be from heaven, instead of persuading, I shall proceed in directing. Reader, if thou hast managed well the former work, thou art got within sight of thy rest; thou believest the truth of it; thou art convinced of its excellencies; thou hast fallen in love with it; thou longest after it; thou hopest for it; and thou art resolved to venture courageously for obtaining it. But is here any work for joy in this? We delight in the good we possess; it is present good that is the object of joy; and thou wilt say, "Alas, I am yet without it!" But think a little further with thyself. Is it nothing to have a deed of gift from God? Are his infallible promises no ground of joy? Is it nothing to live in daily expectation of entering into the kingdom of God? Is not my assurance of being hereafter glorified, a sufficient ground for inexpressible joy? Is it not a delight to the heir of a kingdom to think of what he must soon possess, though at present he little differs from a servant? Have we not both command and example for "rejoicing in hope of the glory of God"?

Here then, reader, take thy heart once more and carry it to the top of the highest mount; show it the kingdom of Christ, and the glory of it; and say to it, "All this will thy Lord give thee, who hast believed in him, and been a worshiper of him. 'It is the Father's good pleasure to give thee this kingdom.' Seest thou this astonishing glory which is above thee? All this is thy own inheritance. This crown is thine, these pleasures are thine; this company, this beautiful place, all are thine; because thou art Christ's, and Christ is thine; when thou wast united to him, thou hadst all these with him." Thus take thy heart into the land of promise; show it the pleasant hills and fruitful valleys; show it the clusters of grapes which thou hast gathered, to convince it that it is a blessed land, flowing with better than milk and honey. Enter the gates of the holy city, walk through the streets of the "New Jerusalem, walk about Sion, and go round about her; tell the towers thereof; mark well her bulwarks; consider her palaces; that thou mayst tell it to" thy soul. Has it not "the glory of God," and is not "her light like unto a stone most precious, even like a jasper stone, clear as crystal"? See the "twelve foundations of her walls, and in them the names of the twelve apostles of the Lamb. The walls of it are of jasper; and the city is pure gold, like unto clear glass; and the foundations are garnished with all manner of precious stones; and the twelve gates are twelve pearls, every several gate is of one pearl, and the street of the city is pure gold, as it were transparent glass; there is no temple in it, for the Lord Almighty, and the Lamb, are the temple of it. It hath no need of the sun, neither of the moon in it, for the glory of God doth lighten it, and the Lamb is the light thereof; and the nations of them which are saved shall walk in the light of it. These sayings are faithful and true; and the Lord God of the holy prophets sent his angels," and his own Son, "to show unto his servants the things which must shortly be done." Say now to all this, "This is thy rest, O my soul! and this must be the place of thy everlasting habitation." Let all the sons of "Sion rejoice; let the daughters of Jerusalem be glad; for great is the Lord, and greatly to be praised in the city of our God, in the mountain of his holiness. Beautiful for situation, the joy of the whole earth. is Mount Sion. God is known in her palaces for a refuge."

Yet proceed on; the soul that loves, ascends frequently, and runs familiarly through the streets of the heavenly Jerusalem, visiting the patriarchs and prophets, saluting the apostles, and admiring the armies of martyrs; so do thou lead on thy heart as from street to street; bring it into the palace of the Great King; lead it, as it were, from chamber to chamber. Say to it,

"Here must I lodge; here must I live; here must I praise, here must I love, and be beloved. I must shortly be one of this heavenly choir, and be better skilled in the music. Among this blessed company must I take up my place; my voice must join to make up the melody. My tears will then be wiped away; my groans be turned to another tune; my cottage of clay be changed to this palace; my prison rags to these splendid robes; and my sordid flesh shall be put off, and such a sunlike, spiritual body be put on; 'for the former things are here passed away.' 'Glorious things are spoken of thee, O city of God!' When I look upon this glorious place, what a dunghill and dungeon methinks is earth! O what difference betwixt a man, feeble, pained, groaning, dying, rotting in the grave, and one of these triumphant, shining saints! Here shall I 'drink of the river of pleasures, the streams whereof make glad the city of God.' Must Israel, under the bondage of the law, 'serve the Lord with joyfulness, and with gladness of heart, for the abundance of all things?' Surely I shall serve him with joyfulness and gladness of heart for the abundance of glory. Did persecuted saints 'take joyfully the spoiling of their goods'? and shall not I take joyfully such a full reparation of all my losses? Was it a celebrated 'day wherein the Jews rested from their enemies,' because it 'was turned unto them from sorrow to joy, and from mourning into a good day'? What a day, then, will that be to my soul, whose rest and change will be inconceivably greater? 'When the wise men saw the star' that led to Christ, 'they rejoiced with exceeding great joy'; but I shall shortly see him, who is himself 'the bright and morning Star.' If the disciples 'departed from the sepulcher with great joy,' when they had but heard that their Lord 'was risen from the dead'; what will be my joy, when I shall see him reigning in glory, and myself raised to a blessed communion with him! Then shall I indeed have 'beauty for ashes, the oil of joy for mourning, and the garment of praise for the spirit of heaviness, and Sion shall be made an eternal excellency, a joy of many generations.' Why, then do I not arise from the dust, and cease my complaints? Why do I not trample on vain delights, and feed on the foreseen delights of glory? Why is not my life a continual joy, and the savor of heaven perpetually upon my spirit?"

Let me here observe, that there is no necessity to exercise these affections, either exactly in this order, or all at one time. Sometimes one of thy affections may need more exciting, or may be more lively than the rest; or, if thy time be short, one may be exercised one day and another the next; all which must be left to thy prudence to determine. Thou hast also an opportunity, if inclined to make use of it, to exercise opposite and more mixed affections, such as hatred of sin, which would deprive thy soul of these immortal joys; godly fear, lest thou shouldst abuse thy mercy; godly shame and grief, for having abused it; unfeigned repentance; self-indignation; jealously over thy heart; and pity for those who are in danger of losing these immortal joys.

Thirdly. We are also to take notice how heavenly contemplation is promoted by SOLILOQUY and PRAYER.

Though consideration be the chief instrument in this work, yet, by itself, it is not so likely to affect the heart. In this respect contemplation is like preaching, where the mere explaining of truths and duties is seldom attended with much success as the lively application of them to the conscience; and especially when a divine blessing is earnestly sought to accompany such application.

1. By *soliloquy,* or a pleading the case with thyself, thou must in thy meditation quicken thy own heart. Enter into a serious debate with it. Plead with it in the most moving and affecting language, and urge it with the most powerful and weighty arguments. It is what holy men of God have practiced in all ages. Thus David: "Why art thou cast down, O my soul? and why art thou disquieted within me? Hope thou in God; for I shall yet praise him, who is the health of my countenance, and my God." And again; "Bless the Lord, O my soul! and forget not all his benefits!" This soliloquy is to be made use of according to the several affections of the soul, and according to its several necessities. It is a preaching to one's self; for as every good master or father of a family is a good preacher to his own family, so every good Christian is a good preacher to his own soul. Therefore the very same method

which a minister should use in his preaching to others, every Christian should endeavor after in speaking to himself. Observe the matter and manner of the most heart-affecting minister; let him be a pattern for your imitation; and the same way that he takes with the hearts of his people, do thou also take with thy own heart. Do this in thy heavenly contemplation; explain to thyself the things on which thou dost meditate; confirm thy faith in them by Scripture; and then apply them to thyself according to their nature and thy own necessity. There is no need to object against this, from a sense of thy own inability. Doth not God command thee to "teach the Scriptures diligently unto thy children, and talk of them when thou sittest in thine house, and when thou walkest by the way, and when thou liest down, and when thou risest up"? And if thou must have some ability to teach thy children, much more to teach thyself; and if thou canst talk of divine things to others, why not also to thy own heart?

2. Heavenly contemplation is also promoted by speaking to God in *prayer,* as well as by speaking to ourselves in soliloquy. Ejaculatory prayer may very properly be mixed with meditation, as a part of the duty. How often do we find David, in the same psalm, sometimes pleading with his soul and sometimes with God! The apostle bids us "speak to ourselves in psalms, and hymns, and spiritual songs"; and no doubt we may also speak to God in them. This keeps the soul sensible of the divine presence, and tends greatly to quicken and raise it. As God is the highest object of our thoughts, so our viewing him, speaking to him and pleading with him, more elevates the soul and excites the affections than any other part of meditation. Though we remain unaffected while we plead the case with ourselves; yet, when we turn our speech to God, it may strike us with awe; and the holiness and majesty of him whom we speak to, may cause both the matter and words to pierce the deeper. When we read that "Isaac went out to meditate in the field," the margin says, "to pray"; for the Hebrew word signifies both. Thus, in our meditations, to intermix soliloquy and prayer, sometimes speaking to our own hearts, and sometimes to God, is, I apprehend, the highest step to which we can advance in this heavenly

work. Nor should we imagine it will be as well to take up with prayer alone, and lay aside meditation; for they are distinct duties, and must both of them be performed. We need one as well as the other, and therefore shall wrong ourselves by neglecting either. Besides, the mixture of them, like music, will be more engaging; as the one serves to put life into the other. And our speaking to ourselves in meditation, should go before our speaking to God in prayer. For want of attending to this due order, men speak to God with far less reverence and affection than they would speak to an angel if he should appear to them; or to a judge, if they were speaking for their lives. Speaking to the God of heaven in prayer, is a weightier duty than most are aware of.

Richard Baxter, 1615–91

Praise

A.A. Bonar

Praise ye the Lord: for it is good to sing praises unto our God; for it is pleasant; and praise is comely – Psalm 147:1. Notice that beautiful scene of worship in Revelation 5:6–13, where the four living beings and the four and twenty elders lifted up their golden vials full of odors, which are the prayers of saints. They did so in the sight of Christ – the Lamb, and yet the Lion of the tribe of Judah – appearing with the seven-sealed book in His possession, His claim to the possession of our earth as its only rightful king. On that occasion they held up their vials of prayer, as if saying, Now, Lord, in this Thy day, remember what has been unanswered hitherto. But on that same occasion we are told that they held in the other hand "every one of them a harp," all the while that they showed him the vials full of odors. And what do we learn from this, taking these four living beings and the four and twenty elders, as showing us the Church of God (the saints, I believe, of the Old Testament and the New Testament in one) every one of them holding a harp, just as really as every one of them had a vial full of odors? Is it not the illustration of the text, "Let us offer to Him the sacrifice of praise continually," just as elsewhere it is written, "Pray without ceasing"?

Let us offer "praise continually, even the fruit of our lips giving thanks to His name" (Heb. 13: 15). The praise we are to offer is lips – ever uttering forth thanks to His name.

In the North of Scotland, in the county of Banffshire, some years ago, there was a remarkable wave of blessing which passed from village to village on the seacoast, as if the Lord had a peculiar love for fishermen, remembering the fisherman of Galilee. At this period, three friends were visiting some of these villages. After they had gone through several of them, they came in the evening to one with a population of about five hundred souls. They said to some of the people, "Might we not have a prayer meeting?" The answer they got took them quite by surprise. "Oh, sir, it is all praise here just now. It is all praise." So the friends say, "How? What has happened to you, especially?" The answer was, "Among the adult population there are only four persons that do not profess to have been brought to Christ, and so it is all praise with us here."

PRAISE BEGINS

You see what gives origin to praise; you see where praise, and when praise, really begins. When God takes the sinner out of the miry clay, and when he sets his feet upon the rock, it is then he begins to sing the new song. You may have joined in many a tune, you may have been delighted with many a hymn, but you have never offered praise all your life long to this moment, unless your feet have been taken out of the miry clay and set upon the rock. The new song begins on THE ROCK. And it is a new song. There is not a believer here but will tell you how differently he felt from the moment he saw his Savior, and how completely different was his song of praise onward from that hour. Have you, then, got into the right position for praise? Are your feet upon the rock? "O, Lord," says Isaiah, "I will praise Thee; though Thou wast angry with me, Thine anger is turned away" (Isa. 12:1). See again where praise begins, and what kindles its flame.

There is a very beautiful incident – I do not know if it is often noticed – in the Second Book of Chronicles, chapter 29, in the history of King Hezekiah. He was led to appoint certain arrangements in regard to what we should call the psalmody of the Temple, and one of them is thus stated, "When the burnt offering began, the song of the Lord began also" (v. 27). He appointed that every morning when the sacrifice should be offered, they should sing and blow the trumpets, that all Jerusalem might know that the atoning sacrifice was now presented on Israel's altar. When the offering began, then the song of the Lord began. Again, you see there that true praise begins when the sinner's eye rests upon the sacrifice, when the guilty conscience has felt the power of the atoning blood, and when the sinner's vacant heart has been filled with the Person of the great Sacrifice, the Great Atoner Himself.

PRAISE IS TO BE CONTINUED

We suggested that praise is to be offered continually. It is so written (Heb. 13:15) "continually." We should count it our privilege to be in this continual frame of praise. Does not Psalm 119:164 put it in this way? "Seven times a day do I praise Thee." David says in another psalm, "I pray to Thee at evening, morning, and at noon"; but here it is, "I will praise Thee seven times a day," as if he would even go beyond the other limit in the matter of praise. At all events, we are to be praising continually.

There is no need to fear that we shall want matter, and yet is it not a fact that we do not keep up the freshness of our new song as years go on? And why is this? Is it not because we are not getting a fresh view of the Lamb of God? You observe in a very memorable chapter, the fifth of Revelation, that when they got that new sight of the Lamb, the Lamb with the Book in His possession, holding it up in their view, it is said they sang a new song. "Thou art worthy, for Thou wast slain." I appeal to believers if this is not the case, that every time they get another view of Christ, of His person, of His offering, of His office, of His words, and of His ways, then it is they feel they can sing afresh with their whole soul to Him. And is there no matter in His varied dealings with you personally, as well as endless variety in His varied manifestations of His name?

PRAISE IS NOT MONOTONOUS

But there is a passage, which, perhaps, might seem to a superficial reader to represent the worship in heaven, the praise in heaven, as if it were somewhat monotonous; for one seraph cried to another, says Isaiah in his sixth chapter, "Holy, holy, holy, Lord God of Hosts," and the living beings in the fourth chapter of the Revelation, full of eyes before and behind (intimating a power to look far into the mystery of godliness), are said to rest not day nor night, singing what? Singing this song, "Holy, holy, holy, Lord God Almighty." Now the question arises, Do they always sing that song? Is there no variety? Here, friends, it is good to get some right idea of what that really teaches. You are to pray without ceasing, and to praise without ceasing, "continually;" that is, your heart is to be in that state. You are filled with the groanings that cannot be uttered, and your heart is at the same time in that state, that if the chord only be touched, it is ready to give forth some utterance of adoration.

Now in the passage I have referred to, we are taught that while there may, and will be, a ceaseless variety of subjects for praise to God, yet there pervades the adoration an undertone, and the undertone is, "Holy, holy, holy." There is no levity in the praise of Heaven, there is no lightness in the hymns; they never forget all their songs to sing to the Holy, Holy, Holy One. Oh, there is glorious solemnity in heaven, glorious solemnity amid the rapturous joy of these adoring multitudes! A model surely for us. There should be no levity in our songs. Let our souls be like the seraphs, and like these living beings, who always keep before them the holy one, while they worship the Lamb.

Now, there are many things that might be said about praise; but you remember the Psalms have given us three statements that may guide us. The Book of Psalms says praise is pleasant; it says again, "it is good to sing praise"; and again it says "praise is comely for the upright."

PRAISE IS "PLEASANT"

You know it is pleasant to yourselves; but "praise is pleasant," means more than that. It means it is pleasant to God; it is something that God is pleased with. I should like to show you how truly God takes pleasure in the praises of His saints. Have you not noticed that though

Solomon offered up that remarkable prayer in the Temple in 2 Chronicles 6, recorded by the Holy Spirit, yet the blessing did not come down then. It was a little later, when the multitude of singers were as one in giving forth their praise, and saying, "The Lord is good; His mercy endureth for ever" (2 Chron. 7:3). The cloud of glory came down and filled the Temple as they uttered the burst of praise. And in the history of King Jehoshaphat (2 Chron. 20) going forth to battle against Ammon, Moab, and Seir, Jehoshaphat's remarkable prayer is recorded at full length. Still, it was not then that the victory, or the assurance of victory came; but as he marched out of Jerusalem down the valley of Tekoa, to where he expected to meet the enemy, they made the valley resound with songs. It is said he consulted with the people, and instead of going forth with common martial music, they agreed they would march down the valley with the Lord's song on their lips: and the burden of it is, "for He is good, for His mercy endureth for ever." Now, it is added, that when the song began "the Lord set an ambushment against Moab, and Ammon, and Seir" (2 Chron. 20:22), and Israel did not need to fight; they just came up and gathered the spoils.

Do you see the honor God put upon true praise rendered to Himself? Prayer must be followed by praise. Prayer by itself (the Lord seems to say) is very well, but He wants praise: He must have the harp as well as the golden vial full of odor. We must now have both, as well as those that stand before the Lamb.

And in the prison of Philippi, what do we find? There were Paul and Silas praying. Yes, but they "sang praises," and the emphasis is put upon the praises, for it is said the prisoners heard them, or more correctly, at least, more emphatically, it is, "and the prisoners were listening." You can, as it were, picture them awakening, and expressing wonder to each other, and each putting his ear to the door of his cell. The prisoners were listening! Songs in a prison? Such songs – songs of Zion – had never been heard there before. And it was then that the earthquake shook the prison; and the Lord came down and converted the jailer, a man memorable in the Church of God, and who will be memorable till the Lord comes.

Praise is "pleasant" to the Lord, as well as pleasing to us.

PRAISE IS "GOOD"

Praise is "good"; it is sanctifying. There is something in it tending to build up the soul in sanctification. How could it be otherwise? Praise is the element of heaven. If so, in this praise there must be much of heaven. What are some of the elements of heaven? Surely one is joy holy joy, joy in the Lord. Now, nothing sanctifies more than this joy. Mere sorrow never sanctifies; sorrow, indeed, turns us away from earthly good, but in itself the sorrow of the world worketh death. What sanctifies?

These light afflictions, which are but for a moment, work out for us an exceeding weight of glory, while we look not at the things that are seen, but at the things that are not seen (2 Cor. 4:17, 18). It is joy to which we are led by sorrow that sanctifies – joy in the Lord, joy that is the element of heaven.

And we can at once see there is something unselfish in praise. You can suppose prayer to have a great deal of selfishness in it, and the Lord is quite aware of that; but He does not object to a kind of selfishness in our prayers, that is, that kind of seeking that we ourselves may be receivers of His blessing. But praise is more unselfish, more heaven-like, more, therefore, like Jesus; it is a giving forth of what we have received. And further – I think you will all agree in this, only sing praise truly, and there will be little discontent. I do not know a better remedy for discontent than praise, true praise. Where are your murmurs when you are singing praise? Oh, if those that fret and are discontented at little things or at great things, if they would only substitute for all that, praise, they would soon know it is good to give thanks! Oh, praise is sanctifying! Praise chases away hard thoughts of God which men call "infirmities," and which saints often call "infirmities," but which are really downright corruption, and dishonoring to God, as much as were the murmurs in the camp of Israel.

PRAISE IS "COMELY"

And then praise is "comely." I will not dwell upon this. But you will at once own that praise is very becoming. Only withhold it and you will see what a position you put yourself into. Ask, Is it right to withhold praise? Would it be grateful? Would you feel as if you were putting yourself in a right position? A good man once said, with something of sarcasm, "I think some Christian people are going to make heaven a place of gratitude, and mean to keep all their gratitude until they get there, they show so little here." Praise is comely. To withhold it is most unseemly. Most unseemly in any circumstances; for it matters not what your position is as a saint of God, or your position in the world, or what your afflictions may be, or what your circumstances, praise is still fitting. Every Christian is expected, in all circumstances, to be able to praise continually. All believers, remember. But yet, it is not the case that all saints always do it. One of our old Scots writers, John Livingstone, said in his day, "A line of praise is worth a page of prayer," because he found it such a rare thing. Do you think he exaggerated? He wanted to stir up believers to praise more. And you notice in the Book of Psalms, as it gets near its close, prayer is "almost" forgotten. The four last Psalms are just a burst of praise. The stream is spread: it is not shallower, it is deeper, but it is just joining the ocean, and it is all praise, praise to God.

I would say further, Are you afflicted? You could not do wrong in singing praise. We heard the story of a Welsh girl whose father had died, and the mother came out of the room weeping. The child said, "Mother, what is the matter?" "Oh, what shall I do, my child? Oh, what shall I do?" "Mother, what is the matter?" "Your father is dead, child, and what shall I do?" The child looked up into the mother's face, and said, "Mother, praise the Lord, praise the Lord." The mother was reproved; she went away, and she tried to praise; and as she began to praise the Lord for what was left to her, she soon found that the burden of her heart was lifted. The Lord was left; the Lord with all His grace was still her possession. She was in the position of Habakkuk, who sings, "Though the fig tree shall not blossom, neither shall fruit be in the vines; the labor of the olive shall fail, and the fields shall yield no meat; the flock shall be cut off from the fold, and there shall be no herd in the stalls, yet I will rejoice in the Lord, I will joy in the God of my salvation" (Heb. 3:17, 18).

And then he inscribed his song, "To the chief singer upon my stringed instruments." Was not that a pattern for us? Afflicted one, praise the Lord, and tell your afflicted friends to try praising the Lord.

I would say again, have you some special duty on hand? Then try praise as a preface. You know what they do when armies march. What did the Germans do lately? What did the French do? Had they not got a military song? Did not the Germans sing the "Watch on the Rhine"? And did not the French sing the "Marseillaise"? What should Christian armies do? What did our Captain do before He went to the Mount of Olives, and as He went to the Garden of Gethsemane, the sorest of His conflicts? He sang a hymn – the Master sang a hymn with His disciples. We are almost sure what it was; it was the 118th Psalm, for that was the Psalm with which the Passover service concluded; in that Psalm you find this burst of praise (think of the Master singing it): "The right hand of the Lord doeth valiantly. The right hand of the Lord is exalted: the right hand of the Lord doeth valiantly. I shall not die but live" (Ps. 118: 16, 17). Oh, try that when going out to battle, to duties! In facing difficulties, try praise.

Again, are there anxious souls present today? I wish you to notice, anxious soul, that this subject speaks to you. Try praise! But I want to guard myself against being misunderstood, for I thoroughly agree with what has been sometimes so well stated, that in our day, there are many persons prayed into peace, and there are a great number sung into peace, and the peace is worth nothing. It is excitement; it is not peace founded on the Word, it is peace founded on the feelings. That kind of peace, whether you got it in one way or the other, if it is not founded on the testimony of God concerning His Son, if it is not founded upon what the Father testifies regarding the accepted offering of His beloved Son, is not a solid peace. Tell anxious souls to try praise, notwithstanding; only point out to them this aspect of the matter – tell them to praise the Lamb; tell them to praise Him because He offered Himself as the sacrifice: tell them to fix their eye upon His blood. For, you notice, in the very act of so doing they have forgotten self. Self forgotten, it is the Lamb that is remembered. Worthy is the Lamb! I am all unworthiness; worthy is the Lamb! They have received what they sought.

PRAISE AT CHRIST'S RETURN

I have to make a closing remark. There is a song in reserve for us; Christ is coming, and there is to be a song then, such as we have never yet sung – at least, I suppose very likely that is what is meant by "the song of the Lamb." The song of Moses we know something of, but it is at the Sea of Glass that we shall sing this song of the Lamb. Christ used to sing when He was on earth. We referred to His singing before He went out to the Mount of Olives; and it is said of His people that they too, shall have a song on that very day when Christ comes (Isa. 30:27, 29), a song as in the night, when a holy solemnity is kept. Now, what may we think regarding that song? If the Lord Jesus, at His First Coming, in the night in which He instituted the Lord's Supper, Himself gave thanks in the name of God's Church for after ages, did He not also sing that song for His people, for none could sing as He did? Would you have liked to have heard Him singing it in the upper room?

In the narrative given by Mark, of this story of Gethsemane (14:51), we are told of a young man who seems to have crept under the bushes, wishing to listen to what went on. Perhaps that young man heard some of Christ's strong crying and unutterable groanings. And I think many of us would like to have gone into that upper room, and to have heard Him sing that song, before He went to the Garden. We cannot, however. The time is past; but there is a song in reserve for us which Christ will lead. Yes! we believe that Christ will sing this song Himself. It is written in Psalm 22:22, 25, "In the midst of the congregation will I praise Thee," "My praise shall be of Thee in the great congregation." Oh, what will it be to hear Christ singing then, leading the song of praise, and inviting all His ransomed to join Him! Our voices are only now being tuned for that day when we shall join Him in "The Song of the Lamb" – a song which will be forever, and ever.

A.A. Bonar, 1810–92

Follow the Lamb
Horatius Bonar

Keep company with God, and with the people of God
Intimacy with God is the very essence of religion, and the foundation of discipleship. It is in intercourse with Father, Son, and Spirit that the most real parts of our lives are lived; and all parts that are not lived in fellowship with Him, "in whom we live, and move, and have our being," are unreal, untrue, unsuccessful, and unsatisfying. The understanding of doctrine is one thing, and intimacy with God is another. They ought always to go together; but they are often seen asunder; and, when there is the former without the latter, there is a hard, proud, hollow religion. Get your teaching from God (Job 36:22; Jer 23:30); take your doctrine from His lips; learn truth upon your knees. Beware of opinions and speculations: they become idols, and nourish pride of intellect; they furnish no food to the soul; they make you sapless and heartless; they are like winter frost-work on your windowpane, shutting out the warm sun.

Let God be your companion, your bosom-friend, your instructor, your counselor. Take Him into the closet with you, into the study, into the shop, into the market-place, into the railway carriage, into the boat. When you make a feast and call guests, invite Him as one of them. He is always willing to come; and there is no company like His. When you are in perplexity, and are taking advice from friends, let Him be one of your "friends in counsel." When you feel lonely, make Him the "companion of your solitude." And if you are known to be one given to the divine companionship, you will be saved from much idle and wasteful society and conversation. You will not feel at home with worldly men, nor they with you. You will not choose the half-and-half Christian, or the formalist, or the servant of two masters, for your friend; nor will any of these seek your fellowship. When thrown into worldly society, from your business or your relationships, as you may sometimes be, do not cease to be the Christian; nor try to make excuses for the worldliness of those with whom you are obliged to associate; for that is just making excuses for yourself in associating with them. Do not try to make yourself or them believe that they are religious when they are not; but show them whose disciples you are; not necessarily in words, but by a line of conduct more expressive and efficacious than words. Do not conform to the world in order to please men or to save yourself from their taunt or jest. Be not afraid to ask a blessing at meals, or to have family worship, or to enter into religious conversation, because a worldly man is present. Keep constant company with the great God of heaven and earth; and let every other companionship be regulated by His. Go where you please, if you can take Him with you; go nowhere if He cannot be admitted, or if you are obliged for the time to conceal or disguise your divine discipleship. When Joseph went down to Egypt, he took the young child with him (Matt 2:21); so, wherever you go, take the young child with you.

Beware of declension in prayer. – Whenever you feel the closet becoming a dull place, you may be sure something is wrong. Backsliding has begun. Go straight to God that He may "heal it" (Hosea 14:4). Do not trifle with it; nor resort to other expedients to relieve the dullness, such as shortening the time, or getting some lively religious books to take off the weariness; go at once to the Great Quickener with the cry, "Quicken us, and we will call on Thy name" (Psa 80:18). Beware of going through prayer in a careless or perfunctory way, like a hireling doing his work in order to get done with it. "Pray in the Holy Ghost" (Jude 20). "Pray without ceasing." Pray with honest fervor and simple faith, as men who really want what they ask for, and expect to get it all. Few things tend more to deaden the soul, to harden the heart, to drive out spirituality, than cold, formal prayer. It will eat as doth a canker. Dread it and shun it. Do not mock God by asking what you don't want, or by pretending to desire what you don't care for. "The end of all things is at hand; be ye therefore sober, and watch unto prayer" (1 Peter 4:7).

Be much alone with God. Do not put Him off with a quarter of an hour morning and evening. Take time to get thoroughly acquainted. Converse over everything with Him. Unbosom yourself wholly – every thought, feeling, wish, plan, doubt – to Him. He wants converse with His creatures; shall His creatures not want converse with Him? He wants, not merely to be on "good terms" with you, if one may use man's phrase, but to be intimate; shall you decline the intimacy, and be satisfied with mere acquaintance? What! intimate with the world, with friends, with neighbors, with politicians, with philosophers, with naturalists, or with poets; but not with God! That would look ill indeed. Folly, to prefer the clay to the potter, the marble to the sculptor, this little earth and its lesser creatures to the mighty Maker of the universe, the great "All and in all!"

Do not shrink from being alone. Much of a true man's true life must be so spent. David Brainerd thus writes: – "My state of solitude does not make the hours hang heavy upon my hands. Oh, what reason of thankfulness have I on account of this retirement! I find that I do not, and it seems I cannot, lead a Christian life when I am abroad, and cannot spend time in devotion, in conversation, and serious meditation, as I should do. These weeks that I am obliged now to be from home, in order to learn the Indian tongue, are mostly spent in perplexity and barrenness, without much relish of divine things; and I feel myself a stranger at the throne of grace for want of a more frequent and continued retirement." Do not suppose that such retirement for divine converse will hinder work. It will greatly help it. Much private fellowship with God will give you sevenfold success. Pray much if you would work much; and if you want to work more, pray more. Luther used to say, when an unusual press of business came upon him, "I must pray more to-day." Be like him in the day of work or trial. Do not think that mere working will keep you right or set you right. The watch won't go till the spring is mended. Work will do nothing for you till you have gone to God for a working heart. Trying to work yourself into a better frame of feeling is not only hopeless, but injurious. You say, I want to feel more and to love more. It is well. But you can't work yourself into these. I do not say to any one who feels his coldness, "Go and work." Work, if done heartlessly, will only make you colder. You must go straight to Jesus with that cold heart, and warm it at His cross; then work will be at once a necessity, a delight, and a success.

Horatius Bonar, 1808–82

How the Spirit Enables Us to Pray

Thomas Boston

It is by the help of the Holy Spirit that we are able to pray, Gal 4:6, "And because you are sons, God has sent forth the Spirit of His Son into your hearts, crying out, 'Abba, Father!'" Rom 8:26, "Likewise the Spirit also helps in our weaknesses. For we do not know what we should pray for as we ought, but the Spirit Himself makes intercession for us with groanings which cannot be uttered."

THERE ARE TWO SORTS OF PRAYERS

Firstly, A prayer wrought out by virtue of a gift of knowledge and utterance. This is bestowed on many reprobates, and that gift may be useful to others, and to the church. But as it is merely of that sort, it is not accepted, nor does Christ put it in before the Father for acceptance.

For, secondly, There is a prayer wrought in men by virtue of the Holy Spirit, Zech. 12:10, "And I will pour on the house of David and on the inhabitants of Jerusalem the Spirit of grace and supplication," and that is the only acceptable prayer to God. James 5:16, "Confess your trespasses to one another, and pray for one another, that you may be healed. The effective, fervent prayer of a righteous man avails much." The word "effective" is from the Greek word "inwrought." Right praying is praying in the Spirit. It is a gale blowing from heaven, the breathing of the Spirit in the saints, that carries them out in the prayer, and which comes the length of the throne.

THE SPIRIT HELPS US TO PRAY IN TWO WAYS

1. As a teaching and instructing Spirit, furnishing proper matter of prayer, causing us to know what we pray for, Rom. 8:26, enlightening the mind in the knowledge of our needs, and those of others. The Spirit brings into our remembrance these things, suggesting them to us according to the word, together with the promises of God, on which prayer is grounded, John 14:26, "But the Helper, the Holy Spirit, whom the Father will send in My name, He will teach you all things, and bring to your remembrance all things that I said to you." Hence it is that the saints are sometimes carried out in prayer for things which they had no view of before, and carried by some things they had.

2. As a quickening, exciting Spirit, Rom. 8:26; the Spirit qualifying the soul with praying graces and affections, working in the praying person sense of needs, faith, fervency, humility, etc. Psa 10:17, "Lord, You have heard the desire of the humble; You will prepare their heart; You will cause Your ear to hear."

The man may go to his knees in a very unprepared attitude for prayer, yet the Spirit blows, he is helped. It is for this reason the Spirit is said to make intercession for us, namely, in so far as he teaches and quickens, puts us in a praying frame of mind, and draws out our petitions, as it were, which the Mediator presents.

SPECIAL GIFTEDNESS IN PRAYER?

This praying with the help of the Spirit is particular to the saints, Jam. 5:16; yet they do not have that help at all times, nor always in the same measure; for sometimes the Spirit, being provoked, departs, and they are left in a withered condition. So there is great need to look for a breathing, and pant for it, when we are to go to duty: for if there be not a gale, we will tug at the oars but heartlessly.

Let no man think that a readiness and flowing of expression in prayer, is always the effect of the Spirit's assistance. For that may be the product of a gift, and of the common operations of the Spirit, removing the impediment of the exercise of it. And it is evident one may be scarce of words, and have groans instead of them, while the Spirit helps him to pray, Rom. 8:26. Neither is every flood of emotions in prayer, the effect of the Spirit of prayer. There are of those which puff up a man, but make him never a whit more holy, tender in his walk, etc. But the influences of the Spirit never miss to be humbling but sanctifying. Hence, says David, "But who am I, and who are my people, That we should be able to offer so willingly as this? For all things come from You, and of Your own we have given You," 1 Chr. 29:14; and, says the apostle, "We have no confidence in the flesh," Phil. 3:3.

Thomas Boston, 1676–1723

Praying in the Name of Christ

Thomas Boston

1. NEGATIVELY

It is not a bare faithless mentioning of his name in our prayers, nor finishing our prayers with them, Matt. 7:21. The saints use the words, "through Jesus Christ our Lord," 1 Cor. 15:57, but often is that scabbard produced, while the sword of the Spirit is not in it. The words are said, but the faith is not exercised.

2. POSITIVELY

To pray in the name of Christ is to pray, first, At his command, to go to God by his order, John 16:24, "Until now you have asked nothing in My name. Ask, and you will receive." Christ as God commands all men to pray, to offer that piece of natural duty to God; but that is not the command meant. But Christ as Mediator sends his own to his Father to ask supply of their wants, and allows them to tell that he sent them, as one recommends a poor body to a friend, John 16:24, just cited. So to pray in the name of Christ is to go to God as sent by the poor man's friend. So it implies:

1. The soul's having come to Christ in the first place, John 15:7, "If you abide in Me, and My words abide in you, you will ask what you desire, and it shall be done for you." He that would pray aright, must do as those who made Blastus the king's chamberlain their friend first, and then made their plea to their king, Acts 12:20.

2. The soul's taking its encouragement to pray from Jesus Christ, Heb 4:14, "Seeing then that we have a great High Priest who has passed through the heavens, Jesus the Son of God, let us hold fast our confession. For we do not have a High Priest who cannot sympathize with our weaknesses, but was in all points tempted as we are, yet without sin. Let us therefore come boldly to the throne of grace, that we may obtain mercy and find grace to help in time of need."

The way to the throne in heaven is blocked up by our sins. And sinners have no confidence to seek the Lord. Jesus Christ came down from heaven, died for the criminals, and gathers them to himself by effectual calling. He, as having all interest with his Father, bids them go to his Father in his name, and ask what they need, assuring them of acceptance. And from thence they take their encouragement, viz. from his promises in the word. And he gives them his token with them, which the Father will own, and that is his own Spirit, Rom 8:26,27, "Likewise the Spirit also helps in our weaknesses. For we do not know what we should pray for as we ought, but the Spirit Himself makes intercession for us with groanings which cannot be uttered. Now He who searches the hearts knows what the mind of the Spirit is, because He makes intercession for the saints according to the will of God."

PRAYING TO GOD THROUGH CHRIST

Secondly, it is to direct our prayers to God through Jesus Christ, Heb 7:25, "Therefore He is also able to save to the uttermost those who come to God through Him, since He always lives to make intercession for them," and in chapter 13:15, "Therefore by Him let us continually offer the sacrifice of praise to God, that is, the fruit of our lips, giving thanks to His name."

Praying Christ's name is depending wholly on Christ's merit and intercession for access, acceptance, and a gracious return:

1. Depending on Christ for access to God, Eph 3:12, "In whom we have boldness and access with confidence through faith in Him." There is no access to God but through him, John 14:6, "No one comes to the Father except through Me." They that attempt otherwise to come to God, will get the door thrown in their face. But we must take hold of the Mediator, and come in at his side, who is the Secretary of heaven.

2. Depending on him for acceptance of our prayers, Eph 1:6, "He has made us accepted in the Beloved." Our Lord Christ is the only altar that can sanctify our gift. If one lay the stress of the acceptance of his prayers on his attitude, feelings, tenderness, and so on, the prayer will not be accepted. A crucified Christ only can bear the weight of the acceptance of either our persons or performances.

3. Depending on him for a gracious answer, 1 John 5:14, "Now this is the confidence that we have in Him, that if we ask anything according to His will, He hears us." No prayers are heard and answered but for the Mediator's sake; and

whatever petitions agreeable to God's will are put up to God, in this dependence, are heard.

WHY MUST WE PRAY IN THE NAME OF CHRIST?

The reason of this may be taken up in these two things:

1. There is no access for a sinful creature to God without a Mediator, Isa 59:2, "But your iniquities have separated you from your God: And your sins have hidden His face from you, So that He will not hear." John 14:6, "I am the way, the truth, and the life. No one comes to the Father except through Me." Sin has set us at a distance from God, and has bolted the door of our access to him, that it is beyond our power, or that of any creature, to open it for us. His justice rejects the criminal, his holiness the unclean creature, unless there be an acceptable person to go between him and us. Our God is a consuming fire: and so there is no immediate access for a sinner to him.

2. And there is none appointed nor fit for that work but Christ, 1 Tim. 2:5. It is he alone who is our great High Priest. None but he has satisfied justice for our sins. And as he is the only Mediator of redemption, so he is the only Mediator of intercession, 1 John 2:1, "If anyone sins, we have an Advocate with the Father, Jesus Christ the righteous." The sweet savor of his merit alone is capable to procure acceptance to our prayers, in themselves unworthy, Rev. 8:3,4.

Thomas Boston, 1676–1723

The Ministry of Prayer

E.M. Bounds

The story of prayer is the story of great achievements. Prayer is a wonderful power placed by Almighty God in the hands of His saints, which may be used to accomplish great purposes and to achieve unusual results. Prayer reaches to everything, takes in all things great and small which are promised by God to the children of men. The only limits to prayer are the promises of God and His ability to fulfill those promises.

"Prayer should be the breath of our breath-ing, the thought of our thinking, the soul of our feeling, and the life of our living, the sound of our hearing, the growth of our growing." Prayer in its magnitude is length without end, width without bounds, height without top, and depth without bottom. Illimitable in its breadth, exhaustless in height, fathomless in depths and infinite in extension" (Homer W. Hodge).

The ministry of prayer has been the peculiar distinction of all of God's saints. This has been the secret of their power. The energy and the soul of their work has been the closet. The need of help outside of man being so great, man's natural inability to always judge kindly, justly, and truly, and to act the Golden Rule, so prayer is enjoined by Christ to enable man to act in all these things according to the Divine will. By prayer, the ability is secured to feel the law of love, to speak according to the law of love, and to do everything in harmony with the law of love. God can help us. God is a Father. We need God's good things to help us to "do justly, to love mercy, and to walk humbly before God." We need Divine aid to act brotherly, wisely, and nobly, and to judge truly, and charitably. God's help to do all these things in God's way is secured by prayer. "Ask, and ye shall receive; seek, and ye shall find; knock, and it shall be opened unto you."

In the marvelous output of Christian graces and duties, the result of giving ourselves wholly to God, recorded in the twelfth chapter of Romans, we have the words, "Continuing instant in prayer," preceded by "rejoicing in hope, patient in tribulation," followed by, "Distributing to the necessity of the saints, given to hospitality." Paul thus writes as if these rich and rare graces and unselfish duties, so sweet, bright, generous, and unselfish, had for their center and source the ability to pray. This is the same word which is used of the prayer of the disciples which ushered in Pentecost with all of its rich and glorious blessings of the Holy Spirit. In Colossians, Paul presses the word into the service of prayer again, "Continue in prayer, and watch in the same with thanksgiving."

The word in its background and root means strong, the ability to stay, and persevere stead-fast, to hold fast and firm, to give constant attention to. In Acts, chapter six, it is translated, "Give ourselves continually to prayer." There is in it constancy, courage, unfainting perseverance. It means giving such marked attention to, and such deep concern to a thing, as will make it conspicuous and controlling. This is an advance in demand on "continue." Prayer is to be incessant, without intermission, assiduously, no check in desire, in spirit or in act, the spirit and the life always in the attitude of prayer. The knees may not always be bended, the lips may not always be vocal with words of prayer, but the spirit is always in the act and intercourse of prayer.

There ought to be no adjustment of life or spirit for closet hours. The closet spirit should sweetly rule and adjust all times and occasions. Our activities and work should be performed in the same spirit which makes our devotion and which makes our closet time sacred. "Without intermission, incessantly, assiduously," describes an opulence, and energy, and unabated and ceaseless strength and fullness of effort; like the full and exhaustless and spontaneous flow of an artesian stream. Touch the man of God who thus understands prayer, at any point, at any time, and a full current of prayer is seen flowing from him.

But all these untold benefits, of which the Holy Spirit is made to us the conveyor, go back in their disposition and results to prayer. Not on a little process and a mere performance of prayer is the coming of the Holy Spirit and of His great grace conditioned, but on prayer set on fire, by an unquenchable desire, with such a sense of need as cannot be denied, with a fixed determination which will not let go, and which will never faint till it wins the greatest good and gets the best and last blessing God has in store for us.

The First Christ, Jesus, our Great High Priest, forever blessed and adored be His Name, was a gracious Comforter, a faithful Guide, a gifted Teacher, a fearless Advocate, a devoted Friend, and an all powerful Intercessor. The other, "another Comforter," the Holy Spirit, comes into all these blessed relations of fellowship, authority and aid, with all the tenderness, sweetness, fullness and efficiency of the First Christ. Was the First Christ the Christ of prayer? Did He offer prayers and supplications, with strong crying and tears unto God? Did He

seek the silence, the solitude and the darkness that He might pray unheard and unwitnessed save by heaven, in His wrestling agony, for man with God? Does He ever live, enthroned above at the Father's right hand, there to pray for us?

Then how truly does the other Christ, the other Comforter, the Holy Spirit, represent Jesus Christ as the Christ of prayer! This other Christ, the Comforter, plants Himself not in the waste of the mountain nor far into the night, but in the chill and the night of the human heart, to rouse it to the struggle, and to teach it the need and form of prayer. How the Divine Comforter, the Spirit of Truth, puts into the human heart the burden of earth's almighty need, and makes the human lips give voice to its mute and unutterable groanings!

What a mighty Christ of prayer is the Holy Spirit! How He quenches every flame in the heart but the flame of heavenly desire! How He quiets, like a weaned child, all the self-will, until in will, in brain, and in heart, and by mouth, we pray only as He prays. "Making intercession for the saints, according to the will of God."

E.M. Bounds, The Possibilities of Prayer

Power Through Prayer
E.M. Bounds

CONTENTS

"Recreation to a minister must be as whetting is with the mower – that is, to be used only so far as is necessary for his work. May a physician in plague-time take any more relaxation or recreation than is necessary for his life, when so many are expecting his help in a case of life and death? Will you stand by and see sinners gasping under the pangs of death, and say: 'God doth not require me to make myself a drudge to save them'? Is this the voice of ministerial or Christian compassion or rather of sensual laziness and diabolical cruelty."

Richard Baxter

"Misemployment of time is injurious to the mind. In illness I have looked back with self-reproach on days spent in my study; I was wading through history and poetry and monthly journals, but I was in my study! Another man's trifling is notorious to all observers, but what am I doing? Nothing, perhaps, that has reference to the spiritual good of my congregation. Be much in retirement and prayer. Study the honor and glory of your Master."

Richard Cecil

1. MEN OF PRAYER NEEDED

"Study universal holiness of life. Your whole usefulness depends on this, for your sermons last but an hour or two; your life preaches all the week. If Satan can only make a covetous minister a lover of praise, of pleasure, of good eating, he has ruined your ministry. Give yourself to prayer, and get your texts, your thoughts, your words from God. Luther spent his best three hours in prayer."

Robert Murray McCheyne

We are constantly on a stretch, if not on a strain, to devise new methods, new plans, new organizations to advance the Church and secure enlargement and efficiency for the gospel. This trend of the day has a tendency to lose sight of the man or sink the man in the plan or organization. God's plan is to make much of the man, far more of him than of anything else. Men are God's method. The Church is looking for better methods; God is looking for better men. "There was a man sent from God whose name was John." The dispensation that heralded and prepared the way for Christ was bound up in that man John. "Unto us a child is born, unto us a son is given." The world's salvation comes out of that cradled Son. When Paul appeals to the personal character of the men who rooted the gospel in the world, he solves the mystery of their success. The glory and efficiency of the gospel is staked on the men who proclaim it. When God declares that "the eyes of the Lord run to and fro throughout the whole earth, to show himself strong in the behalf of them whose heart is perfect toward him," he declares the necessity of men and his dependence on them as a channel through which to exert his power upon the world. This vital, urgent truth is one that this age of machinery is apt to forget. The forgetting of it is as baneful on the work of God as would be the striking of the sun from his sphere. Darkness, confusion, and death would ensue.

What the Church needs to-day is not more machinery or better, not new organizations or more and novel methods, but men whom the Holy Ghost can use – men of prayer, men mighty in prayer. The Holy Ghost does not flow through methods, but through men. He does not come on machinery, but on men. He does not anoint plans, but men – men of prayer.

An eminent historian has said that the accidents of personal character have more to do with the revolutions of nations than either philosophic historians or democratic politicians will allow. This truth has its application in full to the gospel of Christ, the character and conduct of the followers of Christ – Christianize the world, transfigure nations and individuals. Of the preachers of the gospel it is eminently true.

The character as well as the fortunes of the gospel is committed to the preacher. He makes or mars the message from God to man. The preacher is the golden pipe through which the divine oil flows. The pipe must not only be golden, but open and flawless, that the oil may have a full, unhindered, unwasted flow.

The man makes the preacher. God must make the man. The messenger is, if possible, more than the message. The preacher is more than the sermon. The preacher makes the sermon. As the life-giving milk from the mother's bosom is but the mother's life, so all the preacher says is tinctured, impregnated by what the preacher is. The treasure is in earthen vessels, and the taste of the vessel impregnates and may discolor. The man, the whole man, lies behind the sermon. Preaching is not the performance of an hour. It is the outflow of a life. It takes twenty years to make a sermon, because it takes twenty years to make the man. The true sermon is a thing of life. The sermon grows because the man grows. The sermon is forceful because the man is forceful. The sermon is holy because the man is holy. The sermon is full of the divine unction because the man is full of the divine unction.

Paul termed it "My gospel"; not that he had degraded it by his personal eccentricities or diverted it by selfish appropriation, but the gospel was put into the heart and lifeblood of the man Paul, as a personal trust to be executed by his Pauline traits, to be set aflame and empowered by the fiery energy of his fiery soul. Paul's sermons – what were they? Where are they? Skeletons, scattered fragments, afloat on the sea of inspiration! But the man Paul, greater than his sermons, lives forever, in full form, feature and stature, with his molding hand on the Church. The preaching is but a voice. The voice in silence dies, the text is forgotten, the sermon fades from memory; the preacher lives.

The sermon cannot rise in its life-giving forces above the man. Dead men give out dead sermons, and dead sermons kill. Everything depends on the spiritual character of the preacher. Under the Jewish dispensation the high priest had inscribed in jeweled letters on a golden frontlet: "Holiness to the Lord." So every preacher in Christ's ministry must be molded into and mastered by this same holy motto. It is a crying shame for the Christian ministry to fall lower in holiness of character and holiness of aim than the Jewish priesthood. Jonathan Edwards said: "I went on with my eager pursuit after more holi-

ness and conformity to Christ. The heaven I desired was a heaven of holiness." The gospel of Christ does not move by popular waves. It has no self-propagating power. It moves as the men who have charge of it move. The preacher must impersonate the gospel. Its divine, most distinctive features must be embodied in him. The constraining power of love must be in the preacher as a projecting, eccentric, an all-commanding, self-oblivious force. The energy of self-denial must be his being, his heart and blood and bones. He must go forth as a man among men, clothed with humility, abiding in meekness, wise as a serpent, harmless as a dove; the bonds of a servant with the spirit of a king, a king in high, royal, in dependent bearing, with the simplicity and sweetness of a child. The preacher must throw himself, with all the abandon of a perfect, self-emptying faith and a self-consuming zeal, into his work for the salvation of men. Hearty, heroic, compassionate, fearless martyrs must the men be who take hold of and shape a generation for God. If they be timid time servers, place seekers, if they be men pleasers or men fearers, if their faith has a weak hold on God or his Word, if their denial be broken by any phase of self or the world, they cannot take hold of the Church nor the world for God.

The preacher's sharpest and strongest preaching should be to himself. His most difficult, delicate, laborious, and thorough work must be with himself. The training of the twelve was the great, difficult, and enduring work of Christ. Preachers are not sermon makers, but men makers and saint makers, and he only is well-trained for this business who has made himself a man and a saint. It is not great talents nor great learning nor great preachers that God needs, but men great in holiness, great in faith, great in love, great in fidelity, great for God – men always preaching by holy sermons in the pulpit, by holy lives out of it. These can mold a generation for God.

After this order, the early Christians were formed. Men they were of solid mold, preachers after the heavenly type – heroic, stalwart, soldierly, saintly. Preaching with them meant self-denying, self-crucifying, serious, toilsome, martyr business. They applied themselves to it in a way that told on their generation, and formed in its womb a generation yet unborn for God. The preaching man is to be the praying man. Prayer is the preacher's mightiest weapon. An almighty force in itself, it gives life and force to all.

The real sermon is made in the closet. The man – God's man – is made in the closet. His life and his profoundest convictions were born in his secret communion with God. The burdened and tearful agony of his spirit, his weightiest and sweetest messages were got when alone with God. Prayer makes the man; prayer makes the preacher; prayer makes the pastor.

The pulpit of this day is weak in praying. The pride of learning is against the dependent humility of prayer. Prayer is with the pulpit too often only official – a performance for the routine of service. Prayer is not to the modern pulpit the mighty force it was in Paul's life or Paul's ministry. Every preacher who does not make prayer a mighty factor in his own life and ministry is weak as a factor in God's work and is powerless to project God's cause in this world.

2. OUR SUFFICIENCY IS OF GOD

"But above all he excelled in prayer. The inwardness and weight of his spirit, the reverence and solemnity of his address and behavior, and the fewness and fullness of his words have often struck even strangers with admiration as they used to reach others with consolation. The most awful, living, reverend frame I ever felt or beheld, I must say, was his prayer. And truly it was a testimony. He knew and lived nearer to the Lord than other men, for they that know him most will see most reason to approach him with reverence and fear."

William Penn of George Fox

The sweetest graces by a slight perversion may bear the bitterest fruit. The sun gives life, but sunstrokes are death. Preaching is to give life; it may kill. The preacher holds the keys; he may lock as well as unlock. Preaching is God's great institution for the planting and maturing of spiritual life. When properly executed, its benefits are untold; when wrongly executed, no evil can exceed its damaging results. It is an easy matter to destroy the flock if the shepherd be unwary or the pasture be destroyed, easy to capture the citadel if the watchmen be asleep or the food and water be poisoned. Invested with such gracious prerogatives, exposed to so great evils, involving so many grave responsibilities, it would be a parody on the shrewdness of the devil and a libel on his character and reputation if he did not bring his master influences to adulterate the preacher and the preaching. In face of all this, the exclamatory interrogatory of Paul, "Who is sufficient for these things?" is never out of order.

Paul says: "Our sufficiency is of God, who also hath made us able ministers of the new testament; not of the letter, but of the spirit: for the letter killeth, but the spirit giveth life." The true ministry is God-touched, God-enabled, and God-made. The Spirit of God is on the preacher in anointing power, the fruit of the Spirit is in his heart, the Spirit of God has vitalized the man and the word; his preaching gives life, gives life as the spring gives life; gives life as the resurrection gives life; gives ardent life as the summer gives ardent life; gives fruitful life as the autumn gives fruitful life. The life-giving preacher is a man of God, whose heart is ever athirst for God, whose soul is ever following hard after God, whose eye is single to God, and in whom by the power of God's Spirit the flesh and the world have been crucified and his ministry is like the generous flood of a life-giving river.

The preaching that kills is non-spiritual preaching. The ability of the preaching is not from God. Lower sources than God have given to it energy and stimulant. The Spirit is not evident in the preacher nor his preaching. Many kinds of forces may be projected and stimulated by preaching that kills, but they are not spiritual forces. They may resemble spiritual forces, but are only the shadow, the counterfeit; life they may seem to have, but the life is magnetized. The preaching that kills is the letter; shapely and orderly it may be, but it is the letter still, the dry, husky letter, the empty, bald shell. The letter may have the germ of life in it, but it has no breath of spring to evoke it; winter seeds they are, as hard as the winter's soil, as icy as the winter's air, no thawing nor germinating by them. This letter-preaching has the truth. But even divine truth has no life-giving energy alone; it must be energized by the Spirit, with all God's forces at its back. Truth unquickened by God's Spirit deadens as much as, or more than, error. It may be the truth without admixture; but without the Spirit its shade and touch are deadly, its truth error, its light darkness. The letter-preaching is unctionless, neither mellowed nor oiled by the Spirit. There may be tears, but tears cannot run God's machinery; tears may be but summer's breath on a snow-covered iceberg, nothing but surface slush. Feelings and earnestness there may be, but it is the emotion of the actor and the earnestness of the attorney. The preacher may feel from the kindling of his own sparks, be eloquent over his own exegesis, earnest in delivering the product of his own brain; the professor may usurp the place and imitate the fire of the apostle; brains and nerves may serve the place and feign the work of God's Spirit, and by these forces the letter may glow and sparkle like an illumined text, but the glow and sparkle will be as barren of life as the field sown with pearls. The death-dealing element lies back of the words, back of the sermon, back of the occasion, back of the manner, back of the action. The great hindrance is in the preacher himself. He has not in himself the mighty life-creating forces. There may be no discount on his orthodoxy, honesty, cleanness, or earnestness; but somehow the man, the inner man, in its secret places has never broken down and surrendered to God, his inner life is not a great highway for the transmission of God's message, God's power. Somehow self and not God rules in the holy of holiest. Somewhere, all unconscious to himself, some spiritual nonconductor has touched his inner being, and the divine current has been arrested. His inner being has never felt its thorough spiritual bankruptcy, its utter powerlessness; he has never learned to cry out with an ineffable cry of self-despair and self-helplessness till God's power and God's fire comes in and fills, purifies, empowers. Self-esteem, self-ability in some pernicious shape has defamed and violated the temple which should be held sacred for God. Life-giving preaching costs the preacher much – death to self, crucifixion to the world, the travail of his own soul. Crucified preaching only can give life. Crucified preach-

ing can come only from a crucified man.

3. THE LETTER KILLETH

"During this affliction I was brought to examine my life in relation to eternity closer than I had done when in the enjoyment of health. In this examination relative to the discharge of my duties toward my fellow creatures as a man, a Christian minister, and an officer of the Church, I stood approved by my own conscience; but in relation to my Redeemer and Savior the result was different. My returns of gratitude and loving obedience bear no proportion to my obligations for redeeming, preserving, and supporting me through the vicissitudes of life from infancy to old age. The coldness of my love to Him who first loved me and has done so much for me overwhelmed and confused me; and to complete my unworthy character, I had not only neglected to improve the grace given to the extent of my duty and privilege, but for want of improvement had, while abounding in perplexing care and labor, declined from first zeal and love. I was confounded, humbled myself, implored mercy, and renewed my covenant to strive and devote myself unreservedly to the Lord."

Bishop McKendree

The preaching that kills may be, and often is, orthodox – dogmatically, inviolably orthodox. We love orthodoxy. It is good. It is the best. It is the clean, clear-cut teaching of God's Word, the trophies won by truth in its conflict with error, the levees which faith has raised against the desolating floods of honest or reckless misbelief or unbelief; but orthodoxy, clear and hard as crystal, suspicious and militant, may be but the letter well-shaped, well-named, and well-learned, the letter which kills. Nothing is so dead as a dead orthodoxy, too dead to speculate, too dead to think, to study, or to pray.

The preaching that kills may have insight and grasp of principles, may be scholarly and critical in taste, may have every minutia of the derivation and grammar of the letter, may be able to trim the letter into its perfect pattern, and illume it as Plato and Cicero may be illumined, may study it as a lawyer studies his textbooks to form his brief or to defend his case, and yet be like a frost, a killing frost. Letter-preaching may be eloquent, enameled with poetry and rhetoric, sprinkled with prayer spiced with sensation, illumined by genius and yet these be but the massive or chaste, costly mountings, the rare and beautiful flowers which coffin the corpse. The preaching which kills may be without scholarship, unmarked by any freshness of thought or feeling, clothed in tasteless generalities or vapid specialties, with style irregular, slovenly, savoring neither of closet nor of study, graced neither by thought, expression, or prayer. Under such preaching how wide and utter the desolation! how profound the spiritual death!

This letter-preaching deals with the surface and shadow of things, and not the things themselves. It does not penetrate the inner part. It has no deep insight into, no strong grasp of, the hidden life of God's Word. It is true to the outside, but the outside is the hull which must be broken and penetrated for the kernel. The letter may be dressed so as to attract and be fashionable, but the attraction is not toward God nor is the fashion for heaven. The failure is in the preacher. God has not made him. He has never been in the hands of God like clay in the hands of the potter. He has been busy about the sermon, its thought and finish, its drawing and impressive forces; but the deep things of God have never been sought, studied, fathomed, experienced by him. He has never stood before "the throne high and lifted up," never heard the seraphim song, never seen the vision nor felt the rush of that awful holiness, and cried out in utter abandon and despair under the sense of weakness and guilt, and had his life renewed, his heart touched, purged, inflamed by the live coal from God's altar. His ministry may draw people to him, to the Church, to the form and ceremony; but no true drawings to God, no sweet, holy, divine communion induced. The Church has been frescoed but not edified, pleased but not sanctified. Life is suppressed; a chill is on the summer air; the soil is baked. The city of our God becomes the city of the dead; the Church a graveyard, not an embattled army. Praise and prayer are stifled; worship is dead. The preacher and the preaching have helped sin, not holiness; peopled hell, not heaven.

Preaching which kills is prayerless preaching. Without prayer the preacher creates death, and not life. The preacher who is feeble in prayer is feeble in life-giving forces. The preacher who has retired prayer as a conspicuous and largely prevailing element in his own character has shorn his preaching of its distinctive life-giving power. Professional praying there is and will be, but professional praying helps the preaching to its deadly work. Professional praying chills and kills both preaching and praying. Much of the lax devotion and lazy, irreverent attitudes in congregational praying are attributable to professional praying in the pulpit. Long, discursive, dry, and inane are the prayers in many pulpits. Without unction or heart, they fall like a killing frost on all the graces of worship. Death-dealing prayers they are. Every vestige of devotion has perished under their breath. The deader they are the longer they grow. A plea for short praying, live praying, real heart praying, praying by the Holy Spirit – direct, specific, ardent, simple, unctuous in the pulpit – is in order. A school to teach preachers how to pray, as God counts praying, would be more beneficial to true piety, true worship, and true preaching than all theological schools.

Stop! Pause! Consider! Where are we? What are we doing? Preaching to kill? Praying to kill? Praying to God! the great God, the Maker of all worlds, the Judge of all men! What reverence! what simplicity! what sincerity! what truth in the inward parts is demanded! How real we must be! How hearty! Prayer to God the noblest exercise, the loftiest effort of man, the most real thing! Shall we not discard forever accursed preaching that kills and prayer that kills, and do the real thing, the mightiest thing – prayerful praying, life-creating preaching, bring the mightiest force to bear on heaven and earth and draw on God's exhaustless and open treasure for the need and beggary of man?

4. TENDENCIES TO BE AVOIDED

"Let us often look at Brainerd in the woods of America pouring out his very soul before God for the perishing heathen without whose salvation nothing could make him happy. Prayer – secret fervent believing prayer – lies at the root of all personal godliness. A competent knowledge of the language where a missionary lives, a mild and winning temper, a heart given up to God in closet religion – these, these are the attainments which, more than all knowledge, or all other gifts, will fit us to become the instruments of God in the great work of human redemption."

Carey's Brotherhood, Serampore

There are two extreme tendencies in the ministry. The one is to shut itself out from intercourse with the people. The monk, the hermit were illustrations of this; they shut themselves out from men to be more with God. They failed, of course. Our being with God is of use only as we expend its priceless benefits on men. This age, neither with preacher nor with people, is much intent on God. Our hankering is not that way. We shut ourselves to our study, we become students, bookworms, Bible worms, sermon makers, noted for literature, thought, and sermons; but the people and God, where are they? Out of heart, out of mind. Preachers who are great thinkers, great students must be the greatest of prayers, or else they will be the greatest of backsliders, heartless professionals, rationalistic, less than the least of preachers in God's estimate.

The other tendency is to thoroughly popularize the ministry. He is no longer God's man, but a man of affairs, of the people. He prays not, because his mission is to the people. If he can move the people, create an interest, a sensation in favor of religion, an interest in Church work – he is satisfied. His personal relation to God is no factor in his work. Prayer has little or no place in his plans. The disaster and ruin of such a ministry cannot be computed by earthly arithmetic. What the preacher is in prayer to God, for himself, for his people, so is his power for real good to men, so is his true fruitfulness, his true fidelity to God, to man, for time, for eternity.

It is impossible for the preacher to keep his spirit in harmony with the divine nature of his high calling without much prayer. That the preacher by dint of duty and laborious fidelity to the work and routine of the ministry can keep himself in trim and fitness is a serious mistake. Even sermon-making, incessant and taxing as an art, as a duty, as a work, or

as a pleasure, will engross and harden, will estrange the heart, by neglect of prayer, from God. The scientist loses God in nature. The preacher may lose God in his sermon.

Prayer freshens the heart of the preacher, keeps it in tune with God and in sympathy with the people, lifts his ministry out of the chilly air of a profession, fructifies routine and moves every wheel with the facility and power of a divine unction.

Mr. Spurgeon says: "Of course the preacher is above all others distinguished as a man of prayer. He prays as an ordinary Christian, else he were a hypocrite. He prays more than ordinary Christians, else he were disqualified for the office he has undertaken. If you as ministers are not very prayerful, you are to be pitied. If you become lax in sacred devotion, not only will you need to be pitied but your people also, and the day cometh in which you shall be ashamed and confounded. All our libraries and studies are mere emptiness compared with our closets. Our seasons of fasting and prayer at the Tabernacle have been high days indeed; never has heaven's gate stood wider; never have our hearts been nearer the central Glory."

The praying which makes a prayerful ministry is not a little praying put in as we put flavor to give it a pleasant smack, but the praying must be in the body, and form the blood and bones. Prayer is no petty duty, put into a corner; no piecemeal performance made out of the fragments of time which have been snatched from business and other engagements of life; but it means that the best of our time, the heart of our time and strength must be given. It does not mean the closet absorbed in the study or swallowed up in the activities of ministerial duties; but it means the closet first, the study and activities second, both study and activities freshened and made efficient by the closet. Prayer that affects one's ministry must give tone to one's life. The praying which gives color and bent to character is no pleasant, hurried pastime. It must enter as strongly into the heart and life as Christ's "strong crying and tears" did; must draw out the soul into an agony of desire as Paul's did; must be an inwrought fire and force like the "effectual, fervent prayer" of James; must be of that quality which, when put into the golden censer and incensed before God, works mighty spiritual throes and revolutions.

Prayer is not a little habit pinned on to us while we were tied to our mother's apron strings; neither is it a little decent quarter of a minute's grace said over an hour's dinner, but it is a most serious work of our most serious years. It engages more of time and appetite than our longest dinings or richest feasts. The prayer that makes much of our preaching must be made much of. The character of our praying will determine the character of our preaching. Light praying will make light preaching. Prayer makes preaching strong, gives it unction, and makes it stick. In every ministry weighty for good, prayer has always been a serious business.

The preacher must be preeminently a man of prayer. His heart must graduate in the school of prayer. In the school of prayer only can the heart learn to preach. No learning can make up for the failure to pray. No earnestness, no diligence, no study, no gifts will supply its lack.

Talking to men for God is a great thing, but talking to God for men is greater still. He will never talk well and with real success to men for God who has not learned well how to talk to God for men. More than this, prayerless words in the pulpit and out of it are deadening words.

5. PRAYER, THE GREAT ESSENTIAL

"You know the value of prayer: it is precious beyond all price. Never, never neglect it."

Sir Thomas Buxton

"Prayer is the first thing, the second thing, the third thing necessary to a minister. Pray, then, my dear brother: pray, pray, pray."

Edward Fayson

Prayer, in the preacher's life, in the preacher's study, in the preacher's pulpit, must be a conspicuous and an all-impregnating force and an all-coloring ingredient. It must play no secondary part, be no mere coating. To him it is given to be with his Lord "all night in prayer." The preacher, to train himself in self-denying prayer, is charged to look to his Master, who, "rising up a great while before day, went out, and departed into a solitary place, and there prayed." The preacher's study ought to be a closet, a Bethel, an altar, a vision, and a ladder, that every thought might ascend heavenward ere it went manward; that every part of the sermon might be scented by the air of heaven and made serious, because God was in the study.

As the engine never moves until the fire is kindled, so preaching, with all its machinery, perfection, and polish, is at a dead standstill, as far as spiritual results are concerned, till prayer has kindled and created the steam. The texture, fineness, and strength of the sermon is as so much rubbish unless the mighty impulse of prayer is in it, through it, and behind it. The preacher must, by prayer, put God in the sermon. The preacher must, by prayer, move God toward the people before he can move the people to God by his words. The preacher must have had audience and ready access to God before he can have access to the people. An open way to God for the preacher is the surest pledge of an open way to the people.

It is necessary to iterate and reiterate that prayer, as a mere habit, as a performance gone through by routine or in a professional way, is a dead and rotten thing. Such praying has no connection with the praying for which we plead. We are stressing true praying, which engages and sets on fire every high element of the preacher's being – prayer which is born of vital oneness with Christ and the fullness of the Holy Ghost, which springs from the deep, overflowing fountains of tender compassion, deathless solicitude for man's eternal good; a consuming zeal for the glory of God; a thorough conviction of the preacher's difficult and delicate work and of the imperative need of God's mightiest help. Praying grounded on these solemn and profound convictions is the only true praying. Preaching backed by such praying is the only preaching which sows the seeds of eternal life in human hearts and builds men up for heaven.

It is true that there may be popular preaching, pleasant preaching, taking preaching, preaching of much intellectual, literary, and brainy force, with its measure and form of good, with little or no praying; but the preaching which secures God's end in preaching must be born of prayer from text to exordium, delivered with the energy and spirit of prayer, followed and made to germinate, and kept in vital force in the hearts of the hearers by the preacher's prayers, long after the occasion has past.

We may excuse the spiritual poverty of our preaching in many ways, but the true secret will be found in the lack of urgent prayer for God's presence in the power of the Holy Spirit. There are preachers innumerable who can deliver masterful sermons after their order; but the effects are short-lived and do not enter as a factor at all into the regions of the spirit where the fearful war between God and Satan, heaven and hell, is being waged because they are not made powerfully militant and spiritually victorious by prayer.

The preachers who gain mighty results for God are the men who have prevailed in their pleadings with God ere venturing to plead with men. The preachers who are the mightiest in their closets with God are the mightiest in their pulpits with men.

Preachers are human folks, and are exposed to and often caught by the strong driftings of human currents. Praying is spiritual work; and human nature does not like taxing, spiritual work. Human nature wants to sail to heaven under a favoring breeze, a full, smooth sea. Prayer is humbling work. It abases intellect and pride, crucifies vainglory, and signs our spiritual bankruptcy, and all these are hard for flesh and blood to bear. It is easier not to pray than to bear them. So we come to one of the crying evils of these times, maybe of all times – little or no praying. Of these two evils, perhaps little praying is worse than no praying. Little praying is a kind of make-believe, a salvo for the conscience, a farce and a delusion.

The little estimate we put on prayer is evident from the little time we give to it. The time given to prayer by the average preacher scarcely counts in the sum of the daily aggregate. Not infrequently the preacher's only praying is by his bedside in his nightdress, ready for bed and soon in it, with, perchance the addition of a few hasty snatches of prayer ere he is dressed in the morning. How feeble, vain, and little is such praying compared with the time and energy devoted to praying by

holy men in and out of the Bible! How poor and mean our petty, childish praying is beside the habits of the true men of God in all ages! To men who think praying their main business and devote time to it according to this high estimate of its importance does God commit the keys of his kingdom, and by them does he work his spiritual wonders in this world. Great praying is the sign and seal of God's great leaders and the earnest of the conquering forces with which God will crown their labors.

The preacher is commissioned to pray as well as to preach. His mission is incomplete if he does not do both well. The preacher may speak with all the eloquence of men and of angels; but unless he can pray with a faith which draws all heaven to his aid, his preaching will be "as sounding brass or a tinkling cymbal" for permanent God-honoring, soul-saving uses.

6. A PRAYING MINISTRY SUCCESSFUL

"The principal cause of my leanness and unfruitfulness is owing to an unaccountable backwardness to pray. I can write or read or converse or hear with a ready heart; but prayer is more spiritual and inward than any of these, and the more spiritual any duty is the more my carnal heart is apt to start from it. Prayer and patience and faith are never disappointed. I have long since learned that if ever I was to be a minister faith and prayer must make me one. When I can find my heart in frame and liberty for prayer, everything else is comparatively easy."

Richard Newton

It may be put down as a spiritual axiom that in every truly successful ministry prayer is an evident and controlling force – evident and controlling in the life of the preacher, evident and controlling in the deep spirituality of his work. A ministry may be a very thoughtful ministry without prayer; the preacher may secure fame and popularity without prayer; the whole machinery of the preacher's life and work may be run without the oil of prayer or with scarcely enough to grease one cog; but no ministry can be a spiritual one, securing holiness in the preacher and in his people, without prayer being made an evident and controlling force.

The preacher that prays indeed puts God into the work. God does not come into the preacher's work as a matter of course or on general principles, but he comes by prayer and special urgency. That God will be found of us in the day that we seek him with the whole heart is as true of the preacher as of the penitent. A prayerful ministry is the only ministry that brings the preacher into sympathy with the people. Prayer as essentially unites to the human as it does to the divine. A prayerful ministry is the only ministry qualified for the high offices and responsibilities of the preacher. Colleges, learning, books, theology, preaching cannot make a preacher, but praying does. The apostles' commission to preach was a blank till filled up by the Pentecost which praying brought. A prayerful minister has passed beyond the regions of the popular, beyond the man of mere affairs, of secularities, of pulpit attractiveness; passed beyond the ecclesiastical organizer or general into a sublimer and mightier region, the region of the spiritual. Holiness is the product of his work; transfigured hearts and lives emblazon the reality of his work, its trueness and substantial nature. God is with him. His ministry is not projected on worldly or surface principles. He is deeply stored with and deeply schooled in the things of God. His long, deep communings with God about his people and the agony of his wrestling spirit have crowned him as a prince in the things of God. The iciness of the mere professional has long since melted under the intensity of his praying.

The superficial results of many a ministry, the deadness of others, are to be found in the lack of praying. No ministry can succeed without much praying, and this praying must be fundamental, ever-abiding, ever-increasing. The text, the sermon, should be the result of prayer. The study should be bathed in prayer, all its duties so impregnated with prayer, its whole spirit the spirit of prayer. "I am sorry that I have prayed so little," was the deathbed regret of one of God's chosen ones, a sad and remorseful regret for a preacher. "I want a life of greater, deeper, truer prayer," said the late Archbishop Tait. So may we all say, and this

may we all secure.

God's true preachers have been distinguished by one great feature: they were men of prayer. Differing often in many things, they have always had a common center. They may have started from different points, and traveled by different roads, but they converged to one point: they were one in prayer. God to there was the center of attraction, and prayer was the path that led to God. These men prayed not occasionally, not a little at regular or at odd times; but they so prayed that their prayers entered into and shaped their characters; they so prayed as to affect their own lives and the lives of others; they so prayed as to make the history of the Church and influence the current of the times. They spent much time in prayer, not because they marked the shadow on the dial or the hands on the clock, but because it was to them so momentous and engaging a business that they could scarcely give over.

Prayer was to them what it was to Paul, a striving with earnest effort of soul; what it was to Jacob, a wrestling and prevailing; what it was to Christ, "strong crying and tears." They "prayed always with all prayer and supplication in the Spirit, and watching thereunto with all perseverance." "The effectual, fervent prayer" has been the mightiest weapon of God's mightiest soldiers. The statement in regard to Elijah – that he "was a man subject to like passions as we are, and he prayed earnestly that it might not rain: and it rained not on the earth by the space of three years and six months. And he prayed again, and the heaven gave rain, and the earth brought forth her fruit" – comprehends all prophets and preachers who have moved their generation for God, and shows the instrument by which they worked their wonders.

7. MUCH TIME SHOULD BE GIVEN TO PRAYER

"The great masters and teachers in Christian doctrine have always found in prayer their highest source of illumination. Not to go beyond the limits of the English Church, it is recorded of Bishop Andrews that he spent five hours daily on his knees. The greatest practical resolves that have enriched and beautified human life in Christian times have been arrived at in prayer."

Canon Liddon

While many private prayers, in the nature of things, must be short; while public prayers, as a rule, ought to be short and condensed; while there is ample room for and value put on ejaculatory prayer – yet in our private communions with God time is a feature essential to its value. Much time spent with God is the secret of all successful praying. Prayer which is felt as a mighty force is the mediate or immediate product of much time spent with God. Our short prayers owe their point and efficiency to the long ones that have preceded them. The short prevailing prayer cannot be prayed by one who has not prevailed with God in a mightier struggle of long continuance. Jacob's victory of faith could not have been gained without that all-night wrestling. God's acquaintance is not made by pop calls. God does not bestow his gifts on the casual or hasty comers and goers. Much with God alone is the secret of knowing him and of influence with him. He yields to the persistency of a faith that knows him. He bestows his richest gifts upon those who declare their desire for and appreciation of those gifts by the constancy as well as earnestness of their importunity. Christ, who in this as well as other things is our Example, spent many whole nights in prayer. His custom was to pray much. He had his habitual place to pray. Many long seasons of praying make up his history and character. Paul prayed day and night. It took time from very important interests for Daniel to pray three times a day. David's morning, noon, and night praying were doubtless on many occasions very protracted. While we have no specific account of the time these Bible saints spent in prayer, yet the indications are that they consumed much time in prayer, and on some occasions long seasons of praying was their custom.

We would not have any think that the value of their prayers is to be measured by the clock, but our purpose is to impress on our minds the necessity of being much alone with God; and that if this feature has not been produced by our faith, then our faith is of a feeble and surface type.

The men who have most fully illustrated Christ in their character, and have most powerfully affected the world for him, have been men who spent so much time with God as to make it a notable feature of their lives. Charles Simeon devoted the hours from four till eight in the morning to God. Mr. Wesley spent two hours daily in prayer. He began at four in the morning. Of him, one who knew him well wrote: "He thought prayer to be more his business than anything else, and I have seen him come out of his closet with a serenity of face next to shining." John Fletcher stained the walls of his room by the breath of his prayers. Sometimes he would pray all night; always, frequently, and with great earnestness. His whole life was a life of prayer. "I would not rise from my seat," he said, "without lifting my heart to God." His greeting to a friend was always: "Do I meet you praying?" Luther said: "If I fail to spend two hours in prayer each morning, the devil gets the victory through the day. I have so much business I cannot get on without spending three hours daily in prayer." He had a motto: "He that has prayed well has studied well."

Archbishop Leighton was so much alone with God that he seemed to be in a perpetual meditation. "Prayer and praise were his business and his pleasure," says his biographer. Bishop Ken was so much with God that his soul was said to be God-enamored. He was with God before the clock struck three every morning. Bishop Asbury said: "I propose to rise at four o'clock as often as I can and spend two hours in prayer and meditation." Samuel Rutherford, the fragrance of whose piety is still rich, rose at three in the morning to meet God in prayer. Joseph Alleine arose at four o'clock for his business of praying till eight. If he heard other tradesmen plying their business before he was up, he would exclaim: "O how this shames me! Doth not my Master deserve more than theirs?" He who has learned this trade well draws at will, on sight, and with acceptance of heaven's unfailing bank.

One of the holiest and among the most gifted of Scotch preachers says: "I ought to spend the best hours in communion with God. It is my noblest and most fruitful employment, and is not to be thrust into a corner. The morning hours, from six to eight, are the most uninterrupted and should be thus employed. After tea is my best hour, and that should be solemnly dedicated to God. I ought not to give up the good old habit of prayer before going to bed; but guard must be kept against sleep. When I awake in the night, I ought to rise and pray. A little time after breakfast might be given to intercession." This was the praying plan of Robert McCheyne. The memorable Methodist band in their praying shame us. "From four to five in the morning, private prayer; from five to six in the evening, private prayer."

John Welch, the holy and wonderful Scotch preacher, thought the day ill spent if he did not spend eight or ten hours in prayer. He kept a plaid that he might wrap himself when he arose to pray at night. His wife would complain when she found him lying on the ground weeping. He would reply: "O woman, I have the souls of three thousand to answer for, and I know not how it is with many of them!"

8. EXAMPLES OF PRAYING MEN

"The act of praying is the very highest energy of which the human mind is capable; praying, that is, with the total concentration of the faculties. The great mass of worldly men and of learned men are absolutely incapable of prayer."

Samuel Taylor Coleridge

Bishop Wilson says: "In H. Martyn's journal the spirit of prayer, the time he devoted to the duty, and his fervor in it are the first things which strike me."

Payson wore the hard-wood boards into grooves where his knees pressed so often and so long. His biographer says: "His continuing instant in prayer, be his circumstances what they might, is the most noticeable fact in his history, and points out the duty of all who would rival his eminence. To his ardent and persevering prayers must no doubt be ascribed in a great measure his distinguished and almost uninterrupted success."

The Marquis DeRenty, to whom Christ was most precious, ordered his servant to call him from his devotions at the end of half an hour. The servant at the time saw his face through an aperture. It was marked with such holiness that he hated to arouse him. His lips were moving, but he was perfectly silent. He waited until three half hours had passed; then he called to him, when he arose from his knees, saying that the half hour was so short when he was communing with Christ.

Brainerd said: "I love to be alone in my cottage, where I can spend much time in prayer."

William Bramwell is famous in Methodist annals for personal holiness and for his wonderful success in preaching and for the marvelous answers to his prayers. For hours at a time he would pray. He almost lived on his knees. He went over his circuits like a flame of fire. The fire was kindled by the time he spent in prayer. He often spent as much as four hours in a single season of prayer in retirement.

Bishop Andrewes spent the greatest part of five hours every day in prayer and devotion.

Sir Henry Havelock always spent the first two hours of each day alone with God. If the encampment was struck at 6 a.m., he would rise at four.

Earl Cairns rose daily at six o'clock to secure an hour and a half for the study of the Bible and for prayer, before conducting family worship at a quarter to eight.

Dr. Judson's success in prayer is attributable to the fact that he gave much time to prayer. He says on this point: "Arrange thy affairs, if possible, so that thou canst leisurely devote two or three hours every day not merely to devotional exercises but to the very act of secret prayer and communion with God. Endeavor seven times a day to withdraw from business and company and lift up thy soul to God in private retirement. Begin the day by rising after midnight and devoting some time amid the silence and darkness of the night to this sacred work. Let the hour of opening dawn find thee at the same work. Let the hours of nine, twelve, three, six, and nine at night witness the same. Be resolute in his cause. Make all practicable sacrifices to maintain it. Consider that thy time is short, and that business and company must not be allowed to rob thee of thy God." Impossible, say we, fanatical directions! Dr. Judson impressed an empire for Christ and laid the foundations of God's kingdom with imperishable granite in the heart of Burmah. He was successful, one of the few men who mightily impressed the world for Christ. Many men of greater gifts and genius and learning than he have made no such impression; their religious work is like footsteps in the sands, but he has engraven his work on the adamant. The secret of its profundity and endurance is found in the fact that he gave time to prayer. He kept the iron red-hot with prayer, and God's skill fashioned it with enduring power. No man can do a great and enduring work for God who is not a man of prayer, and no man can be a man of prayer who does not give much time to praying.

Is it true that prayer is simply the compliance with habit, dull and mechanical? A petty performance into which we are trained till tameness, shortness, superficiality are its chief elements? "Is it true that prayer is, as is assumed, little else than the half-passive play of sentiment which flows languidly on through the minutes or hours of easy reverie?" Canon Liddon continues: "Let those who have really prayed give the answer." They sometimes describe prayer with the patriarch Jacob as a wrestling together with an Unseen Power which may last, not unfrequently in an earnest life, late into the night hours, or even to the break of day. Sometimes they refer to common intercession with St. Paul as a concerted struggle. They have, when praying, their eyes fixed on the Great Intercessor in Gethsemane, upon the drops of blood which fall to the ground in that agony of resignation and sacrifice. Importunity is of the essence of successful prayer. Importunity means not dreaminess but sustained work. It is through prayer especially that the kingdom of heaven suffereth violence and the violent take it by force. It was a saying of the late Bishop Hamilton that "No man is likely to do much good in prayer who does not begin by looking upon it in the light of a work to be prepared for and persevered in with all the earnestness which we bring to bear upon subjects which are in our opinion at once most interesting and most necessary."

9. BEGIN THE DAY WITH PRAYER

"I ought to pray before seeing any one. Often when I sleep long, or meet with others early, it is eleven or twelve o'clock before I begin secret prayer. This is a wretched system. It is unscriptural. Christ arose before day and went into a solitary place. David says: 'Early will I seek thee'; 'Thou shalt early hear my voice.' Family prayer loses much of its power and sweetness, and I can do no good to those who come to seek from me. The conscience feels guilty, the soul unfed, the lamp not trimmed. Then when in secret prayer the soul is often out of tune, I feel it is far better to begin with God – to see his face first, to get my soul near him before it is near another."

Robert Murray McCheyne

The men who have done the most for God in this world have been early on their knees. He who fritters away the early morning, its opportunity and freshness, in other pursuits than seeking God will make poor headway seeking him the rest of the day. If God is not first in our thoughts and efforts in the morning, he will be in the last place the remainder of the day.

Behind this early rising and early praying is the ardent desire which presses us into this pursuit after God. Morning listlessness is the index to a listless heart. The heart which is behindhand in seeking God in the morning has lost its relish for God. David's heart was ardent after God. He hungered and thirsted after God, and so he sought God early, before daylight. The bed and sleep could not chain his soul in its eagerness after God. Christ longed for communion with God; and so, rising a great while before day, he would go out into the mountain to pray. The disciples, when fully awake and ashamed of their indulgence, would know where to find him. We might go through the list of men who have mightily impressed the world for God, and we would find them early after God.

A desire for God which cannot break the chains of sleep is a weak thing and will do but little good for God after it has indulged itself fully. The desire for God that keeps so far behind the devil and the world at the beginning of the day will never catch up.

It is not simply the getting up that puts men to the front and makes them captain generals in God's hosts, but it is the ardent desire which stirs and breaks all self-indulgent chains. But the getting up gives vent, increase, and strength to the desire. If they had lain in bed and indulged themselves, the desire would have been quenched. The desire aroused them and put them on the stretch for God, and this heeding and acting on the call gave their faith its grasp on God and gave to their hearts the sweetest and fullest revelation of God, and this strength of faith and fullness of revelation made them saints by eminence, and the halo of their sainthood has come down to us, and we have entered on the enjoyment of their conquests. But we take our fill in enjoyment, and not in productions. We build their tombs and write their epitaphs, but are careful not to follow their examples.

We need a generation of preachers who seek God and seek him early, who give the freshness and dew of effort to God, and secure in return the freshness and fullness of his power that he may be as the dew to them, full of gladness and strength, through all the heat and labor of the day. Our laziness after God is our crying sin. The children of this world are far wiser than we. They are at it early and late. We do not seek God with ardor and diligence. No man gets God who does not follow hard after him, and no soul follows hard after God who is not after him in early morn.

10. Prayer and Devotion United

"There is a manifest want of spiritual influence on the ministry of the present day. I feel it in my own case and I see it in that of others. I am afraid there is too much of a low, managing, contriving, maneuvering temper of mind among us. We are laying ourselves out more than is expedient to meet one man's taste and another man's prejudices. The ministry is a grand and holy affair, and it should find in us a simple habit of spirit and a holy but humble indifference to all consequences. The leading defect in Christian ministers is want of a devotional habit."

Richard Cecil

Never was there greater need for saintly men and women; more imperative still is the call for saintly, God-devoted preachers. The world moves with gigantic strides. Satan has his hold and rule on the world, and labors to make all its movements subserve his ends. Religion must do its best work, present its most attractive and perfect models. By every means, modern sainthood must be inspired by the loftiest ideals and by the largest possibilities through the Spirit. Paul lived on his knees, that the Ephesian Church might measure the heights, breadths, and depths of an unmeasurable saintliness, and "be filled with all the fullness of God." Epaphras laid himself out with the exhaustive toil and strenuous conflict of fervent prayer, that the Colossian Church might "stand perfect and complete in all the will of God." Everywhere, everything in apostolic times was on the stretch that the people of God might each and "all come in the unity of the faith, and of the knowledge of the Son of God, unto a perfect man, unto the measure of the stature of the fullness of Christ." No premium was given to dwarfs; no encouragement to an old babyhood. The babies were to grow; the old, instead of feebleness and infirmities, were to bear fruit in old age, and be fat and flourishing. The divinest thing in religion is holy men and holy women.

No amount of money, genius, or culture can move things for God. Holiness energizing the soul, the whole man aflame with love, with desire for more faith, more prayer, more zeal, more consecration – this is the secret of power. These we need and must have, and men must be the incarnation of this God-inflamed devotedness. God's advance has been stayed, his cause crippled: his name dishonored for their lack. Genius (though the loftiest and most gifted), education (though the most learned and refined), position, dignity, place, honored names, high ecclesiastics cannot move this chariot of our God. It is a fiery one, and fiery forces only can move it. The genius of a Milton fails. The imperial strength of a Leo fails. Brainerd's spirit can move it. Brainerd's spirit was on fire for God, on fire for souls. Nothing earthly, worldly, selfish came in to abate in the least the intensity of this all-impelling and all-consuming force and flame.

Prayer is the creator as well as the channel of devotion. The spirit of devotion is the spirit of prayer. Prayer and devotion are united as soul and body are united, as life and the heart are united. There is no real prayer without devotion, no devotion without prayer. The preacher must be surrendered to God in the holiest devotion. He is not a professional man, his ministry is not a profession; it is a divine institution, a divine devotion. He is devoted to God. His aim, aspirations, ambition are for God and to God, and to such prayer is as essential as food is to life.

The preacher, above everything else, must be devoted to God. The preacher's relations to God are the insignia and credentials of his ministry. These must be clear, conclusive, unmistakable. No common, surface type of piety must be his. If he does not excel in grace, he does not excel at all. If he does not preach by life, character, conduct, he does not preach at all. If his piety be light, his preaching may be as soft and as sweet as music, as gifted as Apollo, yet its weight will be a feather's weight, visionary, fleeting as the morning cloud or the early dew. Devotion to God – there is no substitute for this in the preacher's character and conduct. Devotion to a Church, to opinions, to an organization, to orthodoxy – these are paltry, misleading, and vain when they become the source of inspiration, the animus of a call. God must be the mainspring of the preacher's effort, the fountain and crown of all his toil. The name and honor of Jesus Christ, the advance of his cause, must be all in all. The preacher must have no inspiration but the name of Jesus Christ, no ambition but to have him glorified, no toil but for him. Then prayer will be a source of his illuminations, the means of perpetual advance, the gauge of his success. The perpetual aim, the only ambition, the preacher can cherish is to have God with him.

Never did the cause of God need perfect illustrations of the possibilities of prayer more than in this age. No age, no person, will be examples of the gospel power except the ages or persons of deep and earnest prayer. A prayerless age will have but scant models of divine power. Prayerless hearts will never rise to these Alpine heights. The age may be a better age than the past, but there is an infinite distance between the betterment of an age by the force of an advancing civilization and its betterment by the increase of holiness and Christlikeness by the energy of prayer. The Jews were much better when Christ came than in the ages before. It was the golden age of their Pharisaic religion. Their golden religious age crucified Christ. Never more praying, never

less praying; never more sacrifices, never less sacrifice; never less idolatry, never more idolatry; never more of temple worship, never less of God worship; never more of lip service, never less of heart service (God worshiped by lips whose hearts and hands crucified God's Son!); never more of churchgoers, never less of saints.

It is prayer-force which makes saints. Holy characters are formed by the power of real praying. The more of true saints, the more of praying; the more of praying, the more of true saints.

11. AN EXAMPLE OF DEVOTION

"I urge upon you communion with Christ a growing communion. There are curtains to be drawn aside in Christ that we never saw, and new foldings of love in him. I despair that I shall ever win to the far end of that love, there are so many plies in it. Therefore dig deep, and sweat and labor and take pains for him, and set by as much time in the day for him as you can. We will be won in the labor."

Samuel Rutherford

God has now, and has had, many of these devoted, prayerful preachers – men in whose lives prayer has been a mighty, controlling, conspicuous force. The world has felt their power, God has felt and honored their power, God's cause has moved mightily and swiftly by their prayers, holiness has shone out in their characters with a divine effulgence.

God found one of the men he was looking for in David Brainerd, whose work and name have gone into history. He was no ordinary man, but was capable of shining in any company, the peer of the wise and gifted ones, eminently suited to fill the most attractive pulpits and to labor among the most refined and the cultured, who were so anxious to secure him for their pastor. President Edwards bears testimony that he was "a young man of distingushed talents, had extraordinary knowledge of men and things, had rare conversational powers, excelled in his knowledge of theology, and was truly, for one so young, an extraordinary divine, and especially in all matters relating to experimental religion. I never knew his equal of his age and standing for clear and accurate notions of the nature and essence of true religion. His manner in prayer was almost inimitable, such as I have very rarely known equaled. His learning was very considerable, and he had extraordinary gifts for the pulpit."

No sublimer story has been recorded in earthly annals than that of David Brainerd; no miracle attests with diviner force the truth of Christianity than the life and work of such a man. Alone in the savage wilds of America, struggling day and night with a mortal disease, unschooled in the care of souls, having access to the Indians for a large portion of time only through the bungling medium of a pagan interpreter, with the Word of God in his heart and in his hand, his soul fired with the divine flame, a place and time to pour out his soul to God in prayer, he fully established the worship of God and secured all its gracious results. The Indians were changed with a great change from the lowest besotments of an ignorant and debased heathenism to pure, devout, intelligent Christians; all vice reformed, the external duties of Christianity at once embraced and acted on; family prayer set up; the Sabbath instituted and religiously observed; the internal graces of religion exhibited with growing sweetness and strength. The solution of these results is found in David Brainerd himself, not in the conditions or accidents but in the man Brainerd. He was God's man, for God first and last and all the time. God could flow unhindered through him. The omnipotence of grace was neither arrested nor straightened by the conditions of his heart; the whole channel was broadened and cleaned out for God's fullest and most powerful passage, so that God with all his mighty forces could come down on the hopeless, savage wilderness, and transform it into his blooming and fruitful garden; for nothing is too hard for God to do if he can get the right kind of a man to do it with.

Brainerd lived the life of holiness and prayer. His diary is full and monotonous with the record of his seasons of fasting, meditation, and retirement. The time he spent in private prayer amounted to many hours daily. "When I return home," he said, "and give myself to meditation, prayer, and fasting, my soul longs for mortification, self-denial, humility, and divorcement from all things of the world." "I have nothing to do," he said, "with earth but only to labor in it honestly for God. I do not desire to live one minute for anything which earth can afford." After this high order did he pray: "Feeling somewhat of the sweetness of communion with God and the constraining force of his love, and how admirably it captivates the soul and makes all the desires and affections to center in God, I set apart this day for secret fasting and prayer, to entreat God to direct and bless me with regard to the great work which I have in view of preaching the gospel, and that the Lord would return to me and show me the light of his countenance. I had little life and power in the forenoon. Near the middle of the afternoon God enabled me to wrestle ardently in intercession for my absent friends, but just at night the Lord visited me marvelously in prayer. I think my soul was never in such agony before. I felt no restraint, for the treasures of divine grace were opened to me. I wrestled for absent friends, for the ingathering of souls, for multitudes of poor souls, and for many that I thought were the children of God, personally, in many distant places. I was in such agony from sun half an hour high till near dark that I was all over wet with sweat, but yet it seemed to me I had done nothing. O, my dear Savior did sweat blood for poor souls! I longed for more compassion toward them. I felt still in a sweet frame, under a sense of divine love and grace, and went to bed in such a frame, with my heart set on God." It was prayer which gave to his life and ministry their marvelous power.

The men of mighty prayer are men of spiritual might. Prayers never die. Brainerd's whole life was a life of prayer. By day and by night he prayed. Before preaching and after preaching he prayed. Riding through the interminable solitudes of the forests he prayed. On his bed of straw he prayed. Retiring to the dense and lonely forests, he prayed. Hour by hour, day after day, early morn and late at night, he was praying and fasting, pouring out his soul, interceding, communing with God. He was with God mightily in prayer, and God was with him mightily, and by it he being dead yet speaketh and worketh, and will speak and work till the end comes, and among the to glorious ones of that glorious day he will be with the first.

Jonathan Edwards says of him: "His life shows the right way to success in the works of the ministry. He sought it as the soldier seeks victory in a siege or battle; or as a man that runs a race for a great prize. Animated with love to Christ and souls, how did he labor? Always fervently. Not only in word and doctrine, in public and in private, but in prayers by day and night, wrestling with God in secret and travailing in birth with unutterable groans and agonies, until Christ was formed in the hearts of the people to whom he was sent. Like a true son of Jacob, he persevered in wrestling through all the darkness of the night, until the breaking of the day!"

12. HEART PREPARATION NECESSARY

"For nothing reaches the heart but what is from the heart or pierces the conscience but what comes from a living conscience."

William Penn

"In the morning was more engaged in preparing the head than the heart. This has been frequently my error, and I have always felt the evil of it especially in prayer. Reform it then, O Lord! Enlarge my heart and I shall preach."

Robert Murray McCheyne

"A sermon that has more head infused into it than heart will not borne home with efficacy to the hearers."

Richard Cecil

Prayer, with its manifold and many-sided forces, helps the mouth to utter the truth in its fullness and freedom. The preacher is to be prayed for, the preacher is made by prayer. The preacher's mouth is to be prayed for; his mouth is to be opened and filled by prayer. A holy mouth is made by praying, by much praying; a brave mouth is made by praying, by much praying. The Church and the world, God and heaven, owe much to Paul's mouth; Paul's mouth owed its power to prayer.

How manifold, illimitable, valuable, and helpful prayer is to the preacher in so many ways, at so many points, in every way! One great value is, it helps his heart.

Praying makes the preacher a heart preach-

er. Prayer puts the preacher's heart into the preacher's sermon; prayer puts the preacher's sermon into the preacher's heart.

The heart makes the preacher. Men of great hearts are great preachers. Men of bad hearts may do a measure of good, but this is rare. The hireling and the stranger may help the sheep at some points, but it is the good shepherd with the good shepherd's heart who will bless the sheep and answer the full measure of the shepherd's place.

We have emphasized sermon-preparation until we have lost sight of the important thing to be prepared – the heart. A prepared heart is much better than a prepared sermon. A prepared heart will make a prepared sermon.

Volumes have been written laying down the mechanics and taste of sermon-making, until we have become possessed with the idea that this scaffolding is the building. The young preacher has been taught to lay out all his strength on the form, taste, and beauty of his sermon as a mechanical and intellectual product. We have thereby cultivated a vicious taste among the people and raised the clamor for talent instead of grace, eloquence instead of piety, rhetoric instead of revelation, reputation and brilliancy instead of holiness. By it we have lost the true idea of preaching, lost preaching power, lost pungent conviction for sin, lost the rich experience and elevated Christian character, lost the authority over consciences and lives which always results from genuine preaching.

It would not do to say that preachers study too much. Some of them do not study at all; others do not study enough. Numbers do not study the right way to show themselves workmen approved of God. But our great lack is not in head culture, but in heart culture; not lack of knowledge but lack of holiness is our sad and telling defect – not that we know too much, but that we do not meditate on God and his word and watch and fast and pray enough. The heart is the great hindrance to our preaching. Words pregnant with divine truth find in our hearts nonconductors; arrested, they fall shorn and powerless.

Can ambition, that lusts after praise and place, preach the gospel of Him who made himself of no reputation and took on Him the form of a servant? Can the proud, the vain, the egotistical preach the gospel of him who was meek and lowly? Can the bad-tempered. passionate, selfish, hard, worldly man preach the system which teems with long-suffering, self-denial, tenderness, which imperatively demands separation from enmity and crucifixion to the world? Can the hireling official, heartless, perfunctory, preach the gospel which demands the shepherd to give his life for the sheep? Can the covetous man, who counts salary and money, preach the gospel till he has gleaned his heart and can say in the spirit of Christ and Paul in the words of Wesley: "I count it dung and dross; I trample it under my feet; I (yet not I, but the grace of God in me) esteem it just as the mire of the streets, I desire it not, I seek it not?" God's revelation does not need the light of human genius, the polish and strength of human culture, the brilliancy of human thought, the force of human brains to adorn or enforce it; but it does demand the simplicity, the docility, humility, and faith of a child's heart.

It was this surrender and subordination of intellect and genius to the divine and spiritual forces which made Paul peerless among the apostles. It was this which gave Wesley his power and radicated his labors in the history of humanity. This gave to Loyola the strength to arrest the retreating forces of Catholicism.

Our great need is heart-preparation. Luther held it as an axiom: "He who has prayed well has studied well." We do not say that men are not to think and use their intellects; but he will use his intellect best who cultivates his heart most. We do not say that preachers should not be students; but we do say that their great study should be the Bible, and he studies the Bible best who has kept his heart with diligence. We do not say that the preacher should not know men, but he will be the greater adept in human nature who has fathomed the depths and intricacies of his own heart. We do say that while the channel of preaching is the mind, its fountain is the heart; you may broaden and deepen the channel, but if you do not look well to the purity and depth of the fountain, you will have a dry or polluted channel. We do say that almost any man of common intelligence has sense enough to preach the gospel, but

very few have grace enough to do so. We do say that he who has struggled with his own heart and conquered it; who has taught it humility, faith, love, truth, mercy, sympathy, courage; who can pour the rich treasures of the heart thus trained, through a manly intellect, all surcharged with the power of the gospel on the consciences of his hearers – such a one will be the truest, most successful preacher in the esteem of his Lord.

13. GRACE FROM THE HEART RATHER THAN THE HEAD

"Study not to be a fine preacher. Jerichos are blown down with rams' horns. Look simply unto Jesus for preaching food; and what is wanted will be given, and what is given will be blessed, whether it be a barley grain or a wheaten loaf, a crust or a crumb. Your mouth will be a flowing stream or a fountain sealed, according as your heart is. Avoid all controversy in preaching, talking, or writing; preach nothing down but the devil, and nothing up but Jesus Christ."

Berridge

The heart is the Savior of the world. Heads do not save. Genius, brains, brilliancy, strength, natural gifts do not save. The gospel flows through hearts. All the mightiest forces are heart forces. All the sweetest and loveliest graces are heart graces. Great hearts make great characters; great hearts make divine characters. God is love. There is nothing greater than love, nothing greater than God. Hearts make heaven; heaven is love. There is nothing higher, nothing sweeter, than heaven. It is the heart and not the head which makes God's great preachers. The heart counts much every way in religion. The heart must speak from the pulpit. The heart must hear in the pew. In fact, we serve God with our hearts. Head homage does not pass current in heaven.

We believe that one of the serious and most popular errors of the modern pulpit is the putting of more thought than prayer, of more head than of heart in its sermons. Big hearts make big preachers; good hearts make good preachers. A theological school to enlarge and cultivate the heart is the golden desideratum of the gospel. The pastor binds his people to him and rules his people by his heart. They may admire his gifts, they may be proud of his ability, they may be affected for the time by his sermons; but the stronghold of his power is his heart. His scepter is love. The throne of his power is his heart.

The good shepherd gives his life for the sheep. Heads never make martyrs. It is the heart which surrenders the life to love and fidelity. It takes great courage to be a faithful pastor, but the heart alone can supply this courage. Gifts and genius may be brave, but it is the gifts and genius of the heart and not of the head.

It is easier to fill the head than it is to prepare the heart. It is easier to make a brain sermon than a heart sermon. It was heart that drew the Son of God from heaven. It is heart that will draw men to heaven. Men of heart is what the world needs to sympathize with its woe, to kiss away its sorrows, to compassionate its misery, and to alleviate its pain. Christ was eminently the man of sorrows, because he was preeminently the man of heart.

"Give me thy heart," is God's requisition of men. "Give me thy heart!" is man's demand of man.

A professional ministry is a heartless ministry. When salary plays a great part in the ministry, the heart plays little part. We may make preaching our business, and not put our hearts in the business. He who puts self to the front in his preaching puts heart to the rear. He who does not sow with his heart in his study will never reap a harvest for God. The closet is the heart's study. We will learn more about how to preach and what to preach there than we can learn in our libraries. "Jesus wept" is the shortest and biggest verse in the Bible. It is he who goes forth *weeping* (not preaching great sermons), bearing precious seed, who shall come again rejoicing, bringing his sheaves with him.

Praying gives sense, brings wisdom, broadens and strengthens the mind. The closet is a perfect school-teacher and schoolhouse for the preacher. Thought is not only brightened and clarified in prayer, but thought is born in prayer. We can learn more in an hour praying, when praying indeed, than from many hours in the study. Books are in the closet which can be found and read nowhere else. Revelations are made in the closet which are made nowhere else.

14. Unction a Necessity
"One bright benison which private prayer brings down upon the ministry is an indescribable and inimitable something – an unction from the Holy One … If the anointing which we bear come not from the Lord of hosts, we are deceivers, since only in prayer can we obtain it. Let us continue instant constant fervent in supplication. Let your fleece lie on the thrashing floor of supplication till it is wet with the dew of heaven."

Charles Haddon Spurgeon

Alexander Knox, a Christian philosopher of the days of Wesley, not an adherent but a strong personal friend of Wesley, and with much spiritual sympathy with the Wesleyan movement, writes: "It is strange and lamentable, but I verily believe the fact to be that except among Methodists and Methodist clergyman, there is not much interesting preaching in England. The clergy, too generally have absolutely lost the art. There is, I conceive, in the great laws of the moral world a kind of secret understanding like the affinities in chemistry, between rightly promulgated religious truth and the deepest feelings of the human mind. Where the one is duly exhibited, the other will respond. Did not our hearts burn within us? – but to this devout feeling is indispensable in the speaker. Now, I am obliged to state from my own observation that this *onction*, as the French not unfitly term it, is beyond all comparison more likely to be found in England in a Methodist conventicle than in a parish Church. This, and this alone, seems really to be that which fills the Methodist houses and thins the Churches. I am, I verily think, no enthusiast; I am a most sincere and cordial churchman, a humble disciple of the School of Hale and Boyle, of Burnet and Leighton. Now I must aver that when I was in this country, two years ago, I did not hear a single preacher who taught me like my own great masters but such as are deemed Methodistical. And I now despair of getting an atom of heart instruction from any other quarter. The Methodist preachers (however I may not always approve of all their expressions) do most assuredly diffuse this true religion and undefiled. I felt real pleasure last Sunday. I can bear witness that the preacher did at once speak the words of truth and soberness. There was no eloquence – the honest man never dreamed of such a thing – but there was far better: a cordial communication of vitalized truth. I say vitalized because what he declared to others it was impossible not to feel he lived on himself."

This unction is the art of preaching. The preacher who never had this unction never had the art of preaching. The preacher who has lost this unction has lost the art of preaching. Whatever other arts he may have and retain – the art of sermon-making, the art of eloquence, the art of great, clear thinking, the art of pleasing an audience – he has lost the divine art of preaching. This unction makes God's truth powerful and interesting, draws and attracts, edifies, convicts, saves.

This unction vitalizes God's revealed truth, makes it living and life-giving. Even God's truth spoken without this unction is light, dead, and deadening. Though abounding in truth, though weighty with thought, though sparkling with rhetoric, though pointed by logic, though powerful by earnestness, without this divine unction it issues in death and not in life. Mr. Spurgeon says: "I wonder how long we might beat our brains before we could plainly put into word what is meant by preaching with unction. Yet he who preaches knows its presence, and he who hears soon detects its absence. Samaria, in famine, typifies a discourse without it. Jerusalem, with her feast of fat things, full of marrow, may represent a sermon enriched with it. Every one knows what the freshness of the morning is when orient pearls abound on every blade of grass, but who can describe it, much less produce it of itself? Such is the mystery of spiritual anointing. We know, but we cannot tell to others what it is. It is as easy as it is foolish, to counterfeit it. Unction is a thing which you cannot manufacture, and its counterfeits are worse than worthless. Yet it is, in itself, priceless, and beyond measure needful if you would edify believers and bring sinners to Christ."

15. UNCTION, THE MARK OF TRUE GOSPEL PREACHING
"Speak for eternity. Above all things, cultivate your own spirit. A word spoken by you when your conscience is clear and your heart full of God's Spirit is worth ten thousand words spoken in unbelief and sin. Remember that God, and not man, must have the glory. If the veil of the world's machinery were lifted off, how much we would find is done in answer to the prayers of God's children."

Robert Murray McCheyne

Unction is that indefinable, indescribable something which an old, renowned Scotch preacher describes thus: "There is sometimes somewhat in preaching that cannot be ascribed either to matter or expression, and cannot be described what it is, or from whence it cometh, but with a sweet violence it pierceth into the heart and affections and comes immediately from the Word; but if there be any way to obtain such a thing, it is by the heavenly disposition of the speaker."

We call it unction. It is this unction which makes the word of God "quick and powerful, and sharper than any two-edged sword, piercing even to the dividing asunder of soul and spirit, and of the joints and marrow, and a discerner of the thoughts and intents of the heart." It is this unction which gives the words of the preacher such point, sharpness, and power, and which creates such friction and stir in many a dead congregation. The same truths have been told in the strictness of the letter, smooth as human oil could make them; but no signs of life, not a pulse throb; all as peaceful as the grave and as dead. The same preacher in the meanwhile receives a baptism of this unction, the divine inflatus is on him, the letter of the Word has been embellished and fired by this mysterious power, and the throbbings of life begin – life which receives or life which resists. The unction pervades and convicts the conscience and breaks the heart.

This divine unction is the feature which separates and distinguishes true gospel preaching from all other methods of presenting the truth, and which creates a wide spiritual chasm between the preacher who has it and the one who has it not. It endues revealed truth with all the energy of God. Unction is simply putting God in his own word and on his own preachers. By mighty and great prayerfulness and by continual prayerfulness, it is all potential and personal to the preacher; it inspires and clarifies his intellect, gives insight and grasp and projecting power; it gives to the preacher heart power, which is greater than head power; and tenderness, purity, force flow from the heart by it. Enlargement, freedom, fullness of thought, directness and simplicity of utterance are the fruits of this unction.

Often earnestness is mistaken for this unction. He who has the divine unction will be earnest in the very spiritual nature of things, but there may be a vast deal of earnestness without the least mixture of unction.

Earnestness and unction look alike from some points of view. Earnestness may be readily and without detection substituted or mistaken for unction. It requires a spiritual eye and a spiritual taste to discriminate.

Earnestness may be sincere, serious, ardent, and persevering. It goes at a thing with good will, pursues it with perseverance, and urges it with ardor; puts force in it. But all these forces do not rise higher than the mere human. The *man* is in it – the whole man, with all that he has of will and heart, of brain and genius, of planning and working and talking. He has set himself to some purpose which has mastered him, and he pursues to master it. There may be none of God in it. There may be little of God in it, because there is so much of the man in it. He may present pleas in advocacy of his earnest purpose which please or touch and move or overwhelm with conviction of their importance; and in all this earnestness may move along earthly ways, being propelled by human forces only, its altar made by earthly hands and its fire kindled by earthly flames. It is said of a rather famous preacher of gifts, whose construction of Scripture was to his fancy or purpose, that he "grew very eloquent over his own exegesis." So men grow exceeding earnest over their own plans or movements. Earnestness may be selfishness simulated.

What of unction? It is the indefinable in preaching which makes it preaching. It is that which distinguishes and separates preaching from all mere human addresses. It is the divine in preaching. It makes the preaching sharp to those who need sharpness. It distills as the dew to those who need to he refreshed. It is well described as:

A two-edged sword
Of heavenly temper keen,
And double were the wounds it made
Wherever it glanced between.
'Twas death to silt; 'twas life
To all who mourned for sin.
It kindled and it silenced strife,
Made war and peace within.

This unction comes to the preacher not in the study but in the closet. It is heaven's distillation in answer to prayer. It is the sweetest exhalation of the Holy Spirit. It impregnates, suffuses, softens, percolates, cuts, and soothes. It carries the Word like dynamite, like salt, like sugar; makes the Word a soother, an arranger, a revealer, a searcher; makes the hearer a culprit or a saint, makes him weep like a child and live like a giant; opens his heart and his purse as gently, yet as strongly as the spring opens the leaves. This unction is not the gift of genius. It is not found in the halls of learning. No eloquence can woo it. No industry can win it. No prelatical hands can confer it. It is the gift of God – the signet set to his own messengers. It is heaven's knighthood given to the chosen true and brave ones who have sought this anointed honor through many an hour of tearful, wrestling prayer.

Earnestness is good and impressive: genius is gifted and great. Thought kindles and inspires, but it takes a diviner endowment, a more powerful energy than earnestness or genius or thought to break the chains of sin, to win estranged and depraved hearts to God, to repair the breaches and restore the Church to her old ways of purity and power. Nothing but this holy unction can do this.

16. MUCH PRAYER THE PRICE OF UNCTION
"All the minister's efforts will be vanity or worse than vanity if he have not unction. Unction must come down from heaven and spread a savor and feeling and relish over his ministry; and among the other means of qualifying himself for his office, the Bible must hold the first place, and the last also must be given

to the Word of God and prayer."

Richard Cecil

In the Christian system unction is the anointing of the Holy Ghost, separating unto God's work and qualifying for it. This unction is the one divine enablement by which the preacher accomplishes the peculiar and saving ends cf preaching. Without this unction there are no true spiritual results accomplished; the results and forces in preaching do not rise above the results of unsanctified speech. Without unction the former is as potent as the pulpit.

This divine unction on the preacher generates through the Word of God the spiritual results that flow from the gospel; and without this unction, these results are not secured. Many pleasant impressions may be made, but these all fall far below the ends of gospel preaching. This unction may be simulated. There are many things that look like it, there are many results that resemble its effects; but they are foreign to its results and to its nature. The fervor or softness excited by a pathetic or emotional sermon may look like the movements of the divine unction, but they have no pungent, perpetrating heart-breaking force. No heart-healing balm is there in these surface, sympathetic, emotional movements; they are not radical, neither sin-searching nor sin-curing.

This divine unction is the one distinguishing feature that separates true gospel preaching from all other methods of presenting truth. It backs and interpenetrates the revealed truth with all the force of God. It illumines the Word and broadens and enrichens the intellect and empowers it to grasp and apprehend the Word. It qualifies the preacher's heart, and brings it to that condition of tenderness, of purity, of force and light that are necessary to secure the highest results. This unction gives to the preacher liberty and enlargement of thought and soul – a freedom, fullness, and directness of utterance that can be secured by no other process.

Without this unction on the preacher the gospel has no more power to propagate itself than any other system of truth. This is the seal of its divinity. Unction in the preacher puts God in the gospel. Without the unction, God is absent, and the gospel is left to the low and unsatisfactory forces that the ingenuity, interest, or talents of men can devise to enforce and project its doctrines.

It is in this element that the pulpit oftener fails than in any other element. Just at this all-important point it lapses. Learning it may have, brilliancy and eloquence may delight and charm, sensation or less offensive methods may bring the populace in crowds, mental power may impress and enforce truth with all its resources; but without this unction, each and all these will be but as the fretful assault of the waters on a Gibraltar. Spray and foam may cover and spangle; but the rocks are there still, unimpressed and unimpressible. The human heart can no more be swept of its hardness and sin by these human forces than these rocks can be swept away by the ocean's ceaseless flow.

This unction is the consecration force, and its presence the continuous test of that consecration. It is this divine anointing on the preacher that secures his consecration to God and his work. Other forces and motives may call him to the work, but this only is consecration. A separation to God's work by the power of the Holy Spirit is the only consecration recognized by God as legitimate.

The unction, the divine unction, this heavenly anointing, is what the pulpit needs and must have. This divine and heavenly oil put on it by the imposition of God's hand must soften and lubricate the whole man – heart, head, spirit – until it separates him with a mighty separation from all earthly, secular, worldly, selfish motives and aims, separating him to everything that is pure and Godlike.

It is the presence of this unction on the preacher that creates the stir and friction in many a congregation. The same truths have been told in the strictness of the letter, but no ruffle has been seen, no pain or pulsation felt. All is quiet as a graveyard. Another preacher comes, and this mysterious influence is on him; the letter of the Word has been fired by the Spirit, the throes of a mighty movement are felt, it is the unction that pervades and stirs the conscience and breaks the heart. Unctionless preaching makes everything hard, dry, acrid, dead.

This unction is not a memory or an era of the past only; it is a present, realized, conscious fact. It belongs to the experience of the man as well as to his preaching. It is that which transforms him into the image of his divine Master, as well as that by which he declares the truths of Christ with power. It is so much the power in the ministry as to make all else seem feeble and vain without it, and by its presence to atone for the absence of all other and feebler forces.

This unction is not an inalienable gift. It is a conditional gift, and its presence is perpetuated and increased by the same process by which it was at first secured; by unceasing prayer to God, by impassioned desires after God, by estimating it, by seeking it with tireless ardor, by deeming all else loss and failure without it.

How and whence comes this unction? Direct from God in answer to prayer. Praying hearts only are the hearts filled with this holy oil; praying lips only are anointed with this divine unction.

Prayer, much prayer, is the price of preaching unction; prayer, much prayer, is the one, sole condition of keeping this unction. Without unceasing prayer the unction never comes to the preacher. Without perseverance in prayer, the unction, like the manna overkept, breeds worms.

17. PRAYER MARKS SPIRITUAL LEADERSHIP

"Give me one hundred preachers who fear nothing but sin and desire nothing but God, and I care not a straw whether they be clergymen or laymen; such alone will shake the gates of hell and set up the kingdom of heaven on earth. God does nothing but in answer to prayer."

John Wesley

The apostles knew the necessity and worth of prayer to their ministry. They knew that their high commission as apostles, instead of relieving them from the necessity of prayer, committed them to it by a more urgent need; so that they were exceedingly jealous else some other important work should exhaust their time and prevent their praying as they ought; so they appointed laymen to look after the delicate and engrossing duties of ministering to the poor, that they (the apostles) might,

unhindered, "give themselves continually to prayer and to the ministry of the word." Prayer is put first, and their relation to prayer is put most strongly – "give themselves to it," making a business of it, surrendering themselves to praying, putting fervor, urgency, perseverance, and time in it.

How holy, apostolic men devoted themselves to this divine work of prayer! "Night and day praying exceedingly," says Paul. "We will give ourselves continually to prayer" is the consensus of apostolic devotion to prayer. How these New Testament preachers laid themselves out in prayer for God's people! How they put God in full force into their Churches by their praying! These holy apostles did not vainly fancy that they had met their high and solemn duties by delivering faithfully God's word, but their preaching was made to stick and tell by the ardor and insistence of their praying. Apostolic praying was as taxing, toilsome, and imperative as apostolic preaching. They prayed mightily day and night to bring their people to the highest regions of faith and holiness. They prayed mightier still to hold them to this high spiritual altitude. The preacher who has never learned in the school of Christ the high and divine art of intercession for his people will never learn the art of preaching, though homiletics be poured into him by the ton, and though he be the most gifted genius in sermon-making and sermon-delivery.

The prayers of apostolic, saintly leaders do much in making saints of those who are not apostles. If the Church leaders in after years had been as particular and fervent in praying for their people as the apostles were, the sad, dark times of worldliness and apostasy had not marred the history and eclipsed the glory and arrested the advance of the Church. Apostolic praying makes apostolic saints and keeps apostolic times of purity and power in the Church.

What loftiness of soul, what purity and elevation of motive, what unselfishness, what self-sacrifice, what exhaustive toil, what ardor of spirit, what divine tact are requisite to be an intercessor for men!

The preacher is to lay himself out in prayer for his people; not that they might be saved, simply, but that they be mightily saved. The apostles laid themselves out in prayer that their saints might be perfect; not that they should have a little relish for the things of God, but that they "might be filled with all the fullness of God." Paul did not rely on his apostolic preaching to secure this end, but "for this cause he bowed his knees to the Father of our Lord Jesus Christ." Paul's praying carried Paul's converts farther along the highway of sainthood than Paul's preaching did. Epaphras did as much or more by prayer for the Colossian saints than by his preaching. He labored fervently always in prayer for them that "they might stand perfect and complete in all the will of God."

Preachers are preeminently God's leaders. They are primarily responsible for the condition of the Church. They shape its character, give tone and direction to its life.

Much every way depends on these leaders. They shape the times and the institutions. The Church is divine, the treasure it incases is heavenly, but it bears the imprint of the human. The treasure is in earthen vessels, and it smacks of the vessel. The Church of God makes, or is made by, its leaders. Whether it makes them or is made by them, it will be what its leaders are; spiritual if they are so, secular if they are, conglomerate if its leaders are. Israel's kings gave character to Israel's piety. A Church rarely revolts against or rises above the religion of its leaders. Strongly spiritual leaders; men of holy might, at the lead, are tokens of God's favor; disaster and weakness follow the wake of feeble or worldly leaders. Israel had fallen low when God gave children to be their princes and babes to rule over them. No happy state is predicted by the prophets when children oppress God's Israel and women rule over them. Times of spiritual leadership are times of great spiritual prosperity to the Church.

Prayer is one of the eminent characteristics of strong spiritual leadership. Men of mighty prayer are men of might and mold things. Their power with God has the conquering tread.

How can a man preach who does not get his message fresh from God in the closet? How can he preach without having his faith quickened, his vision cleared, and his heart warmed by his closeting with God? Alas, for the pulpit lips which are untouched by this closet flame. Dry and unctionless they will ever be, and truths divine will never come with power from such lips. As far as the real interests of religion are concerned, a pulpit without a closet will always be a barren thing.

A preacher may preach in an official, entertaining, or learned way without prayer, but between this kind of preaching and sowing God's precious seed with holy hands and prayerful, weeping hearts there is an immeasurable distance.

A prayerless ministry is the undertaker for all God's truth and for God's Church. He may have the most costly casket and the most beautiful flowers, but it is a funeral, notwithstanding the charmful array. A prayerless Christian will never learn God's truth; a prayerless ministry will never be able to teach God's truth. Ages of millennial glory have been lost by a prayerless Church. The coming of our Lord has been postponed indefinitely by a prayerless Church. Hell has enlarged herself and filled her dire caves in the presence of the dead service of a prayerless Church.

The best, the greatest offering is an offering of prayer. If the preachers of the twentieth century will learn well the lesson of prayer, and use fully the power of prayer, the millennium will come to its noon ere the century closes. "Pray without ceasing" is the trumpet call to the preachers of the twentieth century. If the twentieth century will get their texts, their thoughts, their words, their sermons in their closets, the next century will find a new heaven and a new earth. The old sin-stained and sin-eclipsed heaven and earth will pass away under the power of a praying ministry.

18. PREACHERS NEED THE PRAYERS OF THE PEOPLE

"If some Christians that have been complaining of their ministers had said and acted less before men and had applied themselves with all their might to cry to God for their ministers – had, as it were, risen and stormed heaven with their humble, fervent and incessant prayers for them – they would have been much more in the way of success."

Jonathan Edwards

Somehow the practice of praying in particular for the preacher has fallen into disuse or become discounted. Occasionally have we heard the practice arraigned as a disparagement of the ministry, being a public declaration by those who do it of the inefficiency of the ministry. It offends the pride of learning and self-sufficiency, perhaps, and these ought to be offended and rebuked in a ministry that is so derelict as to allow them to exist.

Prayer, to the preacher, is not simply the duty of his profession, a privilege, but it is a necessity. Air is not more necessary to the lungs than prayer is to the preacher. It is absolutely necessary for the preacher to pray. It is an absolute necessity that the preacher be prayed for. These two propositions are wedded into a union which ought never to know any divorce: *the preacher must pray; the preacher must be prayed for.* It will take all the praying he can do, and all the praying he can get done, to meet the fearful responsibilities and gain the largest, truest success in his great work. The true preacher, next to the cultivation of the spirit and fact of prayer in himself, in their intensest form, covets with a great covetousness the prayers of God's people.

The holier a man is, the more does he estimate prayer; the clearer does he see that God gives himself to the praying ones, and that the measure of God's revelation to the soul is the measure of the soul's longing, importunate prayer for God. Salvation never finds its way to a prayerless heart. The Holy Spirit never abides in a prayerless spirit. Preaching never edifies a prayerless soul. Christ knows nothing of prayerless Christians. The gospel cannot be projected by a prayerless preacher. Gifts, talents, education, eloquence, God's call, cannot abate the demand of prayer, but only intensify the necessity for the preacher to pray and to be prayed for. The more the preacher's eyes are opened to the nature, responsibility, and difficulties in his work, the more will he see, and if he be a true preacher the more will he feel, the necessity of prayer; not only the increasing demand to pray himself, but to call on others to help him by their prayers.

Paul is an illustration of this. If any man could project the gospel by dint of personal force, by brain power, by culture, by personal

grace, by God's apostolic commission, God's extraordinary call, that man was Paul. That the preacher must be a man given to prayer, Paul is an eminent example. That the true apostolic preacher must have the prayers of other good people to give to his ministry its full quota of success, Paul is a preeminent example. He asks, he covets, he pleads in an impassioned way for the help of all God's saints. He knew that in the spiritual realm, as elsewhere, in union there is strength; that the concentration and aggregation of faith, desire, and prayer increased the volume of spiritual force until it became overwhelming and irresistible in its power. Units of prayer combined, like drops of water, make an ocean which defies resistance. So Paul, with his clear and full apprehension of spiritual dynamics, determined to make his ministry as impressive, as eternal, as irresistible as the ocean, by gathering all the scattered units of prayer and precipitating them on his ministry. May not the solution of Paul's preeminence in labors and results, and impress on the Church and the world, be found in this fact that he was able to center on himself and his ministry more of prayer than others? To his brethren at Rome he wrote: "Now I beseech you, brethren, for the Lord Jesus Christ's sake, and for the love of the Spirit, that ye strive together with me in prayers to God for me." To the Ephesians he says: "Praying always with all prayer and supplication in the Spirit, and watching thereunto with all perseverance and supplication for all saints; and for me, that utterance may be given unto me, that I may open my mouth boldly, to make known the mystery of the gospel." To the Colossians he emphasizes: "Withal praying also for us, that God would open unto us a door of utterance, to speak the mystery of Christ, for which I am also in bonds: that I may make it manifest as I ought to speak." To the Thessalonians he says sharply, strongly: "Brethren, pray for us." Paul calls on the Corinthian Church to help him: "Ye also helping together by prayer for us." This was to be part of their work. They were to lay to the helping hand of prayer. He in an additional and closing charge to the Thessalonian Church about the importance and necessity of their prayers says: "Finally, brethren, pray for us, that the word of the Lord may have free course, and be glorified, even as it is with you: and that we may be delivered from unreasonable and wicked men." He impresses the Philippians that all his trials and opposition can be made subservient to the spread of the gospel by the efficiency of their prayers for him. Philemon was to prepare a lodging for him, for through Philemon's prayer Paul was to be his guest.

Paul's attitude on this question illustrates his humility and his deep insight into the spiritual forces which project the gospel. More than this, it teaches a lesson for all times, that if Paul was so dependent on the prayers of God's saints to give his ministry success, how much greater the necessity that the prayers of God's saints be centered on the ministry of to-day!

Paul did not feel that this urgent plea for prayer was to lower his dignity, lessen his influence, or depreciate his piety. What if it did? Let dignity go, let influence be destroyed, let his reputation be marred – he must have their prayers. Called, commissioned, chief of the Apostles as he was, all his equipment was imperfect without the prayers of his people. He wrote letters everywhere, urging them to pray for him. Do you pray for your preacher? Do you pray for him in secret? Public prayers are of little worth unless they are founded on or followed up by private praying. The praying ones are to the preacher as Aaron and Hur were to Moses. They hold up his hands and decide the issue that is so fiercely raging around them.

The plea and purpose of the apostles were to put the Church to praying. They did not ignore the grace of cheerful giving. They were not ignorant of the place which religious activity and work occupied an the spiritual life; but not one nor all of these, in apostolic estimate or urgency, could at all compare in necessity and importance with prayer. The most sacred and urgent pleas were used, the most fervid exhortations, the most comprehensive and arousing words were uttered to enforce the all-important obligation and necessity of prayer.

"Put the saints everywhere to praying" is the burden of the apostolic effort and the keynote of apostolic success. Jesus Christ had striven to do this in the days of his personal ministry. As he was moved by infinite compassion at the ripened fields of earth perishing for lack of laborers and pausing in his own praying – he tries to awaken the stupid sensibilities of his disciples to the duty of prayer as he charges them, "Pray ye the Lord of the harvest that he will send forth laborers into his harvest." "And he spake a parable unto them to this end, that men ought always to pray and not to faint."

19. DELIBERATION NECESSARY TO LARGEST RESULTS FROM PRAYER

"This perpetual hurry of business and company ruins me in soul if not in body. More solitude and earlier hours! I suspect I have been allotting habitually too little time to religious exercises, as private devotion and religious meditation, Scripture-reading, etc. Hence I am lean and cold and hard. I had better allot two hours or an hour and a half daily. I have been keeping too late hours, and hence have had but a hurried half hour in a morning to myself. Surely the experience of all good men confirms the proposition that without a due measure of private devotions the soul will grow lean. But all may be done through prayer – almighty prayer, I am ready to say – and why not? For that it is almighty is only through the gracious ordination of the God of love and truth. O then, pray, pray, pray!"

William Wilberforce

Our devotions are not measured by the clock, but time is of their essence. The ability to wait and stay and press belongs essentially to our intercourse with God. Hurry, everywhere unseeming and damaging, is so to an alarming extent in the great business of communion with God. Short devotions are the bane of deep piety. Calmness, grasp, strength, are never the companions of hurry. Short devotions deplete spiritual vigor, arrest spiritual progress, sap spiritual foundations, blight the root and bloom of spiritual life. They are the prolific source of backsliding, the sure indication of a superficial piety; they deceive, blight, rot the seed, and impoverish the soil.

It is true that Bible prayers in word and print are short, but the praying men of the Bible were with God through many a sweet and holy wrestling hour. They won by few words but long waiting. The prayers Moses records may be short, but Moses prayed to

God with fastings and mighty cryings forty days and nights.

The statement of Elijah's praying may be condensed to a few brief paragraphs, but doubtless Elijah, who when "praying he prayed," spent many hours of fiery struggle and lofty intercourse with God before he could, with assured boldness, say to Ahab, "There shall not be dew nor rain these years, but according to my word." The verbal brief of Paul's prayers is short, but Paul "prayed night and day exceedingly." The "Lord's Prayer" is a divine epitome for infant lips, but the man Christ Jesus prayed many an all-night ere his work was done; and his all-night and long-sustained devotions gave to his work its finish and perfection, and to his character the fullness and glory of its divinity.

Spiritual work is taxing work, and men are loath to do it. Praying, true praying, costs an outlay of serious attention and of time, which flesh and blood do not relish. Few persons are made of such strong fiber that they will make a costly outlay when surface work will pass as well in the market. We can habituate ourselves to our beggarly praying until it looks well to us, at least it keeps up a decent form and quiets conscience – the deadliest of opiates! We can slight our praying, and not realize the peril till the foundations are gone. Hurried devotions make weak faith, feeble convictions, questionable piety. To be little with God is to be little for God. To cut short the praying makes the whole religious character short, scrimp, niggardly, and slovenly.

It takes good time for the full flow of God into the spirit. Short devotions cut the pipe of God's full flow. It takes time in the secret places to get the full revelation of God. Little time and hurry mar the picture.

Henry Martyn laments that "want of private devotional reading and shortness of prayer through incessant sermon-making had produced much strangeness between God and his soul." He judged that he had dedicated too much time to public ministrations and too little to private communion with God. He was much impressed to set apart times for fasting and to devote times for solemn prayer. Resulting from this he records: "Was assisted this morning to pray for two hours." Said William Wilberforce, the peer of kings: "I must secure

more time for private devotions. I have been living far too public for me. The shortening of private devotions starves the soul; it grows lean and faint. I have been keeping too late hours." Of a failure in Parliament he says: "Let me record my grief and shame, and all, probably, from private devotions having been contracted, and so God let me stumble." More solitude and earlier hours was his remedy.

More time and early hours for prayer would act like magic to revive and invigorate many a decayed spiritual life. More time and early hours for prayer would be manifest in holy living. A holy life would not be so rare or so difficult a thing if our devotions were not so short and hurried. A Christly temper in its sweet and passionless fragrance would not be so alien and hopeless a heritage if our closet stay were lengthened and intensified. We live shabbily because we pray meanly. Plenty of time to feast in our closets will bring marrow and fatness to our lives. Our ability to stay with God in our closet measures our ability to stay with God out of the closet. Hasty closet visits are deceptive, defaulting. We are not only deluded by them, but we are losers by them in many ways and in many rich legacies. Tarrying in the closet instructs and wins. We are taught by it, and the greatest victories are often the results of great waiting – waiting till words and plans are exhausted, and silent and patient waiting gains the crown. Jesus Christ asks with an affronted emphasis, "Shall not God avenge his own elect which cry day and night unto him?"

To pray is the greatest thing we can do: and to do it well there must be calmness, time, and deliberation; otherwise it is degraded into the littlest and meanest of things. True praying has the largest results for good; and poor praying, the least. We cannot do too much of real praying; we cannot do too little of the sham. We must learn anew the worth of prayer, enter anew the school of prayer. There is nothing which it takes more time to learn. And if we would learn the wondrous art, we must not give a fragment here and there – "A little talk with Jesus," as the tiny saintlets sing – but we must demand and hold with iron grasp the best hours of the day for God and prayer, or there will be no praying worth the name.

This, however, is not a day of prayer. Few men

there are who pray. Prayer is defamed by preacher and priest. In these days of hurry and bustle, of electricity and steam, men will not take time to pray. Preachers there are who "say prayers" as a part of their program, on regular or state occasions; but who "stirs himself up to take hold upon God?" Who prays as Jacob prayed – till he is crowned as a prevailing, princely intercessor? Who prays as Elijah prayed – till all the locked-up forces of nature were unsealed and a famine-stricken land bloomed as the garden of God? Who prayed as Jesus Christ prayed as out upon the mountain he "continued all night in prayer to God?" The apostles "gave themselves to prayer" – the most difficult thing to get men or even the preachers to do. Laymen there are who will give their money – some of them in rich abundance – but they will not "give themselves" to prayer, without which their money is but a curse. There are plenty of preachers who will preach and deliver great and eloquent addresses on the need of revival and the spread of the kingdom of God, but not many there are who will do that without which all preaching and organizing are worse than vain – pray. It is out of date, almost a lost art, and the greatest benefactor this age could have is the man who will bring the preachers and the Church back to prayer.

20. A PRAYING PULPIT BEGETS A PRAYING PEW

"I judge that my prayer is more than the devil himself; if it were otherwise, Luther would have fared differently long before this. Yet men will not see and acknowledge the great wonders or miracles God works in my behalf. If I should neglect prayer but a single day, I should lose a great deal of the fire of faith."

Martin Luther

Only glimpses of the great importance of prayer could the apostles get before Pentecost. But the Spirit coming and filling on Pentecost elevated prayer to its vital and all-commanding position in the gospel of Christ. The call now of prayer to every saint is the Spirit's loudest and most exigent call. Sainthood's piety is made, refined, perfected, by prayer. The gospel moves with slow and timid pace when the saints are not at their prayers early and late and long.

Where are the Christly leaders who can teach the modern saints how to pray and put them at it? Do we know we are raising up a prayerless set of saints? Where are the apostolic leaders who can put God's people to praying? Let them come to the front and do the work, and it will be the greatest work which can be done. An increase of educational facilities and a great increase of money force will be the direst curse to religion if they are not sanctified by more and better praying than we are doing. More praying will not come as a matter of course. The campaign for the twentieth or thirtieth century fund will not help our praying but hinder if we are not careful. Nothing but a specific effort from a praying leadership will avail. The chief ones must lead in the apostolic effort to radicate the vital importance and *fact* of prayer in the heart and life of the Church. None but praying leaders can have praying followers. Praying apostles will beget praying saints. A praying pulpit will beget praying pews. We do greatly need some body who can set the saints to this business of praying. We are not a generation of praying saints. Non-praying saints are a beggarly gang of saints who have neither the ardor nor the beauty nor the power of saints. Who will restore this breach? The greatest will he be of reformers and apostles, who can set the Church to praying.

We put it as our most sober judgment that the great need of the Church in this and all ages is men of such commanding faith, of such unsullied holiness, of such marked spiritual vigor and consuming zeal, that their prayers, faith, lives, and ministry will be of such a radical and aggressive form as to work spiritual revolutions which will form eras in individual and Church life.

We do not mean men who get up sensational stirs by novel devices, nor those who attract by a pleasing entertainment; but men who can stir things, and work revolutions by the preaching of God's Word and by the power of the Holy Ghost, revolutions which change the whole current of things.

Natural ability and educational advantages do not figure as factors in this matter; but capacity for faith, the ability to pray, the power of thorough consecration, the ability of self-littleness, an absolute losing of one's self in

God's glory, and an ever-present and insatiable yearning and seeking after all the fullness of God – men who can set the Church ablaze for God; not in a noisy, showy way, but with an intense and quiet heat that melts and moves everything for God.

God can work wonders if he can get a suitable man. Men can work wonders if they can get God to lead them. The full endowment of the spirit that turned the world upside down would be eminently useful in these latter days. Men who can stir things mightily for God, whose spiritual revolutions change the whole aspect of things, are the universal need of the Church.

The Church has never been without these men; they adorn its history; they are the standing miracles of the divinity of the Church; their example and history are an unfailing inspiration and blessing. An increase in their number and power should be our prayer.

That which has been done in spiritual matters can be done again, and be better done. This was Christ's view. He said "Verily, verily, I say unto you, He that believeth on me, the works that I do shall he do also; and greater works than these shall he do; because I go unto my Father." The past has not exhausted the possibilities nor the demands for doing great things for God. The Church that is dependent on its past history for its miracles of power and grace is a fallen Church.

God wants elect men – men out of whom self and the world have gone by a severe crucifixion, by a bankruptcy which has so totally ruined self and the world that there is neither hope nor desire of recovery; men who by this insolvency and crucifixion have turned toward God perfect hearts.

Let us pray ardently that God's promise to prayer may be more than realized.

E.M. Bounds, 1835–1913

Instructions to be Observed Concerning Prayer

John Bradford

There are nine things that pertain to the knowledge of true prayer:
1. To know what prayer is
2. How many sorts of prayer there are

3. The necessity of prayer
4. To Whom we ought to pray
5. By Whom we must pray
6. Where to pray
7. What to pray
8. The excellency of prayer
9. What we must do, that our prayers may be heard

1. WHAT PRAYER IS
Prayer is a simple, unfeigned, humble, and ardent opening of the heart before God; wherein we either ask things needful, or give thanks for benefits received. Paul (1 Tim. ii) calls it by four sundry names in one sentence, namely, prayer, supplication, intercession, and thanksgiving: whereof the first is, for the avoiding and preventing of evil; the second is an earnest and fervent calling upon God for any thing; the third is an intercession for others; the fourth is a praising of God for things received.

2. THERE ARE TWO MANNER OF WAYS HOW WE SHOULD PRAY
First, publicly, and that is called common prayer; second, privately, us when men pray alone, and that is called private prayer; and how both these two are allowed before God, the Scripture bears testimony by the example of all the holy men and women before and after Christ.

3. OF THE NECESSITY OF PRAYER
There are four things that provoke us to pray: first, the commandment of God; secondly, sin in us, which drives us, from necessity, to God for succor, life, and mercy; thirdly, our weak nature being unable to do any good, requires prayer to strengthen it, even as a house requires principal pillars for the upholding of it; fourthly the subtlety of the enemy (who privily lurks in the inward parts, waiting to overthrow us even in those things we think are best done) stirs us vehemently thereunto.

4. TO WHOM WE OUGHT TO PRAY
Three things pertain to Him that must be prayed unto: first, that he have such ears as may hear all the world at once; secondly, that he be in all places at once; thirdly that he have

such power that he may be able to help, and such mercy that he will deliver.

5. BY WHOM WE SHOULD PRAY
Christ is the only way by whom we have free access unto the Father, and for whom our prayers are accepted (our infirmities notwithstanding,) without whom all our prayers are abominable.

6. WHERE TO PRAY
As touching the place where we should pray, seeing all places are one, there is none forbidden; only the common prayer must be made in what place soever the congregation of Christ assembles.

7. WHAT TO PRAY
This is according to the necessity of every man; and forasmuch as we need both spiritual and corporeal things, we may boldly ask them both: for as to ask spiritual gifts, is profitable and commanded, so to ask corporeal, is necessary and allowed.

8. OF THE EXCELLENCY OF PRAYER
The worthiness of prayer consists in two things; in the dignity of the commander, who is God, the fountain of all goodness, who commands only good things; and in the effect that follows it, which is the obtaining of whatsoever we desire faithfully, according to the will off God.

9. WHAT TO DO THAT WE MAY BE HEARD
First, we must put off our own righteousness, pride, and estimation of ourselves, and put on Christ with his righteousness; secondly, an earnest faith and fervent love, with the putting off all rancor, malice, and envy, is required; finally, true repentance knits up the knot, for in it are contained all the virtues before named.

John Bradford, c.1510–55

Preparations for the Christian Ministry: Habits of Special Prayer
Charles Bridges

Luther long since has said – "Prayer, meditation, and temptation, make a Minister." No one will hesitate to admit the importance of the first of these qualifications, who has ever realized the weight of Ministerial responsibility, who has been led to know that his "sufficiency is of God," and that prayer is the appointed channel of heavenly communications. The student's conscious need of wisdom, humility and faith, to ascertain the pure simplicity of his purpose, his necessary qualifications, and his Divine call to the holy office – will bring him a daily suppliant to the throne of grace. In his General Studies, abstracted from this spirit of prayer, he will find a dryness – a want of power to draw his resources to this one center of the Ministry – or perhaps a diversion from the main object into some track of self-indulgence. And even in this special duty of the Scriptures he will feel himself, (as Witsius says) "like a blind man contemplating the heavens," – or as when the world in its original confusion "was without form and void, and darkness was upon the face of the deep." God must speak to his heart – "Let there be light;" and "for this he will be inquired of to do it unto him."

Wickliff's judgment of the main qualification of an expositor of Scripture is equally striking and accurate. He should be a man of prayer – he needs the internal instruction of the primary Teacher. Dr. Owen observes with his usual impressiveness – "For a man solemnly to undertake the interpretation of any portion of Scripture without invocation of God, to be taught and instructed by his Spirit, is a high provocation of him; nor shall I expect the discovery of truth from any one, who thus proudly engages in a work so much above his ability. But this is the sheet anchor of a faithful expositor in all difficulties; nor can he without this be satisfied, that he hath attained the mind of the Spirit in any Divine revelation. When all other helps fail, as they frequently do, this will afford him the best relief. The labors of former expositors are of excellent use: but they are far from having discovered the depth of this vein of wisdom; nor will the best of our endeavors prescribe limits to our successors; and the reason why the generality go in the same track, except in some excursions of curiosity, is – not giving themselves up to the conduct of the Holy Spirit in the diligent performance of their duty."

Let the probationer then seriously calculate the cost of the work. Many are the painful exercises of faith and patience superadded to the daily difficulties of the Christian life. Need we therefore remind him, what an awakening call there is for prayer, for additional supplies of heavenly influence – that his knowledge may grow "unto all the riches of the full assurance of understanding" – that his heart may be constrained to a cheerful and ready obedience – that all his powers may be consecrated to this sole object – and that the whole work of preparation may be sealed by an abundant blessing? George Herbert justly remarks of "some in a preparatory way," that their "aim and labor must be, not only to get knowledge, but to subdue and mortify all lusts and affections, and not to think, that, when they have read the fathers or school-men, a Minister is made, and the thing done. The greatest and hardest preparation is within." And indeed, to bring the heart to the work, and to keep it there – to exchange the indulgence of ease for labor and self-denial, the esteem of the world for the reproach of Christ and of his cross – to endure the prospect of successive disappointment and discouragement – this it is that raises within the "evil spirit" of despondency: "which kind can come forth by nothing but by prayer and fasting."

The first Ministers of the Gospel were prepared for their work (unconsciously indeed to themselves) by their Master's retirement for the continuance of a whole night of prayer to God. With the same holy preparation the first Missionaries to the Gentiles were sent forth ; and thus – instead of "returning (like the nobles of Judah) with their vessels empty, ashamed and confounded, and covering their heads" – they gladdened the hearts of their brethren with tidings of the great things "that God had done with them." Indeed an entrance upon this great work without the spirit of prayer, would be to "go a" most fearful "warfare at our own charges." The kingdom of Satan would have little to apprehend from an attack of literature, or from any systematic mechanism of external forms. The outworks might be stormed, but the citadel would remain impregnable. "The prey" will never be "taken from the mighty, nor the lawful captives delivered," by any other

power than the Ministry of the Gospel clothed with Almighty energy. By this means the first attack was made by the servants of Christ, waiting in earnest prayer for the fulfillment of the faithful promises. The Christian Ministry is a work of faith; and, that it may be a work of faith, it must be a work of prayer. Prayer obtains faith, while faith in its reaction quickens to increasing earnestness of prayer. Thus spiritual, enlightened, and encouraging views of the Ministry flow from the habit of diligent waiting on God. If then the candidate for the sacred office should never bow his knee, without making the momentous work before him a subject of large supplication, he will do well. But if he should add to his customary times of prayer seasons of retirement, consecrated to the sole purpose of contemplating the work, and separating himself to its service, he will do better. A man of special prayer will be a man of special faith: and faith enables "the worm to thresh the mountains," and, in holy triumph, to cast them down before him – "Who art thou, O great mountain? before Zerubbabel thou shalt become a plain."

Charles Bridges, 1794–1869

Training of the Twelve
A.B. Bruce

LESSONS ON PRAYER
Matt. 6:5–13; 7:7–11; Luke 11:1–13; 18:1–5.

It would have been matter for surprise if, among the manifold subjects on which Jesus gave instruction to His disciples, prayer had not occupied a prominent place. Prayer is a necessity of spiritual life, and all who earnestly try to pray soon feel the need of teaching how to do it. And what theme more likely to engage the thoughts of a Master who was Himself emphatically a man of prayer, spending occasionally whole nights in prayerful communion with His heavenly Father?

We find, accordingly, that prayer was a subject on which Jesus often spoke in the hearing of His disciples. In the Sermon on the Mount, for example, He devoted a paragraph to that topic, in which He cautioned His hearers against pharisaic ostentation and heathenish repetition, and recited a form of devotion as a model of simplicity, comprehensiveness, and brevity (Matthew 6.2–4.). At other times He directed attention to the necessity, in order to acceptable and prevailing prayer, of perseverance, concord, strong faith, and large expectation.

The passage cited from the eleventh chapter of Luke's Gospel gives an account of what may be regarded as the most complete and comprehensive of all the lessons communicated by Jesus to His disciples on the important subject to which it relates. The circumstances in which this lesson was given are interesting. The lesson on prayer was itself an answer to prayer. A disciple, in all probability one of the twelve, after hearing Jesus pray, made the request: "Lord, teach us to pray, as John also taught his disciples." The request and its occasion taken together convey to us incidentally two pieces of information. From the latter we learn that Jesus, besides praying much alone, also prayed in company with His disciples, practicing family prayer as the head of a household, as well as secret prayer in personal fellowship with God His Father. From the former we learn that the social prayers of Jesus were most impressive. Disciples hearing them were made painfully conscious of their own incapacity, and after the Amen were ready instinctively to proffer the request, "Lord, teach us to pray," as if ashamed any more to attempt the exercise in their own feeble, vague, stammering words.

When this lesson was given we know not, for Luke introduces his narrative of it in the most indefinite manner, without noting either time or place. The reference to John in the past tense might seem to indicate a date subsequent to his death; but the mode of expression would be sufficiently explained by the supposition that the disciple who made the request had previously been a disciple of the Baptist. Nor can any certain inference be drawn from the contents of the lesson. It is a lesson which might have been given to the twelve at any time during their disciplehood, so far as their spiritual necessities were concerned. It is a lesson for children, for spiritual minors, for Christians in the crude stage of the divine life, afflicted with confusion of mind, dumbness, dejection, unable to pray for want of clear thought, apt words, and above all, of faith that

knows how to wait in hope; and it meets the wants of such by suggesting topics, supplying forms of language, and furnishing their weak faith with the props of cogent arguments for perseverance. Now such was the state of the twelve during all the time they were with Jesus; till He ascended to heaven, and power descended from heaven on them, bringing with it a loosed tongue and an enlarged heart. During the whole period of their discipleship, they needed prompting in prayer such as a mother gives her child, and exhortations to perseverance in the habit of praying, even as do the humblest followers of Christ. Far from being exempt from such infirmities, the twelve may even have experienced them in a superlative degree. The heights correspond to the depths in religious experience. Men who are destined to be apostles must, as disciples, know more than most of the chaotic, speechless condition, and of the great, irksome, but most salutary business of Waiting on God for light, and truth, and grace, earnestly desired but long withheld.

It was well for the church that her first ministers needed this lesson on prayer; for the time comes in the case of most, if not all, who are spiritually earnest, when its teaching is very seasonable. In the spring of the divine life, the beautiful blossom-time of piety, Christians may be able to pray with fluency and fervor, unembarrassed by want of words, thoughts, and feelings of a certain kind. But that happy stage soon passes, and is succeeded by one in which prayer often becomes a helpless struggle, an inarticulate groan, a silent, distressed, despondent waiting on God, on the part of men who are tempted to doubt whether God be indeed the hearer of prayer, whether prayer be not altogether idle and useless. The three wants contemplated and provided for in this lesson – the want of ideas, of words, and of faith – are as common as they are grievous. How long it takes most to fill even the simple petitions of the Lord's Prayer with definite meanings! the second petition, e.g., "Thy kingdom come," which can be presented with perfect intelligence only by such as have formed for themselves a clear conception of the ideal spiritual republic or commonwealth. How difficult, and therefore how rare, to find out acceptable words for precious thoughts slowly reached! How many, who have never got any thing on which their hearts were set without needing to ask for it often, and to wait for it long (no uncommon experience), have been tempted by the delay to give up asking in despair! And no wonder; for delay is hard to bear in all cases, especially in connection with spiritual blessings, which are in fact, and are by Christ here assumed to be, the principal object of a Christian man's desires. Devout souls would not be utterly confounded by delay, or even refusal, in connection with mere temporal goods; for they know that such things as health, wealth, wife, children, home, position, are not unconditionally good, and that it may be well sometimes not to obtain them, or not easily and too soon. But it is most confounding to desire with all one's heart the Holy Ghost, and yet seem to be denied the priceless boon; to pray for light, and to get instead deeper darkness; for faith, and to be tormented with doubts which shake cherished convictions to their foundations; for sanctity, and to have the mud of corruption stirred up by temptation from the bottom of the well of eternal life in the heart. Yet all this, as every experienced Christian knows, is part of the discipline through which scholars in Christ's school have to pass ere the desire of their heart be fulfilled.

The lesson on prayer taught by Christ, in answer to request, consists of two parts, in one of which thoughts and words are put into the mouths of immature disciples, while the other provides aids to faith in God as the answerer of prayer. There is first a form of prayer, and then an argument enforcing perseverance in prayer.

The form of prayer commonly called the Lord's Prayer, which appears in the Sermon on the Mount as a sample of the right kind of prayer, is given here as a summary of the general heads under which all special petitions may be comprehended. We may call this form the alphabet of all possible prayer. It embraces the elements of all spiritual desire, summed up in a few choice sentences, for the benefit of those who may not be able to bring their struggling aspirations to birth in articulate language. It contains in all six petitions, of which three

– the first three, as was meet – refer to God's glory, and the remaining three to man's good. We are taught to pray, first for the advent of the divine kingdom, in the form of universal reverence for the divine name, and universal obedience to the divine will; and then, in the second place, for daily bread, pardon, and protection from evil for ourselves. The whole is addressed to God as Father, and is supposed to proceed from such as realize their fellowship one with another as members of a divine family, and therefore say, "Our Father." The prayer does not end, as our prayers now commonly do, with the formula, "for Christ's sake"; nor could it, consistently with the supposition that it proceeded from Jesus. No prayer given by Him for the present use of His disciples, before His death, could have such an ending, because the plea it contains was not intelligible to them previous to that event. The twelve did not yet know what Christ's sake (sache) meant, nor would they till after their Lord had ascended, and the Spirit had descended and revealed to them the true meaning of the facts of Christ's earthly history. Hence we find Jesus, on the eve of His passion, telling His disciples that up to that time they had asked nothing in His name, and representing the use of His name as a plea to be heard, as one of the privileges awaiting them in the future. "Hitherto," He said, "have ye asked nothing in my name; ask, and ye shall receive, that your joy may be full". And in another part of His discourse: "Whatsoever ye shall ask in my name, that will I do, that the Father may be glorified in the Son".

To what extent the disciples afterwards made use of this beautifully simple yet profoundly significant form, we do not know; but it may be assumed that they were in the habit of repeating it as the disciples of the Baptist might repeat the forms taught them by their master. There is, however, no reason to think that the "Lord's Prayer," though of permanent value as a part of Christ's teaching, was designed to be a stereotyped, binding method of addressing the Father in heaven. It was meant to be an aid to inexperienced disciples, not a rule imposed upon apostles. Even after they had attained to spiritual maturity, the twelve might use this form if they pleased, and possibly they did occasionally use it; but

Jesus expected that by the time they came to be teachers in the church they should have outgrown the need of it as an aid to devotion. Filled with the Spirit, enlarged in heart, mature in spiritual understanding, they should then be able to pray as their Lord had prayed when He was with them; and while the six petitions of the model prayer would still enter into all their supplications at the throne of grace, they would do so only as the alphabet of a language enters into the most extended and eloquent utterances of a speaker, who never thinks of the letters of which the words he utters are composed.

In maintaining the provisional, pro tempore character of the Lord's Prayer, so far as the twelve were concerned, we lay no stress on the fact already adverted to, that it does not end with the phrase, "for Christ's sake." That defect could easily be supplied afterwards mentally or orally, and therefore was no valid reason for disuse. The same remark applies to our use of the prayer in question. To allow this form to fall into desuetude merely because the customary concluding plea is wanting, is as weak on one side as the too frequent repetition of it is on the other. The Lord's Prayer is neither a piece of Deism unworthy of a Christian, nor a magic charm like the "Pater noster" of Roman Catholic devotion. The most advanced believer will often find relief and rest to his spirit in falling back on its simple, sublime sentences, while mentally realizing the manifold particulars which each of them includes; and he is but a tyro in the art of praying, and in the divine life generally, whose devotions consist exclusively, or even mainly, in repeating the words which Jesus put into the mouths of immature disciples.

The view now advocated regarding the purpose of the Lord's Prayer is in harmony with the spirit of Christ's whole teaching. Liturgical forms and religious methodism in general were much more congenial to the strict ascetic school of the Baptist than to the free school of Jesus. Our Lord evidently attached little importance to forms of prayer, any more than to fixed periodic fasts, else He would not have waited till He was asked for a form, but would have made systematic provision for the wants of His followers, even as the Baptist did,

by, so to speak, compiling a book of devotion or composing a liturgy. It is evident, even from the present instructions on the subject of praying, that Jesus considered the form He supplied of quite subordinate importance: a mere temporary remedy for a minor evil, the want of utterance, till the greater evil, the want of faith, should be cured; for the larger portion of the lesson is devoted to the purpose of supplying an antidote to unbelief.

The second part of this lesson on prayer is intended to convey the same moral as that which is prefixed to the parable of the unjust judge — "that men ought always to pray, and not to faint." The supposed cause of fainting is also the same, even delay on the part of God in answering our prayers. This is not, indeed, made so obvious in the earlier lesson as in the later. The parable of the ungenerous neighbor is not adapted to convey the idea of long delay: for the favor asked, if granted at all, must be granted in a very few minutes. But the lapse of time between the presenting and the granting of our requests is implied and presupposed as a matter of course. It is by delay that God seems to say to us what the ungenerous neighbor said to his friend, and that we are tempted to think that we pray to no purpose.

Both the parables spoken by Christ to inculcate perseverance in prayer seek to effect their purpose by showing the power of importunity in the most unpromising circumstances. The characters appealed to are both bad — one in ungenerous, and the other unjust; and from neither is any thing to be gained except by working on his selfishness. And the point of the parable in either case is, that importunity has a power of annoyance which enables it to gain its Objection.

It is important again to observe what is supposed to be the leading subject of prayer in connection with the argument now to be considered. The thing upon which Christ assumes His disciples to have set their hearts is personal sanctification. This appears from the concluding sentence of the discourse: "How much more shall your heavenly Father give the Holy Spirit to them that ask Him!" Jesus takes for granted that the persons to whom He addresses Himself here seek first the kingdom of God and His righteousness. Therefore, though He inserted a petition for daily bread in the form of prayer, He drops that object out of view in the latter part of His discourse; both because it is by hypothesis not the chief object of desire, and also because, for all who truly give God's kingdom the first place in their regards, food and raiment are thrown into the bargain.

To such as do not desire the Holy Spirit above all things, Jesus has nothing to say. He does not encourage them to hope that they shall receive any thing of the Lord; least of all, the righteousness of the kingdom, personal sanctification. He regards the prayers of a double-minded man, who has two chief ends in view, as a hollow mockery – mere words, which never reach Heaven's ear.

The supposed cause of fainting being delay, and the supposed object of desire being the Holy Spirit, the spiritual situation contemplated in the argument is definitely determined. The Teacher's aim is to succor and encourage those who feel that the work of grace goes slowly on within them, and wonder why it does so, and sadly sigh because it does so. Such we conceive to have been the state of the twelve when this lesson was given them. They had been made painfully conscious of incapacity to perform aright their devotional duties, and they took that incapacity to be an index of their general spiritual condition, and were much depressed in consequence.

The argument by which Jesus sought to inspire His discouraged disciples with hope and confidence as to the ultimate fulfillment of their desires, is characterized by boldness, geniality, wisdom, and logical force. Its boldness is evinced in the choice of illustrations . Jesus has such confidence in the goodness of His cause, that He states the case as disadvantageously for Himself as possible, by selecting for illustration not good samples of men, but persons rather below than above the ordinary standard of human virtue. A man who, on being applied to at any hour of the night by a neighbor for help in a real emergency, such as that supposed in the parable, or in a case of sudden sickness, should put him off with such an answer as this, "Trouble me not, the door is now shut, and my children are with me in bed; I cannot rise and give thee," would justly incur the contempt of his acquaintances, and become a byword among them for all that is ungenerous and heartless. The same readiness to take an extreme case is observable in the second argument, drawn from the conduct of fathers towards their children. "If a son shall ask bread of any of you" – so it begins. Jesus does not care what father may be selected; He is willing to take any one they please: He will take the very worst as readily as the best; nay, more readily, for the argument turns not on the goodness of the parent, but rather on his want of goodness, as it aims to show that no special goodness is required to keep all parents from doing what would be an outrage on natural affection, and revolting to the feelings of all mankind.

The genial, kindly character of the argument is manifest from the insight and sympathy displayed therein. Jesus divines what hard thoughts men think of God under the burden of unfulfilled desire; how they doubt His goodness, and deem Him indifferent, heartless, unjust. He shows His intimate knowledge of their secret imaginations by the cases He puts; for the unkind friend and unnatural father, and we may add, the unjust judge, are pictures not indeed of what God is, or of what He would have us believe God to be, but certainly of what even pious men sometimes think Him to be. And He cannot only divine, but sympathize. He does not, like Job's friends, find fault with those who harbor doubting and apparently profane thoughts, nor chide them for impatience, distrust, and despondency. He deals with them as men compassed with infirmity, and needing sympathy, counsel, and help. And in supplying these, He comes down to their level of feeling, and tries to show that, even if things were as they seem, there is no cause for despair. He argues from their own thoughts of God, that they should still hope in Him. "Suppose," He says in effect, "God to be what you fancy, indifferent and heartless, still pray on; see, in the case I put, what perseverance can effect. Ask as the man who wanted loaves asked, and ye shall also receive from Him who seems at present deaf to your petitions. Appearances, I grant, may be very unfavorable, but they cannot be more so in your case than in that of the petitioner in the parable; and yet you observe how he fared through not being too easily disheartened."

Jesus displays His wisdom in dealing with the doubts of His disciples, by avoiding all elaborate explanations of the causes or reasons of delay in the answering of prayer, and using only arguments adapted to the capacity of persons weak in faith and in spiritual understanding. He does not attempt to show why sanctification is a slow, tedious work, not a momentary act: why the Spirit is given gradually and in limited measure, not at once and without measure. He simply urges His hearers to persevere in seeking the Holy Spirit, assuring them that, in spite of trying delay, their desires will be fulfilled in the end. He teaches them no philosophy of waiting on God, but only tells them that they shall not wait in vain.

This method the Teacher followed not from necessity, but from choice. For though no attempt was made at explaining divine delays in providence and grace, it was not because explanation was impossible. There were many things which Christ might have said to His disciples at this time if they could have borne them; some of which they afterwards said themselves, when the Spirit of Truth had come, and guided them into all truth, and made them acquainted with the secret of God's way. He might have pointed out to them, e.g., that the delays of which they complained were according to the analogy of nature, in which gradual growth is the universal law; that time was needed for the production of the ripe fruits of the Spirit, just in the same way as for the production of the ripe fruits of the field or of the orchard; that it was not to be wondered at if the spiritual fruits were peculiarly slow in ripening, as it was a law of growth that the higher the product in the scale of being, the slower the process by which it is produced; that a momentary sanctification, though not impossible, would be as much a miracle in the sense of a departure from law, as was the immediate transformation of water into wine at the marriage in Cana; that if instantaneous sanctification were the rule instead of the rare exception, the kingdom of grace would become too like the imaginary worlds of children's dreams, in which trees, fruits, and palaces spring into being full-grown, ripe, and

furnished, in a moment as by enchantment, and too unlike the real, actual world with which men are conversant, in which delay, growth, and fixed law are invariable characteristics.

Jesus might further have sought to reconcile His disciples to delay by descanting on the virtue of patience. Much could be said on that topic. It could be shown that a character cannot be perfect in which the virtue of patience has no place, and that the gradual method of sanctification is best adapted for its development, as affording abundant scope for its exercise. It might be pointed out how much the ultimate enjoyment of any good thing is enhanced by its having to be waited for; how in proportion to the trial is the triumph of faith; how, in the quaint words of one who was taught wisdom in this matter by his own experience, and by the times in which he lived, "It is fit we see and feel the shaping and sewing of every piece of the wedding garment, and the framing and molding and fitting of the crown of glory for the head of the citizen of heaven"; how "the repeated sense and frequent experience of grace in the ups and downs in the way, the falls and risings again of the traveler, the revolutions and changes of the spiritual condition, the new moon, the darkened moon, the full moon in the Spirit's ebbing and flowing, raiseth in the heart of saints on their way to the country a sweet smell of the fairest rose and lily of Sharon"; how, "as travelers at night talk of their foul ways, and of the praises of their guide, and battle being ended, soldiers number their wounds, extol the valor, skill, and courage of their leader and captain," so "it is meet that the glorified soldiers may take loads of experience of free grace to heaven with them, and there speak of their way and their country, and the praises of Him that hath redeemed them out of all nations, tongues, and languages".

Such considerations, however just, would have been wasted on men in the spiritual condition of the disciples. Children have no sympathy with growth in any world, whether of nature or of grace. Nothing pleases them but that an acorn should become an oak at once, and that immediately after the blossom should come the ripe fruit. Then it is idle to speak of the uses of patience to the inexperienced; for the moral value of the discipline of trial cannot be appreciated till the trial is past. Therefore, as before stated, Jesus abstained entirely from reflections of the kind suggested, and adopted a simple, popular style of reasoning which even a child could understand.

The reasoning of Jesus, while very simple, is very cogent and conclusive. The first argument – that contained in the parable of the ungenerous neighbor – is fitted to inspire hope in God, even in the darkest hour, when He appears indifferent to our cry, or positively unwilling to help, and so to induce us to persevere in asking. "As the man who wanted the loaves knocked on louder and louder, with an importunity that knew no shame, and would take no refusal, and thereby gained his object, the selfish friend being glad at last to get up and serve him out of sheer regard to his own comfort, it being simply impossible to sleep with such a noise; so (such is the drift of the argument), so continue thou knocking at the door of heaven, and thou shalt obtain thy desire if it were only to be rid of thee. See in this parable what a power importunity has, even at a most unpromising time – midnight – and with a most unpromising person, who prefers his own comfort to a neighbor's good: ask, therefore, persistently, and it shall be given unto you also; seek, and ye shall find; knock, and it shall be opened unto you."

At one point, indeed, this most pathetic and sympathetic argument seems to be weak. The petitioner in the parable had the selfish friend in his power by being able to annoy him and keep him from sleeping. Now, the tried desponding disciple whom Jesus would comfort may rejoin: "What power have I to annoy God, who dwelleth on high, far beyond my reach, in imperturbable felicity? 'Oh that I knew where I might find Him, that I might come even to His seat! But, behold, I go forward, but He is not there; and backward, but I cannot perceive Him: on the left hand, where He doth work, but I cannot behold Him: He hideth Himself on the right hand, that I cannot see Him'". The objection is one which can hardly fail to occur to the subtle spirit of despondency, and it must be admitted that it is not frivolous. There is really a failure of the analogy at this point. We can annoy a man,

like the ungenerous neighbor in bed, or the unjust judge, but we cannot annoy God. The parable does not suggest the true explanation of divine delay, or of the ultimate success of importunity. It merely proves, by a homely instance, that delay, apparent refusal, from whatever cause it may arise, is not necessarily final, and therefore can be no good reason for giving up asking.

This is a real if not a great service rendered. But the doubting disciple, besides discovering with characteristic acuteness what the parable fails to prove, may not be able to extract any comfort from what it does prove. What is he to do then? Fall back on the strong asseveration with which Jesus follows up the parable: "And I say unto you." Here, doubter, is an oracular dictum from One who can speak with authority; One who has been in the bosom of the eternal God, and has come forth to reveal His inmost heart to men groping in the darkness of nature after Him, if haply they might find Him. When He addresses you in such emphatic, solemn terms as these, "I say unto you, Ask, and it shall be given you; seek, and ye shall find; knock, and it shall be opened unto you," you may take the matter on His word, at least pro tempore. Even those who doubt the reasonableness of prayer, because of the constancy of nature's laws and the unchangeableness of divine purposes, might take Christ's word for it that prayer is not vain, even in relation to daily bread, not to speak of higher matters, until they arrive at greater certainty on the subject than they can at present pretend to. Such may, if they choose, despise the parable as childish, or as conveying crude anthropopathic ideas of the Divine Being, but they cannot despise the deliberate declarations of One whom even they regard as the wisest and best of men.

The second argument employed by Jesus to urge perseverance in prayer is of the nature of a *reductio ad absurdum*, ending with a conclusion [hungarumlaut]*fortiori*. "If," it is reasoned, "God refused to hear His children's prayers, or, worse still, if He mocked them by giving them something bearing a superficial resemblance to the things asked, only to cause bitter disappointment when the deception was discovered, then were He not only as bad as, but far worse than, even the most depraved of mankind. For, take fathers at random, which of them, if a son were to ask bread, would give him a stone? or if he asked a fish, would give him a serpent? or if he asked an egg, would offer him a scorpion? The very supposition is monstrous. Human nature is largely vitiated by moral evil; there is, in particular, an evil spirit of selfishness in the heart which comes into conflict with the generous affections, and leads men ofttimes to do base and unnatural things. But men taken at the average are not diabolic; and nothing short of a diabolic spirit of mischief could prompt a father to mock a child's misery, or deliberately to give him things fraught with deadly harm. If, then, earthly parents, though evil in many of their dispositions, give good, and, so far as they know, only good, gifts to their children, and would shrink with horror from any other mode of treatment, is it to be credited that the Divine Being, that Providence, can do what only devils would think of doing? On the contrary, what is only barely possible for man is for God altogether impossible, and what all but monsters of iniquity will not fail to do God will do much more. He will most surely give good gifts, and only good gifts, to His asking children; most especially will He give His best gift, which His true children desire above all things, even the Holy Spirit, the enlightener and the sanctifier. Therefore again I say unto you: Ask, and ye shall receive; seek, and ye shall find; knock, and it shall be opened."

Yet it is implied in the very fact that Christ puts such cases as a stone given for bread, a serpent for a fish, or a scorpion for an egg, that God seems at least sometimes so to treat His children. The time came when the twelve thought they had been so treated in reference to the very subject in which they were most deeply interested, after their own personal sanctification, viz., the restoration of the kingdom to Israel. But their experience illustrates the general truth, that when the Hearer of prayer seems to deal unnaturally with His servants, it is because they have made a mistake about the nature of good, and have not known what they asked. They have asked for a stone, thinking it bread, and hence the true bread seems a stone; for a shadow, thinking it a substance, and hence the substance seems a shadow. The kingdom for which the twelve

prayed was a shadow, hence their disappointment and despair when Jesus was put to death: the egg of hope, which their fond imagination had been hatching, brought forth the scorpion of the cross, and they fancied that God had mocked and deceived them. But they lived to see that God was true and good, and that they had deceived themselves, and that all which Christ had told them had been fulfilled. And all who wait on God ultimately make a similar discovery, and unite in testifying that "the Lord is good unto them that wait for Him, to the soul that seeketh Him".

For these reasons should all men pray, and not faint. Prayer is rational, even if the Divine Being were like men in the average, not indisposed to do good when self-interest does not stand in the way – the creed of heathenism. It is still more manifestly rational if, as Christ taught and Christians believe, God be better than the best of men – the one supremely good Being – the Father in heaven. Only in either of two cases would prayer really be irrational: if God were no living being at all, – the creed of atheists, with whom Christ holds no argument; or if He were a being capable of doing things from which even bad men would start back in horror, i.e., a being of diabolic nature, – the creed, it is to be hoped, of no human being.

A.B. Bruce, 1831–99

The Spirit of Prayer
James Buchanan

In the Scriptures a special operation of the Spirit is mentioned, by which he aids his people in the exercise of prayer; and it is spoken of as one that is common to all believers, and permanent through all ages of the Church. This cheering truth is implied in God's promise of old, "I will pour upon the house of David, and the inhabitants of Jerusalem, the Spirit of grace and of supplications"; and it is implied also in the declared duty of all believers, which is described in the apostle's exhortation, "Praying always with all prayer and supplication in the Spirit." But the most emphatic testimony on the subject is contained in the words of the apostle (Rom. viii. 26), "Likewise the Spirit also helpeth our infirmities; for we know not what we should pray for as we ought; but the Spirit itself maketh intercession for us with groanings that cannot be uttered." That the Spirit of God does in some way 'make intercession for the saints," is abundantly evident from these passages; but it may be useful to inquire, first, In what sense this is to be understood, or in what way the Spirit acts as a Spirit of grace and supplication; and secondly, What lessons, whether of warning, direction, or encouragement, may be deduced from the doctrine of his agency in prayer.

1. In explanation of this doctrine, it is not to be understood as importing that the Holy Spirit makes intercession for us in his own person, or that he directly addresses his prayer to the Father on our behalf. Christ, as Mediator, prayed for his disciples while he was yet on earth, and he still makes continual intercession for them in heaven, by appearing in the presence of God for them; but the Holy Spirit is never represented in Scripture as interceding in the same way, either by offering up his own personal request, or by appearing for us at the throne. He does intercede, however, in another way, by "dwelling in us" as "the Spirit of grace and supplication," disposing and enabling us to pray for ourselves. He is the Spirit of supplication, just as he is the Spirit of faith, and repentance, and hope. He is the author of these spiritual graces, the source whence they flow, and by which they are continually sustained. Yet they exist in the believer, and are exercised by him, so as to form part of his own personal character; and just so the Spirit is said to make intercession for us, when he stirs us up to intercede for ourselves, and gives us grace to desire and to ask what blessings we severally require. That this is the sense in which the doctrine is to be understood appears from several expressions, which imply that, by the Spirit's grace, believers are taught and enabled to offer up their own supplications at the throne; for, first of all, it is not the Spirit considered as a distinct person of the Godhead that is said to intercede, but "the Spirit that dwelleth in you," even the Spirit of adoption, whereby we cry, "Abba, Father". And, secondly, it is expressly said, that the Spirit helpeth our infirmities; for we know not what we should pray for as we ought – our own prayers being directly referred to, and his interposition designed to remove those hindrances, and supply those defects in us, which would otherwise impair or interrupt our communion with God: – and thirdly, it is added, that "he maketh intercession for us with groanings which cannot be uttered"; an expression which cannot be applied personally to the Spirit, but is aptly descriptive of that moral earnestness and deep concern which he awakens in our own hearts; and accordingly it is added, "He that searcheth the hearts knoweth the mind of the Spirit."'These various expressions are sufficient to show, that, by the intercession of the Spirit, we are to understand the earnest supplication and prayer which we are disposed and enabled, by his grace, to offer up at the throne.

If any one doubt the necessity of the Spirit's aid in the exercise of prayer, there is enough in the words of the apostle to convince him of his error; for even an inspired man, classing himself along with other believers, says, "The Spirit also helpeth our infirmities; for we know not what we should pray for as we ought."'This humbling confession of our own infirmity and ignorance, and of our simple dependence on the grace and strength of the Spirit, is, indeed, much at variance with the natural feelings of the human heart, which is prone to self-sufficiency and presumptuous confidence in its own unaided powers; but there is reason to fear that those who have never felt their need of the Spirit's grace in the exercise of prayer have either never prayed at all, or if they have observed the outward form, are still strangers to its spiritual nature, as the greatest work, the highest and holiest service of the soul, by which it holds communion with God, in the exercise of those graces of faith, and love, and hope, which are all inspired and sustained by the Holy Spirit. The careless and presumptuous sinner, or the cold and formal professor, may be conscious of no difficulty in prayer which cannot be overcome by the power of his own natural faculties: he may content himself with a repetition of a form of words, such as his memory can easily retain and recall, and caring for no further communion with God than what may be implied in the occasional or regular use of that form, he is not sensible of any infirmity such as calls for the aid of the Spirit. But not such are the feelings of any true believer, for never is he more sensible of his own infirmity, and of his absolute dependence on the Spirit's grace, than when he seeks, in the hour of prayer, to spread his case before the Lord, and to hold communion and fellowship with him as his Father in heaven. Having some idea, however inadequate, of the greatness and majesty of God; and some sense, however feeble, of the spirituality of his service; knowing that "God is a Spirit, and that they that worship him must worship him in spirit and in truth'; but conscious at the same time of much remaining darkness, of the corruptions which still cleave to him, and of the manifold distractions to which his mind is subject, even in the most solemn exercises, he knows what those "infirmities" are of which the apostle speaks, and will be ready to join with him in the humbling confession, "We know not what things we should pray for as we ought." His own experience teaches him that the spirit of prayer is not the natural and spontaneous product of his own heart; that it was implanted there, and that it must be continually sustained by grace from on high; and long after he has been enabled to come with comfort to the throne of grace, and to pour out his heart with much of the peace which a spirit of adoption imparts, he may be reminded, by the variations of his own experience, that he must be dependent, from first to last, on the Spirit's grace for all his earnestness and all his enjoyment in prayer. Oh! what believer has not occasionally felt his own utter emptiness, and the barrenness even of this precious privilege, when, left to himself, he attempted to pray, while the spirit of prayer was withheld! You may have retired at your usual hour to your closets, and fallen upon your knees, and used even your accustomed words; but you felt that your affections were cold, your desires languid, and your whole heart straitened and oppressed. You strove once more to renew your request, and with greater urgency than before; but in spite of all your efforts your thoughts began to wander even in God's immediate presence; and as you rose from your knees, you were ready to exclaim, "Oh that it were with me as in months past! Oh, that I knew where I might find him!

that I might come even to his seat! I would order my cause before him, and fill my mouth with arguments." On such occasions you complain of unbelief, of a wandering mind, of a hard and insensible heart; and these complaints are frequently heard amongst God's people, for I believe that he often visits them with such experiences for the very purpose of impressing them with a humbling sense of their own infirmity, and reminding them of their dependence on the Spirit for the right use and enjoyment of all the means of grace.

The grace of the Holy Ghost, then, is indispensable, if we would maintain the spirit and enjoy the exercise of prayer; but we must ever remember, that in this, as in every other part of his work, he acts by the use of means, and in a way that is wisely adapted to the rational and moral nature with which we are endowed. He acts upon us, not as mere machines, but as moral agents; and by various considerations and motives, he teaches and disposes us to pray. Every part of his work as the Spirit of grace has a tendency to prepare us for this exercise; for whether he act as a reprover, convincing us of sin, – or as a sanctifier, subduing our corruptions, or as a comforter, giving us peace and joy in believing, or as a teacher, enlarging our views of divine truth, and confirming our faith in it, all the operations of his grace are subservient more or less directly to the exercise of prayer. But that we may have a clear and distinct idea of the Spirit's agency as "the Spirit of grace and supplication," it may be observed more particularly, that –

I. He enables us for prayer, by disclosing to us our necessities and wants, our sins and shortcomings, so as to impress us with a deep sense of our absolute dependence on God. This is intimated when it is said, "The Spirit also helpeth our infirmities; for we know not what we should pay for as we ought." Self-ignorance is a great hindrance to fervent prayer. We are not duly sensible of our wants, and hence we have no earnest desire for those supplies of grace which we really need: we are apt to say with the Laodiceans, "I am rich and increased with goods, and have need of nothing"; not knowing that "we are wretched, and miserable, and poor, and blind, and naked."

Our prayers have respect either to our

temporal or our spiritual wants, and with reference to both we need the enlightening and directing grace of the Spirit. In respect to our temporal wants, it might seem that we could have little difficulty in understanding them, and in praying for what things we need; but I apprehend every experienced believer will be ready to acknowledge his ignorance on this subject, and to confess that he often knows not what is really good for him. Every condition of life has its peculiar snares, and temptations, and trials; and one of the most precious fruits of the Spirit is a disposition to resign ourselves to the will of God, and to pray for temporal blessings only insofar as they may be consistent with, or conducive to, our spiritual welfare. This resigned and spiritual frame of mind is beautifully expressed in the prayer of Agur: "Give me neither poverty nor riches: feed me with food convenient for me: lest I be full, and deny thee, and say, Who is the Lord? or lest I be poor, and steal, and take the name of my God in vain." This is so far from being the natural disposition of our hearts, that the apostle represents the very opposite spirit as prevailing among professing Christians, and breathing in their very prayers: "Ye ask and receive not, because ye ask amiss, that ye may consume it on your lusts."

In reference, again, to our spiritual wants, we are often lamentably ignorant of their nature and extent; and they who have paid most attention to the state of their hearts will be the first to feel how much they need the grace of the Spirit to direct them to a discovery of their sins. Thus David exclaims, "Who can understand his errors? cleanse thou me from secret faults"; "Search me, O God, and know my heart: try me, and know my thoughts: and see if there be any wicked way in me, and lead me in the way everlasting." Nothing is more necessary to prayer than to know the "plague of our hearts."

2. The Holy Spirit, besides disclosing to us our wants, our weaknesses, and our sins, makes known the rich provision of all needful grace which is treasured up in Christ; and this is as useful for our direction and encouragement as the discovery of our necessities is for awakening our desires, since it is, in a great measure, owing to our ignorance or unbelief

in regard to the rich provision of the Gospel, that we "know not what we should pray for as we ought." The Holy Spirit makes known to the believer, in all their fullness and variety, the inestimable blessings of redemption; for "he takes of the things, of Christ, and shows them unto us"; and he is sent that we may "know the things which are freely given to us of God."

A clear discovery of the rich and glorious privileges which Christ has purchased for his people, is at once a means of direction and a source of encouragement in prayer: when they are placed before us in all their variety and extent, we feel how much we need them, how suitable they are to our real wants, and how infinitely precious and desirable in themselves. Pardon, repentance, holiness, peace of conscience, eternal life – when these and similar blessings are vividly conceived of as having been purchased by the Savior for his people, and offered to all without exception in the Gospel, we see what we should pray for; and we feel also that we have a free right and warrant to pray for them, infinitely great and precious though they be. Ignorance of the gracious provisions of the Gospel, or a dim and indistinct apprehension, either of the nature of these blessings, or of the method by which they were provided, or of the terms on which they are offered, is a great hindrance to prayer; but prayer becomes free and lively in proportion as we are taught by the Spirit to know the things which are "freely given to us of God." These are great blessings, and when we pray for them we may well feel that we make a great request of God; but when we know that they are all treasured up for us in the fullness that is in Christ, and that they are freely tendered to us in the Gospel, "we come boldly to the throne of grace, that we may obtain mercy, and find grace to help in every time of need."

3. The Holy Spirit assists us in prayer, by working in us such dispositions and desires as make us to seek for those supplies of grace which we need, with earnest, importunate, and persevering supplication: "As the hart panteth after the water brooks, so panteth my soul after thee, O God. My soul thirsteth for God, for the living God: when shall I come and appear before God?"

Naturally we have no such disposition

or desire. The carnal mind which is enmity against God, is naturally averse from those spiritual blessings of which it stands in need. True, it is desirous of exemption from pain and punishment and danger; but whatever is spiritual is obnoxious to its taste, insomuch that were an unrenewed mind supposed (if we may suppose a case which is never realized in actual experience) to be sensible, on the one hand, of its sin and misery and danger, and enabled to perceive, on the other, the number and variety of the blessings which have been purchased and offered by Christ; it would, if left to follow its own inclination without the restraining and renewing grace of the Spirit, refuse to accept God's great salvation!

The awakening of spiritual desire in the heart is the work of God's Spirit; and that desire must be kept alive by his continued agency: "Blessed are they that hunger and thirst after righteousness; for they shall be filled." This new disposition or desire makes prayer natural, easy, and delightful to the people of God. Just as a natural man hungers and thirsts for food and drink, so the renewed man hungers and thirsts after righteousness. He has a new spiritual appetite, which naturally and spontaneously seeks its proper spiritual aliment. And hence those commands and observances which are a burden and bondage to mere formalists are an easy yoke to every living Christian.

4. The Holy Spirit helps us in prayer by strengthening and exciting into lively exercise those spiritual graces which are essentially implied in communion with God. Prayer properly consists in the exercise of these graces: it is not the mere utterance of words, nor is it even the mere expression of natural feeling; it is an exercise of repentance, of faith, of love, of trust and delight in God; of repentance, which is expressed in the language of confession; of faith, for he that cometh to God must believe that he is the rewarder of them that "diligently seek him"; of love, for we call him "Abba, Father," "our Father which art in heaven"; of trust, for we commit our case into his hands; and of delight, for the promise is, "Delight thyself in the Lord, and he will give thee the desires of thine heart." These graces are not only presupposed or implied in prayer, but

prayer properly consists in the lively exercise of them, insomuch, that where these graces are awanting, there is no prayer, whatever forms may be observed, and whatever words employed. Now let it be remembered, that all these graces are the fruits of the Spirit, that they are at first implanted, and must ever afterwards be nourished, by the Spirit, and you will perceive at once how the Spirit may assist us in prayer simply by strengthening and exciting into lively exercise all the gracious affections of the soul. By this means he gives us freedom and comfort in prayer: for where these graces are absent, prayer is a mere form; where they are weak, prayer is cold and languid; but where they abound, prayer is the soul's communion with God.

5. The Spirit aids us in this exercise, by helping our infirmities, when he either removes the hindrances to prayer, or stirs us up to watch against them, and to rise above them.

There are many hindrances to prayer, some of them external, arising from the body, or the world, others of them internal, arising from the state of our own hearts. Of the latter, I may mention ignorance, unbelief, indifference, despondency, and such like; which are removed by the Holy Spirit, as he is the enlightener, the sanctifier, and the comforter of God's people: and of the former, bodily infirmities, the cares and business of life, the dissipating influence of society, and such like, from which the Spirit promises no exemption to any of his people, but which he strengthens them to resist, and enables them to overcome. But if we would overcome these hindrances to prayer, we must avail ourselves of those helps which the Spirit of God has provided for us, remembering that he acts in the use of ordinary means, and that his grace is to be sought in the way of duty.

II. Many lessons might be deduced from the doctrine of the Spirit's agency as "the Spirit of grace and supplication," applicable alike for our warning, our direction, and our encouragement in prayer.

We learn from it that prayer is a very solemn exercise, an exercise in which we not only hold direct converse with God whom we address, but in which God also holds converse with us by the operation of his Spirit in our hearts; and as this reflection is fitted to rebuke and humble us on account of the carelessness with which we have too often approached his throne, so it should warn us against the guilt and danger of calling on his name without some suitable feelings of reverence and godly fear.

We learn from it that prayer is an exercise far beyond our natural power, and demands the exercise of graces which can only be imparted by the Spirit of God; and this reflection, again, should direct us to look to the Spirit of all grace, and to implore his aid, as often as we come to the throne.

We learn from it that God has made the most ample provision for our being restored to his communion and fellowship: for not only is he revealed as the hearer and the answerer of prayer, sitting on the throne of grace, and waiting to be gracious; and not only is Christ revealed as our advocate and intercessor, standing beside the throne, and ready to present our requests, perfumed with the incense of his own merits; but lest, when all outward impediments were removed, there might still remain some hindrance in our own hearts, the Holy Spirit is also revealed as "the Spirit of grace and supplication," "who intercedeth for the saints according to the will of God"; and as this precious truth should encourage us to ask his grace to help our infirmities, so should it inspire the hope of an answer in peace; for every prayer that is prompted by the Spirit is a pledge of its own fulfillment, seeing that "God who searcheth the hearts knoweth what is the mind of the Spirit, because he maketh intercession for the saints according to the will of God." And although we should feel as if we were at a loss for words to express our desires to God, even this should not discourage us; the desire of the heart is prayer, although it should find no fit utterance; for Moses' heart spake only, when God said, "Wherefore criest thou unto me"; and Hannah's, when "she spake in her heart"; her lips moved, but her voice was not heard, yet without words "she poured out her heart before the Lord"; and the very want of suitable expressions may only show that the Spirit is making intercession for us "with groanings that cannot be uttered."

But while we are warned, and directed, and encouraged by this precious truth, we must habitually bear in mind that the Spirit's grace is to be sought in the path of duty; that his influence is not designed to supersede but to stimulate our industry; and that if we would overcome the hindrances which prevent or mar our communion with God, we must diligently avail ourselves of the helps which he has provided for our use. Where prayer is prevented or abridged by any necessary cause, and especially by bodily infirmity, the words of Christ himself show that he will make every reasonable allowance for our weakness: for on that memorable night, when he was in an agony in the garden, and when his soul was exceeding sorrowful, even unto death, and his sweat was as it were great drops of blood falling to the ground, his disciples, whom he commanded to watch, began to sleep; he gently rebuked them, saying, "What! couldest thou not watch one hour?" and exhorted them, "Watch and pray, lest ye enter into temptation"; yet no sooner was the warning uttered, than he himself suggested their excuse, "The spirit truly is willing, but the flesh is weak." But there are other hindrances to prayer, for which no such allowance can be made, and which we must watch against and overcome in the use of every appointed means, if we would expect the blessing of the Spirit. Our bodily infirmities themselves, when they proceed, as they often do, from sloth and self-indulgence, and from the fullness of a pampered appetite, are reasons for deep self-humiliation, when they mar our communion with God; and we should watch unto prayer, and even fast, if need be, remembering the apostle's words, "I keep under my body, and bring it into subjection, lest by any means, having preached the Gospel to others, I should myself be cast away." And in like manner, the necessary business of life must be attended to; but the absorbing cares, the idle amusements, the mere vanities of the world, which so often abridge the time and destroy the comfort of prayer, should be watchfully guarded against, and steadily resisted, if we would enjoy the communion of the Spirit in our fellowship with God.

James Buchanan

On Praying in the Spirit

John Bunyan

I will Pray with the Spirit and with the Understanding also
or
A Discourse Touching Prayer; Wherein Is Briefly Discovered

CONTENTS

1. What Prayer Is
2. What It Is To Pray With The Spirit
3. What It Is To Pray With The Spirit And With The Understanding Also

"For we know not what we should pray for as we ought: – the Spirit – helpeth our infirmities" (Rom 8:26).

"I will pray with the Spirit, and I will pray with the understanding also" – (1 Cor 14:15).

Prayer is an ordinance of God, and that to be used both in public and private; yea, such an ordinance as brings those that have the spirit of supplication into great familiarity with God; and is also so prevalent in action, that it getteth of God, both for the person that prayeth, and for them that are prayed for, great things. It is the opener of the heart of God, and a means by which the soul, though empty, is filled. By prayer the Christian can open his heart to God, as to a friend, and obtain fresh testimony of God's friendship to him. I might spend many words in distinguishing between public and private prayer; as also between that in the heart, and that with the vocal voice. Something also might be spoken to distinguish between the gifts and graces of prayer; but eschewing this method, my business shall be at this time only to show you the very heart of prayer, without which, all your lifting up, both of hands, and eyes, and voices, will be to no purpose at all. "I will pray with the Spirit."

The method that I shall go on in at this time shall be,

FIRST. To show you what true prayer is.

SECOND. To show you what it is to pray with the Spirit.

THIRD. What it is to pray with the Spirit and understanding also. And so,

FOURTHLY. To make some short use and application of what shall be spoken.

WHAT PRAYER IS

First,.What [true] prayer is.

Prayer is a sincere, sensible, affectionate pouring out of the heart or soul to God, through Christ, in the strength and assistance of the Holy Spirit, for such things as God hath promised, or according to the Word, for the good of the church, with submission, in faith, to the will of God.

In this description are these seven things.

First, It is a sincere;

Second, A sensible;

Third, An affectionate, pouring out of the soul to God, through Christ;

Fourth, By the strength or assistance of the Spirit;

Fifth, For such things as God hath promised, or, according to his word;

Sixth, For the good of the church;

Seventh, With submission in faith to the will of God.

FIRST. For the first of these, it is a *sincere* pouring out of the soul to God. Sincerity is such a grace as runs through all the graces of God in us, and through all the actings of a Christian, and hath the sway in them too, or else their actings are not any thing regarded of God, and so of and in prayer, of which particularly David speaks, when he mentions prayer. "I cried unto him," the Lord "with my mouth, and he was extolled with my tongue. If I regard iniquity in my heart, the Lord will not hear" my prayer (Psa 66:17, 18). Part of the exercise of prayer is sincerity, without which God looks not upon it as prayer in a good sense (Psa 16:1–4). Then "ye shall seek me and find me, when ye shall search for me with all your heart" (Jer 29:12–13). The want of this made the Lord reject their prayers in Hosea 7:14, where he saith, "They have not cried unto me with their heart," that is, in sincerity, "when they howled upon their beds." But for a pretence, for a show in hypocrisy, to be seen of men, and applauded for the same, they prayed. Sincerity was that which Christ commended in Nathaniel, when he was under the fig tree. "Behold, an Israelite indeed, in whom is no guile." Probably this good man was pouring out of his soul to God in prayer under the fig tree, and that in a sincere and unfeigned spirit before the Lord. The prayer that hath this in it as one of the principal ingredients, is the prayer that God looks at. Thus, "The prayer of the upright is his delight" (Prov 15:8).

And why must sincerity be one of the essentials of prayer which is accepted of God, but because sincerity carries the soul in all simplicity to open its heart to God, and to tell him the case plainly, without equivocation; to condemn itself plainly, without dissembling; to cry to God heartily, without complimenting. "I have surely heard Ephraim bemoaning himself thus; Thou has chastised me, and I was chastised, as a bullock unaccustomed to the yoke" (Jer 31:18). Sincerity is the same in a corner alone, as it is before the face of the world. It knows not how to wear two vizards, one for an appearance before men, and another for a short snatch in a corner; but it must have God, and be with him in the duty of prayer. It is not lip-labor that it doth regard, for it is the heart that God looks at, and that which sincerity looks at, and that which prayer comes from, if it be that prayer which is accompanied with sincerity.

SECOND. It is a sincere and *sensible* pouring out of the heart or soul. It is not, as many take it to be, even a few babbling, prating, complimentary expressions, but a sensible feeling there is in the heart. Prayer hath in it a sensibleness of diverse things; sometimes sense of sin, sometimes of mercy received, sometimes of the readiness of God to give mercy, etc.

1. A sense of the want of mercy, by reason of the danger of sin. The soul, I say, feels, and from feeling sighs, groans, and breaks at the heart. For right prayer bubbleth out of the heart when it is overpressed with grief and bitterness, as blood is forced out of the flesh by reason of some heavy burden that lieth upon it (1 Sam 1:10; Psa 69:3). David roars, cries, weeps, faints at heart, fails at the eyes, loseth his moisture, etc., (Psa 38:8–10). Hezekiah mourns like a dove (Isa 38:14). Ephraim bemoans himself (Jer 31:18). Peter weeps bitterly (Matt 26:75). Christ hath strong cryings and tears (Heb 5:7). And all this from a sense of the justice of God, the guilt of sin, the pains of hell and destruction. "The sorrows of death compassed me, and the pains of hell gat hold upon me: I found trouble and sorrow." Then cried I unto the Lord (Psa 116:3, 4). And in another place, "My sore ran in the night" (Psa 77:2). Again, "I am bowed down greatly; I go mourning all the day long" (Psa 38:6). In all these instances, and in hundreds more that might be named, you may see that prayer carrieth in it a sensible feeling disposition, and that first from a sense of sin.

2. Sometimes there is a sweet sense of mercy received; encouraging, comforting, strengthening, enlivening, enlightening mercy, etc. Thus David pours out his soul, to bless, and praise, and admire the great God for his loving-kindness to such poor vile wretches. "Bless the Lord, O my soul; and all that is within me bless his holy name. Bless the Lord, O my soul, and forget not all his benefits. Who forgiveth all thine iniquities, who healeth all thy diseases; who redeemeth thy life from destruction; who crowneth thee with loving-kindness and tender mercies; who satisfieth thy mouth with good things, so that thy youth is renewed like the eagle's" (Psa 103:1–5). And thus is the prayer of saints sometimes turned into praise and thanksgiving, and yet are prayers still. This is a mystery; God's people pray with their praises, as it is written, "Be careful for nothing, but in every thing by prayer, and supplication, with thanksgiving, let your request be made known unto God" (Phil 4:6). A sensible thanksgiving, for mercies received, is a mighty prayer in the sight of God; it prevails with him unspeakably.

3. In prayer there is sometimes in the soul a sense of mercy to be received. This again sets the soul all on a flame. "Thou, O lord of hosts," saith David, "hast revealed to thy servant, saying I will build thee an house; therefore hath thy servant found in his heart to pray – unto thee" (2 Sam 7:27). This provoked Jacob, David, Daniel, with others – even a sense of mercies to be received – which caused them, not by fits and starts, nor yet in a foolish frothy way, to babble over a few words written in a paper; but mightily, fervently, and continually, to groan out their conditions before the Lord, as being sensible, sensible, I say, of their wants, their misery, and the willingness of God to show mercy (Gen 32:10, 11; Dan 9:3, 4).

A good sense of sin, and the wrath of God, with some encouragement from God to come unto him, is a better Common-prayer-book than that which is taken out of the Papistical mass-book, being the scraps and fragments of the devices of some popes, some friars, and I wot not what.

THIRD. Prayer is a sincere, sensible, and an *affectionate* pouring out of the soul to God. O! the heat, strength, life, vigor, and affection, that is in right prayer! "As the hart panteth after the water-brooks, so panteth my soul after thee, O God" (Psa 42:1). "I have longed after thy precepts" (Psa 119:40). "I have longed for thy salvation" (ver 174). "My soul longeth, yea, even fainteth, for the courts of the Lord; my heart and my flesh crieth out for the living God" (Psa 84:2). "My soul breaketh for the longing that it hath unto thy judgments at all times" (Psa 119:20). Mark ye here, "My soul longeth," it longeth, it longeth, etc. O what affection is here discovered in prayer! The like you have in Daniel. "O Lord, hear; O Lord, forgive; O Lord, hearken and do; defer not, for thine own sake, O my God" (Dan 9:19). Every syllable carrieth a mighty vehemency in it. This is called the fervent, or the working prayer, by James. And so again, "And being in an agony, he prayed more earnestly" (Luke 22:44). Or had his affections more and more drawn out after God for his helping hand. O! How wide are the most of men with their prayers from this prayer, that is, prayer in God's account! Alas! The greatest part of men make no conscience at all of the duty; and as for them that do, it is to be feared that many of them are very great strangers to a sincere, sensible, and affectionate pouring out their hearts or souls to God; but even content themselves with a little lip-labor and bodily exercise, mumbling over a few imaginary prayers. When the affections are indeed engaged in prayer, then, then the whole man is engaged, and that in such sort, that the soul will spend itself to nothing, as it were, rather than it will go without that good desired, even communion and solace with Christ. And hence it is that the saints have spent their strengths, and lost their lives, rather than go without the blessing (Psa 69:3; 38:9, 10; Gen 32:24, 26).

All this is too, too evident by the ignorance, profaneness, and spirit of envy, that reign in the hearts of those men that are so hot for the forms, and not the power of praying. Scarce one of forty among them know what it is to be born again, to have communion with the

Father through the Son; to feel the power of grace sanctifying their hearts: but for all their prayers, they still live cursed, drunken, whorish, and abominable lives, full of malice, envy, deceit, persecuting of the dear children of God. O what a dreadful after-clap is coming upon them! which all their hypocritical assembling themselves together, with all their prayers, shall never be able to help them against, or shelter them from.

Again, It is a pouring out of the heart or soul. There is in prayer an unbosoming of a man's self, an opening of the heart to God, an affectionate pouring out of the soul in requests, sighs, and groans. "All my desire is before thee," saith David, "and my groaning is not hid from thee" (Psa 38:9). And again, "My soul thirsteth for God, for the living God. When shall I come and appear before God? When I remember these things, I pour out my soul in me" (Psa 42:2, 4). Mark, "I pour out my soul." It is an expression signifying, that in prayer there goeth the very life and whole strength to God. As in another place, "Trust in him at all times; ye people, – pour out your heart before him" (Psa 62:8). This is the prayer to which the promise is made, for the delivering of a poor creature out of captivity and thralldom. "If from thence thou shalt seek the Lord thy God, thou shalt find him, if thou seek him with all thy heart and with all thy soul" (Deut 4:29).

Again, It is a pouring out of the heart or soul to God. This showeth also the excellency of the spirit of prayer. It is the great God to which it retires. "When shall I come and appear before God?" And it argueth, that the soul that thus prayeth indeed, sees an emptiness in all things under heaven; that in God alone there is rest and satisfaction for the soul. "Now she that is a widow indeed, and desolate, trusteth in God" (1 Tim 5:5). So saith David, "In thee, O Lord, do I put my trust; let me never be put to confusion. Deliver me in thy righteousness, and cause me to escape; incline thine ear to me, and save me. Be thou my strong habitation, whereunto I may continually resort: – for thou art my rock and my fortress; deliver me, O my God, – out of the hand of the unrighteous and cruel man. For thou art my hope, O Lord God, thou art my trust from my youth" (Psa 71:1–5). Many in a wording way speak of God; but right prayer makes God his hope, stay, and all. Right prayer sees nothing substantial, and worth the looking after, but God. And that, as I said before, it doth in a sincere, sensible, and affectionate way.

Again, It is a sincere, sensible, affectionate pouring out of the heart or soul to God, through Christ. This through Christ must needs be added, or else it is to be questioned, whether it be prayer, though in appearance it be never so eminent or eloquent.

Christ is the way through whom the soul hath admittance to God, and without whom it is impossible that so much as one desire should come into the ears of the Lord of Sabaoth (John 14:6). "If ye shall ask anything in my name"; "whatsoever ye shall ask the Father in my name, I will do it" (John 14:13, 14). This was Daniel's way in praying for the people of God; he did it in the name of Christ. "Now therefore, O our God, hear the prayer of thy servant, and his supplications, and cause thy face to shine upon thy sanctuary that is desolate, for the Lord's sake" (Dan 9:17). And so David, "For thy name's sake," that is, for thy Christ's sake, "pardon mine iniquity, for it is great" (Psa 25: 11). But now, it is not every one that maketh mention of Christ's name in prayer, that doth indeed, and in truth, effectually pray to God in the name of Christ, or through him. This coming to God through Christ is the hardest part that is found in prayer. A man may more easily be sensible of his works, ay, and sincerely too desire mercy, and yet not be able to come to God by Christ. That man that comes to God by Christ, he must first have the knowledge of him; "for he that cometh to God, must believe that he is" (Heb 11:6). And so he that comes to God through Christ, must be enabled to know Christ. Lord, saith Moses, "show me now thy way, that I may know thee" (Exo 33:13).

This Christ, none but the Father can reveal (Matt 11:27). And to come through Christ, is for the soul to be enabled of God to shroud itself under the shadow of the Lord Jesus, as a man shroudeth himself under a thing for safeguard (Matt 16:16). Hence it is that David so often terms Christ his shield, buckler, tower, fortress, rock of defense, etc., (Psa 18:2; 27:1; 28:1). Not only because by him he overcame his enemies, but because through him he found favor with God the Father. And so he saith to Abraham, "Fear not, I am thy shield," etc., (Gen 15:1). The man then that comes to God through Christ, must have faith, by which he puts on Christ, and in him appears before God. Now he that hath faith is born of God, born again, and so becomes one of the sons of God; by virtue of which he is joined to Christ, and made a member of him (John 3:5, 7; 1:12). And therefore, secondly he, as a member of Christ, comes to God; I say, as a member of him, so that God looks on that man as a part of Christ, part of his body, flesh, and bones, united to him by election, conversion, illumination, the Spirit being conveyed into the heart of that poor man by God (Eph 5:30). So that now he comes to God in Christ's merits, in his blood, righteousness, victory, intercession, and so stands before him, being "accepted in his Beloved" (Eph 1:6). And because this poor creature is thus a member of the Lord Jesus, and under this consideration hath admittance to come to God; therefore, by virtue of this union also, is the Holy Spirit conveyed into him, whereby he is able to pour out himself, to wit, his soul, before God, with his audience. And this leads me to the next, or fourth particular.

FOURTH. Prayer is a sincere, sensible, affectionate, pouring out of the heart or soul to God through Christ, by the strength or *assistance of the Spirit*. For these things do so depend one upon another, that it is impossible that it should be prayer, without there be a joint concurrence of them; for though it be never so famous, yet without these things, it is only such prayer as is rejected of God. For without a sincere, sensible, affectionate pouring out of the heart to God, it is but lip-labor; and if it be not through Christ, it falleth far short of ever sounding well in the ears of God. So also, if it be not in the strength and assistance of the Spirit, it is but like the sons of Aaron, offering with strange fire (Lev 10:1, 2). But I shall speak more to this under the second head; and therefore in the meantime, that which is not petitioned through the teaching and assistance of the Spirit, it is not possible that it should be "according to the will of God (Rom 8:26, 27).

FIFTH. Prayer is a sincere, sensible, affectionate pouring out of the heart, or soul, to God, through Christ, in the strength and assistance of the Spirit, *for such things as God hath promised*, etc., (Matt 6:6–8). Prayer it is, when it is within the compass of God's Word; and it is blasphemy, or at best vain babbling, when the petition is beside the book. David therefore still in his prayer kept his eye on the Word of God. "My soul," saith he, "cleaveth to the dust; quicken me according to thy word." And again, "My soul melteth for heaviness, strengthen thou me according unto thy word" (Psa 119: 25–28; see also 41, 42, 58, 65, 74, 81, 82, 107, 147, 154, 169, 170). And, "remember thy word unto thy servant, upon which thou hast caused me to hope" (ver 49). And indeed the Holy Ghost doth not immediately quicken and stir up the heart of the Christian without, but by, with, and through the Word, by bringing that to the heart, and by opening of that, whereby the man is provoked to go to the Lord, and to tell him how it is with him, and also to argue, and supplicate, according to the Word; thus it was with Daniel, that mighty prophet of the Lord. He understanding by books that the captivity of the children of Israel was hard at an end; then, according unto that word, he maketh his prayer to God. "I Daniel," saith he, "understood by books," viz., the writings of Jeremiah, "the number of the years whereof the word of the Lord came to Jeremiah, – that he would accomplish seventy years in the desolations of Jerusalem. And I set my face to the Lord God, to seek by prayer and supplications, with fasting, and sackcloth, and ashes" (Dan 9:2, 3). So that I say, as the Spirit is the helper and the governor of the soul, when it prayeth according to the will of God; so it guideth by and according to, the Word of God and his promise. Hence it is that our Lord Jesus Christ himself did make a stop, although his life lay at stake for it. I could now pray to my Father, and he should give me more than twelve legions of angels; but how then must the scripture be fulfilled that thus it must be? (Matt 26:53, 54). As who should say, Were there but a word for it in the scripture, I should soon be out of the hands of mine enemies, I should be helped by angels; but the scripture will not warrant this kind of praying, for that saith otherwise. It is a praying then according to the Word and promise. The Spirit by the Word must direct, as well in the manner, as in the matter of prayer. "I will pray with the Spirit,

and I will pray with the understanding also" (1 Cor 14:15). But there is no understanding without the Word. For if they reject the word of the Lord, "what wisdom is in them?" (Jer 8:9).

SIXTH. *For the good of the church.* This clause reacheth in whatsoever tendeth either to the honor of God, Christ's advancement, or his people's benefit. For God, and Christ, and his people are so linked together that if the good of the one be prayed for, to wit, the church, the glory of God, and advancement of Christ, must needs be included. For as Christ is in the Father, so the saints are in Christ; and he that toucheth the saints, toucheth the apple of God's eye; and therefore pray for the peace of Jerusalem, and you pray for all that is required of you. For Jerusalem will never be in perfect peace until she be in heaven; and there is nothing that Christ doth more desire than to have her there. That also is the place that God through Christ hath given to her. He then that prayeth for the peace and good of Zion, or the church, doth ask that in prayer which Christ hath purchased with his blood; and also that which the Father hath given to him as the price thereof. Now he that prayeth for this, must pray for abundance of grace for the church, for help against all its temptations; that God would let nothing be too hard for it; and that all things might work together for its good, that God would keep them blameless and harmless, the sons of God, to his glory, in the midst of a crooked and perverse nation. And this is the substance of Christ's own prayer in John 17. And all Paul's prayers did run that way, as one of his prayers doth eminently show. "And this I pray, that your love may abound yet more and more in knowledge, and in all judgment; that ye may approve things that are excellent; that ye may be sincere, and without offence, till the day of Christ. Being filled with the fruits of righteousness, which are by Jesus Christ unto the glory and praise of God" (Phil 1:9–11). But a short prayer, you see, and yet full of good desires for the church, from the beginning to the end; that it may stand and go on, and that in the most excellent frame of spirit, even without blame, sincere, and without offence, until the day of Christ, let its temptations or persecutions be what they will (Eph 1:16–21; 3:14–19; Col 1:9–13).

SEVENTH. And because, as I said, prayer doth *submit to the will of God*, and say, Thy will be done, as Christ hath taught us (Matt 6:10); therefore the people of the Lord in humility are to lay themselves and their prayers, and all that they have, at the foot of their God, to be disposed of by him as he in his heavenly wisdom seeth best. Yet not doubting but God will answer the desire of his people that way that shall be most for their advantage and his glory. When the saints therefore do pray with submission to the will of God, it doth not argue that they are to doubt or question God's love and kindness to them. But because they at all times are not so wise, but that sometimes Satan may get that advantage of them, as to tempt them to pray for that which, if they had it, would neither prove to God's glory nor his people's good. "Yet this is the confidence that we have in him, that if we ask anything according to his will, he heareth us; and if we know that he hear us, whatsoever we ask, we know that we have the petitions that we desired of him," that is, we asking in the Spirit of grace and supplication (1 John 5:14, 15). For, as I said before, that petition that is not put up in and through the Spirit, it is not to be answered, because it is beside the will of God. For the Spirit only knoweth that, and so consequently knoweth how to pray according to that will of God. "For what man knoweth the things of a man, save the spirit of man which is in him? even so the things of God knoweth no man but the Spirit of God" (1 Cor 2:11). But more of this hereafter. Thus you see, first, what prayer is. Now to proceed.

WHAT IT IS TO PRAY WITH THE SPIRIT

Second. I will pray with the Spirit. Now to pray with the Spirit − for that is the praying man, and none else, so as to be accepted of God − it is for a man, as aforesaid, sincerely and sensibly, with affection, to come to God through Christ, etc.; which sincere, sensible, and affectionate coming must be by the working of God's Spirit.

There is no man nor church in the world that can come to God in prayer, but by the assistance of the Holy Spirit. "For through Christ we all have access by one Spirit unto the Father" (Eph 2:18). Wherefore Paul saith, "For we know not what we should pray for as we ought; but the Spirit itself maketh intercession for us with groanings which cannot be uttered. And he that searcheth the hearts, knoweth what is the mind of the Spirit, because he maketh intercession for the saints according to the will of God" (Rom 8:26, 27). And because there is in this scripture so full a discovery of the spirit of prayer, and of man's inability to pray without it; therefore I shall in a few words comment upon it.

"For we." Consider first the person speaking, even Paul, and, in his person, all the apostles. We apostles, we extraordinary officers, the wise master-builders, that have some of us been caught up into paradise (Rom 15:16; 1 Cor 3:10; 2 Cor 12:4). "We know not what we should pray for." Surely there is no man but will confess, that Paul and his companions were as able to have done any work for God, as any pope or proud prelate in the church of Rome, and could as well have made a Common Prayer Book as those who at first composed this; as being not a whit behind them either in grace or gifts.

"For we know not what we should pray for." We know not the matter of the things for which we should pray, neither the object to whom we pray, nor the medium by or through whom we pray; none of these things know we, but by the help and assistance of the Spirit. Should we pray for communion with God through Christ? should we pray for faith, for justification by grace, and a truly sanctified heart? none of these things know we. "For what man knoweth the things of a man, save the spirit of man which is in him? even so the things of God knoweth no man, but the Spirit of God" (1 Cor 2:11). But here, alas! the apostles speak of inward and spiritual things, which the world knows not (Isa 29:11).

Again, as they know not the matter, etc., of prayer, without the help of the Spirit; so neither know they the manner thereof without the same; and therefore he adds, "We know not what we should pray for as we ought"; but the Spirit helpeth our infirmities, with sighs and groans which cannot be uttered. Mark here, they could not so well and so fully come off in the manner of performing this duty, as these in our days think they can.

The apostles, when they were at the best, yea, when the Holy Ghost assisted them, yet then they were fain to come off with sighs and groans, falling short of expressing their mind, but with sighs and groans which cannot be uttered.

But here now, the wise men of our days are so well skilled as that they have both the manner and matter of their prayers at their finger-ends; setting such a prayer for such a day, and that twenty years before it comes. One for Christmas, another for Easter, and six days after that. They have also bounded how many syllables must be said in every one of them at their public exercises. For each saint's day, also, they have them ready for the generations yet unborn to say. They can tell you, also, when you shall kneel, when you shall stand, when you should abide in your seats, when you should go up into the chancel, and what you should do when you come there. All which the apostles came short of, as not being able to compose so profound a manner; and that for this reason included in this scripture, because the fear of God tied them to pray as they ought.

"For we know not what we should pray for as we ought." Mark this, "as we ought." For the not thinking of this word, or at least the not understanding it in the spirit and truth of it, hath occasioned these men to devise, as Jeroboam did, another way of worship, both for matter and manner, than is revealed in the Word of God (1 Kings 12:26–33). But, saith Paul, we must pray as we ought; and this WE cannot do by all the art, skill, and cunning device of men or angels. "For we know not what we should pray for as we ought, but the Spirit"; nay, further, it must be "the Spirit itself" that helpeth our infirmities; not the Spirit and man's lusts; what man of his own brain may imagine and devise, is one thing, and what they are commanded, and ought to do, is another. Many ask and have not, because they ask amiss; and so are never the nearer the enjoying of those things they petition for (James 4:3). It is not to pray at random that will put off God, or cause him to answer. While prayer is making, God is searching the heart, to see from what root and spirit it doth arise (1 John 5:14). "And he that searcheth the heart knoweth,"

that is, approveth only, the meaning "of the Spirit, because he maketh intercession for the saints according to the will of God." For in that which is according to his will only, he heareth us, and in nothing else. And it is the Spirit only that can teach us so to ask; it only being able to search out all things, even the deep things of God. Without which Spirit, though we had a thousand Common Prayer Books, yet we know not what we should pray for as we ought, being accompanied with those infirmities that make us absolutely incapable of such a work. Which infirmities, although it is a hard thing to name them all, yet some of them are these that follow.

FIRST. Without the Spirit man is so infirm that he cannot, with all other means whatsoever, be enabled to think one right saving thought of God, of Christ, or of his blessed things; and therefore he saith of the wicked, "God is not in all his thoughts," (Psa 10:4); unless it be that they imagine him altogether such a one as themselves (Psa 50:21). For "every imagination of the thoughts of his heart was only evil," and that "continually" (Gen 6:5; 8:21). They then not being able to conceive aright of God to whom they pray, of Christ through whom they pray, nor of the things for which they pray, as is before showed, how shall they be able to address themselves to God, without the Spirit help this infirmity? Peradventure you will say, By the help of the Common Prayer Book; but that cannot do it, unless it can open the eyes, and reveal to the soul all these things before touched. Which that it cannot, it is evident; because that is the work of the Spirit only. The Spirit itself is the revealer of these things to poor souls, and that which doth give us to understand them; wherefore Christ tells his disciples, when he promised to send the Spirit, the Comforter, "He shall take of mine and show unto you"; as if he had said, I know you are naturally dark and ignorant as to the understanding any of my things; though ye try this course and the other, yet your ignorance will still remain, the veil is spread over your heart, and there is none can take away the same, nor give you spiritual understanding but the Spirit. The Common Prayer Book will not do it, neither can any man expect that it should be instrumental that way, it being none of God's ordinances; but a thing since the Scriptures were written, patched together one piece at one time, and another at another; a mere human invention and institution, which God is so far from owning of, that he expressly forbids it, with any other such like, and that by manifold sayings in his most holy and blessed Word. (See Mark 7:7, 8, and Col 2:16–23; Deut 12:30–32; Prov 30:6; Deut 4:2; Rev 22:18). For right prayer must, as well in the outward part of it, in the outward expression, as in the inward intention, come from what the soul doth apprehend in the light of the Spirit; otherwise it is condemned as vain and an abomination, because the heart and tongue do not go along jointly in the same, neither indeed can they, unless the Spirit help our infirmities (Mark 7; Prov 28:9; Isa 29:13). And this David knew full well, which did make him cry, "Lord, open thou my lips, and my mouth shall show forth thy praise" (Psa 51:15). I suppose there is none can imagine but that David could speak and express himself as well as others, nay, as any in our generation, as is clearly manifested by his word and his works. Nevertheless when this good man, this prophet, comes into God's worship, then the Lord must help, or he can do nothing. "Lord, open thou my lips, and" then "my mouth shall show forth thy praise." He could not speak one right word, except the Spirit itself gave utterance. "For we know not what we should pray for as we ought, but the Spirit itself helpeth our infirmities." But,

SECOND. It must be a praying with the Spirit, that is, the effectual praying; because without that, as men are senseless, so hypocritical, cold, and unseemly in their prayers; and so they, with their prayers, are both rendered abominable to God (Matt 23:14; Mark 12:40; Luke 18:11, 12; Isa 58:2, 3). It is not the excellency of the voice, nor the seeming affection, and earnestness of him that prayeth, that is anything regarded of God without it. For man, as man, is so full of all manner of wickedness, that as he cannot keep a word, or thought, so much less a piece of prayer clean, and acceptable to God through Christ; and for this cause the Pharisees, with their prayers, were rejected. No question but they were excellently able to express themselves in words, and also for length of time, too, they were very notable; but

they had not the Spirit of Jesus Christ to help them, and therefore they did what they did with their infirmities or weaknesses only, and so fell short of a sincere, sensible, affectionate pouring out of their souls to God, through the strength of the Spirit. That is the prayer that goeth to heaven, that is sent thither in the strength of the Spirit. For,

THIRD. Nothing but the Spirit can show a man clearly his misery by nature, and so put a man into a posture of prayer. Talk is but talk, as we use to say, and so it is but mouth-worship, if there be not a sense of misery, and that effectually too. O the cursed hypocrisy that is in most hearts, and that accompanieth many thousands of praying men that would be so looked upon in this day, and all for want of a sense of their misery! But now the Spirit, that will sweetly show the soul its misery, where it is, and what is like to become of it, also the intolerableness of that condition. For it is the Spirit that doth effectually convince of sin and misery, without the Lord Jesus, and so puts the soul into a sweet, sensible, affectionate way of praying to God according to his word (John 16:7–9).

FOURTH. If men did see their sins, yet without the help of the Spirit they would not pray. For they would run away from God, with Cain and Judas, and utterly despair of mercy, were it not for the Spirit. When a man is indeed sensible of his sin, and God's curse, then it is a hard thing to persuade him to pray; for, saith his heart, "There is no hope," it is in vain to seek God (Jer 2:25; 18:12). I am so vile, so wretched, and so cursed a creature, that I shall never be regarded! Now here comes the Spirit, and stayeth the soul, helpeth it to hold up its face to God, by letting into the heart some small sense of mercy to encourage it to go to God, and hence it is called "the Comforter" (John 14:26).

FIFTH. It must be in or with the Spirit; for without that no man can know how he should come to God the right way. Men may easily say they come to God in his Son: but it is the hardest thing of a thousand to come to God aright and in his own way, without the Spirit. It is "the Spirit" that "searcheth all things, yea, the deep things of God" (1 Cor 2:10). It is the Spirit that must show us the way of coming to God, and also what there is in God that makes him desirable: "I pray thee," saith Moses, "show me now thy way, that I may know thee" (Exo 33:13). And, He shall take of mine, and "show it unto you" (John 16:14).

SIXTH. Because without the Spirit, though a man did see his misery, and also the way to come to God; yet he would never be able to claim a share in either God, Christ, or mercy, with God's approbation. O how great a task is it, for a poor soul that becomes sensible of sin and the wrath of God, to say in faith, but this one word, "Father!" I tell you, however hypocrites think, yet the Christian that is so indeed finds all the difficulty in this very thing, it cannot say God is its Father. O! saith he, I dare not call him Father; and hence it is that the Spirit must be sent into the hearts of God's people for this very thing, to cry Father: it being too great a work for any man to do knowingly and believingly without it (Gal 4:6). When I say knowingly, I mean, knowing what it is to be a child of God, and to be born again. And when I say believingly, I mean, for the soul to believe, and that from good experience, that the work of grace is wrought in him. This is the right calling of God Father; and not as many do, to say in a babbling way, the Lord's prayer (so called) by heart, as it lieth in the words of the book. No, here is the life of prayer, when in or with the Spirit, a man being made sensible of sin, and how to come to the Lord for mercy; he comes, I say, in the strength of the Spirit, and crieth Father. That one word spoken in faith, is better than a thousand prayers, as men call them, written and read, in a formal, cold, lukewarm way. O how far short are those people of being sensible of this, who count it enough to teach themselves and children to say the Lord's prayer, the creed, with other sayings; when, as God knows, they are senseless of themselves, their misery, or what it is to be brought to God through Christ! Ah, poor soul! Study your misery, and cry to God to show you your confused blindness and ignorance, before you be so rife in calling God your Father, or teaching your children either so to say. And know, that to say God is your Father, in a way of prayer or conference, without any experiment of the work of grace on your souls, it is to say you are Jews and are not, and so to lie. You say, Our Father; God saith, You blaspheme! You say you are Jew, that is, true Christians; God

saith, You lie! "Behold I will make them of the synagogue of Satan, which say they are Jews, and are not, but do lie" (Rev 3:9). "And I know the blasphemy of them that say they are Jews, and are not, but are the synagogue of Satan" (Rev 2:9). And so much the greater the sin is, by how much the more the sinner boasts it with a pretended sanctity, as the Jews did to Christ, in the 8th of John, which made Christ, even in plain terms, to tell them their doom, for all their hypocritical pretences (John 8:41–45). And yet forsooth every cursed whoremaster, thief, and drunkard, swearer, and perjured person; they that have not only been such in times past, but are even so still: these I say, by some must be counted the only honest men, and all because with their blasphemous throats, and hypocritical hearts, they will come to church, and say, "Our Father!" Nay further, these men, though every time they say to God, Our Father, do most abominably blaspheme, yet they must be compelled thus to do. And because others that are of more sober principles, scruple the truth of such vain traditions; therefore they must be looked upon to be the only enemies of God and the nation: when as it is their own cursed superstition that doth set the great God against them, and cause him to count them for his enemies (Isa 53:10). And yet just like to Bonner, that blood-red persecutor, they commend, I say, these wretches, although never so vile, if they close in with their traditions, to be good churchmen, the honest subjects; while God's people are, as it hath always been, looked upon to be a turbulent, seditious, and factious people (Ezra 4:12–16).

Therefore give me leave a little to reason with thee, thou poor, blind, ignorant sot.

(1.) It may be thy great prayer is to say, "Our Father which art in heaven," etc. Dost thou know the meaning of the very first words of this prayer? Canst thou indeed, with the rest of the saints, cry, Our Father? Art thou truly born again? Hast thou received the spirit of adoption? Dost thou see thyself in Christ, and canst thou come to God as a member of him? Or art thou ignorant of these things, and yet darest thou say, Our Father? Is not the devil thy father? (John 8:44). And dost thou not do the deeds of the flesh? And yet darest thou say to God, Our Father? Nay, art thou not a desperate persecutor of the children of God? Hast thou not cursed them in thine heart many a time? And yet dost thou out of thy blasphemous throat suffer these words to come, even our Father? He is their Father whom thou hatest and persecutest. But as the devil presented himself amongst the sons of God, (Job 1), when they were to present themselves before the Father, even our Father, so is it now; because the saints were commanded to say, Our Father, therefore all the blind ignorant rabble in the world, they must also use the same words, Our Father.

(2.) And dost thou indeed say, "Hallowed be thy name" with thy heart? Dost thou study, by all honest and lawful ways, to advance the name, holiness, and majesty of God? Doth thy heart and conversation agree with this passage? Dost thou strive to imitate Christ in all the works of righteousness, which God doth command of thee, and prompt thee forward to? It is so, if thou be one that can truly with God's allowance cry, "Our Father." Or is it not the least of thy thoughts all the day? And dost thou not clearly make it appear, that thou art a cursed hypocrite, by condemning that with thy daily practice, which thou pretendest in thy praying with thy dissembling tongue?

(3.) Wouldst thou have the kingdom of God come indeed, and also his will to be done in earth as it is in heaven? Nay, notwithstanding, thou according to the form, sayest, Thy kingdom come, yet would it not make thee ready to run mad, to hear the trumpet sound, to see the dead arise, and thyself just now to go and appear before God, to reckon for all the deeds thou hast done in the body? Nay, are not the very thoughts of it altogether displeasing to thee? And if God's will should be done on earth as it is in heaven, must it not be thy ruin? There is never a rebel in heaven against God, and if he should so deal on earth, must it not whirl thee down to hell? And so of the rest of the petitions. Ah! How sadly would even those men look, and with what terror would they walk up and down the world, if they did but know the lying and blaspheming that proceedeth out of their mouth, even in their most pretended sanctity? The Lord awaken you, and teach you, poor souls, in all humility, to take heed that you be not rash and unadvised with

your heart, and much more with your mouth! When you appear before God, as the wise man saith, "Be not rash with thy mouth, and let not thine heart be hasty to utter any thing" (Eccl 5:2); especially to call God Father, without some blessed experience when thou comest before God. But I pass this.

SEVENTH. It must be a praying with the Spirit if it be accepted, because there is nothing but the Spirit that can lift up the soul or heart to God in prayer: "The preparations of the heart in man, and the answer of the tongue, is from the Lord" (Prov 16:1). That is, in every work for God, and especially in prayer, if the heart run with the tongue, it must be prepared by the Spirit of God. Indeed the tongue is very apt, of itself, to run without either fear or wisdom: but when it is the answer of the heart, and that such a heart as is prepared by the Spirit of God, then it speaks so as God commands and doth desire.

They are mighty words of David, where he saith, that he lifteth his heart and his soul to God (Psa 25:1). It is a great work for any man without the strength of the Spirit, and therefore I conceive that this is one of the great reasons why the Spirit of God is called a Spirit of supplications, (Zech 12:10), because it is that which helpeth the heart when it supplicates indeed to do it; and therefore saith Paul, "Praying with all prayer and supplication in the Spirit" (Eph 6:18). And so in my text, "I will pray with the Spirit." Prayer, without the heart be in it, is like a sound without life; and a heart, without it be lifted up of the Spirit, will never pray to God.

EIGHTH. As the heart must be lifted up by the Spirit, if it pray aright, so also it must be held up by the Spirit when it is up, if it continue to pray aright. I do not know what, or how it is with others' hearts, whether they be lifted up by the Spirit of God, and so continued, or no: but this I am sure of, First, That it is impossible that all the prayer-books that men have made in the world, should lift up, or prepare the heart; that is the work of the great God himself. And, in the second place, I am sure that they are as far from keeping it up, when it is up. And indeed here is the life of prayer, to have the heart kept with God in the duty. It was a great matter for Moses to keep his hands lifted up to God in prayer; but how much more then to keep the heart in it! (Exo 17:12).

The want of this is that which God complains of; that they draw nigh to him with their mouth, and honor him with their lips, but their hearts were far from him (Isa 29:13; Eze 33), but chiefly that they walk after the commandments and traditions of men, as the scope of Matthew 15:8, 9 doth testify. And verily, may I but speak my own experience, and from that tell you the difficulty of praying to God as I ought, it is enough to make your poor, blind, carnal men to entertain strange thoughts of me. For, as for my heart, when I go to pray, I find it so loth to go to God, and when it is with him, so loth to stay with him, that many times I am forced in my prayers, first to beg of God that he would take mine heart, and set it on himself in Christ, and when it is there, that he would keep it there. Nay, many times I know not what to pray for, I am so blind, nor how to pray, I am so ignorant; only, blessed be grace, the Spirit helps our infirmities (Psa 86:11).

O! the starting-holes that the heart hath in the time of prayer; none knows how many bye-ways the heart hath, and back-lanes, to slip away from the presence of God. How much pride also, if enabled with expressions. How much hypocrisy, if before others. And how little conscience is there made of prayer between God and the soul in secret, unless the Spirit of supplication be there to help? When the Spirit gets into the heart, then there is prayer indeed, and not till then.

NINTH. The soul that doth rightly pray, it must be in and with the help and strength of the Spirit; because it is impossible that a man should express himself in prayer without it. When I say, it is impossible for a man to express himself in prayer without it, I mean, that it is impossible that the heart, in a sincere and sensible affectionate way, should pour out itself before God, with those groans and sighs that come from a truly praying heart, without the assistance of the Spirit. It is not the mouth that is the main thing to be looked at in prayer, but whether the heart is so full of affection and earnestness in prayer with God, that it is impossible to express their sense and desire; for then a man desires indeed, when his desires are so strong, many, and mighty,

that all the words, tears, and groans that can come from the heart, cannot utter them: "The Spirit – helpeth our infirmities, – and maketh intercession for us with [sighs and] groanings which cannot be uttered" (Rom 8:26).

That is but poor prayer which is only discovered in so many words. A man that truly prays one prayer, shall after that never be able to express with his mouth or pen the unutterable desires, sense, affection, and longing that went to God in that prayer.

The best prayers have often more groans than words: and those words that it hath are but a lean and shallow representation of the heart, life, and spirit of that prayer. You do not find any words of prayer, that we read of, come out of the mouth of Moses, when he was going out of Egypt, and was followed by Pharaoh, and yet he made heaven ring again with his cry (Exo 14:15). But it was inexpressible and unsearchable groans and cryings of his soul in and with the Spirit. God is the God of spirits, and his eyes look further than at the outside of any duty whatsoever (Num 16:22). I doubt this is but little thought on by the most of them that would be looked upon as a praying people (1 Sam 16:7).

The nearer a man comes in any work that God commands him to the doing of it according to his will, so much the more hard and difficult it is; and the reason is, because man, as man, is not able to do it. But prayer, as aforesaid, is not only a duty, but one of the most eminent duties, and therefore so much the more difficult: therefore Paul knew what he said, when he said, "I will pray with the Spirit." He knew well it was not what others writ or said that could make him a praying person; nothing less than the Spirit could do it.

TENTH. It must be with the Spirit, or else as there will be a failing in the act itself, so there will be a failing, yea, a fainting, in the prosecution of the work. Prayer is an ordinance of God, that must continue with a soul so long as it is on this side glory. But, as I said before, it is not possible for a man to get up his heart to God in prayer; so it is as difficult to keep it there, without the assistance of the Spirit. And if so, then for a man to continue from time to time in prayer with God, it must of necessity be with the Spirit.

Christ tells us, that men ought always to pray, and not to faint (Luke 18:1). And again tells us, that this is one definition of a hypocrite, that either he will not continue in prayer, or else if he do it, it will not be in the power, that is, in the spirit of prayer, but in the form, for a pretence only (Job 27:10; Matt 23:14). It is the easiest thing of a hundred to fall from the power to the form, but it is the hardest thing of many to keep in the life, spirit, and power of any one duty, especially prayer; that is such a work, that a man without the help of the Spirit cannot so much as pray once, much less continue, without it, in a sweet praying frame, and in praying, so to pray as to have his prayers ascend into the ears of the Lord God of Sabaoth.

Jacob did not only begin, but held it: "I will not let thee go, unless thou bless me" (Gen 32). So did the rest of the godly (Hosea 12:4). But this could not be without the spirit of prayer. It is through the Spirit that we have access to the Father (Eph 2:18).

The same is a remarkable place in Jude, when he stirreth up the saints by the judgment of God upon the wicked to stand fast, and continue to hold out in the faith of the gospel, as one excellent means thereto, without which he knew they would never be able to do it. Saith he, "Building up yourselves on your most holy faith, praying in the Holy Ghost" (Jude 20). As if he had said, Brethren, as eternal life is laid up for the persons that hold out only, so you cannot hold out unless you continue praying in the Spirit. The great cheat that the devil and antichrist delude the world withal, it is to make them continue in the form of any duty, the form of preaching, of hearing, or praying, etc. These are they that have "a form of godliness, but denying the power thereof; from such turn away" (2 Tim 3:5).

Here followeth the third thing; to wit,

WHAT IT IS TO PRAY WITH THE SPIRIT, AND WITH THE UNDERSTANDING

THIRD. And now to the next thing, what it is to pray with the Spirit, and to pray with the understanding also. For the apostle puts a clear distinction between praying with the Spirit, and praying with the Spirit and understanding: therefore when he saith, "he will pray with the Spirit," he adds, "and I will pray with the understanding also." This distinction was occasioned through the Corinthians not observing that it was their duty to do what they did to the edification of themselves and others too: whereas they did it for their own commendations. So I judge: for many of them having extraordinary gifts, as to speak with divers tongues, etc., therefore they were more for those mighty gifts than they were for the edifying of their brethren; which was the cause that Paul wrote this chapter to them, to let them understand, that though extraordinary gifts were excellent, yet to do what they did to the edification of the church was more excellent. For, saith the apostle, "if I pray in an unknown tongue, my spirit prayeth, but my understanding," and also the understanding of others, "is unfruitful" (1 Cor 14:3, 4, 12, 19, 24, 25. Read the scope of the whole chapter). Therefore, "I will pray with the Spirit, and I will pray with the understanding also."

It is expedient then that the understanding should be occupied in prayer, as well as the heart and mouth: "I will pray with the Spirit, and I will pray with the understanding also." That which is done with understanding, is done more effectually, sensibly, and heartily, as I shall show farther anon, than that which is done without it; which made the apostle pray for the Colossians, that God would fill them "with the knowledge of his will, in all wisdom and spiritual understanding" (Col 1:9). And for the Ephesians, that God would give unto them "the spirit of wisdom and revelation, in the knowledge of him" (Eph 1:17). And so for the Philippians, that God would make them abound "in knowledge, and in all judgment" (Phil 1:9). A suitable understanding is good in everything a man undertakes, either civil or spiritual; and therefore it must be desired by all them that would be a praying people. In my speaking to this, I shall show you what it is to pray with understanding.

Understanding is to be taken both for speaking in our mother-tongue, and also experimentally. I pass the first, and treat only on the second.

For the making of right prayers, it is to be required that there should be a good or spiritual understanding in all them who pray to God.

FIRST. To pray with understanding, is to pray as being instructed by the Spirit in the understanding of the want of those things which the soul is to pray for. Though a man be in never so much need of pardon of sin, and deliverance from wrath to come, yet if he understand not this, he will either not desire them at all, or else be so cold and lukewarm in his desires after them, that God will even loathe his frame of spirit in asking for them. Thus it was with the church of the Laodiceans, they wanted knowledge or spiritual understanding; they knew not that they were poor, wretched, blind, and naked. The cause whereof made them, and all their services, so loathsome to Christ, that he threatens to spew them out of his mouth (Rev 3:16, 17). Men without understanding may say the same words in prayer as others do; but if there be an understanding in the one, and none in the other, there is, O there is a mighty difference in speaking the very same words! The one speaking from a spiritual understanding of those things that he in words desires, and the other words it only, and there is all.

SECOND. Spiritual understanding espieth in the heart of God a readiness and willingness to give those things to the soul that it stands in need of. David by this could guess at the very thoughts of God towards him (Psa 40:5). And thus it was with the woman of Canaan; she did by faith and a right understanding discern, beyond all the rough carriage of Christ, tenderness and willingness in his heart to save, which caused her to be vehement and earnest, yea, restless, until she did enjoy the mercy she stood in need of (Matt 15:22–28).

And understanding of the willingness that is in the heart of God to save sinners, there is nothing will press the soul more to seek after God, and to cry for pardon, than it. If a man should see a pearl worth an hundred pounds lie in a ditch, yet if he understood not the value of it, he would lightly pass it by: but if he once get the knowledge of it, he would venture up to the neck for it. So it is with souls concerning the things of God: if a man once get an understanding of the worth of them, then his heart, nay, the very strength of his soul, runs after them, and he will never leave crying till he have them. The two blind men in the gospel,

because they did certainly know that Jesus, who was going by them, was both able and willing to heal such infirmities as they were afflicted with: therefore they cried, and the more they were rebuked, the more they cried (Matt 20:29–31).

THIRD. The understanding being spiritually enlightened, hereby there is the way, as aforesaid, discovered, through which the soul should come unto God; which gives great encouragement unto it. It is else with a poor soul, as with one who hath a work to do, and if it be not done, the danger is great; if it be done, so is the advantage. But he knows not how to begin, nor how to proceed; and so, through discouragement, lets all alone, and runs the hazard.

FOURTH. The enlightened understanding sees largeness enough in the promises to encourage it to pray; which still adds to it strength to strength. As when men promise such and such things to all that will come for them, it is great encouragement to those that know what promises are made, to come and ask for them.

FIFTH. The understanding being enlightened, way is made for the soul to come to God with suitable arguments, sometimes in a way of expostulation, as Jacob (Gen 32:9). Sometimes in way of supplication, yet not in a verbal way only, but even from the heart there is forced by the Spirit, through the understanding, such effectual arguments as moveth the heart of God. When Ephraim gets a right understanding of his own unseemly carriages towards the Lord, then he begins to bemoan himself (Jer 31:18–20). And in bemoaning of himself, he used such arguments with the Lord, that it affects his heart, draws out forgiveness, and makes Ephraim pleasant in his eyes through Jesus Christ our Lord: "I have surely heard Ephraim bemoaning himself thus," saith God, "Thou hast chastised me, and I was chastised; as a bullock unaccustomed to the yoke; turn thou me, and I shall be turned; for thou art the Lord my God. Surely after that I was turned, I repented, and after that I was instructed," or had a right understanding of myself, "I smote upon my thigh, I was ashamed; yea, even confounded; because I did bear the reproach of my youth." These be Ephraim's complaints and bemoanings of himself; at which the Lord breaks forth into these heart-melting expressions, saying, "Is Ephraim my dear son? Is he a pleasant child? For since I spake against him, I do earnestly remember him still; therefore my bowels are troubled for him; I will surely have mercy upon him, saith the Lord." Thus, you see, that as it is required to pray with the Spirit, so it is to pray with the understanding also. And to illustrate what hath been spoken by a similitude: – set the case, there should come two a-begging to your door; the one is a poor, lame, wounded, and almost starved creature, the other is a healthful lusty person; these two use the same words in their begging; the one saith he is almost starved, so doth the other: but yet the man that is indeed the poor, lame, or maimed person, he speaks with more sense, feeling, and understanding of the misery that is mentioned in their begging, than the other can do; and it is discovered more by his affectionate speaking, his bemoaning himself. His pain and poverty make him speak more in a spirit of lamentation than the other, and he shall be pitied sooner than the other, by all those that have the least dram of natural affection or pity. Just thus it is with God: there are some who out of custom and formality go and pray; there are others who go in the bitterness of their spirits: the one he prays out of bare notion and naked knowledge; the other hath his words forced from him by the anguish of his soul. Surely that is the man that God will look at, "even to him that is poor," of an humble "and of a contrite spirit, and trembleth at my word" (Isa 66:2).

SIXTH. An understanding well enlightened is of admirable use also, both as to the matter and manner of prayer. He that hath his understanding well exercised, to discern between good and evil, and in it placed a sense either of the misery of man, or the mercy of God; that soul hath no need of the writings of other men to teach him by forms of prayer. For as he that feels the pain needs not to be taught to cry O! even so he that hath his understanding opened by the Spirit needs not so to be taught of other men's prayers, as that he cannot pray without them. The present sense, feeling, and pressure that lieth upon his spirit, provokes him to groan out his request unto the Lord. When

David had the pains of hell catching hold on him, and the sorrows of hell compassing him about, he needs not a bishop in a surplice to teach him to say, "O Lord, I beseech thee, deliver my soul" (Psa 116:3, 4). Or to look into a book, to teach him in a form to pour out his heart before God. It is the nature of the heart of sick men, in their pain and sickness, to vent itself for ease, by dolorous groans and complainings to them that stand by. Thus it was with David, in Psalm 38:1–12. And thus, blessed be the Lord, it is with them that are endued with the grace of God.

SEVENTH. It is necessary that there be an enlightened understanding, to the end that the soul be kept in a continuation of the duty of prayer.

The people of God are not ignorant how many wiles, tricks, and temptations the devil hath to make a poor soul, who is truly willing to have the Lord Jesus Christ, and that upon Christ's terms too; I say, to tempt that soul to be weary of seeking the face of God, and to think that God is not willing to have mercy on such a one as him. Ay, saith Satan, thou mayest pray indeed, but thou shalt not prevail. Thou seest thine heart is hard, cold, dull, and dread; thou dost not pray with the Spirit, thou dost not pray in good earnest, thy thoughts are running after other things, when thou pretendest to pray to God. Away hypocrite, go no further, it is but in vain to strive any longer! Here now, if the soul be not well informed in its understanding, it will presently cry out, "the Lord hath forsaken me, and my Lord hath forgotten me" (Isa 49:14). Whereas the soul rightly informed and enlightened saith, Well, I will seek the Lord, and wait; I will not leave off, though the Lord keep silence, and speak not one word of comfort (Isa 40:27). He loved Jacob dearly, and yet he made him wrestle before he had the blessing (Gen 32:25–27). Seeming delays in God are no tokens of his displeasure; he may hide his face from his dearest saints (Isa 8:17). He loves to keep his people praying, and to find them ever knocking at the gate of heaven; it may be, says the soul, the Lord tries me, or he loves to hear me groan out my condition before him.

The woman of Canaan would not take seeming denials for real ones; she knew the

Lord was gracious, and the Lord will avenge his people, though he bear long with them (Luke 18:1–6). The Lord hath waited longer upon me than I have waited upon him; and thus it was with David, "I waited patiently," saith he; that is, it was long before the Lord answered me, though at the last "he inclined" his ear "unto me, and heard my cry" (Psa 40:1). And the most excellent remedy for this is, an understanding well informed and enlightened. Alas, how many poor souls are there in the world, that truly fear the Lord, who, because they are not well informed in their understanding, are oft ready to give up all for lost, upon almost every trick and temptation of Satan! The Lord pity them, and help them to "pray with the Spirit, and with the understanding also." Much of mine own experience could I here discover; when I have been in my fits of agony of spirit, I have been strongly persuaded to leave off, and to seek the Lord no longer; but being made to understand what great sinners the Lord hath had mercy upon, and how large his promises were still to sinners; and that it was not the whole, but the sick, not the righteous, but the sinner, not the full, but the empty, that he extended his grace and mercy unto. This made me, through the assistance of his Holy Spirit, to cleave to him, to hang upon him, and yet to cry, though for the present he made no answer; and the Lord help all his poor, tempted, and afflicted people to do the like, and to continue, though it be long, according to the saying of the prophet (Hab 2:3). And to help them (to that end) to pray, not by the inventions of men, and their stinted forms, but "with the Spirit, and with the understanding also."

QUERIES AND OBJECTIONS ANSWERED
And now to answer a query or two, and so to pass on to the next thing.

QUERY FIRST. But what would you have us poor creatures to do that cannot tell how to pray? The Lord knows I know not either how to pray, or what to pray for.

ANSWER. Poor heart! thou canst not, thou complainest, pray. Canst thou see thy misery? Hath God showed thee that thou art by nature under the curse of his law? If so, do not mistake, I know thou dost groan and that most bitterly. I am persuaded thou canst scarcely be found doing any thing in thy calling, but prayer breaketh from thy heart. Have not thy groans gone up to heaven from every corner of thy house? (Rom 8:26). I know it is thus; and so also doth thine own sorrowful heart witness thy tears, thy forgetfulness of thy calling, etc. Is not thy heart so full of desires after the things of another world, that many times thou dost even forget the things of this world? Prithee read this scripture, Job 23:12.

QUERY SECOND. Yea, but when I go into secret, and intend to pour out my soul before God, I can scarce say anything at all.

ANSWER. 1. Ah! Sweet soul! It is not thy words that God so much regards, as that he will not mind thee, except thou comest before him with some eloquent oration. His eye is on the brokenness of thine heart; and that it is that makes the very bowels of the Lord to run over. "A broken and a contrite heart, O God, thou wilt not despise" (Psa 51:17).

2. The stopping of thy words may arise from overmuch trouble in thy heart. David was so troubled sometimes, that he could not speak (Psa 77:3, 4). But this may comfort all such sorrowful hearts as thou art, that though thou canst not through the anguish of thy spirit speak much, yet the Holy Spirit stirs up in thine heart groans and sighs, so much the more vehement: when the mouth is hindered, yet the spirit is not. Moses, as aforesaid, made heaven ring again with his prayers, when (that we read of) not one word came out of his mouth (Exo 14:15). But,

3. If thou wouldst more fully express thyself before the Lord, study, first, Thy filthy estate; secondly, God's promises; thirdly, The heart of Christ. Which thou mayest know or discern,

(1.) By his condescension and bloodshed.

(2.) By the mercy he hath extended to great sinners formerly, and plead thine own vileness, by way of bemoaning; Christ's blood by way of expostulation; and in thy prayers, let the mercy that he hath extended to other great sinners, together with his rich promises of grace, be much upon thy heart. Yet let me counsel thee, (a.) Take heed that thou content not thyself with words. (b.) That thou do not think that God looks only at them neither. But, (c.) However, whether thy words be few or many, let thine heart go with them; and then shalt thou seek him, and find him, when thou shalt seek him with thy whole heart (Jer 29:13).

OBJECTION. But though you have seemed to speak against any other way of praying but by the Spirit, yet here you yourself can give direction how to pray.

ANSWER. We ought to prompt one another forward to prayer, though we ought not to make for each other forms of prayer. To exhort to pray with Christian direction is one thing, and to make stinted forms for the tying up the Spirit of God to them is another thing. The apostle gives them no form to pray withal, yet directs to prayer (Eph 6:18; Rom 15:30–32). Let no man therefore conclude, that because we may with allowance give instructions and directions to pray, that therefore it is lawful to make for each other forms of prayer.

OBJECTION. But if we do not use forms of prayer, how shall we teach our children to pray?

ANSWER. My judgment is, that men go the wrong way to teach their children to pray, in going about so soon to teach them any set company of words, as is the common use of poor creatures to do.

For to me it seems to be a better way for people betimes to tell their children what cursed creatures they are, and how they are under the wrath of God by reason of original and actual sin; also to tell them the nature of God's wrath, and the duration of the misery; which if they conscientiously do, they would sooner teach their children to pray than they do. The way that men learn to pray, it is by conviction for sin; and this is the way to make our sweet babes do so too. But the other way, namely, to be busy in teaching children forms of prayer, before they know any thing else, it is the next way to make them cursed hypocrites, and to puff them up with pride. Teach therefore your children to know their wretched state and condition; tell them of hell-fire and their sins, of damnation, and salvation; the way to escape the one, and to enjoy the other, if you know it yourselves, and this will make tears run down your sweet babes' eyes, and hearty groans flow from their hearts; and then also you may tell them to whom they should pray, and through whom they should pray: you may tell them also of God's promises, and his former grace

extended to sinners, according to the word.

Ah! Poor sweet babes, the Lord open their eyes, and make them holy Christians. Saith David, "Come ye children, hearken unto me; I will teach you the fear of the Lord" (Psa 34:11). He doth not say, I will muzzle you up in a form of prayer; but "I will teach you the fear of the Lord"; which is, to see their sad states by nature, and to be instructed in the truth of the gospel, which doth through the Spirit beget prayer in every one that in truth learns it. And the more you teach them this, the more will their hearts run out to God in prayer. God never did account Paul a praying man, until he was a convinced and converted man; no more will it be with any else (Acts 9:11).

OBJECTION. But we find that the disciples desired that Christ would teach them to pray, as John also taught his disciples; and that thereupon he taught them that form called the Lord's Prayer.

ANSWER. 1. To be taught by Christ, is that which not only they, but we desire; and seeing he is not here in his person to teach us, the Lord teach us by his Word and Spirit; for the Spirit it is which he hath said he would send to supply in his room when he went away, as it is (John 14:16; 16:7).

2. As to that called a form, I cannot think that Christ intended it as a stinted form of prayer. (1.) Because he himself layeth it down diversely, as is to be seen, if you compare Matthew 6 and Luke 11. Whereas if he intended it as a set form, it must not have been so laid down, for a set form is so many words and no more. (2.) We do not find that the apostles did ever observe it as such; neither did they admonish others so to do. Search all their epistles, yet surely they, both for knowledge to discern and faithfulness to practice, were as eminent as any he ever since in the world which would impose it.

3. But, in a word, Christ by those words, "Our Father," etc., doth instruct his people what rules they should observe in their prayers to God. (1.) That they should pray in faith. (2.) To God in the heavens. (3.) For such things as are according to his will, etc. Pray thus, or after this manner.

OBJECTION. But Christ bids pray for the Spirit; this implieth that men without the Spirit may notwithstanding pray and be heard. (See

Luke 11:9–13).

ANSWER. The speech of Christ there is directed to his own (verse 1). Christ's telling of them that God would give his Holy Spirit to them that ask him, is to be understood of giving more of the Holy Spirit; for still they are the disciples spoken to, which had a measure of the Spirit already; for he saith, "when ye pray, say, Our Father," (verse 2) I say unto you (verse 8). And I say unto you, (verse 9) "If ye then, being evil, know how to give good gifts unto your children, how much more shall your heavenly Father give the Holy Spirit to them that ask him," (verse 13). Christians ought to pray for the Spirit, that is, for more of it, though God hath endued them with it already.

QUESTION. Then would you have none pray but those that know they are the disciples of Christ?

ANSWER. Yes.

1. Let every soul that would be saved pour out itself to God, though it cannot through temptation conclude itself a child of God. And,

2. I know if the grace of God be in thee, it will be as natural to thee to groan out thy condition, as it is for a sucking child to cry for the breast. Prayer is one of the first things that discovers a man to be a Christian (Acts 9:12). But yet if it be right, it is such prayer as followeth. (1.) To desire God in Christ, for himself, for his holiness, love, wisdom, and glory. For right prayer, as it runs only to God through Christ, so it centers in him, and in him alone. "Whom have I in heaven but thee? And there is none upon earth that I desire," long for, or seek after, "beside thee" (Psa 73:25). (2.) That the soul might enjoy continually communion with him, both here and hereafter. "I shall be satisfied, when I awake with" thine image, or in "thy likeness," (Psa 17:15). "For in this we groan earnestly," etc., (2 Cor 5:2). (3.) Right prayer is accompanied with a continual labor after that which is prayed for. "My soul waiteth for the Lord more than they that watch for the morning" (Psa 130:6). "I will rise now, I will seek him whom my soul loveth" (Song 3:2). For mark, I beseech you, there are two things that provoke to prayer. The one is a detestation to sin, and the things of this life; the other is a longing desire after communion with God, in a holy and undefiled state and inheritance. Compare

but this one thing with most of the prayers that are made by men, and you shall find them but mock prayers, and the breathings of an abominable spirit; for even the most of men either do pray at all, or else only endeavor to mock God and the world by so doing; for do but compare their prayer and the course of their lives together, and you may easily see that the thing included in their prayer is the least looked after by their lives. O sad hypocrites!

Thus have I briefly showed you, FIRST, What prayer is; SECOND, What it is to pray with the Spirit; THIRD, What it is to pray with the Spirit, and with the understanding also.

USE AND APPLICATION
Fourth, I shall now speak a word or two of application, and so conclude with,
First, A word of information;
Second, A word of encouragement;
Third, A word of rebuke.

FIRST, A WORD OF INFORMATION
For the first to inform you; as prayer is the duty of every one of the children of God, and carried on by the Spirit of Christ in the soul; so every one that doth but offer to take upon him to pray to the Lord, had need be very wary, and go about that work especially with the dread of God, as well as with hopes of the mercy of God through Jesus Christ.

Prayer is an ordinance of God, in which a man draws very near to God; and therefore it calleth for so much the more of the assistance of the grace of God to help a soul to pray as becomes one that is in the presence of him. It is a shame for a man to behave himself irreverently before a king, but a sin to do so before God. And as a king, if wise, is not pleased with an oration made up with unseemly words and gestures, so God takes no pleasure in the sacrifice of fools (Eccl 5:1, 4). It is not long discourses, nor eloquent tongues, that are the things which are pleasing in the ears of the Lord; but a humble, broken, and contrite heart, that is sweet in the nostrils of the heavenly Majesty (Psa 51:17; Isa 57:15). Therefore for information, know that there are these five things that are obstructions to prayer, and even make void the requests of the creature.

1. When men regard iniquity in their hearts,

at the time of their prayers before God. "If I regard iniquity in my heart, the Lord will not hear" my prayer (Psa 66:18). For the preventing of temptation, that by the misunderstanding of this may seize thy heart, when there is a secret love to that very thing which thou with thy dissembling lips dost ask for strength against. For this is the wickedness of man's heart, that it will even love, and hold fast, that which with the mouth it prays against: and of this sort are they that honor God with their mouth, but their heart is far from him (Isa 29:13; Eze 33:31). O! how ugly would it be in our eyes, if we should see a beggar ask an alms, with an intention to throw it to the dogs! Or that should say with one breath, Pray, you bestow this upon me; and with the next, I beseech you, give it me not! And yet thus it is with these kind of persons; with their mouth they say, "Thy will be done"; and with their hearts nothing less. With their mouth say, "Hallowed be thy name"; and with their hearts and lives thy delight to dishonor him all the day long. These be the prayers that become sin (Psa 109:7), and though they put them up often, yet the Lord will never answer them (2 Sam 22:42).

2. When men pray for a show to be heard, and thought somebody in religion, and the like; these prayers also fall far short of God's approbation, and are never like to be answered, in reference to eternal life. There are two sorts of men that pray to this end.

(1.) Your trencher chaplains, that thrust themselves into great men's families, pretending the worship of God, when in truth the great business is their own bellies; and were notably painted out by Ahab's prophets, and also Nebuchadnezzar's wise men, who, though they pretended great devotion, yet their lusts and their bellies were the great things aimed at by them in all their pieces of devotion.

(2.) Them also that seek repute and applause for their eloquent terms, and seek more to tickle the ears and heads of their hearers than anything else. These be they that pray to be heard of men, and have all their reward already (Matt 6:5). These persons are discovered thus, (a.) They eye only their auditory in their expressions. (b.) They look for commendation when they have done. (c.) Their hearts either rise or fall according to their praise or enlargement.

(d.) The length of their prayer pleaseth them; and that it might be long, they will vainly repeat things over and over (Matt 6:7). They study for enlargements, but look not from what heart they come; they look for returns, but it is the windy applause of men. And therefore they love not to be in their chamber, but among company: and if at any time conscience thrusts them into their closet, yet hypocrisy will cause them to be heard in the streets; and when their mouths have done going their prayers are ended; for they wait not to hearken what the Lord will say (Psa 85:8).

3. A third sort of prayer that will not be accepted of God, it is, when either they pray for wrong things, or if for right things, yet that the thing prayed for might be spent upon their lusts, and laid out to wrong ends. Some have not, because they ask not, saith James, and others ask and have not, because they ask amiss, that they may consume it on their lusts (James 4:2–4). Ends contrary to God's will is a great argument with God to frustrate the petitions presented before him. Hence it is that so many pray for this and that, and yet receive it not. God answers them only with silence; they have their words for their labor; and that is all. Objection. But God hears some persons, though their hearts be not right with him, as he did Israel, in giving quails, though they spent them upon their lusts (Psa 106:14). Answer. If he doth, it is in judgment, not in mercy. He gave them their desire indeed, but they had better have been without it, for he "sent leanness into their soul" (Psa 106:15). Woe be to that man that God answereth thus.

4. Another sort of prayers there are that are not answered; and those are such as are made by men, and presented to God in their own persons only, without their appearing in the Lord Jesus. For though God hath appointed prayer, and promised to hear the prayer of the creature, yet not the prayer of any creature that comes not in Christ. "If ye shall ask anything in my name." And whether ye eat or drink, or whatsoever ye do, do all in the name of the Lord Jesus Christ (Col 3:17). "If ye shall ask anything in my name," etc., (John 14:13, 14), though you be never so devout, zealous, earnest and constant in prayer, yet it is in Christ only that you must be heard and

accepted. But, alas! the most of men know not what it is to come to him in the name of the Lord Jesus, which is the reason they either live wicked, pray wicked, and also die wicked. Or else, that they attain to nothing else but what a mere natural man may attain unto, as to be exact in word and deed betwixt man and man, and only with the righteousness of the law to appear before God.

5. The last thing that hindereth prayer is, the form of it without the power. It is an easy thing for men to be very hot for such things as forms of prayer, as they are written in a book; but yet they are altogether forgetful to inquire with themselves, whether they have the spirit and power of prayer. These men are like a painted man, and their prayers like a false voice. They in person appear as hypocrites, and their prayers are an abomination (Prov 28:9). When they say they have been pouring out their souls to God he saith they have been howling like dogs (Hosea 7:14).

When therefore thou intendest, or art minded to pray to the Lord of heaven and earth, consider these following particulars. 1. Consider seriously what thou wantest. Do not, as many who in their words only beat the air, and ask for such things as indeed they do not desire, nor see that they stand in need thereof. 2. When thou seest what thou wantest, keep to that, and take heed thou pray sensibly.

OBJECTION. But I have a sense of nothing; then, by your argument, I must not pray at all.

ANSWER. 1. If thou findest thyself sense-less in some sad measure, yet thou canst not complain of that senselessness, but by being sensible there is a sense of senselessness. According to thy sense, then, that thou hast of the need of anything, so pray; (Luke 8:9), and if thou art sensible of thy senselessness, pray the Lord to make thee sensible of whatever thou findest thine heart senseless of. This was the usual practice of the holy men of God. "Lord, make me to know mine end," saith David (Psa 39:4). "Lord, open to us this parable," said the disciples (Luke 8:9). And to this is annexed the promise, "Call unto me and I will answer thee, and show thee great and mighty things which thou knowest not," that thou art not sensible of (Jer 33:3). But,

ANSWER. 2. Take heed that thy heart go to God as well as thy mouth. Let not thy mouth go any further than thou strivest to draw thine heart along with it. David would lift his heart and soul to the Lord; and good reason; for so far as a man's mouth goeth along without his heart, so far it is but lip-labor only; and though God calls for, and accepteth the calves of the lips, yet the lips without the heart argueth, not only senselessness, but our being without sense of our senselessness; and therefore if thou hast a mind to enlarge in prayer before God, see that it be with thy heart.

ANSWER. 3. Take heed of affecting expressions, and so to please thyself with the use of them, that thou forget not the life of prayer.

I shall conclude this use with a caution or two.

CAUTION 1. And the first is, take heed thou do not throw off prayer, through sudden persuasions that thou hast not the Spirit, neither prayest thereby. It is the great work of the devil to do his best, or rather worst, against the best prayers. He will flatter your false dissembling hypocrites, and feed them with a thousand fancies of well-doing, when their very duties of prayer, and all other, stink in the nostrils of God, when he stands at a poor Joshua's hand to resist him, that is, to persuade him, that neither his person nor performances are accepted of God (Isa 65:5; Zech 3:1). Take heed, therefore, of such false conclusions and groundless discouragements; and though such persuasions do come in upon thy spirit, be so far from being discouraged by them, that thou use them to put thee upon further sincerity and restlessness of spirit, in thy approaching to God.

CAUTION 2. As such sudden temptations should not stop thee from prayer, and pouring out thy soul to God; so neither should thine own heart's corruptions hinder thee. (Let not thy corruptions stop thy prayers). It may be thou mayest find in thee all those things before mentioned, and that they will be endeavoring to put forth themselves in thy praying to him. Thy business then is to judge them, to pray against them, and to lay thyself so much the more at the foot of God, in a sense of thy own vileness, and rather make an argument from thy vileness and corruption of heart, to plead with God for justifying and sanctifying grace, than an argument of discouragement and despair. David went this way. "O Lord," saith he, "pardon mine iniquity, for it is great" (Psa 25:11).

SECOND. A WORD OF ENCOURAGEMENT

And therefore, secondly, to speak a word by way of encouragement, to the poor, tempted, and cast down soul, to pray to God through Christ. Though all prayer that is accepted of God in reference to eternal life must be in the Spirit – for that only maketh intercession for us according to the will of God, (Rom 8:27) – yet because many poor souls may have the Holy Spirit working on them, and stirring of them to groan unto the Lord for mercy, though through unbelief they do not, nor, for the present, cannot believe that they are the people of God, such as he delights in; yet forasmuch as the truth of grace may be in them, therefore I shall, to encourage them, lay down further these few particulars.

1. That scripture in Luke 11:8 is very encouraging to any poor soul that doth hunger after Christ Jesus. In verses 5–7, he speaketh a parable of a man that went to his friend to borrow three loaves, who, because he was in bed, denied him; yet for his importunity-sake, he did arise and give him, clearly signifying that though poor souls, through the weakness of their faith, cannot see that they are the friends of God, yet they should never leave asking, seeking, and knocking at God's door for mercy. Mark, saith Christ, "I say unto you, though he will not rise and give him, because he is his friend; yet because of his importunity," or restless desires, "he will rise and give him as many as he needeth." Poor heart! thou criest out that God will not regard thee, thou dost not find that thou art a friend to him, but rather an enemy in thine heart by wicked works (Col 1:21). And thou art as though thou didst hear the Lord saying to thee, Trouble me not, I cannot give unto thee, as he in the parable; yet I say, continue knocking, crying, moaning, and bewailing thyself. I tell thee, "though he will not rise and give thee, because thou art his friend; yet, because of thy importunity, he will arise and give thee as many as thou needest." The same in effect you have discovered, Luke 18, in the parable of the unjust judge and

the poor widow; her importunity prevailed with him. And verily, mine own experience tells me, that there is nothing that doth more prevail with God than importunity. Is it not so with you in respect of your beggars that come to your door? Though you have no heart to give them anything at their first asking, yet if they follow you, bemoaning themselves, and will take no nay without an alms, you will give them; for their continual begging overcometh you. Are there bowels in you that are wicked, and will they be wrought upon by an importuning beggar? Go thou and do the like. It is a prevailing motive, and that by good experience, he will arise and give thee as many as thou needest (Luke 11:8).

2. Another encouragement for a poor trembling convinced soul is to consider the place, throne, or seat, on which the great God hath placed himself to hear the petitions and prayers of poor creatures; and that is a "throne of grace" (Heb 4:16). "The mercy-seat" (Exo 25: 22). Which signifieth that in the days of the gospel God hath taken up his seat, his abiding-place, in mercy and forgiveness; and from thence he doth intend to hear the sinner, and to commune with him, as he saith (Exo 25:22), – speaking before of the mercy-seat – "And there I will meet with thee," mark, it is upon the mercy-seat: "There I will meet with thee, and" there "I will commune with thee, from above the mercy-seat." Poor souls! They are very apt to entertain strange thoughts of God, and his carriage towards them: and suddenly to conclude that God will have no regard unto them, when yet he is upon the mercy-seat, and hath taken up his place on purpose there, to the end he may hear and regard the prayers of poor creatures. If he had said, I will commune with thee from my throne of judgment, then indeed you might have trembled and fled from the face of the great and glorious Majesty. But when he saith he will hear and commune with souls upon the throne of grace, or from the mercy-seat, this should encourage thee, and cause thee to hope, nay, to "come boldly unto the throne of grace, that thou mayest obtain mercy, and find grace to help in time of need" (Heb 4:16).

3. There is yet another encouragement to continue in prayer with God: and that is this:

As there is a mercy-seat, from whence God is willing to commune with poor sinners; so there is also by his mercy-seat, Jesus Christ, who continually besprinkleth it with his blood. Hence it is called "the blood of sprinkling" (Heb 12:24). When the high-priest under the law was to go into the holiest, where the mercy-seat was, he might not go in "without blood" (Heb 9:7).

Why so? Because, though God was upon the mercy-seat, yet he was perfectly just as well as merciful. Now the blood was to stop justice from running out upon the persons concerned in the intercession of the high-priest, as in Leviticus 16:13–17, to signify that all thine unworthiness that thou fearest should not hinder thee from coming to God in Christ for mercy. Thou criest out that thou art vile, and therefore God will not regard thy prayers; it is true, if thou delight in thy vileness, and come to God out of a mere pretence. But if from a sense of thy vileness thou do pour out thy heart to God, desiring to be saved from the guilt, and cleansed from the filth, with all thy heart; fear not, thy vileness will not cause the Lord to stop his ear from hearing of thee. The value of the blood of Christ which is sprinkled upon the mercy-seat stops the course of justice, and opens a floodgate for the mercy of the Lord to be extended unto thee. Thou hast therefore, as aforesaid, "boldness to enter into the holiest by the blood of Jesus," that hath made "a new and living way" for thee, thou shalt not die (Heb 10:19, 20).

Besides, Jesus is there, not only to sprinkle the mercy-seat with his blood, but he speaks, and his blood speaks; he hath audience, and his blood hath audience; insomuch that God saith, when he doth but see the blood, he "will pass over you, and the plague shall not be upon you," etc., (Exo 12:13).

I shall not detain you any longer. Be sober and humble; go to the Father in the name of the Son, and tell him your case, in the assistance of the Spirit, and you will then feel the benefit of praying with the Spirit and with the understanding also.

THIRD. A WORD OF REPROOF

1. This speaks sadly to you who never pray at all. "I will pray," saith the apostle, and so saith the heart of them that are Christians. Thou then art not a Christian that art not a praying person. The promise is that every one that is righteous shall pray (Psa 32:6). Thou then art a wicked wretch that prayest not. Jacob got the name of Israel by wrestling with God (Gen 32). And all his children bare that name with him (Gal 6:16). But the people that forget prayer, that call not on the name of the Lord, they have prayer made for them, but it is such as this, "Pour out thy fury upon the heathen," O Lord, "and upon the families that call not on thy name" (Jer 10:25). How likest thou this, O thou that art so far off from pouring out thine heart before God, that thou goest to bed like a dog, and risest like a hog, or a sot, and forgettest to call upon God? What wilt thou do when thou shalt be damned in hell, because thou couldst not find in thine heart to ask for heaven? Who will grieve for thy sorrow, that didst not count mercy worth asking for? I tell thee, the ravens, the dogs, etc., shall rise up in judgment against thee, for they will, according to their kind, make signs, and a noise for something to refresh them when they want it; but thou hast not the heart to ask for heaven, though thou must eternally perish in hell, if thou hast it not.

2. This rebukes you that make it your business to slight, mock at, and undervalue the Spirit, and praying by that. What will you do, when God shall come to reckon for these things? You count it high treason to speak but a word against the king, nay, you tremble at the thought of it; and yet in the meantime you will blaspheme the Spirit of the Lord. Is God indeed to be dallied with, and will the end be pleasant unto you? Did God send his Holy Spirit into the hearts of his people, to that end that you should taunt at it? Is this to serve God? And doth this demonstrate the reformation of your church? Nay, is it not the mark of implacable reprobates? O fearful! Can you not be content to be damned for your sins against the law, but you must sin against the Holy Ghost?

Must the holy, harmless, and undefiled Spirit of grace, the nature of God, the promise of Christ, the Comforter of his children, that without which no man can do any service acceptable to the Father – must this, I say, be the burthen of your song, to taunt, deride, and mock at? If God sent Korah and his company headlong to hell for speaking against Moses and Aaron, do you that mock at the Spirit of Christ think to escape unpunished? (Num 16; Heb 10:29). Did you never read what God did to Ananias and Sapphira for telling but one lie against it? (Acts 5:1–8). Also to Simon Magus for but undervaluing of it? (Acts 8:18–22). And will thy sin be a virtue, or go unrewarded with vengeance, that makest it thy business to rage against, and oppose its office, service, and help, that it giveth unto the children of God? It is a fearful thing to do despite unto the Spirit of grace (Compare Matt 12:31, with Mark 3:28–30).

3. As this is the doom of those who do openly blaspheme the Holy Ghost, in a way of disdain and reproach to its office and service: so also it is sad for you, who resist the Spirit of prayer, by a form of man's inventing. A very juggle of the devil, that the traditions of men should be of better esteem, and more to be owned than the Spirit of prayer. What is this less than that accursed abomination of Jeroboam, which kept many from going to Jerusalem, the place and way of God's appointment to worship; and by that means brought such displeasure from God upon them, as to this day is not appeased? (1 Kings 12:26–33). One would think that God's judgments of old upon the hypocrites of that day should make them that have heard of such things take heed and fear to do so. Yet the doctors of our day are so far from taking of warning by the punishment of others, that they do most desperately rush into the same transgression, viz., to set up an institution of man, neither commanded nor commended of God; and whosoever will not obey herein, they must be driven either out of the land or the world.

Hath God required these things at your hands? If he hath, show us where? If not, as I am sure he hath not, then what cursed presumption is it in any pope, bishop, or other, to command that in the worship of God which he hath not required? Nay further, it is not that part only of the form, which is several texts of Scripture that we are commanded to say, but even all must be confessed as the divine worship of God, notwithstanding those absurdities contained therein, which because they are at large discovered by others, I omit the rehearsal of them. Again, though a man be willing to live never so peaceably, yet because he cannot, for conscience sake, own that for one of the most eminent parts of God's worship, which he never commanded, therefore must that man be looked upon as factious, seditious, erroneous, heretical – a disparagement to the church, a seducer of the people, and what not? Lord, what will be the fruit of these things, when for the doctrine of God there is imposed, that is, more than taught, the traditions of men? Thus is the Spirit of prayer disowned, and the form imposed; the Spirit debased, and the form extolled; they that pray with the Spirit, though never so humble and holy, counted fanatics; and they that pray with the form, though with that only, counted the virtuous! And how will the favorers of such a practice answer that Scripture, which commandeth that the church should turn away from such as have "a form of godliness, and deny the power thereof"? (2 Tim 3:5). And if I should say that men that do these things aforesaid, do advance a form of prayer of other men's making, above the spirit of prayer, it would not take long time to prove it. For he that advanceth the book of Common Prayer above the Spirit of prayer, he doth advance a form of men's making above it. But this do all those who banish, or desire to banish, them that pray with the Spirit of prayer; while they hug and embrace them that pray by that form only, and that because they do it. Therefore they love and advance the form of their own or others' inventing, before the Spirit of prayer, which is God's special and gracious appointment.

If you desire the clearing of the minor, look into the jails in England, and into the alehouses of the same; and I trow you will find those that plead for the Spirit of prayer in the jail, and them that look after the form of men's inventions only in the alehouse. It is evident also by the silencing of God's dear ministers, though never so powerfully enabled by the Spirit of prayer, if they in conscience cannot admit of that form of Common Prayer. If this be not an exalting the Common Prayer Book above either praying by the Spirit, or preaching the Word, I have taken my mark amiss. It is not pleasant for me to dwell on this. The Lord in mercy turn the hearts of the people to seek more after the Spirit of prayer; and in the strength of that, to pour out their souls before the Lord. Only let me say it is a sad sign, that that which is one of the most eminent parts of the pretended worship of God is Antichristian, when it hath nothing but the tradition of men, and the strength of persecution, to uphold or plead for it.

THE CONCLUSION

I shall conclude this discourse with this word of advice to all God's people.

1. Believe that as sure as you are in the way of God you must meet with temptations.

2. The first day therefore that thou dost enter into Christ's congregation, look for them.

3. When they do come, beg of God to carry thee through them.

4. Be jealous of thine own heart, that it deceive thee not in thy evidences for heaven, nor in thy walking with God in this world.

5. Take heed of the flatteries of false brethren.

6. Keep in the life and power of truth.

7. Look most at the things which are not seen.

8. Take heed of little sins.

9. Keep the promise warm upon thy heart.

10. Renew thy acts of faith in the blood of Christ.

11. Consider the work of thy generation.

12. Count to run with the foremost therein. Grace be with thee.

John Bunyan, 1628–88, written in prison in 1662 and published in 1663

Temporal Things Spiritualized
or
A Book for Boys and Girls
or
Divine Emblems
John Bunyan
To the reader
Courteous reader

The title page will show, if there thou look,
Who are the proper subjects of this book.

They're boys and girls of all sorts and degrees,
From those of age to children on the knees.

Thus comprehensive am I in my notions,
They tempt me to it by their childish motions.

We now have boys with beards, and girls that be
Big as old women, wanting gravity.

Then do not blame me, 'cause I thus describe them.
Flatter I may not, lest thereby I bribe them

To have a better judgment of themselves,
Than wise men have of babies on their shelves.

Their antic tricks, fantastic modes, and way,
Show they, like very boys and girls, do play

With all the frantic fopperies of this age,
And that in open view, as on a stage;

Our bearded men do act like beardless boys;
Our women please themselves with childish toys.

Our ministers, long time, by word and pen,
Dealt with them, counting them not boys, but men.

Thunderbolts they shot at them and their toys,
But hit them not, 'cause they were girls and boys.

The better charg'd, the wider still they shot,
Or else so high, these dwarfs they touched not.

Instead of men, they found them girls and
    boys,
Addict to nothing as to childish toys.

Wherefore, good reader, that I save them may,
I now with them the very dotterel play;

And since at gravity they make a tush,
My very beard I cast behind a bush;

And like a fool stand fing'ring of their toys,
And all to show them they are girls and boys.

Nor do I blush, although I think some may
Call me a baby, 'cause I with them play.

I do't to show them how each fingle-fangle
On which they doting are, their souls
    entangle,

As with a web, a trap, a gin, or snare;
And will destroy them, have they not a care.

Paul seemed to play the fool, that he might
    gain
Those that were fools indeed, if not in grain;

And did it by their things, that they might
    know
Their emptiness, and might be brought unto

What would them save from sin and vanity,
A noble act, and full of honesty.

Yet he nor I would like them be in vice,
While by their playthings I would them entice,

To mount their thoughts from what are
    childish toys,
To heaven, for that's prepared for girls and
    boys.

Nor do I so confine myself to these,
As to shun graver things; I seek to please

Those more compos'd with better things than
    toys;
Though thus I would be catching girls and
    boys.

Wherefore, if men have now a mind to look,

Perhaps their graver fancies may be took

With what is here, though but in homely
    rhymes:
But he who pleases all must rise betimes.

Some, I persuade me, will be finding fault,
Concluding, here I trip, and there I halt:

No doubt some could those groveling notions
    raise
By fine-spun terms, that challenge might the
    bays.

But should all men be forc'd to lay aside
Their brains that cannot regulate the tide

By this or that man's fancy, we should have
The wise unto the fool become a slave.

What though my text seems mean, my morals
    be
Grave, as if fetch'd from a sublimer tree.

And if some better handle can a fly,
Than some a text, why should we then deny

Their making proof, or good experiment,
Of smallest things, great mischiefs to prevent?

Wise Solomon did fools to piss-ants send,
To learn true wisdom, and their lies to mend.

Yea, God by swallows, cuckoos, and the ass,
Shows they are fools who let that season pass,

Which he put in their hand, that to obtain
Which is both present and eternal gain.

I think the wiser sort my rhymes may slight,
But what care I, the foolish will delight

To read them, and the foolish God has chose,
And doth by foolish things their minds
    compose,

And settle upon that which is divine;
Great things, by little ones, are made to shine.

I could, were I so pleas'd, use higher strains:
And for applause on tenters stretch my brains.

But what needs that? the arrow, out of sight,
Does not the sleeper, nor the watchman
   fright;

To shoot too high doth but make children
   gaze,
'Tis that which hits the man doth him amaze.

And for the inconsiderableness
Of things, by which I do my mind express,

May I by them bring some good thing to pass,
As Samson, with the jawbone of an ass;

Or as brave Shamgar, with his ox's goad
(Both being things not manly, nor for war in
   mode),

I have my end, though I myself expose
To scorn; God will have glory in the close.
                                                John Bunyan

I.
UPON THE BARREN FIG-TREE IN GOD'S
VINEYARD.

What, barren here! in this so good a soil?
The sight of this doth make God's heart recoil
From giving thee his blessing; barren tree,
Bear fruit, or else thine end will cursed be!
Art thou not planted by the water-side?
Know'st not thy Lord by fruit is glorified?
The sentence is, Cut down the barren tree:
Bear fruit, or else thine end will cursed be.
Hast thou been digg'd about and dunged too,
Will neither patience nor yet dressing do?
The executioner is come, O tree,
Bear fruit, or else thine end will cursed be!
He that about thy roots takes pains to dig,
Would, if on thee were found but one good fig,
Preserve thee from the axe: but, barren tree,
Bear fruit, or else thy end will cursed be!
The utmost end of patience is at hand,
'Tis much if thou much longer here doth
   stand.
O cumber-ground, thou art a barren tree.
Bear fruit, or else thine end will cursed be!
Thy standing nor they name will help at all;
When fruitful trees are spared, thou must fall.
The axe is laid unto thy roots, O tree!
Bear fruit, or else thine end will cursed be.

II.
UPON THE LARK AND THE FOWLER.

Thou simple bird, what makes thou here to
   play?
Look, there's the fowler, pr'ythee come away.
Do'st not behold the net? Look there, 'tis
   spread,
Venture a little further, thou art dead.
Is there not room enough in all the field
For thee to play in, but thou needs must yield
To the deceitful glitt'ring of a glass,
Plac'd betwixt nets, to bring thy death to pass?
Bird, if thou art so much for dazzling light,
Look, there's the sun above thee; dart upright;
Thy nature is to soar up to the sky,
Why wilt thou come down to the nets and die?
Take no heed to the fowler's tempting call;
This whistle, he enchanteth birds withal.
Or if thou see'st a live bird in his net,
Believe she's there, 'cause hence she cannot
   get.
Look how he tempteth thee with is decoy,
That he may rob thee of thy life, thy joy.
Come, pr'ythee bird, I pr'ythee come away,
Why should this net thee take, when 'scape
   thou may?
Hadst thou not wings, or were thy feathers
   pull'd,
Or wast thou blind, or fast asleep wer't lull'd,
The case would somewhat alter, but for thee,
Thy eyes are ope, and thou hast wings to flee.
Remember that thy song is in thy rise,
Not in thy fall; earth's not thy paradise.
Keep up aloft, then, let thy circuits be
Above, where birds from fowler's nets are
   free.

Comparison.
This fowler is an emblem of the devil,
His nets and whistle, figures of all evil.
His glass an emblem is of sinful pleasure,
And his decoy of who counts sin a treasure.
This simple lark's a shadow of a saint,
Under allurings, ready now to faint.

This admonisher a true teacher is,
Whose works to show the soul the snare and
   bliss,
And how it may this fowler's net escape,
And not commit upon itself this rape.

III.
UPON THE VINE-TREE.

What is the vine, more than another tree?
Nay most, than it, more tall, more comely be.
What workman thence will take a beam or
    pin,
To make ought which may be delighted in?
Its excellency in its fruit doth lie:
A fruitless vine, it is not worth a fly.

Comparison.
What are professors more than other men?
Nothing at all. Nay, there's not one in ten,
Either for wealth, or wit, that may compare,
In many things, with some that carnal are.
Good are they, if they mortify their sin,
But without that, they are not worth a pin.

IV.
MEDITATIONS UPON AN EGG.

1.
The egg's no chick by falling from the hen;
Nor man a Christian, till he's born again.
The egg's at first contained in the shell;
Men, afore grace, in sins and darkness dwell.
The egg, when laid, by warmth is made a
    chicken,
And Christ, by grace, those dead in sin doth
    quicken.
The egg, when first a chick, the shell's its
    prison;
So's flesh to the soul, who yet with Christ is
    risen.
The shell doth crack, the chick doth chirp and
    peep,
The flesh decays, as men do pray and weep.
The shell doth break, the chick's at liberty,
The flesh falls off, the soul mounts up on high
But both do not enjoy the self-same plight;
The soul is safe, the chick now fears the kite
    [bird of prey].

2.
But chicks from rotten eggs do not proceed,
Nor is a hypocrite a saint indeed.
The rotten egg, though underneath the hen,
If crack'd, stinks, and is loathsome unto men.
Nor doth her warmth make what is rotten
    sound;

What's rotten, rotten will at last be found.
The hypocrite, sin has him in possession,
He is a rotten egg under profession.

3.
Some eggs bring cockatrices; and some men
Seem hatch'd and brooded in the viper's den.
Some eggs bring wild-fowls; and some men
    there be
As wild as are the wildest fowls that flee.
Some eggs bring spiders, and some men
    appear
More venom'd than the worst of spiders are.
Some eggs bring piss-ants [archaic for "ants"],
    and some seem to me
As much for trifles as the piss-ants be.
Thus divers eggs do produce divers shapes,
As like some men as monkeys are like apes.
But this is but an egg, were it a chick,
Here had been legs, and wings, and bones to
    pick.

V.
OF FOWLS FLYING IN THE AIR.

Methinks I see a sight most excellent,
All sorts of birds fly in the firmament:

Some great, some small, all of a divers kind,
Mine eye affecting, pleasant to my mind.
Look how they tumble in the wholesome air,
Above the world of worldlings, and their care.
And as they divers are in bulk and hue,
So are they in their way of flying too.

So many birds, so many various things
Tumbling i' the element upon their wings.

Comparison.
These birds are emblems of those men that
    shall
Ere long possess the heavens, their all in all.
They are each of a diverse shape and kind,
To teach we of all nations there shall find.
They are some great, some little, as we see,
To show some great, some small, in glory be.

Their flying diversely, as we behold,
Do show saints' joys will there be manifold;

Some glide, some mount, some flutter, and
  some do,
In a mix'd way of flying, glory too.

And all to show each saint, to his content,
Shall roll and tumble in that firmament.

VI.
UPON THE LORD'S PRAYER.

Our Father which in heaven art,
Thy name be always hallowed;
Thy kingdom come, thy will be done;
Thy heavenly path be followed
By us on earth as 'tis with thee,
We humbly pray;
And let our bread us given be,
From day to day.

Forgive our debts as we forgive
Those that to us indebted are:
Into temptation lead us not,
But save us from the wicked snare.
The kingdom's thine, the power too,
We thee adore;
The glory also shall be thine
For evermore.

VII.
MEDITATIONS UPON PEEP OF DAY.

I oft, though it be peep of day, don't know
Whether 'tis night, whether 'tis day or no.
I fancy that I see a little light,
But cannot yet distinguish day from night;
I hope, I doubt, but steady yet I be not,
I am not at a point, the sun I see not.

Thus 'tis with such who grace but now possest,
They know not yet if they be cursed or blest.

VIII.
UPON THE FLINT IN THE WATER.

This flint, time out of mind, has there abode,
Where crystal streams make their continual
  road.
Yet it abides a flint as much as 'twere
Before it touched the water, or came there
Its hard obdurateness is not abated,
'Tis not at all by water penetrated.

Though water hath a soft'ning virtue in't,
This stone it can't dissolve, for 'tis a flint.
Yea, though it in the water doth remain,
It doth its fiery nature still retain.

If you oppose it with its opposite,
At you, yea, in your face, its fire 'twill spit.

Comparison.
This flint an emblem is of those that lie,
Like stones, under the Word, until they die.
Its crystal streams have not their nature
  changed,
They are not, from their lusts, by grace
  estranged.

IX.
UPON THE FISH IN THE WATER.

1.
The water is the fish's element;
Take her from thence, none can her death
  prevent;
And some have said, who have transgressors
  been,
As good not be, as to be kept from sin.

2.
The water is the fish's element:
Leave her but there, and she is well content.
So's he, who in the path of life doth plod,
Take all, says he, let me but have my God.

3.
The water is the fish's element,
Her sportings there to her are excellent;
So is God's service unto holy men,
They are not in their element till then.

X.
UPON THE SWALLOW.

This pretty bird, O! how she flies and sings,
But could she do so if she had not wings?
Her wings bespeak my faith, her songs my
  peace;
When I believe and sing my doubtings cease.

XI.
UPON THE BEE.

The bee goes out, and honey home doth
    bring,
And some who seek that honey find a sting.
Now would'st thou have the honey, and be
    free
From stinging, in the first place kill the bee.

Comparison.
This bee an emblem truly is of sin,
Whose sweet, unto a many, death hath been.
Now would'st have sweet from sin and yet
    not die,
Do thou it, in the first place, mortify.

XII.
UPON A LOWERING MORNING.

Well, with the day I see the clouds appear,
And mix the light with darkness everywhere;
This threatening is, to travelers that go
Long journeys, slabby rain they'll have, or
    snow.
Else, while I gaze, the sun doth with his beams
Belace the clouds, as 'twere with bloody
    streams;
This done, they suddenly do watery grow,
And weep, and pour their tears out where
    they go.

Comparison.
Thus 'tis when gospel light doth usher in
To us both sense of grace and sense of sin;
Yea, when it makes sin red with Christ's
    blood,
Then we can weep till weeping does us good.

XIII.
UPON OVER-MUCH NICENESS.

'Tis much to see how over nice some are
About the body and household affair,

While what's of worth they slightly pass it by,
Not doing, or doing it slovenly.

Their house must be well furnished, be in
    print,
Meanwhile their soul lies ley, has no good in't.

Its outside also they must beautify,
When in it there's scarce common honesty.
Their bodies they must have tricked up and
    trim,
Their inside full of filth up to the brim.
Upon their clothes there must not be a spot,
But is their lives more than one common blot.
How nice, how coy are some about their diet,
That can their crying souls with hogs'-meat
    quiet.
All drest must to a hair be, else 'tis naught,
While of the living bread they have no
    thought.
Thus for their outside they are clean and nice,
While their poor inside stinks with sin and
    vice.

XIV.
MEDITATIONS UPON A CANDLE.

Man's like a candle in a candlestick,
Made up of tallow and a little wick;

And as the candle when it is not lighted,
So is he who is in his sins benighted.

Nor can a man his soul with grace inspire,
More than can candles set themselves on fire.
Candles receive their light from what they are
    not;
Men grace from Him for whom at first they
    care not.
We manage candles when they take the fire;
God men, when he with grace doth them
    inspire.
And biggest candles give the better light,
As grace on biggest sinners shines most
    bright.
The candle shines to make another see,
A saint unto his neighbor light should be.
The blinking candle we do much despise,
Saints dim of light are high in no man's eyes.
Again, though it may seem to some a riddle,
We use to light our candles at the middle.

True light doth at the candle's end appear,
And grace the heart first reaches by the ear.
But 'tis the wick the fire doth kindle on,
As 'tis the heart that grace first works upon.
Thus both do fasten upon what's the main,
And so their life and vigor do maintain.

The tallow makes the wick yield to the fire,
And sinful flesh doth make the soul desire
That grace may kindle on it, in it burn;
So evil makes the soul from evil turn.

But candles in the wind are apt to flare,
And Christians, in a tempest, to despair.
The flame also with smoke attended is,
And in our holy lives there's much amiss.
Sometimes a thief will candle-light annoy,
And lusts do seek our graces to destroy.
What brackish is will make a candle sputter;
'Twixt sin and grace there's oft' a heavy
    clutter.
Sometimes the light burns dim, 'cause of the
    snuff,
Sometimes it is blown quite out with a puff;
But watchfulness preventeth both these evils,
Keeps candles light, and grace in spite of
    devils.
Nor let not snuffs nor puffs make us to doubt,
Our candles may be lighted, though puffed
    out.
The candle in the night doth all excel,
Nor sun, nor moon, nor stars, then shine so
    well.
So is the Christian in our hemisphere,
Whose light shows others how their course
    to steer.
When candles are put out, all's in confusion;
Where Christians are not, devils make
    intrusion.
Then happy are they who such candles have.
All others dwell in darkness and the grave.
But candles that do blink within the socket,
And saints, whose eyes are always in their
    pocket,
Are much alike; such candles make us fumble,
And at such saints good men and bad do
    stumble.

Good candles don't offend, except sore eyes,
Nor hurt, unless it be the silly flies.

Thus none like burning candles in the night,
Nor ought to holy living for delight.
But let us draw towards the candle's end:
The fire, you see, doth wick and tallow spend,
As grace man's life until his glass is run,
And so the candle and the man is done.

The man now lays him down upon his bed,
The wick yields up its fire, and so is dead.
The candle now extinct is, but the man
By grace mounts up to glory, there to stand.

XV.
UPON THE SACRAMENTS.

Two sacraments I do believe there be,
Baptism and the Supper of the Lord;
Both mysteries divine, which do to me,
By God's appointment, benefit afford.

But shall they be my God, or shall I have
Of them so foul and impious a thought,
To think that from the curse they can me
    save?
Bread, wine, nor water, me no ransom bought.

XVI.
UPON THE SUN'S REFLECTION
UPON THE CLOUDS IN A FAIR MORNING.

Look yonder, ah! methinks mine eyes do see
Clouds edged with silver, as fine garments be;
They look as if they saw that golden face
That makes black clouds most beautiful with
    grace.
Unto the saints' sweet incense, or their prayer,
These smoky curdled clouds I do compare.
For as these clouds seem edged, or laced with
    gold,
Their prayers return with blessings manifold.

XVII.
UPON APPAREL.

God gave us clothes to hide our nakedness,
And we by them do it expose to view.

Our pride and unclean minds to an excess,
By our apparel, we to others show.

XVIII.
THE SINNER AND THE SPIDER.

Sinner.
What black, what ugly crawling thing art thou?

Spider.
I am a spider —

Sinner.
A spider, ay, also a filthy creature.

Spider.
Not filthy as thyself in name or feature.
My name entailed is to my creation,
My features from the God of thy salvation.

Sinner.
I am a man, and in God's image made,
I have a soul shall neither die nor fade,
God has possessed me with human reason,
Speak not against me lest thou speakest
    treason.
For if I am the image of my Maker,
Of slanders laid on me He is partaker.

Spider.
I know thou art a creature far above me,
Therefore I shun, I fear, and also love thee.
But though thy God hath made thee such a
    creature,
Thou hast against him often played the traitor.
Thy sin has fetched thee down: leave off to
    boast;
Nature thou hast defiled, God's image lost.
Yea, thou thyself a very beast hast made,
And art become like grass, which soon doth
    fade.
Thy soul, thy reason, yea, thy spotless state,
Sin has subjected to th' most dreadful fate.
But I retain my primitive condition,
I've all but what I lost by thy ambition.

Sinner.
Thou venomed thing, I know not what to call
    thee,
The dregs of nature surely did befall thee,
Thou wast made of the dross and scum of all,
Man hates thee; doth, in scorn, thee spider
    call.

Spider.
My venom's good for something, 'cause God
    made it,
Thy sin hath spoiled thy nature, doth degrade
    it.
Of human virtues, therefore, though I fear
    thee,
I will not, though I might, despise and jeer
    thee.

Thou say'st I am the very dregs of nature,
Thy sin's the spawn of devils, 'tis no creature.
Thou say'st man hates me 'cause I am a spider,
Poor man, thou at thy God art a derider;
My venom tendeth to my preservation,
Thy pleasing follies work out thy damnation.
Poor man, I keep the rules of my creation,
Thy sin has cast thee headlong from thy
    station.
I hurt nobody willingly, but thou
Art a self-murderer; thou know'st not how
To do what good is; no, thou lovest evil;
Thou fliest God's law, adherest to the devil.

Sinner.
Ill-shaped creature, there's antipathy
'Twixt man and spiders, 'tis in vain to lie;
I hate thee, stand off, if thou dost come nigh
    me,
I'll crush thee with my foot; I do defy thee.

Spider.
They are ill-shaped, who warped are by sin,
Antipathy in thee hath long time been
To God; no marvel, then, if me, his creature,
Thou dost defy, pretending name and feature.
But why stand off? My presence shall not
    throng thee,
'Tis not my venom, but thy sin doth wrong
    thee. Come,
I will teach thee wisdom, do but hear me,
I was made for thy profit, do not fear me.
But if thy God thou wilt not hearken to,
What can the swallow, ant, or spider do?
Yet I will speak, I can but be rejected,
Sometimes great things by small means are
    effected.
Hark, then, though man is noble by creation,
He's lapsed now to such degeneration,
Is so besotted and so careless grown,
As not to grieve though he has overthrown
Himself, and brought to bondage everything
Created, from the spider to the king.
This we poor sensitives do feel and see;
For subject to the curse you made us be.
Tread not upon me, neither from me go;
'Tis man which has brought all the world to
    woe,
The law of my creation bids me teach thee;
I will not for thy pride to God impeach thee.
I spin, I weave, and all to let thee see,

Thy best performances but cobwebs be.
Thy glory now is brought to such an ebb,
It doth not much excel the spider's web;
My webs becoming snares and traps for flies,
Do set the wiles of hell before thine eyes;
Their tangling nature is to let thee see,
Thy sins too of a tangling nature be.
My den, or hole, for that 'tis bottomless,
Doth of damnation show the lastingness.
My lying quiet until the fly is catch'd,
Shows secretly hell hath thy ruin hatch'd.
In that I on her seize, when she is taken,
I show who gathers whom God hath forsaken.
The fly lies buzzing in my web to tell
Thee how the sinners roar and howl in hell.
Now, since I show thee all these mysteries,
How canst thou hate me, or me scandalize?

Sinner.
Well, well; I no more will be a derider,
I did not look for such things from a spider.

Spider.
Come, hold thy peace; what I have yet to say,
If heeded, help thee may another day.
Since I an ugly ven'mous creature be,
There is some semblance 'twixt vile man and
    me.
My wild and heedless runnings are like those
Whose ways to ruin do their souls expose.
Daylight is not my time, I work in th' night,
To show they are like me who hate the light.
The maid sweeps one web down, I make
    another,
To show how heedless ones convictions
    smother;
My web is no defense at all to me,
Nor will false hopes at judgment be to thee.

Sinner.
O spider, I have heard thee, and do wonder
A spider should thus lighten and thus thunder.

Spider.
Do but hold still, and I will let thee see
Yet in my ways more mysteries there be.
Shall not I do thee good, if I thee tell,
I show to thee a four-fold way to hell;
For, since I set my web in sundry places,
I show men go to hell in divers traces.
One I set in the window, that I might

Show some go down to hell with gospel light.
One I set in a corner, as you see,
To show how some in secret snared be.
Gross webs great store I set in darksome
    places,
To show how many sin with brazen faces;
Another web I set aloft on high,
To show there's some professing men must
    die.
Thus in my ways God wisdom doth conceal,
And by my ways that wisdom doth reveal.
I hide myself when I for flies do wait,
So doth the devil when he lays his bait;
If I do fear the losing of my prey,
I stir me, and more snares upon her lay:
This way and that her wings and legs I tie,
That, sure as she is catch'd, so she must die.
But if I see she's like to get away,
Then with my venom I her journey stay.
All which my ways the devil imitates
To catch men, 'cause he their salvation hates.

Sinner.
O spider, thou delight'st me with thy skill!
I pr'ythee spit this venom at me still.

Spider.
I am a spider, yet I can possess
The palace of a king, where happiness
So much abounds. Nor when I do go thither,
Do they ask what, or whence I come, or
    whither
I make my hasty travels; no, not they;
They let me pass, and I go on my way.
I seize the palace, do with hands take hold
Of doors, of locks, or bolts; yea, I am bold,
When in, to clamber up unto the throne,
And to possess it, as if 'twere mine own.
Nor is there any law forbidding me
Here to abide, or in this palace be.
Yea, if I please, I do the highest stories
Ascend, there sit, and so behold the glories
Myself is compassed with, as if I were
One of the chiefest courtiers that be there.
Here lords and ladies do come round about
    me,
With grave demeanor, nor do any flout me
For this, my brave adventure, no, not they;
They come, they go, but leave me there to stay.
Now, my reproacher, I do by all this
Show how thou may'st possess thyself of bliss:

Thou art worse than a spider, but take hold
On Christ the door, thou shalt not be
  controll'd.
By him do thou the heavenly palace enter;
None chide thee will for this thy brave
  adventure;
Approach thou then unto the very throne,
There speak thy mind, fear not, the day's thine
  own;
Nor saint, nor angel, will thee stop or stay,
But rather tumble blocks out of the way.
My venom stops not me; let not thy vice
Stop thee; possess thyself of paradise.
Go on, I say, although thou be a sinner,
Learn to be bold in faith, of me a spinner.
This is the way the glories to possess,
And to enjoy what no man can express.
Sometimes I find the palace door uplock'd,
And so my entrance thither has upblock'd.
But am I daunted? No, I here and there
Do feel and search; so if I anywhere,
At any chink or crevice, find my way,
I crowd, I press for passage, make no stay.
And so through difficulty I attain
The palace; yea, the throne where princes
  reign.
I crowd sometimes, as if I'd burst in sunder;
And art thou crushed with striving, do not
  wonder.
Some scarce get in, and yet indeed they enter;
Knock, for they nothing have, that nothing
  venture.
Nor will the King himself throw dirt on thee,
As thou hast cast reproaches upon me.
He will not hate thee, O thou foul backslider!
As thou didst me, because I am a spider.
Now, to conclude since I such doctrine bring,
Slight me no more, call me not ugly thing.
God wisdom hath unto the piss-ant given,
And spiders may teach men the way to
  heaven.

Sinner.
Well, my good spider, I my errors see,
I was a fool for railing upon thee.
Thy nature, venom, and thy fearful hue,
Both show that sinners are, and what they do.
Thy way and works do also darkly tell,
How some men go to heaven, and some to
  hell.
Thou art my monitor, I am a fool;

They learn may, that to spiders go to school.

XIX.
MEDITATIONS UPON THE DAY BEFORE THE
SUN-RISING.

But all this while, where's he whose golden
  rays
Drives night away and beautifies our days?
Where's he whose goodly face doth warm and
  heal,
And show us what the darksome nights
  conceal?
Where's he that thaws our ice, drives cold
  away?
Let's have him, or we care not for the day.
Thus 'tis with who partakers are of grace,
There's naught to them like their Redeemer's
  face.

XX.
OF THE MOLE IN THE GROUND.

The mole's a creature very smooth and slick,
She digs i' th' dirt, but 'twill not on her stick;
So's he who counts this world his greatest
  gains,
Yet nothing gets but's labor for his pains.
Earth's the mole's element, she can't abide
To be above ground, dirt heaps are her pride;
And he is like her who the worldling plays,
He imitates her in her work and ways.

Poor silly mole, that thou should'st love to be
Where thou nor sun, nor moon, nor stars can
  see.
But O! how silly's he who doth not care
So he gets earth, to have of heaven a share!

XXI.
OF THE CUCKOO.

Thou booby, say'st thou nothing but Cuckoo?
The robin and the wren can thee outdo.

They to us play through their little throats,
Taking not one, but sundry pretty taking
  notes.
But thou hast fellows, some like thee can do
Little but suck our eggs, and sing Cuckoo.
Thy notes do not first welcome in our spring,

Nor dost thou its first tokens to us bring.
Birds less than thee by far, like prophets, do
Tell us, 'tis coming, though not by Cuckoo.
Nor dost thou summer have away with thee,
Though thou a yawling bawling Cuckoo be.
When thou dost cease among us to appear,
Then doth our harvest bravely crown our
   year.
But thou hast fellows, some like thee can do
Little but suck our eggs, and sing Cuckoo.
Since Cuckoos forward not our early spring,
Nor help with notes to bring our harvest in;
And since, while here, she only makes a noise,
So pleasing unto none as girls and boys,
The Formalist we may compare her to,
For he doth suck our eggs, and sing Cuckoo.

XXII.
OF THE BOY AND BUTTERFLY.

Behold how eager this our little boy
Is for this Butterfly, as if all joy,
All profits, honors, yea, and lasting pleasures,
Were wrapt up in her, or the richest treasures,
Found in her, would be bundled up together,
When all her all is lighter than a feather.
He halloos, runs, and cries out, Here, boys,
   here,
Nor doth he brambles or the nettles fear.
He stumbles at the mole-hills, up he gets,
And runs again, as one bereft of wits;
And all this labor and this large outcry,
Is only for a silly butterfly.

Comparison.
This little boy an emblem is of those
Whose hearts are wholly at the world's
   dispose,
The butterfly doth represent to me,
The world's best things at best but fading be.
All are but painted nothings and false joys,
Like this poor butterfly to these our boys.
His running through nettles, thorns, and
   briars,
To gratify his boyish fond desires;

His tumbling over mole-hills to attain
His end, namely, his butterfly to gain;
Doth plainly show what hazards some men
   run.
To get what will be lost as soon as won.

Men seem in choice, than children far more
   wise,
Because they run not after butterflies;
When yet, alas! for what are empty toys,
They follow children, like to beardless boys.

XXIII.
OF THE FLY AT THE CANDLE.

What ails this fly thus desperately to enter
A combat with the candle? Will she venture
To clash at light? Away, thou silly fly;
Thus doing thou wilt burn thy wings and die.
But 'tis a folly her advice to give,
She'll kill the candle, or she will not live.
Slap, says she, at it; then she makes retreat,
So wheels about, and doth her blows repeat.
Nor doth the candle let her quite escape,
But gives some little check unto the ape:
Throws up her heels it doth, so down she falls,
Where she lies sprawling, and for succor calls.
When she recovers, up she gets again,
And at the candle comes with might and
   main,
But now behold, the candle takes the fly,
And holds her, till she doth by burning die.

Comparison.
This candle is an emblem of that light
Our gospel gives in this our darksome night.
The fly a lively picture is of those
That hate and do this gospel light oppose.
At last the gospel doth become their snare,
Doth them with burning hands in pieces tear.

XXIV.
ON THE RISING OF THE SUN.

Look, look, brave Sol doth peep up from
   beneath,
Shows us his golden face, doth on us breathe;
He also doth compass us round with glories,
Whilst he ascends up to his highest stories.
Where he his banner over us displays,
And gives us light to see our works and ways.
Nor are we now, as at the peep of light,
To question, is it day, or is it night?

The night is gone, the shadows fled away,
And we now most sure are that it is day.
Our eyes behold it, and our hearts believe it;

Nor can the wit of man in this deceive it.
And thus it is when Jesus shows his face,
And doth assure us of his love and grace.

XXV.
UPON THE PROMISING FRUITFULNESS OF A
TREE.

A comely sight indeed it is to see
A world of blossoms on an apple-tree:
Yet far more comely would this tree appear,
If all its dainty blooms young apples were.
But how much more might one upon it see,
If all would hang there till they ripe should be.
But most of all in beauty 'twould abound,
If then none worm-eaten should there be
    found.
But we, alas! do commonly behold
Blooms fall apace, if mornings be but cold.
They too, which hang till they young apples
    are,
By blasting winds and vermin take despair,
Store that do hang, while almost ripe, we see
By blust'ring winds are shaken from the tree,
So that of many, only some there be,
That grow till they come to maturity.

Comparison.
This tree a perfect emblem is of those
Which God doth plant, which in his garden
    grows,
Its blasted blooms are motions unto good,
Which chill affections do nip in the bud.
Those little apples which yet blasted are,
Show some good purposes, no good fruits
    bear.
Those spoiled by vermin are to let us see,
How good attempts by bad thoughts ruin'd be.
Those which the wind blows down, while
    they are green,
Show good works have by trials spoiled been.
Those that abide, while ripe upon the tree,
Show, in a good man, some ripe fruit will be.
Behold then how abortive some fruits are,
Which at the first most promising appear.
The frost, the wind, the worm, with time doth
    show,
There flows, from much appearance, works
    but few.

XXVI.
UPON THE THIEF.

The thief, when he doth steal, thinks he doth
    gain;
Yet then the greatest loss he doth sustain.
Come, thief, tell me thy gains, but do not
    falter.
When summ'd, what comes it to more than
    the halter?
Perhaps, thou'lt say, The halter I defy;
So thou may'st say, yet by the halter die.
Thou'lt say, Then there's an end; no, pr'ythee,
    hold,
He was no friend of thine that thee so told.
Hear thou the Word of God, that will thee tell,
Without repentance thieves must go to hell.
But should it be as thy false prophet says,
Yet naught but loss doth come by thievish
    ways.
All honest men will flee thy company,
Thou liv'st a rogue, and so a rogue will die.
Innocent boldness thou hast none at all,
Thy inward thoughts do thee a villain call.

Sometimes when thou liest warmly on thy
    bed,
Thou art like one unto the gallows led.
Fear, as a constable, breaks in upon thee,
Thou art as if the town was up to stone thee.
If hogs do grunt, or silly rats do rustle,
Thou art in consternation, think'st a bustle
By men about the door, is made to take thee,
And all because good conscience doth forsake
    thee.
Thy case is most deplorably so bad,
Thou shunn'st to think on't, lest thou
    should'st be mad.
Thou art beset with mischiefs every way,
The gallows groaneth for thee every day.
Wherefore, I pr'ythee, thief, thy theft forbear,
Consult thy safety, pr'ythee, have a care.
If once thy head be got within the noose,
'Twill be too late a longer life to choose.
As to the penitent thou readest of,
What's that to them who at repentance scoff.
Nor is that grace at thy command or power,
That thou should'st put it off till the last hour.
I pr'ythee, thief, think on't, and turn betime;
Few go to life who do the gallows climb.

XXVII.
OF THE CHILD WITH THE BIRD AT THE BUSH.

My little bird, how canst thou sit
And sing amidst so many thorns?
Let me a hold upon thee get,
My love with honor thee adorns.

Thou art at present little worth,
Five farthings none will give for thee,
But pr'ythee, little bird, come forth,
Thou of more value art to me.

'Tis true it is sunshine to-day,
To-morrow birds will have a storm;
My pretty one come thou away,
My bosom then shall keep thee warm.

Thou subject are to cold o'nights,
When darkness is thy covering;
At days thy danger's great by kites,
How can'st thou then sit there and sing?

Thy food is scarce and scanty too,
'Tis worms and trash which thou dost eat;
Thy present state I pity do,
Come, I'll provide thee better meat.

I'll feed thee with white bread and milk,
And sugar plums, if them thou crave.
I'll cover thee with finest silk,
That from the cold I may thee save.

My father's palace shall be thine,
Yea, in it thou shalt sit and sing;
My little bird, if thou'lt be mine,
The whole year round shall be thy spring.

I'll teach thee all the notes at court,
Unthought-of music thou shalt play;
And all that thither do resort,
Shall praise thee for it every day.

I'll keep thee safe from cat and cur,
No manner o' harm shall come to thee;
Yea, I will be thy succourer,
My bosom shall thy cabin be.

But lo, behold, the bird is gone;
These charmings would not make her yield;
The child's left at the bush alone,
The bird flies yonder o'er the field.

Comparison.

This child of Christ an emblem is,
The bird to sinners I compare,
The thorns are like those sins of his
Which do surround him everywhere.

Her songs, her food, and sunshine day,
Are emblems of those foolish toys,
Which to destruction lead the way,
The fruit of worldly, empty joys.

The arguments this child doth choose
To draw to him a bird thus wild,
Shows Christ familiar speech doth use
To make's to him be reconciled.

The bird in that she takes her wing,
To speed her from him after all,
Shows us vain man loves any thing
Much better than the heavenly call.

XXVIII.
OF MOSES AND HIS WIFE.

This Moses was a fair and comely man,
His wife a swarthy Ethiopian;
Nor did his milk-white bosom change her sin.
She came out thence as black as she went in.

Now Moses was a type of Moses' law,
His wife likewise of one that never saw
Another way unto eternal life;
There's mystery, then, in Moses and his wife.

The law is very holy, just, and good,
And to it is espoused all flesh and blood;
But this its goodness it cannot bestow
On any that are wedded thereunto.

Therefore as Moses' wife came swarthy in,
And went out from him without change of
    skin,
So he that doth the law for life adore,
Shall yet by it be left a black-a-more.

XXIX.
OF THE ROSE-BUSH.

This homely bush doth to mine eyes expose
A very fair, yea, comely ruddy rose.

This rose doth also bow its head to me,
Saying, Come, pluck me, I thy rose will be;
Yet offer I to gather rose or bud,
Ten to one but the bush will have my blood.
This looks like a trapan, or a decoy,
To offer, and yet snap, who would enjoy;
Yea, the more eager on't, the more in danger,
Be he the master of it, or a stranger.

Bush, why dost bear a rose if none must have
　it.
Who dost expose it, yet claw those that crave
　it?
Art become freakish? dost the wanton play,
Or doth thy testy humor tend its way?

Comparison.
This rose God's Son is, with his ruddy looks.
But what's the bush, whose pricks, like tenter-
　hooks,
Do scratch and claw the finest lady's hands,
Or rend her clothes, if she too near it stands?
This bush an emblem is of Adam's race,
Of which Christ came, when he his Father's
　grace
Commended to us in his crimson blood,
While he in sinners' stead and nature stood.
Thus Adam's race did bear this dainty rose,
And doth the same to Adam's race expose;
But those of Adam's race which at it catch,
Adam's race will them prick, and claw, and
　scratch.

XXX.
OF THE GOING DOWN OF THE SUN.

What, hast thou run thy race, art going down?
Thou seemest angry, why dost on us frown?
Yea, wrap thy head with clouds and hide thy
　face,
As threatening to withdraw from us thy
　grace?
O leave us not! When once thou hid'st thy
　head,
Our horizon with darkness will be spread.
Tell who hath thee offended, turn again.
Alas! too late, intreaties are in vain.

Comparison.
Our gospel has had here a summer's day,
But in its sunshine we, like fools, did play;

Or else fall out, and with each other wrangle,
And did, instead of work, not much but
　jangle.
And if our sun seems angry, hides his face,
Shall it go down, shall night possess this
　place?
Let not the voice of night birds us afflict,
And of our misspent summer us convict.

XXXI.
UPON THE FROG.

The frog by nature is both damp and cold,
Her mouth is large, her belly much will hold;
She sits somewhat ascending, loves to be
Croaking in gardens, though unpleasantly.

Comparison.
The hypocrite is like unto this frog,
As like as is the puppy to the dog.
He is of nature cold, his mouth is wide
To prate, and at true goodness to deride.
He mounts his head as if he was above
The world, when yet 'tis that which has his
　love.
And though he seeks in churches for to croak,
He neither loveth Jesus nor his yoke.

XXXII.
UPON THE WHIPPING OF A TOP.

'Tis with the whip the boy sets up the top,
The whip makes it run round upon its toe;
The whip makes it hither and thither hop:
'Tis with the whip the top is made to go.

Comparison.
Our legalist is like unto this top,
Without a whip he doth not duty do;
Let Moses whip him, he will skip and hop;
Forbear to whip, he'll neither stand nor go.

XXXIII.
UPON THE PISMIRE.

Must we unto the pismire go to school,
To learn of her in summer to provide
For winter next ensuing. Man's a fool,
Or silly ants would not be made his guide.

But, sluggard, is it not a shame for thee

To be outdone by pismires? Pr'ythee hear:
Their works, too, will thy condemnation be
When at the judgment-seat thou shalt appear.
But since thy God doth bid thee to her go,
Obey, her ways consider, and be wise;
The piss-ant tell thee will what thou must do,
And set the way to life before thine eyes.

XXXIV.
UPON THE BEGGAR.

He wants, he asks, he pleads his poverty,
They within doors do him an alms deny.
He doth repeat and aggravate his grief,
But they repulse him, give him no relief.
He begs, they say, Begone; he will not hear,
But coughs, sighs, and makes signs he still is
  there;
They disregard him, he repeats his groans;
They still say nay, and he himself bemoans.
They grow more rugged, they call him
  vagrant;
He cries the shriller, trumpets out his want.
At last, when they perceive he'll take no nay,
An alms they give him without more delay.

Comparison.

This beggar doth resemble them that pray
To God for mercy, and will take no nay,

But wait, and count that all his hard gainsays
Are nothing else but fatherly delays;

Then imitate him, praying souls, and cry:
There's nothing like to importunity.

XXXV.
UPON THE HORSE AND HIS RIDER.

There's one rides very sagely on the road,
Showing that he affects the gravest mode.
Another rides tantivy, or full trot,
To show much gravity he matters not.

Lo, here comes one amain, he rides full speed,
Hedge, ditch, nor miry bog, he doth not heed.
One claws it up-hill without stop or check,
Another down as if he'd break his neck.

Now every horse has his especial guider;
Then by his going you may know the rider.

Comparison.

Now let us turn our horse into a man,
His rider to a spirit, if we can.
Then let us, by the methods of the guider,
Tell every horse how he should know his rider.
Some go, as men, direct in a right way,
Nor are they suffered to go astray;
As with a bridle they are governed,
And kept from paths which lead unto the
  dead.
Now this good man has his especial guider,
Then by his going let him know his rider.
Some go as if they did not greatly care,
Whether of heaven or hell they should be heir.
The rein, it seems, is laid upon their neck,
They seem to go their way without a check.
Now this man too has his especial guider,
And by his going he may know his rider.

Some again run as if resolved to die,
Body and soul, to all eternity.
Good counsel they by no means can abide;
They'll have their course whatever them
  betide.
Now these poor men have their especial
  guider,
Were they not fools they soon might know
  their rider.
There's one makes head against all godliness,
Those too, that do profess it, he'll distress;
He'll taunt and flout if goodness doth appear,
And at its countenancers mock and jeer.
Now this man, too, has his especial guider,
And by his going he might know his rider.

XXXVI.
UPON THE SIGHT OF A POUND OF CANDLES
FALLING TO THE GROUND.

But be the candles down, and scattered too,
Some lying here, some there? What shall we
  do?
Hold, light the candle there that stands on
  high,
It you may find the other candles by.

Light that, I say, and so take up the pound
You did let fall and scatter on the ground.

Comparison.

The fallen candles do us intimate

The bulk of God's elect in their laps'd state;
Their lying scattered in the dark may be
To show, by man's lapsed state, his misery.
The candle that was taken down and lighted,
Thereby to find them fallen and benighted,
Is Jesus Christ; God, by his light, doth gather
Who he will save, and be unto a Father.

XXXVII.
UPON A PENNY LOAF.

Thy price one penny is in time of plenty,
In famine doubled, 'tis from one to twenty.
Yea, no man knows what price on thee to set
When there is but one penny loaf to get.

Comparison.
This loaf's an emblem of the Word of God,
A thing of low esteem before the rod
Of famine smites the soul with fear of death,
But then it is our all, our life, our breath.

XXXVIII.
THE BOY AND WATCHMAKER.

This watch my father did on me bestow,
A golden one it is, but 'twill not go,
Unless it be at an uncertainty:
But as good none as one to tell a lie.

When 'tis high day my hand will stand at nine;
I think there's no man's watch so bad as mine.
Sometimes 'tis sullen, 'twill not go at all,
And yet 'twas never broke nor had a fall.

Watchmaker.
Your watch, though it be good, through want
    of skill
May fail to do according to your will.
Suppose the balance, wheels, and springs be
    good,
And all things else, unless you understood
To manage it, as watches ought to be,
Your watch will still be at uncertainty.
Come, tell me, do you keep it from the dust,
Yea, wind it also duly up you must?

Take heed, too, that you do not strain the
    spring;
You must be circumspect in every thing,
Or else your watch, were it as good again,

Would not with time and tide you entertain.

Comparison.
This boy an emblem is of a convert,
His watch of the work of grace within his
    heart,
The watchmaker is Jesus Christ our Lord,
His counsel, the directions of his Word;
Then convert, if thy heart be out of frame,
Of this watchmaker learn to mend the same.
Do not lay ope' thy heart to worldly dust,
Nor let thy graces over-grow with rust,

Be oft' renewed in the' spirit of thy mind,
Or else uncertain thou thy watch wilt find.

XXXIX.
UPON A LOOKING-GLASS

In this see thou thy beauty, hast thou any,
Or thy defects, should they be few or many.
Thou may'st, too, here thy spots and freckles
    see,
Hast thou but eyes, and what their numbers be.
But art thou blind? There is no looking-glass
Can show thee thy defects, thy spots, or face.

Comparison.
Unto this glass we may compare the Word,
For that to man advantage doth afford
(Has he a mind to know himself and state),
To see what will be his eternal fate.

But without eyes, alas! how can he see?
Many that seem to look here, blind men be.
This is the reason they so often read
Their judgment there, and do it nothing dread.

XL.
OF THE LOVE OF CHRIST.

The love of Christ, poor I! may touch upon;
But 'tis unsearchable. O! there is none
Its large dimensions can comprehend
Should they dilate thereon world without end.
When we had sinned, in his zeal he sware,
That he upon his back our sins would bear.
And since unto sin is entailed death,
He vowed for our sins he'd lose his breath.
He did not only say, vow, or resolve,
But to astonishment did so involve

Himself in man's distress and misery,
As for, and with him, both to live and die.
To his eternal fame in sacred story,
We find that he did lay aside his glory,
Stepped from the throne of highest dignity,
Became poor man, did in a manger lie;

Yea, was beholden unto his for bread,
Had, of his own, not where to lay his head;
Though rich, he did for us become thus poor,
That he might make us rich for evermore.
Nor was this but the least of what he did,
But the outside of what he suffered?
God made his blessed son under the law,
Under the curse, which, like the lion's paw,
Did rent and tear his soul for mankind's sin,
More than if we for it in hell had been.
His cries, his tears, and bloody agony,
The nature of his death doth testify.

Nor did he of constraint himself thus give,
For sin, to death, that man might with him
    live.
He did do what he did most willingly,
He sung, and gave God thanks, that he must die.
But do kings use to die for captive slaves?
Yet we were such when Jesus died to save's.
Yea, when he made himself a sacrifice,
It was that he might save his enemies.

And though he was provoked to retract
His blest resolves for such so good an act,
By the abusive carriages of those
That did both him, his love, and grace oppose;
Yet he, as unconcerned with such things,
Goes on, determines to make captives kings;
Yea, many of his murderers he takes
Into his favor, and them princes makes.

XLI.
ON THE CACKLING OF A HEN.

The hen, so soon as she an egg doth lay,
(Spreads the fame of her doing what she may.)
About the yard she cackling now doth go,
To tell what 'twas she at her nest did do.
Just thus it is with some professing men,
If they do ought that good is, like our hen
They can but cackle on't where e'er they go,
What their right hand doth their left hand
    must know.

XLII.
UPON AN HOUR-GLASS.

This glass, when made, was, by the workman's
    skill,
The sum of sixty minutes to fulfill.
Time, more nor less, by it will out be spun,
But just an hour, and then the glass is run.
Man's life we will compare unto this glass,
The number of his months he cannot pass;
But when he has accomplished his day,
He, like a vapor, vanisheth away.

XLIII.
UPON A SNAIL.

She goes but softly, but she goeth sure,
She stumbles not, as stronger creatures do.
Her journey's shorter, so she may endure
Better than they which do much farther go.
She makes no noise, but stilly seizeth on
The flower or herb appointed for her food,
The which she quietly doth feed upon
While others range and glare, but find no
    good.
And though she doth but very softly go,
However, 'tis not fast nor slow, but sure;
And certainly they that do travel so,
The prize they do aim at they do procure.

Comparison.
Although they seem not much to stir, less go,
For Christ that hunger, or from wrath that
    flee,
Yet what they seek for quickly they come to,
Though it doth seem the farthest off to be.
One act of faith doth bring them to that
    flower
They so long for, that they may eat and live,
Which, to attain, is not in others power,
Though for it a king's ransom they would
    give.
Then let none faint, nor be at all dismayed
That life by Christ do seek, they shall not fail
To have it; let them nothing be afraid;
The herb and flower are eaten by the snail.

XLIV.
OF THE SPOUSE OF CHRIST.

Who's this that cometh from the wilderness,

Like smokey pillars thus perfum'd with myrrh,
Leaning upon her dearest in distress,
Led into's bosom by the Comforter?

She's clothed with the sun, crowned with
      twelve stars,
The spotted moon her footstool she hath
      made.
The dragon her assaults, fills her with jars,
Yet rests she under her Beloved's shade,
But whence was she? what is her pedigree?
Was not her father a poor Amorite?
What was her mother but as others be,
A poor, a wretched, and a sinful Hittite.
Yea, as for her, the day that she was born,
As loathsome, out of doors they did her cast;
Naked and filthy, stinking and forlorn;
This was her pedigree from first to last.
Nor was she pitied in this estate,
All let her lie polluted in her blood:
None her condition did commiserate,
There was no heart that sought to do her good.
Yet she unto these ornaments is come,
Her breasts are fashioned, her hair is grown;
She is made heiress of the best kingdom;
All her indignities away are blown.

Cast out she was, but now she home is taken,
Naked (sometimes), but now, you see, she's
      cloth'd;
Now made the darling, though before forsaken,
Barefoot, but now as princes' daughters shod.
Instead of filth, she now has her perfumes;
Instead of ignominy, her chains of gold:
Instead of what the beauty most consumes,
Her beauty's perfect, lovely to behold.

Those that attend and wait upon her be
Princes of honor, clothed in white array;
Upon her head's a crown of gold, and she
Eats wheat, honey, and oil, from day to day.
For her beloved, he's the high'st of all,
The only Potentate, the King of kings:
Angels and men do him Jehovah call,
And from him life and glory always springs.
He's white and ruddy, and of all the chief:
His head, his locks, his eyes, his hands, and
      feet,
Do, for completeness, out-go all belief;
His cheeks like flowers are, his mouth most
      sweet.

As for his wealth, he is made heir of all;
What is in heaven, what is on earth is his:
And he this lady his joint-heir doth call,
Of all that shall be, or at present is.

Well, lady, well, God has been good to thee;
Thou of an outcast, now art made a queen.
Few, or none, may with thee compared be,
A beggar made thus high is seldom seen.

Take heed of pride, remember what thou art
By nature, though thou hast in grace a share,
Thou in thyself dost yet retain a part
Of thine own filthiness; wherefore beware.

XLV.
UPON A SKILFUL PLAYER OF AN INSTRUMENT.

He that can play well on an instrument,
Will take the ear, and captivate the mind
With mirth or sadness; for that it is bent
Thereto, as music in it place doth find.
But if one hears that hath therein no skill,
(As often music lights of such a chance)
Of its brave notes they soon be weary will:
And there are some can neither sing nor
      dance.

Comparison.
Unto him that thus skilfully doth play,
God doth compare a gospel-minister,
That rightly preacheth, and doth godly pray,
Applying truly what doth thence infer.

This man, whether of wrath or grace he preach,
So skilfully doth handle every word;
And by his saying doth the heart so reach,
That it doth joy or sigh before the Lord.
But some there be, which, as the brute, doth
      lie
Under the Word, without the least advance
Godward; such do despise the ministry;
They weep not at it, neither to it dance.

XLVI.
OF MAN BY NATURE.

From God he's a backslider,
Of ways he loves the wider;
With wickedness a sider,
More venom than a spider.

In sin he's a considerer,
A make-bate and divider;
Blind reason is his guider,
The devil is his rider.

XLVII.
UPON THE DISOBEDIENT CHILD.

Children become, while little, our delights!
When they grow bigger, they begin to fright's.
Their sinful nature prompts them to rebel,
And to delight in paths that lead to hell.
Their parents' love and care they overlook,
As if relation had them quite forsook.

They take the counsels of the wanton's, rather
Than the most grave instructions of a father.
They reckon parents ought to do for them,
Though they the fifth commandment do
    contemn;
They snap and snarl if parents them control,
Though but in things most hurtful to the soul.
They reckon they are masters, and that we
Who parents are, should to them subject be!
If parents fain would have a hand in choosing,
The children have a heart will in refusing.
They'll by wrong doings, under parents gather,
And say it is no sin to rob a father.

They'll jostle parents out of place and power,
They'll make themselves the head, and them
    devour.
How many children, by becoming head,
Have brought their parents to a piece of bread!
Thus they who, at the first, were parents joy,
Turn that to bitterness, themselves destroy.
But, wretched child, how canst thou thus
    requite
Thy aged parents, for that great delight
They took in thee, when thou, as helpless, lay
In their indulgent bosoms day by day?

Thy mother, long before she brought thee
forth,
Took care thou shouldst want neither food
    nor cloth.
Thy father glad was at his very heart,
Had he to thee a portion to impart.

Comfort they promised themselves in thee,
But thou, it seems, to them a grief wilt be.

How oft, how willingly brake they their sleep,
If thou, their bantling, didst but winch or
    weep.
Their love to thee was such they could have
    giv'n,
That thou mightst live, almost their part of
    heav'n.
But now, behold how they rewarded are!
For their indulgent love and tender care;
All is forgot, this love he doth despise.
They brought this bird up to pick out their
    eyes.

XLVIII.
UPON A SHEET OF WHITE PAPER.

This subject is unto the foulest pen,
Or fairest handled by the sons of men.

'Twill also show what is upon it writ,
Be it wisely, or nonsense for want of wit,
Each blot and blur it also will expose
To thy next readers, be they friends or foes.

Comparison.
Some souls are like unto this blank or sheet,
Though not in whiteness.
The next man they meet,
If wise or fool, debauched or deluder,
Or what you will, the dangerous intruder
May write thereon, to cause that man to err
In doctrine or in life, with blot and blur.
Nor will that soul conceal from who observes,
But show how foul it is, wherein it swerves.
A reading man may know who was the writer,
And, by the hellish nonsense, the inditer.

XLIX.
UPON FIRE.

Who falls into the fire shall burn with heat;
While those remote scorn from it to retreat.
Yea, while those in it, cry out, O! I burn,
Some farther off those cries to laughter turn.

Comparison.
While some tormented are in hell for sin;
On earth some greatly do delight therein.
Yea, while some make it echo with their cry,
Others count it a fable and a lie.
                    John Bunyan, 1628–88

Daniel's Prayer

John Calvin

Daniel relates how he was clothed in the boldness of the Spirit of God to offer his life as a sacrifice to God, because he knew he had no hope of pardon left, if his violation of the king's edict had been discovered; he knew the king himself to be completely in shackles even if he wished to pardon him – as the event proved. If death had been before the Prophet's eyes, he preferred meeting it fearlessly rather than ceasing from the duty of piety. We must remark that the internal worship of God is not treated here, but only the external profession of it. If Daniel had been forbidden to pray, this fortitude with which he was endued might seem necessary; but many think he ran great risks without sufficient reason, since he increased the chance of death when only outward profession was prohibited. But as Daniel here is not the herald of his own virtue, but the Spirit speaks through his mouth, we must suppose that this magnanimity in the holy Prophet was pleasing to God. And his liberation shewed how greatly his piety was approved, because he had rather lose his life than change any of his habits respecting the worship of God. We know the principal sacrifice which God requires, is to call upon his name. For we hereby testify him to be the author of all good things; next we shew forth a specimen of our faith; then we fly to him, and cast all our cares into his bosom, and offer him our prayers. Since, therefore, prayer constitutes the chief part of our adoration and worship of God, it was certainly a matter of no slight moment when the king forbade any one to pray to God; it was a gross and manifest denial of piety.

And here, again, we collect how blind was the king's pride when he could sign so impious and foul an edict! Then how mad were the nobles who, to ruin Daniel as far as they possibly could, endeavored to abolish all piety, and draw down God from heaven! For what remains, when men think they can free themselves from the help of God, and pass him over with security? Unless he prop us up by his special aid, we know how entirely we should be reduced to nothing. Hence the king forbade any one to offer up any prayer during a whole month – that is, as I have said, he exacts from every one a denial of God! But Daniel could not obey the edict without committing an atrocious insult against God and declining from piety; because, as I have said, God exacts this as a principal sacrifice. Hence it is not surprising if Daniel cordially opposed the sacrilegious edict. Now, with respect to the profession of piety, it was necessary to testify before men his perseverance in the worship of God. For if he had altered his habits at all, it would have been a partial abjuration; he would not have said that he openly despised God to please Darius; but that very difference in his conduct would have been a proof of perfidious defection. We know that God requires not only faith in the heart and the inward affections, but also the witness and confession of our piety.

Daniel, therefore, was obliged to persevere in the holy practice to which he was accustomed, unless he wished to be the very foulest apostate! He was in the habit of praying with his windows open: hence he continued in his usual course, lest any one should object that he gratified his earthly king for a moment by omitting the worship of God. I wish this doctrine was now engraven on the hearts of all men as it ought to be; but this example of the Prophet is derided by many, not perhaps openly and glaringly, but still clearly enough, the Prophet seems to them too inconsiderate and simple, since he incurs great danger, rashly, and without any necessity. For they so separate faith from its outward confession as to suppose it can remain entire even if completely buried, and for the sake of avoiding the cross. they depart a hundred times from its pure and sincere profession. We must maintain, therefore, not only the duty of offering to God the sacrifice of prayer in our hearts, but that our open profession is also required, and thus the reality of our worship of God may clearly appear.

I do not say that our hasty thoughts are to be instantly spread abroad, rendering us subject to death by the enemies of God and his gospel; but I say these things ought to be united and never to be separated, namely, faith and its profession. For confession is of two kinds: first, the open and ingenuous testimony to our inward feelings; and secondly, the necessary maintenance of the worship of God, lest we shew any sign of a perverse and perfidious hypocrisy, and thus reject the pursuit of piety. With regard to the first kind, it is neither always nor everywhere necessary to profess our faith; but the second kind ought to be perpetually practiced, for it can never be necessary for us to pretend either disaffection or apostasy. For although Daniel did not send for the Chaldeans by the sound of a trumpet whenever he wished to pray, yet he framed his prayers and his vows in his couch as usual, and did not pretend to be forgetful of piety when he saw his faith put to the test, and the experiments made whether or not he would persevere in his constancy. Hence he distinctly says, he went home, after being made acquainted with the signing of the decree. Had he been admitted to the council, he would doubtless have spoken out, but the rest of the nobles cunningly excluded him, lest he should interfere with them, and they thought the remedy would be too late, and utterly in vain as soon as he perceived the certainty of his own death. Hence, had he been admitted to the king's council, he would there have discharged his duty, and heartily interposed; but after the signing of the edict, and the loss of all opportunity for advising the king, he retired to his house.

We must here notice the impossibility of finding an excuse for the king's advisers, who purposely escape when they see that unanimity of opinion cannot be obtained, and think God will be satisfied in this way, if they only maintain perfect silence. But no excuse can be admitted for such weakness of mind. And, doubtless, Daniel is unable to defend them by his example, since, as we have already said, he was excluded by the cunning and malice of the nobles from taking his place among them as usual, and thus admonishing the king in time. He now says, His windows were open towards Jerusalem. The question arises, Whether it was necessary for Daniel thus to open his windows? For some one may object – he did this under a mistaken opinion; for if God fills heaven end earth, what signified his windows being open towards Jerusalem? There is no doubt that the Prophet used this device as a stimulus to his fervor in prayer. For when

praying for the liberation of his people, he directed his eyes towards Jerusalem, and that sight became a stimulus to enflame his mind to greater devotion. Hence the opening of the Prophet's windows has no reference to God, as if he should be listened to more readily by having the open heaven between his dwelling and Judea; but he rather considered himself and his natural infirmity. Now, if the holy Prophet, so careful in his prayers, needed this help, we must see whether or not our sloth in these days has need of more stimulants! Let us learn, therefore, when we feel ourselves to be too sluggish and cold in prayer, to collect all the aids which can arouse our feelings and correct the torpor of which we are conscious. This, then, was the Prophet's intention in opening his windows towards Jerusalem. Besides, he wished by this symbol to shew his domestics his perseverance, in the hope and expectation of the promised redemption. When, therefore, he prayed to God, he kept Jerusalem in sight, not that his eyes could penetrate to so distant a region, but he directed his gaze towards Jerusalem to shew himself a stranger among the Chaldeans, although he enjoyed great power among them, and was adorned with great authority, and excelled in superior dignity. Thus he wished all men to perceive how he longed for the promised inheritance, although for a time he was in exile. This was his second reason for opening his windows.

He says, He prayed three times a day. This is worthy of observation, because, unless we fix certain hours in the day for prayer, it easily slips from our memory. Although, therefore, Daniel was constant in pouring forth prayers, yet he enjoined upon himself the customary rite of prostrating himself before God three times a day. When we rise in the morning, unless we commence the day by praying to God, we shew a brutish stupidity, so also when we retire to rest, and when we take our food and at other times, as every one finds most advantageous to himself. For here God allows us liberty, but we ought all to feel our infirmities, and to apply the proper remedies. Therefore, for this reason, Daniel was in the habit of praying thrice. A proof of his fervor is also added, when he says, He prostrated himself on his knees; not that bending the knee is necessary in prayer, but while we need aids to devotion, as we have said, that posture is of importance. First of all, it reminds us of our inability to stand before God, unless with humility and reverence; then, our minds are better prepared for serious entreaty, and this symbol of worship is pleasing to God. Hence Daniel's expression is by no means superfluous: He, fell upon his knees whenever he wished to pray to God. He now says, he uttered prayers and confessions before God, or he praised God, for we must diligently notice how many in their prayers mutter to God. For although they demand either one thing or another, yet they are carried along by an immoderate impulse, and, as I have said, they are violent in their requests unless God instantly grants their petitions.

This is the reason why Daniel joins praises or the giving of thanks with prayers; as, also, Paul exhorts us respecting both. Offer up, says he, your prayers to God, with thanksgiving, (Philippians 4:6), as if he had said, We cannot rightly offer vows and prayers to God unless when we bless his holy name, although he does not immediately grant our petitions. In Daniel's case we must remark another circumstance: he had been an exile for a long time, and tossed about in many troubles and changes; still he celebrates God's praises. Which of us is endued with such patience as to praise God, if afflicted with many trials through three or four years? Nay, scarcely a day passes without our passions growing warm and instigating us to rebel against God! Since Daniel, then, could persevere in praising God, when oppressed by so many sorrows, anxieties, and troubles – this was a remarkable proof of invincible patience. By noticing the time, he marks, as I have said before, a perseverance, since he was not only accustomed to pray once or twice, but by a regular constancy he exercised himself in this duty of piety every day.

John Calvin, 1509–64

Of Prayer
John Calvin

INSTITUTES OF THE CHRISTIAN RELIGION
BOOK III, CHAPTER XX

OF PRAYER: A PERPETUAL EXERCISE OF
FAITH
THE DAILY BENEFITS DERIVED FROM IT

The principal divisions of this chapter are:
I. Connection of the subject of prayer with the previous chapters. The nature of prayer, and its necessity as a Christian exercise, sec. 1, 2.
II. To whom prayer is to be offered. Refutation of an objection which is too apt to present itself to the mind, sec. 3.
III. Rules to be observed in prayer, sec. 4–16.
IV. Through whom prayer is to be made, sec. 17–19.
V. Refutation of an error as to the doctrine of our Mediator and Intercessor, with answers to the leading arguments urged in support of the intercession of saints, sec. 20–27.
VI. The nature of prayer, and some of its accidents, sec. 28–33.
VII. A perfect form of invocation, or an exposition of the Lord's Prayer, sec. 34–50.
VIII. Some rules to be observed with regard to prayer, as time, perseverance, the feeling of the mind, and the assurance of faith, sec. 50–52.

OUTLINE.
1. A general summary of what is contained in the previous part of the work. A transition to the doctrine of prayer. Its connection with the subject of faith.
2. Prayer defined. Its necessity and use.
3. Objection, that prayer seems useless, because God already knows our wants. Answer, from the institution and end of prayer. Confirmation by example. Its necessity and propriety. Perpetually reminds us of our duty, and leads to meditation on divine providence. Conclusion. Prayer a most useful exercise. This proved by three passages of Scripture.
4. Rules to be observed in prayer. First, reverence to God. How the mind ought to be composed.
5. All giddiness of mind must be excluded, and all our feelings seriously engaged. This

confirmed by the form of lifting the hand in prayer. We must ask only in so far as God permits. To help our weakness, God gives the Spirit to be our guide in prayer. What the office of the Spirit in this respect. We must still pray both with the heart and the lips.

6. Second rule of prayer, a sense of our want. This rule violated, 1. By perfunctory and formal prayer 2. By hypocrites who have no sense of their sins. 3. By giddiness in prayer. Remedies.

7. Objection, that we are not always under the same necessity of praying. Answer, we must pray always. This answer confirmed by an examination of the dangers by which both our life and our salvation are every moment threatened. Confirmed farther by the command and permission of God, by the nature of true repentance, and a consideration of impenitence. Conclusion.

8. Third rule, the suppression of all pride. Examples. Daniel, David, Isaiah, Jeremiah, Baruch.

9. Advantage of thus suppressing pride. It leads to earnest entreaty for pardon, accompanied with humble confession and sure confidence in the Divine mercy. This may not always be expressed in words. It is peculiar to pious penitents. A general introduction to procure favor to our prayers never to be omitted.

10. Objection to the third rule of prayer. Of the glorying of the saints. Answer. Confirmation of the answer.

11. Fourth rule of prayer, – a sure confidence of being heard animating us to prayer. The kind of confidence required, viz., a serious conviction of our misery, joined with sure hope. From these true prayer springs. How diffidence impairs prayer. In general, faith is required.

12. This faith and sure hope regarded by our opponents as most absurd. Their error described and refuted by various passages of Scripture, which show that acceptable prayer is accompanied with these qualities. No repugnance between this certainty and an acknowledgment of our destitution.

13. To our unworthiness we oppose, 1. The command of God. 2. The promise. Rebels and hypocrites completely condemned. Passages of Scripture confirming the command to pray.

14. Other passages respecting the prom-

ises which belong to the pious when they invoke God. These realized though we are not possessed of the same holiness as other distinguished servants of God, provided we indulge no vain confidence, and sincerely betake ourselves to the mercy of God. Those who do not invoke God under urgent necessity are no better than idolaters. This concurrence of fear and confidence reconciles the different passages of Scripture, as to humbling ourselves in prayer, and causing our prayers to ascend.

15. Objection founded on some examples, viz., that prayers have proved effectual, though not according to the form prescribed. Answer. Such examples, though not given for our imitation, are of the greatest use. Objection, the prayers of the faithful sometimes not effectual. Answer confirmed by a noble passage of Augustine. Rule for right prayer.

16. The above four rules of prayer not so rigidly exacted, as that every prayer deficient in them in any respect is rejected by God. This shown by examples. Conclusion, or summary of this section.

17. Through whom God is to be invoked, viz., Jesus Christ. This founded on a consideration of the divine majesty, and the precept and promise of God himself. God therefore to be invoked only in the name of Christ.

18. From the first all believers were heard through him only: yet this specially restricted to the period subsequent to his ascension. The ground of this restriction.

19. The wrath of God lies on those who reject Christ as a Mediator. This excludes not the mutual intercession of saints on the earth.

20. Refutation of errors interfering with the intercession of Christ. 1. Christ the Mediator of redemption; the saints mediators of intercession. Answer confirmed by the clear testimony of Scripture, and by a passage from Augustine. The nature of Christ's intercession.

21. Of the intercession of saints living with Christ in heaven. Fiction of the Papists in regard to it. Refuted. 1. Its absurdity. 2. It is nowhere mentioned by Scripture. 3. Appeal to the conscience of the superstitious. 4. Its blasphemy. Exception. Answers.

22. Monstrous errors resulting from this fiction. Refutation. Exception by the advocates of this fiction. Answer.

23. Arguments of the Papists for the intercession of saints. 1. From the duty and office of angels. Answer. 2. From an expression of Jeremiah respecting Moses and Samuel. Answer, retorting the argument. 3. The meaning of the prophet confirmed by a similar passage in Ezekiel, and the testimony of an apostle.

24. 4. Fourth papistical argument from the nature of charity, which is more perfect in the saints in glory. Answer.

25. Argument founded on a passage in Moses. Answer.

26. Argument from its being said that the prayers of saints are heard. Answer, confirmed by Scripture, and illustrated by examples.

27. Conclusion, that the saints cannot be invoked without impiety.
1. It robs God of his glory.
2. Destroys the intercession of Christ.
3. Is repugnant to the word of God.
4. Is opposed to the due method of prayer.
5. Is without approved example.
6. Springs from distrust. Last objection. Answer.

28. Kinds of prayer.
Vows.
Supplications.
Petitions.
Thanksgiving.
Connection of these, their constant use and necessity. Particular explanation confirmed by reason, Scripture, and example. Rule as to supplication and thanksgiving.

29. The accidents of prayer, viz., private and public, constant, at stated seasons, etc. Exception in time of necessity. Prayer without ceasing. Its nature. Garrulity of Papists and hypocrites refuted. The scope and parts of prayer. Secret prayer. Prayer at all places. Private and public prayer.

30. Of public places or churches in which common prayers are offered up. Right use of churches. Abuse.

31. Of utterance and singing. These of no avail if not from the heart. The use of the voice refers more to public than private prayer.

32. Singing of the greatest antiquity, but not universal. How to be performed.

33. Public prayers should be in the vulgar, not in a foreign tongue. Reason:
1. The nature of the Church.

2. Authority of an apostle.
Sincere affection always necessary. The tongue not always necessary. Bending of the knee, and uncovering of the head.

34. The form of prayer delivered by Christ displays the boundless goodness of our heavenly Father. The great comfort thereby afforded.

35. Lord's Prayer divided into six petitions. Subdivision into two principal parts, the former referring to the glory of God, the latter to our salvation.

36. The use of the term Father implies:
1. That we pray to God in the name of Christ alone.
2. That we lay aside all distrust.
3. That we expect everything that is for our good.

37. Objection, that our sins exclude us from the presence of him whom we have made a Judge, not a Father. Answer, from the nature of God, as described by an apostle, the parable of the prodigal son, and from the expression, *Our Father.* Christ the earnest, the Holy Spirit the witness, of our adoption.

38. Why God is called generally, Our Father.

39. We may pray specially for ourselves and certain others, provided we have in our mind a general reference to all.

40. In what sense God is said to be *in heaven.* A threefold use of this doctrine for our consolation. Three cautions. Summary of the preface to the Lord's Prayer.

41. The necessity of the first petition a proof of our unrighteousness. What meant by the name of God. How it is hallowed. Parts of this hallowing. A deprecation of the sins by which the name of God is profaned.

42. Distinction between the first and second petitions. The kingdom of God, what. How said to come. Special exposition of this petition. It reminds us of three things. Advent of the kingdom of God in the world.

43. Distinction between the second and third petitions. The will here meant not the secret will or good pleasure of God, but that manifested in the word. Conclusion of the three first petitions.

44. A summary of the second part of the Lord's Prayer. Three petitions. What contained in the first. Declares the exceeding kindness of

God, and our distrust. What meant by bread. Why the petition for bread precedes that for the forgiveness of sins. Why it is called ours. Why to be sought this day, or daily. The doctrine resulting from this petition, illustrated by an example. Two classes of men sin in regard to this petition. In what sense it is called, our bread. Why we ask God to give it to us.

45 Close connection between this and the subsequent petition. Why our sins are called debts. This petition violated:

1. By those who think they can satisfy God by their own merits, or those of others.

2. By those who dream of a perfection which makes pardon unnecessary.

Why the elect cannot attain perfection in this life. Refutation of the libertine dreamers of perfection. Objection refuted. In what sense we are said to forgive those who have sinned against us. How the condition is to be understood.

46. The sixth petition reduced to three heads.

1. The various forms of temptation.

The depraved conceptions of our minds.

The wiles of Satan, on the right hand and on the left.

2. What it is to be led into temptation. We do not ask not to be tempted of God. What meant by evil, or the evil one. Summary of this petition. How necessary it is. Condemns the pride of the superstitious. Includes many excellent properties. In what sense God may be said to lead us into temptation.

47. The three last petitions show that the prayers of Christians ought to be public. The conclusion of the Lord's Prayer. Why the word Amen is added.

48. The Lord's Prayer contains everything that we can or ought to ask of God. Those who go beyond it sin in three ways.

49. We may, after the example of the saints, frame our prayers in different words, provided there is no difference in meaning.

50. Some circumstances to be observed. Of appointing special hours of prayer. What to be aimed at, what avoided. The will of God, the rule of our prayers.

51. Perseverance in prayer especially recommended, both by precept and example. Condemnatory of those who assign to God a time and mode of hearing.

52. Of the dignity of faith, through which we always obtain, in answer to prayer, whatever is most expedient for us. The knowledge of this most necessary.

1. From the previous part of the work we clearly see how completely destitute man is of all good, how devoid of every means of procuring his own salvation. Hence, if he would obtain succor in his necessity, he must go beyond himself, and procure it in some other quarter. It has farther been shown that the Lord kindly and spontaneously manifests himself in Christ, in whom he offers all happiness for our misery, all abundance for our want, opening up the treasures of heaven to us, so that we may turn with full faith to his beloved Son, depend upon him with full expectation, rest in him, and cleave to him with full hope. This, indeed, is that secret and hidden philosophy which cannot be learned by syllogisms: a philosophy thoroughly understood by those whose eyes God has so opened as to see light in his light (Ps. 36:9). But after we have learned by faith to know that whatever is necessary for us or defective in us is supplied in God and in our Lord Jesus Christ, in whom it hath pleased the Father that all fullness should dwell, that we may thence draw as from an inexhaustible fountain, it remains for us to seek and in prayer implore of him what we have learned to be in him. To know God as the sovereign disposer of all good, inviting us to present our requests, and yet not to approach or ask of him, were so far from availing us, that it were just as if one told of a treasure were to allow it to remain buried in the ground. Hence the Apostle, to show that a faith unaccompanied with prayer to God cannot be genuine, states this to be the order: As faith springs from the Gospel, so by faith our hearts are framed to call upon the name of God (Rom. 10:14). And this is the very thing which he had expressed some time before, viz., that the Spirit of adoption, which seals the testimony of the Gospel on our hearts, gives us courage to make our requests known unto God, calls forth groanings which cannot be uttered, and enables us to cry, Abba, Father (Rom. 8:26). This last point, as we have hitherto only touched upon it slightly in passing, must now be treated more fully.

2. To *prayer*, then, are we indebted for penetrating to those riches which are treasured up for us with our heavenly Father. For there is a kind of intercourse between God and men, by which, having entered the upper sanctuary, they appear before Him and appeal to his promises, that when necessity requires they may learn by experiences that what they believed merely on the authority of his word was not in vain. Accordingly, we see that nothing is set before us as an object of expectation from the Lord which we are not enjoined to ask of Him in prayer, so true it is that prayer digs up those treasures which the Gospel of our Lord discovers to the eye of faith. The necessity and utility of this exercise of prayer no words can sufficiently express. Assuredly it is not without cause our heavenly Father declares that our only safety is in calling upon his name, since by it we invoke the presence of his providence to watch over our interests, of his power to sustain us when weak and almost fainting, of his goodness to receive us into favor, though miserably loaded with sin; in fine, call upon him to manifest himself to us in all his perfections. Hence, admirable peace and tranquility are given to our consciences; for the straits by which we were pressed being laid before the Lord, we rest fully satisfied with the assurance that none of our evils are unknown to him, and that he is both able and willing to make the best provision for us.

3. But some one will say, Does he not know without a monitor both what our difficulties are, and what is meet for our interest, so that it seems in some measure superfluous to solicit him by our prayers, as if he were winking, or even sleeping, until aroused by the sound of our voice? Those who argue thus attend not to the end for which the Lord taught us to pray. It was not so much for his sake as for ours. He wills indeed, as is just, that due honor be paid him by acknowledging that all which men desire or feel to be useful, and pray to obtain, is derived from him. But even the benefit of the homage which we thus pay him redounds to ourselves. Hence the holy patriarchs, the more confidently they proclaimed the mercies of God to themselves and others felt the stronger incitement to prayer. It will

be sufficient to refer to the example of Elijah, who being assured of the purpose of God had good ground for the promise of rain which he gives to Ahab, and yet prays anxiously upon his knees, and sends his servant seven times to inquire (1 Kings 18:42); not that he discredits the oracle, but because he knows it to be his duty to lay his desires before God, lest his faith should become drowsy or torpid. Wherefore, although it is true that while we are listless or insensible to our wretchedness, he wakes and watches for use and sometimes even assists us unasked; it is very much for our interest to be constantly supplicating him; first, that our heart may always be inflamed with a serious and ardent desire of seeking, loving and serving him, while we accustom ourselves to have recourse to him as a sacred anchor in every necessity; secondly, that no desires, no longing whatever, of which we are ashamed to make him the witness, may enter our minds, while we learn to place all our wishes in his sight, and thus pour out our heart before him; and, lastly, that we may be prepared to receive all his benefits with true gratitude and thanksgiving, while our prayers remind us that they proceed from his hand. Moreover, having obtained what we asked, being persuaded that he has answered our prayers, we are led to long more earnestly for his favor, and at the same time have greater pleasure in welcoming the blessings which we perceive to have been obtained by our prayers. Lastly, use and experience confirm the thought of his providence in our minds in a manner adapted to our weakness, when we understand that he not only promises that he will never fail us, and spontaneously gives us access to approach him in every time of need, but has his hand always stretched out to assist his people, not amusing them with words, but proving himself to be a present aid. For these reasons, though our most merciful Father never slumbers nor sleeps, he very often seems to do so, that thus he may exercise us, when we might otherwise be listless and slothful, in asking, entreating, and earnestly beseeching him to our great good. It is very absurd, therefore, to dissuade men from prayer, by pretending that Divine Providence, which is always watching over the government of the universes is in vain importuned by our supplications, when, on the contrary, the Lord himself declares, that he is "nigh unto all that call upon him, to all that call upon him in truth" (Ps. 145:18). No better is the frivolous allegation of others, that it is superfluous to pray for things which the Lord is ready of his own accord to bestow; since it is his pleasure that those very things which flow from his spontaneous liberality should be acknowledged as conceded to our prayers. This is testified by that memorable sentence in the psalms to which many others corresponds: "The eyes of the Lord are upon the righteous, and his ears are open unto their cry" (Ps. 34: 15). This passage, while extolling the care which Divine Providence spontaneously exercises over the safety of believers, omits not the exercise of faith by which the mind is aroused from sloth. The eyes of God are awake to assist the blind in their necessity, but he is likewise pleased to listen to our groans, that he may give us the better proof of his love. And thus both things are true, "He that keepeth Israel shall neither slumber nor sleep" (Ps. 121:4); and yet whenever he sees us dumb and torpid, he withdraws as if he had forgotten us.

4. Let the first rule of right prayer then be, to have our heart and mind framed as becomes those who are entering into converse with God. This we shall accomplish in regard to the mind, if, laying aside carnal thoughts and cares which might interfere with the direct and pure contemplation of God, it not only be wholly intent on prayer, but also, as far as possible, be borne and raised above itself. I do not here insist on a mind so disengaged as to feel none of the gnawings of anxiety; on the contrary, it is by much anxiety that the fervor of prayer is inflamed. Thus we see that the holy servants of God betray great anguish, not to say solicitude, when they cause the voice of complaint to ascend to the Lord from the deep abyss and the jaws of death. What I say is, that all foreign and extraneous cares must be dispelled by which the mind might be driven to and fro in vague suspense, be drawn down from heaven, and kept groveling on the earth. When I say it must be raised above itself, I mean that it must not bring into the presence of God any of those things which our blind and stupid reason is wont to devise, nor keep itself confined within the little measure of its own vanity, but rise to a purity worthy of God.

5. Both things are specially worthy of notice. First, let every one in professing to pray turn thither all his thoughts and feelings, and be not (as is usual) distracted by wandering thoughts; because nothing is more contrary to the reverence due to God than that levity which bespeaks a mind too much given to license and devoid of fear. In this matter we ought to labor the more earnestly the more difficult we experience it to be; for no man is so intent on prayer as not to feel many thoughts creeping in, and either breaking off the tenor of his prayer, or retarding it by some turning or digression. Here let us consider how unbecoming it is when God admits us to familiar intercourse to abuse his great condescension by mingling things sacred and profane, reverence for him not keeping our minds under restraint; but just as if in prayer we were conversing with one like ourselves forgetting him, and allowing our thoughts to run to and fro. Let us know, then, that none duly prepare themselves for prayer but those who are so impressed with the majesty of God that they engage in it free from all earthly cares and affections. The ceremony of lifting up our hands in prayer is designed to remind us that we are far removed from God, unless our thoughts rise upward: as it is said in the psalm, "Unto thee, O Lord, do I lift up my soul" (Psalm 25:1). And Scripture repeatedly uses the expression to *raise our prayers* meaning that those who would be heard by God must not grovel in the mire. The sum is, that the more liberally God deals with us, condescendingly inviting us to disburden our cares into his bosom, the less excusable we are if this admirable and incomparable blessing does not in our estimation outweigh all other things, and win our affection, that prayer may seriously engage our every thought and feeling. This cannot be unless our mind, strenuously exerting itself against all impediments, rise upward.

Our second proposition was, that we are to ask only in so far as God permits. For though he bids us pour out our hearts (Ps. 62:8), he does not indiscriminately give loose reins to foolish and depraved affections; and when he promises that he will grant believers their wish, his indulgence does not proceed so far as to submit to their caprice. In both matters grievous delinquencies are everywhere committed. For not only do many without modesty, without reverence, presume to invoke God concerning their frivolities, but impudently bring forward their dreams, whatever they may be, before the tribunal of God. Such is the folly or stupidity under which they labor, that they have the hardihood to obtrude upon God desires so vile, that they would blush exceedingly to impart them to their fellow men. Profane writers have derided and even expressed their detestation of this presumption, and yet the vice has always prevailed. Hence, as the ambitious adopted Jupiter as their patron; the avaricious, Mercury; the literary aspirants, Apollo and Minerva; the warlike, Mars; the licentious, Venus: so in the present day, as I lately observed, men in prayer give greater license to their unlawful desires than if they were telling jocular tales among their equals. God does not suffer his condescension to be thus mocked, but vindicating his own light, places our wishes under the restraint of his authority. We must, therefore, attend to the observation of John: "This is the confidence that we have in him, that if we ask anything according to his will, he heareth us" (1 John 5:14).

But as our faculties are far from being able to attain to such high perfection, we must seek for some means to assist them. As the eye of our mind should be intent upon God, so the affection of our heart ought to follow in the same course. But both fall far beneath this, or rather, they faint and fail, and are carried in a contrary direction. To assist this weakness, God gives us the guidance of the Spirit in our prayers to dictate what is right, and regulate our affections. For seeing "we know not what we should pray for as we ought," "the Spirit itself maketh intercession for us with groanings which cannot be uttered" (Rom. 8:26) not that he actually prays or groans, but he excites in us sighs, and wishes, and confidence, which our natural powers are not at all able to conceive. Nor is it without cause Paul gives the name of *groanings which cannot be uttered* to the prayers which believers send forth under the guidance of the Spirit. For those who are truly

exercised in prayer are not unaware that blind anxieties so restrain and perplex them, that they can scarcely find what it becomes them to utter; nay, in attempting to lisp they halt and hesitate. Hence it appears that to pray aright is a special gift. We do not speak thus in indulgence to our sloths as if we were to leave the office of prayer to the Holy Spirit, and give way to that carelessness to which we are too prone. Thus we sometimes hear the impious expression, that we are to wait in suspense until he take possession of our minds while otherwise occupied. Our meaning is, that, weary of our own heartlessness and sloth, we are to long for the aid of the Spirit. Nor, indeed, does Paul, when he enjoins us to pray *in the Spirit* (1 Cor. 14:15), cease to exhort us to vigilance, intimating, that while the inspiration of the Spirit is effectual to the formation of prayer, it by no means impedes or retards our own endeavors; since in this matter God is pleased to try how efficiently faith influences our hearts.

6. Another rule of prayer is, that in asking we must always truly feel our wants, and seriously considering that we need all the things which we ask, accompany the prayer with a sincere, nay, ardent desire of obtaining them. Many repeat prayers in a perfunctory manner from a set form, as if they were performing a task to God, and though they confess that this is a necessary remedy for the evils of their condition, because it were fatal to be left without the divine aid which they implore, it still appears that they perform the duty from custom, because their minds are meanwhile cold, and they ponder not what they ask.

A general and confused feeling of their necessity leads them to pray, but it does not make them solicitous as in a matter of present consequence, that they may obtain the supply of their need. Moreover, can we suppose anything more hateful or even more execrable to God than this fiction of asking the pardon of sins, while he who asks at the very time either thinks that he is not a sinner, or, at least, is not thinking that he is a sinner; in other words, a fiction by which God is plainly held in derision? But mankind, as I have lately said, are full of depravity, so that in the way of perfunctory service they often ask many things of God which they think come to them without his beneficence, or from some other quarter, or are already certainly in their possession. There is another fault which seems less heinous, but is not to be tolerated. Some murmur out prayers without meditation, their only principle being that God is to be propitiated by prayer. Believers ought to be specially on their guard never to appear in the presence of God with the intention of presenting a request unless they are under some serious impression, and are, at the same time, desirous to obtain it. Nay, although in these things which we ask only for the glory of God, we seem not at first sight to consult for our necessity, yet we ought not to ask with less fervor and vehemency of desire. For instance, when we pray that his name be hallowed – that hallowing must, so to speak, be earnestly hungered and thirsted after.

7. If it is objected, that the necessity which urges us to pray is not always equal, I admit it, and this distinction is profitably taught us by James: "Is any among you afflicted? let him pray. Is any merry? let him sing psalms" (James 5:13). Therefore, common sense itself dictates, that as we are too sluggish, we must be stimulated by God to pray earnestly whenever the occasion requires. This David calls a time when God "may be found" (a seasonable time); because, as he declares in several other passages, that the more hardly grievances, annoyances, fears, and other kinds of trial press us, the freer is our access to God, as if he were inviting us to himself. Still not less true is the injunction of Paul to pray "always" (Eph. 6: 18); because, however prosperously according to our view, things proceed, and however we may be surrounded on all sides with grounds of joy, there is not an instant of time during which our want does not exhort us to prayer. A man abounds in wheat and wine; but as he cannot enjoy a morsel of bread, unless by the continual bounty of God, his granaries or cellars will not prevent him from asking for daily bread. Then, if we consider how many dangers impend every moment, fear itself will teach us that no time ought to be without prayer. This, however, may be better known in spiritual matters. For when will the many sins of which we are conscious allow us

to sit secure without suppliantly entreating freedom from guilt and punishment? When will temptation give us a truce, making it unnecessary to hasten for help? Moreover, zeal for the kingdom and glory of God ought not to seize us by starts, but urge us without intermission, so that every time should appear seasonable. It is not without cause, therefore, that assiduity in prayer is so often enjoined. I am not now speaking of perseverance, which shall afterwards be considered; but Scripture, by reminding us of the necessity of constant prayer, charges us with sloth, because we feel not how much we stand in need of this care and assiduity. By this rule hypocrisy and the device of lying to God are restrained, nay, altogether banished from prayer. God promises that he will be near to those who call upon him in truth, and declares that those who seek him with their whole heart will find him: those, therefore, who delight in their own pollution cannot surely aspire to him.

One of the requisites of legitimate prayer is repentance. Hence the common declaration of Scripture, that God does not listen to the wicked; that their prayers, as well as their sacrifices, are an abomination to him. For it is right that those who seal up their hearts should find the ears of God closed against them, that those who, by their hardheartedness, provoke his severity should find him inflexible. In Isaiah he thus threatens: "When ye make many prayers, I will not hear: your hands are full of blood" (Isaiah 1:15). In like manner, in Jeremiah, "Though they shall cry unto me, I will not hearken unto them" (Jer. 11:7, 8, 11); because he regards it as the highest insult for the wicked to boast of his covenant while profaning his sacred name by their whole lives. Hence he complains in Isaiah: "This people draw near to me with their mouth, and with their lips do honor me; but have removed their heart far from men" (Isaiah 29:13). Indeed, he does not confine this to prayers alone, but declares that he abominates pretense in every part of his service. Hence the words of James, "Ye ask and receive not, because ye ask amiss, that ye may consume it upon your lusts" (James 4:3). It is true, indeed (as we shall again see in a little), that the pious, in the prayers which they utter, trust not to their own worth; still the admonition of John is not superfluous: "Whatsoever we ask, we receive of him, because we keep his commandments" (1 John 3:22); an evil conscience shuts the door against us. Hence it follows, that none but the sincere worshipers of God pray aright, or are listened to. Let every one, therefore, who prepares to pray feel dissatisfied with what is wrong in his condition, and assume, which he cannot do without repentance, the character and feelings of a poor suppliant.

8. The third rule to be added is: that he who comes into the presence of God to pray must divest himself of all vainglorious thoughts, lay aside all idea of worth; in short, discard all self-confidence, humbly giving God the whole glory, lest by arrogating anything, however little, to himself, vain pride cause him to turn away his face. Of this submission, which casts down all haughtiness, we have numerous examples in the servants of God. The holier they are, the more humbly they prostrate themselves when they come into the presence of the Lord. Thus Daniel, on whom the Lord himself bestowed such high commendation, says, "We do not present our supplications before thee for our righteousness but for thy great mercies. O Lord, hear; O Lord, forgive; O Lord, hearken and do; defer not, for thine own sake, O my God: for thy city and thy people are called by thy name." This he does not indirectly in the usual manner, as if he were one of the individuals in a crowd: he rather confesses his guilt apart, and as a suppliant betaking himself to the asylum of pardon, he distinctly declares that he was confessing his own sin, and the sin of his people Israel (Dan. 9:18–20). David also sets us an example of this humility: "Enter not into judgment with thy servant: for in thy sight shall no man living be justified" (Psalm 143:2). In like manner, Isaiah prays, "Behold, thou art wroth; for we have sinned: in those is continuance, and we shall be saved. But we are all as an unclean thing, and all our righteousness is as filthy rags; and we all do fade as a leaf; and our iniquities, like the wind, have taken us away. And there is none that calleth upon thy name, that stirreth up himself to take hold of thee: for thou hast hid thy face from us, and hast consumed us, because of our iniquities.

But now, O Lord, thou art our Father; we are the clay, and thou our potter; and we all are the work of thy hand. Be not wroth very sore, O Lord, neither remember iniquity for ever: Behold, see, we beseech thee, we are all thy people." (Isa. 64:5–9). You see how they put no confidence in anything but this: considering that they are the Lord's, they despair not of being the objects of his care. In the same way, Jeremiah says, "O Lord, though our iniquities testify against us, do thou it for thy name's sake" (Jer. 14:7). For it was most truly and piously written by the uncertain author (whoever he may have been) that wrote the book which is attributed to the prophet Baruch, "But the soul that is greatly vexed, which goeth stooping and feeble, and the eyes that fail, and the hungry soul, will give thee praise and righteousness, O Lord. Therefore, we do not make our humble supplication before thee, O Lord our God, for the righteousness of our fathers, and of our kings." "Hear, O Lord, and have mercy; for thou art merciful: and have pity upon us, because we have sinned before thee" (Baruch 2:18, 19; 3:2).

9. In fine, supplication for pardon, with humble and ingenuous confession of guilt, forms both the preparation and commencement of right prayer. For the holiest of men cannot hope to obtain anything from God until he has been freely reconciled to him. God cannot be propitious to any but those whom he pardons. Hence it is not strange that this is the key by which believers open the door of prayer, as we learn from several passages in The Psalms. David, when presenting a request on a different subject, says, "Remember not the sins of my youth, nor my transgressions; according to thy mercy remember me, for thy goodness sake, O Lord" (Psalm 25:7). Again, "Look upon my affliction and my pain, and forgive my sins" (Psalm 25:18). Here also we see that it is not sufficient to call ourselves to account for the sins of each passing day; we must also call to mind those which might seem to have been long before buried in oblivion. For in another passage the same prophet, confessing one grievous crime, takes occasion to go back to his very birth, "I was shapen in iniquity, and in sin did my mother conceive

me" (Psalm 51:5); not to extenuate the fault by the corruption of his nature, but as it were to accumulate the sins of his whole life, that the stricter he was in condemning himself, the more placable God might be. But although the saints do not always in express terms ask forgiveness of sins, yet if we carefully ponder those prayers as given in Scripture, the truth of what I say will readily appear; namely, that their courage to pray was derived solely from the mercy of God, and that they always began with appeasing him. For when a man interrogates his conscience, so far is he from presuming to lay his cares familiarly before God, that if he did not trust to mercy and pardon, he would tremble at the very thought of approaching him. There is, indeed, another special confession. When believers long for deliverance from punishment, they at the same time pray that their sins may be pardoned; for it were absurd to wish that the effect should be taken away while the cause remains. For we must beware of imitating foolish patients who, anxious only about curing accidental symptoms, neglect the root of the disease. Nay, our endeavor must be to have God propitious even before he attests his favor by external signs, both because this is the order which he himself chooses, and it were of little avail to experience his kindness, did not conscience feel that he is appeased, and thus enable us to regard him as altogether lovely. Of this we are even reminded by our Savior's reply. Having determined to cure the paralytic, he says, "Thy sins are forgiven thee"; in other words, he raises our thoughts to the object which is especially to be desired, viz. admission into the favor of God, and then gives the fruit of reconciliation by bringing assistance to us. But besides that special confession of present guilt which believers employ, in supplicating for pardon of every fault and punishment, that general introduction which procures favor for our prayers must never be omitted, because prayers will never reach God unless they are founded on free mercy. To this we may refer the words of John, "If we confess our sins, he is faithful and just to forgive us our sins and to cleanse us from all unrighteousness" (1 John 1:9). Hence, under the law it was necessary to consecrate prayers by the expiation of blood, both that they might

be accepted, and that the people might be warned that they were unworthy of the high privilege until, being purged from their defilements, they founded their confidence in prayer entirely on the mercy of God.

10. Sometimes, however, the saints in supplicating God, seem to appeal to their own righteousness, as when David says, "Preserve my soul; for I am holy" (Ps. 86:2). Also Hezekiah, "Remember now, O Lord, I beseech thee how I have walked before thee in truth, and with a perfect heart, and have done that which is good in thy sight" (Is. 38:2). All they mean by such expressions is, that regeneration declares them to be among the servants and children to whom God engages that he will show favor. We have already seen how he declares by the Psalmist that his eyes "are upon the righteous, and his ears are open unto their cry" (Ps. 34:16:) and again by the apostle, that "whatsoever we ask of him we obtain, because we keep his commandments" (John 3:22). In these passages he does not fix a value on prayer as a meritorious work, but designs to establish the confidence of those who are conscious of an unfeigned integrity and innocence, such as all believers should possess. For the saying of the blind man who had received his sight is in perfect accordance with divine truth, And God heareth not sinners (John 9:31); provided we take the term sinners in the sense commonly used by Scripture to mean those who, without any desire for righteousness, are sleeping secure in their sins; since no heart will ever rise to genuine prayer that does not at the same time long for holiness. Those supplications in which the saints allude to their purity and integrity correspond to such promises, that they may thus have, in their own experience, a manifestation of that which all the servants of God are made to expect. Thus they almost always use this mode of prayer when before God they compare themselves with their enemies, from whose injustice they long to be delivered by his hand. When making such comparisons, there is no wonder that they bring forward their integrity and simplicity of heart, that thus, by the justice of their cause, the Lord may be the more disposed to give them succor. We rob not the pious breast of

the privilege of enjoying a consciousness of purity before the Lord, and thus feeling assured of the promises with which he comforts and supports his true worshipers, but we would have them to lay aside all thought of their own merits and found their confidence of success in prayer solely on the divine mercy.

11. The fourth rule of prayer is, that notwithstanding of our being thus abased and truly humbled, we should be animated to pray with the sure hope of succeeding. There is, indeed, an appearance of contradiction between the two things, between a sense of the just vengeance of God and firm confidence in his favor, and yet they are perfectly accordant, if it is the mere goodness of God that raises up those who are overwhelmed by their own sins. For, as we have formerly shown (chap. iii. sec. 1, 2) that repentance and faith go hand in hand, being united by an indissoluble tie, the one causing terror, the other joy, so in prayer they must both be present. This concurrence David expresses in a few words: "But as for me, I will come into thy house in the multitude of thy mercy, and in thy fear will I worship toward thy holy temple" (Ps. 5:7). Under the goodness of God he comprehends faith, at the same time not excluding fear; for not only does his majesty compel our reverence, but our own unworthiness also divests us of all pride and confidence, and keeps us in fear. The confidence of which I speak is not one which frees the mind from all anxiety, and soothes it with sweet and perfect rest; such rest is peculiar to those who, while all their affairs are flowing to a wish are annoyed by no care, stung with no regret, agitated by no fear. But the best stimulus which the saints have to prayer is when, in consequence of their own necessities, they feel the greatest disquietude, and are all but driven to despair, until faith seasonably comes to their aid; because in such straits the goodness of God so shines upon them, that while they groan, burdened by the weight of present calamities, and tormented with the fear of greater, they yet trust to this goodness, and in this way both lighten the difficulty of endurance, and take comfort in the hope of final deliverance. It is necessary therefore, that the prayer of the believer should be the result of both feelings, and exhibit the influence of both; namely, that while he groans under present and anxiously dreads new evils, he should, at the same times have recourse to God, not at all doubting that God is ready to stretch out a helping hand to him. For it is not easy to say how much God is irritated by our distrust, when we ask what we expect not of his goodness. Hence, nothing is more accordant to the nature of prayer than to lay it down as a fixed rule, that it is not to come forth at random, but is to follow in the footsteps of faith. To this principle Christ directs all of us in these words, "Therefore, I say unto you, What things soever ye desire, when ye pray, believe that ye receive them, and ye shall have them" (Mark 11:24). The same thing he declares in another passage, "All things, whatsoever ye shall ask in prayer, believing, ye shall receive" (Matth. 21:22). In accordance with this are the words of James, "If any of you lack wisdom, let him ask of God, that giveth to all men liberally, and upbraideth not, and it shall be given him. But let him ask in faith, nothing wavering" (James 1:5). He most aptly expresses the power of faith by opposing it to wavering. No less worthy of notice is his additional statement, that those who approach God with a doubting, hesitating mind, without feeling assured whether they are to be heard or not, gain nothing by their prayers. Such persons he compares to a wave of the sea, driven with the wind and tossed. Hence, in another passage he terms genuine prayer "the prayer of faith" (James 5:15). Again, since God so often declares that he will give to every man according to his faith he intimates that we cannot obtain anything without faith. In short, it is faith which obtains everything that is granted to prayer. This is the meaning of Paul in the well known passage to which dull men give too little heed, "How then shall they call upon him in whom they have not believed? and how shall they believe in him of whom they have not heard?" "So then faith cometh by hearing, and hearing by the word of God" (Rom. 10:14, 17). Gradually deducing the origin of prayer from faith, he distinctly maintains that God cannot be invoked sincerely except by those to whom, by the preaching of the Gospel, his mercy and willingness have been made known, nay, familiarly explained.

12. This necessity our opponents do not at all consider. Therefore, when we say that believers ought to feel firmly assured, they think we are saying the absurdest thing in the world. But if they had any experience in true prayer, they would assuredly understand that God cannot be duly invoked without this firm sense of the Divine benevolence. But as no man can well perceive the power of faith, without at the same time feeling it in his heart, what profit is there in disputing with men of this character, who plainly show that they have never had more than a vain imagination? The value and necessity of that assurance for which we contend is learned chiefly from prayer. Every one who does not see this gives proof of a very stupid conscience. Therefore, leaving those who are thus blinded, let us fix our thoughts on the words of Paul, that God can only be invoked by such as have obtained a knowledge of his mercy from the Gospel, and feel firmly assured that that mercy is ready to be bestowed upon them. What kind of prayer would this be? "O Lord, I am indeed doubtful whether or not thou art inclined to hear me; but being oppressed with anxiety I fly to thee that if I am worthy, thou mayest assist me." None of the saints whose prayers are given in Scripture thus supplicated. Nor are we thus taught by the Holy Spirit, who tells us to "come boldly unto the throne of grace, that we may obtain mercy, and find grace to help in time of need" (Heb. 4:16); and elsewhere teaches us to "have boldness and access with confidence by the faith of Christ" (Eph. 3:12). This confidence of obtaining what we ask, a confidence which the Lord commands, and all the saints teach by their example, we must therefore hold fast with both hands, if we would pray to any advantage. The only prayer acceptable to God is that which springs (if I may so express it) from this presumption of faith, and is founded on the full assurance of hope. He might have been contented to use the simple name of faith, but he adds not only confidence, but liberty or boldness, that by this mark he might distinguish us from unbelievers, who indeed like us pray to God, but pray at random. Hence, the whole Church thus prays "Let thy mercy O Lord, be upon us, according as we hope in thee" (Ps. 33:22). The same condition is set down by the Psalmist in another passage, "When I cry unto thee, then shall mine enemies turn back: this I know, for God is for me" (Ps. 56:9). Again, "In the morning will I direct my prayer unto thee, and will look up" (Ps. 5:3). From these words we gather, that prayers are vainly poured out into the air unless accompanied with faith, in which, as from a watchtower, we may quietly wait for God. With this agrees the order of Paul's exhortation. For before urging believers to pray in the Spirit always, with vigilance and assiduity, he enjoins them to take "the shield of faith," "the helmet of salvation, and the sword of the Spirit, which is the word of God" (Eph. 6:16–18).

Let the reader here call to mind what I formerly observed, that faith by no means fails though accompanied with a recognition of our wretchedness, poverty, and pollution. How much soever believers may feel that they are oppressed by a heavy load of iniquity, and are not only devoid of everything which can procure the favor of God for them, but justly burdened with many sins which make him an object of dread, yet they cease not to present themselves, this feeling not deterring them from appearing in his presence, because there is no other access to him. Genuine prayer is not that by which we arrogantly extol ourselves before God, or set a great value on anything of our own, but that by which, while confessing our guilt, we utter our sorrows before God, just as children familiarly lay their complaints before their parents. Nay, the immense accumulation of our sins should rather spur us on and incite us to prayer. Of this the Psalmist gives us an example, "Heal my soul: for I have sinned against thee" (Ps. 41:4). I confess, indeed, that these stings would prove mortal darts, did not God give succor; but our heavenly Father has, in ineffable kindness, added a remedy, by which, calming all perturbation, soothing our cares, and dispelling our fears he condescendingly allures us to himself; nay, removing all doubts, not to say obstacles, makes the way smooth before us.

13. And first, indeed in enjoining us to pray, he by the very injunction convicts us of impious contumacy if we obey not. He could not give a more precise command than that which

is contained in the psalms: "Call upon me in the day of trouble" (Ps. 50:15). But as there is no office of piety more frequently enjoined by Scripture, there is no occasion for here dwelling longer upon it. "Ask," says our Divine Master, "and it shall be given you; seek, and ye shall find; knock, and it shall be opened unto you" (Matth. 7:7). Here, indeed, a promise is added to the precept, and this is necessary. For though all confess that we must obey the precept, yet the greater part would shun the invitation of God, did he not promise that he would listen and be ready to answer. These two positions being laid down, it is certain that all who cavilingly allege that they are not to come to God directly, are not only rebellious and disobedient but are also convicted of unbelief, inasmuch as they distrust the promises. There is the more occasion to attend to this, because hypocrites, under a pretense of humility and modesty, proudly contemn the precept, as well as deny all credit to the gracious invitation of God; nay, rob him of a principal part of his worship. For when he rejected sacrifices, in which all holiness seemed then to consist, he declared that the chief thing, that which above all others is precious in his sight, is to be invoked in the day of necessity. Therefore, when he demands that which is his own, and urges us to alacrity in obeying, no pretexts for doubt, how specious soever they may be, can excuse us. Hence, all the passages throughout Scripture in which we are commanded to pray, are set up before our eyes as so many banners, to inspire us with confidence. It were presumption to go forward into the presence of God, did he not anticipate us by his invitation. Accordingly, he opens up the way for us by his own voice, "I will say, It is my people: and they shall say, The Lord is my God" (Zech. 13:9). We see how he anticipates his worshipers, and desires them to follow, and therefore we cannot fear that the melody which he himself dictates will prove unpleasing. Especially let us call to mind that noble description of the divine character, by trusting to which we shall easily overcome every obstacle: O thou that hearest prayer, unto thee shall all flesh come" (Ps. 65:2). What can be more lovely or soothing than to see God invested with a title which assures us that nothing is more proper to his nature than to listen

to the prayers of suppliants? Hence the Psalmist infers, that free access is given not to a few individuals, but to all men, since God addresses all in these terms, "Call upon me in the day of trouble: I will deliver thee, and thou shalt glorify me" (Ps. 50:15). David, accordingly, appeals to the promise thus given in order to obtain what he asks: "Thou, O Lord of hosts, God of Israel, hast revealed to thy servant, saying, I will build thee an house: therefore hath thy servant found in his heart to pray this prayer unto thee" (2 Sam. 7:27). Here we infer, that he would have been afraid but for the promise which emboldened him. So in another passage he fortifies himself with the general doctrine, "He will fulfill the desire of them that fear him" (Ps. 145:19). Nay, we may observe in The Psalms how the continuity of prayer is broken, and a transition is made at one time to the power of God, at another to his goodness, at another to the faithfulness of his promises. It might seem that David, by introducing these sentiments, unseasonably mutilates his prayers; but believers well know by experience, that their ardor grows languid unless new fuel be added, and, therefore, that meditation as well on the nature as on the word of God during prayer, is by no means superfluous. Let us not decline to imitate the example of David, and introduce thoughts which may reanimate our languid minds with new vigor.

14. It is strange that these delightful promises affect us coldly, or scarcely at all, so that the generality of men prefer to wander up and down, forsaking the fountain of living waters, and hewing out to themselves broken cisterns, rather than embrace the divine liberality voluntarily offered to them (Jer. 2:13). "The name of the Lord," says Solomon, "is a strong tower; the righteous runneth into it, and is safe" (Pr. 18:10). Joel, after predicting the fearful disaster which was at hand, subjoins the following memorable sentence: "And it shall come to pass, that whosoever shall call on the name of the Lord shall be delivered" (Joel 2:32). This we know properly refers to the course of the Gospel. Scarcely one in a hundred is moved to come into the presence of God, though he himself exclaims by Isaiah, "And it shall come to pass, that before they call, I will answer; and

while they are yet speaking, I will hear" (Is. 65:24). This honor he elsewhere bestows upon the whole Church in general, as belonging to all the members of Christ: "He shall call upon me, and I will answer him: I will be with him in trouble; I will deliver him, and honor him" (Ps. 91:15). My intention, however, as I already observed, is not to enumerate all, but only select some admirable passages as a specimen how kindly God allures us to himself, and how extreme our ingratitude must be when with such powerful motives our sluggishness still retards us. Wherefore, let these words always resound in our ears: "The Lord is nigh unto all them that call upon him, to all that call upon him in truth" (Ps. 145:18). Likewise those passages which we have quoted from Isaiah and Joel, in which God declares that his ear is open to our prayers, and that he is delighted as with a sacrifice of sweet savor when we cast our cares upon him. The special benefit of these promises we receive when we frame our prayer, not timorously or doubtingly, but when trusting to his word whose majesty might otherwise deter us, we are bold to call him Father, he himself deigning to suggest this most delightful name. Fortified by such invitations it remains for us to know that we have therein sufficient materials for prayer, since our prayers depend on no merit of our own, but all their worth and hope of success are founded and depend on the promises of God, so that they need no other support, and require not to look up and down on this hand and on that. It must therefore be fixed in our minds, that though we equal not the lauded sanctity of patriarchs, prophets, and apostles, yet as the command to pray is common to us as well as them, and faith is common, so if we lean on the word of God, we are in respect of this privilege their associates. For God declaring, as has already been seen, that he will listen and be favorable to all, encourages the most wretched to hope that they shall obtain what they ask; and, accordingly, we should attend to the general forms of expression, which, as it is commonly expressed, exclude none from first to last; only let there be sincerity of heart, self-dissatisfaction, humility, and faith, that we may not, by the hypocrisy of a deceitful prayer, profane the name of God. Our most merciful Father will not reject those whom he not only encourages to come, but urges in every possible way. Hence David's method of prayer to which I lately referred: "And now, O Lord God, thou art that God, and thy words be true, and thou hast promised this goodness unto thy servant, that it may continue for ever before thee" (2 Sam. 7:28). So also, in another passage, "Let, I pray thee, thy merciful kindness be for my comfort, according to thy word unto thy servant" (Psalm 119:76). And the whole body of the Israelites, whenever they fortify themselves with the remembrance of the covenant, plainly declare, that since God thus prescribes they are not to pray timorously (Gen. 32:13). In this they imitated the example of the patriarchs, particularly Jacob, who, after confessing that he was unworthy of the many mercies which he had received of the Lord's hand, says, that he is encouraged to make still larger requests, because God had promised that he would grant them. But whatever be the pretexts which unbelievers employ, when they do not flee to God as often as necessity urges, nor seek after him, nor implore his aid, they defraud him of his due honor just as much as if they were fabricating to themselves new gods and idols, since in this way they deny that God is the author of all their blessings.

On the contrary, nothing more effectually frees pious minds from every doubt, than to be armed with the thought that no obstacle should impede them while they are obeying the command of God, who declares that nothing is more grateful to him than obedience. Hence, again, what I have previously said becomes still more clear, namely, that a bold spirit in prayer well accords with fear, reverence, and anxiety, and that there is no inconsistency when God raises up those who had fallen prostrate. In this way forms of expression apparently inconsistent admirably harmonize. Jeremiah and David speak of humbly laying their supplications before God (Jer. 42:9; Dan. 9:18). In another passage Jeremiah says "Let, we beseech thee, our supplication be accepted before thee, and pray for us unto the Lord thy God, even for all this remnant" (Jer. 42:2). On the other hand, believers are often said to *lift up prayer*. Thus Hezekiah speaks, when asking the prophet to undertake the office of interceding (2 Kings

19:4). And David says, "Let my prayer be set forth before thee as incense; and the lifting up of my hands as the evening sacrifice" (Ps. 141:2). The explanation is, that though believers, persuaded of the paternal love of God, cheerfully rely on his faithfulness, and have no hesitation in imploring the aid which he voluntarily offers, they are not elated with supine or presumptuous security; but climbing up by the ladder of the promises, still remain humble and abased suppliants.

15. Here, by way of objection, several questions are raised. Scripture relates that God sometimes complied with certain prayers which had been dictated by minds not duly calmed or regulated. It is true, that the cause for which Jotham imprecated on the inhabitants of Shechem the disaster which afterwards befell them was well founded; but still he was inflamed with anger and revenge (Judges 9:20); and hence God, by complying with the execration, seems to approve of passionate impulses. Similar fervor also seized Samson, when he prayed, "Strengthen me, I pray thee, only this once, O God, that I may be at once avenged of the Philistines for my two eyes" (Judges 16:28). For although there was some mixture of good zeal, yet his ruling feeling was a fervid, and therefore vicious longing for vengeance. God assents, and hence apparently it might be inferred that prayers are effectual, though not framed in conformity to the rule of the word.

But I answer, *first*, that a perpetual law is not abrogated by singular examples; and, *secondly*, that special suggestions have sometimes been made to a few individuals, whose case thus becomes different from that of the generality of men. For we should attend to the answer which our Savior gave to his disciples when they inconsiderately wished to imitate the example of Elias, "Ye know not what manner of spirit ye are of" (Luke 9:55). We must, however, go farther and say, that the wishes to which God assents are not always pleasing to him; but he assents, because it is necessary, by way of example, to give clear evidence of the doctrine of Scripture, viz., that he assists the miserable, and hears the groans of those who unjustly afflicted implore his aid: and, accordingly, he executes his judgments when

the complaints of the needy, though in themselves unworthy of attention, ascend to him. For how often, in inflicting punishment on the ungodly for cruelty, rapine, violence, lust, and other crimes, in curbing audacity and fury, and also in overthrowing tyrannical power, has he declared that he gives assistance to those who are unworthily oppressed though they by addressing an unknown deity only beat the air? There is one psalm which clearly teaches that prayers are not without effect, though they do not penetrate to heaven by faith (Ps. 107:6, 13, 19). For it enumerates the prayers which, by natural instinct, necessity extorts from unbelievers not less than from believers, and to which it shows by the event, that God is, notwithstanding, propitious. Is it to testify by such readiness to hear that their prayers are agreeable to him? Nay; it is, first, to magnify or display his mercy by the circumstance, that even the wishes of unbelievers are not denied; and, secondly, to stimulate his true worshipers to more urgent prayer, when they see that sometimes even the wailings of the ungodly are not without avail. This, however, is no reason why believers should deviate from the law divinely imposed upon them, or envy unbelievers, as if they gained much in obtaining what they wished. We have observed (chap. iii. sec. 25), that in this way God yielded to the feigned repentance of Ahab, that he might show how ready he is to listen to his elect when, with true contrition, they seek his favor. Accordingly, he upbraids the Jews, that shortly after experiencing his readiness to listen to their prayers, they returned to their own perverse inclinations. It is also plain from the Book of Judges that, whenever they wept, though their tears were deceitful, they were delivered from the hands of their enemies. Therefore, as God sends his sun indiscriminately on the evil and on the good, so he despises not the tears of those who have a good cause, and whose sorrows are deserving of relief. Meanwhile, though he hears them, it has no more to do with salvation than the supply of food which he gives to other despisers of his goodness.

There seems to be a more difficult question concerning Abraham and Samuel, the one of whom, without any instruction from the word of God, prayed in behalf of the people of Sodom, and the other, contrary to an express prohibition, prayed in behalf of Saul (Gen. 18:23; 1 Sam. 15:11). Similar is the case of Jeremiah, who prayed that the city might not be destroyed (Jer. 32:16ff). It is true their prayers were refused, but it seems harsh to affirm that they prayed without faith. Modest readers will, I hope, be satisfied with this solution, viz., that leaning to the general principle on which God enjoins us to be merciful even to the unworthy, they were not altogether devoid of faith, though in this particular instance their wish was disappointed. Augustine shrewdly remarks, "How do the saints pray in faith when they ask from God contrary to what he has decreed? Namely, because they pray according to his will, not his hidden and immutable will, but that which he suggests to them, that he may hear them in another manner; as he wisely distinguishes" (August. *de Civit. Dei*, Lib. xxii. c. 2). This is truly said: for, in his incomprehensible counsel, he so regulates events, that the prayers of the saints, though involving a mixture of faith and error, are not in vain. And yet this no more sanctions imitation than it excuses the saints themselves, who I deny not exceeded due bounds. Wherefore, whenever no certain promise exists, our request to God must have a condition annexed to it. Here we may refer to the prayer of David, "Awake for me to the judgment that thou hast commanded" (Ps. 7:6); for he reminds us that he had received special instruction to pray for a temporal blessing.

16. It is also of importance to observe, that the four laws of prayer of which I have treated are not so rigorously enforced, as that God rejects the prayers in which he does not find perfect faith or repentance, accompanied with fervent zeal and wishes duly framed. We have said (sec. 4), that though prayer is the familiar intercourse of believers with God, yet reverence and modesty must be observed: we must not give loose reins to our wishes, nor long for anything farther than God permits; and, moreover, lest the majesty of God should be despised, our minds must be elevated to pure and chaste veneration. This no man ever performed with due perfection. For, not to speak of the generality of men, how often do David's complaints savor of intemperance?

Not that he actually means to expostulate with God, or murmur at his judgments, but failing, through infirmity, he finds no better solace than to pour his griefs into the bosom of his heavenly Father. Nay, even our stammering is tolerated by God, and pardon is granted to our ignorance as often as anything rashly escapes us: indeed, without this indulgence, we should have no freedom to pray. But although it was David's intention to submit himself entirely to the will of God, and he prayed with no less patience than fervor, yet irregular emotions appear, nay, sometimes burst forth, – emotions not a little at variance with the first law which we laid down. In particular, we may see in a clause of the thirty-ninth Psalm, how this saint was carried away by the vehemence of his grief, and unable to keep within bounds. "O spare me, that I may recover strength, before I go hence, and be no more" (Ps. 39:13). You would call this the language of a desperate man, who had no other desire than that God should withdraw and leave him to relish in his distresses. Not that his devout mind rushes into such intemperance, or that, as the reprobate are wont, he wishes to have done with God; he only complains that the divine anger is more than he can bear. During those trials, wishes often escape which are not in accordance with the rule of the word, and in which the saints do not duly consider what is lawful and expedient. Prayers contaminated by such faults, indeed, deserve to be rejected; yet provided the saints lament, administer self-correction and return to themselves, God pardons.

Similar faults are committed in regard to the second law (as to which, see sec. 6), for the saints have often to struggle with their own coldness, their want and misery not urging them sufficiently to serious prayer. It often happens, also, that their minds wander, and are almost lost; hence in this matter also there is need of pardon, lest their prayers, from being languid or mutilated, or interrupted and wandering, should meet with a refusal. One of the natural feelings which God has imprinted on our mind is, that prayer is not genuine unless the thoughts are turned upward. Hence the ceremony of raising the hands, to which we have adverted, a ceremony known to all ages and nations, and still in common use. But who, in lifting up his hands, is not conscious of sluggishness, the heart cleaving to the earth? In regard to the petition for remission of sins (sec. 8), though no believer omits it, yet all who are truly exercised in prayer feel that they bring scarcely a tenth of the sacrifice of which David speaks, "The sacrifices of God are a broken spirit: a broken and a contrite heart, O God, thou wilt not despise" (Ps. 51:17). Thus a twofold pardon is always to be asked; first, because they are conscious of many faults the sense of which, however, does not touch them so as to make them feel dissatisfied with themselves as they ought; and, secondly, in so far as they have been enabled to profit in repentance and the fear of God, they are humbled with just sorrow for their offenses, and pray for the remission of punishment by the judge. The thing which most of all vitiates prayer, did not God indulgently interpose, is weakness or imperfection of faith; but it is not wonderful that this defect is pardoned by God, who often exercises his people with severe trials, as if he actually wished to extinguish their faith. The hardest of such trials is when believers are forced to exclaim, "O Lord God of hosts, how long wilt thou be angry against the prayer of thy people?" (Ps. 80:4), as if their very prayers offended him. In like manner, when Jeremiah says "Also when I cry and shout, he shutteth out my prayers (Lam. 3:8), there cannot be a doubt that he was in the greatest perturbation. Innumerable examples of the same kind occur in the Scriptures, from which it is manifest that the faith of the saints was often mingled with doubts and fears, so that while believing and hoping, they, however, betrayed some degree of unbelief. But because they do not come so far as were to be wished, that is only an additional reason for their exerting themselves to correct their faults, that they may daily approach nearer to the perfect law of prayer, and at the same time feel into what an abyss of evils those are plunged, who, in the very cures they use, bring new diseases upon themselves: since there is no prayer which God would not deservedly disdain, did he not overlook the blemishes with which all of them are polluted. I do not mention these things that believers may securely pardon themselves in any faults which they commit,

but that they may call themselves to strict account, and thereby endeavor to surmount these obstacles; and though Satan endeavors to block up all the paths in order to prevent them from praying, they may, nevertheless, break through, being firmly persuaded that though not disencumbered of all hindrances, their attempts are pleasing to God, and their wishes are approved, provided they hasten on and keep their aim, though without immediately reaching it.

17. But since no man is worthy to come forward in his own name, and appear in the presence of God, our heavenly Father, to relieve us at once from fear and shame, with which all must feel oppressed, has given us his Son, Jesus Christ our Lord, to be our Advocate and Mediator, that under his guidance we may approach securely, confiding that with him for our Intercessor nothing which we ask in his name will be denied to us, as there is nothing which the Father can deny to him (1 Tim. 2:5; 1 John 2:1; see sec. 36, 37). To this it is necessary to refer all that we have previously taught concerning faith; because, as the promise gives us Christ as our Mediator, so, unless our hope of obtaining what we ask is founded on him, it deprives us of the privilege of prayer. For it is impossible to think of the dread majesty of God without being filled with alarm; and hence the sense of our own unworthiness must keep us far away, until Christ interpose, and convert a throne of dreadful glory into a throne of grace, as the Apostle teaches that thus we can "come boldly unto the throne of grace, that we may obtain mercy, and find grace to help in time of need" (Heb. 4:16). And as a rule has been laid down as to prayer, as a promise has been given that those who pray will be heard, so we are specially enjoined to pray in the name of Christ, the promise being that we shall obtain what we ask in his name. "Whatsoever ye shall ask in my name," says our Savior, "that will I do; that the Father may be glorified in the Son;" "Hitherto ye have asked nothing in my name; ask, and ye shall receive, that your joy may be full" (John 14:13; 16:24). Hence it is incontrovertibly clear that those who pray to God in any other name than that of Christ contumaciously falsify his orders, and regard

his will as nothing, while they have no promise that they shall obtain. For, as Paul says "All the promises of God in him are yea, and in him amen" (2 Cor. 1:20), that is, are confirmed and fulfilled in him.

18. And we must carefully attend to the circumstance of time. Christ enjoins his disciples to have recourse to his intercession after he shall have ascended to heaven: "At that day ye shall ask in my name" (John 16:26). It is certain, indeed, that from the very first all who ever prayed were heard only for the sake of the Mediator. For this reason God had commanded in the Law, that the priest alone should enter the sanctuary, bearing the names of the twelve tribes of Israel on his shoulders, and as many precious stones on his breast, while the people were to stand at a distance in the outer court, and thereafter unite their prayers with the priest. Nay, the sacrifice had even the effect of ratifying and confirming their prayers. That shadowy ceremony of the Law therefore taught, first, that we are all excluded from the face of God, and, therefore, that there is need of a Mediator to appear in our name, and carry us on his shoulders and keep us bound upon his breast, that we may be heard in his person; And secondly, that our prayers, which, as has been said, would otherwise never be free from impurity, are cleansed by the sprinkling of his blood. And we see that the saints, when they desired to obtain anything, founded their hopes on sacrifices, because they knew that by sacrifice all prayers were ratified: "Remember all thy offerings," says David, "and accept thy burnt sacrifice" (Ps. 20:3). Hence we infer, that in receiving the prayers of his people, God was from the very first appeased by the intercession of Christ. Why then does Christ speak of a new period ("at that day") when the disciples were to begin to pray in his name, unless it be that this grace, being now more brightly displayed, ought also to be in higher estimation with us? In this sense he had said a little before, "Hitherto ye have asked nothing in my name; ask." Not that they were altogether ignorant of the office of Mediator (all the Jews were instructed in these first rudiments), but they did not clearly understand that Christ by his ascent to heaven would be more the advo-

cate of the Church than before. Therefore, to solace their grief for his absence by some more than ordinary result, he asserts his office of advocate, and says, that hitherto they had been without the special benefit which it would be their privilege to enjoy, when aided by his intercession they should invoke God with greater freedom. In this sense the Apostle says that we have "boldness to enter into the holiest by the blood of Jesus, by a new and living way, which he hath consecrated for us" (Heb. 10:19, 20). Therefore, the more inexcusable we are, if we do not with both hands (as it is said) embrace the inestimable gift which is properly destined for us.

19. Moreover since he himself is the only way and the only access by which we can draw near to God, those who deviate from this way, and decline this access, have no other remaining; his throne presents nothing but wrath, judgment, and terror. In short, as the Father has consecrated him our guide and head, those who abandon or turn aside from him in any way endeavor, as much as in them lies, to sully and efface the stamp which God has impressed. Christ, therefore, is the only Mediator by whose intercession the Father is rendered propitious and exorable (1 Tim. 2:5). For though the saints are still permitted to use intercessions, by which they mutually beseech God in behalf of each other's salvation, and of which the Apostle makes mention (Eph. 6:18, 19; 1 Tim. 2:1); yet these depend on that one intercession, so far are they from derogating from it. For as the intercessions which, as members of one body we offer up for each other, spring from the feeling of love, so they have reference to this one head. Being thus also made in the name of Christ, what more do they than declare that no man can derive the least benefit from any prayers without the intercession of Christ? As there is nothing in the intercession of Christ to prevent the different members of the Church from offering up prayers for each other, so let it be held as a fixed principle, that all the intercessions thus used in the Church must have reference to that one intercession. Nay, we must be specially careful to show our gratitude on this very account, that God pardoning our unworthiness, not only allows each individual to pray

for himself, but allows all to intercede mutually for each other. God having given a place in his Church to intercessors who would deserve to be rejected when praying privately on their own account, how presumptuous were it to abuse this kindness by employing it to obscure the honor of Christ?

20. Moreover, the Sophists are guilty of the merest trifling when they allege that Christ is the Mediator of *redemption*, but that believers are mediators of *intercession*; as if Christ had only performed a temporary mediation, and left an eternal and imperishable mediation to his servants. Such, forsooth, is the treatment which he receives from those who pretend only to take from him a minute portion of honor. Very different is the language of Scripture, with whose simplicity every pious man will be satisfied, without paying any regard to those importers. For when John says, "If any man sin, we have an advocate with the Father, Jesus Christ the righteous" (1 John 2:1), does he mean merely that we once had an advocate; does he not rather ascribe to him a perpetual intercession? What does Paul mean when he declares that he "is even at the right hand of God, who also maketh intercession for us"? (Rom. 8:32). But when in another passage he declares that he is the only Mediator between God and man (1 Tim. 2:5), is he not referring to the supplications which he had mentioned a little before? Having previously said that prayers were to be offered up for all men, he immediately adds, in confirmation of that statement, that there is one God, and one Mediator between God and man. Nor does Augustine give a different interpretation when he says, "Christian men mutually recommend each other in their prayers. But he for whom none intercedes, while he himself intercedes for all, is the only true Mediator. Though the Apostle Paul was under the head a principal member, yet because he was a member of the body of Christ, and knew that the most true and High Priest of the Church had entered not by figure into the inner veil to the holy of holies, but by firm and express truth into the inner sanctuary of heaven to holiness, holiness not imaginary, but eternal (Heb 9:11, 24), he also commends himself to the prayers of the faithful (Rom. 15:30; Eph. 6:19; Col. 4:3). He does not make himself a mediator between God and the people, but asks that all the members of the body of Christ should pray mutually for each other, since the members are mutually sympathetic: if one member suffers, the others suffer with it (1 Cor. 12:26). And thus the mutual prayers of all the members still laboring on the earth ascend to the Head, who has gone before into heaven, and in whom there is propitiation for our sins. For if Paul were a mediator, so would also the other apostles, and thus there would be many mediators, and Paul's statement could not stand, 'There is one God, and one Mediator between God and men, the man Christ Jesus' (1 Tim. 2:5) in whom we also are one (Rom. 12:5) if we keep the unity of the faith in the bond of peace (Eph. 4:3)," (August. *Contra Parmenian*, Lib. ii. cap. 8). Likewise in another passage Augustine says, "If thou requirest a priest, he is above the heavens, where he intercedes for those who on earth died for thee" (August. in Ps. 94). We imagine not that he throws himself before his Father's knees, and suppliantly intercedes for us; but we understand with the Apostle, that he appears in the presence of God, and that the power of his death has the effect of a perpetual intercession for us; that having entered into the upper sanctuary, he alone continues to the end of the world to present the prayers of his people, who are standing far off in the outer court.

21. In regard to the saints who having died in the body live in Christ, if we attribute prayer to them, let us not imagine that they have any other way of supplicating God than through Christ who alone is the way, or that their prayers are accepted by God in any other name. Wherefore, since the Scripture calls us away from all others to Christ alone, since our heavenly Father is pleased to gather together all things in him, it were the extreme of stupidity, not to say madness, to attempt to obtain access by means of others, so as to be drawn away from him without whom access cannot be obtained. But who can deny that this was the practice for several ages, and is still the practice, wherever Popery prevails? To procure the favor of God, human merits are ever and anon obtruded, and very frequently while Christ is passed by, God

is supplicated in their name. I ask if this is not to transfer to them that office of sole intercession which we have above claimed for Christ? Then what angel or devil ever announced one syllable to any human being concerning that fancied intercession of theirs? There is not a word on the subject in Scripture. What ground then was there for the fiction? Certainly, while the human mind thus seeks help for itself in which it is not sanctioned by the word of God, it plainly manifests its distrust (see s. 27). But if we appeal to the consciences of all who take pleasure in the intercession of saints, we shall find that their only reason for it is, that they are filled with anxiety, as if they supposed that Christ were insufficient or too rigorous. By this anxiety they dishonor Christ, and rob him of his title of sole Mediator, a title which being given him by the Father as his special privilege, ought not to be transferred to any other. By so doing they obscure the glory of his nativity and make void his cross; in short, divest and defraud of due praise everything which he did or suffered, since all which he did and suffered goes to show that he is and ought to be deemed sole Mediator. At the same time, they reject the kindness of God in manifesting himself to them as a Father, for he is not their Father if they do not recognize Christ as their brother. This they plainly refuse to do if they think not that he feels for them a brother's affection; affection than which none can be more gentle or tender. Wherefore Scripture offers him alone, sends us to him, and establishes us in him. "He," says Ambrose, "is our mouth by which we speak to the Father; our eye by which we see the Father; our right hand by which we offer ourselves to the Father. Save by his intercession neither we nor any saints have any intercourse with God" (Ambros. *Lib. de Isaac et Anima*). If they object that the public prayers which are offered up in churches conclude with the words, *through Jesus Christ our Lord*, it is a frivolous evasion; because no less insult is offered to the intercession of Christ by confounding it with the prayers and merits of the dead, than by omitting it altogether, and making mention only of the dead. Then, in all their litanies, hymns, and proses where every kind of honor is paid to dead saints, there is no mention of Christ.

22. But here stupidity has proceeded to such a length as to give a manifestation of the genius of superstition, which, when once it has shaken off the rein, is wont to wanton without limit. After men began to look to the intercession of saints, a peculiar administration was gradually assigned to each, so that, according to diversity of business, now one, now another, intercessor was invoked. Then individuals adopted particular saints, and put their faith in them, just as if they had been tutelar deities. And thus not only were gods set up according to the number of the cities (the charge which the prophet brought against Israel of old, Jer. 2:28; 11:13), but according to the number of individuals. But while the saints in all their desires refer to the will of God alone, look to it, and acquiesce in it, yet to assign to them any other prayer than that of longing for the arrival of the kingdom of God, is to think of them stupidly, carnally, and even insultingly. Nothing can be farther from such a view than to imagine that each, under the influence of private feeling, is disposed to be most favorable to his own worshipers. At length vast numbers have fallen into the horrid blasphemy of invoking them not merely as helping but presiding over their salvation. See the depth to which miserable men fall when they forsake their proper station, that is, the word of God. I say nothing of the more monstrous specimens of impiety in which, though detestable to God, angels, and men, they themselves feel no pain or shame. Prostrated at a statue or picture of Barbara or Catherine, and the like, they mutter a *Pater Noster;* and so far are their pastors from curing or curbing this frantic course, that, allured by the scent of gain, they approve and applaud it. But while seeking to relieve themselves of the odium of this vile and criminal procedure, with what pretext can they defend the practice of calling upon Eloy (Eligius) or Medard to look upon their servants, and send them help from heaven, or the Holy Virgin to order her Son to do what they ask? The Council of Carthage forbade direct prayer to be made at the altar to saints. It is probable that these holy men, unable entirely to suppress the force of depraved custom, had recourse to this check, that public prayers might not be vitiated with such forms of expression as *Sancte Petre, ora pro*

nobis – St Peter, pray for us. But how much farther has this devilish extravagance proceeded when men hesitate not to transfer to the dead the peculiar attributes of Christ and God?

23. In endeavoring to prove that such intercession derives some support from Scripture they labor in vain. We frequently read (they say) of the prayers of angels, and not only so, but the prayers of believers are said to be carried into the presence of God by their hands. But if they would compare saints who have departed this life with angels, it will be necessary to prove that saints are ministering spirits, to whom has been delegated the office of superintending our salvation, to whom has been assigned the province of guiding us in all our ways, of encompassing, admonishing, and comforting us, of keeping watch over us. All these are assigned to angels, but none of them to saints. How preposterously they confound departed saints with angels is sufficiently apparent from the many different offices by which Scripture distinguishes the one from the other. No one unless admitted will presume to perform the office of pleader before an earthly judge; whence then have worms such license as to obtrude themselves on God as intercessors, while no such office has been assigned them? God has been pleased to give angels the charge of our safety. Hence they attend our sacred meetings, and the Church is to them a theater in which they behold the manifold wisdom of God (Eph. 3:10). Those who transfer to others this office which is peculiar to them, certainly pervert and confound the order which has been established by God and ought to be inviolable. With similar dexterity they proceed to quote other passages. God said to Jeremiah, "Though Moses and Samuel stood before me, yet my mind could not be toward this people" (Jer. 15:1). How (they ask) could he have spoken thus of the dead but because he knew that they interceded for the living? My inference, on the contrary, is this: since it thus appears that neither Moses nor Samuel interceded for the people of Israel, there was then no intercession for the dead. For who of the saints can be supposed to labor for the salvation of the peoples while Moses who, when in life, far surpassed all others in this matter, does

nothing? Therefore, if they persist in the paltry quibble, that the dead intercede for the living, because the Lord said, *"If they stood before me,"* (*intercesserint*), I will argue far more speciously in this way: Moses, of whom it is said, *"if he interceded,"* did not intercede for the people in their extreme necessity: it is probable, therefore, that no other saint intercedes, all being far behind Moses in humanity, goodness, and paternal solicitude. Thus all they gain by their caviling is to be wounded by the very arms with which they deem themselves admirably protected. But it is very ridiculous to wrest this simple sentence in this manner; for the Lord only declares that he would not spare the iniquities of the people, though some Moses or Samuel, to whose prayers he had shown himself so indulgent, should intercede for them. This meaning is most clearly elicited from a similar passage in Ezekiel: "Though these three men, Noah, Daniel, and Job, were in it, they should deliver but their own souls by their righteousness, saith the Lord God" (Ezek. 14:14). Here there can be no doubt that we are to understand the words as if it had been said, If two of the persons named were again to come alive; for the third was still living, namely, Daniel, who it is well known had then in the bloom of youth given an incomparable display of piety. Let us therefore leave out those whom Scripture declares to have completed their course. Accordingly, when Paul speaks of David, he says not that by his prayers he assisted posterity, but only that he "served his own generation" (Acts 13:36).

24. They again object, Are those, then, to be deprived of every pious wish, who, during the whole course of their lives, breathed nothing but piety and mercy? I have no wish curiously to pry into what they do or meditate; but the probability is, that instead of being subject to the impulse of various and particular desires, they, with one fixed and immoveable will, long for the kingdom of God, which consists not less in the destruction of the ungodly than in the salvation of believers. If this be so, there cannot be a doubt that their charity is confined to the communion of Christ's body, and extends no farther than is compatible with the nature of that communion. But though I grant that in

this way they pray for us, they do not, however, lose their quiescence so as to be distracted with earthly cares: far less are they, therefore, to be invoked by us. Nor does it follow that such invocation is to be used because, while men are alive upon the earth, they can mutually commend themselves to each other's prayers. It serves to keep alive a feeling of charity when they, as it were, share each other's wants, and bear each other's burdens. This they do by the command of the Lord, and not without a promise, the two things of primary importance in prayer. But all such reasons are inapplicable to the dead, with whom the Lord, in withdrawing them from our society, has left us no means of intercourse (Eccles. 9:5, 6), and to whom, so far as we can conjecture, he has left no means of intercourse with us. But if any one allege that they certainly must retain the same charity for us, as they are united with us in one faith, who has revealed to us that they have ears capable of listening to the sounds of our voice, or eyes clear enough to discern our necessities? Our opponents, indeed, talk in the shade of their schools of some kind of light which beams upon departed saints from the divine countenance, and in which, as in a mirror, they, from their lofty abode, behold the affairs of men; but to affirm this with the confidence which these men presume to use, is just to desire, by means of the extravagant dreams of our own brain, and without any authority, to pry and penetrate into the hidden judgments of God, and trample upon Scripture, which so often declares that the wisdom of our flesh is at enmity with the wisdom of God, utterly condemns the vanity of our mind, and humbling our reason, bids us look only to the will of God.

25. The other passages of Scripture which they employ to defend their error are miserably wrested. Jacob (they say) asks for the sons of Joseph, "Let my name be named on them, and the name of my fathers, Abraham and Isaac" (Gen. 48:16). First, let us see what the nature of this invocation was among the Israelites. They do not implore their fathers to bring succor to them, but they beseech God to remember his servants, Abraham, Isaac, and Jacob. Their example, therefore, gives no countenance to

those who use addresses to the saints themselves. But such being the dullness of these blocks, that they comprehend not what it is to invoke the name of Jacob, nor why it is to be invoked, it is not strange that they blunder thus childishly as to the mode of doing it. The expression repeatedly occurs in Scripture. Isaiah speaks of women being called by the name of men, when they have them for husbands and live under their protection (Isa. 4:1). The calling of the name of Abraham over the Israelites consists in referring the origin of their race to him, and holding him in distinguished remembrance as their author and parent. Jacob does not do so from any anxiety to extend the celebrity of his name, but because he knows that all the happiness of his posterity consisted in the inheritance of the covenant which God had made with them. Seeing that this would give them the sum of all blessings, he prays that they may be regarded as of his race, this being nothing else than to transmit the succession of the covenant to them. They again, when they make mention of this subject in their prayers, do not betake themselves to the intercession of the dead, but call to remembrance that covenant in which their most merciful Father undertakes to be kind and propitious to them for the sake of Abraham, Isaac, and Jacob. How little, in other respects, the saints trusted to the merits of their fathers, the public voice of the Church declares in the prophets "Doubtless thou art our Father, though Abraham be ignorant of us, and Israel acknowledge us not; thou, O Lord, art our Father, our Redeemer" (Isa. 63:16). And while the Church thus speaks, she at the same time adds, "Return for thy servants' sake," not thinking of anything like intercession, but adverting only to the benefit of the covenant. Now, indeed, when we have the Lord Jesus, in whose hand the eternal covenant of mercy was not only made but confirmed, what better name can we bear before us in our prayers? And since those good Doctors would make out by these words that the Patriarchs are intercessors, I should like them to tell me why, in so great a multitude, no place whatever is given to Abraham, the father of the Church? We know well from what a crew they select their intercessors. Let them then tell me what consistency there is in neglecting and rejecting

Abraham, whom God preferred to all others, and raised to the highest degree of honor. The only reason is, that as it was plain there was no such practice in the ancient Church, they thought proper to conceal the novelty of the practice by saying nothing of the Patriarchs: as if by a mere diversity of names they could excuse a practice at once novel and impure. They sometimes, also, object that God is entreated to have mercy on his people "for David's sake" (Ps. 132:10; see Calv. *Com.*). This is so far from supporting their error, that it is the strongest refutation of it. We must consider the character which David bore. He is set apart from the whole body of the faithful to establish the covenant which God made in his hand. Thus regard is had to the covenant rather than to the individual. Under him as a type the sole intercession of Christ is asserted. But what was peculiar to David as a type of Christ is certainly inapplicable to others.

26. But some seem to be moved by the fact, that the prayers of saints are often said to have been heard. Why? Because they prayed. "They cried unto thee" (says the Psalmist), "and were delivered: they trusted in thee, and were not confounded" (Ps. 22:5). Let us also pray after their example, that like them we too may be heard. Those men, on the contrary, absurdly argue that none will be heard but those who have been heard already. How much better does James argue, "Elias was a man subject to like passions as we are, and he prayed earnestly that it might not rain: and it rained not on the earth by the space of three years and six months. And he prayed again and the heaven gave rain, and the earth brought forth her fruit" (James 5:17, 18). What? Does he infer that Elias possessed some peculiar privilege, and that we must have recourse to him for the use of it? By no means. He shows the perpetual efficacy of a pure and pious prayer, that we may be induced in like manner to pray. For the kindness and readiness of God to hear others is malignantly interpreted, if their example does not inspire us with stronger confidence in his promise, since his declaration is not that he will incline his ear to one or two, or a few individuals, but to all who call upon his name. In this ignorance they are the less excusable, because they seem as it

were avowedly to contemn the many admonitions of Scripture. David was repeatedly delivered by the power of God. Was this to give that power to him that we might be delivered on his application? Very different is his affirmation: "The righteous shall compass me about; for thou shalt deal bountifully with me" (Ps. 142:7). Again, "The righteous also shall see, and fear, and shall laugh at him" (Ps. 52:6). "This poor man cried, and the Lord heard him, and saved him out of all his troubles" (Ps. 34:6). In The Psalms are many similar prayers, in which David calls upon God to give him what he asks, for this reason, viz., that the righteous may not be put to shame, but by his example encouraged to hope. Here let one passage suffice, "For this shall every one that is godly pray unto thee in a time when thou mayest be found" (Ps. 32:6, Calv. *Com.*). This passage I have quoted the more readily, because those ravers who employ their hireling tongues in defense of the Papacy, are not ashamed to adduce it in proof of the intercession of the dead. As if David intended anything more than to show the benefit which he shall obtain from the divine clemency and condescension when he shall have been heard. In general, we must hold that the experience of the grace of God, as well towards ourselves as towards others, tends in no slight degree to confirm our faith in his promises. I do not quote the many passages in which David sets forth the loving-kindness of God to him as a ground of confidence, as they will readily occur to every reader of The Psalms. Jacob had previously taught the same thing by his own example, "I am not worthy of the least of all thy mercies, and of all the truth which thou hast showed unto thy servant: for with my staff I passed over this Jordan; and now I am become two bands" (Gen. 32:10). He indeed alleges the promise, but not the promise only; for he at the same time adds the effect, to animate him with greater confidence in the future kindness of God. God is not like men who grow weary of their liberality, or whose means of exercising it become exhausted; but he is to be estimated by his own nature, as David properly does when he says, "Thou hast redeemed me, O Lord God of truth" (Ps. 31:5). After ascribing the praise of his salvation to God, he adds that he is true: for were he not ever like himself, his past favor would not be an infallible ground for confidence and prayer. But when we know that as often as he assists us, he gives us a specimen and proof of his goodness and faithfulness, there is no reason to fear that our hope will be ashamed or frustrated.

27. On the whole, since Scripture places the principal part of worship in the invocation of God (this being the office of piety which he requires of us in preference to all sacrifices), it is manifest sacrilege to offer prayer to others. Hence it is said in the psalm: "If we have forgotten the name of our God, or stretched out our hands to a strange god, shall not God search this out?" (Ps. 44:20, 21). Again, since it is only in faith that God desires to be invoked, and he distinctly enjoins us to frame our prayers according to the rule of his word: in fine, since faith is founded on the word, and is the parent of right prayer, the moment we decline from the word, our prayers are impure. But we have already shown, that if we consult the whole volume of Scripture, we shall find that God claims this honor to himself alone. In regard to the office of intercession, we have also seen that it is peculiar to Christ, and that no prayer is agreeable to God which he as Mediator does not sanctify. And though believers mutually offer up prayers to God in behalf of their brethren, we have shown that this derogates in no respect from the sole intercession of Christ, because all trust to that intercession in commending themselves as well as others to God. Moreover, we have shown that this is ignorantly transferred to the dead, of whom we nowhere read that they were commanded to pray for us. The Scripture often exhorts us to offer up mutual prayers; but says not one syllable concerning the dead; nay, James tacitly excludes the dead when he combines the two things, to "confess our sins one to another, and to pray one for another" (James 5:16). Hence it is sufficient to condemn this error, that the beginning of right prayer springs from faith, and that faith comes by the hearing of the word of God, in which there is no mention of fictitious intercession, superstition having rashly adopted intercessors who have not been divinely appointed. While the Scripture abounds in various forms of prayer, we find no

example of this intercession, without which Papists think there is no prayer. Moreover, it is evident that this superstition is the result of distrust, because they are either not contented with Christ as an intercessor, or have altogether robbed him of this honor. This last is easily proved by their effrontery in maintaining, as the strongest of all their arguments for the intercession of the saints, that we are unworthy of familiar access to God. This, indeed, we acknowledge to be most true, but we thence infer that they leave nothing to Christ, because they consider his intercession as nothing, unless it is supplemented by that of George and Hypolyte, and similar phantoms.

28. But though prayer is properly confined to vows and supplications, yet so strong is the affinity between petition and thanksgiving, that both may be conveniently comprehended under one name. For the forms which Paul enumerates (1 Tim. 2:1) fall under the first member of this division. By prayer and supplication we pour out our desires before God, asking as well those things which tend to promote his glory and display his name, as the benefits which contribute to our advantage. By thanksgiving we duly celebrate his kindnesses toward us, ascribing to his liberality every blessing which enters into our lot. David accordingly includes both in one sentence, "Call upon me in the day of trouble: I will deliver thee, and thou shalt glorify me" (Ps. 50:15). Scripture, not without reason, commands us to use both continually. We have already described the greatness of our want, while experience itself proclaims the straits which press us on every side to be so numerous and so great, that all have sufficient ground to send forth sighs and groans to God without intermission, and suppliantly implore him. For even should they be exempt from adversity, still the holiest ought to be stimulated first by their sins, and, secondly, by the innumerable assaults of temptation, to long for a remedy. The sacrifice of praise and thanksgiving can never be interrupted without guilt, since God never ceases to load us with favor upon favor, so as to force us to gratitude, however slow and sluggish we may be. In short, so great and widely diffused are the riches of his liberality

towards us, so marvelous and wondrous the miracles which we behold on every side, that we never can want a subject and materials for praise and thanksgiving.

To make this somewhat clearer: since all our hopes and resources are placed in God (this has already been fully proved), so that neither our persons nor our interests can prosper without his blessing, we must constantly submit ourselves and our all to him. Then whatever we deliberate, speak, or do, should be deliberated, spoken, and done under his hand and will; in fine, under the hope of his assistance. God has pronounced a curse upon all who, confiding in themselves or others, form plans and resolutions, who, without regarding his will, or invoking his aid, either plan or attempt to execute (James 4:14; Isaiah 30:1; 31:1). And since, as has already been observed, he receives the honor which is due when he is acknowledged to be the author of all good, it follows that, in deriving all good from his hand, we ought continually to express our thankfulness, and that we have no right to use the benefits which proceed from his liberality, if we do not assiduously proclaim his praise, and give him thanks, these being the ends for which they are given. When Paul declares that every creature of God "is sanctified by the word of God and prayers" (1 Tim. 4:5), he intimates that without the word and prayers none of them are holy and pure, *word* being used metonymically for *faith*. Hence David, on experiencing the loving-kindness of the Lord, elegantly declares, "He hath put a new song in my mouth" (Ps. 40:3); intimating, that our silence is malignant when we leave his blessings unpraised, seeing every blessing he bestows is a new ground of thanksgiving. Thus Isaiah, proclaiming the singular mercies of God, says, "Sing unto the Lord a new song" (Is. 42:10). In the same sense David says in another passage, "O Lord, open thou my lips; and my mouth shall show forth thy praise" (Ps. 41:15). In like manner, Hezekiah and Jonah declare that they will regard it as the end of their deliverance "to celebrate the goodness of God with songs in his temple" (Is. 38:20; Jonah 2:10). David lays down a general rule for all believers in these words, "What shall I render unto the Lord for all his benefits toward me? I will take the cup of salvation, and

call upon the name of the Lord" (Ps. 116:12, 13). This rule the Church follows in another psalm, "Save us, O Lord our God, and gather us from among the heathen, to give thanks unto thy holy name, and to triumph in thy praise" (Ps. 106:47). Again, "He will regard the prayer of the destitute, and not despise their prayer. This shall be written for the generation to come: and the people which shall be created shall praise the Lord." "To declare the name of the Lord in Zion, and his praise in Jerusalem" (Ps. 102:18, 21). Nay, whenever believers beseech the Lord to do anything *for his own name's sake*, as they declare themselves unworthy of obtaining it in their own name, so they oblige themselves to give thanks, and promise to make the right use of his loving-kindness by being the heralds of it. Thus Hosea, speaking of the future redemption of the Church, says, "Take away all iniquity, and receive us graciously; so will we render the calves of our lips" (Hos. 14:2). Not only do our tongues proclaim the kindness of God, but they naturally inspire us with love to him. "I love the Lord, because he hath heard my voice and my supplications" (Ps. 116:1). In another passage, speaking of the help which he had experienced, he says, "I will love thee, O Lord, my strength" (Ps. 18:1). No praise will ever please God that does not flow from this feeling of love. Nay, we must attend to the declaration of Paul, that all wishes are vicious and perverse which are not accompanied with thanksgiving. His words are, "In everything by prayer and supplication with thanksgiving let your requests be made known unto God" (Phil. 4:6). Because many, under the influence of moroseness, weariness, impatience, bitter grief and fear, use murmuring in their prayers, he enjoins us so to regulate our feelings as cheerfully to bless God even before obtaining what we ask. But if this connection ought always to subsist in full vigor between things that are almost contrary, the more sacred is the tie which binds us to celebrate the praises of God whenever he grants our requests. And as we have already shown that our prayers, which otherwise would be polluted, are sanctified by the intercession of Christ, so the Apostle, by enjoining us "to offer the sacrifice of praise to God continually" by Christ (Heb. 13:15), reminds us, that without the intervention of his priesthood our lips are not pure enough to celebrate the name of God. Hence we infer that a monstrous delusion prevails among Papists, the great majority of whom wonder when Christ is called an intercessor. The reason why Paul enjoins, "Pray without ceasing; in everything give thanks" (1 Thess. 5:17, 18), is, because he would have us with the utmost assiduity, at all times, in every place, in all things, and under all circumstances, direct our prayers to God, to expect all the things which we desire from him, and when obtained ascribe them to him; thus furnishing perpetual grounds for prayer and praise.

29. This assiduity in prayer, though it specially refers to the peculiar private prayers of individuals, extends also in some measure to the public prayers of the Church. These, it may be said, cannot be continual, and ought not to be made, except in the manner which, for the sake of order, has been established by public consent. This I admit, and hence certain hours are fixed beforehand, hours which, though indifferent in regard to God, are necessary for the use of man, that the general convenience may be consulted, and all things be done in the Church, as Paul enjoins, "decently and in order" (1 Cor. 14:40). But there is nothing in this to prevent each church from being now and then stirred up to a more frequent use of prayer and being more zealously affected under the impulse of some greater necessity. Of perseverance in prayer, which is much akin to assiduity, we shall speak towards the close of the chapter (sec. 51, 52). This assiduity, moreover, is very different from the BATTOLOGIAN (Greek – English "yammering"), *vain speaking*, which our Savior has prohibited (Matth. 6:7). For he does not there forbid us to pray long or frequently, or with great fervor, but warns us against supposing that we can extort anything from God by importuning him with garrulous loquacity, as if he were to be persuaded after the manner of men. We know that hypocrites, because they consider not that they have to do with God, offer up their prayers as pompously as if it were part of a triumphal show. The Pharisee, who thanked God that he was not as other men, no doubt proclaimed his praises before men, as if he had wished to

gain a reputation for sanctity by his prayers. Hence that vain speaking, which for a similar reason prevails so much in the Papacy in the present day, some vainly spinning out the time by a reiteration of the same frivolous prayers, and others employing a long series of verbiage for vulgar display. This childish garrulity being a mockery of God, it is not strange that it is prohibited in the Church, in order that every feeling there expressed may be sincere, proceeding from the inmost heart.

Akin to this abuse is another which our Savior also condemns, namely, when hypocrites for the sake of ostentation court the presence of many witnesses, and would sooner pray in the market-place than pray without applause. The true object of prayer being, as we have already said (sec. 4, 5), to carry our thoughts directly to God, whether to celebrate his praise or implore his aid, we can easily see that its primary seat is in the mind and heart, or rather that prayer itself is properly an effusion and manifestation of internal feeling before Him who is the searcher of hearts. Hence, when our divine Master was pleased to lay down the best rule for prayer, his injunction was, "Enter into thy closet, and when thou hast shut thy door, pray to thy Father which is in secret, and thy Father which seeth in secret shall reward thee openly" (Matth. 6:6). Dissuading us from the example of hypocrites, who sought the applause of men by an ambitious ostentation in prayer, he adds the better course – enter thy chamber, shut thy door, and there pray. By these words (as I understand them) he taught us to seek a place of retirement which might enable us to turn all our thoughts inwards and enter deeply into our hearts, promising that God would hold converse with the feelings of our mind, of which the body ought to be the temple. He meant not to deny that it may be expedient to pray in other places also, but he shows that prayer is somewhat of a secret nature, having its chief seat in the mind, and requiring a tranquility far removed from the turmoil of ordinary cares. And hence it was not without cause that our Lord himself, when he would engage more earnestly in prayer, withdrew into a retired spot beyond the bustle of the world, thus reminding us by his example that we are not to neglect those helps which enable the mind, in itself too much disposed to wander, to become sincerely intent on prayer. Meanwhile, as he abstained not from prayer when the occasion required it, though he were in the midst of a crowd, so must we, whenever there is need, lift up "pure hands" (1 Tim. 2:8) at all places. And hence we must hold that he who declines to pray in the public meeting of the saints, knows not what it is to pray apart, in retirement, or at home. On the other hand, he who neglects to pray alone and in private, however sedulously he frequents public meetings, there gives his prayers to the wind, because he defers more to the opinion of man than to the secret judgment of God. Still, lest the public prayers of the Church should be held in contempt, the Lord anciently bestowed upon them the most honorable appellation, especially when he called the temple the *"house of prayer"* (Isa. 56:7). For by this expression he both showed that the duty of prayer is a principal part of his worship, and that to enable believers to engage in it with one consent his temple is set up before them as a kind of banner. A noble promise was also added, "Praise waiteth for thee, O God, in Sion: and unto thee shall the vow be performed" (Ps. 65:1). By these words the Psalmist reminds us that the prayers of the Church are never in vain; because God always furnishes his people with materials for a song of joy. But although the shadows of the law have ceased, yet because God was pleased by this ordinance to foster the unity of the faith among us also, there can be no doubt that the same promise belongs to us – a promise which Christ sanctioned with his own lips, and which Paul declares to be perpetually in force.

30. As God in his word enjoins common prayer, so public temples are the places destined for the performance of them, and hence those who refuse to join with the people of God in this observance have no ground for the pretext, that they enter their chamber in order that they may obey the command of the Lord. For he who promises to grant whatsoever two or three assembled in his name shall ask (Matth. 18:20), declares, that he by no means despises the prayers which are publicly offered up, provided there be no ostentation, or catching at human applause, and provided there

be a true and sincere affection in the secret recesses of the heart. If this is the legitimate use of churches (and it certainly is), we must, on the other hand, beware of imitating the practice which commenced some centuries ago, of imagining that churches are the proper dwellings of God, where he is more ready to listen to us, or of attaching to them some kind of secret sanctity, which makes prayer there more holy. For seeing we are the true temples of God, we must pray in ourselves if we would invoke God in his holy temple. Let us leave such gross ideas to the Jews or the heathen, knowing that we have a command to pray without distinction of place, "in spirit and in truth" (John 4:23). It is true that by the order of God the temple was anciently dedicated for the offering of prayers and sacrifices, but this was at a time when the truth (which being now fully manifested, we are not permitted to confine to any material temple) lay hid under the figure of shadows. Even the temple was not represented to the Jews as confining the presence of God within its walls, but was meant to train them to contemplate the image of the true temple. Accordingly, a severe rebuke is administered both by Isaiah and Stephen, to those who thought that God could in any way dwell in temples made with hands (Isa. 66:2; Acts 7:48).

31. Hence it is perfectly clear that neither words nor singing (if used in prayer) are of the least consequence, or avail one iota with God, unless they proceed from deep feeling in the heart. Nay, rather they provoke his anger against us, if they come from the lips and throat only, since this is to abuse his sacred name, and hold his majesty in derision. This we infer from the words of Isaiah, which, though their meaning is of wider extent, go to rebuke this vice also: "Forasmuch as this people draw near me with their mouth, and with their lips do honor me, but have removed their heart far from me, and their fear toward me is taught by the precept of men: therefore, behold, I will proceed to do a marvelous work among this people, even a marvelous work and a wonder: for the wisdom of their wise men shall perish, and the understanding of their prudent men shall be hid" (Isa. 29:13). Still we

do not condemn words or singing, but rather greatly commend them, provided the feeling of the mind goes along with them. For in this way the thought of God is kept alive on our minds, which, from their fickle and versatile nature, soon relax, and are distracted by various objects, unless various means are used to support them. Besides, since the glory of God ought in a manner to be displayed in each part of our body, the special service to which the tongue should be devoted is that of singing and speaking, inasmuch as it has been expressly created to declare and proclaim the praise of God. This employment of the tongue is chiefly in the public services which are performed in the meeting of the saints. In this way the God whom we serve in one spirit and one faith, we glorify together as it were with one voice and one mouth; and that openly, so that each may in turn receive the confession of his brother's faith, and be invited and incited to imitate it.

32. It is certain that the use of singing in churches (which I may mention in passing) is not only very ancient, but was also used by the Apostles, as we may gather from the words of Paul, "I will sing with the spirit, and I will sing with the understanding also" (1 Cor. 14:15). In like manner he says to the Colossians, "Teaching and admonishing one another in psalms, and hymns, and spiritual songs, singing with grace in your hearts to the Lord" (Col. 3:16). In the former passage, he enjoins us to sing with the voice and the heart; in the latter, he commends spiritual Songs, by which the pious mutually edify each other. That it was not an universal practice, however, is attested by Augustine (Confess. Lib. ix. cap. 7), who states that the church of Milan first began to use singing in the time of Ambrose, when the orthodox faith being persecuted by Justina, the mother of Valentinian, the vigils of the people were more frequent than usual; and that the practice was afterwards followed by the other Western churches. He had said a little before that the custom came from the East. He also intimates (Retract. Lib. ii). that it was received in Africa in his own time. His words are, "Hilarius, a man of tribunitial rank, assailed with the bitterest invectives he could use the custom which then began to exist at Carthage,

of singing hymns from the book of Psalms at the altar, either before the oblation, or when it was distributed to the people; I answered him, at the request of my brethren." And certainly if singing is tempered to a gravity befitting the presence of God and angels, it both gives dignity and grace to sacred actions, and has a very powerful tendency to stir up the mind to true zeal and ardor in prayer.

We must, however, carefully beware, lest our ears be more intent on the music than our minds on the spiritual meaning of the words. Augustine confesses (Confess. Lib. x. cap. 33) that the fear of this danger sometimes made him wish for the introduction of a practice observed by Athanasius, who ordered the reader to use only a gentle inflection of the voice, more akin to recitation than singing. But on again considering how many advantages were derived from singing, he inclined to the other side. If this moderation is used, there cannot be a doubt that the practice is most sacred and salutary. On the other hand, songs composed merely to tickle and delight the ear are unbecoming the majesty of the Church, and cannot but be most displeasing to God.

33. It is also plain that the public prayers are not to be couched in Greek among the Latins, nor in Latin among the French or English (as hitherto has been every where practiced), but in the vulgar tongue, so that all present may understand them, since they ought to be used for the edification of the whole Church, which cannot be in the least degree benefitted by a sound not understood. Those who are not moved by any reason of humanity or charity, ought at least to be somewhat moved by the authority of Paul, whose words are by no means ambiguous: "When thou shalt bless with the spirit, how shall he that occupieth the room of the unlearned say, Amen, at thy giving of thanks, seeing he understandeth not what thou sayest? For thou verily givest thanks, but the other is not edified" (1 Cor. 14: 16, 17). How then can one sufficiently admire the unbridled license of the Papists, who, while the Apostle publicly protests against it, hesitate not to bawl out the most verbose prayers in a foreign tongue, prayers of which they themselves sometimes do not understand

one syllable, and which they have no wish that others should understand? Different is the course which Paul prescribes, "What is it then? I will pray with the spirit, and I will pray with the understanding also; I will sing with the spirit, and I will sing with the understanding also": meaning by the *spirit* the special gift of tongues, which some who had received it abused when they dissevered it from the mind, that is, the understanding. The principle we must always hold is, that in all prayer, public and private, the tongue without the mind must be displeasing to God. Moreover, the mind must be so incited, as in ardor of thought far to surpass what the tongue is able to express. Lastly, the tongue is not even necessary to private prayer, unless in so far as the internal feeling is insufficient for incitement, or the vehemence of the incitement carries the utterance of the tongue along with it. For although the best prayers are sometimes without utterance, yet when the feeling of the mind is overpowering, the tongue spontaneously breaks forth into utterance, and our other members into gesture. Hence that dubious muttering of Hannah (1 Sam. 1:13), something similar to which is experienced by all the saints when concise and abrupt expressions escape from them. The bodily gestures usually observed in prayer, such as kneeling and uncovering of the head (Calv. in Acts 20:36), are exercises by which we attempt to rise to higher veneration of God.

34. We must now attend not only to a surer method, but also form of prayer, that, namely, which our heavenly Father has delivered to us by his beloved Son, and in which we may recognize his boundless goodness and condescension (Matth. 6:9; Luke 11:2). Besides admonishing and exhorting us to seek him in our every necessity (as children are wont to betake themselves to the protection of their parents when oppressed with any anxiety), seeing that we were not fully aware how great our poverty was, or what was right or for our interest to ask, he has provided for this ignorance; that wherein our capacity failed he has sufficiently supplied. For he has given us a form in which is set before us as in a picture everything which it is lawful to wish,

everything which is conducive to our interest, everything which it is necessary to demand. From his goodness in this respect we derive the great comfort of knowing, that as we ask almost in his words, we ask nothing that is absurd, or foreign, or unseasonable; nothing, in short, that is not agreeable to him. Plato, seeing the ignorance of men in presenting their desires to God, desires which if granted would often be most injurious to them, declares the best form of prayer to be that which an ancient poet has furnished: "O king Jupiter, give what is best, whether we wish it or wish it not; but avert from us what is evil even though we ask it" (Plato, *Alcibiad.* ii). This heathen shows his wisdom in discerning how dangerous it is to ask of God what our own passion dictates; while, at the same time, he reminds us of our unhappy condition in not being able to open our lips before God without dangers unless his Spirit instruct us how to pray aright (Rom. 8:26). The higher value, therefore, ought we to set on the privilege, when the only begotten Son of God puts words into our lips, and thus relieves our minds of all hesitation.

35. This form or rule of prayer is composed of *six petitions.* For I am prevented from agreeing with those who divide it into *seven* by the adversative mode of diction used by the Evangelist, who appears to have intended to unite the two members together; as if he had said, Do not allow us to be overcome by temptation, but rather bring assistance to our frailty, and deliver us that we may not fall. Ancient writers also agree with us, that what is added by Matthew as a seventh head is to be considered as explanatory of the sixth petition. But though in every part of the prayer the first place is assigned to the glory of God, still this is more especially the object of the three first petitions, in which we are to look to the glory of God alone, without any reference to what is called our own advantage. The three remaining petitions are devoted to our interest, and properly relate to things which it is useful for us to ask. When we ask that the name of God may be hallowed, as God wishes to prove whether we love and serve him freely, or from the hope of reward, we are not to think at all of our own interest; we must set his glory before

our eyes, and keep them intent upon it alone. In the other similar petitions, this is the only manner in which we ought to be affected. It is true, that in this way our own interest is greatly promoted, because, when the name of God is hallowed in the way we ask, our own sanctification also is thereby promoted. But in regard to this advantage, we must, as I have said, shut our eyes, and be in a manner blind, so as not even to see it; and hence were all hope of our private advantage cut off, we still should never cease to wish and pray for this hallowing, and everything else which pertains to the glory of God. We have examples in Moses and Paul, who did not count it grievous to turn away their eyes and minds from themselves, and with intense and fervent zeal long for death, if by their loss the kingdom and glory of God might be promoted (Exod. 32:32; Rom. 9:3). On the other hand, when we ask for daily bread, although we desire what is advantageous for ourselves, we ought also especially to seek the glory of God, so much so that we would not ask at all unless it were to turn to his glory. Let us now proceed to an exposition of the Prayer. OUR FATHER WHICH ART IN HEAVEN.

36. The first thing suggested at the very outset is, as we have already said (sec. 17–19), that all our prayers to God ought only to be presented in the name of Christ, as there is no other name which can recommend them. In calling God our Father, we certainly plead the name of Christ. For with what confidence could any man call God his Father? Who would have the presumption to arrogate to himself the honor of a son of God were we not gratuitously adopted as his sons in Christ? He being the true Son, has been given to us as a brother, so that that which he possesses as his own by nature becomes ours by adoption, if we embrace this great mercy with firm faith. As John says, "As many as received him, to them gave he power to become the sons of God, even to them that believe in his name" (John 1:12). Hence he both calls himself our Father, and is pleased to be so called by us, by this delightful name relieving us of all distrust, since nowhere can a stronger affection be found than in a father. Hence, too, he could not have given us a stronger testimony of his boundless love than in calling us

his sons. But his love towards us is so much the greater and more excellent than that of earthly parents, the farther he surpasses all men in goodness and mercy (Isaiah 63:16). Earthly parents, laying aside all paternal affection, might abandon their offspring; he will never abandon us (Ps. 27:10), seeing he cannot deny himself. For we have his promise, "If ye then, being evil, know how to give good gifts unto your children, how much more shall your Father which is in heaven give good things to them that ask him?" (Matth. 7:11). In like manner in the prophet, "Can a woman forget her sucking child, that she should not have compassion on the son of her womb? Yea, they may forget, yet will not I forget thee" (Isaiah 49:15). But if we are his sons, then as a son cannot betake himself to the protection of a stranger and a foreigner without at the same time complaining of his father's cruelty or poverty, so we cannot ask assistance from any other quarter than from him, unless we would upbraid him with poverty, or want of means, or cruelty and excessive austerity.

37. Nor let us allege that we are justly rendered timid by a consciousness of sin, by which our Father, though mild and merciful, is daily offended. For if among men a son cannot have a better advocate to plead his cause with his father, and cannot employ a better intercessor to regain his lost favor, than if he come himself suppliant and downcast, acknowledging his fault, to implore the mercy of his father, whose paternal feelings cannot but be moved by such entreaties, what will that "Father of all mercies, and God of all comfort," do? (2 Cor. 1:3). Will he not rather listen to the tears and groans of his children, when supplicating for themselves (especially seeing he invites and exhorts us to do so), than to any advocacy of others to whom the timid have recourse, not without some semblance of despair, because they are distrustful of their father's mildness and clemency? The exuberance of his paternal kindness he sets before us in the parable (Luke 15:20; see Calv. *Comm.*) when the father with open arms receives the son who had gone away from him, wasted his substance in riotous living, and in all ways grievously sinned against him. He waits not till pardon is asked in words,

but, anticipating the request, recognizes him afar off, runs to meet him, consoles him, and restores him to favor. By setting before us this admirable example of mildness in a man, he designed to show in how much greater abundance we may expect it from him who is not only a Father, but the best and most merciful of all fathers, however ungrateful, rebellious, and wicked sons we may be, provided only we throw ourselves upon his mercy. And the better to assure us that he is such a Father if we are Christians, he has been pleased to be called not only a Father, but our Father, as if we were pleading with him after this manner, O Father, who art possessed of so much affection for thy children, and art so ready to forgive, we thy children approach thee and present our requests, fully persuaded that thou hast no other feelings towards us than those of a father, though we are unworthy of such a parent. But as our narrow hearts are incapable of comprehending such boundless favor, Christ is not only the earnest and pledge of our adoption, but also gives us the Spirit as a witness of this adoption, that through him we may freely cry aloud, Abba, Father. Whenever, therefore, we are restrained by any feeling of hesitation, let us remember to ask of him that he may correct our timidity, and placing us under the magnanimous guidance of the Spirit, enable us to pray boldly.

38. The instruction given us, however, is not that every individual in particular is to call him Father, but rather that we are all in common to call him Our Father. By this we are reminded how strong the feeling of brotherly love between us ought to be, since we are all alike, by the same mercy and free kindness, the children of such a Father. For if He from whom we all obtain whatever is good is our common Father (Matth. 23:9), everything which has been distributed to us we should be prepared to communicate to each other, as far as occasion demands. But if we are thus desirous as we ought, to stretch out our hands and give assistance to each other, there is nothing by which we can more benefit our brethren than by committing them to the care and protection of the best of parents, since if He is propitious and favorable nothing more can be desired.

And, indeed, we owe this also to our Father. For as he who truly and from the heart loves the father of a family, extends the same love and good-will to all his household, so the zeal and affection which we feel for our heavenly Parent it becomes us to extend towards his people, his family, and, in fine, his heritage, which he has honored so highly as to give them the appellation of the "fullness" of his only begotten Son (Eph. 1:23). Let the Christian, then, so regulate his prayers as to make them common, and embrace all who are his brethren in Christ; not only those whom at present he sees and knows to be such, but all men who are alive upon the earth. What God has determined with regard to them is beyond our knowledge, but to wish and hope the best concerning them is both pious and humane. Still it becomes us to regard with special affection those who are of the household of faith, and whom the Apostle has in express terms recommended to our care in everything (Gal. 6:10). In short, all our prayers ought to bear reference to that community which our Lord has established in his kingdom and family.

39. This, however, does not prevent us from praying specially for ourselves, and certain others, provided our mind is not withdrawn from the view of this community, does not deviate from it, but constantly refers to it. For prayers, though couched in special terms, keeping that object still in view, cease not to be common. All this may easily be understood by analogy. There is a general command from God to relieve the necessities of all the poor, and yet this command is obeyed by those who with that view give succor to all whom they see or know to be in distress, although they pass by many whose wants are not less urgent, either because they cannot know or are unable to give supply to all. In this way there is nothing repugnant to the will of God in those who, giving heed to this common society of the Church, yet offer up particular prayers, in which, with a public mind, though in special terms, they commend to God themselves or others, with whose necessity he has been pleased to make them more familiarly acquainted.

It is true that prayer and the giving of our

substance are not in all respects alike. We can only bestow the kindness of our liberality on those of whose wants we are aware, whereas in prayer we can assist the greatest strangers, how wide soever the space which may separate them from us. This is done by that general form of prayer which, including all the sons of God, includes them also. To this we may refer the exhortation which Paul gave to the believers of his age, to lift up "holy hands without wrath and doubting" (1 Tim. 2:8). By reminding them that dissension is a bar to prayer, he shows it to be his wish that they should with one accord present their prayers in common.

40. The next words are, WHICH ART IN HEAVEN. From this we are not to infer that he is enclosed and confined within the circumference of heaven, as by a kind of boundaries. Hence Solomon confesses, "The heaven of heavens cannot contain thee" (1 Kings 8:27); and he himself says by the Prophet, "The heaven is my throne, and the earth is my footstool" (Isa. 56:1); thereby intimating, that his presence, not confined to any region, is diffused over all space. But as our gross minds are unable to conceive of his ineffable glory, it is designated to us by *heaven*, nothing which our eyes can behold being so full of splendor and majesty. While, then, we are accustomed to regard every object as confined to the place where our senses discern it, no place can be assigned to God; and hence, if we would seek him, we must rise higher than all corporeal or mental discernment. Again, this form of expression reminds us that he is far beyond the reach of change or corruption, that he holds the whole universe in his grasp, and rules it by his power. The effect of the expressions therefore, is the same as if it had been said, that he is of infinite majesty, incomprehensible essence, boundless power, and eternal duration. When we thus speak of God, our thoughts must be raised to their highest pitch; we must not ascribe to him anything of a terrestrial or carnal nature, must not measure him by our little standards, or suppose his will to be like ours. At the same time, we must put our confidence in him, understanding that heaven and earth are governed by his providence and power. In short, under the name of Father is

set before us that God, who hath appeared to us in his own image, that we may invoke him with sure faith; the familiar name of Father being given not only to inspire confidence, but also to curb our minds, and prevent them from going astray after doubtful or fictitious gods. We thus ascend from the only begotten Son to the supreme Father of angels and of the Church. Then when his throne is fixed in heaven, we are reminded that he governs the world, and, therefore, that it is not in vain to approach him whose present care we actually experience. "He that cometh to God," says the Apostle, "must believe that he is, and that he is a rewarder of them that diligently seek him" (Heb. 11:6). Here Christ makes both claims for his Father, *first*, that we place our faith in him; and, *secondly*, that we feel assured that our salvation is not neglected by him, inasmuch as he condescends to extend his providence to us. By these elementary principles Paul prepares us to pray aright; for before enjoining us to make our requests known unto God, he premises in this way, "The Lord is at hand. Be careful for nothing" (Phil. 4:5, 6). Whence it appears that doubt and perplexity hang over the prayers of those in whose minds the belief is not firmly seated, that "the eyes of the Lord are upon the righteous" (Ps. 34:15).

41. The first petition is, HALLOWED BE THY NAME. The necessity of presenting it bespeaks our great disgrace. For what can be more unbecoming than that our ingratitude and malice should impair, our audacity and petulance should as much as in them lies destroy, the glory of God? But though all the ungodly should burst with sacrilegious rage, the holiness of God's name still shines forth. Justly does the Psalmist exclaim, "According to thy name, O God, so is thy praise unto the ends of the earth" (Ps. 48:10). For wherever God hath made himself known, his perfections must be displayed, his power, goodness, wisdom, justice, mercy, and truth, which fill us with admiration, and incite us to show forth his praise. Therefore, as the name of God is not duly hallowed on the earth, and we are otherwise unable to assert it, it is at least our duty to make it the subject of our prayers. The sum of the whole is, It must be our desire that God

may receive the honor which is his due: that men may never think or speak of him without the greatest reverence. The opposite of this reverence is profanity, which has always been too common in the world, and is very prevalent in the present day. Hence the necessity of the petition, which, if piety had any proper existence among us, would be superfluous. But if the name of God is duly hallowed only when separated from all other names it alone is glorified, we are in the petition enjoined to ask not only that God would vindicate his sacred name from all contempt and insult, but also that he would compel the whole human race to reverence it. Then since God manifests himself to us partly by his word, and partly by his works, he is not sanctified unless in regard to both of these we ascribe to him what is due, and thus embrace whatever has proceeded from him, giving no less praise to his justice than to his mercy. On the manifold diversity of his works he has inscribed the marks of his glory, and these ought to call forth from every tongue an ascription of praise. Thus Scripture will obtain its due authority with us, and no event will hinder us from celebrating the praises of God, in regard to every part of his government. On the other hand, the petition implies a wish that all impiety which pollutes this sacred name may perish and be extinguished, that everything which obscures or impairs his glory, all detraction and insult, may cease; that all blasphemy being suppressed, the divine majesty may be more and more signally displayed.

42. The second petition is, THY KINGDOM COME. This contains nothing new, and yet there is good reason for distinguishing it from the first. For if we consider our lethargy in the greatest of all matters, we shall see how necessary it is that what ought to be in itself perfectly known should be inculcated at greater length. Therefore, after the injunction to pray that God would reduce to order, and at length completely efface every stain which is thrown on his sacred name, another petition, containing almost the same wish, is added, viz., Thy kingdom come. Although a definition of this kingdom has already been given, I now briefly repeat that God reigns when men, in denial of themselves and contempt of the world and this

earthly life, devote themselves to righteousness and aspire to heaven (see Calvin, Harm. Matth. 6). Thus this kingdom consists of two parts; the first is, when God by the agency of his Spirit corrects all the depraved lusts of the flesh, which in bands war against Him; and the second, when he brings all our thoughts into obedience to his authority. This petition, therefore, is duly presented only by those who begin with themselves; in other words, who pray that they may be purified from all the corruptions which disturb the tranquility and impair the purity of God's kingdom. Then as the word of God is like his royal scepter, we are here enjoined to pray that he would subdue all minds and hearts to voluntary obedience. This is done when by the secret inspiration of his Spirit he displays the efficacy of his word, and raises it to the place of honor which it deserves. We must next descend to the wicked, who perversely and with desperate madness resist his authority. God, therefore, sets up his kingdom, by humbling the whole world, though in different ways, taming the wantonness of some, and breaking the ungovernable pride of others. We should desire this to be done every day, in order that God may gather churches to himself from all quarters of the world, may extend and increase their numbers, enrich them with his gifts, establish due order among them; on the other hand, beat down all the enemies of pure doctrine and religion, dissipate their counsels, defeat their attempts. Hence it appears that there is good ground for the precept which enjoins daily progress, for human affairs are never so prosperous as when the impurities of vice are purged away, and integrity flourishes in full vigor. The completion, however, is deferred to the final advent of Christ, when, as Paul declares, "God will be all in all" (1 Cor. 15:28). This prayer, therefore, ought to withdraw us from the corruptions of the world which separate us from God, and prevent his kingdom from flourishing within us; secondly, it ought to inflame us with an ardent desire for the mortification of the flesh; and, lastly, it ought to train us to the endurance of the cross; since this is the way in which God would have his kingdom to be advanced. It ought not to grieve us that the outward man decays provided the inner man is renewed. For such is the nature of the kingdom of God, that while we submit to his righteousness he makes us partakers of his glory. This is the case when continually adding to his light and truth, by which the lies and the darkness of Satan and his kingdom are dissipated, extinguished, and destroyed, he protects his people, guides them aright by the agency of his Spirit, and confirms them in perseverance; while, on the other hand, he frustrates the impious conspiracies of his enemies, dissipates their wiles and frauds, prevents their malice and curbs their petulance, until at length he consume Antichrist "with the spirit of his mouth," and destroy all impiety "with the brightness of his coming" (2 Thess. 2:8, Calv. *Comm.*).

43. The third petition is, THY WILL BE DONE ON EARTH AS IT IS IN HEAVEN. Though this depends on his kingdom, and cannot be disjoined from it, yet a separate place is not improperly given to it on account of our ignorance, which does not at once or easily apprehend what is meant by God reigning in the world. This, therefore, may not improperly be taken as the explanation, that God will be King in the world when all shall subject themselves to his will. We are not here treating of that secret will by which he governs all things, and destines them to their end (see chap. xxiv. s. 17). For although devils and men rise in tumult against him, he is able by his incomprehensible counsel not only to turn aside their violence, but make it subservient to the execution of his decrees. What we here speak of is another will of God, namely, that of which voluntary obedience is the counterpart; and, therefore, heaven is expressly contrasted with earth, because, as is said in The Psalms, the angels "do his commandments, hearkening unto the voice of his word" (Ps. 103:20). We are, therefore, enjoined to pray that as everything done in heaven is at the command of God, and the angels are calmly disposed to do all that is right, so the earth may be brought under his authority, all rebellion and depravity having been extinguished. In presenting this request we renounce the desires of the flesh, because he who does not entirely resign his affections to God, does as much as in him lies to oppose the divine will, since everything which proceeds

from us is vicious. Again, by this prayer we are taught to deny ourselves, that God may rule us according to his pleasure; and not only so, but also having annihilated our own may create new thoughts and new minds so that we shall have no desire save that of entire agreement with his will; in short, wish nothing of ourselves, but have our hearts governed by his Spirit, under whose inward teaching we may learn to love those things which please and hate those things which displease him. Hence also we must desire that he would nullify and suppress all affections which are repugnant to his will.

Such are the three first heads of the prayer, in presenting which we should have the glory of God only in view, taking no account of ourselves, and paying no respect to our own advantage. And though all the events prayed for must happen in their own time, without being either thought of, wished, or asked by us, it is still our duty to wish and ask for them. And it is of no slight importance to do so, that we may testify and profess that we are the servants and children of God, desirous by every means in our power to promote the honor due to him as our Lord and Father, and truly and thoroughly devoted to his service. Hence if men, in praying that the name of God may be hallowed, that his kingdom may come, and his will be done, are not influenced by this zeal for the promotion of his glory, they are not to be accounted among the servants and children of God; and as all these things will take place against their will, so they will turn out to their confusion and destruction.

44. Now comes the second part of the prayer, in which we descend to our own interests, not, indeed, that we are to lose sight of the glory of God (to which, as Paul declares, we must have respect even in meat and drink, 1 Cor. 10:31), and ask only what is expedient for ourselves; but the distinction, as we have already observed, is this: God claiming the three first petitions as specially his own, carries us entirely to himself, that in this way he may prove our piety. Next he permits us to look to our own advantage, but still on the condition, that when we ask anything for ourselves it must be in order that all the benefits which he

confers may show forth his glory, there being nothing more incumbent on us than to live and die to him.

By the first petition of the second part, GIVE US THIS DAY OUR DAILY BREAD, we pray in general that God would give us all things which the body requires in this sublunary state, not only food and clothing, but everything which he knows will assist us to eat our bread in peace. In this way we briefly cast our care upon him, and commit ourselves to his providence, that he may feed, foster, and preserve us. For our heavenly Father disdains not to take our body under his charge and protection, that he may exercise our faith in those minute matters, while we look to him for everything, even to a morsel of bread and a drop of water. For since, owing to some strange inequality, we feel more concern for the body than for the soul, many who can trust the latter to God still continue anxious about the former, still hesitate as to what they are to eat, as to how they are to be clothed, and are in trepidation whenever their hands are not filled with corn, and wine, and oil (Ps. 4:8): so much more value do we set on this shadowy, fleeting life, than on a blessed immortality. But those who, trusting to God, have once cast away that anxiety about the flesh, immediately look to him for greater gifts, even salvation and eternal life. It is no slight exercise of faith, therefore, to hope in God for things which would otherwise give us so much concern; nor have we made little progress when we get quit of this unbelief, which cleaves, as it were, to our very bones.

The speculations of some concerning super-substantial bread seem to be very little accordant with our Savior's meaning; for our prayer would be defective were we not to ascribe to God the nourishment even of this fading life. The reason which they give is heathenish, viz., that it is inconsistent with the character of sons of God, who ought to be spiritual, not only to occupy their mind with earthly cares, but to suppose God also occupied with them. As if his blessing and paternal favor were not eminently displayed in giving us food, or as if there were nothing in the declaration that godliness hath "the promise of the life that now is, and of that which is to come" (1 Tim. 4:8). But although the forgiveness of sins

is of far more importance than the nourishment of the body, yet Christ has set down the inferior in the prior place, in order that he might gradually raise us to the other two petitions, which properly belong to the heavenly life, – in this providing for our sluggishness. We are enjoined to ask *our bread*, that we may be contented with the measure which our heavenly Father is pleased to dispense, and not strive to make gain by illicit arts. Meanwhile, we must hold that the title by which it is ours is donation, because, as Moses says (Levit. 26: 20, Deut. 8:17), neither our industry, nor labor, nor hands, acquire anything for us, unless the blessing of God be present; nay, not even would abundance of bread be of the least avail were it not divinely converted into nourishment. And hence this liberality of God is not less necessary to the rich than the poor, because, though their cellars and barns were full, they would be parched and pine with want did they not enjoy his favor along with their bread.

The terms *this day*, or, as it is in another Evangelist, *daily*, and also the epithet *daily*, lay a restraint on our immoderate desire of fleeting good – a desire which we are extremely apt to indulge to excess, and from which other evils ensue: for when our supply is in richer abundance we ambitiously squander it in pleasure, luxury, ostentation, or other kinds of extravagance. Wherefore, we are only enjoined to ask as much as our necessity requires, and as it were for each day, confiding that our heavenly Father, who gives us the supply of to-day, will not fail us on the morrow. How great soever our abundance may be, however well filled our cellars and granaries, we must still always ask for daily bread, for we must feel assured that all substance is nothing, unless in so far as the Lord, by pouring out his blessing, make it fruitful during its whole progress; for even that which is in our hand is not ours except in so far as he every hour portions it out, and permits us to use it. As nothing is more difficult to human pride than the admission of this truth, the Lord declares that he gave a special proof for all ages, when he fed his people with manna in the desert (Deut. 8:3), that he might remind us that "man shall not live by bread alone, but by every word that proceedeth out of the mouth of God" (Matth. 4:4). It is thus intimated, that by his power alone our life and strength are sustained, though he ministers supply to us by bodily instruments.

In like manner, whenever it so pleases, he gives us a proof of an opposite description, by breaking the strength, or, as he himself calls it, the *staff* of bread (Levit. 26:26), and leaving us even while eating to pine with hunger, and while drinking to be parched with thirst. Those who, not contented with daily bread, indulge an unrestrained insatiable cupidity, or those who are full of their own abundance, and trust in their own riches, only mock God by offering up this prayer. For the former ask what they would be unwilling to obtain, nay, what they most of all abominate, namely, daily bread only, and as much as in them lies disguise their avarice from God, whereas true prayer should pour out the whole soul and every inward feeling before him. The latter, again, ask what they do not at all expect to obtain, namely, what they imagine that they in themselves already possess. In its being called *ours*, God, as we have already said, gives a striking display of his kindness, making that to be ours to which we have no just claim. Nor must we reject the view to which I have already adverted, viz., that this name is given to what is obtained by just and honest labor, as contrasted with what is obtained by fraud and rapine, nothing being our own which we obtain with injury to others. When we ask God to *give us*, the meaning is, that the thing asked is simply and freely the gift of God, whatever be the quarter from which it comes to us, even when it seems to have been specially prepared by our own art and industry, and procured by our hands, since it is to his blessing alone that all our labors owe their success.

45. The next petition is, FORGIVE US OUR DEBTS. In this and the following petition our Savior has briefly comprehended whatever is conducive to the heavenly life, as these two members contain the spiritual covenant which God made for the salvation of his Church, "I will put my law in their inward parts, and write it on their hearts." "I will pardon all their iniquities" (Jer. 31:33; 33:8). Here our Savior begins with the forgiveness of sins, and then adds the subsequent blessing, viz., that God would

protect us by the power, and support us by the aid of his Spirit, so that we may stand invincible against all temptations. To sins he gives the name of *debts*, because we owe the punishment due to them, a debt which we could not possibly pay were we not discharged by this remission, the result of his free mercy, when he freely expunges the debt, accepting nothing in return; but of his own mercy receiving satisfaction in Christ, who gave himself a ransom for us (Rom. 3:24). Hence, those who expect to satisfy God by merits of their own or of others, or to compensate and purchase forgiveness by means of satisfactions, have no share in this free pardon, and while they address God in this petition, do nothing more than subscribe their own accusation, and seal their condemnation by their own testimony. For they confess that they are debtors, unless they are discharged by means of forgiveness. This forgiveness, however, they do not receive, but rather reject, when they obtrude their merits and satisfactions upon God, since by so doing they do not implore his mercy, but appeal to his justice. Let those, again, who dream of a perfection which makes it unnecessary to seek pardon, find their disciples among those whose itching ears incline them to imposture, (see Calv. on Dan. 9: 20); only let them understand that those whom they thus acquire have been carried away from Christ, since he, by instructing all to confess their guilt, receives none but sinners, not that he may soothe, and so encourage them in their sins, but because he knows that believers are never so divested of the sins of the flesh as not to remain subject to the justice of God. It is, indeed, to be wished, it ought even to be our strenuous endeavor, to perform all the parts of our duty, so as truly to congratulate ourselves before God as being pure from every stain; but as God is pleased to renew his image in us by degrees, so that to some extent there is always a residue of corruption in our flesh, we ought by no means to neglect the remedy.

But if Christ, according to the authority given him by his Father, enjoins us, during the whole course of our lives, to implore pardon, who can tolerate those new teachers who, by the phantom of perfect innocence, endeavor to dazzle the simple, and make them believe that they can render themselves completely free from guilt? This, as John declares, is nothing else than to make God a liar (1 John 1:10). In like manner, those foolish men mutilate the covenant in which we have seen that our salvation is contained by concealing one head of it, and so destroying it entirely; being guilty not only of profanity in that they separate things which ought to be indissolubly connected; but also of wickedness and cruelty in overwhelming wretched souls with despair – of treachery also to themselves and their followers, in that they encourage themselves in a carelessness diametrically opposed to the mercy of God. It is excessively childish to object, that when they long for the advent of the kingdom of God, they at the same time pray for the abolition of sin. In the former division of the prayer absolute perfection is set before us; but in the latter our own weakness. Thus the two fitly correspond to each other – we strive for the goal, and at the same time neglect not the remedies which our necessities require.

In the next part of the petition we pray to be forgiven, *"as we forgive our debtors"*; that is, as we spare and pardon all by whom we are in any way offended, either in deed by unjust, or in word by contumelious treatment. Not that we can forgive the guilt of a fault or offence; this belongs to God only; but we can forgive to this extent: we can voluntarily divest our minds of wrath, hatred, and revenge, and efface the remembrance of injuries by a voluntary oblivion. Wherefore, we are not to ask the forgiveness of our sins from God, unless we forgive the offenses of all who are or have been injurious to us. If we retain any hatred in our minds, if we meditate revenge, and devise the means of hurting; nay, if we do not return to a good understanding with our enemies, perform every kind of friendly office, and endeavor to effect a reconciliation with them, we by this petition beseech God not to grant us forgiveness. For we ask him to do to us as we do to others. This is the same as asking him not to do unless we do also. What, then, do such persons obtain by this petition but a heavier judgment? Lastly, it is to be observed that the condition of being forgiven as we forgive our debtors, is not added because by forgiving others we deserve forgiveness, as if the cause of forgiveness were expressed; but

by the use of this expression the Lord has been pleased partly to solace the weakness of our faith, using it as a sign to assure us that our sins are as certainly forgiven as we are certainly conscious of having forgiven others, when our mind is completely purged from all envy, hatred, and malice; and partly using as a badge by which he excludes from the number of his children all who, prone to revenge and reluctant to forgive, obstinately keep up their enmity, cherishing against others that indignation which they deprecate from themselves; so that they should not venture to invoke him as a Father. In the Gospel of Luke, we have this distinctly stated in the words of Christ.

46. The sixth petition corresponds (as we have observed) to the promise of *writing the law upon our hearts*; but because we do not obey God without a continual warfare, without sharp and arduous contests, we here pray that he would furnish us with armor, and defend us by his protection, that we may be able to obtain the victory. By this we are reminded that we not only have need of the gift of the Spirit inwardly to soften our hearts, and turn and direct them to the obedience of God, but also of his assistance, to render us invincible by all the wiles and violent assaults of Satan. The forms of temptation are many and various. The depraved conceptions of our minds provoking us to transgress the law – conceptions which our concupiscence suggests or the devil excites, are temptations; and things which in their own nature are not evil, become temptations by the wiles of the devil, when they are presented to our eyes in such a way that the view of them makes us withdraw or decline from God. These temptations are both on the right hand and on the left. On the right, when riches, power, and honors, which by their glare, and the semblance of good which they present, generally dazzle the eyes of men, and so entice by their blandishments, that, caught by their snares, and intoxicated by their sweetness, they forget their God: on the left, when offended by the hardship and bitterness of poverty, disgrace, contempt, afflictions, and other things of that description, they despond, cast away their confidence and hope, and are at length totally estranged from God. In regard to

both kinds of temptation, which either enkindled in us by concupiscence, or presented by the craft of Satan's war against us, we pray God the Father not to allow us to be overcome, but rather to raise and support us by his hand, that strengthened by his mighty power we may stand firm against all the assaults of our malignant enemy, whatever be the thoughts which he sends into our minds; next we pray that whatever of either description is allotted us, we may turn to good, that is, may neither be inflated with prosperity, nor cast down by adversity. Here, however, we do not ask to be altogether exempted from temptation, which is very necessary to excite, stimulate, and urge us on, that we may not become too lethargic.

It was not without reason that David wished to be tried, nor is it without cause that the Lord daily tries his elect, chastising them by disgrace, poverty, tribulation, and other kinds of cross. But the temptations of God and Satan are very different: Satan tempts, that he may destroy, condemn, confound, throw headlong; God, that by proving his people he may make trial of their sincerity, and by exercising their strength confirm it; may mortify, tame, and cauterize their flesh, which, if not curbed in this manner, would wanton and exult above measure. Besides, Satan attacks those who are unarmed and unprepared, that he may destroy them unawares; whereas whatever God sends, he "will with the temptation also make a way to escape, that ye may be able to bear it." Whether by the term evil we understand the devil or sin, is not of the least consequence. Satan is indeed the very enemy who lays snares for our life, but it is by sin that he is armed for our destruction.

Our petition, therefore, is, that we may not be overcome or overwhelmed with temptation, but in the strength of the Lord may stand firm against all the powers by which we are assailed; in other words, may not fall under temptation: that being thus taken under his charge and protection, we may remain invincible by sin, death, the gates of hell, and the whole power of the devil; in other words, be delivered from evil. Here it is carefully to be observed, that we have no strength to contend with such a combatant as the devil, or to sustain the violence of his assault. Were it otherwise, it

would be mockery of God to ask of him what we already possess in ourselves. Assuredly those who in self-confidence prepare for such a fight, do not understand how bold and well-equipped the enemy is with whom they have to do. Now we ask to be delivered from his power, as from the mouth of some furious raging lion, who would instantly tear us with his teeth and claws, and swallow us up, did not the Lord rescue us from the midst of death; at the same time knowing that if the Lord is present and will fight for us while we stand by, through him "we shall do valiantly" (Ps. 60:12). Let others if they will confide in the powers and resources of their free will which they think they possess; enough for us that we stand and are strong in the power of God alone. But the prayer comprehends more than at first sight it seems to do. For if the Spirit of God is our strength in waging the contest with Satan, we cannot gain the victory unless we are filled with him, and thereby freed from all infirmity of the flesh. Therefore, when we pray to be delivered from sin and Satan, we at the same time desire to be enriched with new supplies of divine grace, until completely replenished with them, we triumph over every evil. To some it seems rude and harsh to ask God not to lead us into temptation, since, as James declares (James 1:13), it is contrary to his nature to do so. This difficulty has already been partly solved by the fact that our concupiscence is the cause, and therefore properly bears the blame of all the temptations by which we are overcome. All that James means is, that it is vain and unjust to ascribe to God vices which our own consciousness compels us to impute to ourselves. But this is no reason why God may not when he sees it meet bring us into bondage to Satan, give us up to a reprobate mind and shameful lusts, and so by a just, indeed, but often hidden judgment, lead us into temptation. Though the cause is often concealed from men, it is well known to him. Hence we may see that the expression is not improper, if we are persuaded that it is not without cause he so often threatens to give sure signs of his vengeance, by blinding the reprobate, and hardening their hearts.

47. These three petitions, in which we specially commend ourselves and all that we

have to God, clearly show what we formerly observed (sec. 38, 39), that the prayers of Christians should be public, and have respect to the public edification of the Church and the advancement of believers in spiritual communion. For no one requests that anything should be given to him as an individual, but we all ask in common for daily bread and the forgiveness of sins, not to be led into temptation, but delivered from evil. Moreover, there is subjoined the reason for our great boldness in asking and confidence of obtaining (sec. 11, 36). Although this does not exist in the Latin copies, yet as it accords so well with the whole, we cannot think of omitting it.

The words are, THINE IS THE KINGDOM, AND THE POWER, AND THE GLORY, FOR EVER. Here is the calm and firm assurance of our faith. For were our prayers to be commended to God by our own worth, who would venture even to whisper before him? Now, however wretched we may be, however unworthy, however devoid of commendation, we shall never want a reason for prayer, nor a ground of confidence, since the kingdom, power, and glory, can never be wrested from our Father. The last word is AMEN, by which is expressed the eagerness of our desire to obtain the things which we ask, while our hope is confirmed, that all things have already been obtained and will assuredly be granted to us, seeing they have been promised by God, who cannot deceive. This accords with the form of expression to which we have already adverted: "Grant, O Lord, for thy name's sake, not on account of us or of our righteousness." By this the saints not only express the end of their prayers, but confess that they are unworthy of obtaining did not God find the cause in himself and were not their confidence founded entirely on his nature.

48. All things that we ought, indeed all that we are able, to ask of God, are contained in this formula, and as it were rule, of prayer delivered by Christ, our divine Master, whom the Father has appointed to be our teacher, and to whom alone he would have us to listen (Matth. 17:5). For he ever was the eternal wisdom of the Father, and being made man, was manifested as the Wonderful, the Counselor (Isa. 11:2;

9:6). Accordingly, this prayer is complete in all its parts, so complete, that whatever is extraneous and foreign to it, whatever cannot be referred to it, is impious and unworthy of the approbation of God. For he has here summarily prescribed what is worthy of him, what is acceptable to him, and what is necessary for us; in short, whatever he is pleased to grant. Those, therefore, who presume to go further and ask something more from God, first seek to add of their own to the wisdom of God (this it is insane blasphemy to do); secondly, refusing to confine themselves within the will of God, and despising it, they wander as their cupidity directs; lastly, they will never obtain anything, seeing they pray without faith. For there cannot be a doubt that all such prayers are made without faith, because at variance with the word of God, on which if faith do not always lean it cannot possibly stand. Those who, disregarding the Master's rule, indulge their own wishes, not only have not the word of God, but as much as in them lies oppose it. Hence Tertullian (*De Fuga in Persequutione*) has not less truly than elegantly termed it *Lawful Prayer*, tacitly intimating that all other prayers are lawless and illicit.

49. By this, however, we would not have it understood that we are so restricted to this form of prayer as to make it unlawful to change a word or syllable of it. For in Scripture we meet with many prayers differing greatly from it in word, yet written by the same Spirit, and capable of being used by us with the greatest advantage. Many prayers also are continually suggested to believers by the same Spirit, though in expression they bear no great resemblance to it. All we mean to say is, that no man should wish, expect, or ask anything which is not summarily comprehended in this prayer. Though the words may be very different, there must be no difference in the sense. In this way, all prayers, both those which are contained in the Scripture, and those which come forth from pious breasts, must be referred to it, certainly none can ever equal it, far less surpass it in perfection. It omits nothing which we can conceive in praise of God, nothing which we can imagine advantageous to man, and the whole is so exact that all hope of improving it

may well be renounced. In short, let us remember that we have here the doctrine of heavenly wisdom. God has taught what he willed; he willed what was necessary.

50. But although it has been said above (sec. 7, 27, etc.), that we ought always to raise our minds upwards towards God, and pray without ceasing, yet such is our weakness, which requires to be supported, such our torpor, which requires to be stimulated, that it is requisite for us to appoint special hours for this exercise, hours which are not to pass away without prayer, and during which the whole affections of our minds are to be completely occupied; namely, when we rise in the morning, before we commence our daily work, when we sit down to food, when by the blessing of God we have taken it, and when we retire to rest. This, however, must not be a superstitious observance of hours, by which, as it were, performing a task to God, we think we are discharged as to other hours; it should rather be considered as a discipline by which our weakness is exercised, and ever and anon stimulated. In particular, it must be our anxious care, whenever we are ourselves pressed, or see others pressed by any strait, instantly to have recourse to him not only with quickened pace, but with quickened minds; and again, we must not in any prosperity of ourselves or others omit to testify our recognition of his hand by praise and thanksgiving. Lastly, we must in all our prayers carefully avoid wishing to confine God to certain circumstances, or prescribe to him the time, place, or mode of action. In like manner, we are taught by this prayer not to fix any law or impose any condition upon him, but leave it entirely to him to adopt whatever course of procedure seems to him best, in respect of method, time, and place. For before we offer up any petition for ourselves, we ask that his will may be done, and by so doing place our will in subordination to his, just as if we had laid a curb upon it, that, instead of presuming to give law to God, it may regard him as the ruler and disposer of all its wishes.

51. If, with minds thus framed to obedience, we allow ourselves to be governed by the laws of Divine Providence, we shall easily learn to persevere in prayer, and suspending our own desires wait patiently for the Lord, certain, however little the appearance of it may be, that he is always present with us, and will in his own time show how very far he was from turning a deaf ear to prayers, though to the eyes of men they may seem to be disregarded. This will be a very present consolation, if at any time God does not grant an immediate answer to our prayers, preventing us from fainting or giving way to despondency, as those are wont to do who, in invoking God, are so borne away by their own fervor, that unless he yield on their first importunity and give present help, they immediately imagine that he is angry and offended with them and abandoning all hope of success cease from prayer. On the contrary, deferring our hope with well tempered equanimity, let us insist with that perseverance which is so strongly recommended to us in Scripture. We may often see in The Psalms how David and other believers, after they are almost weary of praying, and seem to have been beating the air by addressing a God who would not hear, yet cease not to pray because due authority is not given to the word of God, unless the faith placed in it is superior to all events. Again, let us not tempt God, and by wearying him with our importunity provoke his anger against us. Many have a practice of formally bargaining with God on certain conditions, and, as if he were the servant of their lust, binding him to certain stipulations; with which if he do not immediately comply, they are indignant and fretful, murmur, complain, and make a noise. Thus offended, he often in his anger grants to such persons what in mercy he kindly denies to others. Of this we have a proof in the children of Israel, for whom it had been better not to have been heard by the Lord, than to swallow his indignation with their flesh (Num. 11:18, 33).

52. But if our sense is not able till after long expectation to perceive what the result of prayer is, or experience any benefit from it, still our faith will assure us of that which cannot be perceived by sense, viz., that we have obtained what was fit for us, the Lord having so often and so surely engaged to take an interest in all our troubles from the moment they have been

deposited in his bosom. In this way we shall possess abundance in poverty, and comfort in affliction. For though all things fail, God will never abandon us, and he cannot frustrate the expectation and patience of his people. He alone will suffice for all, since in himself he comprehends all good, and will at last reveal it to us on the day of judgment, when his kingdom shall be plainly manifested. We may add, that although God complies with our request, he does not always give an answer in the very terms of our prayers but while apparently holding us in suspense, yet in an unknown way, shows that our prayers have not been in vain. This is the meaning of the words of John, "If we know that he hear us, whatsoever we ask, we know that we have the petitions that we desired of him" (1 John 5:15). It might seem that there is here a great superfluity of words, but the declaration is most useful, namely, that God, even when he does not comply with our requests, yet listens and is favorable to our prayers, so that our hope founded on his word is never disappointed. But believers have always need of being supported by this patience, as they could not stand long if they did not lean upon it. For the trials by which the Lord proves and exercises us are severe, nay, he often drives us to extremes, and when driven allows us long to stick fast in the mire before he gives us any taste of his sweetness. As Hannah says, "The Lord killeth, and maketh alive; he bringeth down to the grave, and bringeth up" (1 Sam. 2:6). What could they here do but become dispirited and rush on despair, were they not, when afflicted, desolate, and half dead, comforted with the thought that they are regarded by God, and that there will be an end to their present evils. But however secure their hopes may stand, they do not stop praying, since prayer unaccompanied by perseverance leads nowhere.

John Calvin, 1509–64

A Discourse of Delight In Prayer

Stephen Charnock

"Delight thyself also in the Lord; and he shall give the desires of thine heart." Psalm 37:4

The beginning of this psalm is a heap of instructions: The great lesson intended in it is placed in verse 1. "Fret not thyself because of evil-doers, neither be thou envious against the workers of iniquity." It is resumed, verses 7, 8, where many reasons are asserted to enforce it.

Fret not.

1. Do not envy them. Be not troubled at their prosperity.

2. Do not imitate them. Be not provoked by their glow-worm happiness, to practice the same wickedness to arrive to the same prosperity.

3. Be not sinfully impatient, and quarrel not with God, because he hath not by his providence allowed thee the same measures of prosperity in the world. Accuse him not of injustice and cruelty, because he afflicts the good, and is indulgent to the wicked. Leave him to dispense his blessings according to his own mind.

4. Condemn not the way of piety and religion wherein thou art. Think not the worse of thy profession, because it is attended with affliction.

The reason of this exhortation is rendered, verse 2. "For they shall soon be cut down like the grass, and wither as the green herb"; amplified by a similitude or resemblance of their prosperity to grass: their happiness hath no stability. It hath, like grass, more of color and show, than strength and substance. Grass nods this and that way with every wind. The mouth of a beast may pull it up, or the foot of a beast may tread it down; the scorching sun in summer, or the fainting sun in winter, will deface its complexion.

The Psalmist then proceeds to positive duties, verse 3.

1. Faith. Trust in the Lord. This is a grace most fit to quell such impatience. The stronger the faith, the weaker the passion. Impatient motions are signs of a flagging faith. Many times men are ready to cast off their help in Jehovah, and address to the God of Ekron multitudes of friends or riches. But trust thou in the Lord; in the promises of God, in the providence of God.

2. Obedience. Do good. Trust in God's

promises, and observance of his precepts, must be linked together. It is but a pretended trust in God, where there is a real walking in the paths of wickedness. Let not the glitter of the world render thee faint and feeble in a course of piety.

3. The keeping our station. Do good. Because wicked men flourish, hide not thyself therefore in a corner, but keep thy sphere, run thy race. "And verily thou shalt be fed"; have every thing needful for thee. And now, because men delight in that wherein they trust, the Psalmist diverts us from all other objects of delight, to God as the true Objection. "Delight thyself in the Lord"; place all thy pleasure and joy in him. And because the motive expresseth the answer of prayer, the duty enjoined seems to respect the act of prayer, as well as the object of prayer; prayer coming from a delight in God, and a delight in seeking him. Trust is both the spring of joy and the spring of supplication. When we trust him for sustenance and preservation, we shall receive them; so when we delight in seeking him, we shall be answered by him.

1. The duty. In the act, delight. In the object, the Lord.

2. The motive. "He shall give thee the desires of thy heart"; the most substantial desires, those desires which he approves of; the desire of thy heart as gracious, though not the desire of thy heart as carnal: the desire of thy heart as a Christian, though not the desire of thy heart as a creature. He shall give; God is the object of Our joy, and the author of our comfort.

Doctrine. Delight in God, in seeking him only, procures gracious answers; or, without cheerful prayers, we cannot have gracious answers. There are two parts. 1. Cheerfulness on our parts. 2. Grants on God's part.

1. Cheerfulness and delight on our parts. Joy is the tuning the soul. The command to rejoice precedes the command to pray. "Rejoice evermore: pray without ceasing," 1 Thess. 5:16, 17. Delight makes the melody, otherwise prayer will be but a harsh sound. God accepts the heart only, when it is a gift given, not forced. Delight is the marrow of religion.

1. Dullness is not suitable to the great things we are chiefly to beg for. The things revealed in the Gospel are a feast, Isa. 25:6. Dullness

becomes not such a solemnity. Manna must not be sought for with a lumpish heart. With joy we are to draw water out of the wells of salvation, Isa. 12:3. Faith is the bucket, but joy and love are the hands that move it. They are the Hur and Aaron that hold up the hands of this Moses. God doth not value that man's service, who accounts not his service a privilege and a pleasure.

2. Dullness is not suitable to the duty. Gospel-duties are to be performed with a gospel-disposition. God's people ought to be a willing people, Psalm 110:3, a people of willingness: as though in prayer no other faculty of the soul had its exercise but the will. This must breathe fully in every word; as the spirit in Ezekiel's wheels. Delight, like the angel, Judges 13:20, must ascend in the smoke and flame of the soul. Though there be a kind of union by contemplations yet the real union is by affection. A man cannot be said to be a spiritual king, if he doth not present his performances with a royal and prince-like spirit. It is for vigorous wrestling that Jacob is called a prince, Gen. 32:28.

This disposition is essential to grace. Natural men are described to be of a heavy and weary spirit in the offering of sacrifices, Mal. 1:13. It was but a sickly lame lamb they brought for an offering, and yet they were weary of it; that which was not fit for their table, they thought fit for the altar.

In the handling this doctrine I shall shew,
1. What this delight is.
2. Whence it springs.
3. The reasons of the doctrine.
4. The use.

1. WHAT THIS DELIGHT IS.

Delight properly is an affection of the mind that springs from the possession of the good which hath been ardently desired. This is the top stone, the highest step; delight is but an embryo till it come to fruition, and that certain and immutable: otherwise, if there be probability or possibility of losing that which we have present possession of, the fear of it is as a drop of gall that infects the sweetness of this passion; delight properly is a silencing of desire, and the banquet of the soul on the presence of its desired Objection.

But there is a delight of a lower stamp.

1. In desires. There is a delight in desire, as
well as in fruition. A cheerfulness in labor, as
well as in attainment. The desire of Canaan
made the good Israelites cheerful in the wilderness. There is an beginning delight in motion,
but a consummate delight in rest and fruition.

2. In hopes. Desired happiness affects the
soul; much more expected happiness. "We
rejoice in the hope of the glory of God," Rom.
5:2. Joy is the natural issue of a well-grounded
hope. A tottering expectation will engender
but a tottering delight: such a delight will mad
men have, which is rather to be pitied than
desired. But if an imaginary hope can affect the
heart with some real joy, much more a hope
settled upon a sure bottom, and raised upon a
good foundation, there may be joy in a title as
well as in possession.

3. In contemplation. The consideration and
serious thoughts of heaven do affect a gracious
heart, and fill it with pleasure, though itself be
as if in a wilderness. The near approach to
a desired good doth much affect the heart.
Moses was surely more pleased with the sight
of Canaan from Pisgah, than with the hopes
of it in the desert. A traveler's delight is more
raised when he is nearest his journey's end, and
a hungry stomach hath a greater joy when he
sees the meat approaching which must satisfy
the appetite. As the union with the object is
nearer, so the delight is stronger. Now this
delight the soul hath in duty, is not a delight of
fruition, but of desire, hope, or contemplation;
Gaudium viae, not *patriae* [a delight of the journey, not of the home].

1. We may consider delight as active or passive.

1. Active: which is an act of our souls in our
approaches to God. When the heart, like the
sun, rouseth up itself as a giant to run a spiritual race.

2. Passive: which is God's dispensation in
approaches to us, and often met with in our
cheerful addresses to God, "Thou meetest him
that rejoiceth and worketh righteousness," Isa.
64:5. When we delightfully draw close about
the throne of grace, God doth often cast his
arms about our necks: especially when cheerful prayer is accompanied with a cheerful

obedience. This joy is, when Christ meets us
in prayer with a "Be of good cheer, thy sins
are forgiven," thy request granted. The active
delight is the health of the soul, the passive is
the good complexion of the soul. The one is
man's duty, the other God's peculiar gift. The
one is the inseparable property of the new
birth, the other a separable privilege. There
may be a joy in God when there is little joy
from God. There may be gold in the mine,
when no flowers are on the surface.

2. We may consider delight as settled or transient: As spiritual or sensitive.

1. A settled delight. In strong and grown
Christians, when prayer proceeds out of a
thankfulness to God, a judicious knowledge
and apprehension of God. The nearer to God
the more delight; as the motion of a stone is
most speedy when nearest its center.

2. A sensitive delight. As in persons troubled
in mind, there may be a kind of delight in
prayer, because there is some sense of ease in
the very venting itself; and in some, because
of the novelty of a duty they were not accustomed to before. Many prayers may be put up
by persons in necessity without any spiritual
delight in them; as crazy persons take more
medicine than those that are healthy, yet they
delight not in that medicine. The Pharisee
could pray longer, and perhaps with some
delight too, but upon a sensual ground, with
a proud and a vaunting kind of cheerfulness,
a delight in himself, when the publican had
a more spiritual delight; though a humble
Sorrow in the consideration of his own vileness, yet a delight in the consideration of
God's mercy.

This sensitive delight may be more sensible
in a young, than in a grown Christian. There
is a more sensible affection at the first meeting of friends, though more solid after some
converse; as there is a love which is called the
love of the espousals. As it is in sorrow for
sin, so in this delight: a young convert hath
a greater torrent, a grown Christian a more
constant stream; as at the first conversion of
a sinner there is an overflowing joy among
the angels, which we read not of after, though,
without question, there is a settled joy in them
at the growth of a Christian. An elder son may

have a delight in his father's presence, more rooted, firm, and rational, than a younger child that clings more about him with affectionate expressions. As sincerity is the soul of all graces and duties, so this delight is the luster and embroidery of them.

Now this delight in prayer,

1. It is an inward and hearty delight. As to the subject of it, it is seated in the heart. A man in prayer may have a cheerful countenance and a drowsy spirit. The Spirit of God dwells in the heart, and love and joy are the first-fruits of it. Gal. 5:22. Love to duty, and joy in it; joy as a grace, not as a mere comfort. As God is hearty in offering mercy, so is the soul in petitioning for it. There is a harmony between God and the heart. Where there is delight, there is great pains taken with the heart; a gracious heart strikes itself again and again, as Moses did the rock twice. Those ends which God hath in giving, are a Christian's end in asking. Now the more of our hearts in the requests, the more of God's heart in the grants. The emphasis of mercy is God's whole heart and whole soul in it, Jer. 32:41. So the emphasis of duty is our whole heart and whole soul. As without God's cheerful answering, a gracious soul would not relish a mercy, so without our hearty asking, God doth not relish our prayer.

2. It is a delight in God, who is the object of prayer. The glory of God, communion with him, enjoyment of him, is the great end of a believer in his supplications. That delight which is in prayer, is chiefly in it as a means conducing to such an end, and is but a spark of that delight which the soul hath in the object of prayer. God is the center wherein the soul rests, and the end which the soul aims at. According to our apprehensions of God are our desires for him; when we apprehend him as the chiefest good, we shall desire him, and delight in him as the chiefest good. There must first be a delight in God, before there can be a spiritual delight, or a permanency in duty. "Will he delight himself in the Almighty? Will he always call upon God?" Job 27:10. Delight is a grace; and as faith, desire, and love, have God for their object, so hath this. And according to the strength of our delight in the object or end, is the strength of our delight in the means of

attainment. When we delight in God as glorious, we shall delight to honor him; when we regard him as good, we shall delight to pursue and enjoy him, and delight in that which brings us to an intercourse with him. He that rejoices in God, will rejoice in every approach to him. "The joy of the Lord is our strength," Neh. 8:10. The more joy in God, the more strength to come to him. The lack of this is the reason of our snail-like motion to him. Men have no sweet thoughts of God, and therefore no mind to converse with him. We cannot judge our delight in prayer to be right, if we have not a delight in God; for natural men may have a delight in prayer, when they have corrupt and selfish ends; they may have a delight in a duty, as it is a means, according to their apprehensions, to gain such an end: As Balaam and Balak offered their sacrifice cheerfully, hoping to ingratiate themselves with God, and to have liberty to curse his people.

3. A delight in the precepts and promises of God, which are the ground and rules of prayer. First, David delights in God's testimonies, and then calls upon him with his whole heart. A gracious heart must first delight in precepts and promises, before it can turn them into prayers: for prayer is nothing else but a presenting God with his own promise, desiring to work that in us and for us which he hath promised to us. None was more cheerful in prayer than David, because none was more rejoicing in the statutes of God. God's statutes were his songs, Psalm 119:54. And the divine Word was sweeter to him than the honey and the honey-comb. If our hearts leap not at divine promises, we are like to have but drowsy souls in desiring them. If our eye be not upon the dainties God sets before us, our desires cannot be strong for him. If we have no delight in the great charters of heaven, the rich legacies of God, how can we sue for them? If we delight not in the covenant of grace, we shall not delight in prayers for grace. It was the hopes of reward made Moses so valiant in suffering, and the joy set before Christ in a promise, made him so cheerful in enduring the shame, Heb. 12:1, 2.

4. A delight in prayer itself. A Christian's heart is in secret ravished into heaven. There is a delight in coming near God, and warming the soul by the fire of his love.

The angels are cheerful in the act of praise; their work is their glory. A holy soul doth so delight in this duty, that if there were no command to engage him, no promise to encourage him, he would be stepping into God's courts. He thinks it not a good day that passeth without some intercourse with God. David would have taken up his lodgings in the courts of God, and regards it as the only blessedness, Psalm 65:4. And so great a delight he had in being in God's presence, that he envies the birds the happiness of building their nests near his tabernacle. A delight there is in the holiness of prayer; a natural man under some troubles may delight in God's comforting and easing presence, but not in his sanctifying presence. He may delight to pray to God as a store-house to supply his wants, but not as a refiner's fire to purge away his dross. "Prayer, as praise, is a melody to God in the heart," Eph. 5:19. And the soul loves to be fingering the instrument and touching the strings.

5. A delight in the things asked. This heavenly cheerfulness is most in heavenly things. What delight others have in asking worldly goods, a gracious heart hath in begging the light of God's countenance. That soul cannot be dull in prayer that seriously considers he prays for no less than heaven and happiness; no less than the glory of the great God. A gracious man is never weary of spiritual things, as men are never weary of the sun, but though it is enjoyed every day, yet long for the rising of it again. From this delight in the matter of prayer it is that the saints have redoubled and repeated their petitions, and redoubled the Amen at the end of prayer, to manifest the great affections to those things they have asked. The soul loves to think of those things the heart is set upon; and frequent thoughts express a delight.

6. A delight in those graces and affections which are exercised in prayer. A gracious heart is most delighted with that prayer wherein grace hath been more stirring, and gracious affections have been boiling over. The soul desires not only to speak to God, but to make melody to God; the heart is the instrument, but graces are the strings, and prayer the touching them, and therefore he is more displeased with the flagging of his graces than with missing an answer. There may he a delight in gifts, in a man's own gifts, in the gifts of another, in the pomp and varnish of devotion; but a delight in exercising spiritual graces is an ingredient in this true delight. The Pharisees are marked by Christ to make long prayers; vaunting in an outward bravery of words, as if they were playing the courtiers with God, and complimenting him: but the publican had a short prayer, but more grace, "Lord be merciful to me a sinner"; there is reliance and humility. A gracious heart labors to bring flaming affections; and if he cannot bring flaming grace, he will bring smoking grace: he desires the preparation of his heart as well as the answer of his prayer, Psalm 10:17.

2. WHENCE THIS DELIGHT SPRINGS

1. From the Spirit of God. Not a spark of fire upon our own hearth is able to kindle this spiritual delight; it is the Holy Ghost that breathes such a heavenly heat into our affections. The Spirit is the fire that kindles the soul, the spring that moves the watch, the wind that drives the ship. The swiftest ship with spread sails will be but sluggish in its motion, unless the wind fills its sails; without this Spirit we are but in a weak and sickly condition, our breath but short, a heavy and troublesome asthma is upon us. "When I cried unto thee, thou didst strengthen me with strength in my soul." Psalm 138:3. As prayer is the work of the Spirit in the heart, so doth delight in prayer owe itself to the same author. God will make them joyful in his house of prayer, Isa. 56:7.

2. From grace. The Spirit kindles, but gives us the oil of grace to make the lamp burn clear. There must not only be wind to drive, but sails to catch it; a prayer without grace is a prayer without wings. There must be grace to begin it. A dead man cannot rejoice in his land, money, or food; be cannot act, and therefore cannot be cheerful in action. Cheerfulness supposeth life; dead men cannot perform a duty, "The dead praise not the Lord," (Psalm 115:17), nor dead souls a cheerful duty. There must not only be grace infused, but grace actuated. No man in a sleep or swoon can rejoice. There must not only be a living principle, but a lively operation. If the sap lurk only in the root, the branches can bring forth no fruit: our best prayers without the sap of grace diffusing

itself, will be but as withered branches. Grace actuated puts heat into performances, without which they are but benumbed and frozen, (Reynolds). Just as a rusty key will not unlock a door, rusty grace will not enlarge the heart. There must be grace to maintain it. There is not only need of fire to kindle the lamp, but of oil to preserve the flame. Natural men may have their affections kindled in a way of common working, but they will presently faint and die, as the flame of cotton will dim and vanish, if there be no oil to nourish it. There is a temporary joy in hearing the word; and if in one duty, why not in another? Why not in prayer? Like a fire of thorns that makes a great blaze but a short stay, Matt. 13:20.

3. From a good conscience. "A good heart is a continual feast," Prov. 15:15. He that hath a good conscience must needs be cheerful in his religious and civil duties. Guilt will come trembling, and with a sad countenance, into the presence of God's majesty. A guilty child cannot with cheerfulness come into a displeased father's presence. A soul smoked with hell, cannot with delight approach to he heaven. Guilty souls, in regard of the injury they have done to God, will be afraid to come; and in regard of the soot of sin wherewith they are defiled, and the blackness they have contracted, they will be ashamed to come. They know that by their sins they should provoke his anger, not allure his love. A soul under conscience of sin cannot up to God, Psalm 40:12. Nor will God with favor look down upon it, Psalm 59:8. It must be a pure heart that must see him with pleasure, Matt. 5:8. And pure hands must be lifted up to him, 1 Tim. 2:8. Jonah was asleep after his sin, and was outdone in readiness to pray even by idolaters. The mariners jog him, but could not get him, that we read of, to call upon that God whom he had offended, Jonah chap. 1. Where there is corruption, the sparks of sin will kindle that tinder, and weaken a spiritual delight. A perfect heart and a willing mind are put together, 1 Chron. 29:9. There cannot be willingness without sincerity, nor sincerity without willingness.

4. From a holy and frequent familiarity with God. Where there is a great familiarity there is a great delight; delight in one anoth-er's company, and delight in one another's converse; strangeness contracts, and familiarity enlarges the soul. There is more swiftness in going to a God with whom we are acquainted, than to a God to whom we are strangers. This encourages the soul to go to God; I go to a God whose face I have seen, whose goodness I have tasted, with whom I have often met in prayer. Frequent familiarity makes us more understanding of the excellency of another; an excellency understood will be beloved, and being beloved, will be delighted in.

5. From hopes of receiving. There is an delight which ariseth from hopes of enjoying. "Rejoicing in hope," Rom. 12:12. There cannot be a pleasant motion where there is a paralysis of doubts. How full of delight must that soul be that can plead a promise, and carry God's hand and seal to heaven, and shew him his own bond; when it can be pleaded not only as a favor to engage his mercy, but in some sense a debt to engage his truth and righteousness! Christ in his prayer, which was his swan-like song (John 17), pleads the terms of the covenant between his Father and himself; "I have glorified thee on earth, glorify me with that glory I had with thee before the world was." This is the case of a delightful approach, when we carry a covenant of grace with us for ourselves, and a promise of security and perpetuity for the church. Upon this account we have more cause of a pleasant motion to God than the ancient believers had. Fear motivated them under the law; love motivates us under the gospel. He cannot but delight in prayer that hath arguments Of God's own framing to plead with God, who cannot deny his own arguments and reasonings. Little comfort can be sucked from a perhaps. But when we come to seek covenant-mercies, God's faithfulness to his covenant puts the mercy past a perhaps. We come to a God sitting upon a throne of grace, upon Mount Sion, not on Mount Sinai; to a God that desires our presence, more than we desire his assistance.

6. From a sense of former mercies. If manna be rained down, it doth not only take off our thoughts from Egyptian garlic, but quickens our desires for a second shower. A sense of God's majesty will make us lose our showy self-satisfaction; and a sense of God's love

will make us lose our dumpishness. We may as well come again with a merry heart, when God accepts our prayers, as go away and eat our bread with joy when God accepts our works, Eccles. 9:7. The doves will readily fly to the windows where they have formerly found shelter; and the beggar to the door where he hath often received alms. "Because he hath inclined his ear to hear me, therefore will I call upon him as long as I live," Psalm 116:2. I have found refuge with God before; I have found my wants supplied, my soul raised, my temptations checked, my doubts answered, and my prayers accepted, therefore I will repeat my appeals with cheerfulness.

I might also add other causes; as a love to God, a heavenliness of spirit, a consideration of Christ's intercession, a deep humiliation. The more unpleasant sin is to our relish, the more delightful will God be, and the more cheerful our souls in addresses to him. The more unpleasant sin is to us, the more spiritual our souls are; and the more spiritual our souls, the more spiritual our affections; the more stony, the more lumpish and unable to move; the more contrite, the more supple. Another cause is a spiritual taste: a report of a thing may give some pleasure, but a taste greater.

3. REASONS

Without cheerful seeking we cannot have a gracious answer.

1. God will not give an answer to those prayers that dishonor him. A flat and dumpish attitude is not for his honor. The heathens themselves thought their gods should not be put off with a sacrifice dragged to the altar. We do not read of lead, that lumpish earthly metal, employed about the tabernacle or temple, but the purer and most glittering sorts of metals. God will have the most excellent service, because he is the most excellent being. He will have the most delightful service, because he bestows the most delightful and excellent gifts. All sacrifices were to be offered up with fire, which is the quickest and most active element. It is a dishonor to so great, so glorious a majesty, to put him off with such low and dead-hearted services. Those petitions cannot expect an answer, which are offered in a manner injurious to the person we address them to. It is

not for the credit of our great Master to have his servants dejected in his work: As though His service were an uncomfortable thing; as though God were a wilderness, and the world a paradise.

2. Dull and lumpish prayer doth not reach him, and therefore cannot expect an answer. Such desires are as arrows that sink down at our feet; there is no force to carry them to heaven: The heart is an unbent bow that hath no strength. When God will hear, he makes first a prepared heart, Psalm 10:17. He first strings the instrument, and then receives the sound. An enlarged heart only runs, Psalm 119:32. A contracted heart moves slowly, and often faints in the journey.

3. Lumpishness speaks an unwillingness that God should hear us. It speaks a kind of a fear that God should grant our petitions. He that puts up a petition to a prince coldly and dully, gives him good reason to think that he doth not care for an answer. That husbandman hath no great mind to harvest, that is lazy in tilling his ground and sowing his seed. How can we think God should delight to read over our petitions, when we take so little delight in presenting them? God gives not mercy to an unwilling person. The first thing God doth, is to make his people willing. Dull spirits seek God as if they did not care for finding him: such tempers either account not God real, or their petitions unnecessary.

4. Without delight we are not fit to receive a mercy. Delight in a mercy wanted, makes room for desire; and large desires make room for mercy. If no delight in begging, there will be no delight in enjoying. If there be no cheerfulness to quicken our prayers when we need a blessing, there will be little joy to quicken our praise when we receive a blessing. A weak, sickly stomach, is not fit to be seated at a plentiful table. Where there is a dull asking supply, there is none, or a very dull sense of wants. Now, God will not send His mercies but to a soul that will welcome them. The deeper the sense of our wants, the higher the estimation of our supplies. A cheerful soul is fit to receive the least, and fit to receive the greatest mercy. He will more prize a little mercy, than a dull petitioner shall prize a greater, because he hath a sense of his wants. If Zaccheus had not a

great joy at the news of Christ's coming by his door, he would not have so readily entertained and welcomed him.

USE 1. OF INFORMATION

1. There is a great pleasure in the ways of God, if rightly understood. Prayer, which is a duty wherein we express our wants, is delightful. There is more sweetness in a Christian's asking, than in a wicked man's enjoying blessings.

2. What delight will there be in heaven! If there be such sweetness in desire, what will there be in a full fruition! If there is joy in seeking, what is there then in finding! Duty hath its sweets, its thousands; but glory its ten thousands. If the pleasure of the seed-time be so great, what will the pleasure of the harvest be!

3. The miserable condition of those who can delight in any thing but prayer. It is an aggravation of our enmity to God, when we can sin cheerfully and pray dully: when duty is more loathsome than iniquity.

USE 2. OF EXAMINATION

We pray; but how are our hearts? If it be for what concerns our momentary being, is not our running like the running of Ahimaaz? But when for spiritual things, do not our hearts sink within us, like Nabal's? Let us, therefore, observe our hearts closely; allow them not to give us the slip in our examination of them; resolve not to take the first answer, but search to the bottom.

1. Whether we delight at all in prayer.

1. How do we prize the opportunities of duty? There is an opportunity of an earthly, and an opportunity of a heavenly gain; consider which our hearts more readily close with. Can we with much pleasure follow a vain world, and heartlessly welcome an opportunity of duty, delight more with Judas in bags, than in Christ's company? This is sad! But are praying opportunities our festival times? Do we go to the house of God with the voice of joy and praise?

2. Whether we seek excuses to avoid a present duty, when conscience and opportunity urge and invite us to it? Are our souls more skilful in delays than in performances? Are there no excuses when sin calls us, and studied put-offs

when God invites us? Like the sluggard, folding our arms, yet a little while longer? Or do our hearts rise and beat quick against frivolous excuses that step in to hinder us from prayer?

3. How are our hearts affected in prayer? Are we more ready to pray ourselves asleep, than into a vigorous frame? Do we enter into it with some life, and find our hearts quickly tire and fatigue us? Are we more awake when we are up, than we were all the time upon our knees? Are our hearts in prayer like withered sapless things, and very quick afterwards if any worldly business invite us? Are we like logs and blocks in prayer, and like a roe upon the mountains in earthly concerns? Surely what our pulse beats quickest to, is the object most delighted in.

4. What time is it we choose for prayer? Is it not our drowsiest and laziest time, when our nods are as many, or more than our petitions; as though the dullest time, and the deadest state of mind were most suitable to a rising God? Do we come with our hearts full of the world, to pray for heaven? Or do we pick out the most lively seasons? Luther chose those hours for prayer and meditation wherein he found himself most lively for study.

5. Do we not often wish a duty over? As those in the prophet that were glad when the Sabbath was over, that they might run to their buying and selling? Or, are we of Peter's temper, and express Peter's language? It is good to be here with Christ on the mount.

6. Do we prepare ourselves by delightful and enlivening considerations? Do we think of the precept of God, which should spur us, and of the promise of God which should allure us? Do we rub our souls to heat them, Do we blow them to kindle them into a flame? Do we send up quick prayers for a quickening spirit? If thoughts of God be a burden, requests to him will not be a pleasure. If we have a coldness in our thoughts of God and duty, we can have no warmth in our desire, no delight in our petitions.

7. Do we content ourselves with dull motions, or do we give check to them? Can we, though our hearts be never so lazy, stroke ourselves at the end, and call ourselves good and faithful servants? Do we take our souls to task afterwards, and examine why they are so lazy, why

644 THE ENCYCLOPEDIA OF PRAYER AND PRAISE

so heavy? Do we inquire into the causes of our deadness? A gracious soul is more troubled at its dullness in prayer, than a natural conscience is at the omission of prayer. He will complain of his sluggishness and mend his pace.

2. If we find we have a delight, let us examine whether it be a delight of the right kind.

1. Do we delight in it because of the gift we have ourselves, or the gift of others we join with? A man may rejoice in hearing the word, not because of the holiness and spirituality of the matter, but because of the goodness of the dress, and the elegancy of the expression. Ezek. 33:32; The prophet was unto them as a lovely song; as one that kind a pleasant voice. He may, upon the same ground, delight in prayer. But this is a temper not kindled by the true fire of the sanctuary. Or, do we delight in it, not when our tongues are most quick, but our hearts most warm; not because we have the best words, but the most spiritualized affections? We may have angels' gifts in prayer, without an angel's spirit.

2. Is there a delight in all parts of a duty? Not only in asking temporal blessings, or some spiritual, as pardoning mercy, but in begging for refining grace? Are we earnest only when we have bosom quarrels and conscience-convulsions, but tire when we come to pray for sanctifying mercy? The cause of this is a sense of discomfort with the trouble and danger, not with the sin and cause.

3. Doth our delight in prayer and spiritual things outdo our delight in outward things? The Psalmist's joy in God was more than his delight in the harvest of vintage, Psalm 4:7. Are we like ravens that delight to hover in the air sometimes, but our greatest delight is to feed upon carrion? Though we have, and may have a sensible delight in worldly things, yet is it as solid and rational as that we have in duty?

4. Is our delight in prayer a humble delight? Is it a rejoicing with humbling? "Serve the Lord with gladness, and rejoice before him with trembling," Psalm 2:11. If our service be right, it will be cheerful, and if truly cheerful, it will be humble.

5. Is our delight in prayer accompanied with a delight in waiting? Do we, like merchants, not only delight in the first launching of a ship, or the setting it out of the haven with a full freight; but also in expectations of a rich return of spiritual mercies? Do we delight to pray, though God for the present doth not delight to give, and wait, like David, with an owning God's wisdom in delaying? Or do we shoot them only as arrows at random, and never look after them where they strike, or where to find them?

6. Is our delight in praising God when mercy comes, answerable to the delight in praying when a wanted mercy was begged? The ten lepers desired mercy with an equal cheerfulness, in hopes of having their leprosy cured; but only the one who returned expressed genuine delight. As he prayed with a loud voice, so he praised with a loud voice, Luke, 17:13, 15. And Christ tells him, his faith had made him whole. As he had an answer in the way of grace, so he had before a gracious delight in his asking; the others had a natural delight, and so a return in the way of common providence.

USE 3. OF EXHORTATION.

Let us delight in prayer. God loves a cheerful giver in alms, and a cheerful petitioner in prayer. God would have his children free with him. He takes special notice of a spiritual frame, "who hath engaged his heart" Jer. 30:21. The more delight we have in God, the more delight he will have in us. He takes no pleasure in a lumpish service. It is an uncomely sight to see a joyful sinner and a dumpish petitioner. Why should we not exercise as much joy in holy duties, as formerly we did in sinful practices? How delightfully will men sit at their games, and spend their days in gluttony and luxury? And shall not a Christian find much more delight in applying himself to God? We should delight that we can, and have hearts to ask such gifts, that thousands in the world never dream of begging. To be dull, is a discontentedness with our own petitions. Delight in prayer is the way to gain assurance. To seek God, and treat him as our chiefest good, endears the soul to him. Delighting in accesses to him, will enflame our love. And there is no greater sign of an interest in him than a powerful estimation of him. God casts off none that affectionately clasp about his throne.

To this purpose,

1. Pray for quickening grace. How often do we find David upon his knees for it? God only gives this grace, and God only stirs this grace.

2. Meditate on the promises you intend to plead. Unbelief is the great root of all dumpishness. It was by the belief of the word we had life at first, and by an exercise of that belief we gain liveliness. What maintains our love will maintain our delight; the amiableness of God, and the excellency of the promises, are the incentives and fuel both of the one and of the other. Think that they are eternal things you are to pray for and that you have as much invitation to beg them, and as good a promise to attain them, as David, Paul, or any other ever had. How would this awaken our drowsy souls, and elevate our heavy hearts, and open the lazy eye-lids to look up! And whatever meditation we find begin to kindle our souls, let us follow it on, that the spark may not go out.

3. Choose the time when your hearts are most revived. Observe when God sends an invitation, and hoist up the sails when the wind begins to blow. There is no Christian but hath one time or an another a greater activeness of spirit. Choose none of those seasons which may quench the heat, and dull the sprightliness of your affection. Resolve beforehand this, to delight yourselves in the Lord, and thereby you shall gain the desire of your hearts.

Stephen Charnock, 1628–80

Homily on the Lord's Prayer
John Chrysostom

"Take heed that ye do not your alms before men, to be seen of them." [Matt. 6:1]

1. He roots out in what remains the most tyrannical passion of all, the rage and madness with respect to vainglory, which springs up in them that do right.

For at first He had not at all discoursed about it; it being indeed superfluous, before He had persuaded them to do any of the things which they ought, to teach in which way they should practice and pursue them.

But after He had led them on to self-command, then He proceeds to purge away also the alloy which secretly subsists with it.

For this disease is by no means of random birth; but when we have duly performed many of the commandments. It behooved therefore first to implant virtue, and then to remove the passion which mars its fruit.

And see with what He begins, with fasting, and prayer, and almsgiving: for in these good deeds most especially is it wont to make its haunt. The Pharisee, for instance, was hereby puffed up, who saith, "I fast twice a week, I give tithes of my substance" (Luke 19:12). And he was vainglorious too in his very prayer, making it for display. For since there was no one else present, he pointed himself out to the publican, saying, "I am not as the rest of men, nor even as this publican."

And mark how Christ began, as though He were speaking of some wild beast, hard to catch, and crafty to deceive him who was not very watchful. Thus, "take heed," saith He, "as to your alms." So Paul also speaks to the Philippians; "Beware of dogs" (Philippians 3:2). And with reason, for the evil beast comes in upon us secretly, and without noise puffs all away, and unobservedly carries out all that is within.

Forasmuch then as He had made much discourse about almsgiving, and brought forward God, "Who maketh His sun to rise on the evil and the good" (Matt. 5:45), and by motives from all quarters had urged them on to this, and had persuaded them to exult in the abundance of their giving; He finishes by taking away also all things that encumber this fair olive tree. For which same cause He saith, "Take heed that ye do not your alms before men," for that which was before mentioned, is "God's" almsgiving.

2. And when He had said, "not to do it before men," He added, "to be seen of them."

And though it seems as if the same thing were said a second time, yet if any one give particular attention, it is not the same thing, but one is different from the other; and it hath great security, and unspeakable care and tenderness. For it may be, both that one doing alms before men may not do it to be seen of them, and again that one not doing it before men may do it to be seen of them. Wherefore it is not simply the thing, but the intent, which He both punishes and rewards. And unless such exactness were employed, this would make many more backward about the giving of alms, because it is not on every occasion altogether possible to do it secretly. For this cause, setting thee free from this restraint, He defines both the penalty and the reward not by the result of the action, but by the intention of the doer.

That is, that thou mayest not say, "What? am I then the worse, should another see?" – "it is not this," saith He, "that I am seeking, but the mind that is in thee, and the tone of what thou doest." For His will is to bring our soul altogether into frame, and to deliver it from every disease. Now having, as you see, forbidden men's acting for display, and having taught them the penalty thence ensuing, namely, to do it vainly, and for naught, He again rouses their spirits by putting them in mind of the Father, and of Heaven, that not by the loss alone He might sting them, but also shame them by the recollection of Him who gave them being. "For ye have no reward," saith He, "with your Father which is in Heaven." (Matt. 6:1).

Nor even at this did He stop, but proceeds yet further, by other motives also increasing their disgust. For as above He set forth publicans and heathens, by the quality of the person shaming their imitators, so also in this place the hypocrites. "Therefore when thou doest thine alms," saith He, "do not sound a trumpet before thee, as the hypocrites do" (Matt. 6:2). Not that they had trumpets, but He means to display the greatness of their frenzy, by the use of this figure of speech, deriding and making a shows of them hereby.

And well hath He called them "hypocrites" for the mask was of mercy, but the spirit of cruelty and inhumanity. For they do it, not because they pity their neighbors, but that they themselves may enjoy credit; and this came of the utmost cruelty; while another was perishing with hunger, to be seeking vainglory, and not putting an end to his suffering.

It is not then the giving alms which is required, but the giving as one ought, the giving for such and such an end.

Having then amply derided those men, and having handled them so, that the hearer should be even ashamed of them, He again corrects thoroughly the mind which is so distempered: and having said how we ought not to act, He signifies on the other hand how we ought to act. How then ought we to do our alms? "Let not thy left hand know," saith He, "what thy right hand doeth." (Matt. 6:3).

Here again His enigmatical meaning is not of the hands, but He hath put the thing hyperbolically. As thus: "If it can be," saith He, "for thyself not to know it, let this be the object of thine endeavor; that, if it were possible, it may be concealed from the very hands that minister." It is not, as some say, that we should hide it from wrong-headed men, for He hath here commanded that it should be concealed from all.

And then the reward too; consider how great it is. For after He had spoken of the punishment from the one, He points out also the honor derived from the other; from either side urging them, and leading them on to high lessons. Yea, for He is persuading them to know that God is everywhere present, and that not by our present life are our interests limited, but a yet more awful tribunal will receive us when we go hence, and the account of all our doings, and honors, and punishments: and that no one will be hid in doing anything either great or small, though he seem to be hid from men. For all this did He darkly signify, when He said, "Thy Father which seeth in secret shall reward thee openly" (Matt. 6:4). Setting for him a great and august assemblage of spectators, and what He desires, that very thing bestowing on him in great abundance. "For what," saith He, "dost thou wish? is it not to have some to be spectators of what is going on? Behold then, thou hast some; not angels, nor archangels, but the God of all." And if thou desire to have men also as spectators, neither of this desire doth He deprive thee at the fitting season, but rather in greater abundance affords it unto thee. For, if thou shouldest now make a display, thou wilt be able to make it to ten only, or twenty, or (we will say) a hundred persons: but if thou take pains to lie hid now, God Himself will then proclaim thee in the presence of the whole universe. Wherefore above all, if thou wilt have men see thy good deeds, hide them now, that then all may look on them with the more honor, God making them manifest, and extolling them, and proclaiming them before all. Again, whereas now they that behold will rather condemn thee as vainglorious; when they see thee crowned, so far from condemning, they will even admire thee, all of them. When therefore by waiting a little, thou mayest both receive a reward, and reap greater admiration; consider what folly it is to cast thyself out of both these; and while thou art seeking thy reward from God, and while God is beholding, to summon men for the display of what is going on. Why, if display must be made of our love, to our Father above all should we make it; and this most especially, when our Father hath the power both to crown and to punish.

And let me add, even were there no penalty, it were not meet for him who desires glory, to let go this our theatre, and take in exchange that of men. For who is there so wretched, as that when the king was hastening to come and see his achievements, he would let him go, and make up his assembly of spectators of poor men and beggars? For this cause then, He not only commands to make no display, but even to take pains to be concealed: it not being at all the same, not to strive for publicity, and to strive for concealment.

3. "And when ye pray," saith He, "ye shall not be as the hypocrites, for they love to pray standing in the synagogues, and in the corners of the streets. Verily I say unto you, they have their reward" (Matt. 6:5). "But thou, when thou prayest, enter into thy closet, and when thou hast shut thy door, pray to thy Father which is in secret." (Matt. 6:6).

These too again He calls "hypocrites," and very fitly; for while they are feigning to pray to God, they are looking round after men; wearing the garb not of suppliants, but of ridiculous persons. For he, who is to do a suppliant's office, letting go all other, looks to him alone, who hath power to grant his request. But if thou leave this one, and go about wandering and casting around thine eyes everywhere, thou wilt depart with empty hands. For this was thine own will. Wherefore He said not, "such shall not receive a reward," but, "they have it out:" that is, they shall indeed receive one, but from those of whom they themselves desire to have it. For God wills not this: He rather for His part was willing to bestow

on men the recompense that comes from Himself; but they seeking that which is from men, can be no longer justly entitled to receive from Him, for whom they have done nothing.

But mark, I pray thee, the loving-kindness of God, in that He promises to bestow on us a reward, even for those good things which we ask of Him. Having then discredited them, who order not this duty as they ought, both from the place and from their disposition of mind, and having shown that they are very ridiculous: He introduces the best manner of prayer, and again gives the reward, saying, "Enter into thy closet."

"What then," it may be said, "ought we not to pray in church?" Indeed we ought by all means, but in such a spirit as this. Because everywhere God seeks the intention of all that is done. Since even if thou shouldest enter into thy closet, and having shut the door, shouldest do it for display, the doors will do thee no good.

It is worth observing in this case also, how exact the definition, which He made when He said, "That they may appear unto men." So that even if thou shut the doors, this He desires thee duly to perform, rather than the shutting of the doors, even to shut the doors of the mind. For as in everything it is good to be freed from vainglory, so most especially in prayer. For if even without this, we wander and are distracted, when shall we attend unto the things which we are saying, should we enter in having this disease also? And if we who pray and beseech attend not, how do we expect God to attend?

4. But yet some there are, who after such and so earnest charges, behave themselves so unseemly in prayer, that even when their person is concealed, they make themselves manifest to all by their voice, crying out disorderly, and rendering themselves objects of ridicule both by gesture and voice.

Seest thou not that even in a market place, should any one come up doing like this, and begging clamorously, he wilt drive away him whom he is petitioning; but if quietly, and with the proper gesture, then he rather wins over him that can grant the favor?

Let us not then make our prayer by the

gesture of our body, nor by the loudness of our voice, but by the earnestness of our mind: neither with noise and clamor and for display, so as even to disturb those that are near us, but with all modesty, and with contrition in the mind, and with inward tears.

But art thou pained in mind, and canst not help crying aloud? yet surely it is the part of one exceedingly pained to pray and entreat even as I have said. Since Moses too was pained, and prayed in this way and was heard; for this cause also God said unto him, "Wherefore criest thou unto me" (Exodus 14:15). And Hannah too again, her voice not being heard, accomplished all she wished, forasmuch as her heart cried out. But Abel prayed not only when silent, but even when dying, and his blood sent forth a cry more clear than a trumpet.

Do thou also then groan, even as that holy one, I forbid it not. "Rend," as the prophet commanded, "thine heart, and not thy garments" (Joel 2:13). Out of deeps call upon God, for it is said, "Out of the depths have I cried to Thee, O Lord" (Psalm 129 (130):1). From beneath, out of the heart, draw forth a voice, make thy prayer a mystery. Seest thou not that even in the houses of kings all tumult is put away, and great on all sides is the silence? Do thou also therefore, entering as into a palace, – not that on the earth, but what is far more awful than it, that which is in heaven, – show forth great seemliness. Yea, for thou art joined to the choirs of angels, and art in communion with archangels, and art singing with the seraphim. And all these tribes show forth much goodly order, singing with great awe that mystical strain, and their sacred hymns to God, the King of all. With these then mingle thyself, when thou art praying, and emulate their mystical order.

For not unto men art thou praying, but to God, who is everywhere present, who hears even before the voice, who knows the secrets of the mind. If thou so pray, great is the reward thou shalt receive.

"For thy Father," saith He, "who seeth in secret, shall reward thee openly" (Matt. 6: 4, 6, 18). He said not, "shall freely give thee," but, "shall reward thee;" yea, for He hath made Himself a debtor to thee, and even from this hath honored thee with great honor. For

because He Himself is invisible, He would have thy prayer be so likewise.

5. Then He speaks even the very words of the prayer. "When ye pray," saith He, "use no vain repetitions, even as the heathen do" (Matt. 6:7).

You see that when He was discoursing of almsgiving, He removed only that mischief which comes of vainglory, and added nothing more; neither did He say whence one should give alms; as from honest labor, and not from rapine nor covetousness: this being abundantly acknowledged among all. And also before that, He had thoroughly cleared up this point, when He blessed them "that hunger after righteousness."

But touching prayer, He adds somewhat over and above; "not to use vain repetitions." And as there He derides the hypocrites, so here the heathen; shaming the hearer everywhere most of all by the vileness of the persons. For since this, in most cases, is especially biting and stinging, I mean our appearing to be likened to outcast persons; by this topic He dissuades them; calling frivolousness, here, by the name of "vain repetition:" as when we ask of God things unsuitable, kingdoms, and glory, and to get the better of enemies, and abundance of wealth, and in general what does not at all concern us. "For He knoweth," saith He, "what things ye have need of" (Matt. 6:8). And herewith He seems to me to command in this place, that neither should we make our prayers long; long, I mean, not in time, but in the number and length of the things mentioned. For perseverance indeed in the same requests is our duty: His word being, "continuing instant in prayer" (Rom. 12:12). And He Himself too, by that example of the widow, who prevailed with the pitiless and cruel ruler, by the continuance of her intercession; and by that of the friend, who came late at night time, and roused the sleeper from his bed, not for his friendship's, but for his importunity's sake; what did He, but lay down a law, that all should continually make supplication unto Him? He doth not however bid us compose a prayer of ten thousand clauses, and so come to Him and merely repeat it. For this He obscurely signified when He said, "They think that they shall be heard for their much speaking" (Matt. 6:7).

"For He knoweth," saith He, "what things ye have need of." And if He know, one may say, what we have need of, wherefore must we pray? Not to instruct Him, but to prevail with Him; to be made intimate with Him, by continuance in supplication; to be humbled; to be reminded of thy sins.

6. "After this manner, therefore, pray ye," saith He: "Our Father, which art in heaven" (Matt. 6:9).

See how He straightway stirred up the hearer, and reminded him of all God's bounty in the beginning. For he who calls God Father, by him both remission of sins, and taking away of punishment, and righteousness, and sanctification, and redemption, and adoption, and inheritance, and brotherhood with the Only-Begotten, and the supply of the Spirit, are acknowledged in this single title. For one cannot call God Father, without having attained to all those blessings. Doubly, therefore, doth He awaken their spirit, both by the dignity of Him who is called on, and by the greatness of the benefits which they have enjoyed. But when He saith, "in Heaven," He speaks not this as shutting up God there, but as withdrawing him who is praying from earth, and fixing him in the high places, and in the dwellings above.

He teaches, moreover, to make our prayer common, in behalf of our brethren also. For He saith not, "my Father, which art in Heaven," but, "our Father," offering up his supplications for the body in common, and nowhere looking to his own, but everywhere to his neighbor's good. And by this He at once takes away hatred, and quells pride, and casts out envy, and brings in the mother of all good things, even charity, and exterminates the inequality of human things, and shows how far the equality reaches between the king and the poor man, if at least in those things which are greatest and most indispensable, we are all of us fellows. For what harm comes of our kindred below, when in that which is on high we are all of us knit together, and no one hath aught more than another; neither the rich more than the poor, nor the master than the servant, neither the ruler than the subject, nor the king than the

common soldier, nor the philosopher than the barbarian, nor the skillful than the unlearned? For to all hath He given one nobility, having vouchsafed to be called the Father of all alike.

7. When therefore He hath reminded us of this nobility, and of the gift from above, and of our equality with our brethren, and of charity; and when He hath removed us from earth, and fixed us in Heaven; let us see what He commands us to ask after this.

Not but, in the first place, even that saying alone is sufficient to implant instruction in all virtue. For he who hath called God Father, and a common Father, would be justly bound to show forth such a conversation, as not to appear unworthy of this nobility, and to exhibit a diligence proportionate to the gift. Yet is He not satisfied with this, but adds, also another clause, thus saying, "Hallowed be Thy name" (Matt. 6:9).

Worthy of him who calls God Father, is the prayer to ask nothing before the glory of His Father, but to account all things secondary to the work of praising Him. For "hallowed" is glorified. For His own glory He hath complete, and ever continuing the same, but He commands him who prays to seek that He may be glorified also by our life. Which very thing He had said before likewise, "Let your light so shine before men, that they may see your good works, and glorify your Father which is in heaven" (Matt. 5:16). Yea, and the seraphim too, giving glory, said on this wise, "Holy, holy, holy" (Isa. 6:3). So that "hallowed" means this, viz. "glorified." That is, "vouchsafe," saith he, "that we may live so purely, that through us all may glorify Thee." Which thing again appertains unto perfect self-control, to present to all a life so irreprehensible, that every one of the beholders may offer to the Lord the praise due to Him for this.

"Thy kingdom come" (Matt. 6:10). And this again is the language of a right-minded child, not to be rivetted to things that are seen, neither to account things present some great matter; but to hasten unto our Father, and to long for the things to come. And this springs out of a good conscience, and a soul set free from things that are on earth. This, for instance, Paul himself was longing after every day: wherefore he also said, that "even we ourselves, who have the first-fruits of the Spirit, groan, waiting for an adoption, the redemption of our body" (Rom. 8:23). For he who hath this fondness, can neither be puffed up by the good things of this life, nor abashed by its sorrows; but as though dwelling in the very heavens, is freed from each sort of irregularity. "Thy will be done in earth, as it is in Heaven" (Matt. 6:10).

Behold a most excellent train of thought! in that He bade us indeed long for the things to come, and hasten towards that sojourn; and, till that may be, even while we abide here, so long to be earnest in showing forth the same conversation as those above. For ye must long, saith He, for heaven, and the things in heaven; however, even before heaven, He hath bidden us make the earth a heaven and do and say all things, even while we are continuing in it, as having our conversation there; insomuch that these too should be objects of our prayer to the Lord. For there is nothing to hinder our reaching the perfection of the powers above, because we inhabit the earth; but it is possible even while abiding here, to do all, as though already placed on high. What He saith therefore is this: "As there all things are done without hindrance, and the angels are not partly obedient and partly disobedient, but in all things yield and obey (for He saith, "Mighty in strength, performing His word"); so vouchsafe that we men may not do Thy will by halves, but perform all things as Thou willest."

Seest thou how He hath taught us also to be modest, by making it clear that virtue is not of our endeavors only, but also of the grace from above? And again, He hath enjoined each one of us, who pray, to take upon himself the care of the whole world. For He did not at all say, "Thy will be done" in me, or in us, but everywhere on the earth; so that error may be destroyed, and truth implanted, and all wickedness cast out, and virtue return, and no difference in this respect be henceforth between heaven and earth. "For if this come to pass," saith He, "there will be no difference between things below and above, separated as they are in nature; the earth exhibiting to us another set of angels."

8. "Give us this day our daily bread" (Matt. 6:11).

What is "daily bread"? That for one day. For because He had said thus, "Thy will be done in earth as it is in heaven" (Matt. 6:10), but was discoursing to men encompassed with flesh, and subject to the necessities of nature, and incapable of the same impassibility with the angels: — while He enjoins the commands to be practiced by us also, even as they perform them; He condescends likewise, in what follows, to the infirmity of our nature. Thus, "perfection of conduct," saith He, "I require as great, not however freedom from passions; no, for the tyranny of nature permits it not: for it requires necessary food." But mark, I pray thee, how even in things that are bodily, that which is spiritual abounds. For it is neither for riches, nor for delicate living, nor for costly raiment, nor for any other such thing, but for bread only, that He hath commanded us to make our prayer. And for "daily bread," so as not to "take thought for the morrow" (Matt. 6:34). Because of this He added, "daily bread," that is, bread for one day.

And not even with this expression is He satisfied, but adds another too afterwards, saying, "Give us this day;" so that we may not, beyond this, wear ourselves out with the care of the following day. For that day, the intervals before which thou knowest not whether thou shalt see, wherefore dost thou submit to its cares?

This, as He proceeded, he enjoined also more fully, saying, "Take no thought for the morrow" (Matt. 6:34). He would have us be on every hand unencumbered and winged for flight, yielding just so much to nature as the compulsion of necessity requires of us.

9. Then forasmuch as it comes to pass that we sin even after the washing of regeneration, He, showing His love to man to be great even in this case, commands us for the remission of our sins to come unto God who loves man, and thus to say, "Forgive us our debts, as we also forgive our debtors" (Matt. 6:12).

Seest thou surpassing mercy? After taking away so great evils, and after the unspeakable greatness of His gift, if men sin again, He counts them such as may be forgiven. For that this prayer belongs to believers, is taught us both by the laws of the church, and by the beginning of the prayer. For the uninitiated could not call God Father. If then the prayer belongs to believers, and they pray, entreating that sins may be forgiven them, it is clear that not even after the laver is the profit of repentance taken away. Since, had He not meant to signify this, He would not have made a law that we should so pray. Now He who both brings sins to remembrance, and bids us ask forgiveness, and teaches how we may obtain remission and so makes the way easy; it is perfectly clear that He introduced this rule of supplication, as knowing, and signifying, that it is possible even after the font to wash ourselves from our offenses; by reminding us of our sins, persuading us to be modest; by the command to forgive others, setting us free from all revengeful passion; while by promising in return for this to pardon us also, He holds out good hopes, and instructs us to have high views concerning the unspeakable mercy of God toward man. But what we should most observe is this, that whereas in each of the clauses He had made mention of the whole of virtue, and in this way had included also the forgetfulness of injuries (for so, that "His name be hallowed," is the exactness of a perfect conversation; and that "His will be done," declares the same thing again: and to be able to call God "Father," is the profession of a blameless life; in all which things had been comprehended also the duty of remitting our anger against them that have transgressed): still He was not satisfied with these, but meaning to signify how earnest He is in the matter, He sets it down also in particular, and after the prayer, He makes mention of no other commandment than this, saying thus: "For if ye forgive men their trespasses, your heavenly Father also will forgive you" (Matt. 6:14).

So that the beginning is of us, and we ourselves have control over the judgment that is to be passed upon us. For in order that no one, even of the senseless, might have any complaint to make, either great or small, when brought to judgment; on thee, who art to give account, He causes the sentence to depend; and "in what way soever thou hast judged for thyself, in the same," saith He, "do I also judge

thee." And if thou forgive thy fellow servant, thou shalt obtain the same favor from me; though indeed the one be not equal to the other. For thou forgivest in thy need, but God, having need of none: thou, thy fellow slave; God, His slave: thou liable to unnumbered charges; God, being without sin. But yet even thus doth He show forth His loving-kindness towards man. Since He might indeed, even without this, forgive thee all thine offenses; but He wills thee hereby also to receive a benefit; affording thee on all sides innumerable occasions of gentleness and love to man, casting out what is brutish in thee, and quenching wrath, and in all ways cementing thee to him who is thine own member.

For what canst thou have to say? that thou hast wrongfully endured some ill of thy neighbor? (For these only are trespasses, since if it be done with justice, the act is not a trespass.) But thou too art drawing near to receive forgiveness for such things, and for much greater. And even before the forgiveness, thou hast received no small gift, in being taught to have a human soul, and in being trained to all gentleness. And herewith a great reward shall also be laid up for thee elsewhere, even to be called to account for none of thine offenses. What sort of punishment then do we not deserve, when after having received the privilege, we betray our salvation? And how shall we claim to be heard in the rest of our matters, if we will not, in those which depend on us, spare our own selves?

10. "And lead us not into temptation; but deliver us from the evil one: for Thine is the kingdom, and the power, and the glory, for ever. Amen" (Matt. 6:13).

Here He teaches us plainly our own vileness, and quells our pride, instructing us to deprecate all conflicts, instead of rushing upon them. For so both our victory will be more glorious, and the devil's overthrow more to be derided. I mean, that as when we are dragged forth, we must stand nobly; so when we are not summoned, we should be quiet, and wait for the time of conflict; that we may show both freedom from vainglory, and nobleness of spirit. And He here calls the devil "the wicked one," commanding us to wage against him a war that knows no truce, and implying that he is not such by nature. For wickedness is not of those things that are from nature, but of them that are added by our own choice. And he is so called pre-eminently, by reason of the excess of his wickedness, and because he, in no respect injured by us, wages against us implacable war. Wherefore neither said He, "deliver us from the wicked ones," but, "from the wicked one"; instructing us in no case to entertain displeasure against our neighbors, for what wrongs soever we may suffer at their hands, but to transfer our enmity from these to him, as being himself the cause of all our wrongs.

Having then made us anxious as before conflict, by putting us in mind of the enemy, and having cut away from us all our remissness; He again encourages and raises our spirits, by bringing to our remembrance the King under whom we are arrayed, and signifying Him to be more powerful than all.

"For Thine," saith He, "is the kingdom, and the power, and the glory."

Doth it not then follow, that if His be the kingdom, we should fear no one, since there can be none to withstand, and divide the empire with him. For when He saith, "Thine is the kingdom," He sets before us even him, who is warring against us, brought into subjection, though he seem to oppose, God for a while permitting it. For in truth he too is among God's servants, though of the degraded class, and those guilty of offense; and he would not dare set upon any of his fellow servants, had he not first received license from above. And why say I, "his fellow servants"? Not even against swine did he venture any outrage, until He Himself allowed him; nor against flocks, nor herds, until he had received permission from above.

"And the power," saith He. Therefore, manifold as thy weakness may be, thou mayest of right be confident, having such a one to reign over thee, who is able fully to accomplish all, and that with ease, even by thee.

"And the glory, for ever. Amen." Thus He not only frees thee from the dangers that are approaching thee, but can make thee also glorious and illustrious. For as His power is great, so also is His glory unspeakable, and they are all boundless, and no end of them.

Seest thou how He hath by every means anointed His Champion, and hath framed Him to be full of confidence?

11. Then, as I said before, meaning to signify, that of all things He most loathes and hates bearing malice, and most of all accepts the virtue which is opposite to that vice; He hath after the prayer also again put us in mind of this same point of goodness; both by the punishment set, and by the reward appointed, urging the hearer to obey this command.

"For if ye forgive men," saith He, "your heavenly Father will also forgive you. But if ye forgive not, neither will He forgive you" (Matt. 6:15).

With this view He hath again mentioned heaven also, and their Father; to abash the hearer by this topic likewise; that he of all people, being of such a Father, should be made a wild beast of; and summoned as he is to heaven, should cherish an earthly and ordinary sort of mind. Since not by grace only, you see, ought we to become His children, but also by our works. And nothing makes us so like God, as being ready to forgive the wicked and wrong-doers; even as indeed He had taught before, when He spake of His "making the sun to shine on the evil and on the good."

For this same cause again in every one of the clauses He commands us to make our prayers common, saying, "Our Father," and "Thy will be done in earth as it is in heaven," and "Give us the bread, and forgive us our debts," and "lead us not into temptation," and "deliver us;" everywhere commanding us to use this plural word, that we may not retain so much as a vestige of anger against our neighbor.

How great punishment then must they deserve, who after all this, so far from themselves forgiving, do even entreat God for vengeance on their enemies, and diametrically as it were transgress this law; and this while He is doing and contriving all, to hinder our being at variance one with another? For since love is the root of all that is good, He removing from all sides whatever mars it, brings us together, and cements us to each other. For there is not, there is not one, be he father, or mother, or friend, or what you will, who so loved us as the God who created us. And this, above all things, both His daily benefits and His precepts make manifest. But if thou tell me of the pains, and of the sorrows, and of the evils of life; consider in how many things thou offendest Him every day, and thou wilt no longer marvel, though more than these evils should come upon thee, but if thou shouldest enjoy any good, then thou wilt marvel, and be amazed. But as it is, we look upon the calamities that come upon us, but the offenses, whereby we offend daily, we consider not: therefore we are perplexed. Since if we did but reckon up with strictness our sins of one day only, in that case we should know well how great evils we must be liable to. And to let pass the other misdoings of which we have been guilty, each one for himself, and to speak of what have been committed this day; although of course I know not in what each of us may have sinned, yet such is the abundance of our misdoings, that not even he who knew all exactly would be able to choose from among these only. Which of us, for instance, hath not been careless in his prayers? Which hath not been insolent, or vainglorious? Who hath not spoken evil of his brother, hath not admitted a wicked desire, hath not looked with unchaste eyes, hath not remembered things with hostile feeling, even till he made his heart swell?

And if while we are in church, and in a short time we have become guilty of so great evils; what shall be when we are gone out from hence? If in the harbor the waves are so high, when we are gone forth into the channel of wickednesses, the forum I mean, and to public business, and our cares at home, shall we indeed be able so much as to know ourselves again?

But yet from our so great and so many sins, God hath given us a short and easy way of deliverance, and one that is free from all toil. For what sort of toil is it to forgive him that hath grieved us? Nay, it is a toil not to forgive, but to keep up our enmity: even as to be delivered from the anger, both works in us a great refreshment, and is very easy to him that is willing. For there is no sea to be crossed, nor long journey to be traveled, nor summits of mountains to be passed over, nor money to be spent, no need to torment thy body; but it suffices to be willing only, and all our sins are done away.

But if so far from forgiving him thyself, thou makest intercession to God against him, what hope of salvation wilt thou then have, if at the very time when thou oughtest rather to appease God, even then thou provokest Him; putting on the garb of a suppliant, but uttering the cries of a wild beast, and darting out against thyself those shafts of the wicked one? Wherefore Paul also, making mention of prayer, required nothing so much as the observance of this commandment; for He saith, "lifting up holy hands without wrath and doubting" (1 Tim. 2:8). And if when thou hast need of mercy, not even then wilt thou let go thine anger, but art rather exceedingly mindful of it, and that, although thou knowest thou art thrusting the sword into thyself; when will it be possible for thee to become merciful, and to spew out the evil venom of this wickedness? But if thou hast not yet seen this outrageousness in its full extent, suppose it happening among men, and then thou wilt perceive the excess of the insolence. As thus: should one approach thee who are a man, seeking to obtain mercy, and then, in the midst of his lying on the ground, should see an enemy, and leaving off to supplicate thee, begin to beat him; wouldest thou not make thyself more angry with him? This do thou consider as taking place with regard to God also. For so thou likewise, making supplication unto God, leavest thy supplication in the midst, and smitest thine enemy with thy words, and insultest the laws of God. Him who made a law to dismiss all anger, thou art summoning against those that have vexed thee, and requiring Him to do things contrary to His own commandments. Is it not enough for thee in the way of revenge, that thou thyself transgressed the law of God, but entreatest thou Him likewise to do so? What? hath He forgotten what He commanded? What? is He a man who spake these things? It is God, who knows all things, and whose will is, that His own laws be kept with the utmost exactness, and who, so far from doing these things which thou art requiring of Him, doth even regard thee who sayest these things, merely because thou sayest them, with aversion and hatred, and exacts of thee the most extreme penalty. How then seekest thou to obtain of Him things, from which He very seriously bids thee refrain?

Yet some there are, who have come to such a point of brutishness, as not only to make intercession against their enemies, but even to curse their children, and to taste, if only it might be, of their very flesh; or rather they are even tasting thereof. For tell me not this, that thou hast not fixed thy teeth in the body of him that vexed thee; since thou hast done, at least as far as concerned thee, what is much more grievous; in claiming that wrath from above should fall upon him, and that he should be delivered over to undying punishment, and be overthrown with his whole house.

Why, what sort of bites are as ferocious as this? what kind of weapons as bitter? Not so did Christ instruct thee; not so did He command thee to stain thy mouth with blood. Nay, mouths made bloody with human flesh are not so shocking as tongues like these.

How then wilt thou salute thy brother? how wilt thou touch the sacrifice? how taste the Lord's blood, when thou hast so much venom upon thy mind? Since when thou sayest, "Rend him in pieces, and overthrow his house, and destroy all," when thou art imprecating on him ten thousand deaths, thou art in nothing different from a murderer, or rather from a wild beast that devours men. Let us cease then from this disease and madness, and that kindliness which He commanded let us show forth towards them that have vexed us: that we may become like "our Father which is in heaven." And we shall cease therefrom, if we call to mind our own sins; if we strictly search out all our misdeeds at home, abroad, and in the market, and in church.

12. For if for nothing else, surely for our disrespectfulness here we are worthy to undergo the utmost punishment. For when prophets are chanting, and apostles singing hymns, and God is discoursing, we wander without, and bring in upon us a turmoil of worldly business. And we do not afford to the laws of God so great stillness, even as the spectators in the theatres to the emperor's letters, keeping silence for them. For there, when these letters are being read, deputies at once, and governors, and senate, and people, stand

all upright, with quietness hearkening to the words. And if amid that most profound silence any one should suddenly leap up and cry out, he suffers the utmost punishment, as having been insolent to the emperor. But here, when the letters from heaven are being read, great is the confusion on all sides. And yet both He who sent the letters is much greater than this our king, and the assembly more venerable: for not men only, but angels too are in it; and these triumphs, of which the letters bear us the good tidings, are much more awful than those on earth. Wherefore not men only, but angels also and archangels; both the nations of heaven, and all we on the earth, are commanded to give praise. For, "Bless the Lord," it is said, "all His works." Yea, for His are no small achievements, rather they surpass all speech, and thought, and understanding of man.

And these things the prophets proclaim every day, each of them in a different way publishing this glorious triumph. For one saith, "Thou hast gone up on high, Thou hast led captivity captive, and hast received gifts amongst men. (Eph. 4:8). And, "The Lord strong and mighty in battle" (Psalm 23 (24):8). And another saith, "He shall divide the spoils of the strong" (Isa. 53:12 LXX). For indeed to this purpose He came, that He might "preach deliverance to captives, and recovery of sight to the blind" (Isa. 61:1 LXX; Luke 4:18). And raising aloud the cry of victory over death, he said, "Where, O Death, is thy victory? Where, O Grave, is thy sting?" (1 Cor. 15:55). And another again, declaring glad tidings of the most profound peace, said, "They shall beat their swords into ploughshares, and their spears into pruning hooks" (Isaiah 2:4; Micah 4:3). And while one calls on Jerusalem, saying, "Rejoice greatly, O daughter of Sion, for lo! thy King cometh to thee meek, riding upon an ass, and a young colt" (Zech. 9:9; Matt. 21:5). another proclaims His second coming also, saying on this wise, "The Lord, whom ye seek, will come, and who will abide the day of His coming? (Mal. 3:1, 2). Leap ye as calves set free from bonds" (Mal. 4:2 variant). And another again, amazed at such things, said, "This is our God; there shall none other be accounted of in comparison of Him" (Baruch 3:35). Yet, nevertheless, while both these and many more sayings than these are being uttered, while we ought to tremble, and not so much as account ourselves to be on the earth; still, as though in the midst of a forum, we make an uproar and disturbance, and spend the whole time of our solemn assembly in discoursing of things which are nothing to us. When therefore both in little things, and in great, both in hearing, and in doing, both abroad, and at home, in the church, we are so negligent; and together with all this, pray also against our enemies: whence are we to have any hope of salvation, adding to so great sins yet another grievous enhancement, and equivalent to them all, even this unlawful prayer?

Have we then hereafter any right to marvel, if aught befall us of the things which are unexpected and painful? whereas we ought to marvel when no such thing befalls us. For the former is in the natural order of things, but the latter were beyond all reason and expectation. For surely it is beyond reason, that they who are become enemies of God, and are provoking Him to anger, should enjoy sunshine and showers, and all the rest; who being men surpass the barbarity of wild beasts, setting themselves one against another, and by the biting of their neighbors staining their own tongues with blood: after the spiritual table, and His so great benefits, and His innumerable injunctions.

Therefore, considering these things, let us cast up that venom; let us put an end to our enmities, and let us make the prayers that become such as we are. Instead of the brutality of devils, let us take upon us the mildness of angels; and in whatsoever things we may have been injured, let us, considering our own case, and the reward appointed us for this commandment, soften our anger; let us assuage the billows, that we may both pass through the present life calmly, and when we have departed thither, may find our Lord such as we have been towards our fellow-servants. And if this be a heavy and fearful thing, let us make it light and desirable; and let us open the glorious gates of confidence towards Him; and what we had not strength to effect by abstaining from sin, that let us accomplish by becoming gentle to them who have sinned against us (for this surely is not grievous, nor

burdensome); and let us by doing kindnesses to our enemies, lay up beforehand much mercy for ourselves.

For so both during this present life all will love us, and above all others, God will both befriend and crown us, and will count us worthy of all the good things to come; unto which may we all attain, by the grace and love towards man of our Lord Jesus Christ, to whom be glory and might for ever and ever. Amen.

John Chrysostom, c. 345–407, Homily 19 On St. Matthew: On the Lord's Prayer

Jesus Praying for Himself
John Chrysostom

Homily LXXX.

"These words spake Jesus, and lifted up His eyes to heaven, and saith, Father, the hour is come; glorify Thy Son, that Thy Son also may glorify Thee." John xvii. 1

"*He that hath done and taught,*" it saith, "*the same shall be called great in the Kingdom of heaven.*" And with much reason; for to show true wisdom in words, is easy, but the proof which is by works is the part of some noble and great one. Wherefore also Christ, speaking of the endurance of evil, putteth Himself forth, bidding us take example from Him. On this account too, after this admonition, He betaketh Himself to prayer, teaching us in our temptations to leave all things, and flee to God. For because He had said, "In the world ye shall have tribulation," and had shaken their souls, by the prayer He raiseth them again. As yet they gave heed unto Him as to a man; and for their sake He acteth thus, just as He did in the case of Lazarus, and there telleth the reason; "Because of the people that stand by I said it, that they might believe that Thou hast sent Me" (c. xi. 42). "Yea," saith some one, "this took place with good cause in the case of the Jews; but wherefore in that of the disciples?" With good cause in the case of the disciples also. For they who, after all that had been said and done, said, "Now we know that Thou knowest" (c. xvi. 30), most of all needed to be established. Besides, the Evangelist doth not even call the action prayer; but what saith he? "He lifted up His eyes to heaven," and saith rather that it was a discoursing with the Father. And if elsewhere he speaks of prayer, and at one time shows Him kneeling on His knees, at another lifting His eyes to heaven, be not thou troubled; for by these means we are taught the earnestness which should be in our petitions, that standing we should look up, not with the eyes of the flesh only, but of the mind, and that we should bend our knees, bruising our own hearts. For Christ came not merely to manifest Himself, but also about to teach virtue ineffable. But it behooveth the teacher to teach, not by words only, but also by actions. Let us hear then what He saith in this place.

"Father, the hour is come; glorify Thy Son, that Thy Son also may glorify Thee."
Again He showeth us, that not unwilling He cometh to the Cross. For how could He be unwilling, who prayed that this might come to pass, and called the action "glory," not only for Himself the Crucified, but also for the Father? since this was the case, for not the Son only, but the Father also was glorified. For before the Crucifixion, not even the Jews knew Him; Israel," it saith, "hath not known Me" (Isa. i. 3); but after the Crucifixion, all the world ran to Him. Then He speaketh also of the manner of the glory, and how He will glorify Him.

VER. 2
"As Thou hast given Him power over all flesh," "that nothing which Thou hast given Him should perish." For to be always doing good, is glory to God. But what is, "As Thou hast given Him power over all flesh"? He now showeth, that what belongs to the preaching is not confined to the Jews alone, but is extended to all the world, and layeth down beforehand the first invitations to the Gentiles. And since He had said, "Go not into the way of the Gentiles" (Matt. x. 5), and after this time is about to say, "Go ye, and make disciples of all nations" (Matt. xxviii. 19), He showeth that the Father also willeth this. For this greatly offended the Jews, and the disciples too; nor indeed after this did they easily endure to lay hold on the Gentiles, until they received the teaching of the Spirit; because hence arose no small stumblingblock

for the Jews. Therefore, when Peter after such a manifestation of the Spirit came to Jerusalem, he could scarcely, by relating the vision of the sheet, escape the charges brought against him. But what is, "Thou hast given Him power over all flesh"? I will ask the heretics, "When did He receive this power? was it before He formed them, or after?" He himself saith, that it was after that He had been crucified, and had risen again; at least then He said, "All power is given unto Me" (Matt. xxviii. 18), and, "Go ye and make disciples of all nations." What then, had He not authority over His own works? Did He make them, and had He not authority over them after having made them? Yet He is seen doing all in times of old, punishing some as sinners, (for, "Surely I will not hide," it saith, "from My servant Abraham, that which I am about to do" – Gen. xviii. 17, LXX), and honoring others as righteous. Had He then the power at that time, and now had He lost it, and did He again receive it? What devil could assert this? But if His power was the same both then and now, (for, saith He, "as the Father raiseth up the dead and quickeneth them, even so the Son quickeneth whom He will" – c. v. 21), what is the meaning of the words? He was about to send them to the Gentiles; in order therefore that they might not think that this was an innovation, because He had said, "I am not sent, save unto the lost sheep of the house of Israel" (Matt. xv. 24), He showeth that this seemeth good to the Father also. And if He saith this with great meanness of circumstance, it is not wonderful. For so He edified both those at that time, and those who came afterwards; and as I have before said, He always by the excess of meanness firmly persuaded them that the words were those of condescension.

But what is, "Of all flesh"?
For certainly not all believed. Yet, for His part, all believed; and if men gave no heed to His words, the fault was not in the teacher, but in those who received them not.
"That He should give eternal life to as many as Thou hast given Him."
If here also He speaketh in a more human manner, wonder not. For He doth so both on account of the reasons I have given, and to avoid the saying anything great concerning

Himself; since this was a stumblingblock to the hearers because as yet they imagined nothing great concerning Him. John, for example, when He speaks in his own person, doth not so, but leadeth up his language to greater sublimity, saying, "All things were made by Him, and without Him was not anything made" (c. i. 3, 4, 9, 11); and that He was "Life"; and that He was "Light"; and that "He came to His own": he saith not, that He would not have had power, had He not received it, but that He gave to others also "power to become sons of God." And Paul in like manner calleth Him equal with God. But He Himself asketh in a more human way, saying thus, "That He should give eternal life to as many as Thou hast given Him" (Philip. ii. 6).

VER. 3

"And this is life eternal, that they might know Thee the only true God, and Jesus Christ whom Thou hast sent."

"The only true God," He saith, by way of distinction from those which are not gods; for He was about to send them to the Gentiles. But if they will not allow this, but on account of this word "only" reject the Son from being true God, in this way as they proceed they reject Him from being God at all. For He also saith, "Ye seek not the glory which is from the only God" (c. v. 44). Well then; shall not the Son be God? But if the Son be God, and the Son of the Father who is called the Only God, it is clear that He also is true, and the Son of Him who is called the Only true God. Why, when Paul saith, "Or I only and Barnabas" (1 Cor. ix. 6,) doth he exclude Barnabas? Not at all; for the "only" is put by way of distinction from others. And, if He be not true God, how is He "Truth"? for truth far surpasses what is true. What shall we call the not being a "true" man, tell me? shall we not call it the not being a man at all? so if the Son is not true God, how is He God? And how maketh He us gods and sons, if He is not true? But on these matters we have spoken more particularly in another place; wherefore let us apply ourselves to what follows.

VER. 4

"I have glorified Thee on the earth." Well said He, "on the earth"; for in heaven He had been already glorified, having His own natural

glory, and being worshiped by the Angels. Christ then speaketh not of that glory which is bound up with His Essence, (for that glory, though none glorify Him, He ever possesseth in its fullness,) but of that which cometh from the service of men. And so the, "Glorify Me," is of this kind; and that thou mayest understand that He speaketh of this manner of glory, hear what follows.

"I have finished the work which Thou gavest Me that I should do it."

And yet the action was still but beginning, or rather was not yet beginning. How then said He, "I have finished"? Either He meaneth, that "I have done all My part"; or He speaketh of the future, as having already come to pass; or, which one may say most of all, that all was already effected, because the root of blessings had been laid, which fruits would certainly and necessarily follow, and from His being present at and assisting in those things which should take place after these. On this account He saith again in a condescending way, "Which Thou gavest Me." For had He indeed waited to hear and learn, this would have fallen far short of His glory. For that He came to this of His own will, is clear from many passages. As when Paul saith, that "He so loved us, as to give Himself for us" (Eph. v. 2;) and, "He emptied Himself, and took upon Him the form of a servant" (Philip. ii. 7); and, "As the Father hath loved Me, so have I loved you" (c. xv. 9).

VER. 5

"And now, O Father, glorify Thou Me with Thine Own Self, with the glory which I had with Thee before the world was."

Where is that glory? For allowing that He was with reason unhonored among men, because of the covering which was put around Him; how seeketh He to be glorified with the Father? What then saith He here? The saying refers to the Dispensation; since His fleshly nature had not yet been glorified, not having as yet enjoyed incorruption, nor shared the kingly throne. Therefore He said not "on earth," but "with Thee."

This glory we also shall enjoy according to our measure, if we be sober.
Wherefore Paul saith, "If so be that we suffer

with Him, that we may also be glorified together." (Rom. viii. 17). Ten thousand tears then do they merit, who through sluggishness and sleep plot against themselves when such glory is set before them; and, were there no hell, they would be more wretched than any, who, when it is in their power to reign and to be glorified with the Son of God, deprive themselves of so great blessings. Since if it were necessary to be cut in pieces, if to die ten thousand deaths, if to give up every day ten thousand lives and as many bodies, ought we not to submit to such things for such glory? But now we do not even despise money, which hereafter, though unwilling, we shall leave: we do not despise money, which brings about us ten thousand mischiefs, which remains here, which is not our own. For we are but stewards of that which is not our own, although we receive it from our fathers. But when there is hell besides, and the worm that dieth not, and the fire that is not quenched, and the gnashing of teeth, how, tell me, shall we bear these things? How long will we refuse to see clearly, and spend our all on daily fightings, and contentions, and unprofitable talk, feeding, cultivating earth, fattening the body and neglecting the soul, making no account of necessary things, but much care about things superfluous and unprofitable? And we build splendid tombs, and buy costly houses, and draw about with us herds of all kinds of servants, and devise different stewards, appointing managers of lands, of houses, of money, and managers of those managers; but as to our desolate soul, we care nothing for that. And what will be the limit to this? Is it not one belly that we fill, is it not one body that we clothe? What is this great bustle of business? Why and wherefore do we cut up and tear to pieces the one soul, which we have had assigned to us, in attending to the service of such things, contriving for ourselves a grievous slavery? For he who needs many things is the slave of many things, although he seem to be their master. Since the lord is the slave even of his domestics, and brings in another and a heavier mode of service; and in another way also he is their slave, not daring without them to enter the agora, nor the bath, nor the field, but they frequently go about in all directions without him. He who seems to be master,

dares not, if his slaves be not present, to go forth from home, and if whilst unattended he do but put his head out of his house, he thinks that he is laughed at. Perhaps some laugh at us when we say this, yet on this very account they would be deserving of ten thousand tears. For to show that this is slavery, I would gladly ask you, wouldest thou wish to need some one to put the morsel to thy mouth, and to apply the cup to thy lips? Wouldest thou not deem such a service worthy of tears? What if thou didst require continually supporters to enable thee to walk, wouldest thou not think thyself pitiable, and in this respect more wretched than any? So then thou oughtest to be disposed now. For it matters nothing whether one is so treated by irrational things, or by men.

Why, tell me, do not the Angels differ from us in this respect, that they do not want so many things as we do? Therefore the less we need, the more we are on our way to them; the more we need, the more we sink down to this perishable life. And that thou mayest learn that these things are so, ask those who have grown old which life they deem happiest, that when they were helplessly mastered, or now when they are masters of these things? We have mentioned these persons, because those who are intoxicated with youth, do not even know the excess of their slavery. For what of those in fever, do they call themselves happy when, thirsting much, they drink much and need more, or when, having recovered their health, they are free from the desire? Seest thou that in every instance the needing much is pitiable, and far apart from true wisdom, and an aggravation of slavery and desire? Why then do we voluntarily increase to ourselves wretchedness? For, tell me, if it were possible to live uninjured without roof or walls, wouldest thou not prefer this; wherefore then dost thou increase the signs of thy weakness? Do we not for this call Adam happy, that he needed nothing, no house, no clothes? "Yes," saith some one, "but now we are in need of them." Why then do we make our need greater? If many persons curtail many of the things actually needed, (servants, I mean, and houses, and money,) what excuse can we have if we overstep the need? The more thou puttest about thee, the more slavish dost thou become; for by whatever proportion thou requirest more, in that proportion thou hast trenched upon thy freedom. For absolute freedom is, to want nothing at all; the next is, to want little; and this the Angels and their imitators especially possess. But for men to succeed in this while tarrying in a mortal body, think how great praise this hath. This also Paul said, when writing to the Corinthians, "But I spare you," and, "lest such should have trouble in the flesh" (1 Cor. vii. 28). Riches are called "usables," that we may "use" them rightly, and not keep and bury them; for this is not to possess them, but to be possessed by them. Since if we are going to make this our aim how to multiply them, not that we may employ them rightly, the order is reversed, and they possess us, not we them. Let us then free ourselves from this grievous bondage, and at last become free. Why do we devise ten thousand different chains for ourselves? Is not the bond of nature enough for thee, and the necessity of life, and the crowd of ten thousand affairs, but dost thou twine also other nets for thyself, and put them about thy feet? And when wilt thou lay hold on heaven, and be able to stand on that height? For a great thing, a great thing is it, that even having cut asunder all these cords, thou shouldest be able to lay hold on the city which is above. So many other hindrances are there; all which that we may conquer, let us keep to the mean estate [and having put away superfluities, let us keep to what is necessary.] Thus shall we lay hold on eternal life, through the grace and loving-kindness of our Lord Jesus Christ, to whom be glory for ever and ever. Amen.

John Chrysostom, c.347–407

Rejoice

John Chrysostom

Philippians 4:4–7. "Rejoice in the Lord always: again I will say, Rejoice. Let your forbearance be known unto all men. The Lord is at hand. In nothing be anxious; but in everything by prayer and supplication with thanksgiving let your requests be made known unto God. And the peace of God, which passeth all under-standing, shall guard your hearts and your thoughts through Christ Jesus."

"Blessed they that mourn," and "woe unto them that laugh" (Matt. 5:4; Luke 6:25), saith Christ. How then saith Paul, "Rejoice in the Lord always"? "Woe to them that laugh," said Christ, the laughter of this world which ariseth from the things which are present He blessed also those that mourn, not simply for the loss of relatives, but those who are pricked at heart, who mourn their own faults, and take count of their own sins, or even those of others. This joy is not contrary to that grief, but from that grief it too is born. For he who grieveth for his own faults, and confesseth them, rejoiceth. Moreover, it is possible to grieve for our own sins, and yet to rejoice in Christ. Since then they were afflicted by their sufferings, "for to you it is given not only to believe in him, but also to stiffer for him" (Phil. 1:29), therefore he saith, "Rejoice in the Lord." For this can but mean, If you exhibit such a life that you may rejoice. Or when your communion with God is not hindered, rejoice. Or else the word "in" may stand for "with": as if he had said, with the Lord. "Always; again I will say, Rejoice." These are the words of one who brings comfort; as, for example, he who is in God rejoiceth always. Yea though he be afflicted, yea whatever he may suffer, such a man always rejoiceth. Hear what Luke saith, that "they returned from the presence of the Council, rejoicing that they were counted worthy to be scourged for His name." (Acts 5:41) If scourging and bonds, which seem to be the most grievous of all things, bring forth joy, what else will be able to produce grief in us? "Again I will say, Rejoice." Well hath he repeated. For since the nature of the things brought forth grief, he shows by repeating, that they should by all means rejoice." Let your forbearance be known unto all men." He said above, "Whose god is the belly, and whose glory is in their shame," and that they "mind earthly things." (Phil. 3:19) It was probable that they would be at enmity with the wicked; he therefore exhorted them to have nothing in common with them, but to use them with all forbearance, and that not only their brethren, but also their enemies and opposers. "The Lord is at hand, in nothing be anxious." For why, tell me? do they ever rise in opposition? And if ye see them living in luxury, why are ye in affliction? Already the judgment is nigh; shortly will they give account of their actions. Are ye in affliction, and they in luxury? But these things shall shortly receive their end. Do they plot against you, and threaten you? "In nothing be anxious." The judgment is already at hand, when these things shall be reversed. "In nothing be anxious." If ye are kindly affected toward those who prepare evil against you, yet it shall not at last turn out to their profit. Already the recompense is at hand, if poverty, if death, if aught else that is terrible be upon you. "But in everything, by prayer and supplication, with thanksgiving, let your requests be made known unto God." There is this for one consolation, "the Lord is at hand." And again, "I will be with you always, even unto the end of the world." (Matt. 28:20) Behold another consolation, a medicine which healeth grief, and distress, and all that is painful. And what is this? Prayer, thanksgiving in all things. And so He wills that our prayers should not simply be requests, but thanksgivings too for what we have. For how should he ask for future things, who is not thankful for the past? "But in everything by prayer and supplication." Wherefore we ought to give thanks for all things, even for those which seem to be grievous, for this is the part of the truly thankful man. In the other case the nature of the things demands it; but this springs from a grateful soul, and one earnestly affected toward God. God acknowledgeth these prayers, but others He knoweth not. Offer up such prayers as may be acknowledged; for He disposeth all things for our profit, though we know it not. And this is a proof that it greatly profiteth, namely, that we know it not. "And the peace of God which pusseth all understanding shall guard your hearts and your thoughts in Christ Jesus." What meaneth this? "The peace of God" which He hath wrought toward men, surpasseth all understanding. For who could have expected, who could have hoped, that such good things would have come? They exceed all man's understanding, not his speech alone. For His enemies, for those who hated Him, for those who determined to turn themselves away, for these, he refused not to deliver up His Only Begotten Son, that He might make peace with us. This peace then, i.e. the reconciliation, the love of God, shall guard your hearts and your

thoughts. For this is the part of a teacher, not only to exhort, but also to pray, and to assist by supplication, that they may neither be overwhelmed by temptations, nor carried about by deceit. As if he had said, May He who hath delivered you in such sort as mind cannot comprehend, may He Himself guard yon, and secure you, so that you suffer no ill. Either he means this, or that that peace of which Christ saith, "Peace I leave with you, My peace I give unto you" (John 14:27): this shall guard you, for this peace exceedeth all man's understanding. How? When he tells us to be at peace with our enemies, with those who treat us unjustly, with those who are at war and enmity toward us; is it not beyond man's understanding? But rather let us look to the former. If the peace surpasseth all understanding, much more doth God Himself, who giveth peace, pass all understanding, not ours only, but also that of Angels, and the Powers above. What meaneth "in Christ Jesus"? Shall guard us in Him, so that ye may remain firm, and not fall from His faith.

VER. 8.
"Finally, brethren, whatsoever things are honorable, whatsoever things are true, whatsoever things are just." What is "Finally "? It stands for, "I have said all." It is the word of one that is in haste, and has nothing to do with present things.

"Finally, brethren, whatsoever things are honorable, whatsoever things are true, whatsoever things are just, whatsoever things are pure, whatsoever things are lovely, whatsoever things are of good report, if there be any virtue, and if there be any praise, think on these things."

VER. 9.
"The things which ye both learned and received, and heard and saw in me." What meaneth, "whatsoever things are lovely"? Lovely to the faithful, lovely to God. "Whatsoever things are true." Virtue is really true, vice is falsehood. For the pleasure of it is a falsehood, and its glory is falsehood, and all things of the world are falsehood. "Whatsoever things are pure." This is opposed to the words "who mind earthly things." "Whatsoever things

are honorable." This is opposed to the words "whose god is their belly." "Whatsoever things are just," i.e. saith he, "whatsoever things are of good report." "If there be any virtue, if there be any praise." Here he willeth them to take thought of those things too which regard men. "Think on these things," saith he. Seest thou, that he desires to banish every evil thought from our souls; for evil actions spring from thoughts. "The things which ye both learned and received." This is teaching, in all his exhortations to propose himself for a model: as he saith in another place, "even as ye have us for an example" (Phil. 3:17). And again here, "What things ye learned and received," i.e. have been taught by word of mouth, "and heard and saw in me": both in respect of my words and actions and conduct. Seest thou, how about everything he lays these commands on us? For since it was not possible to make an accurate enumeration of all things, of our coming in, and going out, and speech, and carriage, and intercourse (for of all these things it is needful that a Christian should have thought), he said shortly, and as it were in a summary, "ye heard and saw in me." I have led yon forward both by deeds and by words. "These things do," not only in words, but do them also. "And the God of peace shall be with you," i.e. ye shall be in a calm, in great safety, ye shall suffer nothing painful, nor contrary to your will. For when we are at peace with Him, and we are so through virtue, much more will He be at peace with us. For He who so loved us, as to show favor to us even against our will, will He not, if He sees us hastening toward Him, Himself yet much more exhibit His love toward us?

Nothing is such an enemy of our nature as vice. And from many things it is evident, how vice is at enmity with us, and virtue friendly toward us. What will ye? That I should speak of fornication? It makes men subject to reproach, poor, objects of ridicule, despicable to all, just as enemies treat them. Ofttimes it hath involved men in disease and danger; many men have perished or been wounded in behalf of their mistresses. And if fornication produces these things, much rather doth adultery. But doth almsgiving so? By no means. But as a loving mother setteth her son in great propriety, in good order, in good report, and

gives him leisure to engage in necessary work, thus alms-giving doth not release us nor lead us away from our necessary work, but even renders the soul more wise. For nothing is more foolish than a mistress.

But what willest thou? To look upon covetousness? It too treats us like an enemy. And how? It makes us hated by all. It prepareth all men to vaunt themselves against us; both those who have been treated unjustly by us, and those who have not, who share the grief of the former, and are in fear for themselves. All men look upon us as their common foes, as wild beasts, as demons. Everywhere are there innumerable accusations, plots against us, envyings, all which are the acts of enemies. But justice, on the contrary, makes all men friends, all men sociable, all men well disposed towards us, by all men prayers are made in our behalf; our affairs are in perfect safety, there is no danger, there is no suspicion. But sleep also fearlessly comes over us with perfect safety, no care is there, no lamenting.

How much better this sort of life is! And what? Is it best to envy, or to rejoice with one another? Let us search out all these things, and we shall find that virtue, like a truly kind mother, places us in safety, while vice is a treacherous thing, and full of danger. For hear the prophet, who saith, "The Lord is a stronghold of them that fear Him, and His covenant is to show them" (Ps. 25:14, Sept.). He feareth no one, who is not conscious to himself of any wickedness; on the contrary, he who liveth in crime is never confident, but trembles at his domestics, and looks at them with suspicion. Why say, his domestics? He cannot bear the tribunal of his own conscience. Not only those who are without, but his inward thoughts affect him likewise, and suffer him not to be in quiet. What then, saith Paul? Ought we to live dependent on praise? He said not, look to praise, but do praiseworthy actions, yet not for the sake of praise.

"Whatsoever things are true," for the things we have been speaking of are false. "Whatsoever things are honorable." That which is "honorable" belongs to external virtue, that which is "pure" to the soul. Give no cause of stumbling, saith he, nor handle of accusation. Because he had said, "Whatsoever things are of good report," lest you should think that he means only those things which are so in the sight of men, he proceeds, "if there be any virtue, and if there be any praise, think on these things" – do these things. He wills us ever to be in these things, to care for these things, to think on these things. For if we will be at peace with each other, God too will be with us, but if we raise up war, the God of peace will not be with us. For nothing is so hostile to the soul as vice. That is, peace and virtue place it in safety. Wherefore we must make a beginning on our part, and then we shall draw God toward us.

God is not a God of war and fighting. Make war and fighting to cease, both that which is against Him, and that which is against thy neighbor. Be at peace with all men, consider with what character God saveth thee. "Blessed are the peacemakers, for they shall be called sons of God" (Matt. 5:9). Such always imitate the Son of God: do thou imitate Him too. Be at peace. The more thy brother warreth against thee, by so much the greater will be thy reward. For hear the prophet who saith, "With the haters of peace I was peaceful" (Ps. 120:7, Sept.). This is virtue, this is above man's understanding, this maketh us near God; nothing so much delighteth God as to remember no evil. This sets thee free from thy sins, this looseth the charges against thee: but if we are fighting and buffeting, we become far off from God: for enmities are produced by conflict, and from enmity springs remembrance of evil.

Cut out the root, and there will be no fruit. Thus shall we learn to despise the things of this life, for there is no conflict, none, in spiritual things, but whatever thou seest, either conflicts or envy, or whatever a man can mention, all these spring from the things of this life. Every conflict hath its beginning either in covetousness, or envy, or vainglory. If therefore we are at peace, we shall learn to despise the things of the earth. Hath a man stolen our money? He hath not injured us, only let him not steal our treasure which is above. Hath he hindered thy glory? Yet not that which is from God, but that which is of no account. For this is no glory, but a mere name of glory, or rather a shame. Hath he stolen thy honor? Rather not thine but his own. For as he who committeth injustice doth not so much inflict as receive injustice, thus

too he who plots against his neighbor, first destroyeth himself.

For "he who diggeth a pit for his neighbor, falleth into it" (Prov. 26:27). Let us then not plot against others, lest we injure ourselves. When we supplant the reputation of others, let us consider that we injure ourselves, it is against ourselves we plot. For perchance with men we do him harm, if we have power, but we injure ourselves in the sight of God, by provoking Him against us. Let us not then harm ourselves. For as we injure ourselves when we injure our neighbors, so by benefiting them we benefit ourselves. If then thy enemy harm thee, he hath benefited thee if thou art wise, and so requite him not with the same things, but even do him good. But the blow, you say, remains severe. Consider then that thou dost not benefit, but punishest him, and benefitest thyself, and quickly you will come to do him good. What then? Shall we act from this motive? We ought not to act on this motive, but if thy heart will not hear other reason, induce it, saith he, even by this, and thou wilt quickly persuade it to dismiss its enmity, and wilt for the future do good to thine enemy as to a friend, and wilt obtain the good things which are to come, to which God grant that we may all attain in Christ Jesus. Amen.

John Chrysostom, Homily 14, c.347–407

The Lord's Prayer
Cyprian

1. The evangelical precepts, beloved brethren, are nothing else than divine teachings, – foundations on which hope is to be built, supports to strengthen faith, nourishments for cheering the heart, rudders for guiding our way, guards for obtaining salvation, – which, while they instruct the docile minds of believers on the earth, lead them to heavenly kingdoms.

God, moreover, willed many things to he said and to be heard by means of the prophets His servants; but how much greater are those which the Son speaks, which the Word of God who was in the prophets testifies with His own voice; not now bidding to prepare the way for His coming, but Himself coming and opening and showing to us the way, so that we who have before been wandering in the darkness of death, without forethought and blind, being enlightened by the light of grace, might keep the way of life, with the Lord for our ruler and guide!

2. He, among the rest of His salutary admonitions and divine precepts wherewith He counsels His people for their salvation, Himself also gave a form of praying – Himself advised and instructed us what we should pray for. He who made us to live, taught us also to pray, with that same benignity, to wit, wherewith He has condescended to give and confer all things else; in order that while we speak to the Father in that prayer and supplication which the Son has taught us, we may be the more easily heard.

Already He had foretold that the hour was coming "when the true worshippers should worship the Father in spirit and in truth" (Jn. 4:23); and He thus fulfilled what He before promised, so that we who by His sanctification (or, "satisfaction") have received the Spirit and truth, may also by His teaching worship truly and spiritually. For what can be a more spiritual prayer than that which was given to us by Christ, by whom also the Holy Spirit was given to us? What praying to the Father can be more truthful than that which was delivered to us by the Son who is the Truth, out of His own mouth? So that to pray otherwise than He taught is not ignorance alone, but also sin; since He Himself has established, and said, "Ye reject the commandments of God, that ye may keep your own traditions" (Mk. 7:9).

3. Let us therefore, brethren beloved, pray as God our Teacher has taught us. It is a loving and friendly prayer to beseech God with His own word, to come up to His ears in the prayer of Christ. Let the Father acknowledge the words of His Son when we make our prayer, and let Him also who dwells within in our breast Himself dwell in our voice. And since we have Him as an Advocate with the Father for our sins, let us, when as sinners we petition on behalf of our sins, put forward the words of our Advocate. For since He says, that "whatsoever we shall ask of the Father in His name, He will give us" (Jn. 16:23), how much more effectually do we obtain what we ask in Christ's name, if we ask for it in His own

prayer! (Cf. Jn. 14:6).

4. But let our speech and petition when we pray be under discipline, observing quietness and modesty. Let us consider that we are standing in God's sight. We must please the divine eyes both with the habit of body and with the measure of voice. For as it is characteristic of a shameless man to be noisy with his cries, so, on the other hand, it is fitting to the modest man to pray with moderated petitions.

Moreover, in His teaching the Lord has bidden us to pray in secret – in hidden and remote places, in our very bed-chambers – which is best suited to faith, that we may know that God is everywhere present, and hears and sees all, and in the plenitude of His majesty penetrates even into hidden and secret places, as it is written, "I am a God at hand, and not a God afar off. If a man shall hide himself in secret places, shall I not then see him? Do not I fill heaven and earth?" (Jr. 23:23,24). And again: "The eyes of the Lord are in every place, beholding the evil and the good" (Pr. 15:3).

And when we meet together with the brethren in one place, and celebrate divine sacrifices with God's priest, we ought to be mindful of modesty and discipline – not to throw abroad our prayers indiscriminately, with unsubdued voices, nor to cast to God with tumultuous wordiness a petition that ought to be commended to God by modesty; for God is the hearer, not of the voice, but of the heart. Nor need He be clamorously reminded, since He sees men's thoughts, as the Lord proves to us when He says, "Why think ye evil in your hearts?" (Mt. 9:4). And in another place: "And all the churches shall know that I am He that searcheth the hearts and reins" (Rv. 2:23).

5. And this Hannah in the first book of Kings, who was a type of the Church, maintains and observes, in that she prayed to God not with clamorous petition, but silently and modestly, within the very recesses of her heart. She spoke with hidden prayer, but with manifest faith. She spoke not with her voice, but with her heart, because she knew that thus God hears; and she effectually obtained what she sought, because she asked it with belief. Divine Scripture asserts this, when it says, "She spake in her heart, and her lips moved, and her voice was not heard; and God did hear her" (1 Sm. 1:13).

We read also in the Psalms, "Speak in your hearts, and in your beds, and be ye pierced" (Ps 4:4).

6. And let not the worshiper, beloved brethren, be ignorant in what manner the publican prayed with the Pharisee in the temple. Not with eyes lifted up boldly to heaven, nor with hands proudly raised; but beating his breast, and testifying to the sins shut up within, he implored the help of the divine mercy. And while the Pharisee was pleased with himself, this man who thus asked, the rather deserved to be sanctified, since he placed the hope of salvation not in the confidence of his innocence, because there is none who is innocent; but confessing his sinfulness he humbly prayed, and He who pardons the humble heard the petitioner.

And these things the Lord records in His Gospel, saying, "Two men went up into the temple to pray; the one a Pharisee, and the other a publican. The Pharisee stood, and prayed thus with himself: God, I thank Thee that I am not as other men are, unjust, extortioners, adulterers, even as this publican. I fast twice in the week, I give tithes of all that I possess. But the publican stood afar off, and would not so much as lift up his eyes unto heaven, but smote upon his breast, saying, God, be merciful to me a sinner. I say unto you, this man went down to his house justified rather than the Pharisee: for every one that exalteth himself shall be abased; and whosoever humbleth himself shall be exalted" (Lk. 18:10–14).

7. These things, beloved brethren, when we have learnt from the sacred reading, and have gathered in what way we ought to approach to prayer, let us know also from the Lord's teaching what we should pray. "Thus," says He, "pray ye: – "Our Father, which art in heaven, Hallowed be Thy name. Thy kingdom come. Thy will be done, as in heaven so in earth. Give us this day our daily bread. And forgive us our debts, as we forgive our debtors. And suffer us not to be led into temptation; but deliver us from evil. Amen" (Mt. 6:9).

8. Before all things, the Teacher of peace and the Master of unity would not have prayer to be made singly and individually, as for one who prays to pray for himself alone. For we say not "My Father, which art in heaven," nor

"Give me this day my daily bread"; nor does each one ask that only his own debt should be forgiven him; nor does he request for himself alone that he may not be led into temptation, and delivered from evil. Our prayer is public and common; and when we pray, we pray not for one, but for the whole people, because we the whole people are one. The God of peace and the Teacher of concord, who taught unity, willed that one should thus pray for all, even as He Himself bore us all in one.

This law of prayer the three children observed when they were shut up in the fiery furnace, speaking together in prayer, and being of one heart in the agreement of the spirit; and this the faith of the sacred Scripture assures us, and in telling us how such as these prayed, gives an example which we ought to follow in our prayers, in order that we may be such as they were: "Then these three," it says, "as if from one mouth sang an hymn, and blessed the Lord" (Dn. 3:51 LXX (3 Youths 28)). They spoke as if from one mouth, although Christ had not yet taught them how to pray. And therefore, as they prayed, their speech was availing and effectual, because a peaceful, and sincere, and spiritual prayer deserved well of the Lord.

Thus also we find that the apostles, with the disciples, prayed after the Lord's ascension: "They all," says the Scripture, "continued with one accord in prayer, with the women, and Mary who was the mother of Jesus, and with His brethren" (Ac. 1:14). They continued with one accord in prayer, declaring both by the urgency and by the agreement (or, "both the urgency and the agreement") of their praying, that God, "who maketh men to dwell of one mind in a house" (Ps. 67(68):6), only admits into the divine and eternal home those among whom prayer is unanimous.

9. But what matters of deep moment are contained in the Lord's prayer! How many and how great, briefly collected in the words, but spiritually abundant in virtue! so that there is absolutely nothing passed over that is not comprehended in these our prayers and petitions, as in a compendium of heavenly doctrine.

"After this manner," says He, "pray ye: Our Father, which art in heaven." The new man, born again and restored to his God by His grace, says "Father," in the first place because he has now begun to be a son. "He came," He says, "to His own, and His own received Him not. But as many as received Him, to them gave He power to become the sons of God, even to them that believe in His name" (Jn. 1:11). The man, therefore, who has believed in His name, and has become God's son, ought from this point to begin both to give thanks and to profess himself God's son, by declaring that God is his Father in heaven; and also to bear witness, among the very first words of his new birth, that he has renounced an earthly and carnal father, and that he has begun to know as well as to have as a father Him only who is in heaven, as it is written: "They who say unto their father and their mother, I have not known thee, and who have not acknowledged their own children; these have observed Thy precepts and have kept Thy covenant" (Dt. 33:9).

Also the Lord in His Gospel has bidden us to call "no man our father upon earth, because there is to us one Father, who is in heaven" (Mt. 23:9). And to the disciple who had made mention of his dead father, He replied, "Let the dead bury their dead" (Mt. 8:22); for he had said that his father was dead, while the Father of believers is living.

10. Nor ought we, beloved brethren, only to observe and understand that we should call Him Father who is in heaven; but we add to it, and say our Father, that is, the Father of those who believe – of those who, being sanctified by Him, and restored by the nativity of spiritual grace, have begun to be sons of God.

A word this, moreover, which rebukes and condemns the Jews, who not only unbelievingly despised Christ, who had been announced to them by the prophets, and sent first to them, but also cruelly put Him to death; and these cannot now call God their Father, since the Lord confounds and confutes them, saying, "Ye are born of your father the devil, and the lusts of your father ye will do. For he was a murderer from the beginning, and abode not in the truth, because there is no truth in him" (Jn. 8:44). And by Isaiah the prophet God cries in wrath, "I have begotten and brought up children; but they have despised me. The ox knoweth his owner, and the ass his master's

crib; but Israel hath not known me, and my people hath not understood me. Ah sinful nation, a people laden with sins, a wicked seed, corrupt (or, "lawlesss") children! Ye have forsaken the Lord; ye have provoked the Holy One of Israel to anger" (Is. 1:3). In repudiation of these, we Christians, when we pray, say Our Father; because He has begun to be ours, and has ceased to be the Father of the Jews, who have forsaken Him. Nor can a sinful people be a son; but the name of sons is attributed to those to whom remission of sins is granted, and to them immortality is promised anew, in the words of our Lord Himself: "Whosoever committeth sin is the servant of sin. And the servant abideth not in the house for ever, but the son abideth ever" (Jn. 8:34).

11. But how great is the Lord's indulgence! how great His condescension and plenteousness of goodness towards us, seeing that He has wished us to pray in the sight of God in such a way as to call God Father, and to call ourselves sons of God, even as Christ is the Son of God, – a name which none of us would dare to venture on in prayer, unless He Himself had allowed us thus to pray! We ought then, beloved brethren, to remember and to know, that when we call God Father, we ought to act as God's children; so that in the measure in which we find pleasure in considering God as a Father, He might also be able to find pleasure in us.

Let us converse as temples of God, that it may be plain that God dwells in us. Let not our doings be degenerate from the Spirit; so that we who have begun to be heavenly and spiritual, may consider and do nothing but spiritual and heavenly things; since the Lord God Himself has said, "Them that honor me I will honor; and he that despiseth me shall be despised" (1 Sm. 2:30). The blessed apostle also has laid down in his epistle: "Ye are not your own; for ye are bought with a great price. Glorify and bear about God in your body" (1 Co. 6:20).

12. After this we say, "Hallowed be Thy name;" not that we wish for God that He may be hallowed by our prayers, but that we beseech of Him that His name may be hallowed in us. But by whom is God sanctified, since He Himself sanctifies? Well, because He says, "Be

ye holy, even as I am holy" (Lv. 20:7), we ask and entreat, that we who were sanctified in baptism may continue in that which we have begun to be. And this we daily pray for; for we have need of daily sanctification, that we who daily fall away may wash out our sins by continual sanctification. And what the sanctification is which is conferred upon us by the condescension of God, the apostle declares, when he says, "neither fornicators, nor idolaters, nor adulterers, nor effeminate, nor abusers of themselves with mankind, nor thieves, nor deceivers, nor drunkards, nor revilers, nor extortioners, shall inherit the kingdom of God. And such indeed were you; but ye are washed; but ye are justified; but ye are sanctified in the name of our Lord Jesus Christ, and by the Spirit of our God" (1 Co. 6:9). He says that we are sanctified in the name of our Lord Jesus Christ, and by the Spirit of our God. We pray that this sanctification may abide in us and because our Lord and Judge warns the man that was healed and quickened by Him, to sin no more lest a worse thing happen unto him, (Jn. 5:14), we make this supplication in our constant prayers, we ask this day and night, that the sanctification and quickening which is received from the grace of God may be preserved by His protection.

13. There follows in the prayer, Thy kingdom come. We ask that the kingdom of God may be set forth to us, even as we also ask that His name may be sanctified in us. For when does God not reign, or when does that begin with Him which both always has been, and never ceases to be? We pray that our kingdom, which has been promised us by God, may come, which was acquired by the blood and passion of Christ; that we who first are His subjects in the world, may hereafter reign with Christ when He reigns, as He Himself promises and says, "Come, ye blessed of my Father, receive the kingdom which has been prepared for you from the beginning of the world" (Mt. 25:34).

Christ Himself, dearest brethren, however, may be the kingdom of God, whom we day by day desire to come, whose advent we crave to be quickly manifested to us. For since He is Himself the (or, "our") Resurrection, since in Him we rise again, so also the kingdom of God may be understood to be Himself, since in Him we shall reign. But we do well in seeking the kingdom of God, that is, the heavenly kingdom, because there is also an earthly kingdom. But he who has already renounced the world, is moreover greater than its honors and its kingdom. And therefore he who dedicates himself to God and Christ, desires not earthly, but heavenly kingdoms. But there is need of continual prayer and supplication, that we fall not away from the heavenly kingdom, as the Jews, to whom this promise had first been given, fell away; even as the Lord sets forth and proves: "Many," says He, "shall come from the east and from the west, and shall recline with Abraham, and Isaac, and Jacob in the kingdom of heaven. But the children of the kingdom shall be cast out into outer darkness: there shall be weeping and gnashing of teeth" (Mt. 8:11). He shows that the Jews were previously children of the kingdom, so long as they continued also to be children of God; but after the name of Father ceased to be recognized among them, the kingdom also ceased; and therefore we Christians, who in our prayer begin to call God our Father, pray also that God's kingdom may come to us.

14. We add, also, and say, "Thy will be done, as in heaven so in earth"; not that God should do what He wills, but that we may be able to do what God wills. For who resists God, that He may not do what He wills? But since we are hindered by the devil from obeying with our thought and deed God's will in all things, we pray and ask that God's will may be done in us; and that it may be done in us we have need of God's good will, that is, of His help and protection, since no one is strong in his own strength, but he is safe by the grace and mercy of God. And further, the Lord, setting forth the infirmity of the humanity which He bore, says, "Father, if it be possible, let this cup pass from me'" and affording an example to His disciples that they should do not their own will, but God's, He went on to say, "Nevertheless not as I will, but as Thou wilt" (Mt. 26:39). And in another place He says, "I came down from heaven not to do my own will, but the will of Him that sent me" (Jn. 6:38). Now if the Son was obedient to do His Father's will, how much more should the servant be obedient to do his Master's will! as in his epistle John also exhorts and instructs us to do the will of God, saying,

"Love not the world, neither the things that are in the world. If any man love the world, the love of the Father is not in him. For all that is in the world is the lust of the flesh, and the lust of the eyes, and the ambition of life, which is not of the Father, but of the lust of the world. And the world shall pass away, and the lust thereof: but he that doeth the will of God abideth for ever, even as God also abideth for ever" (1 Jn. 2:15–17). We who desire to abide for ever should do the will of God, who is everlasting.

15. Now that is the will of God which Christ both did and taught. Humility in conversation; steadfastness in faith; modesty in words; justice in deeds; mercifulness in works; discipline in morals; to be unable to do a wrong, and to be able to bear a wrong when done; to keep peace with the brethren; to love God with all one's heart; to love Him in that He is a Father; to fear Him in that He is God; to prefer nothing whatever to Christ, because He did not prefer anything to us; to adhere inseparably to His love; to stand by His cross bravely and faithfully; when there is any contest on behalf of His name and honor, to exhibit in discourse that constancy wherewith we make confession; in torture, that confidence wherewith we do battle; in death, that patience whereby we are crowned; – this is to desire to be fellow-heirs with Christ; this is to do the commandment of God; this is to fulfill the will of the Father.

16. Moreover, we ask that the will of God may be done both in heaven and in earth, each of which things pertains to the fulfillment of our safety and salvation. For since we possess the body from the earth and the spirit from heaven, we ourselves are earth and heaven; and in both – that is, both in body and spirit – we pray that God's will may be done. For between the flesh and spirit there is a struggle; and there is a daily strife as they disagree one with the other, so that we cannot do those very things that we would (Rm. 7:16–20), in that the spirit seeks heavenly and divine things, while the flesh lusts after earthly and temporal things; and therefore we ask that, by the help and assistance of God, agreement may be made between these two natures, so that while the will of God is done both in the spirit and in the flesh, the soul which is new-born by Him may be preserved.

This is what the Apostle Paul openly and manifestly declares by his words: "The flesh," says he, "lusteth against the spirit, and the spirit against the flesh: for these are contrary the one to the other; so that ye cannot do the things that ye would. Now the works of the flesh are manifest, which are these; adulteries, fornications, uncleanness, lasciviousness, idolatry, witchcraft, murders, hatred, variance, emulations, wraths, strife, seditions, dissensions, heresies, envyings, drunkenness, reveling, and such like: of the which I tell you before, as I have also told you in times past, that they which do such things shall not inherit the kingdom of God. But the fruit of the spirit is love, joy, peace, magnanimity, goodness, faith, gentleness, continence, chastity" (Gal. 5:17–22). And therefore we make it our prayer in daily, yea, in continual supplications, that the will of God concerning us should be done both in heaven and in earth; because this is the will of God, that earthly things should give place to heavenly, and that spiritual and divine things should prevail.

17. And it may be thus understood, beloved brethren, that since the Lord commands and admonishes us even to love our enemies, and to pray even for those who persecute us, we should ask, moreover, for those who are still earth, and have not yet begun to be heavenly, that even in respect of these God's will should be done, which Christ accomplished in preserving and renewing humanity. For since the disciples are not now called by Him earth, but the salt of the earth, and the apostle designates the first man as being from the dust of the earth, but the second from heaven, we reasonably, who ought to be like God our Father, who maketh His sun to rise upon the good and bad, and sends rain upon the just and the unjust, so pray and ask by the admonition of Christ as to make our prayer for the salvation of all men; that as in heaven – that is, in us by our faith – the will of God has been done, so that we might be of heaven; so also in earth – that is, in those who believe not (some editions omit the not) – God's will may be done, that they who as yet are by their first birth of earth, may, being born of water and of the Spirit, begin to be of heaven.

18. As the prayer goes forward, we ask and say, "Give us this day our daily bread." And

this may be understood both spiritually and literally, because either way of understanding it is rich in divine usefulness to our salvation. For Christ is the bread of life; and this bread does not belong to all men, but it is ours. And according as we say, "Our Father," because He is the Father of those who understand and believe; so also we call it "our bread," because Christ is the bread of those who are in union with His body. [Or, "According as we say Our Father, so also we call Christ our bread, because He is ours as we come in contact with His body.")

And we ask that this bread should be given to us daily, that we who are in Christ, and daily receive the Eucharist for the food of salvation, may not, by the interposition of some heinous sin, by being prevented, as withheld and not communicating, from partaking of the heavenly bread, be separated from Christ's body, as He Himself predicts, and warns, "I am the bread of life which came down from heaven. If any man eat of my bread, he shall live for ever: and the bread which I will give is my flesh, for the life of the world" (Jn. 6:58) .When, therefore, He says, that whoever shall eat of His bread shall live for ever; as it is manifest that those who partake of His body and receive the Eucharist by the right of communion are living, so, on the other hand, we must fear and pray lest any one who, being withheld from communion, is separate from Christ's body should remain at a distance from salvation; as He Himself threatens, and says, "Unless ye eat the flesh of the Son of man, and drink His blood, ye shall have no life in you" (Jn. 6:53). And therefore we ask that our bread – that is, Christ – may be given to us daily, that we who abide and live in Christ may not depart from His sanctification and body.

19. But it may also be thus understood, that we who have renounced the world, and have cast away its riches and pomps in the faith of spiritual grace, should only ask for ourselves food and support, since the Lord instructs us, and says, "Whosoever forsaketh not all that he hath, cannot be my disciple" (Lk. 14:33). But he who has begun to be Christ's disciple, renouncing all things according to the word of his Master, ought to ask for his daily food, and not to extend the desires of his petition

to a long period, as the Lord again prescribes, and says, "'Take no thought for the morrow, for the morrow itself shall take thought for itself. Sufficient for the day is the evil thereof" (Mt. 6:34). With reason, then, does Christ's disciple ask food for himself for the day, since he is prohibited from thinking of the morrow; because it becomes a contradiction and a repugnant thing for us to seek to live long in this world, since we ask that the kingdom of God should come quickly. Thus also the blessed apostle admonishes us, giving substance and strength to the steadfastness of our hope and faith: "We brought nothing," says he, "into this world, nor indeed can we carry anything out. Having therefore food and raiment, let us be herewith content. But they that will be rich fall into temptation and a snare, and into many and hurtful lusts, which drown men in perdition and destruction. For the love of money is the root of all evil; which while some coveted after, they have made shipwreck from the faith, and have pierced themselves through with many sorrows" (1 Tm. 6:7).

20. He teaches us that riches are not only to be contemned, but that they are also full of peril; that in them is the root of seducing evils, that deceive the blindness of the human mind by a hidden deception. Whence also God rebukes the rich fool, who thinks of his earthly wealth, and boasts himself in the abundance of his overflowing harvests, saying, "Thou fool, this night thy soul shall be required of thee; then whose shall those things be which thou hast provided?" (Lk. 12:20). The fool who was to die that very night was rejoicing in his stores, and he to whom life already was failing, was thinking of the abundance of his food. But, on the other hand, the Lord tells us that he becomes perfect and complete who sells all his goods, and distributes them for the use of the poor, and so lays up for himself treasure in heaven. He says that that man is able to follow Him, and to imitate the glory of the Lord's passion, who, free from hindrance, and with his loins girded, is involved in no entanglements of worldly estate, but, at large and free himself, accompanies his possessions, which before have been sent to God. For which result, that every one of us may be able to prepare himself, let him thus learn to pray, and know, from the

character of the prayer, what he ought to be.

21. For daily bread cannot be wanting to the righteous man, since it is written, "The Lord will not slay the soul of the righteous by hunger" (Pr. 10:3); and again "I have been young and now am old, yet have I not seen the righteous forsaken, nor his seed begging their bread." [Ps. 36(37):25) And the Lord moreover promises and says, "Take no thought, saying, "What shall we eat, or what shall we drink, or wherewithal shall we be clothed? For after all these things do the nations seek. And your Father knoweth that ye have need of all these things. Seek ye first the kingdom of God and His righteousness, and all these things shall be added unto you" (Mt. 6:31). To those who seek God's kingdom and righteousness, He promises that all things shall be added. For since all things are God's, nothing will be wanting to him who possesses God, if God Himself be not wanting to him. Thus a meal was divinely provided for Daniel: when he was shut up by the king's command in the den of lions, and in the midst of wild beasts who were hungry, and yet spared him, the man of God was fed. Thus Elijah in his flight was nourished both by ravens ministering to him in his solitude, and by birds bringing him food in his persecution. And – oh detestable cruelty of the malice of man! – the wild beasts spare, the birds feed, while men lay snares, and rage!

22. After this we also entreat for our sins, saying, "And forgive us our debts, as we also forgive our debtors." After the supply of food, pardon of sin is also asked for, that he who is fed by God may live in God, and that not only the present and temporal life may be provided for, but the eternal also, to which we may come if our sins are forgiven; and these the Lord calls debts, as He says in His Gospel, "I forgave thee all that debt, because thou desiredst me" (Mt. 18:32). And how necessarily, how providently and salutarily, are we admonished that we are sinners, since we are compelled to entreat for our sins, and while pardon is asked for from God, the soul recalls its own consciousness of sin! Lest any one should flatter himself that he is innocent, (some manuscripts add "although none is innocent") and by exalting himself should more deeply perish, he is instructed and taught that he sins daily, in that he is bidden to

entreat daily for his sins. Thus, moreover, John also in his epistle warns us, and says, "If we say that we have no sin, we deceive ourselves, and the truth is not in us; but if we confess our sins, the Lord is faithful and just to forgive us our sins" (1 Jn.1:8). In his epistle he has combined both, that we should entreat for our sins, and that we should obtain pardon when we ask. Therefore he said that the Lord was faithful to forgive sins, keeping the faith of His promise; because He who taught us to pray for our debts and sins, has promised that His fatherly mercy and pardon shall follow.

23. He has clearly joined herewith and added the law, and has bound us by a certain condition and engagement, that we should ask that our debts be forgiven us in such a manner as we ourselves forgive our debtors, knowing that that which we seek for our sins cannot be obtained unless we ourselves have acted in a similar way in respect of our debtors. Therefore also He says in another place, "With what measure ye mete, it shall be measured to you again" (Mt. 7:2). And the servant who, after having had all his debt forgiven him by his master, would not forgive his fellow-servant, is cast back into prison; because he would not forgive his fellow-servant, he lost the indulgence that had been shown to himself by his lord (Mt. 18:32).

And these things Christ still more urgently sets forth in His precepts with yet greater power of His rebuke. "When ye stand praying," says He, "forgive if ye have aught against any, that your Father which is in heaven may forgive you your trespasses. But if ye do not forgive, neither will your Father which is in heaven forgive you your trespasses" (Mk. 11:25). There remains no ground of excuse in the day of judgment, when you will be judged according to your own sentence; and whatever you have done, that you also will suffer. For God commands us to be peacemakers, and in agreement, and of one mind in His house (Ps. 67(68):6 Vulgate); and such as He makes us by a second birth, such He wishes us when new-born to continue, that we who have begun to be sons of God may abide in God's peace, and that, having one spirit, we should also have one heart and one mind. Thus God does not receive the sacrifice of a person who is in disagreement, but commands him to go back from the altar and first be reconciled to his brother, that so God also may be appeased by the prayers of a peace-maker. Our peace and brotherly agreement is the greater sacrifice to God, – and a people united in one in the unity of the Father, and of the Son, and of the Holy Spirit.

24. For even in the sacrifices which Abel and Cain first offered, God looked not at their gifts, but at their hearts, so that he was acceptable in his gift who was acceptable in his heart. Abel, peaceable and righteous in sacrificing in innocence to God, taught others also, when they bring their gift to the altar, thus to come with the fear of God, with a simple heart, with the law of righteousness, with the peace of concord. With reason did he, who was such in respect of God's sacrifice, become subsequently himself a sacrifice to God; so that he who first set forth martyrdom, and initiated the Lord's passion by the glory of his blood, had both the Lord's righteousness and His peace (Gn. 4:1–16).

Finally, such are crowned by the Lord, such will be avenged (or, "will judge") with the Lord in the day of judgment; but the quarrelsome and disunited, and he who has not peace with his brethren, in accordance with what the blessed apostle and the Holy Scripture testifies, even if he have been slain for the name of Christ, shall not be able to escape the crime of fraternal dissension, because, as it is written, "He who hateth his brother is a murderer" (1 Jn. 3:15) and no murderer attains to the kingdom of heaven, nor does he live with God. He cannot be with Christ, who had rather be an imitator of Judas than of Christ. How great is the sin which cannot even be washed away by a baptism of blood – how heinous the crime which cannot be expiated by martyrdom!

25. Moreover, the Lord of necessity admonishes us to say in prayer, "And suffer us not to be led into temptation." In which words it is shown that the adversary can do nothing against us except God shall have previously permitted it; so that all our fear, and devotion, and obedience may be turned towards God, since in our temptations nothing is permitted to evil unless power is given from Him. This is proved by divine Scripture, which says,

"Nebuchadnezzar king of Babylon came to Jerusalem, and besieged it; and the Lord delivered it into his hand" (2 Kg. 24:11). But power is given to evil against us according to our sins, as it is written, "Who gave Jacob for a spoil, and Israel to those who make a prey of Him? Did not the Lord, against whom they sinned, and would not walk in His ways, nor hear His law? and He has brought upon them the anger of His wrath" (Is. 42:24). And again, when Solomon sinned, and departed from the Lord's commandments and ways, it is recorded, "And the Lord stirred up Satan against Solomon himself" (1 Kg. 11:14).

26. Now power is given against us in two modes: either for punishment when we sin, or for glory when we are proved, as we see was done with respect to Job; as God Himself sets forth, saying, "Behold, all that he hath I give unto thy hands; but be careful not to touch himself" (Jb. 1:12). And the Lord in His Gospel says, in the time of His passion, "Thou couldest have no power against me unless it were given thee from above" (Jn. 19:11). But when we ask that we may not come into temptation, we are reminded of our infirmity and weakness in that we thus ask, lest any should insolently vaunt himself, lest any should proudly and arrogantly assume anything to himself, lest any should take to himself the glory either of confession or of suffering as his own, when the Lord Himself, teaching humility, said, "Watch and pray, that ye enter not into temptation; the spirit indeed is willing, but the flesh is weak" (Mk. 14:38); so that while a humble and submissive confession comes first, and all is attributed to God, whatever is sought for suppliantly with fear and honor of God, may be granted by His own loving-kindness.

27. After all these things, in the conclusion of the prayer comes a brief clause, which shortly and comprehensively sums up all our petitions and our prayers. For we conclude by saying, "But deliver us from evil," comprehending all adverse things which the enemy attempts against us in this world, from which there may be a faithful and sure protection if God deliver us, if He afford His help to us who pray for and implore it. And when we say, Deliver us from evil, there remains nothing further which ought to be asked. When we have once asked

for God's protection against evil, and have obtained it, then against everything which the devil and the world work against us we stand secure and safe. For what fear is there in this life, to the man whose guardian in this life is God?

28. What wonder is it, beloved brethren, if such is the prayer which God taught, seeing that He condensed in His teaching all our prayer in one saving sentence? This had already been before foretold by Isaiah the prophet, when, being filled with the Holy Spirit, he spoke of the majesty and loving-kindness of God, "consummating and shortening His word," He says, "in righteousness, because a shortened word will the Lord make in the whole earth" (Is. 10:22). For when the Word of God, our Lord Jesus Christ, came unto all, and gathering alike the learned and unlearned, published to every sex and every age the precepts of salvation, He made a large compendium of His precepts, that the memory of the scholars might not be burdened in the celestial learning, but might quickly learn what was necessary to a simple faith. Thus, when He taught what is life eternal, He embraced the sacrament of life in a large and divine brevity, saying, "And this is life eternal, that they might know Thee, the only and true God, and Jesus Christ, whom Thou hast sent" (Jn. 17:3). Also, when He would gather from the law and the prophets the first and greatest commandments, He said, "Hear, O Israel; the Lord thy God is one God: and thou shalt love the Lord thy God with all thy heart, and with all thy mind, and with all thy strength. This is the first commandment. And the second is like unto it, Thou shalt love thy neighbor as thyself" (Mt. 12:29–31). "On these two commandments hang all the law and the prophets" (Mt. 22:40). And again: "Whatsoever good things ye would that men should do unto you, do ye even so to them. For this is the law and the prophets" (Mt. 7:12).

29. Nor was it only in words, but in deeds also, that the Lord taught us to pray, Himself praying frequently and beseeching, and thus showing us, by the testimony of His example, what it behoved us to do, as it is written, "But Himself departed into a solitary place, and there prayed" (Lk. 5:16). And again: "He went out into a mountain to pray, and continued all night in prayer to God" (Lk. 6:12). But if He prayed who was with-

out sin, how much more ought sinners to pray; and if He prayed continually, watching through the whole night in uninterrupted petitions, how much more ought we to watch nightly in constantly repeated prayer!

30. But the Lord prayed and besought not for Himself – for why should He who was guiltless pray on His own behalf? – but for our sins, as He Himself declared, when He said to Peter, "Behold, Satan hath desired that he might sift you as wheat. But I have prayed for thee, that thy faith fail not" (Lk. 22:31). And subsequently He beseeches the Father for all, saying, "Neither pray I for these alone, but for them also which shall believe on me through their word; that they all may be one; as Thou, Father, art in me, and I in Thee, that they also may be one in us" (Jn. 17:20). The Lord's loving-kindness, no less than His mercy, is great in respect of our salvation, in that, not content to redeem us with His blood, He in addition also prayed for us. Behold now what was the desire of His petition, that like as the Father and Son are one, so also we should abide in absolute unity; so that from this it may be understood how greatly he sins who divides unity and peace, since for this same thing even the Lord besought, desirous doubtless that His people should thus be saved and live in peace, since He knew that discord cannot come into the kingdom of God

31. Moreover, when we stand praying, beloved brethren, we ought to be watchful and earnest with our whole heart, intent on our prayers. Let all carnal and worldly thoughts pass away, nor let the soul at that time think on anything but the object only of its prayer. For this reason also the priest, by way of preface before his prayer, prepares the minds of the brethren by saying, "Lift up your hearts," that so upon the people's response, "We lift them up unto the Lord," he may be reminded that he himself ought to think of nothing but the Lord. Let the breast be closed against the adversary, and be open to God alone; nor let it suffer God's enemy to approach to it at the time of prayer. For frequently he steals upon us, and penetrates within, and by crafty deceit calls away our prayers from God, that we may have one thing in our heart and another in our voice, when not the sound of the voice, but the soul and mind, ought to be praying to the Lord with a simple intention. But what carelessness

it is, to be distracted and carried away by foolish and profane thoughts when you are praying to the Lord, as if there were anything which you should rather be thinking of than that you are speaking with God! How can you ask to be heard of God, when you yourself do not hear yourself? Do you wish that God should remember you when you ask, if you yourself do not remember yourself? This is absolutely to take no precaution against the enemy; this is, when you pray to God, to offend the majesty of God by the carelessness of your prayer; this is to be watchful with your eyes, and to be asleep with your heart, while the Christian, even though he is asleep with his eyes, ought to be awake with his heart, as it is written in the person of the Church speaking in the Song of Songs, "I sleep, yet my heart waketh" (Ca. 5:2). Wherefore the apostle anxiously and carefully warns us, saying, "Continue in prayer, and watch in the same" (1 Co. 1:2); teaching, that is, and showing that those are able to obtain from God what they ask, whom God sees to be watchful in their prayer.

32. Moreover, those who pray should not come to God with fruitless or naked prayers. Petition is ineffectual when it is a barren entreaty that beseeches God. For as every tree that bringeth not forth fruit is cut down and cast into the fire; assuredly also, words that do not bear fruit cannot deserve anything of God, because they are fruitful in no result. And thus Holy Scripture instructs us, saying, "Prayer. is good with fasting and almsgiving" (Tb. 20:8). For He who will give us in the day of judgment a reward for our labors and alms, is even in this life a merciful hearer of one who comes to Him in prayer associated with good works. Thus, for instance, Cornelius the centurion, when he prayed, had a claim to be heard. For he was in the habit of doing many alms-deeds towards the people, and of ever praying to God. To this man, when he prayed about the ninth hour, appeared an angel bearing testimony to his labors, and saying, "Cornelius, thy prayers and thine alms are gone up in remembrance before God" (Ac. 10:2,4).

33. Those prayers quickly ascend to God which the merits of our labors urge upon God. Thus also Raphael the angel was a witness to the constant prayer and the constant good works of Tobias, saying, "It is honorable to reveal and confess the works of God. For when thou didst pray, and Sarah, I did bring the remembrance of your prayers before the holiness of God. And when thou didst bury the dead in simplicity, and because thou didst not delay to rise up and to leave thy dinner, but didst go out and cover the dead, I was sent to prove thee; and again God has sent me to heal thee, and Sarah thy daughter-in-law. For I am Raphael, one of the seven holy angels which stand and go in and out before the glory of God" (Tb. 12:12–15). By Isaiah also the Lord reminds us, and teaches similar things, saying, "Loosen every knot of iniquity, release the oppressions of contracts which have no power, let the troubled go into peace, and break every unjust engagement. Break thy bread to the hungry, and bring the poor that are without shelter into thy house. When thou seest the naked, clothe him; and despise not those of the same family and race as thyself. Then shall thy light break forth in season, and thy raiment shall spring forth speedily; and righteousness shall go before thee, and the glory of God shall surround thee. Then shalt thou call, and God shall hear thee; and while thou shalt yet speak, He shall say, Here I am" (Is. 58:6–9). He promises that He will be at hand, and says that He will hear and protect those who, loosening the knots of unrighteousness from their heart, and giving alms among the members of God's household according to His commands, even in hearing what God commands to be done, do themselves also deserve to be heard by God. The blessed Apostle Paul, when aided in the necessity of affliction by his brethren, said that good works which are performed are sacrifices to God. "I am full," saith he. "having received of Epaphroditus the things which were sent from you, an odor of a sweet smell, a sacrifice acceptable, well pleasing to God" (Ph. 4:18). For when one has pity on the poor, he lends to God; and he who gives to the least gives to God – sacrifices spiritually to God an odor of a sweet smell.

34. And in discharging the duties of prayer, we find that the three children with Daniel, being strong in faith and victorious in captivity (Dn. 1–3), observed the third, sixth, and ninth hour, as it were, for a sacrament of the Trinity, which in the last times had to be manifested. For

both the first hour in its progress to the third shows forth the consummated number of the Trinity, and also the fourth proceeding to the sixth declares another Trinity; and when from the seventh the ninth is completed, the perfect Trinity is numbered every three hours, which spaces of hours the worshipers of God in time past having spiritually decided on, made use of for determined and lawful times for prayer. And subsequently the thing was manifested, that these things were of old Sacraments, in that anciently righteous men prayed in this manner. For upon the disciples at the third hour the Holy Spirit descended, who fulfilled the grace of the Lord's promise(Ac. 2:15). Moreover, at the sixth hour, Peter, going up unto the house-top, was instructed as well by the sign as by the word of God admonishing him to receive all to the grace of salvation, whereas he was previously doubtful of the receiving of the Gentiles to baptism (Ac. 10:9). And from the sixth hour to the ninth, the Lord, being crucified, washed away our sins by His blood; and that He might redeem and quicken us, He then accomplished His victory by His passion.

35. But for us, beloved brethren, besides the hours of prayer observed of old, both the times and the sacraments have now increased in number. For we must also pray in the morning, that the Lord's resurrection may be celebrated by morning prayer. And this formerly the Holy Spirit pointed out in the Psalms, saying, "My King, and my God, because unto Thee will I cry; O Lord, in the morning shalt Thou hear my voice; in the morning will I stand before Thee, and will look up to Thee" (Ps. 5:2). And again, the Lord speaks by the mouth of the prophet: "Early in the morning shall they watch for me, saying, Let us go, and return unto the Lord our God"(Ho. 6:1). Also at the sun setting and at the decline of day, of necessity we must pray again. For since Christ is the true sun and the true day, as the worldly sun and worldly day depart, when we pray and ask that light may return to us again, we pray for the advent of Christ, which shall give us the grace of everlasting light. Moreover, the Holy Spirit in the Psalms manifests that Christ is called the day. "The stone," says He, "which the builders rejected, is become the head of the corner. This is the Lord's doing; and it is

marvelous in our eyes. This is the day which the Lord hath made; let us walk and rejoice in it" (Ps. 117(118):22). Also the prophet Malachi testifies that He is called the Sun, when he says, "But to you that fear the name of the Lord shall the Sun of righteousness arise, and there is healing in His wings" (Ml. 4:2). But if in the Holy Scriptures the true sun and the true day is Christ, there is no hour excepted for Christians wherein God ought not frequently and always to be worshipped; so that we who are in Christ – that is, in the true Sun and the true Day – should be instant throughout the entire day in petitions, and should pray; and when, by the law of the world, the revolving night, recurring in its alternate changes, succeeds, there can be no harm arising from the darkness of night to those who pray, because the children of light have the day even in the night. For when is he without light who has light in his heart? or when has not he the sun and the day, whose Sun and Day is Christ?

36. Let not us, then, who are in Christ – that is, always in the light – cease from praying even during night. Thus the widow Anna, without intermission praying and watching, persevered in deserving well of God, as it is written in the Gospel: "She departed not," it says, "from the temple, serving with fastings and prayers night and day" (Lk. 2:37). Let the Gentiles look to this, who are not yet enlightened, or the Jews who have remained in darkness by having forsaken the light. Let us, beloved brethren, who are always in the light of the Lord, who remember and hold fast what by grace received we have begun to be, reckon night for day; let us believe that we always walk in the light, and let us not be hindered by the darkness which we have escaped. Let there be no failure of prayers in the hours of night – no idle and reckless waste of the occasions of prayer. New-created and newborn of the Spirit by the mercy of God, let us imitate what we shall one day be. Since in the kingdom we shall possess day alone, without intervention of night, let us so watch in the night as if in the daylight. Since we are to pray and give thanks to God for ever, let us not cease in this life also to pray and give thanks.

Cyprian, c.200–258, Treatise IV: On the Lord's Prayer, translated by Ernest Wallis, 1886

Family Prayer

Philip Doddridge

This address may come into the hands of many, who have long been exemplary for their diligence and zeal in the duties I am about to recommend, such, I hope, will be confirmed, by what they read, in pursuing the good resolutions they have taken and the good customs they have formed, and will also be excited more earnestly to endeavor to contribute towards introducing the like into other families over which they have any influence, and especially into those which may branch out from their own, by the settlement of children or servants.

But I have those principally in view, who have hitherto lived in the omission of family-prayer.

While I write this, I have that awakening scripture before me: "Pour out my fury upon the heathen that know thee not, and upon the families that call not on thy name" (Jer. 10:25). I appeal to you, whether this does not strongly imply, that every family, which is not a heathen family, which is not quite ignorant of the living and true God, will call upon his name.

Well may it then pain my heart, to think that there should be a professedly Christian family, whom this dreadful character suits: well may it pain my heart, to think of the divine fury, which may be poured out on the heads and on the members of it: and well may it make me desirous to do my utmost to secure you and yours, from every appearance and possibility of such danger. Excuse the earnestness with which I may address you. I really fear lest while you delay, the fire of the divine pleasure should fall upon you (Gen. 19:16, 17). And as I adore the patience of God in having thus suspended the storm, I am anxious about every hour's delay, lest it should fall the heavier.

What I desire and intreat of you is, that you proportion honor and acknowledge God in your families, by calling them together every day to hear some part of his word read to them, and to join for a few minutes at least in your confessions, prayers, and praises to him. And is this a cause, that should need to be pleaded at large by a great variety of united motives? Truly the petition seems so reasonable, and a

compliance with it from one who has not quite renounced religion might seem so natural, that one would think worship the bare proposing of it must suffice. Yet experience tells, it is much otherwise. Some who maintain a public profession of religion have refused, and will continue to refuse year after year.

Reflect, Sir, (for I address myself to every particular person) seriously reflect on the reasonableness of family religion. Must not your consciences presently tell you, it is fit that persons who receive so many mercies together, should acknowledge them together? Can you in your mind be satisfied that you and your nearest relatives should pay no joint-homage to that God, who hath set you in your family, and who hath given to you, and to the several members of it, so many domestic enjoyments? Can it be right, if you have any sense of these things each of you in your own hearts, that the sense of them should be concealed and smothered there, and that you should never join in your grateful acknowledgments to him? Can you imagine it reasonable, that when you have a constant dependence upon him for so many mercies, without the concurrence of which your family would be a scene of misery, you should never present yourselves together in his presence to ask them at his hand? Upon what principles is public worship to be recommended and urged, if not by such as have their proportionable weight here?

Indeed the force of these considerations hath not only been known and acknowledged by the people of God in all ages; we have not only Noah and Abraham, Joshua and David, Job and Daniel, each under a much darker dispensation than ours, as examples of it; but even the poor heathen had their household images, some of them in private chapels, and others about the common hearth, where the family used to worship them by frequent prayers and sacrifices. And the brass, and wood, and stone, of which they consisted, shall (as it were) cry out against you, shall rise up against you and condemn you, if while you call yourselves the worshipers of the one living and eternal God, and beast in the revelation you have received by his prophets and by his Son, you presume to omit a homage, which the stupid worshipers of such vanities as these failed not to present to them, while they called them their Gods. Be persuaded then, I beseech you, to be consistent in your conduct. Either give up all pretences to religion, or maintain a steady and uniform regard to it, at home as well as abroad, in the family, as well as in the closet, or at church.

1. Consider the happy influence which the duty I am recommending might have upon the young members of your family, the children and servants committed to your care. For I now consider you, as a parent and a master. The father of a family is a phrase that comprehends both these relations; and with great propriety, as humanity obliges us to endeavor to take a parental care of all under our roof. And indeed, you ought to consider your servants, in this view, with a tender regard. They are probably in the flower of life, for that is the age which is commonly spent in service; and you should recollect how possible it is, that this may be, if rightly improved, the best opportunity their whole life may afford them for learning religion, and being brought under the power of it. Let them not, if they should finally perish, have cause to testify before God in the day of their condemnation, that "under your roof they learn the neglect and forgetfulness of God and all that their pious parents, perhaps in a much inferior station of life to you, had in earlier days been attempting to teach them." Or, if they come to you quite ignorant of religion, (as if they come from prayerless families, it is very probable that they do,) have compassion upon them, I intreat you, and endeavor to give them those advantages which they never yet had; and which it is too probable, as things are generally managed, they never will have, if you will not afford them.

But I would especially, if I might be allowed to borrow the pathetic words of Job, intreat you by the children of your own body (Job, 19:17). I would now as it were present them all before you, and beseech you by the bowels of parental affection, that to all the other tokens of tenderness and love, you would not refuse to add this, without which many of the rest may be worse than in vain.

Give me leave to plead with you, as the instruments of introducing them into being. O remember, it is indeed a debased and corrupted nature you have conveyed to them. Consider, that the world, into which you have been the means of bringing them, is a place in which they are surrounded with many temptations, and in which, as they advance in life, they must expect many more; so that it is much to be feared, that they will remain ignorant and forgetful of God, if they do not learn from you to love and serve him. For how can it be expected they should learn this at all, if you give them no advantages for receiving and practicing the lesson at home?

And let me further urge and intreat you to remember, that these dear children are committed to your special care by God their Creator, who has made them thus dependent upon you, that you might have an opportunity of forming their minds, and of influencing them to a right temper and conduct. And can this by any means be effectually done, if you do not at proper times call them together, to attend to the instructions of the word of God, and to join in solemn prayers and supplications to him? At least, is it possible it should be done any other way, with equal advantage, if this be not added to the rest?

Family-worship is a most proper way of teaching children religion, as you teach them language by insensible degrees; a little one day, and a little another; for to them line must be upon line, and precept upon precept. They may learn to conceive aright of the divine perfections, when they hear you daily acknowledging and adoring them: their hearts may be early touched with remorse for sin, when they hear your confessions poured out before God: they will know what mercies they are to ask for themselves, by observing what turn your petitions take: your intercession, may diffuse into their minds a spirit of love to mankind, a concern for the interest of the church and of their country, and what is not, I think, by any means to be neglected, sentiments of loyalty towards our sovereign and his family, when they hear you often invoking the divine blessing upon them: and your solemn thanksgivings for the bounties of Providence, and for benefits of a spiritual nature, may affect their hearts with those gracious impressions towards the gracious Author of all, which may excite in their little breasts love to him, the most noble and genuine principle or all true and acceptable religion: thus they may become Christians by insensible degrees, and grow in the knowledge and love of truth, as they do in stature.

Indeed were this duty properly attended to, it might be expected, that all Christian families would, according to their respective sizes and circumstances, become nurseries of piety; and you would see, in the most convincing view, the wisdom of providence, in making human infants so much more dependent on their parents, and so much more incapable to shift for themselves, than the offspring of inferior creatures are.

Let me then intreat you, my dear friend, to look on your children the very next time you see them, and ask your own heart, how you can answer it to God, and to them, that you deprive them of such advantages as these – advantages, without which, it is to be feared, your care of them in other respects will turn to but little account, should they be ever so prosperous in life. For what is prosperity in life without the knowledge, and fear, and love of God? What, but the poison of the soul, which swells and kills it? What, but the means of making it more certainly, more deeply, more intolerably miserable? In short, not mention the happy influence family devotion may have on their temporal affairs, by drawing down the divine blessing, and by forming their minds to those virtues, which pave the way to wealth and reputation, health and contentment which make no enemies, and attract many friends; it is, with respect to the eternal world, the greatest cruelty to your children to neglect giving them those advantages, which no other attentions in education exclusive of these can afford, and it is impossible you should ever be able to give them any other equivalent. If you do your duty in this respect, they will have reason to bless you living and dying, and if you neglect it, take care that you and they come not, in consequence of that neglect, into a world where (horrid as the thought may seem), you will be for ever cursing each other.

2. Let me now press you to consider, how much your own interest is concerned in the matter.

Your spiritual interest is concerned. Let me seriously ask you, do you not need those advantages for religion, which the performance of family-duty will give you, added to those of a more secret and a more public nature, if peradventure they are regarded by you? These instructions, these adorations, these confessions, these supplications, these intercessions, these thanksgivings, which may be so useful to your children and servants, may they not be useful to yourselves? May not your own hearts have some peculiar advantage for being impressed, when you are the mouth of others in these domestic devotions, beyond what in a private station of life it is otherwise possible you should have? Nay, the remoter influence they may have on your conduct, in other respects, and at other times, when considered, merely in the general as religious exercises performed by you in your family, is to be recollected as an argument of vast importance.

A sense of common decency would engage you, if you pray with your family, to avoid a great many evils, which would appear doubly evil in a father or a master, who kept up such religious exercises in his house. Do you imagine, that if reading the scripture, and family prayer were introduced into the houses of some of your neighbors – drunkenness, and lewdness, and cursing and swearing, and profaning the Lord's day, would not like so many evil demons, be quickly driven out? The master of a family would not, for shame, indulge them, if he had nothing more than the form of duty kept up; and his reformation, though only external, and at first on a kind of constraint, would carry with it the reformation of many more who have such a dependence on his favor as they would not sacrifice, though, by a madness very prevalent among the children of men, they can venture to sacrifice their souls to every trifle.

And may it not perhaps be your more immediate concern, to recollect, that if you prayed with your family, you would yourself be more careful to abstain from all appearance of evil? (1 Thess. 5:22). You would find out a way to suppress that turbulency of passion, which may now be ready to break out before you are aware, and other imprudences, in which your own heart would check you by saying, "Does this become one, that is by and by to kneel down with his domestics, his children, and servants, and adore God with them, and pray against every thing which displeases God, and makes us unfit for the heavenly world?" I will not say, this will cure every thing that is wrong, but I believe you are already persuaded it would often have a very good influence. And I fear it is the secret desire of indulging some irregularities without such a restraint, that, shameful as such a conduct is, hath driven out family-prayer from several houses where it was once maintained, and hath prevented its introduction into others. But if you have any secret disinclination of heart rising against it in this view, it becomes you seriously to take the alarm; for, to speak plainly, I hardly know a blacker symptom of damnation, than a fear of being restrained in the commission of sin.

After this, it may seem a matter of smaller importance, to urge the good influence which a proper discharge of family-duty may have upon your own temporal affairs; both by restraining you from many evils, and engaging you to a proper conduct yourself, and also by impressing your children and servants with a sense of religion. And it is certain, the more careful they are of their duty to God, the more likely they will be to perform their duty to you. Nor can any thing strengthen your natural authority among them more, than your presiding in such solemnities, if supported by a suitable conduct. But I would hope, nobler motives will have a superior weight. And therefore waiving this topic, I intreat you as the last argument to consider,

3. The influence it may have on a general reformation and on the propagation of religion to those who are yet unborn. You ought to consider every child and servant in your family, as one who may be a source, not only of life, but (in some degree) of character and happiness, to those who are hereafter to arise into being; yea, whose conduct may in part affect those that are to descend from them in a remote generation. If they grow up, while under your eye, ignorant of religion, they will certainly be much less capable of teaching it to others; for these are the years of discipline, and

if they be neglected now, there is little probability of their receiving after-instruction. Nor is this all the evil consequence; for it is highly probable, that they will think themselves sanctioned by your example in a like negligence, and so you may entail heathenism under the name of Christianity, on your descendants and theirs in ages to come. Whereas your diligence and zeal might be remembered, and imitated by them, perhaps when you are in your grave; and the stock which they first received from you, might with rich improvements be communicated to great numbers, so that one generation after another might learn to fear and serve the Lord. On the whole, God only knows what a church may arise from one godly family, what a harvest may spring up from a single seed; and on the other hand, it is impossible to say, how many souls may at length perish by the treacherous neglect of a single person, and to speak plainly, by your own.

These, Sir, are the arguments I have to plead with you, and which I have selected out of many more: And now give me leave seriously to ask you, as in the presence of God, whether there be not on the whole, an unanswerable force in them? And if there be, what follows, but that you immediately yield to that force, and set up Family-Worship this very day. For methinks, I would hardly thank you for a resolution to do it to morrow, so little do I expect from that resolution. How can you excuse yourself in the continued omission? Bring the matter before God: He will be the final Judge of it, and if you cannot debate the question as in his presence, it is a sign of a bad cause, and of a bad heart too, which is conscious of the badness of the cause, and yet will not give it up, not comply with a duty, of your obligations to which, you are secretly convinced, while in effect you say, "I will go on in this sin, and venture the consequence." O! it is a dreadful venture, and will be found provoking the Lord to jealously, as if you were stronger than he (1 Cor. 10:22). God is represented as giving this reason to his angels for a particular favor to bestowed on Abraham – I know that he will command his children and household to keep the way of the Lord, that he may obtain the blessing promised. (Gen. 18:19). Did he not hereby intend to declare his approbation of the care which Abraham took to support religion in his family? And can it be supported in a total neglect of prayer? – Again, Do you not in your conscience think, that the Spirit of God meant that we should take Joshua for an example, when he tells us, that he resolved (and publicly declared the resolution,) that he and his house would serve the Lord (Josh. 24: 15). which must express a religious care of his family too? – Do you not believe, that this blessed Spirit meant it as a commendation of Job that he offered sacrifices for all his children (Job 1:5); sacrifices, undoubtedly attended with prayers: when he feared least the gaiety of their hearts in their successive feastings might have betrayed them into some moral evil? – And was it not to do an honor to David, that the scripture informs us, that he "went home to bless his household," (2 Sam. 6:20), that is, to perform some solemn act of domestic worship, when he had been spending the whole day in public devotion? – And do you think, when our blessed Lord, whose life was employed in religious services, so frequently took his disciples apart to pray with them, that he did not intend this as an example to us, of praying with those under our special care, or in other words, with the members of our own family, who are most immediately so? – Or can you by any imaginable artifice delude yourself so far as to think, that when we are solemnly charged and commanded to pray "with all prayer and supplication" (Eph. 6:18), this kind of prayer is not included in that apostolical injunction? Were there not one praying family in the whole world, methinks it should instigate you to the practice, rather than tempt you to neglect it, and you should press on as ambitions of the glory of leading the way: For what could be a nobler object of ambition, than to be pointed out by the blessed God himself, as Job was; of whom he said, with a kind of triumph, "Hast thou considered my servant Job, that there is none like him in the land, or even on the earth?" (Job 1:8). But blessed be God, the neglect we have supposed is far from being universal. Let it however rejoice us, if God may say, "There are such and such families, distinguishable from those in their neighborhood on this account; as prevalent as the neglect of family-prayer is, they have the resolution to practice it, and, like my servant Daniel, fear not the reproach and contempt which profane and ungodly men may cast upon them, if they may but honor me and engage my favor; I know them; I hearken and hear, and a book of remembrance is written before me for them that fear me, and think on my name."

Say not, you have no time. How many hours in a week do you find for amusement, while you have none for devotion in your family? And do you indeed hold the blessing of God so very cheap, and think it a matter of so little importance, that you conclude your business must succeed the worse, if a few minutes were daily taken to implore it before your family? Let me rather admonish you, that the greater your business is, the more need you have to pray earnestly, that your hearts may not be engrossed by it. And I would beg leave further to remind you, that if your hurry of business were indeed so great as the objection supposes, (which I believe is seldom the case) prudence alone might suggest, that you should endeavor to contract it. For there are certain boundaries, beyond which a wise and faithful care cannot extend;. and as an attempt to go beyond these boundaries has generally its foundation in avarice, it often has its end in poverty and ruin. But if you were ever so secure of succeeding for this world, how dear might you and your children pay for that success, it all the blessed consequences of family-religion, for time, and for eternity, were to be given up as the price of that very small part of your gains, which is owing to the minutes you take from these exercises, that you may give them to the world? For you plainly perceive the question is only about them, and by no means about a strenuous application to the proper duties of your secular, calling through the day. And if you will be rich upon such profane terms as are here supposed, (for truly I can call them no better than profane,) you will probably plunge yourself into final perdition, and may in the mean time pierce yourself through with many sorrows (1 Tim. 6:9, 10). while religious families learn by happy experience, that the blessing of the Lord, which they are so often imploring together, "maketh rich, and addeth no sorrow with it" (Prov. 10:22). or that "a little with the fear of the Lord is better than great treasure, with that intermingled trouble, Prov. 15:16. which in the neglect of God must necessarily be expected.

As for ability, where the heart is rightly disposed, it does not require any uncommon abilities to discharge family-worship in a decent and edifying manner. "The heart of a wise and good Man, in this respect, teacheth his mouth, and addeth knowledge to his lips" (Prov. 16:23) "and out of the fullness of it, when it is indeed full of pious affections, the mouth will naturally speak" (Luke 6:45) There is no need at all of speaking elegantly. The plainest and simplest language, in addresses to the Majesty of heaven, appears to me far preferable to labored, pompous, and artificial expressions. Plain, short sentences, uttered just as they rise in the mind, will be best understood by them that join with you; and they will be more pleasing to God than any thing which should proceed from ostentation and parade.

I must also desire you to consider, how many helps you may easily procure. The scripture is a large and noble magazine of the most proper sentiments, and most expressive language; which, if you will attend to with a becoming regard, will soon furnish you for this good work. We have too in our language a great variety of excellent forms of prayer for families as well as for private persons; which you may use, at least at first, with great profit. And if it be too laborious to you to learn them by heart, or if having learnt them, you dare not trust your memory, what should forbid your reading them reverently and devoutly? I hope the main thing is, that God be reverently and sincerely adored, that suitable blessings, temporal and spiritual, be sought from him for ourselves and others, and cordial thanksgivings returned to him for the various gifts of his continual bounty. I know in a great variety of instances, that it is very possible for Christians of no extraordinary genius, and with a very low education, to acquit themselves honorably in prayer without the assistance of forms: And they who at first need them, may, and probably, if they seriously set about it, would soon out-grow that need. But if they not, God might be glorified, and families edified by the continued use of such helps.

If opposition be made in your family, you ought to let any in whom you discover it know, that your measures are fixed, and that you cannot and will not resign that just authority, which the laws of God and men give you in your own house, to their unhappy temper, or daring impiety. Make the trial, whether they will dare to break with you, rather than submit to so easy a condition, as that of being present at your hours of family-worship. If it be a servant that disputes it, you will no doubt think it a great blessing to your family to rid it of so detestable a member, in that relation. And if a child grown up to years, that should be years of discretion, should set himself against this reformation, though it is certain that, wherever such a son of Belial be, he must be a great grief to your heart, you will be delivered from a great deal of distress which the sight of his wickedness must daily give you, by refusing him a place in your own family, which he would only disgrace and corrupt, and leaving him to practice those irregularities and scandals which always go along with such a presumptuous contempt of religion, any where else rather than under your own roof.

May God give you resolution immediately to make the attempt! And may he assist and accept you, and scatter down every desirable blessing of providence and of grace on you and yours! So that this day may become memorable in your lives, as a season from whence you may date a prosperity and a joy hitherto unknown, how happy soever you may have been in former years; For, very imperfect, I am sure, must that domestic happiness be, in which domestic religion has no part.

But if after all, you will not be persuaded, but will hearken to the voice of cowardice, and sloth, and irreligion, in defiance of so many awakening and affecting reasons, you must answer it at large If your children and servants grow up in the neglect of God, and pierce your hearts with those sorrows, which such servants, and especially such children, are like to occasion: if they raise profane and profligate families; if they prove the curse of their country, as well as the torment and ruin of those most intimately related to them; the guilt is in part yours, and (I repeat again,) you must answer it to God at the great day, that you have omitted the proper and appointed method of preventing such fatal evils. In the mean time, you must answer the omission to your own conscience; which probably has not been easy in former days, and in future days may be yet more unquiet. Yet, Sir, the memory of this address may continue to torment you, if it cannot reform you: and if you do not forsake the house of God as well as exclude God and his worship from your own house, you will meet with new wounds; for new exhortations and admonitions will arm reflection with new reproaches. And in this uncomfortable manner you will probably go on, till what has been the grief and shame of your life, become the affliction of your dying bed; nor dare I presume to assure you, that God will answer your last cries for pardon. The best you can expect under the consciousness of this guilt, is to pass trembling to your final doom; – But whatever that doom be, you must acquit the friend who has given you faithful warning; and this address, transcribed as it were in the records of the divine omniscience, shall testify, that a matter of so great importance hath not been kept out of your view, nor slightly urged on your conscience.

Philip Doddridge, 1702–51, originally part of a letter

Prayer

M.G. Easton

Prayer – is converse with God; the intercourse of the soul with God, not in contemplation or meditation, but in direct address to him.

Prayer may be oral or mental, occasional or constant, ejaculatory or formal. It is a "beseeching the Lord" (Ex. 32:11); "pouring out the soul before the Lord" (1 Sam. 1:15); "praying and crying to heaven" (2 Chr. 32:20); "seeking unto God and making supplication" (Job 8:5); "drawing near to God" (Ps. 73:28); "bowing the knees" (Eph. 3:14).

Prayer presupposes a belief in the personality of God, his ability and willingness to hold intercourse with us, his personal control of all things and of all his creatures and all their actions.

Acceptable prayer must be sincere (Heb. 10:22), offered with reverence and godly fear, with a humble sense of our own insignificance as creatures and of our own unworthiness as sinners, with earnest importunity, and with unhesitating submission to the divine will. Prayer must also be offered in the faith that God is, and is the hearer and answerer of prayer, and that he will fulfill his word, "Ask, and ye shall receive" (Matt. 7:7, 8; 21:22; Mark 11:24; John 14:13, 14), and in the name of Christ (16:23, 24; 15:16; Eph. 2:18; 5:20; Col. 3:17; 1 Pet. 2:5). Prayer is of different kinds, secret (Matt. 6:6); social, as family prayers, and in social worship; and public, in the service of the sanctuary.

Intercessory prayer is enjoined (Num. 6:23; Job 42:8; Isa. 62:6; Ps. 122:6; 1 Tim. 2:1; James 5:14), and there are many instances on record of answers having been given to such prayers, e.g., of Abraham (Gen. 17:18, 20; 18:23–32; 20:7, 17, 18), of Moses for Pharaoh (Ex. 8:12, 13, 30, 31; Ex. 9:33), for the Israelites (Ex. 17:11, 13; 32:11–14, 31–34; Num. 21:7, 8; Deut. 9:18, 19, 25), for Miriam (Num. 12:13), for Aaron (Deut. 9:20), of Samuel (1 Sam. 7: 5–12), of Solomon (1 Kings 8; 2 Chr. 6), Elijah (1 Kings 17:20–23), Elisha (2 Kings 4:33–36), Isaiah (2 Kings 19), Jeremiah (42:2–10), Peter (Acts 9:40), the church (12:5–12), Paul (28:8).

No rules are anywhere in Scripture laid down for the manner of prayer or the attitude to be assumed by the suppliant. There is mention made of kneeling in prayer (1 Kings 8: 54; 2 Chr. 6:13; Ps. 95:6; Isa. 45:23; Luke 22:41; Acts 7:60; 9:40; Eph. 3:14, etc.); of bowing and falling prostrate (Gen. 24:26, 52; Ex. 4:31; 12:27; Matt. 26:39; Mark 14:35, etc.); of spreading out the hands (1 Kings 8:22, 38, 54; Ps. 28:2; 63:4; 88:9; 1 Tim. 2:8, etc.); and of standing (1 Sam. 1:26; 1 Kings 8:14, 55; 2 Chr. 20:9; Mark 11:25; Luke 18:11, 13).

If we except the "Lord's Prayer" (Matt. 6: 9–13), which is, however, rather a model or pattern of prayer than a set prayer to be offered up, we have no special form of prayer for general use given us in Scripture.

Prayer is frequently enjoined in Scripture (Ex. 22:23, 27; 1 Kings 3:5; 2 Chr. 7:14; Ps. 37:4; Isa. 55:6; Joel 2:32; Ezek. 36:37, etc.), and we have very many testimonies that it has been answered (Ps. 3:4; 4:1; 6:8; 18:6; 28:6; 30:2; 34:4; 118:5; James 5:16–18, etc.).

Abraham's servant prayed to God, and God

directed him to the person who should be wife to his master's son and heir (Gen. 24:10–20).

Jacob prayed to God, and God inclined the heart of his irritated brother, so that they met in peace and friendship (Gen. 32:24–30; 33:1–4).

Samson prayed to God, and God showed him a well where he quenched his burning thirst, and so lived to judge Israel (Judg. 15:18–20).

David prayed, and God defeated the counsel of Ahithophel (2 Sam. 15:31; 16:20–23; 17:14–23).

Daniel prayed, and God enabled him both to tell Nebuchadnezzar his dream and to give the interpretation of it (Dan. 2: 16–23).

Nehemiah prayed, and God inclined the heart of the king of Persia to grant him leave of absence to visit and rebuild Jerusalem (Neh. 1:11; 2:1–6).

Esther and Mordecai prayed, and God defeated the purpose of Haman, and saved the Jews from destruction (Esther 4:15–17; 6:7, 8).

The believers in Jerusalem prayed, and God opened the prison doors and set Peter at liberty, when Herod had resolved upon his death (Acts 12:1–12).

Paul prayed that the thorn in the flesh might be removed, and his prayer brought a large increase of spiritual strength, while the thorn perhaps remained (2 Cor. 12:7–10).

Prayer is like the dove that Noah sent forth, which blessed him not only when it returned with an olive-leaf in its mouth, but when it never returned at all. (Robinson's Job).

M.G. Easton, *Easton's Bible Dictionary*

Concerts of Prayer

Jonathan Edwards
or

"A humble attempt to promote the agreement and union of God's people throughout the world in extraordinary prayer for a revival of religion and the advancement of God's kingdom on earth, according to Scriptural promises and prophecies of the last time."

THE FUTURE GLORIOUS STATE OF CHRIST'S CHURCH

"This is what the LORD Almighty says: "Many peoples and the inhabitants of many cities will yet come, and the inhabitants of one city will go to another and say, 'Let us go at once to entreat the LORD and seek the LORD Almighty. I myself am going.' And many peoples and powerful nations will come to Jerusalem to seek the LORD Almighty and to entreat him"(Zech. 8:20–22).

In this chapter Zechariah prophecies of the future, glorious advancement of the Church. It is evident there is more intended than was ever fulfilled in the Jewish nation during Old Testament times. Here are plain prophecies describing things that were never fulfilled before the coming of Messiah, particularly what is said in the two last verses in the chapter where Zechariah speaks of "many people and strong nations worshiping and seeking the true God," and of so great an addition of Gentiles to the Church that the majority of visible worshipers consist of Gentiles, outnumbering the Jews ten to one.

Nothing ever happened, from the time of Zechariah to the coming of Christ, to fulfill this prophecy. It's fulfillment can only be in the calling of the Gentiles during and following apostolic times, or in the future, glorious enlargement of God's Church in the end times, so often foretold by Old Testament prophets, particularly by Zechariah. It is most likely that the Spirit of God speaks here of the greatest revival and the most glorious advancement of the Church on earth, the blessings of which will benefit the Jewish nation.

Indeed, there is great agreement on this point, between this prophecy of Zechariah, and other prophecies concerning the Church's latter day glory. Consider Isaiah 60:2–4, "See, darkness covers the earth and thick darkness is over the peoples, but the Lord rises upon you and his glory appears over you. Nations will come to your light, and kings to the brightness of your dawn. Lift up your eyes and look about you: All assemble and come to you; your sons come from afar, and your daughters are carried on the arm."

Without doubt, this entire chapter foretells the most glorious state of the God's Church on earth, as does Isaiah 66:8, Micah 4:1–3 and Isaiah 2:1–4: "In the last days the mountain of the LORD's temple will be established as chief among the mountains; it will be raised above the hills, and peoples will stream to it."

"Many nations will come and say, 'Come, let us go up to the mountain of the LORD, to the house of the God of Jacob. He will teach us his ways, so that we may walk in his paths.'

"The law will go out from Zion, the word of the LORD from Jerusalem. He will judge between many peoples and will settle disputes for strong nations far and wide. They will beat their swords into plowshares and their spears into pruning hooks. Nation will not take up sword against nation, nor will they train for war anymore." Nothing whatsoever has happened to fulfill these prophecies. Moreover, since the prophecy in my text (Zech. 8:20–22) and the following verse agrees with them, there is reason to think it addresses the same times. Indeed, there is remarkable agreement in the description given throughout this chapter with the representations of those times elsewhere in the prophetic books.

Though the prophet is at times referring to the future smiles of heaven on the Jewish nation, yet the Spirit of God doubtless refers to events far greater than these, of which these are but faint resemblances. The Jews had just returned from the Babylonian captivity, Chaldea and other countries, and resettled in Canaan where they were experiencing great increase of both numbers and wealth.

We find it common in the prophecies of the Old Testament that when the prophets are speaking of the favors and blessings of God on the Jews, attending or following their return from the Babylonian captivity, the Spirit of God takes the opportunity from there to speak of the incomparably greater blessings on the Church, that will attend and follow her deliverance from the spiritual Babylon, of which those were a type. The prophet, in this chapter, speaks of God's bringing his people again from the east and west to Jerusalem (vs. 7–8), and multitudes of all nations taking hold of the skirts of the Jews. Although this prophecy literally refers to the Jews return from Babylon, its fulfillment cannot be seen there for no such things spoken of here attended their return.

Therefore, it must refer to the great calling and gathering of Jews into the fold of Christ, and to them receiving the blessings of His kingdom, after the fall of the Antichrist and the destruction of the spiritual Babylon.

THE POWER OF PRAYER
In Zechariah 8:20–22 we have an account of how this future advancement of the Church should occur. It would come to fruition as multitudes from different towns resolve to unite in extraordinary prayer, seeking God until He manifests Himself and grants the fruits of his presence. We may observe several things in particular:

1. The Necessity Of Prayer
Some suppose that prayer includes the whole of worship to God and that prayer is a part of worship during the days of the gospel when sacrifices are abolished. Therefore, this can be understood as a prophecy of a great revival of religion with true worship of God among His people, repentance from idolatry, and growth of the Church.

However, it seems reasonable to me to suppose that something even more special is intended regarding prayer given that prayer is not only repeatedly mentioned, but that this prophecy parallels many other prophecies that speak of an extraordinary spirit of prayer preceding that glorious day of revival and advancement of the Church's peace and prosperity. It particularly parallels what the prophet later speaks of the "pouring out of a spirit of grace and supplications" as that which introduces the great religious revival (Zech. 12:10).

2. The Good Which Shall Be Brought By Prayer: God Himself
Scripture says, "They shall go to pray before the Lord, and to seek the Lord of Hosts." The good that they seek for is "The Lord of Hosts," Himself. If "seeking God" means no more than seeking the favor or mercy of God then "praying before the Lord," and "seeking the Lord of Hosts" must be looked upon as synonymous. However, "seeking the Lord" is commonly used to mean something far more than seeking something from God. Surely it implies

that God Himself is what is desired and sought after.

Thus, the Psalmist desired God, thirsted after Him and sought after Him: "O God, thou art my God; early will I seek thee. My flesh longeth for thee, in a dry and thirsty land, where no water is, to see thy power and thy glory, so as I have seen thee in the sanctuary ... My soul followeth hard after thee ... Whom have I in heaven by thee? And there is none upon earth that I desire besides thee. "The Psalmist earnestly pursued after God; his soul thirsted after Him, he stretched forth his hands unto Him. All of God's saints have this in common: they are those that seek God. "This is the generation of them that seek Him." "Your heart shall live that seek God," etc.

If this be the true sense of this phrase "seeking the Lord of Hosts," then we must understand that God who had withdrawn Himself, or, as it were, hid Himself, would return to His Church, granting the fruits of His presence and communion with His people, which He so often promised, and for which His Church had so long waited.

In short, it seems reasonable to understand the phrase, "seeking the Lord of Hosts" means not merely praying to God, but seeking the promised restoration of the Church of God after the Babylonian captivity and the great apostasy occasioning it is called their "seeking God, and searching for Him;" and God's granting this promised revival and restoration called His being "found of them." (See Jer. 29:10–14.)

The prophets occasionally represent God as being withdrawn and hiding Himself: "Verily thou art a God that hideth thyself, O God of Israel, the Savior. I hid me, and was wroth." The prophets then go on to represent God's people seeking Him, searching and waiting for and calling after Him. When God answers their prayers and restores and advances His people, according to His promise, then He is said to come and say, "Here am I" and to show Himself, and they are said to find Him and see Him plainly. "Then you will call, and the Lord will answer; you will cry for help, and he will say: Here am I ..." "But Israel will be saved by the Lord with an everlasting salvation ... I have not said to Jacob's descendants, 'Seek me

in vain.' I, the Lord, speak the truth; I declare what is right."

"The Sovereign Lord will wipe away the tears from all faces; he will remove the disgrace of his people from all the earth. In that day they will say, 'Surely this is our God; we trusted in him, and he saved us. This is the Lord, we trusted in him; let us rejoice and be glad in his salvation.' We wait for you; your name and renown are the desire of our hearts" (Isa. 58:9; Isa. 45:17, 19; Isa. 25:8–9).

3. We May Observe Who It Is That Will Be United In Seeking The Lord

"The inhabitants of many cities ... yea, many people and strong nations." Many people from all over the world will unite to seek the Lord.

From the prophecy, it seems reasonable to assume that this will be fulfilled in the following manner: First, God's people will be given a spirit of prayer, inspiring them to come together and pray in an extraordinary manner, that He would help his Church, show mercy to mankind in general, pour out his Spirit, revive His work, and advance His kingdom in the world as He promised.

Moreover, such prayer would gradually spread and increase more and more, ushering in a revival of religion. This would be characterized by greater worship and service of God among believers. Others will be awakened to their need for God, motivating them to earnestly cry out to God for mercy. They will be led to join with God's people in that extraordinary seeking and serving of God which they see around them. In this way the revival will grow until the awakening reaches whole nations and those in the highest positions of influence. The Church will grow to be ten times larger than it was before. Indeed, at length, all the nations of the world will be converted unto God.

Thus, ten men, out of all languages and nations, will "take hold of the skirt of" the Jew (in the sense of the Apostle), saying "We will go with you, for we have heard that God is with you." Thus will be fulfilled, "O thou that heareth prayer, unto thee shall all flesh come."

4. We May Also Observe The Manner Of Their Unity In Prayer

It is a visible and voluntary union that was first proposed by some of God's people with others readily joining in over time. Those who live in one city will declare to those of another city, "Let us go" etc. Many of those who hear their declaration will not only join with them but will make the call for the unity in prayer known to still others. As a result, the movement will grow, prevail and spread among God's people. Some suppose that the words, "I will go also," are to be taken as words spoken by the one making the proposal. He states this expressing his willingness and desire to do what he is asking his hearer to do. But this is to suppose no more than is expressed in the phrase, "Come and let us go ..." itself. It seems more natural to me to understand these words as being the consent or reply of the one to whom the proposal is made. This is much more agreeable to the flow of the text which represents the compliance of great numbers of people in this movement. And though if these words are thus understood, we must suppose something understood in the text that is not expressed: Those of other cities will say, "I will go also." Yet, this is not difficult to conceive of as such figures of speech are common in the Scripture (Jer. 3:22; Ps. 1:6, 7).

5. Next, We Can Observe The Manner In Which They Agree To Pray

"Let us go speedily to pray," or, as it says in the margin: let us go continually. Literally translated this means, "let us go in going." The Hebrew language often doubles words for emphasis (e.g., the holy of holies signifies that which is most holy). Such doubling of words also denotes the certainty of an event coming to pass. For example, when God said to Abraham, "in multiplying, I will multiply thy seed," God implies that He would certainly multiply his seed, and multiply it exceedingly.

6. Finally, This Prophecy Gives Us A Picture Of This Union In Prayer Being An Inviting And A Happy Thing

We sense God's pleasure, and the results prove tremendously successful. From the whole of this prophecy we may infer that it is well pleasing to God for many people, in different parts of the world, to voluntarily come into a visible union to pray in an extraordinary way for those great outpourings of the Holy Spirit which shall advance the Kingdom of our Lord Jesus Christ that God has so often promised shall be in the latter ages of the world.

AN EXAMPLE FROM HISTORY

Let me relate a brief history of what has happened in Scotland. In October of 1744, a number of ministers in Scotland, considering the state of God's Church, and mankind in general, believed that God was calling those concerned for the welfare of the Church to unite in extraordinary prayer. They knew God was the Creator and source of all blessings and benefits in the Church so they earnestly prayed that He would appear in His glory, and strengthen the Church, and manifest His compassion to the world of mankind by an abundant outpouring of His Holy Spirit. They desired a true revival in all parts of Christendom, and to see nations delivered from their great and many calamities, and to bless them with the unspeakable benefits of the Kingdom of our glorious Redeemer, and to fill the whole earth with His glory.

These ministers consulted with one another on this subject and concluded that they were obliged to begin such prayer and attempt to persuade others to do the same. After seeking God for direction, they determined that for the next two years they would set apart some time on Saturday evenings and Sunday mornings every week for prayer as one's other duties would allow. More importantly, it was decided that the first Tuesday of each quarter (beginning with the first Tuesday of November) would be time to be spent in prayer. People were to pray for either the entire day or part of the day, as they found themselves disposed, or as circumstances allowed. They would meet in either private prayer groups or in public meetings, whichever was found to be most convenient.

It was determined that none should make any promises or feel under strict obligation to observe every one of these days without fail; for these days were not holy or established by sacred authority. However, to prevent negligence, and the temptation to make excuses for trivial reasons, it was proposed that if those who resolve to pray cannot take part on the agreed upon day, they would use the next available day for the purpose of prayer.

The primary reason for this cooperation in prayer was to maintain, among the people of God, that necessity of prayer for the coming of Christ's Kingdom, which Christ directed his followers to do. We are, unfortunately, too little inclined to pray because of our laziness and immaturity, or because of the distraction of our own worldly, private affairs. We have prayed at times, but without special seasons for prayer, we are, likely, to neglect it either partially or totally. But when we set aside certain times for prayer, resolving to fulfill this commission unless extraordinarily hindered, we are less likely to neglect it.

The return of each new season will naturally refresh the memory and will cause us to remember these teachings of our Lord Jesus Christ, and the obligations we have as His followers. We will be renewed in the importance, necessity and unspeakable value of the mercy we seek from God, and by frequent renovation, the vision to pray will be kept alive in our hearts at all times. Therefore, those ministers from Scotland determined that such gatherings would help encourage greater prayerfulness among God's people for revival throughout the year. They also believed that the quarterly gathering would encourage and strengthen people to pray, especially if they knew that many other Christians in so many distant places were praying for the same things at a same time.

It was thought that two years would be a sufficient trial period, after which time would be given to evaluate fruitfulness of the endeavor. It was not known but thought best to allow some time to make some adjustments if necessary. The time period, though short, was thought sufficient to judge its fruitfulness. Those involved would have the opportunity to communicate their thoughts, and perhaps improve, on this manner of prayer. As for promulgating this concert of prayer, the ministers decided to simply pass the word through personal conversation, and correspondence with others far away, rather than any formal advertisement in the press. At first it was intended that some formal paper outlining

the proposal should be sent around for proper amendments and improvements, and then agreement. But after more thoughtful deliberation, it was concluded that this would only give rise to objections which they thought best to avoid in the beginning. Great success seems to have met their labors for great numbers in Scotland and England, and even some in North America joined with them. As to Scotland, many people in the four chief cities, Edinburgh, Glasgow, Aberdeen, and Dundee joined. There were also many country towns and congregations in various other areas that participated. A Mr. Robe, of Kilsyth, stated that "There were then above thirty societies of young people there, newly erected, some of which consisted of upwards of thirty members."

The two years ended last November. Just prior to this, a number of ministers in Scotland agreed on a letter, to be printed and sent abroad to their brethren, proposing to them, and requesting of them, to join with them in continuing this concert of prayer, and in the endeavors to promote it. Almost five hundred copies of this letter were sent over to New England, with instructions to distribute them to the Massachusetts-Bay area, Connecticut, New Hampshire, Rhode Island, New York, New Jersey, Pennsylvania, Maryland, Virginia, Carolina and Georgia. Most were sent to a congregational minister in Boston along with a letter from twelve ministers in Scotland. Other copies were sent to other ministers in Boston, and some to a minister in Connecticut.

The proposal, dated August 26, 1746, opens with an explanation of the purpose and times for the concerts of prayer, and an entreaty to the ministers to communicate their opinions after the two year period had completed.

The ministers then go on to assure their Bostonian brethren that the concerts are not to be seen as binding; men are not expected to set apart days from secular affairs, or "fix on any part of ... precise days, whether it be convenient or not." Nor are they to be seen as "absolute promises, but as friendly, harmonious resolutions, with liberty to alter circumstances as shall be found expedient." Because of such liberty these prayer times cannot be judged to infringe upon those "religious times" appointed by men.

The letter also asked ministers to consider composing and publishing short "persuasive directions" regarding the necessity of prayer, either by particular authors or several joining together. Without such repeated reminders men are apt to become weary and begin to neglect their duty. Ministers are also asked to preach frequently on the importance and necessity of prayer for the coming of the Lord's Kingdom, particularly near or on the quarterly times.

The Boston ministers are to understand that these prayer concerts are not restricted to any particular denomination, but is extended to all who have "at heart the interest of vital Christianity, and the power of godliness; and who, however differing about other things, are convinced of the importance of fervent prayer ..."

It was proposed that the prayer should extend for seven more years and the ministers agreed to this. However there was concern that zeal for spreading news of the concert would wane because of the length proposed. Nevertheless, it was agreed that the first period of time (two years) was too short.

If persons who formerly agreed to this concert should discontinue it, would it not look like that fainting in prayer Scripture so ardently warned against? Would this not be particularly unsuitable given the need of public reformation? Those ministers in Boston said of this proposal: "The motion seems to come from above, and to be wonderfully spreading in Scotland, England, Wales, Ireland and North America."

Jonathan Edwards, 1703–58

Prevailing Prayer
Charles G. Finney

The effectual fervent prayer of a righteous man availeth much. James 5:16.

There are two kinds of means requisite to promote a revival: the one to influence man, the other to influence God. The truth is employed to influence men, and prayer to move God. When I speak of moving God, I do not mean that God's mind is changed by prayer, or that His disposition or character is changed. But prayer produces such a change in us as renders it consistent for God to do as it would not be consistent for Him to do otherwise. When a sinner repents, that state of feeling makes it proper for God to forgive him. God has always been ready to forgive him on that condition, so that when the sinner changes his feelings and repents, it requires no change of feeling in God to pardon him. It is the sinners repentance that renders His forgiveness proper, and is the occasion of God's acting as he does. So when Christians offer effectual prayer, their state of feeling renders it proper for God to answer them. He was never unwilling to bestow the blessing – on the condition that they felt aright, and offered the right kind of prayer.

Prayer is an essential link in the chain of causes that lead to a revival, as much so as truth is. Some have zealously used truth to convert men, and laid very little stress on prayer. They have preached, and talked, and distributed tracts with great zeal, and then wondered that they had so little success. And the reason was, that they forgot to use the other branch of the means, effectual prayer. They overlooked the fact that truth, by itself, will never produce the effect, without the Spirit of God, and that the Spirit is given in answer to prayer.

Sometimes it happens that those who are the most engaged in employing truth are not the most engaged in prayer. This is always unhappy. For unless they have the spirit of prayer (or unless some one else has), the truth, by itself will do nothing but harden men in impenitence. Probably in the Day of Judgment it will be found that nothing is ever done by the truth, used ever so zealously, unless there is a spirit of prayer somewhere in connection with the presentation of truth.

Others err in the reverse direction. Not that they lay too much stress on prayer. But they overlook the fact that prayer might be offered for ever, by itself, and nothing would be done. Because sinners are not converted by direct contact of the Holy Ghost, but by the truth, employed as a means.

To expect the conversion of sinners by prayer alone, without the employment of truth, is to tempt God.

Our subject being Prevailing Prayer, I propose:
I. To show what is effectual or prevailing prayer.
II. To state some of the most essential attributes of prevailing prayer.
III. To give some reasons why God requires this kind of prayer.
IV. To show that such prayer will avail much.

I. WHAT PREVAILING PRAYER IS

1. Effectual, prevailing prayer, does not consist in benevolent desires alone. Benevolent desires are doubtless pleasing to God. Such desires pervade heaven and are found in all holy beings. But they are not prayer. Men may have these desires as the angels and glorified spirits have them. But this is not the effectual, prevailing prayer spoken of in the text. Prevailing prayer is something more than this.

2. Prevailing, or effectual prayer, is that prayer which attains the blessing that it seeks. It is that prayer which effectually moves God. The very idea of effectual prayer is that it achieves its goal.

II. ESSENTIAL ATTRIBUTES OF PREVAILING PRAYER

I cannot detail in full all the things that go to make up prevailing prayer. But I will mention some things that are essential to it; some things which a person must do in order to prevail in prayer.

1. He must pray for a definite Objection. He need not expect to offer such prayer if he prays at random, without any distinct or definite Objection. He must have an object distinctly before his mind. I speak now of secret prayer. Many people go away into their rooms alone "to pray," simply because "they must say their prayers." The time has come when they are in the habit of going by themselves for prayer – in the morning, or at noon, or at whatever time of day it may be. But instead of having anything to say, any definite object before their mind, they fall down on their knees and pray for just what comes into their minds – for everything that floats in the imagination at the time, and when they have done they can hardly tell a word of what they have been praying for. This is not effectual prayer. What should we think of anybody who should try to move a Legis-

lature so, and should say: "Now it is winter, and the Legislature is in session, and it is time to send up petitions," and should go up to the Legislature and petition at random, without any definite object? Do you think such petitions would move the Legislature?

A man must have some definite object before his mind. He cannot pray effectually for a variety of objects at once. The mind is so constituted that it cannot fasten its desires intensely upon many things at the same time. All the instances of effectual prayer recorded in the Bible are of this kind.

Wherever you see that the blessing sought for in prayer was attained, you will find that the prayer which was offered was prayer for that definite Objection.

2. Prayer, to be effectual, must be in accordance with the revealed will of God. To pray for things contrary to the revealed will of God, is to tempt God. There are three ways in which God's will is revealed to men for their guidance in prayer.

(a) By express promises or predictions in the Bible, that He will give or do certain things; promises in regard to particular things, or in general terms, so that we may apply them to particular things. For instance, there is this promise: "What things soever ye desire when ye pray, believe that ye receive them, and ye shall have them" (Mark 11:24).

(b) Sometimes God reveals His will by His Providence. When He makes it clear that such and such events are about to take place, it is as much a revelation as if He had written it in His Word. It would be impossible to reveal everything in the Bible. But God often makes it clear to those who have spiritual discernment that it is His will to grant such and such blessings.

(c) By His Spirit. When God's people are at a loss what to pray for, agreeable to His will, His Spirit often instructs them. Where there is no particular revelation, and Providence leaves it dark, and we know not what to pray for as we ought, we are expressly told that "the Spirit also helpeth our infirmities," and "the Spirit itself maketh intercession for us with groanings which cannot be uttered" (Romans 8:26). A great deal has been said on the subject of praying in faith for things not revealed. It is objected that this doctrine implies a new revelation. I answer that, new or old, it is the very revelation that Jehovah says He makes. It is just as plain here as if it were now revealed by a voice from heaven, that the Spirit of God helps the people of God to pray according to the will of God, when they themselves know not what they ought to pray for. "And He that searcheth the hearts knoweth what is the mind of the Spirit, because He maketh intercession for the saints according to the will of God" (Romans 8:27); and He leads Christians to pray for just those things, "with groanings which cannot be uttered." When neither the Word nor Providence enables them to decide, let them be "filled with the Spirit," as God commands them to be. He says: "Be filled with the Spirit" (Ephesians 5:18). And He will lead their minds to such things as God is willing to grant.

3. To pray effectually you must pray with submission to the will of God. Do not confound submission with indifference. No two things are more unlike. I once knew an individual come where there was a revival. He himself was cold, and did not enter into the spirit of it, and had no spirit of prayer; and when he heard the brethren pray as if they could not be denied, he was shocked at their boldness, and kept all the time insisting on the importance of praying with submission; when it was as plain as anything could be that he confounded submission with indifference.

Again, do not confound submission in prayer with a general confidence that God will do what is right. It is proper to have this confidence that God will do right in all things. But this is a different thing from submission. What I mean by submission in prayer is, acquiescence in the revealed will of God. To submit to any command of God is to obey it.

Submission to some supposable or possible, but secret, decree of God is not submission. To submit to any dispensation of Providence is impossible till it comes. For we never can know what the event is to be, till it takes place. Take a case: David, when his child was sick, was distressed, and agonized in prayer, and refused to be comforted. He took it so much to heart that when the child died his servants were afraid to tell him. But as soon as he heard that the child was dead, he laid aside his grief, and arose, and asked for food, and ate and

drank as usual. While the child was yet alive he did not know what was the will of God, and so he fasted and prayed, and said: "Who can tell whether God will be gracious to me, that my child may live?" He did not know but that his prayer, his agony, was the very thing on which it turned, whether the child was to live or not. He thought that if he humbled himself and entreated God, perhaps God would spare him this blow. But as soon as God's will appeared, and the child was dead, he bowed like a saint. He seemed not only to acquiesce, but actually to take a satisfaction in it. "I shall go to him, but he shall not return to me" (2 Samuel 12:15–23). This was true submission. He reasoned correctly in the case. While he had no revelation of the will of God he did not know but that the child's recovery depended on his prayer. But when he had a revelation of the will of God he submitted. While the will of God is not known, to submit, without prayer, is tempting God. Perhaps, and for aught you know, the fact of your offering the right kind of prayer may be the thing on which the event turns. In the case of an impenitent friend, the very condition on which he is to be saved from hell may be the fervency and importunity of your prayer for that individual.

4. Effectual prayer for an object implies a desire for that object commensurate with its importance. If a person truly desires any blessing, his desires will bear some proportion to the greatness of the blessing. The desires of the Lord Jesus Christ for the blessing He prayed for were amazingly strong, amounting even to agony. If the desire for an object is strong, and is a benevolent desire, and the thing is not contrary to the will and providence of God, the presumption is that it will be granted. There are two reasons for this presumption:

(a) From the general benevolence of God. If it is a desirable object; if, so far as we can see, it would be an act of benevolence in God to grant it, His general benevolence is presumptive evidence that He will grant it.

(b) If you find yourself exercised with benevolent desires for any object, there is a strong presumption that the Spirit of God is exciting these very desires, and stirring you up to pray for that object, so that it may be granted in answer to prayer. In such a case no degree of desire or importunity in prayer is improper. A Christian may come up, as it were, and take hold of the hand of God. See the case of Jacob, when he exclaimed, in an agony of desire: "I will not let Thee go except Thou bless me" (Genesis 32:26). Was God displeased with his boldness and importunity? Not at all; but He granted him the very thing he prayed for.

So in the case of Moses. God said to him: "Let Me alone, that My wrath may wax hot against them, and that I may consume them; and I will make of thee a great nation" (Exodus 32:10). What did Moses do? Did he stand aside and let God do as He said? No; his mind runs back to the Egyptians, and he thinks how they will triumph. "Wherefore should the Egyptians say, For mischief did He bring them out?" It seemed as if he took hold of the uplifted hand of God, to avert the blow. Did God rebuke him and tell him he had no business to interfere? No; it seemed as if He was unable to deny anything to such importunity, and so Moses stood in the gap, and prevailed with God.

Prevailing prayer is often offered in the present day, when Christians have been wrought up to such a pitch of importunity and such a holy boldness afterwards when they looked back upon it, they were frightened and amazed at themselves, to think they should have dared to exercise such importunity with God. And yet these prayers have prevailed, and obtained the blessing. And many of these persons, with whom I am acquainted, are among the holiest persons I know in the world

5. Prayer, to be effectual, must be offered from right motives. Prayer should not be selfish, but should be dictated by a supreme regard for the glory of God. A great deal is offered from pure selfishness. Women sometimes pray for their husbands, that they may be converted, because, they say: "It would be so much more pleasant to have my husband go to Church with me," and all that. And they seem never to lift up their thoughts above self at all. They do not seem to think how their husbands are dishonoring God by their sins, nor how God would be glorified in their conversion. So it is very often with parents. They cannot bear to think that their children should be lost. They pray for them very earnestly indeed. But

if you talk with them upon the subject they are very tender about it and tell you how good their children are – how they respect religion, and how they are, indeed, "almost Christians now"; and so they talk as if they were afraid you would hurt their children by simply telling them the truth. They do not think how such amiable and lovely children are dishonoring God by their sins; they are only thinking what a dreadful thing it will be for them to go to hell. Unless their thoughts rise higher than this, their prayers will never prevail with a holy God.

The temptation to selfish motives is so strong that there is reason to fear a great many parental prayers never rise above the yearnings of parental tenderness. And that is the reason why so many prayers are not answered and why so many pious, praying parents have ungodly children. Much of the prayer for the heathen world seems to be based on no higher principle than sympathy. Missionary agents and others are dwelling almost exclusively upon the six hundred millions of heathens going to hell, while little is said of their dishonoring God. This is a great evil, and until the Church learns to have higher motives for prayer and missionary effort than sympathy for the heathen, her prayers and efforts will never amount to much.

Prayer, to be effectual, must be by the intercession of the Spirit. You never can expect to offer prayer according to the will of God without the Spirit. In the first two cases, it is not because Christians are unable to offer such prayer, where the will of God is revealed in His Word or indicated by His providence. They are able to do it, just as they are able to be holy. But the fact is, that they are so wicked that they never do offer such prayer, unless they are influenced by the Spirit of God. There must be a faith, such as is produced by the effectual operation of the Holy Ghost.

It must be persevering prayer. As a general thing, Christians who have backslidden and lost the spirit of prayer, will not get at once into the habit of persevering prayer. Their minds are not in a right state, and they cannot fix their thoughts so as to hold on till the blessing comes. If their minds were in that state in which they would persevere till the answer came, effectual prayer might be offered at once, as well as after praying ever so many times for an Objection. But they have to pray again and again, because their thoughts are so apt to wander away and are so easily diverted from the Objection.

Most Christians come up to prevailing prayer by a protracted process. Their minds gradually become filled with anxiety about an object, so that they will even go about their business sighing out their desires to God.

Just as the mother whose child is sick goes round her house sighing as if her heart would break. And if she is a praying mother, her sighs are breathed out to God all the day long. If she goes out of the room where her child is, her mind is still on it; and if she is asleep, still her thoughts are on it, and she starts in her dreams, thinking that perhaps it may be dying. Her whole mind is absorbed in that sick child. This is the state of mind in which Christians offer prevailing prayer.

For what reason did Jacob wrestle all night in prayer with God? He knew that he had done his brother Esau a great injury, in getting away the birthright, a long time before. And now he was informed that his injured brother was coming to meet him with an armed force, altogether too powerful to contend with. And there was great reason to suppose that Esau was coming with a purpose of revenge. There were two reasons then why Jacob should be distressed. The first was that he had done this great injury and had never made any reparation. The other was that Esau was coming with a force sufficient to crush him. Now what does he do? He first arranges everything in the best manner he can to placate and meet his brother: sending his present first, then his property, then his family, putting those he loved most farthest behind. And by this time his mind was so exercised that he could not contain himself. He goes away alone over the brook and pours out his very soul in an agony of prayer all night.

And just as the day was breaking, the Angel of the Covenant said: "Let me go"; and Jacob's whole being was, as it were, agonized at the thought of giving up, and he cried out: "I will not let Thee go, except Thou bless me."

His soul was wrought up into an agony, and he obtained the blessing, but he always bore the marks of it, and showed that his body had been greatly affected by this mental struggle. This is prevailing prayer.

Now, do not deceive yourselves with thinking that you offer effectual prayer, unless you have this intense desire for the blessing. I do not believe in it. Prayer is not effectual unless it is offered up with an agony of desire. The apostle Paul speaks of it as a travail of the soul. Jesus Christ, when he was praying in the garden, was in such an agony that "His sweat was as it were great drops of blood falling down to the ground" (Luke 22:44). I have never known a person sweat blood; but I have known a person pray till the blood started from his nose. And I have known persons pray till they were all wet with perspiration, in the coldest weather in winter. I have known persons pray for hours, till their strength was all exhausted with the agony of their minds. Such prayers prevailed with God.

This agony in prayer was prevalent in President Edwards' day, in the revivals which then took place. It was one of the great stumbling blocks in those days to persons who were opposed to the revival, that people used to pray till their body was overpowered with their feelings. I will give a paragraph of what President Edwards says on the subject, to let you see that this is not a new thing in the Church, but has always prevailed wherever revivals prevailed with power. It is from his "Thoughts on Revivals":

"We cannot determine that God shall never give any person so much of a discovery of Himself, not only as to weaken their bodies, but to take away their lives. It is supposed by very learned and judicious divines, that Moses' life was taken away after this manner, and this has also been supposed to be the case with some other saints.

"If God gives a great increase of discoveries of Himself and of love to Him, the benefit is infinitely greater than the calamity, though the life should presently after be taken away …

"There is one particular kind of exercise and concern of mind that many have been empowered by, that has been especially stumbling to some; and that is, the deep concern and distress that they have been in for the souls of others. I am sorry that any put us to the trouble of doing that which seems so needless, as defending such a thing as this. It seems like mere trifling in so plain a case, to enter into a formal and particular debate, in order to determine whether there be anything in the greatness and importance of the case that will answer and bear a proportion to the greatness of the concern that some have manifested. Men may be allowed, from no higher a principle than common ingenuousness and humanity, to be very deeply concerned, and greatly exercised in mind, at seeing others in great danger of no greater a calamity than drowning or being burned up in a house on fire. And if so, then doubtless it will be allowed to be equally reasonable, if they saw them in danger of a calamity ten times greater, to be still much more concerned: and so much more still, if the calamity were still vastly greater. And why, then, should it be thought unreasonable and looked upon with a very suspicious eye, as if it must come from some bad cause, when persons are extremely concerned at seeing others in very great danger of suffering the wrath of Almighty God to all eternity? And besides, it will doubtless be allowed that those that have very great degrees of the Spirit of God, that is, a spirit of love, may well be supposed to have vastly more of love and compassion to their fellow creatures than those that are influenced only by common humanity.

"Why should it be thought strange that those that are full of the Spirit of Christ should be proportionally in their love to souls, like Christ? – who had so strong a love for them, and concern for them, as to be willing to drink the dregs of the cup of God's fury for them; and at the same time that He offered up His blood for souls, offered up also, as their High Priest, strong crying and tears, with an extreme agony, wherein the soul of Christ was, as it were, in travail for the souls of the elect; and, therefore in saving them He is said to 'see of the travail of His soul.' As such a spirit of love to, and concern for, souls was the spirit of Christ, so it is the spirit of the Church; and therefore the Church, in desiring and seeking that Christ might be brought forth in the world, and in the souls of men, is represented (Revelation 12:1,

2) as 'a woman crying, travailing in birth, and pained to be delivered.' The spirit of those that have been in distress for the souls of others, so far as I can discern, seems not to be different from that of the apostle, who travailed for souls, and was ready to wish himself accursed from Christ for others (Romans 9:3). Nor from that of the Psalmist (Psalm 119:53): 'Horror hath taken hold upon me, because of the wicked that forsake Thy law.' And (ver. 136): 'Rivers of waters run down mine eyes, because they keep not Thy law.' Nor from that of the prophet Jeremiah (4:19): 'My bowels, my bowels! I am pained at my very heart; my heart maketh a noise in me: I cannot hold my peace, because Thou hast heard, O my soul, the sound of the trumpet, the alarm of war.' And so chapter 9:1, and 13:17, and Isaiah 22:4. We read of Mordecai, when he saw his people in danger of being destroyed with a temporal destruction (Esther 4:1), that he 'rent his clothes, and put on sackcloth with ashes, and went out into the midst of the city, and cried with a loud and a bitter cry.' And why then should persons be thought to be distracted when they cannot forbear crying out at the consideration of the misery of those that are going to eternal destruction?"

I have quoted this to show that this thing was common in the great revivals of those days. It has always been so in all great revivals, and has been more or less common in proportion to the greatness, and extent, and depth of the work. It was so in the great revivals in Scotland, and multitudes used to be overpowered, and some almost died, by the depth of their agony.

So also, prayer prevailed at Cambuslang, 1741–2, in the revival under William McCulloch and Whitefield. When Whitefield reached Cambuslang he immediately preached, on the braeside, to a vast congregation (on a Tuesday at noon). At six o'clock he preached again, and a third time at nine. Then McCulloch took up the parable and preached till one in the morning, and still the people were unwilling to leave. So many were convicted, crying to God for mercy, that Whitefield described the scene as "a very field of battle." On the ensuing Communion Sunday, Whitefield preached to twenty thousand people; and again on the Monday, when, he said: "you might have seen thousands bathed in tears, some at the same time wringing their hands, others almost swooning, and others crying out and mourning over a pierced Savior. It was like the Passover in Josiah's time." On the voyage from London to Scotland, prior to this campaign, Whitefield had "spent most of his time on board ship in secret prayer." (See Gledstone's "George Whitefield, M.A., Field Preacher.")

If you mean to pray effectually, you must pray a great deal. It was said of the Apostle James that after he was dead it was found that his knees were callous, like a camel's knees, by praying so much. Ah, here was the secret of the success of those primitive ministers! They had callous knees!

If you intend prayer to be effectual, you must offer it in the name of Christ. You cannot come to God in your own name. You cannot plead your own merits. But you can come in a name that is always acceptable.

You all know what it is to use the name of a man. If you should go to the bank with a draft or note, endorsed by John Jacob Astor, that would be giving you his name, and you know you could get the money from the bank just as well as he could himself. Now, Jesus Christ gives you the use of His name. And when you pray in the name of Christ the meaning of it is, that you can prevail just as well as He could Himself, and receive just as much as God's well beloved Son would if He were to pray Himself for the same things. But you must pray in faith.

You cannot prevail in prayer without renouncing all your sins. You must not only recall them to mind, and repent of them, but you must actually renounce them, and leave them off, and in the purpose of your heart renounce them all for ever.

You must pray in faith. You must expect to obtain the things for which you ask. You need not look for an answer to prayer, if you pray without any expectation of obtaining it. You are not to form such expectations without any reason for them. In the cases I have supposed, there is a reason for the expectation. In case the thing is revealed in God's Word, if you pray without an expectation of receiving the blessings, you just make God a liar. If the will of God is indicated by His providence, you ought

to depend on it, according to the clearness of the indication, so far as to expect the blessing if you pray for it. And if you are led by His Spirit to pray for certain things, you have as much reason to expect those things to be done as if God had revealed it in His Word.

But some say: "Will not this view of the leadings of the Spirit of God lead people into fanaticism?" I answer that I know not but many may deceive themselves in respect to this matter. Multitudes have deceived themselves in regard to all the other points of religion. And if some people should think they are led by the Spirit of God, when it is nothing but their own imagination, is that any reason why those who know that they are led by the Spirit should not follow the Spirit? Many people suppose themselves to be converted when they are not. Is that any reason why we should not cleave to the Lord Jesus Christ? Suppose some people are deceived in thinking they love God, is that any reason why the pious saint who knows he has the love of God shed abroad in his heart should not give vent to his feelings in songs of praise? Some may deceive themselves in thinking they are led by the Spirit of God. But there is no need of being deceived. If people follow impulses, it is their own fault. I do not want you to follow impulses. I want you to be sober minded, and follow the sober, rational leadings of the Spirit of God. There are those who understand what I mean, and who know very well what it is to give themselves up to the Spirit of God in prayer.

III. WHY GOD REQUIRES SUCH PRAYER

I will state some of the reasons why these things are essential to effectual prayer. Why does God require such prayer, such strong desires, such agonizing supplications?

1. These strong desires strongly illustrate the strength of God's feelings.

They are like the real feelings of God for impenitent sinners. When I have seen, as I sometimes have, the amazing strength of love for souls that has been felt by Christians, I have been wonderfully impressed with the amazing love of God, and His desires for their salvation. The case of a certain woman, of whom I read, in a revival, made the greatest impression on my mind. She had such an unutterable compassion and love for souls, that she actually panted for breath. What must be the strength of the desire which God feels, when His Spirit produces in Christians such amazing agony, such throes of soul, such travail – God has chosen the best word to express it: it is travail – travail of the soul.

I have seen a man of as much strength of intellect and muscle as any man in the community fall down prostrate, absolutely overpowered by his unutterable desires for sinners. I know this is a stumbling block to many; and it always will be as long as there remain in the Church so many blind and stupid professors of religion. But I cannot doubt that these things are the work of the Spirit of God. Oh, that the whole Church could be so filled with the Spirit as to travail in prayer, till a nation should be born in a day!

It is said in the Word of God that "as soon as Zion travailed, she brought forth" (Isaiah 66: 8). What does that mean? I asked a professor of religion this question once. He was taking exception to our ideas of effectual prayer, and I asked what he supposed was meant by Zion's travailing.

"Oh," said he, "it means that as soon as the Church shall walk together in the fellowship of the Gospel, then it will be said that Zion travels! This walking together is called traveling." Not the same term, you see.

2. These strong desires that I have described are the natural results of great benevolence and clear views regarding the danger of sinners.
It is perfectly reasonable that it should be so. If the women who are present should look up yonder and see a family burning to death in a fire and hear their shrieks, and behold their agony, they would feel distressed, and it is very likely that many of them would faint away with agony. And nobody would wonder at it, or say they were fools or crazy to feel so much distressed at such an awful sight. It would be thought strange if there were not some expressions of powerful feeling. Why is it any wonder, then, if Christians should feel as I have described when they have clear views of the state of sinners, and the awful danger they are in? The fact is, that those individuals who

never have felt so have never felt much real benevolence, and their piety must be of a very superficial character. I do not mean to judge harshly, or to speak unkindly, but I state it as a simple matter of fact; and people may talk about it as they please, but I know such piety is superficial. This is not censoriousness, but plain truth.

People sometimes "wonder at Christians having such feelings." Wonder at what? Why, at the natural, and philosophical, and necessary results of deep piety towards God, and deep benevolence towards man, in view of the great danger they see sinners to be in.

3. The soul of a Christian, when it is thus burdened, must have relief.
God rolls this weight upon the soul of a Christian, for the purpose of bringing him nearer to Himself. Christians are often so unbelieving that they will not exercise proper faith in God till He rolls this burden upon them so heavily that they cannot live under it, but must go to Him for relief. It is like the case of many a convicted sinner. God is willing to receive him at once, if he will come right to Him, with faith in Jesus Christ. But the sinner will not come. He hangs back, and struggles, and groans under the burden of his sins, and will not throw himself upon God, till his burden of conviction becomes so great that he can live no longer; and when he is driven to desperation, as it were, and feels as if he were ready to sink into hell, he makes a mighty plunge, and throws himself upon God's mercy as his only hope. It was his duty to come before. God had no delight in his distress, for its own sake.

So, when professors of religion get loaded down with the weight of souls, they often pray again and again, and yet the burden is not gone, nor their distress abated, because they have never thrown it all upon God in faith.

But they cannot get rid of the burden. So long as their benevolence continues, it will remain and increase; and unless they resist and quench the Holy Ghost, they can get no relief, until, at length, when they are driven to extremity, they make a desperate effort, roll the burden upon the Lord Jesus Christ, and exercise a child-like confidence in Him. Then they feel relieved; then they feel as if the soul they were praying for would be saved. The burden is gone, and God seems in kindness to soothe the mind with a sweet assurance that the blessing will be granted. Often, after a Christian has had this struggle, this agony in prayer, and has obtained relief in this way, you will find the sweetest and most heavenly affections flow out – the soul rests sweetly and gloriously in God, and rejoices "with joy unspeakable and full of glory."

Do any of you think that there are no such things now in the experience of believers? If I had time, I could show you, from President Edwards and other approved writers, cases and descriptions just like this. Do you ask why we never have such things here? I tell you it is not at all because you are so much wiser than Christians are in rural districts, or because you have so much more intelligence or more enlarged views of the nature of religion, or a more stable and well regulated piety. I tell you, no; instead of priding yourselves in being free from such extravagances, you ought to hide your heads, because Christians in the city are so worldly, and have so much starch, and pride, and fashion, that they cannot come down to such spirituality as this. I wish it could be so. Oh, that there might be such a spirit in this city and in this Church! I know it would make a noise if we had such things done here. But I would not care for that. Let them say, if they please, that the folks in Chatham Chapel 20 are getting deranged. We need not be afraid of that, if we live near enough to God to enjoy His Spirit in the manner I have described.

4. These effects of the spirit of prayer upon the body are themselves no part of religion.
It is only that the body is often so weak that the feelings of the soul overpower it. These bodily effects are not at all essential to prevailing prayer; but are only a natural or physical result of highly excited emotions of the mind. It is not at all unusual for the body to be weakened, and even overcome, by any powerful emotion of the mind, on other subjects besides religion. The doorkeeper of Congress, in the time of the Revolution, fell down dead on the reception of some highly cheering intelligence. I knew a woman in Rochester who was in a great agony of prayer for the conversion of her son-in-law.

One morning he was at an anxious meeting, and she remained at home praying for him. At the close of the meeting he came home a convert, and she was so rejoiced that she fell down and died on the spot. It is no more strange that these effects should be produced by religion than by strong feeling on any other subject. It is not essential to prayer, but is the natural result of great efforts of the mind.

5. Doubtless one great reason why God requires the exercise of this agonizing prayer is, that it forms such a bond of union between Christ and the Church.
It creates such a sympathy between them. It is as if Christ came and poured the overflowings of His own benevolent heart into His people, and led them to sympathize and to cooperate with Him as they never do in any other way. They feel just as Christ feels – so full of compassion for sinners that they cannot contain themselves. Thus it is often with those ministers who are distinguished for their success in preaching to sinners; they often have such compassion, such overflowing desires for their salvation, that these are shown in their speaking, and their preaching, just as though Jesus Christ spoke through them. The words come from their lips fresh and warm, as if from the very heart of Christ. I do not mean that He dictates their words; but He excites the feelings that give utterance to them. Then you see a movement in the hearers, as if Christ Himself spoke through lips of clay.

6. This travailing in birth for souls creates also a remarkable bond of union between warm-hearted Christians and the young converts.
Those who are converted appear very dear to the hearts that have had this spirit of prayer for them. The feeling is like that of a mother for her first-born. Paul expresses it beautifully when he says: "My little children!" His heart was warm and tender to them. "My little children, of whom I travail in birth again" – they had backslidden, and he has all the agonies of a parent over a wandering child – "I travail in birth again until Christ be formed in you" (Galatians 4:19); "Christ, the hope of glory" (Colossians 1:27). In a revival, I have often noticed how those who had the spirit of prayer,

loved the young converts. I know this is all so much algebra to those who have never felt it. But to those who have experienced the agony of wrestling, prevailing prayer, for the conversion of a soul, you may depend upon it, that soul, after it is converted, appears as dear as a child is to the mother. He has agonized for it, received it in answer to prayer, and can present it before the Lord Jesus Christ, saying: "Behold, I and the children whom the Lord hath given me" (Isaiah 8:18. See also Hebrews 2:13).

7. Another reason why God requires this sort of prayer is, that it is the only way in which the Church can be properly prepared to receive great blessings without being injured by them.
When the Church is thus prostrated in the dust before God, and is in the depth of agony in prayer, the blessing does them good. While at the same time, if they had received the blessing without this deep prostration of soul, it would have puffed them up with pride. But as it is, it increases their holiness, their love, their humility.

IV. SUCH PRAYER WILL AVAIL MUCH

The prophet Elijah mourned over the declensions of the house of Israel, and when he saw that no other means were likely to be effectual, to prevent a perpetual going away into idolatry, he prayed that the judgments of God might come upon the guilty nation. He prayed that it might not rain, and God shut up the heavens for three years and six months, till the people were driven to the last extremity. And when he sees that it is time to relent what does he do? See him go up to the mountain and bow down in prayer. He wished to be alone; and he told his servant to go seven times, while he was agonizing in prayer. The last time, the servant told him that a little cloud had appeared, like a man's hand, and he instantly arose from his knees – the blessing was obtained. The time had come for the calamity to be turned back. "Ah, but," you say, "Elijah was a prophet." Now, do not make this objection. They made it in the apostle's days, and what does the apostle say? Why he brought forward this very instance, and the fact that Elijah was a man of like passions with ourselves, as a case of prevailing prayer, and insisted that they should pray so

too (1 Kings 17:1; 18:41–5; James 5:17).

John Knox was a man famous for his power in prayer, so that Queen Mary of England used to say that she feared his prayers more than all the armies of Europe. And events showed that she had reason to do it. He used to be in such an agony for the deliverance of his country, that he could not sleep. He had a place in his garden where he used to go to pray.

One night he and several friends were praying together, and as they prayed, Knox spoke and said that deliverance had come. He could not tell what had happened, but he felt that something had taken place, for God had heard their prayers. What was it? Why, the next news they had was, that Mary was dead!

Take a fact which was related in my hearing by a minister. He said that in a certain town there had been no revival for many years; the Church was nearly extinct, the youth were all unconverted, and desolation reigned unbroken. There lived in a retired part of the town, an aged man, a blacksmith by trade, and of so stammering a tongue that it was painful to hear him speak. On one Friday, as he was at work in his shop, alone, his mind became greatly exercised about the state of the Church and of the impenitent. His agony became so great that he was induced to lay by his work, lock the shop door, and spend the afternoon in prayer.

He prevailed, and on the Sabbath called on the minister and desired him to appoint a "conference meeting." After some hesitation, the minister consented; observing however, that he feared but few would attend. He appointed it the same evening at a large private house. When evening came, more assembled than could be accommodated in the house. All were silent for a time, until one sinner broke out in tears, and said, if any one could pray, would he pray for him? Another followed, and another, and still another, until it was found that persons from every quarter of the town were under deep conviction. And what was remarkable was, that they all dated their conviction at the hour that the old man was praying in his shop. A powerful revival followed. Thus this old stammering man prevailed, and as a prince had power with God.

REMARKS

1. A great deal of prayer is lost, and many people never prevail in prayer, because, when they have desires for particular blessings, they do not follow them up. They may have desires, benevolent and pure, which are excited by the Spirit of God; and when they have them, they should persevere in prayer, for if they turn off their attention, they will quench the Spirit. When you find these holy desires in your minds:

(a) Do not quench the Spirit;

(b) Do not be diverted to other objects.

Follow the leadings of the Spirit till you have offered that "effectual fervent prayer" that "availeth much" (James 5:16).

2. Without the spirit of prayer, ministers will do but little good. A minister need not expect much success unless he prays for it. Sometimes others may have the spirit of prayer and obtain a blessing on his labors. Generally, however, those preachers are the most successful who have most of the spirit of prayer themselves.

3. Not only must ministers have the spirit of prayer, but it is necessary that the Church should unite in offering that effectual fervent prayer which can prevail with God. "I will yet for this be inquired of by the house of Israel, to do it" (Ezekiel 36:37).

Now I have only to ask you, in regard to what I have set forth: "Will you do it?" Have you done what I said to you at the last Lecture? Have you gone over your sins, and confessed them, and got them all out of the way?

Can you pray now? And will you join and offer prevailing prayer that the Spirit of God may come down here?

Charles G. Finney, Revival Lectures

The Soul of Prayer

P.T. Forsyth

CONTENTS

DEDICATION

To Mrs. Waterhouse

Lomberdale Hall, in the High Peak

There is, high among the hills, a garden with a walk – a terraced walk. The moors lie round it, and the heights face it; and below the village drowses; while far, far afield, the world agonizes in a solemn tragedy of righteousness (where you, too, have your sepulchers) – a tragedy not quite divorced from the war in heaven, nor all unworthy of the glorious cusp of sky that roofs the riot of the hills.

The walk begins with a conservatory of flowers and it ends in an old Gothic arch – rising, as it were, from beauty natural and frail to beauty spiritual and eternal. And it curves and twines between rocky plants, as if to suggest how arduous the passage from the natural to the spiritual is. And it has, half-way, a little hermitage on it, like a wayside chapel, of old carved and inscribed stones. And the music and the pictures! Close by, the mowers whir upon the lawn, and the thrust flutes in the birch hedge; beyond, in the gash of the valley, the stream purrs up through the steep woods; still farther, the limestone rocks rise fantastic, like castles in the air; and, over all, the lark still soars and sings in the sun (as he does even in Flanders), and makes melody in his heart to the Lord.

That terrace was made with a purpose and a welcome at will. And it is good to pace the Italian paving, to tread the fragrance from the alyssum in the seams, to brood upon the horizons of the far, long wolds, with their thread of road rising and vanishing into busy Craven, and all the time to think greatly of God and kindly of men – faithfully of the past, lovingly of the present, and hopefully of the future.

So in our soul let us make a cornice road for God to come when He will, and walk upon our high places. And a little lodge and shelter let us have on it, of sacred stones, a shrine of ancient writ and churchly memories. Let us make an eyrie there of large vision and humane, a retreat of rest and refitting for a dreadful world. May He show us, up there apart, transfigured things in a noble light. May He prepare us for the sorrows of the valley by a glorious peace, and for the action of life by a fellowship gracious, warm, and noble (as even earthly friendships may be). So may we face all the harsh realisms of Time in the reality, power, and kindness of the Eternal, whose Mercy is as His Majesty for ever.

1. THE INWARDNESS OF PRAYER

It is difficult and even formidable thing to write on prayer, and one fears to touch the Ark. Perhaps no one ought to undertake it unless he has spent more toil in the practice of prayer than on its principle. But perhaps also the effort to look into its principle may be graciously regarded by Him who ever liveth to make intercession as itself a prayer to know better how to pray. All progress in prayer is an answer to prayer – our own or another's. And all true prayer promotes its own progress and increases our power to pray.

The worst sin is prayerlessness. Overt sin, or crime, or the glaring inconsistencies which often surprise us in Christian people are the effect of this, or its punishment. We are left by God for lack of seeking Him. The history of the saints shows often that their lapses were the fruit and nemesis of slackness or neglect in prayer. Their life, at seasons, also tended to become inhuman by their spiritual solitude. They left men, and were left by men, because they did not in their contemplation find God; they found but the thought or the atmosphere of God. Only living prayer keeps loneliness humane. It is the great producer of sympathy. Trusting the God of Christ, and transacting with Him, we come into tune with men. Our egoism retires before the coming of God, and into the clearance there comes with our Father our brother. We realize man as he is in God and for God, his Lover. When God fills our heart He makes more room for man than the humanist heart can find. Prayer is an act, indeed *the* act, of fellowship. We cannot truly pray even for ourselves without passing beyond ourselves and our individual experience. If we should begin with these the nature of prayer carries us beyond them, both to God and to man. Even private prayer is common prayer – the more so, possibly, as it retires from being public prayer.

Not to want to pray, then, is the sin behind sin. And it ends in not being able to pray. That is its punishment – spiritual dumbness, or at least aphasia, and starvation. We do not take our spiritual food, and so we falter, dwindle, and die. "In the sweat of your brow ye shall eat your bread." That has been said to be true both of physical and spiritual labor. It is true both of the life of bread and of the bread of life.

Prayer brings with it, as food does, a new sense of power and health. We are driven to it by hunger, and, having eaten, we are refreshed and strengthened for the battle which even our physical life involves. For heart and flesh cry out for the living God. God's gift is free; it is, therefore, a gift to our freedom, i.e. renewal to our moral strength, to what makes men of us. Without this gift always renewed, our very freedom can enslave us. The life of every organism is but the constant victory of a higher energy, constantly fed, over lower and more elementary forces. Prayer is the assimilation of a holy God's moral strength.

We must work for this living. To feed the soul we must toil at prayer. And what a labor it is! "He prayed in an agony." We must pray even to tears if need be. Our cooperation with God is our receptivity; but it is an active, a laborious receptivity, an importunity that drains our strength away if it do not tap the sources of the Strength Eternal. We work, we slave, at receiving. To him that hath this laborious expectancy it shall be given. Prayer is the powerful appropriation of power, of divine power. It is therefore creative.

Prayer is not mere wishing. It is asking – with a will. Our will goes into it. It is energy. *Orare est laborare*. We turn to an active Giver; therefore we go into action. For we could not pray without knowing and meeting Him in kind. If God has a controversy with Israel, Israel must wrestle with God. Moreover, He is the Giver not only of the answer, but first of the prayer itself. His gift provokes ours. He beseeches us, which makes us beseech Him. And what we ask for chiefly is the power to ask more and to ask better. We pray for more prayer. The true "gift of prayer" is God's grace before it is our facility.

Thus prayer is, for us, paradoxically, both a gift and a conquest, a grace and a duty. But does that not mean, is it not a special case of the truth, that all duty is a gift, every call on us a blessing, and that the task we often find a burden is really a boon? When we look up from under it it is a load, but those who look down to it from God's side see it as a blessing. It is like great wings – they increase the weight but also the flight. If we have no duty to do God has shut Himself from us. To be denied duty is to be denied God. No cross no Christ. "When pain ends gain ends too."

We are so egoistically engrossed about God's giving of the answer that we forget His gift of the prayer itself. But it is not a question simply of willing to pray, but of accepting and using as God's will the gift and the power to pray. In every act of prayer we have already begun to do God's will, for which above all things we pray. The prayer within all prayer is "Thy will be done." And has that petition not a special significance here? "My prayer is Thy Will. Thou didst create it in me. It is Thine more than mine. Perfect Thine own will" – all that is the paraphrase, from this viewpoint, of "Hear my prayer." "The will to pray," we say, "is Thy will. Let that be done both in my petition and in Thy perfecting of it." The petition is half God's will. It is God's will inchoate. "Thy will" (in my prayer) "be done" (in Thy answer). It is Thine both to will and to do. Thy will be done in heaven – in the answer, as it is done upon earth – in the asking."

Prayer has its great end when it lifts us to be more conscious and more sure of the gift than the need, of the grace than the sin. As petition rises out of need or sin, in our first prayer it comes first; but it may fall into a subordinate place when, at the end and height of our worship, we are filled with the fullness of God. "In that day ye shall ask Me nothing." Inward sorrow is fulfilled in the prayer of petition; inward joy in the prayer of thanksgiving. And this thought helps to deal with the question as to the hearing of prayer, and especially its answer. Or rather as to the place and kind of answer. We shall come one day to a heaven where we shall gratefully know that God's great refusals were sometimes the true answers to our truest prayer. Our soul is fulfilled if our petition is not.

When we begin to pray we may catch and surprise ourselves in a position like this. We feel to be facing God from a position of independence. If He start from His end we do from ours. We are His vis-a-vis; He is ours. He is an object so far as we are concerned; and we are the like to Him. Of course, He is an object of worship. We do not start on equal terms, march up to Him, as it were, and put our case. We do more than approach Him erect, with courteous self-respect shining through our poverty. We bow down to Him. We worship. But still it is a voluntary, an independent, submission and tribute, so to say. It is a reverence which we make an offer. We present something which is ours to give. If we ask Him to give we feel that we begin the giving in our worship. We are outside each other; and we call, and He graciously comes.

But this is not Christian idea, it is only a crude stage of it (if the New Testament is to guide us). We are there taught that only those things are perfected in God which He begins, that we seek only because He found, we beseech Him because He first besought us (2 Cor. v. 20). If our prayer reach or move Him it is because He first reached and moved us to pray. The prayer that reached and moved us to pray. The prayer that reached heaven began there, when Christ went forth. It began when God turned to beseech us in Christ – in the appealing Lamb slain before the foundation of the world. The Spirit went out with the power and function in it to return with our soul. Our prayer is the answer to God's. Herein is prayer, not that we prayed Him, but that He first prayed us, in giving His Son to be a propitiation for us. The heart of the Atonement is prayer – Christ's great self-offering to God in the Eternal Spirit. The whole rhythm of Christ's soul, so to say, was Godhead going out and returning on itself. And so God stirs and inspires all prayer which finds and moves Him. His love provokes our sacred forwardness. He does not compel us, but we cannot help it after that look, that tone, that turn of His. All say, "I am yours if you will"; and when we will it is prayer. Any final glory of human success or destiny rises from man being God's continual creation, and destined by Him for Him. So we pray because we were made for prayer, and God draws us out by breathing Himself in.

We feel this especially as prayer passes upwards into praise. When the mercy we besought comes home to us its movement is reversed in us, and it returns upon itself as thanksgiving. "Great blessings which we won with prayer are worn with thankfulness." Praise is the converted consecration of the egoism that may have moved our prayer. Prayer may spring from self-love, and be so far natural; for nature is all of the craving and taking kind. But praise is supernatural. It is of pure grace. And it is a sign that the prayer was more than natural at heart. Spare some leisure, therefore, from petition for thanksgiving. If the Spirit move conspicuously to praise, it shows that He also moved latently the prayer, and that within nature is that which is above it. "Prayer and thanks are like the double motion of the lungs; the air that is drawn in by prayer is breathed forth again by thanks."

Prayer is turning our will on God either in the way of resignation or of impertration. We yield to His Will or He to ours. Hence religion is above all things prayer, according as it is a religion of will and conscience, as it is an ethical religion. It is will and Will. To be religious is to pray. Bad prayer is false religion. Not to pray is to be irreligious. "The battle for religion is the battle for prayer; the theory of religion is the philosophy of prayer." In prayer we do not think out God; we draw Him out. Prayer is where our thought of God passes into action, and becomes more certain than thought. In all thought which is not mere dreaming or brooding there is an element of will; and in earnest (which is intelligent) prayer we give this element the upper hand. We do not simply spread our thought our before God, but we *offer* it to Him, turn it on Him, bring it to bear on Him, press it on Him. This is our great and first sacrifice, and it becomes pressure on God. We can offer God nothing so great and effective as our obedient acceptance of the mind and purpose and work of Christ. It is not easy. It is harder than any idealism. But then it is very mighty. And it is a power that grows by exercise. At first it groans, at last it glides. And it comes to this, that, as there are thoughts that seem to think themselves in us, so there are prayers that pray themselves in us. And, as those are the best thoughts, these are the best prayers. For it is the Christ at prayer who lives in us, and we are conduits of the Eternal Intercession.

Prayer is often represented as the great means of the Christian life. But it is no mere means, it is the great end of that life. It is, of course, not untrue to call it a means. It is so, especially at first. But at last it is truer to say that we live the Christian life in order to pray than that we pray in order to live the Christian life. It is at least as true. Our prayer prepares for our work and sacrifice, but all our work and sacrifice still more prepare for prayer. And we are, perhaps, oftener wrong in our work, or even our sacrifice, than we are in our prayer – and that for want of its guidance. But to reach this height, to make of prayer our great end, and to order life always in view of such a solemnity, in this sense to pray without ceasing and without pedantry – it is a slow matter. We cannot move fast to such a fine product of piety and feeling. It is a growth in grace. And the whole history of the world shows that nothing grows so slowly as grace, nothing costs as much as free grace; a fact which drives us to all kinds of apologies to explain what seems the absence of God from His world, and especially from His world of souls. If God, to our grief, seems to us far absent from history, how does He view the distance, the absence, of history from Him?

A chief object of all prayer is to bring us to God. But we may attain His presence and come closer to Him by the way we ask Him for other things, concrete things or things of the Kingdom, than by direct prayer for union with Him. The prayer for deliverance from personal trouble or national calamity may bring us nearer Him than mere devout aspiration to be lost in Him. The poor woman's prayer to find her lost sovereign may mean more than the prayer of many a cloister. Such distress is often meant by God as the initial means and exercise to His constant end of reunion with Him. His patience is so long and kind that He is willing to begin with us when we are no farther on than to use Him as a means of escape or relief. The holy Father can turn to His own account at last even the exploiting egoism of youth. And He gives us some answer, though the relief does not come, if He keep us praying, and ever more instant and purified in prayer. Prayer is never rejected so long as we do not cease to pray. The chief failure of prayer is its cessation.

Our importunity is a part of God's answer, both of His answer to us and ours to Him. He is sublimating our idea of prayer, and realizing the final purpose in all trouble of driving us farther in on Himself. A homely image has been used. The joiner, when he glues together two boards, keeps them tightly clamped till the cement sets, and the outward pressure is no more needed; then he unscrews. So with the calamities, depressions, and disappointments that crush us into close contact with God. The pressure on us is kept up till the soul's union with God is set. Instant relief would not establish the habit of prayer, though it might make us believe in it with a promptitude too shallow to last or to make it the principle of our soul's life at any depth. A faith which is based chiefly on impetration might become more of a faith in prayer than a faith in God. If we got all we asked for we should soon come to treat Him as a convenience, or the request as a magic. The reason of much bewilderment about prayer is that we are less occupied about faith in God than about faith in prayer. In a like way we are misled about the question of immortality because we become more occupied with the soul than with God, and with its endless duration more than its eternal life, asking if we shall be in eternity more than eternity in us.

In God's eyes the great object of prayer is the opening or restoring of free communion with Himself in a kingdom of Christ, a life communion which may even, amid our duty and service, become as unconscious as the beating of our heart. In this sense every true prayer brings its answer with it; and that not "reflexly" only, in our pacification of soul, but objectively in our obtaining a deeper and closer place in God and His purpose. If prayer is God's great gift, it is one inseparable from the giver; who, after all, is His own great gift, since revelation is His Self-donation. He is actively with us, therefore, as we pray, and we exert His will in praying. And, on the other hand, prayer makes us to realize how far from God we were, i.e. it makes us realize our worst trouble and repair it. The outer need kindles the sense of the inner, and we find that the complete answer to prayer is the Answerer, and the hungry soul comes to itself in the fullness of Christ.

Prayer is the highest use to which speech can be put. It is the highest meaning that can be put into words. Indeed, it breaks through language and escapes into action. We could never be told of what passed in Christ's mountain midnights. Words fail us in prayer oftener than anywhere else; and the Spirit must come in aid of our infirmity, set out our case to God, and give to us an unspoken freedom in prayer, the possession of our central soul, the reality of our inmost personality in organic contact with His. We are taken up from human speech to the region of the divine Word, where Word is deed. We are integrated into the divine consciousness, and into the dual soliloquy of Father and Son, which is the divine give and take that upholds the world. We discover how poor a use of words it is to work them into argument and pursue their dialectic consequences. There is a deeper movement of speech than that, and a more inward mystery, wherein the Word does not spread out to wisdom, nor broods in dream, but gathers to power and condenses to action. The Word becomes Flesh, Soul, Life, the active conquering kingdom of God. Prayer, as it is spoken, follows the principle of the Incarnation with its twofold movement, down and up. It is spirit not in expression only, but in deed and victory. It is speech become not only movement, but moral action and achievement; it is word become work; as the Word from being Spirit became flesh, as Christ from prophet became priest, and then Holy Spirit. It is the principle of the Incarnation, only with the descending movement reversed. "Ye are gods." God became man in His Son's outgoing that man might become divine; and prayer is in the train of the Son's return to the Father, a function of the Ascension and Exaltation, in which (if we may not say man becomes God) we are made partakers of the divine nature, not ontologically, but practically, experimentally. It is the true response, and tribute, and trophy to Christ's humiliation. Man rises to be a co-worker with God in the highest sense. For it is only action, it is not by dream or rapture, far less in essence, that we enter communion with an active being – above all with the eternal Act of God in Christ that upholds the world. As such communion prayer is no mere rapport, no mere contact. It is the central act of the soul, organic with Christ's; it is that which brings it into tune with the whole universe as God's act, and answers the beating of its central heart. It is a part and function of the creative, preservative, and consummatory energy of the world.

What is true religion? It is not the religion which contains most truth in the theological sense of the word. It is not the religion most truly thought out, not that which most closely fits with thought. It is religion which comes to itself most powerfully in prayer. It is the religion in which the soul becomes very sure of God and itself in prayer. Prayer contains the very heart and height of truth, but especially in the Christian sense of truth – reality and action. In prayer the inmost truth of our personal being locks with the inmost reality of things, its energy finds a living Person acting as their unity and life, and we escape the illusions of sense, self, and the world. Prayer, indeed, is the great means for appropriating, out of the amalgam of illusion which means so much for our education, the pure gold of God as He wills, the Spirit as He works, and things as they are. It is the great school both of proficiency and of veracity of soul. (How few court and attain proficiency of soul!) It may often cast us down, for we are reduced by this contact to our true dimensions – but to our great peace.

Prayer, true prayer, does not allow us to deceive ourselves. It relaxes the tension of our self-inflation. It produces a clearness of spiritual vision. Searching with a judgment that begins at the house of God, it ceases not to explore with His light our own soul. If the Lord is our health He may need to act on many men, or many moods, as a lowering medicine. At His coming our self-confidence is shaken. Our robust confidence, even in grace, is destroyed. The pillars of our house tremble, as if they were ivy-covered in a searching wind. Our lusty faith is refined, by what may be a painful process, into a subtler and more penetrating kind; and its outward effect is for the time impaired, though in the end it is increased. The effect of the prayer which admits God into the recesses of the soul is to destroy that spiritual density, not to say stupidity, which made our religion cheery or vigorous because it knew no better, and which was the condition of getting many obvious things done, and producing palpable effect on the order of the day. There are fervent prayers which, by making people feel good, may do no more than foster the delusion that natural vigor or robust religion, when flushed enough, can do the work of the kingdom of God. There is a certain egoist self-confidence which is increased by the more elementary forms of religion, which upholds us in much of our contact with men, and which even secures us an influence with them. But the influence is one of impression rather than permeation, it overbears rather than converts, and it inflames rather than inspires. This is a force which true and close prayer is very apt to undermine, because it saps our self-deception and its Pharisaism. The confidence was due to a lack of spiritual insight which serious prayer plentifully repairs. So by prayer we acquire our true selves. If my prayer is not answered, I am. If my petition is not fulfilled, my person, my soul, is; as the artist comes to himself and his happiness in the exercise of the talent he was made for, in spite of the delay and difficulty of turning his work to money. If the genius is happy who gets scope, the soul is blessed that truly comes to itself in prayer.

Blessed, yet not always happy. For by prayers we are set tasks sometimes which (at first, at least) may add to life's burden. Our eyes being opened, we see problems to which before we were blind, and we hear calls that no more let us alone. And I have said that we are shown ourselves at times in a way to dishearten us, and take effective dogmatism out of us. We lose effect on those people who take others at their own emphatic valuation, who do not try the spirits, and who have acquired no skill to discern the Lord in the apostle. True searching prayer is incompatible with spiritual dullness or self-complacency. And, therefore, such stupidity is not a mere defect, but a vice. It grew upon us because we did not court the searching light, nor haunt the vicinity of the great white Throne. We are chargeable with it because of our neglect of what cures it. Faith is a quickening spirit, it has insight; and religious density betrays its absence, being often the victim of the sermon instead of the alumnus of the gospel. It is not at all the effect of ignorance. Many ignorant people escape it by the exercise of themselves unto godliness; and they not only show wonderful spiritual acumen, but they turn it upon themselves; with a result, often, of great but vigilant humility, such axis apt to die out of an aggressive religion more eager to bring in a kingdom coming than to trust a Kingdom come. They are self-sufficient in a godly sort, and can even carry others, in a way which reveals the action of a power in them beyond all natural and unschooled force. We can feel in them the discipline of the Spirit. We can read much habitual prayer between their lines. They have risen far above religion. They are in the Spirit, and live in a long Lord's day. We know that they are not trying to serve Christ with the mere lustiness of natural religion, nor expecting to do the Spirit's work with the force of native temperament turned pious. There are, even amongst the religious, people who judge heavenly things with an earthly mind. And, outside the religious, among those who are but interested in religion, there may be a certain gifted stupidity, a witty obtuseness; as among some writers who *sans gene* turn what they judge to be the spirit of the age upon the realities of Eternity, and believe that it dissolves them in spray. Whether we meet this type within the Church or without, we can mostly feel that it reveals the prayerless temper whatever the zeal or vivacity may be. Not to pray is not to discern – not to discern the things that really matter, and the powers that really rule. The mind may see acutely and clearly, but the personality perceives nothing subtle and mighty; and then it comforts and deludes itself by saying it is simple and not sophisticated; and it falls a victim to the Pharisaism of the plain man. The finer (and final) forces, being unfelt, are denied or decried. The eternal motives are misread, the spell of the Eternal disowned. The simplicity in due course becomes merely bald. And all because the natural powers are unschooled, unchastened, and unempowered by the energy of prayer; and yet they are turned, either, in one direction, to do Christian work, active but loveless, or, on the other, to discuss and renounce Christian truth. It is not always hard to tell among Christian men those whose thought is matured in prayer, whose theology there becomes a hymn, whose energy is disciplined there, whose work there becomes love poured out, as by many a Salvationist lass, and whose

temper is there subdued to that illuminated humility in which a man truly finds his soul. "The secret of the Lord is with them that fear Him, and He will show them His covenant." The deeper we go into things the more do we enter a world where the mastery and the career is not to talent but to prayer.

In prayer we do not ask God to do things contrary to Nature. Rather here ascending Nature takes its true effect and arrives. For the God we invoke is the Lord and Destiny of the whole creation; and in our invocation of Him Nature ends on its own key-note. He created the world at the first with a final and constant reference to the new creation, whose native speech is prayer. The whole creation thus comes home and finds itself in our prayer; and when we ask from the God of the whole Creation we neither do not expect an arbitrary thing. We petition a God in whom all things are fundamentally working together for good to such a congenial cry. So far from crossing Nature, we give it tongue. We lift it to its divinest purpose, function, and glory. Nature excels itself in our prayer. The Creation takes its true effect in personality, which at once resists it, crowns it, and understands it; and personality takes true effect in God – in prayer. If there be a divine teleology in Nature at all, prayer is the *telos*. The world was made to worship God, for God's glory. And this purpose is the world's providence, the principle of creation. It is an end present all along the line and course of natural evolution; for we deal in prayer most closely with One to whom is no after nor before. We realize the simultaneity of Eternity.

When we are straitened in prayer we are yet not victims of Nature, we are yet free in the grace of God – as His own freedom was straitened in Christ's incarnation, not to say His dereliction, to the finishing of His task. It is hard, it is often impossible, for us to tell whether our hour of constriction or our hour of expansion contributes more to the divine purpose and its career. Both go to make real prayer. They are the systole and diastole of the world's heart. True prayer is the supreme function of the personality which is the world's supreme product. It is personality with this function that God seeks above all to rear – it is neither particular moods of its experience, nor influential relations of it with the world. The praying personality has an eternal value for God as an end in itself. This is the divine fullness of life's time and course, the one achievement that survives with more power in death than in life. The intercession of Christ in heaven is the continuity and consummation of His supreme work on earth. To share it is the meaning of praying in the Spirit. And it has more effect on history than civilization has. This is a hard saying, but a Christian can say no otherwise without in so far giving up his Christianity.

"There is a budding morrow in midnight." And every juncture, every relation, and every pressure of life has in it a germ of possibility and promise for our growth in God and grace; which germ to rear is the work of constant and progressive prayer. (For as a soul has a history, prayer has its progress.) This germ we do not always see, nor can we tend it as if we did. It is often hidden up under the earthly relations, and may there be lost – our soul is lost. (It can be lost even through love.) But also it may from there be saved – and we escape from the fowler's net. It's growth is often visible only to the Savior whom we keep near by prayer, whose search we invoke, and for whose action we make room in prayer. Our certainty of Him is girt round with much uncertainty, about His working, about the steps of His process. But in prayer we become more and more sure that He is sure, and knows all things to His end. All along Christ is being darkly formed within us as we pray; and our converse with God goes on rising to become an element of the intercourse of the Father and the Son, whom we overhear, as it were, at converse in us. Yet this does not insulate us from our kind; for other people are then no more alien to us, but near in a Lord who is to them what He is to us. Private prayer may thus become more really common prayer that public prayer is.

And so also with the universe itself as we rise in Christ to prayer. Joined with its Redeemer, we are integrated into its universality. We are made members of its vast whole. We are not detained and cramped in a sectional world. We are not planted in the presence of an outside, alien universe, nor in the midst

of a distraught, unreconciled universe, which speaks like a crowd, in many fragments and many voices, and drags us from one relation with it to another, with a Lo, here is Christ, or there. But it is a universe wholly vocal to us, really a universe, and vocal as a whole, one congenial and friendly, as it comes to us in its Christ and ours. It was waiting for us – for such a manifestation of the Son of God as prayer is. This world is not now a desert haunted by demons. And it is more than a vestibule to another; it is its prelude in the drama of all things. We know it in another knowledge now than its own. Nature can never be understood by natural knowledge. We know it as science never can – as a whole, and as reality. We know it as we are known of God – altogether, and not in pieces. Having nothing, and praying for everything, we possess all things. The faith that energizes in Christian prayer sets us at the center of that whole of which Nature is the overture part. The steps of thought and its processes of law fade away. They do not cease to act, but they retire from notice. We grasp the mobile organization of things deep at its constant and trusty heart. We receive the earnest of our salvation – Christ in us.

There, where one center reconciles all things,
The world's profound heart beats.

We are planted there. And all the mediation of process becomes immediate in its eternal ground. As we are going there we feel already there. "They were willing to receive Him into the boat, and straightway the boat was at the land whither they were going." We grasp that eternal life to which all things work, which gives all the waxing organization its being and meaning – for a real organism only grows because it already is. That is the mark of a real life. And soul and person is the greatest organism of all. We apprehend our soul as it is apprehended of God and in God, the timeless God – with all its evolution, past or future, converted into a divine present. We are already all that we are to be. We possess our souls in the prayer which is real communion with God. We enter by faith upon that which to sight and history is but a far future reversion. When He comes to our prayer He brings with Him all that He purposes to make us. We are already the "brave creature" He means us to be. More than our desire is fulfilled – our soul is. In such hour or visitation we realize our soul or person at no one stage of it, but in its fullness, and in the context of its whole and final place in history, the world, and eternity. A phase which has no meaning in itself, yet carries, like the humble mother of a great genius, an eternal meaning in it. And we can seize that meaning in prayer; we can pierce to what we are at our true course and true destiny, i.e. what we are to God's grace. Laws and injunctions such as "Love your neighbor," even "Love your enemy," then become life principles, and they are law pressures no more. The yoke is easy. Where all is forgiven to seventy times seven there is no friction and no grief any more. We taste love and joy. All the pressure of life then goes to form the crystals of faith. It is God making up His jewels.

When we are in God's presence by prayer we are *right,* our will is morally right, we are doing His will. However unsure we may be about other acts and efforts to serve Him we know we are right in this. If we ask truly but ask amiss, it is not a sin, and He will in due course set us right in that respect. We are sure that prayer is according to His will, and that we are just where we ought to be. And that is a great matter for the rightness of our thought, and of the aims and desires proposed by out thoughts. It means much both as to their form and their passion. If we realize that prayer is the acme of our right relation to God, if we are sure that we are never so right with Him in anything we do as in prayer, then prayer must have the greatest effect and value for our life, both in its purpose and its fashion, in its spirit and its tenor. What puts us right morally, right with a Holy God (as prayer does), must have a great shaping power on every part and every juncture of life. And, of course, especially upon the spirit and tenor of our prayer itself, upon the form and complexion of our petition.

The effect of our awful War will be very different on the prayerful and the prayerless. It will be a sifting judgment. It will turn to prayer those who did not pray, and increase the prayer of those who did. But some, whose belief in God grew up only in fair weather and not at the Cross, it will make more skeptical and prayerless than ever, and it will present them with a world more confused and more destitute of a God than before; which can only lead to renewed outbreaks of the same kind as soon as the nations regain strength. The prayerless spirit saps a people's moral strength because it blunts their thought and conviction of the Holy. It must be so if prayer is such a moral blessing and such a shaping power, if it pass, by its nature, from the vague volume and passion of devotion to formed petition and effort. Prayerlessness is an injustice and a damage to our own soul, and therefore to its history, both in what we do and what we think. The root of all deadly heresy is prayerlessness. Prayer finds our clue in a world otherwise without form and void. And it draws a magic circle round us over which the evil spirits may not pass. "Prayer," says Vinet, "is like the air of certain ocean isles, which is so pure that there vermin cannot live. We should surround ourselves with this atmosphere, as the diver shuts himself into his bell ere he descends into the deep."

If there must be in the Church a communion of belief, there must be there also a communion of prayer. For the communion of prayer is the very first form the communion of belief takes. It is in this direction that Church unity lies. It lies behind prayer, in something to which prayer gives effect, in that which is the source and soul of prayer – in our relation with God in Christ, in our new creation. Prayer for Church unity will not bring that unity; but that which stirs, and founds, and wings prayer will. And prayer is its chief exercise. The true Church is just as wide as the community of Christian prayer, i.e. of due response to the gospel of our reconcilement and communion with God. And it is a thing almost dreadful that Christians who pray to the same God, Christ, and Savior should refuse to unite in prayer because of institutional differences.

A prayer is also a promise. Every true prayer carries with it a vow. If it do not, it is not in earnest. It is not of a piece with life. Can we pray in earnest if we do not in the act commit ourselves to do our best to bring about the answer? Can we escape some king of hypocrisy? This is especially so with intercession. What is the value of praying for the poor if all the rest of our time and interest is given only to becoming rich? Where is the honesty of praying for our country if in our most active hours we are chiefly occupied in making something out of it, if we are strange to all sacrifice for it? Prayer is one form of sacrifice, but if it is the only form it is vain oblation. If we pray for our child that he may have God's blessing, we are really promising that nothing shall be lacking on our part to be a divine blessing to him. And if we have no kind of religious relation to him (as plenty of Christian parents have none), our prayer is quite unreal, and its failure should not be a surprise. To pray for God's kingdom is also so engage ourselves to service and sacrifice for it. To begin our prayer with a petition for the hallowing of God's name and to have no real and prime place for holiness in our life or faith is not sincere. The prayer of the vindictive for forgiveness is mockery, like the prayer for daily bread from a wheat-cornered. No such man could say the Lord's Prayer but to his judgment. What would happen to the Church if the Lord's Prayer became a test for membership as thoroughly as the Creeds have been? The Lord's Prayer is also a vow to the Lord. None but a Christian can pray it, or should. Great worship of God is also a great engagement of ourselves, a great committal of our action. To begin the day with prayer is but a formality unless it go on in prayer, unless for the rest of it we pray in deed what we began in word. One has said that while prayer is the day's best beginning it must not be like the handsome title-page of a worthless book.

"Thy will be done." Unless that were the spirit of all our prayer, how should we have courage to pray if we know ourselves at all, or if we have come to a time when we can have some retrospect on our prayers and their fate? Without this committal to the wisdom of God, prayer would be a very dangerous weapon in proportion as it was effective. No true God could promise us an answer to our every prayer. No Father of mankind could. The rain that saved my crop might ruin my neighbor's. It would paralyze prayer to be sure that it would prevail as it is offered, certainly and at once. We should be terrified at the power put into our foolish hands. Nothing would do more to cure us of a belief in our own wisdom

than the granting of some of our eager prayers. And nothing could humiliate us more than to have God say when the fulfillment of our desire brought leanness to our souls. "Well, you have it." It is what He has said to many. But He said more, "My grace is sufficient for thee."

2. THE NATURALNESS OF PRAYER

We touch the last reality directly in prayer. And we do this not by thought's natural research, yet by a quest not less laborious. Prayer is the atmosphere of revelation, in the strict and central sense of that word. It is the climate in which God's manifestation bursts open into inspiration. All the mediation of Nature and of things sinks here to the rear, and we are left with God in Christ as His own Mediator and His own Revealer. He is directly with us and in us. We transcend there two thousand years as if they were but one day. By His Spirit and His Spirit's creative miracle God becomes Himself our new nature, which is yet our own, our destined Nature; for we were made with His image for our "doom of greatness." It is no mere case of education or evolution drawing out our best. Prayer has a creative action in its answer. It does more than present us with our true, deep, latent selves. It lays hold on God, and God is not simply our magnified self. Our other self is, in prayer, our Creator still creating. Our Maker it is that is our Husband. He is Another. We feel, the more we are united with Him in true prayer, the deep, close difference, the intimate otherness in true love. Otherwise prayer becomes mere dreaming; it is spiritual extemporizing and not converse. The division runs not simply between us and Nature, but it parts us within our spiritual self, where union is most close. It is a spiritual distinction, like the distinction of Father and Son in heaven. But Nature itself, our natural selves, are involved in it; because Nature for the Christian is implicated in Redemption. It "arrives." It is read in a new script. The soul's conflict is found in a prelude in it. This may disturb our pagan joy. It may quench the consolations of Nature. The ancient world could take refuge in Nature as we cannot. It could escape there from conscience in a way impossible to us, because for us body runs up into soul, and Nature has become organic with spirit, an arena and even (in human nature) an experience of God's will. It groans to come to itself in the sons of God. Redemption is cosmic. We do not evade God's judgment there; and we put questions about His equity there which did not trouble the Greek. It we take the wings of the morning and dwell in the uttermost parts of the earth, God still besets us behind and before. We still feel the collision of past and future, of conduct and conscience. If we try to escape from His presence there, we fail; the winds are His messengers, the fires His ministers, wars and convulsions instruments of His purpose. He is always confronting us, judging us, saving us in a spiritual world, which Nature does not stifle, but only makes it more universal and impressive than our personal strife. In Nature our *vis-a-vis* is still the same power we meet as God in our soul.

>   The voice that rolls the stars along
>   Speaks all His promises.

Our own natural instincts turn our scourges, but also our blessings, according as they mock God or serve Him. So Nature becomes our chaperone for Christ, our tutor whose duty is daily to deliver us at Christ's door. It opens out into a Christ whose place and action are not historic only, but also cosmic. The cosmic place of Christ in the later epistles is not apostolic fantasy, extravagant speculation, nor groundless theosophy. It is the ripeness of practical faith, faith which by action comes to itself and to its own.

Especially is this pointed where faith has its most pointed action as prayer. If cosmic Nature runs up into man, man rises up into prayer; which thus fulfils Nature, brings its inner truth to pass, and crowns its bias to spirit. Prayer is seen to be the opening secret of creation, its destiny, that to which it all travails. It is the burthen of evolution. The earnest expectation of the creation waits, and all its onward thrust works, for the manifestation of the sons of God. Nature comes to itself in prayer. Prayer realizes and brings to a head the truth of Nature, which groans being burdened with the passion of its deliverance, its relief in prayer. "*Magna ars est conversari cum Deo.*" "The art of prayer is Nature gone to heaven." We become in prayer Nature's true artists (if we may so say), the vehicles of its finest and inmost

passion. And we are also its true priests, the organs of its inner commerce with God, where the Spirit immanent in the world meets the Spirit transcendent in obedient worship. The sum of things for ever speaking is heard in heaven to pray without ceasing. It is speaking not only to us but in us to God. Soliloquy here is dialogue. In our prayer God returns from His projection in Nature to speak with Himself. When we speak to God it is really the God who lives in us speaking through us to Himself. His Spirit returns to Him who gave it; and returns not void, but bearing our souls with Him. The dialogue of grace is really the monologue of the divine nature in self-communing love. In prayer, therefore, we do true and final justice to the world. We give Nature to itself. We make it say what it was charged to say. We make it find in thought and word its own soul. It comes to itself not in man but in the praying man, the man of Christian prayer. The Christian man at prayer is the secretary of Creation's praise. So prayer is the answer to Nature's quest, as God is the answer to prayer. It is the very nature of nature; which is thus miraculous or nothing at its core.

Here the friction vanishes, therefore, between prayer and natural law. Nature and all its plexus of law is not static, but dynamic. It is not interplay, but evolution. It has not only to move, but to arrive. Its great motive power is not a mere instinct, but a destiny. Its system is not a machine, but a procession. It is dramatic. It has a close. Its ruling power is not what it rises from, but what it moves to. Its impulse is its goal immanent. All its laws are overruled by the comprehensive law of its destination. It tends to prayer. The laws of Nature are not like iron. If they are fixed they are only fixed as the composition is fixed at H_2O of the river which is so fluid and moving that I can use it at any time to bear me to its sea. They are fixed only in so far as makes reliable, and not fatal, to man's spirit. Their nature is constant, but their function is not stiff. What is fixed in the river is the constancy of its fluidity. "Still glides the stream, and shall for ever glide." The greatest law of Nature is thus its bias to God, its *nisus* to return to His rest. This comes to light chiefly in man's gravitation to Him, when His prodigal comes home to Him. The forwardest creation comes to itself in our passion for God and in our finding of Him in prayer. In prayer, therefore, we do not ask God to do things contrary to Nature, though our request may seem contrary to sections of it which we take for the whole. We ask Him to fulfill Nature's own prayer.

The atmosphere of prayer seems at first to be the direct contrary of all that goes with such words as practical or scientific. But what do we mean by practical at last but that which contributes to the end for which the world and mankind were made? The whole of history, as the practical life of the race, is working out the growth, the emancipation of the soul, the enrichment and fortifying of the human spirit. It is doing on the large scale what every active life is doing on the small – it is growing soul. There is no reality at last except soul, except personality. This alone has eternal meaning, power, and value, since this alone develops or hampers the eternal reality, the will of God. The universe has its being and its truth for a personality, but for one at last which transcends individual limits. To begin with the natural plane, our egoism constructs there a little world with a definite teleology converging on self, one which would subdue everybody and everything to the tributary to our common sensible self. On a more spiritual (yet not on the divine) plane the race does the like with its colossal ego. It views and treats the universe as contributory to itself, to the corporate personality of the race. Nature is here for man, man perhaps for the superman. We are not here for the glory of God, but God is here for the aid and glory of man. But either way all things are there to work together for personality, and to run up into a free soul. Man's practical success is then what makes for the enhancement of this ego, small or great. But, on the Christian plane, man himself, as part of a creation, has a meaning and an end; but it is in God; he does not return on himself. God is his nisus and drift. God works in him; he is not just trying to get his own head out. But God is Love. All the higher science of Nature which is the milieu and the machinery that give the soul its bent to love, and turn it out its true self in love. All the practice and science of the world is there, therefore, to reveal and realize love and

love's communion. It is all a stage, a scenery, a plot, for a denouement where beings mingle, and each is enriched by all and all by each. It all goes to the music of that love which binds all things together in the cosmic dance, and which makes each stage of each thing prophetic of its destined fullness only in a world so bound. So science itself is practical if prayer end and round all. It is the theory of a cosmic movement with prayer for its active end. And it is an ethical science at last, it is a theology, if the Christian end is the real end of the whole world. All knowledge serves love and love's communion. For Christian faith a universe is a universe of souls, an organism of persons, which is the expression of an Eternal Will of love. This love is the real presence which gives meaning, and movement, and permanence to a fleeting world of sense. And it is by prayer that we come into close and conscious union with this universe and power of love, this living reality of things. Prayer (however miraculous) is, therefore, the most natural things in the world. It is the effectuation of all Nature, which comes home to roost there, and settles to its rest. It is the last word of all science, giving it contact with a reality which, as science alone, it cannot reach. And it is also the most practical things in all man's action and history, as doing most to bring to pass the spiritual object for which all men and all things exist and strive.

Those who feel prayer stifled by the organization of law do not consider that law itself, if we take a long enough sweep, keeps passing us on to prayer. Law rises from Nature, through history, to heaven. It is integrated historically, i.e. by Christ's cross and the Church's history, with the organization of love. But that is the organization of Eternity in God, and it involves the interaction of all souls in a communion of ascending prayer. Prayer is the native movement of the spiritual life that receives its meaning and its soul only in Eternity, that works in the style and scale of Eternity, owns its principles, and speaks its speech. It is the will's congenial surrender to that Redemption and Reconciliation between loving wills which is God's Eternity acting in time. We beseech God because He first besought us.

So not to pray on principle means that thought has got the better of the will. The question is whether thought includes will or will thought; and thought wins if prayer is suppressed. Thought and not personality is then in command of the universe. If will is but a function of the idea, then prayer is but a symptom, it is not a power. It belongs to the phenomenology of the Infinite, it is not among its controls.

Prayer is doing God's will. It is letting Him pray in us. We look for answer because His fullness is completely equal to His own prayers. Father and Son are perfectly adequate to each other. That is the Holy Spirit and self-sufficiency of the Godhead.

If God's will is to be done on earth as it is in heaven, prayer begins with adoration. Of course, it is thanks and petition; but before we give even our prayer we must first receive. The Answerer provides the very prayer. What we do here rests on what God has done. What we offer is drawn from us by what He offers. Our self-oblation stands on His; and the spirit of prayer flows from the gift of the Holy Ghost, the great Intercessor. Hence praise and adoration of His work in itself comes before even our thanksgiving for blessings to us. At the height of prayer, if not at its beginning, we are preoccupied with the great and glorious thing God has done for His own holy name in Redemption, apart from its immediate and particular blessing to us. We are blind for the time to ourselves. We cover our faces with our wings and cry "Holy, holy, holy is the Lord God of hosts; the fullness of the earth is His glory." Our full hearts glorify. We magnify His name. His perfections take precedence of our occasions. We pray for victory in the present was, for instance, and for deliverance from all war, for the sake of God's kingdom – in a spirit of adoration for the deliverance there that is not destroyed, or foiled, even by a devilry like this. If the kingdom of God not only got over the murder of Christ, but made it its great lever, there is nothing that it cannot get over, and nothing it cannot turn to eternal blessing and to the glory of the holy name. But to the perspective of this faith, and to its vision of values so alien to human standards, we can rise only in prayer.

But it would be unreal prayer which was adoration only, with no reference to special boons or human needs. That would be as if God recognized no life but His own – which is very undivine egoism, and its collective form is the religion of mere nationalism. In true prayer we do two things. We go out of ourselves, being lost in wonder, love and praise; but also, and in the same act, we go in upon ourselves. We stir up all that is within us to bless and hallow God's name. We examine ourselves keenly in that patient light, and we find ourselves even when our sin finds us out. Our nothingness is not burned and branded into us as if we had above only the starry irony of heaven. Our heart comes again. Our will is braced and purified. We not only recall our needs, but we discover new ones, of a more and more intimate and spiritual kind. The more spiritual we grow, the more we rise out of the subconscious or the unconscious. We never realize ourselves as we do when we forget ourselves after this godly sort in prayer. Prayer is not falling back upon the abyss below the soul; even as the secret of the Incarnation is sought in vain in that non-moral zone. Prayer is not what might be called the increased drone or boom of an unspeakable Om. But we rise in it to more conscious and positive relation with God the Holy – the God not abysmal but revealed, in whose revelation the thoughts of many hearts are revealed also, and whose fullness makes need almost as fast as it satisfies it.

After adoration, therefore, prayer is thanksgiving and petition. When we thank God our experience "arrives." It finds what it came for. It fulfills the greatest end of experience. It comes to its true self, comes to its own, and has its perfect work. It breathes large, long, and free, *sublimi anbelitu*. The soul runs its true normal course back to God its Creator, who has stamped the destiny of this return upon it, and leaves it no peace till it finds its goal in Him. The gift we thank for becomes sacramental because it conveys chiefly the Giver, and is lost in Him and in His praise. It is He that chiefly comes in His saints and His boons. In real revelation we rise for above a mere interpretation of life, a mere explanation of events; we touch their Doer, the Life indeed, and we can dispense with interpretations, having Him. An occurrence thus becomes a revelation. It gives us God, in a sacrament. And where there is real revelation there is thanksgiving, there is Eucharist; for God Himself is in the gift, and strikes His own music from the soul. If we think most of the gift, prayer may subtly increase our egoism. We praise for a gift to us. We are tempted to treat God as an asset, and to exploit him. But true prayer, thinking most of the Giver, quells the egoism and dissolves it in praise. What we received came for another end than just to gratify us. It came to carry God to us, and to lift us to Him and to the consent of His glory. The blessing in it transcends the enjoyment of it, and the Spirit of the outgoing God returns to Him not void, but bringing our souls as sheaves with Him.

So also with the petition in our prayer. It also is purified by adoration, praise, and thanksgiving. We know better what to pray for as we ought. We do not only bring to God desires that rise apart from Him, and that we present by an act of our own; but our desires, our will, as they are inspired are also formed in God's presence, as requests. They get shape. In thanks we spread out before Him and offer Him our past and present, but in petition it is our future.

But has petition a true place in the highest and purest prayer? Is it not lost in adoration and gratitude? Does adoration move as inevitably to petition as petition rises to adoration? In reply we might ask whether the best gratitude and purest thanks are not for answered petitions. Is there not this double movement in all spiritual action which centers in the Incarnation, where man ascends as God comes down? Does not man enlarge in God as God particularizes upon men? But, putting that aside, is the subsidence of petition not due to a wrong idea of God; as if our only relation were dependence, as if, therefore, will-lessness before Him were the devout ideal — as if we but acknowledge Him and could not act on Him? Ritschl, for example, following Schleiermacher, says, "Love to God has no sphere of action outside love to our brother." If that were so, there would be no room for petition, but only for worship of God and service of man without intercession. The position is not unconnected with Ritschl's neglect of the Spirit and His intercession, or with his aversion to the Catholic type of piety. If suffering were the only occasion of prayer, then resignation, and not petition, might be the true spirit of prayer. But our desires and wills do not rise out of our suffering only, nor out of our passivity and dependence, but also out of our duty and our place in life; and therefore our petition is as due to God and as proper as our life's calling. If we may not will nor love, no doubt petition, especially for others, is a mistake. Of course, also, our egoism, engrossed with our happiness influences our prayer too often and too much. But we can never overcome our self-will by will-lessness, nor our greed of happiness by apathy. Petitions that are less than pure can only be purified by petition. Prayer is the salvation of prayer. We pray for better prayer. We can rise above our egoism only as we have real dealing with the will of God in petitionary prayer which does change His detailed intentions toward us though not His great will of grace and Salvation.

The element of adoration has been missed from worship by many observers of our public prayer. And the defect goes with the individualism of the age just past. Adoration is a power the egoist and individualist loses. He loses also the power both of thanksgiving and of petition, and sinks, through silence before God, to His neglect. For our blessings are not egoistically meant, nor do they remain blessings if so taken. They contemplate more than ourselves, as indeed does our whole place and work in the gift of life. We must learn to thank God not only for the blessings of others, but for the power to convey to others gifts which make them happier than they make us – as the gifts of genius so often do. One Church should praise Him for the prosperity of other Churches, for that is to the good of the gospel. And, as for petition, how can a man or a Church pray for their own needs to the omission of others? God's fundamental relation to us is one that embraces and blesses all. We are saved in a common salvation. The atmosphere of prayer is communion. Common prayer is the inevitable fruit of a gospel like Christ's.

Public prayer, therefore, should be in the main liturgical, with room for free prayer. The more it really is common prayer, and the more our relation with men extend and deepen (as prayer with and for men does extend them), the more we need forms which proceed from the common and corporate conscience of the Church. Even Christ did. As He rose to the height of His great world-work on the cross His prayer fell back on the liturgy of His people – on the Psalms. It is very hard for the ordinary minister to come home to the spiritual variety of a large congregation without those great forms which arose out of the deep soul of the Church before it spread into sectional boughs or individual twigs.

Common prayer is not necessarily public. To recite the Litany on a sick-bed is common prayer. Christ felt the danger of common prayer as public prayer (Matt. vi. 5,6). And this is specially so when the public prayer is "extempore." To keep that real calls for an amount of private prayer which perhaps is not for every one. "Extempore" prayers are apt to be private prayers in public, like the Pharisee's in the temple, with too much idiosyncrasy for public use; or else they lose the spontaneity of private prayer, and turn as formal as a liturgy can be, though in another (and perhaps deadlier) way. The prayers of the same man inevitably fall more or less into the same forms and phrases. But private prayer may be more common in its note than public prayer should be private in its tone. Our private prayer should be common in spirit. We are doing in the act what many are doing. In the retired place we include in sympathy and intercession a world of other men which we exclude in fact. The world of men disappears from around us but not from within. We are not indifferent to its weal or woe in our seclusion. In the act of praying for ourselves we pray for others, for no temptation befalls us but what is common to man; and in praying for others we pray with them. We pray for their prays and the success of their prayers. It is an act of union. We can thus be united even with churches that refuse to pray or unite with us.

Moreover, it is common prayer, however solitary, that prevails most, as being most in tune with the great first goal of God's grace – the community. So this union in prayer gives to prayer an ethical note of great power and value. If we really pray with others, it must clear, and consolidate, and exalt our moral relations with them everywhere. Could we best the man with whom and for whom we really pray? There is a great democratic note in common prayer which is also true prayer. "Eloquence and ardor have not done so much for Christ's cause as the humble virtues, the united activity, and the patient prayers of thousands of faithful people whose names are quite unknown." And we are united thus not only to the living but to the long dead. "He who prays is nearer Christ than even the apostles were," certainly than the apostles before the Cross and Resurrection.

We have been warned by a man of genius that the bane of so much religion is that it clings to God with its weakness and not with its strength. This is very true of that supreme act of religion of which our critics know least – of the act of prayer. So many of us pray because we are driven by need rather than kindled by grace. Our prayer is a cry rather than a hymn. It is a quest rather than a tryst. it trembles more than it triumphs. It asks for strength rather than exerts it. How different was the prayer of Christ! All the divine power of the Eternal Son went to it. It was the supreme form taken by His Sonship in its experience and action. Nothing is more striking in Christ's life than His combination of selflessness and power. His consciousness of power was equal to anything, and egoism never entered Him. His prayer was accordingly. It was the exercise of His unique power rather than of His extreme need. It came from His uplifting and not His despair. It was less His duty than His joy. It was more full of God's gift of grace than of man's poverty of faith, of a holy love than of a seeking heart. In His prayer He poured out neither His wish nor His longing merely, but His will. And He knew He was heard always. He knew it with such power and certainty that He could distribute His value, bless with His overflow, and promise His disciples they would be heard in His name. It was by His prayer that He countered and foiled the godless power in the world, the kingdom of the devil. "Satan hath desired to have thee – but I have prayer for thee." His prayer means so much for the weak because it arose out of this strength and its exercise. It was chiefly in His prayer that He was the Messiah, and the Revealer and Wielder of the power and kingship of God. His power with

God was so great that it made His disciples feel it could only be the power of God; He prayer in the Eternal Spirit whereby He offered Himself to God. And it was so great because it was spent on God alone. So true is it that the kingdom of God comes not with observation, that the greatest things Christ did for it were done in the night and not in the day; His prayers meant more than His miracles. And His great triumph was when there were none to see, as they all forsook Him and fled. He was mightest in His action for men not when He was acting on men but on God. He felt the dangers of the publicity where His work lay, and He knew that they were only to be met in secrecy. He did most for His public in entire solitude; there He put forth all His power. His nights were not always the rest of weakness from the day before, but often the storing of strength for the day to come. Prayer (if we let Christ teach us of it) is mightiest in the mightiest. It is the ether round the throne of the Most High. Its power answers to the omnipotence of grace. And those who feel they owe everything to God's grace need have no difficulty about the range of prayer. They may pray for everything.

A word, as I close this chapter, to the sufferers. We pray for the removal of pain, pray passionately, and then with exhaustion, sick from hope deferred and prayer's failure. But there is a higher prayer than that. It is a greater thing to pray for pain's conversion than for its removal. It is more of grace to pray that God would make a sacrament of it. The sacrament of pain! That we partake not simply, nor perhaps chiefly, when we say, or try to say, with resignation, "Thy will be done." It is not always easy for the sufferer, if he remain clear-eyed to see that it is God's will. It may have been caused by an evil mind, or a light fool, or some stupid greed. But, now it is there, a certain treatment of it is God's will; and that is to capture and exploit it for Him. It is to make it serve the soul and glorify God. It is to consecrate its elements and make it sacramental. It is to convert it into prayer.

God has blessed pain even in causing us to pray for relief from it, or profit. Whatever drives us to Him, and even nearer Him, has a blessing in it. And, if we are to go higher still, it is to turn pain to praise, to thank Him in the fires, to review life and use some of the energy we spend in worrying upon recalling and tracing His goodness, patience, and mercy. If much open up to us in such a review we may be sure there is much more we do not know, and perhaps never may. God is the greatest of all who do good by stealth and do not crave for every benefit to be acknowledged. Or we may see how our pain becomes a blessing to others. And we turn the spirit of heaviness to the garment of praise. We may stop grousing and get our soul into its Sunday clothes. The sacrament of pain becomes then a true Eucharist and giving of thanks.

And if there were a higher stage than all it would be Adoration – when we do not think of favors or mercies to us or ours at all, but of the perfection and glory of the Lord. We feel to His Holy Name what the true artist feels towards an unspeakable beauty. As Wordsworth says:

> I gazed and gazed,
> And did not wish her mine.

There was a girl of 15, tall, sweet, distinguished beyond her years. And this is how Heine ran into English at the sight of her:

> No flower is half so lovely,
> So dear, and fair, and kind.
> A boundless tide of tenderness
> Flows over my heart and mind.
>
> And I pray. (There is no answer
> To beauty unearthly but prayer.)
> God answered my prayer, and keep you
> So dear, and fine, and fair.

3. THE MORAL REACTIONS OF PRAYER

All religion is founded on prayer, and in prayer it has its test and measure. To be religious is to pray, to be irreligious is to be incapable of prayer. The theory of religion is really the philosophy of prayer; and the best theology is compressed prayer. The true theology is warm, and it steams upward into prayer. Prayer is access to whatever we deem God, and if there is no such access there is no religion; for it is not religion to resign ourselves to be crushed by a brute power so that we can no more remonstrate than resist. It is in prayer that our real idea of God appears, and in prayer that our real relation to God shows itself. On the first levels of our religion we go to our God for help and boon in the junctures of our natural life; but, as we rise to supernatural religion, gifts becomes less to us than the Giver; they are not such as feed our egoism. We forget ourselves in a godly sort; and what we court and what we receive in our prayer is not simply a boon but communion – or if a boon, it is the boon which Christians call the Holy Spirit, and which means, above all else, communion with God. But lest communion subside into mere meditation it must concentrate in prayer. We must keep acquiring by such effort the grace so freely given. There is truly a subconscious communion, and a godliness that forgets God well, in the hourly life of taxing action and duty; but it must rise to seasons of colloquy, when our action is wholly with the Father, and the business even of His kingdom turns into heart converse, where the yoke is easy and the burden light. Duty is then absorbed in love – the deep, active union of souls outwardly distinct. Their connection is not external and (as we might say) inorganic; it is inward, organic, and reciprocal. There is not only action but interplay, not only need and gift but trust and love. The boon is the Giver Himself, and its answer is the self of the receiver. *Cor ad cor loquitor.* All the asking and having goes on in a warm atmosphere, where soul passes into soul without fusion, person is lost in person without losing personality, and thought about prayer becomes thought in prayer. The greatest, deepest, truest thought of God is generated in prayer, where right thought has its essential condition in a right will. The state and act of true prayer contains the very substance and summit of Christian truth, which is always there in solution, and becomes increasingly explicit and conscious. To grow in grace is to become more understanding in prayer. We make for the core of Christian reality and the source of Christian power.

Our atonement with God is the pregnant be-all and end-all of Christian peace and life; and what is that atonement but the head and front of the Savior's perpetual intercession, of the outpouring of His sin-laden soul unto death? Unto death! That is to say, it is its outpouring utterly. So that His entire self-emptying and His perfect and prevailing prayer is one. In this intercession our best prayer, broken, soiled, and feeble as it is, is caught up and made prayer indeed and power with God. This intercession prays for our very prayer, and atones for the sin in it. This is praying in the Holy Ghost, which is not necessarily a matter either of intensity or elation. This is praying "for Christ's sake." If it be true that the whole Trinity is in the gospel of our salvation, it is also true that all theology lies hidden in the prayer which is our chief answer to the gospel. And the bane of so much theology, old and new, is that it has been denuded of prayer and prepared in a vacuum.

Prayer draws on our whole personality; and not only so, but on the whole God. And it draws on a God who really comes home nowhere else. God is here, not as a mere presence as He is in Nature, nor is He a mere pressure as He closes in upon us in the sobering of life. We do not face Him in mere meditation, nor do we cultivate Him as life's most valuable asset. But He is here as our Lover, our Seeker, our Visitant, our Interlocutor; He is our Savior, our Truth, our Power, nay, our Spiritual World. In this supreme exercise of our personality He is at once our Respondent and our Spiritual Universe. Nothing but the experience of prayer can solve paradoxes like these. On every other level they are absurd. But here deep answers deep. God becomes the living truth of our most memorable and shaping experience, not its object only but its essence. He who speaks to us also hears in us, because He opens our inward ear (Rom. viii. 15; Gal. iv. 6). And yet He is Another, who so fully lives in us as to give us but the more fully to ourselves. So that our prayer is a soliloquy with God, a monologue *a deux.*

There is no such engine for the growth and command of the moral soul, single, or social, as prayer. Here, above all, he who will do shall know. It is the great organ of Christian knowledge and growth. It plants us at the very center of our own personality, which gives the soul the true perspective of itself; it sets us also at the very center of the world in God, which gives us the true hierarchy of things. Nothing, therefore, develops such "inwardness" and yet such self-knowledge and self-control. Private prayer, when it is made a serious business, when it is formed prayer, when we pray audibly in our chamber, or when we write our prayers, guided always by the day's record, the passion of piety, and above all the truths of Scripture, is worth more for our true and grave and individual spirituality than gatherings of greater unction may be. Bible searching and searching prayer go hand in hand. What we receive from God in the Book's message we return to Him with interest in prayer. Nothing puts us in living contact with God but prayer, however facile our mere religion may be. And therefore nothing does so much for our originality, so much to make us our own true selves, to stir up all that is in us to be, and hallow all we are. In life it is not hard work; it is faculty, insight, gift, talent, genius. And what genius does in the natural world prayer does in the spiritual. Nothing can give us so much power and vision. It opens a fountain perpetual and luminous at the center of our personality, where we are sustained because we are created anew and not simply refreshed. For here the springs of life continually rise. And here also the eye discerns a new world because it has second sight. It sees two worlds at once. Hence, the paradoxes I spoke of. Here we learn to read the work of Christ which commands the world unseen. And we learn to read even the strategy of Providence in the affairs of the world. To pray to the Doer must help us to understand what is done. Prayer, as our greatest work, breeds in us the flair for the greatest work of God, the instinct of His kingdom and the sense of His track in Time.

Here, too, we acquire that spiritual veracity which we so constantly tend to lose; because we are in contact with the living and eternal reality. Our very love is preserved from dissimulation, which is a great danger when we love men and court their love. Prayer is a greater school and discipline of divine love than the service of man is. But not if it is cut off from it.

And no less also is it the school of repentance, which so easily can grow morbid. We are taught to be not only true to reality, but sincere with ourselves. We cannot touch God thus without having a light no less searching than saving shed upon our own hearts; and we are thus protected from Pharisaism in our judgment of either self or friend or foe – especially at present of our foe. No companion of God can war in His name against man without much self-searching and self-humiliation, however reserved. But here humility turns into moral strength.

Here we are also regathered in soul from the fancies that bewilder us and the distractions that dissolve us into the dust of the world. We are collected into peace and power and sound judgment, and we have a heart for any fate, because we rest in the Lord whose judgments are salvation. What gives us our true stay gives us our true self; and it protects us from the elations and despairs which alternate in ourselves by bringing home to us a Savior who is more to us than we are to ourselves. We become patient with ourselves because we realize the patience of God. We get rid of illusions about ourselves and the world because our intimacy is with the real God, and we know that we truly are just what we are before Him. We thus have a great peace, because in prayer, as the crowning act of faith, we lay hold of the grace of God the Savior. Prayer alone prevents our receiving God's grace in vain. Which means that it establishes the soul of a man or a people, creates the moral personality day by day, spreads outward the new heart through society, and goes to make a new ethos in mankind. We come out with a courage and a humanity we had not when we went in, even though our old earth remove, and our familiar hills are cast into the depth of the sea. The true Church is thus co-extensive with the community of true prayer.

It is another paradox that combines the vast power of prayer both on the lone soul and on the moral life, personal and social, with the soul's shyness and aloofness in prayer. Kant (whose genius in this respect reflected his race) has had an influence upon scientific thought and its efficiency far greater than upon religion, though he is well named the philosopher of Protestantism. He represent (again like his race) intellectual power and a certain stiff moral insight, but not spiritual atmosphere, delicacy, or flexibility, which is rather the Catholic tradition. Intellectualism always tends to more force than finish, and always starves or perverts ethic. And nowhere in Kant's work does this limitation find such expression as in his treatment of prayer, unless it be in his lack of any misgivings about treating it at all with his equipment or the equipment of his age. Even his successors know better now – just as we in England have learned to find in Milton powers and harmonies hidden from the too great sagacity of Dr. Johnson or his time. Kant, then, speaks of prayer thus. If we found a man (he says) given to talking to himself we should begin to suspect him of some tendency to mental aberration. Yet the personality of such a man is a very real thing. It is a thing we can be more sure of than we can of the personality of God, who, if He is more than a conclusion for intellectual thought, is not more than a postulate for moral. No doubt in time of crisis it is an instinct to pray which even cultivated people do not, and need not, lose. But if any such person were surprised even in the attitude of private prayer, to say nothing of its exercise, he would be ashamed. He would think he had been discovered doing something unworthy of his intelligence, and would feel about it as educated people do when found out to be yielding to a superstition about the number thirteen.

A thinker of more sympathy and delicacy would have spoken less bluntly. Practical experience would have taught him discrimination. He would have realized the difference between shame and shyness, between confusion at an unworthy thing and confusion at a thing too fine and sacred for exposure. And had his age allowed him to have more knowledge and taste in history, and especially the history of religion, he would have gone, not to the cowardice of the ordinary cultivated man, but to the power and thoroughness of the great saints or captains of the race – to Paul, to Thomas a Kempis, to Cromwell with his troops, or Gustavus Adolphus with his. I do but humbly allude to Gethsemane. But Kant belonged to a time which had not realized, as even our science does now, the final power of the subtler forces, and the overwhelming effect in the long run of the impalpable and elusive influences of life. Much might be written about the effect of prayer on the great history of the world.

4. THE TIMELINESS OF PRAYER

Let him pray now that never prayed before,

And him that prayed before but pray the more.

The nearer we are driven to the God of Christ, the more we are forced on paradox when we begin to speak. I have been led to allude to this more than once. The *magnalia dei* are not those great simplicities of life on which some orders of genius lay a touch so tender and sure; but they are the great reconciliations in which life's tragic collisions come to lie "quiet, happy and supprest." Such are the peaceful paradoxes (the paradox at last of grace and nature in the Cross) which make the world of prayer such a strange and difficult land to the lucid and rational interpreters of life. It is as miraculous as it is real that the holy and the guilty should live together in such habitual communion as the life of prayer. And it is another paradox that combines the vast power of prayer for the active soul, whether single or social, with the same soul's shyness and aloofness in prayer.

There is a tendency to lose the true balance and adjustment here. When all goes well we are apt to overdo the aloofness that goes with spiritual engagement, and so to sacrifice some of its power and blessing for the soul. Prayer which becomes too private may become too remote, and is apt to become weak. (Just as when it is too intimate it becomes really unworthy, and may become absurd even to spiritual men; it does so in the trivialities associated sometimes with the answer to prayer.) It is neither seemly nor healthy to be nothing but shy about the greatest powers in life. If we felt them as we should, and if we had their true vitality in us, we could not be so reserved about them. Some churches suffer much from extempore prayer, but perhaps those suffer more that exclude it. It at least gives a public consecration to prayer private and personal, which prayer, from the nature of it, must be extempore and "occasional." The bane of extempore prayer is that it is confused with prayer unprepared; and the greatest preparation for prayer is to pray. The leader of prayer should be a man of prayer – so long as prayer does not become for him a luxury which really unfits him for liturgy, and private devotion does not indispose him for public worship. Delicacy and propriety in prayer are too dearly bought if they are there at the cost of its ruling power in life, private and public, and of its prevailing power with God.

It is one of the uses of our present dreadful adversity that we are driven to bring the great two-handed engine of prayer frankly to the fore. There is probably a greater volume of personal prayer to-day than for generations we have had in this somewhat silent people, and there is less embarrassment in owning it. One hears tales of the humor in the trenches, but not so much of the prayer which appears, from accounts, to be at least equally and visibly there. And it is not the prayer of fear, either at home or abroad, but of seriousness, of a new moral exaltation, or at least deepening, a new sense of realities which are clouded by the sunshine of normal life. How can we but pray when we send, or our hearts go out to those who send, the dearest to the noble peril, or lose them in a noble death; or when we melt to those who are cast into unspeakable anxiety by the indirect effects of such a war upon mind or estate? We are helpless then unless we can pray. Or how can we but pray as we regain, under the very hand and pressure of God, the sense of judgment which was slipping from our easy and amiable creed? Above the aircraft we hear the wings of the judgment angel; their wind is on our faces; how should we not pray? We now discuss with each other our prayers as we have seldom done before; and we do it for our practical guidance, and not merely our theological satisfaction. We ask our neighbors' judgment if we may pray for victory when we can be so little sure as we are in the increased complexity of modern issues that all the right is on one side; or when our enemy is a great nation to which the Christianity and the culture of the world owe an unspeakable debt, whether for reformation or illumination. And if Christian faith and prayer is a supernatural, and therefore an international rivalries and tutelary gods?

Truly the course of events has been the answer to this question easier than at first. We are driven by events to believe that a great moral blindness has befallen Germany; that its God, ceasing to be Christian, has become but Semitic; that it has lost the sense of the great imponderables; that the idolatry of the State has barrack-bound the conscience of the Church and stilled that witness of the kingdom of God which beards kings and even beheads them. We are forced to think that the cause of righteousness has passed from its hands with the passing from them of humanity, with the submersion of the idea of God's kingdom in nationality or the cult of race, with the worship of force, mammon, fright, and ruthlessness, with the growth of national cynicism in moral things, and with the culture of a withering, self-searing hate which is the nemesis of mortal sin, and which even God cannot use as He can use anger, but must surely judge. This people has sinned against its own soul, and abjured the kingdom of God. That settles our prayer for victory. We must pray for the side more valuable for the kingdom of God – much as we have to confess.

It would more than repay much calamity if we were moved and enlarged to a surer sense, a greater use, and a franker confession of the power of prayer for life, character, and history. There is plenty of discussion of the present situation, historic, ethical, or political, and much of it is competent, and even deep. There is much speculation about the situation after the War, at home and abroad. But its greatest result may be the discredit of elegant, paltering, and feeble types of religion, the end of the irreligious wits and fribbles, and the rise of a new moral seriousness and a new spiritual realism. Many will be moved, in what seems the failure of civilization, to a new reliance on the Church, and especially on the more historic, ethical, and positive Churches, which have survived the paganism of culture and which ride the waves of storm. Yet even these impressions can evaporate unless they are fixed by action. And the action that fixes them in their own kind is prayer – prayer which is really action. A religion of prosperity grows dainty, petty, sentimental, and but pseudo-heroic. We unlearn our fathers' creed that religion is, above all things, an act, that worship is the greatest act of which man is capable, and that true worship culminates in the supreme labor, and even sorrow, of real prayer. This is man at his utmost; and it has for it near neighbors all the great things that men or nations do. But when a nation must go to righteous war it embarks on one of the very greatest acts of its life, especially if its very existence as a servant of God's kingdom hang on it. A state of war is really the vast and prolonged act of a corporate soul, with a number of minor acts organized into it. It is capable of being offered to a God whose kingdom is a public campaign moving through history, and coming by the faith, toil, peril, sacrifice, grief, and glory of nations, as well as the hearts and souls. It is not possible to separate moral acts so great and solemn as the act of prayer (especially common and corporate prayer) and the act of war; nor to think them severed in the movement, judgment, and purpose of the Eternal. And we are forced into paradox again. The deeper we go down into the valley of decision the higher we must rise (if we are to possess and command our souls) into the mount of prayer, and we must hold up the hands of those whose chief concern is to prevail with God. If we win we shall have a new sense of power amid all our loss and weakness; but what we shall need most of all if the power to use that power, and to protest us from our victory and its perilous sequels, whether of pride or poverty. And if we do not win we shall need it more. There will be much to sober us either way, more perhaps than ever before in our history.

But that is not all, and it is not enough. As Christian people we need something to sanctify that very sobering and to do for the new moral thoughtfulness itself what that does for the peace-bred levity of the natural man. For such a purpose there is no agent like prayer – serious, thinking, private prayer, or prayer in groups, in small, grave, congenial, understanding groups – prayer with the historic sense, church-nurtured and Bible-fed. Public prayer by all means, but, apart from liturgical form, the more open the occasions and the larger the company the more hard it may be to secure for such prayer the right circumstances or the right lead. Public facility is apt to outstrip the real intimacy and depth with God. While on the other hand, the prayer that freely rises and aptly flows in our audience of God may be paralyzed in an audience of men. So that public prayer does not always reflect the practice of private petition as the powerful factor it is in Christian life and history. It does not always suggest a door opened in heaven, the insight or fellowship of eternal yet historic

powers in awful orbits. It does not always do justice to our best private prayer, to private prayer made a business and suffused with as much sacred mind as goes to the more secular side even of the Christian life. Should ministers enlist? it is asked. But to live in true and concrete prayer is to be a combatant in the War, as well as a statesman after it, if statesmen ought to see the whole range of forces at work. The saintly soldier still needs the soldier saint. Yet so much prayer has ceased to be a matter of thought, will, or conflict, and religion therefore has become so otiose, that it is not easy even for the Christian public to take such a saying as more than a phrase. This is but one expression of a general skepticism, both in the Church and out, about prayer, corporate or private, as power with God, and therefore as momentous in the affairs of life and history. But momentous and effectual it must be. Other things being equal, a voluntary and convinced army is worth more than a conscript one. So to know that we are morally right means worlds for our shaping of the things that face us and must be met; and we are never so morally right as in proficient prayer with the Holy One and the Just. It has, therefore, a vast effect on the course of things if we believe at all in their moral destiny. It is a power behind thrones, and it neutralizes, at the far end, the visible might of armies and their victories. It settles at last whether morality or machinery is to rule the world. If it lose battles, it wins in the long historic campaign. Whereas, if we have no such action with God, we lose delicacy of perception in the finer forces of affairs; we are out of touch and understanding with the final control in things, the power that is working to the top always; we become dense in regard to the subtle but supreme influences that take the generals and chancellors by surprise; and we are at the mercy of the sleepless action of the kingdom of evil on the world. It is a fatal thing to under estimate the enemy; and it is in Christian prayer, seriously and amply pursued, that the soul really learns to gauge evil's awful and superhuman power in affairs. I am speaking not only of the single soul, perhaps at the moment not chiefly, but of the soul and prayer of a society like the true Church or a sobered people. The real power of prayer in history is not a fusillade of praying units of whom Christ is the chief, but it is the corporate action of a Savior-Intercessor and His community, a volume and energy of prayer organized in a Holy Spirit and in the Church the Spirit creates. The saints shall thus judge the world and control life. Neither for the individual nor for the Church is true prayer an enclave in life's larger and more actual course. It is not a sacred enclosure, a lodge in some vast wilderness. That is the weak side of pietism. But, however intimate, it is in the most organic and vital context of affairs, private and public, if all things work together, deeply and afar, for the deep and final kingdom of God. Its constant defeat of our egoism means the victory of our social unity and its weal. For the egoist neither prays nor loves. On the other hand, such prayer recalls us from a distraught altruism, teeming with oddities, and frayed down to atomism by the variety of calls upon it; because the prayer is the supreme energy of a loving will and believing soul engaged with the Love that binds the earth, the sun, and all the stars. So far it is from being the case that love to God has no sphere outside love to man that our love to man perishes unless it is fed by the love that spends itself on God in prayer, and is lifted thereby to a place and a sway not historic only, but cosmic.

Our communion with God in Christ rose, and it abides, in a crisis which shook not the earth only, but also heaven, in a tragedy and victory more vast, awful, and pregnant than the greatest war in history could be. Therefore the prayer which gives us an ever-deeper interest and surer insight into that eternal moral crisis of the Cross gives us also (though it might take generations) a footing that commands all the losses or victories of earth, and a power that rules both spirit and conscience in the clash and crash of worlds. As there is devoted thought which ploughs its way into the command of Nature, there is thought, still more devoted, that prays itself into that moral interior of the Cross, where the kingdom of God is founded once for all on the last principle and power of the universe, and set up, not indeed amid the wreck of civilization, but by its new birth and a baptism so as by fire. Prayer of the right kind, with heart and soul and strength and mind,

unites any society in which it prevails with those last powers of moral and social regeneration that settle history and that reside in the creative grace of the Cross, which is God's true omnipotence in the world. "O God, who showiest Thine almighty power most chiefly in having mercy and forgiving." Such speech as this may to some appear tall and rhetorical; but it would have so seemed to no father of the church, ancient or modern, taking apostolic measure of the place and moment of Christ in society, history, or the universe.

If war is in any sense God's judgment on sin, and if sin was destroyed by the judgment in Christ and on Him, let us pray with a new depth and significance to-day, "O Lamb of God, that took away the sin of the world, grant us Thy peace. Send us the peace that honors in act and deed that righteous and final judgment in Thy Cross of all historic things, and that makes therein for Thy Kingdom on earth as in heaven. Give peace in our time, O Lord, but, peace or war, Take the crown of this poor world."

5. The Ceaselessness of Prayer

Prayer as Christian freedom, and prayer as Christian life – these are two points I would now expand.

I. First, as to the moral freedom involved and achieved in prayer.

Prayer has been described as religion in action. But that as it stands is not a sufficient definition of the prayer which lives on the Cross. The same thing might be said about the choicest forms of Christian service to humanity. It is true enough, and it may carry us far; but only if we become somewhat clear about the nature of the religion at work. Prayer is certainly not the action of a religion mainly subjective. It is the effective work of a religion which hangs upon the living God, of a soul surer of God than of itself, and living not its own life, but the life of the Son of God. To say prayer is faith in action would be better; for the word "faith" carries a more objective reference than the word "religion." Faith is faith in another. In prayer we do not so much work as interwork. We are fellow workers with God in a reciprocity. And as God is the freest Being in existence, such co-operant prayer is the freest things that man can do. It we were free in sinning, how much more free in the praying which undoes sin! If we were free to break God's will, how much more free to turn it or to accept it! Petitionary prayer is man's cooperation in kind with God amidst a world He freely made for freedom. The world was made by a freedom which not only left room for the kindred freedom of prayer, but which so ordered all things in its own interest that in their deepest depths they conspire to produce prayer. To pray in faith is to answer God's freedom in its own great note. It means we are taken up into the fundamental movement of the world. It is to realize that for which the whole world, the world as a whole, was made. It is an earnest of the world's consummation. We are doing what the whole world was created to do. We overleap in the spirit all between now and then, as in the return to Jesus we overleap the two thousand years that intervene. The object the Father's loving purpose had in appointing the whole providential order was intercourse with man's soul. That order of the world is, therefore, no rigid fixture, nor is it even a fated evolution. It is elastic, adjustable, flexible, with margins for freedom, for free modification in God and man; always keeping in view that final goal of communion, and growing into it be a spiritual interplay in which the whole of Nature is involved. The goal of the whole cosmic order is the "manifestation of the sons of God," the realization of complete sonship, its powers and its confidences.

Thus we rise to say that our prayer is the momentary function of the Eternal Son's communion and intercession with the Eternal Father. We are integrated in advance into the final Christ, for whom, and to whom, all creation moves. Our prayer is more than the acceptance by us of God's will; it is its assertion in us. The will of God is that men should pray everywhere. He wills to be entreated. Prayer is that will of God's making itself good. When we entreat we give effect to His dearest will. And in His will is our eternal liberty. In this will of His our finds itself, and is at home. It ranges the liberties of the Father's house. But here prayer must draw from the Cross, which is the frontal act of our emancipation as well as

the central revelation of God's own freedom in grace. The action of the Atonement and of its release of us is in the nature of prayer. It is the free return of the Holy upon the Holy in the Great Reconciliation.

II. Then, secondly, as to prayer being the expression of the perennial new life of faith in the Cross. The Christian life is prayer without ceasing.

When we are told to pray without ceasing, it seems to many tastes to-day to be somewhat extravagant language. And no doubt that is true. Why should we be concerned to deny it? Measured language and the elegant mean is not the note of the New Testament at least. But can we love or trust God too much? Christian faith is one that overcomes and commands the world in a passion rather than balances it. It triumphs in a conclusive bliss, it does not play off one part against another. The grace of Christ is not but graciousness of nature, and He does not rule His Church by social act. The peace of God is not the calm of culture, it is not the charm of breeding. Every great forward movement in Christianity is associated with much that seems academically extravagant. Erasmus is always shocked with Luther. It is only an outlet of that essential extravagance which makes the paradox of the Cross, and keeps it as the irritant, no less than the life of the world – perhaps because it is the life of the world. There is nothing so abnormal, so unworldly, so supernatural, in human life as prayer, nothing that is more of an instinct, it is true, but also nothing that is less rational among all the things that keep above the level of the silly. The whole Christian life in so far as it is lived from the Cross and by the Cross is rationally an extravagance. For the Cross is the paradox of all things; and the action of the Spirit is the greatest miracle in the world; and yet it is the principle of the world. Paradox is but the expression of that dualism which is the moral foundation of a Christian world. I live who die daily. I live another's life.

To pray without ceasing is not, of course, to engage in prayer without break. That is an impossible literalism. True, "They rest not day and night, saying, Holy, holy, holy, Lord God Almighty, who wert, and art, and art to come." But it is mere poverty of soul to think of this as the iteration of a doxology. It is deep calling unto deep, eternity greeting eternity. The only answer to God's eternity is an eternal attitude of prayer.

Nor does the phrase mean that the Church shall use careful means that the stream and sound of prayer shall never cease to flow at some spots of the earth, as the altar lamp goes not out. It does not mean the continuous murmur of the mass following the sun round the world, incessant relays of adoring priests, and functions going on day and night.

But it means the constant bent and drift of the soul – as the Word which was from the beginning (John i. 1). All the current of its being set towards Him. It means being "in Christ," being in such a moving, returning Christ – reposing in this godward, and not merely godlike life. The note of prayer becomes the habit of the heart, the tone and tension of its new nature; in such a way that when we are released from the grasp of our occupations the soul rebounds to its true bent, quest, and even pressure upon God. It is the soul's habitual appetite and habitual food. A growing child of God is always hungry. Prayer is not identical with the occasional act of praying. Like the act of faith, it is a whole life thought of as action. It is the life of faith in its purity, in its vital action. Eating and speaking are necessary to life, but they are not living. And how hidden prayer may be – beneath even gaiety! If you look down on Portland Race you see but a shining sea; only the pilot knows the tremendous current that pervades the smiling calm.

So far this "pray without ceasing" from being absurd because extravagant that every man's life is in some sense a continual state of prayer. For what is his life's prayer but its ruling passion? All energies, ambitions and passions are but expressions of a standing nisus in life, of a hunger, a draft, a practical demand upon the future, upon the unattained and the unseen. Every life is a draft upon the unseen. If you are not praying towards God you are towards something else. You pray as your face is set – towards Jerusalem or Babylon. The very egotism of craving life is prayer. The great difference is the object of it. To whom, for what, do we pray? The man whose passion is habitually set upon pleasure, knowledge,

wealth, honor, or power is in a state of prayer to these things or for them. He prays without ceasing. These are his real gods, on whom he waits day and night. He may from time to time go on his knees in church, and use words of Christian address and petition. He may even feel a momentary unction in so doing. But it is a flicker; the other devotion is his steady flame. His real God is the ruling passion and steady pursuit of his life taken as a whole. He certainly does not pray in the name of Christ. And what he worships in spirit and in truth is another God than he addresses at religious times. He prays to an unknown God for a selfish boon. Still, in a sense, he prays. The set and drift of his nature prays. It is the prayer of instinct, not of faith. It is prayer that needs total conversion. But he cannot stop praying either to God or to God's rival – to self, society, world, flesh, or even devil. Every life that is not totally inert is praying either to God or God's adversary.

What do we really mean, whom do we mean, when we say, "My God"? In what sense mine? May our God not be but an idol we exploit, and in due course our doom?

There is a fearful and wonderful passage in Kierkegaard's *Entweder-Oder* which, if we transfer it to this connection, stirs thoughts deeper than its own tragedy. The seduced, heart-broken, writes to the seducer.

"John! I do not say my John. That I now see you never were. I am heavily punished for ever letting such an idea be my joy. Yet – yet, mine you are – my seducer, my deceiver, my enemy, my murderer, the spring of my calamity, the grave of my joy, the abyss of my misery. I call you mine, and I am yours – your curse for ever. Oh, do not think I will slay you and put a dagger into you. But flee where you will, I am yours, to the earth's end yours. Love a hundred others but I am yours. I am yours in your last hour, I am yours, yours, yours – your curse."

Beware lest the whole trend of the soul fix on a deity that turns a doom. There is the prayer which makes God our judgment as well as one which makes Him our joy.

Prayer is the nature of our hell as well as our heaven.

Our hell is ceaseless, passionate, fruitless, hopeless, gnawing prayer. It is the heart churning, churning grinding itself out in misery. It is life's passion and struggle surging back on itself like a barren, salt, corroding sea. It is the heart's blood rising like a fountain only to fall back on us in red rain. It is prayer which we cannot stop, addressed to nothing, and obtaining nothing. It calls into space and night. Or it is addressed to self, and it aggravates the wearing action of self on self. Our double being revolves on itself, like two millstones with nothing to grind.

And prayer is our heaven. It goes home to God, and attains there, and rests there. We are "in Christ," whose whole existence is prayer. He is there to extinguish our hell and make our heaven – far more to quench our wrath and our seething than God's.

To cultivate the ceaseless spirit of prayer, use more frequent acts of prayer. To learn to pray with freedom, force yourself to pray. The great liberty begins in necessity.

Do not say, "I cannot pray, I am not in the spirit." Pray till you are in the spirit. Think of analogies from lower levels. Sometimes when you need rest most you are too restless to lie down and take it. Then compel yourself to lie down, and to lie still. Often in ten minutes the compulsion fades into consent, and you sleep, and rise a new man.

Again, it is often hard enough to take up the task which in half an hour you enjoy. It is often against the grain to turn out of an evening to meet the friends you promised. But once you are in their midst you are in your element.

Sometimes, again, you say, "I will not go to church. I do not feel that way." That is where the habit of an ordered religious life comes in aid. Religion is the last region for chance desires. Do it as a duty, and it may open out as a blessing. Omit it, and you may miss the one thing that would have made an eternal difference. You stroll instead, and return with nothing but appetite – when you might have come back with an inspiration. Compel yourself to meet your God as you would meet your promises, your obligations, your fellow men.

So if you are averse to pray, pray the more. Do not call it lip-service. That is not the lip-service God disowns. It is His Spirit acting in your self-coercive will, only not yet in your heart. What is unwelcome to God is lip-service which is untroubled at not being more.

As appetite comes with eating, so prayer with praying. Our hearts learn the language of the lips.

Compel yourself often to shape on your lips the detailed needs of your soul. It is not needful to inform God, but to deepen you, to inform yourself before God, to enrich that intimacy with ourself which is so necessary to answer the intimacy of God. To common sense the fact that God knows all we need, and wills us all good, the fact of His infinite Fatherhood, is a reason for not praying. Why tell Him what He knows? Why ask what He is more than willing to give? But to Christian faith and to spiritual reason it is just the other way. Asking is polar cooperation. Jesus turned the fact to a use exactly the contrary of its deistic sense. He made the all-knowing Fatherhood the ground of true prayer. We do not ask as beggars but as children. Petition is not mere receptivity, nor is it mere pressure; it is filial reciprocity. Love loves to be told what it knows already. Every lover knows that. It wants to be asked for what it longs to give. And that is the principle of prayer to the all-knowing Love. As God knows all, you may reckon that your brief and humble prayer will be understood (Matt. vi. 8). It will be taken up into the intercession of the Spirit stripped of its dross, its inadequacy made good, and presented as prayer should be. That is praying in the Holy Ghost. Where should you carry your burden but to the Father, where Christ took the burden of all the world? We tell God, the heart searcher, our heavy thoughts to escape from brooding over them. "When my spirit was overwhelmed within me, Thou knewest my path" (Ps. cxlii. 3). So Paul says the Spirit intercedes for us and gives our broken prayer divine effect (Rom. viii. 26). To be sure of God's sympathy is to be inspired to prayer, where His mere knowledge would crush it. There is no father who would be satisfied that his son should take everything and ask for nothing. It would be thankless. To cease asking is to cease to be grateful. And what kills petition kills praise.

Go into your chamber, shut the door, and cultivate the habit of praying audibly. Write prayers and burn them. Formulate your soul. Pay no attention to literary form, only to spiritual reality. Read a passage of Scripture and then sit down and turn it into prayer, written or spoken. Learn to be particular, specific, and detailed in your prayer so long as you are not trivial. General prayers, literary prayers, and stately phrases are, for private prayer, traps and sops to the soul. To formulate your soul is one valuable means to escape formalizing it. This is the best, the wholesome, kind of self-examination. Speaking with God discovers us safely to ourselves We "find" ourselves, come to ourselves, in the Spirit. Face your special weaknesses and sins before God. Force yourself to say to God exactly where you are wrong. When anything goes wrong, do not ask to have it set right, without asking in prayer what is was in you that made it go wrong. It is somewhat fruitless to ask for a general grace to help specific flaws, sins, trials, and griefs. Let prayer be concrete, actual, a direct product of life's real experiences. Pray as your actual self, not as some fancied saint. Let it be closely relevant to your real situation. Pray without ceasing in this sense. Pray without a break between your prayer and your life. Pray so that there is a real continuity between your prayer and your whole actual life. But I will bear round upon this point again immediately.

Meantime, let me say this. Do not allow your practice in prayer to be arrested by scientific or philosophic considerations as to how answer is possible. That is a valuable subject for discussion, but it is not entitled to control our practice. Faith is at least as essential to the soul as science, and it has a foundation more independent. And prayer is not only a necessity of faith, it is faith itself in action.

Criticism of prayer dissolves in the experience of it. When the soul is at close quarters with God it becomes enlarged enough to hold together in harmony things that oppose, and to have room for harmonious contraries. For instance: God, of course, is always working for His Will and Kingdom. But man is bound to pray for its coming, while it is coming all the time. Christ laid stress on prayer as a necessary means of bringing the Kingdom to pass. And it cannot come without our praying. Why? Because its coming is the prayerful frame of soul. So again with God's freedom. It is absolute. But it reckons on ours. Our prayer does not force His hand; it answers His freedom

in kind. We are never so active and free as in prayer to an absolutely free God. We share His freedom when we are "in Christ."

If I must choose between Christ, who bids me pray for everything, and the servant, who tells me certain answers are physically and rationally impossible, must I not choose Christ? Because, while the savant knows much about nature and its action (and much more than Christ did), Christ knew everything about the God of nature and His reality. He knew more of what is possible to God than anybody has ever known about what is possible in nature. On such a subject as prayer, anyone is a greater authority who wholly knows the will of God than he who only knows God's methods, and knows them but in part. Prayer is not an act of knowledge but of faith. It is not a matter of calculation but of confidence – "that our faith should not stand in the wisdom of men, but in the power of God." Which means that in this region we are not to be regulated by science, but by God's self-revelation. Do not be so timid about praying wrongly if you pray humbly. If God is really the Father that Christ revealed, then the principle is – take everything to Him that exercises you. Apart from frivolity, such as praying to find the stud you lost, or the knife, or the umbrella, there is really no limitation in the New Testament on the contents of petition. Any regulation is as to the spirit of the prayer, the faith it springs from. In all distress which mars your peace, petition must be the form your faith takes – petition for rescue. Keep close to the New Testament Christ, and then ask for anything you desire in that contact. Ask for everything you can ask in Christ's name, i.e. everything desirable by a man who is in Christ's kingdom of God, by a man who lives for it at heart, everything in tune with the purpose and work of the kingdom in Christ. If you are in that kingdom, then pray freely for whatever you need or wish to keep you active and effective for it, from daily bread upwards and outwards. In all things make your requests known. At least you have laid them on God's heart; and faith means confidences between you and not only favors. And there is not confidence if you keep back what is hot or heavy on your heart. If prayer is not a play of the religious fantasy, or a routine task, it must be the application of faith to a concrete actual and urgent situation. Only remember that prayer does not work by magic, and that stormy desire is not fervent, effectual prayer. You may be but exploiting a mighty power; whereas you must be in real contact with the real God. It is the man that most really has God that most really seeks God.

I said a little while ago that to pray without ceasing also meant to pray without a breach with your actual life and the whole situation in which you are. This is the point at which to dwell on that. If you may not come to God with the occasions of your private life and affairs, then there is some unreality in the relation between you and Him. If some private crisis absorbs you, some business or family anxiety of little moment to others but of much to you, and if you may not bring that to God in prayer, then one of two things. Either it is not you, in your actual reality, that came to God, but it is you in a pose – you in some role which you are trying with poor success to play before Him. You are trying to pray as another person than you are, – a better person, perhaps, as some great apostle, who should have on his worshiping mind nothing but the grand affairs of the Church and Kingdom, and not be worried by common cares. You are praying in court-dress. You are trying to pray as you imagine one should pray to God, i.e. as another person than you are, and in other circumstances. You are creating a self and a situation to place before God. Either that or you are not praying to a God who loves, helps, and delivers you in every pinch of life, but only to one who uses you as a pawn for the victory of His great kingdom. You are not praying to Christ's God. You are praying to a God who cares only for the great actions in His kingdom, for the heroic people who cherish nothing but the grand style, or for the calm people who do not deeply feel life's trials. The reality of prayer is bound up with the reality and intimacy of life.

And its great object is to get home as we are to God as He is, and to win response even when we get no compliance. The prayer of faith does not mean a prayer absolutely sure that it will receive what it asks. That is not faith. Faith is that attitude of soul and self to God which is the root and reservoir of prayer apart from

all answer. It is what turns need into request. It is what moves your need to need God. It is what makes you sure your prayer is heard and stored, whether granted or not. "He putteth all my tears in His bottle." God has old prayers of yours long maturing by Him. What wine you will drink with Him in His kingdom! Faith is sure that God refuses with a smile; that He says No in the spirit of Yes, and He gives or refuses always in Christ, our Great Amen. And better prayers are stirred by the presence of the Deliverer than even by the need of deliverance.

It is not sufficiently remembered that before prayer can expect an answer it must be itself an answer. That is what is meant by prayer in the name of Christ. It is prayer which answers God's gift in Christ, with Whom are already given us all things. And that is why we must pray without ceasing, because in Christ God speaks without ceasing. Natural or instinctive prayer is one thing; supernatural prayer is another; it is the prayer not of instinct but of faith. It is our word answering God's. It is more the prayer of fullness even than of need, of strength than of weakness – though it be "a strength girt round with weakness." Prayer which arises from mere need is flung out to a power which is only remembered, or surmised, or unknown. It is flung into darkness and uncertainty. But in Christian prayer we ask for what we need because we are full of faith in God's power and word, because need becomes petition at the touch of His word. (I always feel that in the order of our public worship prayer should immediately follow the lesson, without the intrusion on an anthem. And for the reason I name – that Christian prayer is our word answering God's.) We pray, therefore, in Christ's name, or for His sake, because we pray as answering the gift in Christ. Our prayer is the note the tremulous soul utters when its chords are smitten by Him. We then answer above all things God's prayer to us in His cross that we would be reconciled. God so beseeches us in Christ. So that, if we put it strongly, we may say that our prayer to God in Christ is our answer to God's prayer to us there. "The best thing in prayer is faith," says Luther.

And the spirit of prayer in Christ's name is the true child-spirit. A certain type of religion is fond of dwelling on faith as the spirit of divine childhood; and its affinities are all with the tender and touching element in childhood. But one does not always get from the prophets of such piety the impression of a life breathed in prayer. And the notion is not the New Testament sense of being children of God. That is a manlier, a maturer thing. It is being sons of God by faith, and by faith's energy of prayer. It is not the sense of being as helpless as a child that clings, not the sense of weakness, ignorance, gentleness, and all that side of things. But it is the spirit of a prayer which is a great act of faith, and therefore a power. Faith is not simply surrender, but adoring surrender, not a mere sense of dependence, but an act of intelligent committal, and the confession of a holiness which is able to save, keep, and bless for ever.

How is it that the experience of life is so often barren of spiritual culture for religious people? They become stoic and stalwart, but not humble; they have been sight, but no insight. Yet it is not the stalwarts but the saints that judge the world, i.e. that take the true divine measure of the world and get to its subtle, silent, and final powers. Whole sections of our Protestantism have lost the virtue of humility or the understanding of it. It means for them no more than modesty or diffidence. It is the humility of weakness, not of power. To many useful, and even strong, people no experience seems to bring this subtle, spiritual intelligence, this finer discipline of the moral man. No rebukes, no rebuffs, no humiliations, no sorrows, seem to bring it to them. They have no spiritual history. Their spiritual biography not even an angel could write. There is no romance in their soul's story. At sixty they are, spiritually, much where they were at twenty-six. To calamity, to discipline of any kind, they are simply resilient. Their religion is simply elasticity. It is but lusty life. They rise up after the smart is over, or the darkness fades away, as self-confident as if they were but seasoned politicians beaten at one election, but sure of doing better at the next. They are to the end just irrepressible, or persevering, or dogged. And they are as juvenile in moral insight, as boyish in spiritual perception, as ever.

Is it not because they have never really had personal religion? That is, they have never really prayed with all their heart; only, at most, with all their fervor, certainly not with strength and mind. They have never "spread out" their whole soul and situation to a god who knows. They have never opened the petals of their soul in the warm sympathy of His knowledge. They have not become particular enough in their prayer, faithful with themselves, or relevant to their complete situation. They do not face themselves, only what happens to them. They pray with their heart and not with their conscience. They pity themselves, perhaps they spare themselves, they shrink from hurting themselves more than misfortune hurts them. They say, "If you knew all you could not help pitying me." They do not say, "God knows all, and how can He spare me?" For themselves, or for their fellows, it is the prayer of pity, not of repentance. We need the prayer of self-judgment more than the prayer of fine insight.

We are not humble in God's sight, partly because in our prayer there is a point at which we cease to pray, where we do not turn everything out into God's light. It is because there is a chamber or two in our souls where we do not enter in and take God with us. We hurry Him by the door as we take Him along the corridors of our life to see our tidy places or our public rooms. We ask from our prayers too exclusively comfort, strength, enjoyment, or tenderness and graciousness, and not often enough humiliation and its fine strength. We want beautiful prayers, touching prayers, simple prayers, thoughtful prayers; prayers with a quaver or a tear in them, or prayers with delicacy and dignity in them. But searching prayer, humbling prayer, which is the prayer of the conscience, and not merely of the heart or taste; prayer which is bent on reality, and to win the new joy goes through new misery if need by – are such prayers as welcome and common as they should be? Too much of our prayer is apt to leave us with the self-complacency of the sympathetically incorrigible, of the benevolent and irremediable, of the breezy octogenarian, all of whose yesterdays look backward with a cheery and exasperating smile.

It is an art – this great and creative prayer – this intimate conversation with God. "*Magna ars est conversari cum Deo,*" says Thomas a Kempis. It has to be learned. In social life we learn that conversation is not mere talk. There is an art in it, if we are not to have a table of gabblers. How much more is it so in the conversation of heaven! We must learn that art by practice, and by keeping the best society in that kind. Associate much with the great masters in this kind; especially with the Bible; and chiefly with Christ. Cultivate His Holy Spirit. He is the grand master of God's art and mystery in communing with man. And there is no other teacher, at least, of man's art of communion with God.

6. THE VICARIOUSNESS OF PRAYER

The work of the ministry labors under one heavy disadvantage when we regard it as a profession and compare it with other professions. In these, experience brings facility, a sense of mastery in the subject, self-satisfaction, self-confidence; but in our subject the more we pursue it, the more we enter into it, so much the more are we cast down with the overwhelming sense, not only of our insufficiency, but of our unworthiness. Of course, in the technique of our work we acquire a certain ease. We learn to speak more or less freely and aptly. We learn the knack of handling a text, of conducting church work, or dealing with men, and the life. If it were only texts or men we had to handle! But we have to handle the gospel. We have to lift up Christ – a Christ who is the death of natural self-confidence – a humiliating, even a crushing Christ; and we are not always alive to our uplifting and resurrection in Him. We have to handle a gospel that is a new rebuke to us every step we gain in intimacy with it. There is no real intimacy with the gospel which does not mean a new sense of God's holiness, and it may be long before we realize that the same holiness that condemns is that which saves. There is no new insight into the Cross which does not bring, whatever else come with it, a deeper sense of the solemn holiness of the love that meets us there. And there is no new sense of the holy God that does not arrest His name upon our unclean lips. If our very repentance is to be repented of, and we should be forgiven much in our very prayers, how shall we be proud, or even pleased, with what we may think a success in our preaching? So that we are not surprised that some

preachers, after what the public calls a most brilliant and impressive discourse, retire (as the emperor retired to close his life in the cloister) to humble themselves before God, to ask forgiveness for the poor message, and to call themselves most unprofitable servants – yea, even when they knew themselves that they had "done well." The more we grasp our gospel the more it abashes us.

Moreover, as we learn more of the seriousness of the gospel for the human soul, we feel the more that every time we present it we are adding to the judgment of some as well as to the salvation of others. We are not like speakers who present a matter that men can freely take or leave, where they can agree or differ with us without moral result. No true preacher can be content that his flock should believe in him. That were egoism. They must believe with him. The deeper and surer our gospel is the more is our work a judgment on those to whom it is not a grace. This was what bore upon the Savior's own soul, and darkened His very agony into eclipse. That He, who knew Himself to be the salvation of His own beloved people, should, by His very love, become their doom! And here we watch and suffer with Him, however sleepily. There is put into our charge our dear people's life or death. For to those to whom we are not life we are death, in proportion as we truly preach, not ourselves, but the real salvation of Christ.

How solemn our place is! It is a sacramental place. We have not simply to state our case, we have to convey our Christ, and to convey Him effectually as the soul's final fate. We are sacramental elements, broken often, in the Lord's hands, as He dispenses His grace through us. We do not, of course, believe that orders are an ecclesiastical sacrament, as Rome does. But we are forced to realize the idea underlying that dogma – the sacramental nature of our person, work, and vocation for the gospel. We are not saviors. There is only one Savior. But we are His sacraments. We do not believe in an ecclesiastical priesthood; but we are made to feel how we stand between God and the people as none of our flock do. We bring Christ to them, and them to Christ, in sacrificial action in a way far more moral, inward, and taxing than official priesthood can be. As ministers we lead the sacerdotal function of the whole Church in the world – its holy confession and sacrifice for the world in Christ.

We ought, indeed, to feel the dignity of the ministry; we must present some protest against the mere fraternal conception which so easily sinks into an unspiritual familiarity. But still more than the dignity of the ministry do its elect feel its solemnity. How can it be otherwise? We have to dwell much with the everlasting burnings of God's love. We have to tend that consuming fire. We have to feed our life where all the tragedy of life is gathered to an infinite and victorious crisis in Christ. We are not the fire, but we live where it burns. The matter we handle in our theological thought we can only handle with some due protection for our face. It is one of the dangerous industries. It is continually acting on us, continually searching our inner selves that no part of us may be unforgiven, unfed, or unsanctified. We cannot hold it and examine it at arm's length. It enters into us. It evokes the perpetual comment of our souls, and puts us continually on self-judgment. Our critic, our judge, is at the door. Self-condemnation arrests denunciation. And the true apostle can never condemn but in the spirit of self-condemnation.

But, after all, our doom is our blessing. Our Judge is on our side. For if humiliation be wrung from us, still more is faith, hope, and prayer. Everything that rebukes our self-satisfaction does still more to draw out our faith. When we are too tired or doubtful to ask we can praise and adore. When we are weary of confessing our sin we can forget ourselves in a godly sort and confess our Savior. We can say the creed when we cannot raise the song. He also hath given us the reconciliation. The more judgment we see in the holy cross the more we see it is judgment unto salvation. The more we are humbled the more we "roll our souls upon Christ." And we recover our self-possession only by giving our soul again and again to Christ to keep. We win a confidence in self-despair. Prayer is given us as wings wherewith to mount, but also to shield our face when they have carried us before the great white throne. It is in prayer that the holiness comes home as love, and the love is established as holiness. At every step our thought is transformed to prayer, and our prayer opens new ranges of thought. His great revelation is His holiness, always outgoing in atoning love. The Christian revelation is not "God is love" so much as "love is God." That is, it is not God's love, but the infinite power of God's love, its finality, omnipotence, and absoluteness. It is not passionate and helpless love, but it has power to subdue everything that rises against it. And that is the holiness of love – the eternal thing in it. We receive the last reconciliation. Then the very wrath of God becomes a glory. The red in the sky is the new dawn. Our self-accusation becomes a new mode of praise. Our loaded hearts spring light again. Our heavy conscience turns to grave moral power. A new love is born for our kind. A new and tender patience steals upon us. We see new ways of helping, serving, and saving. We issue into a new world. We are one with the Christ not only on His cross, but in His resurrection. Think of the resurrection power and calm, of that solemn final peace, that infinite satisfaction in the eternal thing eternally achieved, which filled His soul when He had emerged from death, when man's worst had been done, and God's best had been won, for ever and for all. We have our times of entrance into that Christ. As we were one with Him in the likeness of His death, so we are in the likeness of His resurrection. And the same Eternal Spirit which puts the preacher's soul much upon the cross also raises it continually from the dead. We overcome our mistakes, negligences, sins; nay, we rise above the sin of the whole world, which will not let our souls be as good as they are. We overcome the world, and take courage, and are of new cheer. We are in the Spirit. And then we can preach, pray, teach, heal. And even the unclean lips then put a new thrill into our sympathy and a new tremor into our praise.

If it be not so, how shall our dangerous work not demoralize us, and we perish from our too much contact with holy things.

The minister's holiest prayer is hardly lawful to utter. Few of his public would comprehend it. Some would dismiss it with their most opprobrious word. They would call it theological. When he calls to God in his incomprehensible extremity they would translate it into an appeal to Elijah (Matt. xxvii. 47). For to them theology is largely mythology.

We are called at the present day to a recon-struction of the old theology, a restatement of the old gospel. We have to reappropriate and remint the truth of our experienced Christianity. But what a hardship it is that this call should search us at a time when the experimental power of our Christianity has abated, and the evangelical experience is so low and so confused as it often is! It must be the minister's work to recover and deepen this experience for the churches, in the interest of faith, and of the truth in which faith renders account of itself. Theological inadequacy, and especially antagonism to theology, means at root religious defect. For the reformation of belief we must have a restoration of faith. And a chief engine for such recovery of faith is for us what it was for Luther and his like – prayer. And it is not mindless prayer, but that prayer which is the wrestling of the conscience and not merely the cry of the heart, the prayer for reconciliation and redemption and not merely for guidance and comfort, the prayer of faith and not merely of love.

I saw in a friend's house a photograph from (I think) Dürer – just two tense hands, palms together, and lifted in prayer. It was most eloquent, most subduing. I wish I could stamp the picture on the page here and fit it to Milton's line:

The great two-handed engine at our door.

Public prayer is, on the whole, the most difficult part of the work of the minister. To help the difficulty I have always claimed that pulpit notes of prayer may be used. "The Lord's Prayer" itself is of this nature. It is not a prayer, but a scheme of prayer, heads of prayer, or buoys in the channel. But even with the use of all helps there are perils enough. There are prayers that, in the effort to become real, are much too familiar in their fashion of speech. A young man began his prayer, in my own hear-ing, with the words, "O God, we have come to have a chat with Thee." It was gruesome. Think of it as a sample of modern piety for the young! No prayers, certainly no public prayers, should be "chats with God." Again, other prayers are sentimental prayers. George Dawson's volume has this fault. The prayers of the Church should not be exposures of the affectional man. The

public prayer of the Church, as the company of grace, is the saved soul returning to God that gave it; it is the sinner coming to the Savior, or the ransomed of the Lord returning to Zion; it is the sanctified with the sancti-fier; it is not primarily the child talking to the Father – though that note may prevail in more private prayers. We are more than stray sheep reclaimed. We are those whose defiant iniquity has lain upon Christ for us all.

But the root of the difficulty of public prayer lies further back than in the matter of style. It lies in the difficulty of private prayer, in its spiritual poverty, its inertia, its anemia. What culture can deal with the rooted diffi-culty that resides there, out of sight, in the inner man of the heart, for lack of the cour-age of faith, for sheer spiritual fecklessness? Yet the preparation for prayer is to pray. The prayer is the practice of prayer. It is only prayer that teaches to pray. The minister ought never to speak before men in God's name without himself first speaking to God in man's name, and making intercession as for himself so for his people.

Intercession! We are properly vigilant that the minister do not sever himself from his people in any sacerdotal way. But for all that, is the minister's personal and private prayer on exactly the same footing as a layman's? It is a question that leads to the distinction between intercessory and vicarious prayer. The person-al religion of the minister is vicarious even when it is not intercessory. Great indeed is the spiritual value of private intercession. The intercessory private prayer of the minister is the best corrective of the critical spirit or the grumbling spirit which so easily besets and withers us to-day. That reconciliation, that pacification of heart, which comes by prayer opens in us a fountain of private interces-sion, especially for our antagonists. Only, of course, it must be private. But the minister is also praying to his people's good even when he is not interceding on their behalf, or lead-ing them in prayer. What he is for his Church he is with his whole personality. And so his private and personal prayers are vicarious for his people even when he does not know it. No Christian man lives for himself, nor believes for himself. And if the private Christian in his private prayers does not pray, any more than he lives, unto himself alone, much more is this true for the minister. His private prayers make a great difference to his people. They may not know what makes his spell and blessing; even he may not. But it is his most private prayers; which, thus, are vicarious even where not intercessory.

What he is for his Church, I have said, he is with his whole personality. And nothing gives us personality like true prayer. Nothing makes a man so original. We cannot be true Christians without being original. Living faith destroys the commonplaceness, the monotony of life. Are not all men original in death? *"Je mourrai seul."* Much more are they original and their true selves in Christ's death, and in their part and lot in that. For true originality we must be one, and closely one, with God. To be creative we must learn with the Creator. The most effectual man in history was he who said, "I live; yet not I, but Christ liveth in me." What a reflection on our faith that so much piety should be humdrum, and deadly dull! Private prayer, when it is real action, is the greatest forge of personality. It places a man in direct and effective contact with God the Creator, the source of originality, and especially with God the Redeemer as the source of the new creation. For the minister personality is everything – not geniality, as it is the day's fashion to say, but personality; and prayer is the spring of personality. This impressive personality, due to prayer, you may often have in "the peasant saint." And in some cases its absence is as palpable. Hence comes vulgarity in prayer, essential vulgarity underlying much possible fineness of phrase or manner. Vulgarity in prayer lies not so much in its offenses to good taste in style as in its indications of the absence of spiritual habit and reality. If the theology of rhetoric destroys the theology of reality in the sermon, how much more in prayer!

Prayer is for the religious life what original research is for science – by it we get direct contact with reality. The soul is brought into union with its own vaster nature – God. Therefore, also, we must use the Bible as an original; for indeed, the Bible is the most copious spring of prayer, and of power, and of range. If we learn to pray from the Bible, and

avoid a mere recitation of its phrases, we shall cultivate in our prayer the large humane note of a universal gospel. Let us nurse our prayer on our study of our Bible; and let us, therefore, not be too afraid of theological prayer. True Christian prayer must have theology in it; no less than true theology must have prayer in it and must be capable of being prayed. "Your theology is too difficult," said Charles V to the Reformers; "it cannot be understood without much prayer." Yes, that is our arduous puritan way. Prayer and theology must interpenetrate to keep each other great, and wide, and mighty. The failure of the habit of prayer is at the root of much of our light distaste for theology. There is a conspiracy of influences round us whose effect is to belittle our great work. Earnest ministers suffer more from the smallness of their people than from their sins, and far more than from their unkindness. Our public may kill by its triviality a soul which could easily resist the assaults of opposition or wickedness. And our newspapers will greatly aid their work. Now, to resist this it is not enough to have recourse to prayer and to cultivate devotion. Unfortunately, there are signs in the religious world to show that prayer and piety alone do not save men from pettiness of interest, thinness of soul, spiritual volatility, the note of insincerity, or foolishness of judgment, or even vindictiveness. The remedy is not prayer alone, but prayer on the scale of the whole gospel and at the depth of searching faith. It is considered prayer – prayer which rises above the childish petitions that disfigure much of our public pietism, prayer which issues from the central affairs of the kingdom of God. It is prayer with the profound Bible as its book of devotion, and a true theology of faith for half of its power. It is the prayer of a mind that moves in Bible passion, and ranges with Bible scope, even when it eschews Bible speech and "the language of Canaan."

And yet, with all its range, it is prayer with concentration. It has not only thought but will in it. The great reason why so many will not decide for Christ is that Christ requires from the world concentration; not seclusion and not renunciation merely, but concentration. And we ministers have our special form of that need. I am speaking not of our share in the common troubles of life, but of those specially that arise from the ministerial office and care. No minister can live up to his work on the casual or interjectional kind of prayer that might be sufficient for many of his flock. He must think, of course, in his prayers – in his private prayers – and he must pray his faith's thought. But, still more, in his praying he must act. Prayer is not a frame of mind, but a great energy. He must rise to conceive his work as an active function of the work of Christ; and he must link his faith, therefore, with the intercession which covers the whole energy of Christ in His kingdom. In this, as in many ways, he must remember, to his great relief and comfort, that it is not he who is the real pastor of his church, but Christ, and that he is but Christ's curate. The final responsibility is not his, but Christ's, who bears the responsibility of all the sins and frets, both of the world and, especially, of the Church.

The concentration, moreover, should correspond to the positivity of the gospel and the Bible. Prayer should rise more out of God's Word and concern for His kingdom than even out of our personal needs, trials, or desires. That is implied in prayer in Christ's name or for Christ's sake, prayer from His place in the midst of the Kingdom. Our Prayer-book, the Bible, does not prescribe prayer, but it does more – it inspires it. And prayer in Christ's name is prayer inspired by His first interest – the gospel. Do not use Christ simply to countersign your egoist petition by a closing formula, but to create, inspire, and glorify it. Prayer in Christ's name is prayer for Christ's object – for His Kingdom, and His promise of the Holy Ghost.

It we really pray for that and yet do not feel we receive it, probably enough we have it; and we are looking for some special form of it not ours, or not ours yet. We may be mistaking the fruits of the Spirit for His presence. Fruits come late. They are different from signs. Buds are signs, and so are other things hard to see. It is the Spirit that keeps us praying for the Spirit, as it is grace that keeps us in grace. Remember the patience of the missionaries who waited in the Spirit fifteen years for their first convert. If God gave His Son unasked, how much more will He give His Holy Spirit to them that ask

it! But let us not prescribe the form in which He comes.

The true close of prayer is when the utterance expires in its own spiritual fullness. That is the true Amen. Such times there are. We feel we are at last laid open to God. We feel as though we "did see heaven opened, and the holy angels, and the great God Himself." The prayer ends itself; we do not end it. It mounts to its heaven and renders its spirit up to God, saying, "It is finished." It has its perfect consummation and bliss, its spiritually natural close and fruitation, whether it has answer or not.

7. THE INSISTENCY OF PRAYER

In all I have said I have implied that prayer should be strenuously importunate. Observe, not petitionary merely, nor concentrated, nor active alone, but importunate. For prayer is not only meditation or communion. Nor ought it to be merely submissive in tone, as the "quietist" ideal is. We need not begin with "Thy will be done" if we but end with it. Remember the stress that Christ laid on importunity. Strenuous prayer will help us to recover the masculine type of religion – and then our opponents will at least respect us.

I would speak a little more fully on this matter of importunity. It is very closely bound up with the reality both of prayer and of religion. Prayer is not really a power till it is importunate. And it cannot be importunate unless it is felt to have a real effect on the Will of God. I may slip in here my conviction that far less of the disbelief in prayer is due to a scientific view of nature's uniformity than to the slipshod kind of prayer that men hear from us in public worship; it is often but journalese sent heavenwards, or phrase-making to carry on. And I would further say that by importunity something else is meant than passionate dictation and stormy pertinacity – imposing our egoist will on God, and treating Him as a mysterious but manageable power that we may coerce and exploit.

The deepening of the spiritual life is a subject that frequently occupies the attention of religious conferences and of the soul bent on self-improvement. But it is not certain that the great saints would always recognize the ideal of some who are addicted to the use of the phrase. The "deepening of the spiritual life" they would find associated with three unhappy things.

1. They would recoil from a use of Scripture prevalent to those circles, which is atomistic individualist, subjective, and fantastic.

2. And what they would feel most foreign to their own objective and penetrating minds might be the air of introspection and self-measurement too often associated with the spiritual thus "deepened" – a spiritual egoism.

3. And they would miss the note of judgment and Redemption.

We should distinguish at the outset *the deepening of spiritual life* from the *quickening of spiritual sensibility*. Christ on the cross was surely deepened in spiritual experience, but was not the essence of that dereliction, and the concomitant of that deepening, the dulling of spiritual sensibility?

There are many plain obstacles to the deepening of spiritual life, amid which I desire to name here only one; it is prayer conceived merely, or chiefly, as submission, resignation, quietism. We say too soon, "Thy will be done"; and too ready acceptance of a situation as His will often means feebleness or sloth. It may be His will that we surmount His will. It may be His higher will that we resist His lower. Prayer is an act of will much more than of sentiment, and its triumph is more than acquiescence. Let us submit when we must, but let us keep the submission in reserve rather than in action, as a ground tone rather than the stole effort. Prayer with us has largely ceased to be wrestling. But is that not the dominant scriptural idea? It is not the sole idea, but is it not the dominant? And is not our subdued note often but superinduced and unreal?

I venture to enlarge on this last head, by way of meeting some who hesitate to speak of the power of prayer to alter God's will. I offer two points:

I. Prayer may really change the will of God, or, if not His will, His intention.
II. It may, like other human energies of godly sort, take the form of resisting the will of God. Resisting His will may be doing His will.

I. As to the first point. If this is not believed the earnestness goes out of prayer. It becomes either a ritual, or a soliloquy only overheard by God; just as thought with the will out of it degenerates into dreaming or brooding, where we are more passive than active. Prayer is not merely the meeting of two moods or two affections, the laying of the head on a divine bosom in trust and surrender. That may have its place in religion, but it is not the nerve and soul of prayer. Nor is it religious reverie. Prayer is an encounter of wills – till one will or the other give way. It is not a spiritual exercise merely, but in its maturity it is a cause acting on the course of God's world. It is, indeed, by God's grace that prayer is a real cause, but such it is. And of course there must be in us a faith corresponding to the grace. Of course also there is always, behind all, the readiness to accept God's will without a murmur when it is perfectly evident and final. "My grace is sufficient for thee." Yes, but there is also the repeated effort to alter its form according to our sanctified needs and desires. You will notice that in Paul's case the power to accept the sufficiency of God's grace only came in the course of an importunate prayer aiming to turn God's hand. Paul ended, rather than began, with "Thy will be done." The peace of God is an end and not a beginning.

"Thy will be done" was no utterance of mere resignation; thought it has mostly come to mean this in a Christianity which tends to canonize the weak instead of strengthening them. As prayer it was a piece of active cooperation with God's will. It was a positive part of it. It is one thing to submit to a stronger will, it is another to be one with it. We submit because we cannot resist it; but when we are one with it we cannot succumb. It is not a power, but our power. But the natural will is not one with God's; and so we come to use these words in a mere negative way, meaning that we cease to resist. Our will does not accept God's, it just stops work. We give in and lie down. But is that the sense of the words in the Lord's Prayer? Do they mean that we have no objection to God's will being done? or that we do not withstand any more? or even that we accept it gladly? Do they not mean something far more positive – that we actively will God's will and aid it, that it is the whole content of our own, that we put into it all the will that there can be in prayer, which is at last the great will power of the race? It is our heart's passion that God's will be done and His kingdom come. And can His kingdom come otherwise than as it is a passion with us? Can His will be done? God's will was not Christ's consent merely, nor His pleasure, but His meat and drink, the source of His energy and the substance of His work.

Observe, nothing can alter God's grace, His will in that sense, His large will and final purpose – our racial blessing, our salvation, our redemption in Jesus Christ. But for that will He is an infinite opportunist. His ways are very flexible. His intentions are amenable to us if His will is changeless. The steps of His process are variable according to our freedom and His.

We are living, let us say, in a careless way; and God proposes a certain treatment of us according to our carelessness. But in the exercise of our spiritual freedom we are by some means brought to pray. We cease to be careless. We pray God to visit us as those who hear. Then He does another thing. He acts differently, with a change caused by our freedom and our change. The treatment for deafness is altered. God adopts another treatment – perhaps for weakness. We have by prayer changed His action, and, so far, His will (at any rate His intention) concerning us. As we pray, the discipline for the prayerless is altered to that for the prayerful. We attain the thing God did not mean to give us unless He had been affected by our prayer. We change the conduct, if not the will, of God to us, the *Verhalten* if not the *Verhaltniss*.

Again, we pray and pray, and no answer comes. The boon does not arrive. Why? Perhaps we are not spiritually ready for it. It would not be a real blessing. But the persistence, the importunity of faith, is having a great effect on our spiritual nature. It ripens. A time comes when we are ready for answer. We then present ourselves to God in a spiritual condition which reasonably causes His to yield. The new spiritual state is not the answer to our prayer, but it is its effect; and it is the condition which makes the answer possible. It makes the prayer effectual. The gift can be

a blessing now. So God resists us no more. Importunity prevails, not as mere importunity (for God is not bored into answer), but as the importunity of God's own elect, i.e. as obedience, as a force of the Kingdom, as increased spiritual power, as real moral action, bringing corresponding strength and fitness to receive. I have often found that what I sought most I did not get at the right time, not till it was too late, not till I had learned to do without it, till I had renounced it in principle (though not in desire). Perhaps it had lost some of its zest by the time it came, but it meant more as a gift and a trust. That was God's right time – when I could have it as though I had it not. If it came, it came not to gratify me, but to glorify Him and be a means of serving Him.

One recalls here that most pregnant saying of Schopenhauer: "All is illusion – the hope or the thing hoped." If it is not true for all it is true for very many. Either the hope is never fulfilled or else its fulfillment disappoints. God gives the hoped for thing, but sends leanness into the soul. The mother prays to have a son – and he breaks her heart, and were better dead. Hope may lie to us, or the thing hoped may dash us. But though He slay me I will trust. God does not fail. Amid the wreck of my little world He is firm, and I in Him. I justify God in the ruins; in His good time I shall arrive. More even than my hopes may go wrong. I may go wrong. But my Redeemer liveth; and, great though God is as my Fulfiller, He is greater as my Redeemer. He is great as my hope, but He is greater as my power. What is the failure of my hope from Him compared with the failure of His hope in me? If He continue to believe in me I may well believe in Him.

God's object with us is not to give just so many things and withhold so many; it is to place us in the tissue of His kingdom. His best answer to us is to raise us to the power of answering Him. The reason why He does not answer our prayer is because we do not answer Him and His prayer. And His prayer was, as though Christ did beseech us, "Be ye reconciled." He would lift us to confident business with Him, to commerce of loving wills. The painter wrestles with the sitter till he gives him back himself, and there is a speaking likeness. So man with God, till God surrender

His secret. He gives or refuses things, therefore, with a view to that communion alone, and on the whole. It is that spiritual personal end, and not an iron necessity, that rules His course. Is there not a constant spiritual interaction between God and man as free spiritual beings? How that can be is one of the great philosophic problems. But the fact that it is is of the essence of faith. It is the unity of our universe. Many systems try to explain how human freedom and human action are consistent with God's omnipotence and omniscience. None succeed. How secondary causes like man are compatible with God as the Universal and Ultimate Cause is not rationally plain. But there is no practical doubt that they are compatible. And so it is with the action of man on God in prayer. We may perhaps, for the present, put it thus, that we cannot change the will of God, which is grace, and which even Christ never changed but only revealed or effected; but we can change the intention of God, which is a manner of treatment, in the interest of grace, according to the situation of the hour.

If we are guided by the Bible we have much ground for this view of prayer. *Does not Christ set more value upon importunity than on submission?* "Knock, and it shall be opened." I would refer also not only to the parable of the unjust judge, but to the incident of the Syrophenician woman, where her wit, faith, and importunity together did actually change our Lord's intention and break His custom. Then there is Paul beseeching the Lord thrice for a boon; and urging us to be instant, insistent, continual in prayer. We have Jacob wrestling. We have Abraham pleading, yea, haggling, with God for Sodom. We have Moses interceding for Israel and asking God to blot his name out of the book of life, if that were needful to save Israel. We have Job facing God, withstanding Him, almost bearding Him, and extracting revelation. And we have Christ's own struggle with the Father in Gethsemane.

It is a wrestle on the greatest scale – all manhood taxed as in some great war, or some great negotiation of State. And the effect is exhaustion often. No, the result of true, prayer is not always peace.

II. As to the second point. This wrestle is in a certain sense a resisting of God. You cannot have wrestling otherwise; but you may have Christian fatalism. It is not mere wrestling with ourselves, our ignorance, our self-will. That is not prayer, but self-torment. Prayer is wrestling with God. And it is better to fall thus into the hands of God than of man – even than our own. It is a resistance that God loves. It is quite foreign to the godless, self-willed defiant resistance. In love there is a kind of resistance that enhances it. The resistance of love is a quite different thing from the resistance of hostility. The yielding to one you love is very different from capitulating to an enemy:

Two constant lovers, being joined in one,

Yielding unto each other yield to none –

i.e. to no foreign force, no force foreign to the love which makes them one.

So when God yields to prayer in the name of Christ, to the prayer of faith and love, He yields to Himself who inspired it, as He swore by Himself since none was greater. Christian prayer is the Spirit praying in us. It is prayer in the solidarity of the Kingdom. It is a continuation of Christ's prayer, which in Gethsemane was wrestling with the Father. But if so, it is God pleading with God, God dealing with God – as the true atonement must be. And when God yields it is not to an outside influence He yields, but to Himself.

Let me make it still more plain. When we resist the will of God we may be resisting what God wills to be temporary and to be resisted, what He wills to be intermediary and transcended. We resist because God wills we should. We are not limiting God's will, any more than our moral freedom limits it. That freedom is the image of His, and, in a sense, part of His. We should defraud Him and His freedom if we did not exercise ours. So the prayer which resists His dealing may be part of His will and its fulfillment.

Does God not will the existence of things for us to resist, to grapple with? Do we ourselves not appoint problems and make difficulties for those we teach, for the very purpose of their overcoming them? We set questions to children of which we know the answer quite well. The real answer to our will and purpose is not the solution but the grappling, the wrestling. And we may properly give a reward not for the correct answer, but for the hard and honest effort. That work is the prayer; and it has its reward apart from the solution.

That is a principle of education with us. So it may be with God. But I mean a good deal more by this than what is called the reflex action of prayer. It that were all it would introduce an unreality into prayer. We should be praying for exercise, not for action. It would be prayer with a theological form, which yet expects no more than a psychological effect. It would be a prayer which is not sure that God is really more interested in us than we are in Him. But I mean that God's education has a lower stage for us and a higher. He has a lower will and a higher, a prior and a posterior. And the purpose of the lower will is that it be resisted and struggled through to the higher. By God's will (let us say) you are born in a home where your father's earnings are a few shillings a week, like many an English laborer. Is it God's will that you acquiesce in that and never strive out of it? It is God's will that you are there. Is it God's will that you should not resist being there? Nay, it may be His will that you should wisely resist it, and surmount His lower, His initial, will, which is there for the purpose. That is to say, it is His will that you resist, antagonize, His will. And so it is with the state of childhood altogether.

Again: Is disease God's will? We all believe it often is – even if man is to blame for it. It may be, by God's will, the penalty on human ignorance, negligence, or sin. But let us suppose there were only a few cases where disease is God's will. It was so in the lower creatures, before man lived, blundered, or sinned. Take only one such case. Is it God's will that we should lie down and let the disease have its way? Why, a whole profession exists to say no. Medicine exists as an antagonism to disease, even when you can say that disease is God's will and His punishment of sin. A doctor will tell you that resignation is one of his foes. He begins to grow hopeless if the patient is so resigned from the outset as to make no effort, if there be no will to live. Resistance to this ordinance of God's is the doctor's business and the doctor's ally. And why? Because God ordained disease for the purpose of being resisted; He ordained the resistance, that from the conflict man might come out the stronger, and more full of resource and dominion over nature.

Again, take death. It is God's will. It is in the very structure of man, in the divine economy. It is not the result of sin; it was there before sin. Is it to be accepted without demur? Are doctors impious who resist it? Are we sinning when we shrink from it? Does not the life of most people consist in the effort to escape it, in the struggle for a living? So also when we pray and wrestle for another's life, for our dear one's life. "Sir, come down ere my child die." The man was impatient. How familiar we are with his kind! "Do, please, leave your religious talk, which I don't understand; get doing something; cure my child." But was that an impious prayer? It was ignorant, practical, British, but not quite faithless. And it was answered, as many a similar prayer has been. But, then, if death be God's will, to resist it is to resist God's will. Well, it is His will that we should. Christ, who always did God's will, resisted His own death, slipped away from it often, till the hour came; and even then He prayed with all his might against it when it seemed inevitable. "If it be possible, release Me." He was ready to accept it, but only in the last resort, only if there was no other way, only after every other means had been exhausted. To the end He cherished the fading hope that there might be some other way. He went to death voluntarily, freely, but – shall we say reluctantly? – resisting the most blessed act of God's will that ever was performed in heaven or on earth; resisting, yet sure to acquiesce when that was God's clear will.

The whole nature, indeed, is the will of God, and the whole of grace is striving with nature. It is our nature to have certain passions. That is God's will. But it is our calling of God to resist them as much as to gratify them. There are there as God's will to be resisted as much as indulged. The redemption from the natural man includes the resistance to it, and the release of the soul from what God Himself appointed as its lower stages – never as its dwelling place, and never its tomb. So far prayer is on the lines of evolution.

Obedience is the chief end. But obedience is not mere submission, mere resignation. It is not always acquiescence, even in prayer. We obey God as much when we urge our suit, and make a real petition of it, as when we accept

His decision; as much when we try to change His will as when we bow to it. The kingdom cf heaven suffereth violence. There is a very fine passage in Dante, Pard. xx. 94 (Longfellow):

Regnum coelorum suffereth violence
From fervent love, and from that living hope
That overcometh the divine volition.
Not in the way that man o'ercometh man;
We conquer it because it will be conquered,
And, conquered, conquers by benignity.

It is His will – His will of grace – that prayer should prevail with Him and extract blessings. And how we love the grace that so concedes them! The answer to prayer is not the complaisance of a playful power lightly yielding to the playful egoism of His favorites. "Our antagonist is our helper." To struggle with Him is one way of doing His will. To resist is one way of saying, "Thy will be done." It was God's will that Christ should deprecate the death God required. It pleased God as much as His submission to death. But could it have been pleasing to Him that Christ should pray so, if no prayer could ever possibly change God's will? Could Christ have prayed so in that belief? Would faith ever inspire us to pray if the God of our faith must be unmoved by prayers? The prayer that goes to an inflexible God, however good He is, is prayer that rises more from human need than from God's own revelation, or from Christian faith (where Christian prayer should rise). It is His will, then, that we should pray against what seems His will, and what, for the lower stage of our growth, is His will. And all this without any unreality whatever.

Let us beware of a pietist fatalism which thins the spiritual life, saps the vigor of character, makes humility mere acquiescence, and piety only feminine, by banishing the will from prayer as much as thought has been banished from it. "The curse of so much religion" (I have quoted Meredith) "is that men cling to God with their weakness rather than with their strength."

The popularity of much acquiescence is not because it is holier, but because it is easier. And an easy gospel is the consumption that attacks Christianity. It is the phthisis to faith.

Once come to think that we best say "Thy will be done" when we acquiesce, when we resign, and not also when we struggle and wrestle, and in time all effort will seem less pious than submission. And so we fall into the ecclesiastical type of religion, drawn from an age whose first virtue was submission to outward superiors. We shall come to canonize decorum and subduedness in life and worship (as the Episcopal Church with its monarchical ideas of religion has done). We shall think more of order than of effort, more of law than of life, more of fashion than of faith, of good form than of great power. But was subduedness the mark of the New Testament men? Our religion may gain some beauty in this way, but it loses vigor. It may gain style, but it loses power. It is good form, but mere aesthetic piety. It may consecrate manners, but it improverishes the mind. It may regulate prayer by the precepts of intelligence instead of the needs and faith of the soul. It may feed certain pensive emotions, but it may emasculate will, secularize energy, and empty character. And so we decline to a state of things in which we have no shocking sins – yes, and no splendid souls; when all souls are dully correct, as like as shillings, but as thin, and as cheap.

All our forms and views of religion have their test in prayer. Lose the importunity of prayer, reduce it to soliloquy, or even to colloquy, with God, lose the real conflict of will and will, lose the habit of wrestling and the hope of prevailing with God, make it mere walking with God in friendly talk; and, precious as that is, yet you tend to lose the reality of prayer at last. In principle you make it mere conversation instead of the soul's great action. You lose the food of character, the renewal of will. You may have beautiful prayers – but as ineffectual as beauty so often is, and as fleeting. And so in the end you lose the reality of religion. Redemption turns down into mere revelation, faith to assent, and devotion to a phase of culture. For you lose the power of the Cross and so of the soul.

Resist God, in the sense of rejecting God, and you will not be able to resist any evil. But resist God in the sense of closing with God, cling to Him with your strength, not your weakness only, with your active and not only your passive faith, and He will give you strength. Cast yourself into His arms not to be caressed but to wrestle with Him. He loves that holy war. He may be too many for you, and lift you from your feet. But it will be to lift you from earth, and set you in the heavenly places which are their who fight the good fight and lay hold of God as their eternal life.

P.T. Forsyth, 1848–1921

Introduction to the Devout Life

Francis de Sales

CONTENTS
Five meditations:
    Creation
    Why we were created
    Gifts of God
    Sin
    Death

FIRST MEDITATION
OF CREATION

Preparation
1. PLACE yourself in the Presence of God.
2. Ask Him to inspire your heart.

Considerations
1. Consider that but a few years since you were not born into the world, and your soul was as yet non-existent. Where wert thou then, O my soul? the world was already old, and yet of thee there was no sign.
2. God brought you out of this nothingness, in order to make you what you are, not because He had any need of you, but solely out of His Goodness.
3. Consider the being which God has given you; for it is the foremost being of this visible world, adapted to live eternally, and to be perfectly united to God's Divine Majesty.

Affections and Resolutions
1. Humble yourself utterly before God, saying with the Psalmist, O Lord, I am nothing in respect of Thee – what am I, that Thou

shouldst remember me? O my soul, thou wert yet lost in that abyss of nothingness, if God had not called thee forth, and what of thee in such a case?
2. Give God thanks. O Great and Good Creator, what do I not owe Thee, Who didst take me from out that nothingness, by Thy Mercy to make me what I am? How can I ever do enough worthily to praise Thy Holy Name, and render due thanks to Thy Goodness?
3. Confess your own shame. But alas, O my Creator, so far from uniting myself to Thee by a loving service, I have rebelled against Thee through my unruly affections, departing from Thee, and giving myself up to sin, and ignoring Thy Goodness, as though Thou hadst not created me.
4. Prostrate thyself before God. O my soul, know that the Lord He is thy God, it is He that hath made thee, and not thou thyself. O God, I am the work of Thy Hands; henceforth I will not seek to rest in myself, who am naught. Wherein hast thou to glory, who art but dust and ashes? how canst thou, a very nothing, exalt thyself? In order to my own humiliation, I will do such and such a thing, – I will endure such contempt: – I will alter my ways and henceforth follow my Creator, and realize that I am honored by His calling me to the being He has given; I will employ it solely to obey His Will, by means of the teaching He has given me ...

Conclusion
1. Thank God. Bless the Lord, O my soul, and praise His Holy Name with all thy being, because His Goodness called me forth from nothingness, and His Mercy created me.
2. Offer. O my God, I offer Thee with all my heart the being Thou hast given me, I dedicate and consecrate it to Thee.
3. Pray. O God, strengthen me in these affections and resolutions. Dear Lord, I commend me, and all those I love, to Thy never failing Mercy. OUR FATHER, etc.

At the end of your meditation linger a while, and gather, so to say, a little spiritual bouquet from the thoughts you have dwelt upon, the sweet perfume whereof may refresh you through the day.

SECOND MEDITATION
OF THE END FOR WHICH WE WERE CREATED

Preparation
1. PLACE yourself before God.
2. Ask Him to inspire your heart.

Considerations
1. God did not bring you into the world because He had any need of you, useless as you are; but solely that He might show forth His Goodness in you, giving you His Grace and Glory. And to this end He gave you understanding that you might know Him, memory that you might think of Him, a will that you might love Him, imagination that you might realize His mercies, sight that you might behold the marvels of His works, speech that you might praise Him, and so on with all your other faculties.

2. Being created and placed in the world for this intent, all contrary actions should be shunned and rejected, as also you should avoid as idle and superfluous whatever does not promote it.

Consider how unhappy they are who do not think of all this, – who live as though they were created only to build and plant, to heap up riches and amuse themselves with trifles.

Affections and Resolutions
1. Humble yourself in that hitherto you have so little thought upon all this. Alas, my God, of what was I thinking when I did not think of Thee? what did I remember when I forgot Thee? what did I love when I loved Thee not? Alas, when I ought to have been feeding on the truth, I was but filling myself with vanity, and serving the world, which was made to serve me.

2. Abhor your past life. I renounce ye, O vain thoughts and useless cogitations, frivolous and hateful memories: I renounce all worthless friendships, all unprofitable efforts, and miserably ungrateful self-indulgence, all pitiful compliances.

3. Turn to God. Thou, my God and Savior shalt henceforth be the sole object of my thoughts; no more will I give my mind to ideas which are displeasing to Thee. All the days of my life I will dwell upon the greatness of Thy Goodness, so lovingly poured out upon me.

Thou shalt be henceforth the delight of my heart, the resting-place of all my affections. From this time forth I will forsake and abhor the vain pleasures and amusements, the empty pursuits which have absorbed my time; – the unprofitable ties which have bound my heart I will loosen henceforth, and to that end I will use such and such remedies.

Conclusion
1. Thank God, Who has made you for so gracious an end. Thou hast made me, O Lord, for Thyself, that I may eternally enjoy the immensity of Thy Glory; when shall I be worthy thereof when shall I know how to bless Thee as I ought?

2. Offer. O Dearest Lord, I offer Thee all my affections and resolutions, with my whole heart and soul.

3. Pray. I entreat Thee, O God, that Thou wouldest accept my desires and longings, and give Thy Blessing to my soul, to enable me to fulfill them, through the Merits of Thy Dear Son's Precious Blood shed upon the Cross for me. OUR FATHER, etc. Gather your little spiritual bouquet.

THIRD MEDITATION
OF THE GIFTS OF GOD

Preparation
1. PLACE yourself in the Presence of God.
2. Ask Him to inspire your heart.

Considerations
1. Consider the material gifts God has given you – your body, and the means for its preservation; your health, and all that maintains it; your friends and many helps. Consider too how many persons more deserving than you are without these gifts; some suffering in health or limb, others exposed to injury, contempt and trouble, or sunk in poverty, while God has willed you to be better off.

2. Consider the mental gifts He has given you. Why are you not stupid, idiotic, insane like many you wot of? Again, God has favored you with a decent and suitable education, while many have grown up in utter ignorance.

3. Further, consider His spiritual gifts. You are a child of His Church, God has taught

you to know Himself from your youth. How often has He given you His Sacraments? what inspirations and interior light, what reproofs, He has given to lead you aright; how often He has forgiven you, how often delivered you from occasions of falling; what opportunities He has granted for your soul's progress! Dwell somewhat on the detail, see how Loving and Gracious God has been to you.

Affections and Resolutions

1. Marvel at God's Goodness. How good He has been to me, how abundant in mercy and plenteous in loving-kindness! O my soul, be thou ever telling of the great things the Lord has done for thee!

2. Marvel at your own ingratitude. What am I, Lord, that Thou rememberest me? How unworthy am I! I have trodden Thy Mercies under root, I have abused Thy Grace, turning it against Thy very Self; I have set the depth of my ingratitude against the deep of Thy Grace and Favor.

3. Kindle your gratitude. O my soul, be no more so faithless and disloyal to thy mighty Benefactor! How should not my whole soul serve the Lord, Who has done such great things in me and for me?

4. Go on, my daughter, to refrain from this or that material indulgence; let your body be wholly the servant of God, Who has done so much for it: set your soul to seek Him by this or that devout practice suitable thereto. Make diligent use of the means provided by the Church to help you to love God and save your soul. Resolve to be constant in prayer and seeking the Sacraments, in hearing God's Word, and in obeying His inspirations and counsels.

Conclusion

1. Thank God for the clearer knowledge He has given you of His benefits and your own duty.

2. Offer your heart and all its resolutions to Him.

3. Ask Him to strengthen you to fulfill them faithfully by the Merits of the Death of His Son. OUR FATHER, etc. Gather the little spiritual bouquet.

FOURTH MEDITATION
ON SIN

Preparation

1. PLACE yourself in the Presence of God.
2. Ask Him to inspire your heart.

Considerations

1. Consider how long it is since you first began to commit sin, and how since that first beginning sin has multiplied in your heart; how every day has added to the number of your sins against God, against yourself and against your neighbor, by deed, word, thought and desire.

2. Consider your evil tendencies, and how far you have followed them. These two points will show you that your sins are more in number than the hairs of your head, or the sand on the seashore.

3. Apart from sin, consider your ingratitude towards God, which is in itself a sin enfolding all the others, and adding to their enormity: consider the gifts which God has given you, and which you have turned against the Giver; especially the inspirations you have neglected, and the promptings to good which you have frustrated. Review the many Sacraments you have received, and see where are their fruits. Where are the precious jewels wherewith your Heavenly Bridegroom decked you? with what preparation have you received them? Reflect upon the ingratitude with which, while God sought to save you, you have fled from Him and rushed upon destruction.

Affections and Resolutions

1. Humble yourself in your wretchedness. O my God, how dare I come before Thine Eyes? I am but a corrupt being, a very sink of ingratitude and wickedness. Can it be that I have been so disloyal, that not one sense, not one faculty but has been sullied and stained; – not one day has passed but I have sinned before Thee? Was this a fitting return for all my Creator's gifts, for my Redeemer's Blood?

2. Ask pardon; – throw yourself at the Lord's Feet as the prodigal son, as the Magdalene, as the woman convicted of adultery. Have mercy, Lord, on me a sinner! O Living Fountain of Mercy, have pity on me, unworthy as I am.

3. Resolve to do better. Lord, with the help of Thy Grace I will never again give myself up to sin. I have loved it too well; – henceforth I would abhor it and cleave to Thee. Father of Mercy, I would live and die to Thee.

4. In order to put away past sin, accuse yourself bravely of it, let there not be one sinful act which you do not bring to light.

5. Resolve to make every effort to tear up the roots of sin from your heart, especially this and that individual sin which troubles you most.

6. In order to do this, resolve steadfastly to follow the advice given you, and never think that you have done enough to atone for your past sin.

Conclusion

1. Thank God for having waited till now for you, and for rousing these good intentions in your heart.

2. Offer Him all your heart to carry them to good effect.

3. Pray that He would strengthen you.

FIFTH MEDITATION
OF DEATH

Preparation

1. PLACE yourself in the Presence of God.

2. Ask His Grace.

3. Suppose yourself to be on your deathbed, in the last extremity, without the smallest hope of recovery.

Considerations

1. Consider the uncertainty as to the day of your death. One day your soul will quit this body – will it be in summer or winter? in town or country? by day or by night? will it be suddenly or with warning? will it be owing to sickness or an accident? will you have time to make your last confession or not? will your confessor or spiritual father be at hand or will he not? Alas, of all these things we know absolutely nothing: all that we do know is that die we shall, and for the most part sooner than we expect.

2. Consider that then the world is at end as far as you are concerned, there will be no more of it for you, it will be altogether overthrown for you, since all pleasures, vanities, worldly joys, empty delights will be as a mere fantastic vision to you. Woe is me, for what mere trifles and unrealities I have ventured to offend my God? Then you will see that what we preferred to Him was naught. But, on the other hand, all devotion and good works will then seem so precious and so sweet: – Why did I not tread that pleasant path? Then what you thought to be little sins will look like huge mountains, and your devotion will seem but a very little thing.

3. Consider the universal farewell which your soul will take of this world. It will say farewell to riches, pleasures, and idle companions; to amusements and pastimes, to friends and neighbors, to husband, wife and child, in short to all creation. And lastly it will say farewell to its own body, which it will leave pale and cold, to become repulsive in decay.

4. Consider how the survivors will hasten to put that body away, and hide it beneath the earth – and then the world will scarce give you another thought, or remember you, any more than you have done to those already gone. "God rest his soul!" men will say, and that is all. O death, how pitiless, how hard thou art!

5. Consider that when it quits the body the soul must go at once to the right hand or the left. To which will your soul go? what side will it take? none other, be sure, than that to which it had voluntarily drawn while yet in this world.

Affections and Resolutions

1. Pray to God, and throw yourself into His Arms. O Lord, be Thou my stay in that day of anguish! May that hour be blessed and favorable to me, if all the rest of my life be full of sadness and trial.

2. Despise the world. Forasmuch as I know not the hour in which I must quit the world, I will not grow fond of it. O dear friends, beloved ones of my heart, be content that I cleave to you only with a holy friendship which may last for ever; why should I cling to you with a tie which must needs be broken?

I will prepare for the hour of death and take every precaution for its peaceful arrival; I will thoroughly examine into the state of my conscience, and put in order whatever is wanting.

Conclusion

Thank God for inspiring you with these resolutions: offer them to His Majesty: entreat Him anew to grant you a happy death by the Merits of His Dear Son's Death ...

> Francis de Sales, 1567–1622,
> *Introduction to the Devout Life*

Pray always

William Gurnall

"Praying always with all prayer and supplication," etc. (Eph. 6:18).

"Praying always."
This points to the time of performing the duty of prayer – "always." This word "always" hath a threefold importance.

FIRST. To pray "always" is as much as if he had said, "pray in everything," according to that of the same apostle in another epistle – "In every thing by prayer and supplication with thanksgiving let your requests be made known unto God."

SECOND. To pray "always" may import as much as to pray in all conditions.

THIRD. To pray "always" is to pray daily.

Threefold import of the expression "praying always."

FIRST. TO PRAY ALWAYS IS TO PRAY IN EVERYTHING

Prayer is a catholic duty, with which, like a girdle, we are to compass in all our affairs. It is to be as bread and salt on our table; whatever else we have to our meal, these are not forgot to be set on: whatever we do, or would have, prayer is necessary, be it small or great. Not as the heathen, who prayed for some things to their gods, and not for other. If poor, they prayed for riches; if sick, for health; but as for the good things of the mind, such as patience, contentment, and other virtues, they thought they could carve well enough in these for themselves, without troubling their gods to help them. The poet it seems was of this mind –

It is enough,
To pray of Jove who gives and takes away

That he may give me life and wealth:
I will myself prepare the equal soul.
How proud is ignorance! let God give the less, and man will do the greater.

But their folly is not so much to wondered at, as the irreligion of many among ourselves, who profess to know the true God, and have the light of his word to direct them what worship to give him. Some are so brutish in their knowledge, that they hardly pray to God for anything others for everything. May be they look upon pardon of sin, and salvation of their souls – as fruit on the top branches of a tree – out of the reach of their own arm, and therefore now and then put up some slighty prayers to God for them. But as for temporals, which seem to hang lower, they think they can pluck them by their own industry, without setting up the ladder of prayer to come at them. They that should see some – how busy they are in laying their plots, and how seldom in prayer – could not but think they expected their safety from their own policy, and not God's providence. Or, should they observe how hard they work in their shop, and how seldom and lazy they are at prayer for God's blessing on their labor in their closet, they must conclude these men promise themselves their estates more from their own labor than the divine bounty.

In a word, it is some great occasion that must bring them upon their knees before God in prayer. May be, when they have an extraordinary enterprise in hand, wherein they look for strong opposition or great difficulty, in such a case God shall have them knocking at his door – for now they are at their wits" end and know not how to turn them; but the more ordinary and common actions of their lives they think they can please their master at their pleasures, and so pass by God's door without bespeaking his presence or assistance. Thus, one runs into his shop, and another into the field, and takes no notice that God is concerned in their employments. If to take a long journey by the sea or land, where eminent dangers and hazards present themselves unto their thoughts, then God hath their company; but if to stay at home, or walk to and fro in their ordinary employments, they bespeak not the providential wing of God to overshadow them. This is not to "pray always." If thou wilt, therefore, be a Christian, do not thus part stakes with God, committing the greater transactions of thy life to him, and trusting thyself with the less: but "acknowledge God in all thy ways, and lean not to thine own understanding" in any. By this thou shalt give him the glory of his universal providence, with which he encircles all his creatures and all their actions. As nothing is too great to be above his power, so nothing is too little to be beneath his care. He is the God of the valleys as well as of the mountains. The sparrow on the hedge and the hair on our head are cared for by him; and this is no more derogatory to his glorious majesty than it was to make them at first. Nay, thou shalt, by this, not only give God his glory, but secure thyself, for there is no passage in thy whole life so minute and inconsiderable, which – if God should withdraw his care and providence – might not be an occasion of a sin or danger to thee. And that which exposeth thee to these calls upon thee to engage God for thy defense.

FIRST. The least passage in thy life may prove an occasion of sin to thee. At what a little wicket, many times, a great sin enters, we daily see. David's eye did but casually light on Bath-sheba, and the good man's foot was presently in the devil's trap. Hast thou not then need to pray that God would set a guard about thy senses wherever thou goest? and to cry with him, "Keep back mine eyes from beholding vanity?" Dinah went but to give her neighbors, "the daughters of the land," a visit – which was but an ordinary civility – and we may imagine that she little thought, when she went out, of playing the strumpet before she came home; yet, alas! we read how she was deflowered! What need then hast thou, before thou goest forth, to charge God with the keeping of thee, that so thou mayest be in his fear from morning till night!

SECOND. No passage of thy life so small wherein thou mayest not fall into some great danger. How many have been choked with their food at their own table? – received their deadly wound by a beam from their own house? Knowest thou what will be the end of any action when thou beginnest it? Joseph was sent by his father to see his brethren in the field, and neither of them thought of a longer journey; yet this proved the sad occasion of his captivity in a strange land. Job's servants were destroyed with lightning from heaven when they were abroad about their master's business. Where canst thou be safe if heaven's eye be not on thee? A slip of thy foot as thou walkest, or a trip of thy horse as thou ridest, may break thy bones, yea thy neck. O what need, then, of a God to make thy path plain before thee! It is he that "preserveth man and beast"; and canst thou have faith to expect his protection when thou hast not a heart to bespeak it in thy humble prayers at his hand? What reason hath God to care for thy safety, who carest no more for his honor?

SECOND. TO PRAY ALWAYS MAY IMPORT AS MUCH AS TO PRAY IN ALL CONDITIONS; THAT IS, IN PROSPERITY AS WELL AS IN ADVERSITY

So Calvin takes it: *omni tempore perinde valet, atque tam prosperis quâm adversis* – it holds at all times equally, and as much in prosperity as in adversity. Indeed, when God doth afflict, he puts an especial season for prayer into our hands; but when he enlargeth our state, he doth not discharge us of the duty, as if we might then lay it aside, as the traveler doth his cloak when the weather is warm. Prayer is not a winter garment. It is then to be warn indeed; but not to be left off in the summer of prosperity. If you would find some at prayer you must stay till it thunders and lightens; not go to them except it be in a storm or tempest. These are like some birds that are never heard to cry or make a noise but in or against foul weather. This is not to pray always; not to serve God, but to serve ourselves of God; to visit God, not as a friend for love of his company, but as a mere beggar for relief of our present necessity; using prayer as that pope is said to have used preaching, for a net to compass in some mercy we want, and when the fish is got then to throw away the duty. Well, Christian, take heed of this; thou hast arguments enough to keep this duty always on its wheels, let thy condition be what it will.

Why we should pray in all conditions

FIRST. Pray in prosperity, that thou mayest speed when thou prayest in adversity. Own

God now, that he may acknowledge thee then. Shall that friend be welcome to us that never gives us a visit but when he comes to borrow? This is a right beggar's trick, but not a friend's part.

SECOND. Pray in prosperity, to clear thyself that thou didst not pray in hypocrisy when thou wert afflicted. One prayer now will be a better evidence for thy sincerity than a whole bundle of duties performed in adversity. Colors are better discerned and distinguished by daylight than by the candle in the night. I am sure the truth and plainness of our hearts in duty will be best discovered in prosperity. In affliction, even gracious souls have scruples upon their spirits that they seek themselves. Smart and pain, they fear, makes them cry till they remember that their acquaintance with God did not begin in their affliction, but that they took delight in his company before these straits drove them to him.

THIRD. Pray in prosperity, that thou mayest not be ensnared by thy prosperity. Ephraim and Manasseh were brethren, and so are plenty and forgetfulness – the signification of their names. Prosperity is no friend to the memory; therefore we are cautioned so much to beware when we are full, lest then we forget God: *magnus vir est cui præsens fælicitas si arrisit non irrisit* (Bern.) – he is a holy man indeed whose present prosperity doth not mock and abuse him when it smiles most pleasingly on him. O how hard it is to be pleased with it and not be ensnared by it! "Wine," Solomon saith, "is a mocker;" it soon puts him that is too bold with it to shame. Prosperity doth the same. A little of it makes us drunk, and then we know not what we do. This hath proved often an hour of temptation to the best of men. You shall find in Scripture the saints have got their saddest falls on the evenest ground. Noah, who had seen the whole world drowned in water, no sooner was he almost come to safe shore but himself is drowned in wine. David's heart was fixed in the wilderness; but his wanton eye wandered when upon the terrace of his palace. Health, honor, riches, and pleasures, with the rest of this world's enjoyments, they are like luscious wine. We cannot drink little of them, they are so sweet to our carnal palate; and we cannot bear much of them, because they are strong and heady, fuming up in pride and carnal confidence. Now prayer is an excellent preservative against the evil of this state.

1. As it spiritualizes our joy into thankfulness. It is carnal joy that is dreggy, and therefore soon putrefies. Now, as prayer in affliction refines the Christian's sorrow by breathing it forth into holy groans to God, whereby he is kept from sinful complaints of God and murmurings against him, thus here the Christian, by giving a spiritual vent to his joy in thanksgiving and praises to his God, is preserved from the degeneracy of carnal joy, that betrays the soul to many foul sins, if itself be not one. For this purpose it is that the apostle James cuts out this twofold channel for this double affection to run in: "Is any among you afflicted? let him pray. Is any merry? let him sing psalms," James 5:13. As if he should say, "Let the afflicted soul pray, that he may not murmur. Let the joyous saint sing psalms, that his joy turns not sensual." A carnal heart can easily be merry and jocund when he prospers; the saint alone is praiseful. The psalmist, speaking of the mariners delivered from storms at sea, which threatened their wreck, saith, "Then are they glad because they be quiet," Ps. 107:30. But this they may be and yet not thankful. Wherefore he adds his holy option, "O that men would praise the Lord for his goodness!"

2. By prayer the soul is led into the acquaintance of higher delights than are to be found in all his temporal enjoyments, and thereby is taken off from an inordinate valuation of them, because he knows where better are to be had. The true reason why men are puffed up with too high an opinion of worldly felicities is their ignorance of {the} spiritual.

3. Prayer is God's ordinance to sanctify our creature-comforts. Everything is "sanctified by the word of God and prayer," 1 Tim. 4:5. Now, this obtained, the Christian may safely drink of these streams. The unicorn hath now put in his horn to heal them; Satan shall not have such power to corrupt him in the use of them as another that bespeaks not God's blessing on them. There is a vanity and flatulency in every creature, which, if not corrected by prayer, breeds indigested humors in him that feeds on it.

FOURTH. In thy prosperity, Pray to show

thy dependence on God for what thou enjoyest. "Thou hidst thy face," saith David, "and I was troubled." Truly it is time for God to withdraw his hand when thou goest about to cut off his title. That enjoyment comes but as a guest which is not entertained by prayer. Solomon tells us of wings that our temporal mercies have. Now if anything can clip these and keep them from fleeing away, it is prayer. God would often have destroyed Israel, but Moses stood in the gap; their mercies were oft upon the wing, but that holy man's prayers stayed their flight. God's heart would not serve him to come over the back of his prayer and put that to shame. No; they shall live. But let them say, Moses" prayer begged their life. Now, if the prayer of a holy person could avail for others, and obtain a new lease for their lives, that were, many of them, none of the best; surely, then, the prayer of a saint may have great power with God for his own. Long life is promised to him that honors his earthly father. Prayer gives our heavenly Father the greatest honor. If, therefore, thou wouldst have thy life, or the life of any mercy, prolonged, forget not to pay him this tribute. Yea, would you transmit what God hath blessed you with to your posterity, the best way thou canst take is to lock thy estate up in God's hand by prayer. Whatever will thou makest, God is sure to be thy executor. Man may propose and purpose, but God disposeth. Engage him, and the care is taken for thy posterity.

FIFTH. Pray now, that thou mayest outlive the loss of thy prosperity. When prayer cannot prevail to keep a temporal mercy alive with thee, yet it will have a powerful influence to keep thy heart alive when that dies. O it is sad when a man's estate and comfort are buried in the same grave together! None will bear the loss of an enjoyment so patiently as he that was exercised in prayer while he had it. When Job was in his flourishing estate, his children alive, and all his other enjoyments, then was he a great trader with God in this duty. He "sanctified" his children every day. He did not bless himself in them, but sought the blessing of God for them; and see how comfortably he bears all: "The Lord gave, and the Lord hath taken away; blessed be the name of the Lord." The more David prayed for his child while

alive the fewer tears he shed for it when it was dead.

THIRD. TO PRAY ALWAYS IS TO PRAY DAILY
When the Christian keeps a constant daily exercise of this duty, prayer is not a holiday, but everyday work: "Every day will I bless thee; and I will praise thy name for ever and ever," Ps. 145:2. This was typified by "the daily sacrifice," called therefore "the continual burnt offering," Ex. 29:38; whereby was signified our daily need of seeking mercy at God's hands through Christ. When our Lord taught his disciples to pray, he bade them not to ask bread for a week, no, not for a morrow, but for the present day: "Give us this day our daily bread" – plainly signifying our duty to seek our bread every day of God. This surely was also the end why God gave the manna in such a portion as should not stuff their cupboards, and furnish them with a store for a month or a week, but be a just demensum – measure and sufficient allowance for a day, that so they might be kept in a daily dependence on God, and look up to him daily who carried the key of their pantry for them. And have not we the same necessities upon us with them? Our bodies are as weak as theirs, and cannot be preserved without a daily repast. Do we not depend on him for the bread of the day and the rest of the night? And he hath too good an opinion of his soul's constitution, who thinks it can live or thrive with yesterday's meal, without renewing his communion with God to-day. The mother would think her sucking child not well, if it should forsake the breast a whole day; so mayest thou conclude thy soul is not right, that can pass a day without craving any spiritual repast in prayer. If thy wants be not sufficient to keep the chariot of this duty on its wheels, yet the sins which thou daily renewest would drive thee every day to confess and beg pardon for them.

We are under a law not to let the sun go down upon our wrath against our brother. And dare we, who every day deserve God's wrath, let the sun go down before that controversy is taken up between God and us? In a word, every day hath its new mercies. "His compassions fail not; they are new every morning," Lam. 3:23. These new mercies contract a new debt, and God hath told us the way of payment, viz. a tribute of praise. Without this, we cannot expect a sanctified use of them. He is branded by all for a profane person that eats his meat and gives not thanks. And it would be thought a ridiculous excuse, should he say he gave thanks yesterday, and that should serve for this meal also. We have more mercies every day to bless God for than what is set on our tables. We wear mercies; we breathe mercies; we walk upon mercies; our whole life is but a passage from one mercy, to be entertained by another. As one cloth is drawn, another is laid for a new feast to be set on. Now, doth God every day anoint our head with fresh oil, and shall not we crown him with new praises? I will not enter into a discourse how oft a Christian should in a day pray. At least it must be twice, i.e. morning and night. Prayer must be the key of the morning and lock of the night. We show not ourselves Christians, if we do not open our eyes with prayer when we rise, and shut them again with the same key when we lie down at night. This answers to the morning and evening sacrifice in the law, which yet was so commanded as to leave room for those other free-will offerings which their zeal might prompt them to. Pray as oft as you please besides, so that your devotions justle not with the necessary duties of your particular callings; the oftener the more welcome. We read of David's "seven times a day." But be sure thou dost not retrench and cut God short of thy stated hours. "It is a good thing," saith the psalmist, "to give thanks unto the Lord, to shew forth thy lovingkindness in the morning, and thy faithfulness every night," Ps. 92:1, 2. God is alpha and omega. It is fit we should begin and end the day with his praise, who begins and ends it for us with his mercy.

Well, Christian, thou seest thy duty plainly laid before thee. As thou wouldst have God prosper thy labor in the day, and sweeten thy rest in the night, clasp them both together with thy morning and evening devotions. He that takes no care to set forth God's portion of time in the morning, doth not only rob God of his due, but is a thief to himself all the day after, by losing the blessing which a faithful prayer might bring from heaven on his undertakings. And he that closeth his eyes at night without

prayer, lies down before his bed is made. He is like a foolish captain in a garrison, who betakes himself to his rest before he hath set the watch for the city's safeguard. God is his people's keeper; but can he expect to be kept by him, that chargeth not the divine providence with his keeping? The angels, at his command, pitch their tents about his saints" dwellings. But as the drum calls the watch together, so God looks that, by humble prayer, we should beg of him their ministry and attendance about us. I shall shut up this discourse with one caution to be observed in your daily exercise of this duty.

Caution
Beware that thy constant daily performance of this duty doth not degenerate into a lifeless formality. What we do commonly, we are prone to be but ordinary and slighty in the doing. He is a rare Christian that keeps his course in prayer, and yet grows not customary to pray of mere course. The power of religion cannot be preserved without an outward form and order observed in its exercises; and yet very hard it is not to grow formal in those duties which we are daily conversant with. Many that are very neat and nice when their holiday suit is on their back, are yet too slovenly in wearing their everyday apparel. Thus, at a fast or on a Sabbath, our hearts haply are stirred up to some solemnity and spirituality becoming the duty of prayer, as being awed with the sacredness of the time and extraordinary weight of the work; but alas! in our everyday duties we are too slighty and slovenly.

Now, set thyself, Christian, with all thy might, to keep up the life and vigor of thy spirit in thy daily approaches to God. Be as careful to set an edge on thy graces before thy prayer, as on thy stomach before thy meal. Labor to come as hungry to this duty, as to eat thy dinner and supper. Now no expedient for this like a holy watch set about thy heart in the whole course of thy life. He that watcheth his heart all day, is most likely to find it at hand and in time for prayer at night. Whereas, loose walking breeds lazy praying. Be oft in the day putting thyself in mind what work waits for thee at night. Thou art to draw near unto thy God, and this will make thee afraid of doing anything in the day that will indispose thee, or make thee fear a chide from thy God, when thou appearest before him. That of the apostle is observable: "If ye call on the Father, who without respect of persons judgeth according to every man's work, pass the time of your sojourning here in fear," 1 Peter 1:17. As if he had said, "Do you mean to pray? then look to the whole course of your walking, that it be in the fear of God, or else you will have little heart to go about that work, and as little hope that he will bid you welcome, for he judgeth all persons that pray, not only by their prayers, but by their works and walking."

William Gurnall, 1617–79, A Directory for Prayer

Prayer and Thanksgiving

William Gurnall

"Be careful for nothing; but in everything by prayer and supplication with thanksgiving let your requests be made known unto God." Philippians 4:6

Prayer and supplication
"Praying ... with all perseverance and supplication for all saints." In praying for saints you must pray for all: I do not mean for quick and dead; prayer is a means to wait upon them in their way; at death, when they are at their journey's end, prayers are useless, and the wicked in that estate are beneath, the saints above, our prayers; we cannot help the wicked, the tree is fallen, and so it must lie. We read of a change the body shall have after death. Vile bodies may, but filthy souls cannot after death be made glorious: if they leave the body filthy, so shall they meet it at the resurrection. As the wicked are beyond our help, so the saints are above all need of our help ... We are to love all saints, therefore to pray for all. The new creature never wants its new nature; if God loves all His children, then wilt thou all thy brethren, or not one of them. When Paul commends Christians for this grace of love, he doth it thus: (Eph. i. 15) "After I heard of your faith in the Lord Jesus, and love unto all the saints." Now, if we love all, we cannot but pray for all.

Though we are to pray for all saints, yet some call for a more special remembrance at our hands: for instance, those that are near to us by bond of nature as well as of grace. "A brother beloved, specially to me, but how much more unto thee, both in the flesh, and in the Lord" (Philemon 16). You are. to pray particularly for those that are in distress: whoever you forget, remember these: this is a fit season for love. A friend for adversity is as proper as fire for a winter's day: Job's friends chose the right time to visit him, but took not the right course of improving their visit: had they spent the time in praying for him which they did in hot disputes with him, they had profited him, and pleased God more.

Prayer and thanksgiving
Prayer is a means to dispose the heart to praise. When David begins a psalm with prayer, he commonly ends it with praise. That Spirit which leads a soul out of itself to God for supply, will direct it to the same God with His praise. We do not borrow money of one man and return it to another. If God hath been thy strength, surely thou wilt make Him thy song. The thief comes not to thank a man for what he steals out of his yard. Mercies ill got are commonly as ill spent, because they are not sanctified, and so become fuel to feed lusts.

As a necessary ingredient in all our prayers: Let your requests be made known with thanksgiving (Phil. iv. 6). This spice must be in all our offerings. He that prays for a mercy he wants, and is not thankful for mercies received, may seem mindful of himself, but is forgetful of God, and so takes the right course to shut his prayers out of doors. God will not put His mercies into a rent purse; and such is an unthankful heart.

Daniel, when in the very shadow of death, the plot being laid to take away his life, prayed three times a day, and gave thanks before his God (Dan. vi. 10). To have heard him pray in that great strait would not have afforded so much matter for wonder; but to have his heart in tune for giving thanks in such a sad hour was admirable.

William Gurnall, The Christian in Complete Armor, Volume 1

When ye Pray

William Guthrie

"Therefore I say unto you, What thingsoever ye desire, when ye pray, believe that ye receive them, and ye shall have them." – Mark xi. 24.

I will now speak of those qualifications requisite in acceptable prayer – there being a vast difference between prayer and acceptable prayer – between our uttering words to God and praying by a gift, and praying by the promised Spirit of grace and supplication, in such a way and manner as to be accepted of God in what we pray for. This is the thing that doth so much take up the thoughts of the tender and serious Christian: Am I accepted of God in what I do? The words of the mouth many times run this way; and if ye heard the language of their heart, ye would hear much unto this purpose.

Now, the first requisite qualification of acceptable prayer to God is true and saving faith. And it is so requisite in prayer, that no man or woman can put up a suitable desire without it. And the having of this grace makes anything that they do in this exercise of a sweet smelling savor unto God. Hence, I shall observe, That in order to acceptance with God in all our addresses unto Him sound, saving, and justifying faith is very requisite and necessary. And the method is the following:

CONTENTS

1. I shall show you from Scripture that this is the thing that God requires in prayer to make it acceptable.

2. Show you what it is to pray in faith.

3. Show you what is faith's work in prayer.

4. Show you what is the nature and properties of this grace, which is so necessary in prayer, that without it God will not accept of prayer.

1. For the first of these, the Scripture makes this very clear and plain, in the words of the text: "Whatsoever ye desire, when ye pray, believe that ye receive them, and ye shall have them." As ever ye would be accepted of God, believe, and so, "Whatsoever thing ye shall ask in prayer believing, ye shall receive." "I will

therefore that men pray everywhere, lifting up holy hands, without wrath and doubting." That is, let faith be acted and exercised in our prayers. "Let us, therefore, come boldly unto the throne of grace, that we may obtain mercy, and find grace to help in time of need. Let us draw near with a true heart in full assurance of faith, having our hearts sprinkled from an evil conscience, and our bodies washed with pure water." So that the way to draw near to God acceptably is by faith. The apostle James allows any that lack wisdom, to ask it by faith. "If any of you lack wisdom, let him ask of God. But let him ask in faith, nothing wavering." So if you would obtain anything from me, says God, seek it in faith. And says the same apostle, "And the prayer of faith shall save the sick, and the Lord shall raise him up; and if he hath committed sins, they shall be forgiven him." Now, that which gives being and life to prayer is faith. Thus, for the first head, these Scriptures hold out that, in acceptable prayer, faith is requisite and altogether necessary.

2. The second thing is: To show what it is to pray in faith. I shall take it up in these six things, which ye may endeavor to keep in remembrance.

1. To pray in faith is to be endued with saving grace from the Lord. This grace of faith must be infused into the person that approaches unto God. For it is impossible that the person that wants faith can be acceptable to God – I mean not faith of miracles, or an historical faith, but true and justifying faith. This shows that all that are destitute of this grace are in a bad case. "For without faith it is impossible to please God." And this is the woeful case they are in that want faith, that never anything they do is acceptable to God; and this, again, is the noble privilege of those that have it, that all they do in duty is accepted of Him.

2. To pray in faith is not only to have this grace infused into you, but it is to have that grace in exercise in and about the particular petition ye would put up to God. Whatsoever thing ye ask, ye must have faith exercised about that particular, whether it be for soul or body; for yourself or for the Church; for spiritual or for temporal things.

3. To pray in faith is to make use of the grounds

of faith in our praying, viz., the word of promise; for the promises are the ground of our suit. So that in acceptable prayer faith makes use of this and that promise and turns the promise into a petition. This is faith's work. It is neither humility, nor self-denial that can do this. But faith takes this and the other promise, and holds it up to God, that He may make it out. "Remember the word unto thy servant, upon which thou hast caused me to hope."

4. To pray in faith is to make use of and to employ Christ the Mediator. So that the soul will never go to God but in the Mediator; and it looks for a return to its suits or petitions, only in and through the Mediator, Jesus Christ, and Him crucified. Says He Himself, "Whatsoever ye shall ask in my name, that will I do." That is, "Expect access to the Father in and through my name; look for a return in and through my name." We pray in faith when in all our addressee we are actually endeavoring to improve the merit and mediation of Him who is at the right hand of God the Father.

5. To pray in faith is to pray over the belly of all opposition. When, in human appearance, there is nothing but anger and wrath from God, and when the soul is under the apprehensions of His wrath, yet faith will come over all these unto God. When He is inflicting some judgment upon the person, and seems to be angry with the person, then faith goes over all and presses in unto God; that is to pray in faith. For instance, "I cried by reason of my affliction; I said, I am cast out of thy presence." Yet what does faith when in sense he is cast out of God's presence! Faith puts him upon supplicating God again. "Yet will I look again to thy holy temple."

6. To pray in faith is this: When the soul promises to itself on the ground of God's word an answer to the particular petition it is putting up to God. To pray in faith is not only to know well that the thing ye are seeking is warrantable and according to His will, but in some measure to have assurance (or endeavor after it) of an answer in absolute things, that is, if it be absolutely necessary they believe it shall be granted. As to conditional petitions, they believe that if it be good for them, they shall have what they ask. If they present a petition for those things that are absolutely necessary, whether in respect of themselves or His Church, it shall be sure unto them; and if their petition is for things conditional, either to themselves or the Church, if it be for their good it shall not be wanting. Ye see an instance to this purpose in Mic. vii. 7. All was then going wrong, yet, says he, "I will look unto the Lord; I will wait for the God of my salvation; my God will hear me :" as if he had said, "What then! I answer myself that God will hear me." Remember these six things which show what it is to pray in faith.

3. The third thing is: What is faith's work in prayer, or what is the work of this grace in a believer in his suits and supplications?

1. It instructs the person of his own need of the unsearchable riches that are in Christ. It makes him cry out, "O sinful man that I am? I have destroyed and undone myself." And, on the other hand, it informs the soul of its relief and outgate from that misery, and of the soul's portion that is to be had in Christ, and of the fullness thereof; so that there is not the least want, but there is a perfect and complete fullness in Christ, as ye may see in the case of the publican. What was the thing he prayed for? Says he, "God be merciful to me a sinner." Faith instructs as to his sin, and then as to the way of his relief and help from sin, viz., in Christ; so that faith's first work in prayer is to instruct a sinner of its own condition, and then of its supply, and help. And poor, poor are they that want this grace of faith; and rich, rich are they that have it.

2. Faith's work in prayer is to be the hand by which the soul takes hold of the remedy and relief that is in Christ, and offered by Him to us in the gospel. It is the soul's hand to lay hold of Christ and His fullness, as He is offered and held forth to us. As a poor man puts forth his hand to take that which is offered unto him, so it is with faith in prayer. It is called a receiving, and it is the very hand whereby Christ, and all that is to be had in Him, is to be received or laid hold of. This is an excellent mark in prayer.

3. The work of faith in prayer is, to enable the soul to wait patiently on God for a return of the petition it hath put up. Faith says, "Ye have prayed, and that is your duty; but see, Sirs, that ye stay still at His door until ye get an answer. Be not like those who shoot blunt-shot, and

never look where it goes. 'I will hear what God the Lord will speak.'" "I will stand on my watch, and set me on the tower to see what He will say to me," says faith to the soul. This is a good work of faith in prayer, to make our souls wait patiently on Him, while He is trying them with delays. It is faith that puts strength into our souls to make them patiently wait on, till God send an answer unto them.

4. It is true faith's work in prayer to make them judge aright of all the Lord's dispensations towards them, appeciably in or about the exercise of prayer. Faith says, "Look that ye construct aright of Him, and entertain not wrong thoughts of Him: although He gives you not His presence now, yet He will come." "He that will come, shall come, and shall not tarry." If He give you not in that measure that ye propose, see that ye fret not. If He seem to frown, you are then to abase yourselves as miserable wretches. What says David, "O my God, I cry in the day time, and thou hearest not. But thou art holy, O thou that inhabitest the praises of Israel." There is faith's work; he cried to God, and is not heard; but says he, "Thou art holy." As if he had said, "I aver that He is holy, if He should shut out my prayers, as it were, with hewn stone, and refuse to answer me till my dying day, yet Thou art holy." That is faith's work in prayer.

5. Faith's work in prayer is to take hold of the least meaning, may-be, or intimation from the Lord, and to lay hold of the least ground of hope of mercy; as a poor man takes hold of the least meaning of mercy from man. It was the exercise of the woman of Canaan in her prayer, when Christ upbraided her, saying, "What have I to do with thee? Should I give the children's bread to dogs?" "Truth, Lord," says she, "Thou hast given me some ground to expect help from Thee." "Truth, Lord, I acknowledge that I am a dog; but it is as true that dogs eat of the crumbs which fall from their master's table." Whereupon Christ says unto her, "O woman, great is thy faith. Thy faith hath taken hold of the least intimation, or may-be, as a ground of hope. Be it unto thee even an thou wilt." And this reproves those who fret if they get not what dish of meat they please; or if it pleases them not – they cast it from them. But if thou knewest what thou art, and how little thou

deservest, thou wouldst bless God, that thou art not in hell already.

6. Faith's work in prayer is to enjoin every praying faculty, or all that is within the soul, before God. For faith sets its desires in order. Faith makes it desire nothing but what God hath allowed in His word, and it will be nothing short of this. Again, it orders our zeal, so that it is not blind and preposterous: where faith rules it orders humility, so that the soul does not say in a sullen fit, "Lord, depart from me for; I am a sinful man." It orders sorrow for sin neither to be too little nor too great. It is faith's work to make the soul sorrow heartily before God: on the other hand it makes us guard against anxious sorrow. Then it orders hope that the soul may wait patiently for the answer or accomplishment of prayer. Thus it is faith's work to order all things within the soul, and put all things in a composed temper. So commanding is the grace of faith in a soul where it is, that it will let nothing be out of order.

7. Faith's work in a soul in prayer is to make it importunate in pressing for that which it prays for. Having the word of God for its ground, and the name of Christ for its encouragement, it importunately presses for the thing desired, and when He seems to say, "Ye shall not have it" it says, "I will not let Thee go." It was faith that made Jacob wrestle that night with God; says the angel, "Let me go, for the day breaketh. And he said, I will not let thee go, except thou bless me." And, "Moses," says the Lord, "will ye let me alone, that I may destroy this people." But says Moses, "If thou wilt forgive their sins; and if not, blot me out of thy book, which thou hast written." And the woman of Samaria, say what He would, harped still upon this string, "Lord, have mercy upon me."

8. Faith's work in prayer is to undertake for the soul to God, and for God to the soul. This is the very kernel of prayer. Faith says to the soul, "I assure thee that whatsoever God hath promised in His word, that He will give and perform." Faith says to the soul, "There is not a promise made to the Church, but it shall be accomplished; nor to itself in particular, but it shall be performed." So that this is the work of faith in prayer, to engage for the Lord that all the promises that He hath given shall be made

out and fulfilled unto them. On the other hand, faith engages the soul to wait patiently on for the accomplishment of all that the Lord bath promised. So that this is one of the mysteries of God; and it is lamentable that so many souls live strangers to God and to this work of faith, and do not consider the worth and excellency of this grace of faith. I dare say that we, His Church and people, would be as far above trouble this day as we are under it if we had faith and the lively exercise thereof. Those that have this are of all men the most happy, and those that want it are of all men the most miserable.

9. Faith's work is to make the soul to plead with God upon Scripture argument. Faith looks to what God hath promised, and makes use of all these promises in its approaches unto God in prayer. This ye may see in Moses pleading for the people. He pleads upon all the promises the Lord had made unto them, when they had provoked His anger to burn against them. And so Jeremiah pleads upon scriptural arguments, not for himself only, but for the people of his time, that the Lord would do some great thing for them. So that this is faith's work, to gather all the arguments contained in Scripture, and to pray that the Lord would do this and that according to His promise.

10. The work of faith in prayer in, to turn over all the suits that the supplicant puts up into the hand of Christ the Mediator, that for His sake, intercession, and mediation they may be accepted of God, and answered in things according to His will; which implies a disclaiming of any works or merit in the person's self that is praying. Says Daniel: "Cause thy face to shine upon thy sanctuary that is desolate, for the Lord's sake." Not for my sake, nor the people's sake, nor for anything that we can do, but for the Lord Jesus Christ's sake. He puts all the suits upon Christ's account, that in His name they may come before the Father and be accepted.

11. This is faith's work in prayer, to make the person praying keep at a due distance from God. Faith makes the person keep its own due room as unworthy – as dust and ashes. It teaches persons to give God His due room, as He is the high and lofty one; to have low thoughts of themselves, and high thoughts of God. Faith says to the soul, "Carry in subordination unto God; let not your words be rash, nor your thoughts and conceptions of Him unsuitable." Faith made Abraham say, "I have taken upon me to speak unto the Lord, which am but dust and ashes." It is an excellent work of faith, to make us to ascribe to Him that which is due to Him – glory, honor, and dominion for ever, and to take shame and confusion of face unto ourselves.

12. Faith's work in prayer is to furnish the supplicant with subject-matter of prayer, viz., to gather the promises that are here and there in the Bible. And then it not only furnishes matter, but it furnishes a mouth to speak unto God; it opens the mouth to speak unto God that which the soul hath gathered. Nay, it furnishes feet to go unto God with the matter gathered. Nor does faith only furnish matter, and a mouth to speak it, and feet to go to God with it, but it is as wings unto the soul, whereby it flies as it were with wings unto heaven with the petition that it hath to put up to Him for itself, or for His work, or for His Zion. Oh, hut this is an excellent work of faith! It makes them that wait upon the Lord "mount up as on eagles wings; and walk, and not be weary; and run, and not be faint."

13. It is faith's work in prayer to enable the soul to wait patiently till God give an answer to prayer. Faith is still petitioning and supplicating the Lord till He give a gracious return. To renew the self-same thing in prayer again and again, it being according to His will and warranted in His word, in the exercise of the self-same faith, is no tautology, though it were a hundred times to have the self-same suit. It was the way of the woman of Canaan. "I am not sent to thee," says Christ; yet she prays still, "Have mercy upon me, Lord." And it made Paul return his suit again and again. "For this thing I besought the Lord thrice." This is also an excellent work of faith. Nay, I may say, they never can do anything in the exercise of prayer that want this grace. Their prayers have no bones, strength, nor edge. They will never pierce heaven.

14. Faith's work in prayer is, to make the petitioner take up God aright as the object of prayer, and Christ Jesus as the only Mediator, and take up their own condition aright, that they may apply the promises accordingly. For

faith's work is to apprehend aright our Lord Jesus Christ the Angel of the covenant, and to apprehend our own soul's case and condition aright; as in Isa. xli. it is called a looking; as it makes them take up Him whom they are seeking, and themselves aright. This is faith's work in prayer. And,

Lastly, I shall add this. It is faith's work in prayer to enable the soul to prevail over, and, as it were, to command the Lord. The prayer of faith has a prevailing and commanding over the great and dreadful Lord. Hence it is said by James, "The fervent prayer of the righteous availeth much." And it healeth the sick. It is said of Jacob, "He had power over the angel, and prevailed." Says the Lord, "Concerning my sons and my daughters, command ye me." Thus the Almighty Maker of heaven and earth is content to be commanded by Him own creatures praying in faith, and in a manner prevailing over Him. This is only prayer animated by faith. Were it not so, your prayers would not go above the crown of your heads. It was faith that made Him yield to the woman of Canaan – "Be it unto thee, even as thou wilt." For I cannot keep it from thee. Thy faith has prevailed over Me." Now from all these, you may see the woeful case they are in, who want this grace; and the good and desirable case they are in, whom God hath endued with it.

4. The fourth thing is, What is the nature of this faith, which is a necessary and requisite qualification in prayer? That we may show you the worth and excellency of this grace, and the need folk have of it, I shall in these particulars hold it out, that ye may know it, and how to come by it.

1. This grace of saving faith is one of the main, choice and principal graces peculiar to the elect, and is the very root of all other graces. It in a manner, the kernel and life of all the rest, it being the only grace that closeth with Christ. "Add to your faith virtue; and to your virtue, knowledge." It is the first ground stone, and then add to it all the rest. All that folk go about, all the moral duties that some professed Christians perform, are but mere shadows for want of this.

2. This grace is one in all the elect, but not in a like measure in all. It is the self-same grace in all the elect. But you will say, How is that? For then one's faith would serve all. No, there are as many faiths, as particular persons of the elect; for it is not one in the elect as to the measure of it; for some may have a less, and some a greater degree of faith. But in this respect, it is one as to its closing with Christ, and embracing of Him as offered unto them in the gospel. it in the very self-same faith in all the elect. It was the self-same faith that was in Abraham, Isaac, and Jacob, that is in all the believers after them. The smallest as well as the greatest hath the self-same faith in substance. If this were considered, it might be comfortable to us. You will say, "The apostle Paul, and the rest of these worthy men, might plead confidently with God in their own behalf, and in the behalf of others." But, I say, if ye have fled to Christ, and closed with Him, ye may with confidence draw near to the throne of grace, to plead with God on your own, and on the behalf of others also.

3. This grace of faith may, yea, ought to increase in the saints of God. See Mark ix. 2., 2 Cor. x. 15, where the increase of faith is mentioned. And, "Remembering without ceasing your work of faith, and labor of love." This grace is said to grow. "The righteousness of God revealed in the gospel from faith to faith." It is a sin and a shame for Christians to be and continue at the same degree that at the first they were at. Where it is sound and real, it grows. And oh, but the Lord's people should endeavor much for the increase of faith, that they be not as children, ever doubting and staggering, so that they cannot live without sensible manifestations of God's favorable presence unto them.

4. Ye should know that as it ought to grow, so sometimes it may come under decay, as to the exercise of it; though there cannot be a decay of it as to its foundation. But I say, it may come under a decay as to its exercise; which proceeds either from security, or from Christians being too much elated in duty. When these give a stroke to faith, it may come under a decay. Christians, beware of security, for it is the bane of faith. Beware of uplifting in duties, for it likewise is the bane of faith. And in your afflictions pray to God for the increase of your faith, for trials and rods of affliction are for trials to faith, therefore ye ought to pray for faith that

are bearing the burden in the heat of the day.

5. The grace of faith is that which renders all that ye do acceptable unto God, "For without faith it is impossible to please God."

6. This grace of faith hath always with it obedience, and the bringing forth of good fruit to the glory of God and the edification of others, which fruit is called "the obedience of faith." Wherever it is, it leads still to sincere endeavors to keep up all the commandments of God By this, folk may know whether they have this grace or not.

7. This grace of faith apprehends things altogether beyond the reach of human reason, and brings these things home unto the man's own bosom. It makes things that are absent as if they were present; it brings that into the man's heart that he shall have to all eternity; it brings in God to the man; it brings in Christ to his bosom; it brings in the joys of heaven to his soul – hence it is said to be "the substance of things not seen." It was this that made Moses see Him that is invisible, and the eternal glory and happiness of the saints in heaven, whereupon he refused to be preferred in Pharaoh's court; and this is the nature of this grace which is so necessary and requisite a qualification in the duty of prayer. And,

8. This grace of faith is a most sincere cordial grace. It is called "faith unfeigned." It knows not what it is to have the winding by-gates that carnal reason and hellish policy find out. This grace of faith is downright and without guile.

9. The nature of this grace is, that it is firm, stable, and steadfast, and renders the person steadfast in whom it is: "Rooted and built up in him, and stablished in the faith." They are like growing trees that cannot be shaken; they are like mount Zion, that cannot be removed. When they are in a right frame, let the world turn upside down, they will not be afraid. But folk destitute of this grace, like weather-cocks, will never hold out in the storm. They may bear it a little, but will not endure unto the end. But they that trust in the Lord shall be stable as mount Zion; rooted and built up in Him, they can never be removed.

10. This grace of faith is altogether supernatural. It is wholly of God, and hath nothing of our own power in it. "Faith is not of ourselves, it is the gift of God." It descends from the Father

of lights, and by this ye may know where to find it; and if it he once infused into you, it can never be plucked out of your hearts again. They are fools that think to believe, without knowing God the Author of faith.

11. This grace hath the Word of God for its ground. It is not this or that minister said it; not this great man, nor that great man that said it; no, nothing will serve the believer until he gets this, "Thus saith the Lord."

12. This grace of faith is a knowing and intelligent grace, so that they, in whom it is, know somewhat of God, and of Jesus Christ, who is the immediate object of faith, and of the promises of the Gospel, and of their own case and condition. Says Christ, "And have known surely that I came out from thee, and have believed that thou didst send me," – hence sometimes it is called knowledge.

13. This grace is a lively, operative, and working grace. It makes the soul in which it is lively, diligent, and active in working the work of God. It is called "the work of faith." It puts folk upon working. Ye shall never see one who hath true faith, though he discerns it not, but he is busy; even though believers were not bidden – yea, though they were forbidden – they would read the Scripture, pray unto God, speak and confer with the Lord's people when under trouble or disquiet of mind, if they know them to be such as they might safely communicate their mind unto.

14. This grace is a most precious grace in respect of God, the author of it; in respect of Christ, the object of it; and in respect of the Gospel, the means of attaining to it; and in respect of salvation, the end of it. Oh, but it is precious, and makes those that have it precious unto God.

15. It is a most conquering and overcoming grace; "It overcometh the world and the devil;" it is the shield that quenches all his fiery darts.

16. I shall add that it is a purifying and cleansing grace, for it gives the person no rest until he has recourse unto the fountain of His blood. Says John, "He that hath this hope in him, purifieth himself, even as he is pure." Not only to be reformed outwardly, but inwardly. By these things ye may see what this grace of faith is; and by some of them ye may know if ye have it, and how ye may get it. Withal ye may

see the need ye have of it. If ye would go to God acceptably – if ye would bear a storm – if ye would have life – then study faith. If ye get it not, ye shall never see life, and nothing that ye do shall be acceptable to God. Remember these things, lay them to heart, and do not think that it will he enough to hear them; for how will ye look death in the face who never studied this grace! How will ye wade the fords of Jordan to eternity? And how shall ye be able to answer God in the great day of accounts? If ye would get safe through all these, labor to obtain this grace of faith. The Lord help you so to do.

William Guthrie, 1620–65

A Short and Very Easy Method of Prayer

Madame Guyon

A short and very easy method of prayer; which all can practice with the greatest facility, and arrive in a short time, by its means, at a high degree of perfection.

"Walk before me and be thou perfect." – Gen. xvii.

1. THE AUTHOR'S PREFACE

This little treatise, conceived in great simplicity, was not originally intended for publication. It was written for a few individuals, who were desirous of loving God with all their heart. Many, however, because of the profit they received in reading the manuscript, wished to obtain copies, and, on this account alone, it was committed to the press. It still remains in its original simplicity. It contains no censure on the various divine leadings of others; on the contrary, it enforces the received teachings. The whole is submitted to the judgment of the learned and experienced; requesting them, however, not to stop at the surface, but to enter into the main design of the author, which is to induce the whole world to love God, and to serve Him with comfort and success, in a simple and easy manner, adapted to those little ones who are unqualified for learned and deep researches, but who earnestly desire to be truly devoted to God. An unprejudiced reader will find, hidden under the most common expressions, a secret unction, which will excite him to seek after that happiness which all should wish to enjoy. In asserting that perfection is easily attained, the word facility, is used; because God is, indeed found with facility, when we seek Him within ourselves. But some, perhaps, may urge that passage in St. John "Ye shall seek me, and shall not find me," (vii. 34); this apparent difficulty, however, is removed by another passage, where He, who cannot contradict himself, has said to all, "Seek and ye shall find," (Matt. vii. 7). It is true, indeed, that he who would seek God, seeks Him where He is not; and, therefore, it is added, "Ye shall die in your sins." But he, who will take some trouble to seek God in his own heart, and sincerely forsake his sin, that he may draw near unto Him, shall infallibly find Him. A life of piety appears so frightful to many, and prayer of such difficult attainment, that they are discouraged from taking a single step towards it. But as the apprehended difficulty of an undertaking often causes despair of succeeding and reluctance in commencing, so its desirableness, and the idea that it is easy to accomplish, induce us to enter upon its pursuit with pleasure, and to pursue it with vigor. The advantages and facility of this way are therefore set forth in the following treatise. O were we once persuaded of the goodness of God toward his poor creatures, and of his desire to communicate Himself to them, we should not create ideal monsters, nor so easily despair of obtaining that good which He is so earnest to bestow: "He that spared not his own Son, but delivered him up for us all; how shall He not, with him, also freely give us all things?" (Rom. viii. 32). It needs only a little courage and perseverance; we have enough of both in our temporal concerns, but none at all in the one thing needful, (Luke x. 42). If any think that God is not easily to be found in this way, let them not on my testimony alter their minds, but let them try it, and their own experience will convince them, that the reality far exceeds all my representations of it. Beloved reader, pursue this little tract with a sincere and candid spirit, in lowliness of mind, and not with an inclination to criticize, and you will not fail to reap profit from it. It was written with a desire that you might wholly devote yourself to God; receive it then with a like desire: for it has no other design than to invite the simple and the child-like to approach their father, who delights in the humble confidence of his children, and is greatly grieved at their distrust. With a sincere desire, therefore, for your salvation, seek nothing from the unpretending method here proposed, but the love of God, and you shall assuredly obtain it. Without setting up our opinions above those of others, we mean only with sincerity to declare, from our own experience and the experience of others, the happy effects produced by thus simply following after the Lord. As this treatise was intended only to instruct in prayer, nothing is said of many things which we esteem, because they do not immediately relate to our main subject. It is, however, beyond a doubt, that nothing will be found herein to offend, provided it be read in the spirit with which it was written. And it is still more certain, that those who in right earnest make trial of the way, will find we have written the truth. It is Thou alone, O holy Jesus, who lovest simplicity and innocence, "and whose delight is to dwell with the children of men," (Prov. viii. 31), with those who are, indeed, willing to become "little children," (Matt. xviii. 3); it is Thou alone, who canst render this little work of any value, by imprinting it on the heart, and leading those who read it to seek Thee within themselves, where Thou reposest as in the manger, waiting to receive proofs of their love, and to give them testimony of thine. They lose these advantages by their own fault. But it belongeth unto thee, O child Almighty! uncreated Love! silent and all-containing Word! to make thyself loved, enjoyed and understood. Thou canst do it; and I know Thou wilt do it by this little work, which belongeth entirely to Thee, proceedeth wholly from Thee, and tendeth only to Thee!

CHAPTER 1
INTRODUCTION

1. That all are called to prayer, and by the aid of ordinary grace may put up the prayer of the heart, which is the great means of salvation, and which can be offered at all times, and by the most uninstructed. All are capable of prayer, and it is a dreadful misfortune that almost all the world have conceived the idea that they are not called to prayer. We are all called to prayer, as we are all called to salvation. Prayer is nothing but the application of the heart to God, and the internal exercise of love. St. Paul has enjoined us to "pray without ceasing" (1 Thess. v. 17); and our Lord bids us watch and pray, (Mark xiii. 33,37): all therefore may, and all ought to practice prayer. I grant that meditation is attainable but by few, for few are capable of it; and therefore, my beloved brethren who are athirst for salvation, meditative prayer is not the prayer which God requires of you, nor which we would recommend.

2. Let all pray: you should live by prayer, as you should live by love. "I counsel you to buy of me gold tried in the fire, that ye may be rich" (Rev. iii. 18). This is very easily obtained, much more easily than you can conceive. Come all ye that are athirst to the living waters, nor lose your precious moments in hewing our cisterns that will hold no water (John vii. 37; Jer. ii. 13). Come ye famishing souls, who find naught to satisfy you; come, and ye shall be filled! Come, ye poor afflicted ones, bending beneath your load of wretchedness and pain, and ye shall be consoled! Come, ye sick, to your physician, and be not fearful of approaching him because ye are filled with diseases; show them, and they shall be healed! Children, draw near to your Father, and he will embrace you in the arms of love! Come ye poor, stray, wandering sheep, return to your Shepherd! Come, sinners, to your Savior! Come ye dull, ignorant, and illiterate, ye who think yourselves the most incapable of prayer! ye are more peculiarly called and adapted thereto. Let all without exception come, for Jesus Christ hath called ALL. Yet let not those come who are without a heart; they are excused; for there must be a heart before there can be love. But who is without a heart? O come, then, give this heart to God; and here learn how to make the donation.

3. All who are desirous of prayer, may easily pray, enabled by those ordinary graces and gifts of the Holy Spirit which are common to all men. Prayer is the key to perfection, and the sovereign good; it is the means of delivering us from every vice, and obtaining us every virtue; for the one great means of becoming perfect, is to walk in the presence of God. He himself hath said, "Walk before me, and be thou perfect"

(Gen. xvii. 1). It is by prayer alone that we are brought into his presence, and maintained in it without interruption.

4. You must, then, learn a species of prayer which may be exercised at all times; which does not obstruct outward employments; which may be equally practiced by princes, kings, prelates, priests and magistrates, soldiers and children, tradesmen, laborers, women, and sick persons; it is not the prayer of the head, but of the heart. It is not a prayer of the understanding alone, for the mind of man is so limited in its operations that it can have but one object at a time; but it is the prayer of the heart which is not interrupted by the exercises of reason. Nothing can interrupt this prayer but disordered affections; and when once we have enjoyed God, and the sweetness of his love, we shall find it impossible to relish aught but himself.

5. Nothing is so easily obtained as the possession and enjoyment of God. He is more present to us than we are to ourselves. He is more desirous of giving Himself to us than we are to possess Him; we only need to know how to seek Him, and the way is easier and more natural to us than breathing. Ah! ye who think yourselves so dull and fit for nothing, by prayer you may live on God himself with less difficulty or interruption that you live on the vital air. Will it not then be highly sinful to neglect prayer? But doubtless you will not, when you have learnt the method, which is the easiest in the world.

CHAPTER 2

1. First degree of prayer, practiced in two ways; one by reading and meditation, the other by meditation alone.

2,3. Rules and methods of meditation.

4. Remedies for its difficulties.

1. There are two ways of introducing some important practical or speculative truth, always preferring the practical, and proceeding thus: whatever truth you have chosen, read only a small portion of it, endeavoring to taste and digest it, to extract the essence and substance of it, and proceed no farther while any savor or relish remains in the passage: then take up your book again, and proceed as

before, seldom reading more than half a page at a time. It is not the quantity that is read, but the manner of reading, that yields us profit. Those who read fast, reap no more advantage, than a bee would by only skimming over the surface of the flower, instead of waiting to penetrate into it, and extract its sweets. Much reading is rather for scholastic subjects, than divine truths; to receive profit from spiritual books, we must read as I have described; and I am certain that if that method were pursued, we should become gradually habituated to pray by our reading, and more fully disposed for its exercise.

2. Meditation, which is the other method, is to be practiced at an appropriated season, and not in the time of reading. I believe that the best manner of meditating is as follows: When by an act of lively faith, you are placed in the presence of God, read some truth wherein there is substance; pause gently thereon, not to employ the reason, but merely to fix the mind; observing that the principal exercise should ever be the presence of God, and that the subject, therefore, should rather serve to stay the mind, than exercise it in reasoning. Then let a lively faith in God immediately present in our inmost souls, produce an eager sinking into ourselves, restraining all our senses from wandering abroad: this serves to extricate us, in the first instance, from numerous distraints, to remove us far from external objects, and to bring us nigh to God, who is only to be found in our inmost center, which is the Holy of Holies wherein he dwells. He has even promised to come and make his abode with him that doeth his will. (John xiv. 23.) St. Augustine blames himself for the time he lost in not having sought God, from the first, in this manner of prayer.

3. When we are thus fully entered into ourselves, and warmly penetrated throughout with a lively sense of the Divine presence; when the senses are all recollected, and withdrawn from the circumference to the center, and the soul is sweetly and silently employed on the truths we have read, not in reasoning, but in feeding thereon, and animating the will by affection, rather than fatiguing the understanding by study; when, I say, the affections are in this state, (which, however difficult it

may appear at first, is, as I shall hereafter show, easily attainable,) we must allow them sweetly to repose, and, as it were, swallow what they have tasted. For as a person may enjoy the flavor of the finest viands in mastication, yet receive no nourishment from them, if he does not cease the action and swallow the food; so when our affections are enkindled, if we endeavor to stir them up yet more, we extinguish the flame, and the soul is deprived of its nourishment. We should, therefore, in a repose of love, full of respect and confidence, swallow the blessed food we have received. This method is highly necessary, and will advance the soul more in a short time, than any other in years.

4. But as I have said that our direct and principal exercise should consist in the contemplation of the Divine presence, we should be exceedingly diligent in recalling our dissipated senses, as the most easy method of overcoming distractions; for a direct contest only serves to irritate and augment them; whereas, by sinking within, under a view by faith, of a present God, and simply recollecting ourselves, we wage insensibly very successful, though indirect war with them. It is proper here to caution beginners against wandering from truth to truth, and from subject to subject; the right way to penetrate every divine truth, to enjoy its full relish, and to imprint it on the heart, is to dwell upon it whilst its savor continues. Though recollection is difficult in the beginning, from the habit the soul has acquired of being always abroad, yet, when by the violence it has done itself, it becomes a little accustomed to it, the process is soon render perfectly easy; and this partly from the force of habit, and partly because God, whose one will towards his creatures is to communicate himself to them, imparts abundant grace, and an experimental enjoyment of his presence, which very much facilitate it.

CHAPTER 3

1. Method of meditative prayer for those who cannot read;

2,3. Applied to the Lord's Prayer and to some of the attributes of God.

4. Transition from the first to the second degree of prayer.

1. Those who cannot read books, are not, on that account, excluded from prayer. The great book which teaches all things, and which is written all over, within and without, is Jesus Christ himself. The method they should practice is this: they should first learn this fundamental truth, that "the kingdom of God is within them," (Luke xvii. 21), and that it must be sought there only. It is as incumbent on the clergy to instruct their parishioners in prayer, as in their catechism. It is true they tell them the end of their creation; but they do not give them sufficient instructions how they may attain it. They should be taught to begin by an act of profound adoration and annihilation before God, and closing the corporeal eyes, endeavor to open those of the soul; they should then collect themselves inwardly, and by a lively faith in God, as dwelling within them, pierce into the divine presence; not suffering the senses to wander abroad, but holding them as much as may be in subjection.

2. They should then repeat the Lord's prayer in their native tongue; pondering a little upon the meaning of the words, and the infinite willingness of that God who dwells within them to become, indeed, "their father." In this state let them pour out their wants before him; and when they have pronounced the word, "father," remain a few moments in a reverential silence, waiting to have the will of this their heavenly Father made manifest to them. Again, the Christian, beholding himself in the state of a feeble child, soiled and sorely bruised by repeated falls, destitute of strength to stand, or of power to cleanse himself, should lay his deplorable situation open to his Father's view in humble confusion; occasionally intermingling a word or two of love and grief, and then again sinking into silence before Him. Then, continuing the Lord's prayer, let him beseech this King of Glory to reign in him, abandoning himself to God, that He may do it, and acknowledging his right to rule over him. If they feel an inclination to peace and silence, let them not continue the words of the prayer so long as this sensation holds; and when it subsides, let them go on with the second petition, "thy will be done on earth as it is in heaven!" upon which let these humble suppliants beseech God to accomplish in them, and

by them, all his will, and let them surrender their hearts and freedom into his hands, to be disposed of as He pleases. When they find that the will should be employed in loving, they will desire to love, and will implore Him for his love; but all this will take place sweetly and peacefully: and so of the rest of the prayer, in which the clergy may instruct them. But they should not burthen themselves with frequent repetitions of set forms, or studied prayers; for the Lord's prayer once repeated as I have just described, will produce abundant fruit.

3. At other times, they may place themselves as sheep before their Shepherd, looking up to Him for their true food: O divine Shepherd, Thou feedest thy flock with Thyself, and art indeed their daily bread. They may also represent to him the necessities of their families: but let all be done from this principal and one great view of faith, that God is within them. All our imaginations of God amount to nothing; a lively faith in his presence is sufficient. For we must not form any image of the Deity, though we may of Jesus Christ, beholding him in his birth, or his crucifixion, or in some other state or mystery, provided the soul always seeks Him in its own center. On other occasions, we may look to him as a physician, and present for his healing virtue all our maladies; but always without perturbation, and with pauses from time to time, that the silence, being mingled with action, may be gradually extended, and our own exertion lessened; till at length, by continually yielding to God's operations, He gains the complete ascendancy, as shall be hereafter explained.

4. When the divine presence is granted us, and we gradually begin to relish silence and repose, this experimental enjoyment of the presence of God introduces the soul into the second degree of prayer, which, by proceeding in the manner I have described, is attainable as well by the illiterate as by the learned; some privileged souls, indeed, are favored with it even from the beginning.

CHAPTER 4

1. Second degree of prayer, called here "The prayer of simplicity." At what time we reach it.

2. How to offer and continue it.

3. Requisites to offering it acceptably.

1. Some call the second degree of prayer Contemplation, The prayer of faith and stillness, and others call it The prayer of simplicity. I shall here use this latter appellation, as being more just than that of contemplation, which implies a more advanced state than that I am now treating of. When the soul has been for some time exercised in the way I have mentioned, it gradually finds that it is enabled to approach God with facility; that recollection is attended with much less difficulty, and that prayer becomes easy, sweet, and delightful: it recognizes that this is the true way of finding God, and feels that " his name is as ointment poured forth" (Cant. i. 3). The method must now be altered, and that which I describe must be pursued with courage and fidelity, without being disturbed at the difficulties we may encounter in the way.

2. First, as soon as the soul by faith places itself in the presence of God, and becomes recollected before Him, let it remain thus for a little time in respectful silence. But if, at the beginning, in forming the act of faith, it feels some little pleasing sense of the Divine presence, let it remain there without being troubled for a subject, and proceed no farther, but carefully cherish this sensation while it continues. When it abates, it may excite the will by some tender affection; and if, by the first moving thereof, it finds itself reinstated in sweet peace, let it there remain; the fire must be gently fanned, but as soon as it is kindled, we must cease our efforts, lest we extinguish it by our activity.

3. I would warmly recommend to all, never to finish prayer without remaining some little time afterward in a respectful silence. It is also of the greatest importance for the soul to go to prayer with courage, and to bring with it such a pure and disinterested love, as seeks nothing from God, but to please Him, and to do his will; for a servant who only proportions his diligence to his hope of reward, is unworthy of any recompense. Go then to prayer, not desiring to enjoy spiritual delights, but to be just as it pleases God; this will preserve your spirit tranquil in aridities as well as in consolation, and prevent your being surprised at the apparent repulses or absence of God.

CHAPTER 5

On various matters occurring in or belonging to the degree of prayer, that is to say,

1. On aridities; which are caused by deprivation of the sensible presence of God for an admirable end, and which are to be met by acts of solid and peaceful virtue of mind and soul.

2. Advantages of this course.

1. Though God has no other desire than to impart Himself to the loving soul that seeks Him, yet He frequently conceals Himself from it, that it may be roused from sloth, and impelled to seek Him with fidelity and love. But with what abundant goodness does He recompense the faithfulness of his beloved! And how often are these apparent withdrawings of Himself succeeded by the caresses of love! At these seasons we are apt to believe that it proves our fidelity, and evinces a greater ardor of affection to seek Him by an exertion of our own strength and activity; or that such a course will induce Him the more speedily to revisit us. No, dear souls, believe me, this is not the best way in this degree of prayer; with patient love, with self-abasement and humiliation, with the reiterated breathings of an ardent but peaceful affection, and with silence full of veneration, you must await the return of the Beloved.

2. Thus only can you demonstrate that it is Himself alone, and his good pleasure, that you seek; and not the selfish delights of your own sensations in loving Him. Hence it is said (Eccles. ii. 2,3): "Be not impatient in the time of dryness and obscurity; suffer the suspensions and delays of the consolations of God; cleave unto him, and wait upon him patiently, that thy life may increase and be renewed." Be patient in prayer, though during your whole lifetime you should do nothing else than wait the return of the Beloved in a spirit of humiliation, abandonment, contentment, and resignation. Most excellent prayer! and it may be intermingled with the sighings of plaintive love! This conduct indeed is most pleasing to the heart of God, and will, above all others, compel his return.

CHAPTER 6

1, 2. On the abandonment of self to God, its fruit, and its irrevocableness.

3. Its nature; God requires it.

4. Its practice.

1. Here we must begin to abandon and give up our whole existence to God, from the strong and positive conviction, that the occurrences of every moment result from his immediate will and permission, and are just such as our state requires. This conviction will make us content with everything; and cause us to regard all that happens, not from the side of the creature, but from that of God. But, dearly beloved, whoever you are who sincerely wish to give yourselves up to God, I conjure you, that after having once made the donation, you take not yourselves back again; remember, a gift once presented, is no longer at the disposal of the giver.

2. Abandonment is a matter of the greatest importance in our progress; it is the key to the inner court; so that he who knows truly how to abandon himself, will soon become perfect. We must therefore continue steadfast and immovable therein, without listening to the voice of natural reason. Great faith produces great abandonment; we must confide in God, "hoping against hope" (Rom. iv. 18).

3. Abandonment is the casting off all selfish care, that we may be altogether at the divine disposal. All Christians are exhorted to abandonment; for it is said to all; "Take no thought for the morrow; for your Heavenly Father knoweth that ye have need of all these things (Matt. vi. 32–34). "In all thy ways acknowledge him, and he shall direct thy paths" (Prov. iii. 6.) "Commit thy works unto the Lord and thy thoughts shall be established" (Prov. xvi. 3). "Commit thy way unto the Lord; trust also in Him and He will bring it to pass" (Psalm xxxvii. 5). Our abandonment, then, should be, both in respect to external and internal things, an absolute giving up of all our concerns into the hands of God, forgetting ourselves and thinking only of Him; by which the heart will remain always disengaged, free, and at peace.

4. It is practiced by continually losing our own will in the will of God; renouncing every private inclination as soon as it arises, however good it may appear, that we may stand in indifference with respect to ourselves, and only

will what God has willed from all eternity; resigning ourselves in all things, whether for soul or body, for time or eternity; forgetting the past, leaving the future to Providence, and devoting the present to God; satisfied with the present moment, which brings with it God's eternal order in reference to us, and is as infallible a declaration of his will, as it is inevitable and common to all; attributing nothing that befalls us to the creature, but regarding all things in God, and looking upon all, excepting only our sins, as infallibly proceeding from Him. Surrender yourselves then to be led and disposed of just as God pleases, with respect both to your outward and inward state.

CHAPTER 7

1. On suffering: that it should be accepted from the hand of God.

2. Its use and profit.

3. Its practice.

1. Be patient under all the sufferings God sends; if your love to Him be pure, you will not seek Him less on Calvary, than on Tabor; and surely, He should be as much loved on that as on this, since it was on Calvary that he made the greatest display of love. Be not like those who give themselves to Him at one season, only to withdraw from Him at another. They give themselves only to be caressed, and wrest themselves back again, when they are crucified; or at least turn for consolation to the creature.

2. No, beloved souls, you will not find consolation in aught but in the love of the cross, and in total abandonment; who savoreth not the cross, savoreth not the things that be of God. (See Matt. xvi. 23.) It is impossible to love God without loving the cross; and a heart that savors the cross, finds the bitterest things to be sweet; "To the hungry soul every bitter thing is sweet" (Prov. xxvii. 7): because it finds itself hungering for God, in proportion as it is hungering for the cross. God gives us the cross, and the cross gives us God. We may be assured that there is an internal advancement, when there is progress in the way of the cross; abandonment and the cross go hand in hand together.

3. As soon as anything is presented in the form of suffering, and you feel a repugnance, resign yourself immediately to God with respect to it, and give yourself up to Him in sacrifice: you will then find, that when the cross arrives, it will not be so very burthensome, because you have yourself desired it. This, however does not prevent you from feeling its weight, as some have imagined; for when we do not feel the cross, we do not suffer. A sensibility to suffering is one of the principal parts of suffering itself. Jesus Christ himself chose to endure its utmost rigors. We often bear the cross in weakness, at other times in strength; all should be alike to us in the will of God.

CHAPTER 8

1. On mysteries; God gives them in this state in reality.

2,3. We must let Him bestow or withhold as seems good to Him, with a loving regard to his will.

1. It will be objected, that, by this method, we shall have no mysteries imprinted on our minds; but so far is this from bring the case, that it is the peculiar means of imparting them to the soul. Jesus Christ, to whom we are abandoned, and whom we follow as the way, whom we hear as the truth, and who animates us as the life (John xiv. 6), in imprinting himself on the soul, impresses there the characters of his different states. To bear all the states of Jesus Christ, is a much greater thing, than merely to meditate about them. St. Paul bore in his body the states of Jesus Christ; "I bear in my body," says he, "the marks of the Lord Jesus" (Gal. vi. 17); he does not say that he reasoned thereon.

2. In this state of abandonment Jesus Christ frequently communicates some peculiar views, or revelations of his states: these we should thankfully accept, and dispose ourselves for what appears to be his will; receiving equally whatever frame He may bestow, and having no other choice, but that of ardently reaching after Him, of dwelling ever with Him, and of sinking into nothingness before Him, and accepting indiscriminately all his gifts, whether darkness or illumination, fecundity or barrenness, weakness or strength, sweetness or bitterness,

temptations, distractions, pain, weariness, or uncertainty; and none of all these should, for one moment, retard our course.

3. God engages some, for whole years, in the contemplation and enjoyment of a single mystery, the simple view or contemplation of which recollects the soul; let them be faithful to it; but as soon as God is pleased to withdraw this view from the soul, let it freely yield to the deprivation. Some are very uneasy at their inability to meditate on certain mysteries; but without reason, since an affectionate attachment to God includes in itself every species of devotion, and whoever is calmly united to God alone, is, indeed, most excellently and effectually applied to every divine mystery. Whoever loves God loves all that appertains to him.

CHAPTER 9

1.2. On virtue. All virtues come with God and are solidly and deeply implanted in the soul in this degree of the prayer of the heart.

3. This takes place without difficulty.

1. It is thus that we acquire virtue with facility and certainty; for as God is the principle of all virtues, we inherit all in the possession of Himself; and in proportion as we approach toward his possession, in like proportion do we receive the most eminent virtues. For all virtue is but as a mask, an outside appearance mutable as our garments, if it be not bestowed from within; then, indeed, it is genuine, essential, and permanent: "The King's daughter is all glorious within," says David (Psalm xlv. 13). These souls, above all others, practice virtue in the most eminent degree, though they advert not to any particular virtue. God, to whom they are united, leads them to the most extensive practice of it; He is exceedingly jealous over them, and permits them not the least pleasure.

2. What a hungering for sufferings have those souls, who thus glow with divine love! How would they precipitate themselves into excessive austerities, where they permitted to pursue their own inclinations! They think of naught save how they may please their Beloved; and they begin to neglect and forget themselves; and as their love to God increases, so do self-detestation and disregard of the creature.

3. O were this simple method once acquired, a way so suited to all, to the dull and ignorant as well as to the most learned, how easily would the whole church of God be reformed! Love only is required: "Love," says St. Augustine, "and then do what you please." For when we truly love, we cannot have so much as a will to do anything that might offend the object of our affections.

CHAPTER 10

1. On mortification: that it is never perfect when it is solely exterior.

2. But it must be accomplished by dwelling upon God within.

3. Which, however, does not dispense with its outward practice to some degree.

4. Hence, a sound conversion.

1. I say further, that, in any other way, it is next to impossible to acquire a perfect mortification of the senses and passions. The reason is obvious: the soul gives vigor and energy to the senses, and the senses raise and stimulate the passions; a dead body has neither sensations nor passions, because its connection with the soul is dissolved. All endeavors merely to rectify the exterior impel the soul yet farther outward into that about which it is so warmly and zealously engaged. Its powers are diffused and scattered abroad; for, its whole attention being immediately directed to austerities and other externals, it thus invigorates those very senses it is aiming to subdue. For the senses have no other spring whence to derive their vigor than the application of the soul to themselves, the degree of their live and activity being proportioned to the degree of attention which the soul bestows upon them. This life of the senses stirs up and provokes the passions, instead of suppressing or subduing them; austerities may indeed enfeeble the body, but for the reasons just mentioned, can never take off the keenness of the senses, nor lessen their activity.

2. The only method of effecting this, is inward recollection, by which the soul is turned wholly and altogether inward, to possess a present God. If it direct all its vigor and energy within, this simple act separates it from the senses, and, employing all its powers

internally, it renders them faint; and the nearer it draws to God, the farther is it separated from self. Hence it is, that those in whom the attractions of grace are very powerful, find the outward man altogether weak and feeble, and even liable to faintings.

3. I do not mean by this, to discourage mortification; for it should ever accompany prayer, according to the strength and state of the person, or as obedience demands. But I say, that mortification should not be our principal exercise; nor should we prescribe to ourselves such and such austerities, but simply following the internal attractions of grace, and being occupied with the divine presence, without thinking particularly on mortification, God will enable us to perform every species of it. He gives those who abide faithful to their abandonment to Him, no relaxation until He has subdued everything in them that remains to be mortified. We have only, then, to continue steadfast in the utmost attention to God, and all things will be perfectly done. All are not capable of outward austerities, but all are capable of this. In the mortification of the eye and ear, which continually supply the busy imagination with new subjects, there is little danger of falling into excess; but God will teach us this also, and we have only to follow his Spirit.

4. The soul has a double advantage by proceeding thus; for, in withdrawing from outward objects, it constantly draws nearer to God; and besides the secret sustaining and preserving power and virtue which it receives, it is farther removed from sin the nearer it comes to Him; so that its conversion becomes firmly established as a matter of habit.

CHAPTER 11

1. On the perfect conversion which is the result of this kind of prayer; how it is accomplished.

2,3. Two of its aids; the drawing of God, and the tendency of the soul to its center.

4. Its practice.

1. "Turn ye unto Him from whom the children of Israel have so deeply revolted" (Isa. xxxi. 6). Conversion is nothing more than turning from the creature in order to return to God. It is not perfect (however good and essential to salvation) when it consists simply in turning from sin to grace. To be complete, it should take place from without inwardly. When the soul is once turned toward God, it finds a wonderful facility in continuing steadfast in conversion; and the longer it remains thus converted, the nearer it approaches and the more firmly it adheres to God; and the nearer it draws to Him, it is of necessity the farther removed from the creature, which is so contrary to Him; so that it is so effectually established in conversion, that the state becomes habitual, and as it were natural. Now, we must not suppose that this is effected by a violent exertion of its own powers; for it is not capable of, nor should it attempt any other co-operation with divine grace, than that of endeavoring to withdraw itself from external objects, and to turn inwards; after which it has nothing farther to do, than to continue firm in its adherence to God.

2. God has an attractive virtue which draws the soul more and more powerfully to Himself, and in attracting, He purifies; just as it is with a gross vapor exhaled by the sun, which, as it gradually ascends, is rarified and rendered pure; the vapor, indeed, contributes to its ascent only by its passivity; but the soul co-operates freely and voluntarily. This kind of introversion is very easy and advances the soul naturally, and without effort, because God is our center. The center always exerts a very powerful attractive virtue; and the more spiritual and exalted it is, the more violent and irresistible are its attractions.

3. But besides the attracting virtue of the center, there is, in every creature, a strong tendency to reunion with its center, which is vigorous and active in proportion to the spirituality and perfection of the subject. As soon as anything is turned towards its center, it is precipitated towards it with extreme rapidity, unless it be withheld by some invincible obstacle. A stone held in the hand is no sooner disengaged than by its own weight it falls to the earth as to its center; so also water and fire, when unobstructed, flow incessantly towards their center. Now, when the soul by its efforts to recollect itself, is brought into the influence of the central tendency, it falls gradually, with-

out any other force than the weight of love, into its proper center; and the more passive and tranquil it remains, the freer from self-motion, the more rapidly it advances, because the energy of the central attractive virtue is unobstructed, and has full liberty for action.

4. All our care should therefore be directed towards acquiring the greatest degree of inward recollection; nor should we be discouraged by the difficulties we encounter in this exercise, which will soon be recompensed on the part of God, by such abundant supplies of grace, as will render it perfectly easy, provided we are faithful in meekly withdrawing our hearts from outward distractions and occupations, and returning to our center, with affections full of tenderness and serenity. When at any time the passions are turbulent, a gentle retreat inwards to a present God, easily deadens them; any other way of opposing rather irritates than appeases them.

CHAPTER 12

1. Another and more exalted degree of prayer, the prayer of the simple presence of God, or of Active Contemplation, of which very little is said, the subject being reserved for another treatise.

2,3,4. How selfish activity merges here in an activity lively, full, abundant, divine, easy, and as it were natural; a state far different from that idleness and passivity objected to by the opponents of the inner life. The subject illustrated by several comparisons.

5. Transition to Infused Prayer, in which the fundamental, vital activity of the soul is not lost, but is more abundantly and powerfully influenced (as are the faculties) by that of God. 6. The facility of these methods of coming to God, and an exhortation to self abandonment.

1. The soul that is faithful in the exercise of love and adherence to God, as above described, is astonished to feel Him gradually taking possession of its whole being; it now enjoys a continual sense of that presence which is become as it were natural to it; and this, as well as prayer, becomes a matter of habit. It feels an unusual serenity gradually diffusing itself over all its faculties. Silence now constitutes its whole prayer; whilst God communicates an infused love, which is the beginning of ineffable blessedness. O that I were permitted to pursue this subject, and describe some degrees of the endless progression of subsequent states? But I now write only for beginners; and shall therefore proceed no farther, but wait our Lord's time for developing what may be applicable to every state.

2. We must, however, urge it as a matter of the highest import, to cease self-action and self-exertion, that God himself may act alone: He says by the mouth of his prophet David, "Be still and know that I am God" (Psalm xlvi. 10). But the center is so infatuated with love and attachment to its own working, that it does not believe that it works at all unless it can feel, know, and distinguish all its operations. It is ignorant that its inability minutely to observe the manner of its motion, is occasioned by the swiftness of its progress; and that the operations of God, abounding more and more, absorb those of the creature; just as we see that the stars shine brightly before the sun rises, but gradually vanish as his light advances, and become invisible, not from want of light in themselves, but from the excess of it in him. The case is similar here; for there is a strong and universal light which absorbs all the little distinct lights of the soul; they grow faint and disappear under its powerful influence, and self-activity is now no longer distinguishable.

3. Those greatly err, who accuse this prayer of inactivity, a charge that can only arise from inexperience. O! if they would but make some efforts towards the attainment of it, they would soon become full of light and knowledge in relation to it. This appearance of inaction is, indeed, not the consequence of sterility, but of abundance, as will be clearly perceived by the experienced soul, who will recognize that the silence is full and unctuous by reason of plenty.

4. There are two kinds of people that keep silence; the one because they have nothing to say, the other because they have too much: the latter is the case in this state; silence is occasioned by excess and not by defect. To be drowned, and to die of thirst, are deaths widely different; yet water may be said to be the cause of both; abundance destroys in one case, and want in the other. So here the fullness of grace

stills the activity of self; and therefore it is of the utmost importance to remain as silent as possible. The infant hanging at its mother's breast, is a lively illustration of our subject; it begins to draw the milk, by moving its little lips; but when its nourishment flows abundantly, it is content to swallow without effort; by any other course it would only hurt itself, spill the milk, and be obliged to quit the breast. We must act in like manner in the beginning of prayer, by moving the lips of the affections; but as soon as the milk of divine grace flows freely, we have nothing to do, but, in stillness, sweetly to imbibe it, and when it ceases to flow, again stir up the affections as the infant moves its lips. Whoever acts otherwise, cannot make the best use of this grace, which is bestowed to allure the soul into the repose of Love, and not to force it into the multiplicity of self.

5. But what becomes of the babe that thus gently and without exertion, drinks in the milk? Who would believe that it could thus receive nourishment? Yet the more peacefully it feeds, the better it thrives. What, I say, becomes of this infant? It drops asleep on its mother's bosom. So the soul that is tranquil and peaceful in prayer, sinks frequently into a mystic slumber, wherein all its powers are at rest, till it is wholly fitted for that state, of which it enjoys these transient anticipations. You see that in this process the soul is led naturally, without trouble, effort, art or study. The interior is not a strong hold, to be taken by storm and violence; but a kingdom of peace, which is to be gained only by love. If any will thus pursue the little path I have pointed out, it will lead them to infused prayer. God demands nothing extraordinary nor too difficult; on the contrary, He is greatly pleased by a simple and child-like conduct.

6. The most sublime attainments in religion, are those which are easiest reached; the most necessary ordinances are the least difficult. It is thus also in natural things; if you would reach the sea, embark on a river, and you will be conveyed to it insensibly and without exertion. Would you go to God, follow this sweet and simple path, and you will arrive at the desired object, with an ease and expedition that will amaze you. O that you would but once make the trial! how soon would you find that all I have said is too little, and that your own experience will carry you infinitely

beyond it! What is it you fear? why do you not instantly cast yourself into the arms of Love, who only extended them on the cross that He might embrace you? What risk do you run in depending solely on God, and abandoning yourself wholly to Him? Ah! he will not deceive you, unless by bestowing an abundance beyond your highest hopes; but those who expect all from themselves, may hear this rebuke of God by his prophet Isaiah, "Ye have wearied yourselves in the multiplicity of your ways, and have not said, let us rest in peace" (Isa. lvii. 10, Vulgate).

CHAPTER 13
1. On the rest before God present in the soul in a wonderful way.
2. Fruits of this peaceful presence.
3. Practical advice.

1. The soul advanced thus far, has no need of any other preparation than its quietude: for now the presence of God, during the day, which is the great effect, or rather continuation of prayer, begins to be infused, and almost without intermission. The soul certainly enjoys transcendent blessedness, and finds that God is more intimately present to it than it is to itself. The only way to find him is by introversion. No sooner do the bodily eyes close, than the soul is wrapt in prayer: it is amazed at so great a blessing, and enjoys an internal converse, which external matters cannot interrupt.
2. The same may be said of this species of prayer, that is said of wisdom: "all good things come together with her" (Wisdom vii. 11). For virtues flow from this soul into exercise with so much sweetness and facility, that they appear natural to it, and the living spring within breaks forth abundantly into a facility for all goodness, and an insensibility to all evil.
3. Let it then remain faithful in this state; and beware of choosing or seeking any other disposition whatever than this simple rest, as a preparative either to confession or communion, to action or prayer; for its sole business is to suffer itself to be filled with this divine effusion. I would not be understood to speak of the preparations necessary for ordinances, but of the most interior disposition in which they can be received.

CHAPTER 14

1,2. On interior silence; its reason; God recommends it.

3. Exterior silence, retirement and recollection contribute to it.

1. "The Lord is in his holy temple; let all the earth keep silence before him" (Hab. ii. 20). The reason why inward silence is so indispensable, is, because the Word is essential and eternal, and necessarily requires dispositions in the soul in some degree correspondent to His nature, as a capacity for the reception of Himself. Hearing is a sense formed to receive sounds, and is rather passive than active, admitting, but not communicating sensation; and if we would hear, we must lend the ear for that purpose. Christ, the eternal Word, who must be communicated to the soul to give it new life, requires the most intense attention to his voice, when He would speak within us.

2. Hence it is so frequently enjoined upon us in sacred writ, to listen and be attentive to the voice of God; I quote a few of the numerous exhortations to this effect: "Hearken unto me, my people, and give ear unto me, O my nation!" (Isa. li. 4), and again "Hear me, all ye whom I carry in my bosom, and bear within my bowels" (Isa. xlvi. 3), and further by the Psalmist, "Hearken, O daughter! and consider, and incline thine ear; forget also thine own people, and thy father's house; so shall the king greatly desire thy beauty" (Ps. xlv. 10, 11). We must forget ourselves, and all self-interest, and listen and be attentive to God; these two simple actions, or rather passive dispositions, produce the love of that beauty, which He himself communicates.

3. Outward silence is very requisite for the cultivation and improvement of inward; and, indeed, it is impossible we should become truly interior, without loving silence and retirement. God saith by the mouth of his prophet, "I will lead her into solitude, and there will I speak to her heart (Hos. ii. 14, Vulg.); and unquestionably the being internally engaged with God is wholly incompatible with being externally busied about a thousand trifles. When, through weakness, we become as it were uncentered, we must immediately turn again inward; and this process we must repeat as often as our distractions recur. It is a small matter to be devout and recollected for an hour or half hour, if the unction and spirit of prayer do not continue with us during the whole day.

CHAPTER 15

1,2. On the examination of conscience; how it is performed in this state, and that by God himself.

3,4. On the confession, contrition, and forgetfulness or remembrance of faults in this state.

5. This is not applicable to the previous degree, Communion.

1. Self-examination should always precede confession, but the manner of it should be conformable to the state of the soul. The business of those that are advanced to the degree of which we now treat, is to lay their whole souls open before God, who will not fail to enlighten them, and enable them to see the peculiar nature of their faults. This examination, however, should be peaceful and tranquil; and we should depend on God for the discovery and knowledge of our sins, rather than on the diligence of our own scrutiny. When we examine with effort, we are easily deceived, and betrayed by self-love into error: "We call the evil good, and the good evil," (Isa. v. 20); but when we lie in full exposure before the Sun of Righteousness, his divine beams render the smallest atoms visible. We must, then, forsake self, and abandon our souls to God, as well in examination as confession.

2. When souls have attained to this species of prayer, no fault escapes the reprehension of God; no sooner are they committed than they are rebuked by an inward burning and tender confusion. Such is the scrutiny of Him who suffers no evil to be concealed; and the only way is to turn simply to God, and bear the pain and correction He inflicts. As He becomes the incessant examiner of the soul, it can now no longer examine itself; and if it be faithful in its abandonment, experience will prove that it is much more effectually explored by his divine light, than by all its own carefulness.

3. Those who tread these paths should be informed of a matter respecting their confusion, in which they are apt to err. When they begin to give an account of their sins, instead

of the regret and contrition they had been accustomed to feel, they find that love and tranquility sweetly pervade and take possession of their souls: now those who are not properly instructed are desirous of resisting this sensation, and forming an act of contrition, because they have heard, and with truth, that this is requisite. But they are not aware that they thereby lose the genuine contrition, which is this infused love, and which infinitely surpasses any effect produced by self-exertion, comprehending the other acts in itself as in one principal act, in much higher perfection than if they were distinctly perceived. Let them not be troubled to do otherwise, when God acts so excellently in and for them. To hate sin in this manner, is to hate it as God does. The purest love is that which is of his immediate operation in the soul; why should we then be so eager for action? Let us remain in the state He assigns us, agreeably to the instructions of the wise man: "Put your confidence in God; remain in quiet where he hath placed you" (Eccles. xi. 22).

4. The soul will also be amazed at finding a difficulty in calling its faults to remembrance. This, however, should cause no uneasiness, first, because this forgetfulness of our faults is some proof of our purification from them, and, in this degree of advancement, it is best to forget whatever concerns ourselves that we may remember only God. Secondly, because, when confession is our duty, God will not fail to make known to us our greatest faults; for then He himself examines; and the soul will feel the end of examination more perfectly accomplished, than it could possibly have been by all our own endeavors.

5. These instructions, however, would be altogether unsuitable to the preceding degrees, while the soul continues in its active state, wherein it is right and necessary that it should an all things exert itself, in proportion to its advancement. As to those who have arrived at this more advanced state, I exhort them to follow these instructions, and not to vary their simple occupations even on approaching the communion; let them remain in silence, and suffer God to act freely. He cannot be better received than by Himself.

CHAPTER 16

1. On reading and vocal prayers; they should be limited.

2. Not to be used against our interior drawing, unless they are of obligation.

1. The method of reading in this state, is to cease when you feel yourself recollected, and remain in stillness, reading but little, and always desisting when thus internally attracted.

2. The soul that is called to a state of inward silence, should not encumber itself with vocal prayers; whenever it makes use of them, and finds a difficulty therein, and an attraction to silence, let it not use constraint by persevering, but yield to the internal drawing, unless the repeating such prayers be a matter of obligation. In any other case, it is much better not to set forms, but wholly given up to the leadings of the Holy Spirit; and in this way every species of devotion is fulfilled in a most eminent degree.

CHAPTER 17

1. On petitions; those which are self-originated cease; and their place is supplied by those of the Spirit of God.

2. Abandonment and faith necessary here.

1. The soul should not be surprised at feeling itself unable to offer up to God such petitions as had formerly been made with facility; for now the Spirit maketh intercession for it according to the will of God; that Spirit which helpeth our infirmities; "for we know not what we should pray for as we ought; but the Spirit itself maketh intercession for us with groanings which cannot be uttered" (Rom. viii. 26). We must second the designs of God, which tend to divest us of all our own operations, that his may be substituted in their place.

2. Let this, then, be done in you; and suffer not yourself to be attached to anything, however good it may appear; it is no longer such to you, if it in any measure turns you aside from what God desires of you. For the divine will is preferable to every other good. Shake off, then, all self-interest, and live by faith and abandonment; here it is that genuine faith begins truly to operate.

CHAPTER 18

1. On faults committed in the state. We must turn from them to God without trouble or discouragement.

2. The contrary course weakens us and is opposed to the practice of humble souls.

1. Should we either wander among externals, or commit a fault, we must instantly turn inwards; for having departed thereby from God, we should as soon as possible turn toward Him, and suffer the penalty which He inflicts. It is of great importance to guard against vexation on account of our faults; it springs from a secret root of pride, and a love of our own excellence; we are hurt at feeling what we are.

2. If we become discouraged, we are the more enfeebled; and from our reflections on our imperfections, a chagrin arises, which is often worse than the imperfection themselves. The truly humble soul is not surprised at its defects or failings; and the more miserable it beholds itself, the more it abandons itself to God, and presses for a more intimate alliance with Him, seeing the need it has of his aid. We should the rather be induced to act thus, as God himself has said, "I will instruct thee and teach thee in the way which thou shalt go; I will guide thee with mine eye" (Psalm xxxii. 8).

CHAPTER 19

1. On distractions and temptations; the remedy for them is to turn to God.

2. This is the practice of the saints, and there is danger in any other way.

1. A direct struggle with distractions and temptations rather serves to augment them, and withdraws the soul from that adherence to God, which should ever be its sole occupation. We should simply turn away from the evil, and draw yet nearer to God. A little child, on perceiving a monster, does not wait to fight with it, and will scarcely turn its eyes toward it, but quickly shrinks into the bosom of its mother, in assurance of its safety. "God is in the midst of her," says the Psalmist, "she shall not be moved; God shall help her, and that right early" (Psalm xlvi. 5).

2. If we do otherwise, and in our weakness attempt to attack our enemies, we shall frequently find ourselves wounded, if not totally defeated: but, by remaining in the simple presence of God, we shall find instant supplies of strength for our support. This was the resource of David: "I have set," says he, "the Lord always before me; because he is at my right hand, I shall not be moved. Therefore my heart is glad, and my glory rejoiceth; my flesh also shall rest in hope." (Psalm xvi. 8,9.) And it is said in Exodus, "The Lord shall fight for you, and ye shall hold your peace" (Exod. xiv. 14).

CHAPTER 20

1,2. Prayer divinely explained as a devotional sacrifice, under the similitude of incense.

3. Our annihilation in this sacrifice.

4,5. Solidity and fruit of this prayer according to the Gospel.

1. Both devotion and sacrifice are comprehended in prayer, which, according to St. John is an incense, the smoke whereof ascendeth unto God; therefore it is said in the Apocalypse, that "unto the angel was given much incense, that he should offer it with the prayers of all saints" (Rev. viii. 3). Prayer is the effusion of the heart in the presence of God: "I have poured out my soul before the Lord," said the mother of Samuel (1 Sam. i. 15). The prayer of the wise men at the feet of Christ in the stable of Bethlehem, was signified by the incense they offered.

2. Prayer is a certain warmth of love, melting, dissolving, and sublimating the soul, and causing it to ascend unto God, and, as the soul is melted, odors rise from it; and these sweet exhalations proceed from the consuming fire of love within. This is illustrated in the Canticles, (i. 12), where the spouse says, "While the king sitteth at his table, my spikenard sendeth forth the smell thereof." The table is the center of the soul; and when God is there, and we know how to dwell near, and abide with Him, the sacred presence gradually dissolves the hardness of the soul, and, as it melts, fragrance issues forth; hence it is, that the Beloved says of his spouse, in seeing her soul melt when he spoke, "Who is this that cometh out of the wilderness, like pillars of smoke perfumed with myrrh and frankincense?" (Cant. v. 6; iii. 6).

3. Thus does the soul ascend to God, by giving up self to the destroying and annihilating power of divine love. This is a state of sacrifice essential to the Christian religion, in which the soul suffers itself to be destroyed and annihilated, that it may pay homage to the sovereignty of God; as it is written, "The power of the Lord is great, and he is honored only by the humble" (Eccles. iii. 20). By the destruction of self, we acknowledge the supreme existence of God. We must cease to exist in self, in order that the Spirit of the Eternal Word may exist in us: it is by the giving up of our own life, that we give place to his coming; and in dying to ourselves, He himself lives in us. We must surrender our whole being to Christ Jesus, and cease to live any longer in ourselves, that He may become our life; "that being dead, our life may be hid with Christ in God" (Col. iii. 3). "Pass ye into me," sayeth God, "all ye who earnestly seek after me" (Eccles. xxi. 16). But how is it we pass into God? In no way but by leaving and forsaking ourselves, that we may be lost in Him; and this can be effected only by annihilation, which, being the true prayer of adoration, renders unto God alone, all blessing, honor, glory, and power, forever and ever" (Rev. v. 13).

4. This prayer of truth; it is "worshipping God in spirit and in truth" (John iv. 23). "In spirit," because we enter into the purity of that Spirit which prayeth within us, and are drawn forth from our own carnal and human method; "in truth," because we are thereby placed in the truth of the all of God, and the nothing of the creature. There are but these two truths, the All and the Nothing; everything else is falsehood. We can pay due honor to the All of God, only in our own Annihilation; which is no sooner accomplished, that He, who never suffers a void in nature, instantly fills us with Himself. Ah! did we but know the virtues and the blessings which the soul derives from this prayer, we should not be willing to do anything else; It is the pearl of great price; the hidden treasure, (Matt. xiii. 44, 45), which, whoever findeth, selleth freely all that he hath to purchase it; it is the well of living water, which springeth up unto everlasting life. It is the adoration of God "in spirit and in truth" (John iv. 14–23): and it is the full performance of the purest evangelical precepts.

5. Jesus Christ assures us, that the "kingdom of God is within us" (Luke xvii. 21): and this is true in two senses: first, when God becomes so fully Savior and Lord in us, that nothing resists his domination, then our interior is his kingdom; and again, when we possess God, who is the Supreme Good, we possess his kingdom also, wherein there is fullness of joy, and where we attain the end of our creation. Thus it is said, "to serve God is to reign." The end of our creation, indeed, is to enjoy God, even in this life; but, alas! who thinks of it?

CHAPTER 21

The objections of slothfulness and inactivity made to this form of prayer fully met, and the truth shown that the soul acts nobly, forcibly, calmly, quickly, freely, simply, sweetly, temperately, and certainly; but in dependence upon God, and moved by his Holy Spirit: the restless and selfish activity of nature being destroyed, and the life of God communicated by union with Him.

1. Some persons, when they hear of the prayer of silence, falsely imagine that the soul remains stupid, dead, and inactive; but it unquestionably acts more nobly and more extensively than it had ever done before; for God himself is its mover, and it now acts by the agency of his Spirit. St. Paul would have us led by the Spirit of God (Rom. viii. 14). It is not meant that we should cease from action; but that we should act through the internal agency of his grace. This is finely represented by the prophet Ezekiel's vision of the wheels, which had a living Spirit; and whithersoever the Spirit was to go, they went; they ascended and descended as they were moved; for the Spirit of life was in them, and they returned not when they went (Ezek. i. 18). Thus the soul should be equally subservient to the will of that vivifying Spirit which is in it, and scrupulously faithful to follow only as that moves. These motions never tend to return in reflections on the creatures or self; but go forward in an incessant approach toward the end.

2. This activity of the soul is attended with the utmost tranquility. When it acts of itself, the act is forced and constrained, and, therefore, it is more easily distinguished; but when the action is under the influence of the Spirit of grace, it

is so free, so easy, and so natural, that it almost seems as if we did not act at all. "He brought me forth also into a large place; He delivered me, because He delighted in me" (Ps. xviii. 19). When the soul is in its central tendency, or in other words, is returned through recollection into itself, from that moment, the central attraction becomes a most potent activity, infinitely surpassing in energy every other species. Nothing, indeed, can equal the swiftness of this tendency to the center; and though an activity, yet it is so noble, so peaceful, so full of tranquility, so natural, and so spontaneous, that it appears to the soul as if it were none at all. When a wheel rolls slowly we can easily perceive its parts; but when its motion is rapid, we can distinguish nothing. So the soul which rests in God, has an activity exceedingly noble and elevated, yet altogether peaceful; and the more peaceful it is, the swifter is its course; because it is given up to that Spirit by whom it is moved and directed.

3. This attracting Spirit is no other than God himself, who, in drawing us, causes us to run to Him. How well did the spouse understand this, when she said, "Draw me, we will run after thee" (Cant. i. 4). Draw me unto Thee, O my divine center, by the secret springs of my existence, and all my powers and senses shall follow Thee! This simple attraction is both an ointment to heal and a perfume to allure: we follow, saith she, the fragrance of thy perfumes; and though so powerful an attraction, it is followed by the soul freely, and without constraint; for it is equally delighted as forcible; and whilst it attracts by its power, it carries us away by its sweetness. "Draw me," says the spouse, "and we will run after thee." She speaks of and to herself: "draw me," – behold the unity of the center which is drawn! "we will run," – behold the correspondence and course of all the senses and powers in following the attraction of the center!

4. Instead, then, of encouraging sloth, we promote the highest activity, by inculcating a total dependence of the Spirit of God, as our moving principle; for it is in Him, and by Him alone, that we live and move, and have our being (Acts xvii. 28). This meek dependence on the Spirit of God is indispensably necessary, and causes the soul shortly to attain the unity and simplicity in which it was created. We must, therefore, forsake our multifarious activity, to enter into the simplicity and unity of God, in whose image we were originally formed (Gen. i. 27). "The Spirit is one and manifold, (Wisdom vii. 22), and his unity does not preclude his multiplicity. We enter into his unity when we are united to his Spirit, and by that means have one and the same spirit with Him; and we are multiplied in respect to the outward execution of his will, without any departure from our state of union. In this way, when we are wholly moved by the divine Spirit, which is infinitely active, our activity must, indeed, be more energetic than that which is merely our own. We must yield ourselves to the guidance of "wisdom, which is more moving than any motion," (Wisdom vii. 24), and by abiding in dependence upon its action, our activity will be truly efficient.

5. "All things were made by the Word, and without Him was not anything made, that was made" (John i. 3). God originally formed us in his own image and likeness; He breathed into us the Spirit of his Word, that breath of Life (Gen. ii. 7) which He gave us at our creation, in the participation whereof the image of God consisted. Now, this Life is one, simple, pure, intimate, and always fruitful. The devil having broken and deformed the divine image in the soul by sin, the agency of the same Word whose Spirit was inbreathed at our creation, is absolutely necessary for its renovation. It was necessary that it should be He, because He is the express image of his Father; and no image can be repaired by its own efforts, but must remain passive for that purpose under the hand of the workman. Our activity should, therefore, consist in placing ourselves in a state of susceptibility to divine impressions, and pliability to all the operations of the Eternal Word. Whilst tablet is unsteady, the painter is unable to produce a correct picture upon it, and every movement of self is productive of erroneous lineaments; it interrupts the work and defeats the design of this adorable Painter. We must then remain in peace, and move only when He moves us. Jesus Christ hath life in himself, (John v. 26), and He must give life to every living thing. The spirit of the church of God is the spirit of the divine movement. Is she

idle, barren, or unfruitful? No; she acts, but her activity is in dependence upon the Spirit of God, who moves and governs her. Just so should it be in her members; that they may be spiritual children of the Church, they must be moved by the Spirit.

6. As all action is estimable only in proportion to the grandeur and dignity of the efficient principle, this action is incontestably more noble than any other. Actions produced by a divine principle, are divine; but creaturely actions, however good they appear, are only human, or at least virtuous, even when accompanied by grace. Jesus Christ says that He has life in Himself: all other beings have only a borrowed life; but the Word has life in Himself; and being communicative of his nature, He desires to bestow it upon man. We should therefore make room for the influx of this life, which can only be done by the ejection and loss of the Adamical life, and the suppression of the activity of self. This is agreeable to the assertion of St. Paul, "If any man be in Christ, he is a new creature; old things are passed away; behold, all things are become new," (2 Cor. v. 17); but this state can be accomplished only by dying to ourselves, and to all our own activity, that the activity of God may be substituted in its place. Instead, therefore, of prohibiting activity, we enjoin it; but in absolute dependence on the Spirit of God, that his activity may take the place of our own. This can only be effected by the consent of the creature; and this concurrence can only be yielded by moderating our own action, that the activity of God may, little by little, be wholly substituted for it.

7. Jesus Christ has exemplified this in the Gospel. Martha did what was right; but because she did it in her own spirit, Christ rebuked her. The spirit of man is restless and turbulent; for which reason he does little, though he seems to do a great deal. "Martha," says Christ, "thou art careful and troubled about many things; but one thing is needful; and Mary hath chosen that good part which shall not be taken away from her" (Luke x. 41, 42). And what was it Mary had chosen? Repose, tranquility, and peace. She had apparently ceased to act, that the Spirit of Christ might act in her; she had ceased to live, that Christ might be her life.

This shows how necessary it is to renounce ourselves, and all our activity, to follow Christ; for we cannot follow Him, if we are not animated by his Spirit. Now that his Spirit may gain admittance, it is necessary that our own should be expelled: "He that is joined unto the Lord," says St. Paul, "is one spirit" (1 Cor. vi. 17). And David said it was good for him to draw near unto the Lord, and to put his trust in him (Psalm lxxiii. 28). What is this drawing near? it is the beginning of union.

8. Divine union has its commencement, its progress, its achievement, and its consummation. It is at first an inclination towards God. When the soul is introverted in the manner before described, it gets within the influence of the central attraction, and acquires an eager desire after union; this is the beginning. It then adheres to Him when it has got nearer and nearer, and finally becomes one, that is, one spirit with Him; and then it is that spirit which had wandered from God, returns again to its end.

9. Into this way, then, which is the divine motion, and the spirit of Jesus Christ, we must necessarily enter. St. Paul says, "If any man have not the spirit of Christ, he is none of his" (Rom. viii. 9): therefore, to be Christ's, we must be filled with his Spirit, and emptied of our own. The Apostle, in the same passage, proved the necessity of this divine influence. "As many," says he, "as are led by the Spirit of God, they are the sons of God" (Rom. viii. 14). The spirit of divine filiation is, then, the spirit of divine motion: he therefore adds, "Ye have not received the spirit of bondage again to fear; but ye have received the spirit of adoption whereby ye cry Abba, Father." This spirit is no other than the spirit of Christ, through which we participate in his filiation; "The Spirit beareth witness with our spirit that we are the children of God." When the soul yields itself to the influence of this blessed Spirit, it perceives the testimony of its divine filiation; and it feels also, with superadded joy, that it has received, not the spirit of bondage, but of liberty, even the liberty of the children of God; it then finds that it acts freely and sweetly, though with vigor and infallibility.

10. The spirit of divine action is so necessary in all things, that St. Paul, in the same passage,

founds that necessity on our ignorance with respect to what we pray for: "The Spirit," says he, "also helpeth our infirmities: for we know not what we should pray for as we ought; but the Spirit itself maketh intercession for us, with groanings which cannot be uttered." This is plain enough; if we know not what we stand in need of, nor how to pray as we ought for those things which are necessary, and if the Spirit which is in us, and to which we resign ourselves, must ask for us, should we not permit Him to give vent to his unutterable groanings in our behalf? This Spirit is the Spirit of the Word, which is always heard, as He says himself: "I knew that thou hearest me always" (John xi. 42); and if we freely admit this Spirit to pray and intercede for us, we also shall be always heard. And why? Let us learn from the same great Apostle, that skillful Mystic, and Master of the interior life, where he adds, "He that searcheth the heart, knoweth what is the mind of the Spirit; because he maketh intercession for the saints, according to the will of God" (Rom. viii. 27): that is to say, the Spirit demands only what is conformable to the will of God. The will of God is that we should be saved, and that we should become perfect: He, therefore, intercedes for all that is necessary for our perfection.

11. Why, then, should we be burthened with superfluous cares, and weary ourselves in the multiplicity of our ways, without ever saying, let us rest in peace. God himself invites us to cast all our care upon Him; and He complains in Isaiah, with ineffable goodness, that the soul had expended its powers and its treasures on a thousand external objects, when there was so little to do to attain all it need desire. "Wherefore," saith God, "do you spend money for that which is not bread; and your labor for that which satisfieth not? Hearken diligently unto me, and eat ye that which is good, and let your soul delight itself in fatness" (Isa. lv. 2). Oh! did we but know the blessedness of thus hearkening to God, and how greatly the soul is strengthened by such a course! "Be silent, O all flesh, before the Lord" (Zech. ii. 13); all must cease as soon as He appears. But to engage us still farther to an abandonment without reservation, God assures us, by the same Prophet, that we need fear nothing, because he takes a very special care of us; "Can a woman forget her sucking child, that she should not have compassion on the son of her womb? Yes, she may forget; yet will not I forget thee" (Isa. xlix. 15). O words full of consolation! Who after that will fear to abandon himself wholly to the guidance of God?

CHAPTER 22

1–6. Distinction between inward and outward acts; in this state the acts of the soul are inward, but habitual, continued, direct, lasting, deep, simple, unconscious, and resembling a gentle and perpetual sinking into the ocean of Divinity.

7,8. A comparison.

9. How to act when we perceive no attraction.

1. Acts are distinguished into external and internal. External acts are those which appear outwardly, and bear relation to some sensible object, and have no moral character, except such as they derive from the principle from which they proceed. I intend here to speak only of internal acts, those energies of the soul, by which it turns internally towards some objects, and away from others.

2. If during my application to God, I should form a will to change the nature of my act, I should thereby withdraw myself from God and turn to created objects, and that in a greater or less degree according to the strength of the act: and if, when I am turned towards the creature, I would return to God, I must necessarily form an act for that purpose; and the more perfect this act is, the more complete is the conversion. Till conversion is perfected, many reiterated acts are necessary; for it is with some progressive, though with others it is instantaneous. My act, however, should consist in a continual turning to God, an exertion of every faculty and power of the soul purely for Him, agreeably to the instructions of the son of Sirach: "Re-unite all the motions of thy heart in the holiness of God" (Eccles. xxx. 24); and to the example of David, "I will keep my whole strength for thee," (Psalm lix. 9, Vulg.). For we have strayed from our heart by sin, and it is our heart only that God requires: "My son give me thine heart, and let thine eye observe my

ways" (Prov. xxiii. 26). To give the heart to God, is to have the whole energy of the soul ever centering in Him, that we may be rendered conformable to his will. We must, therefore, continue invariably turned to God, from our first application to Him. But the spirit being unstable, and the soul accustomed to turn to external objects, it is easily distracted. This evil, however, will be counteracted if, on perceiving the wandering, we, by a pure act of return to God, instantly replace ourselves in Him; and this act subsists as long as the conversion lasts, by the powerful influence of a simple and unfeigned return to God.

3. As many reiterated acts form a habit, the soul contracts the habit of conversion; and that act which was before interrupted and distinct becomes habitual. The soul should not, then, be perplexed about forming an act which already subsists, and which, indeed, it cannot attempt to form without very great difficulty; it even finds that it is withdrawn from its proper state, under pretence of seeking that which is in reality acquired, seeing the habit is already formed, and it is confirmed in habitual conversion and habitual love. It is seeking one act by the help of many, instead of continuing attached to God by one simple act alone. We may remark, that at times we form with facility many distant yet simple acts; which shows that we have wandered, and that we re-enter our heart after having strayed from it; yet when we have re-entered, we should remain there in peace. We err, therefore, in supposing that we must not form acts; we form them continually: but let them be conformable to the degree of our spiritual advancement.

4. The great difficulty with most spiritual people arises from their not clearly comprehending this matter. Now, some acts are transient and distinct, others are continued, and again, some are direct, and others reflective. All cannot form the first, neither are all in a state suited to form the others. The first are adapted to those who have strayed, and who require a distinct exertion, proportioned to the extent of their deviation; if the latter be inconsiderable, an act of the most simple kind is sufficient.

5. By the continued act, I mean that whereby the soul is altogether turned toward God by a direct act, always subsisting, and which it does not renew unless it has been interrupted. The soul being thus turned, is in charity, and abides therein; "and he that dwelleth in love, dwelleth in God" (1 John iv. 16). The soul then, is it were, exists and rests in the habitual act. It is, however, free from sloth; for there is still an uninterrupted act subsisting, which is a sweet sinking into the Deity, whose attraction becomes more and more powerful. Following this potent attraction, and dwelling in love and charity, the soul sinks continually deeper into that Love, maintaining an activity infinitely more powerful, vigorous, and effectual than that which served to accomplish its first return.

6. Now the soul that is thus profoundly and vigorously active, being wholly given up to God, does not perceive this act, because it is direct and not reflective. This is the reason why some, not expressing themselves properly, say, that they make no acts; but it is a mistake, for they were never more truly or nobly active; they should say, that they did not distinguish their acts, and not that they did not act. I grant that they do not act in themselves; but they are drawn, and they follow the attraction. Love is the weight which sinks them. As one falling into the sea, would sink from one depth to another to all eternity, if the sea were infinite, so they, without perceiving their descent, drop with inconceivable swiftness into the lowest deeps. It is, then, improper to say that we do not make acts; all form acts, but the manner of their formation is not alike in all. The mistake arises from this, that all who know they should act, are desirous of acting distinguishably and perceptibly; but this cannot be: sensible acts are for beginners; there are others for those in a more advanced state. To stop in the former, which are weak and of little profit, is to declare ourselves of the latter; as to attempt the latter without having passed through the former, is a no less considerable error.

7. "To everything there is a season" (Eccles. iii. 1): every state has its commencement, its progress, and its consummation, and it is an unhappy error to stop in the beginning. There is no art but what has its progress; at first, we labor with toil, but at last we reap the fruit of our industry. When the vessel is in port, the

mariners are obliged to exert all their strength, that they may clear her thence, and put to sea; but they subsequently turn her with facility as they please. In like manner, while the soul remains in sin and the creature, many endeavors are requisite to effect its freedom; the cables which hold it must be loosed, and then by strong and vigorous efforts it gathers itself inward, pushes off gradually from the old port of Self, and, leaving that behind, proceeds to the interior, the haven so much desired.

8. When the vessel is thus started, as she advances on the sea, she leaves the shore behind; and the farther she departs from the land, the less labor is requisite in moving her forward. At length she begins to get gently under sail, and now proceeds so swiftly in her course, that the oars, which are become useless, are laid aside. How is the pilot now employed? he is content with spreading the sails and holding the rudder. To spread the sails, is to lay ourselves before God in the prayer of simple exposition, to be moved by his Spirit; to hold the rudder, is to restrain our heart from wandering from the true course, recalling it gently, and guiding it steadily by the dictates of the Spirit of God, which gradually gains possession of the heart, just as the breeze by degrees fills the sails and impels the vessel. While the winds are fair, the pilot and the mariners rest from their labors. What progress do they not now secure, without the least fatigue! They make more way now in one hour, while they rest and leave the vessel to the wind, than they did in a length of time by all their former efforts; and even were they now to attempt using the oars, besides greatly fatiguing themselves, they would only retard the vessel by their useless exertions. This is our proper course interiorly, and a short time will advance us by the divine impulsion farther than many reiterated acts of self-exertion. Whoever will try this path, will find it the easiest in the world.

9. If the wind be contrary and blow a storm, we must cast anchor in the sea, to hold the vessel. This anchor is simply trust in God and hope in his goodness, waiting patiently the calming of the tempest and the return of a favorable gale; thus did David: "I waited patiently for the Lord, and he inclined unto me,

and heard my cry" (Ps. xl. 1). We must therefore be resigned to the Spirit of God, giving ourselves up wholly to his divine guidance.

CHAPTER 23

1,2. The barrenness of preaching, vice, error, heresies, and all sorts of evils arise from the fact that the people are not instructed in the prayer of the heart;

3–5. Although the way is surer, easier, and fitter for the simple minded.

6–8. Exhortation to pastors to set their flocks upon the practice of it, without employing them in studied forms and methodical devotion.

1. If all who labored for the conversion of others sought to reach them by the heart, introducing them immediately into prayer and the interior life, numberless and permanent conversions would ensue. On the contrary, few and transient fruits must attend that labor which is confined to outward matters, such as burdening the disciple with a thousand precepts for external exercises, instead of leading the soul to Christ by the occupation of the heart in Him. If ministers were solicitous thus to instruct their parishioners, shepherds, while they watched their flocks, would have the spirit of the primitive Christians, and the husbandman at the plough maintain a blessed intercourse with his God; the manufacturer, while he exhausted his outward man with labor, would be renewed with inward strength; every species of vice would shortly disappear, and every parishioner become spiritually minded.

2. O when once the heart is gained, how easily is all the rest corrected! this is why God, above all things, requires the heart. By this means alone, we may extirpate the dreadful vices which so prevail among the lower orders, such as drunkenness, blasphemy, lewdness, enmity and theft. Jesus Christ would reign everywhere in peace, and the face of the church would be renewed throughout. The decay of internal piety is unquestionably the source of the various errors that have appeared in the world; all would speedily be overthrown, were inward devotion re-established. Errors take possession of no soul, except such as are deficient in faith and prayer; and if, instead of

engaging our wandering brethren in constant disputations, we would but teach them simply to believe, and diligently to pray, we should lead them sweetly to God. O how inexpressibly great is the loss sustained by mankind from the neglect of the interior life! And what an account will those have to render who are entrusted with the care of souls, and have not discovered and communicated to their flock this hidden treasure!

3. Some excuse themselves by saying, that there is danger in this way, or that simple persons are incapable of comprehending the things of the Spirit. But the oracles of truth affirm the contrary: "The Lord loveth those who walk simply" (Prov. xii. 22, Vulg.). But what danger can there be in walking in the only true way, which is Jesus Christ, giving ourselves up to Him, fixing our eye continually on Him, placing all our confidence in his grace, and tending with all the strength of our soul to his purest love?

4. The simple ones, so far from being incapable of this perfection, are, by their docility, innocence, and humility, peculiarly qualified for its attainment; and, as they are not accustomed to reasoning, they are less tenacious of their own opinions. Even from their want of learning, they submit more freely to the teachings of the divine Spirit; whereas others, who are cramped and blinded by self-sufficiency, offer much greater resistance to the operations of grace. We are told in Scripture that "unto the simple, God giveth the understanding of his law" (Psalm cxviii. 130, vulg.): and we are also assured, that God loves to communicate with them: "The Lord careth for the simple; I was reduced to extremity and He saved me" (Psalm cxvi. 6, cxv. 6, Vulg.). Let spiritual fathers be careful how they prevent their little ones from coming to Christ; He himself said to his apostles, "Suffer little children to come unto me, for of such is the kingdom of heaven" (Matt. xix. 14). It was the endeavor of the apostles to prevent children from going to our Lord, which occasioned this command.

5. Man frequently applies a remedy to the outward body, whilst the disease lies at the heart. The cause of our being so unsuccessful in reforming mankind, especially those of the lower classes, is our beginning with external matters; all our labors in this field, do but produce such fruit as endures not; but if the key of the interior be first given, the exterior would be naturally and easily reformed. Now this is very easy. To teach man to seek God in his heart, to think of Him, to return to Him whenever he finds he has wandered from Him, and to do and suffer all things with a single eye to please Him, is leading the soul to the source of all grace, and causing it to find there everything necessary for sanctification.

6. I therefore beseech you all, O ye that have the care of souls, to put them at once into this way, which is Jesus Christ; nay, it is He himself that conjures you, by all the blood he has shed for those entrusted to you. "Speak to the heart of Jerusalem!" (Isa. xl. 2, vulg.) O ye dispensers of his grace! preachers of his word! ministers of his sacraments! establish his kingdom! – and that it may indeed be established, make Him ruler over the heart! For as it is the heart alone that can oppose his sovereignty, it is by the subjection of the heart that his sovereignty is most highly honored: "Give glory to the holiness of God, and he shall become your sanctification" (Isa. viii. 13, Vulg.). Compose catechisms expressly to teach prayer, not by reasoning nor by method, for the simple are incapable of that; but to teach the prayer of the heart, not of the understanding; the prayer of God's Spirit, not of man's invention.

7. Alas! by directing them to pray in elaborate forms, and to be curiously critical therein, you create their chief obstacles. The children have been led astray from the best of fathers, by your endeavoring to teach them too refined a language. Go, then, ye poor children, to your heavenly Father, speak to him in your natural language; rude and barbarous as it may be, it is not so to Him. A father is better pleased with an address which love and respect have made confused, because he sees that it proceeds from the heart, than he is by a dry and barren harangue, though never so elaborate. The simple and undisguised emotions of love are infinitely more expressive than all language, and all reasoning.

8. Men have desired to love by formal rules, and have thus lost much of that love. O how unnecessary is it to teach an art of loving! The language of love is barbarous to him that does

not love, but perfectly natural to him that does; and there is no better way to learn how to love God, than to love him. The most ignorant often become the most perfect, because they proceed with more cordiality and simplicity. The Spirit of God needs none of our arrangements; when it pleases Him, He turns shepherds into Prophets, and, so far from excluding any from the temple of prayer, he throws wide the gates that all may enter; while wisdom is directed to cry aloud in the highways, "Whoso is simple let him turn in hither" (Prov. ix. 4); and to the fools she saith, "Come eat of my bread, and drink of the wine which I have mingled" (Prov. ix. 5). And doth not Jesus Christ himself thank his Father for having "hid these things from the wise and prudent, and revealed them unto babes"? (Matt. xi. 25).

CHAPTER 24

On the passive way to Divine Union. It is impossible to attain Divine Union, solely by the way of meditation, or of the affections, or by any devotion, no matter how illuminated. There are many reasons for this, the chief of which are those which follow.

1. According to Scripture, "no man shall see God and live" (Exod. xxxiii. 20). Now all the exercises of discursive prayer, and even of active contemplation, regarded as an end, and not as a mere preparative to that which is passive, are still living exercises, by which we cannot see God; that is to say, be united with him. All that is of man and of his doing, be it never so noble, never so exalted, must first be destroyed. St. John relates that there was silence in heaven (Rev. viii. 1). Now heaven represents the ground and center of the soul, wherein all must be hushed to silence when the majesty of God appears. All the efforts, nay, the very existence, of self, must be destroyed; because nothing is opposite to God, but self, and all the malignity of man is in self-appropriation, as the source of its evil nature; insomuch that the purity of a soul increases in proportion as it loses this self-hood; and that which was a fault while the soul lived in self-appropriation, is no longer such, after it has acquired purity and innocence, by departing from that self-hood, which caused the dissimilitude between

it and God.

2. To unite two things so opposite as the purity of God and the impurity of the creature, the simplicity of God and the multiplicity of man, much more is requisite than the efforts of the creature. Nothing less than an efficacious operation of the Almighty can ever accomplish this; for two things must have some relation or similarity before they can become one; as the impurity of dross cannot be united with the purity of gold.

3. What, then, does God do? He sends his own Wisdom before Him, as fire shall be sent upon the earth, to destroy by its activity all that is impure; and as nothing can resist the power of that fire, but it consumes everything, so this Wisdom destroys all the impurities of the creature, in order to dispose it for divine union. The impurity which is so fatal to union consists in self-appropriation and activity. Self-appropriation; because it is the source and fountain of all that defilement which can never be allied to essential purity; as the rays of the sun may shine, indeed, upon mire, but can never be united with it. Activity; for God being in an infinite stillness, the soul, in order to be united to Him, must participate of his stillness, else the contrariety between stillness and activity would prevent assimilation. Therefore, the soul can never arrive at divine union but in the rest of its will; nor can it ever become one with God, but by being re-established in central rest and in the purity of its first creation.

4. God purifies the soul by his Wisdom, as refiners do metals in the furnace. Gold cannot be purified but by fire, which gradually consumes all that is earthy and foreign, and separates it from the metal. It is not sufficient to fit it for use that the earthy part should be changed into gold; it must then be melted and dissolved by the force of fire, to separate from the mass every drossy or alien particle; and must be again and again cast into the furnace, until it has lost every trace of pollution, and every possibility of being farther purified. The goldsmith cannot now discover any adulterate mixture, because of its perfect purity and simplicity. The fire no longer touches it; and were it to remain an age in the furnace, its spotlessness would not be increased, nor its substance diminished. It is then fit for the most

exquisite workmanship, and if, thereafter, this gold seem obscured or defiled, it is nothing more than an accidental impurity occasioned by the contact of some foreign body, and is only superficial; it is no hindrance to its employment, and is widely different from its former debasement, which was hidden in the ground of its nature, and, as it were, identified with it. Those, however, who are uninstructed, beholding the pure gold sullied by some external pollution, would be disposed to prefer an impure and gross metal, that appeared superficially bright and polished.

5. Farther, the pure and the impure gold are not mingled; before they can be united, they must be equally refined; the goldsmith cannot mix dross and gold. What will he do, then? He will purge out the dross with fire, so that the inferior may become as pure as the other, and then they may be united. This is what St. Paul means, when he declares that "the fire shall try every man's work of what sort it is" (1 Cor. iii 3); he adds, "If any man's work be burnt, he shall suffer loss, but he himself shall be saved, yet so as by fire." He here intimates, that there are works so degraded by impure mixtures, that though the mercy of God accepts them, yet they must pass through the fire, to be purged from self; and it is in this sense that God is said to examine and judge our righteousness, because that by the deeds of the law there shall no flesh be justified; but by the righteousness of God, which is by faith in Jesus Christ (Rom. iii. 20, etc.).

6. Thus we may see that the divine justice and wisdom, like a pitiless and devouring fire, must destroy all that is earthly, sensual, and carnal, and all self-activity, before the soul can be united to its God. Now, this can never be accomplished by the industry of the creature; on the contrary, he always submits to it with reluctance; because, as I have said, he is so enamored of self, and so fearful of its destruction, that did not God act upon him powerfully and with authority, he would never consent.

7. It may, perhaps, be objected here, that as God never robs man of his free will, he can always resist the divine operations; and that I therefore err in saying God acts absolutely, and without the consent of man. Let me, however, explain. By man's giving a passive consent, God, with-

out usurpation, may assume full power and an entire guidance; for having, in the beginning of his conversion, made an unreserved surrender of himself to all that God wills of him or by him, he thereby gave an active consent to whatever God might afterwards require. But when God begins to burn, destroy, and purify, the soul does not perceive that these operations are intended for its good, but rather supposes the contrary; and, as the gold at first seems rather to blacken than brighten in the fire, so it conceives that its purity is lost; insomuch, that if an active and explicit consent were then required, the soul could scarcely give it, nay would often withhold it. All it does is to remain firm in its passive consent, enduring as patiently as possible all these divine operations, which it is neither able nor desirous to obstruct.

8. In this manner, therefore, the soul is purified from all its self-originated, distinct, perceptible, and multiplied operations, which constitute a great dissimilitude between it and God; it is rendered by degrees conform, and then uniform; and the passive capacity of the creature is elevated, ennobled, and enlarged, though in a secret and hidden manner, hence called mystical; but in all these operations the soul must concur passively. It is true, indeed, that in the beginning its activity is requisite; from which, however, as the divine operations become stronger, it must gradually cease; yielding itself up to the impulse of the divine Spirit, till it is wholly absorbed in Him. But this is a process which lasts a long time.

9. We do not, then, say, as some have supposed, that there is no need of activity; since, on the contrary, it is the gate; at which, however, we should not always tarry, since we ought to tend towards ultimate perfection, which is impracticable except the first helps are laid aside; for however necessary they may have been at the entrance of the road, they afterwards become greatly detrimental to those who adhere to them obstinately, preventing them from ever attaining the end. This made St. Paul say, "Forgetting those things which are behind, and reaching forth to those which are before, I press toward the mark, for the prize of the high calling of God in Christ Jesus" (Phil. iii. 13). Would you not

say that he had lost his senses, who, having undertaken a journey, should fix his abode at the first inn, because he had been told that many travelers had come that way, that some had lodged there, and that the masters of the house dwelt there? All that we wish, then, is, that souls would press toward the end, taking the shortest and easiest road, and not stopping at the first stage. Let them follow the counsel and example of St. Paul, and suffer themselves to be led by the Spirit of God, (Rom. viii. 14), which will infallibly conduct them to the end of their creation, the enjoyment of God.

10. But while we confess that the enjoyment of God is the end for which alone we were created, and that every soul that does not attain divine union and the purity of its creation in this life, can only be saved as by fire, how strange it is, that we should dread and avoid the process; as if that could be the cause of evil and imperfection in the present life, which is to produce the perfection of glory in the life to come.

11. None can be ignorant that God is the Supreme Good; that essential blessedness consists in union with Him; that the saints differ in glory, according as the union is more or less perfect; and that the soul cannot attain this union by the mere activity of its own powers, since God communicates Himself to the soul, in proportion as its passive capacity is great, noble and extensive. We can only be united to God in simplicity and passivity, and as this union is beatitude itself, the way that leads us in this passivity cannot be evil, but must be the most free from danger, and the best.

12. This way is not dangerous. Would Jesus Christ have made this the most perfect and necessary of all ways, had it been so? No! all can travel it; and as all are called to happiness, all are likewise called to the enjoyment of God, both in this life and the next, for that alone is happiness. I say the enjoyment of God himself, and not of his gifts; these latter do not constitute essential beatitude, as they cannot fully content the soul; it is so noble and so great, that the most exalted gifts of God cannot make it happy, unless the Giver also bestows Himself. Now the whole desire of the Divine Being is to give Himself to every creature, according to

the capacity with which it is endowed; and yet, alas! how reluctantly man suffers himself to be drawn to God! how fearful is he to prepare for divine union!

13. Some say, that we must not place ourselves in this state. I grant it; but I say also, that no creature could ever do it; since it would not be possible for any, by all their own efforts, to unite themselves to God; it is He alone must do it. It is altogether idle, then, to exclaim against those who are self-united, as such a thing cannot be. They say again, that some may feign to have attained this state. None can any more feign this, than the wretch who is on the point of perishing with hunger can, for any length of time at least, feign to be full and satisfied. Some wish or word, some sigh or sign, will inevitably escape him, and betray that he is far from being satisfied. Since then none can attain this end by their own labor, we do not pretend to introduce any into it, but only to point out the way that leads to it: beseeching all not to become attached to the accommodations on the road, external practices, which must all be left behind when the signal is given. The experienced instructor knows this, points to the water of life, and lends his aid to obtain it. Would it not be an unjustifiable cruelty to show a spring to a thirsty man, then bind him so that he could not reach it, and suffer him to die of thirst?

14. This is just what is done every day. Let us all agree in the way, as we all agree in the end, which is evident and incontrovertible. The way has its beginning, process, and termination; and the nearer we approach the consummation, the farther is the beginning behind us; it is only by leaving the one, that we can arrive at the other. You cannot get from the entrance to a distant place, without passing over the intermediate space, and, if the end be good, holy, and necessary, and the entrance also good, why should the necessary passage, the direct road leading from the one to the other, be evil? O the blindness of the greater part of mankind, who pride themselves on science and wisdom! How true is it, O my God, that thou hast hid these things from the wise and prudent, and hast revealed them unto babes!

Madame Guyon, 1617–79

The Communion of Saints

A.A. Hodge

The Westminster Confession of Faith
Chapter 26
Of the Communion of Saints

SECTION 1

All saints, that are united to Jesus Christ their Head, by his Spirit, and by faith, have fellowship with him in his graces, sufferings, death, resurrection, and glory:[1] and, being united to one another in love, they have communion in each other's gifts and graces,[2] and are obliged to the performance of such duties, public and private, as do conduce to their mutual good, both in the inward and outward man.[3]

[1] 1 John 1:3; Eph. 2:5–6; 3:16–18; John 1:16; Phil. 3:10; Rom. 6:5–6; 8:17; 2 Tim. 2:12

[2] Eph. 4:15–16; 1 Cor. 3:21–23; 12:7, 12; Col. 2:19

[3] 1 Thess. 5:11, 14; Rom. 1:11–12, 14; 1 John 3:16–18; Gal. 6:10

SECTION 2

Saints by profession are bound to maintain an holy fellowship and communion in the worship of God, and in performing such other spiritual services as tend to their mutual edification;[4] as also in relieving each other in outward things, according to their several abilities and necessities. Which communion, as God offereth opportunity, is to be extended unto all those who, in every place, call upon the name of the Lord Jesus.[5]

[4] Heb. 10:24–25; Acts 2:42, 46; Isa. 2:3; 1 Cor. 11:20

[5] 1 John 3:17; 2 Cor. ch. 8–9; Acts 2:44–45; 11:29–30

SECTION 3

This communion which the saints have with Christ, doth not make them in any wise partakers of the substance of his Godhead; or to be equal with Christ in any respect: either of which to affirm is impious and blasphemous.[6] Nor doth their communion one with another, as saints, take away, or infringe the title or propriety which each man hath in his goods and possessions.[7]

[6] Col. 1:18–19; 1 Cor. 8:6; Psa. 45:6–7; Heb.

1:6–9; John 1:14; 20:17

[7] Exod. 20:15; Eph. 4:28; Acts 5:4

Communion is a mutual interchange of offices between parties, which flows from a common principle in which they are united. The nature and degree of the communion will depend upon the nature and intimacy of the union from which it proceeds.

This chapter teaches:

1. Of the union of Christ and his people.

2. The fellowship between him and them resulting therefrom.

3 The union between the true people of Christ growing out of their union with him.

4. The communion of saints growing out of their union with each other.

5. The mutual duties of all who profess to be saints with regard to all their fellow-professors.

1. All saints are united to the Lord Jesus. We need to know what is the foundation and what is the nature of this union, and how it is established.

(1.) As to the foundation of the union subsisting between the true believer and the Lord Jesus, the Scriptures teach that it rests in the eternal purpose of the Triune God, expressed in the decree of election (we were "chosen in him before the foundation of the world," Eph. i. 4), and the eternal covenant of grace formed between the Father and his Word as the mediatorial head of his people, treating with the Head for the members, and with the members in the Head, and providing for their salvation in him. John xvii. 2, 6.

(2.) As to the nature of this union of the believer with Christ, the Scriptures teach –

(a.) That it is federal and representative, whereby Christ acts in all things as our federal Head, in our stead, and for our benefit. Hence our legal status is determined by his, and his rights, honors, relations, all are made ours in copartnership with him.

(b.) That it is a vital and spiritual union. Its actuating source and bond is the Spirit of the Head, who dwells and works in the members. 1 Cor. vi. 17; xii. 13; 1 John iii. 24; iv. 13. Hence our spiritual life is derived from him and sustained and determined by his life, which we share.

Gal. ii. 20.

(c.) That it is a union between our entire persons and Christ, and therefore one involving our bodies through our souls. 1 Cor. vi. 15, 19.

(3.) As to the manner in which this union is established, the Scriptures teach that the elect, having been in the divine idea comprehended under the headship of Christ from eternity, are in time actually united to him –

(a.) By the powerful operation of his Spirit, whereby they are "quickened together with Christ" (Eph. ii. 5); which Spirit evermore dwells in them as the organ of Christ's presence with them, the infinite medium through which the fullness of his love and life, and all the benefits purchased by his blood, pass over freely from the Head to the members.

(b.) By the actings of faith upon their part, whereby they grasp Christ and appropriate him and his grace to themselves, and whereby they ever continue to live in him and to draw their resources from him. Eph. iii. 17.

This union is illustrated in Scripture by the relation subsisting between a foundation and its superstructure (1 Pet. ii. 4–6); a tree and its branches (John xv. 5); the members of the body and the head (Eph. iv. 15, 16); a husband and wife (Eph. v. 31, 32); Adam and his descendants (Rom. v. 12–19).

This union has been called by theologians a "mystical" union, because, it never could have been known unless revealed by the Lord himself, and because it is so incomparably intimate and excellent that it transcends all other unions of which we have experience. Nevertheless it is not mysterious in the sense of involving any confusion between Christ's personality and ours, nor does it make us in any wise partakers of his Godhead or to be equal with him in any respect. It is a union between persons in which each retains his separate identity, and in which the believer, although immeasurably exalted and blessed, nevertheless is entirely subordinated to and continues dependent upon his Lord.

2. On the basis of this union a most intimate fellowship or interchange of mutual offices ever continues to be sustained between believers and Christ.

(1.) They have fellowship with Christ:

(a.) In all the covenant merits of his active and passive obedience. Forensically they are "complete in him." Col. ii. 10. His Father, his inheritance, his throne, his crown, are theirs. As their mediatorial Head he acts as prophet, priest, and king. In union with him they are also prophets, priests, and kings. 1 John ii. 27; 1 Peter ii. 5; Rev. iii. 21; v. 10. They have fellowship with Christ also:

(b.) In the transforming, assimilating power of his life. "Of his fullness have all we received, and grace for grace." John i. 16. Thus they have the "Spirit," and "the mind" of Christ, and bear his "likeness "or "image." Rom. viii. 9; Phil. ii. 5; 1 John iii. 2. This includes the bodies also, making them temples of the Holy Ghost; and in the resurrection our glorified bodies are to be like his. 1 Cor. vi. 19; xv. 43, 49. They have fellowship with Christ:

(c.) In all their experiences, inward and outward, in their joys and victories, in their labors, sufferings, temptations, and death. Rom. viii. 37; 2 Cor. xii. 9; Gal. vi. 17; Phil. iii. 10; Heb. xii. 3; 1 Pet. iv. 13.

(2.) Christ has fellowship with them. They belong to him as the purchase of his blood. They are devoted to his service. They are coworkers together with him in building up his kingdom. They bear fruit to his praise, and shine as stars in his crown. Their hearts, their lives, their possessions, are all consecrated to him, and are held by them in trust for him. Prov. xix. 17; Rom. xiv. 8; 1 Cor. vi. 19, 20.

3. Since all true believers are thus intimately united to Christ as the common Head of the whole body, and the Source of a common life, it follows that they must be intimately united together. If they have but one Head, and are all members of one body, they must have one common life, and be all members one of another.

The Romish and Ritualistic view is, that individuals are united to the Church through the sacraments, and through the Church to Christ. The true view is, that the individual is united to Christ the Head by the Holy Ghost and by faith; and by being united to Christ he is, *ipso facto*, united to all Christ's members, the Church. The holy catholic Church is the product of the Holy

Ghost. Wherever the Spirit is, there the Church is. The presence of the Spirit is known by his fruits, which are "love, joy, peace," etc. Gal. v. 22, 23. All believers receiving the same Spirit are by him baptized into "one body;" and thus they all become, "though many members," but "one body," "the body of Christ "and "members in particular." 1 Cor. xii. 13–27.

4. Hence true believers, all being united in one living body, sustain many intimate relations, and discharge many important offices for one another, which are summarily expressed by the general phrase, "The communion of saints."

5. The mutual duties of all who profess to be saints with regard to all their fellow-professors. (1.) They have a common Head, and common duties with respect to him; a common profession, a common system of faith to maintain, a common gospel to preach, a common worship and service to maintain.
(2.) They have a common life, and one Holy Ghost dwelling in and binding together in one the whole body. Hence they are involved in the ties of sympathy and identity of interest. One cannot prosper without all prospering with him – one cannot suffer without all suffering with him.
(3.) As they constitute one body in the eyes of the world, they have a common reputation, and are all severally and collectively honored or dishonored with each other. Hence all schisms in the body, injurious controversies, malignant representations of Christian by Christian, are self-defaming as well as wicked.
(4.) The body of saints is like the natural body in this also, that, although one body, each several member is an organ of the Holy Ghost for a special function, and has his own individual difference of qualification, and consequently of duty. Hence, in the economy of the body, each member is to contribute his special function and his special grace or beauty, and has in his turn fellowship in the gifts and complementary graces of all the rest. Eph. iv. 11–16; 1 Cor. xii. 4–21. This shall be perfectly realized in heaven. John x. 16; xvii. 22.
(5.) Since this is the union of all true believers with the Lord and with each other, and since, consequently, a "communion of saints" so

intimate necessarily nourishes among true believers in proportion to their intelligence and their advancement in grace, it follows that all branches of the visible Church, and all the individual members thereof, should do all within their power to act upon the principle of the "communion of saints" in their intercourse with all who profess the true religion. If the Church is one, the churches are one. If all saints are one, and are embraced in this holy "communion," then all who profess to be saints should regard and treat all their fellow-professors on the presumption that they are saints and "heirs together with them of the grace of life." Think of it! In spite of all controversies and jealousies, one in the eternal electing love of God! – one in the purchase of Christ's sacrificial blood! – one in the beatifying indwelling of the Holy Ghost! – one in the eternal inheritance of glory! Surely we should be also one in all the charities, sympathies, and helpful offices possible, in these short and evil days of earthly pilgrimage. These mutual duties are, of course, some of them public – as between different evangelical churches – and may of them private and personal. Many of them relate to the souls, and many also to the bodies of the saints. The rule is, the law of love in the heart, and the principles and examples of saints recorded in Scripture applied to the special circumstances of every individual case. But while these mutual relations and offices of the saints sanctify, they are not designed to supersede the fundamental principles of human society, as the rights of property and the family tie.

A.A. Hodge, 1823–86

The Imitation of Christ
Thomas à Kempis

BOOK II
THE INTERIOR LIFE

"The kingdom of God is within you," says the Lord.

Turn, then, to God with all your heart. Forsake this wretched world and your soul shall find rest. Learn to despise external things, to devote yourself to those that are within, and you will see the kingdom of God come unto you, that kingdom which is peace and joy in the Holy Spirit, gifts not given to the impious.

Christ will come to you offering His consolation, if you prepare a fit dwelling for Him in your heart, whose beauty and glory, wherein He takes delight, are all from within. His visits with the inward man are frequent, His communion sweet and full of consolation, His peace great, and His intimacy wonderful indeed.

Therefore, faithful soul, prepare your heart for this Bridegroom that He may come and dwell within you; He Himself says: "If any one love Me, he will keep My word, and My Father will love him, and We will come to him, and will make Our abode with him."

Give place, then, to Christ, but deny entrance to all others, for when you have Christ you are rich and He is sufficient for you. He will provide for you. He will supply your every want, so that you need not trust in frail, changeable men. Christ remains forever, standing firmly with us to the end.

Do not place much confidence in weak and mortal man, helpful and friendly though he be; and do not grieve too much if he sometimes opposes and contradicts you. Those who are with us today may be against us tomorrow, and vice versa, for men change with the wind. Place all your trust in God; let Him be your fear and your love. He will answer for you; He will do what is best for you.

You have here no lasting home. You are a stranger and a pilgrim wherever you may be, and you shall have no rest until you are wholly united with Christ.

Why do you look about here when this is not the place of your repose? Dwell rather upon heaven and give but a passing glance to all earthly things. They all pass away, and you together with them. Take care, then, that you do not cling to them lest you be entrapped and perish. Fix your mind on the Most High, and pray unceasingly to Christ.

If you do not know how to meditate on heavenly things, direct your thoughts to Christ's passion and willingly behold His sacred wounds. If you turn devoutly to the wounds and precious stigmata of Christ, you will find great comfort in suffering, you will

mind but little the scorn of men, and you will easily bear their slanderous talk.

When Christ was in the world, He was despised by men; in the hour of need He was forsaken by acquaintances and left by friends to the depths of scorn. He was willing to suffer and to be despised; do you dare to complain of anything? He had enemies and defamers; do you want everyone to be your friend, your benefactor? How can your patience be rewarded if no adversity test it? How can you be a friend of Christ if you are not willing to suffer any hardship? Suffer with Christ and for Christ if you wish to reign with Him.

Had you but once entered into perfect communion with Jesus or tasted a little of His ardent love, you would care nothing at all for your own comfort or discomfort but would rejoice in the reproach you suffer; for love of Him makes a man despise himself.

A man who is a lover of Jesus and of truth, a truly interior man who is free from uncontrolled affections, can turn to God at will and rise above himself to enjoy spiritual peace.

He who tastes life as it really is, not as men say or think it is, is indeed wise with the wisdom of God rather than of men.

He who learns to live the interior life and to take little account of outward things, does not seek special places or times to perform devout exercises. A spiritual man quickly recollects himself because he has never wasted his attention upon externals. No outside work, no business that cannot wait stands in his way. He adjusts himself to things as they happen. He whose disposition is well ordered cares nothing about the strange, perverse behavior of others, for a man is upset and distracted only in proportion as he engrosses himself in externals.

If all were well with you, therefore, and if you were purified from all sin, everything would tend to your good and be to your profit. But because you are as yet neither entirely dead to self nor free from all earthly affection, there is much that often displeases and disturbs you. Nothing so mars and defiles the heart of man as impure attachment to created things. But if you refuse external consolation, you will be able to contemplate heavenly things and often to experience interior joy.

Thomas à Kempis, 1379 – 1471

Prayer and the Consciousness

Abraham Kuyper

"Call upon Me in the day of trouble; I will deliver thee, and thou shalt glorify Me." – Psalm 1. 15.

The form of prayer does not affect its character. It may be a mere groaning in thought, or a sigh in which the oppressed soul finds relief; it may consist of a single cry, a flow of words, or an elaborate invocation of the Eternal. It may even turn into speaking or singing. But so long as the soul, in the consciousness that God lives and hears its cry, addresses itself directly to Him as tho it stood in His immediate presence, the character of prayer remains intact. However, discrimination between these various forms of prayer is necessary in order to discover, in the root of prayer itself, the work of the Holy Spirit.

The suppliant is you; your ego; neither your body nor your soul, but your person. It is true, both body and soul are engaged in prayer, but yet in such a way that your person, your ego, your self, pours out the soul; in the soul becomes conscious of your prayer, and through the body gives it utterance.

This will become clear when we consider the part which the body takes in prayer; for no one will deny that the body has something to do with prayer. Mutual prayer is simply impossible without the aid of the body, for that requires a voice to utter prayer in one, and hearing ears in the others. Moreover, prayer without words rarely satisfies the soul. Mere mental prayer is necessarily imperfect; earnest, fervent prayer constrains us to express it in words. There maybe a depth of prayer that cannot be expressed, but then we are conscious of the lack; and the fact that the Holy Spirit prays for us with groans that can not be uttered is to us source of very great comfort.

When the soul is perfectly composed, mere mental meditation may be very sweet and blessed; but no sooner do the waters of the soul heave with broader swell than we feel irresistibly constrained to utter prayer in words; and altho in the solitude of the closet yet the silent prayer becomes an audible and sometimes a loud invocation of the mercies of our God. Even Christ in Gethsemane prayed, not in silent meditation nor in unuttered groans, but with strong words which still seem to sound in our ears.

And not only in this, but in other ways, the body largely affects our prayer.

There is, in the first place, a natural desire to make the whole body partake of it. For this reason we kneel when we humble ourselves before the majesty of God. We close the eyes not to be distracted by the world. We lift up the hands as invoking His grace. The agonized wrestler in prayer prostrates himself on the ground. We uncover the head in token of reverence. In the assembly of the saints the men stand on their feet, as they would if the King of Glory should come in.

In the second place, the effect of the body upon prayer is evident from the influence which bodily conditions frequently exert upon it. Depressing headache, muscular or nervous pains, congestive disorders causing undue excitement, often prevent not the sigh, but the full outpouring of: prayer. Every one knows what effect drowsiness has upon the exercise of warm and earnest prayer. While, on the other hand, a vigorous constitution, clear head, and tranquil mind are peculiarly conducive to prayer. For this reason the Scripture and the example of the fathers speak of fasting as means to assist the saints in this exercise.

Lastly, bodily distress prior to distress of the soul has often opened mute lips in prayer before God. Families that were strangers to prayer have learned to pray in times of serious illness. In threatening dangers of fire or 'water, lips that were used to cursing have frequently cried aloud in supplication. Compelled by war, famine, and pestilence, godless cities have frequently appointed days of prayer with the same zeal wherewith formerly they appointed days of rejoicing.

Hence the significance of the body in this respect is very great in fact, so great that when abnormal conditions cause the bond between body and soul to become inactive, prayer ceases at the same time. However, mere bodily exercise is not prayer, but lip-service. Mere imitation of the form, mere sounds of prayer tolling from the lips, mere words addressed to the Eternal One without conscious purpose in the soul, are the form of prayer, but not the power thereof.

And this is not all. To trace the work of the Holy Spirit in prayer we must enter more deeply into this matter. According to the ordinary representation, which is partly correct, prayer is impossible without an act of the memory, by which we recall our sins and the mercies of God; without an act of the mind, choosing the words to express our adoration of the divine virtues; without an act of the consciousness, to represent our needs in prayer; without an act of love, enabling us to enter into the needs of our country, church, and place of habitation, of our relatives, children, and friends; and lastly, without meditating upon the fundamentals of prayer, recalling the promises of God, the experiences of the fathers, and the conditions of the Kingdom.

All these are activities of the brain, which is the seat of the thinking mind; as soon as this is disturbed by abnormal conditions, the consciousness is obscured and the thinking ceases or becomes confused. Without the brain, therefore, there can be no thinking; without thinking there can be no thoughts; without thoughts there can be no accumulation of thoughts in the memory; and without meditation, which is the result of the former two, there can be no prayer in the proper sense of the word. From which it is evident that prayer depends upon the exercise of bodily functions much more largely than is generally supposed.

And yet, let us be on our guard not to push this too far; and imagine that the root of prayer is in the brain, i.e., in a member of the body; for it is not. Our own experience in prayer teaches us, agreeably to the Scripture, that it is in the heart. As from the heart are the issues of life, so are also the issues of prayer. Unless the heart compels us to pray, all our cries are in vain. Men with magnificent brains but cold hearts have never been men of prayer; and, on the contrary, among the men of poor mental development, but with large, warm hearts, are found a number of souls mighty in prayer.

And even this is not all; for the heart itself is a bodily organ. In proportion as the blood circulates through the heart with strong or feeble pulsation, in that proportion is the soul's vital expression strong and overwhelming, or weak and weary; and, dependent upon

this, prayer is warm and animated, or cold and formal. When the heart is weak and suffering, the life of prayer generally loses something of its freshness and power.

We are men, and not spirits; and, unlike angels, we can not exist without the body. God created us body and soul. The former belongs to our being essentially and forever. Hence an utterance of our life like prayer must necessarily be dependent upon soul and body, and that in much stronger sense than we usually suppose.

However, the fact must be emphasized that prayer's dependence upon the body is not absolute. Otherwise there could be no prayer among the angels, nor in the Holy Spirit. Our prayer depends upon the consciousness; when that is lost, prayer ceases. And, since we are men, consisting of body and soul, the human consciousness is, in the ordinary sense, related also to the body. But that this dependence is not absolute is evident from the fact that the Eternal Being, whose divine consciousness is but dimly reflected in that of man, has no body. "God is Spirit." And the same is true of the world of spirits, who, altho incorporeal, yet possess a consciousness and of the three Persons of the Trinity, especially of the Holy Spirit.

Hence the question arises whether man separated by death from the body loses consciousness. To this we reply in the affirmative. Our human consciousness, as we possess it in our present earthly existence, is lost in death, to be restored to us in the resurrection, in a form stronger, purer, and holier. St. Paul says: "We," – that is, our human consciousness, – "now know in part, but then we, the same human consciousness shall know face to face, even as we are known."

But from this it does not follow that in the intermediate state the soul must be denied all self-consciousness. The Scripture teaches the very contrary. Of course, for this knowledge we, depend upon the Scripture alone. The dead can not tell us anything of their state after death. No one but God, who ordained the conditions of life in the intermediate state, can reveal to us what those conditions are. And He has revealed to us that immediately after death the redeemed are with Jesus. St.

Paul says: "I have a desire to depart and to be with Christ." And, since a friend's presence does not afford us pleasure except we are conscious of it, it follows that the souls of the saints, in the intermediate state, must possess some sort of consciousness different from that which we now possess, but sufficient to realize and enjoy the presence of Christ. For which reasons the fathers rejected every representation of death as a sleep; as tho our persons from the moment of death to that of the resurrection should sleep in perfect forgetfulness of the glorious things of God; altho they, denied not the intermediate state in which the soul is separated from the body.

Wherefore it seems possible for the soul to be conscious in a higher sense, without the aid of the body, independently of the heart and the brains – a consciousness which enables us to realize the glorious things of God and the presence of the Lord Jesus Christ.

How this higher consciousness operates is a deep mystery; nor is the nature of its operation revealed. And since we can have no other representations than those formed by means of the brain, it is impossible for us to have the slightest idea of this higher consciousness. Its existence is revealed, but no more.

The following may be considered as settled, and this is the principal thing in our present inquiry: In that temporary consciousness in which we will work in the intermediate state, the same person will become self-conscious who now is conscious by means of heart and brain. Even after death it shall be our own person that shall be bearer of that consciousness, and by it I shall be conscious of myself. It can not be otherwise; or else consciousness after death is impossible, for the simple reason that consciousness alone can not exist without a person. And another person it can not be. Hence my own person shall be bearer of that consciousness; and thus shall I be enabled to enjoy the presence of Jesus.

From this we draw the following important conclusion: that so far as the form of the ordinary consciousness is concerned, it is dependent upon the body; while essentially it is not so dependent. Essentially it continues to exist, even when sleep obscures the thought, or insanity estranges me from myself, or a swoon makes me lose consciousness; essentially it continues to exist even when death temporarily separates me from the body. From which it follows that the root and seat of the consciousness must be looked for in the soul, and that heart and brain are but the vehicles, conductors, which our person uses to manifest that consciousness in ideas and representations.

And since prayer is a speaking to the Eternal, i.e., a conscious standing before Him, it follows that the root of prayer has its seat in our person and in our spiritual being; and, altho bound also to the body, so far as the germ is concerned rests in our personal ego, in so far as the ego, conscious of the existence of the divine Persons and of the bond that unites it to them, allows that bond to operate. And thus we come to this final conclusion: that the possibility of prayer finds its deepest ground in the fact of our being created after the image of God. Not only is our self-consciousness a result of that fact, for God is eternally self-conscious, but from it also springs that other mighty fact that I, as a man, can be conscious of the existence of the. Eternal, and of the intimate bond which unites me, to Him. The consciousness of this bond and relation manifests itself in prayer as soon as we address ourselves to God. Hence the work of the Holy Spirit in prayer must be looked for in His work of the creation of man. And since; in our former study, on this point, we discovered that it is God the Holy Spirit who in man's creation caused this consciousness to awake, carrying into it, and maintaining by it the consciousness of the existence of God and of the bond which unites man to Him, it is evident that prayer, as a phenomenon in man's spiritual life, finds its basis directly in the work of the Holy Spirit in man's creation.

Abraham Kuyper, 1837–1920

A Serious Call to a Devout and Holy Life

William Law

The times and hours of prayer

CHAPTER 14

Concerning that part of devotion which relates to times and hours of prayer. Of daily early prayer in the morning. How we are to improve our forms of prayer, and how to increase the spirit of devotion.

Having in the foregoing chapters shown the necessity of a devout spirit, or habit of mind, in every part of our common life, in the discharge of all our business, in the use of all the gifts of God; I come now to consider that part of devotion, which relates to times and hours of prayer.

I take it for granted, that every Christian, that is in health, is up early in the morning; for it is much more reasonable to suppose a person up early, because he is a Christian, than because he is a laborer, or a tradesman, or a servant, or has business that wants him.

We naturally conceive some abhorrence of a man that is in bed when he should be at his labor or in his shop. We cannot tell how to think anything good of him, who is such a slave to drowsiness as to neglect his business for it.

Let this therefore teach us to conceive how odious we must appear in the sight of Heaven, if we are in bed, shut up in sleep and darkness, when we should be praising God; and are such slaves to drowsiness, as to neglect our devotions for it.

For if he is to be blamed as a slothful drone, that rather chooses the lazy indulgence of sleep, than to perform his proper share of worldly business; how much more is he to be reproached, that would rather lie folded up in a bed, than be raising up his heart to God in acts of praise and adoration!

Prayer is the nearest approach to God, and the highest enjoyment of Him, that we are capable of in this life.

It is the noblest exercise of the soul, the most exalted use of our best faculties, and the highest imitation of the blessed inhabitants of Heaven.

When our hearts are full of God, sending up holy desires to the throne of grace, we are then in our highest state, we are upon the utmost heights of human greatness; we are not before kings and princes, but in the presence and audience of the Lord of all the world, and can be no higher, till death is swallowed up in glory.

On the other hand, sleep is the poorest, dullest refreshment of the body, that is so far from being intended as an enjoyment, that we are forced to receive it either in a state of insensibility, or in the folly of dreams.

Sleep is such a dull, stupid state of existence, that even amongst mere animals, we despise them most which are most drowsy.

He, therefore, that chooses to enlarge the slothful indulgence of sleep, rather than be early at his devotions to God, chooses the dullest refreshment of the body, before the highest, noblest employment of the soul; he chooses that state which is a reproach to mere animals, rather than that exercise which is the glory of Angels.

You will perhaps say, though you rise late, yet you are always careful of your devotions when you are up.

It may be so. But what then? Is it well done of you to rise late, because you pray when you are up?

Is it pardonable to waste great part of the day in bed, because some time after you say your prayers?

It is as much your duty to rise to pray, as to pray when you are risen. And if you are late at your prayers, you offer to God the prayers of an idle, slothful worshiper, that rises to prayers as idle servants rise to their labor.

Farther; if you fancy that you are careful of your devotions when you are up, though it be your custom to rise late, you deceive yourself; for you cannot perform your devotions as you ought. For he that cannot deny himself this drowsy indulgence, but must pass away good part of the morning in it, is no more prepared for prayer when he is up, than he is prepared for fasting, abstinence, or any other self-denial. He may indeed more easily read over a form of prayer, than he can perform these duties; but he is no more disposed to enter into the true spirit of prayer than he is disposed to fasting. For sleep thus indulged gives a softness and idleness to all our tempers, and makes us unable to relish anything but what suits with an idle state of mind, and gratifies our natural tempers, as sleep does. So that a person who is a slave to this idleness is in the same temper when he is up; and though he is not asleep, yet he is under the effects of it; and everything that is idle, indulgent, or sensual, pleases him for the same reason that sleep pleases him; and, on the other hand, everything that requires care, or trouble, or self-denial, is hateful to him, for the same reason that he hates to rise. He that places any happiness in this morning indulgence, would be glad to have all the day made happy in the same manner; though not with sleep, yet with such enjoyments as gratify and indulge the body in the same manner as sleep does; or, at least, with such as come as near to it as they can. The remembrance of a warm bed is in his mind all the day, and he is glad when he is not one of those that sit starving in a church.

Now you do not imagine that such a one can truly mortify that body which he thus indulges: yet you might as well think this, as that he can truly perform his devotions; or live in such a drowsy state of indulgence, and yet relish the joys of a spiritual life.

For surely no one will pretend to say that he knows and feels the true happiness of prayer, who does not think it worth his while to be early at it.

It is not possible in nature for an epicure to be truly devout: he must renounce this habit of sensuality, before he can relish the happiness of devotion.

Now he that turns sleep into an idle indulgence, does as much to corrupt and disorder his soul, to make it a slave to bodily appetites, and keep it incapable of all devout and heavenly tempers, as he that turns the necessities of eating into a course of indulgence.

A person that eats and drinks too much does not feel such effects from it, as those do who live in notorious instances of gluttony and intemperance: but yet his course of indulgence, though it be not scandalous in the eyes of the world, nor such as torments his own conscience, is a great and constant hindrance to his improvement in virtue; it gives him eyes that see not, and ears that hear not; it creates a sensuality in the soul, increases the power of bodily passions, and makes him incapable of entering into the true spirit of religion.

Now this is the case of those who waste their time in sleep; it does not disorder their lives, or wound their consciences, as notorious acts of intemperance do; but, like any other more moderate course of indulgence, it

silently, and by smaller degrees, wears away the spirit of religion, and sinks the soul into a state of dullness and sensuality.

If you consider devotion only as a time of so much prayer, you may perhaps perform it, though you live in this daily indulgence; but if you consider it as a state of the heart, as a lively fervor of the soul, that is deeply affected with a sense of its own misery and infirmities, and desires the Spirit of God more than all things in the world: you will find that the spirit of indulgence, and the spirit of prayer, cannot subsist together. Mortification of all kinds is the very life and soul of piety; but he that has not so small a degree of it, as to be able to be early at his prayers, can have no reason to think that he has taken up his cross, and is following Christ.

What conquest has he got over himself; what right hand has he cut off; what trials is he prepared for; what sacrifice is he ready to offer unto God, who cannot be so cruel to himself as to rise to prayer at such time as the drudging part of the world are content to rise to their labor?

Some people will not scruple to tell you, that they indulge themselves in sleep, because they have nothing to do; and that; if they had either business or pleasure to rise to, they would not lose so much of their time in sleep. But such people must be told that they mistake the matter; that they have a great deal of business to do; they have a hardened heart to change; they have the whole spirit of religion to get. For surely he that thinks devotion to be of less moment than business or pleasure; or that he has nothing to do because nothing but his prayers want him, may be justly said to have the whole spirit of religion to seek.

You must not therefore consider how small a crime it is to rise late, but you must consider how great a misery it is to want the spirit of religion, to have a heart not rightly affected with prayer; and to live in such softness and idleness, as makes you incapable of the most fundamental duties of a truly Christian and spiritual life.

This is a right way of judging of the crime of wasting great part of your time in bed.

You must not consider the thing barely in itself, but what it proceeds from; what virtues it shows to be wanting; what vices it naturally strengthens. For every habit of this kind discovers the state of the soul, and plainly shows the whole turn of your mind.

If our blessed Lord used to pray early before day; if He spent whole nights in prayer; if the devout Anna was day and night in the temple (Luke ii. 36, 37); if St. Paul and Silas at midnight sang praises unto God (Acts xvi. 35); if the primitive Christians, for several hundred years, besides their hours of prayers in the daytime, met publicly in the churches at midnight, to join in psalms and prayers; is it not certain that these practices showed the state of their heart? Are they not so many plain proofs of the whole turn of their minds?

And if you live in a contrary state, wasting great part of every day in sleep, thinking any time soon enough to be at your prayers; is it not equally certain, that this practice as much shows the state of your heart, and the whole turn of your mind?

So that if this indulgence is your way of life, you have as much reason to believe yourself destitute of the true spirit of devotion, as you have to believe the Apostles and saints of the primitive Church were truly devout. For as their way of life was a demonstration of their devotion, so a contrary way of life is as strong a proof of a want of devotion.

When you read the Scriptures, you see a religion that is all life, and spirit, and joy, in God; that supposes our souls risen from earthly desires, and bodily indulgences, to prepare for another body, another world, and other enjoyments. You see Christians represented as temples of the Holy Ghost, as children of the day, as candidates for an eternal crown, as watchful virgins, that have their lamps always burning, in expectation of the bridegroom. But can he be thought to have this joy in God, this care of eternity, this watchful spirit, who has not zeal enough to rise to his prayers?

When you look into the writings and lives of the first Christians, you see the same spirit that you see in the Scriptures. All is reality, life, and action. Watching and prayers, self-denial and mortification, was the common business of their lives.

From that time to this, there has been no person like them, eminent for piety, who has not, like them, been eminent for self-denial and mortification. This is the only royal way that leads to a kingdom.

But how far are you from this way of life, or rather how contrary to it, if, instead of imitating their austerity and mortification, you cannot so much as renounce so poor an indulgence, as to be able to rise to your prayers! If self-denials and bodily sufferings, if watchings and fastings, will be marks of glory at the day of judgment, where must we hide our heads, that have slumbered away our time in sloth and softness?

You perhaps now find some pretenses to excuse yourselves from that severity of fasting and self-denial, which the first Christians practiced. You fancy that human nature is grown weaker, and that the difference of climates may make it not possible for you to observe their methods of self-denial and austerity in these colder countries.

But all this is but pretense: for the change is not in the outward state of things, but in the inward state of our minds. When there is the same spirit in us that there was in the Apostles and primitive Christians, when we feel the weight of religion as they did, when we have their faith and hope, we shall take up our cross, and deny ourselves, and live in such methods of mortification as they did.

Had St. Paul lived in a cold country, had he had a constitution made weak with a sickly stomach, and often infirmities, he would have done as he advised Timothy, he would have mixed a little wine with his water. But still he would have lived in a state of self-denial and mortification. He would have given this same account of himself: – "I therefore so run, not as uncertainly; so fight I, not as one that beateth the air: but I keep under my body, and bring it into subjection: lest that by any means, when I have preached to others, I myself should be a castaway" (1 Cor. ix. 26, 27).

After all, let it now be supposed, that you imagine there is no necessity for you to be so sober and vigilant, so fearful of yourself, so watchful over your passions, so apprehensive of danger, so careful of your salvation, as the Apostles were. Let it be supposed, that you imagine that you want less self-denial and mortification, to subdue your bodies, and purify your souls, than they wanted; that you need not have your loins girt, and your lamps burning, as they had; will you therefore live in a quite contrary state? Will you make your life as constant a course of softness and indulgence, as theirs was of strictness and self-denial?

If therefore you should think that you have time sufficient, both for prayer and other duties, though you rise late; yet let me persuade you to rise early, as an instance of self-denial. It is so small a one, that, if you cannot comply with it, you have no reason to think yourself capable of any other.

If I were to desire you not to study the gratifications of your palate, in the niceties of meats and drinks, I would not insist much upon the crime of wasting your money in such a way, though it be a great one; but I would desire you to renounce such a way of life, because it supports you in such a state of sensuality and indulgence, as renders you incapable of relishing the most essential doctrines of religion.

For the same reason, I do not insist much on the crime of wasting so much of your time in sleep, though it be a great one; but I desire you to renounce this indulgence, because it gives a softness and idleness to your soul, and is so contrary to that lively, zealous, watchful, self-denying spirit, which was not only the spirit of Christ and His Apostles, the spirit of all the saints and martyrs which have ever been amongst men, but must be the spirit of all those who would not sink in the common corruption of the world.

Here, therefore, we must fix our charge against this practice; we must blame it, not as having this or that particular evil, but as a general habit, that extends itself through our whole spirit, and supports a state of mind that is wholly wrong.

It is contrary to piety; not as accidental slips and mistakes in life are contrary to it, but in such a manner, as an ill habit of body is contrary to health.

On the other hand, if you were to rise early every morning, as an instance of self-denial, as a method of renouncing indulgence, as a means of redeeming your time, and fitting your spirit for prayer, you would find mighty advantages from it. This method, though it seems such a small circumstance of life, would in all probability be a means of great piety. It would keep

it constantly in your head, that softness and idleness were to be avoided, that self-denial was a part of Christianity. It would teach you to exercise power over yourself, and make you able by degrees to renounce other pleasures and tempers that war against the soul.

This one rule would teach you to think of others: it would dispose your mind to exactness, and would be very likely to bring the remaining part of the day under rules of prudence and devotion.

But above all, one certain benefit from this method you will be sure of having, it will best fit and prepare you for the reception of the Holy Spirit. When you thus begin the day in the spirit of religion, renouncing sleep, because you are to renounce softness, and redeem your time; this disposition, as it puts your heart into a good state, so it will procure the assistance of the Holy Spirit: what is so planted and watered will certainly have an increase from God. You will then speak from your heart, your soul will be awake, your prayers will refresh you like meat and drink, you will feel what you say, and begin to know what saints and holy men have meant, by fervor of devotion.

He that is thus prepared for prayer, who rises with these dispositions, is in a very different state from him who has no rules of this kind; who rises by chance, as he happens to be weary of his bed, or is able to sleep no longer. If such a one prays only with his mouth, – if his heart feels nothing of that which he says, – if his prayers are only things of course, – if they are a lifeless form of words, which he only repeats because they are soon said, – there is nothing to be wondered at in all this; for such dispositions are the natural effect of such a state of life.

Hoping, therefore, that you are now enough convinced of the necessity of rising early to your prayers, I shall proceed to lay before you a method of daily prayer.

I do not take upon me to prescribe to you the use of any particular forms of prayer, but only to show you the necessity of praying at such times, and in such a manner.

You will here find some helps, how to furnish yourself with such forms of prayer as shall be useful to you. And if you are such a proficient in the spirit of devotion, that your heart is always ready to pray in its own language, in this case I press no necessity of borrowed forms.

For though I think a form of prayer very necessary and expedient for public worship, yet if any one can find a better way of raising his heart unto God in private, than by prepared forms of prayer, I have nothing to object against it; my design being only to assist and direct such as stand in need of assistance.

Thus much, I believe, is certain, that the generality of Christians ought to use forms of prayer at all the regular times of prayer. It seems right for every one to begin with a form of prayer; and if, in the midst of his devotions, he finds his heart ready to break forth into new and higher strains of devotion, he should leave his form for a while, and follow those fervor of his heart, till it again wants the assistance of his usual petitions.

This seems to be the true liberty of private devotion; it should be under the direction of some form; but not so tied down to it, but that it may be free to take such new expressions, as its present fervor happen to furnish it with; which sometimes are more affecting, and carry the soul more powerfully to God, than any expressions that were ever used before.

All people that have ever made any reflections upon what passes in their own hearts, must know that they are mighty changeable in regard to devotion. Sometimes our hearts are so awakened, have such strong apprehensions of the Divine Presence, are so full of deep compunction for our sins, that we cannot confess them in any language but that of tears.

Sometimes the light of God's countenance shines so bright upon us, we see so far into the invisible world, we are so affected with the wonders of the love and goodness of God, that our hearts worship and adore in a language higher than that of words, and we feel transports of devotion, which only can be felt.

On the other hand, sometimes we are so sunk into our bodies, so dull and unaffected with that which concerns our souls, that our hearts are as much too low for our prayers; we cannot keep pace with our forms of confession, or feel half of that in our hearts which we have in our mouths; we thank and praise God with forms of words, but our hearts have little or no share in them.

It is therefore highly necessary to provide against this inconstancy of our hearts, by having at hand such forms of prayer as may best suit us when our hearts are in their best state, and also be most likely to raise and stir them up when they are sunk into dullness. For, as words have a power of affecting our hearts on all occasions, as the same thing differently expressed has different effects upon our minds, so it is reasonable that we should make this advantage of language, and provide ourselves with such forms of expression as are most likely to move and enliven our souls, and fill them with sentiments suitable to them.

The first thing that you are to do, when you are upon your knees, is to shut your eyes, and with a short silence let your soul place itself in the presence of God; that is, you are to use this, or some other better method, to separate yourself from all common thoughts, and make your heart as sensible as you can of the Divine presence.

Now if this recollection of spirit is necessary, — as who can say it is not? — then how poorly must they perform their devotions, who are always in a hurry; who begin them in haste, and hardly allow themselves time to repeat their very form, with any gravity or attention! Theirs is properly saying prayers, instead of praying.

To proceed: if you were to use yourself (as far as you can) to pray always in the same place; if you were to reserve that place for devotion, and not allow yourself to do anything common in it; if you were never to be there yourself, but in times of devotion; if any little room, or (if that cannot be) if any particular part of a room was thus used, this kind of consecration of it as a place holy unto God, would have an effect upon your mind, and dispose you to such tempers, as would very much assist your devotion. For by having a place thus sacred in your room, it would in some measure resemble a chapel or house of God. This would dispose you to be always in the spirit of religion, when you were there; and fill you with wise and holy thoughts, when you were by yourself. Your own apartment would raise in your mind such sentiments as you have when you stand near an altar; and you would be afraid of thinking or doing anything that was foolish near that place, which is the place of prayer and holy intercourse with God.

When you begin your petitions, use such various expressions of the attributes of God, as may make you most sensible of the greatness and power of the Divine Nature.

Begin, therefore, in words like these: O Being of all beings, Fountain of all light and glory, gracious Father of men and Angels, whose universal Spirit is everywhere present, giving life, and light, and joy, to all Angels in Heaven, and all creatures upon earth, etc.

For these representations of the Divine attributes, which show us in some degree the Majesty and greatness of God, are an excellent means of raising our hearts into lively acts of worship and adoration.

What is the reason that most people are so much affected with this petition in the Burial Service of our Church: Yet, O Lord God most holy, O Lord most mighty, O holy and most merciful Savior, deliver us not into the bitter pains of eternal death? It is, because the joining together of so many great expressions gives such a description of the greatness of the Divine Majesty, as naturally affects every sensible mind.

Although, therefore, prayer does not consist in fine words, or studied expressions; yet as words speak to the soul, as they have a certain power of raising thoughts in the soul; so those words which speak of God in the highest manner, which most fully express the power and presence of God, which raise thoughts in the soul most suitable to the greatness and providence of God, are the most useful and most edifying in our prayers.

When you direct any of your petitions to our blessed Lord, let it be in some expressions of this kind: O Savior of the world, God of God, Light of Light; Thou that art the brightness of Thy Father's glory, and the express Image of His Person; Thou that art the Alpha and Omega, the Beginning and End of all things; Thou that hast destroyed the power of the devil; that hast overcome death; Thou that art entered into the Holy of Holies, that sittest at the right hand of the Father, that art high above all thrones and principalities, that makest intercession for all the world; Thou that art the Judge of the quick

and dead; Thou that wilt speedily come down in Thy Father's glory, to reward all men according to their works, be Thou my Light and my Peace, etc.

For such representations, which describe so many characters of our Savior's nature and power, are not only proper acts of adoration, but will, if they are repeated with any attention, fill our hearts with the highest fervor of true devotion.

Again; if you ask any particular grace of our blessed Lord, let it be in some manner like this: O Holy Jesus, Son of the most High God, Thou that wast scourged at a pillar, stretched and nailed upon a cross, for the sins of the world, unite me to Thy cross, and fill my soul with Thy holy, humble, and suffering spirit. O Fountain of mercy, Thou that didst save the thief upon the cross, save me from the guilt of a sinful life; Thou that didst cast seven devils out of Mary Magdalene, cast out of my heart all evil thoughts and wicked tempers. O Giver of life, Thou that didst raise Lazarus from the dead, raise up my soul from the death and darkness of sin. Thou that didst give to Thy Apostles power over unclean spirits, give me power over my own heart. Thou that didst appear unto Thy disciples when the doors were shut, do Thou appear unto me in the secret apartment of my heart. Thou that didst cleanse the lepers, heal the sick, and give sight to the blind, cleanse my heart, heal the disorders of my soul, and fill me with heavenly light.

Now these kind of appeals have a double advantage; first, as they are so many proper acts of our faith, whereby we not only show our belief of the miracles of Christ, but turn them at the same time into so many instances of worship and adoration.

Secondly, as they strengthen and increase the faith of our prayers, by presenting to our minds so many instances of that power and goodness, which we call upon for our own assistance.

For he that appeals to Christ, as casting out devils and raising the dead, has then a powerful motive in his mind to pray earnestly, and depend faithfully upon His assistance.

Again: in order to fill your prayers with excellent strains of devotion, it may be of use to you to observe this farther rule:

When at any time, either in reading the Scripture or any book of piety, you meet with a passage that more than ordinarily affects your mind, and seems, as it were, to give your heart a new motion towards God, you should try to turn it into the form of a petition, and then give it a place in your prayers. By this means you will be often improving your prayers, and storing yourself with proper forms of making the desires of your heart known unto God.

At all the stated hours of prayer, it will be of great benefit to you to have something fixed, and something at liberty, in your devotions.

You should have some fixed subject, which is constantly to be the chief matter of your prayer at that particular time; and yet have liberty to add such other petitions, as your condition may then require.

For instance: as the morning is to you the beginning of a new life; as God has then given you a new enjoyment of yourself, and a fresh entrance into the world; it is highly proper that your first devotions should be a praise and thanksgiving to God, as for a new creation; and that you should offer and devote body and soul, all that you are, and all that you have, to His service and glory.

Receive, therefore, every day as a resurrection from death, as a new enjoyment of life; meet every rising sun with such sentiments of God's goodness, as if you had seen it, and all things, new created upon your account: and under the sense of so great a blessing, let your joyful heart praise and magnify so good and glorious a Creator.

Let, therefore, praise and thanksgiving, and oblation of yourself unto God, be always the fixed and certain subject of your first prayers in the morning; and then take the liberty of adding such other devotions, as the accidental difference of your state, or the accidental difference of your heart, shall then make most needful and expedient for you.

For one of the greatest benefits of private devotion consists in rightly adapting our prayers to those two conditions, – the difference of our state, and the difference of our hearts.

By the difference of our state, is meant the difference of our external state or condition, as of sickness, health, pains, losses, disap-pointments, troubles, particular mercies, or judgments, from God; all sorts of kindnesses, injuries, or reproaches, from other people.

Now as these are great parts of our state of life, as they make great difference in it by continually changing; so our devotion will be made doubly beneficial to us, when it watches to receive and sanctify all these changes of our state, and turns them all into so many occasions of a more particular application to God of such thanksgiving, such resignation, such petitions, as our present state more especially requires.

And he that makes every change in his state a reason of presenting unto God some particular petitions suitable to that change, will soon find that he has taken an excellent means not only of praying with fervor, but of living as he prays.

The next condition, to which we are always to adapt some part of our prayers, is the difference of our hearts; by which is meant the different state of the tempers of our hearts, as of love, joy, peace, tranquility, dullness and dryness of spirit, anxiety, discontent, motions of envy and ambition, dark and disconsolate thoughts, resentments, fretfulness, and peevish tempers.

Now as these tempers, through the weakness of our nature, will have their succession, more or less, even in pious minds; so we should constantly make the present state of our heart the reason of some particular application to God.

If we are in the delightful calm of sweet and easy passions, of love and joy in God, we should then offer the grateful tribute of thanksgiving to God for the possession of so much happiness, thankfully owning and acknowledging Him as the bountiful Giver of it all.

If, on the other hand, we feel ourselves laden with heavy passions, with dullness of spirit, anxiety, and uneasiness, we must then look up to God in acts of humility, confessing our unworthiness, opening our troubles to Him, beseeching Him in His good time to lessen the weight of our infirmities, and to deliver us from such passions as oppose the purity and perfection of our souls.

Now by thus watching and attending to the present state of our hearts, and suiting some of our petitions exactly to their wants, we shall not only be well acquainted with the disorders of our souls, but also be well exercised in the method of curing them.

By this prudent and wise application of our prayers, we shall get all the relief from them that is possible: and the very changeableness of our hearts will prove a means of exercising a greater variety of holy tempers.

Now, by all that has here been said, you will easily perceive, that persons careful of the greatest benefit of prayer ought to have a great share in the forming and composing their own devotions.

As to that part of their prayers which is always fixed to one certain subject, in that they may use the help of forms composed by other persons; but in that part of their prayers which they are always to suit to the present state of their life, and the present state of their heart, there they must let the sense of their own condition help them to such kinds of petition, thanksgiving, or resignation, as their present state more especially requires.

Happy are they who have this business and employment upon their hands!

And now, if people of leisure, whether men or women, who are so much at a loss how to dispose of their time, who are forced into poor contrivances, idle visits, and ridiculous diversions, merely to get rid of hours that hang heavily upon their hands; if such were to appoint some certain spaces of their time to the study of devotion, searching after all the means and helps to attain a devout spirit; if they were to collect the best forms of devotion, to use themselves to transcribe the finest passages of Scripture-prayers; if they were to collect the devotions, confessions, petitions, praises, resignations, and thanksgivings, which are scattered up and down in the Psalms, and range them under proper heads, as so much proper fuel for the flame of their own devotion; if their minds were often thus employed, sometimes meditating upon them, sometimes getting them by heart, and making them as habitual as their own thoughts, how fervently would they pray, who came thus prepared to prayer! And how much better would it be, to make this benefit of leisure time, than to be dully and idly lost in the poor impertinences

of a playing, visiting, wandering life!

How much better would it be, to be thus furnished with hymns and anthems of the saints, and teach their souls to ascend to God, than to corrupt, bewilder, and confound their hearts with the wild fancies, the lustful thoughts of lewd poets!

Now though people of leisure seem called more particularly to this study of devotion, yet persons of much business or labor must not think themselves excused from this, or some better method of improving their devotion.

For the greater their business is, the more need they have of some such method as this, to prevent its power over their hearts, to secure them from sinking into worldly tempers, and preserve a sense and taste of heavenly things in their minds. And a little time regularly and constantly employed to any one use or end, will do great things, and produce mighty effects.

And it is for want of considering devotion in this light, as something that is to be nursed and cherished with care, as something that is to be made part of our business, that is to be improved with care and contrivance, by art and method, and a diligent use of the best helps; it is for want of considering it in this light that so many people are so little benefitted by it and live and die strangers to that spirit of devotion, which, by a prudent use of proper means, they might have enjoyed in a high degree.

For though the spirit of devotion is the gift of God, and not attainable by any mere power of our own, yet it is mostly given to, and never withheld from, those who, by a wise and diligent use of proper means, prepare themselves for the reception of it.

And it is amazing to see how eagerly men employ their parts, their sagacity, time, study, application, and exercise: how all helps are called to their assistance, when anything is intended and desired in worldly matters; and how dull, negligent, and unimproved they are; how little they use their parts, sagacity, and abilities, to raise and increase their devotion!

Mundanus (worldly-wise man) is a man of excellent parts, and clear apprehension. He is well advanced in age, and has made a great figure in business. Every part of trade and business that has fallen in his way has had some improvement from him; and he is always contriving to carry every method of doing anything well to its greatest height. Mundanus aims at the greatest perfection in everything. The soundness and strength of his mind, and his just way of thinking upon things, make him intent upon removing all imperfections.

He can tell you all the defects and errors in all the common methods, whether of trade, building, or improving land or manufactures. The clearness and strength of his understanding, which he is constantly improving by continual exercise in these matters, by often digesting his thoughts in writing, and trying everything every way, has rendered him a great master of most concerns in human life.

Thus has Mundanus gone on, increasing his knowledge and judgment, as fast as his years came upon him.

The one only thing which has not fallen under his improvement, nor received any benefit from his judicious mind, is his devotion: this is just in the same poor state it was, when he was only six years of age, and the old man prays now in that little form of words which his mother used to hear him repeat night and morning.

This Mundanus, that hardly ever saw the poorest utensil, or ever took the meanest trifle into his hand, without considering how it might be made or used to better advantage, has gone all his life long praying in the same manner as when he was a child; without ever considering how much better or oftener he might pray; without considering how improbable the spirit of devotion is, how many helps a wise and reasonable man may call to his assistance, and how necessary it is, that our prayers should be enlarged, varied, and suited to the particular state and condition of our lives.

If Mundanus sees a book of devotion, he passes it by, as he does a spelling-book, because he remembers that he learned to pray, so many years ago, under his mother, when he learned to spell.

Now how poor and pitiable is the conduct of this man of sense, who has so much judgment and understanding in everything, but that which is the whole wisdom of man!

And how miserably do many people, more or less, imitate this conduct!

All which seems to be owing to a strange, infatuated state of negligence, which keeps people from considering what devotion is. For if they did but once proceed so far as to reflect about it, or ask themselves any questions concerning it, they would soon see that the spirit of devotion was like any other sense or understanding, that is only to be improved by study, care, application, and the use of such means and helps as are necessary to make a man a proficient in any art or science.

Classicus (i.e., a classical scholar) is a man of learning, and well versed in all the best authors of antiquity. He has read them so much, that he has entered into their spirit, and can very ingeniously imitate the manner of any of them. All their thoughts are his thoughts, and he can express himself in their language. He is so great a friend to this improvement of the mind, that if he lights on a young scholar, he never fails to advise him concerning his studies.

Classicus tells his young man, he must not think that he has done enough when he has only learned languages; but that he must be daily conversant with the best authors, read them again and again, catch their spirit by living with them, and that there is no other way of becoming like them, or of making himself a man of taste and judgment.

How wise might Classicus have been, and how much good might he have done in the world, if he had but thought as justly of devotion, as he does of learning!

He never, indeed, says anything shocking or offensive about devotion, because he never thinks, or talks, about it. It suffers nothing from him but neglect and disregard.

The two Testaments would not have had so much as a place amongst his books, but that they are both to be had in Greek.

Classicus thinks that he sufficiently shows his regard for the Holy Scripture, when he tells you, that he has no other books of piety besides them.

It is very well, Classicus, that you prefer the Bible to all other books of piety: he has no judgment, that is not thus far of your opinion.

But if you will have no other book of piety besides the Bible, because it is the best, how comes it, Classicus, that you do not content yourself with one of the best books amongst the Greeks and Romans? How comes it that you are so greedy and eager after all of them? How comes it that you think the knowledge of one is a necessary help to the knowledge of the other? How comes it that you are so earnest, so laborious, so expensive of your time and money, to restore broken periods, and scraps of the ancients?

How comes it that you read so many commentators upon Cicero, Horace, and Homer, and not one upon the Gospel? How comes it that you love to read a man? How comes it that your love of Cicero and Ovid makes you love to read an author that writes like them; and yet your esteem for the Gospel gives you no desire, nay, prevents your reading such books as breathe the very spirit of the Gospel?

How comes it that you tell your young scholar, he must not content himself with barely understanding his authors, but must be continually reading them all, as the only means of entering into their spirit, and forming his own judgment according to them?

Why then must the Bible lie alone in your study? Is not the spirit of the saints, the piety of the holy followers of Jesus, as good and necessary a means of entering into the spirit and taste of the gospel, as the reading of the ancients is of entering into the spirit of antiquity?

Is the spirit of poetry only to be got by much reading of poets and orators? And is not the spirit of devotion to be got in the same way, by frequently reading the holy thoughts, and pious strains of devout men?

Is your young poet to search after every line that may give new wings to his fancy, or direct his imagination? And is it not as reasonable for him who desires to improve in the Divine life, that is, in the love of heavenly things, to search after every strain of devotion that may move, kindle, and inflame the holy ardor of his soul?

Do you advise your orator to translate the best orations, to commit much of them to memory, to be frequently exercising his talent in this manner, that habits of thinking and speaking justly may be formed in his mind? And is there not the same benefit and advantage to be made by books of devotion? Should not a man use them in the same way, that habits on devotion, and aspiring to God in holy thoughts, may be well formed in his soul?

Now the reason why Classicus does not think and judge thus reasonably of devotion, is owing to his never thinking of it in any other manner than as the repeating a form of words. It never in his life entered his head, to think of devotion as a state of the heart, as an improvable talent of the mind, as a temper that is to grow and increase like our reason and judgment, and to be formed in us by such a regular, diligent use of proper means, as are necessary to form any other wise habit of mind.

And it is for want of this, that he has been content all his life with the bare letter of prayer, and eagerly bent upon entering into the spirit of heathen poets and orators.

And it is much to be lamented, that numbers of scholars are more or less chargeable with this excessive folly; so negligent of improving their devotion, and so desirous of other poor accomplishments; as if they thought it a nobler talent to be able to write an epigram in the turn of Martial, than to live, and think, and pray to God, in the spirit of St. Austin.

And yet, to correct this temper, and fill a man with a quite contrary spirit, there seems to be no more required, than the bare belief in the truth of Christianity.

And if you were to ask Mundanus and Classicus, or any man of business or learning, whether piety is not the highest perfection of man, or devotion the greatest attainment in the world, they must both be forced to answer in the affirmative, or else give up the truth of the Gospel.

For to set any accomplishment against devotion, or to think anything, or all things in this world, bears any proportion to its excellency, is the same absurdity in a Christian, as it would be in a philosopher to prefer a meal's meat to the greatest improvement in knowledge.

For as philosophy professes purely the search and inquiry after knowledge, so Christianity supposes, intends, desires, and aims at nothing else but the raising fallen man to a Divine life, to such habits of holiness, such degrees of devotion, as may fit him to enter amongst the holy inhabitants of the kingdom of heaven.

He that does not believe this of Christianity, may be reckoned an infidel; and he that believes thus much has faith enough to give him a right judgment of the value of things, to support him in a sound mind, and enable him to conquer all the temptations which the world shall lay in his way.

To conclude this chapter. Devotion is nothing else but right apprehensions and right affections towards God.

All practices, therefore, that heighten and improve our true apprehensions of God, all ways of life that tend to nourish, raise, and fix our affections upon Him, are to be reckoned so many helps and means to fill us with devotion.

As Prayer is the proper fuel of this holy flame, so we must use all our care and contrivance to give prayer its full power: as by alms, self-denial, frequent retirements, and holy readings, composing forms for ourselves, or using the best we can get, adding length of time, and observing hours of prayer: changing, improving, and suiting our devotions to the condition of our lives, and the state of our hearts.

Those who have most leisure seem more especially called to a more eminent observance of these holy rules of a devout life. And they, who, by the necessity of their state, and not through their own choice, have but little time to employ thus, must make the best use of that little they have. For this is the certain way of making devotion produce a devout life.

William Law, 1686–1761

The Practice of the Presence of God: The Best Rule of a Holy Life

Conversations and Letters of Brother Lawrence

Good when He gives, supremely good;
Nor less when He denies:
Afflictions, from His sovereign hand,
Are blessings in disguise.

PREFACE
"I believe in the … communion of saints." Surely if additional proof of its reality were needed, it might be found in the universal oneness of experimental Christianity in all ages and in all lands. The experiences of Thomas à Kempis, of

Tauler and of Madame Guyon, of John Woolman and Hester Ann Rogers, how marvelously they agree, and how perfectly they harmonize! And Nicholas Herman, of Lorraine, whose letters and converse are here given, testifies to the same truth! In communion with Rome, a lay brother among the Carmelites, for several years a soldier, in an irreligious age, amid a skeptical people, yet in him the practice of the presence of GOD was as much a reality as the "watch" of the early Friends, and the "holy seed" in him and others was the "stock" (Isa. vi. 16) from which grew the household and evangelistic piety of the eighteenth century, of Epworth and of Moorfields.

"When unadorned, adorned the most" is the line which deters from any interpolations or interpretations other than the few "contents" headings which are given. May the "Christ in you" be the "hope of glory" to all who read.

CONVERSATIONS
FIRST CONVERSATION
Conversion and precious employment. Satisfaction in God's presence. Faith our duty. Resignation the fruit of watchfulness.

The first time I saw Brother Lawrence was upon the 3rd of August, 1666. He told me that GOD had done him a singular favor, in his conversion at the age of eighteen.

That in the winter, seeing a tree stripped of its leaves, and considering that within a little time, the leaves would be renewed, and after that the flowers and fruit appear, he received a high view of the Providence and Power of GOD, which has never since been effaced from his soul. That this view had perfectly set him loose from the world, and kindled in him such a love for GOD, that he could not tell whether it had increased in above forty years that he had lived since.

That he had been footman to M. Fieubert, the treasurer, and that he was a great awkward fellow who broke everything.

That he had desired to be received into a monastery, thinking that he would there be made to smart for his awkwardness and the faults he should commit, and so he should sacrifice to GOD his life, with its pleasures: but that GOD had disappointed him, he having met with nothing but satisfaction in that state.

That we should establish ourselves in a sense of God's Presence, by continually conversing with Him. That it was a shameful thing to quit His conversation, to think of trifles and fooleries.

That we should feed and nourish our souls with high notions of GOD; which would yield us great joy in being devoted to Him.

That we ought to quicken, i.e., to enliven, our faith. That it was lamentable we had so little; and that instead of taking faith for the rule of their conduct, men amused themselves with trivial devotions, which changed daily. That the way of Faith was the spirit of the Church, and that it was sufficient to bring us to a high degree of perfection.

That we ought to give ourselves up to GOD, with regard both to things temporal and spiritual, and seek our satisfaction only in the fulfilling His will, whether He lead us by suffering or by consolation, for all would be equal to a soul truly resigned. That there needed fidelity in those drynesses, or insensibilities and irksomenesses in prayer, by which GOD tries our love to Him; that then was the time for us to make good and effectual acts of resignation, whereof one alone would oftentimes very much promote our spiritual advancement.

That as for the miseries and sins he heard of daily in the world, he was so far from wondering at them, that, on the contrary, he was surprised there were not more, considering the malice sinners were capable of: that for his part, he prayed for them; but knowing that GOD could remedy the mischiefs they did, when He pleased, he gave himself no further trouble.

That to arrive at such resignation as GOD requires, we should watch attentively over all the passions which mingle as well in spiritual things as those of a grosser nature: that GOD would give light concerning those passions to those who truly desire to serve Him. That if this was my design, viz., sincerely to serve GOD, I might come to him (Bro. Lawrence) as often as I pleased, without any fear of being troublesome; but if not, that I ought no more to visit him.

SECOND CONVERSATION
Love the motive of all. Once in fear, now in joy.

Diligence and love. Simplicity the key to Divine assistance. Business abroad as at home. Times of prayer and self-mortification not essential for the practice. All scruples brought to God.

That he had always been governed by love, without selfish views; and that having resolved to make the love of GOD the end of all his actions, he had found reasons to be well satisfied with his method. That he was pleased when he could take up a straw from the ground for the love of GOD, seeking Him only, and nothing else, not even His gifts.

That he had been long troubled in mind from a certain belief that he should be damned; that all the men in the world could not have persuaded him to the contrary; but that he had thus reasoned with himself about it: I did not engage in a religious life but for the love of GOD, and I have endeavored to act only for Him; whatever becomes of me, whether I be lost or saved, I will always continue to act purely for the love of GOD. I shall have this good at least, that till death I shall have done all that is in me to love Him. That this trouble of mind had lasted four years; during which time he had suffered much.

That since that time he had passed his life in perfect liberty and continual joy. That he placed his sins betwixt him and GOD, as it were, to tell Him that he did not deserve His favors, but that GOD still continued to bestow them in abundance.

That in order to form a habit of conversing with GOD continually, and referring all we do to Him; we must at first apply to Him with some diligence: but that after a little care we should find His love inwardly excite us to it without any difficulty.

That he expected after the pleasant days GOD had given him, he should have his turn of pain and suffering; but that he was not uneasy about it, knowing very well, that as he could do nothing of himself, GOD would not fail to give him the strength to bear them.

That when an occasion of practicing some virtue offered, he addressed himself to GOD, saying, LORD, I cannot do this unless You enable me; and that then he received strength more than sufficient.

That when he had failed in his duty, he only confessed his fault, saying to GOD, I shall never do otherwise, if You leave me to myself; 'tis You must hinder my falling, and mend what is amiss. That after this, he gave himself no further uneasiness about it.

That we ought to act with GOD in the greatest simplicity, speaking to Him frankly and plainly, and imploring His assistance in our affairs, just as they happen. That GOD never failed to grant it, as he had often experienced.

That he had been lately sent into Burgundy, to buy the provision of wine for the society, which was a very unwelcome task for him, because he had no turn for business and because he was lame, and could not go about the boat but by rolling himself over the casks. That however he gave himself no uneasiness about it, nor about the purchase of the wine. That he said to GOD, It was His business he was about, and that he afterwards found it very well performed. That he had been sent into Auvergne the year before upon the same account; that he could not tell how the matter passed, but that it proved very well.

So, likewise, in his business in the kitchen (to which he had naturally a great aversion), having accustomed himself to do everything there for the love of GOD, and with prayer, upon all occasions, for His grace to do his work well, he had found everything easy, during the fifteen years that he had been employed there.

That he was very well pleased with the post he was now in; but that he was as ready to quit that as the former, since he was always pleasing himself in every condition, by doing little things for the love of GOD.

That with him the set times of prayer were not different from other times: that he retired to pray, according to the directions of his Superior, but that he did not want such retirement, nor ask for it, because his greatest business did not divert him from GOD.

That as he knew his obligation to love GOD in all things, and as he endeavored so to do, he had no need of a director to advise him, but that he needed much a confessor to absolve him. That he was very sensible of his faults, but not discouraged by them; that he confessed them to GOD, and did not plead against Him to excuse them. When he had so done, he peaceably resumed his usual practice of love and adoration.

That in his trouble of mind, he had consulted nobody, but knowing only by the light of faith that GOD was present, he contented himself with directing all his actions to Him, i.e., doing them with a desire to please Him, let what would come of it.

That useless thoughts spoil all: that the mischief began there; but that we ought to reject them, as soon as we perceived their impertinence to the matter in hand, or our salvation; and return to our communion with GOD.

That at the beginning he had often passed his time appointed for prayer, in rejecting wandering thoughts, and falling back into them. That he could never regulate his devotion by certain methods as some do. That nevertheless, at first he had meditated for some time, but afterwards that went off, in a manner that he could give no account of.

That all bodily mortifications and other exercises are useless, but as they serve to arrive at the union with GOD by love; that he had well considered this, and found it the shortest way to go straight to Him by a continual exercise of love, and doing all things for His sake.

That we ought to make a great difference between the acts of the understanding and those of the will; that the first were comparatively of little value, and the others all.

That our only business was to love and delight ourselves in GOD.

That all possible kinds of mortification, if they were void of the love of GOD, could not efface a single sin. That we ought, without anxiety, to expect the pardon of our sins from the Blood of JESUS CHRIST, only endeavoring to love Him with all our hearts. That GOD seemed to have granted the greatest favors to the greatest sinners, as more signal monuments of His mercy.

That the greatest pains or pleasures, of this world, were not to be compared with what he had experienced of both kinds in a spiritual state: so that he was careful for nothing and feared nothing, desiring but one only thing of GOD, viz., that he might not offend Him.

That he had no scruples; for, said he, when I fail in my duty, I readily acknowledge it, saying, I am used to do so: I shall never do otherwise, if I am left to myself. If I fail not, then I give

GOD thanks, acknowledging that it comes from Him.

THIRD CONVERSATION
Faith working by love. Outward business no detriment. Perfect resignation the sure way.

He told me, that the foundation of the spiritual life in him had been a high notion and esteem of GOD in faith; which when he had once well conceived, he had no other care at first, but faithfully to reject every other thought, that he might perform all his actions for the love of GOD. That when sometimes he had not thought of GOD for a good while, he did not disquiet himself for it; but after having acknowledged his wretchedness to GOD, he returned to Him with so much the greater trust in Him, by how much he found himself more wretched to have forgot Him.

That the trust we put in GOD honors Him much, and draws down great graces.

That it was impossible, not only that GOD should deceive, but also that He should long let a soul suffer which is perfectly resigned to Him, and resolved to endure everything for His sake.

That he had so often experienced the ready succors of Divine Grace upon all occasions, that from the same experience, when he had business to do, he did not think of it beforehand; but when it was time to do it, he found in GOD, as in a clear mirror, all that was fit for him to do. That of late he had acted thus, without anticipating care; but before the experience above mentioned, he had used it in his affairs.

When outward business diverted him a little from the thought of GOD, a fresh remembrance coming from GOD invested his soul, and so inflamed and transported him that it was difficult for him to contain himself.

That he was more united to GOD in his outward employments, than when he left them for devotion in retirement.

That he expected hereafter some great pain of body or mind; that the worst that could happen to him was, to lose that sense of GOD, which he had enjoyed so long; but that the goodness of GOD assured him He would not forsake him utterly, and that He would give him strength to bear whatever evil He permitted to happen to him; and therefore that he feared nothing, and had no occasion to consult with anybody about his state. That when he had attempted to do it, he had always come away more perplexed; and that as he was conscious of his readiness to lay down his life for the love of GOD, he had no apprehension of danger. That perfect resignation to GOD was a sure way to heaven, a way in which we had always sufficient light for our conduct.

That in the beginning of the spiritual life, we ought to be faithful in doing our duty and denying ourselves; but after that unspeakable pleasures followed: that in difficulties we need only have recourse to JESUS CHRIST, and beg His grace, with which everything became easy.

That many do not advance in the Christian progress, because they stick in penances, and particular exercises, while they neglect the love of GOD, which is the end. That this appeared plainly by their works, and was the reason why we see so little solid virtue.

That there needed neither art nor science for going to GOD, but only a heart resolutely determined to apply itself to nothing but Him, or for His sake, and to love Him only.

FOURTH CONVERSATION
The manner of going to God. Hearty renunciation. Prayer and praise prevent discouragement. Sanctification in common business. Prayer and the presence of God. The whole substance of religion. Self-estimation. Further personal experience.

He discoursed with me very frequently, and with great openness of heart, concerning his manner of going to GOD, whereof some part is related already.

He told me, that all consists in one hearty renunciation of everything which we are sensible does not lead to GOD; that we might accustom ourselves to a continual conversation with Him, with freedom and in simplicity. That we need only to recognize GOD intimately present with us, to address ourselves to Him every moment, that we may beg His assistance for knowing His will in things doubtful, and for rightly performing those which we plainly see He requires of us, offering them to Him before we do them, and giving Him thanks when we have done.

That in this conversation with GOD, we are also employed in praising, adoring, and loving him incessantly, for His infinite goodness and perfection.

That, without being discouraged on account of our sins, we should pray for His grace with a perfect confidence, as relying upon the infinite merits of our LORD. That GOD never failed offering us His grace at each action; that he distinctly perceived it, and never failed of it, unless when his thoughts had wandered from a sense of God's Presence, or he had forgot to ask His assistance.

That GOD always gave us light in our doubts, when we had no other design but to please Him.

That our sanctification did not depend upon changing our works, but in doing that for God's sake, which we commonly do for our own. That it was lamentable to see how many people mistook the means for the end, addicting themselves to certain works, which they performed very imperfectly, by reason of their human or selfish regards.

That the most excellent method he had found of going to GOD, was that of doing our common business without any view of pleasing men (Gal. i. 10; Eph. vi. 5, 6), and (as far as we are capable) purely for the love of GOD.

That it was a great delusion to think that the times of prayer ought to differ from other times. That we are as strictly obliged to adhere to GOD by action in the time of action, as by prayer in its season.

That his prayer was nothing else but a sense of the presence of GOD, his soul being at that time insensible to everything but Divine love: and that when the appointed times of prayer were past, he found no difference, because he still continued with GOD, praising and blessing Him with all his might, so that he passed his life in continual joy; yet hoped that GOD would give him somewhat to suffer, when he should grow stronger.

That we ought, once for all, heartily to put our whole trust in GOD, and make a total surrender of ourselves to Him, secure that He would not deceive us.

That we ought not to be weary of doing little things for the love of GOD, who regards not the greatness of the work, but the love with which it is performed. That we should not wonder if, in the beginning, we often failed in our endeavors, but that at last we should gain a habit, which will naturally produce its acts in us, without our care, and to our exceeding great delight.

That the whole substance of religion was faith, hope, and charity; by the practice of which we become united to the will of GOD: that all beside is indifferent and to be used as a means, that we may arrive at our end, and be swallowed up therein, by faith and charity.

That all things are possible to him who believes, that they are less difficult to him who hopes, they are more easy to him who loves, and still more easy to him who perseveres in the practice of these three virtues.

That the end we ought to propose to ourselves is to become, in this life, the most perfect worshipers of GOD we can possibly be, as we hope to be through all eternity.

That when we enter upon the spiritual we should consider, and examine to the bottom, what we are. And then we should find ourselves worthy of all contempt, and such as do not deserve the name of Christians, subject to all kinds of misery, and numberless accidents, which trouble us, and cause perpetual vicissitudes in our health, in our humors, in our internal and external dispositions: in fine, persons whom GOD would humble by many pains and labors, as well within as without. After this, we should not wonder that troubles, temptations, oppositions and contradictions, happen to us from men. We ought, on the contrary, to submit ourselves to them, and bear them as long as GOD pleases, as things highly advantageous to us.

That the greater perfection a soul aspires after, the more dependent it is upon Divine grace.

Being questioned by one of his own society (to whom he was obliged to open himself) by what means he had attained such an habitual sense of GOD, he told him that, since his first coming to the monastery, he had considered GOD as the end of all his thoughts and desires, as the mark to which they should tend, and in which they should terminate.

That in the beginning of his novitiate he spent the hours appointed for private prayer in thinking of GOD, so as to convince his mind of, and to impress deeply upon his heart, the Divine existence, rather by devout sentiments, and submission to the lights of faith, than by studied reasonings and elaborate meditations. That by this short and sure method, he exercised himself in the knowledge and love of GOD, resolving to use his utmost endeavor to live in a continual sense of His Presence, and, if possible, never to forget Him more.

That when he had thus in prayer filled his mind with great sentiments of that infinite Being, he went to his work appointed in the kitchen (for he was cook to the society); there having first considered severally the things his office required, and when and how each thing was to be done, he spent all the intervals of his time, as well before as after his work, in prayer.

That, when he began his business, he said to GOD, with a filial trust in Him, "O my GOD, since You art with me, and I must now, in obedience to Your commands, apply my mind to these outward things, I beseech You to grant me the grace to continue in Your Presence; and to this end do You prosper me with Your assistance, receive all my works, and possess all my affections."

As he proceeded in his work, he continued his familiar conversation with his Maker, imploring His grace, and offering to Him all his actions.

When he had finished, he examined himself how he had discharged his duty; if he found well, he returned thanks to GOD; if otherwise, he asked pardon; and without being discouraged, he set his mind right again, and continued his exercise of the presence of GOD, as if he had never deviated from it. "Thus," said he, "by rising after my falls, and by frequently renewed acts of faith and love, I am come to a state, wherein it would be as difficult for me not to think of GOD, as it was at first to accustom myself to it."

As Bro. Lawrence had found such an advantage in walking in the presence of GOD, it was natural for him to recommend it earnestly to others; but his example was a stronger inducement than any arguments he could propose. His very countenance was edifying; such a sweet and calm devotion appearing in it, as could not but affect the beholders. And it was observed, that in the greatest hurry of business in the kitchen, he still preserved his recollection and heavenly-mindedness. He was never hasty nor loitering, but did each thing in its season, with an even uninterrupted composure and tranquility of spirit. "The time of business," said he, "does not with me differ from the time of prayer; and in the noise and clutter of my kitchen, while several persons are at the same time calling for different things, I possess GOD in as great tranquility as if I were upon my knees at the Blessed Sacrament."

LETTERS
FIRST LETTER
How the habitual sense of God's Presence was found.

Since you desire so earnestly that I should communicate to you the method by which I arrived at that habitual sense of God's Presence, which our LORD, of His mercy, has been pleased to vouchsafe to me; I must tell you, that it is with great difficulty that I am prevailed on by your importunities; and now I do it only upon the terms, that you show my letter to nobody. If I knew that you would let it be seen, all the desire that I have for your advancement would not be able to determine me to it. The account I can give you is:

Having found in many books different methods of going to GOD, and divers practices of the spiritual life, I thought this would serve rather to puzzle me, than facilitate what I sought after, which was nothing but how to become wholly God's.

This made me resolve to give the all for the All: so after having given myself wholly to GOD, to make all the satisfaction I could for my sins, I renounced, for the love of Him, everything that was not He; and I began to live as if there was none but He and I in the world. Sometimes I considered myself before Him as a poor criminal at the feet of his judge; at other times I beheld Him in my heart as my FATHER, as my GOD: I worshiped Him the oftenest that I could, keeping my mind in His holy Presence, and recalling it as often as I found it wandered from Him. I found no small pain in this exercise, and yet I continued it, notwithstanding all the difficulties that occurred, without troubling or disquieting myself when my mind had wandered involuntarily. I made this my business, as much all the day long as at the appointed times of prayer; for at all times, every hour, every minute, even in the height of my business, I drove away from my mind everything that was capable of interrupting my thought of GOD.

Such has been my common practice ever since I entered into religion; and though I have done it very imperfectly, yet I have found great advantages by it. These, I well know, are to be imputed to the mere mercy and goodness of GOD, because we can do nothing without Him; and I still less than any. But when we are faithful to keep ourselves in His holy Presence, and set Him always before us, this not only hinders our offending Him, and doing anything that may displease Him, at least willfully, but it also begets in us a holy freedom, and if I may so speak, a familiarity with GOD, wherewith we ask, and that successfully, the graces we stand in need of. In fine, by often repeating these acts, they become habitual, and the presence of GOD is rendered as it were natural to us. Give Him thanks, if you please, with me, for His great goodness towards me, which I can never sufficiently admire, for the many favors He has done to so miserable a sinner as I am. May all things praise Him. Amen.

SECOND LETTER
Difference between himself and others. Faith alone consistently and persistently. Deprecates this state being considered a delusion.

Not finding my manner of life in books, although I have no difficulty about it, yet, for greater security, I shall be glad to know your thoughts concerning it.

In a conversation some days since with a person of piety, he told me the spiritual life was a life of grace, which begins with servile fear, which is increased by hope of eternal life, and which is consummated by pure love; that each of these states had its different stages, by which one arrives at last at that blessed consummation.

I have not followed all these methods. On the contrary, from I know not what instincts, I found they discouraged me. This was the reason why, at my entrance into religion, I took

a resolution to give myself up to GOD, as the best satisfaction I could make for my sins; and, for the love of Him, to renounce all besides.

For the first years, I commonly employed myself during the time set apart for devotion, with the thoughts of death, judgment, hell, heaven, and my sins. Thus I continued some years applying my mind carefully the rest of the day, and even in the midst of my business, to the presence of GOD, whom I considered always as with me, often as in me.

At length I came insensibly to do the same thing during my set time of prayer, which caused in me great delight and consolation. This practice produced in me so high an esteem for GOD, that faith alone was capable to satisfy me in that point. [I suppose he means that all distinct notions he could form of GOD were unsatisfactory, because he perceived them to be unworthy of GOD, and therefore his mind was not to be satisfied but by the views of faith, which apprehends GOD as infinite and incomprehensible, as He is in Himself, and not as He can be conceived by human ideas.]

Such was my beginning; and yet I must tell you, that for the first ten years I suffered much: the apprehension that I was not devoted to GOD, as I wished to be, my past sins always present to my mind, and the great unmerited favors which GOD did me, were the matter and source of my sufferings. During this time I fell often, and rose again presently. It seemed to me that the creatures, reason, and GOD Himself were against me; And faith alone for me. I was troubled sometimes with thoughts, that to believe I had received such favors was an effect of my presumption, which pretended to be at once where others arrive with difficulty; at other times that it was a willful delusion, and that there was no salvation for me.

When I thought of nothing but to end my days in these troubles (which did not at all diminish the trust I had in GOD, and which served only to increase my faith), I found myself changed all at once; and my soul, which till that time was in trouble, felt a profound inward peace, as if she were in her center and place of rest.

Ever since that time I walk before GOD simply, in faith, with humility and with love; and I apply myself diligently to do nothing and think nothing which may displease Him. I hope that when I have done what I can, He will do with me what He pleases.

As for what passes in me at present, I cannot express it. I have no pain or difficulty about my state, because I have no will but that of GOD, which I endeavor to accomplish in all things, and to which I am so resigned, that I would not take up a straw from the ground against His order, or from any other motive but purely that of love to Him.

I have quitted all forms of devotion and set prayers but those to which my state obliges me. And I make it my business only to persevere in His holy presence, wherein I keep myself by a simple attention, and a general fond regard to GOD, which I may call an actual presence of GOD; or, to speak better, an habitual, silent, and secret conversation of the soul with GOD, which often causes in me joys and raptures inwardly, and sometimes also outwardly, so great that I am forced to use means to moderate them, and prevent their appearance to others.

In short, I am assured beyond all doubt, that my soul has been with GOD above these thirty years. I pass over many things, that I may not be tedious to you, yet I think it proper to inform you after what manner I consider myself before GOD, whom I behold as my King.

I consider myself as the most wretched of men, full of sores and corruption, and who has committed all sorts of crimes against his King; touched with a sensible regret I confess to Him all my wickedness, I ask His forgiveness, I abandon myself in His hands, that He may do what He pleases with me. This King, full of mercy and goodness, very far from chastising me, embraces me with love, makes me eat at His table, serves me with His own hands, gives me the key of His treasures; He converses and delights Himself with me incessantly, in a thousand and a thousand ways, and treats me in all respects as His favorite. It is thus I consider myself from time to time in His holy presence.

My most usual method is this simple attention, and such a general passionate regard to GOD; to whom I find myself often attached with greater sweetness and delight than that of an infant at the mother's breast: so that if I dare use the expression, I should choose to call this state the bosom of GOD, for the inexpressible sweetness which I taste and experience there. If sometimes my thoughts wander from it by necessity or infirmity, I am presently recalled by inward motions, so charming and delicious that I am ashamed to mention them.

I desire your reverence to reflect rather upon my great wretchedness, of which you are fully informed, than upon the great favors which GOD does me, all unworthy and ungrateful as I am.

As for my set hours of prayer, they are only a continuation of the same exercise. Sometimes I consider myself there, as a stone before a carver, whereof he is to make a statue: presenting myself thus before GOD, I desire Him to make His perfect image in my soul, and render me entirely like Himself.

At other times, when I apply myself to prayer, I feel all my spirit and all my soul lift itself up without any care or effort of mine; and it continues as it were suspended and firmly fixed in GOD, as in its center and place of rest.

I know that some charge this state with inactivity, delusion, and self-love: I confess that it is a holy inactivity, and would be a happy self-love, if the soul in that state were capable of it; because in effect, while she is in this repose, she cannot be disturbed by such acts as she was formerly accustomed to, and which were then her support, but would now rather hinder than assist her.

Yet I cannot bear that this should be called delusion; because the soul which thus enjoys GOD desires herein nothing but Him. If this be delusion in me, it belongs to GOD to remedy it. Let Him do what He pleases with me: I desire only Him, and to be wholly devoted Him.

You will, however, oblige me in sending me your opinion, to which I always pay a great deference, for I have a singular esteem for your reverence, and am yours in our Lord.

THIRD LETTER
For a soldier friend whom he encourages to trust in God.

We have a GOD who is infinitely gracious, and knows all our wants. I always thought that He would reduce you to extremity. He will come in His own time, and when you least expect it. Hope in Him more than ever: thank Him with me for the favors He does you, particularly for the fortitude and patience which He gives you in your afflictions: it is a plain mark of the care He takes of you; comfort yourself then with Him, and give thanks for all.

I admire also the fortitude and bravery of M. GOD has given him a good disposition, and a good will; but there is in him still a little of the world, and a great deal of youth. I hope the affliction which GOD has sent him will prove a wholesome remedy to him, and make him enter into himself; it is an accident very proper to engage him to put all his trust in Him, who accompanies him everywhere: let him think of Him the oftenest he can, especially in the greatest dangers. A little lifting up the heart suffices; a little remembrance of GOD, one act of inward worship, though upon a march, and sword in hand, are prayers which, however short, are nevertheless very acceptable to GOD; and far from lessening a soldier's courage in occasions of danger, they best serve to fortify it.

Let him then think of GOD the most he can; let him accustom himself, by degrees, to this small but holy exercise; nobody perceives it, and nothing is easier than to repeat often in the day these little internal adorations. Recommend to him, if you please, that he think of GOD the most he can, in the manner here directed; it is very fit and most necessary for a soldier, who is daily exposed to dangers of life, and often of his salvation. I hope that GOD will assist him and all the family, to whom I present my service, being theirs and yours.

FOURTH LETTER
Writes of himself as of a third person, and encourages his correspondent to press on to fuller practicing of the Presence of God.

I have taken this opportunity to communicate to you the sentiments of one of our society concerning the admirable effects and continual assistances which he receives from the presence of GOD. Let you and me both profit by them.

You must know, his continual care has been, for above forty years past that he has spent in religion, to be always with GOD; and to do nothing, say nothing, and think nothing which may displease Him; and this without any other view than purely for the love of Him, and because He deserves infinitely more.

He is now so accustomed to that Divine presence, that he receives from it continual succors upon all occasions. For about thirty years, his soul has been filled with joys so continual, and sometimes so great, that he is forced to use means to moderate them, and to hinder their appearing outwardly.

If sometimes he is a little too much absent from that Divine presence, GOD presently makes Himself to be felt in his soul to recall him; which often happens when he is most engaged in his outward business: he answers with exact fidelity to these inward drawings, either by an elevation of his heart towards GOD, or by a meek and fond regard to Him, or by such words as love forms upon these occasions; as for instance, My GOD, here I am all devoted to You: LORD, make me according to Your heart. And then it seems to him (as in effect he feels it) that this GOD of love, satisfied with such few words, reposes again, and rests in the depth and center of his soul. The experience of these things gives him such an assurance that GOD is always in the depth or bottom of his soul, and renders him incapable of doubting it, upon any account whatever.

Judge by this what content and satisfaction he enjoys, while he continually finds in himself so great a treasure: he is no longer in an anxious search after it, but has it open before him, and may take what he pleases of it.

He complains much of our blindness; and cries often that we are to be pitied who content ourselves with so little. GOD, says he, has infinite treasure to bestow, and we take up with a little sensible devotion which passes in a moment. Blind as we are, we hinder GOD, and stop the current of His graces. But when He finds a soul penetrated with a lively faith, He pours into it His graces and favors plentifully; there they flow like a torrent, which, after being forcibly stopped against its ordinary course, when it has found a passage, spreads itself with impetuosity and abundance.

Yes, we often stop this torrent, by the little value we set upon it. But let us stop it no more: let us enter into ourselves and break down the bank which hinders it. Let us make way for grace; let us redeem the lost time, for perhaps we have but little left; death follows us close, let us be well prepared for it; for we die but once, and a miscarriage there is irretrievable.

I say again, let us enter into ourselves. The time presses: there is no room for delay; our souls are at stake. I believe you have taken such effectual measures, that you will not be surprised. I commend you for it, it is the one thing necessary: we must, nevertheless, always work at it, because not to advance, in the spiritual life, is to go back. But those who have the gale of the HOLY SPIRIT go forward even in sleep. If the vessel of our soul is still tossed with winds and storms, let us awake the LORD, who reposes in it, and He will quickly calm the sea.

I have taken the liberty to impart to you these good sentiments, that you may compare them with your own: they will serve again to kindle and inflame them, if by misfortune (which GOD forbid, for it would be indeed a great misfortune) they should be, though never so little, cooled. Let us then both recall our first favors. Let us profit by the example and the sentiments of this brother, who is little known of the world, but known of GOD, and extremely caressed by Him. I will pray for you; do you pray instantly for me, who am yours in our LORD.

FIFTH LETTER
Prayer for a sister who is about to make a vow and profession. A fresh insisting upon the necessity and virtue of practicing the Presence of God.

I received today two books and a letter from Sister, who is preparing to make her profession, and upon that account desires the prayers of your holy society, and yours in particular. I perceive that she reckons much upon them; pray do not disappoint her. Beg of GOD that she may make her sacrifice in the view of His love alone, and with a firm resolution to be wholly devoted to Him.

I will send you one of those books which treat of the presence of GOD; a subject which, in my opinion, contains the whole spiritual life; and it seems to me that whoever duly practices it will soon become spiritual.

I know that for the right practice of it, the heart must be empty of all other things; because GOD will possess the heart alone; and as He cannot possess it alone, without empty-

ing it of all besides, so neither can He act there, and do in it what He pleases, unless it be left vacant to Him.

There is not in the world a kind of life more sweet and delightful, than that of a continual conversation with GOD: those only can comprehend it who practice and experience it; yet I do not advise you to do it from that motive; it is not pleasure which we ought to seek in this exercise; but let us do it from a principle of love, and because GOD would have us.

Were I a preacher, I should above all other things preach the practice of the presence of GOD; and were I a director, I should advise all the world to do it: so necessary do I think it, and so easy too.

Ah! knew we but the want we have of the grace and assistance of GOD, we should never lose sight of Him, no, not for a moment. Believe me; make immediately a holy and firm resolution never more willfully to forget Him, and to spend the rest of your days in His sacred presence, deprived for the love of Him, if He thinks fit, of all consolations.

Set heartily about this work, and if you do it as you ought, be assured that you will soon find the effects of it. I will assist you with my prayers, poor as they are: I recommend myself earnestly to yours, and those of your holy society.

SIXTH LETTER
To a member of the order who had received from him a book, and to whom he again enlarges on his favorite topic. Encouragement to persevere.

I have received from Mrs. – the things which you gave her for me. I wonder that you have not given me your thoughts of the little book I sent to you, and which you must have received. Pray set heartily about the practice of it in your old age; it is better late than never.

I cannot imagine how religious persons can live satisfied without the practice of the presence of GOD. For my part I keep myself retired with Him in the depth of center of my soul as much as I can; and while I am so with Him I fear nothing; but the least turning from Him is insupportable.

This exercise does not much fatigue the body: it is, however, proper to deprive it sometimes, nay often, of many little pleasures which are innocent and lawful: for GOD will not permit that a soul which desires to be devoted entirely to Him should take other pleasures than with Him; that is more than reasonable.

I do not say that therefore we must put any violent constraint upon ourselves. No, we must serve GOD in a holy freedom, we must do our business faithfully, without trouble or disquiet; recalling our mind to GOD mildly and with tranquility, as often as we find it wandering from Him.

It is, however, necessary to put our whole trust in GOD, laying aside all other cares, and even some particular forms of devotion, though very good in themselves, yet such as one often engages in unreasonably: because those devotions are only means to attain to the end; so when by this exercise of the presence of GOD we are with Him who is our end, it is then useless to return to the means; but we may continue with Him our commerce of love, persevering in His holy presence: one while by an act of praise, of adoration, or of desire; one while by an act of resignation, or thanksgiving; and in all the manner which our spirit can invent.

Be not discouraged by the repugnance which you may find in it from nature; you must do yourself violence. At the first, one often thinks it lost time; but you must go on, and resolve to persevere in it to death, notwithstanding all the difficulties that may occur. I recommend myself to the prayers of your holy society, and yours in particular. I am yours in our LORD.

SEVENTH LETTER

At the age of nearly fourscore exhorts his correspondent, who is sixty-four, to live and die with God and promises and asks for prayer.

I pity you much. It will be of great importance if you can leave the care of your affairs to, and spend the remainder of your life only in worshiping GOD. He requires no great matters of us; a little remembrance of Him from time to time, a little adoration: sometimes to pray for His grace, sometimes to offer Him your sufferings, and sometimes to return Him thanks for the favors He has given you, and still gives you, in the midst of your troubles, and to console yourself with Him the oftenest you can. Lift up your heart to Him, sometimes even at your meals, and when you are in company: the least little remembrance will always be acceptable to Him. You need not cry very loud; He is nearer to us than we are aware of.

It is not necessary for being with GOD to be always at church; we may make an oratory of our heart, wherein to retire from time to time, to converse with Him in meekness, humility, and love. Every one is capable of such familiar conversation with GOD, some more, some less: He knows what we can do. Let us begin then; perhaps He expects but one generous resolution on our part. Have courage. We have but little time to live; you are near sixty-four, and I am almost eighty. Let us live and die with GOD: sufferings will be sweet and pleasant to us, while we are with Him: and the greatest pleasures will be, without Him, a cruel punishment to us. May He be blessed for all. Amen.

Use yourself then by degrees thus to worship Him, to beg His grace, to offer Him your heart from time to time, in the midst of your business, even every moment if you can. Do not always scrupulously confine yourself to certain rules, or particular forms of devotion; but act with a general confidence in GOD, with love and humility. You may assure – of my poor prayers, and that I am their servant, and yours particularly.

EIGHTH LETTER

Concerning wandering thoughts in prayer.

You tell me nothing new: you are not the only one that is troubled with wandering thoughts. Our mind is extremely roving; but as the will is mistress of all our faculties, she must recall them, and carry them to GOD, as their last end.

When the mind, for want of being sufficiently reduced by recollection, at our first engaging in devotion, has contracted certain bad habits of wandering and dissipation, they are difficult to overcome, and commonly draw us, even against our wills, to the things of the earth.

I believe one remedy for this is, to confess our faults, and to humble ourselves before GOD. I do not advise you to use multiplicity of words in prayer; many words and long discourses being often the occasions of wandering: hold yourself in prayer before GOD, like a dumb or paralytic beggar at a rich man's gate: let it be your business to keep your mind in the presence of the LORD. If it sometimes wander, and withdraw itself from Him, do not much disquiet yourself for that; trouble and disquiet serve rather to distract the mind, than to re- collect it; the will must bring it back in tranquility; if you persevere in this manner, GOD will have pity on you.

One way to re-collect the mind easily in the time of prayer, and preserve it more in tranquility, is not to let it wander too far at other times: you should keep it strictly in the presence of GOD; and being accustomed to think of Him often, you will find it easy to keep your mind calm in the time of prayer, or at least to recall it from its wanderings.

I have told you already at large, in my former letters, of the advantages we may draw from this practice of the presence of GOD: let us set about it seriously and pray for one another.

NINTH LETTER
Enclosing a letter to a corresponding sister, whom he regards with respect tinged with fear. His old theme concisely put.

The enclosed is an answer to that which I received from − ; pray deliver it to her. She seems to me full of good will, but she would go faster than grace. One does not become holy all at once. I recommend her to you: we ought to help one another by our advice, and yet more by our good examples. You will oblige me to let me hear of her from time to time, and whether she be very fervent and very obedient.

Let us thus think often that our only business in this life is to please GOD, that perhaps all besides is but folly and vanity. You and I have lived above forty years in religion [i.e., a monastic life]. Have we employed them in loving and serving GOD, who by His mercy has called us to this state and for that very end? I am filled with shame and confusion, when I reflect on the one hand upon the great favors which GOD has done, and incessantly continues to do, me; and on the other, upon the ill use I have made of them, and my small advancement in the way of perfection.

Since by His mercy He gives us still a little time, let us begin in earnest, let us repair the lost time, let us return with a full assurance to that FATHER of mercies, who is always ready to receive us affectionately. Let us renounce, let us generously renounce, for the love of Him, all that is not Himself; He deserves infinitely more. Let us think of Him perpetually. Let us put all our trust in Him: I doubt not but we shall soon find the effects of it, in receiving the abundance of His grace, with which we can do all things, and without which we can do nothing but sin.

We cannot escape the dangers which abound in life, without the actual and continual help of GOD; let us then pray to Him for it continually. How can we pray to Him without being with Him? How can we be with Him but in thinking of Him often? And how can we often think of Him, but by a holy habit which we should form of it? You will tell me that I am always saying the same thing: it is true, for this is the best and easiest method I know; and as I use no other, I advise all the world to it. We must know before we can love. In order to know GOD, we must often think of Him; and when we come to love Him, we shall then also think of Him often, for our heart will be with our treasure. This is an argument which well deserves your consideration.

TENTH LETTER
Has difficulty, but sacrifices his will, to write as requested. The loss of a friend may lead to acquaintance with the Friend.

I have had a good deal of difficulty to bring myself to write to M. − , and I do it now purely because you and Madam desire me. Pray write the directions and send it to him. I am very well pleased with the trust which you have in GOD: I wish that He may increase it in you more and more: we cannot have too much in so good and faithful a Friend, who will never fail us in this world nor in the next.

If M. − makes his advantage of the loss he has had, and puts all his confidence in GOD, He will soon give him another friend, more powerful and more inclined to serve him. He disposes of hearts as He pleases. Perhaps M. − was too much attached to him he has lost. We ought to love our friends, but without encroaching upon the love of GOD, which must be the principal.

Pray remember what I have recommended to you, which is, to think often on GOD, by day, by night, in your business, and even in your diversions. He is always near you and with you; leave Him not alone. You would think it rude to leave a friend alone, who came to visit you: why then must GOD be neglected? Do not then forget Him, but think on Him often, adore Him continually, live and die with Him; this is the glorious employment of a Christian; in a word, this is our profession, if we do not know it we must learn it. I will endeavor to help you with my prayers, and am yours in our LORD.

ELEVENTH LETTER

To one who is in great pain. God is the Physician of body and of soul. Feels that he would gladly suffer at His wish.

I do not pray that you may be delivered from your pains; but I pray GOD earnestly that He would give you strength and patience to bear them as long as He pleases. Comfort yourself with Him who holds you fastened to the cross: He will loose you when He thinks fit. Happy those who suffer with Him: accustom yourself to suffer in that manner, and seek from Him the strength to endure as much, and as long, as He shall judge to be necessary for you. The men of the world do not comprehend these truths, nor is it to be wondered at, since they suffer like what they are, and not like Christians: they consider sickness as a pain to nature, and not as a favor from GOD; and seeing it only in that light, they find nothing in it but grief and distress. But those who consider sickness as coming from the hand of GOD, as the effects of His mercy, and the means which He employs for their salvation, commonly find in it great sweetness and sensible consolation.

I wish you could convince yourself that GOD is often (in some sense) nearer to us and more effectually present with us, in sickness than in health. Rely upon no other Physician, for, according to my apprehension, He reserves your cure to Himself. Put then all your trust in Him, and you will soon find the effects of it in your recovery, which we often retard, by putting greater confidence in physic than in GOD.

Whatever remedies you make use of, they will succeed only so far as He permits. When pains come from GOD, He only can cure them. He often sends diseases of the body, to cure those of the soul. Comfort yourself with the sovereign Physician both of soul and body.

I foresee that you will tell me that I am very much at my ease, that I eat and drink at the table of the LORD. You have reason: but think you that it would be a small pain to the greatest criminal in the world, to eat at the king's table, and be served by him, and notwithstanding such favors to be without assurance of pardon? I believe he would feel exceeding great uneasiness, and such as nothing could moderate, but only his trust in the goodness of his sovereign. So I assure you, that whatever pleasures I taste at the table of my King, yet my sins, ever present before my eyes, as well as the uncertainty of my pardon, torment me, though in truth that torment itself is pleasing.

Be satisfied with the condition in which GOD places you: however happy you may think me, I envy you. Pains and suffering would be a paradise to me, while I should suffer with my GOD; and the greatest pleasure would be hell to me, if I could relish them without Him; all my consolation would be to suffer something for His sake.

I must, in a little time, go to GOD. What comforts me in this life is, that I now see Him by faith; and I see Him in such a manner as might make me say sometimes, I believe no more, but I see. I feel what faith teaches us, and, in that assurance and that practice of faith, I will live and die with Him.

Continue then always with GOD: 'this the only support and comfort for your affliction. I shall beseech Him to be with you. I present my service.

TWELFTH LETTER

To the same correspondent probably, and expresses his own abiding comfort through faith.

If we were well accustomed to the exercise of the presence of GOD, all bodily diseases would be much alleviated thereby. GOD often permits that we should suffer a little, to purify our souls, and oblige us to continue with Him. Take courage, offer Him your pains incessantly, pray to Him for strength to endure them. Above all, get a habit of entertaining yourself often with GOD, and forget Him the least you can. Adore Him in your infirmities, offer yourself to Him from time to time; and, in the height of your sufferings, beseech Him humbly and affectionately (as a child his father) to make you conformable to His holy will. I shall endeavor to assist you with my poor prayers.

GOD has many ways of drawing us to Himself. He sometimes hides Himself from us: but faith alone, which will not fail us in time of need, ought to be our support, and the foundation of our confidence, which must be all in GOD.

I know not how GOD will dispose of me: I am always happy: all the world suffer; and I, who deserve the severest discipline, feel joys so continual, and so great, that I can scarce contain them.

I would willingly ask of GOD a part of your sufferings, but that I know my weakness, which is so great, that if He left me one moment to myself, I should be the most wretched man alive. And yet I know not how He can leave me alone, because faith gives me as strong a conviction as sense can do, that He never forsakes us, till we have first forsaken Him. Let us fear to leave Him. Let us be always with Him. Let us live and die in His presence. Do you pray for me, as I for you.

THIRTEENTH LETTER
To the same he exhorts for fuller and entire confidence in God, for body and soul.

I am in pain to see you suffer so long; what gives me some ease, and sweetens the feeling I have of your griefs, is that they are proofs of God's love towards you: see them in that view, and you will bear them more easily. As your case is, 'this my opinion that you should leave off human remedies, and resign yourself entirely to the providence of GOD; perhaps He stays only for that resignation and a perfect trust in Him to cure you. Since notwithstanding all your cares, physic has hitherto proved unsuccessful, and your malady still increases, it will not be tempting GOD to abandon yourself in His hands, and expect all from Him.

I told you, in my last, that He sometimes permits bodily diseases to cure the distempers of the soul. Have courage then: make a virtue of necessity: ask of GOD, not deliverance from your pains, but strength to bear resolutely, for the love of Him, all that He should please, and as long as He shall please.

Such prayers, indeed, are a little hard to nature, but most acceptable to GOD, and sweet to those that love Him. Love sweetens pains; and when one loves GOD, one suffers for His sake with joy and courage. Do you so, I beseech you; comfort yourself with Him, who is the only Physician of all our maladies. He is the FATHER of the afflicted, always ready to help us. He loves us infinitely more than we imagine: love Him then, and seek not consolation elsewhere: I hope you will soon receive it. Adieu. I will help you with my prayers, poor as they are, and shall be, always, yours in our LORD.

FOURTEENTH LETTER
Gratitude, for mercies to his correspondent, and measure of relief while he has himself been near death, but with consolation in his suffering.

I render thanks to our LORD, for having relieved you a little, according to your desire. I have been often near expiring, though I was never so much satisfied as then. Accordingly I did not pray for any relief, but I prayed for strength to suffer with courage, humility, and love. Ah, how sweet is it to suffer with GOD! However great the sufferings may be, receive them with love. 'This paradise to suffer and be with Him; so that if in this life we would enjoy the peace of paradise, we must accustom ourselves to a familiar, humble, affectionate conversation with Him: we must hinder our spirits wandering from Him upon any occasion: we must make our heart a spiritual temple, wherein to adore Him incessantly: we must watch continually over ourselves, that we may not do, nor say, nor think anything that may displease Him. When our minds are thus employed about GOD, suffering will become full of unction and consolation.

I know that to arrive at this state, the beginning is very difficult; for we must act purely in faith. But though it is difficult, we know also that we can do all things with the grace of GOD, which He never refuses to them who ask it earnestly. Knock, persevere in knocking, and I answer for it that He will open to you in

His due time, and grant you all at once what He has deferred during many years. Adieu. Pray to Him for me, as I pray to Him for you. I hope to see Him quickly.

FIFTEENTH LETTER
From his death-bed. Repeats the same exhortation to knowledge, that we may love.

God knows best what is needful for us, and all that He does is for our good. If we knew how much He loves us, we should be always ready to receive equally and with indifference from His hand the sweet and the bitter; all would please that came from Him. The sorest afflictions never appear intolerable, but when we see them in the wrong light. When we see them in the hand of GOD, who dispenses them: when we know that it is our loving FATHER, who abases and distresses us: our sufferings will lose their bitterness, and become even matter of consolation.

Let all our employment be to know GOD: the more one knows Him, the more one desires to know Him. And as knowledge is commonly the measure of love, the deeper and more extensive our knowledge shall be, the greater will be our love: and if our love of GOD were great we should love Him equally in pains and pleasures.

Let us not amuse ourselves to seek or to love GOD for any sensible favors (however elevated) which He has or may do us. Such favors, though never so great, cannot bring us so near to GOD as faith does in one simple act. Let us seek Him often by faith: He is within us; seek Him not elsewhere. Are we not rude and deserve blame, if we leave Him alone, to busy ourselves about trifles, which do not please Him and perhaps offend Him? 'This to be feared these trifles will one day cost us dearly.

Let us begin to be devoted to Him in good earnest. Let us cast everything besides out of our hearts; He would possess them alone. Beg this favor of Him. If we do what we can on our parts, we shall soon see that change wrought in us which we aspire after. I cannot thank Him sufficiently for the relaxation He has vouchsafed you. I hope from His mercy the favor to see Him within a few days. Let us pray for one another.

[He took to his bed two days after and died within the week.]

Brother Lawrence, 1611–91

The Large Catechism
Martin Luther

CHAPTER 11
OF PRAYER

No man can perfectly keep the Ten Commandments, even though he have begun to believe, and since the devil with all his power together with the world and our own flesh, resists our endeavors, nothing is so necessary as that we should continually resort to the ear of God, call upon Him, and pray to Him, that He would give, preserve, and increase in us faith and the fulfillment of the Ten Commandments, and that He would remove everything that is in our way and opposes us therein. But that we might know what and how to pray, our Lord Christ has Himself taught us both the mode and the words, as we shall see.

But before we explain the Lord's Prayer part by part, it is most necessary first to exhort and incite people to prayer, as Christ and the apostles also have done. And the first matter is to know that it is our duty to pray because of God's commandment. For thus we heard in the Second Commandment: Thou shalt not take the name of the lord, thy God, in vain, that we are there required to praise that holy name, and call upon it in every need, or to pray. For to call upon the name of God is nothing else than to pray. Prayer is therefore as strictly and earnestly commanded as all other commandments: to have no other God, not to kill, not to steal, etc. Let no one think that it is all the same whether he pray or not, as vulgar people do, who grope in such delusion and ask Why should I pray? Who knows whether God heeds or will hear my prayer? If I do not pray, some one else will. And thus they fall into the habit of never praying, and frame a pretext, as though we taught that there is no duty or need of prayer, because we reject false and hypocritical prayers.

But this is true indeed that such prayers as have been offered hitherto when men were babbling and bawling in the churches were no prayers. For such external matters, when they are properly observed, may be a good exercise for young children, scholars, and simple persons, and may be called singing or reading, but not really praying. But praying, as the Second Commandment teaches, is to call upon

God in every need. This He requires of us, and has not left it to our choice. But it is our duty and obligation to pray if we would be Christians, as much as it is our duty and obligation to obey our parents and the government; for by calling upon it and praying the name of God is honored and profitably employed. This you must note above all things, that thereby you may silence and repel such thoughts as would keep and deter us from prayer. For just as it would be idle for a son to say to his father, "Of what advantage is my obedience? I will go and do what I can; it is all the same"; but there stands the commandment, Thou shalt and must do it, so also here it is not left to my will to do it or leave it undone, but prayer shall and must be offered at the risk of God's wrath and displeasure.

This is therefore to be understood and noted before everything else, in order that thereby we may silence and repel the thoughts which would keep and deter us from praying, as though it were not of much consequence if we do not pray, or as though it were commanded those who are holier and in better favor with God than we; as, indeed, the human heart is by nature so despondent that it always flees from God and imagines that He does not wish or desire our prayer, because we are sinners and have merited nothing but wrath. Against such thoughts (I say) we should regard this commandment and turn to God, that we may not by such disobedience excite His anger still more. For by this commandment He gives us plainly to understand that He will not cast us from Him nor chase us away, although we are sinners, but rather draw us to Himself, so that we might humble ourselves before Him, bewail this misery and plight of ours, and pray for grace and help. Therefore we read in the Scriptures that He is angry also with those who were smitten for their sin, because they did not return to Him and by their prayers assuage His wrath and seek His grace.

Now, from the fact that it is so solemnly commanded to pray, you are to conclude and think, that no one should by any means despise his prayer, but rather set great store by it, and always seek an illustration from the other commandments. A child should by no means despise his obedience to father and mother, but should always think: This work is a work

of obedience, and what I do I do with no other intention than that I may walk in the obedience and commandment of God, on which I can settle and stand firm, and esteem it a great thing, not on account of my worthiness, but on account of the commandment. So here also, what and for what we pray we should regard as demanded by God and done in obedience to Him, and should reflect thus: On my account it would amount to nothing; but it shall avail, for the reason that God has commanded it. Therefore everybody, no matter what he has to say in prayer, should always come before God in obedience to this commandment.

We pray, therefore, and exhort every one most diligently to take this to heart and by no means to despise our prayer. For hitherto it has been taught thus in the devil's name that no one regarded these things, and men supposed it to be sufficient to have done the work, whether God would hear it or not. But that is staking prayer on a risk, and murmuring it at a venture, and therefore it is a lost prayer. For we allow such thoughts as these to lead us astray and deter us: I am not holy or worthy enough; if I were as godly and holy as St. Peter or St. Paul, then I would pray. But put such thoughts far away, for just the same commandment which applied to St. Paul applies also to me; and the Second Commandment is given as much on my account as on his account, so that he can boast of no better or holier commandment.

Therefore you should say: My prayer is as precious, holy, and pleasing to God as that of St. Paul or of the most holy saints. This is the reason: For I will gladly grant that he is holier in his person, but not on account of the commandment; since God does not regard prayer on account of the person, but on account of His word and obedience thereto. For on the commandment on which all the saints rest their prayer I, too, rest mine. Moreover I pray for the same thing for which they all pray and ever have prayed; besides, I have just as great a need of it as those great saints, yea, even a greater one than they.

Let this be the first and most important point, that all our prayers must be based and rest upon obedience to God, irrespective of our person, whether we be sinners or saints, worthy or unworthy. And we must know that God will not have it treated as a jest, but be angry, and punish all who do not pray, as surely as He punishes all other disobedience; next, that He will not suffer our prayers to be in vain or lost. For if He did not intend to answer your prayer, He would not bid you pray and add such a severe commandment to it.

In the second place, we should be the more urged and incited to pray because God has also added a promise, and declared that it shall surely be done to us as we pray, as He says Ps. 50, 15: Call upon Me in the day of trouble: I will deliver thee. And Christ in the Gospel of St. Matthew, 7, 7: Ask, and it shall be given you. For every one that asketh receiveth. Such promises ought certainly to encourage and kindle our hearts to pray with pleasure and delight, since He testifies with His [own] word that our prayer is heartily pleasing to Him, moreover, that it shall assuredly be heard and granted, in order that we may not despise it or think lightly of it, and pray at a venture.

This you can hold up to Him and say: Here I come, dear Father, and pray, not of my own purpose nor upon my own worthiness, but at Thy commandment and promise, which cannot fail or deceive me. Whoever, therefore, does not believe this promise must know again that he excites God to anger as a person who most highly dishonors Him and reproaches Him with falsehood.

Besides this, we should be incited and drawn to prayer because in addition to this commandment and promise God anticipates us, and Himself arranges the words and form of prayer for us, and places them upon our lips as to how and what we should pray, that we may see how heartily He pities us in our distress, and may never doubt that such prayer is pleasing to Him and shall certainly be answered; which [the Lord's Prayer] is a great advantage indeed over all other prayers that we might compose ourselves. For in them the conscience would ever be in doubt and say: I have prayed, but who knows how it pleases Him, or whether I have hit upon the right proportions and form? Hence there is no nobler prayer to be found upon earth than the Lord's Prayer which we daily pray because it has this excellent testimony, that God loves to hear it, which we ought not to surrender for all the riches of the world.

And it has been prescribed also for this reason that we should see and consider the distress which ought to urge and compel us to pray without ceasing. For whoever would pray must have something to present, state, and name which he desires; if not, it cannot be called a prayer.

Therefore we have rightly rejected the prayers of monks and priests, who howl and growl day and night like fiends; but none of them think of praying for a hair's breadth of anything. And if we would assemble all the churches, together with all ecclesiastics, they would be obliged to confess that they have never from the heart prayed for even a drop of wine. For none of them has ever purposed to pray from obedience to God and faith in His promise, nor has any one regarded any distress, but (when they had done their best) they thought no further than this, to do a good work, whereby they might repay God, as being unwilling to take anything from Him, but wishing only to give Him something.

But where there is to be a true prayer there must be earnestness. Men must feel their distress, and such distress as presses them and compels them to call and cry out then prayer will be made spontaneously, as it ought to be, and men will require no teaching how to prepare for it and to attain to the proper devotion. But the distress which ought to concern us most, both as regards ourselves and every one, you will find abundantly set forth in the Lord's Prayer. Therefore it is to serve also to remind us of the same, that we contemplate it and lay it to heart, lest we become remiss in prayer. For we all have enough that we lack, but the great want is that we do not feel nor see it. Therefore God also requires that you lament and plead such necessities and wants, not because He does not know them, but that you may kindle your heart to stronger and greater desires, and make wide and open your cloak to receive much.

Therefore, every one of us should accustom himself from his youth daily to pray for all his wants, whenever he is sensible of anything affecting his interests or that of other people among whom he may live, as for preachers, the government, neighbors, domestics, and always (as we have said) to hold up to God His commandment and promise, knowing that He will not have them disregarded. This I say because I would like to see these things brought home again to the people that they might learn to pray truly, and not go about coldly and indifferently, whereby they become daily more unfit for prayer; which is just what the devil desires, and for what he works with all his powers. For he is well aware what damage and harm it does him when prayer is in proper practice. For this we must know, that all our shelter and protection rest in prayer alone. For we are far too feeble to cope with the devil and all his power and adherents that set themselves against us, and they might easily crush us under their feet. Therefore we must consider and take up those weapons with which Christians must be armed in order to stand against the devil. For what do you think has hitherto accomplished such great things, has checked or quelled the counsels, purposes, murder, and riot of our enemies, whereby the devil thought to crush us, together with the Gospel, except that the prayer of a few godly men intervened like a wall of iron on our side? They should else have witnessed a far different tragedy, namely, how the devil would have destroyed all Germany in its own blood. But now they may confidently deride it and make a mock of it, however, we shall nevertheless be a match both for themselves and the devil by prayer alone, if we only persevere diligently and not become slack. For whenever a godly Christian prays: Dear Father let Thy will be done, God speaks from on high and says: Yes, dear child, it shall be so, in spite of the devil and all the world.

Let this be said as an exhortation, that men may learn, first of all, to esteem prayer as something great and precious, and to make a proper distinction between babbling and praying for something. For we by no means reject prayer, but the bare, useless howling and murmuring we reject, as Christ Himself also rejects and prohibits long palavers. Now we shall most briefly and clearly treat of the Lord's Prayer. Here there is comprehended in seven successive articles, or petitions, every need which never ceases to relate to us, and each so great that it ought to constrain us to keep praying it all our lives.

CHAPTER 12
HALLOWED BE THY NAME
This is, indeed, somewhat obscure, and not expressed in good German, for in our mother-tongue we would say: Heavenly Father, help that by all means Thy name may be holy. But what is it to pray that His name may be holy? Is it not holy already? Answer: Yes, it is always holy in its nature, but in our use it is not holy. For God's name was given us when we became Christians and were baptized, so that we are called children of God and have the Sacraments by which He so incorporates us in Himself that everything which is God's must serve for our use.

Here now the great need exists for which we ought to be most concerned, that this name have its proper honor, be esteemed holy and sublime as the greatest treasure and sanctuary that we have; and that as godly children we pray that the name of God, which is already holy in heaven, may also be and remain holy with us upon earth and in all the world.

But how does it become holy among us? Answer, as plainly as it can be said: When both our doctrine and life are godly and Christian. For since in this prayer we call God our Father, it is our duty always to deport and demean ourselves as godly children, that He may not receive shame, but honor and praise from us.

Now the name of God is profaned by us either in words or in works. (For whatever we do upon the earth must be either words or works, speech or act.) In the first place, then, it is profaned when men preach, teach, and speak in the name of God what is false and misleading, so that His name must serve to adorn and to find a market for falsehood. That is, indeed, the greatest profanation and dishonor of the divine name. Furthermore, also when men, by swearing, cursing, conjuring, etc., grossly abuse the holy name as a cloak for their shame. In the second place also by an openly wicked life and works, when those who are called Christians and the people of God are adulterers, drunkards, misers, envious, and slanderers. Here again must the name of God come to shame and be profaned because of us. For just as it is a shame and disgrace to a natural father to have a bad perverse child that opposes him in words and deeds, so that on its account he suffers contempt and reproach, so also it brings dishonor upon God if we who are called by His name and have all manner of goods from Him teach, speak, and live in any other manner except as godly and heavenly children, so that people say of us that we must be not God's, but the devil's children.

Thus you see that in this petition we pray just for that which God demands in the Second Commandment; namely, that His name be not taken in vain to swear, curse, lie, deceive, etc., but be usefully employed to the praise and honor of God. For whoever employs the name of God for any sort of wrong profanes and desecrates this holy name, as aforetime a church was considered desecrated when a murder or any other crime had been committed in it, or when a pyx or relic was desecrated, as being holy in themselves, yet become unholy in use. Thus this point is easy and clear if only the language is understood, that to hallow is the same as in our idiom to praise, magnify, and honor both in word and deed.

Here, now, learn how great need there is of such prayer. For because we see how full the world is of sects and false teachers, who all wear the holy name as a cover and sham for their doctrines of devils, we ought by all means to pray without ceasing, and to cry and call upon God against all such as preach and believe falsely and whatever opposes and persecutes our Gospel and pure doctrine, and would suppress it, as bishops, tyrants, enthusiasts, etc. Likewise also for ourselves who have the Word of God, but are not thankful for it, nor live as we ought according to the same. If now you pray for this with your heart, you can be sure that it pleases God; for He will not hear anything more dear to Him than that His honor and praise is exalted above everything else, and His Word is taught in its purity and is esteemed precious and dear.

THY KINGDOM COME

As we prayed in the First Petition concerning the honor and name of God that He would prevent the world from adorning its lies and wickedness with it, but cause it to be esteemed sublime and holy both in doctrine and life, so that He may be praised and magnified in us, so here we pray that His kingdom also may come.

But just as the name of God is in itself holy, and we pray nevertheless that it be holy among us, so also His kingdom comes of itself, without our prayer, yet we pray nevertheless that it may come to us, that is, prevail among us and with us, so that we may be a part of those among whom His name is hallowed and His kingdom prospers.

But what is the kingdom of God? Answer: Nothing else than what we learned in the Creed, that God sent His Son Jesus Christ our Lord, into the world to redeem and deliver us from the power of the devil, and to bring us to Himself, and to govern us as a King of righteousness, life and salvation against sin death, and an evil conscience, for which end He has also bestowed His Holy Ghost, who is to bring these things home to us by His holy Word, and to illumine and strengthen us in the faith by His power.

Therefore we pray here in the first place that this may become effective with us, and that His name be so praised through the holy Word of God and a Christian life that both we who have accepted it may abide and daily grow therein, and that it may gain approbation and adherence among other people and proceed with power throughout the world, that many may find entrance into the Kingdom of Grace, be made partakers of redemption, being led thereto by the Holy Ghost, in order that thus we may all together remain forever in the one kingdom now begun.

For the coming of God's Kingdom to us occurs in two ways; first, here in time through the Word and faith; and secondly, in eternity forever through revelation. Now we pray for both these things, that it may come to those who are not yet in it, and, by daily increase, to us who have received the same, and hereafter in eternal life. All this is nothing else than saying: Dear Father, we pray, give us first Thy Word, that the Gospel be preached properly throughout the world; and secondly, that it be received in faith, and work and live in us, so that through the Word and the power of the Holy Ghost Thy kingdom may prevail among us, and the kingdom of the devil be put down, that he may have no right or power over us, until at last it shall be utterly destroyed, and sin, death, and hell shall be exterminated, that we may live forever in perfect righteousness and blessedness.

From this you perceive that we pray here not for a crust of bread or a temporal, perishable good, but for an eternal inestimable treasure and everything that God Himself possesses; which is far too great for any human heart to think of desiring if He had not Himself commanded us to pray for the same. But because He is God, He also claims the honor of giving much more and more abundantly than any one can comprehend, – like an eternal, unfailing fountain, which, the more it pours forth and overflows, the more it continues to give, – and He desires nothing more earnestly of us than that we ask much and great things of Him, and again is angry if we do not ask and pray confidently.

For just as when the richest and most mighty emperor would bid a poor beggar ask whatever he might desire, and were ready to give great imperial presents, and the fool would beg only for a dish of gruel, he would be rightly considered a rogue and a scoundrel who treated the command of his imperial majesty as a jest and sport, and was not worthy of coming into his presence: so also it is a great reproach and dishonor to God if we, to whom He offers and pledges so many unspeakable treasures, despise the same, or have not the confidence to receive them, but scarcely venture to pray for a piece of bread.

All this is the fault of the shameful unbelief which does not look to God for as much good as will satisfy the stomach, much less expects without doubt such eternal treasures of God. Therefore we must strengthen ourselves against it, and let this be our first prayer; then, indeed, we shall have all else in abundance, as Christ teaches (Matt. 6, 33): Seek ye first the kingdom of God and His righteousness and all these things shall be added unto you. For how could He allow us to suffer want and to be straitened in temporal things when He promises that which is eternal and imperishable?

THY WILL BE DONE ON EARTH AS IT IS IN HEAVEN

Thus far we have prayed that God's name be honored by us, and that His kingdom prevail among us; in which two points is compre-

hended all that pertains to the honor of God and to our salvation, that we receive as our own God and all His riches. But now a need just as great arises, namely, that we firmly keep them, and do not suffer ourselves to be torn therefrom. For as in a good government it is not only necessary that there be those who build and govern well, but also those who make defense, afford protection and maintain it firmly, so here likewise, although we have prayed for the greatest need, for the Gospel, faith, and the Holy Ghost, that He may govern us and redeem us from the power of the devil, we must also pray that His will be done. For there will be happenings quite strange if we are to abide therein, as we shall have to suffer many thrusts and blows on that account from everything that ventures to oppose and prevent the fulfillment of the two petitions that precede.

For no one believes how the devil opposes and resists them, and cannot suffer that any one teach or believe aright. And it hurts him beyond measure to suffer his lies and abominations, that have been honored under the most specious pretexts of the divine name, to be exposed, and to be disgraced himself, and, besides, be driven out of the heart, and suffer such a breach to be made in his kingdom. Therefore he chafes and rages as a fierce enemy with all his power and might, and marshals all his subjects, and, in addition enlists the world and our own flesh as his allies. For our flesh is in itself indolent and inclined to evil, even though we have accepted and believe the Word of God. The world, however, is perverse and wicked; this he incites against us, fans and stirs the fire, that he may hinder and drive us back, cause us to fall, and again bring us under his power. Such is all his will, mind, and thought, for which he strives day and night, and never rests a moment, employing all arts, wiles, ways, and means whichever he can invent.

If we would be Christians, therefore, we must surely expect and reckon upon having the devil with all his angels and the world as our enemies, who will bring every possible misfortune and grief upon us. For where the Word of God is preached, accepted, or believed, and produces fruit, there the holy cross cannot be wanting. And let no one think that he shall have peace; but he must risk what whatever he has upon earth – possessions, honor. house and estate, wife and children, body and life. Now, this hurts our flesh and the old Adam; for the test is to be steadfast and to suffer with patience in whatever way we are assailed, and to let go whatever is taken from us.

Hence there is just as great need, as in all the others, that we pray without ceasing: "Dear Father, Thy will be done, not the will of the devil and of our enemies, nor of anything that would persecute and suppress Thy holy Word or hinder Thy kingdom; and grant that we may bear with patience and overcome whatever is to be endured on that account, lest our poor flesh yield or fall away from weakness or sluggishness."

Behold, thus we have in these three petitions, in the simplest manner, the need which relates to God Himself, yet all for our sakes. For whatever we pray concerns only us, namely, as we have said, that what must be done anyway without us, may also be done in us. For as His name must be hallowed and His kingdom come without our prayer, so also His will must be done and succeed although the devil with all his adherents raise a great tumult, are angry and rage against it, and undertake to exterminate the Gospel utterly. But for our own sakes we must pray that even against their fury His will be done without hindrance also among us, that they may not be able to accomplish anything and we remain firm against all violence and persecution, and submit to such will of God.

Such prayer, then, is to be our protection and defense now, is to repel and put down all that the devil, Pope, bishops, tyrants, and heretics can do against our Gospel. Let them all rage and attempt their utmost, and deliberate and resolve how they may suppress and exterminate us, that their will and counsel may prevail: over and against this one or two Christians with this petition alone shall be our wall against which they shall run and dash themselves to pieces. This consolation and confidence we have, that the will and purpose of the devil and of all our enemies shall and must fail and come to naught, however proud, secure, and powerful they know themselves to be. For if their will were not broken and hindered, the

kingdom of God could not abide on earth nor His name be hallowed.

GIVE US THIS DAY OUR DAILY BREAD

Here, now, we consider the poor breadbasket, the necessaries of our body and of the temporal life. It is a brief and simple word, but it has a very wide scope. For when you mention and pray for daily bread, you pray for everything that is necessary in order to have and enjoy daily bread and, on the other hand, against everything which interferes with it. Therefore you must open wide and extend your thoughts not only to the oven or the flour-bin but to the distant field and the entire land, which bears and brings to us daily bread and every sort of sustenance. For if God did not cause it to grow, and bless and preserve it in the field, we could never take bread from the oven or have any to set upon the table.

To comprise it briefly, this petition includes everything that belongs to our entire life in the world, because on that account alone do we need daily bread. Now for our life it is not only necessary that our body have food and covering and other necessaries, but also that we spend our days in peace and quiet among the people with whom we live and have intercourse in daily business and conversation and all sorts of doings, in short, whatever pertains both to the domestic and to the neighborly or civil relation and government. For where these two things are hindered (intercepted and disturbed) that they do not prosper as they ought, the necessaries of life also are impeded, so that ultimately life cannot be maintained. And there is, indeed, the greatest need to pray for temporal authority and government, as that by which most of all God preserves to us our daily bread and all the comforts of this life. For though we have received of God all good things in abundance we are not able to retain any of them or use them in security and happiness, if He did not give us a permanent and peaceful government. For where there are dissension, strife, and war, there the daily bread is already taken away, or at least checked.

Therefore it would be very proper to place in the coat-of-arms of every pious prince a loaf of bread instead of a lion, or a wreath of rue, or to stamp it upon the coin, to remind both them and their subjects that by their office we have protection and peace, and that without them we could not eat and retain our daily bread. Therefore they are also worthy of all honor, that we give to them for their office what we ought and can, as to those through whom we enjoy in peace and quietness what we have, because otherwise we would not keep a farthing; and that, in addition, we also pray for them that through them God may bestow on us the more blessing and good.

Let this be a very brief explanation and sketch, showing how far this petition extends through all conditions on earth. Of this any one might indeed make a long prayer, and with many words enumerate all the things that are included therein, as that we pray God to give us food and drink, clothing, house, and home, and health of body; also that He cause the grain and fruits of the field to grow and mature well; furthermore, that He help us at home towards good housekeeping, that He give and preserve to us a godly wife, children, and servants, that He cause our work, trade, or whatever we are engaged in to prosper and succeed, favor us with faithful neighbors and good friends, etc. Likewise, that He give to emperors, kings, and all estates, and especially to the rulers of our country and to all counselors, magistrates, and officers, wisdom, strength, and success that they may govern well and vanquish the Turks and all enemies; to subjects and the common people, obedience, peace, and harmony in their life with one another, and on the other hand, that He would preserve us from all sorts of calamity to body and livelihood, as lightning, hail, fire, flood, poison, pestilence, cattle-plague, war and bloodshed, famine, destructive beasts, wicked men, etc. All this it is well to impress upon the simple, namely, that these things come from God, and must be prayed for by us.

But this petition is especially directed also against our chief enemy, the devil. For all his thought and desire is to deprive us of all that we have from God, or to hinder it; and he is not satisfied to obstruct and destroy spiritual government in leading souls astray by his lies and bringing them under his power, but he also prevents and hinders the stability of all government and honorable, peaceable relations on earth. There he causes so much contention, murder, sedition, and war also lightning and hail to destroy grain and cattle, to poison the air, etc. In short, he is sorry that any one has a morsel of bread from God and eats it in peace; and if it were in his power, and our prayer (next to God) did not prevent him, we would not keep a straw in the field, a farthing in the house, yea, not even our life for an hour, especially those who have the Word of God and would like to be Christians.

Behold, thus God wishes to indicate to us how He cares for us in all our need, and faithfully provides also for our temporal support. and although He abundantly grants and preserves these things even to the wicked and knaves, yet He wishes that we pray for them, in order that we may recognize that we receive them from His hand, and may feel His paternal goodness toward us therein. For when He withdraws His hand, nothing can prosper nor be maintained in the end, as, indeed, we daily see and experience. How much trouble there is now in the world only on account of bad coin, yea, on account of daily oppression and raising of prices in common trade, bargaining and labor on the part of those who wantonly oppress the poor and deprive them of their daily bread! This we must suffer indeed; but let them take care that they do not lose the common intercession, and beware lest this petition in the Lord's Prayer be against them.

AND FORGIVE US OUR TRESPASSES, AS WE FORGIVE THOSE WHO TRESPASS AGAINST US This part now relates to our poor miserable life, which, although we have and believe the Word of God, and do and submit to His will, and are supported by His gifts and blessings is nevertheless not without sin. For we still stumble daily and transgress because we live in the world among men who do us much harm and give us cause for impatience, anger, revenge, etc. Besides, we have Satan at our back, who sets upon us on every side, and fights (as we have heard) against all the foregoing petitions, so that it is not possible always to stand firm in such a persistent conflict.

Therefore there is here again great need to call upon God and to pray: Dear Father, forgive us our trespasses. Not as though He did not forgive sin without and even before our prayer (for He has given us the Gospel, in which is pure forgiveness before we prayed or ever thought about it). But this is to the intent that we may recognize and accept such forgiveness. For since the flesh in which we daily live is of such a nature that it neither trusts nor believes God, and is ever active in evil lusts and devices, so that we sin daily in word and deed, by commission and omission by which the conscience is thrown into unrest, so that it is afraid of the wrath and displeasure of God, and thus loses the comfort and confidence derived from the Gospel; therefore it is ceaselessly necessary that we run hither and obtain consolation to comfort the conscience again.

But this should serve God's purpose of breaking our pride and keeping us humble. For in case any one should boast of his godliness and despise others, God has reserved this prerogative to Himself, that the person is to consider himself and place this prayer before his eyes, and he will find that he is no better than others, and that in the presence of God all must lower their plumes, and be glad that they can attain forgiveness. And let no one think that as long as we live here he can reach such a position that he will not need such forgiveness. In short, if God does not forgive without ceasing, we are lost.

It is therefore the intent of this petition that God would not regard our sins and hold up to us what we daily deserve, but would deal graciously with us, and forgive, as He has promised, and thus grant us a joyful and confident conscience to stand before Him in prayer. For where the heart is not in right relation towards God, nor can take such confidence, it will nevermore venture to pray. But such a confident and joyful heart can spring from nothing else than the (certain) knowledge of the forgiveness of sin.

But there is here attached a necessary, yet consolatory addition: As we forgive. He has promised that we shall be sure that everything is forgiven and pardoned, yet in the manner that we also forgive our neighbor. For just as we daily sin much against God and yet He forgives everything through grace, so we, too, must ever forgive our neighbor who does us injury, violence, and wrong, shows malice

toward us, etc. If, therefore you do not forgive, then do not think that God forgives you; but if you forgive, you have this consolation and assurance, that you are forgiven in heaven, not on account of your forgiving, – for God forgives freely and without condition, out of pure grace, because He has so promised, as the Gospel teaches, – but in order that He may set this up for our confirmation and assurance for a sign alongside of the promise which accords with this prayer, Luke 6, 37: Forgive, and ye shall be forgiven. Therefore Christ also repeats it soon after the Lord's Prayer, and says, Matt. 6, 14: For if ye forgive men their trespasses, your heavenly Father will also forgive you, etc.

This sign is therefore attached to this petition, that, when we pray, we remember the promise and reflect thus: Dear Father, for this reason I come and pray Thee to forgive me, not that I can make satisfaction, or can merit anything by my works, but because Thou hast promised and attached the seal thereto that I should be as sure as though I had absolution pronounced by Thyself. For as much as Baptism and the Lord's Supper appointed as external signs, effect, so much also this sign can effect to confirm our consciences and cause them to rejoice. And it is especially given for this purpose, that we might use and practice it every hour, as a thing that we have with us at all times.

AND LEAD US NOT INTO TEMPTATION

We have now heard enough what toil and labor is required to retain all that for which we pray, and to persevere therein, which, however, is not achieved without infirmities and stumbling. Besides, although we have received forgiveness and a good conscience and are entirely acquitted, yet is our life of such a nature that one stands to-day and to-morrow falls. Therefore, even though we be godly now and stand before God with a good conscience, we must pray again that He would not suffer us to relapse and yield to trials and temptations.

Temptation, however, or (as our Saxons in olden times used to call it) Bekoerunge, is of three kinds, namely, of the flesh, of the world and of the devil. For in the flesh we dwell and carry the old Adam about our neck, who exerts himself and incites us daily to unchastity, laziness, gluttony and drunkenness, avarice and deception, to defraud our neighbor and to overcharge him, and, in short, to all manner of evil lusts which cleave to us by nature, and to which we are incited by the society, example and what we hear and see of other people, which often wound and inflame even an innocent heart.

Next comes the world, which offends us in word and deed, and impels us to anger and impatience. In short, there is nothing but hatred and envy, enmity, violence and wrong, unfaithfulness, vengeance, cursing, raillery slander, pride and haughtiness, with superfluous finery, honor, fame, and power, where no one is willing to be the least, but every one desires to sit at the head and to be seen before all.

Then comes the devil, inciting and provoking in all directions, but especially agitating matters that concern the conscience and spiritual affairs, namely, to induce us to despise and disregard both the Word and works of God to tear us away from faith, hope, and love and bring us into misbelief, false security, and obduracy, or, on the other hand, to despair, denial of God, blasphemy, and innumerable other shocking things. These are indeed snares and nets, yea, real fiery darts which are shot most venomously into the heart, not by flesh and blood, but by the devil.

Great and grievous, indeed, are these dangers and temptations which every Christian must bear, even though each one were alone by himself, so that every hour that we are in this vile life where we are attacked on all sides, chased and hunted down, we are moved to cry out and to pray that God would not suffer us to become weary and faint and to relapse into sin, shame, and unbelief. For otherwise it is impossible to overcome even the least temptation.

This, then, is leading us not into temptation, to wit, when He gives us power and strength to resist, the temptation, however, not being taken away or removed. For while we live in the flesh and have the devil about us, no one can escape temptation and allurements; and it cannot be otherwise than that we must endure trials, yea, be engulfed in them; but we pray for this, that we may not fall and be drowned in them.

To feel temptation is therefore a far different thing from consenting or yielding to it.

We must all feel it, although not all in the same manner, but some in a greater degree and more severely than others; as, the young suffer especially from the flesh, afterwards, they that attain to middle life and old age, from the world, but others who are occupied with spiritual matters, that is, strong Christians, from the devil. But such feeling, as long as it is against our will and we would rather be rid of it, can harm no one. For if we did not feel it, it could not be called a temptation. But to consent thereto is when we give it the reins and do not resist or pray against it.

Therefore we Christians must be armed and daily expect to be incessantly attacked, in order that no one may go on in security and heedlessly, as though the devil were far from us, but at all times expect and parry his blows. For though I am now chaste, patient, kind, and in firm faith, the devil will this very hour send such an arrow into my heart that I can scarcely stand. For he is an enemy that never desists nor becomes tired, so that when one temptation ceases, there always arise others and fresh ones.

Accordingly, there is no help or comfort except to run hither and to take hold of the Lord's Prayer, and thus speak to God from the heart: Dear Father, Thou hast bidden me pray; let me not relapse because of temptations. Then you will see that they must desist, and finally acknowledge themselves conquered. Else if you venture to help yourself by your own thoughts and counsel, you will only make the matter worse and give the devil more space. For he has a serpent's head, which if it gain an opening into which he can slip, the whole body will follow without check. But prayer can prevent him and drive him back.

BUT DELIVER US FROM EVIL. AMEN.
In the Greek text this petition reads thus: Deliver or preserve us from the Evil One, or the Malicious One; and it looks as if He were speaking of the devil, as though He would comprehend everything in one so that the entire substance of all our prayer is directed against our chief enemy. For it is he who hinders among us everything that we pray for: the name or honor of God, God's kingdom and will, our daily bread, a cheerful good

conscience, etc.

Therefore we finally sum it all up and say: Dear Father pray, help that we be rid of all these calamities. But there is nevertheless also included whatever evil may happen to us under the devil's kingdom – poverty, shame, death, and, in short, all the agonizing misery and heartache of which there is such an unnumbered multitude on the earth. For since the devil is not only a liar, but also a murderer, he constantly seeks our life, and wreaks his anger whenever he can afflict our bodies with misfortune and harm. Hence it comes that he often breaks men's necks or drives them to insanity, drowns some, and incites many to commit suicide, and to many other terrible calamities. Therefore there is nothing for us to do upon earth but to pray against this arch enemy without ceasing. For unless God preserved us, we would not be safe from him even for an hour.

Hence you see again how God wishes us to pray to Him also for all the things which affect our bodily interests, so that we seek and expect help nowhere else except in Him. But this matter He has put last; for if we are to be preserved and delivered from all evil, the name of God must first be hallowed in us, His kingdom must be with us, and His will be done. After that He will finally preserve us from sin and shame, and, besides, from everything that may hurt or injure us.

Thus God has briefly placed before us all the distress which may ever come upon us, so that we might have no excuse whatever for not praying. But all depends upon this, that we learn also to say Amen, that is, that we do not doubt that our prayer is surely heard and (what we pray) shall be done. For this is nothing else than the word of undoubting faith, which does not pray at a venture, but knows that God does not lie to him, since He has promised to grant it. Therefore, where there is no such faith, there cannot be true prayer either.

It is, therefore, a pernicious delusion of those who pray in such a manner that they dare not from the heart say yea and positively conclude that God hears them, but remain in doubt and say, How should I be so bold as to boast that God hears my prayer? For I am but a poor sinner, etc.

The reason for this is, they regard not the promise of God, but their own work and worthiness, whereby they despise God and reproach Him with lying, and therefore they receive nothing. As St. James says (1, 6): But let him ask in faith, nothing wavering; for he that wavereth is like a wave of the sea, driven with the wind and tossed. For let not that man think that he shall receive anything of the Lord. Behold, such importance God attaches to the fact that we are sure we do not pray in vain, and that we do not in any way despise our prayer.

Martin Luther, 1483–1546

Table Talk
Martin Luther

OF PRAYER

328

None can believe how powerful prayer is, and what it is able to effect, but those who have learned it by experience.

It is a great matter when in extreme need, to take hold on prayer. I know, whenever I have earnestly prayed, I have been amply heard, and have obtained more than I prayed for; God, indeed, sometimes delayed, but at last he came.

Ecclesiasticus says: "The prayer of a good and godly Christian availeth more to health, than the physician's physic."

O how great a thing, how marvelous, a godly Christian's prayer is! how powerful with God; that a poor human creature should speak with God's high Majesty in heaven, and not be affrighted, but, on the contrary, know that God smiles upon him for Christ's sake, his dearly beloved Son. The heart and conscience, in this act of praying, must not fly and recoil backwards by reason of our sins and unworthiness, or stand in doubt, or be scared away. We must not do as the Bavarian did, who, with great devotion, called upon St Leonard, an idol set up in a church in Bavaria, behind which idol stood one who answered the Bavarian, and said: Fie on thee, Bavarian; and in that sort often repulsed and would not hear him, till at last, the Bavarian went away, and said: Fie on thee, Leonard.

When we pray, we must not let it come to: Fie upon thee; but certainly hold and believe, that we are already heard in that for which we pray, with faith in Christ. Therefore the ancients ably defined prayer an *Accensus mentis ad Deum*, a climbing up of the heart unto God.

329

Our Savior Christ as excellency as briefly comprehends in the Lord's prayer all things needful and necessary. Except under troubles, trials, and vexations, prayer cannot rightly be made. God says: "Call on me in the time of trouble;" without trouble it is only a bald prattling, and not from the heart; 'tis a common saying: "Need teaches to pray." And though the papists say that God well understands all the words of those that pray, yet St Bernard is far of another opinion, who says: God hears not the words of one that prays, unless he that prays first hears them himself. The pope is a mere tormentor of the conscience. The assemblies of his greased crew, in prayer, were altogether like the croaking of frogs, which edified nothing at all; mere sophistry and deceit, fruitless and unprofitable. Prayer is a strong wall and fortress of the church; it is a godly Christian's weapon, which no man knows or finds, but only he who has the spirit of grace and of prayer.

The three first petitions in our Lord's prayer comprehend such great and celestial things, that no heart is able to search them out. The fourth contains the whole policy and economy of temporal and house government, and all things necessary for this life. The fifth fights against our own evil consciences, and against original and actual sins, which trouble them. Truly that prayer was penned by wisdom itself; none but God could have done it.

330

Prayer in popedom is mere tongue-threshing; not prayer, but a work of obedience. Thence a confused sea of *Horae Canonicae*, the howling and babbling in cells and monasteries, where they read and sing the psalms and collects, without any spiritual devotion, understanding neither the words, sentences, nor meaning.

How I tormented myself with those Horae Canonicae before the Gospel came, which by reason of much business I often intermitted, I cannot express. On the Saturdays, I used to lock myself up in my cell, and accomplish what the whole week I had neglected. But at last I was troubled with so many affairs, that I was fain often to omit also my Saturday's devotions. At length, when I saw that Amsdorf and others derided such devotion, then I quite left it off.

From this great torment we are now delivered by the Gospel. Though I had done no more but only freed people from that torment, they might well give me thanks for it.

331

We cannot pray without faith in Christ, the Mediator. Turks, Jews, and papists may repeat the words of prayer, but they cannot pray. And although the Apostles were taught this Lord's prayer by Christ, and prayed often, yet they prayed not as they should have prayed; for Christ says: "Hitherto ye have not prayed in my name"; whereas, doubtless, they had prayed much, speaking the words. But when the Holy Ghost came, then they prayed aright in the name of Christ. If praying and reading of prayer be but only a bare work, as the papists hold, then the righteousness of the law is nothing worth. The upright prayer of the godly Christian is a strong hedge, as God himself says: "And I sought for a man among them that should make up the hedge, and stand in the gap before me for the land, that I should not destroy it, but I found none."

332

When Moses, with the children of Israel, came to the Red Sea, then he cried with trembling and quaking; yet he opened not his mouth, neither was his voice heard on earth by the people; doubtless he cried and sighed in his heart, and said: Ah, Lord God! what course shall I now take? Which way shall I now turn myself? How am I come to this strait? No help or counsel can save us; before us is the sea; behind us are our enemies the Egyptians; on both sides high and huge mountains; I am the cause that all this people shall now be destroyed. Then answered God, and said: "Wherefore criest thou unto me?" as if God should say: What an alarm dost thou make, that the whole heavens ring! Human reason is not able to search this passage out. The way through the Red Sea is full as broad and wide, if not wider, than Wittenberg lies from Coburg; that so, doubtless, the people were constrained in the night season to rest and to eat therein; for six hundred thousand men, besides women and children, would require a good time to pass through, though they went one hundred and fifty abreast.

333
It is impossible that God should not hear the prayers which with faith are made in Christ, though he give not according to the measure, manner, and time we dictate, for he will not be tied. In such sort dealt God with the mother of St. Augustine; she prayed to God that her son might be converted, but as yet it would not be; then she ran to the learned, entreating them to persuade and advise him thereunto. She propounded unto him a marriage with a Christian virgin, that thereby he might be drawn and brought to the Christian faith, but all would not do as yet. But when our Lord God came thereto, he cam to purpose, and made of him such an Augustine, that he became a great light to the church. St James says: "Pray one for another, for the prayer of the righteous availeth much." Prayer is a powerful thing, for God has bound and tied himself thereunto.

334
Christ gave the Lord's prayer, according to the ideas of the Jews – that is, he directed it only to the Father, whereas they that pray, should pray as though they were to be heard for the Son's sake. This was because Christ would not be praised before his death.

335
Justice Jonas asked Luther if these sentences in Scripture did not contradict each other; where God says to Abraham: "If I find ten in Sodom, I will not destroy it"; and where Ezekiel says: "Though these three men, Noah, Daniel, and Job, were in it, yet would I not hear," etc.; and where Jeremiah says: "Therefore pray not thou for this people." Luther answered; No, they are not against one another; for in Ezekiel it was forbidden them to pray, but it was not so with Abraham. Therefore we must have regard to

the Word; when God says: thou shalt not pray, then we may well cease.

336
When governors and rulers are enemies to God's Word, then our duty is to depart, to sell and forsake all we have; to fly from one place to another, as Christ commands. We must make for ourselves no tumults, by reason of the Gospel, but suffer all things.

337
Upright Christians pray without ceasing; though they pray not always with their mouths, yet their hearts pray continually, sleeping and waking; for the sigh of a true Christian is a prayer. As the Psalm saith: "Because of the deep sighing of the poor, I will up, saith the Lord," etc. In like manner a true Christian always carried the cross, though he feel it not always.

338
The Lord's prayer binds the people together, and knits them one to another, so that one prays for another, and together one with another; and it is so strong and powerful that it even drives away the fear of death.

339
Prayer preserves the church, and hitherto has done the best for the church; therefore, we must continually pray. Hence Christ says: "Ask, and ye shall have; seek, and ye shall find; knock, and it shall be opened unto you."

First, when we are in trouble, he will have us to pray; for God often, as it were, hides himself, and will not hear; yea, will not suffer himself to be found. Then we must seek him; that is, we must continue in prayer. When we seek him, he often locks himself up, as it were, in a private chamber; if we intend to come in unto him, then we must knock, and when we have knocked once or twice, then he begins a little to hear. At last, when we make much knocking, then he opens, and says: What will ye have? Lord, say we, we would have this or that; then, say he, Take it unto you. In such sort must we persist in praying, and waken God up.

Martin Luther, 1483–1546

The Way Into The Holiest

F.B. Meyer

GETHSEMANE

"Who in the days of his flesh, when he had offered up prayers and supplications with strong crying and tears unto him that was able to save him from death, and was heard in that he feared: though he were a Son, yet learned he obedience by the things which he suffered." Hebrews v. 7, 8.

Eight ancient olive trees still mark the site of Gethsemane; not improbably they witnessed that memorable and mysterious scene referred to here. And what a scene was that! It had stood alone in unique and unapproachable wonder, had it not been followed by fifteen hours of even greater mystery.

The strongest words in Greek language are used to tell of the keen anguish through which the Savior passed within those Garden walls. "He began to be sorrowful"; as if in all his past experiences he had never known what sorrow was! "lie was sore amazed"; as if his mind were almost dazed and overwhelmed. "He was very heavy," his spirit stooped beneath the weight of his sorrows, as afterward his body stooped beneath the weight of his cross; or the word may mean that he was so distracted with sorrow, as to be almost beside himself. And the Lord himself could not have found a stronger word than he used when he said, "My soul is exceeding sorrowful, even unto death."

But the evangelist Luke gives us the most convincing proof of his anguish when he tells us that his sweat, like great beads of blood, fell upon the ground, touched by the slight frost, and in the cold night air. The finishing touch is given in these words, which tell of his "strong crying and tears."

THE THINGS WHICH HE SUFFERED

What were they? They were not those of the Substitute. The tenor of Scripture goes to show that the work of substitution was really wrought out upon the cross. There the robe of our completed righteousness was woven from the top through-out. It was on the free that he bare our sins in his own body. It was by his blood that he brought us nigh to God. It was by the death of God's Son that we have been reconciled to God; and the repeated references of Scripture, and especially of this epistle, to sacrifice, indicate that in the act of dying, that was done which magnifies the law, and makes it honorable, and removes every obstacle that had otherwise prevented the love of God from following out its purposes of mercy.

We shall never fully understand here how the Lord Jesus made reconciliation for the sins of the world, or how that which he bore could be an equivalent for the penalty due from a sinful race. We have no standard of comparison; we have no line long enough to let us down into the depths of that unexplored mystery; but we may thankfully accept it as a fact stated on the page of Scripture perpetually, that he did that which put away the curse, atoned for human guilt, and was more than equivalent to all those sufferings which a race of sinful men must otherwise have borne. The mystery defies our language, but it is apprehended by faith; and as she stands upon her highest pinnacles, love discerns the meaning of the death of Christ by a spiritual instinct, though as yet she has not perfectly learned the language in which to express her conceptions of the mysteries that circle around the cross. It may be that in thousands of unselfish actions, she is acquiring the terms in which some day she will be able to understand and explain all.

But all that we need insist on here, and now, is that the sufferings of the Garden are not to be included in the act of Substitution, though, as we shall see, they were closely associated with it. Gethsemane was not the altar, but the way to it.

Our Lord's suffering in Gethsemane could hardly arise from the fear of his approaching physical sufferings. Such a supposition seems wholly inconsistent with the heroic fortitude, the majestic silence, the calm ascendancy over suffering with which he bore himself till he breathed out his spirit, and which drew from a hardened and worldly Roman expressions of respect.

Besides, if the mere prospect of scourging and crucifixion drew from our Lord these strong crying and tears and bloody sweat, he surely would stand on a lower level than that to which multitudes of his followers attained through faith in him. Old men like Polycarp, tender maidens like Blandina, timid boys like Attalus, have contemplated beforehand with unruffled composure, and have endured with unshrinking fortitude, deaths far more awful, more prolonged, more agonizing. Degraded criminals have climbed the scaffold without a tremor or a sob; and surely the most exalted faith ought to bear itself as bravely as the most brutal indifference in the presence of the solemnities of death and eternity. It has been truly said that there is no passion in the mind of man, however weak, which cannot master the fear of death; and it is therefore impossible to suppose that the fear of physical suffering and disgrace could have so shaken our Savior's spirit.

But he anticipated the sufferings that he was to endure as the propitiation for sin. He knew that he was about to be brought into the closest association with the sin which was devastating human happiness and grieving the divine nature. He knew, since he had so identified himself with our fallen race, that, in a very deep and wonderful way, he was to be made sin and to bear our curse and shame, cast out by man, and apparently forsaken by God. He knew, as we shall never know, the exceeding sinfulness and horror of sin; and what it was to be the meeting-place where the iniquities of our race should converge, to become the scapegoat charged with guilt not his own, to bear away the sins of the world. All this was beyond measure terrible to one so holy and sensitive as he.

He had long foreseen it. He was the Lamb slain from before the foundation of the world. Each time a lamb was slain by a conscience-stricken sinner, or a scapegoat let go into the wilderness, or a pigeon dipped into the flowing water encrimsoned by the blood of its mate, he had been reminded of what was to be. He knew before his incarnation where in the forest the seedling was growing to a sapling from the wood of which his cross would be made. He even nourished it with his rain and sun. Often during his public ministry he was evidently looking beyond the events that were transpiring around him to that supreme event, which he called his "hour." And as it came nearer, his human soul was overwhelmed at the prospect of having to sustain the weight of a world's sin.

His human nature did not shrink from death as death; but from the death which he was to die as the propitiation for our sins, and not for ours only, but for those of the whole world.

Six months before his death he had set his face to go to Jerusalem, with such a look of anguish upon it as to fill the hearts of his disciples with consternation. When the questions of the Greeks reminded him that he must shortly fall into the ground and die, his soul became so troubled that he cried, "Father, save me from this hour!" And now, with strong cryings and tears, he made supplication to his Father, as king that, if it were possible, the cup might pass from him. In this his human soul spoke. As to his divinely wrought purpose of redemption, there was no vacillation or hesitation. But, as man, he asked whether there might not be another way of accomplishing the redemption on which he had set his heart.

But there was no other way. The Father's will, which he had come down from heaven to do, pointed along the rugged, flinty road that climbed Calvary, and passed over it, and down to the grave. And at once he accepted his destiny, and with the words "If this cup may not pass from me except I drink it, thy will be done," he stepped forth on the flints that were to cut those blessed feet, drawing from them streams of blood.

HIS STRONG CRYING AND TEARS

Our Lord betook himself to that resource which is within the reach of all, and which is peculiarly precious to those who are suffering and tempted, he prayed. His heart was overwhelmed within him; and he poured out all his anguish into his Father's ears, with strong cryings and tears. Let us note the characteristics of that prayer, that we too may be able to pass through our dark hours, when they come.

It was secret prayer. Leaving the majority of his disciples at the Garden gate, he took with him the three who had stood beside Jairus's dead child, and had beheld the radiance that steeped him in his transfiguration. They alone might see him tread the winepress: but even they were left at a stone's cast, whilst he went forward alone into the deeper shadow. We are told that they became overpowered with sleep;

so that no mortal ear heard the whole burden of that marvelous prayer, some fitful snatches of which are reserved in the Gospels.

It was humble prayer. The evangelist Luke says that he knelt. Another says that he fell on his face. Being formed in fashion as a man, he humbled himself and became obedient to death, even the death of the cross. And it may be that even then he began to recite that marvelous Psalm, which was so much on his lips during those last hours, saying, "I am a worm, and no man; a reproach of men and despised of the people."

It was filial prayer. Matthew describes our Lord as saying, "O my Father"; and Mark tells us that he used the endearing term which was often spoken by the prattling lips of little Jewish children, Abba. For the most part, he probably spoke Greek; but Aramaic was the language of his childhood, the language of the dear home in Nazareth. In the hour of mortal agony, the mind ever reverts to the associations of its first awakening. The Savior, therefore, appearing to feel that the more stately Greek did not sufficiently express the deep yearnings of his heart, substituted for it the more tender language of earlier years. Not "Father" only, but "Abba, Father!"

It was earnest prayer. "He prayed more earnestly," and one proof of this appears in his repetition of the same words. It was as if his nature were too oppressed to be able to express itself in a variety of phrase; such as might indicate a certain leisure and liberty of thought. One strong current of anguish running at its highest could only strike one monotone of grief, like the note of the storm or the flood. Back, and back again, came the words, cup … pass … will … Father. And the sweat of blood, pressed from his forehead, as the red juice of the grape beneath the heavy foot of the peasant, witnessed to the intensity of his soul.

It was submissive prayer. Matthew and Mark quote this sentence, "Nevertheless not what I will, but what thou wilt." Luke quotes this, "Father, if thou be willing, remove this cup from me; nevertheless, not my will, but thine be done."

Jesus was the Father's Fellow's co-equal in his divine nature; but for the purpose of redemption it was needful that he should temporarily divest himself of the use of the attributes of his deity, and live a truly human life. As man, he carefully marked each symptom of his Father's will, from the day when it prompted him to linger behind his parents in the temple; and he always instantly fulfilled his behests. "I came down from heaven," he said, "not to do mine own will, but the will of him that sent me." This was the yoke he bore, and in taking it, he found rest unto his soul. Whatever was the danger or difficulty into which such obedience might carry him, he ever followed the beacon-cloud of the divine will; sure that the manna of daily strength would fall, and that the deep sweet waters of peace would follow where it led the way. That way now seemed to lead through the heart of a fiery furnace. There was no alternative than to follow; and he elected to do so, nay, was glad, even then, with a joy that the cold waters of death could not extinguish. At the same time, he learnt what obedience meant, and gave an example of it, that shone out with unequaled majesty, purity, and beauty, unparalleled in the annals of the universe. As man, our Lord then learnt how much was meant by that word obedience. "He learned obedience." And now he asks that we should obey him, as he obeyed God. "Unto them that obey him."

Sometimes the path of the Christian's obedience becomes very difficult. It climbs upward; the gradient is continually steeper; the foothold ever more difficult; and, as the evening comes, the nimble climber of the morning creeps slowly forward on hands and knees. The day is never greater than the strength; but as the strength grows by use, the demands upon it are greater, and the hours longer. At last a moment may come, when we are called for God's sake to leave some dear circle; to risk the loss of name and fame; to relinquish the cherished ambition of a life; to incur obloquy, suffering, and death; to drink the bitter cup; to enter the brooding cloud; to climb the smoking mount. Ah! then we too learn what obedience means; and have no resource but in strong cryings and tears.

In such hours pour out thy heart in audible cries. Plentifully mingle the name "Father" with thine entreaties. Fear not to repeat the same words. Look not to man, he cannot understand thee; but to him who is nearer to thee than thy dearest. So shalt thou get calmer and quieter, until thou rest in his will; as a child, worn out by a tempest of passion, sobs itself to sleep on its mother's breast.

The Answer

"He was heard for his godly fear." His holy reverence and devotion to his Father's will made it impossible that his prayers should be unanswered; although, as it so often happens, the answer came in another way than his fears had suggested. The cup was not taken away, but the answer came. It came in the mission of the angel that stood beside him. It came in the calm serenity with which he met the brutal crowd, that soon filled that quiet Garden with their coarse voices and trampling feet. It came in his triumph over death and the grave. It came in his being perfected as mediator, to become unto all them that obey him the Author of eternal salvation, and the High-Priest forever after the order of Melchizedek.

Prayers prompted by love and in harmony with godly fear are never lost. We may ask for things which it would be unwise and unkind of God to grant; but in that case, his goodness shows itself rather in the refusal than the assent. And yet the prayer is heard and answered. Strength is instilled into the fainting heart. The faithful and merciful High-Priest does for us what the angel essayed to do for him; but how much better, since he has learnt so much of the art of comfort in the school of suffering! And out of it the way finally emerges into life, though we have left the right hand and foot in the grave behind us. We also discover that we have learnt the art of becoming channels of eternal salvation to those around us. Ever since Jesus suffered there, Gethsemane has been threaded by the King's highway that passes through it to the New Jerusalem. And in its precincts God has kept many of his children, to learn obedience by the things that they suffer, and to learn the divine art of comforting others as they themselves have been comforted by God.

There are comparatively few, to whom Jesus does not say, at some time in their lives, "Come and watch with me." He takes us with him into the darksome shadows of the winepress, though there are recesses of shade, at a stone's cast, where he must go alone. Let us not misuse the precious hours in the heavy slumbers of insensibility. There are lessons to be learnt there which can be acquired nowhere else; but if we heed not his summons to watch with him, it may be that he will close the precious opportunity by bidding us sleep on and take our rest; because the allotted term has passed, and the hour of a new epoch has struck. If we fail to use for prayer and preparation the sacred hour, that comes laden with opportunities for either; if we sleep instead of watching with our Lord: what hope have we of being able to play a noble part when the flashing lights and the trampling feet announce the traitor's advent? Squander the moments of preparation, and you may have to rue their loss through all the coming years!

F.B. Meyer, 1847–1929

Helps to Intercession

Andrew Murray

1. Pray Without Ceasing

Pray Without Ceasing. – Who can do this? How can one do it who is surrounded by the cares of daily life? How can a mother love her child without ceasing? How can the eyelid without ceasing hold itself ready to protect the eye? How can I breathe and feel and hear without ceasing? Because all these are the functions of a healthy, natural life. And so, if the spiritual life be healthy, under the full power of the Holy Spirit, praying without ceasing will be natural. Pray Without Ceasing. – Does it refer to continual acts of prayer, in which we are to persevere till we obtain, or to the spirit of prayerfulness that should animate us all the day? It includes both. The example of our Lord Jesus shows us this. We have to enter our closet for special seasons of prayer; we are at times to persevere there in importunate prayer. We are also all the day to walk in God's presence, with the whole heart set upon heavenly things. Without set times of prayer, the spirit of prayer will be dull and feeble. Without the continual prayerfulness, the set times will not avail.

Pray Without Ceasing. – Does that refer to prayer for ourselves or others? To both. It is because many confine it to themselves that they fail so in practicing it. It is only when the branch gives itself to bear fruit, more fruit, much fruit, that it can live a healthy life, and expect a rich inflow of sap. The death of Christ brought Him to the place of everlasting intercession. Your death with Him to sin and self sets you free from the care of self, and elevates you to the dignity of intercessor – one who can get life and blessing from God for others. Know your calling; begin this your work. Give yourself wholly to it, and before you know it you will be finding something of this "Praying always" within you.

Pray Without Ceasing. – How can I learn it? The best way of learning to do a thing – in fact the only way – is to do it. Begin by setting apart some time every day, say ten or fifteen minutes, in which you say to God and to yourself, that you come to Him now as an intercessor for others. Let it be after your morning or evening prayer, or any other time. If you cannot secure the same time every day, do not be troubled. Only see that you do your work. Christ chose you and appointed you to pray for others. If at first you do not feel any special urgency or faith or power in your prayers, do not let that hinder you. Quietly tell your Lord Jesus of your feebleness; believe that the Holy Spirit is in you to teach you to pray, and be assured that if you begin, God will help you. God cannot help you unless you begin and keep on.

Pray Without Ceasing. – How do I know what to pray for? If once you begin, and think of all the needs around you, you will soon find enough. But to help you, this little book is issued with subjects and hints for prayer for a month. It is meant that we should use it month by month, until we know more fully how to follow the Spirit's leading, and have learned, if need be, to. make our own list of subjects, and then can dispense with it. In regard to the use of these helps, a few words may be needed.

1. HOW TO PRAY

You notice for every day two headings – the one What to Pray; the other, How to Pray. If the subjects only were given, one might fall into the routine of mentioning names and things before God, and the work would become a burden. The hints under the heading How to Pray, are meant to remind you of the spiritual nature of the work, of the need of Divine help, and to encourage faith in the certainty that God, through the Spirit, will give us grace to pray aright and will also hear our prayer. One does not at once learn to take his place boldly, and to dare to believe that he will be heard. Therefore take a few moments each day to listen to God's voice reminding you of how certainly even you will be heard, and calling on you to pray in that faith in your Father, to claim and take the blessing you plead for. And let these words about How to Pray, enter your hearts and occupy your thoughts at other times, too. The work of intercession is Christ's great work on earth, entrusted to Him because He gave Himself a sacrifice to God for men. The work of intercession is the greatest work a Christian can do. Give yourself as a sacrifice to God for men, and the work will become your glory and your joy, too.

2. WHAT TO PRAY

Scripture calls us to pray for many things: for all saints; for all men, for kings and all rulers; for all who are in adversity; for the sending forth of laborers; for those who labor in the gospel; for all converts; for believers who have fallen into sin; for one another in our own immediate circles. The Church is now so much larger than when the New Testament was written; the number of forms of work and workers is so much greater; the needs of the Church and the world are so much better known, that we need to take time and thought to see where prayer is needed, and to what our hearts are most drawn out. The Scriptural calls to prayer demand a large heart, taking in all saints, and all men, and all needs. An attempt has been made in these helps to indicate what the chief subjects are that need prayer, and that ought to interest every Christian.

It will be felt difficult by many to pray for such large spheres as are sometimes mentioned. Let it be understood that in each case we may make special intercession for our own circle of interest coming under that heading. And it is hardly needful to say, further, that where one subject appears of more special interest or urgency than another we are free for a time, day after day, to take up that subject. If only time be really given to intercession, and the spirit of believing intercession be cultivated, the object is attained. While, on the one hand, the heart must be enlarged at times to take in all, the more pointed and definite our prayer can be, the better. With this view paper is left blank on which we can write down special petitions we desire to urge before God.

3. ANSWERS TO PRAYER
More than one little book has been published in which Christians may keep a register of their petitions, and note when they are answered. Room has been left on every page for this, so that more definite petitions with regard to individual souls or special spheres of work may be recorded, and the answer expected. When we pray for all saints, or for missions in general, it is difficult to know when or how our prayer is answered, or whether our prayer has had any part in bringing the answer. It is of extreme importance that we should prove that God hears us, and to this end take note of what answers to look for, and when they come. On the day of praying for all saints, take the saints of your congregation, or in your prayer meeting, and ask for a revival among them. Take, in connection with missions, some special station or missionary you are interested in, or more than one, and plead for blessing. And expect and look for its coming, that you may praise God.

4. PRAYER CIRCLES
In publishing this invitation to intercession, there is no desire to add another to the many existing prayer unions or praying bands. The first object is to stir the many Christians who practically, through ignorance of their calling or unbelief as to their prayer availing much, take but very little part in the work of intercession; and then to help those who do pray to some fuller apprehension of the greatness of the work, and the need of giving their whole strength to it. There is a circle of prayer which asks for prayer on the first day of every month for the fuller manifestation of the power of the Holy Spirit throughout the Church. I have given the words of that invitation as subject for the first day, and taken the same thought as keynote throughout. The more one thinks of the need and the promise, and the greatness

of the obstacles to be overcome in prayer, the more one feels it must become our life work day by day, that to which every other interest is subordinated.

But while not forming a large prayer union, it is suggested that it may be found helpful to have small prayer circles to unite in prayer, either for one month, with some special object introduced daily along with the others, or through a year or longer, with the view of strengthening each other in the grace of intercession. If a minister were to invite some of his neighboring brethren to join for some special requests along with the printed subjects for supplication, or a number of the more earnest members of his congregation to unite in prayer for revival, some might be trained to take their place in the great work of intercession, who now stand idle because no man hath hired them.

5. WHO IS SUFFICIENT FOR THESE THINGS?
The more we study and try to practice this grace of intercession, the more we become overwhelmed by its greatness and our feebleness. Let every such impression lead us to listen: My grace is sufficient for thee, and to answer truthfully: Our sufficiency is of God. Take courage; it is in the intercession of Christ you are called to take part. The burden and the agony, the triumph and the victory are all His. Learn from Him, yield to His Spirit in you, to know how to pray. He gave Himself a sacrifice to God for men, that He might have the right and power of intercession. "He bare the sin of many, and made intercession for the transgressors." Let your faith rest boldly on His finished work. Let your heart wholly identify itself with Him in His death and His life. Like Him, give yourself to God a sacrifice for men; it is your highest nobility; it is your true and full union with Him; it will be to you, as to Him, your power of intercession. Beloved Christian! come and give your whole heart and life to intercession, and you will know its blessedness and its power. God asks nothing less; the world needs nothing less; Christ asks nothing less; let us offer to God nothing less.

FIRST DAY
What to Pray – For the Power of the Holy Spirit.

I bow my Knees unto the Father, that He would grant you that ye may be strengthened with power through His Spirit. – Eph. 3:14–16.
Wait for the promise of the Father. – Acts 1: 4."the fuller manifestation of the grace and energy of the blessed Spirit of God, in the removal of all that is contrary to God's revealed will, so that we grieve not the Holy Spirit, but that He may work in mightier power in the Church, for the exaltation of Christ and the blessing of souls."

God has one promise to and through His exalted Son; our Lord has one gift to His Church; the Church has one need; all prayer unites in the one petition – the power of the Holy Spirit. Make it your one prayer.

How to Pray – As a Child Asks a Father
If a son ask bread of any of you that is a father, will he give him a stone! How much more shall your Heavenly Father give the Holy Spirit to them that ask Him? – Luke 11:11, 13.

Ask as simply and trustfully as a child asks bread. You can do this because "God hath sent forth the Spirit of his Son into your hearts crying, Abba, Father. " This Spirit is in you to give you childlike confidence. In the faith of His praying in you, ask for the power of that Holy Spirit everywhere. Mention places or circles where you specially ask it to be seen.

SECOND DAY
What to Pray – For the Spirit of Supplication
The Spirit Himself maketh intercession for us. – Rom. 8:26.
I will pour out the Spirit of Supplication. – Zech. 12:10.

"The evangelization of the world depends first of all upon a revival of prayer. Deeper than the need of men – aye, deep down at the bottom of our spiritless life – is the need for the forgotten secret of prevailing, world-wide prayer."

Every child of God has the Holy Spirit in him to pray. God waits to give the Spirit in full measure. Ask for yourself, and all who join, the outpouring of the Spirit of Supplication. Ask it for your own prayer circle.

How to Pray – In the Spirit
With all prayer and supplication, praying at all seasons in the Spirit. – Eph 6:18.
Praying in the Holy Spirit. – Jude 20.

Our Lord gave His disciples on His resurrection day the Holy Spirit to enable them to wait for the full outpouring on the day of Pentecost. It is only in the power of the Spirit already in us, acknowledged and yielded to, that we can pray for His fuller manifestation. Say to the Father, it is the Spirit of His Son in you urging you to plead His promise.

THIRD DAY
What to Pray – For All Saints
With all prayer and supplication praying at all seasons, and watching thereunto in all perseverance and supplication for all saints. – Eph. 6:18.

Every member of a body is interested in the welfare of the whole, and exists to help and complete the others. Believers are one body, and ought to pray, not so much for the welfare of their own church or society, but, first of all, for all saints. This large, unselfish love is the proof that Christ's Spirit and Love are teaching them to pray. Pray first for all and then for the believers around you.

How to Pray – In the Love of the Spirit
By this shall all men know that ye are My disciples, if ye have love one to another. – John 13:35. I pray that they all may be one, that the world may believe that Thou didst send Me. – John 17:21.

I beseech you, brethren, by the love of the Spirit, that ye strive together with me in your prayers to God for me. – Rom. 15:30.
Above all things being fervent in your love among yourselves. – 1 Pet. 4:8.

If we are to pray we must love. Let us say to God we do love all His saints; let us say we love specially every child of His we know. Let us pray with fervent love, in the love of the Spirit.

FOURTH DAY
What to Pray – For the Spirit Holiness
God is the Holy One. His people is a holy people. He speaks: I am holy: I am the Lord which make you holy. Christ prayed: Sanctify them. Make them holy through Truth. Paul prayed: God establish your hearts unblameable in holiness. God sanctify you wholly!

Pray for all saints – God's holy ones – throughout the Church, that the Spirit of holiness may rule them. Specially for new converts. For the saints in your own neighborhood or congregation. For any you are specially interested in. Think of their special need, weakness, or sin, and pray that God may make them holy.

How to Pray – Trusting in God's Omnipotence
The things that are impossible with men are possible with God. When we think of the great things we ask for, of how little likelihood there is of their coming, of our own insignificance, prayer is not only wishing, or asking, but believing and accepting. Be still before God and ask Him to let you know Him as the Almighty One, and leave your petitions with Him Who doeth wonders.

FIFTH DAY
What to Pray – That God's People May Be Kept from the World
Holy Father, keep through Thine own name those whom Thou hast given Me. I pray not that Thou shouldest take them out of the world, but that Thou shouldest Keep them from the evil. They are not of the world, even as I am not of the world. – John 17:11, 15, 16.

In the last night Christ asked three things of His disciples: that they might be kept as those who are not of the world; that they might be sanctified; that they might be one in love. You cannot do better than pray as Jesus prayed. Ask for God's people that they may be kept separate from the world and its spirit; that they, by the Spirit, may live as those who are not of the world.

How to Pray – Having Confidence before God
Beloved, if our heart condemn us not, then have we confidence toward God. And whatsoever we ask, we receive of Him, because we keep His commandments, and do those things that are pleasing in His sight. – 1 John 3:21, 22.
Learn these words by heart. Get them into your heart. Join the ranks of those who, with John, draw near to God with an assured heart, that does not condemn them, having confidence toward God. In this spirit pray for your brother who sins (1 John 5:16). In the quiet confidence of an obedient child, plead for

those of your brethren who may be giving way to sin. Pray for all to be kept from the evil. And say often, "What we ask, we receive, because we keep and do."

SIXTH DAY
What to Pray – For the Spirit of Love in the Church
I pray that they may be one, even as we are one: I in them and Thou in Me; that the world may know that Thou hast sent Me, and hast loved them, as Thou hast loved Me . . that the love wherewith Thou hast loved Me may be in them, and I in them. – John 17:22, 23, 26.
The fruit of the Spirit is love. – Gal. 5:22.
Believers are one in Christ, as He is one with the Father. The love of God rests on them, and can dwell in them. Pray that the power of the Holy Ghost may so work this love in believers, that the world may see and know God's love in them. Pray much for this.

How to Pray – As One of God's Remembrancers
I have set watchmen on thy walls, which shall never hold their peace day nor night: ye that are the Lord's remembrancers, keep not silence, and give Him no rest. – Isa. 62:6.
Study these words until your whole soul be filled with the consciousness, I am appointed intercessor. Enter God's presence in that faith. Study the world's need with that thought – it is my work to intercede; the Holy Spirit will teach me for what and how. Let it be an abiding consciousness: My great at lifework, like Christ's, is intercession – to pray for believers and those who do not yet know God.

SEVENTH DAY
What to Pray – For the Power of the Holy Spirit on Ministers
I beseech you that ye strive together with me in your prayers to God for me. – Rom. 15:30.
He will deliver us; ye also helping together on our behalf by your supplication. – 2 Cor. 1:10, 11.
What a great host of ministers there is in Christ's Church. What need they have of prayer. What a power they might be, if they were all clothed with the power of the Holy Ghost. Pray definitely for this; long for it. Think of your minister, and ask it very specially for

him. Connect every thought of the ministry, in your town or neighborhood or the world, with the prayer that all may be filled with the Spirit.

Plead for them the promise, "Tarry until ye be clothed with power from on high." Luke 24:49. "Ye shall receive power, when the Holy Ghost is come upon you." Acts 1:8.

How to Pray – In Secret
But thou, when thou prayest, enter into thy inner chamber, and having shut thy door, pray to thy Father which is in secret. – Matt. 6:6.
He withdrew again into the mountain to pray, Himself alone. – Matt. 14:23; John 6:15.

Take time and realize, when you are alone with God: Here am I now, face to face with God, to intercede for His servants. Do not think you have no influence, or that your prayer will not be missed. Your prayer and faith will make a difference. Cry in secret to God for His ministers.

EIGHTH DAY
What to Pray – For the Spirit on All Christian Workers
Ye also helping together on our behalf that for the gift bestowed upon us by means of many, thanks may be given by many on our behalf. – 2 Cor. 1:11.

What multitudes of workers in connection with our churches and missions, our railways and postmen, our soldiers and sailors, our young men and young women, our fallen men and women, our poor and sick! God be praised for this! What could they not accomplish if each were living in the fullness of the Holy Spirit? Pray for them; it makes you a partner in their work, and you will praise God each time you hear of blessing anywhere.

How to Pray – With Definite Petitions
What wilt thou that I should do unto thee? – Luke 18:41.

The Lord knew what the man wanted, and yet He asked him. The utterance of our wish gives point to the transaction in which we are engaged with God, and so awakens faith and expectation. Be very definite in your petitions, so as to know what answer you may look for. Just think of the great host of workers, and ask and expect God definitely to bless them in

answer to the prayer of His people. Then ask still more definitely for workers around you. Intercession is not the breathing out of pious wishes; its aim is – in believing, persevering prayer – to receive and bring down blessing.

NINTH DAY
What to Pray – For God's Spirit on Our Mission Work
The evangelization of the world depends first of all upon a revival of prayer. Deeper than the need for men – aye, deep down at the bottom of our spiritless life, is the need for the forgotten secret of prevailing, world-wide prayer.
As they ministered to the Lord, and fasted, the Holy Ghost said, Separate Me Barnabas and Saul. Then when they had fasted and prayed, they sent them away. So they being sent forth by the Holy Ghost, departed. – Acts 13:3, 4.

Pray that our mission work may all be done in this spirit – waiting on God, hearing the voice of the Spirit, sending forth men with fasting and prayer. Pray that in our churches our mission interest and mission work may be in the power of the Holy Spirit and of prayer. It is a Spirit-filled, praying Church that will send out Spirit-filled missionaries, mightily in prayer.

How to Pray – Take Time
I give myself unto prayer. – Ps. 109:4.
We will give ourselves continually to prayer. – Acts 6:4.
Be not rash with thy mouth, and let not thine heart be hasty to utter anything before God. – Eccles. 5:2.
And He continued all night in prayer to God. – Luke 6:12.

Time is one of the chief standards of value. The time we give is a proof of the interest we feel. We need time with God – to realize His presence; to wait for Him to make Himself known; to consider and feel the needs we plead for; to take our place in Christ; to pray till we can believe that we have received. Take time in prayer, and pray down blessing on the mission work of the Church.

TENTH DAY
What to Pray – For God's Spirit on Our Missionaries

What the world needs today is not only more missionaries, but the outpouring of God's Spirit on everyone whom He has sent out to work for Him in the foreign field.

Ye shall receive power, when the Holy Ghost is come upon you: and ye shall be My witnesses unto the uttermost part of the earth. – Acts 1:8.

God always gives His servants power equal to the work He asks of them. Think of the greatness and difficulty of this work, – casting Satan out of his strongholds – and pray that everyone who takes part in it may receive and do all his work in the power of the Holy Ghost. Think of the difficulties of your missionaries, and pray for them.

How to Pray – Trusting God's Faithfulness

He is faithful that promised. She counted Him faithful who promised. – Heb. 10:23; 11:11.

Just think of God's promises to His Son, concerning His kingdom; to the Church, concerning the heathen; to His servants, concerning their work; to yourself, concerning your prayer; and pray in the assurance that He is faithful, and only waits for prayer and faith to fulfill them.

"Faithful is He that calleth you" (to pray), "who also will do it" (what He has promised). 1 Thess. 5:24.

Take up individual missionaries, make yourself one with them, and pray till you know that you are heard. Oh, begin to live for Christ's kingdom as the one thing worth living for!

ELEVENTH DAY

What to Pray – For More Laborers

Pray ye therefore the Lord of the harvest, that He send forth laborers into His harvest. – Matt. 9:38.

What a remarkable call of the Lord Jesus for help from His disciples in getting the need supplied. What an honor put upon prayer. What a proof that God wants prayer and will hear it.

Pray for laborers, for all students in theological seminaries, training homes, Bible institutes, that they may not go, unless He fits them and sends them forth; that our churches may train their students to seek for the sending forth of the Holy Spirit; that all believers may

hold themselves ready to be sent forth, or to pray for those who can go.

How to Pray – In Faith, Nothing Doubting

Jesus saith unto them, Have faith in God. Whosoever shall say unto this mountain, Be thou removed, and be thou cast into the sea; and shall not doubt in his heart, but shall believe that what he saith shall come to pass, he shall have it. – Mark 11:22, 23.

Have faith in God! Ask Him to make Himself known to you as the faithful mighty God, who worketh all in all; and you will be encouraged to believe that He can give suitable and sufficient laborers, however impossible this appears. But, remember, in answer to prayer and faith. Apply this to every opening where a good worker is needed. The work is God's. He can give the right workman. But He must be asked and waited on.

TWELFTH DAY

What to Pray – For the Spirit to Convince the World of Sin

I will send the Comforter to you. And He, when He is come, will convict the world in respect of sin. – John 1:7, 8.

God's one desire, the one object of Christ's being manifested, is to take away sin. The first work of the Spirit on the world is conviction of sin. Without that, no deep or abiding revival, no powerful conversion. Pray for it, that the gospel may be preached in such power of the Spirit, that men may see that they have rejected and crucified Christ, and cry out, What shall we do?

Pray most earnestly for a mighty power of conviction of sin wherever the gospel is preached.

How to Pray – Stir Up Yourself to Take Hold of God's Strength

Let him take hold of My strength, that he may make peace with Me. – Isa. 27:5.

There is none that calleth upon Thy name, that stirreth up himself to take hold of Thee. – Isa. 64:7.

Stir up the gift of God which is in thee. – 2 Tim. 1:6.

First, take hold of God's strength. God is a Spirit. I cannot take hold of Him, and hold

Him fast, but by the Spirit. Take hold of God's strength, and hold on till it has done for you what He has promised. Pray for the power of the Spirit to convict of sin.

Second, stir up yourself – the power is in you by the Holy Spirit – to take hold. Give your whole heart and will to it, and say, I will not let Thee go except Thou bless me.

THIRTEENTH DAY
What to Pray – For the Spirit of Burning

And it shall come to pass, that he that is left in Zion shall be called holy: when the Lord shall have washed away the filth of the daughters of Zion, by the Spirit of Judgment and the Spirit of Burning. – Isa. 4:3.

A washing by fire! a cleansing by judgment! He that has passed through this shall be called holy. The power of blessing for the world, the power of work and intercession that will avail, depends upon the spiritual state of the Church; and that can only rise higher as sin is discovered and put away. Judgment must begin at the house of God. There must be conviction of sin for sanctification. Beseech God to give His Spirit as a Spirit of Judgment and a Spirit of Burning – to discover and burn out sin in His people.

How to Pray – In the Name of Christ

Whatsoever ye shall ask in My name, that will I do. If ye shall ask Me anything in My name, that will I do. – John 4:13, 14.

Ask in the name of your Redeemer God, who sits upon the throne. Ask what He has promised, what He gave His blood for, that sin may be put away from among His people, Ask – the prayer is after His own heart – for the spirit of deep conviction of sin to come among His people. Ask for the spirit of burning. Ask in the faith of His name – the faith of what He wills, of what He can do – and look for the answer. Pray that the Church may be blessed, to be made a blessing in the world.

FOURTEENTH DAY
What to Pray – For the Church of the Future

That the children might not be as their fathers, a generation that set not their heart aright, and whose spirit was not steadfast with God. – Ps. 78:8.

I will pour My Spirit upon thy seed, and My blessing upon thy offspring. – Isa. 44:3.

Pray for the rising generation, who are to come after us. Think of the young men and women and children of this age, and pray for all the agencies at work among them; that in associations and societies and unions, in homes and schools, Christ may be honored, and the Holy Spirit get possession of them. Pray for the young of your neighborhood.

How to Pray – With the Whole Heart

The Lord grant thee according to thine own heart. – Ps. 20:4.
Thou hast given him his heart's desire. – Ps. 21:2.
I cried with my whole heart; hear me, O Lord. – Ps. 119:145.

God lives, and listens to every petition with His whole heart. Each time we pray the whole Infinite God is there to hear. He asks that in each prayer the whole man shall be there too; that we shall cry with our whole heart. Christ gave Himself to God for men; and so He takes up every need into His intercession. If once we seek God with our whole heart, the whole heart will be in every prayer with which we come to this God. Pray with your whole heart for the young.

FIFTEENTH DAY
What to Pray – For Schools and Colleges

As for Me, this is My Covenant with them, saith the Lord: My Spirit that is upon thee and My Words which I have put in thy mouth, shall not depart out of thy mouth, nor out of the mouth of thy seed, nor out of the mouth of thy seed's seed, saith the Lord, from henceforth and for ever. – Isa. 59:21.

The future of the Church and the world depends, to an extent we little conceive, on the education of the day. The Church may be seeking to evangelize the heathen, and be giving up her own children to secular and materialistic influences. Pray for schools and colleges, and that the Church may realize and fulfill its momentous duty of caring for its children. Pray for godly teachers.

How to Pray – Not Limiting God

They limited the Holy One of Israel. – Ps. 78:41.

He did not many mighty works there because of their unbelief. – Matt. 13:5.

Is anything too hard for the Lord! – Gen. 18. 14. Ah, Lord God! Thou hast made the heaven and the earth by Thy great power; there is nothing too hard for Thee. Behold, I am the Lord: is there anything too hard for Me! – Jer. 32:17, 27.

Beware, in your prayer, above everything, of limiting God, not only by unbelief, but by fancying that you know what He can do. Expect unexpected things, above all that we ask or think. Each time you intercede, be quiet first and worship God in His glory. Think of what He can do, of how He delights to hear Christ, of your place in Christ, and expect great things.

SIXTEENTH DAY
What to Pray – For the Power of the Holy Spirit in Our Sunday Schools
Thus saith the Lord, Even the captives of the mighty shall be taken away, and the prey of the terrible shall be delivered: for I will contend with him that contendeth with thee, and will save thy children. – Isa. 49:25.

Every part of the work of God's Church is His work. He must do it. Prayer is the confession that He will – the surrender of ourselves into His hands to let Him – work in us and through us. Pray for the hundreds of thousands of Sunday School teachers, that those who know God may be filled with His Spirit. Pray for your own Sunday School. Pray for the salvation of the children.

How to Pray – Boldly
We have a great High Priest, Jesus the Son of God. Let us therefore come boldly unto the throne of grace. – Heb. 4:14, 16.

These hints to help us in our work of intercession – what are they doing for us? Making us conscious of our feebleness in prayer? Thank God for this. It is the very first lesson we need on the way to pray the effectual prayer that availeth much. Let us persevere, taking each subject boldly to the throne of grace. As we pray we shall learn to pray and to believe and to expect with increasing boldness. Hold fast your assurance: it is at God's command you come as an intercessor. Christ will give you grace to pray aright.

SEVENTEENTH DAY
What to Pray – For Kings and Rulers
I exhort therefore, first of all, that supplications, prayers, intercessions, thanksgiving, be made for all men; for kings and all that are in high places; that we may lead a tranquil and quiet life in all godliness and gravity. – 1 Tim. 2:1, 2.

What a faith in the power of prayer! A few feeble and despised Christians are to influence the mighty Roman emperors, and help in securing peace and quietness. Let us believe that prayer is a power that is taken up by God in His rule of the world. Let us pray for our country and its rulers; for all the rulers of the world; for rulers in cities or districts in which we are interested. When God's people unite in this, they may count upon their prayers effecting in the unseen world more than they know. Let faith hold this fast.

How to Pray – The Prayer before God as Incense
And another angel came and stood at the altar, having a golden censer; and there was given unto him much incense, that he should add it unto the prayers of all the saints upon the golden altar which was before the throne. And the smoke of the incense, with the prayers of the saints, went up before God out of the angel's hand. And the angel taketh the censer; and he filled it with the fire upon the altar, and cast it upon the earth: and there followed thunder, and voices, and lightning, and an earthquake. – Rev. 8:3–5.

The same censer brings the prayer of the saints before God and casts fire upon the earth. The prayers that go up to heaven have their share in the history of this earth. Be sure that thy prayers enter God's presence.

EIGHTEENTH DAY
What to Pray – For Peace
I exhort therefore first of all, that supplications be made for Kings and all that are in high places; that we may lead a tranquil and quiet life in all godliness and gravity. For this is good and acceptable in the sight of God our Savior. – 1 Tim. 2:1–3.

He maketh wars to cease unto the end of the earth. – Ps. 46:9.

What a terrible sight! – the military armaments in which the nations find their pride. What a terrible thought!. – the evil passions that may at any moment bring on war. And what a prospect for suffering and desolation that must come. God can, in answer to the prayer of His people, give peace. Let us pray for it, and for the rule of righteousness on which alone it can be stablished.

How to Pray – With the Understanding
What is it then will pray with the spirit, and I will pray with the understanding. – 1 Cor. 14:15.
We need to pray with the spirit, as the vehicle of the intercession of God's Spirit, if we are to take hold of God in faith and power. We need to pray with the understanding, if we are really to enter deeply into the needs we bring before Him. Take time to apprehend intelligently, in each subject, the nature, the extent, the urgency of the request, the ground and way and certainty of God's promise as revealed in His Word. Let the mind affect the heart. Pray with the understanding and with the spirit.

NINETEENTH DAY
What to Pray – For the Holy Spirit on Christendom
Having a form of godliness, but denying the power thereof. – 2 Tim. 3:5.
Thou hast a name that thou livest, and thou art dead. – Rev. 3:1.

There are five hundred million nominal Christians. The state of the majority is unspeakably awful. Formality, worldliness, ungodliness, rejection of Christ's service, ignorance, and indifference – to what an extent does all this prevail. We pray for the heathen – oh! do let us pray for those bearing Christ's name – many in worse than heathen darkness. Does not one feel as if one ought to begin to give up his life, and to cry day and night to God for souls? In answer to prayer God gives the power of the Holy Ghost.

How to Pray – In Deep Stillness of Soul
My soul is silent unto God: from Him cometh my salvation. – Ps. 62:1.

Prayer has its power in God alone. The nearer a man comes to God Himself, the deeper he enters into God's will; the more he takes hold of God, the more power in prayer.

God must reveal Himself. If it please Him to make Himself known, He can make the heart conscious of His presence. Our posture must be that of holy reverence, of quiet waiting and adoration.

As your month of intercession passes on, and you feel the greatness of your work, be still before God. Thus you will get power to pray.

TWENTIETH DAY
What to Pray – For God's Spirit on the Heathen
Behold, these shall come from far; and these from the land of Sinim. – Isa. 49:12.
Princes shall come out of Egypt; Ethiopia shall haste to stretch out her hands to God. – Ps. 68:31.
I the Lord will hasten it in his time. – Isa. 60:22. Pray for the heathen, who are yet without the Word. Think of China, with her three hundred millions – a million a month dying without Christ. Think of Dark Africa, with its two hundred millions. Think of thirty millions a year going down into the thick darkness. If Christ gave His life for them, will you not do so? You can give yourself up to intercede for them. Just begin, if you have never yet begun, with this simple monthly school of intercession. The ten minutes you give will make you feel this is not enough. God's Spirit will draw you on. Persevere, however feeble you are. Ask God to give you some country or tribe to pray for. Can anything be nobler than to do as Christ did? Give your life for the heathen.

How to Pray – With Confident Expectation of an Answer
Call unto me, and I will answer thee, and will shew thee great things and difficult, which thou knowest not. – Jer. 33:3.
Thus saith the Lord God: I will yet be inquired of, that I do it. – Ezek. 3:37.

Both texts refer to promises definitely made, but their fulfillment would depend upon prayer: God would be inquired of to do it.

Pray for God's fulfillment of His promises to His Son and His Church, and expect the answer. Plead for the heathen: plead God's promises.

TWENTY-FIRST DAY
What to Pray – For God's Spirit on the Jews

I will pour out upon the house of David, and the inhabitants of Jerusalem, the Spirit of grace and supplications; and they shall look unto Me whom they pierced. – Zech. 12:10.

Brethren, my heart's desire and my supplication to God is for them, that they may be saved. – Rom. 10:1.

Pray for the Jews. Their return to the God of their fathers stands connected, in a way we cannot tell, with wonderful blessing to the Church, and with the coming of our Lord Jesus. Let us not think that God has foreordained all this, and that we cannot hasten it. In a divine and mysterious way God has connected his fulfillment of His promise with our prayer. His Spirit's intercession in us is God's forerunner of blessing. Pray for Israel and the work done among them. And pray too: Amen. Even so, come Lord Jesus!

How to Pray – With the Intercession of the Holy Spirit

We know not how to pray as we ought; but the Spirit Himself maketh intercession for us with groanings which cannot be uttered. – Rom. 8:26.

In your ignorance and feebleness believe in the secret indwelling and intercession of the Holy Spirit within you. Yield yourself to His life and leading habitually. He will help your infirmities in prayer. Plead the promises of God even where you do not see how they are to be fulfilled. God knows the mind of the Spirit, because He maketh intercession for the saints according to the will of God. Pray with the simplicity of a little child; pray with the holy awe and reverence of one in whom God's Spirit dwells and prays.

TWENTY-SECOND DAY
What to Pray – For All Who Are in Suffering

Remembering them that are in bonds, as bound with them; them that are evil entreated, as being yourselves in the body. – Heb. 13:3.

What a world of suffering we live in! How Jesus sacrificed all and identified Himself with it! Let us in our measure do so too. The persecuted, the Jews, the famine-stricken millions of India, the hidden slavery of Africa, the poverty and wretchedness of our great cities – and so much more: what suffering among those who

know God and who know Him not. And then in smaller circles, in ten thousand homes and hearts, what sorrow. In our own neighborhood, how many needing help or comfort. Let us have a heart for, let us think of the suffering. It will stir us to pray, to work, to hope, to love more. And in a way and time we know not God will hear our prayer.

How to Pray – Praying always and not fainting

He spake unto them a parable to the end that they ought always to pray, and not to faint. – Luke 18:1.

Do you not begin to feel prayer is really the help for this sinful world? What a need there is of unceasing prayer! The very greatness of the task makes us despair! What can our ten minutes intercession avail? It is right we feel this: this is the way in which God is calling and preparing us to give our life to prayer. Give yourself wholly to God for men, and amid all your work, your heart will be drawn out to men in love, and drawn up to God in dependence and expectation. To a heart thus led by the Holy Spirit, it is possible to pray always and not to faint.

TWENTY-THIRD DAY
What to Pray – For the Holy Spirit in Your Own Work

I labor, striving according to His working, which worketh in me mightily. – Col. 1:29.

You have your own special work; make it a work of intercession. Paul labored, striving according to the working of God in him. Remember, God is not only the Creator, but the Great Workman, who worketh all in all. You can only do your work in His strength, by His working in you through the Spirit. Intercede much for those among whom you work, till God gives you life for them. Let us all intercede too for each other, for every worker throughout God's Church, however solitary or unknown.

How to Pray – In God's Very Presence

Draw nigh to God, and He will draw nigh to you. – Jas. 4:8.

The nearness of God gives rest and power in prayer. The nearness of God is given to him who makes it his first object. "Draw nigh to

God" seek the nearness to Him, and He will give it; "He will draw nigh to you." Then it becomes easy to pray in faith.

Remember that when first God takes you into the school of intercession it is almost more for your own sake than that of others. You have to be trained to love, and wait, and pray, and believe. Only persevere. Learn to set yourself in His presence, to wait quietly for the assurance that He draws nigh. Enter His holy presence, tarry there, and spread your work before Him. Intercede for the souls you are working among. Get a blessing from God, His Spirit into your own heart, for them.

TWENTY-FOURTH DAY
What to Pray – For the Spirit on Your Own Congregation
Beginning at Jerusalem. – Luke 24:47.

Each one of us is connected with some congregation or circle of believers, who are to us the part of Christ's body with which we come into most direct contact. They have a special claim on our intercession. Let it be a settled matter between God and you that you are to labor in prayer on its behalf. Pray for the minister and all leaders or workers in it. Pray for the believers according to their needs. Pray for conversions. Pray for the power of the Spirit to manifest itself. Band yourself with others to join in secret in definite petitions. Let intercession be a definite work, carried on as systematically as preaching or Sunday School. And pray, expecting an answer.

How to Pray – Continually
Watchmen, that shall never hold their peace day or night. – Isa. 62:6.
His own elect, that cry to Him day and night. – Luke 18:7
Night and day praying exceedingly that we may perfect that which is lacking in your faith. – 1 Thess. 3:10.
A widow indeed, hath her hope set in God, and continueth in supplications night and day. – 1 Tim. 5:5.

When the glory of God, and the love of Christ, and the need of souls are revealed to us, the fire of this unceasing intercession will begin to burn in us for those who are near and those who are far off.

TWENTY-FIFTH DAY
What to Pray – For More Conversions
He is able to save completely, seeing He ever liveth to make intercession. – Heb. 7:25.
We will give ourselves continually to prayer and the ministry of the Word ... And the Word of God increased; and the number of the disciples multiplied exceedingly. – Acts 6:4, 7.

Christ's power to save, and save completely, depends on His unceasing intercession. The apostles' withdrawing themselves from other work to give themselves continually to prayer was followed by the number of the disciples multiplying exceedingly. As we, in our day, give ourselves to intercession, we shall have more and mightier conversions. Let us plead for this. Christ is exalted to give repentance. The Church exists with the Divine purpose and promise of having conversions. Let us not be ashamed to confess our sins and feebleness, and cry to God for more conversions in Christian and heathen lands, of those too whom you know and love. Plead for the salvation of sinners.

How to Pray – In Deep Humility
Truth, Lord: yet the dogs eat of the crumbs ... O woman, great is thy faith: be it unto thee even as thou wilt. – Matt. 15:27, 28.

You feel unworthy and unable to pray aright. To accept this heartily, and to be content still to come and be blest in your unworthiness, is true humility. It proves its integrity by not seeking for anything, but simply trusting His grace. And so it is the very strength of a great faith, and gets a full answer. "Yet the dogs" – let that be your plea as you persevere for someone possibly possessed of the devil. Let not your littleness hinder you for a moment.

TWENTY-SIXTH DAY
What to Pray – For the Holy Spirit on Young Converts
Peter and John prayed for them, that they might receive the Holy Ghost; for as yet He was fallen upon none of them: only they had been baptized into the name of the Lord Jesus. – Acts 8:15, 16.
Now He which establisheth us with you in Christ, and anointed us, is God; who also gave us the earnest of the Spirit in our hearts. – 2 Cor. 1:21, 22.

How many new converts who remain feeble; how many who fall into sin; how many who backslide entirely. If we pray for the Church, its growth in holiness and devotion to God's service, pray especially for the young converts. How many stand alone, surrounded by temptation; how many have no teaching on the Spirit in them, and the power of God to establish them; how many in heathen lands, surrounded by Satan's power. If you pray for the power of the Spirit in the Church, pray especially that every young convert may know that he may claim and receive the fullness of the Spirit.

How to Pray – Without Ceasing

As for me, God forbid that I should sin against the Lord in ceasing to pray for you. – 1 Sam. 12:23.

It is sin against the Lord to escape praying for others. When once we begin to see how absolutely indispensable intercession is, just as much a duty as loving God or believing in Christ, and how we are called and bound to it as believers, we shall feel that to cease intercession is grievous sin. Let us ask for grace to take up our place as priests with joy, and give our lives to bring down the blessing of Heaven.

Twenty-seventh day
What to Pray – That God's People May Realize Their Calling

I will bless thee; and be thou a blessing: IN THEE shall ALL THE FAMILIES OF THE EARTH be blessed. – Gen. 12:2, 3.

God be merciful UNTO US, and bless US, and cause His face to shine UPON US. That Thy way may be known UPON EARTH, Thy saving health AMONG ALL NATIONS. – Ps. 67:1, 2.

Abraham was only blessed that he might be a blessing to all the earth. Israel prays for blessing, that God may be known among all nations. Every believer, just as much as Abraham, is only blessed that he may carry God's blessing to the world.

Cry to God that His people may know this, that every believer is only to live for the interests of God and His kingdom. If this truth were preached and believed and practiced, what a revolution it would bring in our mission work. What a host of willing intercessors we should

have. Plead with God to work it by the Holy Spirit.

How to Pray – As One Who Has Accepted for Himself What He Asks for Others

Peter said What I have, I give unto thee ... The Holy Ghost fell on them, as on us at the beginning ... God gave them the like gift, as He gave unto us. – Acts 3:6; 9:15, 17.

As you pray for this great blessing on God's people, the Holy Spirit taking entire possession of them for God's service, yield yourself to God, and claim the gift anew in faith. Let each thought of feebleness or shortcoming only make you the more urgent in prayer for others; as the blessing comes to them, you too will be helped. With every prayer for conversions or mission work, pray that God's people may know wholly they belong to Him.

Twenty-eighth day
What to Pray – That all God's People May Know the Holy Spirit

The Spirit of Truth, Whom the world knoweth not; but ye know Him; for He abideth with you, and shall be in you. – John 14:17.

Know ye not that your body is the temple of the Holy Ghost? – 1 Cor. 6: 19.

The Holy Spirit is the power of God for the salvation of men. He only works as He dwells in the Church. He is given to enable believers to live wholly as God would have them live, in the full experience and witness of Him who saves completely. Pray God that everyone of His people may know the Holy Spirit! That He, in all His fullness, is given to them! That they cannot expect to live as their Father would have, without having Him in His fullness, without being filled with Him! Pray that all God's people, even away in churches gathered out of heathendom, may learn to say: I believe in the Holy Ghost.

How to Pray – Laboring Fervently in Prayer

Who is one of you, saluteth you, always reverently you in prayers, that ye may stand perfect and complete in all the will of God. – Col. 4:12.

To a healthy man labor is a delight; in what interests him he labors fervently. The believer who is in full health, whose heart is filled with God's Spirit, labors fervently in prayer. For what? That his brethren may stand perfect and complete in all the will of God; that they may know what God wills for them how He calls them to live, and be led and walk by the Holy Ghost. Labor fervently in prayer that all God's children may know this, as possible, as divinely sure.

TWENTY-NINTH DAY
What to Pray – For the Spirit of Intercession
I chose you, and appointed you, that ye should go and bear fruit; that whatsoever ye shall ask of the Father in My name, He may give it to you. – John 15:16.
Hitherto have ye asked nothing in My name, In that day ye shall ask in My name. – John 6:24, 26.

Has not our school of intercession taught us how little we have prayed in the name of Jesus? He promised His disciples: In that day, when the Holy Spirit comes upon you, ye shall ask in My name. Are there not tens of thousands with us mourning the lack of the power of intercession? Let our intercession today be for them and all God's children, that Christ may teach us that the Holy Spirit is in us; and what it is to live in His fullness, and to yield ourselves to His intercessional work within us. The Church and the world need nothing so much as a mighty Spirit of Intercession to bring down the power of God on earth. Pray for the descent from heaven of the Spirit of Intercession for a great prayer revival.

How to Pray – Abiding in Christ
If ye abide in Me, and My words abide in you, ask whatsoever ye will, and it shall be done to you. – John 15:7.

Our acceptance with God, our access to Him, is all in Christ. As we consciously abide in Him we have the liberty, not a liberty to our old nature or self-will, but the Divine liberty from all self-will, to ask what we will, in the power of the new nature, and it shall be done. Let us keep this place, and believe even now that our intercession is heard, and that the Spirit of Supplication will be given all around us.

THIRTIETH DAY
What to Pray – For the Holy Spirit with the Word of God

Our Gospel came not unto you in word only, but also in power, and in the Holy Ghost, and in much assurance. – 1 Thess. 1:5.

Those who preached unto you the Gospel with the Holy Ghost sent forth from Heaven. – 1 Pet. 1:12.

What numbers of Bibles are being circulated. What numbers of sermons on the Bible are being preached. What numbers of Bibles are being read in home and school. How little blessing when it comes "in word" only; what Divine blessing and power when it comes "in the Holy Ghost," when it is preached "with the Holy Ghost sent forth from Heaven." Pray for Bible circulation, and preaching and teaching and reading, that it may all be in the Holy Ghost, with much prayer. Pray for the power of the Spirit with the Word in your own neighborhood, wherever it is being read or heard. Let every mention of "The Word of God" waken intercession.

How to Pray – Watching and Praying
Continue steadfastly in prayer watching therein with thanksgiving; withal praying for us also, that God may open unto us a door for the Word. – Col. 4:2, 3.

Do you not see how all depends upon God and prayer? As long as He lives and loves, and hears and works, as long as there are souls with hearts closed to the Word, as long as there is work to be done in carrying the Word – Pray without ceasing. Continue steadfastly in prayer, watching therein with thanksgiving. These words are for every Christian.

THIRTY-FIRST DAY
What to Pray – For the Spirit of Christ in His people
I am the Vine, ye are the branches. – John 15:5.
That ye should do as I have done to you. – John 13:15.

As branches we are to be so like the Vine, so entirely identified with it, that all may see that we have the same nature, and life, and Spirit. When we pray for the Spirit, let us not only think of a Spirit of power, but the very disposition and temper of Christ Jesus. Ask and expect nothing less: for yourself, and all God's children, cry for it.

How to Pray – Striving in Prayer
That ye strive together with me in your prayers to God for me. – Rom. 15:30.
I would ye knew what great conflict I have for you. – Col. 2:1.

All the powers of evil seek to hinder us in prayer. Prayer is a conflict with opposing forces. It needs the whole heart and all our strength. May God give us grace to strive in prayer till we prevail.

Andrew Murray, 1828–1917

Prayer and Fasting

Andrew Murray

Then came the disciples to Jesus apart, and said, Why could not we cast him out? And Jesus said unto them, Because of your unbelief: for verily I say unto you, If ye have faith as a grain of mustard seed, nothing shall be impossible to you. Howbeit this kind goeth not out but by prayer and fasting. Matthew xvii. 19–21.

When the disciples saw Jesus cast the evil spirit out of the epileptic whom "they could not cure,' they asked the Master for the cause of their failure. He had given them "power and authority over all devils, and to cure all diseases.' They had often exercised that power, and joyfully told how the devils were subject to them. And yet now, while He was on the Mount, they had utterly failed. That there had been nothing in the will of God or in the nature of the case to render deliverance impossible, had been proved: at Christ's bidding the evil spirit had gone out. From their expression, "Why could we not?' it is evident that they had wished and sought to do so; they had probably used the Master's name, and called upon the evil spirit to go out. Their efforts had been vain, and in presence of the multitude, they had been put to shame. "Why could we not?'

Christ's answer was direct and plain: "Because of your unbelief.' The cause of His success and their failure, was not owing to His having a special power to which they had no access. No; the reason was not far to seek. He had so often taught them that there is one power, that of faith, to which, in the kingdom of darkness, as in the kingdom of God, every-thing must bow; in the spiritual world failure has but one cause, the want of faith. Faith is the one condition on which all Divine power can enter into man and work through him. It is the susceptibility of the unseen: man's will yielded up to, and molded by, the will of God. The power they had received to cast out devils, they did not hold in themselves as a permanent gift or possession; the power was in Christ, to be received, and held, and used by faith alone, living faith in Himself. Had they been full of faith in Him as Lord and Conqueror in the spirit-world, had they been full of faith in Him as having given them authority to cast out in His name, this faith would have given them the victory. "Because of your unbelief' was, for all time, the Master's explanation and reproof of impotence and failure in His Church.

But such want of faith must have a cause too. Well might the disciples have asked: "And why could we not believe? Our faith has cast out devils before this: why have we now failed in believing? "The Master proceeds to tell them ere they ask: "This kind goeth not out but by fasting and prayer." As faith is the simplest, so it is the highest exercise of the spiritual life, where our spirit yields itself in perfect receptivity to God's Spirit and so is strengthened to its highest activity. This faith depends entirely upon the state of the spiritual life; only when this is strong and in full health, when the Spirit of God has full sway in our life, is there the power of faith to do its mighty deeds. And therefore Jesus adds: "Howbeit this kind goeth not out but by fasting and prayer." The faith that can overcome such stubborn resistance as you have just seen in this evil spirit, Jesus tells them, is not possible except to men living in very close fellowship with God, and in very special separation from the world – in prayer and fasting. And so He teaches us two lessons in regard to prayer of deep importance. The one, that faith needs a life of prayer in which to grow and keep strong. The other, that prayer needs fasting for its full and perfect development.

Faith needs a life of prayer for its full growth. In all the different parts of the spiritual life, there is such close union, such unceasing action and re-action, that each may be both cause and effect. Thus it is with faith. There can be no true prayer without faith; some measure of faith must precede prayer. And yet prayer is also the way to more faith; there can be no higher degrees of faith except through much prayer. This is the lesson Jesus teaches here. There is nothing needs so much to grow as our faith. "Your faith groweth exceedingly," is said of one Church. When Jesus spoke the words, "According to your faith be it unto you," He announced the law of the kingdom, which tells us that all have not equal degrees of faith, that the same person has not always the same degree, and that the measure of faith must always determine the measure of power and of blessing. If we want to know where and how our faith is to grow, the Master points us to the throne of God. It is in prayer, in the exercise of the faith I have, in fellowship with the living God, that faith can increase. Faith can only live by feeding on what is Divine, on God Himself.

It is in the adoring worship of God, the waiting on Him and for Him, the deep silence of soul that yields itself for God to reveal Himself, that the capacity for knowing and trusting God will be developed. It is as we take His word from the Blessed Book, and bring it to Himself, asking him to speak it to us with His living loving voice, that the power will come fully to believe and receive the word as God's own word to us. It is in prayer, in living contact with God in living faith, that faith, the power to trust God, and in that trust, to accept everything He says, to accept every possibility He has offered to our faith will become strong in us. Many Christians cannot understand what is meant by the much prayer they sometimes hear spoken of: they can form no conception, nor do they feel the need, of spending hours with God. But what the Master says, the experience of His people has confirmed: men of strong faith are men of much prayer.

This just brings us back again to the lesson we learned when Jesus, before telling us to believe that we receive what we ask, first said, "Have faith in God." It is God, the living God, into whom our faith must strike its roots deep and broad; then it will be strong to remove mountains and cast out devils. "If ye have faith, nothing shall be impossible to you." Oh! if we do but give ourselves up to the work God has for us in the world, coming into contact with the mountains and the devils there are to be cast away and cast out, we should soon comprehend the need there is of much faith, and of much prayer, as the soil in which alone faith can be cultivated. Christ Jesus is our life, the life of our faith too. It is His life in us that makes us strong, and makes us simple to believe. It is in the dying to self which much prayer implies, in closer union to Jesus, that the spirit of faith will come in power. Faith needs prayer for its full growth.

And prayer needs fasting for its full growth: this is the second lesson. Prayer is the one hand with which we grasp the invisible; fasting, the other, with which we let loose and cast away the visible. In nothing is man more closely connected with the world of sense than in his need of food, and his enjoyment of it. It was the fruit, good for food, with which man was tempted and fell in Paradise. It was with bread to be made of stones that Jesus, when an hungered, was tempted in the wilderness, and in fasting that He triumphed. The body has been redeemed to be a temple of the Holy Spirit; it is in body as well as spirit, it is very specially, Scripture says, in eating and drinking, we are to glorify God. It is to be feared that there are many Christians to whom this eating to the glory of God has not yet become a spiritual reality. And the first thought suggested by Jesus' words in regard to fasting and prayer, is, that it is only in a life of moderation and temperance and self-denial that there will be the heart or the strength to pray much.

But then there is also its more literal meaning. Sorrow and anxiety cannot eat: joy celebrates its feasts with eating and drinking. There may come times of intense desire, when it is strongly felt how the body, with its appetites, lawful though they be, still hinder the spirit in its battle with the powers of darkness, and the need is felt of keeping it under. We are creatures of the senses: our mind is helped by what comes to us embodied in concrete form; fasting helps to express, to deepen, and to confirm the resolution that we are ready to sacrifice anything, to sacrifice ourselves, to attain what we seek for the kingdom of God. And He who accepted the fasting and sacrifice of the Son, knows to value and accept and reward with spiritual power the soul that is thus ready to give up all for Christ and His kingdom.

And then follows a still wider application. Prayer is the reaching out after God and the unseen; fasting, the letting go of all that is of the seen and temporal. While ordinary Christians imagine that all that is not positively forbidden and sinful is lawful to them, and seek to retain as much as possible of this world, with its property, its literature, its enjoyments, the truly consecrated soul is as the soldier who carries only what he needs for the warfare. Laying aside every weight, as well as the easily besetting sin, afraid of entangling himself with the affairs of this life, he seeks to lead a Nazarite life, as one specially set apart for the Lord and His service. Without such voluntary separation, even from what is lawful, no one will attain power in prayer: this kind goeth not out but by fasting and prayer.

Disciples of Jesus! who have asked the Master to teach you to pray, come now and accept His lessons. He tells you that prayer is the path to faith, strong faith, that can cast out devils. He tells you: "If ye have faith, nothing shall be impossible to you;" let this glorious promise encourage you to pray much. Is the prize not worth the price? Shall we not give up all to follow Jesus in the path He opens to us here; shall we not, if need be, fast? Shall we not do anything that neither the body nor the world around hinder us in our great life-work, – having intercourse with our God in prayer, that we may become men of faith, whom He can use in His work of saving the world.

Andrew Murray, 1828–1917

With Christ in the School of Prayer

Andrew Murray

GEORGE MÜLLER AND THE SECRET OF HIS POWER IN PRAYER

When God wishes anew to teach His Church a truth that is not being understood or practiced, He mostly does so by raising some man to be in word and deed a living witness to its blessedness. And so God has raised up in this nineteenth century, among others, George Müller to be His witness that He is indeed the Hearer of prayer. I know of no way in which the principal truths of God's word in regard to prayer can be more effectually illustrated and established than a short review of his life and of what he tells of his prayer-experiences.

He was born in Prussia on 25th September 1805, and is thus now eighty years of age. His early life, even after having entered the University of Halle as a theological student, was wicked in the extreme. Led by a friend one evening, when just twenty years of age, to a prayer meeting, he was deeply impressed, and soon after brought to know the Savior. Not long after he began reading missionary papers, and in course of time offered himself to the London Society for promoting Christianity to the Jews. He was accepted as a student, but soon found that he could not in all things submit to the rules of the Society, as leaving too little liberty for the leading of the Holy Spirit. The connection was dissolved in 1830 by mutual consent, and he became the pastor of a small congregation at Teignmouth. In 1832 he was led to Bristol, and it was as pastor of Bethesda Chapel that he was led to the Orphan Home and other work, in connection with which God has so remarkably led him to trust His word and to experience how God fulfils that word.

A few extracts in regard to his spiritual life will prepare the way for what we specially wish to quote of his experiences in reference to prayer.

"In connection with this I would mention, that the Lord very graciously gave me, from the very commencement of my divine life, a measure of simplicity and of childlike disposition in spiritual things, so that whilst I was exceedingly ignorant of the Scriptures, and was still from time to time overcome even by outward sins, yet I was enabled to carry most minute matters to the Lord in prayer. And I have found 'godliness profitable unto all things, having promise of the life that now is, and of that which is to come.' Though very weak and ignorant, yet I had now, by the grace of God, some desire to benefit others, and he who so faithfully had once served Satan, sought now to win souls for Christ."

It was at Teignmouth that he was led to know how to use God's word, and to trust the Holy Spirit as the Teacher given by God to make that word clear. He writes: –

"God then began to show me that the word of God alone is our standard of judgment in spiritual things; that it can be explained only by the Holy Spirit; and that in our day, as well as in former times. He is the Teacher of His people. The office of the Holy Spirit I had not experimentally understood before that time.

"It was my beginning to understand this latter point in particular, which had a great effect on me; for the Lord enabled me to put it to the test of experience, by laying aside commentaries, and almost every other book and simply reading the word of God and studying it.

"The result of this was, that the first evening that I shut myself into my room, to give myself to prayer and meditation over the Scriptures, I learned more in a few hours than I had done during a period of several months previously.

"But the particular difference was that I received real strength for my soul in so doing. I now began to try by the test of the Scriptures the things which I had learned and seen, and found that only those principles which stood the test were of real value."

Of obedience to the word of God, he writes as follows, in connection with his being baptized: –

"It had pleased God, in His abundant mercy, to bring my mind into such a state, that I was willing to carry out into my life whatever I should find in the Scriptures. I could say, 'I will do His will,' and it was on that account, I believe, that I saw which 'doctrine is of God.' – And I would observe here, by the way, that the passage to which I have just alluded (John vii. 17) has been a most remarkable comment to me on many doctrines and precepts of our most holy faith. For instance: 'Resist not evil; but whosoever shall smite thee on thy right cheek, turn to him the other also. And if any man will sue thee at the law, and take away thy coat, let him have thy cloak also. And whosoever shall compel thee to go a mile, go with him twain. Give to him that asketh thee, and from him that would borrow of thee, turn not thou away. Love your enemies, bless them that curse you, do good to them that hate you, and pray for them which despitefully use you, and persecute you' (Matt. v. 39–44). 'Sell that ye have, and give alms' (Luke xii. 33). 'Owe no man any thing, but to love one another' (Rom. xii. 8). It may be said, 'Surely these passages cannot be taken literally, for how then would the people of God be able to pass through the world?' The state of mind enjoined in John vii. 17 will cause such objections to vanish. WHOSOEVER IS WILLING TO ACT OUT these commandments of the Lord LITERALLY, will, I believe, be led with me to see that to take them LITERALLY is the will of God. – Those who do so take them will doubtless often be brought into difficulties, hard to the flesh to bear, but these will have a tendency to make them constantly feel that they are strangers and pilgrims here, that this world is not their home, and thus to throw them more upon God, who will assuredly help us through any difficulty into which we may be brought by seeking to act in obedience to His word."

This implicit surrender to God's word led him to certain views and conduct in regard to money, which mightily influenced his future life. They had their root in the conviction that money was a Divine stewardship, and that all money had therefore to be received and dispensed in direct fellowship with God Himself. This led him to the adoption of the following four great rules: 1. Not to receive any fixed salary, both because in the collecting of it there was often much that was at variance with the freewill offering with which God's service is to be maintained, and in the receiving of it a danger of placing more dependence on human sources of income than in the living God Himself. 2. Never to ask any human being for help, however great the need might be, but to make his wants known to the God who has promised to care for His servants and to hear their prayer. 3. To take this command (Luke xii. 33) literally, "Sell that thou hast and give alms," and never to save up money, but to spend all God entrusted to him on God's poor, on the work of His kingdom. 4. Also to take Rom. xiii. 8, "Owe no man anything," literally, and never to buy on credit, or be in debt for anything, but to trust God to provide.

This mode of living was not easy at first. But Müller testifies it was most blessed in bringing the soul to rest in God, and drawing it into closer union with Himself when inclined to backslide. "For it will not do, it is not possible, to live in sin, and at the same time, by communion with God, to draw down from heaven everything one needs for the life that now is."

Not long after his settlement at Bristol, "THE SCRIPTURAL KNOWLEDGE INSTITUTION FOR HOME AND ABROAD" was established for aiding in Day, Sunday School, Mission and Bible work. Of this Institution the Orphan Home work, by which Mr. Müller is best known, became a branch. It was in 1834 that his heart was touched by the case of an orphan brought to Christ in one of the schools, but who had to go to a poorhouse where its spiritual wants would not be cared for. Meeting shortly after with a life of Franke, he writes (Nov. 20, 1835): "Today I have had it very much laid on my heart no longer merely to think about the establishment of an Orphan Home, but actually to set about it, and I have been very much in prayer respecting it, in order to ascertain the Lord's mind. May God make it plain." And again, Nov. 25: "I have been again much in prayer yesterday and today about the Orphan Home, and am more and more convinced that it is of God. May He in mercy guide me. The three chief reasons are – 1. That God may be glorified, should He be pleased to furnish me with the means, in its being seen that it is not a vain thing to trust Him; and that thus the faith of His children may be strengthened. 2. The spiritual welfare of fatherless and motherless children. 3. Their temporal welfare."

After some months of prayer and waiting on God, a house was rented, with room for thirty children , and in course of time three more, containing in all 120 children. The work was carried on it this way for ten years, the supplies for the needs of the orphans being asked and received of God alone. It was often a time of sore need and much prayer, but a trial of faith more precious than of gold was found unto praise and honor and glory of God. The Lord was preparing His servant for greater things. By His providence and His Holy Spirit, Mr. Müller was led to desire, and to wait upon God till he received from Him, the sure promise of £15,000 for a Home to contain 300 children. This first Home was opened in 1849. In 1858, a second and third Home, for 950 more orphans, was opened, costing £35,000. And in

1869 and 1870, a fourth and a fifth Home, for 850 more, at an expense of £50,000, making the total number of the orphans 2100.

In addition to this work, God has given him almost as much as for the building of the Orphan Homes, and the maintenance of the orphans, for other work, the support of schools and missions, Bible and tract circulation. In all he has received from God, to be spent in His work, during these fifty years, more than one million pounds sterling. How little he knew, let us carefully notice, that when he gave up his little salary of £35 a year in obedience to the leading of God's word and the Holy Spirit, what God was preparing to give him as the reward of obedience and faith; and how wonderfully the word was to be fulfilled to him: "Thou hast been faithful over few things; I will set thee over many things."

And these things have happened for an ensample to us. God calls us to be followers of George Müller, even as he is of Christ. His God is our God; the same promises are for us; the same service of love and faith in which he labored is calling for us on every side. Let us in connection with our lessons in the school of prayer study the way in which God gave George Müller such power as a man of prayer: we shall find in it the most remarkable illustration of some of the lessons which we have been studying with the blessed Master in the word. We shall specially have impressed upon us His first great lesson, that if we will come to Him in the way He has pointed out, with definite petitions, made known to us by the Spirit through the word as being according to the will of God, we may most confidently believe that whatsoever we ask it shall be done.

PRAYER AND THE WORD OF GOD

We have more than once seen that God's listening to our voice depends upon our listening to His voice. (See Lessons 22 and 23.) We must not only have a special promise to plead, when we make a special request, but our whole life must be under the supremacy of the word: the word must be dwelling in us. The testimony of George Müller on this point is most instructive. He tells us how the discovery of the true place of the word of God, and the teaching of the Spirit with it, was the commencement of a new era in his spiritual life. Of it he writes: –

"Now the scriptural way of reasoning would have been: God Himself has condescended to become an author, and I am ignorant about that precious book which His Holy Spirit has caused to be written through the instrumentality of His servants, and it contains that which I ought to know, and the knowledge of which will lead me to true happiness; therefore I ought to read again and again this most precious book, this book of books, most earnestly, most prayerfully, and with much meditation; and in this practice I ought to continue all the days of my life. For I was aware, though I read it but little, that I knew scarcely anything of it. But instead of acting thus and being led by my ignorance of the word of God to study it more, my difficulty in understanding it, and the little enjoyment I had in it, made me careless of reading it (for much prayerful reading of the word gives not merely more knowledge, but increases the delight we have in reading it); and thus, like many believers, I practically preferred, for the first four years of my divine life, the works of uninspired men to the oracles of the living God. The consequence was that I remained a babe, both in knowledge and grace. In knowledge, I say; for all true knowledge must be derived, by the Spirit, from the word. And as I neglected the word, I was for nearly four years so ignorant, that I did not clearly know even the fundamental points of our holy faith. And this lack of knowledge most sadly kept me back from walking steadily in the ways of God. For when it pleased the Lord in August 1829 to bring me really to the Scriptures, my life and walk became very different. And though ever since that I have very much fallen short of what I might and ought to be, yet by the grace of God I have been enabled to live much nearer to Him than before. If any believers read this who practically prefer other books to the Holy Scriptures, and who enjoy the writings of men much more than the word of God, may they be warned by my loss. I shall consider this book to have been the means of doing much good, should it please the Lord, through its instrumentality, to lead some of His people no longer to neglect the Holy Scriptures, but to give them that preference which they have

hitherto bestowed on the writings of men.

"Before I leave this subject, I would only add: If the reader understands very little of the word of God, he ought to read it very much; for the Spirit explains the word by the word. And if he enjoys the reading of the word little, that is just the reason why he should read it much; for the frequent reading of the Scriptures creates a delight in them, so that the more we read them, the more we desire to do so.

"Above all, he should seek to have it settled in his own mind that God alone by His Spirit can teach him, and that therefore, as God will be inquired of for blessings, it becomes him to seek God's blessing previous to reading, and also whilst reading.

"He should have it, moreover, settled in his mind that although the Holy Spirit is the best and sufficient Teacher, yet that this Teacher does not always teach immediately when we desire it, and that therefore we may have to entreat Him again and again for the explanation of certain passages; but that He will surely teach us at last, if indeed we are seeking for light prayerfully, patiently, and with a view to the glory of God."

We find in his journal frequent mention made of his spending two and three hours in prayer over the word for the feeding of his spiritual life. As the fruit of this, when he had need of strength and encouragement in prayer, the individual promises were not to him so many arguments from a book to be used with God, but living words which he had heard the Father's living voice speak to him, and which he could now bring to the Father in living faith.

PRAYER AND THE WILL OF GOD
One of the greatest difficulties with young believers is to know how they can find out whether what they desire is according to God's will. I count it one of the most precious lessons God wants to teach through the experience of George Müller, that He is willing to make know, of things of which His word says nothing directly, that they are His will for us, and that we may ask them. The teaching of the Spirit, not without or against the word, but as something above and beyond it, in addition to it, without which we cannot see God's will,

is the heritage of every believer. It is through THE WORD, AND THE WORD ALONE, that the Spirit teaches, applying the general principles or promises to our special need. And it is THE SPIRIT, AND THE SPIRIT ALONE, who can really make the word a light on our path, whether the path of duty in our daily walk, or the path of faith in our approach to God. Let us try and notice in what childlike simplicity and teachableness it was that the discovery of God's will was so surely and so clearly made known to His servant.

With regard to the building of the first Home and the assurance he had of its being God's will, he writes in May 1850, just after it had been opened, speaking of the great difficulties there were, and how little likely it appeared to nature that they would be removed: "But while the prospect before me would have been overwhelming had I looked at it naturally, I was never even for once permitted to question how it would end. For as from the beginning I was sure it was the will of God that I should go to the work of building for Him this large Orphan Home, so also from the beginning I was as certain that the whole would be finished as if the Home had been already filled."

The way in which he found out what was God's will, comes out with special clearness in his account of the building of the second Home; and I ask the reader to study with care the lesson the narrative conveys: –

"Dec. 5, 1850. – Under these circumstances I can only pray that the Lord in His tender mercy would not allow Satan to gain an advantage over me. By the grace of God my heart says: Lord, if I could be sure that it is Thy will that I should go forward in this matter, I would do so cheerfully; and, on the other hand, if I could be sure that these are vain, foolish, proud thoughts, that they are not from Thee, I would, by Thy grace, hate them, and entirely put them aside.

"My hope is in God: He will help and teach me. Judging, however, from His former dealings with me, it would not be a strange thing to me, nor surprising, if He called me to labor yet still more largely in this way.

"The thoughts about enlarging the Orphan work have not yet arisen on account of an abundance of money having lately come in; for

I have had of late to wait for about seven weeks upon God, whilst little, very little comparatively, came in, i.e. about four times as much was going out as came in; and, had not the Lord previously sent me large sums, we should have been distressed indeed.

"Lord! how can Thy servant know Thy will in this matter? Wilt Thou be pleased to teach him!

"December 11. – During the last six days, since writing the above, I have been, day after day, waiting upon God concerning this matter. It has generally been more or less all the day on my heart. When I have been awake at night, it has not been far from my thoughts. Yet all this without the least excitement. I am perfectly calm and quiet respecting it. My soul would be rejoiced to go forward in this service, could I be sure that the Lord would have me to do so; for then, notwithstanding the numberless difficulties, all would be well; and His Name would be magnified.

"On the other hand, were I assured that the Lord would have me to be satisfied with my present sphere of service, and that I should not pray about enlarging the work, by His grace I could, without an effort, cheerfully yield to it; for He has brought me into such a state of heart, that I only desire to please Him in this matter. Moreover, hitherto I have not spoken about this thing even to my beloved wife, the sharer of my joys, sorrows, and labors for more than twenty years; nor is it likely that I shall do so for some time to come: for I prefer quietly to wait on the Lord, without conversing on this subject, in order that thus I may be kept the more easily, by His blessing, from being influenced by things from without. The burden of my prayer concerning this matter is, that the Lord would not allow me to make a mistake, and that He would teach me to do His will.

"December 26. – Fifteen days have elapsed since I wrote the preceding paragraph. Every day since then I have continued to pray about this matter, and that with a goodly measure of earnestness, by the help of God. There has passed scarcely an hour during these days, in which, whilst awake, this matter has not been more or less before me. But all without even a shadow of excitement. I converse with no one about it. Hitherto have I not even done so with my dear wife. For this I refrain still, and deal with God alone about the matter, in order that no outward influence and no outward excitement may keep me from attaining unto a clear discovery of His will. I have the fullest and most peaceful assurance that He will clearly show me His will. This evening I have had again an especial solemn season for prayer, to seek to know the will of God. But whilst I continue to entreat and beseech the Lord, that He would not allow me to be deluded in this business, I may say I have scarcely any doubt remaining on my mind as to what will be the issue, even that I should go forward in this matter. As this, however, is one of the most momentous steps that I have ever taken, I judge that I cannot go about this matter with too much caution, prayerfulness, and deliberation. I am in no hurry about it. I could wait for years, by God's grace, were this His will, before even taking one single step toward this thing, or even speaking to anyone about it; and, on the other hand, I would set to work tomorrow, were the Lord to bid me do so. This calmness of mind, this having no will of my own in the matter, this only wishing to please my Heavenly Father in it, this only seeking His and not my honor in it; this state of heart, I say, is the fullest assurance to me that my heart is not under a fleshly excitement, and that, if I am helped thus to go on, I shall know the will of God to the full. But, while I write this, I cannot but add at the same time, that I do crave the honor and the glorious privilege to be more and more used by the Lord.

"I desire to be allowed to provide scriptural instruction for a thousand orphans, instead of doing so for 300. I desire to expound the Holy Scriptures regularly to a thousand orphans, instead of doing so to 300. I desire that it may be yet more abundantly manifest that God is still the Hearer and Answerer of prayer, and that He is the living God now as He ever was and ever will be, when He shall simply, in answer to prayer, have condescended to provide me with a house for 700 orphans and with means to support them. This last consideration is the most important point in my mind. The Lord's honor is the principal point with me in this whole matter; and just because this is the case, if He would be more glorified

by not going forward in this business, I should by His grace be perfectly content to give up all thoughts about another Orphan House. Surely in such a state of mind, obtained by the Holy Spirit, Thou, O my Heavenly Father, wilt not suffer Thy child to be mistaken, much less deluded. By the help of God I shall continue further day by day to wait upon Him in prayer, concerning this thing, till He shall bid me act.

"Jan. 2, 1851. – A week ago I wrote the preceding paragraph. During this week I have still been helped day by day, and more than once every day, to seek the guidance of the Lord about another Orphan House. The burden of my prayer has still been, that He in His great mercy would keep me from making a mistake. During the last week the book of Proverbs has come in the course of my Scripture reading, and my heart has been refreshed in reference to this subject by the following passages: 'Trust in the Lord with all thine heart; and lean not unto thine own understanding. In all thy ways acknowledge Him, and He shall direct thy paths' (Prov. iii. 5, 6). By the grace of God I do acknowledge the Lord in all my ways, and in this thing in particular; I have therefore the comfortable assurance that He will direct my paths concerning this part of my service, as to whether I shall be occupied in it our not. Further: "The integrity of the upright shall preserve them" (Prov. xi. 3). By the grace of God I am upright in this business. My honest purpose is to get glory to God. Therefore I expect to be guided aright. Further: 'Commit thy works unto the Lord, and thy thoughts shall be established' (Prov. xvi. 3). I do commit my works unto the Lord, and therefore expect that my thoughts will be established. My heart is more and more coming to a calm, quiet, and settled assurance, that the Lord will condescend to use me still further in the orphan work. Here Lord is Thy servant."

When later he decided to build two additional houses, Nos. 4 and 5, he writes thus again: –

"Twelve days have passed away since I wrote the last paragraph. I have still day by day been enabled to wait upon the Lord with reference to enlarging the Orphan work, and have been during the whole of this period also in perfect peace, which is the result of seeking in this thing only the Lord's honor and the temporal and spiritual benefit of my fellow-men. Without an effort could I by His grace put aside all thoughts about this whole affair, if only assured that it is the will of God that I should do so; and, on the other hand, would at once go forward, if He would have it be so. I have still kept this matter entirely to myself. Though it be now about seven weeks, since day by day, more or less, my mind has been exercised about it, and since I have been daily praying about it, yet not one human being knows of it. As yet I have not even mentioned it to my dear wife in order that thus, by quietly waiting upon God, I might not be influenced by what might be said to me on the subject. This evening has been particularly set apart for prayer, beseeching the Lord once more not to allow me to be mistaken in this thing, and much less to be deluded by the devil. I have also sought to let all the reasons against building another Orphan House, and all the reasons for doing so pass before my mind: and now for the clearness and definiteness, write them down …

"Much, however, as the nine previous reasons weigh with me, yet they would not decide me were there not one more. It is this. After having for months pondered the matter, and having looked at it in all its bearings and with all its difficulties, and then having been finally led, after much prayer, to decide on this enlargement, my mind is at peace. The child who has again and again besought His Heavenly Father not to allow him to be deluded, nor even to make a mistake, is at peace, perfectly at peace concerning this decision; and has thus the assurance that the decision come to, after much prayer during weeks and months, is the leading of the Holy Spirit; and therefore purposes to go forward, assuredly believing that he will not be confounded, for he trusts in God. Many and great may be his difficulties; thousands and ten thousands of prayers may have ascended to God, before the full answer may be obtained; much exercise of faith and patience may be required; but in the end it will again be seen, that His servant, who trusts in Him, has not been confounded."

PRAYER AND THE GLORY OF GOD

We have sought more than once to enforce the truth, that while we ordinarily seek the reasons of our prayers not being heard in the thing we ask not being according to the will of God, Scripture warns us to find the cause in ourselves, in our not being in the right state or not asking in the right spirit. The thing may be in full accordance with His will, but the asking, the spirit of the supplicant, not; then we are not heard. As the great root of all sin is self and self-seeking, so there is nothing that even in our more spiritual desires so effectually hinders God in answering as this: we pray for our own pleasure or glory. Prayer to have power and prevail must ask for the glory of God; and he can only do this as he is living for God's glory.

In George Müller we have one of the most remarkable instances on record of God's Holy Spirit leading a man deliberately and systematically, at the outset of a course of prayer, to make the glorifying of God his first and only object. Let us ponder well what he says, and learn the lesson God would teach us through him: –

"I had constantly cases brought before me, which proved that one of the especial things which the children of God needed in our day, was to have their faith strengthened.

"I longed, therefore, to have something to point my brethren to, as a visible proof that our God and Father is the same faithful God as ever He was; as willing as ever to PROVE Himself to be the LIVING GOD in our day as formerly, to all who put their trust in Him.

"My spirit longed to be instrumental in strengthening their faith, by giving them not only instances from the word of God, of His willingness and ability to help all who rely upon Him, but to show them by proofs that He is the same in our day. I knew that the word of God ought to be enough, and it was by grace enough for me; but still I considered I ought to lend a helping hand to my brethren.

"I therefore judged myself bound to be the servant of the Church of Christ, in the particular point in which I had obtained mercy; namely, in being able to take God at His word and rely upon it. The first object of the work was, and is still: that God might be magnified by the fact that the orphans under my care are provided with all they need, only by prayer and faith, without any one being asked; thereby it may be seen that God is FAITHFUL STILL, AND HEARS PRAYER STILL.

"I have again these last days prayed much about the Orphan House, and have frequently examined my heart; that if it were at all my desire to establish it for the sake of gratifying myself, I might find it out. For as I desire only the Lord's glory, I shall be glad to be instructed by the instrumentality of my brother, if the matter be not of Him.

"When I began the Orphan work in 1835, my chief object was the glory of God, by giving a practical demonstration as to what could be accomplished simply through the instrumentality of prayer and faith, in order thus to benefit the Church at large, and to lead a careless world to see the reality of the things of God, by showing them in this work, that the living God is still, as 4000 years ago, the living God. This my aim has been abundantly honored. Multitudes of sinners have been thus converted, multitudes of the children of God in all parts of the world have been benefitted by this work, even as I had anticipated. But the larger the work as grown, the greater has been the blessing, bestowed in the very way in which I looked for blessing: for the attention of hundreds of thousands has been drawn to the work; and many tens of thousands have come to see it. All this leads me to desire further and further to labor on in this way, in order to bring yet greater glory to the Name of the Lord. That He may be looked at, magnified, admired, trusted in, relied on at all times, is my aim in this service; and so particularly in this intended enlargement. That it may be seen how much one poor man, simply by trusting in God, can bring about by prayer; and that thus other children of God may be led to carry on the work of God in dependence upon Him; and that children of God may be led increasingly to trust in Him in their individual positions and circumstances, therefore I am led to this further enlargement."

PRAYER AND TRUST IN GOD

There are other points on which I would be glad to point out what is to be found in Mr. Müller's narrative, but one more must suffice. It is the lesson of firm and unwavering trust in God's promise as the secret of persevering prayer. If once we have, in submission to the teaching of the Spirit in the word, taken hold of God's promise, and believed that the Father has heard us, we must not allow ourselves by any delay or unfavorable appearances be shaken in our faith.

"The full answer to my daily prayers was far from being realized; yet there was abundant encouragement granted by the Lord, to continue in prayer. But suppose, even, that far less had come in than was received, still, after having come to the conclusion, upon scriptural grounds, after much prayer and self-examination, I ought to have gone on without wavering, in the exercise of faith and patience concerning this object; and thus all the children of God, when once satisfied that anything which they bring before God in prayer, is according to His will, ought to continue in believing, expecting, persevering prayer until the blessing is granted. Thus am I myself now waiting upon God for certain blessings, for which I have daily besought Him for ten years and six months without one day's intermission. Still the full answer is not yet given concerning the conversion of certain individuals, though in the meantime I have received many thousands of answers to prayer. I have also prayed daily without intermission for the conversion of other individuals about ten years, for others six or seven years, for others from three or two years; and still the answer is not yet granted concerning those persons, while in the meantime many thousands of my prayers have been answered, and also souls converted, for whom I had been praying. I lay particular stress on this for the benefit of those who may suppose that I need only to ask of God, and receive at once; or that I might pray concerning anything, and the answer would surely come. One can only expect to obtain answers to prayers which are according to the mind of God; and even then, patience and faith may be exercised for many years, even as mine are exercised, in the matter to which I have referred; and yet am I daily continuing in prayer, and expecting the answer, and so surely expecting the answer, that I have often thanked God that He will surely give it, though now for nineteen years faith and patience have thus been exercised. Be encouraged, dear Christians, with fresh earnestness to give yourselves to prayer, if you can only be sure that you ask things which are for the glory of God.

"But the most remarkable point is this, that £6, 6s. 6d. from Scotland supplied me, as far as can be known now, with all the means necessary for fitting up and promoting the New Orphan Houses. Six years and eight months I have been day by day, and generally several times daily, asking the Lord to give me the needed means for this enlargement of the Orphan work, which, according to calculations made in the spring of 1861, appeared to be about fifty thousand pounds: the total of this amount I had now received. I praise and magnify the Lord for putting this enlargement of the work into my heart, and for giving me courage and faith for it; and above all, for sustaining my faith day by day without wavering. When the last portion of the money was received, I was no more assured concerning the whole, that I was at the time I had not received one single donation towards this large sum. I was at the beginning, after once having ascertained His mind, through most patient and heart-searching waiting upon God, as fully assured that He would bring it about, as if the two houses, with their hundreds of orphans occupying them, had been already before me. I make a few remarks here for the sake of young believers in connection with this subject: 1. Be slow to take new steps in the Lord's service, or in your business, or in your families: weigh everything well; weigh all in the light of the Holy Scriptures and in the fear of God. 2. Seek to have no will of your own, in order to ascertain the mind of God, regarding any steps you propose taking, so that you can honestly say you are willing to do the will of God, if He will only please to instruct you. 3. But when you have found out what the will of God is, seek for His help, and seek it earnestly, perseveringly, patiently, believingly, expectantly; and you will surely in His own time and way obtain it.

"To suppose that we have difficulty about money only would be a mistake: there occur hundreds of other wants and of other difficulties. It is a rare thing that a day occurs without some difficulty or some want; but often there are many difficulties and many wants to be met and overcome the same day. All these are met by prayer and faith, our universal remedy; and we have never been confounded. Patient, persevering, believing prayer, offered up to God, in the Name of the Lord Jesus, has always, sooner or later, brought the blessing. I do not despair, by God's grace, of obtaining any blessing, provided I can be sure it would be for any real good, and for the glory of God.

Andrew Murray. With Christ in the School of Prayer [The extracts are from a work in four volumes, *The Lord's Dealings with George Müller*. J. Nisbet & Co., London.]

Public Prayer

John Newton

It is much to be desired, that our hearts might be so affected with a sense of divine things and so closely engaged when we are worshiping God, that it might not be in the power of little circumstances to interrupt and perplex us, and to make us think the service wearisome and the time which we employ in it tedious. But as our infirmities are many and great, and the enemy of our souls is watchful to discompose us, if care is not taken by those who lead in social prayer, the exercise which is approved by the judgment may become a burden and an occasion of sin …

LENGTH OF PRAYERS

The chief fault of some good prayers is, that they are too long; not that I think we should pray by the clock, and limit ourselves precisely to a certain number of minutes; but it is better of the two, that the hearers should wish the prayer had been longer, than spend half the time in wishing it was over. This is frequently owing to an unnecessary enlargement upon every circumstance that offers, as well as to the repetition of the same things. If we have been copious in pleading for spiritual blessings, it may be best to be brief and summary in the article of intercession for others, or if the frame of our spirits, or the circumstances of affairs, lead us to be more large and particular in laying the cases of others before the Lord respect should be had to this intention in the former part of the prayer.

There are, doubtless, seasons when the Lord is pleased to favor those who pray with a peculiar liberty: they speak because they feel; they have a wrestling spirit and hardly know how to leave off. When this is the case, those who join with them are seldom wearied, though the prayer should be protracted something beyond the usual limits. But I believe it sometimes happens, both in praying and in preaching, that we are apt to spin out our time to the greatest length, when we have in reality the least to say. Long prayers should in general be avoided, especially where several persons are to pray successively; or else even spiritual hearers will be unable to keep up their attention. And here I would just notice an impropriety we sometimes meet with, that when a person gives expectation that he is just going to conclude his prayer, something not thought of in its proper place occurring that instant to his mind, leads him as it were to begin again. But unless it is a matter of singular importance, it would be better omitted for that time.

PREACHING IN PRAYERS
The prayers of some good men are more like preaching than praying. They rather express the Lord's mind to the people, than the desires of the people to the Lord. Indeed this can hardly be called prayer. It might in another place stand for part of a good sermon, but will afford little help to those who desire to pray with their hearts. Prayer should be sententious, and made up of breathings to the Lord, either of confession, petition, or praise. It should be not only Scriptural and evangelical, but experimental, a simple and unstudied expression of the wants and feelings of the soul. It will be so if the heart is lively and affected in the duty, it must be so if the edification of others is the point in view.

METHOD IN PRAYER
Several books have been written to assist in the gift and exercise of prayer, and many useful hints may be borrowed from them. But a too close attention to the method therein recommended, gives an air of study and formality, and offends against that simplicity which is so essentially necessary to a good prayer, that

no degree of acquired abilities can compensate for the want of it. It is possible to learn to pray mechanically, and by rule; but it is hardly possible to do so with acceptance and benefit to others. When the several parts of invocation, adoration, confession, petition, etc., follow each other in a stated order, the hearer's mind generally goes before the speaker's voice, and we can form a tolerable conjecture what is to come next. On this account we often find that unlettered people who have had little or no help from books, or rather have not been fettered by them, can pray with an unction and savor in an unpremeditated way, while the prayers of persons of much superior abilities, perhaps even of ministers themselves, are, though accurate and regular, so dry and starched, then they afford little either of pleasure or profit to spiritual mind. The spirit of prayer is the fruit and token of the Spirit of adoption.

The studied addresses with which some approach the throne of grace remind us of a stranger's coming to a great man's door; he knocks and waits, sends in his name, and goes through a course of ceremony, before he gains admittance, while a child of the family uses no ceremony at all, but enters freely when he pleases, because he knows he is at home. It is true, we ought always to draw near the Lord with great humiliation of spirit, and a sense of our unworthiness. But this spirit is not always best expressed or promoted by a pompous enumeration of the names and titles of the God with whom we have to do, or by fixing in our minds beforehand the exact order in which we propose to arrange the several parts of our prayer. Some attention to method may be proper, for the prevention of repetitions; and plain people may be a little defective in it sometimes; but this defect will not be half so tiresome and disagreeable as a studied and artificial exactness.

PECULIARITIES OF MANNER
Many – perhaps most – people who pray in public have some favorite word or expression which recurs too often in their prayers, and is frequently used as a mere expletive, having no necessary connection with the sense of what they are speaking. The most disagreeable of

these is when the name of the blessed God, with the addition perhaps of one or more epithets, as Great, Glorious, Holy, Almighty, etc., is introduced so often and without necessity, as seems neither to indicate a due reverence in the person who uses It, nor suited to excite reverence in those who hear. I will not say that this is taking the Name of God in vain, in the usual sense of the phrase: it is, however, a great impropriety, and should be guarded against. It would be well if they who use redundant expressions had a friend to give them a caution so that they might with a little care be retrenched; and hardly any person can be sensible of the little peculiarities he may inadvertently adopt, unless he is told of them.

There are several things likewise respecting the voice and manner of prayer, which a person may with due care correct in himself, and which, if generally corrected, would make meetings for prayer more pleasant than sometimes they are … Very loud speaking is a fault, when the size of the place and the number of the hearers do not render it necessary. The end of speaking (in public) is to be heard: and when that end is attained a greater elevation of the voice is frequency hurtful to the speaker, and is more likely to confuse a hearer than fix his attention. I do not deny but allowance must be made for constitution, and the warmth of the passions, which dispose some persons to speak louder than others. Yet such will do well to restrain themselves as much as they can. It may seem indeed to indicate great earnestness, and that the heart is much affected; yet it is often but false fire. It may be thought speaking "with power," but a person who is favored with the Lord's presence may pray with power in a moderate voice; and there may be very little of the power of the Spirit, though the voice should be heard in the street and neighborhood.

The other extreme of speaking too low is not so frequent; but, if we are not heard, we might as well altogether hold our peace. It exhausts the spirits and wearies the attention, to be listening for any length of time to a very low voice. Some words or sentences will be lost, which will render what is heard less intelligible and agreeable. If the speaker can be heard by the person furthest distant from him,

the rest will hear of course.

The tone of the voice is likewise to be regarded. Some have a tone in prayer so very different from their usual way of speaking, that their nearest friends, if not accustomed to them, could hardly know them by their voice. Sometimes the tone is changed, perhaps more than once, so that if our eyes did not give us more certain information than our ears, we might think two or three persons had been speaking by turns. It is a pity that when we approve what is spoken we should be so easily disconcerted by an awkwardness of delivery: yet so it often is, and probably so it will be, in the present weak and imperfect state of human nature. It is more to be lamented than wondered at, that sincere Christians are sometimes forced to confess: "He is a good man, and his prayers as to their substance are spiritual and judicious, but there is something so displeasing in his manner that I am always uneasy when I hear him."

INFORMALITY IN PRAYER

Contrary to this, and still more offensive, is a custom that some have of talking to the Lord in prayer. It is their natural voice indeed, but it is that expression of it which they use upon the most familiar and trivial occasions. The human voice is capable of so many inflections and variations, that it can adapt itself to the different sensations of the mind, as joy, sorrow, fear, desire, etc. If a man was pleading for his life, or expressing his thanks to the king for a pardon, common sense and decency would teach him a suitableness of manner; and anyone who could not understand his language might know by the sound of his words that he was not making a bargain or telling a story. How much more, when we speak to the King of kings, should the consideration of his glory and our own vileness, and of the important concerns we are engaged in before him, impress us with an air of seriousness and reverence, and prevent us from speaking to him as if he was altogether such an one as ourselves! The liberty to which we are called by the gospel does not at all encourage such a pertness and familiarity as would be unbecoming to use towards a fellow-worm, who was a little advanced above us in worldly dignity.

I shall be glad if these hints may be of any service to those who desire to worship God in spirit and in truth, and who wish that whatever has a tendency to damp the spirit of devotion, either in themselves or in others, might be avoided.

John Newton, 1725–1807

The Content of Prayer and the Recipient of Prayer

Origen

THE CONTENT OF PRAYER: ITS FOUR MOODS

After thus interpreting the benefactions which have accrued to saints through their prayers, let us turn our attention to the words "ask for the great things and the little shall be added unto you: and ask for the heavenly things and the earthly shall be added unto you." All symbolical and typical things may be described as little and earthly in comparison with the true and the spiritual.

And, I believe, the divine Word, in urging us on to imitate the prayers of the saints, speaks of the heavenly and great things set forth through those concerned with the earthly and little, in order that we may make our requests according to the reality of which their achievements were typical. He says in effect: Do you who would be spiritual ask for the heavenly and great, in order that obtaining in them heavenly things you may inherit a kingdom of heaven, and as obtaining great things you may enjoy the greatest blessings, while as for the earthly and little that you require by reason of your bodily necessities, your Father will supply them to you in due measure.

In the first Epistle to Timothy the Apostle has employed four terms corresponding to four things in close relation to the subject of devotion and prayer. It will therefore be of service to cite his language and see whether we can satisfactorily determine the strict meaning of each of the four. He says, "I exhort therefore first of all that requests, prayers, intercessions, thanksgivings be made on behalf of all men," and so on.

Request I take to be that form of prayer which a man in some need offers with suppli-

cation for its attainment; prayer, that which a man offers in the loftier sense for higher things with ascription of glory; intercession, the addressing of claim to God by a man who possesses a certain fuller confidence; thanksgiving, the prayerful acknowledgment of the attainment of blessings from God, he who returns the acknowledgment being impressed by the greatness, or what seems to the recipient the greatness, of the benefactions conferred. Of the first, examples are found in Gabriel's speech to Zechariah who, it is likely, had prayed for the birth of John: "Fear not, Zechariah, because your request hath been heard and your wife Elizabeth shall beget you a Son and you shall call his name John"; in the account in Exodus of the making of the Calf: "And Moses made request before the Lord God, and said: To what purpose, Lord, art you in anger wroth with your people whom you hast brought out of the land of Egypt in great might?"

In Deuteronomy: "And I made request before the Lord a second time even as also the former time forty days and forty nights bread I ate not and water I drank not for all your sins that you sinned"; and in Esther: "Mordecai made request of God, recalling all the works of the Lord, and said; Lord, Lord, King Almighty," and Esther herself "made request of the Lord God of Israel and said: Lord our King ..." Of the second, examples are found in Daniel: "And Azariah drew himself up and prayed thus, and opening his mouth amid the fire said ... "; and in Tobit: "And with anguish I prayed saying, 'Righteous art you, O Lord, and all your works; all your ways are mercy and truth, and judgment true and righteous dost you judge forever.'" Since however, the circumcised have marked the passage in Daniel spurious as not standing in the Hebrew, and dispute the Book of Tobit as not within the Testament, I shall cite Hannah's case from the first book of Kings.

"And she prayed unto the Lord, and wept exceedingly, and vowed a vow, and said, 'O Lord of Hosts, if you will indeed have regard unto the humiliation of your bondmaid,'" and so on; and in Habakkuk: "A prayer of Habakkuk the prophet, set to song. O Lord, I have hearkened to your voice and was afraid; I did mark your works and was in ecstasy. In the midst of two living beings you shall be known;

as the years draw nigh you shall be fully known"; a prayer which eminently illustrates what I said in defining prayer that it is offered with ascription of glory by the suppliant. And in Jonah also, Jonah prayed unto the Lord his God from the belly of the monster, and said, "I cried in my affliction unto the Lord my God, and he heard me. You heard my wail from the belly of death, my cry; you flung me away into the depths of the heart of the sea, and streams encircled me."

Of the third, we have an example in the Apostle where he with good reason employs prayer in our case, but intercession in that of the Spirit as excelling us and having confidence in approaching Him with whom He intercedes; for as to what we are to pray, he says, "as we ought we know not, but the Spirit Himself more than intercedes with God in sighs unspeakable, and He that searches hearts knows what is the mind of the Spirit because His intercession on behalf of saints is according to God"; for the Spirit more than intercedes, and intercedes, whereas we pray.

What Joshua said concerning the sun's making a stand over against Gabaoth is, I think, also intercession: Then spake Joshua to the LORD in the day when the LORD delivered up the Amorites before the children of Israel, "Here spoke Joshua to the Lord in the day when God delivered up the Amorites before the children of Israel, and he said in the sight of Israel, Sun, stand thou still upon Gibeon; and thou, Moon, in the valley of Ajalon"; and in Judges, it is, I think, in intercession that Samson said, "Let my soul die together with the aliens" when he leaned in might and the house fell upon the princes and upon all the people in it. Even though it is not explicitly said that Joshua and Samson interceded but that they said, their language seems to be intercession, which, if we accept the terms in their strict sense, is in our opinion distinct from prayer.

Of thanksgiving an example is our Lord's utterance when He says: "I make acknowledgment to you, O Father, Lord of heaven and earth, that you did hide these things from the wise and understanding and reveal them to infants"; for I make acknowledgment is equivalent to I give thanks.

THE RECIPIENT OF PRAYER IN ITS FOUR MOODS

Now request and intercession and thanksgiving, it is not out of place to offer even to men – the two latter, intercession and thanksgiving, not only to saintly men but also to others. But request to saints alone, should some Paul or Peter appear, to benefit us by making us worthy to obtain the authority which has been given to them to forgive sins – with this addition indeed that, even should a man not be a saint and we have wronged him, we are permitted our becoming conscious of our sin against him to make request even of such, that he extend pardon to us who have wronged him.

Yet if we are offer thanksgiving to men who are saints, how much more should we give thanks to Christ, who has under the Father's will conferred so many benefactions upon us? Yes and intercede with Him as did Stephen when he said, "Lord, set not this sin against them." In imitation of the father of the lunatic we shall say, "I request, Lord, have mercy" either on my son, or myself, or as the case may be. But if we accept prayer in its full meaning, we may not ever pray to any begotten being, not even to Christ himself, but only to the God and Father of All to whom our Savior both prayed himself, as we have already instanced, and teaches us to pray.

For when He has heard one say. "Teach you us to pray," He does not teach men to pray to Himself but to the Father saying, "Our Father in heaven," and so on. For if, as is shown elsewhere, the Son is other than the Father in being and essence, prayer is to be made either to the Son and not the Father or to both or to the Father alone.

That prayer to the Son and not the Father is most out of place and only to be suggested in defiance of manifest truth, one and all will admit. In prayer to both it is plain that we should have to offer our claims in plural form, and in our prayers say, "Grant you both, Bless you both, Supply you both, Save you both," or the like, which is self-evidently wrong and also incapable of being shown by anyone to stand in the scriptures as spoken by any.

It remains, accordingly, to pray to God alone, the Father of All, not however apart from the High Priest who has been appointed by the Father with swearing of an oath, according to the words He hath sworn and shall not repent, "You art a priest forever after the order of Melchizedek." In thanksgiving to God, therefore, during their prayers, saints acknowledge His favors through Christ Jesus.

Just as the man who is scrupulous about prayer ought not to pray to one who himself prays but to the Father upon whom our Lord Jesus has taught us to call in our prayers, so we are not to offer any prayer to the Father apart from Him. He clearly sets this forth himself when He says, "Verily, verily, I tell you, whatsoever you may ask of my Father He shall give you in my house. Until but now you have not asked aught in my name. Ask and you shall receive, that your joy may be fulfilled."

He did not say, "Ask of me," nor yet simply "Ask of the father," but "Whatsoever you may ask of the Father, He will give you in my name." For until Jesus taught this, no one had asked of the Father in the name of the Son. True was the saying of Jesus, "Until but now you have not asked aught in my name"; and true also the words, "Ask and you shall receive, that your joy may be fulfilled." Should anyone, however who believes that prayer ought to be made to Christ himself, confused by the sense of the expression make obeisance, confront us with that acknowledged reference to Christ in Deuteronomy, "Let all God's angels make obeisance to Him," we may reply to him that the church, called Jerusalem by the prophet, is also said to have obeisance made to her by kings and queens who become her foster sires and nurses, in the words, "Behold, I lift up my hand upon the nations, and upon the isles will I lift up my sign: and they shall bring your sons in their bosom and your daughters they shall lift up on their shoulders; and kings shall be your foster sires, their queens they nurses: to the face of the earth shall they make obeisance to you, and the dust of your feet shall they lick: and you shall know that I am the Lord and shall not be ashamed."

And how does it not accord with Him who said, "Why callest you me good? None is good save One – God the Father" to suppose that He would say, "Why pray you to me? To the Father alone ought you to pray, to whom I also pray, as indeed you learn from the holy Scriptures. For you ought not to pray to one who has been appointed high priest for you by the Father and has received it from the Father to be advocate, but through a high priest and advocate able to sympathize with your weaknesses, having been tried in all points like you but, by reason of the Father's free gift to me, tried without sin.

Learn you therefore how great a free gift you have received from my Father in having received through regeneration in me the Spirit of adoption, that you may be called sons of God and my brethren. For you have read my utterance spoken through David to the Father concerning you, "I will proclaim your name to my brethren; in the midst of the church will I sing hymns to you." It is not reasonable that those who have been counted worthy of one common Father should pray to a brother. To the Father alone ought you, with me and through me, to send up prayer."

So then hearing Jesus speak to such effect, let us pray to God through Him, all with one accord and without division concerning the manner of prayer. Are we not indeed divided if we pray some to the Father, others to the Son – those who pray to the Son, whether with the Father or without the Father, committing a crude error in all simplicity for lack of discrimination and examination?

Let us therefore pray as to God, intercede as with a Father, request as of a Lord, give thanks as to God and Father and Lord, though in no way as to a servant's lord; for the Father may reasonably be considered Lord not only of the Son but also of those who through Him are become sons also, though, just as He is not God of dead but of living men, so He is not Lord of baseborn servants but of such as at the first are ennobled by means of fear because they are as infants, but serve thereafter according to love in a service more blessed than that which is in fear. For within the soul itself, visible to the Seer of Hearts alone, these are distinctive characters of servants and sons of God.

Origen, 185 – 254

Our Father in Heaven

Origen

OUR FATHER IN HEAVEN

It deserves a somewhat careful observation of the so-called Old Testament to discover whether it is possible to find anywhere in it a prayer of one who addresses God as Father. For though I have made examination to the best of my ability, I have up to the present failed to find one. I do not say that God is not spoken of as Father or that accounted believers in God are not called sons of God, but that I have not yet found in prayer that confidence in calling God Father which the Savior has proclaimed.

That God is spoken of as Father and those who have waited on God's word as sons, may be seen in many places, as in Deuteronomy, "You have forsaken God your parent and forgotten God your nourisher," and again, "Is He not your Father himself that got you and made you and created you?" and again, "Sons who have not faith in them." And in Isaiah, "I have nourished and brought up children, and they have rebelled against me"; and in Malachi, "A son honors his father, and a servant his master: if then I be a father, where is my honor? and if I be a master, where is my fear?" So then, even though God is termed Father and their Sons who have been begotten by reason of their faith in Him, yet sure and unchangeable sonship is not to be seen in the ancient people.

The very passages I have cited since the subjection of those so-called sons, since according to the apostle "the heir, as long as he is a child, differs nothing from a servant, though he be lord of all; But is under tutors and governors until the time appointed of the father." But the fullness of time is in the sojourn of our Lord Jesus Christ, when they who desire receive adoption as sons, as Paul teaches in the words, "For you did not receive a spirit of slavery unto fear, but you received a spirit of adoption as sons, wherein we cry 'Abba Father'"; and as it is in the Gospel according to John, "To as many as received Him He gave authority to become children of God if believers on His name"; and it is by reason of this Spirit of adoption as sons, we learn in the Catholic Epistle of John regarding the begotten of God, that

"Everyone that is begotten of God does no sin because His seed abides in him, and he cannot sin because he is begotten of God."

And yet if we think of the meaning of the words which are written in Luke, "When you pray say: Father … ," we shall hesitate to address this expression to Him unless we have become genuine sons in case, in addition to our other sins, we should also become liable to a charge of impiety. My meaning is as follows. In the first Epistle to Corinthians Paul says, "No one can say 'Jesus is Lord' save in a holy spirit, and no one that speaks in God's spirit says 'cursed be Jesus' calling the same thing a holy spirit and God's spirit." What is meant by speaking in a holy spirit of Jesus as Lord is not quite clear, as countless actors and numbers of heterodox people, and at times even demons conquered by the power in the name, utter the expression.

No one therefore will venture to declare that anyone of these calls Jesus "Lord" in a holy spirit. For the same reason, indeed, they could not be shown to call Jesus Lord at all, since they alone call Jesus Lord who express it from inward disposition in service to the word of God and in proclaiming no other Lord than Him in all their conduct. And if it be such who say Jesus is Lord, it may be that everyone who sins, in that he curses the divine Word through his transgression, has through his actions called out, "Cursed be Jesus."

And accordingly, as the one type of man says "Jesus is Lord," and the man of opposite disposition "Cursed be Jesus," "so everyone that hath been begotten of God and does not sin" because he is partaker of God's seed which turns him from all sin, says through his conduct "Our Father in Heaven," the spirit himself witnessing with their spirit that they are children of God and heirs to Him and joint heirs with Christ, since as suffering with Him they reasonably hope with Him also to be glorified. But in order that theirs may be no one-sided utterance of the words "Our Father," in addition to their actions they have a heart – a fountain and source of good actions – believing unto righteousness, in harmony with which their mouth makes acknowledgment unto salvation.

So then their every act and word and

thought, formed by the only begotten word in accord with Him, imitates the image of the invisible God and has come to be "in accordance with the image of the Creator" who makes "the sun to rise upon evil men and good and rains upon righteous and unrighteous," that there may be in them the image of the heavenly One who is himself also an image of God. Saints, therefore, as an image of an Image himself, a son, receive the impress of Sonship, becoming conformed not only to the glorified body of Christ but also to Him who is in that body, and they become conformed to Him who is in a glorified body through being transformed by the renewing of their mind.

And if such men through out the whole of life voice the words "Our Father in the Heavens," plainly he that does sin, as John says in the Catholic Epistle, "is of the devil because the devil sins from the beginning" and just as God's seed abiding in the begotten of God produces inability to sin in him who is formed in accordance with the only begotten Word, so the devil's seed is in everyone that does sin, to the extent in which it is present within the soul – not suffering its possessor to have power to prosper. But since "for this end was the Son of God manifested that He might undo the actions of the devil," it is possible, through the undoing of the actions of the devil by the sojourn of the Word of God within our Soul, for the evil seed implanted in us to be utterly removed and for us to become children of God.

Let us, therefore, not think that it is words we are taught to say in any appointed season of prayer. On the contrary, if we understand our former consideration of prayer without ceasing, let our whole life of prayer without ceasing speak the words "Our Father in the Heavens," having its commonwealth in no wise on earth but in every way in heaven, which is God's throne because of the foundation of the kingdom of God in all who wear the image of the Heavenly One and therefore become heavenly. When the Father of saints is said to be in the heavens, we are not to suppose that He is circumscribed by material form and dwells in heaven.

Since, in that case, as contained God will be formed to be less than the heavens because they contain Him, whereas the ineffable might of His godhead demands our belief that all things are contained and held together by Him. And, in general, passages which taken literally are thought by the simpler order of minds to assert that God is in space are to be otherwise taken in a sense more becoming to great spiritual concepts of God.

Such are those passages in the Gospel according to John: Before the feast of the Passover, Jesus, knowing that His hour had come that He should pass from this world to the Father, as He had loved His own who were in the world, loved them to the end; and shortly after: knowing that the Father had given all into His hands, and that He had come forth from God and was returning to God; and later: you heard that I said to you: I return and come unto you. If you loved me you would have rejoiced that I go to the Father; and again later; Now I return to Him that sent me and none of you asks me: Where do you return?

If these things are to be taken spacially, so also plainly is: Jesus answered and said to them, "If any one love me he will keep my word and my Father will love him and we shall come unto him and make abode with him." But surely the words do not imply a spacial transition of the Father and the Son to the lover of the word of Jesus and are therefore not to be taken spacially.

On the contrary, the Word of God, in condescension for us and, in regard to His proper desert, in humiliation while among men, is said to pass from this world unto the Father so that we also may behold Him perfectly there in reversion to His proper fullness from the emptiness among us whereby He emptied himself – where we also, enjoying His guidance, shall be filled and freed from all emptiness. To such an end the Word of God well may leave the world and depart to Him that sent Him, and go to the Father! And as for that passage near the end of the Gospel according to John, "Cling not to me, for I am not yet gone up unto my Father," let us seek to conceive it in the more mystical sense:

Let ours be the more reverent conception of the ascension of the Son to the Father with sanctified insight, an ascension rather of soul than of body. I think it right to have linked these considerations to the clause Our Father in the Heavens for the sake of doing away with a low conception of God held by those who think that He is in heaven spacially, and of preventing anyone from saying God is in material space since it follows that He also is physical, which leads to opinions most impious\ – to belief that He is divisible and material and corruptible. For every material thing is divisible and corruptible.

Or else let them tell us, not on the strength of vague sensation but with a claim to clear understanding, how it can be of any other than a material nature. Since, then, in writings before Christ's bodily sojourn there are also many statements which seem to say that God is in physical space, it appears to me to be not out of place to cite a few of them also for the sake of doing away with any doubt in those who, because they know no better, confine God, who is over all, within small and scanty space on their own scale. First, in Genesis it says Adam and Eve heard the sound of the lord God walking at evening in the garden, and both Adam and his wife hid themselves from the Lord God amid the wood of the Garden.

I shall put the question to those who not only refuse to enter into the treasures of the passage but do not so much as knock at all at its door, whether they are able to imagine the Lord God, who fills the heaven and the earth, who as they themselves suppose in the more physical sense uses heaven as throne and the earth as a footstool for His feet, as contained by so scanty a space in comparison with the whole heaven and the earth that a garden which they suppose to be material is not filled by God but so far exceeds Him in greatness as to hold Him even when walking while a sound from the tread of His feet is heard? Absurder still on their interpretation is the hiding of Adam and Eve, in fear of God by reason of their transgression, from before God amid the wood of the Garden.

For it is not even said that they merely desired to hide but that they actually hid themselves. And how is it in their view that God inquires of Adam saying: Where are you? I have discussed these matters at greater length in my examination of the contents of Genesis, yet here, too – in order not to pass by so grave

a subject in complete silence – it will suffice if I recall what is said by God in Deuteronomy: I will dwell in them and walk in them. For as is His walk in saints such is His walk in the Garden also, since everyone that sins hides from God and shuns His oversight and renounces his confidence with Him. So it was that Cain also went out from before God and dwelt in the land of Nod over against Eden. In the same way, therefore, as He dwells in saints.

So also does He dwell in heaven (that is, in every saint who wears the image of the Heavenly One, or Christ, in whom all who are being saved are luminaries and stars of heaven, or else because saints are in heaven) according to the saying: Unto you who dwells in heaven have I lifted up my eyes. And yet the passage in Ecclesiastes: Be not in haste to utter speech before God, because God is in heaven above, and you on Earth below, means to show the interval which separates those who are in the body of humiliation from Him who is with the angels and holy powers who are being exalted by the help of the Word also and with Christ himself. For it is not unreasonable that He should be strictly at the Father's throne, allegorically called heaven, while His church, termed Earth, is a footstool at His feet.

I have cited a few Old Testament utterances, thought to represent God in space, for the sake of urging the reader by every means within the power given me to accept the divine scripture in the higher and more spiritual sense whenever it seems to teach that God is in space. And it was fitting that these considerations should be linked to the clause Our Father in the Heavens inasmuch as it distinguishes the essence of God from all created beings. For it is upon such as do not share in that essence that a certain glory of God and a power from Him, an outflow of the deity, comes.

Origen, 185 – 254

Principles of Effective Intercession
Arthur T. Pierson

We venture to suggest a few thoughts on prayer, which embody some of our most mature convictions upon this great subject, and are suggested alike by Scripture teaching and by the experience of praying saints.

Give yourself to the Lord anew as an intercessor, to undertake and fulfill in yourself all the conditions requisite to your becoming a perfect channel of blessing; and to put to the proof the promise: "If you abide in Me and My words abide in you, you shall ask what you desire, and it shall be done for you." (John 15:7).

Consider well before you put any object or person before you in prayer; whether it is according to the will of God; whether you can claim for your request a definite promise, whether it is laid as a burden on your heart by the spirit of prayer, and having so determined, never cease praying till you have the answer, or at least the assurance of answer.

Unite with you in prayer, one or more of the most devout disciples, especially in critical cases. One great advantage is that selfishness is apt to color our supplications, and when others are united with us, they are less affected by motives that may unduly influence us.

You may be sure that there is no truer index of what you are spiritually than is found in what you habitually desire and yearn for, and this will naturally find expression in your secret prayer habit.

No matter what prayer has secured, attained or achieved for us, boundless possibilities still lie before us. It may be doubted whether we have yet touched more than the fringe of the garment of a prayer-hearing God. We come timid and trembling, when we ought to come boldly and confidently. We ask but little, where we should only honor God by making large demands.

In praying do not think of yourself as knocking at a closed door. Christ's dying cry rent the veil in two, and opened up both to vision and entrance the holy of holies with the mercy seat. Let us come boldly to a throne of grace. God is not a reluctant God, needing to be besieged like a walled city, which must be compelled to capitulate. Let us not spell beseech, besiege.

Do not forget that others for whom you are praying may get more comfort from your intercession than you get out of it.

The injunction to pray is not one but seven. It is in effect a command to acquaint thyself with God, to be conformed to His image, to keep yourself in His love, to study to show thyself approved unto Him, to be a co-worker together with God, to taste and see that the Lord is good, to commission Him concerning the work of His hands.

The greatest obstacle to the conversion of men is not any barrier in them so much as a barrier in us. The church as a corporate body, have never yet accepted, intelligently, lovingly, joyfully and confidently, the promises of God to praying souls.

The true intercessor learns to claim blessing. He sees all good provided and ready, and he comes to it as a hungry child to his father's table, not to ask to be fed, but to help himself to what his father's love has spread before him.

Seek first the kingdom of God and His righteousness, Put first things first, and God will add the secondary things without you seeking them. In such a sublime transaction as giving yourself to God – body, soul and spirit, He throws in "all these things" as if not even worthy to be counted or mentioned (Mt 6:33).

Cultivate a holy calm as a preparation for private prayer, as a lake while it is ruffled, can not reflect the over-arching heavens; so your heart while disturbed and distracted, can not reflect the face of God. Wait before God until you are at peace.

Spiritual guides for those who yearn for greater power to prevail in prayer. First, we call renewed attention to the great fundamental conditions of acceptable and effective supplication, which should always be kept before them:

Renunciation of all known sin. "If I regard iniquity in my heart, the Lord will not hear me," Psalm 66:18.

A spirit of forgiveness. "When you stand praying, forgive, if you have aught against any," Mark 11:25.

The confidence of faith. "Whatever things you desire when you pray, believe that you receive them," Mark 11:24.

A spiritual motive. "You ask and receive not, because you ask amiss, that you may consume it upon your lusts," James 4:3.

"In Jesus' name." "If you shall ask anything in my name, I will do it," John 14:13, 14; 16:23.

According to God's will. "If we ask anything according to His will He hears us," 1 John 5:14.

Some conspicuous promises which fortify our feeble faith!

The promptness of Divine help. "Before they call I will answer; and while they are yet speaking, I will hear," Isaiah 65:24.

The possibilities of faith. "If thou will believe, all things are possible to him that believes," Mark 9:23.

Abiding union with Christ. "If you abide in me, and my words abide in you, you shall ask what you will, and it shall be done unto you," John 15:7.

God's immeasurable ability. "Able to do exceedingly abundantly above all we ask or think," Eph. 3:20.

The riches in glory. "My God shall supply all your need according to His riches in glory by Christ Jesus," Phil. 4:19.

Agreement in prayer. "If two of you agree on earth as touching anything that they shall ask, it shall be done for them by my Father who is in heaven," Matt. 18:19.

A. T. Pierson

A Call to Prayer

J.C. Ryle

"Men ought always to pray" Luke 18:1.
"I will that men pray everywhere" 1 Timothy 2:8.

Prayer is the most important subject in practical religion. All other subjects are second to it. Reading the Bible, keeping the Sabbath, hearing sermons, attending public worship, going to the Lord's Table, all these are very weighty matters. But none of them are so important as private prayer.

I propose in this paper to offer plain reasons why I use such strong language about prayer. I invite to these reasons the attention of every thinking man into whose hands this paper may fall. I venture to assert with confidence that they deserve serious consideration.

1. IN THE FIRST PLACE, PRAYER IS ABSOLUTELY NEEDFUL TO A MAN'S SALVATION

I say absolutely needful, and I say so advisedly.

I am not speaking now of infants and idiots. I am not settling the state of the heathen. I remember that where little is given, there little will be required. I speak especially of those who call themselves Christians, in a land like our own. And of such I say no man or woman can expect to be saved who does not pray.

I hold salvation by grace as strongly as any one. I would gladly offer a free and full pardon to the greatest sinner that ever lived. I would not hesitate to stand by his dying bed, and say, "Believe on the Lord Jesus Christ even now, and you shall he saved." But that a man can have salvation without asking for it, I cannot see in the Bible. That a man will receive pardon of his sins, who will not so much as lift up his heart inwardly, and say, "Lord Jesus, give it to me," this I cannot find. I can find that nobody will be saved by his prayers, but I cannot find that without prayer anybody will be saved.

There will be many at Christ's right hand in the last day. The saints gathered from North and South, and East and West, will be "a multitude that no man can number" (Rev. 7:9). The song of victory that will burst from their mouths, when their redemption is at length complete, will be a glorious song indeed. It will be far above the noise of many waters, and of mighty thunders. But there will be no discord in that song. They that sing will sing with one heart as well as one voice. Their experience will be one and the same. All will have believed. All will have been washed in the blood of Christ. All will have been born again. All will have prayed. Yes, we must pray on earth, or we shall never praise in heaven. We must go through the school of prayer, or we shall never be fit for the holiday of praise. In short, to be prayerless is to be without God, – without Christ, – without grace, – without hope, – and without heaven. It is to be in the road to hell.

2. IN THE SECOND PLACE, A HABIT OF PRAYER IS ONE OF THE SUREST MARKS OF A TRUE CHRISTIAN

All the children of God on earth are alike in this respect. From the moment there is any life and reality about their religion, they pray. Just as the first sign of life in an infant when born into the world, is the act of breathing, so the first act of men and women when they are born again, is praying.

This is one of the common marks of all the elect of God; "They cry unto Him day and night" (Luke 18:1). The Holy Spirit, who makes them new creatures, works in them the feeling of adoption, and makes them cry, "Abba, Father" (Rom. 7:15). The Lord Jesus, when He quickens them, gives them a voice and a tongue, and says to them, "Be dumb no more." God has no dumb children. It is as much a part of their new nature to pray, as it is of a child to cry. They see their need of mercy and grace. They feel their emptiness and weakness. They cannot do otherwise than they do. They must pray.

I have looked carefully over the lives of God's saints in the Bible. I cannot find one of whose history much is told us, from Genesis to Revelation, who was not a man of prayer. I find it mentioned as a characteristic of the godly, that "they call on the Father," that "they call on the name of the Lord Jesus Christ." I find it recorded as a characteristic of the wicked, that "they call not upon the Lord" (1 Peter 1:17; 1 Cor. 1:2; Psalm 14:4).

I have read the lives of many eminent Christians who have been on earth since the Bible days. Some of them, I see, were rich, and some poor. Some were learned, and some unlearned. Some of them were Episcopalians, some Presbyterians, some Baptists, some Independents. Some were Calvinists, and some Arminians. Some have loved to use a liturgy, and some to use none. But one thing, I see, they all had in common. They have all been men of prayer.

I study the reports of Missionary Societies in our own times. I see with joy that heathen men and women are receiving the Gospel in various parts of the globe. There are conversions in Africa, in New Zealand, in Hindostan, in America. The people converted are naturally unlike one another in every respect. But one striking thing I observe at all the Missionary stations. The converted people always pray.

I do not deny that a man may pray without heart, and without sincerity. I do not for a moment pretend to say that the mere fact of a person praying proves everything about his soul. As in every other part of religion, so also in this, there is plenty of deception and hypocrisy.

But this I do say, – that not praying is a clear proof that a man is not yet a true Christian. He cannot really feel his sins. He cannot love God. He cannot feel himself a debtor to Christ. He cannot long after holiness. He cannot desire heaven. He has yet to be born again. He has yet to be made a new creature. He may boast confidently of election, grace, faith, hope, and knowledge, and deceive ignorant people. But you may rest assured it is all vain talk if he does not pray.

And I say furthermore, that of all the evidences of real work of the Spirit, a habit of hearty private prayer is one of the most satisfactory that can be named. A man may preach from false motives. A man may write books, and make fine speeches, and seem diligent in good works, and yet be a Judas Iscariot. But a man seldom goes into his closet, and pours out his soul before God in secret, unless he is in earnest. The Lord Himself has set His stamp on prayer as the best proof of a true conversion. When He sent Ananias to Saul in Damascus, He gave him no other evidence of his change of heart than this, – "Behold, he prayeth" (Acts 9:11).

I know that much may go on in a man's mind before he is brought to pray. He may have many convictions, desires, wishes, feelings, intentions, resolutions, hopes, and fears. But all these things are very uncertain evidences. They are to be found in ungodly people, and often come to nothing. In many a case they are not more lasting than "the morning cloud, and the dew that goeth away" (Hos. 6: 4). A real hearty prayer, flowing from a broken and contrite spirit, is worth all these things put together.

I know that the elect of God are chosen to salvation from all eternity. I do not forget that the Holy Spirit, who calls them in due time, in many instances leads them by very slow degrees to acquaintance with Christ. But the eye of man can only judge by what it sees. I cannot call any one justified until he believes. I dare not say that any one believes until he prays. I cannot understand a dumb faith. The first act of faith will be to speak to God. Faith is to the soul what life is to the body. Prayer is to faith what breath is to life. How a man can live and not breathe is past my comprehension, and how a man can believe and not pray is past my comprehension too.

Let no one be surprised if he hears ministers of the Gospel dwelling much on the importance of prayer. This is the point we want to bring you to, – we want to know that you pray. Your views of doctrine may be correct. Your love of Protestantism may be warm and unmistakable. But still this may be nothing more than head knowledge and party spirit. The great point is this, – whether you can speak to God as well as speak about God.

(1) Let me speak a word to those who do not pray

I dare not suppose that all who read these pages will be praying people. If you are a prayerless person, suffer me to speak to you this day on God's behalf.

Prayerless friend, I can only warn you; but I do warn you most solemnly. I warn you that you are in a position of fearful danger. If you die in your present state you are a lost soul. You will only rise again to be eternally miserable. I warn you that of all professing Christians you are most utterly without excuse. There is not a single good reason that you can show for living without prayer.

It is useless to say you know not how to pray. Prayer is the simplest act in all religion. It is simply speaking to God. It needs neither learning, nor wisdom, nor book-knowledge to begin it. It needs nothing but heart and will. The weakest infant can cry when he is hungry. The poorest beggar can hold out his hand for an alms, and does not wait to find fine words. The most ignorant man will find something to say to God, if he has only a mind.

It is useless to say you have no convenient place to pray in. Any man can find a place private enough, if he is disposed. Our Lord prayed on a mountain; Peter on the house-top; Isaac in the field; Nathanael under the fig-tree; Jonah in the whale's belly. Any place may become a closet, an oratory, and a Bethel, and be to us the presence of God.

It is useless to say you have no time. There is plenty of time, if men will only employ it. Time may be short, but time is always long enough for prayer. Daniel had all the affairs of a kingdom on his hands, and yet he prayed three times a day. David was ruler over a mighty nation, and yet he says, "Evening and morning and at noon will I pray" (Psalm 55:17). When time is really wanted, time can always be found.

It is useless to say you cannot pray till you have faith and a new heart, and that you must sit still and wait for them. This is to add sin to sin. It is bad enough to be unconverted and going to hell. It is even worse to say, "I know it, but I will not cry for mercy." This is a kind of argument for which there is no warrant in Scripture. " Call ye upon the Lord," saith Isaiah, "while He is near" (Isaiah 55:6). "Take with you words, and come unto the Lord," says Hosea (Hosea 14:1). "Repent and pray," says Peter to Simon Magus (Acts 8:22); if you want faith and a new heart, go and cry to the Lord for them. The very attempt to pray has often been the quickening of a dead soul. Alas, there is no devil so dangerous as a dumb devil.

Oh, prayerless man, who and what are you that you will not ask anything of God? Have you made a covenant with death and hell? Are you at peace with the worm and the fire? Have you no sins to be pardoned? Have you no fear of eternal torment? Have you no desire after heaven? Oh, that you would awake from your present folly! Oh, that you would consider your latter end! Oh, that you would arise and call upon God! Alas, there is a day coming when men shall pray loudly, "Lord, Lord, open to us," but all too late; – when many shall cry to the rocks to fall on them, and the hills to cover them, who would never cry to God. In all affection I warn you. Beware lest this be the end of your soul. Salvation is very near you. Do not lose heaven for want of asking.

(2) Let me speak, lastly, to those who do pray

I trust that some who read this paper know well what prayer is, and have the Spirit of adoption. To all such I offer a few words of brotherly counsel and exhortation. The incense offered in the tabernacle was ordered to be made in a particular way. Not every kind of incense would do. Let us remember this, and be careful about the matter and manner of our prayers.

If I know anything of a Christian's heart, you to whom I now speak are often sick of your own prayers. You never enter into the

Apostle's words, "When I would do good, evil is present with me" (Rom. 7:21), so thoroughly as you sometimes do upon your knees. You can understand David's words, "I hate vain thoughts." You can sympathize with that poor converted Hottentot, who was overheard praying, "Lord, deliver me from all my enemies; and, above all, from that bad man myself!" – There are few children of God who do not often find the season of prayer a season of conflict. The devil has special wrath against us when he sees us on our knees. Yet I believe that prayers which cost us no trouble should be regarded with great suspicion. I believe we are very poor judges of the goodness of our prayers, and that the prayer which pleases us least often pleases God most. Suffer me then, as a companion in the Christian warfare, to offer you a few words of exhortation. One thing, at least, we all feel, – we must pray. We cannot give it up: we must go on.

(a) I commend, then, to your attention the importance of reverence and humility in prayer. Let us never forget what we are, and what a solemn thing it is to speak with God. Let us beware of rushing into His presence with carelessness and levity. Let us say to ourselves, "I am on holy ground. This is no other than the gate of heaven. If I do not mean what I say, I am trifling with God. If I regard iniquity in my heart, the Lord will not hear me." Let us keep in mind the words of Solomon: "Be not rash with thy mouth, and let not thine heart be hasty to utter anything before God; for God is in heaven, and thou on earth" (Eccles. 5:2). When Abraham spoke to God, he said, "I am dust and ashes." When Job spoke, he said, "I am vile" (Gen. 18:27; Job 40:4). Let us do likewise.

(b) I commend to you, in the next place, the importance of praying spiritually. I mean by this that we should labor always to have the direct help of the Spirit in our prayers, and beware above all things of formality. There is nothing so spiritual but that it may become a form, and this is specially true of private prayer. We may insensibly get into the habit of using the fittest possible words, and offering the most Scriptural petitions; and yet we may do it all by rote, without feeling it, and walk daily round an old beaten path, like a horse in a mill. I desire to touch this point with caution and delicacy. I know that there are certain great things we daily want, and that there is nothing necessarily formal in asking for these things in the same words. The world, the devil, and our hearts, are daily the same. Of necessity we must daily go over old ground. But this I say, – we must be very careful on this point. If the skeleton and outline of our prayers be by habit almost a form, let us strive that the clothing and filling up of our prayers be as far as possible of the Spirit. As to praying out of a book, it is a habit I cannot praise. If we can tell our doctors the state of our bodies without a book, we ought to be able to tell the state of our souls to God. I have no objection to a man using crutches, when he is first recovering from a broken limb. It is better to use crutches than not to walk at all. But if I saw him all his life on crutches, I should not think it matter for congratulation. I should like to see him strong enough to throw his crutches away.

(c) I commend to you, in the next place, the importance of making prayer a regular business of life. I might say something of the value of regular times in the day for prayer. God is a God of order. The hours for morning and evening sacrifice in the Jewish temple were not fixed as they were without a meaning. Disorder is eminently one of the fruits of sin. But I would not bring any under bondage. This only I say, that it is essential to your soul's health to make praying a part of the business of every twenty-four hours in your life. Just as you allot time to eating, sleeping, and business, so also allot time to prayer. Choose your own hours and seasons. At the very least, speak with God in the morning, before you speak with the world; and speak with God at night, after you have done with the world. But settle it down in your minds that prayer is one of the great things of every day. Do not drive it into a corner. Do not give it the scraps, and leavings, and parings of your day. Whatever else you make a business of, make a business of prayer.

(d) I commend to you, in the next place, the importance of perseverance in prayer. Once having begun the habit, never give it up. Your heart will sometimes say, "We have had family prayers; what mighty harm if we leave private prayer undone?" – Your body will sometimes say. "You are unwell, or sleepy, or weary; you need not pray." – Your mind will sometimes say, "You have important business to attend to to-day: cut short your prayers." Look on all such suggestions as coming direct from the devil. They are all as good as saying, "Neglect your soul." I do not maintain that prayers should always be of the same length; – but I do say, let no excuse make you give up prayer. It is not for nothing that Paul said, "Continue in prayer," and "Pray without ceasing" (Colos. 4:2; 1 Thess. 5:17). He did not mean that men should be always on their knees, as an old sect, called the Euchite, supposed. But he did mean that our prayers should be like the continual burnt offering, – a thing steadily persevered in every day; – that it should be like seed-time and harvest, and summer and winter, – a thing that should unceasingly come round at regular seasons; – that it should be like the fire on the altar, not always consuming sacrifices, but never completely going out. Never forget that you may tie together morning and evening devotions by an endless chain of short ejaculatory prayers throughout the day. Even in company, or business, or in the very streets, you may be silently sending up little winged messengers to God, as Nehemiah did in the very presence of Artaxerxes (Neh. 2:4). And never think that time is wasted which is given to God. A nation does not become poorer because it loses one year of working days in seven by keeping the Sabbath. A Christian never finds he is a loser in the long run by persevering in prayer.

(e) I commend to you, in the next place, the importance of earnestness in prayer. It is not necessary that a man should shout, or scream, or be very loud, in order to prove that he is in earnest. But it is desirable that we should be hearty, and fervent, and warm, and ask as if we were really interested in what we were doing. It is the "effectual fervent" prayer that "availeth much," and not the cold, sleepy, lazy, listless one. This is the lesson that is taught us by the expressions used in Scripture about prayer. It is called, "crying, knocking, wrestling, laboring, striving." This is the lesson taught us by Scripture examples. Jacob is one. He said to the angel at Peniel, "I will not let thee go, except thou bless me" (Gen. 32:26). Daniel is another.

Hear how he pleaded with God: "O Lord, hear; O Lord, forgive; O Lord, hearken and do; defer not, for thine own sake, O my God" (Dan. 9:19). Our Lord Jesus Christ is another. It is written of Him, "In the days of His flesh He offered up prayer and supplication, with strong crying and tears" (Heb. 5:7). Alas, how unlike is this to many of our supplications! How tame and lukewarm they seem by comparison! How truly might God say to many of us, "You do not really want what you pray for!" Let us try to amend this fault. Let us knock loudly at the donor of grace, like Mercy in "Pilgrim's Progress," as if we must perish unless heard. Let us settle it down in our minds, that cold prayers are a sacrifice without fire. Let us remember the story of Demosthenes, the great orator, when one came to him, and wanted him to plead his cause. He heard him without attention, while he told his story without earnestness. The man saw this, and cried out with anxiety that it was all true. "Ah!" said Demosthenes, "I believe you now."

(f) I commend to you, in the next place, the importance of praying with faith. We should endeavor to believe that our prayers are always heard, and that if we ask things according to God's will, we shall always be answered. This is the plain command of our Lord Jesus Christ: "Whatsoever things ye desire, when ye pray, believe that ye receive them, and ye shall have them" (Mark 11:24). Faith is to prayer what the feather is to the arrow; without it prayer will not hit the mark. We should cultivate the habit of pleading promises in our prayers. We should take with us some promise, and say, "Lord, here is Thine own word pledged. Do for us as Thou hast said" (2 Sam. 7:25) .This was the habit of Jacob, and Moses, and David. The 119th Psalm is full of things asked, "according to Thy word." Above all, we should cultivate the habit of expecting answers to our prayers. We should do like the merchant who sends his ships to sea. We should not be satisfied unless we see some return. Alas, there are few points on which Christians come short so much as this. The Church at Jerusalem made prayer without ceasing for Peter in prison; but when the prayer was answered, they would hardly believe it (Acts 12:15). It is a solemn saying of old Traill's, "There is no surer mark of trifling in prayer, than when men are careless what they get by prayer."

(g) I commend to you, in the next place, the importance of boldness in prayer. There is an unseemly familiarity in some men's prayers, which I cannot praise. But there is such a thing as a holy boldness, which is exceedingly to be desired. I mean such boldness as that of Moses, when he pleads with God not to destroy Israel: Wherefore," says he, "should the Egyptians speak and say, For mischief did He bring them out, to slay them in the mountains? Turn from Thy fierce anger" (Exod. 32:12). I mean such boldness as that of Joshua, when the children of Israel were defeated before Ai: "What," says he, "wilt Thou do unto Thy great name?" (Josh. 7:9). This is the boldness for which Luther was remarkable. One who heard him praying said, "What a spirit, – what a confidence was in his very expressions! With such a reverence he sued, as one begging of God, and yet with such hope and assurance as if he spake with a loving father or friend." This is the boldness which distinguished Bruce, a great Scotch divine of the 17th century. His prayers were said to be "like bolts shot up into heaven." Here also I fear we sadly come short. We do not sufficiently realize the believer's privileges. We do not plead as often as we might, "Lord, are we not Thine own people? Is it not for Thy glory that we should be sanctified? Is it not for Thine honor that thy Gospel should increase?"

(h) I commend to you, in the next place, the importance of fullness in prayer. I do not forget that our Lord warns us against the example of the Pharisees, who for pretense made long prayers, and commands us, when we pray, not to use vain repetitions. But I cannot forget, on the other hand, that He has given His own sanction to large and long devotions, by continuing all night in prayer to God. At all events we are not likely in this day to err on the side of praying too much. Might it not rather be feared that many believers in this generation pray too little? Is not the actual amount of time that many Christians give to prayer in the aggregate very small? I am afraid these questions cannot be answered satisfactorily. I am afraid the private devotions of many are most painfully scanty and limited, – just enough to prove they are alive, and no more.

They really seem to want little from God. They seem to have little to confess, little to ask for, and little to thank Him for. Alas, this is altogether wrong! Nothing is more common than to hear believers complaining that they do not get on. They tell us that they do not grow in grace, as they could desire. Is it not rather to be suspected that many have quite as much grace as they ask for? Is it not the true account of many, that they have little, because they ask little? The cause of their weakness is to be found in their own stunted, dwarfish, clipped, contracted, hurried, little, narrow, diminutive prayers. They have not because they ask not. Oh, reader, we are not straitened in Christ, but in ourselves. The Lord says, "Open thy mouth wide, and I will fill it." But we are like the king of Israel who smote on the ground thrice and stayed, when he ought to have smitten five or six times (Psalm 81:10; 2 Kings 13:18, 19).

(i) I commend to you, in the next place, the importance of particularity in prayer. We ought not to be content with great general petitions. We ought to specify our wants before the throne of grace. It should not be enough to confess we are sinners. We should name the sins of which our conscience tells us we are most guilty. It should not be enough to ask for holiness. We should name the graces in which we feel most deficient. It should not be enough to tell the Lord we are in trouble. We should describe our trouble and all its peculiarities. This is what Jacob did, when he feared his brother Esau. He tells God exactly what it is that he fears (Gen. 32:11). This is what Abraham's servant did, when he sought a wife for his master's son. He spreads before God precisely what he wants (Gen. 24:12). This is what Paul did, when he had a thorn in the flesh. He besought the Lord (2 Cor. 12:8). This is true faith and confidence. We should believe that nothing is too small to be named before God. What should we think of the patient who told his doctor he was ill, but never went into particulars? What should we think of the wife who told her husband she was unhappy, but did not specify the cause? What should we think of the child who told his father he was in trouble, but nothing more? Let us never forget that Christ is the true bridegroom of the soul, – the true physician of the heart, – the real father of all His people. Let us show that we feel this, by being unreserved in our communications with Him. Let us hide no secrets from Him. Let us tell Him all our hearts.

(j) I commend to you, in the next place, the importance of intercession in our prayers. We are all selfish by nature, and our selfishness is very apt to stick to us, even when we are converted. There is a tendency in us to think only of our own souls, – our own spiritual conflict, – our own progress in religion, and to forget others. Against this tendency we have all need to watch and strive, and not least in our prayers. We should study to be of a public spirit. We should stir ourselves up to name other names beside our own before the throne of grace. We should try to bear in our hearts the whole world, – the heathen, – the Jews, – the Roman Catholics, – the body of true believers, – the professing Protestant Churches, – the country in which we live, – the congregation to which we belong, – the household in which we sojourn, – the friends and relations we are connected with. For each and all of these we should plead. This is the highest charity. He loves me best who loves me in his prayers. This is for our soul's health. It enlarges our sympathies and expands our hearts. This is for the benefit of the Church. The wheels of all machinery for extending the Gospel are oiled by prayer. They do as much for the Lord's cause who intercede like Moses on the mount, as they do who fight like Joshua in the thick of the battle. This is to be like Christ. He bears the names of His people on His breast and shoulders as their High Priest before the Father. Oh, the privilege of being like Jesus! This is to be a true helper to ministers. If I must needs choose a congregation, give me a people that prays.

(k) I commend to you, in the next place, the importance of thankfulness in prayer. I know well that asking God is one thing, and praising God is another. But I see so close a connection between prayer and praise in the Bible, that I dare not call that true prayer in which thankfulness has no part. It is not for nothing that Paul says, "By prayer and supplication, with thanksgiving, let your request be made known unto God" (Phil. 4:6). "Continue in prayer, and watch in the same with thanksgiving (Coloss. 4:2). It is of mercy that we are not in hell. It is of mercy that we have the hope of heaven. It is of mercy that we live in a land of spiritual light. It is of mercy that we have been called by the Spirit, and not left to reap the fruit of our own ways. It is of mercy that we still live, and have opportunities of glorifying God actively or passively. Surely, these thoughts should crowd on our minds whenever we speak with God. Surely, we should never open our lips in prayer without blessing God for that free grace by which we live, and for that loving-kindness which endureth for ever. Never was there an eminent saint who was not full of thankfulness. St. Paul hardly ever writes an Epistle without beginning with thankfulness. Men like Whitfield in the last century, and Bickersteth, and Marsh, and Haldane Stewart, in our own time, were ever running over with thankfulness. Oh, if we would be bright and shining lights in our day, we must cherish a spirit of praise! And above all, let our prayers be thankful prayers.

(l) I commend to you, in the last place, the importance of watchfulness over your prayers. Prayer is that point of all others in religion at which you must be on your guard. Here it is that true religion begins: here it flourishes, and here it decays. Tell me what a man's prayers are, and I will soon tell you the state of his soul. Prayer is the spiritual pulse: by this the spiritual health may always be tested. Prayer is the spiritual weather-glass: by this we may always know whether it is fair or foul with our hearts. Oh, let us keep an eye continually upon our private devotions! Here is the pith, and marrow, and backbone of our practical Christianity. Sermons, and books, and tracts, and committee meetings, and the company of good men, are all good in their way; but they will never make up for the neglect of private prayer. Mark well the places, and society, and companions, that unhinge your hearts for communion with God, and make your prayers drive heavily. There be on your guard. Observe narrowly what friends and what employments leave your soul in the most spiritual frame, and most ready to speak with God. To these cleave and stick fast. If you will only take care of your prayers, I will engage that nothing shall go very wrong with your soul.

I offer these points for private consideration. I do it in all humility. I know no one who needs to be reminded of them more than I do myself. But I believe them to be God's own truth, and I should like myself and all I love to feel them more.

I want the times we live in to be praying times. I want the Christians of our day to be praying Christians. I want the Church of our age to be a praying Church. My heart's desire and prayer in sending forth this paper is to promote a spirit of prayerfulness. I want those who never prayed yet, to arise and call upon God; and I want those who do pray, to improve their prayers every year, and to see that they are not getting slack, and praying amiss.

J.C. Ryle, 1816–1900, Practical Religion

Praying for Your Children
William Scribner

Although praying for our children is clearly a biblical duty it is too frequently neglected. Often this arises from a secret unbelief in regard to the likelihood, or possibility, of conversion and real religion in childhood and early youth. This has arrested and prevented prayer and effort for this great blessing.

The early conversion of all the children of the Church should be intensely desired and incessantly prayed for. Many who are converted only as adults suffer from evil habits developed in their youth. Not only would these be prevented, but habits which none but a true Christian prizes – habits such as daily and systematic prayer, determined fighting with sin in its various forms, generosity, watchfulness over self, and others of a similar kind – are usually formed strongest when young.

In addition, we should expect the conversion of the children of believers as much as, if not more than, others who attend the church and who are not yet believers. The same means of grace have been enjoyed and the exhortations and warnings of the gospel are as understandable to a child as to an adult.

The biblical evidence that it is God's will that the children in the Church should be born again at an early age, is found in Matthew 19:14: "Let the little children to come to Me."

Often children are not converted because parents leave their work to others. valuable though Sunday school teachers are, no parent can be released from the obligation of striving by his own personal efforts to lead his children to Christ. We are commanded to bring our children up "in the fear and nurture of the Lord." In the case of the children of believers, parental training should be the first and usual means of their salvation.

The work to be done by parents includes:
a. Instructing them in the faith.
b. Setting them a holy example.
c. Restraining them.
d. Praying for them.
It is this last aspect which is the focus here.

I. PRAYING FOR YOUR CHILDREN'S SALVATION
You should pray for your children's conversion because:
1. Their salvation is so great a prize that it is worth all the pains which your prayer to secure it for them may cost you.

The fact that their souls are precious beyond all thought, that the loss of their souls would be inconceivably dreadful, that eternal life would be an infinite gain to them, and that your prayers may be instrumental in saving them, should stir you up to offer constant requests on their behalf.

2. Few will pray for them if you do not.

Though we are commanded to intercede for all men (1 Tim. 2:1), few engage in this duty as they should. When it is done, those who are prayed for are often those who are considered important in the Church's or the world's estimation.

3. No one else can pray for them as you do.

The genuine love you have for your children, the tenderness you feel for them and your knowledge of their make-up, needs and problems, qualify you to plead with God on their behalf with an urgency and earnestness which can take no refusal. When God wants to convince us of his willingness to hear prayer, he bases his argument on his parental love:

"If you then, being evil, know how to give good gifts to your children, how much more will your heavenly Father give the Holy Spirit to those who ask Him!" (Luke 11:13).

4. Your omitting to do so will be perilous to them and to you.

God notes our attempts to fulfill our parental obligations. It is not to unfaithful, prayerless parents that his exceeding great and precious promises are addressed:

"But the mercy of the LORD is from everlasting to everlasting on those who fear Him, and His righteousness to children's children, to such as keep His covenant, and to those who remember His commandments to do them." (Ps. 103:17–18)

Your children are surrounded by evil influences and they are fallen creatures. They need to be protected by the power of God, and no less do they need to be inwardly restrained, enlightened, controlled, purified, and guided by the Holy Spirit.

5. You will then find it easier to perform other parental duties on the performance of which God has conditioned their salvation.

God commended Abraham for being one who would fulfill his parental duties (Gen. 18:18–19):

"For I have known him, in order that he may command his children and his household after him, that they keep the way of the LORD, to do righteousness and justice, that the LORD may bring to Abraham what He has spoken to him."

God's will for you as a parent is clear: "And these words which I command you today shall be in your heart. You shall teach them diligently to your children, and shall talk of them when you sit in your house, when you walk by the way, when you lie down, and when you rise up (Deut. 6:6–7). It is a great work, and nothing can sustain you under the burden like praying for your children, believingly, earnestly and perseveringly. in giving attention to instruction and discipline, do not neglect prayer! Some blessings seldom come except in answer to heartfelt prayer. One of these is the early conversion of our children.

6. Prayer alone can call into exercise that divine power in their behalf, which is absolutely necessary in order that the prayers which you may employ for their salvation may not be used in vain.

Only God's mighty power can effect the great change necessary, raising them to life from a state of spiritual death. Your child is absolutely dependent upon the influences of God's all-powerful Spirit. Though you persevere in the use of means, without the Spirit it will be in vain. Nothing but believing prayer can secure his power to effect the change.

7. By their salvation, granted in answer to your prayers, your Savior will be glorified

Not merely the salvation of your children, but the glory of your dear Savior in their salvation, should impel you to pray for them. This motive should be stronger than any other which can influence you to seek their salvation.

8. You have a strong encouragement and incentive to do so in the explicit promise of God that, if you are faithful to your trust, he will be their God.

The words which God spoke to Abraham, when he entered into covenant with him and his seed, may be regarded as addressed to every believer individually, and therefore to you (cf. Gen. 17:7; also Isa. 59:21, Acts 2:38). God's promises to you take into account your responsibility as a parent. Because God loves his own people with a love which passes knowledge, they cannot earnestly plead for such a thing as the salvation of their children without having power with him. In addition to this, his love for them causes him to have tenderness for their children. They also are beloved by him and are dear to him for their parents' sake.

II. PRAYING FOR YOUR CHILDREN'S WELFARE

Do not consider only your children's salvation but pray also for your children's welfare because:

1. You my then expect, as a result of your prayers, that the power of God will counteract in some measure the evil you have done them.

Even the best of parents sometimes do their children harm. This may be as a result of undue severity in discipline, partiality or injustice, but equally by misguided tenderness and lack of conscientious in exercising authority. Unceasing prayer will enable you to avoid these sins. Thoughtful love for them, and an earnest desire for their real good, would take replace mere fondness, and you would be led to avoid the extremes of harshness and hurtful indulgence.

2. There will be critical periods in their lives when without your incessant prayers, offered with reference to such times, they my be left to act most unwisely if not disastrously.

Pray for them in the momentous decisions concerning matters such as their future career and possible marriage. Do not put off praying over these because they might be in the distant future. Consider, you may not be alive when they face these decisions.

3. It will lead you to a better understanding of them. Fervent prayer, continuously offered for them, in which their special wants, as far as you know them, are spread before God, will be sure to lead to a greater watchfulness over them. It will lead to a closer study of their character and to more exact understanding of their traits and wants. You should know what motives most easily influence them and what temptations are most likely to lead them into wrongdoing. You should also be familiar with their sorrows and circumstances, knowing intimately each one's character. If you are praying for them you will be compelled to note these things.

4. It will increase your holy desires for them.

If we cannot pray, even for strangers, without learning to love them, surely the more we commend our children to God, the stronger will our love for their souls become. This steady increase of holy desires in your heart, with reference to you children, will prove an unspeakable blessing both to them and to you.

5. No other means will be so effectual in enabling you to overcome the difficulty you experience in talking with then on religious subjects.

Out of the abundance of your heart your mouth will speak. We are often too reserved when it comes to speaking of spiritual matters with our children, despite the scriptural command (Deut. 6:7). Nothing is so suited to remove this as earnest, persistent prayer, in which your child's needs are spread before God and specific requests are offered in its behalf.

6. You will thereby secure for then God's aid in the efforts they my make to yield you their obedience God requires of children submission to the parent's will and implicit obedi-ence. Children need more than mere human assistance, even though that assistance may come from wise and affectionate parents. They can no more perform their duties as children without such help from God, than you, without such help, can perform your parental duties. You are solemnly bound to think of the dependence of your children on God's help, and earnestly to pray that that help may be given them in their endeavors to honor and obey you.

7. Other parents seeing your example, may be led to imitate you.

Others may be challenged by your diligence and may be inspired to be more zealous in their parental duties.

8. They will often, should they continue in the world, have their times of need when the power of God alone can avail to help them.

Disappointments, sickness, losses, cares, in short, adversity in various forms, will be sure to overtake them sooner or later, and well will it be for them if you have anticipated these times of need by much prayer offered on their behalf. There will be times of temptation when they will be in fearful danger. The evil one will seek to lay snares for them and at such times earthly friends will be of no help. Ask the Savior to defend them from the spite, power and wiles of evil spirits, the agents of Satan, who are constantly around them.

In closing, never approach the throne of grace with your own wants without remembering your children's. who are no less helpless and needy than you. Let us resolve that we will give ourselves more intently to the work of interceding for our children. Whether we pray for our offspring or not must decide what our distant decedents are to be, and what kind of influence they will exert. Surely our fervent prayers for God's blessing on our children would be offered without ceasing were we able to fully comprehend the far-reaching results of such prayers.

William Scribner

Divine Meditations

Richard Sibbes

Prayer exercises all the graces of the Spirit; we cannot pray, unless our faith is exercised, our love, our patience, which makes us set a high price upon that we seek after and to use it well.

It is not so easy a matter to pray as men think, and that in regard of the unspiritualness of our nature compared with the duty itself which is to draw near to a holy God; we cannot endure to sever ourselves from our lusts. There is also a great rebellion in our hearts against anything that is good. Satan also is a special enemy. When we go to God by prayer, the devil knows we go to fetch help and strength against him, and therefore he opposes all he can; but though many men mumble over a few prayers, yet indeed no man can pray as he ought but he that is within the covenant of grace and by the Holy Ghost.

A child of God may pray and not be heard, because at that time he may be a child under displeasure. If any sin lie unrepented of we are not in a fit state to pray. Will a king regard the petition of a traitor that purposes to go on in his rebellion, or a father hear a disobedient child? Therefore when we come to God, we should renew our repentance, faith and purposes of better pleasing Him, and then remember the Scripture and search all the promises as part of our best riches, and when we have them, we should humbly challenge God with His own promises. This will make us strong and faithful in our prayers when we know we never pray to Him in vain.

In prayer we tempt God if we ask that which we labor not for; our faithful endeavors must second our devotion, for to ask maintenance and not put our hands to the work is only to knock at the door and yet pull the door to us that it might not open. In this case, if we pray for grace and neglect the spring from whence it comes, how can we speed? It was a rule in ancient time, "Lay your hand to the plough and then pray." No man should pray without ploughing, nor plough without prayer.

When we pray God oftentimes refuses to give us comfort because we are not on good terms with Him; therefore we should still look back to our past life. Perhaps God sees you running to this or that sin, and before He will hear you, you must renew your repentance for that sin, for our nature is such that it will knock at every door and seek every corner before we will come to God, like the woman in the Gospel – she sold all before she came to Christ – so that God will not hear before we forsake all helps and all false dependence upon the creature, and then He gets the greatest glory and we have the greatest sweetness to our souls. That water which comes from the fountain is the sweetest, and so divine comfort is the sweetest when we see nothing in the creature, and God is the best discerner of the fittest time to bestow His own consolations.

When God means to bestow any blessing on His church or children He will pour out upon them the spirit of prayer and, as all pray for everyone, so everyone prays for all; this is a great comfort to weak Christians when they cannot pray, that the prayers of others shall prevail for them.

When we shoot an arrow, we look to the fall of it; when we send a ship to sea, we look for its return; and when we sow seed, we look for a harvest; so likewise when we sow our prayers, through Christ, in God's bosom, shall we not look for an answer and observe how we speed? It is a seed of atheism to pray and not to look how we speed. But a sincere Christian will pray and wait, and strengthen his heart with promises out of the Word, and never leave praying and looking up till God gives him a gracious answer.

Richard Sibbes

Order and Argument in Prayer

C.H. Spurgeon

"Oh that I knew where I might find him! that I might come even to his seat! I would order my cause before him, and fill my mouth with arguments." Job 23:3,4

In Job's uttermost extremity he cried after the Lord. The longing desire of an afflicted child of God is once more to see his Father's face. His first prayer is not, "Oh that I might be healed of the disease which now festers in every part of my body!" nor even, "Oh that I might see my children restored from the jaws of the grave, and my property once more brought from the hand of the spoiler!" but the first and uppermost cry is, "Oh that I knew where I might find HIM – who is my God! that I might come even to his seat!" God's children run home when the storm comes on. It is the heaven-born instinct of a gracious soul to seek shelter from all ills beneath the wings of Jehovah. "He that hath made his refuge God," might serve as the title of a true believer. A hypocrite, when he feels that he has been afflicted by God, resents the infliction, and, like a slave, would run from the master who has scourged him; but not so the true heir of heaven, he kisses the hand which smote him, and seeks shelter from the rod in the bosom of that very God who frowned upon him. You will observe that the desire to commune with God is intensified by the failure of all other sources of consolation. When Job first saw his friends at a distance, he may have entertained a hope that their kindly counsel and compassionate tenderness would blunt the edge of his grief; but they had not long spoken before he cried out in bitterness, "Miserable comforters are ye all." They put salt into his wounds, they heaped fuel upon the flame of his sorrow, they added the gall of their upbraiding to the wormwood of his griefs. In the sunshine of his smile they once had longed to sun themselves, and now they dare to cast shadows upon his reputation, most ungenerous and undeserved. Alas for a man when his wine-cup mocks him with vinegar, and his pillow pricks him with thorns! The patriarch turned away from his sorry friends and looked up to the celestial throne, just as a traveler turns from his empty skin bottle and betakes himself with all speed to the well. He bids farewell to earthborn hopes, and cries, "Oh that I knew where I might find my God!" My brethren, nothing teaches us so much the preciousness of the Creator as when we learn the emptiness of all besides. When you have been pierced through and through with the sentence, "Cursed is he that trusteth in man, and maketh flesh his arm," then will you suck unutterable sweetness from the divine assurance, "Blessed is he that trusteth in the Lord,

and whose hope the Lord is." Turning away with bitter scorn from earth's hives, where you found no honey, but many sharp stings, you will rejoice in him whose faithful word is sweeter than honey or the honeycomb.

It is further observable that though a good man hastens to God in his trouble, and runs with all the more speed because of the unkindness of his fellow men, yet sometimes the gracious soul is left without the comfortable presence of God. This is the worst of all griefs; the text is one of Job's deep groans, far deeper than any which came from him on account of the loss of his children and his property: "Oh that I knew where I might find HIM!" The worst of all losses is to lose the smile of my God. He now had a foretaste of the bitterness of his Redeemer's cry, "My God, my God, why hast thou forsaken me?" God's presence is always with his people in one sense, so far as secretly sustaining them is concerned, but his manifest presence they do not always enjoy. Like the spouse in the song, they seek their beloved by night upon their bed, they seek him but they find him not; and though they wake and roam through the city they may not discover him, and the question may be sadly asked again and again, "Saw ye him whom my soul loveth?" You may be beloved of God, and yet have no consciousness of that love in your soul. You may be as dear to his heart as Jesus Christ himself, and yet for a small moment he may forsake you, and in a little wrath he may hide himself from you. But, dear friends, at such times the desire of the believing soul gathers yet greater intensity from the fact of God's light being withheld. Instead of saying with proud lip, "Well, if he leaveth me I must do without him; if I cannot have his comfortable presence I must fight on as best may be," the soul saith, "No, it is my very life; I must have my God. I perish, I sink in deep mire where there is no standing, and nothing but the arm of God can deliver me." The gracious soul addresseth itself with a double zeal to find out God, and sends up its groans, its entreaties, its sobs and sighs to heaven more frequently and fervently. "Oh that I knew where I might find him!" Distance or labor are is nothing; if the soul only knew where to go she would soon overleap the distance. She makes no stipulation about mountains or rivers, but vows that if she knew where, she would come even to his seat. My soul in her hunger would break through stone walls, or scale the battlements of heaven to reach her God, and though there were seven hells between me and him, yet would I face the flame if I might reach him, nothing daunted if I had but the prospect of at last standing in his presence and feeling the delight of his love. That seems to me to be the state of mind in which Job pronounced the words before us.

But we cannot stop upon this point, for the object of this morning's discourse beckons us onward. It appears that Job's end, in desiring the presence of God, was that he might pray to him. He had prayed, but he wanted to pray as in God's presence. He desired to plead as before one whom he knew would hear and help him. He longed to state his own case before the seat of the impartial Judge, before the very face of the all-wise God; he would appeal from the lower courts, where his friends judged unrighteous judgment, to the Court of King's Bench – the High Court of heaven – there, saith he, "I would order my cause before him, and fill my mouth with arguments."

In this latter verse Job teaches us how he meant to plead and intercede with God. He does, as it were, reveal the secrets of his closet, and unveils the art of prayer. We are here admitted into the guild of suppliants; we are shown the art and mystery of pleading; we have here taught to us the blessed handicraft and science of prayer, and if we can be bound apprentice to Job this morning, for the next hour, and can have a lesson from Job's Master, we may acquire no little skill in interceding with God.

There are two things here set forth as necessary in prayer – *ordering of our cause, and filling our mouth with arguments*. We shall speak of those two things, and then if we have rightly learned the lesson, a blessed result will follow.

1. FIRST, IT IS NEEDFUL THAT OUR SUIT BE ORDERED BEFORE GOD

There is a vulgar notion that prayer is a very easy thing, a kind of common business that may be done anyhow, without care or effort. Some think that you have only to reach a book

down and get through a certain number of very excellent words, and you have prayed and may put the book up again; others suppose that to use a book is superstitious, and that you ought rather to repeat extemporaneous sentences, sentences which come to your mind with a rush, like a herd of swine or a pack of hounds, and that when you have uttered them with some little attention to what you have said, you have prayed. Now neither of these modes of prayer were adopted by ancient saints. They appear to have thought a great deal more seriously of prayer than many do now-a-days. It seems to have been a mighty business with them, a long-practiced exercise, in which some of them attained great eminence, and were thereby singularly blest. They reaped great harvests in the field of prayer, and found the mercy seat to be a mine of untold treasures.

The ancient saints were wont, with Job, to order their cause before God; that is to say, as a petitioner coming into Court does not come there without thought to state his case on the spur of the moment, but enters into the audience chamber with his suit well prepared, having moreover learned how he ought to behave himself in the presence of the great One to whom he is appealing. It is well to approach the seat of the King of kings as much as possible with pre-meditation and preparation, knowing what we are about, where we are standing, and what it is which we desire to obtain. In times of peril and distress we may fly to God just as we are, as the dove enters the cleft of the rock, even though her plumes are ruffled; but in ordinary times we should not come with an unprepared spirit, even as a child comes not to his father in the morning till he has washed his face. See yonder priest; he has a sacrifice to offer, but he does not rush into the court of the priests and hack at the bullock with the first pole-axe upon which he can lay his hand, but when he rises he washes his feet at the brazen laver, he puts on his garments, and adorns himself with his priestly vestments; then he comes to the altar with his victim properly divided according to the law, and is careful to do according to the command, even to such a simple matter as the placing of the fat, and the liver, and the kidneys, and he taketh the blood in a bowl and poureth it in an appropriate place at the foot of the altar, not throwing it just as may occur to him, and kindles the fire not with common flame, but with the sacred fire from off the altar. Now this ritual is all superseded, but the truth which it taught remains the same; our spiritual sacrifices should be offered with holy carefulness. God forbid that our prayer should be a mere leaping out of one's bed and kneeling down, and saying anything that comes first to hand; on the contrary, may we wait upon the Lord with holy fear and sacred awe. See how David prayed when God had blessed him – he went in before the Lord. Understand that; he did not stand outside at a distance, but he went in before the Lord and he sat down – for sitting is not a bad posture for prayer, let who will speak against it – and sitting down quietly and calmly before the Lord he then began to pray, but not until first he had thought over the divine goodness, and so attained to the spirit of prayer. Then by the assistance of the Holy Ghost did he open his mouth. Oh that we oftener sought the Lord in this style! Abraham may serve us as a pattern; he rose up early – here was his willingness; he went three days journey – here was his zeal; he left his servants at the foot of the hill – here was his privacy; he carried the wood and the fire with him – here was his preparation; and lastly, he built the altar and laid the wood in order, and then took the knife – here was the devout carefulness of his worship. David puts it, "In the morning will I direct my prayer unto thee, and will look up"; which I have frequently explained to you to mean that he marshaled his thoughts like men of war, or that he aimed his prayers like arrows. He did not take the arrow and put it on the bowstring and shoot, and shoot, and shoot anywhere; but after he had taken out the chosen shaft, and fitted it to the string, he took deliberate aim. He looked – looked well – at the white of the target; kept his eye fixed on it, directing his prayer, and then drew his bow with all his strength and let the arrow fly; and then, when the shaft had left his hand, what does he say? "I will look up." He looked up to see where the arrow went, to see what effect it had; for he expected an answer to his prayers, and was not as many who scarcely think of their prayers after they have uttered them.

David knew that he had an engagement before him which required all his mental powers; he marshaled up his faculties and went about the work in a workmanlike manner, as one who believed in it and meant to succeed. We should plough carefully and pray carefully. The better the work the more attention it deserves. To be anxious in the shop and thoughtless in the closet is little less than blasphemy, for it is an insinuation that anything will do for God, but the world must have our best.

If any ask what order should be observed in prayer, I am not about to give you a scheme such as many have drawn out, in which adoration, confession, petition, intercession, and ascription are arranged in succession. I am not persuaded that any such order is of divine authority. It is to no mere mechanical order I have been referring, for our prayers will be equally acceptable, and possibly equally proper, in any form; for there are specimens of prayers, in all shapes, in the Old and New Testament. The true spiritual order of prayer seems to me to consist in something more than mere arrangement. It is most fitting for us first to feel that we are now doing something that is real; that we are about to address ourselves to God, whom we cannot see, but who is really present; whom we can neither touch nor hear, nor by our senses can apprehend, but who, nevertheless, is as truly with us as though we were speaking to a friend of flesh and blood like ourselves. Feeling the reality of God's presence, our mind will be led by divine grace into an humble state; we shall feel like Abraham, when he said, "I have taken upon myself to speak unto God, I that am but dust and ashes." Consequently we shall not deliver ourselves of our prayer as boys repeating their lessons, as a mere matter of rote, much less shall we speak as if we were rabbis instructing our pupils, or as I have heard some do, with the coarseness of a highwayman stopping a person on the road and demanding his purse of him; but we shall be humble yet bold petitioners, humbly importuning mercy through the Savior's blood. We shall not have the reserve of a slave but the loving reverence of a child, yet not an impudent, impertinent child, but a teachable obedient child, honoring his Father, and therefore asking earnestly, but with deferential submission to his Father's will. When I feel that I am in the presence of God, and take my rightful position in that presence, the next thing I shall want to recognize will be that I have no right to what I am seeking, and cannot expect to obtain it except as a gift of grace, and I must recollect that God limits the channel through which he will give me mercy – he will give it to me through his dear Son. Let me put myself then under the patronage of the great Redeemer. Let me feel that now it is no longer I that speak but Christ that speaketh with me, and that while I plead, I plead his wounds, his life, his death, his blood, himself. This is truly getting into order.

The next thing is to consider what I am to ask for? It is most proper in prayer, to aim at great distinctness of supplication. There is much reason to complain of some public prayers, that those who offer them do not really ask God for anything. I must acknowledge I fear to having so prayed myself, and certainly to having heard many prayers of the kind, in which I did not feel that anything was sought for from God – a great deal of very excellent doctrinal and experimental matter uttered, but little real petitioning, and that little in a nebulous kind of state, chaotic and unformed. But it seems to me that prayer should be distinct, the asking for something definitely and distinctly because the mind has realized its distinct need of such a thing, and therefore must plead for it. It is well not to beat round the bush in prayer, but to come directly to the point. I like that prayer of Abraham's, "Oh that Ishmael might live before thee!" There is the name and the person prayed for, and the blessing desired, all put in a few words, – "Ishmael might live before thee!" Many persons would have used a roundabout expression of this kind, "Oh that our beloved offspring might be regarded with the favor which thou bearest to those who," etc. Say "Ishmael," if you mean "Ishmael"; put it in plain words before the Lord. Some people cannot even pray for the minister without using such circular descriptives that you might think it were the parish beadle, or somebody whom it did not do to mention too particularly. Why not be distinct, and say what we mean as well as mean what we say? Ordering our cause would bring us to greater distinctness of mind. It is not necessary, my dear brethren, in the closet to ask for every supposable good thing; it is not necessary to rehearse the catalogue of every want that you may have, have had, can have, or shall have. Ask for what you now need, and, as a rule, keep to present need; ask for your daily bread – what you want now – ask for that. Ask for it plainly, as before God, who does not regard your fine expressions, and to whom your eloquence and oratory will be less than nothing and vanity. Thou art before the Lord; let thy words be few, but let thy heart be fervent.

You have not quite completed the ordering when you have asked for what you want through Jesus Christ. There should be a looking round the blessing which you desire, to see whether it is assuredly a fitting thing to ask; for some prayers would never be offered if men did but think. A little reflection would show to us that some things which we desire were better let alone. We may, moreover, have a motive at the bottom of our desire which is not Christ-like, a selfish motive, which forgets God's glory and caters only for our own case and comfort. Now although we may ask for things which are for our profit, yet still we must never let our profit interfere in any way with the glory of God. There must be mingled with acceptable prayer the holy salt of submission to the divine will. I like Luther's saying, "Lord, I will have my will of thee at this time." "What!" say you, "Like such an expression as that?" I do, because of the next clause, which was, "I will have my will, *for I know that my will is thy will.*" That is well spoken, Luther; but without the last words it would have been wicked presumption. When we are sure that what we ask for is for God's glory, then, if we have power in prayer, we may say, "I will not let thee go except thou bless me": we may come to close dealings with God, and like Jacob with the angel we may even put it to the wrestle and seek to give the angel the fall sooner than be sent away without the benediction. But we must be quite clear, before we come to such terms as those, that what we are seeking is really for the Master's honor.

Put these three things together, the deep spirituality which recognizes prayer as being real conversation with the invisible God – much distinctness which is the reality of prayer, asking for what we know we want – and withal much fervency, believing the thing to be necessary, and therefore resolving to obtain it if it can be had by prayer, and above all these complete submission, leaving it still with the Master's will; – commingle all these, and you have a clear idea of what it is to order your cause before the Lord.

Still prayer itself is an art which only the Holy Ghost can teach us. He is the giver of all prayer. Pray for prayer – pray till you can pray; pray to be helped to pray, and give not up praying because thou canst not pray, for it is when thou thinkest thou canst not pray that thou art most praying; and sometimes when thou hast no sort of comfort in thy supplications, it is then that thy heart all broken and cast down is really wrestling and truly prevailing with the Most High.

2. THE SECOND PART OF PRAYER IS FILLING THE MOUTH WITH ARGUMENTS

– not filling the mouth with words nor good phrases, nor pretty expressions, but filling the mouth with arguments are the knocks of the rapper by which the gate is opened.

Why are arguments to be used at all? is the first inquiry; the reply being, Certainly not because God is slow to give, not because we can change the divine purpose, not because God needeth to be informed of any circumstance with regard to ourselves or of anything in connection with the mercy asked: the arguments to be used are for our own benefit, not for his. He requires for us to plead with him, and to bring forth our strong reasons, as Isaiah saith, because this will show that we feel the value of the mercy. When a man searches for arguments for a thing it is because he attaches importance to that which he is seeking. Again, our use of arguments teaches us the ground upon which we obtain the blessing. If a man should come with the argument of his own merit, he would never succeed; the successful argument is always founded upon grace, and hence the soul so pleading is made to understand intensely that it is by grace and by grace alone that a sinner obtaineth anything of the Lord. Besides, the use of arguments is intended to stir up our fervency. The man who uses one argument with God will get more force

in using the next, and will use the next with still greater power, and the next with more force still. The best prayers I have ever heard in our prayer meetings have been those which have been fullest of argument. Sometimes my soul has been fairly melted down when I have listened to brethren who have come before God feeling the mercy to be really needed, and that they must have it, for they first pleaded with God to give it for this reason, and then for a second, and then for a third, and then for a fourth and a fifth, until they have awakened the fervency of the entire assembly. My brethren, there is no need for prayer at all as far as God is concerned, but what a need there is for it on our own account! If we were not constrained to pray, I question whether we could even live as Christians. If God's mercies came to us unasked, they would not be half so useful as they now are, when they have to be sought for; for now we get a double blessing, a blessing in the obtaining, and a blessing in the seeking. The very act of prayer is a blessing. To pray is as it were to bathe one's-self in a cool purling stream, and so to escape from the heats of earth's summer sun. To pray is to mount on eagle's wings above the clouds and get into the clear heaven where God dwelleth. To pray is to enter the treasure-house of God and to enrich one's-self out of an inexhaustible storehouse. To pray is to grasp heaven in one's arms, to embrace the Deity within one's soul, and to feel one's body made a temple of the Holy Ghost. Apart from the answer prayer is in itself a benediction. To pray, my brethren, is to cast off your burdens, it is to tear away your rags, it is to shake off your diseases, it is to be filled with spiritual vigor, it is to reach the highest point of Christian health. God give us to be much in the holy art of arguing with God in prayer.

The most interesting part of our subject remains; it is a very rapid summary and catalogue of a few of the arguments which have been used with great success with God. I cannot give you a full list; that would require a treatise such as Master John Owen might produce. It is well in prayer to plead with Jehovah *his attributes*. Abraham did so when he laid hold upon God's justice. Sodom was to be pleaded for, and Abraham begins, "Peradventure there be fifty righteous within the city: wilt thou also destroy and not spare the place for the fifty righteous that are therein? that be far from thee to do after this manner, to slay the righteous with the wicked: and that the righteous should be as the wicked, that be far from thee: Shall not the Judge of all the earth do right?" Here the wrestling begins. It was a powerful argument by which the patriarch grasped the Lord's left hand, and arrested it just when the thunderbolt was about to fall. But there came a reply to it. It was intimated to him that this would not spare the city, and you notice how the good man, when sorely pressed, retreated by inches; and at last, when he could no longer lay hold upon justice, grasped God's right hand of mercy, and that gave him a wondrous hold when he asked that if there were but ten righteous there the city might be spared. So you and I may take hold at any time upon the justice, the mercy, the faithfulness, the wisdom, the long-suffering, the tenderness of God, and we shall find every attribute of the Most High to be, as it were, a great battering-ram, with which we may open the gates of heaven.

Another mighty piece of ordinance in the battle of prayer is *God's promise*. When Jacob was on the other side of the brook Jabbok, and his brother Esau was coming with armed men, he pleaded with God not to suffer Esau to destroy the mother and the children, and as a master reason he pleaded, "And thou saidst, surely I will do thee good." Oh the force of that plea! He was holding God to his word: "Thou saidst." The attribute is a splendid horn of the altar to lay hold upon; but the promise, which has in it the attribute and something more, is yet a mightier holdfast. "Thou saidst." Remember how David put it. After Nathan had spoken the promise, David said at the close of his prayer, "Do as thou hast said." That is a legitimate argument with every honest man, and has *he* said, and shall he not do it? "Let God be true, and every man a liar." Shall not *he* be true? Shall *he* not keep his word? Shall not every word that cometh out of his lips stand fast and be fulfilled? Solomon, at the opening of the temple, used this same mighty plea. He pleads with God to remember the word which he had spoken to his father David, and to bless

that place. When a man gives a promissory note his honor is engaged. He signs his hand, and he must discharge it when the due time comes, or else he loses credit. It shall never be said that God dishonors his bills. The credit of the Most High never was impeached, and never shall be. He is punctual to the moment; he never is before his time, but he never is behind it. You shall search this Book through, and you shall compare it with the experience of God's people, and the two tally from the first to the last; and many a hoary patriarch has said with Joshua in his old age, "Not one good thing hath failed of all that the Lord God hath promised: all hath come to pass." My brother, if you have a divine promise, you need not plead it with an "if" in it; you may plead with a certainty. If for the mercy which you are now asking, you have God's solemnly pledged word, there will scarce be any room for the caution about submission to his will. You know his will: that will is in the promise; plead it. Do not give him rest until he fulfill it. He meant to fulfill it, or else he would not have given it. God does not give his words merely to quiet our noise, and to keep us hopeful for awhile, with the intention of putting us off at last; but when he speaks, he speaks because he means to act.

A third argument to be used is that employed by Moses, *the great name of God*. How mightily did he argue with God on one occasion upon this ground! "What wilt thou do for thy great name? The Egyptians will say, Because the Lord could not bring them into the land, therefore he slew them in the wilderness." There are some occasions when the name of God is very closely tied up with the history of his people. Sometimes in reliance upon a divine promise, a believer will be led to take a certain course of action. Now, if the Lord should not be as good as his promise, not only is the believer deceived, but the wicked world looking on would say, "Aha! aha! Where is your God?" Take the case of our respected brother, Mr. Muller, of Bristol. These many years he has declared that God hears prayer, and firm in that conviction, he has gone on to build house after house for the maintenance of orphans. Now, I can very well conceive that, if he were driven to a point of want of means for the maintenance of those thousand or two thousand children, he might very well use the plea, "What wilt thou do for thy great name?" And you, in some severe trouble, when you have fairly received the promise, may say, "Lord, thou hast said, 'In six troubles I will be with thee, and in seven I will not forsake thee.' I have told my friends and neighbors that I put my trust in thee, and if thou do not deliver me now, where is thy name? Arise, O God, and do this thing, lest thy honor be cast into the dust." Coupled with this, we may employ the further argument of *the hard things said by the revilers*. It was well done of Hezekiah, when he took Rabshakeh's letter and spread it before the Lord. Will that help him? It is full of blasphemy, will that help him? "Where are the gods of Arphad and Sepharvaim? Where are the gods of the cities which I have overthrown? Let not Hezekiah deceive you, saying that Jehovah will deliver you." Does that have any effect? Oh! yes, it was a blessed thing that Rabshakeh wrote that letter, for it provoked the Lord to help his people. Sometimes the child of God can rejoice when he sees his enemies get thoroughly out of temper and take to reviling. "Now," he says, "they have reviled the Lord himself; not me alone have they assailed, but the Most High himself. Now it is no longer the poor insignificant Hezekiah with his little band of soldiers, but it is Jehovah, the King of angels, who has come to fight against Rabshakeh. Now what wilt thou do, O boastful soldier of proud Sennacherib? Shalt not thou be utterly destroyed, since Jehovah himself has come into the fray? All the progress that is made by Popery, all the wrong things said by speculative atheists and so on, should be by Christians used as an argument with God, why he should help the gospel. Lord; see how they reproach the gospel of Jesus! Pluck thy right hand out of thy bosom! O God, they defy thee! Anti-Christ thrusts itself into the place where thy Son once was honored, and from the very pulpits where the gospel was once preached Popery is now declared. Arise, O God, wake up thy zeal, let thy sacred passions burn! Thine ancient foe again prevails. Behold the harlot of Babylon once more upon her scarlet-colored beast rides forth in triumph! Come, Jehovah, come, Jehovah, and once again show what thy bare arm can do! This is a legitimate mode of pleading with God, for his great name's sake.

So also may we plead *the sorrows of his people*. This is frequently done. Jeremiah is the great master of this art. He says, "Her Nazarites were purer than snow, they were whiter than milk, they were more ruddy in body than rubies, their polishing was of sapphire: their visage is blacker than a coal." "The precious sons of Zion, comparable to fine gold, how are they esteemed as earthen pitchers, the work of the hands of the potter!" He talks of all their griefs and straitnesses in the siege. He calls upon the Lord to look upon his suffering Zion; and ere long his plaintive cries are heard. Nothing so eloquent with the father as his child's cry; yes, there is one thing more mighty still, and that is a moan, – when the child is so sick that it is past crying, and lies moaning with that kind of moan which indicates extreme suffering and intense weakness. Who can resist that moan? Ah! and when God's Israel shall be brought very low so that they can scarcely cry but only their moans are heard, then comes the Lord's time of deliverance, and he is sure to show that he loveth his people. Dear friends, whenever you also are brought into the same condition you may plead your moanings, and when you see a church brought very low you may use her griefs as an argument why God should return and save the remnant of his people.

Brethren, it is good to plead with God *the past*. Ah, you experienced people of God, you know how to do this. Here is David's specimen of it: "Thou *hast* been my help. Leave me not, neither forsake me." He pleads God's mercy to him from his youth up. He speaks of being cast upon his God from his very birth, and then he pleads, "Now also, when I am old and grayheaded, O God, forsake me not." Moses also, speaking with God, says, "Thou *didst* bring this people up out of Egypt." As if he would say, "Do not leave thy work unfinished; thou hast begun to build, complete it. Thou hast fought the first battle; Lord, end the campaign! Go on till thou gettest a complete victory." How often have we cried in our trouble, "Lord, thou didst deliver me in such and such a sharp trial, when it seemed as if no help were near; thou hast never forsaken me yet. I have set up my Ebenezer in thy name. If thou hadst intended to leave me why hast thou showed me such things? Hast thou brought thy servant to this place to put him to shame?" Brethren, we have to deal with an unchanging God, who will do in the future what he has done in the past, because he never turns from his purpose, and cannot be thwarted in his design; the past thus becomes a very mighty means of winning blessings from him.

We may even use *our own unworthiness* as an argument with God. "Out of the eater comes forth meat, and out of the strong comes forth sweetness." David in one place pleads thus: "Lord, have mercy upon mine iniquity, for it is great." That is a very singular mode of reasoning; but being interpreted it means, "Lord, why shouldest thou go about doing little things? Thou art a great God, and here is a great sinner. Here is a fitness in me for the display of thy grace. The greatness of my sin makes me a platform for the greatness of thy mercy. Let the greatness of thy love be seen in me." Moses seems to have the same on his mind when he asks God to show his great power in sparing his sinful people. The power with which God restrains himself is great indeed. O brothers and sisters, there is such a thing as creeping down at the foot of the throne, crouching low and crying, "O God, break me not – I am a bruised reed. Oh! tread not on my little life, it is now but as the smoking flax. Wilt thou hunt me? Wilt thou come out, as David said, "after a dead dog, after a flea?" Wilt thou pursue me as a leaf that is blown in the tempest? Wilt thou watch me, as Job saith, as though I were a vast sea, or a great whale? Nay, but because I am so little, and because the greatness of thy mercy can be shown in one so insignificant and yet so vile, therefore, O God, have mercy upon me."

There was once an occasion when the very Godhead of Jehovah made a triumphant plea for the prophet Elijah. On that august occasion, when he had bidden his adversaries see whether their god could answer them by fire, you can little guess the excitement there must have been that day in the prophet's mind. With what stern sarcasm did he say, "Cry aloud: for he is a god; either he is talking, or he is pursuing, or he is in a journey, or peradventure he sleepeth, and must be awakened." And as they cut themselves with knives, and leaped upon the altar, oh the scorn with which that man of

God must have looked down upon their impotent exertions, and their earnest but useless cries! But think of how his heart must have palpitated, if it had not been for the strength of his faith, when he repaired the altar of God that was broken down, and laid the wood in order, and killed the bullock. Hear him cry, "Pour water on it. You shall not suspect me of concealing fire; pour water on the victim." When they had done so, he bids them, "Do it a second time"; and they did it a second time; and then he says, "Do it a third time." And when it was all covered with water, soaked and saturated through, then he stands up and cries to God, "O God, let it be known that thou only art God." Here everything was put to the test. Jehovah's own existence was now put, as it were, at stake, before the eyes of men by this bold prophet. But how well the prophet was heard! Down came the fire and devoured not only the sacrifice, but even the wood, and the stones, and even the very water that was in the trenches, for Jehovah God had answered his servant's prayer. We sometimes may do the same, and say unto him, "Oh, by thy Deity, by thine existence, if indeed thou be God, now show thyself for the help of thy people!"

Lastly, the grand Christian argument is *the sufferings, the death, the merit, the intercession of Christ Jesus.* Brethren, I am afraid we do not understand what it is that we have at our command when we are allowed to plead with God for Christ's sake. I met with this thought the other day: it was somewhat new to me, but I believe it ought not to have been. When we ask God to hear us, pleading Christ's name, we usually mean, "O Lord, thy dear Son deserves this of thee; do this unto me because of what he merits." But if we knew it we might go in the city, "Sir, call at my office, and use my name, and say that they are to give you such a thing." I should go in and use your name, and I should obtain my request as a matter of right and a matter of necessity. This is virtually what Jesus Christ says to us. "If you need anything of God, all that the Father has belongs to me; go and use my name." Suppose you should give a man your check-book signed with your own name and left blank, to be filled up as he chose; that would be very nearly what Jesus has done in these words, "If ye ask anything in my name,

I will give it you." If I had a good name at the bottom of the check, I should be sure that I should get it cashed when I went to the banker with it; so when you have got Christ's name, to whom the very justice of God hath become a debtor, and whose merits have claims with the Most High, when you have Christ's name there is no need to speak with fear and trembling and bated breath. Oh, waver not and let not faith stagger! When thou pleadest the name of Christ thou pleadest that which shakes the gates of hell, and which the hosts of heaven obey, and God himself feels the sacred power of that divine plea.

Brethren, you would do better if you sometimes thought more in your prayers of Christ's griefs and groans. Bring before the Lord his wounds, tell the Lord of his cries, make the groans of Jesus cry again from Gethsemane, and his blood speak again from that frozen Calvary. Speak out and tell the Lord that with such griefs, and cries, and groans to plead, thou canst not take a denial: such arguments as these will speed you.

3. IF THE HOLY GHOST SHALL TEACH US HOW TO ORDER OUR CAUSE, AND HOW TO FILL OUR MOUTH WITH ARGUMENTS, THE RESULT SHALL BE THAT WE SHALL HAVE OUR MOUTH FILLED WITH PRAISES

The man who has his mouth full of arguments in prayer shall soon have his mouth full of benedictions in answer to prayer. Dear friend, thou hast thy mouth full this morning, has thou? What of? Full of complaining? Pray the Lord to rinse thy mouth out of that black stuff, for it will little avail thee, and it will be bitter in thy bowels one of these days. Oh, have thy mouth full of prayer, full of it, full of arguments so that there is room for nothing else. Then come with this blessed mouthful, and you shall soon go away with whatsoever you have asked of God. Only delight thou thyself in him, and he will give thee the desire of thy heart.

It is said – I know not how truly – that the explanation of the text, "Open thy mouth wide and I will fill it," may be found in a very singular Oriental custom. It is said that not many years ago – I remember the circumstance being reported – the King of Persia ordered the

chief of his nobility, who had done something or other which greatly gratified him, to open his mouth, and when he had done so he began to put into his mouth pearls, diamonds, rubies, and emeralds, till he had filled it as full as it could hold, and then he bade him go his way. This is said to have been occasionally done in Oriental Courts towards great favorites. Now certainly whether that be an explanation of the text or not it is an illustration of it. God says, "Open thy mouth with arguments," and then he will fill it with mercies priceless, gems unspeakably valuable. Would not a man open his mouth wide when he had to have it filled in such a style? Surely the most simple-minded among you would be wise enough for that. Oh! let us then open wide our mouth when we have to plead with God. Our needs are great, let our askings be great, and the supply shall be great too. You are not straitened in him; you are straitened in your own bowels. The Lord give you large mouths in prayer, great potency, not in the use of language, but in employing arguments.

What I have been speaking to the Christian is applicable in great measure to the unconverted man. God give thee to see the force of it, and to fly in humble prayer to the Lord Jesus Christ and to find eternal life in him.

C.H. Spurgeon, 1834–92

The Prayer of Jabez
C.H. Spurgeon

"Oh that thou wouldest bless me indeed!" – 1 Chronicles 4:10.

We know very little about Jabez, except that he was more honorable than his brethren, and that he was called Jabez because his mother bare him with sorrow. It will sometimes happen that where there is the most sorrow in the antecedents, there will be the most pleasure in the sequel. As the furious storm gives place to the clear sunshine, so the night of weeping precedes the morning of joy. Sorrow the harbinger; gladness the prince it ushers in. Cowper says:
    "The path of sorrow, and that path alone,

Leads to the place where sorrow is unknown."

To a great extent we find that we must sow in tears before we can reap in joy. Many of our works for Christ have cost us tears. Difficulties and disappointments have wrung our soul with anguish. Yet those projects that have cost us more than ordinary sorrow, have often turned out to be the most honorable of our undertakings. While our grief called the offspring of desire "Benoni," the son of my sorrow, our faith has been afterwards able to give it a name of delight, "Benjamin," the son of my right hand. You may expect a blessing in serving God if you are enabled to persevere under many discouragements. The ship is often long coming home, because detained on the road by excess of cargo. Expect her freight to be the better when she reaches the port. More honorable than his brethren was the child whom his mother bore with sorrow. As for this Jabez, whose aim was so well pointed, his fame so far sounded, his name so lastingly embalmed – he was a man of prayer. The honor he enjoyed would not have been worth having if it had not been vigorously contested and equitably won. His devotion was the key to his promotion. Those are the best honors that come from God, the award of grace with the acknowledgment of service. When Jacob was surnamed Israel, he received his princedom after a memorable night of prayer. Surely it was far more honorable to him than if it had been bestowed upon him as a flattering distinction by some earthly emperor. The best honor is that which a man gains in communion with the Most High. Jabez, we are told, was more honorable than his brethren, and his prayer is forthwith recorded, as if to intimate that he was also more prayerful than his brethren. We are told of what petitions his prayer consisted. All through it was very significant and instructive. We have only time to take one clause of it – indeed, that one clause may be said to comprehend the rest: "Oh that thou wouldest bless me indeed!" I commend it as a prayer for yourselves, dear brethren and sisters; one which will be available at all seasons; a prayer to begin Christian life with, a prayer to end it with, a prayer which would never be unseasonable in your joys or in your sorrows.

Oh that thou, the God of Israel, the covenant God, would bless me indeed! The very pith of the prayer seems to lie in that word, "indeed." There are many varieties of blessing. Some are blessings only in name: they gratify our wishes for a moment, but permanently disappoint our expectations. They charm the eye, but pall on the taste. Others are mere temporary blessings: they perish with the using. Though for awhile they regale the senses, they cannot satisfy the higher cravings of the soul. But, "Oh that thou wouldest bless me indeed!" I wot whom God blesseth shall be blessed. The thing good in itself is bestowed with the good-will of the giver, and shall be productive of so much good fortune to the recipient that it may well be esteemed as a blessing "indeed," for there is nothing comparable to it. Let the grace of God prompt it, let the choice of God appoint it, let the bounty of God confer it, and then the endowment shall be something godlike indeed; something worthy of the lips that pronounce the benediction, and verily to be craved by every one who seeks honor that is substantial and enduring. "Oh that thou wouldest bless me indeed!" Think it over, and you will see that there is a depth of meaning in the expression.

We may set this in contrast with human blessings: "Oh that thou wouldest bless me indeed!" It is very delightful to be blessed by our parents, and those venerable friends whose benedictions come from their hearts, and are backed up by their prayers. Many a poor man has had no other legacy to leave his children except his blessing, but the blessing of an honest, holy, Christian father is a rich treasure to his son. One might well feel it were a thing to be deplored through life if he had lost a parent's blessing. We like to have it. The blessing of our spiritual parents is consolatory. Though we believe in no priestcraft, we like to live in the affections of those who were the means of bringing us to Christ, and from whose lips we were instructed in the things of God. And how very precious is the blessing of the poor! I do not wonder that Job treasured that up as a sweet thing. "When the ear heard me, then it blessed me." If you have relieved the widow and the fatherless, and their thanks are returned to you in benediction, it is no mean reward. But, dear friends, after all – all that parents, relatives, saints, and grateful persons can do in the way of blessing, falls very far short of what we desire to have. O Lord, we would have the blessings of our fellow-creatures, the blessings that come from their hearts; but, "Oh that Thou wouldest bless me indeed!" for thou canst bless with authority. Their blessings may be but words, but thine are effectual. They may often wish what they cannot do, and desire to give what they have not at their own disposal, but thy will is omnipotent. Thou didst create the world with but a word. O that such omnipotence would now bespeak me thy blessing! Other blessings may bring us some tiny cheer, but in thy favor is life. Other blessings are mere tittles in comparison with thy blessing; for thy blessing is the title "to an inheritance incorruptible" and unfading, to "a kingdom which cannot be moved." Well therefore might David pray in another place, "With thy blessing let the house of thy servant be blessed for ever." Perhaps in this place, Jabez may have put the blessing of God in contrast with the blessings of men. Men will bless thee when thou doest well for thyself. They will praise the man who is successful in business. Nothing succeeds like success. Nothing has so much the approval of the general public as a man's prosperity. Alas! they do not weigh men's actions in the balances of the sanctuary, but in quite other scales. You will find those about you who will commend you if you are prosperous; or like Job's comforters, condemn you if you suffer adversity. Perhaps there may be some feature about their blessings that may please you, because you feel you deserve them. They commend you for your patriotism: you have been a patriot. They commend you for your generosity: you know you have been self-sacrificing. Well, but after all, what is there in the verdict of man? At a trial, the verdict of the policeman who stands in the court, or of the spectators who sit in the court-house, amounts to just nothing. The man who is being tried feels that the only thing that is of importance at all will be the verdict of the jury, and the sentence of the judge. So it will little avail us whatever we may do, how others commend or censure. Their blessings are not of any great value. But, "Oh that thou wouldest bless me,"

that thou wouldest say, "Well done, good and faithful servant." Commend thou the feeble service that through thy grace my heart has rendered. That will be to bless me indeed.

Men are sometimes blessed in a very fulsome sense by flattery. There are always those who, like the fox in the fable, hope to gain the cheese by praising the crow. They never saw such plumage, and no voice could be so sweet as yours. The whole of their mind is set, not on you, but on what they are to gain by you. The race of flatterers is never extinct, though the flattered usually flatter themselves it is so. They may conceive that men flatter others, but all is so palpable and transparent when heaped upon themselves, that they accept it with a great deal of self-complacency, as being perhaps a little exaggerated, but after all exceedingly near the truth. We are not very apt to take a large discount off the praises that others offer us; yet, were we wise, we should press to our bosom those who censure us; and we should always keep at arm's length those who praise us, for those who censure us to our face cannot possibly be making a market of us; but with regard to those who extol us, rising early, and using loud sentences of praise, we may suspect, and we shall very seldom be unjust in the suspicion, that there is some other motive in the praise which they render to us than that which appears on the surface. Young man, art thou placed in a position where God honors thee? Beware of flatterers. Or hast thou come into a large estate? Hast thou abundance? There are always flies where there is honey. Beware of flattery. Young woman, art thou fair to look upon? There will be those about thee that will have their designs, perhaps their evil designs, in lauding thy beauty. Beware of flatterers. Turn thou aside from all these who have honey on their tongue, because of the poison of asps that is under it. Bethink thee of Solomon's caution, "meddle not with him that flattereth with his lips." Cry to God, "Deliver thou me from all this vain adulation, which nauseates my soul." So shalt thou pray to him the more fervently, "Oh that thou wouldest bless me indeed!" Let me have thy benediction, which never says more than it means; which never gives less than it promises. If you take then the prayer of Jabez as being put in contrast with the benedictions which come from men, you see much force in it.

But we may put it in another light, and compare the blessing Jabez craved with those blessings that are temporal and transient. There are many bounties given to us mercifully by God for which we are bound to be very grateful; but we must not set too much store by them. We may accept them with gratitude, but we must not make them our idols. When we have them we have great need to cry, "Oh that thou wouldest bless me indeed, and make these inferior blessings real blessings"; and if we have them not, we should with greater vehemence cry, "Oh that we may be rich in faith, and if not blessed with these external favors, may we be blessed spiritually, and then we shall be blessed indeed."

Let us review some of these mercies, and just say a word or two about them.

One of the first cravings of men's hearts is wealth. So universal the desire to gain it, that we might almost say it is a natural instinct. How many have thought if they once possessed it they should be blessed indeed! but there are ten thousand proofs that happiness consists not in the abundance which a man possesseth. So many instances are well known to you all, that I need not quote any to show that riches are not a blessing indeed. They are rather apparently than really so. Hence, it has been well said, that when we see how much a man has we envy him; but could we see how little he enjoys we should pity him. Some that have had the most easy circumstances have had the most uneasy minds. Those who have acquired all they could wish, had their wishes been at all sane, have been led by the possession of what they had to be discontented because they had not more.

"Thus the base miser starves amidst his store,

Broods o'er his gold, and griping still at more,

Sits sadly pining, and believes he's poor."

Nothing is more clear to any one who chooses to observe it, than that riches are not the chief good at whose advent sorrow flies, and in whose presence joy perennial springs. Full often wealth cozens the owner. Dainties are spread on his table, but his appetite

fails, minstrels wait his bidding, but his ears are deaf to all the strains of music; holidays he may have as many as he pleases, but for him recreation has lost all its charms: or he is young, fortune has come to him by inheritance, and he makes pleasure his pursuit till sport becomes more irksome than work, and dissipation worse than drudgery. Ye know how riches make themselves wings; like the bird that roosted on the tree, they fly away. In sickness and despondency these ample means that once seemed to whisper, "Soul, take thine ease," prove themselves to be poor comforters. In death they even tend to make the pang of separation more acute, because there is the more to leave, the more to lose. We may well say, if we have wealth, "My God, put me not off with these husks; let me never make a god of the silver and the gold, the goods and the chattels, the estates and investments, which in thy providence thou hast given me. I beseech thee, bless me indeed. As for these worldly possessions, they will be my bane unless I have thy grace with them." And if you have not wealth, and perhaps the most of you will never have it, say, "My Father, thou hast denied me this outward and seeming good, enrich me with thy love, give me the gold of thy favor, bless me indeed; then allot to others whatever thou wilt, thou shalt divide my portion, my soul shall wait thy daily will; do thou bless me indeed, and I shall be content."

Another transient blessing which our poor humanity fondly covets and eagerly pursues is fame. In this respect we would fain be more honorable than our brethren, and outstrip all our competitors. It seems natural to us all to wish to make a name, and gain some note in the circle we move in at any rate, and we wish to make that circle wider if we can. But here, as of riches, it is indisputable that the greatest fame does not bring with it any equal measure of gratification. Men, in seeking after notoriety or honor, have a degree of pleasure in the search which they do not always possess when they have gained their object. Some of the most famous men have also been the most wretched of the human race. If thou hast honor and fame, accept it; but let this prayer go up, "My God, bless thou me indeed, for what profit were it, if my name were in a thousand mouths, if thou shouldest spew it out of thy mouth? What matter, though my name were written on marble, if it were not written in the Lamb's Book of Life? These blessings are only apparently blessings, windy blessings, blessings that mock me. Give me thy blessing: then the honor which comes of thee will make me blessed indeed." If you happen to have lived in obscurity, and have never entered the lists for honors among your fellow-men, be content to run well your own course and fulfill truly your own vocation. To lack fame is not the most grievous of ills; it is worse to have it like the snow, that whitens the ground in the morning, and disappears in the heat of the day. What matters it to a dead man that men are talking of him? Get thou the blessing indeed.

There is another temporal blessing which wise men desire, and legitimately may wish for rather than the other two – the blessing of health. Can we ever prize it sufficiently? To trifle with such a boon is the madness of folly. The highest eulogiums that can be passed on health would not be extravagant. He that has a healthy body is infinitely more blessed than he who is sickly, whatever his estates may be. Yet if I have health, my bones well set, and my muscles well strung, if I scarcely know an ache or pain, but can rise in the morning, and with elastic step go forth to labor, and cast myself upon my couch at night, and sleep the sleep of the happy, yet, oh let me not glory in my strength! In a moment it may fail me. A few short weeks may reduce the strong man to a skeleton. Consumption may set in, the cheek may pale with the shadow of death. Let not the strong man glory in his strength. The Lord "delighteth not in the strength of the horse: he taketh not pleasure in the legs of a man." And let us not make our boast concerning these things. Say, thou that are in good health, "My God, bless me indeed. Give me the healthy soul. Heal me of my spiritual diseases. Jehovah Rophi come, and purge out the leprosy that is in my heart by nature: make me healthy in the heavenly sense, that I may not be put aside among the unclean, but allowed to stand amongst the congregation of thy saints. Bless my bodily health to me that I may use it rightly, spending the strength I have in thy service and to thy glory; otherwise, though blessed with health, I may not be blessed indeed." Some of you, dear friends, do not possess the great treasure of health. Wearisome days and nights are appointed you. Your bones are become an almanac, in which you note the changes of the weather. There is much about you that is fitted to excite pity. But I pray that you may have the blessing indeed, and I know what that is. I can heartily sympathies with a sister that said to me the other day, "I had such nearness to God when I was sick, such full assurance, and such joy in the Lord, and I regret to say I have lost it now; that I could almost wish to be ill again, if thereby I might have a renewal of communion with God." I have oftentimes looked gratefully back to my sick chamber. I am certain that I never did grow in grace one half so much anywhere as I have upon the bed of pain. It ought not to be so. Our joyous mercies ought to be great fertilizers to our spirit; but not unfrequently our griefs are more salutary than our joys. The pruning knife is best for some of us. Well, after all, whatever you have to suffer, of weakness, of debility, of pain, and anguish, may it be so attended with the divine presence, that this light affliction may work out for you a far more exceeding and eternal weight of glory, and so you may be blessed indeed.

I will only dwell upon one more temporal mercy, which is very precious – I mean the blessing of home. I do not think any one can ever prize it too highly, or speak too well of it. What a blessing it is to have the fireside, and the dear relationships that gather round the word "Home," wife, children, father, brother, sister! Why, there are no songs in any language that are more full of music than those dedicated to "Mother." We hear a great deal about the German "Fatherland" – we like the sound. But the word, "Father," is the whole of it. The "land" is nothing: the "Father" is key to the music. There are many of us, I hope, blessed with a great many of these relationships. Do not let us be content to solace our souls with ties that must ere long be sundered. Let us ask that over and above them may come the blessing indeed. I thank thee, my God, for my earthly father; but oh, be thou my Father, then am I blessed indeed. I thank thee, my God, for a mother's love; but comfort thou my soul as one whom a mother comforteth, then am I blessed indeed. I thank thee, Savior, for the marriage bond; but be thou the bridegroom of my soul. I thank thee for the tie of brotherhood; but be thou my brother born for adversity, bone of my bone, and flesh of my flesh. The home thou hast given me I prize, and thank thee for it; but I would dwell in the house of the Lord for ever, and be a child that never wanders, wherever my feet may travel, from my Father's house with its many mansions. You can thus be blessed indeed. If not domiciled under the paternal care of the Almighty, even the blessing of home, with all its sweet familiar comforts, does not reach to the benediction which Jabez desired for himself. But do I speak to any here that are separated from kith and kin? I know some of you have left behind you in the bivouac of life graves where parts of your heart are buried, and that which remains is bleeding with just so many wounds. Ah, well! the Lord bless you indeed! Widow, thy maker is thy husband. Fatherless one, he hath said, "I will not leave you comfortless: I will come to you." Oh, to find all your relationships made up in him, then you will be blessed indeed! I have perhaps taken too long a time in mentioning these temporary blessings, so let me set the text in another light. I trust we have had human blessings and temporary blessings, to fill our hearts with gladness, but not to foul our hearts with worldliness, or to distract our attention from the things that belong to our everlasting welfare.

Let us proceed, thirdly, to speak of imaginary blessings. There are such in the world. From them may God deliver us. "Oh that thou wouldest bless me indeed!" Take the Pharisee. He stood in the Lord's house, and he thought he had the Lord's blessing, and it made him very bold, and he spoke with unctuous self-complacency, "God, I thank thee, that I am not as other men are," and so on. He had the blessing, and well indeed he supposed himself to have merited it. He had fasted twice in the week, paid tithes of all that he possessed, even to the odd farthing on the mint, and the extra halfpenny on the cumin he had used. He felt he had done everything. His the blessing of a quiet or a quiescent conscience; good, easy man. He was a pattern to the parish. It was a pity everybody did not live as he did; if they

had, they would not have wanted any police. Pilate might have dismissed his guards, and Herod his soldiers. He was just one of the most excellent persons that ever breathed. He adored the city of which he was a burgess! Ay; but he was not blessed indeed. This was all his own overweening conceit. He was a mere wind-bag, nothing more and the blessing which he fancied had fallen upon him, had never come. The poor publican whom he thought accursed, went to his home justified rather than he. The blessing had not fallen on the man who thought he had it. Oh, let every one of us here feel the sting of this rebuke, and pray: "Great God, save us from imputing to ourselves a righteousness which we do not possess. Save us from wrapping ourselves up in our own rags, and fancying we have put on the wedding garments. Bless me indeed. Let me have the true righteousness. Let me have the true worthiness which thou canst accept, even that which is of faith in Jesus Christ."

Another form of this imaginary blessing is found in persons who would scorn to be thought self-righteous. Their delusion, however, is near akin. I hear them singing –

"I do believe, I will believe
That Jesus died for me,
And on his cross he shed his blood,
From sin to set me free."

You believe it, you say. Well, but how do you know? Upon what authority do you make so sure? Who told you? "Oh, I believe it." Yes, but we must mind what we believe. Have you any clear evidence of a special interest in the blood of Jesus? Can you give any spiritual reasons for believing that Christ has set you free from sin? I am afraid that some have got a hope that has not got any ground, like an anchor without any fluke – nothing to grasp, nothing to lay hold upon. They say they are saved, and they stick to it they are, and think it wicked to doubt it; but yet they have no reason to warrant their confidence. When the sons of Kohath carried the ark, and touched it with their hands, they did rightly; but when Uzzah touched it he died. There are those who are ready to be fully assured; there are others to whom it will be death to talk of it. There is a great difference between presumption and full assurance. Full assurance is reasonable: it is based on solid ground. Presumption takes for granted, and with brazen face pronounces that to be its own to which it has no right whatever. Beware, I pray thee, of presuming that thou art saved. If with thy heart thou dost trust in Jesus, then art thou saved; but if thou merely sayest, "I trust in Jesus," it doth not save thee. If thy heart be renewed, if thou shalt hate the things that thou didst once love, and love the things that thou didst once hate; if thou hast really repented; if there be a thorough change of mind in thee; if thou be born again, then hast thou reason to rejoice: but if there be no vital change, no inward godliness; if there be no love to God, no prayer, no work of the Holy Spirit, then thy saying, "I am saved," is but thine own assertion, and it may delude, but it will not deliver thee. Our prayer ought to be, "Oh that thou wouldest bless me indeed, with real faith, with real salvation, with the trust in Jesus that is the essential of faith; not with the conceit that begets credulity. God preserve us from imaginary blessings!" I have met with persons who said, "I believe I am saved, because I dreamt it." Or, "Because I had a text of Scripture that applied to my own case. Such and such a good man said so and so in his sermon." Or, "Because I took to weeping and was excited, and felt as I never felt before." Ah! but nothing will stand the trial but this, "Dost thou abjure all confidence in everything but the finished work of Jesus, and dost thou come to Christ to be reconciled in him to God?" If thou dost not, thy dreams, and visions, and fancies, are but dreams, and visions, and fancies, and will not serve thy turn when most thou needest them. Pray the Lord to bless thee indeed, for of that sterling verity in all thy walk and talk there is a great scarcity.

Too much I am afraid, that even those who are saved – saved for time and eternity – need this caution, and have good cause to pray this prayer that they may learn to make a distinction between some things which they think to be spiritual blessings, and others which are blessings indeed. Let me show you what I mean. Is it certainly a blessing to get an answer to your prayer after your own mind? I always like to qualify my most earnest prayer with, "Not as I will, but as thou wilt." Not only ought I to do it, but I would like to do it, because

otherwise I might ask for something which it would be dangerous for me to receive. God might give it me in anger, and I might find little sweetness in the grant, but much soreness in the grief it caused me. You remember how Israel of old asked for flesh, and God gave them quails; but while the meat was yet in their mouths the wrath of God came upon them. Ask for the meat, if you like, but always put in this: "Lord, if this is not a real blessing, do not give it me." "Bless me indeed." I hardly like to repeat the old story of the good woman whose son was ill – a little child near death's door – and she begged the minister, a Puritan, to pray for its life. He did pray very earnestly, but he put in, "If it be thy will, save this child." The woman said, "I cannot bear that: I must have you pray that the child shall live. Do not put in any ifs or buts." "Woman," said the minister, "it may be you will live to rue the day that ever you wished to set your will up against God's will." Twenty years afterwards, she was carried away in a fainting fit from under Tyburn gallows-tree, where that son was put to death as a felon. Although she had lived to see her child grow up to be a man, it would have been infinitely better for her had the child died, and infinitely wiser had she left it to God's will. Do not be quite so sure that what you think an answer to prayer is any proof of divine love. It may leave much room for thee to seek unto the Lord, saying, "Oh that thou wouldest bless me indeed!" So sometimes great exhilaration of spirit, liveliness of heart, even though it be religious joy, may not always be a blessing. We delight in it, and oh, sometimes when we have had gatherings for prayer here, the fire has burned, and our souls have glowed! We felt at the time how we could sing:

> "My willing soul would stay
> In such a frame as this,
> And sit and sing herself away
> To everlasting bliss."

So far as that was a blessing we are thankful for it; but I should not like to set such seasons up, as if my enjoyments were the main token of God's favor; or as if they were the chief signs of his blessing. Perhaps it would be a greater blessing to me to be broken in spirit, and laid low before the Lord at the present time. When you ask for the highest joy, and pray to be on the mountain with Christ, remember it may be as much a blessing; yea, a blessing indeed to be brought into the Valley of Humiliation, to be laid very low, and constrained to cry out in anguish,

"Lord, save, or I perish!"

"If to-day he deigns to bless us
With a sense of pardon'd sin,
He to-morrow may distress us,
Make us feel the plague within,
All to make us
Sick of self, and fond of him."

These variable experiences of ours may be blessings indeed to us, when, had we been always rejoicing, we might have been like Moab, settled on our lees, and not emptied from vessel to vessel. It fares ill with those who have no changes; they fear not God. Have we not, dear friends, sometimes envied those persons that are always calm and unruffled, and are never perturbed in mind? Well, there are Christians whose evenness of temper deserves to be emulated. And as for that calm repose, that unwavering assurance which comes from the Spirit of God, it is a very delightful attainment; but I am not sure that we ought to envy anybody's lot because it is more tranquil or less exposed to storm and tempest than our own. There is a danger of saying, "Peace, peace," where there is no peace, and there is a calmness which arises from callousness. Dupes there are who deceive their own souls. "They have no doubts," they say, but it is because they have little heart searching. They have no anxieties, because they have not much enterprise or many pursuits to stir them up. Or it may be they have no pains, because they have no life. Better go to heaven, halt and maimed, than go marching on in confidence down to hell. "Oh that thou wouldest bless me indeed!" My God, I will envy no one of his gifts or his graces, much less of his inward mood or his outward circumstances, if only thou wilt "bless me indeed." I would not be comforted unless thou comfortest me, nor have any peace but Christ my peace, nor any rest but the rest which cometh from the sweet savor of the sacrifice of Christ. Christ shall be all in all, and none shall be anything to me save himself. O that we might always feel that we are not to judge as to the manner of the bless-

ing, but must leave it with God to give us what we would have, not the imaginary blessing, the superficial and apparent blessing, but the blessing indeed!

Equally too with regard to our work and service, I think our prayer should always be, "Oh that thou wouldest bless me indeed!" It is lamentable to see the work of some good men, though it is not ours to judge them, how very pretentious, but how very unreal it is. It is really shocking to think how some men pretend to build up a church in the course of two or three evenings. They will report, in the corner of the newspapers, that there were forty-three persons convinced of sin, and forty-six justified, and sometimes thirty-eight sanctified; I do not know what besides of wonderful statistics they give as to all that is accomplished. I have observed congregations that have been speedily gathered together, and great additions have been made to the church all of a sudden. And what has become of them? Where are those churches at the present moment? The dreariest deserts in Christendom are those places that were fertilized by the patent manures of certain revivalists. The whole church seemed to have spent its strength in one rush and effort after something, and it ended in nothing at all. They built their wooden house, and piled up the hay, and made a stubble spire that seemed to reach the heavens, and there fell one spark, and all went away in smoke; and he that came to labor next time – the successor of the great builder – had to get the ashes swept away before he could do any good. The prayer of every one that serves God should be, "Oh that thou wouldest bless me indeed." Plod on, plod on. If I only build one piece of masonry in my life, and nothing more, if it be gold, silver, or precious stones, it is a good deal for a man to do; of such precious stuff as that, to build even one little corner which will not show, is a worthy service. It will not be much talked of, but it will last. There is the point: it will last. "Establish thou the work of our hands upon us; yea, the work of our hands establish thou it." If we are not builders in an established church, it is of little use to try at all. What God establishes will stand, but what men build without his establishment will certainly come to nought. "Oh that thou wouldest bless me indeed!"

Sunday-school teacher, be this your prayer. Tract distributor, local preacher, whatever you may be, dear brother or sister, whatever your form of service, do ask the Lord that you may not be one of those plaster builders using sham compo that only requires a certain amount of frost and weather to make it crumble to pieces. Be it yours, if you cannot build a cathedral, to build at least one part of the marvelous temple that God is piling for eternity, which will outlast the stars.

I have one thing more to mention before I bring this sermon to a close. The blessings of God's grace are blessings indeed, which in right earnest we ought to seek after. By these marks shall ye know them. Blessings indeed, are such blessings as come from the pierced hand; blessings that come from Calvary's bloody tree, streaming from the Savior's wounded side – thy pardon, thine acceptance, thy spiritual life: the bread that is meat indeed, the blood that is drink indeed – thy oneness to Christ, and all that comes of it – these are blessings indeed. Any blessing that comes as the result of the Spirit's work in thy soul is a blessing indeed; though it humble thee, though it strip thee, though it kill thee, it is a blessing indeed. Though the harrow go over and over thy soul, and the deep plough cut into thy very heart; though thou be maimed and wounded, and left for dead, yet if the Spirit of God do it, it is a blessing indeed. If he convinceth thee of sin, of righteousness, and of judgment, even though thou hast not hitherto been brought to Christ, it is a blessing indeed. Anything that he does, accept it; do not be dubious of it; but pray that he may continue his blessed operations in thy soul. Whatsoever leads thee to God is in like manner a blessing indeed. Riches may not do it.

There may be a golden wall between thee and God. Health will not do it: even the strength and marrow of thy bones may keep thee at a distance from thy God. But anything that draws thee nearer to him is a blessing indeed. What though it be a cross that raiseth thee? Yet if it raise thee to God it shall be a blessing indeed. Anything that reaches into eternity, with a preparation for the world to come, anything that we can carry across the river, the holy joy that is to blossom in those fields beyond the swelling flood, the pure cloudless love of the brotherhood which is to be the atmosphere of truth for ever – anything of this kind that has the eternal broad arrow on it – the immutable mark – is a blessing indeed. And anything which helps me to glorify God is a blessing indeed. If I be sick, and that helps me to praise him, it is a blessing indeed. If I be poor, and I can serve him better in poverty than in wealth, it is a blessing indeed. If I be in contempt, I will rejoice in that day and leap for joy, if it be for Christ's sake – it is a blessing indeed. Yea, my faith shakes off the disguise, snatches the visor from the fair forehead of the blessing, and counts it all joy to all into divers trials for the sake of Jesus and the recompense of reward that he has promised. "Oh that we may be blessed indeed!"

Now, I send you away with these three words: "Search." See whether the blessings are blessings indeed, and be not satisfied unless you know that they are of God, tokens of his grace, and earnests of his saving purpose. "Weigh" – that shall be the next word. Whatever thou hast, weigh it in the scale, and ascertain if it be a blessing indeed, conferring such grace upon you as causeth you to abound in love, and to abound in every good word and work. And lastly, "Pray." So pray that this prayer may mingle with all thy prayers, that whatsoever God grants or whatever he withholds thou mayest be blessed indeed. Is it a joy-time with thee? O that Christ may mellow thy joy, and prevent the intoxication of earthly blessedness from leading thee aside from close walking with him! In the night of sorrow, pray that he will bless thee indeed, lest the wormwood also intoxicate thee and make thee drunk, lest thy afflictions should make thee think hardly of him. Pray for the blessing, which having, thou art rich to all the intents of bliss, or which lacking, thou art poor and destitute, though plenty fill thy store. "If thy presence go not with me, carry us not up hence." But "Oh that thou wouldest bless me indeed!"

C.H. Spurgeon, 1834–92

Holy Living

Jeremy Taylor

Of Prayer

CONTENTS
Motives to Prayer.
Rules for the Practice of Prayer.
Caution for making Vows.
Remedies against Wandering Thoughts in Prayer.
Signs of Tediousness of Spirit in our Prayers and all Actions of Religion.
Remedies against Tediousness of Spirit.

There is no greater argument in the world of our spiritual danger and unwillingness to religion, than the backwardness which most men have always, and all men have sometimes, to say their prayers – so weary of their length, so glad when they are done, so witty to excuse and frustrate an opportunity: and yet all is nothing but a desiring of God to give us the greatest and the best things we can need, and which can make us happy – it is a work so easy, so honorable, and to so great purpose, that in all the instances of religion and providence (except only the incarnation of his Son) God hath not given us a greater argument of his willingness to have us saved, and of our unwillingness to accept it, his goodness and our gracelessness, his infinite condescension and our carelessness and folly, than by rewarding so easy a duty with so great blessings.

MOTIVES TO PRAYER

I cannot say anything beyond this very consideration and its appendages to invite Christian people to pray often. But we may consider that,

1. It is a duty commanded by God and his holy Son.

2. It is an act of grace and highest honor, that we, dust and ashes, are admitted to speak to the eternal God, to run to him as to a father, to lay open our wants, to complain of our burdens, to explicate our scruples, to beg remedy and ease, support and counsel, health and safety, deliverance and salvation: and,

3. God hath invited us to it by many gracious promises of hearing us.

4. He hath appointed his most glorious Son to be the precedent of prayer, and to make continual intercession for us to the throne of grace.

5. He hath appointed an angel to present the prayers of his servants: and,

6. Christ unites them to his own, and sanctifies them, and makes them effective and prevalent: and,

7. Hath put it into the hands of men to rescind, or alter, all the decrees of God, which are of one kind, (that is, conditional, and concerning ourselves and our final estate, and many instances of our intermedial or temporal,) by the power of prayers.

8. And the prayers of men have saved cities and kingdoms from ruin: prayer hath raised cities and kingdoms from ruin: prayer hath raised dead men to life, hath stopped the violence of fire and shut the mouths of wild beasts, hath altered the course of nature, caused rain in Egypt, and drought in the sea: it made the sun to go from west to east, and the moon to stand still, and it cures diseases without physic, and makes physic to do the work of nature, and nature to do the work of grace, and grace to do the work of God; and it does miracles of accident and event; and yet prayer, that does all this, is, of itself, nothing but an ascent of the mind to God, a desiring things fit to be desired, and an expression of this desire to God as we can, and as becomes us. And our unwillingness to pray is nothing else but a not desiring what we ought passionately to long for; or, if we do desire it, it is a choosing rather to miss our satisfaction and felicity than to ask for it.

There is no more to be said in this affair, but that we reduce it to practice, according to the following rules:

RULES FOR THE PRACTICE OF PRAYER

1. We must be careful that we never ask anything of God that is sinful, or that directly ministers to sin; for that is to ask God to dishonor himself, and to undo us. We had need consider what we pray; for before it returns in blessing it must be joined with Christ's intercession, and presented to God. Let us principally ask of God power and assistances to do our duty, to glorify God, to do good works, to

live a good life, to die in the fear and favor of God and eternal life: these things God delights to give, and commands that we shall ask, and we may with confidence expect to be answered graciously; for these things are promised without any reservations of a secret condition: if we ask them, and do our duty towards the obtaining them, we are sure never to miss them

2. We may lawfully pray to God for the gifts of the Spirit that minister to holy ends; such as are the gift of preaching, the spirit of prayer, good expression, a ready and unloosed tongue, good understanding, learning, opportunities to publish them, etc., with these only restraints: (1.) That we cannot be so confident of the event of those prayers as of the former. (2.) That we must be curious to secure our intention in these desires, that we may not ask them to serve our own ends, but only for God's glory; and then we shall have them, or a blessing for desiring them. In order to such purposes our intentions in the first desires cannot be amiss; because they are able to sanctify other things, and therefore cannot be unhallowed themselves. (3.) We must submit to God's will, desiring him to choose our employment, and to furnish our persons as he shall see expedient.

3. Whatsoever we may lawfully desire of temporal things, we may lawfully ask of God in prayer, and we may expect them, as they are promised. (1.) Whatsoever is necessary to our life and being is promised to us; and therefore we may, with certainty, expect food and raiment, food to keep us alive, clothing to keep us from nakedness and shame; so long as our life is permitted to us, so long all things necessary to our life shall be ministered. We may be secure of maintenance, but not secure of our life – for that is promised, not this: only concerning food and raiment we are not to make accounts by the measure of our desires, but by the measure of our needs. (2.) Whatsoever is convenient for us; pleasant, and modestly delectable, we may pray for, so we do it, 1. With submission to God's will. 2. Without impatient desires. (3.) That it be not a trifle and inconsiderable, but a matter so grave and concerning as to be a fit matter to be treated on between God and our souls. (4.) That we ask not to spend upon our lusts, but for ends

of justice, or charity, or religion, and that they be employed with sobriety.

4. He that would pray with effect must live with care and piety. For although God gives to sinners and evil persons the common blessings of life and chance, yet either they want the comfort and blessing of those blessings, or they become occasions of sadder accidents to them, or serve to upbraid them in their ingratitude or irreligion: and in all cases, they are not the effects of prayer, or the fruits of promise, or instances of a father's love; for they cannot be expected with confidence, or received without danger, or used without a curse and mischief in their company. But as all sin is an impediment to prayer, so some have a special indisposition towards acceptation; such are uncharitableness and wrath, hypocrisy in the present action, pride and lust; because these, by defiling the body or the spirit, or by contradicting some necessary ingredient in prayer, (such as are mercy, humility, purity, and sincerity,) do defile the prayer, and make it a direct sin, in the circumstances or formality of the action.

5. All prayer must be made with faith and hope, that is, we must certainly believe we shall receive the grace which God hath commanded us to ask; and we must hope for such things which he hath permitted us to ask, and our hope shall not be vain, though we miss what is not absolutely promised; because we shall at least have an equal blessing in the denial as in the grant. And, therefore, the former conditions must first be secured; that is, that we ask things necessary, or at least good and innocent and profitable, and that our persons be gracious in the eyes of God: or else, what God hath promised to our natural needs he may, in many degrees, deny to our personal incapacity; but the thing being secured, and the person disposed, there can be no fault at all; for whatsoever else remains is on God's part, and that cannot possibly fail. But because the things which are not commanded cannot possibly be secured, (for we are not sure they are good in all circumstances,) we can but hope for such things, even after we have secured our good intentions. We are sure of a blessing, but in what instance we are not yet assured.

6. Our prayers must be fervent, intense, earnest, and importunate, when we pray

for things of high concernment and necessity. "Continuing instant in prayer; striving in prayer; laboring fervently in prayer; night and day, praying exceedingly; praying always with all prayer": so St. Paul calls it. "Watching unto prayer": so St. Peter. "Praying earnestly": so St. James. And this is not at all to be abated in matters spiritual and of duty: for, according as our desires are, so are our prayers; and as our prayers are, so shall be the grace; and as that is, so shall be the measure of glory. But this admits of degrees according to the perfection or imperfection of our state of life; but it hath no other measures, but ought to be as great as it can, the bigger the better: we must make no positive restraints upon ourselves. In other things they are to use a bridle; and as we must limit our desires with submission to God's will, so also we must limit the importunity of our prayers by the moderation and term of our desires. Pray for it as earnestly as you may desire it.

7. Our desires must be lasting, and our prayers frequent, assiduous, and continual; not asking for a blessing once, and then leaving it, but daily renewing our suits, and exercising our hope, and faith, and patience, and long-suffering, and religion, and resignation, and self-denial, in all the degrees we shall be put to. This circumstance of duty our blessed Savior taught, saying, that "men ought always to pray, and not to faint." Always to pray, signifies the frequent doing of the duty in general; but because we cannot always ask several things, and those are such as concern our great interest, the precept comes home to this very circumstance; and St. Paul calls it "praying without ceasing"; and himself in his own case gave a precedent – "For this cause I besought the Lord thrice." And so did our blessed Lord; he went thrice to God on the same errand, with the same words, in a short space-about half a night; for his time to solicit his suit was but short. And the Philippians were remembered by the apostle, their spiritual father, 'always pray for the pardon of our sins, for the assistance of God's grace, for charity, for life eternal, never giving over till we die"; and thus also we pray for supply of great temporal needs in their several proportions; in all cases being curious we do not give over out of weariness or impatience; for God oftentimes defers to grant our suit, because he loves to hear us beg it, and hath a design to give us more than we ask, even a satisfaction of our desires, and a blessing for the very importunity.

8. Let the words of our prayers be pertinent, grave, material, not studiously many, but according to our need, sufficient to express our wants, and to signify our importunity. God hears us not the sooner for our many words, but much the sooner for an earnest desire; to which let apt and sufficient words minister, be they few or many, according as it happens. A long prayer and a short differ not in their capacities of being accepted, for both of them take their value according to the fervency of spirit, and the charity of the prayer. That prayer, which is short by reason of an impatient spirit, or dullness, or despite of holy things, or indifferency of desires, is very often criminal, always imperfect; and that prayer which is long out of ostentation, or superstition, or a trifling spirit, is as criminal and imperfect as the other in their several instances. This rule relates to private prayer. In public, our devotion is to be measured by the appointed office, and we are to support our spirit with spiritual arts, that our private spirit may be a part of the public spirit, and be adopted into the society and blessings of the communion of saints.

9. In all forms of prayer mingle petition with thanksgiving, that you may endear the present prayer and the future blessing, by returning praise and thanks for what we have already received. This is St. Paul's advice – "Be careful for nothing; but in everything, by prayer and supplication with thanksgiving, let your requests be made known unto God."

10. Whatever we beg of God, let us also work for it, if the thing be matter of duty, or a consequent to industry; for God loves to bless labor and to reward it, but not to support idleness. And therefore our blessed Savior in his sermons joins watchfulness with prayer, for God's graces are but assistances, not new creations of the whole habit, in every instant or period of our life. Read Scriptures, and then pray to God for understanding. Pray against temptation; but you must also resist the devil, and then he will flee from you. Ask of God

competency of living; but you must also work with your hands the things that are honest, that ye may have to supply in time of need. We can but do our endeavor, and pray for blessing, and then leave the success with God; and beyond this we cannot deliberate, we cannot take care – but, so far, we must.

11. To this purpose let every man study his prayers and read his duty in his petitions. For the body of our prayer is the sum of our duty; and as we must ask of God whatsoever we need, so we must labor for all that we ask. Because it is our duty, therefore we must pray for God's grace; but because God's grace is necessary, and without it we can do nothing, we are sufficiently taught, that in the proper matter or our religious prayers is the just matter of our duty; and if we shall turn our prayers into precepts, we shall the easier turn our hearty desires into effective practices.

12. In all our prayers we must be careful to attend our present work, having a present mind, not wandering upon impertinent things, not distant from our words, much less contrary to them; and if our thoughts do at any time wander, and divert upon other objects, bring them back again with prudent and severe arts – by all means striving to obtain a diligent, a sober, an untroubled, and a composed spirit.

13. Let your posture and gesture of body in prayers be reverend, grave, and humble – according to public order, or the best examples, if it be in public – if it be in private, either stand or kneel, or lie flat upon the ground on your face, in your ordinary and more solemn prayers, but in extraordinary, casual, and ejaculatory prayers, the reverence and devotion of the soul, and the lifting up the eyes and hands to God with any other posture not indecent, is usual and commendable; for we may pray in bed, on horseback, "everywhere," and at all times, and in all circumstances; and it is well if we do so; and some servants have not opportunity to pray so often as they would, unless they supply the appetites of religion by such accidental devotions.

14. "Let prayers and supplications and giving of thanks be made for all men; for kings, and all that are in authority; for this is good and acceptable in the sight of God our Savior." We, who must love our neighbors as ourselves,

must also pray for them as for ourselves, with this only difference, that we may enlarge in our temporal desires for kings, and pray for secular prosperity to them with more importunity than for ourselves; because they need more to enable their duty and government, and for the interests of religion and justice. This part of prayer is by the apostle called intercession; in which, with special care, we are to remember our relatives, our family, our charge, our benefactors, our creditors, not forgetting to beg pardon and charity for our enemies, and protection against them.

15. Rely not on a single prayer in matters of great concernment; but make it as public as you can, by obtaining of others to pray for you – this being the great blessing of the communion of saints, that a prayer united is strong, like a well-ordered army; and God loves to be tied fast with such cords of love, and constrained by a holy violence.

16. Every time that is not seized upon by some other duty is seasonable enough for prayer; but let it be performed as a solemn duty morning and evening, that God may begin and end all our business; that the outgoing of the morning and evening may praise him; for so we bless God, and God blesses us. And yet fail not to find or make opportunities to worship God at some other times of the day, at least by ejaculations and short addresses, more or less, longer or shorter, solemnly or without solemnity, privately or publicly, as you can, or are permitted, always remembering, that as every sin is a degree of danger and unsafety, so every pious prayer and well-employed opportunity is a degree of return to hope and pardon.

CAUTION FOR MAKING VOWS

A vow to God is an act of prayer, and a great degree and instance of opportunity, and an increase of duty by some new uncommanded instance, or some more eminent degree of duty, or frequency of action, or earnestness of spirit in the same. And because it hath pleased God, in all ages of the world, to admit of intercourse with his servants in the matters of vows, it is not ill advice that we make vows to God in such cases in which we have great need or great danger. But let it be done according to these rules and by these cautions:

1. That the matter of the vow be lawful.

2. That it be useful in order to religion or charity.

3. That it be grave, not trifling or impertinent; but great in our proportion of duty towards the blessing.

4. That it be an uncommanded instance, that is, that it be of something, or in some manner, or in some degree, to which formerly we were not obliged, or which we might have omitted without sin.

5. That it be done with prudence; that is, that it be safe in all the circumstances of person, lest we beg a blessing and fall into a snare.

6. That every vow of a new action be also accompanied with a new degree and enforcement of our essential and unalterable duty – such as was Jacob's vow, that (besides the payment of the tithe) God should be his God; that so he might strengthen his duty to him, first in essentials and precepts, and then in additionals and accidentals. For it is but an ill tree that spends more in leaves and suckers and gums than in fruit; and that thankfulness and religion is best that first secures duty and then enlarges in counsels. Therefore, let every great prayer and great need and great danger draw us nearer to God by the approach of a pious purpose to live more strictly, and let every mercy of God answering that prayer produce a real performance of it.

7. Let not young beginners in religion enlarge their hearts and straighten their liberty by vows of long continuance; nor, indeed, any one else, without a great experience of himself and of all accidental dangers. Vows of single actions are safest, and proportionable to those single blessings ever begged in such cases of sudden and transient importunities.

8. Let no action which is matter of question and dispute in religion ever become the matter of a vow. He vows foolishly that promises to God to live and die in such an opinion in an article not necessary nor certain; or that, upon confidence of his present guide, binds himself for ever to the profession of what he may afterwards more reasonably contradict, or may find not to be useful, or not profitable, but of some danger or of no necessity.

If we observe the former rules we shall pray piously and effectually; but because even this duty hath in it some special temptations, it is necessary that we are armed by special remedies against them. The dangers are, 1. Wandering thoughts; 2. Tediousness of spirit. Against the first these advices are profitable:

REMEDIES AGAINST WANDERING THOUGHTS IN PRAYER.

If we feel our spirits apt to wander in our prayers, and to retire into the world, or to things unprofitable, or vain and impertinent:

1. Use prayer to be assisted in prayer; pray for the spirit of supplication, for a sober, fixed, and recollected spirit; and when to this you add a moral industry to be steady in your thoughts, whatsoever wanderings after this do return irremediably are a misery of nature and an imperfection, but no sin, while it is not cherished and indulged to.

2. In private it is not amiss to attempt the cure by reducing your prayers into collects and short forms of prayer, making voluntary interruptions, and beginning again, that the want of spirit and breath may be supplied by the short stages and periods.

3. When you have observed any considerable wanderings of your thoughts, bind yourself to repeat thy prayer again with actual attention, or else revolve the full sense of it in your spirit, and repeat it in all the effect and desires of it; and, possibly, the tempter may be driven away with his own art, and may cease to interpose his trifles when he perceives they do but vex the person into carefulness and piety; and yet he loses nothing of his devotion, but doubles the earnestness of his care.

4. If this be not seasonable or opportune, or apt to any man's circumstances, yet be sure, with actual attention, to say a hearty Amen to the whole prayer with one united desire, earnestly begging the graces mentioned in the prayer; for that desire does the great work of the prayer, and secures the blessing, if the wandering thoughts were against our will, and disclaimed by contending against them.

5. Avoid multiplicity of businesses of the world, and in those that are unavoidable, labor for an evenness and tranquility of spirit, that you may be untroubled and smooth in all tempests of fortune; for so we shall better tend religion when we are not torn in pieces with

the cares of the world, and seized upon with low affections, passions, and interest.

6. It helps much to attention and actual advertisement in our prayers, if we say our prayers silently, without the voice, only by the spirit. For, in mental prayer, if our thoughts wander we only stand still; when our mind returns we go on again – there is none of the prayer lost, as it is if our mouths speak and our hearts wander.

7. To incite you to the use of these, or any other counsels you shall meet with, remember that it is a great indecency to desire of God to hear those prayers, a great part whereof we do not hear ourselves. If they be not worthy of our attention they are far more unworthy of God's.

SIGNS OF TEDIOUSNESS OF SPIRIT IN OUR PRAYERS AND ALL ACTIONS OF RELIGION

The second temptation in our prayer is a tediousness of spirit or a weariness of the employment; like that of the Jews, who complained that they were weary of the new moons, and their souls loathed the frequent return of their Sabbaths: so do very many Christians, who first pray without fervor or earnestness of spirit; and, secondly, meditate but seldom, and that without fruit, or sense, or affection; or, thirdly, who seldom examine their consciences, and when they do it, they do it but sleepily, slightly, without compunction, or hearty purpose, or fruits of amendment. They enlarge themselves in the thoughts and fruitation of temporal things, running for comfort to them only in any sadness and misfortune. They love not to frequent the sacraments, nor any the instruments of religion, as sermons, confessions, prayers in public, fastings; but love ease and a loose undisciplined life. They obey not their superiors, but follow their own judgment when their judgment follows their affections, and their affections follow sense and worldly pleasures. They neglect, or dissemble, or defer, or do not attend to the motions and inclinations to virtue which the Spirit of God puts into their soul. They repent them of their vows and holy purposes, not because they discover any indiscretion in them, or intolerable inconvenience, but because they have within them labor (as the case now stands)

to them displeasure. They content themselves with the first degrees and necessary parts of virtue; and when they are arrived thither, they sit down as if they were come to the mountain of the Lord, and care not to proceed on toward perfection. They inquire into all cases in which it may be lawful to omit a duty; and, though they will not do less than they are bound to, yet they will do no more than needs must; for they do out of fear and self-love, not out of the love of God, or the spirit of holiness and zeal. The event of which will be this: he that will do no more than needs must, will soon be brought to omit something of his duty, and will be apt to believe less to be necessary than is.

REMEDIES AGAINST TEDIOUSNESS OF SPIRIT.

The remedies against this temptation are these:

1. Order your private devotions so that they become not arguments and causes of tediousness by their indiscreet length, but reduce your words into a narrow compass, still keeping all the matter; and what is cut off in the length of your prayers supply in the earnestness of your spirit; for so nothing is lost, while the words are changed into matter, and length of time into fervency of devotion. The forms are made not the less perfect, and the spirit is more, and the scruple is removed.

2. It is not imprudent, if we provide variety of forms of prayer to the same purposes, that the change, by consulting with the appetites of fancy, may better entertain the spirit; and, possibly, we may be pleased to recite a hymn when a collect seems flat to us and unpleasant; and we are willing to sing rather than to say, or to sing this rather than that: we are certain that variety is delightful; and whether that be natural to us, or an imperfection, yet if it be complied with, it any remove some part of the temptation.

3. Break your office and devotion into fragments, and make frequent returnings by ejaculations and abrupt intercourses with God; for so no length can oppress your tenderness and sickliness of spirit; and, by often praying in such manner and in all circumstances, we shall habituate our souls to prayer by making it the business of many lesser portions of our time; and by thrusting in between all our

other employments, it will make everything relish of religion, and by degrees turn all into its nature.

4. Learn to abstract your thoughts and desires from pleasures and things of the world; for nothing is a direct cure to this evil but cutting off all other loves and adherences. Order your affairs so that religion may be propounded to you as a reward, and prayer as your defense, and holy actions as your security and charity and good works as your treasure. Consider that all things else are satisfactions but to the brutish part of a man; and that these are the refreshments and relishes of that noble part of us by which we are better than beasts; and whatsoever other instrument, exercise, or consideration, is of use to take our loves from the world, the same is apt to place them upon God.

5. Do not seek for deliciousness and sensible consolations in the actions of religion, but only regard the duty and the conscience of it; for although in the beginning of religion most frequently, and at some other times irregularly, God complies with our infirmity, and encourages our duty with little overflowings of spiritual joy, and sensible pleasure, and delicacies in prayer, so as we seem to feel some little beam of heaven, and great refreshments from the spirit of consolation, yet this is not always safe for us to have, neither safe for us to expect and look for; and when we do, it is apt to make us cool in our inquires and waitings upon Christ when we want them: it is a running after him, not for the miracles but for the loaves; not for the wonderful things of God, and the desires of pleasing him, but for the pleasures of pleasing ourselves. And as we must not judge our devotion to be barren or unfruitful when we want the overflowings of joy running over, so neither must we cease for want of them. If our spirits can serve God choosingly and greedily out of pure conscience of our duty, it is better in itself and more safe for us.

6. Let him use to soften his spirit with frequent meditation upon sad and dolorous objects, as of death, the terrors of the day of judgment, fearful judgments upon sinners, strange horrid accidents, fear of God's wrath, the pains of hell, the unspeakable amazements of the damned, the intolerable load of a sad

eternity: for whatsoever creates fear, or makes the spirit to dwell in a religious sadness, is apt to entender the spirit, and make it devout and pliant to any part of duty; for a great fear, when it is ill-managed, is the parent of superstition; but a discreet and well-guided fear produces religion.

7. Pray often, and you shall pray oftener; and when you are accustomed to a frequent devotion, it will so insensibly unite to your nature and affections, that it will become a trouble to omit your usual or appointed prayers; and what you obtain at first by doing violence to your inclinations, at last will not be left without as great unwillingness as that by which at first it entered. This rule relies not only upon reason derived from the nature, of habits, which turn into a second nature, and make their actions easy, frequent, and delightful' but it relies upon a reason depending upon the nature and constitution of grace, whose productions are of the same nature with the parent, and increases itself, naturally growing from grains to huge trees, from minutes to vast proportions, and from moments to eternity. But be sure not to omit your usual prayers without great reason, though without sin it may be done; because after you have omitted something, in a little while you will be past the scruple of that, and begin to be tempted to leave out more. Keep yourself up to your usual forms – you may enlarge when you will; but do not contract or lesson them without a very probable reason.

8. Let a man frequently and seriously, by imagination, place himself upon his death-bed, and consider what great joys he shall have for the remembrance of every day well spent, and what then he would give that he had so spent all his days. He may guess at it by proportions; for it is certain he shall have a joyful and prosperous night who hath spent his day holily; and he resigns his soul with peace into the hands of God, who hath lived in the peace of God and the works of religion in his lifetime. This consideration is of a real event; it is of a thing that will certainly come to pass. 'It is appointed for all men once to die;' and after death comes judgment; the apprehension of which is dreadful, and the presence of it is intolerable; unless, by religion and sanctity, we are disposed for so

venerable an appearance.

9. To this may be useful that we consider the easiness of Christ's yoke, the excellences and sweetnesses that are in religion, the peace of conscience, the joy of the Holy Ghost, the rejoicing in God, the simplicity and pleasure of virtue, the intricacy, trouble, and business of sin; the blessings and health and reward of that; the curses the sicknesses and sad consequences of this; and that, if we are weary of the labors of religion, we must sit still and do nothing; for whatsoever we do contrary to it is infinitely more full of labor, care, difficulty, and vexation.

10. Consider this also, that tediousness of spirit is the beginning of the most dangerous condition and estate in the whole world. For it is a great disposition to the sin against the Holy Ghost: it is apt to bring a man to backsliding and the state of unregeneration; to make him return to his vomit and his sink; and either to make the man impatient, or his condition scrupulous, unsatisfied, irksome, and desperate: and it is better that he had never known the way of godliness, than, after the knowledge of it, that he should fall away. There is not in the world a greater sign that the spirit of reprobation is beginning upon a man than when he is habitually and constantly, or very frequently, weary, and slights or loathes holy offices.

11. The last remedy that preserves the hope of such a man, and can reduce him to the state of zeal and the love of God, is a pungent, sad, and a heavy affliction; not desperate, but recreated with some intervals of kindness, or little comforts, or entertained with hopes of deliverance; which condition if a man shall fall into, by the grace of God he is likely to recover; but if this help him not, it is infinite odds but he will quench the spirit.

Jeremy Taylor, 1613–67

On Prayer

Tertullian

CONTENTS

CHAPTER 1. GENERAL INTRODUCTION
The Spirit of God, and the Word of God, and the Reason of God – Word of Reason, and Reason and Spirit of Word – Jesus Christ our Lord, namely, who is both the one and the other, – has determined for us, the disciples of the New Testament, a new form of prayer; for in this particular also it was needful that new wine should be laid up in new skins, and a new breadth be sewn to a new garment. Besides, whatever had been in bygone days, has either been quite changed, as circumcision; or else supplemented, as the rest of the Law; or else fulfilled, as Prophecy; or else perfected, as faith itself. For the new grace of God has renewed all things from carnal unto spiritual, by superinducing the Gospel, the obliterator of the whole ancient bygone system; in which our Lord Jesus Christ has been approved as the Spirit of God, and the Word of God, and the Reason of God: the Spirit, by which He was mighty; the Word, by which He taught; the Reason, by which He came. So the prayer composed by Christ has been composed of three parts. In speech, by which *prayer* is enunciated, in spirit, by which alone it prevails, even John had taught his disciples to pray, but all John's doings were laid as groundwork for Christ, until, when "He had increased" – just as the same John used to announce "that it was needful" that "He should increase and himself decrease" – the whole

work of the forerunner passed over, together with his spirit itself, unto the Lord. Therefore, after what form of words John taught to pray is not extant, because earthly things have given place to heavenly. "He who is from the earth," says John, "speaketh earthly things; and He who is here from the heavens speaketh those things which He hath seen." And what is the Lord Christ's – as this method of praying is – that is not heavenly? And so, blessed *brethren*, let us consider His heavenly wisdom: first, touching the precept of praying secretly, whereby He exacted man's faith, that he should be confident that the sight and hearing of Almighty God are present beneath roofs, and extend even into the secret place; and required modesty in faith, that it should offer its religious homage to Him alone, whom it believed to see and to hear everywhere. Further, since wisdom succeeded in the following precept, let it in like manner appertain unto faith, and the modesty of faith, that we think not that the Lord must be approached with a train of words, who, we are certain, takes unsolicited foresight for His own. And yet that very brevity – and let this make for the third grade of wisdom – is supported on the substance of a great and blessed interpretation, and is as diffuse in meaning as it is compressed in words. For it has embraced not only the special duties of prayer, be it veneration of God or petition for man, but almost every discourse of the Lord, every record of *His* Discipline; so that, in fact, in the Prayer is comprised an epitome of the whole Gospel.

CHAPTER 2. THE FIRST CLAUSE

The prayer begins with a testimony to God, and with the reward of faith, when we say, "Our Father who art in the heavens"; for (in so saying), we at once pray to God, and commend faith, whose reward this appellation is. It is written, "To them who believed on Him He gave power to be called sons of God." However, our Lord very frequently proclaimed God as a Father to us; nay, even gave a precept "that we call no one on earth father, but the Father whom we have in the heavens": and so, in thus praying, we are likewise obeying the precept. Happy they who recognize their Father! This is the reproach that is brought against Israel,

to which the Spirit attests heaven and earth, saying, "I have begotten sons, and they have not recognized me." Moreover, in saying "Father," we also call Him "God." That appellation is one both of filial duty and of power. Again, in the Father the Son is invoked; "for I," saith He, "and the Father are One." Nor is even our mother the Church passed by, if, that is, in the Father and the Son is recognized the mother, from whom arises the name both of Father and of Son. In one general term, then, or word, we both honor God, together with His own, and are mindful of the precept, and set a mark on such as have forgotten their Father.

CHAPTER 3. THE SECOND CLAUSE

The name of "God the Father" had been published to none. Even Moses, who had interrogated Him on that very point, had heard a different name. To us it has been revealed in the Son, for the Son is now the Father's new name. "I am come," saith He, "in the Father's name"; and again, "Father, glorify Thy name"; and more openly, "I have manifested Thy name to men." That *name*, therefore, we pray may "be hallowed." Not that it is becoming for men to *wish* God *well*, as if there were any other by whom He may be wished well, or as if He would suffer unless we do so wish. Plainly, it is universally becoming for God to be *blessed* in every place and time, on account of the memory of His benefits ever due from every man. But this petition also serves the turn of a blessing. Otherwise, when is the name of God not "holy," and "hallowed" through Himself, seeing that of Himself He sanctifies all others – He to whom that surrounding circle of angels cease not to say, "Holy, holy, holy"? In like wise, therefore, we too, candidates for angelhood, if we succeed in deserving it, begin even here on earth to learn by heart that strain hereafter to be raised unto God, and the function of future glory. So far, for the glory of God. On the other hand, for our own petition, when we say, "Hallowed be Thy name," we pray this; that it may be hallowed *in us* who are in Him, as well in all others for whom the grace of God is still waiting; that we may obey this precept, too, in "praying for all," even for our personal enemies. And therefore with suspended utterance, not saying, "Hallowed be it *in us*," we say, "*in all*."

CHAPTER 4. THE THIRD CLAUSE

According to this model, we subjoin, "Thy will be done in the heavens and on the earth"; not that there is some power withstanding to prevent God's will being done, and we pray for Him the successful achievement of His will; but we pray for His will to be done *in all*. For, by figurative interpretation of *flesh* and *spirit, we* are "heaven" and "earth"; albeit, even if it is to be understood simply, still the sense of the petition is the same, that *in us* God's will be done on earth, to make it possible, namely, for it to be done also in the heavens. What, moreover, *does* God will, but that we should walk according to His Discipline? We make petition, then, that He supply us with the substance of His will, and the capacity to do it, that we may be saved both in the heavens and on earth; because the sum of His will is the salvation of them whom He has adopted. There is, too, that will of God which the Lord accomplished in preaching, in working, in enduring: for if He Himself proclaimed that He did not His own, but the Father's will, without doubt those things which He used to do *were* the Father's will; unto which things, as unto exemplars, we are now provoked; to preach, to work, to endure even unto death. And we *need* the will of God, that we may be able to fulfill these duties. Again, in saying, "Thy will be done," we are even wishing well to ourselves, in so far that there is nothing of *evil* in the will of God; even if, proportionably to each one's deserts, somewhat other is imposed on us. So by this expression we premonish our own selves unto patience. The Lord also, when He had wished to demonstrate to us, even in His own flesh, the flesh's infirmity, by the reality of suffering, said, "Father, remove this Thy cup"; and remembering Himself, *added*, "save that not my will, but Thine be done." Himself *was* the Will and the Power of the Father: and yet, for the demonstration of the patience which was due, He gave Himself up *to* the Father's Will.

CHAPTER 5. THE FOURTH CLAUSE

"Thy kingdom come" has also reference to that whereto "Thy will be done" refers – *in us,* that is. For when does God not reign, in whose hand is the heart of all kings? But whatever we wish for ourselves we augur for Him, and *to*

Him we attribute what *from* Him we expect. And so, if the *manifestation* of the Lord's kingdom pertains unto the will of God and unto our anxious expectation, how do some pray for some protraction of the age, when the kingdom of God, which we pray may arrive, tends unto the consummation of the age? Our wish is, that our reign be hastened, not our servitude protracted. Even if it had not been prescribed in the Prayer that we should ask for the advent of the kingdom, we should, unbidden, have sent forth that cry, hastening toward the realization of our hope. The souls of the martyrs beneath the altar cry in jealousy unto the Lord "How long, Lord, dost Thou not avenge our blood on the inhabitants of the earth?" for, of course, their avenging is regulated by the end of the age. Nay, Lord, Thy kingdom come with all speed, – the prayer of Christians the confusion of the heathen, the exultation of angels, for the sake of which we suffer, nay, rather, for the sake of which we pray!

CHAPTER 6. THE FIFTH CLAUSE

But how gracefully has the Divine Wisdom arranged the order of the prayer; so that *after* things heavenly – that is, after the "Name" of God, the "Will" of God, and the "Kingdom" of God – it should give earthly necessities also room for a petition! For the Lord had withal issued His edict, "Seek ye first the kingdom, and then even these shall be added": albeit we may rather understand, "Give us this day our daily bread," *spiritually*. For *Christ* is our Bread; because Christ is Life, and bread is life. "I am," saith He, "the Bread of Life"; and, a little above, "The Bread is the Word of the living God, who came down from the heavens." Then *we find*, too, that His body is reckoned in bread: "This is my body." And so, in petitioning for "daily bread," we ask for perpetuity in Christ, and indivisibility from His body. But, because that word is admissible in a carnal sense too, it cannot be so used without the religious remembrance withal of spiritual Discipline; for (the Lord) commands that *bread* be prayed for, which is the only *food* necessary for believers; for "all other things the nations seek after." The like lesson He both inculcates by examples, and repeatedly handles in parables, when He says, "Doth a father take away *bread* from his children, and hand it to dogs?" and again, "Doth a father give his son a stone when he asks for *bread*?" For He *thus* shows what it is that sons expect from their father. Nay, even that nocturnal knocker knocked for "*bread.*" Moreover, He Justly added, "Give us *this day*," seeing He had previously said, "Take no careful thought about the morrow, what ye are to eat." To which subject He also adapted the parable of the man who pondered on an enlargement of his barns for his forthcoming fruits, and on seasons of prolonged security; but that very night he dies.

CHAPTER 7. THE SIXTH CLAUSE

It was suitable that, after contemplating the liberality of God, we should likewise address His clemency. For what will aliments profit us, if we are really *consigned* to them, as it were a bull destined for a victim? The Lord knew Himself to be the only guiltless One, and so He teaches that we beg "to have our debts remitted us." A petition for pardon is a full confession; because he who begs for pardon fully admits his guilt. Thus, too, penitence is demonstrated acceptable to God who desires it rather than the death of the sinner. Moreover, *debt* is, in the Scriptures, a figure of *guilt*; because it is equally due to the sentence of judgment, and is exacted by it: nor does it evade the justice of exaction, unless the exaction be remitted, just as the lord remitted to that slave *in the parable* his debt; for hither does the scope of the whole parable tend. For the fact withal, that the same servant, after liberated by his lord, does not equally spare his own debtor; and, being on that account impeached before his lord, is made over to the tormentor to pay the uttermost farthing – that is, every guilt, however small: corresponds with our profession that "we also remit to our debtors"; indeed elsewhere, too, in conformity with this Form of Prayer, He saith, "Remit, and it shall be remitted you." And when Peter had put the question whether remission were to be granted to a brother seven times, "Nay," saith He, "seventy-seven times"; in order to remold the Law for the better; because in Genesis *vengeance* was assigned "seven times" in the case of Cain, but in that of Lamech "seventy-seven times."

CHAPTER 8. THE SEVENTH OR FINAL CLAUSE

For the completeness of so brief a prayer He added – in order that we should supplicate not touching the remitting merely, but touching the entire averting, of acts of guilt "Lead us not into temptation": that is, suffer us not to be led into it, by him (of course) who tempts; but far be the thought that the Lord should seem to tempt, as if He either were ignorant of the faith of any, or else were eager to overthrow it. Infirmity and malice are characteristics of the devil. For *God* had commanded even Abraham to make a sacrifice of his son, for the sake not of tempting, but proving, his faith; in order through him to make an example for that precept of His, whereby He was, by and by, to enjoin that he should hold no pledges of affection dearer than God. He Himself, when tempted by the devil, demonstrated who it is that presides over and is the originator of temptation. This passage He confirms by subsequent ones, saying, "Pray that ye be not tempted"; yet they *were* tempted", (as they showed) by de-setting their Lord, because they had given way rather to sleep than prayer. The final clause, therefore, is consonant, and interprets the sense of "Lead us not into temptation"; for this *sense* is, "But convey us away from the Evil One."

CHAPTER 9. RECAPITULATION

In summaries of so few words, how many utterances of the prophets, the Gospels, the apostles – how many discourses, examples, parables of the Lord, are touched on! How many duties are simultaneously discharged! The honor of God in the "Father"; the testimony of faith in the "Name; "the offering of obedience in the "Will"; the commemoration of hope in the "Kingdom"; the petition for life in the "Bread"; the full acknowledgment of debts in the prayer for their "Forgiveness"; the anxious dread of temptation in the request for "Protection." What wonder? God alone could teach how he wished Himself prayed to. The religious rite of prayer therefore, ordained by Himself, and animated, even at the moment when it was issuing out of the Divine mouth, by His own Spirit, ascends, by its own prerogative, into heaven, commending to the Father what the Son has taught.

CHAPTER 10. WE MAY SUPERADD PRAYERS OF OUR OWN TO THE LORD'S PRAYER

Since, however, the Lord, the Foreseer of human necessities, said separately, after delivering His Rule of Prayer, "Ask, and ye shall receive"; and *since* there are petitions which are made according to the circumstances of each individual; our additional wants have the right – after beginning with the legitimate and customary prayers as a foundation, as it were – of rearing an outer superstructure of petitions, yet with remembrance of the Master's precepts.

CHAPTER 11. WHEN PRAYING THE FATHER, YOU ARE NOT TO BE ANGRY WITH A BROTHER

That we may not be as far from the ears of God as we are from His precepts, the memory of His precepts paves for our prayers a way unto heaven; of which *precepts* the chief is, that we go not up unto God's altar before we compose whatever of discord or offence we have contracted with our brethren. For what sort of deed is it to approach the peace of God without peace? the remission of debts while you retain them? How will he appease his *Father* who is angry with his *brother*, when from the beginning "all anger" is forbidden us? For even Joseph, when dismissing his brethren for the purpose of fetching their father, said, "And be not angry in the way." He warned *us*, to be sure, at that time (for elsewhere our Discipline is called "the Way"), that when, set in "the way" of prayer, we go not unto "the Father" with anger. After that, the Lord, "amplifying the Law," openly adds *the prohibition of* anger against a brother to *that of* murder. Not even by an evil word does He permit it to be vented. Ever if we *must* be angry, our anger must not be maintained beyond sunset, as the apostle admonishes. But how rash is it either to pass a day without prayer, while you refuse to make satisfaction to your brother; or else, by perseverance in anger, to lose your prayer?

CHAPTER 12. WE MUST BE FREE LIKEWISE FROM ALL MENTAL PERTURBATION

Nor merely from anger, but altogether from *all* perturbation of mind, ought the exercise of prayer to be free, uttered from a spirit such as the Spirit unto whom it is sent. For a defiled spirit cannot be acknowledged by a holy Spirit, nor a sad by a joyful, nor a lettered by a free. No one grants reception to his adversary: no one grants admittance except to his compeer …

CHAPTER 13. OF KNEELING

In the matter of *kneeling* also prayer is subject to diversity of observance, through the act of some few who abstain from kneeling on the Sabbath; and since this dissension is particularly on its trial before the churches, the Lord will give His grace that the dissentients may either yield, or else indulge their opinion without offence to others. We, however (just as we have received), only on the day of the Lord's Resurrection ought to guard not only against kneeling, but every posture and office of solicitude; deferring even our businesses lest we give any place to the devil. Similarly, too, in the period of Pentecost; which period we distinguish by the same solemnity of exultation. But who would hesitate *every* day to prostrate himself before God, at least in the first prayer with which we enter on the daylight? At fasts, moreover, and Stations, no prayer should be made without kneeling, and the remaining customary marks of humility; for (then) we are not only *praying*, but *deprecating*, and making satisfaction to God our Lord. Touching *times* of prayer nothing at all has been prescribed, except clearly "to pray at every time and every place."

CHAPTER 14. OF PLACE FOR PRAYER

But how "in every place," since we are prohibited (from praying) in public? In every place, he means, which opportunity or even necessity, may have rendered suitable: for that which was done by the apostles (who, in gaol, in the audience of the prisoners, "began praying and singing to God") is not considered to have been done contrary to the precept; nor yet that which was done by Paul, who in the ship, in presence of all, "made thanksgiving to God."

CHAPTER 15. OF TIME FOR PRAYER

Touching the *time*, however, the extrinsic observance of certain hours will not be unprofitable – those common hours, I mean, which mark the intervals of the day – the third, the sixth, the ninth – which we may find in the Scriptures to have been more solemn than the rest. The first infusion of the Holy Spirit into the congregated disciples took place at "the third hour." Peter, on the day on which he experienced the vision of Universal Community, (exhibited) in that small vessel, had ascended into the more lofty parts *of the house*, for prayer's sake "at the sixth hour." The same (apostle) was going into the temple, with John, "at the ninth *hour*," when he restored the paralytic to his health. Albeit these *practices* stand simply without any *precept* for their observance, still it may be granted a good thing to establish some definite presumption, which may both add stringency to the admonition to, pray, and may, as it were by a law, tear us out from our businesses unto such a duty; so that – what we read to have been observed by Daniel also, in accordance (of course) with Israel's discipline – we pray at least not less than thrice in the day, debtors as we are to Three – Father, Son, and Holy Spirit: of course, in addition to our regular prayers which are due, without any admonition, on the entrance of light and of night. But, withal, it becomes believers not to take food, and not to go to the bath, before interposing a prayer; for the refreshments and nourishments of the spirit are to be held prior to those of the flesh, and things heavenly prior to things earthly.

CHAPTER 16. OF THE PARTING OF BRETHREN

You will not dismiss a brother who has entered your house without prayer. "Have you seen," says *Scripture*, "a brother? you have seen your Lord;" – especially "a stranger," lest perhaps he be "an angel." But again, when received yourself by brethren, you will not make earthly refreshments prior to heavenly, for your faith will forthwith be judged. Or else how will you – according to the precept – say, "Peace to this *house*," unless you exchange mutual peace with them who are *in* the house?

CHAPTER 17. OF SUBJOINING A PSALM

The more diligent in prayer are wont to subjoin in their prayers the "Hallelujah," and such kind of psalms, in the closes of which the company respond. And, of course, every institution is excellent which, for the extolling and honoring of God, aims unitedly to bring Him enriched prayer as a choice victim.

CHAPTER 18. OF THE SPIRITUAL VICTIM, WHICH PRAYER IS

For this is the spiritual victim which has abolished the pristine sacrifices. "To what purpose," saith He, "(bring ye) me the multitude of your sacrifices? I am full of holocausts of rams, and I desire not the fat of rams, and the blood of bulls and of goats. For who hath required these from your hands?" What, then, God *has* required the Gospel teaches. "An hour will come," saith He, "when the true adorers shall adore the Father in spirit and truth. For God is a Spirit, and accordingly requires His adorers to be such." We are the true adorers and the true priests, who, praying in spirit, sacrifice, in spirit, prayer, – a victim proper and acceptable to God, which assuredly He has required, which He has looked forward to for Himself! This *victim*, devoted from the whole heart, fed on faith, tended by truth, entire in innocence, pure in chastity, garlanded with love, we ought to escort with the pomp of good works, amid psalms and hymns, unto God's altar, to obtain for us all things from God.

CHAPTER 19. OF THE POWER OF PRAYER

For what has God, who exacts it *ever* denied to prayer coming from "spirit and truth"? How mighty specimens of its efficacy do we read, and hear, and believe! *Old-world* prayer, indeed, used to free from fires, and from beasts, and from famine; and yet it had not (then) received its form from Christ. But how far more amply operative is *Christian* prayer! It does not station the angel of dew in mid-fires, nor muzzle lions, nor transfer to the hungry the rustics' bread; it has no delegated grace to avert any sense of suffering; but it supplies the suffering, and the feeling, and the grieving, with endurance: it amplifies grace by virtue, that faith may know what she obtains from the Lord, understanding what – for God's name's sake – she suffers. But in days gone by, withal prayer used to call down plagues, scatter the armies of foes, withhold the wholesome influences of the showers. Now, however, the prayer of righteousness avers all God's anger, keeps bivouac on behalf of personal enemies, makes supplication on behalf of persecutors. Is it wonder if *it* knows how to extort the *rains* of heaven – (prayer) which was *once* able to procure its *fires*? Prayer is alone that which vanquishes God. But Christ has willed that it be operative for no evil: He had conferred on it all its virtue in the cause of good. And so it knows nothing save how to recall the souls of the departed from the very path of death, to transform the weak, to restore the sick, to purge the possessed, to open prison-bars, to loose the bonds of the innocent. Likewise it washes away faults, repels temptations, extinguishes persecutions, consoles the faint-spirited, cheers the high-spirited, escorts travelers, appeases waves, makes robbers stand aghast, nourishes the poor, governs the rich, upraises the fallen, arrests the falling, confirms the standing. Prayer is the wall of faith: her arms and missiles against the foe who keeps watch over us on all sides. And, so never walk we unarmed. By day, be we mindful of Station; by night, of vigil. Under the arms of prayer guard we the standard of our General; await we in prayer the angel's trump. The angels, likewise, all pray; every creature prays; cattle and wild beasts pray and bend their knees; and when they issue from their layers and lairs, they look up heavenward with no idle mouth, making their breath vibrate after their own manner. Nay, the birds too, rising out of the nest, upraise themselves heavenward, and, instead of hands, expand the cross of their wings, and say somewhat to seem like prayer. What more then, touching the office of prayer? Even the Lord Himself prayed; to whom be honor and virtue unto the ages of the ages!

Tertullian, c.160–225, On Prayer

Praise
R.A. Torrey

Praise
God is worthy of, 2 Sa 22:4.
Christ is worthy of, Re 5:12.
God is glorified by, Ps 22:23; 50:23.
Offered to Christ, Joh 12:13.
Acceptable through Christ, Heb 13:15.

Is due to God on account of
His majesty, Ps 96:1, 6; Isa 24:14.
His glory, Ps 138:5; Eze 3:12.

His excellency, Ex 15:7; Ps 148:13.
His greatness, 1Ch 16:25; Ps 145:3.
His holiness, Ex 15:11; Isa 6:3.
His wisdom, Da 2:20; Jude 1:25.
His power, Ps 21:13.
His goodness, Ps 107:8; 118:1; 136:1; Jer 33:11.
His mercy, 2 Ch 20:21; Ps 89:1; 118:1–4; 136:1–26.
His loving-kindness and truth, Ps 138:2.
His faithfulness and truth, Isa 25:1.
His salvation, Ps 18:46; Isa 35:10; 61:10; Lu 1: 68, 69.
His wonderful works, Ps 89:5; 150:2; Isa 25:1.
His consolation, Ps 42:5; Isa 12:1.
His judgment, Ps 101:1.
His counsel, Ps 16:7; Jer 32:19.
Fulfilling of his promises, 1 Ki 8:56.
Pardon of sin, Ps 103:1–3; Ho 14:2.
Spiritual health, Ps 103:3.
Constant preservation, Ps 71:6–8.
Deliverance, Ps 40:1–3; 124:6.
Protection, Ps 28:7; 59:17.
Answering prayer, Ps 28:6; 118:21.
The hope of glory, 1 Pe 1:3,4.
All spiritual blessings, Ps 103:2; Eph 1:3.
All temporal blessings, Ps 104:1, 14; 136:25.
The continuance of blessings, Ps 68:19.

Is obligatory upon
Angels, Ps 103:20; 148:2.
Saints, Ps 30:4; 149:5.
Gentiles, Ps 117:1; Ro 15:11.
Children, Ps 8:2; Mt 21:16.
High and low, Ps 148:1, 11.
Young and old, Ps 148:1, 12.
Small and great, Re 19:5.
All men, Ps 107:8; 145:21.
All creation, Ps 148:1–10; 150:6.

Is good and comely, Ps 33:1; 147:1.

Should be offered
With the understanding, Ps 47:7; 1 Co 14:15.
With the soul, Ps 103:1; 104:1, 35.
With the whole heart, Ps 9:1; 111:1; 138:1.
With uprightness of heart, Ps 119:7.
With the lips, Ps 63:3; 119:171.
With the mouth, Ps 51:15; 63:5.
With joy, Ps 63:5; 98:4.
With gladness, 2Ch 29:30; Jer 33:11.
With thankfulness, 1Ch 16:4; Ne 12:24; Ps 147:7.
Continually, Ps 35:28; 71:6.

During life, Ps 104:33.
More and more, Ps 71:14.
Day and night, Re 4:8.
Day by day, 2Ch 30:21.
For ever and ever, Ps 145:1, 2.
Throughout the world, Ps 113:3.
In psalms and hymns &c, Ps 105:2; Eph 5:19;
   Col 3:16.

Accompanied with musical instruments
   1Ch 16:41,42; Ps 150:3,5.
Is a part of public worship Ps 9:14; 100:4; 118:
   19,20; Heb 2:12.

Saints should
Show forth, Isa 43:21; 1 Pe 2:9.
Be endued with the spirit of, Isa 61:3.
Render, under affliction, Ac 16:25.
Glory in, 1 Ch 16:35.
Triumph in, Ps 106:47.
Express their joy by, Jas 5:13.
Declare, Isa 42:12.
Invite others to, Ps 34:3; 95:1.
Pray for ability to offer, Ps 51:15; 119:175.
Posture suited to, 1 Ch 23:30; Ne 9:5.

Called the
Fruit of the lips, Heb 13:15.
Voice of praise, Ps 66:8.
Voice of triumph, Ps 47:1.
Voice of melody, Isa 51:3.
Voice of a psalm, Ps 98:5.
Garment of praise, Isa 61:3.
Sacrifice of praise, Heb 13:15.
Sacrifices of joy, Ps 27:6.
Calves of the lips, Ho 14:2.

The heavenly host engage in, Isa 6:3; Lu 2:13;
   Re 4:9–11; 5:12.

Exemplified
Melchizedek, Ge 14:20.
Moses, Ex 15:1–21.
Jethro, Ex 18:10.
Israelites, 1 Ch 16:36.
David, 1 Ch 29:10–13; Ps 119:164.
Priests and Levites, Ezr 3:10–11.
Ezra, Ne 8:6.
Hezekiah, Isa 38:19.
Zacharias, Lu 1:64.
Shepherds, Lu 2:20.

Simeon, Lu 2:28.
Anna, Lu 2:38.
Multitudes, Lu 18:43.
Disciples, Lu 19:37, 38.
The Apostles, Lu 24:53.
First converts, Ac 2:47.
Lame man, Ac 3:8.
Paul and Silas, Ac 16:25.

R.A. Torrey, 1856–1928, Torrey's
New Topical Textbook

Prayer
R.A. Torrey

Prayer, Intercessory
Christ set an example of ,Lu 22:32; 23:34; Joh
   17:9–24.
Commanded, 1 Ti 2:1; Jas 5:14,16.

Should be offered up for
Kings, 1 Ti 2:2.
All in authority, 1Ti 2:2.
Ministers, 2 Co 1:11; Php 1:19.
The Church, Ps 122:6; Isa 62:6, 7.
All saints, Eph 6:18.
All men, 1 Ti 2:1.
Masters, Ge 24:12–14.
Servants, Lu 7:2,3.
Children, Ge 17:18; Mt 15:22.
Friends, Job 42:8.
Fellow-countrymen, Ro 10:1.
The sick, Jas 5:14.
Persecutors, Mt 5:44.
Enemies among whom we dwell, Jer 29:7.
Those who envy us, Nu 12:13.
Those who forsake us, 2 Ti 4:16.
Those who murmur against God, Nu 11:1, 2;
   14:13, 19.

By ministers for their people, Eph 1:16; 3:14–19;
   Php 1:4.
Encouragement to, Jas 5:16; 1 Jo 5:16.
Beneficial to the offerer, Job 42:10.
Sin of neglecting, 1 Sa 12:23.
Seek an interest in, 1 Sa 12:19; Heb 13:18.
Unavailing for the obstinately-impenitent, Jer
   7:13–16; 14:10, 11.

Exemplified
Abraham, Ge 18:23–32.

Abraham's servant, Ge 24:12–14.

Moses, Ex 8:12; 32:11–13.
Samuel, 1 Sa 7:5.
Solomon, 1 Ki 8:30–36.
Elisha, 2 Ki 4:33.
Hezekiah, 2 Ch 30:18.
Isaiah, 2 Ch 32:20.
Nehemiah, Ne 1:4–11.
David, Ps 25:22.
Ezekiel, Eze 9:8.
Daniel, Da 9:3–19.
Stephen, Ac 7:60.
Peter and John, Ac 8:15.
Church of Jerusalem, Ac 12:5.
Paul, Col 1:9–12; 2Th 1:11.
Epaphras, Col 4:12.
Philemon, Phm 1:22.

Prayer, Private
Christ was constant in, Mt 14:23; 26:36, 39; Mr 1:35; Lu 9:18, 29.
Commanded, Mt 6:6.

Should be offered
At evening, morning, and noon, Ps 55:17.
Day and night, Ps 88:1.
Without ceasing, 1 Th 5:17.

Shall be heard, Job 22:27.
Rewarded openly, Mt 6:6.
An evidence of conversion, Ac 9:11.
Nothing should hinder, Da 6:10.

Exemplified
Lot, Ge 19:20.
Eliezer, Ge 24:12.
Jacob, Ge 32:9–12.
Gideon, Jdj 6:22,36, 39.
Hannah, 1 Sa 1:10.
David, 2 Sa 7:18–29.
Hezekiah, 2 Ki 20:2.
Isaiah, 2 Ki 20:11.
Manasseh, 2 Ch 33:18,19.
Ezra, Ezr 9:5,6.
Nehemiah, Ne 2:4.
Jeremiah, Jer 32:16–25.
Daniel, Da 9:3,17.
Jonah, Jon 2:1.
Habakkuk, Hab 1:2.
Anna, Lu 2:37.
Paul, Ac 9:11.

Peter, Ac 9:40; 10:9.
Cornelius, Ac 10:30.

Prayer, Public
Acceptable to God, Isa 56:7.
God promises to hear, 2 Ch 7:14,16.
God promises to bless in Ex 20:24.

Christ
Sanctifies by his presence, Mt 18:20.
Attended, Mt 12:9; Lu 4:16.
Promises answers to, Mt 18:19.

Instituted form of, Lu 11:2.
Should not be made in an unknown language, 1 Co 14:14–16.
Saints delight in, Ps 42:4; 122:1.
Exhortation to, Heb 10:25.
Urge others to join in, Ps 95:6; Zec 8:21.

Exemplified
Joshua, Jos 7:6–9.
David, 1 Ch 29:10–19.
Solomon, 2 Ch 6:1–42.
Jehoshaphat, 2 Ch 20:5–13.
Jeshua, Ne 9:1–38.
Jews, Lu 1:10.
The Christians, Ac 2:46; 4:24; 12:5, 12.
Peter, Ac 3:1.
Teachers and Prophets, at Antioch, Ac 13:3.
Paul, Ac 16:16.

Prayer, Social and Family
Promise of answers to, Mt 18:19.
Christ promises to be present at, Mt 18:20.
Punishment for neglecting Jer 10:25.

Exemplified
Abram, Ge 12:5, 8.
Jacob, Ge 35:2, 3, 7.
Joshua, Jos 24:15.
David, 2Sa 6:20.
Job, Job 1:5.
The Disciples, Ac 1:13, 14.
Cornelius, Ac 10:2.
Paul and Silas, Ac 16:25.
Paul, Ac 20:36; 21:5.

R.A. Torrey, 1856–1928, Torrey's
New Topical Textbook

Prayer and Revival

R.A. Torrey

THE NEED OF PRAYER BEFORE AND DURING REVIVALS

If we are to pray aright in such a time as this, much of our prayer should be for a general revival. If there was ever a time in which there was need to cry unto God in the words of the Psalmist, "Wilt Thou not revive us again, that Thy people may rejoice in Thee?" (Ps. 85:6) it is this day in which we live. It is surely time for the Lord to work, for men have made void His law (Ps. 199:126). The voice of the Lord given in the written Word is set at naught both by the world and the church. Such a time is not a time for discouragement – the man who believes in God and believes in the Bible can never be discouraged; but it is a time for Jehovah Himself to step in and word. The intelligent Christian, the wide-awake watchman on the walls of Zion, may well cry with the Psalmist of old, "It is time for Jehovah to work, for they have made void Thy law" (Ps. 119:126, Am.RV). The great need of the day is a general revival. Let us consider first of all what a general revival is. A revival is a time of quickening or impartation of life. As God alone can give life, a revival is a time when God visits His people and by the power of His Spirit imparts new life to them, and through them imparts life to sinners dead in trespasses and sins. We have religious excitements gotten up by the cunning methods and hypnotic influence of the mere professional evangelist; but these are not revivals and are not needed. They are the devil's imitations of a revival. NEW LIFE FROM GOD – that is a revival. A general revival is a time when this new life from God is not confined to scattered localities, but is general throughout Christendom and the earth. The reason why a general revival is needed is that spiritual dearth and desolation and death is general. It is not confined to any one country, though it may be more manifest in some countries than in others. It is found in foreign mission fields as well as in home fields. We have had local revivals. The life-giving Spirit of God has breathed upon this minister and that, this church and that, this community and that; but we need, we sorely need, a revival that shall be widespread and general. Let us look for a few moments at the results of a revival. These results are apparent in ministers, in the church and in the unsaved.

1. The results of a revival in a minister are:

(1) The minister has a new love for souls. We ministers as a rule have no such love for souls as we ought to have, no such love for souls as Jesus had, no such love for souls as Paul had. But when God visits His people the hearts of ministers are greatly burdened for the unsaved. They go out in great longing for the salvation of their fellow men. They forget their ambition to preach great sermons and for fame, and simply long to see men brought to Christ.

(2) When true revivals come ministers get a new love for God's Word and a new faith in God's Word. They fling to the winds their doubts and criticisms of the Bible and of the creeds, and go to preaching the Bible and especially Christ crucified. Revivals make ministers who are loose in their doctrines orthodox. A genuine wide-sweeping revival would do more to turn things upside down and thus get them right side up than all the heresy trials ever instituted.

(3) Revivals bring to ministers new liberty and power in preaching. It is no week-long grind to prepare a sermon, and no nerve-consuming effort to preach it after it has been prepared. Preaching is a joy and a refreshment, and there is power in it in times of revival.

2. The results of a revival on Christians generally are as marked as its results upon the ministry.

(1) In times of revival Christians come out from the world and live separated lives. Christians who have been dallying with the world, who have been playing cards and dancing and going to the theater and indulging in similar follies, give them up. These things are found to be incompatible with increasing life and light.

(2) In times of revival Christians get a new spirit of prayer. Prayer-meetings are no longer a duty, but become the necessity of a hungry, importunate heart. Private prayer is followed with new zest. The voice of earnest prayer to God is heard day and night. People no longer ask, "Does God answer prayer?" They know He does, and besiege the throne of grace day

and night.

(3) In times of revival Christians go to work for lost souls. They do not go to meeting simply to enjoy themselves and get blessed. They go to meeting to watch for souls and to bring them to Christ. They talk to men on the street and in the stores and in their homes. The cross of Christ, salvation, heaven and hell become the subjects of constant conversation. Politics and the weather and new bonnets and the latest novels are forgotten.

(4) In times of revival Christians have new joy in Christ. Life is joy, and new life is new joy. Revival days are glad days, days of heaven on earth.

(5) In times of revival Christians get a new love for the Word of God. They want to study it day and night. Revivals are bad for saloons and theaters, but they are good for bookstores and Bible agencies.

3. But revivals also have a decided influence on the unsaved world.

(1) First of all, they bring deep conviction of sin. Jesus said that when the Spirit was come He would convince the world of sin (Jn. 16:7, 8). Now we have seen that a revival is a coming of the Holy Spirit, and therefore there must be a new conviction of sin, and there always is. If you see something men call a revival, and there is no conviction of sin, you may know at once that it is bogus. It is a sure mark.

(2) Revivals bring also conversion and regeneration. When God refreshes His people, He always converts sinners also. The first result of Pentecost was new life and power to the one hundred and twenty disciples in the upper room; the second result was three thousand conversions in a single day. It is always so. I am constantly reading of revivals here and there, where Christians were greatly helped but there were no conversions. I have my doubts about that kind. If Christians are truly refreshed, they will get after the unsaved by prayer and testimony and persuasion, and there will be conversions.

WHY A GENERAL REVIVAL IS NEEDED

We see what a general revival is, and what it does; let us now face the question why it is needed at the present time. I think that the mere description of what it is and what it does shows that it is needed, sorely needed, but let us look at some specific conditions that exist to-day that show the need of it. In showing these conditions one is likely to be called a pessimist. If facing the facts is to be called a pessimist, I am willing to be called a pessimist. If in order to be an optimist one must shut his eyes and call black white, and error truth, and sin righteousness, and death life, I don't want to be called an optimist. But I am an optimist all the same. Pointing out the real condition will lead to a better condition.

1. Look first at the ministry.

(1) Many of us who are professedly orthodox ministers are practically infidels. That is plain speech, but it is also indisputable fact. There is no essential difference between the teachings of Tom Paine and Bob Ingersoll and the teachings of some of our theological professors. The latter are not so blunt and honest about it; they phrase it in more elegant and studied sentences; but it means the same. Much of the so-called new learning and higher criticism is simply Tom Paine infidelity sugar-coated. Prof. Howard Osgood, who is a real scholar and not a mere echo of German infidelity, once read a statement of some positions, and asked if they did not fairly represent the scholarly criticism of to-day, and when it was agreed that they did, he startled his audience by saying: "I am reading from Tom Paine's 'Age of Reason.'" There is little new in the higher criticism. Our future ministers oftentimes are being educated under infidel professors, and being immature boys when they enter the college or seminary, they naturally come out infidels in many cases, and then go forth to poison the church.

(2) Even when our ministers are orthodox – as thank God so very many are! – they are oftentimes not men of prayer. How many modern ministers know what it is to wrestle in prayer, to spend a good share of a night in prayer? I do not know how many, but I do know that many do not.

(3) Many of us who are ministers have no love for souls. How many preach because they MUST preach, because they feel that men every where are perishing, and by preaching they hope to save some? And how many follow up

their preaching as Paul did, by beseeching men everywhere to be reconciled to God? Perhaps enough has been said about us ministers; but it is evident that a revival is needed for our sake or some of us will have to stand before God overwhelmed with confusion in an awful day of reckoning that is surely coming.

2. Look now at the church:

(1) Look at the doctrinal state of the church. It is bad enough. Many do not believe in the whole Bible. The book of Genesis is a myth, Jonah is an allegory, and even the miracles of the Son of God are questioned. The doctrine of prayer is old-fashioned, and the work of the Holy Spirit is sneered at. Conversion is unnecessary, and hell is no longer believed in. Then look at the fads and errors that have sprung up out of this loss of faith, Christian Science, Unitarianism, Spiritualism, Universalism, Babism, Metaphysical Healing, etc., etc., a perfect pandemonium of doctrines of devils.

(2) Look at the spiritual state of the church. Worldliness is rampant among church members. Many church members are just as eager as any in the rush to get rich. They use the methods of the world in the accumulation of wealth, and they hold just as fast to it as any when they have gotten it. Prayerlessness abounds among church members on every hand. Some one has said that Christians on the average do not spend more than five minutes a day in prayer. Neglect of the Word of God goes hand in hand with neglect of prayer to God. Very many Christians spend twice as much time every day wallowing through the more of the daily papers as they do bathing in the cleansing laver of God's Holy Word. How many Christians average an hour a day spent in Bible study? Along with neglect of prayer and neglect of the Word of God goes a lack of generosity. The churches are rapidly increasing in wealth, but the treasuries of the missionary societies are empty. Christians do not average a dollar a year for foreign missions. It is simply appalling. Then there is the increasing disregard for the Lord's Day. It is fast becoming a day of worldly pleasure, instead of a day of holy service. The Sunday newspaper with its inane twaddle and filthy scandal takes the place of the Bible; and visiting and golf and bicycle, the place of the Sunday-school and church service.

Christians mingle with the world in all forms of questionable amusements. The young man and young woman who does not believe in dancing with its rank immodesties, the card table with its drift toward gambling, and the theater with its ever-increasing appeal to lewdness, is counted an old fogy. Then how small a proportion of our membership has really entered into fellowship with Jesus Christ in His burden for souls! Enough has been said of the spiritual state of the church.

3. Now look at the state of the world.

(1) Note how few conversions there are. The Methodist church, which has led the way in aggressive work has actually lost more members than it has gained the last year. Here and there a church has a large number of accessions upon confession of faith, but these churches are rare exceptions; and where there are such accessions, in how few cases are the conversions deep, thorough and satisfactory.

(2) There is lack of conviction of sin. Seldom are men overwhelmed with a sense of their awful guilt in trampling under foot the Son of God. Sin is regarded as a "misfortune" or as "infirmity," or even as "good in the making"; seldom as enormous wrong against a holy God.

(3) Unbelief is rampant. Many regard it as a mark of intellectual superiority to reject the Bible, and even faith in God and immortality. It is about the only mark of intellectual superiority many possess, and perhaps that is the reason they cling to it so tenaciously.

(4) Hand in hand with this widespread infidelity goes gross immorality, as has always been the case. Infidelity and immorality are Siamese twins. They always exist and always grow and always fatten together. This prevailing immorality is found everywhere. Look at the legalized adultery that we call divorce. Men marry one wife after another, and are still admitted into good society; and women do likewise. There are thousands of supposedly respectable men in America living with other men's wives, and thousands of supposedly respectable women living with other women's husbands. This immorality is found in the theater. The theater at its best is bad enough, but now "Sapphos," and the "Degenerates,"

and all the unspeakable vile accessories of the stage rule the day, and the women who debauch themselves by appearing in such plays are defended in the newspapers and welcomed by supposedly respectable people. Much of our literature is rotten, but decent people will read books as bad as "Trilby" because it is the rage. Art is oftentimes a mere covering for shameless indecency. Women are induced to cast modesty to the winds that the artist may perfect his art and defile his morals. Greed for money has become a mania with rich and poor. The multi-millionaire will often sell his soul and trample the rights of his fellow men under foot in the mad hope of becoming a billionaire, and the laboring man will often commit murder to increase the power of the union and keep up wages. Wars are waged and men shot down like dogs to improve commerce, and to gain political prestige for unprincipled politicians who parade as statesmen. The licentiousness of the day lifts its serpent head everywhere. You see it in the newspapers, you see it on the bill-boards, you see it on the advertisements of cigars, shoes, bicycles, patent medicines, corsets and everything else. You see it on the streets at night. You see it just outside the church door. You find it not only in the awful cesspools set apart for it in the great cities, but it is crowding further and further up our business streets and into the residence portions of our cities. Alas! now and then you find it, if you look sharp, in supposedly respectable homes; indeed it will be borne to your ears by the confessions of broken-hearted men and women. The moral condition of the world in our day is disgusting, sickening, appalling. We need a revival, deep, widespread, general, in the power of the Holy Ghost. It is either a general revival or the dissolution of the church, of the home, of the state. A revival, new life from God, is the cure, and the only cure. That will stem the awful tide of immorality and unbelief. Mere argument will not do it; but a sign from heaven, a new outpouring of the Spirit of God, It was not discussion but the breath of God that relegated Tom Paine, Voltaire, Volney and other of the old infidels to the limbo of forgetfulness; and we need a new breath from God to send the Wellhausens and the Kuenens and the Grafs and the parrots they have trained to occupy chairs and pulpits in England and America to keep them company. I believe that breath from God is coming. The great need of to-day is a general revival. The need is clear. It admits of no honest difference of opinion. What then shall we do? Pray. Take up the Psalmist's prayer, "Revive us again, that Thy people may rejoice in Thee." Take up Ezekiel's prayer, "Come from the four winds, O breath (breath of God), and breathe upon these slain that they may live." Hark, I hear a noise! Behold a shaking! I can almost feel the breeze upon my cheek. I can almost see the great living army rising to their feet. Shall we not pray and pray and pray and pray, till the Spirit comes, and God revives His people?

THE PLACE OF PRAYER BEFORE AND DURING REVIVALS

No treatment of the subject How to Pray would be at all complete if it did not consider the place of prayer in revivals. The first great revival of Christian history had its origin on the human side in a ten-days' prayer-meeting. We read of that handful of disciples, "These all with one accord continued steadfastly in prayer." (Acts 1:14, RV) The result of that prayer-meeting we read of in the 2nd chapter of the Acts of the Apostles, "They were all filled with the Holy Ghost, and began to speak with other tongues, as the Spirit gave them utterance" (v.4). Further on in the chapter we read that "there were added unto them in that day about three thousand souls" (v.41, RV). This revival proved genuine and permanent. The converts "continued steadfastly in the apostles' teaching and fellowship, in the breaking of bread and the prayers" (v.42, RV). "And the Lord added to them day by day those that were being saved" (v.47, RV). Every true revival from that day to this has had its earthly origin in prayer.

The great revival under Jonathan Edwards in the 18th century began with his famous call to prayer. The marvelous work of grace among the Indians under Brainerd had its origin in the days and nights that Brainerd spent before God in prayer for an endowment of power from on high for this work. A most remarkable and widespread display of God's reviving power was that which broke out at Rochester, New York, in 1830, under the labors of Charles G.

Finney. It not only spread throughout the State but ultimately to Great Britain as well. Mr. Finney himself attributed the power of this work to the spirit of prayer that prevailed. He describes it in his autobiography in the following words: "When I was on my way to Rochester, as we passed through a village, some thirty miles east of Rochester, a brother minister whom I knew, seeing me on the canal-boat, jumped aboard to have a little conversation with me, intending to ride but a little way and return. He, however, became interested in conversation, and upon finding where I was going, he made up his mind to keep on and go with me to Rochester. We had been there but a few days when this minister became so convinced that he could not help weeping aloud at one time as we passed along the street. The Lord gave him a powerful spirit of prayer, and his heart was broken. As he and I prayed together, I was struck with his faith in regard to what the Lord was going to do there. I recollect he would say, 'Lord, I do not know how it is; but I seem to know that Thou art going to do a great work in this city.' The spirit of prayer was poured out powerfully, so much so that some persons stayed away from the public services to pray, being unable to restrain their feelings under preaching.

"And here I must introduce the name of a man, whom I shall have occasion to mention frequently, Mr. Abel Clary. He was the son of a very excellent man, and an elder of the church where I was converted. He was converted in the same revival in which I was. He had been licensed to preach; but his spirit of prayer was such, he was so burdened with the souls of men, that he was not able to preach much, his whole time and strength being given to prayer. The burden of his soul would frequently be so great that he was unable to stand, and he would writhe and groan in agony. I was well acquainted with him, and knew something of the wonderful spirit of prayer that was upon him. He was a very silent man, as almost all are who have that powerful spirit of prayer.

"The first I knew of his being in Rochester, a gentleman who lived about a mile west of the city, called on me one day and asked me if I knew a Mr. Abel Clary, a minister. I told him that I knew him well. 'Well,' he said, 'he is at my house, and has been there for some time, and I don't know what to think of him.' I said, 'I have not seen him at any of our meetings.' 'No,' he replied, 'he cannot go to meeting, he says. He prays nearly all the time, day and night, and in such agony of mind that I do not know what to make of it. Sometimes he cannot even stand on his knees, but will lie prostrate on the floor, and groan and pray in a manner that quite astonishes me.' I said to the brother, 'I understand it: please keep still. It will all come out right; he will surely prevail.'

"I knew at the time a considerable number of men who were exercised in the same way. A Deacon P –, of Camden, Oneida county; a Deacon T – , of Rodman, Jefferson county; a Deacon B –, of Adams, in the same county; this Mr. Clary and many others among the men, and a large number of women partook of the same spirit, and spent a great part of their time in prayer. Father Nash, as we called him, who in several of my fields of labor came to me and aided me, was another of those men that had such a powerful spirit of prevailing prayer. This Mr. Clary continued in Rochester as long as I did, and did not leave it until after I had left. He never, that I could learn, appeared in public, but gave himself wholly to prayer.

"I think it was the second Sabbath that I was at Auburn at this time, I observed in the congregation the solemn face of Mr. Clary. He looked as if he was borne down with an agony of prayer. Being well acquainted with him, and knowing the great gift of God that was upon him, the spirit of prayer, I was very glad to see him there. He sat in the pew with his brother, the doctor, who was also a professor of religion, but who had nothing by experience, I should think, of his brother Abel's great power with God.

"At intermission, as soon as I came down from the pulpit, Mr. Clary, with his brother, met me at the pulpit stairs, and the doctor invited me to go home with him and spend the intermission and get some refreshments. I did so.

"After arriving at his house we were soon summoned to the dinner table. We gathered about the table, and Dr. Clary turned to his brother and said, 'Brother Abel, will you ask the blessing?' Brother Abel bowed his head and began, audibly, to ask a blessing. He had uttered but a sentence or two when he broke instantly down, moved suddenly back from the table, and fled to his chamber. The doctor supposed he had been taken suddenly ill, and rose up and followed him. In a few moments he came down and said, 'Mr. Finney, brother Abel wants to see you.' Said I, 'What ails him?' Said he, 'I do not know but he says, you know. He appears in great distress, but I think it is the state of his mind.' I understood it in a moment, and went to his room. He lay groaning upon the bed, the Spirit making intercession for him, and in him, with groanings that could not be uttered. I had barely entered the room, when he made out to say, 'Pray, brother Finney.' I knelt down and helped him in prayer, by leading his soul out for the conversion of sinners. I continued to pray until his distress passed away, and then I returned to the dinner table.

"I understood that this was the voice of God. I saw the spirit of prayer was upon him, and I felt his influence upon myself, and took it for granted that the work would move on powerfully. It did so. The pastor told me afterward that he found that in the six weeks that I was there, five hundred souls had been converted."

Mr. Finney in his lectures on revivals tells of other remarkable awakenings in answer to the prayers of God's people. He says in one place, "A clergyman in W—n told me of a revival among his people, which commenced with a zealous and devoted woman in the church. She became anxious about sinners, and went to praying for them; she prayed, and her distress increased; and she finally came to her minister, and talked with him, and asked him to appoint an anxious meeting, for she felt that one was needed. The minister put her off, for he felt nothing of it. The next week she came again, and besought him to appoint an anxious meeting, she knew there would be somebody to come, for she felt as if God was going to pour out His Spirit. He put her off again. And finally she said to him, 'If you do not appoint an anxious meeting I shall die, for there is certainly going to be a revival.' The next Sabbath he appointed a meeting, and said that if there were any who wished to converse with him about the salvation of their souls, he would meet them on such an evening.

He did not know of one, but when he went to the place, to his astonishment he found a large number of anxious inquirers."

In still another place he says, "The first ray of light that broke in upon the midnight which rested on the churches in Oneida county, in the fall of 1825, was from a woman in feeble health, who, I believe had never been in a powerful revival. Her soul was exercised about sinners. She was in agony for the land. She did not know what ailed her, but she kept praying more and more, till it seemed as if her agony would destroy her body. At length she became full of joy and exclaimed, 'God has come! God has come! There is no mistake about it, the work is begun, and is going over all the region!' And sure enough the work began, and her family were almost all converted, and the work spread all over that part of the country."

The great revival of 1857 in the United States began in prayer and was carried on by prayer more than by anything else. Dr. Cuyler in an article in a religious newspaper some years ago said, "Most revivals have humble beginnings, and the fire starts in a few warm hearts. Never despise the day of small things. During all my own long ministry, nearly every work of grace had a similar beginning. One commenced in a meeting gathered at a few hour's notice in a private house. Another commenced in a group gathered for Bible study by Mr. Moody in our mission chapel. Still another – the most powerful of all – was kindled on a bitter January evening at a meeting of young Christians under my roof. Dr. Spencer, in his 'Pastor's Sketches', (the most suggestive book of its kind I have ever read), tells us that a remarkable revival in his church sprang from the fervent prayers of a godly old man who was confined to his room by lameness. That profound Christian, Dr. Thomas H. Skinner, of the Union Theological Seminary, once gave me an account of a remarkable coming together of three earnest men in his study when he was the pastor of the Arch Street Church in Philadelphia. They literally wrestled in prayer. They made a clean breast in confession of sin, and humbled themselves before God. One and another church officer came in and joined them. The heaven-kindled flame soon spread through the whole congregation in one of the most powerful revivals ever known in that city."

In the early part of the seventeenth century there was a great religious awakening in Ulster, Ireland. The lands of the rebel chiefs which had been forfeited to the British crown, were settled up by a class of colonists who for the most part were governed by a spirit of wild adventure. Real piety was rare. Seven ministers, five from Scotland and two from England, settled in that country, the earliest arrivals being in 1613. Of one of these ministers named Blair it is recorded by a contemporary, "He spent many days and nights in prayer, alone and with others, and was vouchsafed great intimacy with God." Mr. James Glendenning, a man of very meager natural gifts, was a man similarly minded as regards prayer. The work began under this man Glendenning. The historian of the time says, "He was a man who never would have been chosen by a wise assembly of ministers nor sent to begin a reformation in this land. Yet this was the Lord's choice to begin with him the admirable work of God which I mention on purpose that all may see how the glory is only the Lord's in making a holy nation in this profane land, and that it was 'not by might, nor by power, nor by man's wisdom, but by My Spirit, saith the Lord.'" In his preaching at Oldstone multitudes of hearers felt in great anxiety and terror of conscience. They looked on themselves as altogether lost and damned, and cried out, "Men and brethren, what shall we do to be saved?" They were stricken into a swoon by the power of His Word. A dozen in one day were carried out of doors as dead. These were not women, but some of the boldest spirits of the neighborhood; "some who had formerly feared not with their swords to put a whole market town into a fray." Concerning one of them, then a mighty strong man, now a mighty Christian, say that his end in coming into church was to consult with his companions how to work some mischief. This work spread throughout the whole country. By the year 1626 a monthly concert of prayer was held in Antrim. The work spread beyond the bounds of Down and Antrim to the churches of the neighboring counties. So great became the religious interest that Christians would come thirty or forty miles to the communions, and continue from the time they came until they returned without wearying or making use of sleep. Many of them neither ate nor drank, and yet some of them professed that they "went away most fresh and vigorous, their souls so filled with the sense of God." This revival changed the whole character of northern Ireland.

Another great awakening in Ireland in 1859 had a somewhat similar origin. By many who did not know, it was thought that this marvelous work came without warning and preparation, but Rev. William Gibson, the moderator of the General Assembly of the Presbyterian Church in Ireland in 1860, in his very interesting and valuable history of the work tells how there had been preparation for two years. There had been constant discussion in the General Assembly of the low estate of religion, and of the need of a revival. There had been special sessions for prayer. Finally four young men, who became leaders in the origin of the great work, began to meet together in an old schoolhouse in the neighborhood of Kells. About the spring of 1858 a work of power began to manifest itself. It spread from town to town, and from county to county. The congregations became too large for the buildings, and the meetings were held in the open air, oftentimes attended by many thousands of people. Many hundreds of persons were frequently convicted of sin in a single meeting. In some places the criminal courts and jails were closed for lack of occupation. There were manifestations of the Holy Spirit's power of a most remarkable character, clearly proving that the Holy Spirit is as ready to work to-day as in apostolic days, when ministers and Christians really believe in Him and begin to prepare the way by prayer.

Mr. Moody's wonderful work in England and Scotland and Ireland that afterwards spread to America had its origin on the manward side in prayer. Mr. Moody made little impression until men and women began to cry to God. Indeed his going to England at all was in answer to the importunate cries to God of a bed-ridden saint. While the spirit of prayer continued the revival abode in strength, but in the course of time less and less was made of prayer and the work fell off very perceptibly in power. Doubtless one of the great secrets of the unsatisfactoriness and superficiality and unreality of many of our modern so-called revivals, is that more dependence is put upon man's machinery than upon God's power, sought and obtained by earnest, persistent, believing prayer. We live in a day characterized by the multiplication of man's machinery and the diminution of God's power. The great cry of our day is work, work, work, new organizations, new methods, new machinery; the great need of our day is prayer. It was a master stroke of the devil when he got the church so generally to lay aside this mighty weapon of prayer. The devil is perfectly willing that the church should multiply its organizations, and deftly contrive machinery for the conquest of the world for Christ if it will only give up praying. He laughs as he looks at the church to-day and says to himself: "You can have your Sunday-schools and your Young People's Societies, your Young Men's Christian Associations and your Women's Christian Temperance Unions, your Institutional Churches and your Industrial Schools, and your Boy's Brigades, your grand choirs and your fine organs, your brilliant preachers and your revival efforts too, if you don't bring the power of Almighty God into them by earnest, persistent, believing, mighty prayer."

Prayer could work as marvelous results today as it ever could, if the church would only betake itself to it. There seem to be increasing signs that the church is awakening to this fact. Here and there God is laying upon individual ministers and churches a burden of prayer that they have never known before. Less dependence is being put upon machinery and more dependence upon God. Ministers are crying to God day and night for power. Churches and portions of churches are meeting together in the early morning hours and the late night hours crying to God for the latter rain. There is every indication of the coming of a mighty and widespread revival. There is every reason why, if a revival should come in any country at this time, it should be more widespread in its extent than any revival of history. There is the closest and swiftest communication by travel, by letter, and by cable between all parts of the world. A true fire of God kindled in America would soon spread to the uttermost parts of the earth. The only thing needed to bring this fire is prayer. It is not necessary that the whole church get to praying to begin with. Great revivals always begin first in the hearts of a few men and women whom God arouses by His Spirit to believe in Him as a living God, as a God who answers prayer, and upon whose heart He lays a burden from which no rest can be found except in importunate crying unto God. May God use this book to arouse many others to pray that the greatly-needed revival may come, and come speedily.

R.A. Torrey, 1856–1928

Praying in the Spirit
R.A. Torrey

1. Over and over again in what has already been said, we have seen our dependence upon the Holy Spirit in prayer. This comes out very definitely in Eph. 6:18, "Praying always with all prayer and supplication IN THE SPIRIT," and in Jude 20, "Praying IN THE HOLY GHOST." Indeed the whole secret of prayer is found in these three words, "in the Spirit." It is the prayer that God the Holy Spirit inspires that God the Father answers. The disciples did not know how to pray as they ought, so they came to Jesus and said, "Lord teach us to pray." We know not how to pray as we ought, but we have another Teacher and Guide right at hand to help us (John 14:16, 17), "The Spirit helpeth our infirmity" (Rom. 8:26, RV). He teaches us how to pray. True prayer is prayer in the Spirit; that is, the prayer the Spirit inspires and directs. When we come into God's presence we should recognize "our infirmity," our ignorance of what we should pray for or how we should pray for it, and in the consciousness of our utter inability to pray aright we should look up to the Holy Spirit, casting ourselves utterly upon Him to direct our prayers, to lead out our desires and to guide our utterance of them. Nothing can be more foolish in prayer than to rush heedlessly into God's presence, and ask the first thing that comes into our mind, or that some thoughtless friend has asked us to pray for. When we

first come into God's presence we should be silent before Him. We should look up to Him to send His Holy Spirit to teach us how to pray. We must wait for the Holy Spirit, and surrender ourselves to the Spirit, then we shall pray aright. Oftentimes when we come to God in prayer, we do not feel like praying. What shall one do in such a case? cease praying until he does feel like it? Not at all. When we feel least like praying is the time when we most need to pray. We should wait quietly before God and tell Him how cold and prayerless our hearts are, and look up to Him and trust Him and expect Him to send the Holy Spirit to warm our hearts and draw them out in prayer. It will not be long before the glow of the Spirit's presence will fill our hearts, and we will begin to pray with freedom, directness, earnestness and power. Many of the most blessed seasons of prayer I have ever known have begun with a feeling of utter deadness and prayerlessness, but in my helplessness and coldness I have cast myself upon God, and looked to Him to send His Holy Spirit to teach me to pray, and He has done it. When we pray in the Spirit, we will pray for the right things and in the right way. There will be joy and power in our prayer.

2. If we are to pray with power we must pray WITH FAITH. In Mark 11:24 Jesus says, "Therefore I say unto you, What things soever ye desire, when ye pray, believe that ye receive them, and ye shall have them." No matter how positive any promise of God's Word may be, we will not enjoy it in actual experience unless we confidently expect its fulfillment in answer to our prayer. "If any of you lack wisdom," says James, "let him ask of God that giveth to all men liberally, and upbraideth not; and it shall be given him." Now that promise is as positive as a promise can be, but the next verse adds, "But let him ask in faith, nothing doubting: for he that doubteth is like the surge of the sea driven by the wind and tossed. For let not that man think that he shall receive anything of the Lord" (RV). There must then be confident unwavering expectation. But there is a faith that goes beyond expectation, that believes that the prayer is heard and the promise granted. This comes out in the Revised Version of Mark 11:24, "Therefore I say unto you, All things whatsoever ye pray and ask for, believe

that ye HAVE received them, and ye shall have them." But how can one get this faith? Let us say with all emphasis, it cannot be pumped up. Many a one reads this promise about the prayer of faith, and then asks for things that he desires and tries to make himself believe that God has heard the prayer. This ends only in disappointment, for it is not real faith and the thing is not granted. It is at this point that many people make a collapse of faith altogether by trying to work up faith by an effort of their will, and as the thing they made themselves believe they expected to get is not given, the very foundation of faith is oftentimes undermined. But how does real faith come? Rom 10:17 answers the question: "So then faith cometh by hearing, and hearing BY THE WORD OF GOD." If we are to have real faith, we must study the Word of God and find out what is promised, then simply believe the promises of God. Faith must have a warrant. Trying to believe something that you want to believe is not faith. Believing what God says in His Word is faith. If I am to have faith when I pray, I must find some promise in the Word of God on which to rest my faith. Faith furthermore comes through the Spirit. The Spirit knows the will of God, and if I pray in the Spirit, and look to the Spirit to teach me God's will, He will lead me out in prayer along the line of that will, and give me faith that the prayer is to be answered; but in no case does real faith come by simply determining that you are going to get the thing that you want to get. If there is no promise in the Word of God, and no clear leading of the Spirit, there can be no real faith, and there should be no upbraiding of self for lack of faith in such a case. But if the thing desired is promised in the Word of God, we may well upbraid ourselves for lack of faith if we doubt; for we are making God a liar by doubting His Word.

R.A. Torrey, 1856–1928

Prayer as a Means of Grace
B.B. Warfield

Acts 9:11: – "For behold, he prayeth."
We read these words, "For behold, he prayeth," of Saul of Tarsus, immediately after the account

of how, when he was journeying from Jerusalem to Damascus on his persecuting errand, he was smitten to the ground by the Divine hand and raised again by those gracious words – how gracious, how inexplicably gracious they must have seemed to him! – which promised him service for the very One whom he was now persecuting.

And when we read them our first thought is likely to turn on the appropriateness of prayer in the circumstances. Thus the theme is obviously suggested of prayer as the appropriate expression of the renewed sinner's heart. On this subject I shall not, however, speak to you just now. I wish to call your attention, rather, to another subject for meditation which also lies in our passage, though perhaps not so prominently. That is, Prayer as a means of Grace.

If we look closely at this verse we shall see that it suggests prayer as a means of grace. You will notice that it reads, "For behold, he prayeth, and he hath seen" a vision of Ananaias coming to him, to restore him to sight. "For behold he prayeth and"; that is, this statement is given as a reason, and as a reason why Ananaias should now go to him. And the reason is that Paul is now prepared for the visit. And the preparation consists of the two items that he is praying and that he has seen in a vision Ananaias coming. In other words, that he is in a state of preparedness for the reception of grace in general is evidenced by his being in prayer; while he is prepared for Ananaias' coming in particular through the vision. The passage thus represents prayer as the state of preparedness for the reception of grace; and, therefore, in the strictest sense as a means of grace. We purpose to look at it for a few moments in this light.

Even if we should not rise above the naturalistic plane, I think we might be able to see that the attitude into which the act of prayer brings the soul is one which especially softens the soul and lays it open to gracious influences. Say that we hold with those who believe in prayer, but do not believe in answer to prayer. Well, is not the mental attitude assumed in prayer, at least, a humble attitude, a softening attitude, a beneficial attitude? Do we not see that thus the very act of prayer by its reflex influence alone – could we believe in no more – will tend to quiet the soul, break down its

pride and resistance, and fit it for a humble walk in the world? In its very nature, prayer is a confession of weakness, a confession of need, of dependence, a cry for help, a reaching out for something stronger, better, more stable and trustworthy than ourselves, on which to rest and depend and draw. No one can take this attitude once without an effect on his character; no one can take it in a crisis of his life without his whole subsequent life feeling the influence in its sweeter, humbler, more devout and restful course; no one can take it habitually without being made, merely by its natural, reflex influence, a different man, in a very profound sense, from what he otherwise would have been. Prayer, thus, in its very nature, because it is an act of self-abnegation, a throwing of ourselves at the feet of One recognized as higher and greater than we, and as One on whom we depend and in whom we trust, is a most beneficial influence in this hard life of ours. It places the soul in an attitude of less self-assertion and predisposes it to walk simply and humbly in the world.

The significance of all this is, of course, vastly increased, when we rise above the region of naturalism into that of supernaturalism. If when we believe only in prayer but not in its answer, if when we look only for a natural, reflex influence on our life of the attitude into which prayer brings us, we can recognize in it a softening, blessing effect; how much more when we perceive a Divine person above who hears and answers the prayer. If there were no God, we can see that it would be a blessing to men to think there was a God and throw themselves at His feet in prayer. If there is a God who sits aloft and hears and answers, do we not see that the attitude into which prayer brings the soul is the appropriate attitude which the soul should occupy to Him, and is the truest and best preparation of the soul for the reception of His grace? The soul in the attitude of prayer is like the flower turned upwards towards the sky and opening for the reception of the life-giving rain. What is prayer but an adoring appearing before God with a confession of our need and helplessness and a petition for His strength and blessing? What is prayer but a recognition of our dependence and a proclamation that all that we dependent creatures need is found abundantly and to spare in God, who gives to all men liberally and upbraids not? What is prayer but the very adjustment of the heart for the influx of grace? Therefore it is that we look upon the prayerful attitude as above all others the true Christian attitude – just because it is the attitude of devout and hopeful dependence on God. And, therefore, it is that we look upon that type of religious teaching as, above all others, the true Christian type which has as its tendency to keep men in the attitude of prayer, through all their lives.

Every type of religious teaching will inevitably beget its corresponding type of religious life. And that teaching alone which calls upon man to depend wholly on the Lord God Almighty – our loving Father who has given His Son to die for us – for all the exercises of grace, will make Christians whose whole life is a prayer. Not that other Christians do not pray. But only of these Christians can it be said that their life is an embodied prayer. In so far as any Christian's life is a prayerful life, pervaded by and made up out of prayer, it approaches in its silent witness the ideal of this type of teaching. What other attitude is possible to a Christian on his knees before God but an attitude of entire dependence on God for His gifts, and of humble supplication to Him for His favor? But are we to rise from our knees only to take up a different attitude towards God? Says one of the greatest thinkers of modern times:

"On his knees before God, every one that has been saved will recognize the sole efficiency of the Holy Spirit in every good work ... In a word, whoever truly prays ascribes nothing to his own will or power except the sin that condemns him before God, and knows of nothing that could endure the judgment of God except it be wrought within him by the Divine love. But whilst all other tendencies in the Church preserve this attitude so long as their prayer lasts, to lose themselves in radically different conceptions as soon as the Amen has been pronounced, the Calvinist adheres to the truth of his prayer, in his confession, in his theology, in his life, and the Amen that has closed his petition re-echoes in the depths of his consciousness and throughout the whole of his existence."

That is to say, for us Calvinists the attitude of prayer is the whole attitude of our lives. Certainly this is the true Christian attitude, because it is the attitude of dependence, and trust. But just because this is the attitude of prayer, prayer puts the soul in the attitude for receiving grace and is essentially a means of grace. But once again, prayer is a means of grace because it is a direct appeal to God for grace. It is in its very innermost core a petition for help and that is – proportionately to its sphere – for grace. The means – the most direct and appropriate, the most prevailing and sure means of obtaining aid from a superior, is to ask for it. If a community desires a boon from the government, it petitions for it. The means above all others by which we are to obtain God's blessing is naturally and properly to petition for it. It is true that all prayer is not petition. The Apostle gives us a list of the aspects of prayer in 1 Tim. ii:1 sq. under the names of "supplications, prayers, intercessions, thanksgivings." All these elements enter into prayer. Prayer in its full conception is then, not merely asking from God, but all intercourse with God. Intercourse, indeed, is the precise connotation of the standing word for prayer in the New Testament – the second in the list of 1 Tim. ii:1, translated in our version simply "prayers," The sacred idea of prayer per se is, therefore, to put it sharply, just communion with God, the meeting of the soul with God, and the holding of converse with Him. Perhaps we would best define it as conscious intercourse or communion with God. God may have communion with us without prayer; He may enter our souls beneath consciousness, and deal with us from within; and because He is within us we can be in communion with Him apart from prayer. But conscious communion with Him is just prayer. Now, I think we may say, emphatically, that prayer is a means of grace above everything else because it is in all its forms conscious communion with God. This is the source of all grace. When the soul is in contact with God, in intercourse with God, in association with Him, it is not only in an attitude to receive grace; it is not only actually seeking grace; it is already receiving and possessing grace. And intercourse with God is the very essence of prayer.

It is impossible to conceive of a praying

man, therefore, as destitute of grace. If he prays, really prays, he draws near to God with heart open for grace, humbly depending on Him for its gift. And he certainly receives it. To say, Behold he prayeth! is equivalent, then, to saying, Behold a man in Christ! Dr. Charles Hodge used to startle us by declaring that no praying soul ever was lost. It seemed to us a hard saying. Our difficulty was that we did not conceive "praying" purely enough. We can, no doubt, go through the motions of prayer and not be saved souls. Our Savior tells us of those who love to pray on the street corners and in the synagogues, to be seen of men. And He tells us that they have their reward. Their purpose in praying is to be seen of men, and they are seen of men. What can they ask more? But when we really pray – we are actually in enjoyment of communion with God. And is not communion with God salvation? The thing for us to do is to pray without ceasing; once having come into the presence of God, never to leave it; to abide in His presence and to live, steadily, unbrokenly, continuously, in the midst of whatever distractions or trials, with and in Him. God grant such a life to every one of us!

B.B. Warfield, 1851-1921

The Way of Salvation: Prayer

Thomas Watson

"But I give myself unto prayer." Psa 109:4.
It is one thing to pray, and another thing to be given to prayer: he who prays frequently, is said to be given to prayer; as he who often distributes alms, is said to be given to charity. Prayer is a glorious ordinance, it is the soul's trading with heaven. God comes down to us by his Spirit, and we go up to him by prayer.

WHAT IS PRAYER?

It is an offering up of our desires to God for things agreeable to his will, in the name of Christ.

"Prayer is offering up our desires;" and therefore called making known our requests. Phil 4:6. In prayer we come as humble petitioners, begging to have our suit granted. It is "offering up of our desires to God." Prayer is

not to be made to any but God. The Papists pray to saints and angels, who know not our grievances. "Abraham be ignorant of us." Isa 63:16. All angel-worship is forbidden. Col 2: 18, 19. We must not pray to any but whom we may believe in. "How shall they call on him in whom they have not believed?" Rom 10:14. We cannot believe in an angel, therefore we must not pray to him.

WHY MUST PRAYER BE MADE TO GOD ONLY?

Because he only hears prayer. "Oh thou that hearest prayer." Psa 65:2. Hereby God is known to be the true God, in that he hears prayer. "Hear me, O Lord, hear me, that this people may know that thou art the Lord God" 1 Kings 18:37. Because God only can help. We may look to second causes, and cry, as the woman did, "Help, my lord, O king." And he said, "If the Lord do not help thee, whence shall I help thee?" 2 Kings 6:26, 27. If we are in outward distress, God must send from heaven and save; if we are in inward agonies, he only can pour in the oil of joy; therefore prayer is to be made to him only.

We are to pray "for things agreeable to his will." When we pray for outward things, for riches or children, perhaps God sees these things not to be good for us; and our prayers should comport with his will. We may pray absolutely for grace; "For this is the will of God, even your sanctification." 1 Thess 4:3. There must be no strange incense offered. Exod 30:9. When we pray for things which are not agreeable to God's will, it is offering strange incense.

WE ARE TO PRAY "IN THE NAME OF CHRIST"

To pray in the name of Christ, is not only to mention Christ's name in prayer, but to pray in the hope and confidence of his merits. "Samuel took a sucking lamb and offered it," &c. 1 Sam 7:9. We must carry the lamb Christ in the arms of our faith, and so shall we prevail in prayer. When Uzziah would offer incense without a priest, God was angry, and struck him with leprosy, 2 Chron 26:16. When we do not pray in Christ's name, in the hope of his mediation, we offer up incense without a priest; and what can we expect but to meet with rebukes, and to have God answer us by terrible things?

WHAT ARE THE SEVERAL PARTS OF PRAYER?

There is the confessors part, which is the acknowledgement of sin.

The supplicatory part, when we either deprecate and pray against some evil, or request the obtaining of some good.

The congratulatory part, when we give thanks for mercies received, which is the most excellent part of prayer. In petition, we act like men; in giving thanks, we act like angels.

WHAT ARE THE SEVERAL SORTS OF PRAYER?

There is mental prayer, in the mind. 1 Sam 1:13. Vocal. Psa 77:1. Ejaculatory, which is a sudden and short elevation of the heart to God. "So I prayed to the God of heaven." Neh 2:4. Inspired prayer, when we pray for those things which God puts into our heart. The Spirit helps us with sighs and groans. Rom 8:26. Both the expressions of the tongue, and the impressions of the heart, so far as they are right, are from the Spirit.

PRESCRIBED PRAYER

Our Savior has set us a pattern of prayer. God prescribed a set form of blessing for the priests. Numb 6:23. Public prayer, when we pray in the audience of others. Prayer is more powerful when many join and unite their forces. *Vis unita fortior* [A united force is stronger], Matt 18:19. Private prayer; when we pray by ourselves. "Enter into thy closet." Matt 6:6.

That prayer is most likely to prevail with God which is rightly qualified. That is a good medicine which has the right ingredients; and that prayer is good, and most likely to prevail with God, which has these seven ingredients in it:

It must be mixed with faith. "But let him ask in faith." James 1:6. Believe that God hears, and will in due time grant, believe his love and truth; believe that he is love, and therefore will not deny you; believe that he is truth, and therefore will not deny himself. Faith sets prayer to work. Faith is to prayer what the feather is to the arrow; it feathers the arrow of prayer, and makes it fly swifter, and pierce

the throne of grace. The prayer that is faithless is fruitless.

IT MUST BE A MELTING PRAYER

"The sacrifices of God are a broken spirit." Psa 51:17. The incense was to be beaten to typify the breaking of the heart in prayer. Oh! says a Christian, I cannot pray with such gifts and elocution as others; as Moses said, "I am not eloquent;" but can't thou weep? Does thy heart melt in prayer? Weeping prayer prevails. Tears drop as pearls from the eye. Jacob wept and made supplication; and "had power over the angel." Hosea 12:4. Prayer must be fired with zeal and fervency. "Effectual fervent prayer availeth much" James 5:16. Cold prayer, like cold suitors, never speed. Prayer without fervency, is like a sacrifice without a fire. Prayer is called a "pouring out of the soul," to signify vehemence 1 Sam 1:15. Formality starves prayer. Prayer is compared to incense. "Let my prayer be set forth as incense" Psa 141:2. Hot coals were to be put to the incense, to make it odoriferous and fragrant; so fervency of affection is like coals to the incense; it makes prayer ascend as a sweet perfume. Christ prayed with strong cries, Heb 5:7. *Clamor iste penetrat nubes* [Such a cry pierces the clouds], Luther. Fervent prayer, like a powder engine set against heaven's gates, makes them fly open. To cause holy fervor and ardor of soul in prayer, consider,

Prayer without fervency is no prayer; it is speaking, not praying. Lifeless prayer is no more prayer than the picture of a man is a man. One may say as Pharaoh, "I have dreamed a dream," Gen 41:15. It is dreaming, not praying. Life and fervency baptize a duty, and give it a name.

Consider in what need we stand of those things which we ask in prayer. We come to ask the favor of God; and if we have not his love all we enjoy is cursed to us. We pray that our souls may be washed in Christ's blood; if he wash us not we have no part in him, John 13:8. When will we be in earnest, if not when we are praying for the life of our souls?

It is only fervent prayer that has the promise of mercy affixed to it. "Ye shall find me, when ye shall search for me with all your heart" Jer 29:13. It is dead praying without a promise; and the promise is made only to ardency. The a tiles among the Romans, had their doors always standing open, that all who had petitions might have free access to them; so God's heart is ever open to fervent prayer.

PRAYER MUST BE SINCERE

Sincerity is the silver thread which must run through the whole duties of religion. Sincerity in prayer is when we have gracious holy ends; when our prayer is not so much for temporal mercies as for spiritual. We send out prayer as our merchant ship, that we may have large returns of spiritual blessings. Our aim in it is, that our hearts may be more holy, that we may have more communion with God and that we may increase our stock of grace. The prayer which wants a good aim, wants a good issue.

The prayer that will prevail with God must have a fixedness of mind. "My heart is fixed, O God" Psa 57:7. Since the fall the mind is like quicksilver, which will not fix; it has *principium motus*, but *non quietus* [a principle of restlessness, not of peace]. The thoughts will be roving and dancing up and down in prayer, just as if a man who is traveling to a certain place should run out of the road, and wander he knows not whither. In prayer we are traveling to the throne of grace, but how often do we, by vain cogitations, turn out of the road! This is rather wandering than praying.

How shall we cure these vain impertinent thoughts, which distract us in prayer, and, we fear, hinder its acceptance?

Be very apprehensive in prayer of the infiniteness of God's majesty and purity. His eye is upon us in prayer, and we may say as David, "Thou tellest my wanderings," Psa 56:8. The thoughts of this would make us *hoc agere*, mind the duty we are about. If a man were to deliver a petition to an earthly prince, would he at the same time be playing with a feather? Set yourselves, when you pray, as in God's presence. Could you but look through the keyhole of heaven, and see how devout and intent the angels are in their worshiping God, surely you would be ready to blush at your vain thoughts and vile impertinences in prayer.

If you would keep your mind fixed in prayer, keep your eye fixed. "Unto thee lift I up mine eyes, O thou that dwellest in the heavens," Psa 123:1. Much vanity comes in at the eye. When the eye wanders in prayer, the heart wanders. To think to keep the heart fixed in prayer, and yet let the eye gaze, is as if one should think to keep his house safe, and yet let the windows be open.

If you would have your thoughts fixed in prayer, get more love to God. Love is a great fixer of the thoughts. He who is in love cannot keep his thoughts off the object. He who loves the world has his thoughts upon the world. Did we love God more, our minds would be more intent upon him in prayer. Were there more delight in duty, there would be less distraction.

Implore the help of God's Spirit to fix your minds, and make them intent and serious in prayer. The ship without a pilot rather floats than sails. That our thoughts do not float up and down in prayer, we need the blessed Spirit to be our pilot to steer us. Only God's Spirit can bound the thoughts. A shaking hand may as well write a line steadily, as we can keep our hearts fixed in prayer without the Spirit of God.

Make holy thoughts familiar to you in your ordinary course of life. David was often musing on God. "When I am awake, I am still with thee" Psa 139:18. He who gives himself liberty to have vain thoughts out of prayer, will scarcely have other thoughts in prayer.

If you would keep your mind fixed on God, watch your hearts, not only after prayer, but in prayer. The heart will be apt to give you the slip, and have a thousand vagaries in prayer. We read of angels ascending and descending on Jacob's ladder; so in prayer you shall find your hearts ascending to heaven, and in a moment descending upon earthly objects. O Christians, watch your hearts in prayer. What a shame is it to think, that when we are speaking to God our hearts should be in the fields, or in our counting-houses, or one way or other, running upon the devil's errand!

Labor for larger degrees of grace. The more ballast the ship has the better it sails; so the more the heart is ballasted with grace, the steadier it will sail to heaven in prayer.

PRAYER THAT IS LIKELY TO PREVAIL WITH GOD MUST BE ARGUMENTATIVE

God loves to have us plead with him, and use

arguments in prayer. See how many arguments Jacob used in prayer. "Deliver me, I pray thee, from the hand of my brother," Gen 32:11. The arguments he used are from God's command "Thou saidst to me, Return to thy country;" ver 9; as if he had said, I did not take this journey of my own head, but by thy direction; therefore thou canst not but in honor protect me. And he uses another argument. "Thou saidst, I will surely do thee good;" ver 12. Lord, wilt thou go back from thy own promise? Thus he was argumentative in prayer; and he got not only a new blessing, but a new name. "Thy name shall be called no more Jacob, but Israel: for as a prince hast thou power with God, and hast prevailed"; ver 28. God loves to be overcome with strength of argument. Thus, when we come to God in prayer for grace, let us be argumentative. Lord, thou callest thyself the God of all grace; and whither should we go with our vessel, but to the fountain? Lord, thy grace may be imparted, yet not impaired. Has not Christ purchased grace for poor indigent creatures? Every drachm of grace costs a drop of blood. Shall Christ die to purchase grace for us, and shall not we have the fruit of his purchase? Lord, it is thy delight to milk out the breast of mercy and grace, and wilt thou abridge thyself of thy own delight? Thou hast promised to give thy Spirit to implant grace; can truth lie? can faithfulness deceive? God loves thus to be overcome with arguments in prayer.

Prayer that would prevail with God, must be joined with reformation. "If thou stretch out thy hands toward him; if iniquity be in thy hand, put it far away," Job 11:13, 14. Sin, lived in, makes the heart hard, and God's ear deaf. It is foolish to pray against sin, and then sin against prayer. "If I regard iniquity in my heart, the Lord will not hear me," Psa 66:18. The loadstone loses its virtue when bespread with garlic; so does prayer when polluted with sin. The incense of prayer must be offered upon the altar of a holy heart.

Thus you see what is the prayer which is most likely to prevail with God.

Use one

It reproves such as pray not at all. It is made the note of a reprobate, that he calls not upon God. Psa 14:4. Does he think to have an alms who never asks it? Do they think to have mercy from God who never seek it? Then God would befriend them more than he did his own Son. Christ offered up prayers with strong cries, Heb 5:7. None of God's children are born dumb, Gal 4:6.I t reproves such as have left off prayer, which is a sign that they never felt the fruit and comfort of it. He that leaves off prayer leaves off to fear God. "Thou castest off fear, and restrainest prayer before God," Job 15:4. A man that has left off prayer, is fit for any wickedness. When Saul had given over inquiring after God he went to the witch of Endor.

Use two

Be persons given to prayer. "I give myself," says David, "to prayer." Pray for pardon and purity. Prayer is the golden key that opens heaven. The tree of the promise will not drop its fruit unless shaken by the hand of prayer. All the benefits of Christ's redemption are handed over to us by prayer.

I have prayed a long time for mercy, and have no answer. "I am weary of crying," Ps 69:3.

God may hear us when we do not hear from him; as soon as prayer is made, God hears it, though he does not presently answer. A friend may receive our letter, though he does not presently send us an answer.

GOD MAY DELAY PRAYER, YET HE WILL NOT DENY IT

Why does God delay an answer to prayer?

Because he loves to hear the voice of prayer. "The prayer of the upright is his delight," Prov 15:8. You let the musician play a great while ere you throw him down money, because you love to hear his music, Cant 2:14.God may delay prayer when he will not deny it, that he may humble us. He has spoken to us long in his word to leave our sins, but we would not hear him; therefore he lets us speak to him in prayer and seems not to hear us.

He may delay to answer prayer when he will not deny it, because he sees we are not yet fit for the mercy we ask. Perhaps we pray for deliverance when we are not fit for it; our scum is not yet boiled away. We would have God swift to deliver, and we are slow to repent.

God may delay to answer prayer, that the

mercy we pray for may be more prized, and may be sweeter when it comes. The longer the merchant's ships stay abroad, the more he rejoices when they come home laden with spices and jewels; therefore be not discouraged, but follow God with prayer. Though God delays, he will not deny. Prayer vincit invincibilem [conquers the invincible], it overcomes the Omnipotent, Hos 12:4. The Syrians tied their god Hercules fast with a golden chain, that he should not remove. The Lord was held by Moses" prayer as with a golden chain. "Let me alone;" why, what did Moses? he only prayed, Exod 32:10. Prayer ushers in mercy. Be thy case never so sad, if thou canst but pray thou needest not fear, Psa 10:17. Therefore give thyself to prayer.

Thomas Watson, c.1620–1686

Upon Our Lord's Sermon on the Mount

John Wesley

The Lord's Prayer is the model and standard of all our prayers

1. After having taught the true nature and ends of prayer, our Lord subjoins an example of it; even that divine form of prayer which seems in this place to be proposed by way of pattern chiefly, as the model and standard of all our prayers: "After this manner therefore pray ye." Whereas, elsewhere he enjoins the use of these very words: "He said unto them, When ye pray, say –" (Luke 11:2).

2. We may observe, in general, concerning this divine prayer,

First, that it contains all we can reasonably or innocently pray for. There is nothing which we have need to ask of God, nothing which we can ask without offending him, which is not included, either directly or indirectly, in this comprehensive form.

Secondly, that it contains all we can reasonably or innocently desire; whatever is for the glory of God, whatever is needful or profitable, not only for ourselves, but for every creature in heaven and earth. And, indeed, our prayers are the proper test of our desires; nothing being fit to have a place in our desires which is not fit to

have a place in our prayers: What we may not pray for, neither should we desire.

Thirdly, that it contains all our duty to God and man; whatsoever things are pure and holy, whatsoever God requires of the children of men, whatsoever is acceptable in his sight, whatsoever it is whereby we may profit our neighbor, being expressed or implied therein.

3. It consists of three parts, – the preface, the petitions, and the doxology, or conclusion. The preface, "Our Father which art in heaven," lays a general foundation for prayer; comprising what we must first know of God, before we can pray in confidence of being heard. It likewise points out to us all those tempers with which we are to approach to God, which are most essentially requisite, if we desire either our prayers or our lives should find acceptance with him.

4. "Our Father:" – If he is a Father, then he is good, then he is loving, to his children. And here is the first and great reason for prayer. God is willing to bless; let us ask for a blessing. "Our Father"; – our Creator; the Author of our being; He who raised us from the dust of the earth; who breathed into us the breath of life, and we became living souls. But if he made us, let us ask, and he will not withhold any good thing from the work of his own hands. "Our Father"; – our Preserver; who, day by day, sustains the life he has given; of whose continuing love we now and every moment receive life and breath and all things. So much the more boldly let us come to him, and we shall "obtain mercy, and grace to help in time of need." Above all, the Father of our Lord Jesus Christ, and of all that believe in him; who justifies us "freely by his grace, through the redemption that is in Jesus"; who hath "blotted out all our sins, and healed all our infirmities"; who hath received us for his own children, by adoption and grace; and, "because" we "are sons, hath sent forth the Spirit of his Son into" our "hearts, crying, Abba, Father"; who "hath begotten us again of incorruptible seed," and "created us anew in Christ Jesus." Therefore we know that he heareth us always; therefore we pray to him without ceasing. We pray, because we love; and "we love him because he first loved us."

5. "Our Father": – Not mine only who now

cry unto him, but ours in the most extensive sense. The God and "Father of the spirits of all flesh"; the Father of angels and men: So the very Heathens acknowledged him to be, the Father of the universe, of all the families both in heaven and earth. Therefore with him there is no respect of persons. He loveth all that he hath made. "He is loving unto every man, and his mercy is over all his works." And the Lord's delight is in them that fear him, and put their trust in his mercy; in them that trust in him through the Son of his love, knowing they are "accepted in the Beloved." But "if God so loved us, we ought also to love one another"; yea, all mankind; seeing "God so loved the world, that he gave his only-begotten Son," even to die the death, that they "might not perish, but have everlasting life"

6. "Which art in heaven": – High and lifted up; God over all, blessed for ever: Who, sitting on the circle of the heavens, beholdeth all things both in heaven and earth; whose eye pervades the whole sphere of created being; yea, and of uncreated night; unto whom "are known all his works," and all the works of every creature, not only "from the beginning of the world," from all eternity, from everlasting to everlasting; who constrains the host of heaven, as well as the children of men, to cry out with wonder and amazement, O the depth! "The depth of the riches, both of the wisdom and of the knowledge of God!" "Which art in heaven": – The Lord and Ruler of all, superintending and disposing all things; who art the King of kings, and Lord of lords, the blessed and only Potentate; who art strong and girded about with power, doing whatsoever pleaseth thee; the Almighty; for whensoever thou willest, to do is present with thee.

"In heaven": – Eminently there. Heaven is thy throne, "the place where thine honor" particularly "dwelleth." But not there alone; for thou fillest heaven and earth, the whole expanse of space. "Heaven and earth are full of thy glory. Glory be to thee, O Lord, most high!"

Therefore should we "serve the Lord with fear, and rejoice unto him with reverence." Therefore should we think, speak, and act, as continually under the eye, in the immediate presence, of the Lord, the King.

7. "Hallowed be thy name." – This is the first of the six petitions, whereof the prayer itself is composed. The name of God is God himself; the nature of God, so far as it can be discovered to man. It means, therefore, together with his existence, all his attributes or perfections; His Eternity, particularly signified by his great and incommunicable name, JEHOVAH, as the Apostle John translates it: "the Alpha and Omega, the beginning and the end; He which is, and which was, and which is to come"; – His Fullness of Being, denoted by his other great name, I AM THAT I AM! – His omnipresence; – His omnipotence; who is indeed the only Agent in the material world; all matter being essentially dull and inactive, and moving only as it is moved by the finger of God; and he is the spring of action in every creature, visible and invisible, which could neither act nor exist, without the continual influx and agency of his almighty power; – His wisdom, clearly deduced from the things that are seen, from the goodly order of the universe; – His Trinity in Unity, and Unity in Trinity, discovered to us in the very first line of his written word; *bara' 'elohim* – literally, the Gods created, a plural noun joined with a verb of the singular number; as well as in every part of his subsequent revelations, given by the mouth of all his holy Prophets and Apostles; – His essential purity and holiness; – and, above all, his love, which is the very brightness of his glory.

In praying that God, or his name, may "be hallowed" or glorified, we pray that he may be known, such as he is, by all that are capable thereof, by all intelligent beings, and with affections suitable to that knowledge; that he may be duly honored, and feared, and loved, by all in heaven above and in the earth beneath; by all angels and men, whom for that end he has made capable of knowing and loving him to eternity.

8. "Thy kingdom come." – This has a close connection with the preceding petition. In order that the name of God might be hallowed, we pray that his kingdom, the kingdom of Christ, may come. This kingdom then comes to a particular person, when he "repents and believes the gospel"; when he is taught of God, not only to know himself, but to know Jesus Christ and him crucified. As "this is life eternal,

to know the only true God, and Jesus Christ whom he hath sent"; so it is the kingdom of God begun below, set up in the believer's heart; "the Lord God Omnipotent" then "reigneth," when he is known through Christ Jesus. He taketh unto himself his mighty power, that he may subdue all things unto himself. He goeth on in the soul conquering and to conquer, till he hath put all things under his feet, till "every thought is brought into captivity to the obedience of Christ."

When therefore God shall "give his Son the Heathen for his inheritance, and the uttermost parts of the earth for his possession"; when "all kingdoms shall bow before him, and all nations shall do him service"; when "the mountain of the Lord's house," the Church of Christ, "shall be established in the top of the mountains"; when "the fullness of the Gentiles shall come in, and all Israel shall be saved"; then shall it be seen, that "the Lord is King, and hath put on glorious apparel," appearing to every soul of man as King of kings, and Lord of lords. And it is meet for all those who love his appearing, to pray that he would hasten the time; that this his kingdom, the kingdom of grace, may come quickly, and swallow up all the kingdoms of the earth; that all mankind, receiving him for their King, truly believing in his name, may be filled with righteousness, and peace, and joy, with holiness and happiness, – till they are removed hence into his heavenly kingdom, there to reign with him for ever and ever.

For this also we pray in those words, "Thy kingdom come": We pray for the coming of his everlasting kingdom, the kingdom of glory in heaven, which is the continuation and perfection of the kingdom of grace on earth. Consequently this, as well as the preceding petition, is offered up for the whole intelligent creation, who are all interested in this grand event, the final renovation of all things, by God's putting an end to misery and sin, to infirmity and death, taking all things into his own hands, and setting up the kingdom which endureth throughout all ages.

Exactly answerable to this are those awful words in the prayer at the burial of the dead: "Beseeching thee, that it may please thee of thy gracious goodness, shortly to accomplish the number of thine elect, and to hasten thy king-

dom: That we, with all those that are departed in the true faith of thy holy name, may have our perfect consummation and bliss, both in body and soul, in thy everlasting glory."

9. "Thy will be done in earth, as it is in heaven." – This is the necessary and immediate consequence wherever the kingdom of God is come; wherever God dwells in the soul by faith, and Christ reigns in the heart by love.

It is probable, many, perhaps the generality of men, at the first view of these words, are apt to imagine they are only an expression of, or petition for, resignation; for a readiness to suffer the will of God, whatsoever it be concerning us. And this is unquestionably a divine and excellent temper, a most precious gift of God. But this is not what we pray for in this petition; at least, not in the chief and primary sense of it. We pray, not so much for a passive, as for an active, conformity to the will of God, in saying, "Thy will be done in earth, as it is in heaven."

How is it done by the angels of God in heaven, – those who now circle his throne rejoicing? They do it willingly; they love his commandments, and gladly hearken to his words. It is their meat and drink to do his will; it is their highest glory and joy. They do it continually; there is no interruption in their willing service. They rest not day nor night, but employ every hour (speaking after the manner of men; otherwise our measures of duration, days, and nights, and hours, have no place in eternity) in fulfilling his commands, in executing his designs, in performing the counsel of his will. And they do it perfectly. No sin, no defect belongs to angelic minds. It is true, "the stars are not pure in his sight," even the morning-stars that sing together before him. "In his sight," that is, in comparison of Him, the very angels are not pure. But this does not imply, that they are not pure in themselves. Doubtless they are; they are without spot and blameless. They are altogether devoted to his will, and perfectly obedient in all things.

If we view this in another light, we may observe, the angels of God in heaven do all the will of God. And they do nothing else, nothing but what they are absolutely assured is his will. Again they do all the will of God as he willeth; in the manner which pleases him, and no other. Yea, and they do this, only because it is his will; for this end, and no other reason.

10. When therefore we pray, that the will of God may "be done in earth as it is in heaven," the meaning is, that all the inhabitants of the earth, even the whole race of mankind, may do the will of their Father which is in heaven, as willingly as the holy angels; that these may do it continually, even as they, without any interruption of their willing service; yea, and that they may do it perfectly, – that "the God of peace, through the blood of the everlasting covenant, may make them perfect in every good work to do his will, and work in them all "which is well-pleasing in his sight."

In other words, we pray that we and all mankind may do the whole will of God in all things; and nothing else, not the least thing but what is the holy and acceptable will of God. We pray that we may do the whole will of God as he willeth, in the manner that pleases him: And, lastly, that we may do it because it is his will; that this may be the sole reason and ground, the whole and only motive, of whatsoever we think, or whatsoever we speak or do.

11. "Give us this day our daily bread." – In the three former petitions we have been praying for all mankind. We come now more particularly to desire a supply for our own wants. Not that we are directed, even here, to confine our prayer altogether to ourselves; but this, and each of the following petitions, may be used for the whole Church of Christ upon earth.

By "bread" we may understand all things needful, whether for our souls or bodies; the things pertaining to life and godliness: We understand not barely the outward bread, what our Lord terms "the meat which perisheth"; but much more the spiritual bread, the grace of God, the food "which endureth unto everlasting life." It was the judgment of many of the ancient Fathers, that we are here to understand the sacramental bread also; daily received in the beginning by the whole Church of Christ, and highly esteemed, till the love of many waxed cold, as the grand channel whereby the grace of his Spirit was conveyed to the souls of all the children of God.

"Our daily bread." – The word we render daily has been differently explained by different commentators. But the most plain and natural sense of it seems to be this, which is retained in almost all translations, as well ancient as modern; – what is sufficient for this day; and so for each day as it succeeds.

12. "Give us": – For we claim nothing of right, but only of free mercy. We deserve not the air we breathe, the earth that bears, or the sun that shines upon, us. All our desert, we own, is hell: But God loves us freely; therefore, we ask him to give, what we can no more procure for ourselves, than we can merit it at his hands.

Not that either the goodness or the power of God is a reason for us to stand idle. It is his will that we should use all diligence in all things, that we should employ our utmost endeavors, as much as if our success were the natural effect of our own wisdom and strength: And then, as though we had done nothing, we are to depend on Him, the giver of every good and perfect gift.

"This day": – For we are to take no thought for the morrow. For this very end has our wise Creator divided life into these little portions of time, so clearly separated from each other, that we might look on every day as a fresh gift of God, another life, which we may devote to his glory; and that every evening may be as the close of life, beyond which we are to see nothing but eternity.

13. "And forgive us our trespasses, as we forgive them that trespass against us." – As nothing but sin can hinder the bounty of God from flowing forth upon every creature, so this petition naturally follows the former; that, all hindrances being removed, we may the more clearly trust in the God of love for every manner of thing which is good.

"Our trespasses": – The word properly signifies our debts. Thus our sins are frequently represented in Scripture; every sin laying us under a fresh debt to God, to whom we already owe, as it were, ten thousand talents. What then can we answer when he shall say, "Pay me that thou owest"? We are utterly insolvent; we have nothing to pay; we have wasted all our substance. Therefore, if he deal with us according to the rigor of his law, if he exact what he justly may, he must command us to be "bound hand and foot, and delivered over to the tormentors."

Indeed we are already bound hand and

foot by the chains of our own sins. These, considered with regard to ourselves, are chains of iron and fetters of brass. They are wounds wherewith the world, the flesh, and the devil, have gashed and mangled us all over. They are diseases that drink up our blood and spirits, that bring us down to the chambers of the grave. But considered, as they are here, with regard to God, they are debts, immense and numberless. Well, therefore, seeing we have nothing to pay, may we cry unto him that he would "frankly forgive" us all!

The word translated forgive implies either to forgive a debt, or to unloose a chain. And if we attain the former, the latter follows of course: if our debts are forgiven, the chains fall off our hands. As soon as ever, through the free grace of God in Christ, we "receive forgiveness of sins," we receive likewise "a lot among those which are sanctified, by faith which is in him." Sin has lost its power; it has no dominion over those who "are under grace," that is, in favor with God. As "there is now no condemnation for them that are in Christ Jesus," so they are freed from sin as well as from guilt. "The righteousness of the law is fulfilled in" them, and they "walk not after the flesh, but after the Spirit."

14. "As we forgive them that trespass against us." – In these words our Lord clearly declares both on what condition, and in what degree or manner, we may look to be forgiven of God. All our trespasses and sins are forgiven us, if we forgive, and as we forgive, others. (First, God forgives us if we forgive others.) This is a point of the utmost importance. And our blessed Lord is so jealous lest at any time we should let it slip out of our thoughts, that he not only inserts it in the body of his prayer, but presently after repeats it twice over. "If," saith he, "ye forgive men their trespasses, your heavenly Father will also forgive you: But if ye forgive not men their trespasses, neither will your Father forgive your trespasses" (Matt. 6:14, 15) Secondly, God forgives us as we forgive others. So that if any malice or bitterness, if any taint of unkindness or anger remains, if we do not clearly, fully, and from the heart, forgive all men their trespasses, we far cut short the forgiveness of our own: God cannot clearly and fully forgive us: He may show us some degree of mercy; but we will not suffer him to blot out all our sins, and forgive all our iniquities.

In the mean time, while we do not from our hearts forgive our neighbor his trespasses, what manner of prayer are we offering to God whenever we utter these words? We are indeed setting God at open defiance: we are daring him to do his worst. "Forgive us our trespasses, as we forgive them that trespass against us!" That is, in plain terms, "Do not thou forgive us at all; we desire no favor at thy hands. We pray that thou wilt keep our sins in remembrance, and that thy wrath may abide upon us." But can you seriously offer such a prayer to God? And hath he not yet cast you quick into hell?' O tempt him no longer! Now, even now, by his grace, forgive as you would be forgiven! Now have compassion on thy fellow-servant, as God hath had and will have pity on thee!

15. "And lead us not into temptation, but deliver us from evil." – "[And] lead us not into temptation." The word translated temptation means trial of any kind. And so the English word temptation was formerly taken in an indifferent sense, although now it is usually understood of solicitation to sin. St. James uses the word in both these senses; first, in its general, then in its restrained, acceptation. He takes it in the former sense when he saith, "Blessed is the man that endureth temptation; For when he is tried," or approved of God, "he shall receive the crown of life" (James 1:12, 13). He immediately adds, taking the word in the latter sense, "Let no man say when he is tempted, I am tempted of God; for God cannot be tempted with evil, neither tempteth he any man. But every man is tempted, when he is drawn away of his own lust," or desire, drawn out of God, in whom alone he is safe, – "and enticed"; caught as a fish with a bait. Then it is, when he is thus drawn away and enticed, that he properly "enters into temptation." Then temptation covers him as a cloud; it overspreads his whole soul. Then how hardly shall he escape out of the snare! Therefore, we beseech God "not to lead us into temptation," that is, (seeing God tempteth no man,) not to suffer us to be led into it. "But deliver us from evil": Rather "from the evil one," is unquestionably the wicked one, emphatically so called, the prince and god

of this world, who works with mighty power in the children of disobedience. But all those who are the children of God by faith are delivered out of his hands. He may fight against them; and so he will. But he cannot conquer, unless they betray their own souls. He may torment for a time, but he cannot destroy; for God is on their side, who will not fail, in the end, to "avenge his own elect, that cry unto him day and night." Lord, when we are tempted, suffer us not to enter into temptation! Do thou make a way for us to escape, that the wicked one touch us not!

16. The conclusion of this divine prayer, commonly called the Doxology, is a solemn thanksgiving, a compendious acknowledgement of the attributes and works of God. "For thine is the kingdom" – the sovereign right of all things that are or ever were created; yea, thy kingdom is an everlasting kingdom, and thy dominion endureth throughout all ages. "The power" – the executive power whereby thou governest all things in thy everlasting kingdom, whereby thou dost whatsoever pleaseth thee, in all places of thy dominion. "And the glory" – the praise due from every creature, for thy power, and the mightiness of thy kingdom, and for all thy wondrous works which thou workest from everlasting, and shalt do, world without end, "for ever and ever! Amen!" So be it!

I believe it will not be unacceptable to the serious reader, to subjoin

A Paraphrase On The Lord's Prayer

Father of all, whose powerful voice
Call'd forth this universal frame;
Whose mercies over all rejoice,
Through endless ages still the same.
Thou, by thy word, upholdest all;
Thy bounteous love to all is show'd,
Thou hear'st thy every creature's call,
And fillest every mouth with good.

In heaven thou reign'st, enthroned in light,
Nature's expanse beneath thee spread;
Earth, air, and sea before thy sight,
And hell's deep gloom are open laid.
Wisdom, and might, and love are thine:
Prostrate before thy face we fall,

Confess thine attributes divine,
An hail the Sovereign Lord of All.

Thee, sovereign Lord, let all confess
That moves in earth, or air, or sky
Revere thy power, thy goodness bless,
Tremble before thy piercing eye.
All ye who owe to Him your birth,
In praise your every hour employ:
Jehovah reigns! Be glad, O earth!
And shout, ye morning stars, for joy!

Son of thy Sire's eternal love,
Take to thyself thy mighty power;
Let all earth's sons thy mercy prove,
Let all thy bleeding grace adore.
The triumphs of thy love display;
In every heart reign thou alone;
Till all thy foes confess thy sway,
And glory ends what grace begun.

Spirit of grace, and health, and power,
Fountain of light and love below,
Abroad thine healing influence shower,
O'er all the nations let it flow.
Inflame our hearts with perfect love;
In us the work of faith fulfill;
So not heaven's hosts shall swifter move
Than we on earth to do thy will.

Father, 'tis thine each day to yield
Thy children's wants a fresh supply:
Thou cloth'st the lilies of the field,
And hearest the young ravens cry.
On thee we cast our care; we live
Through thee, who know'st our every need;
O feed us with thy grace, and give
Our souls this day the living bread!

Eternal, spotless Lamb of God,
Before the world's foundation slain,
Sprinkle us ever with thy blood;
O cleanse and keep us ever clean.
To every soul (all praise to Thee!)
Our bowels of compassion more:
And all mankind by this may see
God is in us; for God is love.

Giver and Lord of life, whose power
And guardian care for all are free;
To thee, in fierce temptation's hour,

From sin and Satan let us flee.
Thine, Lord, we are, and ours thou art;
In us be all thy goodness show'd;
Renew, enlarge, and fill our heart
With peace, and joy, and heaven, and God.

Blessing and honor, praise and love,
Co-equal, co-eternal Three,
In earth below, in heaven above,
By all thy works be paid to thee.
Thrice Holy! thine the kingdom is,
The power omnipotent is thine;
And when created nature dies,
Thy never-ceasing glories shine.

John Wesley, 1703–91

What is Prayer?

Westminster Larger Catechism

Question 178: What is prayer?

Answer: Prayer is an offering up of our desires unto God, in the name of Christ, by the help of his Spirit; with confession of our sins, and thankful acknowledgment of his mercies.

Question 179: Are we to pray unto God only?

Answer: God only being able to search the hearts, hear the requests, pardon the sins, and fulfill the desires of all; and only to be believed in, and worshiped with religious worship; prayer, which is a special part thereof, is to be made by all to him alone, and to none other.

Question 180: What is it to pray in the name of Christ?

Answer: To pray in the name of Christ is, in obedience to his command, and in confidence on his promises, to ask mercy for his sake; not by bare mentioning of his name, but by drawing our encouragement to pray, and our boldness, strength, and hope of acceptance in prayer, from Christ and his mediation.

Question 181: Why are we to pray in the name of Christ?

Answer: The sinfulness of man, and his distance from God by reason thereof, being so great, as that we can have no access into his presence without a mediator; and there being none in heaven or earth appointed to, or fit for, that glorious work but Christ alone, we are to pray in no other name but his only.

Question 182: How does the Spirit help us to pray?

Answer: We not knowing: What to pray for as we ought, the Spirit helps our infirmities, by enabling us to understand both for whom, and: What, and: How prayer is to be made; and by working and quickening in our hearts (although not in all persons, nor at all times, in the same measure) those apprehensions, affections, and graces which are requisite for the right performance of that duty.

Question 183: For whom are we to pray?

Answer: We are to pray for the whole church of Christ upon earth; for magistrates, and ministers; for ourselves, our brethren, yea, our enemies; and for all sorts of men living, or that shall live hereafter; but not for the dead, nor for those that are known to have sinned the sin unto death.

Question 184: For what things are we to pray?

Answer: We are to pray for all things tending to the glory of God, the welfare of the church, our own or others good; but not for anything that is unlawful.

Question 185: How are we to pray?

Answer: We are to pray with an awful apprehension of the majesty of God, and deep sense of our own unworthiness, necessities, and sins; with penitent, thankful, and enlarged hearts; with understanding, faith, sincerity, fervency, love, and perseverance, waiting upon him, with humble submission to his will.

Question 186: What rule has God given for our direction in the duty of prayer?

Answer: The whole Word of God is of use to direct us in the duty of prayer; but the special rule of direction is that form of prayer which our Savior Christ taught his disciples, commonly called the Lord's Prayer.

Question 187: How is the Lord's Prayer to be used?

Answer: The Lord's Prayer is not only for direction, as a pattern, according to which we are to make other prayers; but may also be used as a prayer, so that it be done with understanding, faith, reverence, and other graces necessary to the right performance of the duty of prayer.

Question 188: Of how many parts does the Lord's Prayer consist?

Answer: The Lord's Prayer consists of three parts; a preface, petitions, and a conclusion.

Question 189: What does the preface of the Lord's Prayer teach us?

Answer: The preface of the Lord's Prayer (contained in these words, Our Father which art in heaven), teaches us, when we pray, to draw near to God with confidence of his fatherly goodness, and our interest therein; with reverence, and all other childlike dispositions, heavenly affections, and due apprehensions of his sovereign power, majesty, and gracious condescension: as also, to pray with and for others.

Question 190: What do we pray for in the first petition?

Answer: In the first petition (which is, Hallowed be Thy name), acknowledging the utter inability and indisposition that is in ourselves and all men to honor God aright, we pray, that God would by his grace enable and incline us and others to know, to acknowledge, and highly to esteem him, his titles, attributes, ordinances, Word, works, and: Whatsoever he is pleased to make himself known by; and to glorify him in thought, word, and deed: that he would prevent and remove atheism, ignorance, idolatry, profaneness, and: Whatsoever is dishonorable to him; and, by his overruling providence, direct and dispose of all things to his own glory.

Question 191: What do we pray for in the second petition?

Answer: In the second petition (which is, Thy kingdom come), acknowledging ourselves and all mankind to be by nature under the dominion of sin and Satan, we pray, that the kingdom of sin and Satan may be destroyed, the gospel propagated throughout the world, the Jews called, the fullness of the Gentiles brought in; the church furnished with all gospel officers and ordinances, purged from corruption, countenanced and maintained by the civil magistrate: that the ordinances of Christ may be purely dispensed, and made effectual to the converting of those that are yet in their sins, and the confirming, comforting, and building up of those that are already converted: that Christ would rule in our hearts here, and hasten the time of his second coming, and our reigning with him forever: and that he

would be pleased so to exercise the kingdom of his power in all the world, as may best conduce to these ends.

Question 192: What do we pray for in the third petition?

Answer: In the third petition (which is, Thy will be done in earth, as it is in heaven), acknowledging, that by nature we and all men are not only utterly unable and unwilling to know and do the will of God, but prone to rebel against his Word, to repine and murmur against his providence, and wholly inclined to do the will of the flesh, and of the devil: we pray, that God would by his Spirit take away from ourselves and others all blindness, weakness, indisposedness, and perverseness of heart; and by his grace make us able and willing to know, do, and submit to his will in all things, with the like humility, cheerfulness, faithfulness, diligence, zeal, sincerity, and constancy, as the angels do in heaven.

Question 193: What do we pray for in the fourth petition?

Answer: In the fourth petition (which is, Give us this day our daily bread), acknowledging, that in Adam, and by our own sin, we have forfeited our right to all the outward blessings of this life, and deserve to be wholly deprived of them by God, and to have them cursed to us in the use of them; and that neither they of themselves are able to sustain us, nor we to merit, or by our own industry to procure them; but prone to desire, get, and use them unlawfully: we pray for ourselves and others, that both they and we, waiting upon the providence of God from day to day in the use of lawful means, may, of his free gift, and as to his fatherly wisdom shall seem best, enjoy a competent portion of them; and have the same continued and blessed unto us in our holy and comfortable use of them, and contentment in them; and be kept from all things that are contrary to our temporal support and comfort.

Question 194: What do we pray for in the fifth petition?

Answer: In the fifth petition (which is, Forgive us our debts, as we forgive our debtors), acknowledging, that we and all others are guilty both of original and actual sin, and thereby become debtors to the justice of God;

and that neither we, nor any other creature, can make the least satisfaction for that debt: we pray for ourselves and others, that God of his free grace would, through the obedience and satisfaction of Christ, apprehended and applied by faith, acquit us both from the guilt and punishment of sin, accept us in his Beloved; continue his favor and grace to us, pardon our daily failings, and fill us with peace and joy, in giving us daily more and more assurance of forgiveness; which we are the rather emboldened to ask, and encouraged to expect, when we have this testimony in ourselves, that we from the heart forgive others their offenses.

Question 195: What do we pray for in the sixth petition?

Answer: In the sixth petition (which is, And lead us not into temptation, but deliver us from evil), acknowledging, that the most wise, righteous, and gracious God, for divers holy and just ends, may so order things, that we may be assaulted, foiled, and for a time led captive by temptations; that Satan, the world, and the flesh, are ready powerfully to draw us aside, and ensnare us; and that we, even after the pardon of our sins, by reason of our corruption, weakness, and want of watchfulness, are not only subject to be tempted, and forward to expose ourselves unto temptations, but also of ourselves unable and unwilling to resist them, to recover out of them, and to improve them; and worthy to be left under the power of them: we pray, that God would so overrule the world and all in it, subdue the flesh, and restrain Satan, order all things, bestow and bless all means of grace, and quicken us to watchfulness in the use of them, that we and all his people may by his providence be kept from being tempted to sin; or, if tempted, that by his Spirit we may be powerfully supported and enabled to stand in the hour of temptation: or when fallen, raised again and recovered out of it, and have a sanctified use and improvement thereof: that our sanctification and salvation may be perfected, Satan trodden under our feet, and we fully freed from sin, temptation, and all evil, forever.

Question 196: What does the conclusion of the Lord's Prayer teach us?

Answer: The conclusion of the Lord's Prayer (which is, For thine is the kingdom, and the power, and the glory, forever. Amen.), teaches us to enforce our petitions with arguments, which are to be taken, not from any worthiness in ourselves, or in any other creature, but from God; and with our prayers to join praises, ascribing to God alone eternal sovereignty, omnipotency, and glorious excellency; in regard whereof, as he is able and willing to help us, so we by faith are emboldened to plead with him that he would, and quietly to rely upon him, that he will fulfill our requests. And, to testify this our desire and assurance, we say, Amen.

Westminster Larger Catechism

Intercession: Every Christian's Duty
George Whitefield

"Brethren, pray for us" 1 Thessalonians 5:25.

If we inquire, why there is so little love to be found amongst Christians, why the very characteristic, by which every one should know that we are disciples of the holy Jesus, is almost banished out of the Christian world, we shall find it, in a great measure, owing to a neglect or superficial performance of that excellent part of prayer, INTERCESSION, or imploring the divine grace and mercy in behalf of others.

Some forget this duty of praying for others, because they seldom remember to pray for themselves: and even those who are constant in praying to their Father who is in heaven, are often so selfish in their addresses to the throne of grace, that they do not enlarge their petitions for the welfare of their fellow Christians as they ought; and thereby fall short of attaining that Christian charity, that unfeigned love to their brethren, which their sacred profession obliges them to aspire after, and without which, though they should bestow all their goods to feed the poor, and even give their bodies to be burned, yet it would profit them nothing.

Since these things are so, I shall from the words of the text (though originally intended to be more confined) endeavor, to show,

I. FIRST, That it is every Christian's duty to pray for others as well as for himself.

II. SECONDLY, Show, whom we ought to

pray for, and in what manner we should do it. And,

III. THIRDLY, I shall offer some motives to excite all Christians to abound in this great duty of intercession.

I. FIRST, I SHALL ENDEAVOR TO SHOW, THAT IT IS EVERY CHRISTIAN'S DUTY TO PRAY FOR OTHERS, AS WELL AS FOR HIMSELF

Now PRAYER is a duty founded on natural religion; the very heathens never neglected it, though many Christian heathens amongst us do: and it is so essential to Christianity, that you might as reasonably expect to find a living man without breath, as a true Christian without the spirit of prayer and supplication. Thus, no sooner was St. Paul converted, but "behold he prayeth," saith the Lord Almighty. And thus will it be with every child of God, as soon as he becomes such: prayer being truly called, The natural cry of the new-born soul.

For in the heart of every true believer there is a heavenly tendency, a divine attraction, which as sensibly draws him to converse with God, as the lodestone attracts the needle.

A deep sense of their own weakness, and of Christ's fullness; a strong conviction of their natural corruption, and of the necessity of renewing grace; will not let them rest from crying day and night to their Almighty Redeemer, that the divine image, which they lost in Adam, may through his all-powerful mediation, and the sanctifying operation of his blessed spirit, be begun, carried on, and fully perfected both in their souls and bodies.

Thus earnest, thus importunate, are all sincere Christians in praying for themselves: but then, not having so lively, lasting, and deep a sense of the wants of their Christian brethren, they are for the most part too remiss and defective in their prayers for them. Whereas, was the love of God shed abroad in our hearts, and did we love our neighbor in that manner, in which the Son of God our savior loved us, and according to his command and example, we could not but be as importunate for their spiritual and temporal welfare, as for our own; and as earnestly desire and endeavor that others should share in the benefits of the death and passion of Jesus Christ, as we ourselves.

Let not any one think, that this is an uncommon degree of charity; an high pitch of perfection, to which not every one can attain: for, if we are all commanded to "love our neighbor (that is every man) even as ourselves," nay to "lay down our lives for the brethren"; then, it is the duty of all to pray for their neighbors as much as for themselves, and by all possible acts and expressions of love and affection towards them, at all times, to show their readiness even to lay down their lives for them, if ever it should please God to call them to it.

Our blessed Savior, as "he hath set us an example, that we should follow his steps" in every thing else, so hath he more especially in this: for in that divine, that perfect and inimitable prayer (recorded in the 17th of St. John) which he put up just before his passion, we find but few petitions for his own, though many for his disciples welfare: and in that perfect form which he has been pleased to prescribe us, we are taught to say, not MY, but "OUR Father," thereby to put us in mind, that, whenever we approach the throne of grace, we ought to pray not for ourselves alone, but for all our brethren in Christ.

Intercession then is certainly a duty incumbent upon all Christians.

II. WHOM WE ARE TO INTERCEDE FOR, AND HOW THIS DUTY IS TO BE PERFORMED, COMES NEXT TO BE CONSIDERED

1. And first, our intercession must be UNIVERSAL. "I will, (says the apostle) that prayers, supplications and intercessions be made for all men." For as God's mercy is over all his works, as Jesus Christ died to redeem a people out of all nations and languages; so we should pray, that "all men may come to the knowledge of the truth, and be saved." Many precious promises are made in holy writ, that the gospel shall be published through the whole world, that "the earth shall be covered with the knowledge of the Lord, as the waters cover the sea": and therefore it is our duty not to confine our petitions to our own nation, but to pray that all those nations, who now sit in darkness and in the shadow of death, may have the glorious gospel shine out upon them, as well as upon us. But you need not that any man should teach you this, since ye yourselves

are taught of God, and of Jesus Christ himself, to pray, that his kingdom may come; part of the meaning of which petition is, that "God's ways may be known upon earth, and his saving health among all nations."

2. Next to the praying for all men, we should, according to St. Paul's rule, pray for KINGS; particularly for our present sovereign King George, and all that are put in authority under him: that we may lead quiet lives, in all godliness and honesty. For, if we consider how heavy the burden of government is, and how much the welfare of any people depends on the zeal and godly conversation of those that have the rule over them: if we set before us the many dangers and difficulties, to which governors by their station are exposed, and the continual temptations they be under to luxury and self-indulgence; we shall not only pity, but pray for them: that he who preserved Esther, David, and Josiah, "unspotted from the world," amidst the grandeur of a court, and gave success to their designs, would also preserve them holy and unblameable, and prosper all the works of their hands upon them. But

3. THIRDLY, you ought, in a more especial manner, to pray for those, whom "the Holy Ghost hath made OVERSEERS over you." This is what St. Paul begs, again and again, of the churches to whom he writes: Says he in the text, "Brethren, pray for us"; and again, in his epistle to the Ephesians, "praying always, with all manner of supplication; and for me also, that I may open my mouth boldly, to declare the mystery of the gospel." And in another place, to express his earnestness in this request, and the great importance of their prayers for him, he bids the church "strive, (or, as the original word signifies, be in a agony) together with him in their prayers." And surely, if the great St. Paul, that chosen vessel, that favorite of heaven, needed the most importunate prayers of his Christian converts; much more do the ordinary ministers of the gospel stand in need of the intercession of their respective flocks.

And I cannot but in a more especial manner insist upon this branch of your duty, because it is a matter of such importance: for, no doubt, much good is frequently withheld from many, by reason of their neglecting to pray for their ministers, and which they would

have received, had they prayed for them as they ought. Not to mention, that people often complain of the want of diligent and faithful pastors. But how do they deserve good pastors, who will not earnestly pray to God for such? If we will not pray to the Lord of the harvest, can it be expected he will send forth laborers into his harvest?

Besides, what ingratitude is it, not to pray for your ministers! For shall they watch and labor in the word and doctrine for you, and your salvation, and shall not you pray for them in return? If any bestow favors on your bodies, you think it right, meet, and your bounden duty, to pray for them; and shall not they be remembered in your prayers, who daily feed and nourish your souls? Add to all this, that praying for your ministers, will be a manifest proof of your believing, that though Paul plant, and Apollos water, yet it is God alone who giveth the increase. And you will also find it the best means you can use, to promote your own welfare; because God, in answer to your prayers, may impart a double portion of his Holy Spirit to them, whereby they will be qualified to deal out to you larger measures of knowledge in spiritual things, and be enabled more skillfully to divide the word of truth.

Would men but constantly observe this direction, and when their ministers are praying in their name to God, humbly beseech him to perform all their petitions: or, when they are speaking in God's name to them, pray that the Holy Ghost may fall on all them that hear the word; we should find a more visible good effect of their doctrine, and a greater mutual love between ministers and their people. For ministers hands would then be hold up by the people's intercessions, and the people will never dare to vilify or traduce those who are the constant subjects of their prayers.

4. Next to our ministers, OUR FRIENDS claim a place in our intercessions; but then we should not content ourselves with praying in general terms for them, but suit our prayers to their particular circumstances. When Miriam was afflicted with a leprosy from God, Moses cried and said, "Lord, heal her." And when the nobleman came to apply to Jesus Christ, in behalf of his child, he said, "Lord, my little daughter lieth at the point of death, I pray thee

to come and heal her." In like manner, when our friends are under any afflicting circumstances, we should endeavor to pray for them, with a particular regard to those circumstances. For instance, is a friend sick? We should pray, that if it be God's good pleasure, it may not be unto death; but is otherwise, that he would give him grace so to take his visitation, that, after this painful life ended, he may dwell with him in life everlasting. Is a friend in doubt in an important matter? We should lay his case before God, as Moses did that of the daughters of Zelophehad, and pray, that God's Holy Spirit may lead him into all truth, and give all seasonable direction. Is he in want? We should pray, that his faith may never fail, and that in God's due time he may be relieved. And in all other cases, we should not pray for our friends only in generals, but suit our petitions to their particular sufferings and afflictions; for otherwise, we may never ask perhaps for the things our friends most want.

It must be confessed, that such a procedure will oblige some often to break from the forms they use; but if we accustom ourselves to it, and have a deep sense of what we ask for, the most illiterate will want proper words to express themselves.

We have many noble instances in holy scripture of the success of this kind of particular intercession; but none more remarkable than that of Abraham's servant, in the book of Genesis, who being sent to seek a wife for his son Isaac, prayed in a most particular manner in his behalf. And the sequel of the story informs us, how remarkably his prayer as answered. And did Christians now pray for their friends in the same particular manner, and with the same faith as Abraham's servant did for his master; they would, no doubt, in many instances, receive as visible answers, and have as much reason to bless God for them, as he had. But

5. As we ought thus to intercede for our friends, so in like manner must we also pray for OUR ENEMIES. "Bless them that curse you, (says Jesus Christ) and pray for them that despitefully use you, and persecute you." Which commands he enforced in the strongest manner by his own example: in the very agonies and pangs of death, he prayed even for his murderers, "Father, forgive them, for they know not what they do!" This, it must needs be confessed, is a difficult duty, yet not impracticable, to those who have renounced the things of this present life, (from an inordinate love of which all enmities arise) and who knowing the terrible woes denounced against those who offend Christ's little ones, can, out of real pity, and a sense of their danger, pray for those by whom such offenses come.

6. Lastly, and to conclude this head, we should intercede for all that are any ways AFFLICTED in mind, body, or estate; for all who desire, and stand in need of our prayers, and for all who do not pray for themselves.

And Oh! That all who hear me, would set apart some time every day for the due performance of this most necessary duty! In order to which, I shall now proceed,

III. To show the advantages, and offer some considerations to excite you to the practice of daily intercession

1. FIRST, It will fill your hearts with love one to another. He that every day heartily intercedes at the throne of grace for all mankind, cannot but in a short time be filled with love and charity to all: and the frequent exercise of his love in this manner, will insensibly enlarge his heart, and make him partaker of that exceeding abundance of it which is in Christ Jesus our Lord! Envy, malice, revenge, and such like hellish tempers, can never long harbor in a gracious intercessor's breast; but he will be filled with joy, peace, meekness, long-suffering, and all other graces of the Holy Spirit. By frequently laying his neighbor's wants before God, he will be touched with a fellow-feeling of them; he will rejoice with those that do rejoice, and weep with those that weep. Every blessing bestowed on others, instead of exciting envy in him, will be looked on as an answer to his particular intercession, and fill his soul with joy unspeakable and full of glory.

Abound therefore in acts of general and particular intercessions; and when you hear of your neighbor's faults, instead of relating them to, and exposing them before others, lay them in secret before God, and beg of him to correct and amend them. When you hear of a notorious sinner, instead of thinking you do well to be angry, beg of Jesus Christ to convert, and make him a monument of his free grace; you cannot imagine what a blessed alteration this practice will make in your heart, and how much you will increase day by day in the spirit of love and meekness towards all mankind!

But farther, to excite you to the constant practice of this duty of intercession, consider the many instances in holy scripture, of the power and efficacy of it. Great and excellent things are there recorded as the effects of this divine employ. It has stopped plagues, it has opened and shut heaven; and has frequently turned away God's fury from his people. How was Abimelech's house freed from the disease God sent amongst them, at the intercession of Abraham! When "Phineas stood up and prayed," how soon did the plague cease! When Daniel humbled and afflicted his soul, and interceded for the Lord's inheritance, how quickly was an angel dispatched to tell him, "his prayer was heard!" And, to mention but one instance more, how does God own himself as it were overcome with the importunity of Moses, when he was interceding for his idolatrous people, "Let me alone," says God!

This sufficiently shows, I could almost say, the omnipotency of intercession, and how we may, like Jacob, wrestle with God, and by an holy violence prevail both for ourselves and others. And no doubt it is owing to the secret and prevailing intercessions of the few righteous souls who still remain among us, that God has yet spared this miserably sinful nation: for were there not some such faithful ones, like Moses, left to stand in the gap, we should soon be destroyed, even as was Sodom, and reduced to ashes like unto Gomorrah.

But, to stir you up yet farther to this exercise of intercession, consider, that in all probability, it is the frequent employment even of the glorified saints: for though they are delivered from the burden of the flesh, and restored to the glorious liberty of the sons of God, yet as their happiness cannot be perfectly consummated till the resurrection of the last day, when all their brethren will be glorified with them, we cannot but think they are often importunate in beseeching our heavenly Father, shortly to accomplish the number of his elect, and to hasten his kingdom. And shall now we, who are on earth, be often exercised in this divine employ with the glorious company of the spirits of just men made perfect? Since our happiness is so much to consist in the communion of saints in the church triumphant above, shall we not frequently intercede for the church militant here below; and earnestly beg, that we may all be one, even as the Holy Jesus and his Father are one, that we may also be made perfect in one?

To provoke you to this great work and labor of love, remember, that it is the never ceasing employment of the holy and highly exalted Jesus himself, who sits at the right hand of God, to hear all our prayers, and to make continual intercession for us! So that he who is constantly employed in interceding for others, is doing that on earth, which the eternal Son of God is always doing in heaven.

Imagine therefore, when you are lifting up holy hands in prayer for one another, that you see the heavens opened, and the Son of God in all his glory, as the great high-priest of your salvation, pleading for you the all-sufficient merit of his sacrifice before the throne of his heavenly Father! Join then your intercessions with his, and beseech him, that they may, through him, come up as incense, and be received as a sweet-smelling favor, acceptable in the sight of God! This imagination will strengthen your faith, excite a holy earnestness in your prayers, and make you wrestle with God, as Jacob did, when he saw him face to face, and his life was preserved; as Abraham, when he pleaded for Sodom; and as Jesus Christ himself, when he prayed, being in an agony, so much the more earnestly the night before his bitter passion.

And now, brethren, what shall I say more, since you are taught of Jesus Christ himself, to abound in love, and in this good work of praying one for another. Though ever so mean, though as poor as Lazarus, you will then become benefactors to all mankind; thousands, and twenty times ten thousands, will then be blessed for your sakes! And after you have employed a few years in this divine exercise here, you will be translated to that happy place, where you have so often wished others might be advanced; and be exalted to sit at the right hand of our All-powerful, All-prevailing Intercessor, in the kingdom of his heavenly Father hereafter.

However, I cannot but in an especial manner press this upon you now, because all ye, amongst whom I have now been preaching, in all probability will see me no more: for I am now going (I trust under the conduct of God's most Holy Spirit) from you, knowing not what shall befall me: I need therefore your most importunate intercessions, that nothing may move me from my duty, and that I may not "count even my life dear unto myself, so that I may finish my course with joy, and the ministry I have received of the Lord Jesus, to testify the gospel of the grace of God!"

Whilst I have been here, to the best of my knowledge, I have not failed to declare unto you the whole will of God: and though my preaching may have been a savor of death unto death to some; yet I trust it has been also a savor of life unto life to others; and therefore I earnestly hope that those will not fail to remember me in their prayers. As for my own part, the many unmerited kindnesses I have received from you, will not suffer me to forget you: out of the deep, therefore, I trust shall my cry come unto God; and whilst the winds and storms are blowing over me, unto the Lord will I make my supplication for you. For it is but a little while, and "we must all appear before the judgment seat of Christ"; where I must give a strict account of the doctrine I have preached, and you of your improvement under it. And O that I may never be called out as a swift witness, against any of those, for whose salvation I have sincerely, though too faintly, longed and labored!

It is true, I have been censured by some as acting out of sinister and selfish views; "but it is a small matter with me to be judged by man's judgment"; I hope my eye is single; but I beseech you, brethren, by the mercies of God in Christ Jesus, pray that it may be more so! And that I may increase with the increase of grace in the knowledge and love of God through Jesus Christ our Lord.

And now, brethren, what shall I say more? I could wish to continue my discourse much longer; for I can never fully express the desire of my soul towards you! Finally, therefore, brethren, "whatsoever things are holy, whatsoever things are pure, whatsoever things are honest, what soever things are of good report: if there be any consolation in Christ, if any fellowship of the spirit," if any hopes of our appearing to the comfort of each other at the awful tribunal of Jesus Christ, "think of the things that you have heard," and of those which your pastors have declared, and will yet declare unto you; and continue under their ministry to "work out your own salvation with fear and trembling": so that whether I should never see you any more, or whether it shall please God to bring me back again at any time, I may always have the satisfaction of knowing that your conversation is such "as becometh the gospel of Christ."

I almost persuade myself, that I could willingly suffer all things, so that it might any ways promote the salvation of your precious and immortal souls; and I beseech you, as my last request, "obey them that have the rule over you in the Lord"; and be always ready to attend on their ministry, as it is your bounden duty. Think not that I desire to have myself exalted at the expense of another's character; but rather think this, not to have any man's person too much in admiration; but esteem all your ministers highly in love, as they justly deserve for their work's sake.

And now, "brethren, I commend you to god, and to the word of his grace, which is able to build you up, and give you an inheritance amongst all them that are sanctified." May God reward you for all your works of faith, and labors of love, and make you to abound more and more in every good word and work towards all men. May he truly convert all that have been convinced, and awaken all that are dead in trespasses and sins! May he confirm all that are wavering! And may you all go on from one degree of grace unto another, till you arrive unto the measure of the stature of the fullness of Christ; and thereby be made meet to stand before that God, "in whose presence is the fullness of joy, and at whose right-hand there are pleasures for evermore!" Amen! Amen!

George Whitefield, 1714–70

The Pharisee and the Publican

George Whitefield

Luke 18:14 – "I tell you, this man went down to his house justified rather than the other: For every one that exalteth himself, shall be abased; and he that humbleth himself, shall be exalted."

Though there be some who dare to deny the Lord Jesus, and disbelieve the revelation he has been pleased to give us, and thereby bring upon themselves swift destruction; yet I would charitably hope there are but few if any such among you, to whom I am now to preach the kingdom of God. Was I to ask you, how you expect to be justified in the sight of an offended God? I suppose you would answer, only for the sake of our Lord Jesus Christ. But, was I to come more home to your consciences, I fear that most would make the Lord Jesus but in part their Savior, and go about, as it were, to establish a righteousness of their own. And this is not thinking contrary to the rules of Christian charity: for we are all self-righteous by nature; it is as natural for us to turn to a covenant of works, as for the sparks to fly upwards. We have had so many legal and so few free-grace preachers, for these many years, that most professors now seem to be settled upon their lees [residue, remains, grounds, settlings], and rather deserve the title of Pharisees than Christians.

Thus it was with the generality of the people during the time of our Lord's public ministration: and therefore, in almost all his discourses, he preached the gospel to poor sinners, and denounced terrible woes against proud self-justiciaries. The parable, to which the words of the text belong, looks both these ways: For the evangelist informs us (ver. 9) that our Lord "spake it unto certain who trusted in themselves that they were righteous, and despised others." And a notable parable it is; a parable worthy of your most serious attention. "He that hath ears to hear, let him hear," what Jesus Christ speaks to all visible professors in it.

Ver. 10. "Two men went up to the temple to pray (and never two men of more opposite characters) the one a Pharisee and the other a Publican." The Pharisees were the strictest sect among the Jews. "I was of the strictest sect, of the Pharisees," says Paul. They prayed often; not only so, but they made long prayers; and, that they might appear extraordinary devout, they would pray at the corners of the street, where two ways met, that people going or coming, both ways, might see them. "They made broad (as our Lord informs us) the borders of their phylacteries," they had pieces of parchment sown to their long robes, on which some parts of the Scripture were written, that people might from thence infer, that they were lovers of the law of God. They were so very punctual and exact in outward purifications, that they washed at their going out and coming in. They held the washing of pots, brazen vessels and tables, and many other such-like things they did. They were very zealous for the traditions of the fathers, and for the observation of the rites and ceremonies of the church, notwithstanding they frequently made void the law of God by their traditions. And they were so exceedingly exact in the outward observation of the Sabbath, that they condemned our Lord for making a little clay with his spittle; and called him a sinner, and said, he was not of God, because he had given sight to a man born blind, on the Sabbath-day. For these reasons they were had in high veneration among the people, who were sadly misled by these blind guides: they had the uppermost places in the synagogues, and greetings in the market-places (which they loved dearly) and were called of men, Rabbi; in short, they had such a reputation for piety, that it became a proverb among the Jews, that, if there were but two men saved, the one of them must be a Pharisee.

As for the Publicans, it was not so with them. It seems they were sometimes Jews, or at least proselytes of the gate; for we find one here coming up to the temple; but for the generality, I am apt to think they were Gentiles; for they were gatherers of the Roman taxes, and used to amass much wealth (as appears by the confession of Zaccheus, one of the chief of them) by wronging men with false accusations. They were so universally infamous, that our Lord himself tells his disciples, "the excommunicated man should be to them as a heathen man, or a Publican." And the

Pharisees thought it a sufficient impeachment of our Lord's character, that he was a friend to Publicans and sinners, and went to sit down with them at meat.

But, however they disagreed in other things, they agreed in this, that public worship is a duty incumbent upon all: for they both came up to the temple. The very heathens were observers of temple-worship. We have very early notice of men's sacrificing to, and calling upon the name of the Lord, in the Old Testament; and I find it no where contradicted in the New. Our Lord, and his apostles, went up to the temple; and we are commanded by the apostle, "not to forsake the assembling ourselves together," as the manner of too many is in our days; and such too, as would have us think well of them, though they seldom or never tread the courts of the Lord's house. But, though our devotions begin in our closets, they must not end there. And, if people never show their devotions abroad, I must suspect they have little or none at home. "Two men went up to the temple." And what went they thither for? Not (as multitudes amongst us do) to make the house of God a house of merchandise, or turn it into a den of thieves; much less to ridicule the preacher, or disturb the congregation; no, they came to the temple, says our Lord, "to pray." Thither should the tribes of God's spiritual Israel go up, to talk with, and pour out their hearts before the mighty God of Jacob.

"Two men went up to the temple to pray." I fear one of them forgot his errand. I have often been at a loss what to call the Pharisee's address; it certainly does not deserve the name of a prayer: he may rather be said to come to the temple to boast, than to pray; for I do not find one word of confession of his original guilt; not one single petition for pardon of his past actual sins, or for grace to help and assist him for the time to come: he only brings to God, as it were, a reckoning of his performances; and does that, which no flesh can justly do, I mean, glory in his presence.

Ver. 11. "The Pharisee stood, and prayed thus with himself; God, I thank thee that I am not as other men are, extortioners, unjust, adulterers, or even as this Publican."

Our Lord first takes notice of his posture; "the Pharisee stood," he is not to be condemned for that; for standing, as well as kneeling, is a proper posture for prayer. "When you stand praying," says our Lord; though sometimes our Lord kneeled, nay, lay flat on his face upon the ground; his apostles also kneeled, as we read in the Acts, which has made me wonder at some, who are so bigoted to standing in family, as well as public prayer, that they will not kneel, notwithstanding all kneel that are around them. I fear there is something of the Pharisee in this conduct. Kneeling and standing are indifferent, if the knee of the soul be bent, and the heart upright towards God. We should study not to be particular in indifferent things, lest we offend weak minds. What the Pharisee is remarked for, is his "standing by himself": for the words may be rendered, he stood by himself, upon some eminent place, at the upper part of the temple, near the Holy of holies, that the congregation might see what a devout man he was: or it may be understood as we read it, he prayed by himself, or of himself, out of his own heart; he did not pray by form; it was an extempore prayer: for there are many Pharisees that pray and preach too, extempore. I do not see why these may not be acquired, as well as other arts and sciences. A man, with a good elocution [articulation, oratory, speech], ready turn of thought, and good memory, may repeat his own or other men's sermons, and, by the help of Wilkins or Henry, may pray seemingly excellently well, and yet not have the least grain of true grace in his heart; I speak this, not to cry down extempore prayer, or to discourage those dear souls who really pray by the spirit; I only would hereby give a word of reproof to those who are so bigoted to extempore prayer, that they condemn, as least judge, all that use forms, as though not so holy and heavenly, as others who pray without them. Alas! this is wrong. Not every one that prays extempore is a spiritual, nor every one that prays with a form, a formal man. Let us not judge one another; let not him that uses a form, judge him that prays extempore, on that account; and let not him that prays extempore, despise him who uses a form.

"The Pharisee stood, and prayed thus by himself." Which may signify also praying inwardly in his heart; for there is a way (and that an excellent one too) of praying when we cannot speak; thus Anna prayed, when she spoke not aloud, only her lips moved. Thus God says to Moses, "Why criest thou?" when, it is plain, he did not speak a word. This is what the apostle means by the "spirit making intercession (for believers) with groanings which cannot be uttered." For there are times when the soul is too big to speak; when God fills it as it were, and overshadows it with his presence, so that it can only fall down, worship, adore, and lie in the dust before the Lord. Again, there is a time when the soul is benumbed, barren and dry, and the believer has not a word to say to his heavenly Father; and then the heart only can speak. And I mention this for the encouragement of weak Christians, who think they never are accepted but when they have a flow of words, and fancy they do not please God at the bottom, for no other reason but because they do not please themselves. Such would do well to consider, that God knows the language of the heart, and the mind of the spirit; and that we make use of words, not to inform God, but to affect ourselves. Whenever therefore any of you find yourselves in such a frame, be not discouraged: offer yourselves up in silence before God, as clay in the hands of the potter, for him to write and stamp his own divine image upon your souls. But I believe the Pharisee knew nothing of this way of prayer: he was self-righteous, a stranger to the divine life; and therefore either of the former explanations may be best put upon these words.

"He stood, and prayed thus with himself; God, I thank thee that I am not as other men are, extortioners, unjust, adulterer, or even as this Publican." Here is some appearance of devotion, but it is only in appearance. To thank God that we are not extortioners, unjust, adulterers, and as wicked in our practices as other men are, is certainly meet, right, and our bounden duty: for whatever degrees of goodness there may be in us, more than in others, it is owing to God's restraining, preventing, and assisting grace. We are all equally conceived and born in sin; all are fallen short of the glory of God, and liable to all the curses and maledictions of the law; so that "he who glorieth, must glory only in the Lord." For none of us have any thing which we did not receive; and whatever we have received, we did not in the least merit it, nor could we lay the least claim to it on any account whatever: we are wholly indebted to free grace for all. Had the Pharisee thought thus, when he said, "God, I thank thee that I am not as other men are," it would have been an excellent introduction to his prayer: but he was a free-willer, as well as self-righteous (for he that is one must be the other) and thought by his own power and strength, he had kept himself from these vices. And yet I do not see what reason he had to trust in himself that he was righteous, merely because he had to trust in himself that he was righteous, merely because he was not an extortioner, unjust, adulterer; for all this while he might be, as he certainly was (as is also every self-righteous person) as proud as the devil. But he not only boasts, but lies before God (as all self-justiciaries will be found liars here or hereafter). He thanks God that he was not unjust: but is it not an act of the highest injustice to rob God of his prerogative? is it not an act of injustice to judge our neighbor? and yet of both these crimes this self-righteous vaunter is guilty. "Even as this Publican!" He seems to speak with the untmost disdain; this Publican! Perhaps he pointed at the poor man, that others might treat him with the like contempt. Thou proud, confident boaster, what hadst thou to do with that poor Publican? supposing other Publicans were unjust, and extortioners, did it therefore follow that he must be so? or, if he had been such a sinner, how knowest thou but he has repented of those sins? His coming up to the temple to pray, is one good sign of a reformation at least. Thou art therefore inexcusable, O Pharisee, who thus judgest the Publican: for thou that judgest him to be unjust, art, in the very act of judging, unjust thyself: thy sacrifice is only the sacrifice of a fool.

We have seen what the Pharisee's negative goodness comes to; I think, nothing at all. Let us see how far his positive goodness extends; for, if we are truly religious, we shall not only eschew evil, but also do good: "I fast twice in the week, I give tithes of all that I possess."

The Pharisee is not here condemned for his fasting, for fasting is a Christian duty; "when you fast," says our Lord, thereby taking it for granted that his disciples would fast. And "when the bridegroom shall be taken away, then shall they fast in those days." "In fasting often," says the apostle. And all that would not be cast-aways, will take care, as their privilege, without legal constraint, to "keep their bodies under, and bring them into subjection." The Pharisee is only condemned for making a righteousness of his fasting, and thinking that God would accept him, or that he was any better than his neighbors, merely on account of his fasting, and thinking that God would accept him, or that he was any better than his neighbors, merely on account of his fasting: this is what he was blamed for. The Pharisee was not to be discommended for fasting twice in a week; I wish some Christians would imitate him more in this: but to depend on fasting in the least, for his justification in the sight of God, was really abominable. "I give tithes of all that I possess." He might as well have said, I pay tithes. But self-righteous people (whatever they may say to the contrary) think they give something to God. "I give tithes of all that I possess": I make conscience of giving tithes, not only of all that the law requires, but of my mint, annise, and cumin, of all things whatsoever I possess; this was well; but to boast of such things, or of fasting, is pharisaical and devilish. Now then let us sum up all the righteousness of this boasting Pharisee, and see what little reason he had to trust in himself, that he was righteous, or to despise others. He is not unjust (but we have only his bare word for that, I think I have proved the contrary); he is no adulterer, no extortioner; he fasts twice in the week, and gives tithes of all that he possesses; and all this he might do, and a great deal more, and yet be a child of the devil: for here is no mention made of his loving the Lord his God with all his heart, which was the "first and great commandment of the law"; here is not a single syllable of inward religion; and he was not a true Jew, who was only one outwardly. It is only an outside piety at the best; inwardly he is full of pride, self-justification, free-will and great uncharitableness.

Were not the Pharisees, do you think, highly offended at this character? for they might easily know it was spoken against them. And though, perhaps, some of you may be offended at me, yet, out of love, I must tell you, I fear this parable is spoken against many of you: for

are there not many of you, who go up to the temple to pray, with no better spirit than this Pharisee did? And because you fast, it may be in the Lent, or every Friday, and because you do no body any harm, receive the sacrament, pay tithes, and give an alms now and then; you think that you are safe, and trust in yourselves that you are righteous, and inwardly despise those, who do not come up to you in these outward duties? this, I am persuaded, is the case of many of you, though, alas! it is a desperate one, as I shall endeavor to show at the close of this discourse.

Let us now take a view of the Publican, ver. 13. "And the Publican standing afar off, would not lift up so much as his eyes unto heaven, but smote upon his breast, saying, God be merciful to me a sinner."

"The Publican standing afar off." Perhaps in the outward court of the temple, conscious to himself that he was not worthy to approach the Holy of holies; so conscious and so weighed down with a sense of his own unworthiness, that he would not so much as lift up his eyes unto heaven, which he knew was God's throne. Poor heart! what did he feel at this time! none but returning publicans, like himself, can tell. Methinks I see him standing afar off, pensive, oppressed, and even overwhelmed with sorrow; sometimes he attempts to look up; but then, thinks he, the heavens are unclean in God's sight, and the very angels are charged with folly; how then shall such a wretch as I dare to lift up my guilty head! And to show that his heart was full of holy self-resentment, and that he sorrowed after a godly sort, he smote upon his breast; the word in the original implies, that he struck hard upon his breast: he will lay the blame upon none but his own wicked heart. He will not, like unhumbled Adam, tacitly lay the fault of his vileness upon God, and say, The passions which thou gavest me, they deceived me, and I sinned: he is too penitent thus to reproach his Maker; he smites upon his breast, his treacherous, ungrateful, desperately wicked breast; a breast now ready to burst: and at length, out of the abundance of his heart, I doubt not, with many tears, he as last cries out, "God be merciful to me a sinner." Not, God be merciful to yonder proud Pharisee: he found enough in himself to vent his resentment against, without looking abroad upon others. Not, God be merciful to me a saint; for he knew "all his righteousnesses were but filthy rags." Not, God be merciful to such or such a one; but, God be merciful to me, even to me a sinner, a sinner by birth, a sinner in thought, word, and deed; a sinner as to my person, a sinner as to all my performances; a sinner in whom is no health, in whom dwelleth no good thing, a sinner, poor, miserable, blind and naked, from the crown of the head to the sole of the feet, full of wounds, and bruises, and putrefying sores; a self-accused, self-condemned sinner. What think you? would this Publican have been offended if any minister had told him that he deserved to be damned? would he have been angry, if any one had told him, that by nature he was half a devil and half a beast? No: he would have confessed a thousand hells to have been his due, and that he was an earthly, devil-ish sinner. He felt now what a dreadful thing it was to depart from the living God: he felt that he was inexcusable every way; that he could in nowise, upon account of any thing in himself, be justified in the sight of God; and therefore lays himself at the feet of sovereign mercy. "God be merciful to me a sinner." Here is no confidence in the flesh, no plea fetched from fasting, paying tithes, or the performance of any other duty; here is no boasting that he was not an extortioner, unjust, or an adulterer. Perhaps he had been guilty of all these crimes, at least he knew he would have been guilty of all these, had he been left to follow the devices and desires of his own heart; and therefore, with a broken and contrite spirit, he cries out, "God be merciful to me a sinner."

This man came up to the temple to pray, and he prayed indeed. And a broken and contrite heart God will not despise. "I tell you," says our Lord, I who lay in the bosom of the Father from all eternity; I who am God, and therefore know all things; I who can neither deceive, nor be deceived, whose judgment is according to right; I tell you, whatever you may think of it, or think of me for telling you so, "this man," this Publican, this despised, sinful, but broken-hearted man, "went down to his house justified (acquitted, and looked upon as righteous in the sight of God) rather than the other."

Let Pharisees take heed that they do not pervert this text: for when it is said, "This man went down to his house justified rather than the other," our Lord does not mean that both were justified, and that the Publican had rather more justification than the Pharisee: but it implies, either that the Publican was actually justified, but the Pharisee was not; or, that the Publican was in a better way to receive justi-fication, than the Pharisee; according to our Lord's saying, "The Publicans and Harlots enter the kingdom of heaven before you." That the Pharisee was not justified is certain, for "God resisteth the proud"; and that the Publican was at this time actually justified (and perhaps went home with a sense of it in his heart) we have great reason to infer from the latter part of the text, "For every one that exalteth himself shall be abased, and he that humbleth himself shall be exalted."

The parable therefore now speaks to all who hear me this day: for that our Lord intended it for our learning, is evident, from his making such a general application: "For every one that exalteth himself shall be abased, and he that humbleth himself shall be exalted."

The parable of the Publican and Pharisee, is but as it were a glass, wherein we may see the different disposition of all mankind; for all mankind may be divided into two general classes. Either they trust wholly in themselves, or in part, that they are righteous, and then they are Pharisees; or they have no confidence in the flesh, are self-condemned sinners, and then they come under the character of the Publican just now described. And we may add also, that the different reception these men meet with, points out to us in lively colors, the different treatment the self-justiciary and self-condemned criminal will meet with at the terrible day of judgment: "Every one that exalts himself shall be abased, but he that humbleth himself shall be exalted."

"Every one," without exception, young or old, high or low, rich or poor (for God is no respecter of persons) "every one," whosoever he be, that exalteth himself, and not free-grace; every one that trusteth in himself that he is righteous, that rests in his duties, or thinks to join them with the righteousness of Jesus Christ, for justification in the sight of God, though he be no adulterer, not extortioner, though he be not outwardly unjust, nay, though he fast twice in the week, and gives tithes of all that he possess; yet shall he be abased in the sight of all good men who know him here, and before men and angels, and God himself, when Jesus Christ comes to appear in judgment hereafter. How low, none but the almighty God can tell. He shall be abased to live with devils, and make his abode in the lowest hell for evermore.

Hear this, all ye self-justiciaries, tremble, and behold your doom! a dreadful doom, more dreadful than words can express, or thought conceive! If you refuse to humble yourselves, after hearing this parable, I call heaven and earth to witness against you this day, that God shall visit you with all his storms, and pour all the vials of his wrath upon your rebellious heads; you exalted yourselves here, and God shall abase you hereafter; you are as proud as the devil, and with devils shall you dwell to all eternity. "Be not deceived, God is not mocked"; he sees your hearts, he knows all things. And, notwithstanding you may come up to the temple to pray, your prayers are turned into sin, and you go down to your houses unjustified, if you are self-justiciaries; and do you know what it is to be unjustified? why, if you are unjustified, the wrath of God abideth upon you; you are in your blood; all the curses of the law belong to you: cursed are you when you go out, cursed are you when you come in; cursed are your thoughts, cursed are your words, cursed are your deeds; every thing you do, say, or think, from morning to night is only one continued series of sin. However highly you may be esteemed in the sight of men, however you may be honored with the uppermost seats in the synagogues, in the church militant, you will have no place in the church triumphant. "Humble yourselves therefore under the mighty hand of God": pull down every self-righteous thought, and every proud imagination, that now exalteth itself against the perfect, personal, imputed righteousness of the dear Lord Jesus: "For he (and he alone) that humbleth himself shall be exalted."

He that humbleth himself, whatever be he: if, instead of fasting twice in the week, he has been drunk twice in the week; if, instead of giving tithes of all that he possesses, he has cheated the minister of his tithes, and the king of his taxes; notwithstanding he be unjust, an extortioner, an adulterer, nay, notwithstanding the sins of all mankind center and unite in him; yet, if through grace, like the Publican, he is enabled to humble himself, he shall be exalted; not in a temporal manner; for Christians must rather expect to be abased, and to have their names cast out as evil, and to lay down their lives for Christ Jesus in this world: but he shall be exalted in a spiritual sense; he shall be freely justified from all his sins by the blood of Jesus; he shall have peace with God, a peace which passeth all understanding; not only peace, but joy in believing; he shall be translated from the kingdom of Satan, to the kingdom of God's dear Son: he shall dwell in Christ, and Christ in him: he shall be one with Christ, and Christ one with him: he shall drink of divine pleasures, as out of a river: he shall be sanctified throughout in spirit, soul and body; in one word, he shall be filled with all the fullness of God. Thus shall the man that humbleth himself be exalted here; but O, how high shall he be exalted hereafter! as high as the highest heavens, even to the right-hand of God: there he shall sit, happy both in soul and body, and judge angels; high, out of the reach of all sin and trouble, eternally secure from all danger of falling. O sinners, did you but know how highly God intends to exalt those who humble themselves, and believe in Jesus, surely you would humble yourselves, at least beg of God to humble you; for it is he that must strike the rock of your hearts, and cause floods of contrite tears to flow therefrom. O that God would give this sermon such a commission, as he once gave to the rod of Moses! I would strike you through and through with the rod of his word, until each of you was brought to cry out with the poor Publican, "God be merciful to me a sinner." What pleasant language would this be in the ears of the Lord of Sabbaoth!

Are there no poor sinners among you? what, are you all Pharisees? Surely, you cannot bear the thoughts of returning home unjustified; can you? what if a fit of the apoplexy should seize you, and your souls be hurried away before the awful Judge of quick and dead? what will you do without Christ's righteousness? if you go out of the world unjustified, you must remain so for ever. O that you would humble yourselves! then would the Lord exalt you; it may be, that, whilst I am speaking, the Lord might justify you freely by his grace. I observed, that perhaps the Publican had a sense of his justification before he went from the temple, and knew that his pardon was sealed in heaven: and who knows but you may be thus exalted before you go home, if you humble yourselves? O what peace, love and joy, would you then feel in your hearts! you would have a heaven upon earth. O that I could hear any of you say (as I once heard a poor sinner, under my preaching, cry out) He is come, He is come! How would you then, like him, extol a precious, a free-hearted Christ! how would you magnify him for being such a friend to Publicans and sinners? greater love can no man show, than to lay down his life for a friend; but Christ laid down his life for his enemies, even for you, if you are enabled to humble yourselves, as the Publican did. Sinners, I know not how to leave off talking with you; I would fill my mouth with arguments, I would plead with you. "Come, let us reason together"; though your sins be as scarlet, yet, if you humble yourselves, they shall be as white as snow. One act of true faith in Christ, justifies you for ever and ever; he has not promised you what he cannot perform; he is able to exalt you: for God hath exalted, and given him a name above every name; that at the name of Jesus every knee shall bow; nay, God hath exalted him to be not only a Prince, but a Savior. May he be a Savior to you! and then I shall have reason to rejoice; in the day of judgment, that I have not preached in vain, not labored in vain.

George Whitefield, 1714–70

Imagination in Prayer

Alexander Whyte

"Lord, teach us to pray" Luke 11:1.
"Full of eyes" Revelation 4:8.

I never, or hear, or speak, or write the word "imagination" without being arrested and recalled to what Pascal and Butler and Edwards have all said, with such power and with such passion, on the subject of imagination. Pascal – himself all compact of imagination as he is – Pascal sets forth again and again a tremendous indictment against the "deceits" and "deceptions" of the imagination. Butler also, in few but always weighty words, stigmatizes the imagination as "that forward and delusive faculty." While Jonathan Edwards, in his own masterful way, would almost seem to have given the death-blow to the use of the imagination in all matters of personal and experimental religion. But as to Butler, – that great author's latest and best editor, in two paragraphs of really fine criticism, has clearly brought out that what Butler calls "the errors of the imagination" are not errors of the imagination at all, but are the errors of unbridled fancy and caprice, and of an unbalanced and ill-regulated judgment. "It seems probable," so sums up Butler's venerable editor, "that this is one of the rare instances in which Butler, relaxing the firmness of his hold, forgets himself, and assumes a license in the use of words." And then, the editor turns the tables on his admired author by going on to say that, in felicity of imaginative illustration, Butler is the equal of Macaulay himself; while, in some other of the exercises of the imagination, Butler is even above Burke.

What, then, you will ask, – with all that, – what exactly, and in itself, and at its best, is the imagination? Well, come back for a moment to the very beginning of all things, if you would have the best answer to that question. And, then, I will answer that question by asking and answering another question. "How did God create man?" – "God created man," I am answered, "male and female, after His own image, in knowledge, righteousness, and holiness, with dominion over the creatures." Our understanding, then, our mind and our memory, are both so many images to us of the Divine Mind. Our conscience, again, is an inward voice to us, impressing upon us an imprint of the Divine Righteousness, and the Divine Law. Our will, also, and the Divine Will, are of the same Divine Substance. And as for our heart – it is "a copy, Lord, of Thine." And then, in his imagination, man possesses, and exercises in himself, a certain, and hat a not very far-off likeness of the Divine Omnipresence, and the Divine Omniscience. For, by his imagination, a man can look behind, and before, and around, and within, and above. By his imagination a man can go back to the beginning ere ever the earth was. One man has done it. Moses has done it. And what Moses has done to this earth, that one day will not be remembered nor come into mind, – all that John, Moses' fellow in imagination, has done to the new heaven and the new earth. The imagination, then, whatever else it is, is not that "forward, ever-intruding and delusive faculty": it is not that "author of all error," as Butler, so unlike himself, so confuses and miscalls it. Nor is it what Pascal so lashes to death with his splendid invective. Nor is it imagination at all, as we have to do with it to-day, that Edwards so denounces in his Religious Affections.

Imagination, as God in His goodness gave it at first to man, – imagination is nothing less than the noblest intellectual attribute of the human mind. And his imagination is far more to every spiritually-minded man than a merely intellectual attribute of his mind. I shall not need to go beyond Pascal himself, – so splendidly endowed with this splendid gift. "Imagination," says Pascal, "creates all the beauty, and all the justice, and all the happiness that is in the heart of man." The imagination, then, must not be made to bear the blame that really belongs to those men who have prostituted it, and have filled its great inward eyes full of visions of folly and sin: when they should have set the Lord always before their inward eyes, with all His works in nature, and in grace, and in glory. Because there is only one of a city, and two of a family, who ever employ their inward eyes aright, – are the inward eyes of those men to be plucked out who have on their inward eyes an unction from the Holy One? No. A thousand times, No! "Open Thou mine eyes, that I may behold wondrous things out of Thy law. I am a stranger in the earth: hide not Thy commandments from me."

If, then, you would learn to pray to perfection, – that is to say, to pray with all that is within you, – never fail, never neglect, to do this. Never once shut your bodily eyes and bow your knees to begin to pray, without, at the same moment, opening the eyes of your imagination. It is but a bodily service to shut our outward eyes, and not at the same moment open the eyes of our inner man. Do things like this, then, when you would be in the full spirit of prayer. Things, more or less, like this. "I speak as a child." Let your imagination sweep up through the whole visible heavens, up to the heaven of heavens. Let her sweep and soar on her shining wing, up past sun, moon, and stars. Let her leave Orion and the Pleiades far behind her. And let her heart swell and beat as she says such things as these to herself: "He made all these things. He, Whom I now seek. That is His Sun. My Father made them all. My Mediator made them all to the glory of His Father. And He is the heir of all things. Oh, to be at peace with the Almighty! Oh, never again for one moment to forget or disobey, or displease Him! Oh, to be an heir of God, and a joint heir with Jesus Christ! Oh, to be found among the sons and the daughters of God Almighty!"

At another time, as you kneel down, flash, in a moment, – I still speak as a child, – the eyes of your heart back to Adam in his garden, and with the image of God still in all its glory upon him: and to Abraham over Sodom; and to Moses in the cleft of the rock; and to David in the night-watches; and to Jesus Christ all night on the mountain top – and your time will not be lost. For, by such a flash of your imagination, at such a moment, the spirit of grace and supplications will be put in complete possession of your whole soul. Never open your eyes any morning without, that moment, seeing God and saying, "I laid me down and slept; I awaked; for the Lord sustained me." And never lie down without saying, "I will both lay me down in peace, and sleep: for Thou, Lord, only makest me to dwell in safety." Never set out on a journey till you have said to God and to your own soul, "The Lord shall preserve thy going out and thy coming in from this time forth, and even for evermore." And never so much as say grace at table, however short time you have to say it in, without seeing Him: in the twinkling of an eye, be for one moment, if no more, with Him who spreads your table, and makes your cup to run over. In short, be sure to get a true sight and a true hold of God, in some way or other, before you begin either prayer or praise. There is nothing in this world so difficult. The time it takes, sometimes, and the toil, and the devices, and the instrumentalities – you would not believe: because no word in all the Bible better describes us when we are at prayer, and at praise, and at table than this: "Without God"; and this: "Their hearts are far from Me." Be sure, then – with all the help that heaven and earth, that God and man can give you – be sure you get your eyes and your hands on God in your prayer. You may begin and end your prayer without that – if you are in a hurry; and if you have no time or taste to give to Him Who will be honored, and waited on, and well pleased with you. But, if so, you need not begin. It is not prayer at all. In your audience of an earthly sovereign, you would not grudge or count up the time and the pains and the schooling beforehand. You would not begin to speak to him while yet you were in the street, or on the stair, and out among the common crowd. You would keep your cause in your heart till you were in his presence: and then, when you saw him sitting on his throne high up above you, you would then fall down before him, and would fill your mouth with arguments.

Never say any of your idle words to Almighty God. Say your idle words to your equals. Say them to your sovereigns. But, never, as you shall answer for it, – never, all your days, – to God. Set the Lord always before you. Direct your prayer to Him, and look up. Better be somewhat too bold and somewhat unseemly than altogether to neglect and forget Almighty God. Better say that so bold saying, – "I will not let Thee go," than pray with such laziness and sleepiness and stupidity as we now pray. Look for God, and look at God: till you can honestly say to Him, with Dr. Newman, a great genius and a great saint, that there are now, to you, two and two only supreme and luminously self-evident beings in the whole universe, yourself and your Creator. And, when once you begin to pray in that way, you will know it. Every prayer of yours like that will, ever after, leave its lasting mark upon you. You will not long remain the same man. Praying, with the imagination all awake, and all employed – such praying will soon drink up your whole soul into itself. You will then "pray always." It will be to you by far the noblest and

the most blessed of all your employments in this present world. You will pray "without ceasing." We shall have to drag you out of your closet by main force. You will then be prayerful "over much." "Whether in the body I cannot tell; or whether out of the body, I cannot tell: God knoweth." Such will you all become when you accustom your inward eyes to see and to brood continually on the power, and on the greatness, and on the goodness, and on the grace and on the glory of God.

Yes, but all the time, what about this? – you will ask: what about this – that "no man hath seen God at any time"? Well, – that is true, and well remembered, and opportunely and appropriately brought forward. Whatever else is true or false, that is true. That, all the time, abides the deepest and the surest of truths. And thus it was that the Invisible Father sent His Son to take our "opaque and palpable" flesh, and, in it, to reveal the Father. "And the Word was made flesh, and dwelt among us, and we beheld His glory." And it is this being "made flesh" of the Son of God that has enabled us to see God. It is the birth and the whole life, and the words, and the works, and the death, and the resurrection, and the ascension, and the revelation from heaven again of Jesus Christ – it is all this that has for ever opened up such new and boundless worlds which the Christian imagination may visit, and in which she may expatiate and regale herself continually.

The absolute and pure Godhead is utterly and absolutely out of all reach even of the highest flights of the imagination of man. The pure and unincarnated Godhead dwells in light which no man's imagination has ever seen even afar off, or ever can see. But then, hear this. "He that hath seen Me hath seen the Father." Well, if that is true, come now! Awake up, O my baffled and beaten-back imagination! Awake, and look at last upon thy God! Awake, and feast thyself for ever on thy God! Bathe, and sun, and satiate thyself to all eternity, in the sweetness and in the beauty and in the light, and in the glory of thy God! There is nothing, in earth or in heaven, to our imagination now like the Word made flesh. We cannot waste any more, so much as one beat of her wing, or one glance of her eye, or one heave of her heart on any one else, in heaven or earth, but the Word made flesh. "Whom have I in heaven but Thee? And there is none upon earth that I desire beside Thee." There is a cold and heartless proverb among men to this effect: "Out of sight, out of mind." And this cold and heartless proverb would be wholly true – even of believing men – if it were not for the divine offices and the splendid services of the Christian imagination. But the truly Christian imagination never lets Jesus Christ out of her sight. And she keeps Him in her sight and ever before her inward eyes in this way. You open your New Testament – which is her peculiar and most delightful field, – you open that Book of books, say, at the beginning of the Sermon on the Mount. And, by your imagination, that moment you are one of Christ's disciples on the spot, and are at His feet. And all that Sermon you never once lift your eyes off the Great Preacher. You hear nothing else, and you see nothing else, till He shuts the Book and says: "Great was the fall of the house," – and so ends His sermon. All through His sermon you have seen the working of His face. In every word of His sermon, you have felt the beating of His heart. Your eye has met His eye, again and again, till you are in chains of grace and truth to Him ever after. And then, no sooner has He risen up, and come down the hill, than a leper, who dared not go up the hill, falls down at His feet, and says, "Lord, if Thou wilt, Thou canst make me clean!" And all your days, ever since that Sermon, you are that leper. All that day you have been more and more like that leper, till now, as that day closes, you are like him nigh unto death. You worship Christ like the leper. He is beside you. He stands over you. You feel, as never before, the leprosy of sin. It fills full your polluted heart. The diseased flesh of that poor leper is the flesh of a little child compared with you and with your heart. Till in a more than leper-like loathing at yourself, and a more than leper-like despair of yourself, you bury your face before His feet, and cry to Him: "But, Lord, if Thou only wilt, Thou canst make me clean!"

And so on – as often as, with your imagination anointed with holy oil, you again open your New Testament. At one time, you are the publican: at another time, you are the prodigal: at another time, you are Lazarus, in his grave, beside whose dead body it was not safe or fit for a living man to come: at another time, you are Mary Magdalene: at another time, Peter in the porch: and then at another time, Judas with the money of the chief priest in his hand, and afterwards with his halter round his neck. Till your whole New Testament is all over autobiographic of you. And till you can say to Matthew, and Mark, and Luke, and to John himself: Now I believe; and not for your sayings so much; for I have seen Him myself, and have myself been healed of Him, and know that this is indeed the Christ of God, and the Savior of the World. Never, then, I implore you, I demand of you – never, now, all the days and nights that are left to you – never open your New Testament till you have offered this prayer to God the Holy Ghost: "Open Thou mine eyes!" And then, as you read, stop and ponder: stop and open your eyes: stop and imagine: stop till you actually see Jesus Christ in the same room with you. "Lo! I am with you alway!" Ask Him, if He hides Himself from you, ask Him aloud, – yes, aloud, – whether these are, indeed, His words to you, or no. Expect Him. Rise up, and open to Him. Salute Him. Put down your book. Put down your light, and then say such things as these – say: "Jesus Christ! Son of David! Son of Mary! Carpenter's Son! Son of God! Savior of Sinners, of whom I am chief!" Speak it out. Do not be afraid that both men and devils hear thee speaking to thy Savior. What about them all when thou art alone with the Son of God? And, besides, all men are asleep. "Art thou, in very truth, here, O Christ? Dost Thou see me? Dost Thou hear me? Yes! Thou art here! I am sure of it. I feel it. O blessed One! O Son of the Highest! I am not worthy that Thou shouldest come under my roof. But Thou art here! Here, of all the houses in the whole city! And, here, with me – O my Savior: with me of all men in the whole city!" Fall at His feet, kiss His feet. Kiss His feet till thy lips come upon an iron nail in them: and, after that, thou wilt know, of a truth, Who He is, that is with thee in the night-watches!

But your absolutely highest, and absolutely best, and absolutely boldest use of your imagination has yet to be told, if you are able to bear it, and are willing to receive it. It is a very high and a very fruitful employment of your imagination to go back and to put yourself by means of it into the place of Adam, and Abraham, and Moses, and Job, and Peter, and Judas, and the Magdalene, and the thief on the cross. But, to put out this magnificent talent to its very best usury, you mistake the highest boldness in all the world, and put yourself in the place of CHRIST HIMSELF. Put yourself and all that is within you into the Hand of the Holy Ghost, and He will help you, most willingly and most successfully, to imagine yourself to be Jesus Christ. Imagine yourself, then, to be back in Nazareth, where He was brought up. Imagine yourself, – and show to your son and your Sunday school scholar the way to imagine himself, – sitting beside Joseph and Mary every Sabbath day in that little synagogue. Imagine yourself to be the carpenter's son, as He was. Imagine yourself at Jordan at John's great awakening of the dry bones, and then at John's Baptism. Imagine yourself fighting the devil in the wilderness with nothing but fasting and praying and the Word of God for weapons. Imagine yourself without where to lay your head. Imagine all your disciples turning against you and forsaking you. Imagine the upper room, and the garden, and the arrest and the Cross, and the darkness, and "My God, My God, why hast Thou forsaken Me?" Did you ever imagine yourself to be crucified? Paul did. And the imagination made him the matchless apostle of the Cross that he was. And then, imagine yourself Christ risen, and in glory, and looking down on your heart, and on your life, and on your closet, and on your bed. Imagine Him seeing you, – your mind, your heart, your inspiration, your motives, your intentions, your thoughts: – all you think, and all you say, and all you do. And then, – I challenge you to imagine what HE must be thinking and feeling, and making up His mind to-day as to what He is to say, and to do, to you; and when! What would you say about yourself, if you were in

His place, – if you had died on the tree for such sins as yours, and then saw yourself what, all this time, you are, having no wish and no intention ever to be otherwise? I think you would throw down your office. I feel sure you would wash your hands of yourself. You would say, "Let him alone!" You would say "Cut it down! Why cumbereth it the ground?" I will tell you literally and exactly what you would say. From God's word I will tell you what any honest and earnest and wearied-out and insulted man would say, and what may this moment, for anything you know, be said over you from the great white throne of God. "Because I have called, and ye refused; I have stretched out My hand, and no man regarded … I will laugh at your calamity; I will mock when your fear cometh; when your fear cometh as desolation, and your destruction cometh as a whirlwind … For that they hated knowledge, and did not choose the fear of the Lord." Imagine the Lamb in His wrath saying that! And imagine yourself dying, and not knowing at threescore and ten how to pray! Imagine yourself at the river, and no one there to meet you – and no one to say to you, "I will be with thee"! Imagine the Judge in His hot anger saying it; – and shutting the door – "I never knew you"! And then, imagine with all your might of imagination – imagine that, by an unparalleled act of God's grace, you are sent back again to this world, just for one more year, just for one more week, just for one more Sabbath day or Sabbath night! O prayer-neglecting sinner! O equally prayer-neglecting child of God! One more Sabbath day of the Mercy-seat, and the Mediator at God's right hand, and the Blood of Christ that speaketh peace!

"I have heard of Thee by the hearing of the ear: but now, mine eye seeth Thee. Wherefore I abhor myself, and repent in dust and ashes."

Alexander Whyte, 1836–1921,
Lord, Teach Us to Pray, Chapter 20

Prayer Collections

Book of Common Prayer: Collection of Prayers

THE ORDER FOR MORNING PRAYER, DAILY THROUGHOUT THE YEAR.

A general Confession

ALMIGHTY and most merciful Father; We have erred, and strayed from thy ways like lost sheep. We have followed too much the devices and desires of our own hearts. We have offended against thy holy laws. We have left undone those things which we ought to have done; And we have done those things which we ought not to have done; And there is no health in us. But thou, O Lord, have mercy upon us, miserable offenders. Spare thou them, O God, who confess their faults. Restore thou those who are penitent; According to thy promises declared unto mankind in Christ Jesu our Lord. And grant, O most merciful Father, for his sake; That we may hereafter live a godly, righteous, and sober life, To the glory of thy holy Name. Amen.

The Absolution, or Remission of sins

ALMIGHTY God, the Father of our Lord Jesus Christ, who desireth not the death of a sinner, but rather that he may turn from his wickedness, and live; and hath given power, and commandment, to his Ministers, to declare and pronounce to his people, being penitent, the Absolution and Remission of their sins: He pardoneth and absolveth all them that truly repent, and unfeignedly believe his holy Gospel. Wherefore let us beseech him to grant us true repentance, and his Holy Spirit, that those things may please him, which we do at this present; and that the rest of our life hereafter may be pure, and holy; so that at the last we may come to his eternal joy; through Jesus Christ our Lord.

The people shall answer here, and at the end of all other prayers,
Amen.

OUR Father, which art in heaven, Hallowed be thy Name. Thy kingdom come. Thy will be done in earth, As it is in heaven. Give us this day our daily bread. And forgive us our trespasses, As we forgive them that trespass against us. And lead us not into temptation, But deliver us from evil. For thine is the kingdom, The power, and the glory, For ever and ever. Amen.

Venite, exultemus Domino

Psalm xcv.

O COME, let us sing unto the Lord: let us heartily rejoice in the strength of our salvation.

Let us come before his presence with thanksgiving: and show ourselves glad in him with Psalms.

For the Lord is a great God: and a great King above all gods.

In his hand are all the corners of the earth: and the strength of the hills is his also.

The sea is his, and he made it: and his hands prepared the dry land.

O come, let us worship and fall down: and kneel before the Lord our Maker.

For he is the Lord our God: and we are the people of his pasture, and the sheep of his hand.

To day if ye will hear his voice, harden not your hearts: as in the provocation, and as in the day of temptation in the wilderness;

When your fathers tempted me: proved me, and saw my works.

Forty years long was I grieved with this generation, and said: It is a people that do err in their heart, and they have not known my ways.

Unto whom I sware in my wrath that they should not enter into my rest.

Glory be to the Father, and to the Son: and to the Holy Ghost;

As it was in the beginning, is now, and ever shall be: world without end. Amen.

Te Deum Laudamus

WE praise thee, O God: we acknowledge thee to be the Lord.

All the earth doth worship thee: the Father everlasting.

To thee all Angels cry aloud: the Heavens, and all the Powers therein.

To thee Cherubim and Seraphim: continually do cry,

Holy, Holy, Holy: Lord God of Sabaoth;

Heaven and earth are full of the Majesty: of thy glory.

The glorious company of the Apostles: praise thee.

The goodly fellowship of the Prophets: praise thee.

The noble army of Martyrs: praise thee.

The holy Church throughout all the world: doth acknowledge thee;

The Father: of an infinite Majesty;

Thine honorable, true: and only Son;

Also the Holy Ghost: the Comforter.

Thou art the King of Glory: O Christ.

Thou art the everlasting Son: of the Father.

When thou tookest upon thee to deliver man: thou didst not abhor the Virgin's womb.

When thou hadst overcome the sharpness of death: thou didst open the Kingdom of Heaven to all believers.

Thou sittest at the right hand of God: in the glory of the Father.

We believe that thou shalt come: to be our Judge.

We therefore pray thee, help thy servants: whom thou hast redeemed with thy precious blood.

Make them to be numbered with thy Saints: in glory everlasting.

O Lord, save thy people: and bless thine heritage.

Govern them: and lift them up for ever.

Day by day: we magnify thee;

And we worship thy Name: ever world without end.

Vouchsafe, O Lord: to keep us this day without sin.

O Lord, have mercy upon us: have mercy upon us.

O Lord, let thy mercy lighten upon us: as our trust is in thee.

O Lord, in thee have I trusted: let me never be confounded.

Or this Canticle
Benedicite, omnia opera

O ALL ye Works of the Lord, bless ye the Lord: praise him, and magnify him for ever.

O ye Angels of the Lord, bless ye the Lord: praise him, and magnify him for ever.

O ye Heavens, bless ye the Lord: praise him, and magnify him for ever.

O ye Waters that be above the firmament, bless ye the Lord: praise him, and magnify him for ever.

O all ye Powers of the Lord, bless ye the Lord: praise him, and magnify him for ever.

O ye Sun and Moon, bless ye the Lord: praise him, and magnify him for ever.

O ye Stars of heaven, bless ye the Lord: praise him, and magnify him for ever.

O ye Showers and Dew, bless ye the Lord: praise him, and magnify him for ever.

O ye Winds of God, bless ye the Lord: praise him, and magnify him for ever.

O ye Fire and Heat, bless ye the Lord: praise him, and magnify him for ever.

O ye Winter and Summer, bless ye the Lord: praise him, and magnify him for ever.

O ye Dews and Frosts, bless ye the Lord: praise him, and magnify him for ever.

O ye Frost and Cold, bless ye the Lord: praise him, and magnify him for ever.

O ye Ice and Snow, bless ye the Lord: praise him, and magnify him for ever.

O ye Nights and Days, bless ye the Lord: praise him, and magnify him for ever.

O ye Light and Darkness, bless ye the Lord: praise him, and magnify him for ever.

O ye Lightnings and Clouds, bless ye the Lord: praise him, and magnify him for ever.

O let the Earth bless the Lord: yea, let it praise him, and magnify him for ever.

O ye Mountains and Hills, bless ye the Lord: praise him, and magnify him for ever.

O all ye Green Things upon the earth, bless ye the Lord: praise him, and magnify him for ever.

O ye Wells, bless ye the Lord: praise him, and magnify him for ever.

O ye Seas and Floods, bless ye the Lord: praise him, and magnify him for ever.

O ye Whales, and all that move in the waters, bless ye the Lord: praise him, and magnify him for ever.

O all ye Fowls of the air, bless ye the Lord: praise him, and magnify him for ever.

O all ye Beasts and Cattle, bless ye the Lord: praise him, and magnify him for ever.

O ye Children of Men, bless ye the Lord: praise him, and magnify him for ever.

O let Israel bless the Lord: praise him, and magnify him for ever.

O ye Priests of the Lord, bless ye the Lord: praise him, and magnify him for ever.

O ye Servants of the Lord, bless ye the Lord: praise him, and magnify him for ever.

O ye Spirits and Souls of the Righteous, bless ye the Lord: praise him, and magnify him for ever.

O ye holy and humble Men of heart, bless ye the Lord: praise him, and magnify him for ever.

O Ananias, Azarias, and Misael, bless ye the Lord: praise him, and magnify him for ever.

Glory be to the Father, and to the Son: and to the Holy Ghost;

As it was in the beginning, is now, and ever shall be: world without end. Amen.

Benedictus
St. Luke i. 68.

BLESSED be the Lord God of Israel: for he hath visited and redeemed his people;

And hath raised up a mighty salvation for us: in the house of his servant David;

As he spake by the mouth of his holy Prophets: which have been since the world began;

That we should be saved from our enemies: and from the hand of all that hate us.

To perform the mercy promised to our forefathers: and to remember his holy Covenant;

To perform the oath which he sware to our forefather Abraham: that he would give us;

That we being delivered out of the hand of our enemies: might serve him without fear;

In holiness and righteousness before him: all the days of our life.

And thou, Child, shalt be called the Prophet of the Highest: for thou shalt go before the face of the Lord to prepare his ways;

To give knowledge of salvation unto his people: for the remission of their sins,

Through the tender mercy of our God: whereby the day-spring from on high hath visited us;

To give light to them that sit in darkness, and in the shadow of death: and to guide our feet into the way of peace.

Glory be to the Father, and to the Son: and to the Holy Ghost;

As it was in the beginning, is now, and ever shall be: world without end. Amen.

Or this Psalm
Jubilate Deo. Psalm c.

O BE joyful in the Lord, all ye lands: serve the Lord with gladness, and come before his presence with a song.

Be ye sure that the Lord he is God; it is he that hath made us, and not we ourselves: we are his people, and the sheep of his pasture.

O go your way into his gates with thanksgiving, and into his courts with praise: be thankful unto him, and speak good of his Name.

For the Lord is gracious, his mercy is everlasting: and his truth endureth from generation to generation.

Glory be to the Father, and to the Son: and to the Holy Ghost;

As it was in the beginning, is now, and ever shall be: world without end. Amen.

The second Collect, for Peace

O GOD, who art the author of peace and lover of concord, in knowledge of whom standeth our eternal life, whose service is perfect freedom; Defend us thy humble servants in all assaults of our enemies; that we, surely trusting in thy defense, may not fear the power of any adversaries, through the might of Jesus Christ our Lord. Amen.

The third Collect, for Grace

O LORD, our heavenly Father, Almighty and everlasting God, who hast safely brought us to the beginning of this day; Defend us in the same with thy mighty power; and grant that this day we fall into no sin, neither run into any kind of danger; but that all our doings may be ordered by thy governance, to do always that is righteous in thy sight; through Jesus Christ our Lord. Amen.

A Prayer for the Queen's Majesty

O LORD, our heavenly Father, the high and mighty, King of kings, Lord of lords, the only Ruler of princes, who dost from thy throne behold all the dwellers upon earth; Most heartily we beseech thee with thy favor to behold our most gracious Sovereign Lady, Queen ELIZABETH; and so replenish her with the grace of thy Holy Spirit, that she may always incline to thy will, and walk in thy way. Endue her plenteously with heavenly gifts; grant her in health and wealth long to live; strengthen her that she may vanquish and overcome all her enemies; and finally, after this life, she may attain everlasting joy and felicity; through Jesus Christ our Lord. Amen.

A Prayer for the Royal Family.

ALMIGHTY God, the fountain of all goodness, we humbly beseech thee to bless Philip Duke of Edinburgh, Charles Prince of Wales, and all the Royal Family: Endue them with thy Holy Spirit; enrich them with thy heavenly grace; prosper them with all happiness; and bring them to thine everlasting kingdom; through Jesus Christ our Lord. Amen.

A Prayer for the Clergy and People

ALMIGHTY and everlasting God, who alone workest great marvels; Send down upon our Bishops, and Curates, and all Congregations committed to their charge, the healthful Spirit of thy grace; and that they may truly please thee, pour upon them the continual dew of thy blessing. Grant this, O Lord, for the honor of our Advocate and Mediator, Jesus Christ. Amen.

A Prayer of St. Chrysostom

ALMIGHTY God, who hast given us grace at this time with one accord to make our common supplications unto thee; and dost promise, that when two or three are gathered together in thy Name thou wilt grant their requests; Fulfill now, O Lord, the desires and petitions of thy servants, as may be most expedient for them; granting us in this world knowledge of thy truth, and in the world to come life everlasting. Amen.

2 Corinthians xiii

THE grace of our Lord Jesus Christ, and the love of God, and the fellowship of the Holy Ghost, be with us all evermore. Amen.

THE ORDER FOR EVENING PRAYER, DAILY THROUGHOUT THE YEAR.

A general Confession

ALMIGHTY and most merciful Father; We have erred, and strayed from thy ways like lost sheep. We have followed too much the devices and desires of our own hearts. We have offended against thy holy laws. We have left undone those things which we ought to have done; And we have done those things which we ought not to have done; And there is no health in us. But thou, O Lord, have mercy upon us, miserable offenders. Spare thou them, O God, who confess their faults. Restore thou those who are penitent; According to thy promises declared unto mankind in Christ Jesu our Lord. And grant, O most merciful Father, for his sake; That we may hereafter live a godly, righteous, and sober life, To the glory of thy holy Name. Amen.

The Absolution or Remission of sins

ALMIGHTY God, the Father of our Lord Jesus Christ, who desireth not the death of a sinner, but rather that he may turn from his wickedness, and live; and hath given power, and commandment, to his Ministers, to declare and pronounce to his people, being penitent, the Absolution and Remission of their sins: He pardoneth and absolveth all them that truly repent, and unfeignedly believe his holy Gospel. Wherefore let us beseech him to grant us true repentance, and his Holy Spirit, that those things may please him, which we do at this present; and that the rest of our life hereafter may be pure, and holy; so that at the last we may come to his eternal joy; through Jesus Christ our Lord.

OUR Father, which art in heaven, Hallowed be thy Name. Thy kingdom come. Thy will be done in earth, As it is in heaven. Give us this day our daily bread. And forgive us our trespasses, As we forgive those who trespass against us. And lead us not into temptation, But deliver us from evil. For thine is the kingdom, The power, and the glory, For ever and ever. Amen.

Magnificat (or the Song of the blessed Virgin Mary)
St. Luke 1.
MY soul doth magnify the Lord: and my spirit hath rejoiced in God my Savior.

For he hath regarded: the lowliness of his handmaiden.

For behold, from henceforth: all generations shall call me blessed.

For he that is mighty hath magnified me: and holy is his Name.

And his mercy is on them that fear him: throughout all generations.

He hath showed strength with his arm: he hath scattered the proud in the imagination of their hearts.

He hath put down the mighty from their seat: and hath exalted the humble and meek.

He hath filled the hungry with good things: and the rich he hath sent empty away.

He remembering his mercy hath holpen his servant Israel: as he promised to our forefathers, Abraham and his seed, for ever.

Glory be to the Father, &c.

As it was in the beginning, &c.

Cantate Domino
Psalm xcviii.
O SING unto the Lord a new song: for he hath done marvelous things.

With his own right hand, and with his holy arm: hath he gotten himself the victory.

The Lord declared his salvation: his righteousness hath he openly showed in the sight of the heathen.

He hath remembered his mercy and truth toward the house of Israel: and all the ends of the world have seen the salvation of our God.

Show yourselves joyful unto the Lord, all ye lands: sing, rejoice, and give thanks.

Praise the Lord upon the harp: sing to the harp with a psalm of thanksgiving.

With trumpets also and shawms: O shew yourselves joyful before the Lord the King.

Let the sea make a noise, and all that therein is: the round world, and that dwell therein.

Let the floods clap their hands, and let the hills be joyful together before the Lord: for he cometh to judge the earth.

With righteousness shall he judge the world: and the peoples with equity.

Glory be to the Father, &c.

As it was in the beginning, &c.

Nunc dimittis (or the Song of Simeon)
St. Luke ii. 29.
LORD, now lettest thou thy servant depart in peace: according to thy word.

For mine eyes have seen: thy salvation,

Which thou hast prepared: before the face of all people;

To be a light to lighten the Gentiles: and to be the glory of thy people Israel.

Glory be to the Father, &c.

As it was in the beginning, &c.

Deus misereatur
Psalm lxvii.
GOD be merciful unto us, and bless us: and shew us the light of his countenance, and be merciful unto us;

That thy way may be known upon earth: thy saving health among all nations.

Let the peoples praise thee, O God: yea, let all the peoples praise thee.

O let the nations rejoice and be glad: for thou shalt judge the folk righteously, and govern the nations upon earth.

Let the people praise thee, O God: yea, let all the people praise thee.

Then shall the earth bring forth her increase: and God, even our own God, shall give us his blessing.

God shall bless us: and all the ends of the world shall fear him.

Glory be to the Father, &c.

As it was in the beginning, &c.

The Second Collect at Evening Prayer

O GOD, from whom all holy desires, all good counsels, and all just works do proceed; Give unto thy servants that peace which the world cannot give; that our hearts may be set to obey thy commandments, and also that by thee, we, being defended from the fear of our enemies, may pass our time in rest and quietness; through the merits of Jesus Christ our Savior. Amen.

The Third Collect, for Aid against all Perils

LIGHTEN our darkness, we beseech thee, O Lord; and by thy great mercy defend us from all perils and dangers of this night; for the love of thy only Son, our Savior, Jesus Christ. Amen.

A Prayer for the Queen's Majesty

O LORD, our heavenly Father, the high and mighty, King of kings, Lord of lords, the only Ruler of princes, who dost from thy throne behold all the dwellers upon earth; Most heartily we beseech thee with thy favor to behold our most gracious Sovereign Lady, Queen ELIZABETH; and so replenish her with the grace of thy Holy Spirit, that she may always incline to thy will, and walk in thy way. Endue her plenteously with heavenly gifts; grant her in health and wealth long to live; strengthen her that she may vanquish and overcome all her enemies; and finally, after this life, she may attain everlasting joy and felicity; through Jesus Christ our Lord. Amen.

A Prayer for the Royal Family

ALMIGHTY God, the fountain of all goodness, we humbly beseech thee to bless Philip Duke of Edinburgh, Charles Prince of Wales, and all the Royal Family: Endue them with thy Holy Spirit; enrich them with thy heavenly grace; prosper them with all happiness; and bring them to thine everlasting kingdom; through Jesus Christ our Lord. Amen.

A Prayer for the Clergy and People

ALMIGHTY and everlasting God, who alone workest great marvels; Send down upon our Bishops, and Curates, and all Congregations committed to their charge, the healthful Spirit of thy grace; and that they may truly please thee, pour upon them the continual dew of thy blessing. Grant this, O Lord, for the honor of our Advocate and Mediator, Jesus Christ. Amen.

A Prayer of St. Chrysostom

ALMIGHTY God, who hast given us grace at this time with one accord to make our common supplications unto thee; and dost promise, that when two or three are gathered together in thy Name thou wilt grant their requests; Fulfill now, O Lord, the desires and petitions of thy servants, as may be most expedient for them; granting us in this world knowledge of thy truth, and in the world to come life everlasting. Amen.

2 Corinthians xiii.

THE grace of our Lord Jesus Christ, and the love of God, and the fellowship of the Holy Ghost, be with us all evermore. Amen.

Here endeth the Order of Evening Prayer throughout the Year.

THE LITANY

O GOD the Father, of heaven: have mercy upon us miserable sinners.

O God the Father, of heaven: have mercy upon us miserable sinners.

O God the Son, Redeemer of the world: have mercy upon us miserable sinners.

O God the Son, Redeemer of the world: have mercy upon us miserable sinners.

O God the Holy Ghost, proceeding from the Father and the Son: have mercy upon us miserable sinners.

O God the Holy Ghost, proceeding from the Father and the Son: have mercy upon us miserable sinners.

O holy, blessed, and glorious Trinity, three Persons and one God: have mercy upon us miserable sinners.

O holy, blessed, and glorious Trinity, three Persons and one God: have mercy upon us miserable sinners.

Remember not, Lord, our offences, nor the offences of our forefathers; neither take thou vengeance of our sins: Spare us, good Lord, spare thy people, whom thou hast redeemed with thy most precious blood, and be not angry with us for ever.

Spare us, good Lord.

From all evil and mischief; from sin; from the
crafts and assaults of the devil; from thy
wrath, and from everlasting damnation,

Spare us, good Lord.

From all blindness of heart; from pride,
vainglory, and hypocrisy; from
envy, hatred, and malice, and all
uncharitableness,

Spare us, good Lord.

From fornication, and all other deadly sin; and
from all the deceits of the world, the flesh,
and the devil,

Spare us, good Lord.

From lightning and tempest; from
earthquake, fire, and flood; from plague,
pestilence, and famine; from battle and
murder, and from sudden death,

Spare us, good Lord.

From all sedition, privy conspiracy, and
rebellion; from all false doctrine,
heresy, and schism; from hardness of
heart, and contempt of thy Word and
Commandment,

Spare us, good Lord.

By the mystery of thy holy Incarnation; by
thy holy Nativity and Circumcision; by thy
Baptism, Fasting, and Temptation,

Spare us, good Lord.

By thine Agony and Bloody Sweat; by thy
Cross and Passion; by thy precious Death
and Burial; by thy glorious Resurrection
and Ascension, and by the Coming of the
Holy Ghost,

Spare us, good Lord.

In all time of our tribulation; in all time of our
prosperity; in the hour of death, and in the
day of judgment,

Spare us, good Lord.

We sinners do beseech thee to hear us, O Lord
God; and that it may please thee to rule
and govern thy holy Church universal in
the right way;

We beseech thee to hear us, good Lord.

That it may please thee to keep and strengthen
in the true worshipping of thee, in
righteousness and holiness of life, thy
Servant ELIZABETH, our most gracious
Queen and Governor;

We beseech thee to hear us, good Lord.

That it may please thee to rule her heart in

thy faith, fear, and love, and that she may
evermore have affiance in thee, and ever
seek thy honor and glory;

We beseech thee to hear us, good Lord.

That it may please thee to be her defender and
keeper, giving her the victory over all her
enemies;

We beseech thee to hear us, good Lord.

That it may please thee to bless and preserve
Philip Duke of Edinburgh, Charles Prince
of Wales, and all the Royal Family;

We beseech thee to hear us, good Lord.

That it may please thee to illuminate all
Bishops, Priests, and Deacons, with true
knowledge and understanding of thy
Word; and that both by their preaching
and living they may set it forth, and show it
accordingly;

We beseech thee to hear us, good Lord.

That it may please thee to endue the Lords
of the Council, and all the Nobility, with
grace, wisdom, and understanding;

We beseech thee to hear us, good Lord.

That it may please thee to bless and keep the
Magistrates, giving them grace to execute
justice, and to maintain truth;

We beseech thee to hear us, good Lord.

That it may please thee to bless and keep all
thy people;

We beseech thee to hear us, good Lord.

That it may please thee to give to all nations
unity, peace, and concord;

We beseech thee to hear us, good Lord.

That it may please thee to give us an heart to
love and dread thee, and diligently to live
after thy commandments;

We beseech thee to hear us, good Lord.

That it may please thee to give to all thy
people increase of grace to hear meekly thy
Word, and to receive it with pure affection,
and to bring forth the fruits of the Spirit;

We beseech thee to hear us, good Lord.

That it may please thee to bring into the way
of truth all such as have erred, and are
deceived;

We beseech thee to hear us, good Lord.

That it may please thee to strengthen such
as do stand; and to comfort and help the
weak-hearted; and to raise up those who
fall; and finally to beat down Satan under
our feet;

We beseech thee to hear us, good Lord.

That it may please thee to succor, help, and comfort, all who are in danger, necessity, and tribulation;

We beseech thee to hear us, good Lord.

That it may please thee to preserve all who travel by land, by water, all women laboring of child, all sick persons, and young children; and to show thy pity upon all prisoners and captives;

We beseech thee to hear us, good Lord.

That it may please thee to defend, and provide for, the fatherless children, and widows, and all who are desolate and oppressed;

We beseech thee to hear us, good Lord.

That it may please thee to have mercy upon all men;

We beseech thee to hear us, good Lord.

That it may please thee to forgive our enemies, persecutors, and slanderers, and to turn their hearts;

We beseech thee to hear us, good Lord.

That it may please thee to give and preserve to our use the kindly fruits of the earth, so that in due time we may enjoy them;

We beseech thee to hear us, good Lord.

That it may please thee to give us true repentance; to forgive us all our sins, negligences, and ignorances; and to endue us with the grace of thy Holy Spirit to amend our lives according to thy holy Word;

We beseech thee to hear us, good Lord.

Son of God: we beseech thee to hear us.

Son of God: we beseech thee to hear us.

O Lamb of God: that takest away the sins of the world;

Grant us thy peace.

O Lamb of God: that takest away the sins of the world;

Have mercy upon us.

O Christ, hear us.

O Christ, hear us.

Lord, have mercy upon us.

Lord, have mercy upon us.

Christ, have mercy upon us.

Christ, have mercy upon us.

Lord, have mercy upon us.

Lord, have mercy upon us.

Priest. O Lord, deal not with us according to our sins.

Answer. Neither reward us according to our iniquities.

Let us pray.

O GOD, merciful Father, that despisest not the sighing of a contrite heart, nor the desire of such as are sorrowful; Mercifully assist our prayers which we make before thee in all our troubles and adversities, whensoever they oppress us; and graciously hear us, that those evils which the craft and subtilty of the devil or man worketh be brought to nought; and by the providence of thy goodness they may be dispersed; that we thy servants, being hurt by no persecutions, may evermore give thanks unto thee in thy holy Church; through Jesus Christ our Lord.

O Lord, arise, help us, and deliver us for thy Name's sake.

O GOD, we have heard with our ears, and our fathers have declared unto us, the noble works that thou didst in their days, and in the old time before them.

O Lord, arise, help us, and deliver us for thine honor.

Glory be to the Father, and to the Son, and to the Holy Ghost;

As it was in the beginning, is now, and ever shall be, world without end. Amen.

From our enemies defend us, O Christ.

Graciously look upon our afflictions.

Pitifully behold the sorrows of our hearts.

Mercifully forgive the sins of thy people.

Favorably with mercy hear our prayers.

O Son of David, have mercy upon us.

Both now and ever vouchsafe to hear us, O Christ.

Graciously hear us, O Christ; graciously hear us, O Lord Christ.

Priest. O Lord, let thy mercy be showed upon us;

Answer. As we do put our trust in thee.

Let us pray.

WE humbly beseech thee, O Father, mercifully to look upon our infirmities; and, for the glory of thy Name, turn from us all those evils that we most justly have deserved; and grant, that in all our troubles we may put our whole trust and confidence in thy mercy, and evermore serve thee in holiness and pureness of living, to thy honor and glory; through our only Mediator and Advocate, Jesus Christ our Lord. Amen.

A Prayer of St. Chrysostom

ALMIGHTY God, who hast given us grace at this time with one accord to make our common supplications unto thee; and dost promise, that when two or three are gathered together in thy Name thou wilt grant their requests; Fulfill now, O Lord, the desires and petitions of thy servants, as may be most expedient for them; granting us in this world knowledge of thy truth, and in the world to come life everlasting. Amen.

2 Corinthians xiii

THE grace of our Lord Jesus Christ, and the love of God, and the fellowship of the Holy Ghost, be with us all evermore. Amen.
Here endeth the Litany.

PRAYERS AND THANKSGIVINGS, Upon Several Occasions, To be used before the two final Prayers of the Litany, or of Morning and Evening Prayer.

PRAYERS
For Rain

O GOD, heavenly Father, who by thy Son Jesus Christ hast promised to all those who seek thy kingdom, and the righteousness thereof, all things necessary to their bodily sustenance; Send us, we beseech thee, in this our necessity, such moderate rain and showers, that we may receive the fruits of the earth to our comfort, and to thy honor; through Jesus Christ our Lord. Amen.

For Fair Weather

O ALMIGHTY Lord God, who for the sin of man didst once drown all the world, except eight persons, and afterward of thy great mercy didst promise never to destroy it so again; We humbly beseech thee, that although we for our iniquities have worthily deserved a plague of rain and waters, yet upon our true repentance thou wilt send us such weather, as that we may receive the fruits of the earth

in due season; and learn both by thy punishment to amend our lives, and for thy clemency to give thee praise and glory; through Jesus Christ our Lord. Amen.

In Time of Dearth and Famine

O GOD, heavenly Father, whose gift it is that the rain doth fall, the earth is fruitful, beasts do increase, and fishes do multiply; Behold, we beseech thee, the afflictions of thy people; and grant that the scarcity and dearth, which we do now most justly suffer for our iniquity, may, through thy goodness be mercifully turned into cheapness and plenty; for the love of Jesus Christ our Lord, to whom, with thee and the Holy Ghost, be all honor and glory, now and for ever. Amen.

Or this

O GOD, merciful Father, who, in the time of Elisha the prophet, didst suddenly in Samaria turn great scarcity and dearth into plenty and cheapness; Have mercy upon us, that we, who are now for our sins punished with like adversity, may likewise find a seasonable relief: Increase the fruits of the earth by thy heavenly benediction; and grant that we, receiving thy bountiful liberality, may use the same to thy glory, the relief of those that are needy, and our own comfort; through Jesus Christ our Lord. Amen.

In the time of War and Tumults

O ALMIGHTY God, King of all kings, and Governor of all things, whose power no creature is able to resist, to whom it belongeth justly to punish sinners, and to be merciful to those who truly repent; Save and deliver us, we humbly beseech thee, from the hands of our enemies; abate their pride, assuage their malice, and confound their devices; that we, being armed with thy defense, may be preserved evermore from all perils, to glorify thee, who art the only giver of all victory; through the merits of thy Son, Jesus Christ our Lord. Amen.

In the time of any common Plague or Sickness

O ALMIGHTY God, who in thy wrath did send a plague upon thine own people in the wilderness, for their obstinate rebellion against Moses and Aaron; and also, in the time of king David, didst slay with the plague of Pestilence three-score and ten thousand, and yet remembering thy mercy didst save the rest; Have pity upon us miserable sinners, who now are visited with great sickness and mortality; that like as thou didst then accept of an atonement, and didst command the destroying Angel to cease from punishing, so it may now please thee to with-draw from us this plague and grievous sick-ness; through Jesus Christ our Lord. Amen.

In the Ember Weeks, to be said every day, for those that are about to be admitted into Holy Orders
ALMIGHTY God, our heavenly Father, who hast purchased to thyself an universal Church by the precious blood of thy dear Son; Merci-fully look upon the same, and at this time so guide and govern the minds of thy servants the Bishops and Pastors of thy flock, that they may lay hands suddenly on no man, but faithfully and wisely make choice of fit persons, to serve in the sacred Ministry of thy Church. And to those which shall be ordained to any holy function, give thy grace and heavenly benedic-tion; that both by their life and doctrine they may show forth thy glory, and set forward the salvation of all men; through Jesus Christ our Lord. Amen.

Or this
ALMIGHTY God, the giver of all good gifts, who of thy divine providence hast appointed divers Orders in thy Church; Give thy grace, we humbly beseech thee, to all those who are to be called to any office and administration in the same; and so replenish them with the truth of thy doctrine, and endue them with innocency of life, that they may faithfully serve before thee, to the glory of thy great Name, and the benefit of thy holy Church; through Jesus Christ our Lord. Amen.

A Prayer that may be said after any of the former
O GOD, whose nature and property is ever to have mercy and to forgive, receive our humble petitions; and though we be tied and bound with the chain of our sins, yet let the pitiful-ness of thy great mercy loose us; for the honor of Jesus Christ, our Mediator and Advocate. Amen.

A Prayer for the High Court of Parliament, to be read during their Session
MOST gracious God, we humbly beseech thee, as for this Kingdom in general, so especially for the High Court of Parliament, under our most religious and gracious Queen at this time assembled: That thou wouldest be pleased to direct and prosper all their consultations, to the advancement of thy glory, the good of thy Church, the safety, honor, and welfare of our Sovereign and her Dominions; that all things may be so ordered and settled by their endeav-ors, upon the best and surest foundations, that peace and happiness, truth and justice, religion and piety, may be established among us for all generations. These and all other necessaries, for them, for us, and thy whole Church, we humbly beg in the Name and Mediation of Jesus Christ, our most blessed Lord and Savior. Amen.

A Collect or Prayer for all Conditions of Men, to be used at such times when the Litany is not appointed to be said
O GOD, the Creator and Preserver of all mankind, we humbly beseech thee for all sorts and conditions of men: that thou would-est be pleased to make thy ways known unto them, thy saving health unto all nations. More especially, we pray for the good estate of the Catholic Church; that it may be so guided and governed by thy good Spirit, that all who profess and call themselves Christians may be led into the way of truth, and hold the faith in unity of spirit, in the bond of peace, and in righteousness of life. Finally, we commend to thy fatherly goodness all those, who are any ways afflicted, or distressed, in mind, body, or estate; [*especially those for whom our prayers are desired;] that it may please thee to comfort and relieve them, according to their several necessities, giving them patience under their sufferings, and a happy issue out of all their afflictions. And this we beg for Jesus Christ his sake. Amen.
* This to be said when any desire the Prayers of the Congregation.

THANKSGIVINGS
A General Thanksgiving
ALMIGHTY God, Father of all mercies, we

thine unworthy servants do give thee most humble and hearty thanks for all thy goodness and loving-kindness to us, and to all men; [*particularly to those who desire now to offer up their praises and thanksgivings for thy late mercies vouchsafed unto them.] We bless thee for our creation, preservation, and all the blessings of this life; but above all, for thine inestimable love in the redemption of the world by our Lord Jesus Christ; for the means of grace, and for the hope of glory. And, we beseech thee, give us that due sense of all thy mercies, that our hearts may be unfeignedly thankful, and that we shew forth thy praise, not only with our lips, but in our lives; by giving up ourselves to thy service, and by walking before thee in holiness and righteousness all our days; through Jesus Christ our Lord, to whom with thee and the Holy Ghost be all honor and glory, world without end. Amen.

* This to be said when any that have been prayed for desire to return praise.

For Rain

O GOD our heavenly Father, who by thy gracious providence dost cause the former and the latter rain to descend upon the earth, that it may bring forth fruit for the use of man; We give thee humble thanks that it hath pleased thee, in our great necessity, to send us at the last a joyful rain upon thine inheritance, and to refresh it when it was dry, to the great comfort of us thy unworthy servants, and to the glory of thy holy Name; through thy mercies in Jesus Christ our Lord. Amen.

For Fair Weather

O LORD God, who hast justly humbled us by thy late plague of immoderate rain and waters, and in thy mercy hast relieved and comforted our souls by this seasonable and blessed change of weather; We praise and glorify thy holy Name for this thy mercy, and will always declare thy loving-kindness from generation to generation; through Jesus Christ our Lord. Amen.

For Plenty

O MOST merciful Father, who of thy gracious goodness hast heard the devout prayers of thy Church, and turned our dearth and scarcity into cheapness and plenty; We give thee humble thanks for this thy special bounty; beseeching thee to continue thy loving-kindness unto us, that our land may yield us her fruits of increase, to thy glory and our comfort; through Jesus Christ our Lord. Amen.

For Peace, and Deliverance from our Enemies

O ALMIGHTY God, who art a strong tower of defense unto thy servants against the face of their enemies; We yield thee praise and thanksgiving for our deliverance from those great and apparent dangers wherewith we were compassed. We acknowledge it thy goodness that we were not delivered over as a prey unto them; beseeching thee still to continue such thy mercies towards us, that all the world may know that thou art our Savior and mighty Deliverer; through Jesus Christ our Lord. Amen.

For restoring Public Peace at Home

O ETERNAL God, our heavenly Father, Who alone makest men to be of one mind in a house, and stillest the outrage of a violent and unruly people; We bless thy holy Name, that it hath pleased thee to appease the seditious tumults which have been lately raised up amongst us; most humbly beseeching thee to grant to all of us grace, that we may henceforth obediently walk in thy holy commandments; and, leading a quiet and peaceable life in all godliness and honesty, may continually offer unto thee our sacrifice of praise and thanksgiving for these thy mercies towards us; through Jesus Christ our Lord. Amen.

For Deliverance from the Plague, or other common Sickness

O LORD God, who has wounded us for our sins, and consumed us for our transgressions, by thy late heavy and dreadful visitation; and now, in the midst of judgment remembering mercy, hast redeemed our souls from the jaws of death; We offer unto thy fatherly goodness ourselves, our souls and bodies which thou hast delivered, to be a living sacrifice unto thee, always praising and magnifying thy mercies in the midst of thy Church; through Jesus Christ our Lord. Amen.

Or this
WE humbly acknowledge before thee, O most merciful Father, that all the punishments which are threatened in thy law might justly have fallen upon us, by reason of our manifold transgressions and hardness of heart: Yet seeing it hath pleased thee of thy tender mercy, upon our weak and unworthy humiliation, to assuage the contagious sickness wherewith we lately have been sore afflicted, and to restore the voice of joy and health into our dwellings; We offer unto thy Divine Majesty the sacrifice of praise and thanksgiving, lauding and magnifying thy preservation and providence over us; through Jesus Christ our Lord. Amen.

THE ORDER OF THE ADMINISTRATION OF THE LORD'S SUPPER, OR HOLY COMMUNION
The Collect
ALMIGHTY God, unto whom all hearts be open, all desires known, and from whom no secrets are hid; Cleanse the thoughts of our hearts by the inspiration of thy Holy Spirit, that we may perfectly love thee, and worthily magnify thy holy Name; through Christ our Lord. Amen.

ALMIGHTY God, whose kingdom is everlasting, and power infinite: Have mercy upon the whole Church; and so rule the heart of thy chosen servant ELIZABETH, our Queen and Governor, that she (knowing whose minister she is) may above all things seek thy honor and glory; and that we, and all her subjects (duly considering whose authority she hath) may faithfully serve, honor, and humbly obey her, in thee, and for thee, according to thy blessed Word and ordinance; through Jesus Christ our Lord, who with thee and the Holy Ghost liveth and reigneth, ever one God, world without end. Amen.

Or,

ALMIGHTY and everlasting God, we are taught by thy Holy Word, that the hearts of Kings are in thy rule and governance, and that thou dost dispose and turn them as it seemeth best to thy godly wisdom: We humbly beseech thee so to dispose and govern the heart of ELIZABETH thy Servant, our Queen and Governor, that, in all her thoughts, words, and works, she may ever seek thy honor and glory, and study to preserve thy people committed to her charge, in wealth, peace, and godliness: Grant this, O merciful Father, for thy dear Son's sake, Jesus Christ our Lord. Amen.

Let us pray for the whole state of Christ's Church militant here in earth
ALMIGHTY and everliving God, who by thy holy Apostle hast taught us to make prayers, and supplications, and to give thanks for all men; We humbly beseech thee most mercifully [*to accept our alms and oblations, and] to receive these our prayers, which we offer unto thy Divine Majesty; beseeching thee to inspire continually the Universal Church with the spirit of truth, unity, and concord: And grant, that all they who do confess thy holy Name may agree in the truth of thy holy Word, and live in unity, and godly love. We beseech thee also to save and defend all Christian Kings, Princes, and Governors; and specially thy Servant ELIZABETH our Queen; that under her we may be godly and quietly governed: And grant unto her whole Council, and to all that are put in authority under her, that they may truly and impartially administer justice, to the punishment of wickedness and vice, and to the maintenance of thy true religion, and virtue. Give grace, O heavenly Father, to all Bishops and Curates, that they may both by their life and doctrine set forth thy true and lively Word, and rightly and duly administer thy holy Sacraments. And to all thy people give thy heavenly grace; and especially to this congregation here present; that, with meek heart and due reverence, they may hear, and receive thy holy Word; truly serving thee in holiness and righteousness all the days of their life. And we most humbly beseech thee, of thy goodness, O Lord, to comfort and succor all those who, in this transitory life, are in trouble, sorrow, need, sickness, or any other adversity. And we also bless thy holy Name for all thy servants departed this life in thy faith and fear; beseeching thee to give us grace so to follow their good examples, that with them we may be partakers of thy heavenly kingdom. Grant this, O Father, for Jesus Christ's sake, our only Mediator and Advocate. Amen.

* If there be no alms or oblations, then the words [of accepting our alms and oblations] be left out unsaid.

YE that do truly and earnestly repent you of your sins, and are in love and charity with your neighbors, and intend to lead a new life, following the commandments of God, and walking from henceforth in his holy ways; Draw near with faith, and take this holy Sacrament to your comfort; and make your humble confession to Almighty God, meekly kneeling upon your knees.

General Confession

ALMIGHTY God, Father of our Lord Jesus Christ, Maker of all things, judge of all men; We acknowledge and bewail our manifold sins and wickedness, Which we, from time to time, most grievously have committed, By thought, word, and deed, Against thy Divine Majesty, Provoking most justly thy wrath and indignation against us. We do earnestly repent, And are heartily sorry for these our misdoings; The remembrance of them is grievous unto us; The burden of them is intolerable. Have mercy upon us, Have mercy upon us, most merciful Father; For thy Son our Lord Jesus Christ's sake, Forgive us all that is past; And grant that we may ever hereafter Serve and please thee In newness of life, To the honor and glory of thy Name; Through Jesus Christ our Lord. Amen.

ALMIGHTY God, our heavenly Father, who of his great mercy hath promised forgiveness of sins to all them that with hearty repentance and true faith turn unto him; Have mercy upon you; pardon and deliver you from all your sins; confirm and strengthen you in all goodness; and bring you to everlasting life; through Jesus Christ our Lord. Amen.

WE do not presume to come to this thy Table, O merciful Lord, trusting in our own righteousness, but in thy manifold and great mercies. We are not worthy so much as to gather up the crumbs under thy Table. But thou art the same Lord, whose property is always to have mercy: Grant us therefore, gracious Lord, so to eat the flesh of thy dear Son Jesus Christ, and to drink his blood, that our sinful bodies may be made clean by his body, and our souls washed through his most precious blood, and that we may evermore dwell in him, and he in us. Amen.

Prayer of Consecration

ALMIGHTY God, our heavenly Father, who of thy tender mercy didst give thine only Son Jesus Christ to suffer death upon the Cross for our redemption; who made there (by his one oblation of himself once offered) a full, perfect, and sufficient sacrifice, oblation, and satisfaction, for the sins of the whole world; and did institute, and in his holy Gospel command us to continue, a perpetual memory of that his precious death, until his coming again; Hear us, O merciful Father, we most humbly beseech thee; and grant that we receiving these thy creatures of bread and wine, according to thy Son our Savior Jesus Christ's holy institution, in remembrance of his death and passion, may be partakers of his most blessed Body and Blood: who, in the same night that he was betrayed, (a) took Bread; and, when he had given thanks, (b) he brake it, and gave it to his disciples, saying, Take, eat, (c) this is my Body which is given for you: Do this in remembrance of me. Likewise after supper he (d) took the Cup; and, when he had given thanks, he gave it to them, saying, Drink ye all of this; for this (e) is my Blood of the New Testament, which is shed for you and for many for the remission of sins: Do this, as oft as ye shall drink it, in remembrance of me. Amen.

(a) Here the Priest is to take the Paten unto his hands: (b) And here to break the Bread: (c) And here to lay his hand upon all the Bread. (d) Here he is to take the Cup into his hand: (e) And here to lay his hand upon every vessel (be it Chalice or Flagon) in which there is any Wine to be consecrated.

THE Body of our Lord Jesus Christ, which was given for thee, preserve thy body and soul unto everlasting life. Take and eat this in remembrance that Christ died for thee, and feed on him in thy heart by faith with thanksgiving.

THE Blood of our Lord Jesus Christ, which was shed for thee, preserve thy body and soul unto everlasting life. Drink this in remembrance that Christ's Blood was shed for thee, and be thankful.

O LORD and heavenly Father, we thy humble servants entirely desire thy fatherly goodness mercifully to accept this our sacrifice of praise and thanksgiving; most humbly beseeching thee to grant, that by the merits and death of thy Son Jesus Christ, and through faith in his blood, we and all thy whole Church may obtain remission of our sins, and all other benefits of his passion. And here we offer and present unto thee, O Lord, ourselves, our souls and bodies, to be a reasonable, holy, and lively sacrifice unto thee; humbly beseeching thee, that all we, who are partakers of this holy Communion, may be fulfilled with thy grace and heavenly benediction. And although we be unworthy, through our manifold sins, to offer unto thee any sacrifice, yet we beseech thee to accept this our bounden duty and service; not weighing our merits, but pardoning our offences, through Jesus Christ our Lord; by whom, and with whom, in the unity of the Holy Ghost, all honor and glory be unto thee, O Father Almighty, world without end. Amen.

Or this.

ALMIGHTY and everliving God, we most heartily thank thee, for that thou dost vouchsafe to feed us, who have duly received these holy mysteries, with the spiritual food of the most precious Body and Blood of thy Son our Savior Jesus Christ; and dost assure us thereby of thy favor and goodness towards us; and that we are very members incorporate in the mystical body of thy Son, which is the blessed company of all faithful people; and are also heirs through hope of thy everlasting kingdom, by the merits of the most precious death and passion of thy dear Son. And we most humbly beseech thee, O heavenly Father, so to assist us with thy grace, that we may continue in that holy fellowship, and do all such good works as thou hast prepared for us to walk in; through Jesus Christ our Lord, to whom, with thee and the Holy Ghost, be all honor and glory, world without end. Amen.

Then shall be said or sung,
GLORY be to God on high, and in earth peace, good will towards men. We praise thee, we bless thee, we worship thee, we glorify thee, we give thanks to thee for thy great glory, O Lord God, heavenly King, God the Father Almighty. O Lord, the only begotten Son Jesu Christ; O Lord God, Lamb of God, Son of the Father, that takest away the sins of the world, have mercy upon us. Thou that takest away the sins of the world, have mercy upon us. Thou that takest away the sins of the world, receive our prayer. Thou that sittest at the right hand of God the Father, have mercy upon us.

For thou only art holy; thou only art the Lord; thou only, O Christ, with the Holy Ghost, art most high in the glory of God the Father. Amen.

Then the Priest (or Bishop if he be present) shall let them depart with this Blessing
THE peace of God, which passeth all understanding, keep your hearts and minds in the knowledge and love of God, and of his son Jesus Christ our Lord: and the blessing of God Almighty, the Father, the Son, and the Holy Ghost, be amongst you and remain with you always. Amen.

ASSIST us mercifully, O Lord, in these our supplications and prayers, and dispose the way of thy servants towards the attainment of everlasting salvation; that, among all the changes and chances of this mortal life, they may ever be defended by thy most gracious and ready help; through Jesus Christ our Lord. Amen.

O ALMIGHTY Lord, and everlasting God, vouchsafe, we beseech thee, to direct, sanctify, and govern, both our hearts and bodies, in the ways of thy laws, and in the works of thy commandments; that through thy most mighty protection, both here and ever, we may be pre-served in body and soul; through our Lord and Savior Jesus Christ. Amen.

GRANT, we beseech thee, Almighty God, that the words, which we have heard this day with our outward ears, may through thy grace be so grafted inwardly in our hearts, that they may bring forth in us the fruit of good living, to the honor and praise of thy Name; through Jesus Christ our Lord. Amen.

PREVENT us O Lord, in all our doings with thy most gracious favor, and further us with thy continual help; that in all our works begun, continued, and ended in thee, we may glorify thy holy Name, and finally by thy mercy obtain everlasting life; through Jesus Christ our Lord. Amen.

ALMIGHTY God, the fountain of all wisdom, who knowest our necessities before we ask, and our ignorance in asking; We beseech thee to have compassion upon our infirmities; and those things, which for our unworthiness we dare not, and for our blindness we cannot ask, vouchsafe to give us, for the worthiness of thy Son Jesus Christ our Lord. Amen.

ALMIGHTY God, who hast promised to hear the petitions of them that ask in thy Son's Name; We beseech thee mercifully to incline thine ears to us that have made now our prayers and supplications unto thee; and grant, that those things, which we have faithfully asked according to thy will, may effectually be obtained, to the relief of our necessity, and to the setting forth of thy glory; through Jesus Christ our Lord. Amen.

THE MINISTRATION OF PUBLIC BAPTISM OF INFANTS TO BE USED IN THE CHURCH
ALMIGHTY and everlasting God, who of thy great mercy didst save Noah and his family in the ark from perishing by water; and also didst safely lead the children of Israel thy people through the Red Sea, figuring thereby thy holy Baptism; and by the Baptism of thy well-beloved Son Jesus Christ, in the river Jordan, didst sanctify Water to the mystical washing away of sin: We beseech thee, for thine infinite mercies, that thou wilt mercifully look upon this Child; wash him and sanctify him with the Holy Ghost; that he, being delivered from thy wrath, may be received into the ark of Christ's Church; and being steadfast in faith, joyful through hope, and rooted in charity, may so pass the waves of this troublesome world, that finally he may come to the land of everlasting life, there to reign with thee world without end, through Jesus Christ our Lord. Amen.

ALMIGHTY and immortal God, the aid of all that need, the helper of all that flee to thee for succor, the life of them that believe, and the resurrection of the dead: We call upon thee for this Infant, that he, coming to thy holy Baptism, may receive remission of his sins by spiritual regeneration. Receive him, O Lord, as thou hast promised by thy well-beloved Son, saying, Ask, and ye shall have; seek, and ye shall find; knock, and it shall be opened unto you: So give now unto us that ask; let us that seek find; open the gate unto us that knock; that this Infant may enjoy the everlasting benediction of thy heavenly washing, and may come to the eternal kingdom which thou hast promised by Christ our Lord. Amen.

ALMIGHTY and everlasting God, heavenly Father, we give thee humble thanks that thou hast vouchsafed to call us to the knowledge of thy grace and faith in thee: Increase this knowledge, and confirm this faith in us evermore. Give thy Holy Spirit to this Infant, that he may be born again, and be made an heir of everlasting salvation, through our Lord Jesus Christ, who liveth and reigneth with thee and the Holy Spirit, now and for ever. Amen.

O MERCIFUL God, grant that the old Adam in this Child may be so buried, that the new man may be raised up in him. Amen.

Grant that all carnal affections may die in him, and that all things belonging to the Spirit may live and grow in him. Amen.

Grant that he may have power and strength, to have victory, and to triumph against the devil, the world, and the flesh. Amen.

Grant that whosoever is here dedicated to thee by our office and ministry may also be endued with heavenly virtues, and everlastingly rewarded, through thy mercy, O blessed Lord God, who dost live, and govern all things, world without end. Amen.

ALMIGHTY everliving God, whose most dearly beloved Son Jesus Christ, for the forgiveness of our sins, did shed out of his most precious side both water and blood; and gave commandment to his disciples, that they should go teach all nations, and baptize them in the Name of the Father, and of the Son, and of the Holy Ghost: Regard, we beseech thee, the supplications of thy congregation; sanctify this Water to the mystical washing away of sin; and grant that this Child now to be baptized therein, may receive the fullness of thy grace, and ever remain in the number of thy faithful and elect children; through Jesus Christ our Lord. Amen.

N. I baptize thee in the Name of the Father, and of the Son, and of the Holy Ghost. Amen.

WE receive this Child into the Congregation of Christ's flock, *and do sign him with the sign of the Cross, in token that hereafter he shall not be ashamed to confess the faith of Christ crucified, and manfully to fight under his banner against sin, the world, and the devil, and to continue Christ's faithful soldier and servant unto his life's end. Amen.

SEEING now, dearly beloved brethren, that this Child is regenerate and grafted into the body of Christ's Church, let us give thanks unto Almighty God for these benefits, and with one accord make our prayers unto him, that this Child may lead the rest of his life according to this beginning.

WE yield thee hearty thanks, most merciful Father, that it hath pleased thee to regenerate this Infant with thy Holy Spirit, to receive him for thine own Child by adoption, and to incorporate him into thy holy Church. And humbly we beseech thee to grant that he being dead unto sin, and living unto righteousness, and being buried with Christ in his death, may crucify the old man, and utterly abolish the whole body of sin; and that, as he is made partaker of the death of thy Son, he may also be partaker of his resurrection; so that finally, with the residue of thy holy Church, he may be an inheritor of thine everlasting kingdom; through Christ our Lord. Amen.

THE MINISTRATION OF PRIVATE BAPTISM OF CHILDREN, IN HOUSES

N. I baptize thee in the Name of the Father, and of the Son, and of the Holy Ghost. Amen.

WE yield thee hearty thanks, most merciful Father, that it hath pleased thee to regenerate this Infant with thy Holy Spirit, to receive him for thine own Child by adoption, and to incorporate him into thy holy Church. And we humbly beseech thee to grant, that as he is now made partaker of the death of thy Son,

so he may be also of his resurrection; and that finally, with the residue of thy Saints, he may inherit thine everlasting kingdom; through the same thy Son Jesus Christ our Lord. Amen.

ALMIGHTY and everlasting God, heavenly Father, we give thee humble thanks, that thou hast vouchsafed to call us to the knowledge of thy grace, and faith in thee: Increase this knowledge, and confirm this faith in us evermore. Give thy Holy Spirit to this Infant, that he, being born again, and being made an heir of everlasting salvation, through our Lord Jesus Christ, may continue thy servant, and attain thy promise; through the same our Lord Jesus Christ thy Son, who liveth and reigneth with thee and the Holy Spirit, now and for ever. Amen.

WE receive this Child into the congregation of Christ's flock, *and do sign him with the sign of the Cross, in token that hereafter he shall not be ashamed to confess the faith of Christ crucified, and manfully to fight under his banner, against sin, the world, and the devil; and to continue Christ's faithful soldier and servant unto his life's end. Amen.

　* Here the Priest shall make a Cross upon the Child's forehead.

WE yield thee most hearty thanks, most merciful Father, that it hath pleased thee to regenerate this Infant with thy Holy Spirit, to receive him for thine own Child by adoption, and to incorporate him into thy holy Church. And humbly we beseech thee to grant, that he being dead unto sin, and living unto righteousness, and being buried with Christ in his death, may crucify the old man, and utterly abolish the whole body of sin; and that, as he is made partaker of the death of thy Son, he may also be partaker of his resurrection; so that finally, with the residue of thy holy Church, he may be an inheritor of thine everlasting kingdom; through Jesus Christ our Lord. Amen.

IF thou art not already baptized, N. I baptize thee in the name of the Father, and of the Son, and of the Holy Ghost. Amen.

THE MINISTRATION OF PUBLIC BAPTISM

TO SUCH AS ARE OF RIPER YEARS, AND
ABLE TO ANSWER FOR THEMSELVES

ALMIGHTY and everlasting God, who of thy great mercy didst save Noah and his family in the ark from perishing by water; and also didst safely lead the children of Israel thy people through the Red Sea, figuring thereby thy holy Baptism; and by the Baptism of thy well-beloved Son Jesus Christ, in the river Jordan, didst sanctify the element of Water to the mystical washing away of sin: We beseech thee, for thine infinite mercies, that thou wilt mercifully look upon these thy servants; wash them and sanctify them with the Holy Ghost, that they, being delivered from thy wrath, may be received into the ark of Christ's Church; and being steadfast in faith, joyful through hope, and rooted in charity, may so pass the waves of this troublesome world, that finally they may come to the land of everlasting life, there to reign with thee world without end; through Jesus Christ our Lord. Amen.

ALMIGHTY and immortal God, the aid of all that need, the helper of all that flee to thee for succor, the life of them that believe, and the resurrection of the dead: We call upon thee for these persons, that they, coming to thy holy Baptism, may receive remission of their sins by spiritual regeneration. Receive them, O Lord, as thou hast promised by thy well-beloved Son, saying, Ask, and ye shall receive; seek, and ye shall find; knock, and it shall be opened unto you: So give now unto us that ask; let us that seek find; open the gate unto us that knock; that these persons may enjoy the everlasting benediction of thy heavenly washing, and may come to the eternal kingdom which thou hast promised by Christ our Lord. Amen.

ALMIGHTY and everlasting God, heavenly Father, we give thee humble thanks, for that thou hast vouchsafed to call us to the knowledge of thy grace, and faith in thee: Increase this knowledge, and confirm this faith in us evermore. Give thy Holy Spirit to these persons, that they may be born again, and be made heirs of everlasting salvation; through our Lord Jesus Christ, who liveth and reigneth with thee and the Holy Spirit, now and for ever. Amen.

O MERCIFUL God, grant that the old Adam in these persons may be so buried, that the new man may be raised up in them. Amen.

Grant that all carnal affections may die in them, and that all things belonging to the Spirit may live and grow in them. Amen.

Grant that they may have power and strength to have victory, and to triumph, against the devil, the world, and the flesh. Amen.

Grant that they, being here dedicated to thee by our office and ministry, may also be endued with heavenly virtues, and everlastingly rewarded, through thy mercy, O blessed Lord God, who dost live, and govern all things, world without end. Amen.

ALMIGHTY, everliving God, whose most dearly beloved Son Jesus Christ, for the forgiveness of our sins, did shed out of his most precious side both water and blood, and gave commandment to his disciples, that they should go teach all nations, and baptize them In the Name of the Father, the Son, and the Holy Ghost: Regard, we beseech thee, the supplications of this congregation; sanctify this Water to the mystical washing away of sin; and grant that the persons now to be baptized therein may receive the fullness of thy grace, and ever remain in the number of thy faithful and elect children, through Jesus Christ our Lord. Amen.

N. I baptize thee In the Name of the Father, and of the Son, and of the Holy Ghost. Amen.

Then shall the Priest say,
WE receive this person into the congregation of Christ's flock; *and do sign *him* with the sign of the Cross, in token that hereafter *he* shall not be ashamed to confess the faith of Christ crucified, and manfully to fight under his banner, against sin, the world, and the devil; and to continue Christ's faithful soldier and servant unto *his* life's end. Amen.

 * Here the Priest shall make a Cross upon the person's forehead.

WE yield thee humble thanks, O heavenly Father, that thou hast vouchsafed to call us to the knowledge of thy grace, and faith in thee;

Increase this knowledge, and confirm this faith in us evermore. Give thy Holy Spirit to these persons; that, being now born again, and made heirs of everlasting salvation, through our Lord Jesus Christ, they may continue thy servants, and attain thy promises; through the same Lord Jesus Christ thy Son, who liveth and reigneth with thee, in the unity of the same Holy Spirit, everlastingly. Amen.

THE ORDER OF CONFIRMATION

Or Laying on of Hands upon Those That Are Baptized and Come to Years of Discretion.

ALMIGHTY and everliving God, who hast vouchsafed to regenerate these thy servants by Water and the Holy Ghost, and hast given unto them forgiveness of all their sins: Strengthen them, we beseech thee, O Lord, with the Holy Ghost the Comforter, and daily increase in them thy manifold gifts of grace; the spirit of wisdom and understanding; the spirit of counsel and ghostly strength; the spirit of knowledge and true godliness; and fill them, O Lord, with the spirit of thy holy fear, now and for ever. Amen.

DEFEND, O Lord, this thy Child [or this thy Servant] with thy heavenly grace, that he may continue thine for ever; and daily increase in thy Holy Spirit more and more, until he come unto thy everlasting kingdom. Amen.

ALMIGHTY and everliving God, who makest us both to will and to do those things that be good and acceptable unto thy divine Majesty; We make our humble supplications unto thee for these thy servants, upon whom (after the example of thy holy Apostles) we have now laid our hands, to certify them (by this sign) of thy favor and gracious goodness towards them. Let thy fatherly hand, we beseech thee, ever be over them, let thy Holy Spirit ever be with them; and so lead them in the knowledge and obedience of thy Word, that in the end they may obtain everlasting life; through our Lord Jesus Christ, who with thee and the Holy Ghost liveth and reigneth, ever one God, world without end. Amen.

O ALMIGHTY Lord, and everlasting God, vouchsafe, we O beseech thee, to direct, sanctify, and govern, both our hearts and bodies, in the ways of thy laws, and in the works of thy commandments; that, through thy most mighty protection both here and ever, we may be preserved in body and soul; through our Lord and Savior Jesus Christ. Amen.

THE Blessing of God Almighty, the Father, the Son, and the Holy Ghost, be upon you, and remain with you for ever. Amen.

THE FORM OF SOLEMNIZATION OF MATRIMONY

O ETERNAL God, Creator and Preserver of all mankind, Giver of all spiritual grace, the Author of everlasting life: Send thy blessing upon these thy servants, this man and this woman, whom we bless in thy Name; that, as Isaac and Rebecca lived faithfully together, so these persons may surely perform and keep the vow and covenant betwixt them made, (whereof this Ring given and received is a token and pledge,) and may ever remain in perfect love and peace together, and live according to thy laws; through Jesus Christ our Lord. Amen.

GOD the Father, God the Son, God the Holy Ghost, bless, preserve, and keep you; the Lord mercifully with his favor look upon you; and so fill you with all spiritual benediction and grace, that ye may so live together in this life, that in the world to come ye may have life everlasting. Amen.

O GOD of Abraham, God of Isaac, God of Jacob, bless these thy servants, and sow the seed of eternal life in their hearts; that whatsoever in thy holy Word they shall profitably learn, they may in deed fulfill the same. Look, O Lord, mercifully upon them from heaven, and bless them. And as thou didst send thy blessing upon Abraham and Sarah, to their great comfort, so vouchsafe to send thy blessing upon these thy servants; that they obeying thy Will, and alway being in safety under thy protection, may abide in thy love unto their lives' end; through Jesus Christ our Lord. Amen.

This Prayer next following shall be omitted, where the Woman is past child-bearing

O MERCIFUL Lord, and heavenly Father, by whose gracious gift mankind is increased: We beseech thee, assist with thy blessing these two persons, that they may both be fruitful in procreation of children, and also live together so long in godly love and honesty, that they may see their children Christianly and virtuously brought up, to thy praise and honor; through Jesus Christ our Lord. Amen.

O GOD, who by thy mighty power hast made all things of nothing; who also (after other things set in order) didst appoint, that out of man (created after thine own image and similitude) woman should take her beginning; and, knitting them together, didst teach that it should never be lawful to put asunder those whom thou by Matrimony hadst made one: O God, who hast consecrated the state of Matrimony to such an excellent mystery, that in it is signified and represented the spiritual marriage and unity betwixt Christ and his Church: Look mercifully upon these thy servants, that both this man may love his wife, according to thy Word, (as Christ did love his spouse the Church, who gave himself for it, loving and cherishing it even as his own flesh,) and also that this woman may be loving and amiable, faithful and obedient to her husband; and in all quietness, sobriety, and peace, be a follower of holy and godly matrons. O Lord, bless them both, and grant them to inherit thy everlasting kingdom; through Jesus Christ our Lord. Amen.

ALMIGHTY God, who at the beginning did create our first parents, Adam and Eve, and did sanctify and join them together in marriage; Pour upon you the riches of his grace, sanctify and bless you, that ye may please him both in body and soul, and live together in holy love unto your lives' end. Amen.

THE ORDER FOR THE VISITATION OF THE SICK

PEACE be to this house, and to all that dwell in it.

REMEMBER not, Lord, our iniquities, nor the iniquities of our forefathers: Spare us, good Lord, spare thy people, whom thou hast redeemed with thy most precious blood, and be not angry with us for ever.

Answer. Spare us, good Lord.

O LORD, look down from heaven, behold, visit, and relieve this thy servant. Look upon him with the eyes of thy mercy, give him comfort and sure confidence in thee, defend him from the danger of the enemy, and keep him in perpetual peace and safety; through Jesus Christ our Lord. Amen.

HEAR us, Almighty and most merciful God and Savior; extend thy accustomed goodness to this thy servant who is grieved with sickness. Sanctify, we beseech thee, this thy fatherly correction to him; that the sense of his weakness may add strength to his faith, and seriousness to his repentance: That, if it shall be thy good pleasure to restore him to his former health, he may lead the residue of his life in thy fear, and to thy glory: or else, give him grace so to take thy visitation, that, after this painful life ended, he may dwell with thee in life everlasting; through Jesus Christ our Lord. Amen.

OUR Lord Jesus Christ, who hath left power to his Church to absolve all sinners who truly repent and believe in him, of his great mercy forgive thee thine offences: And by his authority committed to me, I absolve thee from all thy sins, In the Name of the Father, and of the Son, and of the Holy Ghost. Amen.

And then the Priest shall say the Collect following

Let us pray.

O MOST merciful God, who, according to the multitude of thy mercies, dost so put away the sins of those who truly repent, that thou rememberest them no more: Open thine eye of mercy upon this thy servant, who most earnestly desireth pardon and forgiveness. Renew in him, most loving Father, whatsoever hath been decayed by the fraud and malice of the devil, or by his own carnal will and frailness; preserve and continue this sick member in the unity of the Church; consider his contrition, accept his tears, assuage his pain, as shall seem to thee most expedient for him. And forasmuch as he putteth his full trust only in thy mercy, impute not unto him his former sins, but strengthen him with thy blessed Spirit; and, when thou art pleased to take him hence, take him unto thy favor, through the merits of thy most dearly beloved Son Jesus Christ our Lord. Amen.

O SAVIOR of the world, who by thy Cross and precious Blood hast redeemed us, Save us, and help us, we humbly beseech thee, O Lord.

Then shall the Minister say,
THE Almighty Lord, who is a most strong tower to all them that put their trust in him, to whom all things in heaven, in earth, and under the earth, do bow and obey, be now and evermore thy defense; and make thee know and feel, that there is none other Name under heaven given to man, in whom, and through whom, thou mayest receive health and salvation, but only the Name of our Lord Jesus Christ. Amen.

And after that shall say,
UNTO God's gracious mercy and protection we commit thee. The Lord bless thee, and keep thee. The Lord make his face to shine upon thee, and be gracious unto thee. The Lord lift up his countenance upon thee, and give thee peace, both now and evermore. Amen.

A Prayer for a sick Child
O ALMIGHTY God, and merciful Father, to whom alone belong the issues of life and death: Look down from heaven, we humbly beseech thee, with the eyes of mercy upon this child now lying upon the bed of sickness: Visit him, O Lord, with thy salvation; deliver him in thy good appointed time from his bodily pain, and save his soul for thy mercies' sake: That, if it shall be thy pleasure to prolong his days here on earth, he may live to thee, and be an instrument of thy glory, by serving thee faithfully, and doing good in his generation; or else receive him into those heavenly habitations, where the souls of them that sleep in the Lord Jesus enjoy perpetual rest and felicity. Grant this, O Lord, for thy mercies' sake, in the same thy Son our Lord Jesus Christ, who liveth and

reigneth with thee and the Holy Ghost, ever one God, world without end. Amen.

A Prayer for a sick person, when there appeareth small hope of recovery
O FATHER of mercies, and God of all comfort, our only help in time of need: We fly unto thee for succor in behalf of this thy servant, here lying under thy hand in great weakness of body. Look graciously upon him, O Lord; and the more the outward man decayeth, strengthen him, we beseech thee, so much the more continually with thy grace and Holy Spirit in the inner man. Give him unfeigned repentance for all the errors of his life past, and steadfast faith in thy Son Jesus; that his sins may be done away by thy mercy, and his pardon sealed in heaven, before he go hence, and be no more seen. We know, O Lord, that there is no word impossible with thee; and that, if thou wilt, thou canst even yet raise him up, and grant him a longer continuance amongst us: Yet, forasmuch as in all appearance the time of his dissolution draweth near, so fit and prepare him, we beseech thee, against the hour of death, that after his departure hence in peace, and in thy favor, his soul may be received into thine everlasting kingdom, through the merits and mediation of Jesus Christ, thine only Son, our Lord and Savior. Amen.

A commendatory Prayer for a sick person at the point of departure
O ALMIGHTY God, with whom do live the spirits of just men made perfect, after they are delivered from their earthly prisons: We humbly commend the soul of this thy servant, our dear brother, into thy hands, as into the hands of a faithful Creator, and most merciful Savior; most humbly beseeching thee, that it may be precious in thy sight. Wash it, we pray thee, in the blood of that immaculate Lamb, that was slain to take away the sins of the world; that whatsoever defilements it may have contracted in the midst of this miserable and naughty world, through the lusts of the flesh, or the wiles of Satan, being purged and done away, it may be presented pure and without spot before thee. And teach us who survive, in this and other like daily spectacles of mortality, to see how frail and uncertain our

own condition is; and so to number our days, that we may seriously apply our hearts to that holy and heavenly wisdom, whilst we live here, which may in the end bring us to life everlasting, through the merits of Jesus Christ thine only Son our Lord. Amen.

A Prayer for persons troubled in mind or in conscience

O BLESSED Lord, the Father of mercies, and the God of all comforts: We beseech thee, took down in pity and compassion upon this thy afflicted servant. Thou writest bitter things against him, and makest him to possess his former iniquities; thy wrath lieth hard upon him, and his soul is full of trouble: But, O merciful God, who hast written thy holy Word for our learning, that we, through patience and comfort of thy holy Scriptures, might have hope; give him a right understanding of himself, and of thy threats and promises; that he may neither cast away his confidence in thee, nor place it any where but in thee. Give him strength against all his temptations, and heal all his distempers. Break not the bruised reed, nor quench the smoking flax. Shut not up thy tender mercies in displeasure; but make him to hear of joy and gladness, that the bones which thou hast broken may rejoice. Deliver him from fear of the enemy, and lift up the light of thy countenance upon him, and give him peace, through the merits and mediation of Jesus Christ our Lord. Amen.

THE COMMUNION OF THE SICK
The Collect

ALMIGHTY, everliving God, Maker of mankind, who dost correct those whom thou dost love, and chastise every one whom thou dost receive: We beseech thee to have mercy upon this thy servant visited with thine hand, and to grant that he may take his sickness patiently, and recover his bodily health, (if it be thy gracious will;) and whensoever his soul shall depart from the body, it may be without spot presented unto thee; through Jesus Christ our Lord. Amen.

THE ORDER FOR THE BURIAL OF THE DEAD

FORASMUCH as it hath pleased Almighty God of his great mercy to take unto himself the soul of our dear brother here departed, we therefore commit his body to the ground; earth to earth, ashes to ashes, dust to dust; in sure and certain hope of the Resurrection to eternal life, through our Lord Jesus Christ; who shall change our vile body, that it may be like unto his glorious body, according to the mighty working, whereby he is able to subdue all things to himself.

I HEARD a voice from heaven, saying unto me, Write, From henceforth blessed are the dead which die in the Lord: even so saith the Spirit: for they rest from their labors.

ALMIGHTY God, with whom do live the spirits of them that depart hence in the Lord, and with whom the souls of the faithful, after they are delivered from the burden of the flesh, are in joy and felicity: We give thee hearty thanks, for that it hath pleased thee to deliver this our brother out of the miseries of this sinful world; beseeching thee, that it may please thee, of thy gracious goodness, shortly to accomplish the number of thine elect, and to hasten thy kingdom; that we, with all those that are departed in the true faith of thy holy Name, may have our perfect consummation and bliss, both in body and soul, in thy eternal and everlasting glory; through Jesus Christ our Lord. Amen.

The Collect

O MERCIFUL God, the Father of our Lord Jesus Christ, who is the resurrection and the life; in whom whosoever believeth shall live, though he die; and whosoever liveth, and believeth in him, shall not die eternally; who also hath taught us, by his holy Apostle Saint Paul, not to be sorry, as men without hope, for them that sleep in him: We meekly beseech thee, O Father, to raise us from the death of sin unto the life of righteousness; that, when we shall depart this life, we may rest in him, as our hope is this our brother doth; and that, at the general Resurrection in the last day, we may be found acceptable in thy sight; and receive that blessing, which thy well-beloved Son shall then pronounce to all that love and fear thee, saying, Come, ye blessed children of my Father, receive the kingdom prepared for you from the beginning of the world: Grant this, we beseech thee,

O merciful Father, through Jesus Christ, our Mediator and Redeemer. Amen.

THE grace of our Lord Jesus Christ, and the love of God and the fellowship of the Holy Ghost, be with us all evermore. Amen.

THE THANKSGIVING OF WOMEN AFTER CHILD-BIRTH COMMONLY CALLED CHURCHING OF WOMEN

O ALMIGHTY God, we give thee humble thanks for that thou hast vouchsafed to deliver this woman thy servant from the great pain and peril of Child-birth: Grant, we beseech thee, most merciful Father, that she, through thy help, may both faithfully live, and walk according to thy will, in this life present; and also may be partaker of everlasting glory in the life to come; through Jesus Christ our Lord. Amen.

A COMMINATION, or Denouncing of God's Anger and Judgments against Sinners, With certain Prayers, to be used on the first Day of Lent, and at other times, as the Ordinary shall appoint.

O LORD, we beseech thee, mercifully hear our prayers, and spare all those who confess their sins unto thee; that they, whose consciences by sin are accused, by thy merciful pardon may be absolved; through Christ our Lord. Amen.

O MOST mighty God, and merciful Father, who hast compassion upon all men, and hatest nothing that thou hast made; who wouldest not the death of a sinner, but that he should rather turn from his sin, and be saved: Mercifully forgive us our trespasses; receive and comfort us, who are grieved and wearied with the burden of our sins. Thy property is always to have mercy; to thee only it appertaineth to forgive sins. Spare us therefore, good Lord, spare thy people, whom thou hast redeemed; enter not into judgment with thy servants, who are vile earth, and miserable sinners; but so turn thine anger from us, who meekly acknowledge our vileness, and truly repent us of our faults, and so make haste to help us in this world, that we may ever live with thee in the world to come; through Jesus Christ our Lord. Amen.

Then shall the people say this that followeth, after the Minister

TURN thou us, O good Lord, and so shall we be turned. Be favorable, O Lord, Be favorable to thy people, Who turn to thee in weeping, fasting, and praying. For thou art a merciful God, Full of compassion. Longsuffering, and of great pity. Thou sparest when we deserve punishment, And in thy wrath thinkest upon mercy. Spare thy people, good Lord, spare them, And let not thine heritage be brought to confusion. Hear us, O Lord, for thy mercy is great, And after the multitude of thy mercies look upon us; Through the merits and mediation of thy blessed Son, Jesus Christ our Lord. Amen.

Then the Minister alone shall say,

THE Lord bless us, and keep us; the Lord lift up the light of his countenance upon us, and give us peace, now and for evermore. Amen.

FORMS OF PRAYER TO BE USED AT SEA
The Collect

PREVENT us, O Lord, in all our doings, with thy most gracious favor, and further us with thy continual help; that in all our works begun, continued, and ended in thee, we may glorify thy holy Name, and finally by thy mercy obtain everlasting life; through Jesus Christ our Lord. Amen.

Prayers to be used in Storms at Sea

O MOST powerful and glorious Lord God, at whose command the winds blow, and lift up the waves of the sea, and who stillest the rage thereof. We thy creatures, but miserable sinners, do in this our great distress cry unto thee for help: Save, Lord, or else we perish. We confess, when we have been safe, and seen all things quiet about us, we have forgot thee our God, and refused to hearken to the still voice of thy word, and to obey thy commandments: But now we see, how terrible thou art in all thy works of wonder; the great God to be feared above all: And therefore we adore thy Divine Majesty, acknowledging thy power, and imploring thy goodness. Help, Lord, and save us for thy mercy's sake in Jesus Christ thy Son, our Lord. Amen.

Or this

O MOST glorious and gracious Lord God, who dwellest in heaven, but beholdest all things below: Look down, we beseech thee, and hear us, calling out of the depth of misery, and out of the jaws of this death, which is ready now to swallow us up: Save, Lord, or else we perish. The living, the living, shalt praise thee. O send thy word of command to rebuke the raging winds, and the roaring sea; that we, being delivered from this distress, may live to serve thee, and to glorify thy Name all the days of our life. Hear, Lord, and save us, for the infinite merits of our blessed Savior, thy Son, our Lord Jesus Christ. Amen.

Short Prayers in respect of a Storm

THOU, O Lord, that stillest the raging of the sea, hear, hear us, and save us, that we perish not.

O blessed Savior, that didst save thy disciples ready to perish in a storm, hear us, and save us, we beseech thee.

Lord, have mercy upon us.

Christ, have mercy upon us.

Lord, have mercy upon us.

Lord, hear us.

Christ, hear us.

God the Father, God the Son, God the Holy Ghost, have mercy upon us, save us now and evermore. Amen.

Collects of Thanksgiving

O MOST blessed and glorious Lord God, who art of infinite goodness and mercy: We thy poor creatures, whom thou hast made and preserved, holding our souls in life, and now rescuing us out of the jaws of death, humbly present ourselves again before thy Divine Majesty, to offer a sacrifice of praise and thanksgiving, for that thou heardest us when we called in our trouble, and didst not cast out our prayer, which we made before thee in our great distress: Even when we gave all for lost, our ship, our goods, our lives, then didst thou mercifully look upon us, and wonderfully command a deliverance; for which we, now being in safety, do give all praise and glory to thy holy Name; through Jesus Christ our Lord. Amen.

Or, this:

O MOST mighty and gracious good God, thy mercy is over all thy works, but in special manner hath been extended toward us, whom thou hast so powerfully and wonderfully defended. Thou hast shewed us terrible things, and wonders in the deep, that we might see how powerful and gracious a God thou art; how able and ready to help them that trust in thee. Thou hast shewed us how both winds and seas obey thy command; that we may learn, even from them, hereafter to obey thy voice, and to do thy will. We therefore bless and glorify thy Name, for this thy mercy in saving us, when we were ready to perish. And, we beseech thee, make us as truly sensible now of thy mercy, as we were then of the danger: And give us hearts always ready to express our thankfulness, not only by words, but also by our lives, in being more obedient to thy holy commandments. Continue, we beseech thee, this thy goodness to us; that we, whom thou hast saved, may serve thee in holiness and righteousness all the days of our life; through Jesus Christ our Lord and Savior. Amen.

A Hymn of Praise and Thanksgiving after a dangerous Tempest

O COME, let us give thanks unto the Lord, for he is gracious: and his mercy endureth for ever.

Great is the Lord, and greatly to be praised; let the redeemed of the Lord say so: whom he hath delivered from the merciless rage of the sea.

The Lord is gracious and full of compassion: slow to anger, and of great mercy.

He hath not dealt with us according to our sins: neither rewarded us according to our iniquities.

But as the heaven is high above the earth: so great hath been his mercy towards us.

We found trouble and heaviness: we were even at death's door.

The waters of the sea had well-nigh covered us: the proud waters had well-nigh gone over our soul.

The sea roared: and the stormy wind lifted up the waves thereof.

We were carried up as it were to heaven, and then down again into the deep: our soul melted within us, because of trouble;

Then cried we unto thee, O Lord: and thou didst deliver us out of our distress.

Blessed be thy Name, who didst not despise the prayer of thy servants: but didst hear our cry, and hast saved us.

Thou didst send forth thy commandment: and the windy storm ceased, and was turned into a calm.

O let us therefore praise the Lord for his goodness: and declare the wonders that he hath done, and still doeth for the children of men.

Praised be the Lord daily: even the Lord that helpeth us, and poureth his benefits upon us.

He is our God, even the God of whom cometh salvation: God is the Lord by whom we have escaped death.

Thou, Lord, hast made us glad through the operation of thy hands: and we will triumph in thy praise.

Blessed be the Lord God: even the Lord God, who only doeth wondrous things;

And blessed be the Name of his Majesty for ever: and let every one of us say, Amen, Amen.

Glory be to the Father, and to the Son: and to the Holy Ghost;

As it was in the beginning, is now, and ever shall be: world without end. Amen.

THE FORM OF ORDAINING OR CONSECRATING OF AN ARCHBISHOP OR BISHOP

The Collect

ALMIGHTY God, who by thy Son Jesus Christ didst give to thy holy Apostles many excellent gifts, and didst charge them to feed thy flock; Give grace, we beseech thee, to all Bishops, the Pastors of thy Church, that they may diligently preach thy Word, and duly administer the godly Discipline thereof; and grant to the people, that they may obediently follow the same; that all may receive the crown of everlasting glory; through the same thy Son Jesus Christ our Lord. Amen.

ALMIGHTY God, giver of all good things, who by thy Holy Spirit hast appointed divers Orders of Ministers in thy Church; Mercifully behold this thy servant, now called to the Work and Ministry of a Bishop; and so replenish him with the truth of thy Doctrine, and adorn him with innocency of life, that, both by word and deed, he may faithfully serve thee in this Office, to the glory of thy Name, and the edifying and well-governing of thy Church; through the merits of our Savior Jesus Christ, who liveth and reigneth with thee and the same Holy Spirit, world without end. Amen.

ALMIGHTY God, our heavenly Father, who hath given you a good will to do all these things; Grant also unto you strength and power to perform the same; that, he accomplishing in you the good work which he hath begun, you may be found perfect and irreprehensible at the latter day; through Jesus Christ our Lord. Amen.

Veni, Creator Spiritus

COME, Holy Ghost, our souls inspire,
And lighten with celestial fire.
Thou the anointing Spirit art,
Who dost thy sevenfold gifts impart.
Thy blessed unction from above,
Is comfort, life, and fire of love.
Enable with perpetual light
The dullness of our blinded sight.
Anoint and cheer our soiled face
With the abundance of thy grace.
Keep far our foes, give peace at home;
Where thou art guide, no ill can come.
Teach us to know the Father, Son,
And thee, of both, to be but One;
That, through the ages all along,
This may be our endless song:
Praise to thy eternal merit,
Father, Son, and Holy Spirit.

ALMIGHTY God, and most merciful Father, who, of thine infinite goodness, hast given thy only and dearly beloved Son Jesus Christ, to be our Redeemer, and the Author of everlasting life; who, after that he had made perfect our redemption by his death, and was ascended into heaven, poured down his gifts abundantly upon men, making some Apostles, some Prophets, some Evangelists, some Pastors and Doctors, to the edifying and making perfect his Church; Grant, we beseech thee, to this thy servant, such grace, that he may evermore be ready to spread abroad thy Gospel, the glad tidings of reconciliation with thee; and use the authority given him, not to destruction, but to salvation; not to hurt, but to help: so that, as a wise and faithful servant, giving to thy family their portion in due season, he may at last be received into everlasting joy; through the same Jesus Christ our Lord, who, with thee and the Holy Ghost, liveth and reigneth, one God, world without end. Amen.

Then the Archbishop shall deliver him the Bible, saying
GIVE heed unto reading, exhortation, and doctrine. Think upon the things contained in this Book. Be diligent in them, that the increase coming thereby may be manifest unto all men; for by so doing thou shalt both save thyself and them that hear thee. Be to the flock of Christ a shepherd, not a wolf; feed them, devour them not. Hold up the weak, heal the sick, bind up the broken, bring again the outcasts, seek the lost. Be so merciful, that you be not too remiss; so minister discipline, that you forget not mercy; that when the Chief Shepherd shall appear, you may receive the never-fading crown of glory; through Jesus Christ our Lord. Amen.

MOST merciful Father, send down, we beseech thee, upon this thy servant thy heavenly blessing; and so endue him with thy Holy Spirit, that he, preaching thy Word, may not only be earnest to reprove, beseech, and rebuke, with all patience and doctrine; but also may be, to such as believe, a wholesome example in word, in conversation, in love, in faith, in chastity, and in purity; that, faithfully fulfilling his course, at the latter day he may receive the crown of righteousness, laid up by the Lord Jesus, the righteous Judge, who liveth and reigneth with thee and the same Holy Spirit, one God, world without end. Amen.

PREVENT us, O Lord, in all our doings with thy most gracious favor, and further us with thy continual help; that in all our works begun, continued, and ended in thee, we may glorify thy holy Name, and finally by thy mercy obtain everlasting life; through Jesus Christ our Lord. Amen.

THE Peace of God, which passeth all understanding, keep your hearts and minds in the knowledge and love of God, and of his Son Jesus Christ our Lord: And the Blessing of God Almighty, the Father, the Son, and the Holy Ghost, be amongst you, and remain with you always. Amen.

The Form and Manner of Making of Deacons
O GOD, merciful Father, that despisest not the sighing of a contrite heart, nor the desire of such as are sorrowful; Mercifully assist our prayers which we make before thee in all our troubles and adversities, whensoever they oppress us; and graciously hear us, that those evils which the craft and subtilty of the devil or man worketh be brought to nought; and by the providence of thy goodness they may be dispersed; that we thy servants, being hurt by no persecutions, may evermore give thanks unto thee in thy holy Church; through Jesus Christ our Lord.

WE humbly beseech thee, O Father, mercifully to look upon our infirmities; and, for the glory of thy Name, turn from us all those evils that we most justly have deserved; and grant, that in all our troubles we may put our whole trust and confidence in thy mercy, and evermore serve thee in holiness and pureness of living, to thy honor and glory; through our only Mediator and Advocate, Jesus Christ our Lord. Amen.

The Collect
ALMIGHTY God, who by thy divine providence hast appointed divers Orders of Ministers in thy Church, and didst inspire thine Apostles to choose into the Order of Deacons the first Martyr Saint Stephen, with others; Mercifully behold these thy servants now called to the like Office and Administration: so replenish them with the truth of thy Doctrine, and adorn them with innocency of life, that, both by word and good example, they may faithfully serve thee in this Office, to the glory of thy Name, and the edification of thy Church; through the merits of our Savior Jesus Christ, who liveth and reigneth with thee and the Holy Ghost, now and for ever. Amen.

ALMIGHTY God, giver of all good things, who of thy great goodness hast vouchsafed to accept and take these thy servants unto the Office of Deacons in thy Church; Make them, we beseech thee, O Lord, to be modest, humble, and constant in their Ministration, to have a ready will to observe all spiritual Discipline; that they, having always the testimony of a good conscience, and continuing ever stable and strong in thy Son Christ, may so well behave themselves in this inferior Office, that they may be found worthy to be called unto the higher Ministries in thy Church; through the same thy Son our Savior Jesus Christ, to whom be glory and honor, world without end. Amen.

All the saints and other holy days

O almighty God, who hast knit together thine elect in one communion and fellowship, in the mystical body of thy Son Jesus Christ our Lord: grant us grace so to follow thy blessed saints in all virtuous and godly living, that we may come to those unspeakable joys, which thou has prepared for them that unfeignedly love thee; through Jesus Christ our Lord.

Book of Common Prayer, 1549

Book of Common Prayer: Collection of Collects for the Christian Year

The First Sunday of Advent
The Collect

ALMIGHTY God, give us grace that we may cast away the works of darkness, and put upon us the armor of light, now in the time of this mortal life in which thy Son Jesus Christ came to visit us in great humility; that in the last day, when he shall come again in his glorious majesty to judge both the quick and the dead, we may rise to the life immortal; through him who liveth and reigneth with thee and the Holy Ghost, one God, now and for ever. Amen.

The Second Sunday in Advent.
The Collect.

BLESSED Lord, who hast caused all holy Scriptures to be written for our learning; Grant that we may in such wise hear them, read, mark, learn, and inwardly digest them, that by patience and comfort of thy holy Word, we may embrace, and ever hold fast, the blessed hope of everlasting life, which thou hast given us in our Savior Jesus Christ. Amen.

The Third Sunday in Advent
The Collect

O LORD Jesu Christ, who at thy first coming didst send thy messenger to prepare thy way before thee; Grant that the ministers and stewards of thy mysteries may likewise so prepare and make ready thy way, by turning the hearts of the disobedient to the wisdom of the just, that at thy second coming to judge the world we may be found an acceptable people in thy sight, who livest and reignest with the Father and the Holy Spirit ever, one God, world without end. Amen.

The Fourth Sunday in Advent
The Collect

O LORD, raise up (we pray thee) thy power, and come among us, and with great might succor us; that whereas, through our sins and wickedness, we are sore let and hindered in running the race that is set before us, thy bountiful grace and mercy may speedily help and deliver us; through the satisfaction of thy Son our Lord, to whom with thee and the Holy Ghost be honor and glory, world without end. Amen.

The Nativity of our Lord, or the Birth-day of Christ, Commonly called Christmas-Day
The Collect

ALMIGHTY God, who hast given us thy only-begotten Son to take our nature upon him, and as at this time to be born of a pure Virgin; Grant that we being regenerate, and made thy children by adoption and grace, may daily be renewed by thy Holy Spirit; through the same our Lord Jesus Christ, who liveth and reigneth with thee and the same Spirit, ever one God, world without end. Amen.

Saint Stephen's Day
The Collect

Grant, O Lord, that, in all our sufferings here upon earth for the testimony of thy truth, we may steadfastly look up to heaven, and by faith behold the glory that shall be revealed; and, being filled with the Holy Ghost, may learn to love and bless our persecutors by the example of thy first Martyr Saint Stephen, who prayed for his murderers to thee, O blessed Jesus, who standest at the right hand of God to succor all those that suffer for thee, our only Mediator and Advocate. Amen.

Saint John the Evangelist's Day
The Collect
MERCIFUL Lord, we beseech thee to cast thy bright beams of light upon thy Church, that it being enlightened by the doctrine of thy blessed Apostle and Evangelist Saint John may so walk in the light of thy truth, that it may at length attain to the light of everlasting life; through Jesus Christ our Lord. Amen.

The Innocents' Day
The Collect
O ALMIGHTY God, who out of the mouths of babes and sucklings hast ordained strength, and madest infants to glorify thee by their deaths; Mortify and kill all vices in us, and so strengthen us by thy grace, that by the innocency of our lives, and constancy of our faith even unto death, we may glorify thy holy Name; through Jesus Christ our Lord. Amen.

The Sunday after Christmas-Day
The Collect
ALMIGHTY God, who hast given us thy only-begotten Son to take our nature upon him, and as at this time to be born of a pure Virgin; Grant that we being regenerate, and made thy children by adoption and grace, may daily be renewed by thy Holy Spirit; through the same our Lord Jesus Christ, who liveth and reigneth with thee and the same Spirit, one God, world without end. Amen.

The Circumcision of Christ
The Collect
ALMIGHTY God, who madest thy blessed Son to be circumcised, and obedient to the law for man; Grant us the true Circumcision of the Spirit; that, our hearts, and all our members, being mortified from all worldly and carnal lusts, we may in all things obey thy blessed

will; through the same thy Son Jesus Christ our Lord. Amen.

The Epiphany, or the Manifestation of Christ to the Gentiles
The Collect
O GOD, who by the leading of a star didst manifest thy only-begotten Son to the Gentiles: Mercifully grant, that we, which know thee now by faith, may after this life have the fruition of thy glorious Godhead; through Jesus Christ our Lord. Amen.

The First Sunday after the Epiphany
The Collect
O LORD, we beseech thee mercifully to receive the prayers of thy people which call upon thee; and grant that they may both perceive and know what things they ought to do, and also may have grace and power faithfully to fulfill the same; through Jesus Christ our Lord. Amen.

The Second Sunday after the Epiphany
The Collect
ALMIGHTY and everlasting God, who dost govern all things in heaven and earth; Mercifully hear the supplications of thy people, and grant us thy peace all the days of our life; through Jesus Christ our Lord. Amen.

The Third Sunday after the Epiphany
The Collect
ALMIGHTY and everlasting God, mercifully look upon our infirmities, and in all our dangers and necessities stretch forth thy right hand to help and defend us; through Jesus Christ our Lord. Amen.

The Fourth Sunday after the Epiphany
The Collect
O GOD, who knowest us to be set in the midst of so many and great dangers, that by reason of the frailty of our nature we cannot always stand upright; Grant to us such strength and protection, as may support us in all dangers, and carry us through all temptations; through Jesus Christ our Lord. Amen.

The Fifth Sunday after the Epiphany
The Collect
O LORD, we beseech thee to keep thy Church

and household continually in thy true religion; that they who do lean only upon the hope of thy heavenly grace may evermore be defended by thy mighty power; through Jesus Christ our Lord. Amen.

The Sixth Sunday after the Epiphany
The Collect

O GOD, whose blessed Son was manifested that he might destroy the works of the devil, and make us the sons of God, and heirs of eternal life; Grant us, we beseech thee, that, having this hope, we may purify ourselves, even as he is pure; that, when he shall appear again with power and great glory, we may be made like unto him in his eternal and glorious kingdom; where with thee, O Father, and thee, O Holy Ghost, he liveth and reigneth, ever one God, world without end. Amen.

The Sunday called Septuagesima, or the third Sunday before Lent
The Collect

O LORD, we beseech thee favorably to hear the prayers of thy people; that we, who are justly punished for our offences, may be mercifully delivered by thy goodness, for the glory of thy Name; through Jesus Christ our Savior, who liveth and reigneth with thee and the Holy Ghost, ever one God, world without end. Amen.

The Sunday called Sexagesima, or the second Sunday before Lent
The Collect

O LORD God, who seest that we put not our trust in any thing that we do; Mercifully grant that by thy power we may be defended against all adversity; through Jesus Christ our Lord. Amen.

The Sunday called Quinquagesima, or the next Sunday before Lent
The Collect

O LORD, who hast taught us that all our doings without charity are nothing worth; Send thy Holy Ghost and pour into our hearts that most excellent gift of charity, the very bond of peace and of all virtues, without which whosoever liveth is counted dead before thee; Grant this for thine only Son Jesus Christ's sake. Amen.

The First day of Lent, Commonly called Ash-Wednesday
The Collect

ALMIGHTY and everlasting God, who hatest nothing that thou hast made and dost forgive the sins of all them that are penitent; Create and make in us new and contrite hearts, that we, worthily lamenting our sins, and acknowledging our wretchedness, may obtain of thee, the God of all mercy, perfect remission and forgiveness; through Jesus Christ our Lord. Amen.

The First Sunday in Lent
The Collect

O LORD, who for our sake didst fast forty days and forty nights; Give us grace to use such abstinence, that, our flesh being subdued to the Spirit, we may ever obey thy godly motions in righteousness, and true holiness, to thy honor and glory, who livest and reignest with the Father and the Holy Ghost, one God, world without end. Amen.

The Second Sunday in Lent
The Collect

ALMIGHTY God, who seest that we have no power of ourselves to help ourselves; Keep us both outwardly in our bodies, and inwardly in our souls; that we may be defended from all adversities which may happen to the body, and from all evil thoughts which may assault and hurt the soul; through Jesus Christ our Lord. Amen.

The Third Sunday in Lent
The Collect

WE beseech thee, Almighty God, look upon the hearty desires of thy humble servants, and stretch forth the right hand of thy Majesty, to be our defense against all our enemies; through Jesus Christ our Lord. Amen.

The Fourth Sunday in Lent
The Collect

GRANT, we beseech thee, Almighty God, that we, who for our evil deeds do worthily deserve to be punished, by the comfort of thy grace may mercifully be relieved; through our Lord and Savior Jesus Christ. Amen.

The Fifth Sunday in Lent
The Collect

WE beseech thee, Almighty God, mercifully to look upon thy people; that by thy great goodness they may be governed and preserved evermore, both in body and soul; through Jesus Christ our Lord. Amen.

The Sunday next before Easter
The Collect

ALMIGHTY and everlasting God, who, of thy tender love towards mankind, hast sent thy Son, our Savior Jesus Christ, to take upon him our flesh, and to suffer death upon the cross, that all mankind should follow the example of his great humility; Mercifully grant, that we may both follow the example of his patience, and also be made partakers of his resurrection; through the same Jesus Christ our Lord. Amen.

Good Friday
The Collects

ALMIGHTY God, we beseech thee graciously to behold this thy family, for whom our Lord Jesus Christ was contented to be betrayed, and given up into the hands of wicked men, and to suffer death upon the cross, who now liveth and reigneth with thee and the Holy Ghost, ever one God, world without end. Amen.

ALMIGHTY and everlasting God, by whose Spirit the whole body of the Church is governed and sanctified; Receive our supplications and prayers, which we offer before thee for all estates of men in thy holy Church, that every member of the same, in his vocation and ministry may truly and godly serve thee; through our Lord and Savior Jesus Christ. Amen.

O MERCIFUL God, who hast made all men, and hatest nothing that thou hast made, nor wouldest the death of a sinner, but rather that he should be converted and live; Have mercy upon all Jews, Turks, Infidels, and Heretics, and take from them all ignorance, hardness of heart, and contempt of thy Word; and so fetch them home, blessed Lord, to thy flock, that they may be saved among the remnant of the true Israelites, and be made one fold under one shepherd, Jesus Christ our Lord, who liveth and reigneth with thee and the Holy Spirit, one God, world without end. Amen.

Easter-Even
The Collect

GRANT, O Lord, that as we are baptized into the death of thy blessed Son our Savior Jesus Christ, so by continual mortifying our corrupt affections we may be buried with him; and that through the grave, and gate of death, we may pass to our joyful resurrection; for his merits, who died, and was buried, and rose again for us, thy Son Jesus Christ our Lord. Amen.

Easter-Day
The Collect

ALMIGHTY God, who through thine only-begotten Son Jesus Christ hast overcome death, and opened unto us the gate of everlasting life; We humbly beseech thee, that, as by thy special grace preventing us thou dost put into our minds good desires, so by thy continual help we may bring the same to good effect; through Jesus Christ our Lord, who liveth and reigneth with thee and the Holy Ghost, ever one God, world without end. Amen.

Monday in Easter-Week
The Collect

ALMIGHTY God, who through thy only-begotten Son Jesus Christ hast overcome death, and opened unto us the gate of everlasting life; We humbly beseech thee, that, as by thy special grace preventing us thou dost put into our minds good desires, so by thy continual help we may bring the same to good effect; through Jesus Christ our Lord, who liveth and reigneth with thee and the Holy Ghost, ever one God, world without end. Amen.

Tuesday in Easter-Week
The Collect

ALMIGHTY God, who through thine only-begotten Son Jesus Christ hast overcome death, and opened unto us the gate of everlasting life; We humbly beseech thee, that, as by thy special grace preventing us thou dost put into our minds good desires, so by thy continual help we may bring the same to good effect; through Jesus Christ our Lord, who liveth and reigneth with thee and the Holy Ghost, ever one God, world without en. Amen.

The First Sunday after Easter
The Collect
ALMIGHTY Father, who has given thine only Son to die for our sins, and to rise again for our justification; Grant us so to put away the leaven of malice and wickedness, that we may alway serve thee in pureness of living and truth; through the merits of the same thy Son Jesus Christ our Lord. Amen.

The Second Sunday after Easter
The Collect
ALMIGHTY God, who has given thine only Son to be unto us both a sacrifice for sin, and also an ensample of godly life; Give us grace that we may always most thankfully receive that his inestimable benefit, and also daily endeavor ourselves to follow the blessed steps of his most holy life; through the same Jesus Christ our Lord. Amen.

The Third Sunday after Easter
The Collect
ALMIGHTY God, who shewest to them that be in error the light of thy truth, to the intent that they may return into the way of righteousness; Grant unto all them that are admitted into the fellowship of Christ's Religion, that they may eschew those things that are contrary to their profession, and follow all such things as are agreeable to the same; through our Lord Jesus Christ. Amen.

The Fourth Sunday after Easter
The Collect
O ALMIGHTY God, who alone canst order the unruly wills and affections of sinful men; Grant unto thy people, that they may love the thing which thou commandest, and desire that which thou dost promise; that so, among the sundry and manifold changes of the world, our hearts may surely there be fixed, where true joys are to be found; through Jesus Christ our Lord. Amen.

The Fifth Sunday after Easter
The Collect
O LORD, from whom all good things do come;

Grant to us thy humble servants, that by thy holy inspiration we may think those things that be good, and by thy merciful guiding may perform the same; through our Lord Jesus Christ. Amen.

The Ascension-Day
The Collect
GRANT, we beseech thee, Almighty God, that like as we do believe thy only-begotten Son our Lord Jesus Christ to have ascended into the heavens; so we may also in heart and mind thither ascend, and with him continually dwell, who liveth and reigneth with thee and the Holy Ghost, one God, world without end. Amen.

Sunday after Ascension-Day
The Collect
O GOD the King of glory, who hast exalted thine only Son Jesus Christ with great triumph unto thy kingdom in heaven; We beseech thee, leave us not comfortless; but send to us thine Holy Ghost to comfort us, and exalt us unto the same place whither our Savior Christ is gone before, who liveth and reigneth with thee and the Holy Ghost, one God, world without end. Amen.

Whit-Sunday
The Collect
GOD, who as at this time didst teach the hearts of thy faithful people, by the sending to them the light of thy Holy Spirit; Grant us by the same Spirit to have a right judgment in all things, and evermore to rejoice in his holy comfort; through the merits of Christ Jesus our Savior, who liveth and reigneth with thee, in the unity of the same Spirit, one God, world without end. Amen.

Monday in Whitsun-Week
The Collect
O GOD, who as at this time didst teach the hearts of thy faithful people, by sending to them the light of thy Holy Spirit; Grant us by the same Spirit to have a right judgment in all things, and evermore to rejoice in his holy comfort; through the merits of Christ Jesus our Savior, who liveth and reigneth with thee, in the unity of the same Spirit, one God, world without end. Amen.

Tuesday in Whitsun-Week
The Collect

O GOD, who as at this time didst teach the hearts of thy faithful people, by sending to them the light of thy Holy Spirit; Grant us by the same Spirit to have a right judgment in all things, and evermore to rejoice in his holy comfort; through the merits of Christ Jesus our Savior, who liveth and reigneth with thee, in the unity of the same Spirit, one God, world without end. Amen.

Trinity-Sunday
The Collect

ALMIGHTY and everlasting God, who hast given unto us thy servants grace, by the confession of a true faith to acknowledge the glory of the eternal Trinity, and in the power of thy Divine Majesty to worship the Unity; We beseech thee, that thou wouldst keep us steadfast in this faith, and evermore defend us from all adversities, who livest and reignest, one God, world without end. Amen.

The First Sunday after Trinity
The Collect

O GOD, the strength of all them that put their trust in thee, mercifully accept our prayers; and because through the weakness of our mortal nature we can do no good thing without thee, grand us the help of thy grace, that in keeping of thy commandments we may please thee, both in will and deed; through Jesus Christ our Lord. Amen.

The Second Sunday after Trinity
The Collect

O LORD, who never failest to help and govern them who thou dost bring up in thy steadfast fear and love; Keep us, we beseech thee, under the protection of thy good providence, and make us to have a perpetual fear and love of thy holy Name; through Jesus Christ our Lord. Amen.

The Third Sunday after Trinity
The Collect

O LORD, we beseech thee mercifully to hear us; and grant that we, to whom though hast given an hearty desire to pray, may by thy mighty aid be defended and comforted in all dangers and adversities; through Jesus Christ our Lord. Amen.

The Fourth Sunday after Trinity
The Collect

O GOD, the protector of all that trust in thee, without whom nothing is strong, nothing is holy; Increase and multiply upon us thy mercy; that, thou being our ruler and guide, we may so pass through things temporal, that we finally lose not the things eternal: Grant this, O heavenly Father, for Jesus Christ's sake our Lord. Amen.

The Fifth Sunday after Trinity
The Collect

GRANT, O Lord, we beseech thee, that the course of this world may be so peaceably ordered by thy governance, that thy Church may joyfully serve thee in all godly quietness; through Jesus Christ our Lord. Amen.

The Sixth Sunday after Trinity
The Collect

O GOD, who hast prepared for them that love thee such good things as pass man's understanding; Pour into our hearts such love toward thee, that wee, loving thee above all things, may obtain thy promises, which exceed all that we can desire; through Jesus Christ our Lord. Amen.

The Seventh Sunday after Trinity
The Collect

LORD of all power and might, who art the author and giver of all good things; Graft in our hearts the love of thy Name, increase in us true religion, nourish us with all goodness, and of thy great mercy keep us in the same; through Jesus Christ our Lord. Amen.

The Eighth Sunday after Trinity
The Collect

O GOD, whose never-failing providence ordereth all things both in heaven and earth; We humbly beseech thee to put away from us all hurtful things, and to give us those things which be profitable for us; through Jesus Christ our Lord. Amen.

The Ninth Sunday after Trinity
The Collect
GRANT to us, Lord, we beseech thee, the spirit to think and do always such things as be rightful; that we, who cannot do any thing that is good without thee, may by thee be enabled to live according to thy will; through Jesus Christ our Lord. Amen.

The Tenth Sunday after Trinity
The Collect
LET thy merciful ears, O Lord, be open to the prayers of thy humble servants; and that they may obtain their petitions make them to ask such things as shall please thee; through Jesus Christ our Lord. Amen.

The Eleventh Sunday after Trinity
The Collect
O GOD, who declarest thy almighty power most chiefly in shewing mercy and pity; Mercifully grant unto us such a measure of thy grace, that we, running the way of thy commandments, may obtain thy gracious promises, and be made partakers of thy heavenly treasure; through Jesus Christ our Lord. Amen.

The Twelfth Sunday after Trinity
The Collect
ALMIGHTY and everlasting God, who art always more ready to hear than we are to pray, and art wont to give more than either we desire, or deserve; Pour down upon us the abundance of thy mercy; forgiving us those things whereof our conscience is afraid, and giving us those good things which we are not worthy to ask, but through the merits and mediation of Jesus Christ, thy Son, our Lord. Amen.

The Thirteenth Sunday after Trinity
The Collect
ALMIGHTY and merciful God, of whose only gift it cometh that thy faithful people do unto thee true and laudable service; Grant, we beseech thee, that we may so faithfully serve thee in this life, that we fail not finally to attain thy heavenly promises; through the merits of Jesus Christ our Lord. Amen.

The Fourteenth Sunday after Trinity
The Collect
ALMIGHTY and everlasting God, give unto us the increase of faith, hope, and charity; and, that we may obtain that which thou dost promise, make us to love that which thou dost command; through Jesus Christ our Lord. Amen.

The Fifteenth Sunday after Trinity
The Collect
KEEP, we beseech thee, O Lord, thy Church with thy perpetual mercy: and, because the frailty of man without thee cannot but fall, keep us ever by thy help from all things hurtful, and lead us to all things profitable to our salvation; through Jesus Christ our Lord. Amen.

The Sixteenth Sunday after Trinity
The Collect
O LORD, we beseech thee, let thy continual pity cleanse and defend thy Church; and, because it cannot continue in safety without thy succor, preserve it evermore by thy help and goodness; through Jesus Christ our Lord. Amen.

The Seventeenth Sunday after Trinity
The Collect
LORD, we pray thee that thy grace may always prevent and follow us, and make us continually to be given to all good works; through Jesus Christ our Lord. Amen.

The Eighteenth Sunday after Trinity
The Collect
LORD, we beseech thee, grant thy people grace to withstand the temptations of the world, the flesh, and the devil, and with pure hearts and minds to follow thee the only God; through Jesus Christ our Lord. Amen.

The Nineteenth Sunday after Trinity
The Collect
O GOD, forasmuch as without thee we are not able to please thee; Mercifully grant, that thy Holy Spirit may in all things direct and rule our hearts; through Jesus Christ our Lord. Amen.

The Twentieth Sunday after Trinity
The Collect
O ALMIGHTY and most merciful God, of thy bountiful goodness keep us, we beseech thee, from all things that may hurt us; that we, being ready both in body and soul, may cheerfully accomplish those things that though wouldest have done; through Jesus Christ our Lord. Amen.

The Twenty-first Sunday after Trinity
The Collect
GRANT, we beseech thee, merciful Lord, to thy faithful people pardon and peace, that they may be cleansed from all their sins, and serve thee with a quiet mind; through Jesus Christ our Lord. Amen.

The Twenty-second Sunday after Trinity
The Collect
LORD, we beseech thee to keep thy household the Church in continual godliness; that through thy protection it may be free from all adversities, and devoutly given to serve thee in good works, to the glory of thy Name; through Jesus Christ our Lord. Amen.

The Twenty-third Sunday after Trinity
The Collect
O GOD, our refuge and strength, who art the author of all godliness; Be ready, we beseech thee, to hear the devout prayers of thy Church; and grant that those things which we ask faithfully we may obtain effectually; through Jesus Christ our Lord. Amen.

The Twenty-fourth Sunday after Trinity
The Collect
O LORD, we beseech thee, absolve thy people from their offences; that through thy bountiful goodness we may all be delivered from the bands of those sins, which by our frailty we have committed: Grant this, O heavenly Father, for Jesus Christ's sake, our blessed Lord and Savior. Amen.

The Twenty-fifth Sunday after Trinity
The Collect
STIR up, we beseech thee, O Lord, the wills of thy faithful people; that they, plenteously bringing forth the fruit of good works, may of

thee be plenteously rewarded; through Jesus Christ our Lord. Amen.

Saint Andrew's Day
The Collect
ALMIGHTY God, who didst give such grace unto thy holy Apostle Saint Andrew, that he readily obeyed the calling of thy Son Jesus Christ, and followed him without delay; Grant unto us all, that we, being called by thy holy Word, may forthwith give up ourselves obediently to fulfill the holy commandments; through the same Jesus Christ our Lord. Amen.

Saint Thomas the Apostle
The Collect
ALMIGHTY and everliving God, who for the more confirmation of the faith didst suffer thy holy Apostle Thomas to be doubtful in thy Son's resurrection; Grant us so perfectly, and without all doubt, to believe in thy Son Jesus Christ, that our faith in thy sight may never be reproved. Hear us, O Lord, through the same Jesus Christ, to whom, with thee and the Holy Ghost, be all honor and glory, now and fore evermore. Amen.

The Conversion of Saint Paul
The Collect
O GOD, who, through the preaching of the blessed Apostle Saint Paul, hast caused the light of the Gospel to shine throughout the world; Grant, we beseech thee, that we, having his wonderful conversion in remembrance, may shew forth our thankfulness unto thee for the same, by following the holy doctrine which he taught; through Jesus Christ our Lord. Amen.

The Presentation of Christ in the Temple, Commonly Called, The Purification of Saint Mary the Virgin.
The Collect
ALMIGHTY and everliving God, we humbly beseech thy Majesty, that, as thy only-begotten Son was this day presented in the temple in substance of our flesh, so we may be presented unto thee with pure and clean hearts, by the same thy Son Jesus Christ our Lord. Amen.

Saint Matthais's Day
The Collect

O ALMIGHTY God, who into the place of the traitor Judas didst choose thy faithful servant Matthias to be of the number of the twelve Apostles; Grant that thy Church, being alway preserved from false Apostles, may be ordered and guided by faithful and true pastors; through Jesus Christ our Lord. Amen.

The Annunciation of the Blessed Virgin Mary
The Collect

WE beseech thee, O Lord, pour thy grace into our hearts; that, as we have known the incarnation of thy Son Jesus Christ by the message of an angel, so by his cross and passion we may be brought unto the glory of his resurrection; through the same Jesus Christ our Lord. Amen.

Saint Mark's Day
The Collect

O ALMIGHTY God, who hast instructed thy holy Church with the heavenly doctrine of thy Evangelist Saint Mark; Give us grace, that, being not like children carried away with every blast of vain doctrine, we may be established in the truth of thy holy Gospel; through Jesus Christ our Lord. Amen.

Saint Philip and Saint James's Day
The Collect

O ALMIGHTY God, whom truly to know is everlasting life; Grant us perfectly to know thy Son Jesus Christ to be the way, the truth, and the life; that, following the steps of thy holy Apostles, Saint Philip and Saint James, we may steadfastly walk in the way that leadeth to eternal life; through the same thy Son Jesus Christ our Lord. Amen.

Saint Barnabas the Apostle
The Collect

O LORD God Almighty, who didst endue thy holy Apostle Barnabas with singular gifts of the Holy Ghost; Leave us not, we beseech thee, destitute of thy manifold gifts, nor yet of grace to use them alway to thy honor and glory; through Jesus Christ our Lord. Amen.

Saint John Baptist's Day
The Collect

ALMIGHTY God, by whose providence thy servant John Baptist was wonderfully born, and sent to prepare the way of they Son our Savior, by preaching of repentance; Make us so to follow his doctrine and holy life, that we may truly repent according to his preaching; and after his example constantly speak the truth, boldly rebuke vice, and patiently suffer for the truth's sake; through Jesus Christ our Lord. Amen.

Saint Peter's Day
The Collect

O ALMIGHTY God, who by thy Son Jesus Christ didst give to thy Apostle Saint Peter many excellent gifts, and commandest him earnestly to feed thy flock; Make, we beseech thee, all Bishops and Pastors diligently to preach thy holy Word, and the people obediently to follow the same, that they may receive the crown of everlasting glory; through Jesus Christ our Lord. Amen.

Saint James the Apostle
The Collect

GRANT, O merciful God, that as thine holy Apostle Saint James, leaving his father and all that he had, without delay was obedient unto the calling of thy Son Jesus Christ, and followed him; so we, forsaking all worldly and carnal affections, may be evermore ready to follow thy holy commandments; through Jesus Christ our Lord. Amen.

Saint Bartholomew the Apostle
The Collect

O ALMIGHTY and everlasting God, who didst give to thine Apostle Bartholomew grace truly to believe and to preach thy Word; Grant, we beseech thee, unto thy Church, to love that Word which he believed, and both to preach and receive the same; through Jesus Christ our Lord. Amen.

Saint Matthew the Apostle
The Collect

O ALMIGHTY God, who by thy blessed Son didst call Matthew from the receipt of custom to be an Apostle and Evangelist; Grant us grace to forsake all covetous desires, and inordinate love of riches, and to follow the same thy Son Jesus Christ, who liveth and reigneth with thee and the Holy Ghost, one God, world without end. Amen.

Saint Michael and all Angels
The Collect

O EVERLASTING God, who hast ordained and constituted the services of Angels and men in a wonderful order; Mercifully grant, that as thy holy Angels alway do thee service in heaven, so by thy appointment they may succor and defend us on earth; through Jesus Christ our Lord. Amen.

Saint Luke the Evangelist
The Collect

ALMIGHTY God, who calledst Luke the Physician, whose praise is in the Gospel, to be an Evangelist, and Physician of the soul; May it please thee, that, by the wholesome medicines of the doctrine delivered by him, all the diseases of our souls may be healed; through the merits of thy Son Jesus Christ our Lord. Amen.

Saint Simon and Saint Jude, Apostles
The Collect

O ALMIGHTY God, who hast built thy Church upon the foundation of the Apostles and Prophets, Jesus Christ himself being the head corner-stone; Grant us so to be joined together in unity of spirit by their doctrine, that we may be made an holy temple acceptable unto thee; through Jesus Christ our Lord. Amen.

All Saints' Day
The Collect

O ALMIGHTY God, who hast knit together thine elect in one communion and fellowship, in the mystical body of thy Son Christ our Lord; Grant us grace so to follow thy blessed Saints in all virtuous and godly living, that we may come to those unspeakable joys, which thou hast prepared for them that unfeignedly love thee; through Jesus Christ our Lord. Amen.

Prayer Prescription for every day of the year
D. L. Hammond

A collection of original Christian prayers by Donna L. Hammond, intended for use as part of a Daily Devotional.

Beginning in 1972, Donna L. Hammond was asked to write a series of short inspirational prayers for inclusion in the Sunday bulletins used in a protestant church in Huntsville, Alabama. These prescription prayers (labeled in the bulletins as PRAYER Rx's) have been generated continuously since then.

JANUARY 1

Dear Lord, Saturdays are family days – for some, a day to catch up on things that have been accumulating all week! For others, a day to do things together as a family unit. But whatever, let me not leave You out of this "family day." ... Let me sl-o-o-o-w down. Let me try to show Your love to others in all of my actions. Let me be more sensitive to my spouse, and to our children, for if they do not sense love and concern within me, how will they understand when I try to tell them of Your love? ... Help me, Lord, this New Year's Day to resolve to set an example for my family, for I have a tendency to "fall from grace."
> In Jesus' name.
> Amen.

JANUARY 2

Dear Lord, as I seek Your direction for my life at the beginning of this New Year, do I hear You asking, "What did you do with last year's directions?" ... Oh Lord, help me to humbly take stock of my life and find areas that need to be more consecrated to You. Help me to sincerely want to go deeper into Your Word, to pray for others, and to serve in my own "personal mission field." ... Fill me with Your Holy Spirit that I may have the strength and power to change, so that I may reflect You each day of my life.
> In the name of Jesus I pray.
> Amen.

JANUARY 3

Dear Lord, remind me of the paradoxes of the Bible. I am a sinner and yet I am a child of Yours, an adopted son or daughter. Help me to see that in order to "love my neighbor as myself," I must have a proper sense of self-worth, of who I am in Your sight when I have accepted You as my Lord and Savior. Only then can I love others, wanting for them all that I want for myself in Your love, and in my life.

In Jesus' name I pray.

Amen.

JANUARY 4

Dear Lord Jesus, let me serve others because I love You. Help me not to wait until I feel an affinity for another before I offer kindness, aid or concern. If I truly love You, I will want to serve others in Your behalf. ... Help me to reflect Your love, so that others will desire to know You too.

In Your holy name I pray.

Amen.

JANUARY 5

Dear Lord, sometimes we don't listen, or don't comprehend, or almost subconsciously tune out Your words, thinking, "those words must be for someone else." ... Forgive us Lord, for often being like a flock of ducks that listened to a pastor's sermon, and heard him tell them that they could fly! ... Then on the way out of the church, they said to each other: "Wasn't that a good sermon?" – as they waddled on home. ... Oh Lord, help me to see that unless I listen to Your Word on Sundays, and unless I take it in, seek the Holy Spirit's guidance, and let it penetrate the depths of my spirit, then on Mondays I will be no different than the ducks. If I am to increase my faith, then I must be open to growth, for You have a greater vision for me than to see me aimlessly waddle through my life. ... Open my eyes, Lord, and let me desire all that You have for me.

In the name of Jesus I pray.

Amen.

JANUARY 6

Dear Lord, as we begin to live out this New Year ahead, let us not forget to pray for our nation. More and more we see emphasis being placed on the secular, on the material, and we realize that we are being forced as a nation, and as individuals, to live beyond our means. Let us stop and ask ourselves, "In whom do we believe, and what do we believe?" Help us to ponder these words: "When a man ceases to believe in God, he does not believe in nothing, he believes in anything!" ... We pray that those in leadership positions will lead this country back to our Christian roots, lest they make a god of diversity, and we as a nation desert You, and You desert us! ... Remind us that freedom has its boundaries, and that these boundaries are determined by whatever we as a nation commit ourselves to! Oh Lord, let us pray each day that we and our leaders will commit ourselves to You.

In Jesus' name we pray.

Amen.

JANUARY 7

Dear Lord, forgive us all for letting our pride in our nation's scientific achievements, our economic growth, and our material comforts cloud our thinking. Help us not to be too quick to discard all of the wisdom of former leaders and concerned citizens. Forgive us for our arrogance. ... Let us consider these words of William Penn: "All men must be governed by God or they will be ruled by tyrants!" And also those of President Woodrow Wilson: "The sum of the whole matter is this – that our civilization cannot survive materially unless it can be redeemed spiritually. ... Only then can discontent be driven out and all of the shadows lifted from the road ahead." ... Oh Lord, help us to learn from those before us who have accepted You and tried to live out Your will in their lives. Help us to want that too, for ourselves and our children, and for all citizens of our nation.

We pray this in the name of Your Son, Jesus Christ.

Amen.

JANUARY 8

Dear Lord Jesus, as we reflect on the Christmas holiday just past, we find that more and more groups of individuals are trying to take You out of Christmas. Nativity scenes are questioned, and yet the "reason for the season" was Your divine birth in Bethlehem. ... And yet, surprisingly, we still find Your spirit of love, sharing, and concern for the poor, the hungry, and those in need of comfort. Isn't it strange that those who deny You are often willing to share their love, or to be on the receiving end of love? ... Doesn't this prove that Your teachings were true, Your examples worthy? Could it not also prove that Your ways are best for us all, for our nation, and for our civilization? Could it not be that You are who You said You were – trustworthy and caring? Could it not be? ... Help us all as individuals to see this, before we unknowingly forfeit all that Your sacrifice made possible for us.

In Your holy name I pray.

Amen.

JANUARY 9

Dear Lord Jesus, remind me that there is a time for me to pray in my closet, and a time to come out and stand up for You. ... Now, as everything is being shaken – my values, my beliefs, my faith – and the world is blaspheming You, my commitment to You is being tested, isn't it? ... Help me to walk closely with You each day, to redefine my faith, and to stand boldly for You. Keep me from a "deluding spirit,"* that I may not deny You.

In Your holy name I pray.

Amen.

* (See II Thess. 2:11)

JANUARY 10

Our most gracious heavenly Father, You are my refuge and my fortress, my God in whom I trust! You deliver me from the snare of the trapper and from deadly pestilence. ... You have promised that Your faithfulness will be my shield, and You are indeed trustworthy. ... Remind me that I do not have to be afraid. For even though trying times come, You will see me through them. ... You have said that if I do indeed make You my God, even the Most High my dwelling place, that no real evil can defeat me! You have said that if I truly love You, that I may call upon Your name, and that You will answer! ... Oh Lord, in the New Year ahead, help me to give You honor and praise daily, and to be the means by which others may come to know You. And help me to be as faithful to You in my commitments as Your have promised to be to me.

In the name of Jesus I pray.

Amen.

JANUARY 11

Dear Lord, You never promised that life would be easy, or that patience in parenting would be a "natural." In fact, You never implied that parents and their offspring would always live in harmony, did You? ... But You did promise to be with us and to hear our prayers. Teach us, Lord, to pray together daily, both as a family and separately. Help us each to learn to start the day with prayer, to seek Your guidance, and to sense Your leading, lest we run ahead of You, and bring on our own problems. ... Each day, let us find some blessings to count. Open our eyes to sense Your protection and care. Then when we gather together at night as a family, let us share our experiences of the day, and the many evidences of Your care and kindness. ... Thank You, Lord.

In Jesus' holy name we pray.

Amen.

JANUARY 12

Dear Lord Jesus, how do You love me? Let me count the ways – enough to bless me, to always be with me, to heal my wounds, to strengthen me, to give Your life for me! ... How do I love You? Enough to praise You in all things, to be obedient, to serve You? Enough to commit my life to You? ... Oh Lord, help me to love You enough to never count the cost. ... You didn't.

In Your holy name I pray.

Amen.

JANUARY 13

Dear Heavenly Father, I want to try my wings! I want to fly free! Help me to see that only by committing my life to You can I really be free – free from worry, free from wanting to sin, free from yielding to temptation. Only with Your help, Lord, will I ever be truly free – free to trust everything to You, free to serve, free to become all that You want me to be, free to be joyful! ... I want to try my wings, I want to fly free. ... Help me, Lord.

In Jesus' holy name I pray.

Amen.

JANUARY 14

Dear Lord, mountaintop experiences with You are inspiring! ... It's when You send me to hoe in the vineyard that I have trouble – in the heat, the trials, the temptations, and the decisions of each day – Lord, then the mountaintop seems so far away. ... Remind me to listen for Your still small voice in the midst of the confusion of the day. Remind me that my weakness enables You to reveal Your strength.* ... You are there; I just have to listen more intently. Help me, Lord, for I truly need You.

In Jesus' name I pray.

Amen.

* (See II Cor. 12:9)

JANUARY 15

Dear Lord, though disaster is everywhere and winter storms and floods engulf me, though the economy is in ruins, unemployment is rampant in my world, and brave men everywhere tremble, yet I will rejoice that You are the God of my salvation. Even though Your ways are not my ways, I can trust You. Help me to stand on Your Word, to meet the test, and to discover anew that You are indeed faithful.

In Jesus' name I pray.

Amen.

JANUARY 16

Dear Lord Jesus, forgive me for passing hurriedly over "forgive us our sins," while contentedly thinking, "I have not committed murder, or stolen, or cheated on my income tax, etc." Remind me, Lord, that for a "growing" Christian, worry, doubt, fear, ill temper, despondency, impatience, selfishness, insensitivity, and lack of love are "sins," in that they separate me from You. ... Help me to turn to You in order to receive the insight and strength that I need to walk as You walked. ... Help me to call upon Your name, that I may be saved from my sins.

In Your holy name I pray.

Amen.

JANUARY 17

Dear Lord, help me to realize that humility is not belittling oneself, but rather forgetting oneself. Help me to forget myself, to cease expecting recognition or thanks, but rather to see that I am serving You. ... Let my satisfaction be in pleasing You, and let my heart sing Your praises.

In the name of Jesus I pray.

Amen.

JANUARY 18

Dear Lord, remind me that neither Satan nor You can work within me against my will. You gave me "free will" and the choices are mine, aren't they? ... Oh Lord, let me choose You, Your way, EVERY TIME I make a choice. Help me, for I am often weak.

In Your name I pray.

Amen.

JANUARY 19

Dear Lord, remind us that in a marriage it is important for each partner to have the same goals in life, and to hold to the same high moral standards. If I am to live with my mate "until death do us part," then I must help him/her to be more lovable. How? By being more lovable myself! ... Love must be completely unselfish, sacrificial, each wanting to help to develop his/her mate's uniqueness to the fullest. ... It involves risk, doesn't it? But then Your love was offered with a risk too. Help us to remember to make You the center strand of the cord that will hold our marriage together, for our marriage will be at risk without You.

In Jesus' name I pray.

Amen.

JANUARY 20

Dear Heavenly Father, help me not to fall into the habit of blithely committing a sin and at the same time thinking that I'll come to You later for forgiveness. ... Remind me that sin is not so much an act against Your laws as it is the wrecking of my personal relationship with You. ... Your heart is grieved, so let mine be too, until I truly repent and turn my life around. Help me, Lord.

In Jesus' holy name I pray.

Amen.

JANUARY 21

Dear Lord, forgive me for trusting in my own intelligence and doubting Yours. I seem to have no misgivings about the things that I have reasoned out, but I have trouble trusting and believing in Your almighty power apart from my finite understanding. ... Oh Lord, help me to accept You as a Sovereign Being, fully knowledgeable and worthy of my complete trust!

In the name of Jesus I pray.

Amen.

JANUARY 22

Our most gracious heavenly Father, as we acknowledge Your sovereignty today, help us to remember that as Christians we have committed ourselves to living by Your rules, and not by our generational whims or desires. ... You created us, male and female to procreate, nurture and enjoy our families, that we might continue to be Your people. Through Your Son's sacrifice, You loved us, You taught us, and You saved us. ... Jesus taught that we were to seek and follow Your will, that we were to show sensitivity to sinners, but that we were not to condone their sins! ... Forgive us, Lord, as a nation, as a denomination, as a church, and as individuals for too often condoning what You have called sin.* Give us courage as we try to remain faithful to Your Word.

In Jesus' name we pray.

Amen.

* (See Exod. 20:12–17)

JANUARY 23

Dear Lord Jesus, remind me that although I am busy with acts of service, You really want me to learn to BE a servant. I can serve You and still be egotistical and proud; but to be a servant, I need to humble myself, to put another's needs first, and to be willing to "wash feet" as You did. ... Oh Lord, am I a big enough person for that, secure enough in my own identity? Help me to be all that You want me to be through the power of the Holy Spirit.

In Your holy name I pray.

Amen.

JANUARY 24

Dear Lord, sometimes Your Spirit speaks to me in quiet ways, in a "still small voice," so easily missed while the TV is blaring, the telephone is ringing, and electronic games and "electronic children" are all pulling me in a dozen different directions. ... Quiet me down, Lord, that I in turn may be a quieting influence in my family, and so that we as a family may HEAR You more clearly and be more sensitive to the leading of Your Spirit in this year ahead.

In the name of Jesus I pray.

Amen.

JANUARY 25

Dear Lord, as a nation You have indeed answered our prayers for a new and respected leader, who as our President has promised to seek Your guidance, and who seeks to honestly bring about changes for the good of every citizen. Help us who call ourselves both Christians and citizens to commit ourselves to pray daily for our government leaders, for we must all be concerned about the direction in which they lead our nation. ... Let us see this as an opportunity, not only for our leaders, but for all citizens of good-will, to unite in seeking Your guidance for our nation, our families and our children.

In Jesus' name we pray.

Amen.

JANUARY 26

Dear Lord, in the New Year ahead, help me to remember that wherever I go, I'll be! I can't escape me! Circumstances won't govern my life as much as my attitude toward them. ... Yet, wherever I am, You are! Oh Lord, help me to realize that I cannot deal with me and my problems without You! For You have the answers to all of my needs, if and when I consult You. ... You are my only real security! Help me to KNOW IT, BELIEVE IT, and LIVE IT! ... It's up to me, isn't it? It's my move. Help me Lord, for it is hard for me to change my ways.

In Jesus' name I pray.

Amen.

JANUARY 27

Dear Lord, worship can be holy, sacred, uplifting, and filled with "Praise the Lord" and hosannas. Salvation can be free – accepting Your grace, then repenting and turning Your way. ... But discipleship is costly, isn't it? You called me, not just for my own salvation, but to be a cross-bearer," to share another's burden, to love the unlovable, and to lead others to You! … Oh Lord, for this I was chosen, so fill me with Your Holy Spirit and equip me for this task that I cannot accomplish on my own.

In Jesus' name I pray.

Amen.

January 28

Dear Lord, the Psalmist has said: "It is good for me that I have been afflicted; that I might learn Thy statutes."* Help me to see that sometimes it takes affliction for You to get my full attention and cooperation. … Thank You, Lord, for caring enough and opening my eyes to Your deeper truths. Help me to set my heart on keeping Your statutes, and on discerning Your purpose for my life.

In the name of Jesus I pray.

Amen.

* (Psalm 119:71 – KJV; see also Verse 67)

January 29

Dear Lord, when I come to a Red Sea experience in my life – no way around, or back, no way but through – remind me that "those who wait on the Lord shall renew their strength; they shall mount with wings like eagles, they shall run and not be weary, they shall walk and not faint."* Help me, Lord, to learn to wait until all fear is gone, until Your peace floods my soul, until You tell me to "move on."

In Jesus' name I pray.

Amen.

(Isaiah 40:31 – NKJV)

January 30

Dear Lord, I said that I loved You, but clouds started to gather 'round. … I said I trusted You, then I lost my job. … I said You wanted only good for me, and sickness stalked my family. … Oh Lord, I try so hard to be a Christian – why me? … Then in my despair I cried out to You for help, and You said, "I thought you'd never ask!" … Oh Lord, what lengths You went to, to get my attention! Help me to learn not to lean on my own understanding, but rather to turn to You for the answers to my problems.* … Help me, for often I find that I am unable to help myself. I do need You! Help me to be patient.

In Jesus' name I pray.

Amen.

* (See Prov. 3:5–6)

January 31

Dear Lord, help me to leave spaces in my days for quiet growth, for new ideas, for dreams and new insights, for new perspectives and directions, for listening for Your quiet voice, and sensing Your will for me. … Let me not limit my quiet time with You, lest I miss out on what Your Holy Spirit has uniquely for me! … Let me not be impatient, afraid of being becalmed; let me learn to wait until the breath of the Holy Spirit fills my sails, and I can set forth on a course, secure in the knowledge that it is the one that You have charted for me.

In the name of Jesus I pray.

Amen.

February 1

Dear Lord, the Psalmist has said: "It is good for me that I have been afflicted; that I might learn Thy statutes."* Help us to see that sometimes it takes affliction or severe criticism for You to get our full attention and cooperation. … Such a time is this in our country's present travail. … We pray for our President and his wife as they face both their problems and ours. … Remind us all that we are not who we say we are, but rather it is our actions that define us; yet if we truly repent and turn our lives around, You are ready to forgive our sins. … Can any nation long survive if its leaders can not be trusted? Help us to see that honesty and truth are as necessary in one's private life as in one's public dealings. … How can we expect our children to be honest and truthful if we ourselves are not? Oh Lord, we pray for our nation, our leaders, and ourselves. … Could it be that we all need to take a closer look at Your 10 commandments?

In Jesus' holy name we pray.

Amen.

* (Psalm 119:71)

February 2

Dear Lord, sometimes as a nation we need to pause to get our bearings. First of all, remind us that all wisdom was not arrived at in just this century. … One philosopher observed that those who will not learn from the past are bound to repeat its mistakes. ... Was Edward Gibbon* not wise in 1788, when he set forth these five basic reasons why great civilizations wither and die: (1) the undermining of the dignity and sanctity of the home, which is the basis for human society; (2) higher and higher taxes, and the spending of public money for free bread and circuses for the populace; (3) the mad craze for pleasure, with sports and plays becoming more exciting, more brutal, and more immoral; (4) the building of great armaments, when the real enemy was within – the decay of individual responsibility; and (5) the decay of religion, whose leaders lost touch with life and their power to guide. ... Lord, help us to pause to consider both Gibbon's words and Your ten commandments, and then ask ourselves if we as a nation can find our direction without You?

In Jesus' name we pray.

Amen.

* (From *The Rise and Fall of the Roman Empire* Edward Gibbon)

Note: This is the first of a series of six prayers that are based on a poem of unknown origin.

FEBRUARY 3

Dear Lord, "I asked for strength, that I might achieve; I was made weak, that I might learn humbly to obey." ... How often when we are weak we find ourselves forced to turn to You, to wait upon You. ... It is then in the quietness of one's "aloneness" that one senses Your presence, and Your comforting assurance and peace. ... It is then that one learns, as the Apostle Paul did,* that our weakness is Your opportunity to show Your strength, and that Your strength is indeed sufficient for our needs! ... Once we discover this, and seek to learn Your will, we have only to obey. ... Forgive me, Lord, for running ahead of You, and thinking that I can manage my life without You.

In the name of Jesus I pray.

Amen.

* (II Cor. 12:7–9)

Note: This is the second of a series of six prayers that are based on a poem of unknown origin.

FEBRUARY 4

Dear Lord, "I asked for help, that I might do greater things; I was given infirmity that I might do better things." ... Sometimes in takes an infirmity to make me slow down enough to turn to You. When one is side-tracked, then one has the time to contemplate one's life and its direction. ... Help me, Lord, to see that my life has too often been like driving in the fast lane. I have sped along without looking at a map, so caught up in my own thoughts and everyday demands that I haven't had time to realize where I am headed. ... I wanted to do "greater things," but now You have let infirmity force me to take time-out. ... Inspire me, Lord, to use this time of recovery to see how I might serve You better. Help me to slow down and sort out the important from the merely self-serving. ... Show me how to make my life more meaningful, that others may be encouraged to know You. Thank You, Lord, for this lesson and for Your patience.

In Jesus' name I pray.

Amen.

Note: This is the third of a series of six prayers that are based on a poem of unknown origin.

FEBRUARY 5

Dear Lord, "I asked for riches, that I might be happy; I was given poverty that I might be wise." ... As I am forced to deal with the situation in which I find myself, I realize that I have often learned more in poverty, how to relate to more people in need, both physically and spiritually, than I would have if I only associated with wealthy friends. ... When I suffered unemployment, lack of funds, worry and illness, it was then that I realized that I needed Your help. I needed Your strength, Your encouragement, and the prayers of Christian friends. ... Through these setbacks, I learned to feel another's suffering and pain. ... Oh Lord, in my adversity, You have been my Rock. Help me to encourage others in their times of need, and to share what I have learned, that You are indeed sufficient in times of trouble!

In Jesus' name I pray.

Amen.

Note: This is the fourth of a series of six prayers that are based on a poem of unknown origin.

FEBRUARY 6

Dear Lord, "I asked for power, that I might have the praise of men; I was given weakness, that I might feel the need of God!" ... Oh Lord, we each need to be humbled at times, for it is easy, especially for those in positions of power, to have an excessive estimate of their own self-worth. ... Forgive me, Lord, in my own circumstance, if I get carried away and develop an exaggerated opinion of my authority. Help me, Lord, to keep a proper understanding of WHO YOU ARE, and who I am. ... Remind all who are in positions of leadership, whether in government, business, teaching or parenting, that we each have a duty to lead responsibly, and to set a good example for others to follow. ... Oh Lord, help me in reading this prayer to acknowledge Your sovereignty, Your superior knowledge, Your love and concern for me, and my need to seek Your guidance each day.

In Jesus' name I pray.

Amen.

Note: This is the fifth of a series of six prayers that are based on a poem of unknown origin.

FEBRUARY 7

Dear Lord, "I asked for all things, that I might enjoy life; I was given life, that I might enjoy all things!" ... Forgive us each, Lord, for too often concentrating on what we don't have, and taking for granted what we do have! ... Help me to resolve to start each day counting my blessings: (1) Any day I can get out of bed is a plus, and I thank You, Lord; (2) If I can't get out of bed, I thank You for a bed in which to rest; (3) I thank You for family and friends; (4) If I have neither family nor friends, I thank you for those who lend me a helping hand; (5) I thank You, Lord, for the beauties of nature around me – sunrises, sunsets, mountains or plains, country or city parks, flowers and bird songs – for beauty is often in the eye of the beholder, and help me to be sensitive to Your gift of creation; (6) Thank You for my daily work, and if I am seeking employment, help me not to be above taking temporary employment while seeking Your guidance. ... Oh Lord, help me, while waiting, to learn to enjoy the moment, and to praise You even then.

In Jesus' name I pray.

Amen.

Note: This is the sixth of a series of six prayers that are based on a poem of unknown origin.

FEBRUARY 8

Dear Lord, "I got nothing that I asked for, but everything I hoped for. Almost despite myself, my unspoken prayers were answered. I am, among all men, most richly blessed."* ... I thank You, Lord, for the difference You have made in my life. Help me as a Christian, to be a person who can make this world a better place, because I have learned to seek Your will and be obedient to it.

In the name of Jesus I pray.

Amen.

* Comment: This poem became identified with Max Cleland, who closed many of his speeches with it. Cleland was appointed to head the Veteran's Administration in 1977. He was a Vietnam veteran who lost both of his legs and an arm as the result of a grenade explosion in Vietnam.

FEBRUARY 9

Dear Lord, let us pause to look at how we, as a nation, react to crisis situations or major changes that affect us all. ... When our soldiers, wounded or deceased, are brought home, we turn to You. When the Challenger met its tragic end, we grieved as one, and turned to You. When a beloved entertainer lost his only son in a lamentable roadside shooting, our hearts were united in sympathy as we searched for answers. ... At our President's inauguration, it seemed fitting to turn to You. We invoked Your blessing, and listened to songs of our nation's heritage and religious roots, and of Your AMAZING GRACE. ... Oh Lord, forgive us for ignoring our Christian roots as we too often try to live our daily lives and govern our nation without seeking Your guidance. Help us to realize that we did not make it this far as a nation without Your help and Your blessing. ... Help us to understand that we can not build a "Bridge to the next century" without a strong moral foundation, and a clear identification of right and wrong for our youth and for ourselves. ... Forgive us for our arrogance, in thinking that we have outgrown You, lest we ourselves bring on our nation's downfall!

In the name of Jesus we pray.

Amen.

"All men must be governed by God, or they will be ruled by tyrants." William Penn

FEBRUARY 10

Dear Lord Jesus, forgive me for hurrying through life, often too busy to take time to "know" You, to really listen to the Holy Spirit's leading. Help me to get my priorities straight, then everything else will fall into place, won't it?

In Your holy name I pray.

Amen.

FEBRUARY 11

Dear Heavenly Father, everyone has the same number of hours in a day. How I use mine will determine the person I become. ... Whether or not I take time to read Your Word and to listen to the leading of the Holy Spirit is a choice that I make daily. ... Help me to see that only by choosing Your way can I be transformed into the likeness of Jesus. ... Oh Lord, I want to choose life, and live it on Your terms.

In Your holy name I pray.

Amen.

FEBRUARY 12

Dear Lord, today, as we remember President Lincoln's birthday, help us to re-read his Proclamation of 1863, given to the nation in trying times, and apply his wisdom to our present situation. President Lincoln said: "We have been the recipients of the choicest bounties of Heaven; we have been preserved these many years in peace and prosperity; we have grown in numbers, wealth, and power as no other nation has ever grown. But we have forgotten God. ... We have vainly imagined, in the deceitfulness of our hearts, that all these blessings were produced by some superior wisdom and virtue of our own. ... We have become too self-sufficient to feel the necessity of redeeming and preserving grace; too proud to pray to the God who made us." ... We might add to Lincoln's last sentence: "... and egotistical enough to think that we have outgrown Him!" ... Oh Lord, bring us to our senses, lest we turn

away from You, and by so doing bring on our nation's downfall.

In the name of Jesus we pray.

Amen.

FEBRUARY 13

Dear Lord, I can not catch a butterfly no matter how hard I try, but when I'm not trying, one may come to rest on my shoulder. Help me to realize that happiness is like a butterfly; I'll never find it. But if I love my family and spend time with them, if I try to make my world a better place, and if I serve You and show Your love to others, then happiness will find me!? ... Thank You, Lord, for letting my heart sing today.

In the name of Jesus I pray.

Amen.

FEBRUARY 14

Dear Lord, let this be a day to show love to a dear one. As a husband, remind me to show love for my wife in a special way – some unexpected surprise, time out to especially thank her for the many roles she plays to make our lives together a success. ... This day, as a wife, teach me to be sensitive to the needs of my husband and my children. Sometimes, Lord, I am physically exhausted, but remind me that sometimes their days are like that too. Help me to see that at such times, it is more important that we all take time to share our problems than it is to have a meal on time! ... Oh Lord, help us as a family to appreciate each other, and to express our love for each other. ... Help us as parents to teach our children that we as a family need You as our center; show us how to pray together, that we may seek Your guidance for our lives, as we seek to live in Your will.

In the name of Jesus I pray.

Amen.

FEBRUARY 15

Dear Lord, help us as parents to spend more time with our children, sometimes with each one alone. Help us to get to know each child better, to understand his or her thinking and needs. Let us listen to their opinions, and where they are off the track, their actions threatening to be non-productive or detrimental to their health or safety, let us explain why, and take a stand as parents. Let us pray together, and explain not only the hopes that we as parents have for their lives and conduct, but all that You too envision for them. ... Open their eyes to see that hasty decisions, without seeking Your guidance, could cause life-long consequences. ... Oh Lord, be with all families who love You, as they seek to live according to Your will.

In Jesus' holy name we pray.

Amen.

FEBRUARY 16

Dear Lord Jesus, You have said, "Blessed are the poor in spirit, ..." meaning those who realize that they cannot do it alone. ... Help me to realize that I need You in my life each day; I need Your wisdom, and I need to know that Your love is constant and that Your grace is sufficient to sustain me. ... As I prepare for uncertain times ahead, help me to yield to Your sovereignty, to trust Your faithfulness, and to desire to serve You as I seek Your will for my life.

In Your holy name I pray.

Amen.

FEBRUARY 17

Dear Lord, a grandfather pointed out to his grandchild a tiny bird singing its heart out, not knowing they were there. He asked, "Could you sing in the rain if no one heard you but God?" ... Oh Lord, that is the test of my faith and my love, isn't it? When the going gets rough, can I be counted on to stand for You, to sing Your praises even then? (continued tomorrow)

In Jesus' name I pray.

Amen.

(First of 3)

FEBRUARY 18

Dear Lord, let us each stop to consider the influence that Christianity, when correctly practiced, has had on many civilizations of the last two millennia. ... Remind us as citizens of these United States of America that it was our Judeo-Christian roots that helped us to become a nation worthy of Your blessings. ... No other so-called democracy has lasted as long. And yet today, we are arrogant enough to think that "we can do it better our own way!"

Many give You only lip-service, until the time comes when they face a national catastrophic situation. ... What will You say to those who choose to follow "other gods," often of their own making? (Continued tomorrow)

In the name of Jesus I pray.

Amen.

(Second of 3)

FEBRUARY 19

Dear Lord, what will You say to those who choose to follow their own selfish aims, who do only what they can get away with – whether it be robbing people, cheating on a marriage, killing on the streets, or aborting their babies at a whim, or for convenience? ... What will You say when some people follow their own self-serving gains, legal or not, even those in high places? ... What will Christians say or do while all this is happening; will some remain quiet and close their eyes, trying to take the "high road" and think positive thoughts? ... What will You say, Lord? Will You say, "I never knew you?"* ... Oh Lord, have we changed that much? Have we been too busy with our own lives? Have we been deceived, or blind to the dangers that surround us and can destroy us?

In Jesus' name I pray.

Amen.

* (Matt. 7:23)

(Third of 3)

FEBRUARY 20

Dear Lord, remind us that many men and women of high principles have worked and prayed, and some have sacrificed their lives to preserve the dreams that our founding fathers had for this nation, and You have heard their prayers! ... Bring us to our senses today before we unknowingly lose all that we have inherited! ... Someone once remarked that "Christianity has not been tried and found wanting; rather it has not been tried!" ... Help us to see, Lord, that those who believe that nothing is worth dying for very probably have no beliefs worth living for! ... For those of us who believe You when You said, "I am the way, and the truth, and the life; no one comes to the Father, but through Me,"* we ask that You help us to be Your ambassadors, that we may tell others of Your healing love, Your forgiveness, and Your amazing grace!

... Help us as a nation to realize that You are indeed faithful to Your Word. Help us to return to the faith of our fathers, lest we all become losers and sacrifice the future of our children.

This we pray in Jesus' name.

Amen.

* (John 14:6)

FEBRUARY 21

Dear Lord, in the midst of worldwide confusion, "wars and rumors of wars," moral decay, and political quandary, and when my personal world crashes in around me, remind me that You are God and that You are still in control. ... Help us as a nation to not give way to despondency, but to keep our eyes focused on You, and to recall past times when You have sustained us. ... Help our leaders to prayerfully seek Your will and Your direction before they make world-shaking decisions. ... Bring revival to this nation, and to Christians around the world, and let it begin with me!

In Jesus' name I pray.

Amen.

FEBRUARY 22

Dear Lord, today, as we commemorate the birthday of our nation's first president, George Washington, let us consider his words of wisdom, which helped to lay the foundation of our nation's government: "Reason and experience both forbid us to expect that national morality can prevail in exclusion of religious principle." Help us to read and re-read these words, and then compare them with the trends of today, where we are quick to take down Your ten commandments from our school walls because we don't want to "offend" minority groups. Many of our young people are caught up in the "do your own thing, whatever" philosophy, leading to confusion, crime, and juvenile pregnancies. As we re-read President Washington's words, help us to see that a "no rules" society can only lead to chaos. ... Oh Lord, no nation can long exist without law and order. Help us to demand better government for our families, for our nation's young people, and for ourselves.

In Jesus' holy name we pray.

Amen.

(Texts: Exod. 20:1–17; Judges 21:24–25)

FEBRUARY 23

Dear Lord, it's the "dailyness" of life that tests my Christianity, isn't it? It's the things that I put off doing that tire me the most. It's my preoccupation with living that makes me forget You. Yet only in remembering You is there any real purpose to my life! ... You have said, "I will write my laws upon their hearts."* Oh Lord, slow me down that I may hear Your Holy Spirit speak to my spirit, and discover my heart's true longings.

In Jesus' name I pray.

Amen.

* (see Heb. 8:10)

FEBRUARY 24

Dear Lord, remind me that man can never travel far enough in space to go beyond the boundaries of Your love. ... Even though I cannot see the wind, I can believe it's there because of its effects. ... Just so, I can believe in You because I see Your love and concern in all that You have provided for us in Your creation. ... Help me, Lord, to reflect Your love so that others may desire to know You too, for I often feel inadequate.

In Jesus' name I pray.

Amen.

FEBRUARY 25

Dear Lord, I need mountaintop experiences – quiet times with You. I need Your inspiration and the in-filling of Your Holy Spirit to give me faith, confidence, strength, inner peace, joy and spiritual power! ... But Lord, my work for You has to be done in the valleys of life – in the "hum-drumness" of my daily chores, doesn't it? Help me to remember my mountaintops as You call me to hoe in Your vineyard, and to keep my joy so that others may see You in me.

In Jesus' name I pray.

Amen.

FEBRUARY 26

Dear Lord, I ask for strength, and You give me difficulties that require strength. I pray for courage, and You give me dangers to overcome. I ask for favors, and You give me opportunities. I pray for patience, and You lead me into a traffic tie-up, but You never forsake me. Your love surrounds me, and You give me

both encouragement and hope. ... Help me to remember times in the past when You have stood by me, comforted me, strengthened me, healed me, and blessed me. Thank You, Lord, and help me to be a blessing to others, that they may want to know You.
In Jesus' name I pray.
Amen.

FEBRUARY 27

Dear Heavenly Father, some can pray short prayers and see results. Remind me that they may have spent hours in Your Word and in quiet meditation, awaiting Your guidance. They are "prayed up." When a crisis comes they KNOW how to pray in Your will because they KNOW You. ... Oh Lord, help me to see that I need to spend time in Your Word daily. Help me, lest I give You cause to say, "I never knew you."
In Jesus' name we pray
Amen.

FEBRUARY 28

Dear Lord Jesus, how shall we prepare our hearts in these Lenten days before us as we prepare to celebrate Your resurrection on Easter Sunday? ... First, let us consider the suffering that You endured on the cross when You became the sacrifice for the sins of mankind. ... You died that those who would believe, repent, and accept You as their Lord and Savior might not only be forgiven of their sins, but have eternal life! ... What do You want from me this Lenten Season? ... As I wait for Your answer, somehow I sense that You are not asking me just to give up desserts! ... Are You telling me that You want real, "soul-depth" commitment? And why not? After all, You died for me! Are You asking me to live for You? Every day? ... I'd have to really turn my life around, wouldn't I? I'd have to spend time studying Your Word, and seeking to know Your will too. ... But You did promise* that You would send Your Holy Spirit to lead me into Your truth, to guide me, to comfort me, and to "empower me." I wouldn't be left on my own. You did promise that Your grace would be sufficient for my needs.** It's my move, isn't it?
In Your holy name I pray.
Amen.

* (John 14:12–21)
** (II Cor. 12:9)

FEBRUARY 29

Dear Lord, remind us that Your Word is an account of how lost and miserable we humans become when we forget You. ... In Your severe mercy, You command our attention as You seek to bring us back to You. ... As we prepare for the Lenten Season, let us recognize and confess our sins. Forgive us our tendency to allow Your Word to be rewritten to suit society's permissiveness. ... Help us to recognize Your sovereignty and Your love, for only then can we endure Your justice.
In Jesus' name we pray.
Amen.

MARCH 1

Dear Heavenly Father, help me to realize that You have a purpose for me right where I am, whether happy or depressed, secure or frightened, well or ill, going forward or marking time. There is always something for me to learn, or something I can do for You, Lord. You can use me every day of my life! Show me how, Lord, show me how.
In Jesus' name I pray.
Amen.

MARCH 2

Dear Heavenly Father, help me to see the "nowness" of my Christian faith. The past is past, and put aside, and the future is in Your hands, Lord, but the "now" is up to me. This is where I either reflect You or not – in how I live today. ... Fill me with Your Spirit, enable me to be more than I am, that I may seize this precious time that will not come again, and live today to Your glory.
In Jesus' holy name I pray.
Amen.

MARCH 3

Dear Lord, help me to understand that You have a plan for my life, even beyond my farthest dreams. You want me to trust You and to be obedient, to seek Your will first, and then to use my creativity and intelligence to carry it out. ... Help me not to run ahead of You, deciding on my own what is the best action to take without ever seeking Your advice. ... When I realize that we are to be partners, then I understand that the opportunities You provide me will lead to the greatest fulfillment for my life. ... Let me accept joyfully whatever You give me to do, no matter how small. Let my daily actions be Your gospel.

In the name of Jesus I pray.

Amen.

MARCH 4

Dear Lord, You have said, "Blessed are the poor in spirit,"* – those who realize that they need the Holy Spirit to quicken both Your Word and Your truth for them. ... Help me to realize that I need You each day of my life; I need Your guidance, I need Your wisdom, I need to know that Your love is constant and that Your grace is sufficient to sustain me. ... As I prepare for uncertain times ahead, help me to yield to Your sovereignty, to trust Your faithfulness, and to desire to serve You as I seek Your will for my life.

In Jesus' holy name I pray.

Amen.

* (Matt. 5:3)

MARCH 5

Most Gracious Heavenly Father, if as Watchman Nee has written, "You have indeed chosen this world to be the arena for Your plan, the center of what You have set Yourself to do," then help me to trust You completely. ... Help me to remember that moral excellence, like a good painting, begins by drawing a guide-line; and remind me that You have already drawn that line! You have set limits for mankind's conduct, and for mine. ... Help me to see that it is only when I try to live within Your parameters that I can enjoy my greatest fulfillment and worth. ... Help us as a nation, as a church, and as individuals to try to see things from Your point of view, lest by insisting on our own "guide-lines," we bring on our downfall. ... Help us to wake up before we are overwhelmed by our mistakes.

In Jesus' name I pray.

Amen.

MARCH 6

Dear Lord, could it be, as C. S. Lewis says,

that if I think I have not met Satan it may be because I am going his way? ... Am I oblivious to the real enemy, and the spiritual warfare battling for men's souls in the world today, mine included? Help me to understand that Satan's chief weapon is deception. Remind me that all it takes for evil to succeed is for it to gain acceptance from "good" people. ... Oh Lord, open my eyes before it is too late. Help me to walk more closely with You, and to stay in Your Word daily, that I may have Your truth as my plumb line. ... Surely now is the time for me as a Christian to stand firmly on my convictions. Help me, Lord, for I am often anxious, confused and weak.

In Jesus' name I pray.

Amen.

MARCH 7

Dear Lord, remind me that "man is born broken; he lives by mending, and the grace of God is the glue."* Oh Lord, how often I have needed Your mending when I have been battered and bruised by life's daily trials. ... How often I have felt beaten down by ridicule, broken dreams, physical illness, or unfair circumstances beyond my control. ... Yet through it all, You were there, faithful to Your promises when I turned to You. ... It was then that I found that Your grace is indeed sufficient and able to mend my brokenness. ... Thank You, Lord, for being there for me. In my weakness, I am beginning to discover Your strength! Steady me, for I sometimes forget.

In Jesus' name I pray.

Amen.

* Eugene O'Neill

MARCH 8

Dear Lord, remind me that when I truly commit my life to You, it means that I accept You as Lord of my life, that I am willing to stop going my own way and "doing my own thing," and that I am now ready to commit to seeking Your will for my life. Give me the strength to keep my resolve. ... Remind me too that You do indeed answer prayers, not always as I may desire, but according to what I am ready for, or what is best for me. You may answer: "Yes," "No," "Wait a while," or "I have something better in mind!" ... Oh Lord, help me to realize that I can truly count on You – the question is: "Will You be able to count on me?" … Help me, Lord, for I am often weak.

In Jesus' name I pray.
Amen.

MARCH 9

Dear Lord, a bird does not sing because it has the answer, a bird sings because it has a song! Do I have a song? Have I made You the Lord of my life? Is loving You, seeking Your will and being obedient to it, my song? Help it to be, and help me to sing it each day for Your glory!

In Jesus' name I pray.
Amen.

MARCH 10

Dear Lord, remind me that my prayer-line to You is a two-way one. It is not just for me to call You in a crisis situation, it is also for You to call me! … How can I know Your will for me if I am never "at home," quiet enough, to receive Your calls? … Am I so preoccupied with my worldly cares that I don't hear and recognize Your voice? Do I not take time to be still and to wait upon You, Lord? … Remind me that You don't just call on Sundays "when the rates are less;" You want to be able to reach me any time and any place, when You might need me, or when You know that I need You. … My life could be so much richer and fuller, so much more Christian and worthwhile if I talked with You every day! … Help me to see this, Lord. It's my call, isn't it?

In Jesus' name I pray.
Amen.

MARCH 11

Dear Lord, help me to see these days as a time of testing for all nations, and a time of purifying for Your church. … The questions are: "Will I stand against evil in this spiritual battle as You did in the wilderness, or will I take the easy way out and accommodate and accept it; and will I allow Your Word to be watered down and re-interpreted to extremes in order to embrace society's every desire? Am I willing to sit by while society puts prosperity first and allows sin (by Your definition) to go unchecked?" … Remind me that tolerance can be carried to such extremes that Christians have no convic-

tions or commitments worth defending! … Let us each seek Your will on bended knee, and give us the strength to live it out.

In Jesus' name I pray.
Amen.

MARCH 12

Dear Lord, how we must grieve You, as a nation and as individuals. Let us count the ways: we have changed Your Word to fit our desires; we have stood by while others demean You in art, film and TV; we have remained silent while our children have been taught humanism and the occult, without demanding their freedom to learn Your influence on history; we have ignored the infiltration of New Age philosophies in our churches and seminaries; we have turned to other gods; and we have allowed our unborn to be aborted. … Could it be that we ourselves are the obstacles to the peace for which we so desperately pray? Lord, let Your Holy Spirit convince me of my errors and teach me how to pray, lest my silence and inaction give consent to those who seek to demean both Your teachings and Christians everywhere.

In Jesus' name I pray.
Amen.

MARCH 13

Dear Lord, as flowers lie dormant awaiting the warmth of Your sun, help me to realize that for too long my life has been dormant, awaiting my surrender to You. … "I believe, help Thou my unbelief." Take away the last shreds of doubt that keep me from total commitment, that I too may experience a springtime in my soul. Help me, Lord.

In Jesus' name I pray.
Amen.

MARCH 14

Dear Lord, it's spring! Your glory is everywhere! The blooms of bulbs long dormant, the songs of returning birds, the caressing warmth of the sun, all of these prove once again that You are trustworthy, that You were there even when everything was cold, dark and silent. You were there, planning greater beauty for us than we had dared to dream. … When things are at an impasse, help me to realize that "spring" will return to my life, and that You have more gifts in store for me, greater things for me to do. Help me to trust You while I wait, Lord, and while waiting, let me be content to share another's joy.

In Jesus' name I pray.

Amen.

MARCH 15

Dear Lord, as I find myself living in the rapidly changing and fast-paced society of today, one in which misinformation and temptations to follow "other gods" are rampant, help me to see it all as a test of my own Christian beliefs and of the truth of Your Word. ... Through all the darkness and uncertainty of today, let me live as though all were light! Surely that will be my spirit's greatest test, won't it? ... Help me to remember to keep my eyes on You, for You have declared Yourself to be the LIGHT and the WAY; and while remembering, let me "count it all joy!" *

In Jesus' name I pray.

Amen.

*(James 1:2)

MARCH 16

Dear Lord, help us during this Lenten season, to assess our lives: as Christians, as the Church, and as a Nation. Help us to see our short-comings, and to discover Your vision for us! Let us each ask: ... (1) Do I seek Your will and Your help daily? Do I read Your Word? Do I take time to encourage my family, and to lend a helping hand to someone in need? ... (2) Do I feel that we, as Your church, are adequately teaching Your Word – Your truth? ... Do both our church and our government leaders seek Your will before they make decisions? ... (3) Are we teaching our young people the difference between right and wrong? Do we explain that Your way of living brings joy, blessings, inner strength and peace, while wrong and sinful living brings severe consequences and heartache? ... (4) Am I setting a good example by being a concerned citizen, by trying to do my part in turning our nation around? Do I let my representatives know when I think they are misleading us and ignoring our Christian heritage? ... Oh Lord, forgive me as a Christian for too often standing on the sidelines. Help me to resolve to consecrate my life anew to being a better Christian in all areas of my life.

In Jesus' name I pray.

Amen.

MARCH 17

Dear Lord, we of today's society have allowed, or created, and sometimes abetted easy access to drugs, either by intent or by lack of attention. The resulting situation has made parenting one of today's most difficult tasks! ... Help us to realize that as citizens, and as Christians, we each have a responsibility, through our prayers and our actions, to change this situation. ... Oftentimes, Lord, when we pray for guidance You send it in ways we are apt to miss! ... However, we pray that You will give parents wisdom, understanding, love, strength, and even tough-love when needed for discipline. Help them, Lord, to stay the course, for the life of a son or a daughter is precious to You, to their parents, and to all of us, for our youth will shape the future of our nation.

In Jesus' name we pray.

Amen.

MARCH 18

Dear Lord, help me each day of my life to remember to count my blessings and to concentrate on the positive, for it is not what life does to me, but rather my attitude that determines the amount of peace and joy that I experience. I know that all things work together for the good of those who love You and are called by You. Help me to cling to this and always to praise You.

In Jesus' name I pray.

Amen.

MARCH 19

Most Gracious Heavenly Father, Your Son has set us an example in John 5:19 by saying: "Truly, truly, I say to you, the Son can do nothing of Himself unless it is something He sees the Father doing; for whatever the Father does, these things the Son also does in like manner." ... How often have I said "Thy will be done on earth as it is in heaven" in reciting Your Prayer on Sunday, and then failed to seek and follow Your will for me each day? ... Help me this Lenten Season to truly want to re-commit my life to following Your Son's example, so that both Your sacrifice and His will not have been in vain! ... If each of us who call ourselves Christians, around the world, would daily seek Your guidance and follow it, we could make Your world more as You have envisioned it! ... Help each of us, with Your love and help, to want to make and live up to this commitment each day!

In Jesus' name we pray.

Amen.

MARCH 20

Dear Lord, You did not say how long the prodigal son was away. ... It could have been one, five or ten years, or more. ... It is hard to be a parent, only to be able to stand by when a loved child takes a wrong path; yet it must be his or her "turning about," and all that any parent can do is to pray and to trust You to do the drawing. ... How much more then we begin to understand some of Your heartache, Lord. Even though You first chose us and loved us, You too are helpless unless we choose You, for love must be freely given. Oh Lord, open our hearts to understand this.

In Jesus' name I pray.

Amen.

MARCH 21

Dear Lord, Help me not to look at the magnitude of my problems, but rather at the MAGNITUDE of my God. For You, oh Lord, are able. ... Satan will tempt me to see only my circumstances in order to defeat me; he will mock Your words to enlarge my doubts. ... But my victory will depend upon my keeping my eyes on Your greatness and Your ability, for You are indeed able! ... Satan cannot win unless I choose to go over to his side, for the choice is mine, isn't it? ... Oh Lord, when I cannot see the way ahead, remind me that my faith is in You, and that You know the way. You will be with me as I take one step at a time, for Your will will never take me beyond where Your amazing grace can sustain me! ... Help me, Lord, to trust You completely, for I am often weak and fearful.

In Jesus' name I pray.

Amen.

MARCH 22

Dear Lord, even though our present-day society teaches that there are no "absolutes," remind us that our first president, George Washington, said, "It is impossible to have a public morality without religious principles." ... Could it be that in the USA we have wrongly re-interpreted the "separation of church and state" to exclude our Judeo-Christian principles in the daily conduct of government, politics, business, schools, on our streets, or in our TV and movie programming? ... Have we become a nation that accepts immorality, corruption and crime as normal, and the aborting of innocent lives as our right? ... Oh Lord, help us to see ourselves as You must see us and to weep, for surely, "Our pain is Yours, and Your pain is ours, for we catch each other's tears in the cup of the Father's will."*

In Jesus' name I pray.

Amen.

* (Mother Angelica)

MARCH 23

Dear Lord, without You, I have no moral guidelines – no restraining force to keep my life in order. Without You, I am left to float free, tumbling and turning with no real purpose or direction, borne hither and yon by any current world philosophies or teachings. ... Help me to see that just as life without the law of gravity could be confusing and difficult, just so my life without You would be filled with error, grief and frustration. A life without a compass would soon prove pointless; without purpose and moral guidelines, life would be both chaotic and dangerous. ... Oh Lord, help me to see my need to choose You and to seek Your highest expectations for my life, for You have made me uniquely for Your purpose. I need You as my sovereign God and my redeeming Savior, and I need the special anointing of Your Holy Spirit to reveal Your truth and to empower me to act out Your will for my life. ... Engulf me with Your love and Your peace that I may want to live my life to glorify You, and to enjoy You forever.

In Jesus' name I pray.

Amen.

MARCH 24

Dear Lord, remind us that this nation was once great because it was established on Your Judeo-Christian legacy and by people who held Your Word to be sacred and Your sovereignty to be supreme. ... Help us not to be too quick to destroy our foundations in our haste to build a new global order – an order where diversity is revered and no unifying moral guidelines are offered. ... Forgive us for seeking the quick fix, the surface-surgery, when we need to rebuild our moral base and set limits on our sexual excesses. We need once more to be accountable and responsible for our individual actions and honest in all of our dealings, showing concern for those in need. ... Oh Lord, our nation's leaders and citizens alike must set moral examples for all young people, worldwide. If we won't do it, will You be forced to bring our nation to its knees? ... Forgive us for deserting Your high calling and sabotaging Your plan.

In Jesus' name I pray.

Amen.

MARCH 25

Dear Lord, I want to try my wings, to soar; but first, teach me to walk in Your steps, finding that my only real security lies in being in the center of Your will. Only then can my spirit take wings; only then can I be free to become what You want me to be. Only then will I be able to soar in oneness with You, and find an inner peace that transcends my circumstances.

In Jesus' name I pray.

Amen.

MARCH 26

Dear Lord, You have said: "These things I have spoken to you, that My joy may be in you, and that your joy may be made full."* ... Help me to realize the significance of Your message – all that You really want from me is the joy that You experienced on earth, as You lived out the Father's will; You want me to find that same joy. In short, You want what is best for me, and what will bring me to enjoy eternal life with You! ... I may take wrong turns, or I may have to mark time. You may let me suffer illness, hardships or ridicule. However, You never give

up in trying to help me to discover that my real fulfillment will only be found in You! ... The choice is mine, isn't it? Help me to truly want all that You desire so uniquely for me!

In Jesus' name I pray.

Amen.

* (John 15:11)

MARCH 27

Dear Lord, help me to learn to really listen – to You, to my family, to those around me, and to be sensitive to the "unspoken," for often it is in the "unspoken" that the needs of others are revealed. You are not only heard in a clap of thunder, or in the cry of a newborn infant, but also in the silence of a sunrise and the quiet desperation of an anguished heart. ... Help me to listen, that I may bring Your love and comfort to others. Fill me with Your Holy Spirit that I may develop a "listening heart."

In Jesus' name I pray.

Amen.

MARCH 28

Dear Lord, help me to be aware of Your presence all about me – in the beauties of nature, the smile of a child, the handclasp of a friend, the love of my family. ... Let me not take a "vacation" from this awareness. Your love surrounds me. Help me to come alive and reflect Your love, that others may see You in me.

In Your name I pray.

Amen.

MARCH 29

Dear Lord, remind us that our first president, George Washington, cautioned us that if a democracy is to succeed, it needs to have public morality and a religious base. These are the ties that until now have held our nation together, and You, Lord, were admittedly our strength! ... Open our eyes to see how far we have strayed from our heritage. How much longer will we stand by while minority groups re-interpret our laws regarding our freedom to publicly acknowledge You? How much longer can we tolerate the re-writing of our history, hiding the full knowledge of our Christian roots and the truth of Columbus' Christian background and purposes? ... Oh Lord, how much longer can we expect You to "bless

America" if we fail to reverence You? ... Call us all to repentance; forgive us, Lord, and open our hearts and minds to realize that we have come this far only with Your help and Your tolerance. ... Forgive us, Lord, for deserting You as a nation, and give us the courage to once again be Your people!

In Jesus' name we pray.

Amen.

(See II Chron. 7:14)

MARCH 30

Dear Lord, prayer is necessary if I am to know You, if I am to grow in understanding, isn't it? Prayer is repenting of my sins and seeking forgiveness. Prayer is praising You, not just petitioning You for favors. ... Prayer is seeking Your presence and Your guidance daily in my life. Prayer is trusting that You know best. It is seeking to know Your will for my life, and then being willing to be used by You. ... It is praying and interceding for those who are hurting or ill, or those who are confused and suffering from difficult situations. ... Prayer can make a difference, Lord; teach me how to pray.

In Your name I ask this.

Amen.

MARCH 31

Dear Lord, are my prayers not being answered because I have not followed Your last instructions? Am I not being healed in spirit, mind and body because You told me to forgive and forget, or to give up some willful sin in my life, be it gluttony, lust, rebellion, drugs, self-centeredness, or a critical spirit? ... When I do my part, will signs follow? Is it my move, Lord? And all the time I have been blaming You! Help me, I pray.

In Jesus' name.

Amen.

APRIL 1

Dear Lord, in our nation's present travail, remind us of past times when we have prayed daily for Your guidance. ... Only as we unite in committing ourselves to pray for our leaders and our nation, to seek to learn Your will for the direction that we should take, can we make the right choices! ... When we are both faithful and sincere in trying to follow Your will,

remind us that it will never lead us beyond where Your grace can sustain us! ... We ask that You will be with those who are suffering – the displaced families, the terrorized, the tortured, the heartbroken – and comfort them all. Be also with those who are trying to provide shelter, food and help and protect them; and watch over our own service men and women and keep them ever in Your care.

In Jesus' name we pray.

Amen.

APRIL 2

Dear Lord, help me not to be afraid to admit that this is Your world, Your creation, and that You gave me life. ... Help me not to water down my words because some are non-believers, or because some believe in other gods. ... How will they ever know You if we who believe are coerced into keeping silent by those who make civil liberties their creed? ... Oh Lord, let Your Holy Spirit fill me with a holy boldness, and also the wisdom as to when and how to use it.

In Jesus' name I pray.

Amen.

APRIL 3

Dear Lord, some days I look at my children and wonder how to cope. ... Then there are days when they are pure joy! Help me to remember this when they are ornery. ... Thank You that they love me even when I storm and shout. Help them to know that I love them. ... Teach us all to forgive and to accept forgiveness, and to be patient. It's not easy, Lord, but You didn't promise ease, You promised help. Thank You, I need it.

In Your holy name I pray.

Amen.

APRIL 4

Dear Lord, marriage – "for better or for worse, in sickness or in health, till death do us part" – oh Lord, I promised, didn't I? I didn't know it would be like this, but I did promise. Help me to grow up, to accept my responsibilities, not alone, but with Your help. I need You, Lord, each day. Thank You for being there.

In Your holy name I pray.

Amen.

APRIL 5

Dear Lord, as I reflect on this Easter season, let it be the dawn of a new life for me. Let me realize that because You were victorious over sin, disease and death, I too can manifest victory in my life. These no longer give me reasons to fear. … Give me the faith that comes from reading the Word, and let me seek and receive the infilling of the Holy Spirit, who will lead me into all truth and give me power, comfort and inner peace. Let me find new ways to serve You, to thank You, to praise You. Because You lived and died for me, I can face tomorrow. Because You live in me, today can be worthwhile.

In Jesus' name I pray.

Amen.

APRIL 6

Dear Lord, remind me that my prayer-line to You is a two-way one. It is not just for me to call You in a crisis situation, it is also for You to call me! … How can I know Your will for me if I am never "at home," quiet enough, to receive Your calls? … Am I so preoccupied with my worldly cares that I don't hear and recognize Your voice? Do I not take time to be still and to wait upon You, Lord? … Remind me that You don't just call on Sundays when the rates are less; You want to be able to reach me any time and any place, when You might need me, or when You know that I need You. … My life could be so much richer and fuller, so much more Christian and worthwhile if I talked with You every day! … Help me to see this, Lord. It's my call, isn't it?

In Jesus' name I pray.

Amen.

APRIL 7

Dear Lord, help me to realize that when I accept Your forgiveness for my sins, even though I need no longer to be haunted by guilt, this does not eliminate the results of my sins. I may have to deal with the results for a long time – perhaps forever. … Cause me to stop and think before I carelessly or purposely depart from Your ways. … Draw me closer, Lord, and protect me from myself.

In Jesus' name I pray.

Amen.

APRIL 8

Dear Lord, had I been there when You rode into Jerusalem, would I have been shouting hosannas and waving palm branches? Would I have sanctioned Your teachings, stood up for Your message, proclaimed Your Lordship? … Where do I find myself this Palm Sunday? Am I rejoicing, sharing Your gospel, defending Your Word, Your values, Your absolutes? Or have I withdrawn to my comfortable TV chair, not wanting to get involved or to think about my children's future world? … Forgive me, Lord, if by being apathetic or naive I have inadvertently joined the crowd, mocking Your truths, deserting Your teachings, re-writing the Bible to make today's sins acceptable. … Open my eyes, Lord, to see myself as You see me. Strengthen me to be Your kind of Christian, lest I find myself allied with those who are crucifying You anew.

In Jesus' name I pray.

Amen.

APRIL 9

Dear Lord, help me during this Lenten Season to realize that I need to be willing to surrender every part of my life to You – my worst as well as my best. Then this Easter can be my resurrection too! … Let me be willing to die to my old ways and to start a new life – Your way.

In Your holy name I pray.

Amen.

APRIL 10

Dear Lord, as Easter approaches, let me take time to examine my heart. Your Word says that I am to grow in holiness, that I must "be holy as You are holy" – not an option, but a requirement. … My Easter should not be just lilies and bunnies, or even just hymns and cantatas – a once-a-year commemoration. Rather, Easter should follow a time of personal assessment have I grown this past year, in building a deeper relationship with You, reading Your Word, and seeking to know Your will for my life? Or have I forgotten the commitment that I made, putting my Christianity "on hold," believing that I am "good enough" to suit me? … Remind me that Jesus became the sacrificial Lamb for me that I might be freed from the bondage of sin and have eternal life. Remind me too, that I am to tell others about You. Help me to strive to "be holy as You are holy."

In Jesus' name I pray.

Amen.

APRIL 11

Dear Lord, help me to remember that there is more to confession than just admitting my waywardness. ... In order to warrant Your forgiveness, I must truly repent, being willing to give up my sin, to turn about, and to go Your way. Oh Lord, that takes willingness and determination on my part, doesn't it? It takes perseverance and love, both Yours and mine. Stay close to me, Lord, as I humbly confess my sins to You.

In Jesus' name I pray.

Amen.

APRIL 12

Dear Lord, the question is not how righteous and merciful You are, but rather how righteous and sincere we are. ... Repenting, both as a nation and as an individual does not mean just saying, "I'm sorry to have ignored Your Word." It means turning around, looking at my wrong opinions and actions, and seeking to go Your way. ... Thank You, Lord, that You are indeed merciful and just, and that You do not give us what we deserve, but rather what You know we need to bring us back to You. ... Help me to pray, "Thy will be done," and to mean it. Help me first to truly commit myself to seeking to know Your will, and then give me the courage and strength to live by it daily. Let me be someone else's gospel.

In Jesus' name I pray.

Amen.

APRIL 13

Dear Lord, will I fail You as the disciples did at Gethsemane? Will this day, Good Friday, find me looking the other way while many in films, TV, comedy, the press and the arts choose to blaspheme and ridicule You? ... Will I remain silent while others blatantly interpret their freedom of expression to mean a license to immorality or impropriety, and where reverence and respect are no longer exhibited? ... Oh Lord, by my very silence, will I not become a party to crucifying You again

today? Help me to have the courage to defend You in these trying times lest I become a party to the destruction of everything for which You lived and died, and thereby forfeit my right to eternal life.

In Jesus' name I pray.

Amen.

APRIL 14

Dear Lord, it all happened on the cross, didn't it? Even then, in the darkness of those hours – Your suffering, Your bleeding, Your dying, Your separation from the Father – even then, You were thinking of me! ... You died for my sins, for my diseases, for my healing, and that I might never have to know separation from You. ... Help me, Lord, to live that I may be more worthy of Your sacrifice, and thank You for Your promise of victory in my life!

In Jesus' name I pray.

Amen.

APRIL 15

Dear Lord Jesus, remind us that as Eugene O'Neill once observed, "Man is born broken. He lives by mending, and the grace of God is the glue!" ... This Easter, help me to realize more fully that Your sacrifice on the cross made possible the gift of the Father's grace to all who would believe. ... You lived in trying times too, and yet Your faith in Your heavenly Father never faltered! ... Help us, who call ourselves Christians, to try to grow in faith. Give us the strength we need to stay the course as we each seek daily to discover and live out the Father's will for our lives. ... Only then will Your sacrifice not have been in vain! ... Help us to love You enough not to count the cost! You didn't!

In Your holy name I pray.

Amen.

APRIL 16

Dear Lord, thank You for Easter – Your gift to me: the sunrise of my world, victory over pain, conquest of death, flowers reborn and birds rejoicing, acceptance unqualified, strength unlimited, and the promise of LIFE ETERNAL! ... Easter gives my life meaning. Because of You, I too can LIVE!

In Jesus' name I pray.

Amen.

APRIL 17

Dear Lord, today may be the most important day of my life because the seeds I sow today will determine what I harvest tomorrow. ... If I sow seeds of doubt and cultivate these by sampling the occult, or if I "buy into" the line that I am responsible to no one, free to live my life according to my own gospel and agenda, then I will have no one to blame but myself if my life ends in a quagmire. ... But if I sow seeds of taking time to study Your Word, seeking the Holy Spirit's guidance to understand Your truths, and accepting Your authority, Your love and Your forgiveness, then I will find that I am free indeed, and that Your strength and comfort will be sufficient for my needs. ... Open my eyes and my heart to want all that You have for me.

In Jesus' name I pray.

Amen.

APRIL 18

Dear Lord, it takes two to do anything in life – two to quarrel, two to forgive; two to make a marriage, two to break a marriage; two to enjoy friendship; two to share the beauty of a sunset. ... It also takes You and me, Lord, to make any sense out of life. Help me to want to center my life in You, that I may reflect You in all that I do, so that our world, Yours and mine, will be brighter; and because we met, another's world can be brighter too.

In Your holy name I pray.

Amen.

APRIL 19

Dear Lord Jesus, teach me to roll with the punches when even family and friends seem to delight in pointing out my faults, sometimes in chorus! Perhaps some of their criticism might be justified, but when several at one time point out a person's faults and give unsolicited advice, this is hard to take. ... Remind me that You too often faced criticism and verbal attacks, and yet even in Your time of extreme suffering on the cross You were able to say: "Father, forgive them for they know not what they do!"* ... Help me to learn to forgive and to forget; but often forgetting is the hardest! ... You and I know my faults and shortcomings better than others, and You know my heart.

Teach me to live out Your love even in such trying times. It is my challenge, to "turn the other cheek," isn't it?

In Your holy name I pray.

Amen.

* (Luke 23:34)

APRIL 20

Our Father, who art in heaven, we thank You for Christian believers who defend You as Creator of our universe and our humanity. Whether it took six of our days or six of Your days,* here we are, and apes are still apes! What does matter is that we can enjoy the complex nature and beauty and awesomeness of Your creation. Without building a relationship with You, our "great knowledge" may very well bring on our downfall. ... Forgive us, Lord, for our arrogance, our willfulness or immaturity, and our self-centeredness. Forgive us for thinking that we can manage our lives, our nation, and our world-relations without You. Teach us to want more of You, not less; to see that without You we cannot fulfill Your purposes or our dreams. You alone are our only hope, our sustaining grace.

In Jesus' name I pray.

Amen.

* (2 Peter 3:8)

APRIL 21

Dear Lord, as I study Your Word and ask You to make Your truth and Your guidance concerning our nation's problems known to me, am I hearing You correctly?

"Since when did I ever say that to sin should be a civil right? How can my people call themselves Christians and advocate what I have called 'sin'?"

But Lord, times have changed –

"I have not changed!"

Oh Lord, do You mean –

"Think it over carefully, for you cannot serve two masters,* the world and Me. You have to choose."

Oh Lord, I am often confused and easily influenced by the beliefs of others. Forgive me, for I want to choose You – but, all the way?

"All the way!"

All right, Your way, Lord. But I won't be very popular and I'll lose some friends.

"You will have Me – forever. My grace will sustain you. Trust Me."

Thank You, Lord, I'll try.

In Jesus' name I pray.

Amen.

* (See Matthew 6:24)

APRIL 22

Dear Lord, remind me that You never meant that Christian love and mercy should cohabit with sin. Rather You taught that if I would confess my sin to You and truly repent, that You would forgive me; but You did not say that You would mercifully look the other way and allow me to continue in my sin. ... Lord, help me to understand Your Word as You revealed it to Your committed apostles, for Your truths and Your plan for the family are timeless. Remind me that You created my human sexuality to be a precious blessing. Help me to love You and trust You enough to live by Your rules.

In Jesus' name I pray.

Amen.

APRIL 23

Dear Lord, rescue me from myself, my pride, my self-centeredness, and my "woe is me" attitude. Prod me when I am lazy, and convict me when I am wrong. ... Fill me with Your Holy Spirit, and enable me to be the kind of Christian I want to be, the kind that You know I can be with Your help.

In Jesus' name I pray.

Amen.

APRIL 24

Dear Lord, help me to search my heart today to see if I am really living what I say I believe. Give me the courage to look at the REAL me, and with Your help, the strength to change whatever separates me from You. Create within me such a love for You that I will not count the cost.

In Jesus' name I pray.

Amen.

APRIL 25

Dear Lord, if I am ever to grow toward spiritual maturity, I must grow some each day. Teach me to say "Thank You, Lord" at the moment I notice

a blessing; and let me say "Help me, Lord" when a need arises, confident that You want to be included in both my joys and my problems. Let me be continually aware of Your presence, and receptive to Your Spirit's bidding.

In Jesus' name I pray.

Amen.

APRIL 26

Dear Lord, remind me that there are some things I can do better than others, and some things that others can do better than I. Help me to know my strength, to stay within my "calling," and to give You all the glory. ... Help me not to run ahead of You, but to listen and learn Your will for my life; then give me the courage to act – to speak out. ... Discipleship is often costly, isn't it? ... Help me, Lord, for it is much easier just to watch television.

In the name of Your Son, Jesus Christ, I pray.

Amen.

APRIL 27

Dear Lord, as we search for answers to our problems, we ask how we can acquire faith. Open our eyes to see that we can not live without faith.

In Jesus' name we pray.

Amen.

APRIL 28

Dear Lord, in a recent national poll, 89% of us called ourselves Christians. Today, let us reflect on just how far we have strayed from following Your Word, as we read the words of one of Your disciples. ... William Booth, founder of the Salvation Army once prophesied that a time would come when we would see: (1) Christianity without Christ, (2) salvation without His blood, and (3) religion without the Holy Spirit. ... We need to ask, are too many ministers trying to "sanitize" the Bible so that it won't offend anyone, making it compatible with society's demands? Are too many professors in our universities and seminaries trying to explain the Bible by their own reasoning, leaving out the sovereignty of God and the supernatural spiritual dimension? ... Oh Lord, forgive us all for not reading Your Word for ourselves, and for not allowing the Holy Spirit

to lead us into an understanding of Your truth.*
Save us, Lord, from our own arrogance.

In Jesus' name we pray.

Amen.

* (See John 14:26; 16:13)

APRIL 29

Dear Lord God, help us to see that in Your inspired Word we are warned: "Beloved, do not believe every spirit, but test the spirits to see whether they are from God; because many false prophets have gone out into the world!" * ... C. S. Lewis also recognized that we may face this problem when he observed: "If you haven't met Satan recently, you are probably going his way!" ... Open our eyes to see that perhaps at no other time in our nation's history have we been attacked by such powerful demonic forces, misleading and overcoming so many of our people.

In Jesus' name we pray.

Amen.

* (1 John 4:1)

APRIL 30

Dear Lord, give us the insight to see that New Age philosophies today encourage each person to be his or her "own god," each to decide his or her gender, and she to decide how often and when she wants to abort their babies! ... Surely it must be obvious that we are losing our unity, our center, and our moral guidelines. ... Are the leaders of our government, our schools, our movies and television, and some liberal churches, often following New Age trends and sending mixed messages to our citizens? Have their arrogance and their self-centered aims blinded them as to where they are leading us? ... Open the eyes of our citizens to recognize the demonic forces rampant in our land, and call us to repentance before it is too late; for how can we expect You to hear us in times of national crises if we are worshiping "other gods?" ... On this coming National Day of Prayer let us each repent for his or her part, either by neglect or intent, in weakening our nation. Let us sincerely pray for our nation to repent and become obedient to Your moral laws before it is too late.

In Jesus' holy name we pray.

Amen.

MAY 1

Lord Jesus, how shall we pray?

"Pray to your Father in heaven in this way: 'Our Father who art in heaven, hallowed be Thy name.'" (Matthew 6:9)

We are to reverence His holy name, for He is a sovereign God – Creator and Overseer of the universe, my world, and my life!

"'Thy kingdom come. Thy will be done, on earth as it is in heaven.'" (Verse 10)

If we seek to know Him and His will through His Word and the promptings of the Holy Spirit, and if we are obedient to His commands, then He will help us to fulfill our greatest potential, and we in turn will be filled with His great joy, and will experience His "kingdom on earth"!

"'Give us this day our daily bread.'" (Verse 11)

Help us to learn to trust You for our needs – not our wants – and then to recognize Your surprise blessings as You provide them, remembering always to thank You for them.

In Your holy name we pray.

Amen.

(To be continued tomorrow)

MAY 2

Dear Lord Jesus, continue to teach us how we should pray each day, in the same way that You taught Your disciples –

"'And forgive us our debts, as we also have forgiven our debtors.'" (Matthew 6:12)

Help us to see that we can only experience your forgiveness after we have forgiven those who have wronged us, for our hearts cannot hold Your complete forgiveness if we reserve one section for bitterness. When we forgive others, then we won't be the ones to suffer illness – either mentally, physically, or both. We must not condone another's sin, but we do need to forgive the sinner, because You truly do know what is best for us!

"'And do not lead us into temptation, but deliver us from evil. *[For Thine is the kingdom, and the power, and the glory, forever. Amen]'" (Verse 13)

Do not let us be tempted beyond our strength, Lord. Help us, to resist Satan's entice-ments, as You, Lord Jesus, resisted them in the desert wilderness. Remind us of the commitments that we made when we accepted You as our Lord and Savior – to God the Father, to You, and to the Holy Spirit, who is our connection with You, our comforter, and our guide to Your truth.**

In Your holy name we pray.

Amen.

* (The earliest manuscripts omit this clause.)

** (See John 14:15–21)

MAY 3

Dear Lord, help me to learn not to keep running ahead of You, trying to do it all by myself, solving all my problems and everyone else's, and making "heavy weather." Teach me to turn everything over to You, claiming Your promises, praising Your name, and waiting for Your direction and Your timing. ... My life could be less stressful, couldn't it, Lord, and much more meaningful if only I'd learn. Help me.

In Your holy name I pray.

Amen.

MAY 4

Dear Lord, today across our country, Christians will begin observing a National Week of Prayer. Help us each to commit to pray each day this week for our nation as we seek Your guidance for both our elected and civilian leaders, and also for ourselves. ... Let us remember our heritage, and the prayers of our forefathers as they endured hardships to establish this nation. Help us to be worthy of their sacrifices, and of those who have in later years given their lives to save their nation. ... Let us also pray for Christians around the world, many in dangerous places, and for the people whom they are trying to help in nations suffering from hunger, poverty and sickness. ... Remind us to be informed voters, and to seek Your direction for our nation, for Christian are citizens too, and they have both a right and a duty to become involved, lest we fail to be "one nation under God" as we all recite in our Pledge of Allegiance.

We pray this in Jesus' name.

Amen.

MAY 5

Dear Lord, it isn't "love that makes the world go round," is it? It takes people, people like me, to show Your love so that others will ask, "WHY?" Then I can say, "Because You first loved me." ... Oh Lord, give me courage to mention You, for all my loving cannot give someone salvation, or make anyone a NEW BEING – only You can do that. Give me the words to introduce You to others.

In Your holy name I pray.

Amen.

MAY 6

Dear Lord, on this National Day of Prayer we ask that You open our eyes as responsible citizens, and especially as Christians, to see the situation that we face in our nation today. Remind us about how we have been uninformed, or too busy, or deceived, and so have allowed our nation to erode morally. Make us aware that You are calling us to choose leaders who will help us recover our moral compass.

In Jesus' name we pray.

Amen.

MAY 7

Dear Lord, granted that Christians aren't perfect, but surely You want us to try each day to do something for You – some good Samaritan deed. It need not take too much time or effort; it just takes an awareness, developing a sensitivity to another's needs! ... Lord, forgive me for too often being so engrossed in my own concerns, some of no real importance or urgency, that I forget to notice those around me. ... If all of us who call ourselves Christians would courteously hold a door, or lend a helping hand to a stranger, could it be that we might make our part of the world a better place in which to live? ... Help each of us, Lord, to realize that representing You and being Your "ambassador," is a full-time task.

In Jesus' name I pray.

Amen.

MAY 8

Dear Lord, could it be that if we who call ourselves Christians took our citizenship responsibilities seriously, if we became informed, checking not only what our leaders tell us, but also considering their "track record" for honesty, trustworthiness, or their self-serving deeds, could it be that we could change the nation? ... Could it be that by living and advocating Christian principles, that we might help to create a "brave new nation?" ... Oh Lord, we have prayed for You to raise up righteous leaders; could it be that You are showing us, "we the people," that it is up to us to demand and elect righteous leaders? ... How much more time are You going to give us, before You let us bring on our own destruction? Open our eyes, Lord, and give us wisdom and strength.

In the name of Jesus I pray.

Amen.

MAY 9

Dear Lord, help me to remember that although Your grace and love are free, You really want to build a relationship with me and restore a "oneness" with You. Whether that happens or not depends upon my response, doesn't it? For only if I repent of my sins and shortcomings and want to turn my life around, will I be ready for Kingdom-living now. ... Each time I slip or stray, I need to repent anew, for faith without repentance is not truly sincere, is it?

Help me in the name of Jesus, I pray.

Amen.

MAY 10

Dear Lord, remind me that neither Satan nor You can work within me against my will. You gave me "free will" and the choices are mine, aren't they? ... It is my responsibility to be informed, to read varied news reports, to listen to different commentators, Christian as well as secular, for some may be following a personal agenda. ... Help me to compare my conclusions with Your truth, and Your moral standards. Let me choose Your way, every time I make a choice. I need to know Your will, Lord, for it is so easy to be deceived. ... Help me to pray each day for our nation's leaders, that they may give "seeking Your guidance and knowing Your will for our nation" top priority in their daily agendas.

In Jesus' name I pray.

Amen.

MAY 11

Dear Lord Jesus, remind me that each step that I take in my walk with You counts, not just the goal. If I am to be a Christian, then I must be a Christian person each step of the way. Help me to see that every day of my life contributes something to the person I am becoming, and my conduct influences others around me. Fill me with the Holy Spirit, so that I may stand firm in the trials that I encounter daily.

In Your holy name I pray.

Amen.

MAY 12

Dear Lord, forgive me for too often burying my head in the sand, thinking that what I don't know won't affect my life. ... Help me to be alert to Satan's deceptions, which sometimes cause even the elect to be deceived; as many today seek to destroy our nation, our Christian freedoms, and our families. ... Remind me that I cannot serve "other gods." Let me turn to You, and commit my life to standing on Your Word, trusting that even in my weakness, Your strength will be sufficient for me.* ... Help me, Lord, to look around and see that as a Christian, I need to move from being an ostrich to being a Prayer Warrior, for more changes are brought about through intercessory prayer than this world realizes!

In Jesus' name I pray.

Amen.

* (See II Cor. 12:9–10 – KJV)

MAY 13

Dear Lord, as we pause today to honor mothers everywhere. Oh Lord, bless mothers everywhere as they seek to love and care for their children, and to teach them about You.

In Jesus' name we pray.

Amen.

MAY 14

Dear Lord, teach me that there will be times of concern when I need to turn everything over to You, to relax, and to trust it all to You – to "climb my watchtower and wait to see what answer You will give to my complaint."* Remind me that my weakness is Your opportunity to show me that Your strength is sufficient. ... Forgive me for forgetting that You never asked me to bear ALL of my burdens alone.

In Jesus' name I pray.

Amen.

* (See Hab. 2:1 – TLB)

MAY 15

Dear Lord, Christianity is not blindly following a list of rules, but rather building a relationship with You, isn't it? ... To know You as my Lord and friend, I must spend time with You, study Your Word, know Your plan for my life, experience Your love, recognize Your joys and Your sorrows, and share mine with You. ... Relationships require nurturing, don't they? Help me to do my part, to study Your Word and to understand Your rules. Only then will I understand that You want the best for me, and why You have called some actions sin.

In Your name I pray.

Amen.

MAY 16

"How precious it is, Lord, to realize that You are thinking about me constantly! I can't even count how many times a day Your thoughts turn toward me. And when I waken in the morning You are still thinking of me!"* ... Oh Lord, help my thoughts to turn toward You during the day, that I may know Your will and be obedient to it. Let me praise You daily, and thank You for Your constant care.

In Your holy name I pray.

Amen.

* (Psalm 139:17–18 – TLB)

MAY 17

Dear Lord, there are times in my life when I seem to be getting no where, when I am forced to mark time. Help me to learn the hard lesson of patience, and to put my trust in You. ... Help me to use these times wisely, to sort out my relationship with You, and to gain a new perspective, that I may set more realistic goals, which will be pleasing to You. Give me patience to await Your timing.

In Jesus' name I pray.

Amen.

MAY 18

Dear Lord, so I come to church on Sunday, does that make me a Christian? No, but it may make me smug or comfortable. ... Oh Lord help me to see that You have called me to be a "holy person," set apart from others, seven days a week! ... What have I done this past week that only a Christian would have done? ... Right now, let me resolve to walk more humbly with You, obedient to Your will, and more sensitive to the needs of others. For if my actions do not reflect You, those that I meet may be turned away from You.

In Jesus' name I pray.

Amen.

MAY 19

Dear Lord, remind me that Corrie Ten Boom said that You were more grieved by powerless Christians than by powerful atheists! You said that we were to ask for the Holy Spirit* – that was a promise, wasn't it? Help me to want all that You have for me, that I may truly be an "overcomer," equipped to stand for You and with You in a hostile world.

In Your holy name I pray.

Amen.

* (See Luke 11:13)

MAY 20

Dear Lord, I haven't really understood Your Word until I realize that it is full of paradoxes, and until I truly accept Your sovereignty, have I? ... Sometimes You want me to be healed, and my spirit senses this; other times You may use my illness for Your purposes, or to test the depth of my faith. ... Let me learn to "count it all joy,"* and to trust You completely.

In Jesus' name I pray.

Amen.

* (See James 1:2)

MAY 21

Dear Lord, just as a potter* must have moist and malleable clay to shape his vessels, so too, You need me to be pliable if You are to mold me according to Your will. ... Oh Lord, help me to yield myself completely to You – mind, will and emotions. ... "Melt me, mold me, fill me, use me; Spirit of the Living God, fall afresh on me." Only then can I go forth – in the name of the Father, to celebrate His sovereignty; in the name of His Son, to proclaim His message; and in the name of the Holy Spirit, empowered

to serve.
In Jesus' name I pray.
Amen.
* (See Jeremiah 18:1–6)

MAY 22

Dear Lord, forgive me for hanging a "DO NOT DISTURB" sign on my faith, for being blind to any new insights, deaf to Your Spirit's pleadings, smug in my own self-righteousness, and satisfied with my limited vision. Quicken within me a desire to study Your Word, and open my eyes that I may see glimpses of all that You want for me. … Create in me a desire to want it too.
In Jesus' name I pray.
Amen.

MAY 23

Dear Lord, as one sign said: "You loved the world too much to send a committee," remind me that You seldom speak to committees – You speak to individuals. … If each member of a committee consults You, and LISTENS for the leading of Your Spirit, then the committee should be unanimous in its decisions, shouldn't it? Help me to take time to be in Your presence daily, so that I will more readily recognize Your leading.
In Jesus' name I pray.
Amen.

MAY 23

Dear Lord, as one sign said: "You loved the world too much to send a committee," remind me that You seldom speak to committees – You speak to individuals. … If each member of a committee consults You, and LISTENS for the leading of Your Spirit, then the committee should be unanimous in its decisions, shouldn't it? Help me to take time to be in Your presence daily, so that I will more readily recognize Your leading.
In Jesus' name I pray.
Amen.

MAY 24

Dear Lord, it's hard to face temptation and not give in; it's hard to try to serve You without running ahead, neglecting to seek Your will. It's difficult to "bear fruit"* without staying

attached to the vine, and You have said that You are the Vine.** … Help me to learn soon that I can't be an effective Christian just by my own will power. I need Your strength, Your love, and the guidance and power of the Holy Spirit in my life. … Forgive me for being weak, or lazy, or too blind, too proud, too set in my ways, too independent to see that!
In Your holy name I pray.
Amen.
* (See Gal. 5:22–26)
** (See John 15:1–11)

MAY 25

Dear Lord, if I insist on running my car on molasses when its inventor meant it to run on gasoline, I'll come to grief. … In Your sovereign plan, You have given me FREEDOM to deny You or to choose You, to go my own way and make my own rules, or to go Your way and live by Your rules! … Oh Lord, help me to get beyond my "intelligent reasoning" and realize in my spirit that it's only when I choose to make Your will my will that I find my life's greatest fulfillment. Your high octane fuel is the only way to go! Forgive me, Lord, for thinking I could find the answers without You.
In the name of Jesus I pray.
Amen.

MAY 26

Dear Lord, so much of my suffering is brought about by my being out of harmony with Your will, but there is a quantity of suffering which is necessary for my spiritual growth. … Oh Lord, remind me that even then, You are in the midst of it, sufficient for my strength, and that the beauty of the morning can be appreciated because of the darkness of the night. … Sorrow is ever making channels for joy! Let me learn to praise You always.
In Jesus name I pray.
Amen.

MAY 27

Dear Lord, often I am too hard on myself and others, setting impossible standards and agonizing over past hurts, or over my own past sins of omission and commission. … Remind me that a butterfly would remain earthbound and useless if it tried to hold on to its cocoon.

Teach me not to spoil the opportunities of the day by refusing to surrender the past to You. ... Help me to know that Your love forgives, surrounds and challenges me each day. Set me free, that all my actions and words may more truly glorify You!

In Jesus' name I pray.

Amen.

MAY 28

Dear Lord, help us in the USA to pause this Memorial Day to honor all of those who have sacrificed their lives to preserve our nation's freedom. ... Help us to carefully consider (1) whether we are worthy of their sacrifices, and (2) whether we are in danger of letting this precious freedom slip away. ... To our forefathers, freedom to worship meant accepting Your sovereignty and Your salvation, and being able to pray publicly. ... Today, it means freedom for all religions, cults and "gods," except You, and little public recognition of our Christian roots except in times of crisis. ... Freedom to learn meant having free access to truth. Today, it often means a rewriting of history by those who wish to mold future generations to live in a godless society! ... Forgive us, Lord, for not seeking Your guidance and acting upon it. Help us as Christians to turn again to You before it is too late.

In Jesus' name we pray.

Amen.

MAY 29

Dear Lord, when everything seems to be flying apart in my life and I feel overwhelmed, remind me to stop everything, to sit quietly, to center in on You, and to read Your Word. For only as I return to oneness with You can my harmony be restored. ... Remind me that You are my Shepherd, and I shall not want for inner peace, for strength, for confidence, and for answers, for You have promised that Your Holy Spirit will lead me into all truth and show me where I need to change. ... Thank You, Lord, for always being there for me when I turn to You.

In Your name I pray.

Amen.

MAY 30

Dear Father God, sometimes I bemoan the fact that our society seems to be getting further away from You. ... Many of those in the younger generation seem to believe in a "god" of their own making – some "energy force" out there that surrounds our planet and the universe. However, their "force" has no real substance, no mind, no guide-lines, and no "amazing grace!" ... When I ask, "Why, Lord, why?" Then You answer, "Until people like you, who know that I am authentic and who have felt my sustaining strength and love, until you tell them about Me, they are alone." ... How do I know that I have heard from You? Because the words were so "of God," and in accordance with Your Word; they were in agreement with Jesus' examples and teachings, and He said that He only spoke and acted with Your approval! ... Oh Lord, if we who call ourselves Christians seek Your help as we try to live within Your will and share Your gospel message with others, then together, we can make this a better world!

In the name of Jesus I pray.

Amen.

MAY 31

Dear Lord, Christianity is on trial today. My faith is being tried; deception, false gods, temptations and ridicule surround me. ... Help me, Lord, for I can not stand alone. Help me to center my life in You, then Your strength will be sufficient in my weakness.

In Your name I pray.

Amen.

JUNE 1

Dear Lord Jesus, if and when I as a Christian spend time in quiet meditation, it is then that You can reveal "new insights" through the Holy Spirit to my spirit. ... For example, You did not send Your people – those who have accepted You, Jesus Christ, as Lord and Savior – to bring peace to the world.* Rather, You want Your people to find an "inner peace" within themselves when they faithfully live out Your will as You reveal it to them! ... But Your peace is not a passive peace! You call us to recognize Satan's wiles and the many ways in which we are being misled and deceived. We Christians are expected to "storm the gates of hell" wherever we encounter them; for only then will we have that precious peace that comes from knowing that we have stood against evil as You did in Your day. ... Oh Lord, give all of us, who call ourselves "Your people," the foresight, the strength and the will to stand for Your truth! That will be our real test, won't it?

In Your holy name we pray.

Amen.

* (See Matt. 10:34–40)

JUNE 2
Dear Lord, help me to accept life as a series of shocks – floods, tornadoes, sickness, death – interspersed with moments of shining joy, gentle love, quiet peace, indomitable hope. All this is the fabric of my life. Help me to cling to these moments, sustained by Your strength, secure in Your love. ... Let me remember that Your despair became victory, Your sorrow, joy. Let this be so in my life. Keep me on an even keel, Lord. I need You.

Thank You, Lord Jesus.

Amen.

JUNE 3
Dear Lord, help us each this Pentecost Sunday to desire to understand more fully the purpose of the founding of Your church. ... Even though Your disciples were "born again" in the Upper Room when You breathed the Holy Spirit into them, You told them to wait in Jerusalem for the power of the Holy Spirit to come upon them! ... Forgive us, for too often we have been satisfied with being "reborn," that is, receiving a new spirit and prayer line to You, and Your promise of eternal life. Yet You want us to wait and pray to be empowered too! ... We live in a fractured world as Your first disciples did, for as Christians today we are faced with ridicule and persecution, and our freedoms are endangered. ... We need all that You have for us – the power and the spiritual gifts for the words to witness, the faith to pray for healing and miracles, and the courage to keep Your Word alive. Oh Lord, help us each to sincerely seek Your Pentecost experience* in our lives today.

In Jesus' name we pray.

Amen.

* (See Acts 1:4–5,8; 2:1–19; Luke 11:13)

JUNE 4
Dear Lord Jesus, help me to see that the climax of Your mission on earth was Your Pentecost experience – the establishing of Your church and the arrival of the Holy Spirit. ... You came, not just to offer mankind a "heavenly insurance policy," but also to equip those who would believe for Kingdom-living here and now, so that Your words might continue to be spread abroad. ... You came, not for just one generation, but for all generations to come. ... You promised to baptize us with Your Holy Spirit, to provide the spiritual gifts, the boldness, the courage, and the power to enable Your disciples, then and now, to keep Your message alive. ... You promised all of that if I would but ask,* and I'm asking You now, Lord. Use me, and empower me to be Your witness, so that all I say and do will glorify You!

In Your holy name I pray.

Amen.

* (See Luke 11:13)

JUNE 5
Dear Lord Jesus, yesterday was the birthday of Your church. Before the Holy Spirit entered the disciples at Pentecost, they were timid and afraid. ... Lord, I am often timid and afraid too, but You promised that the Holy Spirit would be our link to You if we would but ask.* I'm asking now, Lord, if not in some flash of lightning, then in the slow clearing of the fog of my fears and uncertainties. ... Seize me with Your Holy Spirit, that I may have the courage to act for You in love, and to praise You no matter what happens, as I strive to live daily within Your will.

In Your holy name I pray.

Amen.

* (Luke 11:13)

JUNE 6
Dear Lord, You know that it is not easy to be a farmer – to raise one's family, flocks or herds, and crops of grain, vegetables or fruit to feed others, while being dependent upon favorable weather conditions to make these crops grow! ... However, you never promised that life would be easy, only that You would be there to help us if we would but believe and trust in You! ... Help me to learn to count my many blessings – the quiet, awesome, breath-taking

beauty of the first rays of a sunrise, or the closing rays of a beautiful sunset after a hard day's work! ... Thank You, Lord God, for all of my blessings, for the chance to raise my family, to be of service to others, and for my special quiet times with You!

In Jesus' name I pray.

Amen.

JUNE 7

Dear Lord, how You must weep for our nation and for the world! Open our eyes that we may see ourselves as You must see us – accepting immorality, fornication, homosexuality, wholesale abortion, drugs, and the break-up of the family, all as a way of life. ... How heartbroken You must be as You see us turning from the faith of our fathers to "other gods" – self-gratification, cults, humanism and materialism. ... Call us to repentance and forgive us, so that our pride will not separate us from You. Remind us anew that our only security comes from being in the center of Your will, and from being obedient and wholly committed to You.

In Jesus' name we pray.

Amen.

(See I Cor. 6:9–11)

JUNE 8

Dear Lord, only if we repent and seek Your forgiveness and turn from our self-centered and self-indulgent ways, only as we turn around and fully dedicate ourselves to discovering Your priorities for our lives, only then can we pray expectantly, "God bless America." Help us, Lord, to do our part and to be faithful to You, as we expect You to be faithful to us.

In Jesus' name I pray.

Amen.

JUNE 9

Dear Lord, today I am surrounded by confusion, false propaganda, misinformation, lies, deceit and hypocrisy in both politics and religion. ... More than ever, I need the guidance of the Holy Spirit to lead me into all truth and show me any errors in my thinking, as You promised to do if I would ask. ... Lord, I'm asking: "Let Your Holy Spirit fill me* – spirit, soul, and body – lest I unknowingly fall into Satan's traps."

In Your holy name I pray.

Amen.

* (Luke 11:13)

JUNE 10

Dear Lord, even though some scholars suggest that the Bible needs to be reinterpreted to appeal to today's reality, remind us, Lord, that although society changes, You do not change. ... You have said that certain acts are sinful. This is Your decision, for this is Your universe. ... Oh Lord, help me to be mindful of Your Word as Your Holy Spirit reveals Your truth to me. ... Help me, lest I be swayed by every ideology or cult, and end up worshiping "another Jesus."*

In Jesus' holy name I pray.

Amen.

* (II Cor. 11:4)

JUNE 11

Dear Lord, if I am to live with my mate "until death do us part," then I must help him/her to be more lovable. How? By being more lovable myself! Love must be completely unselfish, sacrificial, wanting my spouse's uniqueness developed to the fullest. Oh Lord, it's a risk, isn't it? But then Your love was offered with a risk too. Help me, for I am so inadequate without You.

In Jesus' name I pray.

Amen.

JUNE 12

Dear Lord, remind me that as a Christian I need to take time to put myself in another's situation before I form an opinion or criticize. ... Let me first ask myself how I would feel if I were faced with a serious illness, or prolonged unemployment, or had to deal with a wayward son or daughter. How would I react if I were wrongly accused of a crime that I didn't commit? ... Before I make a hurried judgment, let me first ask myself, "Would I have joined the crowd in Jerusalem and shouted, 'Crucify! Crucify!'?" ... Help me to remember that You taught understanding, compassion, love for one's neighbor, and even for one's enemy. Help me, Lord, lest I forget; for I too am not without sin.

In Jesus' name I pray.

Amen.

JUNE 13

Dear Lord Jesus, yesterday was the birthday of Your church. Before the Holy Spirit entered the disciples at Pentecost, they were timid and afraid. ... Lord, I am often timid and afraid too, but You promised that the Holy Spirit would be our link to You if we would but ask.* I'm asking now, Lord, if not in some flash of lightning, then in the slow clearing of the fog of my fears and uncertainties. ... Seize me with Your Holy Spirit, that I may have the courage to act for You in love, and to praise You no matter what happens, as I strive to live daily within Your will.

In Your holy name I pray.

Amen.

* (See Luke 11:13)

JUNE 14

Dear Lord, as we observe Flag Day on this June 14th in the U.S.A., let us revere You as our forefathers did, and honor our flag – the symbol of our freedom, for which so many have given their lives. ... Let us pause to assess our country: we see corruption in high places, and leaders who wink at immorality and thus threaten the very family values that made this nation great. ... Remind us that we still declare that we are "one nation under God," and that as a nation we will be strengthened or weakened by the degree of integrity that we demand of ourselves individually! ... Oh Lord, we sincerely pray that You will raise up righteous leaders for our nation, and that You will give us the wisdom to recognize and support them. Let all that we do be pleasing in Your sight.

In the name of Jesus we pray.

Amen.

JUNE 15

Dear Lord, when I feel helpless, hurt, ridiculed and forsaken, remind me that You have felt that way too. ... There is really NOTHING that I can ever face that You have not experienced. ... If I am a hostage or a prisoner, or if I am in bondage to sin, You were that also when You hung on the cross. ... If I feel helpless when a loved one suffers, or turns away from me, You also knew that sadness when Your love was rejected. ... If there seems to be no one for me in my aloneness, grief or suffering, I should remember that You too must have felt deserted, alone and without hope in the Garden of Gethsemene. ... Oh Lord, only You can really understand my problems. What a friend we have in You! I am not alone, am I? Thank You, Lord, and I ask that You continue to fill my life with Your glorious presence.

In Your holy name I pray.

Amen.

JUNE 16

Dear Lord, some days my cup truly "runneth over;" I feel one with You, and I want to sing Your praises! ... Help me to remember this when life gets hectic, and my nerves get frazzled. Let me find that I have an inner storehouse of joy and strength* to sustain me. ... Thank You, Lord, that this is so, for if it isn't, then my faith is but a hollow mockery, and I have never really known You.

In Your holy name I pray.

Amen.

* (Nehemiah 8:10b)

JUNE 17

Dear Lord, as we pause today to honor our fathers, we are each grateful for our father's patient toil, his steadfast devotion, his moral leadership, and his quiet "goodness," for a loving father reflects Your love and helps his children to know You as a kind and loving Father. Bless each father as he unselfishly sacrifices for his family. Help each of us, whether wife or mother, son or daughter, to show our appreciation in countless ways every day of the year, for fathers too need to be nourished by love.

In Jesus' name we thank You, Lord.

Amen.

JUNE 18

Dear Lord, there is more that You have for me, isn't there? Prod me, and challenge me to move from "square one" in my faith, lest I too long remain a "baby Christian." ... Let me truly desire a greater and more complete infilling of Your Holy Spirit, so that I may gain new insights into Your Word and Your will. ... Only then can I have a "holy boldness" to stand up for You in EVERY AREA of my life. Let Your Spirit flow through me so that others may desire to know You also!

In Your holy name I pray.
Amen.

JUNE 19

Dear Lord, You have said that where a man's treasure is, there his heart will be also,* and that as a man thinketh, so he becomes.** In short, I will become what I love. If I love what is base, I will become base, if noble, I will become noble. ... Oh Lord, help me to be careful of how I spend my time, of what I put into my mind, and of whom I choose as companions. ... Help me, Lord, to desire You and Your will for my life. I cannot serve two masters – You and the world. Help me to choose You.

In Your holy name I pray.
Amen.
* (Luke 12:34)
** (Prov. 23:7)
(Please refer also to Prayer for February 23)

JUNE 20

Dear Lord, open my eyes that I may recognize the evidence of Your love and faithfulness all around me. ... Open my spiritual ears that I may more truly hear Your spoken words, and understand how getting to know You can impact my life for the better. ... Open my heart that I may be more sensitive to the needs and concerns of others. ... Let my spirit sense how You would have me use my time, my talents and my monies for Your glory. ... Help me to abandon my role as a spectator and choose to be a PLAYER for You!

In the name of Jesus I pray.
Amen.

JUNE 21

Dear Lord, what are You asking of me – my time, my talents, my money, my commitment, or MORE? ... Are You asking me to give of myself, and never count the cost? Am I to give, even though misunderstood? Am I to witness, even though it is not received? Am I to help others when it is unsolicited and unacknowledged? ... Lord, are You asking me to act as You would have acted in similar situations? Am I hearing You correctly? ... Help me, Lord, for I am often timid. Fill me with Your Holy Spirit, for I can not do it alone.

In the name of Jesus I pray.
Amen.

JUNE 22

Dear Lord, do I turn to You only in times of crisis, and then complain because I do not "hear" Your voice? Remind me that You have not moved; rather it is I who have distanced myself from You. ... How can I expect to recognize Your Holy Spirit's leading if I spend so little time with You? ... Oh Lord, help me to spend more time with You daily, in reading Your Word and in prayer. Help me to count my blessings, for I always have some. Only then will I be able to recognize Your guidance, to be responsive to Your call, to begin to understand Your plan for my life, and to feel a "oneness" with You.

In Your name I pray.
Amen.

JUNE 23

Dear Lord, here I am on this day, all starched and scrubbed, and ready to sing Your praises; but how about those days when I feel myself drowning in my unsolvable problems, what then? That's the test of my faith, isn't it – when the day is bathed in sunlight but my own world has a cloud? ... Help me to remember to turn my concerns over to You, and to praise You anyhow, for You can make my bleakest cloud bearable, and provide light for my path. I know You can; I just forget sometimes. Thank You, Lord.

In Jesus' name I pray.
Amen.

JUNE 24

Dear Lord, when did You separate the sacred from the secular – in healing the blind man, or feeding the five thousand, or in driving out the money changers? When did You compartmentalize Your life? ... What part of my life is not sacred – my business dealings, my government responsibilities, my family relationships, my time spent in school or college? ... Am I to be a Sunday Christian only? Were You? ... If I truly want to be a Christian in my heart, then there is no time at which I can leave my heart at home on the shelf, is there?

In Your holy name I pray.
Amen.

JUNE 25

Dear Lord, I said that I love You, but clouds started to gather round. ... I said I trusted You, then I lost my job. ... I said that You wanted only good for me, but sickness stalked my family. ... Oh Lord, I try so hard to be a Christian, why me? ... Then in my despair I cried out to You for help and You said, "I thought you'd never ask!" ... Oh Lord, what lengths You went to in order to get my attention! Help me to lean not on my own understanding, but to turn to You. Help me, for at times I can't help myself.

In Jesus' name I pray.

Amen.

JUNE 26

Dear Lord, help me to leave space in my days for quiet growth, for new ideas, for dreams and insights, for new perspectives and directions, for listening for Your quiet voice, and sensing Your will for me. ... Let me not limit my quiet time with You, lest I miss out on what Your Holy Spirit has uniquely for me! ... Let me not be afraid if I feel becalmed; let me learn to wait until the breath of the Holy Spirit fills my sails and I set forth on a course, secure in the knowledge that it is the one You have chosen for me.

In Jesus' name I pray.

Amen.

JUNE 27

Dear Lord, remind me that Corrie Ten Boom said that You were more grieved by powerless Christians than by powerful atheists! You said that we were to ask for the Holy Spirit* – that was a promise, wasn't it? Help me to want all that You have for me, that I may truly be an "overcomer," equipped to stand for You and with You in a hostile world.

In Your holy name I pray.

Amen.

* (Luke 11:13)

JUNE 28

Most gracious Heavenly Father, You are indeed the author of reconciliation! For You sent Your Son, Christ Jesus, to be the means for giving a second chance to any who would accept Him on faith as Your Son and Your messenger! For those who can believe in Him, ask forgiveness for their sins, and truly repent – willing to give up their sinful ways – He promised to provide help now, and eternal life in the future! ... Remind me that Jesus, who was Himself innocent of sin, carried out Your first move toward reconciliation at Your direction! ... Open my heart to better understand Your ways.

In Jesus' name I pray.

Amen.

JUNE 29

Dear Lord, when I find myself in serious opposition to another's thinking, be it a spouse, a relative, companions at work or church, friends or others, help me to realize that You do not want me to give up my convictions when they are in accordance with Your Word; rather You do expect me to show "Christian love" – kindness, friendliness, and understanding. ... However, You expect me to make the first move toward reconciliation! You want me to do what I can to restore broken relationships! Help me to do this, Lord.

In Jesus' name I pray.

Amen.

JUNE 30

Dear Lord, could it be that You want me to make the first move in restoring a broken relationship because You know that for one, like me, to withdraw and leave another harboring resentments will cause each of us to suffer. Not only will I feel withdrawal from those in opposition to my words, but I will also feel estranged from You! ... Remind me that You desire Your Holy Spirit to flow through me to others! ... You want me to be Your Christian representative every day, not just on Sundays! You want me to live Your message by my example! With Your help, I know that I can.

In Jesus' name I pray.

Amen.

JULY 1

Dear Lord, forgive us for thinking that full-time discipleship is only for ministers or other professional Christian workers, for You have called each of us, Your people, to be full-time Christians, haven't You – at home with our families, at our places of employment, while driving to work or to shop, and as we meet those who daily cross our paths? ... Do we reflect You as we wait in a check-out line, and do we stand on Your Word as we face our political concerns and responsibilities? ... Remind us that often our actions or lack of action speak louder than words, and that nations are in danger of falling when good people remain silent. ... Give us wisdom and courage to live every day as Your representatives, for we may be the only "gospel" that some people will ever encounter.

In Jesus' name we pray.

Amen.

JULY 2

Dear Lord, how we must grieve You! You had such plans for this nation. Our founding fathers recognized Your authority, that we were each Your creation. Even those who didn't know You well believed in the sacredness of life. ... Now, because we are so knowledgeable, we want to usurp Your position. We want to rewrite Your Word, and redesign Your family unit according to our own likings. ... Remind us, Lord, that if we who call ourselves Your people do not stand for Your moral principles, then we are no better than the leaders that we either voted for or elected by not voting at all! ... You speak to us in earthquakes, fire, floods, hurricanes and blizzards. How can we fail to see that You are still in charge? How many wake-up calls will You give us? ... Help us to have the courage to be fully Your people, to live holy lives because You are holy and You require holiness of us.*

In Jesus' name I pray.

Amen.

* (See Lev. 19:2; 1 Thess. 4:7–8)

JULY 3

Dear Lord God, the continuation of our nation's freedom depends on how well we understand its history and pass it on to our children, doesn't it? Our forefathers, the founders of our nation, depended on You as our "Creator God," our strength, and our guide. ... Let us pass on these truths, lest we forget, and some not even have the chance to learn of them. ... It is up to each of us, isn't it? Help us, Lord, to realize that in these changing times our nation's very survival is threatened. Give us the courage and wisdom to stand with

You and for You, to pass on Your truths, lest we all fall prey to deception.

In the name of Jesus we pray.

Amen.

JULY 4

Dear Lord, as we observe our nation's Independence Day this July 4th, let us all consider Benjamin Franklin's statement, given in 1787 when the Continental Congress was deadlocked. He stood and addressed George Washington, saying: "Sir, we have not hitherto once thought of humbly appealing to the Father of Lights to illuminate our understanding. In the beginning of the contest with Great Britain, when we were sensible to danger, we had daily prayers in this room for divine protection. Our prayers, Sir, were heard and graciously answered. ... Do we imagine that we no longer need His assistance? I have lived, Sir, a long time, and the longer I live, the more convincing proofs I see in this truth, that God governs the affairs of men. And if a sparrow cannot fall to the ground without His notice,* is it probable that an empire can rise without His aid? ... We have been assured that except the Lord build the house, they labor in vain that build it.** – I firmly believe this." ... Lord, forgive us our arrogance as a nation for thinking that we can survive our present or build a future without You.

In Jesus' name we pray.

Amen.

* (Matt. 10:29)

** (Psalm 127:1)

JULY 5

Dear Lord Jesus, we cry out for peace, but there can be no real peace until You return, because we are caught up in a climaxing "spiritual battle" for men's souls. You have said that even the "elect" may be deceived. ... You are asking us to choose between humanistic philosophies, other gods, and Your unadulterated Word, aren't You? ... Remind us that You set limits when You defended Your Father's house against the money-changers, commanding them not to make it into a den of robbers. ... Forgive us today, and forgive me, for often by my silence I have allowed others to legalize what You have called "immorality." Oh Lord, give me the courage to defend You as Joshua did, and say: "... as for me and my house, we will serve the Lord."*

In Your name I pray.

Amen.

* (Joshua 24:15)

JULY 6

Dear Lord, when a new electric bulb fails to light, I do not say that there must be something wrong with the theory of electricity, but rather that there must be something wrong with its connection to the power source. ... When my prayers seem to go unanswered, help me to realize that it is not Your love or power that is missing, but rather my connection with You. Show me, Lord, what thoughts or deeds of mine are causing the break, and help me to get in "sync" with You.

In Your holy name I pray.

Amen.

JULY 7

Dear Lord, You are willing to accept me just as I am, warts and all – my hurts, my guilt, and my sins. You love me just as I am, but You don't want me to stay that way! ... When I sincerely confess my sins, help me to accept Your forgiveness, believing it, and forgiving myself. Repenting means to reverse my direction, doesn't it? Help me to want to become Your "new creation," letting Your desires become my desires, and realizing that You want only the best for me. Keep me ever in Your care, and help me to grow in my faith.

In Jesus' name I pray.

Amen.

JULY 8

Our most gracious heavenly Father, as we acknowledge Your sovereignty today, help us to remember that as Christians we have committed ourselves to living by Your rules, and not by our generational whims or desires. ... You created us, male and female to procreate, nurture and enjoy our families, that we might continue to be Your people. Through Your Son's sacrifice, You loved us, You taught us, and You saved us. ... Jesus taught that we were to seek and follow Your will, that we were to show sensitivity to sinners, but that we were

not to condone their sins! ... Forgive us, Lord, as a nation, as a denomination, as a church, and as individuals for too often condoning what You have called sin.* Give us courage as we try to remain faithful to Your Word.

In Jesus' name we pray.

Amen.

* (See Romans 1:18–32; Exod. 20:12–17)

JULY 9

Dear Lord, help me to remember that although Your grace is free, discipleship is costly. If I truly accept You as my Lord and Savior, and commit myself to You, then out of love I will want to serve You, seeking to know Your will and to be obedient to it. ... Help me to be a channel of Your love, Your healing, and Your strength that others may see You in me. ... That's what it is all about, isn't it – this being a Christian? You first loved me, and I am to pass Your love on to others. ... And let me count it all joy.

In Your holy name I pray.

Amen.

JULY 10

Dear Lord, where I can change my condition for the better, give me the wisdom and courage to do so. Where I cannot change my circumstances, help me to take control and change my attitude. Let me adopt a positive attitude that will glorify You, and may my problems become opportunities for service. ... "As a man thinketh"* – help me to see, Lord, that how I choose to think will influence my future. Is my cup half empty, or is it half full? I can be optimistic, or I can choose to think negatively and witness to the weakness of my faith, and help to bring on the disaster that I dread. It's up to me, isn't it?

In Jesus' name I pray.

Amen.

* (See Prov. 23:7)

JULY 11

Dear Lord, remind me that discipline is a requirement of discipleship. For how else can I discover the truth of Your declaration to Your disciple Paul: "My strength is made perfect in [your] weakness."* I must prove this in my own life if I am to share it with others. ... Help me, Lord, as I struggle with difficult problems in circumstances that test my faith. Help me to see that I do need You, and remind me to wait for Your leading. In the midst of it all, let me feel Your peace, and then discover that You are indeed adequate for all of my needs.

In Jesus' name I pray.

Amen.

* (II Cor. 12:9)

JULY 12

Dear Lord, You have said that if we will wait upon You, that You will renew our strength; we shall mount up with wings as eagles; we shall run and not be weary; we shall walk and not faint. ... But Lord, it is not always easy to wait. Sometimes I want You to give me patience, right now! ... Help me to remember the times that You have stood with me in the past. Help me to believe that You will renew my strength, and provide for all my needs, as I wait to find a job, or as I start a new one; as I start a new program, make a new beginning, or prepare to go off to college; as I wait for healing – whatever. You will be there with me. Let me remember that You are trustworthy, and learn to praise You in all things!

In Jesus' name I pray.

Amen.

JULY 13

Dear Lord, when days get hectic, and I am feeling overwhelmed with my parenting responsibilities, when everyone is late and starting the day behind schedules has become the norm, forgive me when I lose my cool. ... Help me to reschedule and slow down, and to try not to crowd too much into my children's lives and mine. ... These times are difficult enough for both parents and young people. Help me not to add to the problem – not to run ahead of You. ... Rather teach me to plan quiet times of family togetherness each day so that we can listen to each other, heal our brokenness, count our blessings, experience Your love and Your peace, and sit through at least one meal together daily.

In Jesus' name I pray.

Amen.

JULY 14

Dear Lord, remind me that as Corrie ten Boom once said, "God does not hold me responsible

for success but for faithfulness – Jesus said, 'Well done you good and faithful servant,' not 'well done you good and successful servant.'" ... Help me , Lord, as I strive to be faithful; sometimes it's not easy, sometimes it's not convenient, sometimes it means standing against criticism and ridicule, threats and attacks. ... It may take more courage than I have, but then You have promised not to leave me alone, and that Your strength will be sufficient. ... Help me to endure to the end, and to learn to praise You in all things!

In Jesus' name I pray.

Amen.

JULY 15

Dear Lord, help me to see that the real problem is not what happens to me but rather how I react that makes the difference. Teach me, Oh Lord, to deal with the circumstances in my life so that they will not be able to disturb my "inner peace and joy" in You. ... Help me to come to know You by studying Your Word and building a relationship with You. Remind me to put on Your armor* and to recognize my real enemy. Engrave in my heart that You are greater than any evil that can attack me.** ... As long as I abide in You, You have promised to abide in me. Give me Your gift of faith and help me to remain steadfast.

In Your holy name I pray.

Amen.

* (See Eph. 6)

** (See 1 John 4:4)

JULY 16

Dear Lord, help me to see that love is not the blind acceptance of every sin and sinner; rather love is caring enough to pray for a wayward nation, a decadent society, for family members following false gods or on drugs. ... Love is coming against their spiritual blindness, and seeking Your help for them when they cannot be reached any other way. ... Help me, Lord, to love enough to be a faithful daily intercessor. Truly, as the poet said: "More things are wrought by prayer than this world dreams ..." Let Christians everywhere join together in prayer.

In Your name I pray.

Amen.

JULY 17
Dear Heavenly Father, help me to realize that prayer, as C. H. Dodd has indicated, should not be a device for getting You to use Your resources to grant my desires, but rather a means for me to re-direct my desires to be in accordance with Your will. ... Remind me that Jesus said: "Whatever you ask the Father in My name He will give you,"* meaning something that receives Your approval, and is made possible because I have accepted Jesus as my Lord and Savior. ... So let me think over my requests before I pray in order that they may be according to Your will; this may reduce the number of my requests, but it may also increase the number of Your positive answers. ... Let me take time to study Your Word that I may better understand Your will, and recognize the Holy Spirit's leading.
In Jesus' name I pray.
Amen.
* (John 16:23; also see James 4:3)

JULY 18
Dear Lord, help me to put my own problems in the proper perspective, trusting Your plan for my life. Let me see that the "daily-ness" of my living is a part of the fabric of my eternity. ... Especially in the midst of my despair, let my inner peace and joy be the sign of Your loving Presence in my life. Thank You, Lord.
In Your holy name I pray.
Amen.

JULY 19
Dear Lord, help me to learn that You have a purpose for me right where I am – whether happy or depressed, secure or frightened, well or ill, going forward or marking time – there is something that I can do for You, Lord. ... You can use me every day of my life! Show me how, Lord. ... Help me to take time to listen, and to chip away at my self-centeredness, that I may "know" within me Your Holy Spirit's leading. ... Help me to want to make Your will my will, in both big and little things – such as to encourage another, to show love and kindness, or to lend a helping hand. ... No matter my present circumstances, it is up to me to enlarge the vistas of my life, isn't it? Open my eyes to see the opportunities that You provide for me to reflect You each day.
This I ask in Jesus' name.
Amen.

JULY 20
Dear Lord, You have a way of humbling us, of bringing us as a nation to our knees. Then and only then do we realize how completely we must depend on You. ... Forgive us for forgetting, and for making money, riches, and material gain our top priorities. ... Bring us back to the reality of being Your people, and of walking in FAITH. You alone are our source, our provider, our security, and our God.
In the name of Jesus we pray.
Amen.

JULY 21
Dear Lord, You have said that Your people perish for lack of knowledge.* ... Help me to see that in this time of so much confusion, hype, and disinformation, that as a Christian I must continually seek Your truth. ... I will recognize Your truth because it will be righteous, and because it will be in accordance with Your Word, Your character, and Your will. Disinformation disregards You, Your sovereignty, and Your righteousness. ... Help me, Lord, for Satan "prowls around like a roaring lion, seeking someone to devour,"** and in many disguises. Help me to know You well enough to "know" what is not of You.
In Jesus' name I pray.
Amen.
* (See Hosea 4:6)
** (I Peter 5:8)

JULY 22
Dear Lord, help me to walk closely with You daily, taking time to read Your Word, so that I will come to know You, and recognize Your Spirit's leading, so that I will not be deceived or coerced into following "another Jesus."* ... Give me the courage and wisdom to "pursue righteousness, godliness, faith, love, perseverance, and gentleness." Help me to "fight the good fight of faith,"** that I may be Your true witness.
In Jesus' name I pray.
Amen.
* (See II Cor. 11:4)
** (1 Tim. 6:11–12)

JULY 23

Dear Lord, whether life polishes me or grinds me down depends on what I am made of, doesn't it? And what I am made of depends on where I'm centered. ... Oh Lord, help me to make You my focus, my center, in the days ahead; to daily read Your Word, to be still and reflect on its meaning, so that I may really get to know You. How can I sense Your will for my life unless I first try to build a relationship with You? Only then can I discern how You would respond in my situation, and know intuitively the leading of Your Holy Spirit. ... Help me Lord, for I want to be willing to commit my life totally to You.

In Jesus' name I pray.
Amen.

JULY 24

Dear Lord, as You seek to purify Your church today, staying in my closet to pray and hoping to escape society's problems will not be enough, will it? ... Remind me that You are counting on us who call ourselves by Your name – we Christians – to represent You in this fractured world of today. ... You not only want me to do good deeds and tell others about You, but there comes a time when I must recognize that there is a "spiritual battle" being waged.* Like it or not, I will have to take a stand at some point, either for You, or against You by default. It's my call, isn't it?

In Jesus' name I pray.
Amen.

* (See Eph. 6:10–18)

JULY 25

Dear Lord, remind me, lest I forget, that You came not only to put away sin, not only the guilt and punishment of it, but sin itself. You came to change me so that I would no longer desire to sin. ... Help me Lord, to really understand this, so that I may repent and invite You to take over my life. Only then can You cleanse me, and put Your Spirit within me as You have promised. ... It all depends on me – how sincere I am, doesn't it?

In the name of Jesus I pray.
Amen.

JULY 26

Dear Lord, when has life not been uncertain? Each generation has its own problems, and when Your people have turned away from You, their trials and hardships have intensified. So what do You require of us, and where can we find security? ... You have said that we are "to act justly, and to love mercy, and to walk humbly with You,"* and that "he that shall endure to the end shall be saved."** ... Help me to keep the faith, and to walk closely with You; for You only expect me to be the best that I can be in whatever circumstances I find myself, and to try to reflect You as Your witness. ... Let me never forget that for any Christian the safest place to be is in the center of Your will. ... Help me Lord, for I am often weak and easily discouraged. Remind me to trust You and to walk in faith, and to seek the Holy Spirit's guidance.

In Jesus' name I pray.
Amen.

* (Micah 6:8)
** (Matt. 24:13)

JULY 27

Most gracious Lord, remind us that we who call ourselves "Your people" on Sundays are required to live by Your guidelines seven days a week! Both as Christians and as citizens of this great nation, we need to remember that it was founded on Your moral principles. ... We each need to be honest and trustworthy in all of our daily dealings. No nation, no society, no marriage, and no family can long survive without honesty and trustworthiness! ... Open our eyes to see that too many times we give You honor on Sundays and then accept our daily newscaster's "take" on weekdays as our "gospel." Quite often we are misled and deceived! ... Remind us of our grandparents' truism that "Two wrongs do not make a right!" ... Help us to demand of our leaders the same integrity that You expect each of us to demand of ourselves, whether as Christians, as citizens, or both. Help us to seek the truth and Your guidance, lest we be deceived.

In Jesus' name we pray.
Amen.

JULY 28

Dear Lord, help me to seek You early in the morning that my heart may get its bearings by reading Your Word, and then praying for our country's leaders and interceding for those in need. ... Help me to discover Your direction for my day, lest You get crowded out of my life's difficulties and pleasures, and I am left adrift in a sea of my own choosing.

In Your holy name I pray.

Amen.

JULY 29

Dear Lord, Help us to realize that Christians everywhere are in a spiritual battle, and need to recognize the enemy – those who ridicule and demean You, trying to blot out Your influence. Help me to realize also that "greater is He (God) who is within me, than he (Satan) who is in the world."* ... If I walk in Your will, then You will never desert me, for I can count on You. You will provide strength and courage and guidance, for You are true to Your Word. ... The question is, can You count on me? Oh Lord, I hope so, for I need You, and You need your people to be faithful. ... Help me to keep my connection for I am often weak, and I am helpless without You.

In Jesus' name I pray.

Amen.

* (1 John 4:4)

JULY 30

Dear Lord, in these days when it is difficult to publicly acknowledge my Christian faith, when at times, some "Christians" find it easier to water down their faith and are willing to define "love" as accepting "other gods" as equal to You, give me courage. Give me wisdom to delve more deeply into Your Word, to seek the Holy Spirit's guidance that I may know Your truth. ... Open my eyes that You may reveal to me an understanding of Your justice – that You alone are sovereign, and that we are to have no other God but You! Your justice is fair, for You do indeed punish sinners as You have said You would, while Your mercy is voluntary, for You alone understand the "heart." ... Teach me, O Lord, and help me to bring my heart into alignment with Your will.

In Jesus' name I pray.

Amen.

JULY 31

Dear Lord, help me to accept the fact that life is often filled with trials – earthquakes, floods, fires, tornadoes, lay-offs, accidents, sickness, and loss of loved ones, interspersed with times of joy, gentle love, helping hands, quiet peace, and indomitable hope! ... Help me to remember that others have faced similar problems, and found You. Let my faith never falter, for in the midst of my adversities You are there. ... Let me resolve to put my hand in Yours, for You have said that You are the Way, the Truth, and the Life.* ... New opportunities will come, new doors will open. The sun will shine again! ... Help me to trust You all the way, and to be ready.

In Jesus' name I pray.

Amen.

*(See John 14:6)

AUGUST 1

Dear Lord, remind me that if I am to call myself a truly committed Christian, then I must not leave my Christianity on the church doorstep when I leave the Sunday service. Help me to see that I must stand for You in all of my daily dealings – secular, political and personal. If I don't stand on Your Word, how will others see You in me? ... However, there is more, isn't there, Lord? You want me to go and tell others about You. Otherwise, even though I may live a kind and caring life, no one will know that it is because of You and Your help. You are the "good news," You are the message that God the Father sent. ... Help me, Lord, to be open to Your leading. Give me the wisdom, and the words, and the courage to know what to say and when to say it, so that others may desire to know You.

In Your holy name I pray.

Amen.

AUGUST 2

Dear Lord, as we look around the world we see chaos, discord, and famine. We find our own nation a microcosm of the world and its problems. ... As we face changes proposed to create a "cultural shift" in our nation, help us not to be too quick to discard our past heritage. Instead, let us re-study the dreams, foresight, and the dedication of the founders of our nation, predicated on the Judeo-Christian ethic. ... Give us a desire to know the truth, lest we indeed "perish from lack of knowledge."* ... Help us to ferret out history books written before they were "cleansed" and re-written to fit today's scholars' self-serving agendas. Wake us up as a nation, and as Christians to see that we need to reclaim our Godly heritage. ... Help us to realize that Christianity is always in danger of extinction in every generation unless it is kept viable and passed on to our youth. Oh Lord, give us courage, for it will not be easy. And guide us as we seek to know and to live within Your will.

In Jesus' name we pray.

Amen.

* (See Hosea 4:6)

AUGUST 3

Dear Lord, rescue me from myself, lead me when I become confused, prod me when I am wrong, fill me with Your Holy Spirit, and enable me to be the kind of Christian that You want me to be – the kind that You know that I can be, with Your help.

In Your holy name I pray.

Amen.

AUGUST 4

Dear Lord, let us consider these words written by William Arthur Ward and discover anew that Your presence surrounds us.

"In a garden, I found contentment.

In a seed, I found faith.

In a flower, I found God.

In a tree, I found patience.

In a butterfly, I found beauty.

In a smile, I found acceptance.

In a touch, I found encouragement.

In a friend, I found joy.

In a child, I found trust."

Oh Lord, open my eyes, my mind, and my heart to recognize the reminders of You and Your love that surround me. Forgive me for being so caught up in my worldly concerns that I think You have deserted me, and consequently miss all of the beauty and joy that You have for me, and the evidence of Your presence.

In Jesus' name I pray.

Amen.

AUGUST 5

Dear Lord, in times of trials and suffering, when I feel overwhelmed, and my faith shrinks to the size of a "mustard seed," forgive me! Forgive me for focusing on the magnitude of my problems instead of the magnitude of my God! ... Help me to see that accepting Your sovereignty is no longer just an academic question, but an everyday necessity as the basis of my Christian faith. For if I really accept Your sovereignty, then I must believe that You are adequate for all of my needs. ... I pray that the Holy Spirit will make known to me whether I am to act or to wait. Help me to trust that You can bring something meaningful even out of my crisis-situations, and to learn that Your grace, Your mercy, and Your love are indeed sufficient for all of my needs, for You are faithful to Your Word.

In the name of Jesus I pray.

Amen.

AUGUST 6

Dear Lord, I need a vacation. You know that I've worked hard. I need a rest – but not from You. ... Come with me; let me praise You daily; let me set aside some time each day to read Your Word, to pray, to experience a deeper relationship with You. Then I will return truly rested, refreshed, and renewed. ... Oh Lord, I have expected You always to be there for me in times of crisis; let me never take a vacation from You.

In Your holy name I pray.

Amen.

AUGUST 7

Dear Lord, teach me to follow You, not just to try to do as You did, but to be as You were. That's the core of it, isn't it? ... If I try to be – to become more Christ-like – then my doing will be the fruit, won't it? ... I must have love in my heart – no unforgiveness, no bitterness, no envy, no self-centered agenda – then it will be easy to show love in my actions. I'll need Your help. I can't do it without You, but if I truly seek Your will, and ask for the Holy Spirit's guidance, then I will be able to fulfill Your plan for my life. ... Help me to develop patience, and strength and courage, for Your sake and for mine.

In Jesus' name I pray.
Amen.

AUGUST 8

Dear Lord, why is it that I am always in a hurry and You are not? Remind me that most things that are really worthwhile were not achieved in a day. ... By study and prayer, help me to create the climate for Your miracles. Help me, Lord, to build a day to day relationship with You so that I can recognize Your actions in my life, and give You all the glory.
In Jesus' name I pray.
Amen.

AUGUST 9

Dear Lord, You did not say in Your Word that as a Christian I would not be tempted, but rather that with Your help, I need not be overcome. ... You did not say that I could solve others' problems, but that I could introduce them to You, and that You would provide the answers. ... Oh Lord, help me to study Your Word until knowing Your laws and living by them becomes second nature to me, lest I stumble and cause others to fall.
In Your name I pray.
Amen.

AUGUST 10

Dear Lord, why do bad things happen to good people? ... Help us to realize that nothing happens to us that You do not know about, and allow. ... You may let us make mistakes, and You may let Satan attack us to teach us that we need Your strength and protection. Whatever the source of our problems, You can turn the outcome to good!* ... Oh Lord, forgive us for getting so caught up in trying to run our own lives that we fail to seek Your will; forgive us for often turning to You only in times of crisis; forgive us for being "slow learners;" and forgive us for letting our pride separate us from You. ... Teach us, Lord, that You are indeed faithful and trustworthy, just as You want us to be. Give us faith to see that Your grace is indeed sufficient to sustain us in all situations.
In Jesus' name we pray.
Amen.
* (See Genesis 50:20)

AUGUST 11

Our gracious heavenly Father, if as Watchman Nee has written, "You have indeed chosen this world to be the arena for Your plan, the center of what You have set Yourself to do," then help me to trust You completely. ... Help me to remember that moral excellence, like a good painting, begins by drawing a guide-line; and remind me that You have already drawn that line! You have set limits for mankind's conduct, and for mine. ... Help me to see that it is only when I try to live within Your parameters that I can enjoy my greatest fulfillment and worth. ... Help us as a nation, as a church, and as individuals to try to see things from Your point of view, lest by insisting on our own "guide-lines," we bring on our downfall. ... Help us to wake up before we are overwhelmed by our mistakes.
In Jesus' name I pray.
Amen.

AUGUST 12

Dear Lord, remind me that all of my problems are not always Satan's attacks, but some are Your way of testing me and challenging my faith to grow deeper roots. ... Only if my faith is tested will I be strong enough to stand when my life is in crisis. ... Help me, Lord, to trust You all the way, and never to fail You as Your friends did at Gethsemane and at the time of Your crucifixion. I need Your strength.
In Your name I pray.
Amen.

AUGUST 13

Dear Lord, although some Christians may achieve greatness as leaders, the growth of Christianity has always depended on individuals catching the vision. Help me to be sensitive to the opportunities available to me to act out Your love, Your compassion and concerns for others that I may reflect Your amazing grace. For often it is in the little things – holding a door for someone, lending a helping hand, giving words of encouragement or appreciation that I best represent You. ... Help us, Oh Lord, who call ourselves Your followers, who believe Your message, to remember that we may be the first "gospel in action" that some have ever encountered. ... When the timing is right, give me the words to tell someone about You!

In Your name, Jesus, I pray.

Amen.

AUGUST 14

Dear heavenly Father, You created me to have fellowship with You. Let me come before You with rejoicing – not complaining, not questioning, not asking, not beseeching, but realizing fully the privilege that is mine in being able to honor You with praise and thanksgiving. Help me to seek You for who You are, rather than for just what You can do for me.

In the name of our Lord Jesus I pray.

Amen.

AUGUST 15

Dear Lord, You have said: "If My people who are called by My name will humble themselves, and pray and seek My face, and turn from their wicked ways, then I will hear from heaven, and will forgive their sin and heal their land."* Many of Your people across this land, in cities and towns, in churches, parks and homes, observe a day of prayer each year. ... Open our eyes to see the error of our ways. Forgive us for thinking that we can re-design You to fit today's social changes. Help us to see that Your moral order was meant for all generations and that we are the ones who need to change. ... Forgive us, for we have often denied our Christian heritage. We have been deceived and have allowed others to lead us astray. How we must have grieved You! ... Give us spiritual insight and a desire to seek Your will – for our nation, for Your churches, and for our lives – lest we fail You and fall into a quagmire of our own making.

In Jesus' holy name we pray.

Amen.

* (II Chron. 7:14)

AUGUST 16

Dear Lord, help me to learn to release my yesterdays, especially when I may have lived by my own desires and not by Your Word. Remind me that You want me to sincerely repent, and to commit myself anew. ... Teach me, Lord, to leave my tomorrows in Your hands, knowing that You want the best for me. ... Help me to

look forward to each new day with open arms! Let me learn to seek Your will early in the morning, and to recognize the blessings and opportunities that await me. Every day You show Your love in so many ways; thank You that I can indeed count on You. Help me, Lord, to recognize my many opportunities for sharing Your love with others, and help me to be the faithful servant that You want me to be.

In Jesus' name I pray.

Amen.

AUGUST 17

Dear Lord, the answers that I receive when I pray certainly demonstrate Your faithfulness to me, but they are also dependent upon my being obedient and faithful to You. ... Your Word tells us that we cannot expect to have our prayers answered while we are living in sin and in disobedience to Your commandments.* ... Oh Lord, help me to sincerely repent of any wrong-doing before I come to You with my needs.

In Jesus' name I pray.

Amen.

* (See James 4:1–4)

AUGUST 18

Dear Lord, as we pray for our nation's leadership, help us to realize, both as Christians and as citizens, that each one of us has a responsibility to our country. ... Help us to commit ourselves to pray daily for our leaders and for our nation's welfare. Let us recognize our country's waywardness, and repent and seek Your will that we may return to being bound by Your truths. ... As we pray for Christian revival around the world, let us also pray for Christian revival here at home. ... Open our eyes to see the subtle deceptions of the New Age philosophies that have already invaded our media, entertainment, businesses, schools and universities, and many of our church denominations, where too often freedom has been accepted to mean no boundaries, no absolutes, and no rules. ... Oh Lord, remind us that You are still sovereign; it is Your universe and Your world, and the Bible is Your "manufacturer's handbook." ... Remind us all that no society can long survive which ignores Your guidelines, for the concept of "no rules, no game" is as true in life as it is in football. Help us, Lord, for we are often deceived and misled.

In Jesus' name we pray.

Amen.

AUGUST 19

Our Father who art in heaven, remind us that truth is not what we say it is, it is what You have declared it to be! ... Remind us too that You sent Your beloved Son that we might better understand Your love and desires for all who would accept Him and His teachings, and His sacrifice on the cross, that we might be forgiven our sins, and have the promise of eternal life! ... Jesus said to Thomas, "I am the way, the truth and the life. No one comes to the Father but through Me."* ... "He who has seen Me has seen the Father ... Do you not believe I am in the Father and the Father is in Me? The Words that I say to you I do not speak on My own initiative, but the Father abiding in Me does His work ... He who has My command-ments and keeps them, he is the one who loves Me, and he who loves Me shall be loved by My Father."** ... Help my heart to listen, and my daily life to reflect these words of Jesus.

In His name I pray.

Amen.

* (John 1:1)

** (John 14:6, 9–10)

AUGUST 20

Dear Lord, remind each of us that saying one is sorry is only the beginning of righting the wrongs we have committed. ... Repentance requires that we turn around and not repeat our careless or intentional sins. ... For any of us, turning around is the test of our sincerity, isn't it? ... We each set examples, whether we realize it or not, for we never know when our lives will be used as an example or excuse for someone else's behavior! ... Oh Lord, help us to realize this for Your sake and for ours!

In Jesus' name we pray.

Amen.

* (See Psalm 51:10–13; Prov. 28:13; Romans 6: 1–4)

AUGUST 21

Dear Lord, remind me that there will never be enough ordained ministers and missionar-ies to change the world! Only Christians, by example and word, can contact one on one the unchurched and the agnostic or atheist in the market place. ... Help me, Lord, to truly be Your disciple. Give me the right words at the right time to share Your love, encourage-ment and comfort, so that others will desire to know You.

In Jesus' name I pray.

Amen.

AUGUST 22

Dear Lord, if only the birds with beautiful voic-es sang, the world would often be silent. ... Let me "sing out" Your praises because my spirit is filled with love and gratitude for Your gift of faith, and for Your presence in my life. ... Let me worship You, Lord, for Your faithfulness, and for sending Your Son and the Holy Spirit that I may better understand Your will for my life. Let me in all of my being praise You, Lord.

Amen and Amen.

AUGUST 23

Dear Lord, You have said that as a man thinks, so he becomes. Search me, Oh Lord, and bring my unconscious images and drives before Your judgment and mercy. Cleanse me with Your love, helping me to forgive as I would be forgiven. Let my thoughts be Your thoughts, that I may be re-made in Your likeness. Then my life will take on new meaning, and others will be warmed by its glow, and Your glory will be shown for all to see.

In Your holy name I pray.

Amen.

AUGUST 24

Dear Lord, let me praise You! Let me give You honor and glory and praise! Let my spirit worship You, not just in words or hymns, but with a very real conviction that You are sover-eign, that You are faithful, and that You love me! ... Even when life's problems overwhelm me, remind me that You are in the midst of it all with me. You have it all in Your hands, and You can be trusted.

Praise Your holy name.

Amen.

AUGUST 25

Dear Lord, in the midst of today's fast-paced society, help me to slow down lest I miss all that You have for me. ... There are moments when Your creation crosses my path – a bird's song, a new rose bud after a dry summer, a clear view of the mountains, a child's laughter, a friend's greeting, a stranger's smile – but is my mind on other things? ... Have I missed these moments that You have provided for my enjoyment, my renewal, or my opportunity? Have I neglected to recognize another's need – an encouraging word, a helping hand? ... Have I missed the right time to tell someone about You when I failed to point out that it was not "luck," but You, Lord, when a prayer was answered? Have I forgotten to encourage or express my love to a spouse, an offspring, or a friend? ... Help me to recognize and seize these precious moments that will not come again.

In Jesus' name I pray.

Amen.

AUGUST 26

Dear Lord, when my life seems rudderless, and I find myself floundering without purpose or goals, remind me that You created me for Your own purpose. ... How can I expect to find Your will for me unless I study Your Word and build a relationship with You? ... Without You, I only fall into a sea of worldly temptations – immorality, drugs, cults, self-centeredness – and my only destination is hell, both here and hereafter. ... The choice is mine, isn't it? Help me Lord, to choose You, and Your will for my life.

In the name of Jesus I pray.

Amen.

AUGUST 27

Dear Lord, help me to leave spaces in my days for quiet growth, for new ideas, for dreams and new insights, for perspectives and directions, for listening to Your quiet voice, and sensing Your will for me. ... Let me not limit my quiet time by setting boundaries, lest I miss out on what Your Holy Spirit has uniquely for me!

In Jesus' name I pray.

Amen.

AUGUST 28

Dear Lord, there are times when I feel overwhelmed, caught in a web of insurmountable problems, not knowing where to turn. My heart has needs that my mind cannot answer. Oh Lord, teach me to turn everything over to You, to relax, to trust You, to "climb my watchtower and wait to see what answer You will give to my complaint."* ... Remind me that my weakness is also my opportunity to discover Your strength. Forgive me, Lord, for forgetting that You never expected me to carry my burdens alone. ... I need You every hour, I need You. Do not abandon me.

In Jesus' name I pray.

Amen.

* (See Hab. 2:1 – TLB & NKJ)

AUGUST 29

Dear Lord, just for today, I will try to serve You by putting Your will ahead of my desires. ... Just for today, I will try to think before I speak or act, asking myself, "How would Jesus respond?" ... Just for today, I will try to live out my faith with the help and strength of the Holy Spirit – one day at a time. ... Help me, for I often forget.

In the name of Jesus I pray.

Amen.

AUGUST 30

Dear heavenly Father, help me to review Your truths, that I may have watered down or chosen to ignore. A sin is not "missing the mark" as the Greeks, who had many gods, defined it. It is a sin because You defined it as such, and You are sovereign. ... Fornication, adultery, homosexuality, the killing of the unborn, abusing one's body – all are an abomination to You and grieve Your Spirit. ... Help me to realize that You loved me so much that You sent Your Son to redeem my sins. Help me, for I often I find it hard to forgive myself.

In the name of Jesus I pray.

Amen.

AUGUST 31

Dear Lord, just as each new day brings its own problems, to us as a nation, and to me as an individual, so does each day show our need for You. ... Oh Lord, open my eyes to see that

I need to come to You daily for guidance. I need to come to You in prayer and to study Your Word, in order to be able to recognize Your leading. ... You have said that man does not live by bread alone. ... Forgive us all, for too often we have wanted to go our own way, to "do our own thing." Remind each of us that while enthusiasm is laudable, wisdom is also necessary. Help us, Lord, to seek Your will and Your guidance each morning to be ready for whatever the day brings.

In Jesus' name I pray.

Amen.

SEPTEMBER 1

Most gracious heavenly Father, forgive us, Your people, for standing by while our nation slips further and further from its Christian heritage. ... Each day we find ourselves being misinformed and misled by those who think that our nation's problems can be solved by more taxes, more policemen, and more government spending. Open our eyes, Lord, to see that these are only "patches" on our country's structure, while its moral foundations are being undermined. ... Help us to see that unless we return to living by Your rules for morality – unless we teach each generation the value of being personally accountable, responsible, honest and caring – we will contribute to bringing on the downfall of our nation. ... Oh Lord, help us to see that only repentance will save us – turning around and deciding to go Your way – because You can not and will not bless our sinful ways.

In Jesus' name we pray.

Amen.

SEPTEMBER 2

Dear Lord, we have prayed that You would raise up righteous leaders for our country – men of integrity and moral example who will lead this nation to fulfill Your vision and our dreams. Give us the wisdom to recognize them, for we have often been deceived. ... Remind us that integrity and morality are not just words to be bandied about, but words to be reflected in one's everyday conduct. These are essential in building character. ... Let us demand these qualities for these leaders and for ourselves, for no nation, no society, and no

family can long survive without standards that require honesty and responsibility in all of our actions, dealings, and relationships. Only then will we and our leaders set honorable examples for our youth to follow. Only then can we rightfully sing: "GOD BLESS AMERICA." ... Help us, Lord, to become the nation that You want us to be. Let us reclaim Your vision for our country; with Your help we can!

In Jesus' name we pray.

Amen.

SEPTEMBER 3

Dear Lord, just when I had it all made, then everything fell apart. I lost my job! How could You let this happen, Lord? Where were You? Where are You now? ... My son, I am right here, I haven't moved. The last time I heard from you, you said that you were pressed for time, and only had a minute. ... You sounded as though you had things under your control, and didn't need Me. However, let Me remind you that I never promised you a life of ease. I said that I would be with you if our connection was not broken. ... Think it over, and call Me in the morning. Continued tomorrow

In Jesus' name we pray.

Amen.

SEPTEMBER 4

Dear Lord, slow me down, and let me listen to the language of my heart. Let me sense the quickening of my spirit, and realize that my soul has questions that only You can answer. ... Let me take on fewer tasks so that those I do tackle may be pleasing to You. ... It is not quantity that counts but quality, isn't it? Help me to make my time worth something – encouraging, caring, helpful, productive, at home with family and loved ones, at work with colleagues and associates, and with others encountered throughout the day. Let me make someone's day brighter because our paths crossed. Help me to reflect Your love and concern, trusting You to give me the words to say, when needed to brighten someone's day. Let me not miss the opportunities that cross my path.

In Jesus' name I pray.

Amen.

SEPTEMBER 5

Dear Lord, sometimes life is just too hectic, too fast-paced! I am apt to cry out, "Lord, give me patience, right now!" When will I learn? Often times after such a prayer, I find myself stalled in a traffic jam, or caught in a supermarket line where the person checking out can't find her pen or her identification card. It is getting so that I am almost afraid to pray that prayer, Lord, for You seem to answer it by giving me more opportunities to practice patience! ... Remind me even then, that You didn't tell me to crowd so many activities into my schedule that 24–hour days would not be long enough! In fact, You don't even tell time by hours and minutes, do You? You might even see some things in my schedule that should have been left out. ... Help me Lord, to consult You before I plan my day, and not run ahead of You.

In Jesus' name I pray.

Amen.

SEPTEMBER 6

Dear Lord, are You still there? Forgive me for breaking our connection. I've been thinking of what You said yesterday. Forgive me for thinking that I could manage my life without You. ... I've reread Your Word, where You said through Your Son, Jesus: "Take My yoke upon you, and learn from Me, ... for My yoke is easy, and My load is light."* I realize that if I seek to discover Your will for my life, and to be "yoked" to You, that Your yoke will not chafe if I am truly walking closely with You, and in sync with Your will. ... The two of us together, Lord, will be carrying my load! I need never walk alone! ... I took time to count my blessings – my loving wife, my children – all are helping out and encouraging me. We have our health, but most of all, we are growing closer to You. ... In the years ahead, we may even see that what we considered to be a catastrophe – losing my employment – may be turned into a blessing as we each grow in our faith. Thank You, Lord, for Your very real presence in our lives.

In Jesus' name I pray.

Amen.

* (Matt. 11:28–30)

SEPTEMBER 7

Most gracious heavenly Father, many of us as leaders, ministers and teachers come together in September to consider the year ahead, and the opportunities that it will present to share Your Word with others. We ask Your help as we seek to be Your ambassadors in a hurting and confused world. ... Remind us that we each need to be open to Christian growth, knowledge, and understanding that can only come from spending time in Your Word, and seeking the Holy Spirit's interpretive guidance and direction. ... Remind us too that Your will will never take us beyond where Your grace can sustain us! ... Help us, as church leaders, to truly commit ourselves to pray, and to work diligently to help our local church to become more nearly like the Church that You first envisioned! ... Lord, as we try to grow in faith and knowledge, help us to become more dedicated ambassadors, that others will desire to know You.

In Jesus' holy name we pray.

Amen.

SEPTEMBER 8

Dear Lord, September – a new beginning – in school, in college, in jobs, in programs and meetings; but Lord, in the midst of all these changes, help me not to forget You! Help me to still take time to count my blessings, and to seek Your direction for my life, lest I blunder and make wrong decisions. ... Remind me that it is in my busy-ness that I need You the most. Alert me to the needs of others in war-torn countries, and of those suffering from disasters, earthquakes, or droughts, abroad and in our own nation. ... As a committed Christian, I am called to be an intercessor. My prayers do count! Joined with those of many others, they can indeed change the world for the better. It's up to people like me, Christians, young people, parents and grandparents, isn't it, Lord? Help me to be faithful.

In Jesus' name I pray.

Amen.

SEPTEMBER 9

Dear Lord, if I call myself a Christian, just what kind of Christian am I? Am I a nominal Christian – a Christian in name only? Am I a luke-warm Christian – not really committed? Am I a Sunday Christian only, and on week days giving no one any reason to suspect that I consider myself a Christian? Do I only turn to You in times of crisis, and get upset if You don't answer immediately? Would I be surprised if You said, "Where have you been?" ... In short, have I ever really felt close to You? Could it be because I've been too busy with my worldly life to study Your Word, or to spend time with other Christians? Have I ever understood Your will and Your promises, all that You want for me? ... Oh Lord, how can I get to know You better? Please answer. Amen. Continued tomorrow

    In Jesus' name I pray.

    Amen.

SEPTEMBER 10

"To answer your question, 'How can I get to know You better?' – the same way one gets to know a friend or family member, by spending time together, one on one. If you will read My Book, in the Old Testament, you will learn of Me as Creator, and Sovereign God, 'I AM.' I brought into existence ALL that I have for you to enjoy and use creatively. ... I set forth rules and discipline for man's greatest good. I inspired the writers of the Bible to present both My shepherding love and My severe mercy. ... In the New Testament, I sent My only beloved Son to be the last 'sacrificial Lamb' for the lost sinners of all future generations to find their way back into My fold. It is open to all who choose to accept My Son, Jesus Christ, as their Lord and Savior. I have promised forgiveness and eternal life to those who accept Him as the Way, the Life, and the Truth." ... Thank You, Lord, for Your answer to my question. Help me not forget to seek fellowship with You each day, that I may know Your will for my life and be obedient to Your leading.

    In Jesus' name I pray.

    Amen.

SEPTEMBER 11

Gracious heavenly Father, You have created each of us for Your purposes. ... You have a plan for my life. It is up to me to build a relationship with You, to discover what You want for me. My greatest worth and happiness depend on this. ... Remind me that I am made in Your image, just as Jesus was when "He emptied Himself,"* and became flesh and

blood. ... His Spirit was His connection to You, just as my spirit becomes when I acknowledge You as God and accept Jesus' sacrifice for my sins. ... He had a soul, just as I have – mind, will, and emotions – one's unique personality. ... Jesus chose to always seek Your will, and to be obedient to it. I have the same choice, for I can know Your will through the Word and by Jesus' example, with the Holy Spirit's guidance. ... I have a physical, destructible body, just as Jesus had. How I take care of it, and use it, is a test of my commitment to You, for You have called me "to be holy as You are holy,"** for my greatest fulfillment, and for Your purposes. ... Open my eyes to see this, Lord. Walk with me, and help me to desire to share Your love and Your Word, that together we can make this a better world.

    In the name of Jesus I pray.

    Amen.

    * (Phil. 2:5–7)

    ** (I Peter 1:16)

SEPTEMBER 12

Lord Jesus, help me to understand that when I became a committed Christian, I also became Satan's target, for a lukewarm Christian is no threat to him. I may not always recognize Satan, for as C. S. Lewis wrote, "If one hasn't met Satan, it is probably because one is going his way!" ... Remind me that at Your baptism by John the Baptist, the triune Godhead was there: You, the Son, the Holy Spirit descending like a dove from heaven, and God the Father, whose voice was heard saying, "This is My beloved Son, in whom I am well-pleased."* You were "empowered" in a mighty way for Your ministry. ... But then You, Jesus, were "led up by the Spirit into the wilderness to be tempted by the devil."** ... You were tested, just as we will be; and You passed Your test, just as we can too with Your help, for "He who is in you is greater than he [Satan] who is in the world."*** ... Thank You that You have promised to be with me always, and that Your grace will be sufficient for all of my needs.

    In Your holy name I pray.

    Amen.

    * (Matt. 3:17)

    ** (Matt. 4:1)

    *** (1 John 4:4)

SEPTEMBER 13

Dear Lord, today let me consider Your revelation to Your apostle Paul which is recorded in the twelfth verse of the sixth chapter of his letter to the Ephesian church: "For our struggle is not against flesh and blood, but against rulers, against powers, against world forces of this darkness, against spiritual forces of wickedness in heavenly places." ... Oh Lord, save me from myself! Open my eyes before I become mesmerized by those who would try to lead me astray for their own purposes. ... Help me to realize that Satan often comes disguised as a seducer or temptress, a pretender, a deceiver, or a charming liar. ... Oh Lord, help me to recognize the enemy, lest I be easily taken in. Help me to stand firmly on Your Word and to trust You to put protective angels around me.

   In Jesus' name I pray.
   Amen.

SEPTEMBER 14

Dear Lord, I know that when I have given in faith of my time, You have helped me to accomplish more in less time; when I have given of my meager talent and forgotten my timidity, You have used me and made me adequate; and when I have dared to tithe, You have taken care of all my needs. ... Help me to be a better steward of all that You have given me, rejoicing that I do have more time, talent, and treasure to share than I realized. For this I thank You.

   In Your holy name I pray.
   Amen.

SEPTEMBER 15

Dear Lord, today is Your gift to me! Let me not fret about the past, re-living my mistakes and hurts, rather help me to learn from them. ... Remind me not to live for some tomorrow that may or may not come, lest I miss the NOW. ... Let me treasure every precious experience, large or small, good or bad, for I can enjoy it, or learn from it. ... Let me try to live each day to Your glory, for only then can I be sure that my life is indeed worth while, and precious to You. ... Thank You, Lord, for this moment – that I am here, and that You are with me! This is my joy! At other times this is my comfort,

my faith, and my peace!
   In Jesus' name I pray.
   Amen.

SEPTEMBER 16

Dear Lord, we Your people, who call ourselves Your "church," find ourselves as Christians to be under attack today, both from without and within, with Your deity being questioned, Your sovereignty demeaned, and Your atonement mocked. ... Help us who have committed ourselves to You as our Lord and Savior and who know You as "the Truth" to stand firmly in Your defense, lest the church be redefined to suit the agenda of those who would crucify You anew. ... Oh Lord, we weep at the arrogance of those who want to design their own "gods" to include their pagan beliefs and their favorite sins. ... Open their eyes and ours before it is too late. Help us as Christians to first understand Your will, and then help us to have the courage we will need to be obedient to it during the critical times that we may face in the future.

   In Jesus' name we pray.
   Amen.

SEPTEMBER 17

Dear Lord, how can I be strong enough to stand for You, and for my Christian principles? Remind me that as it is recorded in John 15:1(ff), You said: "I am the true vine, and My Father is the vine dresser. ... As the branch cannot bear fruit of itself, unless it abides in the vine, so neither can you, unless You abide in Me; ... If you abide in Me, and My words abide in you, ask whatever you wish, and it shall be done for you. ... By this is My Father glorified, that you bear much fruit, and so prove to be My disciples. ... These things I have spoken to you, that My joy may be in you, and that your joy be made full!" ... Only by staying attached to the vine, connected to Your life sustaining nourishment, only then will I discover Your guidance, and my strength to live out Your will. Only then can my life bear "fruit," recognizable for all to see, and only then can I be Your witness in a fractured world. It's You and me Lord; help me to stay close to You.

   In Your holy name I pray.
   Amen.

SEPTEMBER 18

Dear Lord God, some people are able to say short prayers and see immediate results. However, I must recognize that they have spent considerable time in studying Your Word, in prayer and meditation, and in seeking to know Your will. In other words, they were already "prayed up!" ... When a crisis comes, they know You! They know that they can trust You, and that You are ready to comfort, strengthen, and sustain them in their time of need. They know that You have said, "My strength is made perfect in weakness."* ... Oh Lord, help me to see that I too, need a close relationship with You in my life. I need to spend time with You each day, and learn that You are indeed faithful to Your Word and that I can count on You! Help me, Lord, for You too want to be able to count on me to share Your love with others.

In Jesus' name I pray.

Amen.

* (II Cor. 12:9)

SEPTEMBER 19

Dear Lord, when we repeat the prayer that You gave Your disciples, we pray: "Thy will be done." Have I concentrated so long on knowing Your will that I have forgotten that it must "be done?" Often it will only be done when a Christian does it; other times, only if I do it! ... Oh Lord, it is not enough to just know Your will, is it? I must be ready to act on it. I ask that You empower me with Your Holy Spirit, that I may carry out Your will more effectively each day.

In Jesus' name I pray.

Amen.

SEPTEMBER 20

Dear Lord Jesus, we sing that old hymn, "What A Friend We Have In Jesus," but how do we define "friend?" I once wrote this definition: "A friend is someone who compliments you enough to encourage you, who is honest enough to keep you humble while being tactful enough to make his honesty acceptable, and who is sensitive enough to your feelings to let you know that he loves you." ... The more I grow in my faith and the better I know You, the more I realize that You are that friend! Now, I can define friend in two words – Jesus Christ!

... How well our parents and grandparents knew You when they sang, "What A Friend We Have In Jesus." Sometimes we only discover this when You are all we have to count on! Thank You for Your loving, caring presence in our lives.

In Your holy name we pray.

Amen.

SEPTEMBER 21

Dear Lord, the answers that I desire when I pray do not hinge so much on Your faithfulness to me, as on my faithfulness to You, do they? ... Help me to see that "whatsoever I ask in Jesus' name" means whatsoever I ask in accordance with Your will, for when Jesus was here in person, He said that He only did what the Father directed. ... Help me to sincerely repent of any wrong-doing before I come to You with my needs.

In Jesus' name I pray.

Amen.

SEPTEMBER 22

Dear Lord, remind me that You are indeed faithful; even in my darkest hour, or in my loneliest moments, I can count on You to sustain me. Help me to know this in my spirit, and in my heart. ... How sincerely I believe this will depend on how closely I have walked with You, won't it? Help me to resolve to spend some quality time with You each day.

In Jesus' name I pray.

Amen.

SEPTEMBER 23

Dear Lord, as we pray for Your guidance for our nation in these critical times, give us the wisdom to measure our decisions by Your yardstick. If we are truthful with ourselves, we will realize that You measure a man or a woman by his or her character. You consider their daily actions and dealings, how they live their lives, how they treat their families and friends; not by their words and promises, but by whether they live by our nation's laws, and whether their word is their bond. ... It is true that You alone are the final judge of one's heart, one's motives, and one's life, but You have called each of us as citizens to decide, not those who are qualified to go to heaven, but rather those who are worthy to hold the high offices of our nation. ... Every day we are expected to make these kinds of judgments, and to decide how our own actions and those of others, the lives we live, and the examples that we set at work and at home will help or hinder our nation, and determine our children's inheritance. ... Can we demand less of our leaders and ourselves? Help us, we pray, for it is our call.

In Jesus' name we pray.

Amen.

SEPTEMBER 24

Dear Lord, let us pause to take stock of our country, for which so many have given their lives. We thank You for such dedication and for our opportunities, made possible through their sacrifices. As we look around at corruption in high places and at leadership that winks at immorality, let us not take this as license, but rather as a challenge for each of us to guard our own integrity. ... Remind us that You are our leader – our God – and that our nation will be strengthened or weakened by the actions of each individual citizen, lest we be held responsible for our short-sightedness and for the destruction of our nation. Help us to seek Your guidance for our immediate families, and for all other families in America, so that our nation's direction may be pleasing to You.

Thank You, Lord.

Amen.

SEPTEMBER 25

Dear Lord, this week, help me to try to see myself as You must see me when measured by Your Word. (Am I a staunch believer, or am I lukewarm? Do I accept Your Word as the truth, or do I pick and choose the parts of the Bible with which I agree? Am I a skeptic, an agnostic, or an atheist?) ... Open my eyes to see that Your ten commandments, as outlined in the book of Exodus, have been the basis for civilization's moral code down through the ages. ... Do I accept this, or do I embrace the new "cultural shift," whose adherents are trying to write their own rules to allow their favorite sins? ... In Exodus, Chapter 20, You began by saying: "I am the Lord your God, who brought you out of the land of Egypt, out

of the house of bondage. You shall have no other Gods before me."* ... Do I really accept Your sovereignty? Must I relive the Old Testament sins, and experience Your punishment? Give me an overwhelming desire to know You through Your Word and through Your Son, Jesus Christ, lest I be led to "strange gods" and to deny You completely. Remind me that the writers of the Bible – both the Old and the New Testaments – were divinely inspired by Your Holy Spirit. Forgive me for thinking that I can manage my life without You.

In His holy name I pray.

Amen.

* (Deut. 5:6–7)

SEPTEMBER 26

Dear Lord, if one doesn't have a view of eternity, if there is no recognition, reverence or respect for You, if nothing is sacred, then there is nothing before, and no future to come – only life in the "now," no value to life, no dreams. ... Yet Your Word clearly tells us that by the power of God we have been saved, and that You have "called us with a holy calling, not according to our works, but according to His own purpose and grace which was granted us in Christ Jesus from all eternity, ..."* Help me to see that I am special in Your sight, someone You need to fulfill a specific task. You have not "called" me to be a lukewarm Christian. You want me to be wholly committed, the best that I can be, with the Holy Spirit's guidance. In short, You want me to live in the center of Your will. Help me to want that too.

In the name of Jesus I pray.

Amen.

* (I1 Timothy 1:9)

SEPTEMBER 27

Dear Lord Jesus, how can I share all that it means to me to have You as the center of my life? How can I explain the joy and the peace that have come into my life since I have known You? ... God drew me to You,* and I accepted You as my Lord and Savior, but it can all be summed up in seven words – You love me, and I love You! What a really "forever" meaning these words can have! ... The only way to experience the depth of their significance is to step out in faith, and to live a life of commitment, honesty, trust and forgiveness – a life of sharing and caring, a life that brings an inner peace and joy! ... When I decided to commit myself to seeking Your will for my life, and then, with Your help, living in obedience to it, then I found that counting my blessings daily was better than counting my "have nots," and that You are indeed adequate to satisfy all of my needs. ... Thank You, Lord, for Your presence in my life; help my daily living to reflect You, as I seek to share You with others.

In Your holy name I pray.

Amen.

* (See John 6:44)

SEPTEMBER 28

Dear Lord, remind me of what Paul told the Philippian church: "Don't worry over anything whatsoever, tell God every detail of your needs in earnest and thankful prayer, and the peace of God which transcends human understanding will keep constant guard over your hearts and minds as they rest in Jesus Christ."* ... Help me to realize that it is easier to accept You as sovereign and Jesus Christ as Your Son, on faith, than to believe in a "happenstance" universe with no divine Designer whose care and love can be experienced by those who believe! ... Remind me, Lord, lest I forget, that You are indeed trustworthy, and that those who trust in You are forever in Your care.

In the name of Jesus I pray.

Amen.

* (Phil. 4:7 – Phillips translation)

SEPTEMBER 29

Dear Lord, if I am to truly serve You in my daily work, help me to see a need and to fill it. ... Let me seek to know Your will for my life, to set goals, and to assess the consequences of my decisions. ... Remind me that I need to spend time in Your Word and in quiet meditation; only then can I recognize the guidance of Your Holy Spirit. Only then can I confidently trust the future to You, as You lead me step by step, one day at a time. ... Thank You, Lord, that when I walk closely with You each day, You are glorified and I am blessed. Help me as I strive to be faithful.

In Jesus' name I pray.

Amen.

SEPTEMBER 30

Dear Lord, help us to think about Ruth Brown's observation that: "We should resolve to be more understanding of the very young, the old, the weak, and the sick. Sometime in life we will each have been all of these." ... Help us to understand our generational differences. Young people have new ideas, new ways to do things, energy, and enthusiasm to offer. Older people have wisdom, learned from years of trial and error. It is hard for older people to stand by and be ignored, and see the next generation make the same mistakes rather than building on knowledge already gained. ... Help us to learn to respect each other's gifts and achievements. ... If we can't do this, why would anyone want to exercise and take vitamins in order to become healthy "senior citizens?" ... Is this generation's answer abortion, and euthanasia next? Oh Lord, help us each to realize that life is Your precious gift for each of us to live wisely, with Your help and within Your will.

In Jesus' name we pray.

Amen.

OCTOBER 1

Dear Lord, remind us lest we forget, and our young people never have an opportunity to learn, that our nation was founded on the religious beliefs of our forefathers. They came to have freedom to worship God in accordance with their Judeo-Christian beliefs, which they had lost in England and Holland. They incorporated Your moral guidelines in our Constitution, in their legal dealings, and in their courts. Later they posted Your ten commandments on the walls of their schools. Our nation weathered its hardships, and it later survived the war between the northern and southern states because You were the third strand of the cord that bound them together. ... And as our nation prospered, You blessed us. Oppressed people came to our shores seeking freedom and safety; some came seeing our nation as a land of opportunity. They were welcomed, absorbed, and they became American citizens. But what of today? Open our eyes that we may see ourselves as You must see us, and weep. Continued tomorrow

In Jesus' name we pray.

Amen.

OCTOBER 2

Dear Lord God, hear our prayers. Help us to see ourselves as You see us, and to weep! … We have tried to usurp Your position and Your authority. How we must grieve You! … You see the arrogance of many of our nation's leaders and opinion formers, both inside and outside of our government. They assume and believe that as a nation we have outgrown You, and so have factored You out of their equations. They seek to replace You with a centrally controlled and "fathering" government that alone knows best. They vision a "new order" that exalts materialism, and legalizes and declares "normal" what You have called sin. … Wake us up as citizens, and wake us up who call ourselves Christians, Your church and Your people. We have together become a party to our nation's downfall by promoting, or accepting these changes, or we have been deceived by our lack of knowledge, and have been reluctant to defend Your truth. … Open our eyes to see what we as a nation have become. Help us to truly seek Your forgiveness, lest we suffer Your severe mercy. … Remind us that You have said that You cannot, and You will not tolerate sin!

In the name of Jesus we pray.

Amen.

OCTOBER 3

Dear Lord God, help me to have a "teachable mind," for that may well be the secret of the Fountain of Youth. Help me to learn more about You, as I seek to walk more closely with You. … These things I have learned: You do not want me to die for You, You want me to live for You! You want each of us to present himself as a "living temple" every day, so that others may see reflections of You in those of us who have committed ourselves to following You. … You have told us that our bodies are to be temples of Your Holy Spirit – teach us that they are "on loan," not to be abused, misused, or drugged, but they are a precious gift to be valued, cared for, and used for Your glory! … Prayer is not just our speaking to You – it is also listening when You speak to us! The more time we spend in building a relationship with You, the better we will recognize Your voice. As one becomes richer in the Spirit, one finds his material desires diminishing. Open our

minds and our hearts to want all that You have for us.

In the name of Jesus we pray.

Amen.

OCTOBER 4

Dear Lord, forgive me for hanging a "DO NOT DISTURB" sign on my faith, for being blind to any new insights, deaf to Your Spirit's pleadings, smug in my own self-righteousness, and satisfied with my limited vision. Quicken within me a desire to study Your Word, and open my eyes that I may see glimpses of all that You want for me. … Create in me a desire to want it too.

In Jesus' name I pray.

Amen.

OCTOBER 5

Dear Lord, help me to accept life as a series of shocks – floods, tornadoes, sickness, death – interspersed with moments of shining joy, gentle love, quiet peace, indomitable hope. All this is the fabric of my life. Help me to cling to these moments, sustained by Your strength, secure in Your love. … Let me remember that Your despair became victory, Your sorrow, joy. Let this be so in my life. Keep me on an even keel, Lord. I need You.

Thank You, Lord.

Amen.

OCTOBER 5

Dear Lord, help me to accept life as a series of shocks-floods, tornadoes, sickness, death – interspersed with moments of shining joy, gentle love, quiet peace, indomitable hope. All this is the fabric of my life. Help me to cling to these moments, sustained by Your strength, secure in Your love. … Let me remember that Your despair became victory, Your sorrow, joy. Let this be so in my life. Keep me on an even keel, Lord. I need You.

Thank You, Lord.

Amen.

OCTOBER 6

Dear Heavenly Father, I pray for blessings, and You send me opportunities! I ask for help, and You send a friend who "just happened to drop by!" In so many ways, Lord, You are there for me, sometimes before I realize that I am in over my head and need Your guidance! In big or little things, You are there. ... Help me to see these encounters as evidence of Your presence, Your love, and Your concern, and help me to remember always to give You thanks. ... More and more I realize that there is no such thing as luck or coincidence; for a believing Christian, it's always Your shepherding presence. ... My life is so much richer, happier, and more peaceful, since I have recognized Jesus as my daily companion and friend! I want to share the "good news," so that others may know Him too. Help us all to continue to grow in our faith, and to learn to praise You in all things.

In Jesus' holy name I pray.

Amen.

OCTOBER 7

Dear Father in heaven, help me to see that I must commit myself to a higher purpose than just gaining personal wealth and material possessions. ... If I concentrate solely on these, and neglect the spiritual, I will have no center, no higher commitment outside of myself! ... Help me to see that such a life is as if one would choose to set out to sea alone in a boat with no compass, no purpose, no port in mind. It might be enjoyable until a crisis arises, and panic sets in. ... Dear Lord, will it take a crisis before I learn that I am not all-sufficient? ... Help me to see that I do need You, and that I need to build a relationship with You before a crisis engulfs me.

In Jesus' name I pray.

Amen.

OCTOBER 8

Dear Lord, many sincere Christians across our nation have long prayed for revival, and we thank you for hearing these prayers, and for raising up the Promise Keepers! ... We thank you for the courage of these men, who publicly repent and dedicate their lives to You, and to their families – husbands, fathers, and sons, each promising to seek Your will and Your help in building better family relationships. ... Remind us to look at ourselves – a society of many broken families and confused youth – in a time of varied destructive influences all around us. ... We find that more and more

government control is being allowed to usurp parental rights and influence in our children's lives and education. ... So let us rejoice that You have heard the prayers of both husbands and wives, as together they seek Your help in strengthening their family togetherness. ... Forgive us, Lord, for too often we have allowed ourselves to be intimidated by those who strive to convince us that Christians should be seen, but not heard! Remind us that Christians are citizens too!

In Jesus' name we pray.

Amen.

OCTOBER 9

Dear Lord, help us to remember that many have chosen to come to this nation to share what we have to offer. We have welcomed them. They too have the freedom to worship in their own way, but that does not mean that we have to give up our Judeo-Christian heritage and teachings to accommodate them! For if we try to amalgamate every religion into ONE, we will likely end up with NONE! ... Help us Lord, to consider this seriously before we abandon our own faith in deference to other religions. Remind us that our Constitution gives every citizen the right to worship in his own way as long as it does not endanger others. Help us as Christians to defend our precious freedom, lest we lose it altogether.

In Jesus' name we pray.

Amen.

OCTOBER 10

Dear Lord God, what, if anything, do we as a nation hold sacred today? Not You, Lord God, and not our flag! For as a nation, we often turn to You only in times of crisis. We hear Your name taken in vain in everyday life, and in movies and on TV. ... We no longer honor our flag and observe the rules for its display and use as we once did. Today we see the flag made into bikinis and other wearing apparel, and we allow it to be burned as a sign of protest. ... Yet in our Pledge of Allegiance, we still say that we are "one nation under God." We have tried to destroy any reference to You in our schools, and have taken the Bible out of many of our school libraries, denying our young people the freedom to learn its contents. ... Our

Senate still opens its sessions with a prayer by its Chaplain, and yet our teenagers must go outside their schools to pray! ... No one should be forced to pray, but to be denied the right to pray shows that we have forsaken You and our Christian heritage. ... Unless we, who call ourselves Your people, unite and stand together to bring us back to sanity, then as a nation that holds nothing sacred, we are in danger of facing the penalty of Your judgment. ... Help us, Lord God, to see this before it is too late!

In Jesus' name we pray.

Amen.

OCTOBER 11

Dear Lord, our nation was founded with Your help on Judeo-Christian religious beliefs. Our moral guidelines were Your ten commandments. Our young people learned right from wrong! ... Today, when a sixteen year-old high school student was asked to define "right," she answered, "I guess whatever makes you feel good, whatever seems right to you!" ... When asked by the interviewer, "If I wanted to murder you, would that be right?" ... The teenager answered, "Well, I suppose you'd have your reasons!" ... And so today, we find ourselves not wanting to offend anyone, and in danger of standing for nothing! ... Remind us, Lord, that the late Catherine Marshall predicted that by taking prayer out of our schools, we would bring on our nation's downfall! ... How can we survive as a nation, as a people, who find their streets, their homes, and their communities unsafe? How much longer can we lock You out of our schools and call ourselves a "free nation?" ... Oh Lord, open our eyes to see the error of our ways, lest we become just another page in history, repeating the sins of Your people as recorded in the Old Testament – denying Your existence and truth, and turning to other "gods." Help us, Lord, before it is too late!

In Jesus' name we pray.

Amen.

OCTOBER 12

Dear Lord Jesus, help me to understand that I need a balance in my life, of work and recreation, of community service and family togetherness, and that all of these areas must

be held together by my Christ centeredness. In everything I do, help me to reflect You. ... Let me listen for the guidance of Your Holy Spirit in all of my activities, so that Your glory may be shown through me.

In Your holy name I pray.

Amen.

OCTOBER 13

Dear Lord, open my eyes to see that more than at any other time in the last 2000 years the world is systematically setting about to deny You. More and more we as a nation are voting You out. ... More and more, as in the Book of Judges, "Everyone did what was right in his own eyes."* ... Oh Lord, before it is too late, open the minds and hearts of Christians everywhere to desire You, and to work to make a difference. Keep us from the deception of Your enemies and ours. Help us not to be just "Sunday-only" Christians.

In Your name I pray.

Amen.

* (Judges 21:25)

OCTOBER 14

Dear Heavenly Father, help us to see that virtue, like bread, is necessary for our nation's meaningful existence. We need to learn to get along with our fellow citizens. We need to develop sensitivity to each other's needs and misfortunes. ... Jesus taught His disciples to be sensitive, to pray for those who are suffering, to speak words of healing and forgiveness. ... This was learned caring, not left up to government-managed welfare, but to neighborly concern – most often, to Christian concern. This is the basis of virtue! ... Help us Lord, to learn this for ourselves and to teach it to our children, lest we lose our lives on streets that are rampant with crime because of our refusal to heed Your commandment to love our neighbor as we love ourselves, and to want for others what we desire for ourselves – the same opportunities, the same encouragement, the same helping hand.

In Jesus' holy name we pray.

Amen.

OCTOBER 15

Dear Heavenly Father, as we continue to reflect

on the way to encourage virtuous living among ourselves, help us to see that it must be rooted in parental example and teaching – right from wrong, respect for life and for others, and respect for the law. This must be expressed in good manners, and in lending a helping hand to someone in need. These attitudes and actions must be reinforced in our schools. … Only then, when we adults, youth, and children act responsibly can we restore safety to our neighborhoods, our streets, and our homes! Only then can we live and enjoy real freedom! … Only then, when we honor and restore virtuous living can we ask and expect You to bless our nation. Only then can we truly be "one nation under God, of the people, by the people, and for the people." Help us, Lord, for we are becoming numb to our sins, and deaf to Your teachings.

In Jesus' holy name we pray.

Amen.

OCTOBER 16

Dear Lord Jesus, the more time I spend with the Holy Spirit's leading in reading Your words, the more I learn! Remind me of these insights I have gleaned – a Christian is a person who is dedicated to Your service, a special person in Your sight, whose calling is to leave this world a better place because of what You have led him to do. … A Christian knows his heavenly Father, and he has forged a relationship with Him. A Christian knows who God the Father is, and he seeks to "enjoy Him forever!" He knows that the safest place to be is in the center of the Father's will. … He seeks to discover the Father's will and, with the help of the Holy Spirit, to be obedient to it. … Help me as I try to live out these things that I am beginning to understand, for I am weak at times. Give me the strength to keep trying, that I may give You glory in all of my actions.

In Your holy name I pray.

Amen.

OCTOBER 17

Dear Lord, help me to remember that even in the depths of my despair, You are there. Help me to remember to rejoice and praise You even then, believing that there is a purpose in everything that happens. Give me the strength to turn my life over completely to You and to mean it, not dictating answers to my prayers, but being willing to listen and to sincerely put You in charge of my life. Give me courage to speak honestly in love, not shying away from reality, or lacking the courage to face the painful. Help me to know that You are my only real security and that You will not fail me. Guide me in the paths that I should walk, both for Your sake and for mine.

In Your holy name I pray.

Amen.

OCTOBER 18

Dear Lord Jesus, You have said, "Blessed are the meek," but how meek, Lord? Sometimes I feel that I am being "used," taken advantage of – do You know what I mean, Lord? … Help me to stop and ask myself, "Am I doing this for John Doe or for You?" If the task will further Your mission, then let me be "meek." Let me forget John Doe and remember only that I said I wanted to serve You.

In Your holy name I pray.

Amen.

OCTOBER 19

Dear Lord, there are days when I am busy with living, snatching little time to praise You and to count my blessings, as I am caught up in my world. … Help me even then to pause and realize that this same day may be dark and tragic for someone else. Let me stop and pray that I may be an instrument of Your healing, always mindful of my brother's needs.

In Jesus' name I pray.

Amen.

OCTOBER 20

Dear Lord, help me to see the "nowness" of my Christian faith. The past is past, and put aside, and the future is in Your hands, Lord, but the "now" is up to me. This is where I either reflect You or not, in how I live today. … Fill me with Your Spirit, and enable me to be more than I am, so that I may seize this precious time that will not come again, and live today to Your glory.

In Jesus' name I pray.

Amen.

OCTOBER 21

Dear Lord God, help me to realize that the "good news" is that You are discoverable, that You are all that Jesus Christ declared You to be. Through Christ I can glimpse the very heart of You, and know that You are a God of love, hope and strength; through Him, I know that I can trust You with my world, and my life. ... Help me in turn to be trustworthy, to let You know in countless ways each day that You can rely on me. For this I thank You.

In Jesus' name I pray.
Amen.

OCTOBER 22

Dear Heavenly Father, let me try each day to serve You a little better, to love others a little more, and the make the world a little better because I am living now. ... At the close of each day, let me realize that where I have failed, or decided unwisely, or lost ground, even these departures were necessary for my spiritual growth. Let me accept myself as I am, as You have accepted me; let me ask Your forgiveness so that I can start anew tomorrow and do better. ... Thank You, Lord, that Your grace makes my living worthwhile, and my short-comings bearable.

In Jesus' holy name I pray.
Amen.

OCTOBER 23

Dear Lord, ... why? Just when I thought I was making some progress in becoming a better Christian, why do I find a house painter who never keeps an appointment on time, who also gets half-way through a job and then loses the code number of his paint? Lord, why is it that I find Your strength and assistance to weather the really serious crises in my life and then dissolve into hysterics over the disarray caused by my three-week's dealings with one elusive painter? ... Could it be, Lord, that there is something I have yet to learn, such as humility, patience, and forgiveness? Could it be that now I can better comprehend the profound way in which You exercised patience at the time of Your crucifixion? ... Even though my problems are small, perhaps I too need to learn to pray, "Father forgive him, even though he seems not to know what he is doing." Thank You for listening, Lord.

In Jesus' name I pray.
Amen.

OCTOBER 24

Dear Lord, when I get out of harmony with You, I am out of harmony with myself! If I let this continue, it is likely to be reflected in my physical being. If I truly want to be whole, then let me seek to restore this inner harmony between us. ... Fill me with Your presence, and let the Holy Spirit guard me from yielding to any temptations to stray. Help me, Lord, to want to be what You know I can be. With Your help, I can be that person!

In Jesus' name I pray.
Amen.

OCTOBER 25

Dear Lord Jesus, help me to search my heart today and see if I am really living what I say I believe. Give me courage to look at the "real me," the strength to change what separates me from You, and love enough to ignore the cost!

This I pray in Your holy name.
Amen.

OCTOBER 26

Dear Lord, how do we see ourselves – as Your lost sheep needing Your guidance, or as an independent generation of citizens and leaders who see no need to consider Your plans for our nation? ... Is it arrogance, or lack of wisdom, that energizes those who think they have "outgrown" You? Is their philosophy driving them to lead our nation to a "point of no return?" ... You warned us in Your Word that there would come a time when many people would be deceived, even some of Your followers.* ... Open our eyes, both as citizens and as Christians, to see that along with our right to be both, we also have a responsibility to be informed and conscientious voters. ... In the days ahead, help us to seek the guidance of Your Holy Spirit in order to discover Your will and direction for our nation, lest we fail You and our children!

In Jesus' holy name we pray.
Amen.

* (See Matt. 24:21–24)

OCTOBER 27

Dear Lord Jesus, this week, help each of us to prepare to consider some serious questions that we face as citizens and voters in our beloved nation. ... Remind us that there is a time to "turn the other cheek," and a time to defend Your moral principles! ... You said that You always consulted God the Father, and then acted according to His will. ... You were seen standing firmly against the money-changers in the temple because they were desecrating Your Father's house! ... Lord Jesus, what of our nation today? Is nothing sacred any more? Is nothing either right or wrong? Is nothing worth the risk of defending? Are honesty and character no longer important? Can a nation long exist without these virtues? ... Help us, Lord Jesus, to humble ourselves individually and to seek the Father's will for our lives and for our nation, and to pray for the courage to make responsible decisions concerning what is best for our nation, and for our children. ... Only then can we be worthy to receive both Your love and Your blessing.

In Your holy name we pray.

Amen.

OCTOBER 28

Dear Lord Jesus, there comes a time of testing when Christians must hold themselves accountable to You, and make hard decisions! Remind us that You too faced such times. ... Today, we face critical decisions at a crucial time in our nation's history, for many of our leaders are usurping the Father's authority, and have not sought His will and His directions. ... Help each of us to seriously and prayerfully consider the course that our nation is taking; do we want a government that advocates more cradle-to-grave control over our lives, a government to be led by "elitists," who consider themselves to be the only ones with sufficient knowledge to lead, and who act on the assumption that the most important "right" of middle class citizens is their "right to pay taxes?" ... Help us, as we prayerfully seek the Father's will, and give us the courage to return this country to the principles and beliefs that made it great.

In Your holy name we pray.

Amen.

OCTOBER 29

Dear Lord, a wise man was once quoted as saying, "Men do not grow in stature unless they align themselves with a noble faith!" Another unknown author observed that: "A nation that does not know its heritage does not understand its present, or know where it is headed!" ... Lord, help us to open our eyes to see the circumstances in which we find ourselves today. Help us to recall that our nation once considered human life to be a precious gift from You, and thus sacred! ... We also believed that You created man to have dominion over the animals. ... Have we so quickly discarded Your Word, and substituted a form of pantheism today? Are nature and animals becoming our "new gods?" ... How can we approve of partial-birth abortions for our human babies when we won't allow such cruelty to animals? Oh Lord, open our eyes to see how we as a nation must grieve You! Help us to realize that our nation is being led away from You, and that it is we who have moved, for You do not change! ... Forgive us for trying to re-write Your Word to suit our desires and our vices! Help us to see that Your ways are best for us and for our nation, before we bring on our own downfall!

In Jesus' holy name we pray.

Amen.

OCTOBER 30

Dear Lord God, You never said that life would be easy, but You did say that if we would believe in You, and commit our ways to Your way, that we could trust You, and that Your will would never take us beyond where Your grace could sustain us! Help us, Lord, to realize that You loved us enough to send Your Son, both as an example and as a sacrifice for our sins. ... Open our eyes to see that today, when we take a stand with You and find society often quick to criticize and put us down, that it is then that we discover Your strength! Just as You told Your apostle Paul, "My grace is sufficient for you, for My power is perfected in [your] weakness."* ... Forgive me Lord, for doubting that You care. Thank You Lord, for Your Holy Spirit's communication line, just as Your Son promised. Help me to always keep the line open, not just in times of need, but to continually praise You and thank You for Your care and Your blessings.

In Jesus' name I pray this prayer.

Amen.

* (I Cor. 12:9)

OCTOBER 31

Dear Lord, if one does not expect much of those who are in leadership positions, then probably that person does not demand much of himself or herself! ... It is true that we are to encourage others – family members, fellow workers, friends, teachers, ministers, and government leaders; however, it is questionable whether anyone should depend on such encouragement for one's sole motivation. If we find ourselves saying, "Lord, I feel so unworthy," we are apt to hear Him say, "For heaven's sake, and yours, get worthy!" ... Remind us that You, Lord, are ready to be our helper, our joy-giver, and the supplier of all our needs! You want us to learn to depend on You, and not others, for our sense of self worth and well being. ... Help me to resolve to spend quality time with You each day in prayer and meditation, so that in my times of trouble we will not be strangers to each other!

In Jesus' name I pray.

Amen.

NOVEMBER 1

Our most gracious Heavenly Father, as we consider the crossroads that our nation faces in our upcoming elections, help us to realize our responsibility both as citizens and as Christians. Let us each first prayerfully seek to know Your will, Your truth, and Your guidance. In short, how would You have us vote? ... Remind us that we can each make a difference! ... By one vote, Texas was admitted to the union in 1845! By one vote, Hitler won leadership in the Nazi Party in 1923! By one vote, Thomas Jefferson became President of the Unites States! ... Help us, Lord, to each prayerfully accept our voting responsibility and Your guidance, lest we become a party to our nation's acceptance of materialism, dishonesty, and immorality as a way of life. For if we no longer choose to consider ourselves "One nation under God," then we can no longer rightfully expect or ask for Your blessing, can we? ... Help us to see

that we need You!

In Jesus' name we pray.

Amen.

NOVEMBER 2

Dear Lord, when everything seems to be flying apart in my life and I feel overwhelmed, remind me to stop everything, to sit quietly, to center in on You, and to read Your Word. For only as I return to oneness with You can my harmony be restored. ... Remind me that You are my Shepherd, and I shall not want for inner peace, for strength, for confidence, and for answers, for You have promised that Your Holy Spirit will lead me into all truth and show me where I need to change. ... Thank You, Lord, for always being there for me when I turn to You.

In Your name I pray.

Amen.

NOVEMBER 3

Dear Lord, as citizens of this special nation which with Your help has survived over 200 years, we each have both a privilege and a responsibility. It is our government – "of the people, by the people, and for the people." We are the ones who choose the future direction for our country. ... Let us put politics aside, as we prayerfully seek Your guidance, let us ask: "Would You want us to choose leaders who will set examples of integrity, dependability, and accountability for our youth and for our citizens? Would You want us to choose leaders who will help us restore the moral climate which our nation has lost?" ... Let us seriously consider whether we really want more government control, leading us to socialism, or whether we want to maintain our freedom. ... Remind us that we are facing a critical time in our history. Let us paraphrase President Kennedy's words: "Let us not ask what our government can do for us, but rather what we can do to improve our government." Help us, Lord, to see that we have often neglected our responsibilities, as citizens, by not seeking Your guidance.

In Jesus' name we pray.

Amen.

NOVEMBER 4

Dear Lord, we ask that You hear our prayers

today for those parents and teachers who are discouraged with our public school system. Many teachers find that they are deterred from teaching as they would like, and many parents are fearful of what their children are learning and much of what they aren't learning. ... Other parents are home schooling and find themselves criticized, and under pressure if they teach Christian ethics. ... To many parents, "it takes a village ..." has come to mean more government control. Parents often feel that they are losing control of their children to the peer-pressure in their schools, where there is often no teaching of right and wrong, or the meaning of virtue. ... Remind us, that Abraham Lincoln said, "The philosophy of the classroom in one generation is the philosophy of the government in the next!" ... Let us prayerfully consider the concerns of these parents and teachers who are facing these problems of our schools today, for as citizens, and as Christians, we too, need to be concerned!

In Jesus' name we pray.

Amen.

NOVEMBER 5

Dear Lord, Your Word says that, "With God all things are possible."* So if I am on Your side, on Your wavelength, living within Your will, then we are on the same side. What more do I need? ... It's up to me to live close to You daily so that I can recognize Your direction for me, isn't it? For then and only then can I step out in faith, trusting that " ... all things work together for good to those who love God, to those who are called according to His purpose."**

Amen, and Amen, and Amen.

* (Matt. 19:26)

** (Romans 8:28)

NOVEMBER 6

Dear Lord, open our eyes as responsible citizens, and especially as Christians, to see the situation that we face in our nation today. Remind us that whether we have been uninformed, or too busy, or deceived, we have allowed our nation to erode morally. Make us aware that You are calling us to choose leaders who will help us recover our moral compass.

In Jesus' name we pray.

Amen.

NOVEMBER 7

Dear Lord, would one snowflake ever admit its part in an avalanche, rushing to its destruction? ... As our nation gains momentum, as it slides deeper and deeper into immorality, crime, and financial debt, am I partly responsible? Have I looked the other way, or have I been deceived by our government's leaders and by a controlled press, who refused to report the truth? ... Oh Lord, forgive me, for I too may have chosen to live in my own "dream world," and by so doing have become a party to this avalanche. ... Oh Lord, You had such a vision for this nation; You have always stood by us in past crises. Will You hear us now? Help us, Lord, save us from ourselves before we go too far to receive Your divine mercy!

In Jesus' name I pray.

Amen.

NOVEMBER 8

Dear Lord, why is it that I am always in a hurry and You are not? Remind me that most things that are really worth while were not achieved in a day! ... By faithful study and prayer, help me to create the climate for Your presence and Your miracles. Help me, Lord, to build a day-to-day relationship with You, so that I can recognize Your actions in my life, and remember to thank You and give You all the credit. It was You who kept me from having an accident as I drove to work today, wasn't it?

In Jesus' name I pray, and give You thanks.

Amen.

NOVEMBER 9

Dear Lord, I can't be considered a true disciple of Yours on Sundays unless I strive EVERY DAY for higher ground in my spiritual walk. ... Help me daily to refuse anything in action or thought that would pull me away from You. Fill me, Lord, with an intense desire to be as righteous as You want me to be.

In Your holy name I pray.

Amen.

NOVEMBER 10

Dear Lord, one morning after studying Your Word I prayed and asked for the Holy Spirit's guidance for my day, and for my life. ... Usually, I am in a hurry, and I do not often wait for Your answers. But that morning I waited, and then these words came to me: "Accept each day's challenges! Remember that I have promised to be with you always! Trust Me! I am closer than a cell phone away!" ... Oh Lord, if I step out in faith and trust You, You will be with me, ready to guide and help and strengthen me. ... Your answer may not be just what I had in mind, but remind me that You see the bigger picture – You know what I need. ... Help me, Lord, to recognize my blessings, and to thank You each day. ... You are trustworthy; help me to be that way too!

In Jesus' name we pray.

Amen.

NOVEMBER 11

Dear Lord, remind me that neither Satan nor You can work within me against my will. Your gave me "free will" and the choices are mine, aren't they? You will hold me responsible for my choices. ... Oh Lord, let me choose You, Your way, EVERY TIME I make a choice. Help me, for I sometimes forget to consult You, and I am often weak.

In Jesus' name I pray.

Amen.

NOVEMBER 12

Dear Lord, on this Veteran's Day, let us pause to remember those who have given their lives for our country or returned home ill or wounded; because of their sacrifices we have blessings to count. ... We have been warned that "if America ceases to be good, she will cease to be great."* ... Oh Lord, help us as a nation not to depart from You. Let us pray daily for our leaders, for we are all truly dependent upon Your mercy and Your guidance.

In the name of Jesus we pray.

Amen.

* (From de Tocque-Ville's "*Democracy in America*, 1832)

NOVEMBER 13

Dear Lord, who doesn't want freedom to pursue happiness? It is our right as US citizens, isn't it? ... Yet as we look around we find many whose ideas of happiness are for each "to do his own thing" – be his own god, have sexual flings, use drugs, fly high! Then when one "crashes"

– can't get it together, can't work, runs out of money, gets sick with Aids – one asks, "Where is my government help, why haven't they been putting more money into finding a cure for Aids, etc.? Lord, where are You, if You really are?" ... "My child, right where I've been all the time, just waiting for your call." ... "Why am I getting this bad rap? Why me?" ... "Because you wanted to be free!" ... "But there is nothing wrong with wanting to be free!" ... "No, except that with freedom comes responsibility; you did not accept responsibility, and you made the choices that brought you down. You chose to ignore My moral laws. I do not tolerate sin, but I can forgive it if you sincerely repent, and change your direction. It's your choice."

In Jesus' name, we ask You to hear the prayers of everyone who sincerely repents, wants to turn his life around, and accepts You as Lord and Savior.

Amen.

NOVEMBER 14

Dear Lord Jesus, remind me that bitterness and hopelessness are not just emotions, but rather choices that I make. Help me each day to count my blessings and to give You thanks, for I can always "choose" my attitude. Help me to choose to walk each day with You, so that I can find an inner joy and the "peace of God which surpasses all understanding."*

In Your Holy name I pray.

Amen.

* (Phil. 4:7)

NOVEMBER 15

Dear Lord, for many generations the churches of our nation were considered "the keepers of our morals." Today, we are seeing many leaders of the hierarchy of some of our mainline denominations re-interpreting Your Word to appease society's "sins." Many of these have not consulted You or their lay constituency. ... Help us all, Lord, who consider ourselves Your people, to see our waywardness and to seek Your forgiveness before it is too late, lest we become a party to bringing down our nation. ... Remind us that You have said: "If My people who are called by My name will humble themselves, and pray and seek My face, and turn from their wicked ways, then I will hear from heaven, and will forgive their sin and heal their land."* ... Help me to prayerfully consider my personal responsibility to encourage and support those religious and government leaders who are trying to lead our people in a direction that will be pleasing to You.

In Jesus' name I pray.

Amen.

* (II Chron. 7:14)

NOVEMBER 16

Our Father, who art in heaven, we thank You for Christian believers who defend You as Creator of our universe and our humanity. Whether it took six of our 24–hour days or six of Your 1,000–year days,* here we are, and apes are still apes! What does matter is that we can enjoy the complex nature, the beauty, and the awesomeness of Your creation. However, without building a relationship with You, our "great knowledge" may very well bring on our downfall. ... Forgive us, Lord, for our arrogance, our willfulness, our immaturity, and our self-centeredness. Forgive us for thinking that we can manage our lives. ... our nation, and our world-relations without seeking Your guidance. Teach us to want more of You, not less; to see that without You we cannot fulfill Your purposes or our dreams. You alone are our only hope, our sustaining grace.

In Jesus' name we pray.

Amen.

* (See II Peter 3:8)

NOVEMBER 17

Dear Lord Jesus, You expressed Your feelings about man's natural tendencies in Your teachings to Your disciples, and for us, known as the Beatitudes. As we read these over we need to look at how our world tends to interpret them. ... You gave Your minister, J. B. Phillips special insight. He believes that You saw "self-love" as man's arch-enemy – self-esteem turned inward and carried to excess – preoccupied with "what's in it for me!" He believes that most people are living by their own "beatitudes" today. Help me, Lord, to seriously consider these erroneous beliefs. Is this the accepted trend in today's society? Is this the way I am living my life? Open my eyes to see me as You must see me.

In Your holy name I pray.

Amen.

NOVEMBER 18

Dear Father God, help me to understand where self-esteem ends and pride begins. ... You must know that today's teaching is that most people don't have enough self-esteem, and that children should be taught to "feel good" about themselves. ... Is it not so that You have created each of us with the gift of life, and an uniqueness in Your sight that comprises individual ability and purpose, to be discovered and developed? ... Parents should help each child to understand this, and encourage each to do his/her best. ... The more talented persons have more responsibility, but everyone has some quality that needs to be developed and used for one's own best interests, and for society's good. These are the blessings; the danger is in letting self-esteem become over-bearing pride! Help me to see this, Father.

In Jesus' name I pray.

Amen.

NOVEMBER 19

Dear Lord Jesus, You, through the Holy Spirit's leading into truth, helped Your servant, J. B. Phillips,* to see that it was PRIDE that caused You the greatest anger. You believed that man, all of us, must recognize this and overcome it if we were ever to follow Your way, Your truth, and Your light. ... Help us to consider this as we read Your beatitudes. Let us prayerfully consider Your teaching as we seek the Holy Spirit's guidance for a better understanding of Your truth.

In the name of Jesus we pray.

Amen.

NOVEMBER 20

Dear Lord Jesus, let us re-read yesterday's prayer, and help us to make important the things You consider important in our lives – the attitudes of our hearts. Let us seek to exhibit the fruit of the Holy Spirit, which can only be developed when we stay attached to You, the "vine,"* for without You we can do nothing.

In Your holy name we pray.

Amen.

* (See John 15:5)

NOVEMBER 21

Gracious Lord God, as we prepare for Thanksgiving Day tomorrow, let us prepare our hearts. As many across the nation are worshipping together, let us join together in praising You and counting our blessings, for we each have some, perhaps more than we realize – we are here! Any day that one can get out of bed is a day to be grateful. We thank You for Your sustaining grace, Your protection, and for Your presence in our lives through good times and through trying times this past year. ... We pray for those in this country, and in other nations around the world, who are suffering and need Your help. ... As You have blessed us, help us to be a blessing to others, in sharing where we can, and in praying that You will sustain them and supply their needs.

In Jesus' name we pray.

Amen.

NOVEMBER 22

Dear Lord, help us to pause to recall our nation's first Thanksgiving as we too give You thanks for our many blessings. Help us today to recognize our blessings and to realize that You are our Provider also! You have watched over our nation, and it is because of Your divine love and care that we have survived this far. Thank You, Lord, and help us each to strive to be worthy of Your amazing grace.

In Jesus' holy name we pray.

Amen.

NOVEMBER 23

Dear Lord, help me to see the "nowness" of my Christian faith. The past is past, and put aside; the future is in Your hands, Lord, but the "now" is up to me. This is where I either reflect You or not, in how I live today. ... Fill me with Your Spirit; enable me to be more than I am, that I may seize this precious time that will not come again, and live today to Your glory.

In Jesus' name I pray.

Amen.

NOVEMBER 24

Dear Lord, help me to see that my first priority is to seek Your will in all things, and then to be obedient to it, no matter what the cost! ... Sacrifice isn't sacrifice unless I give up something important to me, is it? ... Commitment isn't commitment unless I put Your will ahead of my own desires. ... Help me to see that I have a long way to go before I grow out of my complacency, and my sometimes self-righteous arrogance. Help me to get on with my life, and to count You in.

In the name of Jesus I pray.

Amen.

NOVEMBER 25

Most gracious heavenly Father, help us to see that it is truer today than at any other time in our nation's history that we have a generation of citizens who hold nothing to be sacred, and who march to the beat of their own drummer.... Help us, Lord, to be able to recognize our own limitations. If we do not acknowledge You as Creator, and as a higher authority, then we have only our human capabilities to sustain us. ... Remind us that our first president, George Washington, observed that a democracy could not long survive without a religious base. ... Open our eyes and help us to see that we who believe must pray for our nation.

In Jesus' name we pray.

Amen.

NOVEMBER 26

Dear Lord, as we get caught up in the materialism of our fast-paced world today, let us pause to consider some special words of an unknown writer –

Money will buy a bed, but not sleep.

Money will buy books, but not brains.

Money will buy food, but not an appetite.

Money will buy finery, but not beauty.

Money will buy a house, but not a home.

Money will buy medicine, but not health.

Money will buy luxuries, but not happiness.

Money will buy religion, but not salvation.

Money will buy a passport to anywhere but heaven.

Help us each to see that our lives are meaningless without You.

In Jesus' name we pray.

Amen.

NOVEMBER 27

Dear heavenly Father, help us to see how divided we have become as a nation. We were founded by those who sought freedom to worship You as their sovereign God, and as a developing nation we attracted others who came to our shores to find freedom. ... Today, our problem is not with those who bring their own "religion" to our shores. Our problem is with a homegrown group, a generation who writes its own rules based on its desire to go through life pushing its own life-style, unencumbered by any regulations. ... Open our eyes to see the dangers that such a philosophy brings to any society, and especially to ours where there are many of all ages who do put their trust in You and honor their Judeo-Christian roots. ... Help all of us, Lord God, who sincerely believe in faith, family, and freedom. Hear our prayers as we seek to rebuild our nation's religious foundations. Let us pray daily for Your guidance.

In Jesus' holy name we pray.

Amen.

NOVEMBER 28

Dear Lord, I've been thinking that when I commit myself to seeking Your will for my life and then living it, You mean every day! You want me to be morally upright and honest and sensitive to all those who make up "my world" each day! That means at home with my family, at work, at school, in short, in all of my endeavors. You want each one who crosses my path to sense that I am "different," to catch a glimpse of Your love flowing through me! ... You want my everyday living to be a fulfillment of what I say I believe on Sundays! ... Help me not to fail You, for if all who claim to know You would actually live by Your moral laws, we could make a difference, and restore our nation's foundations. Give each of us who makes this commitment to You, Your wisdom, and Your sustaining strength.

In the name of Jesus I pray.

Amen.

NOVEMBER 29

Dear Lord, thank You that You inspired Your apostle Paul to write these words for the encouragement of Your people in every generation: "Delight yourselves in the Lord; yes, find your joy in Him at all times. Have a reputation for gentleness, and NEVER forget the near-ness of your Lord. ... DON'T WORRY OVER ANYTHING WHATEVER; tell God every detail of your needs in earnest and thankful prayer, and the PEACE of God, which transcends human understanding, will keep constant guard over your hearts and minds as they rest in Christ Jesus.* ... Fix your thoughts on what is true and good and right. Think about things that are pure and lovely, and dwell on the fine, good things in others. THINK ABOUT ALL YOU CAN PRAISE GOD FOR AND BE GLAD ABOUT. Keep putting into practice all you have learned from me and saw me doing, and the God of peace will be with you."** ... Oh Lord, help me to remember to read this often and to stay on course with You.

In Jesus' holy name I pray.

Amen.

* (Phil. 4:4–7 – J. B. Phillips Trans.)
** (Phil. 4:8–9 – Tyndale Living Bible)

NOVEMBER 30

Dear Lord, as we get immersed in making material improvements, help us to remember to continually seek Your will and Your guidance. Remind us not to run ahead of You, or to confuse our "wants" with our "needs." ... Let us not forget that our first concern should be how best to encourage people to build a relationship with You, and to grow in their Christian faith. ... Let all that we do in both our material expansion and our spiritual growth be to Your honor and Your glory. ... Let us each ask ourselves, "Today, would any one have known that I was a Christian? Have I told any one about Jesus?

In Jesus' name I pray this.

Amen.

DECEMBER 1

Dear Lord Jesus, as my life seems to pick up speed and is in danger of going into a "spin-cycle," help me to stop and recall the true meaning of this Advent season. ... It is not all this running around, this frantic activity, lists and cards, feasts and festivals; it's You, Lord, isn't it? It's commemorating Your gift to man – Mary's divine visitation, her supreme faith and acceptance of the angel's message, and Your gift forever after to all who will believe. ... Your gift has changed my life! Oh Lord, help me to slow down and remember to make this coming Christmas Your day!

In Your holy name I pray.

Amen.

DECEMBER 2

Dear Heavenly Father, help me to realize that prayer, as C. H. Dodd has indicated, should not be a device for getting You to use Your resources to grant my desires, but rather a means for me to re-direct my desires to be in accordance with Your will. ... Remind me that Jesus said: "Whatever you ask the Father in My name He will give you,"* meaning something that receives Your approval, and is made possible because I have accepted Jesus as my Lord and Savior. ... So let me think over my requests before I pray in order that they may be according to Your will; this may reduce the number of my requests, but it may also increase the number of Your positive answers. ... Let me take time to study Your Word that I may better understand Your will, and recognize the Holy Spirit's leading.

In Jesus' name I pray.

Amen.

* (John 16:23; also James 4:3)

DECEMBER 3

Dear Lord, remind me that You never meant that Christian love and mercy should cohabit with sin. Rather You taught that if I would confess my sin to You and truly repent, that You would forgive me; but You did not say that You would mercifully look the other way and allow me to continue in my sin. ... Lord, help me to understand Your Word as You revealed it to Your committed apostles, for Your truths and Your plan for the family are timeless. Remind me that You created my human sexuality to be a precious blessing. Help me to love You and trust You enough to live by Your rules.

In Your holy name I pray.

Amen.

DECEMBER 4

Dear Lord, help me to realize that when I accept Your forgiveness for my sins, the results of my sins may not disappear immediately. Although I need not be haunted by guilt, I may have to deal with the consequences for a long time – perhaps forever. Cause me to stop and think before I carelessly or purposely depart from Your ways. ... Draw me closer, Lord, and protect me from myself.

In Jesus' name I pray.

Amen.

DECEMBER 5

Dear Lord, help me to weed out the errors in my life, the petty hurts, the small jealousies, and the deep-seated resentments that block the flow of Your Spirit. ... Help me to forgive and to forget. For You have said that You can not forgive me until I first forgive others. It's my move, Lord, isn't it? Help me to be a truly forgiving person.

In Jesus' name I pray.

Amen.

DECEMBER 6

Dear Heavenly Father, remind me that Your Word that I must come as a little child, asking trustingly for Your help, not just in crises but in the "everydayness" of finding lost articles, or a parking space. ... If I think that You would not be interested in such mundane things, am I not making You conform to my own design? If I think that I shouldn't bother You, have I ever really understood Your love, or known You as a real Father? Forgive me, Lord, for not realizing that "living in Your presence" means in all things and at all times.

In Jesus' holy name I pray.

Amen.

DECEMBER 7

Dear Lord, help me in the midst of my life to remember to count my blessings and to concentrate on the positive, for it is not what life does to me but my attitude that determines my peace and joy. All things work for good through You. Help me to cling to this truth and to always praise You.

In Jesus' name I pray.

Amen.

DECEMBER 8

Dear Lord Jesus, calmness can be mine in the "busy-ness" of this Christmas season if I set aside time to be with You. Peace can be mine in my heart when I truly trust You, and joy can be mine when I share Your love with others. … Even though darkness surrounds me, let me remember to walk in Your Light, secure in Your faithfulness. Help me to truly sense this in my spirit.

In Your holy name I pray.

Amen.

DECEMBER 9

Dear Lord Jesus, help me to remember that others have faced similar problems and found You. Let my faith never falter, for in the midst of my adversities, You are there. … If I put my hand in Your hand, You will be the light for my way. … New opportunities will come. New doors will open. The sun will shine again. Help me to trust You and be ready, Lord. Thank You for being my friend and my Savior.

In Your holy name I pray.

Amen.

DECEMBER 10

Dear Lord, the Psalmist has said: "Because you have made the Lord your refuge, the Most High your habitation, no evil shall befall you, no scourge shall come near your tent."* … Help me not to be so busy emphasizing "no evil shall befall you" that I fail to note that it is "because you have made the Lord your refuge." … Only if I truly make You my refuge, the center of my life, only then can You guide me and keep me in Your care.

In the name of Jesus I pray.

Amen.

* (Psalm 91:9–10)

DECEMBER 11

Dear Lord, "as a man thinks in his heart, so he is;"* so then let me always think of You. Let me realize that it is not so much asking You to make me over, as it is living with You, letting You abide in me, talking with You, and letting Your presence permeate my whole being, that will transform my life. … Oh Lord, strengthen my desire to make You the center of my life.

In Jesus' name I pray.

Amen.

* (See Prov. 23:7)

DECEMBER 12

Dear Lord, You were here when I needed You. Your love engulfed me, Your Holy Spirit empowered me, and Your strength sustained me. … Oh Lord, let me be there when You need me – to share Your love with another, to be a tower of strength in someone's weakness, to reflect You in all that I do; for how else can I praise You? How else can I show my heart's thanksgiving? How else can You know that I love You? It is not enough to praise You and say "I love You" on Sunday; it's how I live on Monday and throughout the week, isn't it? Does my life really reflect my love for You in the way I live each day?

In Jesus' name I pray.

Amen.

DECEMBER 13

Dear Lord, You have given me so much! What can I give You? All that I really have to give You is my attention, and all You really want from me is my complete attention. … Lord, help me to want to abide in You and to want You to abide in me at all times. Let Your Holy Spirit touch and empower me, quicken my desire for You, strengthen my faith and dwell within me.

In Jesus' name I pray.

Amen.

(See Eph. 3:14–21)

DECEMBER 14

Dear Lord, if a saint is someone in whom Christ resides, or someone who makes it easier to believe in God, or someone who lets the light shine through, then I want to be a saint. Show me how to walk Your way, each day.

In Jesus' name I pray.

Amen.

DECEMBER 15

Dear Lord Jesus, this is the season for giving, because You first gave to us. What can I give You? … How simple it would be if I could purchase one gift, a really special gift, wrap it, give it, and be through. But no, I can not buy You a gift, can I? It isn't that simple. … You want me to totally surrender my life to You. You want me to re-commit myself to You every day of the year. For You, Christmas was total involvement forever, wasn't it? That too, is the gift You want from me, one that only I can give. Oh Lord, help me to love You enough to want to give You this gift.

In Your holy name I pray.

Amen.

DECEMBER 16

Dear Lord God, people today are looking for someone to love them, and for someone to listen to them. Help each of us to see that we are really looking for You! ... You have known this from the beginning of time, and when You realized that we needed a better understanding of Your love and all that You desired for us, You sent Your Son, Christ Jesus. ... He not only showed us what You are like – our Creator with a Father's deep love and concern for us – but He showed us what we can become! Because of His example, always seeking Your will first, and because of His teachings, we can find purpose for our lives. Because of His sacrifice, making possible our forgiveness, we have the promise of a new spiritual life here and now, and eternal life to come! Oh Lord God, help us to grasp the significance of Jesus' divine birth, for He was Your supreme and loving gift to all who can and will believe in Him.

In the name of Jesus we pray.

Amen.

DECEMBER 17

Dear Lord God, let us indeed commit ourselves to You – as our loving Father, as our provider, as our anchor in times of storms, and as our compass, showing us Your will and leading us to live more worthwhile lives. Help us to remember the commandment that Joshua gave to the Israelites when he said: "... choose for yourselves this day whom you will serve ... But as for me and my house, we will serve the Lord."* ... Let us not ask why the world isn't a better place in which to live, but rather let us ask what we can do to make it better. Oh Lord, You are depending on us to do our part to improve our surroundings, but we must also realize that we are dependent on You! Open our eyes to see this, and our hearts to desire a more meaningful relationship with You.

In the name of Jesus we pray.

Amen.

* (Joshua 24:15)

DECEMBER 18

Dear Lord, if commitment means sacrifice, if commitment means always putting You first, if commitment means promising to grow in Your Word, if commitment means grit and endurance, if it means being a part of the "BODY of CHRIST," and not just being able to quote scripture – then Lord, there is no way that I can make it on my own. Fill me with Your Holy Spirit so that in my life I may find the wisdom, the strength, and the power I need to carry out this commitment that I now make to You.

In Jesus' name I pray.

Amen.

DECEMBER 19

Dear Lord, I hesitated to turn my life over to You for fear of what You might ask me to do – preach a sermon, hand out tracts, take a vow of poverty. But Lord, when I obeyed You, Your Spirit directed me to get my life in order – to clean out the closets of my house and the closets of my heart – to FORGIVE and FORGET, even when I have been right. Lord, what peace and joy are ours when we surrender to You! Help me to be obedient to You and to trust You in all things.

In Jesus' name I pray.

Amen.

DECEMBER 20

Dear Lord Jesus, let me join in the chorus, "Oh come, Oh come, Emmanuel" and really mean it. Let me sing, "Prepare Ye the Way of the Lord," and at the same time prepare my heart for You. Let me seek Your forgiveness, as I also forgive others. Let "Joy to the World" be my song throughout this Advent Season ... that others may know that I am a Christian by my love.

In Your holy name I pray.

Amen.

DECEMBER 21

Dear Lord Jesus, as I prepare for Christmas this year, help me to resolve to make it Your special day. ... In the midst of all the seasonal bustle, the crowded highways and shopping malls, let me take time out to prepare my heart, as I think of Your birth on that first Christmas in

Bethlehem. ... Let me re-read the story of that incredible event when heaven and earth came together to share the glory and the wonder of Your birth on that holy night, and let me read it once again with my family. Help us to make You the center and the reason for our celebration this year.

In Your holy name I pray.

Amen.

DECEMBER 22

Most gracious heavenly Father, help me to slow down in preparing for Christmas. Often I find myself running over my own shadow when hurry, stress, and overload are gaining on me. ... Remind me that Christmas should bring joy; help me to be joyful! ... Christmas should be a time of love; help me to be loving! ... Christmas should be a time of thanksgiving and hope. ... I need to count my blessings, for no matter my present circumstances, I have blessings that others do not have. And because of the significance of Jesus' birth, Your gift to me, I can have hope! ... This Christmas season, let my joy, my love, my thanksgiving, and my hope reflect You, so that others may better understand the real meaning of Christmas and want to know You.

In Jesus' name I pray.

Amen.

DECEMBER 23

Dear Lord Jesus, amidst the hustle and bustle and wrapping of gifts, help me to realize that You are my greatest "GIFT." Let me set aside some quiet time each day to reflect on this. ... Then Christmas will start in my heart, and the glow that warms me will warm all those I meet.

In Your holy name I pray.

Amen.

DECEMBER 24

Dear Lord, I pray so diligently – for others, and for myself! Yet I often concentrate so much on these "wants" that I forget to be thankful for the "haves" – for the blessings and the surprise joys of each day, for family and friends, for bird songs and beautiful sunsets, for expressions of love and opportunities to serve, for near-misses while driving – all of these are evidences of Your answers to prayers that I haven't even

voiced! ... Thank You, Lord, for seeing beyond my wants. Thank You for being with me, now and always.

In Jesus' name I pray.

Amen.

DECEMBER 25

Dear Lord Jesus, slow me down and help me to take time, especially today, to think of the true meaning of Christmas – to experience its peace, to feel its love, to taste its joy, to read of Your birth, to sing of that first silent and holy night. ... Christmas will be what I make it. As for my family and me, help us to make it Your day, Lord.

In Your holy name I pray.

Amen.

DECEMBER 26

Dear Lord, even in my sorrow or sickness You have been there; how can I say thanks? Only by praising You, by sharing Your love, by staying in Your Word, so that my daily life reflects You. How can I say thanks? Oh Lord, let my whole life reflect my gratitude for Your many blessings as I seek to serve You.

In Jesus' name I pray.

Amen.

DECEMBER 27

Dear Lord, let me come before You with praise and thanksgiving ... not always bringing a list of "wants." Help me to remember to truly seek You, the Giver, instead of the gift. For only then will You know that I truly trust You and love You; only then can You bless me.

In Jesus' name I pray.

Amen.

DECEMBER 28

Dear Lord, in this new year ahead, let me not forget that a song isn't my song until I sing it, my joy isn't complete unless I can share it, and my love isn't real love until I give it away! Oh Lord, help me to see that it is in giving that I receive ... that if I try to keep everything to myself I will smother both Your light and mine. Help me, Lord, to remember these things and to let others see You through me.

In Jesus' name I pray.

Amen.

DECEMBER 29

Dear Lord Jesus, what gift can I give You, for You have everything? ... If You want to bring me into union with You, then I must heed Your words – I must deny myself, and take up my cross, and follow You. I must realize that Your words run counter to the world's "Do your own thing." ... What can I give You? I can give myself, my right to independence, so that I can become Your person. ... Oh Lord, this Christmas help me to love You enough to give You me – all of me.

In Your holy name I pray.
Amen.

DECEMBER 30

Dear heavenly Father, as we review the events of this past year, we need to ask Your forgiveness, for too often we who call ourselves Your people must have grieved You! ... We have often stood by silently, or joined with those who oppose the display of Your moral laws in public places. ... Meanwhile our streets, homes, and schools are unsafe. Although our children have been taught Your laws at church and at home, they are often victims of others who are uninformed and undisciplined. ... Help us to see that absolute freedom can only bring chaos to a society, for no nation can long survive with each person doing his or her own thing! ... Help us to see that as Christians we too are citizens, and thus we have a responsibility to speak out on important issues. ... Give us the courage we need, lest we fail You, ourselves, and our children, and become a party to our nation's downfall.

In Jesus' name we pray.
Amen.

DECEMBER 31

Dear Lord, how can I really know You if I don't take time to study Your Word, or to listen for the leading of the Holy Spirit? ... In this coming New Year, help me to spend some time each day in quiet meditation, lest the noise and distractions of my world obscure altogether Your "still small voice."

In Jesus' name I pray.
Amen.

D. L. Hammond, by kind permission

Christian Poetry Collection
George Herbert

DISCIPLINE

THROW away thy rod,
Throw away thy wrath :
my God,
Take the gentle path.
For my hearts desire
Unto thine is bent :
     I aspire
To a full consent.
Nor a word or look
I affect to own,
     But by book,
And thy book alone.
Though I fail, I weep :
Though I halt in pace,
     Yet I creep
To the throne of grace.
Then let wrath remove ;
Love will do the deed :
     For with love
Stonie hearts will bleed.
Love is swift of foot ;
Love's a man of warre,
     And can shoot,
And can hit from farre.
Who can scape his bow ?
That which wrought on thee,
     Brought thee low,
Needs must work on me.
Throw away thy rod ;
Though man frailties hath,
     Thou art God :
Throw away thy wrath.

PRAYER (I)

PRAYER the Churches banquet, Angels age,
God's breath in man returning to his birth,
The soul in paraphrase, heart in pilgrimage,
The Christian plummet sounding heav'n and
     earth;
Engine against th' Almightie, sinner's towre,
Reversed thunder, Christ-side-piercing spear,
The six daies world-transposing in an houre,
A kinde of tune, which all things heare and
     fear;
Softnesse, and peace, and joy, and love, and
     blisse,

Exalted Manna, gladnesse of the best,
Heaven in ordinarie, man well drest,
The milkie way, the bird of Paradise,
Church-bells beyond the stars heard, the souls
    bloud,
The land of spices, something understood.

PRAYER (II)

OF what an easie quick accesse,
My blessed Lord, art thou ! how suddenly
May our requests thine eare invade !
To shew that state dislikes not easinesse,
If I but lift mine eyes, my suit is made :
Thou canst no more not heare, than thou
    canst die.
Of what supreme almightie power
Is thy great arm which spans the east and
    west,
And tacks the center to the sphere !
By it do all things live their measur'd houre :
We cannot ask the thing, which is not there,
Blaming the shallownesse of our request.
Of what unmeasurable love
Art thou possest, who, when thou couldst
    not die,
Wert fain to take our flesh and curse,
And for our sakes in person sinne reprove ;
That by destroying that which ty'd thy purse,
Thou mightst make way for liberalitie!
Since then these three wait on thy throne,
Ease, Power, and Love ; I value prayer so,
That were I to leave all but one,
Wealth, fame, endowments, vertues, all
    should go ;
I and deare prayer would together dwell,
And quickly gain, for each inch lost, an ell.

THE ELIXER

Teach me, my God and King,
In all things Thee to see,
And what I do in any thing
To do it as for Thee.

Not rudely, as a beast,
To runne into an action
But still to make Thee prepossest,
And give it his perfection.

A man that looks on glasse,
On it may stay his eye;

Or if he pleaseth, through it passe,
And then the heav'n espie.

All may of Thee partake:
Nothing can be so mean
Which with his tincture, "for Thy sake,"
Will not grow bright and clean.

A servant with this clause
Makes drudgerie divine;
Who sweeps a room as for Thy law
Makes that and th' action fine.

This is the famous stone
That turneth all to gold;
For that which God doth touch and own
Cannot for lesse be told.

LOVE

Love bade me welcome; yet my soul drew back,
Guilty of dust and sin.
But quick-ey'd Love, observing me grow slack
From my first entrance in,
Drew nearer to me, sweetly questioning,
If I lacked anything.

A guest, I answer'd, worthy to be here:
Love said, You shall be he.
I the unkind, ungrateful? Ah my dear,
I cannot look on thee.
Love took my hand, and smiling did reply,
Who made the eyes but I?

Truth, Lord, but I have marr'd them: let my
    shame
Go where it doth deserve.
And know you not, says Love, who bore the
    blame?
My dear, then I will serve.
You must sit down, says Love, and taste my
    meat:
So I did sit and eat.

REDEMPTION

Having been tenant long to a rich Lord,
Not thriving, I resolved to be bold,
And make a suit unto him, to afford
A new small-rented lease, and cancell th'old.

In heaven at his manor I him sought:
They told me there, that he was lately gone

About some land, which he had dearly bought
Long since on earth, to take possession.

I straight return'd, and knowing his great
   birth,
Sought him accordingly in great resorts;
In cities, theatres, gardens, parks, and courts:
At length a heard a ragged noise and mirth

Of thieves and murderers: there I him espied,
Who straight, Your suit is granted, and died.

THE PULLEY

When God at first made man,
Having a glass of blesings standing by;
Let us, said He, "pour on him all we can:
Let the world's riches, which dispersed lie,
Contract into a span."

So strength first made a way;
The beauty flow'd, then wisdom, honor,
   pleasure:
When almost all was out, God made a stay,
Perceiving that alone of all his treasure
Rest in the bottom lay.

"For if I should," said He,
"Bestow this jewel also on my creature,
He would adore my gifts instead of me,
And rest in Nature, not the God of Nature:
So both should losers be.

"Yet let him keep the rest,
But keep them with repining restlessness;
Let him be rish and weary, that at least,
If goodness lead him not, yet weariness
May toss him to my breast."

EASTER WINGS

Lord, who createdst man in wealth and store,
   Though foolishly he lost the same,
      Decaying more and more,
         Till he became
            Most poor:
            With thee
         O let me rise
      As larks, harmoniously,
   And sing this day thy victories:
Then shall the fall further the flight in me.

My tender age in sorrow did begin:
   And still with sicknesses and shame
      Thou didst so punish sin,
         That I became
            Most thin.
            With thee
         Let me combine
      And feel this day thy victory
   For, if I imp my wing on thine,
Affliction shall advance the flight in me.

THE COLLAR

I struck the board, and cried, No more.
I will abroad.
What? shall I ever sigh and pine?
My lines and life are free; free as the road,
Loose as the wind, as large as store.
Shall I be still in suit?
Have I no harvest but a thorn
To let me blood, and not restore
What I have lost with cordial fruit?
Sure there was wine
Before my sighs did dry it: there was corn
Before my tears did drown it.
Is the year only lost to me?
Have I no bays to crown it?
No flowers, no garlands gay? all blasted?
All wasted?
No so, my heart: but there is fruit,
And thou hast hands.
Recover all thy sigh-blown age
On double pleasures: leave thy cold dispute
Of what is fit, and not forsake thy cage,
Thy rope of sands,
Which petty thoughts have made, and made
   to thee
Good cable, to enforce and draw,
And be thy law,
While thou didst wink and wouldst not see.
Away; take heed:
I will abroad.
Call in thy death's head there: tie up thy fears.
He that forbears
To suit and serve his need,
Deserves his load.
But as I rav'd and grew more fierce and wild
At every word,
Me thoughts I heard one calling, Child:
And I reply'd, My Lord.

SUNDAY

O day most calm, most bright
The fruit of this, the next world's bud,
Th'endorsement of supreme delight,
Writ by a friend, and with his blood;
The couch of time; care's balm and bay:
The week were dark, but for thy light:
Thy torch doth show the way.

The other days and thou
Make up one man; whose face thou art,
Knocking at heaven with thy brow:
The worky-days are the back-part;
The burden of the week lies there,
Making the whole to stoop and bow,
Till thy release appear.

Man had straight forward gone
To endless death: but thou dost pull
And turn us round to look on one,
Whom, if we were not very dull,
We could not choose to look on still;
Since there is no place so alone,
The which he doth not fill.

Sundays the pillars are,
On which heav'n's palace arched lies:
The other days fill up the spare
And hollow room with vanities.
They are the fruitful beds and borders
In God's rich garden: that is bare,
Which parts their ranks and orders.

The Sundays of man's life,
Threaded together on time's string,
Make bracelets to adorn the wife
Of the eternal glorious King.
On Sunday heaven's gate stands ope;
Blessings are plentiful and rife,
More plentiful than hope.

This day my Savior rose,
And did enclose this light for his:
That, as each beast his manger knows,
Man might not of his fodder miss.
Christ hath took in this piece of ground,
And made a garden there for those
Who want herbs for their wound.

The rest of our Creation
Our great Redeemer did remove

With the same shake, which at his passion
Did th'earth and all things with it move.
As Samson bore the doors away,
Christ's hands, though nail'd, wrought our
  salvation,
And did unhinge that day.

The brightness of that day
We sullied by our foul offence:
Wherefore that robe we cast away,
Having a new at his expense,
Whose drops of bloud paid the full price,
That was requir'd to make us gay,
And fit for Paradise.

Thou art a day of mirth:
And where the weekdays trail on ground,
Thy flight is higher, as thy birth.
O let me take thee at the bound,
Leaping with thee from sev'n to sev'n,
Till that we both, being toss'd from earth,
Fly hand in hand to heav'n!

CHURCH MUSICK

Sweetest of sweets, I thank you; when
  displeasure
Did though my body wound my mind,
You took me thence, and in your house of
  pleasure
A dainty lodging me assign'd.

Now I in you with a body move,
Rising and falling with your wings;
We both together sweetly live and love,
Yet say sometimes, God help poor Kings.

Comfort, I'll die; for if you post from me,
Sure I shall do so, and much more;
But if I travel in your company,
You know the way to Heaven's door.

JORDAN

Who says that fictions only and false hair
Become a verse? Is there no truth in beauty?
Is all good structure in a winding stair?
May no lines pass, except they do their duty
Not to a true, but painted chair?

Is it no verse, except enchanted groves
And sudden arbors shadow coarse-spun lines?
Must purling streams refresh a lover's loves?

Must all be veiled, while he that reads, divines,
Catching the sense at two removes?

Shepherds are honest people; let them sing:
Riddle who list, for me, and pull for Prime:
I envy no man's nightingale or spring;
Nor let them punish me with loss of rime,
Who plainly say, My God, My King.

DENIALL
When my devotions could not pierce
Thy silent ears;
Then was my heart broken, as was my verse:
My breast was full of fears
And disorder:

My bent thoughts, like a brittle bow,
Did fly asunder:
Each took his way; some would to pleasures
    go,
Some to the wars and thunder
Of alarms.

As good go any where, they say,
As to benumb
Both knees and heart, in crying night and day,
Come, come, my God, O come,
But no hearing.

O that thou shouldst give dust a tongue
To cry to thee,
And then not hear it crying! all day long
My heart was in my knee,
But no hearing.

Therefore my soul lay out of sight,
Untuned, unstrung:
My feeble spirit, unable to look right,
Like a nipped blossom, hung
Discontented.

O cheer and tune my heartless breast,
Defer no time;
That so thy favors granting my request,
They and my mind may chime,
And mend my rhyme.

VANITY
The fleet astronomer can bore
And thread the spheres with his quick-
    piercing mind:

He views theirs stations, walks from door to
    door,
Surveys, as if he had designed
To make a purchase there: he sees their dances,
And knoweth long before,
Both their full-eyed aspects, and secret
    glances.

The nimble diver with his side
Cuts through the working waves, that he may
    fetch
His dearly-earned pearl, which God did hide
On purpose from the ventrous wretch;
That he might save his life, and also hers,
Who with excessive pride
Her own destruction and his danger wears.

The subtle chymick can devest
And strip the creature naked, till he find
The callow principles within their nest:
There he imparts to them his mind,
Admitted to their bed-chamber, before
They appear trim and drest
To ordinary suitors at the door.

What hath not man sought out and found,
But his dear God? who yet his glorious law
Embosoms in us, mellowing the ground
With showers and frosts, with love and awe,
So that we need not say, Where's this
    command?
Poor man, thou searchest round
To find out death, but missest life at hand.

MAN
My God, I heard this day,
That none doth build a stately habitation,
But he that means to dwell therein.
What house more stately hath there been,
Or can be, than is Man? to whose creation
All things are in decay.

For Man is ev'ry thing,
And more:
He is a tree, yet bears no fruit;
A beast, yet is, or should be more:
Reason and speech we only bring.
Parrots may thank us, if they are not mute,
They go upon the score.

Man is all symmetry,

Full of proportions, one limb to another,
And all to all the world besides:
Each part may call the farthest brother:
For head with foot hath private amity,
And both with moons and tides.

Nothing hath got so far,
But Man hath caught and kept it, as his prey.
His eyes dismount the highest star:
He is in little all the sphere.
Herbs gladly cure our flesh; because that they
Find their acquaintance there.

For us the winds do blow,
The earth doth rest, heav'n move, and
    fountains flow.
Nothing we see, but means our good,
As our delight, or as our treasure:
The whole is, either our cupboard of food,
Or cabinet of pleasure.

The stars have us to bed;
Night draws the curtain, which the sun
    withdraws;
Music and light attend our head.
All things unto our flesh are kind
In their descent and being; to our mind
In their ascent and cause.

Each thing is full of duty:
Waters united are our navigation;
Distinguished, our habitation;
Below, our drink; above, our meat;
Both are our cleanliness.
Hath one such beauty?
Then how are all things neat?

More servants wait on Man,
Than he'll take notice of: in ev'ry path
He treads down that which doth befriend him,
When sickness makes him pale and wan.
Oh mighty love! Man is one world, and hath
Another to attend him.

Since then, my God, thou hast
So brave a palace built; O dwell in it,
That it may dwell with thee at last!
Till then, afford us so much wit;
That, as the world serves us, we may serve
    thee,
And both thy servants be.

LIFE

I made a posie, while the day ran by:
Here will I smell my remnants out, and tie
My life within this band.
But time did beckon to the flowers, and they
By noon most cunningly did steal away,
And wither'd in my hand.

My hand was next to them, and then my
    heart:
I took, without more thinking, in good part
Time's gentle admonition:
Who did so sweetly death's sad taste convey,
Making my mind to smell my fatal day;
Yet sugaring the suspicion.

Farewell, dear flowers, sweetly your time ye
    spent,
Fit, while ye lived, for smell or ornament,
And after death for cures.
I follow straight without complaints or grief,
Since if my scent be good, I care not, if
It be as short as yours.

SIN'S ROUND

Sorry I am, my God, sorry I am,
That my offences course it in a ring.
My thoughts are working like a busy flame,
Until their cockatrice they hatch and bring:
And when they once have perfected their
    draughts,
My words take fire from my inflamed
    thoughts.

My words take fire from my inflamed thoughts,
Which spit it forth like the Sicilian hill.
They vent their wares, and pass them with
    their faults,
And by their breathing ventilate the ill.
But words suffice not, where are lewd
    intentions:
My hands do join to finish the inventions.

My hands do join to finish the inventions:
And so my sins ascend three stories high,
As Babel grew, before there were dissentions.
Let ill deeds loiter not: for they supply
New thoughts of sinning:
wherefore, to my shame,
Sorry I am, my God, sorry I am.

PEACE

Sweet Peace, where dost thou dwell? I humbly
    crave,
Let me once know.
I sought thee in a secret cave,
And ask'd, if Peace were there.
A hollow wind did seem to answer, No:
Go seek elsewhere.

I did; and going did a rainbow note:
Surely, thought I,
This is the lace of Peace's coat:
I will search out the matter.
But while I lookt, the clouds immediately
Did break and scatter.

Then went I to a garden, and did spy
A gallant flower,
The crown Imperial: Sure, said I,
Peace at the root must dwell.
But when I digg'd, I saw a worm devour
What show'd so well.

At length I met a rev'rend good old man,
Whom when for Peace
I did demand; he thus began:
There was a Prince of old
At Salem dwelt, who liv'd with good increase
Of flock and fold.

He sweetly liv'd; yet sweetness did not save
His life from foes.
But after death out of his grave
There sprang twelve stalks of wheat:
Which many wondring at, got some of those
To plant and set.

It prosper'd strangely, and did soon disperse
Through all the earth:
For they that taste it do rehearse,
That virtue lies therein,
A secret virtue bringing peace and mirth
By flight of sin.

"Take of this grain, which in my garden grows,
And grows for you;
Make bread of it: and that repose
And Peace which ev'ry where
With so much earnestness you do pursue,
Is only there."

MAN'S MEDLEY

Hark, how the birds do sing,
and woods do ring.
All creatures have their joy: and man hath his.
Yet if we rightly measure,
Man's joy and pleasure
Rather hereafter, than in present, is.

To this life things of sense
Make their pretense:
In th'other Angels have a right by birth:
Man ties them both alone,
And makes them one,
With th'one hand touching heav'n, with
    th'other earth.

In soul he mounts and flies,
In flesh he dies.
He wears a stuff whose thread is coarse and
    round,
But trimm'd with curious lace
And should take place
After the trimming, not the stuff and ground.

Not that he may not here
Taste of the cheer,
But as birds drink, and straight lift up their
    head,
So must he sip and think
Of better drink
He may attain to, after he is dead.

But as his joys are double,
So is his trouble.
He hath two winters, other things but one:
Both frosts and thoughts do nip,
And bite his lip;
And he of all things fears two deaths alone.

Yet ev'n the greatest griefs
May be reliefs,
Could he but take them right, and in their
ways.
Happy is he, whose heart
Hath found the art
To turn his double pains to double praise.

THE STORM

If as the winds and waters here below
Do fly and flow,
My sighs and tears as busy were above;

Sure they would move
And much affect thee, as tempestuous times
Amaze poor mortals, and object their crimes.

Stars have their storms, ev'n in a high degree,
As well as we.
A throbbing conscience spurred by remorse
Hath a strange force:
It quits the earth, and mounting more and
    more,
Dares to assault, and besiege thy door.

There it stands knocking, to thy musick's
    wrong,
And drowns the song.
Glory and honor are set by till it
An answer get.
Poets have wrong'd poor storms: such days
    are best;
They purge the air without, within the breast.

ARTILLERIE

As I one ev'ning sat before my cell,
Me thoughts a star did shoot into my lap.
I rose, and shook my clothes, as knowing well,
That from small fires comes oft no small
    mishap.
When suddenly I heard one say,
-Do as thou usest, disobey,
Expell good motions from thy breast,
Which have the face of fire, but end in rest-.

I, who had heard of music in the spheres,
But not of speech in stars, began to muse:
But turning to my God, whose ministers
The stars and all things are; if I refuse,
Dread Lord, said I , so oft my good;
Then I refuse not ev'n with blood
To wash away my stubborn thought:
For I will do, or suffer what I ought.

But I have also stars and shooters too,
Born where thy servants both artilleries use.
My tears and prayers night and day do woo,
And work up to thee; yet thou dost refuse.
Not but that I am (I must say still)
Much more oblig'd to do thy will,
Than thou to grant mine: but because
Thy promise now hath ev'n set thee thy laws.

Then we are shooters both, and thou dost

deign
To enter combat with us, and contest
With thine own clay. But I would parley fain:
Shun not my arrows, and behold my breast.
Yet if thou shunnest, I am thine:
I must be so, if I am mine.
There is no articling with thee:
I am but finite, yet thine infinitely.

VIRTUE

Sweet day, so cool, so calm, so bright,
The bridal of earth and sky:
The dew shall weep thy fall tonight;
For thou must die.

Sweet rose, whose hue angry and brave
Bids the rash gazer wipe his eye:
Thy root is ever in its grave,
And thou must die.

Sweet spring, full of sweet days and roses,
A box where sweets compacted lie;
My music shows ye have your closes,
And all must die.

Only a sweet and virtuous soul,
Like seasoned timber, never gives;
But though the whole world turn to coal,
Then chiefly lives.

THE HOLDFAST

I threatened to observe the strict decree
Of my deare God with all my power and
    might:
But I was told by one, "It could not be;
Yet I might trust in God to be my light."

"Then will I trust," said I, "in Him alone."
"Nay, ev'n to trust in Him, was also His:
We must confess that nothing is our own."
"Then I confess that He my succor is."

"But to have nought is ours, not to confess
That we have nought." I stood amaz'd at this,
Much troubled, till I heard a friend expresse
That all things were more ours by being His:

What Adam had, and forfeited for all,
Christ keepeth now, Who cannot fail or fall.
                    George Herbert, 1593–1633

The Genevan Book of Order

The Form of Prayers and Ministration of the Sacraments, etc. Used in the English Congregation at Geneva (1556)

A CONFESSION OF OUR SINS, FRAMED TO OUR TIME, OUT OF THE 9TH CHAPTER OF DANIEL

O Lord God, which art mighty and dreadful, thou that keepest covenant, and shewest mercy to them that love thee and do thy commandments:[a] We have sinned; we have offended;[b] we have wickedly and stubbornly gone back from thy laws and precepts.[c] We would never obey thy servants the prophets that spake in thy name,[d] to our kings and princes, to our forefathers, and to all the people of our land. O Lord, righteousness belongeth unto thee;[e] unto us pertaineth nothing but open shame, as it is come to pass this day unto our miserable country of England; yea unto all our nations, whether they be far or near, through all lands, wherein they are scattered for the offences that they and we have committed against thee,[f] so that the curses and punishments which are written in thy law[g] are now poured upon us; and thou hast performed those words wherewith thou didst menace us and our rulers that governed us, in bringing the same plagues upon us which before were threatened. And yet notwithstanding, both they and we proceed in our iniquity, and cease not to heap sin upon sin. For they which once were well instructed in the doctrine of thy gospel, are now gone back from the obedience of thy truth, and are turned again to that most abominable idolatry,[h] from the which they were once called by the lively preaching of thy word. And we, alas! to this day, do not earnestly repent us of our former wicked ness, neither do we rightly consider the heaviness of thy displeasure.[i] Such is thy just judgment, O Lord, that thou punisheth sin by sin, and man by his own inventions,[k] so that there can be no end of iniquity, except thou prevent us[l] with thy undeserved grace.[m] Therefore convert us, O Lord, and we shall converted;[n] for we do not offer up our prayers trusting in our own righteousness,[o] but in thy manifold mercies. And although thou hast once of thy especial grace delivered us from the miserable thraldom of error and blindness, and called us many times to the sweet liberty of thy gospel,[p] which we notwithstanding have most shamefully abused, in obeying rather our own lusts and affections,[q] than the admonitions of thy prophets;[r] yet we beseech thee once again, for thy name's sake,[s] to pour some comfortable drop of thy accustomed mercies upon us; incline thine ears, and open thine eyes,[t] to behold the grievous plagues of our country, the continual sorrows of our afflicted brethren, and our woeful banishment. And let our afflictions and just punishments be an admonition and warning to other nations among whom we are scattered, that with all reverence they may obey thy holy gospel; lest for like contempt, in the end, like or worse plagues fall upon them.[u] Wherefore, O Lord, hear us! O Lord, forgive us! O Lord, consider and tarry not over long! but for thy dear Son Jesus Christ's sake, be merciful unto us, and deliver us.[x] So shall it be known to all the world, that thou only art the selfsame God, that ever showeth mercy to all such as call upon thy holy name.[y]

a. Neh. 1:5; Job 9, 38–40; Ps. 24, 76, 77:10ff., 139

b. Ex. 20:6; Luke 7:47

c. Gen. 3:6–19; Rom. 5:12ff.; 1 John 1:8–10; Ps. 32:5; 106:6ff.

d. Lev. 26; Deut. 28; Jer. 26:4–6, 29:19; Neh. 1:6–11

e. Ps. 11:7; Jam. 1:13; Job 4:17–19; 9:1ff.; 25:4–6

f. Jer. 26–27

g. Lev. 26:14ff.; Deut. 27–30

h. 2 Pet. 2:20–22; Prov. 26:11; Heb. 6:4–6; 10: 26–31

i. Ps. 19:12–13; Deut. 31:16ff.; 29:20; Ezek. 5: 5–11

k. Rom. 1:18ff.

l. Isa. 65:1

m. Eph. 2:5

n. Ps. 85:4; Jer. 31:18

o. Titus 3:5; 2 Tim. 1:9

p. Gal.4 & 5:1ff.

q. Gal. 5:13–21

r. Zech. 7:8–14

s. Ps. 23:3; 25:11

t. Ps. 71:1ff.

u. Matt. 11:20–24; 12:41; Luke 10:13–16

x. John 16:23–24
y. Ps. 103; 108:4, 136

ANOTHER CONFESSION FOR ALL STATES AND TIMES

O eternal God and most merciful Father, we confess and acknowledge here, before thy divine majesty, that we are miserable sinners,[a] conceived and born in sin and iniquity,[b] so that in us there is no goodness.[c] For the flesh evermore rebels against the spirit,[d] whereby we continually transgress thy holy precepts and commandments, and so purchase to ourselves, through thy just judgment, death and damnation.[e]

Notwithstanding, O heavenly Father, forasmuch as we are displeased with ourselves for the sins that we have committed against thee, and do unfeignedly repent us of the same, we most humbly beseech thee, for Jesus Christ's sake, to show thy mercy upon us, to forgive us all our sins, and to increase thy Holy Spirit in us: that we, acknowledging from the bottom of our hearts our own unrighteousness, may from henceforth not only mortify our sinful lusts and affections,[f] but also bring forth such fruits as may be agreeable to thy most blessed will; not for the worthiness thereof, but for the merits of thy dearly beloved Son Jesus Christ,[g] our only Savior, whom thou hast already given [as] an oblation and offering for our sins, and for whose sake we are certainly persuaded that thou wilt deny us nothing that we shall ask in his name, according to thy will.[h] For thy Spirit does assure our consciences that thou art our merciful Father,[i] and so lovest us thy children through him, that nothing is able to remove thy heavenly grace and favor from us. To thee, therefore, O Father, with the Son and the Holy Ghost, be all honor and glory, world without end. So be it.

a. Rom. 3:9ff.; Ps. 14:1–3
b. Ps. 51:5
c. Rom. 7:15–25
d. Gal. 5:17
e. Rom. 2:1ff.; Jer. 3:23–25; Isa. 40:7 [?]
f. Col. 3:5ff.; Rom. 6:1–7; Eph. 4:20–24; 5:3–5; 1 Pet. 2:11
g. Rom. 5:1ff.; Heb. 9:14; Eph. 2:16ff.
h. John 14:13–14; 16:23; Matt. 7:7–12; Jam. 1: 5–7

i. 1 John 3:24; Rom. 8:9–17, 37–39

A PRAYER FOR THE WHOLE ESTATE OF CHRIST'S CHURCH

Almighty God and most merciful Father, we humbly submit ourselves,[a] and fall down before thy Majesty,[b] beseeching thee from the bottom of our hearts, that this seed of thy word,[c] now sown amongst us, may take such deep root, that neither the burning heat of persecution cause it to wither, neither the thorny cares of this life do choke it, but that as seed sown in good ground, it may bring forth thirty, sixty, and an hundred fold, as thy heavenly wisdom hath appointed. And because we have need continually to crave many things at thy hands, we humbly beseech thee, O heavenly Father, to grant us thy Holy Spirit[d] to direct our petitions, that they may proceed from such a fervent mind as may be agreeable to thy most blessed will.[e]

And seeing that our infirmity is able to do nothing without thy help, and that thou art not ignorant with how many and great temptations[f] we poor wretches are on every side enclosed and compassed, let thy strength, O Lord, sustain our weakness, that we being defended with the force of thy grace, may be safely preserved against all assaults of Satan, who goeth about continually like a roaring lion, seeking to devour us.[g] Increase our faith,[h] O merciful Father, that we do not swerve at any time from thy heavenly word, but augment in us hope and love, with a careful keeping of all thy commandments, that no hardness of heart,[i] no hypocrisy, no concupiscence of the eyes,[k] nor enticements of the world, do draw us away from thy obedience. And seeing we live now in these most perilous times,[l] let thy Fatherly providence defend us against the violence of all our enemies, which do everywhere pursue us; but chiefly against the wicked rage and furious uproars of that Romish idol, enemy to thy Christ.[m]

Furthermore, forasmuch as by thy holy apostle we are taught to make our prayers and supplications for all men,[n] we pray not only for ourselves here present, but beseech thee also, to reduce all such as be yet ignorant, from the miserable captivity of blindness and error, to the pure understanding and knowledge of thy heavenly truth, that we all, with one consent and unity of minds,[o] may worship thee our only God and Savior; and that all pastors, shepherds, and ministers, to whom thou hast committed the dispensation of thy holy word,[p] and charge of thy chosen people,[q] may both in their life and doctrine be found faithful, setting only before their eyes thy glory; and that by them, all poor sheep which wander and go astray, may be gathered and brought home to thy fold.

Moreover, because the hearts of rulers are in thy hands,[r] we beseech thee to direct and govern the hearts of all kings, princes, and magistrates to whom thou hast committed the sword;[s] especially, O Lord, according to our bounden duty, we beseech thee to maintain and increase the honorable estate of this city, into whose defense we are received, the magistrates, the council, and all the whole body of this commonwealth: Let thy Fatherly favor so preserve them, and thy Holy Spirit so govern their hearts, that they may in such sort execute their office, that thy religion may be purely maintained, manners reformed, and sin punished according to the precise rule of thy holy word.[t]

And for that we are all members of the mystical body of Christ Jesus,[u] we make our requests unto thee, O heavenly Father, for all such as are afflicted with any kind of cross or tribulation,[x] as war, plague, famine, sickness, poverty, imprisonment, persecution, banishment, or any other kind of thy rods, whether it be calamity of body, or vexation of mind,[y] that it would please thee to give them patience and constancy, till thou send them full deliverance of all their troubles. And as we are bound to love and honor our parents, kinfolks, friends, and country,[z] so we most humbly beseech thee to show thy pity upon our miserable country of England, which once, through thy mercy, was called to liberty, and now for their and our sins, is brought unto most vile slavery and Babylonian bondage.

Root out from thence, O Lord, all ravening wolves,[a] which to fill their bellies destroy thy flock.[b] And show thy great mercies upon those our brethren which are persecuted, cast in prison, and daily condemned to death for the testimony of thy truth.[c] And though

they be utterly destitute of all men's aid,[d] yet let thy sweet comfort never depart from them, but so inflame their hearts with thy Holy Spirit, that they may boldly and cheerfully abide such trial[e] as thy godly wisdom shall appoint.[f] So that at length, as well by their death as by their life,[g] the kingdom of thy dear Son Jesus Christ may increase and shine through all the world. In whose name we make our humble petitions unto thee, as he hath taught us.

Our Father which art in heaven, etc.

Almighty and ever living God, vouchsafe, we beseech thee, to grant us perfect continuance in thy lively faith, augmenting the same in us daily,[a] till we grow to the full measure of our perfection in Christ,[b] whereof we make our confession, saying,

"I believe in God," etc.

a. 1 Pet. 5:6
b. Num. 16:22; Deut. 9:18; Josh. 7:6
c. Matt. 13:3–8
d. Luke 11:13; Rom. 8:12–17; Jam. 5:16; 1 John 5:14; Rom. 12:11–12; Wisdom 9:17–18
e. 2 Cor. 3:5; John 15:5; Phil. 2:13
f. Ps. 40:12–13, 17; 1 Pet. 1:6
g. 1 Pet. 5:8
h. Luke 17:5
i. Ps. 95:7–8; Heb. 3:7ff.; 4:7
k. 1 John 2:15–17
l. 1 Tim. 4:1ff.; 2 Pet. 3:3ff.; 2 Tim. 3:1ff.; Jude
m. 2 Thess. 2:1ff.; 1 John 2:18; Rev. 13, 17
n. 1 Tim. 2:1ff.
o. Rom. 15:6; 1 Cor. 1:10; Eph. 4:3
p. John 21:15–17; Matt. 28:19–20; 1 Cor. 9:16ff.; Mark 16:15
q. 1 Pet. 5:1–3
r. Prov. 21:1
s. Rom. 13:4; John 19:11
t. 1 Tim. 1:3ff.; Jam. 1:18ff.
u. 1 Cor. 12:12–13; Rom. 12:4–5
x. Jam. 5:13–15
y. 2 Cor. 1:6ff.; Heb. 13:3
z. Ex. 20:12

a. Matt. 7:15; Acts 20:29
b. Ezek. 34:1ff.; Rom. 16:17–18; Phil. 3:2, 18–19
c. Heb. 13:3; Rom. 8:36; Ps. 44:22
d. John 16:33
e. 1 Pet. 1:7
f. Acts 2:23; Matt. 10:35ff.; Luke 21:12ff.
g. Rom. 14:7–8

a. Luke 17:5
b. Eph. 4:12–16

BLESSINGS

The Lord bless you and save you; the Lord make his face shine upon you, and be merciful unto you; the Lord turn his countenance towards you, and grant you his peace.[a]

The grace of our Lord Jesus Christ, the love of God, and communion of the Holy Ghost, be with you all. So be it.[b]

a. Num. 6:24–26
b. 2 Cor. 13:14

The Genevan Book of Order

Collection of prayers in the Orthodox tradition

PRAYER AT DAYBREAK

O Lord Eternal and Creator of all things,
Who of Thy inscrutable goodness called me
    to this life;
Who bestowed on me the grace of Baptism
and the Seal of the Holy Spirit;
Who imbued me with the desire to seek Thee,
the one true God: hear my prayer.
I have no life, no light, no joy or wisdom;
no strength except in Thee, O God.
Because of my unrighteousness I dare not
    raise my eyes to Thee.
But Thou said to Thy disciples,
"Whatsoever you shall ask in prayer believing,
    you shall receive."
and "Whatsoever you shall ask in my name,
    that will I do."
Wherefore I dare to invoke Thee.
Purify me from all taint of flesh and spirit.
Teach me to pray aright.
Bless this day which Thee give unto me, Thy
    unworthy servant.
By the power of Thy blessing enable me at all
    times to speak
and act to Thy glory with a pure spirit, with
    humility, patience,
love, gentleness, peace, courage and wisdom:
aware always of Thy presence.
Of Thy immense goodness, O Lord God,
    show me the path of Thy will,
and grant me to walk in Thy sight without sin.

O Lord, unto Whom all hearts be open,
Thee know what things I have need of.
Thee are acquainted with my blindness and
    my ignorance,
Thee know my infirmity and my soul's
    corruption;
but neither are my pain and anguish hid from
    Thee.
Wherefore I beseech Thee, hear my prayer and
    by Thy Holy Spirit
teach me the way wherein I should walk;
and when my perverted will would lead me
    down other paths
spare me not O Lord, but force me back to
    Thee.
By the power of Thy love, grant me to hold
    fast to that which is good.
Preserve me from every word or deed that
    corrupts the soul;
from every impulse unpleasing in Thy sight
    and hurtful to my brother-man.
Teach me what I should say and how I should
    speak.
If it be Thy will that I make no answer,
inspire me to keep silent in a spirit of peace
that causes neither sorrow nor hurt to my
    fellow man.
Establish me in the path of Thy commandments
and to my last breath let me not stray from
    the light of Thy ordinances,
that Thy commandments may become the
    sole law
of my being on this earth and all eternity.
Yea, Lord, I pray to Thee, have pity on me.
Spare me in my affliction and my misery
and hide not the way of salvation from me.
In my foolishness, O God, I plead with Thee
    for many and great things.
Yet am I ever mindful of my wickedness, my
    baseness, my vileness.
Have mercy upon me.
Cast me not away from your presence because
    of my presumption.
Do Thee rather increase in me this
    presumption,
and grant unto me, the worst of men,
to love Thee as Thee have commanded, with
    all my heart, and with all my soul,
and with all my mind, and with all my
    strength:
with my whole being.

Yea, O Lord, by Thy Holy Spirit, teach me
good judgment and knowledge.
Grant me to know Thy truth before I go down
into the grave.
Maintain my life in this world until I may offer
unto Thee worthy repentance.
Take me not away in the midst of my days,
nor while my mind is still blind.
When Thee shall be pleased to bring my life
to an end,
forewarn me that I may prepare my soul to
come before Thee.
Be with me, O Lord, at that dread hour and
grant me the joy of salvation.
Cleanse me from secret faults, from all
iniquity that is hidden in me;
and give me a right answer before Thy
judgment-seat.
Yea, Lord, of Thy great mercy and
immeasurable love for mankind.
Archimandrite Sophronios, by kind permission

We offer to thee this spiritual worship without
shedding of blood,
and we pray and beseech and implore thee:
send down thy Holy Spirit upon us and upon
these gifts here set forth:
and make this bread the precious Body of thy
Christ,
and what is in this cup the precious Blood of
thy Christ,
transforming them by thy Holy Spirit.
Liturgy of St. Chrysostom, Greek Orthodox
Church, Invocation of the Holy Spirit

EVENING PRAYERS
And now as we lay down to sleep, O Master,
grant us repose both of body and of soul, and
keep us from the dark passions of the night.
Subdue Thou the assaults of passions. Quench
the fiery darts of the Wicked One which are
thrown insidiously at us; calm the commo-
tions of our flesh and put away all thoughts
about worldly and material things as we go to
sleep. Grant us, O god, a watchful mind, chaste
thoughts, a sober heart, and a gentle sleep, free
from all the fantasies of Satan. And raise us up
again at the hour of prayer, established in Thy
commandments and holding steadfast within
ourselves the remembrance of Thy judgments.
Give us the words of Thy glorification all night

long, that we may praise, bless, and glorify
Thy most honorable and magnificent name, O
Father, Son and Holy Spirit, now and ever, and
unto ages of ages. Amen.

O eternal God! Ruler of all creation! Who hast
vouchsafed that I should live even down to the
present hour, forgive the sins I have committed this day by deed, word or thought. Cleanse,
O Lord, my humble soul of all corporal and
spiritual stain. And grant, O Lord, that I may
during this night have a peaceful sleep, so
that on rising from my humble bed, I should
continue to praise Thy holy Name throughout
all the days of my life, and that I be victorious
over all the physical and spiritual enemies
battling against me. Deliver me, O Lord, from
all vain thoughts that defile me, and from evil
desires. For Thine is the Kingdom, and the
Power, and the Glory of the Father, and of the
Son, and of the Holy Spirit, now and ever, and
unto ages of ages. Amen.

O Lord our God, however I have sinned this
day in word, deed or thought, forgive me, for
Thou art gracious and lovest mankind. Grant
me peaceful and undisturbed sleep. Send me
Thy guardian angel to shield me and protect
me from every evil; for Thou art the Guardian of our souls and bodies, and unto Thee we
ascribe glory, to the Father and to the Son and
to the Holy Spirit, now and ever, and unto ages
of ages. Amen.

Into Thy hands, O Lord, Jesus Christ, my God,
I commend my spirit. Bless me, save me and
grant unto me everlasting life. Amen.

PRAYERS OF THANKSGIVING
O Lord my Savior and my Master, I, Thine
unprofitable servant, with fear and trembling
give thanks unto Thy loving goodness for
all Thy benefits which Thou hast poured so
abundantly upon me, Thy servant. I fall down
in adoration before Thee and offer Thee, O
God, my praises; with fervor I cry to Thee: O
God, deliver me henceforth from all adversities and mercifully fulfill in me such of my
desires as may be expedient for me. Hear me,
I entreat Thee, and have mercy, for Thou art
the Hope of all the ends of the earth, and unto

Thee, with the Father, and the Holy Spirit, be ascribed glory, now and ever, and unto ages of ages. Amen.

I praise Thee, O God of our Fathers, I hymn Thee, I bless Thee, I give thanks unto thee for Thy great and tender mercy. To Thee I flee, O merciful and mighty God. Shine into my heart with the True Sun of Thy righteousness. Enlighten my mind and keep all my senses, that henceforth I may walk uprightly and keep Thy commandments, and may finally attain unto eternal life, even to Thee, Who art the source of life, and be admitted to the glorious fruition of Thy inaccessible Light. For Thou art my God, and unto Thee, O Father, Son and Holy Spirit, be ascribed glory, now and ever and unto ages of ages. Amen.

PRAYER OF PHILARET

My Lord, I know not what I ought to ask of
    Thee.
Thou and Thou alone knowest my needs.
Thou lovest me more than I am able to love
    Thee.
O Father, grant unto me, Thy servant, all
    which I cannot ask.
For a cross I dare not ask, nor for consolation;
I dare only to stand in Thy presence.
My heart is open to Thee.
Thou seest my needs of which I myself am
    unaware.
Behold and lift me up!
In Thy presence I stand,
awed and silenced by Thy will and Thy
    judgments,
into which my mind cannot penetrate.
To Thee I offer myself as a sacrifice.
No other desire is mine but to fulfill Thy will.
Teach me how to pray.
Do Thyself pray within me.
Amen.

Philaret, Metropolitan of Moscow

Lord and Master of my life,
take from me the spirit of laziness,
    discouragement,
lust for power and idle talk.
Instead grant to me, Your servant,
the spirit of purity, humility, patience and
    love.

Lord and King, grant me the grace to be aware
    of my own sins
and refrain from judging others;
for You are blessed forever. Amen.

Saint Ephrem the Syrian

EVENING PRAYER OF SAINT BASIL THE GREAT

Lord, O Lord, You delivered us from every arrow that flies in the daylight! Protect us against any difficulty that lurks in the darkness of night. Accept our uplifted hands as an evening sacrifice. Make us worthy to spend the night without blame and fully sheltered against all evil. Protect us against all disturbances or fear of the devil. Grant reverence to our souls and diligence to our minds, that we may understand Your dread and just judgments. Nail down our bodies with fear of You. Let our passions die out, so that in the stillness of this night we may be enlightened by the thought of Your commands. Keep far away from us all indecent dreams and harmful cravings. Awaken us in time for prayer, strengthened in the faith and able to obey Your commands. Through the mercy and kindness of Your only-begotten Son, with whom You are blessed, together with Your all-holy, good and life-giving Spirit, now and ever and forever. Amen.

From the Great Compline

PRAYER OF SAINT BASIL THE GREAT

O God and Lord of the Powers, and Maker of all creation, Who, because of Thy clemency and incomparable mercy, didst send Thine Only-Begotten Son and our Lord Jesus Christ for the salvation of mankind, and with His venerable Cross didst tear asunder the record of our sins, and thereby didst conquer the rulers and powers of darkness; receive from us sinful people, O merciful Master, these prayers of gratitude and supplication, and deliver us from every destructive and gloomy transgression, and from all visible and invisible enemies who seek to injure us. Nail down our flesh with fear of Thee, and let not our hearts be inclined to words or thoughts of evil, but pierce our souls with Thy love, that ever contemplating Thee, being enlightened by Thee, and discerning Thee, the unapproachable and everlasting

Light, we may unceasingly render confession and gratitude to Thee: The eternal Father, with Thine Only-Begotten Son, and with Thine All-Holy, Gracious, and Life-Giving Spirit, now and ever, and unto ages of ages. Amen.

THE JESUS PRAYER
O Lord Jesus Christ, Son of God, have mercy upon me, a sinner.

FROM MATINS
O Lord, our heavenly Father, Almighty and everlasting God, who hast safely brought us to the beginning of this day; Defend us in the same with thy mighty power; and grant that this day we fall into no sin, neither run into any kind of danger; but that all our doings being ordered by thy governance, may be righteous in thy sight; through Jesus Christ our Lord.

FROM EVENSONG
O God, from whom all holy desires, all good counsels, and all just works do proceed; Give unto thy servants that peace which the world cannot give; that our hearts may be set to obey thy commandments, and that also, by thee, we, being defended from the fear of our enemies, may pass our time in rest and quietness; through Jesus Christ our Savior.

FROM EVENSONG
Lighten our darkness, we beseech thee, O Lord; and by thy great mercy defend us from all perils and dangers of this night; for the love of thy only Son, our Savior, Jesus Christ.

CHOIR PRAYER
Take thou good heed that what thou singest with thy lips, thou dost believe in thy heart, and what thou believest in thy heart, thou dost practice in thy life; and may God grant thee grace so to worship and serve Him on earth, that thou mayest praise Him eternally among the redeemed in Heaven.

THE PRAYER OF HUMBLE ACCESS
We do not presume to come to this thy Table, O merciful Lord, trusting in our own righteousness, but in thy manifold and great mercies. We are not worthy so much as to gather up the crumbs under thy Table. But thou art the same Lord, whose property is always to have mercy. Grant us therefore, gracious Lord, so to eat the flesh of thy dear son Jesus Christ, and to drink his blood, that our sinful bodies may be made clean by his body, and our souls washed through his most precious blood, and that we may evermore dwell in him, and he in us. Amen.

The Liturgy of St. Tikhon

A COLLECT FOR EASTER EVEN
Grant, O Lord, that as we are baptized into the death of thy blessed Son, our Savior Jesus Christ, so by continual mortifying of our corrupt affections we may be buried with him; and that through the grave, and gate of death, we may pass to our joyful resurrection; for him, who died, and was buried, and rose again for us, the same thy Son Jesus Christ our Lord. Amen.

SONG OF ST. SYMEON
O heavenly King, the Comforter, the Spirit of Truth
Who art everywhere present and fillest all things,
Treasury of blessings and giver of light,
Come and abide in us and cleans us from every impurity
and save our souls, O Good One.

THE TRISAGION PRAYERS
Holy God, Holy Mighty, Holy Immortal, have mercy on us. (thrice)
Glory to the Father and to the Son and to the Holy Spirit, now and ever and unto ages of ages. Amen.
All Holy Trinity have mercy upon us, Lord cleanse us from our iniquities, O Holy One heal our infirmities, for Thy names sake.
Lord, have mercy (thrice)
Glory to the Father and to the Son and to the Holy Spirit, now and ever and unto ages of ages. Amen.
Our Father, who art in heaven,
hallowed be thy name.
Thy Kingdom come,
Thy will be done on earth as it is in heaven.
Give us this day our daily bread,
and forgive us our trespasses as we forgive those who tresspass against us

And lead us not into temptation, but deliver us from the evil one.

Priest: for thine is the kingdom, and the power and the glory of the Father and the Son and the Holy Spirit, now and ever and unto ages of ages. Amen.

A PRAYER OF THANKSGIVING

Lord Jesus Christ our God, O God of every merciful kindness and compassion, Whose mercy is without measure, and Whose love for mankind is an unfathomable deep: Falling down before Thy greatness, with fear and trembling as unworthy servants, and now humbly rendering thanksgiving unto Thy loving-kindness for Thy benefits bestowed upon us, we glorify, praise, hymn and magnify Thee as Lord, Master, and Benefactor; and falling down again we offer thanks. We implore Thy boundless and ineffable merciful kindness, humbly praying, in that Thou hast now graciously vouchsafed to accept and to fulfill the supplications of Thy servants, so also grant that henceforth we might increase in true love of Thee, and of our neighbors, and in all of the virtues. And enable us to always thank and praise Thee, together with Thine unoriginate Father and Thy most holy and good and consubstantial Spirit. Amen.

Unknown source

Almighty God, Lord, whose name is great, who give us entrance to the Holy of Holies through the coming of your only-begotten Son, our Lord and God and Savior, Jesus Christ, we entreat and implore your goodness. Since we are full of fear and trembling as we are about to stand before your holy altar, send forth your good grace upon us, sanctify our souls, bodies and spirits and change our thoughts to true devotion, so that, with a pure conscience, we may offer you gifts, presents, fruits, for the removal of our sins, for the forgiveness of all your people, by the grace and love for humankind of your only-begotten Son, with whom you are blessed, together with your all-holy, good and life-giving Spirit, now and for ever, and to the ages of ages.

Liturgy of St. James

Defiled as I am by many sins, do not utterly reject me, Master, Lord, our God. For see, I draw near to this divine and heavenly mystery, not as though I were worthy, but, looking to Thy goodness, I raise my voice to Thee, God, be merciful to me, a sinner. For I have sinned against heaven and before Thee, and I am not worthy to lift up my eyes to this Thy sacred and spiritual Table, on which Thy only-begotten Son, our Lord Jesus Christ, is mystically set forth as a sacrifice by me, a sinner stained by every defilement.

Therefore I bring Thee this supplication, that Thy Spirit, the Advocate, may be sent down to me, strengthening and preparing me for this ministry. And grant that without condemnation the word that has been declared by Thee may be proclaimed by me to the people in Christ Jesus our Lord, with whom Thou art blessed, together with Thy all-holy, good, life-giving and consubstantial Spirit, now and for ever, and to the ages of ages. Amen.

Liturgy of St. James

Glory to the Father and to the Son and to the Holy Spirit, the triple and single light of the one Godhead, that exists singly in Trinity and is divided without division. For the one God is Trinity, whose glory the heavens declare, while earth proclaims his dominion, the sea his might and every physical and immaterial creature his greatness. For to him belongs all glory, honor, might, greatness and magnificence, now and for ever, and to the ages of ages.

Liturgy of St. James

Grant us Thy patience, Lord,
in these our woeful days,
The mob's wrath to endure,
The torturer's ire;
Thy unction to forgive
Our neighbors' persecution
And mild, like Thee, to bear
A bloodstained Cross.
And when the mob prevails,
And foes come to despoil us,
To suffer humbly shame,
O Savior aid us!
And when the hour comes
To pass the last dread gate,
Breathe strength in us to pray,
Father forgive them!

Olga Nikolaevna

I know Thee, Savior, as Deliverer, changing the decision about all my ills. Erase my sins, underwrite my remission from sin, bring me amnesty; Engrave my decree, and free me. Thou hast become, O Lord, my King and my God, Thou who dost will that all men be saved.

The Kontakia of Romanos

I pray Thee, compassionate Lord, do not allow me to be condemned because of the unworthy and ungrateful manner in which I contemplate the great mysteries that Thou hast revealed to Thy saints and through them to me, a sinner and Thy unworthy servant. For see, Lord, Thy servant stands before Thee, idle in everything, speechless, as one who is dead; and I do not dare to say anything more or to presumptuously contemplate further. But as always I fall down before Thee, crying from the depths of my soul …

Ephrem the Syrian

Jesus Christ, radiant center of glory, image of our God, the invisible Father, revealer of His eternal designs, prince of peace; Father of the world to come. For our sake he took the likeness of a slave, becoming flesh in the womb of the Virgin Mary, for our sake, wrapped in swaddling bands and laid in a manger adored by the shepherds and hymned by the angelic powers, who sang: Glory to God in the heavens and on earth peace and good to men. Make us worthy, Lord, to celebrate and to conclude in peace the feast which magnifies the rising of Thy light, by avoiding empty words, working with justice, fleeing from the passions, and raising up the spirit above earthly goods. Bless Thy Church, formed long ago to be united with Thou through Thy life-giving blood. Come to the aid of Thy faithful shepherds, of the priests and the teachers of the Gospel. Bless Thy faithful whose only hope is in Thy mercy; Christian souls, the sick, those who are tormented in spirit, and those who have asked us to pray for them. Have pity, in Thy infinite clemency, and preserve us in fitness to receive the future, endless, good things. We celebrate Thy glorious Nativity with the Father who sent thee for our redemption, with the life-giving Spirit, now and for ever and through all ages. Amen

From an ancient Syriac liturgy

Lord God, we can hope for others nothing better than the happiness we desire for ourselves. Therefore I pray Thee, do not separate me after death from those I tenderly loved on earth. Grant that where I am, they may be with me, and that I may enjoy their presence in heaven, after being so often deprived of it on earth. Lord God, I ask Thee to receive Thy beloved children immediately into Thy life-giving heart. After this brief life on earth, give them eternal happiness.

Ambrose of Milan

O Lord, my God, defend me like the pupil of
the eye;
Be Thou my protector, and under Thy wings I
shall be shielded from temptations.
Be a guard to mine eye, That it look not
stealthily;
Be a guard to the ear, That it hear not wickedly.
Be a guard to the mouth, And watch also the
lips'
That my heart incline not to vile sayings,
Nor perform unrighteous deeds.

St. Ephraim the Syrian. From A Prayer to the Trinity

Remember, O my soul, the terrible and frightful wonder: that your Creator for your sake became Man, and deigned to suffer for the sake of your salvation. His angels tremble, the Cherubim are terrified, the Seraphim are in fear, and all the heavenly powers ceaselessly give praise; and you, unfortunate soul, remain in laziness. At least from this time forth arise and do not put off, my beloved soul, holy repentance, contrition of heart and penance for your sins.

St. Paisius Velichkovsky

THE PRAYER OF OFFERING OF ST. JAMES
Master and Lord, who visits us in mercy and compassion and have granted us, humble sinners and Thy unworthy servants the grace to stand at Thy holy Altar and to offer to Thee this dread sacrifice without shedding of blood for our own sins and those committed in ignorance by the people, look on me, Thy unprofitable servant and wipe away my transgressions through Thy compassion and purify my lips and my heart from every defilement of flesh and spirit, and banish from me every

base and unseemly thought, and enable me for this ministry by the power of Thy all-holy Spirit, and accept me through Thy goodness as I approach Thy holy altar, and be well pleased, Lord, for these gifts to be acceptable that are offered through our hands, being gracious to my weaknesses, and do not cast me away from Thy presence. Do not despise my unworthiness, but have mercy on me, O God, in accordance with Thy great mercy and according to the abundance of Thy compassion disregard my offences, so that, coming into the presence of Thy glory with condemnation, I may be found worthy of the protection of Thy only-begotten Son and the illumination of Thy all-holy Spirit, but as Thy servant may I find grace, mercy and forgiveness of sins both in this present age and in the age to come. Yes, Master almighty and all-powerful, listen to my supplication and grant me reprieve from my evil deeds, for it is Thou who workest all in all, and in all things we seek from Thee Thy help and assistance and that of Thy only-begotten Son and Thy good, life-giving and consubstantial Spirit, now and for ever, and to the ages of ages. Amen.

Liturgy of St. James

The demons are sleepless and immaterial, death is at hand, and I am weak. Lord, help me; do not let Thy creature perish, for Thou carest for me in my misery.

St. Peter of Damascus

The wicked one, on the watch, carried me off as booty as I lazily slept. He led my mind into error; he plundered my spirit and snatched away The wealth of Thy grace, this arch robber. So raise me up, as I am fallen, and summon me, Savior, Thou who dost will that all men be saved.

Kontakia of Romanos

Thou, O Lord, hast freed us from the fear of death. Thou hast made the end of this life the beginning to us of true life. Thou for a season restest our bodies in sleep and awakest them again at the last trump. Thou givest our earth, which Thou hast fashioned with Thy hands, to the earth to keep in safety. One day Thou wilt take again what Thou hast given, transfiguring with immortality and grace our mortal and

unsightly remains …

St. Macrina

A PRAYER TO THE ALL-HOLY TRINITY

The Father is my hope; the Son is my refuge; the Holy Spirit is my protector. O All-holy Trinity, glory to thee.

GRACES
BEFORE MEALS

O Christ our God, bless the food and drink of thy servants, for thou art Holy always; now and ever, and unto ages of ages. Amen.

AFTER MEALS

Blessed is God, who is merciful unto us and nourisheth us from His bounteous gifts by His grace and compassion, always, now and ever, and unto ages of ages. Amen.

A PRAYER OF REPENTANCE

O Lord our God, good and merciful, I acknowledge all my sins which I have committed every day of my life, in thought, word and deed; in body and soul alike. I am heartily sorry that I have ever offended thee, and I sincerely repent; with tears I humbly pray thee, O Lord: of thy mercy forgive me all my past transgressions and absolve me from them. I firmly resolve, with the help of Thy Grace, to amend my way of life and to sin no more; that I may walk in the way of the righteous and offer praise and glory to the Name of the Father, Son, and Holy Spirit.
Amen.

A PRAYER IN TIME OF TROUBLE

O God, our help and assistance, who art just and merciful, and who heareth the supplications of thy people; look down upon me. a miserable sinner, have mercy upon me, and deliver me from this trouble that besets me, for which, I know, I am deservedly suffering. I acknowledge and believe, O Lord, that all trials of this life are given by Thee for our chastisement, when we drift away from thee, and disobey thy commandments; deal not with me after my sins, but according to thy bountiful mercies, for I am the work of Thy hands, and thou knowest my weakness. Grant me, I beseech thee, thy divine helping grace, and endow me with patience and strength to endure my tribulations with complete submission to Thy Will. Thou knowest my misery and suffering and to Thee, my only hope and refuge, I flee for relief and comfort; trusting to thine infinite love and compassion, that in due time, when thou knowest best, thou wilt deliver me from this trouble, and turn my distress into comfort, when I shall rejoice in thy mercy, and exalt and praise thy Holy Name, O Father, Son, and Holy Spirit: now and ever, and unto ages of ages. Amen.

THANKSGIVING AFTER DELIVERANCE FROM TROUBLE

Almighty and merciful God, I most humbly and heartily thank thy divine majesty for thy loving kindness and tender mercies, that thou hast heard my humble prayer, and graciously vouchsafed to deliver me from my trouble and misery. Grant me, I beseech thee, thy helping grace, that I may obediently walk in thy holy commandments, and lead a sober, righteous and godly life, ever remembering thy mercies, and the blessings thou hast undeservedly bestowed upon me, that I may continually offer to thee the sacrifice of praise and thanksgiving, O Father, Son, and Holy Spirit. Amen.

A PRAYER OF A SICK PERSON

O Lord Jesus Christ, our Savior, Physician of souls and bodies, who didst become man and suffer death on the Cross for our salvation, and through thy tender love and compassion didst heal all manner of sickness and affliction; do thou O Lord, visit me in my suffering, and grant me grace and strength to bear this sickness with which I am afflicted, with Christian patience and submission to thy will, trusting in thy loving kindness and tender mercy. Bless, I pray thee, the means used for my recovery, and those who administer them. I know O Lord, that I justly deserve any punishment thou mayest inflict upon me for. I have so often offended thee and sinned against thee, in thought, word and deed. Therefore, I humbly pray thee, look upon my weakness, and deal not with me after my sins, but according to the multitude of thy mercies. Have compassion on me, and let mercy and justice meet; and deliver me from this sickness and suffering I am undergoing. Grant that my sickness may be the means of my true repentance and amendment of my life according to thy will, that I may spend the rest of my days in thy love and fear: that my soul, being helped by thy grace and sanctified by thy Holy Mysteries, may be prepared for its passage to the Eternal Life, and there, in the company of thy blessed Saints, may praise and glorify thee with thy Eternal Father and Life-giving Spirit. Amen.

THANKSGIVING AFTER RECOVERY FROM SICKNESS

Almighty God, our heavenly Father, Source of life and Fountain of all good things, I bless thy Holy Name, and offer to thee most hearty thanks for having delivered me from my sickness and restored me to health. Grant me thy continuing grace, I pray thee, that I may keep my good resolutions and correct the errors of my past life, and improve in virtue, and live a new life in dutiful fear of thee, doing thy will in all things, and devoting this new life which thou hast given me to thy service: that thus living for thee, I may be found ready when it pleaseth thee to call me to thee, O heavenly Father, to whom with thine Only-begotten Son, our Lord Jesus Christ, and thine all-holy and Life-giving Spirit, is due all honor, praise, glory, and thanksgiving: now and ever, and unto ages of ages. Amen.

A PRAYER FOR THE SICK

O holy Father, heavenly Physician of our souls and bodies, who hast sent thine Only-begotten Son our Lord Jesus Christ to heal all our ailments and deliver us from death: do thou visit and heal thy servant N., granting him release from pain and restoration to health and vigor, that he may give thanks unto thee and bless thy holy Name, of the Father, and of the Son, and of the Holy Spirit: now and ever, and unto ages of ages. Amen.

SONG OF ST. SYMEON

O heavenly King, the Comforter, the Spirit of
  Truth
Who art everywhere present and fillest all
  things,
Treasury of blessings and giver of light,
Come and abide in us and cleans us from

every impurity
and save our souls, O Good One.

PRAYERS FROM THE AGEPEYA, THE COPTIC ORTHODOX BOOK OF HOURS

THE PRAYER OF THANKSGIVING
Let us give thanks unto the Beneficent and
    Merciful God, the Father of our Lord,
God and Savior, Jesus Christ. For He has
    shielded us, rescued us, kept us,
accepted us unto Him, had compassion on us,
    supported us, and brought us unto
this hour. Let us ask Him also, to keep us this
    holy day and all the days of our
life in all peace, the Almighty Lord our God.
    O Master, Lord, God Almighty,
Father of our Lord, God and Savior Jesus
    Christ; we thank Thee upon every
condition, for any condition, and in whatever
    condition. For Thou hast shielded
us, rescued us, kept us, accepted us unto Thee,
    had compassion on us, supported
us and brought us unto this hour. Therefore
    we ask and entreat Thy goodness, O
Lover-of-man, grant us to complete this holy
    day, and all the days of our life
in all peace with Thy fear. All envy, all
    temptation, all the influence of
Satan, the intrigue of wicked people, the rising
    up of enemies, hidden and
manifest, take away from us, and from all Thy
    people, and from this, Thy holy
place. But as for those things which are good
    and useful provide us with them.
For Thou art the One who gave us the
    authority to trample on serpents and
scorpions and every power of the enemy. And
    lead us not into temptation, but
deliver us from the evil one, through the
    grace, compassion and love of man, of
Thine only begotten Son, our Lord, God and
    Savior, Jesus Christ. Through whom
glory, honor, dominion, and worship befit
    Thee with Him and the Holy Spirit, the
life giver who is of one essence with Thee,
    both now and ever, and unto the ages
of ages. Amen.

Agpeya

THE PRAYER OF EVERY HOUR
Have mercy on us O God, and have mercy on
    us. Thou who, at all times, and at
every hour, in Heaven and on earth art
    worshipped and glorified. O Christ, our
God, who art long-suffering, plenteous in
    mercy and most compassionate, who
loves the righteous and has mercy on sinners,
    of whom I am first. Who does not
wish the death of sinner, but to repent and to
    live. Who calls all to salvation
through the promise of good things to come.
    Receive, O Lord, our prayers at this
hour and at every hour; prosper our way, and
    guide our life toward Thy
commandments. Sanctify our souls, make
    chaste our bodies, correct our thoughts,
purify our intention, heal our sickness, remit
    our sins, and deliver us from
every affliction evil and pain. Compass us
    about with Thy holy angels; that
guided and guarded by their array we may
    attain to the unity of faith and the
knowledge of Thine unapproachable and
    infinite glory for blessed art Thou unto
the ages of ages. Amen.

Agpeya

FOR ENEMIES
Lord Jesus Christ, Who didst command us to love our enemies, and those who defame and injure us, and to pray for them and forgive them; Who Thyself didst pray for Thine enemies, who crucified thee: grant us, we pray, the spirit of Christian reconciliation and meekness, that we may heartily forgive every injury and be reconciled with our enemies. Grant us to overcome the malevolence and offences of people with Christian meekness and true love of our neighbor. We further beseech Thee, O Lord, to grant to our enemies true peace and forgiveness of sins; and do not allow them to leave this life without true faith and sincere conversion. And help us repay evil with goodness, and to remain safe from the temptations of the devil and from all the perils which threaten us, in the form of visible and invisible enemies. Amen.

Source unknown, Orthodox Church

LITURGY OF ST. DIONYSIUS

The prayer before the Pax
PRIEST:
O Lord God,
Who art simplex, not compound,
And hidden in essence sublime!
God the Father,
From Whom all paternity which is in heaven
    and earth is named,
Source of Divinity, of those who participate in
    the Divine Nature,
And Perfector of those who attain perfection;
Good above all good,
And Beautiful above all beautiful;
Peaceful repose,
Peace, Concord and Union of all souls;
Compose the dissensions which divide us
    from one another,
And lead them back to an union with charity,
Which has a kind of similitude to Thy sublime
    essence:
And as Thou art One above all,
And we, one, through the unanimity of a
    good mind;
That we may be found before Thee simplex
    and not divided,
Whilst celebrating this mystery;
And that through the embraces of Charity
    and bonds of Love,
We may be spiritually one,
Both with ourselves and with one another,
Through that Thy Peace pacifying all;
Through the Grace and Compassion and Love
    towards man
Of Thine Only-begotten Son;
Through Whom, and with Whom is due to
    Thee,
Glory, honor and dominion,
With Thy Most Holy Spirit.
R: Amen.
PRIEST: Pax (to all).
R: And with thy spirit.

PRIEST:
Giver of Holiness,
And distributor of every good, O Lord,
Who sanctifiest every rational creature
With sanctification, which is from Thee;
Sanctify, through Thy Holy Spirit,
Us Thy servants, who bow before Thee;

Free us from all servile passions of sin,
From envy, treachery, deceit, hatred, enmities,
And from him, who works the same,
That we may be worthy,
Holily to complete the ministry
Of these life-giving Sacraments,
Through the heavenly Pontiff, Jesus Christ,
Thine Only-begotten Son,
Through Whom, and with Whom, is due to
    Thee,
Glory and honor.
R. Amen.

PRIEST: Essentially existing, and from all ages;
Whose nature is incomprehensible,
Who art near and present to all,
Without any change of Thy sublimity;
Whose goodness every existing thing longs
    for and desires;
The intelligible indeed, and creature endowed
    with intelligence,
Through intelligence;
Those endowed with sense,
Through their senses;
Who, although Thou art One essentially,
Nevertheless art present with us,
And amongst us,
In this hour,
In which Thou hast called and led us to these
    Thy holy mysteries;
And hast made us worthy to stand before the
    sublime throne of Thy majesty,
And to handle the sacred vessels of Thy
    ministry with our impure hands:
Take away from us, O Lord,
The cloke of iniquity in which we are
    enfolded,
As from Jesus, the son of Josedec the High
    Priest,
Thou didst take away the filthy garments,
    [Zech. 3:4],
And adorn us with piety and justice,
As Thou didst adorn him with a vestment of
    glory;
That clothed with Thee alone,
As it were with a garment,
And being like temples crowned with glory,
We may see Thee unveiled
With a mind divinely illuminated,
And may feast,
Whilst we, by communicating therein,

Enjoy this sacrifice set before us;
And render to Thee glory and praise.
R: Amen.

PRIEST (bending low):
For truly the celebration of Thy benefits,
O Lord,
Surpasses the powers of mind, of speech, and
of thought;
Neither is sufficient every mouth, mind and
tongue,
To glorify Thee worthily.
For, by Thy word the heavens were made,
And by the breath of Thy mouth all the
celestial powers;
All the lights in the firmament,
Sun and moon,
Sea and dry land, and whatever is in them.
The voiceless, by their silence,
The vocal by their voices, words, and hymns,
Perpetually bless Thee;
Because Thou art essentially good and beyond
all praise,
Existing in Thy essence incomprehensibly.
This visible and sensible creature praises thee,
And also that intellectual, placed above
sensible perception.
Heaven and earth glorify Thee.
Sea and air proclaim Thee.
The sun, in his course, praises Thee;
The Moon, in her changes, venerates Thee.
Troops of Archangels,
And hosts of Angels;
Those virtues,
More sublime than the world and mental
faculty,
Send benedictions to Thine abode.
Rays of light, eminent and hidden,
Send their sanctus to Thy glory.
Principalities and Orders praise Thee, with
their Jubilate.
Powers and dominions venerate Thee.
Virtues, Thrones, and Seats inaccessible exalt
Thee.
Splendors of light –
Eternal mirrors without flaw –
Holy essences –
Recipients of wisdom sublime, beyond all –
Investigators of the will hidden from all –
In clearest modulations of inimitable tones –
And by voices becoming a rational creature –

Many eyed Cherubim of most subtle
movement, bless Thee.
Seraphim, furnished with six wings
intertwined,
Cry "Sanctus!" unto Thee.
Those very ones,
Who veil their faces with their wings,
And cover their feet with wings,
And flying on every side,
And clapping with their wings,
(That they may not be devoured by Thy
devouring fire)
Sing one to another with equal harmony of
all,
Sweet chants, pure from every thing material,
Rendering to Thee eternal glory;
Crying with one hymn, worthy of God, and
saying:
R: Holy Holy Holy,
Lord of Sabbaoth,
Heaven and Earth are full of Thy Glory.
Blessed is He that cometh in the Lord's Name;
Hosanna in the highest.

PRIEST (bending):
Holy art Thou, O God the Father,
Omnipotent,
Maker and Creator of every creature
Invisible and visible, and sensible;
Holy art Thou, O God, the Only-begotten
Son,
Power and Wisdom of the Father,
Lord and our Savior Jesus Christ;
Holy art Thou, O God, the Holy Spirit,
Perfector and Sanctifier of Saints;
Triad, Holy and Undivided –
Co-essential and of equal glory,
Whose compassion towards our race is most
effusive.
Thou art holy, and making all things holy.
Who didst not leave that our very race in exile
from Paradise,
(Although in the mean-time involved in every
kind of sin),
But wast manifested to it by the Word,
Who, in the presence of the world, suffered
extreme poverty;
It in very truth, He, the Word, took,
Being made like to it in all things, sin
excepted,
That it might make Him prepared beforehand

unto holiness,
And disposed for this life-giving feast.

PRIEST (now raising his voice):
Who being conceived formed and configured
    by the Holy Spirit,
And from virgin blood of the Virgin Mary,
    holy genitrix of God,
Was born indeed Man,
And from the pure and most holy body of the
    same,
And receiving Deity in Flesh,
Whilst the law and properties of nature were
    preserved,
But in a manner beyond nature,
And was acknowledged God in the Spirit, and
    Man in the flesh;
And inasmuch as the Word existed before the
    ages, from Thee,
As was worthy of God,
Was born,
And by power and miracles,
Such as became the Maker of all,
Was testified that He was such,
From the very fact that He has freely imparted
A complete healing and a perfect salvation to
    the whole human race.
Likewise,
In the end and consummation of His
    dispensation on our behalf
And before His saving Cross,
He took bread into His pure and holy hands,
And looked to Thee, O God the Father;
Giving thanks, He blessed, sanctified, brake
And gave to His disciples, the holy Apostles,
    saying,
"Take and eat from it
And believe that it is my body,
That same, which for you and for many is
    broken and given,
For the expiation of faults, the remission of
    sins, and eternal life."
R: Amen.

PRIEST: Likewise, in the same manner,
Over the cup also,
Which He mingled with wine and water,
He gave thanks, blessed, sanctified
And gave to the same disciples and holy
    apostles, saying,
"Take, drink from it, all of you,

And believe that this is My blood of the new
    covenant,
Which is shed and given for you and for many,
For the expiation of faults, remission of sins,
    and eternal life."
R: Amen.

PRIEST: Himself also, through the same holy
    Apostles,
Gave a precept
To the whole company and congregation of
    the faithful saying,
"This do to the memory of Me,
And as oft as ye shall eat this bread
And drink the commixture which is this cup,
And shall celebrate this feast,
Ye shall perform a commemoration of My
    death
Until I come."
R: Of Thy death, O Lord, We perform a
    memorial.

PRIEST: Obeying, then, Thy sovereign
    precept,
And celebrating a commemoration of Thy
    death and resurrection,
Through this sacrifice in perpetual mystery,
We await also Thy second coming,
The renovation of our race,
And the vivification of our mortality.
For, not simply,
But with glory worthy of God,
In Spirit ineffable,
Thou wilt terribly come,
And seated upon the lofty throne of Thy
    majesty,
Thou wilt exact the acknowledgement of Thy
    royal power,
From all things created and made:
And justly, Thou wilt take vengeance for Thy
    image
Upon those who have corrupted it
Through evil passions.
This sacrifice, here celebrated,
We commemorate to Thee, O Lord,
And the sufferings which Thou didst endure
    on the Cross for us.
Be propitious, O Good, and Lover of men,
In that hour full of fear and trembling,
To this congregation of those adoring Thee,
And to all sons of the holy Church,

Bought by Thy precious Blood.
May coals of fire
Be kept from those who are tinged with Thy
    Blood,
And sealed by Thy sacraments in Thy holy
    Name,
As formerly the Babylonian flame
From the youths of the house of Hanania;
For neither do we know others beside Thee,
    O God,
Nor in other have we hope of attaining
    salvation,
Since indeed Thou art the Helper and Savior
    of our race;
And on this account, our wise Church,
Through all our lips and tongues, implores
    Thee,
And through Thee, and with Thee, Thy Father,
    saying:
R: Have mercy.

PRIEST: I invoke Thee, O God the Father,
Have mercy upon us,
And wash away, through Thy grace,
The uncleanness of my evil deeds;
Destroy, through Thy mercy,
What I have done, worthy of wrath;
For I do not extend my hands to Thee with
    presumption,
For I am not able even to look to heaven
On account of the multitude of my iniquities
And the filth of my wickedness.
But, strengthening my mind,
In Thy loving-kindness, grace and long-suffering,
I crave Thy holy Spirit, That Thou wouldst
    send Him upon me,
And upon these oblations, here set forth,
And upon Thy faithful people.

PRIEST: Hear me, O Lord ...
R: Kyrie eleison, (three times).

PRIEST: Through His alighting upon them,
And His overshadowing,
May He make this bread indeed living body,
And procuring life to our souls;
Body salutary –
Body celestial –
Body saving our souls and bodies –
Body of our Lord God and Savior, Jesus Christ
    –

For remission of sins, and eternal life,
For those receiving it.
R: Amen.

PRIEST: And the commixture, which is in this
    cup,
May He make living blood,
And procuring life to all our souls;
Blood salutory –
Blood celestial –
Blood saving our souls and bodies –
Blood of our Lord God and Savior Jesus
    Christ,
For remission of sins to those receiving them.
R: Amen.

PRIEST: Further, according to the tradition,
And Divine recommendation
Of those, who were eye witnesses of Thy
    mysteries,
And interpreters of Thy wonderful acts,
We offer this Eucharist before Thee, O Lord,
And through it we commemorate Thy charity
    towards us,
And the universal dispensation
Of Thine Only-begotten One, in this world,
That Thou wouldst also be reminded through
    it
Of Thy mercy, cognate and natural to Thee,
Which, at all hours, is shed upon Thy
    creatures,
And wouldst snatch us from the wrath,
Reserved for the wicked;
And from the punishments
Of those who work iniquity;
And from the cruel attack of demons,
Who attack our souls, when we shall go
    hence;
And wouldst make us worthy of Thy
    kingdom,
And the habitations of those
Who have kept Thy precepts;
And we will render to Thee,
Glory and the giving of thanks ... (etc.)
R: Amen.

PRIEST (bending): By Thy words, that cannot
    lie,
And by Thy most true teachings,
Thou hast said, O Lord,
That great is the joy in heaven over one sinner

that repenteth.
Rejoice then now, O Lord,
In the conversion of Thy servants, who stand
    here before Thee;
Add also, exultation over us,
To the souls of the pious and just Fathers –
Patriarchs – Prophets – Apostles –
Preachers – Evangelists – Martyrs –
Confessors – Zealots of Divine Worship –
Benefactors – Givers of Alms –
Of those who minister to the necessities of the
    poor –
And from all,
May there be one act of praise today,
Before Thee, at this holy Altar, and in the
    heavenly Jerusalem.

(Elevating his voice).
And on account of these,
And other things of the same kind,
May Thy holy Church,
Which is from one end of the earth to the
    other,
Be established, and preserved in tranquility
    and peace,
In doctrines evangelical and apostolical,
By Divine Hierarchs,
Rightly dispensing the word of truth,
And instructing, by the dogmas of true
    religion:
Through holy Priests,
Who embrace the word of life,
And carry themselves illustriously
In dispensing Thy celestial mysteries:
Through Deacons,
Who are modest,
And perform the pure and royal ministry
    without flaw:
Through true, faithful ones,
Who occupy themselves in words and acts
    worthy of a Christian:
Through choirs of virgins of each sex,
Bearing about in their members
The life-giving mortification of Thy Only-
    begotten Son.
And from hence, in one troop,
May we all be sent to that Church,
The Jerusalem of the firstborn,
Whose names are written in the heavens,
And there let us spiritually glorify Thee,
O God the Father, and Thine Only-begotten

Son, and Thy Holy Spirit.
R: Amen.

Assist also, O Lord,
All those who assist Thy Holy Church,
By offerings – by tenths – by ministry –
And by oblations;
And those also, who ask the prayers of our
    littleness,
Give to them the object of those their prayers,
    O Lord, Lover of men.(raising his voice):
    Send also perfect attention and full health
To all those who have the charge of the poor,
Who provide food for orphans and widows,
And visit the infirm and afflicted.
Restore to them, here indeed abundance and
    goods,
There also delights incorruptible,
Because thou art Lord of each age,
And distributor of immense reward.
And to Thee beseems beneficence,
Both here and there,
And to Thine Only-begotten Son.
R: Amen.

PRIEST (bending): Restrain, O King of Kings,
    the wrath of kings,
Mitigate the fury of soldiers,
Take away wars and seditions,
Cast down the pride of heretics,
And the sentences pronounced against us by
    Justice,
May Thy love for mankind overcome,
And turn into the gentleness of benignity;

(raising his voice): Tranquility and Peace from
    Thee,
Concede to the earth and all its inhabitants;
Visit it with Thy benefits and the care of Thy
    mercy,
With a good and temperate condition of
    atmosphere,
Copiousness of fruits, and abundance of crops,
And variety of flowers;
Preserve it from all pests of fury,
And all unjust attacks of enemies, both
    spiritual and sensible,
That without any injury of passion,
We may sing perpend hymns of praise to Thee
And to Thine Only-begotten Son.
R: Amen.

PRIEST (bending): At this altar,
And at that more exalted one in heaven,
May there be a good remembrance
Of all those, who, out of the world, have
  pleased Thee –
Chiefly indeed of the Holy Genitrix of God,
Of John the Messenger, Baptist and
  Forerunner,
Of Peter and Paul, and of the holy company of
  Apostles,
Of Stephen also,
And of the whole multitude of Martyrs,
And of all those, who,
Before them, with them and after them,
Have pleased, and do please Thee.

(raising his voice).
And since indeed Thou art Omnipotent,
To the company of those beloved ones and to
  Thy family,
Join our weakness, O Lord,
To that blessed congregation
To this Divine part,
That, through them may be received
Our oblations and prayers,
Before the lofty throne of Thy Majesty,
Inasmuch as we are weak and infirm,
And wanting in confidence before Thee.
Forsooth, our sin and our righteousness
Are as nothing
In comparison with the ocean,
Broad and immense,
Of Thy mercy.
Looking then into the hearts of each,
Send to each one good returns for their
  petitions,
That in all and in each
May be adored and praised Thy Majesty,
And that of Thine Only-begotten Son.
R: Amen.

PRIEST (bending): Remember, O Lord, all
  Bishops, Doctors, and Prelates
Of Thy holy Church,
Those, who from James, Apostle, Bishop and
  Martyr,
To this present day,
Have pleased, and do please Thee.

(raising his voice):
Engraft in us, O Lord,

Their true faith and their zeal for the true
  religion;
Their sincere charity without defect;
Their morals without stain;
In order that, adhering to their footsteps,
We may be partakers of their reward,
And of the crowns of victory
Which are prepared for them in Thy heavenly
  kingdom,
And there, together with them,
We may sing to Thee, Glory unceasing,
And to Thy Only-begotten Son.
R: Amen.

PRIEST (bending): Remember, O Lord,
All those who are fallen asleep,
Who have laid themselves down in Thy hope,
In the true faith.
More especially, and by name,
Our Fathers, Brothers and Masters,
And those, on behalf of whom, and by favor
  of whom,
This holy oblation is offered –

(raising his voice):
Join, O Lord, their names,
With the names of Thy Saints
In the blessed habitation of those,
Who feast and rejoice in Thee;
Not recalling against them the memory of
  their sins,
Nor bringing to their memory
The things which they have foolishly done.
For no one is tied to the flesh,
And at the same time, innocent in Thy sight.
For One alone has been seen on earth without
  sin,
Jesus Christ, Thine Only-begotten Son;
Simplex, who came to composition,
Through whom we also have hope of
  obtaining mercy.
R: (Keep quiet)

PRIEST (bending): Remitting our and their
  voluntary sins,
Knowingly or ignorantly committed.
Be propitious, O Lord, Lover of men.

(raising his voice):
And grant to us a peaceful end,
Departure with mercy,

That we may stand without fault on the right
    hand;
And, with open face, and confidence,
Run to meet the arising of Thine Only-
    begotten Son,
and His second and glorious manifestation
    from heaven;
And may hear from Him, that blessed voice,
Which He shall pronounce at the last day to
    the Blessed:
"Blessed of my Father
Receive the inheritance of the heavenly
    kingdom,"
That in this, as in all,
May be glorified and praised, Thy most
    venerated Name.

(The Priest breaks the Host, and says the
    prayer, before "Our Father.")
PRIEST: Father of all,
And Beginning,
Which is above all things –
Light eternal, and Fountain of Light,
Which illuminates all natures endowed with
    reason;
Who callest the poor from the dust,
And raisest the beggar from the dunghill;
And hast called us, lost, rejected and infirm,
To the liberty and household dignity of Thy
    sons,
Through Thy beloved Son, grant to us,
That we may appear in Thy sight, holy sons,
And not unworthy of the name;
And may also perform all our ministry
After a blameless manner;
And with purity of soul,
And cleanliness of intellect,
And with a godly mind,
Whenever we invoke Thee,
God the Father Omnipotent,
Holy and heavenly,
We pray and say,
Our Father, which art in heaven.
R: Hallowed be Thy Name,
Thy Kingdom come,
Thy will be done,
On Earth as it is in Heaven.
Give us this day our daily bread
And forgive us our trepasses
As we forgive those that trespass against us.
And lead us not into temptation,

But deliver us from the evil one.

PRIEST: Free us, Thy servants and sons,
From all temptations,
Most difficult, and surpassing our forces;
And from all griefs,
Which can bring loss to our body or soul.
Guard us, at the same time from the evil one,
And from his universal power,
And from his most pernicious devices.
For Thou art King of all,
And to Thee we render glory.
R: Amen.

PRIEST: Peace.
R: And with thy spirit.

PRIEST: Look, O Lord, upon Thy faithful
    people,
Who bend before Thee,
And await Thy gift,
And contemplate the deposit
Of the Sacraments of Thy Only-begotten,
O God the Father.
Take not away Thy grace from us,
And cast us not away from Thy ministry,
And from participation in Thy sacraments,
But prepare us,
That we may be pure and without flaw,
And worthy of this feast;
And that, with a conscience unblameable,
We may ever enjoy His precious body and
    blood;
And in a life, glorious and endless,
May recline in a spiritual habitation,
And may feast at the table of Thy kingdom,
And may render to Thee glory and praise.
R: Amen.

PRIEST: Peace.
R: And with thy spirit.
DEACON: With fear.
PRIEST: Holy things to holy persons.
R: One holy Father.
DEACON: Let us stand becomingly.
PRIEST: Before Thee.
We give thanks to Thee, O Lord,
And with grateful mind
We acknowledge Thy loving-kindness;
Because, from nothing,
Thou hast led us forth to that which we are,

And hast made us members of Thy
   household,
And sons of Thy sacraments;
And hast entrusted this religious ministry to
   us,
And hast made us worthy of this spiritual
   table.
Preserve in us, O Lord,
The deposit of Thy Divine Mysteries,
That we may frame and complete our life in
   Thy sight,
After the fashion of the angels;
That we may be secured and inseparable
Through the reception of Thy holy
   (mysteries);
Performing Thy great and perfect will,
And may be found ready for that last
   consummation,
And to stand before Thy Majesty,
And may be made worthy of the pleasure of
   Thy kingdom,
Through the grace, mercy and love towards
   man,
Of Thy Only-begotten Son,
Through Whom, and with Whom, is due to
   Thee,
Glory, honor, and dominion,
With Thy Most Holy Spirit.
R: Amen.

PRIEST: O Christ, the King of Glory,
And Father of the Age to come;
Holy Sacrifice;

Heavenly Hierarch;
Lamb of God,
Who takest away the sin of the world,
Spare the sins of Thy people,
And dismiss the foolishness of Thy flock.
Preserve us, through the communication of
   Thy Sacraments,
From every sin,
Whether it be committed by word, or
   thought, or deed;
And from whatever makes us far
From the familiarity of Thy household,
That our bodies may be guarded by Thy body,
And our souls renewed through Thy
   sacraments.
And may Thy benediction, O Lord,
Be in our whole man, within and without;
And may Thou be glorified in us,
And by us,
And may Thy right hand rest upon us,
And that of Thy blessed Father,
And of Thy most holy Spirit.
R: Amen.
DEACON: Bless, O Lord.

Liturgy of St Dionysius, Bishop of the Athenians,
   Liturgiarum Orien. Collectio E. Renaudoti. T. ii.
p. 201, translated by John Parker, The St. Pachomius
   Orthodox Library, By kind permission

Roman Catholics and prayer

1. ROMAN CATHOLIC TEACHING ON PRAYER

Prayer

John. J. Wynne

(Greek *euchesthai*, Latin *precari*, French *prier*, to plead, to beg, to ask earnestly).

An act of the virtue of religion which consists in asking proper gifts or graces from God. In a more general sense it is the application of the mind to Divine things, not merely to acquire a knowledge of them but to make use of such knowledge as a means of union with God. This may be done by acts of praise and thanksgiving, but petition is the principal act of prayer.

The words used to express it in Scripture are: to call up (Gen., iv, 26); to intercede (Job, xxii, 10); to mediate (Is., liii, 10); to consult (I Kings, xxviii, 6); to beseech (Ex., xxxii, 11); and, very commonly, to cry out to. The Fathers speak of it as the elevation of the mind to God with a view to asking proper things from Him (St. John Damascene, "De fide", III, xxiv, in P.G., XCIV, 1090); communing and conversing with God (St. Gregory of Nyssa, "De oratione dom.", in P.G., XLIV, 1125); talking with God (St. John Chrysostom, "Hom. xxx in Gen.", n. 5, in P.G., LIII, 280). It is therefore the expression of our desires to God whether for ourselves or others. This expression is not intended to instruct or direct God what to do, but to appeal to His goodness for the things we need; and the appeal is necessary, not because He is ignorant of our needs or sentiments, but to give definite form to our desires, to concentrate our whole attention on what we have to recommend to Him, to help us appreciate our close personal relation with Him. The expression need not be external or vocal; internal or mental is sufficient.

By prayer we acknowledge God's power and goodness, our own neediness and dependence. It is therefore an act of the virtue of religion implying the deepest reverence for God and habituating us to look to Him for everything, not merely because the thing asked be good in itself, or advantageous to us, but chiefly because we wish it as a gift of God, and not otherwise, no matter how good or desirable it may seem to us. Prayer presupposes faith in God and hope in His goodness. By both, God, to whom we pray, moves us to prayer. Our knowledge of God by the light of natural reason also inspires us to look to Him for help, but such prayer lacks supernatural inspiration, and though it may avail to keep us from losing our natural knowledge of God and trust in Him, or, to some extent, from offending Him, it cannot positively dispose us to receive His graces.

Objects of Prayer

Like every act that makes for salvation, grace is required not only to dispose us to pray, but also to aid us in determining what to pray for. In this "the spirit helpeth our infirmity. For we know not what we should pray for as we ought; but the Spirit himself asketh for us with unspeakable groanings" (Rom., viii, 26). For certain objects we are always sure we should pray, such as our salvation and the general means to it, resistance to temptation, practice of virtue, final perseverance; but constantly we need light and the guidance of the Spirit to know the special means that will most help us in any particular need. That there may be no possibility of misjudgment on our part in such an essential obligation, Christ has taught us what we should ask for in prayer and also in what order we should ask it. In response to the request of His disciples to teach them how to pray, He repeated the prayer commonly spoken of as the Lord's Prayer (q. v.), from which it appears that above all we are to pray that God may be glorified, and that for this purpose men may be worthy citizens of His kingdom, living in conformity with His will. Indeed, this conformity is implied in every prayer: we should ask for nothing unless it be strictly in accordance with Divine Providence in our regard. So much for the spiritual objects of our prayer. We are to ask also for temporal things, our daily bread, and all that it implies, health, strength, and other worldly or temporal goods, not material or corporal only, but mental and moral, every accomplishment that may be a means of serving God and our fellowmen. Finally, there are the evils which we should pray to escape, the penalty of our sins, the dangers of temptation, and every manner of physical or spiritual affliction, so far as these might impede us in God's service.

To whom may we pray

Although God the Father is mentioned in this prayer as the one to whom we are to pray, it is not out of place to address our prayers to the other Divine persons. The special appeal to one does not exclude the others. More commonly the Father is addressed in the beginning of the prayers of the Church, though they close with the invocation, "Through Our Lord Jesus Christ Thy Son who with Thee liveth and reigneth in the unity of the Holy Ghost, world without end". If the prayer be addressed to God the Son, the conclusion is: "Who livest and reignest with God the Father in the unity of the Holy Ghost, God, world without end"; or, "Who with Thee liveth and reigneth in the unity, etc.". Prayer may be addressed to Christ as Man, because He is a Divine Person, not however to His human nature as such, precisely because prayer must always be addressed to a person, never to something impersonal or in the abstract. An appeal to anything impersonal, as for instance to the Heart, the Wounds, the Cross of Christ, must be taken figuratively as intended for Christ Himself.

Who can pray

As He has promised to intercede for us (John,

xiv, 16), and is said to do so (Rom., viii, 34; Heb., vii, 25), we may ask His intercession, though this is not customary in public worship. He prays in virtue of His own merits; the saints intercede for us in virtue of His merits, not their own. Consequently when we pray to them, it is to ask for their intercession in our behalf, not to expect that they can bestow gifts on us of their own power, or obtain them in virtue of their own merit. Even the souls in purgatory, according to the common opinion of theologians, pray to God to move the faithful to offer prayers, sacrifices, and expiatory works for them. They also pray for themselves and for souls still on earth. The fact that Christ knows the future, or that the saints may know many future things, does not prevent them from praying. As they foresee the future, so also they foresee how its happenings may be influenced by their prayers, and they at least by prayer do all in their power to bring about what is best, though those for whom they pray may not dispose themselves for the blessings thus invoked. The just can pray, and sinners also. The opinion of Quesnel that the prayer of the sinned adds to his sin was condemned by Clement XI (Denzinger, 10 ed., n. 1409). Though there is no supernatural merit in the sinner's prayer, it may be heard, and indeed he is obliged to make it just as before he sinned. No matter how hardened he may become in sin, he needs and is bound to pray to be delivered from it and from the temptations which beset him. His prayer could offend God only if it were hypocritical, or presumptuous, as if he should ask God to suffer him to continue in his evil course. It goes without saying that in hell prayer is impossible; neither devils nor lost souls can pray, or be the object of prayer.

For whom we may pray

For the blessed prayers may be offered not with the hope of increasing their beatitude, but that their glory may be better esteemed and their deeds imitated. In praying for one another we assume that God will bestow His favors in consideration of those who pray. In virtue of the solidarity of the Church, that is, of the close relations of the faithful as members of the mystical Body of Christ, any one may benefit by the good deeds, and especially by the prayers of the others as if participating in them. This is the ground of St. Paul's desire that supplications, prayers, intercessions, and thanksgivings be made for all men (Tim., ii, 1), for all, without exception, in high or low station, for the just, for sinners, for infidels; for the dead as well as for the living; for enemies as well as for friends.

Effects of Prayer

In hearing our prayer God does not change His will or action in our regard, but simply puts into effect what He had eternally decreed in view of our prayer. This He may do directly without the intervention of any secondary cause as when He imparts to us some supernatural gift, such as actual grace, or indirectly, when He bestows some natural gift. In this latter case He directs by His Providence the natural causes which contribute to the effect desired, whether they be moral or free agents, such as men; or some moral and others not, but physical and not free; or, again, when none of them is free. Finally, by miraculous intervention, and without employing any of these causes, He can produce the effect prayed for.

The use or habit of prayer redounds to our advantage in many ways. Besides obtaining the gifts and graces we need, the very process elevates our mind and heart to a knowledge and love of Divine things, greater confidence in God, and other precious sentiments. Indeed, so numerous and so helpful are these effects of prayer that they compensate us, even when the special object of our prayer is not granted. Often they are of far greater benefit than what we ask for. Nothing that we might obtain in answer to our prayer could exceed in value the familiar converse with God in which prayer consists. In addition to these effects of prayer, we may (de congruo) merit by it restoration to grace, if we are in sin; new inspirations of grace, increase of sanctifying grace, and satisfy for the temporal punishment due to sin. Signal as all these benefits are, they are only incidental to the proper effect of prayer due to its power based on the infallible promise of God, "Ask, and it shall be given you; seek, and you shall find: knock, and it shall be opened to you" (Matt., vii, 7); "Therefore I say unto you, all things whatsoever you ask when ye pray,

believe that you shall receive" (Mark, xi, 24 – see also Luke, xi, 11; John, xvi, 24, as well as innumerable assurances to this effect in the Old Testament).

Conditions of Prayer

Absolute though Christ's assurances in regard to prayer would seem to be, they do not exclude certain conditions on which the efficacy of prayer depends. In the first place, its object must be worthy of God and good for the one who prays, spiritually or temporally. This condition is always implied in the prayer of one who is resigned to God's will, ready to accept any spiritual favor God may be pleased to grant, and desirous of temporal ones only in so far as they may help to serve God. Next, faith is needed, not only the general belief that God is capable of answering prayer or that it is a powerful means of obtaining His favor, but also the implicit trust in God's fidelity to His promise to hear a prayer in some particular instance. This trust implies a special act of faith and hope that if our request be for our good, God will grant it, or something else equivalent or better, which in His Wisdom He deems best for us. To be efficacious prayer should be humble. To ask as if one had a binding claim on God's goodness, or title of whatever color to obtain some favor, would not be prayer but demand. The parable of the Pharisee and the Publican illustrates this very clearly, and there are innumerable testimonies in Scripture to the power of humility in prayer. "A contrite and humbled heart, O God, thou wilt not despise" (Ps. 1, 19). "The prayer of him that humbleth himself shall pierce the clouds" (Eccl., xxxv, 21). Without sacrifice of humility we may and should try to be sure that our conscience is good, and that there is no defect in our conduct inconsistent with prayer; indeed, we may even appeal to our merits so far as they recommend us to God, provided always that the principal motives of one's confidence are God's goodness and the merits of Christ. Sincerity is another necessary quality of prayer. It would be idle to ask favor without doing all that may be in our power to obtain it; to beg for it without really wishing for it; or, at the same time that one prays, to do anything inconsistent with the prayer. Earnestness or fervor is another such quality, precluding all lukewarm or half-hearted petitions. To be resigned to God's will in prayer does not imply that one should be indifferent in the sense that one does not care whether one be heard or not; on the contrary, true resignation to God's will is possible only after we have desired and earnestly expressed our desire in prayer for such things as seem needful to do God's will. This earnestness is the element which makes the persevering prayer so well described in such parables as the Friend at Midnight (Luke, xi, 5–8), or, the Widow and the Unjust Judge (Luke, xviii, 2–5), and which ultimately obtains the precious gift of perseverance in grace.

Attention in Prayer

Finally, attention is of the very essence of prayer. As an expression of sentiment emanating from our intellectual faculties prayer requires their application, i.e. attention. As soon as this attention ceases, prayer ceases. To begin praying and allow the mind to be wholly diverted or distracted to some other occupation or thought necessarily terminates the prayer, which is resumed only when the mind is withdrawn from the object of distraction. To admit distraction is wrong when one is obliged to apply oneself to prayer; when there is no such obligation, one is at liberty to pass from the subject of prayer, provided it be done without irreverence, to any other proper subject. This is all very simple when applied to mental prayer; but does vocal prayer require the same attention as mental,-in other words, when praying vocally must one attend to the meaning of words, and if one should cease to do so, would one by that very fact cease to pray? Vocal prayer differs from mental precisely in this that mental prayer is not possible without attention to the thoughts that are conceived and expressed whether internally or externally. Neither is it possible to pray without attending to thought and words when we attempt to express our sentiment in our own words; whereas all that is needed for vocal prayer proper is the repetition of certain words, usually a set form with the intention of using them in prayer. So long as the intention lasts, i.e. so long as nothing is done to terminate it or wholly inconsistent with it, so long as one continues to repeat the form of prayer, with proper reverence in disposition and outward manner, with only this general purpose of praying according to the prescribed form, so long as one continues to pray and no thought or external act can be considered a distraction unless it terminate our intention, or by levity or irreverence be wholly inconsistent with the prayer. Thus one may pray in the crowded streets where it is impossible to avoid sights and sounds and consequent imaginations and thoughts.

Provided one repeats the words of the prayer and avoids willful distractions of mind to things in no way pertaining to prayer, one may through mental infirmity or inadvertence admit numerous thoughts not connected with the subject of the prayer, without irreverence. It is true, this amount of attention does not enable one to derive from prayer the full spiritual advantage it should bring; nay, to be satisfied with it as a rule would result in admitting distractions quite freely and wrongfully. For this reason it is advisable not only to keep the mind bent on praying but also to think of the purport of the prayer, and as far as possible to think of the meaning of some at least of the sentiments or expressions of the prayer. As a means of cultivating the habit, it is recommended, notably in the spiritual exercises of St. Ignatius, often to recite certain familiar prayers, the Lord's Prayer, the Angelical Salutation, the Creed, the Confiteor, slowly enough to admit the interval of a breath between the principal words or sentences, so as to have time to think of their meaning, and to feel in one's heart the appropriate emotions. Another practice strongly recommended by the same author is to take each sentence of these prayers as a subject of reflection, not delaying too long on any one of them unless one finds in it some suggestion or helpful thought or sentiment, but then stopping to reflect as long as one finds proper food for thought or emotion, and, when one has dwelt sufficiently on any passage, finishing the prayer without further deliberate reflection.

Necessity of Prayer

Prayer is necessary for salvation. It is a distinct precept of Christ in the Gospels (Matt., vi,

9; vii, 7; Luke, xi, 9; John, xvi, 26; Col., iv, 2; Rom., xii, 12; I Pet., iv, 7). The precept imposes on us only what is really necessary as a means of salvation. Without prayer we cannot resist temptation, nor obtain God's grace, nor grow and persevere in it. This necessity is incumbent on all according to their different states in life, especially on those who by virtue of their office, of priesthood, for instance, or other special religious obligations, should in a special manner pray for their own welfare and for others. The obligation to pray is incumbent on us at all times. "And he spoke also a parable, to them that we ought always to pray, and not to faint" (Luke, xviii, 1); but it is especially pressing when we are in great need of prayer, when without it we cannot overcome some obstacle or perform some obligation; when, to fulfill various obligations of charity, we should pray for others; and when it is specially implied in some obligation imposed by the Church, such as attendance at Mass, and the observance of Sundays and feast-days. This is true of vocal prayer, and as regards mental prayer, or meditation, this, too, is necessary so far as we may need to apply our mind to the study of Divine things in order to acquire a knowledge of the truths necessary for salvation.

The obligation to pray is incumbent on us at all times, not that prayer should be our sole occupation, as the Euchites, or Messalians, and similar heretical sects professed to believe. The texts of Scripture bidding us to pray without ceasing mean that we must pray whenever it is necessary, as it so frequently is necessary; that we must continue to pray until we shall have obtained what we need. Some writers speak of a virtuous life as an uninterrupted prayer, and appeal to the adage "to toil is to pray" (*laborare est orare*). This does not mean that virtue or labor replaces the duty of prayer, since it is not possible either to practice virtue or to labor properly without frequent use of prayer.

The Wyclifites and Waldenses, according to Suarez, advocated what they called vital prayer, consisting in good works, to the exclusion even of all vocal prayer except the Our Father. For this reason Suarez does not approve of the expression, though St. Francis de Sales uses it to mean prayer reinforced by work, or rather work which is inspired by prayer. The practice

of the Church, devoutly followed by the faithful, is to begin and end the day with prayer; and though morning and evening prayer is not of strict obligation, the practice of it so well satisfies our sense of the need of prayer that neglect of it, especially for a long time is regarded as more or less sinful, according to the cause of the neglect, which is commonly some form of sloth.

Vocal Prayer

Prayer may be classified as vocal or mental, private or public. In vocal prayer some outward action, usually verbal expression, accompanies the internal act implied in every form of prayer. This external action not only helps to keep us attentive to the prayer, but it also adds to its intensity. Examples of it occur in the prayer of the Israelites in captivity (Ex., ii, 23); again after their idolatry among the Chanaanites (Judges, iii, 9); the Lord's Prayer (Matt., vi, 9); Christ's own prayer after resuscitating Lazarus (John, xi, 41); and the testimonies in Heb., v, 7, and xiii, 15, and frequently we are recommended to use hymns, canticles, and other vocal forms of prayer. It has been common in the Church from the beginning; nor has it ever been denied, except by the Wyclifites and the Quietists. The former objected to it as unnecessary, as God does not need our words to know what goes on in our souls, and prayer being a spiritual act need be performed by the soul alone without the body. The latter regarded all external action in prayer as an untoward disturbance or interference with the passivity of the soul required, in their opinion, to pray properly. It is obvious that prayer must be the action of the entire man, body as well as soul; that God who created both is pleased with the service of both, and that when the two act in unison they help instead of interfering with one another's activities. The Wyclifites objected not only to all external expression of prayer generally, but to vocal prayer in its proper sense, viz. Prayer expressed in set form of words, excepting only the Our Father. The use of a variety of such forms is sanctioned by the prayer over the first-fruits (Deut., xxvi, 13). If it be right to use one form, that of the Our Father, why not others also? The Litany, Collective and Eucharistic prayers of the early

Church were surely set forms, and the familiar daily prayers, the Our Father, Hail Mary, Apostles' Creed, Confiteor, Acts of Faith, Hope, and Charity, all attest the usage of the Church in this respect and the preference of the faithful for such approved forms to others of their own composition.

Postures in Prayer

Postures in prayer are also an evidence of the tendency in human nature to express inward sentiment by outward sign. Not only among Jews and Christians, but among pagan peoples also, certain postures were considered appropriate in prayer, as, for instance, standing with arms raised among the Romans. The Orante indicates the postures favored by the early Christians, standing with hands extended, as Christ on the Cross, according to Tertullian; or with hands raised towards heaven, with bowed heads, or, for the faithful, with eyes raised toward heaven, and, for the catechumens, with eyes bent on the earth; prostration, kneeling, genuflection, and such gestures as striking the breast are all outward signs of the reverence proper for prayer, whether in public or private.

Mental Prayer

Meditation is a form of mental prayer consisting in the application of the various faculties of the soul, memory, imagination, intellect, and will, to the consideration of some mystery, principle, truth, or fact, with a view to exciting proper spiritual emotions and resolving on some act or course of action regarded as God's will and as a means of union with Him. In some degree or other it has always been practice by God-fearing souls. There is abundant evidence of this in the Old Testament, as, for instance, in Ps. xxxviii, 4; lxii, 7; lxxvi, 13; cxviii throughout; Ecclus., xiv, 22; Is., xxvi, 9; lvii, 1; Jer., xii, 11. In the New Testament Christ gave frequent examples of it, and St. Paul often refers to it, as in Eph., vi, 18; Col., iv, 2; I Tim., iv, 15; I Cor., xiv, 15. It has always been practice in the Church. Among others who have recommended it to the faithful as Chrysostom in his two books on prayer, as also in his "Hom. xxx in Gen." and "Hom. vi. in Isaiam"; Cassian in "Conference ix"; St. Jerome in "Epistola 22 ad

Eustochium"; St. Basil in his "Homily on St. Julitta, M.", and "In regular breviori", 301; St. Cyprian, "In expositione orationis dominicalis"; St. Ambrose, "De sacramentis", VI, iii; St. Augustine, "Epist. 121 ad Probam", cc. v, vi, vii; Boctius, "De spiritu et anima", xxxii; St. Leo, "Sermo viii de jejunio"; St. Bernard, "De consecratione'", I, vii; St. Thomas, II-II, Q. lxxxiii, a. 2.

The writings of the Fathers themselves and of the great theologians are in large measure the fruit of devout meditation as well as of study of the mysteries of religion. There is, however, no trace of methodical meditation before the fifteenth century. Prior to that time, even in monasteries, no regulation seems to have existed for the choir or arrangement of subject, the order, method, and time of the consideration. From the beginning, before the middle of the twelfth century, the Carthusians had times set apart for mental prayer, as appears from Guigo's "Consuetudinary", but no further regulation. About the beginning of the sixteenth century one of the Brothers of the Common Life, Jean Mombaer of Brussels, issued a series of subjects or points for meditation. The monastic rules generally prescribed times for common prayer, usually the recitation of the Office, leaving it to the individual to ponder as he might on one or other of the texts. Early in the sixteenth century the Dominican chapter of Milan prescribed mental prayer for half an hour morning and evening. Among the Franciscans there is record of methodical mental prayer about the middle of that century. Among the Carmelites there was no regulation for it until Saint Theresa introduced it for two hours daily. Although Saint Ignatius reduced meditation to such a definite method in his spiritual exercises, it was not made part of his rule until thirty years after the formation of the Society. His method and that of St. Sulpice have helped to spread the habit of meditating beyond the cloister among the faithful everywhere.

Methods of Meditation

In the method of St. Ignatius the subject of the meditation is chosen beforehand, usually the previous evening. It may be any truth or fact whatever concerning God or the human soul,

God's existence His attributes, such as justice, mercy, love, wisdom, His law, providence, revelation, creation and its purpose, sin and its penalties, death, creation and its purpose, sin and its penalties, death, judgment, hell, redemption, etc. The precise aspect of the subject should be determined very definitely, otherwise its consideration will be general or superficial and of no practical benefit. As far as possible its application to one's spiritual needs should be foreseen, and to work up interest in it, as one retires and rises, one should recall it to mind so as to make it a sleeping and a waking thought. When ready for meditation, a few moments should be given to recollecting what we are about to do so as to begin with quiet of mind and deeply impressed with the sacredness of prayer. A brief act of adoration of God naturally follows, with a petition that our intention to honor Him in prayer may be sincere and persevering, and that every faculty and act, interior and exterior, may contribute to His service and praise. The subject of the meditation is then recalled to mind, and in order to fix the attention, the imagination is here employed to construct some scene appropriate to the subject, e.g. the Garden of Paradise, if the meditation be on Creation, or the Fall of Man; the Valley of Jehosaphat, for the Last Judgment; or, for Hell, the bottomless and boundless pit of fire. This is called the composition of the place, and even when the subject of meditation has no apparent material associations, the imagination can always devise some scene or sensible image that will help to fix or recall one's attention and appreciate the spiritual matter under consideration. Thus, when considering sin, especially carnal sin, as enslaving the soul, the Book of Wisdom, ix, 15, suggests the similarity of the body to the prison house of the soul: "The corruptible body is a load upon the soul, and the earthly habitation presseth down the mind that museth upon many things."

Quite often this initial step, or prelude as it is called, might occupy one profitably the entire time set apart for meditation; but ordinarily it should be made in a few minutes. A brief petition follows for the special grace one hopes to obtain and then the meditation proper begins. The memory recalls the subject as definitely as possible, one point at a time, repeating it over if necessary, always as a matter of intimate personal interest, and with a strong act of faith until the intellect naturally apprehends the truth or the import of the fact under consideration, and begins to conceive it as a matter for careful consideration, reasoning about it and studying what it implies for one's welfare. Gradually an intense interest is aroused in these reflections, until, with faith quickening the natural intelligence one begins to perceive applications of the truth or fact to one's condition and needs and to feel the advantage or necessity of acting upon the conclusions drawn from one's reflections. This is the important moment of meditation. The conviction that we need or should do something in accordance with our consideration begets in us desires or resolutions which we long to accomplish. It we are serious we shall admit of no self-deception either as to the propriety or possibility of such resolutions on our part. No matter what it may cost us to be consistent, we shall adopt them, and the more we appreciate their difficulty and our own weakness or incapacity, the more we shall try to value the motives which prompt us to adopt them, and above all the more we shall pray for grace to be able to carry them out.

If we are in earnest we shall not be satisfied with a superficial process. In the light of the truth we are meditating, our past experience will come to mind and confront us perhaps with memory of failure in previous attempts similar to those we are considering now, or at least with a keen sense of the difficulty to be apprehended, making us more solicitous about the motives animating us and humble in petitioning God's grace. These petitions, as well as all the various emotions that arise from our reflections, find expression in terms of prayer to God which are called colloquies, or conversations with Him. They may occur at any point in the process, whenever our thoughts inspire us to call upon God for our needs, or even for light to perceive and appreciate them and to know the means of obtaining them. This general process is subject to variations according to the character of the matter under consideration. The number of preludes and colloquies may vary, and the time spent in reasoning may be greater or less according to our familiarity with the subject. There is nothing mechanical in the process; indeed, if analyzed, it is clearly the natural operation of each faculty and of all in concert. Roothaan, who has prepared the best summary of it, recommends a remote preparation for it, so as to know whether we are properly disposed to enter into meditation, and, after each exercise, a brief review of each part of it in detail to see how far we may have succeeded. It is strongly advised to select as a means of recalling the leading thought or motive or affection some brief memorandum, preferably couched in the words of some text of Scripture, the "Imitation of Christ", the Fathers of the Church, or of some accredited writer on spiritual things. Meditation made regularly according to this method tends to create an atmosphere or spirit of prayer.

The method in vogue among the Sulpicians and followed by the students in their seminaries is not substantially different from this. According to Chenart, companion of Olier and for a long time director of the Seminary of St. Sulpice, the meditation should consist of three parts: the preparation, the prayer proper, and the conclusion. By way of preparation we should begin with acts of adoration of Almighty God, of self-humiliation, and with fervent petition to be directed by the Holy Spirit in our prayer to know how to make it well and obtain its fruits. The prayer proper consists of considerations and the spiritual emotions or affections that result from such considerations. Whatever the subject of the meditation may be, it should be considered as it may have been exemplified in the life of Christ, in itself, and in its practical importance for ourselves. The simpler these considerations are the better. A long or intricate course of reasoning is not at all desirable. When some reasoning is needed, it should be simple and always in the light of faith. Speculation, subtlety, curiosity are all out of place. Plain, practical reflections, always with an eye to self-examination, in order to see how well or ill our conduct conforms to the conclusions we derive from such reflections, are by means to be sought. The affections are the main object of the meditation. These are to have charity as their aim and norm. They should be few, if possible, one only of such simplicity and intensity that it can inspire the soul to act on the conclusion derived from the consideration and resolve to do something definite in the service of God. To seek too many affections only distracts or dissipates the attention of the mind and weakens the resolution of the will. If it be difficult to limit the emotions to one, it is not well to make much effort to do so, but better to devote our energies to deriving the best fruit we can from such as arise naturally and with ease from our mental reflections. As a means of keeping in mind during the day the uppermost thought or motive of the meditation we are advised to cull a spiritual nosegay, as it is quaintly called, with which to refresh the memory from time to time.

Meditation carefully followed forms habits of recalling and reasoning rapidly and with some ease about Divine things in such a manner as to excite pious affections, which become very ardent and which attach us very strongly to God's will. When prayer is made up chiefly of such affections, it is called by Alvarez de Paz, and other writers since his time, affective prayer, to denote that instead of having to labor mentally to admit or grasp a truth, we have grown so familiar with it that almost the mere recollection of it fills us with sentiments of faith, hope, charity; moves us to practice more generously one or other of the moral virtues; inspires us to make some act of self-sacrifice or to attempt some work for the glory of God. When these affections become more simple, that is, less numerous, less varied, and less interrupted or impeded by reasoning or mental attempts to find expression either for considerations or affections, they constitute what is called the prayer of simplicity by Bossuet and those who follow his terminology, of simple attention to one dominant thought or Divine object without reasoning on it, but simply letting it recur at intervals to renew or strengthen the sentiments which keep the soul united to God.

These degrees of prayer are denoted by various terms by writers on spiritual subjects, the prayer of the heart, active recollection, and by the paradoxical phrases, active repose, active quietude, active silence, as opposed to similar passive states; St. Francis de Sales called it the prayer of simple committal to God, not in the sense of doing nothing or of remaining inert in His sight, but doing all we can to control our own restless and aberrant faculties so as to keep them disposed for His action. By whatever name these degrees of prayer may be called, it is important not to confuse them with any of the modes of Quietism, as also not to exaggerate their importance, as if they were absolutely different from vocal prayers and meditation, since they are only degrees of ordinary prayer. With more than usual attention to the sentiment of a set form of prayer meditation begins; the practice of meditation develops a habit of centering our affections on Divine things; as this habit is cultivated, distractions are more easily avoided, even such as arise from our own varied and complex thoughts or emotions, until God or any truth or fact relating to Him becomes the simple object of our undisturbed attention, and this attention is held steadfast by the firm and ardent affection it excites. St. Ignatius and other masters in the art of prayer have provided suggestions for passing from meditation proper to these further degrees of prayer. In the "Spiritual Exercises" the repetition of previous meditations consists in affective prayer, and the exercises of the second week, the contemplations of the life of Christ, are virtually the same as the prayer of simplicity, which is in its last analysis the same as the ordinary practice of contemplation.

The classification of private and public prayer is made to denote distinction between the prayer of the individual, whether in or out of the presence of others, for his or for others needs, and all prayer offered officially or liturgically whether in public or in secret, as when a priest recites the Divine Office outside of choir. All the liturgical prayers of the Church are public, as are all the prayers which one in sacred orders offers in his ministerial capacity. These public prayers are usually offered in places set apart for this purpose, in churches or chapels, just as in the Old Law they were offered in the Temple and in the synagogue. Special times are appointed for them: the hours for the various parts of the daily Office, days of rogation or of vigil, seasons of Advent and Lent; and occasions of special need, afflic-

tion, thanksgiving, jubilee, on the part of all, or of large numbers of the faithful.

ST. THOMAS, II-II, Q. lxxxv; SUAREZ, De oratione, I, in De religione, IV; PESCH, Praelectiones dogmaticae, IX (Freiburg, 1902); ST. BERNARD, Scala claustralium, attributed to St. Augustine under the title of Scala paradisi in volume IX among his works; ROOTHAAN, The Method of Meditation (New York, 1858); LETOURNEAU, Methode d'oraison mentale du seminaire de St-Sulpice (Paris, 1903); Catechism of the Council of Trent, tr. DONOVAN (Dublin, s. d.); POULAIN, The Graces of Interior Prayer (St. Louis, 1911); CAUSADE, Progress in Prayer, tr. SHEEHAN (St. Louis); FISHER, A Treatise on Prayer (London, 1885); EGGER, Are Our Prayers Heard? (London, 1910); ST. FRANCIS DE SALES, Treatise of the Love of God (tr. London, 1884); ST. PETER OF ALCANTARA, A Golden Treatise on Mental Prayer (tr. Oxford, 1906); FABER, Growth in Holiness (London, 1854). Among the many books of meditation, the following may be mentioned: AVANCINI, Vita et doctrina Jesu Christi ex quatuor evangeliis collectae (Paris, 1850); DE PONTE, Meditationes de praecipuis fidei nostrae mysteriis (St. Louis, 1908–10), tr., Meditations on the Mysteries of Holy Faith (London, 1854); GRANADA, Meditations and Contemplations (New York, 1879); LANCICIUS, Pious Affections towards God and the Saints (London, 1883); SEGNERI, The Manna of the Soul (London, 1892); ST. JOHN BAPTIST DE LA SALLE, Meditations for Sundays and Festivals (New York, 1882); BELLORD, Meditations (London); LUCK, Meditations; CHALLONER, Considerations upon Christian Truths and Christian Doctrines (Philadelphia, 1863); CLARKE, Meditations on the Life, Teaching and Passion of Jesus Christ (New York, 1901); HAMON, Meditations for all the Days in the Year (New York, 1894); MEDAILLE, Meditations on the Gospels, tr. EYRE (New York, 1907); NEWMAN, Meditations and Devotions (New York, 1893); WISEMAN, Daily Meditations (Dublin, 1868); VERCRUYSSE, Practical Meditations (London).

John. J. Wynne, The Catholic Encyclopedia,
Volume XII, 1911

2. CATECHISM OF TRENT ON PRAYER

Importance of Instruction On Prayer

One of the duties of the pastoral office, which is of the highest importance to the spiritual interests of the faithful, is to instruct them on Christian prayer; the nature and efficacy of which must remain unknown to many, if not taught by the pious and faithful diligence of the pastor. To this, therefore, should the care of the pastor be directed in a special manner, that his devout hearers may understand how and for what they are to ask God.

Whatever is necessary to the performance of the duty of prayer is comprised in that divine formula which Christ the Lord deigned to make known to His Apostles, and through them and their successors to all Christians. Its thoughts and words should be so deeply impressed on the mind and memory as to be ever in readiness. To assist pastors, however, in teaching the faithful concerning this prayer, we have set down from those writers who are conspicuous for learning and fullness in this matter, whatever appeared to us most suitable, leaving it to pastors to draw upon the same sources for further information, should they deem it necessary.

Necessity of Prayer

In the first place the necessity of prayer should be insisted upon. Prayer is a duty not only recommended by way of counsel, but also commanded by obligatory precept. Christ the Lord declared this when He said: We should pray always. This necessity of prayer the Church points out in the prelude, if we may so call it, which she prefixes to the Lord's Prayer: Admonished by salutary precepts, and taught by divine instruction, we presume to say, etc.

Therefore, since prayer is necessary to the Christian, the Son of God, yielding to the request of the disciples, Lord, teach us to pray, gave them a prescribed form of prayer, and encouraged them to hope that the objects of their petitions would be granted. He Himself was to them a model of prayer; He not only prayed assiduously, but watched whole nights in prayer.

The Apostles, also, did not omit to recommend this duty to those who had been converted to the faith of Jesus Christ. St. Peter and St. John are most diligent in their admonitions to the devout; and the Apostle, mindful of its nature, frequently admonishes Christians of the salutary necessity of prayer.

Besides, so various are our temporal and spiritual necessities, that we must have recourse to prayer as the best means for communicating our wants and receiving whatever we need. For since God owes nothing to anyone, we must ask of Him in prayer those things we need, seeing that He has constituted prayer as a necessary means for the accomplishment of our desires, particularly since it is clear that there are blessings which we cannot hope to obtain otherwise than through prayer. Thus devout prayer has such efficacy that it is a most powerful means of casting out demons; for there is a certain kind of demon which is not cast out but by prayer and fasting.

Those, therefore, who do not practice assiduous and regular prayer deprive themselves of a powerful means of obtaining gifts of singular value. To succeed in obtaining the object of your desires, it is not enough that you ask that which is good; your entreaties must also be assiduous. Every one that asketh, says St. Jerome, receiveth, as it is written. If, therefore, it is not given you, this is because you do not ask. Ask, therefore, and you shall receive.

The Fruits of Prayer

Moreover, this necessity of prayer is also productive of the greatest delight and usefulness, since it bears most abundant fruits. When it is necessary to instruct the faithful concerning these fruits, pastors will find ample matter in sacred writers. We have made from these sources a selection which appeared to us to suit the present purpose.

Prayer Honors God

The first fruit which we receive is that by praying we honor God, since prayer is a certain act of religion, which is compared in Scripture to a sweet perfume. Let my prayer, says the Prophet, be directed as incense in thy sight. By prayer we confess our subjection to God; we acknowledge and proclaim Him to be the author of all good, in whom alone we center all our hopes, who alone is our refuge, in all dangers and the bulwark of our salvation. Of this fruit we are admonished also in these words: Call upon me in the day of trouble; I ¡will deliver thee, and thou shalt glorify me.

Prayer Obtains What We Request

Another most pleasing and invaluable fruit of prayer is that it is heard by God. Prayer is the key of heaven, says St. Augustine; prayer ascends, and the mercy of God descends. High as are the heavens, and low as is the earth, God hears the voice of man. Such is the utility, such the efficacy of prayer, that through it we obtain a plenitude of heavenly gifts. Thus by prayer we secure the guidance and aid of the Holy Spirit, the security and preservation of the faith, deliverance from punishment, divine protection under temptation, victory over the devil. In a word, there is in prayer an accumulation of spiritual joy; and hence our Lord said: Ask, and you shall receive, that your joy may be full.

Proof

Nor can we, for a moment, doubt that God in His goodness awaits and is at all times ready to hear our petitions. This is a truth to which the Sacred Scriptures bear ample testimony. Since, however, the texts are easy of access, we shall content ourselves with citing as an example the words of Isaias: Then shalt thou call, and the Lord will hear: thou shalt cry, and he will say, "Here I am"; and again, It shall come to pass, that before they call, I will hear: as they are yet speaking, I will hear. With regard to instances of persons, who have obtained from God the objects of their prayers, they are almost innumerable, and too well known to require special mention.

Unwise And Indevout Prayers Unheard

Sometimes, indeed, it happens that what we ask of God we do not obtain. But it is then especially that God looks to our welfare, either because He bestows on us other gifts of higher value and in greater abundance, or because what we ask, far from being necessary or useful, would prove superfluous and injurious. God, says St. Augustine, denies some things in His mercy which He grants in His wrath.

Sometimes, also, such is the remissness and negligence with which we pray, that we ourselves do not attend to what we say. Since prayer is an elevation of the soul to God, if, while we pray, the mind, instead of being fixed upon God, is distracted, and the tongue slurs over the words at random, without attention, without devotion, with what propriety can we give to such empty sounds the name of Christian prayer?

We should not, therefore, be at all surprised, if God does not comply with our requests; either because by our negligence and indifference we almost show that we do not really desire what we ask, or because we ask those things, which, if granted, would be prejudicial to our interests.

To Devout Prayer And Dispositions God Grants More Than Is Asked

On the other hand, to those who pray with devout attention, God grants more than they ask. This the Apostle declares in his Epistle to the Ephesians, and the same truth is unfolded ill the parable of the prodigal son, who would have deemed it a kindness to be admitted into the number of his father's servants.

Nay, God heaps His favors not only on those who seek them, but also on those who are rightly disposed; and this, not only with abundance, but also with readiness. This is shown by the words of Scripture: The Lord hath heard the desire of the poor. For God hastens to grant the inner and hidden desires of the needy without awaiting their utterance.

Prayer Exercises And Increases Faith

Another fruit of prayer is, that it exercises and augments the virtues of the soul, particularly the virtue of faith. As they who have not faith in God, cannot pray as they ought, for how can they call on him, whom they have not believed? so the faithful, in proportion to the fervor of their prayers, possess a stronger and a more assured faith in the protecting providence of God, which requires principally that in all needs we have recourse to Him.

The Scottish Communion Office

God, it is true, might bestow on us all things abundantly, although we did not ask them or even think of them, just as He bestows on the irrational creation all things necessary for the support of life. But our most bountiful Father wishes to be invoked by His children; He wishes that, praying as we ought each day of our lives, we may pray with increased confidence. He wishes that in obtaining our requests we may more and more bear witness to and declare His goodness towards us.

Prayer Increases Charity

Our charity is also augmented. In recognizing God as the author of every blessing and of every good, we are led to cling to Him with the most devoted love. And as those who cherish a mutual affection become more ardently attached by frequent interviews and conversations, so the oftener the soul prays devoutly and implores the divine mercy, thus holding converse with God, the more exquisite is the sense of delight which she experiences in each prayer, and the more ardently is she inflamed to love and adore Him.

Prayer Disposes The Soul For Divine Blessings

Furthermore, God wishes us to make use of prayer, in order that burning with the desire of asking what we are anxious to obtain, we may thus by our perseverance and zeal make such advances in spiritual life, as to be worthy to obtain those blessings which the soul could not obtain before because of its dryness and lack of devotion.

Prayer Makes Us Realize Our Own Needfulness

Moreover, God wishes us to realize, and always keep in mind, that, unassisted by His heavenly grace, we can of ourselves do nothing, and should therefore apply ourselves to prayer with all the powers of our souls.

Prayer Is A Protection Against The Devil

The weapons which prayer supplies are most powerful against our bitterest foes. With the cries of our prayers, says St. Hilary, we must fight against the devil and his armed hosts.

Prayer Promotes A Virtuous Life

From prayer we also derive this important advantage that though we are inclined to evil and to the indulgence of various passions, as a consequence of our natural frailty, God permits us to raise our hearts to Him, in order that while we address Him in prayer, and endeavor to deserve His gifts, we may be inspired with a love of innocence, and, by effacing our sins, be purified from every stain of guilt.

Prayer Disarms The Divine Vengeance

Finally, as St. Jerome observes, prayer disarms the anger of God. Hence, these words of God addressed to Moses: Let me alone, when Moses sought by his prayer to stay the punishments God was about to inflict on His people. Nothing is so efficacious in appeasing God, when His wrath is kindled; nothing so effectually delays or averts the punishments prepared for the wicked as the prayers of men.

The Parts Of Prayer

The necessity and advantages of Christian prayer being explained, the faithful should also know how many, and what are the parts of which it is composed; for that this pertains to the perfect discharge of this duty, we learn from the Apostle. In his Epistle to Timothy, exhorting to pious and holy prayer, he carefully enumerates the parts of which it consists: I desire therefore first of all that supplications, prayers, intercessions, and thanksgivings be made for all men. Although the shades of distinction between these different parts of prayer are delicate, yet the pastor, should he deem the explanation useful to his people, should consult, among others, St. Hilary and St. Augustine.

The Two Chief Parts Of Prayer Petition And Thanksgiving

There are two principal parts of prayer, petition and thanksgiving, and since these are the sources, as it were, from which all the others spring, they appear to us to be of too much importance to be omitted. For we approach God and offer Him the tribute of our worship, either to obtain some favor, or to return Him thanks for those with which His bounty every day enriches and adorns us. God Himself indicated both these most necessary parts of prayer when He declared by the mouth of David: Call upon me in the day of trouble: I will deliver thee, and thou shalt glorify me.

Who does not perceive how much we stand in need of the goodness and beneficence of God, if he but consider the extreme destitution and misery of man?

On the other hand, all that have eyes and understanding know God's loving kindness toward man and the liberal bounty He exercises in our behalf. Wherever we cast our eyes, wherever we turn our thoughts, the admirable light of the divine goodness and beneficence beams upon us. What have we that is not the gift of His bounty? If, then, all things are the gifts and favors bestowed on us by His goodness, why should not everyone, as much as possible, celebrate the praises of God, and thank Him for His boundless beneficence.

Degrees Of Petition And Thanksgiving

Of these duties of petition and thanksgiving each contains many subordinate degrees. In order, therefore, that the faithful may not only pray, but also pray in the best manner, the pastor should propose to them the most perfect mode of praying, and should exhort them to use it to the best of their ability.

The Highest Degree Of Prayer: The Prayer Of The Just

What, then, is the best manner and the most exalted degree of prayer? It is that which is made use of by the pious and the just. Resting on the solid foundation of the true faith, they rise successively from one degree of prayer and virtue to another, until, at length, they reach that height of perfection, whence they can contemplate the infinite power, goodness, and wisdom of God; where, too, they are animated with the assured hope of obtaining not only those blessings which they desire in this life, but also those unutterable rewards which God has pledged Himself to grant to him who piously and religiously implores His assistance.

Soaring, as it were, to heaven, on these two wings, the soul approaches, in fervent desire, the Divinity; adores with supreme praise and thanksgiving Him from whom she has received such inestimable blessings; and, like an only child, animated with singular piety and profound veneration, trustfully tells her most beloved Father all her wants.

This sort of prayer the Sacred Scriptures express by the words pouring out. In his sight, says the Prophet, I pour out my prayer, but before him I declare my trouble. This means that he who comes to pray should conceal or omit nothing, but pour out all, flying with confidence into the bosom of God, his most loving Father. To this the Sacred Scriptures exhort us in these words: Pour out thy heart before him, cast thy care upon the Lord. This is that degree of prayer to which St. Augustine alludes when he says in that book entitled Enchiridion: What faith believes, that hope and charity implore.

The Second Degree Of Prayer: The Prayer Of Sinners

Another degree of prayer is that of those who are weighed down by the guilt of mortal sin, but who strive, with what is called dead faith, to raise themselves from their condition and to ascend to God. But, in consequence of their languid state and the extreme weakness of their faith, they cannot raise themselves from the earth. Recognizing their crimes and stung with remorse of conscience, they bow themselves down with humility, and, far as they are removed from God, implore of Him with penitential sorrow, the pardon of their sins and the peace of reconciliation.

The prayers of such persons are not rejected by God, but are heard by Him. Nay, in His mercy, He generously invites such as these to have recourse to Him, saying: Come to me, all you that labor, and are heavily laden, and I will refresh you, of this class was the publican, who, though he did not dare to raise his eyes towards heaven, left the Temple, as (our Lord) declares, more justified than the Pharisee.

The Third Degree Of Prayer: The Prayer Of Unbelievers

A third degree of prayer is that which is offered by those who have not as yet been illumined with the light of faith; but who, when the divine goodness illumines in their souls the feeble natural light, are strongly moved to the desire and pursuit of truth and most earnestly pray for a knowledge of it.

If they persevere in such dispositions, God, in His mercy, will not neglect their earnest endeavors, as we see verified by the example of Cornelius the centurion. The doors of the divine mercy are closed against none who sincerely ask for mercy.

The Lowest Degree Of Prayer: The Prayer Of The Impenitent

The last degree is that of those who not only do not repent of their sins and enormities, but, adding crime to crime, dare frequently to ask pardon of God for those sins, in which they are resolved to continue. With such dispositions they would not presume to ask pardon from their fellowman.

The prayer of such sinners is not heard by God. It is recorded of Antiochus: Then this wicked man prayed to the Lord, of whom he was not to obtain mercy. Whoever lives in this deplorable condition should be vehemently exhorted to wean himself from all affection to sin, and to return to God in good earnest and from the heart.

What We Should Pray For

Under the head of each Petition we shall point out in its proper place, what is, and what is not a proper object of prayer. Hence it will suffice here to remind the faithful in a general way that they ought to ask of God such things as are just and good, lest, praying for what is not suitable, they may be repelled in these words: You know not what you ask. Whatever it is lawful to desire, it is lawful to pray for, as is proved by the Lord's ample promise: You shall ask whatever you will, and it shall be done unto you, words in which He promises to grant all things.

Spiritual Goods

In the first place, then, the standard which should regulate all our wishes is that we desire above all else God, the supreme Good. After God we should most desire those things which unite us most closely to Him; while those which would separate us from Him, or occasion that separation, should have no share whatever in our affections.

External Goods And Goods Of Body

Taking, then, as our standard the supreme and perfect Good, we can easily infer how we are to desire and ask from God our Father those other things which are called goods. Goods which are called bodily, such as health, strength, beauty and those which are external, such as riches, honors, glory, often supply the means and give occasion for sin; and, therefore, it is not always either pious or salutary to ask for them. We should pray for these goods of life only in so far as we need them, thus referring all to God. It cannot be deemed unlawful to pray for those things for which Jacob and Solomon prayed. If, says Jacob, he shall give me bread to eat and raiment to put on, the Lord shall be my God. Give me, says Solomon, only the necessaries of life.

But when we are supplied by the bounty of God with necessaries and comforts, we should not forget the admonition of the Apostle: Let them that buy, be as if they possessed not, and those that use this world, as if they used it not; for the figure of this world passeth away; and again, If riches abound, set not your heart upon them. God Himself teaches us that only the use and fruit of these things belong to us and that we are obliged to share them with others. If we are blessed with health, if we abound in other external and corporal goods, we should recollect that they are given to us in order to enable us to serve God with greater fidelity, and as the means of lending assistance to others.

Goods Of The Mind

It is also lawful to pray for the goods and adornments of the mind, such as a knowledge of the arts and sciences, provided our prayers are accompanied with this condition, that they serve to promote the glory of God and our own salvation.

The only thing which can be absolutely and unconditionally the object of our wishes, our desires and our prayers, is, as we have already observed, the glory of God, and, next to it, whatever can serve to unite us to that supreme Good, such as faith and the fear and love of God, of which we shall treat at length when we come to explain the Petitions.

For Whom We Ought to Pray

The objects of prayer being known, the faithful are next to be taught for whom they are to pray. Prayer comprehends petition and thanksgiving. We shall first treat of petition.

The Prayer Of Petition Should Be Offered For All

We are to pray for all mankind, without exception of enemies, nation or religion; for every man, be he enemy, stranger or infidel, is our neighbor, whom God commands us to love, and for whom, therefore, we should discharge a duty of love, which is prayer. To the discharge of this duty the Apostle exhort: when he says: I desire that prayer be made for all men. In such prayers we should first ask for those things that concern spiritual interests, and next for what pertains to temporal welfare.

Those For Whom We Should Especially Offer Our Petitions: Pastors

Before all others the pastors of our souls have a right to our prayers, as we learn from the example of the Apostle in his Epistle to the Colossians, in which he asks them to pray for him, that God may open unto him a door of speech, a request which he also makes in his Epistle to the Thessalonians. In the Acts of the Apostles we also read that prayers were offered in the Church without intermission for Peter. St. Basil, in his work On Morals, urges to a faithful compliance with this obligation. We must, he says, pray for those who are charged with preaching the word of truth.

Rulers Of Our Country

In the next place, as the same Apostle teaches, we should pray for our rulers.

Who does not know what a singular blessing a people enjoy in public officials who are just and upright? We should, therefore, beseech God to make them such as they ought to be, fit persons to govern others.

The Just

To offer up our prayers also for the good and pious is a practice taught by the example of holy men. Even the good and the pious need the prayers of others. Providence has wisely ordained it so, in order that the just, realizing the necessity they are under of being aided by the prayers of those who are inferior to them, may not be inflated with pride.

Enemies And Those Outside The Church

The Lord has also commanded us, to pray for those that persecute and calumniate us. The practice of praying for those who are not within the pale of the Church, is, as we know on the authority of St. Augustine, of Apostolic origin. We pray that the faith may be made known to infidels; that idolaters may be rescued from the error of their impiety; that the Jews, emerging from the darkness with which they are encompassed, may arrive at the light of truth; that heretics, returning to soundness of mind, may be instructed in the Catholic faith; and that schismatics may be united in the bond of true charity and may return to the communion of their holy mother, the Church, from which they have separated.

Many examples prove that prayers for such as these are very efficacious when offered from the heart. Instances occur every day in which God rescues individuals of every condition of life from the powers of darkness, and transfers them into the kingdom of His Beloved Son, from vessels of wrath making them vessels of mercy. That the prayers of the pious have very great influence in bringing about this result no one can reasonably doubt.

The Dead

Prayers for the dead, that they may be liberated from the fire of purgatory, are derived from Apostolic teaching. But on this subject we have said enough when explaining the Holy Sacrifice of the Mass.

Sinners

Those who are said to sin unto death derive little advantage from prayers and supplications. It is, however, the part of Christian charity to offer up our prayers and tears for them, in order, if possible, to obtain their reconciliation with God.

With regard to the execrations uttered by holy men against the wicked, it is certain, from the teaching of the Fathers, that they are either prophecies of the evils which are to befall sinners or denunciations of the crimes of which they are guilty, that the sinner may be saved, but sin destroyed.

The Prayer Of Thanksgiving Should Be Offered For All

In the second part of prayer we render most grateful thanks to God for the divine and immortal blessings which He has always bestowed, and still continues to bestow every day on the human race.

Our Thanksgiving Should Especially Be Offered: For The Saints

This duty we discharge especially when we give singular praises to God for the victory and triumph which all the Saints, aided by His goodness, have achieved over their domestic and external enemies.

For The Blessed Virgin Mary

To this sort of prayer belongs the first part of the Angelic Salutation, when used by us as a prayer: Hail Mary, full of grace, the Lord is with thee, blessed art thou among women. For in these words we render to God the highest praise and return Him most gracious thanks, because He has bestowed all His heavenly gifts on the most holy Virgin; and at the same time we congratulate the Virgin herself on her singular privileges.

To this form of thanksgiving the Church of God has wisely added prayers and an invocation addressed to the most holy Mother of God, by which we piously and humbly fly to her patronage, in order that, by her intercession, she may reconcile God to us sinners and may obtain for us those blessings which we stand in need of in this life and in the life to come. We, therefore, exiled children of Eve, who dwell in this vale of tears, should constantly beseech the Mother of mercy, the advocate of the faithful, to pray for us sinners. In this prayer we should earnestly implore her help and assistance; for that she possesses exalted merits with God, and that she is most desirous to assist us by her prayers, no one can doubt without impiety and wickedness.

To Whom We Should Pray

To God

That God is to be prayed to and His name invoked is the language of the law of nature, inscribed upon the human heart. It is also the doctrine of Holy Scripture, in which we hear God commanding: Call upon me in the day of trouble. By the word God, we mean the three Persons (of the adorable Trinity).To The Saints We must also have recourse to the interces-

sion of the Saints who are in glory. That the Saints are to be prayed to is a truth so firmly established in the Church of God, that no pious person can experience a shadow of doubt on the subject. But as this point was explained in its proper place, under a separate head, we refer the pastor and others to that place.

God And The Saints Addressed Differently

To remove, however, the possibility of error on the part of the unlearned it will be found useful to explain to the faithful the difference between these two kinds of invocation. We do not address God and the Saints in the same manner, for we implore God to grant us blessings or to deliver us from evils; while we ask the Saints, since they are the friends of God, to take us under their patronage and to obtain for us from God whatever we need. Hence we make use of two different forms of prayer. To God, we properly say: Have mercy on us, Hear us; but to the Saints, Pray for us. Still we may also ask the Saints, though in a different sense, that they have mercy on us, for they are most merciful. Thus we may beseech them that, touched with the misery of our condition, they would interpose in our behalf their influence and intercession before God.

In the performance of this duty, it is strictly incumbent on all not to transfer to any creature the right which belongs exclusively to God. For instance, when we say the Our Father before the image of a Saint we should bear in mind that we beg of the Saint to pray with us and to obtain for us those favors which we ask of God, in the Petitions of the Lord's Prayer, that he become our interpreter and intercessor with God. That this is an office which the Saints discharge, St. John the Apostle teaches in the Apocalypse.

Preparation for Prayer

In Scripture we read: Before prayer, prepare thy soul, and be not as a man that tempteth God. He tempts God who prays well but acts badly, and while he converses with God allows his mind to wander.

Since, then, the dispositions with which we pray are of such vital importance, the pastor should teach his pious hearers how to pray.

Humility

The first preparation, then, for prayer is an unfeigned humility of soul, an acknowledgment of our sinfulness, and a conviction that, when we approach God in prayer, our sins render us undeserving, not only of receiving a propitious hearing from Him, but even of appearing in His presence.

This preparation is frequently ment'oned in the Scriptures: He hath had regard to the prayer of the humble, and he hath not despised their petitions; the prayer of him that humbleth himself shall pierce the clouds. Many other passages of the same kind will suggest themselves to learned pastors. Hence we abstain from citing more here.

Two examples, however, at which we have already glanced in another place, and which are apposite to our purpose, we shall not pass over in silence. The publican, who, standing afar off, would not so much as lift up his eyes toward heaven, and the woman, a sinner, who, moved with sorrow, washed the feet of Christ the Lord, with her tears, illustrate the great efficacy which Christian humility imparts to prayer.

Sorrow For Sin

The next (preparation) is a feeling of sorrow, arising from the recollection of our past sins, or, at least, some sense of regret, that we do not experience that sorrow. If the sinner bring not with him to prayer both, or, at least one of these dispositions, he cannot hope to obtain pardon.

Freedom From Violence, Anger, Hatred And Inhumanity

There are some crimes, such as violence and murder, which are in a special way obstacles to the efficacy of our prayers, and we must, therefore, preserve our hands unstained by outrage and cruelty. Of such crimes the Lord says by the mouth of Isaias: When you stretch forth your hands, I will turn away my eyes from you; and when you multiply prayer, I will not hear, for your hands are full of blood.

Anger and strife we should also avoid, for they have great influence in preventing our prayers from being heard. Concerning them the Apostle says: 1 will that men pray in every place lifting up pure hands, without anger and contention.

Implacable hatred of any person on account of injuries received we must guard against; for while we are under the influence of such feelings,¡ it is impossible that we should obtain from God the pardon of our sins. When you shall stand to pray, He says, forgive, if you have aught against any man; and, if you will not forgive men, neither will your heavenly Father forgive you your offences.

Hardness and inhumanity to the poor we should also avoid. For concerning men of this kind it was said He that stoppeth his ear against the cry of the poor, shall also cry himself, and shall not be heard.

Freedom From Pride And Contempt Of God's Word

What shall we say of pride? How much it offends God, we learn from these words: God resisteth the proud, and giveth grace to the humble. What of the contempt of the divine oracles? He that turneth away his ears, says Solomon, from hearing the law, his prayer shall be an abomination.

Here, however, we are not to understand that we are forbidden to pray for the forgiveness of the injuries we have done, of murder, anger, insensibility to the wants of the poor, of pride, contempt of God's word, in fine, of any other sin.

Faith And Confidence

Faith is another necessary quality for this preparation of soul. Without faith, we can have no knowledge of the omnipotence or mercy of the supreme Father, which are the sources of our confidence in prayer, as Christ the Lord Himself has taught: All things whatsoever you shall ask in prayer, believing, you shall receive. St. Augustine, speaking of this faith, thus comments on the Lord's words: Without faith prayer is useless.

The chief requisite, therefore, of a good prayer is, as we have already said, a firm and unwavering faith. This the Apostle shows by an antithesis: How shall they call on him whom they have not believed? Believe, then, we must, both in order to pray, and that we be not wanting in that faith which renders prayer fruitful. For it is faith that leads to prayer, and it is prayer that, by removing all doubts, gives strength and firmness to faith. This is the meaning of the exhortation of St. Ignatius to those who would approach God in prayer: Be not of doubtful mind in prayer; blessed is he who hath not doubted. Wherefore, to obtain from God what we ask, faith and an assured confidence, are of first importance, according to the admonition of St. James: Let him ask in faith, nothing wavering.

Motives Of Confidence In Prayer

There is much to inspire us with confidence in prayer. Among these are to be numbered the beneficence and bounty of God, displayed towards us, when He commands us to call Him Father, thus giving us to understand that we are His children. Again there are the numberless instances of those whose prayers have been heard.

Further we have as our chief advocate, Christ the Lord, who is ever ready to assist us, as we read in St. John: If any man sin we have an advocate with the Father, Jesus Christ, the just; and he is the propitiation for our sins.' In like manner Paul the Apostle says: Christ Jesus, that died, yea, that is risen also again, who is at the right hand of God, who also maketh intercession for us. To Timothy he writes: For there is one God, and one mediator of God and men, the man Christ Jesus; and to the Hebrews he writes: Wherefore, it behooved him in all things to be made like unto his brethren, that he might become a merciful and faithful high priest before God. Unworthy, then, as we are, of obtaining our requests, yet considering and resting our claims upon the dignity of our great Mediator and Intercessor, Jesus Christ, we should hope and trust most confidently, that, through His merits, God will grant us all that we ask in the proper way.

Finally, the Holy Ghost is the author of our prayers; and under His guiding influence, we cannot fail to be heard. We have received the spirit of adoption of sons, whereby we cry, "Abba, (Father)." This spirit succors our infirmity and enlightens our ignorance in the discharge of the duty of prayer; nay, even, as the Apostle says, He asketh for us with unspeakable groanings.

Should we, then, at any time waver, not being sufficiently strong in faith, let us say with the Apostles: Lord, increase our faith; and, with the father (of the demoniac): Help my unbelief.

Correspondence With God's Will

But what most ensures the accomplishment of our desires is the union of faith and hope with that conformity of all our thoughts, actions, and prayers to God's law and pleasure. If, He says, you abide in me, and my words abide in you, you shall ask whatever you will, and it shall be done unto you.

Fraternal Charity

In order, however, that our prayers may have this power of obtaining all things from God, we must, as was previously served, forget injuries, cherish sentiments of good will, and practice kindness towards our neighbor.

How to Pray Well

The manner of praying is also a matter of the highest moment. Though prayer in itself is good and salutary, yet if not performed in a proper manner it is unavailing. Often we do not obtain what we ask, because, in the words of St. James, we ask amiss. Pastors, therefore, should instruct the faithful in the best manner of asking well and of making private and public prayer. The rules of Christian prayer have been formed on the teaching of Christ the Lord.

We Must Pray In Spirit And In Truth

We must, then pray in spirit and in truth; for the heavenly Father seeks those who adore Him in spirit and in truth. He prays in this manner whose prayer proceeds from an interior and intense ardor of soul.

Mental Prayer

This spiritual manner of praying does not exclude the use of vocal prayer. Nevertheless, that prayer which is the vehement outpouring of the soul, deservedly holds the first place; and although not uttered with the lips, it is heard by God to whom the secrets of hearts are open. He heard the silent prayer of Anna, the mother of Samuel, of whom we read, that she prayed, shedding many tears and only moving her lips. Such was also the prayer of David, for he says: My heart hath said to thee, my f ace hath sought thee. In reading the Bible one will meet many similar examples.

Vocal Prayer

But vocal prayer has also its advantages and necessity. It quickens the attention of the mind, and kindles the fervor of him who prays. We sometimes, says St. Augustine, in his letter to Proba, animate ourselves to intensify our holy desire by having recourse to words and other signs; filled with vehement ardor and piety, we find it impossible at times not to express our feelings in words; for while the soul exults with joy, the tongue should also give utterance to that exultation. And surely it becomes us to make to God this complete sacrifice of soul and body, a kind of prayer which the Apostles were accustomed to use, as we learn from many passages of the Acts and of the Apostle.

Private And Public Prayer

There are two sorts of prayer, private and public. Private prayer is employed in order to assist interior attention and devotion; whereas in public prayer, which has been instituted to excite the piety of the faithful, and has been prescribed for certain fixed times, the use of words is indispensably required.

Those Who Do Nor Pray In Spirit

This practice of praying in spirit is peculiar to Christians, and is not at all used by infidels. Of these Christ the Lord has said: When you pray, speak not much, as the heathens; for they think that in their much speaking they may be heard. Be not ye, therefore, like to them, for your Father knoweth what is needful for you before you ask him.

But though (our Lord) prohibits loquacity, He is so far from forbidding continuance in prayer which proceeds from the eager and prolonged devotion of the soul that by His own example He exhorts us to such prayer. Not only did He spend whole nights in prayer, but also prayed the third time, saying the selfsame words. The inference, therefore, to be drawn from the prohibition is that prayers consisting of mere empty sounds are not to be addressed to God.

Those Who Do Not Pray In Truth

Neither do the prayers of the hypocrite proceed from the heart; and against the imitation of their example, Christ the Lord warns us in these words: When ye pray, ye shall not be as the hypocrites that love to stand and pray in the synagogues, and corners of the streets, that they may be seen by men. Amen I say, to you they have received their reward. But thou, when thou shalt pray, enter into thy chamber, and having shut the door, pray to thy Father in secret; and thy Father who seeth in secret will repay thee. Here the word chamber may be understood to mean the human heart, which we should not only enter, but should also close against every distraction from without that could deprive our prayer of its perfection. For then will our heavenly Father, who sees perfectly our hearts and secret thoughts, grant our petitions.

We Must Pray With Perseverance

Another necessary condition of prayer is constancy. The great efficacy of perseverance, the Son of God exemplifies by the conduct of the judge, who, while he feared not God, nor regarded man, yet, overcome by the persistence and importunity of the widow, yielded to her entreaties." In our prayers to God we should, therefore, be persevering.

We must not imitate the example of those who become tired of praying, if, after having prayed once or twice, they succeed not in obtaining the object of their prayers. We should never be weary of the duty of prayer, as we are taught by the authority of Christ the Lord and of the Apostle. And should the will at any time fail us, we should beg of God by prayer the strength to persevere.

We Must Pray In The Name Of Jesus Christ

The Son of God would also have us present our prayers to the Father in His name; for, by His merits and the influence of His mediation, our prayers acquire such weight that they are heard by our heavenly Father. For He Himself says in St. John: Amen, Amen, I say unto you, if you ask the Father any thing in my name, he will give it you. Hitherto you have not asked any thing in my name: ask and you shall receive, that your joy may be full; and again: Whatsoever you shall ask the Father in my name, that will I do.

We Must Pray With Fervor, Uniting Petition To Thanksgiving

Let us imitate the fervor of the Saints in prayer; and to petition let us unite thanksgiving, imitating the example of the Apostles, who, as may be seen in the Epistles of St. Paul, always observed this salutary practice.

Fasting And Almsdeeds Should Be Joined To Prayer

To prayer let us unite fasting and almsdeeds. Fasting is most intimately connected with prayer. For the mind of one who is filled with food and drink is so borne down as not to be able to raise itself to the contemplation of God, or even to understand what prayer means.

Almsdeeds have also an intimate connection with prayer. For what claim has he to the virtue of charity, who, possessing the means of affording relief to those who depend on the assistance of others, refuses help to his neighbor and brother? How can he, whose heart is devoid of charity, demand assistance from God unless, while imploring the pardon of his sins, he at the same time humbly beg of God to grant him the virtue of charity?

This triple remedy was, therefore, appointed by God to aid man in the attainment of salvation. For by sin we offend God, wrong our neighbor, or injure ourselves. The wrath of God we appease by pious prayer; our offences against man we redeem by almsdeeds; the stains of our own lives we wash away by fasting. Each of these remedies, it is true, is applicable to every sort of sin; they are, however, peculiarly adapted to those three which we have specially mentioned.

Catechism of Trent on Prayer

3. THE WAY OF PERFECTION
Teresa of Avila

CHAPTER 22
Explains the meaning of mental prayer.

You must know, daughters, that whether or no you are practicing mental prayer has nothing to do with keeping the lips closed. If, while I am speaking with God, I have a clear realization and full consciousness that I am doing so, and if this is more real to me than the words I am uttering, then I am combining mental and vocal prayer. When people tell you that you are speaking with God by reciting the Paternoster and thinking of worldly things—well, words fail me. When you speak, as it is right for you to do, with so great a Lord, it is well that you should think of Who it is that you are addressing, and what you yourself are, if only that you may speak to Him with proper respect. How can you address a king with the deference due to him, or how can you know what ceremonies have to be used when speaking to a grandee, unless you are clearly conscious of the nature of his position and of yours? It is because of this, and because it is the custom to do so, that you must behave respectfully to him, and must learn what the custom is, and not be careless about such things, or you will be dismissed as a simpleton and obtain none of the things you desire. And furthermore, unless you are quite conversant with it, you must get all necessary information, and have what you are going to say written down for you. It once happened to me, when I was not accustomed to addressing aristocrats, that I had to go on a matter of urgent business to see a lady who had to be addressed as "Your Ladyship". I was shown that word in writing; but I am stupid, and had never used such a term before; so when I arrived I got it wrong. So I decided to tell her about it and she laughed heartily and told me to be good enough to use the ordinary form of polite address, which I did.

How is it, my Lord, how is it, my Emperor, that Thou canst suffer this, Prince of all Creation? For Thou, my God, art a King without end, and Thine is no borrowed Kingdom, but Thine own, and it will never pass away. When the Creed says "Whose Kingdom shall have no end" the phrase nearly always makes me feel particularly happy. I praise Thee, Lord, and bless Thee, and all things praise Thee for ever–for Thy Kingdom will endure for ever. Do Thou never allow it to be thought right, Lord, for those who praise Thee and come to speak with Thee to do so with their lips alone. What do you mean, Christians, when you say that mental prayer is unnecessary? Do you understand what you are saying? I really do not think you can. And so you want us all to go wrong: you cannot know what mental prayer is, or how vocal prayers should be said, or what is meant by contemplation. For, if you knew this, you would not condemn on the one hand what you praise on the other.

Whenever I remember to do so, I shall always speak of mental and vocal prayer together, daughters, so that you may not be alarmed. I know what such fears lead to, for I have suffered a certain number of trials in this respect, and so I should be sorry if anyone were to unsettle you, for it is very bad for you to have misgivings while you are walking on this path. It is most important that you should realize you are making progress; for if a traveler is told that he has taken the wrong road, and has lost his way, he begins to wander to and fro and the constant search for the right road tires him, wastes his time and delays his arrival. Who can say that it is wrong if, before we begin reciting the Hours or the Rosary, we think Whom we are going to address, and who we are that are addressing Him, so that we may do so in the way we should? I assure you, sisters, that if you gave all due attention to a consideration of these two points before beginning the vocal prayers which you are about to say you would be engaging in mental prayer for a very long time. For we cannot approach a prince and address him in the same careless way that we should adopt in speaking to a peasant or to some poor woman like ourselves, whom we may address however we like.

The reason we sometimes do so is to be found in the humility of this King, Who, unskilled though I am in speaking with Him, does not refuse to hear me or forbid me to approach Him, or command His guards to throw me out. For the angels in His presence know well that their King is such that He prefers the unskilled language of a humble peasant boy, knowing that he would say more if he had more to say, to the speech of the wisest and most learned men, however elegant may be their arguments, if these are not accompanied by humility. But we must not be unmannerly because He is good. If only to show our gratitude to Him for enduring our foul odor and allowing such a one as myself to come near Him, it is well that we should try to realize His purity and His nature. It is true that we recognize this at once when we approach Him, just as we do when we visit the lords of the earth. Once we are told about their fathers' names and their incomes and dignities, there is no more for us to know about them; for on earth one makes account of persons, and honors them, not because of their merits but because of their possessions.

O miserable world! Give hearty praise to God, daughters, that you have left so wretched a place, where people are honored, not for their own selves, but for what they get from their tenants and vassals: if these fail them, they have no honor left. It is a curious thing, and when you go out to recreation together you should laugh about it, for it is a good way of spending your time to reflect how blindly people in the world spend theirs.

O Thou our Emperor! Supreme Power, Supreme Goodness, Wisdom Itself, without beginning, without end and without measure in Thy works: infinite are these and incomprehensible, a fathomless ocean of wonders, O Beauty containing within Thyself all beauties. O Very Strength! God help me! Would that I could command all the eloquence of mortals and all wisdom, so as to understand, as far as is possible here below, that to know nothing is everything, and thus to describe some of the many things on which we may meditate in order to learn something of the nature of this our Lord and Good.

When you approach God, then, try to think and realize Whom you are about to address and continue to do so while you are addressing Him. If we had a thousand lives, we should never fully understand how this Lord merits that we behave toward Him, before Whom even the angels tremble. He orders all things and He can do all things: with Him to will is to perform. It will be right, then, daughters, for us to endeavor to rejoice in these wondrous qualities of our Spouse and to know Whom we have wedded and what our lives should be. Why, God save us, when a woman in this world is about to marry, she knows beforehand whom she is to marry, what sort of a person he is and what property he possesses. Shall not we, then, who are already betrothed, think about our Spouse, before we are wedded to Him and He takes us home to be with Him? If these thoughts are not forbidden to those who are betrothed to men on earth, how can we be forbidden to discover Who this Man is, Who is His Father, what is the country to which He will take me, what are the riches with which He promises to endow me, what is His rank, how I can best make Him happy, what I can do that will give Him pleasure, and how I can bring my rank into line with His. If a woman is to be happy in her marriage, it is just those things that she is advised to see about, even though her husband be a man of very low station.

Shall less respect be paid to Thee, then, my Spouse, than to men? If they think it unfitting to do Thee honor, let them at least leave Thee Thy brides, who are to spend their lives with Thee. A woman is indeed fortunate in her life if her husband is so jealous that he will allow her to speak with no one but himself; it would be a pretty pass if she could not resolve to give him this pleasure, for it is reasonable enough that she should put up with this and not wish to converse with anyone else, since in him she has all that she can desire. To understand these truths, my daughters, is to practice mental prayer. If you wish to learn to understand them, and at the same time to practice vocal prayer, well and good. But do not, I beg you, address God while you are thinking of other things, for to do that is the result of not understanding what mental prayer is. I think I have made this clear. May the Lord grant us to learn how to put it into practice. Amen.

CHAPTER 23

Describes the importance of not turning back when one has set out upon the way of prayer
Now, as I have said, it is most important that from the first we should be very resolute, and for this there are so many reasons that if I were

to give them all I should have to write at great length. Some of them are given in other books. I will tell you just two or three of them, sisters. One is that when we decide to give anything–such as this slight effort of recollection–to Him Who has given us so much, and Who is continually giving, it would be wrong for us not to be entirely resolute in doing so and to act like a person who lends something and expects to get it back again. (Not that we do not receive interest: on the contrary, we gain a great deal.) I do not call this "giving". Anyone who has been lent something always feels slightly displeased when the lender wants it back again, especially if he is using it himself and has come to look upon it as his own. If the two are friends and the lender is indebted to the recipient for many things of which he has made him free gifts, he will think it meanness and a great lack of affection if he will leave not even the smallest thing in his possession, merely as a sign of love.

What wife is there who, after receiving many valuable jewels from her husband, will not give him so much as a ring–which he wants, not because of its value, for all she has is his, but as a sign of love and a token that she will be his until she dies? Does the Lord deserve less than this that we should mock Him by taking away the worthless gift which we have given Him? Since we have resolved to devote to Him this very brief period of time–only a small part of what we spend upon ourselves and upon people who are not particularly grateful to us for it–let us give it Him freely, with our minds unoccupied by other things and entirely resolved never to take it back again, whatever we may suffer through trials, annoyances or aridities. Let me realize that this time is being lent me and is not my own, and feel that I can rightly be called to account for it if I am not prepared to devote it wholly to God.

I say "wholly", but we must not be considered as taking it back if we should fail to give it Him for a day, or for a few days, because of legitimate occupations or through some indisposition. Provided the intention remains firm, my God is not in the least meticulous; He does not look at trivial details; and, if you are trying to please Him in any way, He will assuredly accept that as your gift. The other way is suitable for ungenerous souls, so mean that they are not large-hearted enough to give but find it as much as they can do to lend. Still, let them make some effort, for this Lord of ours will reckon everything we do to our credit and accept everything we want to give Him. In drawing up our reckoning, He is not in the least exacting, but generous; however large the amount we may owe Him, it is a small thing for Him to forgive us. And, as to paying us, He is so careful about this that you need have no fear He will leave us without our reward if only we raise our eyes to Heaven and remember Him.

A second reason why we should be resolute is that this will give the devil less opportunity to tempt us. He is very much afraid of resolute souls, knowing by experience that they inflict great injury upon him, and, when he plans to do them harm, he only profits them and others and is himself the loser. We must not become unwatchful, or count upon this, for we have to do with treacherous folk, who are great cowards and dare not attack the wary, but, if they see we are careless, will work us great harm. And if they know anyone to be changeable, and not resolute in doing what is good and firmly determined to persevere, they will not leave him alone either by night or by day and will suggest to him endless misgivings and difficulties. This I know very well by experience and so I have been able to tell you about it: I am sure that none of us realize its great importance.

Another reason, very much to the point, is that a resolute person fights more courageously. He knows that, come what may, he must not retreat. He is like a soldier in battle who is aware that if he is vanquished his life will not be spared and that if he escapes death in battle he must die afterwards. It has been proved, I think, that such a man will fight more resolutely and will try, as they say, to sell his life dearly, fearing the enemy's blows the less because he understands the importance of victory and knows that his very life depends upon his gaining it. We must also be firmly convinced from the start that, if we fight courageously and do not allow ourselves to be beaten, we shall get what we want, and there is no doubt that, however small our gains may be, they will make us very rich. Do not be afraid that the Lord Who has called us to

drink of this spring will allow you to die of thirst. This I have already said and I should like to repeat it; for people are often timid when they have not learned by experience of the Lord's goodness, even though they know of it by faith. It is a great thing to have experienced what friendship and joy He gives to those who walk on this road and how He takes almost the whole cost of it upon Himself.

I am not surprised that those who have never made this test should want to be sure that they will receive some interest on their outlay. But you already know that even in this life we shall receive a hundredfold, and that the Lord says: "Ask and it shall be given you." If you do not believe His Majesty in those passages of His Gospel where He gives us this assurance, it will be of little help to you, sisters, for me to weary my brains by telling you of it. Still, I will say to anyone who is in doubt that she will lose little by putting the matter to the test; for this journey has the advantage of giving us very much more than we ask or shall even get so far as to desire. This is a never-failing truth: I know it; though, if you do not find it so, do not believe any of the things I tell you. I can call as witnesses those of you who, by God's goodness, know it from experience.

Teresa of Avila, 1515–82

4 TREASURY OF TRADITIONAL PRAYERS, USED BY CATHOLICS

1. Prayers to almighty God and the Trinity

In the name of the Father, and of the Son, and of the Holy Ghost.

To the king of ages, immortal and invisible, to God alone be honor and glory for ever and ever. Amen.

Holy, holy, holy, Lord God of hosts: the heavens and the earth are full of thy glory.

Thee, God the Father, unbegotten; thee, the only-begotten Son; thee, the Holy Spirit, the Paraclete; the holy and undivided Trinity, we, with all our heart and voice, confess, praise, and bless. May the most just, most high, and most adorable Will of God be in all things done, praised, and magnified forever.

My God and my all!

My God, grant that I may love Thee, and as the sole reward of my love grant that I may ever love Thee more and more.

My God, my only good, Thou art all mine, grant that I may be all Thine.

Blessed be the Name of the Lord!

My God, I give Thee thanks for that which Thou givest, for that which Thou takest away. May Thy Will be done.

My God, unite all minds in the truth and all hearts in charity.

Teach me, O Lord, to do Thy Will, for Thou art my God.

O most holy Trinity, I adore Thee dwelling by Thy grace in my soul.

O most holy Trinity, dwelling by Thy grace in my soul, make me love Thee more and more.

O most holy Trinity, dwelling by Thy grace in my soul, make me more and more holy.

Remain with me, O Lord; be Thou my true joy.

O God, be merciful to me, a sinner.

O God, Thou art all-powerful; make me holy.

Holy God, holy and strong, holy and immortal, have mercy on us.

To Thee be praise, to Thee be glory, to Thee be thanksgiving for ever and ever, O blessed Trinity.

Benediction, and glory, and wisdom, and thanksgiving, honor, power, and strength be to our God for ever and ever. Amen.

Guard me, O Lord, as the pupil of Thy eye; shield me under the shadow of Thy wings.

Into Thy hands, O Lord, I commend my spirit.

O God, come to my assistance; O Lord, make haste to help me.

Vouchsafe, O Lord, this day/night to keep us without sin.

Deliver me, O Lord, from my enemies.

O Lord, repay us not according to the sins which we have committed, nor according to our iniquities.

O Lord, remember not our former iniquities, and forgive us our sins, for Thy Name's sake.

Praise the Lord, all ye nations; praise Him, all ye people, for His mercy is confirmed upon us, and the truth of the Lord remains forever.

My God, I believe in Thee, I hope in Thee, I love Thee above all things with my whole soul, my whole heart, my whole strength; I love Thee because Thou art infinitely good and worthy to be loved; and because I love Thee, it grieves me from my whole heart that I have offended Thee; have mercy on me, a sinner. Amen.

O Lord, increase our faith.

My God, I love Thee.

O blessed Trinity, one God, in Thee I believe, in Thee I hope, Thee I love, Thee I adore, have mercy on me now and at the hour of my death, and save me.

Take, O Lord, and receive all my liberty, my memory, my understanding, and all my will, whatsoever I have and possess. Thou hast given all these things to me; to Thee, O Lord, I restore them; all are Thine, dispose of them all according to Thy Will. Give me Thy love and Thy grace, for this is enough for me.

Omnipotence of the Father, help my frailty, and rescue me from the depths of misery.

Wisdom of the Son, direct all my thoughts,

words, and actions.

Love of the Holy Spirit, be the source of all the operations of my soul, so that they may be entirely conformed to Thy Divine Will.

We give Thee thanks, Almighty God, for all Thy benefits. Who livest and reignest world without end. Amen.

Teach me goodness and knowledge and discipline, O Lord; for I have believed Thy commandments.

O God, the author and lover of peace, to know Whom is to live, to serve Whom is to reign, shield Thy suppliants from all assaults, so that we who trust in Thy protection may fear no foe. Through Christ Our Lord. Amen.

2. Prayers to Jesus

My Jesus, mercy!

Sweetest Jesus, be to me, not a Judge, but a Savior.

Jesus, my God, I love Thee above all things.

Jesus, Son of David, have mercy on me.

O my Jesus, Thou Who art charity itself, kindle in my heart that divine fire that consumes the saints and transforms them into Thee.

Jesus Christ, Son of the living God, light of the world, I adore Thee, for Thee I live, for Thee I die. Amen.

Jesu, for Thee I live—Jesu, for Thee I die—Jesu, I am Thine in life and in death. Amen.

O Jesus, Friend of the little ones, bless the children of the whole world.

Thou art the Christ, the Son of the Living God.

Jesus, for love of Thee I am with Thee and for Thee.

O Jesus, with my whole heart I cling to Thee.

O Jesu be Thou Jesus to me, and save me.

Christ Jesus, be Thou my helper and my redeemer.

O Lord Jesus Christ, Thou alone art holy, Thou alone art the Lord, Thou alone art most high.

O Jesus, grant that I may be Thine, wholly Thine, solely Thine.

Lord Jesus, may I know myself and know Thee.

May I desire nothing save only Thee.

May I hate myself and love Thee.

May I do everything for the sake of Thee.

May I humble myself and exalt Thee.

May I think of nothing except Thee.

May I die to myself and live in Thee.

May I receive whatever happens as from Thee.

May I banish self and follow Thee,
And ever desire to follow Thee.

May I fly from myself and fly to Thee,
That I may deserve to be defended by Thee.

May I fear for myself and fear Thee,
And be among those who are chosen by Thee.

May I distrust myself and trust in Thee.

May I be willing to obey on account of Thee.

May I cling to nothing but to Thee,
And may I be poor for the sake of Thee.

Look upon me, that I may love Thee.

Call me, that I may see Thee,
And ever and ever enjoy Thee. Amen.

Grant me always to will and desire that which is most acceptable to Thee and which pleaseth Thee best.

Let Thy Will be mine, and let my will always follow Thine and agree perfectly with it.

Let me always will or not will the same with Thee; and let me not be able to will or not to will otherwise than as Thou willest or willest not.

O God, Who didst constitute Thine only begotten Son the Savior of mankind and didst bid that He should be called Jesus: mercifully grant that we, who venerate His holy Name on earth, may also be filled with the vision of Him in Heaven. Through the same Christ Our Lord. Amen.

Soul of Christ, sanctify me.

Body of Christ, save me.

Blood of Christ, inebriate me.

Water from the side of Christ, wash me

Passion of Christ, strengthen me.

O good Jesu, hear me.

Within Thy wounds hide me.

Permit me not to be separated from Thee.

From the wicked enemy defend me.

In the hour of my death call me.

And bid me come to Thee,
That with Thy saints I may praise Thee
For ever and ever. Amen.

Hail, saving Victim, offered upon the scaffold of the cross for me and for the whole human race.

Hail, precious blood, streaming from the wounds of our crucified Lord Jesus Christ and washing away the sins of the whole world.

Remember, O Lord, Thy servant, whom Thou hast redeemed with Thy precious blood.

My Lord and my God!

Blessed is He Who cometh in the Name of the Lord: Hosanna in the highest.

Jesu, bread of life, protect us;
Shepherd kind, do not reject us;
In Thy happy fold collect us,
And partakers of the bliss elect us,
Which shall never see an end.
Thou, the wisest and the mightiest,
Who us here with food delightest,
Seat us at Thy banquet brightest
With the blessed Thou invitest
An eternal feast to spend.
Amen.

As the hart panteth after the fountains of water, so my soul panteth after Thee, O God.

Come, O Lord, and do not delay.

Let not the partaking of Thy Body, O Lord Jesus Christ, which I, all unworthy, presume to receive, turn to my judgment and condemnation, but through Thy loving kindness may it be to me a safeguard and remedy for soul and body. Who livest and reignest world without end. Amen.

Lord, I am not worthy that Thou shouldst enter under my roof; but only say the word, and my soul shall be healed.

The cross is my sure salvation.

The cross I ever adore.

The cross of the Lord is with me.

The cross is my refuge.

Hail, O cross, my only hope!

Through the sign of the cross deliver us from our enemies, our God.

We adore Thee, O Christ, and we bless Thee; because by Thy holy cross Thou hast redeemed the world.

I thank Thee, O Lord, for having died upon the cross for my sins.

O good Jesus, hide me within Thy wounds.

Behold, O good and sweetest Jesus, before Thy Face I humbly kneel, and with the greatest fervor of my soul I pray and beseech Thee to fix deep in my heart lively sentiments of faith, hope, and charity, with true contrition for my sins and a most firm purpose of amendment, whilst I contemplate with great sorrow and affection Thy five wounds and ponder them over in my mind, having before my eyes the words which long ago David the prophet spoke in Thy own person concerning Thee, O good Jesus: "They have pierced My hands and My feet, they have numbered all My bones."

Help us, O Lord our God, and defend with perpetual assistance those whom Thou makest to rejoice in the honor of the holy cross. Through Christ Our Lord. Amen.

O God, Who didst will that Thy Son should for us undergo the punishment of the cross in order that Thou mightest drive away the power of the enemy from us, grant to Thy servants that we may attain to the grace of the resurrection. Through the same Christ Our Lord. Amen.

We therefore beseech Thee to help Thy servants, whom Thou hast redeemed with Thy precious Blood.

O Lord, send laborers into Thy harvest.

That Thou wouldst recall all straying sheep into the unity of the Church and wouldst guide all unbelievers into the light of the Gospel, we pray Thee, Lord, hear us.

Savior of the world, save Russia.

Reward O Lord, with eternal life all those who do us good for Thy Name's sake.

Graciously grant, O Lord, peace in our times, that, aided by the help of Thy mercy, we may always be free from sin and secure from all disturbance. Through Christ Our Lord. Amen.

May my heart be spotless, O Lord, that I may not be confounded.

3. Prayers to the Holy Spirit

O Holy Spirit, Spirit of truth, come into our hearts; shed the brightness of Thy light on all peoples, that in the unity of faith they may be pleasing to Thee.

O Holy Spirit, sweet Guest of my soul, remain with me and see that I ever remain with

Thee.

Come, Holy Ghost, fill the hearts of Thy
faithful and kindle in them the fire of Thy
love.

O God, Who by the light of the Holy Ghost
didst instruct the hearts of the faithful,
grant us by the same Spirit to relish what is
right and ever to rejoice in His consolation.
Through Christ Our Lord. Amen.

O Holy Spirit, Creator, be propitious to the
Catholic Church; and by Thy heavenly
power make it strong and secure against
the attacks of its enemies; and renew in
Thy charity and grace the spirit of Thy
servants, whom Thou hast anointed, that
in Thee they may glorify the Father and His
only-begotten Son, Jesus Christ Our Lord.
Amen..

4. Traditional prayers in the Roman Catholic tradition

Signum Crucis (Sign of the Cross)
In the name of the Father, and of the Son, and
of the Holy Spirit. Amen.

By the sign of the cross deliver us from our
enemies, Thou who art our God. In the
name of the Father, and of the Son, and of
the Holy Spirit. Amen.

Old Roman Breviary

DOXOLOGIA MINOR (GLORY BE)
*In this short expression of praise to the Trinity, the first
part may have originated as a baptismal formula and
the second part as an anti-Arian statement.*
Glory be to the Father, and to the Son, and to
the Holy Spirit. As it was in the beginning, is
now, and will be forever. Amen.

THE LORD'S PRAYER
*The Didache teaches that this prayer is prayed by the
faithful three times each day.*
Our Father, who art in heaven, hallowed be
Thy name. Thy kingdom come. Thy will be
done on earth as it is in heaven. Give us this
day our daily bread and forgive us our trespasses as we forgive those who trespass against us.
And lead us not into temptation, but deliver us
from evil. Amen.

ACTUS FIDEI (ACT OF FAITH)
O my God, I firmly believe that Thou art
one God in three divine persons, Father, Son
and Holy Spirit; I believe that Thy divine Son
became man and died for our sins, and that He
shall come to judge the living and the dead. I
believe these and all the truths which the holy
Catholic Church teaches, because Thou hast
revealed them, Who canst neither deceive nor
be deceived. Amen.

ACTUS SPEI (ACT OF HOPE)
O my God, relying on Thy almighty power and
infinite mercy and promises, I hope to obtain
pardon for my sins, the help of Thy grace, and
life everlasting, through the merits of Jesus
Christ, my Lord and Redeemer. Amen.

ACTUS CARITATIS (ACT OF LOVE)
O my God, I love Thee above all things, with
my whole heart and soul, because Thou art all-
good and worthy of all love. I love my neighbor
as myself for the love of Thee. I forgive all who
have injured me, and ask pardon of all whom I
have injured. Amen.

SYMBOLUM APOSTOLORUM (APOSTLES' CREED)
I believe in God, the Father almighty, creator of
heaven and earth. I believe in Jesus Christ, His
only Son, our Lord. He was conceived by the
power of the Holy Spirit and born of the Virgin
Mary. He suffered under Pontius Pilate, was
crucified, died, and was buried. He descended
to the dead. On the third day He rose again. He
ascended into heaven and sits at the right hand
of God, the Father Almighty. From thence He
shall come to judge the living and the dead.
I believe in the Holy Spirit, the holy catholic
Church, the communion of saints, the forgiveness of sins, the resurrection of the body, and
the life everlasting. Amen.

ANGELIC TRISAGION
*This hymn of devotion to the Blessed Trinity is the
official prayer of the Order of the Blessed Trinity,
otherwise known as the Trinitarians. This devotion
has been recited by them and their affiliates for centuries in praise of the Trinity.*
In the name of the Father, and of the Son, and
of the Holy Spirit. Amen.
V. Lord, open my lips.

R. And my mouth shall declare Thy praise.

V. O God, come to my assistance.

R. O Lord, make haste to help me.

V. Glory be to the Father, and to the Son, and to the Holy Spirit,

R. As it was in the beginning, is now and will be forever. Amen.

The decade below is recited three times, once for each member of the Trinity.

All: Holy God! Holy Strong One! Holy Immortal One, have mercy upon us.

V. Our Father, Who art in heaven, hallowed be Thy name. Thy kingdom come. Thy will be done, on earth as it is in heaven. Give us this day our daily bread and forgive us our trespasses as we forgive those who trespass against us. And lead us not into temptation, but deliver us from evil. Amen. The following part of the decade is repeated nine times

V. To Thee, O Blessed Trinity, be praise, and honor, and thanksgiving, for ever and ever!

R. Holy, holy, holy Lord, God of hosts. Heaven and earth are filled with Thy glory.

V. Glory be to the Father, and to the Son, and to the Holy Spirit,

R. As it was in the beginning, is now and will be forever. Amen.

Antiphon

God the Father unbegotten, only-begotten Son, and Holy Spirit, the Comforter; holy and undivided Trinity, with all our hearts we acknowledge Thee: Glory to Thee forever.

V. Let us bless the Father, and the Son with the Holy Spirit.

R. Be praised and exalted above all things forever.

Let us pray,

Almighty, ever-living God, who has permitted us Thy servants, in our profession of the true faith, to acknowledge the glory of the eternal Trinity, and in the power of that majesty to adore the Unity, grant, that by steadfastness in this same faith, we may be ever guarded against all adversity: through Christ our Lord.

All: Amen

All: Set us free, save us, vivify us, O Blessed Trinity!

BENEDICITE DOMINUM (CANTICLE OF THE THREE YOUNG MEN)

Benedicite Dominum, or the Canticle of the Three Young Men is based on words from the Old Testament book of Daniel (Dan. 3, 57–88; 56). It is used at Lauds in the Liturgy of the Hours for Sundays and feast days.

Bless the Lord, all you works of the Lord, praise and exalt him above all forever.

Heavens, bless the Lord; angels of the Lord, bless the Lord.

All you waters that are above the heavens, bless the Lord; let all powers bless the Lord.

Sun and moon, bless the Lord; stars of heaven, bless the Lord.

Every shower and dew, bless the Lord.

All you winds, bless the Lord.

Fire and heat, bless the Lord; cold and chill, bless the Lord.

Dews and hoar frosts, bless the Lord; frost and cold, bless the Lord.

Ice and snow, bless the Lord; nights and days, bless the Lord.

Light and darkness, bless the Lord; lightnings and clouds, bless the Lord.

Let the earth bless the Lord; let it praise and exalt Him above all forever.

Mountains and hills, bless the Lord; everything growing from the earth, bless the Lord.

Seas and rivers, bless the Lord; fountains, bless the Lord.

Whales and all that move in the waters, bless the Lord; all you fowls of the air, bless the Lord.

All you beasts and cattle, bless the Lord; sons of men, bless the Lord.

Israel, bless the Lord; praise and exalt Him above all for ever.

Priests of the Lord, bless the Lord; servants of the Lord, bless the Lord.

Spirits and souls of the just, bless the Lord; holy men of humble heart, bless the Lord.

Ananias, Azaria, and Misael, bless the Lord; praise and exalt Him above all for ever.

Let us bless the Father and the Son, with the Holy Spirit; let us praise and exalt Him above all for ever.

Blessed art Thou, Lord, in the firmament of heaven; and worthy of praise, and glorious above all for ever. Amen.

GLORIA (GLORY TO GOD)

The Gloria is an ancient hymn praising the Trinity. The opening line of the hymn is taken from Luke 2: 14, where the angels announce the birth of Christ to the shepherds. The Gloria dates back to the second century

Glory to God in the highest, and peace on earth to men of good will.

We praise Thee, we bless Thee, we adore Thee, we glorify Thee, we give Thee thanks for Thy great glory, O Lord God, heavenly King, God the Father Almighty.

O Lord Jesus Christ, only begotten Son, Lord God, Lamb of God, Son of the Father, Thou who takest away the sins of the world, have mercy on us; Thou who takest away the sins of the world, receive our prayer.

Thou who sittest at the right hand of the Father, have mercy on us.

For Thou alone art the Holy One, Thou alone art the Lord, Thou alone art the Most High, Jesus Christ, with the Holy Spirit, in the glory of God the Father. Amen.

IN TE CREDO (I BELIEVE IN THEE)

I believe in Thee, I hope in Thee, I love Thee, I adore Thee, O Blessed Trinity, one God; have mercy on me now and at the hour of my death and save me. Amen.

OMNIPOTENS SEMPITERNE DEUS (ALMIGHTY AND EVERLASTING GOD)

Almighty and everlasting God, who hast given unto us Thy servants grace by the profession of the true faith, to acknowledge the glory of the eternal Trinity, and, in the power of Thy divine Majesty, to worship the Unity; we beseech Thee, that by our steadfastness in this same faith, we may evermore be defended from all adversities. Through Christ our Lord. Amen.

SANCTUS (HOLY, HOLY, HOLY)

The first part of the chant is based upon Isaiah 6:3 and Daniel 7:10. The second part is based on Matthew 21:9.

Sanctus, Sanctus, Sanctus, Dominus Deus Sabaoth. Pleni sunt caeli et terra gloria tua. Hosanna in excelsis. Benedictus qui venit in nomine Domini. Hosanna in excelsis.

Holy, holy, holy Lord, God of power and might, heaven and earth are full of Thy glory. Hosanna in the highest. Blessed is He who comes in the name of the Lord. Hosanna in the highest.

TE DEUM

Te Deum, also sometimes called the Ambrosian Hymn because if its association with St. Ambrose, is a traditional hymn of joy and thanksgiving. It is now accredited to Nicetas, Bishop of Remesiana; (4th century).

O God, we praise Thee, and acknowledge Thee to be the supreme Lord.

Everlasting Father, all the earth worships Thee.

All the Angels, the heavens and all angelic powers, All the Cherubim and Seraphim, continuously cry to Thee: Holy, Holy, Holy, Lord God of Hosts! Heaven and earth are full of the Majesty of Thy glory.

The glorious choir of the Apostles, The wonderful company of Prophets, The white-robed army of Martyrs, praise Thee. Holy Church throughout the world acknowledges Thee: The Father of infinite Majesty; Thy adorable, true and only Son; Also the Holy Spirit, the Comforter. O Christ, Thou art the King of glory!

Thou art the everlasting Son of the Father.

When Thou tookest it upon Thyself to deliver man, Thou didst not disdain the Virgin's womb. Having overcome the sting of death, Thou opened the Kingdom of Heaven to all believers.

Thou sitest at the right hand of God in the glory of the Father.

We believe that Thou willst come to be our Judge.

We, therefore, beg Thee to help Thy servants whom Thou hast redeemed with Thy Precious Blood.

Let them be numbered with Thy Saints in everlasting glory.

V. Save Thy people, O Lord, and bless Thy inheritance!

R. Govern them, and raise them up forever.

V. Every day we thank Thee.

R. And we praise Thy Name forever, yes, forever and ever.

V. O Lord, deign to keep us from sin this day.

R. Have mercy on us, O Lord, have mercy on us.

V. Let Thy mercy, O Lord, be upon us, for we

have hoped in Thee.
R. O Lord, in Thee I have put my trust; let me never be put to shame.

CONVERSI AD DOMINUM DEUM (LET US TURN TOWARDS THE LORD GOD)

This prayer concluded one of St. Augustine's sermons, Sermo CLXXXIII.

Let us turn towards the Lord God and Father Almighty, and with a pure heart let us give Him sincere thanks as well as our littleness will allow: Let us with our whole hearts beseech His extraordinary clemency, that He may vouchsafe to hear our prayers according to His good pleasure. May He by His power drive our enemies far from us, lest we fall under the sway of the evil one in act or thought. May He increase our faith, rule our mind, give us spiritual thoughts, and at last lead us to His blessedness, through Jesus Christ His Son. Amen.

DEUS MEUS, CREDO IN TE (MY GOD, I BELIEVE IN THEE)

My God, I believe in Thee, I hope in Thee, I love Thee above all things with all my soul, with all my heart and with all my strength; I love Thee because Thou art infinitely good and worthy of being loved; and because I love Thee, I repent with all my heart of having offended Thee; have mercy on me, a sinner. Amen.

DOMINE SANCTE, PATER OMNIPOTENS (O HOLY LORD, FATHER ALMIGHTY)

O holy Lord, Father almighty, everlasting God, for the sake of Thy bounty and that of Thy Son, who for me endured suffering and death; for the sake of the most excellent holiness of His Mother and the merits of all the Saints, grant unto me a sinner, unworthy of all Thy blessings, that I may love Thee only, may ever thirst for Thy love, may have continually in my heart the benefits of Thy passion, may acknowledge my own wretchedness and may desire to be trampled upon and be despised by all men; let nothing grieve me save guilt. Amen.

St. Bonaventure

O OMNIUM DOMINE (O LORD OF ALL)

O Lord and Creator of all, and especially of this Thy creature! O God and Father and Ruler of Thy people! O Arbiter of life and death! O Guardian and Benefactor of our souls! O Thou who makest all, and in due season transformest all by the power of Thy Word according to Thy wisdom and deep designs, receive now, I beg Thee, those who have gone before us. Receive us too at the opportune time, until Thou hast restrained us in our fleshly life for as long as it will have been to our advantage. Indeed receive us prepared by fear of Thee and not troubled, nor turning back on that day of death, nor unwilling like those who are accustomed to the world and addicted to the flesh. Instead, may we set out eagerly for that everlasting and blessed life which is in Christ Jesus our Lord. To Him be glory for ever and ever. Amen.

Gregory Nazianzen

PERENNE LUMEN IN TEMPLO AETERNI (PERPETUAL LIGHT IN THE ETERNAL TEMPLE)

O Lord, in the name of Jesus Christ, Thy Son and my God, I ask Thee to give me the love that never fails so that my lantern may always be lighted, never failing, burning within me and giving light to others. Thou, O Christ, our sweetest Savior, deign to light our lamps so that they may burn forever in Thy temple, may they receive eternal light from Thee, the Eternal Light, and by it may our darkness be illuminated and the darkness of the world dispelled from us. O my Jesus, I beg Thee to give Thy light to my lantern, so that I may see by its light the Holy of Holies, which has Thee, the eternal High Priest, entering among the great columns of Thy temple. May I see Thee only, look upon Thee, desire Thee; may I gaze lovingly upon Thee alone and before Thee may my lamp always shine, always burn. O Most Loving Savior, I beseech Thee, be pleased to show Thyself to us who knock, that in knowing Thee we may love Thee only, that we may love Thee alone, that we may desire Thee alone, that we may meditate day and night on Thee alone, and that we may always contemplate Thee alone. Deign to inspire in us as much of Thy love as is fitting to be received by Thee as God, so that our whole being may be occupied by Thy love, so that Thy love may posses us completely, so that it may fill our senses, and so that we may not know any other love but for Thee, Who art eternal. May so great a love in us be unable to be extinguished by the many waters of this earth, sea, and sky. Many waters have not been able to extinguish love. May this too be fulfilled in us or at least in part, by Thy gift, our Lord Jesus Christ, to whom be glory forever and ever. Amen.

St. Columban

ADORAMUS TE (WE ADORE THEE)

Shortly before his death in October of 1226, St. Francis; wrote his Testament which contained his last thoughts concerning the order he founded. In it he urged his followers to remain faithful to the rules of the order and the prayer below is taken from this work.

We adore Thee, most holy Lord Jesus Christ, here and in all Thy churches that are in the whole world, and we bless Thee; because by Thy Holy Cross Thou hast redeemed the World. Amen.

St Francis of Assisi

AUFER A ME COR LAPIDEUM (TAKE FROM ME MY HEART OF STONE)

O Lord, take away my heart of stone, my hardened heart, my uncircumcised heart and grant to me a new heart, a heart of flesh, a clean heart! O Thou who purifieth the heart and loveth the clean heart, posses my heart and dwell in it, containing it and filling it, higher than my highest and more intimate than my most intimate thoughts. Thou who art the image of all beauty and the seal of all holiness, seal my heart in Thine image and seal my heart in Thy mercy, O God of my heart and the God of my portion in eternity. Amen.

Baldwin

DOMINE IESU, NOVERIM ME (LORD JESUS, LET ME KNOW MYSELF)

Lord Jesus, let me know myself and know Thee, And desire nothing save only Thee. Let me hate myself and love Thee. Let me do everything for the sake of Thee. Let me humble myself and exalt Thee. Let me think of nothing except Thee. Let me die to myself and live in Thee. Let me accept whatever happens as from Thee. Let me banish self and follow Thee, And ever desire to follow Thee. Let me fly from myself and take refuge in Thee, That I may deserve to be defended by Thee. Let me fear for myself, let me fear Thee, And let me be among those who are chosen by Thee. Let me distrust myself and put my trust in Thee. Let me be willing to obey for the sake of Thee. Let me cling to nothing save only to Thee, And let me be poor because of Thee. Look upon me, that I may love Thee. Call me that I may see Thee, And for ever enjoy Thee. Amen.

St Augustine

LITANIAE LITANIAE SANCTISSIMI NOMINIS IESU (LITANY OF THE MOST HOLY NAME OF JESUS)

In Scripture we read in Paul's letter to the Philipians "Because of this, God greatly exalted him and bestowed on him the name that is above every name, that at the name of Jesus every knee should bend, of those in heaven and on earth and under the earth, and every tongue confess that Jesus Christ is Lord, to the glory of God the Father" (2:9–11). And then again in Revelation 15:4, "Who will not fear you, Lord, or glorify your name?" The 14th century saw the start of veneration of the Holy Name with liturgical celebration. St. Bernardine of Siena (1380–1444) and his followers promoted this devotion.

Lord, have mercy.
Lord, have mercy.
Christ, have mercy.
Christ, have mercy.
Lord, have mercy.
Lord, have mercy.
Jesus, hear us.
Jesus, hear us.
Jesus, graciously hear us.
Jesus, graciously hear us.
God the Father of Heaven, have mercy on us.
God the Son, Redeemer of the world, have mercy on us.
God, the Holy Spirit, have mercy on us.
Holy Trinity, One God, have mercy on us.
Jesus, Son of the living God, have mercy on us.
Jesus, Splendor of the Father, have mercy on us.
Jesus, Brightness of eternal Light, have mercy on us.
Jesus, King of Glory, have mercy on us.
Jesus, Sun of Justice, have mercy on us.
Jesus, Son of the Virgin Mary, have mercy on us.
Jesus, most amiable, have mercy on us.
Jesus, most admirable, have mercy on us.
Jesus, the mighty God, have mercy on us.

Jesus, Father of the world to come, have mercy on us.

Jesus, Angel of Great Council, have mercy on us.

Jesus, most powerful, have mercy on us.

Jesus, most patient, have mercy on us.

Jesus, most obedient, have mercy on us.

Jesus, meek and humble of heart, have mercy on us.

Jesus, Lover of Chastity, have mercy on us.

Jesus, our Lover, have mercy on us.

Jesus, God of Peace, have mercy on us.

Jesus, Author of Life, have mercy on us.

Jesus, Model of Virtue, have mercy on us.

Jesus, zealous for souls, have mercy on us.

Jesus, our God, have mercy on us.

Jesus, our Refuge, have mercy on us.

Jesus, Father of the Poor, have mercy on us.

Jesus, Treasure of the Faithful, have mercy on us.

Jesus, good Shepherd, have mercy on us.

Jesus, true Light, have mercy on us.

Jesus, eternal Wisdom, have mercy on us.

Jesus, infinite Goodness, have mercy on us.

Jesus, our Way and our Life, have mercy on us.

Jesus, joy of the Angels, have mercy on us.

Jesus, King of the Patriarchs, have mercy on us.

Jesus, Master of the Apostles, have mercy on us.

Jesus, Teacher of the Evangelists, have mercy on us.

Jesus, Strength of Martyrs, have mercy on us.

Jesus, Light of Confessors, have mercy on us.

Jesus, Purity of Virgins, have mercy on us.

Jesus, Crown of all Saints, have mercy on us.

Be merciful, spare us O Jesus.

Be merciful, graciously hear us, O Jesus.

From all evil, deliver us, O Jesus. From all sin, deliver us, O Jesus.

From Thy wrath, deliver us, O Jesus.

From the snares of the devil, deliver us, O Jesus.

From the spirit of fornication, deliver us, O Jesus.

From everlasting death, deliver us, O Jesus.

From the neglect of Thy inspirations, deliver us, O Jesus.

Through the mystery of Thy holy Incarnation, deliver us, O Jesus.

Through Thy Nativity, deliver us, O Jesus.

Through Thy Infancy, deliver us, O Jesus.

Through Thy most divine Life, deliver us, O Jesus.

Through Thy Labors, deliver us, O Jesus.

Through Thy Agony and Passion, deliver us, O Jesus.

Through Thy Cross and Dereliction, deliver us, O Jesus.

Through Thy Sufferings, deliver us, O Jesus.

Through Thy Death and Burial, deliver us, O Jesus.

Through Thy Resurrection, deliver us, O Jesus.

Through Thy Ascension, deliver us, O Jesus.

Through Thy Institution of the Most Holy Eucharist, deliver us, O Jesus.

Through Thy Joys, deliver us, O Jesus.

Through Thy Glory, deliver us, O Jesus. Lamb of God, who taketh away the sins of the world, spare us, O Jesu. Lamb of God, who taketh away the sins of the world, graciously hear us, O Jesus.

Lamb of God, who taketh away the sins of the world, have mercy on us, O Jesus.

Jesus hear us. Jesus, graciously hear us.

Let us pray; O Lord Jesus Christ, Thou hast said, "Ask and you shall receive; seek and you shall find; knock, and it shall be opened to you"; mercifully attend to our supplications, and grant us the grace of Thy most divine love, that we may love Thee with all our hearts, and in all our words and actions, and never cease to praise Thee.

Make us, O Lord, to have a perpetual fear and love of Thy holy name, for Thou never failest to govern those who Thou dost solidly establish in Thy love. Amen.

CONCEDE, QUAESUMUS (GRANT, WE BESEECH THEE)

Grant, we beseech Thee, Almighty God, that we may so please Thy Holy Spirit by our earnest entreaties, that we may by His grace both be freed from all temptations and merit to receive the forgiveness of our sins. Through Christ our Lord. Amen.

Roman Missal

O SANCTE SPIRITUS (O HOLY SPIRIT)

O Holy Spirit, who on the solemn day of Pentecost didst suddenly descend upon the Apostles gathered in the Upper Room in parted tongues as it were of fire and didst so enlighten their minds, inflame their hearts, and strengthen their wills, that henceforth they went through the entire world and courageously and confidently proclaimed everywhere the teaching of Christ and sealed it with the shedding of their blood, renew, we beseech Thee, the wondrous outpouring of Thy grace in our hearts also.

How grievously our minds are afflicted with ignorance concerning the nature and dignity of those divine truths which form the object of faith, without which no man may hope for salvation. How far men go astray from a just estimation of earthly goods, which too often are put before the soul itself. How often our hearts do not beat with love of the Creator as they ought, but rather with an ignoble lust for creatures. How often are we led by a false respect for human judgment, when we ought to profess openly the precepts of Jesus Christ and to reduce them to action with a sincere heart and with, if need be, of our worldly substance. What weakness we manifest in embracing and carrying with a serene and willing heart the crosses of this life, which alone can make the Christian a worthy follower of his divine Master.

O Holy Spirit, enlighten our minds, cleanse our hearts, and give new strength to our wills; to such a degree, at least, that we may clearly recognize the value of our soul, and in a like manner, despise the perishable goods of this world; that we may love God above all things, and, for the love of Him, our neighbor as ourselves; that we may not only be free from fear in professing our faith publicly, but rather may glory in it; finally, that we may accept not only prosperity but also adversity as from the hand of the Lord, with all confidence that He will turn all things into good for those who lovingly tend towards Him. Grant, we beseech Thee, that we, by constantly answering the sweet impulses of Thy grace and doing that which is good with a persevering heart, may deserve one day to receive the rich reward of glory everlasting. Amen.

Stories about prayer and people who prayed

1. The Praying Hands

Author unknown

THE STORY BEHIND THE PICTURE OF "THE PRAYING HANDS"

Back in the fifteenth century, in a tiny village near Nuremberg, lived a family with eighteen children. Eighteen! In order merely to keep food on the table for this mob, the father and head of the household, a goldsmith by profession, worked almost eighteen hours a day at his trade and any other paying chore he could find in the neighborhood. Despite their seemingly hopeless condition, two of Albrecht Dürer the Elder's children had a dream. They both wanted to pursue their talent for art, but they knew full well that their father would never be financially able to send either of them to Nuremberg to study at the Academy. After many long discussions at night in their crowded bed, the two boys finally worked out a pact. They would toss a coin. The loser would go down into the nearby mines and, with his earnings, support his brother while he attended the academy. Then, when that brother who won the toss completed his studies, in four years, he would support the other brother at the academy, either with sales of his artwork or, if necessary, also by laboring in the mines. They tossed a coin on a Sunday morning after church. Albrecht Dürer won the toss and went off to Nuremberg.

Albert went down into the dangerous mines and, for the next four years, financed his brother, whose work at the academy was almost an immediate sensation. Albrecht's etchings, his woodcuts, and his oils were far better than those of most of his professors, and by the time he graduated, he was beginning to earn considerable fees for his commissioned works. When the young artist returned to his village, the Dürer family held a festive dinner on their lawn to celebrate Albrecht's triumphant homecoming. After a long and memorable meal, punctuated with music and laughter, Albrecht rose from his honored position at the head of the table to drink a toast to his beloved brother for the years of sacrifice that had enabled Albrecht to fulfill his ambition. His closing words were, "And now, Albert, blessed brother of mine, now it is your turn. Now you can go to Nuremberg to pursue your dream, and I will take care of you."

All heads turned in eager expectation to the far end of the table where Albert sat, tears streaming down his pale face, shaking his lowered head from side to side while he sobbed and repeated, over and over, "No … no …no … no." Finally, Albert rose and wiped the tears from his cheeks. He glanced down the long table at the faces he loved, and then, holding his hands close to his right cheek, he said softly, "No, brother. I cannot go to Nuremberg. It is too late for me. Look … look what four years in the mines have done to my hands! The bones in every finger have been smashed at least once, and lately I have been suffering from arthritis so badly in my right hand that I cannot even hold a glass to return your toast, much less make delicate lines on parchment or canvas with a pen or a brush. No, brother … for me it is too late."

More than 450 years have passed. By now, Albrecht Dürer's hundreds of masterful portraits, pen and silver-point sketches, watercolors, charcoals, woodcuts, and copper engravings hang in every great museum in the world, but the odds are great that you, like most people, are familiar with only one of Albrecht Dürer's works. More than merely being familiar with it, you very well may have a reproduction hanging in your home or office.

One day, to pay homage to Albert for all that he had sacrificed, Albrecht Dürer painstakingly drew his brother's abused hands with palms together and thin fingers stretched skyward. He called his powerful drawing simply "Hands," but the entire world almost immediately opened their hearts to his great masterpiece and renamed his tribute of love "The Praying Hands."

Source unknown

2. Touching Incidents and Remarkable Answers to Prayer

John B. Gough

THE CONVERSION OF HUDSON TAYLOR

Hudson Taylor, founder of China Inland Mission, says that about 1830 his father became so interested in the spiritual condition of China, that he was led to pray that if God ever gave him a son, he might be privileged to labor as a missionary there; a prayer unknown to the son until after seven years of service in that mission field. Though carefully trained to the study of God's word and a life of devotion, yet at the age of fifteen the lad was a skeptic.

Of his conversion he says: "One day, which I shall never forget, when I was about fifteen years old, my dear mother being absent from home some eighty miles away, I had a holiday. I searched through the library for a book to while away time. I selected a gospel tract which looked unattractive, saying, there will be an interesting story at the commencement, and a sermon or moral at the end; I will take the former, and leave the latter for those who like it. I little knew what was going on in the heart of my dear mother. She arose from the dinner-table with an intense yearning for the conversion of her boy, and feeling that, being from home, and having more leisure than she otherwise would, there was a special opportunity afforded her of pleading with God for me. She went to her bedroom, and turned the key in the door, and resolved not to leave the room until her prayers were answered. Hour after hour did that dear mother plead for me, until she could only praise God for the conversion of her son. In the meantime, as I was reading

the tract, 'The Finished Work of Christ,' a light was flashed into my soul by the Holy Spirit, that there was nothing to be done, but to fall on my knees and accept this Savior and his salvation, and praise God forevermore. While my mother was praising God in her closet, I was praising Him in the old warehouse where I had retired to read my book. When I met mother at the door on her return with the glad news, she said: 'I know, my boy; I have been rejoicing for a fortnight in the glad tidings you have to tell me!'"

Many souls are lost for want of persistent pleading with God in their behalf. Time that might be used in prayer is consumed in other ways, and souls and opportunities pass forever from our reach. For those hours of pleading with God, this faithful mother received not only her son for God, but the great work God put into his hands – China Inland Mission. Hudson Taylor has led out into the heart of China more than one hundred and seventy apostolic missionaries, none of whom receive support except through faith in God.

Anna Abrams, in Vanguard

REMARKABLE EXPERIENCE OF C.H. SPURGEON

On his fiftieth birthday, Rev. C. H. Spurgeon was interviewed in reference to his long and eventful ministerial life, especially as to his confidence in the efficacy of prayer. Being asked whether he had in any way modified his views, he replied:

Only in my faith growing far stronger and firmer than ever. It is not a matter of faith with me, but of knowledge and everyday experience. I am constantly witnessing the most unmistakable instances of answers to prayer. My whole life is made up of them. To me they are so familiar as to tease to excite surprise; but to many they would seem marvelous, no doubt. Why, I could no more doubt the efficacy of prayer than I could disbelieve the laws of gravitation. The one is as much a fact as the other, constantly verified every day of my life. Elijah, by the brook Cherith, as he received the daily rations from the ravens, could hardly be a more likely subject for skepticism than I.

Look at my Orphanage. To keep it going entails an annual expenditure of about ten thousand pounds. Only one thousand four hundred is provided for by endowment. The remaining eight thousand six hundred comes to me regularly in answer to prayer. I do not know where I shall get it from day to day. I ask God for it, and he sends it. Mr. Müller, of Bristol, does the same on a far larger scale, and his experience is the same as mine.

The constant inflow of funds – of all the funds necessary to carry on these works – is not stimulated by advertisements, by begging letters, by canvassing, or any of the usual modes of raising the wind. We ask God for the cash, and he sends it. That is a good, material fact, not to be explained away.

But quite as remarkable illustrations of the efficacy of believing faith are constantly occurring in spiritual things. Some two years ago a poor woman, accompanied by her neighbors, came to my vestry in deep distress. Her husband had fled the country; in her sorrow she went to the house of God, and something I said in the sermon made her think I was personally familiar with her case. Of course I had known nothing about her. It was a general illustration that fitted a particular case. She told me her story, and a very sad one it was. I said: "There is nothing we can do but to kneel down and cry to the Lord for the immediate conversion of your husband." We knelt down, and I prayed that the Lord would touch the heart of the deserter, convert his soul, and bring him back to his home. When we rose from our knees , I said to the poor woman: "Do not fret about the matter. I feel sure that your husband will come home, and that he will yet become connected with our church." She went away, and I forgot all about it. Some months after she re-appeared, with her neighbors, and a man, whom she introduced to me as her husband. He had indeed come back, and he had returned a converted man. On making inquiry and comparing notes, we found that the very day on which we had prayed for his conversion, he, being at that time on board a ship far away on the sea, stumbled most unexpectedly upon a stray copy of one of my sermons. He read it. The truth went to his heart. He repented, and sought the Lord, and as soon as possible he returned to his wife and to his daily calling. He was admitted a member,

and last Monday his wife, who up to that time had not been a member, was received among us. That woman does not doubt the power of prayer. All the infidels in the world could not shake her conviction that there is a God that answereth prayer.

I should be the most irrational creature in the world if, with a life every day of which is full of experiences so remarkable, I entertained the slightest doubt on the subject. I do not regard it as miraculous; it is a part and parcel of the established order of the universe, that the shadow of a coming event should fall in advance upon some believing soul in the shape of prayer for its realization. The prayer of faith is a Divine decree commencing its operation.

Faith Made Easy

The Escape Of The Spree

Mr. D. L. Moody and others, who were on the disabled steamer Spree, believe that the vessel was providentially saved in answer to prayer. In the midst of a severe storm, on November 27, 1892, the main shaft broke, and plunged through the bottom of the ship. The waterlogged vessel rolled fearfully, and the decks were washed by the waves. The passengers became greatly alarmed, the indications being that the vessel would sink before help could reach it.

On Sunday, at Mr. Moody's suggestion, a prayer-service was organized. Every person on board attended, except the officers and crew, who could not leave their posts.

Gen. O.O. Howard, who was one of the passengers, says: "It was the most impressive religious gathering any of us ever attended. Jews, Catholics, and all others forgot differences in creeds and denominations. There was no room for them in such an hour. Mr. Moody read the ninety-first and one hundred and seventh Psalms, which one of the Germans translated verse by verse for his countrymen. Mr. Moody offered a most fervent prayer, and made a short address. God heard us and answered us. I went to my stateroom to rest after the meeting, and I was asleep when some one touched me. I awoke to find a sweet, fond little German girl, the daughter of one of the passengers, by my cot. She could not understand a word of English, but my daughter had drilled her to speak four English words, which was the message she brought me, "The steamer is coming,' and then she added her German 'hallelujah.'"

Mr. Moody says of the rescue: "There never was a more earnest prayer to God than that of those seven hundred souls on that helpless, almost sinking ship in mid-ocean, Sunday evening, November 27th, when we met in the saloon to implore God's help; and God answered us, as I knew He would. He sent us a rescuing ship, and He calmed the sea so that for a week it was as smooth as it is in this harbor, though there were storms all around us. It was the grandest test of prayer I ever knew. My son was with me. He is a student in Yale College, and the learned professors there have instilled in him some doubts about God's direct interference in answer to prayer. After we had prayed that Sunday night, I had reached a point where I cared not whether it was God's will that we should go up or down. I determined to go to rest as though we were sailing safely on our way. My boy couldn't rest. We were fast drifting out of the track of vessels, and our peril was extreme. About 2: 15 o'clock he came and woke me, telling me to come on deck. There he pointed out an occasional glimpse of a tiny light that showed over the waves as our ship rolled heavily from side to side. 'It is our star of Bethlehem,' he cried, 'and our prayers are answered.' Before daylight the Huron, whose masthead light it was, had reached us, and the waves were stilled and the winds were hushed by Divine command, while we were drawn out of the direst peril to this safe haven."

The Spree arrived at Queenstown December 2, with her stern thirty feet in the water, notwithstanding her pumps had been steadily worked from the moment of the disaster.

Northwestern Christian Advocate

JOHN WESLEY HEALED IN ANSWER TO PRAYER

An illustrious example of constancy and power in prayer, we find in John Wesley: "It is said that 'as a matter of habit and rule, John Wesley's ordinary private praying consumed two hours a day.' At times he would gather his company and pray all night, or till the power of God came down. Nothing was considered too great or too small to take to the Lord. Seized with a pain in the midst of his preaching, so that he could not speak, 'I know my remedy,' he says, and immediately kneeled down. In a moment the pain was gone, and the voice of the Lord cried aloud to sinners. Being seized with a pain, fever and cough, so that he could scarcely speak, 'I called on Jesus aloud to increase my faith. While I was speaking my pain vanished away, my fever left me, and my bodily strength returned.'

"The elements, as well as sickness, were often in his way, and prayer removed the hindrances. 'Just as I began to preach the sun broke out and shone exceedingly hot on my head. I found if it continued I should not be able to speak long, and I lifted up my heart to God. In a minute or two it was covered with clouds which continued till the service was over.' And he says: 'Let any one who please call this chance, I call it an answer to prayer.' It was raining, and Wesley and his congregation were crowded out of the church, and the rain ceased the moment they came out. He says in regard to this incident: 'How many proofs must we have that there is no petition too little, any more than too great, for God to grant?'

"Wesley moved things mightily, because he moved God mightily. He became the prince of evangelists, because he was the prince of prayers. He stirred the world with the -fire of his zeal, because he had stirred heaven by the fire of his prayers. His pleas had access to men's consciences, because they had access to God. If more men prayed as John Wesley prayed, there would be more of John Wesley's thoroughly spiritual work done."

Prevailing Prayer, by Wigle

PERSECUTORS PUT TO SILENCE, AND CONVERTED

The following is from the Autobiography of that wonderful revivalist, Charles G. Finney. The circumstances as related occurred early in his ministry, at Gouverneur, N.Y.

I have said that there was a Baptist church, and a Presbyterian, each having a meeting-house standing upon the green, not far apart; and that the Baptist church had a pastor, but the Presbyterian had none. As soon as the revival broke out, and attracted general attention, the Baptist brethren began to oppose it. They spoke against it, and used very objectionable means indeed to arrest its progress. This encouraged a set of young men to join hand in hand, to strengthen each other in Opposition to the work. The Baptist Church was quite influential; and the stand that they took greatly emboldened the opposition, and seemed to give it a peculiar bitterness and strength, as might be expected. Those young men seemed to stand like a bulwark in the way of the progress of the work.

In this state of things, Brother Nash and myself, after consultation, made up our minds that that thing must be overcome by prayer, and that it could not be reached in any other way. We therefore retired to a grove, and gave ourselves up to prayer until we prevailed; and we felt confident that no power which earth or hell could interpose, would be allowed permanently to stop the revival.

The next Sabbath, after preaching morning and afternoon myself for I did the preaching altogether, and Brother Nash gave himself up almost continually to prayer – we met at five o'clock in the church, for a prayer-meeting. The meeting-house was filled. Near the close of the meeting, Brother Nash arose, and addressed that company of young men who had joined hand in hand to resist the revival. I believe they were all there, and they sat braced up against the Spirit of God. It was too solemn for them really to make ridicule of what they heard and saw; and yet their brazen-facedness and stiff-neckedness were apparent to everybody.

Brother Nash addressed them very earnestly, and pointed out the guilt and danger of the course they were taking. Toward the close of his address, he waxed exceedingly warm, and said to them: "Now, mark me, young men! God will break your ranks in less than one week, either by converting some of you, or by sending some of you to hell. He will do this as certainly as the Lord is my God!" He was standing where he brought his hand down on the top of the pew before him, so as to make it thoroughly jar. He sat immediately down, dropped his head, and groaned with pain.

The house was as still as death, and most of the people held down their heads. I could see that the young men were agitated. For myself, I regretted that Brother Nash had gone so far. He had committed himself, that God would either take the life of some of them, and send them to hell, or convert some of them, within a week. However, on Tuesday morning of the same week, the leader of these young, men came to me, in the greatest distress of mind. He was all prepared to submit; and as soon as I came to press him, she broke down like a child, confessed, and manifestly gave himself to Christ. Then he said: "What shall I do, Mr. Finney?" I replied: "Go immediately to all your young companions, and pray with them, and exhort them, at once to turn to the Lord." He did so; and before the week was out, nearly if not all of that class of young men, were hoping in Christ.

Charles G. Finney

JOHN KNOX'S PREVAILING PRAYER FOR SCOTLAND

Among the mighty men of faith and prayer whose names will stand forth until this world's history is completed, is that of John Knox. The days of turbulence developed their holy zeal and courage. Summoned before the highest of earth's great ones, true everywhere to God, and a man mighty in prayer, Queen Mary of Scotland once said of Knox that she feared his prayers more than an army of ten thousand men. On England's throne sat Mary, the daughter of Henry VIII., who had been brought up by her mother, Catharine of Aragon, in the dark faith of Rome, a complete tool in the hands of the priests, whose one design was to destroy the Protestants. Soon the jails were filled, the fires kindled in Smithfield, and the whole land was one scene of desolation, and the Protestants were hunted as partridges on the mountains. The great heart of John Knox was stirred. On his knees, on his face for hours together before God, he pleaded for Scotland. "All Scotland for Christ!" was his ceaseless cry.

In one of these seasons of mighty taking hold of God, he sprang to his feet with the cry: "Deliverance has come! Deliverance has come!" As soon as the courier could speed his way from London to the city where John Knox lived, he made the proclamation: "Mary, Queen of England, is dead!"

Pray ye the Lord of the Harvest, to raise up such men in our days, when the tide of worldliness threatens the whole church, and Catholicism is spreading her baneful influence over the free institutions of our land; only waiting for the chance to re-enact the scenes of St. Bartholomew's day in France, or the massacre of ten thousand Protestants in one day as in Ireland, to crush out the religion of our fathers, to burn the Bible, and plunge the whole land into papal darkness.

Sarah A. Cooke

THE SECRET OF JOHN SMITH'S SUCCESS

This extraordinary man died at the early age of thirty-seven He commenced his labors as a Wesleyan minister in England, in 1816, and closed them nearly simultaneously with his life on the 3d of November, 1831. The following, which reveals the secret of his success, is from "Sketches of Wesleyan Preachers," a very interesting work, by Robert A. West:

"Constant communion with God was at the foundation of Mr. Smith's great usefulness. In this he was surpassed by none of any age. Whole nights were often given up to prayer, and always, when in anything like moderate health often, too, when wasted by painful disease-he arose at four o'clock in the morning, and throwing himself before the mercy-seat, for three hours wrestled with God in mighty prayer. The writer has heard, from persons in whose houses he has been temporarily residing, that in the coldest winter morning they have heard him at that hour with suppressed voice pleading with God, while his groans have revealed the intensity of his feelings. Immediately after breakfast and family worship, he would again retire with his Bible into his study, and spend until near noon in the same hallowed employment. Here unquestionably was the great secret of his power in pubic prayer and in preaching – the Lord, who seeth in secret, rewarding him openly. Every sermon was thus sanctified by prayer.

"On one occasion, when at a country appointment, the time for commencing the service had elapsed, and Mr. Smith did not make his appearance. He had left the house where he was a guest about half an hour before, after being some time in his closet. At length he was found in an adjoining barn, wrestling

in prayer for a blessing upon the approaching service; having retired thither, that unobserved he might pour out his full soul before his heavenly Father. He arose, briefly expressed his regret at not having observed the lapse of time, and on the way to the chapel relapsed into silent prayer.

"During the sermon that evening the fervent prayer of the righteous man proved effectual. The Spirit of God descended upon the congregation; the deep, attentive silence observed at the commencement of the discourse was soon interrupted by sobs and moans, and these ere long were followed by loud and piercing cries for mercy, as one after another the hearers were pricked to the heart, and the strongholds of Satan were beaten down; until, so universal was the cry of the broken hearted, that Mr. Smith found it necessary to desist from preaching, and descend into the altar. As he had continued his discourse for some time after its remarkable effects first showed themselves, there was considerable confusion for want of a leading and controlling spirit, and the disorder was rapidly increasing; but when he descended from the pulpit, and took charge of the meeting, his admirable plans and great influence, aided by a yet almost equal to the roar of thunder, soon wrought a change and in perfect order, though not in silence, the meeting continued until midnight. Whatever apparent confusion there might be in these meetings, they were, actually, conducted systematically. Mr. Smith had his method amid the surrounding excitement, and he never delegated control to another, but was the last to retire from the scene of the Redeemer's triumphs."

Anecdotes of the Ministry

HOW WILLIAM TENNENT DEFEATED THE POWERS OF DARKNESS

During the great revival of religion in America, which took place under Mr. Whitefield, and others distinguished for their piety and zeal at that period, Mr. Tennent was laboriously active, and much engaged to help forward the work; in the performance of which he met with strong and powerful temptations. The following is from his own lips:

On the evening preceding public worship, he selected a subject for the discourse intended to be delivered, and made some progress in his preparations. In the morning he resumed the same subject, with an intention to extend his thoughts further on it; but was presently assaulted with a temptation that the Bible was not of Divine authority, but the invention of man. He instantly endeavored to repel the temptation by prayer, but his endeavors proved unavailing. The temptation continued, and fastened upon him with greater strength as the time advanced for public service. He lost all the thoughts which he had prepared on the preceding evening. He tried other subjects, but could get nothing for the people. The whole book of God, under that distressing state of mind, was a sealed book to him; and, to add to his affliction, he was "shut up in prayer"; a cloud, dark as that of Egypt, oppressed his mind.

Thus agonized in spirit, he proceeded to the church, where he found a large congregation assembled, and waiting to hear the word; and then he was more deeply distressed than ever; and especially for the dishonor which he feared would fall upon religion through him that day. He resolved, however, to attempt the service. He introduced it by singing a psalm, during which time his agitation increased to the highest degree. When the moment for prayer commenced, he arose, as one in the most painful and perilous situation, and, with arms extended to heaven, began with this exclamation: "Lord, have mercy upon me!" On the utterance this petition he was heard; the thick cloud instantly broke, away, and light shone upon his soul. The result was a deep solemnity throughout the congregation; and the house, at the end of the prayer, was a place of weeping. He delivered the subject of his evening meditations, which was brought to his full remembrance, with an overflowing abundance of other weighty and solemn matter. The Lord blessed this discourse, so that it proved the happy means of the conversion of about thirty persons. This day he ever afterwards spoke of as his harvest day.

Anecdotes of the Ministry

PRAYER ANSWERED FOR ONE HUNDRED MISSIONARIES AND MONEY TO SUPPORT THEM

Major O. M. Brown, President of the Ohio Christian Alliance, of Cleveland, O.H, furnishes us the following:

In the spring of 1890, Rev. A. B. Simpson, President of the International Christian Alliance, was burdened in prayer for the heathen, who were perishing without the knowledge of the true God. And as he prayed, he began to inquire: "Lord, what can I do about it?" Then he began to ask the Lord to give him that year, one hundred missionaries for the foreign work, and money enough to pay their transit, and support them one year on the field; which would be about one hundred thousand dollars.

At the New York State Convention of the Alliance, held at Round Lake, in July of that same year, Mr. Simpson gave a very stirring address on the subject, and the people pledged $1,800 in a few minutes. At the Ohio Convention, at Beulah Park, near Cleveland, a few days later, $2,200 was pledged. And at the Old Orchard Convention, in Maine, in the month of August, $35,000 was pledged. Afterward, the pledges kept coming in, until there was upwards of $100,000 pledged. Before the year was out, the one hundred missionaries were many of them, in the field, or on the way thither. A few of them had not yet departed, but were ready to sail.

The work nearly doubled during the year 1892. These missionaries are scattered over large portions of the heathen world-in India, China, Japan, Africa, Palestine, South America, and the Islands of the Sea. None of this great force of Christian workers receive any stated salary for their service; and no member of the Mission Board receives any remuneration for his service. God will honor those who ask large things of Him.

Major O. M. Brown

A BLACKSMITH PREVAILED WITH GOD FOR A REVIVAL

A story related by Mr. Finney, will illustrate the power of the mighty prayer of faith, even when every human aid seems withheld, and nothing remains but the burning, throbbing heart, breathing out its longings, and pouring out its groans and tears before the Lord.

In a certain town there had been no revival for many years; the church was nearly run out, the youth were all unconverted, and desolation reigned unbroken. There lived in a retired part of the town, an aged man, a blacksmith by trade, and of so stammering a tongue that it was painful to hear him speak. On one Friday, as he was at work in his shop alone in his mind became greatly exercised about the state of the church, and of the impenitent. His agony became so great that he was induced to lay aside his work, lock the shop door, and spend the afternoon in prayer.

He prevailed and on the Lord's day, called on the minister and desired him to appoint a conference meeting. After some hesitation – the minister consented – observing, however, that he feared but few would attend. He appointed it the same evening, at a large, private house.

The people gathered from far and near, doubtless to surprise of the unbelieving and faint-hearted. A solemn sense of the presence of God seemed to oppress the as feelings too deep for speech were welling up in many hearts. All was silent for a time, until one sinner broke out in and said, if any one could pray, he begged him to pray for him. Another followed, and still another, until it was found that persons from every quarter of the town were under deep conviction. And what was remarkable was, that they all dated their conviction at the hour when the old man was praying in his shop. A powerful revival followed. Thus this old stammering man prevailed, and as a prince had power with God.

Records of Prevailing Prayer
John B. Gough, 1893

3. George Müller of Bristol

A.T. Pierson

A teacher must also be a learner, and therefore only he who continues to learn is competent to continue to teach. Nothing but new lessons, daily mastered, can keep testimony fresh and vitalizing and enable us to give advance lessons. Instead of being always engaged in a sort of review, our teaching and testimony will thus be drawn each day from a new and higher level.

George Müller's experiences of prevailing prayer went on constantly accumulating, and so qualified him to speak to others, not as on a matter of speculation, theory, or doctrinal belief, but of long, varied, and successful personal experiment. Patiently, carefully and frequently, he is to impress on others the conditions of effective supplication. From time to time he met those to whom his courageous, childlike trust in God was a mystery; and, occasionally unbelief's secret misgivings found a voice in the question, what he would do if God did not send help! what, if a meal-time actually came with no food, and no money to procure it; or if clothing were worn out, and nothing to replace it?

To all such questions there was always ready this one answer: that such a failure on God's part is inconceivable, and must therefore be put among the impossibilities. There are, however, conditions necessary on man's part: the suppliant soul must come to God in the right spirit and attitude. For the sake of such readers as might need further guidance as to the proper and acceptable manner of approach to God, he was wont to make very plain the scripture teaching upon this point.

Five grand conditions of prevailing prayer were ever before his mind:

1. Entire dependence upon the merits and mediation of the Lord Jesus Christ, as the only ground of any claim for blessing. (See John xiv.13,14; xv.16, etc.)

2. Separation from all known sin. If we regard iniquity in our hearts, the Lord will not hear us, for it would be sanctioning sin. (Psalm lxvi.18.)

3. Faith in God's word of promise as confirmed by His oath. Not to believe Him is to make Him both a liar and a perjurer. (Hebrews xi.6; vi.13–20.)

4. Asking in accordance with His will. Our motives must be godly: we must not seek any gift of God to consume it upon our own lusts. (1 John v.13; James iv.3.)

5. Importunity in supplication. There must be waiting on God and waiting for God, as the husbandman has long patience to wait for the harvest. (James v.7; Luke xviii.1–10.) The importance of firmly fixing in mind principles such as these cannot be overstated.

The first lays the basis of all prayer, in our oneness with the great High Priest.

The second states a condition of prayer, found in abandonment of sin.

The third reminds us of the need honoring God by faith that He is, and is the Rewarder of the diligent seeker.

The fourth reveals the sympathy with God that helps us to ask what is for our good and His glory.

The last teaches us that, having laid hold of God in prayer, we are to keep hold until His arm is outstretched in blessing.

Where these conditions do not exist, for God to answer prayer would be both a dishonor to Himself and a damage to the suppliant. To encourage those who come to Him in their own name, or in a self-righteous, self-seeking, and disobedient spirit, would be to set a premium upon continuance in sin. To answer the requests of the unbelieving would be to disregard the double insult put upon a word of promise and His oath of confirmation, by consistent doubt of His truthfulness and distrust of His thoughtfulness. Indeed not one condition of prevailing prayer exists which is not such in the very nature of things. These are not arbitrary limitations affixed to prayer by a despotic will; they are necessary alike to God's character and man's good.

All the lessons learned in God's school of prayer made Müller's feelings and convictions about this matter more profound and subduing. He saw the vital relation of prayer to holiness, and perpetually sought to impress it upon both his hearers and readers; and, remembering that for the purpose of persuasion the most effective figure of speech is repetition, he hesitated at no frequency of restatement by which such truths might find root in the minds and hearts of others.

There has never been a saint, from Abel's day to our own, who has not been taught the same essential lessons. All prayer which has ever brought down blessing has prevailed by the same law of success – the inward impulse of God's Holy Spirit. If, therefore, that Spirit's teachings disregarded or disobeyed, or His inward movings be hindered, in just such measure will prayer become formal or be altogether abandoned. Sin, consciously indulged, or duty, knowingly neglected, makes supplication an offence to God.

Again, all prayer prevails only in the measure of our real, even if not conscious, unity with the Lord Jesus Christ as the ground of our approach, and in the degree of our dependence on Him as the medium of our access to God.

Yet again, all prayer prevails only as it is offered in faith; and the answer to such prayer can be recognized and received only on the plane of faith; that is, we must maintain the believing frame, expecting the blessing, and being ready to receive it in God's way and time and form, and not our own.

The faith that thus expects cannot be surprised at answers to prayer. When, in November, 1840, a sister gave ten pounds for the orphans, and at a time specially opportune, Mr. Müller records his triumphant joy in God as exceeding and defying all expression. Yet he was free from excitement and not in the least surprised, because by grace he had been trustfully waiting on God for deliverance. Help had been so long delayed that in one of the houses there was no bread, and in none of them any milk or any money to buy either. It was only a few minutes before the milkman's cart was due, that this money came.

However faithful and trustful in prayer, it behooves us to be none the less careful and diligent in the use of all proper means. Here again Mr. Müller's whole life is a lesson to other believers. For example, when traveling in other lands, or helping other brethren on their way, he besought the Lord's constant guardianship over the conveyances used, and even over the luggage so liable to go astray. But he himself looked carefully to the seaworthiness of the vessel he was to sail in, and to every other condition of safe and speedy transportation for himself and others. In one case where certain German brethren and sisters were departing for foreign shores, he noticed the manner in which the cabman stored away the small luggage in the fly; and observed that several carpetbags were hastily thrust into a hind boot. He also carefully counted the pieces of luggage and took note of the fact that there were seventeen in all. On arriving at the wharf, where there is generally much hurry and flurry, the dishonest cabman would have driven off with a large part of the property belonging to the party, but for this man of God who not only prayed but watched. He who trusted God implicitly, no less faithfully looked to the cabman's fidelity, who, after he pretended to have delivered all the luggage to the porters, was compelled to open that hind boot and, greatly to his own confusion, deliver up the five or six bags hidden away there. Mr. Müller adds in his Narrative that "such a circumstance should teach one to make the very smallest affairs a subject of prayer, as, for instance, that all the luggage might be safely taken out of a fly." May we not add that such a circumstance teaches us that companion lesson, quite as important in its way, that we are to be watchful as well as prayerful, and see that a dishonest cabdriver does not run off with another's goods!

This praying saint, who watched man, most of all watched God. Even in the lesser details of his work, his eye was ever looking for God's unfailing supplies, and taking notice of the divine leadings and dealings; and, afterward, there always followed the fruit of the lips, giving thanks to His name. Here is another secret revealed: prayerfulness and thankfulness – those two handmaidens of God – always go together, each helping the other. "Pray without ceasing: in everything give thanks." (1 Thess. v.17,18.) These two precepts stand side by side where they belong, and he who neglects one will find himself disobeying the other. This man who prayed so much and so well, offered the sacrifice of praise to God continually.

For example, on September 8, 1840, a specific entry was made in the Narrative, so simple, childlike, and in every way characteristic, that every word of it is precious.

"The Lord, to show His continued care over us, raises up new helpers. They that trust in the Lord shall never be confounded. Some who helped for a while may fall asleep in Jesus; others grow cold in the service of the Lord; others be as desirous as ever to help, but no longer able; or, having means, feel it to be His will to lay them out in another way. But in leaning upon God, the Living God alone, we are BEYOND DISAPPOINTMENT and BEYOND being forsaken because of death, or want of means, or want of love, or because of the claims of other work. How precious to have

learned, in any measure, to be content to stand with God alone in the world, and to know that surely no good thing shall be withheld from us, whilst we walk uprightly!"

Among the gifts received during this long life of stewardship for God some deserve individual mention.

To an offering received in March, 1839, a peculiar history attaches. The circumstances attending its reception made upon him a deep impression. He had given a copy of the Annual Report to a believing brother who had been greatly stirred up to prayer by reading it; and knowing his own sister, who was also a disciple, to possess sundry costly ornaments and jewels, such as a heavy gold chain, a pair of gold bracelets, and a superb ring set with fine brilliants, this brother besought the Lord so to show her the uselessness of such trinkets that she should be led to lay them all upon His altar as an offering for the orphan work. This prayer was literally answered. Her sacrifice of jewels proved of service to the work at a time of such pressing need that Mr. Müller's heart specially rejoiced in God. By the proceeds of the sale of these ornaments he was helped to meet the expenses of a whole week, and besides to pay the salaries due to the helpers. But, before disposing of the diamond ring, he wrote with it upon the window-pane of his own room that precious name and title of the Lord – "JEHOVAH JIREH" – and henceforth whenever, in deep poverty, he cast his eyes upon those two words, imperishably written with the point of a diamond upon that pane, he thankfully remembered that "THE LORD WILL PROVIDE."

How many of his fellow believers might find unfailing refreshment and inspiration in dwelling upon the divine promises! Ancient believers were bidden to write God's words on the palms of their hands, the doorposts of their houses, and on their gates, so that the employments of their hands, their goings out and comings in, their personal and home life, might be constant reminders of Jehovah's everlasting faithfulness. He who inscribed this chosen name of God upon the window-pane of his dwelling, found that every ray of sunlight that shone into his room lit up his Lord's promise.

He thus sums up the experiences of the year 1840:

1. Notwithstanding multiplied trials of faith, the orphans have lacked nothing.

2. Instead off being disappointed in his expectations or work, the reverse had been true, such trials being seen to be needful to demonstrate that the Lord was their Helper in times of need.

3. Such a way of living brings the Lord very near, as one who daily inspects the need that He may send the more timely aid.

4. Such constant, instant reliance upon divine help does not so absorb the mind in temporal things as to unfit for spiritual employments and enjoyments; but rather prompts to habitual communion with the Lord and His Word.

5. Other children of God may not be called to a similar work, but are called to a like faith, and may experience similar interposition if they live according to His will and seek His help.

6. The incurring of debt, being unscriptural, is a sin needing confession and abandonment if we desire unhindered fellowship with God, and experience of His interposition.

It was in this year 1840, also, that a further object was embraced in the work of the Scripture Knowledge Institution, namely, the circulation of Christian books and tracts. But, as the continuance and enlargement of these benevolent activities made the needs greater, so, in answer to prayer, the Hand of the great Provider bestowed larger supplies.

Divine interposition will never be doubted by one who, like George Müller, gives himself to prayer, for the coincidences will prove too exact and frequent between demand and supply, times and seasons of asking and answering, to allow of doubt that God has helped.

The "ethics of language" embody many lessons. For example, the term "poetic retribution" describes a visitation of judgment where the penalty peculiarly befits the crime. As poetic lines harmonize, rhyme and rhythm showing the work of a designing hand, so there is often harmony between an offense and its retribution as when Adonibezek, who had afflicted a like injury upon three score and five captive kings, had his own thumbs and great toes cut off, or as when Haman was himself hung on the gallows that he built for Mordecai.

We read in Psalm ix.16:

"The Lord is known by the judgment which He executeth: The wicked is snared in the work of his own hands."

The inspired thought is that the punishment of evil-doers is in such exact correspondence with the character of their evil doings as to show that it is the Lord executing vengeance – the penalty shows a designing hand. He who watches the peculiar retributive judgments of God, how He causes those who set snares and pitfalls for others to fall into them themselves, will not doubt that behind such "poetic retribution" there is an intelligent Judge.

Somewhat so the poetic harmony between prayer and its answer silences all question as to a discriminating Hearer of the suppliant soul. A single case of such answered prayer might be accounted accidental; but, ever since men began to call upon the name of the Lord, there have been such repeated, striking, and marvelous correspondences between the requests of man and the replies of God, that the inference is perfectly safe, the induction has too broad a basis and too large a body of particulars to allow mistake. The coincidences are both too many and too exact to admit the doctrine of chance. We are compelled, not to say justified, to conclude that the only sufficient and reasonable explanation must be found in a God who hears and answers prayer.

Mr. Müller was not the only party to these transactions, nor the only person thus convinced that God was in the whole matter of the work and its support. The donors as well as the receiver were conscious of divine leading.

Frequent were the instances also when those who gave most timely help conveyed to Mr. Müller the knowledge of the experiences that accompanied or preceded their offerings; as, for example, when, without any intimation being given them from man that there was special need, the heart was impressed in prayer to God that there was an emergency requiring prompt assistance.

For example, in June, 1841, fifty pounds were received with these words: "I am not concerned at my having been prevented for so many days from sending this money; I am confident it has not been needed."

"This last sentence is remarkable," says Mr.

Müller. "It is now nearly three years since our funds were for the first time exhausted, and only at this period, since then, could it have been said in truth, so far as I remember, that a donation of fifty pounds was not needed. From the beginning in July, 1838, till now, there never had been a period when we so abounded as when this donation nation came; for there were then, in the orphan fund and the other funds, between two and three hundred pounds! The words of one brother are so much the more remarkable as, on four former occasions, when he likewise gave considerable donations we were always in need, yea, great need, which he afterwards knew from the printed accounts. "Prevailing prayer is largely conditioned on constant obedience.

"Whatsoever we ask we receive of Him, because we keep His commandments, and do those things which are well pleasing in His sight."
(1 John iii.22.)

There is no way of keeping in close touch with God unless a new step is taken in advance whenever new light is given. Here is another of the life-secrets of George Müller. Without unduly counting the cost, he followed every leading of God.

In July, 1841, both Mr. Craik and Mr. Müller were impressed that the existing mode of receiving free-will offerings from those among whom they labored was inexpedient. These contributions were deposited in boxes, over which their names were placed with an explanation of the purpose to which such offerings were applied. But it was felt that this might have the appearance of unduly elevating them above others, as though they were assuming official importance, or excluding others from full and equal recognition as laborers in word and doctrine. They therefore decided to discontinue this mode of receiving such offerings.

Such an act of obedience may seem to some, overscrupulous, but it cost some inward struggles, for it threatened a possible and probable decrease in supplies for their own needs, and the question naturally arose how such lack should be supplied. Happily Mr. Müller had long ago settled the question that to follow a clear sense of duty is always safe. He could say, in every such crisis,

"O God my heart is fixed, my heart is fixed, trusting in Thee."
(Psalm cxii.7.)

Once for all having made such a decision, such apparent risks did not for a moment disturb his peace. Somehow or other the Lord would provide, and all he had to do was to serve and trust Him and leave the rest to His Fatherhood.

In the autumn of 1841 it pleased God that, beyond any previous period, there should be a severe test of faith. For months the supplies had been comparatively abundant, but now, from day to day and from meal to meal, the eye of faith had to be turned to the Lord, and, notwithstanding continuance in prayer, help seemed at times to fail, so much so that it was a special sign of God's grace that, during this long trial of delay, the confidence of Mr. Müller and his helpers did not altogether give way. But he and they were held up, and he unwaveringly rested on the fatherly pity of God.

On one occasion a poor woman gave two pence, adding, "It is but a trifle, but I must give it to you." Yet so opportune was the gift of these "two mites" that one of these two pence was just what was at that time needed to make up the sum required to buy bread for immediate use. At another time eight pence more being necessary to provide for the next meal, but seven pence were in hand; but on opening one of the boxes, one penny only was found deposited, and thus a single penny was traced to the Father's care.

It was in December of this same year, 1841, that, in order to show how solely dependence was placed on a heavenly Provider, it was determined to delay for a while both the holding of any public meeting and the printing of the Annual Report. Mr. Müller was confident that, though no word should be either spoken or printed about the work and its needs, the means would still be supplied. As a matter of fact the report of 1841–2 was thus postponed for five months; and so, in the midst of deep poverty and partly because of the very pressure of such need, another bold step was taken, which, like the cutting away of the ropes that held the life-boat, in that Mediterranean shipwreck, threw Mr. Müller, and all that were with him in the work, more completely on the promise and the providence of God.

It might be inferred that, where such a decision was made, the Lord would make haste to reward at once such courageous confidence. And yet, so mysterious are His ways, that never, up to that time, had Mr. Müller's faith been tried so sharply as between December 12, 1841, and April 12, 1842. During these four months, again, it was as though God were saying, "I will now see whether indeed you truly lean on Me and look to Me." At any time during this trial, Mr. Müller might have changed his course, holding the public meeting and publishing the report, for outside the few who were in his councils, no one knew of the determination, and in fact many children of God looking for the usual year's journal of "The Lord's Dealings," were surprised at the delay. But the conclusion conscientiously reached was, for the glory of the Lord, as steadfastly pursued, and again Jehovah Jireh revealed His faithfulness.

During this four months, on March 9, 1842, the need was so extreme that, had no help come, the work could not have gone on. But, on that day, from a brother living near Dublin, ten pounds came: and the hand of the Lord clearly appeared in this gift, for when the post had already come and no letter had come with it, there was a strong confidence suggested to Mr. Müller's mind that deliverance was at hand; and so it proved, for presently the letter was brought to him, having been delivered at one of the other houses. During this same month, it was necessary once to delay dinner for about a half-hour, because of a lack of supplies. Such a postponement had scarcely ever been known before, and very rarely was it repeated in the entire after-history of the work, though thousands of mouths had to be daily fed.

In the spring of 1843 Mr. Müller felt led to open a fourth orphan house, the third having been opened nearly six years before. This step was taken with his uniform conscientiousness, deliberation, and prayerfulness. He had seen many reasons for such enlargement of the work, but he had said nothing about the matter even to his beloved wife. Day by day he waited on God in prayer, preferring to take counsel only of Him, lest he might do something in haste, move in advance of clear leading, or be biassed unduly by human judgment.

Unexpected obstacles interfered with his securing the premises which had already been offered and found suitable; but he was in no way "discomforted." The burden of his prayer was, "Lord, if Thou hast no need of another orphan house, I have none"; and he rightly judged that the calm deliberation with which he had set about the whole matter, and the unbroken peace with which he met new hindrances, were proofs that he was following the guidance of God and not the motions of self-will.

As the public meeting and the publication of the Annual Report had been purposely postponed to show that no undue dependence was placed even on indirect appeals to man, much special prayer went up to God, that, before July 15, 1844, when the public meeting was to be held, He would so richly supply all need that it might clearly appear that, notwithstanding these lawful means of informing His servants concerning the work had for a time not been used, the prayer of faith had drawn down help from above. As the financial year had closed in May, it would be more than two years since the previous report had been made to the public.

George Müller was jealous for the Lord God of hosts. He desired that "even the shadow of ground might be cut off for persons to say, 'They cannot get any more money; and therefore they now publish another report.'" Hence, while, during the whole progress of the work, he desired to stand with his Master, without heeding either the favorable or unfavorable judgments of men, he felt strongly that God would be much honored and glorified as the prayer-hearing God if, before the public had been at all apprised of the situation, an ample supply might be given. In such case, instead of appearing to ask aid of men, he and his associates would be able to witness to the church and the world, God's faithfulness, and offer Him the praise of joyful and thankful hearts. As he had asked, so was it done unto him. Money and other supplies came in, and, on the day before the accounts were closed, such liberal gifts, that there was a surplus of over twenty pounds for the whole work.

A.T. Pierson, George Müller of Bristol, Chapter 12

Helping children to pray

Fingers of Prayer

Author unknown

1. Your thumb is nearest to you. So begin your prayers by praying for those closest to you. They are the easiest to remember. To pray for our loved ones is, as C.S. Lewis once said, a "sweet duty."

2. The next finger is the pointing finger. Pray for those who teach, instruct, and heal. This includes teachers, doctors, and ministers. They need support and wisdom in pointing others in the right direction. Keep them in your prayers.

3. The next finger is the tallest finger. It reminds us of our leaders. Pray for the President, the Congress, leaders in business and industry, and administrators. These people shape our nation and guide public opinion. They need God's guidance.

4. The fourth finger is the ring finger. Surprising to many is the fact that this is our weakest finger; as any piano teacher will testify. It should remind us to pray for those who are weak, in trouble, or in pain. They need your prayers day and night. You cannot pray too much for them.

5. And lastly comes our little finger; the smallest finger of all. Which is where we should place ourselves in relation to God and others. As the Bible says, "The least shall be the greatest among you." Your pinkie should remind you to pray for yourself. By the time you have prayed for the other four groups, your own needs will be put into proper perspective and you will be able to pray for yourself more effectively.

Author unknown

Quotations about prayer and praise

A

As well might we expect vegetation to spring from the earth without the sunshine and the dew, as the Christian to unfold his grace and advance in his course without patient, persevering, ardent prayer?

Jacob Abbott

There are three steps to overcoming despair: 1. Fervent prayer, 2. Humble down, 3. Selfless activity.

Adrian of New Diveyevo

It is as natural and reasonable for a dependent creature to apply to its Creator for what it needs, as for a child to solicit the aid of a parent who is believed to have the disposition and ability to bestow what it needs.

Archibald Alexander

The primary object of prayer is to know God better; we and our needs should come second.

Florence Allshorn

As regards the place of meditation we can meditate in every place, at home or elsewhere, even in walking and at our work.

Alphonsus

He who prays is certainly saved; he who prays not is certainly lost.

Alphonsus

Know that it is by silence that the saints grew, that it was because of silence that the power of God dwelt in them, because of silence that the mysteries of God were known to them.

Ammonas, a desert father

Prayer is the wing wherewith the soul flies to

Heaven, and meditation the eye wherewith we see God.

Ambrose

Tedium is the grandson of despondency and the daughter of laziness. To drive her away, exert yourself in work and don't be lazy with prayers: then your tedium will pass and zeal will arrive.

Ambrose of Optina

You are most happy. The solitary and contemplative life I hold the most blessed life.

Lancelot Andrewes, said to a man in prison

Horology, a list of times and a list of places for prayer mentioned in the Bible
Always, Our Lord
Without ceasing, Paul
At all times, Paul
He kneeled upon his knees three times a day
 and prayed, Daniel
Evening, and morning, and at noon, will I
 pray, David
Seven times a day do I praise you, a psalmist
In the morning, a great while before day, Our
 Lord
At daybreak, David
The third hour of the day, Peter
About the sixth hour, Peter
The hour of prayer, the ninth, Peter and John
The evening, Isaac
By night, the servants of the Lord
At midnight, David

Lancelot Andrewes

A list of places for prayer mentioned in the Bible
In the assembly of the upright and in the
 congregation, David
Enter into your closet and shut the door, Our
 Lord
They went up into an upper room, the

1119

disciples

He went up upon a housetop to pray, Peter

They went up together into the temple, Peter
and John

We kneeled down on the shore and prayed,
Paul and the church Members at Tyre

He went across the brook Kidron, where there
was a garden, Our Lord

Let them rejoice on their beds, the saints in
Ps. 149

He departed into a desert place and prayed,
Our Lord

In every place, lifting up holy hands, Paul
Lancelot Andrewes

The purpose of prayer is nothing other than to
manifest God and self.
Angela of Foligno

Through perseverance in true prayer, divine
light and grace increase, and these always
make the soul grow deep in humility.
Angela of Foligno

Enter into the inner chamber of your mind.
Shut out all things save God and whatever may
aid you in seeking God; and having barred the
door of your chamber, seek him.
Anselm

In times of any sorrow, illness, poverty, need,
disagreements, and any difficulty, it is better
to spend less time in ruminating and talking
to ourselves, and more often to turn to Christ
our God in prayer, even if it is only a brief one.
Through that, the spirit of bitter despondency
will be driven away, and the heart will be filled
with joy and with hope in God.
Antony of Optina

It is clear that he does not pray, who, far from
uplifting himself to God, requires that God
shall lower Himself to him, and who resorts
to prayer not to stir the man in us to will what
God wills, but only to persuade God to will
what the man in us wills.
Thomas Aquinas

I have no doubt that the world stands because
of the prayers of Christians.
Aristides of Athens

Prayer is a conversation with God, a piece of the
inner, spiritual life, the characteristic and mark
of a faithful Christian's heart, a continual movement of the Holy Spirit, a work of divine healing.
Johann Arndt

Prayer is a precious work and the highest
honor, to be offered to God alone. It must be
done in the love of God and the joy of faith
with total resignation to God's will and certain
expectation of divine help. Prayer strengthens,
unites people with God and brings them into
the community of angels.
Johann Arndt

Jesus prayed for his enemies, and you do not
even pray for your friends.
Johann Arndt

If one draw near to God with praise and prayer
even half a cubit foot, God will go twenty
leagues to meet him.
Sir Edwin Arnold

We should always believe that our prayers will
be answered, even if they are not answered
straight away.
Johann Heinrich Arnold

We need prayer as much as we need water. All
of us need times of quiet before God.
Johann Heinrich Arnold

I sometimes think God would answer our
prayers sooner if they were directed more to
doing his will.
Johann Heinrich Arnold

God desires nothing more than a heart that
detaches itself in silence from everything and
turns and listens to him.
Johann Heinrich Arnold

The child of many prayers shall never perish.
*Author unknown. Said to Monica, Augustine of
Hippo's mother*

Your desire is your prayer; and your desire is
without ceasing; your prayer will also be without ceasing.
Augustine of Hippo

We do not come to God upon our feet, but upon our affections.

Augustine of Hippo

Prayer is the key of heaven.

Augustine of Hippo

When you pray to God in Psalms and hymns, think over in your hearts the words that come from your lips.

Augustine of Hippo

We pray then to him, through him, and in him. We speak along with him, and he speaks along with us.

Augustine of Hippo

What you love you worship; true prayer, real prayer, is nothing but loving: what you love, that you pray to.

Augustine of Hippo

Do what you can and then pray that God will give you the power to do what you cannot.

Augustine of Hippo

Prayer is a great torment to the devil.

Augustine of Hippo

We may pray most when we say least, and we may pray least when we say most.

Augustine of Hippo

When we pray – whether aloud or silently – to God, our cry must come from the heart.

Augustine of Hippo

What can be more excellent than prayer; what is more profitable to our life; what sweeter to our souls; what more sublime, in the course of our whole life, than the practice of prayer!

Augustine of Hippo

Holy prayer is the column of all virtues; a ladder to God; the support of widows, the foundation of faith; the crown of religious; the sweetness of the married life.

Augustine of Hippo

Prayer is the preserver of spiritual health.

Augustine of Hippo

Do you wish to pray in the temple? Pray in your own heart. But begin by being God's temple, for he will listen to those who invoke him in his temple.

Augustine of Hippo

When you pray to God in Psalms and hymns, think over in your hearts the words that come from your lips.

Augustine of Hippo

Be assiduous in prayer.

Augustine of Hippo

As our body cannot live without nourishment, so our soul cannot spiritually be kept alive without prayer.

Augustine of Hippo

As soon as you begin to pray your fleshly weakness starts opposing you – that's the dross from which God wishes to purify you in the furnace.

Augustine of Hippo

He whose attitude towards Christ is correct does indeed ask 'in His Name' and receives what he asks for, if it is something which does not stand in the way of his salvation. He gets it, however, only when he ought to receive it, for certain things are not refused us, but their granting is delayed to a fitting time.

Augustine of Hippo

Prayer is the protection of holy souls; a consolation for the guardian angel; an insupportable torment to the devil; a most acceptable homage to God.

Augustine of Hippo

True, whole prayer is nothing but love.

Augustine of Hippo

Its purpose is to exercise and train our desires, so that we want what he is getting ready to give us.

Augustine of Hippo

The pure prayer that ascends from a faithful heart will be like incense rising from a hallowed altar.

Augustine of Hippo

Prayer is not merely expressing our present desires. Man is a beggar before God.

Augustine of Hippo

He who loves little prays little, and he who loves much prays much.

Augustine of Hippo

God respects not the arithmetic of our prayers, how many they are; nor the rhetoric of our prayers, how elegant they are; nor the music of our prayers, how melodious they are; nor the logic of our prayers, how methodical they are; but the sincerity of our prayers, how heart-sprung they are.

Author unknown

Lord, grant that my last hour may be my best hour.

Author unknown, Old English prayer

Prayer is like the dove that Noah sent forth, which blessed him not only when it returned with an olive-leaf in its mouth, but when it never returned at all.

Author unknown

B

Our prayers must mean something to us if they are to mean anything to God.

Maltbie D. Babcock

A good man's prayers will from the deepest dungeon climb Heaven's height and bring a blessing down.

Joanna Baillie

When prayer is at its highest we wait in silence for God's voice to us.

William Barclay, The Plain Man's Book of Prayers

Real prayer is simply being in the presence of God.

William Barclay

God will not do for me what I can do for myself. Prayer must never be regarded as a labor-saving device.

William Barclay

Prayer is not flight; prayer is power. Prayer does not deliver a man from some terrible situation; prayer enables a man to face and to master the situation.

William Barclay

When we pray and God delays in hearing (our prayer), He does this for our benefit, so as to teach us longsuffering; wherefore we need not become downcast, saying: "We prayed, and were not heard." God knows what is profitable for a person.

Barsanuphius the Great

To clasp the hands in prayer is the beginning of an uprising against the disorder of the world.

Karl Barth

To clasp the hands in prayer is the beginning of an uprising against the disorder of the world.

Karl Barth

The reason why sometimes you have asked and not received, is because you have asked amiss, either inconsistently, or lightly, or because you have asked for what was not good for you, or because you have ceased asking.

Basil the Great

Prayer must carry on our work as much as preaching; he preaches not heartily to his people, who will not pray for them.

Richard Baxter

Let God have your first awaking thoughts.

Richard Baxter

Let prayer be first, before any work of the day.

Richard Baxter

Men may spurn our appeals, reject our message, oppose our arguments, despise our person – but they are helpless against our prayers.

Sidlow Baxter

The greater thy business is, by so much the more thou hast need to pray for God's good speed and blessing upon it, seeing it is certain nothing can prosper without his blessing. The time spent in prayer never hinders, but furthers and prospers a man's journey and business: therefore, though thy haste be never so much, or thy business never so great, yet go not about it, nor out of thy doors, till thou hast prayed.

James Roosevelt Bayley

Prayer covers the whole of a man's life. There is no thought, feeling, yearning, or desire, however low, trifling, or vulgar we may deem it, which, if it affects our real interest or happiness, we may not lay before God and be sure of his sympathy. His nature is such that our often coming does not tire him. The whole burden of the whole life of every man may be rolled on to God and not weary him, though it has wearied the man.

Henry Ward Beecher

Prayer, as the first, second, and third element of the Christian life, should open, prolong, and conclude each day. The first act of the soul in early morning should be a draught at the Heavenly fountain. It will sweeten the taste for the day. A few moments with God at that calm and tranquil season, are of more value than much fine gold. And if you tarry long so sweetly at the throne, you will come out of the closet as the high priest of Israel came from the awful ministry at the altar of incense, suffused all over with the Heavenly fragrance of that communion.

Henry Ward Beecher

It is not well for a man to pray cream and live skim milk.

Henry Ward Beecher

Prayer covers the whole of a man's life.

Henry Ward Beecher

Prayer ought to be short and pure, unless it be prolonged by the inspiration if Divine grace.

Benedict

To pray is to work, to work is to pray.

Motto of the Benedictine Order

He who prays and labors lifts his heart to God with his hands.

Bernard of Clairvaux

I tell you truly that before you have uttered your prayer, it is already recorded in heaven.

Bernard of Clairvaux

Prayer is a wine which makes glad the heart of man.

Bernard of Clairvaux

Wherever you are, pray secretly within yourself. If you are far from a house of prayer, give not yourself trouble to seek for one, for you yourself are a sanctuary designed for prayer. If you are in bed, or in any other place, pray there; your temple is there.

Bernard of Clairvaux

Prayer is a virtue that prevailed against all temptations.

Bernard of Clairvaux

All decays begin in the closet; no heart thrives with out much secret converse with God, and nothing will make amends for the want of it.

John Berridge

God forbid that I should sin against the Lord in ceasing to pray for you.

Bible, 1 Samuel 12:23

The sacrifice of the wicked is an abomination to the LORD: but the prayer of the upright is His delight.

Bible, Proverbs 15:8

The sacrifice of the wicked is an abomination to the LORD: but the prayer of the upright is His delight.

Proverbs 15:8

He that turneth away his ear from hearing the law, even his prayer shall be abomination.

Bible, Proverbs 28:9

Verily I say unto you, Where two or three are gathered together in my name, there am I in the midst of them.

Bible, Matthew 18:20

Men ought always to pray, and not faint.

Bible, Luke 18:1

It is written, My house is the house of prayer: but ye have made it a den of thieves.

Bible, Luke 19:46

Pray without ceasing.

Bible, 1 Thessalonians 5:17

Let us therefore come boldly unto the throne of grace, that we may obtain mercy, and find grace to help in time of need.

Bible, Hebrews 4:16

Submit yourselves therefore to God. Resist the devil, and he will flee from you.

Bible, James 4:7

The effectual fervent prayer of a righteous man availeth much.

Bible, James 5:16

All earthly things with earth will pass away; Prayer grasps eternity. Then pray, always pray!

E.H. Bickersteth

The effectiveness of the prayer program of a church will be in direct proportion to the depth of the individual prayer life of its members. Without a deep devotional life on the part of the participants, the group cannot muster great prayer power.

Paul E. Billheimer

Prayer is an adventure which brings not a thrill but new responsibilities.

Anthony Bloom

To pray aright is right earnest work.

Jakob Boehme

We have not been men of prayer. The spirit of prayer has slumbered among us. The closet has been too little frequented and delighted in. We have allowed business, study or active labor to interfere with our closet-hours. And the feverish atmosphere in which both the church and the nation are enveloped has found its way into our prayer closets.

Andrew Bonar

God will not let me get the blessing without asking. Today I am setting my face to fast and pray for enlightenment and refreshing. Until I can get up to the measure of at least two hours in pure prayer every day, I shall not be contented. Meditation and reading besides.

Andrew Bonar

We must continue in prayer if we are to get an outpouring of the Spirit. Christ says there are some things we shall not get, unless we pray and fast, yes, "prayer and fasting." We must control the flesh and abstain from whatever hinders direct fellowship with God.

Andrew Bonar

Brethren, why so many meetings with our fellow men and so few meetings with God?

Andrew Bonar

Oh brother, pray; in spite of Satan, pray; spend hours in prayer; rather neglect friends than not pray; rather fast, and lose breakfast, dinner, tea, and supper – and sleep too – than not pray.

Andrew Bonar

We must not talk about prayer, we must pray.

Andrew Bonar

Prayer is the mother and origin of every upward striving of the soul.

Bonaventure

Above all, it is not necessary that we should have any unexpected, extraordinary experiences in meditation. This can happen, but if it does not, it is not a sign that the meditation period has been useless.

Dietrich Bonhoeffer

Pray and do right and wait for God's own time.

Dietrich Bonhoeffer

Is prayer your steering wheel or your spare tire?

Corrie ten Boom

Prayerlessness is a sin.

Corrie ten Boom

A man is powerful on his knees.

Corrie Ten Boon

Any concern too small to be turned into a prayer is too small to be made into a burden.

Corrie ten Boom

Don't pray when you feel like it. Have an appointment with the Lord and keep it.

Corrie ten Boom

Depend upon it, if you are bent on prayer, the devil will not leave you alone.

Mary Warburton Booth

You must pray with all your might. That does not mean saying your prayers, or sitting gazing about in church or chapel with eyes wide open while someone else says them for you. It means fervent, effectual, untiring wrestling with God. This kind of prayer be sure the devil and the world and your own indolent, unbelieving nature will oppose. They will pour water on this flame.

William Booth

Pray as if everything depended upon your prayer.

William Booth

Importunate praying is the earnest inward movement of the heart toward God.

E. M. Bounds

Prayer ought to enter into the spiritual habits, but it ceases to be prayer when it is carried on by habit only.

E. M. Bounds

Desire gives fervor to prayer. The soul cannot be listless when some great desire fixes and inflames it. Strong desires make strong prayers. he neglect of prayer is the fearful token of dead spiritual desires. The soul has turned away from God when desire after him no longer presses it into the closet. There can be no true praying without desire.

E.M. Bounds

Prayer thrives in the atmosphere of true devotion.

E.M. Bounds

No principle is more definitely enforced by Christ than that prevailing prayer must have

in it the quality which waits and perseveres, the courage that never surrenders, the patience which never grows tired, the resolution that never wavers.

E.M. Bounds

The word of God is the food by which prayer is nourished and made strong.

E.M. Bounds

Walking with God down the avenue of prayer we acquire something of His likeness, and unconsciously we become witnesses to others of His beauty and His grace.

E.M. Bounds

We can do nothing without prayer. All things can be done by importunate prayer. That is the teaching of Jesus Christ.

E.M. Bounds

Prayer breaks all bars, dissolves all chains, opens all prisons, and widens all straits by which God's saints have been held.

E.M. Bounds

He only can truly pray who is all aglow for holiness, for God, and for heaven.

E.M. Bounds

The stream of praying cannot rise higher than the fountain of living.

E.M. Bounds

Four things let us ever keep in mind: God hears prayer, God heeds prayer, God answers prayer, and God delivers by prayer.

E.M. Bounds

A life growing in its purity and devotion will be a more prayerful life.

E.M. Bounds

Prayer succeeds when all else fails.

E.M. Bounds

We can never expect to grow in the likeness of our Lord unless we follow His example and give more time to communion with the Father. A revival of real praying would produce a spiritual revolution.

E.M. Bounds

Holy living is essential preparation for prayer.
E.M. Bounds

Prayer is the greatest of all forces, because it honors God and brings him into active aid.
E.M. Bounds

The first and last stages of holy living are crowned with praying.
E.M. Bounds

The conditions of praying are the conditions of righteousness, holiness, and salvation.
E.M. Bounds

Sainthood's piety is made, refined, perfected, by prayer.
E.M. Bounds

The gospel moves with slow and timid pace when the saints are not at their prayers early and late and long.
E.M. Bounds

Heaven is too busy to listen to half-hearted prayers.
E.M. Bounds

Praying men must be strong in hope, and faith, and prayer.
E.M. Bounds

Jesus taught that perseverance is the essential element in prayer.
E.M. Bounds

The goal of prayer is the ear of God.
E.M. Bounds

Prayer should not be regarded "as a duty which must be performed, but rather as a privilege to be enjoyed, a rare delight that is always revealing some new beauty."
E.M. Bounds

If God is not first in our thoughts and efforts in the morning, he will be in the last place the remainder of the day.
E.M. Bounds

He who fritters away the early morning, its

opportunity and freshness, in other pursuits than seeking God will make poor headway seeking him the rest of the day.
E.M. Bounds

The pride of learning is against the dependent humility of prayer.
E.M. Bounds

The world needs more true praying to save it from the reign and ruin of Satan.
E.M. Bounds

We are obliged to pray if we are citizens of God's Kingdom.
E.M. Bounds

The gospel cannot live, fight, or conquer without prayer – prayer unceasing, instant, and ardent.
E.M. Bounds

He who is too busy to pray is too busy to live a holy life.
E.M. Bounds

Prayer is the language of a man burdened with a sense of need.
E.M. Bounds

Prayer is an ardent and believing cry to God for some specific thing.
E.M. Bounds

The neglect of prayer is the fearful token of dead spiritual desires.
E.M. Bounds

If prayer puts God to work on earth, then, by the same token, prayerlessness rules God out of the world's affairs, and prevents him from working.
E.M. Bounds

Prayer is the creator as well as the channel of devotion. The spirit of devotion is the spirit of prayer.
E.M. Bounds

God's cause is committed to men; God commits himself to men. Praying men are the vice-regents of God; they do his work and carry out his plans.

E.M. Bounds

Desire gives fervor to prayer.

E.M. Bounds

Talking to men for God is a great thing, but talking to God for men is greater still.

E.M. Bounds

Prayer which costs nothing gets nothing.

E.M. Bounds

[In prayer] no erudition, no purity of diction, no width of mental outlook, no flowers of eloquence, no grace of person can atone for lack of fire.

E.M. Bounds

Prayers are deathless.

E.M. Bounds

That man is the most immortal who has done the most and the best praying.

E.M. Bounds

To pray is the greatest thing we can do.

E.M. Bounds

Be not afraid to pray; to pray is right;
Pray if thou canst with hope, but ever pray,
Though hope be weak or sick with long delay;
Pray in the darkness if there be no light;
And if for any wish thou dare not pray
Then pray to God to cast that wish away.

E.M. Bounds

Prayer can do anything that God can do.

E.M. Bounds

Perhaps little praying is worse than no praying. Little praying is a kind of make-believe, a salve for the conscience, a farce and a delusion.

E.M. Bounds

Nothing is clearer than that prayer has its only worth and significance in the great fact that God hears and answers prayer.

E.M. Bounds

Those who know God the best are the richest and most powerful in prayer. Little acquaintance with God, and strangeness and coldness to Him, make prayer a rare and feeble thing.

E.M. Bounds

God's acquaintance is not made hurriedly. To be much alone with God is the secret of knowing him and of influence with him.

E.M. Bounds

The men who have done the most for God in this world have been early on their knees.

E.M. Bounds

Praying gives sense, brings wisdom, and broadens and strengthens the mind.

E.M. Bounds

The gospel cannot live, fight, or conquer without prayer – prayer unceasing, instant, and ardent.

E.M. Bounds

The more praying there is in the world, the better the world will be.

E.M. Bounds

The story of every great Christian achievement is the history of answered prayer.

E.M. Bounds

God shapes the world by prayer.

E.M. Bounds

The prayers of God's saints strengthen the unborn generation against the desolating waves of sin and evil.

E.M. Bounds

Prayer is weakness leaning on omnipotence.

W.S. Bowden

As the serpent doth cast up all his poison, before he drinks, so we must disgorge our malice before we pray.

John Boys

When I know what I want I always stop on that prayer until I feel that I have pleaded it with God, and until God and I have had dealings with each other upon it.

John Bradford

All great soul-winners have been men of much and mighty prayer, and all great revivals have been preceded and carried out by persevering, prevailing knee-work in the closet.

Samuel Logan Brengle

Intercessory prayer might be defined as loving our neighbor on our knees.

Charles H. Brent

Pray hardest when it is hardest to pray.

Charles H. Brent

A low standard of prayer means a low standard of character and a low standard of service.

Charles H. Brent

It is of the nature of inner prayer to reveal the hidden passions concealed in the human heart and to tame them.

Ignatii Brianchaninov

It is particularly beneficial to practice the Jesus Prayer aloud when assailed by distraction, grief, spiritual despondency and laziness. The vocal Jesus Prayer gradually awakens the soul from the deep moral slumber into which grief and spiritual despair are wont to thrust it.

It is also particularly beneficial to practice the Jesus Prayer aloud when attacked by images, appetites of the flesh, and anger.

It should be practiced when peace and tranquility vanish from the heart, and the mind hesitates, becomes weak, and – so to speak – goes into upheaval because of the multitude of unnecessary thoughts and images.

Ignatius Brainchaninov

The soul of prayer is attentiveness. As the body without a soul is dead, so prayer without attentiveness is dead.

Ignatius Brianchaninov

Some time in February, 1739, I set apart a day for secret fasting and prayer, and spent the day in almost incessant cries to God for mercy, that he would open my eyes to see the evil of sin, and the way of life by Jesus Christ.

David Brainerd

Every true prayer has its background and its foreground. The foreground of prayer is the intense, immediate desire for a certain blessing which seems to be absolutely necessary for the soul to have; the background of prayer is the quiet, earnest desire that the will of God, whatever it may be, should be done.

Phillips Brooks

Pray the largest prayers. You cannot think a prayer so large that God, in answering it, will not wish you had made it larger. Pray not for crutches but for wings!

Phillips Brooks

I do not pray for a lighter load, but for a stronger back.

Phillips Brooks

Do not pray for tasks equal to your powers! Pray for powers equal to your tasks!

Phillips Brooks

If man is man and God is God, to live without prayer is not merely an awful thing: it is an infinitely foolish thing.

Phillips Brooks

Prayer, in its simplest definition, is merely a wish turned God-ward.

Phillips Brooks

Continuing instant in prayer (Rom. 12:12). The Greek is a metaphor taken from hunting dogs that never give over the game till they have their prey.

Thomas Brooks

There is no prayer acknowledged, approved, accepted, recorded, or rewarded by God, but that wherein the heart is sincerely and wholly.

Thomas Brooks

Cold prayers always freeze before they reach heaven.

Thomas Brooks

God's hearing of our prayers doth not depend upon sanctification, but upon Christ's intercession; not upon what we are in ourselves, but what we are in the Lord Jesus.

Thomas Brooks

Prayer crowns God with the honor and glory due to His name, and God crowns prayer with assurance and comfort.

Thomas Brooks

The most praying souls are the most assured souls.

Thomas Brooks

Prayer is nothing but the breathing that out before the Lord, that was first breathed into us by the Spirit of the Lord.

Thomas Brooks

The best and sweetest flowers of paradise God gives to his people when they are on their knees. Prayer is the gate of Heaven the key to let us into paradise.

Thomas Brooks

God hears no more than the heart speaks; and if the heart be dumb, God will certainly be deaf.

Thomas Brooks

God sees us in secret, therefore, let, us seek his face in secret.

Thomas Brooks

God hears no more than the heart speaks; and if the heart be dumb, God will certainly be deaf.

Thomas Brooks

Though our private desires are ever so confused, though our private requests are ever so broken, and though our private groanings are ever so hidden from men, yet God eyes them, records them, and puts them upon the file of heaven, and will one day crown them with glorious answers and returns.

Thomas Brooks

Cold prayers always freeze before they reach heaven.

Thomas Brooks

God looks not at the elegancy of your prayers, to see how neat they are; nor yet at the geometry of your prayers, to see how long they are; nor yet at the arithmetic of your prayers, to see

how many they are; nor yet at the music of your prayers, nor yet at the sweetness of your voice, nor yet at the logic of your prayers; but at the sincerity of your prayers, how hearty they are.

Thomas Brooks

I have resolved to pray more and pray always, to pray in all places where quietness inviteth: in the house, on the highway and on the street; and to know no street or passage in this city that may not witness that I have not forgotten God.

Sir Thomas Browne, M.D., 1605

I purpose to take occasion of praying upon the sight of any church which I may pass, that God may be worshipped there in spirit, and that souls may be saved there; to pray for my sick patients and for the patients of other physicians.

Sir Thomas Browne, M.D., 1605

Every wish
Is like a prayer – with God.

Elizabeth Barrett Browning

Speak low to me, my Savior, low and sweet
From out the hallelujahs, sweet and low,
Lest I should fear and fall, and miss Thee so
Who art not missed by any that entreat.

Elizabeth Barrett Browning

If I forget,
Yet God remembers!
If these hands of mine
Cease from their clinging,
Yet the hands divine
Hold me so firmly that I cannot fall;
And if sometimes I am too tired to call
For him to help me, then he reads the prayer
Unspoken in my heart, and lifts my care.

Robert Browning

Praying is an activity upon which all others depend.

David Bryant

Prayer is action.

David Bryant

Prayer strikes the winning blow. All other missionary efforts simply gather up the fruits of our praying.

David Bryant

Through prayer any of us can directly love the unreached, even to the ends of the earth. As far as God can go, prayer can go.

David Bryant

According to Jesus, by far the most important thing about praying is to keep at it. Be importunate, Jesus says.

Frederick Buechner

In all your prayers forget not to thank the Lord for his mercies.

John Bunyan

When thou prayest, rather let thy heart be without words, than thy words without a heart.

John Bunyan

The spirit of prayer is more precious than treasures of gold and silver.

John Bunyan

Pray often, for prayer is a shield to the soul, a sacrifice to God. and a scourge for Satan."

John Bunyan

Prayer will make a man cease from sin, or sin will entice a man to cease from prayer.

John Bunyan

Thou art not a Christian that art not a praying person.

John Bunyan

When I go aside in order to pray, I find my heart unwilling to approach God; and when I tarry in prayer my heart is unwilling to abide in Him. Therefore I am compelled first to pray to God to move my heart into Himself, and when I am in Him, I pray that my heart remain in Him.

John Bunyan

It is the great work of the devil to do his best, or rather worst, against the best prayers.

John Bunyan

Prayer is a sincere, sensible, affectionate pouring out of the soul to God, through Christ in the strength and assistance of the Spirit, for such things as God has promised.

John Bunyan

Take heed that thy heart go to God as well as thy mouth.

John Bunyan

Let not thy mouth go any further than thou strivest to draw thine heart along with it.

John Bunyan

In prayer it is better to have a heart without words than words without a heart.

John Bunyan

The best prayers have more often groans than words.

John Bunyan

There is no man nor church in the world that can come to God in prayer, but by the assistance of the Holy Spirit.

John Bunyan

Although it be an easy thing to say 'Our Father' with the mouth, yet there are very few that can, in the Spirit, say the two first words in that prayer, that is, that can truly call God their Father, as knowing what it is to be born again, as having experience that they are truly begotten of the Spirit of God.

John Bunyan

It is expedient then that the understanding should be occupied in prayer, as well as the heart and mouth.

John Bunyan

He who runs from God in the morning will scarcely find him the rest of the day.

John Bunyan

By prayer the Christian can open his heart to God, as to a friend, and obtain fresh testimony of God's friendship to him.

John Bunyan

You can do more than pray after you've prayed,

but you cannot do more than pray until you have prayed.

John Bunyan

It is not the mouth that is the main thing to be looked at in prayer, but whether the heart is so full of affection and earnestness in prayer with God that it is impossible to express their sense and desire

John Bunyan

When I go aside in order to pray, I find my heart unwilling to approach God; and when I tarry in prayer my heart is unwilling to abide in Him. Therefore I am compelled first to pray to God to move my heart into Himself, and when I am in Him, I pray that my heart remain in Him.

John Bunyan

Sincerity carries the soul in all simplicity to open its heart to God.

John Bunyan

Let not your mouth go any further than you strive to draw your heart along with it.

John Bunyan

You can do more than pray after you've prayed, but you cannot do more than pray until you have prayed.

John Bunyan

The truths that I know best I have learned on my knees. I never know a thing well, till it is burned into my heart by prayer.

John Bunyan

They never sought in vain that sought the Lord aright!

Robert Burns

I often say my prayers,
But do I ever pray?
And do the wishes of my heart
Go with the words I say?

I may as well kneel down
And worship gods of stone,
As offer to the living God
A prayer of words alone.

For words without the heart
The Lord will never hear;
Nor will he to those lips attend
Whose prayers are not sincere.

John Burton

Prayer is not a substitute for work, thinking, watching, suffering, or giving; prayer is a support for all other efforts.

George Buttrick

You know the value of prayer; it is precious beyond all price. Never, never neglect it.

Thomas Buxton

C

It must be our anxious care, whenever we are ourselves pressed, or see others pressed by any trial, instantly to have recourse to God.

John Calvin, The Institutes of the Christian Religion

God tolerates even our stammering, and pardons our ignorance whenever something inadvertently escapes us – as, indeed, without this mercy there would be no freedom to pray.

John Calvin

There is no time in which God does not invite us to himself.

John Calvin

Now for framing prayer duly and properly let this be the first rule: that we be disposed in mind and heart as befits those who enter conversation with God.

John Calvin

We have short memories in magnifying God's grace. Every blessing that God confers upon us perished through our carelessness, if we are not prompt and active in giving thanks.

John Calvin

The first rule of right prayer is to have our heart and mind framed as becomes those who are entering into converse with God.

John Calvin

Prayer. The chief exercise of faith, by which we

daily receive God's benefits.

John Calvin

Seeing we are the true temples of God, we must pray in ourselves if we would invoke God in his holy temple.

John Calvin

We must understand that the only ones who prepare themselves for prayer adequately are those who are so impressed with God's majesty that they can be free from all earthly worries and affections.

John Calvin

Tears and prayers are our weapons.

John Calvin

Our prayer must not be self-centered. It must arise not only because we feel our own need as a burden we must lay upon God, but also because we are so bound up in love for our fellow men that we feel their need as acutely as our own. To make intercession for men is the most powerful and practical way in which we can express our love for them.

John Calvin

Prayer is ordained to this end that we should confess our needs to God, and bare our hearts to him, as children lay their troubles in full confidence before their parents.

John Calvin

To make intercession for men is the most powerful and practical way in which we can express our love for them.

John Calvin

I do not believe the devil is greatly concerned about getting between us and work. His great concern is getting between us and God.

Duncan Campbell

Prayer – secret, fervent, believing prayer – lies at the root of all personal godliness.

William Carey

Let us often look at Brainerd in the woods of America pouring out his very soul before God for the perishing heathen without whose salva-

tion nothing could make him happy. Prayer – secret fervent believing prayer – lies at the root of all personal godliness

Carey's Brotherhood, Serampore (of David Brainerd)

Our main business in prayer is not to discern what lies dimly in the distance, but to do what clearly lies at hand.

Thomas Carlyle

If I had spent more time with God for souls I should have had more power with souls for God.

Amy Carmichael

Pray that we may enter into that travail of soul with Him. Nothing less is any good. Spiritual children mean travail of soul-spiritual agony.

Amy Carmichael

It is a solemn thing to find oneself drawn out in prayer which knows no relief till the soul it is burdened with is born. It is no less solemn afterwards, until Christ is formed in them.

Amy Carmichael

Prayer takes place in the heart, not in the head.

Carlo Carretto

There is something much greater than human action – prayer.

Carlo Carretto

I am convinced that the really great issues before us will be settled on our knees.

D.A. Carson

We pray best when we are no longer aware of praying.

John Cassian

God is Spirit, and accepts prayer only with the spirit.

John Cassian

I have made a cell in my heart.

Catherine of Siena

The soul must be kept peaceful during prayer and end prayer in peace.

Jean Pierre de Caussade

God loves to see us like little children in his presence.

> Jean-Pierre de Caussade

The Christian will find his parentheses for prayer even in the busiest hours of life.

> David Cecil

The only instance of praying to saints mentioned in the Bible is that of the rich man in torment calling upon Abraham; and let it be remembered, that it was practiced only by a lost soul and without success.

> David Cecil

God denies a Christian nothing, but with a design to give him something better.

> Richard Cecil

God's way of answering the Christian's prayer for more patience, experience, hope and love often is to put him into the furnace of affliction.

> Richard Cecil

Prayer is not a collection of balanced phrases; it is the pouring out of the soul.

> Samuel Chadwick

Prayer is the acid test of devotion.

> Samuel Chadwick

True prayer is a lonely business

> Samuel Chadwick

The Church gives more time, thought, and money to recreation and sport than to prayer.

> Samuel Chadwick

Satan dreads nothing but prayer.

> Samuel Chadwick

The one concern of the devil is to keep Christians from praying. He fears nothing from prayerless studies, prayerless work, and prayerless religion. He laughs at our toil, mocks at our wisdom, but trembles when we pray.

> Samuel Chadwick

There is no power like that of prevailing prayer.

> Samuel Chadwick

Prayer does not enable us to do a greater work for God. Prayer is a greater work for God.

> Thomas Chalmers

Prayer is simple, prayer is supernatural, and to anyone not related to our Lord Jesus Christ, prayer is apt to look stupid.

> Oswald Chambers

Our true character comes out in the way we pray.

> Oswald Chambers

Prayer imparts the power to walk and not faint.

> Oswald Chambers

Prayer is not getting things from God, that is the most initial stage; prayer is getting into perfect communion with God; I tell Him what I know He knows in order that I may get to know it as He does.

> Oswald Chambers

Prayer is the answer to every problem there is.

> Oswald Chambers

Never make the blunder of trying to forecast the way God is going to answer your prayer.

> Oswald Chambers

It will be a wonderful moment for some of us when we stand before God and find that the prayers we clamored for in early days and imagined were never answered, have been answered in the most amazing way, and that God's silence has been the sign of the answer. If we always want to be able to point to something and say, "This is the way God answered my prayer," God cannot trust us yet with His silence.

> Oswald Chambers

Intercessory prayer for one who is sinning prevails, God says so. The will of the man prayed for does not come into question at all, he is connected with God by prayer, and prayer on the basis of the Redemption sets the connection working and God gives life.

> Oswald Chambers

The greatest answer to prayer is that I am brought into a perfect understanding with God, and that alters my view of actual things.
Oswald Chambers

By intercessory prayer we can hold off Satan from other lives and give the Holy Ghost a chance with them. No wonder Jesus put such tremendous emphasis on prayer.
Oswald Chambers

Whenever the insistence is on the point that God answers prayer, we are off the track. The meaning of prayer is that we get hold of God, not of the answer.
Oswald Chambers

Jesus Christ carries on intercession for us in heaven; the Holy Ghost carries on intercession in us on earth; and we the saints have to carry on intercession for all men.
Oswald Chambers

There is nothing to be valued more highly than to have people praying for us; God links up his power in answer to their prayers.
Oswald Chambers

When we discern that people are not going on spiritually and allow the discernment to turn to criticism, we block our way to God. God never gives us discernment in order that we may criticize, but that we may intercede.
Oswald Chambers

It takes a tremendous amount of reiteration on God's part before we understand what prayer is. We do not pray at all until we are at our wits' end.
Oswald Chambers

The revelation of our spiritual standing is what we ask in prayer; sometimes what we ask is an insult to God; we ask with our eyes on the possibilities or on ourselves, not on Jesus Christ.
Oswald Chambers

Our Lord prayed because He was concentrated on God; that is, He did not worship prayer.
Oswald Chambers

In times of declension we are inclined to place the need of prayer instead of penitent approach to God in the fore front.
Oswald Chambers

The purpose of prayer is the maintenance of fitness in an ideal relationship with God amid conditions which ought not to be merely ideal but really actual … by prayer we lay hold on God and He unites us into His consciousness.
Oswald Chambers

The purpose of prayer is to reveal the presence of God equally present all the time in every condition.
Oswald Chambers

Our Lord did not say it was wrong to pray in the corners of the street, but He did say it was wrong to have the motive to "be seen of men."
Oswald Chambers

It is not wrong to pray in the early morning, but it is wrong to have the motive that it should be known.
Oswald Chambers

To pray strenuously needs careful cultivation. We have to learn the most natural methods of expressing ourselves to our Father.
Oswald Chambers

A most beneficial exercise in secret prayer before the Father is to write things down exactly so I see exactly what I think and want to say. Only those who have tried these ways know the ineffable benefit of such strenuous times in secret.
Oswald Chambers

Prayer is not logical, it is a mysterious moral working of the Holy Spirit.
Oswald Chambers

We lean to our own understanding, or we bank on service and do away with prayer, and consequently by succeeding in the external we fail in the eternal, because in the eternal we succeed only by prevailing prayer.
Oswald Chambers

Prayer means that I come in contact with an almighty Christ, and almighty results happen along the lines He laid down.

Oswald Chambers

See that you do not use the trick of prayer to cover up what you know you ought to do.

Oswald Chambers

Learn to be vicarious in public prayer. Allow two rivers to come through you: the river of God, and the river of human interests.

Oswald Chambers

Prayer is God's ordained way, the insignificant way of prayer.

Oswald Chambers

The purpose of prayer is to reveal the Presence of God, equally present at all times and in every condition.

Oswald Chambers

God answers prayer on the ground of Redemption and on no other ground.

Oswald Chambers

The whole meaning of prayer is that we may know God.

Oswald Chambers

If God sees that my spiritual life will be furthered by giving the things for which I ask, then He will give them, but that is not the end of prayer. The end of prayer is that I come to know God Himself.

Oswald Chambers

When we learn to pray in the Holy Ghost, we find there are some things for which we cannot pray, there is a sense of restraint.

Oswald Chambers

We think of prayer as a preparation for work, or a calm after having done work, whereas prayer is the essential work. It is the supreme activity of everything that is noblest in our personality.

Oswald Chambers

The prayer of the feeblest saint who lives in the Spirit and keeps right with God is a terror to Satan.

Oswald Chambers

No spiritualistic séance can succeed in the presence of a humble praying saint.

Oswald Chambers

Satan tries to keep our minds fussy in active work till we cannot think in prayer.

Oswald Chambers

We look upon prayer simply as a means of getting things for ourselves, but the Biblical purpose of prayer is that we may get to know God Himself.

Oswald Chambers

The battle of prayer is against two things in the earthlies: wandering thoughts, and lack of intimacy with God's character as revealed in His word. Neither can be cured at once, but they can be cured by discipline.

Oswald Chambers

Prayer is the vital breath of the Christian; not the thing that makes him alive, but the evidence that he is alive.

Oswald Chambers

Never say you will pray about a thing; pray about it.

Oswald Chambers

Jesus Christ carries on intercession for us in heaven; the Holy Ghost carries on intercession in us on earth; and we the saints have to carry on intercession for all men.

Oswald Chambers

Intercession means that we rouse ourselves up to get the mind of Christ about the one for whom we pray.

Oswald Chambers

The prayer of the saints is never self-important, but always God-important.

Oswald Chambers

Keep praying in order to get a perfect understanding of God himself.

Oswald Chambers

God brings His marvels to pass in lives by means of prayer, and the prayers of the saints are part of God's program.

Oswald Chambers

The key to all of our work for God is that one word – pray.

Oswald Chambers

To say that "prayer changes things" is not as close to the truth as saying, "prayer changes me and then I change things."

Oswald Chambers

How God works in answer to prayer is a mystery that logic cannot penetrate, but that He does work in answer to prayer is gloriously true.

Oswald Chambers

The point of asking is that you may get to know God better.

Oswald Chambers

A great many people do not pray because they do not feel any sense of need.

Oswald Chambers

The reason we do not pray is that we do not own Jesus Christ as Master.

Oswald Chambers

We have to pray with our eyes on God, not on the difficulties.

Oswald Chambers

Prayer is not an exercise. It is the life of the saint.

Oswald Chambers

Prayer is simple, as simple as a child making known its wants to it parents.

Oswald Chambers

It's no use praying unless we are living as children of God.

Oswald Chambers

When a person is at his wits' end, it is not a cowardly thing to pray. It is the only way to get into touch with reality.

Oswald Chambers

Specific times and places and communion with God go together. It is by no haphazard chance that in every age men have risen early to pray. The first thing that marks decline in spiritual life is our relationship to the early morning.

Oswald Chambers

Let our prayers, like the ancient sacrifices, ascend morning and evening. Let our days begin and end with God.

William Ellery Channing

Enter into your prayer by faith, remain in it in hope, and do not abandon it except for that charity which serves and endures.

Jane Frances de Chantal

In prayer, more is accomplished by listening than by talking.

Jane Frances de Chantal

Let us be sure that we understand what an honor it is for us to spend time in prayer, as much as we wish, as intimately as we wish.

Jane Frances de Chantal

A good and perfect prayer requires that we forget self, that we be ready to sacrifice all that we are for God.

Jane Frances de Chantal

Pray as you can, and do not try to pray as you can't.

John Jay Chapman

The less you pray the worse it goes.
The longer one prays, the better it goes.

John Jay Chapman

Whoso will pray, he must fast and be clean,
And fast his soul, and make his body lean.

Geoffrey Chaucer

Nothing you can do will benefit you more than prayer.

Paul Y. Cho

Too busy; O forgive, Dear Lord, that I should ever be, too much engrossed in earthly tasks, to spend an hour with thee.

A.B. Christiansen

It is a very good thing to ask.

John Chrysostom

The just man does not desist from praying until he ceases to be just.

John Chrysostom

No one should give the answer that it is impossible for a man occupied with worldly cares to pray always. You can set up an altar to God in your mind by means of prayer. And so it is fitting to pray at your trade, on a journey, standing at a counter or sitting at your handicraft.

John Chrysostom

It is possible to offer fervent prayer even while walking in public or strolling alone, or seated in your shop, while buying or selling, or even while cooking.

John Chrysostom

Even if we have thousands of acts of great virtue to our credit, our confidence in being heard must be based on God's mercy and God's love for us.

John Chrysostom

Prayer is the root, the fountain, the mother of a thousand blessings.

John Chrysostom

Prayer is a refuge for those who are shaken, an anchor for those tossed by waves, a walking stick for the infirm, a treasure house for the poor, a stronghold for the rich, a destroyer of sicknesses, a preserver of health.

John Chrysostom

Prayer keeps our virtues intact and quickly removes all evil.

John Chrysostom

If temptation overtakes us, prayer easily drives it away; if we lose some property or something else, which causes our soul grief, prayer removes it.

John Chrysostom

Prayer banishes every sorrow, causes good humor, facilitates constant well-being.

John Chrysostom

Prayer is the mother of the love of wisdom.

John Chrysostom

He who can sincerely pray is richer than everyone else, even though he is the poorest of all. On the contrary, he who does not have recourse to prayer, even though he sit on a king's throne, is the poorest of all.

John Chrysostom

Whether or not our prayer is heard depends not on the number of words, but on the fervor of our souls.

John Chrysostom

Prayer is a great weapon, a rich treasure, a wealth that is never exhausted, an undisturbed refuge, a cause of tranquility, the root of a multitude of blessings, and their source.

John Chrysostom

Prayer requires more of the heart than of the tongue.

Adam Clarke

They who pray not, know nothing of God, and know nothing of the state of their own souls.

Adam Clarke

Prayer that runs its course till the last day of life needs a strong and tranquil soul.

Clement of Alexandria

Prayer is conversation with God.

Clement of Alexandria

We know the utility of prayer from the efforts of the wicked spirits to distract us during the divine office; and we experience the fruit of prayer in the defeat of our enemies.

John Climacus

Perseverance in prayer is the annihilation of sloth.

John Climacus

Prayer is communication with God in worship.

E.P. Clowney

Prayer is the living breath of Christ's church.

E.P. Clowney

Wishing will never be a substitute for prayer.

Edwin Louis Cole

Prayer – the very highest energy of which the mind is capable.

Samuel Taylor Coleridge

Prayer is the effort to live in the spirit of the whole.

Samuel Taylor Coleridge

He prayeth best, who loveth best
All things both great and small;
For the dear God who loveth us,
He made and loveth all.

Samuel Taylor Coleridge

To pray as God would have us, with all the heart and strength and reason and will, and to believe that God will listen to our voice through Christ, and verily do the thing he pleaseth thereon, this is the last, the greatest achievement of the Christian's warfare on earth.

Samuel Taylor Coleridge

We should pray with as much earnestness as those who expect everything from God; and should act with as much energy as those who expect everything from themselves.

Charles Caleb Colton

If we address [God] as children, it is because he tells us he is our father.

William Cowper

Have you no words, ah! think again!
Words flow apace when you complain
And fill your fellow creature's ear
With the sad tale of all your care.

Were half the breath thus vainly spent
To heaven in supplication sent,
Your cheerful song would oftener be,
"Hear what the Lord has done for me!"

William Cowper

If we unbosom ourselves to him [God] as a friend, it is because he calls us friends.

William Cowper

And Satan trembles when he sees
The weakest saint upon his knees.

William Cowper

Keep praying, but be thankful that God's answers are wiser than your prayers.

William Culbertson

Only turning God's house into a house of fervent prayer will reverse the power of evil so evident in the world today.

Jim Cymbala

The devil is not terribly frightened of our human efforts and credentials. But he knows his kingdom will be damaged when we begin to lift up our hearts to God.

Jim Cymbala

I learned as never before that persistent calling upon the Lord breaks through every stronghold of the devil, for nothing is impossible with God. For Christians in these troubled times, there is simply no other way.

Jim Cymbala

If He prayed who was without sin, how much more it becometh a sinner to pray.

Cyprian

Christ taught that we should pray alone and silently, and by ourselves; and, so to speak, conversing alone with God alone, with pure and undistracted mind.

Cyril of Alexandria

D

Prayer is the raising of one's mind and heart to God or the requesting of good things from God.

John Damascus

Much prayer much power.

Peter Deyneka

Sometimes the soul is set on fire with the love of God with a force that moves unerringly, but invisibly, so that even the body is, as it were, swept along into the abyss of that unspeakable love. We can experience the force of that holy grace when we are most vigilant, or even, as I have spoken of on other occasions, in the way that sleep starts to affect us. But when you feel this movement, know for certain, and it is a point of utmost importance, that it is the motion of the Holy Spirit of God within us.

Diadochos
of Photike

Prayer is the key to success. Not to pray is to fail. To pray aright is never to fail.

A.C. Dixon

The place of real prayer is the Christian's treasure chamber. He is there in the midst of the treasures of grace which God has given him, and it is there that God enriches him more and more; but in the secret place of the Most High where he dwells, he is rich in love, joy, peace, and all the fruits of the Spirit.

A.C. Dixon

When we rely upon organization, we get what organization can do; when we rely upon education, we get what education can do; when we rely upon eloquence, we get what eloquence can do. And so on. But when we rely upon prayer, we get what God can do.

A.C. Dixon

When I awake in the morning, I address myself to him, and converse with him, speak to him while I am lighting my candle and putting on my clothes.

Philip Doddridge

I throw myself down in my chamber, and I call in and invite God and His Angels thither; and when they are there, I neglect God and His Angels for the noise of a fly, for the rattling of a coach, for the whining of a door.

John Donne

A memory of yesterday's pleasures, a fear of tomorrow's dangers, a straw under my knees, a noise in my ear, a light in my eye, an anything, a nothing, a fancy, a chimera in my brain, troubles me in my prayers.

John Donne

Do not forget prayer. Every time you pray, if your prayer is sincere, there will be new feeling and new meaning in it, which will give your fresh courage.

Fyodor Dostoevsky

Be not forgetful of prayer.

Fyodor Dostoevsky

Every time you pray, if your prayer is sincere, there will be new feeling and new meaning in it which will give you fresh courage, and you will understand that prayer is an education.

Fyodor Dostoevsky

Waiting on God prepares for greater blessing.

Wesley L. Duewel

You are the key to the prayer ministry of your people. Don't expect your people to hunger for what they fail to see in you. They must sense your joy in the Lord, your intimacy with God, your love for Jesus and for themselves. They must sense your vibrant faith as you pray – that you really expect and get answers to your prayers. They must sense these things in your normal public praying; then they will begin to hunger to go deeper in prayer themselves.

Wesley L. Duewel

Prayer has mighty power to move mountains because the Holy Spirit is ready both to encourage our praying and to remove the mountains hindering us. Prayer has the power to change mountains into highways.

Wesley L. Duewel

Prevailing prayer is prayer that pushes right through all difficulties and obstacles, drives back all the opposing forces of Satan, and secures the will of God. Its purpose is to accomplish God's will on earth. Prevailing prayer is prayer that not only takes the initiative but continues on the offensive for God until spiritual victory is won.

Wesley L. Duewel

Many Christians are so spiritually frail, sickly, and lacking in spiritual vitality that they cannot stick to prayer for more than a few minutes at a time.

Wesley L. Duewel

Prayer is the supreme way to be workers together with God.

Wesley L. Duewel

Prayer is the master strategy that God gives for the defeat and rout of Satan.

Wesley L. Duewel

Prayer is God's ordained way to bring His miracle power to bear in human need.

Wesley L. Duewel

All you need to do to learn to pray is to pray.

Wesley L. Duewel

Prayer is the only adequate way to multiply our efforts fast enough to reap the harvest God desires.

Wesley L. Duewel

We can reach our world, if we will. The greatest lack today is not people or funds. The greatest need is prayer.

Wesley Duewel

All the duties of religion are eminently solemn and venerable in the eyes of children. But none will so strongly prove the sincerity of the parent; none so powerfully awaken the reverence of the child; none so happily recommend the instruction he receives, as family devotions, particularly those in which petitions for the children occupy a distinguished place.

Timothy Dwight

E

The greatest hindrance to effective prayer is sin.

Dick Eastman

To pray with bitterness toward fellowmen nullifies hours on our knees.

Dick Eastman

Satan's greatest goal is to keep us from our knees.

Dick Eastman

The greatest blow sent Satan-ward is made by weeping warriors of prayer.

Dick Eastman

If the only prayer we say is "thank you" that would be enough.

Meister Eckhart

The very best and utmost attainment in this life is to remain still and let God act and speak in thee.

Meister Eckhart

I would sooner say five words devoutly in my heart than five thousand words which my soul does not relish with affection and understanding.

Edmund the Martyr

Countless numbers are deceived in multiplying prayers. I would rather say five words devoutly with my heart, than five thousand which my soul does not relish with affection and understanding. "Sing to the Lord wisely," says the Royal Psalmist. What a man repeats by his mouth, that let him feel in his soul.

Edmund the Martyr

Prayer is as natural an expression of faith as breathing is of life.

Jonathan Edwards

But whatever our hopes may be, we must be content to be ignorant of the times and seasons, which the Father hath put in His power; and must be willing that God should answer prayer, and fulfill His own glorious promises, in His own time.

Jonathan Edwards

When God has something very great to accomplish for His church, it is His will that there should precede it, the extraordinary prayers of His people.

Jonathan Edwards

I should think the people of God in this land would be in the way of their duty to do three times as much fasting and prayer as they do.

Jonathan Edwards

He that casts off prayer, in effect casts off all the worship of God, of which prayer is the principal duty.

Jonathan Edwards

The true spirit of prayer is no other than God's own Spirit dwelling in the hearts of the saints.

Jonathan Edwards

There is no way that Christians, in a private capacity, can do so much to promote the work of God and advance the kingdom of Christ as by prayer.

Jonathan Edwards

Never think that God's delays are God's denials. True prayer always receives what it asks, or something better.

Tryon Edwards

God is infinitely great in Himself; we should recognize it in humble adoration: always good; we should acknowledge it by grateful thanksgiving: we have constant need of his blessings; it becomes us to ask them at His hand.

Tryon Edwards

Prayer is as much the instinct of my nature as a Christian, as it is a duty enjoined by the command of God. It is the language of worship, as a man; of dependence, as a creature; of submission, as a subject; of confession, as a sinner; of thankfulness, as the recipient of mercies; of supplication, as a needy being.

Tryon Edwards

The end of our prayers is often gained by an answer very different from what we expect. "Lord, what wilt thou have me to do?" was the question of Paul; and a large part of the answer was, "I will show him how great things he must suffer."

Tryon Edwards

Prayer is the greatest way I know to demonstrate my dependence on God. My greatest declaration of independence would be to stop praying.

Leroy Eims

A Christian's prayer life has two sides. The one is the prayer. The other is the prayer answer.

Ulf Ekman

The mystery of prayer brings the infinite into contact with the infinite, the temporal with the eternal, the seen with the unseen.

Elisabeth Elliot

It is God who gives our prayer its value and its character, not our interior dispositions, not our fervor, not our lucidity.

Jacques Ellul

No man ever prayed heartily without learning something.

Ralph Waldo Emerson

Prayer is the counter poison of pride; the antidote to the passion of hatred; the best rule in making just laws; the best and most powerful means to govern aright; the standard and trophy in war; a stronghold for peace; the seal of virginity; the guard of nuptial fidelity; the safeguard of travelers; the guardian angel during sleep; the source of fertility for the farmer; a safe harbor on the storms of this life; a city of refuge for criminals; the source of all true joy; the best friend and physician of the dying.

Ephrem

Prayer is the source of all true joy.

Ephrem

It is only by sustained prayer that we gain control of our distracted thoughts.

Ephrem

Prayer is the laying aside of thoughts.

Evagrios of Pontus

Persevere with patience in your prayer, and repulse the cares and doubts that arise within you.

Evagrios the Solitary

If you long for prayer, renounce all to gain all.

Evagrios the Solitary

The warfare between us and the demons is waged solely on account of spiritual prayer, for prayer is extremely hateful and offensive to them, though it leads us to salvation and peace.

Evagrios the Solitary

F

As soon as we are with God in faith and in love, we are in prayer.

François Fénelon

The lukewarmness of our prayers is the source of all our other infidelities.

François Fénelon

Of all the duties enjoined by Christianity, none is more essential and yet more neglected, than prayer.

François Fénelon

Of all the duties enjoined by Christianity none is more essential and yet more neglected than prayer.

François Fénelon

Tell God all that is in your heart, as one unloads one's heart, its pleasures and its pains to a dear friend. Tell Him your troubles that He may comfort you; tell Him your joys that He may sober them; tell Him your longings that He may purify them; tell Him your dislikes, that He may help you conquer them; talk to Him of your temptations, that He may shield you from them; show Him the wounds of your heart, that He may heal them; Tell him how self-love makes you unjust to others, how vanity tempts you to be insincere, how pride disguises you to yourself and to others … People who have no secrets from each other never want for subjects of conversation. They do not weigh their words …They talk out of the abundance of the heart; Blessed are they who attain to such familiar, unreserved [conversation] with God.

François Fénelon

Our intercourse with God resembles that with a friend; at first, there are a thousand things to be told, and as many to be asked; but after a time, these diminish, while the pleasure of being together does not. Everything has been said, but the satisfaction of seeing each other, of feeling that one is near the other, or reposing in the enjoyment of a pure and sweet friendship, can be felt without conversation; the silence is eloquent and mutually understood. Each feels that the other is in perfect sympathy with him, and that their two hearts are incessantly pored

one into the other, and constitute but one.

François Fénelon

God never ceases to speak to us, but the noise of the world without and the tumult of our passions within bewilder us and prevent us from listening to him.

François Fénelon

If you are to pray in a profitable way it is best for you, from the start, to think of yourself as a poor, naked, miserable wretch, dying of hunger, who knows about one person who can help you and relieve you of your suffering.

François Fénelon

To realize God's presence is the one sovereign remedy against temptation.

François Fénelon

Accustom yourself gradually to carry prayer into all your daily occupation – speak, act, work in peace, as if you were in prayer, as indeed you ought to be.

François Fénelon

Tell God your troubles, that God may comfort you;
Tell God your joys, that God may sober them;
Tell God your longings, that God may purify them;
Tell God your dislikes, that God may help you conquer them;
Talk to God of your temptations, that God may shield you;
Show God the wounds on your heart, that God may heal them;
Lay bare your indifference to good … your instability.
Tell God how self-love makes you unjust to others, how vanity tempts you to be insincere, and how pride disguises you to yourself as to others.

François Fénelon

You must literally prostrate yourself before him in the quietness of your own room, and through this outward physical action express the humiliation of your soul as you view the terrible sight of your own faults.

François Fénelon

Trouble and perplexity drive me to prayer, and prayer drives away perplexity and trouble.

François Fénelon

I have known persons pray for hours, till their strength was all exhausted with the agony of their minds. Such prayers prevailed with God.

Charles G. Finney

If the spirit of prayer departs, it is a sure indication of a backslidden heart, for while the first love of a Christian continues he is sure to be drawn by the Holy Spirit to wrestle much in prayer.

Charles G. Finney

To pray as a duty and as if obliging God by our prayer, is quite ridiculous, and is certain indication of a backslidden heart.

Charles G. Finney

Probably in the Day of Judgment it will be found that nothing is ever done by the truth, used ever so zealously, unless there is a spirit of prayer somewhere in connection with the presentation of truth.

Charles G. Finney

A prayer-meeting is an index to the state of religion in a Church.

Charles G. Finney

Prevailing, or effectual prayer, is that prayer which attains the blessing that it seeks.

Charles G. Finney

Many persons, being told that God answers prayer for Christ's sake, overlook the condition of obedience.

Charles G. Finney

It is only those that live and walk with God whose prayers are of any avail to themselves, to the church, or to the world.

Charles G. Finney

I have never known a person sweat blood; but I have known a person pray till the blood started from his nose. And I have known persons to pray till they were all wet with perspiration, in the coldest weather in winter. I have known

persons pray for hours, till their strength was all exhausted with the agony of their minds. Such prayers prevailed with God.

Charles G. Finney

That, which begins not with prayer, seldom winds up with comfort.

John Flavel

Take it for a clear truth – that which is not prefaced with prayer will be followed with trouble.

John Flavel

The devil is aware that one hour of close fellowship, hearty converse with God in prayer, is able to pull down what he hath been contriving and building many a year.

John Flavel

Our worst sin is prayerlessness.

P.T. Forsyth

To begin the day with prayer is but a formality unless it go on in prayer, unless for the rest of it we pray in deed what we began in word.

P.T. Forsyth

God save us from the people who would renew the church and bring justice in the world without praying.

P.T. Forsyth

We shall come one day to a heaven where we shall gratefully know that God's great refusals were sometimes the true answers to our truest prayer.

P.T. Forsyth

Do you know why the mighty God of the universe chooses to answer prayer? It is because his children ask.

Richard J. Foster

God receives us just as we are and accepts our prayers just as they are. In the same way that a small child cannot draw a bad picture so a child of God cannot offer a bad prayer.

Richard J. Foster

What happens in meditative prayer is that we create the emotional and spiritual space which allows Christ to construct an inner sanctuary in the heart ... a portable sanctuary which is brought into all we are and do.

Richard J. Foster

In meditative prayer, the truth being meditated upon passes from mouth into the mind and down into the heart, where through quiet rumination it produces in the person praying a loving, faith-filled response.

Richard J. Foster

Real prayer comes not from gritting our teeth, but from falling in love.

Richard J. Foster

To pray is to change.

Richard J. Foster

Petitionary prayer remains primary throughout our lives because we are forever dependent upon God. It is something we never really get beyond, nor should we ever want to.

Richard J. Foster

Prayer catapults us onto the frontier of the spiritual life.

Richard J. Foster

Children do not find it difficult or complicated to talk to their parents, nor do they feel embarrassed to bring the simplest need to their attention. Neither should we hesitate to bring the simplest requests confidently to the Father.

Richard J. Foster

Paul prayed for his people; he asked his people to pray for him.

Richard J. Foster

Real prayer comes not from gritting our teeth, but from falling in love.

Richard J. Foster

Prayer frees us to be controlled by God.

Richard J. Foster

Prayer is the central avenue God uses to transform us.

Richard J. Foster

The Lord hears the cries of the needy, and the sighs and groans of the poor. Judge not that, nor the sighs and groans of the Spirit, which cannot be uttered, lest you judge prayer; for prayer as well lies in sighs and groans to the Lord as otherwise.

George Fox, The Journal of George Fox

When we pray to God we must be seeking nothing – nothing.

Francis of Assisi

Where there is charity and wisdom, there is
    neither fear nor ignorance.
Where there is patience and humility, there is
    neither anger nor vexation.
Where there is poverty and joy, there is
    neither greed nor avarice.
Where there is peace and meditation, there is
    neither anxiety nor doubt.

Francis of Assisi

He prays well who is so absorbed with God that he does not know he is praying.

Francis de Sales

It is truly by means of prayer that we learn the perfection of love of God.

Francis de Sales

All persons, no matter what their state, must pray, for it is principally in prayer that God speaks to us.

Francis de Sales

If you wish to do your duty well, you must pray to God; it is in prayer that we learn to do our work well.

Francis de Sales

Prayer is the warmth of heavenly love.

Francis de Sales

Prayer is the water of blessing which cleanses us of our weaknesses.

Francis de Sales

All creatures were made to praise God. Everyone can pray and not one person can excuse himself/herself from doing so.

Francis de Sales

Prayer is a discussion, a conversation with God, and by it we speak to God and God in turn speaks to us. We aspire to God and breathe in Him; and mutually He breathes into us and in us.

Francis de Sales

Begin every prayer, whether mental or vocal, by recalling the presence of God. Keep to this rule without exception, and you will see in a short time how profitable it will be.

Francis de Sales

Meditation produces good desires in the will and in the heart, such as love of God and neighbor, the desire to please God, to be of service to our neighbor, to be compassionate, to be merciful, and many other good qualities. These desires ought to open themselves up in our hearts and in our actions.

Francis de Sales

Only one thing is necessary for praying well, and this is to have God in our hearts.

Francis de Sales

The secret of secrets in prayer is to follow one's attraction in simplicity of heart.

Francis de Sales

Prayer has forces that triumph over nature.

Francis de Sales

We should go to prayer with deep humility and an awareness of our nothingness.

Francis de Sales

First upon awakening in the morning, turn your thoughts to God present everywhere; place your heart and your entire being in His hands. Then think briefly of the good you will be able to accomplish that day and the evil you can avoid. Then kneel down, adore God from the bottom of your heart and thank Him for all His gifts and benefits He has given you.

Francis de Sales

Aspire to God, with short but frequent outpourings of the heart.

Francis de Sales

I used to think that prayer should have the first place and teaching the second. I now feel it would be truer to give prayer the first, second and third places and teaching the fourth.

James O. Fraser

Satan detests the prayer of faith, for it is an authoritative "notice to quit."

J.O. Fraser

Praying without faith is like trying to cut with a blunt knife – much labor expended to little purpose.

James O. Fraser

Ah, prayer turns trembling saints into great victors!

Henry W. Frost

So many confess their weakness, in denying to confess it, who, refusing to be beholden to a set form of prayer, prefer to say nonsense, rather than nothing, in their extempore expressions. More modesty, and no less piety, it had been for such men to have prayed longer with set forms that they might pray better without them.

Thomas Fuller

Prayer should be the key of the day and the lock of the night.

Thomas Fuller

G

To anxious, prying thought,
And weary, fretting care,
The Highest yieldeth nought;
He giveth all to prayer.

Paul Gerhardt

Pray absolutely for those things you may pray
  for absolutely.
Pray conditionally for those things you may
  pray for conditionally.
For those things you can't pray for – don't.

Paul Gerhardt

Faith and prayer are so inter-linked that faith is prayer and prayer is faith. You cannot separate them. You could not have the one without the other.

A. Lindsay Glegg

To arouse one man or woman to the tremendous power of prayer for others, is worth more than the combined activity of a score of average Christians.

A.J. Gordon

You can do more than pray after you have prayed, but you cannot do more than pray until you have prayed.

A.J. Gordon

Prayer is striking the winning blow. Service is gathering up the results.

S.D. Gordon

The greatest thing anyone can do for God and man is pray.

S.D. Gordon

Prayer is repeating the victor's name (Jesus) into the ears of Satan and insisting on his retreat.

S.D. Gordon

Prayer wonderfully clears the vision; steadies the nerves; defines duty; stiffens the purpose; sweetens and strengthens the spirit.

S.D. Gordon

God's greatest agency; man's greatest agency, for defeating the enemy and winning men back is intercession.

S.D. Gordon

Prayer is not the only thing; but it is the chief thing.

S.D. Gordon

The theme of our generation is: "Get more, know more, and do more," instead of "Pray more, be more, and serve more."

Billy Graham

The only time my prayers are never answered is on the golf course.

Billy Graham

Prayer is simply a two-way conversation between you and God.

Billy Graham

It is not the body's posture, but the heart's attitude that counts when we pray.

Billy Graham

Prayer to God is like a child's conversation with his father. It is natural for a child to ask his father for the things he needs.

Billy Graham

Prayer is spiritual communication between man and God, a two-way relationship in which man should not only talk to God but also listen to Him.

Billy Graham

Prayer is the rope that pulls God and man together. But it doesn't pull God down to us: it pulls us up to him.

Billy Graham

Prayer is your lifeline to God.

Billy Graham

Heaven is full of answers to prayers for which no one ever bothered to ask.

Billy Graham

Avail yourself of the greatest privilege this side of heaven. Jesus Christ died to make this communion and communication with the Father possible.

Billy Graham

I can tell you that God is alive because I talked with Him this morning.

Billy Graham

Prayer is the rope that pulls God and man together. But it doesn't pull God down to us: it pulls us up to him.

Billy Graham

Form the positive habit of starting each day with a few minutes in prayer.

Billy Graham

Remember that you can pray any time, anywhere. Washing dishes, digging ditches, working in the office, in the shop, on the athletic field, even in prison – you can pray and know God hears!

Billy Graham

God has not always answered my prayers. If He had, I would have married the wrong man – several times!

Ruth Graham

Just pray for a tough hide and a tender heart.

Ruth Graham

To be effective, prayer does not have to be long and laborious, but simple and sincere.

Anne Graham Lotz

The Holy Spirit is our personal, invisible prayer partner.

Anne Graham Lotz

We must remember God more often than we draw breath.

Gregory of Nazianzus

If Moses had not received from God the rod of power, he would not have become God to pharaoh and would not have punished both him and Egypt. In the same way the mind, if it does not wield in its hand the power of prayer, will be unable to conquer sin and the powers of the enemy.

Gregory of Sinai

True prayer is not to be found in the words of the mouth, but in the thoughts of the heart.

Gregory I (the Great)

Not only does sin hinder prayer; prayer hinders sin. The two are always opposed. The more careless we are about sin, the less we will pray. The more we pray, the less careless we will be about sin.

Dr. Alvin Vander Griend

Prayer meetings are dead affairs when they are merely asking sessions; there is adventure, hope and life when they are believing sessions, and the faith is corporately, practically and deliberately affirmed.

Norman Grubb

How terrible is the cost of robbing God of time for prayer. When we rob God of time for quiet, we are robbing Him of ourselves. It is only in the quiet that we can really know Him and know ourselves, and be sure that we give ourselves back to Him. Oh, for God's sake, do not risk keeping the windows of Heaven closed by robbing God of time.

Gordon M. Guinness

Furnish thyself with arguments from the promises to enforce thy prayers.

William Gurnall

"Pray." But how? "Without ceasing." "Rejoice." But when? "Evermore." "Give thanks." For what? "In everything."

William Gurnall

Cease to pray and thou wilt begin to sin.

William Gurnall

Prayer is a great heart-easer.

William Gurnall

Prayer is not only a means to prevail for mercy, but also to prevent sin.

William Gurnall

Satan cannot deny but that great wonders have been wrought by prayer. As the spirit of prayer goes up, so his kingdom goes down.

William Gurnall

Never was faithful prayer lost. Some prayers have a longer voyage than others, but then they return with their richer lading at last, so that the praying soul is a gainer by waiting for an answer.

William Gurnall

Sometimes, perhaps, thou hearest another pray with much freedom and fluency, whilst thou canst hardly get out a few broken words. Hence thou art ready to accuse thyself and admire him, as if the gilding of the key made it opens the door the better.

William Gurnall

To pray in the Spirit is the inward principle of prayer. It comprehends both the spirit of the person praying, and the Spirit of God by which our spirits are fitted for, and acted in, prayer.

William Gurnall

The only way to heaven is prayer.

Jeanne Guyon

We are all called to prayer, as we are all called to salvation.

Jeanne Guyon

I would warmly recommend to all, never to finish prayer without remaining some little time afterward in a respectful silence.

Jeanne Guyon

You should live by prayer, as you should live by love.

Jeanne Guyon

The prayer of love softens the heart.

Jeanne Guyon

Prayer is the guide to perfection. For the one way to become perfect is to walk in the presence of God.

Jeanne Guyon

Praying with a believing heart is more important than anything else that has to do with prayer.

Jeanne Guyon

Prayer is nothing but the application of the heart to God.

Jeanne Guyon

Prayer is the overflowing of the heart in the presence of God.

Jeanne Guyon

All are capable of prayer, and it is a dreadful misfortune that almost all the world have conceived the idea that they are not called to prayer.

Jeanne Guyon

H

Satan rocks the cradle when we sleep at our devotions.

Joseph Hall

The prayer of faith is the only power in the universe to which the Great Jehovah yields.

Robert Hall

Prayer is the sovereign remedy.

Robert Hall

To strive in prayer means to struggle through those hindrances which would restrain or even prevent us entirely from continuing in persevering prayer. It means to be so watchful at all times that we can notice when we become slothful in prayer and that we go to the Spirit of prayer to have this remedied. In this struggle, too, the decisive factor is the Spirit of prayer.

O. Hallesby

The more helpless you are, the better you are fitted to pray, and the more answers to prayer you will experience.

O. Hallesby

It is not necessary to maintain a conversation when we are in the presence of God. We can come into His presence and rest our weary souls in quiet contemplation of Him.

O. Hallesby

Our groanings, which cannot be uttered, rise to Him and tell Him better than words how dependent we are upon Him.

O. Hallesby

Speak with God about your daily experiences.

O. Hallesby

The Spirit of prayer makes us so intimate with God that we scarcely pass through an experience before we speak to Him about it, either in supplication, in sighing, in pouring out our woes before Him, in fervent requests, or in thanksgiving and adoration.

O. Hallesby

Prayer is the risen Jesus coming in with His resurrection power, given free rein in our lives, and then using His authority to enter any situation and change things.

O. Hallesby

To pray is to let Jesus come into our hearts. It is not our prayer which moves the Lord Jesus. It is Jesus who moves us to pray.

O. Hallesby

To pray is nothing more involved than to lie in the sunshine of God's grace.

O. Hallesby

Prayer and helplessness are inseparable. Only he who is helpless can truly pray.

O. Hallesby

The quiet hour of prayer is one of the most favorable opportunities God has in which to speak to us seriously. In quietude and solitude before the face of God, our souls can hear better than at any other time.

O. Hallesby

Prayer is the Christian life, reduced to its essence.

Hank Hanegraaff

The weight of a great answer to prayer
Seems almost too much for us.
The grace of it is
Too wonderful for us.

Frances R. Havergal

You may as soon find a living man without breath as a living saint without prayer.

Matthew Henry

The prayers and supplications that Christ offered up were, joined with strong cries and tears, herein setting us example not only to pray, but to be fervent and importunate in prayer. How many dry prayers, how few wet ones, do we offer up to God!

Matthew Henry

When God intends great mercy for His people, the first thing He does is set them a-praying.

Matthew Henry

God's word must be the ground of your expectations in prayer.

Matthew Henry

It is good for us to keep some account of our prayers, that we may not unsay them in our practice.

Matthew Henry

Prayer is the midwife of mercy, that helps to bring it forth.

Matthew Henry

When God is about to give his people the expected good, he pours out a Spirit of prayer, and it is a good sign that he is coming towards them in mercy.

Matthew Henry

Though we cannot by our prayers give God any information, we must by our prayers give Him honor.

Matthew Henry

Let prayer be the key of the morning and the bolt at night. The best way to fight against sin is to fight it on our knees.

Philip Henry

My words and thoughts do both express this
    notion,
That *Life* hath with the sun a double motion.
The first *Is* straight, and our diurnal friend;
The other *Hid*, and doth obliquely bend.
One life is wrapt *In* flesh, and tends to earth:
The other winds towards *Him*, whose happy
    birth
Taught me to live here so *That* still one eye
Should aim and shoot at that which *Is* on
    high;
Quitting with daily labor all *My* pleasure,
To gain at harvest an eternal *Treasure*.

George Herbert

The soul in paraphrase, the heart in
    pilgrimage,
The Christian plummet sounding heav'n and
    earth.

George Herbert

Prayer is the soul's blood.

George Herbert

Who goes to bed and does not pray
Maketh two nights to every day.

George Herbert

If I be bound to pray for all that be in distress, surely I am bound, so far as it is in my power, to practice what I pray for.

George Herbert

In prayer the lips ne'er act the winning part,
Without the sweet concurrence of the heart.

Robert Herrick

If you really wish to achieve spiritual stillness
and to guard your heart successfully, then let
the prayer "Lord Jesus, have mercy upon me"
become one with your breathing, and in a few
days you will see how it can all be achieved.

Hesychios

When I pray for ought, my prayer counts for
    nought;
when I pray for nought, I pray as I ought.

Walter Hilton

Every good and holy desire, though it lacks
the form, hath in itself the substance and force
of a prayer with God, who regardeth the very
moanings, groans, and sighings of the heart.

Herman Hooker

Prayer is the first thing wherewith a righteous
life beginneth, and the last wherewith it doth
end.

Richard Hooker

Prayer is my chief work, and it is by means of it
that I carry on the rest.

Thomas Hooker

Our prayer and God's mercy are like two buck-
ets in a well; while the one ascends, the other
descends.

Alphonso A. Hopkins

It is morally impossible to exercise trust in
God while there is failure to wait upon Him for
guidance and direction.

D.E. Hoste

I am quite sure the rule holds that the more we
pray the more we want to pray; the converse
also being true.

D.E. Hoste

The man who does not learn to wait upon the
Lord and have his thoughts molded by Him
will never possess that steady purpose and
calm trust, which is essential to the exercise of
wise influence upon others, in times of crisis

and difficulty.

D.E. Hoste

I find it a good thing to fast. I do not lay down
rules for anyone in this matter, but I know it has
been a good thing for me to go without meals
to get time for prayer. So many say they have
not sufficient time to pray. We think nothing of
spending an hour or two in taking our meals.

D.E. Hoste

Prayer points us beyond ourselves, beyond our
friendships, to the deepest realization of all:
that God made us to be lovers of God. He is at
the very heart of our hearts.

James Houston

Prayer is not the cunning art of using God,
subjecting Him to one's selfish ends in an effort
to get out of Him what you want.

F.J. Huegel

The most fundamental need, duty, honor and
happiness of mankind is not petition, nor even
contrition, nor again even thanksgiving, but
adoration.

Friedrich von Hügel

I say this prayer very often, because it is a
prayer of complete trust in God: "I cannot
solve this, Lord, but into thy hands I commend
my spirit."

Cardinal Basil Hume

When we fail to wait prayerfully for God's
guidance and strength, we are saying with
our actions if not our lips, that we do not need
him.

Charles Hummel

It's amazing how many coincidences occur
when one begins to pray.

Bill Hybels

Pray as if everything depended on God and act
as if everything depended on oneself.

Ignatius of Loyola

Everything that one turns in the direction of
God is prayer.

Ignatius of Loyola

I have lived to thank God that all my prayers have not been answered.

Jean Ingelow

We pray with words until the words are cut off and we are left is a state of wonder.

Isaac of Antioch

Just as by the rays of the sun the face of the earth is unveiled from the darkness of the atmosphere that enshrouds it, even so is prayer able to dissolve and scatter the clouds of passions from our soul.

Isaac of Antioch

He who neglects prayer, thinking he has another doorway for repentance, is deceived by the devil.

Isaac of Antioch

If you ask God for something and you do not receive it, do not be upset, for you are not wiser than God.

Isaac of Nineveh

The purpose of prayer is for us to acquire love of God, for in prayer can be discovered all sorts of reasons for loving God.

Isaac of Nineveh

When it happens that your soul is inwardly filled with darkness and that, just as the rays of the sun are at times shut off from the earth by clouds, so the soul is deprived for a time of spiritual comfort, and when the light of grace becomes dimmed within because a cloud of passions covers the soul, and because the joy-creating force is weakened in you, so that your mind is shrouded in unaccustomed darkness; let not your thought be troubled, but be patient; read the books of the teachers, force yourself to pray and wait for help. It will be quick in coming.

It will be there before you know it. For as the face of the earth is delivered by rays of the sun from the darkness enshrouding it, so prayer can destroy and disperse the cloud of passions in the soul and illuminate the mind by the light of comfort and joy.

Isaac of Syria

Prayer purifies us, reading instructs us. Both are good when both are possible. Otherwise, prayer is better than reading.

Isidore of Seville

J

Prayer without watching is hypocrisy; and watching without prayer is presumption.

William Jay

We are very specific with our requests and instructions for our babysitters. We want them to know specifics. It should be no different with prayer.

David Jeremiah

To saints their very slumber is a prayer.

Jerome

It is ours to offer what we can, his to supply what we cannot.

Jerome

My spirit is dry within me because it forgets to feed on you.

John of the Cross

He that flees from prayer flees from all that is good.

John of the Cross

When lustful and wicked thoughts war within me, I do what any man would do when pursued by a wild beast. I would climb a tree to be saved. And so I flee to God with prayer, and escape from these wicked thoughts.

John the Dwarf

In prayer you align yourselves to the purpose and power of God and He is able to do things through you that He couldn't do otherwise.

E. Stanley Jones

My best asking falls immeasurably short of my Father's giving; it is beyond that we can ask.

J.H. Jowett

I would rather teach one man to pray than ten men to preach.

J.H. Jowett

It is in the field of prayer that life's critical battles are lost or won.

J.H. Jowett

Endeavor seven times a day to withdraw from business and company and lift up thy soul to God in private retirement.

Adoniram Judson

I never was deeply interested in any subject, I never prayed sincerely for any thing, but it came. At some time, no matter at how distant a day, somehow, in some shape probably the last I should devise it came.

Adoniram Judson

The elements of prayer
Its ground: God, by whose goodness it
    springeth in us.
Its use: to turn our will to His will.
Its end: to be made one with Him and like to
    Him in all things.

Julian of Norwich

Pray inwardly, even if you do not enjoy it.

Julian of Norwich

For God says, "When you are dry, empty, sick, or weak, at such a time is your prayer most pleasing to Me, even though you find little enough to enjoy in it."

Julian of Norwich

Prayer unites the soul to God.

Julian of Norwich

K

Your greatest lack is that you do not know
    how to pray.

Toyohiko Kagawa

You will never learn how to pray until you are moved enough to weep.

Jerry Kaufman

And help us, this and every day,
To live more nearly as we pray.

John Keble

Prayer ... really is a silent surrendering of

everything to God.

Søren Kierkegaard

He who can inwardly lift his mind up to God, and can regard outward things little, needs not to seek for time or place to pray.

Thomas à Kempis

A man prayed, and at first he thought that prayer was talking. But he became more and more quiet until in the end he realized that prayer is listening.

Søren Kierkegaard

Prayer does not change God, but it changes him who prays.

Søren Kierkegaard

Prayer is not hearing yourself talk, but being silent, staying silent and waiting until you hear God.

Søren Kierkegaard

I cannot pray in the name of Jesus to have my own will.

Søren Kierkegaard

No one is a firmer believer in the power of prayer than the devil; not that he practices it, but he suffers from it.

Guy H. King

The very act of prayer honors God and gives glory to God, for it confesses that God is what he is.

Charles Kingsley

All hindrance to prayer arises from ignorance of the teaching of God's Holy Word on the life of holiness He has planned for all His children or from an unwillingness to consecrate ourselves fully to Him.

The Kneeling Christian

A loving spirit is a condition of believing prayer. We cannot be wrong with man and right with God. The spirit of prayer is essentially the spirit of love. Intercession is simply love at prayer.

The Kneeling Christian

We feel sure that the weakness in the spiritual life of many churches is to be traced to an inefficient prayer-meeting, or the absence of meetings for prayer. Can we not make the weekly prayer-meeting a live thing and a living force?"

The Kneeling Christian

We discuss the "problem of prayer"; we are the problem that needs discussing or dissecting!

The Kneeling Christian

The secret of all failure is our failure in secret prayer.

The Kneeling Christian

It is remarkable how often our Lord refers to united prayer.

The Kneeling Christian

We must bear in mind that mere resolutions to take more time for prayer and to conquer reluctance to pray will not prove lastingly effective unless there is a whole hearted and absolute surrender to the Lord Jesus Christ.

The Kneeling Christian

Prayer is an offering up of our desires unto God for things agreeable to His will, in the name of Christ, with confession of our sins and thankful acknowledgment of His mercies.

The Kneeling Christian

Unless the heart is right the prayer must be wrong.

The Kneeling Christian

There is no greater test to spirituality than prayer. The man who tries to pray quickly discovers just where he stands in God's sight.

The Kneeling Christian

Prayer is not given us as a burden to be borne or an irksome duty to fulfill, but to be a joy and power to which there is no limit.

The Kneeling Christian

The only cure for wandering thoughts is to get our minds fixed upon God.

The Kneeling Christian

All that true prayer seeks is God Himself, for with Him we get all we need.

The Kneeling Christian

It would be an immense gain to our spiritual life if we would resolve not to attempt to pray until we had done all in our power to make peace and harmony between ourselves and any with whom we have quarreled.

The Kneeling Christian

No sin is too small to hinder prayer, and perhaps to turn the very prayer itself into sin, if we are not willing to renounce that sin.

The Kneeling Christian

Unbelief is possibly the greatest hindrance to prayer.

The Kneeling Christian

All real growth in the spiritual life,
all victory over temptation,
all confidence and peace in the presence of
    difficulties and dangers,
all repose of spirit in times of great
    disappointment or loss,
all habitual communion with God,
depends upon the practice of secret prayer.

The Kneeling Christian

Surely we must all agree that it is sin in us, and not the unwillingness of Christ to hear, that hinders prayer.

The Kneeling Christian

Intercession is simply love at prayer.

The Kneeling Christian

Prayer is earnest and familiar talking with God.

John Knox

The attributes of prayer must be: love of God, sincerity, and simplicity. We must pray in spirit, because God is a spirit, and not flesh; with truth, and not falsely, because God is the Truth.

John of Kronstadt

All prayers assume the great poverty and misery of our fallen nature; they also assume that the Lord is the ever flowing source of every perfection, every blessing; that He is our inexhaustible treasury. Truly, we must have poverty of spirit during prayer and at all times.

John of Kronstadt

[In our praying] Let us ascribe to the Lord at least the same amount of attention that good parents show to the requests of their children, at least that provident and attentive love which good parents have for their children.

John of Kronstadt

People mostly pray as if there were no God with them, or as if He did not heed their prayers.

John of Kronstadt

Heartfelt prayer is the source of peace of heart, whilst insincere, superficial, inattentive prayer wounds the heart.

John of Kronstadt

When praying, I firmly believe (1) that God alone is and fills everything; (2) that I am His image; (3) that He is an abyss of mercy, the Source of every mercy, and that He Himself has authorized me to pray to Him.

John of Kronstadt

It is necessary to rouse the heart to pray, otherwise it will become quite dry.

John of Kronstadt

During prayer, when our soul is wholly turned towards God, and is united to Him, we feel happy, calm, easy, and joyful, like children resting on their mother's breast;.

John of Kronstadt

The greatest power that God has given to any individual is the power of prayer.

Kathryn Kuhlman

L

He who has a pure heart will never cease to pray; and he who will be constant in prayer, shall know what it is to have a pure heart.

Père La Combe

I have never found any who prayed so well as those who had never been taught how. They who have no master in man, have one in the Holy Spirit.

Père La Combe

A sense of real want is at the very root of prayer.

John Laidlaw

The main lesson about prayer is just this: Do it! Do it! Do it!

John Laidlaw

Beloved, it is not our long prayers but our believing God that gets the answer.

John G. Lake

A short prayer finds its way to heaven.

William Langland

Listening to God is far more important than giving Him your ideas.

Frank C. Laubach

Prayer at its highest is a two-way conversation – and for me the most important part is listening to God's replies.

Frank C. Laubach

I am very sensitive and know whether you are praying for me. If one of you lets me down, I feel it. When you are praying for me, I feel a strange power. When every person in a congregation prays intensely while the pastor is preaching, a miracle happens.

Frank C. Laubach

If you were to rise early every morning, as an instance of self-denial, as a method of renouncing indulgence, as a means of redeeming your time and of fitting your spirit for prayer, you would find mighty advantages from it.

William Law

Perhaps there cannot be a better way of judging of what manner of spirit we are of, than to see whether the actions of our life are such as we may safely commend them to God in our prayers.

William Law

By considering yourself as an advocate with God for your neighbors and acquaintances, you would never find it hard to be at peace with them yourself.

William Law

The spirit of prayer is a stretching with after the life of God, to be one life, one love, one spirit with Christ in God.

William Law

Prayer is the nearest approach to God and the highest enjoyment of Him that we are capable of in this life.

William Law

Prayer is the breath or inspiration of God, stirring, moving and opening itself in the heart.

William Law

There is nothing that makes us love a man so much as praying for him.

William Law

Prayer is my chief work, by it I carry on all else.

William Law

He who has learned to pray has learned the greatest secret of a holy and happy life.

William Law

Prayer is nothing else than a sense of God's presence.

Brother Lawrence

Hold yourself in prayer before God, like a dumb or paralytic beggar at a rich man's gate: let it be your business to keep your mind in the presence of God.

Brother Lawrence

A little remembrance of God, one act of inward worship are prayers which, however short, are nevertheless acceptable to God.

Brother Lawrence

A little lifting of the heart suffices.

Brother Lawrence

Our biggest mistake is to think that a time of

prayer is different from any other time. It is all one.

Brother Lawrence

We can make our heart a chapel where we can go anytime to talk to God privately.

Brother Lawrence

Do not always scrupulously confine yourself to certain rules, or particular forms of devotion; but act with a general confidence in God, with love and humility.

Brother Lawrence

It is a shameful thing to quit our conversation with God to think of trifles and fooleries.

Brother Lawrence

We ought to reject them as soon as we perceive their irrelevance to the matter at hand, or to our salvation, and return to our communion with God.

Brother Lawrence

When I apply myself to prayer, I feel all my spirit and all my soul lift itself up without any care or effort of mine, and it continues as it were suspended and firmly fixed in God, as in its center and place of rest.

Brother Lawrence

Lift up your heart to him, sometimes even at your meals, and when you are in company; the least little remembrance will always be acceptable to him. You need not cry very loud; he is nearer to us than we are aware of.

Brother Lawrence

One way to recall the mind easily in the time of prayer, and preserve it more in tranquility, is not to let it wander too far at other times. You should keep it strictly in the Presence of God; and , being accustomed to think of Him often, you will find it easy to keep your mind calm in the time of prayer, or at least to recall it from its wonderings.

Brother Lawrence

To pray is to drop out in the most profound and positive sense.

Kenneth Leech

The pursuit of a prayerful life of simple love and discipline sets us in isolation from and opposition to the mainstream, mammon-directed culture in which we live.

Kenneth Leech

We become deserters from technocracy, disaffiliating ourselves from its power, rejecting its false values. To pray is to drop out in the most profound and positive sense.

Kenneth Leech

True prayer never comes weeping home: I am sure that I shall get either what I ask, or what I ought to have asked.

Robert Leighton

If God had granted all the silly prayers I've made in my life, where should I be now?

C. S Lewis

Prayer is request.

C.S. Lewis

That wisdom must sometimes refuse what ignorance may quite innocently ask seems to be self-evident.

C.S. Lewis

A few formal, ready-made, prayers serve me as a corrective of – well, let's call it "cheek."

C.S. Lewis

The prayer preceding all prayers is "May it be the real I who speaks."

C.S. Lewis

The most blessed result of prayer would be to rise thinking.

C.S. Lewis

We must lay before him what is in us, not what ought to be in us.

C.S. Lewis

The great masters and teachers in Christian doctrine have always found in prayer their highest source of illumination.

H.P. Liddon

The greatest practical resolves that have

enriched and beautified human life in Christian times have been arrived at in prayer.

H.P. Liddon

I have been driven many times to my knees by the overwhelming conviction that I had nowhere else to go. My own wisdom, and that of all about me, seemed insufficient for the day.

Abraham Lincoln

People may spurn our appeals, reject our messages, oppose our arguments, despise our persons; but they are helpless against our prayers.

Thomas Lindberg

Reformers insisted that access to God was granted to all true believers and from Scripture argued that prayer was available to all at any time.

Thomas Lindberg

It is always too soon to quit praying, even when praying is the last thing we seem able to do.

Harold Lindsell

Prayerlessness is sin.

Harold Lindsell

God uses prayer to educate His people and to produce holiness of character in them.

Harold Lindsell

Nothing so much shows the character of faith as our conduct and attitude after we have prayed. The people of faith not only prayed, but they expected answers. The test of our faith is whether we expect an answer.

D. Martyn Lloyd-Jones

Before we can pray truly we must think spiritually.

D. Martyn Lloyd-Jones

There is a sense in which every man when he begins to pray to God should put his hand upon his mouth.

D. Martyn Lloyd-Jones

The men whose prayers have been answered

have always been those who knew God.

D. Martyn Lloyd-Jones

There is an element of mystery about this question of prayer.

D. Martyn Lloyd-Jones

God's omniscience is no reason for our not telling Him things which He already knows.

D. Martyn Lloyd-Jones

Public prayer should be such that the people who are praying silently and the one who is uttering the words should be no longer conscious of each other, but should be carried on the wings of prayer into the very presence of God.

D. Martyn Lloyd-Jones

There are ideas in our hearts, there are wishes, there are aspirations, there are groanings, there are sighings that the world knows nothing about; but God knows them. So words are not always necessary. When we cannot express our feelings except in wordless groanings, God knows exactly what is happening.

D. Martyn Lloyd-Jones

Pleas and arguments and requests are perfectly legitimate in prayer.

D. Martyn Lloyd-Jones

Always respond to every impulse to pray.

D. Martyn Lloyd-Jones

There is only one way whereby a man can pray with any confidence and assurance, and it is in believing in the cross of our Lord Jesus Christ.

D. Martyn Lloyd-Jones

Pleading the promises of God is the whole secret of prayer, I sometimes think.

D. Martyn Lloyd-Jones

We sometimes think that prayer is simple, but it is not. The great saints of all the centuries are agreed in saying that one of the most difficult things of all is to learn how to pray.

D. Martyn Lloyd-Jones

Prayer means speaking to God who is in heaven, who is all powerful to bless.

D. Martyn Lloyd-Jones

Prayer, in many ways, is the supreme expression of our faith in God.

D. Martyn Lloyd-Jones

Do not claim, you make your requests known.

D. Martyn Lloyd-Jones

Prayer is the highest activity of the human soul, and therefore it is at the same time the ultimate test of a man's true spiritual condition (there is nothing so much as prayer life that tells the truth about us as Christian people.)

D. Martyn Lloyd-Jones

Everything we do in the Christian life is easier than prayer.

D. Martyn Lloyd-Jones

The nearer people are to God, the more they pray to Him.

D. Martyn Lloyd-Jones

Prayer for power is always in evidence in the history of the Church prior to revival.

D. Martyn Lloyd-Jones

The mightiest prayers are often those drenched with the Word of God.

Herbert Lockyer

Take time to be holy;
Speak oft with thy Lord.

W.D. Longstaff

Pray all the time. If necessary, use words.

Max Lucado

Our prayers may be awkward. Our attempts may be feeble. But since the power of prayer is in the one who hears it and not the one who says it, our prayers do make a difference.

Max Lucado

Know answered prayer when you see it, and don't give up when you don't.

Max Lucado

Faith makes our prayer acceptable because it believes that either the prayer will be answered, or that something better will be given instead.

Martin Luther

[When Luther's puppy happened to be at the table, he looked for a morsel from his master, and watched with open mouth and motionless eyes. Luther said,] Oh, if I could only pray the way this dog watches the meat! All his thoughts are concentrated on the piece of meat. Otherwise he has no thought, wish, or hope.

Martin Luther

Prayer is a powerful thing, for God has bound and tied himself thereto.

Martin Luther

None can believe how powerful prayer is, and what it is able to effect, but those who have learned it by experience.

Martin Luther

All who call on God in true faith, earnestly from the heart, will certainly be heard, and will receive what they have asked and desired, although not in the hour or in the measure, or the very thing which they ask; yet they will obtain something greater and more glorious than they had dared to ask.

Martin Luther

The fewer the words, the better the prayer.

Martin Luther

If I fail to spend two hours in prayer each morning, the devil gets the victory through the day. I have so much business I cannot get on without spending three hours daily in prayer.

Martin Luther

To be a Christian without prayer is no more possible than to be alive without breathing.

Martin Luther

As it is the business of tailors to make clothes and of cobblers to mend shoes, so it is the business of Christians to pray.

Martin Luther

Pray, and let God worry.

Martin Luther

Where there is not faith and confidence in prayer, the prayer is dead.

Martin Luther

The Holy Ghost has two offices: first, he is a Spirit of grace, that makes God gracious unto us, and receive us as his acceptable children, for Christ's sake. Secondly, he is a Spirit of prayer, that prays for us, and for the whole world, to the end that all evil may be turned from us, and that all good may happen to us.

Martin Luther

Prayer is the most important thing in my life.

Martin Luther

If I should neglect prayer for a single day, I should lose a great deal of the fire of faith.

Martin Luther

Prayer is a strong wall and fortress of the church; it is a goodly Christian weapon.

Martin Luther

Prayer is the climbing up of the heart into the heart of God.

Martin Luther

To pray well is the better half of study.

Martin Luther

I judge that my prayer is more than the Devil himself; if it were otherwise, Luther would have fared differently long before this. Yet men will not see and acknowledge the great wonders or miracles God works in my behalf.

Martin Luther

Prayer must do the deed.

Martin Luther

The less I pray, the harder it gets; the more I pray, the better it goes.

Martin Luther

I had rather stand against the cannons of the wicked than against the prayers of the righteous.

Thomas Lye

M

Anything big enough to occupy our minds is big enough to hang a prayer on.

George MacDonald

There is a communion with God that asks for nothing, yet asks for everything.

George MacDonald

That man is perfect in faith who can come to God in the utter dearth of his feelings and his desires, without a glow or an aspiration, with the weight of low thoughts, failures, neglects, and wandering forgetfulness, and say to Him, "Thou art my refuge, because Thou art my home". Such a faith will not lead to presumption.

George MacDonald

There are two doorkeepers to the house of prayer, and Sorrow is more on the alert to open than her grandson Joy.

George MacDonald

God will either give you what you ask, or something far better.

Robert Murray M'Cheyne

O believing brethren! what an instrument is this which God hath put into your hands! Prayer moves Him that moves the universe.

Robert Murray McCheyne

God's children should pray. They should cry day and night to Him. God hears every one of your cries in the busy hour of the daytime and in the lonely watches of the night.

Robert Murray McCheyne

A great part of my time is spent in getting my heart in tune for prayer.

Robert Murray M'Cheyne

Give yourselves to prayer and the ministry of the Word. If you do not pray, God will probably lay you aside from your ministry, as He did me, to teach you to pray.

Robert Murray M'Cheyne

It is true friendship to teach one another

to pray.

Robert Murray M'Cheyne

Prayer is the link that connects earth with heaven.

Robert Murray M'Cheyne

If I could hear Christ praying for me in the next room, I would not fear a million enemies. Yet distance makes no difference. He is praying for me.

Robert Murray M'Cheyne

Rose early to seek God and found Him whom my soul loveth. Who would not rise early to meet such company?

Robert Murray M'Cheyne

I ought to pray before seeing any one. Often when I sleep long, or meet with others early, it is eleven or twelve o'clock before I begin secret prayer. This is a wretched system. It is unscriptural. Christ arose before day and went into a solitary place.

Robert Murray M'Cheyne

Prayer is the greatest neglected resource that we have; it's a power that we simply are not using today.

J. Vernon McGee

The greatest need of the present-day church is prayer.

J. Vernon McGee

Maybe one of the reasons the church is not going forward today is because it's not in a position to go forward – - we are not on our knees in prayer.

J. Vernon McGee

The value of consistent prayer is not that He will hear us, but that we will hear Him.

William McGill

In prayer we enter into the caring presence of One who created us and knows us through and through.

Alister McGrath

The prayer that begins with trustfulness, and

passes on into waiting, will always end in thankfulness, triumph, and praise.

Alexander Maclaren

We tell people to pray, but we don't tell them how.

John Mallison

It is prayer, meditation, and converse with God that refreshes, restores, and renews the temper of our minds, at all times, under all trials, after all conflicts with the world.

Henry Edward Manning

Whatever we do without prayer and without hope in God turns out to be harmful and defective.

Mark the Ascetic

It is good to hold fast to the principal commandment, and not to be anxious about particular things or to pray for them specifically, but to seek only the Kingdom and the Word of God (Matthew 6:25–33). If, however, we are still anxious about our particular needs, we need to pray for each of them.

Mark the Ascetic

He who does or plans anything without prayer will not succeed in the end. And this is what the Lord meant when He said, Without Me, you can do nothing (John 15:5).

Mark the Ascetic

There is no perfect prayer unless the intellect invokes God.

Mark the Ascetic

Real power in prayer flows only when man's spirit touches God's spirit.

Catherine Marshall

One can believe intellectually in the efficacy of prayer and never do any praying.

Catherine Marshall

The purpose of all prayer is to find God's will and to make that will our prayer.

Catherine Marshall

We forget that God sometimes has to say "No."

We pray to Him as our heavenly Father, and like wise human fathers, He often says, "No," not from whim or caprice, but from wisdom and from love, and knowing what is best for us.

Peter Marshall

O God, forgive the poverty and the pettiness of our prayers. Listen not to our words but to the yearnings of our hearts. Hear beneath our petitions the crying of our need.

Peter Marshall

Let me burn out for God. After all, whatever God may appoint, prayer is the great thing. Oh, that I might be a man of prayer!

Henry Martyn

I fear John Knox's prayers more than an army of ten thousand men.

Mary Queen of Scots

Pray not to be seen of men but to be heard of God.

John Mason

Prayer does not consist in gifted expressions and a volubility of speech; but in a brokenness of heart.

John Mason

Imperfect broken groans from a broken heart, God will accept.

John Mason

Prayer does not consist in the elegance of the phrase, but in the strength of the affection.

John Mason

A hard heart cannot pray; a broken heart is made up of prayer.

John Mason

When God pours out His Spirit upon man, then will man pour out his heart before God.

John Mason

He that lives without prayer or prays without life, has not the Spirit of God.

John Mason

Where there is a willing heart there will be a continual crying to heaven for help.

John Mason

Prayer, if it be done as a task, is not prayer.

John Mason

Sin quenches prayer, affliction quickens it.

John Mason

The same Spirit of faith which teaches a man to cry earnestly, teaches him to wait patiently.

John Mason

The breath of prayer comes from the life of faith.

John Mason

Prayer is going utterly beyond ourselves, going beyond any words that we could use to describe the experience.

John Mayne

Whatever a man loves he inevitably clings to, and in order not to lose it he rejects everything that keeps him from it. So he who loves God cultivates pure prayer, driving out every passion that keeps him from it.

Maximus the Confessor

Prayer is naught else but a yearning of soul. When it is practiced with the whole heart, it has great power.

Mechthild of Magdeburg

Trouble and perplexity drive me to prayer, and prayer drives away perplexity and trouble.

Philip Melanchthon

Anyone who imagines that he can simply begin meditating without praying for the desire and the grace to do so, will soon give up. But the desire to meditate and the grace to begin meditating should be taken as an implicit promise of further graces.

Thomas Merton

There is always time to look up to Him for His smile.

F.B. Meyer

Fall on your knees and grow there.

F.B. Meyer

There is no burden of the spirit but is lighter by kneeling under it.

F.B. Meyer

Prayer means not always talking to Him, but waiting before Him till the dust settles and the stream runs clear.

F.B. Meyer

The greatest tragedy of life is not unanswered prayer, but unoffered prayer.

F.B. Meyer

Prayer no longer seems like an activity to me; it has become the continuing language of the relationship I believe God designed to fulfill a human life.

Keith Miller

What a man is on his knees before God in secret, that will he be before men: that much and no more.

Fred Mitchell

Prayer is love in need appealing to love in power.

Robert Moffatt

Prayer is the Christian's vital breath,
The Christian's native air,
His watchword at the gates of death:
He enters heaven with prayer.

Prayer is the soul's sincere desire
Uttered or unexpressed
The motion of a hidden fire
That trembles in the breast.

Prayer is the burden of a sigh,
The falling of a tear,
The upward glancing of an eye
When none but God is near.

James Montgomery

When our hearts are comforted, it is all too easy to forget that this contentment comes ultimately only from God.

Douglas Moo

I believe in definite prayer.

D.L. Moody

He who kneels the most stands best.

D.L. Moody

Every work of God can be traced to some kneeling form.

D.L. Moody

Careful for nothing, prayerful for everything, thankful for anything.

D.L. Moody

Spread out your petition before God, and then say, 'Thy will, not mine be done.'

D.L. Moody

Some people's prayers need to be cut off at both ends and set on fire in the middle.

D.L. Moody

If you have so much business to attend to that you have no time to pray, depend upon it, you have more business than God ever intended you should have.

D.L. Moody

Next to the wonder of seeing my Savior will be, I think, the wonder that I made so little use of the power of prayer.

D.L. Moody

Every great movement of God can be traced to a kneeling figure.

D.L. Moody

Prayer is not eloquence, but earnestness; not the definition of helplessness, but the feeling of it; not figures of speech, but earnestness of soul.

Hannah More

So weak is man, so ignorant and blind that did not God sometimes withhold in mercy what we ask, we should be ruined at our own request.

Hannah More

Written forms of prayer are not only useful and proper, but indispensably necessary to

begin with.

Hannah More

The prayer life does not consist of perpetual repetition of petitions. The prayer life consists of life that is always upward and onward and Godward.

George Campbell Morgan

The whole life of the believer should be prayer – and this is the summary and conclusion – every act, every word, every wish. The act that is not prayer in the ultimate, and the word which is not prayer in the last analysis, and the wish that is not prayer in the profoundest depth are to be put away; they do not become the life of faith. They are things that produce fainting.

George Campbell Morgan

Prayer is life passionately wanting, wishing, desiring God's triumph. Prayer is life striving and toiling everywhere and always for that ultimate victory.

George Campbell Morgan

Oh, how strenuous is life! I know a little of it. Men "ought always to pray, and not to faint." How fierce the battle! I know something of the conflict, but I ought not to faint, because I can pray.

George Campbell Morgan

Men ought not to faint because men ought to pray.

George Campbell Morgan

The prayer life does not consist of perpetual repetition of petitions. The prayer life consists of life that is always upward and onward and Godward.

George Campbell Morgan

The men that will change the colleges and seminaries here represented are the men that will spend the most time alone with God.

J.R. Mott

Every other consideration and plan and emphasis is secondary to that of wielding the forces of prayer.

J.R. Mott

Prayer alone will overcome the gigantic difficulties which confront the workers in every field.

J.R. Mott

Hope and confidence should not be placed in the extent and perfection of organizations, nor in the experience which has been accumulated and the agencies and methods which have been devised in a long century of missions, nor in the unusual strength of the missionary body, nor in the multitude who have been gathered from every nation and race and faith into the native Church, nor in the wonderful resources and facilities of the home Church, nor in far-sighted and comprehensive plans, nor in enthusiastic forward movements and inspiring watchwords. It is easy to magnify human personality and agencies. Prayer recognizes that God is the source of life and light and energy.

J.R. Mott

Let methods be changed, therefore, if necessary, that prayer may be given its true place. Let there be days set apart for intercession; let the original purpose of the monthly concert of prayer for missions be given a larger place; let missionary prayer cycles be used by families and by individual Christians; let the best literature on prayer be circulated among the members of the Church; let special sermons on the Subject of intercession be preached. By these and by all other practical means a larger, deeper, wider spirit of prayer should be cultivated in the churches.

J.R. Mott

The Church has not yet touched the fringe of the possibilities of intercessory prayer. Her largest victories will be witnessed when individual Christians everywhere come to recognize their priesthood unto God and day by day give themselves unto prayer.

J.R. Mott

The missionary church is a praying church. The history of missions is a history of prayer. Everything vital to the success of the world's evangelization hinges on prayer. Are thousands of missionaries and tens of thousands of native workers needed? "Pray ye therefore the Lord of the harvest, that He send forth laborers into His harvest."

J.R. Mott

It is possible for the most obscure person in a church, with a heart right toward God, to exercise as much power for the evangelization of the world, as it is for those who stand in the most prominent positions.

J.R. Mott

It takes time for the fires to burn. It takes time for God to draw near and for us to know that He is there. It takes time to assimilate His truth. You ask me, How much time? I do not know. I know it means time enough to forget time.

J.R. Mott

Neither suffering nor ease should find us without a suitable Christian response in prayer and song. Our religion should cover all experience, finding expression in prayer or praise as the occasion may demand.

Alec Motyer

Both in periods of suffering and trouble, and in times of joy, prayer and praise alike acknowledge that he is sufficient. To pray to him is to acknowledge his sovereign power to meet our needs, and to praise is to acknowledge his sovereign power in appointing our circumstances.

Alec Motyer

On the ground of our own goodness we cannot expect to have our prayers answered. But Jesus is worthy, and for His sake we may have our prayers answered. There is nothing too choice, too costly, or too great for God to give Him. He is worthy. He is the spotless, holy Child, who under all circumstances acted according to the mind of God. And if we trust in Him, if we hide in Him, if we put Him forward and ourselves in the background, depend on Him and plead His name, we may expect to have our prayers answered.

George Müller

How truly precious it is that every one who rests alone upon the Lord Jesus for salvation, has in the living God a father, to whom he may fully unburden himself concerning the most minute affairs of his life, and concerning everything that lies upon his heart!

George Müller

I live in the spirit of prayer; I pray as I walk, when I lie down and when I rise, and the answers are always coming.

George Müller

It is not enough for the believer to begin to pray, nor to pray correctly; nor is it enough to continue for a time to pray. We must patiently, believingly continue in prayer until we obtain an answer.

George Müller

I myself have for twenty-nine years been waiting for an answer to prayer concerning a certain spiritual blessing.

George Müller

Prayer is reaching out after the unseen; fasting is letting go of all that is seen and temporal. Fasting helps express, deepen, confirm the resolution that we are ready to sacrifice anything, even ourselves to attain what we seek for the kingdom of God.

Andrew Murray

If the spiritual life be healthy, under the full power of the Holy Spirit, praying without ceasing will be natural.

Andrew Murray

Without set times of prayer, the spirit of prayer will be dull and feeble. Without the continual prayerfulness, the set times will not avail.

Andrew Murray

Scripture calls us to pray for many things: for all saints; for all men; for kings and all rulers; for all who are in adversity; for the sending forth of laborers; for those who labor in the gospel; for all converts; for believers who have fallen into sin; for one another in our immediate circles.

Andrew Murray

Faith in a prayer-hearing God will make a

prayer-loving Christian.

Andrew Murray

A sense of the need of souls;
a Christlike love in the heart;
a consciousness of personal impotence;
faith in the power of prayer;
courage to persevere in spite of refusal;
and the assurance of an abundant reward;
these are the dispositions that constitute a
    Christian an intercessor, and call forth the
    power of prevailing prayer.

Andrew Murray

O, let the place of secret prayer become to me the most beloved spot on earth.

Andrew Murray

May God open our eyes to see what the holy ministry of intercession is, to which, as His royal priesthood, we have been set apart. May He give us a large and strong heart to believe what mighty influence our prayers can exert. And may all fear as to our being able to fulfill our vocation vanish as we see Jesus, living ever to pray, living in us to pray, and standing surety for our prayer life."

Andrew Murray

Through His Spirit, the Spirit of prayer, our life may be one of continual prayer. The Spirit of prayer will help you become an intercessor, asking great things of God for those around you."

Andrew Murray

Without prayer, even though there may be increased interest in missions, more work for them, better success in organization and greater finances, the real growth of the spiritual life and of the love of Christ in the people may be very small.

Andrew Murray

Beware in your prayers, above everything else, of limiting God, not only by unbelief, but by fancying that you know what He can do. Expect unexpected things, "above all that we ask or think.". Each time, before you intercede, be quiet first, and worship God in His glory. Think of what He can do, and how He delights to hear the prayers of His redeemed people. Think of your place and privilege in Christ, and expect great things!

Andrew Murray

Time spent in prayer will yield more that that given to work.

Andrew Murray

Each time, before you intercede, be quiet first, and worship God in his glory.

Andrew Murray

Where there is much prayer, there will be much of the Spirit; where there is much of the Spirit, there will be ever-increasing prayer.

Andrew Murray

We pray for more of the Spirit, and we pray well, if alongside this prayer we set the truth that the Spirit wants more of me.

Andrew Murray

The greatest stumbling block in the way of victory over prayerlessness is the secret feeling that we will never obtain the blessing of being delivered from it.

Andrew Murray

Of all the mysteries of the prayer world the need of persevering prayer is one of the greatest.

Andrew Murray

Prayer is like fire. The fire can only burn brightly if it is supplied with good fuel. That fuel is God's Word.

Andrew Murray

Some people pray just to pray and some people pray to know God.

Andrew Murray

Jesus never taught his disciples how to preach, only how to pray.

Andrew Murray

Beware in your prayer, above everything, of limiting God, not only by unbelief, but by fancying that you know what He can do.

Andrew Murray

Prayer is the highest and holiest work to which man can rise.

Andrew Murray

What a humbling thought it is, that so often there is earnest prayer in which the desire for our own joy or pleasure is far stronger than any desire for God's glory. No wonder there are so many unanswered prayers! Here we have the secret. God cannot be glorified when that glory is not the object of our prayers.

Andrew Murray

Prayer is not monologue, but dialogue. God's voice in response to mine is its most essential part.

Andrew Murray

Prayer is the pulse of life.

Andrew Murray

The coming revival must begin with a great revival of prayer.

Andrew Murray

An increase of secret prayer with ministers will be the sure harbinger of blessing.

Andrew Murray

Prayer is not merely coming to God to ask something from Him. It is, above all, fellowship with God.

Andrew Murray

The glory of the Father must be the aim – the very soul and life – of our prayer.

Andrew Murray

N

Our prayers lay the track down which God's power can come. Like a mighty locomotive, his power is irresistible, but it cannot reach us without rails.

Watchman Nee

Why do so many Christians pray such tiny prayers when their God is so big?

Watchman Nee

I can take my telescope and look millions and

millions of miles into space; but I can lay it aside and go into my room, shut the door, get down on my knees in earnest prayer, and see more of Heaven and get closer to God than I can assisted by all the telescopes and material agencies on earth.

Isaac Newton

God often takes a course for accomplishing His purposes directly contrary to what our narrow views would prescribe. He brings a death upon our feelings, wishes and prospects when He is about to give us the desire of our hearts.

John Newton

I find in my own case an unaccountable backwardness to pray. I can read, I can write, I can converse with a ready will, but…prayer is far more spiritual than any of these. And the more spiritual a duty is the more my carnal heart is apt to start away from it.

John Newton

Thou art coming to a King,
Large petitions with thee bring
For His grace and power are such
None can ever ask too much.

John Newton

I ask'd the Lord, that I might grow
In faith, and love, and ev'ry grace,
Might more of his salvation know,
And seek more earnestly his face.

John Newton

When we speak with God, our power of addressing him, of holding communion with him, and listening to his still small voice, depends on our will being one and the same with his.

Florence Nightingale

Do not grieve if you do not at once receive from God that which you ask. He wishes to benefit you still more by making you persist longer in your patient prayer before Him.

Nilus the elder

Prayer is the seed of gentleness and the absence of anger.

Nilus the elder

Prayer is a remedy against sorrow and depression.

Nilus the elder

Pray firstly to be purified of passions, secondly to be freed from ignorance and forgetfulness, and thirdly to be delivered from all temptation and forsaking.

Nilus the elder

I believe there is one thing for which God is very angry with our land, and for which His Holy Spirit is so little among us, and that is the neglect of united prayer; the appointed means of bringing down the Holy Spirit.

Brownlow North

The neglect of prayer proves to my mind, that there is a large amount of practical infidelity.

Brownlow North

Oh Christians, go more to the prayer-meetings.

Brownlow North

This is our Lord's will, that our prayer and our trust be, alike, large. For I am sure that no man asketh mercy and grace with sincerity, without mercy and grace being given to him first.

Julian of Norwich

Prayer is the breath of your life which gives you the freedom to go and stay where you wish and to find the many signs which point out the way to a new land.

Henry J. Nouwen

We all have a deep desire to pray and a deep resistance against it. We want to be close to God, but also want to keep some distance.

Henri J. Nouwen

Our demon says: "We are too busy to pray; we have too many needs to attend to, too many people to respond to, too many wounds to heal. Prayer is a luxury, something to do during a free hour, a day away from work or on a retreat… ." But to think this way is harmful.

Henry J. Nouwen

Prayer is not a pious decoration of life but the

breath of human existence.

Henry J. Nouwen

The crisis of our prayer life is that our mind may be filled with ideas of God while our heart remains far from him. Real prayer comes from the heart.

Henry J. Nouwen

As we are involved in unceasing thinking, so we are called to unceasing prayer.

Henry J. Nouwen

The idea occurred to me that, instead of excluding, I could include all my thoughts, ideas, plans, projects, worries, and concerns and make them into prayer.

Henry J. Nouwen

Prayer without action grows in powerless pietism, and action without prayer degenerates into questionable manipulation.

Henry J. Nouwen

O

A quiet morning with a loving God puts the events of the upcoming day into proper perspective.

Janette Oke

Every prayer that is really such that is, which flows from the inward necessity of the soul God answers.

Herman Olshausen

Do not attempt to assess the quality of your prayer. God alone can judge its value.

Macarius of Optino

The discussion of prayer is so great that it requires the Father to reveal it, His firstborn Word to teach it, and the Spirit to enable us to think and speak rightly of so great a subject.

Origen

Prayer is one unceasing supplication.

Origen

Prayer, the Church's banquet, Angel's age, God's breath in man returning to his birth,

Give me 15 minutes of prayer every day, and I promise you heaven!

Henry de Ossó

He who prays as he ought will endeavor to live as he prays.

John Owen

There is no duty we perform for God that sin does not oppose. And the more spirituality or holiness there is in what we do, the greater is its enmity to it. Thus those who seek most for God, experience the strongest opposition.

John Owen

No heart can conceive that treasury of mercies which lies in this one privilege, in having liberty and ability to approach unto God at all times, according to His mind and will.

John Owen

He who prays as he ought, will endeavor to live as he prays.

John Owen

If we would talk less and pray more about them, things would be better than they are in the world: at least, we should be better enabled to bear them.

John Owen

P

All our attempts to get our lives into shape need to be soaked in constant, humble, thankful prayer.

J.I. Packer

God may answer the prayer we should have made rather than the prayer we did make.

J.I. Packer

What is the one thing that most often keeps Christians from experiencing God's making a dramatic difference in their lives? Is it carelessness? Lack of good Christian fellowship? Temptation?
May I suggest prayerlessness?

Luis Palau

You can read all the manuals on prayer and

listen to other people pray, but until you begin to pray yourself you will never understand prayer. It's like riding a bicycle or swimming: You learn by doing.

Luis Palau

Make room in your schedule to begin each day alone with God in prayer.

Luis Palau

God has instituted prayer so as to confer upon his creatures the dignity of being causes.

Blaise Pascal

In a single day I have prayed as many as a hundred times, and in the night almost as often.

Patrick of Ireland

Not only does God command us to pray, he permits us to pray. Prayer is both a must and a may, an obligation and a gift.

Ben Patterson

The good fruit visible in the church is planted in prayers prayed in weakness and in secret.

Ben Patterson

We have found no means so much blessed to keep religion alive as FASTING and PRAYER.

Edward Payson

Prayer is the first thing, the second thing, the third thing necessary to a minister. Pray, then, my dear brother; pray, pray, pray.

Edward Payson

Prayer is more than words. It's listening, seeing, feeling.

Norman Vincent Peale

But above all he excelled in prayer. The inwardness and weight of his spirit, the reverence and solemnity of his address and behavior, and the fewness and fullness of his words have often struck even strangers with admiration as they used to reach others with consolation. The most awful, living, reverend frame I ever felt or beheld, I must say, was his prayer. And truly it was a testimony. He knew and lived nearer to the Lord than other men, for they that know

him most will see most reason to approach him with reverence and fear.

William Penn (of George Fox)

For nothing reaches the heart but what is from the heart, or pierces the conscience but what comes from a living conscience.

William Penn

I pray God to keep me from being proud.

Samuel Pepys

Sometimes God delays the answer to our prayer in final form until we have time to build up the strength, accumulate the knowledge, or fashion the character that would make it possible for Him to say yes to what we ask.

Samuel Pepys

Prayer has as much to do with the necessities of this day's living as with the certainties of eternal life.

Eugene H. Peterson

Prayer is elemental, not advanced language. It is the means by which our language becomes honest, true, and personal in response to God. It is the means by which we get everything out in the open before God.

Eugene H. Peterson

Prayer is practical when it affects our outer conduct, but still more when it affects our inward activity.

Maud D. Petre

Daily prayer lifts us out of our selfish concerns to a grander view of the purpose and will and work of God. It invites us to let God work in us as God wills.

Philip. H. Pfatteicher

Teach me how to pray. Pray you yourself in me.

Philaret of Moscow

Remember, whatever warrants you have for praying; you have the same warrant to believe your prayers will be answered.

John Phillips

Anyone who prays should pray having his

heart in touch with his mouth and his mind with his lips.

Philoxenus of Mabbug

God is often moved to delay that we may be led to pray.

A.T. Pierson

How long will it take us to learn that our shortest route to the man next door is by way of God's throne?

A.T. Pierson

Wherever the Church is aroused and the world's wickedness arrested, somebody has been praying.

A.T. Pierson

You must find time or forfeit blessing.

A.T. Pierson

God has no greater controversy with his people today than this, that with boundless promises to believing prayer, there are so few who actually give themselves unto intercession.

A.T. Pierson

Prayer is not intended to change God's purpose, nor is it to move Him to form fresh purposes. God has decreed that certain events shall come to pass through the means He has appointed for their accomplishment.

Arthur W. Pink

Prayer is not so much an act as it is an attitude – an attitude of dependency, dependency upon God.

Arthur W. Pink

We are to fight on our knees!

Arthur W. Pink

The prevailing idea seems to be, that I come to God and ask Him for something that I want, and that I expect Him to give me that which I have asked. But this is a most dishonoring conception. The popular belief reduces God to a servant, our servant: doing our bidding, performing our pleasure, granting our desires. No, prayer is a coming to God, telling Him my need, committing my way unto the Lord, and leaving Him to

deal with it as seemeth Him best.

Arthur W. Pink

Prayer is not appointed for the furnishing of God with the knowledge of what we need, but it is designed as a confession to Him of our sense of the need.

Arthur W. Pink

Prayer is the way and means God has appointed for the communication of the blessings of His goodness to His people.

Arthur W. Pink

Real prayer is communion with God.

Arthur W. Pink

Prayer is a universal duty.

Arthur W. Pink

Nothing is too great and nothing is too small to commit into the hands of the Lord.

Arthur.W. Pink

One seeks God in books; one finds him in prayer.

Padre Pio

Prayer is the open admission that without Christ we can do nothing.

John Piper

Make your life – especially the life of your study – a life of constant communion with God in prayer. The aroma of God will not linger on a person who does not linger in the presence of God ... We are called to the ministry of the word and prayer, because without prayer the God of our studies will be the unfrightening and uninspiring God of insipid academic gamesmanship.

John Piper

A person without prayer is like a tree without roots.

Pius XII

Practice in life whatever you pray for and God will give it to you more abundantly.

E B. Pusey

Have some arrow prayers to pray during the

day, or a psalm. A good watchmaker is one who makes watches and prays: a good house-maid is one who sweeps and prays.

E.B. Pusey

Prayer may be equally with words or without: it may be "Jesu," or, "my God and my all."

E.B. Pusey

Q

Heaven is never deaf but when man's heart is dumb.

Francis Quarles

R

A man who kneels before God will stand before men.

Leonard Ravenhill

God doesn't answer prayer. He answers desperate prayer!

Leonard Ravenhill

For this sin hungry age we need a prayer-hungry Church.

Leonard Ravenhill

The man who has gotten God's word in the prayer closet neither seeks nor expects encouragement from men for the delivery of that word. The Spirit himself bears witness of the approval.

Leonard Ravenhill

The secret of praying is praying in secret.

Leonard Ravenhill

I don't care how colossal his intellect, no man is greater than his prayer life.

Leonard Ravenhill

To stand before men on behalf of God is one thing. To stand before God on behalf of men is something entirely different.

Leonard Ravenhill

A man may study because his brain is hungry for knowledge, even Bible knowledge. But he prays because his soul is hungry for God.

Leonard Ravenhill

Ministers who do not spend two hours a day in prayer are not worth a dime a dozen – degrees or no degrees.

Leonard Ravenhill

The true church lives and moves and has its being in prayer.

Leonard Ravenhill

Notice, we never pray for folks we gossip about, and we never gossip about the folk for whom we pray! For prayer is a great detergent.

Leonard Ravenhill

The church has many organizers, but few agonizers.

Leonard Ravenhill

This much is sure in all churches, forgetting party labels; the smallest meeting numerically is the prayer-meeting. If weak in prayer we are weak everywhere.

Leonard Ravenhill

No man is greater than his prayer life.

Leonard Ravenhill

To stand before men on behalf of God is one thing. To stand before God on behalf of men is something entirely different.

Leonard Ravenhill

The true man of God is grieved at the prayerlessness in the Church.

Leonard Ravenhill

Prayerlessness is disobedience, for God's command is that men ought always to pray and not faint. To be prayerless is to fail God, for He says, "Ask of me."

Leonard Ravenhill

Much of our praying is just asking God to bless some folks that are ill and to keep us plugging along. But prayer is not merely prattle: it is warfare.

Alan Redpath

Effectual prayer is the ordained means that God

uses to accomplish His ordained purposes.

John G. Reisinger

The true motivation for prayer comes from the Holy Spirit of God.

John G. Reisinger

Prayer should never be understood primarily in terms of power but rather as relating to God who is the source of all power.

Van Rheenen

Prayer is the secret of power.

Evan Roberts

The feeling of need and not the force of habit will make thee a sincere suppliant.

Evan Roberts

Prayer is the link between finite man and the infinite purposes of God.

Pat Robertson

In a prayer steeped in silence, we rest in God – body, soul and spirit.

Brother Roger of Taizé

So many Christians find in prayer the courage to take on responsibilities. Rooting themselves in the very wellsprings of Christ, they run the risks of faith.

Brother Roger of Taizé

Well spoke that soldier who asked what he would do if he became too weak to cling to Christ, answered, "Then I will pray him to cling to me."

Christina G. Rossetti

Our greatest victories are won on our knees and with empty stomachs.

Julio C. Ruibal

Words are but the body, the garment, the outside of prayer; sighs are nearer the heart work.

Samuel Rutherford

I urge upon you communion with Christ; a growing communion. There are curtains to be drawn aside in Christ that we never saw,

and new foldings of love in him. I despair that I shall ever win to the far end of that love, there are so many aspects to it. Therefore dig deep, and sweat and labor and take pains for him, and set by as much time in the day for him as you can. We will be won in the labor.

Samuel Rutherford

In the midst of worldly employments, there should be some thoughts of sin, death, judgment, and eternity, with at least a word or two of ejaculatory prayer to God.

Samuel Rutherford

Tears have a tongue, and grammar, and language, that our Father knoweth. Babes have no prayers for the breast, but weeping; the mother can read hunger in weeping.

Samuel Rutherford

I have benefited by my praying for others; for by making an errand to God for them, I have gotten something for myself.

Samuel Rutherford

Even should one rise in prayer higher than Peter or Paul, and hear that a poor man needed a drink of water, he would have to cease from the devotional exercise, sweet though it were, and do the deed of love.

John of Ruysbroeck

Prayer is absolutely necessary to a man's salvation.

J.C. Ryle

There are few children of God who do not often find the season of prayer a season of conflict. The devil has a special rage against us when he sees us on our knees.

J.C. Ryle

Prayer is the surest remedy against the devil and besetting sins.

J.C. Ryle

Fear not because your prayer is stammering, your words feeble, and your language poor. Jesus can understand you.

J.C. Ryle

Bibles read without prayer, sermons heard without prayer, engagements to marriage without prayer, travel undertaken without prayer, homes chosen without prayer, friendships formed without prayer, the daily act of private prayer itself hurried over or gone through without heart – these are the kind of downward steps by which many a Christian descends to a condition of spiritual paralysis, or reaches the point where God allows him to have a tremendous fall.

J.C. Ryle

Prayer obtains fresh and continued outpourings of the Spirit.

J.C. Ryle

Of all the evidences of the real work of the Spirit, a habit of hearty private prayer is one of the most satisfactory that can be named.

J.C. Ryle

There is no part of religion so neglected as private prayer.

J.C. Ryle

Depend on prayer; prayer is powerful.

J.C. Ryle

Words said without heart are as utterly useless to our souls as the drum-beating of the poor heathen before their idols.

J.C. Ryle

In the Bible I can find that nobody will be saved by his prayers, but I cannot find that without prayer anybody will be saved.

J.C. Ryle

To be prayerless is to be without God, without Christ, without grace, without hope, and without heaven.

J.C. Ryle

Neglect of prayer is one great cause of backsliding.

J.C. Ryle

Prayer will consume sin, or sin will choke prayer.

J.C. Ryle, A Call to Prayer

Prayer is the simplest act in all religion. It is simply speaking to God. It needs neither learning, nor wisdom, nor book-knowledge to begin it. It needs nothing but heart and will.

J.C. Ryle

A habit of prayer is one of the surest marks of a true Christian.

J.C. Ryle

Truly we have learn a great lesson when we have learned that "saying prayers" is not praying!

J.C. Ryle

S

In nothing should the leader be ahead of his followers more than in the realm of prayer.

J. Oswald Sanders

Mastering the art of prayer, like any other art, will take time, and the amount of time we allocate to it will be the true measure of our conception of its importance.

*J. Oswald Sander*Those who have truly decided to serve the Lord God should practice the remembrance of God and uninterrupted prayer to Jesus Christ, mentally saying: Lord Jesus Christ, Son of God, have mercy on me, a sinner.

Seraphim of Sarov

Great is the power of prayer, and it brings most of all the Spirit of God and is most easily practiced by everyone.

Seraphim of Sarov

O what peace we often forfeit,
O what needless pain we bear,
All because we do not carry
Everything to God in prayer.

J. M. Scriven

We must pray literally without ceasing – without ceasing; in every occurrence and employment of our lives. You know I mean that prayer of the heart which is independent of place or situation, or which is, rather, a habit of lifting up the heart to God, as in a constant communication with Him.

Elizabeth Ann Seton

The man who thinks only of himself says prayers of petition; he who thinks of his neighbor says prayers of intercession; he who thinks only of loving and serving God says prayers of abandonment to God's will.

Fulton J. Sheen

There are times in my life when I would rather die than pray.

Thomas Shepard

When we go to God by prayer, the devil knows we go to fetch strength against him, and therefore he opposes us all he can.

Richard Sibbes

Prayer is an effort to lay hold of God himself, the author of life.

Sadhu Sundar Singh

Prayer is continual abandonment to God.

Sadhu Sundar Singh

You cannot alter the will of God, but the man of prayer can discover God's will.

Sadhu Sundar Singh

Prayer is the breathing in of the Holy Spirit.

Sadhu Sundar Singh

The essence of prayer does not consist in asking God for something but in opening our hearts to God, in speaking with him, and living with Him in perpetual communion.

Sadhu Sundar Singh

Prayer is the desire to possess God Himself, the Source of all life.

Sadhu Sundar Singh

On the mountains, torrents flow right along, cutting their own courses. But on the plains canals have to be dug out painfully by men so that the water might flow. So among those who live on the heights with God, the Holy Spirit makes its way through of its own accord, whereas those who devote little time to prayer and communion with God have to organize painfully.

Sadhu Sunder Singh

God has created the spiritual food which we need. He has filled the soul of man with desire for this food, with an impulse to cry out for it and to drink it in. The spiritual milk, the nourishment of our souls, we receive through prayer. By means of fervent prayer we must receive it into our souls. As we do this we become stronger day by day, just like the infant at the breast.

Sadhu Sundar Singh

Some people become tired at the end of ten minutes or half an hour of prayer. What will they do when they have to spend Eternity in the presence of God? We must begin the habit here and become used to being with God.

Sadhu Sundar Singh

Prayer must be of the right sort, very humble, very expectant, very persevering. Lord, teach me to pray.

Alexander Smellie

In prayer I must wrestle like Jacob, and pant like David, and hope like Elijah, and be persistent like Bartimeus, and cry with tears like my blessed Lord.

Alexander Smellie

The first basic form of prayer is worship.

Chuck Smith

Prayer is the most important activity a born-again Christian can perform.

Chuck Smith

Oh, how few find time for prayer! There is time for everything else, time to sleep and time to eat, time to read the newspaper and the novel, time to visit friends, time for everything else under the sun, but-no time for prayer, the most important of all things, the one great essential!

Oswald Smith

A prayerless man is proud and independent.

David Smithers

A man can not lead others where he is not willing to go himself. Therefore, beware of the prayerless church leader who no longer readily admits his own need for more of the person and power of Jesus Christ. Only a seeking, praying heart can truly encourage spiritual hunger in others!

David Smithers

Only God's humble and needy children take the time to pray.

David Smithers

To pray is to expose the shores of the mind to the incoming tide of God.

Ralph Sockman

Do not be too easily discouraged. Instead, repeat the Jesus prayer, until it penetrates the depths of your consciousness.

Sophrony of Essex

I know no blessing so small as to be reasonably expected without prayer, nor any so great but may be attained by it.

Robert South

Let not him who prays, suffer his tongue to outstrip his heart; nor presume to carry a message to the throne of grace, while that stays behind.

Robert South

The evangelization of the world in this generation depends first of all upon a revival of prayer. Deeper than the need for men; deeper, far, than the need for money; aye, deep down at the bottom of our spiritless life is the need for the forgotten secret of prevailing, world-wide prayer.

Robert E. Speer

Prayer that is not in the Holy Ghost is in the flesh, and that which is born of the flesh is flesh and cannot please God.

C.H. Spurgeon

Do we sing as much as the birds do? Yet what have birds to sing about, compared with us? Do we sing as much as the angels do? Yet they were never redeemed by the blood of Christ. Birds of the air, shall you excel me? Angels, shall you exceed me? You have done so, but I intend to emulate you, and day by day, and night by night, pour forth my soul in sacred song.

C.H. Spurgeon

The best praying man is the man who is most believingly familiar with the promises of God. After all, prayer is nothing but taking God's promises to Him and saying, "Do as You have said." Prayer is the promise utilized. Prayer not based on a promise has no true foundation.

C.H. Spurgeon

Prayer itself is an art which only the Holy Ghost can teach us. He is the giver of all prayer. Pray for prayer. Pray till you can pray.

C.H. Spurgeon

Prayer girds human weakness with divine strength, turns human folly into heavenly wisdom, and gives to troubled mortals the peace of God. We know not what prayer can do.

C.H. Spurgeon

Continue in prayer, and though the blessing tarry, it must come; in God's own time it must appear to you.

C.H. Spurgeon

He that is never on his knees on earth, shall never stand upon his feet in heaven.

C.H. Spurgeon

If your faith does not make you pray, have nothing to do with it: get rid of it, and God help thee to begin again.

C.H. Spurgeon

The man who, despite the teaching of Scripture, tries to pray without a Savior, insults the deity.

C.H. Spurgeon

True prayer is measured by weight, – not by length. A single groan before God may have more fullness of prayer in it than a fine oration of great length.

C.H. Spurgeon

If you want that splendid power in prayer, you must remain in loving, living, lasting, conscious, practical, abiding union with the Lord Jesus Christ.

C.H. Spurgeon

When God's mercies are coming, their footfalls are our desires to pray.

C.H. Spurgeon

God will hear His people at the beginning of their prayers if the condition of their heart is ready for it.

C.H. Spurgeon

A true prayer is an inventory of needs, a catalog of necessities, an exposure of secret wounds, a revelation of hidden poverty.

C.H. Spurgeon

Prayer plumes the wings of God's young eaglets so that they may learn to mount above the clouds. Prayer brings inner strength to God's warriors and sends them forth to spiritual battle with their muscles firm and their armor in place.

C.H. Spurgeon

Prayer is not a hard requirement it is the natural duty of a creature to its creator, the simplest homage that human need can pay to divine liberality.

C.H. Spurgeon

God's mercy visits every house where night and morning prayers are made, but where these are neglected, sin is incurred.

C.H. Spurgeon

Our prayers may be very beautiful in appearance and might appear to be the very paragon of devotion, but unless there is a secret spiritual force in them, they are vain things.

C.H. Spurgeon

Whether we like it or not, asking is the rule of the Kingdom. If you may have everything by asking in His Name, and nothing without asking, I beg you to see how absolutely vital prayer is.

C.H. Spurgeon

He who knows how to overcome with God in prayer has heaven and earth at his disposal.

C.H. Spurgeon

Learn the secret of praying in the Holy Ghost.

C.H. Spurgeon

Turn everything that is a care into a prayer.

C.H. Spurgeon

Whenever God determines to do a great thing, He first sets His people to pray.

C.H. Spurgeon

We shall never sing, *"Gloria in excelsis"* except we pray to God *de profundis*: out of the depths must we cry, or we shall never behold glory in the highest.

C.H. Spurgeon

As artists give themselves to their models, and poets to their classical pursuits, so must we addict ourselves to prayer.

C.H. Spurgeon

It is interesting to remark how large a portion of Sacred Writ is occupied with the subject of prayer, either in furnishing examples, enforcing precepts, or pronouncing promises.

C.H. Spurgeon

You cannot even truly pray without the Trinity. You cannot draw near to the Father except through the Son and the Holy Spirit.

C.H. Spurgeon

Baptize every prayer into the name of the Father, the Son, and the Holy Spirit, and so make it into a blessing.

C.H. Spurgeon

He who lives without prayer, he who lives with little prayer, he who seldom reads the Word, and he who seldom looks up to heaven for a fresh influence from on high – he will be the man whose heart will become dry and barren.

C.H. Spurgeon

We cannot all argue, but we can all pray. We cannot all be leaders but we can all be pleaders. We cannot all be mighty in rhetoric, but we can all be prevalent in prayer.

C.H. Spurgeon

I would sooner see you eloquent with God than with men.

C.H. Spurgeon

Ten minutes' praying is better than a year's murmuring.

C.H. Spurgeon

All the Christian virtues are locked up in the word prayer.

C.H. Spurgeon

Only the prayer that comes from God can go to God.

C.H. Spurgeon

If there be anything I know, anything that I am quite assured of beyond all question, it is that praying breath is never spent in vain.

C.H. Spurgeon

The more we pray, the more we shall want to
    pray.
The more we pray, the more we can pray.
The more we pray, the more we shall pray.
He who prays little will pray less, but he who
    prays much will pray more.
And he who prays more, will desire to pray
    more abundantly.

C.H. Spurgeon

Where God leads you to pray, he means you to receive.

C.H. Spurgeon

I know of no better thermometer to your spiritual temperature than the intensity of your prayer.

C.H. Spurgeon

Groanings which cannot be uttered are often prayers which cannot be refused.

C.H. Spurgeon

A prayerless soul is a Christless soul.

C.H. Spurgeon

Nothing brings such leanness into a man's soul as lack of prayer.

C.H. Spurgeon

It is well said that neglected prayer is the birthplace of all evil.

C.H. Spurgeon

I commend intercessory prayer, because it opens man's soul, gives a healthy play to his sympathies, constrains him to feel that he is not everybody, and that this wide world and this great universe were not after all made that he might be its petty lord, that everything might bend to his will, and all creatures crouch at his feet.

C.H. Spurgeon

If Jesus needed to pray being what He was, how must we need it, being what we are.

James Stalker

A generous prayer is never presented in vain; the petition may be refused, but the petitioner is always, I believe, rewarded by some gracious visitation.

Robert Louis Stevenson

Prayer among men is supposed a means to change the person to whom we pray; but prayer to God doth not change him, but fits us to receive the things prayed for.

Edward Stillingfleet

Men and women are at their noblest and best when they are on their knees before God in prayer.

John R.W. Stott

Prayer is not a convenient device for imposing our will upon God.

John R.W. Stott

To pray is not only to be truly godly; it is also to be truly human.

John R.W. Stott

We Christians too often substitute prayer for playing the game. Prayer is good; but when used as a substitute for obedience, it is nothing but a blatant hypocrisy, a despicable Pharisaism. To your knees, man!

C. T. Studd

We have taught our people to use prayer too much as a means of comfort – not in the original sense of uplifting, inspiring, strengthening, but in the more modern and baser sense of soothing sorrow, dulling pain, and drying tears – the comfort of the cushion, not the comfort of the Cross.

Geoffrey A. Studdert-Kennedy

If you are strangers to prayer you are strangers to power.

William Ashley (Billy) Sunday

Yank some of the groans out of your prayers, and shove in some shouts.

William Ashley (Billy) Sunday

A teardrop on earth summons the King of heaven.

Charles R. Swindoll

There is a great tendency to think our best work is done at our desk or on our feet.... but it's really done on our knees.

Charles R. Swindoll

Bodily listlessness and sluggishness which affect the soul as a result of our laziness not only make us abandon our normal rule of prayer, but also darken the mind and fill it with despair. Then blasphemous and cowardly thoughts arise in the heart. Indeed, the person tempted by the demon of listlessness cannot even enter his usual place of prayer. He grows sluggish, and absurd thoughts directed against the Creator of all things arise in his mind. Aware of the cause of all this and why it has happened to you, with perseverance enter your normal place of prayer and, falling down before the God of love, ask for a contrite and aching heart, full of tears, to be freed from the weight of listlessness and from your sinful thoughts. If you knock hard and insistently, this release will soon be given to you.

Symeon the New Theologian

T

Like art, like music, like so many other disciplines, prayer can only be appreciated when you actually spend time in it.

Joni Eareckson Tada

Effective prayer is not measured by its length but by its depth.

Joni Eareckson Tada

I have seen many men work without praying, though I have never seen any good come out of it; but I have never seen a man pray without working.

James Hudson Taylor

Brother, if you would enter that Province, you must go forward on your knees.

James Hudson Taylor

Satan will always find you something to do when you ought to be occupied about that [prayer and Bible study], if it is only arranging a window blind.

James Hudson Taylor

Satan, the Hinderer, may build a barrier about us, but he can never roof us in, so that we cannot look up.

James Hudson Taylor

I used to ask God to help me. Then I asked if I might help him. I ended up by asking him to do his work through me.

James Hudson Taylor

Do not have your concert first, and then tune your instrument afterwards. Begin the day with the Word of God and prayer, and get first of all into harmony with Him.

James Hudson Taylor

When we work, we work. When we pray, God works.

James Hudson Taylor

Since the days of Pentecost, has the whole church ever put aside every other work and waited upon Him for ten days, that the Spirit's power might be manifested? We give too much attention to method and machinery and resources, and too little to the source of power.

James Hudson Taylor

It is possible to move men, through God, by prayer alone.

James Hudson Taylor

In Shansi I found Chinese Christians who were accustomed to spend time in fasting and prayer. They recognized that this fasting, which so many dislike, which requires faith in God, since it makes one feel weak and poorly, is really a divinely appointed means of grace. Perhaps the greatest hindrance to our work is our own imagined strength; and in fasting we learn what poor, weak creatures we are – dependent on a meal of meat for the little strength which we are so apt to lean upon.

James Hudson Taylor

When the clock strikes it is good to say a prayer.

Jeremy Taylor

No man can hinder our private addresses to God; every man can build a chapel in his breast, himself the priest, his heart the sacrifice, and the earth he treads on, the altar.

Jeremy Taylor

The body of our prayer is the sum of our duty; and as we must ask of God whatsoever we need, so we must watch and labor for all that we ask.

Jeremy Taylor

The prayers of Holy men appease God's wrath, drive away temptations, resist and overcome the devil, procure the ministry and service of angels, rescind the decrees of God.

Jeremy Taylor

Prayer cures sickness and obtains pardon; it arrests the sun in its course and stays the wheels of the chariot of the moon; it rules over all gods and opens and shuts the storehouses of rain; it unlocks the cabinet of the womb and quenches the violence of fire; it stops the mouths of lions and reconciles our suffering and weak faculties with the violence of torment and violence of persecution; it pleases God and supplies all our need.

Jeremy Taylor

When we pray for any virtue, we should cultivate the virtue as well as pray for it; the form of your prayer should be the rule of your life; every petition to God is a precept to man. Look not, therefore, upon your prayers as a method of good and salvation only, but as a perpetual monition of duty. By what we require of God we see what he requires of us.

Jeremy Taylor

Whatsoever we beg of God, let us also work for it.

Jeremy Taylor

Prayer is the peace of our spirit, the stillness of our thoughts, the evenness of our recollection, the sea of our meditation, the rest of our cares, and the calm of our tempest.

Jeremy Taylor

Prayer is the ascent of the mind to God.

Jeremy Taylor

Do not lie to God.

Jeremy Taylor

When I stop praying, the coincidences stop happening.

William Temple

Battering the gates of heaven with the storms of prayer.

Alfred Tennyson

More things are wrought by prayer than the world dreams of. What are men better than sheep or goats, that nourish a blind life within the brain, if, knowing God, they lift no hands of prayer both for themselves and those who call them friends!

Alfred Tennyson

You pay God a great compliment by asking great things of Him.

Teresa of Avila

There is but one road that reaches God and that is prayer. If anyone shows you another, you are being deceived.

Teresa of Avila

No one is so advanced in prayer that they do not often have to return to the beginning.

Teresa of Avila

The life of prayer is just love to God, and the custom of being ever with him.

Teresa of Avila

Don't let anyone deceive you by showing you a road other than prayer.

Teresa of Avila

Spiritual Communion is very profitable; therefore do not omit it, for by it the Lord learns how much you love Him.

Teresa of Avila

The soul which gives itself to prayer – whether a lot or only a little – must absolutely not have limits set on it.

Teresa of Avila

[In prayer] tears gain everything.

Teresa of Avila

Pray as you can, for prayer doesn't consist of thinking a great deal, but of loving a great deal.

Teresa of Avila

Feel often during the day the need for prayer and pray. Prayer opens the heart, till it is capable of containing God himself. Ask and seek and your heart will be big enough to receive Him and keep Him as Your Own.

Mother Teresa of Calcutta

I always begin my prayer in silence, for it is in the silence of the heart that God speaks. God is the friend of silence-we need to listen to God because it's not what we say but what He says to us and through us that matters.

Mother Teresa of Calcutta

More tears are shed over answered prayers than unanswered ones.

Mother Teresa of Calcutta

God speaks in the silence of the heart. Listening is the beginning of prayer.

Mother Teresa of Calcutta

Prayer is not asking. Prayer is putting oneself in the hands of God.

Mother Teresa of Calcutta

The more you pray, the easier it becomes. The easier it becomes, the more you will pray.

Mother Teresa of Calcutta

My secret is quite simple. I pray.

Mother Teresa of Calcutta

Prayer enlarges the heart until it is capable of containing God's gift of himself.

Mother Teresa of Calcutta

I do not pray for success. I ask for faithfulness.

Mother Teresa of Calcutta

Contemplative prayer is nothing else than a close sharing between friends; it means taking time frequently to be alone with him who we know loves us.

Teresa of Jesus

We pray without a prompter because from the heart.

Tertullian

For me, prayer is a surge of the heart; it is a simple look turned toward heaven. It is a cry of recognition and of love, embracing both trial and joy.

Thérèse of Lisieux

Prayer is a surge of the heart; a simple look turned toward heaven, a cry of recognition and of love, embracing both trial and joy.

Thérèse of Lisieux

Prayer consists not in speaking a lot, but in loving a lot.

Thérèse of Lisieux

Prayer is the test of everything; prayer is also the source of everything; prayer is the driving force of everything; prayer is also the director of everything. If prayer is right, everything is right. For prayer will not allow anything to go wrong.

Theophan the Recluse

In the Bible prayer is worship that includes all the attitudes of the human spirit in its approach to God.

J.G.S.S. Thomson

Prayer is a habit; and the more we pray the better we shall pray.

Mary Wilder Tileston

Prayer is an invisible tool which is wielded in a visible world.

Leo Tolstoy

Out of a very intimate acquaintance with D. L. Moody, I wish to testify that he was a far greater pray-er than he was preacher. Time and time again, he was confronted by obstacles that seemed insurmountable, but he always knew the way to overcome all difficulties. He knew the way to bring to pass anything that needed to be brought to pass. He knew and believed in the deepest depths of his soul that nothing was too hard for the Lord, and that prayer could do anything that God could do.

R.A. Torrey

Prayer is God's appointed way for obtaining things, and the great secret of all lack in our experience, in our life and in our work is neglect of prayer.

R.A. Torrey

The reason why many fail in battle is because they wait until the hour of battle. The reason why others succeed is because they have gained their victory on their knees long before the battle came. Anticipate your battles; fight them on your knees before temptation comes, and you will always have victory.

R.A. Torrey

All the mighty men of God outside the Bible have been men of prayer. They have differed from one another in many things, but in this they have been alike.

R.A. Torrey

God has appointed a way by which we shall seek and obtain mercy and grace. That way is prayer.

R.A. Torrey

Prayer will promote our personal holiness as nothing else, except the study of the Word of God.

R.A. Torrey

One of the great needs of the present day is men and women who will not only start out to pray for things, but pray on and on and on

until they obtain what they seek from God.

R.A. Torrey

When the devil sees a man or woman who really believes in prayer, who knows how to pray, and who really does pray, and, above all, when he sees a whole church on its face before God in prayer, "he trembles" as much as he ever did, for he knows that his day in that church or community is at an end.

R.A. Torrey

Before a word of petition is offered, we should have the definite consciousness that we are talking to God, and should believe that he is listening and is going to grant the thing that we ask of him.

R.A. Torrey

If we are too busy to pray, we are too busy to have power. We have a great deal of activity, but we accomplish little; many services but few conversions; much machinery but few results.

R.A. Torrey

The neglected heart will soon be a heart overrun with worldly thoughts; the neglected life will soon become a moral chaos; the church that is not jealously protected by mighty intercession and sacrificial labors will before long become the abode of every evil bird and the hiding place for unsuspected corruption. The creeping wilderness will soon take over that church that trusts in its own strength and forgets to watch and pray.

A.W. Tozer

When we become too glib in prayer we are most surely talking to ourselves.

A.W. Tozer

Have you noticed how much praying for revival has been going on of late – and how little revival has resulted? I believe the problem is that we have been trying to substitute praying for obeying, and it simply will not work. To pray for revival while ignoring the plain precept laid down in Scripture is to waste a lot of words and get nothing for our trouble. Prayer will become effective when we stop using it as a substitute for obedience.

A. W. Tozer

"Which is more important: reading God's Word or praying?" To which the response is, "Which is more important to a bird: the left or the right wing?"

A.W. Tozer

Prayer is not overcoming God's reluctance; it is laying hold of His highest willingness!

Richard C. Trench

At the profoundest depths in life, men talk not about God but with him.

D. Elton Trueblood

U

Prayer ... is a living and personal relationship, which tends to become more personal and also more simple, as one goes on.

Evelyn Underhill

In prayer, will and grace cooperate.

Evelyn Underhill

V

If I wished to humble anyone, I should question him about his prayers. I know nothing to compare with this topic for its sorrowful self-confessions.

C.J. Vaughan

No one, until he receives the Spirit, can pray in a manner truly pleasing to God.

Innocent Veniaminov

Prayer is the Christian's vital breath: without it you can not move.

George Verwer

Prayer is at the heart of the action and a world-wide prayer movement must run parallel with any kind of world-wide mission movement.

George Verwer

Prayer is nothing else but union with God. In this intimate union, God and the soul are fused together like two bits of wax that no one can every pull apart. This union of God with a tiny creature is a lovely thing. It is a happiness beyond understanding.

John Vianney

W

If you feel stuck, bring your whole self to Christ, not just the problem, but you. Ask God to change your heart. Commit yourself to pray to that end.

Sheila Walsh

However inarticulate, however ignorant or misdirected our prayer may be, however weak in every respect (weak, mind you, even in our ability to believe that it will be heard!) it is the listening of the Lord God which makes our mumble a prayer.

Walter Wangerin, Jr.

Let this be understood above all: the power of prayer is not in us, that we speak. It is in God, that he listens!

Walter Wangerin, Jr.

He that leaves off prayer leaves off the fear of God. "You cast off fear, and restrain prayer before God" (Job 15: 4). A man that leaves off prayer is capable of any wickedness. When Saul had given up inquiring of God he went to the witch of Endor.

Thomas Watson

When prayer leads the van, in due time deliverance brings up the rear.

Thomas Watson

Desires are the soul and life of prayer; words are but the body; now as the body without the soul is dead, so are prayers unless they are animated with our desires.

Thomas Watson

A godly man is a praying man. As soon as grace is poured in, prayer is poured out. Prayer is the soul's traffic with heaven; God comes down to us by his Spirit, and we go up to him by prayer.

Thomas Watson

The Spirit helps faith to turn the key of prayer, and then it unlocks heaven.

Thomas Watson

All that have got to heaven have crept there on their knees.

Thomas Watson

Prayer is the golden key that opens heaven.

Thomas Watson

Prayer is the offering up of our desires to God in the name of Christ, for such things as are agreeable to his will.

Thomas Watson

Prayer is a lifting up of the mind and soul to God.

Thomas Watson

Jesus Christ was more willing to go to the cross, than we are to the throne of grace.

Thomas Watson

The lower the heart descends, the higher the prayer ascends.

Thomas Watson

Those prayers God likes best which come seething hot from the heart.

Thomas Watson

If God does not give us what we crave, he will give us what we need.

Thomas Watson

Christ was in an agony at prayer. Many when they pray are rather in a lethargy, than in an agony. When they are about the world they are all fire; when they are at prayer, they are all ice.

Thomas Watson

Patience in prayer is nothing but faith spun out.

Thomas Watson

The angel fetched Peter out of prison, but it was prayer that fetched the angel.

Thomas Watson

Ceaseless interior prayer is a continual yearning of the human spirit towards God.

The Way of a Pilgrim

The Lord's Prayer contains the sum total of religion and morals.

Arthur Wellesley, Duke of Wellington

Every new victory which a soul gains is the effect of a new prayer.

John Wesley

God's command to "pray without ceasing" is founded on the necessity we have of his grace to preserve the life of God in the soul, which can no more subsist one moment without it, than the body can without air.

John Wesley

Give me one hundred preachers who fear nothing but sin and desire nothing but God, and I care not a straw whether they be clergymen or laymen; such alone will shake the gates of hell and set up the kingdom of heaven on earth. God does nothing but in answer to prayer.

John Wesley

Whether we think of, or speak to, God, whether we act or suffer for him, all is prayer, when we have no other object than his love, and the desire of pleasing him.

John Wesley

All that a Christian does, even in eating and sleeping, is prayer, when it is done in simplicity, according to the order of God, without either adding to or diminishing from it by His choice.

John Wesley

Prayer continues in the desire of the heart, though the understanding be employed on outward things.

John Wesley

In souls filled with love, the desire to please God is continual prayer.

John Wesley

God only requires of his adult children, that their hearts be truly purified, and that they offer him continually the wishes and vows that naturally spring from perfect love. For these desires, being the genuine fruits of love, are the most perfect prayers that can spring from it.

John Wesley

It seems God is limited by our prayer life – that he can do nothing for humanity unless someone ask him.

John Wesley

God does nothing but by prayer, and everything with it.

John Wesley

Prayer continues in the desire of the heart, though the understanding be employed on outward things.

John Wesley

In souls filled with love, the desire to please God is a continual prayer.

John Wesley

Storm the throne of grace and persevere therein, and mercy will come down.

John Wesley

The neglect of prayer is a grand hindrance to holiness.

John Wesley

God does nothing redemptively in the world – except through prayer.

John Wesley

The end of prayer is the perfection of the whole Christian body.

B.F. Westcott

True prayer – the prayer that must be answered – is the personal recognition and acceptance of the divine will.

B.F. Westcott

Prayer is opening up our sluice gates to the mighty ocean of God.

B.F. Westcott

Be much in secret prayer. Converse less with man, and more with God.

George Whitefield

After I have been wearied almost to death in preaching, writing and conversation, and going from place to place, God imparted new life to my soul, and enabled me to intercede with him for an hour and a half and two hours together.

George Whitefield

O prayer! Prayer! It brings and keeps God and man together. It raises man up to God and brings God down to man.

George Whitefield

Often we do not pray because we doubt that anything will actually happen if we pray. Of course, we don't admit this publicly. But if we felt certain of visible results within sixty seconds of every prayer, there would be holes in the knees of every pair of Christian-owned pants in the world!

Donald Whitney

Every chain that spirits wear
Crumbles in the breath of prayer.

John Greenleaf Whittier

The simple heart that freely asks in love, obtains.

John Greenleaf Whittier

If you find your life of prayer to be always so short, and so easy, and so spiritual, as to be without cost and strain and sweat to you, you may depend upon it, you are not yet begun to pray.

Alexander Whyte

Begin to pray as you will wish you had begun when you are on your last bed, and have not all your life on earth learned aright to pray.

Alexander Whyte

The greatest and best talent that God gives to any man or woman in this world is the talent of prayer.

Alexander Whyte

There is nothing that we are so bad at all our days as prayer.

Alexander Whyte

The more passionateness any man puts into his prayer, the more praise the Bible gives to that man.

Alexander Whyte

If prayer is anything at all it is everything.

Alexander Whyte

Prayer is a rising up and a drawing near to God in mind, and in heart, and in spirit.

Alexander Whyte

I can get more out of God by believing Him for one minute than by shouting at Him all night.

Smith Wigglesworth

I must secure more time for private devotions. I have been living far too public for me. The shortening of devotions starves the soul, it grows lean and faint. I have been keeping too late hours.

William Wilberforce

The holy time is quiet
Breathless with adoration
The gentleness of heaven broods o'er the sea;
Listen!

William Wordsworth

X

God does not listen to the prayer of the lazy.

Pope Xystus I

Y

By our prayers, mountains are moved.

Philip Yancey

Z

If a man wants God to hear his prayer quickly, then before he prays for anything else, even his own soul, when he stands and stretches out his hands towards God, he must pray with all his heart for his enemies.

Zeno

True prayer will achieve just as much as it costs us.

Samuel M. Zwemer

The history of missions is the history of answered prayer. From Pentecost to the Haystack meeting in New England and from the days when Robert Morrison landed in China to the martyrdom of John and Betty Stam, prayer has been the source of power and the secret of spiritual triumph.

Samuel M. Zwemer

Prayer is self-discipline.

Samuel M. Zwemer

When we pray for each other on earth we do so believing that all things are given to us through Christ alone.

Huldrych Zwingli